Baseball America
2020
ALMANAC

D0958321

BASEBALL AMERICA INC. · DURHAM, N.C.

Baseball America

ESTABLISHED 1981

P.O. BOX 12877, DURHAM, NC 27709 · PHONE (919) 682-9635

EDITOR AND PUBLISHER B.J. Schecter *@bjschecter*
EXECUTIVE EDITORS J.J. Cooper *@jjcoop36*
Matt Eddy *@MattEddyBA*
CHIEF REVENUE OFFICER Don Hintze
DIRECTOR OF BUSINESS DEVELOPMENT Ben Leigh
DIRECTOR OF DIGITAL STRATEGY Mike Salerno

EDITORIAL

ASSOCIATE EDITORS Kegan Lowe *@KeganLowe*
Josh Norris *@jnorris427*
Justin Coleman *@ElJayColes*
SENIOR WRITER Ben Badler *@benbadler*
NATIONAL WRITERS Teddy Cahill *@tedcahill*
Carlos Collazo *@CarlosACollazo*
Kyle Glaser *@KyleAGlaser*
WEB EDITOR Mark Chiarelli *@Mark_Chiarelli*
SPECIAL CONTRIBUTOR Tim Newcomb *@tdnewcomb*

PRODUCTION

CREATIVE DIRECTOR James Alworth
GRAPHIC DESIGNER James Alworth

BUSINESS

TECHNOLOGY MANAGER Brent Lewis
ACCOUNT EXECUTIVE Kellen Coleman
OFFICE MANAGER & CUSTOMER SERVICE Angela Lewis
CUSTOMER SERVICE Melissa Sunderman

STATISTICAL SERVICE

MAJOR LEAGUE BASEBALL ADVANCED MEDIA

Alliance
>>>> BASEBALL <<<<

BASEBALL AMERICA ENTERPRISES

CHAIRMAN & CEO Gary Green
PRESIDENT Larry Botel
GENERAL COUNSEL Matthew Pace
DIRECTOR OF MARKETING Amy Heart
INVESTOR RELATIONS Michele Balfour
DIRECTOR OF OPERATIONS Joan Disalvo
PARTNERS Jon Ashley
Stephen Alepa
Martie Cordaro
Brian Rothschild
Andrew Fox
Ian Ritchie
Dan Waldman
Sonny Kalsi
Glenn Isaacson
Robert Hernreich
Craig Amazeen
Peter Ruprecht
Beryl Snyder
Tom Steiglehner

3STEP

MANAGING PARTNER David Geaslen
CHIEF CONTENT OFFICER Jonathan Segal
CHIEF FINANCIAL OFFICER Sue Murphy

BASEBALL AMERICA (ISSN 0745-5372/USPS 591-210) August 6, 2019, Vol. 39, No. 8 is published monthly, 12 issues per year, by Baseball America Enterprises, LLC, 4319 South Alston Ave, Suite 103, Durham, NC 27713. Subscription rate is $92.95 for one year; Canada $118.95 (U.S. funds); all other foreign $144.95 per year (U.S. funds). Periodicals postage paid at Durham, NC, & additional mailing offices. Occasionally our subscriber list is made available to reputable firms offering goods and services we believe would be of interest to our readers. If you prefer to be excluded, please send your current address label and a note requesting to be excluded from these promotions to Baseball America Enterprises, LLC, 4319 South Alston Ave, Suite 103, Durham, NC 27713, Attn: Privacy Coordinator. POSTMASTER: Send all UAA to CFS (See DMM 707.4.12.5); NON-POSTAL & MILITARY FACILITIES: send address corrections to Baseball America, P.O. Box 420235, Palm Coast, FL 32142-0235. CANADA POST: Return undeliverable Canadian addresses to IMEX Global Solutions, P.O. Box 25542, London, ON N6C 6B2. Please contact 1-800-381-1288 to start carrying Baseball America in your store.

Baseball America
2020 ALMANAC

Editor
Kegan Lowe

Contributing Editors
Ben Badler, Teddy Cahill, Justin Coleman, Carlos Collazo, J.J. Cooper,
Matt Eddy, Josh Norris

Contributing Writers
M'Lynn Dease, Tyler Henninger, Jared McMasters, Bill Mitchell,
Harvey Sahker, Jeff Sanders, Jon Tayler

Database and Application Development
Brent Lewis

Design & Production
CREATIVE DIRECTOR: James Alworth
GRAPHIC DESIGNER: Leah Tyner

Programming & Technical Development
Brent Lewis

Translation Assistance
Kelly Wong

Cover Photos
MAIN PHOTO: Cody Bellinger.
Photo by oe Robbins/Getty Images

©2019 Baseball America Inc.
No portion of this book may be reprinted or reproduced without
the written consent of the publisher.

For additional copies, visit our Website at
BaseballAmerica.com or call 1-800-845-2726 to order.

US $25.95 / CAN $34.95, plus shipping and handling
per order. Expedited shipping available.

Distributed by Simon & Schuster.
ISBN-13: 1-932391-92-4

**Statistics provided by Major League Baseball Advanced Media
and Compiled by Baseball America.**

EDITOR'S NOTE: Major league statistics are based on final, unofficial 2019 averages.

» The organization statistics, which begin on page 44, include all players who participated in at least one game during the 2019 season.

» Pitchers' batting statistics are not included, nor are the pitching statistics of field players who pitched in less than two games.

» For players who played with more than one team in the same league, the player's cumulative statistics appear on the line immediately after the player's statistics with each team.

» Innings pitched have been rounded off to the nearest full inning.

TABLE OF CONTENTS

Anthony Rendon

DUSTIN BRADFORD/GETTY IMAGES

MAJOR LEAGUES 6

ORGANIZATION STATISTICS 44

**MAJOR
LEAGUES**

Baseball's Power Surge

BY JON TAYLER

There's no way Athletics outfielder Stephen Piscotty could have known at the time, but on March 20, 2019, he helped Major League Baseball take its first step toward a wild and historic year.

The season was less than an hour old when Piscotty stepped into the batter's box against Mariners lefthander Marco Gonzales in Tokyo and launched a fastball nearly 400 feet to center field for a solo home run—the first of his campaign, and the first for the entire league as well. Nor would it be the last. Although Piscotty would collect just 12 more homers in a campaign cut short by injuries, thousands more followed for major league hitters as a whole. From the sluggers down to guys never known for their power, everyone was smashing the ball out of the park in 2019.

This past season featured superstars switching teams, brilliant individual performances, a shocking death, future Hall of Famers burnishing their resumes and much more. But it will be remembered in the history books for one thing above all else: the rise of the home run. Aided by a ball that had less drag and traveled farther than its counterparts from years previous—call it juiced at your own discretion—Major League Baseball smashed its own single-season record for most homers with a staggering 6,776 longballs. That's over 600 more home runs than were hit in 2017, which previously held the top spot for most home runs in a season, and over 1,000 more than 2000, the peak of the Steroid Era, which now sits in a distant third place.

It wasn't just the league that saw records fall, though. Two teams, the Twins and Yankees, cracked the 300-homer barrier, which had never before happened in major league history. Three more teams—the Astros, Dodgers and Athletics—finished the year in the all-time top 10 for most home runs in a single season. In total, 15 teams set franchise records for single-season homers.

Perhaps no team was more emblematic of the league's power surge than Minnesota. The self-dubbed 'Bomba Squad' saw eight of its hitters crank 20 or more homers, with five of them hitting 30 or more. Unsurprisingly, those figures are both new major league records, too.

Despite the home run surge, the biggest record—Barry Bonds' 73 round-trippers in 2001—went unchallenged. No one got even within shouting distance of 60; Mets first baseman Pete Alonso

RON SCHWANE/GETTY IMAGES

Nelson Cruz and the Twins set a major league record with 307 home runs in 2019.

led the majors with 53 and was the only player to reach the half-century mark. While no player reached the top of the mountain, the route to the peak was more crowded than ever. The juiced ball democratized homers: A total of 129 players hit 20 or more homers in 2019, the most ever in a single season. The same is true of 30-plus homers (58, or 11 more than the previous best year).

Everyone became a power threat, and nothing demonstrated that better than the unexpected names crowding the league leader lists. For every established star like Mike Trout, Christian Yelich or Cody Bellinger who hit 40 or more homers, there was also the Royals' Jorge Soler, who led the American League with 48, or the Reds' Eugenio Suarez, who bashed 29 homers in 72 second-half games to finish the season with 49. Yankees infielder Gleyber Torres smashed 38 homers at 22 years old. Twins outfielder Max Kepler, whose career high in dingers was 20 in 2018, hit 36—in 22 fewer games played. D-backs utility infielder Eduardo Escobar hit 35, while teammate Ketel Marte, who weighs 165 pounds, hit 31. The Twins' Mitch Garver, a catcher with all of seven homers to his name in the previous two seasons, smashed

31 as well. Astros slugger and American League Rookie of the Year Yordan Alvarez hit 27 home runs in just 87 regular-season games after making his major league debut in June.

The result of all this power, though, was a game that was increasingly oriented toward the three true outcomes'—walks, strikeouts and home runs. Just over a third of all plate appearances in 2019 ended with one of those results. For the second straight year, there were more strikeouts than hits, and a new record in strikeout rate (23.0%) was set for a 12th straight season. Unsurprisingly, the league's .252 batting average was the 29th lowest in major league history.

In many ways—home runs, strikeouts, velocity, power, wins, losses, and more—major league baseball is ruled by extremes. It's a game full of more talent than has ever been seen before, featuring historically great performances from players barely old enough to drink alcohol. But it feels like it's changing into something fundamentally different. As 2019 enters the record books, it's worth wondering what direction baseball is going and whether this year will go down as a harbinger of what's to come.

New Era Of Moneyball

Baseball isn't just changing on the field. The business of the sport—the economics that underpin the entire enterprise—has also changed dramatically. Few things have shown that better than the last two offseasons, in which owners and front offices have frozen out free agents and focused on cutting costs instead of adding impact players.

The most recent winter was supposed to be different, thanks to the availability of two of the game's best under-30 players: Bryce Harper and Manny Machado. Both free agents for the first time, the belief for years was that they would create massive bidding wars among the league's elite clubs. There were plenty of other top-flight talents available, too: former Cy Young winner Dallas Keuchel; Craig Kimbrel, one of the league's best closers; former AL MVP Josh Donaldson; ace lefthander Patrick Corbin; three-time All-Star Michael Brantley; ageless slugger Nelson Cruz; power-hitting catcher Yasmani Grandal; and a whole host of excellent relievers, including Adam Ottavino, Andrew Miller, and Zack Britton.

But as fall turned into winter and spring training drew closer, most of those players found their markets unexpectedly soft. Several, including Donaldson and Grandal, ended up settling for one-year deals. Cruz and Brantley inked two-year pacts that seemed well below their market value.

And while Corbin managed to score a sizable, six-year contract from the Nationals, both Keuchel and Kimbrel languished on the market all winter, with neither signing a deal until the middle of the season.

The slowdown affected even Machado and Harper. Despite their pedigrees and accolades, the chase for both was curiously slow and devoid of competition. Big-name spenders like the Yankees, Dodgers and Cubs either sat it out or displayed minimal interest. Ultimately, it took until February for both to sign, and each ended up in an unlikely place. For Machado, it was the usually light-spending Padres who reeled him in on a $300 million deal to make him the new centerpiece of their youth movement. As for Harper, he stayed within his division, trading Nationals whites for Phillies red and, in the process, scoring the biggest free agent contract ever handed out in the history of North American professional sports at $330 million.

But while both stars got paid handsomely, there seemed to be little interest in their services, and neither was able to break the $350 million mark that most pundits expected. The quiet surrounding the rest of the market was curious as well.

Whispers of collusion happened both before and after the season. In early November, Braves general manager Alex Anthopoulos was publicly scolded by the Players Union over comments he'd made during a postseason conference call with media members saying he'd spent time during the postseason "(getting) a sense of what the other clubs are going to look to do in free agency, who might be available in trades." The more likely result is that, as more and more teams have not only embraced high-end analytics but also made them the backbone of their operations, player valuations now exist on a narrow and almost identical band. Front offices are increasingly run and staffed by those with finance backgrounds who have brought their experiences at hedge funds and private equity groups into the world of baseball. The result is a league that sticks to hard principles of cost-benefit and market inefficiencies—one in which anything and everything can be quantified, analyzed and priced. Armed with mountains of data, nearly every team has come to the same conclusion: Free agency is for suckers, and handing out big, long-term deals to all but the best of the best is a fool's gambit. And even for the elite players, teams are content to let them sweat, knowing they have all the leverage.

This only works, though, because of the other trend sweeping through baseball over the last few years: tanking. Emboldened by the success of the

JIM McISAAC/GETTY IMAGES

DJ LeMahieu and the Yankees posted an 18-1 record against the lowly Orioles in 2019.

and hit fewer home runs as a team (149) than Alonso, Suarez and Soler combined.

The gap between MLB's haves and have-nots has rarely, if ever, been larger. Yet, even at the top, there seems to be a visible reluctance to take advantage of the league's soft underbelly. Content to contend with what's already in place—young talent still playing on cheap, pre-arbitration contracts—most of the game's elite squads entered 2019 amid a kind of financial retrenchment. The luxury tax threshold evolved into a kind of soft salary cap, with several high-priced squads doing all they could to stay or get below it. Even the Red Sox, whose spending sprees helped build a World Series winner in 2018, decided to chart a new course, even firing the architect of that championship squad, president of baseball operations Dave Dombrowski, in September.

The venerable Dombrowski, who has been a fixture in front offices since the late 1990s, represents a dying breed among front office executives: someone willing to go for it now, no matter the cost in dollars or prospects, and who puts a title above all else. The buzzword for clubs now is sustainability; everyone wants to copy the Astros and Dodgers, the kings of that particular strategy, who marry baseball smarts with a deep, seemingly inexhaustible farm system and a hefty payroll (albeit ones that could easily be much higher). And why not? Los Angeles won its seventh straight division title in 2019, though it fell to Washington in the National League Division Series, while Houston captured its second American League pennant in three years, winning the World Series in 2017.

How successful other teams will be in recreating that particular setup remains to be seen. You can see the seeds sown in places like Baltimore (now run by Mike Elias, formerly the Astros' director of player development) or San Diego, which has built an enviable collection of under-25 talent. Yet, in the present, those teams remain weak if not outright bad, creating an environment in which the apex predators of the league stay at the top of the food chain. And with little competition from the ranks below them, that makes for a decidedly drama-free season. The only divisions that came down to the wire were the AL Central, where upstart Minnesota held off a Cleveland squad that operated with little urgency in the winter and paid for it dearly during the year, and the NL Central. Otherwise, the expected contenders, with the exception of the Indians and Red Sox, cruised to playoff spots. Much like the NBA, the real battle in MLB now happens during the playoffs.

Astros and Cubs, a number of franchises have decided that there's nothing wrong with losing. The Orioles, Blue Jays, Tigers, White Sox, Royals, Mariners, Marlins and Pirates all came into 2019 with no designs on contending and did next to nothing in terms of free agency. With nearly a third of the league essentially sitting out the winter, and other teams more interested in saving money than financing long-shot bids at a title, there was little competition for the upper class of players, allowing the league's best teams to wait them out. Why create a bidding war out of nothing?

The power imbalance created by several teams effectively forfeiting the season before it even started had a visible effect not only on free agency but also on 2019's results. Four teams—the Astros, Yankees, Twins and Dodgers—won 100 or more games; no previous season had ever featured more than three teams accomplish that feat. Similarly, four teams—the Tigers, Orioles, Royals and Marlins—lost 100 or more games, the first time that has happened since 2002 and only the second time the league has seen that many teams lose that many games. The Yankees went 18–1 against the Orioles, and Cleveland went 18–1 against Detroit. The 114-loss Tigers were an abject disaster: They had just one month with double-digit wins (11 in April), won 10 games combined in June and July, lost 56 of their 75 games after the All-Star break,

CONTINUED ON PAGE 11

PLAYER OF THE YEAR

Justin Verlander Getting Better With Age

BY MATT EDDY

John Smoltz knows a thing or two about limiting hard contact. He allowed a lower opponent average in the 1990s than any starter but Randy Johnson, Pedro Martinez, David Cone, Roger Clemens or Curt Schilling.

But even Smoltz couldn't help gushing about the Astros' Justin Verlander during the FS1 broadcast of Game 2 of the American League Championship Series pitting Houston against the Yankees.

"It's hard to find an average that starts with a '2,'" Smoltz said on the telecast, referring to Verlander's historic season in which he limited hits and baserunners like few starting pitchers in history.

Verlander in 2019 recorded the third-lowest WHIP (0.80) and fifth-lowest opponent average (.172) in the modern era, which stretches back to 1901. The names surrounding him on the lists—Pedro Martinez, Walter Johnson, Nolan Ryan, Greg Maddux—signify everything.

Verlander also posted historically low batting averages with runners on base and against lefthanded batters. He was no slouch when he had the platoon advantage, either. The 36-year-old righthander allowed a .182 average to righthanded hitters. While that is the 72nd-stingiest mark ever, it just wasn't as historic as his other achievements, which include leading the major leagues with 21 wins and 223 innings, as well as the aforementioned opponent average and WHIP.

Additionally, Verlander led all major league

Justin Verlander led the majors in wins (21), innings (223) and WHIP (0.80) in 2019.

VAUGHN RIDLEY/GETTY IMAGES

pitchers with 7.8 wins above replacement, according to Baseball Reference. He placed second only to Astros co-ace Gerrit Cole with 300 strikeouts, while his 2.58 ERA was fourth-lowest in the majors but second-best in the DH league only to Cole.

For Verlander's singular 2019 season, in which he helped propel the Astros to a major league high 107 wins, he is the Baseball America Major League Player of the Year.

But Verlander's overall body of work also gave him a boost, because his greatness is not limited to 2019, nor is it limited to the regular season. Only once has Verlander's club been knocked out in the first round, and four times he has helped pitch his team to the World Series—in 2006 and 2012 with Detroit and 2017 and 2019 with Houston.

When Verlander struck out his 3,000th career batter in his final start of 2019, he effectively punched his ticket to Cooperstown. Every eligible pitcher with 3,000 strikeouts is enshrined in the Hall of Fame, except for special cases Roger Clemens and Curt Schilling. Verlander also notched his 225th career win in his final start of 2019. That total doesn't sound historically high, but he trails only 39-year-old CC Sabathia (251) among pitchers who debuted in the 2000s.

PREVIOUS POY WINNERS

2009: Joe Mauer, C, Twins
2010: Roy Halladay, RHP, Phillies
2011: Matt Kemp, OF, Dodgers
2012: Mike Trout, OF, Angels
2013: Mike Trout, OF, Angels
2014: Clayton Kershaw, LHP, Dodgers
2015: Bryce Harper, OF, Nationals
2016: Mike Trout, OF, Angels
2017: Jose Altuve, 2B, Astros
2018: Mike Trout, OF, Angels
Full list: BaseballAmerica.com/awards

CONTINUED FROM PAGE 9

Standing In The Hall Of Fame

Before turning to what happened on the field, it's worth noting the six newest members of the Baseball Hall of Fame. Two were elected by one of the Hall's era-based committees: Harold Baines and Lee Smith. The former spent 22 years as an itinerant DH for five different teams, though most of his career was played out on Chicago's South Side. Baines finished just shy of the 3,000-hit club with 2,866, to go with 384 homers and a 121 career OPS+. Smith, the one-time saves king who finished his career with 478, couldn't crack Cooperstown on the writers' ballot, but the Hall of Fame's hand-picked committee welcomed him in regardless.

The other four came via the BBWAA, which elected the newest quartet in mid-January. The headliner was Mariano Rivera, the greatest closer in the history of baseball who also became the first man elected to the Hall of Fame with 100% of the vote. Joining him was former teammate Mike Mussina, an ace for the Orioles and Yankees in the 1990s and 2000s. In his final year on the ballot, Edgar Martinez finally broke the 75% threshold—a worthy honor for the best DH the game has ever seen. And the final member of that quartet was Roy Halladay, chosen posthumously after a 2018 plane crash that claimed his life. "Your favorite pitcher's favorite pitcher," as Brandon McCarthy called him, Halladay was an indomitable force for the Blue Jays and Phillies in a relatively short yet sterling career.

The Next Generation

Two of the biggest impacts on the 2019 season came from players who weren't expected to be there in the first place. In San Diego, the Padres carved out a roster spot—on the urging of, among others, the newly acquired Machado—for 20-year-old shortstop Fernando Tatis Jr., the son of 13-year veteran Fernando Sr. and one of the top prospects in the sport. Bearing the build and bat speed of Alex Rodriguez and Carlos Correa, the 6-foot-3, 185-pound Tatis Jr. wasted no time making his mark, homering in his fifth career game and batting .300 in his first month in the majors. Overall, Tatis Jr. hit a sterling .317/.379/.590, cracking 22 homers, stealing 16 bases and dazzling with his speed on the bases and his arm at shortstop. Unfortunately, a back injury in mid-August brought an early end to his season.

That also prematurely finished what had been a thrilling Rookie of the Year race with the National League's other super-freshman. Like Tatis Jr., Alonso was, if not a long shot to make the Mets' Opening Day roster, at least an unlikely choice, given that New York could have stolen some future service time by leaving him in the minors through the first few weeks of the season. Instead, the hulking first baseman went north with the big club and amply rewarded the Mets for placing their faith in him. Already mentioned were the 53 homers he clobbered, both leading the league and setting a new rookie record. But the 24-year-old right-hander was also the heart of New York's lineup, leading the team in OPS+ (148) and bWAR (5.0). He had a knack for the dramatic, too, posting a .945 OPS with runners in scoring position and

CONTINUED ON PAGE 13

AMERICAN LEAGUE STANDINGS

East	W	L	PCT	GB	Manager	General Manager	Attendance	Average	Last Penn.
New York Yankees	103	59	.636	—	Aaron Boone	Brian Cashman	3,304,404	40,794	2009
Tampa Bay Rays	96	66	.593	7	Kevin Cash	Erik Neander	1,178,735	14,649	2008
Boston Red Sox	84	78	.519	19	Alex Cora	D. Dombrowski/E. Romero	2,924,627	36,107	2018
Toronto Blue Jays	67	95	.414	36	Charlie Montoyo	Ross Atkins	1,750,144	21,607	1993
Baltimore Orioles	54	108	.333	49	Brandon Hyde	Mike Elias	1,307,807	15,992	1983

Central	W	L	PCT	GB	Manager	General Manager	Attendance	Average	Last Penn.
Minnesota Twins	101	61	.623	—	Rocco Baldelli	Thad Levine	2,294,152	28,323	1991
Cleveland Indians	93	69	.574	8	Terry Francona	Mike Chernoff	1,738,642	21,402	2016
Chicago White Sox	72	89	.447	29	Rick Renteria	Rick Hahn	1,649,775	20,648	2005
Kansas City Royals	59	103	.364	42	Ned Yost	Dayton Moore	1,479,659	18,353	2015
Detroit Tigers	47	114	.292	54	Ron Gardenhire	Al Avila	1,501,430	18,545	2012

West	W	L	PCT	GB	Manager	General Manager	Attendance	Average	Last Penn.
Houston Astros	107	55	.660	—	A.J. Hinch	Jeff Luhnow	2,857,367	35,276	2019
Oakland Athletics	97	65	.599	10	Bob Melvin	David Forst	1,662,211	20,521	1990
Texas Rangers	78	84	.481	29	Chris Woodward	Jon Daniels	2,132,994	26,333	2011
Los Angeles Angels	72	90	.444	35	Brad Ausmus	Billy Eppler	3,019,012	37,272	2002
Seattle Mariners	68	94	.420	39	Scott Servais	Jerry Dipoto	1,791,863	22,122	Never

Wild Card Game: Rays defeated Athletics. **Division Series:** Astros defeated Rays 3-2 and Yankees defeated Twins 3-0 in best-of-five series. **Championship Series:** Astros defeated Yankees 4-2 in a best-of-seven series.

ROOKIE OF THE YEAR

The Powerful Pete Alonso

BY ANTHONY MCCARRON

First baseman Pete Alonso smashed a rookie-record 53 home runs, clicked with a city and its fans well beyond simply blasting moonshots, coined a slogan or two and perhaps inspired a comedy genius to reboot a classic sitcom.

Oh, and the 24-year-old also infused the Mets' clubhouse with a sincere, caring spirit, mauled the club's record book, made the All-Star Game, won the Home Run Derby, showed the scouting community he had been underestimated, bolstered his defense at first base and became the "Polar Bear."

What a first season for Alonso, the unanimous selection as the Rookie of the Year.

"I couldn't have asked for a better rookie year," Alonso said. "This is a fantasy come true."

The reality, though, took hard work, player development and the guts to make a difficult decision. First-year Mets general manager Brodie Van Wagenen could have kept Alonso at Triple-A in April to retain an extra year of contractual control in 2025, but instead he carried Alonso on the Opening Day roster.

"Pete had an extraordinary season," Van Wagenen said. "More importantly, he demonstrated tremendous work ethic and rare leadership qualities for a young player. He genuinely prioritized winning games over his historic personal pursuits. He was a big part of our team's success in 2019, and he is part of a talented core that will impact the Mets for years to come."

Alonso started the season ranked as the No. 48 prospect in baseball, a power hitter with a perhaps suspect glove. But he led the major leagues in home runs, finished third with 348 total bases, tied for third with 85 extra-base hits and was fourth with 120 RBIs.

Along the way, he became the first rookie and the first Mets player to lead the majors in home runs. There was still more than a month left when he broke the club record for homers, 41, which had been shared by Carlos Beltran and Todd Hundley.

And on the second to last day of the

Pete Alonso set an MLB rookie reccord with 53 home runs in 2019.

JIM MCISAAC/GETTY IMAGES

season, Alonso broke Aaron Judge's major league rookie record for homers. Tears sprang to Alonso's eyes when he took the field for the following half-inning.

"To be part of major league baseball history, to be No. 1 out of every single guy to play the game, it's humbling and it's such a ridiculously awesome feeling," Alonso said.

Still, there was some doubt about Alonso's overall potential, even with his power, and Alonso's prospect ratings certainly didn't foreshadow his historic rookie season. In spring training, Baseball America quoted a scout who questioned Alonso's hitting prowess and said he "can't recall him ever hitting a slider."

Alonso clearly relished the vindication his season has brought: "(Scouts) also said I couldn't hit a slider," Alonso said. "That is cool how the tables have turned."

The whole season was cool, worthy of Baseball America's Rookie of the Year award.

PREVIOUS ROY WINNERS

2009: Andrew McCutchen, OF, Pirates
2010: Jason Heyward, OF, Braves
2011: Jeremy Hellickson, RHP, Rays
2012: Mike Trout, OF, Angels
2013: Jose Fernandez, RHP, Marlins
2014: Jose Abreu, 1B, White Sox
2015: Kris Bryant, 3B, Cubs
2016: Corey Seager, SS, Dodgers
2017: Aaron Judge, OF, Yankees
2018: Shohei Ohtani, RHP/DH, Angels
Full list: BaseballAmerica.com/awards

a .956 mark in late and close situations. And he provided the best moment of all-star week, as well, outlasting Vladimir Guerrero Jr. in a titanic Home Run Derby bout that went on long into the night.

Few debuts were as anticipated as that of Guerrero Jr., the son of Hall of Famer Vladimir Guerrero Sr. and the consensus No. 1 prospect in baseball. As a teenager, he demolished the minor leagues in 2018, only to remain stuck in Double-A and Triple-A while the Blue Jays lost games without him. He was injured early in spring training in 2019, so the Blue Jays were able to avoid the controversy that would have come with leaving him in the minor leagues to begin the year. Instead, he opened his season on a rehab stint with high Class A Dunedin in the Florida State League. But after roughly three weeks (but just nine games) at Triple-A Buffalo spent torturing International League pitchers, "Vladito" finally got his chance once enough time had passed to guarantee that the Blue Jays would get one additional year of team control from him. Perhaps the hype was a bit too high, though, as Guerrero Jr. hit .272/.339/.433 with 15 homers and a 106 OPS+ in his first taste of the majors. Then again, those numbers look a little better when you consider that he didn't turn 20 years old until mid-March. In an interesting turn of fate, Guerrero Jr. was also the first of what turned out to be a trio of second-generation stars in Toronto, joined by Cavan Biggio, son of Craig, and Bo Bichette, son of Dante Sr.

Tatis Jr., Alonso and Guerrero Jr.—and the aforementioned Alvarez—weren't the only rookies to stand out, though. Keston Hiura joined the Brewers midway through the year and provided an instant jolt of offense. He led all rookie second basemen with 23 doubles and 19 home runs, hitting .303/.368/.570 in 84 games. Tampa Bay's Brandon Lowe made an early bid for AL Rookie of the Year honors by posting a 124 OPS+ before an injury struck him down in July. Eloy Jimenez, a top-five prospect along with Tatis and Guerrero Jr., found his power stroke late and finished with 31 homers, giving hope to the White Sox's rebuild. Tommy Edman took over as the Cardinals' starting third baseman down the stretch, hitting .304 and helping St. Louis reach the NL Championship Series. Similarly, Will Smith emerged as the Dodgers' top catcher in the second half, cranking 15 homers in 54 games as the Dodgers clinched yet another NL West title. Righthander Chris Paddack emerged as the Padres' ace, posting a 3.33 ERA and 9.8 strikeouts per nine innings at the tender age of 23. Righthander Mike Soroka also topped the Braves' rotation, leading all rookies with a 2.68 ERA, the fifth-best mark in baseball. Soroka proved especially adept at keeping the ball in the park—a trait that can carry a lot of weight in today's game—and his home run rate of 0.72 per nine innings was the second lowest in the majors. And finally, outfielder Bryan Reynolds was one of the few bright spots on a dismal Pirates team, slashing .314/.377/.503 and briefly making a run at becoming the first National League rookie to win a battling title before ultimately coming up short in the season's final month.

Managerial Musical Chairs

NATIONAL LEAGUE STANDINGS

East	W	L	PCT	GB	Manager	General Manager	Attendance	Average	Last Penn.
Atlanta Braves	97	65	.599	—	Brian Snitker	Alex Anthopoulos	2,655,100	32,779	1999
Washington Nationals	93	69	.574	4	Dave Martinez	Mike Rizzo	2,259,781	27,899	2019
New York Mets	86	76	.531	11	Mickey Callaway	Brodie Van Wagenen	2,442,532	30,161	2015
Philadelphia Phillies	81	81	.500	16	Gabe Kapler	Matt Klentak	2,727,421	33,672	2009
Miami Marlins	57	105	.352	40	Don Mattingly	Michael Hill	811,302	10,016	2003
Central	**W**	**L**	**PCT**	**GB**	**Manager**	**General Manager**	**Attendance**	**Average**	**Last Penn.**
St. Louis Cardinals	91	71	.562	—	Mike Shildt	Mike Girsch	3,480,393	42,968	2013
Milwaukee Brewers	89	73	.549	2	Craig Counsell	David Stearns	2,923,333	36,091	1982 (AL)
Chicago Cubs	84	78	.519	7	Joe Maddon	Jed Hoyer	3,094,865	38,208	2016
Cincinnati Reds	75	87	.463	16	David Bell	Nick Krall	1,808,685	22,329	1990
Pittsburgh Pirates	69	93	.426	22	Clint Hurdle	Neal Huntington	1,491,439	18,413	1979
West	**W**	**L**	**PCT**	**GB**	**Manager**	**General Manager**	**Attendance**	**Average**	**Last Penn.**
Los Angeles Dodgers	106	56	.654	—	Dave Roberts	Andrew Friedman	3,974,309	49,066	2018
Arizona Diamondbacks	85	77	.525	21	Torey Lovullo	Mike Hazen	2,135,510	26,364	2001
San Francisco Giants	77	85	.475	29	Bruce Bochy	Farhan Zaidi	2,707,760	33,429	2014
Colorado Rockies	71	91	.438	35	A. Green/R. Barajas	A.J. Preller	2,993,244	36,954	2007
San Diego Padres	70	92	.432	36	Bud Black	Jeff Bridich	2,396,399	29,585	1998

Wild Card Game: Nationals defeated Brewers. **Division Series:** Nationals defeated Dodgers 3-2 and Cardinals defeated Braves 3-2 in best-of-five series. **Championship Series:** Nationals defeated Cardinals 4-0 in a best-of-seven series.

There were new faces leading the charge from the dugouts, as well. After a second straight sub-.500 season in 2018, Minnesota dumped Paul Molitor for Rocco Baldelli, a member of the Rays' front office only a decade removed from his playing days. Despite his lack of time spent drawing up lineups and making pitching changes, Baldelli proved a savvy hire. His revamped coaching staff leaned heavily on analytics and data, which helped transform a middling pitching staff into one of the league's better units. Under Baldelli, the Twins surprisingly took the AL Central, winning 101 games for just the second time in franchise history en route to their first division title since 2010.

The rest of MLB's rookie managers didn't fare as well, though. As part of a complete overhaul, the Orioles said goodbye to veteran skipper Buck Showalter and replaced him with Cubs bench coach and Joe Maddon acolyte Brandon Hyde. In the early stages of what promises to be a long rebuild, the O's handed Hyde the keys to a car missing all its wheels, a few doors, pieces of the engine, and the radio. The result: 108 losses, a last-place finish in the AL East, and a pitching staff that gave up the most home runs in league history—a staggering 305.

Things weren't much better for the division's other first-year manager, with Toronto transitioning from John Gibbons to longtime Rays coach Charlie Montoyo. Despite the presence of those highly talented sons of big leaguers in Guerrero Jr., Biggio and Bichette, the Blue Jays slumped to 95 losses, their most since 2004, due in large part to a thin pitching staff that jettisoned ace Marcus Stroman to the Mets at the trade deadline.

The year started more promisingly for another new addition, with Dodgers third-base coach Chris Woodward taking over for Jeff Banister in Texas and leading the Rangers into the AL's wild card chase. Their luck gave out during a rough summer, as they went 21–32 in July and August to fall out of the race, though they finished 11 games better than 2018's record in the process. Elsewhere in the AL West, the Angels turned to Brad Ausmus to replace Mike Scioscia, hoping the former Tigers boss would see better results in a new city. But the second time didn't prove to be any better than the first for the longtime catcher, who oversaw a team that won just 72 games. Ausmus was fired by the Angels after just one season at the helm in late September.

The National League saw just one new name join the managerial ranks, but he too had a season to forget. In Cincinnati, the accelerated and hopeful jump into contention was entrusted to David

2018 NL MVP Christian Yelich put up yet another MVP-worthy campaign in 2019.

Bell, son of Buddy Bell and formerly high up in San Francisco's front office. But the Reds' attempts to buy their way out of the basement came to naught, as they languished near the bottom of the NL Central for most of the year. Cincinnati finished with 87 losses—an improvement, admittedly, over the last few years, but nowhere near the postseason and the franchise's sixth consecutive losing season.

Baseball At Its Best

The 2019 season wasn't just about home runs for some players. A select few made the jump into the league's top echelon, emerging as elite, MVP-caliber superstars—none moreso than Cody Bellinger and Christian Yelich.

For Bellinger, a sterling first season in which he made the all-star team and won NL Rookie of the Year honors gave way to a disappointing sophomore campaign in 2018, one plagued by strikeouts and a big dip in power. Yet, thanks to a revamped swing more reminiscent of his rookie season, Bellinger rediscovered his stroke, swatting 47 homers and hitting .305/.406/.629. The Dodgers' center fielder, who was hitting .400 or better up until late May, posted a terrific 9.0 bWAR, the best mark on the senior circuit.

Not to be outdone, Yelich proved that his breakout second half in Milwaukee was no fluke, hitting .329/.429/.671 with 44 homers and 30 steals—the first 40-homer/30-steal campaign since teammate Ryan Braun in 2012. He led the NL in batting average, on-base percentage and OPS+ (179), and

ALL-ROOKIE TEAM 2019

Pos	Player, Team	Age	AB	AVG	OBP	SLG	2B	HR	RBI	SB	Rundown
C	Will Smith, Dodgers	24	170	.253	.337	.571	9	15	42	2	Led all rookie catchers with 15 HRs and .571 slugging
1B	Pete Alonso, Mets	24	597	.260	.358	.583	30	53	120	1	Hit rookie-record 53 HRs, led NL in extra-base hits (85)
2B	Keston Hiura, Brewers	22	314	.303	.368	.570	23	19	49	9	Led all rookie 2B with 23 doubles and 19 HRs
3B	Tommy Edman, Cardinals	24	326	.302	.350	.500	17	11	36	15	.850 OPS ranked seventh among rookies with 81+ games
SS	Fernando Tatis Jr., Padres	20	334	.317	.379	.590	13	22	53	16	Hit 22 HRs and stole 16 bases despite playing 84 games
OF	Eloy Jimenez, White Sox	22	468	.267	.315	.513	18	31	79	0	Ranked second among rookies with 31 HRs
OF	Bryan Reynolds, Pirates	24	491	.314	.377	.503	37	16	68	3	Finished top 10 in NL in average (.314) and doubles (37)
OF	Yordan Alvarez, Astros	22	313	.313	.412	.655	26	27	78	0	1.067 OPS ranked fifth in MLB from date of his debut
DH	Vladimir Guerrero Jr., Blue Jays	20	464	.272	.339	.433	26	15	69	0	One of just five rookies with at least 125 hits and 15 HRs

Pos	Pitcher, Team	Age	W	L	SV	ERA	IP	SO	BB	Rundown
SP	Mike Soroka, Braves	21	13	4	0	2.68	175	142	41	2.68 ERA led all rookie starters and ranked fifth in MLB
SP	Dakota Hudson, Cardinals	24	16	7	1	3.35	175	136	86	56.9 percent ground ball rate was highest in the majors
SP	Chris Paddack, Padres	23	9	7	0	3.33	141	153	31	Ranked second among rookies (min. 100 IP) with 3.33 ERA
SP	John Means, Orioles	26	12	11	0	3.60	155	121	38	Baltimore's lone All-Star Game representative; led team in wins
SP	Sandy Alcantara, Marlins	23	6	14	0	3.88	197	151	81	Led all rookies with 197.1 IP; earned first All-Star election
RP	Nick Anderson, Marlins/Rays	28	5	4	0	3.32	65	110	18	Ranked second in MLB with 41.7 strikeout rate

he led the majors in slugging percentage and put up 7.1 bWAR. His odds of winning back-to-back MVP awards, though, took a serious hit when he suffered a fractured kneecap in early September, costing him the last three weeks of the season.

Yelich, though, wasn't alone in marrying power and speed. In Atlanta, outfielder Ronald Acuña Jr. followed up his brilliant first season with an even better second effort, slashing .280/.365/.518, homering 41 times, and leading the NL with 37 stolen bases—all at just 21 years old. Acuña Jr. flirted with becoming the first major league player —and just the fifth all-time—to record 40 or more home runs in a season while also stealing at least 40 bases since the Nationals' Alfonso Soriano in 2006, but a sore hip during the final week of the regular season left him three steals short. And yet Acuña Jr. may not even be the most impressive youngster in his own division, battling as he is with Washington's Juan Soto. At a mere 20 years of age, Soto hit a superb .282/.401/.548 with 34 homers, 12 steals, a 138 OPS+ and 4.7 bWAR. He's just the fifth player ever to post two seasons with an on-base percentage of .400 or better before turning 21, alongside exclusive company such as Mel Ott, Jimmie Foxx and Ted Williams.

The AL wasn't lacking for superstars, either. In Houston, Alex Bregman broke out with his best season to date, hitting .296/.423/.592 with 41 homers, a league-high 119 walks and an AL-best 8.4 bWAR to give the Astros yet another MVP-caliber bat. Third base produced more than its fair share of talent in 2019. In Oakland, Matt Chapman matched his Gold Glove-worthy defense with a career-best 36 homers, while Boston's 23-year-old Rafael Devers topped the AL with 54 doubles, hitting .311/.361/.555 with 32 homers.

And then there was Mike Trout. Rewarded with a $430 million contract extension before the season began that will make him an Angel for life, the best player in baseball was once again, well, the best player in baseball. The 28-year-old center fielder slashed an absurd .291/.438/.645 with a career-high 45 homers, a league-best 183 OPS+, and 8.3 bWAR—the sixth out of eight full seasons in which he's broken the 8.0 mark. Those numbers would have looked even better, too, had Trout not suffered a foot injury that cost him most of September and ended his season prematurely.

All of those terrific performances happened alongside arguably one of the finest pitching years in baseball history, put together by Astros right-hander Gerrit Cole. Over 212.1 innings, the former No. 1 overall pick out of UCLA put up a 2.50 ERA and struck out 326 batters, or 13.8 strikeouts per nine innings—the highest mark any starter has ever recorded in major league history. Likewise with his 39.9% strikeout rate, which was the best figure of any starter ever, some two points better than Pedro Martinez's legendary 1999 season. And from the beginning of June through the end of the season, Cole was arguably the best pitcher who ever lived, posting a 1.73 ERA in 140.2 innings and striking out 214 batters. That stretch included nine straight starts with double-digit strikeouts to wrap up the year—one that's set him up to receive a monster payday when he reaches free agency this winter.

Plenty of other starters—including Cole's Houston teammate Justin Verlander, Mets ace Jacob deGrom, Nationals righthander Max Scherzer and some emerging young arms like the Indians' Shane Bieber, the White Sox's Lucas Giolito and the Cardinals' Jack Flaherty—also had years to remember.

Milestones & More

There was plenty of history made in 2019, starting with a pair of veteran pitchers still capable of making magic even in the late stages of their careers. Amid a campaign that will rank as one of his best ever, Verlander continued to cement himself as a future Hall of Famer by tossing the third no-hitter of his career, blanking the Blue Jays on Sept. 1. Over nine innings in Toronto, the 36-year-old righthander came within a walk of perfection, allowing only one baserunner and striking out 14 batters. It's just the 12th nine-inning no-hitter ever in which a pitcher has struck out 14 or more, and in the process, Verlander became only the sixth pitcher in MLB history to throw three or more no-hitters, joining Nolan Ryan, Cy Young, Bob Feller, Sandy Koufax and Larry Corcoran. This was just a piece of Verlander's season which included a career-high 300 strikeouts in a major league-best 223 innings. He also led the majors in wins (21) for the third time in his career, and his 0.80 WHIP and 5.5 hits allowed per nine innings were the best marks in baseball.

Verlander also picked up career strikeout No. 3,000, accomplishing that feat in his last start of the season on Sept. 28 against the Angels. In doing so, he became the 18th man to reach that number—but not the first in 2019. That honor belonged to CC Sabathia. The 38-year-old lefthander announced before the season that his 19th year in the majors would be his last, bringing an end to a career that had seen him win a Cy Young award and a World Series ring while playing for the Indians, Brewers and Yankees. But before hanging up his spikes, the big southpaw secured his membership into one of the game's most exclusive clubs on April 30, punching out the D-backs' John Ryan Murphy in Arizona for his 3,000th strikeout.

Though Sabathia was saddled with knee troubles that limited him to 107.1 innings and a 4.95 ERA, he was still able to climb the record books before it was all over. His 251 career wins are tied with Bob Gibson for 47th all-time, and his 3,577.1 innings are good for 61st in baseball history. In strikeouts, his 3,093 whiffs are 16th in major league history, just behind Curt Schilling and ahead of John Smoltz, though Verlander is a good bet to pass him before it's all said and done.

Another future Hall of Famer also reached some big round numbers in 2019. Though Albert Pujols' prime is in the past, he can still put a charge in a ball. To an already loaded resume, he added career home run No. 650, which he hit on July 28 against the Orioles—the same day he also reached

CC Sabathia won 251 games and struck out 3,093 batters in his 19-year career.

ELSA/GETTY IMAGES

650 career doubles. That makes him the only player ever to reach both of those marks; only two others—Barry Bonds and Hank Aaron—are even in the 600-600 Club. Pujols, Bonds, Aaron, Alex Rodriguez, Babe Ruth and Willie Mays are the only players to hit 650 or more homers.

On top of that, Pujols also recorded the 2,000th RBI of his long and illustrious career, that coming on May 9 against Detroit. That club is also a small one: Pujols, Rodriguez and Aaron are its only members. And on Aug. 14, he became the all-time hits leader among foreign-born players by collecting No. 3,167, passing fellow Dominican Adrian Beltre in the process. It was an emotional year overall for Pujols, who also made his return to St. Louis for the first time since leaving the Cardinals after the 2011 season.

Joining Pujols in the history books was one of his teammates, Shohei Ohtani. Recovered from Tommy John surgery that put a premature end to his rookie season in 2018, Ohtani was unable to return to being a two-way player, as his elbow was not fully healed enough to resume pitching. He did, however, live up to his billing at the plate, slashing .286/.343/.505 with 18 homers in 106 games. But his biggest moment came against the Rays on June 14, as he hit for the cycle, becoming the first Japanese-born player to accomplish that feat in the majors. Ohtani homered in the first inning, doubled in the third, knocked out the ever-elusive triple in the fifth (after a brief power outage at Tropicana Field, no less) and finished it up with a single in the seventh.

Ohtani's cycle was the second of the year in baseball, following that of Twins shortstop Jorge Polanco on April 5, though it wasn't the last. Four other players joined him and Polanco: Cleveland's Jake Bauers (June 14 against Detroit), Washington's Trea Turner (July 23 against Colorado, and the second of his career), Baltimore's Jonathan Villar (Aug. 5 against the Yankees) and Toronto's Cavan Biggio (Sept. 17 against Baltimore).

In terms of other memorable games, Verlander wasn't the only pitcher to toss a no-hitter. On May 7, Oakland righthander Mike Fiers blanked the Reds at home for the second no-no of his career. There were also combined no-hitters for the Angels (Taylor Cole and Felix Peña on July 12 against the Mariners) and the Astros (Aaron Sanchez, Will Harris, Joe Biagini and Chris Devenski, also against the Mariners, on Aug. 3). It was that kind of year for Seattle, which became the first team to get no-hit twice in the same season since the Mets in 2015.

And from the Department of Perseverance: With his appearance for the Blue Jays on May 15, veteran righthander Edwin Jackson set a new MLB record for most clubs played for in a single career. Toronto represents his 14th different team on a path that's taken him all over the country (and into Canada) over the last 17 years.

Gone, But Not Forgotten

Tragedy struck baseball in the heart of the season. On the afternoon of July 1, Angels pitcher Tyler Skaggs was discovered dead in a Texas hotel room during a road trip to face the Rangers. The 27-year-old lefthander was 7-7, 4.29 on the season before he passed away, and his loss was a huge shock to the baseball community and a massive blow to Los Angeles. With heavy hearts, the Angels and Rangers postponed their scheduled game that day, and the response from around the league was swift and heartfelt. Countless players either wore Skaggs' No. 45, such as his former teammate Patrick Corbin, or wrote it, or his initials, on their jerseys or caps in the days after his death.

As for the Angels, they couldn't grieve for long, returning to the field on July 2 to play Texas. With Skaggs' No. 45 painted on the mound at Globe Life Park and his jersey hanging in the dugout, Los Angeles won its first game without him, beating back tears the whole time. Two weeks later, at home for the first time since his death, the Angels took the field against the Mariners all wearing No.

45 jerseys. With Skaggs' mother, Debbie, throwing out the first pitch, Los Angeles went out that day and no-hit Seattle, on the day before what would've been their teammate's 28th birthday.

CONTINUED ON PAGE 19

AMERICAN LEAGUE BEST TOOLS

A Baseball America survey of American League managers, conducted at midseason 2019, ranked players with the best tools.

Best Hitter
1. Mike Trout, Angels
2. Alex Bregman, Astros
3. Michael Brantley, Astros

Best Power
1. Joey Gallo, Rangers
2. Aaron Judge, Yankees
3. Mike Trout, Angels

Best Bunter
1. Billy Hamilton, Royals
2. Dee Gordon, Mariners
3. Delino DeShields Jr., Rangers

Best Strike-Zone Judgment
1. Mike Trout, Angels
2. Alex Bregman, Astros
3. Carlos Santana, Indians

Best Hit-And-Run Artist
1. Elvis Andrus, Rangers
2. Whit Merrifield, Royals
3. David Fletcher, Angels

Best Baserunner
1. Adalberto Mondesi, Royals
2. Whit Merrifield, Royals
3. Billy Hamilton, Royals

Fastest Baserunner
1. Billy Hamilton, Royals
2. Terrance Gore, Royals
3. Byron Buxton, Twins

Most Exciting Player
1. Mike Trout, Angels
2. Mookie Betts, Red Sox
3. Alex Bregman, Astros

Best Pitcher
1. Justin Verlander, Astros
2. Charlie Morton, Rays
3. Gerrit Cole, Astros

Best Fastball
1. Justin Verlander, Astros
2. Aroldis Chapman, Yankees
3. Gerrit Cole, Astros

Best Curveball
1. Charlie Morton, Rays
2. Trevor Bauer, Indians
3. Blake Snell, Rays

Best Slider
1. Chris Sale, Red Sox
2. Justin Verlander, Astros
3. Ryan Pressly, Astros

Best Changeup
1. Yonny Chirinos, Rays
2. Mike Minor, Rangers
3. John Means, Orioles

Best Control
1. Justin Verlander, Astros
2. Chris Sale, Red Sox
3. Mike Leake, Mariners

Best Pickoff Move
1. Matt Boyd, Tigers
2. Marcus Stroman, Blue Jays
3. Zach Plesac, Indians

Best Reliever
1. Aroldis Chapman, Yankees
2. Brad Hand, Indians
3. Ryan Pressly, Astros

Best Defensive Catcher
1. Christian Vazquez, Red Sox
2. Roberto Perez, Indians
3. Jeff Mathis, Rangers

Best Defensive 1B
1. Matt Olson, Athletics
2. Mitch Moreland, Red Sox
3. Ronald Guzman, Rangers

Best Defensive 2B
1. DJ LeMahieu, Yankees
2. Brandon Lowe, Rays
3. Jose Altuve, Astros

Best Defensive 3B
1. Matt Chapman, Athletics
2. Alex Bregman, Astros
3. Gio Urshela, Yankees

Best Defensive SS
1. Francisco Lindor, Indians
2. Andrelton Simmons, Angels
3. Marcus Semien, Athletics

Best Infield Arm
1. Matt Chapman, Athletics
2. Carlos Correa, Astros
3. Andrelton Simmons, Angels

Best Defensive OF
1. Byron Buxton, Twins
2. Kevin Kiermaier, Rays
3. Jackie Bradley Jr., Red Sox

Best Outfield Arm
1. Ramon Laureano, Athletics
2. Kevin Kiermaier, Rays
3. Jackie Bradley Jr., Red Sox

Best Manager
1. Bob Melvin, Athletics
2. Kevin Cash, Rays
3. A.J. Hinch, Astros

ORGANIZATION OF THE YEAR

Rays Rebuilt Without A Full Teardown

BY J.J. COOPER

In an era when complete teardowns are viewed as the logical first step to build toward playoff success, the Rays took another tack.

Tampa Bay is proving that it's possible to build an exceptional farm system and win in the big leagues without a slew of top five draft picks.

Going into 2020, the Rays have the best prospect in baseball (shortstop Wander Franco), one of the best farm systems in baseball and a 96-win MLB team. And they have done it while picking in the top 10 in the draft only once in the past decade.

The Rays made it back to the postseason for the first time since 2013 with a 96-win season. After beating the Oakland A's in the AL wild card game, the Rays fell to the Astros in five games in the Division Series.

That quick playoff exit should not be a one-time trip. The Rays have the young talent to continue to improve as the 2020s arrive.

They have done by developing homegrown talent, improving their ability to scout and sign international amateurs and a steady stream of creative trades that rely heavily on their pro scouting and analytics departments.

"I think we all realize we do compete in the big-boy division," Rays director of pro scouting Kevin Ibach said. "The lifeblood of the Rays has always been our farm system. The day we start running out of those prospects, we're not going to be able to go out and buy them on the free agent market."

Tampa Bay continues to face severe headwinds. Their stadium situation is one of the

VP of Baseball Operations Erik Neander
and the Rays returned to the playoffs.

worst in baseball, and attempts to build a new one in the St. Petersburg/Tampa area have failed. The team has proposed the idea of splitting their schedule between Montreal and St. Petersburg in future seasons, although such a plan would be difficult to execute.

The Rays have continually ranked near the bottom of baseball in payroll. But while some large-revenue teams tore down their clubs to gather top draft picks in rebuilds, the Rays managed to regroup after their impressive 2008-2013 run without a long run of futility.

The Rays made the World Series in 2008 and they won 90 or more games five times in six seasons from 2008-2013. David Price was traded in 2014 as the team worked to restock the farm system.

The team won only 77 games that year, and they did win only 68 in 2016, but that 2016 season was their only trip to the AL East basement. They finished the decade winning 90 or more games five times.

Time will tell whether the Rays can continue to contend in the difficult AL East, but they are positioned to win 90 or more games next year for a third straight season and perhaps make a deep playoff run.

PREVIOUS WINNERS

2009: Philadelphia Phillies
2010: San Francisco Giants
2011: St. Louis Cardinals
2012: Cincinnati Reds
2013: St. Louis Cardinals
2014: Kansas City Royals
2015: Pittsburgh Pirates
2016: Chicago Cubs
2017: Los Angeles Dodgers
2018: Milwaukee Brewers
Full list: BaseballAmerica.com/awards

The tragedy took an even deeper and sharper turn when it was revealed in October that Skaggs' death had been the result of choking on his own vomit due to an overdose brought on by a combination of oxycodone, fentanyl and alcohol. Even worse, news later emerged that Skaggs had been provided the oxycodone, an illegal opioid, by an Angels team employee.

Skaggs wasn't the only member of the baseball community to pass away in 2019. In February, Frank Robinson—two-time MVP, World Series champion, Hall of Famer, longtime manager and former MLB executive—died at the age of 83. Two weeks later, Don Newcombe, the 1956 NL MVP and Cy Young award winner and a four-time All-Star with the Dodgers, died at the age of 92. In May, former Cubs and Red Sox star Bill Buckner, infamous for his crucial error in Game 6 of the 1986 World Series, passed away at age 69. In July, Jim Bouton, best known for "Ball Four", his controversial and best-selling book on his life in baseball, died at age 80. And in October, the umpiring ranks lost two members: Eric Cooper, who died from a blood clot at age 52, and the retired Chuck Meriwether, dead at 63.

On-Field Ongoings

The season itself played out with little suspense, as the league's elite teams grabbed hold of playoff spots and never surrendered. Most divisions were decided relatively early. The Yankees held off the Rays despite a plethora of injuries, riding career years from Torres and DJ LeMahieu to 103 wins and the franchise's first AL East crown since 2012. In the AL Central, Minnesota outlasted Cleveland for its first division win since 2010. Out west, the Astros cruised to a third straight first-place finish, boosted by a blockbuster trade for D-backs ace righthander Zack Greinke that was finalized in the final minutes of the July 31 deadline. That helped Houston hold off Oakland, which had to settle for the first wild card spot, with Tampa taking the second.

In the NL, the Braves took control of the East in mid-May, wrestling the division away from Harper and the Phillies, who got off to a hot start but fell into a long losing streak that month and never fully recovered. The Dodgers, meanwhile, were never challenged in the NL West, securing that division for the seventh straight year. But in the NL Central, the Cubs, Brewers and Cardinals all battled for first place up until the final week of the season. Chicago bowed out first, falling apart

NATIONAL LEAGUE BEST TOOLS

A Baseball America survey of National League managers, conducted at midseason 2019, ranked players with the best tools.

Best Hitter
1. Christian Yelich, Brewers
2. Cody Bellinger, Dodgers
3. Nolan Arenado, Rockies

Best Power
1. Pete Alonso, Mets
2. Cody Bellinger, Dodgers
3. Christian Yelich, Brewers

Best Bunter
1. Victor Robles, Nationals
2. Kolten Wong, Cardinals
3. Brandon Belt, Giants

Best Strike-Zone Judgment
1. Joey Votto, Reds
2. Freddie Freeman, Braves
3. Anthony Rendon, Nationals

Best Hit-And-Run Artist
1. Yadier Molina, Cardinals
2. Jeff McNeil, Mets
3. Jean Segura, Phillies

Best Baserunner
1. Trea Turner, Nationals
2. Kolten Wong, Cardinals
3. Jarrod Dyson, D-backs

Fastest Baserunner
1. Trea Turner, Nationals
2. Tim Locastro, D-backs
3. Garrett Hampson, Rockies

Most Exciting Player
1. Cody Bellinger, Dodgers
2. Christian Yelich, Brewers
3. Ronald Acuña Jr., Braves

Best Pitcher
1. Max Scherzer, Nationals
2. Jacob deGrom, Mets
3. Zack Greinke, D-backs

Best Fastball
1. Josh Hader, Brewers
2. Walker Buehler, Dodgers
3. Jacob deGrom, Mets

Best Curveball
1. Aaron Nola, Phillies
2. Clayton Kershaw, Dodgers
3. Stephen Strasburg, Nationals

Best Slider
1. Max Scherzer, Nationals
2. Patrick Corbin, Nationals
3. Jacob deGrom, Mets

Best Changeup
1. Luis Castillo, Reds
2. Hyun-Jin Ryu, Dodgers
3. Zack Greinke, D-backs

Best Control
1. Hyun-Jin Ryu, Dodgers
2. Zack Greinke, D-backs
3. Kyle Hendricks, Cubs

Best Pickoff Move
1. Julio Teheran, Braves
2. Eric Lauer, Padres
3. Max Fried, Braves

Best Reliever
1. Josh Hader, Brewers
2. Kirby Yates, Padres
3. Will Smith, Giants

Best Defensive Catcher
1. J.T. Realmuto, Phillies
2. Austin Hedges, Padres
3. Yasmani Grandal, Brewers

Best Defensive 1B
1. Anthony Rizzo, Cubs
2. Paul Goldschmidt, Cardinals
3. Freddie Freeman, Braves

Best Defensive 2B
1. Kolten Wong, Cardinals
2. Ketel Marte, D-backs
3. Ozzie Albies, Braves

Best Defensive 3B
1. Nolan Arenado, Rockies
2. Anthony Rendon, Nationals
3. Manny Machado, Padres

Best Defensive SS
1. Nick Ahmed, D-backs
2. Trevor Story, Rockies
3. Javier Baez, Cubs

Best Infield Arm
1. Javier Baez, Cubs
2. Fernando Tatis Jr., Padres
3. Nolan Arendado, Rockies

Best Defensive OF
1. Harrison Bader, Cardinals
2. Cody Bellinger, Dodgers
3. Lorenzo Cain, Brewers

Best Outfield Arm
1. Cody Bellinger, Dodgers
2. Hunter Renfroe, Padres
3. Starling Marte, Pirates

Best Manager
1. Dave Roberts, Dodgers
2. Craig Counsell, Brewers
3. Bruce Bochy, Giants

in September and missing the playoffs entirely. From there, St. Louis was able to hold off a surging Milwaukee squad that, despite losing Yelich early in September, won 18 of 20 down the stretch.

CONTINUED ON PAGE 21

Mike Trout led the majors in on-base percentage (.438) in 2019.

Gerrit Cole led all MLB pitchers with 326 strikeouts in 2019.

FIRST TEAM

Pos.	Player, Team	AVG	OBP	SLG	AB	R	H	2B	3B	HR	RBI	BB	SO	SB	CS
C	J.T. Realmuto, Marlins	.275	.328	.493	538	92	148	36	3	25	83	41	123	9	1
1B	Pete Alonso, Mets	.260	.358	.583	597	103	155	30	2	53	120	72	183	1	0
2B	Ketel Marte, D-backs	.329	.389	.592	569	97	187	36	9	32	92	53	86	10	2
3B	Alex Bregman, Astros	.296	.423	.592	554	122	164	26	0	41	108	56	131	5	1
SS	Marcus Semien, Athletics	.285	.369	.522	657	123	187	43	7	33	92	87	102	10	8
OF	Cody Bellinger, Dodgers	.305	.406	.629	558	121	170	34	3	47	115	95	108	15	5
OF	Mike Trout, Angels	.291	.438	.645	470	110	137	27	2	45	104	110	120	11	2
OF	Christian Yelich, Brewers	.329	.429	.671	489	100	161	29	3	44	97	80	118	30	2
DH	Nelson Cruz, Twins	.311	.392	.639	454	81	141	26	0	41	108	56	131	0	1

Pos.	Player, Team	W	L	ERA	G	GS	SV	IP	H	R	ER	HR	BB	SO	WHIP
SP	Gerrit Cole, Astros	20	5	2.50	33	33	0	212	142	66	59	29	48	326	0.90
SP	Jacob deGrom, Mets	11	8	2.43	32	32	0	204	154	59	55	19	44	255	0.97
SP	Hyun-Jin Ryu, Dodgers	14	5	2.32	29	29	0	183	160	53	47	17	24	163	1.01
SP	Stephen Strasburg, Nationals	18	6	3.32	33	33	0	209	161	79	77	24	56	251	1.04
SP	Justin Verlander, Astros	21	6	2.58	34	34	0	223	137	66	64	36	42	300	0.80
RP	Kirby Yates, Padres	0	5	1.19	60	0	41	61	41	14	8	2	13	101	0.89

SECOND TEAM

Pos.	Player, Team	AVG	OBP	SLG	AB	R	H	2B	3B	HR	RBI	BB	SO	SB	CS
C	Yasmani Grandal, Brewers	.246	.380	.468	513	79	126	26	2	28	77	109	139	5	1
1B	Freddie Freeman, Braves	.295	.389	.549	597	113	176	34	2	38	121	87	127	6	3
2B	DJ LeMahieu, Yankees	.327	.375	.518	602	109	197	33	2	26	102	46	90	5	2
3B	Anthony Rendon, Nationals	.319	.412	.598	545	117	174	44	3	44	126	80	86	5	1
SS	Xander Bogaerts, Red Sox	.309	.384	.555	614	110	190	52	0	33	117	76	122	4	2
OF	George Springer, Astros	.292	.383	.591	479	96	140	20	3	39	96	67	113	6	2
OF	Ronald Acuña Jr., Braves	.280	.365	.518	626	127	175	22	2	41	101	76	188	37	9
OF	Juan Soto, Nationals	.282	.401	.548	542	110	153	32	5	34	110	108	132	12	1
DH	Jorge Soler, Royals	.265	.354	.569	589	95	156	33	1	48	117	73	178	3	1

Pos.	Player, Team	W	L	ERA	G	GS	SV	IP	H	R	ER	HR	BB	SO	WHIP
SP	Jack Flaherty, Cardinals	11	8	2.75	33	33	1	196	135	62	60	25	55	231	0.97
SP	Sonny Gray, Reds	11	8	2.87	31	31	0	175	122	59	56	17	68	205	1.08
SP	Zack Greinke, D-backs/Astros	18	5	2.93	33	33	0	209	175	73	68	21	30	187	0.98
SP	Charlie Morton, Rays	16	6	3.05	33	33	0	195	154	71	66	15	57	220	1.08
SP	Max Scherzer, Nationals	11	7	2.92	27	27	0	172	144	59	56	18	33	243	1.03
RP	Liam Hendriks, Athletics	4	4	1.80	75	2	25	85	61	18	17	5	21	124	0.97

EXECUTIVE OF THE YEAR

In the 10 years since he was hired as the Nationals general manager, Mike Rizzo stuck to some key tenets.

He's always been willing to be creative when it came to making trades or signing free agents. He's been one who looks to build teams to contend annually rather than sporadically—and he's had ownership willing to spend to help make that possible.

And thanks his scouting background (he's one of the few decision-makers in baseball who has also run drafts as a scouting director), he's also one who trusts his scouts and coaches to do their jobs.

After a slew of quick playoff exits, Rizzo's Nationals won D.C. its first World Series title in nearly a century in 2019. In the past, Rizzo had dealt with plenty of October heartbreak. Now, he's reached the pinnacle.

Mike Rizzo
MITCHELL LAYTON/GETTY IMAGES

PREVIOUS WINNERS

2009: Dan O'Dowd, Rockies
2010: Jon Daniels, Rangers
2011: Doug Melvin, Brewers
2012: Billy Beane, Athletics
2013: Dan Duquette, Orioles
2014: Dan Duquette, Orioles
2015: Sandy Alderson, Mets
2016: Chris Antonetti, Indians
2017: Brian Cashman, Yankees
2018: Dave Dombrowski, Red Sox

Full list: BaseballAmerica.com/awards

MANAGER OF THE YEAR

When a foul ball fractured Christian Yelich's knee cap to end his season on Sept. 10, it was reasonable to suggest that the Brewers' season effectively ended the same day.

At the time, the Brewers were in third place in the NL Central and third place in the wild card race. But Counsell's Brewers didn't let the loss of an MVP candidate derail what was already shaping up as an impressive September.

The Brewers went 13-5 the rest of the way, catching and passing the Cubs for the second NL wild card berth. The Brewers did fall in the wild card game to the eventual World Series champion Nationals, but getting back to the playoffs gave the club back-to-back postseason appearances for only the second time in club history.

Craig Counsell
ALEX TRAUTWIG/MLB VIA GETTY IMAGES

PREVIOUS WINNERS

2009: Mike Scioscia, Angels
2010: Bobby Cox, Braves
2011: Joe Maddon, Rays
2012: Buck Showalter, Orioles
2013: Clint Hurdle, Pirates
2014: Buck Showalter, Orioles
2015: Joe Maddon, Cubs
2016: Terry Francona, Indians
2017: A.J. Hinch, Astros
2018: Bob Melvin, Athletics

Full list: BaseballAmerica.com/awards

CONTINUED FROM PAGE 19

That was enough to secure the Brewers a postseason spot, though, alongside the Nationals, who rebounded from a 19–31 start and played like one of the majors' best teams over the final four-plus months to take the NL's first wild card berth.

For those teams that missed out on the playoffs, there were consequences. Another uneven year from the Mets, coupled with some poor decision-making and a midseason altercation with a reporter, cost Mickey Callaway his job as New York's manager, ending his tenure after just two seasons. He was replaced by former Met Carlos Beltran. A similar fate awaited Gabe Kapler in Philadelphia, as a second straight year in which the Phillies started strong only to fade late sealed his doom; he's since been replaced by former Yankees manager Joe Girardi.

The Angels turned out to have little patience with Ausmus, canning him after just one season. Poor results and a fractious clubhouse spelled the end to Clint Hurdle's tenure in Pittsburgh after nine seasons, as the Pirates collapsed in the second half, going 25–48 after the All-Star break. The poor performance also resulted in Neal Huntington being ousted as the Pirates' general manager. And amid a disappointing year in San Diego, where adding Machado and Tatis Jr. wasn't enough to make the Padres contenders, Andy Green was fired near the end of his fourth season.

The biggest shakeup came in Chicago, where despite guiding the Cubs to the franchise's drought-ending championship in 2016, diminishing returns led to the departure of Joe Maddon (who ended up returning to his old team in Anaheim to take over as the Angels' next skipper). In his place steps longtime catcher and ESPN announcer David Ross, who was an integral part of the Cubs' 2016 World Series team.

Two venerable managers got to go out on their own terms. In San Francisco, Bruce Bochy announced before the season that he would be stepping down at its conclusion, ending a 13-year stint with the Giants that saw him lead the team to three titles. Feted across the league all year long, Bochy went out on a high note, winning his 2,000th career game on Sept. 18, becoming only the 11th manager to reach that mark. Also departing: Bochy's opponent in the 2014 World Series, Kansas City skipper Ned Yost. At season's end, he called it quits after a decade in charge of the Royals, a span that included a championship in 2015 and the most wins of any manager in franchise history.

Retirements & The Rest

Before putting a bow on 2019, let's take a moment to remember those who said goodbye to the game this year. Sabathia has already been mentioned, but a few other players also decided that this season would be their last.

Though Troy Tulowitzki attempted to gut out one more year, this time as a member of the Yankees, injuries limited him to just five games, all in early April. Having barely played since the 2017 season, Tulowitzki announced his retirement on July 25 and, shortly thereafter, took a position as a coach with the University of Texas. That decision brought an end to a career that started in 2006 and featured five all-star selections, two Gold Gloves, two Silver Slugger awards, 225 home runs, a second-place finish in the 2007 NL Rookie of the Year voting, and a starring role on that year's pennant-winning Rockies squad.

During the postseason, two other veterans decided to hang up their spikes. In Atlanta, Brian McCann put a cap on a 15-year career by playing a big role on a division-winning club. The longtime catcher finished with 282 homers across three different teams, mostly with the Braves but also notably with the Yankees and Astros, the last of which he helped guide to a championship in 2017. Also deciding to retire was David Freese, the veteran corner infielder who will forever be known for his clutch heroics for the Cardinals in the 2011 World Series. The 36-year-old played for four teams over an 11-year career and will go down as one of the great postseason performers of his generation.

And in the Pacific Northwest, Mariners fans said goodbye to two franchise icons in Ichiro Suzuki and Felix Hernandez. The 45-year-old Ichiro may have had as close to a perfect ending to his

OTTO GREULE JR/GETTY IMAGES

Ichiro Suzuki retired at the age of 45, ending a highly successful 19-year MLB career.

illustrious as possible, announcing his retirement following the Mariners' early season win over the Athletics in his home country of Japan. Playing in front of a sold-out Tokyo Dome as part of MLB's Japan opening series, Ichiro ran out to his customary position in right field in the bottom of the eighth inning before Seattle manager Scott Servais pulled the rest of his defenders off the field, allowing Ichiro to walk off the field for the final time on his own. At the time of his retirement, Ichiro led all active major leaguers with 3,089 hits across 19 seasons, which came immediately following a professional career in Japan in which he totaled nearly 1,300 hits in his home country. A 10-time All-Star with 10 Gold Gloves to his name, Ichiro was an instant sensation in the majors, winning both the AL MVP and Rookie of the Year awards in 2001.

Meanwhile, the 33-year-old Hernandez hasn't announced any plans to retire, but 2019 was his last season under contract with Seattle, which is unlikely to bring him back after his struggles over the last few seasons. Despite that, King Felix got to go out on a high note, making a final emotional start at Seattle's T-Mobile Park in front of thousands of die-hard fans who spent the night chanting his name and celebrating his brilliant Mariners career. If Hernandez is truly done in Seattle, he leaves as the franchise leader in wins (168), strikeouts (2,439), innings (2,620), ERA (3.32) and numerous other statistical categories.

CONTINUED ON PAGE 24

AL's Young Pitchers Silence NL In 4-3 Win

ALL-STAR GAME

Shane Bieber

JASON MILLER/GETTY IMAGES

BY KYLE GLASER

The National League is overflowing with young stars. So much so that the NL trotted out the youngest starting lineup in All-Star Game history on July 9, with an average age of just under 26.

There was Javier Baez, 26, Cody Bellinger, 23, and Ronald Acuña Jr., 21. Freddie Freeman, 29, was the old man of group. And that's saying nothing of reserves Pete Alonso (24), David Dahl (25) and Trevor Story (26).

The National League held the edge in young stars by a wide margin in the 90th All-Star Game, but it was the American League's young pitchers who proved up to the task.

Jose Berrios, Lucas Giolito and Shane Bieber combined for three scoreless innings and six strikeouts in the critical middle innings, and the AL rode a combined five-hitter to a 4-3 win over the NL in the All-Star Game at Progressive Field in Cleveland.

Bieber, the hometown favorite, struck out the side in a perfect sixth inning and was named Most Valuable Player, becoming the second Indians player to win All-Star Game MVP in his home stadium, following Sandy Alomar Jr. in 1997. The 24-year-old right-hander also became the fifth-youngest player to win All-Star MVP honors behind Ken Griffey Jr., Mike Trout (twice) and Roger Clemens.

"I didn't really know what to think. I kind of lost all feeling in my body," Bieber said of winning MVP. "Just to be able to do it in front of the home crowd in my first All-Star Game is definitely not something I expected."

Bieber led the trio of 20-something arms that helped secure the seventh straight All-Star Game win for the American League.

Berrios, 25, came on in third inning and struck out Acuña and Christian Yelich after the AL took its first lead. Giolito, 24, froze Cody Bellinger on a nasty changeup on his way to a hitless fifth inning. And Bieber, cheered on wildly by the home crowd chanting his name, struck out Willson Contreras, Ketel Marte and Acuña in order in an electrifying sixth inning.

"The way we did it, we did it pretty awesome," Berrios said.

2019 ALL-STAR GAME

JULY 9, 2019
AMERICAN LEAGUE 4,
NATIONAL LEAGUE 3

National	AB	R	H	RBI	American	AB	R	H	RBI
Yelich, LF	2	0	0	0	Springer, RF	2	0	1	0
Bryant, LF	1	0	0	0	Lindor, PH-SS	2	0	0	0
McNeil, LF	1	0	0	0	LeMahieu, 2B	2	0	0	0
Baez, SS	2	0	0	0	Torres, PH-2B	2	0	1	0
Story, SS	1	0	0	0	Trout, CF	2	0	0	0
DeJong, SS	0	0	0	0	Merrifield, CF	2	0	0	0
Freeman, 1B	1	0	0	0	Santana, 1B	3	0	0	0
Blackmon, RF	2	1	1	1	Abreu, 1B	1	0	0	0
Bellinger, RF	2	0	0	0	Martinez, DH	2	0	0	0
Alonso, 1B	2	0	1	2	Vogelbach, PH	1	0	0	0
Arenado, 3B	2	0	0	0	Bregman, 3B	2	1	1	0
Moustakas, 3B	2	0	0	0	Chapman, 3B	0	1	0	0
Bell, DH	2	0	1	0	Sanchez, C	2	1	1	0
Realmuto, PH	2	0	0	0	McCann, C	1	0	1	0
Contreras, C	2	0	0	0	Brantley, LF	1	0	1	1
Muncy, 2B	2	0	0	0	Meadows, LF-RF	1	0	0	0
Marte, 2B	2	0	1	0	Bogaerts, PH	1	0	0	0
Grandal, C	1	1	0	0	Betts, RF	0	0	0	0
Acuña Jr., CF	2	0	0	0	Polanco, SS	2	0	1	1
Dahl, CF	1	1	1	0	Gallo, LF	1	1	1	1
Totals	**32**	**3**	**5**	**3**	**Totals**	**30**	**4**	**8**	**3**

2B: Marte (1, Berrios); Brantley (1, Kershaw), Sanchez (1, Buehler). **HR:** Blackmon (1, Hendriks, 6th inn, 0 on, 2 outs); Gallo (1, Smith, 7th inn, 0 on, 2 outs). **TB:** Blackmon 4, Marte 2, Dahl, Alonso, Bell; Gallo 4, Brantley 2, Sanchez 2, Bregman, Springer, Polanco, McCann, Torres. **RBI:** Alonso 2 (2), Blackmon 1 (1); Polanco 1 (1), Brantley 1 (1), Gallo 1 (1). **2-out RBI:** Alonso 2, Blackmon; Gallo, Brantley. **GIDP:** Bogaerts (1), Abreu (1). **DP:** 2. DeJong-Muncy-Alonso 2. **SB:** Alonso (1, 2nd base off Hand/McCann), DeJong (1, 3rd base off Hand/McCann).

Time of Game: 2:48. **Attendance:** 36,477.

National	IP	H	R	SO	American	IP	H	R	SO
Ryu	1.0	1	0	0	Verlander	1.0	0	0	2
Kershaw	1.0	2	1	1	Tanaka (W)	1.0	1	0	1
deGrom	1.0	0	0	1	Berrios	1.0	1	0	2
Castillo	1.0	0	0	2	Giolito	1.0	0	0	1
Buehler	1.0	2	1	2	Bieber	1.0	0	0	3
Soroka	1.0	0	0	0	Hendriks	1.0	1	1	3
Woodruff	0.2	1	1	0	Greene	1.0	0	0	0
Smith	0.1	1	1	0	Hand	1.0	2	2	1
Alcantara	1.0	1	0	1	Chapman (S)	1.0	0	0	3

CONTINUED FROM PAGE 22

The Future?

So where does baseball go next? The league spent much of the 2019 season seemingly looking both outward and into the future. The game finally touched down on European soil, with the Yankees and Red Sox playing a two-game series in London. Rule changes will be coming into effect for 2020, the biggest of which will be a three-batter minimum for all pitchers—thus either curtailing or eliminating roles such as the lefty specialist—and the end of September roster expansion. Even larger shifts in the sport may be coming soon, too. Throughout the year, MLB utilized the independent Atlantic League as its test kitchen, trying out things like automated strike zones, no mound visits other than pitching changes, and less time between innings. Pitch clocks feel like a near certainty to expand from the minors to the majors sooner rather than later, and in October, news broke that Major League Baseball is eyeing a massive contraction of the minor leagues.

This contraction has to due with the Professional Baseball Agreement (PBA) between MLB and minor league teams expiring at the end of the 2020 season, with a new MLB proposal that was on the table in the fall of 2019 pushing for the elimination of more than 40 minor league teams. If this proposal, or some version of it, were adopted, it would lead to the most dramatic restructuring of the minors in more than half a century. Under the proposal, the remaining leagues would be dramatically reworked, with some leagues getting much smaller, others getting bigger, and teams switching

classification levels all around the country.

Atop it all sits commissioner Rob Manfred, overseeing the game at its economic peak, a business that now brings in an excess of $10 billion in revenue each year. The game's financial health has never been better, with money flowing in from TV deals and the league's wildly profitable digital side, not to mention team valuations that only keep going up. Yet as the rich get richer, the question arises as to whether or not all of this is good for the sport. In-person attendance continues to trend down while ticket prices keep going up as teams continue to target well-off patrons and corporate partners at the expense of the average fan and put the bottom line over wins and losses. Teams now have open license to lose with impunity, while contenders talk about cost control and the bottom line more than they do acquiring stars or titles. Baseball has always been a business, but it increasingly feels like, under Manfred, baseball is first and foremost a business, with the on-field action newly secondary to the profit machine he and the owners have built—one hostile to the very labor that props it up.

The specter looming over all of this is the expiration of the Collective Bargaining Agreement, set for December 2021, the renewal of which promises to be, for the first time in nearly two decades a testy and bitter affair. Players, finding themselves increasingly squeezed in free agency and not reaping the financial benefits of their best years early in their careers, grumble louder and louder about getting a fairer share. They're unlikely, though, to find acquiescence from the owners.

And that is why the 2020's should be momentous for Major League Baseball, although it's not clear at all whether that will be for good or ill.

MLB and MiLB are facing a contentious negotiation to determine the shape of the minor leagues. That needs to be settled before the 2021 season. Before the 2022 season begins, MLB and the MLBPA have to come to agreement on a new Collective Bargaining Agreement, and that negotiation looks to be even more difficult than the discussions between the majors and minors.

The path MLB wants to take is also unclear. Home runs are fun, or at least they can be. So, too, are big strikeouts and pitchers throwing 100 mph. But there can be too much of a good thing, or at least, it can get tiring to hear the same song played so often. Baseball has always changed and grown over the last 150 years, and it will continue to do so into the future. But based on what we saw in 2019, it's worth wondering if we're going to like what we eventually get.

ACTIVE LEADERS

Career leaders among players who played in a game in 2019. Batters require 3,000 plate appearances and pitchers 1,000 innings to qualify for percentage titles.

BATTERS			PITCHERS		
AVG	Miguel Cabrera	.315	ERA	Clayton Kershaw	2.44
OBP	Joey Votto	.421	SO/9	Yu Darvish	11.12
SLG	Mike Trout	.581	BB/9	Masahiro Tanaka	1.79
OPS	Mike Trout	1.000	HR/9	Clayton Kershaw	0.69
R	Albert Pujols	1,828	W	CC Sabathia	251
H	Albert Pujols	3,202	L	CC Sabathia	161
2B	Albert Pujols	661	SV	Craig Kimbrel	346
3B	Curtis Granderson	95	IP	CC Sabathia	3,577
HR	Albert Pujols	656	SO	CC Sabathia	3,093
RBI	Albert Pujols	2,075	BB	CC Sabathia	1,099
BB	Albert Pujols	1,322	AVG	Clayton Kershaw	.208
SO	Mark Reynolds	1,927	G	Fernando Rodney	951
XBH	Albert Pujols	1,333	GS	CC Sabathia	560
SB	Rajai Davis	415	HR	CC Sabathia	382

ARIZONA DIAMONDBACKS

Jon Deuplantier	April 1
Merrill Kelly	April 1
Taylor Clarke	April 20
Kevin Cron	May 24
Domingo Leyba	June 22
Alex Young	June 27
Kevin Ginkel	Aug. 5
Josh Rojas	Aug. 12
Joel Payamps	Aug. 21

ATLANTA BRAVES

Alex Jackson	April 7
Jacob Webb	April 16
Austin Riley	May 15
Huascar Ynoa	June 16
Jeremy Walker	July 26

BALTIMORE ORIOLES

Drew Jackson	March 28
Richie Martin	March 28
Matt Wotherspoon	April 3
Branden Kline	April 20
Tom Eshelman	July 1
Dillon Tate	July 29
Chandler Shepherd	Aug. 13
Hunter Harvey	Aug. 17

BOSTON RED SOX

Michael Chavis	April 20
Darwinzon Hernandez	April 23
Travis Lankins	April 23
Josh Taylor	May 29
Mike Shawaryn	June 7
Trevor Kelley	July 2

CHICAGO CUBS

Adbert Alzolay	June 20
Robel Garcia	July 3
Danny Hultzen	Sept. 8
Nico Hoerner	Sept. 9

CHICAGO WHITE SOX

Eloy Jimenez	March 28
Seby Zavala	May 25
Zack Collins	June 19
Dylan Cease	July 3
Danny Mendick	Sept. 3

CINCINNATI REDS

Nick Senzel	May 3
Josh VanMeter	May 5
Jimmy Herget	July 7
Brian O'Grady	Aug. 8
Joel Kuhnel	Aug. 16

CLEVELAND INDIANS

Eric Stamets	March 28
Oscar Mercado	May 14
Josh Smith	May 25
Zach Plesac	May 28
Aaron Civale	June 22
Bobby Bradley	June 23
Yu Chang	June 28
James Karinchak	Sept. 14

COLORADO ROCKIES

Josh Fuentes	April 6
Yonathan Daza	April 9
Brendan Rodgers	May 17
Jesus Tinoco	May 31
Peter Lambert	June 6
Phillip Diehl	June 11
Dom Nunez	Aug. 13
Rico Garcia	Aug. 27
Sam Hilliard	Aug. 27

DETROIT TIGERS

Reed Garrett	March 29
Eduardo Jimenez	May 7
Gregory Soto	May 11
Nick Ramirez	May 11
David McKay	May 19
Tyler Alexander	July 3
Jake Rogers	July 30
Travis Demeritte	Aug. 2
John Schreiber	Aug. 9
Willi Castro	Aug. 24
Bryan Garcia	Sept. 2

HOUSTON ASTROS

Corbin Martin	May 12
Jack Mayfield	May 27
Garrett Stubbs	May 28
Yordan Alvarez	June 9
Rogelio Armenteros	June 14
Cy Sneed	June 27
Jose Urquidy	July 2
Bryan Abreu	July 31
Abraham Toro	Aug. 22

KANSAS CITY ROYALS

Frank Schwindel	March 28
Chris Ellis	March 31
Kyle Zimmer	March 31
Richard Lovelady	April 9
Kelvin Gutierrez	April 27
Nicky Lopez	May 14
Humberto Arteaga	June 20
Bubba Starling	July 12
Josh Staumont	July 25
Nick Dini	Aug. 7
Ryan McBroom	Sept. 3
Erick Mejia	Sept. 5
Gabe Speier	Sept. 5

LOS ANGELES ANGELS

Luis Rengifo	April 25
Matt Ramsey	April 25
Griffin Canning	April 30
Jared Walsh	May 15
Jose Suarez	June 2
Matt Thaiss	July 3
Jose Rodriguez	July 27
Patrick Sandoval	Aug. 5
Miguel Del Pozo	Aug. 20

LOS ANGELES DODGERS

Matt Beaty	April 30
Kyle Garlick	May 19
Will Smith	May 28
Josh Sborz	June 20
Tony Gonsolin	June 26
Edwin Rios	June 27
Dustin May	Aug. 2
Gavin Lux	Sept. 2

MIAMI MARLINS

Nick Anderson	March 28
Jose Quijada	April 24
Harold Ramirez	May 11
Jordan Yamamoto	June 12
Zac Gallen	June 20
Kyle Keller	Aug. 4
Isan Diaz	Aug. 5
Robert Dugger	Aug. 5
Tyler Heineman	Sept. 4
Brian Moran	Sept. 5

MILWAUKEE BREWERS

Keston Hiura	May 14
Mauricio Dubon	July 7
Trent Grisham	Aug. 1
Devin Williams	Aug. 7
Tyrone Taylor	Sept. 7

MINNESOTA TWINS

Ryne Harper	March 31
Luis Arraez	May 18
Devin Smeltzer	May 28
Ryan Eades	June 8
Sean Poppen	June 19
LaMonte Wade Jr.	June 28
Lewis Thorpe	June 30
Cody Stashak	July 23
Randy Dobnak	Aug. 9
Brusdar Graterol	Sept. 1
Ian Miller	Sept. 4
Jorge Alcala	Sept. 21

NEW YORK METS

Pete Alonso	March 28
Stephen Nogosek	June 19
Chris Mazza	June 29
Sam Haggerty	Sept. 4

NEW YORK YANKEES

Joe Harvey	April 10
Mike Ford	April 18
Thairo Estrada	April 21
Brady Lail	Aug. 12
Adonis Rosa	Aug. 13
Michael King	Sept. 27

OAKLAND ATHLETICS

Skye Bolt	May 3
Sean Murphy	May 19
Sheldon Neuse	May 19
A.J. Puk	Aug. 21
Seth Brown	Aug. 26
Jesus Luzardo	Sept. 11

PHILADELPHIA PHILLIES

Edgar Garcia	May 6
Cole Irvin	May 12
JD Hammer	May 26
Adam Haseley	June 4
Deivy Grullon	Sept. 22

PITTSBURGH PIRATES

Jason Martin	April 6
Bryan Reynolds	April 20
Cole Tucker	April 20
Montana DuRapau	May 9
Geoff Hartlieb	May 18
Mitch Keller	May 27
Dario Agrazal	June 15
Luis Escobar	July 13
James Marvel	Sept. 8

ST. LOUIS CARDINALS

Ryan Helsley	April 16
Lane Thomas	April 17
Genesis Cabrera	May 29
Andrew Knizner	June 2
Tommy Edman	June 8
Rangel Ravelo	June 17
Junior Fernandez	Aug. 11
Randy Arozarena	Aug. 14

SAN DIEGO PADRES

Fernando Tatis Jr.	March 28
Nick Margevicius	March 30
Chris Paddack	March 31
Pedro Avila	April 11
Gerardo Reyes	April 12
Ty France	April 26
Cal Quantrill	May 1
Austin Allen	May 11
Josh Naylor	May 24
Logan Allen	June 18
Andres Munoz	July 12
Adrian Morejon	July 21
Michel Baez	July 23
Eric Yardley	Aug. 21
David Bednar	Sept. 1
Ronald Bolanos	Sept. 3
Seth Mejias-Brean	Sept. 4

SAN FRANCISCO GIANTS

Connor Joe	March 28
Travis Bergen	March 29
Shaun Anderson	May 15
Mike Yastrzemski	May 25
Sam Coonrod	May 26
Conner Menez	July 21
Zach Green	July 21
Sam Selman	Aug. 1
Logan Webb	Aug. 17
Tyler Rogers	Aug. 27
Jaylin Davis	Sept. 4
Enderson Franco	Sept. 18

SEATTLE MARINERS

Dylan Moore	March 20
Braden Bishop	March 21
Brandon Brennan	March 21
Yusei Kikuchi	March 21
Erik Swanson	April 11
R.J. Alaniz	April 12
Shed Long	May 11
Parker Markel	May 12
Taylor Scott	June 8
Austin Nola	June 16
Tim Lopes	July 24
Ryan Court	July 26
Reggie McClain	Aug. 2
Zac Grotz	Aug. 2
Taylor Guilbeau	Aug. 17
Jake Fraley	Aug. 21
Donnie Walton	Sept. 10
Kyle Lewis	Sept. 10
Art Warren	Sept. 12
Justin Dunn	Sept. 12

TAMPA BAY RAYS

Nate Lowe	April 29
Anthony Bemboom	May 12
Colin Poche	June 8
Michael Brosseau	June 23
Brendan McKay	June 29
Ian Gibaut	July 12
Kean Wong	Sept. 5
Cole Sulser	Sept. 6
Johnny Davis	Sept. 11

TEXAS RANGERS

Kyle Bird	March 28
Kyle Dowdy	March 28
Brett Martin	April 19
Wei-Chieh Huang	April 23
Taylor Hearn	April 25
Joe Palumbo	June 8
Phillips Valdez	June 8
Peter Fairbanks	June 9
Locke St. John	June 25
Pedro Payano	July 6
Scott Heineman	Aug. 2
Emmanuel Clase	Aug. 4
Brock Burke	Aug. 20
Nick Solak	Aug. 20
Jonathan Hernandez	Aug. 21

TORONTO BLUE JAYS

Elvis Luciano	March 31
Trent Thornton	March 31
Vladimir Guerrero Jr.	April 26
Cavan Biggio	May 24
Jacob Waguespack	May 27
Jordan Romano	June 12
Bo Bichette	July 29
Yennsy Diaz	Aug. 4
T.J. Zeuch	Sept. 3
Anthony Kay	Sept. 7

WASHINGTON NATIONALS

Jake Noll	March 30
Carter Kieboom	April 26
James Bourque	May 26
Tres Barrera	Sept. 14

CLUB BATTING

	AVG	G	AB	R	H	2B	3B	HR	RBI	BB	SO	SB	OBP	SLG
Houston	.274	162	5613	920	1538	323	28	288	891	645	1166	67	.352	.495
Minnesota	.270	162	5732	939	1547	318	23	307	906	525	1334	28	.338	.494
Boston	.269	162	5770	901	1554	345	27	245	857	590	1382	68	.340	.466
New York	.267	162	5583	943	1493	290	17	306	904	569	1437	55	.339	.490
Chicago	.261	161	5529	708	1443	260	20	182	676	378	1549	63	.314	.414
Tampa Bay	.254	162	5628	769	1427	291	29	217	730	542	1493	94	.325	.431
Cleveland	.250	162	5425	769	1354	286	18	223	731	563	1332	103	.323	.432
Oakland	.249	162	5561	845	1384	292	23	257	800	578	1338	49	.327	.448
Texas	.248	162	5540	810	1374	296	24	223	765	534	1578	131	.319	.431
Kansas City	.247	162	5496	691	1356	281	40	162	655	456	1405	117	.309	.401
Los Angeles	.247	162	5542	769	1368	268	21	220	734	586	1276	65	.324	.422
Baltimore	.246	162	5596	729	1379	252	25	213	698	462	1435	84	.310	.415
Detroit	.240	161	5549	582	1333	292	41	149	556	391	1595	57	.294	.388
Seattle	.237	162	5500	758	1305	254	28	239	730	588	1581	115	.316	.424
Toronto	.236	162	5493	726	1299	270	21	247	697	509	1514	51	.305	.428

CLUB PITCHING

	ERA	G	CG	SHO	SV	IP	H	R	ER	HR	BB	SO	AVG
Tampa Bay	3.65	162	0	12	46	1474	1274	656	598	181	453	1621	.230
Houston	3.66	162	2	14	47	1462	1205	640	595	230	448	1671	.221
Cleveland	3.76	162	6	16	42	1438	1308	657	601	207	450	1508	.240
Oakland	3.97	162	1	12	45	1465	1342	680	646	201	477	1299	.242
Minnesota	4.18	162	1	10	50	1463	1456	754	680	198	452	1463	.257
New York	4.31	162	1	9	50	1443	1374	739	691	248	507	1534	.248
Boston	4.70	162	1	8	33	1471	1423	828	768	215	605	1633	.251
Toronto	4.79	162	1	7	33	1440	1450	828	767	228	604	1332	.259
Chicago	4.90	161	6	7	33	1413	1438	832	769	238	582	1312	.263
Seattle	4.99	162	3	4	34	1439	1484	893	798	260	505	1239	.263
Texas	5.06	162	4	9	33	1438	1515	878	808	241	583	1379	.269
Los Angeles	5.12	162	0	2	32	1443	1417	868	820	267	576	1404	.254
Kansas City	5.20	162	1	7	37	1425	1525	869	824	221	582	1230	.273
Detroit	5.24	161	0	3	31	1433	1555	915	835	250	536	1368	.275
Baltimore	5.59	162	0	5	27	1443	1544	981	897	305	561	1248	.271

CLUB FIELDING

	PCT	PO	A	E	DP		PCT	PO	A	E	DP
Houston	.988	4387	1353	71	97	Baltimore	.982	4329	1408	156	156
Kansas City	.988	4275	1505	73	152	New York	.982	4329	1347	102	135
Oakland	.987	4395	1464	80	123	Texas	.982	4314	1364	105	143
Boston	.985	4413	1436	88	115	Detroit	.981	4299	1452	110	127
Cleveland	.985	4313	1322	83	111	Minnesota	.981	4390	1405	111	129
Tampa Bay	.985	4423	1414	87	129	Chicago	.980	4238	1525	117	170
Los Angeles	.984	4328	1469	92	118	Seattle	.978	4318	1490	132	146
Toronto	.984	4321	1503	96	141						

INDIVIDUAL BATTING LEADERS

	AVG	G	AB	R	H	2B	3B	HR	RBI	BB	SO	SB
Tim Anderson, Chicago	.335	123	498	81	167	32	0	18	56	15	109	17
DJ LeMahieu, New York	.327	145	602	109	197	33	2	26	102	46	90	5
Yoan Moncada, Chicago	.315	132	511	83	161	34	5	25	79	40	154	10
Michael Brantley, Houston	.311	148	575	88	179	40	2	22	90	51	66	3
Rafael Devers, Boston	.311	156	647	129	201	54	4	32	115	48	119	8
Nelson Cruz, Minnesota	.311	120	454	81	141	26	0	41	108	56	131	0
Xander Bogaerts, Boston	.309	155	614	110	190	52	0	33	117	76	122	4
Hanser Alberto, Baltimore	.305	139	524	62	160	21	2	12	51	16	50	4
J.D. Martinez, Boston	.304	146	575	98	175	33	2	36	105	72	138	2
Whit Merrifield, Kansas City	.302	162	681	105	206	41	10	16	74	45	126	20

INDIVIDUAL PITCHING LEADERS

	W	L	ERA	G	GS	CG	SV	IP	H	R	ER	BB	SO
Gerrit Cole, Houston	20	5	2.50	33	33	0	0	212	142	66	59	48	326
Justin Verlander, Houston	21	6	2.58	34	34	2	0	223	137	66	64	42	300
Charlie Morton, Tampa Bay	16	6	3.05	33	33	0	0	195	154	71	66	57	240
Shane Bieber, Cleveland	15	8	3.28	34	33	3	0	214	186	86	78	40	259
Lucas Giolito, Chicago	14	9	3.41	29	29	3	0	177	131	69	67	57	228
Mike Minor, Texas	14	10	3.59	32	32	2	0	208	190	86	83	68	200
Lance Lynn, Texas	16	11	3.67	33	33	0	0	208	195	89	85	59	246
Jose Berrios, Minnesota	14	8	3.68	32	32	1	0	200	194	94	82	51	195
Eduardo Rodriguez, Boston	19	6	3.81	34	34	0	0	203	195	88	86	75	213
Brett Anderson, Oakland	13	9	3.89	31	31	0	0	176	181	80	76	49	90

AWARD WINNERS

Selected by Baseball Writers Association of America

MOST VALUABLE PLAYER

Player	1st	2nd	3rd	Total
Mike Trout, Angels	17	13		355
Alex Bregman, Astros	13	17		335
Marcus Semien, Athletics			22	228
D.J. LeMahieu, Yankees			6	178
Xander Bogaerts, Red Sox			1	147
Matt Chapman, Athletics			4	89
George Springer, Astros			2	69
Mookie Betts, Red Sox				67
Nelson Cruz, Twins				62
Gerrit Cole, Astros				61
Justin Verlander, Astros			1	56
Rafael Devers, Red Sox				40
Jorge Polanco, Twins				20
Francisco Lindor, Indians				13
Carlos Santana, Indians				9
Gleyber Torres, Yankees				8
Eddie Rosario, Twins				6
Jose Abreu, White Sox				5
Max Kepler, Twins				2
J.D. Martinez, Red Sox				1
Yoan Moncada, White Sox				1
Charlie Morton, Rays				1
Matt Olson, Athletics				1
Jorge Soler, Royals				1

CY YOUNG AWARD

Player	1st	2nd	3rd	Total
Justin Verlander, Astros	17	13		171
Gerrit Cole, Astros	13	17		159
Charlie Morton, Rays			18	75
Shane Bieber, Indians			11	64
Lance Lynn, Rangers				18
Eduardo Rodriguez, Red Sox				8
Lucas Giolito, White Sox				8
Mike Minor, Rangers			1	7

ROOKIE OF THE YEAR

Player	1st	2nd	3rd	Total
Yordan Alvarez, Astros	30			150
John Means, Orioles		16	5	53
Brandon Lowe, Rays		6	9	27
Eloy Jiménez, White Sox		4	8	20
Cavan Biggio, Blue Jays		2	1	7
Luis Arraez, Twins		1	2	5
Vladimir Guerrero Jr., Blue Jays		1	2	4
Oscar Mercado, Indians			3	3

MANAGER OF THE YEAR

Player	1st	2nd	3rd	Total
Rocco Baldelli, Twins	13	13	2	106
Aaron Boone, Yankees	13	9	4	96
Kevin Cash, Rays	3	3	9	33
Bob Melvin, Athletics		3	10	19
A.J. Hinch, Astros	1	1	4	12
Terry Francona, Indians		1	1	4

GOLD GLOVE WINNERS

Selected by AL Managers

P—Mike Leake, Mariners. **C**—Roberto Perez, Indians. **1B**—Matt Olson, Athletics. **2B**—Yolmer Sanchez, White Sox. **3B**—Matt Chapman, Athletics. **SS**—Francisco Lindor, Indians. **LF**—Alex Gordon, Royals. **CF**—Kevin Kiermaier, Rays. **RF**—Mookie Betts, Red Sox.

BATTING

GAMES
Whit Merrifield, Kansas City	162
Marcus Semien, Oakland	162
Jorge Soler, Kansas City	162
Jonathan Villar, Baltimore	162
Jose Abreu, Chicago	159

AT-BATS
Whit Merrifield, Kansas City	681
Marcus Semien, Oakland	657
Rafael Devers, Boston	647
Jonathan Villar, Baltimore	642
Jose Abreu, Chicago	634

PLATE APPEARANCES
Marcus Semien, Oakland	747
Whit Merrifield, Kansas City	735
Jonathan Villar, Baltimore	714
Mookie Betts, Boston	706
Jorge Polanco, Minnesota	704

RUNS
Mookie Betts, Boston	135
Rafael Devers, Boston	129
Marcus Semien, Oakland	123
Alex Bregman, Houston	122
Jonathan Villar, Baltimore	111

HITS
Whit Merrifield, Kansas City	206
Rafael Devers, Boston	201
DJ LeMahieu, New York	197
Xander Bogaerts, Boston	190
Marcus Semien, Oakland	187

TOTAL BASES
Rafael Devers, Boston	359
Marcus Semien, Oakland	343
Xander Bogaerts, Boston	341
Jorge Soler, Kansas City	335
Alex Bregman, Houston	328

DOUBLES
Rafael Devers, Boston	54
Xander Bogaerts, Boston	52
Marcus Semien, Oakland	43
Whit Merrifield, Kansas City	41
6 others	40

TRIPLES
Hunter Dozier, Kansas City	10
Whit Merrifield, Kansas City	10
Adalberto Mondesi, Kansas City	9
Mallex Smith, Seattle	8
5 others	7

EXTRA-BASE HITS
Rafael Devers, Boston	90
Xander Bogaerts, Boston	85
Marcus Semien, Oakland	83
Jorge Soler, Kansas City	82
Alex Bregman, Houston	80

HOME RUNS
Jorge Soler, Kansas City	48
Mike Trout, Los Angeles	45
Alex Bregman, Houston	41
Nelson Cruz, Minnesota	41
George Springer, Houston	39

RUNS BATTED IN
Jose Abreu, Chicago	123
Xander Bogaerts, Boston	117
Jorge Soler, Kansas City	117
Rafael Devers, Boston	115
Alex Bregman, Houston	112

Marcus Semien

SACRIFICES
Leury Garcia, Chicago	11
Delino DeShields, Texas	8
Oscar Mercado, Cleveland	7
Roberto Perez, Cleveland	7
Yolmer Sanchez, Chicago	7

SACRIFICE FLIES
Jose Abreu, Chicago	10
Elvis Andrus, Texas	10
Mookie Betts, Boston	9
Josh Reddick, Houston	9
Alex Bregman, Houston	8
Ramon Laureano, Oakland	8
Albert Pujols, Los Angeles	8

HIT BY PITCHES
Alex Gordon, Kansas City	19
Mark Canha, Oakland	18
Shin-Soo Choo, Texas	18
Mike Trout, Los Angeles	16
Jose Abreu, Chicago	13
Robinson Chirinos, Houston	13

WALKS
Alex Bregman, Houston	119
Mike Trout, Los Angeles	110
Carlos Santana, Cleveland	108
Mookie Betts, Boston	97
Daniel Vogelbach, Seattle	92

STOLEN BASES
Mallex Smith, Seattle	46
Adalberto Mondesi, Kansas City	43
Jonathan Villar, Baltimore	40
Elvis Andrus, Texas	32
Tommy Pham, Tampa Bay	25

STOLEN BASE PERCENTAGE
Shin-Soo Choo, Texas	.938
Tommy Pham, Tampa Bay	.938
Adalberto Mondesi, Kansas City	.860
Jose Ramirez, Cleveland	.857
Mookie Betts, Boston	.842

STRIKEOUTS
Rougned Odor, Texas	178
Jorge Soler, Kansas City	178
Jonathan Villar, Baltimore	176
Shin-Soo Choo, Texas	165
Domingo Santana, Seattle	164

Marco Gonzales

AT-BATS PER STRIKEOUT
Hanser Alberto, Baltimore	10.5
David Fletcher, Los Angeles	9.3
Michael Brantley, Houston	8.7
Yuli Gurriel, Houston	8.7
Josh Reddick, Houston	7.6

DOUBLE PLAYS
Jose Abreu, Chicago	24
Trey Mancini, Baltimore	22
Tommy Pham, Tampa Bay	22
Michael Brantley, Houston	21
Albert Pujols, Los Angeles	21
Andrelton Simmons, Los Angeles	21

MULTI-HIT GAMES
DJ LeMahieu, New York	61
Rafael Devers, Boston	60
Whit Merrifield, Kansas City	58
Michael Brantley, Houston	56
Xander Bogaerts, Boston	54
Jorge Polanco, Minnesota	54

ON-BASE PERCENTAGE
Mike Trout, Los Angeles	.438
Alex Bregman, Houston	.423
Carlos Santana, Cleveland	.397
Nelson Cruz, Minnesota	.392
Mookie Betts, Boston	.391

ON-BASE PLUS SLUGGING
Mike Trout, Los Angeles	1.083
Nelson Cruz, Minnesota	1.031
Alex Bregman, Houston	1.015
George Springer, Houston	.974
Xander Bogaerts, Boston	.939

PITCHING

WINS
Justin Verlander, Houston	21
Gerrit Cole, Houston	20
Eduardo Rodriguez, Boston	19
Domingo German, New York	18
Marco Gonzales, Seattle	16
Lance Lynn, Texas	16
Charlie Morton, Tampa Bay	16

LOSSES
Spencer Turnbull, Detroit	17
Reynaldo Lopez, Chicago	15
Jakob Junis, Kansas City	14
Dylan Bundy, Baltimore	14
Brad Keller, Kansas City	14
Aaron Sanchez, Toronto/Houston	14

GAMES
Yusmeiro Petit, Oakland	80
Jake Diekman, Kansas City/Oakland	76
Liam Hendriks, Oakland	75
Buck Farmer, Detroit	73
Adam Ottavino, New York	73
Brandon Workman, Boston	73

GAMES STARTED
Marco Gonzales, Seattle	34
Ivan Nova, Chicago	34
Eduardo Rodriguez, Boston	34
Justin Verlander, Houston	34
7 others	33

GAMES FINISHED
Roberto Osuna, Houston	56
Alex Colome, Chicago	54
Brad Hand, Cleveland	54
Aroldis Chapman, New York	53

Hansel Robles, Los Angeles	51
Ian Kennedy, Kansas City	51

COMPLETE GAMES

Shane Bieber, Cleveland	3
Lucas Giolito, Chicago	3
Mike Leake, Seattle	2
Mike Minor, Texas	2
Ivan Nova, Chicago	2
Justin Verlander, Houston	2

SHUTOUTS

Shane Bieber, Cleveland	2
Lucas Giolito, Chicago	2
Trevor Bauer, Cleveland	1
Carlos Carrasco, Cleveland	1
9 others	1

SAVES

Roberto Osuna, Houston	38
Aroldis Chapman, New York	37
Brad Hand, Cleveland	34
Alex Colome, Chicago	30
Ian Kennedy, Kansas City	30
Taylor Rogers, Minnesota	30

INNINGS PITCHED

Justin Verlander, Houston	223
Shane Bieber, Cleveland	214
Gerrit Cole, Houston	212
Lance Lynn, Texas	208
Mike Minor, Texas	208

HITS ALLOWED

Ivan Nova, Chicago	225
Marco Gonzales, Seattle	210
Reynaldo Lopez, Chicago	203
Rick Porcello, Boston	198
Yusei Kikuchi, Seattle	195
Lance Lynn, Texas	195
Eduardo Rodriguez, Boston	195

RUNS ALLOWED

Reynaldo Lopez, Chicago	119
Rick Porcello, Boston	114
Yusei Kikuchi, Seattle	109
Jakob Junis, Kansas City	108
Ivan Nova, Chicago	107

HOME RUNS ALLOWED

Matthew Boyd, Detroit	39
Yusei Kikuchi, Seattle	36
Justin Verlander, Houston	36

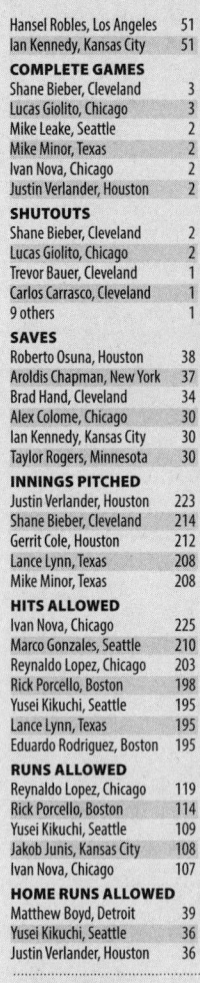

Lucas Giolito

Reynaldo Lopez, Chicago	35
J.A. Happ, New York	34

WALKS ALLOWED

Eduardo Rodriguez, Boston	75
Brad Keller, Kansas City	70
Mike Minor, Texas	68
Aaron Sanchez, Toronto/Houston	68
Martin Perez, Minnesota	67

LOWEST WALKS PER NINE

Shane Bieber, Cleveland	1.7
Justin Verlander, Houston	1.7
Masahiro Tanaka, New York	2.0
Gerrit Cole, Houston	2.0
Ivan Nova, Chicago	2.3

HIT BATTERS

Spencer Turnbull, Detroit	16
Trevor Bauer, Cleveland	14

Chris Bassitt, Oakland	13
Chris Sale, Boston	13
Charlie Morton, Tampa Bay	12

STRIKEOUTS

Gerrit Cole, Houston	326
Justin Verlander, Houston	300
Shane Bieber, Cleveland	259
Lance Lynn, Texas	246
Charlie Morton, Tampa Bay	240

STRIKEOUTS PER NINE

Gerrit Cole, Houston	13.8
Justin Verlander, Houston	12.1
Lucas Giolito, Chicago	11.6
Matthew Boyd, Detroit	11.6
Charlie Morton, Tampa Bay	11.1

STRIKEOUTS PER NINE
(Relievers)

Matt Barnes, Boston	15.4
Josh James, Houston	14.7
Ken Giles, Toronto	14.1
Aroldis Chapman, New York	13.4
Brad Hand, Cleveland	13.2

DOUBLE PLAYS

Ivan Nova, Chicago	30
Mike Minor, Texas	23
Marco Gonzalez, Seattle	22
Brad Keller, Kansas City	22
Eduardo Rodriguez, Boston	20

PICKOFFS

Zach Plesac, Cleveland	6
Matthew Boyd, Detroit	5
Brett Anderson, Oakland	4
Wade Miley, Houston	4
Clayton Richard, Toronto	4
Blake Snell, Tampa Bay	4

WILD PITCHES

Lance Lynn, Texas	18
Trevor Cahill, Los Angeles	14
Matt Barnes, Boston	13
Mike Fiers, Oakland	13
Miguel Castro, Baltimore	11
Blake Snell, Tampa Bay	11

WALKS PLUS HITS PER INNING

Justin Verlander, Houston	0.80
Gerrit Cole, Houston	0.89
Shane Bieber, Cleveland	1.05
Lucas Giolito, Chicago	1.06
Charlie Morton, Tampa Bay	1.08

OPPONENT AVERAGE

Justin Verlander, Houston	.172
Gerrit Cole, Houston	.186
Lucas Giolito, Chicago	.205
Charlie Morton, Tampa Bay	.215
Shane Bieber, Cleveland	.230

WORST ERA

Rick Porcello, Boston	5.52
Reynaldo Lopez, Chicago	5.38
Jakob Junis, Kansas City	5.24
Martin Perez, Minnesota	5.12
Ivan Nova, Chicago	4.72

FIELDING

PITCHER

PCT	11 players	1.000
PO	Justin Verlander, Houston	17
A	Brett Anderson, Oakland	25
DP	Zack Greinke, Houston	4
	Will Harris, Houston	4
E	7 players	3

CATCHER

PCT	Christian Vazquez, Boston	.999
PO	Roberto Perez, Cleveland	1082
A	Christian Vazquez, Boston	71
DP	Roberto Perez, Cleveland	12
E	Gary Sanchez, New York	15
CS	Josh Phegley, Oakland	24
PB	Josh Phegley, Oakland	15

FIRST BASE

PCT	Yuli Gurriel, Houston	.996
PO	Matt Olson, Oakland	1023
A	Matt Olson, Oakland	90
DP	Jose Abreu, Chicago	128
E	Carlos Santana, Cleveland	10

SECOND BASE

PCT	Jason Kipnis, Cleveland	.990
PO	Yolmer Sanchez, Chicago	248
A	Yolmer Sanchez, Chicago	416
DP	Yolmer Sanchez, Chicago	108
E	Rougned Odor, Texas	15

THIRD BASE

PCT	Matt Chapman, Oakland	.981
PO	Matt Chapman, Oakland	146
A	Matt Chapman, Oakland	311
DP	Yoan Moncada, Chicago	37
E	Rafael Devers, Boston	22

SHORTSTOP

PCT	Marcus Semien, Oakland	.981
PO	Elvis Andrus, Texas	205
A	Marcus Semien, Oakland	436
DP	Marcus Semien, Oakland	85
E	Tim Anderson, Chicago	26

OUTFIELD

PCT	3 players	1.000
PO	Mookie Betts, Boston	320
A	Leury Garcia, Chicago	14
DP	Teoscar Hernandez, Toronto	4
E	Domingo Santana, Seattle	12

MAJOR LEAGUES

CLUB BATTING

	AVG	G	AB	R	H	2B	3B	HR	RBI	BB	SO	SB	OBP	SLG
Colorado	.265	162	5660	835	1502	323	41	224	803	489	1503	71	.326	.456
Pittsburgh	.265	162	5657	758	1497	315	38	163	722	425	1213	64	.321	.420
Washington	.265	162	5512	873	1460	298	27	231	824	584	1308	116	.342	.454
Atlanta	.258	162	5560	855	1432	277	29	249	824	619	1467	89	.336	.452
Los Angeles	.257	162	5493	886	1414	302	20	279	861	607	1356	57	.338	.472
New York	.257	162	5624	791	1445	280	17	242	767	516	1384	56	.328	.442
Arizona	.252	162	5633	813	1419	288	40	220	778	540	1360	88	.323	.434
Chicago	.252	162	5461	814	1378	270	26	256	783	581	1460	45	.331	.452
Milwaukee	.246	162	5542	769	1366	279	17	250	744	629	1563	101	.329	.438
Philadelphia	.246	162	5571	774	1369	311	26	215	742	562	1453	78	.319	.427
St. Louis	.245	162	5449	764	1336	246	24	210	714	561	1420	116	.322	.415
Cincinnati	.244	162	5450	701	1328	235	27	227	679	492	1436	80	.315	.422
Miami	.241	162	5512	615	1326	265	18	146	593	395	1469	55	.298	.375
San Francisco	.239	162	5579	678	1332	300	26	167	655	475	1435	47	.302	.392
San Diego	.238	162	5391	682	1281	224	24	219	652	504	1581	70	.308	.410

CLUB PITCHING

	ERA	G	CG	SHO	SV	IP	H	R	ER	HR	BB	SO	AVG
Los Angeles	3.37	162	3	18	44	1446	1201	613	541	185	392	1519	.223
St. Louis	3.80	162	1	14	52	1444	1284	662	609	191	545	1399	.238
Chicago	4.10	162	1	10	38	1442	1376	717	657	195	534	1444	.251
Cincinnati	4.18	162	0	10	46	1438	1270	711	668	214	536	1552	.235
Atlanta	4.19	162	1	8	44	1451	1421	743	675	203	548	1393	.256
New York	4.24	162	3	12	38	1461	1405	737	688	204	500	1520	.251
Arizona	4.25	162	0	11	45	1465	1400	743	691	220	516	1427	.251
Washington	4.27	162	1	13	40	1439	1340	724	683	202	517	1511	.244
San Francisco	4.38	162	1	8	41	1449	1395	773	715	227	519	1368	.249
Milwaukee	4.40	162	0	7	50	1459	1364	766	713	225	572	1497	.246
Philadelphia	4.53	162	3	7	36	1454	1452	794	731	258	546	1392	.251
San Diego	4.60	162	0	6	47	1442	1394	789	732	215	463	1475	.251
Miami	4.74	162	2	8	27	1444	1340	808	760	236	615	1378	.245
Pittsburgh	5.18	162	1	6	31	1440	1511	911	829	241	584	1443	.268
Colorado	5.56	162	1	5	28	1449	1576	958	895	270	589	1264	.277

CLUB FIELDING

	PCT	PO	A	E	DP		PCT	PO	A	E	DP
St. Louis	.989	4332	1578	66	170	Philadelphia	.984	4361	1552	97	139
Atlanta	.987	4352	1522	78	156	Milwaukee	.983	4378	1395	97	135
Arizona	.986	4395	1560	86	138	New York	.983	4383	1435	99	129
San Francisco	.985	4407	1536	90	143	Los Angeles	.982	4337	1428	106	118
Washington	.985	4318	1374	87	112	Chicago	.981	4326	1619	118	142
Cincinnati	.984	4314	1460	91	125	Pittsburgh	.980	4320	1493	121	132
Colorado	.984	4346	1758	97	167	San Diego	.980	4296	1386	116	101
Miami	.984	4333	1364	94	135						

INDIVIDUAL BATTING LEADERS

	AVG	G	AB	R	H	2B	3B	HR	RBI	BB	SO	SB
Christian Yelich, Milwaukee	.329	130	489	100	161	29	3	44	97	80	118	30
Ketel Marte, Arizona	.329	144	569	97	187	36	9	32	92	53	86	10
Anthony Rendon, Washington	.319	146	545	117	174	44	3	34	126	80	86	5
Jeff McNeil, New York	.318	133	510	83	162	38	1	23	75	35	75	5
Nolan Arenado, Colorado	.315	155	588	102	185	31	2	41	118	62	93	3
Charlie Blackmon, Colorado	.314	140	580	112	182	42	7	32	86	40	104	2
Bryan Reynolds, Pittsburgh	.314	134	491	83	154	37	4	16	68	46	121	3
Kevin Newman, Pittsburgh	.308	130	493	61	152	20	6	12	64	28	62	16
Cody Bellinger, Los Angeles	.305	156	558	121	170	34	3	47	115	95	108	15
Trea Turner, Washington	.298	122	521	96	155	37	5	19	57	43	113	35

INDIVIDUAL PITCHING LEADERS

	W	L	ERA	G	GS	CG	SV	IP	H	R	ER	BB	SO
Hyun-Jin Ryu, Los Angeles	14	5	2.32	29	29	1	0	183	160	53	47	24	163
Jacob deGrom, New York	11	8	2.43	32	32	0	0	204	154	59	55	44	255
Mike Soroka, Atlanta	13	4	2.68	29	29	0	0	175	153	56	52	41	142
Jack Flaherty, St. Louis	11	8	2.75	33	33	0	0	196	135	62	60	55	231
Sonny Gray, Cincinnati	11	8	2.87	31	31	0	0	175	122	59	56	68	205
Max Scherzer, Washington	11	7	2.92	27	27	0	0	172	144	59	56	33	243
Clayton Kershaw, Los Angeles	16	5	3.03	29	28	0	0	178	145	63	60	41	189
Patrick Corbin, Washington	14	7	3.25	33	33	1	0	202	169	81	73	70	238
Walker Buehler, Los Angeles	14	4	3.26	30	30	2	0	182	153	77	66	37	215
Stephen Strasburg, Washington	18	6	3.32	33	33	0	0	209	161	79	77	56	251

AWARD WINNERS

Selected by Baseball Writers Association of America

MOST VALUABLE PLAYER

Player	1st	2nd	3rd	Total
Cody Bellinger, Dodgers	19	10		362
Christian Yelich, Brewers	10	18	1	317
Anthony Rendon, Nationals	1	1	24	242
Ketel Marte, D-backs			3	198
Ronald Acuna, Jr., Braves			1	155
Nolan Arenado, Rockies			1	120
Pete Alonso, Mets				102
Freddie Freeman, Braves		1		90
Juan Soto, Nationals				45
Jacob deGrom, Mets				44
Josh Donaldson, Braves				27
Trevor Story, Rockies				26
Jack Flaherty, Cardinals				9
J.T. Realmuto, Phillies				4
Yasmani Grandal, Brewers				4
Max Muncy, Dodgers				4
Stephen Strasburg, Nationals				4
Eugenio Suarez, Reds				4
Hyun-Jin Ryu, Dodgers				3
Kolten Wong, Cardinals				2
Kevin Pillar, Giants				1
Max Scherzer, Nationals				1

CY YOUNG AWARD

Player	1st	2nd	3rd	Total
Jacob deGrom, Mets	29	1		207
Hyun-Jin Ryu, Dodgers	1	10	8	88
Max Scherzer, Nationals		8	8	72
Jack Flaherty, Cardinals		5	11	69
Stephen Strasburg, Nationals		6	1	53
Mike Soroka, Braves			1	9
Sonny Gray, Reds				4
Clayton Kershaw, Dodgers			1	3
Walker Buehler, Dodgers				2
Kirby Yates, Padres				2
Patrick Corbin, Nationals				1

ROOKIE OF THE YEAR

Player	1st	2nd	3rd	Total
Pete Alonso, Mets	29	1		148
Mike Soroka, Braves	1	25	2	82
Fernando Tatis Jr., Padres		2	20	26
Bryan Reynolds, Pirates		1	6	9
Dakota Hudson, Cardinals		1	1	4
Victor Robles, Nationals			1	1

MANAGER OF THE YEAR

Player	1st	2nd	3rd	Total
Mike Shildt, Cardinals	10	14	3	95
Craig Counsell, Brewers	13	6	5	88
Brian Snitker, Braves	3	6	12	45
Dave Roberts, Dodgers	4	1	2	25
Dave Martinez, Nationals		3	6	15
Torey Lovullo, D-backs			2	2

GOLD GLOVE WINNERS

Selected by NL Managers

P—Zack Greinke, D-backs. C—J.T. Realmuto, Phillies. 1B—Anthony Rizzo, Cubs. 2B—Kolten Wong, Cardinals. 3B—Nolan Arenado, Rockies. SS—Nick Ahmed, D-backs. LF—David Peralta, D-backs. CF—J.T. Realmuto, Phillies. RF—Cody Bellinger, Dodgers.

DEPARTMENT LEADERS

BATTING

GAMES
Starlin Castro, Miami	162
Pete Alonso, New York	161
Paul Goldschmidt, St. Louis	161
Cesar Hernandez, Philadelphia	161
3 others	160

AT-BATS
Ozzie Albies, Atlanta	640
Starlin Castro, Miami	636
Eduardo Escobar, Arizona	636
Ronald Acuña Jr., Atlanta	626
Eric Hosmer, San Diego	619

PLATE APPEARANCES
Ronald Acuña Jr., Atlanta	715
Rhys Hoskins, Philadelphia	705
Ozzie Albies, Atlanta	702
Eduardo Escobar, Arizona	699
Pete Alonso, New York	693

RUNS
Ronald Acuña Jr., Atlanta	127
Cody Bellinger, Los Angeles	121
Anthony Rendon, Washington	117
Freddie Freeman, Atlanta	113
Charlie Blackmon, Colorado	112

HITS
Ozzie Albies, Atlanta	189
Ketel Marte, Arizona	187
Nolan Arenado, Colorado	185
Charlie Blackmon, Colorado	182
Amed Rosario, New York	177

TOTAL BASES
Cody Bellinger, Los Angeles	351
Pete Alonso, New York	348
Nolan Arenado, Colorado	343
Ketel Marte, Arizona	337
Charlie Blackmon	334

DOUBLES
Anthony Rendon, Washington	44
Corey Seager, Los Angeles	44
Ozzie Albies, Atlanta	43
Charlie Blackmon, Colorado	42
3 others	38

TRIPLES
Eduardo Escobar, Arizona	10
Ketel Marte, Arizona	9
Ozzie Albies, Atlanta	8
Charlie Blackmon, Colorado	7
5 others	7

EXTRA-BASE HITS
Pete Alonso, New York	85
Cody Bellinger, Los Angeles	84
Charlie Blackmon, Colorado	81
Anthony Rendon, Washington	81
Trevor Story, Colorado	78

HOME RUNS
Pete Alonso, New York	53
Eugenio Suarez, Cincinnati	49
Cody Bellinger, Los Angeles	47
Christian Yelich, Milwaukee	44
Ronald Acuña Jr., Atlanta	41
Nolan Arenado, Colorado	41

RUNS BATTED IN
Anthony Rendon, Washington	126
Freddie Freeman, Atlanta	121
Pete Alonso, New York	120
Nolan Arenado, Colorado	118

Ronald Acuña Jr.

Eduardo Escobar, Colorado	118

SACRIFICES
Clayton Kershaw, Los Angeles	15
Kenta Maeda, Los Angeles	13
Sonny Gray, Cincinnati	12
Hyun-Jin Ryu, Los Angeles	12
German Marquez, Colorado	10

SACRIFICE FLIES
Nick Ahmed, Arizona	12
Eduardo Escobar, Arizona	10
Starlin Castro, Miami	9
Anthony Rendon, Washington	9
Nolan Arenado, Colorado	8
J.T. Realmuto, Philadelphia	8

HIT BY PITCHES
Anthony Rizzo, Chicago	27
Derek Dietrich, Cincinnati	25
Victor Robles, Washington	25
Tim Locastro, Arizona	22
Pete Alonso, New York	21
Jeff McNeil, New York	21

WALKS
Rhys Hoskins, Philadelphia	116
Yasmani Grandal, Milwaukee	109

Juan Soto, Washington	108
Josh Donaldson, Atlanta	100
Bryce Harper, Philadelphia	99

STOLEN BASES
Ronald Acuña Jr., Atlanta	37
Trea Turner, Washington	35
Jarrod Dyson, Arizona	30
Christian Yelich, Milwaukee	30
Victor Robles, Washington	28

STOLEN BASE PERCENTAGE
Tim Locastro, Arizona	1.000
Christian Yelich, Milwaukee	.938
Tommy Edman, St. Louis	.938
Jarrod Dyson, Arizona	.882
Trea Turner, Washington	.875

STRIKEOUTS
Eugenio Suarez, Cincinnati	189
Ronald Acuña Jr., Atlanta	188
Pete Alonso, New York	183
Bryce Harper, Philadelphia	178
Trevor Story, Colorado	174

AT-BATS PER STRIKEOUT
Kevin Newman, Pittsburgh	8.0
Jean Segura, Philadelphia	7.9

Miguel Rojas, Miami	7.8
Adam Frazier, Pittsburgh	7.4
Jose Iglesias, Cincinnati	7.2

DOUBLE PLAYS
Manny Machado, San Diego	24
Starlin Castro, Miami	23
Marcell Ozuna, St. Louis	21
Buster Posey, San Francisco	18
Freedie Freeman, Atlanta	17
Jose Iglesias, Cincinnati	17

MULTI-HIT GAMES
Ketel Marte, Arizona	59
Ozzie Albies, Atlanta	55
Anthony Rendon, Washington	55
Nolan Arenado, Colorado	53
Jeff McNeil, New York	53

ON-BASE PERCENTAGE
Christian Yelich, Milwaukee	.429
Anthony Rendon, Washington	.412
Cody Bellinger, Los Angeles	.406
Anthony Rizzo, Chicago	.405
Juan Soto, Washington	.401

ON-BASE PLUS SLUGGING
Christian Yelich, Milwaukee	1.100
Cody Bellinger, Los Angeles	1.035
Anthony Rendon, Washington	1.010
Ketel Marte, Arizona	.981
Nolan Arenado, Colorado	.962

PITCHING

WINS
Stephen Strasburg, Washington	18
Max Fried, Atlanta	17
Dakota Hudson, St. Louis	16
Clayton Kershaw, Los Angeles	16
Luis Castillo, Cincinnati	15

LOSSES
Merrill Kelly, Arizona	14
Miles Mikolas, St. Louis	14
Sandy Alcantara, Miami	14
Zach Effin, Philadelphia	13
5 others	12

GAMES
Alex Claudio, Milwaukee	83
Wander Suero, Washington	78
Andrew Chafin, Arizona	77
Craig Stammen, San Diego	76
3 others	73

GAMES STARTED
Madison Bumgarner, San Francisco	34
Aaron Nola, Philadelphia	34
Patrick Corbin, Washington	33
Jack Flaherty, St. Louis	33
3 others	33

GAMES FINISHED
Raisel Iglesias, Cincinnati	55
Sean Doolittle, Washington	55
Will Smith, San Francisco	52
Kenley Jansen, Los Angeles	51
Kirby Yates, San Diego	51

COMPLETE GAMES
Zach Eflin, Philadelphia	2
Sandy Alcantara, Miami	2
Walker Buehler, Los Angeles	2
Derek Holland, San Francisco	1
11 others	1

Rhys Hoskins

DEPARTMENT LEADERS

SHUTOUTS
Sandy Alcantara, Miami	2
Zach Eflin, Philadelphia	2
Jason Vargas, New York/Philadelphia	2
Patrick Corbin, Washington	1
6 others	1

SAVES
Kirby Yates, San Diego	41
Josh Hader, Milwaukee	37
Raisel Iglesias, Cincinnati	34
Will Smith, San Francisco	34
Kenley Jansen, Los Angeles	33

INNINGS PITCHED
Stephen Strasburg, Washington	209
Madison Bumgarner, San Francisco	208
Jacob deGrom, New York	204
Aaron Nola, Philadelphia	202
Patrick Corbin, Washington	202

HITS ALLOWED
Jon Lester, Chicago	205
Zack Wheeler, New York	196
Noah Syndergaard, New York	194
Miles Mikolas, St. Louis	193
Madison Bumgarner, San Francisco	191
Jose Quintana, Chicago	191

Jacob deGrom

RUNS ALLOWED
Jon Lester, Chicago	101
Noah Syndergaard, New York	101
Jose Quintana, Chicago	100
Madison Bumgarner, San Francisco	99
Antonio Senzatela, Colorado	99

HOME RUNS ALLOWED
Yu Darvish, Chicago	33
Caleb Smith, Miami	33
Madison Bumgarner, San Francisco	30
Robbie Ray, Arizona	30
3 others	29

WALKS ALLOWED
Dakota Hudson, St. Louis	86
Robbie Ray, Arizona	84
Julio Teheran, Atlanta	83
Sandy Alcantara, Miami	81
Aaron Nola, Philadelphia	80

LOWEST WALKS PER NINE
Hyun-Jin Ryu, Los Angeles	1.2
Miles Mikolas, St. Louis	1.6
Kyle Hendricks, Chicago	1.6

Max Scherzer, Washington	1.7
German Marquez, Colorado	1.8

HIT BATTERS
Julio Teheran, Atlanta	14
Miles Mikolas, St. Louis	12
Aaron Nola, Philadelphia	11
Yu Darvish, Chicago	11
Pablo Lopez, Miami	11

STRIKEOUTS
Jacob deGrom, New York	255
Stephen Strasburg, Washington	251
Max Scherzer, Washington	243
Patrick Corbin, Washington	238
Robbie Ray, Arizona	235

STRIKEOUTS PER NINE
Max Scherzer, Washington	12.7
Robbie Ray, Arizona	12.1
Yu Darvish, Chicago	11.5
Jacob deGrom, New York	11.3
Stephen Strasburg, Washington	10.8

STRIKEOUTS PER NINE
(Relievers)

Josh Hader, Milwaukee	16.4
Edwin Diaz, New York	15.4
Kirby Yates, San Diego	15.0
Felipe Vazquez, Pittsburgh	13.5
Will Smith, San Francisco	13.2

DOUBLE PLAYS
Sandy Alcantara, Miami	23
Miles Mikolas, St. Louis	23
Mike Soroka, Atlanta	23
Dakota Hudson, St. Louis	20
3 others	18

PICKOFFS
Max Fried, Atlanta	5
Patrick Corbin, Washington	4
Joe Musgrove, Pittsburgh	4
Kyle Hendricks, Chicago	3
3 others	3

WILD PITCHES
German Marquez, Colorado	14
Yu Darvish, Chicago	11
Max Fried, Atlanta	11
Jose Quintana, Chicago	11

Joe Kelly, Los Angeles	10

WALKS PLUS HITS PER INNING
Jack Flaherty, St. Louis	0.97
Jacob deGrom, New York	0.97
Hyun-Jin Ryu, Los Angeles	1.01
Max Scherzer, Washington	1.03
Stephen Strasburg, Washington	1.04

OPPONENT AVERAGE
Jack Flaherty, St. Louis	.192
Sonny Gray, Cincinnati	.196
Luis Castillo, Cincinnati	.202
Jacob deGrom, New York	.207
Stephen Strasburg, Washington	.210

WORST ERA
German Marquez, Colorado	4.76
Jose Quintana, Chicago	4.68
Jon Lester, Chicago	4.46
Joe Musgrove, Pittsburgh	4.44
Merrill Kelly, Arizona	4.42

FIELDING

PITCHER
PCT	12 players	1.000
PO	Joe Musgrove, Pittsburgh	30
A	Max Fried, Atlanta	34
DP	Zack Greinke, Arizona	8
E	9 players	4

CATCHER
PCT	Yadier Molina, St. Louis	.999
PO	Yasmani Grandal, Milwaukee	1169
A	Tony Wolters, Colorado	75
DP	J.T. Realmuto, Philadelphia	14
E	Willson Contreras, Chicago	12
	Elias Diaz, Pittsburgh	12
CS	J.T. Realmuto, Philadelphia	43
PB	Tyler Flowers, Atlanta	16

FIRST BASE
PCT	Paul Goldschmidt, St. Louis	.996
PO	Freddie Freeman, Atlanta	1296
A	Christian Walker, Arizona	139
DP	Paul Goldschmidt, St. Louis	146
E	Eric Hosmer, San Diego	14

SECOND BASE
PCT	Ozzie Albies, Atlanta	.994
PO	Ozzie Albies, Atlanta	273
A	Kolten Wong, St. Louis	412
DP	Ozzie Albies, Atlanta	117
E	Keston Hiura, Milwaukee	16

THIRD BASE
PCT	Nolan Arenado, Colorado	.980
PO	Nolan Arenado, Colorado	111
A	Nolan Arenado, Colorado	337
DP	Nolan Arenado, Colorado	43

E	Eugenio Suarez, Cincinnati	17

SHORTSTOP
PCT	Paul DeJong, St. Louis	.989
PO	Paul DeJong, St. Louis	211
A	Paul DeJong, St. Louis	435
DP	Paul DeJong, St. Louis	119
E	Jean Segura, Philadelphia	20

OUTFIELD
PCT	Harold Ramirez, Miami	.996
PO	Victor Robles, Washington	348
A	Bryce Harper, Philadelphia	13
	Hunter Renfroe, San Diego	13
DP	Harrison Bader, St. Louis	4
E	5 players	6

MIKE EHRMANN/GETTY IMAGES

After starting the season 19-31, the Nationals won the franchise's first-ever World Series in 2019.

Nationals Stay Resilient, Finish The Fight

BY JON TAYLER

It almost didn't happen. The dramatic run to the World Series, the first championship in franchise history, the end to almost a century of waiting and futility in Washington, D.C.—came perilously close to falling apart before it even began.

The story of the 2019 Nationals will feature two numbers prominently: 19 and 31. That was their record on May 23, after a sweep at the hands of the Mets lowered them to the fourth-worst record in the majors. All looked lost. Yet amid their rally back to contention and in their wild postseason run, one other number should stand out as well: five. Five times in the playoffs the Nationals faced a deficit in an elimination game. Yet each time, Washington rallied back to save its season, culmi-

nating in back-to-back wins in the World Series to capture that elusive title against a dominant Astros team that, had it won, would likely have gone down as one of the best squads in MLB history.

But the first of those five escapes came right at the beginning for the Nationals, who captured one of the NL's two wild card spots. Hosting a Brewers team that, despite losing Christian Yelich to a knee injury in September, grabbed a postseason place of its own, Washington fell behind from the very start. Staff ace and perennial Cy Young candidate Max Scherzer gave up a two-run home run in the first inning of the wild card game, and a lineup that had finished sixth in the majors in runs scored was able to scratch across only one run in the first seven innings.

Trailing 3–1 in the eighth inning and facing

the Brewers' shutdown closer in Josh Hader, the Nationals looked finished. Yet with one out, pinch-hitter Michael A. Taylor was plunked by a fastball—one that may have caught his bat first, but ruled a hit by pitch nonetheless. Hader struck out Trea Turner for the second out, lowering Washington's chances of victory, per FanGraphs' math, to a meager 11.6 percent. But the Nationals refused to quit. Pinch-hitting for Adam Eaton, venerable veteran Ryan Zimmerman—the last vestige of the franchise's first days in the District—blooped a broken-bat single into center field. A walk to Anthony Rendon followed, loading the bases for Juan Soto, Washington's 20-year-old superstar.

Facing a tiring Hader, Soto laced a ground ball into right field. Rookie Trent Grisham—playing in what would've been Yelich's spot—rushed to retrieve Soto's hit, only to overrun it completely. What would've been at most a game-tying single turned into a bases-clearing double, and a 4–3 lead that the Nationals held to advance.

That was the first Miracle on the Anacostia, though not the last. But the story of the 2019 postseason doesn't belong to just the Nationals. There was plenty of drama across both leagues—surprising defeats, individual heroics, and, sadly for MLB, a plethora of scandals and embarrassments that threatened to tar the entire enterprise. And were it not for Washington's comeback, it's unlikely that this year's World Series would be remembered much if at all outside of southern Texas and the Mid-Atlantic.

The Road To The World Series

To get to the Fall Classic, 10 teams had to be whittled down to two. Though the postseason began with the Nationals' death defiance, things weren't as heart-stopping in the AL wild card game. There, the Rays went to Oakland and easily topped the Athletics by a final score of 5-1 in a game that never really felt in doubt.

That set the Division Series stages. In the AL, the Rays battled the 107-win Astros, the best team in baseball, while the East-winning Yankees clashed with the Central-champion Twins. On the senior circuit, Washington's reward for downing Milwaukee was a date with the Dodgers, owners of 106 regular-season wins and a seventh straight division crown. And in Atlanta, the young and powerful Braves, coming off their second consecutive NL East championship, squared off with a Cardinals squad that had ridden a red-hot second half to its first Central title since 2015.

Following the lead of the wild card game, the

Stephen Strasburg went 5-0 with a 1.98 ERA during the 2019 playoffs.

AL half of the bracket saw few surprises in the first round. New York dispatched of Minnesota in a sweep, extending the Twins' postseason losing streak to a record 16 games (and marking the fourth straight time that their October exit came at the hands of the Yankees). Tampa Bay looked headed to a similar fate after losing the first two against the Astros in Houston, unable to solve the duo of Justin Verlander and Gerrit Cole. But the Rays rallied to win both games at home, sending the series back to Texas for a decisive Game 5—only to be defeated once again by Cole, who struck out 10 batters over eight innings.

The NL playoffs were much more topsy-turvy. Atlanta and St. Louis battled to five games full of bat flips, bad blood, blown leads and late-inning drama before the Cardinals destroyed the Braves with a 10-run first inning in Game 5 to advance. After losing Game 1, the Braves won each of the next two contests, and led the Cardinals late in Game 4, only to have St. Louis icon Yadier Molina hit a game-tying single in the bottom of the eighth inning before lifting a game-winning sacrifice fly in the 10th inning to complete the comeback. Molina's heroics set the stage for Game 5, which was effectively over before the Braves ever stepped to the plate in front of a shocked home crowd.

But the real shock came between the Dodgers and Nationals. Los Angeles easily took Game 1, couldn't solve Stephen Strasburg in Game 2, then beat the soft underbelly of Washington's bullpen in Game 3 to grab a 2–1 series lead.

Once again, the Nationals' backs were against the wall. But in Game 4, Zimmerman saved the day with a home run to make a winner of Scherzer. And despite falling behind early in Game 5, Washington stunned the Dodgers faithful in Chavez Ravine with game-tying solo homers in the eighth inning from Rendon and Soto off of Clayton Kershaw, deployed in relief by a desperate Dave Roberts. The Nats then broke through in the 10th, with Howie Kendrick's grand slam serving as the fatal blow to Los Angeles' championship hopes, and the ticket to get Washington out of the first round for the first time.

The ALCS was a matchup of heavyweights, and it proved a slugfest, as the Yankees and Astros traded punches until Houston finally came out on top in six games. It took heroics from Houston's bullpen, which threw the entirety of Game 6, as well as series MVP Jose Altuve, who walked off Aroldis Chapman in the ninth inning with a massive homer to left field to secure the pennant and his team's second trip to the World Series in three years. There were no such theatrics in the NLCS, where the Nationals not only swept St. Louis, but also never trailed once in any inning of play. Led by a pitching staff that held the Cardinals to just six runs in four games and by series MVP Kendrick, Washington cruised to its first pennant.

Fantastic Finish

While a Houston-Washington matchup offered little history and no rivalry, it carried the sheer joy of pitting the two best rotations in baseball against each other: Verlander, Cole and Zack Greinke versus Scherzer, Strasburg and Patrick Corbin. Game 1 provided a tense, back-and-forth affair that saw Scherzer outduel Cole. But from there, things got sloppy. A close Game 2 devolved after an error-filled seventh inning that saw Washington score six times to blow it open and take a 2–0 series lead. But the Nats couldn't capitalize at home, losing all three games in D.C. and scoring just three runs in the process.

Here was a familiar position for the 2019 Nats: do or die. Needing to win two games in a row against the combo of Verlander and Greinke to stay alive, Washington did just that, blitzing the former in Game 6 with Strasburg pitching masterfully. Game 7 started poorly, though, as Scherzer—scratched from Game 5 due to back and neck spasms—labored through five wobbly innings while Greinke sliced and diced an overmatched Nationals lineup. With nine outs left, Washington trailed, 2–0.

Once again, everything came together late. Rendon crushed a solo shot off Greinke in the seventh to cut the lead in half. A walk to Soto followed, which spelled the end of Greinke's evening. In came Will Harris, the Astros' top setup man, to face Kendrick. The result: a stung line drive to

AMERICAN LEAGUE CHAMPIONS, 1995–2019

American League postseason results in Wild Card Era, 1995-present, where (*) denotes wild card playoff entrant.

YEAR	CHAMPIONSHIP SERIES	ALCS MVP	DIVISION SERIES	DIVISION SERIES
2019	Houston 4, New York 2	José Altuve, 2B, Houston	Houston 3, Tampa Bay* 2	New York 3, Minnesota 0
2018	Boston 4, Houston 1	Jackie Bradley Jr., OF, Boston	Boston 3, New York* 1	Houston 3, Cleveland 0
2017	Houston 4, New York 3	Justin Verlander, RHP, Houston	New York* 3, Cleveland 2	Houston 3, Boston 1
2016	Cleveland 4, Toronto 2	Andrew Miller, LHP, Cleveland	Toronto* 3, Texas 0	Cleveland 3, Boston 0
2015	Kansas City 4, Toronto 2	Alcides Escobar, SS, Kansas City	Kansas City 3, Houston* 2	Baltimore 3, Texas 2
2014	Kansas City 4, Baltimore 0	Lorenzo Cain, OF, Kansas City	Kansas City 3, Los Angeles 0	Baltimore 3, Detroit 0
2013	Boston 4, Detroit 2	Koji Uehara, RHP, Boston	Boston 3, Tampa Bay* 2	Detroit, 3, Oakland 2
2012	Detroit 4, New York 0	Delmon Young, OF, Detroit	New York 3, Baltimore* 2	Detroit 3, Oakland 2
2011	Texas 4, Detroit 2	Nelson Cruz, OF, Texas	Detroit 3, New York 2	Texas 3, Tampa Bay* 1
2010	Texas 4, New York 2	Josh Hamilton, OF, Texas	Texas 3, Tampa Bay 2	New York* 3, Minnesota 0
2009	New York 4, Los Angeles 2	C.C. Sabathia, LHP, New York	New York 3, Minnesota 0	Los Angeles 3, Boston* 0
2008	Tampa Bay 4, Boston 3	Matt Garza, RHP, Tampa Bay	Boston* 3, Los Angeles 1	Tampa Bay 3, Chicago 1
2007	Boston 4, Cleveland 3	Josh Beckett, RHP, Boston	Boston 3, Los Angeles 0	Cleveland 3, New York* 1
2006	Detroit 4, Oakland 0	Placido Polanco, 2B, Detroit	Detroit* 3, New York 1	Oakland 3, Minnesota 0
2005	Chicago 4, Los Angeles 1	Paul Konerko, 1B, Chicago	Chicago 3, Boston* 0	Los Angeles 3, New York 2
2004	Boston 4, New York 3	David Ortiz, DH, Boston	Boston* 3, Anaheim 0	New York 3, Minnesota 1
2003	New York 4, Boston 3	Mariano Rivera, RHP, New York	New York 3, Minnesota 1	Boston* 3, Oakland 2
2002	Anaheim 4, Minnesota 1	Adam Kennedy, 2B, Anaheim	Anaheim* 3, New York 1	Minnesota 3, Oakland 2
2001	New York 4, Seattle 1	Andy Pettitte, LHP, New York	Seattle 3, Cleveland 2	New York 3, Oakland* 2
2000	New York 4, Seattle 2	David Justice, OF, New York	New York 3, Oakland 2	Seattle* 3, Chicago 0
1999	New York 4, Boston 1	Orlando Hernandez, RHP, New York	Boston* 3, Cleveland 2	New York 3, Texas 0
1998	New York 4, Cleveland 2	David Wells, LHP, New York	Cleveland 3, Boston* 1	New York 3, Texas 0
1997	Cleveland 4, Baltimore 2	Marquis Grissom, OF, Cleveland	Cleveland 3, New York* 2	Baltimore 3, Seattle 1
1996	New York 4, Baltimore 1	Bernie Williams, OF, New York	Baltimore* 3, Cleveland 1	New York 3, Texas 1
1995	Cleveland 4, Seattle 2	Orel Hershiser, RHP, Cleveland	Cleveland 3, Boston 0	Seattle 3, New York* 2

right field that pinged off the foul pole, silencing a once-boisterous Houston crowd and giving the Nationals a 3–2 lead.

That advantage grew when Washington teed off on closer Roberto Osuna, deployed despite Houston being behind, while Corbin threw three innings of brilliant relief. Holding a 6–2 lead in the ninth, the Nationals wasted little time in clinching, as closer Daniel Hudson retired the side in order to make them champions. For his efforts, Strasburg was named series MVP, capping a terrific postseason in which he went 5–0, 1.98 and 47 strikeouts in 36.1 innings.

The fantastic finish to what had been a disjointed World Series—one in which, oddly enough, the home team lost each of the seven games for the first time in playoff history—provided the league more than some needed fireworks. It also helped lighten a brutal month of controversies and bad news, most notably the scandal that erupted after Astros assistant general manager Brandon Taubman, during his team's ALCS celebration, taunted a trio of female reporters by saying that he was glad his team had acquired Osuna, who had been suspended for domestic violence a year prior. Although Taubman was eventually fired for his outburst, Houston's ham-fisted handling of the situation—which included an attempt to smear Sports Illustrated's Stephanie Apstein, the reporter who broke the story—cast a pall over the subsequent World Series.

That wasn't the league's only fiasco. After a season that saw a record number of home runs, the ball seemed to go dead in the postseason. A study by Baseball Prospectus showed that, while the regular-season ball had experienced less drag than those in previous years, the October ball was now carrying less. MLB hand-waved away the results, but it was obvious that balls that would've gone over the fence in the summer were now settling into gloves at the warning track. It was yet another controversial event in the seemingly never-ending saga that is currently ongoing between Major League Baseball, its players, and the baseball.

Other problems surfaced throughout the month, including the revelation that Angels pitcher Tyler Skaggs, who died of a drug overdose in July, had bought opioids from a team employee; the unearthing on social media of violent right-wing tweets from umpire Rob Drake; and news that Major League Baseball was planning on drastically shrinking the minor leagues. The fun of the postseason had been overshadowed by a string of unpleasant, avoidable mistakes.

Yet when people look back on October 2019, what they'll remember most is a Nationals team that refused to surrender. "Stay In The Fight" was the team motto created by pugnacious manager Davey Martinez, and that's what they did, all the way through Game 7 of the World Series, when the slogan changed from rallying cry to defiant statement: "Fight Finished."

NATIONAL LEAGUE CHAMPIONS, 1995–2019

National League postseason results in Wild Card Era, 1995-present, where (*) denotes wild card playoff entrant.

YEAR	CHAMPIONSHIP SERIES	NLCS MVP	DIVISION SERIES	DIVISION SERIES
2019	Washington 4, St. Louis 0	Howie Kendrick, 2B, Washington	Washington* 3, Los Angeles 2	St. Louis 3, Atlanta 2
2018	Los Angeles 4, Milwaukee 3	Cody Bellinger, 1B/OF, Los Angeles	Los Angeles 3, Atlanta 1	Milwaukee 3, Colorado 0*
2017	Los Angeles 4, Chicago 1	Justin Turner, 3B/Chris Taylor, CF, L.A.	Los Angeles 3, Arizona* 0	Chicago 3, Washington 2
2016	Chicago 4, Los Angeles 2	Javier Baez, 2B/Jon Lester, LHP, Chicago	Chicago 3, San Francisco* 1	Los Angeles 3, Washington 2
2015	New York 4, Chicago 0	Daniel Murphy, 2B, New York	New York 3, Los Angeles 2	Chicago* 3, St. Louis 1
2014	San Francisco 4, St. Louis 1	Madison Bumgarner, LHP, San Francisco	San Francisco 3, Washington 1	St. Louis 3, Los Angeles 1
2013	St. Louis 4, Los Angeles 2	Michael Wacha, RHP, St. Louis	St. Louis 3, Pittsburgh* 2	Los Angeles 3, Atlanta 1
2012	San Francisco 4, St. Louis 3	Marco Scutaro, 2B, San Francisco	St. Louis* 3, Washington 2	San Francisco 3, Cincinnati 2
2011	St. Louis 4, Milwaukee 2	David Freese, 3B, St. Louis	St. Louis* 3, Philadelphia 2	Milwaukee 3, Arizona 2
2010	San Francisco 4, Philadelphia 2	Cody Ross, OF, San Francisco	Philadelphia 3, Cincinnati 0	San Francisco 3, Atlanta* 1
2009	Philadelphia 4, Los Angeles 1	Ryan Howard, 1B, Philadelphia	Los Angeles 3, St. Louis 0	Philadelphia 3, Colorado* 1
2008	Philadelphia 4, Los Angeles 1	Cole Hamels, LHP, Philadelphia	Los Angeles 3, Chicago 0	Philadelphia 3, Milwaukee* 1
2007	Colorado 4, Arizona 0	Matt Holliday, OF, Colorado	Arizona 3, Chicago 0	Colorado* 3, Philadelphia 0
2006	St. Louis 4, New York 3	Jeff Suppan, RHP, St. Louis	New York 3, Los Angeles* 0	St. Louis 3, San Diego 1
2005	Houston 4, St. Louis 2	Roy Oswalt, RHP, Houston	St. Louis 3, San Diego 0	Houston* 3, Atlanta 1
2004	St. Louis 4, Houston 3	Albert Pujols, 1B, St. Louis	St. Louis 3, Los Angeles 1	Houston* 3, Atlanta 2
2003	Florida 4, Chicago 3	Ivan Rodriguez, C, Florida	Florida* 3, San Francisco 1	Chicago 3, Atlanta 2
2002	San Francisco 4, St. Louis 1	Benito Santiago, C, San Francisco	San Francisco* 3, Atlanta 2	St. Louis 3, Arizona 0
2001	Arizona 4, Atlanta 1	Craig Counsell, SS, Arizona	Atlanta 3, Houston 0	Arizona 3, St. Louis* 2
2000	New York 4, St. Louis 1	Mike Hampton, LHP, New York	St. Louis 3, Atlanta 0	New York* 3, San Francisco 1
1999	Atlanta 4, New York 2	Eddie Perez, C, Atlanta	Atlanta 3, Houston 1	New York* 3, Arizona 1
1998	San Diego 4, Atlanta 2	Sterling Hitchcock, LHP, San Diego	Atlanta 3, Chicago* 0	San Diego 3, Houston 1
1997	Florida 4, Atlanta 2	Livan Hernandez, RHP, Florida	Florida* 3, San Francisco 0	Atlanta 3, Houston 0
1996	Atlanta 4, St. Louis 3	Javy Lopez, C, Atlanta	St. Louis 3, San Diego 0	Atlanta 3, Los Angeles* 0
1995	Atlanta 4, Cincinnati 0	Mike Devereaux, OF, Atlanta	Atlanta 3, Colorado* 1	Cincinnati 3, Los Angeles 0

Year	Winner	Loser	Result
1903	Boston (AL)	Pittsburgh (NL)	5-3
1904	NO SERIES		
1905	New York (NL)	Philadelphia (AL)	4-1
1906	Chicago (AL)	Chicago (NL)	4-2
1907	Chicago (NL)	Detroit (AL)	4-0
1908	Chicago (NL)	Detroit (AL)	4-1
1909	Pittsburgh (NL)	Detroit (AL)	4-3
1910	Philadelphia (AL)	Chicago (NL)	4-1
1911	Philadelphia (AL)	New York (NL)	4-2
1912	Boston (AL)	New York (NL)	4-3-1
1913	Philadelphia (AL)	New York (NL)	4-1
1914	Boston (NL)	Philadelphia (AL)	4-0
1915	Boston (AL)	Philadelphia (NL)	4-1
1916	Boston (AL)	Brooklyn (NL)	4-1
1917	Chicago (AL)	New York (NL)	4-2
1918	Boston (AL)	Chicago (NL)	4-2
1919	Cincinnati (NL)	Chicago (AL)	5-3
1920	Cleveland (AL)	Brooklyn (NL)	5-2
1921	New York (NL)	New York (AL)	5-3
1922	New York (NL)	New York (AL)	4-0
1923	New York (AL)	New York (NL)	4-2
1924	Washington (AL)	New York (NL)	4-3
1925	Pittsburgh (NL)	Washington (AL)	4-3
1926	St. Louis (NL)	New York (AL)	4-3
1927	New York (AL)	Pittsburgh (NL)	4-0
1928	New York (AL)	St. Louis (NL)	4-0
1929	Philadelphia (AL)	Chicago (NL)	4-1
1930	Philadelphia (AL)	St. Louis (NL)	4-2
1931	St. Louis (NL)	Philadelphia (AL)	4-3
1932	New York (AL)	Chicago (NL)	4-0
1933	New York (NL)	Washington (AL)	4-1
1934	St. Louis (NL)	Detroit (AL)	4-3
1935	Detroit (AL)	Chicago (NL)	4-2
1936	New York (AL)	New York (NL)	4-2
1937	New York (AL)	New York (NL)	4-1
1938	New York (AL)	Chicago (NL)	4-0
1939	New York (AL)	Cincinnati (NL)	4-0
1940	Cincinnati (NL)	Detroit (AL)	4-3
1941	New York (AL)	Brooklyn (NL)	4-1
1942	St. Louis (NL)	New York (AL)	4-1
1943	New York (AL)	St. Louis (NL)	4-1
1944	St. Louis (NL)	St. Louis (AL)	4-2
1945	Detroit (AL)	Chicago (NL)	4-3
1946	St. Louis (NL)	Boston (AL)	4-3
1947	New York (AL)	Brooklyn (NL)	4-3
1948	Cleveland (AL)	Boston (NL)	4-2
1949	New York (AL)	Brooklyn (NL)	4-1
1950	New York (AL)	Philadelphia (NL)	4-0
1951	New York (AL)	New York (NL)	4-2
1952	New York (AL)	Brooklyn (NL)	4-3
1953	New York (AL)	Brooklyn (NL)	4-2
1954	New York (NL)	Cleveland (AL)	4-0
1955	Brooklyn (NL)	New York (AL)	4-3
1956	New York (AL)	Brooklyn (NL)	4-3
1957	Milwaukee (NL)	New York (AL)	4-3
1958	New York (AL)	Milwaukee (NL)	4-3
1959	Los Angeles (NL)	Chicago (AL)	4-2
1960	Pittsburgh (NL)	New York (AL)	4-3
1961	New York (AL)	Cincinnati (NL)	4-1
1962	New York (AL)	San Francisco (NL)	4-3
1963	Los Angeles (NL)	New York (AL)	4-0
1964	St. Louis (NL)	New York (AL)	4-3
1965	Los Angeles (NL)	Minnesota (AL)	4-3
1966	Baltimore (AL)	Los Angeles (NL)	4-0
1967	St. Louis (NL)	Boston (AL)	4-3
1968	Detroit (AL)	St. Louis (NL)	4-3
1969	New York (NL)	Baltimore (AL)	4-1
1970	Baltimore (AL)	Cincinnati (NL)	4-1

Juan Soto

Year	Winner	Loser	Result
1971	Pittsburgh (NL)	Baltimore (AL)	4-3
1972	Oakland (AL)	Cincinnati (NL)	4-3
1973	Oakland (AL)	New York (NL)	4-3
1974	Oakland (AL)	Los Angeles (NL)	4-1
1975	Cincinnati (NL)	Boston (AL)	4-3
1976	Cincinnati (NL)	New York (AL)	4-0
1977	New York (AL)	Los Angeles (NL)	4-2
1978	New York (AL)	Los Angeles (NL)	4-2
1979	Pittsburgh (NL)	Baltimore (AL)	4-3
1980	Philadelphia (NL)	Kansas City (AL)	4-2
1981	Los Angeles (NL)	New York (AL)	4-2
1982	St. Louis (NL)	Milwaukee (AL)	4-3
1983	Baltimore (AL)	Philadelphia (NL)	4-1
1984	Detroit (AL)	San Diego (NL)	4-1
1985	Kansas City (AL)	St. Louis (NL)	4-3
1986	New York (NL)	Boston (AL)	4-3
1987	Minnesota (AL)	St. Louis (NL)	4-3
1988	Los Angeles (NL)	Oakland (AL)	4-1
1989	Oakland (AL)	San Francisco (NL)	4-0
1990	Cincinnati (NL)	Oakland (AL)	4-0
1991	Minnesota (AL)	Atlanta (NL)	4-3
1992	Toronto (AL)	Atlanta (NL)	4-2
1993	Toronto (AL)	Philadelphia (NL)	4-2
1994	NO SERIES		
1995	Atlanta (NL)	Cleveland (AL)	4-2
1996	New York (AL)	Atlanta (NL)	4-2
1997	Florida (NL)	Cleveland (AL)	4-3
1998	New York (AL)	San Diego (NL)	4-0
1999	New York (AL)	Atlanta (NL)	4-0
2000	New York (AL)	New York (NL)	4-1
2001	Arizona (NL)	New York (AL)	4-3
2002	Anaheim (AL)	San Francisco (NL)	4-3
2003	Florida (NL)	New York (AL)	4-2
2004	Boston (AL)	St. Louis (NL)	4-0
2005	Chicago (AL)	Houston (NL)	4-0
2006	St. Louis (NL)	Detroit (AL)	4-1
2007	Boston (AL)	Colorado (NL)	4-0
2008	Philadelphia (NL)	Tampa Bay (AL)	4-1
2009	New York (AL)	Philadelphia (NL)	4-2
2010	San Francisco (NL)	Texas (AL)	4-1
2011	St. Louis (NL)	Texas (AL)	4-3
2012	San Francisco (NL)	Detroit (AL)	4-0
2013	Boston (AL)	St. Louis (NL)	4-2
2014	San Francisco (NL)	Kansas City (AL)	4-3
2015	Kansas City (AL)	New York (NL)	4-1
2016	Chicago (NL)	Cleveland (AL)	4-3
2017	Houston (AL)	Los Angeles (NL)	4-3
2018	Boston (AL)	Los Angeles (NL)	4-1
2019	Washington (NL)	Houston (AL)	4-3

WORLD SERIES BOX SCORES

GAME ONE October 22, 2019

WASHINGTON NATIONALS 5, HOUSTON ASTROS 4

	1	2	3	4	5	6	7	8	9	R	H	E
WASHINGTON	0	1	0	1	3	0	0	0	0	5	9	0
HOUSTON	2	0	0	0	0	0	1	1	0	4	10	0

WASHINGTON	AB	R	H	RBI	BB	SO	LOB	AVG
Turner, SS	4	0	1	0	0	1	2	.250
Eaton, RF	4	0	2	1	0	0	1	.500
Rendon, 3B	4	1	0	0	0	1	4	.000
Soto, LF	4	1	3	3	0	1	1	.750
Kendrick, DH	4	0	0	0	0	0	2	.000
Cabrera, A, 2B	4	0	1	0	0	2	1	.250
Zimmerman, 1B	4	1	1	1	0	1	1	.250
Suzuki, C	3	1	0	0	1	1	0	.000
Robles, CF	4	1	1	0	0	1	0	.250
Scherzer, P	0	0	0	0	0	0	0	.000
Corbin, P	0	0	0	0	0	0	0	.000
Rainey, P	0	0	0	0	0	0	0	.000
Hudson, D, P	0	0	0	0	0	0	0	.000
Doolittle, P	0	0	0	0	0	0	0	.000
TOTALS	35	5	9	5	1	8	12	.257

2B: Soto (1, Cole, G). HR: Zimmerman (1, 2nd inning off Cole, G, 0 on, 2 out); Soto (1, 4th inning off Cole, G, 0 on, 0 out). TB: Cabrera, A; Eaton 2; Robles; Soto 7; Turner; Zimmerman 4. RBI: Eaton (1); Soto 3 (3); Zimmerman (1).

HOUSTON	AB	R	H	RBI	BB	SO	LOB	AVG
Springer, CF	3	2	2	2	2	1	1	.667
Altuve, 2B	5	1	1	0	0	1	3	.200
Brantley, LF-RF	4	0	1	0	1	1	3	.250
Bregman, 3B	4	0	0	0	1	3	3	.000
Gurriel, 1B	5	0	2	2	0	1	2	.400
Correa, SS	5	0	1	0	0	3	3	.200
Alvarez, DH	3	0	2	0	1	1	3	.667
Maldonado, C	3	0	0	0	0	0	3	.000
b-Tucker, PH	1	1	1	0	0	0	0	1.000
Chirinos, R, C	0	0	0	0	0	0	0	.000
Reddick, RF	2	0	0	0	0	0	2	.000
a-Díaz, A, PH-LF	2	0	0	0	0	0	2	.000
Cole, G, P	0	0	0	0	0	0	0	.000
Harris, P	0	0	0	0	0	0	0	.000
Smith, J, P	0	0	0	0	0	0	0	.000
TOTALS	37	4	10	4	5	12	25	.270

a-Grounded out for Reddick in the 6th. b-Singled for Maldonado in the 8th. 2B: Gurriel (1, Scherzer); Springer (1, Hudson, D). HR: Springer (1, 7th inning off Rainey, 0 on, 0 out). TB: Altuve; Alvarez 2; Brantley; Correa; Gurriel 3; Springer 6; Tucker. RBI: Gurriel 2 (2); Springer 2 (2).

WASHINGTON	IP	H	R	ER	BB	SO	HR	ERA
Scherzer (W, 1-0)	5.0	5	2	2	3	7	0	3.60
Corbin (H, 1)	1.0	1	0	0	0	2	0	0.00
Rainey (H, 1)	0.1	1	1	1	2	1	1	27.00
Hudson, D (H, 1)	1.1	3	1	1	1	0	0	6.75
Doolittle (S, 1)	1.1	0	0	0	0	1	0	0.00
TOTALS	9.0	10	4	4	5	12	1	4.00

HOUSTON	IP	H	R	ER	BB	SO	HR	ERA
Cole, G (L, 0-1)	7.0	8	5	5	1	6	2	6.43
Harris	1.0	1	0	0	0	1	0	0.00
Smith, J	1.0	0	0	0	0	1	0	0.00
TOTALS	9.0	9	5	5	1	8	2	5.00

WP: Scherzer. Pitches-strikes: Scherzer 112-65; Corbin 21-13; Rainey 19-8; Hudson, D 21-17; Doolittle 13-9; Cole, G 104-70; Harris 18-12; Smith, J 6-5.

GAME TWO October 23, 2019

WASHINGTON NATIONALS 12, HOUSTON ASTROS 3

	1	2	3	4	5	6	7	8	9	R	H	E
WASHINGTON	2	0	0	0	0	0	6	3	1	12	14	2
HOUSTON	2	0	0	0	0	0	0	0	1	3	9	1

WASHINGTON	AB	R	H	RBI	BB	SO	LOB	AVG
Turner, SS	4	2	1	0	0	2	2	.250
Eaton, RF	4	2	2	2	0	0	1	.500
a-Parra, PH-RF	1	0	0	0	0	0	0	.000
Rendon, 3B	4	0	1	2	1	1	2	.125
Soto, LF	3	2	1	0	2	1	2	.571
Kendrick, DH	5	1	2	1	0	0	2	.222
Cabrera, A, 2B	5	1	2	3	0	3	1	.333
Zimmerman, 1B	5	0	2	1	0	1	2	.333
Suzuki, C	5	1	2	1	0	0	2	.250
Robles, CF	3	2	0	0	1	2	2	.143
Taylor, M, CF	1	1	1	1	0	0	0	1.000
Strasburg, P	0	0	0	0	0	0	0	.000
Rodney, P	0	0	0	0	0	0	0	.000
Rainey, P	0	0	0	0	0	0	0	.000
Guerra, Ja, P	0	0	0	0	0	0	0	.000
TOTALS	40	12	14	11	6	10	16	.307

a-Flied out for Eaton in the 9th. 2B: Rendon (1, Verlander); Soto (2, Verlander). HR: Suzuki (1, 7th inning off Verlander, 0 on, 0 out); Eaton (1, 8th inning off James, 1 on, 1 out); Taylor, M (1, 9th inning off Devenski, 0 on, 1 out). TB: Cabrera, A 2; Eaton 5; Kendrick 2; Rendon 2; Soto 2; Suzuki 5; Taylor, M 4; Turner; Zimmerman 2. RBI: Cabrera, A 3 (3); Eaton 2 (3); Kendrick (1); Rendon 2 (2); Suzuki (1); Taylor, M (1); Zimmerman (1).

HOUSTON	AB	R	H	RBI	BB	SO	LOB	AVG
Springer, CF-RF	5	0	0	0	0	1	1	.250
Altuve, 2B	5	0	3	0	0	0	1	.400
Brantley, LF	4	1	2	0	0	0	2	.375
Marisnick, CF	1	0	0	0	0	0	2	.000
Bregman, 3B	4	1	1	2	0	0	2	.125
Gurriel, 1B	4	0	1	0	0	1	0	.333
Alvarez, DH	3	0	1	0	1	1	0	.500
Correa, SS	4	0	0	0	0	3	1	.111
Chirinos, R, C	2	0	0	0	2	1	0	.000
a-Tucker, PH	1	0	0	0	0	1	2	.500
Maldonado, C	1	1	1	1	0	0	0	.250
Reddick, RF-LF	3	0	0	0	1	1	0	.000
Verlander, P	0	0	0	0	0	0	0	.000
Pressly, P	0	0	0	0	0	0	0	.000
James, P	0	0	0	0	0	0	0	.000
Rondón, P	0	0	0	0	0	0	0	.000
Devenski, P	0	0	0	0	0	0	0	.000
TOTALS	37	3	9	3	2	8	14	.257

a-Struck out for Chirinos, R in the 6th. 2B: Altuve (1, Strasburg); Gurriel (2, Strasburg). HR: Bregman (1, 1st inning off Strasburg, 1 on, 1 out); Maldonado (1, 9th inning off Guerra, Ja, 0 on, 1 out). TB: Altuve 4; Alvarez; Brantley 2; Bregman 4; Gurriel 2; Maldonado 4. RBI: Bregman 2 (2); Maldonado (1).

WASHINGTON	IP	H	R	ER	BB	SO	HR	ERA
Strasburg (W, 1-0)	6.0	7	2	2	1	7	1	3.00
Rodney	1.0	0	0	0	1	0	0	0.00
Rainey	1.0	0	0	0	0	1	0	6.75
Guerra, Ja	1.0	2	1	1	0	0	1	9.00
TOTALS	9.0	9	3	3	2	8	2	3.50

HOUSTON	IP	H	R	ER	BB	SO	HR	ERA
Verlander (L, 0-1)	6.0	7	4	4	3	6	1	6.00
Pressly	0.2	3	4	3	2	0	0	40.50
James	1.0	2	3	1	1	3	1	9.00
Rondón	0.1	1	0	0	0	0	0	0.00
Devenski	1.0	1	1	1	0	1	1	9.00
TOTALS	9.0	14	12	9	6	10	3	7.00

Verlander pitched to 2 batters in the 7th. WP: Pressly. IBB: Soto (by Pressly); Alvarez (by Strasburg). Pitches-strikes: Strasburg 114-71; Rodney 21-13; Rainey 12-9; Guerra, Ja 15-9; Verlander 107-69; Pressly 22-13; James 27-18; Rondón 8-5; Devenski 15-11.

GAME 3 October 25, 2019

HOUSTON ASTROS 4, WASHINGTON NATIONALS 1

	1	2	3	4	5	6	7	8	9	R	H	E
HOUSTON	0	1	1	0	1	1	0	0	0	4	11	0
WASHINGTON	0	0	0	1	0	0	0	0	0	1	9	2

HOUSTON	AB	R	H	RBI	BB	SO	LOB	AVG
Springer, CF-RF	4	0	2	0	1	0	2	.333
Altuve, 2B	5	2	2	0	0	0	4	.400
Brantley, LF	4	0	2	2	1	0	1	.417
Osuna, P	0	0	0	0	0	0	0	.000
Bregman, 3B	5	0	0	0	0	1	6	.077
Gurriel, 1B	4	0	0	0	0	1	1	.286
Correa, SS	4	1	1	0	0	1	3	.154
Reddick, RF-LF	4	0	1	1	0	0	0	.111
Chirinos, R, C	4	1	2	1	0	0	1	.333
Greinke, P	1	0	0	0	0	1	0	.000

	AB	R	H	RBI	BB	SO	LOB	AVG
James, P	0	0	0	0	0	0	0	.000
a-Tucker, PH	0	0	0	0	1	0	0	.500
Peacock, P	0	0	0	0	0	0	0	.000
Harris, P	0	0	0	0	0	0	0	.000
b-Alvarez, PH	1	0	0	0	0	0	0	.429
Smith, J, P	0	0	0	0	0	0	0	.000
Marisnick, CF	0	0	0	0	0	0	0	.000
TOTALS	**37**	**4**	**11**	**4**	**3**	**5**	**17**	**.270**

a-Walked for James in the 6th. b-Popped out for Harris in the 8th. **2B:** Correa (1, Sánchez, An); Altuve 2 (3, Sánchez, An, Sánchez, An). **HR:** Chirinos, R (1, 6th inning off Sánchez, An, 0 on, 1 out). **TB:** Altuve 4; Brantley 2; Chirinos, R 5; Correa 2; Gurriel; Reddick; Springer 2. **RBI:** Brantley 2 (2); Chirinos, R (1); Reddick (1).

WASHINGTON	AB	R	H	RBI	BB	SO	LOB	AVG
Turner, SS	5	0	1	0	0	1	3	.231
Eaton, RF	4	0	2	0	1	0	2	.500
Rendon, 3B	5	0	1	0	0	0	4	.154
Soto, LF	4	0	0	0	1	3	3	.364
Cabrera, A, 2B	4	0	2	0	0	1	3	.385
Zimmerman, 1B	3	1	1	0	1	2	2	.333
Suzuki, C	2	0	0	0	0	2	3	.200
a-Parra, PH	1	0	0	0	0	1	0	.000
Ross, J, P	0	0	0	0	0	0	0	.000
c-Kendrick, PH	1	0	1	0	0	0	0	.300
Suero, P	0	0	0	0	0	0	0	.000
Robles, CF	3	0	1	1	1	1	3	.200
Sánchez, An, P	2	0	0	0	0	2	1	.000
Rodney, P	0	0	0	0	0	0	0	.000
b-Adams, M, PH	0	0	0	0	1	0	0	.000
Gomes, C	1	0	0	0	0	0	0	.000
TOTALS	**35**	**1**	**9**	**1**	**5**	**13**	**25**	**.291**

a-Struck out for Suzuki in the 6th. b-Walked for Rodney in the 6th. c-Singled for Ross, J in the 8th. **2B:** Rendon (2, Greinke); Cabrera, A (1, Greinke). **3B:** Robles (1, Greinke). **TB:** Cabrera, A 3; Eaton 2; Kendrick; Rendon 2; Robles 3; Turner; Zimmerman. **RBI:** Robles (1).

HOUSTON	IP	H	R	ER	BB	SO	HR	ERA
Greinke	4.2	7	1	1	3	6	0	1.93
James (W, 1-0)	0.1	0	0	0	0	1	0	6.75
Peacock (H, 1)	0.1	0	0	0	2	1	0	0.00
Harris (H, 1)	1.2	0	0	0	0	2	0	0.00
Smith, J (H, 1)	1.0	1	0	0	0	0	0	0.00
Osuna (S, 1)	1.0	1	0	0	0	1	0	0.00
TOTALS	**9.0**	**9**	**1**	**1**	**5**	**13**	**0**	**5.00**

WASHINGTON	IP	H	R	ER	BB	SO	HR	ERA
Sánchez, An (L, 0-1)	5.1	10	4	4	1	4	1	6.75
Rodney	0.2	0	0	0	2	0	0	0.00
Ross, J	2.0	1	0	0	0	0	0	0.00
Suero	1.0	0	0	0	0	0	0	0.00
TOTALS	**9.0**	**11**	**4**	**4**	**3**	**5**	**1**	**3.67**

IBB: Brantley (by Rodney). **Pitches-strikes:** Greinke 95-60; James 8-5; Peacock 21-10; Harris 25-19; Smith, J 18-12; Osuna 16-9; Sánchez, An 93-57; Rodney 15-9; Ross, J 19-14; Suero 9-8.

GAME 4 October 26, 2019

HOUSTON ASTROS 8, WASHINGTON NATIONALS 1

	1	2	3	4	5	6	7	8	9	R	H	E
HOUSTON	2	0	0	2	0	0	4	0	0	8	13	1
WASHINGTON	0	0	0	0	0	1	0	0	0	1	4	0

HOUSTON	AB	R	H	RBI	BB	SO	LOB	AVG
Springer, RF	4	1	0	0	0	1	2	.250
Altuve, 2B	5	1	2	0	0	0	3	.400
Brantley, LF	5	2	3	0	0	0	1	.471
Bregman, 3B	5	1	3	5	0	0	1	.222
Gurriel, 1B	4	0	1	1	1	2	3	.278
Correa, SS	2	1	0	0	3	0	0	.133
Chirinos, R, C	5	1	2	2	0	0	5	.364
Marisnick, CF	4	0	2	0	1	1	0	.400
Urquidy, P	2	0	0	0	0	1	1	.000
James, P	0	0	0	0	0	0	0	.000
Harris, P	0	0	0	0	0	0	0	.000
a-Tucker, PH	1	1	0	0	0	1	3	.333
Rondón, P	0	0	0	0	0	0	0	.000
Peacock, P	0	0	0	0	0	0	0	.000
b-Alvarez, PH	1	0	0	0	0	0	1	.375
Devenski, P	0	0	0	0	0	0	0	.000
TOTALS	**38**	**8**	**13**	**8**	**7**	**7**	**19**	**.289**

a-Walked for Harris in the 7th. b-Flied out for Peacock in the 9th. **2B:** Chirinos, R (1, Guerra, Ja). **HR:** Chirinos, R (2, 4th inning off Corbin, 1 on, 0 out); Bregman (2, 7th inning off Rodney, 3 on, 1 out). **TB:** Altuve 2; Brantley 3; Bregman 6; Chirinos, R 6; Gurriel; Marisnick 2. **RBI:** Bregman 5 (7); Chirinos, R 2 (3); Gurriel (3).

WASHINGTON	AB	R	H	RBI	BB	SO	LOB	AVG
Turner, SS	5	0	0	0	0	1	5	.167
Eaton, RF	3	0	0	0	1	0	1	.400
Rendon, 3B	4	0	2	0	0	0	0	.235
Soto, LF	3	0	0	1	1	1	3	.286
Kendrick, 2B	4	0	0	0	0	3	4	.214
Zimmerman, 1B	4	0	0	0	0	1	2	.250
Robles, CF	4	0	1	0	0	1	0	.214
Gomes, C	4	0	1	0	0	1	1	.200
Corbin, P	1	0	0	0	0	0	1	.000
a-Parra, PH	0	1	0	0	1	0	0	.000
Rainey, P	0	0	0	0	0	0	0	.000
Rodney, P	0	0	0	0	0	0	0	.000
Suero, P	0	0	0	0	0	0	0	.000
b-Cabrera, A, PH	0	0	0	0	0	0	0	.385
Guerra, Ja, P	0	0	0	0	0	0	0	.000
c-Dozier, B, PH	0	0	0	0	0	1	0	.000
TOTALS	**32**	**1**	**4**	**1**	**5**	**8**	**17**	**.254**

a-Walked for Corbin in the 6th. b-Walked for Suero in the 7th. c-Walked for Guerra, Ja in the 9th. **2B:** Gomes (1, Urquidy). **TB:** Gomes 2; Rendon 2; Robles. **RBI:** Soto (4).

HOUSTON	IP	H	R	ER	BB	SO	HR	ERA
Urquidy (W, 1-0)	5.0	2	0	0	0	4	0	0.00
James	0.1	0	1	1	2	1	0	10.80
Harris (H, 2)	0.2	1	0	0	0	1	0	0.00
Rondón	0.2	1	0	0	1	0	0	0.00
Peacock	1.1	0	0	0	0	1	1	0.00
Devenski	1.0	0	0	0	1	1	0	4.50
TOTALS	**9.0**	**4**	**1**	**1**	**5**	**8**	**0**	**4.00**

WASHINGTON	IP	H	R	ER	BB	SO	HR	ERA
Corbin (L, 0-1)	6.0	7	4	4	2	5	1	5.14
Rainey	0.1	0	2	2	2	0	0	16.20
Rodney	0.1	2	2	2	3	0	1	9.00
Suero	0.1	0	0	0	1	0	0	0.00
Guerra, Ja	2.0	4	0	0	1	2	0	3.00
TOTALS	**9.0**	**13**	**8**	**8**	**7**	**7**	**2**	**4.75**

Pitches-strikes: Urquidy 67-45; James 15-6; Harris 7-5; Rondón 20-14; Peacock 32-18; Devenski 18-9; Corbin 96-59; Rainey 13-4; Rodney 25-10; Suero 5-3; Guerra, Ja 27-17.

GAME 5 October 27, 2019

HOUSTON ASTROS 7, WASHINGTON NATIONALS 1

	1	2	3	4	5	6	7	8	9	R	H	E
HOUSTON	0	2	0	2	0	0	0	1	2	7	10	0
WASHINGTON	0	0	0	0	0	1	0	0	0	1	4	0

HOUSTON	AB	R	H	RBI	BB	SO	LOB	AVG
Springer, CF-RF	3	2	2	2	2	0	0	.316
Altuve, 2B	5	0	1	0	0	0	3	.360
Brantley, RF-LF	3	0	0	0	1	0	1	.400
Bregman, 3B	4	0	0	0	0	0	2	.182
Gurriel, 1B	4	1	2	1	0	0	0	.318
Alvarez, LF	3	2	3	2	0	0	0	.545
1-Marisnick, PR-CF	1	0	0	0	0	0	2	.333
Correa, SS	4	1	1	2	0	1	1	.158
Maldonado, C	3	1	1	0	1	0	0	.286
Cole, G, P	3	0	0	0	0	1	1	.000
Smith, J, P	0	0	0	0	0	0	0	.000
a-Tucker, PH	1	0	0	0	0	1	1	.250
Pressly, P	0	0	0	0	0	0	0	.000
TOTALS	**34**	**7**	**10**	**7**	**4**	**4**	**11**	**.290**

a-Struck out for Smith, J in the 9th. 1-Ran for Alvarez in the 7th. **2B:** Springer (2, Hudson, D). **HR:** Alvarez (1, 2nd inning off Ross, J, 1 on, 1 out); Correa (1, 4th inning off Ross, J, 1 on, 2 out); Springer (2, 9th inning off Hudson, D, 1 on, 2 out). **TB:** Altuve; Alvarez 6; Correa 4; Gurriel 2; Maldonado; Springer 6. **RBI:** Alvarez 2 (2); Correa 2 (2); Gurriel (4); Springer 2 (4).

WASHINGTON	AB	R	H	RBI	BB	SO	LOB	AVG
Turner, SS	4	0	0	0	0	1	1	.136
Eaton, RF	4	0	0	0	0	2	1	.316
Rendon, 3B	3	0	0	0	1	0	0	.200

	AB	R	H	RBI	BB	SO	LOB	AVG
Soto, LF	4	1	2	1	0	1	1	.333
Kendrick, 2B-1B	4	0	1	0	0	1	1	.222
Zimmerman, 1B	2	0	0	0	1	1	2	.222
Hudson, D, P	0	0	0	0	0	0	0	.000
Suero, P	0	0	0	0	0	0	0	.000
Robles, CF	3	0	0	0	0	2	3	.176
Gomes, C	3	0	1	0	0	0	0	.250
Ross, J, P	1	0	0	0	0	0	1	.000
Rainey, P	0	0	0	0	0	0	0	.000
a-Parra, PH	1	0	0	0	0	1	0	.000
Doolittle, P	0	0	0	0	0	0	0	.000
Cabrera, A, 2B	1	0	0	0	1	1	1	.357
TOTALS	30	1	4	1	2	11	10	.233

a-Struck out for Rainey in the 6th. HR: Soto (2, 7th inning off Cole, G, 0 on, 1 out). TB: Gomes; Kendrick; Soto 5. RBI: Soto (5).

HOUSTON	IP	H	R	ER	BB	SO	HR	ERA
Cole, G (W, 1-1)	7.0	3	1	1	2	9	1	3.86
Smith, J	1.0	1	0	0	0	1	0	
Pressly	1.0	0	0	0	0	1	0	16.20
TOTALS	9.0	4	1	1	2	11	1	3.40

WASHINGTON	IP	H	R	ER	BB	SO	HR	ERA
Ross, J (L, 0-1)	5.0	5	4	4	2	1	2	5.14
Rainey	1.0	0	0	0	0	0	0	10.13
Doolittle	1.0	1	0	0	1	1	0	0.00
Hudson, D	1.2	4	3	3	1	2	1	12.00
Suero	0.1	0	0	0	0	0	0	
TOTALS	9.0	10	7	7	4	4	3	5.20

WP: Ross, J. Pitches-strikes: Cole, G 110-71; Smith, J 16-15; Pressly 13-11; Ross, J 78-48; Rainey 9-5; Doolittle 14-8; Hudson, D 36-21; Suero 2-2.

GAME 6 October 29, 2019
WASHINGTON NATIONALS 7, HOUSTON ASTROS 2

	1	2	3	4	5	6	7	8	9	R	H	E
WASHINGTON	1	0	0	0	2	0	2	0	2	7	9	0
HOUSTON	2	0	0	0	0	0	0	0	0	2	6	0

WASHINGTON	AB	R	H	RBI	BB	SO	LOB	AVG
Turner, SS	5	2	2	0	0	0	1	.185
Eaton, RF	2	2	1	1	1	0	1	.333
Rendon, 3B	4	1	3	5	1	0	0	.292
Soto, LF	5	1	1	1	0	0	4	.304
Kendrick, DH	4	0	1	0	0	0	0	.227
Cabrera, A, 2B	4	0	0	0	0	2	1	.278
Zimmerman, 1B	3	0	0	0	1	2	0	.190
Robles, CF	4	0	0	0	0	3	2	.143
Gomes, C	4	1	1	0	0	1	2	.250
Strasburg, P	0	0	0	0	0	0	0	.000
Doolittle, P	0	0	0	0	0	0	0	.000
TOTALS	35	7	9	7	3	8	12	.237

2B: Turner (1, Devenski); Rendon (3, Devenski). HR: Eaton (2, 5th inning off Verlander, 0 on, 1 out); Soto (3, 5th inning off Verlander, 0 on, 2 out); Rendon (1, 7th inning off Harris, 1 on, 2 out). TB: Eaton 4; Gomes; Kendrick; Rendon 7; Soto 4; Turner 3. RBI: Eaton (4); Rendon 5 (7); Soto (6).

HOUSTON	AB	R	H	RBI	BB	SO	LOB	AVG
Springer, CF	4	1	2	0	0	0	0	.348
Altuve, 2B	3	0	0	1	0	1	2	.321
Brantley, LF	4	0	0	0	0	1	2	.333
Bregman, 3B	4	1	2	1	0	0	0	.231
Gurriel, 1B	3	0	0	0	1	0	1	.280
Alvarez, DH	3	0	0	0	1	0	1	.429
Correa, SS	4	0	1	0	0	2	3	.174
Chirinos, R, C	4	0	0	0	0	2	1	.267
Reddick, RF	3	0	1	0	0	1	0	.167
Verlander, P	0	0	0	0	0	0	0	.000
Peacock, P	0	0	0	0	0	0	0	.000
Harris, P	0	0	0	0	0	0	0	.000
Pressly, P	0	0	0	0	0	0	0	.000
Devenski, P	0	0	0	0	0	0	0	.000
TOTALS	32	2	6	2	2	7	10	.274

2B: Springer 2 (4, Strasburg, Strasburg); Correa (2, Doolittle). HR: Bregman (3, 1st inning off Strasburg, 0 on, 2 out). TB: Bregman 5; Correa 2; Reddick; Springer 4. RBI: Altuve (1); Bregman (8).

WASHINGTON	IP	H	R	ER	BB	SO	HR	ERA

	IP	H	R	ER	BB	SO	HR	ERA
Strasburg (W, 2-0)	8.1	5	2	2	2	7	1	2.51
Doolittle	0.2	1	0	0	0	0	0	0.00
TOTALS	9.0	6	2	2	2	7	1	4.67

HOUSTON	IP	H	R	ER	BB	SO	HR	ERA
Verlander (L, 0-2)	5.0	5	3	3	3	3	2	5.73
Peacock	1.1	1	1	1	0	2	0	3.00
Harris	0.2	1	1	1	0	0	1	2.25
Pressly	1.0	0	0	0	0	2	0	10.13
Devenski	1.0	2	2	2	0	1	0	9.00
TOTALS	9.0	9	7	7	3	8	3	4.00

HBP: Eaton (by Devenski). Pitches-strikes: Strasburg 104-65; Doolittle 11-6; Verlander 93-59; Peacock 21-13; Harris 5-4; Pressly 14-8; Devenski 22-14.

GAME 7 October 30, 2019
WASHINGTON NATIONALS 6, HOUSTON ASTROS 2

	1	2	3	4	5	6	7	8	9	R	H	E
WASHINGTON	0	0	0	0	0	0	3	1	2	6	9	0
HOUSTON	0	1	0	0	1	0	0	0	0	2	9	1

WASHINGTON	AB	R	H	RBI	BB	SO	LOB	AVG
Turner, SS	4	0	0	0	1	1	0	.161
Eaton, RF	4	1	1	2	1	0	0	.320
Rendon, 3B	5	1	1	1	0	1	3	.276
Soto, LF	4	1	2	1	1	1	2	.333
Kendrick, DH	3	1	2	2	1	0	1	.280
Cabrera, A, 2B	3	0	1	0	0	0	2	.286
Zimmerman, 1B	3	0	1	0	0	1	0	.208
Gomes, C	3	0	0	0	1	0	3	.188
Robles, CF	4	1	1	0	0	0	2	.160
Scherzer, P	0	0	0	0	0	0	0	.000
Corbin, P	0	0	0	0	0	0	0	.000
Hudson, D, P	0	0	0	0	0	0	0	.000
TOTALS	34	6	9	6	5	3	14	.241

HR: Rendon (2, 7th inning off Greinke, 0 on, 1 out); Kendrick (1, 7th inning off Harris, 1 on, 1 out). TB: Cabrera, A; Eaton; Kendrick 5; Rendon 4; Robles; Soto 2; Zimmerman. RBI: Eaton 2 (6); Kendrick 2 (3); Rendon (8); Soto (7).

HOUSTON	AB	R	H	RBI	BB	SO	LOB	AVG
Springer, CF-RF	4	0	0	0	1	1	3	.296
Altuve, 2B	5	0	1	0	0	3	3	.303
Brantley, LF	4	0	1	0	1	1	1	.321
Bregman, 3B	3	0	0	0	1	1	2	.207
Gurriel, 1B	4	2	2	1	0	0	3	.310
Alvarez, DH	3	0	1	0	1	0	3	.412
Correa, SS	4	0	2	1	0	1	0	.222
Chirinos, R, C	4	0	0	0	0	2	4	.211
Reddick, RF	2	0	1	0	0	0	0	.214
a-Marisnick, PH-CF	2	0	0	0	0	1	0	.375
Greinke, P	0	0	0	0	0	0	0	.000
Harris, P	0	0	0	0	0	0	0	.000
Osuna, P	0	0	0	0	0	0	0	.000
Pressly, P	0	0	0	0	0	0	0	.000
Smith, J, P	0	0	0	0	0	0	0	.000
Urquidy, P	0	0	0	0	0	0	0	.000
TOTALS	35	2	9	2	4	8	21	.272

a-Singled for Reddick in the 6th. HR: Gurriel (1, 2nd inning off Scherzer, 0 on, 0 out). TB: Altuve; Alvarez; Brantley; Correa 2; Gurriel 5; Marisnick; Reddick. RBI: Correa (3); Gurriel (5).

WASHINGTON	IP	H	R	ER	BB	SO	HR	ERA
Scherzer	5.0	7	2	2	4	3	1	3.60
Corbin (W, 1-1)	3.0	2	0	0	0	3	0	3.60
Hudson, D	1.0	0	0	0	0	2	0	9.00
TOTALS	9.0	9	2	2	4	8	1	4.29

HOUSTON	IP	H	R	ER	BB	SO	HR	ERA
Greinke	6.1	2	2	2	2	3	1	2.45
Harris (L, 0-1)(BS, 1)	0.0	2	1	1	0	0	1	4.50
Osuna	1.1	2	1	1	2	0	0	3.86
Pressly	0.1	0	0	0	0	0	0	9.00
Smith, J	0.1	2	2	2	1	0	0	5.40
Urquidy	0.2	1	0	0	0	0	0	0.00
TOTALS	9.0	9	6	6	5	3	2	4.29

Harris pitched to 2 batters in the 7th. Pitches-strikes: Scherzer 103-58; Corbin 44-28; Hudson, D 12-9; Greinke 80-49; Harris 5-3; Osuna 36-19; Pressly 2-1; Smith, J 15-10; Urquidy 10-5.

AMERICAN LEAGUE WILD CARD GAME

TAMPA BAY BAYS 5, OAKLAND ATHLETICS 1

TAMPA BAY	AB	R	H	RBI	BB	SO	LOB	AVG
Díaz, Y, 1B	4	2	3	2	0	0	0	.750
1-Wendle, PR-3B	0	0	0	0	0	0	0	.000
Pham, DH	4	1	2	1	0	1	2	.500
Meadows, LF	3	0	0	0	1	2	1	.000
d'Arnaud, C	4	0	0	0	0	1	2	.000
Duffy, M, 3B	1	1	1	0	0	0	0	1.000
a-Lowe, B, PH-2B	3	0	0	0	0	2	2	.000
García, Av, RF	4	1	1	2	0	2	1	.250
Adames, SS	4	0	0	0	0	2	0	.000
Kiermaier, CF	4	0	0	0	0	0	0	.000
Brosseau, 2B-3B-1B	2	0	0	0	1	1	0	.000
b-Choi, PH-1B	1	0	0	0	0	0	0	.000
Morton, P	0	0	0	0	0	0	0	.000
Castillo, D, P	0	0	0	0	0	0	0	.000
Anderson, N, P	0	0	0	0	0	0	0	.000
Pagán, P	0	0	0	0	0	0	0	.000
TOTALS	34	5	7	5	2	12	8	.206

a-Grounded out for Duffy, M in the 3rd. **b-**Grounded out for Brosseau in the 9th. **1-**Ran for Díaz, Y in the 7th. **HR:** Díaz, Y 2 (2, 1st inning off Manaea, 0 on, 0 out, 3rd inning off Manaea, 0 on, 0 out); García, Av (1, 2nd inning off Manaea, 1 on, 0 out); Pham (1, 5th inning off Petit, 0 on, 2 out). **TB:** Díaz, Y 9; Duffy, M; García, Av 4; Pham 5. **RBI:** Díaz, Y 2 (2); García, Av 2 (2); Pham (1). **2-out RBI:** Pham. **Runners left in scoring position, 2 out:** Pham; Lowe, B. **Team RISP:** 0-for-3. **Team LOB:** 4. **SB:** Pham (1, 2nd base off Petit/Murphy, S). **E:** Brosseau (1, throw). **DP:** 2 (Duffy, M-Brosseau-Díaz, Y; Lowe, B-Brosseau-Díaz, Y).

OAKLAND	AB	R	H	RBI	BB	SO	LOB	AVG
Semien, SS	5	1	1	0	0	2	2	.200
Laureano, RF	3	0	1	1	0	1	1	.333
Chapman, M, 3B	3	0	1	0	1	0	1	.333
Olson, 1B	3	0	1	0	1	3	0	.333
Canha, CF	3	0	0	0	1	2	2	.000
Profar, 2B	4	0	2	0	0	1	4	.500
Davis, K, DH	4	0	0	0	0	3	3	.000
Grossman, LF	4	0	2	0	0	1	1	.500
Murphy, S, C	1	0	0	0	0	0	1	.000
a-Brown, PH	1	0	0	0	0	0	2	.000
Phegley, C	2	0	0	0	0	1	0	.000
Manaea, P	0	0	0	0	0	0	0	.000
Petit, P	0	0	0	0	0	0	0	.000
Diekman, P	0	0	0	0	0	0	0	.000
Luzardo, P	0	0	0	0	0	0	0	.000
Hendriks, P	0	0	0	0	0	0	0	.000
TOTALS	33	1	8	1	3	12	20	.242

a-Grounded into a forceout for Murphy, S in the 4th. **TB:** Chapman, M; Grossman 2; Laureano; Olson; Profar 2; Semien. **RBI:** Laureano (1). **Runners left in scoring position, 2 out:** Profar 2; Semien. **SF:** Laureano. **GIDP:** Murphy, S; Olson. **Team RISP:** 0-for-4. **Team LOB:** 9.

TAMPA BAY	IP	H	R	ER	BB	SO	HR	ERA
Morton (W, 1-0)	5.0	5	1	0	3	4	0	0.00
Castillo, D	2.0	2	0	0	0	3	0	0.00
Anderson, N	1.1	1	0	0	0	4	0	0.00
Pagán	0.2	0	0	0	0	1	0	0.00
TOTALS	9.0	8	1	0	3	12	0	0.00

OAKLAND	IP	H	R	ER	BB	SO	HR	ERA
Manaea (L, 0-1)	2.0	4	4	4	0	5	3	18.00
Petit	2.2	2	1	1	0	2	1	3.38
Diekman	0.1	0	0	0	0	0	0	0.00
Luzardo	3.0	1	0	0	2	4	0	0.00
Hendriks	1.0	0	0	0	1	1	0	0.00
TOTALS	9.0	7	5	5	2	12	4	5.00

Manaea pitched to 1 batter in the 3rd. **Pitches-strikes:** Morton 94-56; Castillo, D 32-22; Anderson, N 22-15; Pagán 6-5; Manaea 46-31; Petit 31-23; Diekman 6-3; Luzardo 46-27; Hendriks 15-9. **Groundouts-flyouts:** Morton 7-2; Castillo, D 1-1; Anderson, N 0-0; Pagán 1-0; Manaea 1-0; Petit 3-3; Diekman 0-0; Luzardo 3-1; Hendriks 1-1. **Batters**

faced: Morton 22; Castillo, D 8; Anderson, N 5; Pagán 2; Manaea 10; Petit 10; Diekman; Luzardo 12; Hendriks 3.

SCORE BY INNING

TAMPA BAY	1	2	1	0	1	0	0	0	0	5	7	1
OAKLAND	0	0	1	0	0	0	0	0	0	1	8	0

AMERICAN LEAGUE DIVISION SERIES

TAMPA BAY RAYS VS. HOUSTON ASTROS

TAMPA BAY	AVG	G	AB	R	H	2B	3B	HR	RBI	BB	SO	SB
Willy Adames, SS	.385	5	13	3	5	1	0	2	2	3	3	0
Ji-Man Choi, 1B	.200	5	15	2	3	0	0	1	1	7	10	0
Travis d'Arnaud, C	.133	5	15	1	2	0	0	0	2	1	5	0
Yandy Díaz, 3B	.000	3	9	0	0	0	0	0	0	0	4	0
Matt Duffy, 3B	.500	2	4	1	2	0	0	0	0	0	0	0
Avisaíl García, RF	.313	4	16	3	5	0	0	0	1	0	3	0
Kevin Kiermaier, CF	.167	5	18	1	3	1	0	1	3	0	6	0
Brandon Lowe, 2B	.250	4	16	1	4	1	0	1	1	1	8	0
Austin Meadows, LF	.150	5	20	2	3	2	0	0	3	2	8	0
Tommy Pham, DH	.333	5	21	1	7	0	0	1	2	1	3	0
Eric Sogard, 2B	.500	2	4	2	2	0	0	1	2	0	1	0
Joey Wendle, 3B	.200	4	10	1	2	1	0	0	1	0	5	0
TOTALS	.236	5	161	18	38	6	0	7	18	15	56	0

TAMPA BAY	W	L	ERA	G	GS	SV	IP	H	R	ER	BB	SO
Nick Anderson	0	0	2.08	3	0	0	4.1	4	1	1	0	4
Diego Castillo	0	0	0.00	3	1	0	3.2	3	0	0	2	5
Oliver Drake	0	0	6.00	2	0	0	3.0	3	2	2	1	4
Tyler Glasnow	0	2	7.71	2	2	0	7.0	9	6	6	3	8
Brendan McKay	0	0	0.00	3	0	0	1.1	2	2	0	0	2
Charlie Morton	1	0	1.80	1	1	0	5.0	3	1	1	2	9
Emilio Pagán	0	0	7.71	3	0	0	2.1	5	3	2	2	1
Colin Poche	0	0	2.08	5	0	0	4.1	2	1	1	0	6
Chaz Roe	0	0	6.75	3	0	0	2.2	3	2	2	1	2
Blake Snell	0	1	1.69	3	1	1	5.1	4	1	1	0	7
Ryan Yarbrough	1	0	0.00	3	0	0	3.0	2	0	0	1	1
TOTALS	2	3	3.43	5	5	1	42	40	19	16	12	49

HOUSTON	AVG	G	AB	R	H	2B	3B	HR	RBI	BB	SO	SB
Jose Altuve, 2B	.350	5	20	4	7	2	0	3	5	1	3	0
Yordan Alvarez, DH	.316	5	19	2	6	3	0	0	1	1	7	0
Michael Brantley, LF	.211	5	19	3	4	0	0	1	1	1	5	0
Alex Bregman, 3B	.353	5	17	6	6	2	0	1	3	3	6	1
Robinson Chirinos, C	.222	4	9	1	2	0	0	1	1	2	4	0
Carlos Correa, SS	.158	5	19	0	3	1	0	0	1	0	9	0
Aledmys Díaz, LF	.000	2	3	0	0	0	0	0	0	0	2	0
Yuli Gurriel, 1B	.316	5	19	1	6	1	0	0	4	1	0	1
Martín Maldonado, C	.400	2	5	0	2	0	0	0	1	1	0	0
Jake Marisnick, CF	—	4	0	0	0	0	0	0	0	0	0	0
Josh Reddick, RF	.100	4	10	1	1	0	0	0	0	1	5	0
George Springer, CF	.143	5	21	1	3	0	0	0	0	1	5	1
Kyle Tucker, RF	.000	2	4	0	0	0	0	0	0	1	2	0
Totals	.242	5	165	19	40	9	0	6	17	12	49	3

HOUSTON	W	L	ERA	G	GS	SV	IP	H	R	ER	BB	SO
Gerrit Cole	2	0	0.57	2	2	0	15.2	6	1	1	3	25
Zack Greinke	0	1	14.73	1	1	0	3.2	5	6	6	1	5
Will Harris	0	0	0.00	3	0	1	2.0	2	0	0	0	3
Josh James	0	0	0.00	2	0	0	1.1	3	0	0	1	2
Wade Miley	0	0	6.75	1	0	0	2.2	4	3	2	1	1
Roberto Osuna	0	0	3.38	3	0	0	2.2	2	1	1	2	4
Ryan Pressly	0	0	18.00	2	0	0	1.0	4	2	2	0	0
Hector Rondón	0	0	—	1	0	0	0.1	1	1	1	0	0
Joe Smith	0	0	0.00	2	0	0	1.2	0	0	0	0	0
Jose Urquidy	0	0	0.00	1	0	0	1.2	3	0	0	1	3
Justin Verlander	1	1	3.38	2	2	0	10.2	8	4	4	6	13
Totals	3	2	3.56	5	5	1	43	38	18	17	15	56

SCORE BY INNING

TAMPA BAY	3	4	1	5	0	1	1	2	1	18
HOUSTON	5	0	0	1	4	2	3	4	0	19

MAJOR LEAGUES

MINNESOTA TWINS VS. NEW YORK YANKEES

MINNESOTA	AVG	G	AB	R	H	2B	3B	HR	RBI	BB	SO	SB
Luis Arraez, 2B	.455	3	11	1	5	4	0	0	1	0	2	0
Jake Cave, LF	.250	2	4	0	1	0	0	0	0	0	2	0
C.J. Cron, 1B	.200	2	5	0	1	0	0	0	0	1	1	0
Nelson Cruz, DH	.200	3	10	2	2	0	0	1	1	4	3	0
Mitch Garver, C	.167	3	12	1	2	0	0	0	1	1	5	0
Marwin Gonzalez, LF	.273	3	11	0	3	1	0	0	0	0	4	0
Max Kepler, CF	.000	3	10	0	0	0	0	0	0	3	3	0
Jorge Polanco, SS	.273	3	11	1	3	0	0	1	2	2	1	1
Eddie Rosario, RF	.308	3	13	1	4	1	0	1	1	0	4	0
Miguel Sano, 3B	.083	3	12	1	1	0	0	1	1	0	8	0
Jonathan Schoop, 2B	.000	2	2	0	0	0	0	0	0	0	2	0
Totals	.218	3	101	7	22	6	0	4	7	11	35	1

MINNESOTA	W	L	ERA	G	GS	SV	IP	H	R	ER	BB	SO
Jose Berrios	0	0	2.25	1	1	0	4.0	4	3	1	3	6
Randy Dobnak	0	1	18.00	1	1	0	2.0	6	4	4	2	0
Tyler Duffey	0	0	21.60	2	0	0	1.2	3	4	4	2	4
Kyle Gibson	0	0	27.00	1	0	0	1.0	1	3	3	3	1
Brusdar Graterol	0	0	0.00	1	0	0	1.0	0	0	0	0	2
Zack Littell	0	1	54.00	2	0	0	0.1	2	2	2	1	0
Trevor May	0	0	0.00	2	0	0	1.0	1	0	0	0	2
Jake Odorizzi	0	1	3.60	1	1	0	5.0	5	2	2	0	5
Taylor Rogers	0	0	4.50	1	0	0	2.0	2	1	1	0	2
Sergio Romo	0	0	9.00	2	0	0	2.0	2	2	2	2	1
Devin Smeltzer	0	0	0.00	1	0	0	3.1	2	0	0	3	4
Cody Stashak	0	0	10.80	2	0	0	1.2	3	2	2	1	0
TOTALS	0	3	7.56	3	3	0	25	29	23	21	17	27

NEW YORK	AVG	G	AB	R	H	2B	3B	HR	RBI	BB	SO	SB
Edwin Encarnacion, DH	.308	3	13	2	4	2	0	0	2	1	2	0
Brett Gardner, CF	.250	3	12	3	3	0	0	1	3	1	5	0
Didi Gregorius, SS	.400	3	10	2	4	0	0	1	6	2	3	0
Aaron Judge, RF	.333	3	9	3	3	0	0	0	0	4	1	0
DJ LeMahieu, 1B	.286	3	14	4	4	2	0	1	4	1	4	0
Cameron Maybin, LF	.333	3	3	2	1	0	0	1	1	0	2	2
Gary Sanchez, C	.125	3	8	1	1	0	0	0	0	3	4	0
Giancarlo Stanton, LF	.167	3	6	0	1	0	0	0	1	4	2	0
Gleyber Torres, 2B	.417	3	12	5	5	3	0	1	4	1	2	2
Gio Urshela, 3B	.250	3	12	1	3	1	0	0	0	0	2	0
TOTALS	.293	3	99	23	29	8	0	5	21	17	27	4

NEW YORK	W	L	ERA	G	GS	SV	IP	H	R	ER	BB	SO
Zack Britton	0	0	3.86	2	0	0	2.1	1	1	1	1	1
Aroldis Chapman	0	0	0.00	2	0	1	2.2	1	0	0	2	4
Chad Green	1	0	0.00	2	0	0	2.0	2	0	0	0	1
J.A. Happ	0	0	0.00	1	0	0	1.0	1	0	0	1	2
Tommy Kahnle	1	0	3.86	3	0	0	2.1	2	1	1	1	3
Jonathan Loaisiga	0	0	9.00	1	0	0	1.0	2	1	1	0	2
Tyler Lyons	0	0	0.00	1	0	0	1.0	0	0	0	0	2
Adam Ottavino	0	0	0.00	3	0	0	1.0	1	0	0	2	1
James Paxton	0	0	5.79	1	1	0	4.2	5	3	3	1	8
Luis Severino	0	0	0.00	1	1	0	4.0	4	0	0	2	4
Masahiro Tanaka	1	0	1.80	1	1	0	5.0	3	1	1	1	7
TOTALS	3	0	2.33	3	3	1	27	22	7	7	11	35

SCORE BY INNINGS

MINNESOTA	1	0	1	1	1	1	0	1	1	7
NEW YORK	1	1	11	0	2	2	4	0	2	23

AMERICAN LEAGUE CHAMPIONSHIP SERIES

NEW YORK YANKEES VS. HOUSTON ASTROS

NEW YORK	AVG	G	AB	R	H	2B	3B	HR	RBI	BB	SO	SB
Edwin Encarnacion, DH	.056	5	18	0	1	1	0	0	0	4	11	0
Brett Gardner, LF	.136	6	22	1	3	0	0	0	1	2	10	0
Didi Gregorius, SS	.217	6	23	2	5	1	0	0	0	0	3	0
Aaron Hicks, CF	.154	5	13	1	2	0	0	1	3	4	5	1
Aaron Judge, RF	.240	6	25	3	6	0	0	1	2	3	10	2
DJ LeMahieu, 1B	.346	6	26	6	9	1	0	2	3	3	2	0
Cameron Maybin, LF	.333	2	3	0	1	0	0	0	0	1	2	0
Gary Sanchez, C	.130	6	23	1	3	0	0	1	3	1	12	0
Giancarlo Stanton, DH	.286	2	7	1	2	0	0	1	1	0	3	0
Gleyber Torres, 2B	.280	6	25	3	7	2	0	2	6	2	4	0
Gio Urshela, 3B	.238	6	21	3	5	0	0	2	2	2	2	0
TOTALS	.214	6	206	21	44	5	0	10	21	22	64	3

NEW YORK	W	L	ERA	G	GS	SV	IP	H	R	ER	BB	SO
Zack Britton	0	0	0.00	5	0	0	5.2	1	0	0	5	5
Luis Cessa	0	0	0.00	2	0	0	4.0	2	0	0	0	4
Aroldis Chapman	0	1	6.75	3	0	1	2.2	1	2	2	2	5
Chad Green	0	1	9.64	4	1	0	4.2	4	5	5	1	5
J.A. Happ	1	0	3.38	2	0	0	2.2	1	1	1	1	1
Tommy Kahnle	0	0	1.59	5	0	0	5.2	2	1	1	2	5
Jonathan Loaisiga	0	0	0.00	3	0	0	1.2	1	1	0	3	1
Tyler Lyons	0	0	0.00	1	0	0	0.2	0	0	0	0	2
Adam Ottavino	0	1	11.57	5	0	0	2.1	6	4	3	1	3
James Paxton	1	0	2.16	2	2	0	8.1	8	2	2	6	12
CC Sabathia	0	0	0.00	2	0	0	1.0	0	0	0	0	0
Luis Severino	0	1	4.15	1	1	0	4.1	5	2	2	3	6
TOTALS	2	4	3.13	6	6	1	54.2	36	22	19	27	54

HOUSTON	AVG	G	AB	R	H	2B	3B	HR	RBI	BB	SO	SB
Jose Altuve, 2B	.348	6	23	6	8	1	0	2	3	4	1	1
Yordan Alvarez, DH	.045	6	22	1	1	0	0	0	0	2	12	0
Michael Brantley, LF	.304	6	23	1	7	0	0	0	1	4	4	0
Alex Bregman, 3B	.167	6	18	4	3	1	0	0	1	7	2	0
Robinson Chirinos, C	.000	4	13	1	0	0	0	0	0	1	6	0
Carlos Correa, SS	.182	6	22	2	4	1	0	2	5	3	9	1
Aledmys Diaz, LF	.000	5	4	0	0	0	0	0	0	1	0	0
Yuli Gurriel, 1B	.125	6	24	1	3	0	0	1	4	1	0	0
Martin Maldonado, C	.250	2	8	0	2	1	0	0	0	0	4	0
Jake Marisnick, CF	.333	5	3	0	1	0	0	0	0	0	2	0
Josh Reddick, RF	.167	5	12	2	2	0	0	1	1	0	2	0
George Springer, CF	.160	6	25	4	4	0	0	2	4	4	10	0
Kyle Tucker, RF	.250	2	4	0	1	0	0	0	0	0	2	0
Totals	.179	6	201	22	36	4	0	8	19	27	54	2

HOUSTON	W	L	ERA	G	GS	SV	IP	H	R	ER	BB	SO
Bryan Abreu	0	1	27.00	1	0	0	0.2	2	2	2	2	0
Gerrit Cole	1	0	0.00	1	1	0	7.0	4	0	0	5	7
Zack Greinke	0	1	3.48	2	2	0	10.1	10	4	4	4	11
Will Harris	0	0	0.00	4	0	0	3.2	1	0	0	1	4
Josh James	1	0	4.91	4	0	0	3.2	3	2	2	3	7
Roberto Osuna	1	0	3.60	4	0	1	5.0	2	2	2	1	4
Brad Peacock	0	0	3.38	2	1	0	2.2	1	1	1	1	3
Ryan Pressly	1	0	10.80	4	0	0	1.2	5	2	2	1	3
Hector Rondon	0	0	0.00	1	0	0	0.1	0	0	0	0	1
Joe Smith	0	0	2.45	4	0	0	3.2	2	1	1	1	3
Jose Urquidy	0	0	3.38	1	0	0	2.2	3	1	1	1	5
Totals	4	2	3.44	6	6	1	55	44	21	21	22	64

SCORE BY INNINGS

NEW YORK	5	1	0	4	0	4	2	1	4	0	0	21
HOUSTON	5	2	3	0	1	4	2	1	3	0	1	22

NATIONAL LEAGUE WILD CARD GAME

WASHINGTON NATIONALS 4, MILWAUKEE BREWERS 3

MILWAUKEE	AB	R	H	RBI	BB	SO	LOB	AVG
Grisham, RF	3	1	0	0	1	2	2	.000
Grandal, C	3	1	1	2	1	1	0	.333
Moustakas, 3B	4	0	0	0	0	1	2	.000
Hiura, 2B	4	0	1	0	0	3	2	.250
Spangenberg, 2B	0	0	0	0	0	0	0	.000
Braun, LF	4	0	1	0	0	0	1	.250
Hader, P	0	0	0	0	0	0	0	.000
Thames, 1B	4	1	2	1	0	1	1	.500
Cain, CF	4	0	1	0	0	1	1	.250
Arcia, SS	4	0	1	0	0	1	2	.250
Woodruff, P	0	0	0	0	0	0	0	.000
a-Shaw, T, PH	0	0	0	0	1	0	0	.000
Suter, P	0	0	0	0	0	0	0	.000
Pomeranz, P	1	0	0	0	0	0	0	.000
Gamel, LF	1	0	0	0	0	1		.000
TOTALS	**32**	**3**	**7**	**3**	**3**	**11**	**12**	**.219**

a-Walked for Woodruff in the 5th. **2B:** Thames (1, Scherzer); Hiura (1, Strasburg). **HR:** Grandal (1, 1st inning off Scherzer, 1 on, 0 out); Thames (1, 2nd inning off Scherzer, 0 on, 0 out). **TB:** Arcia; Braun; Cain; Grandal 4; Hiura 2; Thames 6. **RBI:** Grandal 2 (2); Thames (1). **Runners left in scoring position, 2 out:** Hiura; Grisham; Arcia; Braun. **SAC:** Woodruff. **GIDP:** Thames. **Team RISP:** 0-for-6. **Team LOB:** 6. **E:** Moustakas (1, throw); Grisham (1, fielding). **Outfield assists:** Grisham (Soto at 3rd base).

WASHINGTON	AB	R	H	RBI	BB	SO	LOB	AVG
Turner, SS	4	1	1	1	0	1	3	.250
Eaton, RF	3	0	0	0	0	1	0	.000
c-Zimmerman, PH	1	0	1	0	0	0	0	1.000
1-Stevenson, PR	0	1	0	0	0	0	0	.000
Hudson, D, P	0	0	0	0	0	0	0	.000
Rendon, 3B	3	1	0	0	1	1	0	.000
Soto, LF	4	0	1	2	0	2	0	.250
Kendrick, 1B	3	0	1	0	0	0	0	.333
Cabrera, A, 2B	3	0	0	0	0	1		.000
Suzuki, C	3	0	0	0	0	0	1	.000
Robles, CF	3	0	1	0	0	2	0	.333
Scherzer, P	1	0	0	0	0	0	0	.000
a-Dozier, B, PH	1	0	0	0	0	0	1	.000
Strasburg, P	0	0	0	0	0	0	0	.000
b-Taylor, M, PH-RF	1	0	0	0	0	0	0	.000
TOTALS	**29**	**4**	**5**	**3**	**1**	**7**	**6**	**.172**

a-Reached on error for Scherzer in the 5th. **b-**Hit by pitch for Strasburg in the 8th. **c-**Singled for Eaton in the 8th. **1-**Ran for Zimmerman in the 8th. **HR:** Turner (1, 3rd inning off Woodruff, 0 on, 2 out). **TB:** Kendrick; Robles; Soto; Turner 4; Zimmerman. **RBI:** Soto 2 (2); Turner (1). **2-out RBI:** Turner; Soto 2. **Runners left in scoring position, 2 out:** Turner. **Team RISP:** 1-for-2. **Team LOB:** 3. **DP:** (Rendon-Turner-Kendrick).

MILWAUKEE	IP	H	R	ER	BB	SO	HR	ERA
Woodruff	4.0	2	1	1	0	3	1	2.25
Suter	1.0	1	0	0	0	0	0	0.00
Pomeranz (H, 1)	2.0	0	0	0	0	2	0	0.00
Hader (L, 0-1)(BS, 1)	1.0	2	3	2	1	1	0	18.00
TOTALS	**8.0**	**5**	**4**	**3**	**1**	**7**	**1**	**3.38**

WASHINGTON	IP	H	R	ER	BB	SO	HR	ERA
Scherzer	5.0	4	3	3	3	6	2	5.40
Strasburg (W, 1-0)	3.0	2	0	0	0	4	0	0.00
Hudson, D (S, 1)	1.0	1	0	0	0	1	0	0.00
Totals	9.0	7	3	3	3	11	2	3.00

HBP: Taylor, M (by Hader). **Pitches-strikes:** Woodruff 52-34; Suter 27-16; Pomeranz 30-19; Hader 30-14; Scherzer 77-46; Strasburg 34-26; Hudson, D 11-7. **Groundouts-flyouts:** Woodruff 3-2; Suter 2-1; Pomeranz 3-0; Hader 0-0; Scherzer 4-1; Strasburg 4-0; Hudson, D 0-1. **Batters faced:** Woodruff 14; Suter 5; Pomeranz 6; Hader 6; Scherzer 22; Strasburg 10; Hudson, D 4.

SCORE BY INNINGS

										R	H	E
MILWAUKEE	2	1	0	0	0	0	0	0	0	3	7	2
WASHINGTON	0	0	1	0	0	0	0	3	X	4	5	0

NATIONAL LEAGUE DIVISION SERIES

WASHINGTON NATIONALS VS. LOS ANGELES DODGERS

WASHINGTON	AVG	G	AB	R	H	2B	3B	HR	RBI	BB	SO	SB
Matt Adams, PH	.000	2	2	0	0	0	0	0	0	0	1	0
Asdrubal Cabrera, 2B	.167	4	6	0	1	0	0	0	2	0	1	0
Patrick Corbin, P	.000	3	2	0	0	0	0	0	0	0	2	0
Brian Dozier, 2B	.000	3	4	0	0	0	0	0	0	0	2	0
Adam Eaton, RF	.188	5	16	3	3	0	0	0	1	5	2	0
Yan Gomes, C	.167	3	6	0	1	0	0	0	0	1	4	0
Howie Kendrick, 2B	.250	5	20	2	5	0	0	1	5	1	3	0
Gerardo Parra, PH	.000	2	2	0	0	0	0	0	0	0	0	0
Anthony Rendon, 3B	.412	5	17	5	7	3	0	1	5	3	3	0
Victor Robles, CF	.200	2	5	1	1	0	0	0	0	0	1	0
Anibal Sanchez, P	.000	1	1	0	0	0	0	0	0	0	1	0
Max Scherzer, P	.000	2	3	0	0	0	0	0	0	0	1	0
Juan Soto, LF	.278	5	18	4	5	0	0	2	4	3	4	0
Stephen Strasburg, P	.000	2	3	0	0	0	0	0	0	1	2	0
Kurt Suzuki, C	.000	4	9	0	0	0	0	0	0	3	3	0
Michael A. Taylor, CF	.333	4	12	1	4	0	0	0	1	1	3	0
Trea Turner, SS	.286	5	21	3	6	3	0	0	2	3	0	0
Ryan Zimmerman, 1B	.286	4	14	2	4	1	0	1	3	0	6	0
TOTALS	**.230**	**5**	**161**	**21**	**37**	**8**	**0**	**5**	**20**	**20**	**42**	**0**

WASHINGTON	W	L	ERA	G	GS	SV	IP	H	R	ER	BB	SO
Patrick Corbin	0	2	7.88	3	1	0	8.0	7	8	7	7	14
Sean Doolittle	0	0	2.70	3	0	0	3.1	1	1	1	0	3
Daniel Hudson	1	0	0.00	3	0	1	2.2	3	0	0	2	4
Tanner Rainey	0	0	9.00	3	0	0	2.0	2	2	2	1	1
Fernando Rodney	0	0	0.00	2	0	0	1.2	2	0	0	3	3
Anibal Sanchez	0	0	1.80	1	1	0	5.0	4	1	1	2	9
Max Scherzer	1	0	1.13	2	1	0	8.0	4	1	1	3	10
Stephen Strasburg	1	0	3.00	2	2	0	12.0	9	4	4	1	17
Hunter Strickland	0	0	18.00	2	0	0	1.0	4	4	4	1	3
Wander Suero	0	0	27.00	1	0	0	0.1	2	1	1	0	0
TOTALS	**3**	**2**	**4.20**	**5**	**5**	**1**	**45**	**38**	**22**	**21**	**20**	**64**

LOS ANGELES	AVG	G	AB	R	H	2B	3B	HR	RBI	BB	SO	SB
Matt Beaty, LF	.375	4	8	1	3	0	0	0	0	0	1	0
Cody Bellinger, CF	.211	5	19	2	4	1	0	0	0	2	7	3
Walker Buehler, P	.000	2	4	0	0	0	0	0	0	0	2	0
David Freese, 1B	.500	4	8	2	4	1	0	0	0	0	3	0
Enrique Hernandez, LF	.429	3	7	2	3	1	0	1	3	1	2	0
Rich Hill, P	.000	1	1	0	0	0	0	0	0	0	1	0
Clayton Kershaw, P	.000	2	1	0	0	0	0	0	0	0	0	0
Gavin Lux, 2B	.222	4	9	1	2	0	0	1	1	1	6	0
Russell Martin, C	.500	1	4	2	2	1	0	1	4	1	2	0
Max Muncy, 1B	.263	5	19	4	5	0	0	3	7	4	2	1
Joc Pederson, RF	.267	5	15	3	4	2	0	1	1	2	5	0
A.J. Pollock, LF	.000	5	13	1	0	0	0	0	0	1	11	0
Hyun-Jin Ryu, P	.000	1	2	0	0	0	0	0	0	0	2	0
Corey Seager, SS	.150	5	20	3	3	1	0	0	0	1	8	0
Will Smith, C	.077	4	13	0	1	0	0	0	0	3	5	0
Chris Taylor, LF	.125	5	8	1	1	0	0	0	0	3	4	0
Justin Turner, 3B	.286	5	21	3	6	2	0	2	5	1	2	1
Julio Urias, P	.000	3	1	0	0	0	0	0	0	0	1	0
TOTALS	**.220**	**5**	**173**	**22**	**38**	**9**	**0**	**9**	**21**	**20**	**64**	**5**

LOS ANGELES	W	L	ERA	G	GS	SV	IP	H	R	ER	BB	SO
Pedro Baez	0	0	13.50	2	0	0	0.2	4	1	1	1	1
Walker Buehler	1	0	0.71	2	2	0	12.2	5	1	1	6	15
Rich Hill	0	0	3.38	1	1	0	2.2	2	1	1	4	2
Kenley Jansen	0	0	0.00	2	0	0	1.2	0	0	0	0	2
Joe Kelly	0	1	23.14	3	0	0	2.1	5	6	6	5	4
Clayton Kershaw	0	1	7.11	2	1	0	6.1	8	5	5	1	5
Adam Kolarek	0	0	0.00	3	0	0	1.0	0	0	0	0	2
Kenta Maeda	0	0	0.00	4	0	0	4.2	1	0	0	0	7
Dustin May	0	0	2.70	2	0	0	3.1	3	1	1	1	1

	W	L	ERA	G	GS	SV	IP	H	R	ER	BB	SO
Hyun-Jin Ryu	1	0	3.60	1	1	0	5.0	4	2	2	2	3
Ross Stripling	0	0	9.00	1	0	0	1.0	1	1	1	0	0
Julio Urias	0	1	7.36	3	0	0	3.2	4	3	3	0	0
TOTALS	2	3	4.20	5	5	0	45	37	21	21	20	42

SCORE BY INNINGS

MILWAUKEE	3	2	1	0	4	4	0	3	0	4	21
COLORADO	4	1	0	0	2	8	3	2	2	0	22

ST. LOUIS CARDINALS VS. ATLANTA BRAVES

ST. LOUIS	AVG	G	AB	R	H	2B	3B	HR	RBI	BB	SO	SB
Randy Arozarena, CF	.000	3	3	0	0	0	0	0	0	0	2	0
Harrison Bader, CF	.200	4	10	1	2	0	0	0	1	0	5	1
Matt Carpenter, 3B	.200	4	5	1	1	0	0	0	3	3	2	0
Paul DeJong, SS	.222	5	18	2	4	1	0	0	2	2	8	0
Tommy Edman, 3B	.316	5	19	3	6	3	1	0	2	2	2	0
Jack Flaherty, P	.000	2	5	1	0	0	0	0	1	1	3	0
Dexter Fowler, RF	.091	5	22	3	2	1	0	0	3	2	4	0
Paul Goldschmidt, 1B	.429	5	21	5	9	4	0	2	2	2	2	0
Dakota Hudson, P	.000	1	2	0	0	0	0	0	0	0	2	0
Carlos Martinez, P	.000	3	1	0	0	0	0	0	0	0	1	0
Jose Martinez, PH	.667	3	3	0	2	0	0	0	0	0	1	0
Miles Mikolas, P	1.000	2	1	0	1	0	0	0	0	0	0	0
Yadier Molina, C	.143	5	21	1	3	0	0	0	2	1	2	0
Marcell Ozuna, LF	.429	5	21	6	9	3	0	2	5	1	5	0
Adam Wainwright, P	.000	1	2	0	0	0	0	0	0	0	2	0
Matt Wieters, PH	1.000	1	1	0	0	0	0	0	0	0	0	0
Kolten Wong, 2B	.250	5	20	3	5	3	0	0	4	2	6	0
TOTALS	.251	5	175	26	44	16	1	4	25	16	47	1

LOS ANGELES	W	L	ERA	G	GS	SV	IP	H	R	ER	BB	SO
John Brebbia	0	0	0.00	3	0	0	2.0	3	0	0	0	2
Genesis Cabrera	0	0	0.00	1	0	0	1.0	1	0	0	0	1
Jack Flaherty	1	1	2.77	2	2	0	13.0	12	4	4	2	16
Giovanny Gallegos	0	0	0.00	3	0	0	2.0	1	0	0	2	3
Ryan Helsley	0	0	0.00	2	0	0	1.1	1	0	0	0	3
Dakota Hudson	0	0	1.93	1	1	0	4.2	5	4	1	2	2
Carlos Martinez	1	1	16.20	3	0	0	3.1	6	6	6	3	4
Miles Mikolas	1	0	1.50	2	1	0	6.0	3	1	1	2	2
Andrew Miller	0	0	0.00	3	0	0	2.0	0	0	0	2	1
Adam Wainwright	0	0	0.00	1	1	0	7.2	4	0	0	2	8
Tyler Webb	0	0	4.50	3	0	0	2.0	2	2	1	1	4
Totals	3	2	2.60	5	5	0	45	38	17	13	16	46

ATLANTA	AVG	G	AB	R	H	2B	3B	HR	RBI	BB	SO	SB
Ronald Acuña Jr., CF	.444	5	18	1	8	3	1	1	2	4	5	0
Ozzie Albies, 2B	.250	5	20	3	5	0	0	1	3	2	3	0
Francisco Cervelli, C	.000	2	2	0	0	0	0	0	0	1	1	0
Josh Donaldson, 3B	.158	5	19	2	3	1	0	1	3	2	4	0
Adam Duvall, LF	.273	5	11	2	3	0	0	1	5	1	5	0
Tyler Flowers, C	1.000	2	1	0	1	0	0	0	0	0	1	0
Mike Foltynewicz, P	.000	2	2	0	0	0	0	0	0	0	1	0
Freddie Freeman, 1B	.200	5	20	1	4	1	0	1	1	6	0	
Billy Hamilton, PH	—	2	0	2	0	0	0	0	0	0	1	0
Adeiny Hechavarria, 3B	.000	3	3	0	0	0	0	0	0	0	2	0
Matt Joyce, RF	.100	5	10	0	1	0	0	0	0	1	2	0
Dallas Keuchel, P	.000	2	2	0	0	0	0	0	0	0	1	0
Nick Markakis, RF	.143	5	21	1	3	1	0	0	0	1	4	0
Chris Martin, PR	—	1	0	0	0	0	0	0	0	0	0	0
Brian McCann, C	.188	5	16	1	3	1	0	0	0	1	2	0
Rafael Ortega, PH	.000	4	3	1	0	0	0	0	0	0	1	0
Mike Soroka, P	.000	2	2	0	0	0	0	0	0	0	1	0
Dansby Swanson, SS	.389	5	18	3	7	3	0	0	2	1	6	0
Josh Tomlin, P	.000	2	1	0	0	0	0	0	0	0	1	0
TOTALS	.225	5	169	17	38	10	1	5	16	16	46	1

ATLANTA	W	L	ERA	G	GS	SV	IP	H	R	ER	BB	SO
Mike Foltynewicz	1	1	7.36	2	2	0	7.1	6	7	6	3	7
Max Fried	0	0	9.00	4	0	0	4.0	5	4	4	3	6
Shane Greene	0	0	3.38	2	0	0	2.2	4	1	1	1	3
Luke Jackson	0	0	10.13	3	0	0	2.2	6	4	3	2	6
Dallas Keuchel	0	0	4.50	2	2	0	6.9	4	4	4	4	4
Mark Melancon	0	1	12.00	3	0	2	3.0	8	4	4	2	4
Sean Newcomb	0	0	0.00	4	0	0	3.2	0	0	0	0	4
Darren O'Day	0	0	0.00	4	0	0	2.0	1	0	0	0	2
Mike Soroka	0	0	1.29	1	1	0	7.0	2	1	1	0	7

	W	L	ERA	G	GS	SV	IP	H	R	ER	BB	SO
Julio Teheran	0	1	5.40	2	0	0	1.2	1	1	1	1	2
Josh Tomlin	0	0	0.00	2	0	0	3.2	2	0	0	0	2
TOTALS	1	3	4.76	4	4	1	34	25	20	18	27	35

SCORE BY INNINGS

ST. LOUIS	12	2	2	1	1	0	0	3	4	1	26
ATLANTA	2	0	1	1	3	2	2	0	6	0	17

NATIONAL LEAGUE CHAMPIONSHIP SERIES

WASHINGTON NATIONALS VS. ST. LOUIS CARDINALS

WASHINGTON	AVG	G	AB	R	H	2B	3B	HR	RBI	BB	SO	SB
Matt Adams, PH	1.000	1	1	1	1	0	0	0	0	0	0	0
Patrick Corbin, P	.000	2	1	0	0	0	0	0	0	0	1	0
Brian Dozier, 2B	.000	3	1	0	0	0	0	0	0	0	0	0
Adam Eaton, RF	.235	4	17	3	4	2	1	0	3	1	4	0
Yan Gomes, C	.429	3	7	1	3	1	0	0	3	1	3	0
Howie Kendrick, 2B	.333	4	15	4	5	4	0	0	4	2	4	0
Gerardo Parra, PH	1.000	1	1	0	1	0	0	0	0	0	0	0
Anthony Rendon, 3B	.417	4	12	2	5	1	0	0	2	4	3	0
Victor Robles, CF	.375	2	8	3	3	0	0	1	2	0	2	0
Anibal Sanchez, P	.000	1	4	0	0	0	0	0	0	0	2	0
Max Scherzer, P	.000	1	2	0	0	0	0	0	0	0	1	0
Juan Soto, LF	.188	4	16	2	3	1	0	0	1	1	7	0
Stephen Strasburg, P	.000	1	1	0	0	0	0	0	0	0	1	0
Kurt Suzuki, C	.125	2	8	0	1	0	0	0	0	0	5	0
Michael A. Taylor, CF	.250	2	8	1	2	0	0	1	1	0	4	0
Trea Turner, SS	.294	4	17	2	5	0	0	0	2	1	4	0
Ryan Zimmerman, 1B	.250	4	16	1	4	2	0	0	2	1	3	0
TOTALS	.274	4	135	20	37	11	1	2	20	11	44	0

WASHINGTON	W	L	ERA	G	GS	SV	IP	H	R	ER	BB	SO
Patrick Corbin	1	0	6.75	2	1	0	5.1	4	4	4	3	12
Sean Doolittle	0	0	2.25	3	0	1	4.0	3	1	1	0	3
Daniel Hudson	0	0	0.00	2	0	2	2.0	0	0	0	1	0
Tanner Rainey	0	0	0.00	2	0	0	2.0	0	0	0	0	3
Fernando Rodney	0	0	0.00	1	0	0	1.0	0	0	0	0	2
Anibal Sanchez	1	0	0.00	1	1	0	7.2	1	0	0	1	5
Max Scherzer	1	0	0.00	1	1	0	7.0	1	0	0	2	11
Stephen Strasburg	1	0	0.00	1	1	0	7.0	7	1	0	0	12
TOTALS	4	0	1.25	4	4	3	36	16	6	5	7	48

ST. LOUIS	AVG	G	AB	R	H	2B	3B	HR	RBI	BB	SO	SB
Randy Arozarena, PH	.000	2	1	0	0	0	0	0	0	0	1	1
Harrison Bader, CF	.000	2	2	1	0	0	0	0	0	1	1	0
Matt Carpenter, 3B	.000	4	8	0	0	0	0	0	0	0	4	0
Paul DeJong, SS	.250	4	12	1	3	0	0	0	0	1	6	0
Tommy Edman, RF	.000	4	14	0	0	0	0	0	0	1	5	0
Jack Flaherty, P	.000	1	1	0	0	0	0	0	0	0	1	0
Dexter Fowler, CF	.000	4	11	1	0	0	0	0	0	2	6	0
Paul Goldschmidt, 1B	.063	4	16	0	1	0	0	0	0	0	9	0
Jose Martinez, RF	.500	4	10	1	5	2	0	0	3	0	2	0
Miles Mikolas, P	.000	1	1	0	0	0	0	0	0	0	1	0
Yadier Molina, C	.167	4	12	1	2	0	0	1	1	0	1	0
Yairo Munoz, PH	.000	1	1	0	0	0	0	0	0	0	1	0
Marcell Ozuna, LF	.188	4	16	0	3	1	0	0	0	0	8	0
Adam Wainwright, P	.000	2	2	0	0	0	0	0	0	1	0	0
Matt Wieters, PH	.000	2	2	0	0	0	0	0	0	0	1	0
Kolten Wong, 2B	.143	4	14	1	2	0	0	0	0	2	0	2
TOTALS	.130	4	123	6	16	3	0	1	5	7	48	3

LOS ANGELES	W	L	ERA	G	GS	SV	IP	H	R	ER	BB	SO
John Brebbia	0	0	18.00	2	0	0	1.0	4	2	2	1	1
Genesis Cabrera	0	0	0.00	2	0	0	0.2	0	0	0	0	0
Jack Flaherty	0	1	9.00	1	1	0	4.0	5	4	4	2	6
Giovanny Gallegos	0	0	3.86	2	0	0	2.1	2	1	1	1	3
Ryan Helsley	0	0	0.00	3	0	0	4.0	0	0	0	1	5
Dakota Hudson	0	1	108.00	1	1	0	0.1	5	7	4	1	0
Carlos Martinez	0	0	0.00	1	0	0	0.1	0	0	0	1	1
Miles Mikolas	0	1	1.50	1	1	0	6.0	7	1	1	2	7
Andrew Miller	0	0	0.00	3	0	0	3.0	1	0	0	0	5
Daniel Ponce de Leon	0	0	4.50	1	0	0	2.0	2	1	1	1	4
Adam Wainwright	0	1	3.00	2	1	0	9.0	9	3	3	1	11
Tyler Webb	0	0	6.75	2	0	0	1.1	2	1	1	0	1
TOTALS	0	4	4.50	4	4	0	34.0	37	20	17	11	44

SCORE BY INNINGS

WASHINGTON	7	1	5	0	2	1	2	2	0	20	
ST. LOUIS	0	0	0	1	3	0	1	1	0	6	

ORGANIZATION STATISTICS

Arizona Diamondbacks

SEASON IN A SENTENCE: The D-backs dealt their two biggest stars, Paul Goldschmidt before the season and Zack Greinke at the trade deadline, yet still won 85 games and challenged for the second wild card in the National League.

HIGH POINT: Arizona got as close as 1.5 games out of the wild card on Sept. 7 after winning 11 of 12 games.

LOW POINT: The D-backs went 11-17 in May and looked like they were headed for the cliff, especially after righthander Luke Weaver went on the shelf with a forearm injury on May 31.

NOTABLE ROOKIES: The D-backs had one of the oldest teams in the NL, and that was reflected in the club's Opening Day rookies: 28-year-old first baseman Christian Walker (29 home runs, 111 OPS+) and 30-year-old Merrill Kelly (101 ERA+ in 183 innings). Even reliever Yoan Lopez and outfielder Tim Locastro, the fastest man in baseball, according to StatCast, were 26. But as the season progressed, the face of the typical Arizona rookie got a bit younger, particularly on the pitching side. Homegrown pitchers Alex Young (83 innings), Taylor Clarke (85) and Jon Duplantier (37) all made their big league debuts. Trade deadline acquisition Zac Gallen shined in eight starts for the D-backs down the stretch, recording a 2.89 ERA with 53 strikeouts in 44 innings.

KEY TRANSACTIONS: In December 2018 the D-backs traded Goldschmidt, the best hitter in franchise history, to the Cardinals for a package headlined by young big league righthander Luke Weaver and catcher Carson Kelly. Then at the deadline, Arizona exchanged Greinke for a quartet of Astros prospects, including righthanders Corbin Martin and J.B. Bukauskas and first baseman Seth Beer. The D-backs even consummated a prospect "challenge trade" with the Marlins in which they dealt Double-A shortstop Jazz Chisholm for 24-year-old rookie righthander Zac Gallen.

DOWN ON THE FARM: The D-backs had a banner year on the farm. Three affiliates won their league titles, and D-backs domestic clubs finished with a 422-336 record and .557 winning percentage that placed fourth-best in baseball. Double-A Jackson won the Southern League for the third time in four years—and the second year in a row—while high Class A Visalia won the California League and short-season Hillsboro the Northwest League. Low Class A Kane County gave Arizona a fourth minor league playoff team.

OPENING DAY PAYROLL: $107,584,167 (18th).

PLAYERS OF THE YEAR

ROBERT BINDER

MAJOR LEAGUE	MINOR LEAGUE
Ketel Marte	**Daulton Varsho**
OF/2B	**C/OF**
.329/.389/.592	(Double-A)
Career-high 32 HR	.301/.378/.520,
97 R, 92 RBIs, 10 SB	18 HR, 21 SB

ORGANIZATION LEADERS

Batting		*Minimum 250 AB
MAJORS		
* AVG	Ketel Marte	.329
* OPS	Ketel Marte	.981
HR	Eduardo Escobar	35
RBI	Eduardo Escobar	118
MINORS		
* AVG	Kevin Cron, Reno, AZL D-backs	.329
* OBP	Kevin Cron, Reno, AZL D-backs	.446
* SLG	Kevin Cron, Reno, AZL D-backs	.777
* OPS	Kevin Cron, Reno, AZL D-backs	1.223
R	Andy Young, Jackson, Reno	89
H	Domingo Leyba, Reno	137
TB	Andy Young, Jackson, Reno	247
2B	Domingo Leyba, Reno	37
3B	Juan Batista, DSL D-backs 1, DSL D-backs 2	8
3B	Ben DeLuzio, Jackson, Reno	8
HR	Kevin Cron, Reno, AZL D-backs	39
RBI	Kevin Cron, Reno, AZL D-backs	107
BB	Luis Alejandro Basabe, Visalia	75
SO	Anfernee Grier, Visalia	131
SB	Jose Curpa, AZL D-backs, Missoula	30

Pitching		#Minimum 75 IP
MAJORS		
W	Merrill Kelly	13
# ERA	Zack Greinke	2.90
SO	Robbie Ray	235
SV	Archie Bradley	18
MINORS		
W	Josh Green, Visalia, Jackson	11
L	Matt Koch, Reno	10
# ERA	Kenny Hernandez, Kane County	1.88
G	Lucas Luetge, Jackson, Reno	55
GS	Ryan Weiss, Kane County, Visalia	26
SV	West Tunnell, Visalia, Jackson	19
IP	Jeff Bain, Visalia, Jackson	136
BB	Tyler Mark, Jackson, AZL D-backs, Visalia	47
SO	Jeff Bain, Visalia, Jackson	162
# AVG	Levi Kelly, Kane County	.199

2019 PERFORMANCE

General Manager: Mike Hazen. **Farm Director:** Mike Bell. **Scouting Director:** Deric Ladnier.

Class	Team	League	W	L	PCT	Finish	Manager
Majors	Arizona Diamondbacks	National	85	77	.525	7th (15)	Torey Lovullo
Triple-A	Reno Aces	Pacific Coast	66	74	.471	10th (16)	Chris Cron
Double-A	Jackson Generals	Southern	78	57	.578	3rd (10)	Blake Lalli
High A	Visalia Rawhide	California	83	53	.610	1st (8)	Shawn Roof
Low A	Kane County Cougars	Midwest	81	58	.583	t-2nd (16)	Vince Harrison
Short season	Hillsboro Hops	Northwest	48	28	.632	1st (8)	Javier Colina
Rookie	Missoula Osprey	Pioneer	40	36	.526	2nd (8)	Juan Francia
Rookie	AZL D-backs	Arizona	26	30	.464	13th (21)	Wellington Cepeda
Overall 2019 Minor League Record			422	336	.557	4th (30)	

ORGANIZATION STATISTICS

ARIZONA DIAMONDBACKS
NATIONAL LEAGUE

Batting	B-T	HT	WT	DOB	AVG	vLH	vRH	G	AB	R	H	2B	3B	HR	RBI	BB	HBP	SH	SF	SO	SB	CS	SLG	OBP
Ahmed, Nick	R-R	6-2	195	3-15-90	.254	.312	.234	158	556	79	141	33	6	19	82	52	4	1	12	113	8	2	.437	.316
Almonte, Abraham	B-R	5-9	210	6-27-89	.290	.333	.286	17	31	11	9	3	1	1	4	7	0	0	0	8	0	0	.548	.421
Avila, Alex	L-R	5-11	210	1-29-87	.207	.219	.205	63	164	22	34	8	0	9	24	36	1	0	0	68	1	0	.421	.353
Cron, Kevin	R-R	6-5	250	2-17-93	.211	.222	.208	39	71	12	15	4	0	6	16	4	2	0	1	28	0	1	.521	.269
Dyson, Jarrod	L-R	5-10	165	8-15-84	.230	.326	.218	130	400	65	92	11	2	7	27	47	2	1	2	86	30	4	.320	.313
Escobar, Eduardo	B-R	5-10	185	1-5-89	.269	.298	.256	158	636	94	171	29	10	35	118	50	3	0	10	130	5	1	.511	.321
Flores, Wilmer	R-R	6-3	205	8-6-91	.317	.337	.304	89	265	31	84	18	0	9	37	15	4	0	1	31	0	0	.487	.361
Jones, Adam	R-R	6-2	215	8-1-85	.260	.261	.259	137	485	66	126	25	1	16	67	31	8	0	3	101	2	1	.414	.313
Joseph, Caleb	R-R	6-3	180	6-18-86	.211	.333	.188	20	38	5	8	2	0	0	3	1	1	1	0	10	0	0	.263	.250
Kelly, Carson	R-R	6-2	220	7-14-94	.245	.356	.203	111	314	46	77	19	0	18	47	48	2	0	1	79	0	0	.478	.348
Lamb, Jake	L-R	6-3	215	10-9-90	.193	.304	.177	78	187	26	36	8	2	6	30	32	5	0	2	55	-1	0	.353	.323
Leyba, Domingo	B-R	5-11	160	9-11-95	.280	.333	.273	21	25	6	7	2	1	0	5	4	0	0	1	9	0	0	.440	.367
Locastro, Tim	R-R	6-1	200	7-14-92	.250	.225	.265	91	212	38	53	12	2	1	17	14	22	1	1	44	17	0	.340	.357
Marte, Ketel	B-R	6-1	165	10-12-93	.329	.333	.327	144	569	97	187	36	9	32	92	53	4	0	2	86	10	2	.592	.389
Murphy, John Ryan	R-R	5-11	205	5-13-91	.177	.125	.211	25	62	9	11	3	0	4	7	6	0	1	0	28	0	0	.419	.250
2-team total (1 Braves)					.175	.125	.205	26	63	9	11	3	0	4	7	6	0	1	0	28	0	0	.413	.246
Peralta, David	L-L	6-1	210	8-14-87	.275	.248	.286	99	382	48	105	29	3	12	57	35	5	0	1	87	0	0	.461	.343
Rojas, Josh	L-R	6-1	185	6-30-94	.217	.290	.196	41	138	17	30	7	0	2	16	18	1	0	0	41	4	2	.312	.312
Swihart, Blake	B-R	6-1	200	4-3-92	.136	.133	.137	31	66	9	9	0	0	3	9	4	0	0	0	29	0	0	.273	.186
Tomas, Yasmany	R-R	6-2	250	11-14-90	.000	.000	--	4	6	0	0	0	0	0	0	0	0	0	0	3	0	0	.000	.000
Vargas, Ildemaro	B-R	6-0	170	7-16-91	.269	.340	.243	92	201	25	54	9	1	6	24	9	0	0	1	24	1	0	.413	.299
Walker, Christian	R-R	6-0	220	3-28-91	.259	.241	.266	152	529	86	137	26	1	29	73	67	6	0	1	155	8	1	.476	.348

Pitching	B-T	HT	WT	DOB	W	L	ERA	G	GS	CG	SV	IP	H	R	ER	HR	BB	SO	AVG	vLH	vRH	K/9	BB/9
Andriese, Matt	R-R	6-2	225	8-28-89	5	5	4.71	54	0	0	1	71	72	37	37	8	27	79	.262	.228	.286	10.06	3.44
Avila, Alex	L-R	5-11	210	1-29-87	0	0	4.50	2	0	0	0	2	2	1	1	0	1	1	.286	.500	.000	4.50	4.50
Bradley, Archie	R-R	6-4	225	8-10-92	4	5	3.52	66	1	0	18	72	67	30	28	5	36	87	.246	.267	.231	10.93	4.52
Chafin, Andrew	R-L	6-2	225	6-17-90	2	2	3.76	77	0	0	0	53	52	23	22	6	18	68	.257	.258	.256	11.62	3.08
Clarke, Taylor	R-R	6-4	200	5-13-93	5	5	5.31	23	15	0	1	85	86	55	50	23	30	68	.263	.252	.274	7.23	3.19
Crichton, Stefan	R-R	6-3	200	2-29-92	1	0	3.56	28	0	0	0	30	23	12	12	3	8	33	.204	.146	.236	9.79	2.37
Duplantier, Jon	L-R	6-4	225	7-11-94	1	1	4.42	15	3	0	1	37	39	18	18	2	18	34	.283	.250	.308	8.35	4.42
Gallen, Zac	R-R	6-2	191	8-3-95	2	3	2.89	8	8	0	0	44	37	14	14	5	18	53	.228	.244	.213	10.92	3.71
2-team total (7 Marlins)					3	6	2.81	15	15	0	0	80	62	26	25	8	36	96	.212	.207	.217	10.80	4.05
Ginkel, Kevin	L-R	6-4	210	3-24-94	3	0	1.48	25	0	0	2	24	15	7	4	2	9	28	.174	.200	.152	10.36	3.33
Godley, Zack	R-R	6-3	240	4-21-90	3	5	6.39	27	9	0	2	76	81	55	54	12	35	58	.277	.300	.248	6.87	4.14
Greinke, Zack	R-R	6-2	200	10-21-83	10	4	2.90	23	23	0	0	146	117	48	47	15	21	135	.220	.210	.230	8.32	1.29
Hirano, Yoshihisa	R-R	6-1	185	3-8-84	5	5	4.75	62	0	0	1	53	51	31	28	7	22	61	.249	.250	.248	10.36	3.74
Holland, Greg	R-R	5-10	205	11-20-85	1	2	4.54	40	0	0	17	36	25	18	18	5	24	41	.198	.180	.215	10.35	6.06
Joseph, Caleb	R-R	6-3	180	6-18-86	0	0	0.00	2	0	0	0	1	0	0	0	0	0	0	.000	.000	.000	0.00	0.00
Kelly, Merrill	R-R	6-2	190	10-14-88	13	14	4.42	32	32	0	0	183	184	95	90	29	57	158	.260	.273	.248	7.76	2.80
Koch, Matt	L-R	6-3	215	11-2-90	0	0	9.15	9	0	0	0	21	29	21	21	8	4	9	.333	.400	.262	3.92	1.74
Leake, Mike	R-R	5-10	170	11-12-87	3	3	4.35	10	10	0	0	60	74	36	29	15	8	27	.306	.339	.271	4.05	1.20
Lopez, Yoan	R-R	6-3	185	1-2-93	2	7	3.41	70	0	0	1	61	52	27	23	11	17	42	.232	.211	.246	6.23	2.52
McFarland, T.J.	L-L	6-3	220	6-8-89	0	0	4.82	51	0	0	0	56	71	35	30	6	20	35	.316	.292	.343	5.63	3.21
Murphy, John Ryan	R-R	5-11	205	5-13-91	0	0	27.00	2	0	0	0	3	10	9	9	3	3	0	.526	.385	.833	0.00	9.00
Payamps, Joel	R-R	6-2	200	4-7-94	0	0	4.50	2	0	0	0	4	4	2	2	0	3	3	.308	.375	.200	6.75	6.75
Ray, Robbie	L-L	6-2	195	10-1-91	12	8	4.34	33	33	0	0	174	150	91	84	30	84	235	.234	.209	.241	12.13	4.34
Scott, Robby	R-L	6-3	220	8-29-89	1	0	4.91	11	0	0	0	7	8	4	4	1	7	9	.276	.294	.250	11.05	8.59
Sherfy, Jimmie	R-R	6-0	175	12-27-91	1	0	5.89	17	0	0	1	18	23	12	12	4	5	22	.303	.259	.327	10.80	2.45
Walker, Taijuan	R-R	6-4	235	8-13-92	0	0	0.00	1	1	0	0	1	1	0	0	0	1	1	.250	.000	.500	9.00	0.00
Weaver, Luke	R-R	6-2	170	8-21-93	4	3	2.94	12	12	0	0	64	55	22	21	6	14	69	.227	.225	.230	9.65	1.96
Young, Alex	L-L	6-2	205	9-9-93	7	5	3.56	17	15	0	0	83	72	40	33	14	27	71	.229	.167	.253	7.67	2.92

Fielding

Catcher	PCT	G	PO	A	E	DP	PB
Avila	.995	54	384	29	2	2	2
Joseph	.989	16	87	6	1	2	0
Kelly	.991	101	792	49	8	2	4
Murphy	1.000	18	150	9	0	1	0

First Base	PCT	G	PO	A	E	DP
Cron	.983	12	56	3	1	7
Flores	1.000	16	47	4	0	4
Lamb	.994	24	144	12	1	20
Swihart	1.000	1	2	0	0	0
Walker	.991	142	1042	139	11	95

Second Base	PCT	G	PO	A	E	DP
Escobar	1.000	33	39	64	0	12

	PCT	G	PO	A	E	DP
Flores	.970	64	77	118	6	26
Leyba	.947	8	7	11	1	3
Marte	.990	83	79	122	2	28
Rojas	1.000	1	1	0	0	0
Vargas	.993	48	51	87	1	22

Third Base	PCT	G	PO	A	E	DP
Cron	.000	1	0	0	0	0
Escobar	.978	144	86	219	7	28
Kelly	.000	1	0	0	0	0
Lamb	.985	36	15	50	1	2
Leyba	1.000	1	1	0	0	0
Vargas	.929	14	4	9	1	2

Shortstop	PCT	G	PO	A	E	DP

	PCT	G	PO	A	E	DP
Ahmed	.979	158	207	412	13	79
Leyba	1.000	2	0	4	0	0
Marte	1.000	11	7	20	0	4
Vargas	1.000	4	3	9	0	2

Outfield	PCT	G	PO	A	E	DP
Almonte	.944	12	16	1	1	0
Dyson	.991	118	208	10	2	1
Jones	.972	130	209	2	6	0
Locastro	.991	69	104	1	0	0
Marte	.994	96	163	3	1	0
Peralta	.990	93	201	3	2	1
Rojas	1.000	38	62	2	0	1
Swihart	1.000	18	20	3	0	0
Vargas	1.000	2	1	0	0	0

RENO ACES
PACIFIC COAST LEAGUE

TRIPLE-A

Batting	B-T	HT	WT	DOB	AVG	vLH	vRH	G	AB	R	H	2B	3B	HR	RBI	BB	HBP	SH	SF	SO	SB	CS	SLG	OBP
Almonte, Abraham	B-R	5-9	210	6-27-89	.270	.200	.297	91	319	78	86	33	4	17	59	60	0	0	3	70	12	3	.558	.382
Aplin, Andrew	L-L	6-0	205	3-21-91	.205	.167	.217	28	78	12	16	1	0	2	12	10	1	1	0	19	2	0	.295	.303
Asuaje, Carlos	L-R	5-9	158	11-2-91	.239	.150	.269	59	159	28	38	7	2	5	29	22	3	0	2	32	1	1	.403	.339
Cron, Kevin	R-R	6-5	250	2-17-93	.331	.310	.339	82	305	81	101	20	1	38	105	61	6	0	2	77	1	2	.777	.449
Decker, Cody	R-R	5-11	218	1-17-87	.240	.242	.238	39	96	16	23	6	0	7	21	17	0	0	2	28	0	1	.521	.348
DeLuzio, Ben	R-R	6-3	190	8-9-94	.357	.475	.302	39	126	33	45	12	4	2	20	14	2	0	3	38	3	5	.564	.421
Flores, Wilmer	R-R	6-3	205	8-6-91	.444	.667	.333	2	9	2	4	0	0	0	4	1	0	0	0	1	0	0	.444	.500
Heineman, Tyler	B-R	5-11	205	6-19-91	.325	.304	.333	25	80	16	26	5	1	3	13	9	2	0	0	14	0	0	.525	.407
2-team total (48 New Orleans)					.336	.333	.337	73	244	42	82	17	3	13	38	21	5	3	0	35	4	0	.590	.400
Herbert, Lucas	R-R	6-0	200	11-28-96	.300	.500	.286	8	30	5	9	2	1	1	8	4	0	0	0	8	0	1	.533	.382
Herum, Marty	R-R	6-3	214	12-16-91	.240	.147	.274	51	129	14	31	8	0	4	22	12	2	0	1	40	0	0	.395	.313
Jones, Matt	R-R	6-0	195	4-14-92	.053	.167	.000	7	19	2	1	1	0	0	0	3	0	0	0	7	0	0	.105	.182
Joseph, Caleb	R-R	6-3	180	6-18-86	.265	.315	.241	48	162	29	43	12	1	7	26	13	2	0	2	44	0	0	.482	.324
Lachance, Kevin	R-R	6-3	185	7-2-94	.200	.250	.000	2	5	0	1	0	0	0	0	0	0	0	0	1	0	0	.200	.200
Lamb, Jake	L-R	6-3	215	10-9-90	.180	.167	.185	12	39	5	7	2	0	1	7	7	0	0	0	12	0	0	.308	.304
Leyba, Domingo	B-R	5-11	160	9-11-95	.300	.257	.320	112	457	85	137	37	3	19	77	32	6	0	3	78	0	2	.519	.351
Locastro, Tim	R-R	6-1	200	7-14-92	.301	.359	.274	31	123	35	37	11	2	3	21	10	9	1	0	24	9	1	.618	.394
Marzilli, Evan	L-L	6-0	185	3-13-91	.263	.500	.000	8	19	4	5	1	0	0	2	5	0	0	0	6	0	0	.316	.417
Mathisen, Wyatt	R-R	6-0	225	12-30-93	.283	.309	.269	87	283	72	80	19	1	23	61	39	20	0	3	84	1	0	.601	.403
Murphy, John Ryan	R-R	5-11	205	5-13-91	.250	.311	.215	36	124	26	31	7	0	9	26	12	0	0	0	34	0	0	.524	.316
Murphy, Max	R-R	5-11	195	11-17-92	.222	--	.222	3	9	1	2	0	0	1	1	1	0	0	0	3	0	0	.556	.300
Prince, Josh	R-R	6-0	180	1-26-88	.300	.400	.250	26	60	12	18	6	0	2	18	5	1	1	0	15	2	1	.500	.364
Queliz, Jose	R-R	6-2	224	8-7-92	.250	--	.250	1	4	0	1	0	0	0	0	1	0	0	0	1	0	0	.250	.400
Querecuto, Juniel	B-R	5-9	155	9-19-92	.288	.333	.266	102	386	48	111	19	6	9	51	16	2	1	3	70	7	4	.438	.317
Refsnyder, Rob	R-R	6-0	200	3-26-91	.000	--	.000	1	4	0	0	0	0	0	0	0	0	0	0	1	0	0	.000	.000
Robbins, Joe	R-R	5-9	195	12-8-93	.111	.000	.125	5	9	0	1	0	0	0	0	0	0	0	0	6	0	0	.111	.111
Rojas, Josh	L-R	6-1	185	6-30-94	.514	.546	.500	8	35	11	18	4	1	3	14	5	0	0	0	6	1	0	.943	.575
2-team total (53 Round Rock)					.339	.286	.360	61	245	60	83	20	4	15	53	35	3	0	1	42	20	4	.637	.426
Rosario, Alberto	R-R	6-0	175	1-10-87	.250	.235	.255	42	140	17	35	3	1	1	11	15	1	0	1	27	0	1	.307	.325
Snider, Travis	L-L	6-0	235	2-2-88	.294	.260	.310	93	310	45	91	22	4	11	41	56	1	0	1	84	3	2	.497	.402
Swihart, Blake	B-R	6-1	200	4-3-92	.189	.143	.205	28	106	20	20	2	1	6	22	15	0	0	1	31	0	1	.396	.287
Szczur, Matt	R-R	6-0	200	7-20-89	.322	.273	.351	44	149	34	48	12	1	8	28	19	0	0	4	27	0	3	.577	.390
Tomas, Yasmany	R-R	6-2	250	11-14-90	.301	.395	.257	102	405	63	122	24	3	29	82	22	3	0	1	110	2	0	.590	.341
Tomlinson, Kelby	R-R	6-2	175	6-16-90	.218	.370	.150	30	87	15	19	3	0	1	5	12	1	0	0	25	2	2	.276	.320
2-team total (69 Tacoma)					.242	.306	.215	99	335	45	81	16	2	10	16	27	2	3	2	79	4	3	.302	.301
Vargas, Ildemaro	B-R	6-0	170	7-16-91	.403	.558	.321	28	124	20	50	9	3	2	24	11	1	0	1	5	1	1	.573	.453
Westbrook, Jamie	R-R	5-9	170	6-18-95	.321	.320	.321	30	106	21	34	8	1	4	17	7	0	0	2	15	0	1	.462	.413
Young, Andy	R-R	6-0	195	5-10-94	.280	.261	.288	68	239	53	67	10	3	21	53	24	1	1	1	68	2	1	.611	.373

Pitching	B-T	HT	WT	DOB	W	L	ERA	G	GS	CG	SV	IP	H	R	ER	HR	BB	SO	AVG	vLH	vRH	K/9	BB/9
Atkinson, Ryan	R-R	6-3	218	5-10-93	1	2	10.80	19	0	0	0	25	41	33	30	5	20	28	.360	.277	.418	10.08	7.20
Clarke, Taylor	R-R	6-4	200	5-13-93	3	1	6.63	8	8	0	0	37	41	27	27	6	17	28	.289	.328	.253	6.87	4.17
Crichton, Stefan	R-R	6-3	200	2-29-92	4	3	3.61	36	0	0	1	57	52	24	23	4	15	52	.243	.245	.242	8.16	2.35
De La Rosa, Rubby	R-R	6-0	210	3-4-89	2	0	2.49	18	0	0	1	22	18	7	6	4	7	29	.222	.343	.130	12.05	2.91
Decker, Cody	R-R	5-11	218	1-17-87	0	0	0.00	2	0	0	0	2	0	0	0	0	0	0	.286	.000	.500	0.00	0.00
Donatelli, Justin	R-R	6-6	236	9-16-94	2	2	8.21	9	7	0	0	34	47	33	31	10	17	27	.322	.237	.414	7.15	4.50
Duplantier, Jon	L-R	6-4	225	7-11-94	1	2	5.21	13	11	0	0	38	31	25	22	1	28	44	.233	.264	.213	10.42	6.63
Ginkel, Kevin	L-R	6-4	210	3-24-94	1	0	1.62	15	0	0	6	17	10	3	3	2	8	36	.170	.125	.200	19.44	4.32
Grey, Connor	L-R	6-0	180	5-6-94	0	1	9.39	7	1	0	0	15	26	16	16	4	12	12	.377	.313	.432	7.04	7.04
Hagens, Bradin	R-R	6-3	210	5-12-89	4	2	6.03	22	6	0	0	66	73	52	44	10	37	45	.281	.268	.293	6.17	5.07
Jeter, Bud	R-R	6-3	205	10-27-91	0	0	0.00	3	0	0	0	3	2	0	0	0	3	3	.200	.333	.143	10.13	10.13
Jones, Matt	R-R	6-0	195	4-14-92	0	0	0.00	1	0	0	0	1	0	0	0	0	0	0	.000	.000	.000	0.00	0.00
Joseph, Caleb	R-R	6-3	180	6-18-86	0	0	27.00	1	0	0	0	1	3	3	3	1	0	0	.625	1.000	.400	0.00	0.00
Koch, Matt	L-R	6-3	215	11-2-90	5	10	7.38	21	17	0	0	100	135	86	82	21	30	81	.317	.318	.316	7.29	2.70

ARIZONA DIAMONDBACKS

Name	B-T	HT	WT	DOB	W	L	ERA	G	GS	CG	SV	IP	H	R	ER	HR	BB	SO	AVG	vLH	vRH	SO/9	BB/9
Kohn, Michael	R-R	6-2	200	6-26-86	0	1	9.82	3	0	0	0	4	3	5	4	1	4	3	.250	.000	.429	7.36	9.82
Krehbiel, Joey	R-R	6-2	185	12-20-92	1	4	7.69	51	0	0	1	64	73	62	55	16	45	67	.280	.250	.301	9.37	6.30
Lively, Ben	R-R	6-4	190	3-5-92	2	1	5.04	7	7	0	0	30	36	17	17	7	11	35	.290	.266	.317	10.38	3.26
2-team total (17 Omaha)					6	2	4.48	24	10	0	3	72	77	37	36	14	30	76	.268	.282	.259	9.46	3.73
Luetge, Lucas	L-L	6-4	205	3-24-87	5	2	3.14	33	0	0	1	43	43	22	15	4	14	46	.264	.237	.279	9.63	2.93
Magnifico, Damien	R-R	6-1	205	5-24-91	2	1	7.15	9	0	0	0	11	13	11	9	0	9	12	.277	.280	.273	9.53	7.15
Mathisen, Wyatt	R-R	6-0	225	12-30-93	0	0	34.71	3	0	0	0	2	10	9	9	3	1	1	.625	.500	.833	3.86	3.86
McCanna, Kevin	L-R	6-1	185	2-1-94	0	1	5.40	1	1	0	0	3	5	4	2	1	1	3	.333	.286	.333	8.10	2.70
McFarland, T.J.	L-L	6-3	220	6-8-89	0	0	4.50	3	0	0	0	4	3	2	2	1	1	7	.214	.200	.222	15.75	2.25
Menendez, Bryan	R-R	5-11	215	1-18-96	1	0	4.50	1	0	0	0	2	3	1	1	0	2	2	.375	.375	--	9.00	9.00
Nittoli, Vinny	R-R	6-1	210	11-11-90	0	4	9.50	5	4	0	0	24	21	19		3	9	20	.320	.222	.410	10.00	4.50
Nolasco, Ricky	R-R	6-2	235	12-13-82	1	1	18.00	6	3	0	0	9	15	18	18	3	12	11	.385	.308	.423	11.00	12.00
Payamps, Joel	R-R	6-2	200	4-7-94	2	2	4.97	8	8	0	0	38	41	22	21	6	16	30	.279	.283	.276	7.11	3.79
Prince, Josh	R-R	6-0	180	1-26-88	0	0	13.50	2	0	0	0	1	1	2	2	1	0	0	.200	.000	.333	0.00	0.00
Rzepczynski, Marc	L-L	6-2	220	8-29-85	2	4	5.04	45	0	0	1	45	56	31	25	7	28	36	.304	.271	.333	7.25	5.64
Scott, Robby	R-L	6-3	220	8-29-89	3	0	6.94	41	0	0	1	48	42	40	37	10	35	61	.231	.186	.259	11.44	6.56
Scribner, Troy	L-R	6-3	190	7-2-91	0	1	5.40	1	1	0	0	5	6	3	3	1	1	1	.316	.167	.385	1.80	1.80
Sherfy, Jimmie	R-R	6-0	175	12-27-91	2	3	3.60	35	0	0	12	35	32	17	14	2	21	49	.241	.222	.253	12.60	5.40
Shipley, Braden	R-R	6-1	190	2-22-92	4	5	5.95	30	15	0	0	95	111	69	63	19	37	88	.293	.241	.333	8.31	3.49
Smith, Riley	R-R	6-1	195	1-15-95	2	2	6.89	12	12	0	0	63	85	52	48	15	20	48	.326	.350	.306	6.89	2.87
Snider, Travis	L-L	6-0	235	2-2-88	0	0	9.00	1	0	0	0	1	3	3	1	1	0	0	.429	.667	.250	0.00	0.00
Taylor, Ben	R-R	6-3	225	11-12-92	3	4	5.63	46	0	0	4	56	66	39	35	15	26	70	.286	.231	.321	11.25	4.18
Tonkin, Michael	R-R	6-7	220	11-19-89	0	0	7.71	5	0	0	0	9	12	10	8	2	5	11	.308	.391	.188	10.61	4.82
2-team total (14 San Antonio)					3	0	5.73	19	0	0	0	22	21	17	14	6	14	25	.250	.294	.220	10.23	5.73
Vasquez, Anthony	L-L	6-0	190	9-19-86	4	4	6.99	19	7	0	0	66	102	58	51	17	23	55	.330	.345	.357	7.54	3.15
Vernia, Justin	R-R	6-2	205	9-22-95	0	1	23.40	2	1	0	0	5	13	13	13	3	5	3	.482	.417	.533	5.40	9.00
Widener, Taylor	L-R	6-0	195	10-24-94	6	7	8.10	23	23	0	0	100	133	90	90	23	41	109	.324	.326	.322	9.81	3.69
Young, Alex	L-L	6-2	205	9-9-93	4	3	6.09	20	8	0	0	55	66	38	37	6	26	64	.292	.310	.284	10.54	4.28

Fielding

Catcher	PCT	G	PO	A	E	DP	PB
Heinebert	.990	21	173	20	2	2	4
Herbert	.975	8	73	4	2	0	0
Jones	.960	5	44	4	2	0	3
Joseph	.995	42	347	27	2	2	3
Murphy	.993	31	266	15	2	0	7
Queliz	1.000	1	8	0	0	0	0
Rosario	.989	41	309	36	4	4	5
Swihart	1.000	1	3	0	0	0	0

First Base	PCT	G	PO	A	E	DP
Asuaje	1.000	1	3	0	0	1
Cron	.991	69	496	57	5	40
Decker	.857	2	11	1	2	0
Flores	.917	1	9	2	1	1
Herum	.986	13	63	9	1	9
Joseph	1.000	2	3	0	0	1
Lamb	1.000	5	26	2	0	4
Mathisen	1.000	9	56	4	0	5
Prince	.978	8	44	1	1	2
Querecuto	.955	5	20	1	1	0
Robbins	1.000	1	5	0	0	0
Snider	.972	5	33	2	1	5
Swihart	.958	4	21	2	1	3
Tomas	.979	46	293	27	7	26

Second Base	PCT	G	PO	A	E	DP
Asuaje	.990	35	43	58	1	12

(Second Base, continued)

	PCT	G	PO	A	E	DP
Flores	.000	1	0	0	0	0
Herum	.909	4	12	8	2	1
Lachance	1.000	1	2	5	0	1
Leyba	.994	42	63	112	1	25
Locastro	1.000	1	1	1	0	0
Mathisen	.949	20	29	45	4	11
Prince	1.000	6	6	14	0	2
Querecuto	1.000	14	24	27	0	10
Refsnyder	1.000	1	1	0	0	0
Tomlinson	.978	9	19	25	1	2
Vargas	1.000	6	7	19	0	2
Young	.986	22	27	45	1	7

Third Base	PCT	G	PO	A	E	DP
Asuaje	1.000	12	6	6	0	1
Cron	.971	15	10	23	1	2
Herum	.952	25	9	31	2	2
Joseph	.000	1	0	0	0	0
Lamb	1.000	6	3	3	0	2
Leyba	1.000	2	0	2	0	0
Mathisen	.983	59	36	77	2	9
Prince	.857	4	2	4	1	2
Querecuto	1.000	13	6	16	0	2
Robbins	1.000	1	1	0	0	0
Rojas	1.000	1	0	2	0	0
Tomlinson	1.000	5	1	6	0	1
Vargas	.968	12	6	24	1	3
Young	.898	23	13	31	5	3

Shortstop	PCT	G	PO	A	E	DP
Asuaje	.750	1	1	2	1	1
Leyba	.964	67	70	147	8	25
Querecuto	.974	29	49	65	3	13
Rojas	1.000	2	1	7	0	0
Tomlinson	.971	16	26	40	2	7
Vargas	.982	13	19	35	1	6
Young	.989	25	24	64	1	11

Outfield	PCT	G	PO	A	E	DP
Almonte	.964	86	153	6	6	0
Aplin	.957	26	44	0	2	0
Asuaje	1.000	4	6	0	0	0
Decker	.800	13	8	0	2	0
DeLuzio	.958	38	89	3	4	2
Locastro	1.000	30	63	0	0	0
Marzilli	1.000	7	15	0	0	0
Mathisen	.000	1	0	0	0	0
Murphy	1.000	3	2	0	0	0
Prince	1.000	6	1	0	0	0
Querecuto	1.000	48	70	2	0	0
Rojas	1.000	4	8	1	0	0
Snider	.979	81	137	2	3	0
Swihart	.871	13	26	1	4	0
Szczur	1.000	40	68	4	0	0
Tomas	.961	44	47	2	2	1
Westbrook	1.000	25	41	3	0	1

JACKSON GENERALS

DOUBLE-A

SOUTHERN LEAGUE

Batting	B-T	HT	WT	DOB	AVG	vLH	vRH	G	AB	R	H	2B	3B	HR	RBI	BB	HBP	SH	SF	SO	SB	CS	SLG	OBP
Baez, Jeffrey	R-R	6-0	180	10-30-93	.242	.220	.252	111	360	49	87	20	0	15	55	31	4	1	1	108	9	3	.422	.308
Beer, Seth	L-R	6-3	195	9-18-96	.205	.231	.184	24	88	8	18	7	0	1	17	8	4	0	1	25	0	1	.318	.297
Chisholm, Jazz	L-R	5-11	165	2-1-98	.204	.178	.214	89	314	51	64	6	5	18	44	41	6	0	3	123	13	4	.427	.305
2-team total (23 Jacksonville)					.220	.207	.226	112	395	57	87	10	7	21	54	52	8	0	3	147	16	4	.441	.321
Cribbs Jr., Galli	R-R	6-0	170	10-8-92	.200	.208	.197	88	245	23	49	7	6	2	20	25	3	2	0	99	2	0	.302	.282
DeLuzio, Ben	R-R	6-3	190	8-9-94	.254	.317	.223	79	248	35	63	10	4	2	23	28	9	1	0	59	15	6	.351	.351
Duzenack, Camden	R-R	5-10	170	3-8-95	.147	.194	.108	22	68	8	10	1	0	2	4	14	3	0	0	17	2	0	.250	.318
Ellis, Drew	R-R	6-3	210	12-1-95	.235	.271	.215	118	379	57	89	23	0	14	63	63	3	1	5	109	0	3	.406	.344
Grotjohn, Ryan	L-R	6-2	175	4-25-95	.229	.232	.228	78	227	36	52	10	4	3	19	25	6	1	2	67	3	1	.348	.319
Herbert, Lucas	R-R	6-0	200	11-28-96	.500	--	.500	1	4	1	2	1	1	0	0	0	0	0	0	1	0	0	1.250	.500
Hernandez, Ramon	R-R	6-4	195	3-2-96	.236	.248	.231	98	309	40	73	13	2	11	44	15	8	0	9	77	0	1	.398	.282
Herum, Marty	R-R	6-3	214	12-16-91	.000	.000	.000	4	10	0	0	0	0	0	0	0	0	0	0	3	0	0	.000	.000

Player	B-T	HT	WT	DOB	AVG	vLH	vRH	G	AB	R	H	2B	3B	HR	RBI	BB	HBP	SH	SF	SO	SB	CS	SLG	OBP
Jones, Matt	R-R	6-0	195	4-14-92	.222	1.000	.125	4	9	2	2	0	0	2	2	0	0	0	0	0	0	0	.889	.222
Karaviotis, Mark	R-R	6-1	185	10-12-95	.170	.182	.165	39	112	10	19	2	0	1	16	9	2	0	4	36	0	0	.214	.236
Martinez, Renae	R-R	6-1	185	4-15-94	.222	.286	.182	27	90	9	20	4	0	0	9	7	1	0	2	20	0	0	.267	.280
Marzilli, Evan	L-L	6-0	185	3-13-91	.053	.083	.039	14	38	5	2	0	0	1	1	8	0	0	0	24	0	1	.132	.217
Miroglio, Dominic	R-R	6-0	203	3-10-95	.233	.296	.196	47	146	15	34	8	0	2	12	17	1	0	0	26	0	0	.329	.317
Murphy, Max	R-R	5-11	195	11-17-92	.125	.000	.167	4	8	0	1	0	0	0	0	1	0	0	0	1	0	0	.125	.222
Robbins, Joe	R-R	5-9	195	12-8-93	.091	.000	.143	4	11	0	1	0	0	0	1	3	0	0	1	4	0	0	.091	.267
Smith, Pavin	L-L	6-2	210	2-6-96	.291	.248	.314	123	440	62	128	29	6	12	67	59	0	0	7	61	2	1	.466	.370
Tolbert, L.T.	L-R	6-2	200	6-7-96	.255	.286	.234	31	106	17	27	4	0	1	6	4	2	0	0	19	0	0	.321	.295
Varsho, Daulton	L-R	5-10	190	7-2-96	.301	.277	.312	108	396	85	119	25	4	18	58	42	10	0	4	63	21	5	.520	.378
Westbrook, Jamie	R-R	5-9	170	6-18-95	.269	.362	.221	98	342	51	92	20	1	13	59	32	8	0	6	68	1	1	.447	.340
Wilson, Marcus	R-R	6-2	175	8-15-96	.235	.143	.259	12	34	4	8	2	1	2	7	5	1	0	0	13	3	1	.529	.350
Young, Andy	R-R	6-0	195	5-10-94	.260	.296	.243	65	223	36	58	15	2	8	28	18	19	1	2	53	1	1	.453	.363

Pitching	B-T	HT	WT	DOB	W	L	ERA	G	GS	CG	SV	IP	H	R	ER	HR	BB	SO	AVG	vLH	vRH	K/9	BB/9
Aguilar, Miguel	L-L	5-8	180	9-26-91	1	1	2.12	26	0	0	6	30	22	7	7	1	4	33	.208	.180	.224	10.01	1.21
Atkinson, Ryan	R-R	6-3	218	5-10-93	2	0	3.99	21	0	0	0	29	27	14	13	0	14	38	.243	.214	.261	11.66	4.30
Bain, Jeff	R-R	6-4	200	3-3-96	0	0	3.60	3	3	0	0	15	15	8	6	2	6	10	.254	.265	.240	6.00	3.60
Brill, Matt	R-R	6-2	190	10-25-94	2	5	6.34	32	0	0	4	33	34	33	23	1	20	32	.266	.269	.263	8.82	5.51
Bukauskas, J.B.	R-R	6-0	196	10-11-96	0	1	7.71	2	2	0	0	7	10	6	6	0	5	11	.345	.400	.316	14.14	6.43
Cribbs Jr., Galli	R-R	6-0	170	10-8-92	0	0	0.00	5	0	0	0	4	2	0	0	0	2	1	.154	.200	.125	2.25	4.50
Donatella, Justin	R-R	6-6	236	9-16-94	5	3	4.92	17	7	0	0	53	63	34	29	3	19	42	.289	.400	.218	7.13	3.23
Gann, Cameron	R-R	6-0	203	10-8-92	2	2	2.31	20	0	0	3	23	16	6	6	3	12	24	.203	.233	.184	9.26	4.63
Garcia, Junior	L-L	5-11	220	10-1-95	2	0	2.50	15	0	0	2	18	13	6	5	0	11	21	.203	.304	.146	10.50	5.50
Gibson, Daniel	R-L	6-3	215	10-16-91	0	0	3.60	4	0	0	0	5	5	2	2	0	5	5	.250	.333	.214	9.00	9.00
Ginkel, Kevin	L-R	6-4	210	3-24-94	1	2	2.16	14	0	0	5	17	9	6	4	2	5	26	.158	.200	.135	14.04	2.70
Green, Josh	R-R	6-3	210	8-31-95	2	4	4.28	8	8	0	0	48	61	23	23	2	8	32	.318	.349	.294	5.96	1.49
Grey, Connor	L-R	6-0	180	5-6-94	2	0	2.93	10	3	0	0	31	30	12	10	3	11	23	.256	.222	.296	6.75	3.23
Jeter, Bud	R-R	6-3	205	10-27-91	1	1	4.50	13	0	0	0	20	20	10	10	0	10	18	.253	.250	.255	8.10	4.50
Kohn, Michael	R-R	6-2	200	6-26-86	2	1	2.78	21	0	0	9	23	13	8	7	3	8	41	.161	.229	.109	16.28	3.18
Lewis, Sam	R-R	6-4	195	10-9-91	4	3	2.42	16	8	0	0	48	32	16	13	2	19	50	.192	.239	.156	9.31	3.54
Luetge, Lucas	L-L	6-4	205	3-24-87	4	1	1.08	22	0	0	6	25	14	3	3	0	7	28	.167	.177	.160	10.08	2.52
Magnifico, Damien	R-R	6-1	205	5-24-91	1	0	2.81	41	0	0	4	42	45	15	13	1	18	56	.276	.333	.237	12.10	3.89
Mark, Tyler	R-R	6-1	195	10-18-94	1	1	6.67	21	0	0	0	30	30	23	22	4	30	33	.263	.239	.279	10.01	9.10
Matzek, Tyler	L-L	6-3	230	10-19-90	0	0	6.75	3	0	0	0	3	2	2	2	0	5	3	.200	.000	.400	10.13	16.88
2-team total (1 Mississippi)					0	0	3.60	4	0	0	0	5	2	2	2	0	5	8	.118	.000	.182	14.40	9.00
McCanna, Kevin	L-R	6-1	185	2-1-94	5	5	2.09	30	8	2	1	82	62	21	19	2	27	92	.207	.241	.179	10.14	2.98
McCullough, Mason	R-R	6-4	245	1-7-93	0	1	18.00	5	0	0	0	5	6	11	10	0	9	10	.273	.286	.267	18.00	16.20
McKinley, Jayson	R-R	6-4	210	1-18-94	3	0	1.00	5	0	0	0	9	8	1	1	0	5	17	.235	.158	.333	17.00	5.00
Nolasco, Ricky	R-R	6-2	235	12-13-82	0	0	5.87	2	2	0	0	8	12	6	5	1	4	6	.364	.444	.267	7.04	4.70
Payamps, Joel	R-R	6-2	200	4-7-94	3	4	2.88	7	7	1	0	41	40	17	13	2	2	39	.255	.288	.231	8.63	0.44
Peacock, Matt	R-R	6-1	180	2-27-94	8	4	2.97	21	20	2	0	115	96	41	38	5	43	81	.231	.198	.256	6.32	3.36
Scott, Robby	R-L	6-2	205	8-29-89	0	0	0.00	3	0	0	0	3	0	0	0	0	1	4	.000	.000	.000	3.00	0.00
Smith, Riley	R-R	6-1	195	1-15-95	4	4	2.27	13	13	1	0	71	65	23	18	4	16	62	.242	.213	.271	7.82	2.02
Soriano, Franklyn	L-L	6-5	195	7-21-95	0	0	4.50	1	0	0	0	2	3	1	1	0	1	4	.375	.500	.333	18.00	4.50
Stapler, Cole	R-R	6-4	240	12-22-94	0	0	2.57	11	7	0	1	49	44	16	14	4	11	39	.237	.273	.204	7.16	2.02
Takahashi, Bo	R-R	6-0	197	1-23-97	9	7	3.72	23	23	0	0	119	108	52	49	12	38	104	.247	.274	.224	7.89	2.88
Tunnell, West	L-R	6-1	195	11-20-93	1	1	1.06	16	0	0	6	17	12	2	2	1	4	15	.214	.238	.200	7.94	2.12
Valdez, Bryan	L-L	6-3	180	11-27-94	4	3	4.15	11	7	0	0	48	52	26	22	6	14	22	.271	.340	.245	4.15	2.64
Vargas, Emilio	R-R	6-3	200	8-12-96	5	3	3.78	17	17	0	0	86	74	39	36	10	23	70	.231	.270	.195	7.35	2.42

Fielding

Catcher	PCT	G	PO	A	E	DP	PB
Herbert	1.000	1	10	1	0	0	0
Jones	.000	1	0	0	0	0	0
Martinez	.994	19	154	18	1	2	0
Miroglio	.992	40	328	25	3	5	6
Varsho	.991	76	611	51	6	9	12

First Base	PCT	G	PO	A	E	DP
Beer	.991	14	108	4	1	11
Ellis	.974	6	35	3	1	3
Hernandez	.992	32	224	22	2	26
Jones	1.000	2	18	3	0	1
Karaviotis	1.000	4	23	5	0	3
Smith	.990	79	613	57	7	69
Tolbert	1.000	2	17	2	0	2

Second Base	PCT	G	PO	A	E	DP
Cribbs Jr.	.993	33	55	91	1	21
Duzenack	1.000	12	17	35	0	9
Grotjohn	.960	15	16	32	2	8

Second Base (cont.)	PCT	G	PO	A	E	DP
Hernandez	.933	16	21	35	4	11
Herum	.000	1	0	0	0	0
Robbins	1.000	1	2	3	0	0
Tolbert	.977	21	28	57	2	15
Young	.983	47	68	105	3	21

Third Base	PCT	G	PO	A	E	DP
Cribbs Jr.	1.000	3	1	8	0	1
Duzenack	1.000	1	0	2	0	1
Ellis	.960	107	80	183	11	27
Grotjohn	.833	1	2	3	1	1
Hernandez	.903	19	9	19	3	1
Herum	1.000	1	0	1	0	0
Karaviotis	1.000	2	3	0	0	0
Robbins	.800	2	1	3	1	0
Young	.923	6	5	7	1	1

Shortstop	PCT	G	PO	A	E	DP
Chisholm	.946	88	111	205	18	42
Cribbs Jr.	.961	31	42	82	5	21
Duzenack	.983	13	19	40	1	7
Young	.958	8	11	12	1	2

Outfield	PCT	G	PO	A	E	DP
Baez	.994	93	155	15	1	4
Beer	1.000	10	13	0	0	0
Cribbs Jr.	.962	20	49	2	2	1
DeLuzio	.993	74	148	1	1	0
Grotjohn	.991	53	107	3	1	1
Hernandez	1.000	13	20	1	0	1
Karaviotis	.968	22	28	2	1	1
Marzilli	1.000	13	34	2	0	2
Murphy	1.000	2	4	0	0	0
Smith	.986	41	64	4	1	0
Varsho	1.000	4	7	0	0	0
Westbrook	.975	75	107	10	3	2
Wilson	1.000	10	23	0	0	0

VISALIA RAWHIDE
CALIFORNIA LEAGUE

HIGH CLASS A

Batting	B-T	HT	WT	DOB	AVG	vLH	vRH	G	AB	R	H	2B	3B	HR	RBI	BB	HBP	SH	SF	SO	SB	CS	SLG	OBP
Basabe, Luis Alejandro	B-R	5-10	160	8-26-96	.293	.338	.283	117	420	70	123	21	4	4	51	75	3	0	2	106	16	9	.391	.402
Caballero, Jose	R-R	5-10	185	8-30-96	.268	.290	.262	43	164	36	44	12	0	3	12	24	8	2	0	40	28	7	.396	.388
2-team total (23 Modesto)					.264	.232	.273	66	254	52	67	17	1	3	22	36	10	2	5	55	32	12	.374	.371
Cintron, Jancarlos	R-R	5-8	170	12-1-94	.263	.202	.279	117	476	63	125	26	1	8	56	38	4	0	2	68	9	6	.372	.321
Diaz, Eduardo	R-R	6-2	175	7-19-97	.283	.180	.311	44	187	30	53	11	3	3	27	8	2	0	1	43	5	1	.423	.318
Duzenack, Camden	R-R	5-9	170	3-8-95	.220	.222	.220	91	327	50	72	9	3	18	56	21	6	0	5	95	7	3	.431	.276
Gillette, Joe	R-R	6-4	220	12-15-95	.222	.188	.232	22	72	13	16	3	1	2	7	6	1	0	0	33	0	0	.375	.291
Grier, Anfernee	R-R	6-1	180	10-13-95	.229	.264	.220	107	363	45	83	19	3	9	46	41	4	0	6	131	28	10	.372	.309
Grotjohn, Ryan	L-R	6-2	175	4-25-95	.237	.188	.247	29	93	14	22	7	0	1	10	19	2	1	1	30	1	4	.344	.374
Herbert, Lucas	R-R	6-0	200	11-28-96	.263	.429	.167	5	19	0	5	1	0	0	1	0	0	0	0	5	0	0	.316	.263
Herrera, Jose	B-R	5-10	226	2-24-97	.218	.167	.229	39	133	17	29	6	0	1	15	31	2	0	2	39	1	0	.286	.369
Herum, Marty	R-R	6-3	214	12-16-91	.227	.250	.222	10	44	2	10	2	0	0	1	0	0	0	0	13	0	0	.273	.227
Karaviotis, Mark	R-R	6-1	185	10-12-95	.286	.341	.272	56	206	30	59	8	1	3	33	31	5	0	4	47	2	4	.379	.386
King, Alex	R-R	6-2	200	10-3-95	.243	.327	.220	67	222	29	54	9	1	3	21	29	3	0	1	92	2	3	.333	.337
Lachance, Kevin	R-R	6-3	185	7-2-94	.115	1.000	.080	9	26	3	3	0	0	1	1	0	1	0	0	11	0	0	.115	.143
Martinez, Renae	R-R	6-1	185	4-15-94	.212	.225	.209	73	269	29	57	13	0	8	39	35	5	0	1	70	0	1	.349	.313
McCarthy, Jake	L-L	6-2	195	7-30-97	.277	.244	.286	53	195	29	54	13	3	2	30	17	2	0	0	52	18	2	.405	.341
Murphy, Max	R-R	5-11	195	11-17-92	.307	.438	.261	17	62	9	19	4	0	1	5	3	0	0	0	17	2	1	.419	.339
Perdomo, Geraldo	B-R	6-3	184	10-22-99	.301	.292	.304	26	93	15	28	5	0	1	11	14	4	1	2	11	6	5	.387	.407
Perez, Jorge	L-L	5-8	165	1-18-98	.245	.233	.248	78	245	40	60	11	2	4	28	20	1	3	2	56	10	3	.355	.302
Queliz, Jose	R-R	6-2	224	8-7-92	.250	.333	.200	2	8	0	2	0	0	0	0	0	0	0	0	2	0	0	.250	.250
Robbins, Joe	R-R	5-9	195	12-8-93	.071	.000	.083	5	14	2	1	0	0	1	3	0	0	0	10	0	0	.286	.235
Sanchez, Yan	R-R	6-2	170	8-31-96	.180	.250	.148	13	39	3	7	0	1	0	1	4	0	0	0	13	2	1	.231	.256
Susnara, Tim	L-R	6-1	185	4-17-96	.172	.167	.174	61	203	18	35	5	1	4	20	24	0	0	1	70	2	0	.266	.259
Swihart, Blake	B-R	6-1	200	4-3-92	.211	.000	.235	5	19	6	4	2	0	0	1	1	1	0	0	5	0	0	.316	.286
Thomas, Alek	L-L	5-11	175	4-28-00	.255	.348	.225	23	94	13	24	2	0	2	7	9	1	0	0	33	4	5	.340	.327
Tolbert, L.T.	R-R	6-0	200	6-7-96	.331	.217	.358	62	236	27	78	18	0	2	34	19	4	0	3	32	2	3	.432	.386
Yanqui, Yoel	L-L	6-1	210	4-25-96	.272	.203	.291	84	294	38	80	22	5	6	47	40	1	0	3	76	17	5	.442	.358

Pitching	B-T	HT	WT	DOB	W	L	ERA	G	GS	CG	SV	IP	H	R	ER	HR	BB	SO	AVG	vLH	vRH	K/9	BB/9
Andriese, Matt	R-R	6-2	225	8-28-89	0	0	13.50	2	2	0	0	2	5	3	3	2	1	4	.500	.500	.500	18.00	4.50
Bain, Jeff	R-R	6-4	200	3-3-96	6	8	3.95	23	22	0	0	121	115	63	53	23	38	152	.248	.258	.241	11.34	2.83
Bartlett, Cole	R-R	6-2	189	12-22-94	9	6	3.39	39	0	0	5	82	77	39	31	4	21	61	.244	.202	.267	6.67	2.30
Brill, Matt	R-R	6-2	190	10-25-94	2	0	1.59	10	0	0	4	11	7	3	2	0	7	21	.171	.167	.172	16.68	5.56
Castillo, Luis	R-R	6-3	212	3-10-95	9	0	3.81	43	0	0	2	78	72	36	33	6	20	83	.242	.296	.216	9.58	2.31
Clarke, Taylor	R-R	6-4	200	5-13-93	1	0	0.00	1	1	0	0	6	3	0	0	0	0	3	.150	.200	.100	4.50	0.00
Cuas, Jose	R-R	6-3	195	6-28-94	1	1	2.63	5	0	0	0	14	15	4	4	1	2	11	.289	.304	.276	7.24	1.32
Duplantier, Jon	L-R	6-4	225	7-11-94	0	0	0.00	1	1	0	0	3	2	0	0	0	3	3	.222	.333	.167	9.00	0.00
Fritze, Ryan	R-R	6-2	200	3-5-94	0	0	7.41	10	0	0	0	17	19	14	14	3	13	17	.288	.286	.289	9.00	6.88
Gann, Cameron	R-R	6-0	203	10-8-92	0	2	5.23	9	0	0	1	10	8	10	6	3	5	14	.211	.308	.160	12.19	4.35
Garcia, Junior	L-L	5-11	220	10-1-95	1	1	2.57	9	0	0	0	14	11	4	4	1	5	20	.216	.188	.229	12.86	3.21
Gonzalez, Erbert	R-R	5-10	170	10-21-95	0	0	8.22	4	0	0	0	8	9	7	7	1	6	9	.273	.286	.263	10.57	7.04
Green, Josh	R-R	6-3	210	8-31-95	9	1	1.73	14	14	0	0	78	69	18	15	1	13	69	.247	.237	.255	7.96	1.50
Grey, Connor	L-R	6-0	180	5-6-94	2	1	3.32	7	0	0	0	19	20	8	7	0	1	16	.270	.263	.273	7.58	0.47
Herbert, Lucas	R-R	6-0	200	11-28-96	0	0	27.00	1	0	0	0	1	1	1	1	0	1	1	.500	.000	1.000	27.00	27.00
King, Alex	R-R	6-2	200	10-3-95	0	0	1.80	5	0	0	0	5	3	1	1	0	1	6	.177	.000	.231	10.80	1.80
Lemieux, Mack	L-L	6-3	205	9-6-96	4	1	1.54	33	0	0	1	53	32	9	9	3	22	72	.172	.111	.197	12.30	3.76
Lewis, Justin	R-R	6-2	205	8-10-95	3	2	3.53	12	10	0	0	51	55	23	20	2	13	62	.281	.177	.336	10.94	2.29
Mark, Tyler	R-R	6-1	195	10-18-94	0	0	13.14	12	0	0	0	12	18	23	18	6	16	9	.321	.177	.385	6.57	11.68
McCanna, Kevin	L-R	6-1	185	2-1-94	2	1	4.35	4	1	0	0	10	9	5	5	1	4	13	.225	.222	.227	11.32	3.48
McKinley, Jayson	R-R	6-4	210	1-18-94	4	0	2.84	23	0	0	1	44	27	16	14	1	16	66	.185	.156	.194	13.40	3.25
Menendez, Bryan	R-R	5-11	215	1-18-96	0	0	3.00	1	1	0	0	3	1	3	1	1	0	2	.273	.250	.286	6.00	3.00
Mercer, Matt	R-R	6-2	180	9-1-96	1	2	5.56	12	12	0	0	45	48	29	28	6	28	58	.278	.312	.259	11.51	5.56
Miller, Jared	L-L	6-7	240	8-21-93	0	0	6.48	6	0	0	0	8	8	6	6	0	7	8	.250	.500	.167	8.64	7.56
Moths, Travis	R-R	6-1	190	9-22-95	0	1	4.35	3	3	0	0	10	8	5	5	0	12	9	.211	.240	.154	7.84	10.45
Ratliff, Lane	L-L	6-3	185	3-22-95	1	0	0.64	3	1	0	0	14	9	1	1	0	4	11	.192	.000	.237	7.07	2.57
Soriano, Franklyn	L-L	6-5	195	7-21-95	0	0	8.59	3	0	0	0	7	11	7	7	0	2	12	.333	.200	.357	14.73	2.45
Stapler, Cole	R-R	6-4	240	12-22-94	3	6	3.36	14	14	0	0	75	74	30	28	7	6	87	.256	.271	.246	10.44	0.72
Stout, Kyler	R-R	6-0	195	10-13-94	3	1	4.06	27	0	0	0	38	27	17	17	3	29	54	.203	.255	.174	12.90	6.93
Tunnell, West	L-R	6-1	195	11-20-93	0	0	1.27	27	0	0	13	28	16	6	4	2	17	45	.165	.226	.136	14.29	5.40
Valdez, Bryan	L-L	6-3	180	11-27-94	2	5	4.82	11	9	0	0	52	55	32	28	9	14	43	.266	.266	.266	7.39	2.41
Vernia, Justin	R-R	6-2	205	9-22-95	8	3	3.65	22	18	0	1	113	111	57	46	19	34	103	.259	.242	.266	8.18	2.70
Weiss, Ryan	R-R	6-4	210	12-10-96	1	2	5.97	6	6	0	0	32	42	23	21	2	8	28	.323	.429	.284	7.96	2.27
Williams, Breckin	R-R	6-0	200	9-5-93	6	2	2.94	30	0	0	16	34	31	15	11	1	9	37	.248	.200	.275	9.89	2.41
Yoshikawa, Shumpei	R-R	6-2	175	1-24-95	5	7	3.75	22	21	0	0	103	106	55	43	13	22	123	.265	.272	.262	10.71	1.92

Fielding

Catcher	PCT	G	PO	A	E	DP	PB
Herbert	1.000	5	45	7	0	0	1
Herrera	.986	30	269	14	4	1	2
Martinez	.994	50	468	44	3	3	7
Queliz	1.000	1	9	1	0	1	0
Susnara	.993	51	540	45	4	8	7

First Base	PCT	G	PO	A	E	DP
Gillette	.982	15	97	12	2	10
Grotjohn	1.000	1	1	0	0	0
Herum	.963	3	24	2	1	3

	PCT	G	PO	A	E	DP
Karaviotis	.989	11	84	2	1	7
King	.994	22	159	5	1	12
Robbins	1.000	4	40	5	0	7
Tolbert	1.000	21	146	9	0	15
Yanqui	.996	66	454	30	2	38

Second Base	PCT	G	PO	A	E	DP
Basabe	.947	5	7	11	1	3
Caballero	.978	11	19	25	1	7
Cintron	.985	30	54	79	2	22
Duzenack	.980	48	77	121	4	29
Grotjohn	.969	6	12	19	1	5
Herum	1.000	2	3	0	0	0
King	1.000	4	10	12	0	7
Lachance	1.000	5	4	12	0	3
Sanchez	1.000	3	3	8	0	1
Tolbert	.949	28	36	57	5	14

Third Base	PCT	G	PO	A	E	DP
Basabe	.958	46	24	91	5	11
Caballero	.981	22	12	39	1	3

	PCT	G	PO	A	E	DP
Duzenack	.955	25	12	51	3	4
Gillette	1.000	1	0	1	0	0
Grotjohn	.923	4	2	10	1	3
Herum	1.000	3	1	7	0	1
Karaviotis	1.000	2	1	2	0	0
King	.918	32	12	44	5	4
Lachance	1.000	2	0	2	0	0
Sanchez	.600	2	0	3	2	0
Susnara	.000	1	0	0	0	0
Tolbert	1.000	1	2	1	0	0

Shortstop	PCT	G	PO	A	E	DP
Caballero	.926	9	10	15	2	6
Cintron	.965	88	95	210	11	35
Duzenack	.955	16	26	38	3	12
Perdomo	1.000	26	36	59	0	13

Outfield	PCT	G	PO	A	E	DP
Basabe	.937	37	58	1	4	0
Diaz	1.000	44	85	3	0	0
Duzenack	1.000	3	5	0	0	0
Grier	.995	106	212	3	1	1
Grotjohn	1.000	12	24	2	0	1
Karaviotis	1.000	39	45	5	0	0
Lachance	1.000	1	1	0	0	0
McCarthy	.957	53	109	2	5	1
Murphy	.955	10	17	4	1	0
Perez	.952	75	111	7	6	1
Sanchez	1.000	7	7	0	0	0
Swihart	1.000	2	2	0	0	0
Thomas	1.000	23	65	2	0	0
Yanqui	1.000	14	22	0	0	0

KANE COUNTY COUGARS
MIDWEST LEAGUE

LOW CLASS A

Batting	B-T	HT	WT	DOB	AVG	vLH	vRH	G	AB	R	H	2B	3B	HR	RBI	BB	HBP	SH	SF	SO	SB	CS	SLG	OBP
Alexander, Blaze	R-R	6-0	160	6-11-99	.262	.207	.274	97	343	56	90	12	4	7	47	42	12	0	9	89	14	4	.382	.355
Almond, Zachery	R-B	6-3	210	4-12-96	.217	.258	.207	91	313	35	68	17	0	5	44	43	2	1	9	93	3	1	.320	.308
Dalesandro, Nick	R-R	6-1	175	10-3-96	.313	.250	.327	18	64	9	20	0	0	0	6	9	1	0	0	15	2	0	.313	.405
Diaz, Eduardo	R-R	6-2	175	7-19-97	.283	.256	.287	72	286	48	81	15	3	7	31	26	8	0	4	57	13	4	.430	.355
Fletcher, Dominic	L-L	5-9	185	9-2-97	.318	.323	.317	55	214	33	68	14	1	5	28	22	3	0	0	50	1	1	.463	.389
Garza, David	R-R	6-1	200	2-19-95	.177	.214	.171	29	102	7	18	5	0	0	8	8	6	1	1	28	1	0	.226	.274
Gillette, Joe	R-R	6-4	220	12-15-95	.222	.375	.200	20	63	7	14	2	0	3	7	12	2	0	0	30	4	0	.397	.364
Hernandez, Eddie	B-R	5-9	160	4-18-99	.217	.205	.220	71	267	29	58	13	3	1	28	23	2	1	2	77	2	2	.300	.282
Herrera, Jose	B-R	5-10	226	2-24-97	.278	.333	.272	51	169	23	47	13	1	4	28	35	0	0	4	33	2	1	.438	.394
Holmes, Tra	R-R	6-0	175	7-10-96	.224	.169	.235	118	419	61	94	15	3	3	37	37	17	2	2	122	18	7	.296	.312
January, Ryan	L-R	6-4	200	5-27-97	.273	.000	.333	3	11	4	3	0	0	0	1	0	0	0	0	3	0	0	.273	.333
Kennedy, Buddy	R-R	6-1	190	10-5-98	.262	.267	.262	101	385	50	101	18	4	7	49	47	2	0	4	81	4	4	.384	.343
King, Alex	R-R	6-2	200	10-3-95	.267	.000	.308	14	45	11	12	2	0	3	12	6	3	0	2	18	0	0	.511	.375
Leyton, Steven	R-R	5-10	165	12-17-98	.159	.188	.154	33	107	10	17	3	0	0	4	3	5	2	0	19	1	3	.187	.217
Lynch, Keshawn	R-R	5-9	190	10-12-96	.224	.286	.210	74	237	31	53	9	1	0	22	44	5	3	4	81	2	3	.270	.352
Perdomo, Geraldo	B-R	6-0	184	10-22-99	.268	.291	.263	90	314	48	84	16	3	2	36	56	11	2	2	56	20	8	.357	.394
Perez, Jorge	L-L	5-8	165	1-18-98	.243	.182	.254	19	70	9	17	1	1	2	7	2	0	0	0	13	0	0	.371	.264
Robinson, Kristian	R-R	6-3	190	12-11-00	.217	.313	.197	25	92	14	20	3	1	5	16	8	2	0	0	30	3	2	.435	.294
Rose, Joey	R-R	6-0	205	1-20-98	.199	.321	.176	47	176	16	35	10	0	2	20	13	2	0	2	48	1	0	.290	.259
Shannon, Zack	R-R	6-3	230	6-22-96	.252	.259	.251	94	333	39	84	18	0	12	60	41	4	0	3	94	4	0	.414	.339
Susnara, Tim	L-R	6-1	185	4-17-96	.159	.091	.182	13	44	8	7	0	0	0	4	7	0	0	1	12	0	0	.159	.269
Thomas, Alek	L-L	5-11	175	4-28-00	.312	.234	.324	91	353	63	110	21	7	8	48	43	5	0	1	72	11	6	.479	.393
Tolbert, L.T.	L-R	6-2	200	6-7-96	.313	.375	.292	10	32	6	10	1	0	2	11	5	0	0	1	6	1	0	.531	.395
Wasinger, Daniel	B-R	6-1	205	11-14-95	.115	.000	.150	7	26	1	3	1	0	0	1	3	1	0	0	7	0	0	.154	.233
Yerzy, Andy	L-R	6-3	215	7-5-98	.104	.235	.083	33	125	8	13	5	0	0	9	13	0	0	2	39	0	0	.144	.177

Pitching	B-T	HT	WT	DOB	W	L	ERA	G	GS	CG	SV	IP	H	R	ER	HR	BB	SO	AVG	vLH	vRH	K/9	BB/9
Almonte, Jose	R-R	6-2	185	9-8-95	0	0	54.00	1	0	0	0	0	2	2	2	0	1	0	.667	.500	1.000	0.00	27.00
Baldwin, Erin	R-R	6-5	195	4-22-96	0	1	6.85	10	2	0	0	24	28	19	18	2	12	12	.292	.317	.273	4.56	4.56
Cuas, Jose	R-R	6-3	195	6-28-94	3	2	1.64	14	0	0	7	22	14	6	4	1	9	18	.182	.281	.111	7.36	3.68
Del Moral, Adrian	R-R	6-1	190	2-17-99	4	3	3.09	12	12	0	0	58	58	27	20	1	16	42	.264	.316	.224	6.48	2.47
Frias, Luis	R-R	6-3	180	5-23-98	3	1	4.39	6	6	0	0	27	22	13	13	1	12	29	.225	.182	.246	9.79	4.05
Fritze, Ryan	R-R	6-2	200	3-5-94	0	0	1.62	7	1	0	1	17	8	3	3	1	2	19	.146	.222	.071	10.26	6.48
Gelabert, Michel	L-L	6-3	200	1-7-97	3	2	2.96	10	10	0	0	46	32	24	15	3	19	47	.201	.206	.200	9.26	3.74
Goddard, Jackson	R-R	6-3	220	12-12-96	5	4	2.89	26	20	0	2	103	93	40	33	2	44	92	.244	.241	.246	8.06	3.86
Hernandez, Kenny	L-L	6-1	197	6-24-98	7	3	1.88	30	1	0	3	96	85	29	20	1	31	83	.232	.264	.214	7.78	2.91
Hiraldo, Yaramil	R-R	6-1	180	12-31-95	2	1	1.08	7	0	0	0	17	12	4	2	0	11	14	.194	.174	.205	5.94	2.16
Kelly, Levi	R-R	6-4	205	5-14-99	5	1	2.15	22	22	0	0	100	72	35	24	4	39	126	.199	.234	.172	11.30	3.50
Larrison, Ethan	R-R	6-2	205	8-14-95	3	2	2.89	27	0	0	4	44	41	15	14	2	15	50	.247	.265	.235	10.31	3.09
Lewis, Justin	R-R	6-7	205	8-10-95	3	4	2.23	14	14	0	0	65	51	22	16	2	29	65	.214	.189	.235	9.05	4.04
Lin, Kai-Wei	R-R	5-10	175	3-19-96	5	3	3.95	28	0	0	7	43	39	23	19	3	20	42	.239	.230	.247	8.72	4.15
Lynch, Keshawn	R-R	5-9	190	10-12-96	0	0	0.00	1	0	0	0	1	1	0	0	0	0	2	.250	.000	.333	0.00	0.00
McKenna, Trevor	L-L	6-0	200	1-5-96	0	0	0.00	1	0	0	0	1	0	0	0	0	0	2	.000	--	.000	18.00	18.00
Menendez, Bryan	R-R	5-11	215	1-18-96	0	2	16.20	4	0	0	0	3	7	7	6	0	3	5	.368	.556	.200	13.50	8.10
Miller, Ryan	R-R	6-0	180	3-28-96	4	6	3.62	27	0	0	0	55	60	27	22	7	17	36	.282	.354	.219	5.93	2.80
Pimentel, Chester	R-R	6-5	210	11-12-95	4	6	2.02	36	0	0	9	76	55	26	17	4	27	109	.205	.219	.194	12.96	3.21
Rodriguez, Wesley	R-R	5-10	210	12-4-96	5	1	2.01	35	0	0	1	63	39	16	14	1	29	67	.177	.180	.174	9.62	4.16
Rose, Joey	R-R	6-0	205	1-20-98	0	0	0.00	1	0	0	0	1	0	0	0	0	0	0	.000	--	.000	0.00	0.00
Soriano, Franklyn	L-L	6-5	195	7-21-95	2	2	5.24	9	5	0	0	22	15	15	13	1	15	18	.183	.065	.255	7.25	6.04
Tabor, Matt	R-R	6-2	180	7-14-98	5	4	2.93	21	21	0	0	95	79	34	31	6	16	101	.225	.225	.225	9.53	1.51
Toelken, Andy	R-R	6-2	188	1-15-96	7	3	2.91	35	0	0	1	77	59	32	25	2	14	58	.208	.181	.229	6.75	1.63
Valdez, Bryan	L-L	6-3	180	11-27-94	1	0	2.03	3	3	0	0	13	8	4	3	0	1	11	.167	.200	.152	7.43	0.68
Vernia, Justin	R-R	6-2	205	9-22-95	2	0	2.53	2	2	0	0	11	8	3	3	1	1	4	.195	.143	.250	3.38	0.84
Weiss, Ryan	R-R	6-4	210	12-10-96	7	5	3.44	20	20	0	0	97	108	47	37	5	26	75	.284	.263	.304	6.98	2.42
Workman, Blake	R-R	6-3	195	10-8-97	1	4	1.72	28	0	0	9	52	50	17	10	4	6	67	.249	.241	.254	11.52	1.03

Fielding

Catcher	PCT	G	PO	A	E	DP	PB
Almond	.994	51	430	43	3	5	18
Dalesandro	.994	18	145	17	1	2	5
Herrera	.986	40	341	23	5	4	1
Susnara	.991	12	100	11	1	1	3
Wasinger	.985	6	62	4	1	1	0
Yerzy	.993	17	124	17	1	1	1

First Base	PCT	G	PO	A	E	DP
Almond	.985	26	181	20	3	21
Garza	.987	8	70	6	1	7
Gillette	.947	9	50	4	3	3
Lynch	.000	1	0	0	0	0
Rose	.986	25	195	14	3	23
Shannon	.981	59	442	34	9	41
Tolbert	1.000	3	23	2	0	6
Yerzy	.978	14	86	3	2	9

Second Base	PCT	G	PO	A	E	DP
Alexander	.949	31	61	87	8	24
Garza	.956	13	27	38	3	8
Hernandez	.952	54	95	122	11	28
Kennedy	1.000	5	2	9	0	0
Leyton	.988	21	36	46	1	13
Lynch	.880	8	8	14	3	2
Perdomo	.978	11	21	24	1	8
Tolbert	.833	3	5	5	2	1

Third Base	PCT	G	PO	A	E	DP
Alexander	.885	9	8	15	3	3
Almond	.667	1	0	2	1	0
Garza	.923	5	3	9	1	0
Hernandez	.875	3	1	6	1	1
Kennedy	.900	87	69	146	24	15
King	.912	13	9	22	3	1
Leyton	.750	1	1	5	2	0
Lynch	.867	9	3	10	2	0
Rose	.889	15	14	18	4	3

Shortstop	PCT	G	PO	A	E	DP
Alexander	.954	50	59	126	9	29
Garza	.714	2	1	4	2	1
Leyton	1.000	11	12	23	0	3
Perdomo	.958	80	110	207	14	53

Outfield	PCT	G	PO	A	E	DP
Diaz	.977	67	125	4	3	0
Fletcher	1.000	53	119	4	0	1
Garza	1.000	2	3	0	0	0
Gillette	.929	9	13	0	1	0
Holmes	.987	116	226	5	3	1
January	1.000	2	1	0	0	0
Lynch	1.000	38	59	4	0	2
Perez	.949	18	36	1	2	0
Robinson	.957	25	64	2	3	0
Shannon	.000	1	0	0	0	0
Thomas	.989	90	177	5	2	2

HILLSBORO HOPS
NORTHWEST LEAGUE
SHORT SEASON

Batting	B-T	HT	WT	DOB	AVG	vLH	vRH	G	AB	R	H	2B	3B	HR	RBI	BB	HBP	SH	SF	SO	SB	CS	SLG	OBP
Barrosa, Jorge	B-L	5-9	165	2-17-01	.251	.262	.249	57	223	25	56	12	2	1	26	21	7	1	0	32	8	4	.336	.335
Canzone, Dominic	L-R	6-1	190	8-16-97	.261	.417	.237	21	88	15	23	6	1	3	12	3	1	0	0	16	2	0	.455	.294
Carroll, Corbin	L-L	5-10	165	8-21-00	.326	.333	.325	11	43	13	14	3	4	0	6	5	1	0	2	12	2	0	.581	.408
Dalesandro, Nick	R-R	6-1	175	10-3-96	.194	.111	.225	22	67	4	13	1	0	0	8	14	1	0	1	15	2	0	.209	.337
English, Tristin	R-R	6-3	208	5-14-97	.290	.191	.318	50	193	32	56	12	2	7	30	13	8	0	2	24	1	0	.482	.357
Garza, David	R-R	6-1	200	5-14-97	.274	.280	.272	32	106	23	29	7	0	1	13	16	3	0	0	21	7	0	.368	.384
Gillette, Joe	R-R	6-4	220	12-15-95	.207	.353	.173	27	92	11	19	4	0	2	13	13	0	0	1	39	5	0	.315	.302
Grande, Nick	R-R	5-11	170	2-9-98	.147	.273	.113	31	102	12	15	0	1	0	9	13	2	0	1	23	7	1	.167	.254
Herbert, Lucas	R-R	6-0	200	11-28-96	.333	.571	.214	5	21	3	7	3	1	0	5	1	1	0	0	4	0	0	.571	.391
Hernandez, Eddie	B-R	5-9	160	4-18-99	.242	.125	.266	25	95	12	23	3	3	2	10	10	1	0	0	28	3	1	.400	.321
January, Ryan	L-R	6-4	200	5-27-97	.253	.136	.288	29	95	14	24	7	0	3	21	21	2	0	2	27	1	0	.421	.392
Lachance, Kevin	R-R	6-3	185	7-2-94	.147	.000	.156	12	34	4	5	2	0	0	1	6	1	0	2	7	1	2	.206	.340
Leyton, Steven	R-R	5-10	165	12-17-98	.264	.361	.236	41	159	30	42	7	2	4	16	17	6	0	1	25	3	1	.409	.355
Lin, Lyle	R-R	6-1	200	6-26-97	.205	.192	.209	31	112	8	23	2	0	0	8	3	0	1	1	15	0	0	.223	.274
Marriaga, Jesus	R-R	6-0	170	12-17-98	.244	.204	.254	66	234	51	57	14	4	1	27	45	5	0	2	85	17	6	.350	.374
Martinez, Ricky	R-R	6-0	175	2-22-98	.283	.388	.257	62	240	34	68	10	0	0	16	26	6	0	4	45	15	8	.325	.362
Peguero, Liover	R-R	6-1	160	12-31-00	.262	.333	.253	22	84	13	22	4	2	0	11	8	1	0	0	17	3	1	.357	.333
Robbins, Joe	R-R	5-9	195	12-8-93	.222	.333	.167	3	9	1	2	1	0	0	1	2	1	0	1	5	0	0	.333	.385
Robinson, Kristian	R-R	6-3	190	12-11-00	.319	.371	.305	44	163	29	52	10	1	9	35	23	2	0	1	47	14	3	.558	.407
Wasinger, Daniel	B-R	6-1	205	11-14-95	.202	.381	.163	34	119	9	24	9	0	0	8	5	4	0	2	39	4	0	.277	.254
Yerzy, Andy	L-R	6-3	215	7-5-98	.220	.325	.198	63	232	30	51	11	0	6	34	37	2	0	1	61	1	1	.345	.331

Pitching	B-T	HT	WT	DOB	W	L	ERA	G	GS	CG	SV	IP	H	R	ER	HR	BB	SO	AVG	vLH	vRH	K/9	BB/9
Almonte, Jose	R-R	6-2	185	9-8-95	0	0	4.70	4	0	0	0	8	3	5	4	0	5	8	.125	.333	.095	9.39	5.87
Arroyo, Mailon	B-R	6-0	200	1-2-98	0	0	3.38	11	0	0	0	13	7	5	5	2	6	18	.152	.000	.200	12.15	4.05
Baldwin, Erin	R-R	6-5	195	4-22-96	4	2	5.52	17	1	0	1	31	39	22	19	3	11	24	.300	.239	.333	6.97	3.19
Cruz, Wilfry	R-R	6-2	160	10-22-97	5	2	3.86	12	2	0	0	42	30	22	18	5	23	45	.197	.140	.220	9.64	4.93
Cuas, Jose	R-R	6-3	195	6-28-94	2	0	0.00	7	0	0	3	9	1	0	0	0	2	6	.037	.000	.063	5.79	1.93
Del Moral, Adrian	R-R	6-1	190	2-17-99	1	1	1.93	3	3	0	0	14	9	4	3	0	5	17	.177	.133	.194	10.93	3.21
Frias, Luis	R-R	6-3	180	5-23-98	3	3	1.99	10	10	0	0	50	36	13	11	0	17	72	.205	.197	.210	13.05	3.08
Fuenmayor, Liu	L-L	5-11	170	2-2-99	1	0	1.23	5	0	0	0	7	1	1	1	0	2	7	.044	.000	.053	8.59	2.45
Garcia, Justin	R-R	6-2	175	7-2-95	1	2	2.52	25	0	0	1	36	23	10	10	4	8	42	.178	.083	.215	10.60	2.02
Gelabert, Michel	L-L	6-3	200	1-7-97	4	1	4.97	9	4	0	0	38	41	24	21	0	21	31	.285	.400	.261	7.34	4.97
Grammes, Conor	R-R	6-1	200	7-13-97	0	1	4.11	9	6	0	0	15	11	7	7	0	8	20	.200	.143	.220	11.74	4.70
Henry, Tommy	L-L	6-3	205	7-29-97	0	0	6.00	3	3	0	0	3	4	3	2	0	0	4	.286	.500	.250	12.00	0.00
Herrera, Eduardo	B-R	5-9	155	1-5-00	0	1	5.40	19	0	0	8	20	12	12	12	1	17	27	.174	.158	.180	12.15	7.65
Hiraldo, Yaramil	R-R	6-1	180	12-31-95	0	0	0.95	16	0	0	0	19	6	4	2	0	11	21	.095	.118	.087	9.95	5.21
Holton, Tyler	L-L	6-2	200	6-13-96	3	0	2.23	9	8	0	0	32	22	9	8	2	4	51	.183	.226	.169	14.20	1.11
Jameson, Drey	R-R	6-0	165	8-17-97	0	0	6.17	8	8	0	0	12	14	8	8	1	9	12	.292	.231	.314	9.26	6.94
Larrison, Ethan	R-R	6-2	200	8-14-95	0	0	0.87	8	0	0	0	10	8	1	1	0	4	10	.211	.167	.231	8.71	3.48
Lewis, Sam	R-R	6-4	195	10-9-91	0	0	1.69	4	0	0	0	5	6	1	1	1	1	10	.300	.333	.286	16.88	1.69
Malone, Brennan	R-R	6-4	205	9-8-00	0	0	0.00	1	0	0	0	1	0	0	0	0	0	1	.000	--	.000	9.00	0.00
McKenna, Trevor	L-L	6-0	200	5-17-96	1	2	3.86	13	0	0	0	12	8	6	5	0	12	10	.200	.000	.296	7.71	9.26
Menendez, Bryan	R-R	5-11	215	1-18-96	0	0	2.84	19	0	0	8	19	18	7	6	1	9	29	.250	.238	.255	13.74	4.26
Miller, Jared	L-L	6-7	240	8-21-93	0	0	0.00	3	0	0	0	3	1	0	0	0	5	5	.100	.143	.000	15.00	15.00
Nelson, Ryne	R-R	6-3	184	2-1-98	0	1	2.89	10	7	0	0	19	15	6	6	1	0	26	.227	.250	.217	12.54	4.82
Olivero, Deyni	R-R	6-1	165	1-7-98	8	3	2.09	15	8	0	0	65	50	18	15	3	20	42	.215	.218	.212	5.85	2.77
Polancic, Jake	R-R	6-3	205	6-8-98	2	0	0.92	20	0	0	0	20	10	2	2	0	15	16	.154	.278	.106	7.32	6.86
Reed, Cody	R-L	6-3	245	6-7-96	2	0	0.00	4	0	0	0	9	5	1	0	0	4	10	.156	.167	.154	9.64	3.86
Saalfrank, Andrew	L-L	6-3	205	8-18-97	0	2	3.86	7	5	0	0	12	6	5	5	3	3	21	.146	.125	.152	16.20	2.31

Name	B-T	HT	WT	DOB	W	L	ERA	G	GS	CG	SV	IP	H	R	ER	HR	BB	SO	AVG	vLH	vRH	K/9	BB/9
Sanchez, Yan	R-R	6-2	170	8-31-96	0	0	4.76	6	0	0	0	6	4	3	3	0	5	5	.200	.500	.125	7.94	7.94
Short, Avery	R-L	6-1	205	3-14-01	0	0	0.00	1	0	0	0	1	0	0	0	0	2	2	.000	.000	.000	18.00	18.00
Snyder, Nick	L-L	6-7	220	11-19-97	2	0	0.00	9	0	0	1	16	2	0	0	0	9	27	.042	.125	.025	15.19	5.06
Soriano, Franklyn	L-L	6-5	195	7-21-95	0	0	3.50	8	0	0	0	18	12	7	7	0	11	19	.191	.188	.192	9.50	5.50
Stevens, Jacob	B-R	6-3	225	2-11-96	3	0	2.94	19	0	0	0	34	26	12	11	3	14	32	.210	.161	.226	8.55	3.74
Tineo, Marcos	R-R	6-0	165	3-14-97	6	4	2.57	15	8	0	0	67	62	25	19	1	19	66	.245	.238	.249	8.91	2.57
Walston, Blake	L-L	6-5	175	6-28-01	0	0	3.00	3	3	0	0	6	6	2	2	0	2	6	.261	.500	.238	9.00	3.00

Fielding

C: Dalesandro 17, Herbert 1, January 13, Lin 23, Wasinger 22. **1B:** English 7, Garza 3, Gillette 9, Hernandez 1, Yerzy 56. **2B:** Garza 3, Grande 28, Hernandez 12, Lachance 7, Leyton 8, Martinez 20. **3B:** English 21, Garza 17, Gillette 5, Hernandez 8, Martinez 22, Robbins 3. **SS:** Grande 3, Lachance 2, Leyton 33, Martinez 21, Peguero 18. **OF:** Barrosa 57, Canzone 20, Carroll 11, English 16, Garza 9, Gillette 9, January 5, Marriaga 64, Robinson 40.

MISSOULA OSPREY   ROOKIE ADVANCED
PIONEER LEAGUE

Batting	B-T	HT	WT	DOB	AVG	vLH	vRH	G	AB	R	H	2B	3B	HR	RBI	BB	HBP	SH	SF	SO	SB	CS	SLG	OBP
Andueza, Axel	R-R	6-0	163	10-27-98	.281	.295	.276	54	224	40	63	11	2	1	21	10	1	0	3	29	0	3	.362	.311
Brickhouse, Spencer	L-R	6-4	235	4-10-98	.272	.302	.261	60	224	31	61	14	2	6	34	17	3	0	1	72	2	1	.433	.331
Canzone, Dominic	L-R	6-1	190	8-16-97	.299	.429	.246	25	97	17	29	13	1	5	26	6	0	0	0	13	3	1	.608	.340
Carranza, Tristen	R-R	5-10	200	10-8-96	.252	.200	.270	67	234	41	59	13	1	7	29	31	13	0	1	52	6	1	.406	.369
Castillo, Neyfy	R-R	6-3	175	3-2-01	.125	.000	.200	5	16	3	2	0	0	1	2	5	1	0	0	4	4	0	.313	.364
Coursey, Cam	L-R	5-8	155	8-25-98	.276	.373	.243	51	203	33	56	9	1	1	12	18	2	1	1	24	4	3	.345	.339
Curpa, Jose	R-R	5-9	160	3-9-00	.333	.455	.286	10	39	5	13	1	0	0	3	4	1	0	0	8	2	0	.359	.409
Garcia, Cesar	R-R	6-0	190	4-7-98	.277	.186	.311	59	220	28	61	11	2	3	24	21	2	0	0	40	8	4	.386	.346
Grande, Nick	R-R	5-11	170	2-9-98	.250	.143	.273	13	40	8	10	0	0	1	3	5	1	0	0	9	1	1	.325	.348
Herum, Marty	R-R	6-3	214	12-16-91	.571	.500	.600	2	7	3	4	0	0	2	3	0	0	0	0	0	0	0	1.429	.571
Lachance, Kevin	R-R	6-3	185	7-2-94	.258	.400	.231	10	31	3	8	2	0	1	9	7	0	0		6	1	0	.419	.395
Lanza, Douglas	R-R	6-1	180	3-14-98	.154	.000	.174	8	26	3	4	1	0	1	1	2	0	0		11	1	0	.308	.241
Martinez, Francis	L-R	6-4	250	6-28-97	.246	.220	.256	50	183	28	45	6	2	12	32	16	7	0	1	58	1	2	.497	.329
Maxwell, Carson	R-R	6-4	215	6-30-97	.162	.103	.182	38	117	13	19	3	3	2	7	21	1	0	1	54	0	1	.291	.293
Patino, Wilderd	R-R	6-1	175	7-18-01	.229	.333	.192	10	35	6	8	1	2	0	4	2	2	0	1	14	1	1	.371	.300
Peguero, Liover	R-R	6-1	160	12-31-00	.364	.290	.391	38	143	34	52	7	3	5	27	12	0	0	1	34	8	1	.559	.410
Perez, Leodany	R-R	5-10	160	5-13-00	.083	.000	.100	4	12	1	1	0	0	0	0	2	0	0		3	0	0	.083	.214
Reyes, Jose	L-R	5-9	160	10-11-98	.259	.268	.256	58	220	27	57	11	1	3	25	14	0	0	1	34	9	3	.359	.303
Robbins, Joe	R-R	5-9	195	12-8-93	.177	.167	.182	6	17	1	3	0	0	0	1	3	0	0		5	0	0	.177	.300
Sanchez, David	R-R	6-1	175	1-6-99	.181	.241	.158	29	105	8	19	4	1	1	13	2	0	1		35	1	0	.267	.194
Valbuena, Luvin	R-R	5-9	165	5-7-99	.179	.143	.189	39	134	15	24	5	0	0	10	9	1	0	0	49	1	1	.216	.236
Watson Jr., Kevin	L-R	6-1	190	5-25-99	.217	.214	.217	60	217	26	47	4	7	10	31	15	7	0	0	82	2	2	.438	.289

Pitching	B-T	HT	WT	DOB	W	L	ERA	G	GS	CG	SV	IP	H	R	ER	HR	BB	SO	AVG	vLH	vRH	K/9	BB/9
Almonte, Jose	R-R	6-2	185	9-8-95	0	0	0.00	2	0	0	0	2	0	0	0	0	0	4	.000	.000	.000	18.00	0.00
Arroyo, Mailon	B-R	6-0	200	1-2-98	1	1	1.50	13	0	0	7	18	10	4	3	1	4	30	.159	.222	.133	15.00	2.00
Ay, Bobby	R-R	6-3	190	5-28-97	1	0	4.09	10	10	0	0	11	10	5	5	2	2	14	.238	.350	.136	11.45	1.64
Cruz, Wilfry	R-R	6-2	160	10-22-97	1	0	3.18	3	3	0	0	11	9	8	4	0	7	12	.209	.250	.194	9.53	5.56
De La Cruz, Ezequiel	L-L	6-2	180	1-21-99	2	1	3.81	19	0	0	0	26	32	18	11	1	6	35	.299	.320	.293	12.12	2.08
Fritze, Ryan	R-R	6-2	200	3-5-94	1	2	3.86	14	0	0	5	16	14	9	7	3	7	25	.230	.250	.222	13.78	3.86
Fuenmayor, Liu	L-L	5-11	190		3	2	2.50	14	0	0	0	36	31	11	10	0	14	51	.228	.250	.220	12.75	3.50
Hull, Denson	B-L	6-1	220	10-21-96	2	2	7.89	18	2	0	0	30	30	29	26	7	15	42	.256	.200	.276	12.74	4.55
Lacaze, Dustin	R-R	6-1	207	12-17-96	3	0	3.83	14	7	0	0	56	55	24	24	4	11	47	.259	.301	.233	7.51	1.76
Liebelt, Jared	R-R	6-0	169	1-20-97	1	0	1.69	14	0	0	1	21	17	10	4	1	9	27	.213	.192	.222	11.39	3.80
Marchese, Nick	R-R	6-4	200	10-14-96	3	3	3.97	19	1	0	0	34	34	18	15	2	18	30	.266	.290	.256	7.94	4.76
Martinez, Edgar	R-R	6-0	175	11-2-97	0	2	5.79	9	3	0	0	33	47	22	21	4	5	26	.346	.395	.323	7.16	1.38
Martinez, Justin	R-R	6-3	180	7-30-01	0	0	0.00	3	0	0	0	4	1	1	0	0	4	7	.067	.000	.111	15.79	9.00
McGuff, Patrick	L-R	6-2	200	3-30-94	5	3	4.45	9	9	0	0	55	47	27	27	7	12	61	.224	.254	.212	10.04	1.98
McMinn, Josh	R-R	6-4	205	4-29-96	1	4	3.44	14	13	0	0	55	48	28	21	3	18	65	.230	.192	.250	10.64	2.95
Mieses, Junior	R-R	6-1	168	10-15-99	0	0	1.23	3	0	0	0	7	4	1	1	0	2	11	.148	.000	.222	13.50	2.45
Pope, Austin	R-R	6-3	210	10-26-98	2	2	2.53	13	8	0	0	32	24	11	9	0	12	45	.202	.125	.241	12.66	2.81
Poulin, Tyler	R-R	6-4	220	8-1-96	3	2	5.47	13	11	0	0	49	53	35	30	6	12	46	.292	.298	.261	8.39	2.19
Rosario, Oliver	L-L	6-0	140	6-15-99	1	0	4.81	17	0	0	0	24	20	14	13	3	16	26	.222	.350	.186	9.62	5.92
Stumpo, Mitchell	R-R	6-2	205	6-17-96	1	1	2.81	11	0	0	5	16	10	6	5	1	6	21	.179	.313	.125	11.81	3.38
Swain, Dan	R-R	5-11	200	9-30-96	0	0	18.90	2	0	0	0	3	5	7	7	3	3	6	.333	.333		24.30	8.10
Valdez, Alex	R-R	6-2	185	12-24-99	2	1	8.41	6	6	0	0	20	25	20	19	0	16	30	.309	.250	.356	7.08	2.66
Valdez, Jhonny	R-R	6-3	187	8-10-98	2	1	2.81	10	0	0	2	16	16	8	5	1	5	20	.267	.192	.324	11.25	2.81
Whitson, Landon	R-R	6-3	230	9-11-96	1	2	6.83	21	0	0	0	29	36	23	22	3	9	39	.303	.278	.313	12.10	2.79
Williams, Chris	R-R	5-11	180	8-24-95	1	1	6.00	17	0	0	1	24	32	17	16	3	8	24	.327	.429	.299	9.00	3.00
Zorrilla, Pedro	L-L	6-2	168	4-30-96	4	2	5.67	17	3	0	0	33	28	23	21	4	14	44	.214	.226	.210	11.88	3.78

Fielding

C: Andueza 32, Lanza 6, Valbuena 38. **1B:** Andueza 1, Brickhouse 53, Martinez 22, Maxwell 2. **2B:** Andueza 1, Coursey 47, Curpa 4, Garcia 11, Grande 5, Lachance 2, Reyes 9. **3B:** Andueza 5, Curpa 2, Garcia 17, Herum 2, Maxwell 31, Reyes 21, Robbins 1. **SS:** Coursey 1, Curpa 3, Grande 8, Peguero 37, Reyes 29. **OF:** Canzone 25, Carranza 63, Castillo 5, Garcia 31, Lachance 8, Patino 10, Perez 4, Robbins 4, Sanchez 26, Watson Jr. 56.

ARIZONA DIAMONDBACKS

ARIZONA DIAMONDBACKS

Batting	B-T	HT	WT	DOB	AVG	vLH	vRH	G	AB	R	H	2B	3B	HR	RBI	BB	HBP	SH	SF	SO	SB	CS	SLG	OBP
Almonte, Abraham	B-R	5-9	210	6-27-89	.231	.000	.250	3	13	4	3	0	0	2	3	0	0	0	0	1	1	0	.692	.231
Altavilla, Angelo	R-R	6-1	195	10-11-96	.241	.208	.250	39	116	21	28	3	0	0	12	28	4	2	2	22	14	2	.267	.400
Carroll, Corbin	L-L	5-10	165	8-21-00	.288	.333	.276	31	111	23	32	6	3	2	14	24	0	0	2	29	16	1	.451	.409
Castillo, Neyfy	R-R	6-3	175	3-2-01	.260	.294	.252	45	169	23	44	9	5	1	29	16	3	0	3	46	7	1	.391	.330
Coursey, Cam	L-R	5-8	155	8-25-98	.429	.333	.500	2	7	0	3	1	0	0	1	0	0	1	0	0	1	0	.571	.500
Cron, Kevin	R-R	6-5	250	2-17-93	.200	--	.200	2	5	5	1	0	0	1	2	0	0	0	0	2	0	0	.800	.200
Curpa, Jose	R-R	5-9	160	3-9-00	.294	.250	.307	49	184	33	54	7	2	0	24	24	4	0	1	41	28	9	.353	.385
Dalesandro, Nick	R-R	6-1	175	10-3-96	.500	--	.500	2	2	0	1	1	0	0	4	0	0	0	0	1	0	0	1.000	.833
Espinal, Jeferson	L-L	6-0	180	6-7-02	.286	.200	.300	9	35	6	10	1	0	0	7	8	0	0	0	11	4	1	.314	.419
Estrada, Endy	R-R	5-11	175	4-6-02	.217	--	.217	7	23	3	5	2	0	1	3	2	1	0	0	7	1	0	.435	.308
Flores, Wilmer	R-R	6-3	205	8-6-91	.539	.333	.600	4	13	5	7	4	0	0	1	1	0	0	0	1	0	1	.846	.571
Gutierrez, Sergio	B-R	6-1	195	1-18-01	.242	.143	.271	22	62	4	15	3	0	0	7	7	0	0	2	16	1	1	.290	.310
Hernandez, Eddie	R-R	5-9	160	4-18-99	.125	--	.125	2	8	2	1	0	0	0	1	0	0	0	0	2	1	0	.125	.222
Herum, Marty	R-R	6-3	214	12-16-91	.462	1.000	.417	4	13	2	6	0	0	1	3	2	0	0	0	2	1	0	.692	.533
Hill Jr., Glenallen	B-R	5-9	170	9-30-00	.206	.250	.195	42	160	22	33	4	6	3	18	17	2	1	1	63	19	5	.363	.289
Jaime, Ismael	L-0	179		11-30-99	.257	.269	.255	39	136	14	35	3	0	1	16	19	0	0	1	42	3	4	.302	.346
Jimenez, Rafael	L-R	6-6	215	8-25-99	.193	.091	.218	36	109	11	21	5	0	0	13	12	0	0	2	43	0	3	.239	.268
Joseph, Caleb	R-R	6-3	180	6-18-86	.000	.000	.000	2	5	0	0	0	0	0	0	0	0	0	0	1	0	0	.000	.000
Lanza, Douglas	R-R	6-1	180	3-14-98	.182	.250	.167	8	22	3	4	3	0	1	4	2	2	0	0	10	1	0	.455	.308
Martinez, Sandy	R-R	6-4	195	5-9-00	.239	.250	.237	31	117	8	28	8	2	0	12	1	1	0	0	44	0	0	.342	.252
Mathisen, Wyatt	R-R	6-0	225	12-30-93	.348	.250	.368	8	23	4	8	3	0	0	3	6	2	0	0	3	1	0	.478	.516
Patino, Wilderd	R-R	6-1	175	7-18-01	.349	.200	.384	30	106	18	37	4	3	1	21	11	2	1	5	32	13	3	.472	.403
Peralta, David	L-L	6-1	210	8-14-87	.250	.000	.500	2	4	3	1	0	0	0	4	0	0	0	0	0	0	0	.250	.625
Perez, Leodany	R-R	5-10	160	5-13-00	.227	.217	.229	32	119	25	27	5	2	0	7	5	2	0	2	36	12	3	.303	.282
Ruiz, Roman	R-R	5-11	175	1-3-01	.088	.083	.091	11	34	3	3	0	0	1	6	3	0	0	0	6	2	0	.177	.162
Santos, Oscar	R-R	5-9	175	9-24-00	.218	.321	.183	33	110	13	24	5	0	1	10	13	2	0	1	34	1	2	.291	.310
Szczur, Matt	R-R	6-0	200	7-20-89	.182	.250	.143	3	11	5	2	1	1	0	1	1	0	0	0	1	0	0	.455	.250
Taylor, Marshawn	L-R	5-10	150	8-27-95	.250	.222	.257	45	176	31	44	6	7	0	12	16	3	0	3	29	4	2	.364	.318
Yanqui, Yoel	L-L	6-1	210	4-25-96	.231	.333	.200	4	13	3	3	1	0	0	3	1	0	0	0	3	2	0	.308	.286

Pitching	B-T	HT	WT	DOB	W	L	ERA	G	GS	CG	SV	IP	H	R	ER	HR	BB	SO	AVG	vLH	vRH	K/9	BB/9
Alvarez, Jhosmer	R-R	6-1	155	6-29-01	1	1	6.52	5	1	0	0	10	10	8	7	0	3	15	.270	.177	.350	13.97	2.79
Andriese, Matt	R-R	6-2	225	8-28-89	0	0	27.00	1	1	0	0	2	2	1	0	1	0	.500	1.000	.333	9.00	27.00
Atkinson, Ryan	R-R	6-3	218	5-10-93	1	0	3.00	2	0	0	0	3	1	1	1	1	0	5	.100	.125	.000	15.00	0.00
Beriguete, Francis	L-L	6-3	165	8-11-99	0	1	4.15	13	2	0	0	30	28	22	14	1	19	28	.235	.226	.239	8.31	5.64
Borbolla, Rigoberto	L-L	6-2	170	8-20-01	1	2	4.91	12	4	0	0	37	42	22	20	2	14	37	.290	.325	.276	9.08	3.41
Bravo, Argenis	L-L	5-10	160	1-7-00	0	1	6.06	15	2	0	2	33	34	24	22	1	21	35	.270	.267	.271	9.64	5.79
Cardenas, Antonio	R-R	6-2	165	12-24-99	3	0	0.96	15	0	0	3	28	18	10	3	1	13	33	.178	.250	.139	10.61	4.18
Custodio, Raibel	R-R	6-3	185	9-8-99	1	2	5.40	16	0	0	0	29	19	15	12	2	12	17	.260	.333	.236	7.65	5.40
De Jesus, Henler	L-L	6-4	170	6-15-98	0	0	5.40	2	0	0	0	2	1	1	1	0	2	2	.167	.000	.200	10.80	10.80
Duplantier, Jon	L-R	6-4	225	7-11-94	0	0	18.00	2	2	0	0	2	5	5	4	1	3	3	.455	.500	.400	13.50	13.50
Francis, Harrison	R-R	6-2	195	10-26-98	0	0	0.00	1	0	0	0	1	1	0	0	0	1	0	.333	1.000	.000	9.00	0.00
Ginkel, Kevin	L-R	6-4	210	3-24-94	0	0	0.00	2	0	0	0	2	0	0	0	0	0	1	.000	.000	.000	4.50	4.50
Herrera, Eduardo	B-R	5-9	155	1-5-00	0	0	0.00	3	0	0	3	4	1	0	0	0	0	11	.083	.000	.125	27.00	0.00
Holton, Tyler	L-L	6-2	200	6-13-96	1	0	3.38	4	2	0	0	5	3	2	2	0	4	5	.177	.333	.143	8.44	6.75
Jones, Brock	L-L	6-1	180	6-14-01	0	0	3.18	5	0	0	0	6	3	3	2	0	5	7	.150	.500	.063	11.12	7.94
Kohn, Michael	R-R	6-2	200	6-26-86	0	0	6.75	3	0	0	0	3	1	2	2	0	1	6	.111	.000	.200	20.25	3.38
Larrison, Ethan	R-R	6-2	205	8-14-95	0	0	0.00	1	0	0	0	1	1	1	0	0	1	1	.250	1.000	.000	9.00	9.00
Lewis, Sam	R-R	6-4	195	10-9-91	0	0	0.00	1	0	0	0	1	0	0	0	0	0	2	.000	.000	.000	18.00	0.00
Malone, Brennan	R-R	6-4	205	9-8-00	1	2	5.14	6	3	0	0	7	4	4	4	0	5	7	.167	.308	.000	9.00	6.43
Mark, Tyler	R-R	6-1	195	10-18-94	0	0	4.50	1	0	0	0	2	1	1	1	0	1	3	.143	.250	.000	13.50	4.50
Martinez, Justin	R-R	6-3	180	7-30-01	0	1	3.24	6	2	0	1	17	12	10	6	0	11	23	.191	.217	.175	12.42	5.94
Mendez, Eric	R-R	6-0	171	12-19-98	2	0	4.68	11	0	0	1	25	22	15	13	0	11	35	.227	.212	.234	12.60	3.96
Mercer, Matt	R-R	6-2	180	9-1-96	0	1	2.31	5	4	0	0	12	9	3	3	0	6	10	.225	.250	.208	7.71	4.63
Mieses, Junior	R-R	6-1	168	10-15-99	1	2	3.38	11	7	0	0	35	26	17	13	2	23	44	.210	.224	.197	11.42	5.97
Miller, Jared	L-L	6-7	240	8-21-93	0	0	--	1	0	0	0	1	1	1	0	0	1.000	--	1.000	--	--
Munoz, Jesus	L-L	6-2	160	12-19-98	1	1	0.73	14	0	0	0	12	8	7	1	0	8	15	.178	.083	.212	10.95	5.84
Nolasco, Ricky	R-R	6-2	235	12-13-82	0	0	0.00	3	0	0	0	5	3	0	0	0	2	7	.158	.143	.167	11.81	3.38
Ogando, Gerald	R-R	6-2	180	7-28-00	3	4	3.72	8	6	0	0	29	26	16	12	1	15	31	.248	.159	.312	9.62	4.66
Pacheco, Cristian	R-R	6-2	175	4-23-01	1	2	9.72	3	2	0	0	8	14	11	9	0	7	10	.400	.286	.429	10.80	7.56
Pope, Austin	R-R	6-3	210	10-26-98	0	0	0.00	1	0	0	0	1	0	0	0	0	1	0	.000	--	.000	0.00	9.00
Reed, Cody	R-L	6-3	245	6-7-96	0	1	2.45	3	2	0	0	4	2	1	1	0	3	6	.154	.333	.100	14.73	7.36
Saalfrank, Andrew	L-L	6-3	205	8-18-97	0	0	0.00	1	0	0	0	1	1	0	0	0	0	1	.000	--	.000	9.00	9.00
Sanchez, Yan	R-R	6-2	170	8-31-96	2	3	5.50	14	0	0	1	18	24	14	11	0	10	22	.312	.303	.318	11.00	5.00
Santos, Rael	R-R	6-3	165	3-29-01	1	0	5.79	2	1	0	0	5	6	3	3	0	4	7	.300	.200	.333	13.50	7.71
Sherfy, Jimmie	R-R	6-0	175	12-27-91	1	0	6.75	3	0	0	0	3	2	2	1	0	5	.273	.500	.222	16.88	0.00
Short, Avery	R-L	6-1	175	3-14-01	0	0	2.57	6	1	0	0	7	7	2	2	0	0	7	.259	.500	.158	9.00	0.00
Snyder, Nick	L-L	6-7	220	11-19-97	0	0	9.00	1	0	0	0	1	2	1	1	0	0	3	.333	.333	.333	27.00	0.00
Stroman, Jonathan	R-R	6-2	195	11-1-98	2	1	3.72	13	0	0	0	19	10	9	8	1	10	25	.152	.174	.140	11.64	4.66
Stumpo, Mitchell	R-R	6-2	205	6-17-96	0	0	9.00	2	0	0	0	2	5	2	2	0	0	2	.455	.500	.400	13.50	0.00
Swain, Dan	R-R	5-11	200	9-30-94	0	0	5.40	16	0	0	2	17	18	12	10	1	9	21	.269	.290	.250	11.34	4.86

Name	B-T	HT	WT	DOB	W	L	ERA	G	GS	CG	SV	IP	H	R	ER	BB	SO	AVG	vLH	vRH	K/9	BB/9
Valdez, Alex	R-R	6-2	185	12-24-99	2	1	4.01	10	9	0	0	43	35	20	19	1	17	37	.219	.254	.194	7.80	3.59
Valdez, Jhonny	R-R	6-3	187	8-10-98	0	2	0.00	8	0	0	1	15	9	4	0	0	3	21	.173	.120	.222	12.33	1.76
Vargas, Emilio	R-R	6-3	200	8-12-96	0	2	4.35	3	3	0	0	10	9	5	5	1	2	12	.243	.353	.150	10.45	1.74
Walston, Blake	L-L	6-5	175	6-28-01	0	0	1.80	3	2	0	0	5	2	1	1	0	0	11	.118	.400	.000	19.80	0.00
Williams, Chris	R-R	5-11	180	8-24-95	1	0	2.70	2	0	0	0	3	4	2	1	0	0	2	.286	.000	.308	5.40	0.00

Fielding

C: Dalesandro 2, Gutierrez 15, Joseph 2, Lanza 7, Martinez 20, Santos 19. **1B:** Altavilla 16, Castillo 8, Cron 1, Curpa 1, Estrada 2, Gutierrez 1, Herum 1, Jimenez 34, Lanza 1, Yanqui 2. **2B:** Altavilla 2, Curpa 2, Flores 3, Hill Jr. 39, Mathisen 1, Perez 4, Taylor 9. **3B:** Altavilla 20, Curpa 22, Estrada 3, Hernandez 1, Herum 2, Mathisen 4, Perez 1, Taylor 11. **SS:** Altavilla 3, Coursey 2, Curpa 21, Ruiz 11, Taylor 21. **OF:** Almonte 2, Altavilla 4, Carroll 30, Castillo 3, Curpa 3, Espinal 9, Estrada 3, Herum 2, Jaime 35, Patino 29, Peralta 1, Perez 27, Szczur 3, Taylor 1, Yanqui 1.

DSL D-BACKS   ROOKIE
DOMINICAN SUMMER LEAGUE

Batting	B-T	HT	WT	DOB	AVG	vLH	vRH	G	AB	R	H	2B	3B	HR	RBI	BB	HBP	SH	SF	SO	SB	CS	SLG	OBP
Amador, Alexander	R-R	6-2	180	12-7-00	.211	.000	.222	6	19	2	4	0	1	0	4	6	0	0	0	6	0	0	.316	.400
Aquino, Esteban	L-L	6-3	185	1-8-01	.286	.292	.285	45	161	25	46	12	2	0	18	13	2	0	3	36	10	4	.385	.341
Batista, Juan	R-R	6-1	175	1-9-01	.270	.133	.304	60	226	42	61	9	8	1	25	42	3	0	1	49	26	12	.394	.390
Caldera, Ricardo	R-R	6-1	175	4-6-02	.252	.263	.250	49	163	26	41	8	5	1	26	22	8	0	2	51	2	1	.380	.364
Campo, Cristofer	R-R	6-0	150	1-17-02	.165	.192	.158	42	127	13	21	3	1	0	15	26	2	1	1	27	4	1	.205	.314
Castillo, Neyfy	R-R	6-3	175	3-2-01	.364	1.000	.222	3	11	3	4	2	0	0	6	0	0	0	2	2	0	0	.546	.308
Colina, Angel	R-R	5-11	180	12-15-01	.214	.238	.208	30	98	14	21	6	0	0	11	19	1	0	1	22	2	0	.276	.345
Cuevas, Dairon	B-R	6-1	155	4-5-02	.234	.149	.255	58	231	29	54	9	2	0	16	14	5	1	3	86	13	5	.290	.289
Delgado, Learsi	R-R	5-11	160	3-10-01	.142	.000	.167	44	113	15	16	1	0	1	9	16	8	0	3	45	4	4	.177	.286
Espinal, Jeferson	L-L	6-0	180	6-7-02	.358	.317	.370	47	187	36	67	9	2	2	14	15	2	0	0	45	22	9	.460	.412
Estrada, Endy	R-R	5-11	175	4-6-02	.287	.333	.271	51	192	30	55	13	4	2	28	22	2	0	3	30	12	3	.427	.361
Estrella, Cristian	L-L	6-1	175	11-12-01	.197	.188	.200	37	132	11	26	3	0	0	11	10	1	0	1	38	4	4	.220	.257
Garcia, Manuel	R-R	5-11	170	1-28-00	.269	.333	.252	50	160	20	43	11	2	0	24	23	10	0	3	34	3	6	.363	.388
Goris, Carlos	L-L	5-10	150	12-17-00	.242	.280	.236	57	190	44	46	6	1	3	22	42	1	0	1	41	18	4	.332	.380
Guillermes, Raykel	R-R	6-0	176	1-6-00	.230	.391	.203	49	161	25	37	9	1	0	20	37	3	1	2	40	10	1	.298	.379
Guzman, Alvin	R-R	6-1	166	10-20-01	.226	.226	.226	57	239	39	54	11	3	1	24	16	3	0	4	64	14	3	.310	.279
Hernandez, Alexander	R-R	5-11	150	6-20-99	.264	.325	.250	61	212	45	56	14	3	10	33	37	3	0	5	60	9	3	.500	.374
Leon, Daniel	L-R	6-1	175	11-9-00	.225	.133	.241	32	98	13	22	5	0	0	13	22	5	0	1	30	0	1	.276	.389
Malave, Ramses	R-R	5-11	175	9-29-00	.253	.208	.259	55	194	26	49	15	3	1	35	37	9	0	3	56	13	5	.376	.391
Marcano, Jose	R-R	5-11	160	1-14-02	.203	.235	.198	46	133	17	27	3	1	0	12	23	3	0	3	23	2	2	.241	.327
Martinez, Asdrubal	R-R	5-11	170	1-4-02	.205	.269	.189	44	132	18	27	6	0	0	10	34	5	0	1	28	10	4	.250	.384
Mendez, Mario	L-L	5-11	160	12-30-01	.227	.128	.258	41	163	13	37	10	1	0	18	9	1	0	0	27	6	2	.301	.272
Mendez, Teofilo	R-R	5-11	170	10-8-01	.171	.250	.163	25	88	11	15	3	1	1	7	14	3	0	1	34	2	2	.261	.302
Montas, Manuel	R-R	6-3	180	3-11-01	.000	--	.000	2	5	0	0	0	0	0	0	0	0	0	0	4	0	0	.000	.000
Padron, Juan	R-R	5-10	160	10-17-00	.087	.000	.111	7	23	2	2	0	0	0	3	1	1	0	0	6	0	0	.087	.160
Peguero, Alejandro	B-R	6-0	180	2-28-00	.250	.500	.200	4	12	0	3	1	0	0	1	0	0	0	0	6	0	0	.333	.357
Perez, Leodany	R-R	5-10	160	5-13-00	.222	.000	.244	26	90	18	20	3	1	0	6	23	8	0	0	17	12	5	.278	.422
Rodriguez, Oscar	R-R	6-0	180	9-26-01	.247	.167	.262	24	73	10	18	4	0	0	4	10	7	0	1	12	1	0	.301	.385
Romero, Edward	R-R	5-10	150	5-11-02	.178	.154	.184	58	202	33	36	6	0	0	15	13	6	2	2	49	9	5	.208	.247
Santilien, Osvaldo	R-R	6-3	195	6-23-99	.250	.500	.188	18	60	12	15	3	0	1	7	12	2	0	0	15	0	1	.350	.392
Rubio, Luis	R-R	5-10	155	1-10-02	.297	.419	.278	59	229	39	68	5	5	0	28	40	3	0	2	44	7	5	.362	.405
Ruiz, Roman	R-R	6-1	175	1-10-01	.148	.000	.170	17	61	7	9	2	1	0	6	2	4	0	1	13	1	1	.213	.221
Sanabria, Danyer	L-L	6-1	155	3-7-02	.244	.233	.245	60	246	30	60	13	2	8	39	9	1	0	5	54	6	6	.411	.268
Vegas, Deivis	R-R	5-11	170	2-9-00	.244	.333	.228	56	201	32	49	13	1	0	30	20	6	0	2	29	3	5	.318	.328

Pitching	B-T	HT	WT	DOB	W	L	ERA	G	GS	CG	SV	IP	H	R	ER	BB	SO	AVG	vLH	vRH	K/9	BB/9
Acosta, Enmanuel	R-R	6-2	200	6-6-99	0	3	1.54	8	0	0	4	12	9	4	2	0	3	18	.214	.385	.138	13.89	2.31
Alcantara, Jose	R-R	6-2	180	8-3-99	1	2	1.63	13	1	0	4	28	23	14	5	0	7	32	.217	.182	.226	10.41	2.28
Almonte, Jonathan	R-R	6-0	175	8-9-00	4	1	2.73	18	0	0	0	33	24	18	10	0	11	32	.205	.192	.209	8.73	3.00
Amador, Alexander	R-R	6-1	180	12-7-00	0	0	0.00	3	0	0	0	3	4	0	0	0	0	4	.333	.200	.429	12.00	0.00
Andujar, Hamilton	R-R	6-3	175	9-14-99	4	2	3.63	13	7	0	0	45	37	20	18	1	16	47	.224	.245	.216	9.47	3.22
Arias, Luis	R-R	6-2	170	8-16-01	2	2	3.97	14	3	0	0	34	25	20	15	0	22	35	.268	.177	.326	9.26	5.82
Avendano, Julio	R-R	6-1	175	12-5-00	2	3	6.41	12	0	0	1	27	35	21	19	0	11	30	.315	.321	.313	10.13	3.71
Bascunan, Mauricio	R-R	6-4	170	10-3-01	6	3	2.58	14	2	0	0	38	31	18	11	3	22	22	.214	.220	.212	5.17	5.17
Bohorquez, Jose	R-R	6-1	160	12-12-01	3	2	2.15	14	0	0	1	29	17	7	7	0	13	25	.160	.273	.131	7.67	3.99
Borbolla, Rigoberto	L-L	6-2	170	8-20-01	2	0	0.00	2	1	0	0	9	1	0	0	0	4	14	.037	.000	.044	14.00	4.00
Calzadilla, Abraham	R-R	6-2	170	12-12-01	0	1	9.53	4	3	0	0	6	12	10	6	0	6	5	.444	.125	.579	7.94	9.53
Carvajal, Roaldo	R-R	6-2	180	12-20-00	3	1	4.29	14	3	0	0	36	29	19	17	2	20	27	.218	.111	.235	6.81	5.05
Castillo, Bryan	R-R	6-3	185	1-18-99	1	1	3.20	15	0	0	2	20	11	12	7	0	18	20	.155	.118	.167	9.35	8.24
Cova, Jeanpier	R-R	6-0	175	6-9-00	1	1	6.48	9	0	0	0	8	1	7	6	0	9	5	.039	.000	.053	5.40	9.72
De Dios, Fredely	R-R	6-2	165	11-3-00	0	0	7.71	7	2	0	0	12	12	11	10	0	10	10	.279	.417	.226	7.71	7.71
Del Pozo, Gustavo	R-R	5-9	190	12-17-99	1	3	4.60	13	6	0	0	31	25	27	16	0	34	25	.217	.150	.232	7.18	9.77
Garcia, Jose	L-L	5-11	165	12-4-00	1	2	2.51	20	0	0	5	29	23	11	8	2	10	31	.213	.222	.211	9.73	3.14
Gonzalez, Juan	R-R	6-1	170	3-15-01	0	0	0.00	6	0	0	0	7	4	0	0	0	2	10	.160	.167	.158	12.27	2.45
Isea, Edgar	R-R	6-3	185	8-20-02	0	2	4.30	12	5	0	0	29	24	16	14	0	25	22	.235	.231	.236	6.75	7.67
Marcelino, Jean	R-R	6-2	170	7-19-00	1	4	3.14	15	5	0	2	52	33	25	18	2	17	53	.180	.145	.206	9.23	2.96
Martinez, Justin	R-R	6-3	180	7-30-01	1	2	3.06	9	8	0	0	35	29	14	12	0	22	48	.200	.310	.178	12.23	5.60
Martinez, Victor	L-L	6-1	190	8-16-99	1	1	4.13	17	0	0	1	24	18	15	11	0	23	40	.207	.222	.205	15.00	8.63
Mendoza, Luis	R-R	6-1	190	1-4-02	2	1	3.77	15	7	0	1	45	40	24	19	1	25	33	.245	.222	.254	6.55	4.96
Meran, Andreuris	R-R	6-1	185	8-9-99	0	2	2.41	13	0	0	1	19	12	7	5	1	15	8	.194	.381	.098	3.86	7.23

Name		Ht	Wt	DOB	W	L	ERA	G	GS	CG	SV	IP	H	R	ER	HR	BB	SO	AVG	OBP	SLG		
Morel, Osvaldo	R-R	6-3	195	6-17-01	0	3	9.31	12	3	0	0	29	36	37	30	5	22	33	.305	.342	.288	10.24	6.83
Meza, Carlos	L-L	6-1	155	2-10-01	4	2	4.91	13	1	0	1	29	20	18	16	0	18	36	.192	.267	.180	11.05	5.52
Ogando, Gerald	R-R	6-2	180	7-28-00	1	0	0.00	1	1	0	0	5	1	0	0	0	0	4	.059	.125	.000	7.20	0.00
Pacheco, Cristian	R-R	6-2	175	4-23-01	1	2	3.56	12	12	0	0	48	47	23	19	1	20	43	.257	.213	.279	8.06	3.75
Pena, Bryam	R-R	6-5	170	2-4-01	0	0	4.97	15	6	0	0	38	37	24	21	1	20	36	.255	.200	.280	8.53	4.74
Perez, Jheyson	R-R	6-3	175	2-2-00	6	1	2.81	14	3	0	0	48	40	18	15	2	10	63	.225	.324	.201	11.81	1.88
Pimentel, Pablo	R-R	6-2	175	11-7-99	4	0	4.21	13	1	0	1	26	20	21	12	0	28	24	.213	.318	.181	8.42	9.82
Pimentel, Yoscar	R-R	6-2	160	11-3-01	1	6	6.66	14	13	0	0	49	69	46	36	3	16	46	.345	.391	.339	8.51	2.96
Polanco, Sarlin	R-R	6-1	190	2-23-02	1	0	37.80	6	0	0	0	3	8	14	14	0	12	1	.471	.000	.571	2.70	32.40
Rodriguez, Bernardo	L-L	6-1	170	8-17-98	1	1	6.62	11	0	0	1	18	10	15	13	0	26	27	.175	.154	.182	13.75	13.25
Rodriguez, Victor	L-L	6-1	165	8-14-01	1	1	3.35	13	10	0	0	43	44	19	16	1	12	39	.277	.306	.264	8.16	2.51
Roque, Arturo	R-R	6-1	155	12-2-00	5	1	2.17	10	6	0	0	37	23	12	9	0	16	43	.176	.135	.192	10.37	3.86
Sanchez, Pedro	R-R	5-11	185	9-17-00	2	2	2.91	11	0	0	1	22	17	8	7	2	12	19	.224	.368	.175	7.89	4.98
Santamaria, Jose	R-R	6-2	190	11-26-98	0	1	0.50	11	0	0	3	18	12	6	1	1	4	22	.177	.177	.177	11.00	2.00
Santos, Rael	R-R	6-3	165	3-29-01	4	1	2.63	12	6	0	0	41	31	14	12	0	28	45	.214	.271	.186	9.88	6.15
Sierra, Diomede	L-L	6-2	170	9-11-00	0	2	2.60	14	13	0	0	45	29	23	13	0	34	40	.192	.211	.189	8.00	6.80
Silverio, Aderlyn	R-R	6-1	180	6-5-00	1	2	2.58	13	5	0	0	38	38	13	11	1	15	34	.259	.177	.283	7.98	3.52
Soto, Edinson	R-R	6-4	190	9-17-96	1	1	2.28	19	0	0	10	24	16	9	6	3	15	39	.188	.214	.175	14.83	5.70
Tejeda, Daker	L-L	6-2	170	6-20-01	0	1	18.00	5	1	0	0	3	5	9	6	1	10	3	.357	.250	.400	9.00	30.00
Telleria, Carlos	R-R	6-0	150	11-7-99	4	1	2.15	14	7	0	0	46	39	15	11	1	24	42	.232	.217	.238	8.22	4.70
Valdez, Jose	R-R	6-2	180	11-8-01	0	0	6.43	6	0	0	0	7	7	6	5	0	6	10	.250	.125	.300	12.86	7.71
Vilera, Gabriel	R-R	5-11	175	4-15-00	2	0	10.38	11	0	0	0	13	12	22	15	0	21	11	.226	.182	.238	7.62	14.54

Fielding

C: Caldera 47, Colina 18, Garcia 46, Leon 9, Malave 19, Rodriguez 7, Vegas 1. 1B: Amador 4, Campo 1, Castillo 1, Colina 1, Delgado 5, Estrada 30, Guillermes 4, Leon 11, Malave 30, Marcano 21, Vegas 27. 2B: Campo 14, Cuevas 3, Delgado 32, Guillermes 5, Marcano 17, Mendez 1, Padron 3, Peguero 2, Perez 5, Romero 19, Rubio 41, Vegas 2. 3B: Campo 7, Delgado 4, Estrada 4, Guillermes 12, Hernandez 23, Marcano 9, Mendez 23, Padron 3, Peguero 1, Vegas 9. SS: Cuevas 32, Guillermes 1, Hernandez 8, Mendez 1, Padron 1, Peguero 1, Romero 40, Rubio 21, Ruiz 17. OF: Aquino 28, Batista 39, Campo 16, Castillo 2, Espinal 47, Estrada 17, Estrella 34, Goris 47, Guillermes 1, Guzman 57, Martinez 28, Mendez 32, Montas 1, Perez 21, Sanabria 43, Santilien 3.

Atlanta Braves

SEASON IN A SENTENCE: Any notion that the 2018 Braves were simply a flash in the pan was erased when the 2019 team successfully defended its National League East title, as a young core anchored around Freddie Freeman and Josh Donaldson proved to be one of the strongest teams in baseball with a 97-win season.

HIGH POINT: The Braves rode a nine-game winning streak into early September. That run included sweeps over the White Sox and Blue Jays in interleague play before taking three of four games against the Nationals, which put them up 10 games in the NL East and effectively clinched the division.

LOW POINT: The Dodgers swept the Braves in a three-game series in early May and immediately after that the team lost in walkoff fashion to the Diamondbacks, which put the team at 18-20 and four games out of first place for the division.

NOTABLE ROOKIES: After debuting in 2018, Mike Soroka fully established himself in Atlanta's rotation this season and was the team's best pitcher going 13-4, 2.68 and tying for the team lead with 174.2 innings as a 21-year-old. Former top prospect Austin Riley made his major league debut and got off to an electric start, hitting .356/.397/.746 with seven home runs through his first 15 games in May, but struggled thereafter (.191/.248/.395 with 11 home runs in 65 games) while playing first base, third base and both corner outfield spots.

KEY TRANSACTIONS: Josh Donaldson turned out to be one of the better free agent signings of the offseason after agreeing to a one-year, $23 million contract. He hit .259/.379/.521 with 37 home runs and a 127 OPS+ while playing solid defense at third base. The team also signed Dallas Keuchel several days after the draft for $13 million and he went 8-8, 3.75 over 112.2 innings. Atlanta was also busy at the trade deadline, acquiring relievers Shane Greene, Chris Martin and Mark Melancon, who solidified a previously shaky bullpen.

DOWN ON THE FARM: The Braves continue to push out quality young major league players year after year and should have more on the way in 2020. Outfielders Cristian Pache and Drew Waters reached Triple-A in 2019 and could both make their major league debuts next season, and there's still plenty of upper-level pitching depth with the likes of Ian Anderson, Kyle Wright, Kyle Muller and Bryce Wilson looming. However, lack of depth in the lower minors will surface soon.

OPENING DAY PAYROLL: $110,530,000 (17th).

PLAYERS OF THE YEAR

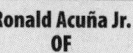

TONY FIRRIOLO

MAJOR LEAGUE

Ronald Acuña Jr.
OF
.280/.365/.518
41 HR, 101 RBIs
37 SB, NL-best 127 R

MINOR LEAGUE

Ian Anderson
RHP
(Double-A/Triple-A)
8-7, 3.38 in 26 GS
172 SO in 135.2 IP

ORGANIZATION LEADERS

Batting		*Minimum 250 AB
MAJORS		
*AVG	Ozzie Albies	.295
*OPS	Freddie Freeman	.938
HR	Ronald Acuna Jr.	41
RBI	Freddie Freeman	121
MINORS		
*AVG	Trey Harris, Rome, Florida, Mississippi	.323
*OBP	Greg Cullen, Rome	.393
*SLG	Adam Duvall, Gwinnett	.602
*OPS	Adam Duvall, Gwinnett	.965
R	Justin Dean, Rome	85
H	Drew Waters, Mississippi, Gwinnett	163
TB	Drew Waters, Mississippi, Gwinnett	242
2B	Drew Waters, Mississippi, Gwinnett	40
3B	Justin Dean, Rome	9
3B	Cristian Pache, Mississippi, Gwinnett	9
3B	Drew Waters, Mississippi, Gwinnett	9
HR	Adam Duvall, Gwinnett	32
RBI	Adam Duvall, Gwinnett	93
BB	Greg Cullen, Rome	71
SO	Drew Lugbauer, Florida	169
SB	Justin Dean, Rome	47

Pitching		#Minimum 75 IP
MAJORS		
W	Max Fried	17
# ERA	Mike Soroka	2.68
SO	Max Fried	173
SV	Luke Jackson	18
MINORS		
W	Kyle Wright, Gwinnett	11
L	Nolan Kingham, Rome, Florida, Mississippi	12
# ERA	Mitch Stallings, Danville, Rome	2.04
G	Jason Creasy, Mississippi, Gwinnett	49
GS	Nolan Kingham, Rome, Florida, Mississippi	27
SV	Jason Creasy, Mississippi, Gwinnett	11
IP	Nolan Kingham, Rome, Florida, Mississippi	165
BB	Kyle Muller, Mississippi	68
SO	Ian Anderson, Mississippi, Gwinnett	172
# AVG	Patrick Weigel, Mississippi, Gwinnett	.184

General Manager: Alex Anthopoulos. **Farm Director:** Dom Chiti. **Scouting Director:** Dana Brown.

Class	Team	League	W	L	PCT	Finish	Manager
Majors	Atlanta Braves	National	97	65	.599	2nd (15)	Brian Snitker
Triple-A	Gwinnett Stripers	International	80	59	.576	2nd (14)	Damon Berryhill
Double-A	Mississippi Braves	Southern	64	75	.460	7th (10)	Chris Maloney
High A	Florida Fire Frogs	Florida State	54	82	.397	12th (12)	Barrett Kleinknecht
Low A	Rome Braves	South Atlantic	65	74	.468	9th (14)	Matt Tuiasosopo
Rookie	Danville Braves	Appalachian	30	38	.441	9th (10)	Anthony Nunez
Rookie	GCL Braves	Gulf Coast	18	31	.367	17th (18)	Nestor Perez
Overall 2019 Minor League Record			311	359	.464	26th (30)	

ORGANIZATION STATISTICS

ATLANTA BRAVES
NATIONAL LEAGUE

Batting	B-T	HT	WT	DOB	AVG	vLH	vRH	G	AB	R	H	2B	3B	HR	RBI	BB	HBP	SH	SF	SO	SB	CS	SLG	OBP
Acuna Jr., Ronald	R-R	6-0	180	12-18-97	.280	.270	.282	156	626	127	175	22	2	41	101	76	9	0	1	188	37	9	.518	.365
Albies, Ozzie	B-R	5-8	165	1-7-97	.295	.389	.267	160	640	102	189	43	8	24	86	54	4	0	4	112	15	4	.500	.352
Camargo, Johan	B-R	6-0	195	12-13-93	.233	.215	.240	98	232	31	54	12	1	7	32	15	0	1	0	43	1	0	.384	.279
Cervelli, Francisco	R-R	6-1	210	3-6-86	.281	.143	.320	14	32	4	9	5	1	2	7	4	1	0	0	10	0	0	.688	.378
2-team total (34 Pittsburgh)					.213	.156	.229	48	141	15	30	8	1	3	12	13	5	1	0	41	1	0	.348	.302
Culberson, Charlie	R-R	6-0	200	4-10-89	.259	.321	.220	108	135	14	35	5	2	5	20	6	1	1	1	44	0	1	.437	.294
Donaldson, Josh	R-R	6-1	210	12-8-85	.259	.215	.271	155	549	96	142	33	0	37	94	100	8	0	2	155	4	2	.521	.379
Duvall, Adam	R-R	6-1	215	9-4-88	.267	.333	.235	41	120	17	32	4	1	10	19	7	2	0	1	39	0	0	.567	.315
Flowers, Tyler	R-R	6-4	260	1-24-86	.229	.155	.262	85	271	36	62	11	3	11	34	31	6	0	2	105	0	0	.413	.319
Freeman, Freddie	L-R	6-5	220	9-12-89	.295	.255	.310	158	597	113	176	34	2	38	121	87	6	0	2	127	6	3	.549	.389
Hamilton, Billy	B-R	6-0	160	9-9-90	.268	.111	.313	26	41	9	11	2	0	0	3	7	0	0	0	13	4	1	.317	.375
Hechavarria, Adeiny	R-R	6-0	195	4-15-89	.328	.400	.314	24	61	14	20	5	1	4	15	6	2	0	1	15	0	0	.639	.400
2-team total (60 New York)					.241	.261	.236	84	203	34	49	12	1	9	33	14	3	0	1	48	3	1	.443	.299
Inciarte, Ender	L-L	5-11	190	10-29-90	.246	.273	.239	65	199	30	49	11	2	5	24	26	4	0	1	41	7	1	.397	.344
Jackson, Alex	R-R	6-2	215	12-25-95	.000	.000	.000	4	13	0	0	0	0	0	0	1	1	0	0	5	0	0	.000	.133
Joyce, Matt	L-R	6-2	200	8-3-84	.295	.273	.298	129	200	32	59	10	0	7	23	38	0	0	4	45	0	0	.450	.408
Markakis, Nick	L-L	6-1	210	11-17-83	.285	.245	.298	116	414	61	118	25	2	9	62	47	2	0	6	59	2	0	.420	.356
McCann, Brian	L-R	6-3	225	2-20-84	.249	.171	.260	85	277	28	69	9	0	12	45	31	2	0	6	53	0	0	.412	.323
Murphy, John Ryan	R-R	5-11	205	5-13-91	.000	--	.000	1	1	0	0	0	0	0	0	0	0	0	0	0	0	0	.000	.000
2-team total (25 Arizona)					.175	.125	.205	26	63	9	11	3	0	4	7	6	0	1	0	28	0	0	.413	.246
Ortega, Rafael	L-R	5-11	160	5-15-91	.205	.083	.224	34	88	7	18	3	0	2	10	8	0	0	0	22	3	0	.307	.271
Riley, Austin	R-R	6-3	220	4-2-97	.226	.262	.215	80	274	41	62	11	1	18	49	16	5	0	2	108	0	2	.471	.280
Swanson, Dansby	R-R	6-1	190	2-11-94	.251	.293	.240	127	483	77	121	26	3	17	65	51	5	1	5	124	10	5	.422	.325

Pitching	B-T	HT	WT	DOB	W	L	ERA	G	GS	CG	SV	IP	H	R	ER	HR	BB	SO	AVG	vLH	vRH	K/9	BB/9
Biddle, Jesse	L-L	6-5	220	10-22-91	0	1	5.40	15	0	0	0	12	18	11	7	1	10	11	.333	.429	.273	8.49	7.71
Blevins, Jerry	L-L	6-6	190	9-6-83	1	0	3.90	45	0	0	1	32	25	15	14	5	16	37	.207	.180	.233	10.30	4.45
Carle, Shane	R-R	6-4	210	8-30-91	0	0	9.64	6	0	0	0	9	11	10	10	3	9	6	.297	.211	.389	5.79	8.68
Culberson, Charlie	R-R	6-0	200	4-10-89	0	0	0.00	2	0	0	0	2	2	0	0	0	2	1	.250	.000	.400	4.50	9.00
Dayton, Grant	L-L	6-2	210	11-25-87	0	1	3.00	14	0	0	0	12	12	5	4	4	14	.255	.250	.258	10.50	3.00
Foltynewicz, Mike	R-R	6-4	200	10-7-91	8	6	4.54	21	21	0	0	117	109	65	59	23	37	105	.244	.228	.258	8.08	2.85
Fried, Max	L-L	6-4	190	1-18-94	17	6	4.02	33	30	1	0	166	174	80	74	21	47	173	.270	.231	.281	9.40	2.55
Gausman, Kevin	L-R	6-3	190	1-6-91	3	7	6.19	16	16	0	0	80	92	60	55	12	27	85	.290	.273	.303	9.56	3.04
2-team total (15 Cincinnati)					3	9	5.72	31	17	0	0	102	113	71	65	15	32	114	.282	.265	.296	10.03	2.81
Greene, Shane	R-R	6-4	197	11-17-88	0	1	4.01	27	0	0	1	25	25	11	11	3	5	21	.269	.394	.200	7.66	1.82
Jackson, Luke	R-R	6-2	210	8-24-91	9	2	3.84	70	0	0	18	73	76	34	31	10	26	106	.266	.157	.332	13.13	3.22
Keuchel, Dallas	L-L	6-3	205	1-1-88	8	8	3.75	19	19	0	0	113	115	50	47	16	39	91	.265	.189	.281	7.27	3.12
Martin, Chris	R-R	6-8	215	6-2-86	1	1	4.08	20	0	0	0	18	17	10	8	1	1	22	.254	.194	.306	11.21	0.51
Melancon, Mark	R-R	6-2	215	3-28-85	1	0	3.86	23	0	0	11	21	22	9	9	1	2	24	.250	.255	.255	10.29	0.86
2-team total (43 San Francisco)					5	2	3.61	66	0	0	12	67	71	28	27	4	18	68	.270	.278	.265	9.09	2.41
Minter, A.J.	L-L	6-0	215	9-2-93	3	4	7.06	36	0	0	5	29	36	23	23	3	23	35	.298	.260	.324	10.74	7.06
Newcomb, Sean	L-L	6-5	255	6-12-93	6	3	3.16	55	4	0	1	68	61	28	24	8	29	65	.236	.250	.230	8.56	3.82
O'Day, Darren	R-R	6-4	220	10-22-82	0	0	1.69	8	0	0	0	5	3	1	1	0	1	6	.158	.200	.143	10.13	1.69
Parsons, Wes	R-R	6-5	204	9-6-92	1	2	3.52	17	0	0	0	15	11	7	6	2	13	12	.229	.294	.194	7.04	7.63
2-team total (15 Colorado)					1	2	5.45	32	0	0	0	35	32	24	21	6	29	26	.265	.255	.270	6.75	7.53
Sobotka, Chad	R-R	6-7	225	7-10-93	0	0	6.21	32	0	0	0	29	28	22	20	6	19	38	.250	.296	.221	11.79	5.90
Soroka, Mike	R-R	6-5	225	8-4-97	13	4	2.68	29	29	0	0	175	153	56	52	14	41	142	.237	.282	.203	7.32	2.11
Swarzak, Anthony	R-R	6-4	215	9-10-85	1	2	4.31	44	0	0	1	40	38	19	19	6	19	35	.252	.292	.233	7.94	4.31
Teheran, Julio	R-R	6-2	205	1-27-91	10	11	3.81	33	33	0	0	175	148	81	74	22	83	162	.230	.215	.240	8.35	4.28
Tomlin, Josh	R-R	6-1	190	10-19-84	2	1	3.74	51	1	0	2	79	82	35	33	14	7	51	.260	.250	.279	5.79	0.79
Toussaint, Touki	R-R	6-3	185	6-20-96	4	0	5.62	24	1	0	0	42	44	28	26	5	26	45	.270	.390	.202	9.72	5.62
Venters, Jonny	L-L	6-3	200	3-20-85	0	0	17.36	9	0	0	1	5	9	13	9	3	8	7	.391	.333	.455	13.50	15.43
2-team total (3 Washington)					0	1	12.38	12	0	0	1	8	12	16	11	3	10	12	.324	.294	.350	13.50	11.25
Vizcaino, Arodys	R-R	6-0	245	11-13-90	1	0	2.25	4	0	0	1	4	3	1	1	1	3	6	.214	.200	.222	13.50	6.75

Name	B-T	HT	WT	DOB	W	L	ERA	G	GS	CG	SV	IP	H	R	ER	HR	BB	SO	AVG	vLH	vRH	K/9	BB/9
Walker, Jeremy	R-R	6-5	205	6-12-95	0	0	1.93	6	0	0	0	9	9	2	2	0	4	6	.265	.286	.259	5.79	3.86
Webb, Jacob	R-R	6-1	200	8-15-93	4	0	1.39	36	0	0	2	32	24	10	5	4	12	28	.205	.180	.218	7.79	3.34
Wilson, Bryse	R-R	6-1	225	12-20-97	1	1	7.20	6	4	0	0	20	26	18	16	5	10	16	.321	.316	.326	7.20	4.50
Winkler, Dan	R-R	6-3	205	2-2-90	3	1	4.98	27	0	0	0	22	18	14	12	5	11	22	.222	.222	.222	9.14	4.57
Wright, Kyle	R-R	6-4	200	10-2-95	0	3	8.69	7	4	0	0	20	24	19	19	4	13	18	.304	.361	.256	8.24	5.95
Ynoa, Huascar	R-R	6-3	175	5-28-98	0	0	18.00	2	0	0	0	3	6	6	6	1	1	3	.400	.375	.429	9.00	3.00

Fielding

Catcher	PCT	G	PO	A	E	DP	PB
Cervelli	.983	9	56	1	1	1	1
Flowers	.996	83	676	37	3	3	16
Jackson	1.000	4	26	3	0	0	0
McCann	.995	83	640	19	3	3	7
Murphy	1.000	1	3	0	0	0	0

First Base	PCT	G	PO	A	E	DP
Camargo	.000	1	0	0	0	0
Cervelli	1.000	2	3	0	0	0
Culberson	.969	10	28	3	1	7
Freeman	.996	158	1296	63	6	128
Riley	.972	6	33	2	1	6

Second Base	PCT	G	PO	A	E	DP
Albies	.994	158	273	384	4	117
Camargo	.950	4	10	9	1	3
Hechavarria	1.000	3	8	4	0	3

Third Base	PCT	G	PO	A	E	DP
Camargo	.862	18	7	18	4	0
Culberson	.000	1	0	0	0	0
Donaldson	.969	148	100	304	13	38
Hechavarria	1.000	1	4	0	0	0
Riley	1.000	5	4	9	0	0

Shortstop	PCT	G	PO	A	E	DP
Camargo	.989	25	27	63	1	14

	PCT	G	PO	A	E	DP
Culberson	.968	7	8	22	1	2
Hechavarria	.975	12	10	29	1	8
Swanson	.976	126	137	347	12	68

Outfield	PCT	G	PO	A	E	DP
Acuna Jr.	.991	156	325	10	3	1
Camargo	.963	16	26	0	1	0
Culberson	1.000	46	27	2	0	1
Duvall	.958	32	44	2	2	0
Hamilton	1.000	24	19	0	0	0
Inciarte	.993	63	143	2	1	1
Joyce	.966	37	54	2	2	1
Markakis	.995	111	191	5	1	1
Ortega	1.000	27	37	0	0	0
Riley	.958	60	89	3	4	1

GWINNETT STRIPERS

INTERNATIONAL LEAGUE

TRIPLE-A

Batting	B-T	HT	WT	DOB	AVG	vLH	vRH	G	AB	R	H	2B	3B	HR	RBI	BB	HBP	SH	SF	SO	SB	CS	SLG	OBP
Blanco, Andres	B-R	5-10	192	4-11-84	.262	.257	.264	118	454	78	119	23	1	19	61	57	17	0	2	109	2	4	.443	.364
Camargo, Johan	B-R	6-0	195	12-13-93	.483	.333	.535	14	58	10	28	6	0	2	15	5	1	0	0	12	0	0	.690	.531
Demeritte, Travis	R-R	6-0	180	9-30-94	.286	.280	.290	96	339	68	97	28	2	20	73	51	6	1	2	106	4	3	.558	.387
Duda, Lucas	L-R	6-4	255	2-3-86	.140	.067	.167	16	57	3	8	1	0	1	5	6	2	0	3	21	0	0	.211	.235
Duvall, Adam	R-R	6-1	215	9-4-88	.266	.323	.244	101	369	74	98	20	4	32	93	48	10	0	2	86	1	0	.602	.364
Florimon, Pedro	B-R	6-2	185	12-10-86	.265	.244	.275	120	407	62	108	15	4	12	68	60	2	0	6	135	2	1	.410	.358
Giardina, Sal	R-R	6-4	215	4-30-92	.260	.222	.283	23	73	9	19	6	0	1	5	4	7	0	1	22	0	0	.384	.353
Inciarte, Ender	L-L	5-11	190	10-29-90	.231	.167	.250	6	26	5	6	1	0	0	1	4	0	0	0	3	0	1	.269	.333
Jackson, Alex	R-R	6-2	215	12-25-95	.229	.250	.220	85	306	52	70	9	0	28	65	20	18	0	1	118	1	0	.533	.313
Kazmar Jr., Sean	R-R	5-9	180	8-5-84	.270	.322	.247	108	381	55	103	21	2	12	61	32	6	0	5	56	1	1	.430	.333
LaMarre, Ryan	R-L	6-1	210	11-21-88	.311	.381	.282	112	405	55	126	24	8	9	53	38	9	0	3	118	19	9	.477	.380
Lien, Connor	R-R	6-3	225	3-15-94	.167	.111	.185	24	36	8	6	0	0	2	6	7	3	0	0	22	1	0	.333	.348
Lopez, Jack	R-R	5-9	165	12-16-92	.273	.316	.258	96	359	62	98	16	0	12	57	19	6	2	4	91	9	2	.418	.317
Lopez, Raffy	L-R	5-9	200	10-2-87	.319	.455	.278	14	47	13	15	4	0	2	7	8	0	0	0	12	0	0	.532	.418
Marte, Luis	R-R	6-1	188	12-15-93	.260	.248	.265	86	312	41	81	12	0	5	33	15	1	0	2	77	5	1	.346	.294
Morales, Jonathan	R-R	5-11	180	1-29-95	.289	.275	.296	34	121	17	35	5	0	2	12	10	0	0	1	25	0	0	.380	.341
Murphy, John Ryan	R-R	5-11	205	5-13-91	.170	.050	.259	14	47	5	8	0	0	1	3	2	1	0	0	13	0	0	.234	.220
Ortega, Rafael	L-R	5-11	160	5-15-91	.285	.254	.300	111	431	83	123	34	3	21	58	59	2	0	1	95	14	7	.524	.373
Pache, Cristian	R-R	6-2	185	11-19-98	.274	.250	.282	26	95	13	26	8	1	1	8	9	0	1	0	18	0	0	.411	.337
Riley, Austin	R-R	6-3	220	4-2-97	.293	.229	.318	44	174	39	51	13	0	15	41	20	0	0	0	39	0	0	.626	.366
Soria, Zack	R-R	5-10	192	10-29-93	.200	.250	.000	5	5	1	1	0	0	0	1	0	0	0	0	0	0	0	.200	.333
Unroe, Riley	B-R	5-10	180	8-3-95	.171	.000	.269	13	41	7	7	1	0	1	3	7	0	0	0	11	1	1	.268	.292
Waters, Drew	B-R	6-2	183	12-30-98	.271	.233	.286	26	107	17	29	5	0	2	11	11	0	0	1	43	3	0	.374	.336

Pitching	B-T	HT	WT	DOB	W	L	ERA	G	GS	CG	SV	IP	H	R	ER	HR	BB	SO	AVG	vLH	vRH	K/9	BB/9
Allard, Kolby	L-L	6-1	190	8-13-97	7	5	4.17	20	20	0	0	110	119	60	51	15	36	98	.284	.245	.297	8.02	2.95
Anderson, Ian	R-R	6-3	170	5-2-98	1	2	6.57	5	5	0	0	25	23	18	18	5	18	25	.242	.205	.268	9.12	6.57
Aro, Jonathan	R-R	6-0	235	10-10-90	3	0	3.72	9	0	0	2	19	22	8	8	1	0	9	.286	.316	.256	4.19	0.00
Biddle, Jesse	L-L	6-5	220	10-22-91	1	0	3.38	4	0	0	0	5	6	2	2	1	1	6	.300	.200	.333	10.13	1.69
Borkovich, Walter	L-R	6-5	217	7-3-95	0	1	18.00	1	0	0	0	2	2	5	4	0	2	0	.286	.500	.200	0.00	9.00
Burrows, Thomas	L-L	6-1	205	9-14-94	1	1	4.75	27	0	0	6	36	31	21	19	3	18	39	.230	.167	.275	9.75	4.50
Carle, Shane	R-R	6-4	210	8-30-91	4	2	5.13	20	1	0	0	33	39	20	19	2	14	31	.289	.259	.312	8.37	3.78
Clouse, Corbin	B-L	6-2	190	6-26-95	0	3	5.65	21	1	0	1	29	29	18	18	6	13	37	.261	.325	.225	11.62	4.08
Creasy, Jason	R-R	6-4	197	5-13-92	3	1	5.59	30	0	0	3	37	37	23	23	7	11	36	.259	.267	.253	8.76	2.68
Davidson, Tucker	L-L	6-2	215	3-25-96	1	1	2.84	4	4	0	0	19	20	8	6	0	9	12	.286	.231	.298	5.68	4.26
Dayton, Grant	L-L	6-2	210	11-25-87	0	1	3.04	22	0	0	0	27	20	9	9	6	4	41	.208	.148	.232	13.84	1.35
De Paula, Jose Rafael	R-R	6-2	215	3-24-91	1	2	4.35	33	0	0	6	39	35	22	19	4	25	45	.247	.297	.205	10.30	5.72
Foltynewicz, Mike	R-R	6-4	200	10-7-91	5	1	3.86	10	10	0	0	51	49	24	22	1	17	45	.253	.290	.213	7.89	2.98
Gausman, Kevin	L-R	6-3	190	1-6-91	0	1	2.57	1	1	0	0	7	6	3	2	1	1	10	.240	.111	.313	12.86	1.29
Giardina, Sal	B-R	6-4	215	4-30-92	0	0	0.00	2	0	0	0	1	1	0	0	0	0	0	.200	.200	--	0.00	0.00
Harrison, Jordan	R-L	6-1	180	4-9-95	1	0	5.79	3	0	0	0	5	5	3	3	0	6	7	.278	.429	.138	13.50	11.57
Hoekstra, Kurt	L-R	6-2	205	6-27-93	0	0	3.24	3	1	0	0	8	10	3	3	1	2	8	.323	.429	.235	8.64	2.16
Johnstone, Connor	R-R	5-10	195	10-4-94	2	0	4.97	7	0	0	0	13	14	8	7	1	6	7	.275	.348	.214	4.97	4.26
Kazmar Jr., Sean	R-R	5-9	180	8-5-84	1	0	0.00	3	0	0	0	3	1	0	0	0	1	1	.111	.000	.143	3.00	3.00
Leyva, Elian	R-R	6-2	210	3-17-89	0	0	5.00	9	2	0	1	18	18	11	10	2	2	16	.243	.300	.177	8.00	1.00
Lopez, Jack	R-R	5-9	165	12-16-92	0	0	27.00	1	0	0	0	1	2	3	3	0	2	0	.500	.500	.500	0.00	18.00
Matzek, Tyler	L-L	6-3	230	10-19-90	0	0	9.00	5	0	0	0	10	11	10	10	1	5	13	.270	.167	.320	11.70	4.50
Minter, A.J.	L-L	6-0	215	9-2-93	2	2	3.57	20	0	0	5	23	24	11	9	4	3	30	.264	.276	.258	11.91	1.19

Name	B-T	HT	WT	DOB	W	L	ERA	G	GS	CG	SV	IP	H	R	ER	HR	BB	SO	AVG	vLH	vRH	K/9	BB/9
Newcomb, Sean	L-L	6-5	255	6-12-93	2	1	2.18	4	3	0	0	21	14	5	5	1	5	20	.192	.222	.182	8.71	2.18
O'Day, Darren	R-R	6-4	220	10-22-82	0	0	0.00	2	0	0	0	2	1	0	0	0	0	3	.143	.200	.000	13.50	0.00
Parsons, Wes	R-R	6-5	204	9-6-92	2	3	2.86	27	0	0	4	57	58	24	18	1	21	54	.276	.370	.217	8.58	3.34
Pfeifer, Philip	L-L	6-0	200	7-15-92	1	0	2.45	3	0	0	0	7	7	2	2	1	3	13	.219	.214	.222	15.95	3.68
Rowen, Ben	R-R	6-4	203	11-15-88	4	3	3.48	31	6	0	0	78	72	30	30	4	11	58	.246	.257	.235	6.72	1.27
Santiago, Andres	R-R	6-1	220	10-26-89	2	2	6.23	11	6	0	0	35	43	26	24	6	19	20	.312	.318	.306	5.19	4.93
Sobotka, Chad	R-R	6-7	225	7-10-93	2	1	4.79	17	0	0	2	21	23	11	11	3	4	32	.274	.367	.222	13.94	1.74
Soroka, Mike	R-R	6-5	225	8-4-97	1	0	3.86	2	2	0	0	9	5	4	4	1	1	10	.156	.067	.235	9.64	0.96
Thielbar, Caleb	R-L	6-0	205	1-31-87	0	0	0.00	1	0	0	1	2	1	0	0	0	0	2	.143	1.000	.000	9.00	0.00
2-team total (50 Toledo)					2	1	3.22	51	0	0	5	78	75	29	28	7	16	94	.252	.255	.250	10.80	1.84
Toussaint, Touki	R-R	6-3	185	6-20-96	1	6	7.49	10	10	0	0	40	51	34	33	5	28	44	.313	.295	.329	9.98	6.35
Venters, Jonny	L-L	6-3	200	3-20-85	0	0	0.00	7	0	0	0	7	3	0	0	0	2	6	.136	.111	.154	7.71	2.57
Walker, Jeremy	R-R	6-5	205	6-12-95	2	1	3.97	11	0	0	1	23	20	10	10	1	6	25	.233	.324	.163	9.93	2.38
Webb, Jacob	R-R	6-1	200	8-15-93	0	1	6.97	10	0	0	1	10	9	8	8	1	9	12	.225	.269	.143	10.45	7.84
Weigel, Patrick	R-R	6-6	240	7-8-94	6	1	2.98	21	11	0	0	63	42	24	21	9	32	55	.194	.158	.221	7.82	4.55
Wilson, Bryse	R-R	6-1	225	12-20-97	10	7	3.42	21	21	0	0	121	120	59	46	12	26	118	.256	.282	.236	8.78	1.93
Winkler, Dan	R-R	6-2	205	2-2-90	0	1	4.86	18	0	0	2	17	16	11	9	1	18	20	.250	.241	.257	10.80	9.72
Wright, Kyle	R-R	6-4	200	10-2-95	11	4	4.17	21	21	0	0	112	107	55	52	13	35	116	.252	.259	.246	9.29	2.80
Ynoa, Huascar	R-R	6-3	175	5-28-98	3	5	5.33	17	14	0	0	73	80	47	43	14	34	79	.275	.278	.273	9.78	4.21

Fielding

Catcher	PCT	G	PO	A	E	DP	PB
Giardina	.979	13	91	4	2	0	0
Jackson	.983	78	646	48	12	3	10
Lopez	1.000	14	117	3	0	1	4
Morales	.996	24	228	14	1	1	1
Murphy	1.000	14	117	9	0	2	3
Soria	1.000	1	11	2	0	0	0
Blanco	.985	95	163	237	6	69	
Camargo	.778	3	2	5	2	0	
Florimon	.000	1	0	0	0	0	
Kazmar Jr.	.985	19	26	39	1	5	
Lopez	1.000	7	5	21	0	5	
Marte	1.000	16	29	37	0	10	
Unroe	1.000	3	6	10	0	4	
Florimon	.976	23	30	51	2	12	
Kazmar Jr.	1.000	6	6	22	0	7	
Lopez	.959	26	35	58	4	16	
Marte	.973	70	95	198	8	44	
Unroe	.000	1	0	0	0	0	

First Base	PCT	G	PO	A	E	DP
Duda	.981	7	48	5	1	3
Florimon	.991	40	297	24	3	32
Giardina	.985	9	62	3	1	4
Kazmar Jr.	.998	69	511	31	1	64
Morales	1.000	9	48	5	0	8
Riley	1.000	4	30	2	0	3
Unroe	.985	8	59	7	1	9

Second Base	PCT	G	PO	A	E	DP

Third Base	PCT	G	PO	A	E	DP
Camargo	1.000	7	1	12	0	1
Florimon	.957	46	22	90	5	7
Kazmar Jr.	.917	6	2	9	1	0
Lopez	.931	55	51	84	10	16
Riley	.947	30	27	45	4	4
Unroe	1.000	1	1	2	0	1

Shortstop	PCT	G	PO	A	E	DP
Blanco	.909	15	13	27	4	4
Camargo	.867	4	5	8	2	2

Outfield	PCT	G	PO	A	E	DP
Demeritte	.969	74	121	4	4	0
Duvall	.972	77	137	4	4	1
Florimon	1.000	3	8	0	0	0
Inciarte	1.000	5	9	1	0	0
LaMarre	.967	89	169	6	6	1
Lien	.944	14	17	0	1	0
Lopez	1.000	8	15	1	0	0
Ortega	.986	100	206	9	3	2
Pache	.980	26	45	3	1	2
Riley	1.000	7	9	0	0	0
Waters	.970	26	63	1	2	0

MISSISSIPPI BRAVES — DOUBLE-A
SOUTHERN LEAGUE

Batting	B-T	HT	WT	DOB	AVG	vLH	vRH	G	AB	R	H	2B	3B	HR	RBI	BB	HBP	SH	SF	SO	SB	CS	SLG	OBP
Adams, Lane	R-R	6-4	220	11-13-89	.077	.100	.053	18	39	1	3	1	0	0	3	5	0	0	0	16	2	1	.103	.182
Alexander, CJ	L-R	6-5	215	7-17-96	.103	.053	.122	24	68	6	7	1	0	2	7	8	0	0	1	25	0	0	.206	.195
Casteel, Ryan	R-R	5-11	205	6-6-91	.263	.235	.272	118	411	47	108	21	2	21	73	43	2	0	2	121	0	1	.477	.334
Contreras, William	R-R	6-0	180	12-24-97	.246	.267	.240	60	191	24	47	9	0	3	17	15	2	0	1	40	0	0	.340	.306
Didder, Ray-Patrick	R-R	6-0	170	10-1-94	.203	.120	.234	114	340	45	69	14	1	4	23	51	15	0	1	120	28	8	.285	.332
Harris, Trey	R-R	5-8	215	1-15-96	.281	.214	.308	41	146	15	41	7	3	2	12	4	4	0	0	33	1	2	.411	.318
Inciarte, Ender	L-L	5-11	190	10-29-90	.400	--	.400	2	5	1	2	0	0	0	0	0	0	0	0	0	1	0	.400	.400
Jenista, Greyson	L-R	6-3	210	12-9-96	.243	.154	.262	74	222	18	54	4	1	5	26	27	2	0	5	75	2	4	.338	.324
Lien, Connor	R-R	6-3	225	3-15-94	.220	.276	.193	57	177	22	39	10	3	9	24	21	1	1	0	91	5	1	.463	.307
Lockhart, Daniel	L-R	5-11	175	11-4-92	.236	.302	.222	83	250	29	59	11	0	5	21	19	5	4	2	54	3	3	.340	.301
Martinez, Carlos	R-R	5-11	204	5-2-95	.198	.244	.185	63	187	11	37	4	0	2	15	12	6	2	0	33	3	0	.251	.268
Michel, Shean	R-R	5-11	180		.000	.250	.000	6	10	0	1	0	1	0	0	2	0	0	0	7	0	0	.300	.250
Morales, Jonathan	R-R	5-11	180	1-29-95	.201	.230	.183	46	154	10	31	8	0	0	13	17	1	2	4	24	0	0	.253	.278
Neslony, Tyler	L-R	6-1	190	2-13-94	.292	.296	.291	58	192	32	56	9	4	5	24	21	3	0	1	43	4	2	.458	.369
Pache, Cristian	R-R	6-2	185	11-19-98	.278	.325	.265	104	392	50	109	28	8	11	53	34	4	1	2	104	8	11	.475	.340
Salazar, Alejandro	R-R	6-0	170	10-5-96	.203	.185	.210	120	408	28	83	10	2	2	19	15	4	2	2	112	10	6	.253	.238
Schwartz, Garrison	L-L	6-0	205	1-22-96	.105	.200	.091	15	38	5	4	0	0	0	0	7	1	0	0	15	1	0	.105	.261
Shewmake, Braden	L-R	6-4	190	11-19-97	.217	.167	.250	14	46	7	10	0	0	0	1	4	1	0	1	11	2	0	.217	.289
Unroe, Riley	B-R	5-10	180	8-25-95	.285	.219	.306	77	270	27	77	12	2	5	37	26	2	3	2	61	9	2	.400	.350
Valenzuela, Luis	L-R	5-10	179	8-25-93	.194	.296	.172	79	247	22	48	12	2	2	24	10	1	0	3	55	0	1	.283	.226
2-team total (17 Birmingham)					.202	.328	.170	96	302	31	61	14	2	3	28	13	1	0	3	66	2	2	.291	.235
Waters, Drew	B-R	6-2	183	12-30-98	.319	.266	.334	108	420	63	134	35	9	5	41	28	4	0	2	121	13	6	.481	.366
Wilkins, Andy	R-L	6-1	225	9-13-88	.204	.177	.215	37	113	11	23	4	0	4	11	17	1	0	2	44	0	0	.345	.308

Pitching	B-T	HT	WT	DOB	W	L	ERA	G	GS	CG	SV	IP	H	R	ER	HR	BB	SO	AVG	vLH	vRH	K/9	BB/9
Anderson, Ian	R-R	6-3	170	5-2-98	7	5	2.68	21	21	1	0	111	82	38	33	8	47	147	.202	.192	.211	11.92	3.81
Aro, Jonathan	R-R	6-0	235	10-10-90	3	3	3.45	22	2	0	1	44	43	20	17	2	9	31	.253	.283	.236	6.29	1.83
Burrows, Thomas	L-L	6-1	205	9-14-94	1	3	3.86	16	0	0	1	21	16	11	9	2	6	24	.205	.185	.216	10.29	2.57
Creasy, Jason	R-R	6-4	197	5-13-92	1	0	2.66	19	0	0	8	24	24	8	7	2	9	25	.261	.263	.259	9.51	3.42
Custodio, Claudio	R-R	5-10	155	10-30-90	5	4	2.61	31	6	0	2	79	60	26	23	2	23	67	.214	.177	.245	7.60	2.61
Davidson, Tucker	L-L	6-2	215	3-25-96	7	6	2.03	21	21	0	0	111	88	34	25	5	45	122	.225	.258	.208	9.92	3.66

Pitching	B-T	HT	WT	DOB	W	L	ERA	G	GS	CG	SV	IP	H	R	ER	HR	BB	SO	AVG	vLH	vRH	K/9	BB/9
De La Cruz, Jasseel	R-R	6-1	215	6-26-97	4	7	3.83	17	16	0	0	87	71	39	37	7	37	73	.223	.238	.211	7.55	3.83
De Paula, Jose Rafael	R-R	6-2	215	3-24-91	0	0	0.00	2	0	0	0	3	2	0	0	0	0	5	.182	.250	.143	15.00	0.00
Gausman, Kevin	L-R	6-3	190	1-6-91	0	0	0.00	1	1	0	0	6	3	1	0	0	0	3	.136	.125	.143	4.50	0.00
Graham, Josh	R-R	6-1	215	10-14-93	4	4	3.55	38	1	0	8	51	41	25	20	6	18	45	.220	.242	.200	7.99	3.20
Harrison, Jordan	R-L	6-1	180	4-9-91	2	4	2.92	35	0	0	2	49	45	17	16	3	18	48	.246	.188	.281	8.76	3.28
Hoekstra, Kurt	L-R	6-2	205	6-27-93	1	2	0.89	11	1	0	0	20	17	8	2	1	12	21	.227	.270	.184	9.30	5.31
Hursh, Jason	R-R	6-2	210	10-2-91	3	3	3.45	34	0	0	2	47	41	21	18	1	15	32	.230	.260	.208	6.13	2.87
Johnstone, Connor	R-R	5-10	195	10-4-94	5	4	4.12	28	7	0	1	79	93	38	36	4	21	50	.299	.300	.298	5.72	2.40
Kelly, Justin	L-L	6-1	175	4-22-93	0	0	0.00	2	0	0	0	5	3	0	0	0	3	3	.158	.231	.000	5.06	5.06
Keuchel, Dallas	L-L	6-3	205	1-1-88	0	0	3.86	1	1	0	0	7	11	3	3	0	1	4	.379	.200	.417	5.14	1.29
Kingham, Nolan	R-R	6-4	210	8-18-96	2	3	3.79	6	6	1	0	36	32	15	15	5	10	25	.235	.283	.197	6.31	2.52
Mader, Michael	L-L	6-2	205	2-18-94	2	2	9.24	7	0	0	0	13	15	15	13	1	11	10	.283	.316	.265	7.11	7.82
Matzek, Tyler	L-L	6-3	230	10-19-90	0	0	0.00	1	0	0	0	2	0	0	0	0	0	5	.000	.000	.000	19.29	0.00
2-team total (3 Jackson)					0	0	3.60	4	0	0	0	5	2	2	2	0	5	8	.118	.000	.182	14.40	9.00
Muller, Kyle	R-L	6-6	225	10-7-97	7	6	3.14	22	22	2	0	112	81	42	39	5	68	120	.208	.211	.207	9.67	5.48
Pfeifer, Philip	L-L	6-0	200	7-15-92	1	2	2.38	11	4	0	0	34	25	12	9	2	16	36	.205	.163	.228	9.53	4.24
Roney, Bradley	R-R	6-1	200	9-1-92	1	0	2.96	20	0	0	3	27	20	9	9	2	11	42	.204	.220	.193	13.83	3.62
Rowen, Ben	R-R	6-4	203	11-15-88	1	0	4.50	9	1	0	0	12	13	8	6	1	4	7	.283	.300	.269	5.25	3.00
Santiago, Andres	R-R	6-1	220	10-26-89	0	0	4.26	8	1	0	0	19	19	9	9	2	11	11	.268	.324	.216	5.21	5.21
Walker, Jeremy	R-R	6-5	205	6-12-95	1	6	2.45	21	1	0	6	59	56	23	16	2	5	57	.245	.277	.209	8.74	0.77
Weigel, Patrick	R-R	6-6	240	7-8-94	0	1	1.72	7	7	0	0	16	8	4	3	0	9	16	.146	.162	.111	9.19	5.17
Wentz, Joey	L-L	6-5	210	10-6-97	5	8	4.72	20	20	0	0	103	90	57	54	13	45	100	.239	.298	.213	8.74	3.93
White, Brandon	R-R	6-2	215	12-21-94	0	0	0.00	1	0	0	0	2	1	0	0	0	1	2	.143	.250	.000	9.00	4.50
Ynoa, Huascar	R-R	6-3	175	5-28-98	1	2	5.27	6	0	0	1	14	17	8	8	2	5	15	.298	.231	.355	9.88	3.29

Fielding

Catcher	PCT	G	PO	A	E	DP	PB
Contreras	.978	53	422	30	10	3	7
Martinez	.988	55	386	31	5	3	2
Morales	1.000	38	327	31	0	2	2

First Base	PCT	G	PO	A	E	DP
Alexander	.943	5	32	1	2	1
Casteel	.995	100	713	48	4	80
Jenista	1.000	2	15	1	0	1
Lockhart	1.000	7	34	2	0	3
Morales	1.000	5	34	3	0	1
Neslony	1.000	1	3	0	0	1
Wilkins	.986	28	199	20	3	23

Second Base	PCT	G	PO	A	E	DP
Lockhart	1.000	8	12	17	0	3

	PCT	G	PO	A	E	DP
Salazar	.981	111	171	285	9	67
Unroe	.895	6	11	6	2	1
Valenzuela	1.000	25	23	56	0	14

Third Base	PCT	G	PO	A	E	DP
Alexander	.926	11	10	15	2	3
Didder	1.000	3	0	5	0	0
Lockhart	.921	59	49	68	10	8
Morales	1.000	3	4	5	0	0
Unroe	.938	37	20	55	5	5
Valenzuela	.929	38	25	53	6	7

Shortstop	PCT	G	PO	A	E	DP
Didder	.957	90	112	198	14	48
Salazar	1.000	4	11	12	0	4
Shewmake	.981	14	16	37	1	6

	PCT	G	PO	A	E	DP
Unroe	.985	34	42	89	2	19
Valenzuela	.960	6	6	18	1	2

Outfield	PCT	G	PO	A	E	DP
Adams	.963	14	24	2	1	0
Didder	.967	20	28	1	1	1
Harris	1.000	36	57	2	0	2
Inciarte	1.000	2	4	0	0	0
Jenista	.989	57	92	1	1	1
Lien	.983	51	109	5	2	0
Lockhart	1.000	3	5	0	0	0
Michel	1.000	1	1	0	0	0
Neslony	1.000	40	62	1	0	0
Pache	.987	103	214	6	3	1
Schwartz	1.000	11	14	1	0	0
Waters	.976	106	237	8	6	2

FLORIDA FIRE FROGS   HIGH CLASS A
FLORIDA STATE LEAGUE

Batting	B-T	HT	WT	DOB	AVG	vLH	vRH	G	AB	R	H	2B	3B	HR	RBI	BB	HBP	SH	SF	SO	SB	CS	SLG	OBP
Alexander, CJ	L-R	6-5	215	7-17-96	.133	.154	.128	19	60	4	8	1	0	0	1	14	0	0	0	18	3	1	.150	.297
Brown, Logan	L-R	6-0	195	9-14-96	.240	.222	.243	48	175	12	42	7	0	0	20	6	1	0	4	44	0	0	.280	.269
Contreras, William	R-R	6-0	180	12-24-97	.263	.158	.290	50	190	26	50	11	0	3	22	14	3	0	4	44	0	0	.368	.324
Cruz, Derian	B-R	6-1	180	10-3-98	.000	.000	.000	3	10	0	0	0	0	0	1	1	0	0	0	5	0	0	.000	.091
Delgado, Riley	R-R	5-10	175	2-22-95	.282	.333	.270	131	511	49	144	15	3	0	33	28	5	3	2	42	1	1	.323	.324
Estrada, Rusber	R-R	6-0	215	6-5-95	.152	.128	.160	49	158	12	24	4	0	1	16	14	8	0	3	56	0	0	.196	.251
Fernandez, Jeremy	R-R	6-1	185	7-11-97	.000	--	.000	2	6	0	0	0	0	0	0	0	0	0	0	2	0	0	.000	.000
Graffanino, AJ	L-R	6-2	170	7-16-97	.000	.000	--	1	1	0	0	0	0	0	0	0	0	0	0	0	0	0	.000	.000
Harris, Trey	R-R	5-8	215	1-15-96	.303	.259	.316	34	122	20	37	5	0	4	17	12	5	0	0	26	3	0	.443	.389
Inciarte, Ender	L-L	5-11	190	10-29-90	.077	.000	.125	5	13	0	1	0	0	0	0	1	0	0	0	2	0	0	.077	.143
Jenista, Greyson	L-R	6-3	210	12-7-96	.223	.196	.231	56	202	24	45	14	1	4	29	27	0	0	2	70	1	4	.361	.312
Josephina, Kevin	R-R	6-0	170	10-24-96	.258	.276	.253	102	372	48	96	20	4	2	34	29	1	1	4	86	4	7	.350	.310
Langhorne, Brett	L-R	6-3	210	6-14-96	.203	.225	.200	117	359	38	73	16	2	3	36	44	2	2	7	146	12	5	.281	.289
Lugbauer, Drew	L-R	6-3	220	8-23-96	.194	.203	.192	127	454	39	88	26	1	16	51	36	1	0	2	169	0	0	.361	.254
Michel, Shean	R-R	5-11	170	9-26-97	.214	.213	.214	73	215	25	46	6	4	0	7	28	0	2	1	63	10	2	.279	.303
Morales, Juan	R-R	6-2	165	11-17-98	.250	.250	.250	6	16	1	4	0	0	0	2	0	0	0	0	6	0	0	.250	.250
Moritz, Andrew	L-R	5-11	180	12-22-96	.287	.219	.302	44	171	18	49	5	0	0	10	9	0	1	0	27	5	3	.316	.322
Owenby, Hagen	R-R	6-1	218	7-21-95	.429	1.000	.333	4	14	1	6	2	0	0	2	1	0	0	0	5	0	0	.571	.467
Ramos, Jefrey	R-R	6-1	185	2-10-99	.241	.290	.229	128	460	49	111	16	4	9	56	30	4	0	4	99	1	1	.352	.291
Rodgers, Jordan	R-R	6-1	185	5-9-95	.204	.432	.138	67	196	18	40	7	0	5	20	6	2	1	1	44	0	2	.316	.234
Schwartz, Garrison	L-L	6-0	205	1-22-96	.216	.200	.222	55	162	15	35	7	0	2	16	16	1	2	1	51	0	2	.296	.289
Soria, Zack	R-R	5-10	192	10-29-93	.162	.191	.155	32	105	3	17	3	0	2	10	10	1	1	1	38	0	0	.248	.239
Unroe, Riley	B-R	5-10	180	8-9-95	.303	.259	.333	38	122	15	42	9	1	3	20	20	3	0	1	34	4	2	.449	.401
Wilkins, Andy	L-R	6-1	225	9-13-88	.136	.167	.130	20	66	5	9	1	0	3	7	11	0	0	1	31	0	0	.288	.256
Wilson, Izzy	L-R	6-3	185	3-6-98	.177	.154	.180	45	124	20	22	5	2	2	6	18	1	0	0	54	7	1	.298	.287
2-team total (20 Charlotte)					.209	.125	.221	65	187	27	39	10	3	3	14	29	1	0	0	73	10	3	.342	.318

Pitching

Pitching	B-T	HT	WT	DOB	W	L	ERA	G	GS	CG	SV	IP	H	R	ER	HR	BB	SO	AVG	vLH	vRH	K/9	BB/9
Bacon, Troy	R-R	6-0	165	9-26-96	4	3	4.13	26	1	0	0	48	49	27	22	5	18	59	.263	.284	.238	11.06	3.38
Beck, Tristan	R-R	6-4	165	6-24-96	2	2	5.65	8	8	0	0	37	45	25	23	2	14	39	.313	.293	.333	9.57	3.44
Borkovich, Walter	L-R	6-5	217	7-3-95	2	5	4.79	28	6	0	1	56	72	38	30	3	20	49	.310	.294	.325	7.83	3.20
Camacho, Alex	R-R	6-7	245	7-30-96	0	0	0.00	2	0	0	0	4	4	0	0	0	0	3	.267	.143	.375	7.36	0.00
De La Cruz, Jasseel	R-R	6-1	215	6-26-97	3	1	1.93	4	4	2	0	28	12	6	6	0	7	26	.128	.130	.125	8.36	2.25
Deal, Hayden	L-L	6-4	210	11-4-94	5	10	3.24	23	22	1	0	119	119	51	43	6	32	99	.260	.226	.277	7.47	2.41
Dirks, Caleb	R-R	6-3	220	6-9-93	2	1	1.69	9	0	0	1	16	11	5	3	0	2	13	.204	.227	.188	7.31	1.13
Dyals, Cutter	R-R	5-11	205	8-10-95	0	1	15.75	6	0	0	0	8	13	14	14	0	3	6	.351	.438	.286	6.75	3.38
Gausman, Kevin	L-R	6-3	190	1-6-91	0	1	5.40	1	1	0	0	5	5	3	3	1	1	6	.263	.400	.111	10.80	1.80
Hartman, Matt	R-R	6-3	220	2-28-96	4	6	3.94	15	11	2	0	75	65	39	33	2	29	45	.227	.227	.228	5.38	3.46
Hernandez, Daysbel	R-R	5-10	220	9-15-96	5	2	1.71	35	0	0	7	53	34	14	10	2	23	70	.184	.174	.196	11.96	3.93
Hoekstra, Kurt	R-R	6-2	205	6-27-93	0	1	3.05	12	0	0	4	21	12	7	7	1	11	24	.169	.273	.079	10.45	4.79
Javier, Odalvi	R-R	6-0	180	9-4-96	1	2	3.28	4	4	0	0	25	19	10	9	2	14	16	.221	.286	.135	5.84	5.11
Kelly, Justin	L-L	6-1	175	4-22-93	1	1	5.93	7	0	0	0	14	13	9	9	0	8	22	.255	.133	.306	14.49	5.27
Kennedy, Jon	L-L	6-5	215	9-20-94	0	1	4.09	7	0	0	1	11	10	6	5	0	4	12	.244	.235	.250	9.82	3.27
Kingham, Nolan	R-R	6-4	210	8-18-96	4	8	4.43	18	18	3	0	114	120	63	56	6	25	84	.274	.299	.242	6.65	1.98
McLaughlin, Sean	L-R	5-11	195	5-16-94	3	5	2.96	35	0	0	4	55	61	29	18	3	20	49	.280	.294	.266	8.07	3.29
O'Day, Darren	R-R	6-4	220	10-22-82	0	0	0.00	1	0	0	0	1	1	0	0	0	0	1	.333	.000	.500	9.00	0.00
Pfeifer, Philip	L-L	6-0	200	7-15-92	4	6	3.23	16	14	1	0	92	81	37	33	7	23	110	.234	.241	.231	10.76	2.25
Roney, Bradley	R-R	6-1	200	9-1-92	0	0	0.00	8	0	0	0	14	7	0	0	0	3	18	.149	.191	.115	11.30	1.88
Shetter, Ryan	R-R	6-3	205	3-5-97	0	1	6.75	3	0	0	0	7	10	7	5	1	1	5	.333	.368	.273	6.75	1.35
Tarnok, Freddy	R-R	6-3	185	11-24-98	3	7	4.87	19	19	1	0	98	105	56	53	6	36	82	.276	.297	.254	7.53	3.31
Weisenberg, Keith	R-R	6-5	195	12-6-95	0	4	10.31	7	5	0	0	18	27	22	21	1	11	19	.342	.297	.381	9.33	5.40
White, Brandon	R-R	6-2	215	12-21-94	3	5	1.40	33	0	0	4	51	44	16	8	1	26	59	.235	.298	.172	10.34	4.56
Wilson, Brooks	L-R	6-2	205	3-15-96	4	3	2.47	24	11	1	0	87	80	31	24	2	25	73	.240	.260	.223	7.52	2.58
Withrow, Matt	R-R	6-5	235	9-23-93	3	3	3.29	15	9	0	0	38	28	15	14	1	20	42	.206	.156	.250	9.86	4.70
Ynoa, Huascar	R-R	6-3	175	5-28-98	0	1	3.27	3	3	0	0	11	10	4	4	0	6	16	.233	.138	.429	13.09	4.91
Young, Lukas	R-R	6-2	210	7-26-96	1	2	4.84	22	0	0	0	35	28	21	19	2	22	32	.219	.228	.211	8.15	5.60

Fielding

Catcher	PCT	G	PO	A	E	DP	PB
Brown	.992	44	328	37	3	2	3
Contreras	.989	43	349	26	4	4	6
Estrada	.995	24	192	14	1	1	6
Soria	1.000	25	212	20	0	3	2
Morales	1.000	3	2	6	0	1	
Rodgers	.959	29	53	65	5	11	
Rodgers	1.000	1	1	0	0	0	
Unroe	.974	37	65	86	4	14	

First Base	PCT	G	PO	A	E	DP
Alexander	.967	4	29	0	1	3
Josephina	.996	31	234	15	1	12
Lugbauer	.988	95	685	49	9	62
Owenby	1.000	1	10	0	0	2
Wilkins	1.000	6	44	1	0	3

Second Base	PCT	G	PO	A	E	DP
Delgado	1.000	8	19	19	0	4
Josephina	.800	4	2	6	2	0
Langhorne	.975	99	158	272	11	54

Third Base	PCT	G	PO	A	E	DP
Alexander	.829	11	8	21	6	2
Cruz	.857	3	6	6	2	0
Delgado	.979	25	13	34	1	2
Josephina	.930	65	43	90	10	10
Lugbauer	.893	12	11	14	3	2
Morales	1.000	3	1	7	0	1
Rodgers	.921	24	15	43	5	9

Shortstop	PCT	G	PO	A	E	DP
Delgado	.975	95	103	213	8	38
Graffanino	1.000	1	1	0	0	0
Langhorne	.867	5	5	8	2	1
Morales	.000	1	0	0	0	0

Outfield	PCT	G	PO	A	E	DP
Alexander	.000	1	0	0	0	0
Fernandez	1.000	2	7	1	0	0
Harris	1.000	29	60	3	0	0
Inciarte	1.000	4	4	0	0	0
Jenista	.988	48	83	2	1	1
Langhorne	.970	11	31	1	1	0
Michel	.976	72	159	5	4	1
Moritz	1.000	44	85	1	0	1
Ramos	.995	114	177	8	1	0
Schwartz	1.000	55	99	0	0	0
Unroe	.500	1	1	0	1	0
Wilson	.920	39	77	3	7	0

ROME BRAVES
SOUTH ATLANTIC LEAGUE

LOW CLASS A

Batting	B-T	HT	WT	DOB	AVG	vLH	vRH	G	AB	R	H	2B	3B	HR	RBI	BB	HBP	SH	SF	SO	SB	CS	SLG	OBP
Ball, Bryce	L-R	6-6	235	7-8-98	.337	.357	.333	21	86	14	29	6	0	4	14	4	0	0	0	20	0	0	.547	.367
Benson, Griffin	B-R	6-5	210	9-28-97	.208	.167	.223	106	375	51	78	22	4	13	60	49	12	0	1	147	1	1	.392	.318
Bermudez, Jose	B-R	6-2	160	7-9-97	.244	.227	.250	75	250	30	61	9	2	1	21	20	4	1	1	88	15	6	.308	.309
Blair, Connor	R-R	6-0	215	5-6-98	.105	.000	.154	6	19	2	2	1	0	1	2	2	0	0	0	6	1	0	.316	.191
Brown, Logan	L-R	6-0	195	9-14-96	.301	.306	.299	51	193	25	58	11	1	1	26	11	4	0	0	39	0	0	.383	.351
Campbell, Drew	L-L	5-11	170	11-10-97	.224	.292	.205	28	107	8	24	4	1	1	7	5	0	2	0	14	1	1	.308	.259
Cruz, Derian	B-R	6-1	180	10-3-98	.195	.200	.193	25	77	11	15	3	1	0	5	10	2	1	1	25	4	1	.260	.300
Cullen, Greg	L-R	5-10	190	11-13-96	.270	.259	.273	130	471	80	127	23	6	9	58	71	25	0	1	100	2	4	.401	.393
Dean, Justin	R-R	5-6	185	12-6-96	.284	.235	.300	109	429	85	122	18	9	9	46	62	10	0	2	115	47	10	.431	.386
Fernandez, Jeremy	R-R	6-1	185	7-11-97	.252	.246	.253	73	290	30	73	9	7	1	22	5	3	0	0	65	7	3	.341	.272
Florentino, Darling	R-R	6-0	210	5-25-01	.198	.229	.187	36	126	8	25	5	0	3	13	7	0	0	1	60	0	1	.310	.239
Harris, Michael	L-L	6-0	195	3-7-01	.183	.125	.197	22	82	11	15	2	1	0	11	9	1	0	1	22	3	0	.232	.269
Harris, Trey	R-R	5-8	215	1-15-96	.366	.368	.366	56	202	38	74	14	4	8	44	20	6	1	1	32	4	5	.594	.437
Langeliers, Shea	R-R	6-0	190	11-18-97	.255	.244	.257	54	216	27	55	13	0	2	34	17	2	0	4	55	0	0	.343	.310
Montesino, Ariel	R-R	5-10	180	9-21-95	.184	.133	.198	43	136	9	25	8	1	1	11	11	3	3	4	45	6	1	.279	.253
Morales, Juan	R-R	6-2	165	11-17-98	.208	.167	.222	7	24	1	5	1	0	0	3	0	0	0	1	8	0	0	.250	.200
Moritz, Andrew	L-R	5-11	180	12-22-96	.231	.146	.264	52	199	20	46	5	1	0	9	3	3	3	3	33	10	2	.266	.271
Owenby, Hagen	R-R	6-1	210	7-21-95	.288	.258	.298	33	125	8	36	3	2	1	8	12	1	0	0	42	1	0	.368	.355
Paraguate, Carlos	R-R	5-10	170	2-2-01	.166	.293	.126	73	241	17	40	11	0	0	18	13	2	2	4	91	4	3	.212	.212
Quintero, Henry	R-R	6-1	193	5-23-94	.266	.219	.281	32	128	19	34	4	2	1	11	7	5	0	1	29	3	0	.352	.326
Riley, Austin	R-R	6-3	220	4-2-97	.200	--	.200	3	10	0	2	0	0	0	0	0	0	0	0	2	0	0	.200	.200
Rodriguez, Ricardo	R-R	5-11	185	12-20-97	.238	.234	.239	67	240	28	57	12	0	0	32	15	5	1	3	50	1	0	.288	.293

Batting	B-T	HT	WT	DOB	AVG	vLH	vRH	G	AB	R	H	2B	3B	HR	RBI	BB	HBP	SH	SF	SO	SB	CS	SLG	OBP
Shewmake, Braden	L-R	6-4	190	11-19-97	.318	.370	.303	51	201	37	64	18	2	3	39	21	3	0	1	29	11	3	.473	.389
Swanson, Dansby	R-R	6-1	190	2-11-94	.400	--	.400	3	10	2	4	0	0	0	1	3	0	0	0	2	0	0	.400	.539
Vasquez, Braulio	R-R	6-0	210	4-13-99	.209	.200	.214	52	153	25	32	4	1	1	13	20	5	4	1	56	2	2	.268	.318
Venter, Brendan	R-R	6-2	215	9-26-96	.220	.188	.234	84	277	31	61	20	0	6	32	22	23	1	2	98	0	0	.357	.327

Pitching	B-T	HT	WT	DOB	W	L	ERA	G	GS	CG	SV	IP	H	R	ER	HR	BB	SO	AVG	vLH	vRH	K/9	BB/9
Cavalieri, Victor	L-L	6-1	180	8-26-95	0	0	8.59	5	0	0	1	7	11	8	7	1	0	7	.355	.182	.450	8.59	0.00
Custodio, Claudio	R-R	5-10	155	10-30-90	2	0	0.00	2	0	0	0	4	2	0	0	0	0	5	.143	.000	.182	11.25	0.00
De La Cruz, Jasseel	R-R	6-1	215	6-26-97	0	1	2.50	4	4	0	0	18	19	5	5	1	5	22	.275	.308	.256	11.00	2.50
DeVito, Ricky	R-R	6-3	195	8-21-98	1	2	3.78	4	4	0	0	17	21	12	7	2	7	11	.309	.389	.280	5.94	3.78
Hartman, Matt	R-R	6-3	220	2-28-96	1	0	2.63	4	1	0	1	14	8	4	4	0	9	15	.174	.158	.185	9.88	5.93
Higginbotham, Jake	L-L	6-0	190	1-11-96	4	4	3.07	33	0	0	4	59	52	27	20	5	26	63	.242	.247	.239	9.66	3.99
Hoekstra, Kurt	L-R	6-2	205	6-27-93	0	2	0.59	12	0	0	4	15	14	6	1	1	5	26	.222	.208	.231	15.26	2.93
Javier, Odalvi	R-R	6-0	180	9-4-96	3	8	3.78	22	22	0	0	121	112	56	51	13	45	101	.242	.237	.247	7.49	3.34
Kalich, Kasey	R-R	6-3	220	4-25-98	1	1	1.31	13	0	0	1	21	9	4	3	0	10	22	.136	.125	.143	9.58	4.35
Keuchel, Dallas	L-L	6-3	205	1-1-88	0	0	0.00	1	1	0	0	7	1	0	0	0	1	9	.046	.000	.071	11.57	1.29
Kingham, Nolan	R-R	6-4	210	8-18-96	1	1	0.56	3	3	0	0	16	12	2	1	0	1	7	.211	.250	.000	3.94	0.56
Lawson, Tanner	L-L	6-1	190	10-25-96	4	6	2.14	30	0	0	2	67	52	24	16	3	23	65	.214	.224	.209	8.69	3.07
Mejia, Dilmer	L-L	5-11	160	7-9-97	8	5	2.66	27	14	0	1	118	108	44	35	8	24	96	.241	.254	.236	7.30	1.83
Montilla, Jose	R-R	6-1	235	6-4-98	3	9	3.03	31	0	0	4	74	77	37	25	6	15	63	.271	.241	.292	7.63	1.82
Mora, Luis	R-R	6-4	210	6-17-95	2	0	3.53	30	0	0	3	43	29	22	17	3	37	62	.192	.190	.194	12.88	7.68
Noguera, Gabriel	L-L	6-2	175	5-31-96	4	5	3.59	24	16	0	2	95	99	59	38	8	44	82	.268	.211	.294	7.74	4.15
Olague, Jose	R-R	6-0	207	12-13-98	10	6	4.02	23	23	1	0	132	147	64	59	8	20	68	.286	.268	.300	4.64	1.36
Rangel, Alan	R-R	6-2	170	8-21-97	10	7	4.51	28	24	1	0	132	142	77	66	10	47	121	.271	.232	.303	8.27	3.21
Riley, Trey	L-R	6-3	205	4-21-98	2	7	7.67	17	12	0	0	59	71	53	50	4	46	41	.317	.370	.280	6.29	7.06
Shetter, Ryan	R-R	6-3	205	3-5-97	4	2	1.81	17	2	0	2	45	33	12	9	0	7	33	.204	.191	.213	6.65	1.41
Stallings, Mitch	L-L	6-2	180	6-30-95	3	0	1.42	3	3	0	0	19	17	3	3	0	5	10	.250	.267	.245	4.74	2.37
Vodnik, Victor	R-R	6-0	200	10-9-99	1	3	2.94	23	3	0	3	67	55	27	22	1	24	69	.223	.204	.239	9.22	3.21
Woods, William	R-R	6-3	190	12-29-98	1	5	3.35	20	7	0	3	51	38	27	19	4	29	58	.208	.177	.231	10.24	5.12
Young, Lukas	R-R	6-2	210	7-26-96	0	0	0.00	11	0	0	5	14	8	2	0	0	6	13	.167	.167	.167	8.36	3.86

Fielding

Catcher	PCT	G	PO	A	E	DP	PB
Brown	.990	42	335	45	4	2	3
Langeliers	.992	42	314	37	3	3	3
Owenby	.977	5	38	4	1	0	0
Rodriguez	.993	54	379	53	3	1	13

First Base	PCT	G	PO	A	E	DP
Ball	.990	11	96	6	1	10
Benson	.998	99	779	41	2	68
Cruz	.667	1	2	0	1	1
Owenby	.974	15	103	8	3	10
Venter	.973	18	138	8	4	19

Second Base	PCT	G	PO	A	E	DP
Cruz	1.000	1	3	3	0	1
Cullen	.976	116	214	317	13	81
Montesino	1.000	13	25	33	0	7

	PCT	G	PO	A	E	DP
Morales	.929	3	6	7	1	1
Paraguate	1.000	2	5	2	0	1
Vasquez	.960	7	11	13	1	4

Third Base	PCT	G	PO	A	E	DP
Cruz	.961	19	13	36	2	2
Florentino	.784	30	14	44	16	4
Montesino	.857	2	4	2	1	0
Morales	1.000	1	0	2	0	0
Paraguate	1.000	1	0	2	0	0
Vasquez	.896	37	17	52	8	4
Venter	.932	56	35	89	9	8

Shortstop	PCT	G	PO	A	E	DP
Florentino	1.000	1	0	2	0	0
Montesino	.920	26	33	71	9	19
Morales	1.000	2	3	4	0	1

	PCT	G	PO	A	E	DP
Paraguate	.954	71	100	188	14	40
Shewmake	.947	39	55	105	9	20
Swanson	1.000	2	5	4	0	1
Vasquez	.900	4	5	13	2	3

Outfield	PCT	G	PO	A	E	DP
Bermudez	.970	72	157	7	5	1
Blair	1.000	6	8	0	0	0
Campbell	.983	27	58	1	1	0
Dean	.985	105	246	14	4	3
Fernandez	.952	69	133	5	7	1
Harris	1.000	22	56	5	0	1
Harris	.986	4	68	3	1	0
Moritz	.987	52	72	2	1	0
Quintero	.981	27	49	2	1	1
Riley	1.000	2	2	0	0	0
Vasquez	1.000	3	5	0	0	0

DANVILLE BRAVES

ROOKIE ADVANCED

APPALACHIAN LEAGUE

Batting	B-T	HT	WT	DOB	AVG	vLH	vRH	G	AB	R	H	2B	3B	HR	RBI	BB	HBP	SH	SF	SO	SB	CS	SLG	OBP
Ball, Bryce	L-R	6-6	235	7-8-98	.324	.290	.336	41	145	37	47	12	0	13	38	22	2	0	4	30	0	0	.676	.410
Berne, Mason	R-R	6-3	225	3-11-96	.341	.143	.378	13	44	7	15	2	0	1	5	5	0	0	1	9	0	0	.455	.400
Birdsong, Cody	R-R	6-2	195	1-19-97	.234	.208	.242	57	209	17	49	10	0	4	22	11	2	1	1	59	0	2	.340	.278
Blair, Connor	R-R	6-0	215	5-6-98	.206	.125	.231	37	136	14	28	5	0	3	19	10	5	0	2	41	2	1	.309	.281
Calandra, Mitch	R-R	5-11	195	1-13-97	.271	.200	.287	28	107	15	29	4	1	0	7	3	1	0	0	18	0	0	.327	.297
Carter, Willie	R-R	6-0	205	4-8-97	.242	.351	.215	52	186	22	45	10	1	4	27	20	5	0	1	50	7	3	.371	.330
Chapman, Brandon	R-R	6-0	200	5-26-96	.245	.182	.262	18	53	3	13	2	1	0	5	7	1	1	0	14	1	0	.321	.344
De Hoyos, Victor	R-R	5-9	175	2-23-98	.131	.130	.131	34	122	8	16	7	0	2	6	9	3	0	0	26	0	1	.238	.209
Hernandez, Ray	R-R	6-3	220	8-19-96	.199	.192	.200	41	141	15	28	6	2	2	21	13	1	0	0	38	0	1	.305	.271
Mateja, Michael	R-R	5-11	190	1-25-97	.256	.214	.266	25	78	17	20	6	0	2	10	8	2	0	2	14	4	4	.410	.333
Milligan, Cody	L-R	5-10	185	12-23-98	.252	.333	.234	59	214	37	54	7	0	1	12	44	3	0	2	54	12	6	.299	.384
Morales, Juan	R-R	6-2	165	11-17-98	.138	.077	.156	18	58	3	8	1	0	0	3	5	0	1	0	15	1	0	.155	.206
Palma, Jose	L-L	6-0	170	6-9-99	.261	.360	.239	45	134	16	35	7	1	0	6	15	1	4	0	27	5	2	.328	.340
Parker, Brandon	R-R	6-1	205	5-27-99	.210	.222	.207	48	176	27	37	5	1	4	22	15	0	5	0	66	4	2	.318	.294
Philip, Beau	R-R	6-0	190	10-30-96	.193	.167	.199	55	207	40	40	6	0	4	20	26	5	0	1	51	5	5	.280	.297
Reyes, Charles	L-R	6-1	165	9-9-99	.235	.278	.226	35	102	12	24	2	0	2	20	11	0	0	0	34	6	3	.314	.310
Saunders, Garrett	R-R	6-0	190	12-3-96	.300	.500	.259	26	70	11	21	1	1	0	3	14	4	2	1	23	3	2	.343	.438
Soderman, Ray	R-R	6-1	200	5-23-97	.077	.000	.111	5	13	0	1	0	0	0	0	0	2	0	0	6	1	1	.077	.200
Vizcaino, Nicholas	R-R	6-1	200	3-19-97	.200	.000	.231	4	15	3	3	2	0	0	0	1	0	0	0	4	0	0	.333	.250

Pitching	B-T	HT	WT	DOB	W	L	ERA	G	GS	CG	SV	IP	H	R	ER	HR	BB	SO	AVG	vLH	vRH	K/9	BB/9
Aquino, Alex	R-R	6-2	165	7-6-96	1	0	3.60	12	0	0	1	20	10	9	8	1	7	22	.152	.194	.100	9.90	3.15

Name	B-T	HT	WT	DOB	W	L	ERA	G	GS	CG	SV	IP	H	R	ER	HR	BB	SO	AVG	vLH	vRH	K/9	BB/9
Barger, Alec	R-R	6-2	201	3-24-98	0	3	5.85	13	13	0	0	40	49	27	26	7	16	43	.308	.329	.291	9.68	3.60
Camacho, Alex	R-R	6-7	245	7-30-96	2	1	3.57	13	0	0	2	23	22	11	9	2	7	28	.256	.250	.261	11.12	2.78
Chapman, Brandon	R-R	6-0	200	5-26-96	0	0	18.00	1	0	0	0	1	3	2	2	0	0	0	.500	.333	.667	0.00	0.00
Crouse, Marrick	R-R	6-3	200	5-2-97	0	0	0.73	10	0	0	0	12	9	3	1	1	10	15	.209	.333	.091	10.95	7.30
Daniels, Zach	L-R	5-11	160	4-21-97	4	2	4.93	15	2	0	0	35	35	23	19	3	13	38	.257	.324	.191	9.87	3.38
De Jesus, Luis	R-R	5-11	170	10-8-98	0	0	12.79	3	1	0	0	6	15	15	9	0	7	5	.417	.571	.318	7.11	9.95
DeVito, Ricky	B-R	6-3	195	8-21-98	0	0	3.32	7	4	0	0	19	13	7	7	1	9	23	.194	.222	.175	10.89	4.26
Gordon, Tanner	L-R	6-5	215	10-26-97	2	1	2.22	13	0	0	0	24	13	6	6	2	12	36	.155	.219	.115	13.32	4.44
Hodgson, Alger	R-R	6-2	190	4-10-99	1	5	5.02	14	4	0	0	38	41	29	21	6	28	36	.275	.292	.260	8.60	6.69
Javier, Ciriaco	R-R	6-3	185	1-1-96	1	0	3.00	2	0	0	1	3	1	1	1	0	4	2	.111	.000	.250	6.00	12.00
Jerez, Miguel	L-L	5-11	180	10-13-97	2	0	4.50	3	0	0	0	8	5	4	4	1	5	13	.185	.200	.182	14.63	5.63
Julian, Deyvis	R-R	6-2	165	4-10-96	1	3	8.31	16	0	0	0	26	27	28	24	3	23	24	.262	.327	.204	8.31	7.96
Kurz, Cameron	R-R	6-0	200	5-10-96	0	0	4.15	3	0	0	1	4	2	2	2	0	1	8	.143	.333	.091	16.62	2.08
Leban, Greg	R-R	6-3	235	5-30-96	1	0	2.04	10	0	0	0	18	13	4	4	1	10	20	.206	.185	.222	10.19	5.09
Owens, Tyler	R-R	5-10	185	1-9-01	0	2	4.63	8	8	0	0	23	17	13	12	2	11	28	.198	.216	.184	10.80	4.24
Polanco, Walner	R-R	6-7	200	12-24-96	0	1	8.22	3	3	0	0	8	7	7	7	3	7	3	.250	.357	.143	3.52	8.22
Reyes, Charles	L-R	6-1	165	9-9-99	0	0	--	1	0	0	0	0	0	3	3	0	3	0	--	--	--	--	--
Sanchez, Filyer	L-L	6-1	175	2-8-97	4	2	3.09	16	3	0	0	44	33	17	15	4	9	27	.204	.179	.217	5.56	1.85
Santos, Lisandro	L-L	6-1	170	7-24-98	2	1	1.14	5	5	0	0	24	21	6	3	0	8	26	.233	.229	.236	9.89	6.46
Segal, Alex	L-L	6-4	190	3-18-98	1	1	4.13	17	1	0	1	28	30	14	13	1	15	35	.275	.265	.280	11.12	4.76
Seipel, Zach	R-R	6-4	210	10-17-96	0	1	5.40	1	1	0	0	5	6	3	3	0	0	4	.300	.333	.273	7.20	0.00
Stallings, Mitch	L-L	6-2	180	6-30-95	3	5	2.25	11	9	0	0	56	53	22	14	1	10	69	.243	.194	.263	11.09	1.77
Vines, Darius	R-R	6-1	190	4-30-98	0	4	6.61	11	11	0	0	31	38	23	23	4	10	33	.297	.333	.265	9.48	2.87
Volquez, Albinson	R-R	6-3	185	8-16-97	1	1	4.82	16	0	0	4	28	21	19	15	3	22	22	.206	.220	.197	7.07	7.07
Wells, Kenny	R-R	6-0	190	4-4-98	0	0	4.86	13	0	0	1	17	11	10	9	1	14	24	.183	.208	.167	12.96	7.56
Williams, Peyton	R-R	6-1	180	5-6-98	2	3	6.32	12	3	0	0	24	22	19	17	4	9	21	.237	.261	.213	7.88	3.38
Yeager, Justin	L-R	6-5	215	1-20-98	2	2	4.24	14	0	0	2	23	23	12	11	3	14	34	.250	.283	.217	13.11	5.40

Fielding

C: Calandra 26, Chapman 12, De Hoyos 29, Soderman 3. 1B: Ball 33, Berne 8, Hernandez 26, Vizcaino 3. 2B: Milligan 56, Morales 5, Saunders 10. 3B: Birdsong 56, Hernandez 4, Morales 5, Saunders 7. SS: Morales 8, Philip 51, Saunders 11. OF: Blair 32, Carter 44, Mateja 19, Palma 40, Parker 44, Reyes 28.

GCL BRAVES   ROOKIE
GULF COAST LEAGUE

Batting	B-T	HT	WT	DOB	AVG	vLH	vRH	G	AB	R	H	2B	3B	HR	RBI	BB	HBP	SH	SF	SO	SB	CS	SLG	OBP
Backstrom, Mahki	L-L	6-5	220	10-10-01	.300	.200	.317	23	70	8	21	5	0	2	8	12	0	0	0	27	1	0	.457	.402
Berne, Mason	R-R	6-3	225	3-11-96	.262	.111	.286	26	65	10	17	1	0	3	12	8	0	0	0	12	0	0	.415	.343
Bryson, Denzel	R-R	5-11	185	9-26-00	.065	.000	.073	27	62	7	4	2	0	0	0	7	2	0	0	31	1	0	.097	.183
Bunnell, Cade	L-R	6-0	182	5-14-97	.141	.083	.154	26	64	17	9	1	0	1	4	25	1	1	0	27	0	0	.203	.385
Cerrato, Wiston	B-R	5-10	170	4-9-99	.235	.071	.269	26	81	8	19	5	1	1	12	5	3	3	1	13	1	0	.358	.300
Encarnacion, Kimberling	R-R	6-0	180	11-22-99	.250	.000	.294	6	20	1	5	1	0	0	2	2	1	0	0	8	0	0	.300	.348
Florentino, Darling	R-R	6-0	210	5-25-01	.202	.261	.185	32	104	16	21	3	0	6	21	7	2	0	3	47	0	0	.404	.259
Grissom, Vaughn	R-R	6-3	180	1-5-01	.288	.310	.282	44	160	22	46	7	1	3	23	16	4	1	3	27	3	0	.400	.361
Guitian, Enmanuel	R-R	5-11	165	9-14-98	.143	.167	.138	18	35	3	5	0	0	0	5	4	0	0	1	10	0	0	.143	.225
Harris, Michael	L-L	6-0	195	3-7-01	.349	.474	.322	31	109	15	38	6	3	2	16	9	1	0	0	20	5	2	.514	.403
Mezquita, Brandol	R-R	6-0	170	7-14-01	.246	.208	.255	34	118	14	29	1	0	1	12	17	2	3	0	40	6	2	.280	.350
Morton, Kadon	R-R	6-2	195	11-19-00	.152	.214	.141	32	99	14	15	5	2	1	9	12	2	0	0	45	1	2	.273	.257
Paolini, Stephen	L-L	6-2	195	11-23-00	.192	.192	.192	35	120	15	23	6	0	0	8	22	0	0	1	37	2	1	.242	.315
Reyes, Joel	R-R	6-0	200	10-3-99	.241	.308	.229	30	83	13	20	5	0	0	8	8	0	1	0	18	5	1	.301	.308
Rojas, Luidemid	B-R	5-11	170	5-4-99	.255	.250	.255	20	55	6	14	4	1	0	3	2	2	1	0	16	0	0	.364	.305
Stevens, Eliezel	R-R	6-0	185	10-8-00	.239	.350	.218	37	130	9	31	6	0	2	19	9	0	0	2	44	7	2	.331	.284
Valdes, Javier	R-R	5-10	195	11-19-98	.088	.000	.111	23	57	3	5	2	0	0	3	11	3	2	0	13	1	0	.123	.268
Wilkins, Andy	L-R	6-1	225	9-13-88	.000	.000	.000	1	3	0	0	0	0	0	0	0	0	0	0	1	0	0	.000	.000
Zamora, Christian	R-R	6-4	210	7-4-01	.206	.273	.192	19	63	7	13	4	2	0	2	6	1	0	0	30	0	0	.333	.286

Pitching	B-T	HT	WT	DOB	W	L	ERA	G	GS	CG	SV	IP	H	R	ER	HR	BB	SO	AVG	vLH	vRH	K/9	BB/9
Asencio, Eudi	R-R	6-3	170	2-28-99	3	3	3.82	12	3	0	1	33	30	18	14	0	10	29	.231	.225	.233	7.91	2.73
Beck, Tristan	R-R	6-4	165	6-24-96	0	0	4.00	2	2	0	0	9	9	6	4	0	4	14	.257	.235	.278	14.00	4.00
Bryant, Chad	R-R	6-0	210	8-3-99	1	1	8.88	11	7	0	0	24	31	24	24	2	13	23	.307	.257	.333	8.51	4.81
Burgess, Brent	R-R	6-0	200	5-2-97	1	0	1.46	8	0	0	1	12	14	2	2	1	8	15	.286	.467	.206	10.95	5.84
Caminero, Carlos	L-L	6-4	185	9-17-97	0	2	7.62	8	0	0	0	13	20	12	11	1	5	12	.339	.500	.314	8.31	3.46
Celedonio, Raulin	R-L	6-6	220	2-8-00	0	1	4.15	9	0	0	0	17	8	12	8	0	18	15	.143	.083	.159	7.79	9.35
Clouse, Corbin	B-L	6-0	230	6-26-95	0	0	3.86	2	0	0	0	2	3	3	1	0	0	2	.273	.000	.300	7.71	0.00
De Jesus, Luis	R-R	5-11	170	10-8-98	0	3	4.79	7	3	0	0	21	20	13	11	2	17	19	.267	.292	.255	8.27	7.40
De La Cruz, Carlos	R-R	6-1	170	9-12-96	2	3	3.65	12	0	0	2	25	25	15	10	0	9	10	.260	.345	.224	3.65	3.28
DeVito, Ricky	B-R	6-3	195	8-21-98	0	0	0.00	1	0	0	0	1	0	0	0	0	0	1	.000	.000	--	9.00	0.00
Diaz, Indigo	R-R	6-5	250	10-14-98	1	0	3.48	6	0	0	0	10	9	4	4	0	2	15	.231	.333	.167	13.06	1.74
Dirks, Caleb	R-R	6-3	220	6-9-93	0	1	2.25	3	0	0	0	4	3	1	1	0	1	6	.235	.333	.125	6.75	2.25
Estes, Joey	R-R	6-2	190	10-8-01	0	1	8.10	5	5	0	0	10	10	10	9	0	7	8	.256	.333	.233	7.20	6.30
Guth, Zach	L-L	6-4	210	4-4-97	0	0	1.93	4	0	0	0	5	1	1	1	0	6	6	.067	.000	.083	11.57	11.57
Javier, Ciriaco	R-R	6-3	185	1-1-96	1	0	7.11	4	0	0	0	6	6	5	5	0	6	6	.300	.300		11.37	8.53
Jerez, Miguel	L-L	5-11	180	10-13-97	0	3	4.30	7	3	0	0	23	23	15	11	1	6	21	.256	.217	.269	8.22	2.35
Johnson, Jared	R-R	6-2	225	3-15-01	0	0	3.52	6	0	0	0	15	15	7	6	0	4	12	.268	.211	.297	7.04	2.35
Kalich, Kasey	R-R	6-3	220	4-25-98	0	0	0.00	1	0	0	0	1	1	0	0	0	1	2	.250	.333	.000	18.00	9.00
Kurz, Cameron	R-R	6-0	200	5-10-96	2	0	0.00	5	0	0	1	7	2	0	0	0	1	4	.095	.143	.071	4.91	1.23

Name	B-T	HT	WT	DOB	W	L	ERA	G	GS	CG	SV	IP	H	R	ER	HR	BB	SO	AVG	vLH	vRH	K/9	BB/9
Leban, Greg	R-R	6-3	235	5-30-96	1	0	9.64	3	0	0	0	5	5	5	5	0	4	9	.263	.250	.267	17.36	7.71
Lopez, Yoeli	R-R	5-10	167	7-31-97	0	0	0.00	1	0	0	0	0	0	0	0	0	0	0	.000	.000	--	0.00	0.00
O'Day, Darren	R-R	6-4	220	10-22-82	0	0	0.00	1	1	0	0	1	0	0	0	0	0	2	.000	.000	.000	18.00	0.00
Owens, Tyler	R-R	5-10	185	1-9-01	0	1	2.25	2	1	0	0	4	1	1	1	0	1	4	.083	.167	.000	9.00	2.25
Pena, Miguel	L-R	6-1	190	11-26-98	0	1	1.88	9	0	0	1	14	16	8	3	1	5	14	.281	.333	.262	8.79	3.14
Polanco, Walner	R-R	6-7	200	12-24-96	1	1	3.20	8	3	0	0	20	20	11	7	0	8	14	.247	.276	.231	6.41	3.66
Rodriguez, Estarlin	R-R	6-0	180	10-24-99	1	2	4.09	8	0	0	0	22	25	13	10	1	11	18	.278	.343	.236	7.36	4.50
Samuelson, Andy	L-L	6-4	185	5-20-99	1	1	6.39	8	0	0	1	13	17	12	9	0	6	21	.298	.333	.289	14.92	4.26
Schwab, Davis	L-L	6-4	230	1-27-97	0	1	3.68	11	1	0	0	22	26	12	9	1	11	20	.299	.200	.319	8.18	4.50
Seipel, Zach	R-R	6-4	210	10-17-96	2	3	3.45	8	4	0	0	31	21	12	12	1	14	33	.186	.216	.171	9.48	4.02
Tarnok, Freddy	R-R	6-3	185	11-24-98	0	1	3.38	3	3	0	0	8	3	3	3	1	1	9	.111	.125	.105	10.13	1.13
Thompson, Ben	R-R	6-5	220	12-21-97	0	0	1.93	2	1	0	0	5	2	1	1	0	1	4	.133	.250	.091	7.71	1.93
Vines, Darius	R-R	6-1	190	4-30-98	0	1	9.00	1	0	0	0	1	1	1	1	0	0	2	.333	--	.333	18.00	0.00
Webb, Jacob	R-R	6-1	200	8-15-93	0	0	0.00	1	0	0	0	1	0	0	0	0	0	1	.000	.000	.000	9.00	0.00
Williams, Peyton	R-R	6-1	180	5-6-98	0	0	4.50	1	1	0	0	2	2	1	1	0	1	3	.250	.500	.167	13.50	4.50
Withrow, Matt	R-R	6-5	235	9-23-93	1	1	7.27	4	1	0	0	9	13	13	7	1	2	9	.325	.368	.286	9.35	2.08
Yeager, Justin	L-R	6-5	215	1-20-98	0	0	0.00	1	0	0	0	2	1	0	0	0	1	3	.143	.000	.167	13.50	4.50

Fielding

C: Bryson 5, Cerrato 24, Guitian 11, Valdes 20. **1B:** Backstrom 22, Berne 24, Bryson 1, Encarnacion 6, Guitian 5. **2B:** Bunnell 7, Rojas 9, Stevens 36. **3B:** Bunnell 12, Florentino 30, Rojas 10. **SS:** Bunnell 7, Grissom 42. **OF:** Harris 23, Mezquita 24, Morton 27, Paolini 34, Reyes 27, Zamora 19.

DSL BRAVES   ROOKIE
DOMINICAN SUMMER LEAGUE

Batting	B-T	HT	WT	DOB	AVG	vLH	vRH	G	AB	R	H	2B	3B	HR	RBI	BB	HBP	SH	SF	SO	SB	CS	SLG	OBP
Celedonio, Jeremy	R-R	6-0	183	12-26-01	.203	.207	.203	59	192	30	39	7	0	4	22	41	8	0	2	72	5	0	.302	.362
Celesten, Nelson	L-R	5-10	160	9-3-99	.214	.263	.202	45	103	11	22	1	1	0	6	15	2	3	1	23	8	5	.243	.322
De La Cruz, Randi	R-R	6-1	180	8-15-01	.209	.188	.212	45	115	18	24	5	0	1	14	23	7	0	0	41	1	1	.278	.372
Dilone, Jose	R-R	6-0	165	10-9-00	.267	.226	.275	63	202	34	54	3	1	1	24	31	4	3	3	45	18	8	.307	.371
Estrada, Deivi	B-R	5-10	155	1-17-01	.307	.259	.314	66	202	36	62	7	1	1	27	42	5	3	3	35	9	6	.366	.433
Floyd, Francisco	R-R	6-1	167	5-25-02	.223	.229	.222	58	220	31	49	4	2	0	18	26	2	2	0	69	14	9	.259	.311
Jimenez, Leomar	R-R	6-1	160	1-9-02	.140	.200	.130	38	107	12	15	3	0	0	5	8	4	1	0	36	8	2	.168	.227
Medina, Yerangel	R-R	6-4	205	3-15-00	.231	.091	.247	31	104	10	24	8	0	2	13	7	3	0	1	26	2	2	.365	.296
Paiva, Carlos	R-R	6-3	185	3-20-02	.167	.125	.177	16	42	2	7	1	0	0	4	5	0	0	0	16	3	2	.191	.255
Pena, Gianfranco	R-R	6-2	180	1-24-00	.250	.222	.257	43	128	16	32	4	0	2	22	10	11	1	4	30	1	0	.328	.346
Pena, Kelvin	R-R	5-11	160	4-10-01	.220	.242	.217	66	236	28	52	15	0	6	40	28	4	0	5	66	1	2	.360	.308
Quintero, Geraldo	B-R	5-8	155	10-10-01	.264	.269	.263	58	197	35	52	10	3	2	22	30	7	2	1	26	21	8	.376	.379
Ruiz, Randy	R-R	5-10	163	12-22-01	.202	.133	.216	39	89	14	18	6	0	0	9	13	6	0	1	20	4	0	.270	.339
Smith, Wilmer	L-R	6-0	185	12-17-00	.219	.133	.232	39	114	19	25	8	0	1	12	21	2	2	2	41	2	0	.316	.345
Then, Alexander	B-R	5-11	156	12-11-01	.204	.432	.149	59	191	32	39	11	2	5	19	19	3	2	5	46	3	8	.246	.271

Pitching	B-T	HT	WT	DOB	W	L	ERA	G	GS	CG	SV	IP	H	R	ER	HR	BB	SO	AVG	vLH	vRH	K/9	BB/9
Alesandro, Ronaldo	R-R	6-0	170	5-7-98	3	1	2.43	18	4	0	6	33	22	13	9	0	11	45	.186	.154	.203	12.15	2.97
Bautista, Jorge	R-R	6-0	155	12-10-00	1	3	3.86	13	12	0	0	54	44	25	23	3	20	46	.218	.136	.257	7.71	3.35
Bennett, Shairon	R-R	6-4	220	12-30-01	1	0	0.00	2	0	0	0	3	0	0	0	0	2	2	.000	.000	.000	6.75	6.75
Bermudez, Nestor	L-L	6-0	160	8-9-01	0	0	11.25	5	0	0	0	4	4	6	5	0	5	4	.222	.000	.250	9.00	11.25
Celedonio, Raulin	R-L	6-6	220	2-8-00	0	2	3.27	4	0	0	0	11	12	7	4	0	1	12	.279	.500	.243	9.82	0.82
Corona, Reibyn	R-R	5-11	175	11-13-01	3	3	5.19	14	9	0	0	43	42	27	25	4	18	29	.264	.289	.254	6.02	3.74
De La Cruz, Carlos	R-R	6-1	170	9-12-96	0	0	2.35	5	0	0	3	8	8	2	2	0	4	6	.267	.333	.238	7.04	4.70
Diaz, Luis	R-R	6-3	200	9-16-99	3	0	3.47	13	0	0	1	23	19	10	9	1	13	20	.229	.191	.242	7.71	5.01
Linares, Ramon	L-L	6-0	160	8-31-01	1	0	2.76	10	0	0	0	16	7	5	5	0	9	17	.125	.222	.106	9.37	4.96
Moreno, Cesari	R-R	6-4	214	12-21-01	2	3	6.08	15	5	0	0	27	24	22	18	1	19	17	.242	.250	.239	5.74	6.41
Moreno, Jose	L-L	5-10	155	9-27-00	0	0	11.57	3	0	0	0	2	1	3	3	0	5	3	.125	.000	.167	11.57	19.29
Munoz, Roddery	R-R	6-3	190	4-14-00	3	5	3.77	14	14	0	0	62	48	39	26	2	29	67	.213	.159	.237	9.73	4.21
Munoz, Rolddy	R-R	6-2	183	4-14-00	0	1	6.23	8	0	0	0	9	8	6	6	0	7	9	.242	.333	.191	9.35	7.27
Nunez, Oscar	R-R	6-0	190	6-16-00	0	1	5.91	8	0	0	0	11	7	8	7	0	16	13	.194	.154	.217	10.97	13.50
Perez, Jordano	R-R	6-0	162	9-2-00	1	0	2.67	16	0	0	3	34	24	15	10	0	13	29	.203	.178	.219	7.75	3.48
Rijo, Orelvis	L-L	6-2	175	10-25-00	1	1	3.57	13	0	0	0	18	19	12	7	1	10	18	.275	.125	.295	9.17	5.09
Rodriguez, Rainiery	B-R	6-2	170	8-28-00	6	1	1.79	15	5	0	2	50	46	14	10	2	15	37	.250	.242	.254	6.62	2.68
Salinas, Royber	R-R	6-3	205	4-10-01	2	3	3.82	17	0	0	0	33	30	19	14	0	22	37	.248	.225	.259	10.09	6.00
Santos, Lisandro	L-L	6-1	170	7-24-98	2	1	2.70	7	5	0	0	30	22	11	9	1	12	29	.208	.167	.210	8.70	3.60
Sierra, Osiris	L-L	6-2	145	2-9-00	1	3	2.21	14	14	0	0	53	41	24	13	1	30	39	.212	.207	.213	6.62	5.09
Solano, Kevin	R-R	6-2	187	4-8-02	4	1	3.29	16	2	1	1	38	30	15	14	2	18	29	.222	.200	.232	6.81	4.23
Vargas, Leonardo	R-R	6-0	170	1-2-01	0	1	1.29	6	0	0	1	7	6	2	1	0	3	4	.231	.286	.211	5.14	3.86
Vargas, Luis	R-R	5-11	196	5-2-02	2	2	3.68	15	0	0	0	22	13	10	9	0	13	18	.173	.160	.180	7.36	5.32
Vidal, Frankelvin	R-R	5-11	201	4-22-02	3	2	2.38	15	0	0	1	23	18	9	6	0	18	22	.240	.294	.224	8.74	7.15

Fielding

C: Pena 30, Pena 18, Ruiz 35. **1B:** Medina 10, Pena 1, Pena 44, Smith 21. **2B:** Celesten 5, Dilone 5, Quintero 27, Then 44. **3B:** Dilone 53, Medina 10, Smith 13, Then 2. **SS:** Dilone 2, Floyd 56, Quintero 9, Then 6. **OF:** Celedonio 48, Celesten 41, De La Cruz 34, Estrada 55, Jimenez 34, Paiva 15, Quintero 20.

Baltimore Orioles

SEASON IN A SENTENCE: The Orioles' rebuild turned a corner in general manager Mike Elias' first year at the helm, when Baltimore improved by eight games—they went 54-108—and didn't even have the worst record in the American League.

HIGH POINT: Draft day was probably the single most significant day of the 2019 season. Picking first overall, Baltimore drafted potential franchise catcher Adley Rutschman out of Oregon State. The decorated collegian ranked as the No. 1 prospect in the short-season New York-Penn League in his pro debut. The Orioles then chose Alabama high school shortstop Gunnar Henderson with the first pick in the second round, and he went on to rank No. 3 in the Rookie-level Gulf Coast League.

LOW POINT: Orioles pitchers set an all-time major league record by allowing 305 home runs, a rate of 1.9 per nine innings.

NOTABLE ROOKIES: A trio of young players positioned themselves for future roles in Baltimore, highlighted by 26-year-old lefthander John Means, an AL all-star who ranked ninth among AL pitchers with 4.5 wins above replacement. Means succeeded on the strength of an outstanding changeup that he learned from minor league pitching coordinator Chris Holt. Righthander Hunter Harvey stayed healthy and took flight after moving to the bullpen. The 24-year-old made seven big league appearances in which he struck out 11, walked four and allowed three hits in six innings before being shut down because of workload. Austin Hays performed well as the everyday center fielder in September. The 23-year-old hit .309/.373/.574 (147 OPS+) with four home runs in 21 games.

KEY TRANSACTIONS: After cashing in Manny Machado, Zack Britton, Kevin Gausman and Jonathan Schoop at the 2018 trade deadline, the Orioles made few trades in 2019. Their most significant deal sent Andrew Cashner to the Red Sox for a pair of Dominican Summer League prospects.

DOWN ON THE FARM: The Orioles cracked the top 10 in organizational winning percentage for the first time since 2015, going 366-333 (.524) to rank ninth. Double-A Bowie reached the Eastern League finals before losing. More significantly, a number of Orioles prospects made developmental strides in 2019, including first baseman Ryan Mountcastle, lefthander Keegan Akin and righthander Mike Baumann. Young guns Grayson Rodriguez and DL Hall, both first-rounders out of high school, dominated the Class A levels.

OPENING DAY PAYROLL: $67,371,100 (27th).

PLAYERS OF THE YEAR

MIKE CARLSON

MAJOR LEAGUE	MINOR LEAGUE
John Means	**Ryan Mountcastle**
LHP	**1B**
12-11, 3.60 in 27 GS	(Triple-A)
121 SO, 155 IP	.312/.344/.527
AL all-star	25 HR, IL MVP

ORGANIZATION LEADERS

Batting		*Minimum 250 AB
MAJORS		
* AVG	Hanser Alberto	.305
* OPS	Trey Mancini	.899
HR	Trey Mancini	35
RBI	Trey Mancini	97
MINORS		
* AVG	Jace Peterson, Norfolk	.313
* OBP	Jace Peterson, Norfolk	.398
* SLG	DJ Stewart, Norfolk, GCL Orioles, Bowie	.550
* OPS	DJ Stewart, Norfolk, GCL Orioles, Bowie	.948
R	Mason McCoy, Frederick, Bowie	81
R	Ryan Mountcastle, Norfolk	81
H	Ryan Mountcastle, Norfolk	162
TB	Ryan Mountcastle, Norfolk	274
2B	Ryan Mountcastle, Norfolk	35
3B	Jaylen Ferguson, Aberdeen, Delmarva	7
3B	Mason McCoy, Frederick, Bowie	7
HR	Ryan Mountcastle, Norfolk	25
RBI	Ryan Mountcastle, Norfolk	83
BB	Cadyn Grenier, Delmarva, Frederick	59
BB	Ryan McKenna, Bowie	59
SO	JC Encarnacion, Delmarva	145
SB	Adam Hall, Delmarva	33
SB	Cedric Mullins, Norfolk, Bowie	33

PITCHING		#Minimum 75 IP
MAJORS		
W	John Means	12
# ERA	John Means	3.60
SO	Dylan Bundy	162
SV	Mychal Givens	11
MINORS		
W	Zac Lowther, Bowie	13
L	Blaine Knight, Delmarva, Frederick	12
# ERA	Gray Fenter, Delmarva	1.81
G	Tim Naughton, Delmarva, Frederick, Bowie	47
GS	Zac Lowther, Bowie	26
SV	Tim Naughton, Delmarva, Frederick, Bowie	20
IP	Zac Lowther, Bowie	148
BB	Hector Guance, Delmarva	66
SO	Zac Lowther, Bowie	154
# AVG	Grayson Rodriguez, Delmarva	.171

2019 PERFORMANCE

General Manager: Mike Elias.

Class	Team	League	W	L	PCT	Finish	Manager
Majors	Baltimore Orioles	American	54	108	.333	14th (15)	Brandon Hyde
Triple-A	Norfolk Tides	International	60	79	.432	12th (14)	Gary Kendall
Double-A	Bowie Baysox	Eastern	76	64	.543	5th (12)	Buck Britton
High A	Frederick Keys	Carolina	53	84	.387	10th (10)	Ryan Minor
Low A	Delmarva Shorebirds	South Atlantic	90	48	.652	1st (14)	Kyle Moore
Short season	Aberdeen IronBirds	New York-Penn	42	33	.560	3rd (14)	Kevin Bradshaw
Rookie	GCL Orioles	Gulf Coast	38	15	.717	1st (18)	Alan Mills
Overall 2019 Minor League Record			359	323	.526	8th (30)	

ORGANIZATION STATISTICS

BALTIMORE ORIOLES
AMERICAN LEAGUE

Batting	B-T	HT	WT	DOB	AVG	vLH	vRH	G	AB	R	H	2B	3B	HR	RBI	BB	HBP	SH	SF	SO	SB	CS	SLG	OBP
Alberto, Hanser	R-R	5-11	215	10-17-92	.305	.398	.238	139	524	62	160	21	2	12	51	16	4	3	3	50	4	4	.422	.329
Broxton, Keon	R-R	6-3	195	5-7-90	.204	.218	.188	37	103	14	21	3	0	4	9	8	0	1	0	49	4	1	.350	.261
2-team total (29 Seattle)					.174	.187	.163	66	155	19	27	3	0	6	14	16	1	1	2	82	6	5	.310	.253
Davis, Chris	L-R	6-3	230	3-17-86	.179	.131	.191	105	307	26	55	9	0	12	36	39	3	0	3	139	0	0	.326	.276
Hays, Austin	R-R	6-1	195	7-5-95	.309	.120	.419	21	68	12	21	6	0	4	13	7	0	0	0	13	2	0	.574	.373
Jackson, Drew	R-R	6-2	200	7-28-93	.000	.000	--	3	3	0	0	0	0	0	0	1	0	0	0	1	0	0	.000	.250
Mancini, Trey	R-R	6-4	215	3-18-92	.291	.278	.297	154	602	106	175	38	2	35	97	63	9	0	5	143	1	0	.535	.364
Martin, Richie	R-R	5-11	190	12-22-94	.209	.243	.170	120	283	29	59	8	3	6	23	14	6	5	1	83	10	1	.322	.260
Mullins, Cedric	B-L	5-8	175	10-1-94	.094	.067	.102	22	64	7	6	2	0	0	4	4	3	2	1	14	1	0	.156	.181
Nunez, Renato	R-R	6-1	220	4-4-94	.244	.270	.229	151	541	72	132	24	0	31	90	44	10	0	4	143	1	1	.460	.311
Peterson, Jace	L-R	6-0	215	5-9-90	.220	.227	.218	29	100	14	22	3	1	2	11	6	1	0	1	24	4	1	.330	.269
Rickard, Joey	R-L	6-1	185	5-21-91	.203	.188	.214	42	118	10	24	7	2	2	6	14	3	0	0	33	3	2	.348	.304
Rondon, Jose	R-R	6-1	195	3-3-94	.000	.000	--	1	1	0	0	0	0	0	0	0	0	0	0	0	0	0	.000	.000
2-team total (55 Chicago)					.196	.250	.134	56	143	10	28	3	0	3	9	11	2	1	0	38	0	0	.280	.263
Ruiz, Rio	L-R	6-1	215	5-22-94	.232	.250	.229	127	370	35	86	13	2	12	46	40	0	1	2	88	0	1	.376	.306
Santander, Anthony	B-R	6-2	190	10-19-94	.261	.272	.254	93	380	46	99	20	1	20	59	19	2	1	3	86	1	2	.476	.297
Severino, Pedro	R-R	6-1	219	7-20-93	.249	.273	.228	96	305	37	76	13	0	13	44	29	4	1	2	73	3	1	.420	.321
Sisco, Chance	L-R	6-2	195	2-24-95	.210	.105	.223	59	167	29	35	7	0	8	20	22	9	0	0	61	0	1	.395	.333
Smith Jr, Dwight	L-R	6-0	210	10-26-92	.241	.212	.252	101	357	46	86	16	3	13	53	26	4	1	4	82	5	1	.412	.297
Stewart, DJ	L-R	6-0	230	11-30-93	.238	.333	.191	44	126	15	30	6	0	4	15	14	1	0	1	26	1	2	.381	.317
Sucre, Jesus	R-R	6-0	200	4-30-88	.210	.217	.205	20	62	3	13	2	0	0	3	4	1	0	0	13	0	0	.242	.269
Trumbo, Mark	R-R	6-4	225	1-16-86	.172	.158	.200	12	29	1	5	3	0	0	3	2	0	0	0	5	0	0	.276	.226
Villar, Jonathan	B-R	6-1	215	5-2-91	.274	.264	.280	162	642	111	176	33	5	24	73	61	4	2	4	176	40	9	.453	.339
Wilkerson, Stevie	B-R	6-1	195	1-11-92	.225	.154	.264	117	329	41	74	18	2	10	35	22	7	1	2	108	3	3	.383	.286
Williams, Mason	L-R	6-1	195	8-21-91	.267	.222	.286	11	30	4	8	1	0	0	2	3	0	0	1	6	1	0	.300	.324
Wynns, Austin	R-R	6-2	205	12-10-90	.214	.188	.222	28	70	8	15	1	0	1	5	3	0	1	0	14	0	0	.271	.247

Pitching	B-T	HT	WT	DOB	W	L	ERA	G	GS	CG	SV	IP	H	R	ER	HR	BB	SO	AVG	vLH	vRH	K/9	BB/9
Alberto, Hanser	R-R	5-11	215	10-17-92	0	0	18.00	1	0	0	0	1	1	2	2	1	2	0	.250	--	.250	0.00	18.00
Araujo, Pedro	R-R	6-3	215	7-2-93	0	0	27.00	1	0	0	0	1	2	2	2	1	1	0	.667	1.000	.500	0.00	13.50
Armstrong, Shawn	R-R	6-2	225	9-11-90	1	1	5.13	51	0	0	4	54	58	32	31	7	26	60	.269	.203	.307	9.94	4.31
2-team total (4 Seattle)					1	1	5.74	55	0	0	4	58	66	38	37	8	29	63	.282	.209	.324	9.78	4.50
Blach, Ty	R-L	6-1	213	10-20-90	1	3	11.32	5	5	0	0	21	32	27	26	6	13	17	.356	.500	.309	7.40	5.66
Bleier, Richard	L-L	6-3	215	4-16-87	3	0	5.37	53	1	0	4	55	65	34	33	6	8	30	.296	.222	.355	4.88	1.30
Brooks, Aaron	R-R	6-4	230	4-27-90	4	5	6.18	14	12	0	0	60	69	43	41	9	20	39	.289	.298	.280	5.88	3.02
2-team total (15 Oakland)					6	8	5.65	29	18	0	0	110	118	72	69	21	34	82	.271	.283	.258	6.71	2.78
Bundy, Dylan	B-R	6-1	200	11-15-92	7	14	4.79	30	30	0	0	162	161	95	86	29	58	162	.256	.274	.239	9.02	3.23
Cashner, Andrew	R-R	6-6	235	9-11-86	9	3	3.83	17	17	0	0	96	86	45	41	11	29	66	.234	.182	.281	6.17	2.71
2-team total (25 Boston)					11	8	4.68	42	23	0	1	150	144	84	78	19	58	108	.253	.223	.279	6.48	3.48
Castro, Miguel	R-R	6-7	205	12-24-94	1	3	4.66	65	0	0	2	73	63	42	38	10	41	71	.232	.258	.218	8.71	5.03
Cobb, Alex	R-R	6-3	205	10-7-87	0	2	10.95	3	3	0	0	12	21	16	15	9	2	8	.362	.292	.412	5.84	1.46
Davis, Chris	L-R	6-3	230	3-17-86	0	0	9.00	1	0	0	0	1	2	1	1	0	1	0	.400	.000	.667	0.00	9.00
Eades, Ryan	R-R	6-2	210	12-15-91	0	1	3.52	6	0	0	0	8	7	3	3	2	4	5	.241	.286	.227	5.87	4.70
2-team total (2 Minnesota)					0	1	2.38	8	0	0	0	11	11	3	3	2	6	10	.256	.333	.226	7.94	4.76
Eshelman, Tom	R-R	6-3	210	6-20-94	1	2	6.50	10	4	0	0	36	47	31	26	12	11	22	.313	.241	.359	5.50	2.75
Fry, Paul	L-L	6-0	190	7-26-92	1	9	5.34	66	0	0	3	57	54	39	34	7	29	55	.247	.250	.244	8.63	4.55
Gilmartin, Sean	L-L	6-2	205	5-8-90	0	1	19.29	1	1	0	0	2	7	5	5	2	2	1	.500	.600	.250	3.86	7.71
Givens, Mychal	R-R	6-0	210	5-13-90	2	6	4.57	58	0	0	11	63	49	35	32	13	26	86	.213	.267	.179	12.29	3.71
Harvey, Hunter	R-R	6-3	175	12-9-94	1	0	1.42	7	0	0	0	6	3	1	1	1	4	11	.136	.143	.133	15.63	5.68
Hess, David	R-R	6-2	180	7-10-93	1	10	7.09	23	14	0	0	80	94	73	63	28	30	68	.288	.266	.301	7.65	3.38
Karns, Nate	R-R	6-3	225	11-25-87	0	1	0.00	4	2	0	0	5	7	1	0	0	3	5	.333	.000	.539	8.44	5.06
Kline, Branden	R-R	6-3	210	9-29-91	1	4	5.93	34	0	0	0	41	44	28	27	9	19	34	.275	.217	.310	7.46	4.17
Lucas, Josh	R-R	6-6	185	11-5-90	0	0	5.74	9	0	0	1	16	14	12	10	2	7	16	.237	.222	.244	9.19	4.02
Means, John	L-L	6-3	230	4-24-93	12	11	3.60	31	27	0	0	155	138	68	62	23	38	121	.234	.184	.249	7.03	2.21

Name	B-T	HT	WT	DOB	W	L	ERA	G	GS	CG	SV	IP	H	R	ER	HR	BB	SO	AVG	vLH	vRH	K/9	BB/9
Ortiz, Luis	R-R	6-3	230	9-22-95	0	1	10.80	1	1	0	0	3	4	4	4	2	5	3	.308	.429	.167	8.10	13.50
Phillips, Evan	R-R	6-2	215	9-11-94	0	1	6.43	25	0	0	0	28	32	20	20	2	20	40	.286	.286	.286	12.86	6.43
Ramirez, Yefry	R-R	6-2	215	11-28-93	0	2	6.97	4	1	0	0	10	11	9	8	2	9	11	.306	.286	.333	9.58	7.84
Rogers, Josh	L-L	6-3	220	7-10-94	0	1	8.79	5	0	0	0	14	18	14	14	7	6	5	.305	.235	.333	3.14	3.77
Scott, Tanner	R-L	6-2	220	7-22-94	1	1	4.78	28	0	0	0	26	28	17	14	4	19	37	.277	.188	.359	12.65	6.49
Scott, Tayler	R-R	6-3	185	6-1-92	0	0	18.69	8	0	0	0	9	20	18	18	5	5	7	.444	.421	.462	7.27	5.19
2-team total (5 Seattle)					0	0	14.33	13	2	0	0	16	31	28	26	6	11	14	.397	.371	.419	7.71	6.06
Shepherd, Chandler	R-R	6-3	185	8-25-92	0	0	6.63	5	3	0	0	19	23	15	14	5	6	17	.303	.267	.326	8.05	2.84
Straily, Dan	R-R	6-2	220	12-1-88	2	4	9.82	14	8	0	0	48	73	53	52	22	22	33	.349	.281	.400	6.23	4.15
Sucre, Jesus	R-R	6-0	200	4-30-88	0	0	0.00	1	0	0	0	1	0	0	0	0	0	0	.000	.000	.000	0.00	0.00
Tate, Dillon	R-R	6-2	195	5-1-94	0	2	6.43	16	0	0	0	21	18	15	15	3	9	20	.231	.192	.250	8.57	3.86
Wilkerson, Stevie	B-R	6-1	195	1-11-92	0	0	6.75	4	0	0	1	5	6	4	4	2	0	1	.273	.300	.250	1.69	0.00
Wojciechowski, Asher	R-R	6-4	235	12-21-88	4	8	4.92	17	16	0	0	82	80	46	45	17	28	80	.248	.253	.243	8.74	3.06
Wotherspoon, Matt	R-R	6-2	215	10-6-91	0	0	15.43	2	0	0	0	5	10	8	8	2	2	2	.435	.429	.444	3.86	3.86
Wright, Mike	R-R	6-6	215	1-3-90	0	1	9.45	10	0	0	1	13	20	14	14	5	7	14	.351	.375	.342	9.45	4.73
2-team total (9 Seattle)					0	1	7.98	19	0	0	1	29	44	30	26	6	12	30	.336	.319	.345	9.20	3.68
Yacabonis, Jimmy	R-R	6-3	205	3-21-92	1	2	6.80	29	4	0	0	41	51	32	31	9	24	33	.307	.281	.321	7.24	5.27
Ynoa, Gabriel	R-R	6-2	205	5-26-93	1	10	5.61	36	13	0	0	111	126	77	69	29	26	67	.280	.274	.286	5.45	2.11

Fielding

Catcher	PCT	G	PO	A	E	DP	PB
Severino	.988	89	655	29	8	5	10
Sisco	.983	52	332	7	6	0	1
Sucre	.991	18	111	5	1	3	3
Wynns	.984	25	173	12	3	1	2

First Base	PCT	G	PO	A	E	DP
Davis	.994	97	671	37	4	86
Mancini	1.000	56	395	40	0	42
Nunez	.983	24	160	10	3	14
Ruiz	1.000	12	34	2	0	0
Sisco	.000	1	0	0	0	0
Sucre	1.000	1	2	0	0	0

Second Base	PCT	G	PO	A	E	DP
Alberto	.990	90	119	169	3	59

	PCT	G	PO	A	E	DP
Peterson	1.000	5	10	18	0	2
Ruiz	1.000	1	0	1	0	0
Villar	.978	111	136	220	8	57
Wilkerson	.967	12	10	19	1	4

Third Base	PCT	G	PO	A	E	DP
Alberto	.960	66	54	115	7	14
Nunez	.947	9	3	15	1	2
Peterson	.909	9	6	14	2	1
Rondon	1.000	1	1	0	0	0
Ruiz	.969	114	70	176	8	26

Shortstop	PCT	G	PO	A	E	DP
Martin	.971	117	108	224	10	46
Villar	.957	97	70	200	12	47

Outfield	PCT	G	PO	A	E	DP
Alberto	1.000	4	6	0	0	0
Broxton	.981	36	104	0	2	0
Davis	.500	1	1	0	1	0
Hays	1.000	20	54	1	0	0
Jackson	1.000	3	3	0	0	0
Mancini	.994	93	167	3	1	1
Mullins	.983	22	58	0	1	0
Nunez	.000	1	0	0	0	0
Peterson	.974	19	37	1	1	0
Rickard	.976	40	83	0	2	0
Santander	.991	90	223	5	2	2
Smith Jr	.969	86	153	3	5	1
Stewart	.964	35	50	3	2	1
Wilkerson	.989	102	179	3	2	1
Williams	.938	9	14	1	1	0

NORFOLK TIDES   TRIPLE-A
INTERNATIONAL LEAGUE

Batting	B-T	HT	WT	DOB	AVG	vLH	vRH	G	AB	R	H	2B	3B	HR	RBI	BB	HBP	SH	SF	SO	SB	CS	SLG	OBP
Bannon, Rylan	R-R	5-7	180	4-22-96	.317	.364	.300	20	82	18	26	10	0	3	17	3	2	0	3	14	0	1	.549	.344
Bostick, Christopher	R-R	5-10	200	3-24-93	.258	.233	.266	106	392	59	101	22	3	12	50	33	7	6	4	99	4	2	.421	.323
Brugman, Jaycob	L-L	6-0	195	1-18-92	.125	.000	.167	3	8	1	1	0	0	1	1	0	0	0	0	3	0	0	.500	.125
Cervenka, Martin	R-R	6-4	225	8-3-92	.372	.600	.303	12	43	3	16	3	0	0	4	5	0	1	0	12	0	0	.442	.438
Clare, Chris	R-R	6-2	175	11-24-94	.500	.500	--	2	2	1	1	0	0	1	2	1	0	0	0	1	0	0	2.000	.667
Feliz, Anderson	B-R	6-0	175	5-11-92	.207	.231	.202	42	135	16	28	7	0	1	14	13	0	1	0	47	0	1	.282	.277
Hays, Austin	R-R	6-1	195	7-5-95	.254	.227	.264	59	240	43	61	16	1	10	27	11	6	0	0	61	6	4	.454	.304
Mountcastle, Ryan	R-R	6-3	195	2-18-97	.312	.349	.297	127	520	81	162	35	1	25	83	24	4	0	5	130	2	1	.527	.344
Mullins, Cedric	B-L	5-8	175	10-1-94	.205	.257	.186	66	268	40	55	8	2	5	24	25	1	6	4	53	13	4	.306	.272
Perez, Carlos	R-R	6-0	210	10-27-90	.125	.167	.111	8	24	2	3	1	0	0	1	0	0	0	0	4	0	0	.167	.160
Peterson, Jace	L-R	6-0	215	5-9-90	.313	.398	.279	90	326	58	102	25	5	10	46	46	2	0	3	56	13	3	.512	.398
Reinheimer, Jack	R-R	6-1	185	7-19-92	.246	.273	.236	106	342	43	84	15	2	4	31	40	2	1	6	77	12	4	.336	.323
Rickard, Joey	R-L	6-1	185	5-21-91	.203	.188	.208	18	64	10	13	5	0	4	10	11	2	0	0	16	1	0	.469	.338
Rifaela, Ademar	L-L	5-10	180	11-20-94	.236	.189	.256	38	127	17	30	6	3	2	11	11	3	0	1	34	0	0	.378	.310
Rondon, Jose	R-R	6-1	195	3-3-94	.219	.167	.236	21	73	9	16	4	0	2	12	10	0	0	0	22	1	0	.356	.313
Ruiz, Rio	R-R	6-2	175	5-21-94	.357	.500	.333	3	14	1	5	0	0	1	7	0	0	0	1	3	0	0	.571	.333
Santander, Anthony	B-R	6-2	190	10-19-94	.259	.333	.240	48	193	30	50	15	0	5	28	13	2	0	1	38	3	2	.415	.311
Sisco, Chance	L-R	6-2	195	2-24-95	.292	.300	.288	45	168	31	49	10	0	10	37	20	7	0	1	44	0	0	.530	.388
Smith Jr, Dwight	L-R	6-0	210	10-26-92	.311	.417	.273	11	45	9	14	2	0	3	12	3	1	0	0	8	0	0	.556	.367
Stewart, DJ	L-R	6-0	230	11-30-93	.291	.318	.281	63	230	42	67	19	2	12	47	38	4	2	3	51	5	4	.548	.396
Sucre, Jesus	R-R	6-0	200	4-30-88	.283	.328	.260	50	184	20	52	15	0	1	19	12	2	0	0	29	0	0	.364	.333
Trumbo, Mark	R-R	6-4	225	1-16-86	.214	.375	.177	12	42	5	9	3	0	4	10	6	0	0	0	15	0	0	.571	.313
Vielma, Engelb	B-R	5-11	155	6-22-94	.204	.205	.203	37	113	13	23	7	1	0	9	14	2	2	0	33	0	1	.283	.308
Vincej, Zach	R-R	6-0	190	5-1-91	.271	.245	.279	101	366	49	99	22	0	8	51	24	3	2	4	64	0	4	.396	.317
Wilkerson, Stevie	B-R	6-1	195	1-11-92	.323	.278	.341	16	62	13	20	0	1	2	10	3	0	2	0	9	3	0	.452	.354
Williams, Mason	L-R	6-1	195	8-21-91	.308	.360	.287	121	442	62	136	15	3	18	67	46	0	3	3	86	4	7	.477	.371
Wynns, Austin	R-R	6-2	205	12-10-90	.264	.377	.213	62	197	26	52	5	0	3	25	25	3	2	3	35	0	0	.335	.351

Pitching	B-T	HT	WT	DOB	W	L	ERA	G	GS	CG	SV	IP	H	R	ER	HR	BB	SO	AVG	vLH	vRH	K/9	BB/9
Akin, Keegan	L-L	6-0	225	4-1-95	6	7	4.73	25	24	0	0	112	109	64	59	10	61	131	.252	.340	.226	10.50	4.89
Araujo, Pedro	R-R	6-3	215	7-2-93	0	1	12.54	4	0	0	0	9	16	15	13	6	5	9	.372	.267	.429	8.68	4.82
Blach, Ty	R-L	6-1	213	10-20-90	0	1	16.88	2	2	0	0	5	17	10	10	1	2	5	.567	1.000	.552	8.44	3.38
Cervenka, Hunter	L-L	6-1	250	1-3-90	1	0	2.25	9	0	0	0	12	7	4	3	0	5	18	.175	.200	.167	13.50	3.75
Chleborad, Tanner	R-R	6-6	185	11-4-92	0	0	7.11	3	0	0	0	6	8	5	5	1	4	4	.308	.188	.568	5.68	

Eades, Ryan	R-R	6-2	210	12-15-91	0	0	0.00	2	0	0	0	2	2	0	0	0	1	1	.333	.500	.250	5.40	5.40
2-team total (29 Rochester)					4	3	5.33	31	2	0	3	52	61	32	31	7	17	64	.291	.286	.294	11.01	2.92
Erwin, Tyler	L-L	6-0	185	8-29-94	0	0	19.29	1	0	0	0	2	5	5	5	1	0	1	.417	.500	.375	3.86	0.00
Eshelman, Tom	R-R	6-3	210	6-20-94	1	2	4.70	7	6	0	0	38	43	21	20	6	7	28	.276	.246	.299	6.57	1.64
2-team total (4 Lehigh Valley)					3	2	3.92	11	10	1	0	64	66	29	28	9	12	51	.261	.237	.287	7.13	1.68
Flaa, Jay	R-R	6-3	225	6-10-92	2	3	5.24	29	3	0	4	55	53	35	32	8	26	43	.252	.266	.241	7.04	4.25
Fry, Paul	L-L	6-0	190	7-26-92	0	0	36.00	1	0	0	0	1	4	4	4	1	1	3	.571	1.000	.500	27.00	9.00
Gilmartin, Sean	L-L	6-2	205	5-8-90	3	3	3.95	32	3	0	0	66	54	32	29	8	23	74	.222	.250	.208	10.09	3.14
Gonzalez, Luis	L-L	6-2	170	1-17-92	1	4	8.69	23	1	0	2	29	43	28	28	8	11	40	.341	.324	.348	12.41	3.41
Harvey, Hunter	R-R	6-3	175	12-9-94	1	1	4.32	12	0	0	0	17	13	8	8	2	5	22	.206	.300	.163	11.88	2.70
Herb, Tyler	R-R	6-3	200	4-28-92	4	8	7.16	16	13	0	0	77	109	66	61	20	37	63	.333	.320	.345	7.40	4.34
Hess, David	R-R	6-2	180	7-10-93	3	2	4.57	13	4	0	1	41	41	21	21	7	12	47	.253	.333	.198	10.23	2.61
Jimenez, Francisco	R-R	6-1	160	10-4-94	1	0	7.71	4	0	0	0	12	14	10	10	4	5	16	.286	.200	.324	12.34	3.86
Karns, Nate	R-R	6-3	225	11-25-87	0	0	81.00	1	0	0	0	0	2	3	3	1	2	0	.667	.500	1.000	0.00	54.00
Kline, Branden	R-R	6-3	210	9-29-91	1	1	6.86	18	0	0	2	21	27	17	16	4	13	27	.307	.290	.320	11.57	5.57
Kremer, Dean	R-R	6-3	180	1-7-96	0	2	8.84	4	4	0	0	19	30	19	19	2	4	21	.366	.303	.408	9.78	1.86
Lee, Chris	L-L	6-3	180	8-17-92	3	2	5.91	18	0	0	2	46	55	35	30	8	22	46	.306	.224	.344	9.07	4.34
Long, Lucas	R-R	6-0	195	10-7-92	0	2	9.53	7	1	0	0	11	19	14	12	1	4	8	.380	.429	.345	6.35	3.18
Lucas, Josh	R-R	6-6	185	11-5-90	0	2	6.85	20	2	0	2	24	29	19	18	4	12	19	.302	.439	.200	7.23	4.56
Muckenhirn, Zach	L-L	6-1	185	2-27-95	0	1	17.18	4	0	0	0	4	9	7	7	1	4	8	.450	.400	.467	19.64	9.82
Ortiz, Luis	R-R	6-3	230	9-22-95	3	7	6.38	14	14	0	0	66	77	56	47	15	31	47	.290	.291	.288	6.38	4.21
Phillips, Evan	R-R	6-2	215	9-11-94	1	2	3.86	27	0	0	1	40	35	18	17	2	17	44	.233	.161	.277	9.98	3.86
Ramirez, Yefry	R-R	6-2	215	11-28-93	1	1	1.50	4	4	0	0	18	11	4	3	2	9	24	.177	.177	.179	12.00	4.50
2-team total (15 Indianapolis)					2	5	4.14	19	9	0	0	63	53	32	29	7	38	82	.228	.208	.244	11.71	5.43
Rogers, Josh	L-L	6-3	220	7-10-94	2	6	8.51	11	11	0	0	55	86	53	52	18	10	33	.357	.338	.365	5.40	1.64
Scott, Tanner	R-L	6-2	220	7-22-94	3	4	2.98	30	0	0	7	45	35	21	15	2	15	57	.211	.159	.230	11.32	2.98
Scott, Tayler	R-R	6-3	185	6-1-92	0	0	0.56	13	0	0	6	16	11	1	1	0	3	21	.193	.294	.150	11.81	1.69
Shepherd, Chandler	R-R	6-3	185	8-25-92	3	5	4.60	14	12	1	0	72	75	41	37	8	23	73	.261	.271	.255	9.08	2.86
2-team total (8 Pawtucket)					3	10	6.18	22	19	1	0	102	128	84	70	19	39	103	.298	.322	.283	9.09	3.44
Straily, Dan	R-R	6-2	220	12-1-88	4	0	2.38	6	6	0	0	34	24	9	9	4	8	38	.195	.237	.177	10.06	2.12
2-team total (6 Lehigh Valley)					5	4	3.76	12	12	0	0	67	57	31	28	9	17	68	.225	.253	.211	9.13	2.28
Tate, Dillon	R-R	6-2	195	5-1-94	2	0	2.00	4	0	0	2	9	7	2	2	1	1	7	.212	.143	.263	7.00	1.00
Wotherspoon, Matt	R-R	6-2	215	10-6-91	5	2	5.54	33	3	0	1	65	65	41	40	10	27	67	.259	.260	.258	9.28	3.74
2-team total (3 Toledo)					5	2	5.32	36	3	0	2	71	70	43	42	11	28	75	.256	.252	.259	9.51	3.55
Yacabonis, Jimmy	R-R	6-3	205	3-21-92	2	2	4.50	17	0	0	2	24	26	15	12	2	15	22	.271	.320	.217	8.25	5.63
Ynoa, Gabriel	R-R	6-2	205	5-26-93	1	0	4.76	3	3	0	0	17	13	9	9	3	6	13	.206	.152	.267	6.88	3.18
Ysla, Luis	L-L	6-1	185	4-27-92	3	6	6.62	22	16	0	0	86	98	68	63	14	55	82	.298	.225	.325	8.61	5.78
Zimmermann, Bruce	L-L	6-2	215	2-9-95	2	3	4.89	7	7	0	0	39	44	22	21	3	18	33	.291	.297	.290	7.68	4.19

Fielding

Catcher	PCT	G	PO	A	E	DP	PB
Cervenka	1.000	11	95	4	0	1	0
Perez	1.000	7	45	8	0	0	0
Sisco	.982	35	267	7	5	0	3
Sucre	.991	37	318	17	3	5	3
Wynns	.996	55	480	33	2	1	4

First Base	PCT	G	PO	A	E	DP
Mountcastle	.994	84	624	43	4	61
Peterson	.990	27	175	15	2	13
Sucre	1.000	2	11	1	0	1
Trumbo	1.000	1	4	0	0	0
Vincej	1.000	28	195	11	0	22
Wilkerson	1.000	1	8	0	0	0

Second Base	PCT	G	PO	A	E	DP
Bostick	.949	66	105	174	15	38
Clare	1.000	1	1	2	0	1
Feliz	.857	1	3	3	1	0
Peterson	1.000	9	14	32	0	6
Reinheimer	.992	31	60	71	1	21

	PCT	G	PO	A	E	DP
Rondon	.800	1	2	2	1	2
Vielma	.889	2	1	7	1	0
Vincej	.986	21	22	47	1	8
Wilkerson	.956	10	12	31	2	6

Third Base	PCT	G	PO	A	E	DP
Bannon	.912	20	14	38	5	9
Feliz	.963	26	7	45	2	2
Mountcastle	.900	9	2	16	2	1
Peterson	.927	38	31	71	8	4
Reinheimer	1.000	1	0	2	0	0
Rondon	.750	3	0	6	2	0
Ruiz	1.000	3	2	5	0	0
Vincej	.928	42	32	58	7	11
Wilkerson	.875	3	2	5	1	0

Shortstop	PCT	G	PO	A	E	DP
Feliz	1.000	2	4	3	0	1
Peterson	1.000	4	5	10	0	5
Reinheimer	.959	73	91	169	11	33
Rondon	.980	14	12	38	1	7

	PCT	G	PO	A	E	DP
Vielma	.983	34	40	73	2	14
Vincej	.978	13	17	27	1	6

Outfield	PCT	G	PO	A	E	DP
Bostick	1.000	2	2	0	0	0
Brugman	1.000	3	5	0	0	0
Feliz	.867	10	13	0	2	0
Hays	.983	55	110	5	2	3
Mountcastle	1.000	26	37	5	0	1
Mullins	.993	62	149	1	1	0
Peterson	1.000	5	4	0	0	0
Rickard	1.000	15	29	3	0	1
Rifaela	1.000	31	40	2	0	0
Rondon	1.000	2	1	0	0	0
Santander	.970	43	93	3	3	0
Smith Jr	1.000	7	18	0	0	0
Stewart	.970	52	95	3	3	0
Trumbo	1.000	2	3	0	0	0
Vielma	.000	1	0	0	0	0
Wilkerson	1.000	2	2	0	0	0
Williams	.988	113	226	12	3	1

BOWIE BAYSOX   *DOUBLE-A*
EASTERN LEAGUE

Batting	B-T	HT	WT	DOB	AVG	vLH	vRH	G	AB	R	H	2B	3B	HR	RBI	BB	HBP	SH	SF	SO	SB	CS	SLG	OBP
Bannon, Rylan	R-R	5-7	180	4-22-96	.255	.272	.249	110	388	45	99	22	4	8	42	47	7	1	1	72	8	4	.394	.345
Billingsley, Cole	L-L	5-10	165	5-29-94	.250	.000	.273	10	24	5	6	2	0	0	2	2	0	0	0	5	0	0	.333	.308
Brockmeyer, Cael	R-R	6-6	245	10-8-91	.107	.143	.095	9	28	3	3	1	0	0	1	2	1	0	1	8	1	0	.143	.188
Cervenka, Martin	R-R	6-4	225	8-3-92	.206	.218	.200	46	160	14	33	1	0	4	17	13	2	0	4	55	2	0	.288	.268
Clare, Chris	R-R	6-2	175	11-24-94	.168	.240	.145	36	101	14	17	4	0	0	4	12	3	0	2	26	1	1	.208	.276
Cumberland, Brett	B-R	5-11	205	6-25-95	.248	.237	.253	41	125	21	31	8	0	4	20	23	8	0	1	34	0	0	.408	.395
Diaz, Yusniel	R-R	6-1	195	10-7-96	.262	.203	.279	76	286	45	75	19	4	11	53	32	1	0	3	67	0	3	.472	.335
Evans, Ian	R-R	5-11	185	7-10-96	.000	.000	.000	3	6	0	0	0	0	0	1	1	0	0	1	2	0	0	.000	.125
Feliz, Anderson	B-R	6-0	175	5-11-92	.285	.294	.282	37	137	19	39	13	0	3	30	17	1	0	2	36	5	2	.445	.363

BALTIMORE ORIOLES

Name	B-T	HT	WT	DOB	AVG	vLH	vRH	G	AB	R	H	2B	3B	HR	RBI	BB	HBP	SH	SF	SO	SB	CS	SLG	OBP
Hays, Austin	R-R	6-1	195	7-5-95	.268	.385	.233	14	56	9	15	5	0	3	11	5	0	0	0	11	3	1	.518	.328
Hoiles, Dalton	R-R	6-1	170	4-30-96	.000	.000	.000	2	4	0	0	0	0	0	0	0	0	0	0	4	0	0	.000	.000
Jarrett, Zach	R-R	6-4	220	12-8-94	.207	.200	.212	26	92	4	19	5	0	0	9	4	1	0	1	25	1	1	.261	.245
Levy, Stuart	R-R	6-2	185	8-21-92	.250	.333	.231	6	16	4	4	0	0	2	3	3	1	0	0	4	0	0	.625	.400
McCoy, Mason	R-R	6-0	175	3-31-95	.266	.227	.281	105	429	60	114	13	7	2	31	36	3	2	1	84	10	3	.343	.326
McKenna, Ryan	R-R	5-11	185	2-14-97	.232	.269	.215	135	488	78	113	26	6	9	54	59	7	9	4	121	25	11	.365	.321
Miller, Sean	R-R	5-11	175	10-10-94	.093	.100	.091	18	54	5	5	0	0	0	1	1	0	1	0	20	0	0	.093	.109
Mullins, Cedric	B-L	5-8	175	10-1-94	.271	.250	.279	51	199	35	54	11	0	5	18	22	1	0	4	31	20	3	.402	.341
Nichting, T.J.	B-R	5-11	188	1-13-95	.256	.247	.259	105	352	40	90	18	3	6	34	16	4	2	4	70	7	2	.375	.293
Palmeiro, Preston	L-R	5-11	180	1-22-95	.237	.284	.220	105	350	50	83	21	1	5	42	26	1	3	4	85	2	1	.346	.289
Perez, Carlos	R-R	6-0	210	10-29-90	.251	.313	.228	94	350	34	88	22	0	14	60	20	8	1	6	52	0	0	.434	.302
Reyes, Jomar	R-R	6-3	220	2-20-97	.000	--	.000	1	1	0	0	0	0	0	0	0	0	0	0	0	0	0	.000	.000
Rifaela, Ademar	L-L	5-10	180	11-20-94	.257	.156	.299	60	218	24	56	12	3	8	33	17	2	0	2	67	1	1	.450	.314
Ripken, Ryan	L-L	6-6	205	7-26-93	.282	.368	.262	30	103	6	29	5	1	1	9	4	1	0	0	24	0	0	.379	.315
Ruiz, Rio	L-R	6-1	215	5-22-94	.000	.000	.000	2	8	0	0	0	0	0	0	0	1	0	0	1	0	0	.000	.111
Stewart, DJ	L-R	6-0	230	11-30-93	.308	.000	.400	4	13	5	4	1	0	1	6	3	1	0	0	2	0	0	.615	.471
Torres, Alexis	R-R	6-0	183	12-12-97	.255	.200	.290	15	51	4	13	1	0	2	7	3	1	0	0	17	0	0	.392	.309
Trumbo, Mark	R-R	6-4	225	1-16-86	.231	.200	.250	3	1	1	3	1	0	0	0	0	0	0	0	3	0	0	.308	.231
Valentin, Jesmuel	B-R	5-9	180	5-12-94	.256	.279	.247	115	403	47	103	24	3	8	46	45	4	1	3	95	10	7	.390	.334
Vielma, Engelb	B-R	5-11	155	6-22-94	.222	.000	.667	3	9	3	2	0	0	1	2	0	1	0	2	0	0	.222	.364
Wynns, Austin	R-R	6-2	205	12-10-90	.294	.200	.333	4	17	2	5	2	0	0	4	3	0	0	1	4	0	0	.412	.400
Yahn, Willy	R-R	5-11	185	11-7-95	.223	.241	.217	32	112	11	25	9	0	0	6	3	0	0	1	23	1	0	.304	.241

Pitching	B-T	HT	WT	DOB	W	L	ERA	G	GS	CG	SV	IP	H	R	ER	HR	BB	SO	AVG	vLH	vRH	K/9	BB/9
Alvarado, Cristian	R-R	6-3	175	9-20-94	3	3	2.66	40	0	0	13	74	51	27	22	7	18	70	.189	.199	.180	8.48	2.18
Araujo, Pedro	R-R	6-3	215	7-2-93	1	3	3.63	24	0	0	0	40	26	20	16	7	19	40	.183	.234	.141	9.08	4.31
Baumann, Michael	R-R	6-4	225	9-10-95	6	2	2.31	13	11	2	1	70	45	19	18	2	21	65	.186	.172	.200	8.36	2.70
Bleier, Richard	L-L	6-3	215	4-16-87	0	0	0.00	2	1	0	0	2	2	0	0	0	1	1	.286	1.000	.167	4.50	4.50
Chleborad, Tanner	R-R	6-6	185	11-4-92	1	2	3.74	11	0	0	0	22	19	12	9	2	6	24	.226	.282	.178	9.97	2.49
Erwin, Tyler	L-L	6-0	185	8-29-94	3	3	2.43	36	0	0	8	41	40	15	11	0	15	35	.255	.318	.209	7.75	3.32
Flaa, Jay	R-R	6-3	225	6-10-92	0	2	2.81	11	0	0	1	16	17	8	5	1	6	28	.270	.214	.314	15.75	3.38
Gonzalez, Brian	R-L	6-3	230	10-25-95	0	2	4.32	18	1	0	1	42	33	21	20	9	11	35	.209	.203	.214	7.56	2.38
Gonzalez, Luis	L-L	6-2	170	1-17-92	2	1	4.19	15	0	0	0	19	19	12	9	2	6	26	.253	.125	.314	12.10	2.79
Grover, Taylor	R-R	6-3	195	4-22-91	0	1	5.27	12	0	0	0	14	17	10	8	2	5	12	.309	.267	.360	7.90	3.29
Harvey, Hunter	R-R	6-3	175	12-9-94	2	5	5.19	14	11	0	1	59	63	40	34	14	21	61	.274	.279	.266	9.31	3.20
Herb, Tyler	R-R	6-3	200	4-28-92	4	3	3.95	10	10	0	0	55	48	30	24	5	20	45	.231	.286	.199	7.41	3.29
Jimenez, Francisco	R-R	6-1	160	10-4-94	5	1	2.82	26	0	0	0	51	48	20	16	6	13	50	.246	.207	.274	8.82	2.29
Karns, Nate	R-R	6-3	225	11-25-87	0	0	9.00	2	1	0	0	3	4	3	3	0	2	1	.444	.500	.333	3.00	6.00
Klimek, Steven	L-R	6-3	205	4-4-94	2	1	1.69	13	1	0	0	21	15	8	4	0	13	22	.192	.097	.255	9.28	5.48
Kline, Branden	R-R	6-3	210	9-29-91	1	0	0.00	3	0	0	0	3	1	0	0	0	2	4	.125	.333	.000	12.00	6.00
Kremer, Dean	R-R	6-3	180	1-7-96	9	4	2.98	15	15	0	0	85	75	29	28	9	29	87	.239	.240	.238	9.25	3.08
Lee, Chris	L-L	6-3	180	8-17-92	0	0	4.50	1	0	0	0	2	1	1	1	1	1	3	.143	.250	.000	13.50	4.50
Lowther, Zac	L-L	6-2	235	4-30-96	13	7	2.55	26	26	0	0	148	102	46	42	8	63	154	.197	.204	.194	9.36	3.83
Molina, Marcos	R-R	6-3	225	3-8-95	4	6	4.36	15	14	0	0	85	85	46	41	15	27	58	.263	.259	.268	6.17	2.87
Muckenhirn, Zach	L-L	6-1	185	2-27-94	3	5	3.21	37	0	0	5	53	39	22	19	3	24	65	.203	.227	.188	10.97	4.05
Naughton, Tim	R-R	6-3	195	11-14-95	0	0	9.00	1	0	0	0	1	1	1	1	0	0	1	.250	.500	.000	9.00	0.00
Pop, Zach	R-R	6-4	220	9-20-96	1	0	0.84	8	0	0	0	11	7	1	1	0	4	11	.184	.177	.191	9.28	3.38
Sedlock, Cody	R-R	6-3	190	6-19-95	1	2	3.71	9	6	0	1	34	30	15	14	3	20	34	.238	.256	.229	9.00	5.29
Tate, Dillon	R-R	6-2	195	5-1-94	2	3	3.48	17	2	0	5	34	28	14	13	4	9	30	.224	.237	.204	8.02	2.41
Wells, Alex	L-L	6-1	190	2-27-97	8	6	2.95	24	24	1	0	137	123	50	45	10	24	105	.236	.225	.242	6.88	1.57
Zimmermann, Bruce	L-L	6-2	215	2-9-95	5	3	2.58	18	17	2	0	101	88	34	29	9	34	101	.227	.188	.246	8.97	3.02

Fielding

Catcher	PCT	G	PO	A	E	DP	PB
Brockmeyer	.967	3	27	2	1	0	0
Cervenka	.987	36	266	37	4	1	1
Cumberland	.995	27	211	4	1	0	1
Levy	.979	6	44	2	1	0	2
Perez	.991	67	584	56	6	2	2
Wynns	1.000	3	22	1	0	0	0

First Base	PCT	G	PO	A	E	DP
Brockmeyer	.978	5	42	2	1	3
Evans	1.000	2	15	1	0	1
Feliz	1.000	1	5	1	0	1
Palmeiro	.994	102	733	56	5	56
Perez	.992	16	115	4	1	8
Ripken	.985	17	128	3	2	7
Valentin	1.000	1	1	1	0	0

Second Base	PCT	G	PO	A	E	DP
Bannon	.981	38	63	90	3	28
Clare	1.000	23	34	52	0	11
Feliz	1.000	20	28	38	0	9
McCoy	1.000	16	29	39	0	5

	PCT	G	PO	A	E	DP
Miller	1.000	5	4	7	0	3
Torres	.912	9	13	18	3	4
Valentin	.935	32	65	51	8	12
Vielma	1.000	1	1	3	0	0
Yahn	1.000	2	3	6	0	2

Third Base	PCT	G	PO	A	E	DP
Bannon	.924	69	42	104	12	3
Clare	1.000	7	6	6	0	1
Feliz	.889	8	5	11	2	2
Reyes	.000	1	0	0	0	0
Ruiz	.800	1	1	3	1	1
Torres	.818	5	6	3	2	0
Valentin	.930	28	22	44	5	4
Vielma	.000	1	0	0	0	0
Yahn	.955	27	11	52	3	6

Shortstop	PCT	G	PO	A	E	DP
Clare	.750	1	1	2	1	1
Feliz	1.000	3	2	2	0	0
McCoy	.973	87	98	192	8	35
Miller	.925	13	18	31	4	10
Torres	1.000	1	0	3	0	1

	PCT	G	PO	A	E	DP
Valentin	.969	38	54	70	4	13
Vielma	1.000	1	0	3	0	1

Outfield	PCT	G	PO	A	E	DP
Billingsley	1.000	8	11	0	0	0
Diaz	.984	60	119	2	2	2
Feliz	1.000	1	4	0	0	0
Hays	1.000	11	27	1	0	0
Hoiles	1.000	2	5	1	0	1
Jarrett	.976	19	40	1	1	0
McKenna	.993	128	286	11	2	1
Mullins	.974	48	110	3	3	0
Nichting	.995	93	194	7	1	2
Rifaela	.989	46	87	1	1	0
Stewart	.000	2	0	0	0	0
Valentin	1.000	17	32	0	0	0
Yahn	.000	2	0	0	0	0

FREDERICK KEYS
CAROLINA LEAGUE

HIGH CLASS A

BALTIMORE ORIOLES

Batting	B-T	HT	WT	DOB	AVG	vLH	vRH	G	AB	R	H	2B	3B	HR	RBI	BB	HBP	SH	SF	SO	SB	CS	SLG	OBP
Billingsley, Cole	L-L	5-10	165	5-29-94	.282	.286	.281	77	287	40	81	15	0	2	22	27	4	5	0	44	15	6	.355	.352
Breazeale, Ben	L-R	6-0	208	10-21-94	.167	.100	.192	12	36	3	6	0	0	0	1	7	0	0	0	9	0	0	.167	.302
Carrillo, Jean	R-R	6-0	200	6-16-97	.205	.258	.181	64	210	18	43	5	0	0	19	23	3	1	1	68	1	0	.229	.291
Clare, Chris	R-R	6-2	175	11-24-94	.231	.167	.265	18	52	5	12	2	0	0	5	7	2	0	0	12	0	0	.269	.344
Craport, Trevor	R-R	5-11	201	8-12-96	.222	.242	.209	68	234	30	52	15	1	4	38	19	5	0	4	41	4	1	.346	.290
Cumberland, Brett	B-R	5-11	205	6-25-95	.273	.273	.273	15	44	7	12	6	0	1	3	7	5	0	0	9	0	0	.477	.429
Diaz, Yusniel	R-R	6-1	195	10-7-96	.273	.600	.177	6	22	0	6	0	0	0	2	3	0	0	0	7	0	0	.273	.360
Dorrian, Patrick	L-R	6-2	188	6-26-96	.233	.130	.266	51	189	22	44	7	1	4	24	13	0	0	2	50	0	0	.344	.279
Escarra, J.C.	L-R	6-3	205	4-24-95	.235	.157	.270	127	442	48	104	16	1	13	57	52	9	0	4	76	2	0	.364	.325
Fajardo, Daniel	R-R	6-1	170	11-19-94	.232	.243	.243	36	112	10	26	6	0	1	12	12	0	0	0	15	0	0	.313	.307
Grenier, Cadyn	R-R	5-11	188	10-31-96	.208	.125	.245	24	77	11	16	4	1	1	4	11	4	0	0	31	2	1	.325	.337
Gudino, Yeltsin	R-R	6-0	150	1-17-97	.256	.195	.288	76	250	27	64	8	0	1	23	22	2	1	1	40	1	0	.300	.320
Hays, Austin	R-R	6-1	195	7-5-95	.162	.118	.200	9	37	3	6	0	0	2	6	1	1	0	1	11	0	0	.324	.200
Jarrett, Zach	R-R	6-4	220	12-8-94	.286	.273	.292	96	353	53	101	14	1	11	39	27	5	0	2	84	7	2	.425	.344
Levy, Stuart	R-R	6-2	185	8-21-92	.187	.267	.148	29	91	8	17	6	0	0	6	9	0	0	0	31	1	0	.253	.260
McCoy, Mason	R-R	6-0	175	3-31-95	.379	.400	.366	27	116	21	44	9	0	2	17	8	0	0	1	16	3	0	.509	.416
Miller, Sean	R-R	5-11	175	10-10-94	.270	.285	.263	96	333	25	90	12	4	0	22	15	1	6	4	68	11	3	.330	.300
Moesquit, Kirvin	B-R	5-8	165	3-10-95	.237	.273	.216	53	177	19	42	11	3	0	11	17	1	1	2	52	11	5	.333	.305
Neustrom, Robert	L-L	6-2	208	11-12-96	.238	.313	.211	31	122	10	29	7	0	2	10	8	0	0	0	30	0	1	.344	.285
Ortega, Irving	R-R	6-2	165	10-30-96	.250	.167	.286	6	21	0	5	1	0	0	1	0	0	0	0	4	1	0	.300	.286
Reyes, Jomar	R-R	6-3	220	2-20-97	.283	.257	.296	100	389	35	110	24	0	8	47	11	10	0	0	73	1	1	.406	.320
Ring, Jake	L-L	5-11	175	8-11-94	.204	.191	.208	53	167	26	34	5	2	6	15	21	3	1	0	58	1	1	.365	.304
Ringhofer, Luke	L-R	6-1	210	2-19-96	--	--	--	1	0	1	0	0	0	0	0	1	0	0	0	0	0	0	--	1.000
Ripken, Ryan	L-L	6-6	205	7-26-93	.273	.280	.270	48	176	18	48	10	1	5	24	8	2	0	1	46	0	1	.426	.310
Robertson, Will	R-R	6-2	190	3-2-95	.205	.275	.148	40	112	15	23	0	3	7	15	3	0	3	34	0	0	.304	.308
Thorburn, Robbie	L-R	5-11	175	3-30-95	.218	.346	.157	49	170	19	37	6	0	2	9	12	2	3	0	49	7	4	.288	.277
Yahn, Willy	R-R	5-11	185	11-7-95	.296	.316	.286	56	216	22	64	13	0	5	35	5	2	1	3	30	1	5	.426	.314

Pitching	B-T	HT	WT	DOB	W	L	ERA	G	GS	CG	SV	IP	H	R	ER	HR	BB	SO	AVG	vLH	vRH	K/9	BB/9
Almengo, Diogenes	R-R	6-2	190	6-2-95	5	5	3.90	35	0	0	13	55	43	27	24	7	40	66	.212	.180	.237	10.73	6.51
Baumann, Michael	R-R	6-4	225	9-10-95	1	4	3.83	11	11	0	0	54	40	24	23	2	24	77	.203	.165	.229	12.83	4.00
Bishop, Cameron	L-L	6-4	215	2-14-96	2	9	4.67	24	22	0	0	114	113	62	59	10	61	109	.261	.243	.269	8.63	4.83
Bleier, Richard	L-L	6-3	215	4-16-87	1	0	4.50	2	0	0	0	2	3	1	1	0	0	1	.333	.250	.400	4.50	0.00
Burke, Scott	R-R	6-3	200	6-2-94	2	2	3.38	32	1	0	2	61	54	25	23	10	18	49	.233	.226	.237	7.19	2.64
Conroy, Ryan	R-R	6-3	190	12-31-96	0	0	0.00	2	0	0	0	3	2	0	0	0	2	1	.200	.000	.333	3.00	6.00
De La Rosa, Matt	L-R	6-2	210	11-15-93	0	1	33.75	1	0	0	0	1	5	5	5	1	1	0	.556	.500	.600	0.00	6.75
Dietz, Matthias	R-R	6-5	220	9-20-95	1	8	10.29	18	2	0	0	35	29	46	40	2	51	39	.223	.242	.206	10.03	13.11
Echevarria, Juan	R-R	6-3	195	6-25-97	0	0	0.00	1	0	0	0	1	0	0	0	0	2	1	.000	.000	.000	9.00	18.00
Hall, DL	L-L	6-2	195	9-19-98	4	5	3.46	19	17	0	1	81	53	33	31	3	54	116	.189	.167	.201	12.94	6.02
Hammonds, Matthew	R-L	6-4	205	5-23-95	0	0	81.00	1	0	0	0	1	1	6	6	0	5	0	.333	1.000	.000	0.00	67.50
Hanifee, Brenan	R-R	6-5	215	5-29-98	9	10	4.60	24	22	2	0	129	126	73	66	12	57	78	.259	.265	.254	5.44	3.98
Hayes, Reed	R-R	6-3	185	3-17-95	1	3	6.19	10	0	0	1	16	21	13	11	2	11	21	.318	.370	.282	11.81	6.19
Jimenez, Francisco	R-R	6-1	160	10-4-94	2	1	1.29	7	0	0	1	21	12	3	3	2	8	15	.167	.177	.158	6.43	3.43
Joyner, Tyler	R-R	6-4	225	5-10-96	0	2	7.50	11	0	0	0	18	17	16	15	3	7	26	.246	.308	.209	13.00	3.50
Karns, Nate	R-R	6-3	225	11-25-87	0	0	10.13	2	2	0	0	3	3	3	3	0	3	1	.300	.000	.375	3.38	10.13
Klimek, Steven	L-R	6-3	205	4-4-94	4	1	2.48	17	0	0	0	33	22	10	9	0	18	31	.190	.184	.194	8.54	4.96
Knight, Blaine	R-R	6-3	165	6-28-96	1	12	6.13	18	17	1	0	84	89	67	57	10	39	56	.273	.247	.298	6.02	4.20
Kremer, Dean	R-R	6-3	180	1-7-96	0	0	0.00	2	0	0	0	10	6	0	0	0	4	14	.177	.188	.167	13.03	3.72
Lebron, David	R-R	5-11	190	9-7-93	2	6	4.57	22	18	0	0	83	85	51	42	6	47	92	.264	.292	.238	10.02	5.12
Lovegrove, Kieran	R-R	6-4	185	7-28-94	0	2	9.95	5	0	0	0	6	5	7	7	0	10	9	.217	.200	.231	12.79	14.21
Matson, Zach	L-L	6-3	225	10-24-95	1	2	5.01	17	0	0	1	32	29	21	18	5	19	35	.236	.241	.234	9.74	5.29
Ming, Cameron	L-L	6-1	177	5-2-96	2	3	5.47	23	0	0	2	49	62	34	30	9	18	41	.310	.213	.353	7.48	3.28
Naughton, Tim	R-R	6-3	195	11-14-95	0	1	2.08	24	0	0	8	22	23	6	5	0	17	30	.267	.241	.281	12.46	7.06
Peluffo, Jhon	R-R	6-3	140	6-16-97	0	0	0.87	3	0	0	0	10	5	1	1	0	4	12	.143	.091	.167	10.45	3.48
Peralta, Ofelky	R-R	6-5	195	4-20-97	3	3	5.48	10	9	0	0	48	51	29	29	6	26	40	.282	.319	.255	7.55	4.91
Perez, Luis	R-R	6-0	175	5-3-95	6	2	2.93	32	3	0	3	80	65	32	26	6	34	69	.224	.225	.224	7.76	3.83
Seabrooke, Travis	R-L	6-6	205	9-16-95	2	2	7.50	14	0	0	2	24	30	23	20	7	11	22	.316	.385	.290	8.25	4.13
Sedlock, Cody	R-R	6-3	190	6-19-95	4	1	2.36	13	10	1	0	61	38	16	16	4	26	66	.181	.149	.207	9.74	3.84
Tate, Dillon	R-R	6-2	195	5-1-94	0	0	5.40	1	1	0	0	2	3	2	1	0	3	.375	.000	.429	16.20	0.00

Fielding

Catcher	PCT	G	PO	A	E	DP	PB
Breazeale	1.000	6	46	1	0	0	1
Carrillo	.992	60	472	47	4	3	7
Cumberland	1.000	8	71	5	0	0	0
Fajardo	.981	36	271	31	6	5	6
Levy	.986	29	266	18	4	1	0

First Base	PCT	G	PO	A	E	DP
Craport	.977	11	81	4	2	8
Dorrian	1.000	1	7	1	0	2
Escarra	.990	112	800	53	9	78
Ripken	1.000	15	114	3	0	9

Second Base	PCT	G	PO	A	E	DP
Clare	.981	16	22	29	1	8

	PCT	G	PO	A	E	DP
Dorrian	1.000	18	33	31	0	8
Gudino	.973	39	61	85	4	23
McCoy	.970	10	11	21	1	4
Miller	.971	34	68	68	4	16
Yahn	.981	25	47	54	2	17

Third Base	PCT	G	PO	A	E	DP
Craport	.000	1	0	0	0	0
Dorrian	.910	30	25	56	8	2
Ortega	.909	5	1	9	1	0
Reyes	.940	81	55	134	12	23
Yahn	.959	25	7	40	2	5

Shortstop	PCT	G	PO	A	E	DP
Dorrian	.875	1	4	3	1	1
Grenier	.964	22	24	56	3	8

	PCT	G	PO	A	E	DP
Gudino	.945	37	41	80	7	20
McCoy	.968	17	25	36	2	9
Miller	.967	61	61	146	7	26

Outfield	PCT	G	PO	A	E	DP
Billingsley	1.000	74	158	7	0	2
Craport	.986	45	61	9	1	1
Diaz	1.000	5	9	0	0	0
Hays	1.000	7	12	0	0	0
Jarrett	.983	89	160	11	3	2
Moesquit	.959	47	69	1	3	0
Neustrom	1.000	28	48	0	0	0
Ring	1.000	49	94	2	0	2
Robertson	1.000	24	39	1	0	1
Thorburn	.990	49	95	7	1	0

DELMARVA SHOREBIRDS   LOW CLASS A
SOUTH ATLANTIC LEAGUE

Batting	B-T	HT	WT	DOB	AVG	vLH	vRH	G	AB	R	H	2B	3B	HR	RBI	BB	HBP	SH	SF	SO	SB	CS	SLG	OBP
Becker, Branden	L-R	6-1	175	9-13-96	.286	.333	.263	8	28	2	8	3	0	0	6	3	0	1	1	5	0	0	.393	.344
Breazeale, Ben	L-R	6-0	208	10-21-94	.221	.193	.230	66	231	25	51	9	0	1	23	29	2	1	0	55	0	1	.273	.313
Curran, Seamus	L-R	6-6	245	9-6-97	.224	.205	.229	119	420	58	94	14	0	17	60	47	4	0	3	125	1	1	.379	.306
Encarnacion, JC	R-R	6-3	195	1-17-98	.240	.255	.236	120	450	53	108	19	3	9	50	28	6	0	1	145	12	3	.356	.293
Fajardo, Daniel	R-R	6-1	170	11-19-94	.258	.393	.228	42	155	15	40	3	0	1	18	5	1	1	0	16	1	0	.297	.286
Ferguson, Jaylen	R-R	6-2	180	7-21-97	.296	.238	.312	24	98	13	29	6	4	0	18	7	0	0	0	25	8	1	.439	.343
Fontana, Shayne	L-L	6-2	195	6-21-97	.254	.222	.259	17	63	10	16	5	3	0	8	6	2	0	0	15	3	1	.429	.338
Fregia, Andrew	R-R	6-1	170	12-18-96	.169	.118	.188	19	65	6	11	1	0	0	2	6	1	0	0	28	4	1	.185	.250
Grenier, Cadyn	R-R	5-11	188	10-31-96	.253	.221	.263	82	308	49	78	18	3	7	39	48	5	0	3	107	5	1	.399	.360
Hall, Adam	R-R	6-0	170	5-22-99	.298	.340	.286	122	463	78	138	22	4	5	45	45	22	1	3	117	33	9	.395	.385
Horvath, Nick	R-L	5-11	200	7-13-96	.200	.265	.176	113	375	53	75	17	2	7	40	53	10	2	3	113	17	8	.312	.313
Lantigua, Edison	L-L	6-0	175	1-9-97	.189	.063	.211	33	111	10	21	6	0	2	12	7	1	0	1	35	0	0	.297	.242
Neustrom, Robert	L-L	6-2	208	11-12-96	.285	.325	.273	47	179	27	51	13	1	5	36	22	2	1	3	37	5	0	.453	.364
Ogren, Ryne	R-R	6-1	180	4-11-97	.253	.200	.268	92	308	37	78	13	2	1	31	33	10	1	2	75	5	1	.318	.343
2-team total (13 West Virginia)					.243	.169	.264	105	354	42	86	14	2	3	36	37	10	1	2	86	5	1	.319	.330
Rizer, Johnny	L-L	6-0	192	11-7-96	.310	.259	.322	36	142	18	44	6	2	1	22	9	2	0	0	27	2	1	.401	.360
Roberts, Cody	R-R	6-1	195	6-16-96	.241	.125	.278	51	166	20	40	4	1	0	21	21	1	0	4	43	0	0	.277	.323
Robertson, Will	R-R	6-2	190	3-2-95	.273	.367	.245	38	132	22	36	10	0	3	18	18	2	0	1	30	0	0	.417	.366
Rutschman, Adley	B-R	6-2	216	2-6-98	.154	.000	.200	12	39	5	6	1	0	2	8	6	0	0	1	9	0	0	.333	.261
Thorburn, Robbie	L-R	5-11	175	3-30-95	.278	.351	.260	47	187	28	52	11	1	4	14	7	4	0	0	51	4	4	.412	.318
Torres, Alexis	R-R	6-0	183	12-12-97	.208	.244	.199	64	212	25	44	14	2	0	13	16	0	0	0	72	0	0	.293	.263
Truitt, Trey	R-R	6-1	190	6-29-96	.000	.000	.000	1	4	0	0	0	0	0	0	0	0	0	0	1	0	0	.000	.000
Turchin, Doran	R-R	6-2	195	7-7-97	.207	.203	.209	88	314	45	65	15	4	6	46	43	9	1	4	106	5	3	.338	.316
Watson, Zach	R-R	6-0	160	6-25-97	.230	.158	.244	16	60	9	13	5	0	3	8	6	1	0	1	13	0	0	.450	.294
Welk, Toby	R-R	6-2	205	5-2-97	.250	.400	.222	9	32	2	8	1	0	0	2	4	0	0	0	8	1	0	.281	.333

Pitching	B-T	HT	WT	DOB	W	L	ERA	G	GS	CG	SV	IP	H	R	ER	HR	BB	SO	AVG	vLH	vRH	K/9	BB/9
Alejandro, Jose	R-R	6-3	200	6-20-95	0	0	0.00	1	0	0	0	2	0	0	0	0	2	0	.000	.000	.000	0.00	9.00
Bautista, Felix	R-R	6-5	190	6-20-95	2	2	3.41	23	0	0	4	32	25	17	12	2	18	43	.214	.325	.156	12.22	5.12
Conroy, Ryan	R-R	6-3	190	12-31-96	1	1	2.70	2	1	0	0	7	7	4	2	0	4	2	.269	.308	.231	2.70	5.40
Constante, Marlon	R-R	5-11	185	7-5-96	0	0	0.00	4	0	0	0	4	0	0	0	0	0	3	.000	.000	.000	6.75	0.00
De La Rosa, Matt	L-R	6-2	210	11-15-93	4	2	3.34	38	0	0	3	65	51	25	24	4	34	74	.219	.195	.232	10.30	4.73
Echevarria, Juan	R-R	6-3	195	6-25-97	0	0	2.43	14	0	0	1	30	23	10	8	2	8	24	.211	.211	.211	7.28	2.43
Fenter, Gray	R-R	6-0	200	1-25-96	8	2	1.81	22	17	0	0	94	61	24	19	4	43	123	.185	.216	.163	11.73	4.10
Garcia, Ruben	R-R	6-4	220	8-2-96	1	3	2.15	18	0	0	8	29	21	8	7	1	10	42	.198	.243	.174	12.89	3.07
Gruener, Nick	R-R	6-0	185	5-16-95	0	1	8.10	11	1	0	0	23	33	23	21	4	10	11	.347	.457	.283	3.86	3.86
Guance, Hector	R-R	6-6	200	7-12-95	9	6	4.33	24	22	0	0	108	87	60	52	4	66	94	.224	.253	.204	7.83	5.50
Hammonds, Matthew	L-L	6-4	205	5-23-95	5	2	3.92	37	1	0	2	85	67	39	37	10	46	82	.216	.226	.212	8.68	4.87
Hayes, Reed	R-R	6-3	185	3-17-95	2	0	1.10	11	0	0	3	16	7	5	2	0	4	12	.125	.083	.156	6.61	2.20
Joyner, Tyler	R-R	6-4	225	5-10-96	5	0	1.98	23	0	0	8	59	36	16	13	2	19	59	.177	.260	.130	9.00	2.90
Knight, Blaine	R-R	6-3	165	6-28-96	3	0	0.68	5	5	0	0	27	11	2	2	1	4	33	.125	.119	.130	11.14	1.35
Litscher, Dallas	R-R	6-8	250	1-10-96	2	2	4.50	7	6	0	0	34	35	20	17	3	15	43	.263	.185	.317	11.38	3.97
Matson, Zach	L-L	6-3	205	10-28-96	4	0	2.55	17	0	0	4	35	21	10	10	3	19	63	.168	.133	.188	16.05	4.84
Miller, Jalen	R-R	5-10	182	3-15-93	0	0	6.75	1	0	0	0	8	7	6	6	0	10	12	.226	.375	.174	13.50	11.25
Naughton, Tim	R-R	6-3	195	11-14-95	3	3	3.10	22	0	0	12	29	24	14	10	1	11	44	.216	.306	.173	13.66	3.41
Peluffo, Jhon	R-R	6-3	140	6-16-97	1	4	2.78	30	0	0	5	58	37	24	18	2	27	55	.228	.205	.163	8.49	4.17
Peralta, Ofelky	R-R	6-5	195	4-20-97	6	3	3.03	15	14	0	1	68	51	26	23	4	33	79	.207	.299	.156	10.40	4.35
Rodriguez, Grayson	L-R	6-5	220	11-16-99	10	4	2.68	20	20	0	0	94	57	30	28	4	36	129	.171	.182	.165	12.35	3.45
Rodriguez, Yelin	L-L	6-3	200	11-3-98	0	0	0.00	1	0	0	0	3	0	2	0	0	3	3	.000	.000	.000	10.13	10.13
Rom, Drew	L-L	6-2	170	12-15-99	6	3	2.93	21	15	0	1	95	83	36	31	5	33	122	.228	.179	.245	11.52	3.12
Roth, Nick	R-R	5-10	175	8-28-96	0	0	4.50	1	0	0	0	2	1	1	1	0	1	2	.167	--	.167	9.00	4.50
Stauffer, Adam	R-R	6-7	240	1-13-99	0	0	0.96	9	3	0	0	19	8	3	2	0	11	31	.118	.172	.077	14.95	5.30
Vespi, Nick	L-L	6-3	215	10-10-95	8	6	3.16	23	16	0	1	91	72	37	32	5	30	100	.215	.149	.241	9.89	2.97
Wilson, Ryan	L-L	6-1	190	11-6-96	6	5	2.80	17	17	0	0	93	73	33	29	6	29	105	.214	.239	.207	10.13	2.80

Fielding

Catcher	PCT	G	PO	A	E	DP	PB
Breazeale	.993	57	545	52	4	0	11
Fajardo	1.000	38	363	36	0	3	5
Ogren	1.000	1	2	0	0	0	0
Roberts	.993	41	390	26	3	0	4
Rutschman	.985	6	60	4	1	0	0

First Base	PCT	G	PO	A	E	DP
Becker	.977	5	42	1	1	5
Breazeale	.957	2	22	0	1	2
Curran	.997	115	831	58	3	62
Fregia	.941	3	16	0	1	0
Ogren	.875	2	13	1	2	2
Roberts	.000	1	0	0	0	0
Torres	1.000	11	86	7	0	4

Second Base	PCT	G	PO	A	E	DP
Becker	.667	1	1	1	1	0
Fregia	1.000	3	6	3	0	2
Grenier	.981	26	48	53	2	10
Hall	.987	39	60	87	2	18
Ogren	.977	42	60	70	3	15
Torres	.925	29	44	54	8	14

Third Base	PCT	G	PO	A	E	DP
Becker	1.000	1	0	3	0	0
Encarnacion	.907	87	65	141	21	10
Fregia	1.000	6	8	6	0	0
Ogren	.981	31	20	33	1	2
Roberts	.000	1	0	0	0	0
Torres	.893	11	5	20	3	0
Welk	.818	6	2	7	2	0

Shortstop	PCT	G	PO	A	E	DP
Grenier	.959	54	62	149	9	28
Hall	.950	79	68	177	13	24
Ogren	.957	6	8	14	1	3

Outfield	PCT	G	PO	A	E	DP
Ferguson	.976	18	39	1	1	0
Fontana	.952	16	19	1	1	0
Fregia	.800	6	4	0	1	0
Horvath	.987	112	228	6	3	2
Lantigua	.977	26	43	0	1	0
Neustrom	1.000	42	70	3	0	0
Ogren	1.000	2	1	0	0	0
Rizer	1.000	35	58	2	0	0
Robertson	1.000	23	27	2	0	0
Thorburn	.969	46	61	2	2	0
Truitt	1.000	1	4	0	0	0
Turchin	1.000	81	157	8	0	1
Watson	1.000	15	28	1	0	0

ABERDEEN IRONBIRDS

SHORT SEASON

NEW YORK-PENN LEAGUE

Batting	B-T	HT	WT	DOB	AVG	vLH	vRH	G	AB	R	H	2B	3B	HR	RBI	BB	HBP	SH	SF	SO	SB	CS	SLG	OBP
Cannon, Jordan	R-R	6-3	210	11-28-96	.205	.600	.129	13	39	4	8	4	1	0	4	2	2	1	1	19	1	0	.359	.273
Carmona, Jean	R-B	6-1	183	10-31-99	.224	.300	.213	25	85	8	19	2	1	0	4	6	2	0	0	31	1	0	.271	.290
Cervenka, Martin	R-R	6-4	225	8-3-92	.125	.000	.133	5	16	1	2	1	0	1	3	3	1	0	0	5	0	0	.375	.300
Cumberland, Brett	B-R	5-11	205	6-25-95	.286	.500	.125	4	14	0	4	0	0	0	1	1	2	0	0	4	0	0	.286	.412
Daschbach, Andrew	R-R	6-3	225	10-22-97	.222	.188	.230	47	158	16	35	8	0	3	25	25	6	0	0	47	0	1	.329	.349
Diaz, Yusniel	R-R	6-1	195	10-7-96	.333	.333	.333	3	9	0	3	3	0	0	1	1	0	0	0	1	0	0	.667	.455
Evans, Ian	R-R	5-11	185	7-10-96	.232	.250	.238	39	125	12	29	3	1	0	12	14	2	0	1	15	2	0	.272	.314
Ferguson, Jaylen	R-R	6-2	180	7-21-97	.274	.333	.266	19	73	17	20	2	3	6	14	6	1	0	0	23	6	2	.630	.338
Fisher, Clay	R-R	6-1	175	3-31-96	.217	.214	.225	48	161	16	35	7	1	3	18	7	9	3	1	45	7	2	.329	.287
Fontana, Shayne	L-L	6-2	195	6-21-97	.250	.000	.300	19	72	13	18	3	1	1	4	6	2	0	1	12	6	0	.361	.321
Fregia, Andrew	R-R	6-1	170	12-18-96	.247	.450	.213	46	142	11	35	9	0	3	20	9	3	0	3	58	4	1	.373	.299
Graham, Tristan	R-R	6-4	215	7-21-95	.229	.300	.217	22	70	9	16	3	1	1	6	5	1	0	0	20	1	0	.343	.290
Handley, Maverick	R-R	5-11	205	3-10-98	.202	.250	.194	41	114	20	23	4	0	0	4	11	5	0	1	47	2	1	.237	.298
Hays, Austin	R-R	6-1	195	7-5-95	.278	.000	.313	5	18	5	5	2	0	2	4	1	0	0	0	1	0	1	.722	.350
Hoiles, Dalton	R-R	6-1	170	4-30-96	.221	.273	.214	32	95	18	21	2	0	3	11	13	9	1	0	22	3	0	.337	.368
Janvrin, Mason	R-R	6-2	180	3-3-98	.254	.250	.255	16	63	10	16	3	0	0	7	1	0	0	0	17	3	3	.302	.266
Lantigua, Edison	L-L	6-0	175	1-9-97	.000	.000	.000	3	9	0	0	0	0	0	0	2	0	0	0	4	1	0	.000	.182
Lewis, Craig	L-L	5-10	190	5-22-97	.216	.000	.229	12	37	4	8	2	0	0	3	1	0	0	1	5	2	0	.270	.231
McLeod, Zach	R-R	6-0	200	1-19-96	.000	.000	.000	3	8	1	0	0	0	0	0	2	1	0	2	3	0	0	.000	.167
Montes, Juan	R-R	6-2	185	5-15-95	.258	.250	.304	14	31	8	8	2	0	0	4	5	3	0	0	7	1	1	.323	.410
Murphy, Alex	R-R	5-11	210	10-5-94	.259	.667	.208	10	27	2	7	1	0	1	5	8	0	0	0	8	0	0	.407	.429
Neustrom, Robert	L-L	6-2	208	11-12-96	.063	.000	.077	4	16	0	1	0	0	0	1	0	0	0	0	5	0	0	.063	.063
Ortega, Irving	R-R	6-2	165	10-30-96	.205	.154	.230	28	78	10	16	3	1	0	4	12	0	0	0	20	4	0	.269	.311
Ortiz, Joseph	R-R	5-11	175	7-14-98	.241	.161	.245	56	195	23	47	2	0	1	17	30	1	2	0	37	2	1	.267	.345
Putzig, Trevor	R-R	5-11	200	8-11-95	.227	.000	.250	7	22	2	5	0	0	0	1	0	0	0	0	6	0	0	.227	.261
Ringhofer, Luke	L-R	6-1	210	2-19-96	.237	.000	.290	15	38	7	9	1	0	0	1	8	1	0	0	12	1	0	.263	.383
Rizer, Johnny	L-L	6-0	192	11-7-96	.305	.250	.299	27	95	16	29	9	2	3	19	6	5	0	1	18	1	1	.537	.374
Roberts, Cody	R-R	6-1	195	6-16-96	.286	.667	.182	4	14	0	4	1	0	0	1	2	0	0	0	3	0	0	.357	.375
Rodriguez, Lenin	R-R	5-9	165	3-26-98	.093	.000	.102	22	54	7	5	0	0	0	0	9	2	0	1	12	1	0	.093	.242
Rutschman, Adley	B-R	6-2	216	2-6-98	.325	.250	.339	20	77	11	25	7	1	1	15	12	1	0	2	16	0	0	.481	.413
Stowers, Kyle	L-L	6-3	200	1-2-98	.216	.143	.229	55	204	19	44	13	1	6	23	20	2	0	2	53	5	1	.378	.290
Truitt, Trey	R-R	6-1	190	6-29-96	.135	.000	.133	13	37	5	5	2	0	1	6	6	1	0	2	13	0	1	.270	.261
Watson, Zach	R-R	6-0	160	6-25-97	.232	.278	.211	20	56	17	13	4	0	2	9	4	1	0	0	17	5	1	.411	.295
Welk, Toby	R-R	6-2	205	5-2-97	.344	.364	.340	48	180	22	62	12	2	4	28	16	3	0	5	42	2	2	.500	.397
Yett, Harris	R-R	6-0	220	3-21-96	.250	.000	.286	2	8	1	2	0	0	0	0	0	0	0	0	2	0	0	.250	.250
Zoellner, Jack	L-R	6-2	205	10-29-94	.000	--	--	2	6	0	0	0	0	0	0	0	0	0	0	0	0	0	.000	.200

Pitching	B-T	HT	WT	DOB	W	L	ERA	G	GS	CG	SV	IP	H	R	ER	HR	BB	SO	AVG	vLH	vRH	K/9	BB/9
Alejandro, Jose	R-R	6-3	200	6-20-95	0	0	5.40	2	0	0	0	2	3	1	1	0	5	3	.429	.500	.400	16.20	27.00
Baca, Tucker	L-L	6-4	193	6-17-96	0	0	--	1	0	0	0	0	0	0	0	0	1	0	--	--	--	--	--
Bautista, Felix	R-R	6-5	190	6-20-95	0	1	3.60	3	0	0	1	5	3	4	2	0	5	5	.167	.000	.231	9.00	9.00
Ciolli, Andrew	R-R	6-5	190	3-28-96	0	0	0.00	3	0	0	0	2	2	0	0	0	1	2	.182	.000	.250	6.75	3.38
Conroy, Ryan	R-R	6-3	190	12-31-96	5	5	2.64	15	15	1	0	78	73	30	23	1	20	71	.252	.233	.260	8.16	2.30
Constante, Marlon	R-R	5-11	185	7-5-96	1	3	3.72	18	0	0	4	29	25	23	12	6	7	34	.240	.265	.229	10.55	2.17
Echevarria, Juan	R-R	6-3	195	6-25-97	1	0	7.71	2	0	0	0	5	8	4	4	0	3	5	.364	.400	.333	5.79	5.79
Emond, Malachi	R-R	6-3	220	7-18-97	3	2	2.66	12	0	0	1	20	19	7	6	1	5	21	.244	.129	.319	9.30	2.21
Garcia, Ruben	R-R	6-4	220	8-2-96	0	0	0.00	2	0	0	0	2	1	0	0	0	2	1	.143	.000	.200	4.50	9.00
Gillispie, Connor	R-R	5-11	185	11-10-97	0	0	1.77	14	0	0	4	20	13	4	4	0	5	21	.191	.211	.184	9.30	2.21
Gonzalez, Brian	R-L	6-3	230	10-25-95	1	0	0.00	4	0	0	1	9	3	0	0	0	5	16	.100	.000	.125	15.58	3.12
Hammer, Dan	R-R	6-2	200	9-10-97	1	2	1.29	10	6	0	1	35	18	6	5	1	13	41	.153	.174	.139	10.54	3.34
Hayes, Reed	R-R	6-3	185	3-17-95	0	0	0.00	1	0	0	0	4	0	0	0	0	2	4	.000	--	.000	9.00	4.50

Name	B-T	HT	WT	DOB	W	L	ERA	G	GS	CG	SV	IP	H	R	ER	HR	BB	SO	AVG	vLH	vRH	K/9	BB/9
Kipper, Jordan	R-R	6-4	185	10-6-92	0	1	1.50	3	0	0	0	6	5	3	1	0	1	6	.238	.500	.133	9.00	1.50
Litscher, Dallas	R-R	6-8	250	1-10-96	4	0	2.23	7	6	0	0	36	23	9	9	1	13	43	.177	.196	.167	10.65	3.22
Lyons, Jake	R-R	6-5	282	8-19-98	2	5	2.87	14	7	0	0	38	32	20	12	1	10	39	.225	.290	.175	9.32	2.39
Magee, Kevin	L-L	6-2	210	1-1-96	5	6	2.04	15	15	1	0	71	59	18	16	5	13	79	.226	.186	.234	10.06	1.66
Martin, Kyle	R-R	6-3	215	3-15-98	2	2	4.12	13	0	0	1	20	22	12	9	0	9	24	.286	.333	.260	10.98	4.12
McFadden, Parker	R-R	6-0	200	6-1-97	0	0	--	2	0	0	0	0	1	1	1	0	4	0	1.000	--	1.000	--	--
McLarty, Griffin	L-R	6-3	185	8-10-98	2	0	2.78	14	0	0	0	23	19	7	7	0	5	25	.238	.256	.220	9.93	1.99
McSweeney, Morgan	R-R	6-4	210	9-21-97	2	0	1.90	15	0	0	0	24	16	6	5	0	12	30	.193	.154	.211	11.41	4.56
Meservey, Nick	L-L	6-5	221	9-10-95	0	0	27.00	2	0	0	0	1	1	3	2	0	3	0	.333	1.000	.000	0.00	40.50
Molina, Marcos	R-R	6-3	225	3-8-95	0	0	4.50	2	2	0	0	4	4	2	2	0	1	2	.250	.250	.250	4.50	2.25
Montville, Jason	L-L	6-2	215	11-16-96	0	0	5.68	2	0	0	0	6	8	4	4	0	2	8	.333	.667	.286	11.37	2.84
Nolasco, Moises	R-R	6-4	170	2-2-97	0	0	6.75	3	0	0	0	7	3	5	5	0	6	3	.143	.000	.188	4.05	8.10
Pendergast, Jonathan	R-R	6-2	200	8-25-97	1	0	0.00	1	0	0	0	3	1	0	0	0	1	1	.111	.000	.143	3.00	3.00
Perkins, Shelton	R-R	5-10	215	1-28-97	1	1	2.04	15	0	0	1	18	4	4	4	2	10	23	.070	.046	.086	11.72	5.09
Prizina, Jake	L-L	6-0	190	1-24-97	0	0	0.00	1	0	0	0	0	1	0	0	0	0	0	.500	--	.500	0.00	0.00
Rodriguez, Leonardo	R-R	6-7	215	11-25-97	2	2	2.65	14	13	0	0	71	47	27	21	4	25	80	.183	.212	.165	10.09	3.15
Rodriguez, Yelin	L-L	6-3	200	11-3-98	1	2	3.54	11	0	0	1	20	17	8	8	1	9	20	.236	.286	.216	8.85	3.98
Roth, Houston	R-B	6-3	220	3-9-98	4	0	1.42	10	4	0	0	32	19	5	5	1	13	39	.174	.195	.162	11.08	3.69
Ryan, James	R-R	6-2	190	11-17-96	0	0	1.04	9	1	0	0	17	18	4	2	0	2	11	.273	.185	.333	5.71	1.04
Stauffer, Adam	R-R	6-7	240	1-13-99	2	1	1.07	5	5	0	0	25	14	5	3	1	8	29	.163	.135	.184	10.30	2.84
Strowd, Kade	R-R	6-2	175	9-17-97	2	0	0.00	13	1	0	3	17	11	1	0	0	7	19	.180	.211	.167	10.06	3.71

Fielding

C: Cannon 7, Cervenka 3, Cumberland 3, Handley 34, Ringhofer 10, Roberts 3, Rodriguez 17, Rutschman 9, Yett 1. **1B:** Cannon 1, Daschbach 35, Evans 32, Montes 5, Murphy 6, Ringhofer 2, Zoellner 1. **2B:** Carmona 23, Fisher 27, Fregia 26, McLeod 2, Ortega 4. **3B:** Fregia 9, Ortega 20, Putzig 7, Welk 42. **SS:** Fisher 22, Fregia 1, Ortiz 55. **OF:** Diaz 2, Ferguson 17, Fontana 18, Fregia 9, Graham 19, Hays 3, Hoiles 30, Janvrin 14, Lantigua 3, Lewis 11, Montes 1, Neustrom 4, Rizer 25, Stowers 50, Truitt 13, Watson 15.

GCL ORIOLES   ROOKIE
GULF COAST LEAGUE

Batting	B-T	HT	WT	DOB	AVG	vLH	vRH	G	AB	R	H	2B	3B	HR	RBI	BB	HBP	SH	SF	SO	SB	CS	SLG	OBP
Alvarez, Yorkislandy	R-R	6-10	170	3-17-99	.000	--	.000	2	4	0	0	0	0	0	0	1	0	0	0	2	1	0	.000	.200
Baez, Carlos	R-R	6-3	175	11-22-97	.248	.222	.256	35	109	13	27	5	1	2	15	5	1	0	1	28	3	1	.367	.285
Brown, Jacob	R-R	5-9	190	2-16-99	.000	.000	.000	1	2	0	0	0	0	0	0	0	0	0	0	0	0	0	.000	.000
Burgess, Christopher	R-R	6-0	220	5-2-97	.286	.200	.304	22	56	9	16	2	0	2	11	10	2	1	0	16	1	0	.429	.412
Cannon, Jordan	R-R	6-3	210	11-28-96	.222	.222	.222	11	27	6	6	2	0	1	5	4	2	0	0	4	0	0	.407	.364
Castro, Ricardo	R-R	6-0	185	12-8-99	.077	.000	.083	5	13	0	1	1	0	0	0	0	1	0	0	2	0	1	.154	.143
Fontana, Shayne	L-L	6-2	195	6-21-97	.349	.333	.351	15	43	11	15	0	1	1	7	9	3	0	1	6	3		.465	.482
Henderson, Gunnar	L-R	6-3	195	6-29-01	.259	.240	.265	29	108	21	28	5	2	1	11	11	1	0	1	28	2	2	.333	.331
Hernaiz, Darell	R-R	6-1	170	8-3-01	.263	.222	.278	29	99	19	26	2	1	2	8	17	0	0	6	25	5	0	.364	.371
Herrera, Josue	R-R	6-5	165	2-3-97	.243	.208	.253	36	103	16	25	8	1	4	25	18	0	0	1	31	2	0	.456	.353
Janvrin, Mason	R-R	6-2	180	3-3-98	.341	.286	.357	26	91	16	31	2	0	0	12	6	0	0	1	22	14	1	.363	.378
Jayne, Andrew	R-R	6-4	195	8-11-99	.097	.286	.052	12	72	15	7	3	0	0	4	3	5	1	0	36	2	0	.139	.188
Kehe, Trevor	R-R	6-0	185	4-6-97	.250	.267	.243	23	52	12	13	3	0	1	7	12	3	2	0	15	5	1	.365	.418
Lewis, Craig	L-L	5-10	190	5-22-97	.417	.500	.400	18	48	7	20	2	0	0	6	4	0	0	1	7	4	2	.458	.453
Lizarraga, Jose	R-R	5-10	170	8-27-97	.224	.214	.227	29	58	4	13	3	0	0	12	4	0	0	0	8	1	0	.276	.274
Martinez, Andrew	R-R	5-11	180	6-17-97	.162	.100	.185	28	74	13	12	0	0	2	8	18	1	0	1	26	0	3	.243	.330
McLeod, Zach	R-R	6-1	200	1-19-96	.235	.313	.212	24	68	12	16	2	1	0	3	10	2	2	0	22	1	0	.294	.350
Montanez, Jose	R-R	6-1	200	7-13-98	.000	.000	.000	5	13	0	0	0	0	0	0	1	2	0	0	2	0	1	.000	.188
Putzig, Trevor	R-R	5-11	200	8-11-95	.290	.263	.297	30	93	15	27	5	2	1	16	12	1	0	0	22	4	0	.419	.431
Rojas, Edisson	L-R	6-3	193	6-6-99	.229	.294	.212	30	83	13	19	4	1	1	12	13	3	1	0	22	6	2	.337	.354
Rutschman, Adley	B-R	6-2	216	2-6-98	.143	.000	.167	5	14	3	2	0	0	1	3	2	0	0	0	2	1	0	.357	.250
Sparks, Lamar	R-R	6-2	170	9-26-98	.240	.273	.232	36	104	16	25	4	0	0	5	14	2	0	0	31	14	5	.279	.342
Stewart, DJ	L-R	6-0	230	11-30-93	.133	.000	.154	5	15	4	2	0	0	2	3	4	1	0	0	5	0	0	.533	.350
Tavarez, Davis	R-R	6-2	190	1-7-99	.314	.333	.308	30	86	13	27	6	1	2	21	11	1	0	0	16	6	1	.477	.398
Tolentino, Frank	R-R	6-1	170	8-5-99	.243	.167	.268	27	74	10	18	3	2	1	14	12	1	0	2	28	5	1	.378	.348
Turchin, Doran	R-R	6-2	195	7-7-97	.200	.500	.000	4	10	0	2	1	0	0	0	1	0	0	0	4	0	0	.300	.273
Yett, Harris	R-R	6-0	220	3-21-96	.340	.333	.342	34	100	18	34	11	0	2	19	17	0	0	2	8	1	0	.510	.429

Pitching	B-T	HT	WT	DOB	W	L	ERA	G	GS	CG	SV	IP	H	R	ER	HR	BB	SO	AVG	vLH	vRH	K/9	BB/9
Alejandro, Jose	R-R	6-3	200	6-20-95	3	0	2.05	12	0	0	1	22	12	8	5	0	11	26	.162	.214	.130	10.64	4.50
Carroll, Cody	R-R	6-5	215	10-15-92	0	0	0.00	2	1	0	0	2	2	0	0	0	0	5	.250	.333	.200	22.50	0.00
Ciolli, Andrew	R-R	6-5	190	3-28-96	1	1	12.27	2	0	0	0	4	7	7	5	0	4	2	.438	.455	.400	4.91	9.82
Daza, Manuel	R-R	6-1	176	9-22-96	2	0	3.00	3	0	0	0	9	7	1	0	0	0	11	.194	.150	.250	10.61	0.00
Denoyer, Noah	B-R	6-5	225	2-17-98	0	0	4.50	3	1	0	0	4	3	2	2	0	1	5	.200	.286	.125	11.25	2.25
Dietz, Matthias	R-R	6-5	220	9-25-95	0	0	0.00	2	0	0	0	2	1	0	0	0	3	2	.167			9.00	13.50
Elliott, Jensen	R-R	6-6	231	4-8-97	0	0	1.40	10	7	0	0	26	16	4	4	0	10	25	.178	.200	.164	8.77	3.51
Farmer, Garrett	R-R	5-11	185	5-14-97	3	2	1.21	14	2	0	0	22	17	5	3	0	2	31	.205	.200	.209	12.49	0.81
Gonzalez, Brian	R-L	6-3	230	10-25-95	1	0	0.00	2	0	0	0	3	3	0	0	0	1	3	.273	.000	.375	9.00	3.00
Hacker, Cody	R-L	5-11	180	6-18-00	0	0	16.20	2	0	0	0	2	4	3	3	0	3	1	.500	.667	.400	5.40	16.20
Karns, Nate	R-R	6-3	225	11-25-87	0	0	2.08	4	4	0	0	4	1	1	1	0	3	3	.071	.167	.000	6.23	6.23
Kipper, Jordan	R-R	6-4	185	10-6-92	2	0	1.50	5	3	0	0	6	2	1	1	0	0	5	.095	.125	.077	7.50	0.00
Lleras, Yeancarlos	R-R	6-0	150	7-22-00	1	0	6.41	11	1	0	1	20	27	18	14	0	10	12	.310	.355	.286	5.49	4.58
Marte, Christopher	R-R	6-1	190	7-9-96	1	0	3.00	1	0	0	0	3	1	1	1	1	0	2	.100	.200	.000	6.00	0.00
McCollough, Dillon	R-L	6-0	205	6-10-96	2	3	2.63	10	0	0	0	14	12	5	4	0	10	13	.245	.333	.225	8.56	6.59

Name	B-T	HT	WT	DOB	W	L	ERA	G	GS	CG	SV	IP	H	R	ER	HR	BB	SO	AVG	vLH	vRH	K/9	BB/9
McGinness, Clayton	R-R	6-1	180	1-13-97	1	1	2.08	11	3	0	2	22	18	5	5	2	3	24	.225	.162	.279	9.97	1.25
Montgomery, J.J.	R-R	6-0	200	6-1-97	3	1	2.70	10	7	0	0	37	22	16	11	1	22	37	.167	.207	.135	9.08	5.40
Montville, Jason	L-L	6-2	215	11-16-96	2	1	2.70	8	1	0	0	17	12	6	5	1	7	15	.203	.308	.174	8.10	3.78
Moore, Xavier	R-R	6-2	175	1-7-99	2	1	5.59	9	4	0	0	19	18	13	12	1	11	16	.240	.214	.255	7.45	5.12
Murphy, Jimmy	R-R	5-11	195	10-14-94	0	0	4.50	5	0	0	0	6	5	3	3	0	2	5	.250	.250	.250	7.50	3.00
Nolasco, Moises	R-R	6-4	170	2-2-97	5	1	1.75	13	0	0	2	26	16	7	5	0	10	25	.188	.125	.226	8.77	3.51
Ortiz, Luis	R-R	6-3	230	9-22-95	0	0	0.00	1	0	0	0	1	0	0	0	0	3		.000	.000	.000	27.00	0.00
Pendergast, Jonathan	R-R	6-2	200	8-25-97	1	1	0.98	12	0	0	5	18	14	7	2	1	7	21	.206	.200	.209	10.31	3.44
Prizina, Jake	L-L	6-0	190	1-24-97	4	1	1.15	10	5	0	0	39	20	5	5	0	5	45	.149	.200	.128	10.38	1.15
Romero, Victor	R-R	6-3	170	2-17-95	0	0	0.00	2	1	0	0	2	0	0	0	0	1		.000	.000	.000	5.40	0.00
Roth, Nick	R-R	5-10	175	8-28-96	1	0	0.92	12	2	0	3	20	16	2	2	1	1	23	.225	.258	.200	10.53	0.46
Ryan, James	R-R	6-2	190	11-17-96	0	1	5.87	5	2	0	0	8	9	5	5	1	7	7	.300	.294	.308	8.22	8.22
Sandridge, Jayvien	L-L	6-5	220	2-11-99	1	0	5.54	11	0	0	0	13	13	14	8	2	13	19	.250	.143	.290	13.15	9.00
Stambaugh, Dalton	R-L	6-0	195	2-11-97	0	0	1.69	10	1	0	2	21	15	7	4	0	7	18	.192	.048	.246	7.59	2.95
Wernet, Gillian	R-R	6-3	210	10-1-98	0	0	162.00	1	0	0	0	0	4	6	6	0	2	1	.800	1.000	.667	27.00	54.00
Zebron, Jake	R-R	6-3	180	2-4-00	2	1	1.31	11	8	0	1	41	35	13	6	0	16	37	.232	.239	.226	8.06	3.48

Fielding

C: Burgess 16, Cannon 9, Herrera 1, Lizarraga 14, Montanez 3, Rutschman 2, Yett 23. **1B:** Herrera 25, Lizarraga 13, Rojas 18, Yett 1. **2B:** Baez 31, Fontana 1, Martinez 25, McLeod 1, Putzig 2. **3B:** Alvarez 2, Herrera 7, McLeod 22, Putzig 28, Rojas 3. **SS:** Baez 5, Burgess 1, Henderson 21, Hernaiz 24, Martinez 3. **OF:** Brown 1, Castro 4, Fontana 13, Janvrin 24, Jayne 25, Kehe 22, Lewis 16, Sparks 18, Stewart 3, Tavarez 29, Tolentino 25, Turchin 3.

DSL ORIOLES   ROOKIE

Batting	B-T	HT	WT	DOB	AVG	vLH	vRH	G	AB	R	H	2B	3B	HR	RBI	BB	HBP	SH	SF	SO	SB	CS	SLG	OBP
Acevedo, Stiven	R-R	6-4	185	8-2-02	.250	.391	.236	61	252	36	63	10	0	1	25	24	9	1	2	55	4	1	.302	.335
Alvarez, Yorkislandy	R-R	6-10	170	3-17-99	.276	.360	.265	56	210	42	58	5	0	0	17	36	5	0	2	17	22	5	.300	.391
Beato, Lians	R-R	5-10	165	9-19-01	.132	.125	.133	17	38	10	5	2	0	0	6	15	2	0	3	13	0	0	.184	.379
Bellony, Isaac	B-R	6-1	180	12-15-01	.239	.143	.249	61	230	41	55	14	1	6	43	34	2	0	5	60	6	7	.387	.336
Castro, Ricardo	R-R	6-0	185	12-8-99	.267	.250	.272	57	206	27	55	7	0	2	28	12	3	1	3	39	6	5	.350	.330
Cruz, Josue	L-L	6-4	175	12-25-00	.253	.259	.252	65	237	43	60	12	6	11	46	40	2	0	2	94	1	1	.494	.363
De La Cruz, Samuel	R-R	5-11	180	10-18-97	.121	.143	.115	18	33	2	4	1	0	0	1	7	0	0	0	11	0	0	.152	.275
De La Rosa, Juan	R-R	6-3	207	6-22-98	.284	.296	.282	49	176	36	50	9	5	2	31	19	10	0	1	49	15	4	.426	.384
Gomez, Angel	R-R	5-11	180	6-17-01	.241	.192	.249	55	203	29	49	6	6	0	23	21	7	0	0	58	6	2	.330	.333
Grullon, Wilkin	R-R	6-0	220	11-28-99	.287	.317	.277	50	178	26	51	11	0	1	32	17	12	0	2	36	0	1	.365	.383
Herrera, Julio	L-R	6-2	180	11-20-00	.221	.261	.212	38	127	13	28	7	0	2	14	7	4	1	1	21	1	2	.323	.281
Infante, Kevin	R-R	6-0	180	7-14-00	.298	.304	.296	60	225	27	67	12	3	3	22	18	6	2	0	40	11	6	.418	.366
Isenia, J'Rudjeanon	R-R	6-1	185	12-7-01	.133	.222	.121	26	75	10	10	3	0	0	4	1	2	2	1	25	3	0	.173	.165
Leon, Carlos	B-R	5-9	171	2-19-01	.193	.250	.180	37	109	15	21	6	0	0	8	5	5	2	1	13	1	4	.248	.258
Lucero, Hector	R-R	6-4	215	4-5-01	.158	.333	.146	31	95	9	15	3	0	1	12	17	2	1	1	31	0	0	.221	.296
Machado, Gilberto	R-R	5-11	160	11-17-00	.221	.143	.233	51	154	30	34	6	2	1	16	22	7	0	0	16	0	1	.305	.344
Mantecon, Michael	R-R	5-10	180	2-2-02	.245	.000	.284	32	94	17	23	4	0	0	8	17	8	0	0	19	4	0	.287	.403
Munoz, Joel	R-R	5-10	155	12-26-96	.200	.400	.164	27	65	9	13	1	0	0	12	7	3	1	3	18	0	1	.215	.295
Nunez, Raily	L-R	6-0	160	7-1-02	.098	.000	.105	14	41	3	4	1	0	0	2	0	0	0	2	22	1	1	.122	.140
Olivares, Oscar	R-R	6-1	223	9-3-98	.230	.317	.196	45	148	25	34	6	0	4	21	17	3	0	1	51	4	1	.351	.320
Placencia, Erison	R-R	6-1	170	12-31-01	.345	.429	.338	26	84	22	29	3	1	0	10	25	1	0	0	19	2	2	.405	.500
Prado, Elio	R-R	6-0	160	11-29-01	.298	.250	.300	26	94	13	28	7	0	0	12	10	7	1	0	15	3	5	.372	.405
2-team total (34 Red Sox2)					.300	.393	.286	60	217	40	65	12	0	3	38	30	9	3	2	36	12	10	.396	.403
Ramirez, Moises	R-R	6-2	211	2-1-02	.243	.105	.271	59	226	37	55	7	4	2	28	22	8	1	1	49	2	2	.336	.331
Reyes, Anyelo	L-R	6-1	170	11-3-01	.206	.261	.187	53	180	25	37	5	1	1	11	9	3	1	0	54	2	2	.261	.255
Rojas, Edidson	L-R	6-3	193	5-14-99	.180	.111	.192	16	61	10	11	3	1	1	9	8	2	0	1	18	2	0	.312	.292
Rolle, James	L-L	6-0	240	10-28-01	.283	.167	.305	34	113	12	32	4	0	5	10	7	3	0	0	36	1	1	.451	.342
Romero, Noelberth	R-R	6-0	145	12-5-01	.279	.294	.276	28	104	15	29	4	0	0	17	7	2	4	0	11	2	1	.317	.336
2-team total (30 Red Sox2)					.273	.267	.275	58	216	29	59	7	1	2	31	18	3	5	0	32	4	2	.343	.338
Santana, Luis	R-R	6-1	160	6-3-99	.161	.071	.191	20	56	6	9	1	0	0	3	0	1	1	0	7	0	0	.179	.175
Santana, Welington	R-R	6-3	182	5-20-01	.220	.320	.194	36	118	16	26	8	0	0	8	5	2	0	1	20	0	0	.288	.262
Sena, Luis	R-R	5-10	140	9-16-01	.237	.316	.217	51	190	34	45	2	2	0	15	21	5	2	1	15	15	6	.268	.327
Valdez, Damian	L-L	6-2	185	2-25-02	.213	.303	.189	47	155	15	33	4	3	1	13	17	1	3	2	49	1	0	.297	.291
Vizcaino, Hector	R-R	6-2	175	3-16-00	.212	.160	.221	55	179	27	38	9	0	0	15	22	11	0	0	60	0	3	.263	.335

Pitching	B-T	HT	WT	DOB	W	L	ERA	G	GS	CG	SV	IP	H	R	ER	HR	BB	SO	AVG	vLH	vRH	K/9	BB/9
Alcantara, Darlin	R-R	6-3	180	9-20-01	0	3	6.28	8	1	0	0	14	11	10	10	0	10	19	.212	.217	.207	11.93	6.28
Angomas, Cesar	L-L	6-2	226	4-19-00	2	5	2.14	14	14	0	0	55	35	29	15	0	32	64	.232	.250	.229	9.14	4.57
Benitez, Joel	R-R	6-2	175	7-21-00	2	7	4.88	14	14	0	0	52	48	39	28	0	34	44	.246	.296	.218	7.66	5.92
Berroa, Johan	L-L	6-2	166	8-27-00	1	2	9.00	6	2	0	0	11	10	11	11	0	7	7	.244	.000	.313	5.73	5.73
Caty, Petter	R-R	6-3	195	6-13-00	1	0	8.68	8	0	0	0	9	16	10	9	0	11	6	.381	.444	.333	6.75	10.61
Chavez, Jesus	L-L	6-1	170	12-23-01	2	4	3.16	14	14	0	0	68	65	28	24	4	21	57	.253	.226	.257	7.51	2.77
Daza, Manuel	R-R	6-1	176	9-22-96	5	3	2.33	15	0	0	4	46	48	19	12	3	11	54	.271	.279	.267	10.49	2.14
De Los Santos, Juan	R-R	6-2	190	5-25-02	0	2	3.63	11	9	0	0	45	48	20	18	0	11	35	.274	.279	.271	7.05	2.22
Del Rosario, Carlos	R-R	6-5	225	6-17-99	2	1	2.79	17	7	0	0	48	31	17	15	0	36	60	.186	.185	.186	11.17	6.70
Duncan, Manuel	R-R	6-1	160	4-1-02	0	0	8.10	6	0	0	0	7	8	6	6	0	5	6	.320	.200	.350	6.75	10.80
Espinal, Andersson	L-L	6-0	184	9-1-99	0	0	5.00	7	0	0	0	9	3	5	5	0	17	11	.103	.143	.091	11.00	17.00
Falconett, Pablo	R-R	6-2	220	10-28-00	0	2	2.67	21	0	0	4	34	32	15	10	1	4	46	.230	.271	.209	12.30	1.07
Frias, Harif	R-R	6-4	163	5-19-01	0	2	4.41	10	0	0	0	16	15	10	8	0	7	12	.259	.400	.209	6.61	3.86
Fulgencio, Orlando	R-R	5-11	168	9-6-00	1	2	3.38	14	5	0	1	48	37	21	18	0	27	42	.214	.254	.186	7.88	5.06
Galva, Claudio	L-L	6-2	169	10-9-96	5	5	1.13	20	0	0	4	48	45	16	6	0	13	47	.245	.182	.258	8.87	2.45

Player	T-B	Ht	Wt	DOB	W	L	ERA	G	GS	CG	SV	IP	H	R	ER	HR	BB	SO	AVG	OBP	SLG		
Genao, Joldanny	R-R	6-4	168	8-1-02	2	0	3.29	9	0	0	0	14	9	6	5	0	11	5	.200	.250	.172	3.29	7.24
Gomez, Jose	R-R	6-3	202	9-23-96	4	2	2.96	13	13	0	0	67	64	28	22	1	16	51	.247	.301	.222	6.85	2.15
Gutierrez, Enmanuel	R-R	6-1	178	9-22-01	1	0	13.50	8	1	0	0	9	7	18	14	1	16	10	.189	.308	.125	9.64	15.43
Lara, Yan	L-L	6-1	178	9-18-99	1	2	6.75	11	6	0	0	33	35	32	25	0	23	27	.269	.136	.296	7.29	6.21
LaRoche, Kelvin	R-R	5-11	170	7-31-99	3	2	2.83	15	7	0	1	64	47	27	20	1	22	31	.205	.128	.245	4.38	3.11
Lopez, Edinson	L-L	6-0	185	6-5-98	2	4	4.55	11	7	0	1	32	31	18	16	0	15	36	.267	.182	.301	10.23	4.26
Lopez, Hector	R-R	6-1	190	10-4-01	2	2	2.05	13	13	0	0	53	37	21	12	1	23	51	.195	.328	.132	8.72	3.93
Manzanillo, Yeudry	R-R	6-3	175	12-7-98	6	0	2.41	20	0	0	2	41	43	20	11	1	8	40	.265	.408	.204	8.78	1.76
Marte, Christopher	R-R	6-1	190	7-9-96	4	6	3.71	13	13	0	0	68	75	36	28	1	8	41	.281	.238	.301	5.43	1.06
Martinez, Joeli	R-R	6-3	180	4-17-00	1	0	12.71	8	0	0	0	11	19	17	16	2	15	5	.365	.429	.342	3.97	11.91
Martinez, Jose	R-R	6-1	174	2-2-00	1	0	4.30	10	0	0	1	23	17	17	11	0	21	17	.200	.115	.237	6.65	8.22
Mendez, Alejandro	R-R	6-4	195	2-28-01	0	0	6.23	4	0	0	0	4	1	4	3	0	6	2	.071	.000	.111	4.15	12.46
Mercedes, Andry	L-L	6-3	185	12-18-00	1	1	0.90	4	1	0	0	10	4	4	1	0	2	17	.114	.167	.103	15.30	1.80
Monroy, Eduard	L-L	5-11	160	10-8-01	1	0	3.98	13	0	0	1	20	21	14	9	0	11	24	.256	.111	.297	10.62	4.87
Morillo, Anthony	R-R	6-2	170	2-7-02	0	0	0.00	2	0	0	0	3	0	0	0	0	1	4	.000	.000	.000	12.00	3.00
Morla, Jorge	R-R	6-3	185	4-13-00	0	3	4.35	10	2	0	0	21	23	14	10	2	11	25	.288	.321	.269	10.89	4.79
Munoz, Joel	R-R	5-10	155	12-26-96	0	0	9.00	1	0	0	0	1	2	1	1	0	1	0	.500	1.000	.000	0.00	9.00
Nolasco, Moises	R-R	6-4	170	2-2-97	0	1	7.50	2	1	0	0	6	9	5	5	1	3	8	.360	.429	.273	12.00	4.50
Rodriguez, Jose A.	R-R	6-1	190	12-27-95	0	1	0.00	5	0	0	1	6	8	3	0	0	3	8	.308	.546	.133	12.00	4.50
Paulino, Adonis	R-R	6-1	165	3-11-00	0	0	4.26	8	0	0	0	13	12	7	6	1	8	10	.250	.167	.300	7.11	5.68
Pierret, Oscar	R-R	6-2	190	3-12-01	1	1	8.26	14	2	0	0	28	36	31	26	1	20	17	.313	.432	.239	5.40	6.35
Pujols, Antonio	L-L	6-3	195	1-27-98	1	1	17.18	4	0	0	0	4	8	10	7	0	3	4	.381	.000	.444	9.82	7.36
Sanchez, Brayner	R-R	6-4	189	6-2-01	4	0	4.18	13	0	0	2	24	20	12	11	1	9	18	.230	.174	.250	6.85	3.42
Solano, Issac	R-R	6-6	195	10-23-01	0	0	20.25	2	0	0	0	1	1	4	3	0	3	1	.167	.000	.200	6.75	20.25
Valencia, Jose	R-R	6-3	204	9-27-00	1	2	3.38	17	0	0	0	37	26	15	14	0	19	33	.196	.208	.188	7.96	4.58
Vargas, Angel	R-R	6-1	173	12-1-01	1	0	3.60	3	0	0	0	5	6	3	2	1	1	7	.273	.375	.214	12.60	1.80
Vasquez, Jairo	R-R	6-1	160	1-16-02	1	0	10.13	13	0	0	0	16	18	19	18	0	11	15	.305	.313	.302	8.44	6.19
Vasquez, Jordany	R-R	6-0	165	1-10-01	4	3	6.69	15	1	0	0	38	46	30	28	1	18	32	.303	.346	.280	7.65	4.30

Fielding

C: Beato 15, De La Cruz 10, Grullon 24, Herrera 31, Lucero 19, Mantecon 25, Munoz 19, Santana 9. **1B:** Beato 1, Cruz 48, De La Cruz 4, De La Rosa 10, Leon 1, Machado 18, Munoz 2, Olivares 34, Rolle 29, Santana 7, Santana 0. **2B:** Alvarez 21, Bellony 1, Leon 18, Machado 17, Mantecon 4, Nunez 6, Reyes 50, Rojas 11, Sena 1, Vizcaino 13. **3B:** Alvarez 19, Leon 10, Machado 17, Olivares 9, Ramirez 25, Rojas 1, Romero 24, Vizcaino 9. **SS:** Alvarez 16, Leon 11, Nunez 2, Placencia 26, Reyes 1, Romero 3, Sena 50, Vizcaino 27. **OF:** Acevedo 54, Alvarez 1, Bellony 56, Castro 52, Cruz 7, De La Rosa 30, Gomez 47, Infante 59, Isenia 17, Munoz 1, Prado 23, Reyes 1, Santana 1, Santana 31, Valdez 43.

Boston Red Sox

SEASON IN A SENTENCE: The Red Sox fell flat in their World Series defense, missing the playoffs for the first time since 2015.

HIGH POINT: The Red Sox beat the Yankees in three straight games in late July to move into second place in the American League East, including a 19-3 victory in the series opener. The 19 runs were the most scored in a game against the Yankees in franchise history.

LOW POINT: The Red Sox shocked the baseball world when they announced the firing of president of baseball operations Dave Dombrowski on Sept. 8. By that point the Red Sox were 17.5 games out of first place in the AL East and there were rumors of front office discord, but Dombrowski's firing still stunned many given the Red Sox were less than a year removed from a World Series.

NOTABLE ROOKIES: Infielder Michael Chavis debuted on April 20 and finished fourth among American League rookies in home runs (18) and RBIs (58). He alternated starting at first and second base before his season ended in August due to shoulder and oblique injuries. Relievers Marcus Walden and Josh Taylor were bright spots in an otherwise miserable year for the Red Sox bullpen. Darwinzon Hernandez, Colten Brewer, Travis Lakins and Mike Shawaryn were all brought up to help the beleaguered relief corps.

KEY TRANSACTIONS: Up against the luxury tax threshold, the Red Sox largely remained on the sidelines during free agency and made few major moves during the season. They traded one-time top prospect Blake Swihart and international bonus pool space to the D-backs for outfield prospect Marcus Wilson in April, and in July they acquired righthander Andrew Cashner from the Orioles for Dominican Summer League prospects Elio Prado and Noelberth Romero.

DOWN ON THE FARM: Red Sox domestic affiliates combined to finish with the fourth-worst combined win percentage (.459) in baseball, but there were individual bright spots. Third baseman Bobby Dalbec hit 27 home runs between Double-A and Triple-A and was selected for Team USA's Olympic qualifying team after the season, as were pitchers Tanner Houck and Noah Song. First baseman Triston Casas and righthander Bryan Mata made great strides and emerged two of the better prospects at their positions. Short-season Lowell reached the New York-Penn League championship series, but fell to Brooklyn (Mets).

OPENING DAY PAYROLL: $213,188,334 (1st).

PLAYERS OF THE YEAR

BRACE HEMMELGARN

BRITA MENG OUTZEN/BOSTON RED SOX

MAJOR LEAGUE	MINOR LEAGUE
Mookie Betts	**Triston Casas**
OF	1B
.295/.391/.524	(Low A/High A)
29 HR, 80 RBIs, 16 SB	.256/.350/.480
AL-best 135 runs	20 HR, 81 RBIs

ORGANIZATION LEADERS

Batting		*Minimum 250 AB
MAJORS		
* AVG	Rafael Devers	.311
* OPS	Xander Bogaerts	.939
HR	J.D. Martinez	36
RBI	Xander Bogaerts	117
MINORS		
* AVG	Jarren Duran, Salem, Portland	.303
* OBP	Jarren Duran, Salem, Portland	.367
* SLG	Marcus Wilson, Salem, Portland	.489
* OPS	Marcus Wilson, Salem, Portland	.847
R	Jarren Duran, Salem, Portland	90
H	Jarren Duran, Salem, Portland	157
TB	Bobby Dalbec, Portland, Pawtucket	217
2B	C.J. Chatham, Portland, Pawtucket	31
3B	Jarren Duran, Salem, Portland	8
3B	Eduardo Lopez, DSL Red Sox 1	8
HR	Bobby Dalbec, Portland, Pawtucket	27
RBI	Triston Casas, Greenville, Salem	81
BB	Josh Ockimey, Pawtucket	82
SO	Gorkys Hernandez, Pawtucket	146
SB	Jarren Duran, Salem, Portland	46

Pitching		#Minimum 75 IP
MAJORS		
W	Eduardo Rodriguez	19
# ERA	Eduardo Rodriguez	3.81
SO	Chris Sale	218
SV	Brandon Workman	16
MINORS		
W	Kyle Hart, Portland, Pawtucket	12
L	Kyle Hart, Portland, Pawtucket	13
# ERA	Daniel McGrath, Portland, Pawtucket	1.98
G	Trevor Kelley, Pawtucket	52
GS	Alex Scherff, Greenville, Salem	27
GS	Jhonathan Diaz, Salem	27
SV	Andrew Schwaab, Portland, Salem	14
IP	Kyle Hart, Portland, Pawtucket	156
BB	Thad Ward, Greenville, Salem	57
SO	Thad Ward, Greenville, Salem	157
# AVG	Andrew Politi, Salem	.197

General Manager: Dave Dombrowski. **Farm Director:** Ben Crockett. **Scouting Director:** Mike Rikard.

Class	Team	League	W	L	PCT	Finish	Manager
Majors	Boston Red Sox	American	84	78	.519	7th (15)	Alex Cora
Triple-A	Pawtucket Red Sox	International	59	81	.421	t-13th (14)	Billy McMillon
Double-A	Portland Sea Dogs	Eastern	62	77	.446	10th (12)	Joe Oliver
High A	Salem Red Sox	Carolina	67	70	.489	6th (10)	Corey Wimberly
Low A	Greenville Drive	South Atlantic	56	82	.406	13th (14)	Iggy Suarez
Short season	Lowell Spinners	New York-Penn	42	34	.553	4th (14)	Luke Montz
Rookie	GCL Red Sox	Gulf Coast	27	25	.519	9th (18)	Tom Kotchman
Overall 2019 Minor League Record			313	369	.459	27th (30)	

ORGANIZATION STATISTICS

BOSTON RED SOX
AMERICAN LEAGUE

Batting	B-T	HT	WT	DOB	AVG	vLH	vRH	G	AB	R	H	2B	3B	HR	RBI	BB	HBP	SH	SF	SO	SB	CS	SLG	OBP
Benintendi, Andrew	L-L	5-10	170	7-6-94	.266	.269	.265	138	541	72	144	40	5	13	68	59	7	3	5	140	10	3	.431	.343
Betts, Mookie	R-R	5-9	180	10-7-92	.295	.271	.304	150	597	135	176	40	5	29	80	97	3	0	9	101	16	3	.524	.391
Bogaerts, Xander	R-R	6-1	210	10-1-92	.309	.291	.316	155	614	110	190	52	0	33	117	76	2	0	6	122	4	2	.555	.384
Bradley Jr., Jackie	L-R	5-10	200	4-19-90	.225	.213	.230	147	494	69	111	28	3	21	62	56	12	3	2	155	8	6	.421	.317
Centeno, Juan	L-R	5-9	195	11-16-89	.133	.250	.091	7	15	0	2	0	0	0	2	2	1	0	0	2	1	0	.133	.278
Chavis, Michael	R-R	5-10	216	8-11-95	.254	.226	.266	95	347	46	88	10	1	18	58	31	4	0	0	127	2	1	.444	.322
Devers, Rafael	L-R	6-0	237	10-24-96	.311	.269	.330	156	647	129	201	54	4	32	115	48	4	1	2	119	8	8	.555	.361
Hernandez, Gorkys	R-R	6-1	196	9-7-87	.143	.042	.240	20	49	5	7	1	2	0	2	5	0	2	1	14	1	0	.245	.218
Hernandez, Marco	L-R	6-0	200	9-6-92	.250	.320	.214	61	148	18	37	7	0	2	11	3	3	1	0	42	1	2	.338	.279
Holt, Brock	L-R	5-10	180	6-11-88	.297	.224	.318	87	259	38	77	14	2	3	31	28	4	0	4	57	1	0	.402	.370
Leon, Sandy	B-R	5-10	225	3-13-89	.192	.187	.196	65	172	14	33	3	0	5	19	13	1	4	1	47	0	0	.297	.251
Lin, Tzu-Wei	L-R	5-9	155	2-15-94	.200	.286	.154	13	20	3	4	2	0	0	1	2	0	0	0	6	1	1	.300	.273
Martinez, J.D.	R-R	6-3	220	8-21-87	.304	.404	.272	146	575	98	175	33	2	36	105	72	4	0	5	138	2	0	.557	.383
Moreland, Mitch	L-L	6-2	230	9-6-85	.252	.204	.262	91	298	48	75	17	1	19	58	34	1	0	2	74	1	0	.507	.328
Nunez, Eduardo	R-R	6-0	195	6-15-87	.228	.200	.247	60	167	13	38	7	0	2	20	4	0	1	2	27	5	1	.305	.243
Owings, Chris	R-R	5-10	185	8-12-91	.156	.261	.046	26	45	4	7	2	0	1	5	6	0	0	0	23	1	1	.267	.255
2-team total (40 Kansas City)					.139	.164	.124	66	180	13	25	6	1	3	14	14	2	0	0	78	5	2	.233	.209
Pearce, Steve	R-R	5-11	200	4-13-83	.180	.200	.163	29	89	9	16	4	0	1	9	7	1	0	1	31	0	0	.258	.245
Pedroia, Dustin	R-R	5-9	175	8-17-83	.100	.000	.118	6	20	1	2	0	0	0	1	1	0	0	0	2	0	0	.100	.143
Swihart, Blake	B-R	6-1	200	4-3-92	.231	.000	.261	12	26	4	6	1	0	1	4	2	1	0	0	7	0	0	.385	.310
Travis, Sam	R-R	6-0	205	8-27-93	.215	.221	.204	59	144	17	31	4	1	6	16	11	1	0	1	36	2	0	.382	.274
Vazquez, Christian	R-R	5-9	195	8-21-90	.276	.285	.272	138	482	66	133	26	1	23	72	33	0	3	3	101	4	2	.477	.321

Pitching	B-T	HT	WT	DOB	W	L	ERA	G	GS	CG	SV	IP	H	R	ER	HR	BB	SO	AVG	vLH	vRH	K/9	BB/9
Barnes, Matt	R-R	6-4	210	6-17-90	5	4	3.78	70	0	0	4	64	51	29	27	8	38	110	.210	.174	.232	15.39	5.32
Brasier, Ryan	R-R	6-0	225	8-26-87	2	4	4.85	62	0	0	7	56	51	33	30	9	21	61	.238	.247	.231	9.86	3.40
Brewer, Colten	R-R	6-4	230	10-09-92	1	2	4.12	58	0	0	0	55	59	26	25	6	34	52	.277	.244	.299	8.56	5.60
Cashner, Andrew	R-R	6-6	235	9-11-86	2	5	6.20	25	6	0	1	54	58	39	37	8	29	42	.287	.303	.274	7.04	4.86
2-team total (17 Baltimore)					11	8	4.68	42	23	0	1	150	144	84	78	19	58	108	.253	.223	.279	6.48	3.48
Chacin, Jhoulys	R-R	6-3	215	1-7-88	0	2	7.36	6	5	0	0	15	16	12	12	6	7	21	.267	.333	.200	12.89	4.30
Eovaldi, Nathan	R-R	6-2	225	2-13-90	2	1	5.99	23	12	0	0	68	72	46	45	16	35	70	.276	.266	.285	9.31	4.66
Hembree, Heath	R-R	6-4	210	1-13-89	1	0	3.86	45	0	0	2	40	34	20	17	7	18	46	.224	.222	.225	10.44	4.08
Hernandez, Darwinzon	L-L	6-2	245	12-17-96	0	1	4.45	29	1	0	0	30	27	18	15	1	26	57	.231	.089	.319	16.91	7.71
Johnson, Brian	L-L	6-4	235	12-7-90	1	3	6.02	21	7	0	0	40	53	29	27	6	23	31	.316	.232	.357	6.92	5.13
Kelley, Trevor	R-R	6-2	210	10-20-93	0	3	8.64	10	0	0	0	8	9	8	8	2	5	6	.290	.333	.273	6.48	5.40
Lakins, Travis	R-R	6-1	180	6-29-94	0	1	3.86	16	3	0	0	23	23	11	10	1	10	18	.258	.231	.280	6.94	3.86
Nunez, Eduardo	R-R	6-0	195	6-15-87	0	0	9.00	1	0	0	0	1	1	1	1	0	1	0	.250	.500	.000	0.00	0.00
Porcello, Rick	R-R	6-5	205	12-27-88	14	12	5.52	32	32	0	0	174	198	114	107	31	45	143	.278	.284	.273	7.38	2.32
Poyner, Bobby	L-L	6-0	205	12-1-92	0	1	6.94	13	1	0	0	12	10	9	9	2	5	11	.233	.235	.231	8.49	3.86
Price, David	L-L	6-5	215	8-26-85	7	5	4.28	22	22	0	0	107	109	57	51	15	32	128	.258	.263	.257	10.73	2.68
Ramirez, Erasmo	R-R	5-10	215	5-2-90	0	0	12.00	1	0	0	0	3	4	4	4	1	3	1	.333	.500	.300	3.00	3.00
Rodriguez, Eduardo	L-L	6-2	220	4-7-93	19	6	3.81	34	34	0	0	203	195	88	86	24	75	213	.253	.264	.250	9.43	3.32
Sale, Chris	L-L	6-6	180	3-30-89	6	11	4.40	25	25	1	0	147	123	80	72	24	37	218	.221	.247	.216	13.32	2.26
Shawaryn, Mike	R-R	6-2	200	9-17-94	0	0	9.74	14	0	0	0	20	26	22	22	5	13	29	.310	.250	.346	12.84	5.75
Smith, Josh A.	R-R	6-2	220	8-7-87	0	3	5.81	18	2	0	1	31	36	22	20	10	8	29	.281	.327	.247	8.42	2.32
Taylor, Josh	L-L	6-5	225	3-2-93	2	2	3.04	52	1	0	0	47	40	17	16	5	16	62	.229	.206	.243	11.79	3.04
Thornburg, Tyler	R-R	5-11	190	9-29-88	0	0	7.71	16	0	0	0	19	21	16	16	4	10	22	.280	.217	.308	10.61	4.82
Velazquez, Hector	R-R	6-0	180	11-26-88	1	4	5.43	34	8	0	0	56	58	40	34	7	28	49	.275	.238	.309	7.83	4.47
Walden, Marcus	R-R	6-0	195	9-13-88	9	2	3.81	70	0	0	2	78	61	38	33	6	32	76	.213	.198	.222	8.77	3.69
Weber, Ryan	R-R	6-1	180	8-12-90	2	4	5.09	18	3	0	0	41	48	25	23	5	8	29	.284	.317	.253	6.42	1.77
Workman, Brandon	R-R	6-5	235	8-13-88	10	1	1.88	73	0	0	16	72	29	18	15	1	45	104	.123	.132	.116	13.06	5.65
Wright, Steven	R-R	6-2	215	8-30-84	0	1	8.53	6	0	0	0	6	11	6	6	3	4	5	.407	.250	.533	7.11	5.68

Fielding

Catcher	PCT	G	PO	A	E	DP	PB
Centeno	1.000	5	25	5	0	1	2
Leon	.995	65	535	30	3	0	4
Swihart	.950	8	55	2	3	0	0
Vazquez	.999	119	994	71	1	6	9

First Base	PCT	G	PO	A	E	DP
Chavis	.989	49	339	24	4	22
Holt	1.000	11	26	5	0	3
Leon	1.000	1	4	0	0	0
Moreland	.995	85	556	48	3	52
Pearce	.972	19	97	9	3	9
Swihart	.000	1	0	0	0	0
Travis	.981	29	149	7	3	14
Vazquez	.982	10	48	6	1	3

Second Base	PCT	G	PO	A	E	DP
Chavis	.975	45	75	81	4	21
Hernandez	.991	48	49	61	1	10
Holt	.991	60	78	136	2	27
Lin	1.000	8	14	9	0	5
Nunez	.973	31	26	47	2	7
Owings	1.000	12	15	21	0	6
Pedroia	1.000	4	9	7	0	3
Vazquez	1.000	2	1	3	0	1

Third Base	PCT	G	PO	A	E	DP
Chavis	1.000	5	1	3	0	1
Devers	.949	152	117	292	22	20
Holt	1.000	4	0	3	0	0
Nunez	.923	8	5	7	1	0
Owings	.000	1	0	0	0	0
Vazquez	1.000	4	0	1	0	0

Shortstop	PCT	G	PO	A	E	DP
Bogaerts	.975	153	165	347	13	70
Devers	.000	1	0	0	0	0
Hernandez	1.000	2	1	2	0	0
Holt	1.000	6	4	16	0	2
Lin	1.000	2	0	3	0	0
Nunez	1.000	6	3	5	0	0
Owings	.941	7	3	13	1	2

Outfield	PCT	G	PO	A	E	DP
Benintendi	.990	136	182	9	2	3
Betts	.994	143	320	10	2	0
Bradley Jr.	.987	145	305	10	4	3
Hernandez	.962	15	24	1	1	0
Holt	.944	9	17	0	1	0
Lin	.000	1	0	0	0	0
Martinez	.959	38	67	4	3	2
Owings	.000	1	0	0	0	0
Pearce	1.000	4	3	1	0	1
Swihart	.000	1	0	0	0	0
Travis	.966	19	26	2	1	0

PAWTUCKET RED SOX

TRIPLE-A
INTERNATIONAL LEAGUE

Batting	B-T	HT	WT	DOB	AVG	vLH	vRH	G	AB	R	H	2B	3B	HR	RBI	BB	HBP	SH	SF	SO	SB	CS	SLG	OBP
Brentz, Bryce	R-R	6-0	215	12-30-88	.216	.267	.196	95	310	47	67	17	0	18	50	39	6	0	2	122	0	2	.445	.314
Castillo, Rusney	R-R	5-9	195	7-9-87	.278	.297	.272	120	460	63	128	25	1	17	64	25	5	0	2	63	5	9	.448	.321
Centeno, Juan	L-R	5-9	195	11-16-89	.248	.192	.269	81	266	27	66	15	0	4	40	24	6	2	3	47	2	0	.350	.321
Chatham, C.J.	R-R	6-3	185	12-22-94	.302	.111	.353	20	86	11	26	5	0	2	10	4	0	0	1	21	0	0	.430	.330
Chavis, Michael	R-R	5-10	216	8-11-95	.257	.429	.238	21	70	11	18	4	0	7	11	8	0	0	1	21	0	0	.614	.329
Dalbec, Bobby	R-R	6-4	225	6-29-95	.257	.308	.250	30	113	12	29	4	0	7	16	5	3	0	2	29	0	2	.478	.301
De La Guerra, Chad	L-R	5-11	190	11-24-92	.288	.278	.291	61	226	35	65	16	1	13	37	24	2	1	0	64	1	2	.540	.361
Hardy, Dylan	R-R	5-11	175	1-20-97	.000	--	.000	1	3	0	0	0	0	0	0	0	0	0	0	2	0	0	.000	.000
Hernandez, Gorkys	R-R	6-1	196	9-7-87	.219	.305	.191	123	430	75	94	14	3	16	53	62	4	2	6	146	20	6	.377	.319
Hernandez, Marco	L-R	6-0	200	9-6-92	.285	.217	.319	35	137	23	39	12	0	2	11	6	0	0	3	32	3	2	.416	.308
Hernandez, Oscar	R-R	6-1	230	7-9-93	.210	.244	.196	47	148	20	31	10	0	6	20	12	3	2	3	33	0	0	.399	.274
Holt, Brock	L-R	5-10	180	6-11-88	.250	.167	.273	9	28	7	7	2	0	1	3	8	1	0	0	12	1	0	.429	.432
Leon, Sandy	B-R	5-10	225	3-13-89	.120	.250	.095	7	25	2	3	0	0	0	1	0	0	0	0	6	0	1	.120	.154
Lin, Tzu-Wei	L-R	5-9	155	2-15-94	.246	.200	.260	59	224	30	55	11	1	4	22	21	0	3	2	58	6	2	.357	.308
Lopez, Deiner	B-R	6-0	165	5-30-94	.130	.200	.111	9	23	1	3	1	0	0	2	0	0	0	0	6	0	1	.174	.200
Lovullo, Nick	R-R	6-0	175	12-1-93	.200	.300	.171	15	45	8	9	1	0	1	5	4	0	1	0	14	1	0	.289	.265
Matheny, Tate	R-R	6-0	185	2-9-94	.083	.000	.100	5	12	2	1	0	0	0	3	3	1	0	0	6	1	0	.083	.313
Miller, Mike	R-R	5-9	170	9-27-89	.256	.220	.272	53	195	29	50	9	0	3	23	22	1	1	2	28	3	4	.349	.332
2-team total (25 Rochester)					.251	.215	.265	78	279	35	70	12	0	3	29	29	1	1	2	46	4	4	.326	.322
Moreland, Mitch	L-L	6-2	230	9-6-85	.000	.000	.000	4	13	0	0	0	0	0	0	1	0	0	0	4	0	0	.000	.071
Nunez, Eduardo	R-R	6-0	195	6-15-87	.133	.333	.000	4	15	1	2	0	0	1	1	0	0	0	0	1	0	0	.333	.133
Ockimey, Josh	L-R	6-1	215	10-18-95	.204	.100	.237	122	377	64	77	17	2	25	57	82	6	0	3	139	0	2	.459	.353
Osinski, Michael	R-R	6-2	195	8-4-95	.000	.000	.000	1	4	0	0	0	0	0	0	0	0	0	0	2	0	0	.000	.000
Owings, Chris	R-R	5-10	185	8-12-91	.325	.226	.373	44	163	26	53	11	0	11	34	15	2	1	2	50	6	4	.595	.385
Pearce, Steve	R-R	5-11	200	4-13-83	.167	.167	.167	7	24	3	4	1	0	0	2	3	2	0	0	10	0	0	.208	.310
Pedroia, Dustin	R-R	5-9	175	8-17-83	.158	.400	.071	5	19	2	3	0	0	0	1	0	0	0	0	6	0	0	.158	.200
Renda, Tony	R-R	5-8	175	1-24-91	.200	.250	.188	5	20	3	4	2	0	1	5	1	0	0	0	3	0	0	.450	.238
Romanski, Jake	R-R	5-11	200	12-22-90	.191	.250	.177	7	21	4	4	2	0	0	2	0	2	0	0	4	0	0	.286	.261
Sturgeon, Cole	L-L	6-0	180	9-17-91	.277	.264	.281	97	343	43	95	17	2	10	43	24	7	2	3	86	6	3	.426	.334
Tobias, Josh	B-R	5-9	195	11-23-92	.291	.289	.292	44	134	16	39	8	1	2	13	13	0	1	2	29	1	1	.410	.349
Travis, Sam	R-R	6-0	205	8-27-93	.275	.348	.246	68	236	36	65	14	1	7	33	31	1	0	0	62	5	1	.432	.362
Witte, Jantzen	R-R	6-2	195	1-4-90	.277	.283	.275	112	393	45	109	22	0	8	49	34	5	0	4	82	8	4	.394	.339

Pitching	B-T	HT	WT	DOB	W	L	ERA	G	GS	CG	SV	IP	H	R	ER	HR	BB	SO	AVG	vLH	vRH	K/9	BB/9
Bleich, Jeremy	L-L	6-2	215	6-18-87	2	2	5.59	12	3	0	0	19	21	13	12	4	8	17	.273	.375	.226	7.91	3.72
2-team total (9 Rochester)					3	3	5.51	21	4	0	0	33	41	21	20	5	11	34	.306	.324	.300	9.37	3.03
Brasier, Ryan	R-R	6-0	225	8-26-87	2	0	0.96	10	0	0	0	9	6	1	1	1	1	13	.182	.083	.238	12.54	0.96
Brewer, Colten	R-R	6-4	230	10-29-92	2	3	4.91	9	0	0	0	11	14	9	6	2	7	10	.304	.250	.346	8.18	5.73
Ellington, Brian	R-R	6-3	215	8-4-90	0	0	9.00	4	0	0	0	4	4	4	4	0	7	5	.308	.286	.333	11.25	15.75
Eovaldi, Nathan	R-R	6-2	225	2-13-90	0	0	0.00	1	1	0	0	1	0	0	0	1	0	3	.000	--	.000	27.00	9.00
Gorst, Matthew	R-R	6-1	205	8-24-94	1	1	2.70	9	1	0	0	13	10	4	4	1	13	8	.222	.263	.192	5.40	8.78
Hart, Kyle	L-L	6-5	170	11-23-92	9	7	3.86	18	15	1	0	100	91	44	43	8	36	80	.251	.284	.241	7.18	3.23
Hembree, Heath	R-R	6-4	210	1-13-89	0	0	0.00	1	0	0	0	1	0	0	0	0	0	2	.000	.000	.000	18.00	0.00
Hernandez, Darwinzon	L-L	6-2	245	12-17-96	1	2	4.76	7	3	0	0	17	10	9	9	2	16	20	.175	.083	.242	10.59	8.47
Houck, Tanner	R-R	6-4	210	6-29-96	0	0	3.24	16	2	0	1	25	19	11	9	3	14	27	.209	.120	.242	9.72	5.04
Jimenez, Dedgar	L-L	6-3	240	3-6-96	0	1	14.09	2	2	0	0	8	10	12	12	2	10	7	.313	.250	.333	8.22	11.74
Johnson, Brian	L-L	6-4	235	12-7-90	1	0	3.68	6	3	0	0	15	13	6	6	1	5	6	.250	.143	.290	11.66	4.91
Kelley, Trevor	R-R	6-2	210	10-20-93	5	5	1.79	52	0	0	12	65	51	18	13	8	21	63	.096		.296	8.68	2.89

Pitching	B-T	HT	WT	DOB	W	L	ERA	G	GS	CG	SV	IP	H	R	ER	HR	BB	SO	AVG	vLH	vRH	K/9	BB/9
Kent, Matthew	L-L	6-0	180	9-13-92	1	4	8.70	6	6	0	0	30	37	29	29	8	15	14	.311	.125	.405	4.20	4.50
Lakins, Travis	R-R	6-1	180	6-29-94	3	4	4.60	40	1	0	6	45	46	25	23	4	23	42	.264	.293	.242	8.40	4.60
Lau, Adam	R-R	6-2	210	7-5-94	1	0	5.79	5	1	0	0	9	8	6	3		11	8	.229	.167	.294	7.71	10.61
Lenik, Kevin	R-R	6-5	225	8-1-91	0	0	4.50	3	0	0	0	4	4	2	2	1	3	4	.250	.667	.154	9.00	6.75
McGrath, Daniel	R-L	6-3	205	7-7-94	0	0	5.23	2	1	0	0	10	13	6	6	1	4	3	.351	.429	.333	2.61	3.48
Mejia, Jenrry	R-R	6-0	205	10-11-89	2	7	6.38	42	0	0	7	48	52	36	34	9	16	49	.277	.264	.285	9.19	3.00
Poyner, Bobby	L-L	6-0	205	12-1-92	2	5	3.77	43	1	0	6	57	47	27	24	9	27	70	.220	.322	.181	10.99	4.24
Ramirez, Erasmo	R-R	5-10	215	5-2-90	6	8	4.74	27	24	1	0	125	125	75	66	18	43	95	.259	.307	.224	6.82	3.09
Runzler, Dan	L-L	6-4	210	3-30-85	1	1	5.40	22	0	0	1	27	26	19	16	3	15	22	.255	.212	.275	7.43	5.06
Shawaryn, Mike	R-R	6-2	200	9-17-94	1	2	4.52	26	14	0	0	90	76	48	45	13	49	76	.235	.246	.227	7.63	4.92
Shepherd, Chandler	R-R	6-3	185	8-25-92	0	5	10.01	8	7	0	0	30	53	43	33	11	16	30	.373	.449	.333	9.10	4.85
2-team total (14 Norfolk)					3	10	6.18	22	19	1	0	102	128	84	70	19	39	103	.298	.322	.289	9.09	3.44
Smith, Josh A.	R-R	6-2	220	8-7-87	5	3	5.48	13	12	1	0	67	82	44	41	9	20	70	.303	.287	.315	9.36	2.67
Stankiewicz, Teddy	R-R	6-4	215	11-25-93	6	7	3.85	24	23	1	0	131	138	62	56	26	39	106	.269	.280	.260	7.28	2.68
Sturgeon, Cole	L-L	6-0	180	9-17-91	0	1	9.00	4	0	0	0	4	7	8	4	1	6	3	.412	.500	.385	6.75	13.50
Tapia, Domingo	R-R	6-3	250	8-4-91	5	4	5.18	44	1	0	2	66	74	47	38	8	32	52	.286	.274	.294	7.09	4.36
Taylor, Josh	L-L	6-5	225	3-2-93	1	1	2.70	20	0	0	3	23	18	9	7	2	11	32	.222	.276	.192	12.34	4.24
Thornburg, Tyler	R-R	5-11	190	9-29-88	0	2	12.66	11	1	0	0	11	17	15	15	5	9	13	.333	.391	.286	10.97	7.59
Velazquez, Hector	R-R	6-0	180	11-26-88	0	0	3.31	12	0	0	1	16	11	6	6	3	11	14	.200	.120	.267	7.71	6.06
Wade, Konner	L-R	6-3	190	12-3-91	0	0	1.80	1	1	0	0	5	8	1	1	0	3	1	.364	.364	.364	1.80	5.40
Walden, Marcus	R-R	6-0	195	9-13-88	0	0	0.00	1	0	0	0	2	1	0	0	0	0	2	.167	.000	.250	10.80	0.00
Weber, Ryan	R-R	6-1	180	8-12-90	1	5	4.50	16	16	1	0	78	86	41	39	9	25	63	.281	.294	.273	7.27	2.88
Weems, Jordan	L-R	6-3	175	11-7-92	0	1	6.17	8	1	0	0	12	14	9	8	1	6	14	.326	.375	.296	10.80	4.63
Witte, Jantzen	R-R	6-2	195	1-4-90	0	0	27.00	1	0	0	0	1	8	7	3	0	0	0	.727	.667	.800	0.00	0.00
Wright, Steven	R-R	6-2	215	8-30-84	1	0	1.86	5	1	0	0	10	6	2	2	1	3	4	.177	.200	.158	3.72	2.79

Fielding

Catcher	PCT	G	PO	A	E	DP	PB
Centeno	.995	81	581	48	3	7	12
Hernandez	.998	47	383	35	1	2	6
Leon	1.000	7	71	6	0	1	0
Romanski	.961	7	47	2	2	0	1

First Base	PCT	G	PO	A	E	DP
Chavis	1.000	4	29	1	0	2
Dalbec	1.000	11	82	0	0	8
Moreland	1.000	3	21	0	0	2
Ockimey	.992	83	568	38	5	67
Pearce	1.000	4	26	4	0	6
Travis	.986	26	198	11	3	17
Witte	1.000	18	127	7	0	11

Second Base	PCT	G	PO	A	E	DP
Chatham	1.000	5	12	10	0	6
Chavis	1.000	7	10	17	0	5
De La Guerra	1.000	16	22	35	0	7
Hernandez	.946	24	38	49	5	12
Holt	1.000	2	3	1	0	1
Lin	1.000	15	28	38	0	12
Lopez	.957	7	8	14	1	3
Lovullo	.976	12	17	24	1	11
Miller	.885	8	13	10	3	4
Nunez	1.000	1	3	4	0	1
Owings	1.000	10	23	33	0	6
Pedroia	1.000	3	4	5	0	1
Renda	.667	1	0	2	1	1
Tobias	.980	39	59	87	3	27
Witte	1.000	6	12	12	0	4

Third Base	PCT	G	PO	A	E	DP
Chavis	.933	7	3	11	1	1
Dalbec	.957	17	13	31	2	2
De La Guerra	.964	13	9	18	1	0
Lin	.000	1	0	0	0	0
Miller	1.000	8	10	13	0	2
Nunez	.500	1	0	1	1	0
Owings	1.000	6	5	10	0	0
Renda	1.000	4	2	5	0	1
Tobias	1.000	6	4	11	0	1
Witte	.964	83	72	145	8	26

Shortstop	PCT	G	PO	A	E	DP
Chatham	.935	15	21	37	4	7
De La Guerra	.960	32	36	61	4	17
Hernandez	1.000	8	7	17	0	3
Holt	1.000	3	3	13	0	0
Lin	.954	27	40	85	6	21
Lopez	1.000	2	4	4	0	0
Lovullo	1.000	3	4	4	0	1
Miller	.943	39	43	73	7	17
Owings	.986	18	28	42	1	7

Outfield	PCT	G	PO	A	E	DP
Brentz	.967	52	83	4	3	1
Castillo	.983	106	226	9	4	1
Hardy	1.000	1	2	0	0	0
Hernandez	.988	118	244	8	3	2
Lin	1.000	11	24	1	0	1
Matheny	1.000	4	5	0	0	0
Osinski	1.000	1	2	0	0	0
Owings	1.000	10	18	1	0	0
Sturgeon	.989	94	182	5	2	1
Travis	1.000	31	43	1	0	0
Witte	1.000	2	5	0	0	0

PORTLAND SEA DOGS

DOUBLE-A

EASTERN LEAGUE

Batting	B-T	HT	WT	DOB	AVG	vLH	vRH	G	AB	R	H	2B	3B	HR	RBI	BB	HBP	SH	SF	SO	SB	CS	SLG	OBP
Asche, Cody	L-R	6-1	205	6-30-90	.208	.167	.217	23	72	9	15	3	0	1	8	17	1	0	1	28	3	0	.292	.363
Chatham, C.J.	R-R	6-3	185	12-22-94	.297	.343	.279	90	350	39	104	26	1	3	36	18	3	1	4	66	7	1	.403	.333
Cubillan, Ricardo	B-R	6-0	155	2-1-98	.286	.200	.333	5	14	1	4	0	0	0	0	3	0	0	0	6	0	0	.286	.412
Curcio, Keith	L-R	5-10	185	12-28-92	.227	.208	.233	29	97	11	22	5	0	2	6	4	1	0	0	22	4	0	.340	.265
Curletta, Joey	R-R	6-4	245	3-8-94	.205	.179	.215	94	312	43	64	18	0	9	44	49	5	0	8	112	3	1	.349	.316
Dalbec, Bobby	R-R	6-4	225	6-29-95	.234	.242	.231	105	359	57	84	15	2	20	57	68	11	0	1	110	6	4	.454	.371
Downs, Jerry	L-L	6-2	215	12-22-93	.177	.000	.237	55	153	10	27	9	0	2	14	13	7	2	1	57	0	0	.275	.270
Duran, Jarren	L-R	6-2	200	9-5-96	.250	.263	.244	82	320	41	80	11	5	1	19	23	5	3	1	84	28	8	.325	.310
Hardy, Dylan	R-R	5-11	175	1-20-97	.143	.091	.161	19	42	3	6	0	0	0	1	3	0	0	0	19	4	0	.143	.200
Hernandez, Oscar	R-R	6-1	230	7-9-93	.083	.200	.053	7	24	3	2	0	0	0	1	2	0	0	0	11	0	0	.083	.154
Holt, Brock	L-R	5-10	180	6-11-88	.000	--	.000	1	2	0	0	0	0	0	0	1	0	0	0	0	0	0	.000	.333
Joseph, Tommy	R-R	6-1	255	7-16-91	.260	.200	.267	13	50	7	13	3	0	0	5	2	2	0	1	17	0	0	.320	.309
Lopez, Deiner	B-R	6-0	165	5-30-94	.169	.152	.179	30	89	7	15	5	0	1	8	2	0	1	0	38	3	0	.258	.187
Lovullo, Nick	R-R	6-0	175	12-1-93	.175	.167	.177	21	63	2	11	0	0	0	3	5	0	0	1	21	0	1	.175	.235
Lucena, Isaias	B-R	5-11	180	11-15-94	.500	.500	--	3	2	0	1	0	0	0	0	0	0	0	0	1	0	0	.500	.667
Madden, Charlie	R-R	6-3	205	9-1-95	.225	.133	.250	24	71	6	16	4	0	5	12	1	1	1	1	28	0	0	.493	.243
Matheny, Tate	R-R	6-0	185	2-9-94	.240	.228	.246	94	329	36	79	16	1	8	42	14	4	4	2	105	11	7	.368	.278
Monge, Joseph	R-R	6-1	190	5-18-95	.188	.250	.150	10	32	5	6	0	0	0	1	0	0	1	0	13	1	0	.188	.235
Netzer, Brett	L-R	6-0	195	4-6-94	.247	.242	.249	130	454	56	112	24	1	8	50	45	5	5	3	128	3	4	.357	.320
Nunez, Jhon	B-R	5-9	165	12-5-94	.280	.196	.310	64	211	26	59	11	1	5	21	13	4	4	0	39	5	3	.412	.333

	B-T	HT	WT	DOB	AVG	vLH	vRH	G	AB	R	H	2B	3B	HR	RBI	BB	HBP	SH	SF	SO	SB	CS	OBP	SLG
Ortega, Jonathan	R-R	5-8	185	9-27-96	.000	--	.000	1	1	1	0	0	0	0	1	1	0	0	0	1	0	0	.000	.500
Osinski, Michael	R-R	6-2	195	8-4-95	.192	.125	.205	17	52	5	10	2	1	0	5	7	1	0	1	18	0	0	.269	.295
Pedroia, Dustin	R-R	5-9	175	8-17-83	.222	.333	.167	6	18	1	4	0	0	0	1	0	0	0	0	3	0	0	.222	.222
Rei, Austin	R-R	6-0	185	10-27-93	.157	.158	.156	26	83	4	13	5	0	1	9	6	0	1	0	29	0	0	.253	.214
Rivera, Jeremy	B-R	5-9	150	1-30-95	.236	.192	.253	101	339	34	80	11	2	6	33	22	3	9	1	70	12	3	.333	.288
Romanski, Jake	R-R	5-11	200	12-22-90	.214	.219	.211	29	89	9	19	3	0	0	3	3	1	2	1	24	0	1	.247	.245
Rusconi, Jagger	B-R	5-11	165	7-18-96	.500	--	.500	2	4	0	2	1	0	0	1	0	0	0	1	0	0	0	.750	.400
Tavarez, Aneury	L-R	5-9	175	4-14-92	.192	.217	.180	20	73	6	14	3	1	0	3	8	0	0	0	18	3	1	.260	.272
Tendler, Luke	L-R	5-11	190	8-25-91	.235	.255	.229	122	413	46	97	23	1	11	58	39	3	1	2	109	4	5	.375	.304
Tobias, Josh	B-R	5-9	195	11-23-92	.309	.200	.344	24	81	11	25	8	0	2	11	9	6	1	0	23	1	7	.482	.417
Wilson, Marcus	R-R	6-2	175	8-15-96	.223	.146	.247	62	206	35	46	14	0	8	22	28	2	0	2	82	6	0	.408	.319
Witte, Jantzen	R-R	6-2	195	1-4-90	.150	.250	.083	6	20	2	3	0	0	1	2	1	0	0	0	9	0	0	.300	.191

Pitching	B-T	HT	WT	DOB	W	L	ERA	G	GS	CG	SV	IP	H	R	ER	HR	BB	SO	AVG	vLH	vRH	K/9	BB/9
Bazardo, Eduard	R-R	6-0	155	9-1-95	4	1	2.78	21	0	0	0	32	27	12	10	2	13	35	.225	.227	.222	9.74	3.62
Cosart, Jake	R-R	6-2	175	2-11-94	1	1	1.59	10	0	0	0	11	6	4	2	0	10	14	.162	.100	.185	11.12	7.94
Crawford, Kutter	R-R	6-1	192	4-1-96	1	3	4.19	5	5	0	0	19	19	10	9	2	15	23	.271	.250	.300	10.71	6.98
Downs, Jerry	L-L	6-2	215	12-22-93	0	0	0.00	1	0	0	0	1	0	0	0	0	0	1	.000	.000	.000	9.00	0.00
Ellington, Brian	R-R	6-3	215	8-4-90	2	0	1.80	12	0	0	1	15	9	5	3	2	13	20	.167	.182	.143	12.00	7.80
Feltman, Durbin	R-R	6-0	205	4-18-97	2	3	5.26	43	0	0	5	51	42	31	30	8	31	54	.223	.245	.198	9.47	5.44
Gomez, Anyelo	R-R	6-1	185	3-1-93	0	0	5.06	4	0	0	0	5	4	3	3	0	4	6	.200	.214	.167	10.13	6.75
Gorst, Matthew	R-R	6-1	205	8-24-94	2	7	4.62	31	2	0	2	49	42	35	25	5	17	45	.236	.306	.150	8.32	3.14
Hart, Kyle	L-L	6-5	170	11-23-92	3	6	2.91	9	9	1	0	56	39	19	18	3	17	60	.199	.225	.181	9.70	2.75
Hernandez, Darwinzon	L-L	6-2	245	12-17-96	1	1	5.13	10	9	0	0	40	33	28	23	2	32	59	.217	.149	.282	13.17	7.14
Houck, Tanner	R-R	6-4	210	6-29-96	8	6	4.25	17	15	1	0	83	86	41	39	4	32	80	.270	.305	.220	8.71	3.48
Jimenez, Dedgar	L-L	6-3	240	3-6-96	4	5	3.78	29	12	0	10	86	75	39	36	9	41	74	.237	.210	.255	7.77	4.31
Johnson, Brian	L-L	6-4	235	12-7-90	1	0	10.50	3	2	0	0	6	11	10	7	1	3	7	.393	.500	.313	10.50	4.50
Kent, Matthew	L-L	6-0	180	9-13-92	5	7	4.19	22	18	0	0	122	134	66	57	3	39	85	.279	.267	.286	6.25	2.87
Lau, Adam	R-R	6-2	210	7-5-94	1	4	3.31	35	0	0	7	52	43	24	19	3	23	62	.236	.245	.224	10.80	4.01
Lenik, Kevin	R-R	6-5	225	8-1-91	1	0	2.70	16	0	0	3	23	10	7	7	2	12	29	.132	.184	.079	11.19	4.63
Leyer, Robinson	R-R	6-2	175	3-13-93	0	1	2.66	15	1	0	0	24	13	8	7	0	17	30	.163	.157	.172	11.41	6.46
LoBrutto, Dominic	L-L	6-1	185	5-31-96	0	2	8.71	7	0	0	1	10	19	11	10	1	6	9	.396	.304	.480	7.84	5.23
Mata, Bryan	R-R	6-3	160	5-3-99	4	6	5.03	11	11	0	0	54	54	32	30	6	24	59	.271	.279	.261	9.89	4.02
McGrath, Daniel	R-L	6-3	205	7-7-94	7	1	1.68	27	15	0	1	112	72	25	21	5	45	113	.184	.180	.187	9.05	3.61
Mejia, Jenrry	R-R	6-0	205	10-11-89	0	0	0.00	1	0	0	0	1	0	0	0	0	2	1	.250	.000	.333	9.00	0.00
Reyes, Denyi	R-R	6-4	209	11-2-96	8	12	4.16	26	26	0	0	151	142	74	70	14	37	116	.243	.267	.214	6.90	2.20
Schellenger, Zach	R-R	6-5	210	1-9-96	0	0	10.38	11	0	0	1	9	8	10	10	1	21	10	.258	.200	.313	10.38	21.81
Schwaab, Andrew	R-R	6-1	205	2-8-93	1	1	5.50	10	0	0	1	18	14	14	11	0	14	22	.209	.235	.182	11.00	7.00
Smith, Hunter	R-R	6-3	195	3-18-94	0	0	0.00	1	0	0	1	3	2	0	0	0	2	1	.200	.000	.286	3.00	6.00
Thompson, Dylan	L-R	6-3	195	9-4-92	1	0	4.50	1	1	0	0	6	8	3	3	0	1	5	.320	.222	.375	7.50	1.50
Wade, Konner	L-R	6-3	190	12-3-91	6	4	2.74	17	13	0	0	95	89	30	29	5	13	64	.246	.262	.228	6.04	1.23
Weems, Jordan	L-R	6-3	175	11-7-92	0	2	3.89	33	0	0	8	44	40	23	19	1	27	55	.244	.221	.264	11.25	5.52

Fielding

Catcher	PCT	G	PO	A	E	DP	PB
Hernandez	1.000	7	69	5	0	1	1
Lucena	1.000	3	10	2	0	0	0
Madden	1.000	23	152	10	0	0	4
Nunez	.983	62	462	56	9	5	13
Rei	.992	26	231	9	2	1	3
Romanski	.987	28	210	20	3	3	2

First Base	PCT	G	PO	A	E	DP
Asche	1.000	1	10	1	0	0
Curletta	.993	70	510	37	4	43
Dalbec	.971	13	58	10	2	3
Downs	.997	44	280	17	1	29
Hernandez	1.000	1	3	0	0	0
Joseph	1.000	7	36	6	0	5
Osinski	1.000	4	21	3	0	1
Tobias	.972	7	34	1	1	3
Witte	.971	5	28	6	1	5

Second Base	PCT	G	PO	A	E	DP
Chatham	1.000	7	10	23	0	3
Lopez	1.000	3	3	7	0	2
Lovullo	.857	4	1	5	1	0
Netzer	.984	110	174	256	7	53
Ortega	.000	1	0	0	0	0
Pedroia	1.000	5	4	9	0	2
Rivera	.978	13	18	27	1	7
Rusconi	1.000	2	2	4	0	1
Tobias	1.000	3	6	8	0	3

Third Base	PCT	G	PO	A	E	DP
Cubillan	1.000	1	1	0	0	0
Dalbec	.928	90	57	137	15	15
Lopez	1.000	3	2	2	0	0
Lovullo	.941	17	13	19	2	2
Osinski	.941	10	10	6	1	1
Rivera	.952	22	10	30	2	1
Tobias	1.000	4	4	5	0	0

Shortstop	PCT	G	PO	A	E	DP
Chatham	.953	78	123	161	14	35
Cubillan	.895	4	8	9	2	3
Holt	1.000	1	1	0	0	0
Lopez	.943	13	13	20	2	6
Lovullo	1.000	1	1	1	0	0
Rivera	.981	48	70	81	3	26

Outfield	PCT	G	PO	A	E	DP
Asche	.975	19	37	2	1	0
Curcio	1.000	27	61	2	0	2
Duran	.984	80	180	1	3	0
Hardy	.952	18	19	1	1	0
Lopez	1.000	12	12	0	0	0
Matheny	.990	94	190	6	2	1
Monge	1.000	9	14	1	0	0
Netzer	1.000	2	3	1	0	0
Nunez	.000	1	0	0	1	0
Rivera	1.000	1	1	0	0	0
Tavarez	.971	18	32	1	1	0
Tendler	.982	91	160	8	3	2
Wilson	.985	61	125	3	2	1

SALEM RED SOX

CAROLINA LEAGUE

Batting	B-T	HT	WT	DOB	AVG	vLH	vRH	G	AB	R	H	2B	3B	HR	RBI	BB	HBP	SH	SF	SO	SB	CS	SLG	OBP
Acosta, Victor	R-R	5-11	160	6-2-96	.274	.229	.291	100	350	45	96	17	1	3	46	38	4	2	2	42	5	4	.354	.350
Batesole, Korby	L-R	6-1	170	2-8-96	.170	.143	.174	25	53	4	9	0	0	0	2	3	1	2	1	12	0	0	.170	.224
Benge, Garrett	L-R	6-0	205	12-28-95	.253	.237	.259	94	336	40	85	16	2	6	35	42	1	1	3	106	6	4	.366	.335
Campana, Marino	R-R	6-4	180	11-28-97	.139	.182	.071	11	36	4	5	1	0	1	4	4	0	0	0	19	0	1	.250	.225
Casas, Triston	L-R	6-4	238	1-15-00	.429	.000	.600	2	7	2	3	1	0	1	3	0	0	0	0	2	0	0	1.000	.429
Castellanos, Pedro	R-R	6-3	195	12-11-97	.276	.278	.275	117	446	61	123	23	2	9	71	22	11	0	7	71	10	7	.397	.321
Corcino, Edgar	R-R	6-1	210	6-7-92	.315	.410	.279	68	219	36	69	18	4	9	46	20	7	0	3	56	2	4	.557	.386
Cottam, Kole	R-R	6-3	220	5-30-97	.256	.267	.250	11	39	5	10	4	0	2	10	1	0	0	1	13	0	1	.513	.262
Curcio, Keith	L-R	5-10	185	12-28-92	.291	.367	.267	70	251	42	73	20	4	1	19	26	1	1	3	46	7	1	.414	.356
Downs, Jerry	L-L	6-2	215	12-22-93	.143	.182	.127	23	77	7	11	4	0	0	1	6	2	0	0	18	0	0	.195	.224
Duran, Jarren	L-R	6-2	200	9-5-96	.387	.458	.347	50	199	49	77	13	3	4	19	23	3	0	1	44	18	5	.543	.456
Esplin, Tyler	L-R	6-4	225	7-6-99	.200	.000	.333	2	5	0	1	0	0	0	1	0	0	0	0	2	0	0	.200	.333
Fitzgerald, Ryan	L-R	6-0	185	6-17-94	.271	.305	.256	127	461	63	125	25	7	3	65	51	6	0	9	107	11	10	.375	.345
Granberg, Devlin	R-R	6-2	224	9-8-95	.222	.188	.241	25	90	9	20	6	0	0	11	4	3	0	2	16	1	1	.289	.273
Hardy, Dylan	R-R	5-11	175	1-20-97	.243	.313	.213	36	107	20	26	4	0	2	11	15	2	2	1	36	2	2	.336	.344
Hernandez, Marco	L-R	6-0	200	9-6-92	.295	.269	.308	21	78	15	23	7	0	0	9	8	3	0	2	9	1	1	.385	.374
Lopez, Deiner	B-R	6-0	165	5-30-94	.176	.261	.137	27	74	5	13	3	1	0	5	7	0	0	0	23	2	3	.243	.247
Lovullo, Nick	R-R	6-0	175	12-1-93	.246	.286	.229	43	138	15	34	11	0	1	13	15	2	0	0	30	0	4	.348	.329
Lucena, Isaias	B-R	5-11	180	11-15-94	.163	.182	.148	16	49	5	8	5	0	0	2	6	0	0	0	10	0	0	.265	.255
Madden, Charlie	R-R	6-3	205	9-1-95	.216	.194	.223	40	134	14	29	6	0	1	22	7	3	1	2	50	1	0	.284	.267
Marrero, Erik	B-R	5-9	185	6-21-97	.192	.357	.121	15	47	3	9	2	0	1	3	3	0	0	0	8	0	0	.298	.240
Miranda, Samuel	R-R	6-1	175	8-21-97	.208	.000	.217	8	24	2	5	1	1	1	3	0	0	0	0	5	0	0	.458	.208
Monge, Joseph	R-R	6-1	190	5-18-95	.256	.143	.320	11	39	4	10	2	0	0	5	2	0	0	0	13	1	0	.308	.293
Nishioka, Tanner	R-R	5-11	180	10-22-94	.250	.263	.244	78	248	21	62	18	0	2	38	13	14	0	7	72	5	1	.347	.316
Ortega, Jonathan	R-R	5-8	185	9-27-96	.242	.429	.188	20	62	9	15	2	0	0	4	6	0	0	1	13	5	3	.274	.329
Osinski, Michael	R-R	6-2	195	8-4-95	.277	.385	.205	29	65	10	18	6	0	0	7	11	1	1	0	15	0	0	.369	.390
Rusconi, Jagger	B-R	5-11	165	7-18-96	.196	.207	.191	107	377	47	74	16	2	3	29	20	4	4	2	112	6	5	.273	.243
Sciortino, Nick	R-R	5-9	197	7-21-95	.163	.200	.147	56	166	13	27	4	1	2	13	20	4	1	2	73	0	2	.235	.266
Suarez, Kervin	B-R	5-11	165	12-19-98	.214	.200	.222	4	14	2	3	1	0	0	1	2	0	0	2	1	0	.286	.313
Williams, Grant	L-R	5-10	180	10-3-95	.333	.143	.400	17	54	4	18	4	0	1	0	3	6	1	0	3	7	2	1	.407	.346
Wilson, Marcus	R-R	6-2	175	8-15-96	.343	.400	.317	45	146	26	50	12	1	8	29	18	1	0	2	47	4	3	.603	.413

Pitching	B-T	HT	WT	DOB	W	L	ERA	G	GS	CG	SV	IP	H	R	ER	HR	BB	SO	AVG	vLH	vRH	K/9	BB/9
Aybar, Yoan	L-L	6-3	165	7-3-97	0	0	1.80	4	0	0	0	5	2	1	1	0	1	3	.125	.167	.100	5.40	1.80
Baker, Robbie	R-R	6-1	185	1-31-95	2	1	5.56	5	0	0	0	11	13	7	7	1	4	8	.296	.235	.333	6.35	3.18
Bazardo, Eduard	R-R	6-0	155	9-1-95	1	1	1.76	17	0	0	4	41	29	10	8	1	9	53	.191	.186	.194	11.63	1.98
Browning, Logan	L-L	5-8	175	9-3-95	2	1	2.81	9	0	0	1	16	16	6	5	2	6	7	.271	.263	.275	3.94	3.38
Cosart, Jake	R-R	6-2	175	2-11-94	0	3	1.83	14	0	0	5	20	13	7	4	1	5	22	.197	.133	.119	10.07	2.29
Crawford, Kutter	R-R	6-1	192	4-1-96	4	5	3.39	14	14	1	0	69	68	29	26	5	30	77	.262	.234	.281	10.04	3.91
De Jesus, Enmanuel	L-L	6-3	190	12-10-96	9	9	3.58	24	24	1	0	131	140	66	52	5	42	122	.275	.239	.288	8.40	2.89
Demchak, Alex	L-L	6-1	220	1-16-95	1	1	6.57	7	0	0	0	12	19	13	9	1	7	13	.352	.273	.372	9.49	5.11
Diaz, Jhonathan	L-L	6-0	170	9-13-96	9	8	3.86	27	27	0	0	128	121	63	55	6	54	118	.249	.232	.256	8.28	3.79
Fisher, Devon	R-R	6-0	215	5-1-96	1	2	10.45	8	0	0	0	10	14	14	12	1	13	13	.311	.304	.318	11.32	11.32
Gomez, Anyelo	R-R	6-1	185	3-1-93	0	0	1.93	7	0	0	0	9	6	2	2	0	5	4	.177	.150	.214	3.86	4.82
Gomez, Rio	L-L	6-0	190	10-20-94	1	2	2.80	25	0	0	2	45	42	18	14	6	20	38	.255	.225	.267	7.60	4.00
Gonzalez, Daniel	R-R	6-5	180	2-9-96	6	10	4.36	26	26	0	0	151	164	78	73	17	31	101	.281	.233	.323	6.03	1.85
Jackson, Kris	R-R	5-11	185	3-20-96	0	1	19.80	4	0	0	0	5	11	11	11	1	4	5	.423	.417	.429	9.00	7.20
LoBrutto, Dominic	L-L	6-1	185	5-31-96	2	1	2.04	23	0	0	3	35	30	10	8	1	5	36	.231	.214	.239	9.17	1.27
Lopez, Deiner	B-R	6-0	165	5-30-94	0	0	0.00	1	0	0	0	1	1	0	0	0	1	0	.250	--	.250	9.00	9.00
Lovullo, Nick	R-R	6-0	175	12-1-93	0	0	0.00	1	0	0	0	1	0	0	0	0	0	0	.000	.000	--	0.00	0.00
Martinez, Algenis	R-R	6-1	185	9-12-93	1	0	2.84	7	0	0	0	13	9	4	4	0	7	10	.209	.188	.222	7.11	4.97
Martinez, Joan	R-R	6-3	195	8-29-96	4	4	3.88	29	0	0	1	49	42	28	21	4	28	58	.232	.254	.219	10.73	5.18
Mata, Bryan	R-R	6-3	160	5-3-99	3	1	1.75	10	10	0	0	51	38	18	10	1	18	52	.201	.234	.179	9.12	3.16
Osinski, Michael	R-R	6-2	195	8-4-95	0	0	0.00	1	0	0	0	1	1	0	0	0	0	1	.500	1.000	1.000	0.00	0.00
Politi, Andrew	R-R	6-0	191	6-4-96	5	2	3.55	33	5	0	1	79	56	37	31	4	37	96	.197	.223	.179	10.98	4.23
Schellenger, Zach	R-R	6-5	210	1-9-96	1	1	5.75	26	0	0	2	36	28	24	23	6	23	51	.214	.200	.224	12.75	5.75
Scherff, Alex	R-R	6-3	205	2-5-98	1	0	1.42	1	1	0	0	6	5	1	1	0	2	3	.227	.250	.222	4.26	2.84
Schwaab, Andrew	R-R	6-1	205	2-8-93	2	1	2.01	34	0	0	13	40	24	13	9	0	15	44	.173	.207	.148	9.82	3.35
Smith, Hunter	R-R	6-3	195	3-18-94	3	4	5.87	23	2	0	0	46	55	37	30	2	23	51	.309	.318	.304	9.98	4.50
Thompson, Dylan	L-R	6-3	195	9-4-92	6	8	5.34	19	16	1	0	86	119	58	51	2	29	53	.335	.301	.362	5.55	3.03
Thompson, Jake	R-R	6-1	200	9-22-94	0	1	3.86	4	0	0	0	7	5	3	3	0	1	5	.208	.111	.267	6.43	1.29
Ward, Thad	R-R	6-3	182	1-16-97	3	3	2.33	12	12	0	0	54	38	15	14	4	32	70	.203	.195	.210	11.67	5.33

Fielding

Catcher	PCT	G	PO	A	E	DP	PB
Cottam	.976	10	73	8	2	1	2
Lucena	1.000	16	132	9	0	1	4
Madden	1.000	39	294	27	0	5	3
Marrero	1.000	15	104	11	0	1	1
Miranda	.986	8	61	9	1	0	0
Osinski	.000	1	0	0	0	0	0
Sciortino	.988	56	445	63	6	3	16

First Base	PCT	G	PO	A	E	DP
Benge	.970	8	61	3	2	7
Casas	1.000	2	17	0	0	2

	PCT	G	PO	A	E	DP	PB
Castellanos	.988	106	794	28	10	79	
Cottam	1.000	1	2	1	0	0	
Downs	1.000	14	108	5	0	13	
Fitzgerald	1.000	1	1	0	0	0	
Granberg	1.000	5	27	3	0	1	
Osinski	.970	7	31	1	1	3	

Second Base	PCT	G	PO	A	E	DP
Acosta	1.000	2	1	0	0	0
Batesole	.938	8	10	5	1	4
Benge	1.000	1	5	3	0	1
Fitzgerald	.977	10	17	26	1	8

	PCT	G	PO	A	E	DP
Hernandez	.905	6	14	5	2	3
Lopez	.889	6	7	9	2	4
Lovullo	.989	22	41	47	1	12
Nishioka	.915	39	62	68	12	15
Ortega	.935	11	13	16	2	3
Rusconi	.987	40	68	87	2	29
Suarez	1.000	2	8	3	0	1
Williams	1.000	9	15	24	0	5

Third Base	PCT	G	PO	A	E	DP
Batesole	.875	10	5	9	2	2
Benge	.948	69	43	159	11	9

Fitzgerald	1.000	5	5	10	0 0
Lopez	.906	13	11	18	3 2
Lovullo	1.000	21	15	31	0 5
Nishioka	.700	5	3	4	3 2
Ortega	1.000	10	6	14	0 1
Osinski	.897	17	10	16	3 1

Shortstop	PCT	G	PO	A	E DP
Batesole	1.000	9	8	15	0 7
Fitzgerald	.960	111	156	274	18 60
Hernandez	.892	11	13	20	4 5

Lopez	1.000	6	2	10	0 1
Lovullo	1.000	2	1	5	0 0
Williams	.944	8	14	20	2 7

Outfield	PCT	G	PO	A	E DP
Acosta	.988	79	153	6	2 1
Campana	.923	10	10	2	1 0
Castellanos	1.000	3	5	0	0 0
Corcino	1.000	60	81	8	0 1
Curcio	.963	69	146	8	6 2

Duran	1.000	50	102	5	0 1
Esplin	1.000	2	4	0	0 0
Granberg	.969	17	28	3	1 0
Hardy	1.000	32	51	3	0 1
Lopez	.000	3	0	0	0 0
Nishioka	.000	1	0	0	0 0
Osinski	1.000	1	1	0	0 0
Rusconi	.976	58	73	8	2 0
Suarez	1.000	1	2	0	0 0
Wilson	.988	41	84	1	1 0

GREENVILLE DRIVE
SOUTH ATLANTIC LEAGUE

LOW CLASS A

Batting	B-T	HT	WT	DOB	AVG	vLH	vRH	G	AB	R	H	2B	3B	HR	RBI	BB	HBP	SH	SF	SO	SB	CS	SLG	OBP
Abreu, Juan Carlos	R-R	6-0	175	5-30-97	.219	.333	.207	10	32	6	7	3	0	0	6	3	1	2	0	14	0	1	.313	.306
Arnold, Jecorrah	R-R	6-2	190	1-6-99	.300	.333	.286	3	10	0	3	0	0	0	1	0	0	0	0	4	0	0	.300	.364
Batesole, Korby	L-R	6-1	170	2-8-96	.200	.208	.198	47	150	15	30	7	0	0	7	4	2	1	0	65	0	5	.247	.231
Brannen, Cole	L-R	6-0	170	8-4-98	.204	.140	.219	114	442	49	90	10	3	1	34	44	2	5	4	128	24	8	.247	.276
Campana, Marino	R-R	6-4	180	11-28-97	.169	.177	.167	19	71	6	12	1	1	1	6	4	0	0	1	26	1	1	.254	.211
Casas, Triston	L-R	6-4	238	1-15-00	.254	.218	.263	118	422	64	107	25	5	19	78	58	7	0	6	116	3	2	.472	.349
Cottam, Kole	R-R	6-3	220	5-30-97	.255	.161	.284	76	263	42	67	21	1	6	34	44	8	0	1	78	0	0	.411	.377
Cubillan, Ricardo	B-R	6-0	155	2-1-98	.100	.000	.111	3	10	1	1	0	0	0	1	0	0	0	0	3	0	0	.100	.182
Dearden, Tyler	L-R	6-2	185	7-6-98	.202	.180	.207	60	208	18	42	7	2	4	21	16	3	5	0	80	0	0	.313	.269
Esplin, Tyler	L-R	6-4	225	7-6-99	.253	.152	.279	100	387	52	98	26	3	5	43	40	4	1	4	107	6	3	.375	.326
Granberg, Devlin	R-R	6-2	224	9-8-95	.286	.229	.303	99	357	57	102	19	5	8	45	45	15	0	3	79	6	4	.434	.386
Hardy, Dylan	R-R	5-11	175	1-20-97	.227	.150	.255	19	75	9	17	2	2	2	8	9	0	1	0	23	3	1	.387	.310
Howlett, Brandon	R-R	6-1	205	9-12-99	.231	.250	.226	113	390	48	90	23	1	8	35	56	12	2	5	144	1	5	.356	.341
Lozada, Everlouis	B-R	5-7	150	11-14-98	.228	.189	.239	65	254	36	58	12	1	6	23	24	0	4	2	63	3	4	.354	.293
Marrero, Alan	R-R	5-10	195	2-25-98	.201	.250	.187	64	214	23	43	10	0	7	22	31	1	0	0	86	0	1	.346	.305
Miranda, Samuel	L-R	6-1	175	8-21-97	.250	.500	.208	9	28	4	7	1	0	1	2	1	0	0	0	8	0	0	.393	.276
Ortega, Jonathan	R-R	5-8	185	9-27-96	.172	.159	.176	56	192	12	33	6	1	2	17	16	0	5	1	57	3	2	.245	.234
Pedroia, Dustin	R-R	5-9	175	8-17-83	.333	.000	.375	3	9	1	3	1	0	0	2	0	0	0	1	0	0	0	.444	.455
Rangel, Oscar	L-R	5-11	175	5-27-98	.167	--	.167	2	6	0	1	0	0	0	0	0	0	0	0	2	0	0	.167	.167
Suarez, Kervin	B-R	5-11	165	12-19-98	.186	.104	.208	60	221	25	41	17	2	2	25	12	1	6	2	80	4	9	.308	.229
Williams, Grant	L-R	5-10	180	10-3-95	.265	.215	.277	104	347	36	92	15	6	1	42	31	6	4	5	43	4	8	.352	.332
Wren, Jordan	L-L	6-1	195	9-23-94	.239	.256	.235	115	423	47	101	20	5	6	43	39	6	0	1	127	31	6	.352	.311

Pitching	B-T	HT	WT	DOB	W	L	ERA	G	GS	CG	SV	IP	H	R	ER	HR	BB	SO	AVG	vLH	vRH	K/9	BB/9
Aybar, Yoan	L-L	6-3	165	7-3-97	1	3	4.88	40	0	0	0	52	34	31	28	1	40	67	.180	.179	.181	11.67	6.97
Baker, Robbie	R-R	6-1	185	1-31-95	0	1	3.92	12	0	0	0	21	16	14	9	4	4	18	.205	.250	.180	7.84	1.74
Batesole, Korby	L-R	6-1	170	2-8-96	0	0	0.00	2	0	0	0	2	0	0	0	1	0		.250	.286	.000	0.00	4.50
Bello, Brayan	R-R	6-1	170	5-17-99	5	10	5.43	25	25	0	0	118	135	77	71	9	38	119	.286	.268	.300	9.10	2.91
Biondic, Kevin	R-R	6-1	215	1-26-96	4	9	4.68	20	14	1	1	100	112	60	52	12	42	52	.292	.278	.302	4.68	3.78
Browning, Logan	L-L	5-8	175	9-3-95	4	1	2.04	33	0	9	0	57	39	17	13	2	11	75	.193	.206	.187	11.77	1.73
Demchak, Alex	L-L	6-1	220	1-16-95	3	1	1.98	22	0	0	3	41	26	9	9	2	14	50	.178	.186	.175	10.98	3.07
Fisher, Devon	R-R	6-0	215	5-1-96	1	2	6.52	13	0	0	1	19	17	15	14	4	8	19	.243	.231	.250	8.84	3.72
Gomez, Rio	L-L	6-0	190	10-20-94	2	0	1.09	14	0	0	5	25	13	4	3	2	4	37	.149	.150	.149	13.50	1.46
Haworth, Hunter	R-R	6-4	210	10-2-96	5	8	4.72	31	10	0	2	103	94	60	54	9	40	124	.241	.301	.205	10.83	3.50
Jackson, Kris	R-R	5-11	185	3-20-96	0	1	3.48	4	0	0	1	10	9	4	4	0	3	6	.237	.000	.360	8.71	2.61
Machamer, Chris	R-R	6-1	180	6-4-97	4	8	6.10	20	20	0	0	93	118	68	63	12	43	55	.308	.316	.302	5.32	4.16
Mosqueda, Oddanier	L-L	5-10	155	5-6-99	2	2	3.29	27	0	0	2	52	44	23	19	4	21	69	.228	.346	.181	11.94	3.63
Nail, Brendan	L-L	6-0	190	10-18-95	0	1	3.96	15	0	0	0	25	21	12	11	3	16	37	.223	.160	.246	13.32	5.76
Ortega, Jonathan	R-R	5-8	185	9-27-96	1	0	0.00	1	0	0	0	2	3	0	0	0	0	0	.250	.200	.286	0.00	0.00
Padron, Angel	L-L	5-11	175	9-16-97	2	7	3.40	28	5	0	1	77	80	44	29	5	33	85	.260	.180	.292	9.98	3.87
Padron-Artilles, Yusniel	R-R	6-0	187	11-12-97	0	2	5.25	6	3	0	0	24	27	14	14	3	7	25	.281	.353	.242	9.38	2.63
Pantoja, Yorvin	L-L	5-11	175	9-22-97	6	3	3.54	36	0	0	1	61	46	29	24	4	30	72	.207	.220	.203	10.62	4.43
Requena, Hildemaro	R-R	6-2	170	7-20-97	0	0	5.40	2	0	0	0	5	8	3	3	1	0	4	.348	.250	.368	0.00	1.80
Santana, Yasel	R-R	6-1	180	12-14-96	0	3	6.05	6	6	0	0	19	25	22	13	4	15	14	.313	.353	.283	6.52	6.98
Scherff, Alex	B-R	6-3	205	2-5-98	5	12	4.83	26	26	0	0	123	144	75	66	14	53	109	.295	.279	.305	7.98	3.88
Shugart, Chase	R-R	5-10	180	10-24-96	4	4	2.81	16	16	1	0	90	89	36	28	4	23	73	.253	.262	.246	7.33	2.31
Suero, Miguel	R-R	6-1	185	1-4-97	0	0	6.97	4	0	0	0	10	13	8	8	2	5	10	.333	.400	.263	8.71	4.35
Sutherland, Casey	R-R	6-3	205	10-18-96	0	0	0.00	1	0	0	0	1	1	0	0	0	2		.250	.000	.333	18.00	0.00
Ward, Thad	R-R	6-3	182	1-16-97	5	2	1.99	13	13	1	0	72	51	24	16	2	25	87	.194	.168	.215	10.82	3.11

Fielding

Catcher	PCT	G	PO	A	E	DP	PB
Cottam	.994	66	598	42	4	4	3
Marrero	.978	63	510	68	13	2	11
Miranda	1.000	9	57	7	0	1	2
Rangel	1.000	2	18	2	0	0	2

First Base	PCT	G	PO	A	E	DP
Batesole	1.000	3	26	2	0	3
Casas	.995	94	710	42	4	52
Cottam	.911	6	38	3	4	2
Cubillan	1.000	1	9	1	0	0
Granberg	.981	36	287	28	6	26

Second Base	PCT	G	PO	A	E	DP
Arnold	.917	2	6	5	1	2
Batesole	.945	19	15	37	3	8
Cubillan	.875	1	2	5	1	0
Lozada	.963	64	87	150	9	29
Ortega	1.000	20	32	51	0	6
Pedroia	1.000	3	5	9	0	4
Suarez	.978	36	48	83	3	11

Third Base	PCT	G	PO	A	E	DP
Batesole	.818	5	3	6	2	2
Casas	.882	8	6	9	2	1

Howlett	.899	105	61	143	23	12
Ortega	.980	21	19	30	1	2

Shortstop	PCT	G	PO	A	E	DP
Batesole	.900	19	32	49	9	7
Cubillan	1.000	1	1	2	0	0
Ortega	.986	15	27	41	1	10
Williams	.975	104	133	261	10	51

BOSTON RED SOX

Outfield	PCT	G	PO	A	E	DP
Abreu	1.000	7	12	0	0	0
Brannen	.982	111	262	16	5	5

	PCT	G	PO	A	E	DP
Campana	.930	17	38	2	3	1
Dearden	.984	43	62	1	1	0
Esplin	.976	93	158	4	4	0
Granberg	1.000	1	2	0	0	0

	PCT	G	PO	A	E	DP
Hardy	.974	19	36	1	1	1
Suarez	.873	27	54	1	8	1
Wren	.985	104	189	5	3	1

LOWELL SPINNERS — SHORT SEASON
NEW YORK-PENN LEAGUE

Batting	B-T	HT	WT	DOB	AVG	vLH	vRH	G	AB	R	H	2B	3B	HR	RBI	BB	HBP	SH	SF	SO	SB	CS	SLG	OBP
Abreu, Juan Carlos	R-R	6-0	175	5-30-97	.265	.429	.222	9	34	6	9	0	1	0	3	1	0	0	0	9	0	0	.324	.286
Arnold, Jecorrah	R-R	6-2	190	1-6-99	.104	.000	.139	19	48	6	5	1	0	1	5	8	2	0	1	28	1	1	.188	.254
Baldwin, Roldani	R-R	5-11	175	3-16-96	.222	.000	.286	3	9	1	2	0	0	0	1	2	0	0	1	2	0	0	.222	.333
Bandy, Luke	R-R	6-0	185	1-5-98	.165	.231	.145	34	109	12	18	5	2	0	8	7	4	2	0	49	1	0	.248	.242
Batesole, Korby	L-R	6-1	170	2-8-96	.333	--	.333	1	3	0	1	0	0	0	0	0	0	1	0	2	0	0	.333	.500
Campana, Marino	R-R	6-4	180	11-28-97	.217	.174	.226	37	129	20	28	5	1	7	23	8	3	0	0	55	4	1	.434	.279
Cannon, Cameron	R-R	5-10	196	10-16-97	.205	.231	.200	42	161	17	33	12	0	3	21	12	7	0	0	37	1	0	.335	.289
Cubillan, Ricardo	B-R	6-0	155	2-1-98	.288	.333	.276	27	73	17	21	3	2	0	17	11	2	2	2	11	4	3	.384	.426
Dalton, Wil	R-R	6-0	190	8-27-97	.203	.080	.237	37	118	19	24	3	3	2	15	14	5	1	1	43	2	1	.331	.312
Davis, Joe	R-R	6-0	230	10-31-96	.281	.423	.250	40	146	18	41	9	0	5	28	6	4	0	4	25	0	0	.445	.319
Decker, Nick	L-L	6-0	200	10-2-99	.247	.226	.252	53	170	23	42	10	5	6	25	21	1	0	3	59	4	5	.471	.328
Diaz, Jonathan	L-R	5-11	170	7-7-99	.243	.231	.247	29	103	15	25	8	3	1	7	9	1	0	2	32	2	1	.408	.310
Erro, Alex	B-R	5-10	180	12-5-97	.277	.130	.305	43	141	16	39	5	0	0	17	9	1	1	2	18	1	1	.312	.320
Flores, Antoni	R-R	6-1	190	10-14-00	.193	.250	.181	55	181	14	35	4	1	0	12	25	1	0	1	59	1	3	.227	.293
Groshans, Jaxx	R-R	6-0	209	7-20-98	.216	.346	.189	44	148	15	32	5	1	4	23	23	0	0	4	34	1	1	.345	.314
Hardy, Dylan	R-R	5-11	175	1-20-97	.200	.000	.222	3	10	1	2	0	0	0	0	0	0	0	0	3	1	0	.200	.200
Jimenez, Gilberto	B-R	5-11	160	7-8-00	.359	.296	.374	59	234	35	84	11	3	3	19	13	2	1	3	38	14	6	.470	.393
LeGrant, Xavier	R-R	6-0	175	4-19-97	.281	.333	.262	17	57	12	16	1	1	1	5	3	1	0	0	20	0	1	.386	.328
Lugo, Matthew	R-R	6-1	185	5-9-01	.250	.000	.500	2	8	0	2	0	0	0	1	0	0	0	0	2	0	0	.250	.250
Marrero, Elih	B-R	5-9	185	6-21-97	.213	.154	.226	20	75	8	16	6	1	0	15	7	1	0	2	14	1	0	.320	.282
Miranda, Samuel	L-R	6-1	175	8-21-97	.053	.000	.063	7	19	2	1	1	0	0	0	2	0	0	0	8	0	0	.105	.143
Northcut, Nicholas	R-R	6-1	200	6-13-99	.211	.186	.219	54	194	20	41	10	2	1	22	20	1	1	1	60	1	1	.299	.287
Pearce, Steve	R-R	5-11	200	4-13-83	.167	.000	.200	2	6	1	1	0	0	0	1	0	0	0	0	3	0	0	.333	.143
Petit, Keibert	R-R	6-1	175	8-3-98	1.000	--	1.000	2	1	0	1	0	0	0	0	0	0	0	0	0	0	0	1.000	1.000
Rafaela, Ceddanne	R-R	5-8	145	9-18-00	.182	.500	.000	3	11	0	2	0	0	0	1	0	0	0	1	3	0	0	.182	.167
Scott, Stephen	L-R	5-11	200	5-23-97	.248	.091	.282	39	125	21	31	10	0	3	12	23	1	0	2	40	3	0	.400	.364
Suarez, Kervin	B-R	5-11	165	12-19-98	.232	.143	.253	34	112	17	26	4	5	1	11	9	3	6	0	43	7	5	.384	.307

Pitching	B-T	HT	WT	DOB	W	L	ERA	G	GS	CG	SV	IP	H	R	ER	HR	BB	SO	AVG	vLH	vRH	K/9	BB/9
Baker, Robbie	R-R	6-1	185	1-31-95	0	0	4.26	8	0	0	0	13	14	10	6	1	5	15	.264	.238	.281	10.66	3.55
Bell, Brock	R-R	6-4	215	3-18-98	0	1	0.00	1	1	0	0	2	3	2	0	0	2	1	.333	.667	.167	5.40	10.80
Bleich, Jeremy	L-L	6-2	215	6-18-87	1	0	0.71	9	0	0	0	13	8	2	1	0	6	16	.178	.231	.156	11.37	4.26
Cellucci, Brendan	L-L	6-4	201	6-30-98	1	0	5.25	8	0	0	0	12	14	7	7	1	7	17	.292	.083	.361	12.75	5.25
Cosart, Jake	R-R	6-2	175	2-11-94	0	0	0.00	1	0	0	0	0	0	0	0	0	0	0	.000	--	.000	0.00	54.00
De La Rosa, Osvaldo	R-R	6-4	210	10-28-97	5	1	1.75	17	0	0	3	26	16	5	5	2	12	27	.180	.214	.164	9.47	4.21
Fernandez, Ryan	R-R	6-0	170	6-11-98	4	1	2.49	17	1	0	4	43	30	15	12	2	11	38	.188	.229	.170	7.89	2.28
Gomez, Anyelo	R-R	6-1	185	3-1-93	0	0	1.17	5	0	0	0	8	2	1	1	0	1	3	.087	.167	.059	3.52	1.17
Groome, Jay	L-L	6-6	220	8-23-98	0	0	4.50	1	1	0	0	2	1	1	1	0	1	3	.300	.500	.167	13.50	4.50
Jackson, Kris	R-R	5-11	185	3-20-96	2	3	1.32	22	0	0	9	27	16	6	4	1	9	27	.168	.300	.108	8.89	2.96
Jimenez, Eddie	R-R	6-2	230	8-9-95	1	0	0.00	1	0	0	0	1	0	0	0	0	1	0	.000	.000	.000	0.00	6.75
Larez, Jose	R-R	6-4	195	1-12-97	1	1	9.28	10	0	0	0	11	14	15	11	1	5	6	.333	.375	.308	5.06	4.22
Lenik, Kevin	R-R	6-5	225	8-1-91	0	0	0.00	1	0	0	0	1	0	0	0	0	0	3	.000	--	.000	27.00	0.00
Leyer, Robinson	R-R	6-2	175	3-13-93	0	1	18.00	3	0	0	0	3	4	6	6	0	2	3	.308	.333	.300	9.00	6.00
Lucas, Bryan	R-R	6-2	160	12-13-97	5	6	5.47	13	10	0	0	54	66	43	33	4	19	44	.296	.313	.289	7.29	3.15
Martinez, Joan	R-R	6-3	195	8-29-96	0	0	6.75	2	0	0	0	3	0	2	2	0	3	4	.000	.000	.000	13.50	10.13
Mejia, Jenrry	R-R	6-0	205	10-11-89	0	1	4.26	6	0	0	1	6	7	3	3	1	1	8	.259	.222	.278	11.37	1.42
Murphy, Chris	L-L	6-1	175	6-5-98	0	1	1.08	10	10	0	0	33	23	6	4	1	7	34	.197	.143	.214	9.18	1.89
Nail, Brendan	R-R	6-0	190	10-18-95	0	0	1.23	8	0	0	4	15	6	3	2	0	6	27	.122	.125	.122	16.57	3.68
Padron-Artiles, Yusniel	R-R	6-0	187	11-12-97	7	1	2.67	13	9	0	0	64	55	22	19	6	14	84	.227	.313	.182	11.81	1.97
Ramirez, Aldo	R-R	6-0	180	5-6-01	2	3	3.94	14	13	0	0	62	59	31	27	5	16	63	.245	.265	.234	9.19	2.34
Requena, Hildemaro	R-R	6-2	170	7-20-97	4	1	3.15	14	1	0	0	34	33	21	12	4	12	21	.260	.275	.253	5.50	3.15
Rodriguez, Jorge	L-L	5-11	170	8-25-00	1	0	3.86	1	0	0	0	5	4	2	2	0	4	2	.211	.000	.267	7.71	0.00
Sanchez, Kelvin	L-L	6-3	196	5-12-97	3	4	4.70	13	5	0	0	44	38	26	23	4	36	38	.245	.212	.254	7.77	7.36
Santana, Yasel	R-R	6-1	180	12-14-96	3	4	3.47	15	5	0	0	57	58	27	22	3	28	57	.260	.271	.255	9.00	4.42
Scroggins, Cody	R-R	6-0	195	8-17-96	0	0	7.30	9	0	0	0	12	8	11	10	1	10	15	.186	.143	.207	10.95	7.30
Song, Noah	R-R	6-4	200	5-28-97	0	0	1.06	7	7	0	0	17	10	2	2	0	5	19	.167	.077	.235	10.06	2.65
Spacke, Dylan	B-R	6-0	180	3-11-98	0	0	3.86	7	0	0	1	12	10	5	5	1	3	16	.233	.250	.222	12.34	2.31
Suero, Miguel	R-R	6-1	185	1-4-97	2	3	2.86	15	0	0	1	44	39	18	14	6	16	36	.245	.200	.273	7.36	3.27
Velazquez, Hector	R-R	6-0	180	11-26-88	0	0	0.00	1	1	0	0	2	1	0	0	0	0	2	.333	.000	.500	18.00	0.00
Windle, Tom	L-L	6-4	215	3-10-92	0	0	0.00	2	0	0	0	2	1	0	0	0	2	1	.125	.333	.000	9.00	0.00
Zeferjahn, Ryan	R-R	6-5	225	2-28-98	0	2	4.50	12	12	0	0	22	24	12	11	2	12	31	.279	.300	.268	12.68	4.91

Fielding

C: Baldwin 2, Diaz 16, Groshans 33, Marrero 20, Miranda 7. **1B:** Cubillan 17, Davis 27, Erro 1, LeGrant 17, Pearce 1, Petit 1, Scott 18. **2B:** Cannon 19, Cubillan 2, Erro 16, Flores 6, Rafaela 2, Suarez 32. **3B:** Cubillan 1, Erro 23, Northcut 53, Rafaela 1. **SS:** Batesole 1, Cannon 18, Cubillan 7, Flores 48, Lugo 2. **OF:** Abreu 3, Arnold 13, Bandy 29, Campana 30, Dalton 34, Decker 52, Hardy 3, Jimenez 58, Scott 14, Suarez 1.

BOSTON RED SOX

GCL RED SOX

ROOKIE

GULF COAST LEAGUE

Batting	B-T	HT	WT	DOB	AVG	vLH	vRH	G	AB	R	H	2B	3B	HR	RBI	BB	HBP	SH	SF	SO	SB	CS	SLG	OBP
Andrade, Fabian	L-L	5-11	162	4-1-99	.206	.385	.160	27	63	8	13	0	0	0	4	7	4	1	0	9	1	0	.206	.324
Bakst, Daniel	R-R	6-2	190	11-14-97	.306	.333	.300	27	98	14	30	8	4	0	15	15	1	0	2	19	0	0	.469	.397
Baldwin, Roldani	R-R	5-11	175	3-16-96	.429	.200	.556	5	14	2	6	0	0	1	3	2	0	0	0	4	0	0	.643	.500
Ball, Trey	L-L	6-6	185	6-27-94	.143	.000	.154	5	14	1	2	1	0	0	6	4	0	0	2	4	0	0	.214	.300
Cannon, Cameron	R-R	5-10	196	10-16-97	.111	.250	.000	3	9	0	1	0	0	0	0	0	1	0	0	5	0	0	.111	.200
Colon, Andre	R-R	6-0	180	2-12-99	.155	.105	.173	24	71	10	11	2	0	0	5	9	3	2	1	15	4	1	.183	.274
D'Alessandro, Dominic	R-R	6-1	223	10-20-96	.292	.185	.320	39	130	18	38	5	1	3	20	27	2	0	0	36	0	0	.415	.421
Diaz, Danny	R-R	6-1	170	1-2-01	.210	.333	.179	26	105	15	22	11	0	1	12	5	2	0	1	30	0	0	.343	.257
Herbert, Jacob	R-R	6-2	220	6-29-00	.143	.154	.140	21	56	4	8	0	0	0	4	5	3	0	0	25	0	0	.143	.250
Joseph, Tommy	R-R	6-1	255	7-16-91	.286	.500	.000	2	7	3	2	1	0	1	2	0	0	0	0	0	0	0	.857	.286
Kemp, Trenton	R-R	6-2	195	9-30-95	.100	.250	.000	6	10	0	1	1	0	0	2	4	1	0	2	6	1	0	.200	.353
Licona, Breiner	R-R	6-1	190	8-14-99	.186	.000	.222	15	43	5	8	1	0	1	1	8	0	1	0	19	0	0	.279	.314
Lugo, Matthew	R-R	6-1	185	5-9-01	.257	.179	.278	39	136	19	35	5	1	1	12	15	3	2	1	36	3	0	.331	.342
Maita, Angel	B-R	5-11	160	5-28-01	.207	.132	.237	41	135	18	28	6	1	0	7	22	3	2	0	42	8	4	.267	.331
Miller, Dean	R-R	6-2	235	1-30-97	.289	.259	.297	37	128	20	37	10	3	4	24	15	2	1	1	40	1	0	.508	.370
Monge, Joseph	R-R	6-1	190	5-18-95	.105	.000	.118	7	19	2	2	0	0	0	2	1	0	0	0	5	0	0	.105	.227
Paulino, Leon	B-R	6-3	205	11-15-00	.153	.231	.136	25	72	8	11	4	0	0	4	11	1	0	0	36	1	1	.208	.274
Perez, Brandon	L-R	6-3	180	12-9-99	.277	.120	.319	34	119	16	33	5	0	1	20	13	2	0	0	35	2	2	.345	.358
Petit, Keibert	R-R	6-1	175	8-3-98	.250	1.000	.000	2	4	2	1	0	0	0	0	0	0	0	0	0	0	0	.250	.250
Rafaela, Ceddanne	R-R	5-8	145	9-18-00	.248	.361	.214	41	153	30	38	1	4	6	17	14	5	3	1	28	9	2	.425	.330
Ramsey, Caleb	L-R	5-10	160	10-29-99	.180	.250	.174	17	50	5	9	2	0	0	6	9	1	0	1	24	3	0	.220	.312
Rangel, Oscar	L-R	5-11	175	5-27-98	.295	.333	.286	21	61	8	18	4	1	0	16	11	2	0	1	15	1	0	.393	.413
Rei, Austin	R-R	6-0	185	10-27-93	.286	.000	.308	7	14	7	4	1	0	0	4	8	2	0	0	5	0	0	.357	.583
Rijo, Nilo	R-R	5-11	165	8-29-98	.214	.231	.209	27	56	10	12	3	0	0	6	14	4	0	0	24	3	4	.268	.405
Rodriguez, Kleiber	B-R	6-2	175	10-8-98	.250	.167	.273	13	28	2	7	2	0	0	9	4	1	0	0	11	0	0	.321	.364
Simas, Karson	R-R	6-6	175	6-2-01	.211	.455	.111	11	38	2	8	0	0	0	4	4	2	0	0	8	0	0	.211	.318

Pitching	B-T	HT	WT	DOB	W	L	ERA	G	GS	CG	SV	IP	H	R	ER	HR	BB	SO	AVG	vLH	vRH	K/9	BB/9
Bell, Brock	R-R	6-4	215	3-18-98	0	1	2.77	8	8	0	0	13	10	4	4	0	4	11	.222	.235	.214	7.62	2.77
Blalock, Bradley	R-R	6-2	190	12-25-00	0	2	6.75	4	3	0	0	7	5	6	5	0	4	4	.208	.143	.235	5.40	5.40
Cepeda, Felix	R-R	6-3	170	7-15-00	2	4	6.16	10	8	0	0	38	39	30	26	4	20	29	.265	.236	.283	6.87	4.74
Duke, Mason	R-R	5-10	210	10-21-96	2	1	2.82	13	0	0	0	22	25	8	7	1	5	17	.281	.306	.264	6.85	2.01
Fisher, Devon	R-R	6-0	215	5-1-96	1	0	0.00	3	0	0	0	4	6	0	0	0	6		.400	.250	.455	13.50	0.00
Gomez, Anyelo	R-R	6-1	185	3-1-93	0	0	7.36	3	0	0	0	4	3	4	3	1	5	6	.200	.000	.300	14.73	12.27
Groome, Jay	L-L	6-6	220	8-23-98	0	0	0.00	2	2	0	0	2	2	0	0	0	0	3	.250	.000	.333	13.50	0.00
Guedez, Yoelvis	R-R	5-11	175	9-8-00	2	1	1.60	14	0	0	3	34	25	6	6	0	5	36	.202	.189	.211	9.62	1.34
Harrington, Reed	R-R	6-5	200	8-8-98	0	0	4.91	4	0	0	0	4	4	2	2	0	2	4	.267	.250	.273	9.82	4.91
Jimenez, Eddie	R-R	6-2	200	8-9-95	1	0	2.89	14	0	0	0	19	18	6	6	1	7	23	.254	.409	.184	11.09	3.38
Jimenez, Richardson	R-R	5-11	173	9-30-99	1	1	6.75	2	0	0	0	4	4	3	3	0	1	6	.250	.333	.200	13.50	2.25
Larez, Jose	R-R	6-4	195	1-12-97	0	3	3.72	7	0	0	0	10	8	4	4	0	7	8	.211	.167	.231	7.45	6.52
LoBrutto, Dominic	L-L	6-1	185	5-31-96	0	0	0.00	2	1	0	0	3	1	0	0	0	4		.111	.333	.000	13.50	0.00
Loubier, Blake	R-R	6-5	190	10-13-00	0	1	5.54	6	6	0	0	13	14	8	8	1	7	15	.286	.261	.308	10.38	4.85
Martinez, Algenis	R-R	6-1	185	9-12-93	0	0	3.00	2	0	0	0	3	2	1	1	0	1	1	.167	.286	.000	3.00	3.00
Montero, Alexander	R-R	6-3	180	9-21-97	0	2	5.75	10	5	0	0	20	25	17	13	1	12	22	.305	.419	.235	9.74	5.31
Perry, Aaron	R-R	5-11	175	6-7-99	0	2	3.00	9	5	0	0	21	11	9	7	0	19	18	.155	.143	.163	7.71	8.14
Reyes, Gregorio	L-L	6-3	170	1-22-99	3	2	3.05	11	8	0	0	41	39	20	14	4	6	36	.244	.182	.267	7.84	1.31
Rodriguez, Jorge	L-L	5-11	170	8-25-00	6	2	1.91	11	6	0	0	47	35	13	10	2	9	58	.202	.167	.216	11.11	1.72
Roedahl, Devon	R-R	6-2	225	11-29-96	0	2	4.09	16	0	0	3	22	20	11	10	2	5	27	.227	.189	.255	11.05	2.05
Schneider, Zach	R-R	6-0	180	1-27-97	1	2	2.28	17	0	0	4	24	20	9	6	1	4	33	.222	.290	.173	12.55	1.52
Spacke, Dylan	B-R	6-0	180	3-11-98	2	1	3.10	12	0	0	0	20	20	10	7	0	3	23	.256	.219	.283	10.18	1.33
Sutherland, Casey	R-R	6-3	205	10-18-96	1	0	0.66	11	0	0	1	27	17	2	2	1	1	26	.174	.118	.234	8.56	0.33
Walter, Brandon	L-L	6-2	200	9-8-96	1	2	2.70	13	0	0	0	33	26	11	10	2	8	39	.208	.241	.198	10.53	2.16

Fielding

C: Baldwin 4, Herbert 17, Licona 15, Rangel 21, Rei 4, Rodriguez 6. **1B:** Andrade 9, D'Alessandro 37, Diaz 1, Joseph 2, Petit 2, Rodriguez 6. **2B:** Bakst 17, Colon 21, Rafaela 13, Rijo 2, Simas 2. **3B:** Diaz 21, Rafaela 15, Rijo 20. **SS:** Cannon 2, Colon 2, Lugo 30, Rafaela 13, Simas 7. **OF:** Andrade 17, Ball 3, Kemp 4, Maita 41, Miller 31, Monge 6, Paulino 21, Perez 33, Ramsey 16.

DSL RED SOX

ROOKIE

Batting	B-T	HT	WT	DOB	AVG	vLH	vRH	G	AB	R	H	2B	3B	HR	RBI	BB	HBP	SH	SF	SO	SB	CS	SLG	OBP
Abreu, Nelfy	B-R	5-10	150	3-2-01	.240	.282	.230	60	200	30	48	3	2	1	23	28	1	2	1	45	17	4	.290	.335
Alvarez, Alixandri	B-R	5-9	152	2-13-02	.216	.360	.188	48	153	33	33	2	1	0	23	28	5	1	4	31	11	3	.242	.347
Astacio, Frank	R-R	5-11	150	10-14-00	.261	.300	.247	35	119	16	31	1	2	1	18	9	1	2	3	19	6	3	.328	.311
Barajas, Moises	R-R	6-0	149	2-14-02	.221	.303	.194	50	136	22	30	6	3	0	13	18	10	3	1	40	2	4	.309	.352
Belen, Darel	R-R	6-4	194	5-21-00	.281	.291	.278	64	242	51	68	11	5	5	39	29	7	0	3	53	14	5	.430	.370
Bonaci, Brainer	B-R	5-10	140	7-9-02	.280	.306	.272	61	229	34	64	14	2	3	37	23	6	0	3	40	18	10	.397	.356
Contreras, Imanol	R-R	5-10	150	10-11-01	.171	.111	.188	31	82	11	14	3	0	0	6	7	3	0	1	28	3	1	.207	.258
Custodio, Gregori	R-R	6-1	165	3-18-01	.210	.192	.215	32	105	14	22	6	0	1	16	13	0	0	2	29	2	1	.295	.292
Daza, Denny	R-R	5-11	160	12-27-00	.216	.167	.234	44	153	26	33	7	0	0	7	16	3	0	3	33	1	1	.261	.297
Diaz, Danny	R-R	6-1	170	1-2-01	.316	.500	.294	12	38	3	12	4	0	1	2	2	3	0	0	7	1	0	.500	.395
Feliz, Albert	R-R	6-2	200	4-13-02	.250	.255	.249	66	236	29	59	15	0	9	47	23	3	0	4	76	3	3	.428	.320

Name	B-T	HT	WT	DOB	AVG	vLH	vRH	G	AB	R	H	2B	3B	HR	RBI	BB	HBP	SH	SF	SO	SB	CS	SLG	OBP
Flores, Erick	L-R	5-9	158	6-10-01	.253	.067	.286	35	99	15	25	5	0	0	11	16	2	0	0	15	2	2	.303	.368
Gari, Andres	L-R	5-11	171	4-27-01	.207	.227	.202	34	111	12	23	5	0	0	11	11	4	0	3	26	2	0	.252	.295
Gonzalez, Bryan	R-R	6-2	212	9-18-01	.251	.324	.225	67	255	43	64	12	4	9	41	30	6	0	2	77	7	3	.435	.341
James, Axel	L-R	5-11	153	1-25-02	.295	.302	.292	48	173	23	51	5	4	2	15	16	1	1	1	42	6	5	.405	.356
Jimenez, Leonel	R-R	5-10	170	11-30-99	.231	.333	.200	5	13	4	3	0	0	0	0	3	3	0	0	3	0	0	.231	.474
Lopez, Eduardo	B-R	6-0	170	5-8-02	.255	.175	.273	60	212	39	54	7	8	0	25	38	2	0	1	38	18	7	.363	.372
Maita, Jesus	B-R	5-10	160	5-28-01	.182	.333	.125	18	44	3	8	2	2	0	6	4	0	0	0	10	1	0	.318	.250
Marcano, Naysbel	R-R	6-0	175	5-23-02	.257	.267	.254	49	175	22	45	11	1	2	28	13	4	0	2	46	1	1	.366	.320
Mejicano, Yorberto	R-R	5-11	185	11-21-00	.274	.364	.258	29	73	11	20	1	1	0	14	12	0	0	2	13	5	0	.315	.368
Morales, Henry	L-R	6-3	185	10-4-01	.211	.125	.244	23	57	7	12	7	0	0	8	13	2	0	0	14	0	0	.333	.375
Mota, Luis	L-R	5-11	150	2-24-01	.267	.297	.258	52	165	29	44	2	0	0	11	38	5	0	0	52	5	6	.279	.418
Navas, Jose	R-R	5-11	160	7-18-00	.293	.308	.288	28	99	15	29	9	0	2	23	8	2	0	1	21	0	0	.444	.355
Paulino, Eddinson	L-R	5-10	155	7-2-02	.287	.240	.301	35	108	17	31	2	4	0	10	18	1	1	0	23	2	6	.380	.394
Pena, Andy	R-R	5-10	165	5-29-02	.333	.400	.250	7	18	1	6	0	0	0	1	2	0	0	0	3	0	3	.333	.400
Perez, Wilmer	L-R	6-2	180	3-21-01	.172	.162	.175	45	151	16	26	3	2	0	14	23	0	1	1	39	1	1	.219	.280
Prado, Elio	R-R	6-0	160	11-29-01	.301	.417	.273	34	123	27	37	5	0	3	26	20	2	2	2	21	9	5	.415	.401
2-team total (26 Orioles1)					.300	.393	.286	60	217	40	65	12	0	3	38	30	9	3	2	36	12	10	.396	.403
Rincones, Brandon	R-R	5-9	145	10-1-00	.264	.225	.272	28	72	12	19	1	1	0	7	9	3	4	0	5	2	3	.306	.369
Rojas, Juan	R-R	6-2	165	4-21-01	.074	.000	.105	15	27	4	2	1	0	0	4	11	3	0	2	16	1	1	.111	.372
Rojas, Miguel	R-R	5-9	157	1-4-02	.240	.222	.244	18	50	9	12	3	1	0	6	7	0	0	1	5	1	0	.340	.328
Romero, Noelberth	R-R	6-0	145	12-5-01	.268	.250	.274	30	112	14	30	3	1	2	14	11	1	1	0	21	2	1	.366	.339
2-team total (28 Orioles2)					.273	.267	.275	58	216	29	59	7	1	2	31	18	3	5	0	32	4	2	.343	.338
Sanchez, Carlos	R-R	6-4	203	9-7-00	.233	.278	.221	32	86	8	20	4	0	2	9	5	5	0	0	21	3	1	.349	.313
Santana, Giancarlos	R-R	6-1	180	11-6-01	.192	.195	.191	50	167	23	32	4	0	0	14	27	5	1	0	46	8	3	.216	.322
Santos, Angeudis	L-R	6-1	165	9-19-01	.184	.171	.188	56	174	30	32	2	2	0	13	55	2	1	1	57	15	4	.218	.384
Vargas, Wilker	L-R	5-9	145	1-8-01	.329	.267	.343	28	82	20	27	4	0	0	7	17	2	0	0	16	7	1	.378	.455
Vaughan, Eduardo	R-R	6-3	160	1-12-02	.268	.250	.272	57	209	31	56	11	0	2	21	17	5	1	1	41	4	3	.349	.336
Zapete, Alex	R-R	6-0	180	9-11-01	.262	.279	.257	47	187	23	49	7	0	0	20	8	3	1	2	19	8	5	.300	.300

Pitching	B-T	HT	WT	DOB	W	L	ERA	G	GS	CG	SV	IP	H	R	ER	HR	BB	SO	AVG	vLH	vRH	K/9	BB/9
Acosta, Armando	R-R	6-1	174	10-11-98	2	0	9.45	11	0	0	1	13	15	16	14	2	16	15	.283	.421	.206	10.13	10.80
Bastardo, Angel	R-R		175	6-18-02	3	1	3.71	12	12	0	0	51	39	24	21	1	12	37	.210	.192	.216	6.53	2.12
Blanco, Royman	R-R	6-1	170	4-17-01	4	1	3.12	16	0	0	0	35	38	14	12	0	12	21	.297	.262	.314	5.45	3.12
Castellanos, Moises	R-R	6-3	193	11-9-01	1	1	3.28	9	2	0	0	25	14	10	9	0	13	22	.167	.160	.170	8.03	4.74
Diaz, Efren	R-R	6-2	178	2-20-02	3	3	3.89	16	1	0	2	39	36	28	17	2	22	38	.235	.283	.215	8.69	5.03
Encarnacion, Juan Daniel	R-R	6-2	170	3-30-01	0	5	3.86	14	14	0	0	56	52	29	24	1	24	49	.257	.259	.256	7.88	3.86
Gomez, Felix	L-L	6-0	155	9-1-99	0	0	4.88	15	0	0	1	24	17	17	13	0	25	20	.205	.143	.226	7.50	9.38
Gonzalez, Wilkelman	R-R	6-0	145	3-25-02	0	3	3.30	14	14	0	0	46	34	22	17	3	24	44	.209	.200	.213	8.55	4.66
Gregorio, Faysel	R-R	6-2	150	5-9-02	3	3	6.98	14	3	0	1	39	41	39	30	3	27	31	.265	.218	.290	7.22	6.28
Hernandez, Adrian	R-R	6-3	185	4-19-02	0	1	1.09	12	1	0	0	33	19	7	4	1	14	22	.164	.118	.183	6.00	3.82
Jackson, Gabriel	R-R	6-2	180	9-7-01	4	3	3.49	14	14	0	0	59	58	32	23	0	27	38	.256	.172	.284	5.76	4.10
Jimenez, Richardson	R-R	5-11	173	9-30-99	1	0	5.23	4	0	0	0	10	7	11	6	0	14	15	.184	.000	.226	13.06	12.19
Maita, Jesus	B-R	5-10	160	5-28-01	0	1	4.15	3	0	0	0	4	3	3	2	0	3	6	.214	.333	.125	12.46	6.23
Martinez, Johan	R-R	6-2	180	4-7-99	0	1	4.57	16	0	0	0	22	12	12	11	0	25	28	.162	.177	.158	11.63	10.38
Montero, Robinson	R-R	5-11	168	11-18-99	4	1	3.53	17	0	0	1	43	33	20	17	0	13	35	.212	.184	.224	7.27	2.70
Munoz, Nixson	L-L	5-10	150	10-8-00	5	2	2.40	14	8	0	0	60	56	19	16	1	6	62	.247	.200	.257	9.30	0.75
Ochoa, Claudio	R-R	6-3	170	9-5-01	1	5	5.91	14	12	0	0	43	47	34	28	1	38	40	.280	.282	.278	8.44	8.02
Ortiz, Emerson	R-R	6-1	180	2-10-97	4	1	4.88	17	0	0	5	28	29	19	15	2	12	30	.257	.255	.258	9.76	3.90
Ortuno, Andres	R-R	6-3	167	9-20-01	2	3	5.01	14	9	0	1	47	48	34	26	1	28	32	.267	.303	.240	6.17	5.40
Ozoria, Isaias	L-L	5-11	180	6-16-98	1	3	4.03	19	0	0	7	22	17	12	10	0	13	25	.215	.333	.200	10.07	5.24
Parra, Robinson	R-R	6-3	190	9-28-98	4	1	1.91	19	0	0	3	38	30	14	8	1	23	30	.242	.261	.231	7.17	5.50
Perez, Railin	R-R	6-3	185	9-2-01	1	1	3.60	13	6	0	0	50	41	26	20	2	19	44	.228	.203	.248	7.92	3.42
Pinales, Isaac	R-R	6-0	172	8-15-95	4	3	3.74	22	0	0	6	34	25	16	14	1	9	29	.205	.242	.191	7.75	2.41
Pineda, Beiker	R-R	6-0	165	4-25-98	2	0	1.47	12	3	0	0	31	28	9	5	0	8	28	.244	.333	.186	8.22	2.35
Ramirez, Jose	R-R	6-0	142	3-28-01	2	3	3.03	17	1	0	1	33	20	21	11	1	38	21	.177	.275	.123	5.79	10.47
Reyes, Carlos	R-R	6-3	190	9-17-01	0	4	5.68	13	7	0	0	38	29	26	24	1	34	36	.215	.170	.244	8.53	8.05
Rosillo, Jesus	R-R	6-3	185	1-19-00	5	1	3.02	16	0	0	2	42	29	17	14	1	30	42	.197	.200	.196	9.07	6.48
Sanchez, Frailyn	R-R	6-4	192	4-23-01	2	6	4.50	13	13	0	0	54	49	32	27	6	20	37	.245	.187	.280	6.17	3.33
Segovia, Gregori	R-R	6-1	175	6-27-00	3	0	2.78	18	0	0	0	36	18	11	11	2	10	39	.255	.233	.288	9.84	2.52
Sena, Reidis	R-R	5-10	160	4-7-01	1	6	4.05	10	10	0	0	40	35	22	18	2	13	32	.241	.203	.267	7.20	2.93
Talavera, Luis	R-R	6-3	175	2-6-02	4	2	4.42	14	7	0	1	57	62	34	28	1	31	40	.288	.218	.329	6.32	4.89
Tineo, Cristofe	R-R	6-0	180	6-17-97	1	2	3.20	17	0	0	0	25	21	13	9	1	26	27	.228	.292	.206	9.59	9.24
Valera, Michael	R-R	6-2	176	2-12-99	0	0	0.00	2	0	0	0	2	1	0	0	0	2	6	.143	.200	.000	13.50	9.00
Velez, Carlos	L-L	6-2	190	5-4-99	2	5	4.50	13	5	0	1	44	35	25	22	1	31	48	.217	.280	.206	9.82	6.34
Villarroel, Irvin	R-R	6-4	180	7-26-01	0	0	4.41	7	0	0	0	16	25	11	8	2	2	10	.362	.250	.408	5.51	1.10

Fielding

C: Flores 34, Gari 20, Marcano 32, Mejicano 28, Navas 23, Pena 7, Rojas 17. **1B:** Belen 15, Custodio 27, Daza 1, Feliz 30, Gari 8, Jimenez 3, Morales 4, Navas 1, Perez 24, Rojas 10, Sanchez 24, Zapete 11. **2B:** Alvarez 31, Astacio 1, Contreras 1, Daza 23, James 5, Mota 38, Paulino 11, Perez 2, Rincones 23, Romero 5, Vargas 10. **3B:** Alvarez 3, Astacio 13, Bonaci 6, Custodio 3, Daza 1, Diaz 10, Jimenez 1, Mota 10, Perez 21, Rincones 3, Romero 23, Vargas 16, Zapete 36. **SS:** Alvarez 11, Astacio 1, Bonaci 49, Daza 19, Mota 3, Paulino 18, Romero 2, Santos 51, Vargas 2. **OF:** Abreu 52, Barajas 50, Belen 34, Contreras 15, Feliz 22, Gonzalez 40, James 34, Lopez 48, Maita 15, Morales 18, Prado 33, Rojas 1, Sanchez 2, Santana 49, Santos 2, Vaughan 56.

Chicago Cubs

SEASON IN A SENTENCE: For the second straight season, the Cubs faltered down the stretch and missed the playoffs.

HIGH POINT: The Cubs held a 3.5-game lead in the division on Aug. 8, and looked to be surging toward the postseason. It was not to be.

LOW POINT: On Sept. 17, the Cubs woke up just two games back in the NL Central, locked in a tie with the Brewers for the second wild card spot. They lost the next nine games. The seventh loss eliminated them from playoff contention, marking two straight late-season slumps that left them watching the playoffs at home. The club then fired manager Joe Maddon and hired former catcher David Ross as his replacement.

NOTABLE ROOKIES: The Cubs aggressively assigned top prospect Nico Hoerner to Double-A to open his first full season. His time with Tennessee was interrupted by a broken wrist, but he still showed enough potential to earn his first big league callup in place of the injured Addison Russell. Hoerner hit .282/.305/.436 with a pair of homers over 20 games. The team also got surprise production from journeyman Robel Garcia, who signed with the Cubs five years after the Indians released him before the 2014 season. He socked five home runs in 31 games.

KEY TRANSACTIONS: The Cubs added veteran closer Craig Kimbrel—who spent the offseason waiting for a big-money contract that never came—on June 7, on a three-year, $43 million deal. He produced 13 saves but went 0-4, 6.53 in the process. They bolstered their lineup with the addition of Nicholas Castellanos from the Tigers—at the cost of minor league righties Paul Richan and Alex Lange—then watched as he got red-hot. He hit .321/.356/.646 with 16 homers after the trade.

DOWN ON THE FARM: Besides Hoerner's ascension to the big leagues, the story of the Cubs' farm system was the left arm of Brailyn Marquez. The 20-year-old Dominican still needs to iron out control and command, but he used a 98-102 mph fastball and a devastating slider to average 11 strikeouts per nine innings at both Class A levels in 2019. Outfielder Brennan Davis showed promise at low Class A before an injury shortened his season, and righthander Riley Thompson was excellent at the same level. The Cubs added Fresno State righthander Ryan Jensen in the first round of the draft.

OPENING DAY PAYROLL: $208,199,143 (2nd).

PLAYERS OF THE YEAR

BLAINE OHIGASHI

MAJOR LEAGUE	MINOR LEAGUE
Anthony Rizzo 1B	**Brailyn Marquez** LHP
.293/.405/.520	(Low A/High A)
27 HR, 94 RBIs, 71 BB	9-5, 3.13 in 22 GS
Won Gold Glove	128 SO in 104 IP

ORGANIZATION LEADERS

Batting		*Minimum 250 AB
MAJORS		
* AVG	Anthony Rizzo	.293
* OPS	Anthony Rizzo	.924
HR	Kyle Schwarber	38
RBI	Anthony Rizzo	94
MINORS		
* AVG	Jim Adduci, Iowa	.301
* OBP	Vimael Machin, Tennessee, Iowa	.390
* SLG	Robel Garcia, Tennessee, Iowa	.586
* OPS	Robel Garcia, Tennessee, Iowa	.954
R	Phillip Evans, Iowa	79
H	Andy Weber, South Bend	134
TB	Phillip Evans, Iowa	219
2B	Andy Weber, South Bend	36
3B	Ronny Simon, DSL Cubs 2	9
HR	Robel Garcia, Tennessee, Iowa	27
RBI	Robel Garcia, Tennessee, Iowa	78
BB	Vimael Machin, Tennessee, Iowa	69
SO	Trent Giambrone, Iowa	131
SB	Zach Davis, Myrtle Beach, Tennessee	40
Pitching		#Minimum 75 IP
MAJORS		
W	Jon Lester	13
W	Jose Quintana	13
# ERA	Kyle Hendricks	3.46
SO	Yu Darvish	229
SV	Craig Kimbrel	13
MINORS		
W	Colin Rea, Iowa	14
L	Alex Lange, Myrtle Beach, Tennessee	12
# ERA	Jack Patterson, South Bend, Myrtle Beach, Tennessee	1.69
G	Jordan Minch, Iowa	45
G	James Norwood, Iowa	45
GS	Cory Abbott, Tennessee	26
GS	Tyson Miller, Tennessee, Iowa	26
GS	Colin Rea, Iowa	26
SV	Ethan Roberts, South Bend, Myrtle Beach	13
IP	Matt Swarmer, Iowa	151
BB	Colin Rea, Iowa	60
SO	Cory Abbott, Tennessee	166
# AVG	Jack Patterson, South Bend, Myrtle Beach, Tennessee	.177

2019 PERFORMANCE

General Manager: Jed Hoyer. **Farm Director:** Jaron Madison. **Scouting Director:** Matt Dorey.

Class	Team	League	W	L	PCT	Finish	Manager
Majors	Chicago Cubs	National	84	78	.519	8th (15)	Joe Maddon
Triple-A	Iowa Cubs	Pacific Coast	75	65	.536	5th (16)	Marty Pevey
Double-A	Tennessee Smokies	Southern	58	81	.417	9th (10)	Jimmy Gonzalez
High A	Myrtle Beach Pelicans	Carolina	55	81	.404	9th (10)	Steve Lerud
Low A	South Bend Cubs	Midwest	76	61	.555	7th (16)	Buddy Bailey
Short season	Eugene Emeralds	Northwest	33	43	.434	6th (8)	Lance Rymel
Rookie	AZL Cubs 1	Arizona	24	31	.436	14th (21)	Carmelo Martinez
Rookie	AZL Cubs 2	Arizona	31	25	.554	t-8th (21)	Ricardo Medina
Overall 2019 Minor League Record			352	387	.476	23rd (30)	

ORGANIZATION STATISTICS

CHICAGO CUBS
NATIONAL LEAGUE

Batting	B-T	HT	WT	DOB	AVG	vLH	vRH	G	AB	R	H	2B	3B	HR	RBI	BB	HBP	SH	SF	SO	SB	CS	SLG	OBP
Adduci, Jim	L-L	6-2	210	5-15-85	.000	--	.000	2	5	0	0	0	0	0	0	0	0	0	0	3	0	0	.000	.000
Almora Jr., Albert	R-R	6-2	190	4-16-94	.236	.213	.247	130	339	41	80	11	1	12	32	16	1	5	2	62	2	1	.381	.271
Baez, Javier	R-R	6-0	190	12-1-92	.281	.304	.275	138	531	89	149	38	4	29	85	28	0	0	2	156	11	7	.531	.316
Bote, David	R-R	6-1	210	4-7-93	.257	.218	.271	127	303	47	78	17	0	11	41	44	7	0	2	93	5	1	.422	.362
Bryant, Kris	R-R	6-5	230	1-4-92	.282	.295	.279	147	543	108	153	35	1	31	77	74	15	0	2	145	4	0	.521	.382
Caratini, Victor	B-R	6-1	215	8-17-93	.266	.250	.270	95	244	31	65	11	0	11	34	29	3	0	3	59	1	0	.447	.348
Castellanos, Nicholas	R-R	6-4	203	3-4-92	.321	.417	.301	51	212	43	68	21	0	16	36	10	2	0	1	47	0	1	.646	.356
Contreras, Willson	R-R	6-1	210	5-13-92	.272	.320	.260	105	360	57	98	18	2	24	64	38	9	0	2	102	1	2	.533	.355
Davis, Taylor	R-R	5-10	200	11-28-89	.167	.000	.214	7	18	2	3	0	0	1	4	2	0	0	0	4	0	0	.333	.250
Descalso, Daniel	L-R	5-10	190	10-19-86	.173	.167	.173	82	168	20	29	5	1	2	15	23	0	1	1	57	2	1	.250	.271
Garcia, Robel	B-R	6-0	168	3-28-93	.208	.111	.241	31	72	8	15	2	2	5	11	7	0	0	1	35	0	0	.500	.275
Gonzalez, Carlos	L-L	6-1	220	10-17-85	.175	.000	.200	15	40	8	7	2	0	1	3	8	0	0	1	19	0	2	.300	.306
Happ, Ian	B-R	6-0	205	8-12-94	.264	.233	.273	58	140	25	37	7	1	11	30	15	0	0	1	39	2	0	.564	.333
Heyward, Jason	L-L	6-5	240	8-9-89	.252	.205	.264	147	513	78	129	20	4	21	62	68	5	0	3	110	8	3	.429	.343
Hoerner, Nico	R-R	5-11	200	5-13-97	.282	.273	.284	20	78	13	22	1	1	3	17	3	0	0	1	11	0	0	.436	.305
Kemp, Tony	L-R	5-6	165	10-31-91	.183	.273	.169	44	82	8	15	3	2	1	12	7	2	0	2	18	0	1	.305	.258
Lucroy, Jonathan	R-R	6-0	200	6-13-86	.189	.286	.154	27	53	2	10	2	0	1	6	6	1	0	0	12	0	0	.283	.283
Maldonado, Martin	R-R	6-0	230	8-16-86	.000	.000	.000	4	11	0	0	0	0	0	0	2	0	0	0	5	0	0	.000	.154
Rizzo, Anthony	L-L	6-3	240	8-8-89	.293	.250	.307	146	512	89	150	29	3	27	94	71	27	0	3	86	5	2	.520	.405
Russell, Addison	R-R	6-0	200	1-23-94	.237	.192	.252	82	215	25	51	4	1	9	23	20	3	1	2	58	2	0	.391	.308
Schwarber, Kyle	L-R	6-0	235	3-5-93	.250	.229	.255	155	529	82	132	29	3	38	92	70	5	0	6	156	2	3	.531	.339
Zagunis, Mark	R-R	6-0	215	2-5-93	.250	.278	.222	30	36	2	9	3	0	0	5	4	0	0	0	16	0	0	.333	.325
Zobrist, Ben	B-R	6-3	210	5-26-81	.260	.191	.271	47	150	24	39	5	0	1	17	23	1	0	2	24	0	0	.313	.358

Pitching	B-T	HT	WT	DOB	W	L	ERA	G	GS	CG	SV	IP	H	R	ER	HR	BB	SO	AVG	vLH	vRH	K/9	BB/9
Alzolay, Adbert	R-R	6-0	179	3-1-95	1	1	7.30	4	2	0	0	12	13	10	10	4	9	13	.260	.321	.182	9.49	6.57
Barnette, Tony	R-R	6-1	190	11-9-83	0	0	6.75	2	0	0	0	1	2	1	1	1	0	0	.400	1.000	.250	0.00	0.00
Brach, Brad	R-R	6-6	215	4-12-86	4	3	6.13	42	0	0	0	40	42	27	27	3	28	45	.284	.412	.217	10.21	6.35
2-team total (16 New York)					5	4	5.47	58	0	0	0	54	57	33	33	4	31	60	.278	.403	.211	9.94	5.13
Caratini, Victor	B-R	6-1	215	8-17-93	0	0	9.00	2	0	0	0	2	2	2	2	1	1	0	.250	.000	.333	0.00	4.50
Cedeno, Xavier	L-L	5-11	210	8-26-86	0	0	0.00	5	0	0	0	2	4	0	0	0	3	1	.400	.500	.375	4.50	13.50
Chatwood, Tyler	R-R	6-0	185	12-16-89	5	3	3.76	38	5	0	2	77	65	33	32	8	37	74	.232	.306	.176	8.69	4.34
Cishek, Steve	R-R	6-6	215	6-18-86	4	6	2.95	70	0	0	7	64	48	22	21	7	29	57	.210	.216	.206	8.02	4.08
Collins, Tim	L-L	5-7	170	8-21-89	0	0	3.12	9	0	0	0	9	9	3	3	1	3	4	.265	.286	.250	4.15	3.12
Darvish, Yu	R-R	6-5	220	8-16-86	6	8	3.98	31	31	0	0	179	140	82	79	33	56	229	.213	.243	.181	11.54	2.82
Davis, Taylor	R-R	5-10	200	11-28-89	0	0	0.00	1	0	0	0	1	3	0	0	0	0	0	.500	.667	.333	0.00	0.00
Descalso, Daniel	L-R	5-10	190	10-19-86	0	0	18.00	1	0	0	0	1	2	2	2	1	0	0	.400	.333	.500	0.00	0.00
Edwards Jr., Carl	R-R	6-3	170	9-3-91	1	1	5.87	20	0	0	0	15	8	11	10	3	9	17	.151	.200	.132	9.98	5.28
2-team total (2 San Diego)					1	1	8.47	22	0	0	0	17	12	17	16	3	13	19	.191	.222	.178	10.06	6.88
Hamels, Cole	L-L	6-4	205	12-27-83	7	7	3.81	27	27	0	0	142	141	64	60	17	56	143	.260	.265	.259	9.08	3.56
Hendricks, Kyle	R-R	6-3	190	12-7-89	11	10	3.46	30	30	1	0	177	168	78	68	19	32	150	.249	.237	.260	7.63	1.63
Holland, Derek	B-L	6-2	213	10-9-86	0	1	6.89	20	1	0	0	16	14	12	12	3	10	11	.246	.227	.257	6.32	5.74
2-team total (31 San Francisco)					2	5	6.08	51	8	1	0	84	82	61	57	20	45	82	.258	.192	.288	8.75	4.80
Hultzen, Danny	L-L	6-3	210	11-28-89	0	0	0.00	6	0	0	0	3	4	0	0	0	2	5	.267	.286	.250	13.50	5.40
Kimbrel, Craig	R-R	6-0	210	5-28-88	0	4	6.53	23	0	0	13	21	21	15	15	9	12	30	.259	.233	.290	13.06	5.23
Kintzler, Brandon	R-R	6-0	194	8-1-84	3	3	2.68	62	0	0	1	57	45	18	17	5	13	48	.215	.163	.248	7.58	2.05
Lester, Jon	L-L	6-4	240	1-7-84	13	10	4.46	31	31	0	0	172	205	101	85	26	52	165	.294	.319	.286	8.65	2.73
Maples, Dillon	R-R	6-2	230	5-9-92	1	0	5.40	14	0	0	0	12	6	7	7	2	10	18	.150	.083	.179	13.89	7.71
Mills, Alec	R-R	6-4	190	11-30-91	1	0	2.75	9	4	0	1	36	31	11	11	5	11	42	.231	.321	.167	10.50	2.75
Montgomery, Mike	L-L	6-5	215	7-1-89	1	2	5.67	20	0	0	0	27	35	18	17	6	13	18	.327	.500	.232	6.00	4.33
Norwood, James	R-R	6-2	215	12-24-93	0	1	2.89	9	0	0	0	9	9	4	3	1	8	11	.250	.200	.269	10.61	7.71
Phelps, David	R-R	6-3	200	10-9-86	2	1	3.18	24	0	0	1	17	17	7	6	2	10	18	.262	.333	.227	9.53	5.29
Quintana, Jose	R-L	6-1	220	1-24-89	13	9	4.68	32	31	0	0	171	191	100	89	20	46	152	.282	.252	.290	8.00	2.42

Rosario, Randy	L-L	6-1	200	5-18-94	1	0	5.91	13	0	0	0	11	12	8	7	2	5	10	.273	.143	.333	8.44	4.22
Ryan, Kyle	L-L	6-5	215	9-25-91	4	2	3.54	73	0	0	0	61	55	26	24	5	29	58	.243	.226	.256	8.56	4.28
Strop, Pedro	R-R	6-1	220	6-13-85	2	5	4.97	50	0	0	10	42	33	24	23	6	20	49	.217	.203	.231	10.58	4.32
Underwood Jr., Duane	R-R	6-2	210	7-20-94	0	0	5.40	12	0	0	0	12	13	7	7	2	3	13	.277	.357	.242	10.03	2.31
Webster, Allen	R-R	6-2	200	2-10-90	0	0	4.91	12	0	0	1	11	14	7	6	2	5	9	.304	.267	.323	7.36	4.09
Wick, Rowan	L-R	6-3	235	11-9-92	2	0	2.43	31	0	0	2	33	22	13	9	0	16	35	.183	.231	.147	9.45	4.32
Wieck, Brad	L-L	6-9	255	10-14-91	2	1	3.60	14	0	0	0	10	2	4	4	1	4	18	.063	.125	.042	16.20	3.60
2-team total (30 San Diego)					2	2	5.71	44	0	0	0	35	28	23	22	8	13	49	.214	.265	.183	12.72	3.38
Zobrist, Ben	B-R	6-3	210	5-26-81	0	0	0.00	1	0	0	0	1	0	0	0	0	2	1	.000	.000	.000	9.00	18.00

Fielding

Catcher	PCT	G	PO	A	E	DP	PB
Caratini	.996	59	460	22	2	1	3
Contreras	.986	99	770	51	12	3	6
Davis	1.000	6	53	2	0	0	1
Lucroy	.985	20	125	9	2	1	0
Maldonado	.973	4	35	1	1	0	0
Schwarber	1.000	1	1	0	0	0	0

First Base	PCT	G	PO	A	E	DP
Bryant	1.000	3	21	1	0	1
Caratini	.990	23	97	7	1	10
Contreras	1.000	2	5	0	0	0
Davis	1.000	1	1	0	0	0
Descalso	.000	1	0	0	0	0
Happ	1.000	7	43	2	0	5
Lucroy	1.000	4	6	0	0	1
Rizzo	.996	146	1140	123	5	120

Second Base	PCT	G	PO	A	E	DP
Bote	.971	50	53	82	4	19
Descalso	.980	45	54	95	3	26
Garcia	.927	18	21	30	4	11
Happ	.970	13	14	18	1	3
Hoerner	1.000	1	0	1	0	0
Kemp	.980	14	19	29	1	7
Russell	.995	63	77	133	1	28
Zobrist	.968	32	36	54	3	16

Third Base	PCT	G	PO	A	E	DP
Baez	1.000	1	2	3	0	0
Bote	.915	67	24	94	11	12
Bryant	.947	115	48	186	13	15
Caratini	1.000	2	0	1	0	0
Descalso	.000	3	0	0	0	0
Happ	.955	8	6	15	1	1

Shortstop	PCT	G	PO	A	E	DP
Baez	.973	129	165	366	15	88
Bote	.917	9	4	7	1	1
Hoerner	.972	17	19	50	2	9
Russell	.924	21	18	43	5	8
Zobrist	.000	1	0	0	0	0

Outfield	PCT	G	PO	A	E	DP
Adduci	1.000	1	5	0	0	0
Almora Jr.	.986	125	201	3	3	0
Bote	1.000	1	1	0	0	0
Bryant	.962	44	50	1	2	0
Castellanos	1.000	51	89	3	0	1
Contreras	1.000	3	2	1	0	0
Garcia	1.000	6	2	0	0	0
Gonzalez	1.000	14	15	0	0	0
Happ	1.000	29	35	1	0	0
Heyward	.981	144	247	6	5	1
Hoerner	1.000	1	2	0	0	0
Kemp	1.000	8	19	0	0	0
Schwarber	.974	140	214	7	6	0
Zagunis	.875	8	7	0	1	0
Zobrist	1.000	17	22	2	0	0

IOWA CUBS   TRIPLE-A
PACIFIC COAST LEAGUE

Batting	B-T	HT	WT	DOB	AVG	vLH	vRH	G	AB	R	H	2B	3B	HR	RBI	BB	HBP	SH	SF	SO	SB	CS	SLG	OBP
Adames, Cristhian	B-R	6-0	185	7-26-91	.256	.111	.300	12	39	9	10	2	0	2	6	8	0	0	1	7	1	0	.462	.375
2-team total (43 Sacramento)					.277	.184	.311	55	184	32	51	14	2	8	31	27	0	0	2	39	2	1	.505	.366
Adduci, Jim	L-L	6-2	210	5-15-85	.301	.260	.311	105	359	59	108	23	0	12	58	21	1	1	4	89	9	4	.465	.338
Almora Jr., Albert	R-R	6-2	190	4-16-94	.225	.300	.205	13	49	6	11	3	1	0	2	4	0	1	0	7	2	1	.327	.283
Arcia, Francisco	L-R	5-11	200	9-14-89	.181	.217	.160	51	160	12	29	5	0	0	14	6	3	1	1	28	0	2	.213	.224
Bernard, Wynton	R-R	6-2	195	9-24-90	.263	.296	.235	41	95	17	25	6	3	1	12	10	0	0	0	21	6	3	.421	.333
Borenstein, Zach	L-R	6-0	225	7-23-90	.244	.286	.222	13	41	4	10	0	0	1	6	2	0	0	0	18	0	0	.317	.279
Bote, David	R-R	6-1	210	4-7-93	.100	.000	.167	3	10	1	1	0	0	0	0	1	0	0	0	5	0	0	.100	.182
Burks, Charcer	R-R	6-0	170	3-9-95	.667	1.000	.500	2	3	0	2	0	0	0	3	1	0	0	0	1	0	0	.667	.750
Caratini, Victor	B-R	6-1	215	8-17-93	.278	.000	.556	4	18	0	5	1	0	0	1	0	0	0	0	1	0	0	.333	.278
Castillo, Erick	R-R	5-11	178	2-25-93	.228	.111	.282	27	57	7	13	3	0	0	8	5	0	1	0	15	0	0	.281	.286
Contreras, Willson	R-R	6-1	210	5-13-92	.143	.000	.167	3	7	3	1	1	0	0	0	1	0	0	0	4	0	0	.286	.333
Davis, Taylor	R-R	5-10	200	11-28-89	.235	.291	.215	61	204	21	48	4	0	5	23	31	1	4	1	38	0	0	.328	.338
Descalso, Daniel	L-R	5-11	190	10-19-86	.148	.125	.158	10	27	5	4	0	0	2	4	5	1	0	0	8	0	0	.370	.303
Dewees, Donnie	L-L	5-11	205	9-29-93	.253	.220	.264	111	368	60	93	18	5	16	52	40	6	3	2	61	6	5	.459	.334
Evans, Phillip	R-R	5-10	210	9-10-92	.283	.349	.258	130	466	79	132	30	3	17	61	57	11	0	5	74	1	4	.470	.371
Field, Johnny	R-R	5-10	195	2-20-92	.234	.256	.224	84	278	39	65	22	3	8	41	21	1	0	3	85	7	4	.421	.287
Garcia, Robel	B-R	6-0	180	3-28-93	.281	.200	.317	76	260	51	73	12	2	21	52	30	4	0	2	98	3	3	.585	.362
Giambrone, Trent	R-R	5-8	175	12-20-93	.241	.239	.243	126	431	66	104	27	0	23	66	42	4	1	0	131	17	4	.464	.315
Gonzalez, Carlos	L-L	6-1	220	10-17-85	.250	--	.250	2	8	1	2	0	0	1	1	0	0	1	0	1	0	0	.625	.250
Hannemann, Jacob	L-L	6-1	200	4-29-91	.248	.230	.253	44	117	21	29	7	1	5	15	15	1	1	2	28	9	3	.453	.333
Happ, Ian	B-R	6-0	205	8-12-94	.242	.270	.230	99	359	66	87	18	1	16	53	65	4	0	1	113	9	2	.432	.364
Higgins, P.J.	R-R	5-10	195	5-10-93	.291	.188	.307	36	117	18	34	8	2	5	19	17	1	1	4	29	0	2	.521	.374
Machado, Dixon	R-R	6-1	190	2-22-92	.261	.305	.244	102	329	53	86	19	1	17	65	54	4	5	1	79	0	2	.480	.371
Machin, Vimael	L-R	5-10	180	9-25-93	.320	.200	.350	12	25	7	8	1	1	1	4	6	0	0	0	5	0	0	.560	.452
Rice, Ian	R-R	6-0	200	8-19-93	.256	.313	.217	12	39	6	10	0	0	2	6	7	0	0	0	8	0	0	.410	.370
Russell, Addison	R-R	6-0	200	1-23-94	.281	.346	.257	27	96	25	27	6	0	7	26	14	5	0	4	25	1	2	.563	.387
Short, Zack	R-R	5-10	180	5-29-95	.211	.103	.240	41	133	22	28	9	0	6	17	21	5	0	1	50	2	1	.414	.338
Vazquez, Luis	R-R	6-1	165	10-10-99	.241	.214	.267	11	29	2	7	1	1	1	1	0	0	0	9	1	0	.448	.267
Zagunis, Mark	R-R	6-0	215	2-5-93	.294	.412	.251	68	255	35	75	26	1	6	43	24	4	0	2	94	6	3	.475	.361
Zobrist, Ben	B-R	6-3	210	5-26-81	.125	.000	.182	5	16	1	2	1	0	0	1	2	0	0	0	0	0	0	.188	.222

Pitching	B-T	HT	WT	DOB	W	L	ERA	G	GS	CG	SV	IP	H	R	ER	HR	BB	SO	AVG	vLH	vRH	K/9	BB/9
Adduci, Jim	L-L	6-2	210	5-15-85	0	0	0.00	1	0	0	0	1	0	0	0	1	0	0	.000	--	.000	0.00	13.50
Alzolay, Adbert	R-R	6-0	179	3-1-95	2	4	4.41	15	15	0	0	65	53	34	32	10	31	91	.215	.238	.199	12.54	4.27
Baldonado, Alberto	L-L	6-4	250	2-1-93	1	0	3.38	8	0	0	0	13	8	5	5	2	10	13	.178	.200	.167	8.78	6.75

Barnette, Tony	R-R	6-1	190	11-9-83	1	0	2.31	13	0	0	0	12	6	3	3	1	2	12	.150	.200	.120	9.26 1.54
Bocchi, Matteo	R-R	6-4	205	7-19-96	0	0	0.00	1	0	0	0	3	0	0	0	0	2	3	.000	.000	.000	10.13 6.75
Brooks, Craig	R-R	5-10	180	9-23-92	2	0	7.62	18	0	0	0	26	29	22	22	12	19	39	.284	.375	.226	13.50 6.58
Carasiti, Matt	R-R	6-3	210	7-23-91	1	1	2.67	16	0	0	1	27	20	11	8	1	11	23	.204	.194	.209	7.67 3.67
2-team total (15 Tacoma)						2	13.53	31	0	0	5	43	39	22	17	4	18	40	.235	.241	.232	8.31 3.74
Cedeno, Xavier	L-L	5-11	210	8-26-86	1	0	3.86	9	0	0	0	7	8	3	3	0	7	3	.296	.000	.444	3.86 9.00
Clifton, Trevor	R-R	6-4	170	5-11-95	4	8	5.18	24	20	0	0	99	98	63	57	20	50	84	.253	.252	.253	7.64 4.55
Collins, Tim	L-L	5-7	170	8-21-89	1	3	4.67	28	0	0	1	27	20	16	14	7	16	37	.202	.108	.258	12.33 5.33
Davis, Taylor	R-R	5-10	200	11-28-89	0	0	108.00	1	0	0	0	0	4	4	4	3	0	0	.800	.500	1.000	0.00 0.00
Dewees, Donnie	L-L	5-11	205	9-29-93	0	0	15.00	5	0	0	1	3	6	5	5	1	4	1	.400	.250	.455	3.00 12.00
Duensing, Brian	L-L	6-0	200	2-22-83	1	1	6.92	12	0	0	1	13	21	10	10	3	5	5	.382	.294	.421	3.46 3.46
Edwards Jr., Carl	R-R	6-3	170	9-3-91	2	0	3.07	14	0	0	0	15	12	6	5	2	6	14	.214	.438	.125	8.59 3.68
2-team total (3 El Paso)					2	1	4.08	17	0	0	0	18	16	9	8	2	7	18	.232	.421	.160	9.17 3.57
Graveman, Kendall	R-R	6-2	200	12-21-90	0	0	3.00	1	1	0	0	3	2	1	1	1	1	2	.200	.000	.286	6.00 3.00
Hamels, Cole	L-L	6-4	205	12-27-83	0	0	5.06	2	2	0	0	5	4	3	3	2	6	6	.235	.400	.167	10.13 10.13
Hannemann, Jacob	L-L	6-1	200	4-29-91	0	1	6.75	2	0	0	0	1	2	1	1	0	1	1	.333	.000	.400	6.75 0.00
Hu, Chih-Wei	R-R	6-0	220	11-4-93	0	1	6.00	2	1	0	0	6	8	4	4	2	6	4	.333	.273	.385	6.00 9.00
Hultzen, Danny	L-L	6-3	210	11-28-89	0	1	1.26	14	0	0	3	14	4	2	2	0	9	23	.087	.050	.115	14.44 5.65
Kimbrel, Craig	R-R	6-0	210	5-28-88	0	0	2.45	4	1	0	0	4	2	1	1	1	1	4	.154	.400	.000	9.82 2.45
Maples, Dillon	R-R	6-2	230	5-9-92	4	4	3.77	38	0	0	7	43	21	19	18	1	36	79	.145	.102	.174	16.53 7.53
Markey, Brad	R-R	5-10	185	3-3-92	0	0	0.00	1	0	0	0	2	0	0	0	0	1	1	.000	.000	.000	4.50 4.50
Mekkes, Dakota	R-R	6-7	275	11-6-94	4	2	5.29	43	0	0	5	49	44	34	29	6	34	61	.235	.343	.171	11.13 6.20
Miller, Tyson	R-R	6-4	215	7-29-95	3	5	7.58	11	11	1	0	49	62	43	41	13	25	43	.304	.382	.244	7.95 4.62
Mills, Alec	R-R	6-4	190	11-30-91	6	4	5.11	19	18	0	0	104	116	62	59	17	30	96	.284	.245	.307	8.31 2.60
Minch, Jordan	L-L	6-3	190	7-16-93	1	0	0.00	1	0	0	0	1	2	0	0	0	2	1	.400	.333	.500	6.75 13.50
Montgomery, Mike	L-L	6-5	215	7-1-89	1	1	2.70	2	2	0	0	10	3	3	3	0	4	8	.086	.000	.097	7.20 3.60
Norwood, James	R-R	6-2	215	12-24-93	3	2	4.21	45	0	0	6	58	40	31	27	9	31	81	.195	.162	.214	12.64 4.84
Passantino, Jeffrey	R-R	5-9	225	9-24-95	0	0	2.00	2	2	0	0	9	7	2	2	0	1	11	.226	.214	.235	11.00 1.00
Rea, Colin	R-R	6-5	235	7-1-90	14	4	3.95	26	26	1	0	148	142	74	65	17	60	120	.255	.268	.246	7.30 3.65
Robinson, Duncan	R-R	6-6	230	12-5-93	1	1	4.76	5	5	0	0	23	24	13	12	1	9	11	.279	.188	.333	4.37 3.57
Rosario, Randy	L-L	6-1	200	5-18-94	1	2	3.11	31	0	0	4	38	46	20	13	5	14	31	.284	.224	.317	7.41 3.35
Rucker, Michael	R-R	6-1	195	4-27-94	0	0	2.25	2	1	0	0	4	4	1	1	0	3	4	.267	.444	.000	9.00 6.75
Ryan, Kyle	L-L	6-5	215	9-25-91	1	0	5.40	1	0	0	0	2	1	1	1	0	0	1	.200	--	.200	5.40 0.00
Short, Wyatt	L-L	5-8	180	10-14-94	0	0	10.80	7	0	0	0	8	10	10	10	2	8	12	.313	.556	.217	12.96 8.64
Strop, Pedro	R-R	6-1	220	6-13-85	1	0	0.00	3	0	0	0	3	1	0	0	0	1	2	.111	.000	.143	6.00 3.00
Swarmer, Matt	R-R	6-5	195	9-25-93	10	11	5.65	27	25	0	0	151	181	96	95	36	44	137	.299	.324	.284	8.15 2.62
Tazawa, Junichi	R-R	5-11	200	6-6-86	1	0	4.00	19	0	0	1	18	20	12	8	2	6	17	.290	.191	.333	8.50 3.00
Underwood Jr., Duane	R-R	6-2	210	7-20-94	3	7	5.07	33	10	0	0	82	84	55	46	8	41	95	.262	.239	.274	10.47 4.52
Webster, Allen	R-R	6-2	200	2-10-90	0	0	0.00	1	0	0	0	1	0	0	0	0	1	0	.250	1.000	.000	9.00 0.00
Wick, Rowan	L-R	6-3	235	11-9-92	1	0	1.80	27	0	0	6	35	25	8	7	3	9	44	.195	.200	.194	11.31 2.31
Wieck, Brad	L-L	6-9	255	10-14-91	1	0	1.59	6	0	0	0	6	4	1	1	0	3	11	.200	.100	.300	17.47 4.76
2-team total (14 El Paso Chihuahuas)					2	1	5.01	20	0	0	2	23	20	13	13	5	9	45	.227	.211	.240	17.36 3.47
Williams, Ryan	R-R	6-4	220	11-1-91	2	0	2.45	3	0	0	0	4	5	1	1	0	1	4	.313	.000	.385	9.82 2.45
Wilson, Alex	R-R	6-0	220	11-3-86	1	2	5.11	10	0	0	1	12	12	7	7	2	2	11	.261	.304	.217	8.03 1.46
2-team total (29 San Antonio Missions)					5	3	2.86	39	0	0	3	50	45	18	16	10	9	42	.242	.235	.246	7.51 1.61

Fielding

Catcher	PCT	G	PO	A	E	DP	PB
Arcia	1.000	46	372	24	0	3	1
Caratini	1.000	2	13	2	0	0	0
Castillo	.981	9	51	2	1	0	0
Contreras	1.000	3	16	1	0	0	0
Davis	.994	51	465	34	3	0	8
Higgins	.989	25	249	16	3	1	4
Rice	1.000	11	92	8	0	0	1

First Base	PCT	G	PO	A	E	DP
Adames	1.000	4	19	2	0	2
Adduci	.997	88	588	23	2	52
Caratini	1.000	2	12	2	0	1
Castillo	.966	7	28	0	1	2
Davis	1.000	6	43	5	0	6
Evans	1.000	15	102	5	0	5
Garcia	1.000	7	40	4	0	6
Giambrone	.991	20	104	9	1	6
Higgins	1.000	6	31	0	0	9
Machado	.956	7	42	1	2	4
Machin	.944	5	17	0	1	2
Underwood Jr.	1.000	1	0	1	0	0

Second Base	PCT	G	PO	A	E	DP
Adames	1.000	3	4	13	0	1
Bote	1.000	4	1	4	0	0
Descalso	1.000	5	8	8	0	4
Evans	.980	15	16	33	1	8
Garcia	.990	29	44	58	1	14
Giambrone	.973	43	55	89	4	15
Happ	1.000	20	17	43	0	12
Machado	1.000	16	21	39	0	12
Machin	.923	3	5	7	1	2
Russell	1.000	7	9	23	0	2
Short	.936	13	19	25	3	9
Zobrist	1.000	5	6	8	0	2

Third Base	PCT	G	PO	A	E	DP
Adames	1.000	6	4	13	0	1
Descalso	1.000	4	1	0	0	
Evans	.948	95	45	138	10	11
Garcia	.884	19	9	29	5	1
Giambrone	.977	25	12	30	1	2
Higgins	1.000	5	3	4	0	0
Machin	1.000	3	5	4	0	0

Shortstop	PCT	G	PO	A	E	DP
Adames	1.000	1	1	1	0	0
Bote	1.000	2	0	2	0	1
Giambrone	.984	19	16	45	1	10
Machado	.978	74	92	179	6	34
Russell	.973	18	26	46	2	9
Short	.923	27	30	66	8	16
Vazquez	.933	11	14	14	2	4

Outfield	PCT	G	PO	A	E	DP
Adduci	.929	11	13	0	1	0
Almora Jr.	1.000	12	29	1	0	0
Bernard	.956	28	41	2	2	1
Borenstein	1.000	8	12	5	0	0
Burks	1.000	2	5	0	0	0
Dewees	.978	102	169	5	4	0
Field	1.000	78	148	2	0	0
Garcia	.951	21	36	3	2	0
Giambrone	.977	32	42	1	1	0
Gonzalez	1.000	2	2	0	0	0
Hannemann	1.000	37	66	1	0	0
Happ	.982	80	160	4	3	1
Underwood Jr.	.000	1	0	0	0	0
Zagunis	.989	53	85	1	1	0
Zobrist	.000	1	0	0	0	0

TENNESSEE SMOKIES

SOUTHERN LEAGUE

DOUBLE-A

Batting	B-T	HT	WT	DOB	AVG	vLH	vRH	G	AB	R	H	2B	3B	HR	RBI	BB	HBP	SH	SF	SO	SB	CS	SLG	OBP
Amaya, Gioskar	R-R	5-11	175	12-13-92	.245	.256	.240	84	269	26	66	18	1	2	24	16	6	2	2	71	1	0	.342	.300
Bernard, Wynton	R-R	6-2	195	9-24-90	.323	.333	.313	11	31	3	10	3	0	1	3	6	0	0	0	4	2	1	.516	.432
Burks, Charcer	R-R	6-0	170	3-9-95	.237	.221	.244	119	384	55	91	16	5	2	41	49	7	3	7	102	16	5	.320	.329
Caro, Roberto	B-R	6-0	185	9-25-93	.239	.213	.252	116	376	57	90	14	4	2	33	60	3	3	4	99	31	13	.314	.345
Castillo, Erick	R-R	5-11	178	2-25-93	.259	.200	.273	10	27	2	7	0	0	0	1	0	2	1	0	3	0	0	.259	.310
Daniel, Clayton	R-R	5-7	170	5-10-95	.304	.429	.259	24	79	9	24	2	2	0	4	5	1	3	0	9	0	1	.380	.353
Davis, Zach	B-R	5-11	175	6-29-94	.227	.200	.236	23	75	17	17	1	1	0	4	11	0	1	0	14	11	1	.267	.324
Donahue, Christian	L-R	5-8	180	5-4-95	.209	.179	.220	106	331	34	69	14	2	3	28	27	1	7	4	76	9	4	.290	.267
Garcia, Robel	B-R	6-0	168	3-28-93	.295	.294	.295	22	78	12	23	5	0	6	26	12	1	0	1	22	1	1	.590	.391
Gonzalez, Eric	R-R	5-10	175	9-2-96	.333	--	.333	1	3	0	1	0	0	0	0	0	0	0	0	0	0	0	.333	.333
Gutierrez, Jose	B-R	5-11	185	11-9-98	.429	.250	.667	2	7	1	3	0	0	0	1	0	0	0	0	0	0	0	.429	.500
Higgins, P.J.	R-R	5-10	195	5-10-93	.276	.272	.278	72	268	31	74	10	0	5	38	25	2	0	4	51	5	2	.369	.338
Hodges, Jesse	R-R	6-1	212	3-29-94	.202	.257	.179	52	119	11	24	5	1	2	24	7	5	1	2	34	0	0	.311	.271
Hoerner, Nico	R-R	5-11	200	5-13-97	.284	.214	.318	70	268	37	76	16	3	3	22	21	4	0	1	31	8	4	.399	.344
Machin, Vimael	L-R	5-10	185	9-25-93	.294	.284	.299	117	422	47	124	26	1	6	61	63	5	1	7	57	8	2	.403	.386
Martinez, Eddy	R-R	6-1	195	1-18-95	.213	.283	.179	39	141	19	30	4	0	3	18	16	1	1	1	30	0	2	.305	.296
Myers, Connor	R-R	5-11	170	2-3-94	.263	.269	.261	118	338	46	89	21	6	3	30	19	9	5	4	111	16	7	.388	.316
Payne, Tyler	R-R	5-11	210	10-25-92	.247	.148	.304	20	73	9	18	5	0	1	10	5	0	0	2	14	0	0	.356	.288
Pereda, Jhonny	R-R	6-1	175	4-18-96	.241	.167	.281	98	344	28	83	16	0	2	39	49	1	2	2	55	2	1	.305	.336
Rice, Ian	R-R	6-0	200	8-19-93	.190	.227	.170	63	184	23	35	9	0	1	13	23	4	0	4	57	0	2	.255	.288
Short, Zack	R-R	5-10	180	5-29-95	.250	.182	.286	16	64	7	16	3	2	0	5	9	0	1	0	18	0	1	.359	.338
Vazquez, Luis	R-R	6-1	165	10-10-99	.207	.357	.177	25	82	8	17	1	0	0	3	4	1	2	0	17	3	0	.220	.253
Young, Jared	L-R	6-1	185	7-9-95	.235	.186	.257	123	455	44	107	21	1	5	57	33	9	2	5	106	5	2	.319	.297
Zobrist, Ben	B-R	6-3	210	5-26-81	.500	--	.500	1	2	2	1	0	0	0	3	0	0	0	1	0	0	01.000	.800

Pitching	B-T	HT	WT	DOB	W	L	ERA	G	GS	CG	SV	IP	H	R	ER	HR	BB	SO	AVG	vLH	vRH	K/9	BB/9
Abbott, Cory	R-R	6-2	220	9-20-95	8	8	3.01	26	26	0	0	147	112	57	49	15	52	166	.210	.204	.214	10.19	3.19
Brooks, Craig	R-R	5-10	180	9-23-92	2	0	0.81	23	0	0	8	33	13	3	3	2	19	55	.117	.191	.073	14.85	5.13
Castillo, Erick	R-R	5-11	178	2-25-93	0	0	0.00	1	0	0	0	1	0	0	0	0	0	2	.000	.000	.000	13.50	0.00
Cedeno, Xavier	L-L	5-11	210	8-26-86	0	1	7.20	7	0	0	0	5	8	4	4	0	4	7	.348	.250	.400	12.60	7.20
Clark, Bailey	R-R	6-4	220	12-3-94	2	1	3.68	33	0	0	4	44	38	25	18	3	25	38	.228	.288	.188	7.77	5.11
Clarkin, Ian	L-L	6-2	215	2-14-95	0	0	3.38	10	0	0	1	13	12	6	5	0	9	5	.250	.250	.250	3.38	6.08
De La Cruz, Oscar	R-R	6-4	200	3-4-95	4	5	4.09	31	8	0	2	81	65	39	37	8	29	88	.220	.194	.238	9.74	3.21
Donahue, Christian	L-R	5-8	180	5-4-95	0	2	9.00	2	0	0	0	1	3	3	1	0	2	1	.500	.667	.333	9.00	18.00
Effross, Scott	R-R	6-2	202	12-28-93	1	2	5.88	17	1	0	0	34	39	23	22	3	9	17	.291	.225	.329	4.54	2.41
Hatch, Thomas	R-R	6-1	200	9-29-94	4	10	4.59	21	21	0	0	100	104	60	51	13	37	93	.274	.298	.256	8.37	3.33
Hecht, Ben	R-R	6-2	170	5-31-95	0	1	3.13	18	1	0	1	23	19	10	8	1	14	25	.238	.108	.349	9.78	5.48
Hedges, Jesse	R-R	6-4	195	10-21-92	1	0	3.18	5	4	0	0	23	21	8	8	2	2	15	.247	.290	.222	5.96	0.79
Hu, Chih-Wei	R-R	6-0	200	11-4-93	2	1	5.73	3	2	0	0	11	18	10	7	2	5	9	.367	.450	.310	7.36	4.09
Lange, Alex	R-R	6-3	197	10-2-95	2	3	3.92	7	7	0	0	39	36	24	17	4	19	28	.252	.215	.282	6.46	4.38
Leal, Erick	R-R	6-3	180	3-17-95	3	5	5.74	11	10	0	0	53	61	36	34	5	23	54	.288	.250	.319	9.11	3.88
Lugo, Luis	L-L	6-5	200	3-5-94	6	0	3.47	13	11	0	0	60	56	24	23	7	25	67	.245	.130	.294	10.11	3.77
Markey, Brad	R-R	5-10	185	3-3-92	1	2	5.60	9	3	0	0	27	34	18	17	4	8	22	.315	.292	.333	7.24	2.63
2-team total (6 Chattanooga)					3	4	5.86	15	9	0	0	55	66	40	36	13	11	48	.299	.262	.333	7.81	1.79
Miller, Tyson	R-R	6-4	215	7-29-95	4	3	2.56	15	15	0	0	88	70	26	25	6	18	80	.219	.217	.221	8.18	1.84
Minch, Jordan	L-L	6-3	190	7-16-93	5	5	4.69	44	0	0	3	56	49	37	29	7	24	52	.229	.267	.209	8.41	3.88
Montgomery, Mike	L-L	6-5	215	7-1-89	0	0	6.75	1	1	0	0	4	3	3	3	1	1	3	.214	.000	.273	6.75	2.25
Nance, Tommy	R-R	6-6	235	3-19-91	2	5	4.24	30	0	0	4	47	42	26	22	2	18	54	.239	.184	.280	10.41	3.47
Passantino, Jeffrey	R-R	5-9	225	9-24-95	1	0	3.60	2	2	0	0	10	14	4	4	1	0	10	.333	.308	.375	9.00	0.00
Patterson, Jack	L-L	6-0	210	8-3-95	1	0	2.63	3	3	0	0	14	11	5	4	1	6	9	.239	.143	.281	5.93	3.95
Peyton, Tyler	R-R	6-3	200	3-31-94	0	0	23.63	2	0	0	0	3	6	7	7	2	3	1	.429	.000	.500	3.38	10.13
Rondon, Manuel	L-L	6-1	165	3-7-95	3	4	4.37	23	0	0	1	35	34	20	17	1	23	20	.272	.270	.273	5.14	5.91
Rucker, Michael	R-R	6-1	195	4-27-94	0	3	4.28	34	0	0	1	76	76	42	36	10	22	89	.263	.256	.268	10.59	2.62
Short, Wyatt	L-L	5-8	180	10-14-94	5	4	1.63	36	0	0	9	50	40	15	9	1	18	54	.224	.179	.244	9.79	3.26
Steele, Justin	L-L	6-2	205	7-11-95	0	6	5.59	11	11	0	0	39	45	24	24	3	20	42	.308	.231	.351	9.78	4.66
Stinnett, Jake	R-R	6-4	205	4-25-92	1	6	5.18	30	5	0	0	57	52	38	33	6	28	66	.246	.234	.256	10.36	4.40
Thompson, Keegan	R-R	6-1	210	3-13-95	0	0	0.00	1	1	0	0	5	0	0	0	0	1	8	.000	.000	.000	14.40	1.80
Uelmen, Erich	R-R	6-2	185	5-19-96	0	3	7.76	6	6	0	0	29	33	25	25	5	19	26	.282	.276	.288	8.07	5.90
Vargas, Alexander	R-R	6-4	203	7-24-97	0	0	7.20	1	1	0	0	5	7	5	4	0	3	0	.368	.357	.400	0.00	5.40
Webster, Allen	R-R	6-2	200	2-10-90	0	1	16.62	6	0	0	0	4	10	8	8	0	1	3	.435	.385	.500	6.23	2.08

Fielding

Catcher	PCT	G	PO	A	E	DP	PB
Castillo	1.000	7	53	4	0	1	0
Gonzalez	1.000	1	6	0	0	0	0
Higgins	.988	25	223	25	3	1	4
Machin	1.000	1	2	0	0	0	0
Payne	1.000	15	130	9	0	1	0
Pereda	.996	85	751	79	3	8	13
Rice	.985	7	59	5	1	1	0

First Base	PCT	G	PO	A	E	DP
Amaya	.990	15	90	11	1	6
Higgins	.988	23	145	13	2	19
Machin	1.000	10	41	3	0	3
Payne	1.000	2	10	2	0	2
Pereda	.979	8	41	5	1	2
Rice	1.000	12	94	3	0	4
Young	.997	84	552	33	2	51

Second Base	PCT	G	PO	A	E	DP
Amaya	.967	9	13	16	1	4
Daniel	1.000	2	4	6	0	1
Donahue	.983	73	121	166	5	38
Garcia	.947	4	7	11	1	5
Higgins	1.000	1	0	1	0	0
Hoerner	.982	16	22	32	1	3
Machin	.989	44	78	95	2	23
Short	1.000	2	2	3	0	1

	PCT	G	PO	A	E	DP
Zobrist	1.000	1	2	1	0	0

Third Base	PCT	G	PO	A	E	DP
Amaya	.948	45	23	50	4	6
Daniel	1.000	4	3	9	0	2
Donahue	.857	19	7	17	4	2
Garcia	.880	18	16	28	6	3
Higgins	.947	23	20	34	3	3
Hodges	.947	26	16	38	3	3
Machin	.927	26	10	28	3	3
Rice	1.000	1	2	3	0	0
Short	1.000	1	2	2	0	0

Shortstop	PCT	G	PO	A	E	DP
Daniel	.962	18	32	44	3	6
Donahue	.750	1	1	2	1	1
Garcia	1.000	1	1	0	0	0
Hoerner	.939	44	62	91	10	20
Machin	.949	47	59	89	8	24
Short	.936	13	15	29	3	4
Vazquez	.935	25	36	51	6	8

Outfield	PCT	G	PO	A	E	DP
Bernard	1.000	7	15	0	0	0

	PCT	G	PO	A	E	DP
Burks	.990	105	201	6	2	3
Caro	.975	107	186	6	5	1
Davis	.974	21	37	0	1	0
Donahue	1.000	11	14	1	0	1
Gutierrez	1.000	1	2	0	0	0
Hoerner	.960	11	21	3	1	1
Machin	1.000	1	1	1	0	0
Martinez	.975	37	75	2	2	0
Myers	.992	106	232	8	2	3
Rice	1.000	10	16	0	0	0
Young	.982	45	52	3	1	1

MYRTLE BEACH PELICANS

HIGH CLASS A

CAROLINA LEAGUE

Batting	B-T	HT	WT	DOB	AVG	vLH	vRH	G	AB	R	H	2B	3B	HR	RBI	BB	HBP	SH	SF	SO	SB	CS	SLG	OBP
Ademan, Aramis	L-R	5-11	160	9-13-98	.221	.212	.224	112	362	40	80	10	8	5	39	48	4	7	1	92	16	9	.334	.318
Amaya, Miguel	R-R	6-1	185	3-9-99	.235	.268	.218	99	341	50	80	24	0	11	57	54	10	5	5	69	2	0	.402	.351
Artis, D.J.	L-L	5-9	165	3-20-97	.250	.231	.259	10	40	3	10	0	0	0	1	2	0	0	0	11	1	3	.250	.286
Balego, Cam	R-R	5-11	205	6-12-95	.247	.268	.237	113	389	53	96	18	0	12	48	58	18	0	3	87	1	4	.386	.368
Bethencourt, Jhonny	R-R	5-11	160	2-12-97	.198	.191	.202	51	157	15	31	6	0	0	14	19	0	3	3	40	7	8	.236	.279
Davis, Zach	B-R	5-11	175	6-29-94	.267	.210	.288	62	225	36	60	9	3	0	12	18	5	3	1	63	29	10	.333	.336
Durna, Tyler	L-L	6-0	205	11-13-96	.253	.308	.230	24	87	14	22	5	0	0	10	4	4	0	0	15	1	0	.310	.316
Fennell, Grant	R-R	6-0	195	10-12-95	.249	.226	.262	97	329	42	82	18	1	5	50	41	5	0	6	102	2	1	.356	.336
Galindo, Wladimir	R-R	6-3	210	11-6-96	.225	.273	.202	51	169	14	38	7	0	2	13	14	1	0	0	51	2	2	.302	.288
Gonzalez, Eric	R-R	5-10	175	9-2-96	.200	.250	.154	9	25	1	5	1	0	0	1	1	0	0	0	3	1	0	.240	.231
Gutierrez, Jose	B-R	5-11	185	11-9-98	.177	.250	.146	26	68	8	12	1	0	0	4	1	0	4	1	18	1	0	.191	.186
Herron, Jimmy	R-L	6-1	195	7-27-96	.220	.183	.236	92	318	35	70	17	4	4	30	44	5	1	5	66	19	7	.337	.320
Mitchell, Kevonte	R-R	6-4	185	8-12-95	.211	.266	.185	104	342	38	72	14	0	14	49	41	7	0	3	104	7	9	.374	.305
Payne, Tyler	R-R	5-11	210	10-25-92	.256	.272	.249	72	254	29	65	15	1	8	30	15	5	0	2	48	0	0	.417	.308
Peguero, Yeiler	B-R	5-10	150	9-20-97	.179	.211	.162	41	112	8	20	3	2	0	5	7	0	6	0	33	6	3	.241	.227
Reynolds, Luke	L-R	6-1	215	3-20-95	.223	.194	.233	81	278	33	62	15	1	6	32	34	6	0	1	96	1	1	.349	.320
Sepulveda, Carlos	L-R	5-10	170	8-27-96	.243	.272	.232	112	379	48	92	12	2	0	36	57	3	4	5	75	14	5	.285	.342
Taylor, Zac	R-R	6-1	185	10-1-95	.098	.154	.040	16	51	3	5	2	1	0	2	2	0	1	0	21	1	2	.177	.132
Wilson, D.J.	L-L	5-8	177	10-8-96	.143	.143	.143	46	140	18	20	3	1	4	15	25	2	1	1	56	9	5	.264	.280
Zinn, Delvin	R-R	5-10	170	5-29-97	.242	.202	.272	53	198	27	48	10	0	0	13	12	5	3	4	40	16	5	.293	.297
Zobrist, Ben	B-R	6-3	210	5-26-81	.200	.143	.333	3	10	3	2	0	0	2	2	2	0	0	0	3	0	0	.800	.333

Pitching	B-T	HT	WT	DOB	W	L	ERA	G	GS	CG	SV	IP	H	R	ER	HR	BB	SO	AVG	vLH	vRH	K/9	BB/9
Alzolay, Adbert	R-R	6-0	179	3-1-95	0	1	11.25	1	1	0	0	4	7	6	5	1	2	3	.389	.500	.375	6.75	4.50
Assad, Javier	R-R	6-1	200	7-30-97	4	10	3.87	22	22	0	0	116	108	53	50	11	41	91	.254	.248	.259	7.04	3.17
Camargo, Jesus	R-R	5-11	170	11-23-95	4	3	3.59	36	0	0	4	73	56	32	29	5	23	68	.212	.198	.221	8.42	2.85
De La Cruz, Oscar	R-R	6-4	200	3-4-95	1	0	1.20	3	3	0	0	15	14	4	2	0	5	17	.246	.308	.194	10.20	3.00
De Los Rios, Enrique	R-R	6-1	175	5-2-95	1	3	2.03	16	2	0	0	40	41	15	9	3	7	29	.266	.263	.269	6.53	1.58
Effross, Scott	R-R	6-2	202	12-28-93	0	0	1.84	8	0	0	0	15	12	3	3	0	1	13	.231	.182	.267	7.98	0.61
Glowicki, Brian	R-R	5-11	190	10-19-94	0	1	7.36	19	0	0	2	33	37	29	27	6	14	33	.272	.245	.289	9.00	3.82
Gonzalez, Eric	R-R	5-10	175	9-2-96	0	0	18.00	1	0	0	0	1	2	2	2	0	1	1	.400	.000	.667	9.00	9.00
Hecht, Ben	R-R	6-2	170	5-31-95	1	2	2.57	24	0	0	4	35	28	10	10	5	14	46	.222	.250	.200	11.83	3.60
Hockin, Chad	R-R	6-2	210	10-7-94	1	1	1.98	11	0	0	0	14	7	5	3	0	6	21	.149	.091	.200	13.83	3.95
Hudson, Bryan	L-L	6-8	220	5-8-97	1	2	5.22	7	7	0	0	29	34	17	17	5	8	24	.288	.310	.281	7.36	2.45
Kellogg, Ryan	R-L	6-6	230	2-4-94	2	8	4.54	23	8	0	0	69	88	40	35	5	15	48	.309	.271	.335	6.23	1.95
Kelly, Garrett	R-R	6-1	210	8-2-94	1	0	3.00	19	0	0	4	27	18	11	9	1	19	30	.186	.195	.179	10.00	6.33
King, Brendan	R-R	6-1	200	7-8-94	0	2	11.17	5	0	0	0	10	14	12	12	1	7	10	.350	.357	.346	9.31	6.52
Lange, Alex	R-R	6-3	197	10-2-95	1	9	7.36	11	11	0	0	48	58	43	39	4	26	51	.290	.247	.324	9.63	4.91
Lawlor, Ryan	R-R	6-1	185	1-8-94	0	2	2.02	21	0	0	3	36	23	10	8	1	13	61	.177	.143	.193	15.39	3.28
Leal, Erick	R-R	6-3	180	3-17-95	1	1	4.31	6	6	0	0	31	24	15	15	3	13	33	.214	.240	.194	9.48	3.73
Little, Brendon	L-L	6-1	195	8-11-96	2	1	5.95	4	4	0	0	20	21	14	13	2	9	23	.269	.261	.273	10.53	4.12
Lugo, Luis	L-L	6-5	200	3-8-94	1	3	3.80	11	7	0	0	47	51	26	20	5	16	45	.279	.354	.252	8.56	3.04
Marquez, Brailyn	L-L	6-4	185	1-30-99	4	1	1.71	5	5	1	0	26	21	6	5	1	7	26	.214	.200	.219	8.89	2.39
Moreno, Erling	R-R	6-3	200	1-13-97	6	5	6.02	16	8	0	0	49	55	34	33	4	36	23	.296	.299	.293	4.20	6.57
Nance, Tommy	R-R	6-6	235	3-19-91	0	0	0.00	1	0	0	1	2	2	0	0	0	0	2	.286	.000	.400	9.00	0.00
Passantino, Jeffrey	R-R	5-9	225	9-24-95	3	1	2.00	7	6	0	0	36	28	8	8	3	6	35	.215	.161	.257	8.75	1.50
Patterson, Jack	L-L	6-0	210	8-3-95	2	0	0.00	5	5	0	0	24	8	1	0	0	8	24	.104	.214	.041	9.13	3.04
Payne, Tyler	R-R	5-11	210	10-25-92	0	1	0.00	2	0	0	0	2	2	1	0	0	0	4	.250	.667	.000	18.00	0.00
Peyton, Tyler	R-R	6-3	200	3-31-94	0	3	5.10	26	0	0	1	48	51	32	27	6	16	34	.267	.261	.271	6.23	3.02
Richan, Paul	R-R	6-2	200	3-26-97	10	5	3.97	17	17	1	0	93	96	47	41	10	18	86	.265	.296	.237	8.32	1.74
Roberts, Ethan	R-R	5-11	170	7-4-97	1	3	2.63	15	0	0	4	24	25	8	7	0	2	23	.269	.286	.259	8.63	0.75
Rodriguez, Manuel	R-R	5-11	205	8-6-96	1	3	3.45	35	0	0	2	47	43	23	18	1	17	65	.242	.233	.248	12.45	3.26
Rondon, Manuel	L-L	6-1	165	3-7-95	0	2	4.80	10	0	0	1	15	19	8	8	0	3	17	.312	.389	.279	10.20	1.80
Stinnett, Jake	R-R	6-4	205	4-25-92	0	0	0.00	1	0	0	0	2	1	2	0	0	1	1	.125	.000	.200	4.50	4.50

	B-T	HT	WT	DOB	W	L	ERA	G	GS	CG	SV	IP	H	R	ER	HR	BB	SO	AVG	vLH	vRH	K/9	BB/9
Uelmen, Erich	R-R	6-2	185	5-19-96	5	3	3.05	11	11	0	0	62	56	23	21	4	18	50	.247	.194	.287	7.26	2.61
Vargas, Alexander	R-R	6-4	203	7-24-97	2	5	4.78	18	13	0	0	79	91	45	42	6	13	47	.292	.248	.329	5.35	1.48

Fielding

Catcher	PCT	G	PO	A	E	DP	PB
Amaya	.989	91	729	78	9	7	13
Balego	1.000	5	21	0	0	1	2
Gonzalez	1.000	8	51	7	0	0	0
Payne	.984	36	280	33	5	1	0

First Base	PCT	G	PO	A	E	DP
Balego	.985	25	181	17	3	28
Durna	.995	24	179	14	1	11
Fennell	1.000	17	109	6	0	9
Galindo	.982	20	159	7	3	18
Payne	1.000	4	22	1	0	3
Reynolds	.990	53	395	22	4	37

Second Base	PCT	G	PO	A	E	DP
Ademan	1.000	7	15	15	0	4
Balego	.875	1	3	4	1	3
Bethencourt	.968	14	30	30	2	7
Peguero	1.000	9	19	24	0	11
Sepulveda	.995	96	153	218	2	61
Zinn	.983	11	26	31	1	7
Zobrist	1.000	2	4	4	0	0

Third Base	PCT	G	PO	A	E	DP
Balego	.955	69	48	123	8	11
Bethencourt	.829	17	9	25	7	2
Galindo	.857	11	5	19	4	2
Peguero	.932	21	14	27	3	6
Reynolds	.917	19	11	33	4	4
Zinn	.875	4	1	6	1	0

Shortstop	PCT	G	PO	A	E	DP
Ademan	.941	102	143	238	24	54
Bethencourt	.908	14	20	39	6	7
Peguero	.923	7	10	14	2	5
Zinn	.919	15	18	39	5	9

Outfield	PCT	G	PO	A	E	DP
Artis	1.000	10	22	0	0	0
Balego	.000	1	0	0	0	0
Davis	1.000	61	124	1	0	1
Fennell	1.000	69	123	8	0	0
Gutierrez	.977	22	39	3	1	1
Herron	.988	85	162	6	2	1
Mitchell	.977	93	162	6	4	0
Taylor	.974	16	37	0	1	0
Wilson	.979	46	89	5	2	0
Zinn	1.000	18	41	1	0	0

SOUTH BEND CUBS
MIDWEST LEAGUE

LOW CLASS A

Batting	B-T	HT	WT	DOB	AVG	vLH	vRH	G	AB	R	H	2B	3B	HR	RBI	BB	HBP	SH	SF	SO	SB	CS	SLG	OBP
Americaan, Edmond	L-L	6-1	170	3-26-97	.160	.000	.191	8	25	0	4	1	0	0	0	3	1	1	0	9	0	0	.200	.276
Artis, D.J.	L-L	5-9	165	3-20-97	.267	.294	.261	49	176	35	47	13	0	2	21	29	7	2	1	52	14	4	.375	.390
Caratini, Victor	B-R	6-1	215	8-17-93	.250	.000	.333	5	12	1	3	1	0	0	1	3	0	0	0	3	0	0	.333	.400
Daniel, Clayton	R-R	5-7	170	5-10-95	.306	.233	.323	43	160	35	49	9	1	2	17	29	2	1	1	20	2	1	.413	.417
Davis, Brennen	R-R	6-4	175	11-2-99	.305	.351	.293	50	177	33	54	9	3	8	30	18	5	2	2	38	4	1	.525	.381
Durna, Tyler	L-L	6-0	205	11-13-96	.304	.341	.297	76	263	33	80	21	1	4	42	31	5	0	1	38	2	6	.437	.387
Gonzalez, Eric	R-R	5-10	175	9-2-96	.218	.227	.216	43	133	12	29	3	1	0	23	14	1	2	2	29	0	0	.256	.293
Hill, Darius	L-L	6-1	190	8-17-97	.224	.222	.224	21	85	10	19	4	0	1	3	7	0	2	0	8	1	1	.306	.283
Jordan, Levi	R-R	5-8	170	9-24-95	.221	.255	.210	66	231	28	51	10	1	1	16	19	3	3	0	48	5	3	.286	.289
Knight, Caleb	R-R	5-11	220	1-2-96	.500	--	.500	2	6	1	3	1	0	0	0	1	0	0	1	0	0	0	.667	.571
Lorenzo, Rafelin	R-R	6-2	200	1-15-97	.258	.270	.255	56	182	17	47	15	1	3	14	9	0	1	3	31	0	0	.401	.289
Maldonado, Nelson	R-R	5-10	195	8-13-96	.311	.364	.293	33	132	20	41	6	2	1	17	8	0	0	1	20	0	0	.409	.348
Mastrobuoni, Marcus	R-R	5-11	205	11-28-93	.261	.333	.240	38	134	19	35	12	0	1	9	7	2	1	1	19	0	0	.373	.306
Mejia, Fidel	B-R	5-11	160	8-30-98	.248	.303	.237	56	202	16	50	9	0	2	24	15	1	2	1	47	0	1	.322	.301
Morel, Christopher	R-R	6-0	140	6-24-99	.284	.245	.294	73	257	36	73	15	7	6	31	11	4	3	3	60	9	6	.467	.320
Narea, Rafael	R-R	5-10	160	4-3-98	.194	.194	.194	51	134	17	26	5	0	0	11	14	4	7	0	31	3	2	.231	.290
Perlaza, Yonathan	B-R	5-10	195	11-10-98	.238	.294	.224	27	84	11	20	5	0	1	11	12	0	1	0	26	0	1	.333	.333
Polanco, Gustavo	R-R	6-0	190	6-13-97	.240	.129	.288	31	104	7	25	2	0	2	7	5	1	0	1	22	0	0	.317	.279
Reynolds, Luke	L-R	6-1	215	3-20-95	.260	.429	.243	22	77	10	20	2	1	2	3	11	1	0	0	22	0	0	.390	.360
Roederer, Cole	L-L	6-0	175	9-24-99	.224	.149	.240	108	384	45	86	19	4	9	60	52	5	0	7	112	16	5	.365	.319
Sierra, Jonathan	L-L	6-3	190	10-17-98	.242	.313	.228	101	380	41	92	18	2	3	40	21	2	1	4	62	2	3	.324	.283
Slaughter, Jake	R-R	6-3	200	10-24-96	.278	.522	.212	29	108	14	30	5	1	1	13	8	2	0	3	22	0	0	.370	.331
Strumpf, Chase	R-R	6-1	191	3-8-98	.125	.167	.111	6	24	3	3	1	0	1	2	1	2	0	1	7	0	0	.292	.214
Taylor, Zac	R-R	6-1	185	10-1-95	.250	.200	.273	4	16	0	4	1	0	0	3	1	0	0	0	4	0	0	.313	.294
Vazquez, Luis	R-R	6-1	165	10-10-99	.269	.333	.250	8	26	4	7	3	0	0	1	1	1	2	0	1	0	0	.385	.321
Velazquez, Nelson	R-R	6-0	190	12-26-98	.286	.302	.282	72	262	33	75	16	4	4	34	21	0	1	1	77	5	3	.424	.338
Weber, Andy	L-R	6-1	190	7-24-97	.275	.291	.272	127	487	65	134	36	8	3	59	43	5	5	4	110	5	0	.400	.338
Zinn, Delvin	R-R	5-10	185	5-29-97	.273	.177	.300	64	231	38	63	11	2	2	14	18	6	3	0	58	14	3	.364	.341
Zobrist, Ben	B-R	6-3	210	5-26-81	.222	.500	.000	3	9	1	2	0	0	0	1	1	0	0	0	2	0	0	.222	.300

Pitching	B-T	HT	WT	DOB	W	L	ERA	G	GS	CG	SV	IP	H	R	ER	HR	BB	SO	AVG	vLH	vRH	K/9	BB/9
Albertos, Jose	R-R	6-1	185	11-7-98	1	0	5.02	8	0	0	0	14	12	10	8	0	13	14	.235	.148	.333	8.79	8.16
Barry, Sean	R-R	6-2	190	5-22-95	0	3	2.38	34	0	0	6	45	40	22	12	1	17	55	.226	.197	.245	10.92	3.38
Carrera, Faustino	L-L	5-10	165	3-9-99	8	7	3.62	22	21	0	0	117	113	57	47	13	29	105	.252	.196	.279	8.08	2.23
Casey, Derek	R-R	6-2	190	2-15-96	5	7	5.02	22	21	0	1	104	112	65	58	13	33	82	.277	.235	.320	7.10	2.86
De Los Rios, Enrique	R-R	6-1	175	5-2-95	0	0	0.00	1	0	0	0	2	1	0	0	0	2	1	.143	.000	.250	3.86	7.71
Franklin, Kohl	R-R	6-4	190	9-9-99	0	0	3.00	1	1	0	0	3	0	2	1	0	5	3	.000	.000	.000	9.00	15.00
Geekie, Dalton	R-R	6-5	200	10-3-94	1	0	5.91	7	0	0	0	11	5	9	7	1	8	13	.139	.167	.125	10.97	6.75
Glowicki, Brian	R-R	5-11	190	10-19-94	2	2	1.38	19	0	0	7	26	19	11	4	0	6	24	.196	.171	.214	8.31	2.08
Guerrero, Fauris	R-R	5-11	180	10-5-96	0	3	5.76	10	0	0	0	25	28	16	16	3	13	26	.280	.244	.309	9.36	4.68
Holland, Derek	B-L	6-2	213	10-9-86	0	0	10.80	1	0	0	0	2	2	2	2	1	0	2	.286	.200	.500	10.80	0.00
Hughes, Brandon	B-L	6-2	215	12-1-95	0	1	2.70	5	0	0	0	7	5	2	2	0	1	9	.200	.214	.182	12.15	1.35
King, Brendan	R-R	6-1	200	7-8-94	5	1	3.90	22	1	0	0	55	50	25	24	7	15	61	.240	.191	.274	9.92	2.44
Lawlor, Ryan	R-L	6-1	185	1-8-94	2	2	1.83	9	0	0	1	20	10	5	4	0	13	14	.156	.160	.150	10.98	5.95
Little, Brendon	L-L	6-1	195	8-11-96	1	1	1.91	6	6	0	0	28	18	7	6	0	13	25	.186	.067	.207	7.94	4.13
Lorenzo, Rafelin	R-R	6-2	200	1-15-97	0	0	0.00	1	0	0	0	1	1	0	0	0	0	0	.250	--	.250	0.00	0.00
Marquez, Brailyn	L-L	6-4	185	1-30-99	5	1	3.61	17	17	0	0	77	64	40	31	4	43	102	.228	.106	.265	11.87	5.00
McCauley, Riley	R-R	6-1	205	12-5-96	1	1	3.31	14	0	0	2	16	7	7	6	1	17	21	.130	.050	.177	11.57	9.37
Medina, Ivan	R-R	6-3	180	2-26-96	0	0	2.08	17	0	0	2	30	27	12	7	2	6	22	.239	.200	.260	6.53	1.78

Name	B-T	HT	WT	DOB	W	L	ERA	G	GS	CG	SV	IP	H	R	ER	HR	BB	SO	AVG	vLH	vRH	K/9	BB/9
Montgomery, Mike	L-L	6-5	215	7-1-89	0	0	0.00	1	1	0	0	2	1	0	0	0	0	4	.143	.500	.000	18.00	0.00
Mort, Zach	R-R	6-1	205	5-22-97	6	2	3.13	18	5	0	0	60	48	32	21	4	27	36	.219	.253	.194	5.37	4.03
Narea, Rafael	R-R	5-10	160	4-3-98	0	0	20.25	3	0	0	0	3	7	6	6	1	1	1	.500	.714	.286	3.38	3.38
Palma, Eugenio	L-L	5-11	170	11-26-96	5	4	3.84	38	0	0	5	68	59	34	29	5	32	61	.236	.170	.276	8.07	4.24
Passantino, Jeffrey	R-R	5-9	225	9-24-95	2	1	4.24	14	0	0	0	34	35	17	16	6	7	48	.267	.196	.313	12.71	1.85
Patterson, Jack	L-L	6-0	210	8-3-95	1	1	2.34	16	1	0	1	42	29	11	11	0	18	47	.195	.212	.186	9.99	3.83
Polanco, Gustavo	R-R	6-0	190	6-13-97	0	0	0.00	4	0	0	0	4	0	0	0	0	4	0	.000	.000	.000	0.00	9.00
Ramos, Eury	R-R	6-3	152	10-10-97	1	3	7.76	7	7	0	0	29	35	26	25	6	15	25	.307	.417	.227	7.76	4.66
Remy, Peyton	L-R	6-2	170	8-20-96	4	4	2.80	23	12	0	2	80	55	28	25	4	35	73	.190	.188	.191	8.18	3.92
Roberts, Ethan	R-R	5-11	170	7-4-97	3	2	2.57	26	0	0	9	35	30	13	10	1	8	31	.222	.222	.222	7.97	2.06
Ryan, Casey	R-R	6-4	230	5-20-94	3	2	4.74	9	0	0	0	19	18	10	10	2	9	11	.257	.296	.233	5.21	4.26
Sanders, Cam	R-R	6-2	175	12-9-96	8	4	2.94	21	20	0	0	101	71	38	33	8	53	84	.198	.201	.195	7.49	4.72
Thompson, Riley	L-R	6-3	205	7-9-96	8	6	3.06	21	21	0	0	94	85	45	32	9	31	87	.239	.226	.248	8.33	2.97
Vega, Carlos	R-R	6-2	220	12-28-95	1	0	3.96	11	3	0	1	25	21	12	11	3	14	28	.219	.270	.186	10.08	5.04
Whitney, Blake	R-R	6-3	185	5-25-96	0	0	6.00	2	0	0	1	3	6	2	2	0	0	4	.400	.750	.273	12.00	0.00

Fielding

Catcher	PCT	G	PO	A	E	DP	PB
Caratini	1.000	4	20	2	0	1	0
Gonzalez	.973	43	361	40	11	0	11
Knight	1.000	2	16	0	0	0	0
Lorenzo	.986	41	303	52	5	2	6
Mastrobuoni	.975	38	276	41	8	2	2
Polanco	.984	16	119	6	2	0	4

First Base	PCT	G	PO	A	E	DP
Durna	.993	70	543	40	4	46
Jordan	.981	10	47	4	1	2
Maldonado	1.000	6	39	3	0	5
Mejia	.990	13	92	4	1	9
Polanco	1.000	2	15	0	0	0
Reynolds	.990	21	185	4	2	11
Slaughter	.993	19	143	9	1	12

Second Base	PCT	G	PO	A	E	DP
Daniel	.987	35	67	82	2	18
Jordan	.992	32	58	72	1	22
Narea	.952	16	33	27	3	8
Slaughter	.947	7	8	10	1	2
Strumpf	1.000	6	12	14	0	2
Vazquez	1.000	3	6	8	0	3
Zinn	.988	44	79	88	2	15
Zobrist	1.000	2	1	5	0	1

Third Base	PCT	G	PO	A	E	DP
Daniel	.941	6	4	12	1	1
Jordan	1.000	14	10	18	0	0
Mejia	.917	33	22	55	7	4
Morel	.922	72	53	124	15	10
Narea	1.000	3	1	1	0	0
Perlaza	.818	9	5	13	4	3
Slaughter	1.000	2	1	1	0	0
Vazquez	1.000	4	5	6	0	0
Zinn	1.000	3	2	2	0	0

Shortstop	PCT	G	PO	A	E	DP
Daniel	1.000	1	1	3	0	0
Narea	.961	19	25	49	3	13
Vazquez	1.000	1	2	1	0	0
Weber	.935	115	139	292	30	49
Zinn	.800	2	0	4	1	0

Outfield	PCT	G	PO	A	E	DP
Americaan	1.000	8	20	0	0	0
Artis	1.000	44	54	1	0	0
Davis	1.000	47	92	3	0	0
Hill	.976	21	40	1	1	0
Jordan	1.000	17	36	0	0	0
Morel	1.000	1	3	0	0	0
Narea	.900	9	9	0	1	0
Perlaza	1.000	10	10	1	0	0
Roederer	.977	106	248	4	6	1
Sierra	.958	90	155	4	7	0
Taylor	1.000	4	8	1	0	0
Velazquez	.970	67	126	2	4	0

EUGENE EMERALDS | SHORT SEASON
NORTHWEST LEAGUE

Batting	B-T	HT	WT	DOB	AVG	vLH	vRH	G	AB	R	H	2B	3B	HR	RBI	BB	HBP	SH	SF	SO	SB	CS	SLG	OBP
Americaan, Edmond	L-L	6-1	170	3-26-97	.282	.283	.282	66	255	38	72	17	5	4	32	19	8	1	1	65	16	7	.435	.350
Byrd, Grayson	L-R	6-3	205	6-16-96	.195	.161	.201	49	185	14	36	8	1	2	21	18	1	0	0	39	0	1	.281	.270
Cuevas, Yovanny	R-R	6-0	170	7-28-98	.177	.125	.183	23	68	12	12	5	0	1	4	15	1	0	0	30	4	0	.294	.333
Diaz, Luis	R-R	5-9	160	4-16-99	.116	.056	.130	33	95	11	11	2	0	0	5	12	0	2	0	36	9	1	.137	.215
Garcia, Reivaj	B-R	5-11	175	8-12-01	.162	.143	.167	12	37	3	6	0	0	0	2	2	0	0	0	10	1	0	.162	.205
Guerra, Alexander	R-R	5-11	240	4-8-97	.200	.188	.203	23	85	8	17	5	0	4	13	5	1	0	2	35	1	0	.400	.247
Gutierrez, Jose	B-R	5-11	185	11-9-98	.250	.333	.235	6	20	2	5	0	1	1	4	3	0	0	0	6	0	0	.500	.348
Hill, Darius	L-L	6-1	190	8-17-97	.306	.222	.328	23	85	9	26	3	1	0	13	7	0	1	4	10	1	2	.365	.344
Huma, Josue	B-R	6-1	175	3-17-00	.226	.000	.269	21	62	10	14	3	0	1	8	13	0	1	0	12	0	1	.323	.360
Hurd, Dalton	R-R	5-9	180	12-17-95	.046	.000	.059	8	22	0	1	1	0	0	1	2	0	0	0	7	0	0	.091	.125
Kelli, Fernando	R-R	6-0	180	7-28-98	.229	.271	.218	62	227	35	52	15	4	2	26	15	8	2	2	66	24	7	.357	.298
Knight, Caleb	R-R	5-11	220	1-2-96	.253	.308	.233	32	99	10	25	2	1	2	11	11	6	2	0	20	1	4	.354	.362
Maldonado, Nelson	R-R	5-10	195	8-13-96	.414	.500	.396	15	58	9	24	4	0	1	11	6	1	0	1	9	2	1	.535	.470
Martinez, Pedro	B-R	5-11	165	1-28-01	.265	.273	.263	27	98	15	26	2	3	0	7	12	2	0	0	36	11	5	.347	.357
Mejia, Rafael	R-R	5-11	195	12-12-97	.129	.222	.091	9	31	0	4	1	0	0	4	1	0	0	0	15	0	0	.161	.156
Olson, Jacob	R-R	6-0	200	5-21-97	.225	.182	.236	35	111	17	25	10	2	0	9	8	3	0	1	26	0	2	.351	.293
Perlaza, Yonathan	B-R	5-10	195	11-10-98	.293	.393	.254	25	99	11	29	9	1	1	9	7	0	0	2	27	5	1	.434	.333
Reynolds, Ryan	R-R	6-2	215	7-17-97	.182	.250	.170	15	55	4	10	3	0	0	5	8	0	0	0	21	0	1	.236	.286
Slaughter, Jake	R-R	6-0		10-24-96	.308	.382	.288	42	159	23	49	7	2	3	27	12	6	0	3	36	6	2	.434	.372
Soto, Jonathan	L-R	5-9	143	7-9-98	.196	.188	.198	45	148	16	29	7	0	0	14	8	0	0	0	24	0	0	.243	.237
Strumpf, Chase	R-R		191	3-8-98	.292	.222	.310	26	89	17	26	8	0	2	14	15	4	0	3	28	2	0	.449	.405
Taylor, Zac	R-R	5-11	185	10-1-95	.282	.231	.292	21	78	17	22	5	2	0	7	10	0	0	0	25	5	3	.397	.364
Vazquez, Luis	R-R	6-1	165	11-10-00	.239	.182	.253	62	226	23	54	9	1	1	20	16	4	1	1	44	3	4	.301	.300
Vicens, Brandon	R-R	5-11	195	12-7-95	.132	.133	.130	12	38	3	5	0	0	0	2	9	0	0	1	11	1	1	.132	.292
Washer, Jake	R-R	6-0	220	2-23-96	.258	.200	.275	21	66	10	17	7	1	1	8	9	0	0	0	24	0	0	.439	.347
Zardon, Danny	R-R	6-0		9-30-94	.162	.000	.207	12	37	4	6	0	0	0	0	7	1	0	0	7	0	0	.243	.311

Pitching	B-T	HT	WT	DOB	W	L	ERA	G	GS	CG	SV	IP	H	R	ER	HR	BB	SO	AVG	vLH	vRH	K/9	BB/9
Aguiar, Maikel	R-R	6-0	185	11-20-96	2	2	5.50	9	0	0	0	18	14	13	11	0	14	21	.212	.192	.225	10.50	7.00
Allen, Chris	L-L	6-4	180	6-13-98	2	0	3.00	11	2	0	1	36	37	18	12	2	7	23	.253	.389	.209	5.75	1.75
Bigge, Hunter	R-R	6-0	195	6-12-98	2	0	1.20	8	0	0	0	15	6	2	2	1	8	20	.120	.143	.111	12.00	4.80
Bocchi, Matteo	R-R	6-4	205	7-19-96	1	0	2.03	7	0	0	0	13	9	3	3	1	4	16	.180	.333	.114	10.80	2.70
Bryant, Zach	R-R	6-1	210	6-5-98	0	1	1.35	7	0	0	1	13	13	3	2	0	4	13	.255	.294	.235	8.78	2.70

CHICAGO CUBS

	W	L	ERA	G	GS	CG	SV	IP	H	R	ER	HR	BB	SO	AVG	vLH	vRH	K/9	BB/9
Burgmann, Josh R-R 6-0 205 1-27-98	0	3	3.79	9	9	0	0	19	18	10	8	4	3	22	.237	.238	.236	10.42	1.42
Clarke, Chris R-R 6-7 212 5-13-98	0	1	1.96	9	8	0	0	23	20	5	5	2	4	26	.230	.303	.185	10.17	1.57
Colorado, Alfredo R-R 6-1 170 6-22-96	0	1	7.94	4	0	0	0	6	6	5	5	1	2	5	.273	.286	.267	7.94	3.18
Cruz, Yovanny R-R 6-1 190 8-23-99	1	2	7.98	5	3	0	0	15	13	17	13	3	12	21	.220	.300	.180	12.89	7.36
Dalton, Tanner R-R 6-2 195 8-25-96	1	0	3.38	12	0	0	1	19	19	8	7	0	7	17	.268	.217	.292	8.20	3.38
De Los Rios, Enrique R-R 6-1 175 5-2-95	0	0	0.00	2	0	0	1	4	1	0	0	0	1	4	.091	.000	.125	9.00	2.25
Deppermann, Brad R-R 6-0 190 6-15-96	0	1	4.50	4	0	0	0	8	9	5	4	1	4	9	.281	.300	.273	10.13	4.50
Estrada, Jeremiah B-R 6-1 185 11-1-98	0	1	5.91	3	1	0	0	11	8	8	7	0	6	15	.211	.222	.200	12.66	5.06
Franklin, Kohl R-R 6-4 190 9-9-99	1	3	2.31	10	10	0	0	39	31	11	10	2	14	49	.214	.232	.202	11.31	3.23
Gallardo, Richard R-R 6-1 187 9-6-01	0	0	2.25	2	1	0	0	4	2	1	1	0	2	2	.154	.286	.000	4.50	4.50
Guerrero, Fauris R-R 5-11 180 10-5-96	1	0	0.68	6	0	0	1	13	5	1	1	0	7	15	.116	.188	.074	10.13	4.73
Hughes, Brandon B-L 6-2 215 12-1-95	0	1	3.86	9	0	0	0	16	10	7	7	1	5	16	.175	.182	.174	8.82	2.76
Jensen, Ryan R-R 6-0 180 11-23-97	0	0	2.25	6	6	0	0	12	7	3	3	0	14	19	.171	.167	.172	14.25	10.50
Kachmar, Chris R-R 6-3 180 9-3-96	4	0	1.56	10	0	0	0	17	11	3	3	1	11	24	.183	.071	.217	12.46	5.71
King, Bryan R-L 6-1 184 11-5-96	2	1	3.07	9	0	0	0	15	10	5	5	0	11	11	.196	.111	.214	6.75	6.75
McAvene, Michael R-R 6-3 210 8-24-97	0	0	1.42	6	6	0	0	13	5	2	2	0	4	20	.119	.150	.091	14.21	2.84
McCauley, Riley R-R 6-1 205 12-5-96	0	1	2.73	17	0	0	6	26	18	9	8	3	16	44	.192	.242	.164	15.04	5.47
Medina, Ivan R-R 6-3 180 2-26-96	1	0	3.00	2	0	0	1	3	3	1	1	0	1	6	.250	.333	.222	18.00	3.00
Mort, Zach R-R 6-1 205 5-22-97	3	3	3.72	9	7	0	0	46	43	24	19	3	10	40	.252	.218	.267	7.83	1.96
Nahas, Joe R-R 6-1 185 11-14-97	0	1	3.21	9	0	0	1	14	14	8	5	0	9	16	.280	.278	.281	10.29	5.79
Nunez, Eduarniel R-R 6-2 174 6-7-99	1	5	6.93	15	9	0	0	38	49	30	29	3	27	38	.318	.356	.303	9.08	6.45
Orta, Raidel R-R 5-9 180 3-4-96	1	2	4.50	11	0	0	0	24	27	13	12	5	7	11	.281	.275	.286	4.13	2.63
Perez, Yunior R-R 6-4 190 12-19-98	2	3	4.73	13	3	0	0	27	21	14	14	0	21	30	.226	.256	.200	10.13	7.09
Pomeroy, John L-R 6-5 210 10-9-94	0	2	7.84	7	0	0	1	10	16	10	9	2	0	7	14	.364	.250	.406	12.19	6.10
Reindl, Jake R-R 6-1 190 1-15-97	0	1	2.08	9	0	0	0	13	12	8	3	1	4	13	.226	.188	.243	9.00	2.77
Reyes, Ruben L-L 5-11 170 10-1-95	1	0	0.00	2	0	0	0	2	2	0	0	2	2	.333	.000	.400	10.80	10.80
Rosario, Aneuris R-R 6-0 165 3-4-95	0	2	3.27	7	0	0	0	11	10	9	4	1	7	10	.238	.200	.273	8.18	5.73
Ryan, Casey R-R 6-4 230 5-20-94	0	0	5.40	4	0	0	1	7	6	5	4	0	2	10	.231	.111	.294	13.50	2.70
Stone, Niels L-R 6-1 190 2-10-99	1	1	8.53	3	2	0	0	6	9	7	6	1	4	4	.300	.250	.333	5.68	5.68
Tejada, Jesus R-R 6-1 168 10-24-96	0	0	6.23	6	0	0	0	13	12	9	9	1	9	10	.250	.250	.250	6.92	6.23
Vargas, Didier R-L 6-0 175 3-13-99	1	5	6.26	15	9	0	0	46	51	40	32	2	38	25	.283	.212	.299	4.89	7.43
Vega, Carlos R-R 6-2 220 12-28-95	1	0	0.00	2	0	0	1	3	1	1	0	0	1	4	.100	.000	.143	12.00	3.00
Whitney, Blake R-R 6-3 185 5-25-96	4	0	3.19	18	0	0	1	54	44	21	19	3	18	62	.222	.274	.192	10.40	3.02
Zardon, Danny R-R 6-0 200 9-30-94	0	0	18.00	1	0	0	0	1	2	2	2	1	0	0	.333	.333	--	0.00	0.00

Fielding

C: Guerra 7, Knight 25, Soto 41, Washer 8, Zardon 4. 1B: Byrd 44, Guerra 3, Knight 1, Maldonado 2, Mejia 6, Reynolds 2, Slaughter 18, Zardon 3. 2B: Diaz 14, Garcia 12, Huma 10, Martinez 15, Perlaza 7, Strumpf 24. 3B: Diaz 13, Huma 10, Martinez 1, Perlaza 17, Reynolds 13, Slaughter 23. SS: Diaz 4, Huma 1, Martinez 11, Vazquez 62. OF: Americaan 66, Cuevas 20, Gutierrez 3, Hill 23, Hurd 7, Kelli 59, Olson 32, Taylor 17, Vicens 10.

AZL CUBS 1 — ROOKIE
ARIZONA LEAGUE

Batting	B-T	HT	WT	DOB	AVG	vLH	vRH	G	AB	R	H	2B	3B	HR	RBI	BB	HBP	SH	SF	SO	SB	CS	SLG	OBP
Adames, Cristhian	B-R	6-0	185	7-26-91	.286	.250	.294	6	21	3	6	0	2	2	8	3	0	0	1	4	0	0	.762	.360
Bautista, Flemin	B-R	5-10	170	3-10-00	.194	.053	.245	19	72	9	14	3	1	2	13	6	0	1	1	31	2	4	.347	.253
Collier, Manny	R-R	5-10	170	12-19-00	.182	.000	.250	3	11	2	2	0	0	0	1	1	0	0		7	2	0	.182	.308
Cuevas, Yovanny	R-R	6-0	170	7-28-98	.329	.478	.268	24	79	19	26	5	0	4	10	15	4	2	0	22	7	2	.544	.459
Diaz, Luis	R-R	5-9	160	4-16-99	.156	.333	.115	9	32	5	5	0	0	0	2	9	0	0	0	11	4	0	.156	.342
Field, Johnny	R-R	5-10	195	2-20-92	.222	.200	.250	3	9	1	2	0	0	0	3	1	0	0	1	2	0	0	.222	.273
Hearn, Ethan	L-R	6-0	200	8-31-00	.160	.111	.175	21	75	9	12	2	0	2	11	12	2	0	3	35	1	1	.267	.283
2-team total (2 Cubs 2)					.163	.105	.180	23	80	10	13	3	0	2	14	13	2	0	3	36	1	1	.275	.286
Hinirio, Albert	B-R	6-2	170	5-15-98	.250	.222	.264	26	80	8	20	8	0	0	7	2	2	1	1	30	1	2	.350	.282
Joaquin, Widimer	R-R	6-2	180	9-8-00	.344	.714	.240	9	32	7	11	1	0	1	9	4	0	0	2	4	0	0	.469	.395
2-team total (31 Cubs 2)					.290	.407	.260	40	131	18	38	4	0	2	21	10	4	0	4	35	1	2	.366	.331
Maldonado, Nelson	R-R	5-10	195	8-13-96	.278	.250	.286	8	36	7	10	3	1	1	9	3	0	0	0	6	1	0	.500	.333
Marchan, Ervis	L-L	5-11	175	8-16-99	.333	.364	.319	30	105	24	35	6	0	1	20	8	2	0	0	14	1	2	.419	.391
Martinez, Eddy	R-R	6-1	195	1-18-95	.250	.000	.333	5	16	4	4	1	0	1	3	3	0	0	0	2	0	0	.500	.368
Martinez, Pedro	B-R	5-11	165	1-28-01	.352	.353	.351	27	108	12	38	6	3	2	17	12	0	1	0	27	8	5	.519	.417
Moreno, Kevin	R-R	6-3	200	6-19-00	.276	.167	.304	9	29	7	8	3	0	2	8	9	0	0	0	8	0	1	.586	.447
2-team total (27 Cubs 2)					.187	.105	.205	36	107	18	20	8	0	2	17	19	1	1	0	41	1	1	.318	.315
Nunez, Orian	R-R	5-10	160	9-3-98	.313	.125	.375	8	32	3	10	2	0	0	2	2	0	0	1	4	2	0	.375	.343
2-team total (22 Cubs 2)					.236	.191	.250	30	89	7	21	5	0	0	4	10	1	0	1	16	2	1	.292	.317
Nunez, Richard	R-R	5-10	170	3-14-95	.208	.200	.211	7	24	6	5	2	0	0	2	3	1	0	1	6	0	1	.292	.310
2-team total (20 Cubs 2)					.271	.200	.292	27	85	16	23	6	0	2	16	15	1	0	1	17	1	0	.412	.382
Olson, Jacob	R-R	6-0	200	5-21-97	.290	.375	.267	9	38	8	11	1	1	1	4	2	2	0	1	10	2	1	.447	.349
Pacheco, Carlos	R-R	5-11	195	4-2-99	.256	.278	.250	46	164	37	42	11	1	4	29	19	1	0	2	57	7	2	.409	.333
Pagan, Ezequiel	L-R	6-1	163	7-8-00	.287	.271	.294	41	174	30	50	6	0	1	26	16	3	3	1	37	18	6	.339	.356
2-team total (9 Cubs 2)					.283	.309	.274	50	212	37	60	6	0	1	28	21	4	3	1	45	19	8	.326	.357
Pena, Brailin	L-L	5-11	160	5-2-01	.148	.250	.111	18	61	6	9	3	0	0	4	7	2	0	1	22	1	2	.197	.254
Pena, Raymond	R-R	5-10	160	4-7-97	.281	.429	.233	18	57	11	16	3	1	0	8	9	1	1	1	20	0	3	.368	.382
Perez, Herson	R-R	5-11	160	11-6-00	.222	.238	.217	24	81	18	18	5	0	0	6	11	1	1	1	15	1	0	.284	.319
Perez, Herson	B-R	5-11	175	12-19-96	.214	.200	.220	25	56	12	12	1	1	0	7	11	4	1	0	12	4	1	.268	.380
Pertuz, Fabian	R-R	6-0	156	9-1-00	.340	.349	.336	40	162	28	55	12	1	2	19	7	3	0	3	38	7	3	.463	.371
2-team total (9 Cubs 2)					.325	.327	.324	49	197	33	64	14	1	2	25	9	3	0	3	46	9	4	.437	.359
Pina, Oswaldo	R-R	5-10	170	8-9-98	.275	.261	.282	45	149	30	41	6	3	1	26	21	3	1	1	38	10	3	.376	.374

Name	B-T	HT	WT	DOB	AVG	vLH	vRH	G	AB	R	H	2B	3B	HR	RBI	BB	HBP	SH	SF	SO	SB	CS	SLG	OBP
Reynolds, Ryan	B-R	6-2	215	7-17-97	.248	.207	.260	35	129	19	32	10	2	1	19	19	0	0	1	45	4	3	.380	.342
Short, Zack	R-R	5-10	180	5-29-95	.375	.667	.200	6	16	5	6	2	0	0	3	8	1	0	0	4	0	0	.500	.600
Taylor, Zac /	R-R	6-1	185	10-1-95	.400	.333	.429	9	40	11	16	1	1	5	15	3	1	0	1	8	6	0	.850	.444

Pitching	B-T	HT	WT	DOB	W	L	ERA	G	GS	CG	SV	IP	H	R	ER	HR	BB	SO	AVG	vLH	vRH	K/9	BB/9
Almanzar, Elian	L-R	6-4	210	2-1-00	0	2	9.35	8	0	0	0	9	10	10	9	0	11	10	.313	.357	.278	10.38	11.42
Bigge, Hunter	R-R	6-0	205	6-12-98	0	0	0.00	1	0	0	0	1	1	0	0	0	2	2	.250	.500	.000	18.00	18.00
Colorado, Alfredo	R-R	6-1	170	6-22-96	0	0	5.63	6	0	0	0	8	10	5	5	1	4	11	.294	.273	.304	12.38	4.50
Combs, Shane	R-R	6-2	219	1-14-97	1	2	5.28	10	0	0	0	15	13	10	9	0	9	18	.236	.286	.185	10.57	5.28
Ferrebus, Emilio	R-R	6-2	165	11-25-97	1	0	5.58	16	0	0	0	31	31	22	19	1	19	34	.279	.313	.254	9.98	5.58
Gallardo, Richard	R-R	6-1	187	9-6-01	0	2	4.15	11	9	0	0	30	32	15	14	1	12	23	.267	.315	.227	6.82	3.56
Garcia, Misael	L-L	6-2	196	4-18-01	0	4	9.36	11	5	0	0	34	41	44	35	4	22	22	.295	.300	.294	5.88	5.88
Graveman, Kendall	R-R	6-2	200	12-21-90	0	0	3.00	1	1	0	0	3	3	1	1	0	0	6	.250	1.000	.100	18.00	0.00
Guante, Julio	R-R	6-3	180	5-29-97	1	0	3.68	3	0	0	0	7	8	3	3	0	0	5	.276	.333	.261	6.14	0.00
2-team total (13 Cubs 2)					2	1	4.66	16	0	0	0	39	48	23	20	4	7	34	.302	.273	.313	7.91	1.63
Hedges, Zach	R-R	6-4	195	10-21-92	0	0	9.00	2	0	0	0	2	4	2	2	0	0	1	.444	.333	.500	4.50	0.00
Herrera, Elias	R-R	6-1	172	9-23-97	3	2	4.15	17	0	0	1	35	26	18	16	1	7	40	.203	.275	.171	10.38	1.82
Hinirio, Albert	R-R	6-2	170	5-15-98	0	0	9.00	1	0	0	0	1	1	1	1	0	1	1	.286	.500	.000	4.50	13.50
Hockin, Chad	R-R	6-2	210	10-7-94	1	0	3.60	5	0	0	0	5	5	2	2	0	2	11	.227	.300	.167	19.80	3.60
Hodge, Porter	R-R	6-4	230	2-21-01	0	0	10.13	5	4	0	0	8	10	9	9	0	8	4	.303	.250	.333	4.50	9.00
Hudson, Bryan	L-L	6-8	220	5-8-97	1	0	2.45	4	2	0	0	7	6	2	2	0	0	8	.200	.000	.222	9.82	0.00
Hughes, Brandon	B-L	6-2	215	12-1-95	2	0	2.79	7	0	0	2	10	2	5	3	1	5	17	.061	.000	.091	15.83	4.66
Kachmar, Chris	R-R	6-3	180	9-3-96	1	0	2.25	4	0	0	0	8	4	2	2	0	4	12	.160	.400	.100	13.50	4.50
Little, Brendon	L-L	6-1	195	8-11-96	0	0	3.68	2	2	0	0	7	4	3	3	2	4	9	.160	.333	.136	11.05	4.91
Marchan, Ervis	L-L	5-11	175	8-16-99	0	0	0.00	1	0	0	0	1	0	0	0	0	1	1	.000	—	.000	9.00	9.00
Nahas, Joe	R-R	6-1	185	11-14-97	0	1	27.00	2	2	0	0	2	4	5	5	0	2	4	.444	.500	.400	21.60	10.80
Nunez, Richard	R-R	5-10	170	3-14-95	0	0	0.00	1	0	0	0	1	0	0	0	0	3	1	.000	.000	—	9.00	27.00
Ochoa, Pablo	L-L	6-0	180	1-11-98	2	0	13.79	9	0	0	0	16	29	26	24	4	10	16	.392	.227	.462	9.19	5.74
Orta, Raidel	R-R	5-9	180	3-4-96	3	0	0.45	9	0	0	0	20	15	7	1	1	2	28	.195	.129	.239	12.60	0.90
Paula, Carlos	R-R	6-0	195	1-29-00	2	1	4.70	7	0	0	0	23	20	12	12	1	15	28	.233	.294	.217	10.96	5.87
Perez, Herson	B-R	5-11	175	12-19-96	0	0	24.30	2	0	0	0	3	9	9	9	0	3	2	.474	.375	.546	5.40	8.10
Pina, Oswaldo	R-R	5-10	170	8-9-98	0	0	40.50	1	0	0	0	1	1	3	3	0	4	1	.333	1.000	.000	13.50	54.00
Reindl, Jake	R-R	6-1	190	1-15-97	0	0	0.00	4	0	0	0	5	2	0	0	0	2	9	.125	.167	.100	16.20	3.60
Remon, Jorge	R-R	6-2	160	2-3-01	0	3	7.94	11	7	0	1	28	21	26	25	1	32	28	.208	.250	.192	8.89	10.16
Rodriguez, Benjamin	R-R	5-11	175	7-27-99	2	3	3.58	12	0	0	0	50	44	30	20	4	17	38	.232	.216	.241	6.79	3.04
Rodriguez, Luis	L-L	6-1	190	9-10-99	2	4	3.61	11	9	0	0	47	44	24	19	2	24	44	.249	.333	.222	8.37	4.56
Rosario, Aneuris	R-R	6-0	165	3-4-95	1	1	1.42	5	0	0	0	6	6	1	1	0	1	10	.261	.333	.214	14.21	1.42
Silva, Luis	L-L	5-11	165	6-6-97	0	1	12.34	9	0	0	1	12	24	16	16	2	10	9	.421	.222	.513	6.94	7.71
Stone, Niels	L-R	6-1	190	2-10-99	1	2	8.76	9	1	0	0	25	33	28	24	2	11	29	.311	.289	.328	10.58	4.01
Thompson, Keegan	R-R	6-1	210	3-13-95	0	2	7.20	2	2	0	0	5	4	4	4	1	0	5	.200	.182	.222	9.00	0.00
Ueckert, Cayne	R-R	6-3	195	5-28-96	0	1	1.37	12	0	0	2	20	17	6	3	1	10	21	.230	.167	.260	9.61	4.58
2-team total (3 Cubs 2)					0	1	1.90	15	0	0	3	24	20	8	5	1	12	26	.230	.143	.271	9.89	4.56
Webster, Allen	R-R	6-2	200	2-10-90	0	0	5.40	2	1	0	0	2	1	1	1	0	0	2	.143	.000	.250	10.80	0.00

Fielding

C: Hearn 16, Nunez 4, Nunez 3, Pena 17, Perez 20. 1B: Hearn 3, Joaquin 1, Maldonado 4, Marchan 26, Nunez 4, Nunez 1, Pena 6, Pertuz 1, Reynolds 14. 2B: Adames 4, Bautista 8, Diaz 4, Martinez 9, Perez 17, Pina 19, Short 2. 3B: Adames 1, Diaz 3, Joaquin 5, Perez 1, Pertuz 21, Pina 9, Reynolds 19. SS: Bautista 7, Martinez 16, Perez 1, Pertuz 16, Pina 19, Short 3. OF: Collier 2, Cuevas 23, Field 2, Hinirio 22, Marchan 3, Martinez 4, Moreno 9, Olson 9, Pacheco 41, Pagan 39, Pena 13, Perez 1, Taylor 8.

AZL CUBS 2   ROOKIE
ARIZONA LEAGUE

Batting	B-T	HT	WT	DOB	AVG	vLH	vRH	G	AB	R	H	2B	3B	HR	RBI	BB	HBP	SH	SF	SO	SB	CS	SLG	OBP
Artis, D.J.	L-L	5-9	165	3-20-97	.188	.667	.077	5	16	3	3	0	0	0	1	4	0	0	0	4	4	0	.188	.350
Bethencourt, Jhonny	R-R	5-11	160	2-12-97	.286	.250	.308	6	21	3	6	1	0	0	4	1	0	0	1	7	0	0	.333	.304
Byrd, Grayson	L-R	6-3	205	6-16-96	.286	.250	.296	8	35	3	10	2	0	1	7	1	0	0	0	8	1	0	.429	.306
Cardona, Jose	R-R	6-1	175	3-16-94	.147	.167	.143	10	34	5	5	0	0	0	4	7	2	0	0	12	3	1	.147	.326
Cruz, Rochest	L-R	5-11	150	6-24-99	.206	.000	.244	42	107	20	22	2	0	0	6	12	4	2	1	31	14	0	.224	.307
Garcia, Reivaj	B-R	5-11	175	8-12-01	.247	.150	.277	23	85	7	21	5	0	0	10	2	2	2	0	10	3	0	.306	.281
Guerra, Alexander	R-R	5-11	160	5-8-97	.298	.500	.264	24	84	20	25	4	2	10	32	15	1	0	1	26	0	0	.750	.406
Gutierrez, Jose	B-R	5-11	185	11-9-98	.438	1.000	.357	6	16	6	7	4	0	0	2	3	0	0	0	4	1	0	.688	.526
Hearn, Ethan	L-R	6-0	200	8-31-00	.200	.000	.250	2	5	1	1	0	0	0	3	1	0	0	0	1	0	0	.400	.333
2-team total (21 Cubs 1)					.163	.105	.180	23	80	10	13	3	0	2	14	13	2	0	3	36	1	1	.275	.286
Hill, Darius	L-L	6-1	190	8-17-97	.306	.500	.250	8	36	5	11	1	1	1	3	1	0	0	0	3	1	1	.472	.324
Hoerner, Nico	R-R	5-11	200	5-13-97	.400	.571	.308	5	20	2	8	1	0	0	1	0	0	0	1	1	0	0	.450	.429
Huma, Josue	B-R	6-1	175	3-17-00	.271	.280	.269	36	129	22	35	4	1	2	22	27	2	1	2	29	5	1	.364	.400
Joaquin, Widimer	B-R	6-2	180	9-8-00	.273	.300	.266	31	99	11	27	3	0	1	12	6	0	0	2	31	1	2	.333	.308
2-team total (9 Cubs 1)					.290	.407	.260	40	131	18	38	4	0	2	21	10	0	0	4	35	1	2	.366	.331
Mejia, Fidel	B-R	5-11	160	8-30-98	.231	.400	.191	8	26	2	6	1	1	3	3	0	0	0	0	6	0	0	.462	.310
Moreno, Kevin	R-R	6-3	200	6-19-00	.154	.077	.169	27	78	11	12	5	0	0	9	10	1	1	0	33	1	0	.218	.258
2-team total (9 Cubs 1)					.187	.105	.205	36	107	18	20	8	0	2	17	19	1	1	0	41	1	1	.318	.315
Morfa, Carlos	R-R	6-2	190	12-20-00	.171	.227	.161	43	146	13	25	10	1	1	15	4	2	0	2	62	1	0	.260	.201
Nunez, Orian	R-R	5-10	160	9-3-98	.193	.231	.182	22	57	6	11	3	0	0	2	8	1	0	0	12	0	1	.246	.303
2-team total (8 Cubs 1)					.236	.191	.250	30	89	7	21	5	0	0	4	10	1	0	1	16	2	1	.292	.317
Nunez, Richard	R-R	5-10	170	3-14-95	.295	.200	.326	20	61	10	18	4	0	2	14	12	0	0	0	11	1	0	.459	.411

	B-T	HT	WT	DOB	AVG	vLH	vRH	G	AB	R	H	2B	3B	HR	RBI	BB	HBP	SH	SF	SO	SB	CS	SLG	OBP
2-team total (7 Cubs 1)					.271	.200	.292	27	85	16	23	6	0	2	16	15	1	0	1	17	1	0	.412	.382
Pagan, Ezequiel	L-R	6-1	163	7-8-00	.263	.571	.194	9	38	7	10	0	0	0	2	5	1	0	0	8	1	2	.263	.364
2-team total (41 Cubs 1)					.283	.309	.274	50	212	37	60	6	0	1	28	21	4	3	1	45	19	8	.326	.357
Pertuz, Fabian	R-R	6-0	156	9-1-00	.257	.222	.269	9	35	5	9	2	0	0	6	2	0	0	0	8	2	1	.314	.297
2-team total (40 Cubs 1)					.325	.327	.324	49	197	33	64	14	1	2	25	9	3	0	3	46	9	4	.437	.359
Rodriguez, Abraham	L-L	5-11	175	3-9-99	.204	.306	.176	44	167	22	34	7	1	4	24	10	1	0	4	29	2	1	.329	.247
Strumpf, Chase	R-R	6-1	191	3-8-98	.182	.000	.286	7	22	5	4	3	0	0	1	7	2	0	1	7	0	0	.318	.406
Velazquez, Nelson	R-R	6-0	190	12-26-98	.316	.667	.250	6	19	4	6	1	0	2	5	2	0	0	0	5	0	0	.684	.381
Verdugo, Luis	R-R	6-0	172	10-12-00	.305	.242	.317	53	197	40	60	9	2	5	38	19	2	0	3	39	8	2	.447	.367
Verenzuela, Ricardo	L-R	6-0	170	1-14-00	.268	.172	.301	32	112	20	30	2	2	0	9	9	0	3	1	37	4	3	.321	.320
Vicens, Brandon	R-R	5-11	195	12-7-95	.198	.208	.196	39	116	20	23	8	2	1	14	20	2	2	1	27	4	0	.328	.324
Washer, Jake	R-R	6-0	220	2-23-96	.250	--	.250	1	4	0	1	0	0	0	0	0	0	0	0	0	0	0	.250	.250
Windham, Bryce	L-R	6-1	190	9-25-96	.325	.208	.355	35	117	32	38	9	1	0	19	30	0	0	1	19	3	1	.419	.460

Pitching	B-T	HT	WT	DOB	W	L	ERA	G	GS	CG	SV	IP	H	R	ER	HR	BB	SO	AVG	vLH	vRH	K/9	BB/9
Aguiar, Maikel	R-R	6-0	185	11-20-96	1	1	3.15	10	0	0	1	20	13	8	7	0	9	24	.194	.207	.184	10.80	4.05
Bocchi, Matteo	R-R	6-4	205	7-19-96	1	2	4.40	8	0	0	1	14	15	7	7	1	4	16	.278	.333	.250	10.05	2.51
Bryant, Zach	R-R	6-2	210	6-5-98	1	0	1.13	5	0	0	1	8	4	2	1	0	4	11	.148	.300	.059	12.38	4.50
Cedeno, Xavier	L-L	5-11	210	8-26-86	0	0	0.00	1	0	0	0	1	0	0	0	0	0	1	.000	.000	.000	9.00	0.00
Cruz, Yovanny	R-R	6-1	190	8-23-99	0	0	4.00	4	4	0	0	9	7	4	4	0	7	7	.212	.286	.158	7.00	7.00
Dalton, Tanner	R-R	6-2	195	8-25-96	0	0	3.00	3	0	0	0	6	5	2	2	0	1	9	.227	.375	.143	13.50	1.50
Deppermann, Brad	R-R	6-0	190	6-15-96	2	0	2.45	3	0	0	0	4	1	1	2	1	0	4	.286	.400	.222	9.82	2.45
Effross, Scott	R-R	6-2	202	12-28-93	1	0	0.00	3	0	0	0	4	1	0	0	0	0	3	.083	.143	.000	7.36	0.00
Espinoza, Manuel	R-R	6-0	175	11-17-00	5	2	2.49	11	7	0	0	47	52	21	13	1	9	37	.280	.294	.271	7.09	1.72
Fermin, Francisco	R-R	6-4	175	11-19-98	0	0	5.73	6	0	0	0	11	12	8	7	1	3	8	.267	.188	.310	6.55	2.45
Galazin, Jamie	R-R	6-4	200	5-20-96	4	0	5.14	14	0	0	4	21	22	16	12	2	10	32	.253	.375	.182	13.71	4.29
Gomez, Jose	R-R	6-2	165	3-15-97	2	2	6.14	8	0	0	0	22	23	15	15	1	13	21	.274	.130	.328	8.59	5.32
Gonzalez, Jose Miguel	R-R	6-3	173	12-5-97	0	1	3.47	12	12	0	0	36	35	17	14	3	15	29	.195	.232	.167	7.18	3.72
Guante, Julio	R-R	6-3	180	5-29-97	1	1	4.88	13	0	0	1	31	40	20	17	4	7	29	.308	.263	.326	8.33	2.01
2-team total (3 Cubs 1)					2	1	4.66	16	0	0	1	39	48	23	20	4	7	34	.302	.273	.313	7.91	1.63
Heredia, Manuel	R-R	6-4	195	2-16-97	2	3	3.25	14	0	0	1	28	28	17	10	1	14	38	.244	.277	.221	12.36	4.55
Herz, Davidjohn	R-L	6-2	175	1-4-01	0	1	2.61	6	6	0	0	10	8	3	3	0	8	8	.238	.133	.296	6.97	6.97
Joaquin, Widimer	R-R	6-2	180	9-8-00	0	0	0.00	1	0	0	0	1	3	0	0	0	1	1	.167	.000	.200	9.00	9.00
King, Bryan	R-L	6-1	184	11-5-96	0	1	0.00	5	0	0	0	9	5	4	0	0	4	11	.161	.000	.217	10.61	3.86
Lee, Chi-Feng	R-R	5-11	190	10-14-97	2	3	5.03	11	5	0	0	48	58	35	27	3	9	44	.289	.274	.297	8.19	1.68
Moore, Alex	R-R	6-3	205	10-25-96	1	1	3.75	10	0	0	0	12	16	9	5	0	11	14	.302	.259	.346	10.50	8.25
Moreno, Kevin	R-R	6-3	200	6-19-00	0	0	0.00	1	0	0	0	0	0	0	0	0	0	0	.000	.000	--	0.00	0.00
Ocampo, Carlos	R-R	6-2	181	9-3-98	3	3	3.28	12	11	0	0	47	32	23	17	2	23	48	.191	.170	.202	9.26	4.44
Pomeroy, John	L-R	6-5	210	10-9-94	0	0	1.35	4	0	0	1	6	5	2	1	0	1	11	.261	.182	.333	14.85	1.35
Ramos, Eury	R-R	6-3	152	10-10-97	0	0	3.00	1	1	0	0	3	3	1	1	0	1	5	.250	.500	.000	15.00	3.00
Ramos, Luis	R-R	6-5	205	12-23-97	2	3	5.18	11	10	0	0	49	44	33	28	1	34	30	.257	.301	.225	5.55	6.29
Schlaffer, Tyler	R-R	6-1	180	5-24-01	0	0	3.38	3	0	0	0	5	6	3	2	0	1	5	.261	.200	.278	8.44	1.69
Ueckert, Cayne	R-R	6-3	195	5-28-96	0	0	4.50	3	0	0	1	4	3	2	2	0	2	5	.231	.000	.333	11.25	4.50
2-team total (12 Cubs 1)					0	1	1.90	15	0	0	3	24	20	8	5	1	12	26	.230	.143	.271	9.89	4.56
Ventura, Omar	R-R	6-2	190	9-10-96	2	1	2.70	16	0	0	3	30	18	10	9	0	16	35	.173	.143	.188	10.50	4.80
Verenzuela, Ricardo	L-R	6-0	170	1-14-00	0	0	0.00	1	0	0	0	1	0	0	0	0	0	0	.000	.000	.000	0.00	0.00
Zardon, Danny	R-R	6-0	200	9-30-94	1	0	0.00	3	0	0	0	4	1	0	0	0	0	5	.077	.000	.111	11.25	0.00

Fielding

C: Guerra 16, Hearn 1, Nunez 13, Nunez 11, Washer 1, Windham 22. **1B:** Byrd 4, Guerra 5, Joaquin 13, Nunez 8, Nunez 9, Rodriguez 27. **2B:** Bethencourt 3, Cruz 26, Garcia 19, Hoerner 1, Huma 7, Joaquin 1, Mejia 1, Strumpf 5. **3B:** Bethencourt 1, Byrd 1, Cruz 9, Huma 18, Joaquin 14, Mejia 5, Pertuz 5, Verdugo 15. **SS:** Bethencourt 2, Cruz 1, Hoerner 3, Huma 12, Pertuz 4, Verdugo 38. **OF:** Artis 4, Byrd 3, Cardona 8, Cruz 1, Gutierrez 6, Hill 8, Moreno 24, Morfa 34, Nunez 1, Pagan 9, Rodriguez 15, Velazquez 4, Verenzuela 31, Vicens 38, Windham 2.

DSL CUBS   ROOKIE

Batting	B-T	HT	WT	DOB	AVG	vLH	vRH	G	AB	R	H	2B	3B	HR	RBI	BB	HBP	SH	SF	SO	SB	CS	SLG	OBP
Acevedo, Augusto	R-R	5-10	165	8-22-00	.229	.222	.231	33	109	18	25	5	1	2	14	17	4	1	1	35	2	1	.349	.351
Aliendo, Pablo	R-R	6-0	155	5-29-01	.203	.125	.221	49	128	25	26	4	1	1	10	22	6	4	1	39	11	5	.273	.344
Alvarez, Ezequiel	B-R	5-11	150	4-10-02	.247	.235	.249	58	190	32	47	7	5	0	19	24	2	4	5	40	23	6	.337	.330
Bautista, Flemin	B-R	5-10	180	3-10-00	.289	.444	.265	37	135	31	39	7	4	6	37	23	0	2	2	35	10	3	.533	.399
Berelleza, Luis	R-R	5-9	180	3-6-00	.200	.000	.238	8	25	2	5	1	0	0	3	3	0	0	0	11	3	0	.240	.286
Brete, Jeinser	R-R	6-0	180	11-26-99	.259	.296	.247	37	108	12	28	8	1	0	12	7	4	1	0	24	6	2	.352	.328
Castillo, Edwin	L-R	6-0	160	10-20-99	.217	.000	.260	23	60	9	13	3	0	0	7	13	0	0	1	16	2	3	.267	.351
Chacon, Miller	R-R	6-0	189	6-17-98	.179	.063	.203	38	95	10	17	3	0	0	8	13	11	0	0	13	3	2	.211	.345
Duarte, Samuel	R-R	5-11	175	1-20-01	.219	.167	.230	50	137	22	30	10	2	5	25	13	5	3	1	23	5	3	.431	.308
Espinal, Christhian	R-R	6-0	180	9-25-00	.187	.333	.164	44	134	22	25	2	0	4	24	23	4	0	2	53	6	4	.291	.319
Fabian, Elias	R-R	5-11	169	3-15-01	.235	.263	.228	31	98	13	23	5	2	2	14	14	1	0	1	24	2	2	.388	.269
Fabrizio, Miguel	R-R	5-11	178	9-26-00	.270	.316	.262	43	126	11	34	6	2	2	18	16	0	0	1	20	1	2	.397	.350
Fernandez, Josue	R-R	6-3	180	2-9-01	.158	.161	.157	52	152	16	24	6	0	1	12	26	2	0	1	67	11	5	.217	.287
Gamargo, Edgar	R-R	5-10	172	2-1-02	.333	.000	.500	3	3	1	1	0	0	0	0	0	0	0	0	1	0	0	.333	.333
Guzman, Orlando	L-R	6-0	160	5-13-02	.239	.333	.212	19	67	8	16	3	2	0	8	7	0	0	0	18	4	2	.343	.311
Heredia, Nestor	R-R	6-1	179	11-25-00	.313	.387	.295	48	160	19	50	8	2	3	17	15	5	2	2	27	14	5	.444	.385
Herrera, Rafael	R-R	5-11	170	9-18-00	.326	.310	.329	61	187	42	61	9	4	2	27	33	2	1	2	35	14	6	.449	.429
Hidalgo, Kelvin	R-R	6-3	190	12-16-00	.091	.000	.118	8	22	4	2	0	1	0	3	1	1	0	1	11	0	0	.182	.160
Lopez, Jose	L-R	5-10	172	1-4-02	.201	.261	.191	44	154	23	31	4	4	2	13	42	0	1	2	53	15	3	.318	.369

CHICAGO CUBS

CHICAGO CUBS

Batting	B-T	HT	WT	DOB	AVG	vLH	vRH	G	AB	R	H	2B	3B	HR	RBI	BB	HP	SH	SF	SO	SB	CS	OBP	SLG
Mancilla, Brayan	R-R	5-10	186	10-28-99	.211	.172	.219	51	175	23	37	8	1	2	21	20	8	0	2	37	10	6	.303	.317
Mateo, Starlin	R-R	6-1	180	7-15-02	.239	.333	.233	19	46	7	11	5	0	1	7	5	1	0	0	18	1	2	.413	.327
Miranda, Kevin	L-R	5-11	168	10-2-99	.159	.250	.139	16	44	9	7	1	0	0	2	7	1	0	0	12	6	2	.182	.289
Mora, Juan	R-R	5-9	176	9-30-99	.271	.256	.274	63	207	50	56	8	5	6	26	34	10	0	3	34	19	4	.444	.394
More, Cristian	L-L	5-10	170	8-11-01	.252	.200	.262	31	127	18	32	2	0	0	8	5	0	0	2	25	13	6	.268	.326
Morel, Rafael	R-R	5-11	165	11-22-01	.283	.405	.259	60	230	50	65	16	5	4	32	26	9	0	3	38	23	9	.448	.373
Pena, Brailin	L-L	5-11	160	5-2-01	.226	.238	.222	27	93	19	21	3	1	2	15	16	2	0	1	19	3	5	.344	.348
Pinango, Yohendrick	L-L	5-11	170	5-7-02	.358	.395	.352	62	240	43	86	20	0	0	36	27	4	0	3	20	27	7	.442	.427
Quintero, Malcom	R-R	6-0	165	7-29-00	.320	.000	.359	40	103	17	33	4	0	0	15	23	3	2	2	30	10	5	.359	.450
Rodriguez, Jonathan	R-R	6-2	190	10-9-00	.235	.119	.261	60	226	37	53	14	0	6	33	17	8	0	2	64	12	6	.376	.308
Ruiz, Lizardo	R-R	5-11	165	8-20-02	.185	.192	.184	53	173	13	32	3	0	1	15	17	1	3	4	49	12	12	.220	.256
Simon, Ronny	B-R	5-9	150	4-17-00	.333	.150	.358	54	168	31	56	13	9	3	28	21	2	4	1	25	14	8	.571	.412
Stevens, Felix	R-R	6-4	235	7-30-99	.280	.286	.279	51	175	36	49	15	2	6	31	26	6	0	3	62	7	3	.491	.386
Tatis, Esmarly	B-R	5-10	165	4-11-00	.267	.423	.233	47	146	28	39	2	1	0	21	34	1	1	0	13	26	2	.295	.409
Valenzuela, Marco	L-R	6-1	170	1-14-00	.200	.118	.214	39	120	16	24	2	3	1	12	24	4	0	0	46	7	7	.292	.351
Vasquez, Juan	R-R	5-11	180	9-7-99	.265	.222	.275	42	98	15	26	3	0	1	18	16	0	1	1	15	4	3	.327	.365
Zapata, Orlando	L-R	5-11	160	2-23-99	.298	.241	.307	61	205	31	61	8	0	0	24	29	2	3	2	28	6	5	.337	.387

Pitching	B-T	HT	WT	DOB	W	L	ERA	G	GS	CG	SV	IP	H	R	ER	HR	BB	SO	AVG	vLH	vRH	K/9	BB/9
Alvarez, Jonathan	R-R	6-1	160	3-16-00	0	1	10.80	2	1	0	0	2	2	3	2	1	4	2	.400	.500	.333	10.80	21.60
Arellano, Jorge	R-R	5-11	162	11-17-98	1	1	4.97	7	0	0	1	13	17	10	7	1	4	16	.298	.250	.311	11.37	2.84
Arredondo, Keiber	R-R	6-0	178	10-9-97	3	1	2.80	18	2	0	4	45	42	17	14	2	23	45	.247	.239	.250	9.00	4.60
Auguste, Donato	R-R	6-2	201	1-19-98	3	2	5.18	14	0	0	2	24	28	19	14	2	9	32	.280	.217	.299	11.84	3.33
Beard, Aneudis	R-R	6-1	185	1-30-98	0	0	0.87	8	0	0	3	10	3	2	1	0	6	9	.088	.000	.130	7.84	5.23
Blanco, Emir	R-R	6-2	240	10-3-01	1	0	11.25	5	0	0	0	4	6	9	5	1	6	3	.353	.167	.455	6.75	13.50
Brete, Jeinser	R-R	6-0	180	11-26-99	0	0	54.00	1	0	0	0	1	2	2	2	0	2	0	.500	.000	1.000	0.00	54.00
Cabrera, Yovanny	R-R	6-2	180	3-22-01	3	3	4.32	19	5	0	0	42	21	22	20	1	32	48	.156	.118	.168	10.37	6.91
Carreno, Kleiber	R-R	6-5	170	10-11-98	2	3	8.68	18	0	0	2	37	56	45	36	3	28	36	.339	.375	.328	8.68	6.75
Carrillo, Alejandro	L-L	5-10	168	2-5-00	7	0	2.28	17	2	0	0	47	44	19	12	3	12	35	.239	.148	.255	6.65	2.28
Castillo, Edwin	L-R	6-0	160	10-20-99	0	0	54.00	1	0	0	0	1	0	4	4	0	5	0	.000	--	.000	0.00	67.50
De La Cruz, Enmanuel	R-R	6-2	168	4-7-02	1	2	10.59	12	0	0	1	17	22	20	20	1	16	5	.328	.143	.377	2.65	8.47
Devers, Luis	R-R	6-3	178	4-24-00	4	4	2.66	14	14	0	0	64	60	28	19	2	14	61	.248	.176	.280	8.53	1.96
Diaz, Moises	R-R	6-0	195	4-27-01	2	6	4.57	14	14	0	0	63	76	42	32	4	19	41	.303	.365	.265	5.86	2.71
Encarnacion, Marcos	R-R	6-2	180	11-28-95	5	0	0.87	17	0	0	5	31	13	7	3	2	2	40	.123	.174	.108	11.61	0.58
Feliz, Anderson	R-R	6-3	165	11-26-01	0	0	10.64	9	0	0	0	11	16	13	11	1	11	12	.370	.412	.345	9.82	9.00
Feliz, Kelvin	R-R	6-1	165	9-30-00	2	2	2.12	13	13	0	0	59	50	17	14	1	27	54	.239	.146	.273	8.19	4.10
Fermin, Francisco	R-R	6-4	175	11-19-98	1	0	1.30	14	1	0	1	35	30	10	5	1	8	41	.227	.184	.253	10.64	2.08
Figuereo, Wilfri	R-R	5-6	171	5-11-01	1	2	3.98	10	0	0	0	20	10	12	9	1	18	16	.159	.167	.156	7.08	7.97
Garcia, Rodrigo	R-R	6-2	192	3-13-99	0	2	3.24	4	0	0	1	8	11	8	3	1	3	11	.333	.167	.370	11.88	3.24
Gomez, Jesus	L-L	6-2	190	4-9-99	0	5	4.04	14	14	0	0	56	54	32	25	2	37	38	.258	.171	.280	6.14	5.98
Gomez, Jose	R-R	6-2	165	3-15-97	3	2	1.69	7	6	0	0	37	27	12	7	1	9	38	.203	.148	.241	9.16	2.17
Gonzalez, Edmar	R-R	6-0	190	8-17-98	2	2	5.05	22	0	0	5	36	26	27	20	3	34	45	.193	.170	.211	11.36	8.58
Green, Ricardo	R-R	6-2	188	12-1-00	0	0	2.25	5	0	0	0	8	10	2	2	0	2	5	.294	.250	.318	5.63	2.25
Grullon, Darling	R-R	6-4	200	11-6-99	3	2	5.08	18	0	0	0	39	35	34	22	2	37	29	.235	.200	.262	6.69	8.54
Heredia, Ferrol	L-L	5-11	200	11-7-98	2	2	4.23	15	7	0	0	55	49	32	26	2	32	50	.258	.233	.230	8.13	5.20
Hernandez, Andy	R-R	6-1	178	11-29-99	2	7	4.13	15	15	0	0	65	70	38	30	2	23	42	.268	.237	.293	5.79	3.17
Herrera, Rafael	R-R	5-11	170	9-18-00	1	0	0.00	3	0	0	0	2	0	0	0	0	0	1	.000	.000	.000	3.86	0.00
Jimenez, Joel	R-R	6-0	160	7-23-00	1	0	9.11	17	0	0	1	27	23	31	27	2	38	29	.232	.306	.191	9.79	12.83
Lopez, Johan	L-L	6-6	203	8-31-98	3	0	6.75	9	0	0	0	16	14	12	11	0	17	17	.255	.111	.283	10.43	10.43
Mancilla, Brayan	R-R	5-10	186	10-28-99	0	0	0.00	1	0	0	0	2	1	0	0	0	1	0	.167	.000	.333	0.00	5.40
Marte, Luis	R-R	6-0	200	2-13-01	0	3	19.18	12	1	0	0	13	18	30	27	1	36	6	.333	.241	.440	4.26	25.58
Miranda, Kevin	L-R	5-11	168	10-2-99	0	0	0.00	3	0	0	0	3	0	0	0	0	1	0	.000	.000	.000	3.00	3.00
Montano, Gregori	R-R	5-11	175	8-18-99	0	4	4.08	8	7	0	0	29	28	21	13	0	6	25	.248	.353	.203	7.85	1.88
Montero, Yander	R-R	6-2	175	10-18-99	0	0	3.44	6	6	0	0	18	20	12	7	0	11	14	.290	.250	.298	6.87	5.40
Mora, Juan	R-R	5-9	176	9-30-99	0	0	6.75	2	0	0	0	1	1	3	1	0	2	0	.250	.500	.000	0.00	13.50
Parra, Anderson	L-L	6-2	185	4-17-99	4	4	3.24	16	0	0	0	36	36	23	12	5	10	33	.261	.125	.290	8.91	2.70
Paula, Carlos	R-R	6-0	195	1-29-00	0	0	1.54	7	7	0	0	35	16	6	6	0	9	36	.137	.179	.124	9.26	2.31
Prieto, Marco	R-R	6-2	165	7-29-99	4	0	0.71	13	0	0	1	25	13	2	2	0	16	26	.148	.152	.146	9.24	5.68
Ramirez, Jorge	R-R	6-2	160	7-12-97	4	0	1.98	19	0	0	1	41	29	11	9	0	15	38	.200	.042	.231	8.34	3.29
Rodriguez, Dawel	R-R	6-3	200	12-15-98	0	0	27.00	1	0	0	0	1	2	2	2	0	2	0	.500	--	.500	0.00	27.00
Salvador, Andricson	L-L	5-11	180	7-24-00	2	5	2.93	13	8	0	0	46	42	29	15	3	12	56	.219	.177	.228	10.96	2.35
Sojo, Alberto	R-R	5-11	170	9-23-00	0	3	3.12	14	13	0	0	49	46	20	17	4	10	45	.241	.229	.248	8.27	1.84
Valenzuela, Luis	R-R	6-1	170	10-23-01	3	0	3.66	11	0	0	0	16	11	8	6	0	14	11	.152	.056	.188	6.41	7.78
Vasquez, Edward	R-R	6-3	180	7-7-97	4	0	1.93	7	7	0	0	37	29	10	8	1	8	22	.223	.314	.190	5.30	1.93
Vasquez, Juan	R-R	5-11	180	9-7-99	0	0	27.00	1	0	0	0	0	2	1	1	0	0	0	.667	1.000	.000	0.00	0.00
Vasquez, Willians	R-R	6-1	200	5-7-97	1	2	2.67	13	0	0	3	30	37	18	9	0	11	28	.301	.160	.337	8.31	3.26
Zapata, Orlando	L-R	5-11	160	2-23-99	0	0	0.00	1	0	0	0	1	0	0	0	0	0	3	.000	--	.000	27.00	0.00

Fielding

C: Aliendo 47, Chacon 16, Fabrizio 30, Gamargo 1, Mancilla 18, Quintero 36, Vasquez 38. 1B: Aliendo 3, Brete 17, Chacon 2, Duarte 2, Espinal 34, Fabrizio 4, Heredia 2, Herrera 19, Mancilla 38, Mateo 1, Mora 2, Pena 10, Quintero 7, Rodriguez 2, Ruiz 2, Vasquez 6, Zapata 10. 2B: Acevedo 14, Bautista 21, Castillo 21, Espinal 5, Heredia 6, Herrera 6, Mora 38, Morel 1, Ruiz 2, Simon 39, Tatis 9, Vasquez 1, Zapata 6. 3B: Acevedo 11, Bautista 7, Brete 18, Castillo 1, Espinal 6, Heredia 22, Herrera 1, Mateo 1, Mora 26, Morel 2, Ruiz 17, Tatis 9, Zapata 44. SS: Acevedo 10, Bautista 6, Castillo 1, Heredia 18, Morel 48, Ruiz 36, Simon 2, Tatis 32, Zapata 3. OF: Alvarez 47, Berelleza 3, Duarte 44, Fabian 22, Fernandez 52, Guzman 15, Herrera 33, Hidalgo 4, Lopez 40, Mateo 14, Miranda 14, More 28, Pena 18, Pinango 51, Rodriguez 30, Simon 1, Stevens 37, Valenzuela 37.

Chicago White Sox

SEASON IN A SENTENCE: A dud bloomed into an ace, a talented shortstop reached new heights, more talented rookies hit the scene, and a bright future became even clearer.

HIGH POINT: For a team that finished 72-89, there are a surprising number of candidates for this category. Top prospect Eloy Jimenez signed an eight-figure contract and eschewed the typical service-time manipulation that often befalls young, talented players. Shortstop Tim Anderson, the team's first-round pick in 2013, rapped out four hits on Sept. 25, and in doing so all but wrapped up the batting title. And on the mound, Lucas Giolito went from the worst ERA (6.13) among qualifiers in 2018 to a 14-9, 3.41 record that placed him among the game's best starters.

LOW POINT: The team went through a seven-game losing streak from Aug. 27-Sept. 2 that marked its longest skid of the season.

NOTABLE ROOKIES: The two key pieces of the 2017 Jose Quintana trade with the Cubs made their debuts. Jimenez was signed to a six-year, $43 million deal before Opening Day and finished the year with 31 home runs in 122 games. He was particularly potent in the second half, when he slashed .292/.328/.542 over 60 games. Righthander Dylan Cease joined club on July 3 and showed flashes of potential. He had particular trouble in the early innings, but seemed to settle down in the middle frames. He finished with an average of 10 strikeouts per nine innings over the course of 14 starts. Catcher Zack Collins homered in his first big league at-bat, but otherwise struggled in his first taste of the major leagues.

KEY TRANSACTIONS: Jimenez's contract was probably the most significant move the White Sox made all season. They made one trade at the deadline, sending reliever Nate Jones to the Rangers for a pair of low-level minor leaguers.

DOWN ON THE FARM: The pipeline to Chicago isn't dry yet. Cuban standout Luis Robert was one of two minor leaguers to hit 30 home runs and steal 30 bases and looks primed to make an impact early in 2020. The team's last two first-rounders, Nick Madrigal and Andrew Vaughn, each showed tremendous offensive potential. Madrigal displayed classic table-setter skills, while Vaughn's tool set hints at mid-lineup thump. Righthander Jonathan Stiever had a breakout year and finished second in the system with 154 strikeouts. Plus, talented righthander Michael Kopech is still lurking.

OPENING DAY PAYROLL: $96,697,001 (22nd).

PLAYERS OF THE YEAR

DAVE DUROCHIK | LAURA WOLFF

MAJOR LEAGUE	MINOR LEAGUE
Lucas Giolito	**Luis Robert**
RHP	**OF**
14-9, 3.41 in 29 GS	(High A / AA / AAA)
228 SO in 177 IP	.328/.376/.624
1.06 WHIP, 134 ERA+	32 HR, 36 SB

ORGANIZATION LEADERS

Batting		*Minimum 250 AB
MAJORS		
* AVG	Tim Anderson	.335
* OPS	Yoan Moncada	.915
HR	Jose Abreu	33
RBI	Jose Abreu	123
MINORS		
* AVG	Luis Robert, Winston-Salem, Birmingham, Charlotte	.328
* OBP	Ryan Goins, Charlotte	.406
* SLG	Luis Robert, Winston-Salem, Birmingham, Charlotte	.624
* OPS	Luis Robert, Winston-Salem, Birmingham, Charlotte	1.001
R	Luis Robert, Winston-Salem, Birmingham, Charlotte	108
H	Luis Robert, Winston-Salem, Birmingham, Charlotte	165
TB	Luis Robert, Winston-Salem, Birmingham, Charlotte	314
2B	Ian Dawkins, Kannapolis	38
3B	Luis Robert, Winston-Salem, Birmingham, Charlotte	11
HR	Luis Robert, Winston-Salem, Birmingham, Charlotte	32
RBI	Luis Robert, Winston-Salem, Birmingham, Charlotte	92
BB	Jameson Fisher, Winston-Salem	72
BB	Daniel Palka, Charlotte	72
SO	Luis Curbelo, Kannapolis, Great Falls	181
SB	Luis Robert, Winston-Salem, Birmingham, Charlotte	36

Pitching		#Minimum 75 IP
MAJORS		
W	Lucas Giolito	14
# ERA	Lucas Giolito	3.41
SO	Lucas Giolito	228
SV	Alex Colome	30
MINORS		
W	Kyle Kubat, Winston-Salem, Birmingham, Charlotte	11
L	Jason Bilous, Kannapolis	10
L	Jonathan Stiever, Kannapolis, Winston-Salem	10
# ERA	Matt Tomshaw, Birmingham, Charlotte	2.90
G	Zach Thompson, Charlotte, Birmingham	45
GS	Davis Martin, Kannapolis	27
SV	Austin Conway, Kannapolis, Winston-Salem	13
IP	John Parke, Winston-Salem, Birmingham	145
BB	Jason Bilous, Kannapolis	61
SO	Davis Martin, Kannapolis	156
# AVG	Sam Long, Kannapolis	.205

2019 PERFORMANCE

General Manager: Rick Hahn. **Farm Director:** Chris Getz. **Scouting Director:** Nick Hostetler.

Class	Team	League	W	L	PCT	Finish	Manager
Majors	Chicago White Sox	American	72	89	.447	9th (15)	Rick Renteria
Triple-A	Charlotte Knights	International	75	64	.540	t-3rd (14)	Mark Grudzielanek
Double-A	Birmingham Barons	Southern	64	72	.471	6th (10)	Omar Vizquel
High A	Winston-Salem Dash	Carolina	72	61	.541	3rd (10)	Justin Jirschele
Low A	Kannapolis Intimidators	South Atlantic	64	74	.464	t-10th (14)	Ryan Newman
Rookie	Great Falls Voyagers	Pioneer	34	40	.459	5th (8)	Tim Esmay
Rookie	AZL White Sox	Arizona	22	34	.393	t-17th (21)	Ever Magallanes
Overall 2019 Minor League Record			331	345	.490	19th (30)	

ORGANIZATION STATISTICS

CHICAGO WHITE SOX
AMERICAN LEAGUE

Batting	B-T	HT	WT	DOB	AVG	vLH	vRH	G	AB	R	H	2B	3B	HR	RBI	BB	HBP	SH	SF	SO	SB	CS	SLG	OBP
Abreu, Jose	R-R	6-3	255	1-29-87	.284	.360	.257	159	634	85	180	38	1	33	123	36	13	0	10	152	2	2	.503	.330
Alonso, Yonder	L-R	6-1	230	4-8-87	.178	.261	.156	67	219	23	39	6	0	7	27	29	1	0	2	53	0	1	.301	.275
Anderson, Tim	R-R	6-1	185	6-23-93	.335	.326	.339	123	498	81	167	32	0	18	56	15	3	0	2	109	17	5	.508	.357
Castillo, Welington	R-R	5-10	220	4-24-87	.209	.222	.201	72	230	19	48	12	0	12	41	16	3	0	2	74	0	0	.417	.267
Collins, Zack	L-R	6-3	220	2-6-95	.186	.136	.203	27	86	10	16	3	1	3	12	14	1	0	0	39	0	0	.349	.307
Cordell, Ryan	R-R	6-4	195	3-31-92	.221	.217	.225	97	217	22	48	8	0	7	24	19	3	6	2	69	3	1	.355	.291
Delmonico, Nicky	L-R	6-3	230	7-12-92	.206	.222	.204	21	63	6	13	2	0	1	6	4	1	0	0	25	0	1	.286	.265
Engel, Adam	R-R	6-2	210	12-9-91	.242	.313	.201	89	227	26	55	10	2	6	26	14	6	1	0	78	3	3	.383	.304
Garcia, Leury	B-R	5-8	180	3-18-91	.279	.312	.264	140	577	93	161	27	3	8	40	21	6	11	3	139	15	5	.378	.310
Goins, Ryan	L-R	5-10	180	2-13-88	.250	.406	.205	52	144	13	36	6	1	2	10	17	1	1	0	44	0	1	.347	.333
Jay, Jon	L-L	5-11	195	3-15-85	.267	.263	.269	47	165	12	44	8	0	0	9	8	3	5	1	30	0	0	.315	.311
Jimenez, Eloy	R-R	6-4	205	11-27-96	.267	.259	.270	122	468	69	125	18	2	31	79	30	4	0	2	134	0	0	.513	.316
McCann, James	R-R	6-3	225	6-13-90	.273	.295	.265	118	439	62	120	26	1	18	60	30	6	1	0	137	4	1	.460	.328
Mendick, Danny	R-R	5-10	189	9-28-93	.308	.235	.364	16	39	6	12	0	0	2	4	1	0	0	0	11	0	0	.462	.325
Moncada, Yoan	B-R	6-2	205	5-27-95	.315	.299	.322	132	511	83	161	34	5	25	79	40	4	1	3	154	10	3	.548	.367
Palka, Daniel	L-L	6-2	220	10-28-91	.107	.091	.110	30	84	4	9	0	0	2	4	8	1	0	0	35	0	1	.179	.194
Reed, AJ	L-L	6-4	275	5-10-93	.136	.250	.125	14	44	1	6	0	0	1	4	4	0	0	1	21	0	0	.205	.204
Rondon, Jose	R-R	6-1	195	3-3-94	.197	.253	.134	55	142	10	28	3	0	3	9	11	2	1	0	38	0	1	.282	.265
2-team total (1 Baltimore)					.196	.250	.134	56	143	10	28	3	0	3	9	11	2	1	0	38	0		0.280	.263
Sanchez, Yolmer	B-R	5-11	185	6-29-92	.252	.292	.239	149	496	59	125	20	4	2	43	44	5	7	3	117	5	4	.321	.318
Skole, Matt	L-R	6-4	220	7-30-89	.208	.250	.203	27	72	7	15	2	0	6	7	0	0	1	31	0	0		.236	.275
Tilson, Charlie	L-L	6-0	185	12-2-92	.229	.130	.248	54	144	16	33	5	0	1	12	10	3	0	0	38	4	0	.285	.293
Zavala, Seby	R-R	5-11	215	8-28-93	.083	.000	.091	5	12	1	1	0	0	0	0	0	0	0	0	9	0	0	.083	.083

Pitching	B-T	HT	WT	DOB	W	L	ERA	G	GS	CG	SV	IP	H	R	ER	HR	BB	SO	AVG	vLH	vRH	K/9	BB/9
Banuelos, Manny	R-L	5-10	215	3-13-91	3	4	6.93	16	8	0	0	51	60	39	39	12	33	44	.303	.321	.296	7.82	5.86
Bummer, Aaron	L-L	6-3	200	9-21-93	0	0	2.13	58	0	0	1	68	43	17	16	4	24	60	.184	.178	.188	7.98	3.19
Burr, Ryan	R-R	6-4	225	5-28-94	1	1	4.58	16	1	0	0	20	17	13	10	3	8	20	.227	.294	.171	9.15	3.66
Cease, Dylan	R-R	6-2	190	12-28-95	4	7	5.79	14	14	0	0	73	78	51	47	15	35	81	.271	.285	.257	9.99	4.32
Colome, Alex	R-R	6-1	220	12-31-88	4	5	2.80	62	0	0	30	61	42	28	19	7	23	55	.191	.190	.192	8.11	3.39
Cordero, Jimmy	R-R	6-4	222	10-19-91	1	0	2.75	30	0	0	0	36	24	11	11	3	11	31	.189	.170	.200	7.75	2.75
2-team total (1 Toronto)					1	1	2.89	31	0	0	0	37	26	12	12	4	11	31	.197	.163	.217	7.47	2.65
Covey, Dylan	R-R	6-1	220	8-14-91	1	8	7.98	18	12	0	0	59	75	54	52	12	28	41	.306	.385	.243	6.29	4.30
Despaigne, Odrisamer	R-R	6-0	200	4-4-87	0	2	9.45	3	3	0	0	13	24	14	14	3	7	7	.407	.476	.368	4.73	4.73
Detwiler, Ross	R-L	6-5	210	3-6-86	3	5	6.59	18	12	0	0	70	86	54	51	20	27	46	.305	.265	.318	5.94	3.49
Frare, Caleb	L-L	6-1	210	7-8-93	0	0	10.13	5	0	0	0	3	2	3	3	1	4	3	.200	.250	.000	10.13	13.50
Fry, Jace	L-L	6-1	190	7-9-93	3	4	4.75	68	0	0	0	55	44	33	29	7	43	68	.218	.193	.235	11.13	7.04
Fulmer, Carson	R-R	6-0	195	12-13-93	1	2	6.26	20	2	0	0	27	26	22	19	5	20	25	.243	.241	.244	8.23	6.59
Giolito, Lucas	R-R	6-6	245	7-14-94	14	9	3.41	29	29	3	0	177	131	69	67	24	57	228	.205	.172	.235	11.62	2.90
Herrera, Kelvin	R-R	5-10	200	12-31-89	3	3	6.14	57	0	0	1	51	60	36	35	8	23	53	.289	.296	.284	9.29	4.03
Jones, Nate	R-R	6-5	220	1-28-86	0	1	3.48	13	0	0	1	10	10	4	4	2	7	10	.256	.154	.308	8.71	6.10
Lopez, Reynaldo	R-R	6-1	200	1-4-94	10	15	5.38	33	33	1	0	184	203	119	110	35	65	169	.279	.290	.267	8.23	3.18
Marshall, Evan	R-R	6-2	225	4-18-90	4	2	2.49	55	0	0	0	51	42	16	14	5	24	41	.228	.221	.233	7.28	4.26
Minaya, Juan	R-R	6-4	210	9-18-90	0	0	3.90	22	0	0	0	28	31	13	12	4	12	27	.277	.279	.275	8.78	3.90
Nova, Ivan	R-R	6-5	250	1-12-87	11	12	4.72	34	34	2	0	187	225	107	98	30	47	114	.303	.293	.313	5.49	2.26
Osich, Josh	L-L	6-3	232	9-3-88	4	0	4.66	57	0	0	0	68	62	38	35	15	15	61	.242	.171	.297	8.11	2.00
Reed, AJ	L-L	6-4	275	5-10-93	0	0	0.00	1	0	0	0	1	0	0	0	0	0	0	.000	--	.000	0.00	0.00
Rodon, Carlos	L-L	6-3	235	12-10-92	3	2	5.19	7	7	0	0	35	33	22	20	4	17	46	.239	.077	.256	11.94	4.41
Rondon, Jose	R-R	6-1	195	3-3-94	0	0	0.00	1	0	0	0	1	0	0	0	0	0	0	.000	.000	.500	0.00	0.00
Ruiz, Jose	R-R	6-1	190	10-21-94	1	4	5.63	40	1	0	0	40	56	27	25	6	24	35	.335	.273	.366	7.88	5.40
Santana, Ervin	R-R	6-2	175	12-12-82	0	2	9.45	3	3	0	0	13	19	14	14	6	6	5	.339	.300	.385	3.38	4.05
Santiago, Hector	R-L	6-0	215	12-16-87	0	1	6.66	11	2	0	0	26	32	20	19	7	17	34	.299	.290	.303	11.92	5.96
Vieira, Thyago	R-R	6-2	210	7-1-93	1	0	9.00	6	0	0	0	7	11	8	7	0	5	8	.344	.385	.316	10.29	6.43

Fielding

Catcher	PCT	G	PO	A	E	DP	PB
Castillo	.989	48	354	19	4	4	9
Collins	1.000	10	75	1	0	0	1
McCann	.992	106	884	39	7	8	3
Zavala	.962	3	22	3	1	0	0

First Base	PCT	G	PO	A	E	DP
Abreu	.993	125	1012	74	8	128
Alonso	.986	21	137	7	2	14
Collins	1.000	1	5	0	0	0
Delmonico	.000	1	0	0	0	0
Goins	1.000	2	3	0	0	1
Palka	1.000	1	4	0	0	0
Reed	.974	4	31	6	1	6
Rondon	1.000	1	2	0	0	0

Skole	1.000	9	59	1	0	9

Second Base	PCT	G	PO	A	E	DP
Garcia	1.000	2	4	5	0	2
Mendick	1.000	3	5	10	0	1
Rondon	.982	18	18	36	1	8
Sanchez	.987	149	248	416	9	108

Third Base	PCT	G	PO	A	E	DP
Garcia	1.000	1	1	1	0	0
Goins	.962	23	31	45	3	9
Mendick	1.000	3	3	6	0	1
Moncada	.962	129	120	256	15	37
Rondon	.963	12	9	17	1	2

Shortstop	PCT	G	PO	A	E	DP
Anderson	.951	122	182	324	26	75

Garcia	.944	19	21	46	4	14
Goins	.950	14	10	28	2	11
Mendick	1.000	5	6	10	0	5
Rondon	.951	15	12	27	2	5

Outfield	PCT	G	PO	A	E	DP
Cordell	.981	91	153	2	3	2
Delmonico	.970	21	30	2	1	1
Engel	.982	86	159	2	3	0
Garcia	.968	120	196	14	7	0
Goins	1.000	8	4	1	0	1
Jay	.984	45	60	2	1	0
Jimenez	.985	114	190	6	3	1
Palka	1.000	23	26	2	0	0
Rondon	1.000	2	1	0	0	0
Tilson	.970	51	94	4	3	0

CHARLOTTE KNIGHTS   TRIPLE-A
INTERNATIONAL LEAGUE

Batting	B-T	HT	WT	DOB	AVG	vLH	vRH	G	AB	R	H	2B	3B	HR	RBI	BB	HBP	SH	SF	SO	SB	CS	SLG	OBP
Anderson, Tim	R-R	6-1	185	6-23-93	.348	.500	.316	5	23	3	8	1	0	1	4	0	0	0	0	2	0	0	.522	.348
Booker, Joel	R-R	6-1	190	11-1-93	.203	.111	.250	26	79	8	16	3	1	1	3	6	2	2	0	24	2	2	.304	.276
Castillo, Wellington	R-R	5-10	220	4-24-87	.286	.000	.333	3	14	1	4	0	0	1	5	0	0	0	0	4	0	0	.500	.286
Collins, Zack	L-R	6-3	220	2-6-95	.282	.224	.306	88	294	56	83	19	1	19	74	62	3	0	8	98	0	0	.548	.403
Cordell, Ryan	R-R	6-4	195	3-31-92	.275	.333	.242	14	51	8	14	5	1	1	6	4	0	0	0	17	1	1	.471	.327
De Jesus Jr., Ivan	R-R	5-11	200	5-1-87	.238	.214	.245	22	63	6	15	2	0	1	5	11	0	1	1	14	0	1	.318	.347
2-team total (9 Rochester)					.242	.174	.263	31	99	11	24	4	0	1	7	13	0	1	1	26	0	2	.313	.327
Delmonico, Nicky	L-R	6-3	230	7-12-92	.286	.417	.255	17	63	13	18	7	0	3	10	10	1	0	2	12	1	0	.540	.382
Engel, Adam	R-R	6-2	210	12-9-91	.270	.333	.255	64	248	43	67	13	4	9	29	22	7	0	0	62	13	3	.464	.347
Escobar, Alcides	R-R	6-1	205	12-16-86	.286	.247	.298	96	367	52	105	28	0	10	70	32	2	0	4	64	6	2	.444	.343
Goins, Ryan	L-R	5-10	180	2-13-88	.322	.383	.310	83	273	47	88	23	2	10	48	39	1	1	2	77	3	3	.531	.406
Gonzalez, Alfredo	R-R	6-0	220	7-13-92	.205	.333	.156	13	44	4	9	1	0	1	5	5	0	0	0	12	0	0	.296	.286
Gonzalez, Daniel	R-R	6-1	190	12-6-95	.111	.000	.125	5	9	0	1	0	0	0	2	0	0	0	2	0	0		.111	.273
Guyer, Brandon	R-R	6-2	210	1-28-86	.244	.154	.286	16	41	10	10	3	1	0	6	5	3	0	0	10	0	0	.366	.367
Jay, Jon	L-L	5-11	195	3-15-85	.359	.385	.350	13	53	8	19	2	0	0	6	2	0	0	0	10	1	0	.396	.382
Jimenez, Eloy	R-R	6-4	205	11-27-96	.318	.250	.333	5	22	3	7	1	0	1	0	0	0	0	0	5	0	0	.500	.318
Madrigal, Nick	R-R	5-7	165	3-5-97	.331	.302	.347	29	118	26	39	6	1	1	12	13	1	1	1	5	4	3	.424	.399
Mendick, Danny	R-R	5-10	189	9-28-93	.279	.281	.278	133	477	75	133	26	1	17	64	66	5	3	7	96	19	8	.444	.368
Mercedes, Yermin	R-R	5-11	225	2-14-93	.310	.310	.310	53	187	35	58	12	0	17	62	24	3	0	6	42	0	0	.647	.386
Michalczewski, Trey	B-R	6-4	220	2-27-95	.224	.200	.233	30	85	10	19	3	0	1	10	12	1	0	0	32	1	1	.365	.327
Moncada, Yoan	B-R	6-2	205	5-27-95	.409	.167	.500	5	22	6	9	1	0	2	6	0	0	0	0	3	0	0	.727	.409
Nolan, Nate	R-R	6-1	210	10-11-94	.000	.000	.000	3	6	2	0	0	0	0	0	1	0	0	0	5	0	0	.000	.143
Orlando, Paulo	R-R	6-2	215	11-1-85	.242	.269	.233	69	256	38	62	15	1	10	32	14	8	0	3	69	5	1	.426	.299
Palka, Daniel	L-L	6-2	220	10-28-91	.263	.182	.299	106	395	83	104	23	0	27	72	72	0	0	4	109	2	0	.527	.374
Peterson, D.J.	R-R	6-1	210	12-31-91	.185	.171	.190	38	130	19	24	5	0	6	16	11	3	1	1	38	1	0	.362	.262
Reed, AJ	L-L	6-4	275	5-10-93	.180	.200	.172	10	39	3	7	1	0	1	2	2	1	0	0	17	0	0	.282	.238
Robert, Luis	R-R	6-3	185	8-3-97	.297	.324	.282	47	202	44	60	10	5	16	39	11	5	0	5	55	7	3	.634	.341
Scavuzzo, Jacob	R-R	6-4	185	1-15-94	.224	.316	.193	23	76	9	17	4	1	1	3	8	0	0	0	26	1	0	.342	.298
Skole, Matt	L-R	6-2	220	7-30-89	.248	.264	.244	92	314	65	78	15	0	21	56	70	2	0	5	99	0	0	.497	.384
Tilson, Charlie	L-L	6-0	185	12-2-92	.288	.314	.277	61	236	36	68	13	2	3	34	19	2	0	1	43	4	3	.398	.345
Tomscha, Damek	R-R	6-2	200	8-27-91	.143	.000	.250	2	7	0	1	0	0	0	0	0	0	0	0	2	0	0	.143	.143
2-team total (53 Lehigh Valley)					.216	.235	.209	55	190	23	41	9	0	8	19	16	6	0	1	57	0	2	.390	.296
Torres, Ramon	B-R	5-11	190	1-22-93	.343	.346	.342	21	67	16	23	4	1	4	16	2	0	0	2	12	0	0	.612	.352
Tucker, Preston	L-L	6-0	210	7-6-90	.277	.263	.281	25	83	14	23	8	0	1	10	9	0	0	1	0	1	0	.410	.344
Zavala, Seby	R-R	5-11	215	8-28-93	.222	.202	.231	82	297	49	66	14	0	20	45	26	6	0	2	116	1	1	.471	.296

Pitching	B-T	HT	WT	DOB	W	L	ERA	G	GS	CG	SV	IP	H	R	ER	HR	BB	SO	AVG	vLH	vRH	K/9	BB/9
Adams, Spencer	R-R	6-3	171	4-13-96	0	1	8.00	5	3	0	0	18	35	21	16	4	8	10	.412	.385	.435	5.00	4.00
Banks, Tanner	L-L	6-1	210	10-24-91	1	0	2.70	2	0	0	0	3	5	2	1	0	1	3	.357	.750	.200	8.10	2.70
Banuelos, Manny	R-L	5-10	215	3-13-91	0	1	15.75	1	1	0	0	4	7	7	7	3	1	2	.389	.400	.385	4.50	2.25
Bummer, Aaron	L-L	6-3	200	9-21-93	0	0	2.35	5	0	0	0	8	7	2	2	0	2	6	.259	.200	.273	7.04	2.35
Cease, Dylan	R-R	6-2	190	12-28-95	5	2	4.48	15	15	0	0	68	75	39	34	4	32	73	.284	.276	.291	9.61	4.21
Cordero, Jimmy	R-R	6-4	222	10-19-91	3	1	0.51	13	0	0	4	18	14	1	1	0	2	14	.215	.222	.211	7.13	1.02
2-team total (1 Buffalo)					4	1	0.48	14	0	0	4	19	14	1	1	0	2	16	.206	.214	.200	7.71	0.96
Covey, Dylan	R-R	6-1	220	8-14-91	2	1	2.82	13	11	0	0	51	59	19	16	6	9	46	.286	.255	.317	8.12	1.59
Despaigne, Odrisamer	R-R	6-0	200	4-4-87	5	4	3.25	16	14	0	0	83	83	31	30	6	28	84	.264	.296	.233	9.11	3.04
2-team total (8 Louisville)					8	6	3.47	24	22	0	0	124	123	52	48	11	44	124	.260	.294	.229	8.98	3.18
Detwiler, Ross	R-L	6-5	210	3-6-86	1	2	3.98	8	8	1	0	43	44	19	19	11	11	35	.273	.188	.310	7.33	2.30
Foster, Matt	R-R	6-0	205	1-27-95	4	1	3.76	37	0	0	4	55	46	23	23	9	19	62	.229	.225	.231	10.15	3.11
Frare, Caleb	L-L	6-1	210	7-8-93	2	1	7.66	21	0	0	1	22	20	19	19	5	19	34	.253	.292	.238	13.70	7.66
Fulmer, Carson	R-R	6-0	195	12-13-93	1	2	4.76	24	0	0	1	34	31	21	18	2	21	51	.239	.271	.220	13.50	5.56
Guerrero, Jordan	L-L	6-3	195	5-31-94	3	7	7.27	20	12	0	0	73	109	62	59	19	44	66	.347	.390	.329	8.14	5.42
Hamilton, Ian	R-R	6-0	200	6-16-95	0	2	9.92	16	0	0	3	16	28	18	18	4	3	20	.378	.400	.364	11.02	1.65
Herrera, Kelvin	R-R	5-10	200	12-31-89	0	1	12.00	3	1	0	0	3	5	4	4	2	0	2	.357	.400	.333	6.00	0.00

CHICAGO WHITE SOX

Name	B-T	HT	WT	DOB	W	L	ERA	G	GS	CG	SV	IP	H	R	ER	HR	BB	SO	AVG	vLH	vRH	K/9	BB/9
Kubat, Kyle	L-L	6-1	195	12-4-92	5	3	5.63	12	12	0	0	56	60	37	35	9	17	35	.278	.206	.307	5.63	2.73
Marshall, Evan	R-R	6-2	225	4-18-90	3	0	0.00	9	0	0	2	10	8	0	0	0	1	13	.229	.333	.150	11.70	0.90
Minaya, Juan	R-R	6-4	210	9-18-90	4	3	3.71	24	0	0	6	34	32	18	14	4	15	41	.250	.183	.309	10.85	3.97
Nicolino, Justin	L-L	6-3	195	11-22-91	7	6	6.28	20	19	1	0	116	134	90	81	34	33	84	.290	.326	.276	6.52	2.56
2-team total (4 Rochester)					8	7	6.12	24	22	1	0	135	156	102	92	36	41	97	.291	.324	.279	6.45	2.73
Nin, Jose	R-R	6-3	220	6-20-95	0	0	10.80	1	0	0	0	2	4	2	2	2	1	1	.500	.333	.600	5.40	5.40
Osich, Josh	L-L	6-3	232	9-3-88	0	0	2.25	3	0	0	0	4	3	1	1	0	2	4	.214	.000	.333	9.00	4.50
Roach, Donn	R-R	6-0	195	12-14-89	3	6	7.83	18	16	0	0	79	127	77	69	16	26	53	.362	.376	.346	6.01	2.95
Ruiz, Jose	R-R	6-1	190	10-21-94	0	0	1.26	11	0	0	7	14	9	2	2	0	7	15	.180	.191	.172	9.42	4.40
Santiago, Hector	R-L	6-0	215	12-16-87	1	4	5.84	7	7	0	0	37	45	25	24		9	33	.310	.238	.340	8.03	2.19
2-team total (8 Syracuse Mets)					4	5	4.50	15	14	0	0	80	77	42	40	14	32	71	.255	.244	.259	7.99	3.60
Schryver, Hunter	L-L	6-1	200	4-3-95	0	0	8.56	11	0	0	1	14	16	13	13	2	12	23	.291	.261	.313	15.15	7.90
Stephens, Jordan	R-R	6-1	190	9-12-92	3	4	8.60	9	6	0	0	38	57	38	36	8	14	27	.350	.355	.345	6.45	3.35
2-team total (6 Columbus Clippers)					4	8	8.95	15	12	0	0	66	96	71	66	17	28	53	.338	.362	.318	7.19	3.80
Thompson, Zach	R-R	6-7	230	10-23-93	5	2	5.50	41	0	0	0	70	79	46	43	15	23	78	.277	.287	.271	9.98	2.94
Tomshaw, Matt	R-L	6-1	205	12-17-88	4	2	3.93	11	5	0	0	37	34	18	16	2	11	32	.271	.233	.289	7.85	2.70
Turner, Colton	L-L	6-3	215	1-17-91	4	4	5.48	37	9	0	0	94	101	59	57	15	35	102	.278	.240	.298	9.80	3.36
Vieira, Thyago	R-R	6-2	210	7-1-93	6	4	5.70	39	0	0	8	47	53	33	30	7	22	51	.288	.350	.240	9.70	4.18
Walsh, Connor	L-R	6-2	190	10-18-92	2	1	4.86	33	0	0	4	46	47	27	25	5	26	48	.263	.291	.240	9.32	5.05

Fielding

Catcher	PCT	G	PO	A	E	DP	PB
Castillo	1.000	3	28	1	0	0	0
Collins	.989	50	404	28	5	3	9
Gonzalez	.991	12	99	9	1	1	1
Gonzalez	.950	3	18	1	1	0	0
Mercedes	.975	24	179	16	5	2	6
Nolan	1.000	1	11	1	0	0	0
Zavala	.993	52	407	29	3	5	5

First Base	PCT	G	PO	A	E	DP
Collins	.985	20	120	9	2	15
Delmonico	.950	4	35	3	2	5
Mercedes	1.000	4	36	1	0	4
Michalczewski	1.000	8	57	0	0	4
Palka	.992	13	112	7	1	14
Peterson	1.000	6	40	3	0	3
Reed	1.000	8	61	8	0	7
Skole	.996	64	525	30	2	54
Tomscha	1.000	1	6	0	0	0
Zavala	1.000	18	149	6	0	18

Second Base	PCT	G	PO	A	E	DP
De Jesus Jr.	.968	9	9	21	1	2
Goins	.984	56	89	154	4	47
Madrigal	.992	28	35	82	1	26
Mendick	1.000	48	82	133	0	30
Michalczewski	1.000	1	1	2	0	0

Third Base	PCT	G	PO	A	E	DP
De Jesus Jr.	1.000	12	5	17	0	1
Escobar	.953	41	25	76	5	10
Mendick	.969	38	25	70	3	10
Mercedes	1.000	2	3	1	0	1
Michalczewski	.881	19	15	22	5	3
Moncada	.833	3	1	4	1	1
Peterson	.930	22	10	30	3	2
Skole	.955	10	5	16	1	1

Shortstop	PCT	G	PO	A	E	DP
Anderson	.889	3	3	5	1	4
Escobar	.972	49	65	143	6	31

	PCT	G	PO	A	E	DP
Goins	.963	28	32	71	4	10
Mendick	.994	42	41	113	1	25
Torres	.976	21	25	55	2	15

Outfield	PCT	G	PO	A	E	DP
Booker	.962	25	50	0	2	0
Cordell	1.000	13	26	1	0	0
Delmonico	.875	12	13	1	2	0
Engel	.986	64	140	5	2	1
Guyer	1.000	14	23	0	0	0
Jay	1.000	11	16	0	0	0
Jimenez	.667	4	2	0	1	0
Mendick	1.000	9	20	1	0	0
Orlando	.964	65	103	5	4	1
Palka	.982	66	107	4	2	0
Robert	.991	47	113	2	1	1
Scavuzzo	.970	21	31	1	1	0
Tilson	.972	60	105	1	3	0
Tomscha	1.000	1	2	0	0	0
Tucker	1.000	17	24	1	0	0

BIRMINGHAM BARONS

DOUBLE-A

SOUTHERN LEAGUE

Batting	B-T	HT	WT	DOB	AVG	vLH	vRH	G	AB	R	H	2B	3B	HR	RBI	BB	HBP	SH	SF	SO	SB	CS	SLG	OBP
Adolfo, Micker	R-R	6-4	255	9-11-96	.205	.250	.197	23	78	5	16	7	0	0	9	14	2	0	1	36	0	3	.295	.337
Basabe, Luis Alexander	B-R	6-0	160	8-26-96	.246	.338	.205	69	256	31	63	12	1	3	30	29	1	4	1	85	9	4	.336	.324
Booker, Joel	R-R	6-1	190	11-1-93	.257	.171	.291	76	272	37	70	10	0	3	33	18	7	2	2	65	17	2	.327	.318
Castillo, Welington	R-R	5-10	220	4-24-87	.143	--	.143	2	7	0	1	1	0	0	0	0	0	0	0	2	0	0	.286	.143
Forbes, Ti'Quan	R-R	6-3	220	8-26-96	.242	.191	.261	116	392	42	95	18	3	3	41	45	9	2	1	106	4	4	.327	.333
Gonzalez, Alfredo	R-R	6-0	220	7-13-92	.238	.240	.237	54	164	28	39	10	0	1	18	26	0	3	2	40	0	3	.317	.339
Gonzalez, Daniel	R-R	6-1	190	12-6-95	.100	.000	.111	3	10	0	1	0	0	0	0	0	0	0	0	2	0	0	.100	.100
Gonzalez, Luis	L-L	6-1	195	9-10-95	.247	.263	.241	126	473	63	117	18	4	9	59	47	5	0	10	89	17	9	.359	.316
Jay, Jon	L-L	5-11	195	3-15-85	.200	.333	.143	3	10	0	2	0	0	0	1	0	0	0	0	2	0	0	.200	.200
Madrigal, Nick	R-R	5-7	165	3-5-97	.342	.220	.382	42	164	30	56	11	2	1	16	14	2	0	0	5	14	6	.451	.400
Mercedes, Yermin	R-R	5-11	225	2-14-93	.327	.436	.287	42	147	19	48	7	0	6	18	17	0	0	3	25	2	0	.497	.389
Michalczewski, Trey	B-R	6-4	220	2-27-95	.208	.227	.200	48	149	13	31	9	0	1	18	20	0	1	0	56	0	1	.309	.300
Nicholas, Brett	L-R	6-2	220	7-18-88	.071	.250	.000	4	14	1	1	1	0	0	0	0	0	0	1	4	0	0	.143	.071
Nolan, Nate	R-R	6-1	210	10-11-94	.189	.231	.168	47	159	20	30	9	0	4	17	11	3	0	1	64	0	0	.321	.253
Quinteiro, Camilo	R-R	5-11	180	4-11-97	.000	--	.000	2	6	0	0	0	0	0	0	0	0	0	0	3	0	0	.000	.000
Remillard, Zach	R-R	6-1	200	2-21-94	.232	.211	.246	27	95	16	22	3	0	2	6	13	0	0	1	36	2	0	.326	.321
Rivera, Laz	R-R	6-1	185	9-20-94	.248	.267	.240	121	424	43	105	22	1	2	39	17	7	5	2	81	10	11	.318	.287
Robert, Luis	R-R	6-3	185	8-3-97	.314	.304	.318	56	226	43	71	16	3	8	29	13	4	1	0	54	21	6	.518	.362
Roman, Mitch	R-R	6-0	190	3-22-95	.165	.185	.160	40	121	14	20	3	1	0	12	15	2	0	1	37	1	1	.231	.266
Rutherford, Blake	L-R	6-2	210	5-2-97	.265	.216	.286	118	438	50	116	17	3	7	49	37	0	0	5	118	9	2	.365	.319
Sheets, Gavin	L-L	6-4	230	4-23-96	.267	.237	.280	126	464	56	124	16	1	16	83	54	4	0	5	99	3	1	.414	.345
Tomscha, Damek	R-R	6-2	200	8-27-91	.269	.236	.287	42	156	16	42	8	1	4	29	11	5	0	2	34	2	0	.410	.333
Torres, Ramon	B-R	5-11	190	1-22-93	.210	.173	.229	58	157	13	33	11	3	0	9	6	1	2	0	26	0	3	.319	.244
Valenzuela, Luis	L-R	5-10	179	8-25-93	.236	.412	.158	17	55	9	13	2	0	1	4	3	0	0	0	11	2	1	.327	.276
2-team total (79 Mississippi)					.202	.328	.170	96	302	31	61	14	2	3	28	13	1	0	3	66	2	2	.291	.235

Pitching	B-T	HT	WT	DOB	W	L	ERA	G	GS	CG	SV	IP	H	R	ER	HR	BB	SO	AVG	vLH	vRH	K/9	BB/9
Arobio, Vince	R-R	5-11	185	3-31-95	3	2	6.11	17	1	0	0	28	27	20	19	3	12	35	.250	.163	.322	11.25	3.86
Banks, Tanner	L-L	6-1	210	10-24-91	5	7	4.23	28	21	0	1	123	131	67	58	12	21	85	.271	.260	.277	6.20	1.53

Name	B-T	HT	WT	DOB	W	L	ERA	G	GS	CG	SV	IP	H	R	ER	HR	BB	SO	AVG	vLH	vRH	K/9	BB/9
Battenfield, Blake	R-R	6-3	220	8-22-94	5	5	4.52	19	19	0	0	96	107	49	48	13	25	69	.287	.299	.278	6.49	2.35
Burdi, Zack	R-R	6-3	205	3-9-95	0	3	6.41	17	0	0	3	20	24	16	14	5	13	24	.289	.227	.312	10.98	5.95
Burns, Wyatt	R-R	5-11	185	11-6-94	0	0	9.82	6	0	0	0	7	11	8	8	2	4	5	.367	.357	.375	6.14	4.91
Cabrera, Mauricio	R-R	6-3	240	9-22-93	4	3	4.50	41	1	0	1	48	52	28	24	2	47	67	.277	.265	.283	12.56	8.81
Clark, Brian	R-L	6-3	235	4-27-93	0	0	15.00	2	0	0	0	3	6	5	5	0	3	3	.462	.600	.375	9.00	9.00
Dopico, Danny	R-R	6-2	210	12-18-93	3	2	2.59	43	0	0	6	63	36	20	18	0	35	73	.168	.145	.183	10.48	5.03
Elliott, Jake	R-R	6-7	230	3-22-95	1	0	3.00	2	0	0	0	3	5	1	1	0	1	3	.455	.500	.444	9.00	3.00
Flores, Bernardo	L-L	6-2	190	8-23-95	3	8	3.33	15	15	0	0	78	74	37	29	10	15	69	.243	.198	.264	7.93	1.72
Foster, Matt	R-R	6-0	205	1-27-95	0	0	0.00	6	0	0	1	10	3	0	0	0	2	12	.097	.083	.105	11.17	1.86
Hansen, Alec	R-R	6-7	235	10-10-94	1	2	5.45	30	1	0	1	40	43	29	24	5	37	45	.281	.339	.245	10.21	8.39
Henzman, Lincoln	R-R	6-2	205	7-4-95	4	6	5.56	15	15	1	0	79	96	57	49	5	18	44	.301	.294	.307	4.99	2.04
Heuer, Codi	R-R	6-5	195	7-3-96	2	3	1.84	22	0	0	9	29	25	11	6	0	7	22	.236	.294	.208	6.75	2.15
Johnson, Tyler	R-R	6-2	205	8-21-95	2	0	3.44	12	0	0	0	18	10	7	7	3	6	23	.154	.156	.152	11.29	2.95
Kubat, Kyle	L-L	6-1	195	12-4-92	4	2	2.42	8	8	1	0	48	43	19	13	0	7	35	.239	.244	.237	6.52	1.30
Lambert, Jimmy	R-R	6-2	190	11-18-94	3	4	4.55	11	11	0	0	59	62	31	30	11	27	70	.272	.262	.280	10.62	4.10
Martinez, Luis	R-R	6-6	200	1-29-95	5	2	4.26	39	0	0	4	61	54	30	29	5	25	73	.241	.292	.207	10.71	3.67
Medeiros, Kodi	L-L	6-2	205	5-25-96	4	8	5.10	28	9	0	0	83	80	56	47	11	51	75	.257	.220	.275	8.13	5.53
Nolin, Sean	L-L	6-4	250	12-26-89	1	1	8.10	4	4	0	0	17	26	16	15	5	6	16	.356	.600	.264	8.64	3.24
Parke, John	L-L	6-4	205	1-3-95	3	4	2.59	14	14	0	0	76	69	31	22	5	18	43	.242	.231	.247	5.07	2.12
Paulino, Felix	R-R	6-1	200	3-24-95	3	2	3.86	6	5	0	0	35	36	16	15	5	13	30	.265	.268	.263	7.71	3.34
Schryver, Hunter	L-L	6-1	200	4-3-95	3	2	2.77	30	0	0	3	49	47	19	15	2	17	39	.261	.258	.263	7.21	3.14
Sousa, Bennett	L-L	6-3	185	4-6-95	0	0	0.00	2	0	0	0	3	2	0	0	0	1	3	.222	.000	.333	10.13	3.38
Thompson, Zach	R-R	6-7	230	10-23-93	0	0	1.69	4	0	0	0	5	5	1	1	0	1	6	.250	.222	.273	10.13	1.69
Tomshaw, Matt	R-L	6-1	205	12-17-88	5	5	2.40	15	12	0	0	75	62	23	20	7	9	86	.218	.241	.208	10.32	1.08
Torres, Ramon	B-R	5-11	190	1-22-93	0	0	0.00	1	0	0	0	0	0	0	0	0	0	1	.000	.000	--	27.00	0.00
Walsh, Connor	L-R	6-2	190	10-18-92	0	1	5.87	11	0	0	1	15	14	12	10	0	11	16	.237	.238	.237	9.39	6.46

Fielding

Catcher	PCT	G	PO	A	E	DP	PB
Castillo	1.000	1	3	0	0	0	0
Gonzalez	.983	53	362	46	7	2	7
Gonzalez	.958	3	21	2	1	0	0
Mercedes	.989	34	244	29	3	6	10
Nicholas	1.000	3	22	0	0	1	0
Nolan	.976	47	381	31	10	0	5

First Base	PCT	G	PO	A	E	DP
Forbes	1.000	1	1	0	0	0
Michalczewski	1.000	10	74	6	0	9
Remillard	1.000	2	12	0	0	1
Sheets	.997	110	839	68	3	79
Tomscha	.984	15	118	7	2	15
Torres	1.000	4	4	0	0	1

Second Base	PCT	G	PO	A	E	DP

	PCT	G	PO	A	E	DP
Forbes	.950	6	12	7	1	2
Madrigal	1.000	39	67	92	0	30
Michalczewski	.973	8	18	18	1	7
Quinteiro	.875	2	1	6	1	1
Rivera	.988	16	31	51	1	12
Roman	.972	39	58	82	4	18
Torres	.971	21	27	40	2	10
Valenzuela	1.000	10	8	19	0	2

Third Base	PCT	G	PO	A	E	DP
Forbes	.935	105	79	180	18	14
Michalczewski	.929	11	10	16	2	3
Remillard	.926	11	3	22	2	1
Tomscha	.867	5	4	9	2	1
Torres	.882	6	3	12	2	2
Valenzuela	1.000	2	0	2	0	0

Shortstop	PCT	G	PO	A	E	DP
Remillard	.943	15	14	36	3	8
Rivera	.966	102	154	244	14	62
Torres	.938	16	19	42	4	7
Valenzuela	1.000	5	7	21	0	4

Outfield	PCT	G	PO	A	E	DP
Basabe	.966	66	137	5	5	1
Booker	.961	73	146	2	6	0
Gonzalez	.985	106	255	7	4	1
Jay	1.000	3	6	0	0	0
Michalczewski	1.000	12	21	0	0	0
Remillard	.000	1	0	0	0	0
Robert	.983	45	115	4	2	1
Rutherford	.978	97	175	6	4	5
Tomscha	1.000	6	11	1	0	0
Torres	1.000	8	6	2	0	0

WINSTON-SALEM DASH

HIGH CLASS A

CAROLINA LEAGUE

Batting	B-T	HT	WT	DOB	AVG	vLH	vRH	G	AB	R	H	2B	3B	HR	RBI	BB	HBP	SH	SF	SO	SB	CS	SLG	OBP
Allen, Jonathan	L-R	6-3	200	3-24-97	.556	.333	.667	2	9	3	5	0	0	2	5	0	0	0	0	2	1	1	1.222	.556
Blackman, Tate	R-R	6-0	195	9-7-94	.193	.229	.177	87	275	35	53	11	0	4	28	39	6	3	5	108	1	1	.276	.302
Cruz, Johan	R-R	6-2	188	10-8-95	.239	.149	.287	37	134	20	32	9	0	1	12	11	1	2	1	43	1	0	.328	.299
Dedelow, Craig	L-R	6-4	195	11-15-94	.246	.259	.241	127	479	61	118	21	10	18	63	37	7	1	4	133	3	6	.445	.307
Destino, Alex	L-L	6-2	215	10-24-95	.143	.000	.182	4	14	2	2	0	0	0	0	2	0	0	0	5	0	0	.143	.250
Fisher, Jameson	L-R	6-2	200	12-18-93	.242	.240	.243	127	459	62	111	30	2	9	44	72	3	1	8	130	7	4	.375	.343
Frost, Tyler	L-R	5-10	183	11-21-95	.247	.276	.235	104	413	56	102	26	3	12	47	35	11	3	5	146	11	7	.412	.319
George, Jordan	B-R	6-2	200	7-16-92	.213	.188	.226	48	141	18	30	7	0	3	19	33	3	0	0	26	0	1	.326	.373
Gonzalez, Daniel	R-R	6-1	190	12-6-95	.179	.200	.154	10	28	3	5	1	0	0	1	2	0	0	1	9	0	0	.214	.226
Madrigal, Nick	R-R	5-7	165	3-5-97	.272	.300	.260	49	191	20	52	10	2	2	27	17	6	1	3	6	17	4	.377	.346
Moniot, Travis	B-R	6-1	190	6-9-97	.125	.000	.143	3	8	1	1	0	0	0	0	1	0	0	0	4	0	0	.125	.222
Muno, JJ	R-R	5-11	190	12-21-93	.238	.206	.250	77	223	42	53	7	6	4	34	31	10	1	4	55	14	6	.377	.351
Nolan, Nate	R-R	6-1	210	10-11-94	.250	--	.250	1	4	0	1	0	0	0	0	0	0	0	0	2	0	0	.500	.250
Perez, Carlos	R-R	5-10	160	9-10-96	.263	.270	.259	89	312	42	82	14	0	2	33	24	2	0	4	26	0	0	.327	.316
Remillard, Zach	R-R	6-1	200	2-21-94	.289	.304	.281	95	357	50	103	15	1	5	37	33	6	3	1	89	6	3	.378	.358
Robert, Luis	R-R	6-3	185	8-3-97	.453	.515	.405	19	75	21	34	5	3	8	24	4	5	0	0	20	8	2	.920	.512
Roman, Mitch	R-R	6-0	190	3-22-95	.269	.259	.273	69	268	29	72	11	1	1	21	21	2	2	1	75	9	7	.328	.325
Skoug, Evan	L-R	5-11	200	10-21-95	.165	.080	.185	44	133	15	22	7	1	5	21	21	0	0	0	52	1	0	.346	.279
Vaughn, Andrew	R-R	6-0	214	4-3-98	.252	.240	.256	29	107	16	27	8	0	3	21	16	1	0	2	17	0	1	.411	.349
Walker, Steele	L-L	5-11	190	7-30-96	.269	.216	.292	100	383	59	103	26	2	10	51	42	6	1	6	63	9	5	.426	.346
Yrizarri, Yeyson	R-R	6-0	175	2-2-97	.218	.294	.185	107	358	33	78	17	1	3	36	17	5	1	1	90	5	1	.296	.263

Pitching	B-T	HT	WT	DOB	W	L	ERA	G	GS	CG	SV	IP	H	R	ER	HR	BB	SO	AVG	vLH	vRH	K/9	BB/9
Arobio, Vince	R-R	5-11	185	3-31-95	0	0	0.00	6	0	0	0	9	4	0	0	0	3	13	.143	.000	.222	13.50	3.12
Banuelos, Manny	R-L	5-10	215	3-13-91	0	0	4.15	2	2	0	0	9	14	4	4	1	4	10	.368	.167	.462	10.38	4.15

Pitching	B-T	HT	WT	DOB	W	L	ERA	G	GS	CG	SV	IP	H	R	ER	HR	BB	SO	AVG	vLH	vRH	K/9	BB/9
Battenfield, Blake	R-R	6-3	220	8-22-94	1	2	2.83	6	6	0	0	35	31	14	11	3	9	25	.240	.273	.216	6.43	2.31
Burns, Wyatt	R-R	5-11	185	11-6-94	3	1	2.78	18	0	0	3	36	29	16	11	0	13	33	.225	.196	.241	8.33	3.28
Castillo, Cristian	L-L	6-0	190	9-25-94	4	5	3.49	11	11	0	0	57	65	27	22	7	13	54	.286	.271	.291	8.58	2.06
Cavanerio, Jorgan	R-R	6-1	155	8-18-94	9	3	3.13	20	19	0	0	112	102	43	39	7	22	73	.242	.263	.230	5.87	1.77
Conway, Austin	R-R	6-1	210	1-16-95	0	0	18.00	3	0	0	0	3	6	6	6	0	5	3	.375	.333	.429	9.00	15.00
Elliott, Jake	R-R	6-7	230	3-22-95	4	2	4.83	33	4	0	2	63	58	44	34	7	26	54	.243	.245	.241	7.67	3.69
Escorcia, Kevin	L-L	6-1	170	1-5-95	2	2	4.33	29	0	0	0	35	38	20	17	2	21	37	.286	.136	.360	9.42	5.35
Frare, Caleb	L-L	6-1	210	7-8-93	0	0	0.00	3	0	0	0	3	1	0	0	0	2	3	.091	.250	.000	8.10	5.40
Hansen, Alec	R-R	6-7	235	10-10-94	1	0	2.13	9	0	0	0	13	1	3	3	0	7	21	.025	.000	.037	14.92	4.97
Henzman, Lincoln	R-R	6-2	205	7-4-95	3	2	4.61	9	9	0	0	41	46	24	21	4	10	18	.288	.309	.266	3.95	2.20
Heuer, Codi	R-R	6-5	195	7-3-96	4	1	2.82	20	0	0	2	38	34	14	12	0	8	43	.233	.232	.233	10.10	1.88
Johnson, Tyler	R-R	6-2	205	8-21-95	0	1	1.80	7	0	0	0	10	6	3	2	1	4	15	.162	.143	.188	13.50	3.60
Kincanon, Will	L-R	6-3	202	10-27-95	3	3	1.86	42	0	0	8	58	45	23	12	4	26	71	.208	.197	.214	11.02	4.03
Kubat, Kyle	L-L	6-1	195	12-4-92	2	0	1.23	4	4	0	0	22	11	4	3	0	5	19	.145	.083	.173	7.77	2.05
Ledo, Luis	R-R	6-4	208	5-28-95	4	1	1.83	34	0	0	8	44	35	11	9	2	21	41	.227	.210	.239	8.32	4.26
Lewis, Zach	R-R	6-3	205	5-24-95	6	8	5.83	28	18	1	0	110	126	80	71	9	41	97	.292	.305	.283	7.96	3.36
Lindgren, Jacob	R-L	5-11	210	3-12-93	1	2	1.53	12	0	0	1	18	17	4	3	0	4	17	.258	.435	.163	8.66	2.04
McClure, Kade	R-R	6-7	230	2-12-96	2	3	3.39	12	12	0	0	66	64	25	25	8	17	49	.252	.256	.250	6.65	2.31
Muno, JJ	L-R	5-11	190	12-21-93	0	0	10.80	3	0	0	0	3	7	6	4	2	2	2	.389	.333	.417	5.40	5.40
Nin, Jose	R-R	6-3	220	6-20-95	5	3	3.93	40	0	0	9	55	57	29	24	4	22	44	.269	.206	.302	7.20	3.60
Parke, John	L-L	6-4	205	1-3-95	4	2	3.65	12	12	0	0	69	71	34	28	6	20	32	.265	.309	.250	4.17	2.61
Perez, Andrew	L-L	6-2	196	7-25-97	2	2	1.15	22	0	0	1	31	25	9	4	0	17	34	.208	.250	.191	9.77	4.88
Pilkington, Konnor	L-L	6-3	225	9-12-97	4	9	4.99	19	19	0	0	96	99	56	53	7	39	96	.270	.273	.269	9.03	3.67
Sousa, Bennett	L-L	6-3	185	4-6-95	1	3	2.70	20	0	0	5	30	22	11	9	4	5	32	.210	.167	.232	9.60	1.50
Stephens, Jordan	R-R	6-1	190	9-12-92	0	0	4.50	1	1	0	0	2	1	1	1	0	4	1	.143	1.000	.000	18.00	0.00
Stiever, Jonathan	R-R	6-2	205	5-12-97	6	4	2.15	12	12	0	0	71	56	17	17	7	13	77	.216	.178	.248	9.76	1.65
Varnell, Taylor	L-L	6-1	190	5-5-95	1	2	3.38	4	4	0	0	21	20	9	8	1	10	21	.263	.200	.286	8.86	4.22

Fielding

Catcher	PCT	G	PO	A	E	DP	PB
Gonzalez	1.000	9	65	8	0	0	0
Nolan	1.000	1	10	0	0	0	2
Perez	.988	87	616	58	8	4	7
Skoug	.995	44	337	35	2	2	4

First Base	PCT	G	PO	A	E	DP
Fisher	.989	108	908	53	11	94
George	.955	8	60	3	3	6
Remillard	1.000	2	19	0	0	5
Vaughn	1.000	16	153	3	0	7

Second Base	PCT	G	PO	A	E	DP
Blackman	.963	53	88	119	8	32
Cruz	.895	4	9	8	2	2
Madrigal	.986	41	82	126	3	39

(Catcher)	PCT	G	PO	A	E	DP
Moniot	1.000	1	3	2	0	1
Muno	.979	21	43	50	2	17
Remillard	.000	1	0	0	0	0
Roman	.971	16	29	39	2	11

Third Base	PCT	G	PO	A	E	DP
Blackman	.857	7	8	10	3	2
Moniot	1.000	1	3	0	0	0
Remillard	1.000	4	4	9	0	4
Roman	.931	25	18	49	5	2
Yrizarri	.897	97	48	221	31	26

Shortstop	PCT	G	PO	A	E	DP
Cruz	.939	30	43	81	8	15
Muno	1.000	7	10	24	0	5
Remillard	.951	81	116	232	18	47

(Outfield)	PCT	G	PO	A	E	DP
Roman	.909	13	6	34	4	3
Yrizarri	.909	3	3	7	1	4

Outfield	PCT	G	PO	A	E	DP
Allen	.875	2	7	0	1	0
Blackman	1.000	2	2	0	0	0
Dedelow	.986	116	203	12	3	3
Destino	1.000	2	6	0	0	0
Fisher	.955	13	20	1	1	0
Frost	.977	92	164	4	4	2
George	.956	26	43	0	2	0
Moniot	.000	1	0	0	0	0
Muno	.988	44	82	0	1	0
Robert	.974	13	37	1	1	0
Roman	1.000	11	18	3	0	1
Walker	1.000	81	176	7	0	2

KANNAPOLIS INTIMIDATORS

LOW CLASS A

SOUTH ATLANTIC LEAGUE

Batting	B-T	HT	WT	DOB	AVG	vLH	vRH	G	AB	R	H	2B	3B	HR	RBI	BB	HBP	SH	SF	SO	SB	CS	SLG	OBP
Alfaro, Jhoandro	B-R	6-1	180	11-4-97	.149	.158	.146	24	74	6	11	1	1	1	6	5	2	2	0	25	3	0	.230	.222
Basabe, Luis Alexander	B-R	6-0	160	8-26-96	.300	.500	.250	5	20	2	6	0	1	0	1	4	0	0	0	7	1	1	.400	.417
Beltre, Ramon	R-R	5-11	160	10-18-96	.207	.162	.220	125	454	45	94	23	6	4	33	13	4	1	0	130	8	3	.311	.236
Bush, Bryce	R-R	6-0	200	12-14-99	.201	.105	.228	67	254	29	51	12	5	5	33	27	4	0	3	92	4	1	.347	.285
Cruz, Johan	R-R	6-2	188	10-8-95	.296	.375	.276	45	159	25	47	9	1	6	26	20	2	2	2	36	0	0	.478	.377
Curbelo, Luis	R-R	6-3	185	11-10-97	.169	.213	.153	64	237	17	40	11	1	5	30	13	2	1	3	105	0	2	.287	.216
Dawkins, Ian	R-R	5-11	195	7-6-95	.298	.339	.288	131	533	75	159	38	1	4	36	37	15	4	0	95	23	8	.396	.361
Destino, Alex	L-L	6-2	215	10-24-95	.298	.274	.304	112	420	63	125	20	2	17	64	49	5	0	2	116	0	1	.476	.376
Gonzalez, Romy	R-R	6-1	210	9-6-96	.244	.269	.239	101	352	35	86	22	4	4	45	38	8	4	3	108	11	3	.364	.329
Hickman, Michael	L-R	6-1	215	11-5-96	.209	.171	.217	64	215	22	45	13	0	6	24	12	5	1	1	71	0	0	.354	.266
Moniot, Travis	B-R	6-1	190	6-9-97	.180	.167	.184	16	50	2	9	2	0	0	3	6	0	0	0	20	3	1	.220	.268
Nunez, Amado	R-R	6-2	178	10-10-97	.206	.197	.209	86	301	35	62	8	2	8	33	19	2	1	2	105	5	1	.326	.256
Osik, Tyler	R-R	5-10	203	11-15-96	.278	.393	.232	26	97	14	27	10	1	5	19	10	1	0	0	30	0	1	.557	.352
Quintero, Camilo	R-R	5-11	180	4-11-97	.181	.316	.147	30	94	9	17	4	0	0	5	20	1	2	1	29	3	1	.223	.328
Simmons, Cameron	R-R	6-4	200	9-22-96	.243	.286	.221	32	103	9	25	6	0	3	14	8	2	0	3	37	4	3	.388	.302
Skoug, Evan	L-R	5-11	200	10-21-95	.172	.231	.157	18	64	6	11	3	1	1	3	11	0	0	0	21	1	0	.297	.293
Sosa, Lenyn	R-R	6-0	180	1-25-00	.252	.368	.217	122	501	72	126	35	2	7	51	27	3	2	3	102	6	6	.371	.292
Sowers, Logan	R-R	6-5	230	1-11-96	.140	.083	.158	15	50	4	7	1	0	1	4	1	2	0	0	23	0	0	.220	.189
Troutwine, Gunnar	R-R	6-1	230	3-6-96	.240	.245	.238	61	200	26	48	15	0	2	14	31	0	1	1	76	1	0	.345	.341
Vaughn, Andrew	R-R	6-0	214	4-3-98	.253	.244	.255	23	83	14	21	7	0	2	11	14	5	0	1	18	0	0	.410	.388
Walker, Steele	L-L	5-11	190	7-30-96	.365	.286	.383	20	74	6	27	10	3	0	11	8	3	0	2	15	4	2	.581	.437
Zangari, Corey	R-R	6-4	240	5-7-97	.203	.197	.205	85	290	44	59	18	1	15	38	44	5	0	5	115	2	1	.428	.314

Pitching	B-T	HT	WT	DOB	W	L	ERA	G	GS	CG	SV	IP	H	R	ER	HR	BB	SO	AVG	vLH	vRH	K/9	BB/9
Arobio, Vince	R-R	5-11	185	3-31-95	2	2	2.63	13	0	0	1	27	17	12	8	2	5	36	.179	.143	.194	11.85	1.65

Name	B-T	HT	WT	DOB	W	L	ERA	G	GS	CG	SV	IP	H	R	ER	HR	BB	SO	AVG	vLH	vRH	K/9	BB/9
Beltre, Ramon	R-R	5-11	160	10-18-96	0	0	0.00	1	0	0	0	0	1	0	0	0	0	0	.500	--	.500	0.00	0.00
Bilous, Jason	R-R	6-2	185	8-11-97	6	10	3.70	31	17	0	0	105	85	47	43	12	61	113	.220	.184	.242	9.72	5.25
Burdi, Zack	R-R	6-3	205	3-9-95	1	1	9.00	3	0	0	0	3	4	3	3	0	1	6	.308	.333	.286	18.00	3.00
Burns, Wyatt	R-R	5-11	185	11-6-94	2	2	5.82	10	0	0	1	17	17	16	11	0	14	14	.246	.240	.250	7.41	7.41
Butler, Hansen	R-R	5-11	180	10-30-95	1	2	7.71	7	0	0	0	9	16	10	8	0	5	16	.381	.417	.333	15.43	4.82
Conway, Austin	R-R	6-1	210	1-16-95	1	1	1.59	26	0	0	13	34	18	8	6	2	17	48	.155	.157	.154	12.71	4.50
Cronin, Declan	R-R	6-4	225	9-24-97	1	2	3.70	13	0	0	0	24	16	10	10	2	9	16	.198	.211	.186	5.92	3.33
Destino, Alex	L-L	6-2	215	10-24-95	0	0	3.38	3	0	0	0	3	2	1	1	0	1	3	.182	.000	.333	10.13	3.38
Dominguez, Johan	R-R	6-4	190	1-18-96	6	5	2.98	24	15	0	0	91	83	41	30	2	33	90	.239	.213	.259	8.93	3.28
Flores, Bernardo	L-L	6-2	190	8-23-95	0	0	9.00	1	1	0	0	3	6	3	3	0	1	0	.462	.000	.500	0.00	3.00
Folman, Kevin	R-R	6-2	215	10-23-94	0	4	5.04	17	10	0	0	70	73	45	39	8	29	71	.261	.286	.238	9.17	3.75
Freeman, Caleb	R-R	6-1	190	2-23-98	0	0	4.15	2	0	0	0	4	3	2	2	1	2	5	.214	.222	.200	10.38	4.15
Lindgren, Jacob	R-L	5-11	210	3-12-93	0	0	0.00	3	0	0	1	3	2	0	0	0	1	3	.182	--	.182	8.10	2.70
Long, Sam	L-L	6-1	185	7-8-95	8	5	3.06	30	15	0	0	97	73	39	33	7	28	112	.205	.273	.183	10.39	2.60
Martin, Davis	L-R	6-2	200	1-4-97	9	9	5.04	27	27	0	0	145	152	94	81	17	38	156	.266	.266	.267	9.71	2.36
McClure, Kade	R-R	6-7	230	2-12-96	2	3	3.09	10	10	1	0	55	56	28	19	3	12	50	.256	.293	.236	8.13	1.95
O'Conner, Justin	R-R	6-0	201	3-31-92	1	0	6.00	9	0	0	1	9	12	6	6	0	1	9	.333	.211	.471	9.00	1.00
Olson, J.B.	R-R	6-2	195	2-15-95	1	2	5.83	26	0	0	3	42	47	29	27	4	19	39	.285	.250	.309	8.42	4.10
Perez, Andrew	L-L	6-2	196	7-25-97	0	3	2.25	19	0	0	2	36	38	10	9	1	12	52	.264	.281	.259	13.00	3.00
Perez, Devon	R-R	6-5	200	5-15-96	1	2	3.20	21	2	0	3	56	47	24	20	5	15	55	.227	.283	.183	8.79	2.40
Perez, Wilber	R-R	6-2	170	11-3-97	4	1	2.83	32	1	0	4	70	36	24	22	5	45	74	.149	.148	.149	9.51	5.79
Pilkington, Konnor	L-L	6-3	225	9-12-97	1	0	1.62	6	6	0	0	33	15	6	6	2	11	42	.132	.261	.099	11.34	2.97
Ramsey, Lane	R-R	6-9	245	7-16-96	4	6	2.75	31	0	0	4	52	42	32	16	2	20	44	.215	.298	.153	7.57	3.44
Sousa, Bennett	L-L	6-3	185	4-6-95	2	3	2.51	21	0	0	3	32	38	14	9	3	7	39	.282	.256	.292	10.86	1.95
Stiever, Jonathan	R-R	6-2	205	5-12-97	4	6	4.74	14	14	0	0	74	88	43	39	10	14	77	.293	.310	.283	9.36	1.70
Varnell, Taylor	L-L	6-1	190	5-5-95	7	4	3.23	20	20	0	0	106	86	44	38	5	34	115	.221	.221	.220	9.76	2.89
Watson, Tyler	L-L	5-11	200	6-9-93	0	1	9.88	10	0	0	1	14	16	16	15	1	7	13	.286	.381	.229	8.56	4.61

Fielding

Catcher	PCT	G	PO	A	E	DP	PB
Alfaro	.986	24	189	18	3	1	5
Hickman	.989	48	403	41	5	0	10
Skoug	1.000	13	125	10	0	0	0
Troutwine	.982	58	558	47	11	6	23

	PCT	G	PO	A	E	DP
Curbelo	.950	4	12	7	1	2
Gonzalez	.967	7	11	18	1	5
Nunez	.908	37	44	64	11	10
Quinteiro	1.000	5	4	10	0	0
Sosa	1.000	3	3	6	0	0

	PCT	G	PO	A	E	DP
Cruz	.985	14	18	47	1	4
Curbelo	1.000	6	6	19	0	2
Quinteiro	1.000	2	1	2	0	0
Sosa	.970	117	158	288	14	59

First Base	PCT	G	PO	A	E	DP
Gonzalez	.990	14	97	5	1	8
Hickman	.984	9	57	4	1	5
Nunez	.978	33	247	17	6	26
Osik	1.000	4	21	1	0	1
Vaughn	.987	19	147	9	2	6
Zangari	.981	64	451	14	9	43

Third Base	PCT	G	PO	A	E	DP
Beltre	.897	34	17	44	7	1
Bush	.679	10	4	15	9	0
Cruz	.944	25	23	45	4	3
Curbelo	.820	46	27	55	18	8
Gonzalez	.875	4	3	4	1	1
Nunez	.000	1	0	0	0	0
Quinteiro	.898	24	12	32	5	3

Outfield	PCT	G	PO	A	E	DP
Basabe	1.000	5	5	1	0	1
Beltre	.962	10	24	1	1	0
Bush	.968	33	59	1	2	0
Dawkins	.993	131	278	9	2	2
Destino	.968	92	143	10	5	3
Gonzalez	.980	71	146	4	3	1
Moniot	.968	16	28	2	1	1
Osik	1.000	5	11	0	0	0
Simmons	1.000	30	56	1	0	1
Sowers	1.000	14	20	0	0	0
Walker	1.000	20	40	0	0	0

Second Base	PCT	G	PO	A	E	DP
Beltre	.960	85	141	192	14	47
Cruz	1.000	3	9	6	0	2

Shortstop	PCT	G	PO	A	E	DP
Beltre	1.000	1	4	1	0	1

CHICAGO WHITE SOX

GREAT FALLS VOYAGERS
PIONEER LEAGUE

ROOKIE ADVANCED

Batting	B-T	HT	WT	DOB	AVG	vLH	vRH	G	AB	R	H	2B	3B	HR	RBI	BB	HBP	SH	SF	SO	SB	CS	SLG	OBP
Abbott, Sam	L-R	6-4	225	4-9-99	.238	.212	.243	58	181	30	43	13	0	9	27	26	8	0	2	79	0	0	.459	.355
Allen, Jonathan	L-R	6-3	200	3-9-97	.250	.188	.266	22	80	12	20	5	1	1	8	3	1	0	0	28	2	0	.375	.286
Archer, Tom	R-R	5-9	175	12-10-96	.217	.286	.188	16	46	3	10	2	0	0	5	2	0	0	0	2	1	0	.261	.250
Comas, Anderson	L-L	6-3	185	2-10-00	.222	.209	.225	54	194	19	43	7	6	2	33	7	1	0	1	58	0	2	.351	.251
Connell, Bryan	R-R	6-3	195	11-9-98	.163	.087	.188	29	92	13	15	2	0	6	13	7	2	0	0	45	0	0	.380	.238
Curbelo, Luis	R-R	6-3	185	11-10-97	.262	.204	.279	56	221	37	58	9	6	8	24	11	0	0	3	76	1	0	.466	.294
Delgado, Lency	R-R	6-3	215	6-20-99	.274	.214	.289	57	215	23	59	14	1	2	32	14	2	1	0	87	1	2	.377	.325
Goldfarb, Jakob	L-R	6-1	196	6-23-96	.154	.000	.177	14	39	7	6	1	0	1	3	9	3	0	0	13	1	0	.256	.353
Gonzalez, Ivan	R-R	5-9	190	10-28-96	.213	.188	.220	22	75	5	16	2	0	0	4	4	1	0	0	12	0	0	.240	.263
Greene, Ty	L-R	6-0	185	5-4-97	.325	.316	.328	23	77	13	25	4	1	0	6	5	2	0	0	5	1	1	.403	.381
Maldonado, Kelvin	R-R	5-11	160	2-21-00	.253	.256	.253	58	229	24	58	11	1	0	17	9	2	1	0	55	2	4	.310	.288
Mendoza, Harvin	L-L	6-2	185	2-18-99	.278	.192	.301	62	230	35	64	17	3	6	29	27	3	0	0	49	0	0	.457	.362
Mieses, Luis	L-L	6-3	185	5-31-00	.241	.277	.231	59	220	24	53	14	0	4	28	7	1	0	3	46	0	1	.359	.264
Quinteiro, Camilo	R-R	5-11	180	4-11-97	.361	.462	.304	10	36	7	13	1	0	0	6	4	0	1	0	11	1	1	.389	.425
Rivera, Joshua	R-R	5-11	185	1-30-99	.221	.206	.227	41	122	20	27	3	4	2	14	12	4	0	1	43	0	0	.361	.303
Sanchez, Kleyder	R-S	5-10	170	12-13-99	.218	.059	.262	23	78	7	17	4	0	0	10	4	0	0	2	25	0	1	.269	.250
Simmons, Cameron	R-R	6-4	200	9-22-96	.359	.353	.364	12	39	6	14	5	0	2	7	5	1	0	0	10	1	0	.641	.444
Weaver, Cabera	R-R	6-3	180	12-1-99	.254	.235	.260	62	236	30	60	13	5	2	18	18	4	2	1	85	10	4	.377	.317

Pitching	B-T	HT	WT	DOB	W	L	ERA	G	GS	CG	SV	IP	H	R	ER	HR	BB	SO	AVG	vLH	vRH	K/9	BB/9
Beer, Allan	R-R	6-2	200	8-26-95	1	0	6.06	12	0	0	1	16	17	11	11	3	5	19	.270	.292	.256	10.47	2.76
Butler, Hansen	R-R	5-11	180	10-30-95	0	0	0.00	1	0	0	0	1	0	0	0	0	0	3	.000	.000	.000	27.00	0.00
Fernandez, Rigo	L-L	6-0	190	11-27-97	3	2	4.91	19	0	0	1	33	28	21	18	2	20	45	.228	.242	.222	12.27	5.45
Freeman, Caleb	R-R	6-1	190	2-23-98	1	1	0.00	5	0	0	2	7	3	2	0	0	1	12	.125	.154	.091	16.20	1.35

Name	B-T	HT	WT	DOB	W	L	ERA	G	GS	CG	SV	IP	H	R	ER	HR	BB	SO	AVG	vLH	vRH	K/9	BB/9
Herrera, Brayan	R-R	6-2	185	4-5-98	2	2	5.27	10	0	0	0	14	18	12	8	3	2	13	.295	.063	.378	8.56	1.32
Jeans, Trey	L-L	5-10	195	1-31-96	1	0	5.40	3	0	0	0	5	8	3	3	0	0	10	.348	1.000	.286	18.00	0.00
Johnson, Nick	R-R	6-3	215	7-21-95	1	2	9.49	21	0	0	3	25	42	27	26	2	17	26	.368	.390	.356	9.49	6.20
Love, Carter	R-R	6-6	225	11-27-95	1	3	7.90	4	4	1	0	14	22	13	12	2	2	13	.361	.438	.333	8.56	1.32
Maynard, Jack	R-R	5-11	195	7-26-96	0	1	7.36	4	0	0	1	7	8	6	6	1	2	5	.286	.375	.250	6.14	2.45
Mercedes, Felix	R-R	6-2	185	2-13-97	0	0	1.13	5	0	0	0	8	2	2	1	0	8	5	.080	.000	.095	5.63	9.00
Metzdorf, Dan	L-L	5-10	165	5-28-96	0	2	3.60	14	14	0	0	40	44	21	16	3	8	36	.286	.156	.320	8.10	1.80
Milto, Pauly	R-R	6-3	245	3-6-97	0	0	1.88	19	0	0	5	29	22	6	6	1	7	26	.214	.268	.177	8.16	2.20
Moore, McKinley	R-R	6-6	225	8-24-98	0	0	0.00	2	0	0	0	3	2	0	0	0	0	5	.182	.250	.143	15.00	0.00
Morgan, Jason	R-R	6-5	175	2-17-96	3	6	4.68	14	14	1	0	75	83	52	39	10	20	33	.285	.327	.262	3.96	2.40
Patel, Karan	R-R	6-0	215	1-2-97	3	3	3.90	18	0	0	1	32	34	20	14	1	7	38	.264	.316	.242	10.58	1.95
Pawelczyk, Nate	R-R	6-1	190	6-9-97	2	0	3.81	21	0	0	1	26	30	13	11	0	8	26	.303	.143	.366	9.00	2.77
Peralta, Sammy	L-L	6-2	205	5-10-98	2	1	2.37	14	3	0	3	30	22	11	8	2	8	45	.191	.267	.165	13.35	2.37
Pineda, Ramon	R-R	6-0	200	2-3-98	2	1	2.22	17	0	0	0	24	17	11	6	0	8	23	.193	.118	.241	8.51	2.96
Reich, Connor	R-R	6-0	225	8-21-95	1	2	5.89	12	0	0	0	18	22	15	12	2	6	17	.293	.296	.292	8.35	2.95
Roper, Kaleb	R-R	6-0	193	11-22-95	4	0	2.65	14	2	0	0	34	22	11	10	0	12	43	.193	.088	.238	11.38	3.18
Silven, Yoelvin	R-R	6-1	176	6-26-99	0	0	6.43	3	0	0	1	7	9	5	5	0	2	8	.333	.286	.350	10.29	2.57
Solesky, Chase	R-R	6-3	201	9-26-97	0	4	6.17	14	13	0	0	42	47	30	29	6	12	45	.280	.357	.225	9.57	2.55
Thompson, Sean	R-R	6-3	190	9-8-95	3	7	6.08	14	14	2	0	80	101	59	54	9	15	66	.301	.321	.287	7.43	1.69
Weems, Avery	R-L	6-2	205	6-6-97	4	3	2.47	10	10	0	0	47	43	17	13	1	7	60	.239	.200	.248	11.41	1.33

Fielding

C: Goldfarb 13, Gonzalez 21, Greene 17, Sanchez 23. 1B: Abbott 28, Mendoza 47. 2B: Archer 14, Maldonado 30, Quinteiro 5, Rivera 26. 3B: Curbelo 49, Delgado 15, Quinteiro 4, Rivera 7. SS: Delgado 41, Maldonado 28, Quinteiro 1, Rivera 5. OF: Allen 21, Comas 51, Connell 25, Mieses 55, Simmons 12, Weaver 61.

AZL WHITE SOX   ROOKIE
ARIZONA LEAGUE

Batting	B-T	HT	WT	DOB	AVG	vLH	vRH	G	AB	R	H	2B	3B	HR	RBI	BB	HBP	SH	SF	SO	SB	CS	SLG	OBP
Adolfo, Micker	R-R	6-4	255	9-11-96	.260	.091	.308	13	50	8	13	5	0	2	3	7	1	0	0	21	0	0	.480	.362
Allen, Jonathan	L-R	6-3	200	3-24-97	.230	.158	.262	16	61	8	14	8	0	0	9	6	1	0	0	16	3	1	.361	.309
Archer, Tom	R-R	5-9	175	12-10-96	.100	.000	.111	2	10	2	1	0	1	0	2	0	0	0	1	0	0		.300	.100
Beard, James	R-R	5-10	170	9-24-00	.213	.321	.182	31	127	19	27	4	1	2	12	8	2	1	0	54	9	3	.307	.270
Bush, Bryce	R-R	6-0	200	12-14-99	.000	.000	.000	4	9	0	0	0	0	0	0	0	0	0	0	2	0	0	.000	.000
Coronado, Anthony	R-R	6-1	180	1-21-00	.307	.345	.292	28	101	18	31	7	2	2	14	5	3	0	0	27	0	0	.475	.358
Diaz, Harold	R-R	5-10	170	1-8-00	.215	.182	.233	19	65	13	14	3	1	1	6	4	2	0	1	17	1	0	.339	.278
Gladney, DJ	R-R	6-3	195	7-10-01	.264	.283	.258	50	201	27	53	5	2	8	25	10	5	0	4	82	1	0	.428	.309
Glass, Logan	R-R	6-4	215	4-9-01	.284	.100	.316	17	67	13	19	5	0	1	9	2	4	0	0	23	1	0	.403	.343
Goldfarb, Jakob	L-R	6-1	196	6-23-96	.250	.167	.286	6	20	2	5	0	0	2	8	2	1	0	0	7	1	0	.550	.348
Gonzalez, Ivan	R-R	5-9	190	10-28-96	.460	.300	.519	10	37	10	17	4	0	0	8	6	1	0	0	6	0	0	.568	.546
Gonzalez, Misael	R-R	6-0	175	5-23-01	.195	.217	.190	36	118	8	23	5	0	0	6	8	0	1	0	52	1	1	.237	.246
Guerrero, Josue	R-R	6-2	190	11-23-99	.240	.244	.238	43	146	16	35	9	0	5	20	13	2	3	2	55	0	0	.404	.307
Krogman, Chase	L-L	5-11	180	2-27-01	.191	.000	.267	7	21	2	4	0	0	0	1	1	0	0	0	6	0	0	.191	.227
Millwee, Daniel	R-R	5-10	205	8-2-95	.256	.100	.310	12	39	4	10	3	0	0	4	8	2	1	0	10	1	0	.333	.408
Ortiz, Gabriel	L-R	6-0	210	3-15-00	.276	.200	.316	7	29	0	8	1	0	0	0	0	0	0	0	6	0	0	.310	.276
Osik, Tyler	R-R	5-10	203	11-15-96	.271	.346	.250	31	118	22	32	10	1	0	18	11	3	0	1	39	1	0	.373	.346
Pimentel, Sidney	B-R	6-1	160	10-27-00	.181	.130	.195	27	105	11	19	4	0	0	8	10	3	0	0	40	0	2	.219	.271
Polanco, Samil	B-R	6-0	160	2-21-00	.290	.311	.282	40	176	19	51	7	2	1	12	5	1	1	0	35	11	5	.369	.313
Ramos, Bryan	R-R	6-2	190	3-12-02	.277	.400	.238	51	188	36	52	10	2	4	26	19	6	0	5	44	3	4	.415	.353
Rodriguez, Jose	R-R	5-11	175	5-13-01	.293	.423	.243	44	188	28	55	7	3	9	31	9	1	2	0	45	7	1	.505	.328
Torres, Victor	R-R	6-0	180	7-29-00	.219	.067	.247	26	96	5	21	2	0	0	9	3	0	0	1	28	2	2	.240	.240
Vaughn, Andrew	R-R	6-0	214	4-3-98	.600	.857	.375	3	15	3	9	2	0	1	4	1	0	0	3	0	0		.933	.625

Pitching	B-T	HT	WT	DOB	W	L	ERA	G	GS	CG	SV	IP	H	R	ER	HR	BB	SO	AVG	vLH	vRH	K/9	BB/9
Acosta, Hector	L-L	6-4	200	10-24-98	1	8	6.32	12	10	0	0	47	74	52	33	5	18	23	.346	.362	.338	4.40	3.45
Allen, Jonathan	L-R	6-3	200	3-24-97	1	0	0.00	1	0	0	0	2	3	2	0	0	0	2	.429	.333	.500	9.00	0.00
Alston, Garvin	R-L	6-4	175	3-12-97	0	1	3.00	13	0	0	1	18	18	8	6	2	4	22	.254	.238	.260	11.00	2.00
Banuelos, Manny	R-L	5-10	215	3-13-91	0	1	4.76	2	2	0	0	6	5	6	3	1	3	8	.227	.000	.250	12.71	4.76
Beer, Allan	R-R	6-2	200	8-26-95	0	0	9.00	1	0	0	0	1	2	1	1	0	0	3	.400	.000	.500	27.00	0.00
Bradford, Cooper	R-R	5-11	180	4-13-98	0	2	4.80	8	8	0	0	30	37	18	16	4	9	35	.303	.318	.295	10.50	2.70
Burke, Jeremiah	R-R	6-2	195	5-16-98	1	2	4.33	12	8	0	0	54	63	29	26	5	18	42	.288	.329	.266	7.00	3.00
Butler, Hansen	R-R	5-11	180	10-30-95	0	0	1.29	6	0	0	0	7	2	1	1	0	2	11	.087	.200	.000	14.14	2.57
Cronin, Declan	R-R	6-4	225	3-24-97	1	0	0.90	7	0	0	0	10	9	1	1	0	2	13	.231	.333	.185	11.70	1.80
Dalquist, Andrew	R-R	6-1	175	11-13-00	0	0	0.00	3	3	0	0	3	2	0	0	0	2	6	.182	.000	.222	6.00	6.00
Flores, Bernardo	L-L	6-2	190	8-23-95	0	0	3.75	4	4	0	0	12	17	5	5	2	1	13	.354	.421	.310	9.75	0.75
Frare, Caleb	L-L	6-1	210	7-8-93	0	0	3.38	3	0	0	0	3	2	2	1	0	2	5	.200	.000	.250	16.88	6.75
Freeman, Caleb	R-R	6-1	190	2-23-98	3	1	2.63	10	0	0	2	14	9	6	4	1	6	21	.180	.071	.222	13.83	3.95
Friedman, Justin	R-R	6-2	200	7-15-97	3	4	5.17	13	5	0	0	47	59	31	27	1	9	51	.294	.338	.265	9.77	1.72
Jarneski, Joseph	R-R	6-0	170	10-28-99	0	0	7.45	8	0	0	0	10	9	10	8	1	10	6	.243	.167	.316	5.59	9.31
2-team total (10 Rangers)					2	0	3.76	18	0	0	0	26	17	13	11	1	22	18	.199		.200	7.52	7.18
Jeans, Trey	L-L	5-10	195	1-31-96	1	0	1.99	18	0	0	2	23	20	9	5	1	5	33	.227	.192	.242	13.10	1.99
Johnson, Tyler	R-R	6-2	205	8-21-95	0	0	0.00	3	0	0	0	3	5	0	0	0	0	5	.385	.500	.333	15.00	0.00
Lindgren, Jacob	R-L	5-11	210	3-12-93	1	0	7.04	6	1	0	0	8	11	7	6	1	2	8	.324	.200	.375	9.39	2.35
Messer, Tyson	R-R	6-0	215	1-7-97	1	1	13.78	17	0	0	0	16	16	37	25	5	32	25	.250	.320	.205	13.78	17.63
Moore, McKinley	R-R	6-6	225	8-24-98	2	1	5.59	20	0	0	3	19	21	15	12	0	17	27	.276	.304	.264	12.57	7.91

CHICAGO WHITE SOX

Pitching	B-T	HT	WT	DOB	W	L	ERA	G	GS	CG	SV	IP	H	R	ER	HR	BB	SO	AVG	vLH	vRH	K/9	BB/9
Nunez, Vladimir	R-R	6-2	240	3-25-97	0	3	4.97	15	0	0	0	29	36	20	16	4	11	35	.305	.389	.268	10.86	3.41
O'Conner, Justin	R-R	6-0	201	3-31-92	1	0	1.80	5	0	0	0	5	1	1	1	1	0	8	.063	.000	.083	14.40	0.00
Peralta, Sammy	L-L	6-2	205	5-10-98	0	0	0.00	4	0	0	1	6	3	0	0	0	2	13	.136	.167	.125	18.47	2.84
Rodriguez, Luis	R-R	6-6	220	4-15-00	1	4	6.54	9	7	0	0	32	39	28	23	4	19	24	.300	.263	.315	6.82	5.40
Silva, Nick	R-R	6-2	205	12-17-96	1	1	3.96	19	0	0	0	25	29	13	11	1	13	23	.293	.364	.258	8.28	4.68
Silven, Yoelvin	R-R	6-1	176	6-26-99	0	2	3.48	15	2	0	0	44	49	20	17	6	5	51	.287	.342	.242	10.43	1.02
Thompson, Matthew	R-R	6-3	195	8-11-00	0	0	0.00	2	2	0	0	2	2	1	0	0	0	2	.250	.500	.000	9.00	0.00
Weems, Avery	R-L	6-2	205	6-6-97	1	1	0.69	4	4	0	0	13	10	4	1	0	3	14	.217	.167	.235	9.69	2.08
Welsh, Mac	R-R	6-4	202	11-3-95	2	2	0.00	12	0	0	3	12	9	4	0	0	2	19	.196	.177	.207	13.86	1.46

Fielding

C: Goldfarb 5, Gonzalez 10, Millwee 8, Ortiz 7, Torres 26. 1B: Gladney 3, Millwee 4, Osik 30, Pimentel 11, Ramos 6, Vaughn 2. 2B: Archer 2, Diaz 17, Pimentel 5, Polanco 24, Rodriguez 10. 3B: Gladney 26, Pimentel 1, Ramos 30, Rodriguez 1. SS: Pimentel 9, Polanco 16, Rodriguez 32. OF: Allen 16, Beard 31, Bush 4, Coronado 28, Glass 17, Goldfarb 1, Gonzalez 35, Guerrero 43, Krogman 7.

DSL WHITE SOX

ROOKIE

DOMINICAN SUMMER LEAGUE

Batting	B-T	HT	WT	DOB	AVG	vLH	vRH	G	AB	R	H	2B	3B	HR	RBI	BB	HBP	SH	SF	SO	SB	CS	SLG	OBP
Bailey, Benyamin	R-R	6-4	215	9-18-01	.324	.231	.349	55	185	41	60	12	3	2	19	52	4	0	2	40	10	2	.454	.477
Benavides, Ruben	R-R	6-1	178	8-9-01	.349	.318	.364	22	66	15	23	8	0	3	12	9	2	0	3	14	2	0	.606	.425
Bernal, Alberto	R-R	6-1	215	6-13-02	.167	.121	.183	43	126	23	21	5	1	2	16	33	7	1	3	55	1	1	.270	.361
Betancourt, Jhoneiker	R-R	6-1	174	5-2-00	.314	.250	.329	32	105	27	33	7	1	1	16	14	10	0	0	19	1	3	.429	.442
Espinoza, Anthony	R-R	5-10	165	9-27-01	.263	.211	.276	55	190	36	50	6	2	1	32	20	7	1	5	25	7	7	.332	.347
Garcia, Richard	R-R	6-1	185	9-20-98	.278	.546	.230	26	72	7	20	1	0	1	11	11	3	0	2	13	0	1	.333	.386
Gutierrez, Roberth	R-R	6-0	170	11-8-01	.274	.294	.267	47	135	26	37	4	5	0	15	21	0	2	3	33	7	4	.378	.365
Jimenez, Cesar	R-R	5-10	160	11-8-00	.208	.174	.222	29	77	12	16	3	0	0	6	8	0	1	0	15	4	3	.247	.282
Laureano, Johnabiell	R-R	6-0	180	10-11-00	.357	.319	.368	59	210	43	75	15	3	6	36	28	4	1	3	43	6	8	.543	.437
Leal, Lazaro	R-R	6-2	210	1-30-97	.225	.191	.236	55	182	22	41	13	1	3	23	38	5	0	1	29	2	1	.357	.372
Mendoza, Jefferson	R-R	6-0	170	1-16-01	.305	.304	.306	33	95	14	29	8	0	3	21	10	4	0	1	28	1	0	.484	.391
Mercedes, Juan	R-R	6-2	190	6-4-00	.223	.133	.248	41	139	15	31	7	1	0	13	16	3	0	0	33	2	0	.288	.317
Mercedes, Matthew	R-R	6-1	195	8-26-98	.328	.280	.339	40	134	24	44	10	1	1	30	16	2	0	3	14	0	0	.440	.400
Peralta, Edwin	R-R	6-3	175	5-10-01	.241	.261	.234	54	170	30	41	9	1	0	16	34	2	0	1	46	10	6	.306	.372
Pineda, Luis	R-R	6-1	209	3-9-01	.185	.188	.185	24	81	12	15	4	1	2	12	9	1	0	0	33	1	0	.333	.275
Rosario, Andres	R-R	6-3	190	3-11-99	.182	.250	.172	11	33	8	6	0	0	1	1	8	0	0	0	19	1	1	.273	.342
Sanchez, Wilber	R-R	5-10	160	2-21-02	.288	.238	.304	52	177	32	51	13	3	0	25	28	2	0	0	33	13	5	.396	.391
Sanchez, Yolbert	R-R	5-11	176	3-2-97	.297	.296	.298	29	111	19	33	8	1	2	12	15	1	0	0	12	3	3	.441	.386
Tatis, Elijah	R-R	5-11	155	9-27-01	.187	.095	.222	25	75	15	14	2	0	0	10	13	0	0	2	16	5	1	.213	.300

Pitching	B-T	HT	WT	DOB	W	L	ERA	G	GS	CG	SV	IP	H	R	ER	HR	BB	SO	AVG	vLH	vRH	K/9	BB/9
Benitez, Francisco	R-R	6-2	187	9-15-00	0	1	8.06	11	6	0	0	22	19	24	20	1	21	14	.238	.167	.268	5.64	8.46
Caraballo, Jendersson	R-R	6-3	190	10-27-99	0	1	12.71	5	1	0	0	6	4	10	8	0	11	5	.211	.286	.167	7.94	17.47
Castro, Oriel	L-L	6-0	175	5-5-01	1	2	4.73	15	6	0	0	40	30	28	21	2	40	38	.216	.250	.202	8.55	9.00
Castro, Ray	R-R	6-3	165	5-9-97	1	1	2.00	3	2	0	0	9	7	2	2	0	2	13	.206	.167	.250	13.00	2.00
2-team total (9 Rangers1)					5	1	2.01	12	9	0	0	45	30	11	10	0	17	41	.183	.169	.194	8.26	3.43
Cruz, Homer	R-R	6-0	175	9-21-99	5	4	3.86	16	14	0	0	63	57	36	27	2	25	65	.237	.278	.208	9.29	3.57
Ferrer, Jorge	L-L	6-3	180	9-5-00	0	1	2.79	7	1	0	0	9	8	3	2	4	10	8	.243	.167	.280	9.31	3.72
Guzman, Ronaldo	L-L	6-0	180	8-23-02	2	3	4.53	14	12	0	0	52	43	29	26	3	29	76	.221	.171	.234	13.24	5.05
Jimenez, Dionicio	R-R	6-4	190	1-7-01	2	5	4.82	10	9	0	0	37	39	27	20	0	15	30	.273	.300	.266	7.23	3.62
Jimenez, Jose	L-L	6-3	195	8-31-02	1	0	12.71	5	1	0	0	6	7	10	8	1	6	5	.292	.429	.235	7.94	9.53
Lagrange, Daneuris	R-R	6-3	175	6-17-98	2	0	4.02	11	1	0	0	16	13	10	7	1	6	18	.210	.316	.163	10.34	3.45
Mercedes, Matthew	R-R	6-1	195	8-26-98	0	0	27.00	1	0	0	0	1	1	3	3	0	3	1	.250	.000	.500	9.00	27.00
Mola, Carlos	R-R	6-4	190	12-20-00	3	5	5.31	16	7	0	0	59	65	40	35	4	13	56	.285	.369	.236	8.49	1.97
Navarro, Edgar	R-R	6-1	180	2-5-98	3	2	4.20	23	2	0	7	56	65	33	26	2	18	68	.296	.353	.270	10.99	2.91
Nin, Luis	R-R	6-2	185	11-30-96	2	1	3.48	8	0	0	0	21	15	9	8	0	6	23	.211	.111	.245	10.02	2.61
Perez, Erick	R-R	6-1	175	12-9-98	3	0	1.92	23	0	0	4	52	36	15	11	2	24	59	.202	.231	.186	10.28	4.18
Rodriguez, Luis	R-R	6-6	220	4-15-00	3	4	4.34	7	6	0	0	29	30	20	14	1	9	29	.256	.345	.227	9.00	2.79
Rondon, Jesus	R-R	6-3	178	9-22-99	4	2	3.67	22	0	0	1	34	28	23	14	2	25	39	.219	.214	.221	10.22	6.55
Valdez, Cristopher	R-R	6-2	175	9-11-00	0	0	11.57	17	1	0	0	28	30	43	36	2	42	26	.263	.286	.256	8.36	13.50
Veloz, Manuel	R-R	6-2	185	1-28-01	5	0	0.91	15	1	0	3	40	25	11	4	0	7	42	.179	.204	.163	9.53	1.59
Veras, Frander	L-R	6-5	185	10-8-98	2	3	4.32	20	0	0	0	33	35	20	16	0	22	36	.276	.222	.297	9.72	5.94

Fielding

C: Benavides 12, Betancourt 13, Garcia 25, Mendoza 21, Pineda 19. 1B: Bernal 3, Leal 13, Mercedes 28. 2B: Betancourt 1, Espinoza 26, Jimenez 24, Sanchez 21, Tatis 12. 3B: Betancourt 5, Espinoza 20, Jimenez 3, Peralta 48, Rosario 3. SS: Espinoza 12, Peralta 7, Sanchez 30, Sanchez 23, Tatis 11. OF: Bailey 51, Gutierrez 43, Laureano 57, Leal 31, Mercedes 40, Mercedes 1, Rosario 9.

Cincinnati Reds

SEASON IN A SENTENCE: The Reds recorded a winning record in only one month (May, 15-13), and as a result they went on to post their sixth consecutive losing season despite a pitching staff that ranked among the top 10 in the majors in team ERA (4.18).

HIGH POINT: The Reds' offense was the catalyst for the 15-13 record the team compiled during May. They posted nine runs or more in seven games that month, which was a clear bright spot in a season that saw them finish 16 games out of first place in the NL Central. The team also rattled off a season-high six game winning streak in June.

LOW POINT: After posting their first loss of the season on March 31, the Reds lost another seven games in a row to start the month of April. Cincinnati failed to score a run in four of those games. After playing sub-.500 ball from June through the end of the season, the Reds secured the No. 12 overall pick in the 2020 draft.

NOTABLE ROOKIES: Slugging outfielder Aristides Aquino became the first player in major league history to hit 13 homers in his first 100 career plate appearances. He continued to mash, posting a .891 OPS in 56 games for the Reds. Top prospect Nick Senzel saw action in the outfield for Cincinnati, but he ended up on the shelf in September due to a torn right labrum. He finished the year with 12 home runs and a .742 OPS.

KEY TRANSACTIONS: The Reds sent prospects Josiah Gray and Jeter Downs as well as veteran righthander Homer Bailey to the Dodgers in December 2018 for outfielders Matt Kemp and Yasiel Puig, infielder Kyle Farmer and lefthander Alex Wood. Later, the Reds sent Puig and minor league lefty Scott Moss to Cleveland while also sending top prospect Taylor Trammell to San Diego in exchange for Trevor Bauer. The righthander made 10 starts in the second half of the season with Cincinnati. The Reds acquired starter Tanner Roark from the Nationals in exchange for Tanner Rainey, as well as pitchers Sonny Gray and Reiver Sanmartin from the Yankees in exchange for Shed Long and a competitive balance pick before the 2019 season began.

DOWN ON THE FARM: It was a struggle in the minors for Cincinnati. The DSL Reds and Rookie-level Billings were the only two affiliates to qualify for their respective league playoffs. Triple-A Louisville tied for the worst record in the International League at 59-81.

OPENING DAY PAYROLL: $128,815,238 (15th).

PLAYERS OF THE YEAR

ALEX TRAUTWIG

ALEX TRAUTWIG

MAJOR LEAGUE	MINOR LEAGUE
Eugenio Suarez	**Aristides Aquino**
3B	**OF**
.271/.358/.572	(Triple-A)
Led Reds in HR (49),	.299/.356/.636
RBIs (103), OPS (.930)	28 HR, 53 RBIs

ORGANIZATION LEADERS

Batting — *Minimum 250 AB

MAJORS

* AVG	Jose Iglesias	.288
* OPS	Eugenio Suarez	.930
HR	Eugenio Suarez	49
RBI	Eugenio Suarez	103

MINORS

* AVG	Rob Refsnyder, Louisville, AZL Reds	.316
* OBP	Rob Refsnyder, Louisville, AZL Reds	.378
* SLG	Aristides Aquino, Louisville	.636
* OPS	Aristides Aquino, Louisville	.992
R	Michael Siani, Dayton	75
H	Christian Colon, Louisville	149
TB	Brian O'Grady, Louisville	236
2B	Christian Colon, Louisville	37
2B	Jose Garcia, Daytona	37
3B	Narcisco Crook, Chattanooga, Louisville	8
HR	Aristides Aquino, Louisville	28
HR	Brian O'Grady, Louisville	28
RBI	Brian O'Grady, Louisville	77
BB	Bruce Yari, Daytona	66
SO	Jose Siri, Chattanooga, Louisville	165
SB	Michael Siani, Dayton	45

Pitching — #Minimum 75 IP

MAJORS

W	Luis Castillo	15
# ERA	Sonny Gray	2.87
SO	Luis Castillo	226
SV	Raisel Iglesias	34

MINORS

W	Packy Naughton, Daytona, Chattanooga	11
W	Tejay Antone, Chattanooga, Louisville	11
L	Keury Mella, Louisville	14
# ERA	Connor Curlis, Dayton, Daytona	2.92
G	Connor Bennett, Dayton, Daytona	48
G	Andy Cox, Dayton, Daytona, Chattanooga	48
G	Jimmy Herget, Louisville	48
GS	Packy Naughton, Daytona, Chattanooga	28
SV	Andry Cuevas, DSL Reds	15
IP	Packy Naughton, Daytona, Chattanooga	157
BB	Jared Solomon, Dayton, Daytona	61
SO	Tejay Antone, Chattanooga, Louisville	133
# AVG	Adrian Rodriguez, Dayton, Daytona	.226

2019 PERFORMANCE

General Manager: Dick Williams/Nick Krall. **Farm Director:** Jeff Graupe. **Scouting Director:** Chris Buckley.

Class	Team	League	W	L	PCT	Finish	Manager
Majors	Cincinnati Reds	National	75	87	.463	11th (15)	David Bell
Triple-A	Louisville Bats	International	59	81	.421	t-13th (14)	Jody Davis
Double-A	Pensacola Blue Wahoos	Southern	61	75	.449	8th (10)	Pat Kelly
High A	Daytona Tortugas	Florida State	66	68	.493	7th (12)	Ricky Gutierrez
Low A	Dayton Dragons	Midwest	58	82	.414	13th (16)	Luis Bolivar
Rookie	Greeneville Reds	Appalachian	26	41	.388	10th (10)	Gookie Dawkins
Rookie	Billings Mustangs	Pioneer	39	37	.513	4th (8)	Bryan LaHair
Rookie	AZL Reds	Arizona	27	29	.482	t-10th (21)	Jose Nieves
Overall 2019 Minor League Record			336	413	.449	28th (30)	

ORGANIZATION STATISTICS

CINCINNATI REDS
NATIONAL LEAGUE

Batting	B-T	HT	WT	DOB	AVG	vLH	vRH	G	AB	R	H	2B	3B	HR	RBI	BB	HBP	SH	SF	SO	SB	CS	SLG	OBP
Aquino, Aristides	R-R	6-4	220	4-22-94	.259	.265	.256	56	205	31	53	8	0	19	47	16	2	0	2	60	7	0	.576	.316
Barnhart, Tucker	L-R	5-11	192	1-7-91	.231	.133	.247	114	316	32	73	14	0	11	40	44	2	1	1	83	1	0	.380	.328
Blandino, Alex	R-R	6-0	190	11-6-92	.250	.269	.200	23	36	6	9	1	0	1	3	10	2	0	2	14	0	0	.361	.420
Casali, Curt	R-R	6-3	225	11-9-88	.251	.241	.258	84	207	24	52	9	0	8	32	25	1	0	3	59	0	0	.411	.331
Colon, Christian	R-R	5-10	195	5-14-89	.500	.500	.500	8	6	1	3	0	0	0	1	0	2	0	0	0	0	0	.500	.625
Dietrich, Derek	L-R	6-0	205	7-18-89	.187	.160	.190	113	251	41	47	8	2	19	43	28	25	0	1	74	1	1	.462	.328
Ervin, Phillip	R-R	5-10	207	7-15-92	.271	.349	.227	94	236	30	64	11	7	7	23	18	4	0	2	63	4	3	.466	.331
Farmer, Kyle	R-R	6-0	214	8-17-90	.230	.274	.207	97	183	22	42	6	0	9	27	10	3	0	1	59	4	1	.410	.279
Galvis, Freddy	B-R	5-10	185	11-14-89	.234	.300	.218	32	107	12	25	4	0	5	16	7	1	0	1	33	0	1	.411	.285
Gennett, Scooter	L-R	5-10	185	5-1-90	.217	.154	.232	21	69	4	15	3	0	0	5	1	1	0	1	20	0	0	.261	.236
2-team total (21 San Francisco)					.226	.172	.240	42	133	15	30	7	0	2	11	2	2	0	2	41	0	0	.323	.245
Graterol, Juan	R-R	6-1	205	2-14-89	.222	.500	.188	6	18	1	4	0	0	0	1	0	0	0	0	4	0	0	.222	.222
Iglesias, Jose	R-R	5-11	194	1-5-90	.288	.271	.293	146	504	62	145	21	3	11	59	20	3	1	2	70	6	6	.407	.318
Kemp, Matt	R-R	6-4	225	9-23-84	.200	.286	.174	20	60	4	12	2	0	1	5	1	0	0	1	19	0	0	.283	.210
Lavarnway, Ryan	R-R	6-4	240	8-7-87	.278	.000	.333	5	18	4	5	2	0	2	7	1	0	0	0	5	0	0	.722	.316
O'Grady, Brian	L-R	6-2	215	5-17-92	.191	.400	.162	28	42	4	8	2	1	2	3	4	2	0	0	17	0	0	.429	.292
Peraza, Jose	R-R	6-0	196	4-30-94	.239	.287	.220	141	376	37	90	18	2	6	33	17	8	0	2	58	7	6	.346	.285
Puig, Yasiel	R-R	6-2	240	12-7-90	.252	.263	.249	100	373	51	94	15	1	22	61	23	5	0	3	89	14	5	.475	.302
Schebler, Scott	L-R	6-0	228	10-6-90	.124	.154	.118	30	81	11	10	2	0	2	7	14	0	0	0	27	0	1	.222	.253
Senzel, Nick	R-R	6-1	205	6-29-95	.256	.316	.236	104	375	55	96	20	4	12	42	30	3	0	1	101	14	5	.427	.315
Suarez, Eugenio	R-R	5-11	213	7-18-91	.271	.276	.270	159	575	87	156	22	2	49	103	70	11	0	6	189	3	2	.572	.358
VanMeter, Josh	L-R	5-11	165	3-10-95	.237	.125	.250	95	228	33	54	13	1	8	23	29	2	0	1	56	9	3	.408	.327
Votto, Joey	L-R	6-2	220	9-10-83	.261	.243	.268	142	525	79	137	32	1	15	47	76	4	0	3	123	5	0	.411	.357
Winker, Jesse	L-L	6-3	215	8-17-93	.269	.163	.285	113	338	51	91	17	2	16	38	38	8	0	0	60	0	2	.473	.357

Pitching	B-T	HT	WT	DOB	W	L	ERA	G	GS	CG	SV	IP	H	R	ER	HR	BB	SO	AVG	vLH	vRH	K/9	BB/9
Alaniz, R.J.	R-R	6-4	219	6-14-91	1	0	5.40	8	0	0	0	12	8	7	7	0	4	7	.195	.200	.191	5.40	3.09
Bauer, Trevor	R-R	6-1	205	1-17-91	2	5	6.39	10	10	0	0	56	57	42	40	12	19	68	.262	.257	.266	10.86	3.04
Bowman, Matt	R-R	6-0	185	5-31-91	2	0	3.66	27	0	0	0	32	27	15	13	2	13	25	.221	.283	.174	7.03	3.66
Castillo, Luis	R-R	6-2	190	12-12-92	15	8	3.40	32	32	0	0	191	139	76	72	22	79	226	.202	.210	.194	10.67	3.73
DeSclafani, Anthony	R-R	6-1	195	4-18-90	9	9	3.89	31	31	0	0	167	151	77	72	29	49	167	.238	.246	.230	9.02	2.65
Duke, Zach	L-L	6-2	210	4-19-83	3	1	5.01	30	0	0	0	23	21	13	13	4	18	18	.250	.250	.250	6.94	6.94
Farmer, Kyle	R-R	6-0	214	8-17-90	0	0	0.00	1	0	0	0	1	1	0	0	0	0	0	.200	.250	.000	0.00	0.00
Garrett, Amir	R-L	6-5	228	5-3-92	5	3	3.21	69	0	0	0	56	44	22	20	7	35	78	.213	.202	.221	12.54	5.63
Gausman, Kevin	L-R	6-3	190	1-6-91	0	2	4.03	15	1	0	0	22	21	11	10	3	5	29	.250	.238	.262	11.69	2.01
2-team total (16 Atlanta)					3	9	5.72	31	17	0	0	102	113	71	65	15	32	114	.282	.265	.296	10.03	2.81
Gray, Sonny	R-R	5-10	192	11-7-89	11	8	2.87	31	31	0	0	175	122	59	56	17	68	205	.196	.196	.197	10.52	3.49
Herget, Jimmy	R-R	6-3	170	9-9-93	0	0	4.26	5	0	0	0	6	8	3	3	2	3	6	.348	.364	.333	0.00	4.26
Hernandez, David	R-R	6-3	245	5-13-85	2	5	8.02	47	0	0	2	43	53	39	38	7	20	53	.306	.351	.273	11.18	4.22
Hughes, Jared	R-R	6-7	240	7-4-85	3	4	4.10	47	0	0	1	48	41	27	22	6	19	34	.236	.220	.244	6.33	3.54
2-team total (25 Philadelphia)					5	5	4.04	72	0	0	1	57	57	37	32	13	27	54	.224	.193	.238	6.81	3.41
Iglesias, Raisel	R-R	6-2	188	1-4-90	3	12	4.16	68	0	0	34	67	61	31	31	12	21	89	.240	.241	.240	11.96	2.82
Kuhnel, Joel	R-R	6-5	260	2-19-95	1	0	4.66	11	0	0	0	10	8	5	5	1	5	9	.216	.267	.182	8.38	4.66
Lorenzen, Michael	R-R	6-3	217	1-4-92	1	4	2.92	73	0	0	7	83	68	29	27	9	28	85	.222	.195	.240	9.18	3.02
Mahle, Tyler	R-R	6-3	210	9-29-94	3	12	5.14	25	25	0	0	130	136	82	74	25	34	129	.266	.282	.252	8.95	2.36
Mella, Keury	R-R	6-2	200	8-2-93	0	0	7.36	2	0	0	0	4	5	3	3	0	2	4	.313	.400	.167	9.82	4.91
Peralta, Wandy	L-L	6-0	220	7-27-91	1	1	6.09	39	0	0	0	34	36	23	23	10	15	27	.275	.266	.284	7.15	3.97
2-team total (8 San Francisco)					1	1	5.67	47	0	0	0	40	40	25	25	11	16	32	.265	.237	.293	7.26	3.63
Peraza, Jose	R-R	6-0	196	4-30-94	0	0	0.00	2	0	0	0	1	1	0	0	0	0	0	.250	1.000	.000	0.00	0.00
Reed, Cody	L-L	6-5	230	4-15-93	0	0	1.42	3	0	0	0	6	6	1	1	0	1	7	.250	.231	.273	9.95	1.42
Roark, Tanner	R-R	6-2	245	10-5-86	6	7	4.24	21	21	0	0	110	119	55	52	14	38	108	.273	.320	.230	8.81	3.12
Romano, Sal	L-R	6-5	255	10-12-93	1	0	7.71	12	0	0	2	16	22	14	14	4	8	16	.328	.387	.278	8.82	4.41
Sims, Lucas	R-R	6-2	225	5-10-94	2	1	4.60	24	4	0	0	43	31	22	22	8	19	57	.201	.172	.222	11.93	3.98
Stephenson, Robert	R-R	6-3	215	2-24-93	3	2	3.76	57	0	0	0	65	43	30	27	9	24	81	.182	.214	.159	11.27	3.34
Wood, Alex	R-L	6-4	215	1-12-91	1	3	5.80	7	7	0	0	36	41	25	23	11	9	30	.291	.296	.290	7.57	2.27

Fielding

Catcher	PCT	G	PO	A	E	DP	PB
Barnhart	.998	102	812	46	2	2	5
Casali	.995	67	572	31	3	4	3
Farmer	.988	15	78	3	1	0	0
Graterol	1.000	5	46	1	0	1	1
Lavarnway	.980	5	46	3	1	1	1

First Base	PCT	G	PO	A	E	DP
Aquino	.000	1	0	0	0	0
Barnhart	1.000	3	12	1	0	2
Blandino	1.000	1	4	0	0	0
Casali	1.000	4	3	1	0	0
Dietrich	.985	21	119	13	2	8
Farmer	.984	18	58	4	1	6
O'Grady	1.000	2	8	1	0	0
VanMeter	.985	17	55	11	1	4
Votto	.993	133	944	118	7	93

Second Base	PCT	G	PO	A	E	DP
Blandino	.962	10	10	15	1	4
Colon	1.000	3	0	1	0	0
Dietrich	.994	58	63	105	1	28
Farmer	.984	41	25	36	1	7
Galvis	.988	27	31	50	1	7
Gennett	1.000	19	27	39	0	13
Peraza	.972	78	80	126	6	33
Senzel	1.000	1	0	1	0	0
VanMeter	1.000	18	13	22	0	4

Third Base	PCT	G	PO	A	E	DP
Blandino	1.000	4	3	2	0	1
Dietrich	.000	1	0	0	0	0
Farmer	1.000	12	2	9	0	0
Peraza	1.000	5	3	5	0	2
Suarez	.954	158	106	246	17	26
VanMeter	1.000	6	2	4	0	1

Shortstop	PCT	G	PO	A	E	DP
Farmer	1.000	1	1	0	0	0
Galvis	1.000	7	3	9	0	2
Iglesias	.980	144	122	324	9	62
Peraza	.975	39	23	56	2	11

Outfield	PCT	G	PO	A	E	DP
Aquino	.980	54	97	3	2	0
Dietrich	1.000	16	9	0	0	0
Ervin	.982	88	107	2	2	0
Kemp	1.000	17	16	0	0	0
Lorenzen	1.000	29	27	1	0	0
O'Grady	1.000	16	23	0	0	0
Peraza	.963	35	26	0	1	0
Puig	.982	98	160	5	3	1
Schebler	.983	25	57	0	1	0
Senzel	.978	97	177	4	4	1
VanMeter	.952	48	58	1	3	0
Votto	.000	1	0	0	0	0
Winker	.981	93	145	6	3	2

LOUISVILLE BATS   TRIPLE-A
INTERNATIONAL LEAGUE

Batting	B-T	HT	WT	DOB	AVG	vLH	vRH	G	AB	R	H	2B	3B	HR	RBI	BB	HBP	SH	SF	SO	SB	CS	SLG	OBP
Aquino, Aristides	R-R	6-4	220	4-22-94	.299	.313	.294	78	294	56	88	13	1	28	53	23	4	0	2	81	5	1	.636	.356
Barnhart, Tucker	L-R	5-11	192	1-7-91	.333	--	.333	1	3	1	1	0	0	0	0	0	0	0	0	1	0	0	.667	.333
Blandino, Alex	R-R	6-0	190	11-6-92	.247	.279	.229	70	239	36	59	13	1	5	24	40	14	0	0	73	1	3	.372	.386
Brown, Cassidy	R-R	6-3	215	7-21-94	.200	.000	.286	7	20	1	4	0	0	1	3	0	0	0	0	6	0	0	.350	.273
Casali, Curt	R-R	6-3	225	11-9-88	.214	.250	.200	5	14	1	3	0	0	1	1	1	0	0	0	3	0	0	.429	.267
Chavez, Alberti	R-R	5-10	170	7-21-95	.222	.191	.233	30	81	14	18	1	1	1	5	8	1	0	3	19	1	1	.296	.290
Ciuffo, Nick	L-R	6-0	200	3-7-95	.250	.143	.308	7	20	4	5	3	0	1	5	3	0	0	0	6	0	0	.550	.400
2-team total (34 Durham)					.231	.170	.274	41	143	18	33	10	1	3	19	14	0	0	2	43	1	1	.378	.296
Colon, Christian	R-R	5-10	195	5-14-89	.300	.331	.287	136	497	63	149	37	2	10	70	57	7	9	12	58	24	13	.443	.372
Crook, Narciso	R-R	6-3	220	7-12-95	.273	.229	.292	84	275	38	75	16	6	10	35	19	4	0	0	84	9	2	.484	.329
Dietrich, Derek	L-R	6-0	205	7-18-89	.182	.667	.000	3	11	2	2	0	0	0	0	1	0	0	0	2	0	0	.182	.250
Ervin, Phillip	R-R	5-10	207	7-15-92	.290	.258	.298	40	145	27	42	8	1	6	26	19	5	0	3	34	6	4	.483	.384
Farmer, Kyle	R-R	6-0	214	8-17-90	.000	.000	.000	1	4	1	0	0	0	0	0	0	0	0	0	2	0	0	.000	.000
Gennett, Scooter	L-R	5-10	185	5-1-90	.167	.000	.182	3	12	0	2	1	0	0	0	0	0	0	0	2	0	0	.250	.167
Gonzalez, Luis	R-R	6-0	175	7-28-94	.263	.385	.200	13	38	8	10	2	0	0	3	4	0	0	0	9	0	1	.316	.333
Graterol, Juan	R-R	6-1	205	3-24-89	.249	.296	.232	58	209	19	52	8	1	2	26	14	2	0	1	18	0	1	.325	.301
Hawkins, Courtney	R-R	6-3	245	11-12-93	.167	.118	.189	15	54	5	9	4	0	2	4	1	1	0	0	21	0	1	.352	.196
Johnson, Sherman	L-R	5-10	190	7-15-90	.241	.281	.226	71	203	32	49	9	1	4	15	34	1	3	0	55	4	4	.355	.353
Lavarnway, Ryan	R-R	6-4	240	8-7-87	.225	.154	.259	13	40	6	9	2	0	3	7	6	0	0	1	9	0	0	.500	.319
3-team total (4 Columbus, 35 Scranton/Wilkes-Barre)					.226	.275	.204	52	159	21	36	5	0	6	28	25	3	0	3	36	0	0	.371	.337
Longhi, Nick	R-L	6-2	205	8-16-95	.283	.339	.259	111	389	51	110	28	3	12	51	30	2	1	2	102	0	1	.463	.336
Martinez, Valentin	R-R	6-0	175	9-21-96	.222	.250	.200	3	9	1	2	2	0	0	1	0	0	0	0	2	0	0	.444	.300
Nay, Mitch	R-R	6-3	200	9-20-93	.210	.333	.157	32	100	12	21	3	0	4	19	9	0	0	0	26	0	0	.360	.275
O'Grady, Brian	L-R	6-2	215	5-17-92	.280	.316	.264	112	429	71	120	30	1	28	77	51	4	0	4	136	20	4	.550	.359
Okey, Chris	R-R	5-11	200	12-29-94	.121	.250	.048	9	33	2	4	1	0	0	3	0	0	0	0	13	0	0	.152	.121
Peraza, Jose	R-R	6-0	196	4-30-94	.600	.500	.636	4	15	3	9	2	0	0	1	0	0	0	0	2	1	1	.733	.600
Refsnyder, Rob	R-R	6-0	205	3-26-91	.315	.361	.297	85	298	42	94	21	2	10	45	31	1	0	4	86	0	2	.500	.377
Rodriguez, Alfredo	R-R	6-0	190	6-17-94	.169	.167	.170	23	77	5	13	4	0	0	9	7	3	0	1	13	3	0	.221	.261
Schebler, Scott	L-R	6-0	228	10-6-90	.217	.158	.241	53	194	18	42	6	0	5	17	12	4	0	2	51	0	1	.325	.274
Senzel, Nick	R-R	6-1	205	6-29-95	.257	.308	.227	8	35	7	9	1	0	1	2	3	0	0	0	10	0	0	.371	.316
Siri, Jose	R-R	6-2	175	7-22-95	.186	.194	.182	30	102	16	19	4	1	0	3	9	0	1	0	39	5	2	.245	.252
Sparks, Taylor	R-R	6-4	200	4-3-93	.000	.000	.000	1	3	0	0	0	0	0	1	0	0	0	0	3	0	0	.000	.250
Trahan, Blake	R-R	5-9	180	5-9-93	.226	.245	.218	101	354	34	80	14	2	5	29	22	5	2	3	84	3	5	.319	.279
Tromp, Chadwick	R-R	5-9	205	3-21-95	.286	.160	.346	26	77	15	22	2	1	7	21	11	2	0	0	25	0	1	.610	.389
Turner, Stuart	R-R	6-2	220	12-27-91	.156	.214	.132	28	96	8	15	2	0	1	11	4	0	2	0	28	0	0	.208	.190
VanMeter, Josh	L-R	5-11	165	3-10-95	.348	.359	.344	49	181	43	63	14	1	14	43	24	3	1	2	37	8	3	.669	.429
Wren, Kyle	L-L	5-10	180	4-23-91	.220	.000	.333	19	50	7	11	2	1	0	1	7	0	1	0	15	1	2	.300	.316

Pitching	B-T	HT	WT	DOB	W	L	ERA	G	GS	CG	SV	IP	H	R	ER	HR	BB	SO	AVG	vLH	vRH	K/9	BB/9
Alaniz, R.J.	R-R	6-4	219	6-14-91	1	2	2.93	25	0	0	4	28	25	11	9	1	11	31	.238	.333	.182	10.08	3.58
Antone, Tejay	R-R	6-4	205	12-5-93	4	8	4.65	14	13	0	0	72	93	42	37	7	31	70	.322	.357	.295	8.79	3.89
Archer, Tristan	R-R	6-2	200	10-18-90	0	0	6.75	10	0	0	0	13	21	11	10	4	5	10	.368	.367	.370	6.75	3.38
Bass, Anthony	R-R	6-2	200	11-1-87	1	1	2.21	19	0	0	9	20	13	7	5	1	6	19	.181	.240	.149	8.41	2.66
Bautista, Wendolyn	R-R	6-0	185	3-27-93	0	0	4.50	5	0	0	1	8	10	4	4	0	3	7	.303	.412	.188	7.88	3.38
Bowman, Matt	R-R	6-0	185	5-31-91	1	1	2.08	29	0	0	4	39	28	11	9	1	18	35	.204	.250	.173	8.08	4.15
Boxberger, Brad	R-R	6-2	205	5-27-88	0	0	11.81	5	0	0	0	5	10	8	7	2	5	8	.385	.600	.250	13.50	8.44
Chavez, Alberti	R-R	5-10	170	7-21-95	0	0	7.20	3	0	0	0	5	11	7	4	2	6	0	.423	.286	.583	0.00	10.80
Collins, Tim	L-L	5-7	170	8-21-89	1	0	6.75	5	0	0	0	4	5	3	3	1	3	3	.333	.444	.167	6.75	6.75
Colon, Christian	R-R	5-10	195	5-14-89	0	0	9.00	1	0	0	0	2	3	2	2	0	1	0	.300	.500	.250	0.00	4.50
Despaigne, Odrisamer	R-R	6-0	200	4-4-87	3	2	3.92	8	8	0	0	41	40	21	18	5	16	40	.253	.290	.220	8.71	3.48

	B-T	HT	WT	DOB																
2-team total (16 Charlotte)					8	6	3.47	24	22	0	0	124	123	52	48	11	44	124	.260	.294 .229 8.98 3.18
Grimm, Justin	R-R	6-3	210	8-16-88	2	0	4.50	17	0	0	0	24	14	12	12	3	17	28	.165	.156 .170 10.50 6.38
Gutierrez, Vladimir	R-R	6-0	190	9-18-95	6	11	6.04	27	27	0	0	137	144	100	92	26	48	117	.266	.282 .256 7.69 3.15
Hawkins, Courtney	R-R	6-3	245	11-12-93	0	0	0.00	1	0	0	0	1	1	0	0	0	0	0	.333	.000 1.000 0.00 0.00
Herget, Jimmy	R-R	6-3	170	9-9-93	3	4	2.91	48	0	0	2	59	41	22	19	7	36	68	.193	.189 .196 10.43 5.52
Jiminian, Johendi	R-R	6-3	170	10-14-92	0	0	9.00	1	0	0	0	5	9	5	5	1	2	2	.391	.333 .455 3.60 3.60
Krol, Ian	L-L	6-1	210	5-9-91	1	3	5.33	28	0	0	1	25	27	16	15	2	12	28	.278	.313 .245 9.95 4.26
2-team total (18 Rochester)					1	4	5.28	46	0	0	9	46	54	29	27	3	22	58	.295	.257 .321 11.35 4.30
Kuhnel, Joel	R-R	6-5	260	2-19-95	2	1	2.00	16	0	0	4	18	13	5	4	1	8	20	.200	.250 .171 10.00 4.00
Lopez, Jose	R-R	6-1	205	9-1-93	2	4	6.84	11	10	1	0	50	63	40	38	13	26	44	.309	.360 .270 7.92 4.68
Mahle, Tyler	R-R	6-3	210	9-29-94	1	2	4.00	3	3	0	0	9	8	4	4	0	3	13	.242	.300 .154 13.00 3.00
Mantiply, Joe	R-L	6-4	215	3-1-91	0	0	3.72	18	0	0	1	29	26	12	12	2	3	26	.241	.188 .263 8.07 0.93
2-team total (6 Scranton/Wilkes-Barre)					0	0	3.99	24	0	0	1	38	37	18	17	5	4	33	.252	.191 .276 7.75 0.94
Markey, Brad	R-R	5-10	185	3-3-92	3	7	7.49	11	5	0	0	34	41	30	28	4	15	13	.295	.299 .292 3.48 4.01
Martinez, Juan	L-L	6-2	175	7-15-92	0	0	23.40	2	1	0	0	5	15	13	13	4	4	4	.517	.500 .526 7.20 7.20
Mella, Keury	R-R	6-2	200	8-2-93	8	14	5.05	27	27	0	0	143	160	93	80	22	56	102	.281	.379 .214 6.43 3.53
Peralta, Wandy	L-L	6-0	220	7-27-91	0	0	3.27	12	0	0	0	11	11	4	4	0	1	7	.262	.200 .318 5.73 0.82
Powers, Alex	R-R	6-4	205	2-26-92	0	0	1.98	23	1	0	2	27	24	6	6	1	12	33	.238	.244 .232 10.87 3.95
Reed, Cody	L-L	6-5	230	4-15-93	1	2	2.61	18	0	0	0	21	13	6	6	1	8	25	.183	.182 .184 10.89 3.48
Reyes, Jesus	R-R	6-2	180	2-21-93	1	6	5.03	43	7	0	0	77	75	52	43	11	54	64	.258	.271 .249 7.48 6.31
Romano, Sal	L-R	6-5	255	10-12-93	4	8	4.28	43	5	0	1	69	72	38	33	6	26	76	.269	.300 .250 9.87 3.38
Sims, Lucas	R-R	6-2	225	5-10-94	5	0	4.56	16	16	0	0	79	69	43	40	9	36	102	.235	.241 .230 11.62 4.10
Stephens, Jackson	R-R	6-2	220	5-11-94	8	4	5.14	47	2	0	0	84	93	54	48	6	37	80	.285	.279 .290 8.57 3.96
Stephenson, Robert	R-R	6-3	215	2-24-93	0	1	4.50	2	0	0	2	3	1	1	0	1	3	.333	.333 .333 13.50 4.50
Stout, Eric	L-L	6-3	205	3-27-93	2	2	6.27	20	9	0	0	60	68	43	42	15	37	52	.286	.371 .250 7.76 5.52
Tazawa, Junichi	R-R	5-11	200	6-6-86	0	0	0.00	2	0	0	0	3	1	0	0	1	0	.111	.000 .200 0.00 3.00
Wood, Alex	R-L	6-4	215	1-12-91	0	1	5.06	3	3	0	0	5	8	4	3	0	2	7	.333	.250 .375 11.81 3.38
Wooten, Rob	R-R	6-1	200	7-21-85	0	1	13.50	3	3	0	0	7	12	11	11	0	4	6	.375	.500 .214 7.36 4.91

Fielding

Catcher	PCT	G	PO	A	E	DP	PB
Barnhart	1.000	1	4	1	0	1	0
Brown	.962	7	47	3	2	0	0
Casali	1.000	3	21	1	0	1	2
Ciuffo	1.000	6	64	3	0	0	0
Farmer	1.000	1	3	0	0	0	0
Graterol	.990	58	472	29	5	4	1
Lavarnway	1.000	11	96	5	0	1	1
Martinez	1.000	3	29	2	0	0	1
Okey	.988	9	78	6	1	1	2
Tromp	1.000	22	174	5	0	1	1
Turner	.986	27	196	11	3	0	2

First Base	PCT	G	PO	A	E	DP
Colon	1.000	6	20	2	0	4
Dietrich	1.000	1	1	0	0	0
Graterol	1.000	1	1	0	0	0
Longhi	.994	50	335	25	2	38
Nay	.988	23	159	4	2	16
O'Grady	.985	64	494	35	8	52
VanMeter	.990	13	91	10	1	12

Second Base	PCT	G	PO	A	E	DP
Blandino	.981	35	70	83	3	30
Chavez	.975	12	16	23	1	5
Colon	1.000	7	9	10	0	2
Dietrich	1.000	1	5	2	0	1
Gennett	1.000	1	3	7	9	0 2
Gonzalez	1.000	8	17	16	0	9
Johnson	.984	48	53	126	3	24
Peraza	1.000	2	3	6	0	2
Trahan	.987	27	29	46	1	12
VanMeter	.973	22	26	46	2	14

Third Base	PCT	G	PO	A	E	DP
Blandino	.951	15	9	30	2	0
Chavez	1.000	5	2	8	0	2
Colon	.963	105	69	192	10	27
Gonzalez	1.000	1	1	0	0	0
Johnson	.000	1	0	0	0	0
Nay	.857	8	5	7	2	0
O'Grady	.800	3	3	1	1	0
Sparks	1.000	1	0	1	0	0
VanMeter	.923	10	10	14	2	2

Shortstop	PCT	G	PO	A	E	DP
Blandino	.943	18	24	42	4	6
Chavez	.983	15	16	41	1	12
Colon	.980	15	18	32	1	6
Gonzalez	1.000	3	4	6	0	2
Peraza	1.000	1	1	1	0	0
Rodriguez	.964	23	23	58	3	9
Trahan	.990	73	86	213	3	47
VanMeter	1.000	1	1	0	0	0

Outfield	PCT	G	PO	A	E	DP
Aquino	.945	69	130	8	8	3
Crook	.991	61	108	4	1	0
Ervin	1.000	34	71	2	0	1
Hawkins	1.000	11	12	0	0	0
Longhi	1.000	52	69	2	0	0
O'Grady	.991	47	107	3	1	0
Peraza	1.000	1	2	0	0	0
Refsnyder	.973	71	106	3	3	1
Schebler	.990	44	98	1	1	1
Senzel	.938	8	15	0	1	0
Siri	.982	30	51	5	1	1
Trahan	1.000	5	5	0	0	0
VanMeter	1.000	6	3	0	0	0
Wren	.966	14	28	0	1	0

CHATTANOOGA LOOKOUTS

DOUBLE-A

SOUTHERN LEAGUE

Batting	B-T	HT	WT	DOB	AVG	vLH	vRH	G	AB	R	H	2B	3B	HR	RBI	BB	HBP	SH	SF	SO	SB	CS	SLG	OBP
Bell, Brantley	R-R	6-3	185	11-16-94	.243	.220	.251	115	358	42	87	19	0	6	36	30	7	1	2	63	10	5	.346	.312
Beltre, Michael	L-R	6-3	220	7-3-95	.234	.174	.249	80	231	28	54	6	2	3	29	29	2	3	3	57	3	2	.316	.321
Brown, Cassidy	R-R	6-3	215	7-21-94	.250	.375	.167	6	20	5	5	2	0	1	4	4	0	1	0	7	0	0	.500	.375
Chavez, Alberti	R-R	5-10	170	7-21-95	.225	.308	.194	33	98	9	22	4	0	0	8	7	2	0	1	25	0	1	.265	.287
Crook, Narciso	R-R	6-3	220	7-12-95	.296	.182	.347	24	71	11	21	6	2	0	6	5	0	0	0	18	1	1	.437	.342
Daal, Calten	R-R	6-1	180	8-1-93	.301	.338	.289	82	279	27	84	7	3	0	32	9	0	2	1	52	5	3	.348	.322
Duenez, Samir	L-R	6-1	230	6-11-96	.270	.462	.220	17	63	6	17	2	0	1	9	5	0	0	2	12	0	0	.349	.314
Fairchild, Stuart	R-R	6-0	190	3-17-96	.275	.394	.242	42	153	25	42	12	1	4	17	19	7	0	0	23	3	2	.444	.380
Flete, Bryant	L-R	5-10	146	1-31-93	.071	.000	.083	8	14	0	1	0	0	0	0	1	0	0	0	6	0	0	.071	.133
Friedl, TJ	L-L	5-10	180	8-14-95	.235	.200	.246	65	226	38	53	11	4	5	28	29	11	1	2	50	13	4	.385	.347
Gonzalez, Luis	R-R	6-0	175	7-28-94	.326	.214	.375	17	46	9	15	5	1	0	8	3	1	1	0	7	0	0	.478	.380
Hawkins, Courtney	R-R	6-3	245	11-12-93	.222	.000	.333	3	9	0	2	0	0	0	1	0	0	0	0	5	0	0	.222	.222
India, Jonathan	R-R	6-0	200	12-15-96	.270	.310	.256	34	111	24	30	3	3	14	22	8	0	4	26	4	0	.378	.414
Isabel, Ibandel	R-R	6-4	225	6-20-95	.243	.330	.207	91	334	52	81	12	1	26	69	26	6	0	2	153	0	0	.518	.307
LaValley, Gavin	R-R	6-3	235	12-28-94	.254	.337	.227	119	394	58	100	22	2	10	56	47	5	1	2	111	2	2	.396	.339
Mendoza, Yonathan	B-R	5-11	167	2-10-94	.233	.182	.263	10	30	4	7	2	0	0	3	3	0	0	0	6	0	0	.300	.303
Nay, Mitch	R-R	6-3	200	9-20-93	.304	.254	.323	82	253	48	77	22	2	13	54	25	2	0	4	48	1	0	.561	.366

	B-T	HT	WT	DOB	AVG	vLH	vRH	G	AB	R	H	2B	3B	HR	RBI	BB	HBP	SH	SF	SO	SB	CS	SLG	OBP
O'Neill, Michael	R-R	6-1	195	6-12-92	.302	.200	.333	22	86	15	26	2	0	1	4	6	1	2	0	20	0	0	.361	.355
2-team total (57 Biloxi)					.291	.290	.292	79	292	42	85	7	1	5	23	22	3	2	0	82	15	3	.373	.347
Okey, Chris	R-R	5-11	200	12-29-94	.228	.290	.212	49	149	21	34	6	1	7	25	19	1	1	1	52	0	0	.423	.318
Rodriguez, Alfredo	R-R	6-0	190	6-17-94	.286	.255	.297	104	409	50	117	18	2	1	25	22	2	2	1	62	13	9	.347	.325
Siri, Jose	R-R	6-2	175	7-22-95	.251	.227	.262	101	366	46	92	15	1	11	50	33	1	2	3	126	21	6	.388	.313
Stephenson, Tyler	R-R	6-4	225	8-16-96	.285	.329	.270	89	312	47	89	19	1	6	44	37	9	0	5	60	0	0	.410	.372
Trammell, Taylor	L-L	6-2	215	9-13-97	.236	.286	.216	94	318	47	75	8	3	6	33	54	4	0	5	86	17	4	.337	.349

Pitching	B-T	HT	WT	DOB	W	L	ERA	G	GS	CG	SV	IP	H	R	ER	HR	BB	SO	AVG	vLH	vRH	K/9	BB/9
Antone, Tejay	R-R	6-4	205	12-5-93	7	4	3.38	13	13	0	0	75	63	38	28	4	22	63	.227	.226	.228	7.59	2.65
Bautista, Wendolyn	R-R	6-0	185	3-27-93	2	4	6.64	12	7	0	0	39	64	33	29	5	10	36	.368	.337	.398	8.24	2.29
Boyles, Ty	R-L	6-3	270	9-30-95	2	2	4.36	47	0	0	1	66	65	33	32	9	34	64	.258	.239	.273	8.73	4.64
Cox, Andy	R-L	6-2	194	10-23-93	0	0	0.00	2	0	0	0	2	2	0	0	0	1	4	.250	.167	.500	18.00	4.50
Finnegan, Brandon	L-L	5-11	198	4-14-93	1	0	6.60	13	0	0	0	15	14	11	11	1	10	17	.255	.174	.313	10.20	6.00
Flete, Bryant	L-R	5-10	146	1-31-93	0	0	18.00	1	0	0	0	1	2	2	2	1	0	0	.400	.000	.667	0.00	9.00
Fossas, Aaron	R-R	6-2	200	9-2-92	4	3	6.70	28	0	0	0	46	53	37	34	4	15	36	.280	.282	.280	7.09	2.96
Hendrix, Ryan	R-R	6-3	185	12-16-94	3	0	2.33	16	0	0	2	19	14	6	5	0	8	23	.200	.214	.191	10.71	3.72
Howard, Nick	R-R	6-4	215	4-6-93	0	1	10.80	3	0	0	0	3	8	7	4	0	3	2	.471	.500	.455	5.40	8.10
Jay, Tyler	L-L	6-1	185	4-19-94	0	0	3.03	18	0	0	0	33	34	11	11	1	12	33	.281	.218	.333	9.09	3.31
2-team total (17 Pensacola)					1	2	3.86	35	0	0	1	61	70	30	26	2	31	60	.294	.198	.354	8.90	4.60
Jiminian, Johendi	R-R	6-3	170	10-14-92	5	5	4.29	28	15	0	0	94	104	53	45	8	37	72	.281	.295	.270	6.87	3.53
Johnson, Jordan	R-R	6-3	200	9-15-93	0	6	6.98	9	9	0	0	39	40	36	30	3	29	39	.258	.229	.292	9.08	6.75
Kuhnel, Joel	R-R	6-5	260	2-19-95	3	2	2.27	25	0	0	10	36	26	10	9	5	8	30	.202	.138	.254	7.57	2.02
Lillie, Ryan	R-R	6-0	210	5-1-96	1	4	8.39	6	5	0	0	25	33	25	23	4	11	20	.314	.191	.397	7.30	4.01
Mantiply, Joe	R-R	6-4	215	3-1-91	1	0	13.50	1	0	0	0	3	2	2	2	0	2	0	.429	.667	.250	0.00	13.50
Markey, Brad	R-R	5-10	185	3-3-92	2	2	6.11	6	0	0	0	28	32	22	19	9	3	26	.283	.237	.333	8.36	0.96
2-team total (9 Tennessee)					3	4	5.86	15	9	0	0	55	66	40	36	13	11	48	.299	.262	.333	7.81	1.79
Martinez, Juan	L-L	6-2	175	7-15-92	3	3	3.60	34	1	0	11	45	43	21	18	5	17	34	.253	.214	.280	6.80	3.40
Mendoza, Yonathan	B-R	5-11	167	2-10-94	0	0	0.00	2	0	0	0	2	3	3	0	1	0	0	.333	.400	.250	0.00	0.00
Moss, Scott	L-L	6-6	225	10-6-94	6	5	3.44	20	20	2	0	102	84	45	39	7	57	123	.227	.277	.200	10.85	5.03
Naughton, Packy	R-L	6-2	195	4-16-96	6	10	3.66	19	19	0	0	106	109	51	43	8	26	81	.266	.299	.251	6.90	2.21
Nutof, Ryan	L-R	6-2	190	11-2-95	3	0	5.89	15	0	0	0	18	22	12	12	2	9	17	.301	.313	.293	8.35	4.42
Payano, Victor	L-L	6-5	185	10-17-92	2	0	4.70	16	0	0	0	23	28	12	12	2	4	18	.304	.270	.327	7.04	1.57
Powers, Alex	R-R	6-4	205	2-26-92	2	0	1.23	17	0	0	6	22	10	3	3	2	6	33	.133	.107	.074	13.50	2.45
Sanmartin, Reiver	L-L	6-2	160	4-15-96	2	7	4.34	12	12	0	0	58	61	41	28	6	17	54	.260	.208	.285	8.38	2.64
Santillan, Tony	R-R	6-3	240	4-15-97	2	8	4.84	21	21	0	0	102	110	59	55	8	54	92	.280	.228	.335	8.09	4.75
Stallings, Jesse	R-R	6-2	194	10-27-94	0	3	6.00	30	0	0	2	33	41	24	22	2	4	19	.302	.294	.306	5.18	1.09
Stout, Eric	L-L	6-3	205	3-27-93	0	0	0.00	1	0	0	0	2	1	0	0	0	0	2	.143	.000	.333	9.00	0.00
Strahan, Wyatt	R-R	6-3	220	4-18-93	0	3	7.74	35	1	0	0	55	68	49	47	6	27	44	.304	.362	.262	7.24	4.45
Thompson, Cory	R-R	5-11	180	9-23-94	2	1	4.21	33	0	0	0	36	44	22	17	8	14	27	.291	.321	.276	6.69	3.47
Wood, Alex	R-L	6-4	215	1-12-91	1	0	1.50	1	1	0	0	6	4	1	1	0	4	5	.191	.000	.250	6.00	0.00
Wooten, Rob	R-R	6-1	200	7-21-85	1	2	4.40	6	0	0	0	29	31	16	14	5	4	24	.267	.281	.250	7.53	1.26

Fielding

Catcher	PCT	G	PO	A	E	DP	PB
Brown	1.000	6	58	6	0	0	0
Okey	.984	44	328	30	6	7	3
Stephenson	.992	87	653	54	6	5	5
Gonzalez	.944	5	5	12	1	1	
LaValley	1.000	1	0	1	0	0	
Mendoza	1.000	1	2	4	0	1	
Flete	1.000	2	1	7	0	0	
Gonzalez	.941	7	5	11	1	1	
Mendoza	1.000	5	10	15	0	4	
Rodriguez	.981	99	123	233	7	39	

First Base	PCT	G	PO	A	E	DP
Duenez	1.000	6	34	3	0	4
Isabel	.997	51	348	16	1	27
LaValley	.993	41	279	16	2	23
Nay	.991	45	313	26	3	25

Second Base	PCT	G	PO	A	E	DP
Bell	.960	60	80	134	9	20
Chavez	.889	3	5	3	1	0
Daal	.945	73	126	151	16	37
Flete	1.000	1	1	1	0	0

Third Base	PCT	G	PO	A	E	DP
Bell	.864	13	7	12	3	0
Chavez	1.000	2	1	1	0	0
Gonzalez	1.000	5	0	1	0	1
India	.908	33	20	49	7	4
LaValley	.918	71	47	99	13	8
Mendoza	1.000	2	1	3	0	0
Nay	1.000	20	16	28	0	4
Rodriguez	1.000	2	3	3	0	0

Shortstop	PCT	G	PO	A	E	DP
Bell	.765	3	6	7	4	2
Chavez	.949	28	29	65	5	16

Outfield	PCT	G	PO	A	E	DP
Bell	.927	20	36	2	3	1
Beltre	.986	67	139	2	2	0
Crook	.925	15	37	0	3	0
Fairchild	1.000	42	107	3	0	1
Friedl	.959	62	112	5	5	0
Isabel	1.000	15	26	0	0	0
O'Neill	.971	21	31	2	1	1
Okey	1.000	1	2	0	0	0
Siri	.989	99	271	9	3	4
Trammell	.952	91	171	7	9	1

DAYTONA TORTUGAS HIGH CLASS A

FLORIDA STATE LEAGUE

Batting	B-T	HT	WT	DOB	AVG	vLH	vRH	G	AB	R	H	2B	3B	HR	RBI	BB	HBP	SH	SF	SO	SB	CS	SLG	OBP
Beltre, Michael	L-R	6-3	220	7-3-95	.319	.500	.302	13	47	7	15	2	0	1	8	7	0	0	0	11	1	1	.426	.407
Cedrola, Lorenzo	R-R	5-8	152	1-12-98	.277	.273	.278	102	343	41	95	10	7	1	28	17	12	5	4	43	18	10	.356	.330
Clementina, Hendrik	R-R	6-0	250	6-17-97	.249	.254	.247	91	338	30	84	13	0	14	54	19	5	0	3	92	1	0	.411	.296
Fairchild, Stuart	R-R	6-0	190	3-17-96	.258	.164	.285	67	248	32	64	17	2	8	37	25	5	0	3	60	3	5	.440	.335
Flete, Bryant	L-R	5-10	146	1-31-93	.277	.231	.283	32	112	18	31	2	0	3	9	18	6	1	0	26	0	0	.375	.404
Garcia, Jose	R-R	6-2	175	4-5-98	.280	.291	.277	104	404	58	113	37	1	8	55	25	17	0	6	83	15	2	.436	.343
Gennett, Scooter	L-R	5-10	185	5-1-90	.143	.200	.111	4	14	1	2	1	0	0	1	0	0	0	3	0	0	0	.214	.200
Gordon, Miles	L-R	6-1	175	12-3-97	.206	.125	.218	19	63	4	13	1	3	0	6	5	0	2	0	15	2	0	.318	.265
Hannah, Jameson	L-L	5-9	185	8-10-97	.224	.125	.255	18	67	6	15	3	1	0	6	9	1	1	0	16	2	1	.299	.325
Harris, Dylan	R-R	5-11	199	1-27-95	.214	.111	.263	7	28	2	6	1	0	0	2	0	1	0	0	7	0	0	.250	.241
India, Jonathan	R-R	6-0	200	12-15-96	.256	.286	.247	87	317	50	81	15	5	8	30	37	9	0	4	84	7	5	.410	.346
Kolozsvary, Mark	R-R	5-8	180	9-4-95	.188	.259	.167	79	234	26	44	11	1	6	21	38	17	1	1	78	0	4	.321	.341
Liberatore, Ernesto	R-R	6-0	210	3-26-96	.091	.000	.100	4	11	0	1	0	0	0	0	0	0	1	8	0	0	.182	.083

CINCINNATI REDS

	B-T	HT	WT	DOB	AVG	vLH	vRH	G	AB	R	H	2B	3B	HR	RBI	BB	HBP	SH	SF	SO	SB	CS	SLG	OBP
Lopez, Alejo	B-R	5-10	170	5-5-96	.287	.253	.295	124	481	67	138	17	3	2	50	38	14	1	5	80	9	6	.347	.353
Manzanero, Pabel	R-R	6-3	236	1-30-96	.224	.188	.232	22	85	6	19	2	0	0	4	0	2	0	1	29	0	0	.247	.239
Mendoza, Yonathan	B-R	5-11	167	2-10-94	.237	.215	.243	80	279	34	66	6	1	3	25	27	0	2	1	53	1	4	.298	.303
Mount, Drew	L-R	5-11	205	3-24-96	.253	.143	.272	76	281	33	71	12	4	1	33	13	2	0	1	84	17	7	.335	.290
Munroe, Shard	L-L	6-0	189	6-15-96	.152	.000	.194	16	46	5	7	0	0	1	8	6	0	0	1	14	2	0	.217	.245
Rey, Brian	R-R	5-11	170	2-22-98	.146	.143	.147	16	48	3	7	2	0	0	6	2	2	0	0	5	1	0	.188	.212
Rivero, Carlos	L-R	6-0	175	4-30-97	.140	.143	.140	14	50	2	7	1	0	1	3	0	0	1	0	20	1	2	.220	.140
Santana, Leandro	R-R	6-2	200	2-19-97	.091	.000	.143	3	11	1	1	1	0	0	3	1	0	0	0	5	0	0	.182	.167
Sugilio, Andy	R-R	6-2	170	10-26-96	.294	.235	.307	118	456	57	134	11	5	3	39	24	2	1	2	92	23	11	.360	.331
Ventura, Randy	B-R	5-9	165	7-11-97	.226	.111	.253	31	93	11	21	2	0	0	8	17	1	0	3	29	3	0	.247	.342
Yari, Bruce	L-L	6-3	224	12-9-94	.225	.238	.222	120	418	54	94	18	6	7	54	66	2	0	5	130	2	2	.347	.330

Pitching	B-T	HT	WT	DOB	W	L	ERA	G	GS	CG	SV	IP	H	R	ER	HR	BB	SO	AVG	vLH	vRH	K/9	BB/9
Bautista, Wendolyn	R-R	6-0	185	3-27-93	4	3	3.58	18	8	1	5	60	52	26	24	8	13	64	.228	.272	.184	9.55	1.94
Bennett, Connor	R-R	5-9	212	4-10-97	0	2	2.08	15	0	0	1	17	13	5	4	2	7	25	.200	.280	.150	12.98	3.63
Byrne, Michael	R-R	6-3	205	4-16-97	7	3	4.27	37	6	0	3	65	72	34	31	7	15	60	.278	.265	.290	8.27	2.07
Cox, Andy	R-L	6-2	194	10-23-93	3	4	2.45	35	0	0	9	37	34	13	10	1	20	49	.248	.250	.247	12.03	4.91
Curlis, Connor	L-L	6-1	180	11-29-96	1	0	0.96	2	2	0	0	9	12	1	1	0	3	7	.324	.571	.267	6.75	2.89
Diaz, Carlos	L-L	6-3	190	2-3-92	0	1	6.00	5	0	0	1	3	1	2	2	0	6	4	.100	.500	.000	12.00	18.00
Fossas, Aaron	R-R	6-2	200	9-2-92	1	2	5.10	8	8	0	0	42	55	27	24	0	14	24	.322	.330	.311	5.10	2.98
Ghyzel, John	R-R	6-5	200	5-18-96	5	2	5.89	38	0	0	2	55	58	37	36	2	33	49	.276	.303	.256	8.02	5.40
Jordan, Andrew	R-R	6-3	180	8-3-97	0	0	0.00	1	1	0	0	5	3	0	0	0	4	6	.200	.167	.222	10.80	7.20
Lillie, Ryan	R-R	6-0	210	5-1-96	3	8	3.74	20	20	0	0	111	100	54	46	15	33	90	.240	.260	.220	7.32	2.68
Lopez, Diomar	R-R	5-11	165	12-15-96	4	1	2.72	28	0	0	2	43	40	17	13	1	9	53	.244	.253	.236	11.09	1.88
Machorro, Carlos	R-R	6-2	175	9-20-96	0	0	10.13	1	0	0	0	3	4	3	3	0	1	2	.333	.400	.286	6.75	3.38
Moreta, Dauri	R-R	6-2	185	4-15-96	1	0	2.35	35	0	0	2	57	46	18	15	6	9	64	.223	.189	.250	10.05	1.41
Naughton, Packy	R-L	6-2	195	4-16-96	5	2	2.63	9	9	0	0	51	49	16	15	2	9	50	.248	.281	.231	8.77	1.58
Nutof, Ryan	L-R	6-2	190	11-2-95	4	1	2.61	25	0	0	10	31	21	10	9	1	8	39	.193	.140	.237	11.32	2.32
Olson, Ryan	R-R	6-2	195	11-22-94	1	3	4.91	9	0	0	0	15	15	9	8	1	8	17	.254	.367	.138	10.43	4.91
Orewiler, Austin	R-R	6-2	220	5-18-93	8	11	4.56	27	26	0	0	126	138	74	64	11	46	90	.284	.293	.277	6.41	3.28
Pinto, Julio	R-R	6-3	223	11-18-95	2	3	5.51	31	0	0	3	47	57	31	29	3	29	49	.303	.337	.275	9.32	5.51
Rodriguez, Adrian	R-R	6-1	233	8-8-96	0	0	8.10	3	0	0	0	3	3	3	3	1	1	2	.231	.500	.111	5.40	2.70
Romero, Wennington	L-L	5-11	175	1-29-98	1	2	4.34	6	6	0	0	29	34	15	14	5	9	26	.296	.393	.264	8.07	2.79
Sanmartin, Reiver	L-R	6-2	160	4-15-96	2	5	3.78	13	13	0	0	64	68	32	27	5	14	60	.264	.190	.285	8.39	1.96
Sceroler, Mac	R-R	6-3	200	4-9-95	5	4	3.69	26	20	0	0	117	101	54	48	13	29	127	.229	.243	.216	9.77	2.23
Schmidt, Clate	R-R	6-1	190	12-10-93	1	1	9.00	11	0	0	0	14	24	16	14	3	10	10	.387	.286	.439	6.43	6.43
2-team total (4 Lakeland)					1	1	7.32	15	0	0	0	20	31	19	16	3	11	14	.369	.286	.411	6.41	5.49
Solomon, Jared	R-R	6-2	192	6-10-97	2	8	4.30	15	15	0	0	73	74	38	35	5	34	65	.265	.282	.250	7.98	4.17
Stallings, Jesse	R-R	6-2	194	10-27-94	0	0	2.51	8	0	0	0	14	7	5	4	1	3	14	.146	.200	.107	8.79	1.88
Thompson, Cory	R-R	5-11	180	9-23-94	5	0	1.96	12	0	0	0	23	13	6	5	2	4	25	.165	.143	.182	9.78	1.57
Zabala, Aneurys	R-R	6-3	259	12-21-96	1	2	5.63	39	0	0	0	54	57	39	34	3	27	48	.265	.255	.273	7.95	4.47

Fielding

Catcher	PCT	G	PO	A	E	DP	PB
Clementina	.985	59	475	42	8	4	2
Kolozsvary	.990	75	602	60	7	8	0
Liberatore	1.000	3	24	4	0	1	0

First Base	PCT	G	PO	A	E	DP
Clementina	1.000	1	1	0	0	0
Lopez	1.000	1	3	0	0	0
Manzanero	.983	15	111	7	2	11
Mendoza	.988	12	84	0	1	4
Munroe	1.000	1	4	0	0	0
Santana	1.000	1	9	1	0	0
Yari	.992	110	842	57	7	83

Second Base	PCT	G	PO	A	E	DP
Gennett	1.000	3	2	4	0	2
Harris	.800	3	3	5	2	0
India	.941	5	7	9	1	4
Lopez	.980	86	137	211	7	46
Mendoza	.978	27	32	58	2	13
Rey	.967	8	11	18	1	4
Ventura	1.000	10	13	18	0	6

Third Base	PCT	G	PO	A	E	DP
Flete	.962	32	25	51	3	6
India	.936	74	47	114	11	7
Lopez	.962	9	9	16	1	0
Mendoza	.918	23	16	40	5	6
Santana	1.000	1	0	2	0	0

Shortstop	PCT	G	PO	A	E	DP
Garcia	.943	100	154	263	25	60
Lopez	1.000	2	2	7	0	2
Mendoza	.976	20	25	56	2	15
Rivero	.919	14	26	31	5	7

Outfield	PCT	G	PO	A	E	DP
Beltre	.857	11	10	2	2	0
Cedrola	.976	98	199	6	5	1
Fairchild	.992	54	123	0	1	0
Gordon	1.000	18	27	2	0	0
Hannah	1.000	16	34	2	0	0
Mount	.969	70	152	3	5	0
Munroe	1.000	12	24	0	0	0
Rey	1.000	5	5	0	0	0
Sugilio	.972	110	196	13	6	2
Ventura	1.000	14	22	1	0	0

DAYTON DRAGONS
MIDWEST LEAGUE

LOW CLASS A

Batting	B-T	HT	WT	DOB	AVG	vLH	vRH	G	AB	R	H	2B	3B	HR	RBI	BB	HBP	SH	SF	SO	SB	CS	SLG	OBP
Bautista, Mariel	R-R	6-3	194	10-15-97	.233	.284	.213	103	386	43	90	10	2	8	33	28	13	1	5	88	19	11	.332	.303
Farmer, Kyle	R-R	6-0	214	8-17-90	.000	--	.000	1	2	0	0	0	0	0	0	1	0	0	0	0	0	0	.000	.333
Finol, Claudio	R-R	5-11	171	4-13-00	.218	.237	.208	53	179	17	39	5	4	1	14	13	4	1	0	33	0	3	.307	.286
Gordon, Miles	L-R	6-1	175	12-3-97	.208	.240	.199	63	226	23	47	6	2	3	25	16	2	6	4	67	13	4	.292	.262
Harris, Dylan	R-R	5-11	199	1-27-95	.133	.154	.125	14	45	2	6	0	0	0	5	1	0	0	7	0	1	.133	.235
Hernandez, Miguel	R-R	6-0	194	4-13-99	.245	.298	.231	127	445	47	109	22	2	5	43	25	1	9	4	94	7	3	.337	.284
Liberatore, Ernesto	R-R	6-0	210	3-26-96	.267	.143	.304	8	30	3	8	1	0	1	2	0	0	0	0	10	0	0	.400	.267
Lloyd, Matt	L-R	6-1	205	3-17-96	.224	.278	.207	23	76	11	17	6	0	3	11	10	1	0	0	21	1	2	.421	.322
Lofstrom, Morgan	L-R	6-1	185	8-17-95	.258	.211	.269	64	213	23	55	15	2	3	23	8	5	2	2	82	0	0	.390	.298
Manzanero, Pabel	R-R	6-3	236	1-30-96	.280	.282	.280	86	386	38	95	25	1	10	44	8	4	0	2	77	1	0	.450	.304
Martinez, Juan	R-R	6-0	219	11-8-98	.238	.254	.232	129	441	49	105	22	4	8	50	51	10	1	1	112	1	2	.361	.330
Munroe, Shard	L-L	6-0	189	6-15-96	.197	.115	.216	47	142	20	28	3	4	3	15	29	1	0	2	45	4	5	.338	.333
Ozuna, Reniel	R-R	6-2	202	7-29-98	.157	.125	.169	40	121	8	19	2	1	2	10	16	0	0	0	33	0	1	.240	.256

	B-T	HT	WT	DOB	AVG	vLH	vRH	G	AB	R	H	2B	3B	HR	RBI	BB	HBP	SH	SF	SO	SB	CS	SLG	OBP
Plaz, Peterson	L-L	5-10	155	3-6-99	.000	--	.000	2	4	0	0	0	0	0	0	1	0	0	0	0	0	1	0	.000	.000
Rey, Brian	R-R	5-11	170	2-22-98	.281	.324	.264	66	235	31	66	16	0	9	40	11	7	1	5	35	1	0	.464	.326
Rivero, Carlos	L-R	6-0	175	4-30-97	.172	.067	.191	38	99	11	17	0	2	1	3	14	0	4	1	51	3	1	.242	.272
Scantlin, Nate	L-R	6-1	180	2-17-99	.071	.000	.100	6	14	2	1	0	0	0	0	3	1	0	0	5	0	0	.071	.278
Schuyler, Jay	R-R	6-1	194	4-11-97	.260	.245	.266	109	388	50	101	16	2	5	50	41	5	2	4	75	5	5	.351	.336
Siani, Michael	L-L	6-1	188	7-16-99	.253	.257	.252	121	466	75	118	10	6	6	39	46	10	8	1	109	45	15	.339	.333
Spillane, Bren	R-R	6-4	223	9-21-96	.207	.218	.203	62	213	31	44	10	0	5	19	28	1	1	0	104	5	2	.324	.302
Ventura, Randy	B-R	5-9	165	7-11-97	.234	.163	.253	70	231	22	54	3	2	0	12	17	1	1	2	57	10	1	.264	.287
Warren, Cameron	R-R	6-3	230	6-15-95	.237	.154	.266	42	148	18	35	7	0	2	13	16	2	1	1	30	0	0	.324	.317
White, Zeek	R-R	6-0	170	1-7-97	.046	.000	.091	8	22	0	1	0	0	0	2	0	0	0	0	10	1	0	.046	.046
Willems, Jonathan	R-R	5-11	190	11-7-98	.214	.154	.231	33	117	12	25	7	0	2	12	2	3	0	1	30	3	1	.325	.244

Pitching	B-T	HT	WT	DOB	W	L	ERA	G	GS	CG	SV	IP	H	R	ER	HR	BB	SO	AVG	vLH	vRH	K/9	BB/9
Bennett, Connor	R-R	5-9	212	4-10-97	3	4	2.27	33	0	0	12	40	35	14	10	1	17	63	.235	.228	.239	14.29	3.86
Byrd, Alec	L-L	6-3	175	3-31-95	0	0	5.40	2	0	0	0	2	5	1	1	0	1	2	.556	.500	.571	10.80	5.40
Campbell, Ryan	R-R	6-3	217	1-11-96	1	1	5.11	7	0	0	0	12	15	7	7	0	5	14	.294	.350	.258	10.22	3.65
Cox, Andy	R-L	6-2	194	10-23-93	0	1	6.60	11	0	0	1	15	14	15	11	0	17	21	.237	.286	.211	12.60	10.20
Curlis, Connor	L-L	6-1	180	11-29-96	4	6	3.16	17	13	0	0	74	68	35	26	9	32	72	.237	.223	.244	8.76	3.89
D'Andrea, Jerry	L-L	6-1	192	5-23-96	0	4	5.12	30	0	0	4	51	46	35	29	3	22	32	.236	.275	.214	12.71	5.65
De Jesus, Jhon	R-R	6-4	203	1-9-97	2	13	5.08	23	23	0	0	96	116	68	54	12	36	68	.301	.349	.255	6.40	3.39
Demurias, Eddy	R-R	6-0	184	8-1-97	3	4	4.50	40	0	0	4	78	85	42	39	4	24	70	.281	.286	.277	8.08	2.77
Diaz, Alexis	R-R	6-2	224	9-28-96	7	4	5.18	25	4	0	0	57	52	34	33	4	28	74	.232	.237	.228	11.62	4.40
Fisher, Andy	L-L	6-1	185	1-21-94	3	3	2.73	10	1	0	0	26	18	10	8	2	4	32	.190	.174	.204	10.94	1.37
Garcia, Pedro	R-R	5-11	220	3-21-95	0	0	0.00	1	0	0	0	1	0	0	0	0	0	2	.000	.000	.000	13.50	0.00
Gibson, Tyler	R-R	6-4	185	9-23-94	1	1	6.48	6	0	0	0	8	15	6	6	0	4	5	.405	.421	.389	5.40	4.32
Harris, Dylan	R-R	5-11	199	1-27-95	0	0	0.00	1	0	0	0	0	0	0	0	0	1	0	.000	--	.000	0.00	27.00
Heatherly, Jacob	L-L	6-1	215	5-20-98	1	2	8.31	4	4	0	0	9	12	9	8	0	6	10	.300	.333	.286	10.38	6.23
Johnson, Jordan	R-R	6-3	200	9-15-93	0	1	9.53	2	2	0	0	6	9	6	6	1	1	3	.360	.400	.300	4.76	1.59
Lodolo, Nick	L-L	6-6	202	2-5-98	0	0	2.57	2	2	0	0	7	6	2	2	0	0	9	.222	.250	.200	11.57	0.00
Machorro, Carlos	R-R	6-2	175	9-20-96	2	0	3.61	24	0	0	0	42	29	17	17	2	22	48	.196	.227	.171	10.20	4.68
Marinan, James	R-R	6-5	239	10-10-98	2	9	5.56	17	17	1	0	79	96	53	49	10	30	48	.306	.318	.295	5.45	3.40
McDonald, Andrew	R-R	6-6	225	12-24-94	0	2	9.33	9	0	0	0	18	31	21	19	4	13	11	.388	.382	.391	5.40	6.38
Nova, Moises	R-R	6-3	190	8-2-95	1	1	4.65	27	0	0	0	41	45	30	21	1	23	50	.280	.250	.306	11.07	5.09
Pidich, Matt	R-R	6-2	220	12-25-94	4	3	2.22	39	0	0	7	65	42	25	16	6	20	75	.179	.184	.175	10.38	2.77
Pinto, Julio	R-R	6-3	223	11-18-95	1	0	4.11	11	0	0	2	15	13	8	7	2	11	22	.217	.200	.229	12.91	6.46
Richardson, Lyon	B-R	6-2	192	1-18-00	3	9	4.15	26	26	0	0	113	126	66	52	10	33	106	.278	.275	.281	8.47	2.64
Rodriguez, Adrian	R-R	6-1	233	8-8-96	6	4	3.18	29	6	0	0	79	67	35	28	9	28	70	.226	.227	.225	7.94	3.18
Salazar, Eduardo	R-R	6-2	177	5-5-98	6	3	3.81	35	11	0	0	106	105	52	45	9	36	81	.259	.229	.283	6.86	3.05
Salinas, Ricky	R-R	6-2	220	3-26-96	4	3	4.13	15	15	0	0	72	70	39	33	7	28	67	.252	.280	.231	8.38	3.50
Schmidt, Clate	R-R	6-1	190	12-10-93	2	1	2.55	15	4	0	2	42	31	13	12	3	21	36	.201	.230	.183	7.65	4.46
Solomon, Jared	R-R	6-2	192	6-10-97	1	3	3.43	11	11	0	0	42	49	19	16	0	27	46	.258	.243	.269	9.86	5.79
Stallings, Jesse	R-R	6-2	194	10-27-94	0	0	0.00	3	0	0	2	4	2	0	0	0	1	5	.125	.167	.100	10.38	2.08
Wynne, Randy	R-R	6-1	180	3-9-93	1	0	4.50	3	1	0	0	12	14	7	6	2	0	14	.280	.222	.313	10.50	0.00

Fielding

Catcher	PCT	G	PO	A	E	DP	PB
Farmer	1.000	1	6	1	0	0	0
Liberatore	.969	8	51	12	2	0	1
Lofstrom	.987	51	408	35	6	1	9
Manzanero	.991	33	298	29	3	1	4
Schuyler	.983	51	430	41	8	1	1

First Base	PCT	G	PO	A	E	DP
Harris	1.000	2	14	1	0	3
Lloyd	.960	6	43	5	2	4
Lofstrom	1.000	4	21	2	0	1
Manzanero	.989	34	261	18	3	27
Martinez	1.000	3	11	0	0	1
Munroe	.947	9	52	2	3	7
Schuyler	.987	9	70	6	1	7
Spillane	.990	43	277	16	3	25
Warren	.973	34	246	7	7	28

Second Base	PCT	G	PO	A	E	DP
Finol	1.000	31	34	95	0	19
Harris	1.000	2	1	4	0	0
Hernandez	.929	2	7	6	1	3
Rey	.948	15	28	27	3	4
Rivero	.957	20	42	47	4	14
Ventura	.969	50	72	117	6	24
Willems	.936	31	45	57	7	12

Third Base	PCT	G	PO	A	E	DP
Finol	.929	13	5	21	2	0
Harris	.750	2	0	3	1	0
Martinez	.866	122	66	180	38	9
Rivero	.923	9	2	10	1	3
Spillane	.750	2	3	3	2	2
Ventura	.500	2	1	0	1	0

Shortstop	PCT	G	PO	A	E	DP
Finol	.956	13	21	22	2	3
Hernandez	.942	122	170	267	27	67
Rivero	.952	11	15	25	2	5

Outfield	PCT	G	PO	A	E	DP
Bautista	.960	90	164	6	7	1
Gordon	.984	59	120	6	2	2
Harris	.000	1	0	0	0	0
Lloyd	1.000	14	24	2	0	0
Munroe	.982	31	53	1	1	0
Ozuna	1.000	39	58	1	0	0
Plaz	1.000	2	4	1	0	0
Rey	.963	46	72	5	3	1
Scantlin	1.000	4	9	0	0	0
Schuyler	1.000	10	27	0	0	0
Siani	.988	118	314	18	4	6
Spillane	.938	8	15	0	1	0
Ventura	1.000	8	18	2	0	0
White	.909	7	20	0	2	0

BILLINGS MUSTANGS   ROOKIE ADVANCED
PIONEER LEAGUE

Batting	B-T	HT	WT	DOB	AVG	vLH	vRH	G	AB	R	H	2B	3B	HR	RBI	BB	HBP	SH	SF	SO	SB	CS	SLG	OBP
Amador, Ranser	R-R	6-2	165	3-15-99	.180	.200	.171	14	50	7	9	2	0	0	4	3	0	0	0	19	2	1	.220	.226
Boselli, Robert	R-R	6-4	240	4-17-96	.308	.200	.375	4	13	1	4	1	0	1	4	3	3	0	0	6	0	0	.615	.526
Callihan, Tyler	L-R	6-1	205	6-22-00	.400	1.000	.368	5	20	3	8	0	1	1	7	1	0	0	0	4	2	0	.650	.429
Case, Cash	L-R	6-1	190	5-12-99	.214	.138	.235	41	131	20	28	4	4	2	12	15	5	3	1	34	0	2	.351	.316
Cotton, Quin	R-R	5-11	200	3-31-98	.283	.282	.283	61	237	37	67	14	2	4	27	34	2	0	1	49	8	8	.409	.376
Finol, Claudio	R-R	5-11	171	4-13-00	.226	.100	.286	8	31	2	7	1	1	0	4	0	0	2	2	4	0	0	.323	.212
Free, James	R-R	6-2	205	4-14-98	.245	.250	.243	43	155	30	38	9	1	7	24	18	3	0	1	38	0	0	.452	.333
Hopkins, TJ	R-R	6-0	195	1-16-97	.267	.389	.223	54	202	40	54	11	3	5	30	19	2	2	3	52	12	2	.426	.332

Batting	B-T	HT	WT	DOB	AVG	vLH	vRH	G	AB	R	H	2B	3B	HR	RBI	BB	HBP	SH	SF	SO	SB	CS	SLG	OBP
Lloyd, Matt	L-R	6-1	205	3-17-96	.245	.200	.253	27	98	14	24	5	0	5	12	13	0	0	0	28	0	0	.449	.333
Martinez, Valentin	R-R	6-0	175	9-21-96	.225	.000	.297	16	49	4	11	1	0	0	2	5	3	1	0	14	0	0	.245	.333
McAfee, Quincy	R-R	5-11	185	9-16-97	.291	.245	.308	60	196	30	57	10	0	1	23	17	6	2	4	25	4	3	.357	.359
Ozuna, Reniel	R-R	6-2	202	7-29-98	.235	.226	.238	62	217	28	51	6	5	5	37	18	3	0	4	59	3	0	.378	.298
Reina, Carlos	B-R	6-0	175	12-11-98	.000	.000	.000	3	7	1	0	0	0	0	0	0	0	0	0	4	0	0	.000	.125
Reyes, Reyny	R-R	6-2	185	3-20-99	.252	.375	.205	35	115	14	29	4	1	0	10	7	0	2	1	25	0	1	.304	.293
Ruiz, Victor	R-R	6-1	190	10-20-99	.270	.270	.271	60	233	19	63	14	1	1	30	14	2	2	5	49	1	2	.352	.311
Scantlin, Nate	L-R	6-1	180	2-17-99	.312	.444	.289	16	61	14	19	5	2	1	5	5	2	0	0	5	3	1	.508	.382
Seminati, Leonardo	R-R	6-2	210	1-2-99	.270	.242	.282	58	204	24	55	8	0	9	27	20	4	0	3	80	1	0	.441	.342
Van Blake, Caleb	L-R	6-0	195	10-20-96	.000	.000	.000	3	9	2	0	0	0	0	0	0	0	0	0	4	0	0	.000	.100
Willems, Jonathan	R-R	5-11	190	11-7-98	.300	.288	.304	60	230	29	69	12	4	0	26	10	1	1	1	41	2	1	.387	.331
Wolforth, Garrett	B-R	6-4	220	10-13-97	.238	.333	.200	6	21	2	5	1	0	1	3	1	0	0	0	6	0	0	.429	.273
Yang, Eric	R-R	5-11	185	3-26-98	.290	.317	.281	51	162	27	47	9	0	4	29	23	19	1	4	44	0	0	.420	.428
Yon, Edwin	R-R	6-5	180	7-24-98	.287	.381	.241	35	129	23	37	6	1	4	10	11	0	0	0	61	0	0	.442	.343

Pitching	B-T	HT	WT	DOB	W	L	ERA	G	GS	CG	SV	IP	H	R	ER	HR	BB	SO	AVG	vLH	vRH	K/9	BB/9
Adames, Jose	R-R	6-2	165	1-17-93	0	0	0.00	3	0	0	1	3	2	0	0	0	0	5	.182	.200	.167	15.00	0.00
Aranguren, Frainger	R-R	6-2	190	3-17-97	3	1	3.16	20	0	0	0	31	35	15	11	5	6	20	.280	.333	.239	5.74	1.72
Byrd, Alec	L-L	6-3	175	3-31-95	0	0	1.93	10	0	0	0	19	17	5	4	1	3	19	.250	.278	.240	9.16	1.45
Cachutt, Manuel	R-R	6-0	185	6-7-97	0	1	6.62	15	0	0	0	18	22	13	13	1	8	16	.324	.333	.316	8.15	4.08
Carreno, Carlos	R-R	6-2	174	9-4-98	4	6	5.37	15	15	0	0	62	70	46	37	8	27	51	.285	.253	.306	7.40	3.92
Conoropo, Omar	B-L	5-10	165	5-27-98	5	0	3.36	16	3	0	0	59	49	24	22	4	13	55	.226	.221	.228	8.39	1.98
D'Andrea, Jerry	L-L	6-1	192	5-23-96	0	1	2.35	5	0	0	1	8	9	3	2	0	3	13	.310	.286	.318	15.26	3.52
Davis, Noah	R-R	6-2	195	4-22-97	1	1	2.10	8	8	0	0	34	27	10	8	4	13	30	.218	.265	.187	7.86	3.41
Dunne, Ryan	R-R	6-3	220	3-17-95	6	4	3.98	23	0	0	0	32	23	19	14	4	17	46	.207	.262	.174	13.07	4.83
Gonzalez, Alberto	R-R	6-1	180	7-26-99	0	0	5.96	11	1	0	0	23	17	15	15	5	11	29	.213	.243	.186	11.51	4.37
Karcher, Ricky	L-R	6-4	195	9-18-97	0	0	4.61	4	4	0	0	14	8	7	7	4	9	17	.163	.222	.129	11.20	5.93
Koch, Ian	R-R	6-4	220	8-18-97	5	0	3.38	15	0	0	1	35	33	13	13	2	8	32	.254	.208	.286	8.31	2.08
Lodolo, Nick	L-L	6-6	202	2-5-98	0	1	2.38	6	6	0	0	11	12	5	3	1	0	21	.261	.188	.300	16.68	0.00
Martinez, Valentin	R-R	6-0	175	9-21-96	0	0	18.00	2	0	0	0	2	3	4	4	0	3	2	.333	.667	.167	9.00	13.50
McDonald, Andrew	R-R	6-6	225	12-24-94	1	0	4.24	10	0	0	0	17	20	10	8	1	4	15	.286	.360	.244	7.94	2.12
McGregor, Justin	R-R	6-1	185	12-13-95	3	6	4.78	15	14	0	0	70	95	52	37	4	7	56	.313	.269	.345	7.23	0.90
Medrano, Miguel	R-R	6-0	165	1-4-98	3	4	3.13	14	14	0	0	60	52	24	21	8	14	66	.230	.253	.215	9.85	2.09
Nino, Jeffry	R-R	6-4	170	9-26-96	2	2	2.45	19	0	0	0	26	21	11	7	0	10	39	.214	.297	.164	13.68	3.51
Peguero, Francis	R-R	6-1	185	8-11-97	1	3	4.00	22	0	0	6	27	23	13	12	4	3	45	.226	.268	.197	15.00	1.00
Raby, Patrick	R-R	6-3	230	5-22-97	0	0	8.64	5	0	0	0	8	7	8	8	1	7	10	.212	.083	.286	10.80	7.56
Rodriguez, Orlando	R-R	6-2	195	12-16-95	0	3	4.42	10	0	0	0	37	35	22	18	3	15	49	.241	.267	.224	12.03	3.68
Salvador, Jose	L-L	6-2	170	9-21-99	0	0	3.86	3	3	0	0	12	5	5	5	1	3	15	.213	.357	.152	11.57	2.31
Schneider, Johnnie	R-R	6-5	180	6-30-97	3	2	3.34	22	0	0	2	32	24	15	12	3	16	36	.203	.208	.200	10.02	4.45
Stevenson, Jake	R-R	6-4	225	3-24-97	1	1	3.10	18	0	0	5	20	18	12	7	1	14	31	.225	.194	.250	13.72	6.20
Travieso, Nick	R-R	6-3	235	1-31-94	0	1	9.00	3	0	0	0	3	3	6	3	0	5	4	.273	.167	.400	12.00	15.00
Van Blake, Caleb	L-R	6-0	195	10-20-96	0	0	0.00	1	0	0	0	2	1	1	0	0	1	2	.200	.000	.333	9.00	4.50

Fielding

C: Boselli 3, Free 18, Martinez 15, Reina 2, Yang 42. 1B: Boselli 1, Free 10, Lloyd 21, Martinez 2, Seminati 46, Wolforth 2. 2B: Callihan 2, Finol 1, McAfee 23, Reyes 2, Willems 53. 3B: Finol 4, McAfee 9, Ruiz 59, Seminati 9, Van Blake 1, Willems 1. SS: Amador 13, Finol 3, McAfee 31, Reyes 33. OF: Case 36, Cotton 59, Hopkins 52, Lloyd 2, Ozuna 52, Scantlin 10, Seminati 7, Wolforth 4, Yon 15.

GREENEVILLE REDS — ROOKIE ADVANCED
APPALACHIAN LEAGUE

Batting	B-T	HT	WT	DOB	AVG	vLH	vRH	G	AB	R	H	2B	3B	HR	RBI	BB	HBP	SH	SF	SO	SB	CS	SLG	OBP
Amador, Ranser	R-R	6-2	165	3-15-99	.142	.135	.145	30	106	5	15	0	1	0	5	6	0	1	0	40	0	3	.160	.188
Berryhill, Luke	R-R	6-1	227	5-28-98	.240	.333	.188	8	25	5	6	1	0	1	5	5	0	0	2	4	0	0	.400	.344
Boselli, Robert	R-R	6-4	240	4-17-96	.182	.200	.174	9	33	2	6	0	0	1	5	2	1	0	2	14	0	0	.273	.237
Bumpass, AJ	L-R	6-3	195	5-30-96	.250	.175	.280	41	140	24	35	10	3	5	27	14	4	1	1	44	4	0	.471	.333
Callihan, Tyler	L-R	6-1	205	6-22-00	.250	.239	.253	52	204	27	51	10	5	5	26	9	2	0	2	46	9	3	.422	.286
Castro, Fidel	L-R	6-3	175	12-26-98	.313	.600	.182	5	16	2	5	0	0	1	2	1	0	0	0	7	0	1	.500	.353
Cerda, Allan	R-R	6-3	170	11-24-99	.220	.200	.224	39	132	22	29	6	0	9	27	20	10	1	2	56	2	2	.470	.360
Gomez, Justin	L-R	5-10	195	4-29-97	.263	.360	.216	25	76	8	20	3	1	2	11	9	1	1	1	24	1	0	.408	.345
Hinds, Rece	R-R	6-4	215	9-5-00	.000	.000	.000	3	8	1	0	0	0	0	1	2	0	0	0	3	0	0	.000	.200
Johnson, Ivan	B-R	6-0	190	10-11-98	.255	.255	.256	46	188	27	48	10	1	6	22	18	2	2	0	46	11	4	.415	.327
Juarez, Raul	R-R	6-1	165	5-21-98	.203	.194	.207	35	123	17	25	5	0	6	15	7	7	0	1	32	0	0	.390	.283
Lantigua, Danny	R-R	6-1	165	3-7-99	.185	.232	.166	53	195	19	36	6	5	3	18	7	2	1	1	97	1	2	.313	.220
Oliver, Hunter	R-R	6-1	195	10-21-97	.231	.143	.333	4	13	2	3	1	0	0	1	0	0	0	0	3	0	0	.308	.286
Olivo, Cristian	L-L	6-2	170	9-30-98	.252	.231	.256	42	147	19	37	6	0	1	14	6	3	0	0	57	1	1	.313	.295
Plaz, Peterson	L-L	5-10	155	3-6-99	.203	.091	.222	25	74	10	15	2	0	0	9	4	0	2	1	10	1	1	.230	.241
Reina, Carlos	R-R	6-0	175	12-11-98	.194	.303	.160	43	139	22	27	13	0	2	15	26	3	0	0	40	3	2	.331	.333
Remy, Danielito	B-R	6-1	170	5-5-98	.192	.178	.198	45	156	16	30	5	1	1	6	7	1	3	0	45	4	1	.256	.232
Reyes, Reyny	R-R	6-2	185	3-20-99	.233	.286	.222	12	43	3	10	3	1	0	6	4	0	0	0	8	0	0	.349	.250
Spooner, Mike	L-R	6-3	204	2-17-97	.223	.185	.239	33	94	14	21	3	1	0	8	16	1	1	0	30	2	0	.277	.342
Tello, Jose	R-R	6-0	170	5-21-98	.371	.250	.474	11	35	6	13	2	1	2	9	4	1	0	0	5	0	0	.657	.450
Trahan, Blake	R-R	5-9	180	9-5-93	.267	1.000	.214	4	15	0	4	1	0	0	0	0	0	0	0	3	0	0	.333	.313
Van Blake, Caleb	L-R	6-0	195	10-20-96	.231	.400	.125	4	13	1	3	2	0	0	1	0	0	0	0	6	0	0	.385	.286
Warren, Cameron	R-R	6-3	230	6-15-95	.333	.313	.348	10	39	6	13	0	1	1	11	4	0	0	0	10	3	2	.462	.395
Wolforth, Garrett	B-R	6-4	220	10-13-97	.242	.283	.222	16	53	4	13	2	0	1	6	4	7	9	2	5	12	1	.302	.167

Pitching	B-T	HT	WT	DOB	W	L	ERA	G	GS	CG	SV	IP	H	R	ER	HR	BB	SO	AVG	vLH	vRH	K/9	BB/9
Abril, Juan Manuel	R-R	6-0	160	3-11-98	1	7	6.99	12	12	0	0	37	45	32	29	3	21	32	.289	.278	.294	7.71	5.06

Name	B-T	HT	WT	DOB	W	L	ERA	G	GS	CG	SV	IP	H	R	ER	HR	BB	SO	AVG	vLH	vRH	K/9	BB/9
Ashcraft, Graham	L-R	6-2	217	2-11-98	2	4	4.53	13	13	0	0	54	51	33	27	2	21	60	.243	.262	.230	10.06	3.52
Byrd, Alec	L-L	6-3	175	3-31-95	3	0	2.25	9	0	0	0	16	12	4	4	0	4	19	.211	.136	.257	10.69	2.25
Cachutt, Manuel	R-R	6-0	185	6-7-97	0	2	11.88	6	0	0	0	8	12	14	11	1	10	7	.324	.313	.333	7.56	10.80
Cooper, Tanner	R-R	6-3	215	9-8-99	1	0	2.21	15	0	0	2	37	23	11	9	1	12	42	.180	.173	.184	10.31	2.95
Fisher, Andy	L-L	6-1	185	1-9-96	0	0	0.87	6	1	0	0	21	13	4	2	0	3	26	.173	.111	.193	11.32	1.31
Garbee, Tyler	R-R	6-3	210	10-8-96	2	2	3.83	15	5	0	2	47	48	23	20	3	11	52	.265	.264	.266	9.96	2.11
Gibson, Tyler	R-R	6-4	185	9-23-94	1	2	2.25	6	0	0	1	12	9	8	3	0	0	16	.209	.250	.185	12.00	0.00
Gilbert, Jake	R-R	6-7	220	12-1-96	0	3	6.18	8	6	0	1	28	31	19	19	2	8	37	.277	.302	.254	12.04	2.60
Gill, Matt	L-R	6-5	240	4-22-98	2	3	7.09	18	0	0	2	27	44	31	21	1	9	25	.355	.370	.346	8.44	3.04
Gonzalez, Alberto	R-R	6-1	180	7-26-99	0	0	7.36	7	0	0	0	11	12	10	9	0	8	12	.273	.300	.250	9.82	6.55
Keys, JC	R-R	5-10	173	10-9-96	1	1	3.77	5	3	0	0	14	12	7	6	0	7	21	.222	.273	.188	13.19	4.40
Kravetz, Evan	L-L	6-8	240	12-19-96	0	0	0.00	1	1	0	0	1	0	0	0	0	0	0	.000	.000	.000	0.00	0.00
Moreno, Jose	R-R	6-5	200	3-8-98	0	0	0.00	1	0	0	0	1	2	3	0	0	2	5	.286	.333	.000	6.75	13.50
Noriega, Orlando	R-R	6-0	175	5-15-99	2	3	5.28	7	7	0	0	31	35	21	18	5	9	24	.285	.271	.297	7.04	2.64
Pucheu, Jacques	L-L	6-2	210	1-1-97	2	0	1.50	4	2	1	0	18	13	3	3	1	6	19	.203	.167	.225	9.50	3.00
Raby, Patrick	R-R	6-3	230	5-22-97	2	1	8.03	7	0	0	0	12	14	13	11	3	9	19	.280	.292	.269	13.86	6.57
Salvador, Jose	L-L	6-2	170	9-21-99	2	3	5.05	11	11	0	0	46	50	27	26	6	16	57	.273	.364	.245	11.07	3.11
Sefcik, Quinten	L-R	6-1	215	11-26-95	0	0	4.15	3	0	0	1	4	6	3	2	1	1	3	.300	.200	.333	6.23	2.08
Serreino, Dan	R-R	6-3	225	6-18-96	0	1	6.75	13	0	0	1	19	15	14	14	2	12	18	.231	.219	.242	8.68	5.79
Soto, Ronard	R-R	6-2	185	5-18-99	0	0	9.00	1	0	0	0	1	4	2	1	0	2	1	.667	.667	.667	9.00	18.00
Stockton, Spencer	B-R	6-3	210	4-24-96	2	1	1.96	4	3	0	0	23	10	5	5	2	3	28	.125	.128	.122	10.96	1.17
Tripp, Johnathon	R-R	6-4	210	5-25-94	0	0	0.00	5	0	0	1	9	4	0	0	0	0	14	.125	.177	.067	13.50	0.00
Wallace, Raul	R-R	6-2	215	8-19-95	0	2	3.50	11	0	0	0	18	10	8	7	1	9	23	.159	.250	.116	11.50	4.50
Wynne, Randy	R-R	6-1	180	3-9-93	3	3	3.04	12	3	0	0	53	45	19	18	4	2	54	.223	.203	.236	9.11	0.34
Zimmerman, Anthony	R-R	6-5	250	9-9-96	0	2	7.94	12	0	0	1	17	18	16	15	2	9	20	.257	.188	.316	10.59	4.76
Zorrilla, Jose	B-L	6-1	180	10-2-98	0	1	8.84	14	0	0	0	19	30	21	19	3	10	26	.337	.241	.383	12.10	4.66

Fielding

C: Berryhill 6, Boselli 6, Gomez 20, Oliver 1, Reina 33, Tello 4. **1B:** Juarez 8, Reina 8, Tello 5, Van Blake 2, Warren 7, Wolforth 40. **2B:** Callihan 20, Johnson 11, Remy 38, Van Blake 1. **3B:** Callihan 31, Hinds 3, Juarez 27, Reyes 4, Van Blake 1, Wolforth 3. **SS:** Amador 27, Johnson 34, Reyes 6, Trahan 3. **OF:** Bumpass 34, Castro 5, Cerda 39, Lantigua 47, Olivo 25, Plaz 24, Remy 2, Spooner 30, Wolforth 7.

AZL REDS   ROOKIE
ARIZONA LEAGUE

Batting	B-T	HT	WT	DOB	AVG	vLH	vRH	G	AB	R	H	2B	3B	HR	RBI	BB	HBP	SH	SF	SO	SB	CS	SLG	OBP
Acosta, Jose	B-R	5-10	170	3-20-00	.370	.556	.324	10	46	10	17	5	0	0	8	1	1	2	0	9	2	1	.478	.396
Aleixo, Axel	L-L	6-1	172	9-11-99	.217	.200	.231	10	23	7	5	2	0	0	3	5	1	0	0	4	1	2	.304	.379
Almonte, Sebastian	R-R	6-0	185	10-22-99	.272	.219	.287	40	147	23	40	10	3	3	22	13	1	1	1	46	8	2	.442	.333
Bautista, Mariel	R-R	6-3	194	10-15-97	.368	.000	.500	5	19	6	7	3	0	0	1	2	0	0	0	3	4	1	.526	.429
Castro, Fidel	L-R	6-3	175	12-26-98	.290	.333	.278	43	169	33	49	10	5	6	30	17	3	0	1	64	9	3	.515	.363
Ciuffo, Nick	L-R	6-0	200	3-7-95	.231	.000	.250	5	13	2	3	3	0	0	1	3	0	0	0	4	0	0	.462	.375
Contreras, Yan	R-R	6-2	185	1-30-01	.145	.158	.140	20	69	8	10	1	2	0	2	14	1	0	0	25	4	1	.217	.298
Creal, Ashton	R-R	6-1	205	3-23-99	.276	.257	.281	48	174	33	48	12	3	0	14	32	6	1	0	48	8	3	.379	.406
Franco, Rafael	R-R	6-2	155	6-20-01	.232	.333	.214	39	138	21	32	1	2	1	13	8	4	0	2	31	6	1	.290	.290
Gomez, Elvis	R-R	6-0	170	5-27-99	.186	.316	.157	36	102	17	19	1	2	0	9	6	3	1	1	25	1	0	.235	.250
Guzman, Edward	R-R	6-1	195	9-30-99	.173	.143	.184	16	52	6	9	1	0	0	4	5	3	0	0	27	0	0	.192	.283
Lopez, Jose	R-R	5-11	165	11-30-99	.232	.179	.250	30	108	12	25	6	3	2	16	1	7	0	3	41	2	2	.398	.277
Marrero, Wendell	L-L	6-2	195	11-28-00	.324	.261	.342	30	102	18	33	4	2	3	21	12	6	0	0	33	0	0	.490	.425
Nieves, Yamil	R-R	6-0	190	7-13-01	.222	.000	.273	12	27	2	6	1	0	0	3	1	0	0	0	9	0	0	.259	.250
Oliver, Hunter	R-R	6-1	195	10-21-97	.125	.000	.167	6	16	2	2	1	0	0	2	5	0	0	1	8	0	1	.188	.318
Palacios, Aiverson	B-R	6-0	150	4-13-00	.136	.143	.133	8	22	4	3	0	1	0	1	2	0	0	0	13	1	0	.227	.208
Pineda, Jose	R-R	6-3	185	2-10-98	.064	.000	.073	14	47	5	3	0	1	0	2	7	0	0	0	35	0	0	.106	.185
Pino, Yassel	R-R	6-2	200	10-4-99	.253	.200	.263	24	91	11	23	2	0	0	11	4	4	0	0	25	0	1	.275	.313
Refsnyder, Rob	R-R	6-0	200	3-26-91	.333	.400	.250	2	9	1	3	1	0	0	1	0	0	0	1	0	0		.444	.400
Santana, Debby	R-R	6-2	185	8-24-00	.310	.360	.293	25	100	13	31	3	2	1	13	3	0	1	1	30	0	0	.410	.327
Schebler, Scott	L-R	6-0	228	10-6-90	.500	--	.500	1	4	1	2	0	0	0	1	0	0	0	0	0	0	0	.500	.500
Sequera, Jorge	R-R	6-0	175	9-30-99	.326	.316	.328	28	86	15	28	6	0	0	8	5	2	0	2	21	4	1	.395	.368
Tejada, Luis	R-R	6-0	160	9-3-99	.208	.154	.219	26	77	11	16	5	0	2	10	10	1	0	0	17	3	2	.351	.307
Tello, Jose	R-R	6-0	170	5-21-98	.296	.303	.294	35	142	24	42	4	3	6	24	7	3	0	1	21	0	0	.493	.34
Thomas, Rylan	R-R	5-11	235	6-25-97	.077	.000	.091	7	13	3	1	1	0	0	1	0	0	0	0	7	0	0	.154	.143
Tromp, Chadwick	R-R	5-9	205	3-21-95	.271	.231	.286	16	48	10	13	5	0	2	16	11	1	0	1	10	0	0	.500	.410
Van Blake, Caleb	L-R	6-0	195	10-20-96	.342	.192	.381	32	123	23	42	7	3	6	26	7	3	0	0	22	1	2	.594	.391

Pitching	B-T	HT	WT	DOB	W	L	ERA	G	GS	CG	SV	IP	H	R	ER	HR	BB	SO	AVG	vLH	vRH	K/9	BB/9
Adames, Jose	R-R	6-2	165	1-17-93	0	0	0.00	1	0	0	0	1	1	2	0	0	0	5	.200	.000	.333	40.50	0.00
Beltre, Allan	R-R	6-4	195	9-12-99	0	2	15.22	7	1	0	0	18	39	34	31	5	15	17	.415	.310	.500	8.35	7.36
Campbell, Ryan	R-R	6-3	217	1-11-96	0	0	3.00	2	2	0	0	3	3	1	1	0	0	1	.250	.286	.200	3.00	0.00
Davis, Noah	R-R	6-2	195	4-22-97	0	2	7.88	5	5	0	0	8	13	7	7	4	0	5	.351	.214	.435	5.63	0.00
Diaz, Alexis	R-R	6-2	224	9-28-96	0	0	5.40	2	1	0	0	2	5	4	1	0	1	3	.556	.500	.667	16.20	5.40
Diaz, Yoel	R-R	6-1	190	1-9-99	1	0	6.75	3	0	0	0	7	6	5	5	0	6	7	.250	.375	.188	9.45	8.10
Falcon, Andres	R-R	6-3	165	10-22-99	3	1	3.75	17	0	0	2	50	35	25	21	3	20	43	.191	.139	.225	7.69	3.58
Garcia, Pedro	R-R	5-11	220	3-21-95	1	0	0.00	5	2	0	0	14	12	1	0	0	4	14	.226	.286	.205	8.79	2.51
Gilbert, Jake	R-R	6-7	220	12-1-96	1	1	2.25	5	0	0	0	8	5	2	1		3	13	.194	.300	.143	14.63	3.38
Hendrix, Ryan	R-R	6-3	185	12-16-94	1	0	0.00	4	2	0	0	5	1	1	0	0	0	8	.059	.000	.111	14.40	0.00
Jay, Tyler	L-L	6-1	185	4-19-94	0	0	9.00	2	1	0	0	2	3	2	2	0	0	5	.333	.000	.500	22.50	0.00
Johnson, Jordan	R-R	6-3	200	9-15-93	0	0	3.00	4	4	0	0	6	7	2	2	0	0	6	.318	.444	.231	9.00	0.00
Koch, Ian	R-R	6-4	220	8-18-97	0	1	13.50	1	1	0	0	1	3	5	1	1	1	0	.500	.500	.500	0.00	13.50

Name	B-T	HT	WT	DOB	W	L	ERA	G	GS	CG	SV	IP	H	R	ER	HR	BB	SO	AVG	vLH	vRH	K/9	BB/9
Lane, Thomas	L-R	6-5	260	11-2-96	1	0	4.26	12	0	0	4	19	17	14	9	1	12	31	.236	.391	.163	14.68	5.68
Lar, Miguel	R-R	6-1	170	10-3-99	4	3	4.31	14	5	0	0	54	60	34	26	4	29	41	.278	.271	.281	6.79	4.80
Lopez, Jefferson	R-R	6-1	185	2-18-01	0	0	10.13	2	0	0	1	3	4	3	3	0	4	2	.400	.250	.500	6.75	13.50
Lopez, Jose	R-R	6-1	205	9-1-93	0	0	0.00	2	0	0	0	2	2	0	0	0	1	4	.222	.333	.167	15.43	3.86
Manuel, Maiker	R-R	6-2	175	7-29-98	3	0	6.53	13	6	0	0	51	67	42	37	7	7	52	.303	.288	.310	9.18	1.24
Mey, Luis	R-R	6-2	160	6-24-01	0	5	8.39	13	12	0	0	40	64	51	37	4	28	28	.370	.300	.407	6.35	6.35
Mojica, Ariel	R-R	6-2	185	9-20-98	1	5	2.87	16	0	0	3	31	35	18	10	1	12	32	.278	.318	.256	9.19	3.45
Moreno, Pedro	R-R	6-5	200	3-8-98	0	2	4.35	16	0	0	1	31	41	24	15	2	12	31	.323	.349	.310	9.00	3.48
Mota, Reinardo	R-R	6-2	165	11-14-98	0	1	19.89	6	0	0	1	6	6	15	14	0	12	8	.250	.182	.308	11.37	17.05
Noriega, Orlando	R-R	6-0	175	5-15-99	0	0	1.59	3	2	0	0	6	5	4	1	0	3	9	.217	.000	.357	14.29	4.76
Nunez, Ruben	L-L	6-3	176	1-24-98	0	0	8.84	13	0	0	0	18	22	18	18	3	29	28	.306	.643	.224	13.75	14.24
Peralta, Jose	R-R	6-1	170	10-2-99	0	0	5.56	8	4	0	0	11	13	8	7	2	5	9	.277	.318	.240	7.15	3.97
Pucheu, Jacques	L-L	6-2	210	1-1-97	3	1	4.08	11	3	0	1	35	29	18	16	1	10	42	.215	.147	.238	10.70	2.55
Sequera, Jorge	R-R	6-0	175	3-20-99	0	0	18.00	1	0	0	0	1	3	2	2	0	0	1	.600	1.000	.333	9.00	0.00
Soto, Ronard	R-R	6-2	185	5-18-99	1	1	2.31	8	0	0	1	12	9	4	3	0	3	13	.220	.263	.182	10.03	2.31
Stockton, Spencer	B-R	6-3	210	4-24-96	3	1	2.14	6	4	0	0	34	31	10	8	0	5	41	.244	.213	.263	10.96	1.34
Tavarez, Dannysmel	R-R	6-3	190	3-10-98	3	2	6.61	8	0	0	0	16	17	13	12	1	14	10	.274	.231	.286	5.51	7.71
Tazawa, Junichi	R-R	5-11	200	6-6-86	0	1	27.00	1	1	0	0	1	2	3	2	1	0	0	.333	.000	.500	0.00	0.00
Wynne, Randy	R-R	6-1	180	3-9-93	1	0	4.50	1	0	0	0	2	2	1	1	0	0	1	.250	.333	.200	4.50	0.00

Fielding

C: Ciuffo 4, Gomez 34, Guzman 8, Nieves 5, Oliver 3, Tello 8, Tromp 10. **1B:** Gomez 1, Guzman 7, Nieves 2, Oliver 1, Sequera 13, Tello 20, Thomas 2, Van Blake 17. **2B:** Acosta 9, Almonte 11, Lopez 7, Palacios 2, Pino 9, Sequera 7, Tejada 9, Van Blake 6. **3B:** Acosta 1, Almonte 22, Pino 9, Santana 23, Sequera 2, Tejada 1, Thomas 4, Van Blake 2. **SS:** Almonte 9, Contreras 20, Lopez 21, Palacios 5, Pino 2. **OF:** Aleixo 10, Bautista 3, Castro 41, Creal 48, Franco 38, Marrero 26, Pineda 8, Refsnyder 2, Schebler 1, Sequera 4.

DSL REDS   ROOKIE
DOMINICAN SUMMER LEAGUE

Batting	B-T	HT	WT	DOB	AVG	vLH	vRH	G	AB	R	H	2B	3B	HR	RBI	BB	HBP	SH	SF	SO	SB	CS	SLG	OBP
Acosta, Jose	B-R	5-10	170	3-20-00	.403	.525	.358	43	149	48	60	12	5	3	24	30	2	1	2	32	24	0	.611	.503
Alcantara, Wilmer	L-L	6-0	180	12-20-01	.209	.121	.238	51	134	40	28	2	1	8	18	32	2	0	0	60	14	3	.418	.369
Cabrera, Luis	R-R	6-3	180	1-18-02	.217	.174	.230	33	97	12	21	5	2	0	13	19	3	2	1	35	3	1	.309	.358
Colmenarez, Samuel	B-R	5-10	160	7-23-99	.254	.238	.260	40	142	23	36	0	5	0	12	20	2	2	0	36	7	4	.324	.354
De La Cruz, Elly	B-R	6-2	150	1-11-02	.285	.333	.268	43	165	24	47	11	1	1	26	14	1	1	2	45	3	6	.382	.351
Fernandez, Ilvin	R-R	6-1	160	9-8-01	.274	.231	.290	40	146	17	40	4	0	0	16	18	3	1	2	27	5	6	.301	.361
Geraldo, Jeferson	R-R	6-3	183	7-31-02	.158	.162	.156	40	133	20	21	9	1	0	7	17	9	0	2	65	4	1	.241	.292
Guzman, Darlin	L-L	6-1	165	9-27-00	.357	.327	.368	47	185	40	66	18	6	6	41	10	2	0	1	44	5	3	.616	.394
Lora, Thomas	R-R	5-11	170	11-2-01	.238	.316	.214	41	164	34	39	11	1	1	19	20	2	0	2	33	16	5	.335	.325
Lozano, Deybert	L-R	6-1	165	11-15-99	.208	.171	.222	36	125	14	26	8	2	1	16	6	4	0	2	21	5	3	.328	.263
Melo, Junior	R-R	6-2	175	5-10-97	.307	.304	.308	43	163	27	50	14	3	3	31	12	4	0	2	16	2	2	.485	.365
Ovalles, Edison	L-R	5-11	150	1-31-02	.196	.400	.146	16	51	10	10	0	1	1	9	6	1	0	1	14	2	0	.294	.288
Perez, Lenniell	R-R	6-0	170	2-3-02	.202	.167	.212	28	84	14	17	6	2	2	12	9	4	1	1	26	2	1	.393	.306
Rodriguez, Fraudy	R-S	5-9	163	9-6-01	.169	.200	.161	25	71	5	12	3	0	1	8	9	1	0	2	16	1	2	.254	.265
Sencion, Jorge	R-R	6-3	225	10-3-98	.238	.546	.173	18	63	7	15	2	0	1	9	4	0	0	0	28	3	0	.318	.284
Tamares, Junior	L-R	6-0	165	9-26-01	.278	.293	.273	54	169	35	47	5	4	1	17	24	2	1	2	45	13	5	.373	.371
Torres, Esmil	R-R	6-0	150	1-18-02	.260	.395	.214	42	150	17	39	4	2	3	26	35	2	2	1	26	16	9	.373	.404
Vellojin, Daniel	B-R	5-11	180	3-15-00	.314	.227	.344	51	175	40	55	9	3	3	42	31	10	0	0	24	8	5	.451	.444

Pitching	B-T	HT	WT	DOB	W	L	ERA	G	GS	CG	SV	IP	H	R	ER	HR	BB	SO	AVG	vLH	vRH	K/9	BB/9
Aguilera, Gabriel	R-R	6-0	165	8-19-00	2	3	4.33	14	7	0	0	44	44	24	21	3	9	35	.256	.217	.270	7.21	1.85
Alcantara, Eddy	L-L	6-5	180	2-11-00	3	2	3.92	15	1	0	0	39	31	19	17	4	22	39	.218	.267	.213	9.00	5.08
Aquino, Luis	R-R	6-2	160	6-19-01	2	4	5.94	13	9	0	0	33	24	25	22	3	34	28	.211	.275	.176	7.56	9.18
Beltre, Allan	R-R	6-4	195	9-12-99	0	0	2.40	6	0	0	2	15	15	8	4	0	11	12	.254	.308	.239	7.20	6.60
Castillo, Zamil	L-L	5-10	160	10-17-99	4	0	4.31	19	0	0	0	31	27	17	15	1	23	40	.233	.313	.220	11.49	6.61
Chirinos, Elkyn	R-R	6-1	160	9-20-00	1	0	2.84	7	0	0	1	13	12	8	4	1	6	22	.245	.250	.242	8.53	4.26
Cuevas, Andry	R-R	6-4	185	8-4-98	6	2	2.27	28	0	0	15	44	19	15	11	2	19	56	.136	.154	.132	11.54	3.92
Diaz, Yoel	R-R	6-1	190	1-9-99	1	1	3.06	18	0	0	5	35	29	17	12	1	21	32	.230	.174	.243	8.15	5.35
Franco, Jose	R-R	6-2	175	11-25-00	3	1	2.20	14	14	0	0	57	50	19	14	1	14	59	.239	.128	.265	9.26	2.20
Lantigua, Israel	R-R	6-3	190	2-9-99	1	0	6.00	20	0	0	1	30	31	26	20	1	35	25	.270	.222	.284	7.50	10.50
Lorant, Nestor	R-R	6-2	175	5-4-02	0	1	4.43	6	4	0	0	20	25	11	10	1	6	20	.317	.286	.328	8.85	2.66
Mendez, Willy	R-R	6-0	180	3-27-00	3	1	6.98	18	0	0	0	30	26	26	23	0	34	23	.234	.250	.232	9.18	10.31
Mota, Reinardo	R-R	6-2	165	11-14-98	2	0	7.82	6	0	0	0	13	14	13	11	0	13	11	.311	.273	.324	7.82	9.24
Ortega, Jose	R-R	6-3	190	11-8-99	1	0	0.00	3	0	0	0	3	1	0	0	0	1	2	.125	--	.125	6.75	3.38
Ramirez, Marwin	R-R	6-2	175	9-10-00	1	1	6.26	11	1	0	0	27	22	20	19	3	13	27	.216	.191	.222	8.89	4.28
Rojas, Jesus	R-R	6-3	185	3-22-02	3	4	3.88	15	13	0	1	53	59	29	23	2	16	34	.277	.211	.291	5.74	2.70
Salazar, Martin	R-R	6-2	175	5-27-00	5	1	2.93	14	14	0	0	58	57	27	19	3	10	55	.253	.231	.260	8.49	1.54
Santos, Carlos	R-R	6-1	180	7-12-98	2	0	5.79	6	0	0	1	9	10	7	6	1	6	17	.256	.455	.179	16.39	5.79
Soto, Ronard	R-R	6-2	185	5-18-99	3	0	3.18	8	0	0	1	23	21	8	8	0	5	28	.247	.269	.237	11.12	1.99
Tavarez, Dannysmel	R-R	6-3	190	3-10-98	1	2	6.39	8	8	0	0	31	34	33	22	0	14	24	.279	.346	.260	6.97	4.06
Yanez, Williams	R-R	6-2	175	11-7-01	3	1	3.12	6	0	0	0	17	18	6	6	0	3	10	.281	.300	.278	5.19	1.56

Fielding

C: Melo 7, Ovalles 7, Rodriguez 23, Vellojin 45. **1B:** Cabrera 26, Melo 36, Rodriguez 1, Sencion 13, Vellojin 1. **2B:** Acosta 3, Colmenarez 10, De La Cruz 13, Fernandez 3, Lora 22, Torres 25. **3B:** Acosta 35, Colmenarez 20, Lora 17, Torres 1. **SS:** Colmenarez 1, De La Cruz 26, Fernandez 31, Torres 14. **OF:** Acosta 2, Alcantara 50, Geraldo 33, Guzman 47, Lozano 36, Perez 19, Tamares 52.

Cleveland Indians

SEASON IN A SENTENCE: The Indians entered the year favored to win their fourth straight American League Central title, but injuries to Francisco Lindor and Jose Ramirez and a fast start by the Twins kept the Indians in second place for most of the year and out of the playoffs.

HIGH POINT: The Indians spent most of the season chasing the Twins, but Cleveland managed to pull ahead of them and into first place in dramatic fashion on Aug. 12. A day after beating Minnesota in 10 innings to pull into a tie for first place, Carlos Santana hit a walk-off home run in the bottom of the ninth for a 6-5 win over the Twins that put Cleveland all alone in first place in the AL Central.

LOW POINT: The Indians had long fallen out of the division title race by the final week of the season, but they were still just 0.5 games out of a AL wild card spot with five games remaining. Instead of finishing strong, the Indians lost all five games to miss out on the playoffs for the first time since 2015.

NOTABLE ROOKIES: Oscar Mercado made his major league debut May 14 and quickly took over as the Indians' starting center fielder. He finished as one of just three rookies with at least 15 home runs and 15 stolen bases. Righthanders Zach Plesac (8-6, 3.81) and Aaron Civale (3-4, 2.34) helped keep the Indians' rotation afloat after Corey Kluber, Mike Clevinger and Carlos Carrasco all suffered injuries or illness.

KEY TRANSACTIONS: The Indians swung a pair of three-way deals primarily aimed at improving their offense. They acquired Carlos Santana from the Phillies and Jake Bauers from the Rays in a three-way deal during the Winter Meetings, and they made the biggest splash of the trade deadline as well. The Indians traded Trevor Bauer to the Reds on July 29 in a three-way deal involving the Padres and received young masher Franmil Reyes, top lefthanded pitching prospect Logan Allen and outfielder Victor Nova from San Diego and lefthander Scott Moss from Cincinnati.

DOWN ON THE FARM: Triple-A Columbus won the International League championship with a three-game sweep of Durham (Rays). Outfielder Ka'ai Tom went 5-for-12 with a double, two home runs, five RBIs and four runs scored during the series and was named playoff MVP. AZL Indians Blue reached the Rookie-level Arizona League championship series but lost to the Rangers.

OPENING DAY PAYROLL: $107,345,783 (19th).

PLAYERS OF THE YEAR

ALEX TRAUTWIG

DAVID MONSEUR

MAJOR LEAGUE

Shane Bieber
RHP
15-8, 3.28 in 33 GS
144 ERA+, 1.05 WHIP
AL-best 1.7 BB/9

MINOR LEAGUE

Nolan Jones
3B
(High A/Double-A)
.272/.409/.442, 15 HR
96 BB led minors

ORGANIZATION LEADERS

Batting		*Minimum 250 AB
MAJORS		
* AVG	Tyler Naquin	.288
* OPS	Carlos Santana	.911
HR	Carlos Santana	34
RBI	Carlos Santana	93
MINORS		
* AVG	Wilbis Santiago, Lake County, Lynchburg	.312
* OBP	Nolan Jones, Lynchburg, Akron	.409
* SLG	Bobby Bradley, Columbus	.567
* OPS	Ka'ai Tom, Akron, Columbus	.912
R	Tyler Freeman, Lake County, Lynchburg	89
H	Tyler Freeman, Lake County, Lynchburg	151
TB	Ka'ai Tom, Akron, Columbus	255
2B	Daniel Johnson, Akron, Columbus	34
3B	Bo Naylor, Lake County	10
3B	Ka'ai Tom, Akron, Columbus	10
HR	Bobby Bradley, Columbus	33
RBI	Ka'ai Tom, Akron, Columbus	86
BB	Nolan Jones, Lynchburg, Akron	96
SO	Quentin Holmes, Lake County	159
SB	Jose Fermin, Lake County	28

Pitching		#Minimum 75 IP
MAJORS		
W	Shane Bieber	15
# ERA	Mike Clevinger	2.71
SO	Shane Bieber	259
SV	Brad Hand	34
MINORS		
W	Jake Paulson, Akron, Columbus	11
L	Adam Scott, Lynchburg, Akron	13
L	Sam Hentges, Akron	13
# ERA	Zach Draper, Lake County, Lynchburg, Akron	3.37
G	Argenis Angulo, Akron, Columbus	48
GS	Adam Scott, Lynchburg, Akron	26
GS	Sam Hentges, Akron	26
GS	Tanner Tully, Akron, Columbus	26
GS	Shao-Ching Chiang, Akron	26
SV	Dalbert Siri, Akron, Columbus	10
IP	Michael Peoples, Columbus	145
BB	Sam Hentges, Akron	64
SO	Adam Scott, Lynchburg, Akron	148
# AVG	Asher Wojciechowski, Columbus	.217

General Manager: Mike Chernoff. **Farm Director:** James Harris. **Scouting Director:** Scott Barnsby.

Class	Team	League	W	L	PCT	Finish	Manager
Majors	Cleveland Indians	American	93	69	.574	6th (15)	Terry Francona
Triple-A	Columbus Clippers	International	81	59	.579	1st (14)	Tony Mansolino
Double-A	Akron Rubberducks	Eastern	61	79	.436	11th (12)	Rouglas Odor
High A	Lynchburg Hillcats	Carolina	62	73	.459	8th (10)	Jim Pankovits
Low A	Lake County Captains	Midwest	74	64	.536	8th (16)	Luke Carlin
Short season	M. Valley Scrappers	New York-Penn	37	39	.487	9th (14)	Dennis Malave
Rookie	AZL Indians Blue	Arizona	35	21	.625	3rd (21)	Larry Day
Rookie	AZL Indians Red	Arizona	27	29	.482	t-10th (21)	Jerry Owens
Overall 2019 Minor League Record			377	364	.509	11th (30)	

ORGANIZATION STATISTICS

CLEVELAND INDIANS
AMERICAN LEAGUE

Batting	B-T	HT	WT	DOB	AVG	vLH	vRH	G	AB	R	H	2B	3B	HR	RBI	BB	HBP	SH	SF	SO	SB	CS	SLG	OBP
Allen, Greg	B-R	6-0	185	3-15-93	.229	.186	.248	89	231	30	53	9	3	4	27	11	9	4	1	53	8	2	.346	.290
Bauers, Jake	L-L	6-1	195	10-6-95	.226	.231	.224	117	372	46	84	16	1	12	43	45	3	0	3	115	3	3	.371	.312
Bradley, Bobby	L-R	6-1	225	5-29-96	.178	.167	.182	15	45	4	8	5	0	1	4	4	0	0	0	20	0	0	.356	.245
Chang, Yu	R-R	6-1	180	8-18-95	.178	.115	.213	28	73	8	13	2	1	1	6	11	0	0	0	22	0	0	.274	.286
Flaherty, Ryan	L-R	6-3	205	7-27-86	.143	.000	.177	14	21	4	3	2	0	0	1	0	0	1	0	7	0	0	.238	.143
Freeman, Mike	L-R	6-0	195	8-4-87	.277	.304	.265	75	177	27	49	8	0	4	24	22	4	6	4	61	1	2	.390	.362
Gonzalez, Carlos	L-L	6-1	220	10-17-85	.210	.133	.240	30	105	13	22	1	0	2	7	10	1	0	1	33	0	1	.276	.282
Haase, Eric	R-R	5-10	210	12-18-92	.063	.100	.000	10	16	1	1	0	0	1	3	1	0	0	0	8	0	0	.250	.118
Kipnis, Jason	L-R	5-11	200	4-3-87	.245	.245	.244	121	458	52	112	23	1	17	65	40	2	5	6	88	7	2	.411	.304
Lindor, Francisco	B-R	5-11	190	11-14-93	.284	.258	.298	143	598	101	170	40	2	32	74	46	3	1	6	98	22	5	.518	.335
Luplow, Jordan	R-R	6-1	195	9-26-93	.276	.320	.217	85	225	42	62	15	1	15	38	33	2	0	1	61	3	2	.551	.372
Martin, Leonys	L-R	6-2	200	3-6-88	.199	.155	.218	65	236	32	47	7	0	9	19	21	4	3	0	78	4	5	.343	.276
Mercado, Oscar	R-R	6-2	197	12-16-94	.269	.263	.273	115	438	70	118	25	3	15	54	28	5	7	4	84	15	4	.443	.318
Miller, Brad	L-R	6-2	215	10-18-89	.250	.200	.258	13	36	4	9	3	0	1	4	4	0	0	0	10	1	0	.417	.325
Moroff, Max	B-R	5-10	190	5-13-93	.125	.000	.182	20	32	3	4	1	0	1	4	2	0	1	0	16	1	0	.250	.177
Naquin, Tyler	L-R	6-2	195	4-24-91	.288	.286	.289	89	274	34	79	19	0	10	34	14	2	2	2	66	4	2	.467	.325
Perez, Roberto	R-R	5-11	220	12-23-88	.239	.264	.227	119	389	46	93	9	1	24	63	45	4	7	4	127	0	0	.452	.321
Plawecki, Kevin	R-R	6-2	220	2-26-91	.222	.200	.232	59	158	13	35	10	0	3	17	12	3	0	1	31	0	1	.342	.287
Puig, Yasiel	R-R	6-2	240	12-7-90	.297	.304	.294	49	182	25	54	15	1	2	23	21	3	0	1	44	5	2	.423	.377
Ramirez, Hanley	R-R	6-2	235	12-23-83	.184	.177	.188	16	49	4	9	1	0	2	8	8	0	0	0	17	0	0	.327	.298
Ramirez, Jose	B-R	5-9	190	9-17-92	.255	.269	.249	129	482	68	123	33	3	23	83	52	2	0	6	74	24	4	.479	.327
Reyes, Franmil	R-R	6-5	275	7-7-95	.237	.305	.202	51	173	26	41	10	0	10	35	18	0	0	3	63	0	0	.468	.304
Santana, Carlos	B-R	5-11	210	4-8-86	.281	.324	.260	158	573	110	161	30	1	34	93	108	3	0	2	108	4	0	.515	.397
Stamets, Eric	R-R	6-0	190	9-25-91	.049	.091	.033	15	41	4	2	1	0	0	2	5	0	1	0	24	0	0	.073	.149
Velazquez, Andrew	B-R	5-8	170	7-14-94	.091	.250	.000	5	11	1	1	1	0	0	0	1	0	0	0	7	1	0	.182	.167
2-team total (10 Tampa Bay)					.087	.143	.063	15	23	3	2	2	0	0	0	1	0	0	0	13	1	0	.174	.125
Zimmer, Bradley	L-R	6-5	220	11-27-92	.000	.000	.000	9	13	1	0	0	0	0	0	1	0	0	0	7	0	0	.000	.071

Pitching	B-T	HT	WT	DOB	W	L	ERA	G	GS	CG	SV	IP	H	R	ER	HR	BB	SO	AVG	vLH	vRH	K/9	BB/9
Allen, Logan	R-L	6-3	200	5-23-97	0	0	0.00	1	0	0	0	2	3	0	0	0	0	3	.333	.500	.200	11.57	0.00
Anderson, Cody	R-R	6-4	240	9-14-90	0	1	9.35	5	2	0	0	9	12	9	9	1	8	9	.333	.235	.421	9.35	8.31
Bauer, Trevor	R-R	6-1	205	1-17-91	9	8	3.79	24	24	1	0	157	127	76	66	22	63	185	.218	.243	.199	10.63	3.62
Bieber, Shane	R-R	6-3	200	5-31-95	15	8	3.28	34	33	3	0	214	186	86	78	31	40	259	.230	.228	.231	10.88	1.68
Carrasco, Carlos	R-R	6-4	224	3-21-87	6	7	5.29	23	12	1	1	80	92	48	47	18	16	96	.288	.274	.301	10.80	1.80
Cimber, Adam	R-R	6-4	195	8-15-90	6	3	3.45	68	0	0	1	57	56	29	28	6	19	41	.257	.296	.244	6.51	3.02
Civale, Aaron	R-R	6-2	215	6-12-95	3	4	2.34	10	10	0	0	58	44	18	15	4	16	46	.216	.235	.203	7.18	2.50
Clevinger, Mike	R-R	6-4	215	12-21-90	13	4	2.71	21	21	0	0	126	96	38	38	10	37	169	.209	.219	.198	12.07	2.64
Clippard, Tyler	R-R	6-3	200	2-14-85	1	0	2.90	53	3	0	0	62	38	20	20	8	15	64	.176	.123	.227	9.29	2.18
Cole, A.J.	R-R	6-5	238	1-5-92	3	1	3.81	25	0	0	1	26	31	16	11	4	8	30	.290	.317	.273	10.38	2.77
Edwards, Jon	R-R	6-5	240	1-8-88	2	0	2.25	9	0	0	0	8	5	2	2	2	6	5	.179	.222	.158	5.63	6.75
Freeman, Mike	L-R	6-0	195	8-4-87	0	0	9.00	1	0	0	0	2	2	2	2	1	0	0	.250	.333	.200	0.00	0.00
Goody, Nick	R-R	5-11	200	7-6-91	3	2	3.54	39	0	0	0	41	30	18	16	7	22	50	.201	.226	.188	11.07	4.87
Hand, Brad	L-L	6-3	220	3-20-90	6	4	3.30	60	0	0	34	57	53	21	21	6	18	84	.242	.196	.258	13.19	2.83
Hoyt, James	R-R	6-6	230	9-30-86	0	0	2.16	8	0	0	0	8	6	2	2	2	2	10	.200	.333	.067	10.80	2.16
Karinchak, James	R-R	6-3	230	9-22-95	0	0	1.69	5	0	0	0	5	3	1	1	0	1	8	.150	.091	.222	13.50	1.69
Kluber, Corey	R-R	6-4	215	4-10-86	2	3	5.80	7	7	0	0	36	44	26	23	4	15	38	.297	.286	.306	9.59	3.79
Maton, Phil	R-R	6-3	220	3-25-93	0	0	2.92	9	0	0	0	12	4	5	4	1	6	13	.098	.059	.125	9.49	4.38
Olson, Tyler	R-L	6-3	205	10-2-89	1	1	4.40	39	0	0	0	31	34	15	15	3	16	28	.281	.245	.306	8.22	4.70
Otero, Dan	R-R	6-3	205	2-19-85	0	0	4.85	25	0	0	0	30	42	17	16	6	3	16	.331	.271	.367	4.85	0.91
Perez, Oliver	L-L	6-3	225	8-15-81	2	4	3.98	67	0	0	1	41	38	20	18	5	12	48	.242	.207	.286	10.62	2.66
Plawecki, Kevin	R-R	6-2	220	2-26-91	0	0	0.00	2	0	0	0	2	0	0	0	0	0	0	.000	.000	.000	0.00	0.00
Plesac, Zach	R-R	6-3	220	1-21-95	8	6	3.81	21	21	1	0	116	102	52	49	19	40	88	.237	.216	.253	6.85	3.11
Plutko, Adam	R-R	6-3	215	10-3-91	7	5	4.86	21	20	0	0	109	115	61	59	22	26	78	.267	.283	.252	6.42	2.14

CLEVELAND INDIANS

	B-T	HT	WT	DOB			ERA	G	GS	CG	SV	IP	H	R	ER	HR	BB	SO	AVG	vLH	vRH	K/9	BB/9
Ramirez, Neil	R-R	6-4	215	5-25-89	0	1	5.40	16	0	0	0	17	18	11	10	5	9	18	.281	.286	.278	9.72	4.86
2-team total (6 Toronto)					0	1	5.40	22	1	0	0	25	26	16	15	7	15	24	.274	.296	.255	8.64	5.40
Rodriguez, Jefry	R-R	6-6	232	7-26-93	1	5	4.63	10	8	0	0	47	48	26	24	5	21	33	.270	.237	.294	6.36	4.05
Salazar, Danny	R-R	6-0	195	1-11-90	0	1	4.50	1	1	0	0	4	4	2	2	3	2	.286	.167	.375	4.50	6.75
Smith, Josh D.	L-L	6-3	200	10-11-89	0	0	5.40	8	0	0	0	8	8	5	5	0	8	12	.242	.313	.177	12.96	8.64
Wittgren, Nick	R-R	6-2	216	5-29-91	5	1	2.81	55	0	0	4	58	47	22	18	10	15	60	.218	.241	.203	9.36	2.34
Wood, Hunter	R-R	6-1	175	8-12-93	0	0	3.86	17	0	0	0	16	20	9	7	3	5	15	.286	.313	.263	8.27	2.76
2-team total (19 Tampa Bay Rays)					1	1	2.98	36	2	0	1	45	46	20	15	7	12	39	.256	.257	.255	7.74	2.38

Fielding

Catcher	PCT	G	PO	A	E	DP	PB
Haase	1.000	8	27	2	0	0	1
Perez	.997	118	1082	52	3	12	0
Plawecki	.995	57	418	19	2	2	1

First Base	PCT	G	PO	A	E	DP
Bauers	.990	31	184	8	2	13
Bradley	.951	5	39	0	2	3
Plawecki	1.000	1	1	1	0	0
Santana	.990	135	951	73	10	77

Second Base	PCT	G	PO	A	E	DP
Flaherty	1.000	2	1	4	0	0
Freeman	.981	33	31	75	2	13
Kipnis	.990	117	150	253	4	51

	PCT	G	PO	A	E	DP
Miller	.935	13	7	22	2	2
Moroff	1.000	10	7	7	0	1
Velazquez	1.000	3	6	7	0	3

Third Base	PCT	G	PO	A	E	DP
Chang	1.000	25	10	32	0	1
Flaherty	1.000	11	5	9	0	0
Freeman	.914	18	8	24	3	1
Moroff	1.000	2	1	2	0	0
Ramirez	.959	126	108	222	14	21

Shortstop	PCT	G	PO	A	E	DP
Chang	1.000	8	1	2	0	1
Freeman	.950	9	7	12	1	1
Lindor	.979	137	159	312	10	68
Moroff	1.000	10	6	10	0	2

	PCT	G	PO	A	E	DP
Stamets	.950	15	10	28	2	3

Outfield	PCT	G	PO	A	E	DP
Allen	.985	84	125	7	2	0
Bauers	.988	53	79	3	1	0
Freeman	1.000	6	10	0	0	0
Gonzalez	.979	20	46	0	1	0
Luplow	1.000	76	117	5	0	1
Martin	.993	65	148	3	1	0
Mercado	.976	110	236	6	6	0
Naquin	1.000	80	165	11	0	3
Puig	.967	48	84	3	3	1
Reyes	1.000	3	4	0	0	0
Velazquez	.000	2	0	0	0	0
Zimmer	1.000	5	5	0	0	0

COLUMBUS CLIPPERS

INTERNATIONAL LEAGUE

TRIPLE-A

Batting	B-T	HT	WT	DOB	AVG	vLH	vRH	G	AB	R	H	2B	3B	HR	RBI	BB	HBP	SH	SF	SO	SB	CS	SLG	OBP
Allen, Greg	B-R	6-0	185	3-15-93	.268	.236	.286	48	198	37	53	9	3	5	17	20	8	0	0	44	10	5	.419	.358
Barnes, Brandon	R-R	6-2	210	5-15-86	.271	.228	.293	94	376	64	102	25	0	24	77	33	6	0	5	109	9	1	.529	.336
2-team total (26 Rochester)					.253	.225	.266	120	478	77	121	30	0	30	95	42	7	0	5	150	11	1	.504	.320
Bauers, Jake	L-L	6-1	195	10-6-95	.247	.238	.250	24	89	13	22	7	0	3	15	14	0	0	0	26	8	2	.427	.350
Bradley, Bobby	L-R	6-1	225	5-29-96	.264	.295	.249	107	402	65	106	23	0	33	74	46	4	0	1	153	0	0	.567	.344
Chang, Yu	R-R	6-1	180	8-18-95	.253	.283	.245	68	253	45	64	15	1	9	39	26	1	0	3	67	4	1	.427	.322
Clement, Ernie	R-R	6-0	170	3-22-96	.546	1.000	.500	3	11	3	6	1	0	0	4	2	0	0	0	1	1	0	.636	.615
Federowicz, Tim	R-R	5-10	215	8-5-87	.278	.200	.317	26	90	7	25	6	0	2	13	11	0	1	1	23	0	0	.411	.353
Flaherty, Ryan	L-R	6-3	205	7-27-86	.263	.244	.272	113	414	66	109	23	2	19	73	65	3	1	3	121	2	2	.466	.365
Freeman, Mike	L-R	6-0	195	8-4-87	.208	1.000	.174	9	24	6	5	0	0	3	3	9	0	0	0	7	1	0	.583	.424
Gonzalez, Carlos	L-L	6-1	220	10-17-85	.316	.500	.316	6	23	1	8	1	0	1	3	6	0	0	0	5	0	0	.522	.483
Haase, Eric	R-R	5-10	210	12-18-92	.226	.248	.216	102	350	67	79	12	3	28	60	42	5	1	3	142	1	1	.517	.315
Johnson, Daniel	L-L	5-10	200	7-11-95	.306	.235	.335	84	337	51	103	27	5	9	44	34	4	0	5	79	6	7	.496	.371
Kipnis, Jason	L-R	5-11	200	4-3-87	.136	.000	.143	6	22	1	3	2	0	0	2	2	0	0	0	6	0	0	.227	.208
Krieger, Tyler	R-R	6-2	185	1-16-94	.196	.136	.250	13	46	4	9	1	0	1	3	2	0	0	0	13	2	0	.283	.289
Lavarnway, Ryan	R-R	6-4	240	8-7-87	.364	.000	.400	4	11	2	4	1	0	0	2	2	0	0	1	1	0	0	.455	.429
3-team total (13 Louisville, 35 Scranton/Wilkes-Barre)					.226	.275	.204	52	159	21	36	5	0	6	28	25	3	0	3	36	0	0	.371	.337
Lindor, Francisco	B-R	5-11	190	11-14-93	.417	--	.417	3	12	4	5	1	0	2	2	1	0	0	0	1	0	0	1.000	.462
Luplow, Jordan	R-R	6-1	195	9-26-93	.311	.385	.281	13	45	12	14	3	0	2	7	10	2	0	0	14	2	1	.511	.456
Marabell, Connor	L-L	6-1	195	3-28-94	.203	.167	.212	20	64	6	13	3	0	1	7	5	0	0	0	5	1	1	.297	.261
Mathias, Mark	R-R	6-0	200	8-24-94	.269	.279	.266	115	412	62	111	31	2	12	59	51	7	2	6	91	13	2	.442	.355
Maybin, Cameron	R-R	6-3	215	4-4-87	.216	.273	.200	14	51	4	11	3	0	0	5	13	2	0	1	20	1	2	.275	.388
2-team total (3 Scranton/Wilkes-Barre)					.266	.273	.264	17	64	8	17	5	0	1	7	14	2	0	1	22	1	2	.391	.407
Mercado, Oscar	R-R	6-2	197	12-16-94	.294	.300	.292	30	119	24	35	10	1	4	15	16	4	1	0	32	14	3	.496	.396
Moroff, Max	B-R	5-10	190	5-13-93	.213	.191	.218	34	108	20	23	4	0	4	8	26	2	0	0	34	1	2	.361	.375
Naquin, Tyler	L-R	6-2	195	4-24-91	.333	.455	.143	4	18	4	6	1	1	3	6	0	0	0	0	4	0	0	1.000	.333
Navarro, Dioner	B-R	5-9	215	2-9-84	.211	.200	.213	29	95	8	20	3	0	1	11	18	1	0	1	21	0	0	.274	.339
Papi, Mike	L-R	6-3	215	9-19-92	.202	.208	.200	27	89	10	18	5	0	0	10	10	1	0	2	25	0	1	.258	.290
Rosales, Adam	R-R	6-2	200	5-20-83	.215	.310	.176	56	200	29	43	8	0	7	19	12	3	0	0	62	1	0	.360	.270
2-team total (20 Rochester)					.210	.262	.186	76	272	34	57	10	0	7	26	19	3	0	1	84	1	0	.324	.268
Stamets, Eric	R-R	6-0	190	9-25-91	.244	.272	.232	90	295	40	72	10	5	6	39	27	3	0	2	83	14	1	.373	.312
Thompson, Trayce	R-R	6-3	205	3-15-91	.219	.253	.205	89	334	51	73	10	3	24	56	33	3	0	1	134	8	3	.482	.294
Tom, Ka'ai	L-R	5-9	190	5-29-94	.298	.311	.294	51	188	33	56	15	4	9	44	21	1	0	1	53	2	3	.564	.370
Velazquez, Andrew	B-R	5-8	170	7-14-94	.244	.400	.200	12	45	5	11	4	1	0	5	0	1	0	0	9	1	1	.378	.261
2-team total (34 Durham)					.264	.273	.261	46	174	25	46	13	2	4	21	10	2	1	0	39	3	5	.431	.312
Wakamatsu, Luke	B-R	6-3	185	10-10-96	.000	.000	.000	1	3	0	0	0	0	0	0	0	0	0	0	1	0	0	.000	.000
Zimmer, Bradley	L-R	6-5	220	11-27-92	.364	.000	.381	6	22	5	8	1	1	1	2	3	0	1	0	6	2	0	.636	.440

Pitching	B-T	HT	WT	DOB	W	L	ERA	G	GS	CG	SV	IP	H	R	ER	HR	BB	SO	AVG	vLH	vRH	K/9	BB/9
Allen, Logan	R-L	6-3	200	5-23-97	1	1	7.66	5	5	0	0	22	31	20	19	6	12	18	.341	.529	.297	7.25	4.84
Anderson, Cody	R-R	6-4	230	9-14-90	0	2	4.56	6	6	0	0	24	25	12	12	3	7	21	.284	.271	.300	7.99	2.66
Angulo, Argenis	R-R	6-3	225	2-26-94	1	0	5.20	22	1	0	3	28	24	18	16	7	16	25	.231	.156	.288	8.13	5.20
Barnes, Brandon	R-R	6-2	210	5-15-86	0	0	0.00	3	0	0	0	5	3	0	0	0	1	1	.200	.143	.250	1.93	1.93
Brady, Sean	L-L	6-0	210	6-9-94	1	0	5.23	2	2	0	0	10	12	6	6	1	6	7	.308	.286	.320	6.10	5.23
Carrasco, Carlos	R-R	6-4	224	3-21-87	0	0	3.86	2	0	0	0	2	2	1	1	0	1	3	.250	.000	.286	11.57	3.86

Chiang, Shao-Ching	R-R	6-0	185	11-10-93	9	9	5.15	26	26	1	0	131	144	86	75	19	57	128	.273	.279	.269	8.79	3.92
Civale, Aaron	R-R	6-2	215	6-12-95	3	1	2.13	8	8	0	0	42	38	13	10	4	9	46	.233	.210	.248	9.78	1.91
Clevinger, Mike	R-R	6-4	215	12-21-90	0	0	18.00	1	1	0	0	2	3	4	4	1	2	4	.333	.000	.429	18.00	9.00
Clippard, Tyler	R-R	6-3	200	2-14-85	0	0	3.00	3	0	0	0	3	2	1	1	0	0	4	.182	.143	.250	12.00	0.00
Cole, A.J.	R-R	6-5	238	1-5-92	0	1	3.18	13	0	0	2	17	10	6	6	2	5	21	.179	.261	.121	11.12	2.65
Edwards, Jon	R-R	6-5	240	1-8-88	6	1	4.22	41	0	0	3	49	43	25	23	7	26	62	.228	.250	.214	11.39	4.78
Flaherty, Ryan	L-R	6-3	205	7-27-86	0	0	9.00	1	0	0	0	1	3	1	1	1	0	0	.500	.333	.667	0.00	0.00
Goody, Nick	R-R	5-11	200	7-6-91	0	1	7.77	21	0	0	0	24	28	23	21	8	13	34	.286	.209	.346	12.58	4.81
Hernandez, Hector	B-L	6-1	190	2-20-91	1	1	2.08	3	0	0	0	4	3	1	1	0	1	7	.188	.000	.300	14.54	2.08
Hill, Cam	R-R	6-1	185	5-24-94	2	2	4.74	21	0	0	1	25	23	13	13	5	12	36	.250	.242	.254	13.14	4.38
Hoyt, James	R-R	6-6	230	9-30-86	2	0	3.43	40	2	0	4	42	46	17	16	3	20	48	.279	.308	.260	10.29	4.29
Hu, Chih-Wei	R-R	6-0	220	11-4-93	1	4	7.95	15	7	0	0	49	60	43	43	16	18	41	.305	.289	.318	7.58	3.33
Kaminsky, Rob	R-L	5-11	200	9-2-94	1	0	5.11	23	0	0	1	25	26	16	14	3	14	31	.265	.261	.267	11.31	5.11
Karinchak, James	R-R	6-3	230	9-22-95	1	1	4.67	17	0	0	2	17	14	10	9	2	13	42	.215	.118	.250	21.81	6.75
Kluber, Corey	R-R	6-4	215	4-10-86	0	0	4.50	2	2	0	0	4	2	2	2	2	3	2	.143	.200	.111	4.50	6.75
Krauth, Ben	L-L	6-0	190	3-10-94	0	0	0.00	1	0	0	0	0	0	0	0	0	3	0	.000	.000	--	0.00	81.00
Martinez, Henry	R-R	6-1	180	4-27-94	2	2	5.61	36	0	0	4	43	48	29	27	4	19	37	.286	.319	.260	7.68	3.95
Maton, Phil	R-R	6-3	220	3-25-93	0	1	2.53	9	0	0	3	11	5	3	3	1	4	17	.143	.267	.050	14.34	3.38
Mitchell, Evan	R-R	6-2	185	3-18-92	0	2	11.74	3	2	0	0	8	17	11	10	1	4	5	.447	.471	.429	5.87	4.70
Morgan, Eli	R-R	5-10	190	5-13-96	1	1	5.40	1	1	0	0	5	5	3	3	0	2	2	.278	.250	.300	3.60	3.60
Moss, Scott	L-L	6-6	225	10-6-94	2	1	1.93	4	4	0	0	19	12	4	4	1	8	23	.179	.400	.140	11.09	3.86
Navarro, Dioner	B-R	5-9	215	2-9-84	0	0	13.50	2	0	0	0	2	6	3	3	1	0	0	.500	.500	.000	0.00	0.00
Nelson, Kyle	L-L	6-1	175	7-8-96	2	0	2.25	11	1	0	1	12	8	3	3	2	5	16	.191	.273	.161	12.00	3.75
Olson, Tyler	R-L	6-3	205	10-2-89	0	0	0.00	1	0	0	0	1	0	0	0	0	0	1	.500	--	.500	27.00	0.00
Orlan, R.C.	R-L	6-0	215	9-28-90	0	2	7.53	11	0	0	1	14	18	13	12	2	13	11	.321	.286	.343	6.91	8.16
Otero, Dan	R-R	6-3	205	2-19-85	0	0	0.73	11	0	0	0	12	5	1	1	1	1	8	.119	.125	.115	5.84	0.73
Paulson, Jake	R-R	6-7	225	2-17-92	1	0	6.75	2	2	0	0	11	10	8	8	3	9	7	.256	.333	.191	5.91	7.59
Peoples, Michael	R-R	6-5	190	9-5-91	10	6	3.98	25	22	0	0	145	157	67	64	17	29	122	.279	.263	.291	7.59	1.80
Plesac, Zach	R-R	6-3	220	1-21-95	3	1	2.73	4	4	0	0	26	19	8	8	2	3	31	.198	.146	.250	10.59	1.03
Plutko, Adam	R-R	6-3	215	10-3-91	1	3	7.47	4	4	0	0	16	21	13	13	1	4	16	.318	.333	.300	9.19	2.30
Pounders, Brooks	R-R	6-5	265	9-26-90	2	1	2.31	24	0	0	1	35	19	9	9	4	11	46	.161	.217	.125	11.83	2.83
2-team total (19 Syracuse)					3	3	4.31	43	1	0	1	56	48	28	27	8	20	66	.233	.307	.191	10.54	3.20
Ramirez, Neil	R-R	6-4	215	5-25-89	2	1	4.91	25	0	0	2	29	28	17	16	7	11	45	.244	.170	.294	13.81	3.38
2-team total (1 Buffalo)					2	1	4.75	26	0	0	2	30	29	17	16	7	11	47	.244	.163	.300	13.95	3.26
Robinson, Jared	R-R	6-0	190	11-20-94	2	1	6.50	10	0	0	0	18	17	13	13	4	14	23	.266	.138	.371	11.50	7.00
Rodriguez, Jefry	R-R	6-6	232	7-26-93	1	0	4.15	5	3	0	0	22	16	10	10	1	11	16	.208	.200	.213	6.65	4.57
Salazar, Danny	R-R	6-0	195	1-11-90	0	0	0.00	2	2	0	0	7	4	0	0	0	2	11	.154	.231	.077	13.50	2.45
Sandlin, Nick	R-R	5-11	175	1-10-97	1	0	4.00	7	0	0	0	9	5	4	4	2	7	11	.172	.300	.105	11.00	7.00
Siri, Dalbert	R-R	6-2	215	7-19-95	0	0	0.00	1	0	0	0	2	2	0	0	0	0	4	.222	.000	.286	15.43	0.00
Smith, Josh D.	L-L	6-3	200	10-11-89	8	1	2.73	41	0	0	6	53	32	17	16	7	24	74	.170	.191	.160	12.65	4.10
Speer, David	L-L	6-1	210	8-14-92	0	0	9.00	1	0	0	0	2	2	2	2	1	2	0	.222	.333	.167	0.00	9.00
Stephens, Jordan	R-R	6-1	190	9-12-92	1	4	9.42	6	6	0	0	29	39	33	30	9	14	26	.322	.370	.284	8.16	4.40
2-team total (9 Charlotte)					4	8	8.95	15	12	0	0	66	96	71	66	17	28	53	.338	.362	.318	7.19	3.80
Talbot, Mitch	R-R	6-1	180	10-17-83	3	3	5.37	12	11	0	1	59	65	37	35	10	10	37	.281	.220	.328	5.68	1.53
Tully, Tanner	L-L	6-0	200	11-30-94	1	1	4.91	3	3	0	0	15	15	8	8	2	2	14	.263	.214	.279	8.59	1.23
Valladares, Randy	L-L	5-11	155	7-6-94	0	0	0.00	1	0	0	0	2	0	0	0	0	1	2	.000	.000	.000	10.80	5.40
Whitehouse, Matt	L-L	6-1	200	4-13-91	1	1	9.69	9	0	0	0	13	16	17	14	5	9	16	.302	.133	.368	11.08	6.23
Wittgren, Nick	R-R	6-2	216	5-29-91	0	0	3.86	2	0	0	0	2	3	2	1	0	2	4	.273	.000	.375	15.43	7.71
Wojciechowski, Asher	R-R	6-4	235	12-21-88	8	2	3.61	15	15	0	0	85	67	35	34	19	31	82	.217	.209	.222	8.72	3.30
Wood, Hunter	R-R	6-1	175	8-12-93	0	0	6.75	1	0	0	0	1	1	1	1	1	0	3	.200	.000	.250	20.25	0.00
2-team total (8 Durham)					1	0	7.50	9	0	0	1	12	17	12	10	4	5	17	.321	.333	.313	12.75	3.75

Fielding

Catcher	PCT	G	PO	A	E	DP	PB
Federowicz	.995	22	207	11	1	1	3
Haase	.990	93	821	52	9	7	11
Lavarnway	1.000	3	24	2	0	0	0
Navarro	.993	26	261	10	2	0	3
Stamets	.959	22	28	43	3	4	
Velazquez	.833	1	3	2	1	2	
Velazquez	1.000	5	6	11	0	3	
Wakamatsu	1.000	1	0	1	0	0	

First Base	PCT	G	PO	A	E	DP
Barnes	1.000	16	119	5	0	10
Bauers	1.000	6	42	4	0	8
Bradley	.988	98	669	58	9	63
Flaherty	1.000	11	87	7	0	4
Rosales	.991	13	103	7	1	7

Second Base	PCT	G	PO	A	E	DP
Barnes	1.000	3	1	1	0	0
Chang	.950	23	29	47	4	13
Clement	1.000	2	6	2	0	0
Federowicz	.000	1	0	0	0	0
Flaherty	.982	15	26	30	1	8
Freeman	1.000	2	6	4	0	1
Kipnis	.962	6	11	14	1	4
Mathias	1.000	52	73	128	0	27
Moroff	.976	11	17	23	1	5
Rosales	1.000	17	22	43	0	12

Third Base	PCT	G	PO	A	E	DP
Chang	.943	17	8	25	2	2
Federowicz	.000	1	0	0	0	0
Flaherty	.940	32	17	52	5	9
Freeman	.800	2	1	3	1	0
Krieger	.905	9	7	12	2	0
Mathias	.954	47	30	73	5	7
Moroff	1.000	5	4	5	0	0
Rosales	1.000	18	12	29	0	4
Stamets	.829	15	7	22	6	2

Shortstop	PCT	G	PO	A	E	DP
Chang	.988	22	27	56	1	9
Clement	1.000	1	2	5	0	3
Flaherty	.992	40	49	78	1	16
Freeman	1.000	4	2	15	0	1
Lindor	1.000	2	0	5	0	0
Mathias	.889	3	5	11	2	1
Moroff	1.000	14	21	37	0	9
Rosales	1.000	2	2	1	0	1
Stamets	.972	51	56	120	5	22

Outfield	PCT	G	PO	A	E	DP
Allen	.988	42	79	4	1	1
Barnes	1.000	63	114	6	0	0
Bauers	1.000	15	25	2	0	1
Gonzalez	1.000	6	14	1	0	0
Johnson	.969	78	149	5	5	2
Krieger	1.000	3	3	0	0	0
Lavarnway	.000	1	0	0	0	0
Luplow	1.000	12	23	0	0	0
Marabell	1.000	17	30	3	0	0
Maybin	.917	11	22	0	2	0
Mercado	.986	28	70	3	1	1
Moroff	1.000	2	1	0	0	0
Naquin	1.000	3	7	1	0	0
Papi	1.000	21	32	3	0	0
Thompson	.987	75	145	4	2	0
Tom	1.000	45	74	3	0	0
Velazquez	1.000	6	10	1	0	0
Zimmer	1.000	6	11	0	0	0

AKRON RUBBERDUCKS

DOUBLE-A

EASTERN LEAGUE

Batting	B-T	HT	WT	DOB	AVG	vLH	vRH	G	AB	R	H	2B	3B	HR	RBI	BB	HBP	SH	SF	SO	SB	CS	SLG	OBP
Brooks, Trenton	L-L	6-0	180	7-3-95	.274	.267	.276	65	241	28	66	22	3	9	36	20	2	0	1	38	1	0	.502	.333
Calica, Andrew	L-R	6-1	195	3-5-94	.200	.000	.217	8	25	4	5	1	1	0	4	4	3	0	0	9	0	1	.320	.375
Call, Alex	R-R	6-0	188	9-27-94	.205	.211	.203	81	293	30	60	13	3	5	31	22	4	2	4	93	5	5	.321	.266
Chu, Li-Jen	R-R	5-11	230	3-13-94	.229	.279	.204	60	210	19	48	12	0	5	25	16	3	0	2	68	0	0	.357	.290
Clement, Ernie	R-R	6-0	170	3-22-96	.261	.309	.243	98	394	46	103	15	3	1	24	26	7	4	6	33	16	10	.322	.314
Friis, Tyler	B-R	5-9	180	2-12-96	.250	.177	.316	26	72	11	18	3	0	1	5	9	1	0	0	12	4	1	.333	.342
Garcia, Wilson	B-R	5-11	227	1-11-94	.269	.256	.275	69	257	29	69	23	0	10	46	15	1	1	1	35	0	0	.475	.310
Gonzalez, Gianpaul	R-R	6-0	185	1-11-96	.128	.143	.121	16	47	3	6	1	0	0	1	7	0	5	0	19	0	0	.149	.241
Gonzalez, Oscar	R-R	6-2	180	1-10-98	.188	.091	.216	29	96	7	18	5	0	1	9	3	0	0	1	17	0	0	.271	.210
Ice, Logan	B-R	5-10	190	5-27-95	.180	.092	.213	79	239	21	43	4	1	4	22	36	3	2	1	74	0	0	.255	.294
Johnson, Daniel	L-L	5-10	200	7-11-95	.253	.255	.253	39	146	25	37	7	2	10	33	16	3	1	1	39	6	3	.534	.337
Jones, Nolan	L-R	6-2	185	5-7-98	.253	.167	.290	49	178	33	45	10	2	8	22	31	2	0	0	63	2	0	.466	.370
Krieger, Tyler	B-R	6-2	185	1-16-94	.211	.109	.264	48	161	24	34	6	1	3	17	16	3	3	2	40	8	3	.317	.291
Longo, Mitch	L-R	6-0	195	1-12-95	.248	.226	.255	90	327	43	81	17	4	5	29	30	5	2	1	73	11	2	.370	.320
Lopez, Jonathan	L-R	6-2	175	8-13-99	.000	.000	.000	1	2	0	0	0	0	0	0	1	0	0	0	1	0	0	.000	.333
Marabell, Connor	L-L	6-1	195	3-28-94	.273	.291	.266	111	421	51	115	23	1	8	50	28	3	1	3	52	7	1	.390	.321
Medina, Jose	L-L	6-1	185	2-14-95	.167	.143	.182	5	18	1	3	1	0	0	1	0	0	0	0	7	0	0	.222	.211
Mejia, Gabriel	R-R	5-11	160	7-30-95	.095	.000	.125	7	21	2	2	0	0	0	1	2	0	0	0	6	1	0	.095	.174
Monasterio, Andruw	R-R	6-0	185	5-30-97	.217	.190	.225	70	249	21	54	6	0	1	11	22	1	3	4	57	5	6	.253	.279
Naquin, Tyler	L-R	6-2	195	4-24-91	.200	.333	.000	2	5	0	1	0	0	0	0	0	0	0	0	1	0	0	.400	.200
Pantoja, Alexis	L-R	5-11	186	1-18-96	.257	.223	.270	117	416	45	107	15	2	2	37	28	1	5	3	72	6	8	.317	.304
Rodriguez, Jorma	R-R	5-10	150	3-25-96	.221	.167	.257	34	122	7	27	2	0	0	11	5	0	1	0	40	0	1	.238	.250
Rodriguez, Nellie	R-R	6-2	225	6-12-94	.199	.241	.180	78	277	34	55	13	0	12	42	31	2	1	3	120	0	0	.376	.281
Salters, Daniel	L-R	6-3	225	2-5-93	.100	.200	.067	6	20	1	2	0	0	1	3	2	0	0	0	4	0	0	.250	.182
Smith, Connor	R-R	5-10	180	4-22-97	.140	.083	.161	12	43	4	6	3	0	1	3	1	1	1	0	15	0	0	.279	.178
Stankiewicz, Drew	R-R	5-10	160	6-18-93	.091	.000	.143	10	22	6	2	0	0	0	1	10	0	0	0	6	1	1	.091	.375
Tom, Ka'ai	L-R	5-9	190	5-29-94	.285	.283	.287	81	291	50	83	12	6	14	42	43	6	1	2	73	3	2	.512	.386
Zimmer, Bradley	L-R	6-5	220	11-27-92	.308	--	.308	4	13	2	4	2	0	1	3	0	0	0	0	4	0	0	.692	.308

Pitching	B-T	HT	WT	DOB	W	L	ERA	G	GS	CG	SV	IP	H	R	ER	HR	BB	SO	AVG	vLH	vRH	K/9	BB/9
Angulo, Argenis	R-R	6-3	225	2-26-94	3	2	2.06	26	0	0	2	35	19	8	8	0	22	63	.157	.167	.149	16.20	5.66
Bernardino, Brennan	L-L	6-4	180	1-15-92	0	0	4.15	2	0	0	0	4	4	2	2	1	1	3	.235	.167	.273	6.23	2.08
Brady, Sean	L-L	6-0	210	6-9-94	0	2	9.64	3	3	0	0	14	20	16	15	0	9	8	.323	.300	.333	5.14	5.79
2-team total (22 Altoona)					5	13	4.20	25	25	1	0	152	155	83	71	15	45	90	.265	.233	.281	5.33	2.66
Broom, Robert	R-R	6-1	190	9-17-96	1	2	0.96	25	0	0	1	37	19	5	4	2	14	35	.148	.180	.128	8.44	3.38
Carrasco, Carlos	R-R	6-4	224	3-21-87	0	0	0.00	1	1	0	0	3	0	0	0	0	1	5	.000	.000	.000	16.88	3.38
Civale, Aaron	R-R	6-2	215	6-12-95	4	0	2.67	5	5	0	0	30	26	9	9	3	6	24	.232	.222	.241	7.12	1.78
Clevinger, Mike	R-R	6-4	215	12-21-90	0	0	0.00	1	1	0	0	5	3	0	0	0	0	5	.158	.000	.250	8.44	0.00
Dowdy, Kyle	R-R	6-1	195	2-3-93	1	1	2.48	7	3	0	0	29	25	10	8	2	11	27	.234	.200	.258	8.38	3.41
Draper, Zach	L-L	6-3	200	10-18-94	0	1	1.59	1	1	0	0	6	8	1	1	0	3	5	.348	.222	.429	7.94	4.76
Eubank, Luke	R-R	6-0	180	2-24-94	1	1	7.24	9	0	0	0	14	17	15	11	2	7	17	.298	.208	.364	11.20	4.61
Gomez, Yapson	L-L	5-10	160	10-2-93	1	0	3.38	3	0	0	0	8	8	5	3	0	2	6	.242	.250	.240	6.75	2.25
Gose, Anthony	L-L	6-1	190	8-10-90	0	3	3.50	22	0	0	1	18	13	15	7	0	20	22	.194	.120	.238	11.00	10.00
Hentges, Sam	L-L	6-8	245	7-18-96	2	13	5.11	26	26	0	0	129	148	89	73	11	64	126	.289	.312	.277	8.81	4.48
Hernandez, Hector	B-L	6-1	190	2-20-91	0	0	0.00	2	0	0	1	2	1	0	0	0	2	2	.167	.333	.000	10.80	10.80
Hu, Chih-Wei	R-R	6-0	220	11-4-93	0	1	3.00	3	2	0	0	9	7	3	3	2	5	9	.212	.333	.143	9.00	5.00
Kaminsky, Rob	R-L	5-11	200	9-2-94	2	1	2.30	19	0	0	1	31	22	11	8	2	8	30	.193	.192	.194	8.62	2.30
Karinchak, James	R-R	6-3	230	9-22-95	0	0	0.00	10	0	0	6	10	2	0	0	0	2	24	.061	.000	.125	21.60	1.80
Kluber, Corey	R-R	6-4	215	4-10-86	0	0	2.25	1	1	0	0	4	2	1	1	1	6	.143	.167	.000	13.50	2.25
Krauth, Ben	L-L	6-0	190	3-10-94	1	3	4.66	34	0	0	1	56	50	33	29	9	32	53	.237	.229	.241	8.52	5.14
Lingos, Eli	L-L	6-0	192	5-21-96	0	1	7.20	2	1	0	0	10	9	9	8	2	4	8	.237	.273	.222	3.60	3.60
Martinez, Henry	R-R	6-1	180	4-27-94	0	1	1.10	11	0	0	0	16	6	2	2	0	10	11	.120	.182	.071	6.06	5.51
Mitchell, Evan	R-R	6-2	185	3-18-92	0	2	4.50	2	2	0	0	8	7	5	4	0	7	5	.250	.214	.563	5.63	7.88
Morgan, Eli	R-R	5-10	190	5-13-96	6	4	3.79	19	18	1	0	102	100	47	43	12	33	104	.256	.267	.246	9.18	2.91
Moss, Scott	L-L	6-6	225	10-6-94	2	0	0.00	2	2	0	0	10	3	1	0	0	5	13	.091	.000	.130	11.70	4.50
Nelson, Kyle	L-L	6-1	175	7-8-96	1	3	3.12	23	0	0	3	26	17	12	9	3	9	36	.183	.189	.179	12.46	3.12
Olson, Tyler	R-L	6-3	205	10-2-89	0	0	0.00	1	0	0	0	1	1	0	0	0	1	2	.333	.500	.000	27.00	13.50
Otero, Dan	R-R	6-3	205	2-19-85	0	0	9.00	3	0	0	0	3	4	3	3	1	1	2	.333	.429	.200	3.00	3.00
Pantoja, Alexis	L-R	5-11	186	1-18-96	0	0	0.00	1	0	0	0	1	0	0	0	0	0	0	.250	.250	--	0.00	0.00
Paulson, Jake	R-R	6-7	225	2-17-92	11	7	3.66	26	18	0	0	120	133	59	49	5	32	73	.282	.332	.237	5.46	2.39
Plesac, Zach	R-R	6-3	220	1-21-95	1	1	0.96	6	6	0	0	37	23	4	4	0	6	34	.176	.174	.177	8.20	1.45
Polanco, Anderson	L-L	6-3	190	6-9-92	0	1	12.27	3	0	0	0	4	5	5	5	1	4	3	.357	.250	.400	7.36	9.82
Robinson, Jared	R-R	6-0	190	11-20-94	1	3	1.57	16	0	0	3	29	16	6	5	1	14	39	.162	.191	.140	12.24	4.40
Rodriguez, Jefry	R-R	6-6	232	7-26-93	0	0	2.45	2	0	0	0	4	2	1	1	0	0	3	.167	.000	.250	7.36	0.00
Salazar, Danny	R-R	6-0	195	1-11-90	0	1	5.40	5	4	0	0	8	8	5	5	1	6	7	.242	.364	.182	7.56	6.48
Sandlin, Nick	R-R	5-11	175	1-10-97	0	0	1.56	15	0	0	2	17	13	4	3	2	8	27	.203	.219	.188	14.02	4.15
Scott, Adam	L-L	6-4	220	10-10-95	4	6	3.94	14	14	0	0	75	70	36	33	9	21	74	.247	.241	.250	8.84	2.51
Siri, Dalbert	R-R	6-2	215	7-19-95	2	2	2.98	45	0	0	10	45	35	20	15	3	29	48	.215	.247	.189	9.53	5.76
Solter, Matt	R-R	6-3	220	6-4-93	1	0	3.51	5	0	0	0	10	26	27	19	16	2	11	.196	.244	.912	3.51	
Speer, David	L-L	6-1	210	8-14-92	3	3	1.81	32	4	0	2	55	42	15	11	4	17	44	.222	.197	.237	7.24	2.80
Stephens, Jordan	R-R	6-1	190	9-12-92	2	1	1.96	9	1	0	0	23	20	6	5	3	5	29	.235	.250	.226	11.35	1.96
Tully, Tanner	L-L	6-0	200	11-30-94	8	11	4.38	23	23	0	0	129	155	71	63	9	27	75	.298	.328	.283	5.22	1.88
Whitehouse, Matt	L-L	6-1	200	4-13-91	3	1	4.50	10	0	0	0	22	18	12	11	0	14	27	.220	.280	.193	11.05	5.73
2-team total (13 Hartford)					4	4	4.66	23	8	0	0	68	71	37	35	3	30	74	.271	.322	.246	9.84	3.99

Fielding

Catcher	PCT	G	PO	A	E	DP	PB
Chu	.987	49	425	28	6	1	7
Gonzalez	.993	16	129	10	1	1	1
Ice	.995	75	574	56	3	5	1
Salters	1.000	3	23	0	0	0	0

	PCT	G	PO	A	E	DP
Monasterio	.985	45	84	119	3	28
Pantoja	.975	41	64	89	4	22
Rodriguez	.960	13	20	28	2	4
Smith	.931	7	11	16	2	5
Stankiewicz	.929	10	13	26	3	6

	PCT	G	PO	A	E	DP
Monasterio	1.000	18	21	29	0	6
Pantoja	.979	35	38	99	3	18
Rodriguez	1.000	2	1	3	0	1

First Base	PCT	G	PO	A	E	DP
Garcia	.995	50	401	21	2	31
Gonzalez	1.000	1	3	0	0	0
Marabell	.995	24	176	14	1	14
Pantoja	1.000	6	32	2	0	3
Rodriguez	.990	64	465	34	5	46

Third Base	PCT	G	PO	A	E	DP
Jones	.947	44	37	70	6	4
Krieger	.921	36	18	52	6	2
Lopez	1.000	1	1	1	0	0
Monasterio	1.000	2	0	9	0	0
Pantoja	.944	36	23	44	4	4
Rodriguez	.933	21	11	31	3	7
Rodriguez	.000	1	0	0	0	0
Smith	1.000	5	4	10	0	2

Outfield	PCT	G	PO	A	E	DP
Brooks	.968	45	86	5	3	0
Calica	1.000	5	7	1	0	0
Call	.995	77	192	4	1	2
Gonzalez	.941	24	45	3	3	0
Johnson	.988	37	78	2	1	0
Krieger	1.000	7	13	1	0	0
Longo	.979	70	135	3	3	2
Marabell	.988	78	157	1	2	0
Medina	1.000	3	4	1	0	0
Mejia	1.000	5	7	0	0	0
Naquin	1.000	2	2	0	0	0
Tom	.965	76	134	2	5	0
Zimmer	1.000	3	2	0	0	0

Second Base	PCT	G	PO	A	E	DP
Clement	1.000	3	6	6	0	2
Friis	1.000	24	38	60	0	14
Krieger	.857	2	3	3	1	0
Mejia	1.000	2	1	0	0	0

Shortstop	PCT	G	PO	A	E	DP
Clement	.941	90	109	239	22	40

LYNCHBURG HILLCATS — HIGH CLASS A
CAROLINA LEAGUE

Batting	B-T	HT	WT	DOB	AVG	vLH	vRH	G	AB	R	H	2B	3B	HR	RBI	BB	HBP	SH	SF	SO	SB	CS	SLG	OBP
Benson, Will	L-L	6-5	225	6-16-98	.189	.197	.185	61	217	29	41	9	2	4	23	31	2	0	5	73	9	2	.304	.290
Brooks, Trenton	L-L	6-0	180	7-3-95	.213	.362	.158	49	174	19	37	11	0	3	18	22	2	3	2	26	0	2	.328	.305
Carter, Jodd	R-R	5-10	170	7-20-96	.243	.273	.231	102	342	48	83	18	1	11	33	52	4	3	2	96	9	5	.398	.348
Collins, Gavin	R-R	5-11	190	7-17-95	.262	.252	.267	100	347	39	91	21	2	7	61	30	5	1	6	52	1	2	.395	.325
Farhat, Cody	R-R	6-1	185	9-26-96	.175	.179	.171	21	63	6	11	2	0	0	4	4	2	1	2	6	0	1	.206	.243
Freeman, Tyler	R-R	6-0	170	5-21-99	.319	.303	.327	62	257	38	82	16	2	0	20	8	7	1	2	25	8	1	.397	.354
Friis, Tyler	B-R	5-9	180	2-12-96	.226	.333	.198	37	133	11	30	9	1	1	17	23	0	0	1	26	5	4	.331	.338
Gonzalez, Oscar	R-R	6-2	180	1-10-98	.320	.394	.296	96	385	46	123	22	3	8	61	12	2	1	2	66	7	5	.455	.342
Jones, Nolan	L-R	6-2	185	5-7-98	.286	.135	.325	77	252	48	72	12	1	7	41	65	4	0	3	85	5	3	.425	.435
Kwan, Steven	L-L	5-9	175	9-5-97	.280	.304	.269	123	479	68	134	26	7	3	39	53	4	1	5	51	11	7	.382	.353
Laureano, Jonathan	R-R	6-1	200	12-21-95	.215	.222	.211	96	340	37	73	16	2	3	30	27	2	2	4	98	1	2	.300	.274
Loopstok, Sicnarf	R-R	5-11	195	4-26-93	.200	.000	.222	3	10	1	2	0	0	0	0	1	0	0	0	4	0	0	.200	.273
Mejia, Gabriel	R-R	5-11	160	7-30-95	.250	.250	.250	14	48	6	12	0	0	0	3	5	0	1	0	17	2	2	.250	.321
Persinger, Dillon	R-R	5-11	180	1-31-96	.163	.130	.175	21	80	9	13	2	0	1	7	6	1	0	1	34	0	1	.225	.227
Pujols, Henry	R-R	6-3	195	12-10-98	.200	--	.200	2	5	1	1	0	0	1	2	0	0	0	0	2	0	0	.800	.200
Reeves, Mitch	R-R	6-2	210	11-18-94	.295	.301	.292	63	227	25	67	16	1	2	29	39	2	1	3	53	1	2	.401	.399
Rivera, Mike	R-R	5-10	200	12-12-95	.201	.227	.194	62	199	22	40	13	1	3	23	20	6	2	2	44	1	1	.322	.291
Rodriguez, Jason	R-R	5-11	180	1-11-95	.292	.387	.220	23	72	4	21	7	0	0	6	3	1	1	0	24	0	0	.389	.329
Santiago, Wilbis	L-R	6-0	180	1-20-96	.310	.196	.340	67	239	22	74	15	4	1	21	6	6	0	2	21	1	3	.418	.340
Smith, Connor	R-R	5-10	180	4-22-97	.244	.344	.180	25	82	7	20	2	0	0	5	12	2	0	1	26	2	0	.268	.351
Vicente, Jose	R-R	5-11	175	11-13-95	.209	.212	.207	27	91	9	19	4	0	3	8	4	1	0	0	16	0	0	.352	.250
Wade, Austen	L-L	6-2	185	2-17-96	.266	.357	.246	23	79	12	21	3	1	1	6	16	0	1	0	19	1	3	.367	.390
Wakamatsu, Luke	B-R	6-3	185	10-10-96	.150	.141	.153	98	314	31	47	16	2	6	26	28	0	5	0	123	7	0	.271	.219

Pitching	B-T	HT	WT	DOB	W	L	ERA	G	GS	CG	SV	IP	H	R	ER	HR	BB	SO	AVG	vLH	vRH	K/9	BB/9
Alvarez, Manuel	R-R	6-3	200	9-17-95	1	0	6.00	11	0	0	0	15	15	10	10	0	12	20	.263	.286	.250	12.00	7.20
Arias, Skylar	L-L	6-3	190	6-30-97	0	0	1.42	5	0	0	0	6	3	1	1	0	2	10	.143	.100	.182	14.21	2.84
Bernardino, Brennan	L-L	6-4	180	1-15-92	1	1	5.14	3	0	0	0	7	9	5	4	0	4	5	.321	.333	.318	6.43	5.14
Broom, Robert	R-R	6-1	190	9-17-96	1	1	0.36	17	0	0	2	25	13	4	1	0	9	35	.149	.229	.096	12.77	3.28
Carter, Jodd	R-R	5-10	170	7-20-96	0	0	0.00	1	0	0	0	1	1	0	0	0	0	0	.200	.000	.333	0.00	0.00
Clemmer, Dakody	R-R	6-2	185	1-19-96	3	1	4.47	28	0	0	0	48	45	25	24	4	20	41	.250	.206	.277	7.63	3.72
Draper, Zach	L-L	6-3	200	10-18-94	0	1	9.53	3	1	0	0	6	16	9	6	1	5	5	.485	.571	.421	4.76	7.94
Echols, Riley	R-R	6-4	205	4-12-95	3	1	3.78	14	0	0	2	17	15	9	7	1	14	10	.246	.154	.314	5.40	7.56
Gallagher, Nick	R-R	6-3	200	9-9-95	1	1	4.89	10	5	0	1	35	25	22	19	2	24	44	.198	.182	.207	11.31	6.17
Garza, Justin	R-R	5-10	170	3-20-94	6	9	4.99	29	20	0	1	119	126	74	66	13	56	109	.275	.312	.254	8.24	4.24
Gomez, Yapson	L-L	5-10	160	10-2-93	2	6	2.27	44	0	0	8	63	51	24	16	3	17	66	.227	.182	.250	9.38	2.42
Gose, Anthony	L-L	6-1	190	8-10-90	1	1	0.82	10	0	0	3	11	3	2	1	0	9	13	.100	.000	.130	10.64	7.36
Hartson, Brock	R-R	6-2	200	8-9-93	2	3	2.91	10	8	0	0	43	36	16	14	4	15	37	.226	.147	.286	7.68	3.12
Hernandez, Hector	B-L	6-1	190	2-20-91	3	3	2.22	14	4	0	0	45	38	14	11	2	15	50	.225	.196	.237	10.07	3.02
Hillman, Juan	L-L	6-2	200	5-15-97	6	12	3.85	25	25	0	0	140	147	77	60	10	41	99	.269	.206	.295	6.35	2.63
Jimenez, Luis	R-R	6-4	170	1-2-95	0	0	3.00	2	0	0	0	3	1	1	1	0	0	4	.200	.250	.167	12.00	0.00
Laureano, Jonathan	R-R	6-1	200	12-21-95	0	0	0.00	1	0	0	0	1	0	0	0	0	0	0	.000	.000	.000	0.00	0.00
McCarty, Kirk	L-L	5-8	185	10-12-95	3	7	5.66	13	13	0	0	56	75	37	35	2	16	60	.326	.393	.288	9.70	2.59
Mejia, Jean Carlos	R-R	6-4	240	8-26-96	3	1	4.09	8	8	0	0	33	28	16	15	0	9	36	.226	.311	.177	9.82	2.45
Mitchell, Evan	R-R	6-2	185	3-18-92	2	2	9.90	7	2	0	0	20	31	23	22	2	7	14	.361	.464	.310	6.30	3.15
Morgan, Eli	R-R	5-10	190	5-13-96	3	1	1.87	6	6	0	0	34	19	7	7	3	5	40	.156	.111	.213	10.69	1.34
Morris, Cody	R-R	6-5	222	11-4-96	2	2	5.52	11	11	0	0	44	54	31	27	6	17	55	.298	.253	.337	11.25	3.48
Mota, Juan	R-R	6-4	190	5-4-96	3	4	3.71	8	8	0	0	44	34	23	18	3	24	41	.213	.229	.200	8.45	4.95
Nelson, Kyle	L-L	6-1	175	7-8-96	1	0	0.00	8	0	0	3	9	3	0	0	0	2	17	.097	.091	.100	16.39	0.00
Pinto, Aaron	L-R	6-0	200	7-3-96	1	0	1.90	25	1	0	3	43	29	12	9	2	13	44	.190	.206	.178	9.28	2.74
Polanco, Anderson	L-L	6-3	190	9-6-92	0	2	4.40	20	3	0	0	47	44	27	23	4	30	52	.249	.275	.238	9.96	5.74

CLEVELAND INDIANS

Name	B-T	HT	WT	DOB	W	L	ERA	G	GS	CG	SV	IP	H	R	ER	HR	BB	SO	AVG	vLH	vRH	K/9	BB/9
Robinson, Jared	R-R	6-0	190	11-20-94	0	3	3.09	14	0	0	5	23	23	13	8	2	7	35	.242	.200	.267	13.50	2.70
Scott, Adam	L-L	6-4	220	10-10-95	3	7	3.45	12	12	0	0	57	58	35	22	4	20	74	.258	.203	.280	11.62	3.14
Solter, Matt	R-R	6-3	220	6-4-93	4	1	3.76	8	8	0	0	41	39	19	17	2	22	36	.248	.208	.269	7.97	4.87
Tati, Felix	R-R	6-2	190	4-1-97	3	1	4.64	32	0	0	0	52	52	31	27	6	19	60	.260	.266	.256	10.32	3.27
Teaney, Jonathan	R-R	6-2	195	1-28-96	3	2	2.77	46	0	0	4	55	53	25	17	6	35	53	.259	.250	.264	8.62	5.69
Valladares, Randy	L-L	5-11	155	7-6-94	1	0	1.50	12	0	0	0	18	15	6	3	0	11	20	.242	.333	.184	10.00	5.50
Vicente, Jose	R-R	5-11	175	11-13-95	0	0	0.00	1	0	0	1	1	1	0	0	0	0	0	.250	.000	.333	0.00	0.00

Fielding

Catcher	PCT	G	PO	A	E	DP	PB
Collins	.992	54	433	42	4	1	9
Laureano	.992	14	113	13	1	0	2
Loopstok	1.000	1	9	0	0	0	0
Rivera	.998	61	522	54	1	5	3
Rodriguez	.982	13	99	9	2	0	0

First Base	PCT	G	PO	A	E	DP
Collins	.981	29	188	17	4	15
Laureano	.996	37	249	22	1	20
Loopstok	1.000	2	15	0	0	2
Persinger	1.000	2	15	1	0	2
Reeves	.985	52	363	21	6	40
Vicente	.971	19	125	8	4	16

Second Base	PCT	G	PO	A	E	DP
Freeman	1.000	3	7	4	0	3
Friis	.991	31	50	65	1	16
Persinger	.981	16	21	31	1	7
Santiago	.957	49	69	88	7	24
Smith	.980	17	19	31	1	12
Wakamatsu	.913	26	42	53	9	11

Third Base	PCT	G	PO	A	E	DP
Collins	1.000	1	1	0	0	0
Friis	1.000	1	0	1	0	0
Jones	.918	72	43	126	15	10
Laureano	.910	42	33	58	9	9
Persinger	.909	3	5	5	1	1
Pujols	1.000	1	0	2	0	0
Santiago	.813	12	4	9	3	0
Smith	.875	10	3	11	2	0

Shortstop	PCT	G	PO	A	E	DP
Freeman	.976	57	89	154	6	28
Friis	.821	5	14	9	5	1
Santiago	.818	3	3	6	2	2
Smith	1.000	1	1	0	0	0
Wakamatsu	.963	72	97	187	11	40

Outfield	PCT	G	PO	A	E	DP
Benson	1.000	54	90	4	0	1
Brooks	.978	40	83	4	2	1
Carter	.978	85	164	13	4	0
Farhat	1.000	19	45	2	0	0
Gonzalez	.977	70	125	5	3	1
Kwan	.988	107	248	8	3	0
Mejia	1.000	12	20	1	0	0
Wade	1.000	19	35	4	0	0

LAKE COUNTY CAPTAINS

LOW CLASS A

MIDWEST LEAGUE

Batting	B-T	HT	WT	DOB	AVG	vLH	vRH	G	AB	R	H	2B	3B	HR	RBI	BB	HBP	SH	SF	SO	SB	CS	SLG	OBP
Benson, Will	L-L	6-5	225	6-16-98	.272	.303	.266	62	217	44	59	12	3	18	55	37	0	0	5	78	18	2	.604	.371
Berardi, Jesse	L-R	5-10	185	1-13-96	.271	.188	.293	66	236	22	64	13	1	3	27	19	1	1	2	39	3	5	.373	.326
Cantu, Ulysses	R-R	5-11	220	5-1-98	.111	.000	.119	15	45	2	5	1	0	0	2	8	1	2	0	10	0	0	.133	.259
Cardenas, Ruben	R-R	6-2	185	10-10-97	.284	.339	.271	84	320	44	91	19	6	10	54	27	3	1	3	69	9	7	.475	.343
2-team total (30 Bowling Green)					.272	.309	.261	114	431	58	117	24	7	13	70	40	5	1	4	90	11	10	.450	.338
Delgado, Raynel	B-R	6-2	185	4-4-00	.250	.091	.283	17	64	7	16	4	0	0	6	2	0	0	1	13	1	0	.313	.269
Engelmann, Jonathan	R-R	6-4	210	9-18-96	.259	.293	.248	49	174	19	45	8	0	3	21	15	6	0	2	36	10	2	.356	.335
Farhat, Cody	R-R	6-1	185	9-26-96	.239	.148	.267	33	117	12	28	6	4	4	16	7	7	0	1	41	5	1	.462	.318
Fermin, Jose	R-R	5-11	160	3-29-99	.293	.290	.293	105	393	75	115	12	2	6	41	42	11	6	3	40	28	9	.379	.374
Freeman, Ike	R-R	5-10	199	6-17-98	.103	.083	.111	12	39	4	4	0	0	0	4	4	1	0	1	13	0	1	.103	.200
Freeman, Tyler	R-R	6-0	170	5-21-99	.292	.388	.267	61	236	51	69	16	3	3	24	18	17	0	1	28	11	4	.424	.382
Gonzalez, Gianpaul	R-R	6-0	185	1-11-96	.065	.250	.037	10	31	0	2	0	0	0	1	0	0	1	0	11	0	0	.065	.094
Gonzalez, Marcos	R-R	5-11	165	10-12-99	.206	.200	.207	11	34	4	7	1	0	1	4	9	0	0	0	11	4	0	.324	.372
Holmes, Quentin	R-R	6-3	175	7-7-99	.175	.141	.184	112	412	54	72	15	4	6	36	5	2	4		159	23	9	.274	.247
Jerez, Miguel	R-R	6-1	178	10-24-97	.176	.172	.177	80	262	30	46	11	0	10	36	33	9	0	2	96	1	0	.332	.288
Kelkboom, Makesiondon	R-R	5-11	152	7-12-00	.163	.231	.151	31	86	6	14	3	1	2	8	7	0	0	1	35	2	4	.291	.223
Lavastida, Bryan	R-R	6-0	200	11-27-98	.333	--	.333	1	3	1	1	0	0	0	0	1	0	0	0	1	0	0	.333	.500
Lopez Alvarez, Angel	R-R	5-10	194	3-14-97	.152	.214	.135	19	66	4	10	4	0	1	7	0	0	0		24	0	1	.258	.233
Naylor, Bo	L-R	6-0	195	2-21-00	.243	.260	.239	107	399	60	97	18	10	11	65	43	1	3	7	104	7	5	.421	.313
Nelson, Hosea	L-L	6-0	210	11-22-96	.206	.257	.197	74	238	45	49	10	4	8	26	32	1	3	2	94	4	5	.382	.300
Pujols, Henry	R-R	6-3	195	12-10-98	.174	.100	.194	15	46	4	8	4	1	1	3	3	1	0	0	26	0	0	.370	.240
Reeves, Mitch	R-R	6-2	210	11-18-94	.257	.191	.273	59	214	32	55	14	0	6	37	28	4	0	2	54	5	2	.407	.351
Rodriguez, Eric	R-R	6-1	188	7-28-98	.138	.000	.191	10	29	3	4	1	0	1	4	4	1	0	0	8	0	0	.276	.265
Rolette, Josh	L-R	5-11	195	5-21-96	.183	.194	.181	64	202	15	37	12	1	1	27	29	3	1	4	62	0	1	.267	.290
Santiago, Wilbis	R-R	6-0	180	1-20-96	.364	.333	.375	3	11	1	4	0	0	0	2	0	0	0	0	0	0	0	.364	.364
Schneemann, Daniel	L-R	6-1	180	12-3-97	.287	.278	.289	70	230	26	66	10	2	2	30	25	5	0	2	50	6	4	.374	.366
Scolamiero, Clark	L-L	6-0	175	1-24-96	.257	.353	.239	31	109	27	28	4	1	4	18	13	2	0	0	29	8	0	.422	.347
Smith, Connor	R-R	5-10	180	4-21-96	.241	.229	.244	53	170	20	41	6	3	0	17	19	6	1	2	33	2	2	.312	.335
Valera, George	L-L	5-10	160	11-13-00	.087	.000	.143	6	23	1	2	0	1	0	2	1	0	0		9	0	0	.174	.192
Wilson, Billy	L-R	5-11	185	5-28-96	.135	.125	.136	17	52	7	7	2	0	1	4	8	2	1	1	28	2	1	.231	.270

Pitching	B-T	HT	WT	DOB	W	L	ERA	G	GS	CG	SV	IP	H	R	ER	HR	BB	SO	AVG	vLH	vRH	K/9	BB/9
Aiken, Brady	L-L	6-4	205	8-16-96	0	0	40.50	2	0	0	0	1	1	3	3	0	6	1	.333	--	.333	13.50	81.00
Alvarez, Manuel	R-R	6-3	190	9-17-95	4	1	2.90	30	0	0	9	40	30	22	13	3	28	47	.204	.175	.220	10.49	6.25
Araujo, Luis	R-R	6-1	155	8-1-96	3	4	4.60	31	0	0	2	47	44	30	24	1	24	57	.246	.258	.239	10.91	4.60
Arias, Skylar	L-R	6-3	190	6-30-97	4	1	1.79	34	1	0	3	60	35	12	12	1	30	71	.173	.197	.162	10.59	4.48
Burgos, Raymond	L-L	6-5	170	11-29-98	2	1	3.44	8	8	0	0	37	40	14	14	3	12	40	.278	.227	.300	9.82	2.95
Clemmer, Dakody	R-R	6-2	185	1-19-96	0	1	3.00	9	0	0	3	15	13	7	5	0	5	14	.245	.250	.243	8.40	3.00
Draper, Zach	L-R	6-3	200	10-18-94	9	4	3.12	26	12	0	0	101	106	42	35	8	36	89	.270	.280	.266	7.93	3.21
Echols, Riley	R-R	6-4	205	4-12-95	0	1	6.00	5	0	0	2	6	9	4	4	1	4	9	.391	.143	.500	13.50	6.00
Gallagher, Nick	R-R	6-3	200	9-9-95	0	0	0.00	4	0	0	0	9	5	0	0	0	4	9	.172	.267	.071	4.00	0.00
Hankins, Ethan	R-R	6-6	200	5-23-00	0	3	4.64	5	5	0	0	21	20	12	11	3	12	20	.250	.290	.214	11.81	5.06
Hartson, Brock	R-R	6-2	200	8-9-93	1	1	18.90	2	1	0	0	3	7	8	7	1	6	3	.438	.571	.333	8.10	16.20
Herrin, Tim	L-L	6-5	225	10-8-96	1	0	4.85	12	0	0	1	26	22	15	14	3	12	19	.234	.195	.264	6.58	4.15

CLEVELAND INDIANS

Pitching	B-T	HT	WT	DOB	W	L	ERA	G	GS	CG	SV	IP	H	R	ER	HR	BB	SO	AVG	vLH	vRH	K/9	BB/9
Hill, Cam	R-R	6-1	185	5-24-94	0	0	0.00	5	0	0	0	6	3	0	0	0	1	8	.136	.125	.143	12.00	1.50
Lingos, Eli	L-L	6-0	192	5-21-96	3	4	3.66	30	10	0	1	98	84	44	40	9	27	95	.226	.261	.206	8.69	2.47
Marman, Kyle	R-R	6-3	195	3-3-97	5	4	3.33	24	0	0	1	46	33	22	17	3	21	58	.200	.141	.238	11.35	4.11
McCarthy, Shane	R-R	6-2	190	7-29-96	4	3	4.14	11	11	0	0	50	42	29	23	4	18	61	.223	.268	.189	10.98	3.24
Meyer, Brendan	L-R	6-5	200	10-8-94	1	0	2.81	16	0	0	1	26	17	8	8	0	10	25	.189	.262	.125	8.77	3.51
Miednik, Jake	L-L	5-10	185	5-1-96	3	1	2.56	20	0	0	4	32	29	12	9	0	12	33	.238	.218	.254	9.38	3.41
Mitchell, Evan	R-R	6-2	185	3-18-92	0	1	7.00	2	2	0	0	9	12	8	7	1	1	6	.316	.375	.300	6.00	1.00
Morris, Cody	R-R	6-5	222	11-4-96	5	2	3.20	10	9	0	0	45	41	20	16	1	10	56	.241	.162	.302	11.20	2.00
Mota, Juan	R-R	6-4	190	5-4-96	3	6	5.45	15	15	1	0	68	71	45	41	10	25	72	.273	.287	.261	9.58	3.33
Oviedo, Luis	R-R	6-4	170	5-15-99	6	6	5.38	19	19	0	0	87	80	54	52	6	40	72	.243	.269	.219	7.45	4.14
Pinto, Aaron	L-R	6-0	200	7-3-96	5	1	1.14	17	0	0	2	32	29	7	4	0	7	38	.240	.239	.240	10.80	1.99
Ponticelli, Thomas	R-R	6-1	195	4-15-97	3	4	5.07	24	12	0	3	92	99	60	52	15	46	73	.276	.302	.259	7.12	4.48
Rholl, Kellen	L-L	6-3	200	5-13-96	3	5	1.62	29	0	0	2	50	44	12	9	0	31	70	.232	.235	.230	12.60	5.58
Royalty, Alex	R-R	6-4	190	3-19-97	6	9	4.54	25	24	2	0	111	110	65	56	7	49	100	.264	.260	.267	8.11	3.97
Turner, Matt	L-L	6-4	180	8-4-99	2	1	2.74	9	0	0	0	43	43	17	13	3	14	29	.254	.243	.263	6.12	2.95
Valdez, Luis	R-R	6-3	170	10-14-96	1	0	2.00	10	0	0	0	18	7	5	4	0	12	16	.117	.154	.088	8.00	6.00
Valladares, Randy	L-L	5-11	155	7-6-94	0	0	0.73	7	0	0	1	12	7	3	1	1	4	13	.159	.177	.148	9.49	2.92

Fielding

Catcher	PCT	G	PO	A	E	DP	PB
Gonzalez	.976	10	71	9	2	0	1
Lavastida	1.000	1	11	0	0	0	0
Lopez Alvarez	.992	14	122	10	1	2	0
Naylor	.985	85	756	79	13	2	14
Rodriguez	1.000	9	75	3	0	1	4
Rolette	.995	25	187	14	1	2	1

First Base	PCT	G	PO	A	E	DP
Cantu	1.000	14	101	11	0	7
Engelmann	.984	18	112	10	2	14
Jerez	.984	70	507	44	9	43
Reeves	.993	36	247	22	2	21
Rolette	.944	2	14	3	1	2

Second Base	PCT	G	PO	A	E	DP
Berardi	.950	10	10	28	2	10
Delgado	1.000	4	7	14	0	2
Fermin	.964	64	108	159	10	32
Freeman	.913	4	4	17	2	1
Freeman	1.000	3	4	6	0	0
Gonzalez	1.000	1	0	3	0	0
Kelkboom	.958	11	18	28	2	5
Santiago	1.000	3	2	4	0	0
Schneemann	.978	22	45	45	2	11
Smith	.979	23	42	51	2	13

Third Base	PCT	G	PO	A	E	DP
Berardi	.910	52	36	65	10	2
Delgado	.929	5	0	13	1	0
Freeman	.917	3	3	8	1	3
Gonzalez	.842	8	3	13	3	3
Kelkboom	.864	20	10	28	6	1
Pujols	.844	15	8	19	5	0
Schneemann	1.000	12	13	25	0	5

	PCT	G	PO	A	E	DP
Smith	.924	29	15	46	5	7

Shortstop	PCT	G	PO	A	E	DP
Delgado	.905	5	7	12	2	1
Fermin	.950	39	42	91	7	16
Freeman	1.000	5	9	10	0	2
Freeman	.949	57	93	151	13	37
Schneemann	.965	34	43	68	4	12

Outfield	PCT	G	PO	A	E	DP
Benson	.969	53	89	4	3	0
Cardenas	.977	72	121	7	3	1
Engelmann	.962	25	50	1	2	0
Farhat	1.000	32	50	7	0	1
Holmes	.965	111	244	4	9	1
Nelson	.978	70	131	1	3	0
Reeves	1.000	3	5	0	0	0
Scolamiero	.985	30	60	4	1	2
Valera	1.000	5	6	3	0	1
Wilson	.967	17	28	1	1	0

MAHONING VALLEY SCRAPPERS   SHORT SEASON
NEW YORK-PENN LEAGUE

Batting	B-T	HT	WT	DOB	AVG	vLH	vRH	G	AB	R	H	2B	3B	HR	RBI	BB	HBP	SH	SF	SO	SB	CS	SLG	OBP
Alfonseca, Pedro	R-R	6-0	178	9-4-97	.143	.222	.115	22	70	7	10	0	0	2	9	6	3	1	0	23	4	1	.229	.241
Bracho, Aaron	B-R	5-11	175	4-24-01	.222	.400	.182	8	27	5	6	1	0	2	4	5	0	0	0	8	0	0	.482	.344
Brennan, Will	L-L	6-0	190	2-2-98	.215	.471	.158	26	93	12	20	4	1	0	10	10	3	1	0	11	4	2	.280	.311
Cantu, Ulysses	R-R	5-11	220	5-1-98	.000	.000	.000	1	4	0	0	0	0	0	0	0	0	0	0	1	0	0	.000	.000
Cooper, Michael	L-R	6-5	180	7-27-99	.238	.255	.233	61	223	29	53	11	4	1	29	17	2	1	2	49	3	0	.336	.295
De Oleo, Henderson	R-R	6-4	210	2-11-98	.177	.323	.125	37	119	10	21	5	0	2	12	14	2	1	0	52	1	2	.269	.274
Delgado, Raynel	B-R	6-2	185	4-4-00	.240	.256	.236	53	200	19	48	11	2	2	17	21	0	0	3	60	5	4	.345	.308
Diaz, Yainer	R-R	6-0	195	9-21-98	.274	.355	.250	34	135	13	37	6	2	2	18	4	0	0	1	22	0	0	.393	.293
Engelmann, Jonathan	R-R	6-4	210	9-18-96	.250	1.000	.200	4	16	3	4	2	0	1	2	1	0	0	0	3	0	0	.563	.294
Escobedo, Julian	L-L	5-11	190	6-10-98	.129	.077	.139	22	85	15	11	4	0	0	8	9	0	1	0	14	0	0	.177	.213
Farhat, Cody	R-R	6-1	185	9-26-96	.500	1.000	.429	3	8	4	4	1	1	0	4	1	0	0	0		1	1	.875	.692
Fernandez, Felix	R-R	6-0	185	12-9-96	.091	.167	.074	12	33	1	3	0	0	1	3	1	0	0	0	14	0	0	.182	.118
Gonzalez, Joab	R-R	5-11	175	12-2-99	.200	.286	.172	37	115	13	23	1	1	1	13	9	0	1	1	38	3	0	.252	.256
Holland, Korey	R-R	5-11	170	1-1-00	.212	.268	.194	48	165	27	35	4	3	1	11	26	4	1	0	53	5	3	.291	.333
Lavastida, Bryan	R-R	6-0	200	11-27-98	.335	.271	.354	58	209	39	70	19	3	2	38	25	3	0	3	27	3	3	.483	.408
Lopez, Jonathan	L-R	6-2	175	8-13-99	.225	.259	.211	32	98	11	22	5	0	0	12	10	4	1	0	26	2	0	.276	.321
Pujols, Rafael	R-R	6-3	195	12-10-98	.148	.067	.174	21	61	2	9	2	0	1	2	5	0	0	0	31	1	0	.230	.212
Rocchio, Brayan	B-R	5-10	150	1-13-01	.250	.270	.244	69	268	33	67	12	3	5	27	20	4	1	2	40	14	8	.373	.310
Rodriguez, Eric	R-R	6-1	188	7-28-98	.140	.250	.097	14	43	2	6	3	0	0	3	4	0	1	1	6	0	0	.209	.208
Rodriguez, Johnathan	R-R	6-3	180	11-4-99	.247	.262	.241	66	231	36	57	15	4	6	27	21	4	0	2	67	4	2	.424	.318
Valera, George	L-L	5-11	160	11-13-00	.236	.158	.261	46	157	22	37	7	1	8	29	29	1	0	1	52	6	2	.446	.356
Wilson, Billy	L-R	5-11	185	5-28-96	.198	.231	.182	24	81	11	16	5	2	1	8	10	3	0	0	40	4	1	.346	.309

Pitching	B-T	HT	WT	DOB	W	L	ERA	G	GS	CG	SV	IP	H	R	ER	HR	BB	SO	AVG	vLH	vRH	K/9	BB/9
Brito, Serafino	R-R	6-0	200	4-28-97	3	2	1.25	9	0	0	0	22	9	5	3	0	7	17	.127	.121	.132	7.06	2.91
Cespedes, Francis	L-L	6-4	185	9-28-94	2	4	6.23	15	0	0	0	26	23	20	18	2	23	30	.230	.232	.229	10.38	7.96
Eichhorn, Brian	R-R	6-1	225	8-15-97	4	3	4.50	14	8	0	0	52	65	33	26	5	17	49	.307	.392	.261	8.48	2.94
Espino, Daniel	R-R	6-2	205	1-5-01	0	2	6.30	3	3	0	0	10	9	8	7	1	5	18	.225	.222	.227	16.20	4.50
Fernandez, Felix	R-R	6-0	185	12-9-96	0	0	0.00	1	0	0	0	0	0	0	0	0	0	1	.000	--	.000	27.00	0.00
Gaddis, Hunter	R-R	6-6	212	4-9-98	0	1	2.30	6	6	0	0	16	11	8	4	0	4	25	.183	.174	.189	15.51	2.30
Gutierrez, Jhonneyver	R-R	6-5	200	12-24-98	2	5	7.31	8	8	0	0	28	36	23	23	1	8	15	.327	.333	.324	4.76	2.54

Name	B-T	HT	WT	DOB	W	L	ERA	G	GS	CG	SV	IP	H	R	ER	HR	BB	SO	AVG	vLH	vRH	K/9	BB/9
Hankins, Ethan	R-R	6-6	200	5-23-00	0	0	1.40	9	8	0	0	39	23	10	6	1	18	43	.178	.280	.114	10.01	4.19
Herrin, Tim	L-L	6-5	225	10-8-96	1	0	0.00	11	0	0	6	17	9	4	0	0	2	10	.150	.174	.135	5.29	1.06
Hill, Cam	R-R	6-1	185	5-24-94	0	0	0.00	2	0	0	0	2	1	0	0	0	4	1	.143	.333	.000	18.00	0.00
Jenkins, Liam	R-R	6-8	225	4-9-97	0	6	4.03	14	11	0	0	58	55	35	26	0	31	44	.255	.238	.270	6.83	4.81
Manzanillo, Maiker	R-R	6-2	190	10-14-96	0	1	7.47	14	0	0	0	16	23	16	13	1	13	10	.338	.344	.333	5.74	7.47
Meyer, Brendan	L-R	6-5	200	10-8-94	0	1	0.00	6	1	0	0	11	6	3	0	0	3	11	.146	.177	.125	8.74	2.38
Miednik, Jake	L-L	5-10	185	5-1-96	0	0	0.00	3	0	0	0	2	2	0	0	0	1	4	.222	.000	.250	15.43	3.86
Mikolajchak, Nick	R-R	6-2	215	11-21-97	1	1	0.47	13	0	0	3	19	10	3	1	0	3	24	.164	.211	.143	11.37	1.42
Misiaszek, Andrew	R-L	6-2	213	8-24-97	2	1	4.85	9	0	0	0	13	16	10	7	2	7	15	.302	.429	.219	10.38	4.85
Mock, Eric	R-R	6-2	220	7-12-96	1	1	3.66	7	0	0	1	20	22	11	8	0	8	18	.279	.308	.264	8.24	3.66
Oca, Jose	R-R	6-0	150	2-28-99	3	2	3.98	18	2	0	1	41	32	23	18	6	19	28	.213	.207	.217	6.20	4.20
Otero, Dan	R-R	6-3	205	2-19-85	0	0	0.00	1	1	0	0	1	1	0	0	0	0	1	.333	.500	.000	13.50	0.00
Paredes, Juan	R-R	6-3	200	9-25-98	1	1	10.38	5	0	0	0	9	14	10	10	0	4	10	.350	.412	.304	10.38	4.15
Perez, Francisco	L-L	6-2	195	7-20-97	1	0	1.80	2	2	0	0	16	6	2	2	1	2	8	.177	.071	.250	7.20	1.80
Ramirez, Jerson	R-R	6-1	185	11-24-98	0	1	0.73	18	0	0	7	25	12	5	2	0	10	28	.148	.152	.146	10.22	3.65
Sanchez, Luis	R-R	6-1	190	3-9-95	1	1	2.70	14	0	0	4	20	6	9	6	1	10	22	.091	.103	.081	9.90	4.50
Scheftz, Jordan	R-R	6-3	190	8-31-95	1	0	16.20	3	0	0	0	3	4	6	6	0	9	2	.308	.000	1.000	5.40	24.30
Turner, Matt	L-L	6-4	180	8-4-99	2	2	2.90	6	6	1	0	31	26	10	10	2	5	23	.222	.290	.198	6.68	1.45
Valdez, Luis	R-R	6-0	170	10-14-96	2	1	3.94	9	0	0	0	16	12	7	7	0	9	20	.203	.191	.211	11.25	5.06
Vargas, Carlos	R-R	6-3	180	10-13-99	6	4	4.52	15	15	1	0	78	73	39	39	4	24	71	.250	.271	.236	8.23	2.78
Vasquez, Gregori	R-R	6-1	185	9-8-97	1	1	4.11	8	4	0	1	31	24	16	14	4	7	27	.216	.238	.203	7.92	2.05
Waldron, Matt	R-R	6-2	185	9-26-96	3	0	3.53	10	1	0	1	36	29	15	14	2	4	40	.218	.196	.230	10.09	1.01

Fielding

C: Diaz 23, Fernandez 5, Lavastida 37, Rodriguez 13. **1B:** Cantu 1, Cooper 60, De Oleo 12, Engelmann 2, Fernandez 1, Wilson 1. **2B:** Bracho 8, Delgado 37, Gonzalez 8, Lopez 19, Rocchio 7. **3B:** De Oleo 23, Delgado 7, Gonzalez 21, Lopez 12, Pujols 17. **SS:** Delgado 9, Gonzalez 7, Lopez 1, Rocchio 62. **OF:** Alfonseca 18, Brennan 24, Engelmann 1, Escobedo 22, Farhat 2, Gonzalez 1, Holland 40, Rodriguez 64, Valera 41, Wilson 17.

AZL INDIANS BLUE   ROOKIE
ARIZONA LEAGUE

Batting	B-T	HT	WT	DOB	AVG	vLH	vRH	G	AB	R	H	2B	3B	HR	RBI	BB	HBP	SH	SF	SO	SB	CS	SLG	OBP
Alfonseca, Pedro	R-R	6-0	178	9-4-97	.303	.231	.333	20	89	24	27	7	0	5	17	4	4	0	1	29	9	1	.551	.357
Amditis, Michael	R-R	5-11	190	8-14-97	.252	.242	.256	36	115	21	29	10	1	1	15	20	1	0	1	25	0	1	.383	.365
Bracho, Aaron	B-R	5-11	175	4-24-01	.296	.444	.247	30	108	25	32	10	2	6	29	23	2	0	4	21	4	1	.593	.416
Brennan, Will	L-L	6-0	190	2-2-98	.306	.400	.275	31	121	26	37	7	3	1	23	15	2	0	2	6	5	4	.438	.386
Cantu, Ulysses	R-R	5-11	220	5-1-98	.324	.500	.200	11	34	8	11	6	0	1	5	9	1	0	0	9	0	0	.588	.477
Cespedes, Cristopher	R-R	6-3	200	5-18-98	.326	.375	.309	48	184	38	60	18	2	6	33	18	2	0	3	54	4	4	.544	.387
Colina, Jose	B-R	6-0	180	3-26-98	.372	.267	.394	29	86	19	32	6	1	8	20	9	2	0	0	17	0	0	.744	.443
Contreras, Jeikol	L-R	6-0	175	4-14-00	.253	.179	.282	29	99	12	25	6	2	2	16	8	0	0	1	42	0	1	.414	.306
2-team total (3 Indians Red)					.252	.172	.284	32	103	13	26	6	2	2	16	9	0	0	1	45	0	1	.408	.310
Escobedo, Julian	L-L	5-11	190	6-10-98	.327	.276	.346	28	107	31	35	8	2	2	16	18	0	0	0	12	8	1	.495	.424
Flores, Jothson	B-R	5-11	160	10-6-98	.346	.615	.256	14	52	10	18	3	0	1	9	8	0	0	0	15	0	0	.462	.433
2-team total (25 Indians Red)					.273	.419	.228	39	132	22	36	4	0	1	16	15	2	3	2	33	2	0	.326	.351
Freeman, Ike	R-R	5-10	199	6-17-98	.217	.308	.196	21	69	7	15	3	0	0	9	3	3	0	0	18	1	1	.261	.280
Gonzalez, Joab	R-R	5-11	175	12-2-99	.375	.308	.421	13	32	7	12	3	0	0	4	4	1	1	1	6	2	1	.469	.447
Jimenez, Pablo	R-R	6-2	175	2-6-99	.150	.241	.115	33	107	18	16	2	3	3	14	10	5	1	2	54	0	0	.308	.250
Kelkboom, Makesiondon	R-R	5-11	152	7-12-00	.111	.500	.063	7	18	0	2	1	0	0	1	0	0	0	0	7	0	1	.167	.111
Lopez Alvarez, Angel	R-R	5-10	194	3-14-97	.290	.250	.316	9	31	2	9	4	0	0	8	6	0	0	0	8	0	0	.419	.405
Maestre, Jesus	R-R	5-10	155	2-4-00	.229	.143	.265	19	48	5	11	0	0	1	8	11	1	0	0	16	3	1	.292	.383
Moroff, Max	B-R	5-10	190	5-13-93	.294	.333	.286	6	17	4	5	2	0	1	6	1	1	0	0	4	0	0	.588	.368
2-team total (1 Indians Red)					.364	.250	.389	7	22	6	8	2	0	1	7	1	1	0	0	5	0	0	.591	.417
Noel, Jhonkensy	R-R	6-1	180	7-15-01	.287	.275	.291	47	178	32	51	12	0	6	42	18	4	0	9	39	5	1	.455	.349
Nova, Victor	L-R	5-9	160	1-6-00	.266		.262	16	57	15	14	1	0	0	3	11	2	1	1	15	2	0	.263	.380
2-team total (26 Padres 1)					.297	.242	.313	42	148	37	44	3	3	1	20	26	2	3	2	37	9	2	.378	.405
Palacio, Gaspar	B-R	5-8	155	3-2-00	.241	.300	.211	8	29	5	7	1	1	1	3	0	0	0		7	0	1	.448	.313
2-team total (22 Indians Red)					.206	.261	.189	30	97	16	20	4	3	2	13	12	1	0	2	25	5	3	.371	.295
Peralta, Wilfri	R-R	6-0	155	12-10-00	.221	.087	.283	44	145	31	32	5	2	2	21	20	2	1	1	44	13	3	.324	.321
Pinorini, Austin	L-R	5-10	185	9-20-96	.158	.400	.071	7	19	2	3	2	0	0	2	0	0	0	0	0			.263	.238
Scolamiero, Clark	L-L	6-0	175	1-24-96	.000	.000	.000	1	2	0	0	0	0	0	0	3	0	0	0	1	0	0	.000	.600
2-team total (8 Indians Red)					.143	.100	.167	9	28	5	4	1	1	3	9	0	0	9	1	0			.286	.351
Tena, Jose	L-R	5-9	159	3-20-01	.325	.458	.280	44	191	30	62	7	6	1	18	6	2	0	0	44	6	2	.440	.352
Velazquez, Andrew	B-R	5-8	170	7-14-94	.429	.200	1.000	3	7	1	3	2	0	0	2	0	0	0	1	0	0		.714	.556
2-team total (6 Indians Red)					.517	.333	.600	9	29	9	15	6	0	2	6	3	1	0	0	0			.931	.576
Zimmer, Bradley	R-R	6-5	220	11-27-92	.500	.333	1.000	3	4	0	2	0	0	0	2	1	0	0	1	1	0		.500	.714
2-team total (2 Indians Red)					.500	.400	.667	5	8	1	4	0	0	1	2	2	1	0	0	2	1	0	.875	.636

Pitching	B-T	HT	WT	DOB	W	L	ERA	G	GS	CG	SV	IP	H	R	ER	HR	BB	SO	AVG	vLH	vRH	K/9	BB/9
De La Cruz, Joel	R-R	6-2	190	11-9-96	0	2	2.84	13	0	0	2	19	17	14	6	0	9	16	.227	.357	.149	7.58	4.26
Enright, Nic	R-R	6-3	205	1-8-97	0	3	0.50	15	0	0	0	18	11	6	1	1	8	26	.177	.160	.189	13.00	4.00
Feliz, Daritzon	L-L	6-2	175	8-19-99	4	5	5.85	12	9	0	0	52	63	41	34	5	18	55	.290	.290	.290	9.46	3.10
Fidel, Chandler	L-L	6-5	225	11-19-97	5	0	5.33	13	1	0	1	27	30	18	16	5	7	27	.270	.115	.318	9.00	2.33
Gaddis, Hunter	R-R	6-6	212	4-9-98	1	2	3.12	7	5	0	0	17	13	8	6	2	3	26	.206	.296	.139	13.50	1.56
Gallagher, Nick	R-R	6-3	200	9-9-95	1	0	0.00	3	0	0	0	3	1	0	0	0	0	6	.100	.000		12.00	0.00
2-team total (3 Indians Red)					1	1	12.71	6	0	0	0	6	8	8	8	1	2	7	.308	.200	.375	11.12	3.18
Garcia, Luis C.	R-R	6-3	180	4-26-97	1	0	2.81	13	0	0	1	16	14	11	5	1	7	21	.233	.250	.229	11.81	3.94

	B-T	HT	WT	DOB	W	L	ERA	G	GS	CG	SV	IP	H	R	ER	HR	BB	SO	AVG	vLH	vRH	K/9	BB/9
Garcia, Luis D.	R-R	6-2	180	6-23-00	7	0	2.58	13	11	0	0	66	53	26	19	2	15	44	.215	.244	.199	5.97	2.04
Gutierrez, Jhonneyver	R-R	6-5	200	12-24-98	2	1	4.20	5	2	0	0	15	14	7	7	2	9	14	.233	.053	.317	8.40	5.40
Hart, Zach	R-R	6-4	235	5-17-97	0	1	12.86	4	1	0	0	7	15	10	10	3	3	7	.469	.500	.455	9.00	3.86
2-team total (9 Indians Red)					2	1	6.04	13	1	0	0	25	33	23	17	4	9	36	.320	.244	.371	12.79	3.20
Janczak, Jared	R-R	6-1	205	6-23-95	1	0	4.02	15	0	0	1	16	16	17	7	0	6	24	.235	.250	.229	13.79	3.45
Jimenez, Diarlin	R-R	6-5	180	3-18-00	1	4	4.66	12	12	0	0	48	60	46	25	1	28	43	.308	.211	.370	8.01	5.21
Jones, Jordan	R-R	6-2	195	10-2-97	3	3	2.17	14	3	0	0	37	30	10	9	1	9	45	.227	.326	.174	10.85	2.17
Karinchak, James	R-R	6-3	230	9-22-95	0	0	0.00	3	0	0	0	3	0	0	0	0	2	8	.000	.000	.000	24.00	6.00
Kelly, Kevin	R-R	6-2	200	11-28-97	1	0	2.70	11	0	0	0	13	14	7	4	1	2	19	.269	.353	.229	12.83	1.35
2-team total (3 Indians Red)					1	0	2.08	14	0	0	2	17	18	7	4	1	2	25	.269	.381	.217	12.98	1.04
Labaut, Randy	L-L	6-1	202	10-1-96	4	0	1.74	11	0	0	1	31	24	9	6	0	5	39	.209	.217	.207	11.32	1.45
Manzanillo, Maiker	R-R	6-2	190	10-14-96	0	0	2.08	3	0	0	1	4	5	1	1	0	1	6	.278	.600	.154	12.46	2.08
McCarthy, Shane	R-R	6-2	190	7-29-96	0	0	0.00	4	4	0	0	12	4	0	0	0	4	15	.105	.087	.133	11.25	3.00
Mejia, Wilmer	R-R	6-2	170	1-15-99	0	2	7.57	9	7	0	0	27	39	25	23	0	10	27	.331	.216	.383	8.89	3.29
Mikolajchak, Nick	R-R	6-2	215	11-21-97	0	0	0.00	4	0	0	2	6	4	1	0	0	0	12	.167	.182	.154	18.00	0.00
Mock, Eric	R-R	6-2	220	7-12-96	1	0	2.57	6	0	0	0	14	11	4	4	1	6	19	.208	.118	.250	12.21	3.86
Ocker, Nate	R-R	6-0	190	12-3-96	0	1	1.50	14	0	0	5	18	18	9	3	1	4	31	.250	.118	.291	15.50	2.00
Paredes, Juan	R-R	6-3	200	9-25-98	1	0	8.18	10	0	0	2	11	12	12	10	0	6	23	.261	.471	.138	18.82	4.91
Salazar, Danny	R-R	6-0	195	1-11-90	0	0	0.00	1	1	0	0	2	3	0	0	0	0	5	.375	1.000	.167	27.00	0.00
2-team total (1 Indians Red)					0	1	6.23	2	2	0	0	4	7	3	3	1	0	11	.350	.556	.182	22.85	0.00
Sanchez, Wilton	R-R	6-4	175	9-8-98	2	0	8.74	8	0	0	0	11	7	11	11	1	11	14	.175	.158	.191	11.12	8.74
Vasquez, Gregori	R-R	6-1	185	9-8-97	0	0	4.50	1	0	0	0	2	1	1	1	0	0	6	.167	.000	.200	0.00	0.00
2-team total (1 Indians Red)					0	0	3.00	2	0	0	0	3	1	1	1	0	2	1	.111	.000	.143	3.00	6.00

Fielding

C: Amditis 33, Colina 21, Lopez Alvarez 8, Pinorini 5. 1B: Cantu 10, Colina 9, Contreras 12, Noel 31, Peralta 1. 2B: Bracho 22, Freeman 1, Gonzalez 4, Maestre 8, Moroff 2, Nova 1, Palacio 8, Peralta 17, Tena 2. 3B: Contreras 4, Freeman 13, Gonzalez 2, Kelkboom 7, Maestre 9, Noel 12, Nova 10, Peralta 3, Tena 4. SS: Freeman 5, Gonzalez 7, Maestre 1, Moroff 2, Peralta 17, Tena 33, Velazquez 1. OF: Alfonseca 20, Brennan 30, Cespedes 42, Escobedo 26, Flores 14, Jimenez 33, Maestre 2, Nova 5, Scolamiero 1, Velazquez 1, Zimmer 1.

AZL INDIANS RED — ROOKIE
ARIZONA LEAGUE

Batting	B-T	HT	WT	DOB	AVG	vLH	vRH	G	AB	R	H	2B	3B	HR	RBI	BB	HBP	SH	SF	SO	SB	CS	SLG	OBP
Bartlett, Will	R-R	6-3	215	2-2-01	.268	.205	.290	44	153	21	41	12	1	1	18	29	1	0	1	48	2	0	.379	.386
Berardi, Jesse	L-R	5-10	185	1-13-96	.250	.286	.231	6	20	4	5	1	0	0	3	1	0	0	0	3	0	0	.300	.286
Brown, Jordan	R-R	6-3	185	9-9-01	.123	.231	.096	26	65	9	8	2	0	0	5	15	4	0	0	32	2	2	.154	.321
Cairo, Christian	R-R	5-10	170	6-11-01	.178	.313	.140	46	146	26	26	3	1	0	9	25	7	0	1	40	7	3	.212	.324
Contreras, Jeikol	L-R	6-0	175	4-14-00	.250	.000	.333	3	4	1	1	0	0	0	1	0	0	0	3	0	0		.250	.400
2-team total (29 Indians Blue)					.252	.172	.284	32	103	13	26	6	2	2	16	9	0	1	45	0	1		.408	.310
Diaz, Yainer	R-R	6-0	195	9-21-98	.451	.214	.500	20	82	15	37	6	0	5	22	4	1	0	1	8	0	0	.707	.477
Flores, Jothson	B-R	5-11	160	10-6-98	.225	.278	.210	25	80	12	18	1	0	0	7	7	2	3	2	18	2	0	.238	.297
2-team total (14 Indians Blue)					.273	.419	.228	39	132	22	36	4	0	1	16	15	2	3	2	33	2	0	.326	.351
Idrogo, Cesar	B-R	5-11	170	3-26-01	.243	.119	.282	49	173	19	42	7	2	0	23	16	0	1	4	31	9	5	.306	.301
Made, Marlin	L-L	5-10	165	4-16-01	.201	.233	.194	47	154	14	31	6	2	4	13	5	1	0	1	46	1	3	.344	.230
Marmol, Roger	R-R	5-11	190	10-5-99	.203	.353	.161	25	79	5	16	2	0	2	8	2	2	0	2	31	0	1	.304	.235
Medina, Jose	L-L	6-1	185	2-14-99	.286	.000	.400	2	7	0	2	0	1	0	4	0	0	0	0	2	0	0	.571	.286
Monasterio, Andruw	R-R	6-0	185	5-30-97	.000		.000	2	7	0	0	0	0	0	0	1	0	0	0	1	0	0	.000	.000
Montero, Jean	R-R	5-11	175	2-26-99	.257	.184	.281	48	152	39	39	3	1	1	10	23	4	0	1	37	27	4	.309	.367
2-team total (6 Indians Blue)					.364	.250	.389	7	22	6	8	2	0	1	7	1	1	0	0	5	0	0	.591	.417
Naranjo, Joe	L-L	6-0	180	5-11-01	.266	.279	.261	48	177	25	47	5	2	1	21	22	0	0	1	44	1	0	.333	.345
Palacio, Gaspar	B-R	5-8	155	3-2-00	.191	.231	.182	22	68	11	13	3	2	1	12	9	1	0	2	18	5	2	.338	.288
2-team total (8 Indians Blue)					.206	.250	.189	30	97	16	20	4	3	2	13	12	1	0	2	25	5	3	.371	.295
Paz, Richard	L-R	5-7	150	6-12-01	.188	.143	.206	15	48	4	9	1	0	0	5	2	0	1	0	7	0	1	.208	.220
Pena, Landy	B-R	6-1	180	11-6-01	.172	.143	.189	20	58	12	10	0	1	0	4	15	0	1	2	22	5	2	.207	.333
Persinger, Dillon	R-R	5-11	180	1-31-96	.182	.000	.286	4	11	2	2	0	0	0	2	5	0	0	0	4	0	1	.182	.438
Planez, Alexfri	R-R	6-2	180	8-17-01	.333	.333	.333	6	24	3	8	2	0	1	3	1	0	0	0	7	0	0	.542	.360
Ramirez, Micael	R-R	5-11	170	6-8-99	.313	.539	.229	16	48	5	15	3	0	0	6	7	0	0	1	12	0	0	.375	.393
Rodriguez, Gabriel	R-R	6-2	174	2-22-02	.215	.120	.275	18	65	7	14	3	0	0	10	4	3	0	1	22	1	1	.262	.288
Scolamiero, Clark	L-L	6-0	175	1-24-96	.154	.111	.177	8	26	5	4	1	0	1	3	6	0	0	0	8	1	0	.308	.313
2-team total (1 Indians Blue)					.143	.100	.167	9	28	5	4	1	0	1	3	9	0	0	0	9	1	0	.286	.351
Valdes, Yordys	B-R	6-0	170	8-16-01	.179	.267	.145	43	162	17	29	3	1	2	11	16	0	2	1	53	15	4	.247	.251
Velazquez, Andrew	B-R	5-8	170	7-14-94	.546	.500	.556	6	22	8	12	4	0	2	6	1	1	0	0	3	0	0	1.000	.583
2-team total (3 AZL Indians Blue)					.517	.333	.600	9	29	9	15	6	0	2	6	3	1	0	0	4	0	0	.931	.576
Weatherford, Zach	R-R	6-2	195	9-27-95	.129	.083	.158	10	31	4	4	1	0	0	4	3	0	0	1	8	1	1	.161	.200
Zimmer, Bradley	L-R	6-5	220	11-27-92	.500	.500	.500	2	4	1	2	0	0	1	2	0	0	0	0	1	0	0	1.250	.500
2-team total (3 Indians Blue)					.500	.400	.667	5	8	1	4	0	0	1	2	2	1	0	2	1	0	0	.875	.636

Pitching	B-T	HT	WT	DOB	W	L	ERA	G	GS	CG	SV	IP	H	R	ER	HR	BB	SO	AVG	vLH	vRH	K/9	BB/9
Bautista, Adenys	R-R	6-3	170	8-6-98	0	0	10.13	4	0	0	0	5	7	7	6	2	5	4	.318	.125	.429	6.75	8.44
Brito, Serafino	R-R	6-0	200	4-28-97	0	0	1.86	6	0	0	0	10	12	3	2	0	0	9	.300	.333	.273	8.38	0.00
Coulter, Kevin	R-R	6-5	227	8-12-96	2	2	2.23	18	0	0	0	36	29	12	9	2	14	47	.216	.216	.217	11.64	3.47
Espino, Daniel	R-R	6-2	205	1-5-01	0	1	1.98	6	6	0	0	14	7	3	3	1	5	16	.152	.200	.115	10.54	3.29
Figueroa, Daniel	R-R	6-0	172	9-25-00	0	0	4.50	1	0	0	0	2	2	1	1	0	0	6	.250	.000	.333	4.50	0.00
Forrester, Jacob	R-R	6-0	185	12-5-95	0	0	4.00	10	0	0	0	9	9	4	4	1	6	15	.257	.286	.250	15.00	6.00

CLEVELAND INDIANS

Name	B-T	HT	WT	DOB	W	L	ERA	G	GS	CG	SV	IP	H	R	ER	HR	BB	SO	AVG	vLH	vRH	K/9	BB/9
Gallagher, Nick	R-R	6-3	200	9-9-95	0	1	27.00	3	0	0	0	3	7	8	8	1	2	3	.438	.400	.455	10.13	6.75
2-team total (3 Indians Blue)					1	1	12.71	6	0	0	0	6	8	8	8	1	2	7	.308	.200	.375	11.12	3.18
Hart, Zach	R-R	6-4	235	5-17-97	2	0	3.44	9	0	0	0	18	18	13	7	1	6	29	.254	.161	.325	14.24	2.95
2-team total (4 Indians Blue)					2	1	6.04	13	1	0	0	25	33	23	17	4	9	36	.320	.244	.371	12.79	3.20
Hartson, Brock	R-R	6-2	200	8-9-93	0	0	9.00	1	1	0	0	2	3	2	2	0	1	4	.375	1.000	.167	18.00	4.50
Hernandez, Allan	R-R	6-5	225	1-19-01	1	0	6.57	11	0	0	0	12	13	15	9	0	15	16	.265	.313	.242	11.68	10.95
Jimenez, Luis	R-R	6-4	170	1-2-95	1	1	1.29	6	0	0	0	7	5	3	1	0	3	11	.200	.167	.231	14.14	3.86
Kelly, Kevin	R-R	6-2	200	11-28-97	0	0	0.00	3	0	0	2	4	4	0	0	0	0	6	.267	.500	.182	13.50	0.00
2-team total (11 Indians Blue)					1	0	2.08	14	0	0	2	17	18	7	4	1	2	25	.269	.381	.217	12.98	1.04
Meza, Wuilson	R-R	5-11	170	10-5-98	1	0	7.36	12	0	0	0	11	14	10	9	0	4	11	.298	.375	.258	9.00	3.27
Miednik, Jake	L-L	5-10	185	5-1-96	0	0	0.00	3	0	0	0	4	2	0	0	0	4	4	.143	.167	.125	9.00	0.00
Misiaszek, Andrew	R-L	6-2	213	8-24-97	2	1	3.77	8	0	0	1	14	14	6	6	0	5	15	.264	.467	.184	9.42	3.14
Munoz, Brauny	R-R	6-1	170	8-20-00	2	4	2.91	12	11	0	0	53	67	35	17	3	13	56	.300	.396	.235	9.57	2.22
Peguero, Luis	R-R	6-1	165	11-15-99	2	0	6.23	16	0	0	0	13	17	15	9	1	16	14	.288	.375	.229	9.69	11.08
Perez, Francisco	L-L	6-2	195	7-20-97	1	1	1.47	6	5	0	0	18	6	5	3	2	6	29	.102	.000	.128	14.24	2.95
Rodriguez, Jefry	R-R	6-6	232	7-26-93	0	0	0.00	1	1	0	0	0	0	0	0	0	1	1	.000	--	.000	9.00	9.00
Rodriguez, Jhan	R-R	6-0	165	7-2-98	3	1	3.86	17	0	0	5	23	20	12	10	2	11	32	.230	.235	.226	12.34	4.24
Salazar, Danny	R-R	6-0	195	1-11-90	0	1	10.13	1	1	0	0	3	4	3	3	1	0	6	.333	.429	.200	20.25	0.00
2-team total (1 Indians Blue)					0	1	6.23	2	2	0	0	4	7	3	3	1	0	11	.350	.556	.182	22.85	0.00
Santana, Christophers	R-R	6-2	195	2-26-98	0	0	2.45	17	0	0	1	22	20	7	6	3	11	33	.238	.250	.233	13.50	4.50
Taveras, Heylin	R-R	5-11	163	8-3-99	0	0	9.00	1	0	0	0	1	2	1	1	0	1	1	.400	1.000	.250	9.00	0.00
Vasquez, Gregori	R-R	6-1	185	9-8-97	0	0	0.00	1	0	0	0	1	0	0	0	0	1	1	.000	.000	.000	9.00	18.00
2-team total (1 Indians Blue)					0	0	3.00	2	0	0	0	3	1	1	1	0	2	1	.111	.000	.143	3.00	6.00
Vasquez, Samuel	R-R		170	9-20-99	2	3	4.21	11	5	0	1	36	24	19	17	2	21	30	.191	.217	.175	7.43	5.20
Vasquez, Wardquelin	R-R	6-3	194	7-25-01	1	1	10.43	10	4	0	0	15	22	20	17	4	24	18	.367	.333	.381	11.05	14.73
Vergara, Jhon	R-R	6-3	170	4-4-00	1	3	5.18	13	4	0	0	40	42	28	23	4	23	29	.280	.270	.287	6.53	5.18
Vinicio, Miguel	R-R	6-3	170	9-1-99	3	2	4.42	10	6	0	1	37	38	21	18	4	18	32	.273	.188	.319	7.85	4.42
Waldron, Matt	R-R	6-2	185	9-26-96	1	0	0.90	4	0	0	0	10	3	1	1	0	1	17	.088	.200	.042	15.30	0.00
Wisely, Alec	R-R	5-9	184	8-13-97	1	1	6.94	7	0	0	0	12	17	9	9	0	6	12	.347	.316	.367	9.26	4.63
Yannuzzi, Yeffersson	L-L	6-2	175	10-4-96	0	0	9.90	8	2	0	0	10	12	12	11	0	16	10	.343	.000	.375	9.00	14.40
Zapata, Juan	R-R	6-1	198	11-19-98	1	6	4.93	12	10	0	0	49	70	32	27	1	13	39	.348	.341	.355	7.11	2.37

Fielding

C: Diaz 15, Marmol 24, Paz 15, Ramirez 9. **1B:** Bartlett 23, Contreras 2, Naranjo 36. **2B:** Berardi 3, Cairo 12, Flores 6, Monasterio 2, Palacio 17, Pena 16, Persinger 1, Valdes 10, Velazquez 1. **3B:** Berardi 2, Brown 18, Cairo 23, Contreras 1, Flores 13, Palacio 4, Persinger 1, Rodriguez 6, Valdes 1. **SS:** Brown 5, Cairo 15, Flores 1, Monasterio 1, Moroff 1, Pena 2, Rodriguez 10, Valdes 32, Velazquez 1. **OF:** Bartlett 11, Flores 7, Idrogo 48, Made 46, Medina 2, Montero 47, Pena 1, Planez 5, Scolamiero 7, Velazquez 2, Weatherford 9, Zimmer 2.

DSL INDIANS   ROOKIE
DOMINICAN SUMMER LEAGUE

Batting	B-T	HT	WT	DOB	AVG	vLH	vRH	G	AB	R	H	2B	3B	HR	RBI	BB	HBP	SH	SF	SO	SB	CS	SLG	OBP
Aguilar, Daniel	L-L	5-8	175	9-16-00	.305	.200	.315	20	59	11	18	5	1	1	5	9	1	0	1	11	5	0	.475	.400
Antunez, Wuilfredo	L-R	6-0	150	5-16-02	.261	.222	.270	15	46	3	12	4	2	0	8	5	2	0	0	10	2	0	.435	.359
Baez, Jose	B-R	5-9	146	8-30-02	.267	.143	.375	5	15	3	4	0	0	0	3	5	0	0	1	4	0	0	.267	.429
2-team total (50 Indians/Brewers)					.230	.273	.216	55	178	21	41	5	1	0	12	29	4	0	2	46	3	2	.270	.347
Burgos, Jorge	L-L	6-0	165	12-26-01	.276	.229	.286	54	196	26	54	16	5	0	14	27	3	1	0	47	10	3	.408	.372
Celesten, Nehemias	R-R	6-1	195	2-3-00	.148	.222	.135	20	61	4	9	5	1	1	7	10	1	0	0	22	0	0	.312	.278
De La Cruz, Moises	B-R	5-8	155	8-9-01	.169	.206	.159	54	166	21	28	3	2	0	15	30	3	1	0	55	9	4	.211	.307
Frias, Dayan	B-R	5-7	140	6-25-02	.216	.300	.192	40	134	25	29	4	3	0	15	37	1	2	3	25	10	5	.291	.383
Lara, Jesus	R-R	5-8	142	6-23-02	.203	.140	.221	58	197	30	40	8	4	2	27	46	12	0	4	25	8	2	.315	.378
Martinez, Angel	B-R	6-0	165	1-27-02	.306	.233	.324	56	222	37	68	10	7	1	27	29	7	2	1	29	11	5	.428	.402
Ostos, Luis	L-L	5-6	136	3-6-02	.216	.167	.222	15	51	10	11	1	0	0	2	7	0	0	0	8	1	1	.235	.310
Paulino, Joseph	R-R	5-11	165	8-5-01	.153	.077	.165	29	98	8	15	3	0	1	7	4	2	0	0	34	0	0	.214	.202
Paz, Richard	L-R	5-7	150	6-12-01	.259	.250	.262	22	81	12	21	5	2	1	16	11	0	0	2	14	0	0	.407	.340
Perez, Derian	L-L	6-3	175	6-8-00	.238	.233	.239	54	164	30	39	7	4	3	17	19	4	0	4	55	5	2	.384	.325
Planchart, Victor	B-R	5-8	165	5-17-01	.267	.286	.263	40	135	19	36	4	1	0	12	24	3	0	0	20	3	3	.311	.389
Ramos, Robinson	R-R	5-11	185	5-24-98	.301	.267	.312	38	123	21	37	7	1	3	25	11	3	0	1	18	1	1	.447	.370
Rodriguez, Gabriel	R-R	6-2	174	2-22-02	.238	.125	.270	38	143	25	34	7	4	3	29	15	8	0	4	27	3	1	.406	.335
Rodriguez, Skeiling	L-R	6-0	175	2-26-01	.279	.281	.278	62	208	32	58	12	8	0	23	26	2	0	3	52	10	3	.414	.360
Romero, Sterling	L-L	5-10	145	3-2-02	.231	.000	.333	5	13	3	3	0	0	0	1	1	0	0	5	1	0	.231	.333
Sanquintin, Junior	B-R	6-0	182	1-8-02	.297	.333	.291	16	64	8	19	5	0	1	11	5	1	0	0	15	0	4	.422	.357
2-team total (35 Indians/Brewers)					.249	.212	.256	51	189	22	47	12	1	3	28	16	3	0	1	51	4	9	.370	.316
Vargas, Adalberto	R-R	5-11	165	9-28-01	.171	.125	.182	13	41	5	7	0	1	0	4	5	2	0	0	12	0	1	.220	.292

Pitching	B-T	HT	WT	DOB	W	L	ERA	G	GS	CG	SV	IP	H	R	ER	HR	BB	SO	AVG	vLH	vRH	K/9	BB/9
Almonte, Luis	R-R	5-10	184	7-19-99	0	1	3.60	14	0	0	1	25	21	14	10	1	15	25	.233	.156	.276	9.00	5.40
Artiles, Reny	R-R	6-0	160	1-17-02	0	0	4.82	6	0	0	0	9	12	5	5	1	6	3	.353	.222	.400	2.89	5.79
2-team total (10 Indians/Brewers)					0	0	6.28	16	0	0	1	29	37	24	20	3	18	23	.322	.244	.365	7.22	5.65
Batista, Dahan	R-R	6-1	170	3-15-00	0	0	5.87	4	0	0	1	8	8	6	5	0	4	7	.258	.300	.238	8.22	4.70
2-team total (14 Indians/Brewers)					1	4	5.46	18	0	0	1	31	37	24	19	1	11	23	.296	.314	.289	6.61	3.16
Bautista, Adenys	R-R	6-3	170	8-6-98	1	1	6.75	7	0	0	0	12	9	13	9	3	10	6	.200	.133	.233	4.50	7.50
Breton, Albert	R-R	6-3	165	10-7-00	0	3	4.46	11	11	0	0	42	35	25	21	0	21	24	.240	.273	.226	5.10	4.46
2-team total (3 Indians/Brewers)					0	3	3.83	14	14	0	0	54	47	28	23	0	24	29	.246	.333	.209	4.83	4.00
Cordones, Miguel	R-R	6-6	180	9-16-99	1	6	4.50	13	13	0	0	46	49	36	23	1	24	36	.278	.323	.254	7.04	4.70
Cruz, Robert	R-R	6-3	170	4-11-00	3	4	4.53	13	13	0	0	52	47	37	26	3	19	31	.237	.229	.242	5.40	3.31

	B-T	HT	WT	DOB	W	L	ERA	G	GS	CG	SV	IP	H	R	ER	HR	BB	SO	AVG	vLH	vRH	K/9	BB/9
Figueroa, Abraham	L-L	6-1	170	2-27-01	1	0	9.87	14	0	0	0	17	22	21	19	3	20	10	.306	.400	.281	5.19	10.38
Figueroa, Daniel	R-R	6-0	172	9-25-00	2	1	5.56	13	0	0	1	23	21	16	14	0	16	20	.247	.265	.235	7.94	6.35
Franco, Logan	R-R	6-3	170	10-11-99	3	3	5.33	14	0	0	0	25	29	20	15	0	14	18	.287	.250	.304	6.39	4.97
Garcia, Yonaiker	R-R	5-11	165	12-15-00	0	1	6.86	13	0	0	0	21	17	21	16	1	20	23	.218	.150	.241	9.86	8.57
Jerez, Elvis	R-R	6-4	185	2-5-00	1	3	6.93	14	0	0	1	38	37	39	29	4	35	40	.253	.273	.245	9.56	8.36
Lopez, Euclides	R-R	5-10	170	10-13-00	0	2	3.57	15	0	0	4	18	16	10	7	0	12	21	.250	.273	.238	10.70	6.11
Perez, Steven	L-L	6-0	155	4-21-01	1	4	2.97	14	14	0	0	58	51	23	19	2	23	48	.239	.308	.224	7.49	3.59
Polanco, Felix	L-L	6-2	190	6-26-00	0	1	5.57	15	0	0	1	21	19	17	13	0	13	24	.235	.267	.227	10.29	5.57
Reyes, Tomas	L-L	5-11	150	9-23-99	5	5	3.05	14	14	1	0	65	52	29	22	3	19	59	.221	.375	.190	8.17	2.63
Sosa, Christian	R-R	6-2	181	1-2-01	2	1	7.01	13	0	0	0	26	26	21	20	2	11	10	.255	.160	.286	3.51	3.86
Taveras, Heylin	R-R	5-11	163	8-3-99	2	2	7.78	14	0	0	1	20	31	21	17	0	12	12	.361	.433	.321	5.49	5.49
Vergara, Jhon	R-R	6-3	170	4-4-00	0	2	8.44	3	3	0	0	11	21	11	10	2	2	10	.412	.353	.441	8.44	1.69
Vicente, Adauri	R-R	6-2	188	12-18-00	1	0	10.80	13	0	0	0	17	22	22	20	0	21	6	.314	.286	.333	3.24	11.34
Villalobos, Hugo	R-R	5-10	170	7-27-01	3	1	3.07	16	0	0	1	29	21	13	10	3	10	35	.196	.069	.244	10.74	3.07

Fielding

C: Paz 17, Planchart 32, Ramos 16, Vargas 8. **1B:** Celesten 15, De La Cruz 1, Paulino 14, Paz 5, Perez 18, Planchart 6, Ramos 21, Vargas 2. **2B:** Baez 1, De La Cruz 9, Frias 16, Lara 28, Martinez 14. **3B:** Baez 2, Celesten 2, De La Cruz 10, Frias 9, Lara 16, Martinez 12, Paulino 10, Rodriguez 9, Sanquintin 3. **SS:** Baez 1, De La Cruz 10, Frias 4, Lara 4, Martinez 17, Rodriguez 25, Sanquintin 12. **OF:** Aguilar 17, Antunez 14, Burgos 54, De La Cruz 25, Frias 3, Ostos 14, Perez 36, Ramos 1, Rodriguez 57, Romero 3.

DSL INDIANS/BREWERS ROOKIE
DOMINICAN SUMMER LEAGUE

Batting	B-T	HT	WT	DOB	AVG	vLH	vRH	G	AB	R	H	2B	3B	HR	RBI	BB	HBP	SH	SF	SO	SB	CS	SLG	OBP
Baez, Jose	B-R	5-9	146	8-30-02	.227	.297	.206	50	163	18	37	5	1	0	9	24	4	0	1	42	3	2	.270	.339
2-team total (5 Indians)					.230	.273	.216	55	178	21	41	5	1	0	12	29	4	0	2	46	3	2	.270	.347
Diaz, Lahiorne	R-R	5-9	190	8-30-00	.108	.048	.125	32	93	5	10	1	0	0	2	6	2	0	0	30	0	0	.118	.178
Gomez, Henyer	B-R	5-7	145	8-26-02	.181	.125	.198	54	205	28	37	6	4	0	12	26	3	1	0	61	14	6	.249	.282
Meza, Alan	L-R	5-9	142	9-24-01	.225	.216	.227	52	169	20	38	4	2	0	8	23	1	0	0	43	12	7	.272	.321
Sanquintin, Junior	B-R	6-0	182	1-8-02	.224	.167	.238	35	125	14	28	7	1	2	17	11	2	0	1	36	4	5	.344	.295
2-team total (16 DSL Indians)					.249	.212	.256	51	189	22	47	12	1	3	28	16	3	0	1	51	4	9	.370	.316

Pitching	B-T	HT	WT	DOB	W	L	ERA	G	GS	CG	SV	IP	H	R	ER	HR	BB	SO	AVG	vLH	vRH	K/9	BB/9
Artiles, Reny	R-R	6-0	160	1-17-02	0	0	6.98	10	0	0	1	19	25	19	15	2	12	20	.309	.250	.347	9.31	5.59
2-team total (6 Indians)					0	0	6.28	16	0	0	1	29	37	24	20	3	18	23	.322	.244	.365	7.22	5.65
Batista, Dahan	R-R	6-1	170	3-15-00	1	4	5.32	14	0	0	0	24	29	18	14	1	7	16	.309	.320	.304	6.08	2.66
2-team total (4 Indians)					1	4	5.46	18	0	0	1	31	37	24	19	1	11	23	.296	.314	.289	6.61	3.16
Breton, Albert	R-R	6-3	165	10-7-00	0	1	1.54	3	3	0	0	12	12	3	2	0	3	5	.267	.539	.156	3.86	2.31
2-team total (11 Indians)					0	3	3.83	14	14	0	0	54	47	28	23	0	24	29	.246	.333	.209	4.83	4.00
Flores, David	L-L	5-10	180	11-2-00	3	1	3.69	18	0	0	2	32	29	15	13	1	12	32	.240	.261	.235	9.09	3.41
Garcia, Frederic	R-R	6-4	195	12-17-00	0	3	7.84	18	4	0	1	31	39	33	27	2	25	20	.320	.296	.333	5.81	7.26
Gervacio, Yeury	L-L	6-1	168	7-1-99	1	4	3.55	12	12	0	0	51	36	24	20	3	24	49	.200	.256	.183	8.70	4.26
Heredia, Erick	R-R	6-4	175	3-17-97	1	0	3.49	17	1	0	3	39	41	18	15	3	9	26	.273	.300	.264	6.05	2.09
Martinez, Daniel	R-R	6-4	150	9-25-99	1	0	8.44	6	0	0	0	11	13	12	10	0	7	11	.317	.357	.296	9.28	5.91
Parra, Ronald	L-L	6-1	160	11-5-98	1	1	10.71	19	0	0	1	21	12	26	25	0	31	26	.169	.267	.143	11.14	13.29
Rodriguez, Adrian	R-R	5-11	155	8-21-00	1	2	6.32	9	0	0	0	16	17	14	11	1	3	13	.274	.267	.281	7.47	1.72
Rubio, Andy	R-R	6-4	175	2-15-01	0	1	7.94	9	0	0	0	11	11	14	10	1	14	15	.250	.286	.233	11.91	11.12
Ruviera, Jose	R-R	6-3	168	9-4-01	0	4	5.11	12	10	0	0	44	42	34	25	2	24	33	.247	.242	.250	6.75	4.91
Santos, Felipito	R-R	6-2	180	7-20-99	0	10	13.93	15	8	0	0	32	52	60	49	4	38	12	.371	.386	.365	3.41	10.80

Fielding

C: Diaz 25. **1B:** Diaz 2. **2B:** Baez 11, Gomez 22, Meza 6, Sanquintin 1. **3B:** Baez 22, Gomez 3, Sanquintin 8, Valderrama 1. **SS:** Baez 18, Gomez 23, Sanquintin 18. **OF:** Dimas 14, Gomez 1, Meza 44.

Colorado Rockies

SEASON IN A SENTENCE: Just one year after finishing tied with the Dodgers for the division title and topping the Cubs in the NL wild card game, the Rockies were one of the league's biggest disappointments in 2019, posting one of the NL's worst road records and finishing 35 games back of the NL West-winning Dodgers.

HIGH POINT: A June 20 win against the D-backs—the Rockies' seventh consecutive win over their NL West rivals—improved Colorado's record to 40-34 and pushed them into the NL's top wild card spot. The win capped a stretch in which the Rockies went 37-22 from mid-April to mid-June—a 102-win pace over a full season—and left Colorado a season-best six games over .500.

LOW POINT: The Rockies struggled with several prolonged losing skids throughout, including a 3-12 start, a six-game losing streak before the All-Star break, and losses in 14 of 16 from Aug. 22 to Sept. 9 to fall a season-worst 24 games under .500.

NOTABLE ROOKIES: The Rockies' top three prospects—middle infielders Brendan Rodgers and Garrett Hampson and righthander Peter Lambert—all saw extended action with Colorado. Rodgers hit just .224/.272/.250 in 25 games before suffering a season-ending shoulder injury, Hampson played in 105 games but was limited to a .686 OPS, and Lambert went 3-7, 7.25 with an eye-popping .321 opponent average in 19 starts.

KEY TRANSACTIONS: After qualifying for the postseason in back-to-back seasons for the first time in franchise history in 2017-18, the Rockies remained relatively quiet in the offseason. Despite losing key contributors DJ LeMahieu, Adam Ottavino and Gerardo Parra in free agency, Colorado's biggest offseason moves were signing Daniel Murphy to a two-year, $24 million contract and agreeing to an eight-year, $260 million extension with face of the franchise Nolan Arenado.

DOWN ON THE FARM: Double-A Hartford was the only one of four Rockies' full-season affiliates to finish above .500, and Rookie-level Grand Junction was the only affiliate to qualify for its league's playoffs. Rodgers tore through the Triple-A Pacific Coast League and made his major league debut on May 17 but underwent season-ending labrum surgery in mid-July after a pedestrian first 25 games. Outfielder Sam Hilliard was a major bright spot, hitting 35 home runs and stealing 22 bases for Triple-A Albuquerque before making his major league debut on Aug. 27.

OPENING DAY PAYROLL: $149,335,166 (11th).

PLAYERS OF THE YEAR

ALEX TRAUTWIG

MAJOR LEAGUE	MINOR LEAGUE
Nolan Arenado	**Sam Hilliard**
3B	OF
.315/.379/.583	(Triple-A)
Led team in hits (185),	.262/.335/.558
HR (41), RBIs (118)	35 HR, 101 RBIs, 22 SB

ORGANIZATION LEADERS

Batting		*Minimum 250 AB
MAJORS		
* AVG	Nolan Arenado	.315
* OPS	Nolan Arenado	.963
HR	Nolan Arenado	41
RBI	Nolan Arenado	118
MINORS		
* AVG	Yonathan Daza, Albuquerque	.364
* OBP	Luis Castro, Lancaster, Hartford	.419
* SLG	Pat Valaika, Albuquerque	.589
* OPS	Roberto Ramos, Albuquerque	.980
R	Sam Hilliard, Albuquerque	109
H	Matt Hearn, Lancaster	160
TB	Sam Hilliard, Albuquerque	279
2B	Brian Mundell, Albuquerque	32
2B	Terrin Vavra, Asheville	32
3B	Elliot Soto, Albuquerque	10
3B	Ryan Vilade, Lancaster	10
HR	Sam Hilliard, Albuquerque	35
RBI	Luis Castro, Lancaster, Hartford	105
RBI	Roberto Ramos, Albuquerque	105
BB	Luis Castro, Lancaster, Hartford	73
SO	Sam Hilliard, Albuquerque	164
SB	Matt Hearn, Lancaster	45

Pitching		#Minimum 75 IP
MAJORS		
W	German Marquez	12
# ERA	Jon Gray	3.84
SO	German Marquez	175
SV	Wade Davis	15
MINORS		
W	Brandon Gold, Hartford	12
L	Jack Wynkoop, Hartford	13
L	Pat Dean, Albuquerque	13
# ERA	Alexander Guillen, Hartford	1.53
G	PJ Poulin, Asheville	54
GS	Lucas Gilbreath, Lancaster	28
SV	Ben Bowden, Hartford	21
IP	Jack Wynkoop, Hartford	149
BB	Lucas Gilbreath, Lancaster	74
SO	Lucas Gilbreath, Lancaster	143
# AVG	Alexander Guillen, Hartford	.183

General Manager: Jeff Bridich. **Farm Director:** Zach Wilson. **Scouting Director:** Bill Schmidt.

Class	Team	League	W	L	PCT	Finish	Manager
Majors	Colorado Rockies	National	71	91	.438	12th (15)	Bud Black
Triple-A	Albuquerque Isotopes	Pacific Coast	60	80	.429	15th (16)	Glenallen Hill
Double-A	Hartford Yard Goats	Eastern	73	66	.525	6th (12)	Warren Schaeffer
High A	Lancaster JetHawks	California	68	70	.493	4th (8)	Scott Little
Low A	Asheville Tourists	South Atlantic	68	72	.486	8th (14)	Robinson Cancel
Rookie	Boise Hawks	Northwest	27	49	.355	8th (8)	Steve Soliz
Rookie	Grand Junction Rockies	Pioneer	38	36	.514	3rd (8)	Jake Opitz
Overall 2019 Minor League Record			334	373	.472	24th (30)	

ORGANIZATION STATISTICS

COLORADO ROCKIES
NATIONAL LEAGUE

Batting	B-T	HT	WT	DOB	AVG	vLH	vRH	G	AB	R	H	2B	3B	HR	RBI	BB	HBP	SH	SF	SO	SB	CS	SLG	OBP
Alonso, Yonder	L-R	6-1	230	4-8-87	.260	.235	.268	54	73	11	19	7	0	3	10	10	1	0	0	17	0	0	.480	.357
Arenado, Nolan	R-R	6-2	215	4-16-91	.315	.315	.315	155	588	102	185	31	2	41	118	62	4	0	8	93	3	2	.583	.379
Blackmon, Charlie	L-L	6-3	220	7-1-86	.314	.307	.318	140	580	112	182	42	7	32	86	40	9	0	5	104	2	5	.576	.364
Butera, Drew	R-R	6-1	205	8-9-83	.163	.160	.167	16	43	6	7	3	0	0	3	4	0	1	1	14	0	0	.233	.229
Cuevas, Noel	R-R	6-2	224	10-2-91	.000	.000	--	1	2	0	0	0	0	0	0	0	0	0	0	0	0	0	.000	.000
Dahl, David	L-R	6-2	200	4-1-94	.302	.319	.295	100	374	67	113	28	5	15	61	28	4	2	5	110	4	4	.524	.353
Daza, Yonathan	R-R	6-2	210	2-28-94	.206	.188	.215	44	97	7	20	1	1	0	3	7	0	0	1	21	1	0	.237	.257
Desmond, Ian	R-R	6-3	220	9-20-85	.255	.297	.226	140	443	64	113	31	4	20	65	34	2	1	2	119	3	3	.479	.310
Fuentes, Josh	R-R	6-2	209	2-19-93	.218	.130	.281	24	55	8	12	1	0	3	7	1	0	0	0	20	1	0	.400	.232
Hampson, Garrett	R-R	5-11	188	10-10-94	.248	.243	.250	105	299	40	74	9	4	8	27	24	0	2	2	88	15	3	.385	.302
Hilliard, Sam	L-L	6-5	238	2-21-94	.273	.267	.274	27	77	13	21	4	2	7	13	9	1	0	0	23	2	0	.649	.356
Iannetta, Chris	R-R	6-0	230	4-8-83	.222	.190	.244	52	144	20	32	10	0	6	21	18	1	0	1	54	0	0	.417	.311
McMahon, Ryan	L-R	6-2	208	12-14-94	.250	.257	.247	141	480	70	120	22	1	24	83	56	1	1	1	160	5	1	.450	.329
Murphy, Daniel	L-R	6-1	221	4-1-85	.279	.320	.263	132	438	56	122	35	1	13	78	32	2	0	4	74	1	1	.452	.328
Nunez, Dom	L-R	6-0	175	1-17-95	.180	.000	.189	16	39	4	7	3	0	2	4	3	0	0	1	17	0	0	.410	.233
Reynolds, Mark	R-R	6-2	220	8-3-83	.170	.169	.172	78	135	13	23	7	0	4	20	22	2	0	3	57	2	0	.311	.290
Rodgers, Brendan	R-R	6-0	180	8-9-96	.224	.208	.231	25	76	8	17	2	0	0	7	4	1	0	0	27	0	0	.250	.272
Story, Trevor	R-R	6-2	214	11-15-92	.294	.314	.286	145	588	111	173	38	5	35	85	58	7	0	3	174	23	8	.554	.363
Tapia, Raimel	L-L	6-3	185	2-4-94	.275	.277	.274	138	426	54	117	23	5	9	44	21	0	0	0	100	9	3	.416	.309
Valaika, Pat	R-R	5-11	208	9-9-92	.190	.238	.135	40	79	11	15	5	1	1	4	7	0	0	0	34	0	0	.317	.256
Wolters, Tony	L-R	5-10	197	6-9-92	.262	.280	.254	121	359	42	94	17	2	1	42	36	8	2	6	68	0	1	.329	.337

Pitching	B-T	HT	WT	DOB	W	L	ERA	G	GS	CG	SV	IP	H	R	ER	HR	BB	SO	AVG	vLH	vRH	K/9	BB/9
Almonte, Yency	B-R	6-5	217	6-4-94	0	1	5.56	28	0	0	0	34	39	22	21	7	14	29	.279	.347	.242	7.68	3.71
Anderson, Tyler	L-L	6-3	215	12-30-89	0	3	11.76	5	5	0	0	21	33	27	27	8	11	23	.363	.348	.368	10.02	4.79
Bettis, Chad	R-R	6-0	201	4-26-89	1	6	6.08	39	3	0	1	64	78	47	43	10	21	42	.301	.303	.300	5.94	2.97
Davis, Wade	R-R	6-5	227	9-7-85	1	6	8.65	50	0	0	15	43	51	42	41	7	29	42	.291	.280	.300	8.86	6.12
Desmond, Ian	R-R	6-3	220	9-20-85	0	0	0.00	1	0	0	0	1	1	0	0	0	0	0	.250	--	.250	0.00	0.00
Diaz, Jairo	R-R	6-0	200	5-27-91	6	4	4.53	56	0	0	5	58	56	34	29	7	19	63	.251	.216	.281	9.83	2.97
Diehl, Phillip	L-L	6-2	180	7-16-94	0	0	7.36	10	0	0	0	7	10	6	6	1	2	8	.313	.200	.412	9.82	2.45
Dunn, Mike	L-L	6-0	212	5-23-85	1	0	7.13	28	0	0	0	18	17	14	14	4	6	15	.262	.212	.313	7.64	3.06
Estevez, Carlos	R-R	6-6	275	12-28-92	2	2	3.75	71	0	0	0	72	70	34	30	12	23	81	.250	.287	.222	10.13	2.88
Freeland, Kyle	L-L	6-4	201	5-14-93	3	11	6.73	22	22	0	0	104	126	85	78	25	39	79	.296	.298	.295	6.81	3.36
Garcia, Rico	R-R	5-11	190	1-10-94	0	1	10.50	2	1	0	0	6	9	7	7	3	5	2	.360	.400	.333	3.00	7.50
Gonzalez, Chi Chi	R-R	6-3	215	1-15-92	2	6	5.29	14	12	0	0	63	59	39	37	11	33	46	.246	.250	.242	6.57	4.71
Gray, Jon	R-R	6-4	227	11-5-91	11	8	3.84	26	25	0	0	150	147	70	64	19	56	150	.259	.272	.248	9.00	3.36
Harvey, Joe	R-R	6-2	235	1-9-92	0	0	5.63	9	0	0	0	8	7	5	5	2	6	6	.241	.111	.300	6.75	6.75
Hoffman, Jeff	R-R	6-5	227	1-8-93	2	6	6.56	15	15	0	0	70	77	51	51	21	34	68	.283	.243	.326	8.74	4.37
Howard, Sam	R-L	6-3	170	3-9-93	2	0	6.63	20	0	0	0	19	21	16	14	5	10	18	.276	.265	.286	10.89	4.74
Johnson, DJ	L-R	6-4	230	8-30-89	0	2	5.04	28	0	0	0	25	23	14	14	1	19	24	.247	.267	.229	8.64	6.84
Lambert, Peter	R-R	6-2	185	4-18-97	3	7	7.25	19	19	0	0	89	119	74	72	18	36	57	.321	.339	.305	5.74	3.63
Marquez, German	R-R	6-1	225	2-22-95	12	5	4.76	28	28	1	0	174	174	96	92	29	35	175	.259	.264	.254	9.05	1.81
McGee, Jake	L-L	6-4	237	8-6-86	0	2	4.35	45	0	0	0	41	47	25	20	11	11	35	.288	.235	.326	7.62	2.40
Melville, Tim	R-R	6-4	225	10-9-89	2	3	4.86	7	7	0	0	33	34	18	18	9	14	24	.274	.269	.281	6.48	3.78
Musgrave, Harrison	L-L	6-1	206	3-3-92	0	0	3.60	10	0	0	0	10	9	4	4	0	7	12	.231	.250	.211	10.80	6.30
Oberg, Scott	R-R	6-2	203	3-13-90	6	1	2.25	49	0	0	5	56	39	18	14	5	23	58	.196	.225	.173	9.32	3.70
Oh, Seunghwan	R-R	5-10	205	7-15-82	3	1	9.33	21	0	0	0	18	29	19	19	6	6	16	.354	.343	.362	7.85	2.95
Parsons, Wes	R-R	6-5	204	9-6-92	0	0	6.98	15	0	0	0	19	21	17	15	4	16	14	.288	.233	.326	6.52	7.45
2-team total (17 Atlanta)					1	2	5.45	32	0	0	0	35	32	24	21	6	29	26	.265	.255	.270	6.75	7.53
Pazos, James	R-L	6-2	235	5-5-91	0	0	1.74	12	0	0	0	10	7	2	2	1	4	10	.200	.200	.200	8.71	3.48
Reynolds, Mark	R-R	6-2	220	8-3-83	0	0	18.00	1	0	0	0	1	2	2	2	0	1	0	.400	.333	.500	0.00	9.00
Rusin, Chris	L-L	6-2	198	10-22-86	0	0	36.00	2	0	0	0	1	5	4	4	1	1	0	.714	.333	1.000	0.00	9.00
Senzatela, Antonio	R-R	6-1	246	1-21-95	11	11	6.71	25	25	0	0	125	161	99	93	19	57	76	.313	.327	.300	5.49	4.11
Shaw, Bryan	B-R	6-1	232	11-8-87	3	2	5.38	70	0	0	1	72	69	44	43	12	29	58	.251	.200	.290	7.25	3.63
Tinoco, Jesus	R-R	6-4	263	4-30-95	0	3	4.75	24	0	0	1	36	36	23	19	12	22	28	.263	.305	.231	7.00	5.50

Fielding

Catcher	PCT	G	PO	A	E	DP	PB
Butera	1.000	14	99	6	0	0	0
Iannetta	.991	45	300	16	3	1	2
Nunez	1.000	14	82	7	0	1	2
Wolters	.999	112	773	75	1	12	4

First Base	PCT	G	PO	A	E	DP
Alonso	1.000	11	83	5	0	6
Butera	1.000	3	7	1	0	0
Fuentes	1.000	11	98	3	0	6
McMahon	.979	19	129	12	3	14
Murphy	.991	110	909	109	9	97
Reynolds	.996	32	217	13	1	29
Valaika	1.000	1	7	1	0	0

Second Base	PCT	G	PO	A	E	DP
Hampson	.974	50	80	109	5	27
McMahon	.972	113	160	295	13	76
Murphy	1.000	3	0	3	0	1
Rodgers	.952	16	19	41	3	10
Valaika	1.000	13	22	32	0	11
Wolters	1.000	8	4	5	0	2

Third Base	PCT	G	PO	A	E	DP
Arenado	.980	154	111	337	9	43
Fuentes	.000	2	0	0	0	0
McMahon	1.000	22	8	21	0	0
Valaika	1.000	3	1	3	0	0
Wolters	1.000	1	1	0	0	0

Shortstop	PCT	G	PO	A	E	DP
Hampson	.976	15	16	25	1	4
Rodgers	.923	9	10	14	2	3
Story	.987	156	214	416	8	90
Valaika	.941	7	4	12	1	3

Outfield	PCT	G	PO	A	E	DP
Blackmon	.983	135	232	5	4	1
Cuevas	.000	1	0	0	0	0
Dahl	.988	93	168	1	2	0
Daza	.964	29	49	4	2	0
Desmond	.974	118	182	5	5	1
Hampson	.982	33	54	0	1	1
Hilliard	.963	25	51	1	2	0
Tapia	.977	106	164	6	4	1

ALBUQUERQUE ISOTOPES   TRIPLE-A
PACIFIC COAST LEAGUE

Batting	B-T	HT	WT	DOB	AVG	vLH	vRH	G	AB	R	H	2B	3B	HR	RBI	BB	HBP	SH	SF	SO	SB	CS	SLG	OBP
Alonso, Yonder	L-R	6-1	230	4-8-87	.419	.364	.450	9	31	7	13	3	1	2	12	5	1	0	1	6	0	0	.774	.500
Azuaje, Jesus	R-R	5-9	165	8-11-97	.179	.417	.000	12	28	5	5	0	0	0	2	8	0	0	0	8	0	0	.179	.361
Blackmon, Charlie	L-L	6-3	220	7-1-86	.286	.000	.500	2	7	0	2	0	0	0	0	0	0	0	0	2	0	0	.286	.286
Butera, Drew	R-R	6-1	205	8-9-83	.300	.294	.303	67	223	38	67	16	2	9	40	33	2	0	4	55	2	0	.511	.389
Cuevas, Noel	R-R	6-2	224	10-2-91	.278	.268	.281	60	205	35	57	12	3	5	33	24	2	1	1	46	3	3	.439	.358
Czinege, Todd	R-R	6-2	204	7-28-94	.500	.000	.667	4	4	2	2	0	0	2	2	0	0	0	1	1	0	0	2.000	.500
Daza, Yonathan	R-R	6-2	210	2-28-94	.364	.358	.367	89	387	67	141	30	4	11	48	25	2	2	2	52	12	9	.548	.404
Fuentes, Josh	R-R	6-2	209	2-19-93	.254	.254	.254	101	402	66	102	23	2	17	64	25	2	4	4	118	1	1	.448	.298
Gentry, Craig	R-R	6-2	190	11-29-83	.539	.500	.556	3	13	3	7	1	0	0	1	0	0	0	0	3	1	0	.615	.539
Gonzalez, Hidekel	R-R	6-0	190	10-7-96	.000	.000	--	1	3	0	0	0	0	0	0	0	0	0	0	2	0	0	.000	.000
Hampson, Garrett	R-R	5-11	188	10-10-94	.266	.320	.250	26	109	15	29	9	1	2	9	5	2	1	0	25	7	2	.422	.310
Hatch, LJ	R-R	5-11	175	5-18-94	.333	.667	.000	2	6	1	2	0	0	0	1	2	0	0	0	3	0	0	.333	.500
Hilliard, Sam	L-L	6-5	238	2-21-94	.262	.268	.259	126	500	109	131	29	7	35	101	54	2	0	3	164	22	5	.558	.335
Isaacs, Todd	R-R	6-0	215	5-22-96	.231	.000	.375	6	13	1	3	1	0	0	0	0	0	0	0	5	1	0	.308	.231
Jones, Mylz	R-R	6-1	185	4-13-94	.080	.000	.133	13	25	1	2	1	0	0	1	1	0	0	0	9	0	0	.120	.115
Metzler, Ryan	R-R	6-3	190	3-20-93	.222	.286	.182	6	18	0	4	0	0	0	3	1	0	0	0	5	0	0	.222	.263
Molina, Nelson	L-R	6-3	175	4-30-95	.150	.000	.171	17	40	5	6	2	0	2	6	2	0	2	1	8	1	0	.350	.186
Mooney, Peter	L-R	5-6	155	8-19-90	.258	.217	.270	102	306	46	79	24	3	5	35	38	2	2	0	55	6	2	.405	.344
Mundell, Brian	R-R	6-3	230	2-28-94	.333	.352	.325	110	390	69	130	32	4	11	61	42	1	1	1	84	1	0	.521	.399
Murphy, Daniel	L-R	6-1	221	4-1-85	.154	.250	.111	3	13	4	2	1	0	0	3	0	0	0	0	3	0	0	.231	.313
Nunez, Dom	L-R	6-0	175	1-17-95	.244	.167	.275	61	213	43	52	14	1	17	42	35	6	0	3	69	2	0	.559	.362
Rabago, Chris	R-R	5-11	185	4-22-93	.259	.455	.209	14	54	7	14	2	0	2	7	3	0	0	0	12	0	1	.407	.298
Ramos, Roberto	L-R	6-3	250	12-28-94	.309	.250	.331	127	431	77	133	27	0	30	105	61	7	0	4	141	0	1	.580	.400
Rodgers, Brendan	R-R	6-0	180	8-9-96	.350	.317	.363	37	143	34	50	10	1	9	21	14	2	0	1	27	0	0	.622	.413
Soto, Elliot	R-R	5-9	160	8-21-89	.305	.323	.296	112	410	79	125	22	10	10	50	45	5	2	1	91	8	5	.481	.380
Story, Trevor	R-R	6-2	214	11-15-92	.333	.333	.333	2	6	0	2	0	0	0	0	0	0	0	0	2	0	0	.333	.333
Valaika, Pat	R-R	5-11	208	9-9-92	.320	.366	.301	84	350	60	112	26	1	22	75	27	0	1	5	90	5	1	.589	.364
Weeks, Drew	R-R	6-2	200	6-9-93	.285	.308	.276	125	396	73	113	23	7	20	75	31	7	3	4	74	6	7	.530	.345

Pitching	B-T	HT	WT	DOB	W	L	ERA	G	GS	CG	SV	IP	H	R	ER	HR	BB	SO	AVG	vLH	vRH	K/9	BB/9
Almonte, Yency	B-R	6-5	217	6-4-94	2	3	4.20	30	0	0	5	30	29	21	14	2	26	32	.246	.240	.250	9.60	7.80
Bowden, Ben	L-L	6-4	235	10-21-94	1	3	5.88	22	0	0	1	26	29	18	17	4	17	37	.274	.139	.343	12.81	5.88
Castellani, Ryan	R-R	6-4	223	4-1-96	2	5	8.31	10	10	0	0	43	54	45	40	14	30	47	.300	.341	.263	9.76	6.23
Cozart, Logan	R-R	6-2	215	1-27-93	0	1	6.35	13	1	0	0	23	30	19	16	7	9	17	.309	.314	.304	6.75	3.57
Dean, Pat	L-L	6-1	195	5-25-89	3	13	7.54	18	17	0	0	91	147	90	76	34	25	59	.365	.406	.350	5.86	2.48
Diaz, Jairo	R-R	6-0	200	5-27-91	1	0	0.45	16	0	0	6	20	12	1	1	0	6	22	.171	.222	.118	9.90	2.70
Diehl, Phillip	L-L	6-2	180	7-16-94	2	1	6.75	39	0	0	0	45	54	35	34	16	15	52	.298	.214	.336	10.32	2.98
Fennell, Trent	R-R	6-5	205	11-26-95	1	0	0.00	1	0	0	0	1	0	0	0	0	1	1	.250	.000	.000	6.75	6.75
Freeland, Kyle	L-L	6-4	201	5-14-93	0	4	8.80	6	6	0	0	30	40	31	29	4	16	28	.328	.314	.333	8.49	4.85
Garcia, Rico	R-R	5-11	190	1-10-94	2	4	6.90	13	13	0	0	61	77	52	47	14	28	51	.308	.298	.316	7.48	4.11
Gonzalez, Chi Chi	R-R	6-3	215	1-15-92	4	5	6.10	16	15	0	0	87	105	64	59	15	36	76	.300	.276	.327	7.86	3.72
Gonzalez, Nelson	R-R	6-1	170	2-15-90	2	0	6.20	19	4	0	0	49	55	35	34	13	28	40	.284	.303	.267	7.30	5.11
Grills, Evan	L-L	6-4	210	6-13-92	1	3	5.70	14	3	0	0	43	57	28	27	3	15	33	.330	.400	.297	6.96	3.16
Harvey, Joe	R-R	6-2	235	1-9-92	0	1	10.38	9	0	0	1	9	12	10	10	5	5	10	.333	.250	.438	10.38	5.19
Hoffman, Jeff	R-R	6-5	227	1-8-93	6	8	7.70	17	16	0	0	85	105	73	73	19	30	98	.299	.325	.276	10.34	3.16
Holder, Heath	R-R	6-6	211	8-23-92	0	1	5.00	2	0	0	0	9	13	5	5	2	3	6	.361	.458	.167	6.00	3.00
Holman, David	R-R	6-6	220	5-31-90	1	3	9.93	14	5	0	0	35	54	41	39	7	18	18	.353	.359	.347	4.58	4.58
Horacek, Mitch	L-L	6-5	185	12-3-91	1	1	18.75	12	0	0	0	12	34	25	25	5	8	13	.523	.492	.557	9.75	6.00
Howard, Sam	R-L	6-3	170	3-5-93	4	1	3.91	42	0	0	1	51	50	23	22	5	23	62	.262	.349	.219	11.01	4.09
Johnson, DJ	L-R	6-4	230	8-30-89	4	1	5.63	40	0	0	3	48	62	31	30	8	16	67	.313	.281	.339	12.56	3.00
Koplove, Kenny	R-R	6-2	170	8-2-93	0	0	3.00	1	0	0	0	3	1	1	1	0	1	5	.182	.500	.115	15.00	0.00
Lambert, Peter	R-R	6-2	185	4-18-97	2	2	5.07	11	11	0	0	60	63	34	34	10	16	51	.264	.286	.239	7.61	2.39
Lawrence, Justin	R-R	6-3	218	11-25-94	1	1	8.71	10	0	0	0	10	12	10	10	3	9	6	.308	.333	.278	5.23	7.84
McGee, Jake	L-L	6-4	237	8-6-86	0	0	2.70	3	1	0	0	3	1	1	1	0	2	1	.250	.200	.286	2.70	5.40
Melville, Tim	R-R	6-4	225	10-9-89	10	5	5.42	18	17	0	0	96	113	64	58	24	40	94	.288	.296	.281	8.78	3.74
Meyer, Ben	L-R	6-6	203	1-30-93	0	1	7.59	3	0	0	0	11	15	9	9	2	4	13	.319	.435	.208	10.97	3.38

2-team total (14 New Orleans)				3	6	7.45	17	17	0	0	74	82	62	61	16	43	76	.286	.291	.282	9.29	5.25
Musgrave, Harrison	L-L	6-1	206	3-3-92	0	2	10.13	21	1	0	0	24	51	29	27	5	12	23	.432	.444	.425	8.63	4.50
Pazos, James	R-L	6-2	235	5-5-91	1	3	8.80	39	0	0	1	44	69	45	43	8	23	42	.361	.303	.392	8.59	4.70
Pierpont, Matt	R-R	6-2	215	1-25-91	2	2	2.65	25	0	0	0	34	36	10	10	5	14	33	.269	.310	.237	8.74	3.71
Rusin, Chris	L-L	6-2	198	10-22-86	3	4	4.93	22	10	0	0	66	83	48	36	7	21	42	.309	.361	.284	5.76	2.88
Senzatela, Antonio	R-R	6-1	246	1-21-95	1	1	5.77	7	7	0	0	34	45	23	22	7	10	12	.326	.293	.350	3.15	2.62
Tinoco, Jesus	R-R	6-4	263	4-30-95	3	1	3.97	29	0	0	1	34	33	17	15	4	18	23	.262	.250	.273	6.09	4.76

Fielding

Catcher	PCT	G	PO	A	E	DP	PB
Butera	.990	65	539	43	6	5	6
Gonzalez	.875	1	7	0	1	0	0
Nunez	.994	60	472	36	3	1	4
Rabago	1.000	14	114	14	0	4	1

First Base	PCT	G	PO	A	E	DP
Alonso	1.000	8	70	5	0	6
Fuentes	1.000	1	7	0	0	3
Mundell	.993	20	133	8	1	19
Murphy	1.000	2	19	0	0	1
Ramos	.988	104	809	46	10	81
Valaika	.991	15	101	12	1	17

Second Base	PCT	G	PO	A	E	DP
Azuaje	1.000	8	10	13	0	3
Fuentes	1.000	1	5	2	0	0
Hampson	.974	15	31	44	2	9
Hatch	1.000	2	4	3	0	2
Metzler	1.000	1	3	4	0	1

Molina	1.000	7	13	11	0	4
Mooney	.987	52	97	133	3	44
Rodgers	.967	27	47	70	4	18
Soto	1.000	4	1	4	0	0
Valaika	1.000	36	63	105	0	33

Third Base	PCT	G	PO	A	E	DP
Fuentes	.953	96	64	198	13	25
Hatch	.000	1	0	0	0	0
Jones	1.000	1	1	1	0	1
Metzler	1.000	3	0	9	0	3
Molina	.750	3	1	5	2	2
Mooney	1.000	3	0	3	0	1
Ramos	.000	2	0	0	0	0
Rodgers	1.000	3	4	3	0	1
Soto	.953	19	6	35	2	4
Valaika	.940	18	7	40	3	1

Shortstop	PCT	G	PO	A	E	DP
Azuaje	1.000	1	0	2	0	0
Hampson	.974	10	14	24	1	6
Molina	.000	1	0	0	0	0
Mooney	.954	23	22	61	4	12
Rodgers	.906	6	12	17	3	5
Soto	.968	86	110	227	11	55
Story	1.000	2	4	0	0	0
Valaika	.985	18	21	45	1	7

Outfield	PCT	G	PO	A	E	DP
Blackmon	.800	2	4	0	1	0
Cuevas	.981	52	98	4	2	1
Daza	.977	89	206	5	5	4
Gentry	1.000	3	6	1	0	0
Hilliard	.992	122	255	5	2	0
Isaacs	1.000	2	4	0	0	0
Jones	1.000	5	3	0	0	0
Mundell	1.000	62	64	3	0	0
Weeks	.971	104	160	6	5	1

HARTFORD YARD GOATS
DOUBLE-A
EASTERN LEAGUE

Batting	B-T	HT	WT	DOB	AVG	vLH	vRH	G	AB	R	H	2B	3B	HR	RBI	BB	HBP	SH	SF	SO	SB	CS	SLG	OBP
Abreu, Willie	L-L	6-4	225	3-21-95	.214	.102	.264	50	159	16	34	7	1	2	11	18	2	1	1	49	5	3	.308	.300
Boswell, Bret	L-R	6-0	180	10-4-94	.219	.232	.215	106	365	45	80	20	0	15	39	32	5	0	2	122	5	8	.397	.290
Burcham, Scott	R-R	5-11	185	6-17-93	.200	.200	.200	81	220	26	44	12	0	3	21	25	2	2	0	65	5	2	.296	.287
Castro, Luis	R-R	6-1	187	9-19-95	.220	.364	.188	20	59	13	13	1	0	2	7	12	4	0	1	16	1	1	.339	.382
Fernandez, Vince	L-R	6-3	210	7-25-95	.257	.275	.248	74	230	39	59	15	3	15	35	28	4	0	1	86	1	1	.544	.346
Herrera, Carlos	L-R	6-0	145	9-23-96	.204	.100	.238	55	162	16	33	10	3	1	9	9	2	3	2	46	2	2	.321	.251
Iannetta, Chris	R-R	6-0	230	4-8-83	.000	.000	--	3	8	0	0	0	0	0	1	0	0	0	1	2	0	0	.000	.000
Jones, Mylz	R-R	6-1	185	4-13-94	.239	.184	.260	98	314	40	75	15	2	9	33	22	5	4	2	69	17	7	.385	.297
Melendez, Manuel	L-L	5-11	165	1-10-97	.258	.245	.264	128	500	60	129	22	6	6	47	20	5	8	3	57	18	9	.346	.292
Metzler, Ryan	R-R	6-3	190	3-20-93	.179	.158	.196	29	84	5	15	3	0	1	6	9	1	0	1	31	2	3	.250	.263
Molina, Nelson	L-R	6-3	175	4-30-95	.200	.385	.143	22	55	7	11	4	0	0	5	5	1	0	1	15	1	2	.273	.274
Nevin, Tyler	R-R	6-4	200	5-29-97	.251	.233	.258	130	466	60	117	26	2	13	61	65	4	1	4	90	6	2	.399	.345
Perez, Arvicent	R-R	5-10	180	1-14-94	.258	.237	.264	59	186	13	48	7	0	2	18	7	2	1	7	34	3	5	.328	.268
Rabago, Chris	R-R	5-11	185	4-22-93	.207	.184	.219	46	145	12	30	9	0	2	14	26	1	3	0	40	8	3	.310	.331
Serven, Brian	R-R	6-0	195	5-5-95	.203	.191	.207	77	242	35	49	12	0	9	30	22	7	3	2	61	1	2	.364	.286
Trejo, Alan	R-R	6-2	185	5-30-96	.243	.282	.228	125	437	45	106	20	0	15	49	25	5	7	2	105	5	4	.391	.290
Vizcaino, Vance	L-R	6-3	215	8-1-94	.266	.221	.280	89	304	47	81	14	4	7	36	33	2	2	1	94	32	9	.408	.343
Welker, Colton	R-R	6-1	195	10-9-97	.252	.262	.248	98	353	37	89	23	1	10	53	32	2	1	6	68	2	1	.408	.313

Pitching	B-T	HT	WT	DOB	W	L	ERA	G	GS	CG	SV	IP	H	R	ER	HR	BB	SO	AVG	vLH	vRH	K/9	BB/9
Bowden, Ben	L-L	6-4	235	10-21-94	0	0	1.05	26	0	0	20	26	8	3	3	1	7	42	.096	.065	.115	14.73	2.45
Cozart, Logan	R-R	6-2	215	1-27-93	3	1	1.69	30	0	0	5	32	28	12	6	2	10	35	.239	.238	.241	9.84	2.81
Culbreth, Ty	L-L	5-11	175	4-9-94	3	8	4.26	18	17	0	0	80	92	49	38	10	23	53	.292	.362	.251	5.94	2.58
Dennis, Matt	R-R	6-1	210	1-3-95	5	4	3.29	14	14	0	0	82	90	32	30	11	21	59	.283	.289	.276	6.48	2.30
Diehl, Phillip	L-L	6-2	180	7-16-94	0	0	0.00	11	0	0	0	13	5	0	0	0	3	12	.116	.000	.161	8.10	2.03
Foley, Jordan	R-R	6-4	225	7-12-93	4	5	4.78	42	2	0	2	58	65	35	31	5	27	65	.288	.275	.302	10.03	4.17
Garcia, Rico	R-R	5-11	190	1-10-94	8	2	1.85	13	13	0	0	68	41	16	14	4	23	87	.179	.174	.186	11.51	3.04
Gold, Brandon	R-R	6-3	203	9-16-94	12	6	3.56	26	26	0	0	144	166	64	57	15	22	115	.290	.285	.296	7.19	1.38
Gonzalez, Rayan	R-R	6-4	238	10-18-90	3	1	2.08	44	0	0	4	56	50	17	13	4	27	56	.237	.245	.229	8.98	4.31
Goudeau, Ashton	R-R	6-6	205	7-23-92	3	3	2.07	16	16	0	0	78	60	23	18	4	12	91	.215	.189	.255	10.46	1.38
Griggs, Scott	R-R	6-4	215	5-13-91	1	4	3.97	45	0	0	16	45	37	21	20	5	18	45	.219	.237	.194	8.93	3.57
Guillen, Alexander	R-R	6-2	175	11-23-95	2	2	1.53	37	0	0	1	77	50	20	13	5	21	91	.183	.197	.165	10.68	2.47
Holder, Heath	R-R	6-6	211	8-23-92	8	4	2.64	29	10	0	2	92	69	32	27	7	25	99	.207	.210	.204	9.68	2.45
Horacek, Mitch	L-L	6-5	185	12-3-91	4	0	2.48	34	0	0	0	36	30	10	10	1	19	43	.234	.224	.243	10.65	4.71
Humphreys, Reid	R-R	6-1	205	11-21-94	0	1	15.00	4	0	0	0	3	11	5	5	0	2	2	.579	.667	.500	6.00	6.00
Lawrence, Justin	R-R	6-3	218	11-25-94	0	4	8.78	30	0	0	0	27	35	28	26	1	20	26	.306	.261	.383	8.78	6.75
Meyer, Ben	L-R	6-6	203	1-30-93	1	1	9.00	4	1	0	0	8	11	9	8	6	4	9	.333	.313	.353	10.13	4.50
Rusin, Chris	L-L	6-2	198	10-22-86	1	0	5.14	3	0	0	0	7	8	4	4	0	3	5	.296	.182	.375	6.43	3.86
Santos, Antonio	R-R	6-3	180	10-6-96	3	3	4.93	8	8	0	0	46	47	25	25	3	10	44	.267	.303	.221	8.67	1.97
Scioneaux, Tate	R-R	6-0	219	12-14-92	4	1	3.49	20	0	0	0	28	26	12	11	3	5	38	.245	.313	.190	12.07	1.59
2-team total (13 Altoona)					5	2	6.25	33	0	0	1	40	46	29	28	8	11	54	.288	.367	.210	12.05	2.45
Whitehouse, Matt	L-L	6-0	200	4-13-91	1	3	4.73	13	8	0	0	46	53	25	24	3	16	47	.294	.339	.271	9.26	3.15
2-team total (10 Akron)					4	4	4.66	23	8	0	0	68	71	37	35	3	30	74	.271	.322	.246	9.84	3.99
Wynkoop, Jack	L-L	6-5	200	11-2-93	7	13	3.56	24	24	2	0	149	155	64	59	18	22	99	.272	.241	.286	5.98	1.33

Fielding

Catcher	PCT	G	PO	A	E	DP	PB
Iannetta	1.000	2	15	2	0	0	0
Perez	1.000	17	142	13	0	3	2
Rabago	.990	46	349	48	4	2	3
Serven	.993	76	616	86	5	7	3

Catcher (cont.)	PCT	G	PO	A	E	DP	PB
Metzler	.983	18	27	31	1	8	
Molina	1.000	4	4	10	0	1	
Trejo	.971	25	42	58	3	11	

Shortstop	PCT	G	PO	A	E	DP
Burcham	.939	31	54	69	8	21
Herrera	.938	19	21	39	4	6
Metzler	.857	6	7	5	2	3
Trejo	.962	91	141	188	13	51

First Base	PCT	G	PO	A	E	DP
Burcham	1.000	1	5	0	0	1
Castro	.984	17	113	14	2	10
Nevin	.986	98	703	57	11	72
Welker	1.000	27	182	16	0	14

Third Base	PCT	G	PO	A	E	DP
Boswell	.919	30	14	43	5	10
Burcham	.980	21	20	29	1	5
Metzler	.800	3	2	2	1	0
Molina	.917	9	7	15	2	0
Nevin	.900	12	8	19	3	1
Trejo	.962	7	8	17	1	1
Welker	.971	63	52	80	4	11

Outfield	PCT	G	PO	A	E	DP
Abreu	.958	45	64	5	3	2
Boswell	1.000	22	39	2	0	0
Burcham	1.000	1	1	0	0	0
Fernandez	.977	65	125	3	3	0
Jones	.994	93	168	6	1	3
Melendez	.986	122	269	11	4	4
Molina	1.000	2	4	0	0	0
Nevin	1.000	8	12	1	0	0
Vizcaino	.985	80	192	7	3	3

Second Base	PCT	G	PO	A	E	DP
Boswell	.985	56	80	119	3	29
Burcham	1.000	16	18	24	0	11
Herrera	.990	31	37	66	1	12

LANCASTER JETHAWKS — HIGH CLASS A
CALIFORNIA LEAGUE

Batting	B-T	HT	WT	DOB	AVG	vLH	vRH	G	AB	R	H	2B	3B	HR	RBI	BB	HBP	SH	SF	SO	SB	CS	SLG	OBP
Bernard, Austin	R-B	5-10	195	3-14-96	.212	.097	.248	81	264	39	56	12	4	8	26	52	4	1	1	89	6	1	.379	.349
Bouchard, Sean	R-R	6-3	215	5-16-96	.292	.329	.281	91	349	50	102	28	2	13	68	33	3	1	5	102	8	4	.496	.354
Boyd, LeeMarcus	R-R	5-10	170	10-6-95	.217	.125	.250	16	60	8	13	3	0	0	7	3	0	0	0	20	1	1	.267	.254
Castro, Luis	R-R	6-1	187	9-19-95	.317	.363	.305	106	385	93	122	24	2	25	98	61	19	0	10	98	14	3	.584	.425
Czinege, Todd	R-R	6-2	204	7-28-94	.225	.215	.228	89	342	48	77	14	3	14	51	24	3	0	2	128	1	4	.406	.280
Diaz, Joel	R-R	6-1	195	9-18-95	.293	.333	.281	52	191	19	56	11	0	0	22	14	1	0	1	55	1	2	.351	.343
Golden, Casey	R-R	6-2	185	9-1-94	.253	.229	.263	104	383	74	97	19	2	23	64	48	16	0	7	158	9	4	.494	.355
Gonzalez, Hidekel	R-R	6-0	190	10-7-96	.179	.222	.158	8	28	2	5	1	0	0	2	0	0	0	0	14	0	0	.214	.233
Hatch, LJ	R-R	5-11	175	5-18-94	.238	.286	.214	13	42	7	10	0	0	1	4	3	1	0	1	10	0	0	.310	.298
Hearn, Matt	L-R	5-9	165	2-29-96	.292	.254	.304	130	548	86	160	24	6	1	39	56	4	7	2	97	45	15	.363	.361
Herrera, Carlos	L-R	6-0	145	9-23-96	.262	.212	.276	55	233	37	61	13	0	10	31	16	2	0	5	61	9	4	.446	.309
Herron, Jimmy	R-L	6-1	195	7-27-96	.338	.308	.346	18	68	12	23	0	1	4	13	6	2	0	1	13	2	3	.544	.403
Marcelino, Ramon	L-R	6-1	175	12-23-96	.226	.200	.233	104	380	44	86	26	6	16	57	14	17	0	7	120	3	2	.453	.280
McLaughlin, Matt	R-R	6-1	185	2-2-96	.279	.376	.249	110	398	55	111	20	2	1	42	48	4	4	3	95	12	7	.347	.360
Morgan, Luke	R-R	6-2	195	5-13-96	.261	.189	.288	57	199	34	52	12	4	2	19	26	2	3	2	58	3	1	.392	.349
Motley, Nic	R-R	6-3	210	8-1-96	.182	.000	.286	3	11	1	2	0	0	0	1	1	2	0	0	4	0	0	.182	.357
Snyder, Taylor	R-R	6-2	165	9-28-94	.276	.244	.285	103	388	56	107	19	4	18	69	27	7	0	7	127	16	4	.485	.329
Vilade, Ryan	R-R	6-2	194	2-18-99	.303	.299	.304	128	509	92	154	27	10	12	71	56	3	6	13	95	24	7	.466	.367

Pitching	B-T	HT	WT	DOB	W	L	ERA	G	GS	CG	SV	IP	H	R	ER	HR	BB	SO	AVG	vLH	vRH	K/9	BB/9
Ceja, Moises	R-R	6-0	175	8-17-95	5	3	3.57	40	0	0	1	76	63	35	30	11	15	81	.220	.243	.206	9.63	1.78
Dennis, Matt	R-R	6-1	210	1-3-95	2	3	5.60	16	7	0	0	53	71	35	33	10	18	42	.323	.319	.329	7.13	3.06
Doyle, Tommy	R-R	6-6	235	5-1-96	2	3	3.25	38	0	0	19	36	24	18	13	4	13	48	.185	.214	.171	12.00	3.25
Fennell, Trent	R-R	6-5	205	11-26-95	1	0	0.93	5	0	0	0	10	9	1	1	0	5	13	.243	.167	.280	12.10	4.66
Gaddis, Will	R-R	6-1	185	3-12-96	10	7	5.86	27	27	0	0	146	189	109	95	20	48	79	.312	.285	.328	4.87	2.96
Gilbreath, Lucas	L-L	6-1	185	3-5-96	5	10	5.81	28	28	0	0	144	168	109	93	22	74	143	.292	.287	.293	8.94	4.63
Harris, Nate	R-R	6-0	190	9-7-94	4	6	4.83	41	3	0	0	91	107	59	49	13	17	77	.293	.317	.281	7.59	1.68
Julio, Erick	R-R	6-1	175	9-22-96	0	0	0.00	1	0	0	0	2	0	0	0	0	0	3	.000	.000	.000	16.20	0.00
Justo, Salvador	R-R	6-5	210	10-14-94	3	3	8.88	44	0	0	8	50	68	54	49	14	24	54	.327	.297	.340	9.79	4.35
Kennedy, Nick	R-L	6-1	200	6-20-96	1	3	3.92	37	0	0	2	41	48	27	18	4	14	35	.295	.245	.318	7.62	3.05
Koplove, Kenny	R-R	6-2	170	8-2-93	2	1	3.60	9	0	0	0	15	11	11	6	0	7	16	.193	.286	.163	9.60	4.20
Lorenzini, Braxton	R-R	6-4	172	4-5-95	2	2	6.15	25	0	0	0	34	38	30	23	4	31	24	.290	.324	.277	6.42	8.29
Mejia, Alejandro	L-L	6-1	168	7-2-98	0	0	3.60	2	0	0	0	5	2	3	2	0	6	1	.118	.125	.111	1.80	10.80
Moore, Austin	R-R	6-2	230	6-21-94	6	1	5.07	48	0	0	2	66	70	40	37	6	33	75	.272	.291	.263	10.28	4.52
Ollies, Kyle	R-R	6-3	205	6-7-95	0	1	6.35	2	2	0	0	6	9	5	4	0	3	6	.360	.250	.462	9.53	4.76
Roberts, Hayden	R-R	6-0	187	8-22-95	4	1	6.02	32	0	0	0	40	54	34	27	6	26	34	.321	.300	.333	7.59	5.80
Rolison, Ryan	R-L	6-2	195	7-11-97	6	7	4.87	22	22	0	0	116	129	70	63	22	38	118	.278	.236	.294	9.13	2.94
Santos, Antonio	R-R	6-3	180	10-6-96	3	6	4.35	18	18	0	0	99	116	57	48	11	18	96	.286	.213	.322	8.70	1.63
Schilling, Garrett	R-R	6-2	185	10-25-95	9	8	5.11	25	25	0	0	129	155	82	73	23	47	122	.303	.299	.306	8.53	3.29
Schmidt, Colten	L-L	6-0	175	11-25-95	2	4	7.67	6	6	0	0	32	54	31	27	4	12	21	.386	.500	.355	5.97	3.41
Tyler, Robert	R-R	6-4	226	6-18-95	1	0	8.16	28	0	0	1	29	36	28	26	4	20	36	.298	.326	.282	11.30	6.28
Williams, Hunter	L-L	6-1	220	2-7-96	0	1	14.54	8	0	0	0	9	4	15	14	0	16	11	.129	.091	.150	11.42	16.62

Fielding

Catcher	PCT	G	PO	A	E	DP	PB
Bernard	.982	80	626	67	13	7	7
Diaz	.987	48	426	39	6	5	7
Gonzalez	1.000	8	55	8	0	1	1
Motley	1.000	3	14	0	0	0	0

Catcher (cont.)	PCT	G	PO	A	E	DP	PB
McLaughlin	1.000	7	40	4	0	6	
Snyder	1.000	3	25	3	0	3	

Third Base	PCT	G	PO	A	E	DP
Bouchard	.928	29	24	53	6	0
Boyd	1.000	2	3	1	0	1
Hatch	.920	9	8	15	2	3
McLaughlin	.877	28	15	42	8	5
Snyder	.953	30	11	50	3	8
Vilade	.875	46	27	71	14	5

First Base	PCT	G	PO	A	E	DP
Bouchard	.965	12	78	5	3	14
Castro	.983	73	556	38	10	57
Czinege	.994	44	310	20	2	30
Diaz	1.000	2	13	1	0	3

Second Base	PCT	G	PO	A	E	DP
Boyd	.962	12	25	25	2	12
Hatch	1.000	2	4	5	0	0
Herrera	.959	33	64	78	6	21
McLaughlin	.979	65	134	152	6	43
Snyder	.970	28	45	53	3	16

Shortstop	PCT	G	PO	A	E	DP
Boyd	1.000	3	3	6	0	2
Herrera	.957	22	36	52	4	11

COLORADO ROCKIES

	PCT	G	PO	A	E	DP
Snyder	.957	33	40	71	5	20
Vilade	.936	83	124	215	23	50
Outfield	**PCT**	**G**	**PO**	**A**	**E**	**DP**
Bouchard	.978	48	86	4	2	0

Boyd	.000	1	0	0	0	0
Czinege	.882	9	15	0	2	0
Golden	.971	88	166	4	5	1
Hatch	.000	1	0	0	0	0
Hearn	.964	125	314	7	12	3

Herron	1.000	14	32	0	0	0
Marcelino	.958	79	149	9	7	0
Morgan	.965	54	106	4	4	0
Snyder	1.000	9	24	0	0	0

ASHEVILLE TOURISTS
SOUTH ATLANTIC LEAGUE

LOW CLASS A

Batting	B-T	HT	WT	DOB	AVG	vLH	vRH	G	AB	R	H	2B	3B	HR	RBI	BB	HBP	SH	SF	SO	SB	CS	SLG	OBP
Boyd, LeeMarcus	R-R	5-10	170	10-6-95	.246	.308	.227	17	57	9	14	4	0	2	12	2	1	1	0	10	1	1	.421	.283
Cresto, John	R-R	6-3	225	12-15-96	.280	.133	.314	67	239	30	67	28	0	7	50	14	8	0	1	74	12	1	.485	.340
Datres, Kyle	R-R	6-0	205	1-5-96	.286	.218	.308	96	315	70	90	27	4	15	46	47	12	4	1	81	21	7	.540	.397
Decolati, Niko	R-R	6-1	215	8-12-97	.265	.279	.261	77	291	42	77	13	4	6	38	13	19	5	3	80	15	6	.399	.334
Edgeworth, Danny	L-R	6-3	210	7-26-95	.272	.200	.285	71	235	36	64	9	0	8	32	31	5	3	0	72	6	3	.413	.369
George, Max	R-R	5-10	190	4-7-96	.247	.227	.255	25	77	9	19	3	0	0	7	14	3	2	0	22	8	1	.286	.383
Golsan, Will	R-R	6-1	185	3-6-96	.259	.263	.258	103	390	62	101	19	1	6	39	43	7	3	4	87	12	17	.359	.340
Guevara, Javier	R-R	5-11	165	9-25-97	.199	.094	.225	45	161	19	32	9	0	0	14	6	1	1	1	34	0	0	.255	.231
Harris, Cade	L-R	6-2	195	5-27-97	.220	.225	.219	79	223	43	49	7	0	7	19	41	3	11	2	93	8	5	.345	.346
Hatch, LJ	R-R	5-11	175	5-18-94	.158	.000	.188	5	19	2	3	1	0	0	1	1	0	0	0	6	0	0	.211	.200
Jipping, Daniel	R-R	6-2	215	4-10-96	.097	.000	.143	9	31	4	3	1	0	0	2	0	0	0	0	11	0	0	.129	.152
Jones, Greg	L-R	6-2	220	10-17-94	.050	.000	.059	7	20	2	1	0	0	1	5	3	0	0	0	9	0	1	.200	.174
Lavigne, Grant	L-R	6-4	220	8-27-99	.236	.224	.240	126	440	52	104	19	0	7	64	68	9	4	5	129	8	9	.327	.347
MacIver, Willie	R-R	6-2	205	10-28-96	.252	.269	.246	117	425	60	107	27	3	13	60	34	11	4	6	105	12	4	.421	.319
Mendoza, Shael	L-R	6-0	165	10-15-96	.156	.111	.174	10	32	1	5	1	0	0	2	1	1	0	6	1	2	.188	.229
Metz, Robert	R-R	5-10	185	7-29-96	.357	--	.357	5	14	2	5	1	0	0	2	0	1	0	0	3	1	0	.429	.438
Montano, Daniel	L-R	6-1	204	3-31-99	.218	.146	.236	122	454	59	99	30	3	7	41	35	2	8	5	119	17	7	.344	.274
Montes, Coco	R-R	6-0	200	10-7-96	.258	.286	.249	132	500	56	129	29	3	13	89	29	8	4	8	122	6	11	.406	.305
Morgan, Luke	R-R	6-2	195	5-13-96	.214	.262	.191	36	131	19	28	7	0	0	11	17	1	0	0	33	9	3	.267	.309
Navarro, Cristopher	R-R	6-0	170	6-14-99	.255	.364	.222	17	47	5	12	1	0	0	6	3	1	3	2	7	1	1	.277	.302
Stovall, Hunter	R-R	5-10	170	9-5-96	.281	.300	.277	18	57	9	16	1	1	0	2	12	1	0	0	12	1	3	.439	.414
2-team total (71 Lakewood)					.242	.279	.230	89	285	33	69	15	4	1	25	34	5	2	4	44	8	7	.333	.329
Vavra, Terrin	L-R	6-1	185	5-12-97	.318	.241	.340	102	374	79	119	32	1	10	52	62	2	6	9	62	18	9	.489	.409

Pitching	B-T	HT	WT	DOB	W	L	ERA	G	GS	CG	SV	IP	H	R	ER	HR	BB	SO	AVG	vLH	vRH	K/9	BB/9
Ausua, Miguel	L-L	6-0	190	7-15-96	0	2	7.11	2	1	0	0	6	10	8	5	2	2	4	.385	.500	.364	5.68	2.84
Bird, Jake	R-R	6-3	200	12-4-95	7	2	3.62	40	8	0	2	97	105	48	39	2	42	80	.285	.287	.284	7.42	3.90
Bosiokovic, Jacob	R-R	6-5	240	12-21-93	2	1	4.54	33	0	0	1	42	38	24	21	3	16	42	.238	.213	.253	9.07	3.46
Bush, Nick	L-L	6-0	195	8-23-96	9	9	3.95	26	25	1	0	132	135	66	58	13	26	132	.263	.270	.259	9.00	1.77
Cabrera, Wander	L-L	6-1	185	11-7-97	0	0	3.38	2	0	0	0	3	3	1	1	0	6		.300	.000	.500	20.25	20.25
Feltner, Ryan	R-R	6-4	190	9-2-96	9	9	5.07	25	25	0	0	119	137	73	67	12	46	116	.290	.237	.336	8.77	3.48
Fennell, Trent	R-R	6-5	205	11-26-95	0	2	5.91	9	2	0	0	21	21	16	14	2	10	27	.263	.273	.255	11.39	4.22
Filpo, Eris	R-R	6-3	170	5-3-98	2	3	10.03	6	6	0	0	23	35	27	26	4	12	22	.357	.380	.333	8.49	4.63
Garcia, Alfredo	L-L	6-2	225	7-22-99	2	9	6.28	19	19	0	0	90	109	69	63	11	38	103	.300	.354	.281	10.26	3.79
Harlow, Colton	L-L	5-10	170	9-21-95	1	0	6.14	12	0	0	0	22	26	15	15	3	6	35	.296	.333	.281	14.32	2.45
Hepple, Eric	R-R	6-0	205	3-28-96	0	1	9.58	9	0	0	0	16	16	12	11	1	6	10	.356	.556	.222	8.71	5.23
Johnson, Boby	R-R	6-1	185	4-8-97	1	3	5.84	31	0	0	0	45	58	31	29	6	14	47	.309	.409	.248	9.47	2.82
Kennedy, Nick	R-L	6-1	200	6-20-96	0	3	2.08	12	0	0	0	17	12	4	4	0	1	25	.188	.080	.256	12.98	0.52
Lackey, Shelby	R-R	6-3	190	7-8-97	3	10	5.47	21	21	0	0	100	108	74	61	13	39	113	.270	.314	.231	10.14	3.50
Martinez, Alexander	R-R	6-1	210	12-28-96	6	4	2.48	52	0	0	14	58	54	23	16	5	17	69	.247	.233	.256	10.71	2.64
Nikorak, Mike	R-R	6-5	240	9-16-96	0	0	9.69	16	0	0	0	13	14	17	14	1	20	13	.269	.278	.265	9.00	13.85
Parra, Frederis	R-R	6-2	162	10-22-94	3	5	4.82	12	10	1	0	65	83	38	35	11	5	35	.307	.340	.288	4.82	0.69
Pint, Riley	R-R	6-5	225	11-6-97	0	1	8.66	21	3	0	0	18	12	17	17	0	31	23	.203	.148	.250	11.72	15.79
Poulin, PJ	R-L	6-1	195	7-25-96	3	2	2.90	54	0	0	13	59	58	25	19	1	20	67	.256	.273	.247	10.22	3.05
Rolison, Ryan	R-L	6-2	195	7-11-97	2	1	0.61	3	3	0	0	15	8	3	1	0	2	14	.157	.000	.211	8.59	1.23
Rosa, Raymells	R-R	6-2	180	12-6-98	2	0	3.90	33	0	0	1	58	55	28	25	2	15	58	.254	.287	.231	9.05	2.34
Schmidt, Colten	L-L	6-0	175	11-25-95	6	4	2.18	18	17	1	0	103	97	30	25	6	12	107	.244	.231	.249	9.32	1.05
Todd, Reagan	L-L	6-3	218	8-30-95	2	0	0.71	11	0	0	0	13	9	1	1	1	3	18	.192	.333	.044	12.79	2.13
Tribucher, Will	L-L	6-3	210	9-23-96	1	1	7.02	15	0	0	0	17	25	14	13	1	7	20	.368	.364	.370	10.80	3.78
Watson, Derrik	R-R	6-2	175	8-21-94	4	2	3.28	34	0	0	0	60	40	27	22	1	43	72	.187	.194	.181	10.74	6.41

Fielding

Catcher	PCT	G	PO	A	E	DP	PB
George	.983	19	165	9	3	1	0
Guevara	.983	45	410	40	8	2	9
Jones	1.000	1	9	1	0	0	0
MacIver	.993	78	669	69	5	2	18

First Base	PCT	G	PO	A	E	DP
Cresto	.972	19	128	11	4	8
Edgeworth	1.000	11	74	10	0	12
Jipping	1.000	2	13	0	0	0
Lavigne	.981	112	876	72	18	90
Navarro	.000	1	0	0	0	0

Second Base	PCT	G	PO	A	E	DP
Boyd	.922	10	16	31	4	10
Datres	.992	28	46	72	1	14
Edgeworth	.966	19	19	37	2	10
Montes	1.000	40	59	92	0	17

Navarro	1.000	3	3	5	0	2
Stovall	1.000	7	13	15	0	4
Vavra	.979	41	67	117	4	26

Third Base	PCT	G	PO	A	E	DP
Boyd	.944	7	6	11	1	0
Cresto	.917	31	15	51	6	3
Datres	.918	55	35	110	13	14
Edgeworth	.875	25	14	28	6	1
Hatch	.571	7	2	2	3	0
MacIver	.000	1	0	0	0	0
Metz	1.000	2	1	3	0	0
Montes	.925	18	12	25	3	1
Stovall	.941	4	5	11	1	1

Shortstop	PCT	G	PO	A	E	DP
Datres	.000	1	0	0	0	0
Montes	.978	75	110	198	7	44

Navarro	.952	15	18	41	3	9
Vavra	.950	53	82	146	12	32
Outfield	**PCT**	**G**	**PO**	**A**	**E**	**DP**
Bosiokovic	.000	1	0	0	0	0
Cresto	.500	4	1	0	1	0
Decolati	.973	74	141	5	4	1
Edgeworth	1.000	6	13	0	0	0
Golsan	.981	98	144	8	3	1
Harris	.955	75	116	10	6	1
Hatch	1.000	2	3	0	0	0
Jones	1.000	1	0	0	0	0
Mendoza	1.000	10	12	1	0	0
Metz	1.000	3	4	0	0	0
Montano	.984	114	178	3	3	1
Morgan	.981	34	46	5	1	1
Stovall	1.000	7	4	1	0	0

BOISE HAWKS
NORTHWEST LEAGUE

SHORT SEASON

Batting	B-T	HT	WT	DOB	AVG	vLH	vRH	G	AB	R	H	2B	3B	HR	RBI	BB	HBP	SH	SF	SO	SB	CS	SLG	OBP
Aeilts, Joe	R-R	6-2	200	1-1-98	.259	.195	.273	58	228	21	59	9	5	1	17	10	4	2	2	70	8	2	.355	.299
Azuaje, Jesus	R-R	5-9	165	8-11-97	.241	.083	.286	16	54	2	13	0	0	0	4	4	1	0	0	8	2	3	.241	.305
Boone, Trevor	R-R	6-2	210	9-9-97	.215	.222	.213	60	209	22	45	12	1	4	22	15	7	2	3	98	4	4	.340	.286
Boyd, LeeMarcus	R-R	5-10	170	10-6-95	.286	.000	.333	2	7	1	2	0	0	0	1	0	0	0	0	3	0	0	.286	.286
Brown, Turner	B-R	5-9	160	8-1-97	.250	.200	.333	2	8	0	2	0	0	0	1	0	0	0	0	1	0	0	.250	.250
Collins, Isaac	B-R	5-9	185	7-22-97	.257	.219	.267	37	148	24	38	6	3	0	17	12	2	0	2	26	5	5	.338	.317
Cope, Daniel	R-R	6-0	195	6-15-97	.222	.182	.234	45	144	15	32	7	0	2	11	32	3	1	0	37	2	0	.313	.374
Dilone, Vladimir	R-R	5-9	160	7-19-00	.207	.192	.211	48	140	17	29	6	2	0	11	19	2	1	2	33	3	2	.279	.307
Hall, Zach	L-L	6-0	195	6-26-96	.159	.000	.208	23	63	8	10	3	0	2	10	11	0	1	0	24	2	0	.302	.284
Hatch, LJ	R-R	5-11	175	5-18-94	.241	.111	.265	17	58	7	14	3	0	0	5	10	1	0	0	15	0	2	.293	.362
Jacobs, Trey	L-R	6-2	195	5-13-97	.252	.160	.275	33	127	16	32	8	1	1	12	9	2	0	1	34	1	2	.354	.309
Jipping, Daniel	R-R	6-2	215	4-10-96	.000	.000	.000	2	8	0	0	0	0	0	0	2	0	0	0	3	0	0	.000	.200
Mendoza, Shael	L-R	6-0	165	10-15-96	.044	.000	.048	9	23	2	1	0	0	0	1	2	1	0	0	12	2	0	.044	.154
Metz, Robert	R-R	5-10	185	7-29-96	.200	.167	.208	18	60	6	12	2	0	0	3	1	0	1	0	19	1	1	.233	.246
Motley, Nic	R-R	6-3	210	8-1-96	.209	.462	.148	22	67	7	14	1	0	2	10	4	0	0	0	30	0	0	.313	.254
Plantier, Tyler	R-R	6-4	225	10-3-95	.253	.048	.323	26	83	10	21	3	1	2	12	13	3	1	0	30	0	2	.386	.374
Quijada, Bryant	R-R	5-10	167	7-2-99	.158	.091	.174	37	114	10	18	3	0	1	16	16	2	4	1	22	2	0	.211	.271
Restituyo, Bladimir	R-R	5-10	151	7-2-01	.259	.292	.250	55	228	28	59	13	0	4	25	2	1	2	2	56	16	5	.368	.266
Schunk, Aaron	R-R	6-2	205	7-24-97	.306	.273	.314	46	173	31	53	12	2	6	23	14	4	0	1	25	4	1	.503	.370
Toglia, Michael	B-L	6-5	226	8-16-98	.248	.161	.272	41	145	25	36	7	0	9	26	28	1	0	2	45	1	1	.483	.369
Torrealba, Yorvis	R-R	6-0	195	7-14-97	.228	.256	.220	59	211	25	48	10	1	0	18	20	6	1	4	30	8	6	.284	.307
Tovar, Ezequiel	R-R	6-0	162	8-1-01	.249	.277	.241	55	217	22	54	4	2	2	13	16	2	6	2	52	13	0	.313	.304

Pitching	B-T	HT	WT	DOB	W	L	ERA	G	GS	CG	SV	IP	H	R	ER	HR	BB	SO	AVG	vLH	vRH	K/9	BB/9
Ausua, Miguel	L-L	6-0	190	7-15-96	0	0	5.40	6	0	0	0	7	6	4	4	1	3	10	.231	.143	.263	13.50	4.05
Baayoun, Zak	L-L	6-1	180	5-1-98	0	5	4.65	10	10	0	0	41	54	27	21	4	8	34	.329	.188	.364	7.52	1.77
Cabrera, Wander	L-L	6-1	185	11-7-97	1	2	3.40	18	4	0	0	48	41	22	18	0	30	42	.230	.356	.188	7.93	5.66
Chevalier, Luke	R-R	6-1	200	3-1-96	0	5	4.89	13	7	0	0	35	36	22	19	0	14	25	.259	.351	.195	6.43	3.60
Condreay, Joel	L-R	6-3	185	7-5-96	5	1	3.43	27	0	0	0	39	35	19	15	1	8	39	.230	.196	.248	8.92	1.83
Del Bonta-Smith, Fineas	R-R	6-0	190	2-2-97	1	2	2.97	22	0	0	0	33	26	11	11	1	11	34	.215	.267	.184	9.18	2.97
Enck, Cameron	R-R	6-4	225	1-19-97	1	2	7.02	25	0	0	0	33	44	29	26	3	13	23	.312	.250	.348	6.21	3.51
Ethridge, Will	R-R	6-5	240	12-20-97	0	2	3.82	9	9	0	0	31	29	15	13	1	6	21	.250	.217	.271	6.16	1.76
Eusebio, Breiling	L-L	6-1	175	10-21-96	1	4	5.87	12	12	0	0	38	43	30	25	1	18	27	.285	.324	.272	6.34	4.23
Fennell, Trent	R-R	6-5	205	11-26-95	0	2	3.24	4	0	0	0	8	8	7	3	0	3	13	.229	.111	.269	14.04	3.24
Filpo, Eris	R-R	6-3	170	5-3-98	2	1	4.25	7	4	0	0	36	34	17	17	3	13	27	.246	.232	.256	6.75	3.25
Garcia, Alfredo	L-L	6-2	225	7-22-99	1	1	4.30	3	3	0	0	15	15	7	7	2	7	20	.268	.400	.239	12.27	4.30
Gray, Peyton	R-R	6-3	200	6-2-95	0	0	4.50	1	0	0	0	2	3	1	1	0	3	.333	.000	.429	13.50	0.00
Harlow, Colton	L-L	5-10	170	9-21-95	1	1	9.00	8	0	0	0	6	10	6	6	0	7	11	.345	.429	.318	16.50	10.50
Hathcock, Colton	R-R	6-2	185	11-2-95	0	3	7.59	13	0	0	1	11	15	10	9	1	4	13	.333	.333	.333	10.97	3.38
Johnson, Boby	R-R	6-1	185	4-8-97	1	0	2.57	11	0	0	0	14	12	4	4	0	6	14	.231	.250	.219	9.00	3.86
Jones, Stephen	R-R	6-4	225	7-30-97	2	1	4.35	24	0	0	0	31	40	16	15	0	6	28	.338	.326	.313	8.13	1.74
Kaczor, Micah	R-R	6-1	205	5-21-97	1	3	5.13	6	6	0	0	26	31	18	15	2	5	17	.293	.231	.328	5.81	1.71
Lorenzini, Braxton	R-R	6-4	172	4-5-95	0	1	11.05	10	0	0	0	7	6	12	9	1	13	8	.231	.444	.118	9.82	15.95
Ocando, Jeffri	R-R	6-1	180	5-15-99	1	8	7.62	13	13	0	0	54	79	55	46	9	16	37	.341	.279	.377	6.13	2.65
Olliges, Kyle	R-R	6-3	205	6-7-95	0	0	6.00	2	0	0	0	3	1	2	2	0	3	2	.100	.000	.000	6.00	9.00
Parra, Frederis	R-R	6-3	162	10-22-94	4	0	0.56	6	6	0	0	32	26	3	2	0	3	24	.219	.279	.184	6.75	0.84
Pimentel, Keven	R-R	6-3	230	4-7-96	1	1	8.80	22	0	0	0	30	50	33	29	1	18	20	.376	.479	.318	6.07	5.46
Spicer, Jordan	R-R	6-3	210	6-5-97	0	0	0.00	2	2	0	0	3	3	0	0	0	1	4	.250	.000	.300	12.00	3.00
Stinnett, Jesse	R-R	6-4	225	7-12-95	2	0	2.00	7	0	0	0	9	4	2	2	0	2	8	.125	.200	.091	8.00	2.00
Supple, Rayne	B-R	6-3	185	8-18-97	0	2	9.72	10	0	0	0	17	23	18	18	0	10	17	.329	.400	.300	9.00	5.40
Todd, Reagan	L-L	6-3	218	8-30-95	2	1	2.57	15	0	0	1	21	19	9	6	1	5	29	.241	.227	.246	12.43	2.14
Tribucher, Will	L-L	6-3	210	9-23-96	0	0	4.38	9	0	0	1	12	11	7	6	2	1	13	.239	.250	.235	9.49	0.73
Wallace, Jacob	R-R	6-1	190	8-13-98	0	0	1.29	22	0	0	12	21	9	3	3	1	9	29	.129	.083	.152	12.43	3.86
Williams, Hunter	L-L	6-1	220	2-7-96	0	1	13.50	3	0	0	0	1	2	3	2	0	7	1	.400	--	.400	6.75	47.25

Fielding

C: Cope 24, Motley 19, Quijada 37. 1B: Jacobs 22, Jipping 2, Motley 1, Plantier 15, Toglia 38. 2B: Azuaje 8, Boyd 1, Brown 1, Collins 23, Dilone 8, Hatch 1, Metz 14, Restituyo 18, Tovar 4. 3B: Azuaje 2, Boyd 1, Dilone 19, Hatch 11, Metz 4, Plantier 5, Schunk 37. SS: Azuaje 5, Brown 1, Dilone 20, Hatch 3, Tovar 49. OF: Aeilts 55, Boone 56, Collins 12, Hall 20, Hatch 2, Mendoza 6, Restituyo 35, Torrealba 53.

GRAND JUNCTION ROCKIES
PIONEER LEAGUE

ROOKIE ADVANCED

Batting	B-T	HT	WT	DOB	AVG	vLH	vRH	G	AB	R	H	2B	3B	HR	RBI	BB	HBP	SH	SF	SO	SB	CS	SLG	OBP
Barnwell, Jacob	R-R	6-0	200	8-8-97	.167	.167	.167	17	54	6	9	2	0	0	3	8	0	0	0	27	1	2	.204	.274
Berberet, Reese	R-R	6-3	225	11-1-97	.132	.211	.102	39	136	14	18	4	0	6	15	10	5	0	2	73	0	1	.294	.216
Brown, Turner	B-R	5-9	160	8-1-97	.182	.182	.182	19	55	9	10	1	1	4	11	0	0	0	14	3	3	.273	.318
Cabrera, Walking	R-R	6-3	184	8-26-00	.177	.385	.132	45	147	16	26	6	2	1	17	26	0	0	3	58	2	3	.265	.296
Carreras, Julio	R-R	6-2	190	1-12-00	.294	.245	.306	67	262	51	77	14	8	5	38	25	9	6	5	63	14	8	.466	.369
Diaz, Eddy	R-R	6-0	175	2-14-00	.331	.455	.301	59	166	32	55	12	3	0	10	8	1	2	0	33	20	9	.440	.366
Doyle, Brenton	R-R	6-3	200	5-14-98	.383	.361	.389	51	180	42	69	11	3	8	33	31	2	1	1	47	17	3	.611	.477
George, Max	R-R	5-10	190	4-7-96	.233	.385	.192	17	60	12	14	2	0	4	12	12	1	0	0	14	2	0	.467	.370
Isaacs, Todd	R-R	6-0	215	5-22-96	.282	.345	.266	38	142	21	40	12	1	2	18	5	2	3	2	38	9	2	.423	.311
Koss, Christian	R-R	6-1	182	1-27-98	.332	.219	.354	53	190	45	63	11	4	11	51	35	7	3	3	43	10	4	.605	.447

Name	B-T	HT	WT	DOB	AVG	vLH	vRH	G	AB	R	H	2B	3B	HR	RBI	BB	HBP	SH	SF	SO	SB	CS	OBP	SLG
Mendoza, Shael	L-R	6-0	165	10-15-96	.000	--	.000	2	7	0	0	0	0	0	0	0	0	0	0	2	0	0	.000	.000
Metz, Robert	R-R	5-10	185	7-29-96	.333	--	.333	3	6	0	2	0	0	0	1	1	2	0	0	2	0	1	.333	.556
Navarro, Cristopher	R-R	6-0	170	6-14-99	.302	.357	.288	38	139	24	42	7	0	1	16	11	2	1	2	19	5	2	.374	.357
Palma, Ronaiker	R-R	5-10	180	1-2-00	.218	.226	.216	44	156	15	34	6	1	0	17	7	2	3	0	17	0	2	.269	.261
Pena, Yolki	L-L	6-2	165	3-30-00	.244	.286	.235	36	123	20	30	5	1	3	14	17	2	1	1	45	1	0	.374	.343
Restituyo, Bladimir	R-R	5-10	151	7-2-01	.310	.316	.308	20	84	13	26	4	2	2	14	2	1	1	2	13	6	1	.476	.326
Simpson, Colin	L-R	5-9	228	7-23-96	.309	.512	.256	56	207	47	64	12	4	18	49	25	1	1	2	69	5	2	.667	.383
Taylor, Owen	B-R	6-2	200	6-9-95	.232	.063	.254	45	142	18	33	9	1	3	27	33	1	0	2	44	1	2	.373	.376
Tovar, Ezequiel	R-R	6-0	162	8-1-01	.264	.211	.283	18	72	12	19	2	2	0	3	10	1	2	1	17	4	1	.347	.357
Yalowitz, Jack	L-L	5-11	180	10-19-96	.204	.222	.200	47	162	19	33	7	0	3	21	14	3	2	2	47	7	3	.303	.276

Pitching	B-T	HT	WT	DOB	W	L	ERA	G	GS	CG	SV	IP	H	R	ER	HR	BB	SO	AVG	vLH	vRH	K/9	BB/9
Achtermann, Alex	L-R	6-3	210	4-12-96	0	0	6.00	6	0	0	0	9	11	10	6	0	7	8	.290	.385	.240	8.00	7.00
Amarista, Anderson	R-R	6-1	185	9-15-98	5	4	4.02	13	13	0	0	69	68	34	31	12	17	49	.255	.278	.243	6.36	2.21
Ausua, Miguel	L-L	6-0	190	7-15-96	3	0	4.74	7	2	0	0	25	33	14	13	2	11	9	.317	.200	.354	3.28	4.01
Barlow, Trysten	L-L	6-1	215	12-31-96	2	1	2.33	16	0	0	0	19	16	6	5	0	9	20	.242	.316	.213	9.31	4.19
Bido, Anderson	R-R	6-3	205	5-7-99	6	0	3.62	23	0	0	0	27	22	16	11	1	9	26	.216	.286	.179	8.56	2.96
Calvo, Blair	R-R	6-3	195	2-27-96	1	3	5.93	14	1	0	0	27	31	24	18	4	19	37	.287	.395	.229	12.18	6.26
Filpo, Eris	R-R	6-3	170	5-3-98	0	0	4.50	1	0	0	0	2	1	1	1	0	2	2	.250	.400	.000	9.00	9.00
Gotsis, Noah	R-R	6-0	160	6-17-96	1	1	4.20	6	0	0	0	15	15	10	7	2	4	16	.254	.308	.212	9.60	2.40
Gray, Peyton	R-R	6-3	200	6-2-95	0	0	0.00	1	0	0	0	1	0	0	0	0	0	2	.000	--	.000	18.00	0.00
Guth, Zach	L-L	6-4	210	4-4-97	0	0	11.81	7	0	0	0	5	4	9	7	0	12	8	.191	.333	.133	13.50	20.25
Hatcher, Cayden	R-R	6-5	200	9-9-95	3	4	5.80	14	2	0	1	40	56	30	26	8	10	40	.324	.386	.293	8.93	2.23
Haynes, Alex	R-R	6-3	205	6-24-97	0	2	7.84	7	7	0	0	21	25	19	18	5	15	30	.313	.407	.264	13.06	6.53
Hepple, Eric	R-R	6-0	205	3-28-96	1	2	5.00	25	0	0	5	27	32	17	15	2	8	28	.305	.375	.274	9.33	0.67
Hollowell, Gavin	R-R	6-7	215	11-4-97	3	0	2.89	17	0	0	7	19	14	8	6	2	5	30	.200	.320	.133	14.46	2.41
Horn, Jared	R-R	6-4	225	7-21-98	2	2	3.80	11	11	0	0	45	53	29	19	4	11	33	.291	.333	.271	6.60	2.20
James, Keegan	R-R	6-3	214	4-1-97	0	0	10.38	5	0	0	0	4	8	5	5	2	2	2	.381	.571	.286	4.15	4.15
Johnson, Boby	R-R	6-1	185	4-8-97	0	0	4.91	5	0	0	0	11	13	6	6	0	1	11	.325	.533	.200	9.00	0.82
Julio, Erick	R-R	6-1	175	9-22-96	0	0	67.50	3	0	0	0	1	10	10	10	5	2	3	.714	.800	.667	20.25	13.50
Kilkenny, Mitchell	R-R	6-4	206	3-24-97	3	3	4.50	12	12	0	0	42	44	26	21	3	10	37	.268	.250	.280	7.93	2.14
Kostyshock, Jacob	R-R	6-4	175	1-2-98	2	1	1.65	14	0	0	0	16	11	4	3	1	2	17	.193	.238	.167	9.37	1.10
Mejia, Alejandro	L-L	6-1	168	7-2-98	0	1	8.08	13	1	0	0	39	62	40	35	5	19	25	.376	.256	.413	5.77	4.38
Mejia, Juan	R-R	6-3	200	7-4-00	0	0	2.83	24	0	0	4	29	16	11	9	2	15	28	.158	.121	.177	8.79	4.71
Moya, Ever	L-L	6-5	220	5-25-99	1	1	3.99	23	0	0	1	29	23	14	13	1	17	43	.217	.152	.247	13.19	5.22
Olivarez, Helcris	L-L	6-2	192	8-8-00	3	4	4.82	11	11	0	0	47	47	30	25	9	24	61	.260	.148	.279	11.76	4.63
Olliges, Kyle	R-R	6-3	205	6-7-95	0	0	0.00	1	0	0	0	1	0	0	0	0	0	1	.000	--	.000	13.50	0.00
Pilar, Anderson	R-R	6-2	210	3-2-98	3	3	3.93	24	0	0	0	34	33	16	15	4	6	32	.248	.261	.241	8.39	1.57
Quezada, Andrew	L-R	6-1	185	6-28-97	0	2	7.20	5	5	0	0	15	22	16	12	3	5	10	.344	.344	.344	6.00	3.00
Ruff, Mike	R-R	6-2	212	3-31-98	0	2	5.18	9	9	0	0	24	27	17	14	4	7	30	.281	.270	.288	11.10	2.59

Fielding

C: Barnwell 14, George 13, Palma 41, Simpson 10. **1B:** Berberet 30, Simpson 6, Taylor 39. **2B:** Brown 18, Carreras 9, Diaz 17, Koss 18, Metz 2, Navarro 7, Restituyo 5. **3B:** Berberet 5, Carreras 39, Koss 18, Navarro 15. **SS:** Carreras 16, Diaz 17, Koss 13, Navarro 12, Tovar 18. **OF:** Berberet 1, Cabrera 45, Doyle 44, Isaacs 26, Mendoza 2, Pena 33, Restituyo 13, Simpson 27, Yalowitz 43.

Detroit Tigers

SEASON IN A SENTENCE: The Tigers finished with the majors' worst record at 47-114, missing the postseason for the fifth consecutive season and securing the No. 1 overall pick in the upcoming draft for the second time in three years.

HIGH POINT: The Tigers posted a double-digit win total in April (11), which was the only month they accomplished the feat. Detroit started a five-game winning streak with a victory over the Yankees on April 2, its longest winning streak of the season.

LOW POINT: The Tigers took a plunge starting in May, when they were 10 games below .500. Things didn't get any better as the season progressed, either, as Detroit lost at least 20 games in May, June, July and August. The franchise's 59 home losses in 2019 tied the major league record—previously held by the 1939 St. Louis Browns—for most home losses in a single season.

NOTABLE ROOKIES: Righthander Spencer Turnbull turned into an important piece of the Tigers' rotation, posting a 4.61 ERA with 146 strikeouts and 59 walks in 148.1 innings. Lefthanded-hitting outfielder Christin Stewart showed glimpses of his plus power with 10 home runs in 104 games, but his .693 OPS and 103 strikeouts left something to be desired.

KEY TRANSACTIONS: Detroit made two significant trades just before the July 31 trade deadline. First, the Tigers sent outfielder Nicholas Castellanos to the Cubs in exchange for pitching prospects Alex Lange and Paul Richan, both of whom could profile as back-end starters in the future. Next, Detroit sent closer Shane Greene to the Braves in exchange for lefthanded pitching prospect Joey Wentz and minor league outfielder Travis Demeritte. The two moves continued the Tigers' rebuild as they hope to sell-off major league veterans in return for young, controllable prospects who can make an impact for years to come.

DOWN ON THE FARM: Rookie-level GCL Tigers West and Double-A Erie were the only two Tigers affiliates to post winning records, although neither team qualified for the postseason. Some of that could just be attributed to unfortunate circumstances, however, as the Gulf Coast League playoffs were cancelled due to Hurricane Dorian. The Tigers' minor league affiliates finished a combined 340-386 in the regular season, which placed them as the 25th-best winning percentage among all 30 major league organizations.

OPENING DAY PAYROLL: $96,243,400 (23rd).

PLAYERS OF THE YEAR

SCOTT AUDETTE

MAJOR LEAGUE	MINOR LEAGUE
Miguel Cabrera	**Tarik Skubal**
DH	LHP
.282/.346/.398	(High A/Double-A)
Led team in RBIs (59),	6-8, 2.42 in 24 GS
OBP and hits (139)	179 SO in 122.2 IP

ORGANIZATION LEADERS

Batting		*Minimum 250 AB
MAJORS		
* AVG	Victor Reyes	.304
* OPS	Nicholas Castellanos	.790
HR	Brandon Dixon	15
RBI	Miguel Cabrera	59
MINORS		
* AVG	Dawel Lugo, Toledo	.333
* OBP	Dawel Lugo, Toledo	.370
* SLG	Frank Schwindel, Erie, Lakeland, Toledo	.498
* OPS	Dawel Lugo, Toledo	.859
R	Derek Hill, Erie	78
H	Jose Azocar, Erie	144
TB	Willi Castro, Toledo	217
2B	Willi Castro, Toledo	28
3B	Brock Deatherage, Lakeland	11
3B	Iverson Leonardo, DSL Tigers 2	11
HR	Mikie Mahtook, Toledo	21
RBI	Kody Eaves, Erie, Toledo	70
BB	Daz Cameron, Toledo	62
SO	Daz Cameron, Toledo	152
SB	Brock Deatherage, Lakeland	45

Pitching		#Minimum 75 IP
MAJORS		
W	Matthew Boyd	9
# ERA	Nick Ramirez	4.07
SO	Matthew Boyd	238
SV	Shane Greene	22
MINORS		
W	Elvin Rodriguez, Lakeland	11
W	Tim Adleman, Toledo, Erie	11
W	Matt Manning, Erie	11
L	Jesus Rodriguez, Lakeland, West Michigan	13
L	Tom de Blok, Lakeland	13
# ERA	Garrett Hill, West Michigan, Lakeland	2.25
G	John Schreiber, Erie, Toledo	53
GS	Tarik Skubal, Lakeland, Erie	24
GS	Spenser Watkins, Erie, Toledo, Lakeland	24
GS	Matt Manning, Erie	24
SV	Drew Carlton, Erie	19
IP	Spenser Watkins, Erie, Toledo, Lakeland	138
BB	Anthony Castro, Erie	65
SO	Tarik Skubal, Lakeland, Erie	179
# ERA	Garrett Hill, West Michigan, Lakeland	169

General Manager: Al Avila. **Farm Director:** Dave Owen. **Scouting Director:** Scott Pleis.

Class	Team	League	W	L	PCT	Finish	Manager
Majors	Detroit Tigers	American	47	114	.292	15th (15)	Ron Gardenhire
Triple-A	Toledo Mud Hens	International	66	74	.471	t-9th (14)	Doug Mientkiewicz
Double-A	Erie Seawolves	Eastern	77	61	.558	2nd (12)	Mike Rabelo
High A	Lakeland Flying Tigers	Florida State	65	70	.481	8th (12)	Andrew Graham
Low A	West Michigan Whitecaps	Midwest	49	90	.353	16th (16)	Lance Parrish
Short season	Connecticut Tigers	New York-Penn	34	42	.447	10th (14)	Brayan Pena
Rookie	GCL Tigers East	Gulf Coast	19	29	.396	14th (18)	Luis Lopez
Rookie	GCL Tigers West	Gulf Coast	30	20	.600	3rd (18)	Gary Cathcart
Overall 2019 Minor League Record			340	386	.468	25th (30)	

ORGANIZATION STATISTICS

DETROIT TIGERS
AMERICAN LEAGUE

Batting	B-T	HT	WT	DOB	AVG	vLH	vRH	G	AB	R	H	2B	3B	HR	RBI	BB	HBP	SH	SF	SO	SB	CS	SLG	OBP
Beckham, Gordon	R-R	6-0	190	9-16-86	.215	.158	.235	83	223	29	48	13	2	6	15	13	4	0	0	68	3	1	.372	.271
Cabrera, Miguel	R-R	6-4	249	4-18-83	.282	.340	.268	136	493	41	139	21	0	12	59	48	3	0	5	108	0	0	.398	.346
Candelario, Jeimer	B-R	6-1	221	11-24-93	.203	.193	.206	94	335	33	68	17	2	8	32	43	7	0	1	99	3	1	.337	.306
Castellanos, Nicholas	R-R	6-4	203	3-4-92	.273	.347	.257	100	403	57	110	37	3	11	37	31	3	0	2	96	2	1	.462	.328
Castro, Harold	L-R	6-0	180	11-30-93	.291	.212	.309	97	354	30	103	10	4	5	38	9	0	2	4	86	4	2	.384	.305
Castro, Willi	B-R	6-1	205	4-24-97	.230	.250	.225	30	100	10	23	6	1	1	8	6	2	1	1	34	0	1	.340	.284
Demeritte, Travis	R-R	6-0	180	9-30-94	.225	.244	.218	48	169	24	38	7	2	3	10	14	1	1	1	63	3	0	.343	.287
Dixon, Brandon	R-R	6-2	215	1-29-92	.248	.278	.238	117	391	41	97	20	4	15	52	21	4	0	4	136	5	1	.435	.291
Goodrum, Niko	B-R	6-3	218	2-28-92	.248	.361	.215	112	423	61	105	27	5	12	45	46	1	0	2	138	12	3	.421	.322
Greiner, Grayson	R-R	6-6	239	10-11-92	.202	.139	.215	58	208	18	42	5	1	5	19	13	1	1	1	70	0	0	.308	.251
Harrison, Josh	R-R	5-8	185	7-8-87	.175	.167	.177	36	137	10	24	7	1	1	8	6	2	0	2	27	4	2	.263	.218
Hicks, John	R-R	6-2	230	8-31-89	.210	.241	.199	95	319	29	67	15	0	13	35	13	0	0	1	109	1	1	.379	.240
Jones, JaCoby	R-R	6-2	201	5-10-92	.235	.200	.244	88	298	39	70	19	3	11	26	27	6	1	1	94	7	2	.430	.310
Lugo, Dawel	R-R	6-0	220	12-31-94	.245	.232	.250	77	273	28	67	11	4	6	26	8	3	0	4	59	0	0	.381	.271
Mahtook, Mikie	R-R	6-1	216	11-30-89	.000	.000	.000	9	23	0	0	0	0	0	0	2	0	0	0	11	0	0	.000	.080
Mercer, Jordy	R-R	6-3	210	8-27-86	.270	.328	.251	74	256	24	69	16	0	9	22	13	2	0	0	57	0	0	.438	.310
Peterson, Dustin	R-R	6-2	210	9-10-94	.227	.375	.194	17	44	3	10	4	0	0	6	2	1	0	0	14	1	0	.318	.277
Reyes, Victor	B-R	6-5	215	10-5-94	.304	.292	.309	69	276	29	84	16	5	3	25	14	0	0	2	64	9	3	.431	.336
Rodriguez, Ronny	R-R	6-0	200	4-17-92	.221	.239	.215	84	276	29	61	12	3	14	43	13	0	0	5	82	3	1	.438	.252
Rogers, Jake	R-R	6-1	205	4-18-95	.125	.286	.088	35	112	11	14	3	0	4	8	13	1	2	0	51	0	0	.259	.222
Stewart, Christin	L-R	6-0	205	12-10-93	.233	.236	.232	104	369	32	86	25	1	10	40	34	7	0	6	103	0	1	.388	.305
Wilson, Bobby	R-R	6-0	230	4-8-83	.091	.000	.108	15	44	2	4	1	0	0	2	2	0	0	1	11	0	0	.114	.130

Pitching	B-T	HT	WT	DOB	W	L	ERA	G	GS	CG	SV	IP	H	R	ER	HR	BB	SO	AVG	vLH	vRH	K/9	BB/9
Adams, Austin	R-R	5-11	205	8-19-86	0	0	5.14	13	0	0	0	14	14	8	8	2	10	9	.259	.191	.303	5.79	6.43
2-team total (2 Minnesota)					0	0	7.02	15	0	0	0	17	18	13	13	4	13	14	.273	.267	.278	7.56	7.02
Alcantara, Victor	R-R	6-2	190	4-3-93	3	2	4.85	46	0	0	0	43	45	25	23	8	15	24	.276	.241	.295	5.06	3.16
Alexander, Tyler	R-L	6-2	200	7-14-94	1	4	4.86	13	8	0	0	54	68	30	29	9	7	47	.302	.239	.318	7.88	1.17
Baez, Sandy	R-R	6-2	245	11-25-93	0	0	9.00	1	0	0	0	1	2	1	1	0	0	0	.400	.000	.667	0.00	0.00
Boyd, Matthew	L-L	6-3	234	2-2-91	9	12	4.56	32	32	0	0	185	178	101	94	39	50	238	.247	.231	.250	11.56	2.43
Carpenter, Ryan	L-L	6-5	230	8-22-90	1	6	9.30	9	9	0	0	41	61	46	42	12	13	25	.339	.378	.326	5.53	2.88
Cisnero, Jose	R-R	6-3	245	4-11-89	0	4	4.33	35	0	0	0	35	35	21	17	5	19	40	.257	.298	.228	10.19	4.84
Dixon, Brandon	R-R	6-2	215	1-29-92	0	0	9.00	2	0	0	0	2	1	2	2	1	0	1	.143	.000	.333	4.50	0.00
Farmer, Buck	L-R	6-4	232	2-20-91	6	6	3.72	73	1	0	0	68	62	32	28	8	24	73	.247	.270	.232	9.71	3.19
Fernandez, Jose Manuel	L-L	6-3	215	2-13-93	0	0	17.18	4	0	0	0	4	6	8	7	1	5	2	.375	.333	.400	4.91	12.27
Garcia, Bryan	R-R	6-2	210	4-19-95	0	0	12.15	7	0	0	0	7	9	9	9	1	5	7	.321	.273	.353	9.45	6.75
Garrett, Reed	R-R	6-2	210	1-2-93	0	0	8.22	13	0	0	0	15	24	15	14	3	13	10	.381	.286	.429	5.87	7.63
Greene, Shane	R-R	6-4	197	11-17-88	0	2	1.18	38	0	0	22	38	21	11	5	5	12	43	.153	.197	.118	10.18	2.84
Hall, Matt	L-L	6-0	200	7-23-93	0	1	7.71	16	0	0	0	23	28	20	20	4	15	27	.289	.310	.279	10.41	5.79
Hardy, Blaine	L-L	6-2	218	3-14-87	1	1	4.47	39	0	0	0	44	38	24	22	10	13	29	.232	.235	.230	5.89	2.64
Jackson, Edwin	R-R	6-2	215	9-9-83	2	5	8.47	10	8	0	0	39	56	40	37	11	19	33	.329	.329	.330	7.55	4.35
2-team total (8 Toronto)					3	10	9.58	18	13	0	0	68	105	81	72	23	32	52	.351	.326	.373	6.92	4.26
Jimenez, Eduardo	R-R	6-2	225	4-4-95	0	0	5.91	8	0	0	0	11	12	7	7	1	5	8	.273	.150	.375	6.75	4.22
Jimenez, Joe	R-R	6-3	272	1-17-95	4	7	4.37	66	0	0	9	60	56	33	29	13	23	82	.244	.262	.228	12.37	3.47
McKay, David	R-R	6-3	205	3-31-95	0	0	5.59	18	0	0	0	19	15	12	12	2	9	24	.211	.290	.150	13.50	4.19
2-team total (7 Seattle)					0	0	5.47	25	0	0	0	26	20	17	16	3	17	34	.206	.244	.173	11.62	5.81
Moore, Matt	L-L	6-3	210	6-18-89	0	0	0.00	2	2	0	0	10	3	0	0	0	1	9	.094	.000	.097	8.10	0.90
Norris, Daniel	L-L	6-2	185	4-25-93	3	13	4.49	32	29	0	0	144	154	75	72	25	38	125	.275	.260	.279	7.79	2.37
Ramirez, Nick	L-L	6-3	240	8-11-89	5	4	4.07	46	0	0	0	80	76	45	36	11	36	34	.247	.231	.255	8.36	3.95
Reininger, Zac	B-R	6-3	190	1-28-93	0	3	8.68	25	1	0	0	28	44	28	27	11	16	17	.361	.333	.375	5.46	5.14
Rosenthal, Trevor	R-R	6-2	230	5-29-90	0	0	7.00	10	0	0	0	9	3	8	7	0	11	12	.103	.133	.071	12.00	11.00
Ross, Tyson	R-R	6-6	245	4-22-87	1	5	6.11	7	7	0	0	35	41	28	24	7	18	25	.289	.254	.324	6.37	4.58
Schreiber, John	R-R	6-3	220	3-5-94	2	0	6.23	13	0	0	0	13	16	9	9	3	4	19	.296	.304	.290	13.15	2.77

Name	B-T	HT	WT	DOB	W	L	ERA	G	GS	CG	SV	IP	H	R	ER	HR	BB	SO	AVG	vLH	vRH	K/9	BB/9
Soto, Gregory	L-L	6-1	240	2-11-95	0	5	5.77	33	7	0	0	58	74	39	37	9	33	45	.308	.294	.314	7.02	5.15
Stumpf, Daniel	L-L	6-2	208	1-4-91	1	1	4.34	48	0	0	0	29	35	18	14	5	15	28	.302	.255	.344	8.69	4.66
Torres, Carlos	R-R	6-1	180	10-22-82	0	0	7.50	4	0	0	0	6	9	5	5	2	1	8	.333	.231	.429	12.00	1.50
Turnbull, Spencer	R-R	6-3	215	9-18-92	3	17	4.61	30	30	0	0	148	154	86	76	14	59	146	.267	.298	.234	8.86	3.58
VerHagen, Drew	R-R	6-6	230	10-22-90	4	3	5.90	22	4	0	0	58	70	40	38	9	23	51	.304	.311	.299	7.91	3.57
Zimmermann, Jordan	R-R	6-2	225	5-23-86	1	13	6.91	23	23	0	0	112	145	89	86	19	25	82	.311	.346	.275	6.59	2.01

Fielding

Catcher	PCT	G	PO	A	E	DP	PB
Greiner	.990	58	478	23	5	2	4
Hicks	1.000	60	476	37	0	3	3
Rogers	.997	34	287	13	1	0	9
Wilson	1.000	15	125	6	0	0	0

First Base	PCT	G	PO	A	E	DP
Beckham	1.000	4	11	0	0	0
Cabrera	.995	26	204	5	1	13
Candelario	.993	20	136	11	1	16
Castro	1.000	1	9	0	0	1
Dixon	.991	61	438	28	4	39
Goodrum	.988	18	151	13	2	11
Hicks	.995	29	212	9	1	24
Mercer	1.000	5	28	5	0	3
Peterson	1.000	1	1	0	0	0
Rodriguez	1.000	13	88	7	0	9

Second Base	PCT	G	PO	A	E	DP
Beckham	.992	39	50	81	1	21
Castro	.963	34	58	73	5	14
Dixon	.857	3	1	5	1	0
Goodrum	.967	22	40	47	3	17
Harrison	1.000	34	70	86	0	22
Mercer	1.000	8	11	26	0	6
Rodriguez	.983	31	40	77	2	20

Third Base	PCT	G	PO	A	E	DP
Beckham	.909	5	5	5	1	0
Candelario	.967	69	44	133	6	19
Castro	.960	10	5	19	1	1
Dixon	.917	4	2	9	1	0
Goodrum	1.000	1	0	2	0	0
Lugo	.976	73	66	136	5	11
Mercer	1.000	1	0	1	0	0
Rodriguez	.833	6	2	8	2	0

Shortstop	PCT	G	PO	A	E	DP
Beckham	.958	18	23	46	3	10
Castro	1.000	2	7	6	0	2
Castro	.963	29	36	67	4	17
Goodrum	.952	38	42	117	8	12
Mercer	.968	59	66	149	7	29
Rodriguez	.948	20	19	54	4	10

Outfield	PCT	G	PO	A	E	DP
Castellanos	.990	89	200	3	2	0
Castro	.990	44	94	3	1	1
Demeritte	.990	47	104	0	1	0
Dixon	.961	33	49	0	2	0
Goodrum	.966	32	53	3	2	0
Jones	.980	85	193	1	4	1
Mahtook	.889	8	16	0	2	0
Peterson	1.000	13	16	0	0	0
Reyes	.994	67	147	7	1	1
Rodriguez	1.000	1	1	0	0	0
Stewart	.964	89	133	2	5	1

TOLEDO MUD HENS   TRIPLE-A
INTERNATIONAL LEAGUE

Batting	B-T	HT	WT	DOB	AVG	vLH	vRH	G	AB	R	H	2B	3B	HR	RBI	BB	HBP	SH	SF	SO	SB	CS	SLG	OBP
Cameron, Daz	R-R	6-2	195	1-15-97	.214	.222	.212	120	448	68	96	22	6	13	43	62	16	0	2	152	17	8	.377	.330
Candelario, Jeimer	B-R	6-1	221	11-24-93	.320	.425	.283	39	153	30	49	10	2	9	33	22	3	0	0	35	0	0	.588	.416
Castro, Harold	L-R	6-0	180	11-30-93	.328	.120	.381	31	122	20	40	5	1	4	25	9	0	2	1	26	1	3	.484	.371
Castro, Willi	B-R	6-1	205	4-24-97	.301	.306	.299	119	465	75	140	28	8	11	62	37	14	3	6	110	17	4	.467	.366
Dixon, Brandon	R-R	6-2	215	1-29-92	.174	.111	.189	11	46	6	8	0	0	1	3	0	0	0	0	16	0	0	.239	.174
Eaves, Kody	L-R	6-0	195	7-8-93	.270	.000	.357	11	37	6	10	3	0	1	7	7	0	0	0	17	2	0	.432	.386
Greiner, Grayson	R-R	6-6	239	10-11-92	.250	.250	.250	13	48	8	12	1	0	2	4	4	1	0	0	16	0	0	.396	.321
Harrison, Josh	R-R	5-8	185	7-8-87	.174	.286	.125	7	23	2	4	1	0	0	3	6	0	0	0	4	0	0	.217	.345
Jones, JaCoby	R-R	6-2	201	5-10-92	.429	.250	.471	5	21	4	9	1	1	2	6	1	2	0	0	6	0	0	.571	.500
Kozma, Pete	R-R	6-0	190	4-11-88	.263	.290	.254	88	278	44	73	17	2	7	51	32	4	1	7	49	2	0	.414	.340
Lester, Josh	L-R	6-3	180	7-17-94	.236	.091	.262	18	72	7	17	5	0	2	14	11	1	0	4	26	0	0	.389	.330
Lugo, Dawel	R-R	6-0	220	12-31-94	.333	.394	.315	68	282	46	94	21	4	5	41	15	3	0	3	52	6	3	.489	.370
Mahtook, Mikie	R-R	6-1	216	11-30-89	.260	.229	.268	98	354	64	92	17	1	21	56	51	5	1	4	106	14	7	.492	.358
Mercer, Jordy	R-R	6-3	210	8-27-86	.233	.083	.290	12	43	11	10	3	0	0	4	5	2	0	0	6	0	0	.302	.340
Morgan, Joey	R-R	6-0	185	8-26-96	.100	.333	.000	6	10	1	1	0	0	0	0	2	0	0	0	3	0	0	.100	.250
Numata, Chace	R-R	6-0	200	8-14-92	.300	.250	.313	6	20	3	6	1	0	0	2	2	0	0	0	0	0	0	.350	.364
Peterson, Cole	L-R	5-11	160	8-2-95	.214	.500	.167	4	14	0	3	0	0	0	1	0	0	1	0	5	0	1	.214	.267
Peterson, Dustin	R-R	6-2	210	9-10-94	.286	.312	.277	79	301	31	86	13	0	11	49	14	1	0	3	78	1	1	.439	.317
Pinero, Daniel	R-R	6-5	230	5-2-94	.231	.276	.210	28	91	18	21	6	1	4	18	8	1	0	0	25	4	0	.451	.364
Reyes, Victor	R-B	6-5	215	10-5-94	.305	.273	.316	74	289	50	88	19	1	10	58	14	1	0	4	50	10	6	.481	.334
Robson, Jacob	L-R	5-10	180	11-20-94	.267	.273	.265	112	409	61	109	21	3	9	52	53	3	4	4	132	25	10	.399	.352
Rodriguez, Ronny	R-R	6-0	200	4-17-92	.320	.400	.296	44	172	33	55	9	2	11	31	6	1	0	2	41	5	0	.587	.343
Rogers, Jake	R-R	6-1	205	4-18-96	.223	.222	.224	48	166	29	37	10	1	9	31	18	6	1	0	53	0	0	.458	.321
Rupp, Cameron	R-R	6-2	260	9-28-88	.254	.000	.295	21	71	6	18	5	0	1	6	2	0	0	0	19	0	0	.366	.329
Schwindel, Frank	R-R	6-1	215	6-29-92	.327	.379	.310	28	113	21	37	7	0	9	33	6	0	0	0	19	0	0	.628	.361
Scivicque, Kade	R-R	6-0	225	3-22-93	.254	.241	.258	34	122	13	31	9	1	2	13	6	1	0	0	28	0	0	.393	.295
Sedio, Chad	L-R	6-3	200	3-30-94	.271	.300	.267	20	70	8	19	6	0	3	14	3	3	0	1	22	0	0	.486	.325
Stewart, Christin	L-R	6-0	205	12-10-93	.289	.546	.197	22	83	14	24	2	0	4	14	18	1	0	0	25	1	0	.458	.422
Wilson, Bobby	R-R	6-0	230	4-8-83	.244	.160	.277	28	90	12	22	2	0	5	10	11	0	0	0	25	0	0	.433	.327
Woodrow, Danny	L-R	5-10	170	1-26-95	.274	.247	.282	100	376	58	103	12	5	1	32	41	4	2	3	89	23	5	.340	.349

Pitching	B-T	HT	WT	DOB	W	L	ERA	G	GS	CG	SV	IP	H	R	ER	HR	BB	SO	AVG	vLH	vRH	K/9	BB/9
Adams, Austin	R-R	5-11	205	8-19-86		2	6.66	18	1	0		26	26	20	19	6	10	20	.257	.240	.275	7.01	3.51
2-team total (11 Rochester)					1	3	5.77	29	2	0	2	44	42	29	28	9	16	48	.246	.206	.276	9.89	3.30
Adleman, Tim	R-R	6-5	225	11-13-87	9	4	3.32	18	17	2	0	103	84	41	38	14	34	109	.224	.179	.258	9.52	2.97
Alcantara, Victor	R-R	6-2	190	4-3-93	0	0	5.89	13	2	0	0	18	17	12	12	3	6	16	.254	.321	.205	7.85	2.95
Alexander, Tyler	R-L	6-2	200	7-14-94	5	10	5.13	20	16	0	0	98	112	57	56	18	23	108	.284	.268	.292	9.88	2.11
Baez, Sandy	R-R	6-2	245	11-25-93	1	0	7.36	18	0	0	0	22	27	19	18	1	14	18	.300	.316	.289	7.36	5.73
Blackwood, Nolan	R-R	6-5	185	3-16-95	0	2	21.00	3	0	0	0	3	6	7	7	1	4	3	.462	.000	.546	9.00	12.00
Burrows, Beau	R-R	6-2	215	9-18-96	2	6	5.51	15	15	0	0	65	68	41	40	12	32	61	.267	.222	.304	8.40	4.41
Carpenter, Ryan	L-L	6-5	230	8-22-90	5	7	5.26	14	14	0	0	77	77	45	45	11	26	76	.260	.250	.263	8.88	3.04
Cisnero, Jose	R-R	6-3	245	4-11-89	1	2	2.70	32	2	0	7	40	36	14	12	3	21	49	.235	.186	.277	11.03	4.73

DeCaster, Ethan	R-R	6-3	190	10-27-94	1	1	3.46	10	0	0	1	13	12	5	5	2	3	17	.231	.211	.242	11.77 2.08
Fernandez, Jose Manuel	L-L	6-3	215	2-13-93	1	1	5.97	27	1	0	0	35	40	24	23	5	16	24	.288	.220	.326	6.23 4.15
Funkhouser, Kyle	R-R	6-2	230	3-16-94	3	7	8.53	18	18	0	0	63	79	67	60	3	54	65	.310	.360	.277	9.24 7.67
Garcia, Bryan	R-R	6-1	203	4-19-95	3	0	2.97	31	0	0	0	33	26	12	11	4	14	33	.210	.173	.236	8.91 3.78
Hall, Matt	L-L	6-0	200	7-23-93	5	4	5.30	25	13	0	0	87	102	58	51	16	31	106	.287	.342	.261	11.01 3.22
Houston, Zac	R-R	6-5	260	11-30-94	1	1	10.00	17	1	0	1	18	18	22	20	1	14	19	.257	.242	.270	9.50 7.00
Jackson, Edwin	R-R	6-2	215	9-9-83	0	2	5.87	2	2	0	0	8	11	8	5	1	4	2	.344	.455	.286	2.35 4.70
2-team total (3 Buffalo)					1	2	5.40	5	2	0	0	12	12	10	7	2	5	5	.267	.400	.200	3.86 3.86
Jimenez, Eduardo	R-R	6-2	225	4-4-95	4	3	2.96	41	0	0	2	55	39	23	18	5	18	51	.198	.244	.162	8.40 2.96
Kozma, Pete	R-R	6-0	190	4-11-88	0	0	4.50	1	0	0	0	2	3	1	1	1	0	0	.333	.000	.500	0.00 0.00
McKay, David	R-R	6-3	205	3-31-95	0	0	0.00	1	0	0	0	2	0	0	0	0	0	6	.000	.000	.000	27.00 0.00
Navilhon, Joe	R-R	6-0	200	7-13-93	1	1	5.19	5	0	0	0	9	8	5	5	3	1	9	.235	.235	.235	9.35 1.04
Paredes, Eduardo	R-R	6-1	250	3-6-95	1	1	6.75	9	0	0	0	12	10	11	9	1	9	11	.238	.368	.130	8.25 6.75
Ramirez, Nick	L-L	6-3	240	8-1-89	1	0	2.00	2	2	0	0	9	12	5	2	1	3	10	.308	.417	.259	10.00 3.00
Reininger, Zac	B-R	6-3	190	1-28-93	4	3	4.08	34	4	0	0	57	65	28	26	7	26	51	.286	.218	.329	8.01 4.08
Rosenthal, Trevor	R-R	6-2	230	5-29-90	0	0	10.13	6	0	0	0	5	8	6	6	2	6	9	.333	.333	.333	15.19 10.13
2-team total (1 Scranton/Wilkes-Barre)					0	0	15.88	7	0	0	0	6	8	10	10	2	9	9	.320	.333	.313	14.29 14.29
Schreiber, John	R-R	6-3	220	3-5-94	6	4	2.28	48	0	0	4	59	39	22	15	4	21	70	.187	.221	.167	10.62 3.19
Schwindel, Frank	R-R	6-1	215	6-29-92	0	0	0.00	1	0	0	0	1	0	0	0	0	1	0	.000	.000	--	0.00 9.00
Soto, Gregory	L-L	6-1	240	2-11-95	0	3	6.94	6	5	0	0	23	25	19	18	2	13	30	.266	.200	.290	11.57 5.01
Stumpf, Daniel	L-L	6-2	208	1-4-91	2	1	0.59	14	0	0	4	15	8	2	1	0	4	24	.146	.059	.184	14.09 2.35
Szkutnik, Trent	R-L	6-0	195	8-21-93	0	0	4.84	15	0	0	0	22	24	15	12	3	13	23	.276	.233	.298	9.27 5.24
Thielbar, Caleb	R-L	6-0	205	1-31-87	2	1	3.30	50	0	0	4	76	74	29	28	7	16	92	.254	.247	.258	10.85 1.89
2-team total (1 Gwinnett)					2	1	3.22	51	0	0	5	78	75	29	28	7	16	94	.252	.255	.250	10.80 1.84
Torres, Carlos	R-R	6-1	180	10-22-82	0	0	0.00	5	0	0	0	6	5	0	0	0	0	3	.263	.333	.200	4.76 0.00
2-team total (8 Rochester)					4	1	3.13	13	0	0	0	23	24	8	8	1	8	19	.286	.303	.275	7.43 3.13
Turnbull, Spencer	R-R	6-3	215	9-18-92	0	0	0.00	1	1	0	0	4	1	0	0	0	0	7	.083	.000	.100	17.18 0.00
VerHagen, Drew	R-R	6-6	230	10-22-90	4	2	4.42	11	11	0	0	53	61	29	26	5	13	51	.289	.308	.271	8.66 2.21
Vest, Will	R-R	6-0	180	6-6-95	0	0	2.70	3	0	0	1	7	9	3	2	1	2	3	.360	.364	.357	4.05 2.70
Voelker, Paul	R-R	5-10	190	8-19-92	0	0	10.13	2	0	0	0	5	5	3	3	0	1	2	.455	.750	.286	6.75 3.38
Watkins, Spenser	R-R	6-2	225	8-27-92	5	6	7.98	16	14	0	0	77	105	69	68	22	28	75	.326	.317	.333	8.80 3.29
Wotherspoon, Matt	R-R	6-2	215	10-6-91	0	0	3.00	3	0	0	1	6	5	2	2	1	1	8	.227	.143	.267	12.00 1.50
2-team total (33 Norfolk)					5	2	5.32	36	3	0	2	71	70	43	42	11	28	75	.256	.252	.259	9.51 3.55
Zimmermann, Jordan	R-R	6-2	225	5-23-86	0	1	7.71	1	1	0	0	5	5	4	4	2	0	6	.263	.182	.375	11.57 0.00

Fielding

Catcher	PCT	G	PO	A	E	DP	PB
Greiner	1.000	9	76	3	0	0	0
Morgan	1.000	4	24	0	0	0	0
Numata	1.000	5	54	1	0	1	1
Rogers	.993	48	428	25	3	4	3
Rupp	.985	21	186	12	3	3	2
Scivicque	.997	34	300	17	1	3	0
Wilson	1.000	26	217	9	0	1	1

First Base	PCT	G	PO	A	E	DP
Candelario	.977	7	41	1	1	8
Castro	1.000	2	17	0	0	0
Dixon	1.000	11	72	7	0	3
Kozma	.963	4	23	3	1	2
Lester	.988	11	73	6	1	7
Morgan	1.000	1	1	0	0	0
Peterson	.985	74	498	24	8	48
Pinero	1.000	5	36	6	0	0
Rodriguez	1.000	6	43	0	0	9
Schwindel	.990	25	191	8	2	24

Second Base	PCT	G	PO	A	E	DP
Castro	.964	23	34	46	3	10
Castro	.947	7	6	12	1	0
Eaves	.977	11	10	32	1	6
Harrison	1.000	4	5	9	0	4
Kozma	.986	59	78	141	3	32
Lugo	1.000	6	5	14	0	2
Peterson	.889	4	2	6	1	2
Pinero	.500	1	1	0	1	0
Rodriguez	1.000	24	45	57	0	15
Sedio	1.000	11	19	33	0	9

Third Base	PCT	G	PO	A	E	DP
Candelario	.988	30	22	60	1	7
Castro	1.000	2	1	6	0	0
Castro	1.000	1	1	0	0	0
Kozma	1.000	4	4	10	0	3
Lester	1.000	7	4	7	0	1
Lugo	.956	62	38	93	6	6
Pinero	.978	19	12	33	1	5
Rodriguez	.933	7	4	10	1	0

	PCT	G	PO	A	E	DP
Sedio	.824	10	3	11	3	1
Wilson	.000	1	0	0	1	0

Shortstop	PCT	G	PO	A	E	DP
Castro	1.000	1	0	2	0	0
Castro	.943	111	135	227	22	52
Kozma	1.000	24	30	57	0	15
Mercer	1.000	7	6	10	0	0
Pinero	.875	3	6	8	2	3

Outfield	PCT	G	PO	A	E	DP
Cameron	.989	112	256	9	3	0
Castro	1.000	3	5	1	0	0
Jones	1.000	3	4	0	0	0
Mahtook	1.000	64	120	4	0	1
Numata	1.000	1	0	1	0	0
Reyes	1.000	67	148	3	0	1
Robson	.980	83	146	2	3	1
Schwindel	1.000	3	8	0	0	0
Stewart	1.000	16	13	0	0	0
Woodrow	.981	74	153	6	3	1

ERIE SEAWOLVES   DOUBLE-A
EASTERN LEAGUE

Batting	B-T	HT	WT	DOB	AVG	vLH	vRH	G	AB	R	H	2B	3B	HR	RBI	BB	HBP	SH	SF	SO	SB	CS	SLG	OBP
Alcantara, Sergio	B-R	5-9	170	7-10-96	.247	.196	.272	102	324	46	80	10	0	2	27	48	2	2	2	71	7	6	.296	.346
Azocar, Jose	R-R	6-0	185	5-11-96	.286	.288	.285	129	504	65	144	21	3	10	58	21	5	1	7	132	16	3	.399	.317
Burch, Luke	L-L	6-2	185	4-18-94	.323	.373	.291	43	130	18	42	4	0	0	5	7	0	0	0	48	5	2	.354	.358
Clemens, Kody	L-R	6-1	170	5-15-96	.170	.083	.200	13	47	5	8	2	0	1	4	6	1	0	0	18	0	0	.277	.278
Eaves, Kody	L-R	6-0	195	7-8-93	.239	.154	.270	112	393	54	94	19	7	15	63	34	1	1	5	117	2	1	.438	.298
Gibson, Cam	L-R	6-1	215	2-12-94	.235	.165	.263	117	400	45	94	20	6	9	51	46	7	1	3	102	25	7	.383	.322
Hill, Derek	R-R	6-2	195	12-30-95	.243	.236	.246	120	470	78	114	19	5	14	45	38	10	5	3	147	21	13	.394	.311
Lester, Josh	L-R	6-3	180	7-17-94	.223	.130	.259	106	394	52	88	22	1	17	54	39	1	1	7	103	0	1	.414	.290
MacLaren, Cole	R-R	5-10	180	6-10-97	.333	.500	.000	1	3	1	1	1	0	0	0	0	0	0	0	0	0	0	.667	.333
Maddox, Will	L-R	5-10	180	6-11-92	.154	.000	.191	9	26	4	4	0	0	0	2	2	0	0	1	7	0	2	.154	.207
2-team total (36 Richmond)					.192	.063	.211	45	130	14	25	3	1	1	8	9	0	0	1	27	4	4	.254	.243
Montgomery, Troy	L-L	5-10	185	8-13-94	.151	.158	.147	19	53	7	8	2	0	1	7	8	0	2	0	16	0	1	.245	.262
Morgan, Joey	R-R	6-0	185	8-26-96	.148	.133	.154	18	54	2	8	1	0	0	3	5	1	1	1	16	0	0	.167	.230

DETROIT TIGERS

Name	B-T	HT	WT	DOB	AVG	vLH	vRH	G	AB	R	H	2B	3B	HR	RBI	BB	HBP	SH	SF	SO	SB	CS	SLG	OBP
Motter, Taylor	R-R	6-1	195	9-18-89	.148	.091	.188	10	27	3	4	0	1	0	2	5	1	0	2	8	1	0	.222	.286
Numata, Chace	B-R	6-0	200	8-14-92	.239	.275	.224	71	234	30	56	11	2	4	26	16	3	0	5	48	0	0	.355	.291
Paredes, Isaac	R-R	5-11	225	2-18-99	.282	.254	.294	127	478	63	135	23	1	13	66	57	11	0	6	61	5	3	.416	.368
Peterson, Cole	L-R	5-11	160	8-2-95	.219	.242	.212	41	137	15	30	5	1	0	8	3	0	2	0	28	3	2	.270	.236
Pinero, Daniel	R-R	6-5	230	5-2-94	.237	.279	.214	88	317	34	75	19	1	11	38	32	6	0	2	84	1	6	.407	.317
Rogers, Jake	R-R	6-1	205	4-18-95	.302	.346	.283	28	86	17	26	3	1	5	21	19	3	0	4	26	0	0	.535	.429
Rosa, Dylan	R-R	6-2	200	6-27-96	.140	.143	.139	14	43	6	6	1	0	1	6	2	2	0	1	20	1	0	.233	.208
Rosoff, Jon	L-R	5-9	175	11-14-94	.222	--	.222	5	9	1	2	0	0	0	1	0	0	0	4	1	0	.222	.300
Schwindel, Frank	R-R	6-1	215	6-29-92	.257	.295	.236	46	171	21	44	8	0	5	23	11	3	0	3	27	0	0	.392	.309
Scivicque, Kade	R-R	6-0	225	3-22-93	.333	.390	.308	35	132	14	44	11	0	7	21	8	2	0	1	24	0	0	.576	.378
Sedio, Chad	L-R	6-3	200	3-30-94	.213	.219	.209	23	75	8	16	5	3	1	8	3	5	0	0	16	0	0	.400	.289
Simcox, A.J.	R-R	6-3	185	6-22-94	.154	.000	.222	4	13	0	2	0	1	0	4	0	0	0	1	3	0	0	.308	.143

Pitching	B-T	HT	WT	DOB	W	L	ERA	G	GS	CG	SV	IP	H	R	ER	HR	BB	SO	AVG	vLH	vRH	K/9	BB/9
Adleman, Tim	R-R	6-5	225	11-13-87	2	0	2.57	2	2	0	0	14	10	4	4	1	1	14	.196	.130	.250	9.00	0.64
Baez, Sandy	R-R	6-2	245	11-25-93	0	0	7.71	2	0	0	0	2	7	2	2	0	1	1	.583	.714	.400	3.86	3.86
Blackwood, Nolan	R-R	6-5	185	3-16-95	6	4	1.76	41	0	0	4	66	49	21	13	3	26	61	.211	.268	.158	8.28	3.53
Breto, Liarvis	L-L	5-11	175	4-10-93	1	0	3.38	7	0	0	0	11	8	4	4	1	10	10	.211	.154	.240	8.44	8.44
Burch, Luke	L-L	6-2	185	4-18-94	0	0	27.00	1	0	0	0	0	2	5	1	0	2	0	.500	--	.500	0.00	54.00
Burrows, Beau	R-R	6-2	215	9-18-96	1	0	0.00	1	1	0	0	5	2	0	0	0	2	3	.125	.091	.200	5.40	3.60
Carlton, Drew	R-R	6-1	215	9-8-95	4	3	1.46	45	0	0	19	68	48	20	11	3	18	65	.200	.168	.231	8.60	2.38
Castro, Anthony	R-R	6-2	190	4-13-95	5	3	4.40	27	18	0	1	102	75	55	50	9	65	116	.207	.188	.227	10.20	5.72
DeCaster, Ethan	R-R	6-3	190	10-27-94	3	2	2.28	25	0	0	0	43	36	12	11	1	9	39	.231	.290	.184	8.10	1.87
Ecker, Mark	R-R	6-0	200	5-27-95	1	4	5.85	22	0	0	0	32	41	26	21	5	21	32	.313	.258	.369	8.91	5.85
Faedo, Alex	R-R	6-5	230	11-12-95	6	7	3.90	22	22	0	0	115	104	50	50	17	25	134	.235	.265	.203	10.46	1.95
Fernandez, Jose Manuel	L-L	6-3	215	2-13-93	1	3	4.15	11	3	0	1	26	30	16	12	4	7	19	.289	.303	.282	6.58	2.42
Funkhouser, Kyle	R-R	6-2	230	3-16-94	3	1	1.90	4	4	0	0	24	16	5	5	2	3	29	.195	.191	.200	11.03	1.14
Garcia, Bryan	R-R	6-1	203	4-19-95	0	0	2.25	3	0	0	1	4	1	1	1	1	0	8	.077	.200	.000	18.00	0.00
Houston, Zac	R-R	6-5	260	11-30-94	6	1	2.04	23	0	0	1	40	31	12	9	0	14	49	.215	.196	.227	11.12	3.18
Jimenez, Eduardo	R-R	6-2	225	4-4-95	0	0	3.00	2	0	0	1	3	3	2	1	1	1	1	.300	.600	.000	3.00	3.00
Lange, Alex	R-R	6-3	197	10-2-95	2	1	3.45	9	0	0	0	16	13	7	6	0	8	15	.245	.211	.265	8.62	4.60
Lescher, Billy	R-R	6-4	215	9-17-95	1	0	4.63	6	0	0	0	12	10	6	6	3	4	11	.233	.167	.316	8.49	3.09
Manning, Matt	R-R	6-6	215	1-28-98	11	5	2.56	24	24	0	0	134	93	42	38	7	38	148	.192	.217	.168	9.97	2.56
Mize, Casey	R-R	6-3	220	5-1-97	6	3	3.20	15	15	1	0	79	69	30	28	5	18	76	.234	.246	.224	8.69	2.06
Navilhon, Joe	R-R	6-0	200	7-13-93	1	3	4.73	24	1	0	1	40	40	21	21	4	12	48	.260	.234	.278	10.80	2.70
Numata, Chace	B-R	6-0	200	8-14-92	0	0	0.00	1	0	0	0	1	1	0	0	0	1	0	.500	--	.500	0.00	13.50
Perez, Fernando	R-R	6-3	181	12-17-93	1	1	12.79	4	0	0	0	6	15	9	9	1	3	7	.441	.421	.467	9.95	4.26
Pinto, Wladimir	R-R	5-11	170	2-12-98	0	1	2.57	16	0	0	0	28	25	9	8	2	15	38	.238	.222	.250	12.21	4.82
Ramirez, Nick	L-L	6-3	240	8-1-89	1	0	2.51	3	3	0	0	14	11	4	4	1	2	20	.212	.125	.227	12.56	1.26
Schreiber, John	R-R	6-3	220	3-5-94	0	0	2.57	5	0	0	0	7	4	2	2	1	3	12	.154	.083	.214	15.43	3.86
Shore, Logan	R-R	6-2	215	12-28-94	4	7	3.43	23	16	1	0	97	91	41	37	8	39	58	.254	.217	.284	5.38	3.62
Sittinger, Brandyn	R-R	6-1	200	6-6-94	0	0	9.00	4	0	0	1	6	6	6	6	0	8	3	.261	.200	.308	4.50	12.00
Skubal, Tarik	L-L	6-3	215	11-20-96	2	3	2.13	9	9	0	0	42	25	13	10	2	18	82	.168	.244	.135	17.43	3.83
Soto, Gregory	L-L	6-1	240	2-11-95	0	1	2.03	3	3	0	0	13	10	3	3	2	4	12	.204	.200	.207	8.10	2.70
Szkutnik, Trent	R-L	6-0	195	8-21-93	1	3	4.30	28	4	0	1	46	45	25	22	4	20	44	.254	.234	.266	8.61	3.91
Thompson, Jake	R-R	6-4	225	1-31-94	1	0	2.25	1	1	0	0	8	4	2	2	1	1	13	.154	.182	.133	14.63	1.13
Vest, Will	R-R	6-0	180	6-6-95	2	4	5.33	20	0	0	4	27	31	20	16	4	9	25	.287	.265	.305	8.33	3.00
Watkins, Spenser	R-R	6-2	225	8-27-92	3	1	4.25	8	7	0	0	42	41	20	20	3	10	32	.256	.225	.288	6.80	2.13
Wentz, Joey	L-L	6-5	210	10-6-97	2	0	2.10	5	5	0	0	26	20	6	6	3	4	37	.213	.345	.154	12.97	1.40

Fielding

Catcher	PCT	G	PO	A	E	DP	PB
MacLaren	1.000	1	6	0	0	0	0
Morgan	.995	18	184	16	1	1	0
Numata	.992	69	578	44	5	6	8
Rogers	.995	21	194	16	1	0	2
Rosoff	1.000	4	27	4	0	1	0
Scivicque	.993	28	264	21	2	1	1

First Base	PCT	G	PO	A	E	DP
Lester	.989	73	528	36	6	43
Maddox	.923	2	11	1	1	1
Motter	.970	4	32	0	1	2
Pinero	.991	32	216	9	2	30
Rosa	1.000	2	5	0	0	1
Schwindel	1.000	21	158	10	0	15
Sedio	.983	10	56	3	1	5

Second Base	PCT	G	PO	A	E	DP
Alcantara	.983	29	41	72	2	17
Clemens	.981	13	21	32	1	8
Eaves	.949	63	76	127	11	28
Maddox	.923	4	3	9	1	0
Motter	.000	1	0	0	0	0
Peterson	1.000	15	19	43	0	3
Pinero	1.000	13	13	30	0	3
Rosoff	.667	1	1	1	1	0
Sedio	.900	7	9	9	2	5
Simcox	1.000	1	2	1	0	0

Third Base	PCT	G	PO	A	E	DP
Eaves	.962	19	6	19	1	3
Lester	.955	10	5	16	1	1
Motter	.000	1	0	0	0	0
Paredes	.952	81	52	106	8	12
Peterson	1.000	4	5	5	0	1
Pinero	1.000	24	20	26	0	2
Simcox	.909	3	2	8	1	0

Shortstop	PCT	G	PO	A	E	DP
Alcantara	.973	73	109	177	8	32
Paredes	.967	32	48	70	4	15
Peterson	.976	21	35	48	2	8
Pinero	.925	14	29	33	5	10

Outfield	PCT	G	PO	A	E	DP
Azocar	.982	128	254	12	5	3
Burch	.980	31	46	3	1	0
Gibson	.984	112	183	7	3	1
Hill	.989	120	255	11	3	3
Montgomery	1.000	16	30	3	0	0
Motter	1.000	1	1	0	0	0
Pinero	1.000	5	4	1	0	0
Rosa	1.000	9	19	1	0	0
Sedio	1.000	3	2	0	0	0

FLORIDA STATE LEAGUE

Batting	B-T	HT	WT	DOB	AVG	vLH	vRH	G	AB	R	H	2B	3B	HR	RBI	BB	HBP	SH	SF	SO	SB	CS	SLG	OBP
Ames, Nick	L-R	6-3	240	11-25-96	.232	.308	.217	88	319	30	74	13	0	9	39	21	5	0	1	95	0	0	.357	.289
Athmann, Austin	R-R	6-2	210	4-27-95	.192	.286	.178	13	52	6	10	2	0	1	3	1	0	0	0	18	0	0	.289	.208
Bojarski, Ulrich	R-R	6-3	200	9-15-98	.182	.048	.232	22	77	12	14	4	1	0	7	1	1	0	1	20	1	0	.260	.200
Bortles, Colby	R-R	6-5	225	5-28-95	.125	.143	.122	18	56	8	7	2	0	0	3	12	1	1	1	22	0	0	.161	.286
Brinkman, Clark	R-R	6-2	195	3-6-96	.231	.167	.286	4	13	1	3	0	0	0	1	1	0	0	0	5	0	0	.231	.333
Burch, Luke	L-L	6-2	185	4-18-94	.307	.364	.300	27	101	13	31	3	3	0	8	8	1	1	0	25	6	4	.396	.364
Clemens, Kody	L-R	6-1	170	5-15-96	.238	.197	.246	115	411	43	98	24	7	11	59	45	4	1	8	101	11	3	.411	.314
Deatherage, Brock	L-L	6-1	175	9-12-95	.228	.211	.232	117	451	62	103	15	11	7	41	23	4	6	3	135	45	11	.357	.270
Dugas, Dayton	R-R	6-3	230	6-9-97	.115	.000	.122	15	52	3	6	1	0	0	4	6	1	0	0	23	2	1	.135	.220
Greiner, Grayson	R-R	6-6	239	10-11-92	.000	.000	.000	6	15	2	0	0	0	0	0	3	1	0	0	4	1	0	.000	.211
Hampton, Reece	B-R	5-10		7-19-96	.248	.342	.229	74	226	30	56	6	6	2	26	15	2	7	2	53	7	4	.354	.298
Harrison, Josh	R-R	5-8	185	7-8-87	.273	.000	.375	3	11	0	3	0	0	0	1	0	0	0	0	2	0	0	.273	.333
Jones, JaCoby	R-T	6-2	201	5-10-92	.211	.000	.250	5	19	3	4	2	0	0	2	4	0	0	0	7	0	1	.316	.348
MacLaren, Cole	R-R	5-10	190	6-10-97	.200	1.000	.000	4	5	1	1	0	0	0	1	5	1	1	0	0	0	0	.200	.636
Mercer, Jordy	R-R	6-3	210	8-27-86	.000	--	.000	4	14	1	0	0	0	0	0	2	0	0	0	3	0	0	.000	.125
Morgan, Joey	R-R	6-0	185	8-26-96	.188	.125	.203	28	85	5	16	2	0	1	11	2	3	0	1	27	0	0	.247	.307
Noworyta, David	R-R	6-4	180	5-24-96	.250	--	.250	1	4	0	1	0	0	0	0	0	0	0	0	1	0	0	.250	.250
Packard, Bryant	L-R	6-3	200	10-6-97	.118	.000	.167	5	17	2	2	0	0	0	2	2	1	0	0	5	0	0	.118	.250
Pearce, Jordan	L-R	6-2	225	6-14-96	.206	.091	.226	24	73	7	15	6	0	1	6	11	3	0	1	21	1	2	.329	.330
Peterson, Cole	L-R	5-11	160	8-2-95	.284	.318	.277	77	275	31	78	8	3	1	25	21	2	3	5	26	23	8	.346	.333
Policelli, Brady	R-R	5-11	195	6-24-95	.249	.307	.238	123	449	61	112	20	9	11	54	47	9	0	3	108	18	7	.408	.331
Proctor, Christopher	L-R	6-1	175	3-8-97	.263	.429	.167	13	38	4	10	0	0	0	2	2	0	0	0	6	0	0	.263	.300
Reyes, Daniel	R-R	6-1	200	9-7-96	.151	.143	.154	25	86	8	13	4	1	2	8	6	1	0	0	31	2	0	.291	.215
Rivera, Reynaldo	L-R	6-6	250	6-14-97	.178	.100	.200	28	90	10	16	4	1	3	8	8	1	0	0	34	0	0	.344	.253
Rosa, Dylan	R-R	6-2	200	6-27-96	.259	.157	.278	91	317	40	82	12	2	10	31	22	4	0	3	77	10	1	.404	.312
Rosoff, Jon	L-R	5-9	175	11-14-94	.277	.100	.304	49	155	10	43	6	2	1	11	12	3	0	1	22	2	1	.361	.339
Schwindel, Frank	R-R	6-1	215	6-29-92	.455	1.000	.400	3	11	2	5	1	0	1	4	0	0	0	0	1	0	0	.818	.455
Sedio, Chad	L-R	6-3	200	3-30-94	.275	.136	.295	51	171	22	47	6	1	1	18	13	13	2	1	49	0	1	.339	.369
Shepherd, Zac	R-R	6-3	185	9-14-95	.192	.250	.172	25	78	11	15	4	0	3	12	10	1	0	2	35	2	0	.359	.286
Sherley, Luke	R-R	6-1	190	5-7-96	.236	.143	.248	39	123	12	29	3	0	0	9	9	3	0	0	23	1	3	.260	.304
Simcox, A.J.	R-R	6-3	185	6-22-94	.253	.254	.253	103	371	40	94	13	9	1	28	30	2	3	1	94	16	5	.345	.312
Stewart, Christin	L-R	6-0	205	12-10-93	.350	.429	.308	6	20	2	7	1	0	1	5	3	0	0	2	3	0	0	.550	.400
Valente, John	R-R	5-11	190	6-23-95	.297	.269	.307	31	101	9	30	0	2	0	11	4	3	1	0	11	3	1	.337	.343

Pitching	B-T	HT	WT	DOB	W	L	ERA	G	GS	CG	SV	IP	H	R	ER	HR	BB	SO	AVG	vLH	vRH	K/9	BB/9
Baez, Sandy	R-R	6-2	245	11-25-93	0	0	6.00	2	0	0	0	3	3	2	2	1	0	3	.250	.286	.200	9.00	0.00
Bass, Brad	R-R	6-6	250	2-19-96	0	0	6.17	6	0	0	1	12	15	8	8	1	6	16	.313	.333	.296	12.34	4.63
Bienlien, Michael	R-R	6-3	222	3-19-98	1	0	3.00	1	0	0	0	3	1	1	1	0	2	2	.250	.167	.333	6.00	6.00
Breto, Liarvis	L-L	5-11	175	4-10-93	1	1	2.33	9	0	0	2	19	17	5	5	0	8	24	.233	.269	.213	11.17	3.72
Brieske, Beau	R-R	6-3	200	4-5-98	0	0	3.00	1	0	0	0	3	2	1	1	1	1	3	.222	.400	.000	9.00	3.00
Burrows, Beau	R-R	6-2	215	9-18-96	0	0	0.00	1	1	0	0	4	1	0	0	0	2	5	.083	.167	.000	11.25	4.50
de Blok, Tom	R-R	6-4	240	5-8-96	2	13	4.04	21	20	0	0	111	98	56	50	9	43	85	.233	.280	.187	6.87	3.48
De Jesus, Angel	R-R	6-4	200	2-13-97	3	1	1.46	27	0	0	5	37	25	9	6	1	15	55	.187	.088	.288	13.38	3.65
DeCaster, Ethan	R-R	6-3	190	10-27-94	0	0	3.18	9	0	0	0	17	16	7	6	0	3	12	.250	.233	.265	7.94	1.59
Ecker, Mark	R-R	6-0	200	5-27-95	6	1	3.67	16	0	0	2	27	28	12	11	0	9	25	.275	.390	.197	8.33	3.00
Foley, Jason	R-R	6-4	215	11-1-95	3	3	3.89	36	0	0	2	44	46	25	19	3	17	43	.263	.294	.233	8.80	3.48
Funkhouser, Kyle	R-R	6-2	230	3-16-94	0	0	0.00	1	1	0	0	5	2	0	0	0	1	4	.118	.000	.182	7.20	1.80
Garcia, Bryan	R-R	6-1	203	4-19-95	0	0	4.50	4	0	0	1	4	3	2	2	1	2	6	.214	.200	.222	13.50	4.50
Green, Max	L-L	6-1	175	5-28-96	3	1	2.83	36	0	0	3	60	55	21	19	4	17	40	.239	.216	.250	5.97	2.54
Hardy, Blaine	L-L	6-2	218	3-14-87	0	0	0.00	2	0	0	0	3	0	0	0	0	0	3	.000	.000	.000	9.00	0.00
Hill, Garrett	R-R	6-0	185	1-16-96	6	6	2.63	16	16	2	0	86	53	29	25	3	34	87	.180	.237	.120	9.14	3.57
Kirby, Chance	R-R	5-11	165	7-19-95	0	0	0.00	1	1	0	0	3	3	1	0	0	1	3	.211	.111	.300	5.40	1.80
Lance, Carson	R-R	6-5	245	5-3-95	0	0	7.71	1	0	0	0	2	1	2	2	1	2	5	.125	.167	.000	19.29	7.71
Lescher, Billy	R-R	6-4	215	9-17-95	3	2	2.53	28	4	0	2	53	49	18	15	4	13	60	.245	.300	.200	10.13	2.19
Mize, Casey	R-R	6-3	220	5-1-97	2	0	0.88	6	6	0	0	31	11	3	3	0	5	30	.110	.096	.125	8.80	1.47
Myers, Dane	R-R	6-2	205	3-8-96	4	5	6.54	15	7	0	0	52	55	40	38	6	24	38	.267	.279	.258	6.54	4.13
Navilhon, Joe	R-R	6-0	200	7-13-93	0	1	1.80	9	2	0	0	15	13	4	3	0	4	11	.241	.177	.350	6.60	2.40
Perez, Franklin	R-R	6-3	197	12-6-97	0	0	2.35	2	2	0	0	8	7	2	2	1	5	6	.259	.000	.389	7.04	5.87
Pinto, Wladimir	R-R	5-11	170	2-12-98	3	3	2.14	23	0	0	6	34	16	12	8	2	20	49	.140	.200	.101	13.10	5.35
Richan, Paul	R-R	6-2	200	3-26-97	2	2	4.11	5	5	0	0	31	39	17	14	2	2	29	.317	.338	.291	8.51	0.59
Rodriguez, Elvin	R-R	6-3	160	3-31-98	11	9	3.77	24	23	1	0	134	113	60	56	12	44	112	.228	.224	.233	7.54	2.96
Rodriguez, Jesus	R-R	6-4	190	2-16-98	2	12	5.62	19	19	0	0	98	118	66	61	9	27	76	.296	.315	.279	7.00	2.49
Schmidt, Clate	R-R	6-1	190	12-10-93	0	0	3.18	4	0	0	0	6	7	3	2	2	2	4	.318	.286	.333	6.35	3.18
2-team total (11 Daytona)					1	1	7.32	15	0	0	0	20	31	19	16	5	12	14	.369	.286	.411	6.41	5.49
Sittinger, Brandyn	R-R	6-1	200	6-6-94	0	2	6.95	16	0	0	1	22	28	20	17	2	10	26	.315	.382	.273	10.64	4.09
Skubal, Tarik	L-L	6-3	215	11-20-96	4	5	2.58	15	15	0	0	80	62	29	23	5	19	97	.210	.226	.203	10.87	2.13
Sodders, Austin	L-L	6-4	205	4-29-95	0	1	4.00	8	1	0	0	18	21	8	8	0	6	14	.304	.286	.313	7.00	3.00
Soto, Gregory	L-L	6-1	240	2-11-95	0	0	6.75	1	1	0	0	4	4	3	3	0	2	5	.286	.000	.308	11.25	4.50
Thompson, Jake	R-R	6-4	225	1-31-94	0	0	1.90	6	4	0	0	24	19	7	5	1	11	21	.211	.255	.154	7.99	4.18
Tobey, Jared	R-L	6-4	225	3-11-96	1	0	3.20	11	2	0	0	20	17	7	7	1	10	16	.246	.320	.205	7.32	4.58
VerHagen, Drew	R-R	6-6	230	10-22-90	1	0	0.00	1	0	0	0	1	0	0	0	0	0	0	.000	.000	.000	0.00	0.00

DETROIT TIGERS

	B-T	HT	WT	DOB	W	L	ERA	G	GS	CG	SV	IP	H	R	ER	HR	BB	SO	AVG	vLH	vRH	K/9	BB/9
Vest, Will	R-R	6-0	180	6-6-95	1	1	0.84	14	0	0	3	21	9	2	2	1	7	30	.129	.077	.194	12.66	2.95
Warner, Burris	R-R	6-0	190	10-15-94	1	1	6.55	12	1	0	0	22	30	21	16	3	9	22	.316	.302	.327	9.00	3.68
Watkins, Spenser	R-R	6-2	225	8-27-92	1	0	2.37	3	3	0	0	19	13	5	5	1	6	14	.191	.231	.138	6.63	2.84
Welhaf, Robbie	R-R	6-1	190	5-19-95	0	0	0.00	1	0	0	0	2	2	0	0	0	2	2	.250	.500	.000	9.00	9.00
Zimmermann, Jordan	R-R	6-2	225	5-23-86	0	0	6.75	1	1	0	0	3	3	2	2	1	0	2	.300	.200	.400	6.75	0.00

Fielding

Catcher	PCT	G	PO	A	E	DP	PB
Athmann	1.000	10	89	6	0	0	0
Greiner	1.000	4	25	3	0	1	0
MacLaren	1.000	4	23	1	0	0	0
Morgan	.992	27	218	19	2	2	3
Noworyta	1.000	1	7	1	0	0	0
Policelli	.978	36	278	28	7	2	7
Proctor	.989	11	81	11	1	4	2
Rosoff	.990	47	375	35	4	3	5

First Base	PCT	G	PO	A	E	DP
Ames	.993	64	392	28	3	30
Bortles	1.000	5	38	4	0	1
Pearce	.978	18	132	4	3	14
Rivera	.989	24	173	6	2	18
Schwindel	1.000	3	23	0	0	1
Sedio	.990	13	99	2	1	6
Shepherd	.963	11	75	3	3	9

Second Base	PCT	G	PO	A	E	DP
Clemens	.990	99	161	231	4	49
Harrison	1.000	2	4	4	0	1
Peterson	1.000	2	2	2	0	0
Sedio	1.000	3	4	6	0	3
Simcox	.972	9	19	16	1	4
Valente	.989	22	36	52	1	11

Third Base	PCT	G	PO	A	E	DP
Bortles	.939	13	12	19	2	2
Pearce	.909	7	3	7	1	0
Peterson	.000	1	0	0	0	0
Policelli	.912	27	19	33	5	1
Sedio	1.000	2	2	3	0	0
Shepherd	.824	13	10	18	6	1
Sherley	.970	14	7	25	1	2
Simcox	.938	54	44	76	8	6
Valente	.955	10	5	16	1	0

Shortstop	PCT	G	PO	A	E	DP
Mercer	.833	2	2	3	1	1
Peterson	.964	70	88	153	9	33
Policelli	1.000	1	1	3	0	2
Sherley	.980	25	32	66	2	11
Simcox	.943	39	58	91	9	21

Outfield	PCT	G	PO	A	E	DP
Bojarski	1.000	17	25	2	0	0
Brinkman	1.000	4	4	0	0	0
Burch	1.000	27	47	1	0	0
Deatherage	.992	100	246	3	2	1
Dugas	1.000	10	22	0	0	0
Hampton	.981	73	143	8	3	0
Jones	1.000	3	6	0	0	0
Packard	1.000	2	1	0	0	0
Policelli	.981	45	94	8	2	4
Reyes	.941	11	16	0	1	0
Rosa	.971	85	159	6	5	1
Sedio	1.000	28	72	1	0	0
Stewart	1.000	3	2	0	0	0

WEST MICHIGAN WHITECAPS

LOW CLASS A

MIDWEST LEAGUE

Batting	B-T	HT	WT	DOB	AVG	vLH	vRH	G	AB	R	H	2B	3B	HR	RBI	BB	HBP	SH	SF	SO	SB	CS	SLG	OBP
Ames, Nick	L-R	6-3	240	11-25-96	.348	.200	.380	31	112	18	39	11	0	1	19	16	0	0	1	29	1	0	.473	.426
Bojarski, Ulrich	R-R	6-3	200	9-15-98	.271	.279	.269	104	384	52	104	17	3	10	55	16	6	1	8	87	6	3	.409	.304
Brinkman, Clark	R-R	6-2	195	3-6-96	.214	.167	.233	13	42	6	9	0	0	1	2	1	0	0	1	15	2	0	.286	.227
Burks, Jeremiah	R-R	6-2	215	1-8-97	.178	.111	.207	33	118	16	21	6	1	1	13	16	2	1	0	52	3	3	.271	.287
Dugas, Dayton	R-R	6-3	230	6-9-97	.271	.415	.229	49	181	20	49	11	1	2	19	10	1	0		67	4	6	.376	.305
Esposito, Vinny	R-R	5-11	200	3-10-96	.190	.000	.225	17	58	5	11	3	0	1	6	3	3	0	1	22	2	1	.293	.262
Greene, Riley	L-L	6-3	200	9-28-00	.219	.278	.183	24	96	13	21	2	2	2	13	6	3	0	3	26	4	0	.344	.278
Hampton, Reece	B-R	5-10	170	7-19-96	.313	.278	.320	29	115	18	36	4	3	1	8	15	2	2	1	28	5	2	.426	.399
Johnson, Cooper	R-R	6-0	215	4-25-98	.179	.035	.255	27	84	13	15	4	0	2	11	15	3	0	1	28	0	2	.298	.320
Joyce, Corey	R-R	6-1	190	8-19-98	.180	.095	.241	13	50	6	9	2	0	0	1	4	1	0	0	15	0	0	.220	.255
Kenley, Jack	L-R	6-0	185	10-8-97	.192	.095	.217	31	104	10	20	6	0	3	10	9	6	1	1	38	3	1	.337	.292
King, Jose	L-R	6-0	175	1-16-99	.209	.111	.228	52	172	23	36	7	1	1	11	17	1	2	1	49	8	3	.279	.283
Liniak, Kingston	R-R	6-2	170	11-11-99	.050	.000	.067	6	20	2	1	0	0	0	1	0	1	0	0	5	1	0	.050	.095
Lipcius, Andre	R-R	6-1	190	5-22-98	.273	.239	.285	67	253	32	69	16	0	2	29	27	1	1	1	57	3	2	.360	.344
Malis, Zach	L-R	6-4	190	11-7-96	.235	.268	.223	63	213	21	50	6	1	3	22	17	3	1	2	43	1	1	.315	.298
Martinez, Hector	R-R	5-11	175	11-1-96	.195	.059	.233	22	77	6	15	3	0	3	11	2	3	0	1	23	0	0	.351	.241
McMillan, Sam	R-R	6-0	200	12-1-98	.241	.217	.247	72	220	36	53	10	0	2	19	47	11	1	1	50	6	6	.314	.398
Meadows, Parker	L-R	6-5	205	11-2-99	.221	.239	.216	126	443	52	98	15	2	7	40	47	2	7	5	113	14	8	.312	.296
Packard, Bryant	L-R	6-3	200	10-6-97	.309	.364	.288	23	81	14	25	6	0	3	12	13	0	0	0	24	1	0	.494	.404
Pearce, Jordan	L-R	6-2	225	6-14-96	.217	.296	.201	47	166	17	36	3	1	2	19	23	3	0	0	42	0	1	.283	.323
Perez, Wenceel	B-R	5-11	195	10-30-99	.233	.273	.218	124	459	59	107	16	6	3	30	45	0	8	4	87	21	13	.314	.299
Proctor, Christopher	L-R	6-1	175	3-8-97	.239	.177	.250	56	210	26	52	8	0	2	25	14	0	0	3	40	5	1	.303	.281
Quintana, Nick	R-R	5-10	187	10-13-97	.158	.094	.175	41	146	14	23	5	1	1	13	13	1	0	2	51	3	1	.226	.228
Reyes, Daniel	R-R	6-0	200	9-7-96	.265	.235	.280	42	151	11	40	13	0	4	24	11	4	0	1	38	2	2	.431	.329
Rivera, Reynaldo	L-R	6-6	250	11-4-96	.228	.121	.250	62	197	19	45	7	2	4	19	20	2	1	1	72	3	0	.345	.305
Sherley, Luke	R-R	6-1	190	5-7-96	.100	.000	.125	3	10	1	1	0	0	1	2	2	0	0	0	5	0	0	.400	.250
Tuck, Avery	L-R	6-4	200	12-28-97	.233	.214	.236	48	172	20	40	5	0	3	21	17	0	0	1	79	3	3	.314	.300
Valente, John	R-R	5-11	190	6-23-95	.312	.194	.338	44	170	21	53	3	1	0	20	14	2	2	3	12	6	3	.341	.365

Pitching	B-T	HT	WT	DOB	W	L	ERA	G	GS	CG	SV	IP	H	R	ER	HR	BB	SO	AVG	vLH	vRH	K/9	BB/9
Arriera, Gio	R-R	6-2	220	6-7-98	3	8	6.81	18	18	0	0	79	97	72	60	4	43	79	.305	.258	.339	8.96	4.88
Bass, Brad	R-R	6-6	250	2-15-96	5	4	3.00	10	10	0	0	60	57	20	20	6	14	45	.255	.245	.262	6.75	2.10
Behenna, Kory	L-L	6-2	185	8-2-96	0	0	2.45	7	0	0	0	7	4	4	2	0	6	7	.154	.100	.188	8.59	7.36
Bienlien, Michael	R-R	6-3	232	3-19-98	0	0	3.66	11	0	0	0	20	22	9	8	0	10	20	.272	.316	.233	9.15	4.58
Breto, Liarvis	L-L	5-11	175	4-10-93	0	0	7.50	4	0	0	0	6	5	5	5	1	5	7	.370	.546	.250	10.50	7.50
Chentouf, Yaya	R-R	5-9	205	6-18-97	3	6	3.86	43	0	0	5	79	88	45	34	2	22	54	.279	.279	.280	6.13	2.50
Conger, Maddux	R-R	6-2	235	6-28-96	0	0	6.14	7	1	0	0	7	11	7	5	1	11	6	.333	.222	.375	7.36	13.50
Crosby, Drew	R-L	6-0	205	11-16-95	1	4	5.09	28	0	0	2	69	85	47	39	5	22	53	.298	.308	.294	6.91	2.87
De Jesus, Angel	R-R	6-4	200	2-13-97	1	1	1.85	9	0	0	3	24	12	5	5	1	14	30	.140	.103	.158	11.10	5.18
De La Cruz, Sandel	R-R	6-2	225	8-6-96	4	4	3.86	34	5	0	1	82	75	42	35	6	41	102	.234	.202	.255	11.24	4.52
Gizzi, Michael	R-R	6-4	195	5-15-95	0	0	1.80	7	0	0	0	5	6	4	1	0	3	1	.261	.250	.286	1.80	5.40
Guzman, Carlos	R-R	6-1	185	5-16-98	2	2	2.73	7	7	0	0	33	23	13	10	3	18	27	.197	.235	.167	7.36	4.91

Name	B-T	HT	WT	DOB	W	L	ERA	G	GS	CG	SV	IP	H	R	ER	HR	BB	SO	AVG	vLH	vRH	H/9	BB/9
Hernandez, Wilkel	R-R	6-3	195	4-13-99	9	7	3.73	21	21	0	0	101	97	49	42	5	26	90	.246	.202	.278	7.99	2.31
Hess, Zack	R-R	6-6	219	2-25-97	0	1	2.57	16	0	0	7	21	15	10	6	2	11	22	.197	.281	.136	9.43	4.71
Hill, Garrett	R-R	6-0	185	1-16-96	2	1	1.41	7	7	0	0	38	19	8	6	0	13	42	.143	.135	.146	9.86	3.05
Javier, Xavier	R-R	6-4	225	2-9-98	0	2	8.56	7	1	0	0	14	15	15	13	1	17	8	.294	.375	.257	5.27	11.20
Kirby, Chance	R-R	5-11	165	7-19-95	5	8	4.90	17	13	0	1	83	77	47	45	12	15	61	.246	.240	.250	6.64	1.63
Klinchock, Robert	R-L	6-4	230	10-1-96	0	1	4.30	3	3	0	0	15	19	8	7	1	2	11	.302	.313	.298	6.75	1.23
Lance, Carson	R-R	6-5	245	5-3-95	0	3	9.82	5	2	0	0	15	16	19	16	2	15	14	.271	.286	.263	8.59	9.20
Malis, Zach	L-R	6-4	190	11-7-96	0	0	0.00	2	0	0	0	2	0	0	0	0	0	3	.000	.000	.000	13.50	0.00
Murphy, Kacey	L-L	6-0	210	1-21-97	1	3	6.43	8	8	0	0	35	44	28	25	5	14	23	.310	.394	.284	5.91	3.60
Pearce, Jordan	L-R	6-2	225	6-14-96	0	0	0.00	2	0	0	0	2	1	0	0	0	1	1	.143	.000	.200	4.50	4.50
Reyes, Angel	R-R	6-2	205	10-17-97	0	3	3.60	46	0	0	7	60	48	26	24	4	35	64	.213	.221	.209	9.60	5.25
Rodriguez, Jesus	R-R	6-3	170	2-16-98	0	1	3.52	2	2	0	0	8	7	3	3	0	5	4	.259	.273	.250	4.70	5.87
Shepherd, Zac	R-R	6-3	185	9-14-95	1	1	3.46	7	0	0	0	13	9	7	5	0	7	16	.180	.111	.219	11.08	4.85
Smith, Hugh	R-R	6-10	214	3-25-97	0	4	3.63	10	10	0	0	45	36	21	18	1	20	45	.218	.181	.256	9.07	4.03
Sodders, Austin	L-L	6-4	205	4-29-95	0	2	8.10	4	1	0	0	10	14	11	9	0	11	7	.378	.250	.414	6.30	9.90
Tobey, Jared	R-L	6-4	225	3-11-96	1	2	1.88	21	0	0	2	29	25	6	6	2	11	41	.229	.175	.261	12.87	3.45
Vasquez, Jose	R-R	6-0	175	3-19-96	2	5	5.30	36	0	0	1	53	64	41	31	3	30	62	.292	.282	.299	10.59	5.13
Welhaf, Robbie	R-R	6-1	190	5-19-95	5	7	2.69	18	13	0	0	90	65	30	27	5	9	85	.195	.200	.192	8.47	0.90
Wolf, Adam	L-L	6-6	235	12-26-96	4	10	6.23	17	17	0	0	78	105	58	54	4	30	70	.317	.386	.292	8.08	3.46

Fielding

Catcher	PCT	G	PO	A	E	DP	PB
Johnson	1.000	27	205	25	0	0	3
McMillan	.988	59	469	31	6	0	4
Proctor	.996	54	416	47	2	4	9

First Base	PCT	G	PO	A	E	DP
Ames	1.000	21	137	4	0	12
Malis	.985	56	432	25	7	31
Pearce	.984	26	166	16	3	17
Rivera	.975	42	283	26	8	31

Second Base	PCT	G	PO	A	E	DP
Burks	.956	28	34	74	5	15
Joyce	.980	11	22	27	1	2
Kenley	.947	26	33	57	5	9
King	.944	28	45	56	6	15
Lipcius	.984	26	55	68	2	21

Second Base (cont.)	PCT	G	PO	A	E	DP
Martinez	.977	12	15	27	1	5
Sherley	1.000	1	2	2	0	1
Valente	.980	8	22	27	1	8

Third Base	PCT	G	PO	A	E	DP
Joyce	.750	1	2	1	1	0
King	.864	12	4	15	3	3
Lipcius	.963	27	22	56	3	0
Malis	1.000	5	3	6	0	0
Martinez	.941	7	3	13	1	0
Pearce	.881	19	11	26	5	1
Quintana	.855	39	32	62	16	2
Sherley	.800	2	1	3	1	0
Valente	.941	31	26	54	5	5

Shortstop	PCT	G	PO	A	E	DP
Joyce	1.000	1	2	2	0	0
King	.932	12	9	32	3	4

Shortstop (cont.)	PCT	G	PO	A	E	DP
Lipcius	.976	9	18	23	1	4
Perez	.930	118	175	264	33	64

Outfield	PCT	G	PO	A	E	DP
Bojarski	.973	94	177	4	5	0
Brinkman	.944	13	16	1	1	0
Dugas	.965	37	53	2	2	0
Esposito	1.000	15	30	0	0	0
Greene	1.000	24	63	0	0	0
Hampton	1.000	24	49	1	0	0
Liniak	1.000	6	9	0	0	0
Meadows	.986	117	269	9	4	2
Packard	.950	17	18	1	1	0
Reyes	1.000	22	53	0	0	0
Rivera	.889	4	7	1	1	0
Tuck	.951	46	89	8	5	1
Valente	.857	2	6	0	1	0

CONNECTICUT TIGERS
NEW YORK-PENN LEAGUE

SHORT SEASON

Batting	B-T	HT	WT	DOB	AVG	vLH	vRH	G	AB	R	H	2B	3B	HR	RBI	BB	HBP	SH	SF	SO	SB	CS	SLG	OBP
Alfonzo, Eliezer	B-R	5-10	155	9-23-99	.318	.320	.318	48	179	16	57	7	0	1	24	8	0	1	3	17	2	2	.374	.342
Alvarado, Darwin	L-R	6-1	170	11-10-98	.364	.000	.444	5	11	2	4	1	0	0	1	1	0	0	1	1	0	0	.455	.385
Brinkman, Clark	R-R	6-2	195	3-6-96	.300	.400	.200	3	10	3	3	1	0	0	0	3	1	0	0	5	0	0	.400	.500
Burks, Jeremiah	R-R	6-2	215	1-8-97	.129	.143	.125	10	31	2	4	0	0	0	1	2	1	0	0	13	1	1	.129	.206
Carpenter, Kerry	L-R	6-2	220	9-2-97	.167	.167	.167	4	18	1	3	0	0	0	1	0	0	0	0	3	1	0	.167	.167
De La Rosa, Eric	R-R	6-4	175	6-3-97	.148	.250	.117	46	135	10	20	3	1	0	9	13	6	1	2	51	4	5	.185	.250
Escalona, Ildemaro	R-R	6-0	170	2-12-99	.000	.000	.000	5	15	3	0	0	0	0	2	1	0	0	3	0	0	.000	.167
Garcia, Alexis	B-R	6-2	170	7-1-97	.105	.000	.143	9	19	5	2	0	0	1	4	9	1	0	0	8	0	2	.263	.414
Greene, Riley	L-L	6-3	190	9-28-00	.296	.400	.254	24	88	12	26	3	1	1	7	11	1	0	0	25	1	0	.386	.380
Holton, Jake	R-R	6-0	210	3-2-98	.222	.311	.193	57	180	30	40	7	0	1	17	40	9	0	3	32	1	0	.278	.384
Jarecki, Matthew	R-R	6-2	205	5-12-96	.222	.000	.250	3	9	1	2	1	0	0	3	0	0	0	2	3	0	0	.333	.182
Johnson, Cooper	R-R	6-2	215	4-25-98	.234	.177	.267	14	47	5	11	3	0	0	6	8	1	1	0	15	0	0	.298	.357
Joyce, Corey	R-R	6-1	190	8-19-98	.219	.125	.247	28	105	10	23	1	1	1	15	5	1	1	2	26	2	2	.276	.257
Kenley, Jack	L-R	6-0	185	10-8-97	.160	.250	.118	8	25	3	4	1	1	0	4	1	1	1	0	10	1	0	.280	.214
King, Jake	L-R	6-0	175	1-19-96	.224	.310	.199	53	183	19	41	7	2	0	7	10	1	1	1	48	2	1	.284	.267
Kreidler, Ryan	R-R	6-4	208	11-12-97	.233	.265	.224	60	228	28	53	13	4	2	20	26	6	0	3	61	9	4	.351	.307
Liniak, Kingston	R-R	6-2	170	11-11-99	.205	.309	.166	52	200	22	41	8	1	1	13	17	5	0	0	60	6	5	.270	.284
Martinez, Hector	R-R	5-11	175	11-1-96	.250	.200	.279	19	68	7	17	5	0	1	17	6	0	0	0	13	1	2	.368	.311
Martinez, Julio	R-R	6-2	195	12-15-97	.222	.111	.259	10	36	2	8	1	0	0	3	4	0	0	0	13	0	1	.250	.300
Navigato, Andrew	R-R	5-11	188	5-28-98	.222	.133	.256	19	54	7	12	1	1	0	3	3	0	0	1	19	0	1	.278	.259
Noworyta, David	R-R	6-4	180	5-24-96	.333	--	.333	1	3	0	1	0	0	0	0	0	0	0	0	0	0	0	.333	.333
Nunez, Moises	R-R	6-2	190	2-7-97	.172	.000	.208	9	29	4	5	3	0	1	4	0	0	0	1	11	0	0	.379	.167
Packard, Bryant	L-R	6-2	200	10-6-97	.351	.286	.367	11	37	5	13	2	0	0	2	6	0	0	1	9	1	0	.405	.432
Quero, Jose	L-L	6-0	190	9-5-98	.333	--	.333	4	12	2	4	3	0	0	2	3	1	0	0	1	0	0	.583	.500
Quiggle, Kona	L-L	6-1	200	2-1-98	.194	.209	.189	53	175	17	34	3	0	2	17	23	2	0	2	51	1	2	.246	.292
Quintana, Nick	R-R	5-10	187	10-13-97	.256	.188	.275	21	86	12	22	7	0	1	4	12	0	0	0	31	1	0	.372	.347
Rea, Yoandy	R-R	6-0	165	6-12-00	.238	.200	.250	6	21	1	5	0	0	0	2	0	1	0	0	7	0	2	.238	.273
Silverio, Gresuan	B-R	6-0	175	1-5-99	.148	.250	.118	29	88	8	13	2	0	1	6	13	2	0	2	35	0	0	.205	.267
Smith, Kelvin	R-R	6-1	185	10-30-99	.152	.111	.167	9	33	3	5	2	0	0	5	1	2	0	0	14	2	0	.212	.222
Tuck, Avery	L-R	6-4	200	12-28-97	.175	.174	.175	37	126	10	22	3	3	1	10	6	1	0	0	41	0	1	.270	.218
Verdon, Jordan	L-R	6-3	190	1-7-97	.241	.355	.206	41	133	17	32	11	2	0	17	17	4	0	1	26	1	0	.353	.342

Pitching	B-T	HT	WT	DOB	W	L	ERA	G	GS	CG	SV	IP	H	R	ER	HR	BB	SO	AVG	vLH	vRH	K/9	BB/9
Aguilera, Juan	R-R	6-1	183	9-24-96	0	0	3.00	2	0	0	0	3	2	1	1	0	2	3	.182	.000	.250	9.00	6.00
Anderson, Austin	R-R	5-11	197	11-20-95	2	1	3.64	21	0	0	3	30	27	17	12	3	12	36	.241	.216	.253	10.92	3.64
Baker, Jake	R-L	6-2	200	6-12-98	2	1	3.68	7	0	0	0	15	12	7	6	0	14	24	.226	.231	.225	14.73	8.59
Behenna, Kory	L-L	6-2	185	8-2-96	4	1	6.56	20	0	0	4	23	32	23	17	1	7	28	.311	.353	.290	10.80	2.70
Bergner, Austin	R-R	6-4	200	5-1-97	0	2	6.33	11	2	0	1	21	25	15	15	2	10	11	.309	.333	.296	4.64	4.22
Beyer, Drew	R-R	6-3	200	5-16-96	0	0	0.00	1	0	0	0	1	0	0	0	0	1	1	.000	--	.000	9.00	9.00
Bienlien, Michael	R-R	6-3	222	3-19-98	0	1	4.50	3	0	0	0	6	6	3	3	0	2	6	.250	.333	.222	9.00	3.00
Chentouf, Yaya	R-R	5-9	205	6-18-97	0	0	0.00	5	0	0	4	5	3	0	0	0	6	6	.188	.250	.167	11.57	0.00
Conger, Maddux	R-R	6-2	235	6-28-96	0	1	2.57	5	1	0	0	14	12	5	4	1	9	12	.235	.211	.250	7.71	5.79
De La Rosa, Bairon	R-R	6-0	195	7-17-96	0	2	10.66	10	0	0	0	13	14	16	15	1	19	16	.286	.263	.300	11.37	13.50
De Los Reyes, Raul	R-R	6-4	220	8-24-97	3	3	2.86	21	0	0	0	28	35	12	9	1	5	28	.299	.364	.274	8.89	1.59
Dellinger, Jack	R-R	6-6	225	2-12-98	0	1	6.75	2	2	0	0	9	13	7	7	0	1	6	.333	.450	.211	5.79	0.96
Domnarski, Doug	R-L	5-11	190	7-8-94	0	0	0.00	1	0	0	0	3	2	0	0	0	2	.222	.333	.167	6.75	0.00
Fajardo, Rodolfo	L-L	6-3	165	2-17-00	0	0	9.00	3	1	0	0	5	7	5	5	0	2	5	.350	.500	.313	9.00	3.60
Fernander, Chavez	R-R	6-3	205	7-7-97	2	2	2.31	11	8	0	0	35	28	9	9	3	13	33	.224	.286	.184	8.49	3.34
Hess, Zack	R-R	6-6	219	2-25-97	0	0	0.00	5	0	0	3	6	1	0	0	0	3	10	.056	.000	.077	15.88	4.76
Javier, Xavier	R-R	6-4	225	2-9-98	3	3	3.90	14	14	0	0	55	50	28	24	2	33	39	.243	.203	.263	6.34	5.37
Jimenez, Marco	R-R	6-0	165	12-6-99	3	2	4.13	14	10	0	0	52	50	26	24	8	21	36	.251	.239	.258	6.19	3.61
Lance, Carson	R-R	6-5	245	5-3-95	4	3	2.92	12	12	0	0	52	39	20	17	2	32	56	.206	.236	.194	9.63	5.50
Magno, Andrew	R-L	5-11	190	4-30-98	1	0	2.05	19	0	0	3	22	16	6	5	2	17	19	.200	.158	.213	7.77	6.95
Montero, Keider	R-R	6-1	145	7-6-00	2	2	2.55	5	5	1	0	25	22	7	7	2	5	26	.259	.250	.262	9.49	1.82
Noble, Wes	R-R	5-11	195	5-27-96	1	1	5.82	7	2	0	0	17	21	11	11	2	7	14	.292	.435	.225	7.41	3.71
O'Loughlin, Jack	L-L	6-5	210	3-14-00	2	4	3.13	13	12	0	0	60	57	24	21	1	24	49	.255	.333	.238	7.31	3.58
Perez, Cleiverth	L-L	5-11	167	2-5-00	0	0	0.00	1	1	0	0	5	2	0	0	0	2	3	.118	.000	.133	5.40	3.60
Shepherd, Zac	R-R	6-3	185	9-14-95	1	3	2.70	13	0	0	1	20	20	7	6	1	6	23	.260	.310	.229	10.35	2.70
Silva, Alfredo	L-L	6-3	180	7-27-98	0	1	0.00	8	3	0	0	19	6	2	0	0	16	23	.098	.000	.113	10.89	7.58
Stuka, Ted	R-R	6-7	225	5-13-97	0	2	4.58	10	0	0	2	18	15	11	9	0	9	15	.250	.067	.311	7.64	4.58
Tassin, Bryce	R-R	6-2	212	1-11-97	3	0	2.45	11	0	0	0	18	15	7	5	1	5	24	.221	.263	.204	11.78	2.45
Thomas, Kyle	R-R	6-3	200	3-5-95	0	1	1.54	17	3	0	1	35	22	6	6	2	8	20	.179	.172	.181	5.14	2.06
Tortosa, Cristhian	L-L	6-4	170	10-30-98	1	0	3.62	15	0	0	0	27	13	17	11	1	24	25	.143	.115	.154	8.23	7.90
Walker, Matt	L-L	6-3	203	6-15-98	0	1	67.50	1	0	0	0	1	3	5	5	1	2	2	.600	1.000	.500	27.00	27.00

Fielding

C: Alfonzo 39, Johnson 9, Noworyta 1, Nunez 6, Rea 3, Silverio 18. **1B:** Holton 51, Quero 3, Verdon 22. **2B:** Burks 8, Garcia 2, Joyce 22, Kenley 3, King 30, Martinez 1, Navigato 10. **3B:** Garcia 6, Joyce 1, King 16, Martinez 15, Navigato 7, Quintana 25, Smith 7. **SS:** Escalona 5, Joyce 4, Kenley 5, King 6, Kreidler 57, Smith 1. **OF:** Alvarado 3, Brinkman 3, Carpenter 4, De La Rosa 39, Greene 21, Jarecki 3, Liniak 52, Martinez 7, Packard 11, Quiggle 53, Tuck 35.

GCL TIGERS EAST   ROOKIE
GULF COAST LEAGUE

Batting	B-T	HT	WT	DOB	AVG	vLH	vRH	G	AB	R	H	2B	3B	HR	RBI	BB	HBP	SH	SF	SO	SB	CS	SLG	OBP
Alvarado, Darwin	L-R	6-1	170	11-10-98	.220	.250	.210	40	141	16	31	5	1	1	19	14	1	0	2	25	8	3	.291	.291
Cary, Elliott	L-L	6-3	175	10-1-95	.177	.211	.167	24	79	11	14	2	0	0	12	4	0	0	27	3	1	.203	.316
Chacon, Esney	R-R	6-1	160	3-17-00	.202	.182	.208	24	94	11	19	2	0	0	8	7	0	1	2	15	4	4	.223	.252
2-team total (14 Tigers West)					.185	.200	.181	38	151	20	28	5	0	0	13	17	0	1	3	26	8	4	.219	.263
Dunn, Cordell	R-R	6-0	190	6-25-99	.143	.143	.143	24	77	7	11	4	0	0	5	9	2	0	0	24	1	0	.195	.250
Figueroa, Gustavo	R-R	6-0	170	9-22-98	.333	.667	.167	4	9	0	3	0	0	0	1	0	0	1	0	.333	.400
2-team total (7 Tigers West)					.231	.375	.143	9	13	3	3	1	0	1	1	3	0	0	4	0	0	.539	.375
Gonzalez, Alvaro	R-R	6-0	165	9-16-00	.200	.294	.180	25	95	8	19	5	0	1	5	5	1	0	2	20	1	1	.284	.243
2-team total (15 Tigers West)					.219	.304	.202	40	137	19	30	8	0	1	14	18	4	0	4	28	5	2	.299	.319
Hurtado, Pedro	B-R	5-11	160	3-1-99	.000	.000	--	1	1	0	0	0	0	0	0	1	0	0	0	0	0	.000	.500
2-team total (16 Tigers West)					.212	.231	.205	17	52	3	11	0	0	1	7	4	0	1	14	1	0	.269	.263
Irigoyen, Carlos	R-R	6-2	165	3-21-01	.263	.226	.279	31	99	12	26	4	0	0	10	7	1	1	2	14	2	2	.303	.312
Laurencio, Luis	R-R	6-2	215	10-6-98	.162	.191	.149	21	68	3	11	0	0	0	6	4	1	0	0	25	3	1	.162	.219
MacLaren, Cole	R-S	5-10	190	6-10-97	.267	.375	.227	15	30	6	8	0	0	2	6	1	0	0	3	0	0	.267	.405
Martinez Jr., Pedro	R-R	6-2	185	8-30-00	.217	.258	.200	31	106	14	23	7	0	2	12	10	2	0	0	27	0	0	.340	.297
2-team total (3 Tigers West)					.455	.375	.375	4	11	4	5	1	0	0	2	3	0	0	1	0	0	.546	.625
Mojica, Jimmy	R-R	6-0	175	5-4-00	.271	.206	.293	39	140	19	38	7	1	0	14	9	3	0	3	26	3	3	.336	.323
Noworyta, David	R-R	6-4	180	5-24-96	.000	.000	.000	4	4	1	0	0	0	0	0	0	1	0	0	4	0	0	.000	.200
2-team total (10 Tigers West)					.074	.000	.095	14	27	2	2	0	0	0	1	3	1	0	1	4	0	0	.074	.188
Olivas, Martin	R-R	6-1	170	7-25-01	.182	.100	.211	24	77	7	14	3	0	1	8	8	2	0	0	15	0	1	.260	.276
Perez, Yerjeni	R-R	6-1	165	2-6-00	.231	.231	.231	13	39	9	9	3	0	0	4	1	0	0	14	0	0	.308	.318
2-team total (18 Tigers West)					.227	.231	.225	31	97	19	22	4	0	1	10	12	1	1	0	27	3	0	.299	.318
Perry, Connor	L-L	5-11	185	4-22-97	.236	.182	.250	37	110	25	26	4	1	2	15	30	2	1	1	36	18	2	.346	.406
Quero, Jose	L-L	6-0	190	9-5-98	.280	.273	.282	31	107	8	30	9	1	4	26	16	0	0	2	18	2	0	.495	.368
Rea, Yoandy	R-R	6-0	165	6-12-00	.400	.536	.343	29	95	21	38	9	0	5	25	7	3	0	1	10	1	0	.653	.453
Reyes, Daniel	R-R	6-1	200	9-7-96	.294	.500	.267	6	17	3	5	2	0	0	2	0	0	1	0	0	0	.412	.429
Smith, Kelvin	R-R	6-1	185	10-30-99	.083	.000	.125	4	12	3	1	0	0	0	1	1	1	0	0	5	0	0	.083	.214
2-team total (20 Tigers West)					.206	.357	.170	24	73	12	15	1	0	3	12	6	3	0	0	27	2	0	.343	.293
Valencia, Eduardo	R-R	6-2	180	1-25-00	.500	.500	.500	1	4	0	2	1	0	0	0	0	0	0	0	0	0	.750	.500
2-team total (31 GCL Tigers West)					.229	.360	.194	32	118	17	27	7	0	0	17	8	1	0	3	31	1	0	.288	.277
Valente, John	R-R	5-11	190	6-23-95	.333	.000	.500	1	3	1	1	0	0	0	0	1	0	0	1	0	0	.333	.500

Batting	B-T	HT	WT	DOB	AVG	vLH	vRH	G	AB	R	H	2B	3B	HR	RBI	BB	HBP	SH	SF	SO	SB	CS	SLG	OBP
2-team total (4 Tigers West)					.222	.000	.286	5	18	2	4	0	1	0	1	1	0	0	0	2	1	0	.333	.263
Veliz, Frank	R-R	5-11	160	9-10-99	.207	.136	.231	27	87	13	18	3	1	0	9	8	4	1	2	18	5	1	.264	.297

Pitching	B-T	HT	WT	DOB	W	L	ERA	G	GS	CG	SV	IP	H	R	ER	HR	BB	SO	AVG	vLH	vRH	K/9	BB/9
Beattie, Matt	B-R	6-4	185	1-5-99	1	2	7.80	10	1	0	0	15	20	21	13	2	15	14	.339	.571	.267	8.40	9.00
Brieske, Beau	R-R	6-3	200	4-5-98	3	1	3.12	10	0	0	2	17	11	7	6	1	9	28	.183	.182	.184	14.54	4.67
Burgos, Ronald	R-R	6-3	190	12-22-99	0	1	13.50	5	0	0	0	5	9	8	7	1	5	2	.429	.444	.417	3.86	9.64
2-team total (8 Tigers West)					0	1	10.80	13	0	0	0	15	28	21	18	3	7	11	.406	.320	.455	6.60	4.20
Chavez, Alejandro	R-R	6-2	170	7-14-99	0	4	8.80	11	7	0	0	31	44	35	30	4	26	23	.336	.381	.315	6.75	7.63
Conger, Maddux	R-R	6-2	235	6-28-96	0	0	0.00	1	1	0	0	1	0	0	0	0	0	0	.000	--	.000	0.00	0.00
2-team total (1 Tigers West)					0	0	0.00	2	1	0	0	3	1	0	0	0	0	0	.100	.333	.000	0.00	0.00
Cortes, Maximo	R-R	6-1	170	11-18-99	1	1	5.48	10	0	0	0	21	24	13	13	3	8	21	.279	.222	.305	8.86	3.38
Di Monte, Daniele	R-R	6-2	187	2-16-02	0	0	5.23	9	0	0	0	10	9	6	6	0	12	10	.231	.267	.208	8.71	10.45
Francisco, Roberto	R-R	6-3	190	3-1-99	0	0	4.91	5	0	0	0	7	7	5	4	0	4	8	.250	.364	.177	9.82	4.91
2-team total (7 Tigers West)					1	1	3.71	12	0	0	1	17	15	12	7	0	6	17	.231	.292	.195	9.00	3.18
Ingram, Kolton	L-L	5-9	170	10-21-96	1	1	4.15	15	1	0	1	30	29	14	14	1	11	28	.252	.179	.276	8.31	3.26
Klinchock, Robert	R-L	6-4	230	10-1-96	2	3	4.79	9	4	0	0	36	37	20	19	1	11	32	.262	.296	.254	8.07	2.78
Moreno, Gerson	R-R	6-0	175	9-10-95	0	2	8.10	7	6	0	0	7	8	6	6	0	5	7	.296	.222	.333	9.45	6.75
Moreno, Williander	R-R	6-0	160	3-13-99	0	3	5.40	7	0	0	1	8	6	7	5	2	8	5	.200	.250	.167	5.40	8.64
Paulino, Miguel	R-R	6-1	185	8-21-98	0	2	6.64	11	0	0	1	20	24	16	15	2	13	18	.296	.345	.269	7.97	5.75
Perez, Cleiverth	L-L	5-11	167	2-5-00	1	3	3.54	10	9	0	0	41	44	19	16	2	9	26	.268	.303	.260	5.75	1.99
Pina, Jose	R-R	6-3	170	5-24-01	2	1	6.66	10	7	0	0	26	29	24	19	0	21	9	.282	.222	.313	3.16	7.36
Pinales, Erick	R-R	6-2	185	1-27-99	0	0	0.00	1	1	0	0	5	0	0	0	0	7	4	.000	.000	.000	7.71	13.50
Salazar, Joseph	R-R	6-1	175	9-24-99	2	3	2.25	9	8	0	0	40	39	18	10	1	12	29	.253	.349	.216	6.53	2.70
Santana, Andy	R-R	6-3	190	10-27-99	3	0	4.81	12	0	0	1	24	26	13	13	2	15	17	.283	.267	.290	6.29	5.55
Sommerfeld, Luke	R-R	6-6	235	7-8-96	0	0	3.86	2	0	0	0	2	3	2	1	0	1	3	.300	.250	.333	11.57	3.86
Tassin, Bryce	R-R	6-2	212	1-11-97	1	1	1.32	6	0	0	0	14	10	4	2	1	4	10	.200	.316	.129	6.59	2.63
Terrero, Richard	L-L	6-6	220	9-9-97	1	1	3.00	6	0	0	0	12	4	4	4	0	9	15	.100	.000	.121	11.25	6.75
White, Brendan	R-R	5-11	185	11-18-98	1	1	2.59	12	3	0	1	24	27	12	7	1	10	21	.267	.355	.229	7.77	3.70
2-team total (2 Tigers West)					1	2	3.77	14	5	0	1	31	37	18	13	1	11	29	.287	.386	.235	8.42	3.19

Fielding

C: Dunn 15, Figueroa 4, Girand 2, Hurtado 1, MacLaren 15, Noworyta 4, Rea 21, Valencia 1. 1B: Laurencio 20, Quero 30. 2B: Gonzalez 16, Irigoyen 4, Olivas 7, Veliz 21. 3B: Irigoyen 5, Martinez Jr. 25, Olivas 15, Smith 3, Valente 1, Veliz 1. SS: Gonzalez 9, Irigoyen 21, Perez 13, Smith 1, Veliz 5. OF: Alvarado 28, Cary 22, Chacon 23, Mojica 38, Perry 33, Quero 2, Reyes 3.

GCL TIGERS WEST   ROOKIE
GULF COAST LEAGUE

Batting	B-T	HT	WT	DOB	AVG	vLH	vRH	G	AB	R	H	2B	3B	HR	RBI	BB	HBP	SH	SF	SO	SB	CS	SLG	OBP
Brinkman, Clark	R-R	6-2	195	3-6-96	.262	.300	.244	18	65	17	17	5	1	1	8	10	1	0	4	14	5	1	.415	.350
Burks, Jeremiah	R-R	6-2	215	1-8-97	.256	.300	.241	35	117	22	30	4	1	3	19	22	6	0	2	40	3	1	.385	.395
Carpenter, Kerry	L-R	6-2	220	9-2-97	.319	.216	.350	43	160	33	51	16	3	9	34	22	5	0	4	18	6	0	.625	.408
Chacon, Esney	R-R	6-1	160	3-17-00	.158	.231	.136	14	57	9	9	3	0	0	5	10	0	0	1	11	4	0	.211	.279
2-team total (24 Tigers East)					.185	.200	.181	38	151	20	28	5	0	0	13	17	0	1	3	26	8	4	.219	.263
Dey, Griffin	R-R	6-2	220	7-19-96	.250	.000	.286	2	8	0	2	0	0	0	0	1	0	0	3	0	0		.250	.333
Escalona, Ildemaro	R-R	6-0	170	2-12-99	.244	.308	.214	14	41	6	10	3	0	0	7	12	0	0	1	12	2	0	.317	.407
Esposito, Vinny	R-R	5-11	200	3-10-96	.182	.250	.143	7	22	6	4	0	1	1	2	4	2	0	0	7	1	0	.409	.357
Girand, Jonah	R-R	6-1	175	5-3-95	.300	.000	.500	7	10	1	3	1	0	1	3	3	0	0	0	6	0	0	.700	.462
2-team total (2 Tigers East)					.231	.000	.375	9	13	1	3	1	0	1	3	3	0	0	0	4	0	0	.539	.375
Gonzalez, Alvaro	R-R	6-0	165	9-16-00	.262	.304	.250	15	42	11	11	3	0	0	9	13	3	0	2	8	4	1	.333	.450
2-team total (25 Tigers East)					.219	.304	.202	40	137	19	30	8	0	1	14	18	4	0	4	28	5	2	.299	.319
Greene, Riley	L-L	6-3	200	9-28-00	.351	.333	.355	9	37	9	13	3	0	2	8	5	1	0	0	12	0	0	.595	.442
Hurtado, Pedro	B-R	5-11	160	3-1-99	.216	.250	.205	16	51	3	11	0	0	1	7	3	0	0	1	14	1	0	.275	.255
2-team total (1 Tigers East)					.212	.231	.205	17	52	3	11	0	0	1	7	4	0	0	1	14	1	0	.269	.263
Jarecki, Matthew	R-R	6-2	205	5-12-96	.292	.184	.328	43	154	29	45	15	2	4	31	22	7	0	5	29	3	2	.494	.394
Kenley, Jack	L-R	6-0	185	10-8-97	.438	--	.438	4	16	5	7	0	0	1	2	4	0	0	0	3	1	0	.625	.550
Kerr, Jimmy	L-R	6-2	205	3-21-97	.278	.304	.269	25	90	16	25	5	0	6	19	13	0	0	0	20	0	0	.556	.369
Mang, Jared	R-R	5-9	200	10-30-96	.212	.235	.205	43	151	20	32	9	3	1	22	15	3	0	2	29	0	1	.331	.292
McMillan, Sam	R-R	6-0	200	12-1-98	.375	.667	.200	3	8	4	3	1	0	0	2	2	0	0	1	0	0	0	.500	.583
2-team total (1 Tigers East)					.455	.667	.375	4	11	4	5	1	0	0	2	3	0	0	1	0	0	0	.546	.625
Navigato, Andrew	R-R	5-11	188	5-28-98	.133	.200	.125	15	45	7	6	2	0	0	1	5	4	0	0	12	0	1	.178	.278
Noworyta, David	R-R	6-4	180	5-24-96	.087	.000	.111	10	23	1	2	0	0	0	1	3	0	0	1	3	0	0	.087	.185
2-team total (4 Tigers East)					.074	.000	.095	14	27	2	2	0	0	0	1	3	1	0	1	4	0	0	.074	.188
Parks, Pavin	L-R	6-2	205	12-24-96	.000	.000	.000	7	19	2	0	0	0	0	0	6	0	0	0	7	0	0	.000	.240
Pearce, Jordan	L-R	6-2	205	6-14-96	.217	.357	.174	23	60	13	13	1	0	1	7	18	5	0	0	11	2	0	.283	.434
Perez, Yerjeni	R-R	6-1	165	2-6-00	.224	.231	.222	18	58	10	13	1	0	1	8	8	0	0	0	13	3	0	.293	.318
2-team total (13 Tigers East)					.227	.231	.225	31	97	19	22	4	0	1	10	12	1	1	0	27	3	0	.299	.318
Smith, Kelvin	R-R	6-1	185	10-30-99	.230	.500	.177	20	61	9	14	1	0	3	11	5	2	0	0	22	2	0	.393	.309
2-team total (4 GCL Tigers East)					.206	.357	.170	24	73	12	15	1	0	3	12	6	3	0	0	27	2	0	.343	.293
Valencia, Eduardo	R-R	6-2	180	1-25-00	.219	.348	.187	31	114	17	25	6	0	0	17	8	1	0	3	13	1	0	.272	.270
2-team total (1 Tigers East)					.229	.360	.194	32	118	17	27	7	0	0	17	8	1	0	3	13	1	0	.288	.277
Valente, John	R-R	5-11	190	6-23-95	.200	.000	.250	4	15	1	3	0	1	0	1	0	0	0	0	1	0	0	.333	.200
2-team total (1 Tigers East)					.222	.000	.286	5	18	2	4	0	1	0	1	1	0	0	0	2	1	0	.333	.263
Zabowski, Cole	L-L	6-5	240	11-5-97	.255	.256	.254	45	157	26	40	10	0	2	20	19	7	0	4	28	1	0	.357	.353

Pitching	B-T	HT	WT	DOB	W	L	ERA	G	GS	CG	SV	IP	H	R	ER	HR	BB	SO	AVG	vLH	vRH	K/9	BB/9

Pitching	B-T	HT	WT	DOB	W	L	ERA	G	GS	CG	SV	IP	H	R	ER	HR	BB	SO	AVG	vLH	vRH	K/9	BB/9
Appleton, Jose	R-R	6-3	170	7-2-97	6	2	2.66	11	7	0	0	44	33	17	13	1	25	34	.214	.170	.234	6.95	5.11
Bergner, Austin	R-R	6-4	200	5-1-97	0	1	6.35	4	0	0	0	6	3	5	4	1	2	7	.143	.143	.143	11.12	3.18
Bienlien, Michael	R-R	6-3	222	3-19-98	1	0	4.50	4	0	0	0	8	7	4	4	0	3	9	.219	.200	.227	10.13	3.38
Breto, Liarvis	L-L	5-11	175	4-10-93	0	0	0.00	10	0	0	4	9	8	0	0	0	1	11	.235	.000	.276	11.42	1.04
Burgos, Ronald	R-R	6-3	190	12-22-99	0	0	9.58	8	0	0	0	10	19	13	11	2	2	9	.396	.250	.469	7.84	1.74
2-team total (5 Tigers East)					0	1	10.80	13	0	0	0	15	28	21	18	3	7	11	.406	.320	.455	6.60	4.20
Coburn, Josh	L-L	6-5	195	6-3-98	1	0	3.54	16	0	0	0	20	21	12	8	1	9	12	.280	.177	.310	5.31	3.98
Conger, Maddux	R-R	6-2	235	6-28-96	0	0	0.00	1	0	0	0	2	1	0	0	0	0	0	.143	.333	.000	0.00	0.00
2-team total (1 Tigers East)					0	0	0.00	2	1	0	0	3	1	0	0	0	0	0	.100	.333	.000	0.00	0.00
De La Cruz, Isrrael	B-R	6-0	150	6-15-97	0	0	3.29	12	0	0	2	14	5	5	5	1	5	14	.109	.063	.133	9.22	3.29
Dellinger, Jack	R-R	6-6	225	2-12-98	3	1	1.07	10	4	0	0	34	25	5	4	1	4	28	.214	.250	.192	7.49	1.07
Domnarski, Doug	R-L	5-11	190	7-8-94	1	0	0.95	16	0	0	1	19	16	5	2	1	4	16	.232	.167	.246	7.58	1.89
Fajardo, Rodolfo	L-L	6-3	165	2-17-00	1	1	2.01	9	8	0	0	22	18	5	5	3	4	17	.217	.188	.224	6.85	1.61
Fenelon, Wilmer	R-R	6-3	170	10-18-00	0	0	6.75	1	0	0	0	3	2	2	2	0	3	3	.200	.250	.167	10.13	10.13
Francisco, Roberto	R-R	6-3	190	3-1-99	1	1	2.79	7	0	0	1	10	8	7	3	0	2	9	.216	.231	.208	8.38	1.86
2-team total (5 Tigers East)					1	1	3.71	12	0	0	1	17	15	12	7	0	6	17	.231	.292	.195	9.00	3.18
Gardea, Dario	R-R	6-2	210	1-29-99	2	3	3.82	8	6	0	0	31	30	17	13	1	8	35	.246	.216	.259	10.27	2.35
Hess, Zack	R-R	6-6	219	2-25-97	1	0	18.00	1	0	0	0	1	1	2	2	0	2	1	.333	1.000	.000	9.00	18.00
Jimenez, Francisco	R-R	6-2	194	3-23-99	1	0	4.50	16	0	0	1	22	14	12	11	2	19	20	.184	.233	.152	8.18	7.77
Kessler, Sam	R-R	6-1	192	12-16-97	1	3	3.48	17	0	0	0	21	16	13	8	1	10	20	.205	.235	.197	8.71	4.35
Ledesma, Stevie	R-R	6-5	195	11-22-95	0	0	0.00	1	0	0	0	1	0	0	0	0	0	1	.000	.000	.000	9.00	0.00
Montero, Keider	R-R	6-1	145	7-6-00	2	1	1.57	5	5	0	0	23	22	8	4	0	11	23	.250	.391	.200	9.00	4.03
Parks, Pavin	R-R	6-1	205	12-24-96	0	0	0.00	4	0	0	0	5	6	1	0	0	1	5	.273	.125	.357	9.00	1.80
Quinones, Emmanuel	R-R	6-1	185	4-15-99	4	3	3.47	11	11	0	0	47	47	24	18	2	10	34	.260	.221	.283	6.56	1.93
Reuss, Grant	R-L	6-5	230	5-23-96	1	0	4.15	5	0	0	0	4	2	4	2	0	8	3	.143	.000	.167	6.23	16.62
Richmond, Nick	R-R	6-4	195	4-2-98	0	0	2.70	5	0	0	1	7	8	3	2	1	1	8	.286	.200	.333	10.80	1.35
Silva, Ricardo	L-L	6-1	165	4-14-00	3	2	4.50	13	3	0	0	32	38	19	16	3	4	25	.290	.308	.286	7.03	1.13
Stuka, Ted	R-R	6-7	225	5-13-97	0	1	7.94	4	4	0	0	6	4	5	5	0	3	6	.191	.125	.231	9.53	4.76
Vancena, Jayce	R-R	6-5	225	4-25-96	1	0	1.53	11	0	0	0	18	19	5	3	0	1	16	.275	.375	.222	8.15	0.51
White, Brendan	R-R	5-11	185	11-18-98	0	1	8.10	2	2	0	0	7	10	6	6	0	1	8	.357	.462	.267	10.80	1.35
2-team total (12 Tigers East)					1	2	3.77	14	5	0	1	31	37	18	13	1	11	29	.287	.386	.235	8.42	3.19

Fielding

C: Girand 7, Hurtado 16, McMillan 1, Noworyta 10, Valencia 25. **1B:** Dey 1, Kerr 7, Myers 0, Pearce 6, Zabowski 37. **2B:** Burks 30, Escalona 5, Gonzalez 6, Kenley 3, Navigato 3, Parks 1, Perez 2, Smith 1, Valente 1. **3B:** Burks 5, Gonzalez 4, Kerr 16, Myers 2, Navigato 3, Parks 2, Pearce 12, Smith 10, Valente 1. **SS:** Escalona 9, Gonzalez 7, Kenley 1, Navigato 9, Parks 4, Perez 16, Smith 6. **OF:** Brinkman 17, Carpenter 36, Chacon 12, Esposito 5, Greene 9, Jarecki 34, Mang 37.

DSL TIGERS   ROOKIE
DOMINICAN SUMMER LEAGUE

Batting	B-T	HT	WT	DOB	AVG	vLH	vRH	G	AB	R	H	2B	3B	HR	RBI	BB	HBP	SH	SF	SO	SB	CS	SLG	OBP
Acevedo, Yoneiry	B-R	5-10	150	12-4-00	.255	.135	.292	44	157	28	40	3	3	0	18	21	1	1	2	28	4	8	.312	.343
Adames, Ernesto	L-L	6-1	180	12-29-99	.177	.077	.193	34	96	8	17	2	1	0	5	11	1	1		41	1	1	.219	.266
Batista, Enrique	R-R	5-9	170	2-10-00	.284	.400	.272	38	102	16	29	2	2	0	9	11	1	3	1	34	3	2	.343	.357
Benitez, Lazaro	R-R	6-0	190	10-15-99	.312	.238	.328	61	231	44	72	16	4	5	35	18	1	0	3	32	5	4	.481	.360
Bolivar, Jesus	R-R	6-1	165	3-23-02	.299	.375	.280	35	117	21	35	4	0	0	18	6	5	0	2		6	3	.333	.354
Bravo, Yoan	R-R	6-1	165	10-14-01	.216	.235	.211	57	176	32	38	4	0	2	19	44	5	0	4	65	10	8	.273	.380
Calderon, Cesar	R-R	6-2	170	11-1-01	.271	.359	.253	61	229	45	62	15	5	7	41	25	3	0	4	53	12	5	.472	.345
Calzadilla, Cristian	R-R	5-10	160	10-17-01	.315	.414	.292	47	149	26	47	6	1	0	15	23	9	1	3	16	5	4	.369	.429
Castillo, Rafael	R-R	5-10	155	4-18-02	.157	.154	.157	27	83	11	13	1	0	0	5	9	3	2	0	32	1	2	.169	.263
Cruz, Angel	R-R	5-11	165	9-27-01	.258	.222	.267	57	225	44	58	14	2	1	22	22	4	1	2	42	8	5	.351	.332
De La Cruz, Danuerys	R-R	5-11	160	4-27-01	.283	.333	.270	34	113	22	32	7	0	3	19	14	3	0	3	37	3	3	.425	.368
De La Cruz, Jose	R-R	6-1	195	1-3-02	.307	.359	.296	56	225	55	69	13	5	11	39	18	8	0	2	75	16	8	.556	.376
Estevez, Geury	B-R	6-0	180	2-20-02	.262	.212	.270	66	237	22	62	6	4	0	28	27	6	1	4	29	10	4	.321	.347
Figuereo, Adonis	L-L	6-2	170	5-5-01	.276	.222	.285	53	185	15	51	7	1	3	22	30	2	1	1	36	4	6	.353	.381
Garcia, Pedro	R-R	6-1	170	5-22-01	.234	.346	.215	51	184	27	43	5	3	1	26	17	0	2	1	46	8	1	.310	.297
Jimenez, Jeremy	R-R	6-2	180	3-3-01	.234	.455	.197	22	77	11	18	2	2	0	10	14	0	0	0	19	1	0	.312	.352
Leonardo, Iverson	L-L	6-0	170	8-21-01	.333	.333	.333	58	198	39	66	15	11	3	39	30	5	0	5	44	10	14	.566	.424
Lopez, Edixon	R-R	5-9	165	10-27-00	.149	.211	.137	45	114	20	17	4	0	0	4	17	4	1	0	49	2	2	.184	.282
Marte, Kendry	B-R	6-0	160	5-10-00	.211	.063	.237	39	109	19	23	5	4	0	6	18	0	2	0	36	8	2	.330	.323
Medrano, Carlos	L-R	5-11	170	11-11-99	.234	.235	.233	37	107	25	25	4	0	1	11	25	0	0	3	37	7	1	.299	.370
Mendoza, Carlos	L-R	5-9	165	12-14-99	.296	.333	.291	68	240	55	71	6	7	0	21	46	10	3	1	28	25	14	.379	.428
Montes, Sergio	R-R	5-11	165	12-19-00	.179	.278	.160	34	112	9	20	2	0	1	12	7	1	1	1	39	2	3	.223	.231
Moreno, Jhenrry	L-R	5-11	160	3-28-00	.241	.188	.250	36	108	16	26	6	0	0	12	8	7	1	0	35	7	3	.296	.333
Nivar, Kevin	R-R	5-10	170	9-28-00	.215	.368	.192	46	144	20	31	3	0	0	9	28	5	2	3	17	3	5	.236	.356
Nunez, Alberoni	R-R	6-1	180	2-17-99	.321	.385	.308	22	78	13	25	4	2	4	13	10	1	1	0	16	2	2	.577	.405
Reina, Jose	R-R	6-2	160	2-28-01	.273	.000	.300	11	44	7	12	3	0	0	5	5	2	1	0	6	3	2	.341	.373
Reyes, Adinso	R-R	6-1	195	10-22-01	.331	.290	.338	62	242	44	80	20	1	7	48	14	8	0	5	51	3	6	.508	.379
Rodriguez, Jose	R-R	6-1	190	9-17-01	.243	.077	.266	63	210	21	51	8	4	0	19	14	6	3	1	49	4	11	.319	.307
Sandoval, Jhon	R-R	6-2	172	11-14-99	.193	.267	.176	51	161	20	31	7	3	3	23	28	5	0	1	77	4	4	.329	.328
Soriano, Joswel	B-R	6-0	175	9-29-00	.073	.000	.094	12	41	4	3	0	1	0	2	6	0	0	0	14	1	1	.122	.192
Tapia, Sergio	R-R	5-10	160	8-24-02	.253	.286	.247	34	99	16	25	7	0	0	13	8	3	2	2	21	2	5	.323	.321
Ulloa, Alexis	R-R	5-10	150	12-18-01	.191	.267	.179	37	110	14	21	1	0	0	13	16	1	2	1	27	5	2	.200	.297

Pitching	B-T	HT	WT	DOB	W	L	ERA	G	GS	CG	SV	IP	H	R	ER	HR	BB	SO	AVG	vLH	vRH	K/9	BB/9
Bauza, Adolfo	R-R	6-2	160	9-27-00	0	7	4.66	14	14	0	0	46	53	32	24	2	32	49	.290	.351	.262	9.52	6.22
Calderon, Fernando	R-R	6-0	170	10-22-96	2	2	6.57	19	1	0	1	37	47	35	27	2	16	30	.301	.404	.257	7.30	3.89
Cordero, Juan	R-R	6-0	165	7-24-02	3	2	4.93	18	0	0	3	38	41	26	21	1	14	25	.283	.400	.230	5.87	3.29
Cruz, Jesus	R-R	6-4	185	10-8-00	0	1	5.60	6	6	0	0	18	13	14	11	0	9	16	.197	.222	.188	8.15	4.58
Dacosta, Francarlos	R-R	6-1	175	2-27-00	3	1	3.41	7	5	0	0	29	30	19	11	3	7	16	.254	.189	.284	4.97	2.17
De Leon, Luis	R-R	6-0	170	5-22-00	2	1	3.33	10	2	0	1	24	27	12	9	3	5	15	.281	.212	.318	5.55	1.85
Diaz, Jose	R-R	6-5	200	5-12-00	1	2	3.94	21	0	0	5	32	32	20	14	2	14	38	.254	.342	.216	10.69	3.94
Fenelon, Wilmer	R-R	6-3	170	10-18-00	1	6	4.44	13	13	0	0	51	49	36	25	0	34	58	.251	.269	.245	10.30	6.04
Flesten, Alexis	L-L	6-1	160	4-4-00	1	0	4.05	14	0	0	0	20	14	12	9	0	19	24	.194	.100	.210	10.80	8.55
Guerrero, Yonson	R-R	6-1	175	5-12-00	2	5	6.66	17	7	0	0	51	73	54	38	2	24	38	.319	.333	.312	6.66	4.21
Herrera, Juan	R-R	6-3	170	9-24-01	1	3	5.28	11	3	0	0	29	30	22	17	3	19	27	.270	.346	.247	8.38	5.90
Herrera, Martin	L-R	6-0	175	9-22-00	4	2	2.61	13	13	0	0	59	60	27	17	0	8	48	.259	.250	.263	7.36	1.23
Lopez, Johan	R-R	6-4	190	4-5-99	3	2	5.18	17	0	0	3	40	41	31	23	1	23	39	.275	.214	.299	8.78	5.18
Lopez, Luis	R-R	5-11	170	12-1-00	0	0	9.00	2	0	0	0	2	5	2	2	0	1	2	.500	.500	.500	9.00	4.50
Marin, Jaime	R-R	5-11	165	12-25-00	1	1	4.50	16	0	0	1	28	26	16	14	2	9	25	.255	.302	.220	8.04	2.89
Marin, Lisandro	R-R	6-2	165	9-15-99	1	6	6.26	14	12	0	0	42	52	41	29	4	16	38	.297	.471	.226	8.21	3.46
Marte, Kendry	B-R	6-0	160	5-10-00	0	0	0.00	2	0	0	0	2	1	0	0	0	1	2	.143	.000	.167	9.00	4.50
Medina, Victor	R-R	5-10	170	2-9-00	0	3	6.05	13	0	0	0	19	22	17	13	0	11	17	.293	.348	.269	7.91	5.12
Montes, Sergio	R-R	5-11	165	12-19-00	0	0	0.00	1	0	0	0	2	0	0	0	0	1	1	.000	.000	.000	3.86	3.86
Nunez, Hendry	R-R	6-4	180	7-22-99	4	4	4.48	16	7	0	1	60	60	38	30	4	23	68	.260	.291	.250	10.14	3.43
Ozuna, Angel	R-R	5-10	170	9-25-98	3	0	5.80	17	0	0	3	36	34	29	23	3	21	31	.250	.250	.250	7.82	5.30
Pena, Carlos	L-L	5-11	160	9-7-98	5	0	2.74	15	4	0	0	49	36	17	15	2	17	71	.197	.095	.210	12.95	3.10
Peraza, Jose	R-R	5-11	160	10-29-01	1	5	4.35	13	6	0	0	31	33	23	15	1	25	23	.277	.235	.294	6.68	7.26
Perez, Luis	L-L	6-1	165	10-10-99	0	1	4.61	9	0	0	0	14	14	10	7	0	5	12	.264	.250	.267	7.90	3.29
Pimentel, Yoldi	R-R	5-11	190	9-15-00	1	1	4.50	15	8	0	2	46	41	28	23	4	17	49	.234	.225	.238	9.59	3.33
Pinales, Erick	R-R	6-2	185	1-27-99	0	4	6.21	16	7	0	0	38	44	33	26	1	27	26	.314	.378	.291	6.21	6.45
Polanco, Juan	R-R	6-1	205	12-30-00	5	2	6.08	19	2	0	1	37	41	30	25	3	23	24	.279	.351	.255	5.84	5.59
Raciel, Alfredo	R-R	6-2	165	6-2-00	1	6	7.36	14	14	0	0	37	54	43	30	4	23	33	.344	.383	.320	8.10	5.65
Ramirez, Jose	R-R	6-1	170	8-18-97	0	2	16.88	6	0	0	0	5	7	11	10	0	9	5	.350	.500	.286	8.44	15.19
Reyes, Marcos	R-R	6-0	170	4-4-98	3	3	6.23	18	0	0	1	52	63	48	36	3	22	35	.288	.274	.293	6.06	3.81
Rivas, Jose	R-R	5-11	160	12-20-01	1	1	5.40	8	0	0	0	13	9	8	8	1	7	15	.184	.182	.184	10.13	4.73
Rudecindo, Maximiguel	R-R	6-3	185	3-21-99	4	1	2.70	17	0	0	3	50	47	26	15	1	11	37	.240	.233	.242	6.66	1.98
Sirit, Rolando	R-R	6-3	165	11-12-01	0	2	14.29	5	5	0	0	6	9	10	9	0	8	3	.360	.500	.316	4.76	12.71
Tejeda, Briant	R-R	6-2	185	2-19-00	1	0	3.24	18	0	0	2	25	18	14	9	0	26	31	.196	.080	.239	11.16	9.36
Torres, Oswal	R-R	6-3	185	5-5-00	2	0	5.93	18	0	0	1	30	38	28	20	0	23	26	.297	.234	.333	7.71	6.82
Valdez, Albert	L-L	6-2	165	7-5-99	0	1	7.89	16	0	0	0	22	24	28	19	1	23	17	.282	.455	.257	7.06	9.55
Vazquez, Juan	L-L	6-2	165	7-2-99	3	3	4.97	22	2	0	3	51	62	39	28	1	19	44	.298	.281	.301	7.82	3.38
Yeguez, Enrique	R-R	6-0	165	12-4-00	2	1	12.06	17	0	0	2	31	51	49	42	6	30	26	.364	.310	.388	7.47	8.62
Zambrano, Darwyn	R-R	6-2	175	7-27-00	1	2	3.93	12	8	0	0	34	27	19	15	3	17	51	.218	.219	.217	13.37	4.46

Fielding

C: Calzadilla 27, De La Cruz 34, Garcia 35, Jimenez 21, Medrano 7, Tapia 13. **1B:** Adames 12, Calderon 1, Calzadilla 20, Castillo 11, Garcia 17, Jimenez 3, Marte 24, Medrano 20, Montes 22, Moreno 15, Nunez 9, Soriano 1, Ulloa 8. **2B:** Acevedo 9, Bravo 1, Castillo 7, Cruz 53, Estevez 11, Lopez 9, Marte 2, Mendoza 4, Montes 2, Nivar 44, Soriano 2, Ulloa 6. **3B:** Bravo 13, Calderon 7, Castillo 5, Estevez 47, Lopez 20, Marte 13, Mendoza 1, Montes 9, Nunez 1, Soriano 1, Ulloa 4. **SS:** Acevedo 35, Bravo 14, Calderon 6, Cruz 1, Estevez 2, Lopez 1, Montes 1, Nivar 1, Reyes 39, Soriano 1, Ulloa 10. **OF:** Adames 11, Batista 33, Benitez 55, Bolivar 33, De La Cruz 20, Estevez 1, Figuereo 42, Leonardo 50, Lopez 14, Medrano 1, Mendoza 61, Moreno 24, Nunez 12, Reina 11, Rodriguez 63, Sandoval 41, Tapia 1.

Houston Astros

SEASON IN A SENTENCE: The Astros have built a consistent power, but they need another World Series title to be a dynasty.

HIGH POINT: Justin Verlander struck out 14 as he no-hit the Blue Jays on Sept. 1. It was the Astros' second no-hitter of the year (four Astros pitchers had combined for a no-hitter on Aug. 3). It was also Verlander's third no-hitter and the Astros 13th no-hitter as a franchise.

LOW POINT: Worse than the Astros' World Series Game 7 loss was the leadup to the World Series. Sports Illustrated reported that assistant general manager Brandon Taubman had aimed an outburst at a trio of female reporters during the club's celebration after winning the ALCS. The Astros initially claimed the reporter had fabricated the story. The Astros' version of the story proved to be completely inaccurate. Taubman was fired during the World Series and the Astros eventually retracted their statement, but not until after their actions had brought a loss of respect to the organization.

NOTABLE ROOKIES: Outfielder/DH Yordan Alvarez didn't debut until June 9, but from then to the end of the season he was one of the most productive hitters in baseball. He hit .313/.416/.655 to actually post the highest OPS among all Astros hitters. Righthander Jose Urquidy didn't make his debut until July, but he pitched well enough (3-1, 3.95) to earn a playoff roster spot and picked up a win as the Astros Game 4 World Series starter.

KEY TRANSACTIONS: Two years after acquiring righthander Justin Verlander at the Aug. 31 trade deadline and one year after adding righthander Gerrit Cole in another trade, the Astros traded away righthanders J.B. Bukauskas and Corbin Martin, first baseman Seth Beer and infielder Josh Rojas to acquire righthander Zack Greinke. Greinke added another frontline arm to a thin rotation. Greinke pitched well as the World Series Game 7 starter.

DOWN ON THE FARM: Houston has graduated Alvarez, Urquidy and outfielder Kyle Tucker and has traded away a significant amount of prospect depth to bolster the big league club. The system is thinner than it has been in any time since the rebuild hit full speed in 2012, but righthander Forrest Whitley does give the team a potential frontline starter and the team has a significant number of hard-throwing pitchers in the lower levels of the minors.

OPENING DAY PAYROLL: $177,443,329 (5th).

PLAYERS OF THE YEAR

MAJOR LEAGUE	MINOR LEAGUE
Justin Verlander **RHP**	**Kyle Tucker** **OF**
21-6, 2.58 in 34 GS	(Triple-A)
Led majors in W,	.266/.354/.555
IP (223), WHIP (0.80)	34 HR, 30 SB

ORGANIZATION LEADERS

Batting		*Minimum 250 AB
MAJORS		
* AVG	Yordan Alvarez	.313
* OPS	Yordan Alvarez	1.067
HR	Alex Bregman	41
RBI	Alex Bregman	112
MINORS		
* AVG	Abraham Toro, Corpus Christi, Round Rock	.324
* OBP	Abraham Toro, Corpus Christi, Round Rock	.411
* SLG	Josh Rojas, Corpus Christi, Round Rock	.575
* OPS	Josh Rojas, Corpus Christi, Round Rock	.978
R	Kyle Tucker, Round Rock	92
H	Abraham Toro, Corpus Christi, Round Rock	143
TB	Kyle Tucker, Round Rock	257
2B	Nick Tanielu, Round Rock	39
3B	Stephen Wrenn, Corpus Christi, Round Rock	9
HR	Kyle Tucker, Round Rock	34
RBI	Kyle Tucker, Round Rock	97
BB	Drew Ferguson, Round Rock	68
BB	Taylor Jones, Round Rock	68
SO	Ronnie Dawson, Corpus Christi, Round Rock	152
SB	Josh Rojas, Corpus Christi, Round Rock	32

Pitching		#Minimum 75 IP
MAJORS		
W	Justin Verlander	21
# ERA	Gerrit Cole	2.50
SO	Gerrit Cole	326
SV	Roberto Osuna	38
MINORS		
W	Jolanse Torres, Quad Cities, Fayetteville	12
L	Chad Donato, Fayetteville, Corpus Christi	12
# ERA	Jolanse Torres, Quad Cities, Fayetteville	1.71
G	Carlos Sanabria, Fayetteville, Corpus Christi	43
GS	J.P. France, Fayetteville	20
GS	Brandon Bielak, Corpus Christi, Round Rock	20
GS	Carson LaRue, Corpus Christi, Round Rock	20
SV	Riley Cabral, Quad Cities, Fayetteville	9
IP	Chad Donato, Fayetteville, Corpus Christi	122
BB	Yohan Ramirez, Fayetteville, Corpus Christi	74
SO	Cristian Javier, Fayetteville, Corpus Christi, Round Rock	170
# AVG	Cristian Javier, Fayetteville, Corpus Christi, Round Rock	.130

2019 PERFORMANCE

General Manager: Jeff Luhnow. **Farm Director:** Pete Putila.

Class	Team	League	W	L	PCT	Finish	Manager
Majors	Houston Astros	American	107	55	.660	1st (15)	A.J. Hinch
Triple-A	Fresno Grizzlies	Pacific Coast	84	56	.600	1st (16)	Mickey Storey
Double-A	Corpus Christi Hooks	Texas	66	73	.475	6th (8)	Omar Lopez
High A	Fayetteville Woodpeckers	Carolina	72	67	.518	4th (10)	Nate Shaver
Low A	Quad Cities River Bandits	Midwest	79	57	.581	4th (16)	Ray Hernandez
Short season	Tri-City Valleycats	New York-Penn	32	42	.432	12th (14)	Ozney Guillen
Rookie	GCL Astros	Gulf Coast	25	26	.490	10th (18)	Wladimir Sutil
Overall 2019 Minor League Record			358	321	.527	7th (30)	

ORGANIZATION STATISTICS

HOUSTON ASTROS
AMERICAN LEAGUE

Batting	B-T	HT	WT	DOB	AVG	vLH	vRH	G	AB	R	H	2B	3B	HR	RBI	BB	HBP	SH	SF	SO	SB	CS	SLG	OBP
Altuve, Jose	R-R	5-6	165	5-6-90	.298	.331	.287	124	500	89	149	27	3	31	74	41	3	1	3	82	6	5	.550	.353
Alvarez, Yordan	L-R	6-5	225	6-27-97	.313	.307	.317	87	313	58	98	26	0	27	78	52	1	0	2	94	0	0	.655	.412
Brantley, Michael	L-L	6-2	200	5-15-87	.311	.282	.323	148	575	88	179	40	2	22	90	51	7	0	4	66	3	2	.503	.372
Bregman, Alex	R-R	6-0	180	3-30-94	.296	.350	.274	156	554	122	164	37	2	41	112	119	9	0	8	83	5	1	.592	.423
Chirinos, Robinson	R-R	6-1	210	6-5-84	.238	.274	.227	114	366	57	87	22	1	17	58	51	13	2	5	125	1	2	.443	.347
Correa, Carlos	R-R	6-4	215	9-22-94	.279	.308	.270	75	280	42	78	16	1	21	59	35	2	0	4	75	1	0	.568	.358
Diaz, Aledmys	R-R	6-1	195	8-1-90	.271	.215	.297	69	210	36	57	12	1	9	40	26	5	0	6	28	2	0	.467	.356
Fisher, Derek	L-R	6-3	205	8-21-93	.226	.353	.167	17	53	9	12	2	1	1	5	7	0	0	0	14	4	1	.359	.317
2-team total (40 Toronto)					.185	.245	.155	57	146	23	27	4	1	7	17	21	0	0	0	57	5	1	.370	.287
Gurriel, Yuli	R-R	6-0	190	6-9-84	.298	.241	.320	144	564	85	168	40	2	31	104	37	5	0	6	65	5	3	.541	.343
Kemp, Tony	L-R	5-6	165	10-31-91	.227	.222	.228	66	163	23	37	6	2	7	17	16	4	1	2	29	4	3	.417	.308
Maldonado, Martin	R-R	6-0	230	8-16-86	.202	.310	.146	27	84	20	17	4	0	6	10	13	1	0	0	26	0	0	.464	.316
2-team total (74 Kansas City)					.221	.235	.214	101	322	46	71	19	0	12	27	30	6	2	1	81	0	0	.391	.298
Marisnick, Jake	R-R	6-4	220	3-30-91	.233	.226	.237	120	292	46	68	16	3	10	34	17	6	3	0	95	10	3	.411	.289
Mayfield, Jack	R-R	5-11	190	9-30-90	.156	.208	.125	26	64	8	10	5	0	2	5	1	0	0	0	16	0	0	.328	.169
Reddick, Josh	L-R	6-2	195	2-19-87	.275	.309	.266	141	501	57	138	19	3	14	56	36	0	1	9	66	5	2	.409	.319
Springer, George	R-R	6-3	215	9-19-89	.292	.272	.299	122	479	96	140	20	3	39	96	67	6	0	4	113	6	2	.591	.383
Stassi, Max	R-R	5-10	200	3-15-91	.167	.000	.211	31	90	4	15	1	0	1	3	7	1	0	0	34	0	0	.211	.235
2-team total (20 Los Angeles)					.136	.028	.177	51	132	7	18	1	0	1	5	12	1	0	2	49	0	0	.167	.211
Straw, Myles	R-R	5-10	180	10-17-94	.269	.294	.257	56	108	27	29	4	2	0	7	19	0	1	0	24	8	1	.343	.378
Stubbs, Garrett	L-R	5-10	175	5-26-93	.200	.375	.148	19	35	8	7	3	0	0	2	4	0	0	0	7	1	0	.286	.282
Toro, Abraham	B-R	6-1	190	12-20-96	.218	.087	.273	25	78	13	17	3	2	2	9	9	1	0	1	19	1	1	.385	.303
Tucker, Kyle	L-R	6-4	190	1-17-97	.269	.296	.250	22	67	15	18	6	0	4	11	4	1	0	0	20	5	0	.537	.319
White, Tyler	R-R	5-11	225	10-29-90	.225	.162	.257	71	218	16	49	14	0	3	21	32	0	0	3	74	0	0	.330	.320

Pitching	B-T	HT	WT	DOB	W	L	ERA	G	GS	CG	SV	IP	H	R	ER	HR	BB	SO	AVG	vLH	vRH	K/9	BB/9
Abreu, Bryan	R-R	6-1	204	4-22-97	0	0	1.04	7	0	0	0	9	4	1	1	0	3	13	.138	.071	.200	13.50	3.12
Armenteros, Rogelio	R-R	6-1	215	6-30-94	1	1	4.00	5	2	0	1	18	17	9	8	1	5	18	.243	.303	.189	9.00	2.50
Biagini, Joe	R-R	6-5	235	5-29-90	0	1	7.36	13	0	0	0	15	21	13	12	6	9	10	.350	.423	.294	6.14	5.52
2-team total (50 Toronto)					3	2	4.59	63	0	0	1	65	71	35	33	14	26	60	.281	.320	.253	8.35	3.62
Cole, Gerrit	R-R	6-4	225	9-8-90	20	5	2.50	33	33	0	0	212	142	66	59	29	48	326	.186	.175	.198	13.82	2.03
Devenski, Chris	R-R	6-3	210	11-13-90	2	3	4.83	61	1	0	0	69	69	39	37	13	21	72	.256	.273	.237	9.39	2.74
Greinke, Zack	R-R	6-2	200	10-21-83	8	1	3.02	10	10	0	0	63	58	25	21	6	9	52	.246	.246	.247	7.47	1.29
Guduan, Reymin	L-L	6-4	205	3-16-92	1	0	11.81	7	0	0	0	5	8	7	7	3	4	6	.364	.375	.357	10.13	6.75
Harris, Will	R-R	6-4	240	8-28-84	4	1	1.50	68	0	0	4	60	42	14	10	6	14	62	.196	.207	.183	9.30	2.10
James, Josh	R-R	6-3	206	3-8-93	5	1	4.70	49	1	0	1	61	46	34	32	10	35	100	.203	.193	.212	14.67	5.14
Martin, Corbin	R-R	6-2	200	12-28-95	1	1	5.59	5	5	0	0	19	23	14	12	8	12	19	.288	.268	.308	8.84	5.59
McHugh, Collin	R-R	6-2	190	6-19-87	4	5	4.70	35	8	0	0	75	62	41	39	12	30	82	.221	.174	.264	9.88	3.62
Miley, Wade	L-L	6-0	220	11-13-86	14	6	3.98	33	33	0	0	167	164	83	74	23	61	140	.254	.207	.268	7.53	3.28
Osuna, Roberto	R-R	6-2	215	2-7-95	4	3	2.63	66	0	0	38	65	45	20	19	8	12	73	.190	.150	.231	10.11	1.66
Peacock, Brad	R-R	6-1	210	2-2-88	7	6	4.12	23	15	0	0	92	78	43	42	15	31	96	.227	.279	.179	9.43	3.04
Perez, Cionel	L-L	5-11	170	4-21-96	1	1	10.00	5	0	0	0	9	11	10	10	3	2	7	.290	.300	.286	7.00	2.00
Pressly, Ryan	R-R	6-3	210	12-15-88	2	3	2.32	55	0	0	3	54	37	15	14	6	12	72	.188	.124	.250	11.93	1.99
Rodgers, Brady	R-R	6-2	210	9-17-90	0	0	16.20	3	0	0	0	5	7	9	9	4	3	4	.318	.182	.455	7.20	5.40
Rondon, Hector	R-R	6-3	230	2-26-88	3	2	3.71	62	1	0	0	61	56	25	25	10	20	48	.242	.219	.259	7.12	2.97
Sanchez, Aaron	R-R	6-4	210	7-1-92	2	0	4.82	4	4	0	0	19	14	10	10	5	9	16	.200	.286	.114	7.71	4.34
2-team total (23 Toronto Blue Jays)					5	14	5.89	27	27	0	0	131	145	92	86	20	68	115	.278	.279	.277	7.88	4.66
Smith, Joe	R-R	6-2	205	3-22-84	1	0	1.80	28	0	0	0	25	19	6	5	2	5	22	.209	.229	.196	7.92	1.80
Sneed, Cy	R-R	6-4	215	10-1-92	0	1	5.48	8	0	0	0	21	26	13	13	5	5	23	.299	.310	.289	9.70	2.11
Stassi, Max	R-R	5-10	200	3-15-91	0	0	0.00	1	0	0	0	0	0	0	0	0	0	0	.000	.000	--	0.00	0.00
Urquidy, Jose	R-R	6-0	180	5-1-95	2	1	3.95	9	7	0	0	41	38	18	18	6	7	40	.241	.180	.300	8.78	1.54
Valdez, Framber	L-L	5-11	170	11-19-93	4	7	5.86	26	8	0	0	71	74	51	46	9	44	68	.267	.197	.291	8.66	5.60
Verlander, Justin	R-R	6-5	225	2-20-83	21	6	2.58	34	34	2	0	223	137	66	64	36	42	300	.172	.163	.182	12.11	1.70
White, Tyler	R-R	5-11	225	10-29-90	0	0	21.60	4	0	0	0	3	7	8	8	4	5	2	.438	.571	.333	5.40	13.50

Fielding

Catcher	PCT	G	PO	A	E	DP	PB
Chirinos	.995	112	1078	51	6	5	4
Maldonado	.989	26	265	7	3	1	1
Stassi	.992	26	252	11	2	2	2
Stubbs	.987	11	75	3	1	0	0

First Base	PCT	G	PO	A	E	DP
Diaz	1.000	26	125	7	0	6
Gurriel	.996	110	728	73	3	58
Maldonado	1.000	1	5	0	0	0
Reddick	.800	4	4	0	1	0
Stassi	1.000	3	5	0	0	0
Toro	1.000	1	4	0	0	1
Tucker	.929	4	12	1	1	1
White	1.000	48	293	25	0	22

Second Base	PCT	G	PO	A	E	DP
Altuve	.972	121	128	257	11	49
Diaz	1.000	25	19	33	0	6
Gurriel	.875	4	1	6	1	0
Kemp	1.000	29	33	50	0	6
Mayfield	1.000	5	5	8	0	2
Straw	1.000	4	0	6	0	0

Third Base	PCT	G	PO	A	E	DP
Bregman	.966	99	66	164	8	17
Diaz	.967	19	10	19	1	2
Gurriel	.967	42	25	64	3	7
Mayfield	.000	1	0	0	0	0
Toro	.962	24	14	37	2	4

Shortstop	PCT	G	PO	A	E	DP
Altuve	.000	1	0	0	1	0
Bregman	.986	65	63	144	3	21

	PCT	G	PO	A	E	DP
Correa	.993	75	95	176	2	34
Diaz	.818	5	2	7	2	0
Mayfield	.981	21	18	33	1	4
Straw	1.000	26	14	41	0	4

Outfield	PCT	G	PO	A	E	DP
Alvarez	.909	10	9	1	1	0
Brantley	.983	123	167	3	3	0
Diaz	1.000	4	2	0	0	0
Fisher	1.000	14	13	0	0	0
Kemp	1.000	25	38	0	0	0
Marisnick	.995	109	196	1	1	1
Reddick	.983	133	231	4	4	1
Springer	.991	109	220	5	2	1
Straw	1.000	18	29	0	0	0
Stubbs	1.000	7	5	0	0	0
Tucker	1.000	19	32	1	0	0

ROUND ROCK EXPRESS TRIPLE-A
PACIFIC COAST LEAGUE

Batting	B-T	HT	WT	DOB	AVG	vLH	vRH	G	AB	R	H	2B	3B	HR	RBI	BB	HBP	SH	SF	SO	SB	CS	SLG	OBP
Altuve, Jose	R-R	5-6	165	5-6-90	.191	.333	.167	5	21	3	4	0	1	0	2	0	0	0	7	0	0	.286	.261
Alvarez, Yordan	L-R	6-5	225	6-27-97	.343	.339	.344	56	213	50	73	16	0	23	71	38	1	0	1	50	2	1	.742	.443
Campos, Oscar	R-R	5-10	170	12-8-96	.385	.333	.400	5	13	2	5	2	0	0	3	0	0	0	0	1	0	1	.539	.385
Correa, Carlos	R-R	6-4	215	9-22-94	.333	.308	.375	6	21	2	7	3	0	0	2	3	0	0	0	5	0	0	.476	.417
Dawson, Ronnie	L-R	6-2	225	5-19-95	.147	.250	.115	10	34	1	5	1	0	0	3	3	1	0	1	11	1	0	.177	.231
De Goti, Alex	R-R	5-10	165	8-19-94	.277	.281	.275	125	481	83	133	29	3	15	70	52	5	1	9	105	4	4	.443	.347
Dennis, Austin	R-R	5-11	170	6-6-97	.200	.000	.286	5	10	2	2	1	0	0	2	2	0	0	1	1	0	0	.300	.308
Diaz, Aledmys	R-R	6-1	195	8-1-90	.125	.200	.091	4	16	2	2	0	0	0	1	0	0	0	0	3	0	0	.125	.177
Ferguson, Drew	R-R	5-11	180	8-3-92	.281	.267	.286	115	402	83	113	19	6	11	57	68	10	0	3	105	27	7	.440	.395
Fisher, Derek	L-R	6-3	205	8-21-93	.286	.343	.261	60	224	44	64	9	1	14	36	40	4	1	1	67	8	3	.522	.402
Jones, Taylor	R-R	6-7	225	12-6-93	.291	.350	.269	125	447	86	130	28	0	22	84	68	8	0	8	112	0	1	.501	.388
Mayfield, Jack	R-R	5-11	190	9-30-90	.287	.258	.297	100	380	78	109	26	1	26	79	37	5	0	9	78	7	1	.566	.350
McCormick, Chas	R-L	6-0	190	4-19-95	.262	.293	.248	57	191	39	50	3	3	10	44	28	0	0	6	34	7	1	.466	.347
Quintana, Lorenzo	R-R	5-10	198	3-1-89	.264	.222	.277	31	110	20	29	4	0	6	19	5	4	0	3	24	2	3	.464	.312
Reed, AJ	L-L	6-4	275	5-10-93	.224	.189	.237	56	192	33	43	11	0	12	35	27	4	0	2	67	0	0	.469	.329
Ritchie, Jamie	R-R	6-2	205	4-9-93	.270	.282	.265	79	252	46	68	20	0	5	33	41	4	0	4	56	2	0	.409	.375
Rojas, Josh	R-R	6-1	185	6-30-94	.310	.233	.338	53	210	49	65	16	3	12	39	30	3	0	1	36	19	4	.586	.402
2-team total (8 Reno)					.339	.286	.360	61	245	60	83	20	4	15	53	35	3	0	1	42	20	4	.637	.426
Sierra, Anibal	R-R	6-1	190	2-15-94	.250	.286	.237	15	52	6	13	2	0	1	13	6	1	0	1	12	0	0	.346	.333
Stassi, Max	R-R	5-10	200	3-15-91	.375	1.000	.167	2	8	1	3	1	0	1	3	1	0	0	0	2	0	1	.875	.444
Straw, Myles	R-R	5-10	180	10-17-94	.321	.371	.304	66	277	46	89	11	3	1	33	32	1	1	2	50	19	4	.394	.391
Stubbs, Garrett	L-R	5-10	175	5-26-93	.240	.260	.234	63	204	33	49	11	0	7	23	24	5	0	2	38	12	2	.397	.332
Tanielu, Nick	R-R	5-11	215	9-4-92	.295	.325	.284	125	454	71	134	39	3	19	84	44	3	0	2	86	2	3	.520	.360
Toro, Abraham	B-R	6-1	190	12-20-96	.424	.533	.392	16	66	17	28	9	0	1	10	10	2	0	1	5	0	1	.606	.506
Tucker, Kyle	L-R	6-4	190	1-17-97	.266	.271	.263	125	463	92	123	26	3	34	97	60	6	0	5	116	30	5	.555	.354
Wrenn, Stephen	R-R	6-2	200	10-7-94	.300	.600	.000	3	10	1	3	0	1	0	0	1	0	0	0	3	1	0	.500	.364

Pitching	B-T	HT	WT	DOB	W	L	ERA	G	GS	CG	SV	IP	H	R	ER	HR	BB	SO	AVG	vLH	vRH	K/9	BB/9
Armenteros, Rogelio	R-R	6-1	215	6-30-94	6	7	4.80	19	18	1	0	84	90	48	45	14	31	85	.276	.230	.301	9.07	3.31
Biagini, Joe	R-R	6-5	235	5-29-90	0	0	27.00	1	0	0	0	2	3	5	5	0	3	3	.375	.333	.400	16.20	16.20
Bielak, Brandon	L-R	6-1	210	4-2-96	8	4	4.41	15	14	0	0	86	69	42	42	10	36	86	.220	.206	.229	9.04	3.78
Blanco, Ronel	R-R	6-0	180	8-31-93	2	1	5.74	19	0	0	4	27	29	20	17	7	16	27	.282	.242	.300	9.11	5.40
Bostick, Akeem	R-R	6-6	215	5-4-95	4	5	7.28	21	12	0	0	80	98	70	65	19	42	73	.300	.320	.290	8.18	4.71
Bravo, Jose	R-R	6-3	213	6-10-97	0	0	9.00	1	0	0	0	3	2	2	2	1	1	3	.375	—	.375	13.50	4.50
Campos, Oscar	R-R	5-10	170	12-8-96	0	0	30.86	2	0	0	0	2	9	8	8	3	1	2	.563	.500	.600	7.71	3.86
Castellanos, Humberto	R-R	5-11	218	4-3-98	0	1	1.42	5	0	0	0	13	4	2	2	1	3	10	.103	.091	.118	7.11	2.13
De Goti, Alex	R-R	5-10	165	8-19-94	0	0	0.00	3	0	0	0	4	0	0	0	0	2	0	.000	.000	.000	0.00	4.91
Deetz, Dean	R-R	6-1	195	11-29-93	2	0	7.15	24	0	0	2	34	32	27	27	8	37	51	.254	.296	.232	13.50	9.79
Duncan, Tanner	R-R	6-2	205	8-12-94	3	0	5.89	10	0	0	0	18	16	13	12	2	8	15	.239	.269	.220	7.36	3.93
Emanuel, Kent	L-L	6-4	212	6-4-92	8	2	3.90	28	7	0	1	102	98	47	44	9	23	81	.254	.219	.266	7.17	2.04
Ferrell, Justin	R-R	6-7	200	4-21-94	1	0	13.50	5	0	0	0	7	10	11	11	2	6	8	.323	.059	.643	9.82	7.36
Ferrell, Riley	R-R	6-2	200	10-18-93	0	0	9.00	7	0	0	1	8	10	8	8	1	6	11	.303	.364	.273	12.38	6.75
2-team total (4 New Orleans)					0	0	5.52	11	0	0	1	15	13	9	9	1	10	15	.232	.273	.206	9.20	6.14
Garza, Ralph	R-R	6-2	195	4-6-94	8	1	4.04	42	0	0	5	78	57	37	35	9	28	80	.202	.214	.196	9.23	3.23
Guduan, Reymin	L-L	6-4	205	3-16-92	3	1	2.63	23	0	0	2	27	29	14	8	1	18	32	.269	.192	.293	10.54	5.93
Hartman, Ryan	L-L	6-3	205	4-21-94	6	7	5.84	25	19	1	2	116	135	80	75	27	45	117	.289	.288	.289	9.10	3.50
James, Josh	R-R	6-3	206	3-8-93	0	0	10.80	3	0	0	0	3	4	4	4	0	2	5	.286	.250	.300	13.50	5.40
Javier, Cristian	R-R	6-1	204	3-26-97	0	0	1.64	2	2	0	0	11	5	2	2	1	4	16	.128	.143	.120	13.09	3.27
LaRue, Carson	R-R	6-1	175	3-6-96	2	4	5.40	7	7	1	0	37	39	27	22	9	15	22	.281	.290	.273	5.40	3.68
Martin, Corbin	R-R	6-2	200	12-28-95	2	1	3.13	9	8	0	0	37	33	13	13	2	18	45	.243	.320	.198	10.85	4.34
Martin, Hunter	R-R	6-1	195	12-14-94	0	0	63.00	1	0	0	0	1	8	7	7	1	1	1	.727	.750	.667	9.00	9.00

Name	B-T	HT	WT	DOB	W	L	ERA	G	GS	CG	SV	IP	H	R	ER	HR	BB	SO	AVG	vLH	vRH	K/9	BB/9
McCurry, Brendan	R-R	5-10	170	1-7-92	3	5	4.23	37	1	0	6	55	47	26	26	9	23	68	.227	.233	.224	11.06	3.74
McHugh, Collin	R-R	6-2	190	6-19-87	0	0	27.00	1	0	0	0	1	1	2	2	1	1	1	.333	.000	.500	13.50	13.50
McKee, Colin	R-R	6-3	225	6-21-94	1	1	9.00	6	0	0	0	6	7	7	6	3	9	6	.292	.167	.333	9.00	13.50
Paulino, Felipe	R-R	6-3	270	10-5-83	1	0	9.58	20	0	0	7	21	30	23	22	5	9	22	.333	.333	.333	9.58	3.92
Peacock, Brad	R-R	6-1	210	2-2-88	0	0	22.09	5	1	0	0	4	6	9	9	1	7	4	.353	.444	.250	9.82	17.18
Perez, Cionel	L-L	5-11	170	4-21-96	2	1	5.36	13	10	0	0	47	53	30	28	6	24	43	.288	.186	.319	8.23	4.60
Quintana, Lorenzo	R-R	5-10	198	3-1-89	0	0	0.00	1	0	0	0	1	1	0	0	0	0	0	.250	.000	.500	0.00	0.00
Ritchie, Jamie	R-R	6-2	205	4-9-93	0	1	9.00	2	0	0	1	2	5	4	2	0	0	1	.455	.500	.444	4.50	0.00
Rodgers, Brady	R-R	6-2	210	9-17-90	4	0	3.83	10	8	0	0	49	48	21	21	8	18	35	.253	.262	.248	6.39	3.28
Scheetz, Kit	L-L	5-10	185	5-18-94	0	0	6.04	15	0	0	0	28	35	19	19	5	13	36	.302	.294	.305	11.44	4.13
Smith, Joe	R-R	6-2	205	3-22-84	0	0	0.00	4	0	0	0	4	1	0	0	0	1	5	.077	.000	.100	11.25	2.25
Sneed, Cy	R-R	6-4	215	10-1-92	7	6	4.19	19	9	0	1	82	71	40	38	13	24	71	.238	.292	.213	7.82	2.64
Tanielu, Nick	R-R	5-11	215	9-4-92	0	0	10.13	2	0	0	0	3	5	3	3	1	0	0	.417	.750	.250	0.00	0.00
Urquidy, Jose	R-R	6-0	180	5-1-95	5	3	4.63	13	12	0	0	70	67	37	36	15	16	94	.245	.185	.282	12.09	2.06
Valdez, Framber	L-L	5-11	170	11-19-93	5	2	3.25	10	7	0	1	44	29	18	16	3	17	69	.185	.135	.200	14.01	3.45
Valdez, Gabriel	R-R	6-2	185	10-25-95	1	0	0.00	3	0	0	1	7	3	1	0	0	2	8	.130	.000	.150	10.29	2.57
Whitley, Forrest	R-R	6-7	195	9-15-97	0	3	12.21	8	5	0	0	24	35	33	33	9	15	29	.343	.214	.392	10.73	5.55

Fielding

Catcher	PCT	G	PO	A	E	DP	PB
Campos	1.000	3	21	1	0	1	0
Quintana	.978	19	169	9	4	0	1
Ritchie	.997	68	608	30	2	5	3
Stassi	.960	2	22	1	0	0	0
Stubbs	.998	54	466	26	1	2	2

First Base	PCT	G	PO	A	E	DP
Alvarez	.972	9	67	2	2	4
Diaz	1.000	1	3	0	0	1
Jones	.996	68	472	49	2	56
Quintana	.000	1	0	0	0	0
Reed	.982	40	257	16	5	27
Tanielu	.994	20	146	9	1	14
Toro	1.000	1	12	0	0	1
Tucker	1.000	11	67	5	0	8

Second Base	PCT	G	PO	A	E	DP
Altuve	1.000	4	7	4	0	2
De Goti	.981	53	90	121	4	32
Diaz	1.000	1	4	2	0	0
Mayfield	1.000	33	46	73	0	16
Rojas	1.000	15	31	31	0	14
Sierra	.958	8	12	11	1	2
Straw	.938	5	8	7	1	3
Stubbs	1.000	5	10	2	0	1
Tanielu	.987	24	27	47	1	14
Toro	1.000	4	4	10	0	1

Third Base	PCT	G	PO	A	E	DP
De Goti	.977	14	14	28	1	2
Diaz	.667	2	1	1	1	0
Jones	.974	15	6	32	1	4
Mayfield	.978	24	17	28	1	3
Rojas	.962	11	7	18	1	3
Tanielu	.969	76	40	116	5	24
Toro	.933	8	3	11	1	0

Shortstop	PCT	G	PO	A	E	DP
Correa	1.000	5	3	10	0	4
De Goti	.970	46	43	118	5	18
Diaz	1.000	1	1	0	0	0
Mayfield	.971	43	41	93	4	25
Rojas	1.000	15	18	39	0	6
Sierra	1.000	7	6	16	0	3
Straw	.948	30	36	73	6	13

Outfield	PCT	G	PO	A	E	DP
Alvarez	1.000	29	36	3	0	0
Dawson	1.000	10	20	0	0	0
De Goti	1.000	6	8	0	0	0
Dennis	1.000	5	8	1	0	0
Ferguson	.986	98	208	3	3	2
Fisher	.991	53	108	3	1	1
Jones	1.000	30	45	2	0	0
McCormick	1.000	50	101	2	0	0
Rojas	1.000	14	20	1	0	0
Straw	.976	34	81	2	2	0
Stubbs	1.000	1	1	0	0	0
Tucker	.995	100	178	6	1	0
Wrenn	1.000	3	6	0	0	0

CORPUS CHRISTI HOOKS

DOUBLE-A

Texas League

Batting	B-T	HT	WT	DOB	AVG	vLH	vRH	G	AB	R	H	2B	3B	HR	RBI	BB	HBP	SH	SF	SO	SB	CS	SLG	OBP
Adams, Jake	R-R	6-2	250	12-23-95	.255	.316	.241	27	98	15	25	5	0	7	21	6	2	0	2	31	1	0	.520	.306
Angarita, Alfredo	L-R	5-10	155	11-16-96	.071	.000	.083	14	14	1	1	0	0	0	0	2	0	2	0	6	0	0	.071	.188
Arauz, Jonathan	B-R	6-0	150	8-3-98	.241	.118	.264	28	108	12	26	3	2	3	13	10	1	0	0	19	1	1	.389	.311
Beer, Seth	L-R	6-3	195	9-18-96	.299	.244	.312	63	234	40	70	9	0	16	52	24	20	0	2	58	0	0	.543	.407
Benedetti, Carmen	L-L	6-2	215	10-29-94	.164	.143	.167	21	73	6	12	2	1	0	2	9	0	0	0	33	1	0	.219	.256
Bermudez, Javier	R-R	5-11	155	1-22-98	.091	.000	.100	5	11	2	1	0	0	0	0	1	0	0	0	4	1	0	.091	.231
Canelon, Carlos	R-R	5-11	168	12-14-94	.345	.500	.320	9	29	6	10	0	0	2	6	2	1	0	1	7	0	0	.552	.394
Dawson, Ronnie	L-R	6-2	225	5-19-95	.212	.111	.228	103	392	71	83	20	2	17	50	47	16	3	1	141	13	10	.403	.320
De La Cruz, Bryan	R-R	6-2	175	12-16-96	.283	.286	.282	64	269	45	76	14	4	4	24	24	2	0	5	60	7	5	.409	.340
Diaz, Aledmys	R-R	6-1	195	8-1-90	.000	.000	.000	2	5	0	0	0	0	0	0	0	0	0	0	4	0	0	.000	.375
Duarte, Osvaldo	R-R	5-9	160	1-18-96	.234	.286	.224	123	458	59	107	13	8	12	46	30	7	1	1	149	21	10	.376	.290
Goetzman, Granden	R-R	6-4	200	11-14-92	.226	.317	.211	82	306	44	69	15	0	15	49	34	2	0	5	89	1	2	.422	.303
Julks, Corey	R-R	6-1	185	2-27-96	.162	.400	.074	10	37	3	6	0	0	0	4	4	0	0	0	16	0	0	.162	.244
Martinez, Hector	R-R	6-1	185	7-6-98	.077	.500	.000	5	13	0	1	0	0	0	0	1	0	0	0	5	0	0	.077	.143
Matijevic, J.J.	L-R	6-0	206	11-14-95	.246	.229	.249	73	281	41	69	21	1	9	35	27	2	0	2	97	8	0	.424	.314
McCormick, Chas	R-L	6-0	190	4-19-95	.277	.400	.261	53	177	26	49	3	3	4	22	39	7	0	0	28	9	3	.396	.426
Meyers, Jake	R-L	6-0	200	6-18-96	.214	.133	.230	24	89	9	19	1	1	6	11	0	0	0	20	3	3	.270	.300
Quintana, Lorenzo	R-R	5-10	198	3-1-89	.321	.320	.322	43	168	36	54	12	1	11	37	8	3	0	0	39	1	0	.601	.363
Robinson, Chuckie	R-R	5-11	225	12-14-94	.217	.250	.211	103	374	30	81	17	1	7	36	25	7	0	3	118	9	1	.324	.276
Rodriguez, Ramiro	L-L	5-11	145	2-2-98	.256	.333	.250	12	39	3	10	2	0	0	2	4	0	0	0	14	3	0	.308	.333
Rojas, Josh	L-R	6-1	185	6-30-94	.322	.238	.333	44	171	29	55	13	2	8	30	22	2	0	0	28	13	6	.561	.405
Santana, Luis	R-R	5-8	175	7-20-99	.228	.167	.235	18	57	5	13	2	0	0	6	3	0	0	0	9	0	0	.263	.333
Shaver, Colton	R-R	6-1	210	9-18-95	.223	.094	.250	55	188	33	42	5	1	15	39	34	5	0	0	73	0	0	.500	.357
Sierra, Anibal	R-R	6-1	190	2-15-94	.204	.128	.217	96	324	30	66	11	0	5	25	24	8	0	2	113	2	4	.284	.274
Springer, George	R-R	6-3	215	9-19-89	.400	--	.400	3	10	3	4	0	0	2	5	4	0	0	0	1	1	0	1.000	.571
Stassi, Max	R-R	5-10	200	3-15-91	.375	.667	.200	2	8	1	3	1	0	1	2	0	0	0	0	3	0	0	.875	.375
Toro, Abraham	B-R	6-1	190	12-20-96	.306	.241	.317	98	376	65	115	22	4	16	70	48	8	0	3	77	4	1	.513	.393
Wrenn, Stephen	R-R	6-2	200	10-7-94	.247	.219	.253	102	380	56	94	22	8	8	44	43	10	1	4	109	24	5	.411	.336

Pitching

Pitching	B-T	HT	WT	DOB	W	L	ERA	G	GS	CG	SV	IP	H	R	ER	HR	BB	SO	AVG	vLH	vRH	K/9	BB/9
Abreu, Bryan	R-R	6-1	204	4-22-97	6	2	5.05	20	13	0	2	77	60	45	43	6	48	101	.217	.197	.233	11.86	5.63
Adcock, Brett	L-L	6-1	225	8-28-95	2	8	6.90	23	19	0	0	87	88	73	67	13	50	87	.256	.225	.270	8.97	5.15
Bailey, Brandon	R-R	5-10	175	10-19-94	4	5	3.30	22	17	0	0	93	72	34	34	12	41	103	.212	.191	.232	10.00	3.98
Bermudez, Jonathan	L-L	6-2	237	10-16-95	0	2	0.93	5	0	0	1	10	4	3	1	0	5	14	.125	.167	.100	13.03	4.66
Bielak, Brandon	L-R	6-1	210	4-2-96	3	0	3.75	8	6	0	0	36	29	15	15	3	14	33	.220	.183	.250	8.25	3.50
Blanco, Ronel	R-R	6-0	180	8-31-93	3	0	4.15	9	0	0	2	17	17	8	8	0	8	26	.254	.308	.220	13.50	4.15
Bravo, Jose	R-R	6-3	213	6-10-97	0	0	7.71	1	0	0	0	2	2	2	2	1	1	5	.222	.500	.143	19.29	3.86
Bukauskas, J.B.	R-R	6-0	196	10-11-96	2	4	5.25	20	14	0	1	86	81	57	50	8	54	98	.252	.293	.216	10.30	5.67
Canelon, Carlos	R-R	5-11	168	12-14-94	0	0	27.00	1	0	0	0	1	4	3	3	1	0	0	.571	.333	.750	0.00	9.00
Collado, Willy	R-R	6-2	175	3-30-98	0	3	2.13	18	0	0	4	38	38	12	9	2	7	36	.252	.292	.215	8.53	1.66
Conine, Brett	R-R	6-3	210	10-16-96	1	0	2.00	4	2	0	0	18	20	5	4	1	6	14	.282	.243	.324	7.00	3.00
Daniels, Brett	R-R	6-0	194	2-25-96	1	0	6.75	3	0	0	0	8	8	6	6	2	6	10	.267	.222	.286	11.25	6.75
Deetz, Dean	R-R	6-1	195	11-29-93	0	0	0.00	1	0	0	0	1	1	0	0	0	0	2	.250	.333	.000	18.00	0.00
DeJuneas, Tommy	R-R	6-1	202	10-24-95	2	6	8.31	23	0	0	0	30	33	33	28	5	33	37	.268	.296	.246	10.98	9.79
Donato, Chad	R-R	6-0	210	6-3-95	3	3	3.57	11	6	0	0	53	44	25	21	7	15	60	.218	.210	.227	10.19	2.55
Duncan, Tanner	R-R	6-2	205	8-12-94	1	1	2.25	3	0	0	0	4	7	3	1	0	1	2	.333	.375	.308	4.50	2.25
Feldmann, Brendan	R-R	6-4	205	4-7-94	1	3	4.24	12	0	0	1	17	13	12	8	3	7	15	.213	.207	.219	7.94	3.71
Ferrell, Justin	R-R	6-7	205	4-21-94	1	2	5.96	17	0	0	1	26	24	17	17	2	22	20	.245	.192	.294	7.01	7.71
Ferrell, Riley	R-R	6-2	200	10-18-93	1	1	1.42	5	0	0	0	6	3	1	1	0	4	8	.136	.125	.143	11.37	5.68
Figueroa, Miguel	R-R	6-2	203	3-22-97	0	0	9.53	4	0	0	0	6	5	6	6	0	4	4	.238	.333	.167	6.35	6.35
Henderson, Layne	R-R	6-4	200	6-8-96	1	2	7.62	8	0	0	0	13	15	12	11	2	12	13	.289	.211	.333	9.00	8.31
Hernandez, Nick	R-R	6-1	212	12-30-94	1	3	3.42	18	0	0	1	24	19	11	9	2	13	25	.218	.186	.250	9.51	4.94
Ivey, Tyler	R-R	6-4	195	5-12-96	4	0	1.57	11	8	0	0	46	28	9	8	5	16	61	.170	.182	.159	11.93	3.13
Javier, Cristian	R-R	6-1	204	3-26-97	6	3	2.07	17	11	0	3	74	31	18	17	5	39	114	.124	.127	.121	13.86	4.74
LaRue, Carson	R-R	6-1	175	3-6-96	2	4	5.96	16	13	1	0	71	77	51	47	8	24	64	.281	.265	.293	8.11	3.04
Martin, Hunter	R-R	6-1	195	12-14-94	0	1	6.43	4	0	0	0	7	8	5	5	2	4	4	.286	.364	.235	5.14	0.00
McHugh, Collin	R-R	6-2	190	6-19-87	0	0	3.00	3	0	0	0	3	2	1	1	0	1	4	.182	.400	.000	12.00	3.00
McKee, Colin	R-R	6-3	225	6-21-94	2	2	1.71	34	0	0	7	58	25	15	11	5	35	76	.131	.157	.108	11.79	5.43
Paredes, Enoli	R-R	5-11	168	9-28-95	2	3	3.78	12	6	0	1	50	29	21	21	1	21	69	.167	.183	.152	12.42	3.78
Peacock, Brad	R-R	6-1	210	2-2-88	0	0	0.00	1	1	0	0	2	0	0	0	0	1	4	.000	.000	.000	18.00	4.50
Pinales, Erasmo	R-R	5-11	180	11-25-94	1	1	4.00	12	0	0	1	18	20	9	8	5	12	31	.282	.270	.294	15.50	6.00
Pressly, Ryan	R-R	6-3	210	12-15-88	0	0	0.00	1	0	0	0	1	0	0	0	0	0	2	.333	.333	--	18.00	0.00
Quintana, Lorenzo	R-R	5-10	198	3-1-89	0	0	27.00	2	0	0	0	1	4	3	3	0	0	0	.571	.500	.600	0.00	0.00
Ramirez, Yohan	R-R	6-4	190	5-6-95	3	5	4.76	17	8	0	1	62	42	35	33	5	52	89	.190	.213	.162	12.85	7.51
Rodriguez, Leovanny	R-R	6-0	183	6-13-96	0	0	0.00	1	0	0	0	2	2	0	0	0	3	2	.222	.500	.000	11.57	0.00
Sanabria, Carlos	R-R	6-3	165	1-24-97	4	3	3.11	37	0	0	6	55	36	26	19	4	36	71	.185	.185	.185	11.62	5.89
Scheetz, Kit	L-L	5-10	185	5-18-94	2	0	4.13	16	0	0	3	24	22	12	11	3	7	27	.244	.250	.242	10.13	2.63
Scrubb, Andre	R-R	6-4	265	1-13-95	0	0	3.71	12	0	0	3	17	21	7	7	0	10	20	.292	.300	.281	10.59	5.29
2-team total (29 Tulsa)					6	1	2.78	41	2	0	3	65	56	24	20	3	33	76	.227	.270	.182	10.58	4.59
Shaver, Colton	R-R	6-1	210	9-18-95	0	0	0.00	1	0	0	0	0	0	0	0	0	0	0	.000	.000	--	0.00	0.00
Smith, Joe	R-R	6-2	205	3-22-84	0	0	13.50	2	0	0	0	2	4	3	3	2	0	4	.400	.500	.333	18.00	0.00
Urquidy, Jose	R-R	6-0	180	5-1-95	2	2	4.09	7	6	0	0	33	28	18	15	2	5	40	.222	.154	.270	10.91	1.36
Valdez, Gabriel	R-R	6-2	185	10-25-95	2	2	5.79	9	2	0	0	28	24	19	18	9	17	21	.233	.229	.236	6.75	5.46
Whitley, Forrest	R-R	6-7	195	9-15-97	2	2	5.56	6	6	0	0	23	18	14	14	2	19	36	.222	.170	.294	14.29	7.54

Fielding

Catcher	PCT	G	PO	A	E	DP	PB
Canelon	1.000	8	66	8	0	0	0
Quintana	1.000	23	212	12	0	0	2
Robinson	.993	88	898	71	7	9	18
Shaver	.992	20	245	15	2	2	2
Stassi	1.000	2	21	2	0	0	0

First Base	PCT	G	PO	A	E	DP
Adams	1.000	18	118	7	0	6
Beer	.990	46	291	12	3	19
Diaz	1.000	1	2	0	0	1
Matijevic	.994	48	301	22	2	26
Quintana	.984	10	58	2	1	6
Rojas	1.000	12	80	9	0	10
Shaver	1.000	3	13	0	0	0
Toro	1.000	6	31	2	0	2

Second Base	PCT	G	PO	A	E	DP
Arauz	.961	15	18	31	2	6
Bermudez	1.000	3	3	5	0	1

	.970	45	84	107	6	24
Duarte	.970	45	84	107	6	24
Rojas	.985	30	61	67	2	17
Santana	.978	17	17	27	1	4
Sierra	.964	23	21	32	2	4
Toro	1.000	11	11	21	0	4

Third Base	PCT	G	PO	A	E	DP
Adams	1.000	2	0	5	0	1
Arauz	1.000	6	1	6	0	1
Diaz	1.000	1	1	0	0	0
Duarte	1.000	10	8	20	0	2
Rojas	.429	2	2	1	4	0
Santana	.800	1	1	3	1	0
Shaver	.932	30	15	26	3	3
Sierra	.833	8	1	4	1	1
Toro	.969	85	58	132	6	15

Shortstop	PCT	G	PO	A	E	DP
Arauz	1.000	7	11	15	0	0
Bermudez	.857	2	4	2	1	0
Diaz	.000	1	0	0	0	0

	.941	66	67	123	12	18
Duarte	.941	66	67	123	12	18
Sierra	.970	65	94	135	7	32

Outfield	PCT	G	PO	A	E	DP
Angarita	1.000	4	11	0	0	0
Beer	.875	8	14	0	2	0
Benedetti	.969	15	30	1	1	0
Dawson	.981	90	209	2	4	1
De La Cruz	1.000	61	100	4	0	1
Diaz	.000	1	0	0	0	0
Duarte	1.000	4	7	0	0	0
Goetzman	.970	42	62	3	2	0
Julks	.889	7	8	0	1	0
Martinez	.917	4	10	1	1	0
Matijevic	.962	22	49	1	2	0
McCormick	1.000	48	86	4	0	3
Meyers	.976	21	40	1	1	0
Rodriguez	.958	11	23	0	1	0
Rojas	1.000	1	1	0	0	0
Springer	1.000	2	5	0	0	0
Wrenn	.968	87	174	5	6	0

CAROLINA LEAGUE

Batting	B-T	HT	WT	DOB	AVG	vLH	vRH	G	AB	R	H	2B	3B	HR	RBI	BB	HBP	SH	SF	SO	SB	CS	SLG	OBP
Adams, Jake	R-R	6-2	250	12-23-95	.246	.250	.244	91	321	38	79	12	0	15	66	31	3	0	7	86	4	3	.424	.312
Adolph, Ross	L-R	6-1	203	12-17-96	.236	.121	.270	43	144	24	34	5	1	1	16	24	4	0	0	43	2	1	.306	.361
Angarita, Alfredo	L-R	5-10	155	11-16-96	.159	.261	.119	28	82	11	13	3	0	0	5	16	2	1	1	22	2	0	.195	.307
Arauz, Jonathan	B-R	6-0	150	8-3-98	.252	.204	.272	87	317	41	80	19	0	8	42	30	4	0	3	69	5	4	.388	.322
Beer, Seth	L-R	6-3	195	9-18-96	.328	.250	.346	35	128	24	42	8	0	9	34	14	7	0	3	30	0	3	.602	.415
Castro, Ruben	L-R	5-10	182	7-10-96	.254	.154	.278	24	67	10	17	1	0	2	7	13	1	1	0	24	2	0	.358	.383
Costes, Marty	R-R	5-9	205	12-18-95	.247	.297	.217	29	97	14	24	3	0	3	12	14	4	0	1	15	0	1	.371	.362
De La Cruz, Bryan	R-R	6-2	175	12-16-96	.276	.361	.252	41	163	29	45	14	2	4	19	16	1	0	3	33	5	1	.460	.339
Flores, Alejandro	B-R	6-1	180	12-27-95	.000	.000	.000	2	6	0	0	0	0	0	0	0	0	0	0	1	0	0	.000	.000
Hensley, David	R-R	6-6	190	3-28-96	.327	.346	.319	28	98	10	32	11	0	0	18	11	0	0	2	23	0	2	.439	.387
Julks, Corey	R-R	6-1	185	2-27-96	.266	.315	.248	97	350	48	93	25	3	4	37	52	7	0	3	76	10	5	.389	.369
Manea, Scott	R-R	5-11	205	12-21-95	.235	.218	.242	102	328	41	77	14	0	12	49	36	22	0	3	83	1	4	.387	.347
Matijevic, J.J.	L-R	6-0	206	11-14-95	.333	.500	.250	5	18	3	6	1	0	2	2	2	0	0	0	4	0	0	.722	.400
Meyers, Jake	R-L	6-0	200	6-18-96	.258	.311	.234	87	341	55	88	28	3	8	41	33	8	0	2	84	9	4	.428	.336
Papierski, Michael	B-R	6-4	225	2-26-96	.233	.266	.219	108	374	58	87	11	1	7	38	61	8	1	2	101	2	7	.324	.351
Pena, Jeremy	R-R	6-0	179	9-22-97	.317	.324	.315	43	167	28	53	13	3	2	13	12	5	0	1	33	3	4	.467	.378
Pineda, Juan	R-R	5-10	190	1-31-98	.000	.000	.000	2	8	0	0	0	0	0	0	0	0	0	0	1	0	0	.000	.000
Rodriguez, Ramiro	L-L	5-10	145	2-2-98	.250	.286	.222	6	16	4	4	1	0	1	2	3	0	0	0	4	1	0	.500	.368
Schreiber, Scott	R-R	6-3	230	10-13-95	.210	.195	.218	72	257	30	54	16	2	7	30	15	1	1	1	87	4	4	.370	.256
Shaver, Colton	R-R	6-1	210	9-18-95	.270	.299	.257	58	211	25	57	23	0	6	33	29	3	0	1	56	0	1	.465	.365
Sierra, Miguelangel	R-R	5-11	201	12-2-97	.203	.256	.179	111	369	45	75	10	1	13	46	37	4	0	3	146	3	3	.342	.281
Stevenson, Cal	L-L	5-10	175	9-12-96	.247	.120	.304	23	81	18	20	6	1	0	9	19	0	0	0	13	2	3	.346	.390
Taylor, Chandler	L-L	6-1	210	2-7-96	.223	.189	.235	80	274	40	61	13	2	14	50	50	3	0	3	129	8	7	.438	.346
Valdez, Enmanuel	L-R	5-9	171	12-28-98	.215	.180	.233	67	228	26	49	11	1	5	31	14	2	1	2	61	6	2	.338	.264

Pitching	B-T	HT	WT	DOB	W	L	ERA	G	GS	CG	SV	IP	H	R	ER	HR	BB	SO	AVG	vLH	vRH	K/9	BB/9
Abreu, Bryan	R-R	6-1	204	4-22-97	1	0	3.68	3	3	0	0	15	9	6	6	2	6	25	.177	.200	.171	15.34	3.68
Billingsley, Jacob	R-R	5-11	185	7-27-94	0	2	4.66	20	0	0	3	29	27	20	15	1	16	44	.246	.220	.261	13.66	4.97
Bravo, Jose	R-R	6-3	213	6-10-97	2	1	0.93	4	0	0	1	10	2	1	1	0	0	10	.059	.000	.091	9.31	0.00
Cabral, Riley	R-R	5-11	211	1-25-97	2	1	4.35	13	0	0	3	21	16	10	10	1	5	33	.213	.194	.227	14.37	2.18
Castellanos, Humberto	R-R	5-11	218	4-3-98	1	1	3.16	15	0	0	3	26	30	14	9	1	6	27	.289	.286	.290	9.47	2.10
Castro, Ruben	L-R	5-10	182	7-10-96	0	0	0.00	1	0	0	0	1	0	0	0	0	0	0	.000	.000	--	0.00	0.00
Ceballos, Yeremi	L-L	6-2	165	12-21-98	0	0	0.96	5	0	0	1	9	2	1	1	1	2	10	.065	.083	.053	9.64	1.93
Collado, Willy	R-R	6-2	175	3-30-98	0	3	1.16	13	0	0	3	23	13	5	3	0	11	33	.161	.237	.093	12.73	4.24
Conine, Brett	R-R	6-3	210	10-16-96	4	2	2.42	15	8	0	0	63	52	19	17	3	17	80	.222	.210	.235	11.37	2.42
Conn, Devin	R-R	5-11	169	4-3-97	1	0	3.00	1	0	0	0	3	3	1	1	0	2	1	.300	.500	.250	3.00	6.00
Deason, Cody	R-R	6-4	214	12-26-96	4	3	3.57	9	6	0	1	40	34	19	16	0	14	44	.224	.210	.239	9.82	3.12
DeJuneas, Tommy	R-R	6-1	202	10-24-95	1	2	4.44	17	0	0	8	24	20	15	12	1	12	33	.222	.278	.185	12.21	4.44
Donato, Chad	R-R	6-0	210	6-3-95	3	9	5.84	15	13	0	0	69	81	50	45	9	24	72	.303	.361	.257	9.35	3.12
Dubin, Shawn	R-R	6-1	154	9-6-95	6	5	3.92	22	18	0	1	99	71	46	43	3	42	132	.196	.186	.203	12.04	3.83
Duncan, Tanner	R-R	6-2	205	8-12-94	0	3	4.71	15	0	0	1	21	23	12	11	3	17	24	.281	.400	.192	10.29	7.29
Feldmann, Brendan	R-R	6-4	205	4-7-94	0	0	10.80	1	0	0	0	2	6	4	2	1	0	2	.500	.667	.444	10.80	0.00
Figueroa, Miguel	R-R	6-2	203	3-22-97	0	0	0.00	1	0	0	0	1	0	0	0	0	0	0	.500	.000	1.000	0.00	0.00
France, J.P.	R-R	6-0	216	4-4-95	4	9	4.31	25	20	0	0	100	88	58	48	12	52	100	.235	.250	.223	8.97	4.66
Garcia, Luis	R-R	6-1	216	12-13-96	4	4	3.02	15	12	0	0	66	43	27	22	5	34	108	.185	.160	.201	14.80	4.66
Gonzalez, Joey	R-R	5-11	174	1-10-97	1	1	5.11	13	0	0	1	25	23	14	14	4	10	25	.245	.270	.228	9.12	3.65
Hansen, Austin	R-R	6-0	195	8-25-96	3	2	3.10	14	7	0	1	52	32	22	18	4	32	76	.174	.146	.200	13.07	5.50
Hernandez, Nick	R-R	6-1	212	12-30-94	0	1	5.87	5	0	0	0	8	6	6	5	0	4	12	.231	.143	.263	14.09	4.70
Ivey, Tyler	R-R	6-4	195	5-12-96	0	0	0.00	1	1	0	0	3	0	0	0	0	1	2	.000	.000	.000	6.00	3.00
Javier, Cristian	R-R	6-1	204	3-26-97	2	0	0.94	7	5	0	1	29	15	5	3	1	16	40	.147	.206	.118	12.56	5.02
Martin, Hunter	R-R	6-1	195	12-14-94	1	0	6.52	10	0	0	0	19	15	16	14	0	16	17	.217	.300	.184	7.91	7.45
Mushinski, Parker	L-L	6-0	218	11-22-95	0	1	3.76	11	9	0	1	53	47	27	22	4	16	63	.229	.180	.245	10.77	2.73
Paredes, Enoli	R-R	5-11	168	9-28-95	3	1	1.64	10	6	0	0	44	21	9	8	3	21	59	.141	.115	.159	12.07	4.30
Perez, Cionel	L-L	5-11	170	4-21-96	1	0	0.00	1	0	0	0	2	2	0	0	0	0	1	.250	.333	.200	4.50	0.00
Ramirez, Yohan	R-R	6-4	190	5-6-95	1	2	2.89	10	7	0	0	44	22	18	14	0	22	69	.145	.200	.113	14.22	4.53
Rodriguez, Leovanny	R-R	6-0	183	6-13-96	7	2	4.52	34	0	0	0	64	74	38	32	6	31	72	.300	.365	.250	10.18	4.35
Rodriguez, Nivaldo	R-R	6-1	170	4-16-97	3	5	2.92	18	9	0	2	74	46	27	24	5	31	75	.175	.157	.190	9.12	3.77
Rosado, Cesar	R-R	6-1	172	6-22-96	3	7	4.40	32	0	0	5	47	25	26	23	2	35	61	.157	.141	.171	11.68	6.70
Saldana, Abdiel	R-R	5-11	195	3-13-96	0	0	40.50	1	1	0	0	1	3	3	3	0	0	0	.600	.750	.000	0.00	40.50
Sanabria, Carlos	R-R	6-3	165	1-24-97	2	0	1.54	6	0	0	1	12	6	2	2	1	4	15	.140	.118	.154	11.57	3.09
Sandoval, Edgardo	R-R	6-0	170	7-9-96	0	0	2.45	1	1	0	0	4	4	2	1	0	1	5	.250	.429	.111	12.27	4.70
Sierra, Miguelangel	R-R	5-11	201	12-2-97	0	0	0.00	1	0	0	0	1	0	0	0	0	1	0	.000	.000	.000	9.00	9.00
Solomon, Peter	R-R	6-4	201	8-16-96	0	0	2.35	2	2	0	0	8	7	2	2	1	4	14	.241	.357	.133	16.43	4.70
Torres, Jojanse	R-R	6-1	175	8-4-95	9	0	1.94	17	9	1	1	79	50	19	17	2	38	81	.178	.161	.196	9.27	4.35
Whitley, Forrest	R-R	6-7	195	9-15-97	1	0	2.16	2	2	0	0	8	4	2	2	0	1	11	.138	.177	.083	11.88	1.08

HOUSTON ASTROS

Fielding

Catcher

	PCT	G	PO	A	E	DP	PB
Castro	1.000	4	32	7	0	0	1
Flores	1.000	1	14	2	0	0	1
Manea	.999	59	633	38	1	3	1
Papierski	.999	67	700	70	1	8	6
Shaver	.989	9	80	9	1	2	2

First Base

	PCT	G	PO	A	E	DP
Adams	.991	66	417	31	4	36
Beer	.981	16	98	4	2	5
Hensley	1.000	5	39	1	0	2
Manea	.000	1	0	0	0	0
Matijevic	1.000	2	17	0	0	0
Schreiber	.994	45	319	27	2	17
Shaver	.960	9	67	5	3	4
Sierra	1.000	1	3	0	0	1

Second Base

	PCT	G	PO	A	E	DP
Angarita	.923	23	26	34	5	4
Arauz	1.000	6	8	11	0	5
Castro	.930	19	15	25	3	4
Pena	.957	11	21	24	2	6
Pineda	1.000	2	3	0	0	0
Sierra	.948	46	54	73	7	21
Valdez	.978	36	42	89	3	11

Third Base

	PCT	G	PO	A	E	DP
Adams	.857	19	9	21	5	2
Arauz	.931	18	17	37	4	6
Hensley	.891	23	11	30	5	0
Pena	1.000	1	0	2	0	0
Shaver	.789	39	12	44	15	3
Sierra	1.000	14	6	22	0	1
Valdez	.948	29	16	39	3	8

Shortstop

	PCT	G	PO	A	E	DP
Angarita	.000	1	0	0	0	0
Arauz	.968	62	69	113	6	24
Pena	.964	29	30	50	3	7
Sierra	.940	49	40	85	8	13

Outfield

	PCT	G	PO	A	E	DP
Adolph	.985	42	63	1	1	1
Angarita	1.000	5	11	0	0	0
Beer	.960	15	24	0	1	0
Costes	.971	27	30	3	1	0
De La Cruz	.935	40	55	3	4	0
Julks	.953	87	139	2	7	0
Matijevic	.000	1	0	0	0	0
Meyers	.981	85	198	5	4	3
Rodriguez	1.000	6	11	0	0	0
Schreiber	.978	28	42	2	1	1
Stevenson	.933	22	40	2	3	1
Taylor	.974	65	109	2	3	1
Valdez	1.000	1	1	0	0	0

QUAD CITIES RIVER BANDITS

LOW CLASS A

MIDWEST LEAGUE

Batting

	B-T	HT	WT	DOB	AVG	vLH	vRH	G	AB	R	H	2B	3B	HR	RBI	BB	HBP	SH	SF	SO	SB	CS	SLG	OBP
Abreu, Wilyer	L-L	6-0	180	6-24-99	.271	.313	.264	35	122	13	33	7	2	1	6	14	2	0	0	29	4	5	.385	.355
Adolph, Ross	L-R	6-1	203	12-17-96	.223	.200	.228	71	238	45	53	15	5	6	24	37	12	0	1	99	9	8	.403	.354
Biermann, Zach	L-L	6-3	225	6-2-97	.194	.273	.177	19	62	7	12	4	0	2	8	2	3	0	0	26	0	0	.355	.254
Campos, Oscar	R-R	5-10	170	12-8-96	.295	.313	.292	54	200	21	59	10	0	4	35	7	2	0	2	28	5	1	.405	.322
Castro, Ruben	L-R	5-10	182	7-10-96	.255	.333	.250	17	51	10	13	3	0	0	4	13	0	0	2	15	4	0	.314	.394
Costes, Marty	R-R	5-9	205	12-18-95	.291	.286	.293	28	103	13	30	3	4	2	20	13	2	0	1	16	5	2	.456	.378
Dawson, Trey	R-R	6-0	177	10-2-96	.206	.172	.213	112	378	49	78	16	2	4	47	40	7	0	1	112	11	8	.291	.293
Dennis, Austin	R-R	5-11	170	6-6-97	.240	.222	.243	105	396	60	95	15	5	3	41	38	6	0	4	78	23	7	.326	.313
Hensley, David	R-R	6-6	190	3-28-96	.238	.226	.241	80	290	40	69	11	3	6	28	25	0	0	3	72	11	4	.359	.296
Holderbach, Alex	R-R	6-0	205	12-26-96	.242	.220	.247	64	219	24	53	5	0	6	24	19	0	0	2	69	1	1	.347	.300
Kessinger, Grae	R-R	6-2	200	8-25-97	.224	.160	.235	50	170	25	38	6	0	2	17	26	3	0	2	32	8	2	.294	.333
Lacroix, Jonathan	L-R	6-1	195	2-8-97	.222	.152	.234	65	225	29	50	12	3	1	29	25	5	0	3	69	7	7	.316	.310
Lee, AJ	R-R	6-0	180	5-26-97	.146	.143	.147	15	41	0	6	1	0	0	4	5	1	0	0	20	1	1	.171	.255
Machado, Carlos	R-R	6-2	170	6-5-98	.206	.143	.216	46	160	15	33	4	1	1	15	2	2	0	0	28	12	3	.263	.226
Marquez, Orlando	R-R	5-10	180	3-12-96	.179	.500	.091	9	28	2	5	3	0	0	4	1	0	0	2	10	0	0	.286	.194
McKenna, Alex	R-R	6-2	200	9-6-97	.252	.262	.250	65	238	22	60	7	1	1	20	20	7	0	1	77	7	9	.303	.327
Nix, James	R-R	6-4	220	5-8-98	.000	.000	.000	3	10	1	0	0	0	0	0	2	0	0	0	3	0	0	.000	.167
Nova, Freudis	R-R	6-1	180	1-12-00	.259	.381	.238	75	282	35	73	20	1	3	29	15	2	0	0	68	10	7	.369	.301
Pena, Jeremy	R-R	6-0	179	9-22-97	.293	.245	.306	66	242	44	71	8	4	5	41	35	6	0	5	57	17	6	.422	.389
Pineda, Andy	L-R	6-1	165	11-11-96	.250	.091	.303	13	44	3	11	1	0	0	2	3	0	0	1	14	3	2	.273	.292
Rodriguez, Ramiro	L-L	5-10	145	2-2-98	.217	.150	.227	50	161	24	35	7	3	2	18	35	4	0	7	37	15	10	.335	.358
Salazar, Cesar	L-R	5-9	185	3-15-96	.262	.324	.252	71	248	28	65	16	1	3	39	17	8	0	6	41	5	3	.371	.323
Schreiber, Scott	R-R	6-3	230	10-13-95	.290	.370	.260	29	100	20	29	8	0	3	18	20	1	0	1	25	5	0	.460	.410
Stubbs, C.J.	R-R	6-3	200	11-12-96	.328	.143	.353	16	58	7	19	5	0	4	16	3	1	0	0	15	2	2	.621	.371
Valdez, Enmanuel	L-R	5-9	171	12-28-98	.275	.261	.278	33	120	23	33	11	0	3	20	16	3	0	0	21	2	3	.442	.374
Wielansky, Michael	R-R	6-2	175	3-18-97	.254	.333	.242	61	209	33	53	9	4	2	25	24	5	0	4	43	4	2	.364	.345

Pitching

	B-T	HT	WT	DOB	W	L	ERA	G	GS	CG	SV	IP	H	R	ER	HR	BB	SO	AVG	vLH	vRH	K/9	BB/9
Bellozo, Valente	R-R	5-10	170	1-4-00	0	1	2.77	3	1	0	1	13	10	4	4	0	2	11	.208	.105	.276	7.62	1.38
Bermudez, Jonathan	L-L	6-2	237	10-16-95	6	1	4.10	18	10	0	0	68	63	32	31	4	26	79	.248	.278	.240	10.46	3.44
Billingsley, Jacob	R-R	5-11	185	7-27-94	0	0	4.91	2	0	0	0	4	4	3	2	0	3	7	.250	.286	.222	17.18	7.36
Bravo, Jose	R-R	6-3	213	6-10-97	5	5	3.79	19	15	1	1	93	76	44	39	9	20	83	.219	.193	.238	8.06	1.94
Cabral, Riley	R-R	5-11	211	1-25-97	1	0	3.95	16	0	0	6	27	25	13	12	0	16	26	.255	.308	.220	8.56	5.27
Castellanos, Humberto	R-R	5-11	218	4-3-98	3	0	3.22	14	0	0	4	36	29	16	13	4	6	46	.213	.333	.100	11.39	1.49
Ceballos, Yeremi	L-L	6-2	165	12-21-98	0	0	2.70	2	0	0	0	3	1	1	1	0	6	5	.091	.000	.111	13.50	16.20
Chavez, Lupe	R-R	6-2	150	12-3-97	0	2	4.56	6	5	0	1	26	29	14	13	1	16	24	.287	.250	.327	8.42	5.61
Cody, Danny	R-R	6-3	175	3-6-97	0	1	10.13	2	0	0	0	3	5	4	3	0	5	3	.417	.500	.400	10.13	16.88
Collado, Willy	R-R	6-2	175	3-30-98	1	0	2.35	4	0	0	0	8	5	2	2	1	2	9	.185	.250	.133	10.57	2.35
Conine, Brett	R-R	6-3	210	10-16-96	3	2	1.91	6	5	0	0	33	18	8	7	3	6	40	.162	.098	.212	10.91	1.64
Conn, Devin	R-R	5-11	169	4-3-97	2	2	3.99	33	0	0	5	59	41	31	26	0	41	67	.200	.238	.174	10.28	6.29
Daniels, Brett	R-R	6-0	194	2-25-96	7	6	2.10	21	15	0	2	103	76	27	24	5	44	105	.208	.209	.207	9.20	3.86
De Paula, Luis	R-R	6-0	160	11-15-96	1	0	4.50	11	0	0	1	22	20	12	11	1	14	24	.253	.417	.116	9.82	5.73
Deason, Cody	R-R	6-4	214	12-26-96	5	3	3.84	11	11	0	0	60	42	24	22	3	31	76	.195	.156	.227	11.34	4.62
Dubin, Shawn	R-R	6-1	154	9-6-95	1	0	0.75	3	1	0	2	12	7	2	1	0	4	19	.167	.191	.143	14.25	3.00
Freure, R.J.	R-R	6-1	210	7-6-97	5	7	4.08	21	14	0	3	88	67	48	40	8	61	114	.213	.188	.231	11.62	6.22
Garcia, Luis	R-R	6-1	216	12-13-96	4	0	2.93	9	6	0	1	43	23	17	14	4	16	60	.153	.159	.148	12.56	3.35
Gayle, Garrett	R-R	6-1	208	8-2-97	1	1	2.38	6	0	0	3	11	8	4	3	2	3	14	.200	.177	.217	11.12	2.38
Gonzalez, Joey	R-R	5-11	174	1-10-97	3	1	2.52	15	0	0	1	36	31	13	10	4	15	31	.230	.192	.253	7.82	3.79
Hansen, Austin	R-R	6-0	195	8-25-96	4	1	0.86	9	7	0	1	42	20	4	4	1	19	52	.140	.170	.122	11.23	4.10

Henderson, Layne	R-R	6-4	200	6-8-96	2	2	2.84	15	0	0	1	25	23	10	8	1	10	42	.235	.149	.314	14.92	3.55
Lopez, Juan Pablo	L-L	6-4	170	2-17-99	1	0	2.25	1	0	0	0	4	3	1	1	0	2	3	.200	.167	.222	6.75	4.50
Martes, Francis	R-R	6-1	225	11-24-95	0	1	6.75	1	1	0	0	3	1	2	2	1	3	6	.111	.200	.000	20.25	10.13
Martin, Hunter	R-R	6-1	195	12-14-94	0	1	3.05	12	0	0	1	21	17	12	7	1	12	24	.221	.259	.200	10.45	5.23
Moclair, Mark	R-R	6-2	205	3-13-97	0	2	7.04	3	2	0	0	8	4	6	6	0	9	11	.160	.214	.091	12.91	10.57
Paulino, Hansel	R-R	6-2	170	1-3-96	0	1	2.25	2	0	0	0	4	3	4	1	0	3	4	.188	.143	.222	9.00	6.75
Ramirez, Manny	R-R	5-11	170	11-21-99	0	0	27.00	2	0	0	0	1	1	4	3	0	6	3	.200	.333	.000	27.00	54.00
Rivera, Jose Alberto	R-R	6-3	160	2-14-97	5	5	3.81	18	11	0	1	76	61	38	32	2	36	95	.222	.226	.219	11.30	4.28
Robaina, Julio	L-L	5-11	170	3-23-01	0	1	0.00	2	0	0	1	6	2	2	0	0	8	6	.111	.000	.125	9.53	12.71
Rodriguez, Nivaldo	R-R	6-1	170	4-16-97	3	1	1.16	6	6	1	0	31	23	6	4	2	4	39	.200	.196	.203	11.32	1.16
Ruppenthal, Matt	R-R	6-4	225	10-21-95	5	7	4.33	24	14	0	2	100	82	52	48	7	52	111	.220	.234	.207	10.02	4.70
Saldana, Abdiel	R-R	5-11	195	3-13-96	2	1	0.47	4	3	0	0	19	16	2	1	0	5	20	.232	.179	.268	9.31	2.33
Schroeder, Jayson	R-R	6-2	195	11-14-99	0	1	12.00	3	1	0	0	6	7	8	8	0	9	9	.280	.444	.188	13.50	13.50
Tejada, Felipe	R-R	6-1	190	2-27-98	6	1	2.80	20	7	0	1	71	47	22	22	2	44	78	.187	.164	.206	9.93	5.60
Torres, Jojanse	R-R	6-1	175	8-4-95	3	0	0.56	7	1	0	0	16	9	1	1	1	8	26	.161	.222	.132	14.63	4.50

Fielding

Catcher	PCT	G	PO	A	E	DP	PB
Campos	.996	25	213	24	1	3	1
Castro	.976	12	107	13	3	1	0
Holderbach	.991	41	432	28	4	3	5
Marquez	.946	4	33	2	2	0	0
Salazar	.993	54	517	54	4	2	4
Stubbs	1.000	7	64	3	0	0	1

First Base	PCT	G	PO	A	E	DP
Biermann	.984	15	113	7	2	8
Campos	1.000	11	64	5	0	9
Castro	1.000	2	14	0	0	1
Dawson	1.000	1	2	0	0	0
Hensley	.993	39	283	20	2	25
Holderbach	1.000	9	68	2	0	2
Marquez	1.000	1	2	0	0	0
Salazar	1.000	8	64	4	0	7
Schreiber	.988	23	143	15	2	9
Stubbs	.972	5	32	3	1	3
Wielansky	.995	29	191	12	1	18

Second Base	PCT	G	PO	A	E	DP
Dawson	.973	45	62	81	4	16
Dennis	1.000	17	21	42	0	7
Hensley	.750	1	2	1	1	1
Kessinger	1.000	7	9	13	0	1
Lee	.970	13	9	23	1	2
Nova	1.000	23	37	50	0	11
Pena	1.000	2	2	3	0	2
Valdez	.897	16	9	26	4	2
Wielansky	.984	19	28	33	1	10

Third Base	PCT	G	PO	A	E	DP
Dawson	.946	39	25	63	5	10
Dennis	.946	21	27	43	4	4
Hensley	.940	23	15	32	3	1
Kessinger	.966	19	18	39	2	5
Lee	1.000	1	2	3	0	0
Nova	.861	18	12	19	5	2
Valdez	.889	10	3	13	2	0
Wielansky	.850	10	2	15	3	4

Shortstop	PCT	G	PO	A	E	DP
Dawson	.960	22	18	30	2	6
Hensley	1.000	1	0	3	0	1
Kessinger	.988	23	29	50	1	10
Nova	.916	32	13	66	9	14
Pena	.970	60	83	114	6	19

Outfield	PCT	G	PO	A	E	DP
Abreu	.964	34	51	2	2	0
Adolph	.967	67	110	7	4	2
Biermann	1.000	2	3	0	0	0
Costes	.962	22	22	3	1	1
Dawson	1.000	4	5	0	0	0
Dennis	.974	66	108	4	3	0
Hensley	1.000	1	2	0	0	0
Lacroix	.977	48	81	4	2	2
Machado	.971	42	64	3	2	1
McKenna	.991	57	108	5	1	2
Nix	.750	3	3	0	1	0
Pineda	1.000	13	19	0	0	0
Rodriguez	.965	50	107	3	4	1
Schreiber	1.000	4	2	0	0	0
Stubbs	1.000	1	2	0	0	0
Wielansky	1.000	4	2	0	0	0

TRI-CITY VALLEYCATS
NEW YORK-PENN LEAGUE

SHORT SEASON

Batting	B-T	HT	WT	DOB	AVG	vLH	vRH	G	AB	R	H	2B	3B	HR	RBI	BB	HBP	SH	SF	SO	SB	CS	SLG	OBP
Abreu, Wilyer	L-L	6-0	180	6-24-99	.229	.125	.259	24	70	8	16	4	0	1	7	5	0	0	2	16	2	3	.329	.273
Arias, Bryan	R-R	6-0	205	6-6-97	.234	.083	.276	36	111	14	26	4	1	2	12	10	0	0	2	25	4	2	.342	.293
Barefoot, Matthew	R-L	6-0	205	9-20-97	.155	.077	.172	23	71	5	11	1	0	0	2	8	0	0	0	17	1	1	.169	.241
Biermann, Zach	L-L	6-3	225	6-2-97	.221	.158	.239	26	86	12	19	4	1	3	14	16	3	0	3	20	2	2	.395	.352
Brewer, Jordan	R-R	6-1	195	8-1-97	.130	.000	.156	16	54	5	7	0	0	1	3	2	0	0	0	6	2	0	.185	.161
Carrasco, Deury	L-R	5-9	165	9-20-99	.165	.100	.174	30	79	6	13	2	0	0	3	0	0	0	0	35	2	5	.190	.195
Carrillo, Yefri	R-R	6-2	170	1-13-01	.182	.000	.286	4	11	0	2	0	0	0	1	1	0	0	0	5	1	0	.182	.250
Ceuta, Yorbin	B-R	6-0	165	1-14-00	.083	.250	.000	4	12	0	1	0	0	0	0	1	0	0	0	2	0	0	.083	.154
Guerrero, Luis	R-R	5-11	185	11-9-98	.202	.233	.191	36	119	17	24	3	0	0	7	22	0	0	1	37	6	3	.227	.324
Kessinger, Grae	R-R	6-2	205	8-25-97	.268	.231	.286	12	41	5	11	4	0	0	3	3	1	0	0	4	1	1	.366	.333
Lee, AJ	R-R	6-0	180	5-26-97	.231	.138	.257	41	134	25	31	9	0	5	15	19	5	0	0	47	11	3	.410	.348
Lee, Korey	R-R	6-2	205	7-25-98	.268	.333	.250	64	224	31	60	6	4	3	28	28	5	0	2	49	8	5	.371	.359
Martinez, Hector	R-R	6-1	185	7-6-98	.143	.000	.200	4	14	0	2	0	0	0	1	2	0	0	0	6	2	0	.143	.250
Nix, James	R-R	6-4	220	5-8-98	.250	.333	.240	10	28	2	7	0	0	1	2	6	1	0	0	8	1	1	.250	.400
Paulino, Juan	L-R	5-11	192	12-10-97	.245	.097	.280	51	163	16	40	10	1	2	16	17	1	0	1	48	12	6	.356	.319
Pavlica, Preston	R-R	6-1	210	9-12-96	.132	.130	.132	39	129	12	17	2	0	3	7	13	1	0	1	62	6	5	.217	.215
Perez, Joe	R-R	6-2	215	8-12-99	.188	.093	.217	50	181	23	34	7	2	7	27	11	3	0	0	54	3	1	.365	.246
Perry, Nathan	L-R	6-2	195	7-7-99	.244	.218	.251	67	234	29	57	11	2	12	35	36	4	0	0	62	1	0	.462	.354
Pineda, Juan	R-R	5-10	190	1-31-98	.118	.143	.100	6	17	1	2	0	0	0	2	1	0	0	0	8	0	0	.118	.167
Ramirez, Juan	L-L	5-9	160	4-9-99	.231	.000	.263	20	65	8	15	2	0	0	2	6	0	0	0	10	6	4	.262	.296
Ramirez, Yeuris	R-R	6-0	170	11-28-98	.233	.357	.172	16	43	7	10	1	1	1	3	4	0	0	0	15	4	3	.372	.298
Reese, E.P.	L-R	5-10	175	3-4-98	.194	.238	.181	32	93	5	18	1	0	0	9	7	2	0	1	16	6	3	.204	.262
Santana, Andres	R-R	6-1	180	11-5-98	.156	.000	.172	10	32	2	5	0	0	0	2	0	0	0	0	12	0	0	.156	.156
Santana, Luis	R-R	5-8	175	7-20-99	.267	.226	.276	52	165	19	44	8	0	2	15	14	5	0	2	24	4	2	.352	.339
Stubbs, C.J.	R-R	6-3	200	11-12-96	.213	.211	.214	39	127	18	27	5	1	5	17	19	3	0	1	35	5	3	.386	.327
Urdaneta, Ronaldo	B-R	5-10	155	11-18-98	.000	--	.000	1	2	0	0	0	0	0	0	0	0	0	0	0	0	0	.000	.000

HOUSTON ASTROS

Pitching	B-T	HT	WT	DOB	W	L	ERA	G	GS	CG	SV	IP	H	R	ER	HR	BB	SO	AVG	vLH	vRH	K/9	BB/9
Barry, Shea	R-R	6-2	195	12-22-97	2	1	3.06	13	0	0	2	18	14	14	6	0	16	21	.203	.345	.100	10.70	8.15
Battenfield, Peyton	R-R	6-4	224	8-10-97	2	1	1.60	14	5	0	0	39	23	8	7	0	15	46	.167	.213	.130	10.53	3.43
Bellozo, Valente	R-R	5-10	170	1-4-00	6	0	1.39	11	4	0	0	45	25	7	7	0	10	58	.165	.170	.162	11.51	1.99
Blanco, Ronel	R-R	6-0	180	8-31-93	0	1	3.60	4	2	0	0	5	4	2	2	0	1	4	.235	.000	.333	7.20	1.80
Brown, Hunter	R-R	6-2	203	8-29-98	2	2	4.56	12	6	0	0	24	13	12	12	0	18	33	.157	.184	.133	12.55	6.85
Ceballos, Yeremi	L-L	6-2	165	12-21-98	0	0	8.00	6	0	0	1	9	7	8	8	2	5	11	.206	.100	.250	11.00	5.00
Chavez, Jervic	L-L	6-0	175	2-8-97	1	0	1.23	2	0	0	0	7	1	1	1	0	5	5	.048	.000	.059	6.14	6.14
Chavez, Lupe	R-R	6-2	150	12-3-97	0	1	1.37	5	2	0	1	20	14	4	3	1	6	20	.200	.313	.167	9.15	2.75
Cobos, Franny	R-R	5-9	170	2-1-01	1	0	0.71	4	1	0	0	13	5	4	1	0	8	13	.116	.000	.185	9.24	5.68
Cody, Danny	R-R	6-3	175	3-6-97	0	0	3.29	7	0	0	1	14	12	10	5	0	4	13	.226	.294	.194	8.56	2.63
De Paula, Brayan	L-L	6-3	175	6-25-99	1	0	0.00	2	0	0	0	5	2	1	0	0	2	5	.111	.000	.154	9.00	3.60
De Paula, Luis	R-R	6-0	160	11-15-96	0	1	4.00	5	0	0	0	9	5	5	4	0	7	8	.172	.167	.177	8.00	7.00
Figueroa, Miguel	R-R	6-2	203	3-22-97	1	2	5.40	11	0	0	0	15	14	12	9	3	14	18	.241	.304	.200	10.80	8.40
Gayle, Garrett	R-R	6-1	208	8-2-97	0	0	2.25	5	0	0	1	8	8	2	2	0	6	10	.276	.111	.350	11.25	6.75
Gusto, Ryan	R-R	6-4	205	3-11-99	0	1	1.64	3	2	0	0	11	4	2	2	0	4	13	.114	.333	.094	10.64	3.27
Henley, Blair	R-R	6-3	190	5-14-97	1	1	1.60	11	2	0	1	34	29	9	6	1	8	46	.228	.222	.233	12.30	2.14
Horrell, Michael	R-R	6-3	195	12-18-96	2	0	7.02	14	0	0	1	17	24	16	13	2	8	20	.333	.292	.354	10.80	4.32
Lopez, Jairo	R-R	5-11	150	11-21-00	2	2	1.71	7	2	0	0	26	10	5	5	0	16	36	.116	.147	.096	12.30	5.47
Lopez, Juan Pablo	L-L	6-4	170	2-17-99	2	4	3.64	13	5	0	1	54	44	25	22	5	18	57	.217	.170	.231	9.44	2.98
Macuare, Angel	R-R	6-2	188	3-3-00	1	2	5.87	10	6	0	1	31	27	21	20	1	22	34	.239	.229	.244	9.98	6.46
McDonald, Cole	L-R	6-4	220	3-11-97	1	0	2.59	9	3	0	0	24	17	9	7	3	15	27	.198	.192	.200	9.99	5.55
Mejias, Christian	R-R	6-0	160	5-19-99	2	3	5.72	12	3	0	0	39	36	26	25	2	20	48	.238	.280	.218	10.98	4.58
Mushinski, Parker	L-L	6-0	218	11-22-95	0	1	7.71	2	2	0	0	5	6	5	4	0	3	4	.316	.429	.250	7.71	5.79
Paulino, Hansel	R-R	6-2	170	1-3-96	2	1	1.42	4	0	0	0	6	4	2	1	1	0	10	.182	.250	.167	14.21	0.00
Paulino, Juan	L-R	5-11	192	12-10-97	0	0	0.00	1	0	0	0	2	0	0	0	0	0	0	.000	.000	.000	0.00	0.00
Plumlee, Peyton	R-R	6-3	201	2-10-97	0	1	3.86	9	0	0	2	14	10	7	6	0	7	12	.204	.250	.182	7.71	4.50
Ramirez, Juan	L-L	5-9	160	4-9-99	0	0	0.00	1	0	0	0	1	0	0	0	0	0	1	.000	.000	.000	9.00	0.00
Ramirez, Manny	R-R	5-11	170	11-21-99	0	3	4.38	13	7	0	0	37	28	23	18	0	40	50	.200	.212	.193	12.16	9.73
Robaina, Julio	L-L	5-11	170	3-23-01	0	1	5.14	3	0	0	1	7	8	5	4	0	5	10	.286	.000	.381	12.86	6.43
Saldana, Abdiel	R-R	5-11	195	3-13-96	0	1	27.00	1	1	0	0	2	8	6	6	0	0	2	.571	.667	.400	9.00	0.00
Sandoval, Edgardo	R-R	6-0	170	7-9-96	2	3	8.80	9	2	0	0	31	43	35	30	2	15	28	.328	.237	.403	8.22	4.40
Schroeder, Jayson	R-R	6-2	195	11-14-99	0	4	8.53	6	4	0	0	13	9	12	12	1	23	11	.333	.414	.250	7.82	16.34
Serrano, Kyle	R-R	6-1	190	7-6-95	0	4	7.71	14	13	0	0	14	11	19	12	1	26	23	.208	.250	.189	14.79	16.71
West, Derek	R-R	6-5	230	12-2-96	1	1	6.75	13	2	0	0	29	26	27	22	1	21	25	.250	.261	.241	7.67	6.44

Fielding

C: Lee 30, Paulino 11, Perry 26, Stubbs 13. **1B:** Arias 4, Biermann 20, Kessinger 1, Lee 2, Paulino 17, Perez 8, Perry 18, Stubbs 11. **2B:** Arias 9, Carrasco 4, Ceuta 3, Kessinger 1, Lee 14, Paulino 9, Ramirez 1, Santana 37, Urdaneta 1. **3B:** Arias 9, Carrasco 3, Kessinger 1, Lee 1, Perez 41, Pineda 3, Ramirez 9, Santana 15. **SS:** Arias 14, Carrasco 20, Ceuta 1, Kessinger 10, Lee 27, Ramirez 4, Santana 1. **OF:** Abreu 23, Arias 2, Barefoot 19, Biermann 6, Brewer 13, Carrillo 4, Guerrero 36, Lee 5, Martinez 3, Nix 9, Paulino 10, Pavlica 37, Pineda 3, Ramirez 19, Reese 31, Santana 9, Stubbs 7.

GCL ASTROS   ROOKIE
GULF COAST LEAGUE

Batting	B-T	HT	WT	DOB	AVG	vLH	vRH	G	AB	R	H	2B	3B	HR	RBI	BB	HBP	SH	SF	SO	SB	CS	SLG	OBP
Alvarez, Jose	R-R	6-1	180	6-4-00	.276	.250	.280	38	127	15	35	5	2	1	17	11	2	0	1	25	1	0	.370	.340
Angarita, Alfredo	L-R	5-10	155	11-16-96	.258	.000	.267	8	31	2	8	0	0	0	2	3	0	0	0	6	1	0	.258	.324
Barber, Colin	L-L	6-0	185	12-4-00	.263	.208	.280	28	99	19	26	5	1	2	6	19	1	0	0	29	2	1	.394	.387
Bermudez, Javier	R-R	5-11	155	1-2-99	.385	.000	.417	4	13	3	5	0	0	0	2	0	0	0	0	3	1	0	.385	.467
Carrillo, Yefri	R-R	6-2	170	1-13-01	.149	.000	.170	24	67	11	10	2	0	1	5	8	3	0	1	33	6	1	.224	.266
Castillo, Abraham	R-R	6-0	180	12-5-00	.173	.000	.189	28	81	10	14	2	0	1	9	14	1	0	1	29	1	1	.235	.299
Castillo, Gerry	R-R	5-10	170	10-3-97	.304	.412	.269	23	69	16	21	5	0	1	12	10	12	1	0	11	3	0	.420	.415
Ceuta, Yorbin	R-R	6-0	165	1-14-00	.232	.286	.221	38	125	10	29	7	1	2	19	8	4	1	7	23	1	1	.352	.285
Cortabarria, Yimmi	R-R	6-2	175	1-10-01	.267	.231	.274	22	75	12	20	6	0	3	15	11	2	1	0	27	1	1	.467	.375
Espinosa, Rolando	R-R	6-0	177	1-5-01	.202	.276	.180	42	129	18	26	8	2	1	14	16	5	0	1	43	9	3	.318	.311
Giron, Adonis	R-R	5-10	190	2-22-01	.191	.133	.203	23	84	8	16	4	1	1	4	2	3	0	0	30	1	1	.298	.236
Guerrero, Luis	R-R	5-11	185	11-9-98	.282	.000	.306	11	39	2	11	3	0	1	4	4	2	0	0	11	0	1	.436	.378
Jordan, Dexter	R-R	6-0	193	10-30-99	.121	.071	.135	22	66	10	8	2	0	1	4	12	2	0	0	24	1	0	.197	.275
Krabbe, Tyler	R-R	6-2	220	1-13-97	.267	.231	.273	24	90	12	24	6	0	1	8	7	1	0	0	23	0	0	.367	.327
Mascai, Victor	L-R	6-2	188	2-10-01	.191	.333	.167	7	21	2	4	1	0	1	3	6	0	0	0	10	1	0	.381	.370
Mendoza, Jose	R-R	5-11	165	6-19-01	.224	.200	.225	26	85	9	19	1	0	0	5	14	1	0	0	25	3	2	.235	.340
Mendoza, Sean	B-R	5-8	150	6-2-00	.235	.227	.236	40	132	18	31	6	0	0	9	19	4	0	2	17	10	2	.280	.344
Nix, James	R-R	6-4	220	5-8-98	.261	.000	.300	8	23	3	6	0	0	1	3	2	0	0	0	11	0	0	.391	.393
Pinto, Franklin	R-R	6-1	160	4-26-01	.277	.238	.286	36	112	21	31	5	2	2	21	10	3	1	2	15	4	0	.411	.347
Ramirez, Yeuris	R-R	6-0	170	11-28-98	.184	.333	.156	14	38	9	7	2	0	2	5	8	5	0	0	15	4	1	.395	.392
Rivas, Rainier	L-L	6-3	203	6-29-01	.351	.286	.367	10	37	1	13	1	0	0	6	1	0	0	0	10	0	0	.378	.415
Rodriguez, Nerio	R-R	6-2	205	9-21-99	.263	.143	.284	31	95	17	25	8	0	3	13	19	1	0	0	29	0	0	.442	.391
Urdaneta, Ronaldo	B-R	5-10	155	11-18-98	.250	.000	.273	5	12	0	3	0	0	0	1	2	0	0	0	2	2	1	.250	.357

Pitching	B-T	HT	WT	DOB	W	L	ERA	G	GS	CG	SV	IP	H	R	ER	HR	BB	SO	AVG	vLH	vRH	K/9	BB/9
Bello, Daniel	L-L	6-2	197	1-8-97	2	1	6.30	5	0	0	0	10	9	8	7	1	9	8	.237	.125	.267	7.20	8.10
Billingsley, Jacob	R-R	5-11	185	7-27-94	1	0	0.00	2	1	0	0	1	1	0	0	0	1	4	.100	.167	.000	12.00	3.00
Bojorquez, Gerardo	R-R	6-3	195	10-23-97	0	0	0.00	1	1	0	0	1	3	5	0	1	3	0	.500	.500	.500	0.00	13.50
Casey, Chandler	R-R	6-2	195	5-30-96	0	0	0.00	5	1	0	2	6	2	0	0	0	3	4	.111	.333	.000	6.35	4.76
Ceballos, Yeremi	L-L	6-2	165	12-21-98	0	0	0.00	2	0	0	1	3	1	0	0	0	3	0	.111	.000	.125	0.00	10.13

Name	B-T	HT	WT	DOB	W	L	ERA	G	GS	CG	SV	IP	H	R	ER	HR	BB	SO	AVG	vLH	vRH	K/9	BB/9
Chavez, Jervic	L-L	6-0	175	2-8-97	2	2	2.89	11	0	0	1	28	21	10	9	3	12	31	.202	.185	.208	9.96	3.86
Cobos, Franny	R-R	5-9	170	2-1-01	2	1	2.22	8	1	0	0	24	23	8	6	1	9	18	.258	.278	.254	6.66	3.33
Cody, Danny	R-R	6-3	175	3-6-97	0	0	2.70	4	0	0	0	7	4	4	2	0	4	5	.174	.125	.200	6.75	5.40
De Paula, Brayan	L-L	6-3	175	6-25-99	0	2	6.99	11	3	0	1	28	26	25	22	4	18	34	.241	.281	.224	10.80	5.72
Deetz, Dean	R-R	6-1	195	11-29-93	1	0	3.00	2	0	0	0	3	3	1	1	0	0	5	.273	.250	.286	15.00	0.00
Dickey, Kevin	B-L	6-4	195	3-31-98	2	1	2.70	11	2	0	1	27	18	13	8	2	18	34	.190	.100	.213	11.48	6.08
Drennan, Whit	L-L	6-7	190	2-25-97	1	1	9.45	10	0	0	0	13	14	14	14	0	10	17	.292	.214	.324	11.48	6.75
Ferrell, Justin	R-R	6-7	205	4-21-94	1	0	0.00	2	1	0	0	4	3	0	0	0	0	3	.231	.200	.250	7.36	0.00
Gusto, Ryan	R-R	6-4	205	3-11-99	0	0	2.45	2	1	0	0	4	2	2	1	0	3	6	.143	.111	.200	14.73	7.36
Henley, Blair	R-R	6-3	190	5-14-97	0	0	0.00	1	1	0	0	3	1	0	0	0	1	4	.100	.000	.200	12.00	3.00
Holcomb, Kevin	R-R	6-5	210	1-5-99	0	4	6.30	8	2	0	0	20	21	16	14	3	15	14	.280	.211	.304	6.30	6.75
Ivey, Tyler	R-R	6-4	195	5-12-96	0	0	0.00	2	2	0	0	3	0	0	0	0	3	5	.000	.000	.000	15.00	9.00
Jimenez, Alfredi	R-R	6-1	175	10-19-99	0	0	3.78	7	4	0	0	17	12	7	7	5	3	27	.200	.167	.214	14.58	1.62
Lopez, Jairo	R-R	5-11	150	11-21-00	2	1	1.09	6	2	0	0	25	15	9	3	1	7	25	.163	.273	.148	9.12	2.55
Martes, Francis	R-R	6-1	225	11-24-95	0	1	6.75	2	2	0	0	3	4	3	2	0	2	7	.333	.250	.375	23.63	6.75
McDonald, Cole	L-R	6-1	220	3-11-97	0	0	0.00	1	1	0	0	2	0	0	0	0	0	2	.000	.000	.000	9.00	0.00
Medina, Fredy	R-R	5-10	160	9-26-97	0	2	12.27	7	3	0	0	7	9	14	10	0	11	11	.290	.364	.250	13.50	13.50
Mejias, Christian	R-R	6-0	160	5-19-99	0	0	3.38	2	0	0	1	3	1	1	1	0	1	2	.125	.000	.143	6.75	3.38
Mushinski, Parker	L-L	6-0	218	11-22-95	0	0	7.71	3	2	0	0	5	8	4	4	0	2	7	.348	.364	.333	13.50	3.86
Palmer, Alex	B-R	5-10	160	5-15-98	2	0	2.45	9	2	0	1	22	16	8	6	0	6	27	.200	.130	.228	11.05	2.45
Pereira, Jherson	R-R	6-2	175	1-27-97	2	0	2.00	6	0	0	1	9	3	5	2	0	8	10	.115	.222	.059	10.00	8.00
Perez, Cionel	L-L	5-11	170	4-21-96	0	0	3.18	3	3	0	0	6	6	2	2	0	3	14	.286	.125	.385	22.24	4.76
Robaina, Julio	L-L	5-11	170	3-23-01	3	1	2.48	10	1	0	0	29	21	9	8	0	12	41	.198	.171	.215	12.72	3.72
Rodgers, Brady	R-R	6-2	210	9-17-90	0	0	2.45	3	3	0	0	7	6	2	2	1	0	8	.207	.429	.136	9.82	0.00
Rodriguez, Elian	R-R	6-4	205	3-10-97	0	2	11.32	10	2	0	0	21	30	31	26	4	24	25	.341	.300	.353	10.89	10.45
Saldana, Abdiel	R-R	5-11	195	3-13-96	0	0	1.80	2	1	0	0	5	3	1	1	0	3	3	.167	.286	.091	5.40	5.40
Scheetz, Kit	L-L	5-10	185	5-18-94	0	0	33.75	2	0	0	0	1	6	5	5	0	2	2	.600	.400	.800	13.50	13.50
Schroeder, Jayson	R-R	6-2	195	11-14-99	1	0	0.00	3	1	0	0	6	3	1	0	0	5	5	.167	.143	.182	7.11	7.11
Serrano, Kyle	R-R	6-1	190	7-6-95	0	1	22.50	2	2	0	0	2	2	5	5	0	5	3	.286	.000	.333	13.50	22.50
Tamarez, Misael	R-R	6-1	162	1-16-00	1	2	2.35	7	0	0	0	15	14	8	4	1	11	18	.241	.067	.302	10.57	6.46
Taveras, Diosmerky	R-R	6-3	180	9-23-99	1	2	5.47	12	2	0	2	25	20	18	15	0	28	28	.241	.222	.255	10.22	10.22
Tokar, Heitor	R-R	6-6	256	10-25-00	1	0	2.83	12	2	0	2	35	30	13	11	2	11	29	.233	.282	.211	7.46	2.83
Whitley, Forrest	R-R	6-7	195	9-15-97	0	2	8.31	2	2	0	0	4	2	5	4	0	9	10	.125	.000	.143	20.77	18.69

Fielding

C: Alvarez 19, Castillo 13, Krabbe 9, Rodriguez 20. **1B:** Alvarez 18, Castillo 3, Castillo 9, Ceuta 5, Mascai 5, Mendoza 2, Ramirez 11, Urdaneta 3. **2B:** Angarita 6, Ceuta 7, Espinosa 13, Jordan 18, Mendoza 4, Mendoza 10. **3B:** Ceuta 4, Espinosa 27, Mendoza 2, Mendoza 18, Ramirez 4. **SS:** Bermudez 3, Ceuta 20, Espinosa 2, Mendoza 11, Mendoza 20. **OF:** Angarita 1, Barber 26, Carrillo 21, Castillo 25, Cortabarria 21, Giron 18, Guerrero 9, Mendoza 1, Nix 7, Pinto 34, Rivas 9.

DSL ASTROS   *ROOKIE*
DOMINICAN SUMMER LEAGUE

Batting	B-T	HT	WT	DOB	AVG	vLH	vRH	G	AB	R	H	2B	3B	HR	RBI	BB	HBP	SH	SF	SO	SB	CS	SLG	OBP
Balogh, Ricardo	B-R	6-3	175	7-9-02	.186	.222	.179	47	102	12	19	0	0	0	11	15	5	3	1	38	3	3	.186	.317
Diaz, Omar	L-L	6-1	180	9-23-01	.230	.115	.250	56	174	30	40	6	2	1	15	29	2	1	2	43	6	6	.305	.343
Gonzalez, Cristian	R-R	6-3	180	10-22-01	.214	.114	.234	63	206	32	44	6	3	1	21	19	4	0	3	56	11	2	.286	.289
Grullon, Sebastian	R-R	6-1	170	7-19-01	.222	.172	.237	44	126	15	28	3	2	0	11	17	1	0	0	38	4	5	.278	.319
Guilamo, Freddy	R-R	5-11	160	12-10-00	.247	.286	.241	40	93	18	23	4	1	1	12	13	1	0	0	28	3	2	.344	.402
Hurtado, Carlos	R-R	6-0	160	5-18-01	.262	.333	.248	54	172	22	45	7	3	1	19	15	3	1	2	28	7	0	.355	.328
Jose, Jairo	R-R	6-0	160	5-13-02	.108	.111	.107	21	37	7	4	0	0	0	1	10	1	0	0	23	3	0	.108	.313
Liranzo, Jesus	R-R	6-1	185	12-3-01	.203	.188	.206	30	79	15	16	0	1	4	9	14	4	0	0	30	5	3	.380	.351
Lopez, Jonarkys	R-R	5-11	160	8-13-01	.222	--	.222	7	9	4	2	0	2	0	2	1	0	0	0	2	0	0	.667	.300
Machandy, Roilan	R-R	6-0	170	5-18-01	.127	.111	.130	25	63	12	8	0	0	0	5	14	5	3	0	24	16	2	.127	.329
Marte, Junior	R-R	6-2	165	4-14-00	.145	.200	.132	31	83	9	12	1	1	0	7	19	0	0	2	21	4	0	.181	.298
Martinez, Yohander	R-R	5-10	175	1-8-02	.313	.326	.310	66	214	36	67	6	3	1	25	40	8	0	0	27	19	11	.383	.439
Monzon, Andres	R-R	5-11	152	12-5-01	.191	.061	.217	65	194	33	37	4	4	0	24	19	15	1	3	43	19	5	.253	.307
Morillo, Enmanuel	R-R	6-0	175	12-6-00	.219	.500	.154	14	32	4	7	3	1	0	3	2	0	0	0	11	0	0	.375	.265
Ortiz, Ayendy	B-R	6-1	170	3-9-02	.174	.177	.173	39	98	6	17	4	0	1	10	10	0	0	0	46	4	1	.245	.250
Palma, Miguel	R-R	5-10	170	1-4-02	.228	.400	.198	51	136	22	31	7	1	4	15	19	13	1	1	35	10	5	.382	.373
Perez, Frank	R-R	6-2	180	12-24-01	.151	.200	.136	39	86	10	13	2	0	1	9	6	8	0	2	37	7	3	.209	.265
Ramirez, Tomas	R-R	6-1	172	11-21-01	.183	.063	.227	25	60	6	11	2	0	2	6	9	0	0	2	25	2	2	.317	.290
Toro, Ricardo	R-R	6-1	170	2-24-01	.245	.324	.224	58	159	15	39	4	2	2	24	16	8	0	3	28	6	5	.333	.339

Pitching	B-T	HT	WT	DOB	W	L	ERA	G	GS	CG	SV	IP	H	R	ER	HR	BB	SO	AVG	vLH	vRH	K/9	BB/9
Batista, Edinson	R-R	6-2	185	5-19-02	2	0	4.00	15	0	0	2	36	33	17	16	0	24	44	.241	.244	.239	11.00	6.00
Bello, Daniel	L-L	6-2	197	1-8-97	1	0	2.81	5	2	0	0	16	13	11	5	0	11	17	.217	.222	.216	9.56	6.19
Beltre, Reimy	R-R	6-3	170	1-2-00	1	0	1.69	10	5	0	1	32	14	8	6	1	21	44	.125	.188	.100	12.25	5.85
Betances, Jose	R-R	6-0	170	10-17-99	1	2	11.64	18	0	0	2	19	22	28	25	1	36	17	.310	.333	.302	7.91	16.76
Calderon, Carlos	R-R	6-0	175	10-4-01	4	3	4.20	14	6	0	0	45	42	27	21	0	24	44	.250	.333	.196	8.80	4.80
De Los Santos, Juan	R-R	6-0	140	3-8-00	2	0	0.00	6	2	0	1	14	5	1	0	0	8	8	.111	.188	.069	5.14	5.14
Eusebio, Marcos	R-R	6-1	180	9-5-00	1	1	4.91	3	0	0	0	4	4	2	2	1	4	4	.267	.429	.125	9.82	9.82
Garcia, Ronny	R-R	6-3	170	12-2-99	3	3	2.63	19	1	0	5	38	27	14	11	0	17	29	.208	.279	.172	6.93	4.06
Jose, Jairo	R-R	6-0	160	5-13-02	0	0	0.00	2	0	0	0	1	0	0	0	0	0	1	.000	--	.000	6.75	0.00
Leon, Ricardo	L-L	6-4	165	3-26-01	1	3	7.62	11	5	0	1	26	21	25	22	0	31	31	.223	.154	.235	10.73	10.73
Martinez, Bryan	L-L	6-5	205	5-25-97	1	1	3.86	5	3	0	0	19	22	10	8	0	7	14	.293	.353	.276	6.75	3.38

Melendez, Jaime	L-R	5-8	170	9-26-01	1	3	2.86	11	5	0	0	28	20	9	9	0	16	39	.204	.235	.188	12.39	5.08
Mezquita, Cristofer	L-L	6-0	175	6-6-00	0	1	5.13	18	0	0	5	26	22	19	15	0	25	38	.220	.238	.215	12.99	8.54
Molero, Jeremy	R-R	6-2	170	11-8-99	4	0	2.19	14	8	0	0	49	24	14	12	1	37	80	.142	.143	.142	14.59	6.75
Nodal, Jose	L-L	6-3	195	7-16-02	1	3	3.26	13	6	0	0	39	32	22	14	2	31	42	.230	.143	.252	9.78	7.22
Pacheco, Daniel	R-R	5-10	160	12-4-01	1	2	6.45	8	3	0	0	22	28	18	16	1	15	16	.322	.250	.356	6.45	6.04
Padilla, Miguel	R-R	6-2	180	4-13-02	4	1	2.08	19	0	0	1	26	20	10	6	2	16	26	.222	.161	.254	9.00	5.54
Pereira, Jherson	R-R	6-2	175	1-27-97	2	0	1.60	9	4	0	2	34	20	7	6	1	5	35	.168	.235	.141	9.36	1.34
Ramirez, Johangel	R-R	6-2	193	9-10-01	0	0	27.00	1	0	0	0	1	4	6	4	0	2	1	.444	.000	.800	6.75	13.50
Reina, Fabricio	R-R	6-3	175	2-26-00	1	3	3.80	14	8	0	0	47	38	27	20	0	25	45	.221	.167	.250	8.56	4.75
Subero, Danny	R-R	6-4	194	11-2-01	1	2	3.41	10	5	0	0	29	23	12	11	0	23	25	.228	.326	.155	7.76	7.14
Tamarez, Misael	R-R	6-1	162	1-16-00	2	2	2.70	7	4	0	0	23	20	10	7	0	13	26	.230	.138	.276	10.03	5.01
Vega, Luis	R-R	6-3	165	11-16-01	2	1	2.67	14	2	0	0	30	33	13	9	1	11	33	.287	.436	.211	9.79	3.26

Fielding

C: Balogh 1, Guilamo 24, Hurtado 34, Lopez 3, Palma 21, Quintero 1, Toro 23. **1B:** Balogh 8, Diaz 2, Gonzalez 1, Guilamo 15, Hurtado 10, Marte 1, Morillo 8, Palma 15, Quintero 3, Toro 26. **2B:** Balogh 21, Gonzalez 2, Grullon 30, Lopez 1, Marte 15, Martinez 7, Morillo 3, Ortiz 21, Perez 1. **3B:** Balogh 2, Gonzalez 18, Grullon 5, Marte 13, Martinez 31, Morillo 1, Ortiz 14. **SS:** Balogh 6, Gonzalez 39, Marte 3, Martinez 27, Ortiz 4, Perez 2. **OF:** Diaz 54, Hurtado 1, Jose 18, Liranzo 27, Machandy 24, Marte 2, Monzon 63, Morillo 1, Perez 33, Ramirez 24, Toro 1.

Kansas City Royals

SEASON IN A SENTENCE: The Royals' rebuilding efforts continued with Kansas City losing 103 games in manager Ned Yost's final season, an improvement from its 104-loss season in 2018.

HIGH POINT: The bright spots were limited in 2019, but for an organization attempting to build a winning culture with its young prospects, it was encouraging to see three of the Royals' minor league affiliates—high Class A Wilmington, low Class A Lexington and Rookie-level Idaho Falls—win their respective league championships within a three-day span in September.

LOW POINT: After starting the season 2-0, the Royals immediately went on a season-worst 10-game losing streak and finished April with a 9-20 record. The lack of success in the big leagues showed in the Royals' attendance total of just under 1.5 million—the lowest attendance since 2006, when the Royals also lost 100 games.

NOTABLE ROOKIES: Ranked among the Royals' top five prospects at the beginning of 2019, Nicky Lopez was promoted to Kansas City in mid-May and split time at both middle infield positions while hitting a modest .240/.276/.325 in 103 games. Eight years after being drafted with the No. 5 overall pick and signing with the Royals for $7.5 million, outfielder Bubba Starling finally made his major league debut and hit .215/.255/.317 with four home runs in 56 games.

KEY TRANSACTIONS: Most of the Royals' moves in the offseason involved picking up veterans to fill out the roster. Players such as Billy Hamilton, Brad Boxberger and Homer Bailey were all signed as potential change-of-scenery free agents, but none finished the year in Kansas City. The most significant transactions occurred off the field, however, with David Glass selling the franchise to a group led by local businessman John Sherman for $1 billion, followed by manager Ned Yost announcing his retirement on Sept. 23.

DOWN ON THE FARM: Wilmington, Lexington and Idaho Falls all won their league championships, and it was Lexington's second consecutive South Atlantic League title. After stockpiling pitching depth in the 2018 draft, the Royals were rewarded by seeing righthander Brady Singer and lefthander Kris Bubic selected to this year's Futures Game in Cleveland. An additional premier prospect was added to the system when the Royals drafted prep shortstop Bobby Witt Jr. with the No. 2 overall pick in June.

OPENING DAY PAYROLL: $83,079,283 (25th).

PLAYERS OF THE YEAR

KYLE COOPER

MAJOR LEAGUE

Jorge Soler
OF
.265/.354/.569
Led AL in HR (48)
and SO (178)

MINOR LEAGUE

Kris Bubic
LHP
(Low A/High A)
11-5, 2.23 in 26 GS
0.97 WHIP, 185 SO

ORGANIZATION LEADERS

Batting		*Minimum 250 AB
MAJORS		
* AVG	Whit Merrifield	.303
* OPS	Jorge Soler	.922
HR	Jorge Soler	48
RBI	Jorge Soler	117
MINORS		
* AVG	Clay Dungan, Idaho Falls	.357
* OBP	Clay Dungan, Idaho Falls	.427
* SLG	Brett Phillips, Omaha	.505
* OPS	Clay Dungan, Idaho Falls	.921
R	Erick Mejia, Omaha	83
H	Erick Mejia, Omaha	134
TB	Gabriel Cancel, NW Arkansas	198
2B	Nathan Eaton, Lexington	32
3B	Brett Phillips, Omaha	13
HR	Jorge Bonifacio, Omaha	20
RBI	Eric Cole, Lexington	71
BB	Brett Phillips, Omaha	72
SO	Taylor Featherston, NW Arkansas, Omaha	173
SB	Nick Heath, NW Arkansas, Omaha	60

Pitching		#Minimum 75 IP
MAJORS		
W	Jakob Junis	9
# ERA	Brad Keller	4.19
SO	Jakob Junis	164
SV	Ian Kennedy	30
MINORS		
W	Brady Singer, Wilmington, NW Arkansas	12
L	Gerson Garabito, NW Arkansas	12
# ERA	Kris Bubic, Lexington, Wilmington	2.23
G	Gabe Speier, NW Arkansas, Omaha	47
GS	Charlie Neuweiler, Lexington	27
SV	Tad Ratliff, Wilmington	23
IP	Kris Bubic, Lexington, Wilmington	149
BB	Foster Griffin, Omaha	64
SO	Kris Bubic, Lexington, Wilmington	185
# AVG	Kris Bubic, Lexington, Wilmington	.199

General Manager: Dayton Moore. **Farm Director:** J.J. Picollo. **Scouting Director:** Lonnie Goldberg.

Class	Team	League	W	L	PCT	Finish	Manager
Majors	Kansas City Royals	American	59	103	.364	13th (15)	Ned Yost
Triple-A	Omaha Storm Chasers	Pacific Coast	59	80	.424	16th (16)	Brian Poldberg
Double-A	NW Arkansas Naturals	Texas	57	81	.413	8th (8)	Darryl Kennedy
High A	Wilmington Blue Rocks	Carolina	82	56	.594	2nd (10)	Scott Thorman
Low A	Lexington Legends	South Atlantic	68	70	.493	7th (14)	Brooks Conrad
Rookie	Burlington Royals	Appalachian	39	29	.574	2nd (10)	Chris Widger
Rookie	Idaho Falls Chukars	Pioneer	34	41	.453	6th (8)	Omar Ramirez
Rookie	AZL Royals	Arizona	33	23	.589	t-4th (21)	Tony Pena Jr.
Overall 2019 Minor League Record			372	380	.495	15th (30)	

ORGANIZATION STATISTICS

KANSAS CITY ROYALS
AMERICAN LEAGUE

Batting	B-T	HT	WT	DOB	AVG	vLH	vRH	G	AB	R	H	2B	3B	HR	RBI	BB	HBP	SH	SF	SO	SB	CS	SLG	OBP
Arteaga, Humberto	R-R	6-1	160	1-23-94	.197	.250	.174	41	122	11	24	4	0	0	4	8	2	3	0	28	1	1	.230	.258
Bonifacio, Jorge	R-R	6-1	225	6-4-93	.350	.455	.222	5	20	3	7	3	0	0	3	1	0	0	0	7	0	0	.500	.381
Cuthbert, Cheslor	R-R	6-1	210	11-16-92	.246	.317	.220	87	309	24	76	14	0	9	40	19	2	0	0	67	1	0	.379	.294
Dini, Nick	R-R	5-8	180	7-27-93	.196	.250	.143	20	56	11	11	3	0	2	6	4	1	1	1	18	0	0	.357	.270
Dozier, Hunter	R-R	6-4	220	8-22-91	.279	.281	.279	139	523	75	146	29	10	26	84	55	3	0	5	148	2	2	.522	.348
Duda, Lucas	L-R	6-4	255	2-3-86	.171	.095	.191	39	105	7	18	4	0	4	15	11	1	0	2	32	0	0	.324	.252
Gallagher, Cam	R-R	6-3	230	12-6-92	.238	.222	.244	45	126	14	30	7	0	3	12	11	3	1	1	28	0	1	.365	.312
Gordon, Alex	L-R	6-1	225	2-10-84	.266	.248	.273	150	556	77	148	31	1	13	76	51	19	1	6	100	5	3	.396	.345
Gore, Terrance	R-R	5-7	165	6-8-91	.275	.450	.161	37	51	13	14	2	1	0	1	6	1	0	0	18	13	5	.353	.362
Gutierrez, Kelvin	R-R	6-3	215	8-28-94	.260	.348	.220	20	73	4	19	2	1	1	11	5	0	0	1	24	1	0	.356	.304
Hamilton, Billy	B-R	6-0	160	9-9-90	.211	.192	.221	93	275	32	58	12	2	0	12	25	0	3	2	74	18	5	.269	.275
Lopez, Nicky	L-R	5-11	175	3-13-95	.240	.267	.230	103	379	44	91	22	2	2	30	18	1	4	0	51	1	1	.325	.276
Maldonado, Martin	R-R	6-0	230	8-16-86	.227	.206	.236	74	238	26	54	15	0	6	17	17	5	2	1	55	0	0	.366	.291
2-team total (27 Houston)					.221	.235	.214	101	322	46	71	19	0	12	27	30	6	2	1	81	0	0	.391	.298
McBroom, Ryan	R-L	6-3	235	4-9-92	.293	.280	.300	23	75	8	22	5	0	0	6	7	1	0	0	25	0	0	.360	.361
Mejia, Erick	B-R	5-11	155	11-9-94	.227	.333	.154	9	22	3	5	1	0	0	4	4	0	0	1	7	0	0	.273	.333
Merrifield, Whit	R-R	6-0	195	1-24-89	.303	.280	.312	162	681	105	206	41	10	16	74	45	5	0	4	126	20	10	.463	.348
Mondesi, Adalberto	B-R	6-1	190	7-27-95	.263	.256	.266	102	415	58	109	20	10	9	62	19	0	3	6	132	43	7	.424	.291
O'Hearn, Ryan	L-L	6-3	200	7-26-93	.195	.170	.200	105	328	32	64	13	1	14	38	39	1	0	2	99	0	1	.369	.281
Owings, Chris	R-R	5-10	185	8-12-91	.133	.114	.143	40	135	9	18	4	1	2	9	8	2	0	0	55	4	1	.222	.193
2-team total (26 Boston)					.139	.164	.124	66	180	13	25	6	1	3	14	14	2	0	0	78	5	2	.233	.209
Phillips, Brett	L-R	6-0	185	5-30-94	.139	.200	.127	30	65	7	9	2	0	2	6	10	0	2	2	23	3	0	.262	.247
Schwindel, Frank	R-R	6-1	215	6-29-92	.067	.077	.000	6	15	0	1	0	0	0	0	0	0	0	0	2	0	0	.067	.067
Soler, Jorge	R-R	6-4	230	2-25-92	.265	.259	.267	162	589	95	156	33	1	48	117	73	10	0	4	178	3	1	.569	.354
Starling, Bubba	R-R	6-4	215	8-3-92	.215	.185	.227	56	186	26	40	7	0	4	12	9	1	1	0	56	2	0	.317	.255
Viloria, Meibrys	L-R	5-11	220	2-15-97	.211	.125	.238	42	133	7	28	7	0	1	15	10	0	1	4	44	0	1	.286	.259

Pitching	B-T	HT	WT	DOB	W	L	ERA	G	GS	CG	SV	IP	H	R	ER	HR	BB	SO	AVG	vLH	vRH	K/9	BB/9
Arteaga, Humberto	R-R	6-1	160	1-23-94	0	0	5.40	1	0	0	0	2	2	1	1	1	1	0	.286	.000	.500	0.00	5.40
Bailey, Homer	R-R	6-4	223	5-3-86	7	6	4.80	18	18	0	0	90	89	49	48	12	38	81	.258	.232	.287	8.10	3.80
2-team total (13 Oakland)					13	9	4.57	31	31	0	0	163	162	84	83	21	53	149	.256	.217	.299	8.21	2.92
Barlow, Scott	R-R	6-3	215	12-18-92	3	3	4.22	61	0	0	1	70	64	33	33	6	37	92	.240	.289	.209	11.77	4.73
Barnes, Jacob	R-R	6-2	220	4-14-90	0	4	8.31	15	0	0	0	13	14	13	12	4	11	10	.264	.238	.281	6.92	7.62
Boxberger, Brad	R-R	6-2	205	5-27-88	1	3	5.40	29	0	0	1	27	25	16	16	3	17	27	.243	.222	.265	9.11	5.74
Diekman, Jake	L-L	6-4	200	1-21-87	0	6	4.75	48	0	0	0	42	33	23	22	3	23	63	.212	.213	.211	13.61	4.97
2-team total (28 Oakland)					1	7	4.65	76	0	0	0	62	49	34	32	3	39	84	.215	.224	.210	12.19	5.66
Duffy, Danny	L-L	6-3	205	12-21-88	7	6	4.34	23	23	0	0	131	125	69	63	21	46	115	.251	.257	.249	7.92	3.17
Ellis, Chris	L-R	6-5	205	9-22-92	0	0	0.00	1	0	0	0	1	1	0	0	0	1	0	.250	.000	.500	0.00	9.00
Fillmyer, Heath	R-R	6-1	195	5-16-94	0	2	8.06	12	3	0	0	22	28	20	20	6	12	15	.308	.333	.289	6.04	4.84
Flynn, Brian	L-L	6-7	255	4-19-90	2	2	5.22	11	1	0	0	29	38	18	17	2	17	22	.333	.298	.358	6.75	5.22
Gordon, Alex	L-R	6-1	225	2-10-84	0	0	19.29	2	0	0	0	2	8	5	5	1	2	0	.571	.600	.556	0.00	7.71
Hahn, Jesse	R-R	6-4	215	7-30-89	0	1	13.50	6	0	0	0	5	7	7	7	1	6	7	.333	.000	.438	13.50	11.57
Hill, Tim	R-L	6-2	200	2-10-90	2	0	3.63	46	0	0	1	40	31	17	16	4	13	39	.217	.186	.238	8.85	2.95
Junis, Jakob	R-R	6-2	225	9-16-92	9	14	5.24	31	31	0	0	175	192	108	102	31	58	164	.276	.298	.250	8.42	2.98
Keller, Brad	R-R	6-5	230	7-27-95	7	14	4.19	28	28	0	0	165	154	80	77	15	70	122	.247	.251	.243	6.64	3.81
Kennedy, Ian	R-R	6-0	205	12-19-84	3	2	3.41	63	0	0	30	63	64	24	24	6	17	73	.261	.226	.298	10.37	2.42
Lively, Ben	R-R	6-4	190	3-5-92	0	0	27.00	1	0	0	0	1	3	3	3	1	0	1	.500	.500	.500	9.00	0.00
Lopez, Jorge	R-R	6-3	195	2-10-93	4	9	6.33	39	18	0	1	124	140	94	87	27	42	109	.286	.332	.241	7.93	3.06
Lovelady, Richard	L-L	6-0	175	7-7-95	0	3	7.65	25	0	0	0	20	30	17	17	2	8	17	.353	.341	.366	7.65	3.60
McCarthy, Kevin	R-R	6-3	215	2-22-92	4	2	4.48	56	0	0	1	60	68	31	30	4	21	38	.285	.297	.277	5.67	3.13
Montgomery, Mike	L-L	6-5	215	7-1-89	2	7	4.64	13	13	0	0	64	78	37	33	12	21	51	.310	.413	.286	7.17	2.95
Newberry, Jake	R-R	6-2	195	11-20-94	1	0	3.77	27	0	0	0	31	29	13	13	7	16	29	.248	.354	.174	8.42	4.65
Owings, Chris	R-R	5-10	185	8-12-91	0	0	21.60	1	0	0	0	2	6	4	4	2	1	0	.546	.500	.667	0.00	5.40

Name	B-T	HT	WT	DOB	W	L	ERA	G	GS	CG	SV	IP	H	R	ER	HR	BB	SO	AVG	vLH	vRH	K/9	BB/9
Peralta, Wily	R-R	6-1	255	5-8-89	2	4	5.80	42	0	0	2	40	45	28	26	7	19	24	.296	.304	.289	5.36	4.24
Rosario, Randy	L-L	6-1	200	5-18-94	1	0	0.00	6	0	0	0	4	3	1	0	0	0	3	.214	.167	.250	7.36	0.00
Skoglund, Eric	L-L	6-7	210	10-26-92	0	3	9.00	6	4	0	0	21	30	21	21	5	9	4	.337	.333	.338	1.71	3.86
Sparkman, Glenn	R-R	6-2	210	5-11-92	4	11	6.02	31	23	1	0	136	164	96	91	30	41	81	.296	.280	.313	5.36	2.71
Speier, Gabe	L-L	6-0	175	4-12-95	0	0	7.36	9	0	0	0	7	5	6	6	2	6	10	.185	.250	.133	12.27	7.36
Staumont, Josh	R-R	6-3	200	12-21-93	0	0	3.72	16	0	0	0	19	21	13	8	4	10	15	.273	.263	.282	6.98	4.66
Zimmer, Kyle	R-R	6-3	225	9-13-91	0	1	10.80	15	0	0	0	18	28	22	22	2	19	18	.337	.286	.375	8.84	9.33

Fielding

Catcher	PCT	G	PO	A	E	DP	PB
Dini	.992	20	112	12	1	1	1
Gallagher	.997	44	292	8	1	2	1
Maldonado	.997	73	544	27	2	2	5
Viloria	.997	41	294	21	1	2	3

First Base	PCT	G	PO	A	E	DP
Cuthbert	.983	46	315	24	6	32
Dozier	1.000	7	47	1	0	4
Duda	1.000	19	111	7	0	15
McBroom	1.000	6	47	1	0	2
Merrifield	.968	5	25	5	1	5
O'Hearn	.995	94	707	24	4	80
Schwindel	.968	5	30	0	1	2

Second Base	PCT	G	PO	A	E	DP
Arteaga	1.000	2	3	2	0	1
Lopez	.990	76	116	195	3	46
Mejia	1.000	1	1	2	0	0
Merrifield	.979	82	154	222	8	61
Owings	1.000	13	28	29	0	9

Third Base	PCT	G	PO	A	E	DP
Arteaga	.000	1	0	0	0	0
Cuthbert	.916	40	22	54	7	5
Dozier	.965	100	66	181	9	20
Gutierrez	.951	18	23	35	3	2
Owings	1.000	12	9	23	0	1

Shortstop	PCT	G	PO	A	E	DP
Arteaga	.976	36	42	78	3	13
Lopez	.992	33	37	86	1	22
Mejia	1.000	1	1	0	0	0

	PCT	G	PO	A	E	DP
Mondesi	.984	100	147	286	7	66
Owings	1.000	3	5	6	0	3

Outfield	PCT	G	PO	A	E	DP
Bonifacio	1.000	5	11	0	0	0
Dozier	1.000	20	41	1	0	0
Gordon	.996	146	268	7	1	2
Gore	.971	23	34	0	1	0
Hamilton	1.000	90	198	3	0	0
McBroom	1.000	14	21	1	0	0
Mejia	1.000	7	22	0	0	0
Merrifield	.988	77	155	5	2	0
O'Hearn	.000	2	0	0	0	0
Owings	1.000	14	25	0	0	0
Phillips	1.000	28	58	2	0	1
Soler	.971	56	97	3	3	0
Starling	.992	55	123	5	1	2

OMAHA STORM CHASERS

PACIFIC COAST LEAGUE

TRIPLE-A

Batting	B-T	HT	WT	DOB	AVG	vLH	vRH	G	AB	R	H	2B	3B	HR	RBI	BB	HBP	SH	SF	SO	SB	CS	SLG	OBP
Arteaga, Humberto	R-R	6-1	160	1-23-94	.299	.310	.296	66	284	39	85	10	1	5	26	12	3	2	1	34	11	5	.394	.333
Bonifacio, Jorge	R-R	6-1	225	6-4-93	.222	.178	.237	117	451	67	100	18	5	20	62	38	4	0	7	121	6	4	.417	.284
Bushor, Chase	R-R	6-0	190	10-9-95	.231	.250	.222	4	13	1	3	0	0	0	0	0	0	0	0	3	0	0	.231	.231
Collado, Offerman	L-R	5-10	140	6-10-96	.154	.167	.143	6	13	0	2	1	0	0	1	0	1	1	0	1	0	0	.231	.200
Cuthbert, Cheslor	R-R	6-1	210	11-16-92	.310	.300	.312	51	197	25	61	17	1	8	35	17	3	0	2	46	0	0	.528	.370
d'Arnaud, Chase	R-R	6-1	197	1-21-87	.266	.310	.252	47	169	25	45	5	3	4	17	14	4	0	2	48	7	1	.402	.333
2-team total (46 Nashville)					.218	.282	.195	93	321	45	70	10	3	10	35	35	8	0	4	102	11	3	.361	.307
Dini, Nick	R-R	5-8	180	7-27-93	.296	.259	.311	58	186	34	55	11	0	13	36	21	2	2	2	29	7	2	.565	.370
Duda, Lucas	L-R	6-4	255	2-3-86	.286	.300	.273	12	42	6	12	3	0	1	4	4	0	0	0	13	0	0	.429	.348
Duenez, Samir	L-R	6-1	230	6-11-96	.214	.114	.239	64	224	24	48	9	0	6	33	21	1	1	1	52	0	1	.335	.283
Esposito, Nate	R-R	5-11	180	6-25-93	.114	.077	.129	15	44	5	5	0	0	1	2	3	0	2	0	10	0	0	.182	.170
Featherston, Taylor	R-R	6-1	185	10-8-89	.255	.385	.206	16	47	7	12	0	2	4	9	5	4	0	0	23	2	0	.596	.375
Fernandez, Xavier	R-R	6-1	197	7-15-95	.273	.294	.265	39	132	17	36	6	0	5	19	10	1	2	1	19	0	1	.432	.326
Flores, Jeckson	R-R	5-11	145	10-28-93	.249	.205	.265	116	410	48	102	14	1	8	52	42	6	13	7	75	17	5	.346	.323
Govern, Jimmy	R-R	5-11	190	12-11-96	.333	.600	.250	6	21	3	7	1	0	2	5	0	0	0	0	6	0	0	.667	.333
Gutierrez, Kelvin	R-R	6-3	215	8-28-94	.287	.265	.294	75	286	41	82	9	2	9	43	35	3	0	3	71	12	1	.427	.367
Heath, Nick	L-L	6-1	187	11-27-93	.256	.250	.259	21	78	17	20	4	1	2	9	17	1	0	1	27	10	4	.410	.392
Hernandez, Elier	R-R	6-3	197	11-21-94	.245	.232	.250	112	396	50	97	13	2	10	36	25	4	2	1	116	8	5	.364	.296
Lopez, Nicky	L-R	5-11	175	3-13-95	.353	.310	.368	31	116	27	41	6	1	3	13	20	2	0	0	5	9	3	.500	.457
Martin, Rudy	L-L	5-7	155	1-31-96	.214	.000	.290	12	42	7	9	2	0	2	4	3	1	1	0	12	6	1	.405	.283
Mejia, Erick	B-R	5-11	190	11-9-94	.271	.231	.285	128	495	83	134	22	6	7	63	50	3	5	3	103	19	6	.382	.339
Mondesi, Adalberto	B-R	6-1	190	7-27-95	.242	.250	.238	9	33	5	8	1	1	1	3	4	0	0	0	13	2	1	.424	.324
Moore, Adam	R-R	6-3	220	5-8-84	.175	.133	.200	12	40	5	7	1	0	2	2	3	0	0	0	9	0	0	.350	.233
2-team total (31 Nashville)					.233	.186	.252	43	146	18	34	3	1	4	21	20	1	0	0	54	0	0	.349	.329
O'Hearn, Ryan	L-L	6-3	200	7-26-93	.295	.200	.317	35	129	20	38	10	1	9	28	17	2	0	1	31	0	0	.597	.383
Phillips, Brett	L-R	6-0	185	5-30-94	.240	.231	.244	105	333	75	80	8	13	18	54	72	3	4	2	118	22	1	.505	.378
Rivero, Sebastian	R-R	6-1	195	11-16-98	.375	.000	.429	3	8	3	3	0	0	0	0	0	0	0	0	2	0	0	.375	.375
Schwindel, Frank	R-R	6-1	215	6-29-92	.186	.158	.196	19	70	8	13	4	0	1	10	4	1	0	1	13	0	1	.286	.237
Starling, Bubba	R-R	6-4	215	8-3-92	.310	.347	.296	72	261	34	81	11	2	7	38	21	0	0	3	59	9	3	.448	.358
Susac, Andrew	R-R	6-1	215	3-22-90	.234	.294	.217	26	77	11	18	4	0	4	15	14	2	0	0	24	3	2	.442	.366
Weiss, Erich	L-R	6-2	200	9-11-91	.281	.286	.280	27	96	10	27	5	1	3	12	11	0	1	0	27	0	1	.479	.324

Pitching	B-T	HT	WT	DOB	W	L	ERA	G	GS	CG	SV	IP	H	R	ER	HR	BB	SO	AVG	vLH	vRH	K/9	BB/9
Barlow, Scott	R-R	6-3	215	12-18-92	0	0	0.00	3	0	0	0	3	0	0	0	0	3	5	.158	.000	.177	7.50	4.50
Barnes, Jacob	R-R	6-2	220	4-14-90	0	0	3.38	3	0	0	0	3	4	1	1	0	0	6	.333	.333	.333	20.25	0.00
2-team total (14 San Antonio)					2	0	4.32	17	0	0	1	17	18	8	8	3	2	21	.261	.250	.267	11.34	1.08
Blewett, Scott	R-R	6-6	210	4-10-96	5	8	8.52	18	16	0	0	81	115	82	77	24	46	56	.333	.326	.338	6.20	5.09
Brickhouse, Bryan	R-R	6-0	195	6-6-92	1	0	10.38	14	0	0	0	17	14	20	20	6	19	7	.230	.222	.235	3.63	9.87
d'Arnaud, Chase	R-R	6-1	197	1-21-87	0	0	0.00	1	0	0	0	1	1	0	0	0	0	0	.250	.333	.000	0.00	0.00
Dziedzic, Jonathan	R-L	6-1	190	2-4-91	3	3	5.25	25	5	0	1	58	65	37	34	13	32	35	.286	.338	.264	5.40	4.94
Esposito, Nate	R-R	5-11	180	6-25-93	0	0	0.00	1	0	0	0	0	0	0	0	0	0	0	.000	--	.000	0.00	0.00
Fillmyer, Heath	R-R	6-1	195	5-16-94	2	3	5.11	19	10	1	0	49	48	28	28	8	26	51	.257	.210	.293	9.30	4.74
Flynn, Brian	L-L	6-7	255	4-19-90	4	4	4.78	11	5	0	0	43	47	25	23	7	18	42	.269	.200	.296	8.72	3.74

Name	B-T	HT	WT	DOB	W	L	ERA	G	GS	CG	SV	IP	H	R	ER	HR	BB	SO	AVG	vLH	vRH	SO/9	BB/9
Gomez, Ofreidy	R-R	6-3	190	7-6-95	0	3	6.75	6	2	0	0	13	21	10	10	2	13	8	.368	.250	.432	5.40	8.78
Greene, Conner	R-R	6-3	185	4-4-95	1	0	4.11	8	0	0	0	15	14	7	7	2	16	10	.259	.316	.229	5.87	9.39
Griffin, Foster	R-L	6-3	220	7-27-95	8	6	5.23	25	25	0	0	131	134	86	76	20	64	111	.259	.339	.236	7.65	4.41
Hernandez, Arnaldo	R-R	6-0	175	2-9-96	4	8	6.39	22	20	0	0	106	142	90	75	24	41	65	.327	.337	.321	5.54	3.49
Hill, Tim	R-L	6-2	200	2-10-90	1	1	2.12	27	0	0	3	30	26	7	7	2	6	30	.236	.186	.269	9.10	1.82
Kalish, Jake	B-L	6-2	210	7-9-91	8	8	5.16	24	10	0	1	119	131	77	68	26	25	89	.279	.279	.279	6.75	1.90
Lenik, Kevin	R-R	6-5	225	8-1-91	2	0	9.00	5	0	0	0	6	7	8	6	1	5	5	.269	.750	.182	7.50	7.50
Lively, Ben	R-R	6-4	190	3-5-92	4	1	4.07	17	3	0	3	42	41	20	19	7	19	41	.252	.302	.227	8.79	4.07
2-team total (7 Reno)					6	2	4.48	24	10	0	3	72	77	37	36	14	30	76	.268	.282	.259	9.46	3.73
Lovelady, Richard	L-L	6-0	175	7-7-95	1	2	3.08	24	0	0	4	26	26	11	9	1	7	29	.265	.269	.264	9.91	2.39
Lovvorn, Zach	R-R	6-0	185	5-26-94	4	11	8.84	21	7	0	0	75	115	79	74	19	46	59	.356	.377	.343	7.05	5.50
Machado, Andres	R-R	6-0	220	4-22-93	3	2	2.89	44	0	0	3	75	61	29	24	12	33	65	.218	.226	.214	7.83	3.98
Marte, Yunior	R-R	6-2	180	2-2-95	0	0	6.15	23	0	0	1	26	32	22	18	4	14	37	.291	.333	.273	12.65	4.78
McCarthy, Kevin	R-R	6-3	215	2-22-92	0	0	3.78	13	0	0	3	17	19	7	7	0	5	15	.297	.177	.340	8.10	2.70
Newberry, Jake	R-R	6-2	195	11-20-94	2	2	3.86	22	0	0	0	28	29	13	12	3	14	30	.271	.286	.264	9.64	4.50
Ogando, Emilio	L-L	6-2	180	8-13-93	0	0	12.27	1	0	0	0	4	7	5	5	0	3	4	.412	.000	.438	9.82	7.36
Skoglund, Eric	L-L	6-7	210	10-26-92	2	4	6.14	11	11	0	0	63	79	45	43	12	17	43	.312	.338	.302	6.14	2.43
Sparkman, Glenn	R-R	6-2	210	5-11-92	0	0	0.00	2	1	0	0	6	4	1	0	0	1	4	.182	.333	.125	5.68	1.42
Speier, Gabe	L-L	6-0	175	4-12-95	0	4	5.63	30	0	0	1	40	41	29	25	10	17	45	.263	.161	.320	10.13	3.83
Staumont, Josh	R-R	6-3	200	12-21-93	1	5	3.16	32	12	0	2	51	31	21	18	4	37	74	.172	.270	.120	12.97	6.49
Ynoa, Michael	R-R	6-7	210	9-24-91	1	1	4.57	17	0	0	2	22	19	13	11	3	14	26	.232	.160	.263	10.80	5.82
Zimmer, Kyle	R-R	6-3	225	9-13-91	2	4	4.33	37	12	0	1	54	46	30	26	6	33	52	.230	.270	.206	8.67	5.50

Fielding

Catcher	PCT	G	PO	A	E	DP	PB
Dini	.990	56	391	23	4	6	2
Esposito	1.000	15	108	11	0	0	0
Fernandez	.976	37	278	11	7	2	4
Moore	.978	11	78	9	2	0	0
Rivero	1.000	2	17	0	0	0	1
Susac	.981	25	194	11	4	0	3

First Base	PCT	G	PO	A	E	DP
Cuthbert	1.000	27	242	10	0	18
d'Arnaud	1.000	14	104	7	0	9
Duda	.952	3	17	3	1	3
Duenez	.986	38	276	8	4	31
Fernandez	1.000	1	8	1	0	0
Gutierrez	1.000	7	38	1	0	6
Moore	1.000	1	3	0	0	1
O'Hearn	1.000	25	198	12	0	13
Schwindel	.983	13	106	9	2	8
Weiss	.985	18	124	7	2	13

Second Base	PCT	G	PO	A	E	DP
Arteaga	.990	22	34	64	1	20
Collado	1.000	1	3	3	0	0
d'Arnaud	.971	17	27	40	2	11
Featherston	1.000	8	26	13	0	6
Flores	.986	48	84	122	3	30
Govern	1.000	1	4	2	0	1
Lopez	.984	14	28	34	1	9
Mejia	.963	31	59	70	5	20

Third Base	PCT	G	PO	A	E	DP
Arteaga	.961	16	8	41	2	6
Bushor	1.000	2	0	7	0	1
Cuthbert	.900	9	4	14	2	0
d'Arnaud	.963	9	10	16	1	1
Dini	.667	1	0	2	1	0
Featherston	1.000	4	6	10	0	0
Flores	.971	16	6	28	1	2
Govern	1.000	2	0	5	0	1
Gutierrez	.960	63	52	116	7	15
Mejia	.957	21	12	33	2	3
Weiss	1.000	5	3	7	0	1

Shortstop	PCT	G	PO	A	E	DP
Arteaga	.982	26	27	82	2	17
Collado	1.000	4	5	7	0	3
Featherston	.909	3	3	7	1	1
Flores	.947	50	67	147	12	25
Gutierrez	1.000	1	0	3	0	1
Lopez	.925	17	12	50	5	8
Mejia	.968	35	45	104	5	26
Mondesi	1.000	6	8	15	0	4

Outfield	PCT	G	PO	A	E	DP
Bonifacio	.976	98	192	12	5	3
d'Arnaud	1.000	2	6	0	0	0
Flores	1.000	1	3	0	0	0
Heath	.959	19	47	0	2	0
Hernandez	.949	90	126	5	7	0
Martin	.966	11	28	0	1	0
Mejia	.967	37	83	6	3	2
Phillips	.987	97	228	6	3	2
Starling	.987	69	147	8	2	3

NORTHWEST ARKANSAS NATURALS   DOUBLE-A
TEXAS LEAGUE

Batting	B-T	HT	WT	DOB	AVG	vLH	vRH	G	AB	R	H	2B	3B	HR	RBI	BB	HBP	SH	SF	SO	SB	CS	SLG	OBP
Blanco, Dairon	R-R	6-0	170	4-26-93	.230	.214	.232	32	126	10	29	7	1	0	5	8	1	0	0	42	6	6	.302	.282
2-team total (78 Midland)					.262	.261	.263	110	427	67	112	20	13	7	49	37	3	1	1	137	33	13	.419	.325
Burt, D.J.	R-R	5-9	160	10-13-95	.226	.353	.180	80	257	24	58	7	2	3	13	29	1	6	3	66	26	10	.304	.303
Cancel, Gabriel	R-R	6-0	185	12-8-96	.246	.227	.250	123	464	70	114	30	0	18	69	34	10	0	5	144	15	2	.427	.308
Castellano, Angelo	R-R	6-0	165	1-13-95	.217	.311	.192	72	217	19	47	8	1	5	21	22	3	11	1	57	6	3	.332	.296
Dozier, Hunter	R-R	6-4	220	8-22-91	.357	1.000	.308	3	14	1	5	1	0	0	4	0	0	0	0	2	1	0	.429	.357
Duenez, Samir	L-R	6-1	230	6-11-96	.167	.273	.154	28	102	10	17	3	1	1	19	7	0	0	4	25	0	0	.245	.212
Esposito, Nate	R-R	5-11	180	6-25-93	.210	.250	.203	28	81	6	17	5	0	0	5	3	1	2	2	22	1	0	.272	.275
Featherston, Taylor	R-R	6-1	185	10-8-89	.240	.233	.241	102	359	45	86	12	4	13	49	19	9	1	3	150	3	6	.404	.292
Fermin, Freddy	R-R	5-10	185	5-16-95	.252	.438	.220	32	107	11	27	3	0	3	11	3	0	1	1	23	0	2	.365	.270
Fernandez, Xavier	R-R	5-11	197	7-15-95	.196	.333	.154	15	51	6	10	0	0	2	6	6	1	0	0	13	1	0	.314	.293
George, Jordan	B-R	6-2	200	7-16-92	.275	.546	.238	30	91	5	25	5	0	0	9	20	1	0	0	20	3	2	.330	.411
Heath, Nick	L-L	6-1	187	11-27-93	.255	.259	.254	84	330	55	84	10	7	6	27	39	0	5	1	116	50	9	.382	.332
Hutchins, Nick	R-R	6-1	200	11-17-95	.219	.333	.192	9	32	4	7	1	0	0	3	0	0	1	0	14	1	0	.250	.219
Jones, Travis	R-R	6-4	210	9-29-95	.262	.189	.279	59	195	26	51	8	1	3	18	21	8	1	2	59	16	5	.359	.354
Lee, Khalil	L-L	5-10	170	6-26-98	.264	.268	.263	129	470	74	124	21	3	8	51	65	9	0	2	154	53	12	.372	.363
Merrell, Kevin	L-R	6-1	180	12-14-95	.235	.200	.243	42	166	14	39	5	4	0	13	9	1	0	0	38	9	2	.313	.278
2-team total (82 Midland)					.242	.247	.241	124	455	51	110	18	8	2	47	27	4	3	5	105	22	6	.330	.287
Miller, Anderson	L-L	6-3	208	5-6-94	.248	.231	.251	86	307	33	76	8	3	5	27	19	2	1	1	86	10	6	.342	.295
Mondesi, Adalberto	B-R	6-1	190	7-27-95	.222	--	.222	2	9	0	2	1	0	0	0	0	0	0	0	4	1	0	.333	.222
Perkins, Blake	B-R	5-11	181	9-10-96	.218	.412	.183	36	110	10	24	2	2	2	12	9	2	0	1	30	4	1	.327	.287
Peterson, Kort	L-R	6-1	195	4-29-94	.225	.292	.211	84	294	30	66	10	4	8	39	14	6	1	3	91	4	3	.367	.271
Rivera, Emmanuel	R-R	6-2	195	6-29-96	.258	.337	.241	131	496	59	128	18	2	7	57	25	5	2	6	77	6	2	.345	.297
Viloria, Meibrys	L-R	5-11	220	2-15-97	.264	.135	.290	63	220	21	58	12	0	1	24	24	3	1	0	60	2	0	.332	.344

Pitching

Pitching	B-T	HT	WT	DOB	W	L	ERA	G	GS	CG	SV	IP	H	R	ER	HR	BB	SO	AVG	vLH	vRH	K/9	BB/9
Beckwith, Andrew	R-R	6-0	180	3-22-95	1	0	5.84	26	0	0	0	37	46	30	24	2	15	28	.299	.308	.292	6.81	3.65
Blewett, Scott	R-R	6-6	210	4-10-96	1	3	3.55	5	5	0	0	25	21	11	10	2	8	34	.221	.250	.186	12.08	2.84
Brentz, Jake	L-L	6-1	195	9-14-94	0	0	3.38	5	0	0	0	5	6	2	2	1	2	5	.286	.000	.500	8.44	3.38
Brickhouse, Bryan	R-R	6-0	195	6-6-92	0	0	2.53	7	0	0	0	11	6	3	3	0	5	16	.167	.222	.111	13.50	4.22
Capps, Holden	R-L	6-2	180	3-24-95	0	2	5.11	14	0	0	0	12	21	9	7	1	6	9	.368	.154	.548	6.57	4.38
Cloney, J.C.	L-L	6-1	226	8-3-94	2	6	3.74	22	15	0	1	101	109	52	42	13	26	81	.277	.278	.277	7.22	2.32
Duffy, Danny	L-L	6-3	205	12-21-88	1	0	0.87	2	2	0	0	10	8	2	1	1	0	11	.216	.000	.250	9.58	0.00
Garabito, Gerson	R-R	6-0	160	8-19-95	6	12	3.77	26	26	0	0	141	148	64	59	13	60	113	.268	.293	.242	7.21	3.83
Gavin, Grant	R-R	6-2	185	7-10-95	6	4	3.61	41	0	0	1	52	43	28	21	6	25	73	.223	.238	.211	12.55	4.30
Gomez, Ofreidy	R-R	6-3	190	7-6-95	7	8	4.05	22	20	1	0	116	110	62	52	12	45	111	.251	.243	.258	8.64	3.50
Greene, Conner	R-R	6-3	185	4-4-95	3	9	5.29	21	16	0	1	97	101	73	57	11	38	85	.267	.274	.260	7.89	3.53
Hensley, Bryce	L-L	6-4	215	10-3-95	0	0	0.00	1	0	0	0	2	1	0	0	0	0	1	.200	.500	.000	5.40	0.00
Hernandez, Arnaldo	R-R	6-0	175	2-9-96	2	2	1.96	4	4	0	0	23	21	12	5	2	11	20	.250	.291	.172	7.83	4.30
Kalish, Jake	B-L	6-2	210	7-9-91	0	0	1.00	3	1	0	1	9	6	1	1	0	1	13	.177	.091	.111	13.00	1.00
Kowar, Jackson	R-R	6-5	180	10-4-96	2	7	3.51	13	13	0	0	74	73	32	29	8	21	78	.254	.263	.247	9.44	2.54
Lovvorn, Zach	R-R	6-0	185	5-26-94	1	0	1.38	8	0	0	0	13	6	2	2	0	5	12	.140	.200	.056	8.31	3.46
Marte, Yunior	R-R	6-2	180	2-2-95	3	3	1.59	23	0	0	1	34	22	8	6	1	13	35	.183	.212	.162	9.26	3.44
Ogando, Emilio	L-L	6-2	180	8-13-93	1	3	4.83	36	2	0	1	69	66	38	37	4	20	74	.252	.214	.274	9.65	2.61
Sheller, Walker	R-R	6-3	195	5-21-95	0	2	9.00	13	0	0	1	13	23	21	13	2	12	11	.371	.429	.324	7.62	8.31
Singer, Brady	R-R	6-5	210	8-4-96	7	3	3.47	16	16	1	0	91	86	43	35	8	26	85	.247	.260	.235	8.44	2.58
Skoglund, Eric	L-L	6-7	210	10-26-92	1	1	5.40	2	2	0	0	10	14	7	6	2	6	5	.333	.444	.303	4.50	1.80
Sotillet, Andres	R-R	6-1	175	3-2-97	6	1	3.35	34	4	0	1	75	68	34	28	6	29	63	.239	.264	.219	7.53	3.46
Speier, Gabe	L-L	6-0	175	4-12-95	1	1	2.42	17	0	0	5	22	20	10	6	2	9	28	.233	.167	.296	11.28	3.63
Storen, Drew	B-R	6-1	195	8-11-87	0	1	7.84	9	0	0	0	10	15	9	9	1	5	12	.366	.375	.360	10.45	4.35
Terrero, Franco	R-R	6-0	180	5-20-95	2	5	5.08	43	0	0	7	44	53	30	25	5	24	48	.294	.317	.276	9.74	4.87
Tillo, Daniel	L-L	6-5	215	6-13-96	1	1	3.47	9	3	0	0	23	22	9	9	1	11	21	.256	.207	.281	8.10	4.24
Vines, Jace	R-R	6-3	215	9-4-94	2	5	5.47	11	9	0	0	51	66	43	31	5	21	40	.317	.355	.277	7.06	3.71
Zuber, Tyler	R-R	5-11	175	6-16-95	1	2	2.42	22	0	0	10	26	18	9	7	2	5	30	.205	.271	.125	10.38	1.73

Fielding

Catcher	PCT	G	PO	A	E	DP	PB
Esposito	.996	27	198	25	1	2	1
Fermin	.985	32	298	24	5	5	2
Fernandez	.971	14	130	4	4	1	2
Hutchins	.989	9	88	4	1	1	0
Viloria	.990	58	450	37	5	3	8

First Base	PCT	G	PO	A	E	DP
Cancel	.981	18	151	7	3	13
Castellano	.990	24	188	15	2	26
Duenez	.987	19	140	13	2	15
George	.991	27	202	11	2	23
Jones	.980	52	364	34	8	44

Second Base	PCT	G	PO	A	E	DP
Burt	.929	21	26	52	6	10
Cancel	.980	82	134	202	7	62
Castellano	.988	17	29	55	1	18
Esposito	1.000	1	0	1	0	0
Featherston	.926	19	31	44	6	10
Rivera	.800	1	2	2	1	1

Third Base	PCT	G	PO	A	E	DP
Burt	.852	8	12	11	4	2
Castellano	.950	12	9	29	2	4
Dozier	1.000	2	1	2	0	0
Jones	.857	1	2	4	1	0
Rivera	.928	117	72	185	20	30

Shortstop	PCT	G	PO	A	E	DP
Cancel	.875	6	7	14	3	3
Castellano	.981	14	20	33	1	7
Featherston	.948	82	130	215	19	58
Merrell	.973	37	49	96	4	19
Mondesi	.667	1	1	1	1	0

Outfield	PCT	G	PO	A	E	DP
Blanco	.979	27	45	2	1	1
Burt	.985	36	64	2	1	0
Heath	.972	73	171	0	5	0
Jones	1.000	3	6	0	0	0
Lee	.974	107	180	9	5	2
Miller	.956	69	127	3	6	0
Perkins	1.000	33	71	4	0	0
Peterson	.986	75	128	9	2	3

WILMINGTON BLUE ROCKS   HIGH CLASS A
CAROLINA LEAGUE

Batting	B-T	HT	WT	DOB	AVG	vLH	vRH	G	AB	R	H	2B	3B	HR	RBI	BB	HBP	SH	SF	SO	SB	CS	SLG	OBP
Aracena, Ricky	R-S	5-8	160	10-2-97	.198	.167	.209	83	257	32	51	8	1	1	13	21	3	11	2	73	12	6	.249	.265
Carrasco, Dennicher	R-R	5-11	195	10-12-95	.246	.283	.233	120	411	47	101	29	2	9	58	34	1	1	4	127	7	4	.392	.302
Castellano, Angelo	R-R	6-0	165	1-13-95	.191	.375	.128	25	63	4	12	3	1	0	5	7	3	2	1	12	4	2	.270	.297
Collado, Offerman	L-R	5-10	140	6-10-96	.233	.333	.191	12	30	3	7	1	0	0	1	2	1	0	0	4	0	0	.267	.303
Gasparini, Marten	R-R	6-0	165	5-24-97	.122	.188	.091	16	49	5	6	1	0	1	0	0	0	0	0	26	0	0	.163	.140
Gigliotti, Michael	L-L	6-1	180	2-14-96	.184	.107	.220	24	87	8	16	2	1	0	5	8	2	2	0	23	5	3	.230	.268
Hicklen, Brewer	R-R	6-2	208	2-9-96	.263	.282	.256	125	419	70	110	13	7	14	51	55	13	4	3	140	39	14	.427	.363
Hill, Tyler	R-R	6-0	195	3-4-96	.403	.429	.386	21	72	14	29	4	1	1	9	7	1	0	2	5	2	4	.528	.451
Isbel, Kyle	L-R	5-11	183	3-3-97	.217	.244	.208	52	194	26	42	7	3	5	23	15	3	1	1	44	8	3	.361	.282
Kasser, Kyle	L-R	5-10	180	10-12-95	.303	.286	.309	62	198	22	60	6	1	0	17	17	2	4	1	24	7	6	.343	.362
Marquez, Jose	B-R	6-0	175	10-7-97	.273	.273	.273	6	22	0	6	0	0	0	2	0	0	1	1	7	0	0	.273	.261
Martin, Rudy	L-L	5-7	155	1-31-96	.164	.130	.175	62	183	19	30	3	1	1	7	19	3	5	0	68	16	5	.208	.254
Matias, Seuly	R-R	6-3	198	9-4-98	.148	.184	.136	57	189	23	28	10	4	4	22	25	4	1	2	98	2	4	.307	.259
Melendez, MJ	L-R	6-1	185	11-29-98	.163	.126	.177	110	363	34	59	23	2	9	54	44	5	3	4	165	7	5	.311	.260
Perez, Cristian	R-R	5-10	170	10-26-96	.252	.272	.244	117	389	37	98	11	1	0	42	20	3	7	5	48	5	10	.285	.290
Perkins, Blake	B-R	5-11	181	9-10-96	.226	.250	.216	86	288	43	65	11	4	6	22	52	2	7	3	79	18	7	.354	.345
Pratto, Nick	L-L	6-1	195	10-6-98	.191	.177	.197	124	419	48	80	21	1	9	46	49	2	0	2	164	17	7	.310	.278
Rivero, Sebastian	R-R	6-1	195	11-16-98	.212	.188	.221	91	288	23	61	14	1	1	24	19	6	8	5	75	2	2	.278	.270
Schultz, Colby	L-R	6-0	180	12-13-94	.227	.241	.222	76	234	22	53	10	1	2	22	24	3	3	5	55	4	7	.303	.303
Steel, Bruce	R-R	6-2	195	12-26-96	.000	.000	.000	8	18	1	0	0	0	0	0	1	0	0	0	10	0	0	.000	.053
Vidal, Stephan	R-R	6-1	215	4-4-96	.125	.000	.250	4	8	0	1	0	0	0	0	0	0	0	0	2	0	0	.125	.125

Pitching	B-T	HT	WT	DOB	W	L	ERA	G	GS	CG	SV	IP	H	R	ER	HR	BB	SO	AVG	vLH	vRH	K/9	BB/9
Beckwith, Andrew	R-R	6-0	180	3-22-95	3	0	1.69	9	0	0	2	16	10	4	3	0	5	17	.196	.188	.200	9.56	2.81
Bowlan, Jonathan	R-R	6-6	262	12-1-96	5	3	2.95	13	12	1	0	76	66	25	25	5	13	76	.237	.284	.210	8.96	1.53
Brickhouse, Bryan	R-R	6-0	195	6-6-92	1	0	0.00	4	0	0	0	6	2	0	0	0	5	8	.105	.100	.111	12.71	7.94
Bubic, Kris	L-L	6-3	220	8-19-97	7	4	2.30	17	17	2	0	102	76	28	26	3	27	110	.215	.293	.182	9.74	2.39
Capps, Holden	R-L	6-2	180	3-24-95	3	2	1.83	25	0	0	1	39	39	14	8	1	7	46	.253	.256	.252	10.53	1.60
Cloney, J.C.	L-L	6-1	226	8-3-94	1	1	2.21	6	2	0	0	20	14	7	5	3	4	16	.189	.143	.208	7.08	1.77
Cox, Austin	L-L	6-4	185	3-28-97	3	3	2.77	11	10	0	0	55	53	19	17	6	16	52	.260	.271	.255	8.46	2.60
Duarte, Daniel	R-R	6-0	170	12-4-96	1	0	4.50	10	0	0	0	18	21	9	9	0	5	16	.304	.370	.262	8.00	2.50
Dye, Josh	L-L	6-5	180	9-14-96	4	2	1.25	25	0	0	5	36	24	8	5	1	15	38	.192	.150	.212	9.50	3.75
Eldred, C.J.	R-R	6-2	225	5-6-95	1	0	0.00	4	0	0	0	7	5	1	0	0	1	6	.217	.429	.125	8.10	1.35
Garcia, Robert	R-L	6-4	225	6-14-96	4	2	4.93	35	0	0	1	49	46	28	27	5	21	66	.243	.309	.216	12.04	3.83
Hahn, Jesse	R-R	6-4	215	7-30-89	0	1	3.38	3	2	0	0	3	2	1	1	0	2	4	.222	.000	.286	13.50	6.75
Kowar, Jackson	R-R	6-5	180	10-4-96	5	3	3.53	13	13	0	0	74	68	33	29	4	22	66	.246	.219	.266	8.03	2.68
Lambright, Austin	L-L	6-3	205	8-26-94	0	2	3.57	16	0	0	0	18	19	8	7	0	9	29	.257	.188	.276	14.77	4.58
Lugo, Rito	L-L	5-10	185	11-3-95	4	4	2.34	31	14	0	0	100	88	30	26	2	22	77	.235	.271	.218	6.93	1.98
Lynch, Daniel	L-L	6-6	190	11-17-96	5	2	3.10	15	15	0	0	78	76	28	27	4	23	77	.253	.271	.245	8.85	2.64
Martinez, Marcelo	L-L	6-2	190	8-10-96	6	7	4.23	25	21	0	1	121	112	59	57	16	37	108	.243	.271	.231	8.01	2.74
Mitchell, Josh	R-L	6-2	220	9-8-94	5	0	3.30	27	1	0	0	44	49	22	16	1	13	47	.287	.322	.268	9.69	2.68
Ratliff, Tad	R-R	6-2	240	4-3-96	3	3	2.81	42	0	0	23	51	42	19	16	3	19	55	.230	.246	.219	9.64	3.33
Sheller, Walker	R-R	6-3	195	5-21-95	1	2	7.29	17	0	0	1	21	26	18	17	4	9	12	.310	.313	.308	5.14	3.86
Singer, Brady	R-R	6-5	210	8-4-96	5	2	1.87	10	10	0	0	58	51	20	12	1	13	53	.248	.307	.203	8.27	2.03
Snider, Collin	R-R	6-4	200	10-10-95	5	3	2.25	28	0	0	4	52	44	19	13	2	11	34	.233	.250	.222	5.88	1.90
Tillo, Daniel	L-L	6-5	215	6-13-96	7	8	3.77	20	20	1	0	107	95	55	45	5	43	64	.238	.239	.237	5.37	3.61
Watson, Nolan	R-R	6-2	195	1-25-97	0	0	0.00	1	1	0	0	4	4	1	0	0	1	3	.222	.375	.100	6.23	2.08
Zuber, Tyler	R-R	5-11	175	6-16-95	3	2	1.23	21	0	0	11	29	16	8	4	0	11	38	.160	.189	.143	11.66	3.38

Fielding

Catcher	PCT	G	PO	A	E	DP	PB
Melendez	.991	71	579	74	6	2	12
Rivero	.981	68	562	46	12	4	9
Vidal	1.000	1	2	0	0	0	0

First Base	PCT	G	PO	A	E	DP
Carrasco	.993	18	140	11	1	13
Castellano	.000	1	0	0	0	0
Kasser	1.000	1	2	0	0	0
Pratto	.992	123	936	78	8	100

Second Base	PCT	G	PO	A	E	DP
Aracena	.973	82	148	218	10	61
Castellano	.833	1	2	8	2	4
Collado	1.000	3	3	0	0	1

	PCT	G	PO	A	E	DP	PB
Gasparini	.889	6	5	11	2	5	
Kasser	1.000	36	41	73	0	16	
Marquez	.857	4	10	8	3	3	
Schultz	.976	11	16	25	1	6	

Third Base	PCT	G	PO	A	E	DP
Carrasco	.916	76	44	130	16	13
Castellano	.935	19	8	35	3	6
Collado	1.000	6	2	10	0	0
Kasser	.947	18	12	24	2	3
Marquez	1.000	2	0	2	0	0
Schultz	.864	24	11	46	9	3
Steel	1.000	6	3	6	0	0

Shortstop	PCT	G	PO	A	E	DP
Castellano	.909	4	5	5	1	0

	PCT	G	PO	A	E	DP
Collado	.909	3	4	6	1	1
Perez	.977	116	154	306	11	74
Schultz	1.000	17	14	37	0	6

Outfield	PCT	G	PO	A	E	DP
Castellano	.000	1	0	0	0	0
Gasparini	.950	10	18	1	1	0
Gigliotti	.979	23	46	0	1	0
Hicklen	.979	103	172	11	4	1
Hill	.919	20	34	0	3	0
Isbel	.988	43	83	2	1	0
Kasser	1.000	6	10	0	0	0
Martin	.962	59	97	3	4	0
Matias	.973	51	101	8	3	3
Perkins	.994	80	172	3	1	1
Schultz	1.000	26	41	3	0	1

LEXINGTON LEGENDS   LOW CLASS A
SOUTH ATLANTIC LEAGUE

Batting	B-T	HT	WT	DOB	AVG	vLH	vRH	G	AB	R	H	2B	3B	HR	RBI	BB	HBP	SH	SF	SO	SB	CS	SLG	OBP
Aracena, Ricky	B-R	5-8	160	10-2-97	.231	.250	.222	3	13	1	3	1	0	0	1	0	0	0	0	4	0	0	.308	.286
Bewley, Brhet	R-R	5-11	182	1-30-97	.253	.217	.263	60	202	25	51	6	1	1	17	31	2	8	1	55	1	4	.307	.356
Caraballo, Jose	R-R	6-1	180	1-7-97	.172	.267	.153	26	87	7	15	5	0	2	10	6	2	0	1	28	0	0	.299	.240
Cole, Eric	B-R	5-11	170	1-17-97	.240	.196	.252	127	466	55	112	21	6	11	71	62	3	0	5	90	7	2	.382	.330
Eaton, Nathan	R-R	5-11	185	12-22-96	.233	.269	.224	126	497	64	116	32	2	5	54	46	8	0	6	116	18	1	.336	.305
Fermin, Freddy	R-R	5-10	185	5-16-95	.263	.269	.261	54	209	37	55	11	0	9	30	14	1	1	1	37	2	0	.445	.311
Gigliotti, Michael	L-L	6-2	180	2-14-96	.309	.296	.313	59	236	42	73	19	1	1	23	27	8	5	3	49	29	7	.411	.394
Guzman, Jeison	L-R	6-2	180	10-8-98	.253	.284	.245	121	450	51	114	23	5	7	48	25	3	10	2	98	15	13	.373	.296
Hudgins, Chris	R-R	6-1	190	3-2-96	.247	.304	.227	48	178	30	44	3	2	9	31	16	5	0	3	52	1	0	.438	.322
Hutchins, Nick	R-R	6-1	200	11-17-95	.261	.245	.266	67	245	29	64	18	0	5	24	26	6	0	2	59	2	2	.396	.302
Jaquez, Rubendy	R-R	5-11	174	11-13-99	.243	.241	.244	114	403	65	98	20	3	6	44	44	4	10	5	102	30	5	.352	.320
Kasser, Kyle	L-R	5-10	180	10-12-95	.300	.333	.296	9	30	5	9	0	0	0	3	5	0	0	0	2	3	0	.300	.400
Lueck, Jackson	B-R	6-1	170	2-19-97	.172	.154	.178	95	309	27	53	10	2	3	23	44	4	4	1	132	3	3	.246	.282
Martin, Rudy	L-L	5-7	155	1-31-96	.214	.333	.189	26	89	8	19	4	1	3	12	5	1	2	0	35	4	4	.382	.263
Morales, Matt	R-R	5-11	170	11-26-96	.185	.250	.147	19	54	5	10	2	1	0	5	2	1	0	1	20	3	2	.259	.224
Negret, Juan Carlos	R-R	6-1	190	6-19-99	.172	.167	.173	39	134	20	23	6	0	6	16	15	7	0	2	57	1	1	.351	.285
Rave, John	L-L	6-0	185	12-30-97	.253	.177	.271	46	174	17	44	7	1	2	13	15	3	3	1	58	6	5	.339	.321
Rohlman, Reed	L-L	6-1	190	1-5-95	.244	.244	.244	106	480	56	117	23	3	5	55	31	3	0	1	138	6	2	.335	.293
Steel, Bruce	R-R	6-2	195	12-26-96	.150	.222	.091	7	20	2	3	1	0	1	3	4	0	0	0	10	0	0	.350	.292
Vallot, Chase	R-R	6-0	215	8-21-96	.190	.154	.198	83	279	31	53	11	3	14	44	32	14	1	2	155	0	1	.401	.303

Pitching	B-T	HT	WT	DOB	W	L	ERA	G	GS	CG	SV	IP	H	R	ER	HR	BB	SO	AVG	vLH	vRH	K/9	BB/9
Bowlan, Jonathan	R-R	6-6	262	12-1-96	6	2	3.36	13	11	0	1	70	55	30	26	4	10	74	.216	.207	.222	9.56	1.29
Bubic, Kris	L-L	6-3	220	8-19-97	4	1	2.08	9	9	0	0	48	27	14	11	3	15	75	.164	.232	.142	14.16	2.83
Cillis, Ted	L-L	6-2	225	8-12-94	1	2	3.12	19	0	0	1	35	39	18	12	3	8	21	.283	.189	.317	5.45	2.08
Cox, Austin	L-L	6-4	185	3-28-97	5	3	2.75	13	13	0	0	75	59	30	23	5	22	77	.206	.153	.224	9.20	2.63
Duarte, Daniel	R-R	6-0	170	12-4-96	1	0	15.75	3	0	0	0	4	9	7	7	2	4	4	.429	.667	.333	9.00	9.00

Pitching (continued)

Name	B-T	HT	WT	DOB	W	L	ERA	G	GS	CG	SV	IP	H	R	ER	HR	BB	SO	AVG	vLH	vRH	K/9	BB/9
Dye, Josh	L-L	6-5	180	9-14-96	1	1	3.38	14	0	0	3	27	24	14	10	1	6	43	.229	.129	.270	14.51	2.03
Eldred, C.J.	R-R	6-2	225	5-6-95	0	7	5.92	24	3	0	2	79	112	64	52	10	14	65	.328	.321	.332	7.41	1.59
Garcia, Yerelmy	R-R	6-2	180	11-5-95	0	1	15.30	7	0	0	0	10	17	17	17	3	4	8	.386	.600	.276	7.20	3.60
Gray, Tyler	R-R	6-2	180	3-12-97	4	4	4.65	28	3	0	2	72	72	43	37	6	23	50	.255	.349	.199	6.28	2.89
Haake, Zach	R-R	6-4	186	10-8-96	4	6	2.85	18	18	0	0	76	60	32	24	2	36	90	.221	.182	.239	10.70	4.28
Heasley, Jon	R-R	6-3	215	1-27-97	8	5	3.12	25	20	0	0	113	93	47	39	11	34	120	.222	.209	.231	9.59	2.72
Hellinger, Jaret	R-L	6-4	170	11-18-96	1	2	6.35	11	0	0	0	17	20	15	12	0	7	17	.278	.273	.280	9.00	3.71
Hensley, Bryce	L-L	6-4	215	10-3-95	1	3	3.05	15	5	0	1	65	68	25	22	3	15	37	.268	.237	.281	5.12	2.08
Hernandez, Carlos	R-R	6-4	175	3-11-97	3	3	3.50	7	7	0	0	36	34	16	14	5	9	43	.250	.244	.253	10.75	2.25
Hinton, Kyle	R-R	6-0	200	2-12-97	3	5	3.26	36	0	0	5	58	38	33	21	6	41	60	.185	.190	.183	9.31	6.36
James, Daniel	R-R	6-4	215	1-19-96	4	3	3.83	32	0	0	5	49	35	27	21	6	24	55	.197	.206	.191	10.03	4.38
Lambright, Austin	L-L	6-3	205	8-26-94	2	0	2.43	17	0	0	1	30	15	9	8	1	16	45	.149	.000	.211	13.65	4.85
Marklund, Brandon	R-R	6-2	185	6-10-96	4	0	0.46	24	0	0	6	39	23	7	2	1	19	44	.162	.152	.167	10.07	4.35
Marquez, Emilio	L-L	5-8	170	4-28-98	0	1	2.45	1	0	0	0	4	5	1	1	0	1	4	.313	1.000	.214	9.82	2.45
Martinez, Marcelo	L-L	6-2	190	8-10-96	0	0	2.00	2	0	0	1	9	9	2	2	1	0	10	.250	.571	.172	10.00	0.00
Morel, Yohanse	R-R	6-0	170	8-23-00	2	6	6.02	14	11	0	1	52	64	48	35	7	21	57	.295	.344	.258	9.80	3.61
Neuweiler, Charlie	R-R	6-1	205	2-8-99	7	10	4.36	27	27	1	0	149	136	85	72	17	63	153	.241	.234	.247	9.26	3.81
Nunez, Andres	R-R	6-4	240	9-20-95	3	2	2.21	26	0	0	2	53	46	18	13	3	12	68	.229	.230	.228	11.55	2.04
Steele, Evan	R-L	6-5	210	11-14-96	4	3	2.39	11	11	0	0	49	40	15	13	2	15	56	.235	.221	.229	10.29	2.76

Fielding

Catcher	PCT	G	PO	A	E	DP	PB
Fermin	.991	44	400	49	4	3	6
Hudgins	.992	24	217	29	2	1	2
Hutchins	.997	35	323	27	1	1	3
Vallot	.982	38	300	24	6	1	8
Bewley	.964	32	55	78	5		21
Eaton	.929	8	8	18	2		5
Jaquez	.961	76	138	179	13		43
Kasser	.966	9	9	19	1		2
Morales	.952	12	17	23	2		4
Jaquez	.915	15	26	39	6		9
Morales	.706	5	4	8	5		2
Steel	.950	4	5	14	1		1

First Base	PCT	G	PO	A	E	DP
Bewley	1.000	9	70	6	0	4
Hudgins	.989	9	84	4	1	4
Hutchins	.979	6	46	1	1	5
Rohlman	.990	114	919	62	10	66

Second Base	PCT	G	PO	A	E	DP
Aracena	1.000	3	7	6	0	2

Third Base	PCT	G	PO	A	E	DP
Bewley	.905	8	5	14	2	1
Eaton	.922	113	64	209	23	14
Hudgins	1.000	1	1	3	0	0
Jaquez	.857	15	5	19	4	2
Steel	.667	3	2	4	3	0

Shortstop	PCT	G	PO	A	E	DP
Guzman	.933	116	144	317	33	47

Outfield	PCT	G	PO	A	E	DP
Bewley	1.000	4	6	1	0	0
Caraballo	1.000	26	47	3	0	1
Cole	.990	120	185	9	2	1
Eaton	.500	1	0	1	1	0
Gigliotti	1.000	59	135	1	0	1
Lueck	.959	95	140	2	6	1
Martin	.957	26	42	3	2	0
Negret	.980	30	46	2	1	0
Rave	.972	46	105	1	3	0
Rohlman	.960	8	22	2	1	0

BURLINGTON ROYALS — ROOKIE ADVANCED
APPALACHIAN LEAGUE

Batting	B-T	HT	WT	DOB	AVG	vLH	vRH	G	AB	R	H	2B	3B	HR	RBI	BB	HBP	SH	SF	SO	SB	CS	SLG	OBP
Atencio, Jesus	R-R	5-10	165	8-22-96	.205	.188	.208	25	88	8	18	3	0	2	10	10	0	4	0	26	1	0	.307	.286
Charleston, Jay	R-R	5-10	170	4-20-98	.220	.444	.181	36	123	24	27	3	1	1	11	18	2	3	0	41	16	2	.285	.329
Dixon, Burle	L-L	6-5	185	10-15-98	.204	.156	.215	48	167	23	34	6	3	3	21	20	3	1	0	62	9	4	.329	.300
Familia, Felix	R-R	6-2	205	10-13-98	.200	.000	.250	2	5	0	1	0	0	0	0	0	0	0	0	1	0	0	.200	.200
Filia, Mikey	R-R	5-9	180	11-5-96	.257	.292	.247	33	113	12	29	7	2	0	10	14	7	0	1	26	7	1	.354	.370
Garcia, Maikel	R-R	6-0	145	3-3-00	.286	.180	.309	55	220	41	63	8	4	1	34	25	0	5	4	40	19	8	.373	.353
Gethings, Jack	L-R	5-10	175	10-9-96	.258	.211	.267	39	120	19	31	5	0	0	11	30	0	6	1	27	5	2	.300	.404
Hancock, William	L-R	6-2	200	10-31-96	.262	.212	.273	47	172	16	45	10	2	0	15	19	3	1	1	54	0	0	.343	.344
Hernandez, Diego	L-L	6-0	150	11-21-00	.214	.000	.231	3	14	1	3	0	0	0	1	0	0	0	0	1	1	1	.214	.214
Hollie, David	R-R	6-2	190	10-25-99	.163	.216	.147	45	166	22	27	7	1	6	25	13	8	0	1	87	2	1	.325	.255
Jackson, Kevon	R-R	5-9	180	6-14-00	.154	.065	.178	49	149	28	23	7	1	1	13	29	2	1	1	65	10	3	.235	.298
Lopez, Raymond	B-R	6-1	155	12-4-98	.095	.100	.108	16	42	4	4	0	0	1	6	3	1	0	2	19	1	0	.167	.167
Massey, Michael	L-R	6-0	190	3-22-98	.272	.452	.232	42	173	32	47	7	0	5	25	13	5	0	1	28	4	0	.399	.339
Means, Jake	L-R	6-2	215	4-14-96	.267	.191	.286	60	210	41	56	11	1	5	29	36	17	0	3	51	2	2	.400	.410
Pasquantino, Vinnie	L-L	6-4	245	10-10-97	.294	.163	.327	57	211	43	62	17	2	14	53	27	3	0	7	40	0	0	.592	.371
Porter, Logan	R-R	6-0	200	7-12-95	.352	.323	.360	44	145	26	51	14	1	9	37	31	7	0	2	34	0	0	.648	.481
Rave, John	L-R	6-0	185	12-30-97	.175	.333	.146	15	57	5	10	2	0	1	3	12	2	0	0	17	3	0	.263	.338
Romero, Rafael	R-R	5-10	155	11-14-98	.211	.100	.227	24	76	10	16	2	0	0	7	10	0	3	0	19	0	0	.237	.302

Pitching	B-T	HT	WT	DOB	W	L	ERA	G	GS	CG	SV	IP	H	R	ER	HR	BB	SO	AVG	vLH	vRH	K/9	BB/9
Alcantara, Adrian	R-R	6-1	178	8-29-99	2	4	2.47	12	10	0	0	51	27	17	14	2	17	57	.152	.119	.168	10.06	3.00
Anderson, Elliott	L-L	6-3	212	9-27-97	2	2	0.91	19	0	0	3	30	23	6	3	1	12	34	.211	.256	.186	10.31	3.64
Atencio, Jesus	R-R	5-10	165	8-22-96	0	0	0.00	1	0	0	0	0	0	0	0	0	0	0	.000	.000	--	0.00	0.00
Biasi, Dante	L-L	6-0	205	12-4-97	1	0	2.50	7	0	0	0	18	13	5	5	3	3	24	.200	.200	.200	12.00	1.50
Bryant, Noah	R-R	6-3	200	10-15-98	1	0	3.38	4	0	0	0	5	4	6	2	0	7	3	.211	.125	.273	5.06	11.81
Buck, Donavin	R-R	6-6	240	4-25-96	1	0	2.73	15	0	0	0	26	18	8	8	2	10	25	.194	.180	.204	8.54	3.42
Capellan, Delvin	R-R	6-1	167	12-6-98	4	2	4.99	12	12	0	0	52	53	31	29	7	14	53	.262	.239	.292	9.11	2.41
Dipoto, Jonah	R-R	6-1	225	9-3-96	1	2	0.94	16	0	0	4	29	11	6	3	0	11	34	.112	.143	.089	10.67	3.45
Franklin, A.J.	L-L	6-1	180	8-18-96	1	1	8.06	13	0	0	1	22	22	21	20	4	19	23	.268	.231	.302	9.27	7.66
Frias, Adan	R-R	6-0	200	5-18-99	0	1	3.43	6	4	0	2	21	19	8	8	1	8	21	.241	.238	.241	9.00	3.43
Garcia, Heribert	R-R	6-0	190	10-2-99	1	1	5.54	3	2	0	0	13	15	8	8	0	2	13	.273	.125	.387	8.31	1.38
Hernandez, Carlos	R-R	6-4	175	3-11-97	0	0	9.28	3	3	0	0	11	11	13	11	1	12	13	.262	.231	.276	10.97	10.13
Jimenez, Wilmer	L-L	5-11	162	6-1-98	0	1	4.26	6	0	0	0	13	10	6	6	1	7	15	.227	.263	.200	10.66	4.97
Kaufman, Rylan	L-L	6-4	190	6-23-99	0	1	12.00	1	1	0	0	3	4	4	4	0	5	0	.333	.000	.364	0.00	15.00
Lopez, Raymond	B-R	6-1	155	12-4-98	1	0	0.00	1	0	0	0	2	0	1	0	0	3	0	.000	.000	.000	13.50	13.50

	B-T	HT	WT	DOB	W	L	ERA	G	GS	CG	SV	IP	H	R	ER	HR	BB	SO	AVG	vLH	vRH	K/9	BB/9
Lynch, Daniel	L-L	6-6	190	11-17-96	1	0	4.00	2	2	0	0	9	13	4	4	1	3	7	.361	.286	.379	7.00	3.00
Murdock, Noah	R-R	6-8	190	8-20-98	3	1	2.17	11	6	0	0	37	35	12	9	2	11	43	.247	.203	.282	10.37	2.65
Parrish, Drew	L-L	5-11	200	12-8-97	3	0	2.52	9	4	0	0	25	19	7	7	4	4	39	.211	.172	.230	14.04	1.44
Phillips, Zack	L-L	6-0	170	7-11-98	4	1	2.15	20	0	0	2	38	29	11	9	2	10	29	.212	.250	.200	6.93	2.39
Smith, Alex	L-L	6-3	216	12-29-96	1	3	3.98	14	0	0	0	20	15	12	9	1	14	29	.206	.412	.143	12.84	6.20
Smith, Patrick	L-L	6-2	215	10-14-96	2	0	3.78	21	0	0	1	33	32	17	14	2	15	31	.260	.333	.226	8.37	4.05
Van Buren, Malcolm	R-R	6-4	185	7-5-98	1	5	5.40	12	8	0	0	42	30	28	25	5	32	59	.201	.232	.175	12.74	6.91
Willis, Marlin	L-L	6-4	190	6-5-98	2	1	2.83	11	5	0	0	48	35	17	15	4	28	49	.207	.208	.207	9.25	5.29
Zerpa, Angel	L-L	6-0	175	9-27-99	6	3	3.33	12	11	0	0	51	41	19	19	6	13	51	.218	.162	.232	8.94	2.28

Fielding

C: Atencio 24, Hancock 45. **1B:** Atencio 2, Familia 1, Means 1, Pasquantino 47, Porter 21. **2B:** Charleston 17, Gethings 21, Massey 27, Romero 6. **3B:** Gethings 5, Means 53, Romero 11. **SS:** Garcia 55, Gethings 11, Romero 5. **OF:** Charleston 13, Dixon 46, Filia 33, Hernandez 3, Hollie 40, Jackson 47, Lopez 16, Rave 13.

IDAHO FALLS CHUKARS   ROOKIE ADVANCED
PIONEER LEAGUE

Batting	B-T	HT	WT	DOB	AVG	vLH	vRH	G	AB	R	H	2B	3B	HR	RBI	BB	HBP	SH	SF	SO	SB	CS	SLG	OBP
Aplin, Rhett	L-L	6-2	220	10-10-95	.310	.327	.304	68	239	43	74	14	1	10	42	37	5	0	2	52	0	1	.502	.410
Bradshaw, Montae	R-R	5-10	170	4-29-96	.118	.333	.071	4	17	1	2	1	0	0	1	0	0	0	0	2	1	0	.177	.118
Dungan, Clay	L-R	6-1	190	6-2-96	.357	.429	.337	65	255	57	91	19	5	2	38	28	6	0	4	32	9	1	.494	.427
Emodi, Michael	R-R	6-4	225	4-18-96	.331	.395	.314	48	175	32	58	18	2	12	45	16	8	0	1	53	3	0	.663	.410
Garcia, Maikel	R-R	6-0	145	3-3-00	.222	--	.222	2	9	1	2	0	0	0	1	0	0	0	0	0	0	1	.222	.222
Govern, Jimmy	R-R	5-11	190	12-11-96	.083	.500	.000	3	12	1	1	1	0	0	2	0	0	0	0	4	0	0	.167	.083
Henry, Isaiah	R-R	6-3	185	3-22-99	.232	.227	.233	60	207	27	48	6	4	6	29	26	1	0	1	105	14	5	.387	.319
Hudgins, Chris	R-R	6-1	190	3-2-96	.304	.200	.333	6	23	4	7	2	0	0	3	3	0	0	0	7	0	0	.391	.385
James, Tyler	R-R	5-10	162	9-14-96	.200	.200	.200	49	165	27	33	6	3	3	15	12	4	3	0	58	5	2	.327	.271
Jones, Travis	R-R	6-4	210	9-29-95	.304	.300	.333	7	23	5	7	1	1	1	6	4	2	0	0	7	0	0	.565	.448
Marquez, Jose	B-R	6-0	175	10-7-97	.310	.288	.316	64	252	45	78	12	5	1	28	28	2	3	4	48	13	8	.409	.378
Mascarella, Wyatt	R-R	6-3	215	10-3-96	.194	.188	.196	20	67	11	13	4	0	1	6	9	0	0	1	33	0	0	.299	.286
McConnell, Brady	R-R	6-3	195	5-24-98	.211	.234	.200	38	152	25	32	12	1	4	22	14	2	1	0	66	5	3	.382	.286
Mondesi, Paul	R-R	6-0	235	7-7-98	.143	.000	.167	5	7	0	1	0	0	0	0	0	0	0	0	4	0	0	.143	.143
Nacero, Kember	R-R	5-11	155	3-5-00	.211	.293	.188	55	185	23	39	5	2	1	19	2	0	1		80	13	6	.276	.290
Negret, Juan Carlos	R-R	6-1	190	6-19-96	.240	.241	.240	68	250	36	60	14	0	13	47	16	5	0	6	74	6	0	.452	.292
Pineda, Hector	R-R	5-10	160	8-22-98	.191	.059	.224	32	84	11	16	1	0	1	5	10	3	0	1	27	0	0	.238	.296
Rodriguez, Ismaldo	B-R	6-0	175	7-3-98	.196	.225	.188	59	219	25	43	8	2	8	37	9	3	1	2	111	6	1	.361	.236
Romero, Rafael	R-R	5-10	155	11-14-98	.167	.250	.125	3	12	0	2	0	0	0	1	0	0	0	0	4	1	0	.167	.167
Smith, Isaiah	R-R	6-3	190	6-19-99	.226	.333	.200	9	31	2	7	3	1	0	4	1	3	0	0	12	4	2	.387	.314
Tolbert, Tyler	R-R	6-0	160	1-27-98	.382	.667	.321	9	34	11	13	2	3	0	6	1	0	3	1	8	2	1	.618	.389
Vidal, Stephan	R-R	6-1	215	4-4-96	.222	.177	.236	20	72	10	16	4	0	3	8	7	1	0	0	20	0	0	.403	.300

Pitching	B-T	HT	WT	DOB	W	L	ERA	G	GS	CG	SV	IP	H	R	ER	HR	BB	SO	AVG	vLH	vRH	K/9	BB/9
Adams, Derrick	L-L	6-3	215	3-8-97	2	1	2.54	18	0	0	4	46	50	18	13	0	11	45	.276	.340	.254	8.80	2.15
Alcantara, Adrian	R-R	6-1	178	8-29-99	1	0	3.60	1	1	0	0	5	3	2	2	0	2	4	.188	.000	.231	7.20	3.60
Bonnenfant, Brad	R-R	6-3	200	2-16-96	1	2	3.46	14	0	0	2	26	34	19	10	5	8	24	.312	.200	.354	8.31	2.77
Bryant, Noah	R-R	6-3	200	10-15-98	0	0	0.00	1	0	0	1	1	0	0	0	0	2	0	.000	--	.000	0.00	18.00
Cosby, Christian	R-R	6-5	215	12-21-96	1	1	4.75	11	1	0	0	36	51	23	19	3	13	37	.323	.225	.367	9.25	3.25
Cox, Brady	R-R	6-0	205	10-24-94	1	2	3.72	18	0	0	2	29	26	16	12	4	10	29	.228	.188	.258	9.00	3.10
Davenport, Cody	R-R	6-0	210	7-15-96	3	3	6.11	12	0	0	0	28	36	22	19	1	11	34	.305	.250	.355	10.93	3.54
Gambrell, Grant	L-R	6-4	225	11-21-97	1	6	6.67	11	10	0	0	27	41	25	20	5	11	28	.348	.359	.342	9.33	3.67
Haake, Zach	R-R	6-4	186	10-8-96	0	0	0.00	1	1	0	0	4	2	0	0	0	3	4	.154	.333	.100	8.31	6.23
Hellinger, Jaret	R-L	6-4	170	11-18-96	1	0	12.00	2	0	0	1	3	3	4	4	1	2	2	.273	.000	.300	6.00	6.00
Johnson, Bryar	R-R	6-3	200	8-17-99	2	3	4.35	13	6	0	0	52	55	31	25	5	17	49	.268	.265	.270	8.54	2.96
Kaufman, Rylan	L-L	6-4	190	6-23-99	0	0	3.60	1	1	0	0	5	4	2	2	0	1	3	.222	1.000	.177	5.40	1.80
Lienhard, Joe	R-R	6-5	235	3-21-97	1	1	2.88	13	0	0	1	25	24	10	8	1	9	24	.255	.250	.258	8.64	3.24
Manning, Austin	L-L	5-10	185	9-7-97	1	1	6.97	16	0	0	1	21	30	16	16	2	11	23	.345	.267	.386	10.02	4.79
Marsh, Alec	R-R	6-2	220	5-14-98	0	1	4.05	13	13	0	0	33	30	16	15	5	4	38	.238	.208	.260	10.26	1.08
Pineda, Hector	R-R	5-10	160	8-22-98	0	0	0.00	1	0	0	0	2	1	0	0	0	0	1	.143	.000	.200	4.50	0.00
Ramirez, Jose	R-R	6-2	225	1-10-98	2	3	4.83	18	0	0	1	32	33	19	17	6	15	25	.268	.205	.298	7.11	4.26
Ridings, Stephen	R-R	6-8	220	8-14-95	4	3	5.91	13	11	0	0	56	48	39	37	6	29	88	.225	.174	.260	14.06	4.63
Sylk, Augie	L-L	6-4	190	6-17-98	0	0	12.15	7	0	0	1	7	8	11	9	0	10	13	.286	.200	.304	17.55	13.50
Van Buren, Malcolm	R-R	6-4	185	7-5-98	0	0	2.25	1	0	0	1	4	3	1	1	0	1	6	.200	.000	.250	13.50	2.25
Veneziano, Anthony	L-L	6-5	205	9-1-97	3	4	5.59	13	11	0	1	47	65	35	29	6	13	44	.323	.400	.287	8.49	2.51
Wang, Chih-Ting	L-L	6-1	230	1-24-99	4	1	3.18	15	0	0	0	34	33	15	12	2	9	39	.248	.270	.247	10.32	2.38
Watts, Cole	R-L	6-4	205	11-2-95	1	6	7.71	14	7	0	0	42	59	45	36	6	16	46	.324	.364	.315	9.86	3.43
Webb, Nathan	R-R	6-2	215	8-20-97	4	3	4.55	13	12	1	0	63	72	43	32	6	27	77	.288	.329	.267	10.94	3.84
Willis, Marlin	L-L	6-4	190	6-5-98	1	0	0.00	1	0	0	0	2	0	0	0	0	0	0	.000	.000	.000	0.00	0.00
Zerpa, Angel	L-L	6-0	175	9-27-99	0	0	4.15	1	1	0	0	4	5	2	2	0	1	4	.278	.000	.333	8.31	2.08

Fielding

C: Emodi 36, Hudgins 2, Mascarella 18, Mondesi 2, Vidal 18. **1B:** Aplin 56, Hudgins 1, Jones 4, Pineda 19. **2B:** Dungan 19, James 15, Marquez 28, Nacero 16. **3B:** Govern 3, Marquez 30, Nacero 30, Pineda 13, Romero 3. **SS:** Dungan 44, Garcia 2, McConnell 24, Nacero 6. **OF:** Bradshaw 4, Henry 58, James 34, Negret 57, Rodriguez 55, Smith 9, Tolbert 9.

AZL ROYALS
ARIZONA LEAGUE

Batting	B-T	HT	WT	DOB	AVG	vLH	vRH	G	AB	R	H	2B	3B	HR	RBI	BB	HBP	SH	SF	SO	SB	CS	SLG	OBP
Aracena, Ricky	B-R	5-8	160	10-2-97	.333	.200	.375	6	21	6	7	1	0	2	9	4	1	0	0	2	1	0	.667	.462
Bushor, Chase	R-R	6-0	190	10-9-95	.351	.000	.406	14	37	8	13	1	0	0	4	4	0	0	1	8	1	0	.378	.405
Camarillo, Gary	R-R	6-1	157	7-5-01	.275	.111	.310	14	51	9	14	0	1	1	7	6	0	0	1	12	2	0	.373	.345
Collins, Darryl	L-R	6-2	185	9-16-01	.320	.283	.336	48	181	24	58	7	7	0	25	22	3	1	1	30	1	2	.437	.401
Familia, Felix	R-R	6-2	205	10-13-98	.200	.200	.200	20	60	5	12	4	0	0	2	5	0	0	0	19	1	1	.267	.262
Fernandez, Xavier	R-R	5-11	197	7-15-95	.375	.667	.308	5	16	3	6	2	0	1	6	0	0	0	1	0	1	0	.688	.353
Gethings, Jack	L-R	5-10	175	10-9-96	.000	--	.000	1	4	0	0	0	0	0	0	1	0	0	0	1	1	0	.000	.200
Gigliotti, Michael	L-L	6-1	180	2-14-96	.429	.333	.455	4	14	3	6	1	0	0	2	3	0	1	0	3	2	0	.500	.529
Gonzalez, Herard	B-R	5-11	167	5-16-01	.308	.357	.291	48	159	28	49	1	2	3	24	31	3	2	4	37	3	5	.396	.421
Govern, Jimmy	R-R	5-11	190	12-11-96	.365	.488	.319	46	156	33	57	17	3	6	33	34	7	0	2	20	6	3	.628	.493
Hernandez, Diego	L-L	6-0	150	11-21-00	.283	.211	.306	39	159	20	45	4	1	1	19	10	1	3	1	33	7	5	.340	.328
Hernandez, Omar	R-R	5-11	170	12-10-01	.290	.217	.306	36	131	21	38	7	1	0	16	8	4	2	2	20	2	1	.359	.345
Isbel, Kyle	L-R	5-11	183	3-3-97	.360	.333	.364	7	25	9	9	2	0	2	7	2	0	0	0	5	3	1	.680	.407
Jones, Travis	R-R	6-4	210	9-29-95	.000	--	.000	1	2	0	0	0	0	0	1	1	0	0	0	1	0	0	.000	.500
Maican, Diego	R-R	6-3	180	10-24-00	.233	.256	.227	48	180	27	42	10	1	2	22	23	5	0	4	58	1	0	.333	.330
McConnell, Brady	R-R	6-3	195	5-24-98	.250	.000	.286	2	8	3	2	1	0	1	1	1	0	0	0	2	0	0	.750	.333
Mondesi, Paul	R-R	6-0	235	7-7-98	.286	.333	.273	13	42	5	12	0	0	0	2	1	1	0	1	8	0	0	.286	.311
Sanchez, Ricardo	L-R	5-9	185	5-4-95	.000	.000	.000	3	8	0	0	0	0	0	0	0	0	0	0	2	0	0	.000	.000
Soto, Edickson	R-R	5-11	165	2-28-00	.245	.231	.250	30	106	11	26	4	1	2	19	3	1	1	3	20	1	1	.359	.266
Steel, Bruce	R-R	6-2	195	12-26-96	.300	.500	.250	4	10	1	3	1	0	0	2	0	0	0	0	5	0	0	.400	.417
Tolbert, Tyler	R-R	6-0	160	1-27-98	.221	.200	.227	41	140	26	31	2	1	0	18	22	7	2	3	41	26	0	.250	.349
Valdez, Enrique	L-R	6-0	158	5-15-01	.220	.125	.250	46	164	19	36	8	2	0	23	11	1	3	2	46	4	4	.293	.270
Vicente, Warling	R-R	5-10	165	6-8-99	.224	.231	.222	31	76	18	17	4	0	0	5	12	3	0	1	26	4	0	.276	.348
Witt Jr., Bobby	R-R	6-1	190	6-14-00	.262	.333	.242	37	164	30	43	2	5	1	27	13	1	0	2	35	9	1	.354	.317

Pitching	B-T	HT	WT	DOB	W	L	ERA	G	GS	CG	SV	IP	H	R	ER	HR	BB	SO	AVG	vLH	vRH	K/9	BB/9
Abreu, Brian	R-R	6-2	194	6-3-99	1	0	15.43	9	0	0	0	7	5	14	12	0	18	9	.192	.133	.273	11.57	23.14
Acevedo, Randy	R-R	6-1	155	3-14-97	1	2	3.48	7	7	0	0	21	22	8	8	1	3	21	.282	.324	.250	9.15	1.31
Aquino, Ismael	R-R	6-2	170	9-2-98	1	1	11.45	8	0	0	1	11	16	14	14	2	7	14	.333	.250	.350	11.45	5.73
2-team total (10 Athletics Green)					2	2	7.22	18	1	0	1	29	31	29	23	2	18	34	.272	.258	.277	10.67	5.65
Barroso, Luis	R-R	6-3	165	9-7-98	3	2	3.54	14	6	0	3	56	57	25	22	5	9	67	.264	.261	.266	10.77	1.45
Bonnenfant, Brad	R-R	6-3	200	2-16-96	0	0	0.00	1	0	0	0	2	1	0	0	0	0	2	.143	.250	.000	9.00	0.00
Broughton, Josh	R-R	6-3	175	7-22-97	0	0	9.53	6	0	0	1	6	8	6	6	1	1	5	.348	.500	.231	7.94	1.59
Buck, Donavin	R-R	6-6	240	4-25-96	0	0	0.00	1	0	0	0	2	2	0	0	0	1	3	.333	--	.333	5.40	0.00
Cabrera, Rovaldis	L-L	5-10	176	11-22-99	4	1	3.86	12	2	0	0	37	34	16	16	5	14	38	.239	.323	.216	9.16	3.38
Castillo, Adriam	R-R	6-5	230	11-19-98	0	1	4.73	11	0	0	1	13	15	8	7	1	9	12	.278	.300	.265	8.10	6.08
Chapman, Tyshaun	L-R	6-2	195	11-13-97	0	0	3.38	5	0	0	0	5	2	2	2	0	9	9	.111	.000	.167	15.19	15.19
Dipoto, Jonah	R-R	6-1	225	9-3-96	0	0	27.00	1	0	0	0	1	4	3	3	0	1	1	.571	.600	.500	9.00	9.00
Duarte, Daniel	R-R	6-0	170	12-4-96	0	0	1.69	4	0	0	0	5	6	3	1	0	1	6	.273	.500	.083	10.13	1.69
Fillmyer, Heath	R-R	6-1	195	5-16-94	0	0	0.00	2	2	0	0	3	3	0	0	0	1	1	.273	.400	.167	3.00	3.00
Garcia, Heribert	R-R	6-0	190	10-2-99	4	3	3.28	11	7	0	0	49	51	26	18	5	10	40	.266	.269	.263	7.30	1.82
Hahn, Jesse	R-R	6-4	215	7-30-89	0	0	0.00	1	1	0	0	1	1	0	0	0	0	2	.250	.000	1.000	18.00	0.00
Hernandez, Carlos	R-R	6-4	175	3-11-97	0	2	7.36	5	5	0	0	11	14	9	9	1	3	12	.304	.250	.333	9.82	2.45
Jimenez, Wilmer	L-L	5-11	162	6-19-98	0	0	1.74	7	0	0	2	10	8	4	2	1	6	19	.211	.100	.250	16.55	5.23
Jin, Woo-Young	R-R	6-2	210	2-5-01	6	2	2.35	14	1	0	2	46	33	14	12	3	13	54	.203	.222	.190	10.57	2.54
Lynch, Daniel	L-L	6-6	190	11-17-96	0	0	1.00	3	3	0	0	9	6	1	1	0	3	12	.200	.333	.185	12.00	3.00
Marquez, Emilio	L-L	5-8	170	4-28-98	5	1	2.51	13	6	0	0	47	39	16	13	3	7	63	.217	.167	.232	12.15	1.35
Noriega, Cruz	R-R	6-1	175	10-1-97	3	3	5.11	13	5	0	0	44	55	29	25	2	17	37	.313	.299	.321	7.57	3.48
Paulino, Anderson	R-R	6-2	200	9-12-98	3	0	4.90	14	10	0	0	61	75	38	33	5	24	44	.305	.272	.325	6.53	3.56
Snider, Collin	R-R	6-4	200	10-10-95	0	0	2.08	3	1	0	0	4	3	1	1	0	0	0	.188	.000	.300	0.00	0.00
Solano, Adrian	R-R	6-1	165	10-17-99	1	1	4.45	14	0	0	1	28	31	20	14	1	11	20	.274	.381	.211	6.35	3.49
Sosa, Onliber	R-R	6-1	195	11-4-97	0	1	13.50	4	0	0	0	6	6	6	6	2	5	4	.375	.375	.375	9.00	11.25
Stil, Matt	R-R	6-3	190	7-5-00	0	3	6.30	9	0	0	0	10	9	11	7	2	10	15	.257	.133	.350	13.50	9.00
Sylk, Augie	L-L	6-4	190	6-17-98	1	0	0.00	5	0	0	2	5	3	0	0	0	2	8	.158	.333	.125	13.50	3.38

Fielding

C: Familia 11, Fernandez 3, Hernandez 35, Mondesi 12, Sanchez 3. **1B:** Bushor 1, Familia 9, Jones 1, Maican 47, Steel 1. **2B:** Aracena 3, Bushor 1, Gethings 1, Gonzalez 40, Govern 1, Tolbert 8, Valdez 6. **3B:** Bushor 8, Gonzalez 3, Govern 44, Steel 3. **SS:** Tolbert 5, Valdez 25, Witt Jr. 26. **OF:** Camarillo 12, Collins 46, Gigliotti 3, Hernandez 36, Isbel 6, Soto 25, Tolbert 24, Vicente 27.

DSL ROYALS
DOMINICAN SUMMER LEAGUE

Batting	B-T	HT	WT	DOB	AVG	vLH	vRH	G	AB	R	H	2B	3B	HR	RBI	BB	HBP	SH	SF	SO	SB	CS	SLG	OBP
Almanzar, Luis	B-R	6-1	170	5-11-99	.213	.118	.250	26	61	7	13	2	0	0	3	4	1	0	0	17	0	2	.246	.273
Calderon, Junior	R-R	6-0	175	12-9-01	.251	.208	.258	56	179	34	45	10	2	3	23	32	2	0	2	30	5	4	.380	.367
Candelario, Wilmin	R-R	5-11	165	9-11-01	.315	.216	.340	49	184	33	58	7	8	4	27	23	3	1	2	62	11	11	.505	.396
Carvajal, Jean	R-R	5-10	153	12-8-00	.225	.200	.228	60	147	27	33	6	2	1	11	19	6	1	0	54	15	4	.313	.337
Cruz, Reymond	R-R	6-1	165	4-14-01	.269	.333	.254	29	78	12	21	3	2	1	13	14	3	0	0	28	11	3	.397	.400
De Leon, Pedro	R-R	5-9	175	2-12-01	.167	.167	.167	34	78	15	13	2	3	0	10	13	2	0	0	23	7	1	.269	.301
De Los Santos, Jaswel	L-R	6-1	175	1-28-02	.264	.216	.274	57	227	43	60	12	5	1	23	25	1	0	1	50	13	7	.374	.339
Febres, Nicolas	R-R	5-11	178	10-11-98	.205	.375	.179	43	122	13	25	0	0	0	10	31	1	2	2	17	1	1	.205	.365

Name	B-T	HT	WT	DOB	AVG	vLH	vRH	G	AB	R	H	2B	3B	HR	RBI	BB	HBP	SH	SF	SO	SB	CS	OBP	SLG
Florentino, Omar	B-R	5-9	145	10-26-01	.227	.191	.232	57	185	37	42	8	3	2	9	32	1	1	0	42	14	6	.335	.344
Freites, Jose	R-R	6-1	180	11-25-01	.198	.235	.190	64	197	20	39	8	1	1	12	26	8	0	3	36	4	3	.264	.312
Garcia, Xionel	R-R	6-2	180	12-15-00	.228	.152	.240	66	241	38	55	10	4	3	27	24	3	0	0	62	9	7	.340	.306
Grullon, Francis	B-R	5-10	170	10-13-00	.277	.233	.286	57	177	39	49	8	3	4	29	33	1	4	4	18	15	7	.424	.386
Herrera, Frank	B-R	6-1	170	3-20-01	.259	.152	.280	54	201	23	52	8	1	4	31	11	8	1	3	17	3	5	.368	.318
Marinez, Neyfi	L-R	6-1	175	9-7-00	.266	.195	.281	65	233	35	62	12	5	6	37	39	2	0	2	62	6	5	.438	.373
Martinez, Edgar	R-R	5-10	150	2-14-01	.312	.250	.324	62	202	40	63	8	1	0	24	33	3	4	3	43	22	12	.361	.411
Martinez, Jarvis	L-L	6-2	180	8-18-00	.178	.053	.205	34	107	16	19	3	2	1	11	12	1	1	1	34	3	3	.271	.265
Medina, Yesi	R-R	5-10	185	4-18-00	.264	.500	.242	35	72	11	19	4	0	1	13	12	4	0	1	12	1	0	.361	.393
Meli, Densi	R-R	6-0	170	1-24-01	.201	.259	.191	55	179	25	36	5	0	5	19	20	8	0	1	71	5	2	.313	.308
Moreno, Olivber	R-R	6-1	187	6-28-01	.288	.280	.291	65	229	44	66	13	1	4	32	36	8	2	1	41	13	8	.406	.402
Pena, Deivy	B-R	6-1	165	10-20-00	.149	.259	.126	53	154	18	23	5	1	0	15	23	4	2	2	82	3	4	.195	.273
Pire, Enmanuel	R-R	5-10	165	5-18-01	.309	.258	.324	39	136	20	42	6	1	0	12	13	1	1	3	21	2	2	.368	.366
Quintana, Guillermo	R-R	6-1	180	3-16-01	.284	.382	.263	60	190	22	54	17	0	2	33	32	4	1	3	30	5	2	.405	.393
Ramirez, Jean	L-L	5-10	180	10-25-00	.329	.267	.336	53	161	27	53	2	1	2	28	21	1	2	7	18	29	8	.391	.395
Reyes, Jesus	R-R	5-10	160	9-14-00	.231	.000	.273	7	13	1	3	1	0	0	1	2	0	1	0	3	1	0	.308	.333
Reyes, Kevin	R-R	5-10	160	5-5-02	.197	.125	.191	55	152	26	30	4	0	0	9	17	1	3	0	42	26	9	.224	.282
Rodriguez, Omar	R-R	6-1	190	4-9-00	.272	.333	.260	52	173	8	47	11	0	2	17	21	5	0	0	47	1	1	.370	.367
Rodriguez, Rodrigo	B-R	6-0	170	9-25-00	.192	.056	.222	31	99	8	19	2	0	0	8	12	2	0	0	27	0	3	.212	.292
Salon, Dionmy	R-R	6-2	190	11-18-01	.200	.313	.184	42	130	17	26	3	0	0	9	22	3	0	0	26	1	2	.223	.329
Sanchez, Javier	R-R	5-11	160	10-27-99	.259	.455	.237	37	108	13	28	5	0	0	11	13	3	2	0	31	5	2	.306	.355
Seijas, Rothaikeg	R-R	5-11	170	7-22-02	.220	.333	.205	41	132	19	29	6	1	1	17	27	1	1	3	37	4	1	.303	.354

Pitching	B-T	HT	WT	DOB	W	L	ERA	G	GS	CG	SV	IP	H	R	ER	HR	BB	SO	AVG	vLH	vRH	K/9	BB/9
Almonte, Junior	R-R	6-1	175	4-10-00	2	1	5.81	13	4	0	0	26	20	19	17	0	15	20	.215	.281	.180	6.84	5.13
Arias, Wander	R-R	6-4	220	11-3-99	2	0	0.90	7	3	0	0	20	11	3	2	0	8	22	.167	.182	.159	9.90	3.60
Avila, Luinder	R-R	6-3	170	8-21-01	1	2	6.41	12	2	0	0	27	25	19	19	1	16	22	.263	.200	.300	7.43	5.40
Ballista, Jose	R-R	5-10	168	9-4-00	2	1	2.66	15	0	0	5	24	13	7	7	0	8	24	.159	.182	.143	9.13	3.04
Breton, Fraicy	L-L	6-3	196	6-10-01	1	2	5.97	12	3	0	0	32	31	24	21	1	20	28	.250	.304	.238	7.96	5.68
Brito, Angel	R-R	6-2	165	3-11-01	3	3	3.41	11	5	0	0	34	28	16	13	0	12	15	.222	.211	.227	3.93	3.15
Cabrera, Daury	R-R	6-4	190	10-23-00	1	4	4.54	13	9	0	0	42	44	28	21	4	16	29	.267	.226	.286	6.26	3.46
Camargo, Cesar	R-R	6-1	195	7-21-99	0	0	0.00	1	0	0	0	0	0	0	0	0	1	1	.000	--	.000	27.00	27.00
Catano, Jose	L-L	6-3	180	6-10-01	0	1	4.50	6	0	0	0	10	14	7	5	1	6	17	.350	.400	.343	15.30	5.40
Cepeda, Luis	L-L	6-0	160	10-12-00	5	3	2.37	12	12	0	0	49	42	19	13	4	6	61	.230	.125	.245	11.13	1.09
Cordero, Pedro	R-R	6-3	170	11-29-01	1	4	6.23	13	2	0	0	26	29	28	18	1	18	20	.290	.455	.244	6.92	6.23
Correa, Jean	R-R	6-1	145	2-16-98	1	3	2.01	15	1	0	2	31	27	10	7	0	3	28	.241	.366	.169	8.04	0.86
Cuevas, Frandy	L-L	5-11	180	1-19-02	3	0	4.56	12	0	0	0	24	18	14	12	2	19	27	.220	.188	.227	10.27	7.23
De La Rosa, Luis	R-R	6-1	170	7-6-02	2	1	2.33	12	11	0	0	39	28	10	10	0	7	52	.197	.200	.196	12.10	1.63
De Los Santos, Kelvin	R-R	6-4	215	2-13-98	5	1	2.01	14	0	0	3	22	17	10	5	1	7	22	.207	.200	.210	8.87	2.82
Diaz, Andres	R-R	6-1	155	7-6-01	3	1	1.87	13	13	0	0	53	51	20	11	1	6	43	.249	.211	.269	7.30	1.02
Feliz, Darwin	R-R	6-1	175	9-19-96	2	3	4.57	14	6	0	2	45	56	25	23	4	7	31	.298	.419	.262	6.15	1.39
Gonzalez, Adrian	R-R	6-2	170	9-30-00	2	1	4.56	13	0	0	2	26	27	19	13	1	5	13	.265	.128	.349	4.56	1.75
Guaba, Yordy	R-R	6-3	175	9-8-00	3	2	3.98	15	0	0	1	32	43	20	14	1	9	31	.331	.286	.347	8.81	2.56
Liquet, Johnfi	L-L	5-11	150	11-4-00	2	2	5.40	12	4	0	0	23	27	19	14	3	8	21	.287	.278	.290	8.10	3.09
Maduro, Cal	R-R	6-0	165	10-25-01	0	0	2.56	14	0	0	6	32	27	13	9	1	8	38	.233	.259	.225	10.80	2.27
Martinez, Juan	R-R	5-11	170	4-6-01	0	2	10.35	12	0	0	0	20	35	26	23	2	13	13	.380	.414	.365	5.85	5.85
Matos, Yonathan	R-R	6-3	194	7-6-98	4	5	7.85	14	4	0	1	29	36	27	25	2	16	33	.316	.333	.310	10.36	5.02
Mendez, Leandro	R-R	5-11	181	4-21-00	2	2	4.44	13	0	0	0	24	25	15	12	1	9	14	.281	.265	.291	5.18	3.33
Morales, Austin	R-R	6-2	185	1-23-98	2	0	1.61	15	0	0	5	22	15	5	4	0	12	12	.195	.214	.184	4.84	4.84
Mujica, Pablo	L-L	6-0	171	6-26-01	1	1	3.65	13	0	0	0	37	32	17	15	0	16	44	.234	.167	.244	10.70	3.89
Ovalle, Luilly	R-R	6-3	170	10-13-00	3	1	1.88	12	5	0	0	38	29	13	8	1	7	34	.207	.255	.177	7.98	1.64
Paulino, Christian	L-L	6-1	166	10-2-01	0	2	9.22	11	0	0	0	14	12	18	14	0	22	18	.255	.444	.211	11.85	14.49
Peralta, Dario	R-R	6-1	170	10-12-00	2	2	2.58	12	7	0	0	38	29	14	11	1	14	26	.206	.170	.232	6.10	3.29
Perez, Wanly	B-R	6-1	165	1-4-00	0	2	6.30	14	3	0	2	30	32	27	21	1	17	31	.281	.286	.279	9.30	5.10
Polanco, Gustavo	L-L	6-2	170	5-9-00	1	0	16.20	4	0	0	0	7	15	12	12	1	1	8	.469	.200	.519	10.80	1.35
Polo, Juan	R-R	6-1	182	5-18-01	3	0	6.75	14	0	0	0	21	18	17	16	0	23	36	.225	.208	.232	15.19	9.70
Ramos, Nelcido	R-R	6-2	180	1-17-01	1	0	5.32	14	0	0	0	22	15	17	13	1	16	17	.190	.182	.193	6.95	6.55
Reynoso, Jeffry	R-R	6-2	185	10-11-01	3	0	1.94	12	8	0	0	42	38	20	9	0	9	31	.247	.368	.077	6.70	1.94
Rosario, Wanner	R-R	6-0	160	1-9-01	0	0	8.71	6	0	0	0	10	8	14	10	0	15	7	.229	.182	.250	6.10	13.06
Sanchez, Carlos	R-R	6-0	175	6-20-99	0	0	1.69	3	3	0	0	11	8	4	2	0	4	9	.222	.308	.174	7.59	3.38
Santana, Osiris	R-R	5-11	165	10-11-01	2	0	2.74	13	0	0	1	23	21	12	7	0	9	21	.241	.321	.203	8.22	3.52
Sosa, Onliber	R-R	6-1	195	11-4-97	0	0	0.00	1	0	0	0	1	1	0	0	0	0	1	.200	--	.200	6.75	0.00
Valenzuela, Oscar	R-R	5-11	171	3-2-01	1	4	2.96	14	0	0	2	49	48	22	16	2	10	23	.258	.196	.285	4.25	1.85
Valerio, Samuel	R-R	6-4	220	10-8-01	3	1	4.62	11	4	0	0	25	23	19	13	1	13	31	.240	.200	.262	11.01	4.62
Vasquez, Javier	R-R	6-1	180	1-6-00	3	2	5.13	15	0	0	3	25	15	15	14	0	18	33	.163	.231	.130	12.04	6.57
Vasquez, Richi	R-R	6-1	155	9-18-00	1	2	2.90	15	1	0	0	31	29	14	10	0	11	33	.244	.280	.234	9.58	3.19
Villar, Luis	L-L	5-10	160	11-8-00	0	4	2.59	13	11	0	0	49	47	22	14	0	7	52	.246	.171	.263	9.62	1.29
Vitriago, Daniel	L-L	5-10	155	12-5-00	1	1	1.34	11	5	0	0	34	24	6	5	1	5	41	.202	.222	.198	10.96	1.34

Fielding

C: Medina 25, Pire 29, Quintana 6, Rodriguez 32, Rodriguez 16, Salon 21. **1B:** Almanzar 7, Calderon 1, De Leon 5, Febres 41, Herrera 51, Meli 8, Pena 5, Quintana 3, Sanchez 5. **2B:** Almanzar 5, Carvajal 15, De Leon 24, Florentino 7, Grullon 27, Martinez 6, Pena 16, Reyes 27, Reyes 2. **3B:** Almanzar 7, Calderon 54, Carvajal 14, De Leon 1, Grullon 2, Martinez 19, Meli 17, Pena 33, Sanchez 3. **SS:** Almanzar 3, Candelario 48, Florentino 45, Martinez 9, Meli 1, Reyes 25. **OF:** Almanzar 1, Carvajal 1, Cruz 5, De Leon 1, De Los Santos 39, De Los Santos 1, Freites 13, Garcia 28, Grullon 1, Marinez 7, Martinez 1, Martinez 12, Meli 1, Moreno 47, Ramirez 48, Seijas 39.

Los Angeles Angels

SEASON IN A SENTENCE: The Angels hoped to contend after signing Mike Trout to a record $360 million contract extension, but Justin Upton, Andrelton Simmons, Shohei Ohtani, Zack Cozart, Tommy La Stella and Andrew Heaney all missed more than two months with injuries, pitcher Tyler Skaggs was found dead in his hotel room during a July road trip to Texas after he overdosed on opioids, and the Angels skidded to a 72-90 finish, their worst record in 20 years.

HIGH POINT: On July 12, the Angels played their first home game after Skaggs' death and every player wore a jersey with Skaggs' name and number on the back. After Skaggs' mother threw out the first pitch, Taylor Cole and Felix Peña combined for a no-hitter in a 13-0 win over the Mariners. After the final out, the Angels laid their jerseys on the mound in an impromptu, tearful ceremony honoring their fallen teammate.

LOW POINT: The Angels banded together after Skaggs' death and sat just 4.5 games out of a wild card on July 24, but they dropped five of seven at home to the lowly Tigers and Orioles. The losses began a tailspin that would last through the season.

NOTABLE ROOKIES: Righthander Griffin Canning debuted at the end of April and ranked second among Angels starters with a 4.58 ERA before he was shut down in August with elbow inflammation. Infielder Luis Rengifo showed flashes of promise at second base, and righthander Ty Buttrey emerged as a power-armed setup man before fading in the second half. Lefthanders Jose Suarez and Patrick Sandoval, infielder Matt Thaiss and first baseman/lefthander Jared Walsh all debuted but failed to make much impact.

KEY TRANSACTIONS: The Angels spent $34.35 million on Matt Harvey, Trevor Cahill, Cody Allen, Jonathan Lucroy and Justin Bour in free agency and they all flopped. Just Cahill and Bour remained with the team by the end of the season. La Stella (trade) and Brian Goodwin (waivers) proved astute offseason pickups.

DOWN ON THE FARM: The Angels posted the lowest minor league winning percentage (.407) of any organization and had none of their seven affiliates make the playoffs. Top prospects Jo Adell and Brandon Marsh each hit over .300 at Double-A Mobile in the Southern League, and Walsh led the Triple-A Pacific Coast League with a 1.109 OPS. Infielder Jeremiah Jackson tied the Rookie-level Pioneer League record with 23 home runs.

OPENING DAY PAYROLL: $167,456,465 (7th).

PLAYERS OF THE YEAR

ROBERT BINDER · ROBERT BINDER

MAJOR LEAGUE	MINOR LEAGUE
Mike Trout OF	**Jared Walsh** 1B
.291/.438/.645	(Triple-A)
45 HR, 104 RBIs	.325/.423/.686,
AL-best 1.083 OPS	36 HR, 86 RBIs

ORGANIZATION LEADERS

Batting		*Minimum 250 AB
MAJORS		
* AVG	Tommy La Stella	.295
* OPS	Mike Trout	1.083
HR	Mike Trout	45
RBI	Mike Trout	104
MINORS		
* AVG	Jared Walsh, Salt Lake	.325
* OBP	Taylor Ward, Salt Lake	.427
* SLG	Jared Walsh, Salt Lake	.686
* OPS	Jared Walsh, Salt Lake	1.109
R	Taylor Ward, Salt Lake	102
H	Jose Rojas, Salt Lake	151
TB	Jose Rojas, Salt Lake	297
2B	Jose Rojas, Salt Lake	39
3B	Devin Davis, Inland Empire	9
HR	Jared Walsh, Salt Lake	36
RBI	Jose Rojas, Salt Lake	107
BB	Taylor Ward, Salt Lake	80
SO	Nonnie Williams, Burlington	166
SB	Nonnie Williams, Burlington	23

Pitching		#Minimum 75 IP
MAJORS		
W	Felix Pena	8
# ERA	Tyler Skaggs	4.29
SO	Andrew Heaney	118
SV	Hansel Robles	23
MINORS		
W	Kyle Tyler, Burlington, Inland Empire	10
L	Cristopher Molina, Burlington, Inland Empire	11
# ERA	Jose Soriano, Burlington, AZL Angels	2.51
G	Jeremy Rhoades, Salt Lake	43
GS	Cristopher Molina, Burlington, Inland Empire	22
SV	Jake Jewell, Salt Lake	8
IP	Cristopher Molina, Burlington, Inland Empire	129
BB	Cole Duensing, Burlington, AZL Angels	69
SO	Hector Yan, Burlington	148
# AVG	Hector Yan, Burlington	.190

General Manager: Billy Eppler. **Farm Director:** Mike LaCassa. **Scouting Director:** Matt Swanson.

Class	Team	League	W	L	PCT	Finish	Manager
Majors	Los Angeles Angels	American	72	90	.444	10th (15)	Brad Ausmus
Triple-A	Salt Lake Bees	Pacific Coast	60	79	.432	14th (16)	Lou Marson
Double-A	Mobile BayBears	Southern	50	86	.368	1st (10)	David Newhan
High A	Inland Empire 66ers	California	57	82	.410	8th (8)	Ryan Barba
Low A	Burlington Bees	Midwest	66	74	.471	11th (16)	Jack Howell
Rookie	Orem Owlz	Pioneer	30	46	.395	8th (8)	Jack Santora
Rookie	AZL Angels	Arizona	19	37	.339	20th (21)	Dave Stapleton
Overall 2019 Minor League Record			282	404	.411	30th (30)	

ORGANIZATION STATISTICS

LOS ANGELES ANGELS
AMERICAN LEAGUE

Batting	B-T	HT	WT	DOB	AVG	vLH	vRH	G	AB	R	H	2B	3B	HR	RBI	BB	HBP	SH	SF	SO	SB	CS	SLG	OBP
Bemboom, Anthony	L-R	6-2	200	1-18-90	.102	.200	.091	22	49	2	5	0	0	1	3	1	0	1	0	19	0	0	.163	.120
2-team total (3 Tampa Bay)					.130	.200	.122	25	54	2	7	1	0	1	4	1	0	1	0	21	0	0	.204	.146
Bour, Justin	L-R	6-4	270	5-28-88	.172	.167	.173	52	151	18	26	5	0	8	26	17	1	0	1	52	0	0	.364	.259
Bourjos, Peter	R-R	6-1	190	3-31-87	.091	.077	.111	26	44	4	4	1	0	0	2	1	0	0	1	15	2	0	.114	.109
Calhoun, Kole	L-L	5-10	215	10-14-87	.232	.212	.240	152	552	92	128	29	1	33	74	70	7	0	2	162	4	1	.467	.325
Cowart, Kaleb	B-R	6-3	225	6-2-92	.160	.333	.136	9	25	1	4	3	0	0	1	0	0	0	0	7	1	0	.280	.192
Cozart, Zack	R-R	6-0	205	8-12-85	.124	.119	.127	38	97	4	12	2	0	0	7	5	2	0	3	16	0	0	.144	.178
Fletcher, David	R-R	5-9	185	5-31-94	.290	.276	.296	154	596	83	173	30	4	6	49	55	0	1	1	64	8	3	.384	.350
Garneau, Dustin	R-R	6-2	205	8-13-87	.232	.333	.196	28	69	11	16	3	0	2	7	8	4	0	0	18	0	0	.362	.346
2-team total (7 Oakland)					.244	.300	.214	35	86	14	21	5	0	3	14	10	4	0	0	22	0	0	.407	.350
Goodwin, Brian	L-R	6-0	200	11-2-90	.262	.263	.261	136	413	65	108	29	3	17	47	38	3	1	3	129	7	3	.470	.326
Hermosillo, Michael	R-R	6-0	205	1-17-95	.139	.000	.172	18	36	7	5	1	1	0	3	5	4	0	1	19	2	0	.222	.304
La Stella, Tommy	L-R	5-11	180	1-31-89	.295	.265	.306	80	292	49	86	8	0	16	44	20	3	0	0	28	0	0	.486	.346
Lucroy, Jonathan	R-R	6-0	200	6-13-86	.242	.217	.255	74	240	28	58	8	1	7	30	21	4	0	3	39	0	0	.371	.310
Ohtani, Shohei	L-R	6-4	210	7-5-94	.287	.282	.288	106	384	51	110	20	5	18	62	33	2	0	4	110	12	3	.505	.343
Parker, Jarrett	L-L	6-4	225	1-1-89	.000	--	.000	5	12	1	0	0	0	0	0	3	0	0	0	8	0	0	.000	.200
Puello, Cesar	R-R	6-2	220	4-1-91	.390	.364	.421	12	41	6	16	3	0	3	12	3	6	0	0	8	0	0	.683	.500
Pujols, Albert	R-R	6-3	235	1-16-80	.244	.261	.236	131	491	55	120	22	0	23	93	43	3	0	8	68	3	0	.430	.305
Rengifo, Luis	B-R	5-10	195	2-26-97	.238	.223	.246	108	357	44	85	18	3	7	33	40	5	1	3	93	2	5	.364	.321
Simmons, Andrelton	R-R	6-2	195	9-4-89	.264	.303	.251	103	398	47	105	19	0	7	40	24	2	0	0	37	10	2	.364	.309
Smith, Kevan	R-R	6-4	240	6-28-88	.251	.338	.203	67	191	21	48	12	0	5	20	16	3	0	1	37	2	0	.393	.318
Stassi, Max	R-R	5-10	200	3-15-91	.071	.059	.080	20	42	3	3	0	0	0	2	5	0	0	2	15	0	0	.071	.163
2-team total (31 Houston)					.136	.028	.177	51	132	7	18	1	0	1	5	12	1	0	2	49	0	0	.167	.211
Thaiss, Matt	L-R	6-0	215	5-6-95	.211	.227	.208	53	147	17	31	7	0	8	23	17	0	0	0	52	0	0	.422	.293
Tovar, Wilfredo	R-R	5-7	180	8-11-91	.193	.233	.150	31	83	5	16	5	0	0	5	5	0	0	1	15	0	0	.253	.239
Trout, Mike	R-R	6-2	235	8-7-91	.292	.266	.303	134	470	110	137	27	2	45	104	110	16	0	4	120	11	2	.645	.438
Upton, Justin	R-R	6-1	215	8-25-87	.215	.136	.248	63	219	34	47	8	0	12	40	32	0	0	5	78	1	1	.416	.309
Walsh, Jared	L-L	6-0	210	7-30-93	.203	.250	.197	31	79	6	16	5	1	1	5	6	2	0	0	35	0	0	.329	.276
Ward, Taylor	R-R	6-1	200	12-14-93	.191	.167	.200	20	42	4	8	3	0	1	2	6	0	0	0	23	0	0	.333	.292
Wong, Kean	L-R	5-11	185	4-17-95	.000	.000	.000	1	4	1	0	0	0	0	0	0	0	0	0	1	0	0	.000	.000
2-team total (6 Tampa Bay)					.167	.333	.133	7	18	2	3	0	0	0	0	0	0	0	0	6	0	1	.167	.167

Pitching	B-T	HT	WT	DOB	W	L	ERA	G	GS	CG	SV	IP	H	R	ER	HR	BB	SO	AVG	vLH	vRH	K/9	BB/9
Allen, Cody	R-R	6-1	210	11-20-88	0	2	6.26	25	0	0	4	23	24	16	16	9	20	29	.255	.244	.264	11.35	7.83
Anderson, Justin	L-R	6-3	230	9-28-92	3	0	5.55	54	0	0	1	47	42	32	29	6	32	60	.232	.238	.227	11.49	6.13
Bard, Luke	R-R	6-3	200	11-15-90	3	3	4.78	32	3	0	0	49	41	27	26	8	13	40	.228	.290	.189	7.35	2.39
Barria, Jaime	R-R	6-1	210	7-18-96	4	10	6.42	19	13	0	0	83	92	61	59	24	27	75	.275	.242	.305	8.17	2.94
Bedrosian, Cam	R-R	6-1	225	10-2-91	3	3	3.23	59	7	0	1	61	48	30	22	7	22	64	.207	.172	.241	9.39	3.23
Buttrey, Ty	L-R	6-6	240	3-31-93	6	7	3.98	72	0	0	2	72	69	34	32	8	23	84	.247	.228	.263	10.45	2.86
Cahill, Trevor	R-R	6-4	230	3-1-88	4	9	5.98	37	11	0	0	102	111	71	68	25	39	81	.273	.296	.256	7.12	3.43
Canning, Griffin	R-R	6-2	180	5-11-96	5	6	4.58	18	17	0	0	90	80	46	46	14	30	96	.235	.204	.263	9.56	2.99
Cole, Taylor	R-R	6-1	200	8-20-89	3	4	5.92	38	6	0	0	52	58	35	34	2	24	50	.286	.256	.310	8.71	4.18
Curtiss, John	R-R	6-5	220	4-5-93	0	0	3.86	1	0	0	0	2	2	1	1	0	3	1	.222	.333	.000	3.86	11.57
Del Pozo, Miguel	L-L	6-1	180	10-14-92	1	1	10.61	17	0	0	0	9	10	11	11	3	8	11	.286	.353	.222	10.61	7.71
Freeman, Sam	R-L	5-11	180	6-24-87	0	0	4.50	1	0	0	0	2	3	1	1	1	2	0	.333	.333	.333	0.00	9.00
Garcia, Luis	R-R	6-2	240	1-30-87	2	1	4.35	64	2	0	1	62	61	35	30	13	33	57	.257	.260	.256	8.27	4.79
Harvey, Matt	R-R	6-4	215	3-27-89	3	5	7.09	12	12	0	0	60	63	48	47	13	29	39	.275	.295	.258	5.88	4.37
Heaney, Andrew	L-L	6-2	200	6-5-91	4	6	4.91	18	18	0	0	95	93	53	52	20	30	118	.251	.321	.231	11.14	2.83
Jewell, Jake	R-R	6-3	200	5-16-93	0	0	6.84	18	0	0	0	26	28	20	20	8	8	23	.275	.326	.237	7.86	2.73
Mejia, Adalberto	L-L	6-3	195	6-20-93	0	0	3.46	20	0	0	0	13	9	6	5	1	8	13	.184	.208	.160	9.00	5.54
2-team total (13 Minnesota)					0	2	6.35	33	0	0	0	28	25	22	20	4	20	28	.234	.200	.254	8.89	6.35
Middleton, Keynan	R-R	6-3	215	9-12-93	0	0	1.17	11	0	0	0	8	4	1	1	0	7	6	.154	.000	.200	7.04	8.22
Pena, Felix	R-R	6-2	220	2-25-90	8	3	4.58	22	7	0	0	96	80	56	49	16	34	101	.219	.260	.181	9.44	3.18
Peters, Dillon	L-L	5-11	190	8-31-92	4	4	5.38	17	12	0	0	72	85	50	43	18	26	55	.290	.232	.313	6.88	3.25

LOS ANGELES ANGELS

Name	B-T	HT	WT	DOB	W	L	ERA	G	GS	CG	SV	IP	H	R	ER	HR	BB	SO	AVG	vLH	vRH	K/9	BB/9
Ramirez, JC	R-R	6-5	250	8-16-88	0	0	4.50	5	0	0	0	8	8	4	4	1	1	4	.250	.286	.222	4.50	1.13
Ramirez, Noe	R-R	6-3	205	12-22-89	5	4	3.99	51	7	0	0	68	59	30	30	9	20	79	.232	.212	.243	10.51	2.66
Ramsey, Matt	R-R	5-11	210	9-24-89	0	0	0.00	1	0	0	0	1	0	0	0	0	0	1	.000	.000	.000	0.00	0.00
Robles, Hansel	R-R	6-0	220	8-13-90	5	1	2.48	71	1	0	23	73	58	20	20	6	16	75	.221	.226	.217	9.29	1.98
Rodriguez, Jose	R-R	6-2	175	8-29-95	0	1	2.75	9	1	0	0	20	17	6	6	5	11	13	.233	.261	.220	5.95	5.03
Sandoval, Patrick	L-L	6-3	190	10-18-96	0	4	5.03	10	9	0	0	39	35	22	22	6	19	42	.240	.306	.218	9.61	4.35
Skaggs, Tyler	L-L	6-4	225	7-13-91	7	7	4.29	15	15	0	0	80	73	41	38	9	28	78	.242	.213	.251	8.81	3.16
Stratton, Chris	R-R	6-2	211	8-22-90	0	2	8.59	7	5	0	0	29	43	28	28	6	18	22	.344	.373	.324	6.75	5.52
Suarez, Jose	L-L	5-10	225	1-3-98	2	6	7.11	19	15	0	0	81	100	67	64	23	33	72	.304	.202	.339	8.00	3.67
Tropeano, Nick	R-R	6-4	205	8-27-90	0	1	9.88	3	1	0	0	14	18	15	15	6	6	10	.316	.333	.300	6.59	3.95
Walsh, Jared	L-L	6-0	210	7-30-93	0	0	1.80	5	0	0	0	5	3	1	1	0	6	5	.177	.375	.000	9.00	10.80

Fielding

Catcher	PCT	G	PO	A	E	DP	PB
Bemboom	1.000	22	136	7	0	0	2
Garneau	.995	27	206	12	1	0	1
Lucroy	.995	67	528	35	3	5	7
Smith	.995	59	392	22	2	0	0
Stassi	1.000	20	118	9	0	0	1

First Base	PCT	G	PO	A	E	DP
Bour	.997	37	264	21	1	24
Garneau	.000	1	0	0	0	0
La Stella	1.000	3	3	0	0	0
Lucroy	1.000	5	6	1	0	1
Pujols	.994	98	719	77	5	70
Thaiss	1.000	13	80	5	0	2
Walsh	1.000	24	139	15	0	12

Second Base	PCT	G	PO	A	E	DP
Bourjos	1.000	1	0	1	0	0
Cowart	1.000	3	5	3	0	2
Cozart	1.000	1	1	0	0	0
Fletcher	.990	42	35	60	1	7
La Stella	.972	46	58	82	4	18
Rengifo	.977	104	165	218	9	58
Wong	1.000	1	2	4	0	1

Third Base	PCT	G	PO	A	E	DP
Bourjos	.000	1	0	0	0	0
Cowart	1.000	6	4	9	0	0
Cozart	.958	31	21	48	3	3
Fletcher	.970	90	41	151	6	17
La Stella	.980	30	10	38	1	4
Pujols	.000	1	0	0	0	0
Thaiss	.909	43	16	54	7	5
Ward	.667	4	2	2	2	1

Shortstop	PCT	G	PO	A	E	DP
Cozart	.917	5	8	3	1	1
Fletcher	.991	39	37	75	1	13
Rengifo	.938	12	17	28	3	2
Simmons	.974	102	137	276	11	56
Tovar	.989	31	29	62	1	12

Outfield	PCT	G	PO	A	E	DP
Bourjos	1.000	23	29	0	0	0
Calhoun	.982	150	312	7	6	2
Fletcher	1.000	23	44	0	0	0
Goodwin	.977	117	207	5	5	1
Hermosillo	1.000	18	32	0	0	0
Parker	1.000	5	5	0	0	0
Puello	1.000	12	25	0	0	0
Trout	.987	122	294	5	4	2
Upton	.957	56	86	2	4	0
Ward	1.000	9	15	0	0	0

SALT LAKE BEES
PACIFIC COAST LEAGUE

TRIPLE-A

Batting	B-T	HT	WT	DOB	AVG	vLH	vRH	G	AB	R	H	2B	3B	HR	RBI	BB	HBP	SH	SF	SO	SB	CS	SLG	OBP
Adell, Jo	R-R	6-3	215	4-8-99	.265	.324	.241	27	121	22	32	11	0	0	8	10	0	0	0	43	1	0	.355	.321
Bemboom, Anthony	L-R	6-2	200	1-18-90	.316	.333	.308	16	57	7	18	1	2	2	10	7	0	0	0	9	0	0	.509	.391
Bour, Justin	L-R	6-4	270	5-28-88	.316	.391	.291	49	187	44	59	12	1	17	43	41	1	0	0	46	2	1	.663	.441
Briceno, Jose	R-R	6-1	225	9-19-92	.215	.167	.230	22	79	8	17	3	0	4	17	3	2	0	0	20	2	0	.405	.262
Cowart, Kaleb	B-R	6-3	225	6-2-92	.289	.338	.271	74	287	42	83	15	4	8	60	25	1	1	3	55	3	4	.453	.345
Franklin, Nick	B-R	6-1	190	3-2-91	.281	.279	.282	41	146	25	41	13	2	3	24	23	1	0	1	28	3	1	.459	.380
Garneau, Dustin	R-R	6-2	205	8-13-87	.229	.182	.246	26	83	16	19	8	0	6	13	11	4	0	0	28	0	0	.542	.347
2-team total (8 Las Vegas)					.248	.258	.244	34	109	18	27	10	1	7	16	14	5	0	1	37	0	0	.551	.357
Hermosillo, Michael	R-R	6-0	205	1-17-95	.243	.351	.198	62	259	51	63	8	3	15	43	26	9	0	2	88	6	4	.471	.331
Kelly, Ty	R-B	6-0	180	7-20-88	.246	.253	.243	79	281	37	69	12	3	1	22	32	2	0	2	80	3	2	.320	.325
Lund, Brennon	L-R	5-9	185	11-27-94	.284	.193	.314	96	352	62	100	26	5	8	51	36	3	0	6	91	6	3	.455	.350
Parker, Jarrett	L-L	6-4	225	1-1-89	.266	.286	.258	96	346	71	92	19	1	24	75	72	3	0	3	125	2	1	.535	.394
Pena, Roberto	R-R	6-0	250	6-8-92	.254	.394	.210	39	138	23	35	9	0	6	25	17	0	0	0	29	1	0	.449	.336
Puello, Cesar	R-R	6-2	220	4-1-91	.296	.229	.320	43	135	25	40	7	0	7	27	22	10	0	0	37	2	1	.504	.431
2-team total (4 New Orleans)					.275	.222	.292	47	149	25	41	7	0	7	29	23	11	0	0	40	2	1	.463	.410
Rengifo, Luis	B-R	5-10	195	2-26-97	.273	.241	.284	27	110	16	30	4	1	5	14	11	0	0	1	24	3	3	.464	.336
Rojas, Jose	L-R	6-0	200	2-24-93	.293	.220	.319	126	515	101	151	39	7	31	107	58	0	0	5	131	4	4	.577	.362
Salcedo, Erick	B-R	5-10	155	6-28-93	.195	.250	.167	24	82	5	16	3	0	1	6	4	0	1	1	9	0	1	.268	.230
Sanjur, Mario	R-R	5-7	174	12-3-95	.261	.333	.250	7	23	4	6	0	0	0	2	0	0	0	0	4	0	0	.261	.261
Scott, Ryan	R-R	6-1	180	2-7-95	.268	.300	.258	11	41	7	11	3	0	1	5	2	0	0	0	10	0	0	.415	.302
Thaiss, Matt	L-R	6-0	215	5-6-95	.274	.195	.305	79	310	63	85	17	2	14	49	59	1	0	2	64	1	0	.477	.390
Thole, Josh	L-R	6-1	230	10-28-86	.241	.129	.304	25	87	10	21	5	0	2	12	16	0	0	0	25	1	0	.368	.359
2-team total (25 Oklahoma City)					.224	.132	.252	50	161	16	53	7	0	3	16	30	1	0	1	44	1	0	.323	.347
Tovar, Wilfredo	R-R	5-7	180	8-11-91	.321	.337	.315	85	327	53	105	17	6	4	57	19	0	0	3	45	3	6	.447	.355
Walsh, Jared	L-L	6-0	210	7-30-93	.325	.367	.305	98	382	90	124	30	0	36	86	59	9	0	4	115	0	0	.686	.423
Ward, Taylor	R-R	6-1	200	12-14-93	.306	.290	.312	106	421	102	129	34	1	27	71	80	9	0	1	101	11	5	.584	.427
Way, Bo	L-L	6-0	180	11-17-91	.226	.083	.268	16	53	7	12	1	0	1	3	4	1	0	0	7	1	1	.321	.293

Pitching	B-T	HT	WT	DOB	W	L	ERA	G	GS	CG	SV	IP	H	R	ER	HR	BB	SO	AVG	vLH	vRH	K/9	BB/9
Alexander, Jason	R-R	6-3	200	3-1-93	3	5	9.36	12	7	0	0	50	88	55	52	6	20	37	.384	.369	.397	6.66	3.60
Anderson, Justin	L-R	6-3	230	9-28-92	0	1	12.27	3	0	0	0	4	2	5	5	2	4	7	.154	.167	.143	17.18	9.82
Ball, Matt	R-R	6-5	200	1-23-95	0	2	5.82	14	7	0	0	43	48	28	28	9	28	43	.291	.284	.297	8.93	5.82
Bard, Luke	R-R	6-3	200	11-13-90	2	4	7.11	16	1	0	1	19	28	20	15	4	10	26	.337	.310	.352	12.32	4.74
Barria, Jaime	R-R	6-1	210	7-18-96	3	3	9.68	10	10	1	0	48	73	53	52	16	10	44	.322	.350	.336	8.19	1.86
Beasley, Jeremy	R-R	6-2	215	11-20-95	1	0	7.90	3	3	0	0	14	19	12	12	1	6	13	.322	.200	.432	8.56	3.95
Bridwell, Parker	R-R	6-4	185	8-2-91	6	6	8.12	22	12	0	1	89	128	92	80	18	44	79	.335	.325	.342	8.02	4.47
Cahill, Trevor	R-R	6-4	230	3-1-88	0	1	27.00	1	1	0	0	2	6	7	7	2	1	5	.462	.833	.143	19.29	3.86
Canning, Griffin	R-R	6-2	180	5-11-96	1	0	0.56	3	3	0	0	16	13	2	1	0	2	17	.224	.333	.129	9.56	1.13
Carpenter, Tyler	R-R	6-5	225	2-25-92	0	2	5.59	2	2	0	0	10	11	12	6	5	4	8	.282	.273	.286	7.45	3.72

Player	B-T	Ht	Wt	DOB	W	L	ERA	G	GS	CG	SV	IP	H	R	ER	HR	BB	SO	AVG	vLH	vRH		
Clark, Ryan	R-R	6-5	220	12-9-93	0	0	9.64	3	0	0	0	5	7	6	5	1	3	3	.318	.364	.273	5.79	5.79
Cole, Taylor	R-R	6-1	200	8-20-89	3	0	5.23	16	0	0	3	21	29	12	12	5	6	24	.333	.324	.340	10.45	2.61
Cowart, Kaleb	B-R	6-3	225	6-2-92	0	1	11.48	13	0	0	0	13	23	19	17	3	11	10	.377	.333	.412	6.75	7.43
Curtiss, John	R-R	6-5	220	4-5-93	2	0	5.91	13	0	0	1	21	20	14	14	4	13	29	.247	.242	.250	12.23	5.48
Custred, Matt	R-R	6-6	240	9-8-93	1	1	4.15	5	0	0	0	9	9	7	4	2	13	7	.310	.222	.350	7.27	13.50
De Horta, Adrian	R-R	6-3	185	3-13-95	0	2	6.75	13	4	0	1	36	32	27	27	10	24	47	.239	.263	.221	11.75	6.00
De Leon, Yoel	L-L	6-2	200	11-23-97	0	1	23.63	1	1	0	0	3	5	7	7	4	3	3	.385	.500	.364	10.13	10.13
Del Pozo, Miguel	L-L	6-1	180	10-14-92	0	0	3.00	2	0	0	1	3	1	1	1	0	3	1	.100	.000	.143	9.00	0.00
2-team total (38 Nashville)					2	3	4.99	40	0	0	2	49	54	28	27	6	21	68	.284	.387	.234	12.58	3.88
Del Rosario, Eduardo	R-R	6-0	145	5-19-95	0	0	3.86	3	0	0	0	2	2	1	1	1	4	1	.222	.000	.286	3.86	15.43
Franklin, Nick	B-R	6-1	190	3-2-91	0	0	0.00	1	0	0	0	1	1	0	0	0	0	1	.333	.500	.000	9.00	0.00
Freeman, Sam	R-L	5-11	180	6-24-87	1	1	7.01	35	0	0	0	53	77	48	41	11	29	42	.350	.319	.365	7.18	4.96
2-team total (5 Fresno)					1	1	6.29	40	0	0	3	59	81	48	41	11	30	53	.336	.308	.350	8.13	4.60
Harvey, Matt	R-R	6-4	220	3-27-89	2	2	16.50	2	2	0	0	6	13	11	11	1	3	10	.419	.222	.500	15.00	4.50
2-team total (5 Las Vegas)					1	2	6.65	7	5	0	0	23	26	17	17	3	8	31	.280	.194	.323	12.13	3.13
Heaney, Andrew	L-L	6-2	200	6-5-91	0	0	0.00	1	1	0	0	4	2	0	0	0	1	10	.133	.143	.125	20.77	2.08
Herrmann, Max	L-L	6-3	210	7-17-93	1	1	2.70	4	2	0	0	17	20	6	5	0	8	15	.318	.200	.340	8.10	4.32
Hofacket, Adam	R-R	6-1	195	2-18-94	0	0	4.73	6	1	0	0	13	13	7	7	1	4	13	.271	.250	.281	8.78	2.70
Hutchison, Drew	L-R	6-3	215	8-22-90	3	0	3.97	4	4	0	0	23	20	10	10	2	9	20	.235	.270	.208	7.94	3.57
Jewell, Jake	R-R	6-3	200	5-16-93	4	4	5.26	34	0	0	8	38	42	25	22	3	17	41	.284	.328	.256	9.80	4.06
Kaelin, Mike	R-R	5-9	185	3-30-94	1	1	9.53	3	1	0	0	6	9	6	6	2	4	6	.375	.400	.357	9.53	6.35
Kelly, Ty	R-R	6-0	180	7-20-88	0	0	0.00	2	0	0	0	2	0	0	0	0	3	1	.000	.000	.000	4.50	13.50
Klonowski, Alex	R-R	6-4	195	4-1-92	1	9	10.54	16	9	0	0	62	107	77	73	15	26	31	.379	.390	.371	4.48	3.75
Krzeminski, Austin	R-R	6-2	210	9-30-96	0	0	10.80	1	0	0	0	3	7	4	4	2	2	3	.438	.444	.429	8.10	5.40
Mahle, Greg	L-L	6-2	230	4-17-93	1	4	6.70	13	6	0	0	43	59	39	32	11	20	40	.322	.318	.324	8.37	4.19
Mathews, Simon	R-R	6-2	180	9-24-95	1	0	4.50	3	0	0	1	8	8	4	4	2	4	11	.250	.286	.222	12.38	4.50
Mattson, Isaac	R-R	6-2	205	7-14-95	0	0	3.86	5	0	0	1	9	9	4	4	0	5	19	.243	.143	.304	18.32	4.82
McCreery, Adam	L-L	6-9	250	12-31-92	0	0	2.00	5	0	0	0	5	2	2	2	0	5	11	.167	.091	.211	11.00	5.00
2-team total (19 Oklahoma City)					0	0	4.55	24	0	0	0	28	33	19	14	4	19	32	.290	.323	.277	10.41	6.18
Mejia, Adalberto	R-L	6-3	195	6-20-93	0	0	0.00	3	0	0	1	2	2	0	0	0	1	2	.222	1.000	.125	7.71	3.86
Middleton, Keynan	R-R	6-3	215	9-12-93	0	0	2.08	5	0	0	4	2	1	1	0	3	5	.125	.100	.167	10.38	6.23	
Pena, Luis	R-R	5-11	190	8-24-95	1	1	9.20	6	0	0	0	15	21	15	15	4	9	18	.362	.450	.316	11.05	5.52
Pena, Roberto	R-R	6-0	250	6-8-92	0	0	27.00	1	0	0	0	1	3	3	3	0	3	0	.500	.333	.667	0.00	27.00
Peters, Dillon	L-L	5-11	190	8-31-92	4	1	6.47	13	11	0	0	57	74	44	41	11	17	55	.316	.368	.299	8.68	2.68
Ramirez, JC	R-R	6-5	250	8-16-88	1	2	6.59	12	8	0	0	41	49	32	30	7	18	26	.299	.284	.309	5.71	3.95
Ramsey, Matt	R-R	5-11	210	9-24-89	0	3	5.27	12	0	0	0	14	16	12	8	0	8	15	.281	.200	.324	9.88	5.27
Rhoades, Jeremy	R-R	6-4	250	2-12-93	3	2	7.02	43	0	0	5	59	60	48	46	11	35	74	.259	.272	.248	11.29	5.34
Rodriguez, Jose	R-R	6-2	175	8-29-95	3	3	6.29	18	2	0	2	44	48	33	31	7	22	45	.274	.319	.245	9.14	4.47
Rojas, Jose	L-R	6-0	200	2-24-93	0	0	0.00	1	0	0	1	0	0	0	0	0	0	0	.000	.000	.333	0.00	9.00
Ryan, Zac	R-R	6-1	201	5-28-94	2	1	4.66	28	0	0	3	37	28	22	19	4	27	48	.207	.175	.231	11.78	6.63
Sandoval, Patrick	L-L	6-3	190	10-18-96	4	4	6.41	15	15	0	0	60	84	62	43	7	35	66	.319	.287	.335	9.85	5.22
Sanjur, Mario	R-R	5-7	174	12-23-95	0	0	27.00	1	0	0	0	1	4	3	3	1	1	0	.571	.500	.600	0.00	9.00
Snow, Forrest	R-R	6-7	250	12-30-88	0	3	6.67	6	5	0	0	28	40	26	21	7	11	29	.328	.208	.405	9.21	3.49
Suarez, Jose	L-L	5-10	225	1-3-98	2	1	3.62	7	6	0	0	32	24	15	13	3	17	31	.202	.194	.205	8.63	4.73
Tropeano, Nick	R-R	6-4	205	8-27-90	4	6	5.87	17	15	0	0	80	90	55	52	12	31	85	.287	.342	.236	9.60	3.50
Walsh, Jared	L-L	6-0	210	7-30-93	1	0	4.15	13	0	0	1	13	16	6	6	0	5	9	.291	.333	.265	6.23	3.46
Way, Bo	L-L	6-0	180	11-17-91	0	1	7.71	3	0	0	0	2	5	3	2	0	3	3	.455	.000	.625	11.57	11.57

Fielding

Catcher	PCT	G	PO	A	E	DP	PB
Bemboom	.993	15	131	7	1	1	0
Briceno	.995	22	185	15	1	0	3
Garneau	.992	26	227	18	2	1	0
Pena	.997	38	327	22	1	4	3
Sanjur	.946	6	50	3	3	1	1
Scott	.990	11	99	1	1	0	2
Thole	.996	25	211	17	1	2	3

First Base	PCT	G	PO	A	E	DP
Bour	.984	26	176	9	3	13
Cowart	1.000	1	4	0	0	0
Franklin	1.000	2	10	0	0	2
Parker	.967	14	80	8	3	9
Pena	1.000	1	8	1	0	0
Rojas	1.000	18	110	11	0	18
Thaiss	1.000	23	169	9	0	23
Tovar	1.000	1	2	0	0	0
Walsh	.995	58	392	40	2	41
Ward	.968	6	30	0	1	3

Second Base	PCT	G	PO	A	E	DP
Cowart	.857	2	3	3	1	1
Franklin	.983	16	20	39	1	13
Kelly	.985	67	117	139	4	43
Rengifo	.963	12	17	35	2	6
Rojas	.969	39	79	78	5	19
Salcedo	1.000	1	2	1	0	0
Tovar	.971	7	12	22	1	8

Third Base	PCT	G	PO	A	E	DP
Cowart	.967	42	31	58	3	3
Franklin	.870	9	8	12	3	2
Rojas	.906	31	15	43	6	6
Thaiss	.924	47	24	85	9	8
Tovar	.000	1	0	0	0	0
Ward	.919	17	10	24	3	0

Shortstop	PCT	G	PO	A	E	DP
Cowart	.987	18	25	52	1	6
Franklin	.902	14	15	31	5	12
Kelly	.929	3	2	11	1	2
Rengifo	.940	12	22	41	4	13
Salcedo	.975	19	26	51	2	14
Tovar	.953	77	87	174	13	37

Outfield	PCT	G	PO	A	E	DP
Adell	.978	26	42	2	1	1
Cowart	.833	8	15	0	3	0
Franklin	1.000	3	8	0	0	0
Hermosillo	.978	61	129	5	3	2
Kelly	1.000	9	12	0	0	0
Lund	.967	96	200	6	7	2
Parker	.976	68	115	6	3	1
Puello	.962	42	76	0	3	0
Rengifo	1.000	3	3	1	0	0
Rojas	.941	12	14	2	1	0
Salcedo	.889	4	7	1	1	0
Walsh	1.000	3	5	0	0	0
Ward	.968	77	143	10	5	0
Way	1.000	16	30	2	0	1

MOBILE BAYBEARS
SOUTHERN LEAGUE

LOS ANGELES ANGELS

Batting	B-T	HT	WT	DOB	AVG	vLH	vRH	G	AB	R	H	2B	3B	HR	RBI	BB	HBP	SH	SF	SO	SB	CS	SLG	OBP
Adell, Jo	R-R	6-3	215	4-8-99	.308	.292	.315	43	159	28	49	15	0	8	23	19	3	0	1	41	6	0	.554	.390
Baldoquin, Roberto	R-R	5-11	199	5-14-94	.232	.239	.228	80	272	25	63	11	1	2	23	18	6	0	3	70	2	2	.302	.291
Cowart, Kaleb	B-R	6-3	225	6-2-92	.180	.286	.120	11	39	4	7	1	0	1	2	2	0	0	1	11	0	0	.282	.214
Gurwitz, Zane	R-R	5-8	185	12-1-94	.204	.125	.228	29	103	10	21	4	0	1	12	11	1	0	1	30	3	0	.272	.285
Houchins, Zach	R-R	6-2	210	9-16-92	.174	.211	.148	13	46	2	8	2	0	0	1	2	0	0	0	12	0	0	.217	.208
Jones, Jahmai	R-R	5-11	205	8-4-97	.234	.252	.227	130	482	66	113	22	3	5	50	50	4	1	7	109	9	11	.324	.308
Justus, Connor	R-R	6-0	190	11-2-94	.184	.155	.196	115	347	40	64	17	0	2	23	39	11	1	2	93	7	4	.251	.286
Kruger, Jack	R-R	6-1	195	10-26-94	.240	.208	.252	92	346	28	83	13	1	3	34	24	7	0	3	69	2	2	.309	.300
Leon, Julian	R-R	5-11	235	1-24-96	.178	.180	.178	68	213	24	38	10	0	5	23	37	7	1	3	89	0	0	.296	.315
Marsh, Brandon	L-R	6-4	215	12-18-97	.300	.323	.292	96	360	48	108	21	2	7	43	47	3	0	2	92	18	5	.428	.384
Morgan, Gareth	R-R	6-4	265	4-12-96	.206	.259	.188	27	107	5	22	3	0	1	10	8	1	0	0	55	1	1	.262	.267
Pena, Roberto	R-R	6-0	250	6-8-92	.258	.278	--	20	62	7	16	4	0	0	4	11	1	0	0	11	0	0	.323	.378
Salcedo, Erick	B-R	5-10	155	6-28-93	.207	.303	.172	76	246	25	51	12	2	2	31	14	0	0	2	38	4	0	.297	.248
Sandoval, Brandon	R-R	6-1	180	6-24-95	.284	.306	.273	77	268	31	76	8	1	2	25	15	4	0	4	66	9	4	.343	.327
Sanger, Brendon	L-R	6-0	195	9-11-93	.203	.184	.209	107	355	38	72	12	1	12	43	47	9	0	2	121	4	0	.344	.310
Sanjur, Mario	R-R	5-7	174	12-23-95	.143	.000	.167	2	7	0	1	0	0	0	1	1	0	0	1	2	0	0	.143	.222
Urena, Jhoan	B-R	6-1	225	9-1-94	.261	.309	.241	127	468	53	122	34	3	9	56	53	1	0	0	140	2	2	.404	.337
Way, Bo	L-L	6-0	180	11-17-91	.260	.221	.273	90	308	34	80	17	3	7	26	27	2	0	1	59	6	3	.403	.323
Weisz, Keaton	R-R	5-8	155	5-30-96	.177	.200	.143	5	17	1	3	1	0	0	0	0	0	0	0	8	0	0	.235	.177
Williams, Cam	R-R	5-11	185	1-16-97	.091	.000	.125	4	11	1	1	0	0	1	2	0	0	0	0	8	0	0	.364	.091
Zimmerman, Jordan	R-R	6-1	175	11-21-94	.272	.361	.236	34	125	13	34	10	1	2	17	9	0	0	0	30	2	0	.416	.321

Pitching	B-T	HT	WT	DOB	W	L	ERA	G	GS	CG	SV	IP	H	R	ER	HR	BB	SO	AVG	vLH	vRH	K/9	BB/9
Alexander, Jason	R-R	6-3	200	3-1-93	1	3	4.03	11	8	0	0	51	47	29	23	4	16	59	.237	.250	--	10.34	2.81
Almeida, Adrian	L-L	6-0	160	2-25-95	1	1	5.79	30	0	0	2	28	35	21	18	1	33	31	.307	.250	.338	9.96	10.61
Ball, Matt	R-R	6-5	200	1-23-95	1	1	3.57	8	8	0	0	35	33	16	14	2	13	45	.243	.239	--	11.46	3.31
Beasley, Jeremy	R-R	6-3	215	11-20-95	6	7	4.06	23	22	0	0	109	110	56	49	13	42	102	.258	.261	.256	8.45	3.48
Beltre, Dario	R-R	6-3	170	11-19-92	1	4	4.78	31	0	0	6	53	48	33	28	3	37	63	.241	--	.250	10.77	6.32
Carpenter, Tyler	R-R	6-5	225	2-25-92	1	2	4.01	12	9	0	0	49	49	25	22	4	14	35	.258	.337	.188	6.39	2.55
Castillo, Jesus	R-R	6-3	205	8-27-95	6	6	2.71	38	12	0	2	100	100	39	30	4	26	80	.261	.277	.246	7.22	2.35
Clark, Ryan	R-R	6-5	220	12-9-93	2	0	2.96	30	0	0	6	46	39	19	15	5	12	64	.232	.205	.256	12.61	2.36
Cowart, Kaleb	B-R	6-3	225	6-2-92	1	1	6.23	4	0	0	1	4	3	4	3	0	4	6	.188	.111	.286	12.46	8.31
De Horta, Adrian	R-R	6-3	185	3-13-95	0	0	2.03	3	2	0	0	13	7	3	3	1	8	23	.156	.160	.150	15.53	5.40
Gatto, Joe	R-R	6-3	220	6-14-95	5	4	4.80	32	0	0	3	54	63	33	29	2	28	57	.293	.237	.339	9.44	4.64
Hanewich, Brett	B-R	6-3	200	12-15-94	0	5	5.12	19	0	0	1	19	21	16	11	2	19	22	.284	.348	.255	10.24	8.84
Herrmann, Max	L-L	6-3	210	7-17-93	1	4	4.94	12	8	1	0	55	57	38	30	1	29	27	.281	.262	.294	4.45	4.77
Hofacket, Adam	R-R	6-1	195	2-18-94	3	3	2.09	30	0	0	6	52	54	17	12	2	17	53	.270	.248	.295	9.23	2.96
Kelly, Zack	R-R	6-3	205	3-3-95	3	6	3.82	20	13	0	0	75	77	42	32	5	29	83	.262	.241	.280	9.92	3.46
Madero, Luis	R-R	6-3	185	4-15-97	5	11	5.72	20	19	0	0	90	117	65	57	11	24	75	.313	.337	.292	7.53	2.41
Mahle, Greg	L-L	6-2	230	4-17-93	3	3	2.22	7	7	1	0	45	48	13	11	3	6	25	.274	.226	.301	5.04	1.21
Mathews, Simon	R-R	6-3	190	9-24-95	0	0	14.54	2	1	0	0	4	8	7	7	1	6	4	.444	.500	.400	8.31	12.46
Mattson, Isaac	R-R	6-2	205	7-14-95	3	3	2.68	24	0	0	0	44	30	16	13	3	13	61	.196	.180	.213	12.57	2.68
Ortega, Oliver	R-R	6-0	165	10-2-96	0	3	8.64	5	5	0	0	17	23	18	16	0	8	14	.319	.294	.342	7.56	4.32
Pena, Luis	R-R	5-11	190	8-24-95	2	1	2.67	18	0	0	2	30	17	13	9	4	12	33	.157	.217	.113	10.58	3.56
Procopio, Daniel	R-R	6-0	190	9-18-95	0	0	5.48	15	0	0	0	23	29	18	14	2	7	17	.309	.282	.327	6.65	2.74
Rodriguez, Jose	R-R	6-2	175	8-29-95	0	2	7.27	5	5	0	0	17	24	15	14	2	6	24	.324	.432	.167	12.46	3.12
Ryan, Zac	R-R	6-1	201	5-28-94	2	2	2.16	10	0	0	3	17	10	5	4	0	7	22	.172	.188	.154	11.88	3.78
Sandoval, Patrick	L-L	6-3	190	10-18-96	0	3	3.60	5	4	0	0	20	14	10	8	1	7	32	.187	.182	.189	14.40	3.15
Santos, Michael	R-R	6-4	205	5-29-95	2	1	4.74	6	1	0	0	19	18	11	10	3	9	12	.261	.333	.182	5.68	4.26
Wantz, Andrew	R-R	6-4	235	10-13-95	0	6	7.13	13	12	0	0	48	59	42	38	12	26	54	.294	.300	.287	10.13	4.88
Warren, Austin	R-R	6-0	170	5-5-96	1	2	2.57	9	0	0	0	14	12	7	4	0	9	14	.218	.364	.121	9.00	5.79
Way, Bo	L-L	6-0	180	11-17-91	0	1	4.09	11	0	0	0	11	9	6	5	0	5	9	.214	.118	.280	7.36	4.09

Fielding

Catcher	PCT	G	PO	A	E	DP	PB
Kruger	.993	75	649	31	5	2	8
Leon	.990	56	435	59	5	4	3
Pena	.977	4	35	8	1	2	0
Sanjur	1.000	2	14	3	0	0	0

First Base	PCT	G	PO	A	E	DP
Baldoquin	.934	9	55	2	4	3
Cowart	1.000	3	12	4	0	1
Houchins	.982	7	50	6	1	7
Leon	1.000	1	6	1	0	0
Pena	.981	12	93	8	2	5
Salcedo	.973	4	34	2	1	3
Urena	.991	92	696	41	7	65
Zimmerman	.990	12	88	7	1	8

Second Base	PCT	G	PO	A	E	DP
Baldoquin	.933	7	10	18	2	3
Cowart	.800	1	1	3	1	0
Jones	.962	110	169	313	19	66
Justus	.908	14	26	33	6	7
Salcedo	.944	5	6	11	1	6
Weisz	1.000	2	3	8	0	0

Third Base	PCT	G	PO	A	E	DP
Baldoquin	.968	44	29	62	3	5
Gurwitz	.942	27	23	42	4	3
Justus	.923	19	6	30	3	1
Salcedo	.826	12	5	14	4	2
Urena	.913	18	5	16	2	0
Weisz	1.000	1	2	0	0	0
Zimmerman	.938	19	7	23	2	1

Shortstop	PCT	G	PO	A	E	DP
Baldoquin	.982	18	20	36	1	8
Justus	.963	81	106	207	12	45
Salcedo	.962	37	56	97	6	22
Weisz	.667	1	0	2	1	0

Outfield	PCT	G	PO	A	E	DP
Adell	.952	41	78	2	4	1
Houchins	1.000	6	4	0	0	0
Jones	1.000	11	15	1	0	0
Marsh	.979	87	179	6	4	2
Morgan	.870	26	39	1	6	0
Salcedo	.967	16	28	1	1	0
Sandoval	.993	71	136	1	1	0
Sanger	.992	85	124	8	1	2
Way	.970	70	126	4	4	1
Williams	1.000	4	6	0	0	0

INLAND EMPIRE 66ERS

CALIFORNIA LEAGUE

HIGH CLASS A

LOS ANGELES ANGELS

Batting	B-T	HT	WT	DOB	AVG	vLH	vRH	G	AB	R	H	2B	3B	HR	RBI	BB	HBP	SH	SF	SO	SB	CS	SLG	OBP
Adams, Jordyn	R-R	6-2	180	10-18-99	.229	.143	.286	9	35	7	8	1	1	1	1	5	0	0	0	14	0	1	.400	.325
Adell, Jo	R-R	6-3	215	4-8-99	.280	.000	.318	6	25	4	7	1	0	2	5	1	1	0	0	10	0	0	.560	.333
Arendas, D.C.	L-R	6-0	190	1-10-94	.170	.133	.179	46	153	20	26	6	3	4	11	20	6	0	0	78	2	0	.327	.291
Bond, Brett	B-R	6-1	216	10-15-95	.208	.125	.250	7	24	2	5	0	0	1	2	1	0	0	0	9	0	0	.333	.240
Cruz, Michael	L-R	5-11	210	1-13-96	.296	.250	.304	23	81	8	24	6	0	3	14	6	1	0	2	18	0	1	.482	.344
Davis, Devin	R-R	6-3	215	2-14-97	.244	.200	.259	91	345	40	84	15	9	7	47	29	5	0	2	102	1	0	.400	.310
Griffin, Spencer	R-R	6-1	170	10-24-96	.234	.308	.210	30	107	15	25	6	2	0	8	17	1	0	0	32	3	0	.327	.344
Gurwitz, Zane	R-R	5-8	185	12-1-94	.288	.398	.234	71	250	41	72	13	3	7	35	27	4	0	2	69	1	0	.448	.364
Hermosillo, Michael	R-R	6-0	205	1-17-95	.222	.250	.200	2	9	0	2	1	0	0	0	1	0	0	0	1	0	0	.333	.300
Hunter Jr., Torii	R-R	6-2	180	6-7-95	.251	.329	.220	73	259	29	65	7	4	1	27	38	7	1	1	76	16	3	.321	.361
Lucroy, Jonathan	R-R	6-0	200	6-13-86	.250	.000	.400	2	8	3	2	1	0	1	1	1	0	0	1	0	0	0	.750	.333
MacKinnon, David	R-R	6-2	200	12-15-94	.140	.177	.125	18	57	5	8	1	0	0	4	19	0	0	1	18	0	0	.158	.351
Martinez, Orlando	L-L	6-0	185	2-17-98	.263	.219	.280	88	380	55	100	21	4	12	49	36	1	0	5	79	5	4	.434	.325
Morgan, Gareth	R-R	6-4	265	4-12-96	.290	.348	.270	44	183	32	53	5	0	20	49	9	2	0	2	95	0	1	.645	.327
2-team total (8 Modesto)					.262	.327	.242	52	210	34	55	5	0	21	52	14	2	0	2	115	1	1	.586	.311
Olmeda, Alexis	R-R	6-0	225	4-5-94	.172	.182	.167	37	134	6	23	5	0	4	10	8	0	0	0	62	1	1	.299	.218
Pina, Keinner	R-R	5-10	175	2-12-97	.173	.095	.226	16	52	1	9	1	0	0	1	7	1	0	0	10	0	0	.192	.283
Pineda, Gleyvin	L-R	5-11	160	8-19-96	.250	.182	.267	89	324	28	81	9	2	2	38	34	3	3	3	93	3	3	.309	.324
Rivas, Leonardo	B-R	5-10	150	10-10-97	.236	.356	.186	73	297	44	70	14	5	6	26	39	2	0	0	90	4	2	.377	.328
Rosario, Rayneldy	L-L	5-8	139	4-30-98	.170	.400	.116	17	53	10	9	0	0	0	2	7	0	1	0	13	0	1	.170	.267
Rubalcaba, Alvaro	R-R	5-8	165	4-24-95	.207	.171	.220	45	135	20	28	6	2	2	12	19	3	0	2	47	2	1	.326	.315
Sanjur, Mario	R-R	5-7	174	12-23-95	.000	.000	.000	7	21	1	0	0	0	0	0	5	0	0	0	9	0	0	.000	.192
Scott, Ryan	R-R	6-1	180	2-7-95	.123	.000	.162	50	154	23	19	1	0	5	14	25	4	2	1	58	0	0	.227	.261
Simmons, Andrelton	R-R	6-2	195	9-4-89	.333	.333	--	1	3	0	1	0	0	0	0	1	0	0	0	0	0	0	.333	.500
Stefanic, Michael	R-R	5-10	180	2-24-96	.270	.247	.278	80	304	44	82	13	1	3	37	24	13	0	1	39	7	3	.349	.348
Survance Jr., Kyle	L-R	6-1	190	12-6-93	.168	.111	.187	45	143	14	24	5	1	1	9	24	5	0	0	62	5	5	.238	.308
Torres, Franklin	R-R	6-0	175	10-27-96	.257	.333	.232	91	346	45	89	17	2	3	32	53	3	1	2	102	1	1	.344	.359
Upton, Justin	R-R	6-1	215	8-25-87	.333	.800	.188	6	21	7	7	1	0	2	6	4	0	0	0	5	0	0	.667	.440
Vega, Ryan	R-R	6-0	190	9-17-96	.220	.242	.210	52	186	15	41	8	0	4	19	26	3	0	1	63	1	1	.328	.324
Williams Jr., Kevin	R-R	6-0	190	6-17-96	.169	.136	.184	51	184	17	31	6	1	4	19	13	3	0	1	74	2	0	.277	.234
Williams, Cam	R-R	5-11	185	1-16-97	.161	.154	.163	17	56	5	9	2	0	1	6	7	2	0	1	25	1	1	.250	.273
Zimmerman, Jordan	R-R	6-1	195	11-21-94	.260	.295	.247	94	338	37	88	14	3	7	32	31	4	0	2	92	6	2	.382	.328

Pitching	B-T	HT	WT	DOB	W	L	ERA	G	GS	CG	SV	IP	H	R	ER	HR	BB	SO	AVG	vLH	vRH	K/9	BB/9
Bates, Nathan	R-R	6-6	205	3-1-94	0	0	2.61	8	1	0	0	10	5	3	3	0	5	16	.132	.154	.120	13.94	4.35
Bertness, Nate	L-L	6-6	205	8-4-95	4	3	4.76	24	2	0	5	62	49	41	33	9	27	70	.216	.129	.255	10.11	3.90
Bond, Brett	B-R	6-1	216	10-15-95	0	0	3.00	2	0	0	0	3	5	1	1	1	1	1	.385	.200	.500	3.00	3.00
Bradish, Kyle	R-R	6-4	190	9-12-96	6	7	4.28	24	18	0	0	101	90	55	48	9	53	120	.235	.257	.222	10.69	4.72
Brady, Denny	R-R	6-1	200	1-18-97	3	9	3.64	17	10	0	0	77	78	40	31	4	25	86	.261	.165	.307	10.10	2.93
Chock, Tanner	B-R	6-1	190	8-8-96	0	1	19.29	1	1	0	0	2	4	5	5	0	3	2	.400	.500	.375	7.71	11.57
Cole, Taylor	R-R	6-1	200	8-20-89	0	0	3.00	2	1	0	0	3	5	3	3	2	2	2	.417	.250	.500	6.75	6.75
Criswell, Cooper	R-R	6-6	200	7-24-96	4	8	4.60	25	21	0	0	117	133	69	60	10	35	111	.289	.322	.269	8.51	2.68
Cruz, Michael	L-R	5-11	210	1-13-96	0	0	13.50	2	0	0	0	1	3	1	1	0	0	1	.600	.500	.667	13.50	0.00
Del Rosario, Eduardo	R-R	6-0	145	5-19-95	0	0	6.14	5	0	0	0	7	9	5	5	0	5	3	.321	.375	.300	3.68	6.14
Garcia, Luis	R-R	6-2	240	1-30-87	0	0	0.00	1	0	0	0	1	1	0	0	0	0	3	.000	.000	.000	27.00	0.00
Gubelman, Jordan	R-R	6-2	225	4-5-97	1	0	0.00	1	0	0	0	1	1	0	0	0	0	1	.250	.000	.500	0.00	9.00
Hanewich, Brett	B-R	6-3	200	12-15-94	1	0	0.93	13	0	0	1	19	8	3	2	1	7	28	.123	.158	.109	13.03	3.26
Harvey, Matt	R-R	6-4	220	3-27-89	0	0	4.50	1	1	0	0	4	4	2	2	1	0	2	.250	.333	.231	4.50	0.00
Hernandez, Aaron	R-R	6-1	170	12-2-96	1	4	4.46	20	15	0	0	73	75	38	36	6	46	81	.269	.258	.275	10.03	5.70
Herrin, Travis	R-R	6-2	220	4-29-95	5	6	5.01	23	14	0	1	106	103	68	59	11	50	106	.256	.254	.258	9.00	4.25
Higgins, Connor	R-L	6-5	240	7-21-96	0	3	5.11	24	0	0	3	37	30	23	21	6	18	48	.224	.195	.237	11.68	4.38
Kelleher, Kevin	R-R	6-3	245	1-24-93	0	0	21.00	3	0	0	0	3	2	9	7	0	10	2	.182	.125	.333	6.00	30.00
Kelly, Zack	R-R	6-3	205	3-3-95	0	1	0.00	1	0	0	0	4	4	1	0	0	0	2	.267	.400	.200	4.50	0.00
Krzeminski, Austin	R-R	6-2	210	9-30-96	0	0	4.82	5	0	0	0	9	5	6	3	0	4	11	.250	.250	.250	10.61	3.86
Lee, Jake	R-R	6-4	215	6-30-95	1	2	4.50	6	4	0	0	24	19	14	12	3	11	34	.209	.180	.231	12.75	4.13
Lind, Luke	L-R	6-6	225	1-26-95	1	2	4.67	11	0	0	3	17	13	11	9	2	8	22	.200	.318	.140	11.42	4.15
Madero, Luis	R-R	6-3	185	4-15-97	1	0	1.13	4	3	0	0	16	15	2	2	0	7	23	.246	.353	.205	12.94	3.94
Manoah Jr., Erik	R-R	6-2	190	12-22-95	1	1	11.70	8	0	0	0	14	13	13	2	8	13	.326	.533	.214	11.70	7.20
Mathews, Simon	R-R	6-2	180	9-24-95	0	2	4.98	21	4	0	0	56	67	34	31	3	24	45	.300	.300	.301	7.23	3.86
Mattson, Isaac	R-R	6-2	205	7-14-95	3	0	0.89	8	0	0	0	20	8	3	2	1	9	30	.121	.130	.116	13.28	3.98
Middleton, Keynan	R-R	6-3	215	9-12-93	0	0	0.00	4	0	0	0	3.2	2	0	0	0	3	9	.143	.250	.100	22.09	7.36
Molina, Cristopher	R-R	6-3	170	6-10-97	2	6	4.55	13	12	0	0	65	75	45	33	7	20	57	.291	.333	.269	7.85	2.76
Morrison, Ben	L-R	5-11	185	1-20-95	1	2	2.75	10	0	0	0	20	17	10	6	0	6	20	.236	.261	.225	9.15	2.75
Ortega, Oliver	R-R	6-0	165	10-2-96	4	5	3.34	21	16	0	2	94	67	44	35	8	49	121	.198	.221	.187	11.54	4.67
Pineda, Gleyvin	L-R	5-11	160	8-19-96	0	0	0.00	1	0	0	0	1	0	0	0	0	1	0	.000	.000	.000	0.00	13.50
Procopio, Daniel	R-R	6-0	190	9-18-95	0	0	0.00	1	0	0	0	1	0	0	0	0	0	0	.000	.000	.000	0.00	10.80
Ramirez, JC	R-R	6-5	250	8-16-88	0	1	6.43	4	2	0	0	7	8	5	5	3	2	7	.286	.417	.188	9.00	2.57
Ramirez, Noe	R-R	6-3	205	12-22-89	0	0	0.00	1	1	0	0	1	0	0	0	0	1	0	.000	.000	.000	9.00	0.00
Robinson, Parker Joe	R-R	6-5	230	8-16-95	0	0	4.91	4	0	0	0	9	6	0	0	0	2	5	.313	.500	.200	4.91	0.00
Rodriguez, Chris	R-R	6-2	185	7-20-98	0	0	0.00	3	3	0	0	9	6	0	0	0	4	13	.188	.133	.235	12.54	3.86
Santos, Michael	R-R	6-4	205	5-29-95	1	3	6.07	8	2	0	1	30	37	24	20	3	7	28	.311	.233	.355	8.49	2.12

Name	B-T	HT	WT	DOB	W	L	ERA	G	GS	CG	SV	IP	H	R	ER	HR	BB	SO	AVG	vLH	vRH	K/9	BB/9
Smith, Tyler	R-R	6-0	230	11-20-95	2	2	3.60	13	0	0	1	25	25	14	10	0	9	30	.272	.233	.290	10.80	3.24
Tavarez, Jorge	R-R	5-10	150	8-4-95	4	2	5.14	40	0	0	4	68	67	41	39	3	29	76	.255	.236	.264	10.01	3.82
Tyler, Kyle	R-R	6-0	185	12-27-96	3	0	2.33	4	2	0	0	19	14	6	5	3	4	19	.197	.250	.182	8.84	1.86
Varela, James	R-R	6-1	210	12-9-96	1	1	9.00	2	0	0	0	3	4	3	3	0	4	1	.333	.200	.500	3.00	12.00
Wantz, Andrew	R-R	6-4	235	10-13-95	5	3	3.56	11	6	0	0	48	40	21	19	4	17	58	.221	.229	.216	10.88	3.19
Warren, Austin	R-R	6-0	170	5-5-96	2	7	3.30	27	0	0	2	44	39	21	16	5	21	63	.242	.224	.252	12.98	4.33
Zimmerman, Jordan	R-R	6-1	195	11-21-94	0	0	6.75	2	0	0	0	1	1	1	1	1	0	1	.200	.000	.250	6.75	0.00

Fielding

Catcher	PCT	G	PO	A	E	DP	PB
Bond	1.000	1	2	0	0	0	0
Cruz	.989	10	77	9	1	0	3
Lucroy	1.000	2	13	1	0	0	0
Olmeda	.986	30	251	32	4	3	3
Pina	.994	15	145	19	1	1	1
Sanjur	.988	7	73	6	1	2	1
Scott	.996	50	492	46	2	1	7
Torres	.975	35	283	29	8	1	17

First Base	PCT	G	PO	A	E	DP
Arendas	.970	21	151	9	5	14
Davis	.987	72	496	45	7	48
MacKinnon	.991	15	102	8	1	5
Torres	1.000	1	2	0	0	0
Zimmerman	.985	33	248	11	4	20

Second Base	PCT	G	PO	A	E	DP
Arendas	1.000	15	20	37	0	6
Gurwitz	.941	14	23	25	3	4
Pineda	.972	28	48	55	3	17
Rivas	1.000	9	21	18	0	8
Rubalcaba	.981	15	23	30	1	7
Stefanic	.980	34	64	83	3	24
Torres	.991	31	52	53	1	7

Third Base	PCT	G	PO	A	E	DP
Arendas	.950	8	3	16	1	2
Gurwitz	.905	34	17	69	9	6
Pineda	.920	33	30	51	7	5
Rivas	1.000	5	3	7	0	3
Torres	1.000	9	7	9	0	1
Zimmerman	.935	54	29	86	8	7

Shortstop	PCT	G	PO	A	E	DP
Pineda	.988	22	32	52	1	11
Rivas	.945	46	54	117	10	26

	PCT	G	PO	A	E	DP
Rubalcaba	.964	31	33	47	3	9
Simmons	1.000	1	1	3	0	0
Stefanic	.962	43	55	96	6	17

Outfield	PCT	G	PO	A	E	DP
Adams	1.000	8	13	2	0	0
Adell	.917	6	11	0	1	0
Griffin	1.000	27	60	0	0	0
Gurwitz	1.000	17	28	1	0	1
Hermosillo	.667	2	2	0	1	0
Hunter Jr.	.977	61	85	0	2	0
Martinez	.990	81	188	5	2	0
Morgan	.933	41	83	0	6	0
Pineda	.857	6	5	1	1	0
Rivas	1.000	9	25	0	0	0
Rosario	.966	16	27	1	1	0
Survance Jr.	.986	39	68	2	1	0
Upton	1.000	5	7	0	0	0
Vega	.984	49	63	0	1	0
Williams Jr.	.970	40	63	2	2	0
Williams	.889	17	40	0	5	0

BURLINGTON BEES
MIDWEST LEAGUE

LOW CLASS A

Batting	B-T	HT	WT	DOB	AVG	vLH	vRH	G	AB	R	H	2B	3B	HR	RBI	BB	HBP	SH	SF	SO	SB	CS	SLG	OBP
Adams, Jordyn	R-R	6-2	180	10-18-99	.250	.197	.261	97	372	52	93	15	2	7	31	50	5	0	1	94	12	5	.358	.346
Arendas, D.C.	L-R	6-0	190	1-10-94	.201	.240	.195	56	184	24	37	9	4	6	24	31	5	0	2	69	2	0	.391	.329
Arias, Kevin	R-R	5-7	160	2-18-99	.135	.429	.067	12	37	4	5	0	1	2	3	2	1	1	0	20	0	0	.351	.200
Del Valle, Francisco	L-L	6-1	187	8-18-98	.205	.246	.196	120	401	47	82	27	4	8	48	63	13	1	2	113	3	3	.352	.330
Fitzsimons, Connor	R-R	5-10	190	8-29-94	.207	.255	.196	80	246	30	51	13	1	6	40	34	15	0	5	116	1	2	.342	.333
Griffin, Spencer	R-R	6-1	170	10-24-96	.243	.350	.220	96	333	55	81	11	6	8	35	36	5	1	3	118	12	4	.384	.346
Jones, Justin	R-R	5-11	185	5-20-96	.260	.373	.238	96	312	36	81	5	3	10	45	42	8	0	2	69	11	3	.391	.360
Maitan, Kevin	B-R	6-2	190	2-12-00	.214	.198	.217	123	486	56	104	11	3	12	46	39	5	0	2	164	7	4	.323	.298
McCullough, Morgan	L-R	5-9	180	12-19-97	.184	.200	.182	13	38	2	7	1	0	0	2	9	2	0	0	9	0	1	.211	.367
Millard, Tim	R-R	6-0	200	5-29-95	.196	.154	.211	37	102	13	20	1	0	2	13	20	3	0	1	31	1	0	.265	.341
Olmeda, Alexis	R-R	6-0	225	4-5-94	.187	.158	.193	31	107	14	20	2	0	2	15	13	1	0	1	40	0	0	.262	.279
Pina, Keinner	R-R	5-10	175	2-12-97	.228	.191	.237	32	114	7	26	3	0	1	13	9	1	0	3	28	0	0	.281	.284
Pineda, Gleyvin	L-R	5-11	160	8-19-96	.272	.250	.276	29	103	18	28	4	1	2	12	15	0	0	0	29	3	0	.388	.364
Rondon, Adrian	R-R	6-1	190	7-7-98	.231	.238	.230	39	156	10	36	4	0	0	8	3	0	1	0	45	3	3	.256	.280
Rosario, Rayneldy	L-L	5-8	139	4-30-98	.136	.100	.143	19	59	3	8	2	0	0	4	2	0	1	0	17	1	1	.170	.164
Rubalcaba, Alvaro	R-R	5-8	165	4-24-95	.155	.233	.141	66	193	22	30	8	0	3	19	44	3	1	0	61	3	5	.244	.321
Sala, Johan	R-R	6-1	175	12-17-97	.200	.333	.177	6	20	2	4	1	0	0	4	2	0	0	0	9	0	0	.250	.273
Sanjur, Mario	R-R	5-7	174	12-23-95	.200	--	.200	2	5	1	1	0	0	0	0	0	0	0	0	3	0	0	.200	.200
Soto, Livan	L-R	6-0	160	6-22-00	.220	.178	.230	64	245	24	54	5	0	1	20	32	1	2	2	40	6	2	.253	.311
Stefanic, Michael	R-R	5-10	180	2-24-96	.333	.267	.351	22	72	5	24	5	1	0	10	6	2	0	0	2	2	2	.431	.400
Vega, Ryan	R-R	6-2	180	9-19-96	.214	.125	.229	33	112	11	24	5	1	1	9	10	3	1	0	27	5	1	.304	.296
Wenson, Harrison	R-R	6-3	235	4-21-95	.191	.156	.198	78	257	38	49	17	0	12	44	44	6	0	1	119	2	1	.397	.321
Williams, Nonie	R-R	6-2	200	5-22-98	.184	.169	.187	119	414	58	76	18	2	6	38	64	7	1	4	166	23	7	.280	.301

Pitching	B-T	HT	WT	DOB	W	L	ERA	G	GS	CG	SV	IP	H	R	ER	HR	BB	SO	AVG	vLH	vRH	K/9	BB/9
Alvarado, Luis	R-R	6-4	210	1-5-97	4	9	3.68	25	16	0	1	100	76	50	41	11	53	108	.213	.216	.211	9.69	4.75
Chatham, Clayton	R-R	6-6	237	6-29-95	2	4	3.59	9	9	0	0	43	42	24	17	0	16	50	.256	.312	.223	10.55	3.38
Clark, Ethan	R-R	6-5	235	10-26-94	1	1	1.84	9	0	0	3	15	13	3	3	0	10	30	.232	.231	.233	18.41	6.14
Del Rosario, Eduardo	R-R	6-0	145	5-19-95	3	1	4.38	20	0	0	2	39	34	19	19	2	17	37	.239	.333	.192	8.54	3.92
Duensing, Cole	R-R	6-4	175	6-6-94	6	7	5.06	25	20	0	1	96	87	62	54	8	65	90	.247	.280	.221	8.44	6.09
Fitzsimons, Connor	R-R	5-10	190	8-29-94	0	0	--	1	0	0	0	0	0	0	0	0	0	0	.000	--	--	0.00	0.00
Higgins, Connor	R-L	6-5	240	7-21-96	3	2	0.46	12	0	0	3	20	12	9	1	0	12	26	.167	.088	.237	11.90	5.49
Kelso, Shane	R-R	6-3	220	8-26-97	0	0	4.15	4	0	0	0	4	2	2	2	0	5	9	.143	.125	.167	18.69	10.38
King, Dylan	R-R	6-3	190	12-5-96	1	1	4.26	11	2	0	0	32	18	20	15	1	24	40	.164	.133	.185	11.37	6.82
Krzeminski, Austin	R-R	6-2	210	9-30-96	1	4	4.45	23	1	0	3	61	76	34	30	4	21	51	.297	.278	.312	7.57	3.12
Lee, Jake	R-R	6-4	215	6-30-95	1	0	3.27	3	2	0	0	11	8	4	4	2	0	15	.205	.217	.188	12.27	0.00
Leon, Matt	R-R	5-11	185	9-25-95	2	0	6.30	9	0	0	0	20	28	15	14	4	11	22	.342	.420	.219	9.90	4.95
Lind, Luke	L-R	6-6	225	1-26-95	3	3	2.50	24	0	0	2	40	38	19	11	2	17	47	.247	.250	.244	10.66	3.86
Millard, Tim	R-R	6-0	200	5-29-95	0	0	0.00	1	0	0	0	2	0	0	0	0	0	1	.667	--	.667	0.00	0.00
Molina, Cristopher	R-R	6-3	170	6-10-97	3	5	2.69	13	10	0	0	64	48	21	19	2	23	65	.208	.207	.209	9.19	3.25
Morrison, Ben	L-R	5-11	185	1-20-95	2	1	0.69	16	0	0	3	26	13	2	2	0	8	34	.141	.113	.180	11.77	2.77
Perez, Mayky	R-R	6-5	235	9-26-96	1	5	5.91	30	0	0	5	46	43	35	30	5	26	52	.249	.232	.260	10.25	5.12

	B-T	HT	WT	DOB	W	L	ERA	G	GS	CG	SV	IP	H	R	ER	HR	BB	SO	AVG	vLH	vRH	K/9	BB/9
Pina, Robinson	R-R	6-4	180	11-26-98	5	8	3.83	26	21	0	1	108	85	58	46	5	61	146	.213	.205	.220	12.17	5.08
Ramirez, Luis	R-R	5-11	175	9-14-97	0	1	2.55	13	0	0	1	25	19	8	7	2	6	28	.209	.161	.233	10.22	2.19
Robinson, Parker Joe	R-R	6-5	230	8-16-95	3	0	4.71	23	0	0	0	42	43	23	22	2	9	45	.274	.339	.232	9.64	1.93
Rogalla, Keith	R-R	6-3	205	9-15-95	1	2	3.80	6	4	0	0	24	22	10	10	1	10	29	.244	.325	.180	11.03	3.80
Rosario, Rayneldy	L-L	5-8	139	4-30-98	0	0	0.00	1	0	0	0	1	0	0	0	0	2	1	.000	.000	.000	9.00	18.00
Smith, Tyler	R-R	6-0	230	11-20-95	5	3	5.05	23	0	0	6	36	33	23	20	3	12	40	.244	.273	.225	10.09	3.03
Soriano, Jose	R-R	6-3	168	10-20-98	5	6	2.55	17	15	0	0	78	53	31	22	5	48	84	.197	.202	.193	9.73	5.56
Swanda, John	R-R	6-2	185	3-18-99	0	1	3.86	4	4	0	0	12	6	5	5	0	5	8	.255	.240	.273	6.17	3.86
Sykes, Chad	R-R	5-11	180	2-11-96	1	1	1.35	11	0	0	0	20	11	3	3	0	8	23	.159	.200	.128	10.35	3.60
Tyler, Kyle	R-R	6-0	185	12-27-96	7	1	2.64	21	16	2	2	102	72	34	30	8	35	87	.196	.169	.219	7.65	3.08
Varela, James	R-R	6-1	210	12-9-96	0	1	18.00	1	0	0	0	1	2	2	2	1	2	0	.250	.000	.333	9.00	18.00
Veliz, Greg	L-R	6-2	200	4-10-97	2	2	4.82	13	0	0	2	19	16	13	10	1	9	21	.235	.241	.231	10.13	4.34
Yan, Hector	L-L	5-11	180	4-26-99	4	5	3.39	26	20	0	1	109	74	45	41	5	52	148	.190	.247	.172	12.22	4.29

Fielding

Catcher	PCT	G	PO	A	E	DP	PB
Olmeda	.987	31	289	22	4	2	6
Pina	.991	30	291	35	3	4	4
Sanjur	1.000	2	7	2	0	0	
Wenson	.989	77	741	72	9	4	3

First Base	PCT	G	PO	A	E	DP
Arendas	.997	41	290	16	1	25
Fitzsimons	.991	62	402	32	4	37
Jones	.984	29	181	9	3	13
Millard	.981	7	49	3	1	6
Rondon	1.000	2	9	0	0	0
Rubalcaba	.000	1	0	0	0	0

Second Base	PCT	G	PO	A	E	DP
Arias	.925	12	17	20	3	4
Jones	.960	26	45	52	4	12

	PCT	G	PO	A	E	DP
Maitan	.900	21	38	34	8	11
McCullough	.969	9	13	18	1	7
Pineda	.941	15	15	33	3	9
Rondon	.933	25	39	45	6	10
Rubalcaba	.979	12	21	25	1	5
Soto	.982	15	28	27	1	8
Stefanic	.947	5	6	12	1	2

Third Base	PCT	G	PO	A	E	DP
Fitzsimons	.857	2	1	5	1	0
Jones	1.000	1	2	2	0	0
Maitan	.910	92	63	119	18	13
McCullough	1.000	5	5	0	0	0
Millard	.891	19	8	33	5	1
Pineda	.947	8	8	10	1	1
Rubalcaba	.882	13	8	22	4	5
Soto	1.000	2	3	3	0	0
Stefanic	1.000	2	0	5	0	1

Shortstop	PCT	G	PO	A	E	DP
Jones	.956	36	52	79	6	18
Pineda	1.000	2	2	1	0	0
Rondon	.943	12	12	21	2	3
Rubalcaba	.936	32	35	82	8	18
Soto	.938	46	55	72	9	12
Stefanic	.985	14	32	35	1	9

Outfield	PCT	G	PO	A	E	DP
Adams	.938	90	189	7	13	1
Del Valle	.981	96	145	9	3	1
Fitzsimons	1.000	1	1	0	0	0
Griffin	.993	84	141	4	1	2
Rosario	1.000	18	44	1	0	1
Sala	1.000	5	3	1	0	1
Vega	1.000	25	32	2	0	0
Williams	.966	105	189	8	7	0

OREM OWLZ

PIONEER LEAGUE — *ROOKIE ADVANCED*

Batting	B-T	HT	WT	DOB	AVG	vLH	vRH	G	AB	R	H	2B	3B	HR	RBI	BB	HBP	SH	SF	SO	SB	CS	SLG	OBP
Arias, Kevin	R-R	5-7	160	2-18-99	.269	.333	.239	26	67	7	18	1	1	1	10	6	6	0	1	27	0	1	.358	.375
Bisay, Edwin	B-R	5-9	156	3-8-00	.250	--	.250	1	4	0	1	0	0	0	0	0	0	0	0	3	0	0	.250	.250
Clawson, David	L-R	6-1	180	5-20-97	.196	.188	.199	59	230	26	45	14	2	6	31	16	2	1	2	76	1	1	.352	.252
Deveaux, Trent	R-R	6-0	160	5-4-00	.172	.000	.200	8	29	4	5	1	0	1	2	2	0	0	0	15	1	0	.310	.226
Flores, Jeans	R-R	5-11	165	3-20-98	.267	.400	.222	19	60	4	16	2	0	2	9	7	2	0	2	15	0	1	.400	.352
Gomez, Cristian	L-R	6-2	205	10-29-96	.281	.200	.296	10	32	6	9	2	2	0	1	3	0	0	0	14	0	0	.469	.343
Guzman, Jose	B-R	5-11	162	9-15-00	.208	.250	.200	6	24	3	5	0	0	1	3	0	0	0	0	6	0	0	.208	.296
Hunter Jr., Torii	R-R	6-2	180	6-7-95	.200	.333	.167	4	15	3	3	1	0	0	2	0	0	0	0	6	1	0	.267	.200
Jackson, Jeremiah	R-R	6-0	165	3-26-00	.266	.297	.255	65	256	47	68	14	2	23	60	24	5	0	6	96	5	1	.606	.333
Knowles, D'Shawn	B-R	6-0	165	1-16-01	.241	.271	.230	64	253	38	61	11	4	6	28	26	3	0	8	76	5	4	.387	.310
Kunz, Justin	R-R	5-9	190	4-4-97	.263	.100	.298	16	57	4	15	4	0	1	7	3	1	0	1	16	0	0	.386	.307
McCullough, Morgan	L-R	5-9	180	12-19-97	.263	.167	.290	47	160	26	42	7	1	4	20	20	1	0	1	50	1	1	.394	.348
Mulrine, Anthony	R-R	6-1	205	3-30-98	.250	.368	.200	44	128	24	32	6	1	5	26	16	14	0	1	33	0	2	.430	.390
Quezada, Jose	R-R	5-9	159	7-26-98	.292	.304	.286	26	72	8	21	4	1	0	4	4	1	0	0	19	3	2	.375	.338
Reyes, Jose	L-R	6-2	180	9-22-00	.263	.100	.321	10	38	6	10	1	0	3	8	4	1	0	0	13	0	0	.526	.349
Rondon, Adrian	R-R	6-1	190	7-7-98	.315	.333	.310	30	111	19	35	7	2	5	19	10	0	0	1	21	2	0	.550	.369
Rosario, Rayneldy	L-L	5-8	139	4-30-98	.000	.000	.000	2	6	1	0	0	0	0	2	0	0	0	2	0	0	.000	.000
Sala, Johan	R-R	6-1	175	12-17-97	.266	.382	.218	52	188	33	50	10	0	4	20	22	6	0	1	52	4	1	.383	.359
Sanjur, Mario	R-R	5-7	174	12-23-95	.368	1.000	.294	6	19	3	7	2	0	0	3	3	0	0	0	3	0	0	.474	.455
Scires, Caleb	L-L	6-0	195	9-1-98	.239	.188	.255	36	130	22	31	7	1	7	19	22	3	0	1	61	3	1	.469	.359
Simmons, Andrelton	R-R	6-2	195	9-4-89	.500	1.000	.250	2	6	1	3	0	0	0	0	0	0	0	0	1	0	0	.500	.500
Verrier, Jose	R-R	6-1	180	12-2-97	.227	.204	.234	65	220	33	50	11	3	11	29	35	13	0	1	98	5	4	.455	.364
White, Brandon	R-R	5-11	160	8-28-97	.281	.353	.257	61	199	33	56	7	4	2	11	22	3	0	0	44	11	5	.387	.362
Williams, Cam	R-R	6-1	185	1-16-97	.182	.333	.125	6	11	5	2	2	0	0	2	5	1	0	0	4	2	1	.364	.471
Williams-Nelson, Drevian	R-R	5-7	175	1-10-00	.233	.000	.280	12	30	6	7	3	0	0	2	4	0	0	0	10	0	0	.333	.343
Wilson, Will	R-R	6-0	184	7-21-98	.275	.286	.271	46	189	23	52	10	3	5	18	14	1	0	0	47	0	0	.439	.328

Pitching	B-T	HT	WT	DOB	W	L	ERA	G	GS	CG	SV	IP	H	R	ER	HR	BB	SO	AVG	vLH	vRH	K/9	BB/9
Aquino, Stiward	R-R	6-6	170	6-20-99	0	1	5.74	4	4	0	0	16	19	11	10	3	6	23	.307	.259	.343	13.21	3.45
Ballew, Seth	L-L	5-10	185	6-13-95	2	2	3.86	6	0	0	0	16	14	8	7	0	5	19	.215	.304	.167	10.47	2.76
Blake, Andrew	R-R	6-5	227	3-24-98	1	0	8.72	17	0	0	1	22	24	22	21	3	18	32	.289	.345	.259	13.29	7.48
Bower, Matt	R-L	6-5	190	6-16-94	1	0	9.00	3	0	0	0	5	9	5	5	2	3	5	.429	.714	.286	9.00	5.40
Chatham, Clayton	R-R	6-6	237	3-29-95	0	2	5.00	3	2	0	0	9	6	5	5	1	9	9	.188	.333	.130	12.00	9.00
Chock, Tanner	R-R	6-1	190	8-8-96	1	2	10.13	7	1	0	2	21	38	28	24	2	10	19	.388	.325	.431	8.02	4.22
Clark, Ethan	R-R	6-5	235	10-26-94	0	1	3.44	10	0	0	1	18	15	7	7	3	11	23	.227	.227	.227	11.29	5.40
Cole, Dazon	R-R	5-11	180	9-3-96	0	1	3.03	20	1	0	2	36	35	14	12	0	22	45	.254	.354	.200	11.36	5.55
De Leon, Yoel	L-L	6-2	200	11-23-97	2	2	5.13	13	0	0	0	47	55	37	27	9	22	53	.287	.339	.262	10.08	4.18
Franco, Sadrac	R-R	6-0	155	6-4-00	0	2	5.04	8	8	0	0	25	28	22	14	5	13	25	.272	.279	.267	9.00	4.68
Gonzalez, Jenrry	L-R	5-10	185	6-7-01	0	1	5.40	2	2	0	0	7	6	5	4	0	5	14	.214	.250	.188	18.90	6.75
Guzman, Emilker	R-R	5-10	160	2-10-99	3	7	4.82	15	12	0	0	62	63	42	33	5	14	59	.263	.310	.229	8.61	2.04

Pitching	B-T	HT	WT	DOB	W	L	ERA	G	GS	CG	SV	IP	H	R	ER	HR	BB	SO	AVG	vLH	vRH	K/9	BB/9
Holmes, William	R-R	6-2	185	12-22-00	0	0	3.86	2	2	0	0	7	4	3	3	2	4	13	.182	.100	.250	16.71	5.14
Kelso, Shane	R-R	6-3	220	8-26-97	2	1	1.65	13	0	0	2	16	12	5	3	0	10	25	.207	.143	.243	13.78	5.51
King, Dylan	R-R	6-3	190	12-5-96	0	1	5.40	2	2	0	0	7	8	7	4	0	3	8	.296	.500	.177	10.80	4.05
Kristofak, Zac	R-R	5-9	185	12-8-97	2	3	6.15	19	0	0	2	26	36	19	18	2	7	24	.330	.425	.275	8.20	2.39
Kunz, Justin	R-R	5-9	190	4-4-97	0	0	0.00	1	0	0	0	1	0	0	0	0	0	0	.500	1.000	.000	0.00	0.00
Leon, Matt	R-R	5-11	185	9-25-95	4	4	3.64	14	11	0	0	64	55	31	26	2	20	68	.230	.222	.234	9.51	2.80
McCullough, Morgan	L-R	5-9	180	12-19-97	0	0	189.00	1	0	0	0	0	6	7	7	3	1	0	.857	1.000	.667	0.00	27.00
Moncion, Kelvin	L-L	6-1	201	12-23-98	3	3	5.64	11	10	0	0	45	47	30	28	7	20	33	.278	.157	.331	6.65	4.03
Mulrine, Anthony	R-R	6-1	205	3-30-98	0	0	0.00	2	0	0	0	1	0	0	0	0	1	0	.000	.000	.000	9.00	0.00
Natera, Jose	R-R	6-1	180	11-30-99	2	3	7.40	6	1	0	0	21	30	20	17	4	9	18	.341	.263	.400	7.84	3.92
Quezada, Jose	R-R	5-9	159	7-26-98	0	0	0.00	1	0	0	0	1	0	0	0	0	2	0	.000	--	.000	0.00	27.00
Randel, Ryan	R-R	6-7	230	8-11-95	0	1	5.03	10	1	0	1	20	22	12	11	5	11	19	.282	.160	.340	8.69	5.03
Rivera, Jerryell	L-L	6-3	180	4-19-99	1	3	6.89	10	9	0	0	33	38	37	25	7	23	31	.290	.207	.314	8.54	6.34
Rogalla, Keith	R-R	6-3	205	9-15-95	0	1	7.94	2	2	0	0	6	10	5	5	0	1	6	.400	.667	.316	9.53	1.59
Rosario, Rayneldy	L-L	5-8	139	4-30-98	0	0	0.00	1	0	0	0	1	1	0	0	0	0	1	.333	1.000	.000	13.50	0.00
Sala, Johan	R-R	6-1	175	12-17-97	0	0	54.00	1	0	0	0	0	3	2	2	1	0	0	.750	.000	1.000	0.00	0.00
Smith, Ryan	L-L	5-11	185	8-13-97	0	2	5.26	19	0	0	0	26	25	17	15	5	12	37	.250	.200	.277	12.97	4.21
Sykes, Chad	R-R	5-11	180	2-11-96	1	0	7.45	7	0	0	1	10	9	10	8	1	5	15	.220	.182	.233	13.97	4.66
Varela, James	R-R	6-1	210	12-9-96	1	0	3.38	7	0	0	0	16	14	7	6	4	6	14	.237	.238	.237	7.88	3.38
Veliz, Greg	L-R	6-2	200	4-10-97	0	0	1.69	6	0	0	0	11	7	5	2	1	0	15	.175	.059	.261	12.66	0.00
Voss, Jacob	R-R	6-9	255	4-20-97	2	0	7.77	20	0	0	1	22	19	23	19	1	31	33	.238	.133	.300	13.50	12.68
Williams, Darrien	R-R	6-3	205	6-24-96	2	3	5.49	21	0	0	2	39	39	31	24	2	24	46	.252	.245	.255	10.53	5.49

Fielding

C: Bisay 1, Flores 19, Kunz 15, Mulrine 38, Sanjur 6. **1B:** Clawson 58, Gomez 10, Rondon 3, Sala 2, Verrier 4. **2B:** Arias 11, Guzman 2, Jackson 21, McCullough 12, Quezada 13, Verrier 3, Williams-Nelson 8, Wilson 13. **3B:** Arias 11, McCullough 27, Quezada 1, Rondon 21, Verrier 22. **SS:** Guzman 4, Jackson 31, McCullough 8, Quezada 1, Rondon 8, Simmons 2, Wilson 28. **OF:** Arias 2, Deveaux 8, Hunter Jr. 4, Knowles 62, Quezada 9, Reyes 10, Rosario 2, Sala 37, Scires 25, Verrier 18, White 59, Williams 5, Williams-Nelson 2.

AZL ANGELS   ROOKIE
ARIZONA LEAGUE

Batting	B-T	HT	WT	DOB	AVG	vLH	vRH	G	AB	R	H	2B	3B	HR	RBI	BB	HBP	SH	SF	SO	SB	CS	SLG	OBP
Adams, Jordyn	R-R	6-2	180	10-18-99	.539	.500	.546	3	13	4	7	1	0	0	4	1	0	0	0	3	4	0	.615	.571
Bisay, Edwin	B-R	5-9	156	3-8-00	.206	.214	.203	24	73	8	15	2	1	0	3	8	0	0	0	27	2	0	.260	.284
Bray, Datren	R-R	5-9	189	4-28-99	.000	--	.000	2	7	1	0	0	0	0	0	1	0	0	0	6	1	0	.000	.125
Brown, Spencer	L-R	5-10	185	7-14-99	.242	.133	.275	23	66	6	16	3	1	0	6	9	1	0	0	22	1	1	.318	.342
Cruz, Michael	L-R	5-11	210	1-13-96	.125	.000	.167	3	8	1	1	0	0	0	1	2	0	0	0	3	0	0	.125	.300
De La Cruz, Julio	R-R	5-11	182	8-3-00	.239	.212	.245	47	180	21	43	9	1	1	19	18	3	0	4	62	1	3	.317	.312
Deveaux, Trent	R-R	6-0	160	5-4-00	.247	.205	.256	52	215	38	53	15	4	6	23	24	4	0	1	76	14	6	.437	.332
Gomez, Cristian	L-R	6-2	205	10-29-96	.265	.225	.275	55	200	35	53	12	4	2	24	22	4	0	2	45	2	0	.395	.347
Guzman, Jose	B-R	5-11	162	9-19-00	.189	.100	.207	49	175	31	33	6	0	1	19	29	2	0	1	56	3	1	.240	.309
Kunz, Justin	R-R	5-9	190	4-4-97	.347	.250	.378	15	49	11	17	0	0	3	9	5	2	0	1	14	0	0	.531	.421
Marcano, Marlon	R-R	5-11	211	9-14-99	.203	.200	.204	21	69	5	14	0	0	0	7	6	1	0	1	24	0	1	.203	.273
Marsh, Brandon	L-R	6-4	215	12-18-97	.048	.100	.000	5	21	1	1	0	0	0	2	0	0	0	0	8	1	0	.048	.048
Moya, Kendy	B-R	5-10	150	12-14-98	.255	.333	.225	18	55	8	14	1	0	0	5	11	0	0	0	9	2	1	.273	.379
Paris, Kyren	R-R	6-0	165	11-11-01	.300	.500	.250	3	10	4	3	1	0	0	2	1	0	0	0	4	0	0	.400	.462
Quezada, Jose	R-R	5-9	159	7-26-98	.167	.000	.200	6	6	1	1	0	0	0	0	1	0	0	0	2	0	0	.167	.375
Reyes, Jose	L-R	6-2	180	9-22-00	.237	.235	.237	47	186	28	44	11	6	1	22	22	1	0	0	59	5	3	.376	.321
Rivas, Leonardo	B-R	5-10	150	10-10-97	.063	.000	.071	7	16	6	1	0	0	0	0	8	0	1	0	4	1	0	.063	.375
Rivas, Rainier	L-L	6-3	220	6-29-01	.260	.000	.317	14	50	9	13	2	2	1	7	4	0	0	1	15	0	0	.440	.309
Rivera, Erik	L-L	6-2	200	2-4-01	.208	.154	.220	21	72	8	15	4	0	0	9	2	0	0	1	31	0	0	.264	.313
Rivera, William	R-R	6-3	184	4-21-00	.194	.111	.213	26	93	18	18	3	0	0	13	11	3	0	0	29	1	2	.226	.299
Soto, Livan	L-R	6-0	160	6-20-00	.214	.200	.217	7	28	4	6	2	0	0	1	1	0	0	0	4	0	2	.286	.241
Uceta, Raider	L-L	6-0	215	1-29-01	.278	.238	.286	32	126	11	35	6	3	0	20	12	0	0	0	36	0	1	.373	.341
Vega, Ryan	R-R	6-2	180	9-17-96	.250	.000	.286	2	8	2	2	0	0	0	0	2	0	0	0	3	0	0	.250	.400
Weisz, Keaton	R-R	5-8	155	5-30-96	.216	.000	.258	13	37	2	8	2	0	0	5	7	1	0	1	14	0	0	.270	.348
Williams-Nelson, Drevian	R-R	5-7	175	1-10-00	.265	.450	.220	30	102	12	27	7	1	1	18	13	2	0	0	30	2	3	.382	.359

Pitching	B-T	HT	WT	DOB	W	L	ERA	G	GS	CG	SV	IP	H	R	ER	HR	BB	SO	AVG	vLH	vRH	K/9	BB/9
Agramonte, Galvi	R-R	5-11	190	5-19-98	0	0	8.44	3	0	0	0	5	6	6	5	0	8	5	.300	.000	.429	8.44	13.50
Aquino, Ewdy	R-R	5-9	170	2-24-00	0	1	4.97	15	0	0	0	25	35	17	14	1	14	31	.330	.361	.314	11.01	4.97
Aquino, Stiward	R-R	5-9	170	9-20-99	0	4	7.71	8	8	0	0	21	27	19	18	1	10	26	.321	.355	.302	11.14	4.29
Ballew, Seth	L-L	5-10	185	6-13-95	4	0	1.38	6	1	0	0	13	6	4	2	0	4	15	.143	.188	.115	10.38	2.77
Bash, Andrew	R-R	6-0	190	8-1-96	1	1	2.81	14	0	0	2	16	13	7	5	1	5	18	.213	.381	.125	10.13	2.81
Bates, Nathan	R-R	6-6	205	3-1-94	0	0	0.00	1	1	0	0	1	0	0	0	0	0	3	.000	.000	.000	27.00	0.00
Bower, Matt	R-L	6-5	190	6-16-94	0	0	0.00	1	1	0	0	1	1	0	0	0	1	0	.250	.000	.500	9.00	0.00
Caceres, Kelvin	R-R	6-1	180	1-26-00	1	0	3.82	10	6	0	0	35	26	22	15	1	26	34	.199	.179	.213	8.66	6.62
Cain, John	L-L	6-10	235	3-17-96	1	0	0.00	2	0	0	0	4	1	0	0	0	2	6	.091	.000	.143	14.73	4.91
Chaney, Chase	R-R	6-1	180	12-16-99	1	5	6.28	11	2	0	0	39	40	40	27	3	35	27	.270	.277	.265	6.28	8.15
Chapman, Ridge	R-R	6-0	210	1-30-97	0	1	12.00	3	3	0	0	3	3	4	4	1	7	4	.333	.333	.333	12.00	21.00
Chatham, Clayton	R-R	6-6	237	6-29-95	0	0	0.00	1	0	0	0	1	0	0	0	0	0	0	.000	.000	.000	9.00	0.00
Contreras, Juan	R-R	6-1	180	9-8-99	0	1	15.43	0	0	0	0	7	8	14	12	0	12	3	.308	.111	.412	3.86	15.43
De Horta, Adrian	R-R	6-3	185	3-13-95	0	0	3.00	2	2	0	0	3	2	1	1	0	1	6	.200	.250	.167	18.00	3.00
Dexter, Jake	R-R	6-2	215	10-10-96	0	1	3.60	7	0	0	0	10	10	5	4	0	5	8	.195	.333	.138	7.20	4.50
Duensing, Cole	R-R	6-4	175	1-6-99	0	0	108.00	1	1	0	0	0	4	4	4	0	0	0	.000	--	.000	0.00	108.00
Duran, Emmanuel	R-R	6-1	182	10-9-00	1	2	6.81	12	2	0	0	37	34	33	28	1	43	40	.256	.276	.240	9.73	10.46
Goff, Julio	R-R	5-10	200	1-11-00	1	2	3.73	9	3	0	0	31	30	16	13	1	15	34	.248	.303	.227	9.77	4.31

Name	B-T	HT	WT	DOB	W	L	ERA	G	GS	CG	SV	IP	H	R	ER	HR	BB	SO	AVG	vLH	vRH	K/9	BB/9
Gonzalez, Jenrry	L-L	5-10	185	6-7-01	3	2	4.34	10	4	0	1	37	32	25	18	1	23	53	.227	.226	.227	12.78	5.54
Gubelman, Jordan	R-R	6-2	225	4-5-97	0	2	6.92	8	0	0	1	13	19	13	10	2	3	11	.352	.444	.306	7.62	2.08
Holmes, William	R-R	6-2	185	12-22-00	0	2	5.71	7	6	0	0	17	15	12	11	2	16	25	.238	.212	.267	12.98	8.31
Lucas, Jean Carlos	R-R	6-3	185	12-2-00	0	0	4.32	7	2	0	0	25	27	23	12	2	13	20	.262	.303	.243	7.20	4.68
Middleton, Keynan	R-R	6-3	215	9-12-93	0	0	0.00	1	1	0	0	1	0	0	0	0	0	2	.000	--	.000	18.00	0.00
Moncion, Kelvin	L-L	6-1	201	12-23-98	1	0	3.38	4	0	0	0	8	7	3	3	0	9	9	.241	.000	.304	10.13	10.13
Moya, Kendy	B-R	5-10	150	12-14-98	0	0	0.00	1	0	0	0	1	1	0	0	0	0	1	.333	.500	.000	5.00	0.00
Natera, Jose	R-R	6-1	180	11-30-99	1	2	6.19	6	2	0	0	16	19	11	11	4	8	22	.275	.233	.308	12.38	4.50
Nunan, Daniel	L-L	6-6	215	5-25-00	1	1	6.11	7	2	0	0	18	19	15	12	0	13	25	.264	.300	.250	12.74	6.62
Quezada, Jose	R-R	5-9	159	7-26-98	0	0	0.00	1	0	0	0	1	2	2	0	1	0	1	.333	.333	.333	9.00	0.00
Randel, Ryan	R-R	6-7	230	8-11-95	0	0	16.20	5	0	0	0	5	15	12	9	1	1	8	.469	.273	.571	14.40	1.80
Rodriguez, Jose M.	R-R	6-3	195	9-8-00	0	0	9.00	1	0	0	0	1	1	1	1	0	1	2	.250	1.000	.000	18.00	9.00
Rogalla, Keith	R-R	6-3	205	9-15-95	0	3	18.47	5	4	0	0	6	14	17	13	0	11	8	.412	.455	.391	11.37	15.63
Santa Maria, Tulio	R-R	6-4	170	6-6-00	0	0	2.70	6	0	0	0	7	3	2	2	0	14	5	.158	.111	.200	6.75	18.90
Soriano, Jose	R-R	6-3	168	10-20-98	0	1	1.93	3	3	0	0	5	5	5	1	0	3	8	.263	.375	.182	15.43	5.79
Van Scoyoc, Connor	R-R	6-6	210	11-26-99	2	2	5.13	12	5	0	0	40	35	29	23	1	36	50	.230	.323	.167	11.16	8.03
Varela, James	R-R	6-1	210	12-9-96	0	1	1.93	6	0	0	0	9	12	5	2	0	3	15	.300	.462	.222	14.46	2.89
Velez, Yeyson	R-R	6-0	165	8-15-98	1	3	4.20	7	0	0	2	15	16	12	7	0	11	22	.267	.261	.270	13.20	6.60
Weisz, Keaton	R-R	5-8	155	5-30-96	0	0	5.40	1	0	0	0	2	2	1	1	0	1	0	.333	1.000	.200	0.00	5.40
Woods, Matthew	R-R	6-2	185	8-31-97	0	1	5.40	9	0	0	1	12	17	7	7	0	3	10	.333	.385	.280	7.71	2.31

Fielding

C: Bisay 24, Cruz 3, Kunz 15, Marcano 21. 1B: Gomez 54, Uceta 2. 2B: Brown 2, De La Cruz 20, Guzman 4, Moya 6, Quezada 5, Soto 4, Weisz 6, Williams-Nelson 17. 3B: Brown 17, De La Cruz 28, Guzman 4, Moya 7, Quezada 1, Weisz 5. SS: Guzman 46, Moya 5, Paris 3, Rivas 6, Soto 3, Weisz 2. OF: Adams 3, Bray 1, Deveaux 51, Marsh 4, Reyes 47, Rivas 13, Rivera 26, Uceta 17, Vega 2, Williams-Nelson 7.

DSL ANGELS · ROOKIE

DOMINICAN SUMMER LEAGUE

Batting	B-T	HT	WT	DOB	AVG	vLH	vRH	G	AB	R	H	2B	3B	HR	RBI	BB	HBP	SH	SF	SO	SB	CS	SLG	OBP
Bonilla, Jose	R-R	6-0	185	4-2-02	.284	.000	.328	20	74	13	21	5	2	0	6	14	2	0	2	19	0	0	.405	.402
Brito, Yohan	L-L	5-9	140	10-20-01	.216	.100	.234	51	148	26	32	1	1	0	12	43	2	1	2	38	10	9	.237	.395
Carreno, Ronald	R-R	6-1	190	4-7-01	.202	.143	.207	34	99	14	20	2	0	3	13	19	2	0	0	31	1	1	.313	.342
Estrada, Jose	R-R	5-10	175	5-5-00	.247	.296	.236	43	154	23	38	7	1	0	14	19	2	0	1	16	2	1	.305	.335
Fana, Willi	L-L	6-0	170	8-20-02	.206	.087	.223	50	180	18	37	6	2	2	22	13	0	0	3	50	3	1	.294	.255
Gill, Starlin	R-R	5-10	150	3-16-00	.303	.273	.309	44	145	29	44	6	1	0	21	18	5	1	0	19	15	6	.359	.399
Jimenez, Jorge	R-R	5-9	150	6-9-02	.296	.263	.300	43	159	28	47	5	2	0	23	28	1	2	2	27	13	4	.352	.400
Mora, Darimel	B-R	5-11	160	7-16-02	.210	.310	.195	57	224	32	47	5	1	1	13	22	1	1	0	39	11	9	.255	.283
Moreno, Darwin	R-R	6-2	175	1-26-02	.188	.500	.177	19	64	14	12	5	0	0	6	18	3	0	0	25	3	0	.266	.388
Nunez, Geison	R-R	6-1	203	7-30-00	.136	.000	.153	23	66	6	9	3	0	0	2	13	4	0	1	20	1	0	.182	.310
Pena, Ysaac	L-R	5-9	180	6-19-98	.295	.292	.296	45	166	22	49	13	4	3	28	16	0	0	4	21	4	3	.476	.350
Puntiel, Jean	R-R	5-11	150	11-13-01	.219	.000	.222	21	64	9	14	1	0	1	4	11	0	1	0	18	5	0	.281	.333
Ramirez, Alexander	R-R	6-2	180	8-29-02	.234	.177	.241	39	154	37	36	8	5	4	19	16	0	1	1	59	6	0	.429	.328
Rijo, Jeison	R-R	6-0	165	10-14-99	.191	.071	.205	42	126	13	24	2	0	2	17	23	7	0	2	31	2	1	.254	.342
Rivas, Rainier	L-L	6-3	222	6-8-99	.400	.333	.406	20	70	15	28	3	2	1	20	14	2	0	0	11	3	2	.543	.512
Santana, Adderlin	R-R	5-8	160	5-31-00	.118	--	.118	8	17	3	2	0	0	1	2	0	0	1	7	1	1	.118	.211
Santana, Natanael	R-R	6-3	190	7-27-01	.258	.286	.255	54	182	34	47	5	1	5	27	34	10	0	2	66	12	4	.379	.399

Pitching	B-T	HT	WT	DOB	W	L	ERA	G	GS	CG	SV	IP	H	R	ER	HR	BB	SO	AVG	vLH	vRH	K/9	BB/9
Alcantara, Jhosua	R-R	6-6	200	9-30-97	0	1	3.68	11	0	0	1	15	15	10	6	1	7	27	.246	.304	.211	16.57	4.30
Aquino, Ewdy	R-R	5-9	170	2-24-00	0	0	5.06	5	0	0	2	5	6	3	3	0	4	5	.286	.364	.200	8.44	6.75
Collado, Christopher	R-R	6-2	190	3-4-00	4	2	4.55	11	3	0	0	32	22	18	16	0	24	33	.196	.103	.247	9.38	6.82
Diaz, Danifer	R-R	6-0	165	7-26-01	2	1	3.33	14	5	0	0	46	37	27	17	1	28	48	.218	.239	.204	9.39	5.48
Duarte, Angel	R-R	5-11	187	1-28-02	3	0	1.10	6	0	0	0	16	9	3	2	0	7	16	.167	.250	.132	8.82	3.86
Duran, Alejandro	R-R	5-11	150	4-10-02	0	0	1.93	7	5	0	0	28	21	7	6	0	5	34	.206	.216	.200	10.93	1.61
Goff, Julio	R-R	5-10	200	1-11-00	1	2	9.24	4	2	0	0	13	21	13	13	3	4	13	.382	.316	.417	9.24	2.84
Gomez, Olivier	R-R	6-1	145	12-4-01	1	3	6.48	6	2	0	0	17	17	15	12	0	8	11	.250	.269	.238	5.94	4.32
Gomez, Victor	R-R	5-11	184	10-19-00	0	1	14.59	9	0	0	0	12	19	22	20	0	14	9	.380	.350	.400	6.57	10.22
Gomez, Wilson	L-L	6-0	177	4-20-01	0	3	22.95	11	0	0	0	7	8	22	17	0	19	7	.296	.375	.263	9.45	25.65
Leon, Jose	L-L	5-10	162	2-6-01	1	4	6.59	17	0	0	1	29	28	28	21	1	19	36	.239	.164	.264	11.30	5.97
Lopez, Nehemias	R-R	5-10	152	5-9-00	1	3	6.60	12	0	0	0	15	12	16	11	0	12	17	.214	.211	.216	10.20	7.20
Nunez, Luis	R-R	6-2	175	9-19-01	1	4	5.56	12	10	0	0	44	54	39	27	1	22	56	.298	.339	.277	11.54	4.53
Pena, Elian	R-R	6-4	171	3-12-00	1	2	3.20	12	7	0	1	39	27	23	14	0	26	32	.188	.196	.184	7.32	5.95
Pena, Ysaac	L-R	5-9	180	6-19-98	0	0	0.00	1	0	0	0	1	0	0	0	0	0	0	.333	.500	.000	0.00	0.00
Perez, Samuel	L-L	5-11	175	11-29-99	1	3	1.26	21	0	0	4	29	18	8	4	1	4	38	.182	.222	.167	11.93	1.26
Pinto, Jean	R-R	5-11	175	1-9-01	0	1	2.25	3	3	0	0	12	12	5	3	0	3	19	.255	.125	.323	14.25	2.25
Rodriguez, Victor	L-L	5-11	160	12-15-00	2	2	2.93	12	4	0	0	40	42	23	13	1	22	41	.266	.313	.254	9.23	4.95
Rojas, Daniel	R-R	6-2	180	10-21-01	0	4	9.20	11	7	0	1	30	32	39	31	5	21	26	.262	.243	.271	7.71	6.23
Tapia, Gabriel	R-R	6-1	160	5-20-02	2	1	2.57	12	8	0	1	49	43	17	14	1	13	47	.234	.219	.242	8.63	2.39
Taveras, Roelis	L-L	5-11	155	6-4-00	1	1	5.40	8	0	0	0	16	14	10	10	0	16	14	.239	.316	.208	6.87	7.85
Tejada, Cristofer	R-R	6-1	175	6-1-01	0	2	6.19	6	3	0	0	16	17	13	11	3	7	17	.254	.333	.209	9.56	3.94
Vargas, Anderson	L-L	5-9	160	10-22-01	0	0	0.00	1	0	0	0	1	2	0	0	0	2	1	.400	--	.400	6.75	13.50
Velez, Yeyson	R-R	6-0	165	8-15-98	2	0	2.88	8	4	0	0	34	30	16	11	0	11	29	.242	.261	.231	7.60	2.88

Fielding

C: Carreno 13, Estrada 34, Nunez 13, Pena 12. 1B: Carreno 21, Nunez 3, Pena 26, Rijo 19. 2B: Estrada 3, Gill 13, Jimenez 19, Mora 19, Puntiel 17, Santana 2. 3B: Bonilla 5, Gill 27, Jimenez 12, Rijo 23, Santana 3. SS: Bonilla 15, Jimenez 15, Mora 35. OF: Brito 49, Fana 38, Gill 5, Moreno 18, Ramirez 27, Rivas

Los Angeles Dodgers

SEASON IN A SENTENCE: The Dodgers won a franchise-record 106 games en route to their seventh straight National League West division title, but their season came to an abrupt end with a gut-wrenching loss to the Nationals in Game 5 of the National League Division Series.

HIGH POINT: The Dodgers' player development was on full display in June when they won three straight games on walk-off home runs by rookies. Matt Beaty hit the game-winning two-run homer in the ninth inning on June 21, Alex Verdugo hit a solo home run in the 11th for the win on June 22, and Will Smith capped it with a three-run, walk-off homer in the bottom of the ninth on June 23.

LOW POINT: The Dodgers were six outs away from advancing to the National League Championship Series, but Clayton Kershaw surrendered back-to-back home runs to Anthony Rendon and Juan Soto to allow the Nationals to pull into a 3-3 tie in the eighth inning of Game 5. Two innings later, Joe Kelly allowed a grand slam to Howie Kendrick to complete the collapse.

NOTABLE ROOKIES: Smith hit 15 home runs in just 54 games and took over as the Dodgers' everyday catcher by the end of July. Verdugo ranked among the rookie leaders in most offensive categories before a back/oblique strain ended his season in early August. Beaty emerged as a key utilityman with a potent bat, and Minor League Player of the Year Gavin Lux received a September callup and homered in his first postseason at-bat. Righthanders Tony Gonsolin (4-2, 2.93) and Dustin May (2-3, 3.63) debuted during the summer and fortified the Dodgers' pitching staff.

KEY TRANSACTIONS: The Dodgers traded Matt Kemp, Yasiel Puig, Alex Wood and Kyle Farmer to the Reds in the offseason for a package driven by prospects Josiah Gray and Jeter Downs. A.J. Pollock signed a five-year, $60 million contract before the season to be the Dodgers' center fielder but was limited to 86 games by an elbow injury and finished the season playing left. The Dodgers mostly stood pat during the season, acquiring lefty specialist Adam Kolarek for prospect Niko Hulsizer in their only major move.

DOWN ON THE FARM: The Dodgers led all National League organizations in minor league winning percentage (.556) for the second straight year. Lux ranked fourth in the minors in both batting average (.347) and OPS (1.028) to win Minor League Player of the Year.

OPENING DAY PAYROLL: $152,863,333 (9th).

PLAYERS OF THE YEAR

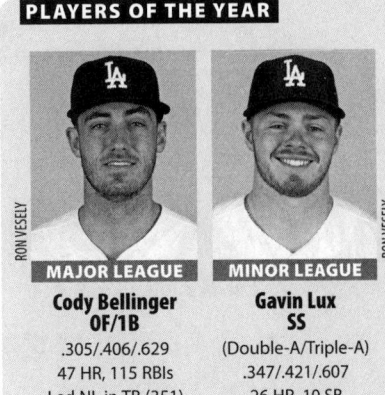

RON VESELY   RON VESELY

MAJOR LEAGUE	MINOR LEAGUE
Cody Bellinger OF/1B	**Gavin Lux** SS
.305/.406/.629	(Double-A/Triple-A)
47 HR, 115 RBIs	.347/.421/.607
Led NL in TB (351)	26 HR, 10 SB

ORGANIZATION LEADERS

Batting		*Minimum 250 AB
MAJORS		
* AVG	Cody Bellinger	.305
* OPS	Cody Bellinger	1.035
HR	Cody Bellinger	47
RBI	Cody Bellinger	115
MINORS		
* AVG	Gavin Lux, Tulsa, Oklahoma City	.347
* OBP	Connor Joe, Oklahoma City	.426
* SLG	Kyle Garlick, Oklahoma City	.675
* OPS	Kyle Garlick, Oklahoma City	1.057
R	Gavin Lux, Tulsa, Oklahoma City	99
H	Gavin Lux, Tulsa, Oklahoma City	159
TB	Gavin Lux, Tulsa, Oklahoma City	278
2B	Miguel Vargas, Great Lakes, Rancho Cucamonga	38
3B	Jeren Kendall, Rancho Cucamonga	10
HR	Edwin Rios, Oklahoma City	31
RBI	Zach Reks, Tulsa, Oklahoma City	93
BB	Dillon Paulson, Great Lakes, Rancho Cucamonga	82
SO	Donovan Casey, Rancho Cucamonga, Tulsa	174
SB	Brayan Morales, Rancho Cucamonga	35

Pitching		#Minimum 75 IP
MAJORS		
W	Clayton Kershaw	16
# ERA	Hyun-Jin Ryu	2.32
SO	Walker Buehler	215
SV	Kenley Jansen	33
MINORS		
W	Jose Chacin, Great Lakes	11
W	Josiah Gray, Great Lakes, Rancho Cucamonga, Tulsa	11
W	Jose Martinez, Great Lakes, Rancho Cucamonga	11
W	Edwin Uceta, Rancho Cucamonga, Tulsa	11
L	Justin De Fratus, Oklahoma City, Tulsa	13
# ERA	Justin Hagenman, Great Lakes	2.24
G	Kevin Quackenbush, Oklahoma City	54
GS	Josiah Gray, Great Lakes, Rancho Cucamonga, Tulsa	25
GS	Andre Jackson, Great Lakes, Rancho Cucamonga	25
GS	Stephen Kolek, Great Lakes	25
SV	Jordan Sheffield, Rancho Cucamonga, Tulsa	13
IP	Justin De Fratus, Oklahoma City, Tulsa	141
BB	J.D. Martin, Tulsa, Oklahoma City	69
SO	Josiah Gray, Great Lakes, Rancho Cucamonga, Tulsa	147
# ERA	Josiah Gray, Great Lakes, Rancho Cucamonga, Tulsa	.207

General Manager: Andrew Friedman. **Farm Director:** Brandon Gomes. **Scouting Director:** Billy Gasparino.

Class	Team	League	W	L	PCT	Finish	Manager
Majors	Los Angeles Dodgers	National	106	56	.654	1st (15)	Dave Roberts
Triple-A	Oklahoma City Dodgers	Pacific Coast	62	77	.446	12th (16)	Travis Barbary
Double-A	Tulsa Drillers	Texas	78	61	.561	2nd (8)	Scott Hennessey
High A	R. Cucamonga Quakes	California	81	57	.587	2nd (8)	Mark Kertenian
Low A	Great Lakes Loons	Midwest	81	55	.596	1st (16)	John Shoemaker
Rookie	Ogden Raptors	Pioneer	54	22	.711	1st (8)	Austin Chubb
Rookie	AZL Dodgers Lasorda	Arizona	27	29	.482	t-10th (21)	Danny Dorn
Rookie	AZL Dodgers Mota	Arizona	33	23	.589	t-4th (21)	Jair Fernandez
Overall 2019 Minor League Record			416	324	.562	2nd (30)	

ORGANIZATION STATISTICS

LOS ANGELES DODGERS
NATIONAL LEAGUE

Batting	B-T	HT	WT	DOB	AVG	vLH	vRH	G	AB	R	H	2B	3B	HR	RBI	BB	HBP	SH	SF	SO	SB	CS	SLG	OBP
Barnes, Austin	R-R	5-10	187	12-28-89	.203	.194	.207	75	212	28	43	12	1	5	25	23	5	0	2	56	3	0	.340	.293
Beaty, Matt	L-R	6-0	215	4-28-93	.265	.125	.286	99	249	36	66	19	1	9	46	17	2	0	0	33	5	0	.458	.317
Bellinger, Cody	L-L	6-4	203	7-13-95	.305	.280	.318	156	558	121	170	34	3	47	115	95	3	0	4	108	15	5	.629	.406
d'Arnaud, Travis	R-R	6-2	210	2-10-89	.000	.000	--	1	1	0	0	0	0	0	0	0	0	0	0	0	0	0	.000	.000
2-team total (10 New York)					.083	.333	.048	11	24	2	2	0	0	0	2	2	0	0	0	5	0	0	.083	.154
Freese, David	R-R	6-2	213	4-28-83	.315	.287	.361	79	162	35	51	13	0	11	29	23	1	0	0	44	0	0	.599	.403
Gale, Rocky	R-R	6-1	185	2-22-88	.133	.333	.083	5	15	1	2	0	0	0	0	0	0	0	0	7	0	0	.133	.133
Garlick, Kyle	R-R	6-1	210	1-26-92	.250	.267	.222	30	48	8	12	4	0	3	6	5	0	0	0	19	0	0	.521	.321
Gyorko, Jedd	R-R	5-10	215	9-23-88	.139	.136	.143	24	36	1	5	1	0	0	2	3	0	0	0	10	0	0	.167	.205
2-team total (38 St. Louis)					.174	.135	.200	62	92	6	16	1	0	2	9	9	0	0	0	24	2	0	.250	.248
Hernandez, Enrique	R-R	5-11	192	8-24-91	.237	.263	.221	130	414	57	98	19	1	17	64	36	6	0	4	97	4	0	.411	.304
Lux, Gavin	L-R	6-2	190	11-23-97	.240	.083	.270	23	75	12	18	4	1	2	9	7	0	0	0	24	2	0	.400	.305
Martin, Russell	R-R	5-10	215	2-15-83	.220	.218	.221	83	209	29	46	5	0	6	20	30	8	0	2	60	1	0	.330	.337
Muncy, Max	L-R	6-0	218	8-25-90	.251	.268	.242	141	487	101	122	22	1	35	98	90	8	0	4	149	4	1	.515	.374
Negron, Kristopher	R-R	6-0	190	2-1-86	.259	.192	.321	30	54	9	14	1	0	2	7	3	0	0	0	17	0	1	.389	.298
Pederson, Joc	L-L	6-1	220	4-21-92	.249	.225	.252	149	450	83	112	16	3	36	74	50	12	0	2	111	1	1	.538	.339
Pollock, A.J.	R-R	6-1	212	12-5-87	.266	.323	.239	86	308	49	82	15	1	15	47	23	7	0	4	74	5	1	.468	.328
Rios, Edwin	L-R	6-3	220	4-21-94	.277	.286	.275	28	47	10	13	2	1	4	8	9	0	0	0	21	0	0	.617	.393
Seager, Corey	L-R	6-4	215	4-27-94	.272	.240	.289	134	489	82	133	44	1	19	87	44	4	0	4	98	1	0	.483	.335
Smith, Will	R-R	5-10	170	3-28-95	.253	.211	.274	54	170	30	43	9	0	15	42	18	5	0	3	52	2	0	.571	.337
Taylor, Chris	R-R	6-1	196	8-29-90	.262	.255	.267	124	366	52	96	29	4	12	52	37	4	2	5	118	8	4	.462	.333
Turner, Justin	R-R	5-11	202	11-23-84	.290	.288	.292	135	479	80	139	24	0	27	67	51	14	0	5	88	2	0	.509	.372
Verdugo, Alex	L-L	6-0	212	5-15-96	.295	.327	.281	106	343	43	101	22	2	12	44	26	2	0	6	49	4	1	.475	.342
White, Tyler	R-R	5-11	225	10-29-90	.046	.067	.000	12	22	2	1	0	0	0	2	4	0	0	0	6	0	0	.046	.192

Pitching	B-T	HT	WT	DOB	W	L	ERA	G	GS	CG	SV	IP	H	R	ER	HR	BB	SO	AVG	vLH	vRH	K/9	BB/9
Alexander, Scott	L-L	6-2	195	7-10-89	3	2	3.63	28	0	0	0	17	17	7	7	2	7	9	.250	.364	.143	4.67	3.63
Baez, Pedro	R-R	6-0	232	3-11-88	7	2	3.10	71	0	0	1	70	43	30	24	6	23	69	.174	.177	.172	8.91	2.97
Buehler, Walker	R-R	6-2	185	7-28-94	14	4	3.26	30	30	2	0	182	153	77	66	20	37	215	.223	.216	.231	10.61	1.83
Chargois, JT	B-R	6-3	200	12-3-90	1	0	6.33	21	0	0	0	21	21	16	15	4	5	28	.273	.235	.283	11.81	2.11
Ferguson, Caleb	R-L	6-3	226	7-2-96	1	2	4.84	46	2	0	0	45	39	26	24	7	27	54	.234	.194	.263	10.88	5.44
Floro, Dylan	L-R	6-2	203	12-27-90	5	3	4.24	50	0	0	0	47	46	25	22	4	14	42	.253	.339	.211	8.10	2.70
Garcia, Yimi	R-R	6-0	205	8-18-90	1	4	3.61	64	0	0	0	62	40	28	25	15	14	66	.178	.182	.176	9.53	2.02
Gonsolin, Tony	R-R	6-3	205	5-14-94	4	2	2.93	11	6	0	1	40	26	15	13	4	15	37	.178	.182	.174	8.33	3.38
Hill, Rich	L-L	6-5	221	3-11-80	4	1	2.45	13	13	0	0	59	48	20	16	10	18	72	.223	.192	.233	11.05	2.76
Jansen, Kenley	B-R	6-5	265	9-30-87	5	3	3.71	62	0	0	33	63	51	28	26	9	16	80	.213	.199	.229	11.43	2.29
Kelly, Joe	R-R	6-1	174	6-9-88	5	4	4.56	55	0	0	1	51	49	31	26	6	22	62	.244	.247	.241	10.87	3.86
Kershaw, Clayton	L-L	6-4	226	3-19-88	16	5	3.03	29	28	0	0	178	145	63	60	28	41	189	.222	.208	.226	9.54	2.07
Kolarek, Adam	L-L	6-3	215	1-14-89	2	0	0.77	26	0	0	0	12	9	3	1	1	2	9	.209	.156	.364	6.94	1.54
Maeda, Kenta	R-R	6-1	184	4-11-88	10	8	4.04	37	26	0	3	154	114	70	69	22	51	169	.202	.247	.158	9.90	2.99
Martin, Russell	R-R	5-10	215	2-15-83	0	0	0.00	4	0	0	0	4	2	0	0	0	2	0	.154	.000	.200	4.50	0.00
May, Dustin	R-R	6-6	180	9-6-97	2	3	3.63	14	4	0	0	35	33	17	14	2	5	32	.250	.346	.188	8.31	1.30
Rosscup, Zac	R-L	6-2	220	6-9-88	0	0	6.00	7	0	0	0	3	6	3	2	1	3	4	.429	.333	.600	12.00	9.00
Ryu, Hyun-Jin	R-L	6-3	255	3-25-87	14	5	2.32	29	29	1	0	183	160	53	47	17	24	163	.234	.199	.245	8.03	1.18
Sadler, Casey	R-R	6-3	205	7-13-90	4	0	2.33	24	1	0	1	27	25	9	7	3	8	20	.248	.235	.260	6.67	2.67
Santana, Dennis	R-R	6-2	190	4-12-96	0	0	7.20	3	0	0	0	5	6	4	4	1	4	6	.300	.571	.154	10.80	7.20
Sborz, Josh	R-R	6-3	215	12-17-93	0	1	8.00	7	0	0	0	9	10	8	8	2	4	7	.286	.333	.250	7.00	4.00
Schultz, Jaime	R-R	5-10	205	6-20-91	0	0	7.20	4	0	0	0	5	6	4	4	1	3	3	.316	.286	.333	5.40	5.40
Stewart, Brock	L-R	6-3	215	10-3-91	0	0	18.00	3	0	0	0	4	9	8	8	2	2	3	.529	.444	.625	6.75	4.50
Stripling, Ross	R-R	6-2	220	11-23-89	4	4	3.47	32	15	0	0	91	84	40	35	11	20	93	.244	.249	.239	9.23	1.99
Urias, Julio	L-L	6-0	225	8-12-96	4	3	2.49	37	8	0	4	80	59	28	22	7	27	85	.201	.198	.203	9.60	3.05

Fielding

Catcher	PCT	G	PO	A	E	DP	PB
Barnes	.990	64	554	12	6	1	2
Gale	.975	4	37	2	1	0	0
Martin	.996	60	512	29	2	0	7
Smith	1.000	46	436	20	0	1	2

First Base	PCT	G	PO	A	E	DP
Beaty	.986	35	197	19	3	15
Bellinger	.995	36	209	9	1	21
Freese	.993	50	287	13	2	18
Gyorko	1.000	7	31	2	0	2
Hernandez	1.000	2	12	0	0	0
Kolarek	1.000	1	1	0	0	1
Muncy	.995	65	356	27	2	36
Pederson	.962	20	142	8	6	9
Rios	1.000	12	46	3	0	4
White	.982	8	51	5	1	6

Second Base	PCT	G	PO	A	E	DP
Barnes	1.000	1	0	4	0	0
Gyorko	1.000	1	0	5	0	3
Hernandez	.980	85	98	152	5	34
Lux	.970	22	27	38	2	9
Muncy	.973	70	75	138	6	38
Negron	1.000	3	4	12	0	2
Taylor	1.000	20	14	23	0	8
Turner	.000	1	0	0	0	0

Third Base	PCT	G	PO	A	E	DP
Beaty	1.000	9	4	7	0	1
Freese	.000	2	0	0	0	0
Gyorko	1.000	9	2	10	0	0
Hernandez	.000	1	0	0	1	0
Martin	1.000	7	1	7	0	1
Muncy	.929	35	13	66	6	1
Negron	1.000	3	1	3	0	0
Rios	.833	5	3	2	1	0

	PCT	G	PO	A	E	DP
Taylor	.917	6	1	10	1	0
Turner	.973	124	67	219	8	22

Shortstop	PCT	G	PO	A	E	DP
Hernandez	1.000	11	13	21	0	4
Negron	1.000	4	2	5	0	3
Seager	.967	132	138	304	15	59
Taylor	.919	39	37	65	9	12

Outfield	PCT	G	PO	A	E	DP
Beaty	1.000	36	46	1	0	0
Bellinger	.988	136	240	10	3	1
Garlick	1.000	15	20	0	0	0
Hernandez	1.000	43	54	1	0	0
Negron	1.000	15	12	0	0	0
Pederson	.987	122	143	5	2	0
Pollock	.983	80	116	3	2	1
Rios	.000	1	0	0	0	0
Taylor	.989	69	92	1	1	0
Verdugo	.989	97	170	6	2	0

OKLAHOMA CITY DODGERS

TRIPLE-A

PACIFIC COAST LEAGUE

Batting	B-T	HT	WT	DOB	AVG	vLH	vRH	G	AB	R	H	2B	3B	HR	RBI	BB	HBP	SH	SF	SO	SB	CS	SLG	OBP
Barnes, Austin	R-R	5-10	187	12-28-89	.264	.214	.274	23	87	19	23	6	0	6	17	14	2	0	1	20	1	1	.540	.375
Beaty, Matt	L-R	6-0	215	4-28-93	.306	.435	.276	32	121	17	37	7	1	3	18	10	4	0	0	12	0	0	.455	.378
Carrera, Ezequiel	L-L	5-11	185	6-11-87	.172	.667	.115	10	29	4	5	1	0	0	2	3	0	0	0	9	1	0	.207	.250
Castro, Daniel	R-R	5-11	201	11-14-92	.244	.188	.267	46	168	18	41	6	0	1	11	13	3	1	2	15	3	0	.298	.307
2-team total (29 Tacoma)					.232	.169	.254	75	280	26	65	9	0	3	18	17	6	2	2	29	3	0	.296	.289
Gailen, Blake	L-L	5-9	180	3-27-85	.250	.250	.250	22	48	6	12	4	0	1	6	5	0	0	0	15	0	0	.396	.321
Gale, Rocky	R-R	6-1	185	2-22-88	.250	.200	.277	30	100	12	25	4	1	2	14	7	1	0	1	24	1	0	.370	.303
Garlick, Kyle	R-R	6-1	210	1-26-92	.314	.305	.316	81	271	54	85	25	2	23	59	25	6	0	2	84	2	1	.675	.382
Gyorko, Jedd	R-R	5-10	215	9-23-88	.273	.286	.267	7	22	5	6	1	0	1	5	3	1	0	0	5	0	0	.455	.385
Jackson, Drew	R-R	6-2	200	7-28-93	.209	.167	.226	85	273	40	57	10	1	6	28	31	5	1	1	92	9	5	.319	.300
Joe, Connor	R-R	6-0	205	8-16-92	.300	.315	.295	105	360	82	108	26	1	15	68	72	10	0	4	81	1	2	.503	.426
Kemmer, Jon	L-L	6-2	230	11-17-90	.252	.125	.284	39	119	24	30	5	0	6	13	16	4	0	0	38	0	0	.445	.360
Landon, Logan	R-R	6-2	180	2-17-93	.154	.400	.000	8	13	0	2	0	0	0	0	4	0	0	0	5	0	0	.154	.353
Lobaton, Jose	B-R	6-1	205	10-21-84	.234	.250	.231	15	47	5	11	4	0	1	5	8	0	0	1	15	0	0	.383	.339
2-team total (75 Tacoma)					.236	.298	.212	90	335	39	79	22	0	14	43	35	2	0	2	98	1	0	.427	.310
Lux, Gavin	L-R	6-2	190	11-23-97	.392	.381	.395	49	199	54	78	18	4	13	39	33	0	0	0	42	3	3	.719	.478
McKinstry, Zach	L-R	6-0	180	4-29-95	.382	.313	.397	26	89	17	34	8	2	7	26	6	0	0	0	18	0	1	.753	.421
Montgomery, Brandon	R-R	6-0		2-12-96	.333	--	.333	1	3	1	1	0	0	1	1	0	0	0	1	0	0	0	1.333	.333
Moore, Ben	R-R	6-1	195	9-22-92	.267	.333	.238	12	30	5	8	0	0	1	2	4	0	0	0	10	0	0	.367	.353
Mora, Angelo	B-R	5-11	150	2-25-93	.231	.268	.214	45	130	15	30	8	2	0	19	6	1	0	2	30	0	0	.323	.266
Orlando, Paulo	R-R	6-2	215	11-1-85	.211	.167	.226	24	71	9	15	5	1	2	7	8	4	0	0	16	1	0	.394	.325
Perkins, Cameron	R-R	6-5	225	9-27-90	.282	.270	.288	84	294	47	83	23	1	9	35	24	7	1	0	49	7	1	.459	.351
Peter, Jake	L-R	6-1	215	4-5-93	.199	.146	.211	92	261	44	52	15	2	7	36	56	2	0	2	89	1	0	.353	.343
Peters, DJ	R-R	6-6	225	12-12-95	.260	.245	.264	57	208	40	54	10	1	12	39	33	12	0	2	75	1	1	.490	.388
Peterson, Shane	L-L	6-1	196	2-11-88	.245	.243	.245	79	278	41	68	14	5	10	38	25	3	0	1	87	4	0	.439	.313
Reks, Zach	L-R	6-2	190	11-12-93	.284	.268	.289	89	331	57	94	19	1	19	71	48	5	0	1	104	2	0	.520	.382
Rios, Edwin	L-R	6-3	220	4-21-94	.270	.271	.269	104	393	72	106	23	2	31	91	37	8	0	6	153	2	2	.575	.340
Robinson, Errol	R-R	5-11	170	10-14-94	.220	.268	.200	61	191	22	42	9	0	2	19	21	2	0	0	45	3	2	.298	.300
Ruiz, Keibert	B-R	6-0	200	7-20-98	.316	.500	.306	9	38	6	12	0	0	2	9	2	0	0	0	1	0	0	.474	.350
Smith, Will	R-R	5-10	195	3-28-95	.268	.281	.264	62	224	48	60	11	2	20	54	40	3	0	3	49	1	0	.603	.382
Thole, Josh	B-R	6-2	230	10-28-86	.203	.200	.203	25	74	8	15	2	0	1	4	14	1	0	1	19	0	0	.270	.333
2-team total (25 Salt Lake)					.224	.152	.252	50	161	18	36	7	0	3	16	30	1	0	1	44	1	0	.323	.347

Pitching	B-T	HT	WT	DOB	W	L	ERA	G	GS	CG	SV	IP	H	R	ER	HR	BB	SO	AVG	vLH	vRH	K/9	BB/9
Allie, Stetson	R-R	6-2	244	3-13-91	0	0	8.16	33	0	0	2	32	29	30	29	8	31	40	.236	.273	.215	11.25	8.72
Bawcom, Logan	R-R	6-2	220	11-2-88	3	3	4.39	8	7	0	0	41	41	20	20	8	15	38	.263	.355	.202	8.34	3.29
Bowden, Michael	R-R	6-3	215	9-9-86	0	0	0.00	1	1	0	0	3	1	0	0	0	3		.100	.333	.000	9.00	0.00
Broussard, Joe	R-R	6-1	225	1-28-91	1	1	6.35	21	0	0	0	28	32	21	20	5	14	25	.283	.419	.232	7.94	4.45
Chargois, JT	B-R	6-3	200	12-3-90	1	2	2.76	27	0	0	0	33	27	12	10	3	16	37	.231	.258	.221	10.19	4.41
Cingrani, Tony	L-L	6-4	217	7-5-89	1	0	2.84	7	0	0	0	6	5	2	2	0	4	15	.238	.222	.250	11.51	5.68
Corcino, Daniel	R-R	5-11	215	8-26-90	8	8	4.90	24	21	1	0	119	112	69	65	25	61	105	.249	.252	.248	7.92	4.60
De Fratus, Justin	B-R	6-4	225	10-21-87	3	5	6.71	10	9	0	0	52	65	43	39	9	17	41	.305	.347	.284	7.05	2.92
Ferguson, Caleb	R-L	6-3	226	7-2-96	0	0	1.76	13	1	0	1	15	9	3	3	1	5	27	.170	.294	.111	15.85	2.93
Floro, Dylan	L-R	6-2	203	12-27-90	0	0	2.08	6	0	0	0	4	3	3	1	0	4	5	.188	.333	.100	10.38	8.31
Gailen, Blake	L-L	5-9	180	3-27-85	1	0	0.00	1	0	0	0	3	1	0	0	0	4	3	.091	.000	.111	8.10	10.80
Gonsolin, Tony	R-R	6-3	205	5-14-94	2	4	4.35	13	13	0	0	41	41	25	20	4	21	50	.249	.167	.282	10.89	4.57
Gonzalez, Victor	L-L	6-0	180	11-16-95	0	0	3.86	15	0	0	0	14	16	7	6	3	4	13	.286	.250	.308	8.36	2.57
Grimm, Justin	R-R	6-3	210	8-16-88	4	4	5.66	35	0	0	1	41	49	28	26	3	15	56	.303	.282	.309	12.19	3.27
Head, Louis	R-R	6-1	180	4-23-90	1	0	8.25	9	0	0	0	12	20	11	11	2	7	14	.392	.400	.389	10.50	5.25

LOS ANGELES DODGERS

Name	B-T	HT	WT	DOB	W	L	ERA	G	GS	CG	SV	IP	H	R	ER	HR	BB	SO	vLH	vRH	AVG	H/9	BB/9
Holmes, Ben	L-L	6-1	195	9-12-91	1	4	6.32	9	9	0	0	37	40	28	26	7	21	40	.276	.265	.279	9.73	5.11
Kemmer, Jon	L-L	6-2	230	11-17-90	0	0	18.00	1	0	0	0	1	5	3	2	0	0	0	.625	.667	.600	0.00	0.00
Kershaw, Clayton	L-L	6-4	226	3-19-88	0	0	4.15	1	1	0	0	4	4	2	2	1	2	6	.267	.000	.333	12.46	4.15
Martin, J.D.	R-R	6-4	220	1-2-83	3	3	5.89	8	8	0	0	44	45	32	29	10	31	31	.262	.234	.278	6.29	6.29
May, Dustin	R-R	6-6	180	9-6-97	3	0	2.30	5	5	0	0	27	21	8	7	0	9	24	.212	.158	.225	7.90	2.46
McAllister, Zach	R-R	6-6	240	12-8-87	0	0	8.03	9	0	0	2	12	19	13	11	5	3	19	.352	.421	.314	13.86	2.19
McCreery, Adam	L-L	6-9	250	12-31-92	0	0	5.79	19	0	0	0	19	28	17	12	4	14	21	.333	.450	.297	10.13	6.75
2-team total (5 Salt Lake)					0	0	4.55	24	0	0	0	28	33	19	14	4	19	32	.290	.323	.277	10.41	6.18
Nunn, Chris	L-L	6-5	200	10-5-90	0	1	8.01	24	0	0	0	30	45	29	27	4	16	39	.344	.379	.333	11.57	4.75
Peterson, Shane	L-L	6-1	196	2-11-88	0	0	0.00	1	0	0	0	1	0	0	0	0	0	0	.000	.000	.000	0.00	0.00
Quackenbush, Kevin	R-R	6-4	235	11-28-88	2	5	5.06	54	0	0	11	59	59	34	33	9	16	85	.257	.329	.219	13.04	2.45
Rosscup, Zac	L-L	6-2	220	6-9-88	0	1	6.23	9	0	0	1	9	8	6	6	1	3	14	.258	.250	.261	14.54	3.12
2-team total (8 Memphis)					0	1	5.40	17	0	0	1	17	15	10	10	1	18	23	.246	.222	.256	12.42	9.72
Sadler, Casey	R-R	6-3	205	7-13-90	0	0	6.00	2	1	0	1	6	8	4	4	1	1	9	.320	.333	.318	13.50	1.50
Santana, Dennis	R-R	6-2	190	4-12-96	5	9	6.94	27	17	0	0	93	111	84	72	16	53	105	.292	.331	.273	10.13	5.11
Sborz, Josh	R-R	6-3	215	12-17-93	4	3	4.68	46	0	0	3	50	56	30	26	2	14	68	.283	.281	.284	12.24	2.52
Schultz, Jaime	R-R	5-10	205	6-20-91	2	3	5.85	47	1	0	4	48	52	38	31	3	27	62	.274	.242	.289	11.71	5.10
Smoker, Josh	L-L	6-1	232	11-26-88	1	2	9.00	12	0	0	0	14	20	15	14	4	9	11	.357	.389	.342	7.07	5.79
Somsen, Layne	R-R	6-0	190	6-5-89	2	0	9.00	5	0	0	0	5	7	6	5	1	8	3	.350	.667	.214	5.40	14.40
Spitzbarth, Shea	R-R	6-1	195	10-4-94	1	0	8.18	20	0	0	0	22	30	20	20	6	8	29	.316	.267	.339	11.86	3.27
Stewart, Brock	L-R	6-3	215	10-3-91	5	7	7.34	17	16	0	0	76	97	67	62	19	40	67	.310	.317	.306	7.93	4.74
Thornburg, Tyler	R-R	5-11	190	9-29-88	0	0	6.00	12	0	0	0	12	11	9	8	3	9	15	.239	.167	.286	11.25	6.75
Vasquez, Luis	R-R	6-4	200	4-3-86	2	0	5.74	12	0	0	0	16	13	15	10	3	16	25	.217	.348	.135	14.36	9.19
White, Mitchell	R-R	6-3	210	12-28-94	3	6	6.50	16	13	0	0	64	73	47	46	13	24	68	.293	.354	.265	9.61	3.39
Zastryzny, Rob	R-L	6-3	205	3-26-92	3	6	6.49	20	16	0	0	94	126	75	68	17	31	84	.326	.337	.323	8.01	2.96

Fielding

Catcher	PCT	G	PO	A	E	DP	PB
Barnes	.953	13	98	4	5	0	1
Gale	.996	24	216	16	1	1	2
Lobaton	.993	14	131	7	1	0	3
Moore	1.000	11	79	6	0	0	1
Ruiz	.989	9	84	4	1	0	0
Smith	.991	52	509	29	5	1	5

Thole	.986	23	199	9	3	3

First Base	PCT	G	PO	A	E	DP
Beaty	1.000	11	72	3	0	6
Gyorko	1.000	4	25	1	0	1
Joe	.992	79	539	45	5	64
Kemmer	1.000	1	5	0	0	1
Perkins	.993	19	125	12	1	15
Peter	1.000	6	27	3	0	5
Rios	.994	25	160	14	1	21
Thole	1.000	1	1	0	0	0

Second Base	PCT	G	PO	A	E	DP
Barnes	1.000	6	9	7	0	0
Castro	1.000	6	7	16	0	3
Jackson	.984	36	53	71	2	24
Lux	.981	12	23	30	1	10
McKinstry	1.000	3	3	9	0	3
Mora	.938	16	23	22	3	8
Peter	.960	59	82	110	8	31
Robinson	1.000	18	29	28	0	11

Third Base	PCT	G	PO	A	E	DP
Beaty	1.000	11	7	21	0	4
Gyorko	1.000	2	1	1	0	0
Jackson	.909	7	5	15	2	4
Joe	.769	6	6	4	3	0
McKinstry	1.000	2	1	3	0	1
Montgomery	1.000	1	1	0	0	0
Mora	.889	22	10	38	6	3
Peter	.955	20	5	37	2	6
Rios	.919	67	42	116	14	10
Robinson	.905	10	6	13	2	0
Smith	1.000	1	1	0	0	0

Shortstop	PCT	G	PO	A	E	DP
Castro	.979	39	43	94	3	24
Jackson	.934	21	22	49	5	10
Lux	.977	36	45	81	3	19
McKinstry	.967	17	19	40	2	11
Mora	.833	2	4	1	1	0
Robinson	.966	33	40	75	4	17

Outfield	PCT	G	PO	A	E	DP
Beaty	1.000	8	12	1	0	0
Carrera	1.000	8	19	0	0	0
Gailen	.929	11	13	0	1	0
Garlick	.972	68	106	0	3	0
Jackson	.972	19	35	0	1	0
Joe	.941	13	15	1	1	0
Kemmer	1.000	26	43	0	0	0
Landon	1.000	3	6	1	0	0
McKinstry	.875	3	7	0	1	0
Orlando	.938	22	29	1	2	0
Perkins	.982	52	105	5	2	0
Peters	.969	56	123	4	4	0
Peterson	.962	63	121	7	5	1
Reks	.964	77	103	5	4	1
Rios	1.000	10	13	1	0	1

TULSA DRILLERS   DOUBLE-A
TEXAS LEAGUE

Batting	B-T	HT	WT	DOB	AVG	vLH	vRH	G	AB	R	H	2B	3B	HR	RBI	BB	HBP	SH	SF	SO	SB	CS	SLG	OBP
Avans, Drew	L-L	5-10	195	6-13-96	.286	.273	.289	65	220	36	63	8	1	6	18	19	1	1	0	64	17	5	.414	.346
Berman, Stevie	R-R	6-2	225	11-28-94	.310	.333	.303	15	42	6	13	0	0	1	7	5	0	0	1	11	0	0	.381	.375
Casey, Donovan	R-R	6-2	190	2-23-96	.213	.118	.234	25	94	13	20	4	0	3	11	7	0	0	0	34	2	0	.351	.267
Downs, Jeter	R-R	5-11	180	7-27-98	.333	.000	.356	12	48	14	16	2	0	5	11	6	2	0	0	10	1	0	.688	.429
Estevez, Omar	R-R	5-10	185	2-25-98	.291	.283	.293	83	299	34	87	24	0	6	36	31	0	1	5	70	0	2	.431	.352
Gale, Rocky	R-R	6-1	185	2-22-88	.214	.000	.231	4	14	0	3	0	0	0	0	0	0	0	0	2	0	0	.214	.214
Gyorko, Jedd	R-R	5-10	215	9-23-88	.600	.667	.500	2	5	2	3	0	0	1	2	1	0	0	0	0	0	0	1.200	.667
Landon, Logan	R-R	6-2	180	2-17-93	.220	.229	.217	79	209	25	46	8	1	5	22	18	2	0	1	59	3	1	.340	.287
Lux, Gavin	L-R	6-2	190	11-23-97	.313	.279	.319	64	259	45	81	7	4	13	37	28	0	0	4	60	7	3	.521	.375
McKinstry, Zach	L-R	6-0	180	4-29-95	.279	.267	.281	95	341	53	95	16	4	12	52	37	3	1	2	74	8	6	.455	.353
McWilliams, Sam	R-R	6-0	175	5-26-98	.000	--	.000	1	3	1	0	0	0	0	0	0	0	0	0	2	0	0	.000	.000
Montgomery, Brandon	R-R	6-0	180	2-12-96	.091	.111	.000	5	11	0	1	0	0	0	1	0	0	0	0	5	0	0	.091	.091
Mora, Angelo	B-R	5-11	150	2-25-93	.291	.410	.254	49	165	26	48	6	1	4	27	17	0	1	1	39	6	2	.412	.355
Parmelee, Chris	L-L	6-1	220	2-24-88	.236	.119	.258	87	271	47	64	10	1	16	52	52	1	0	4	91	0	0	.458	.357
Peters, DJ	R-R	6-6	225	12-12-95	.241	.192	.253	68	249	31	60	10	1	11	42	28	7	0	3	93	1	0	.422	.331
Peterson, Eric	R-R	5-11	190	9-22-93	.245	.385	.194	19	49	7	12	0	1	2	4	7	1	0	0	18	2	0	.408	.351
Procyshen, Jordan	L-R	5-10	185	3-11-93	.165	.125	.169	22	79	11	13	2	0	2	3	6	0	0	0	15	0	0	.266	.224
Reks, Zach	L-R	6-2	190	11-12-93	.310	.231	.320	32	113	29	35	2	1	9	22	15	2	0	2	27	1	1	.584	.394
Rincon, Carlos	R-R	6-3	190	10-14-97	.217	.235	.212	78	254	28	55	11	0	10	20	20	3	0	0	84	1	0	.378	.282

Name	B-T	HT	WT	DOB	AVG	OBP	SLG	G	AB	R	H	2B	3B	HR	RBI	BB	HBP	SH	SF	SO	SB	CS	vLH	vRH
Robinson, Errol	R-R	5-11	170	10-1-94	.310	.323	.307	46	155	23	48	5	0	3	16	20	1	0	1	35	6	4	.400	.390
Ruiz, Keibert	B-R	6-0	200	7-20-98	.254	.250	.254	76	276	33	70	9	0	4	25	28	4	0	2	21	0	0	.330	.329
Santana, Cristian	R-R	6-2	175	2-24-97	.301	.243	.314	102	399	45	120	22	1	10	57	10	2	0	2	88	0	0	.436	.320
Thole, Josh	L-R	6-1	230	10-28-86	.292	.600	.267	22	65	7	19	3	0	0	10	7	1	0	1	16	0	0	.339	.365
Thomas, Cody	L-R	6-4	211	10-8-94	.236	.224	.239	130	474	77	112	17	6	23	76	46	6	0	6	144	5	3	.443	.308
Walker, Jared	L-R	6-2	198	2-4-96	.212	.333	.195	119	321	49	68	8	1	13	34	50	14	1	1	134	4	3	.365	.342
Wong, Connor	R-R	6-1	181	5-19-96	.349	.263	.362	40	149	17	52	9	1	9	31	11	1	0	2	50	2	1	.604	.393

Pitching	B-T	HT	WT	DOB	W	L	ERA	G	GS	CG	SV	IP	H	R	ER	HR	BB	SO	AVG	vLH	vRH	K/9	BB/9
Allie, Stetson	R-R	6-2	244	3-13-91	1	1	10.29	8	0	0	0	7	9	9	8	1	6	10	.300	.286	.304	12.86	7.71
Alvarez, Yadier	R-R	6-3	175	3-7-96	0	2	14.73	2	2	0	0	4	5	4	4	1	4	6	.313	.375	.250	14.73	9.82
Avans, Drew	L-L	5-10	195	6-13-96	1	0	0.00	1	0	0	0	1	1	0	0	0	0	0	.333	--	.333	0.00	0.00
Bawcom, Logan	R-R	6-2	220	11-2-88	1	0	3.91	5	3	0	0	23	26	10	10	4	3	15	.286	.333	.239	5.87	1.17
Bowden, Michael	R-R	6-3	215	9-9-86	1	1	8.15	4	4	0	0	18	26	17	16	7	3	15	.347	.342	.351	7.64	1.53
Boyle, Michael	R-L	6-3	200	4-12-94	2	2	3.02	40	1	0	2	54	44	29	18	8	28	57	.220	.230	.212	9.56	4.70
Cabrera, Yordy	R-R	6-1	205	9-3-90	3	1	3.96	38	4	0	1	61	62	36	27	2	24	53	.261	.238	.278	7.78	3.52
Crawford, Leo	L-L	6-0	180	2-2-97	2	0	2.37	6	5	0	0	30	31	9	8	2	7	28	.265	.320	.250	8.31	2.08
Curry, Parker	R-R	6-0	185	11-21-93	4	5	3.67	24	13	0	0	98	89	44	40	14	20	89	.238	.245	.232	8.17	1.84
De Fratus, Justin	B-R	6-4	225	10-21-87	6	8	4.96	15	13	1	0	89	93	50	49	11	20	57	.270	.276	.264	5.76	2.02
Gonzalez, Victor	L-L	6-0	180	11-16-95	3	1	2.23	15	8	0	2	48	48	15	12	4	14	44	.260	.125	.318	8.19	2.61
Gray, Josiah	R-R	6-1	190	12-21-97	3	2	2.75	9	8	0	0	39	33	14	12	0	11	41	.228	.175	.268	9.38	2.52
Hamilton, Austin	L-L	6-0	185	8-11-93	0	0	3.52	2	2	0	0	8	7	3	3	1	4	4	.250	.222	.263	4.70	4.70
Head, Louis	R-R	6-1	180	4-23-90	2	1	3.38	6	0	0	1	11	9	5	4	1	3	16	.243	.211	.278	13.50	2.53
Holmes, Ben	L-L	6-1	195	9-12-91	1	0	3.75	5	5	0	0	24	29	10	10	5	8	24	.296	.219	.333	9.00	3.00
Kasowski, Marshall	L-R	6-3	215	3-10-95	4	3	2.45	27	0	0	2	29	17	12	8	1	16	46	.162	.216	.111	14.11	4.91
Kershaw, Clayton	L-L	6-4	226	3-19-88	0	0	3.00	1	1	0	0	6	5	2	2	2	0	6	.238	.286	.214	9.00	0.00
Landon, Logan	R-R	6-2	180	2-17-93	0	0	0.00	1	0	0	0	1	0	0	0	0	1	0	.000	--	.000	0.00	9.00
Long, Nolan	R-R	6-10	255	1-19-94	5	1	2.29	40	1	0	6	63	38	21	16	7	39	81	.168	.153	.180	11.57	5.57
Martin, J.D.	R-R	6-4	220	1-2-83	2	7	5.38	14	14	0	0	80	87	57	48	11	38	66	.277	.227	.323	7.39	4.26
May, Dustin	R-R	6-6	180	9-6-97	3	5	3.74	15	15	0	0	79	71	41	33	5	20	86	.237	.254	.222	9.76	2.27
McCreery, Adam	L-L	6-9	250	12-31-92	2	1	2.12	11	0	0	0	17	11	6	4	0	9	18	.180	.107	.242	9.53	4.76
Moseley, Ryan	R-R	6-3	190	10-6-94	4	1	3.18	30	1	0	1	51	46	22	18	4	20	42	.238	.305	.189	7.41	3.53
Nunn, Chris	L-L	6-5	200	10-5-90	2	1	1.33	14	0	0	0	20	15	5	3	2	8	27	.206	.154	.234	11.95	3.54
Paredes, Edward	L-L	6-0	180	9-30-86	1	2	6.75	5	1	0	0	7	10	5	5	0	4	8	.357	.400	.333	10.80	5.40
Parmelee, Chris	L-L	6-1	220	2-24-88	0	0	0.00	1	0	0	0	1	1	0	0	0	0	0	.250	.000	.333	0.00	0.00
Salow, Logan	L-L	6-1	185	9-27-94	0	2	4.19	16	2	0	0	19	16	12	9	0	21	22	.225	.364	.163	10.24	9.78
Schueller, Sven	R-R	6-3	205	1-17-96	0	0	9.00	1	0	0	0	2	3	2	2	1	0	4	.333	1.000	.143	18.00	0.00
Scrubb, Andre	R-R	6-4	265	1-13-95	6	1	2.45	29	2	0	0	48	35	17	13	3	33	56	.200	.256	.146	10.57	4.34
2-team total (12 Corpus Christi)					6	1	2.78	41	2	0	3	65	56	24	20	3	33	76	.227	.270	.182	10.58	4.59
Sheffield, Jordan	R-R	5-10	190	6-1-95	2	3	3.58	34	2	0	6	38	26	16	15	3	32	48	.193	.222	.173	11.47	7.65
Solbach, Markus	R-R	6-5	205	8-26-91	5	1	2.57	8	7	0	0	42	37	18	12	1	8	39	.233	.224	.239	8.36	1.71
Somsen, Layne	R-R	6-0	190	6-5-89	0	1	3.38	9	0	0	3	11	11	8	4	0	4	10	.268	.263	.273	8.44	3.38
Spitzbarth, Shea	R-R	6-1	195	10-4-94	3	3	2.05	32	0	0	1	44	28	12	10	1	17	60	.176	.203	.158	12.27	3.48
Uceta, Edwin	R-R	6-0	155	1-9-98	7	2	3.21	16	14	0	0	73	62	29	26	5	33	76	.238	.202	.265	9.37	4.07
Vasquez, Josh	R-R	6-4	200	4-3-86	0	1	2.70	14	1	0	4	20	13	6	6	1	9	29	.183	.233	.146	13.05	4.05
White, Mitchell	R-R	6-3	210	12-28-94	1	0	2.10	7	7	0	0	30	18	8	7	3	7	37	.165	.164	.167	11.10	2.10
Zastryzny, Rob	R-L	6-3	205	3-26-92	1	2	0.96	3	3	0	0	19	12	7	2	0	8	20	.177	.095	.213	9.64	3.86

Fielding

Catcher	PCT	G	PO	A	E	DP	PB
Berman	.992	15	116	5	1	0	1
Gale	1.000	4	28	4	0	1	0
Procyshen	.990	21	174	17	2	3	1
Ruiz	.995	61	555	34	3	3	5
Thole	.994	19	164	1	1	2	6
Wong	.983	24	211	22	4	2	2

First Base	PCT	G	PO	A	E	DP
Gyorko	1.000	1	4	1	0	0
Mora	1.000	1	5	2	0	0
Parmelee	.990	48	282	29	3	17
Peterson	1.000	1	6	0	0	1
Reks	1.000	6	42	2	0	6
Santana	1.000	14	78	3	0	6
Walker	.989	85	526	31	6	45

Second Base	PCT	G	PO	A	E	DP
Downs	1.000	1	2	1	0	0
Estevez	.951	51	81	113	10	28
Lux	1.000	7	11	16	0	3
McKinstry	.972	49	80	94	5	15
McWilliams	1.000	1	1	0	0	0
Montgomery	1.000	3	1	4	0	0
Mora	.979	13	22	25	1	6
Peterson	.963	7	11	15	1	3
Robinson	.963	9	8	18	1	4
Walker	1.000	7	10	16	0	2
Wong	.846	4	6	5	2	2

Third Base	PCT	G	PO	A	E	DP
Gyorko	1.000	1	1	2	0	0
McKinstry	.889	10	4	12	2	0
Montgomery	1.000	2	1	0	0	0
Mora	.936	24	10	34	3	7
Peterson	.913	10	7	14	2	3
Robinson	.958	10	8	15	1	0
Santana	.906	83	43	120	17	4

	PCT	G	PO	A	E	DP
Walker	.000	2	0	0	1	0
Wong	.900	10	6	12	2	1

Shortstop	PCT	G	PO	A	E	DP
Downs	.935	11	25	18	3	7
Estevez	.923	23	25	35	5	6
Lux	.950	55	79	113	10	23
McKinstry	.930	29	33	74	8	12
Robinson	.979	28	43	52	2	7

Outfield	PCT	G	PO	A	E	DP
Avans	.980	59	95	3	2	0
Casey	.983	24	57	2	1	1
Landon	.993	73	140	3	1	2
McKinstry	.800	7	4	0	1	0
Parmelee	1.000	13	16	1	0	0
Peters	.982	68	154	6	3	0
Reks	.974	19	36	1	1	0
Rincon	.933	64	102	10	8	2
Robinson	1.000	1	2	0	0	0
Thomas	.993	122	269	6	2	4

RANCHO CUCAMONGA QUAKES
CALIFORNIA LEAGUE

HIGH CLASS A

Batting	B-T	HT	WT	DOB	AVG	vLH	vRH	G	AB	R	H	2B	3B	HR	RBI	BB	HBP	SH	SF	SO	SB	CS	SLG	OBP
Amaya, Jacob	R-R	6-0	180	9-3-98	.250	.278	.242	21	80	14	20	3	2	1	13	7	0	1	1	15	1	3	.375	.307
Avans, Drew	L-L	5-10	195	6-13-95	.293	.167	.333	36	123	23	36	7	4	3	19	10	2	1	1	37	3	3	.488	.353
Barbary, Chase	R-R	6-2	180	4-7-97	1.000	1.000	--	1	1	1	1	0	0	0	0	0	0	0	0	0	0	0	1.000	1.000
Barnes, Austin	R-R	5-10	187	12-28-89	.400	.333	.500	2	5	1	2	0	0	0	1	1	0	0	0	1	0	0	.400	.500
Beaty, Matt	L-R	6-0	215	4-28-93	.286	--	.286	2	7	2	2	2	0	0	1	0	0	0	0	2	0	0	.571	.286
Berman, Stevie	R-R	6-2	225	11-28-94	.295	.167	.309	21	61	8	18	4	1	3	13	9	0	1	1	14	2	0	.541	.380
Casey, Donovan	R-R	6-2	190	2-23-96	.271	.289	.265	100	403	80	109	18	9	20	65	37	3	0	2	140	20	3	.509	.335
Chiu, Marcus	R-R	6-2	208	1-13-97	.215	.241	.208	114	376	58	81	13	4	14	44	53	19	1	1	167	5	5	.383	.341
Downs, Jeter	R-R	5-11	180	7-27-98	.269	.348	.247	107	412	78	111	33	4	19	75	54	4	2	7	97	23	8	.507	.354
Feduccia, Hunter	L-R	6-2	215	6-5-97	.239	.188	.255	22	71	8	17	1	1	0	12	9	0	2	0	19	1	2	.282	.325
Heredia, Starling	R-R	6-2	200	2-6-99	.204	.197	.206	101	333	57	68	15	6	10	34	49	5	0	1	147	16	8	.375	.314
Hope, Garrett	R-R	6-3	235	12-27-93	.143	.000	.167	6	21	1	3	0	0	0	1	3	0	0	0	7	0	0	.143	.143
Hulsizer, Niko	R-R	6-2	225	2-1-97	.259	.304	.242	25	85	15	22	6	0	5	18	9	1	0	3	33	3	2	.506	.327
Kendall, Jeren	L-R	5-11	190	2-4-96	.219	.250	.210	96	352	51	77	11	10	19	63	51	3	1	5	147	24	7	.469	.319
Liput, Deacon	L-R	5-10	185	6-27-96	.219	.227	.217	85	306	43	67	11	4	6	34	41	0	3	0	123	10	8	.340	.311
Mann, Devin	R-R	6-3	180	2-11-97	.278	.351	.259	98	367	63	102	19	2	19	63	45	5	0	7	93	5	4	.496	.359
Mendoza, Cesar	R-R	5-11	175	2-28-97	.250	.000	.333	2	4	1	1	0	0	0	0	0	0	1	0	1	0	0	.250	.400
Montgomery, Brandon	R-R	6-0	180	2-12-96	.196	.353	.153	52	158	18	31	6	1	2	14	17	2	3	1	45	8	5	.285	.281
Morales, Brayan	R-L	6-1	170	12-8-95	.228	.182	.241	106	355	40	81	8	7	0	32	23	6	7	4	100	35	13	.290	.284
Paulson, Dillon	L-L	6-3	200	6-10-97	.293	.333	.279	35	116	23	34	10	1	4	14	26	0	0	0	45	3	1	.500	.423
Perez, Moises	R-R	6-0	160	7-18-97	.200	.000	.250	3	10	1	2	0	0	0	1	0	0	0	0	4	1	1	.200	.273
Peterson, Eric	R-R	5-11	190	9-22-93	.429	.500	.421	8	21	5	9	4	0	0	5	1	0	0	0	2	0	0	.619	.455
Pollock, A.J.	R-R	6-1	212	12-5-87	.077	--	.077	5	13	1	1	0	0	1	1	0	0	0	0	5	0	0	.308	.077
Procyshen, Jordan	L-R	5-10	185	3-11-93	.262	.091	.300	16	61	14	16	5	1	6	18	2	0	0	2	9	0	0	.672	.277
Rincon, Carlos	R-R	6-3	190	10-14-97	.231	.250	.218	37	130	25	30	10	0	6	13	21	3	0	0	45	1	1	.446	.351
Rodriguez, Ramon	R-R	5-11	194	10-30-98	.333	.000	.429	3	9	0	3	1	0	0	0	0	0	0	0	2	0	0	.444	.333
Seager, Corey	L-R	6-4	215	4-27-94	.333	--	.333	3	6	0	2	0	0	1	0	0	0	0	0	1	0	0	.333	.333
Suarez, Albert	L-R	5-11	150	11-30-99	.000	--	.000	1	1	0	0	0	0	0	0	0	0	0	0	0	0	0	.000	.000
Taylor, Chris	R-R	6-1	196	8-29-90	.429	.333	.500	4	14	4	6	0	0	1	5	1	0	0	0	2	0	0	.643	.467
Todd, Tre	L-R	6-1	205	9-29-96	.230	.182	.238	29	74	11	17	2	1	2	6	16	1	1	2	28	0	1	.365	.366
Vargas, Miguel	R-R	6-3	205	11-17-99	.284	.296	.281	54	211	23	60	18	1	2	32	20	3	1	1	40	4	3	.408	.353
Wong, Connor	R-R	6-1	181	5-19-96	.245	.222	.251	71	274	39	67	15	6	15	51	21	4	1	2	93	9	2	.507	.306
Yarnall, Nick	L-L	6-0	200	10-17-94	.227	.256	.219	54	176	32	40	8	4	7	28	30	2	0	2	65	2	2	.438	.343

Pitching	B-T	HT	WT	DOB	W	L	ERA	G	GS	CG	SV	IP	H	R	ER	HR	BB	SO	AVG	vLH	vRH	K/9	BB/9
Aleaziz, Reza	R-R	6-4	225	7-11-95	0	0	0.00	2	0	0	0	1	2	2	0	0	1	1	.286	.500	.200	6.75	6.75
Bruihl, Justin	L-L	6-2	215	6-26-97	1	0	3.68	4	0	0	0	7	5	3	3	0	1	9	.179	.200	.174	11.05	1.23
Carrillo, Gerardo	R-R	5-10	154	9-13-98	5	9	5.44	23	21	0	0	86	87	59	52	3	51	86	.263	.301	.240	9.00	5.34
Cespedes, Yeison	R-R	6-1	178	3-5-98	0	1	6.75	2	0	0	0	4	3	3	3	1	4	4	.200	.000	.273	9.00	9.00
Cingrani, Tony	L-L	6-4	217	7-5-89	0	0	0.00	1	0	0	0	1	0	0	0	0	0	1	.000	--	.000	9.00	0.00
Crawford, Leo	L-L	6-0	180	2-2-97	5	4	2.96	19	16	1	0	91	95	33	30	8	20	106	.268	.205	.288	10.45	1.97
de Geus, Brett	R-R	6-2	190	11-4-97	2	0	1.16	20	0	0	4	31	28	4	4	0	7	36	.244	.286	.219	10.45	2.03
Drury, Austin	L-L	5-11	190	8-13-97	1	2	3.58	24	0	0	1	38	39	20	15	0	25	38	.273	.162	.311	9.08	5.97
Ferguson, Caleb	R-L	6-3	226	7-2-96	0	0	0.00	1	0	0	0	1	0	0	0	0	1	2	.000	--	.000	18.00	9.00
Floro, Dylan	L-R	6-2	203	12-27-90	0	0	0.00	2	0	0	0	2	2	0	0	0	1	1	.286	.500	.000	4.50	0.00
Gamboa, Max	R-R	6-5	190	11-22-95	5	5	5.34	43	0	0	1	61	43	44	36	3	49	97	.196	.169	.211	14.39	7.27
Gonzalez, Victor	L-L	6-0	180	11-16-95	2	1	1.65	8	5	0	0	27	17	7	5	0	14	36	.174	.148	.183	11.85	4.61
Gray, Josiah	R-R	6-1	190	12-21-97	7	0	2.14	12	12	0	0	67	52	20	16	3	13	80	.209	.225	.202	10.69	1.74
Grove, Michael	R-R	6-3	200	12-18-96	0	5	6.10	21	21	0	0	52	61	37	35	7	19	73	.293	.194	.346	12.72	3.31
Hamilton, Austin	L-L	6-0	185	8-11-93	6	5	3.97	20	8	0	1	68	85	33	30	6	22	69	.311	.344	.302	9.13	2.91
Helsabeck, Wes	L-L	6-0	195	7-7-92	5	0	4.34	29	0	0	2	46	42	26	22	2	27	61	.239	.212	.250	12.02	5.32
Hemmerich, Devin	R-L	6-1	195	7-14-95	0	0	14.54	3	0	0	0	4	9	8	7	3	2	6	.409	.200	.471	12.46	4.15
Hill, Rich	L-L	6-5	221	3-11-80	0	0	0.00	1	1	0	0	4	2	0	0	0	0	8	.143	.333	.091	18.00	0.00
Jackson, Andre	R-R	6-3	210	5-1-96	3	1	3.66	15	15	0	0	66	61	30	27	5	38	91	.248	.261	.241	12.35	5.16
Jimenez, Melvin	B-R	6-0	170	7-23-99	2	0	3.52	19	0	0	2	31	24	17	12	5	19	46	.207	.189	.215	13.50	5.58
Liput, Deacon	L-R	5-10	185	6-27-96	0	0	0.00	2	0	0	0	1	2	0	0	1	0	2	.500	.500	.500	9.00	13.50
Malisheski, Kevin	R-R	6-3	200	9-7-97	0	0	11.25	2	1	0	0	4	7	5	5	0	4	5	.389	.800	.231	11.25	9.00
Martinez, Jose	R-R	6-0	194	4-23-99	3	0	3.04	5	4	0	0	27	25	9	9	0	6	29	.255	.237	.267	9.79	2.03
Mitchell, Connor	L-L	6-4	180	9-11-95	2	2	2.48	22	0	0	1	29	29	12	8	3	9	38	.244	.267	.236	11.79	2.79
Montgomerie, Wills	R-R	6-3	225	6-2-95	9	3	4.99	24	7	0	0	105	101	67	58	9	59	126	.248	.206	.272	10.83	5.07
Montgomery, Brandon	R-R	6-0	180	2-12-96	0	0	7.94	8	0	0	1	6	8	5	5	1	1	4	.348	.375	.333	6.35	1.59
Moseley, Ryan	R-R	6-3	190	10-6-94	2	2	0.69	17	0	0	4	26	20	11	2	0	15	28	.208	.250	.183	9.69	5.19
Nunez, Darien	L-L	6-2	205	3-19-93	1	0	1.75	19	0	0	2	26	17	5	5	1	10	43	.187	.192	.185	15.08	3.51
Rooney, John	L-L	6-5	235	1-28-97	5	2	3.06	9	9	0	0	50	51	21	17	5	14	45	.276	.341	.255	8.10	2.52
Salow, Logan	L-L	6-1	185	9-27-94	2	0	1.47	27	0	0	5	43	19	8	7	2	22	71	.118	.071	.137	14.86	4.60
Schueller, Sven	R-R	6-3	205	1-17-96	5	3	4.02	34	0	0	3	56	70	32	25	3	21	43	.302	.299	.303	6.91	3.38
Serrano, Elio	R-R	5-11	160	8-2-98	1	0	1.80	3	0	0	0	5	4	1	1	1	2	1	.235	.250	.231	1.80	3.60
Sheffield, Jordan	R-R	5-10	190	6-1-95	2	2	2.60	15	0	0	7	17	6	5	5	2	11	26	.109	.091	.121	13.50	5.71
Strain, Connor	R-R	6-1	180	8-4-94	0	4	3.99	32	0	0	0	38	34	22	17	2	23	44	.238	.159	.273	10.33	5.40
Uceta, Edwin	R-R	6-0	155	1-9-98	4	0	2.15	10	10	0	0	50	47	19	12	6	16	65	.241	.259	.228	11.62	2.86
Urias, Julio	L-L	6-0	225	8-12-96	0	0	9.00	1	1	0	0	3	3	2	0	0	2	3	.300	.333	.286	9.00	0.00

Name	B-T	HT	WT	DOB	W	L	ERA	G	GS	CG	SV	IP	H	R	ER	BB	SO	AVG	vLH	vRH	K/9	BB/9
Warzek, Bryan	L-L	6-0	205	1-17-97	1	3	5.91	26	7	0	0	46	45	32	30	4	49	53	.260	.125	.291	10.45	9.66
Yarnall, Nick	L-L	6-0	200	10-17-94	0	0	0.00	2	0	0	0	2	1	0	0	0	1	1	.143	.500	.000	3.86	3.86
Zuniga, Guillermo	R-R	6-5	230	10-10-98	0	2	4.11	12	0	0	2	15	10	8	7	2	9	22	.182	.087	.250	12.91	5.28

Fielding

Catcher	PCT	G	PO	A	E	DP	PB
Barbary	1.000	1	2	0	0	0	0
Barnes	1.000	2	17	1	0	0	0
Berman	.995	19	172	10	1	2	3
Feduccia	.976	20	192	8	5	2	2
Hope	1.000	6	53	4	0	0	1
Mendoza	1.000	2	16	0	0	0	0
Procyshen	1.000	16	166	10	0	0	2
Rodriguez	1.000	3	24	2	0	0	0
Todd	.991	26	205	7	2	0	5
Wong	.984	59	641	45	11	5	8

First Base	PCT	G	PO	A	E	DP
Beaty	1.000	2	9	2	0	1
Berman	1.000	1	5	0	0	1
Chiu	.990	57	369	13	4	29
Mann	.933	3	13	1	1	4
Paulson	.987	30	208	20	3	22
Vargas	.983	6	52	5	1	6
Yarnall	.984	48	298	18	5	33

Second Base	PCT	G	PO	A	E	DP
Amaya	1.000	4	5	14	0	2
Downs	.971	10	19	14	1	7
Liput	.971	54	89	111	6	28
Mann	.966	51	79	94	6	23
Montgomery	.984	16	32	31	1	12
Perez	1.000	2	3	6	0	1
Suarez	.000	1	0	0	0	0
Taylor	1.000	1	1	3	0	1
Wong	.914	10	12	20	3	2

Third Base	PCT	G	PO	A	E	DP
Amaya	1.000	1	1	5	0	1
Chiu	.789	30	14	46	16	5
Liput	1.000	6	2	16	0	1
Mann	.902	44	29	63	10	8
Montgomery	.947	21	18	36	3	4
Peterson	1.000	4	2	2	0	1
Vargas	.958	43	27	64	4	8
Wong	.000	2	0	0	0	0

Shortstop	PCT	G	PO	A	E	DP
Amaya	.981	14	21	32	1	6
Downs	.945	91	95	196	17	38
Liput	.958	29	31	60	4	14
Montgomery	.931	9	8	19	2	3
Perez	1.000	1	2	3	0	2
Seager	1.000	3	2	3	0	2
Taylor	1.000	1	0	1	0	1

Outfield	PCT	G	PO	A	E	DP
Avans	.982	32	51	4	1	0
Casey	.962	86	162	13	7	4
Chiu	1.000	15	13	0	0	0
Heredia	.941	67	63	1	4	0
Hulsizer	.962	15	22	3	1	1
Kendall	.988	82	160	6	2	2
Montgomery	.846	9	11	0	2	0
Morales	.982	99	211	2	4	0
Peterson	1.000	3	4	0	0	0
Pollock	1.000	4	4	0	0	0
Procyshen	.000	1	0	0	0	0
Rincon	.960	23	23	1	1	0
Todd	1.000	5	1	0	0	0

GREAT LAKES LOONS

MIDWEST LEAGUE

LOW CLASS A

Batting	B-T	HT	WT	DOB	AVG	vLH	vRH	G	AB	R	H	2B	3B	HR	RBI	BB	HBP	SH	SF	SO	SB	CS	SLG	OBP
Amaya, Jacob	R-R	6-0	180	9-3-98	.262	.281	.256	103	386	68	101	25	4	6	58	74	4	0	6	83	4	4	.394	.381
Avans, Drew	L-L	5-10	195	6-13-96	.194	.182	.200	11	36	5	7	1	0	1	3	6	0	0	1	7	4	1	.306	.302
Barbary, Chase	R-R	6-2	180	4-7-97	.000	--	.000	1	3	0	0	0	0	0	0	0	0	0	0	1	0	0	.000	.000
Busch, Michael	L-R	6-0	207	11-9-97	.182	.000	.200	5	11	4	2	0	0	0	2	6	1	0	1	3	0	0	.182	.474
Camargo, Jair	R-R	5-10	150	7-1-99	.236	.241	.235	79	284	38	67	18	0	4	41	21	7	0	4	91	5	3	.342	.301
Cogen, Matt	R-R	6-0	195	8-19-95	.207	.265	.192	51	164	15	34	4	2	0	14	19	2	0	2	43	1	0	.256	.294
Cuadrado, Romer	R-R	6-4	185	9-12-97	.258	.240	.264	82	310	41	80	19	1	7	41	35	6	0	2	87	2	1	.394	.343
Feduccia, Hunter	L-R	6-2	215	6-5-97	.288	.270	.293	50	184	34	53	17	1	4	31	36	0	0	3	42	1	0	.457	.399
Heyer, Luke	R-R	6-0	205	9-26-96	.221	.284	.202	98	349	52	77	17	3	16	60	40	6	0	4	123	5	1	.424	.308
Hoese, Kody	R-R	6-4	200	7-13-97	.264	.333	.247	22	91	15	24	3	1	2	16	8	2	0	2	14	0	0	.385	.330
Hope, Garrett	R-R	6-3	235	12-27-93	.000	.000	.000	2	7	0	0	0	0	0	1	0	0	0	0	5	0	0	.000	.000
Hulsizer, Niko	R-R	6-2	225	2-1-97	.268	.302	.259	58	209	46	56	17	1	15	49	37	8	0	2	75	4	1	.574	.395
Leonard, Eddys	R-R	6-0	160	11-10-00	.250	.000	.333	1	4	1	1	0	0	0	0	0	0	0	0	3	0	0	.250	.250
Lewis, Brandon	R-R	6-3	215	10-23-98	.167	.273	.135	12	48	9	8	2	0	1	5	4	1	0	0	15	0	0	.271	.245
McLain, Josh	R-R	6-1	170	9-23-96	.135	.200	.108	15	52	4	7	3	0	0	5	2	1	0	1	13	2	0	.192	.179
McWilliams, Sam	R-R	6-0	175	5-26-98	.198	.130	.224	22	81	6	16	5	0	1	7	7	1	0	0	26	1	0	.296	.274
Outman, James	L-R	6-3	215	5-14-97	.226	.223	.227	119	442	59	100	15	4	19	56	56	8	0	3	128	20	10	.407	.322
Paulson, Dillon	L-L	6-3	200	6-10-97	.223	.234	.220	82	300	52	67	17	1	12	50	56	1	0	4	88	0	0	.407	.344
Pitre, Gersel	R-R	6-0	203	7-23-96	.284	.143	.321	19	67	7	19	0	0	0	10	1	0	0	2	11	1	0	.284	.286
Robinson, Dan	L-L	6-2	215	10-30-96	.240	.239	.240	94	321	37	77	13	4	2	40	50	2	0	1	68	6	3	.324	.345
Roller, Chris	R-R	6-0	190	10-8-96	.274	.279	.273	88	321	61	88	21	8	7	44	34	10	0	3	77	10	3	.455	.359
Todd, Tre	L-R	6-1	205	9-29-96	.100	.222	.048	10	30	3	3	1	0	1	3	7	1	0	1	11	2	0	.233	.282
Valera, Leonel	R-R	6-1	165	7-9-99	.241	.213	.248	122	449	78	108	15	4	5	42	49	5	0	1	137	27	6	.325	.321
Vargas, Miguel	R-R	6-3	205	11-17-99	.325	.353	.316	70	280	53	91	20	2	5	45	35	3	0	5	43	9	1	.464	.399
Yurchak, Justin	L-R	6-1	204	9-17-96	.292	.276	.296	38	144	24	42	11	1	5	15	14	2	0	2	30	0	1	.486	.358

Pitching	B-T	HT	WT	DOB	W	L	ERA	G	GS	CG	SV	IP	H	R	ER	BB	SO	AVG	vLH	vRH	K/9	BB/9
Alvino, Jasiel	R-R	6-1	180	1-11-97	3	3	4.96	35	2	0	3	49	53	33	27	4	25	50	.276	.261	.289	9.18	4.59
Belge, Jeff	L-L	6-5	225	12-4-97	0	0	1.93	4	0	0	0	5	2	1	1	0	5	3	.143	.000	.250	5.79	9.64
Bruihl, Justin	L-L	6-2	215	6-26-97	4	0	0.79	21	0	0	2	34	23	5	3	0	8	42	.187	.192	.184	11.01	2.10
Castro, Jeronimo	R-R	6-4	200	9-3-96	2	3	4.41	8	8	0	0	35	36	17	17	2	16	42	.267	.267	.267	10.90	4.15
Cespedes, Yeison	R-R	6-1	178	3-5-98	0	0	2.16	5	0	0	0	8	7	2	2	1	1	10	.219	.400	.136	10.80	1.08
Chacin, Jose	R-R	6-4	192	3-25-97	11	8	4.68	26	12	0	1	127	147	72	66	9	26	95	.289	.318	.265	6.73	1.84
Cuello, Edward	R-R	6-0	170	10-20-98	1	0	0.00	7	0	0	3	16	8	1	0	0	5	11	.146	.046	.212	6.19	2.81
de Geus, Brett	R-R	6-2	190	11-4-97	4	2	2.35	19	0	0	4	31	17	11	8	0	6	36	.164	.135	.192	10.57	1.76
Drury, Austin	L-L	5-11	190	8-13-97	1	1	2.39	15	0	0	2	26	26	8	7	2	8	32	.252	.184	.290	10.94	2.73
Finley, Drew	R-R	6-3	200	7-10-96	2	0	4.91	7	0	0	0	11	11	7	6	0	14	11	.268	.333	.241	9.00	11.45
Gray, Josiah	R-R	6-1	190	12-21-97	1	0	1.93	5	5	0	0	23	13	5	5	0	7	26	.165	.194	.140	10.03	2.70
Hagenman, Justin	R-R	6-3	205	10-7-96	6	2	2.24	33	1	0	6	76	64	25	19	2	18	64	.223	.267	.193	7.55	2.12
Heyer, Luke	R-R	6-0	205	9-26-96	1	0	9.00	2	0	0	0	3	7	4	3	0	3	3	.500	1.000	.364	9.00	9.00
Inoa, Joel	R-R	6-2	210	2-21-96	3	3	5.21	35	0	0	5	47	44	32	27	8	21	45	.242	.295	.202	8.68	4.05
Jackson, Andre	R-R	6-3	210	5-1-96	4	1	2.23	10	10	0	0	48	29	13	12	1	19	50	.172	.195	.149	9.31	3.54

Name	B-T	HT	WT	DOB	W	L	ERA	G	GS	CG	SV	IP	H	R	ER	HR	BB	SO	AVG	vLH	vRH	K/9	BB/9
Kolek, Stephen	R-R	6-3	210	4-18-97	7	8	5.00	27	25	0	0	131	143	87	73	7	48	109	.276	.286	.269	7.47	3.29
Little, Jack	L-R	6-4	190	1-10-98	0	1	3.79	9	9	0	0	19	12	11	8	3	14	17	.177	.167	.184	8.05	6.63
Malisheski, Kevin	R-R	6-3	200	9-7-97	0	1	5.40	5	3	0	1	20	16	12	12	0	12	19	.222	.242	.205	8.55	5.40
Martinez, Jose	R-R	6-0	194	4-23-99	8	2	3.34	22	12	0	4	100	85	43	37	9	27	86	.229	.223	.234	7.77	2.44
Ochsenbein, Aaron	R-R	6-3	225	2-29-96	1	1	1.35	13	0	0	2	20	12	4	3	0	5	28	.174	.121	.222	12.60	2.25
Ortiz, Robinson	L-L	6-0	180	1-4-00	4	5	4.59	19	18	0	0	86	73	47	44	10	40	74	.233	.238	.232	7.71	4.17
Pepiot, Ryan	R-R	6-3	215	8-21-97	0	0	2.45	9	9	0	0	18	13	6	5	0	9	21	.197	.207	.189	10.31	4.42
Roller, Chris	R-R	6-0	190	10-8-96	0	0	--	1	0	0	0	0	0	1	0	4	0	--	--	--	--	--
Rooney, John	L-L	6-5	235	1-28-97	5	2	2.63	11	11	0	0	55	44	19	16	2	25	44	.229	.267	.218	7.24	4.12
Tavarez, Alfredo	R-R	6-5	190	11-27-97	1	1	6.75	6	0	0	0	15	18	13	11	2	8	10	.295	.259	.324	6.14	4.91
Washington, Mark	R-R	6-7	205	3-22-96	4	1	2.97	20	0	0	1	39	23	14	13	1	19	43	.170	.196	.155	9.84	4.35
Willeman, Zach	R-R	6-2	175	3-27-96	4	7	5.38	21	6	0	2	80	87	56	48	8	48	55	.275	.311	.242	6.16	5.38
Witt, Nathan	R-R	6-4	210	4-19-96	1	2	5.32	22	0	0	5	24	27	16	14	2	7	31	.276	.300	.259	11.79	2.66
2-team total (15 Bowling Green)					2	5	4.10	37	2	0	6	48	50	31	22	2	20	52	.255	.284	.235	9.68	3.72
Zuniga, Guillermo	R-R	6-5	230	10-10-98	4	1	4.08	21	5	0	3	53	45	26	24	5	22	59	.230	.287	.184	10.02	3.74

Fielding

Catcher	PCT	G	PO	A	E	DP	PB
Barbary	1.000	1	3	0	0	0	0
Camargo	.981	65	463	62	10	4	12
Feduccia	.989	48	426	23	5	4	8
Hope	1.000	2	17	3	0	0	0
Pitre	.992	13	110	9	1	0	0
Todd	.990	10	99	4	1	0	0

First Base	PCT	G	PO	A	E	DP
Cogen	1.000	1	1	0	0	0
Heyer	.989	25	168	7	2	14
Outman	1.000	1	1	0	0	0
Paulson	.987	77	607	51	9	44
Vargas	1.000	2	16	2	0	2
Yurchak	.994	36	327	9	2	28

Second Base	PCT	G	PO	A	E	DP
Amaya	.986	49	79	128	3	28
Busch	1.000	4	6	8	0	2
Heyer	.964	30	39	69	4	9
McWilliams	.964	12	35	45	3	14
Valera	.972	36	42	96	4	17
Vargas	.857	2	1	5	1	2

Third Base	PCT	G	PO	A	E	DP
Amaya	1.000	4	3	6	0	1
Camargo	.864	11	5	14	3	1
Heyer	.969	42	20	75	3	3
Hoese	.938	12	8	22	2	4
Lewis	.947	9	5	13	1	1
Pitre	1.000	3	2	3	0	1
Valera	1.000	2	3	3	0	0
Vargas	.901	59	46	100	16	8

Shortstop	PCT	G	PO	A	E	DP
Amaya	.958	51	72	111	8	18
Heyer	1.000	1	1	1	0	0
Leonard	1.000	1	1	2	0	0
Outman	1.000	1	0	1	0	0
Valera	.936	84	124	213	23	47

Outfield	PCT	G	PO	A	E	DP
Avans	.923	9	12	0	1	0
Cogen	.982	32	54	1	1	0
Cuadrado	.926	59	95	5	8	3
Hulsizer	1.000	33	73	3	0	0
McLain	.964	14	25	2	1	1
Outman	.989	113	262	7	3	2
Robinson	.983	75	113	5	2	0
Roller	.975	84	190	2	5	1

OGDEN RAPTORS
PIONEER LEAGUE
ROOKIE ADVANCED

Batting	B-T	HT	WT	DOB	AVG	vLH	vRH	G	AB	R	H	2B	3B	HR	RBI	BB	HBP	SH	SF	SO	SB	CS	SLG	OBP
Alcantara, Ismael	R-R	6-1	165	9-25-98	.360	.375	.353	8	25	3	9	1	1	2	8	1	1	0	1	9	0	1	.720	.393
Arocho, Jeremy	B-R	5-10	165	10-6-98	.287	.214	.303	48	150	31	43	4	1	1	15	33	0	1	1	28	10	4	.347	.413
Betancourt, Kenneth	R-R	5-8	160	2-5-00	.111	.500	.063	8	18	1	2	0	1	0	3	0	0	0	0	3	1	0	.222	.111
Chalo, Wladimir	R-R	5-8	170	4-21-00	.133	.000	.200	6	15	0	2	0	0	0	1	2	0	1	0	8	0	0	.133	.263
Ching, Zac	R-R	5-9	180	5-29-97	.316	.289	.328	49	177	45	56	13	1	4	38	28	1	0	3	47	1	6	.469	.407
De Jongh, Aldrich	L-R	5-9	160	9-1-98	.280	.222	.288	21	75	14	21	2	1	2	9	2	0	0	2	20	2	1	.413	.291
Hernandez, Marco	R-R	6-2	170	6-24-98	.341	.345	.340	39	135	28	46	8	2	2	20	20	3	0	3	30	2	1	.474	.429
Lao, Sauryn	R-R	6-2	182	8-14-99	.271	.339	.249	61	229	44	62	19	1	9	45	32	3	0	4	78	6	2	.480	.362
Lebron, Rolando	R-R	5-9	170	5-10-98	.500	.333	1.000	3	4	3	2	0	1	1	3	0	0	0	0	1	1	0	1.750	.500
Leonard, Eddys	R-R	6-0	160	11-10-00	.333	.400	.313	8	21	2	7	0	0	1	1	1	1	0	0	9	0	2	.476	.391
Lewis, Brandon	R-R	6-3	215	10-23-98	.369	.500	.323	32	130	32	48	10	0	12	39	10	2	0	0	35	0	2	.723	.423
Littell, Jon	R-R	6-3	218	8-16-95	.261	.235	.268	47	161	29	42	9	2	3	28	24	4	0	2	39	3	2	.398	.367
McLain, Josh	R-R	6-1	170	9-23-96	.214	.000	.273	3	14	3	3	1	0	0	3	0	0	0	0	3	0	0	.286	.214
McWilliams, Sam	R-R	5-11	175	5-26-98	.291	.306	.286	37	148	45	43	9	2	11	29	25	4	0	2	54	6	0	.601	.402
Mendoza, Cesar	R-R	5-11	175	2-28-97	.300	.250	.308	12	30	5	9	2	0	1	4	6	0	0	0	10	0	0	.467	.417
Pages, Andy	R-R	6-1	180	12-8-00	.298	.262	.310	63	235	57	70	22	2	19	55	26	15	0	3	79	7	6	.651	.398
Perez, Moises	R-R	6-1	170	6-24-98	.206	.364	.130	11	34	5	7	0	0	0	3	2	2	0	0	10	0	0	.206	.290
Rodriguez, Ramon	R-R	5-11	194	10-30-98	.279	.290	.274	33	104	11	29	8	0	3	16	12	0	1	1	23	0	0	.442	.350
Shaps, Andrew	L-L	6-1	185	12-5-95	.276	.211	.298	48	152	30	42	11	1	3	21	15	5	1	1	31	2	6	.421	.358
Titus, Jimmy	R-R	6-1	195	1-25-98	.296	.300	.295	40	142	27	42	11	0	6	23	12	4	1	1	40	2	0	.500	.365
Todd, Tre	L-R	6-1	205	9-29-96	.391	.333	.405	13	46	9	18	5	0	4	20	3	1	0	0	9	0	0	.761	.440
Vargas, Imanol	L-R	6-3	185	6-29-98	.250	.000	.313	8	20	5	5	2	1	1	3	2	0	0	0	11	0	0	.600	.318
Verdugo, Alex	L-L	6-0	212	5-15-96	.000	--	.000	1	1	1	0	0	0	0	0	2	0	0	0	0	0	0	.000	.667
Vivas, Jorbit	L-R	5-10	145	3-9-01	.286	.353	.269	24	84	13	24	6	1	1	12	6	6	0	1	16	5	5	.417	.371
Vranesh, Joe	R-R	6-2	200	1-23-98	.320	.400	.300	21	75	19	24	5	0	2	22	15	5	0	1	21	7	1	.467	.458
Ward, Ryan	L-R	5-11	200	2-23-98	.271	.150	.304	49	188	35	51	11	2	4	23	19	1	0	1	30	7	4	.415	.340
Wulff, Brandon	R-R	6-1	225	12-19-96	.148	.077	.167	20	61	16	9	2	2	3	17	19	6	0	0	29	1	1	.393	.395
Yurchak, Justin	L-R	6-1	180	9-17-96	.365	.346	.371	26	96	35	35	8	0	8	31	26	4	0	1	9	0	0	.698	.496

Pitching	B-T	HT	WT	DOB	W	L	ERA	G	GS	CG	SV	IP	H	R	ER	HR	BB	SO	AVG	vLH	vRH	K/9	BB/9
Alcantara, Ismael	R-R	6-1	165	9-25-98	0	0	81.00	1	0	0	0	0	3	3	3	0	1	1	.750	.667	1.000	27.00	27.00
Aleaziz, Reza	R-R	6-4	225	7-11-95	4	0	2.48	23	0	0	5	29	27	9	8	2	15	33	.248	.325	.203	10.24	4.66
Arocho, Jeremy	B-R	5-10	165	10-6-98	0	0	0.00	2	0	0	0	2	0	0	0	0	0	0	.000	.000	.000	10.80	0.00
Belge, Jeff	L-L	6-5	225	12-4-97	2	0	0.53	12	0	0	0	17	10	1	1	0	9	26	.192	.211	.182	13.76	4.76
Cabrera, Jeisson	R-R	6-2	170	9-5-98	0	0	5.68	3	1	0	0	6	5	4	4	1	3	9	.192	.214	.167	12.79	4.26
Cantleberry, Jacob	L-L	6-1	180	8-8-97	2	1	0.69	9	0	0	1	13	6	2	1	0	6	16	.136	.286	.067	11.08	4.15

Castro, Jeronimo	R-R	6-4	200	9-3-96	4	2	3.62	15	15	1	0	70	63	35	28	5	15	74	.235	.212	.250	9.56	1.94
Cespedes, Yeison	R-R	6-1	178	3-5-98	3	1	5.08	15	2	0	0	28	36	20	16	4	10	32	.321	.213	.400	10.16	3.18
Contreras, Nelfri	L-L	6-0	177	12-25-98	1	1	5.04	21	1	0	0	30	42	30	17	1	12	34	.311	.244	.344	10.09	3.56
Cuello, Edward	R-R	6-0	170	10-20-98	4	1	4.37	13	0	0	1	23	19	11	11	2	5	27	.232	.235	.229	10.72	1.99
De La Paz, Franklin	L-L	6-2	190	3-29-99	0	0	7.50	4	0	0	0	6	8	6	5	2	0	8	.308	.273	.333	12.00	0.00
Finley, Drew	R-R	6-3	200	7-10-96	0	1	7.94	18	0	0	0	23	17	26	20	4	31	37	.205	.212	.200	14.69	12.31
Hernandez, Antonio	L-L	5-8	187	9-27-99	4	2	4.94	15	14	0	0	62	71	35	34	8	16	54	.282	.286	.280	7.84	2.32
Hernandez, Ricardo	R-R	6-1	205	2-4-98	2	1	7.36	9	0	0	0	15	18	14	12	1	5	13	.295	.500	.180	7.98	3.07
Jimenez, Melvin	B-R	6-0	170	7-23-99	5	0	2.25	10	1	0	0	20	8	5	5	6	43	.119	.130	.114	19.35	2.70
Malisheski, Kevin	R-R	6-3	200	9-7-97	5	4	4.11	10	10	0	0	50	51	26	23	6	15	58	.263	.288	.246	10.37	2.68
Merrill, Corey	R-R	6-3	210	10-11-94	4	2	2.67	22	0	0	1	30	26	12	9	2	15	37	.228	.200	.250	10.98	4.45
Mixon, Mark	R-R	6-2	180	5-22-97	3	0	2.33	16	0	0	0	19	14	5	5	2	8	17	.212	.321	.132	7.91	3.72
Morillo, Juan	R-R	6-1	150	3-19-99	0	1	4.26	3	3	0	0	13	9	7	6	0	7	17	.192	.154	.206	12.08	4.97
Nunez, Darien	L-L	6-2	205	3-19-93	1	0	4.05	5	0	0	0	7	5	3	3	0	3	12	.200	.250	.177	16.20	4.05
Ochsenbein, Aaron	R-R	6-3	225	2-29-96	1	0	0.00	3	0	0	1	3	1	0	0	0	1	3	.111	.000	.333	9.00	3.00
Ramirez, Adolfo	R-R	6-0	165	6-1-99	0	2	8.59	3	2	0	0	7	10	7	7	1	1	8	.333	.333	.333	9.82	1.23
Robertson, Nick	R-R	6-6	265	7-16-98	0	0	2.45	11	0	0	1	11	7	3	3	0	1	16	.180	.125	.217	13.09	0.82
Serrano, Elio	R-R	5-11	160	8-2-98	5	0	3.47	13	12	0	0	60	47	25	23	7	15	64	.209	.209	.209	9.65	2.26
Shaps, Andrew	L-L	6-1	185	12-5-95	0	0	0.00	2	0	0	0	2	0	0	0	0	1	2	.000	.000	.000	9.00	4.50
Speer, Hunter	R-R	6-0	180	5-18-95	1	0	5.87	24	0	0	4	31	37	20	20	3	14	35	.301	.264	.329	10.27	4.11
Tavarez, Alfredo	R-R	6-5	190	11-27-97	1	3	3.65	15	15	0	0	67	62	32	27	7	26	70	.239	.252	.229	9.45	3.51
Tyranski, Mitchell	L-L	6-2	215	9-2-97	2	0	1.29	11	0	0	2	14	4	2	2	1	2	27	.087	.071	.094	17.36	1.29

Fielding

C: Chalo 5, Hernandez 26, Mendoza 7, Rodriguez 33, Todd 12. **1B:** Hernandez 13, Lao 14, Lewis 13, Littell 12, Mendoza 3, Perez 1, Vargas 4, Yurchak 24. **2B:** Arocho 24, Betancourt 1, Ching 3, Lao 5, Leonard 1, McWilliams 29, Titus 4, Vivas 19. **3B:** Arocho 2, Betancourt 3, Ching 1, Lao 41, Lewis 12, Perez 2, Titus 18, Vivas 1. **SS:** Arocho 17, Betancourt 4, Ching 43, Leonard 7, McWilliams 1, Perez 9, Titus 5. **OF:** Alcantara 8, De Jongh 21, Lebron 2, Littell 31, McLain 3, McWilliams 2, Pages 54, Shaps 40, Vranesh 18, Ward 44, Wulff 18.

AZL DODGERS LASORDA   ROOKIE
ARIZONA LEAGUE

Batting	B-T	HT	WT	DOB	AVG	vLH	vRH	G	AB	R	H	2B	3B	HR	RBI	BB	HBP	SH	SF	SO	SB	CS	SLG	OBP
Allison, Chet	R-R	6-2	215	4-30-99	.148	.235	.127	27	88	8	13	2	0	2	9	14	2	0	1	40	0	0	.239	.276
Barbary, Chase	R-R	6-2	180	4-7-97	.177	.250	.154	7	17	2	3	0	1	0	1	0	0	0	0	8	0	0	.294	.222
Berman, Stevie	R-R	6-2	225	11-28-94	.200	--	.200	2	5	0	1	1	0	0	1	0	0	0	0	0	0	0	.400	.200
2-team total (2 Dodgers Mota)					.300	.333	.286	4	10	1	3	1	0	1	3	0	0	0	0	1	0	0	.700	.300
Busch, Michael	L-R	6-0	207	11-9-97	.077	.000	.167	5	13	1	1	0	0	0	0	1	2	0	0	2	0	0	.077	.250
Carrion, Julio	R-R	6-2	185	12-29-98	.183	.370	.131	40	126	23	23	5	0	2	14	16	5	0	3	41	2	0	.270	.293
Castro, Daniel	R-R	5-11	201	11-14-92	.429	.500	.400	3	7	3	3	0	1	0	1	1	0	0	0	2	0	0	.714	.556
2-team total (1 Dodgers Mota)					.400	.500	.375	4	10	3	4	1	1	0	1	1	0	1	0	2	0	0	.700	.462
Chalo, Wladimir	R-R	5-8	170	4-21-00	.254	.280	.247	36	122	19	31	6	1	4	17	20	2	0	0	26	0	1	.418	.368
Chirinos, Yhostin	R-R	5-10	165	9-29-00	.283	.324	.270	39	145	26	41	1	1	2	10	17	1	0	2	23	2	2	.345	.358
2-team total (3 Dodgers Mota)					.273	.314	.262	42	161	28	44	2	1	2	10	17	1	0	2	29	3	2	.335	.343
Cuadrado, Romer	R-R	6-4	185	9-12-97	.167	.000	.333	3	6	1	1	0	0	0	2	1	0	0	1	0	0	0	.167	.444
2-team total (8 Dodgers Mota)					.270	.200	.296	11	37	7	10	3	0	2	7	4	1	0	0	11	2	0	.514	.357
De Jongh, Aldrich	L-R	5-9	160	9-1-98	.305	.258	.320	32	128	16	39	8	4	1	15	14	1	0	2	30	5	1	.453	.372
Espinoza, Aldo	R-R	6-0	148	9-1-98	.298	.379	.274	34	124	23	37	9	0	2	17	8	2	2	0	22	0	1	.419	.346
Garcia, Yunior	R-R	6-0	198	7-29-01	.236	.174	.265	20	72	8	17	3	0	3	22	1	1	0	1	26	0	1	.403	.253
Guillen, Alfonso	R-R	5-10	161	7-11-99	.000	.000	.000	6	11	0	0	0	0	0	1	4	0	0	1	4	0	0	.000	.250
2-team total (15 Dodgers Mota)					.208	.286	.195	21	48	2	10	1	0	0	3	8	0	0	2	14	0	1	.229	.310
Hernandez, Enrique	R-R	5-11	192	8-24-91	.500	.000	.600	2	6	1	3	1	0	0	0	2	0	0	0	1	0	0	.667	.625
2-team total (1 Dodgers Mota)					.444	.000	.500	3	9	2	4	1	0	1	3	2	0	0	0	1	0	0	.889	.546
Hope, Garrett	R-R	6-3	235	12-27-93	.208	.000	.263	9	24	6	5	1	0	3	6	1	0	0	1	9	0	0	.625	.231
Landry, Meaux	R-R	6-4	230	1-18-98	.180	.240	.165	35	128	14	23	5	0	5	22	7	0	0	1	51	0	0	.336	.221
Lebron, Rolando	R-R	5-9	170	5-10-98	.263	.407	.208	26	99	14	26	6	2	2	17	3	1	0	2	25	5	4	.424	.286
Leonard, Eddys	R-R	6-0	160	11-10-00	.280	.333	.262	46	168	27	47	7	4	3	20	27	2	0	3	48	2	4	.423	.380
Lewis, Brandon	R-R	6-3	215	10-23-98	.220	.286	.185	12	41	5	9	1	0	0	2	5	2	0	1	8	0	0	.244	.327
Mann, Devin	R-R	6-3	180	2-11-97	.539	.667	.500	4	13	2	7	2	0	0	1	1	0	0	0	1	0	1	.692	.571
2-team total (1 Dodgers Mota)					.500	.500	.500	5	14	2	7	2	0	0	1	2	0	0	0	1	0	1	.643	.563
Mateo, Edwin	L-L	5-9	160	11-18-98	.295	.400	.260	38	139	27	41	5	0	4	17	31	3	0	4	33	10	3	.417	.424
McKenzie, Luke	L-R	6-2	210	7-16-98	.180	.125	.194	10	39	6	7	2	0	0	6	4	0	0	1	15	1	0	.231	.250
McLain, Josh	R-R	6-1	170	9-23-96	.207	1.000	.148	7	29	5	6	1	1	0	4	2	1	0	0	12	1	1	.310	.281
2-team total (3 Dodgers Mota)					.180	.429	.125	10	39	6	7	1	1	0	4	4	1	0	0	16	3	1	.256	.273
Mendoza, Cesar	R-R	5-11	175	2-28-97	.000	--	.000	1	3	0	0	0	0	0	0	0	0	0	0	0	0	0	.000	.000
2-team total (3 Dodgers Mota)					.000	.000	.000	4	7	1	0	0	0	0	0	1	0	0	0	1	0	0	.000	.125
Noriega, Andres	R-R	6-1	190	1-3-01	.154	.333	.059	10	26	3	4	1	0	0	5	3	1	1	0	2	0	0	.192	.267
2-team total (19 Dodgers Mota)					.230	.269	.213	29	87	8	20	1	0	1	15	9	3	1	2	16	0	0	.276	.317
Perez, Jaime	R-R	6-1	178	4-5-00	.228	.304	.205	33	101	13	23	6	1	4	10	4	0	2	0	43	0	0	.426	.257
2-team total (1 Dodgers Mota)					.219	.304	.195	34	105	13	23	6	1	4	10	4	0	2	0	45	0	0	.410	.248
Rodriguez, Luis	B-R	6-0	150	3-2-99	.146	.059	.169	26	82	10	12	1	0	1	10	10	0	1	0	33	2	0	.195	.239
Ryan, Tyler	R-R	6-1	210	5-9-96	.240	1.000	.174	10	25	2	6	1	1	0	5	2	1	0	1	8	0	0	.360	.310
2-team total (8 Dodgers Mota)					.192	.400	.167	18	47	3	9	1	2	0	8	3	2	0	1	14	0	0	.298	.264
Sanchez, Frank	R-R	6-3	170	8-25-98	.100	.000	.111	6	10	1	1	0	0	0	1	2	0	0	1	4	0	0	.100	.231
Vivas, Jorbit	L-R	5-10	145	3-9-01	.357	.440	.333	30	115	18	41	11	2	1	20	13	6	0	3	15	5	4	.513	.438

Batting	B-T	HT	WT	DOB	AVG	vLH	vRH	G	AB	R	H	2B	3B	HR	RBI	BB	HBP	SH	SF	SO	SB	CS	SLG	OBP
Wulff, Brandon	R-R	6-1	225	12-19-96	.320	.500	.286	6	25	4	8	1	0	1	2	2	0	0	0	8	3	0	.480	.370
Zabala, Juan	R-R	5-10	170	7-3-99	.278	.333	.250	6	18	5	5	1	1	1	2	1	1	0	0	4	0	0	.611	.350
2-team total (21 Dodgers Mota)					.207	.286	.180	27	82	13	17	3	2	2	6	7	4	0	0	27	1	0	.366	.301

Pitching	B-T	HT	WT	DOB	W	L	ERA	G	GS	CG	SV	IP	H	R	ER	HR	BB	SO	AVG	vLH	vRH	K/9	BB/9
Avila, Igor	L-L	6-1	185	5-17-97	0	1	11.77	6	3	0	0	13	23	21	17	1	9	9	.377	.333	.391	6.23	6.23
2-team total (9 Dodgers Mota)					1	2	8.04	15	3	0	0	28	32	29	25	3	16	24	.283	.192	.310	7.71	5.14
Bawcom, Logan	R-R	6-2	220	11-2-88	0	0	3.60	1	0	0	0	5	5	2	2	0	0	8	.250	.286	.231	14.40	0.00
Belge, Jeff	L-L	6-5	225	12-4-97	0	0	5.40	2	0	0	0	2	1	1	1	0	1	2	.167	1.000	.000	10.80	5.40
Benavides, Gabe	R-L	6-2	180	9-9-96	3	1	4.12	12	0	0	0	20	18	11	9	3	10	12	.257	.300	.250	5.49	4.58
2-team total (3 Dodgers Mota)					3	1	4.84	15	0	0	0	22	22	14	12	3	13	16	.272	.300	.268	6.45	5.24
Berroa, Israiky	R-R	5-11	165	11-17-00	1	4	3.10	10	9	0	0	41	44	19	14	4	16	40	.273	.241	.290	8.85	3.54
Broussard, Joe	R-R	6-1	225	1-28-91	0	0	0.00	2	1	0	0	4	0	0	0	0	0	8	.000	.000	.000	18.00	0.00
2-team total (3 Dodgers Mota)					0	1	2.25	5	3	0	0	8	6	3	2	0	1	10	.207	.091	.278	11.25	1.13
De La Paz, Franklin	L-L	6-2	190	3-29-99	1	3	5.25	17	0	0	0	24	23	15	14	0	10	27	.253	.182	.275	10.13	3.75
De Paula, Reinaldo	R-R	5-11	177	10-20-98	6	1	4.84	19	0	0	1	22	13	17	12	0	16	32	.169	.174	.167	12.90	6.45
Duran, Carlos	R-R	6-7	230	7-30-01	0	4	8.38	8	8	0	0	19	38	23	18	3	10	16	.404	.551	.244	7.45	4.66
Gamboa, Alec	B-L	6-1	205	1-17-97	1	1	2.88	12	7	0	0	25	19	10	8	0	2	33	.209	.368	.167	11.88	0.72
Gilliland, Jacob	R-R	6-2	180	1-16-00	4	0	2.93	8	1	0	0	28	23	9	9	1	15	22	.228	.208	.245	7.16	4.88
2-team total (7 Dodgers Mota)					5	0	3.26	15	1	0	0	39	36	14	14	2	22	39	.245	.206	.279	9.08	5.12
Gonzalez, Juan	R-R	6-0	165	6-24-00	2	3	6.26	16	0	0	0	23	21	18	16	1	13	26	.241	.231	.246	10.17	5.09
Head, Louis	R-R	6-1	180	4-23-90	0	1	9.82	5	2	0	0	7	13	8	8	1	3	8	.419	.231	.556	9.82	3.68
2-team total (2 Dodgers Mota)					0	1	7.20	7	4	0	0	10	15	8	8	1	3	10	.366	.250	.440	9.00	2.70
Hernandez, Ricardo	R-R	6-1	205	2-4-98	1	1	3.45	7	0	0	0	16	12	6	6	0	4	18	.218	.263	.194	10.34	2.30
2-team total (1 Dodgers Mota)					1	2	3.86	8	0	0	0	16	13	7	7	1	4	20	.224	.238	.216	11.02	2.20
Kasowski, Marshall	L-R	6-3	215	3-10-95	0	0	0.00	1	1	0	0	1	0	0	0	0	0	3	.000	.000		27.00	0.00
2-team total (1 Dodgers Mota)					0	0	0.00	2	2	0	0	2	1	0	0	0	0	5	.125	.000	.250	19.29	0.00
Kitagata, Yujo	R-R	6-0	198	1-25-94	0	1	7.20	13	4	0	1	15	13	15	12	1	17	21	.241	.389	.167	12.60	10.20
Little, Jack	L-R	6-4	190	1-10-98	0	0	0.00	1	1	0	0	1	1	0	0	0	0	1	.250	.000	.333	9.00	0.00
2-team total (1 Dodgers Mota)					0	0	0.00	2	2	0	0	3	1	0	0	0	0	4	.100	.000	.143	12.00	0.00
Marcano, Enmanuel	R-R	6-1	185	12-4-98	2	1	2.60	17	0	0	3	28	21	10	8	2	8	34	.204	.226	.194	11.06	2.60
2-team total (1 Dodgers Mota)					2	1	3.10	18	0	0	3	29	22	12	10	3	9	37	.204	.212	.200	11.48	2.79
Martinez, Francisco	L-L	6-1	180	5-4-01	0	0	18.00	1	0	0	0	1	3	2	2	0	0	1	.500	1.000	.000	9.00	0.00
Morillo, Juan	R-R	6-1	150	3-19-99	2	1	2.56	13	1	0	0	46	39	20	13	4	13	58	.222	.193	.235	11.43	2.56
Navarro, Orlandy	R-R	6-2	175	8-3-99	0	0	3.93	13	5	0	0	34	42	16	15	2	8	38	.298	.438	.226	9.96	2.10
Ottesen, Riley	R-R	6-1	185	10-30-94	0	1	3.32	18	0	0	2	22	17	15	8	2	14	31	.207	.161	.235	12.88	5.82
Ramirez, Adolfo	R-R	6-0	165	6-1-99	3	0	0.73	16	0	0	1	49	24	5	4	1	9	61	.146	.153	.142	11.20	1.65
Robertson, Nick	R-R	6-6	265	7-16-98	0	0	0.00	5	0	0	0	5	2	1	0	0	1	7	.105	.000	.133	11.81	0.00
Rodriguez, Luis	R-R	6-0	150	3-2-99	0	0	0.00	3	0	0	0	2	1	0	0	0	0	2	.000	.000	.000	7.71	3.86
Rodulfo, Jose	R-R	6-0	165	8-20-00	1	3	6.41	6	1	0	0	20	22	16	14	1	3	9	.286	.269	.294	4.12	1.37
2-team total (8 Dodgers Mota)					1	5	4.50	14	6	0	0	54	67	36	27	4	9	46	.303	.278	.321	7.67	1.50
Solbach, Markus	R-R	6-5	205	8-26-91	0	0	0.00	1	1	0	0	5	6	0	0	0	0	6	.300	.333	.294	7.20	0.00
2-team total (5 Dodgers Mota)					0	2	4.57	6	4	0	0	22	26	12	11	3	6	20	.289	.281	.293	8.31	2.49
Valdez, Joan	R-R	6-4	175	3-10-99	0	2	8.70	11	10	0	0	30	47	33	29	10	11	23	.364	.289	.405	6.90	3.30

Fielding

C: Barbary 7, Berman 2, Chalo 34, Hope 8, Mendoza 1, Noriega 10, Zabala 6. **1B:** Carrion 15, Espinoza 18, Landry 26, Lewis 3, Sanchez 1. **2B:** Busch 4, Castro 1, Chirinos 4, Espinoza 9, Guillen 3, Hernandez 2, Leonard 20, Mann 1, Rodriguez 1, Vivas 19. **3B:** Carrion 23, Chirinos 17, Lewis 5, Mann 2, Rodriguez 7, Vivas 8. **SS:** Castro 2, Chirinos 17, Leonard 25, Rodriguez 18. **OF:** Allison 22, Cuadrado 1, De Jongh 31, Garcia 14, Guillen 2, Lebron 24, Mateo 37, McKenzie 9, McLain 7, Perez 30, Sanchez 1, Wulff 5.

AZL DODGERS MOTA
ARIZONA LEAGUE
ROOKIE

Batting	B-T	HT	WT	DOB	AVG	vLH	vRH	G	AB	R	H	2B	3B	HR	RBI	BB	HBP	SH	SF	SO	SB	CS	SLG	OBP
Ackerman, Aaron	B-R	6-3	210	5-1-97	.000	--	.000	1	2	0	0	0	0	0	0	0	0	0	0	1	0	0	.000	.000
Alcantara, Ismael	R-R	6-1	165	9-25-98	.301	.448	.268	45	156	31	47	7	3	1	23	27	2	1	2	46	20	0	.404	.406
Aponte, Kevin	R-R	6-2	175	10-26-97	.291	.182	.318	19	55	6	16	0	1	1	8	3	2	0	1	20	3	0	.382	.344
Berman, Stevie	R-R	6-2	225	11-28-94	.400	.333	.500	2	5	1	2	0	0	1	2	0	0	0	0	1	0	1	1.000	.400
2-team total (2 Dodgers Lasorda)					.300	.333	.286	4	10	1	3	1	0	1	3	0	0	0	0	1	0	1	.700	.300
Betancourt, Kenneth	R-R	5-8	160	2-5-00	.219	.360	.188	36	137	16	30	6	2	0	19	10	1	1	1	29	5	2	.292	.275
Cartaya, Diego	R-R	6-2	199	9-7-01	.296	.250	.311	36	135	25	40	10	0	3	13	11	2	0	2	31	1	0	.437	.353
Castro, Daniel	R-R	5-11	201	11-14-92	.333	--	.333	1	3	0	1	0	0	0	0	0	0	0	0	0	0	0	.667	.250
2-team total (3 Dodgers Lasorda)					.400	.500	.375	4	10	3	4	1	0	1	1	1	0	1	0	2	0	0	.700	.462
Chirinos, Yhostin	R-R	5-10	165	9-29-00	.188	.000	.200	3	16	2	3	1	0	0	0	0	0	0	0	6	1	0	.250	.188
2-team total (39 Dodgers Lasorda)					.273	.314	.262	42	161	28	44	2	1	2	10	17	1	0	2	29	3	2	.335	.343
Cuadrado, Romer	R-R	6-4	185	9-12-97	.290	.286	.292	8	31	6	9	3	0	2	7	2	0	0	0	10	2	0	.581	.333
2-team total (3 Dodgers Lasorda)					.270	.200	.296	11	37	7	10	3	0	2	7	4	1	0	0	11	2	0	.514	.357
De Jesus, Alex	R-R	6-2	170	3-22-02	.276	.262	.281	44	163	13	45	8	1	2	25	12	1	0	2	58	5	1	.374	.326
Deluca, Jonny	B-R	5-11	196	7-10-98	.273	.348	.250	26	99	19	27	4	2	1	13	8	4	0	3	7	9	0	.384	.342
Diaz, Luis Carlos	R-R	6-1	155	12-19-99	.375	.000	.400	4	16	4	6	2	0	0	4	1	0	0	0	4	1	1	.500	.412
Diaz, Luis Yanel	R-R	5-10	190	2-6-00	.260	.310	.247	49	192	30	50	6	8	6	34	5	0	0	2	63	9	3	.469	.276
Estevez, Omar	R-R	5-10	185	2-25-98	.300	.250	.313	7	20	7	6	2	0	0	3	2	0	0	0	8	0	0	.400	.364
Guillen, Alfonso	R-R	5-10	161	7-11-99	.270	.400	.250	15	37	2	10	1	0	0	2	4	0	0	1	10	0	1	.297	.333
2-team total (6 Dodgers Lasorda)					.208	.286	.195	21	48	2	10	1	0	0	3	8	0	0	2	14	0	1	.229	.310
Hernandez, Enrique	R-R	5-11	192	8-24-91	.333	--	.333	1	3	1	1	0	0	1	3	0	0	0	0	0	0	0	1.333	.333

Batting	B-T	HT	WT	DOB	AVG	vLH	vRH	G	AB	R	H	2B	3B	HR	RBI	BB	HBP	SH	SF	SO	SB	CS	OBP	SLG
2-team total (2 Dodgers Lasorda)					.444	.000	.500	3	9	2	4	1	0	1	3	2	0	0	0	1	0	0	.889	.546
Hoese, Kody	R-R	6-4	200	7-13-97	.357	.125	.396	19	56	14	20	5	1	3	13	10	1	0	1	11	1	0	.643	.456
Mann, Devin	R-R	6-3	180	2-11-97	.000	.000	--	1	1	0	0	0	0	0	0	1	0	0	0	0	0	0	.000	.500
2-team total (4 Dodgers Lasorda)					.500	.500	.500	5	14	2	7	2	0	0	1	2	0	0	0	1	0	1	.643	.563
McLain, Josh	R-R	6-1	170	9-23-96	.100	.200	.000	3	10	1	1	0	0	0	0	2	0	0	0	4	1	0	.100	.250
2-team total (7 Dodgers Lasorda)					.180	.429	.125	10	39	6	7	1	1	0	4	4	1	0	0	16	3	1	.256	.273
Mendoza, Cesar	R-R	5-11	175	2-28-97	.000	.000	.000	3	4	1	0	0	0	0	0	1	0	0	0	1	0	0	.000	.200
2-team total (1 Dodgers Lasorda)					.000	.000	.000	4	7	1	0	0	0	0	0	1	0	0	0	1	0	0	.000	.125
Noriega, Andres	R-R	6-1	190	1-3-01	.262	.235	.273	19	61	5	16	0	0	1	10	6	2	0	2	14	0	0	.312	.338
2-team total (10 Dodgers Lasorda)					.230	.269	.213	29	87	8	20	1	0	1	15	9	3	1	2	16	0	0	.276	.317
Perez, Jaime	R-R	6-1	178	4-5-00	.000	--	.000	1	4	0	0	0	0	0	0	0	0	0	0	2	0	0	.000	.000
2-team total (33 Dodgers Lasorda)					.219	.304	.195	34	105	13	23	6	1	4	10	4	0	2	0	45	0	0	.410	.248
Ryan, Tyler	R-R	6-1	210	5-9-96	.136	.000	.158	8	22	1	3	0	1	0	3	1	0	0	0	6	0	0	.227	.208
2-team total (10 Dodgers Lasorda)					.192	.400	.167	18	47	3	9	1	2	0	8	3	2	0	1	14	0	0	.298	.264
Sinatro, Danny	L-R	6-0	180	9-18-97	.291	.303	.287	41	141	26	41	6	3	0	16	18	4	1	0	31	15	3	.376	.387
Suarez, Albert	L-R	5-11	150	11-30-99	.267	.268	.267	50	187	24	50	12	2	0	23	9	0	1	2	32	10	5	.353	.298
Vargas, Imanol	L-R	6-3	185	6-29-98	.290	.344	.276	47	155	37	45	9	2	9	25	28	2	1	0	50	4	3	.548	.405
Vison, Jeremiah	R-R	5-4	145	8-27-97	.319	.308	.321	20	69	16	22	2	0	1	5	6	2	0	1	9	8	3	.391	.385
Washington, Justin	R-R	6-4	190	6-19-97	.272	.219	.296	34	103	20	28	6	1	3	10	17	3	1	1	33	5	3	.437	.387
Zabala, Juan	R-R	5-10	170	7-3-99	.188	.267	.163	21	64	8	12	2	1	1	4	6	0	0	0	23	1	0	.297	.288
2-team total (6 Dodgers Lasorda)					.207	.286	.180	27	82	13	17	3	2	2	6	7	4	0	0	27	1	0	.366	.301

Pitching	B-T	HT	WT	DOB	W	L	ERA	G	GS	CG	SV	IP	H	R	ER	HR	BB	SO	AVG	vLH	vRH	K/9	BB/9
Abreu, Jeffry	R-R	6-4	200	1-28-00	2	0	4.66	6	2	0	0	19	19	12	10	2	6	24	.247	.216	.275	11.17	2.79
Acevedo, Axel	R-R	6-2	170	9-23-00	1	0	0.00	6	0	0	1	5	1	0	0	0	2	5	.067	.000	.100	9.00	3.60
Ackerman, Aaron	B-R	6-3	210	5-1-97	0	0	0.00	3	0	0	0	2	0	0	0	0	2	2	.000	.000	.000	0.00	9.00
Acosta, Aldry	R-R	6-4	200	9-7-99	1	0	5.06	8	4	0	0	16	14	9	9	2	7	14	.237	.208	.257	7.88	3.94
Alcantara, Ismael	R-R	6-1	165	9-25-98	0	0	0.00	1	0	0	0	1	0	0	0	0	0	1	.000	--	.000	9.00	0.00
Alejo, Carlos	R-R	6-1	165	8-23-99	1	1	3.42	16	0	0	4	26	24	13	10	0	14	27	.235	.192	.280	9.23	4.78
Andujar, Horacio	R-R	6-2	161	1-14-99	0	0	3.86	4	0	0	0	5	3	2	2	1	4	2	.188	.000	.273	3.86	7.71
Aponte, Kevin	R-R	6-2	175	10-26-97	1	0	0.00	2	0	0	0	1	0	0	0	0	2	1	.000	.000	.000	6.75	13.50
Avila, Igor	L-L	6-1	185	5-17-97	1	1	4.80	9	0	0	0	15	9	8	8	2	7	15	.173	.000	.220	9.00	4.20
2-team total (6 Dodgers Lasorda)					1	2	8.04	15	3	0	0	28	32	29	25	3	16	24	.283	.192	.310	7.71	5.14
Benavides, Gabe	R-L	6-2	180	9-9-96	0	0	10.13	3	0	0	0	3	4	3	3	0	4	3	.364	--	.364	13.50	10.13
2-team total (12 AZL Dodgers Lasorda)					3	1	4.84	15	0	0	0	22	22	14	12	3	13	16	.272	.300	.268	6.45	5.24
Broussard, Joe	R-R	6-1	225	1-28-91	0	0	4.50	3	2	0	0	4	6	3	2	0	1	2	.353	.200	.417	4.50	2.25
2-team total (2 Dodgers Lasorda)					0	1	2.25	5	3	0	0	8	6	3	2	0	1	10	.207	.091	.278	11.25	1.13
Cabrera, Jeisson	R-R	6-2	170	9-5-98	4	2	2.31	14	7	0	0	51	28	16	13	3	25	63	.164	.180	.155	11.19	4.44
Cantleberry, Jacob	L-L	6-1	180	8-8-97	0	0	1.35	10	0	0	0	13	7	2	2	1	3	19	.152	.364	.086	12.83	2.03
Choi, Hyun-il	R-R	6-2	200	5-27-00	5	1	2.63	14	11	0	0	65	57	29	19	6	11	71	.236	.208	.253	9.83	1.52
Cruz, Daniel	R-R	6-3	185	10-5-97	5	2	3.12	17	0	0	4	26	18	11	9	0	10	43	.192	.162	.211	14.88	3.46
De Los Santos, Carlos	R-R	6-2	170	11-18-00	3	1	4.97	15	0	0	0	25	23	18	14	3	15	29	.245	.286	.212	10.30	5.33
Galindo, Harold	R-R	6-2	175	1-22-01	0	0	11.74	4	0	0	0	8	9	12	10	1	3	4	.290	.250	.316	4.70	3.52
Gilliland, Jacob	R-R	6-2	180	1-16-00	1	0	4.09	7	0	0	0	11	13	5	5	1	7	17	.283	.200	.346	13.91	5.73
2-team total (8 Dodgers Lasorda)					5	0	3.26	15	1	0	0	39	36	14	14	2	22	39	.245	.206	.279	9.08	5.12
Head, Louis	R-R	6-1	180	4-23-90	0	0	0.00	2	0	0	0	3	2	0	0	0	2	4	.200	.333	.143	6.75	0.00
2-team total (5 Dodgers Lasorda)					0	1	7.20	7	4	0	0	10	15	8	8	1	3	10	.366	.250	.440	9.00	2.70
Hernandez, Ricardo	R-R	6-1	205	2-4-98	0	1	13.50	1	0	0	0	1	1	1	1	1	0	2	.333	.000	1.000	27.00	0.00
2-team total (7 Dodgers Lasorda)					1	2	3.86	8	0	0	0	16	13	7	7	1	4	20	.224	.238	.216	11.02	2.20
Kasowski, Marshall	L-R	6-3	215	3-10-95	0	0	0.00	1	1	0	0	1	1	0	0	0	0	2	.200	.000	.333	13.50	0.00
2-team total (1 Dodgers Lasorda)					0	0	0.00	2	2	0	0	2	1	0	0	0	0	5	.125	.000	.250	19.29	0.00
Lin, Huei-Sheng	R-R	6-2	198	10-9-98	2	4	7.31	14	3	0	1	32	40	31	26	4	9	39	.294	.353	.259	10.97	2.53
Little, Jack	L-R	6-4	190	1-10-98	0	0	0.00	1	0	0	0	2	0	0	0	0	0	3	.000	.000		13.50	0.00
2-team total (1 Dodgers Lasorda)					0	0	0.00	2	2	0	0	3	1	0	0	0	0	4	.100	.000	.143	12.00	0.00
Marcano, Enmanuel	R-R	6-1	185	12-4-98	0	0	13.50	1	0	0	0	1	1	2	2	1	1	3	.200	.000	.333	20.25	6.75
2-team total (17 Dodgers Lasorda)					2	1	3.10	18	0	0	3	29	22	12	10	3	9	37	.204	.212	.200	11.48	2.79
Martinez, Michael	R-R	6-1	185	7-11-99	2	0	4.58	8	2	0	1	20	18	14	10	1	13	22	.250	.273	.240	10.07	5.95
Martinson, Jordan	L-L	6-0	210	3-7-97	0	0	13.50	2	0	0	0	1	4	2	2	1	1	2	.500	.500	.500	13.50	6.75
Mellen, Sean	L-L	6-2	215	2-20-98	0	0	33.75	3	1	0	0	1	8	5	5	0	1	2	.667	1.000	.500	13.50	6.75
Mendoza, Cesar	R-R	5-11	175	2-28-97	0	0	0.00	1	0	0	0	1	1	0	0	0	0	2	.250	.000	.333	18.00	0.00
Mixon, Mark	R-R	6-2	180	5-22-97	0	0	5.40	3	1	0	0	3	3	2	2	0	1	4	.231	.333	.143	10.80	2.70
Ochsenbein, Aaron	R-R	6-3	225	2-29-96	0	0	4.50	2	0	0	0	4	4	1	1	0	0	4	.444	.500	.400	18.00	0.00
Pepiot, Ryan	R-R	6-3	215	8-21-97	0	0	0.00	2	0	0	0	5	2	0	0	0	4	10	.118	.091	.167	18.00	7.20
Plunkett, Zack	R-R	6-2	225	2-16-96	0	2	0.84	10	1	0	0	11	6	3	1	0	7	18	.154	.167	.143	15.19	5.91
Rodulfo, Jose	R-R	6-0	165	8-20-00	0	2	3.41	8	5	0	0	34	45	20	13	3	6	37	.313	.281	.338	9.70	1.57
2-team total (6 Dodgers Lasorda)					1	5	4.50	14	6	0	0	54	67	36	27	4	9	46	.303	.278	.331	7.67	1.50
Sierra, Yaisel	R-R	6-1	170	6-5-91	0	0	3.00	3	1	0	0	3	5	1	1	0	0	6	.333	.250	.364	18.00	0.00
Smith, Julian	R-L	6-4	190	6-6-97	3	3	5.98	14	6	0	0	47	57	33	31	2	30	46	.307	.138	.338	8.87	5.79
Solbach, Markus	R-R	6-5	205	8-26-91	0	2	5.94	5	5	0	0	17	20	12	11	3	6	16	.286	.276	.293	8.64	3.24
2-team total (2 Dodgers Lasorda)					0	2	4.57	6	6	0	0	22	26	12	11	3	6	21	.280	.289	.281	8.31	2.49
Tyranski, Mitchell	L-L	6-2	215	9-2-97	1	0	1.13	6	0	0	1	8	5	1	1	0	1	13	.185	.125	.211	14.63	1.13
Watson, Cyrillo	R-R	6-1	195	8-10-97	0	0	1.13	9	0	0	1	8	4	1	1	1	1	8	.143	.222	.105	9.00	1.13

LOS ANGELES DODGERS

Fielding

C: Berman 2, Cartaya 28, Mendoza 2, Noriega 14, Ryan 1, Zabala 19. **1B:** Betancourt 13, Guillen 4, Noriega 5, Ryan 4, Vargas 38. **2B:** Betancourt 13, Chirinos 1, De Jesus 2, Guillen 9, Suarez 37. **3B:** Betancourt 11, Chirinos 1, De Jesus 3, Diaz 43, Diaz 1, Guillen 1, Hoese 6, Mann 1. **SS:** Betancourt 7, Castro 1, Chirinos 2, De Jesus 38, Diaz 1, Estevez 4, Suarez 14. **OF:** Alcantara 41, Aponte 14, Cuadrado 8, Deluca 25, Diaz 3, Hernandez 1, McLain 2, Perez 1, Sinatro 32, Vison 18, Washington 33.

DSL DODGERS   ROOKIE
DOMINICAN SUMMER LEAGUE

Batting	B-T	HT	WT	DOB	AVG	vLH	vRH	G	AB	R	H	2B	3B	HR	RBI	BB	HBP	SH	SF	SO	SB	CS	SLG	OBP
Aguilar, Jose	R-R	5-10	170	4-4-01	.250	.227	.256	37	108	18	27	1	4	2	17	13	5	1	2	38	4	4	.389	.352
Alvarez, Oscar	R-R	5-9	145	6-20-00	.200	.500	.140	25	60	5	12	1	0	0	4	6	0	0	1	11	2	0	.217	.269
Arainamo, Darwin	R-R	5-11	160	5-26-02	.127	.182	.114	19	55	6	7	1	0	0	4	7	1	0	1	27	0	0	.146	.234
Avendano, Ender	R-R	5-8	145	3-7-02	.211	.160	.220	51	166	29	35	4	1	1	14	35	3	1	1	51	8	7	.265	.356
Bastardo, Kiumel	R-R	6-0	180	1-12-00	.245	.286	.237	45	159	22	39	5	1	1	16	19	3	3	1	34	7	0	.308	.335
Cairo, Marlon	R-R	6-2	200	1-29-96	.324	.327	.322	59	204	51	66	12	3	10	40	36	7	0	4	64	8	5	.559	.434
Cartaya, Diego	R-R	6-2	199	9-7-01	.240	.400	.222	13	50	11	12	2	2	1	9	5	1	0	1	11	0	0	.420	.316
Cathalina, Mayron	R-R	6-0	145	2-12-01	.103	.158	.082	33	68	12	7	2	1	0	2	15	1	0	0	33	6	2	.162	.274
De Jesus, Alex	R-R	6-2	170	3-22-02	.296	.429	.250	13	54	8	16	5	0	1	9	8	0	0	1	14	0	0	.444	.381
De La Rosa, Bladimir	R-R	6-1	175	10-15-01	.259	.250	.262	48	166	31	43	12	4	5	31	25	3	1	1	59	11	5	.470	.364
Diaz, Juan	B-R	6-2	190	2-20-02	.244	.208	.257	57	201	32	49	13	3	2	32	37	6	0	6	43	2	1	.368	.368
Dominguez, Jesus	L-R	5-9	189	4-6-01	.111	.500	.000	4	9	0	1	0	0	0	1	1	0	0	0	5	0	0	.111	.200
Droz, Miguel	R-R	6-0	170	10-2-01	.183	.067	.222	18	60	6	11	2	1	0	5	14	1	0	1	13	2	2	.250	.342
Enrique, Julio	R-R	6-1	184	2-21-00	.198	.205	.196	56	187	33	37	14	1	2	21	27	11	1	0	67	27	7	.316	.333
Feliz, Francisco	L-R	6-2	180	10-5-00	.163	.056	.188	36	98	15	16	1	0	0	5	30	3	1	1	37	8	3	.174	.371
Fernandez, Alejandro	R-R	5-10	155	3-7-01	.180	.111	.192	23	61	8	11	1	0	0	4	12	1	2	1	11	0	0	.197	.320
Garcia, Jeans	L-R	6-1	185	6-21-01	.159	.267	.125	23	63	4	10	0	0	0	8	12	0	0	1	25	2	2	.159	.290
Garcia, Jose	B-R	6-1	190	10-4-01	.271	.167	.293	20	70	10	19	2	0	0	9	5	0	0	0	21	2	1	.300	.320
Hernandez, Jorge	R-R	5-10	145	1-12-01	.000	--	.000	3	5	0	0	0	0	0	0	1	0	0	0	1	0	0	.000	.167
Hidalgo, Christian	R-R	6-3	186	9-18-01	.131	.000	.165	40	99	12	13	2	1	1	11	25	0	0	4	40	1	0	.202	.297
Ibarra, Joel	R-R	6-0	176	7-10-02	.177	.111	.194	40	130	22	23	7	0	0	10	26	7	0	1	47	9	0	.231	.342
Izturis, Luis	R-R	5-10	155	7-3-00	.203	.036	.256	39	118	28	24	3	0	3	12	34	4	2	0	48	8	4	.305	.397
Jardines, Jenderson	B-R	5-11	160	1-31-01	.206	.077	.221	36	126	16	26	5	0	1	16	18	2	0	2	31	5	1	.270	.311
Machin, Eynar	R-R	5-10	155	10-3-00	.144	.208	.128	39	118	10	17	3	0	2	13	19	5	1	2	28	3	1	.220	.285
Martinez, Hector	R-R	6-0	135	8-22-00	.251	.159	.278	52	195	41	49	8	2	2	15	36	6	1	2	34	10	7	.344	.381
Morales, Luis	R-R	5-9	162	12-6-00	.194	.182	.196	31	108	14	21	7	0	3	18	10	1	0	1	31	8	0	.343	.267
Pereira, Gregory	R-R	5-11	165	5-19-02	.211	.235	.206	37	114	20	24	4	2	0	11	14	5	0	0	35	7	1	.281	.323
Perez, Vladimir	R-R	5-9	138	1-3-01	.235	.200	.244	47	145	20	34	10	1	0	20	11	1	2	46	6	3	.331	.327
Quiroz, Nelson	B-R	5-8	194	11-5-01	.264	.217	.275	37	125	12	33	2	1	1	19	15	2	0	2	21	1	1	.320	.347
Ramos, Jose	R-R	5-11	150	1-1-01	.275	.296	.272	57	207	34	57	15	0	2	27	20	11	0	5	46	9	3	.377	.362
Restituyo, Harold	R-R	6-2	185	9-1-00	.256	.240	.260	41	125	22	32	5	1	1	10	22	8	0	3	34	8	2	.336	.392
Rodriguez, Brayan	R-R	6-4	190	11-23-00	.171	.083	.190	23	70	4	12	3	0	1	9	4	1	0	1	34	0	0	.257	.224
Rodriguez, Frank	R-R	5-11	197	9-28-01	.175	.222	.161	40	114	16	20	4	0	0	8	25	7	0	2	35	0	0	.211	.351
Santiago, Carlos	B-R	5-11	145	7-24-01	.221	.069	.246	58	208	26	46	12	1	5	37	20	6	1	2	52	5	4	.361	.305
Sequera, Yohandry	R-R	5-10	150	1-25-00	.239	.278	.232	40	130	16	31	4	0	1	15	19	3	3	1	29	0	4	.292	.346
Tomsjansen, Rushenten	R-R	5-11	160	5-14-01	.203	.167	.213	49	158	21	32	4	3	2	20	15	7	2	6	37	8	5	.304	.290
Valdez, Amin	L-R	6-0	155	11-18-00	.208	.250	.202	29	106	10	22	2	0	1	11	14	0	0	0	33	1	3	.255	.300
Yan, Luis	B-R	6-3	180	1-1-99	.285	.265	.289	59	214	30	61	10	2	1	30	30	1	1	1	54	13	1	.365	.374

Pitching	B-T	HT	WT	DOB	W	L	ERA	G	GS	CG	SV	IP	H	R	ER	HR	BB	SO	AVG	vLH	vRH	K/9	BB/9
Acevedo, Axel	R-R	6-2	170	9-23-00	5	0	1.14	13	2	0	1	32	17	6	4	0	7	19	.152	.162	.147	5.40	1.99
Alvarez, Oscar	R-R	5-9	145	6-20-00	0	0	13.50	2	0	0	0	1	2	2	2	0	1	1	.333	.000	.500	6.75	6.75
Andujar, Horacio	R-R	6-2	161	1-14-99	0	1	3.52	12	0	0	1	15	13	7	6	0	5	10	.220	.182	.243	5.87	2.93
Avila, Igor	L-L	6-1	185	5-17-97	0	0	3.00	3	3	0	0	12	8	4	4	1	7	10	.191	.000	.200	7.50	5.25
Baez, Wilkin	R-R	6-1	175	11-12-99	1	1	3.00	20	1	0	5	36	22	13	12	0	27	30	.191	.231	.171	7.50	6.75
Baro, Heisell	R-R	6-1	185	2-20-02	1	2	1.22	16	8	0	1	44	23	13	6	3	16	47	.157	.088	.177	9.54	3.25
Beltran, Hugo	R-R	6-1	190	6-13-00	4	5	3.67	15	7	0	0	49	43	23	20	1	5	46	.229	.217	.235	8.45	0.92
Briones, Hendrick	R-R	6-1	167	11-1-01	1	4	1.01	20	1	0	0	36	28	11	4	1	13	22	.231	.172	.250	5.55	3.28
Budier, Andrew	L-L	6-0	165	10-09-04	4	4	1.79	18	5	0	0	50	37	19	10	1	15	53	.204	.200	.205	9.48	2.68
Calzado, Dave	R-R	6-3	190	8-31-00	0	0	9.00	2	0	0	0	2	3	3	2	0	5	0	.333	.600	.000	0.00	22.50
Castillo, Yamil	R-R	6-1	200	8-18-99	0	3	3.33	13	13	0	0	46	43	22	17	0	21	46	.243	.217	.256	9.00	4.11
Castro, Fran	R-R	6-0	175	7-9-00	0	4	3.86	15	0	0	1	21	18	12	9	1	10	13	.240	.115	.306	5.57	4.29
Chacon, Raidel	R-R	6-3	195	9-20-94	0	1	16.31	14	0	0	0	16	25	36	29	2	19	11	.357	.375	.342	6.19	10.69
De Avila, Carlos	R-R	5-11	170	2-11-00	3	1	1.99	23	2	0	3	45	36	18	10	0	5	39	.218	.250	.200	7.74	0.99
De la Cruz, Juan	R-R	5-11	160	8-14-00	4	1	1.70	23	0	0	1	37	28	15	7	0	22	52	.206	.143	.250	12.65	5.35
Duran, Carlos	R-R	6-7	230	7-30-01	1	0	0.43	5	5	0	0	21	8	3	1	0	10	23	.119	.143	.103	9.86	4.29
Feliz, Frankelyn	R-R	6-1	170	12-24-01	0	2	4.55	25	0	0	2	32	32	26	16	1	19	19	.256	.250	.260	5.40	5.40
Galindo, Harold	R-R	6-2	175	1-22-01	3	2	1.48	10	10	0	0	43	33	13	7	0	15	36	.216	.267	.183	7.59	3.16
Gomez, Duany	R-R	6-5	186	9-30-00	2	2	3.19	18	2	0	1	31	33	16	11	2	13	16	.297	.275	.310	4.65	3.77
Gonzalez, Jorge	R-R	6-5	203	8-30-02	1	0	11.25	0	0	0	0	4	3	5	5	0	8	1	.200	.250	.143	2.25	18.00
Gutierrez, Osvanni	R-R	6-1	170	5-24-01	1	2	3.06	9	9	0	0	32	24	12	11	2	9	30	.207	.255	.174	8.35	2.51
Gutierrez, Stiven	R-R	6-1	160	6-21-01	2	1	5.01	13	0	0	0	23	29	13	13	2	9	16	.326	.319	.333	6.17	3.47
Henriquez, Edgardo	R-R	6-4	200	6-24-02	2	2	4.80	18	3	0	0	30	21	22	16	0	28	30	.196	.225	.199	9.00	8.40
Martines, Denverick	L-L	6-0	170	5-31-01	3	0	2.23	16	3	0	0	32	26	12	8	1	20	27	.224	.125	.240	7.52	5.57
Martinez, Michael	R-R	6-1	185	7-11-99	0	1	2.45	2	2	0	0	7	6	2	2	0	3	6	.207	.125	.238	7.36	3.68

Name	B-T	Ht	Wt	DOB	W	L	ERA	G	GS	CG	SV	IP	H	R	ER	HR	BB	SO	AVG	vLH	vRH		
Mendez, Jose	L-L	6-4	180	4-4-01	0	1	8.38	18	0	0	0	19	22	24	18	2	21	16	.282	.316	.271	7.45	9.78
Moron, Eli	R-R	6-0	140	10-7-01	5	2	3.45	15	2	0	0	44	42	21	17	4	14	21	.256	.208	.279	4.26	2.84
Moya, Abel	R-R	6-1	172	6-6-01	2	5	5.57	16	6	0	0	42	45	32	26	4	12	38	.271	.250	.282	8.14	2.57
Paez, Isual	R-R	6-2	180	8-15-99	0	0	40.50	1	0	0	0	1	2	3	3	1	1	0	.667	.000	1.000	0.00	13.50
Peralta, Cristian	L-L	6-3	184	8-18-99	0	0	15.12	9	0	0	0	8	11	15	14	1	20	5	.344	.429	.320	5.40	21.60
Perez, Luisenyer	L-L	5-11	180	11-9-00	2	2	9.14	17	0	0	2	22	29	29	22	0	23	20	.337	.200	.379	8.31	9.55
Portes, Denis	R-R	6-1	170	3-9-02	1	1	5.40	8	0	0	0	10	9	13	6	0	5	5	.214	.313	.154	4.50	4.50
Robles, Benony	L-L	6-4	185	10-1-00	0	3	4.19	15	15	0	0	54	50	30	25	2	27	51	.244	.238	.245	8.55	4.53
Rodriguez, Carlos	R-R	6-2	194	4-2-99	2	1	6.28	12	0	0	1	14	16	13	10	0	7	11	.276	.333	.243	6.91	4.40
Rodriguez, Isaac	L-L	5-10	165	8-3-02	2	1	4.94	20	0	0	0	31	40	23	17	3	18	26	.313	.333	.308	7.55	5.23
Rodriguez, Jeremi	R-R	6-1	165	8-5-01	6	2	2.74	16	3	0	2	43	35	19	13	1	18	35	.212	.158	.241	7.38	3.80
Rosario, Jerming	R-R	6-1	175	5-8-02	0	0	0.79	13	13	0	0	45	28	4	0	15	43		.178	.233	.158	8.54	2.98
Ruben, Samuel	R-R	6-2	151	8-2-00	2	1	3.94	19	2	0	5	32	25	18	14	4	16	24	.210	.146	.266	6.75	4.50
Santana, Dalvinson	L-L	6-0	193	11-4-99	1	0	0.93	4	1	0	0	10	6	3	1	0	4	9	.182	.000	.231	8.38	3.72
Santana, Martin	R-R	6-4	165	1-30-01	0	0	6.35	7	6	0	0	17	18	12	12	1	13	10	.277	.227	.302	5.29	6.88
Suarez, Christian	L-L	5-11	160	11-25-00	6	2	2.28	13	5	0	0	43	41	18	11	1	10	36	.252	.267	.248	7.48	2.08
Tua, Rafael	R-R	5-10	145	10-26-01	3	4	2.22	14	9	0	0	49	36	16	12	3	14	42	.207	.137	.236	7.77	2.59
Turizo, Jesus	R-R	6-2	192	5-9-01	2	2	2.25	22	0	0	4	28	21	11	7	1	11	15	.221	.188	.238	4.82	3.54

Fielding

C: Alvarez 10, Cartaya 9, Dominguez 2, Fernandez 19, Garcia 19, Jardines 4, Quiroz 28, Rodriguez 40. **1B:** Alvarez 14, Bastardo 20, Diaz 31, Feliz 4, Garcia 21, Jardines 2, Perez 10, Yan 46. **2B:** Avendano 36, De La Rosa 9, Droz 9, Feliz 4, Hernandez 1, Ibarra 20, Izturis 14, Machin 8, Martinez 21, Perez 8, Santiago 2, Sequera 6. **3B:** Avendano 10, De Jesus 2, Feliz 28, Hernandez 2, Ibarra 3, Izturis 20, Machin 5, Martinez 7, Perez 27, Santiago 4, Sequera 7. **SS:** Avendano 3, De Jesus 8, De La Rosa 30, Droz 9, Feliz 1, Ibarra 17, Izturis 4, Martinez 24, Santiago 51. **OF:** Aguilar 29, Arainamo 13, Bastardo 17, Cairo 46, Cathalina 28, Diaz 21, Enrique 51, Hidalgo 36, Morales 28, Pereira 35, Ramos 54, Restituyo 21, Rodriguez 13, Tomsjansen 47, Valdez 20, Yan 5.

Miami Marlins

SEASON IN A SENTENCE: Year two of the Marlins' rebuilding efforts didn't draw any more on-field success than year one, as the franchise finished with the National League's worst record for the second consecutive year, this time at 57-105.

HIGH POINT: As was the case in 2018, the Marlins never managed to break above .500 in 2019. They did, however, compile a season-high six-game winning streak from May 17-23 with back-to-back sweeps of the Mets and Tigers by a combined scored of 29-15.

LOW POINT: The Marlins' season-best six-game winning streak came just after the club lost a season-worst seven consecutive games from May 7-15. Miami finished with the NL's worst home record (30-51), road record (25-56) and offense (3.8 runs per game), while also finishing last in attendance (811,302) for the second straight year.

NOTABLE ROOKIES: One year after 26 rookies saw action for the Marlins, there were 17 more first-year players to play for Miami in 2019. Righthander Sandy Alcantara led the team in ERA (3.88), WHIP (1.32) and opponent average (.241) among all qualified pitchers, while also representing the franchise in the All-Star Game. Second baseman Isan Diaz made his major league debut on Aug. 5, hitting a home run off Mets righthander Jacob deGrom in his third career at-bat.

KEY TRANSACTIONS: The Marlins' fire sale continued before the season when they traded catcher J.T. Realmuto to the Phillies in exchange for righthander Sixto Sanchez, lefthander Will Stewart and catcher Jorge Alfaro in February. Sanchez immediately became the Marlins' No. 1 prospect. Prior to the July 31 trade deadline, the Marlins continued to boost their farm system by trading major league talent for prospects Jesus Sanchez (Rays), Jazz Chisholm (D-backs) and Lewin Diaz (Twins)—three position players who all now rank among the Marlins' Top 10 Prospects.

DOWN ON THE FARM: First-year low Class A affiliate Clinton won a system-best 78 games during the regular season before falling to South Bend (Cubs) in the Midwest League championship series. Short-season Batavia also made its league playoffs with a 41-35 regular season record but lost in the first round of the New York-Penn League playoffs to Lowell (Red Sox). Less than two years after having one of the worst prospect pools in baseball, the Marlins' slotted in at No. 8 in BA's farm system talent ranking in Aug. 2019.

OPENING DAY PAYROLL: $62,911,262 (30th).

PLAYERS OF THE YEAR

MAJOR LEAGUE	MINOR LEAGUE
Sandy Alcantara	**Isan Diaz**
RHP	**2B**
6-14, 3.88 in 32 GS	(Triple-A)
197 IP led all rookies	.305/.395/.578
NL all-star	26 HR, 70 RBIs

ORGANIZATION LEADERS

Batting		*Minimum 250 AB
MAJORS		
* AVG	Miguel Rojas	.284
* OPS	Brian Anderson	.811
HR	Starlin Castro	22
RBI	Starlin Castro	86
MINORS		
* AVG	Austin Dean, New Orleans, GCL Marlins	.337
* OBP	Peyton Burdick, Batavia, Clinton	.407
* SLG	Austin Dean, New Orleans, GCL Marlins	.635
* OPS	Austin Dean, New Orleans, GCL Marlins	1.035
R	Isan Diaz, New Orleans	89
H	Magneuris Sierra, Jacksonville, New Orleans	142
TB	Isan Diaz, New Orleans	218
2B	Nic Ready, Batavia	30
3B	Magneuris Sierra, Jacksonville, New Orleans	9
HR	Isan Diaz, New Orleans	26
RBI	Jerar Encarnacion, Clinton, Jupiter	71
BB	Christopher Torres, Clinton	75
SO	Sean Reynolds, Clinton, Batavia	184
SB	Magneuris Sierra, Jacksonville, New Orleans	33

Pitching		#Minimum 75 IP
MAJORS		
W	Caleb Smith	10
# ERA	Sandy Alcantara	3.88
SO	Caleb Smith	168
SV	Sergio Romo	17
MINORS		
W	Hector Noesi, New Orleans	11
L	Will Stewart, Jupiter	12
# ERA	Zac Gallen, New Orleans	1.77
G	R.J. Alvarez, New Orleans	50
GS	Albert Guerrero, Clinton	24
GS	Jorge Guzman, Jacksonville	24
SV	Zach Wolf, Clinton	15
SV	R.J. Alvarez, New Orleans	15
IP	Jorge Guzman, Jacksonville	139
BB	Jorge Guzman, Jacksonville	71
SO	Trevor Rogers, Jupiter, Jacksonville	150
# AVG	Zac Gallen, New Orleans	.153

2019 PERFORMANCE

General Manager: Michael Hill. **Farm Director:** Gary Denbo. **Scouting Director:** D.J. Svihlik.

Class	Team	League	W	L	PCT	Finish	Manager
Majors	Miami Marlins	National	57	105	.352	15th (15)	Don Mattingly
Triple-A	New Orleans Baby Cakes	Pacific Coast	73	65	.529	6th (16)	Keith Johnson
Double-A	Jacksonville Jumbo Shrimp	Southern	66	71	.482	5th (10)	Kevin Randel
High A	Jupiter Hammerheads	Florida State	54	78	.409	11th (12)	Todd Pratt
Low A	Clinton LumberKings	Midwest	78	61	.561	5th (16)	Mike Jacobs
Short season	Batavia Muckdogs	New York-Penn	41	35	.539	5th (14)	Tom Lawless
Rookie	GCL Marlins	Gulf Coast	28	22	.560	5th (18)	Robert Rodriguez
Overall 2019 Minor League Record			340	332	.506	12th (30)	

ORGANIZATION STATISTICS

MIAMI MARLINS
NATIONAL LEAGUE

Batting	B-T	HT	WT	DOB	AVG	vLH	vRH	G	AB	R	H	2B	3B	HR	RBI	BB	HBP	SH	SF	SO	SB	CS	SLG	OBP
Alfaro, Jorge	R-R	6-2	225	6-11-93	.262	.286	.254	130	431	44	113	14	1	18	57	22	10	0	2	154	4	4	.425	.312
Anderson, Brian	R-R	6-3	185	5-19-93	.261	.232	.271	126	459	57	120	33	1	20	66	44	14	0	3	114	5	1	.468	.342
Berti, Jon	R-R	5-10	195	1-22-90	.273	.269	.275	73	256	52	70	14	1	6	24	24	6	0	1	73	17	3	.406	.348
Brinson, Lewis	R-R	6-3	195	5-8-94	.173	.200	.164	75	226	15	39	9	1	0	15	13	6	2	1	74	1	1	.221	.236
Castillo, Wilkin	B-R	6-0	215	6-1-84	.143	.000	.167	2	7	0	1	1	0	0	2	0	0	0	0	3	0	0	.286	.143
Castro, Starlin	R-R	6-2	230	3-24-90	.270	.323	.252	162	636	68	172	31	4	22	86	28	3	0	9	111	2	2	.436	.300
Cooper, Garrett	R-R	6-6	230	12-25-90	.281	.220	.305	107	381	52	107	16	1	15	50	33	5	0	2	110	0	0	.446	.344
Dean, Austin	R-R	6-1	190	10-14-93	.225	.242	.216	64	178	17	40	14	0	6	21	9	0	1	1	47	0	2	.405	.261
Diaz, Isan	L-R	5-10	185	5-27-96	.173	.100	.194	49	179	17	31	5	2	5	23	19	2	0	1	59	0	3	.307	.259
Galloway, Isaac	R-R	6-2	205	10-10-89	.167	.067	.205	19	54	6	9	1	0	0	1	0	0	0	0	17	2	0	.185	.167
Granderson, Curtis	L-R	6-1	200	3-16-81	.183	.245	.172	138	317	44	58	17	1	12	34	41	3	0	2	98	0	3	.357	.281
Heineman, Tyler	B-R	5-11	205	6-19-91	.273	.000	.333	5	11	1	3	1	0	1	2	0	0	1	0	4	0	0	.636	.273
Herrera, Rosell	B-R	6-3	195	10-16-92	.200	.125	.233	63	105	10	21	6	0	2	11	11	2	1	0	27	4	1	.314	.288
Holaday, Bryan	R-R	6-0	214	11-19-87	.278	.258	.286	43	115	12	32	6	0	4	12	11	1	1	1	21	0	1	.435	.344
Marrero, Deven	R-R	6-0	190	8-25-90	.000	.000	.000	5	5	0	0	0	0	0	0	0	0	0	0	3	0	0	.000	.000
O'Brien, Peter	R-R	6-4	235	7-15-90	.167	.067	.222	14	42	2	7	1	0	1	4	1	4	0	0	19	1	0	.262	.255
Prado, Martin	R-R	6-0	215	10-27-83	.233	.268	.210	104	245	26	57	9	0	2	15	12	0	0	3	41	0	0	.294	.265
Puello, Cesar	R-R	6-2	220	4-1-91	.179	.148	.193	32	84	8	15	2	0	1	6	7	5	1	0	30	0	0	.238	.281
Ramirez, Harold	R-R	5-10	220	9-6-94	.276	.263	.281	119	421	54	116	20	3	11	50	18	5	0	1	91	2	1	.416	.312
Riddle, JT	L-R	6-1	180	10-12-91	.189	.240	.178	51	132	15	25	6	0	6	12	5	2	0	0	42	0	0	.371	.230
Rivera, Yadiel	R-R	6-3	185	5-2-92	.183	.214	.156	34	60	8	11	2	0	0	3	6	0	0	0	20	2	0	.217	.258
Rojas, Miguel	R-R	5-11	195	2-24-89	.284	.297	.278	132	483	52	137	29	1	5	46	32	5	1	5	62	9	5	.379	.331
Sierra, Magneuris	L-L	5-11	160	4-7-96	.350	1.000	.316	15	40	5	14	1	1	0	1	2	0	0	0	7	3	3	.425	.381
Walker, Neil	B-R	6-3	210	9-10-85	.261	.275	.259	115	337	37	88	19	1	8	38	42	1	0	1	77	3	0	.395	.344
Wallach, Chad	R-R	6-3	230	11-4-91	.250	.308	.229	19	48	4	12	3	0	1	3	6	0	0	0	12	0	0	.375	.333

Pitching	B-T	HT	WT	DOB	W	L	ERA	G	GS	CG	SV	IP	H	R	ER	HR	BB	SO	AVG	vLH	vRH	K/9	BB/9
Alcantara, Sandy	R-R	6-4	170	9-7-95	6	14	3.88	32	32	2	0	197	179	94	85	23	81	151	.241	.253	.227	6.89	3.69
Anderson, Nick	R-R	6-5	195	7-5-90	2	4	3.92	45	0	0	1	44	40	19	19	5	16	69	.238	.253	.226	14.22	3.30
Brice, Austin	R-R	6-4	235	6-19-92	1	0	3.43	36	0	0	0	45	37	21	17	7	18	46	.214	.246	.192	9.27	3.63
Brigham, Jeff	R-R	6-0	200	2-16-92	3	2	4.46	32	0	0	1	38	36	20	19	8	14	39	.248	.220	.267	9.16	3.29
Chen, Wei-Yin	R-L	6-0	200	7-21-85	0	1	6.59	45	0	0	0	68	87	54	50	15	18	63	.311	.301	.316	8.30	2.37
Conley, Adam	L-L	6-3	200	5-24-90	2	11	6.53	60	0	0	2	61	76	45	44	10	29	53	.308	.336	.286	7.86	4.30
Dugger, Robert	R-R	6-2	180	7-3-95	0	4	5.77	7	7	0	0	34	33	26	22	6	17	25	.254	.300	.214	6.55	4.46
Gallen, Zac	R-R	6-2	191	8-3-95	1	3	2.72	7	7	0	0	36	25	12	11	3	18	43	.191	.162	.222	10.65	4.46
2-team total (8 Arizona)					3	6	2.81	15	15	0	0	80	62	26	25	8	36	96	.212	.207	.217	10.80	4.05
Garcia, Jarlin	L-L	6-3	215	1-18-93	4	2	3.02	53	0	0	0	51	40	17	17	4	16	39	.216	.247	.194	6.93	2.84
Guerrero, Tayron	R-R	6-8	210	1-9-91	1	2	6.26	52	0	0	0	46	42	34	32	7	36	43	.246	.264	.232	8.41	7.04
Hernandez, Elieser	R-R	6-0	210	5-3-95	3	5	5.03	21	15	0	0	82	76	49	46	20	26	85	.242	.260	.226	9.29	2.84
Holaday, Bryan	R-R	6-0	214	11-19-87	0	0	0.00	1	0	0	0	0	0	0	0	0	0	0	.000	--	.000	0.00	0.00
Keller, Kyle	R-R	6-4	200	4-28-93	0	0	3.38	10	0	0	0	11	5	4	4	3	8	11	.139	.000	.115	9.28	6.75
Kinley, Tyler	R-R	6-4	205	1-31-91	3	1	3.65	52	0	0	1	49	43	20	20	5	36	46	.238	.243	.234	8.39	6.57
Lopez, Pablo	L-R	6-3	200	3-7-96	5	8	5.09	21	21	0	0	111	111	64	63	15	27	95	.261	.303	.217	7.68	2.18
Moran, Brian	L-L	6-4	230	9-30-88	1	0	4.26	10	0	0	0	6	6	3	3	1	2	10	.250	.182	.308	14.21	2.84
Noesi, Hector	R-R	6-3	205	1-26-87	0	1	8.46	12	4	0	0	28	30	26	26	7	14	24	.280	.227	.318	7.81	4.55
Quijada, Jose	L-L	5-11	203	11-9-95	2	3	5.76	34	0	0	1	30	27	20	19	10	26	44	.239	.260	.222	13.35	7.89
Richards, Trevor	R-R	6-2	190	5-15-93	3	12	4.50	23	20	0	0	112	104	56	56	16	51	103	.248	.271	.231	8.28	4.10
Romo, Sergio	R-R	5-11	185	3-4-83	2	1	3.58	38	0	0	17	38	34	18	15	4	13	33	.236	.277	.200	7.88	3.11
Smith, Caleb	R-L	6-2	205	7-28-91	10	11	4.52	28	28	0	0	153	128	82	77	33	60	168	.223	.211	.227	9.86	3.52
Smith, Josh D.	L-L	6-3	200	10-11-89	0	0	8.31	6	0	0	0	4	3	4	4	0	3	2	.188	.286	.111	4.15	6.23
Stanek, Ryne	R-R	6-4	225	7-26-91	0	2	5.48	22	0	0	1	21	17	15	13	4	19	28	.215	.167	.256	11.81	8.02
Steckenrider, Drew	R-R	6-5	215	1-10-91	0	2	6.28	15	0	0	0	14	9	10	10	6	5	14	.173	.130	.207	8.79	3.14
Urena, Jose	R-R	6-2	200	9-12-91	4	10	5.21	24	13	0	3	85	99	53	49	13	26	62	.293	.319	.270	6.59	2.76
Yamamoto, Jordan	R-R	6-0	185	5-11-96	4	5	4.46	15	15	0	0	79	54	42	39	11	36	82	.192	.152	.223	9.38	4.12

Fielding

Catcher	PCT	G	PO	A	E	DP	PB
Alfaro	.989	118	930	55	11	8	11
Castillo	1.000	2	20	0	0	0	0
Heineman	1.000	2	26	1	0	0	0
Holaday	.997	38	288	16	1	1	1
Wallach	.993	14	132	7	1	1	1

First Base	PCT	G	PO	A	E	DP
Alfaro	.000	1	0	0	0	0
Cooper	.994	73	444	37	3	39
Dean	1.000	5	27	2	0	3
O'Brien	1.000	1	3	0	0	0
Prado	1.000	40	237	15	0	29
Rivera	1.000	4	22	4	0	3
Rojas	1.000	6	10	0	0	2
Walker	.996	69	441	34	2	45

Second Base	PCT	G	PO	A	E	DP
Castro	.979	117	177	249	9	63
Diaz	.952	48	71	106	9	21
Herrera	1.000	1	1	0	0	0
Rivera	1.000	2	3	0	0	0
Rojas	1.000	3	3	2	0	1
Walker	.000	1	0	0	0	0

Third Base	PCT	G	PO	A	E	DP
Anderson	.977	67	47	126	4	14
Berti	1.000	20	4	30	0	2
Castro	.963	45	27	76	4	8
Herrera	.000	1	0	0	0	0
Marrero	1.000	1	0	1	0	0
Prado	.936	22	16	28	3	5
Rivera	.923	8	2	10	1	1
Walker	.974	26	16	21	1	2

Shortstop	PCT	G	PO	A	E	DP
Berti	.981	32	43	62	2	16
Castro	1.000	3	2	3	0	0
Herrera	1.000	1	0	4	0	2
Marrero	1.000	2	1	2	0	1
Riddle	.917	12	9	13	2	1
Rivera	.833	8	2	3	1	0
Rojas	.977	125	178	287	11	74

Outfield	PCT	G	PO	A	E	DP
Anderson	.972	55	97	9	3	1
Berti	.979	28	46	1	1	0
Brinson	.970	70	157	5	5	2
Cooper	1.000	31	58	4	0	1
Dean	.947	49	69	3	4	0
Galloway	1.000	16	32	1	0	1
Granderson	1.000	89	139	3	0	0
Herrera	.978	48	45	0	1	0
O'Brien	.938	14	14	1	1	0
Puello	.987	28	74	3	1	0
Ramirez	.996	110	252	0	1	0
Riddle	1.000	31	60	3	0	1
Rivera	1.000	4	6	1	0	0
Sierra	1.000	14	23	2	0	1

NEW ORLEANS BABY CAKES

PACIFIC COAST LEAGUE

TRIPLE-A

Batting	B-T	HT	WT	DOB	AVG	vLH	vRH	G	AB	R	H	2B	3B	HR	RBI	BB	HBP	SH	SF	SO	SB	CS	SLG	OBP
Alvarez, Eddy	B-R	5-9	180	1-30-90	.323	.284	.344	66	235	45	76	18	2	12	43	30	4	1	1	53	12	3	.570	.407
Berti, Jon	R-R	5-10	195	1-22-90	.290	.188	.326	22	62	14	18	1	0	4	8	15	1	0	1	11	5	0	.500	.430
Brinson, Lewis	R-R	6-3	195	5-8-94	.270	.281	.266	81	296	56	80	15	4	16	56	32	10	0	0	100	16	5	.510	.361
Brown, Micah	R-R	6-2	200	5-9-96	.174	.167	.177	20	46	4	8	3	0	1	3	3	0	0	0	13	1	0	.304	.225
Castillo, Wilkin	B-R	6-0	215	6-1-84	.250	.191	.278	58	196	23	49	9	2	6	24	16	1	1	0	30	5	1	.408	.310
Dean, Austin	R-R	6-1	190	10-14-93	.337	.308	.348	73	252	48	85	19	1	18	57	28	0	0	2	52	4	3	.635	.401
Diaz, Isan	L-R	5-10	185	5-27-96	.305	.286	.315	102	377	89	115	21	2	26	70	49	7	2	0	96	5	4	.578	.395
Fleming, Billy	R-R	6-1	210	9-20-92	.235	.273	.222	37	85	9	20	4	0	2	4	12	1	1	0	25	0	0	.353	.333
Galloway, Isaac	R-R	6-2	205	10-10-89	.223	.310	.189	32	103	19	23	5	0	7	16	2	2	1	0	41	3	1	.476	.252
Guerrero, Gabriel	R-R	6-3	215	12-11-93	.253	.267	.248	105	324	43	82	17	0	11	48	7	2	0	3	97	5	4	.407	.271
Harrison, Monte	R-R	6-3	220	8-10-95	.274	.327	.258	56	215	41	59	7	2	9	24	25	3	0	1	73	20	2	.451	.357
Heineman, Tyler	B-R	5-11	205	6-19-91	.342	.346	.339	48	164	26	56	12	2	10	25	12	3	3	0	21	4	0	.622	.397
2-team total (25 Reno)					.336	.333	.337	73	244	42	82	17	3	13	38	21	5	3	0	35	4	0	.590	.400
Herrera, Rosell	B-R	6-3	195	10-16-92	.309	.405	.276	48	165	21	51	11	1	5	24	14	1	0	0	32	2	1	.479	.367
Holaday, Bryan	R-R	6-0	214	11-19-87	.247	.214	.253	35	93	8	23	7	0	2	12	17	5	1	2	12	1	1	.387	.385
Marrero, Deven	R-R	6-0	190	8-25-90	.245	.352	.204	112	383	55	94	16	2	15	42	43	1	3	1	100	10	1	.415	.322
Millan, J.C.	R-R	6-0	185	1-18-96	.400	.250	.500	7	10	0	4	2	0	0	1	0	1	0	1	3	0	0	.600	.417
O'Brien, Peter	R-R	6-4	235	7-15-90	.220	.217	.220	75	255	41	56	8	0	17	45	36	0	0	0	107	0	1	.451	.316
Puello, Cesar	R-R	6-2	220	4-1-91	.071	.000	.077	4	14	0	1	0	0	0	2	1	1	0	0	3	0	0	.071	.188
2-team total (43 Salt Lake)					.275	.222	.292	47	149	25	41	7	0	7	29	23	11	0	0	40	2	1	.463	.410
Ramirez, Harold	R-R	5-10	220	9-6-94	.355	.367	.350	31	110	19	39	12	1	4	14	6	4	0	0	19	1	1	.591	.408
Riddle, JT	L-R	6-1	180	10-12-91	.240	.136	.263	32	121	22	29	11	1	4	19	6	1	1	2	20	3	0	.438	.277
Rivera, Yadiel	R-R	6-3	185	5-2-92	.293	.258	.303	82	300	38	88	11	1	14	46	6	2	2	2	81	15	6	.477	.310
Rojas, Miguel	R-R	5-11	195	2-24-89	.364	.500	.333	3	11	1	4	1	0	1	1	1	0	0	0	0	0	0	.727	.417
Sanchez, Jesus	L-R	6-3	230	10-7-97	.246	.308	.231	17	65	11	16	1	0	4	9	9	1	1	2	15	0	0	.446	.338
Santos, Jhonny	R-R	6-0	160	10-2-96	.200	--	.200	2	5	0	1	1	0	0	0	0	0	0	0	1	0	0	.400	.200
Sierra, Magneuris	L-L	5-11	160	4-7-96	.271	.269	.272	81	336	56	91	11	7	6	21	15	1	0	0	58	26	10	.399	.304
Snyder, Matt	L-R	6-5	230	6-17-90	.270	.235	.275	51	148	15	40	10	0	5	32	13	7	0	2	39	1	1	.439	.353
Solarte, Yangervis	B-R	5-11	205	7-3-87	.314	.200	.361	15	51	7	16	2	1	1	9	3	0	0	1	7	0	0	.451	.346
Vigil, Rodrigo	R-R	6-0	165	1-3-93	.150	.143	.152	15	40	2	6	0	0	0	2	3	1	1	0	6	1	0	.150	.227
Wallach, Chad	R-R	6-3	230	11-4-91	.200	--	.200	2	5	2	1	0	0	0	0	1	1	0	0	3	0	0	.200	.429

Pitching	B-T	HT	WT	DOB	W	L	ERA	G	GS	CG	SV	IP	H	R	ER	HR	BB	SO	AVG	vLH	vRH	K/9	BB/9
Alvarez, R.J.	R-R	6-2	225	6-8-91	2	8	4.70	50	0	0	15	54	46	36	28	12	28	65	.235	.267	.215	10.90	4.70
Beggs, Dustin	R-R	6-3	180	6-14-93	6	4	4.86	13	13	0	0	74	81	41	40	13	26	55	.285	.284	.286	6.69	3.16
Brigham, Jeff	R-R	6-0	200	2-16-92	0	1	1.50	17	0	0	2	24	9	5	4	0	8	30	.115	.059	.159	11.25	3.00
Bugg, Parker	R-R	6-6	210	10-26-94	3	4	7.68	24	0	0	1	36	38	32	31	9	21	40	.270	.362	.223	9.91	5.20
Dugger, Robert	R-R	6-2	180	7-3-95	2	4	7.59	10	10	0	0	53	74	49	45	12	17	49	.332	.325	.336	8.27	2.87
Eveld, Tommy	R-R	6-5	195	12-30-93	1	4	7.71	18	0	0	1	23	24	24	20	9	13	24	.267	.136	.309	9.26	5.01
Ferrell, Riley	R-R	6-2	200	10-18-93	0	0	1.35	4	0	0	0	7	3	1	1	0	4	4	.130	.182	.083	5.40	5.40
2-team total (7 Round Rock)					0	0	5.52	11	0	0	1	15	13	9	9	1	10	15	.232	.273	.206	9.20	6.14
Gallen, Zac	R-R	6-2	191	8-3-95	9	1	1.77	14	14	1	0	91	48	21	18	10	17	112	.153	.121	.174	11.04	1.68
Garcia, Jarlin	L-L	6-3	215	1-18-93	2	0	1.93	7	0	0	0	9	6	2	2	1	4	11	.188	.000	.375	10.61	3.86
Graves, Brett	R-R	6-1	170	1-30-93	3	1	3.63	13	0	0	5	17	12	8	7	3	10	21	.197	.111	.233	10.90	5.19
Guerrero, Tayron	R-R	6-8	210	1-9-91	0	0	20.25	1	0	0	0	1	4	4	3	0	1	1	.571	.667	.500	6.75	6.75

				W	L	ERA	G	GS	CG	SV	IP	H	R	ER	HR	BB	SO	AVG	vLH	vRH	BB/9	SO/9
Gunkel, Joe	R-R	6-5 225	12-30-91	8	2	3.80	19	15	0	1	88	91	41	37	11	15	61	.268	.268	.269	6.26	1.54
Hernandez, Elieser	R-R	6-0 210	5-3-95	3	1	1.13	9	9	0	0	48	35	8	6	0	14	69	.194	.212	.184	12.94	2.63
Keller, Kyle	R-R	6-4 200	4-28-93	2	3	4.50	37	0	0	10	54	44	31	27	8	21	73	.218	.164	.244	12.17	3.50
Kickham, Mike	L-L	6-4 220	12-12-88	5	5	4.27	31	13	0	0	86	89	46	41	10	36	84	.264	.262	.265	8.76	3.75
Kinley, Jeff	L-L	6-1 195	2-15-92	0	0	11.48	8	0	0	0	13	26	17	17	4	6	11	.419	.455	.400	7.43	4.05
Kinley, Tyler	R-R	6-4 205	1-31-91	0	1	1.72	14	0	0	2	16	4	3	3	1	7	19	.082	.083	.081	10.91	4.02
Lee, Dylan	L-L	6-4 210	8-1-94	1	3	4.71	13	0	0	0	21	28	14	11	3	9	24	.329	.304	.339	10.29	3.86
Lopez, Pablo	L-R	6-3 200	3-7-96	0	0	1.93	2	2	0	0	9	10	3	2	0	3	10	.278	.294	.263	9.64	2.89
Mahoney, Kolton	R-R	6-1 195	5-20-92	2	1	3.74	4	3	0	0	22	22	9	9	3	5	23	.268	.265	.271	9.55	2.08
Meyer, Ben	L-R	6-6 203	1-30-93	3	5	7.43	14	14	0	0	63	67	53	52	14	39	63	.279	.255	.295	9.00	5.57
2-team total (3 Albuquerque)				3	6	7.45	17	17	0	0	74	82	62	61	16	43	76	.286	.291	.282	9.29	5.25
Milbrath, Jordan	R-R	6-6 215	8-1-91	1	2	4.50	26	1	0	1	52	51	34	26	8	22	56	.255	.261	.252	9.69	3.81
Moran, Brian	L-L	6-4 230	9-30-88	2	3	3.15	43	1	0	0	60	45	25	21	6	26	77	.207	.086	.252	11.55	3.90
Neidert, Nick	R-R	6-1 202	11-20-96	3	4	5.05	9	9	0	0	41	45	25	23	4	22	37	.280	.175	.347	8.12	4.83
Noesi, Hector	R-R	6-3 205	1-26-87	11	4	3.82	21	21	0	0	125	112	54	53	27	30	133	.240	.228	.248	9.58	2.16
Poteet, Cody	R-R	6-1 190	7-30-94	2	3	5.68	10	10	0	0	52	55	33	33	13	19	34	.319	.294	.331	5.85	3.27
Quijada, Jose	L-L	5-11 203	11-9-95	1	0	4.30	22	0	0	4	29	27	18	14	5	12	35	.237	.297	.208	10.74	3.68
Roeder, Josh	R-R	6-0 175	12-2-92	0	1	5.93	3	3	0	0	14	20	9	9	5	4	9	.351	.320	.375	5.93	2.63
Stevens, Tyler	R-R	6-0 215	4-4-96	1	0	4.41	9	0	0	0	16	14	8	8	4	7	14	.241	.185	.290	7.71	3.86
Urena, Jose	R-R	6-2 200	9-12-91	0	0	0.00	2	0	0	0	2	2	3	0	1	0	2	.250	.000	.400	10.80	0.00

Fielding

Catcher	PCT	G	PO	A	E	DP	PB
Castillo	.986	53	481	24	7	3	2
Heineman	.995	44	376	27	2	2	5
Holaday	1.000	34	315	20	0	2	1
Vigil	.981	12	94	10	2	0	1
Wallach	1.000	2	7	1	0	0	0

First Base	PCT	G	PO	A	E	DP
Brown	1.000	1	6	0	0	1
Dean	.988	26	162	9	2	25
Fleming	1.000	14	83	8	0	6
Guerrero	.984	9	57	6	1	5
Heineman	1.000	3	16	1	0	1
Marrero	.955	6	19	2	1	3
O'Brien	.984	45	287	16	5	32
Rivera	1.000	9	39	1	0	4
Snyder	.983	42	261	21	5	27
Solarte	1.000	6	45	3	0	6

Second Base	PCT	G	PO	A	E	DP
Alvarez	1.000	10	15	13	0	2
Brown	1.000	1	2	1	0	0

	PCT	G	PO	A	E	DP
Diaz	.978	99	180	217	9	65
Herrera	.953	11	21	20	2	9
Marrero	.972	11	18	17	1	6
Riddle	1.000	1	0	4	0	2
Rivera	.963	14	23	29	2	10

Third Base	PCT	G	PO	A	E	DP
Alvarez	.924	33	28	57	7	5
Berti	.947	9	8	10	1	0
Brown	1.000	2	0	4	0	1
Fleming	.947	10	4	14	1	1
Herrera	.957	21	13	32	2	3
Marrero	.947	43	32	76	6	8
Millan	1.000	3	0	2	0	0
Riddle	.000	1	0	0	0	0
Rivera	.894	24	14	28	5	4
Solarte	1.000	5	3	6	0	2

Shortstop	PCT	G	PO	A	E	DP
Alvarez	.975	19	34	45	2	16
Berti	.941	5	5	11	1	3
Brown	.826	9	7	12	4	3
Herrera	1.000	2	2	2	0	2

Marrero	.968	50	47	137	6	32
Riddle	.955	23	25	59	4	9
Rivera	.969	35	36	91	4	16
Rojas	1.000	3	3	6	0	0

Outfield	PCT	G	PO	A	E	DP
Alvarez	.667	1	2	0	1	0
Berti	1.000	7	8	1	0	1
Brinson	.979	77	179	6	4	1
Dean	.984	33	59	4	1	0
Galloway	1.000	28	49	2	0	0
Guerrero	.970	79	120	9	4	2
Harrison	.969	51	91	4	3	1
Herrera	1.000	14	21	0	0	0
Millan	.000	1	0	0	0	0
O'Brien	.973	21	32	4	1	1
Puello	1.000	4	9	0	0	0
Ramirez	1.000	23	35	1	0	0
Riddle	1.000	8	13	1	0	1
Rivera	1.000	4	3	0	0	0
Sanchez	1.000	16	33	4	0	1
Santos	1.000	1	1	0	0	0
Sierra	.972	77	138	3	4	0

JACKSONVILLE JUMBO SHRIMP   DOUBLE-A
SOUTHERN LEAGUE

Batting	B-T	HT	WT	DOB	AVG	vLH	vRH	G	AB	R	H	2B	3B	HR	RBI	BB	HBP	SH	SF	SO	SB	CS	SLG	OBP
Alonso, Lazaro	L-R	6-3	220	12-17-94	.147	.000	.172	13	34	6	5	0	0	1	2	4	0	0	0	11	0	0	.235	.237
Alvarez, Eddy	B-R	5-9	180	1-30-90	.333	--	.333	1	3	0	1	0	0	0	0	0	1	0	0	1	0	0	.333	.500
Bird, Corey	L-L	6-1	185	8-11-95	.232	.259	.221	95	298	26	69	6	2	3	29	20	3	1	1	51	15	3	.295	.286
Brigman, Bryson	R-R	5-11	180	6-19-95	.250	.192	.275	98	312	25	78	17	1	2	24	36	4	4	1	62	2	3	.330	.334
Chavez, Santiago	R-R	5-11	175	8-5-95	.173	.182	.169	79	248	17	43	5	0	1	16	18	2	4	0	84	0	0	.206	.235
Chisholm, Jazz	L-R	5-11	165	2-1-98	.284	.290	.280	23	81	6	23	4	2	3	10	11	2	0	0	24	3	0	.494	.383
2-team total (89 Jackson)					.220	.207	.226	112	395	57	87	10	7	21	54	52	8	3		147	16	4	.441	.321
Diaz, Lewin	L-L	6-4	225	11-19-96	.200	.119	.247	31	115	16	23	6	0	8	14	11	2	0	1	28	0	1	.461	.279
2-team total (33 Pensacola)					.253	.227	.268	64	241	28	61	22	1	14	40	19	3	0	4	51	0	1	.527	.311
Dunand, Joe	R-R	6-2	205	9-20-95	.242	.246	.241	130	462	44	112	25	1	5	42	38	15	0	10	119	2	1	.333	.314
Fleming, Billy	R-R	6-1	210	9-20-92	.344	.467	.304	18	61	14	21	5	0	2	8	1	0	1	0	16	0	0	.525	.423
Garrett, Stone	R-R	6-2	195	11-22-95	.243	.202	.262	119	412	55	100	20	4	14	63	18	9	0	0	126	15	7	.413	.289
Guerrero, Gabriel	R-R	6-3	215	12-11-93	.257	.462	.136	9	35	5	9	1	1	0	3	0	0	0	0	7	0	0	.343	.257
Lopez, B.J.	R-R	5-9	185	9-29-94	.194	.333	.167	12	36	4	7	0	0	0	1	3	0	0	0	6	0	0	.194	.256
Mahan, Riley	L-R	6-3	185	12-31-95	.222	.205	.227	61	207	21	46	11	1	6	30	8	3	2	2	62	0	0	.372	.259
Mesa, Victor Victor	R-R	5-10	165	7-20-96	.178	.265	.137	27	107	8	19	2	0	0	3	3	0	3	0	16	3	0	.196	.200
Millan, J.C.	R-R	6-0	185	1-18-96	.268	.236	.283	84	269	27	72	13	0	5	34	21	1	0	1	47	1	3	.372	.322
Miller, Brian	L-R	6-1	186	8-20-95	.265	.271	.262	120	449	52	119	24	5	2	39	37	5	1	3	81	22	9	.354	.326
Nieto, Adrian	B-R	5-10	205	11-12-89	.170	.222	.160	18	59	4	10	0	0	2	5	4	0	1	1	12	1	0	.271	.219
Prado, Martin	R-R	6-0	215	10-27-83	.200	.333	.000	3	5	1	1	0	0	0	0	5	1	0	0	2	1	0	.200	.636
Seymour, Anfernee	B-R	5-11	165	6-24-95	.261	.279	.254	103	276	30	72	13	2	1	28	20	2	4	1	85	17	7	.333	.314
Sierra, Magneuris	L-L	5-11	160	4-7-96	.282	.282	.282	48	181	21	51	8	2	1	7	13	2	1	0	32	7	1	.365	.337
Silviano, John	L-R	5-11	190	7-11-94	.151	.133	.156	65	205	16	31	9	0	4	14	20	1	0	1	81	0	0	.254	.229
Twine, Justin	R-R	5-11	205	10-7-95	.240	.260	.232	105	359	34	86	12	4	1	32	24	6	0	3	93	6	5	.304	.296
Vigil, Rodrigo	R-R	6-0	165	1-3-93	.207	.167	.217	38	116	9	24	3	0	1	11	6	5	1	0	24	2	0	.259	.276

MIAMI MARLINS

Pitching	B-T	HT	WT	DOB	W	L	ERA	G	GS	CG	SV	IP	H	R	ER	HR	BB	SO	AVG	vLH	vRH	K/9	BB/9
Aiello, Vincenzo	R-R	6-2	220	8-6-94	1	1	1.45	15	0	0	0	19	8	4	3	1	4	25	.127	.111	.139	12.05	1.93
Araujo, Elvis	L-L	6-7	275	7-15-91	2	1	7.64	19	0	0	0	18	19	16	15	6	15	25	.260	.167	.306	12.74	7.64
Beggs, Dustin	R-R	6-3	180	6-14-93	1	0	2.79	3	2	0	0	10	12	3	3	1	4	5	.324	.235	.400	4.66	3.72
Bugg, Parker	R-R	6-6	210	10-26-94	1	1	2.38	17	0	0	0	23	10	7	6	3	6	35	.128	.100	.146	13.90	2.38
Cabrera, Edward	R-R	6-4	175	4-13-98	4	1	2.56	8	8	0	0	39	28	12	11	6	13	43	.200	.197	.203	10.01	3.03
Carter, C.J.	R-R	6-0	165	5-27-97	0	1	45.00	1	0	0	0	1	4	5	5	2	2	2	.667	.750	.500	18.00	18.00
Castano, Daniel	L-L	6-4	230	9-17-94	7	2	3.35	18	11	1	0	86	82	34	32	2	16	73	.247	.287	.231	7.64	1.67
Dugger, Robert	R-R	6-2	180	7-3-95	6	6	3.31	13	13	0	0	71	57	31	26	6	21	73	.219	.241	.201	9.30	2.67
Eveld, Tommy	R-R	6-5	195	12-30-93	2	3	2.77	24	0	0	11	26	19	10	8	3	4	36	.207	.214	.200	12.46	1.38
Ferrell, Riley	R-R	6-2	200	10-18-93	0	0	0.00	2	0	0	0	3	0	0	0	0	2	3	.000	.000	.000	10.13	6.75
Garrett, Braxton	L-L	6-3	190	8-5-97	0	1	16.20	1	1	0	0	2	4	4	3	0	3	1	.444	.500	.429	5.40	16.20
Graves, Brett	R-R	6-1	170	1-30-93	2	4	2.20	32	0	0	3	45	27	15	11	3	21	52	.172	.141	.198	10.40	4.20
Guerrero, Jordan	L-L	6-3	195	5-31-94	1	0	1.50	7	0	0	0	12	6	3	2	1	6	12	.150	.167	.143	9.00	4.50
Guzman, Jorge	R-R	6-2	182	1-28-96	7	11	3.50	25	24	1	0	139	96	54	54	13	71	127	.201	.188	.214	8.24	4.61
Keller, Kyle	R-R	6-4	200	4-28-93	0	0	0.00	2	0	0	1	3	1	0	0	0	0	4	.100	.000	.167	12.00	0.00
Kinley, Jeff	L-L	6-1	195	2-15-92	0	0	2.93	25	0	0	2	31	27	12	10	1	13	42	.237	.146	.288	12.33	3.82
Lee, Dylan	L-L	6-4	210	8-1-94	0	3	1.91	32	0	0	13	38	23	9	8	4	12	32	.176	.286	.124	7.65	2.87
Lopez, Pablo	L-R	6-3	200	3-7-96	0	3	21.60	3	3	0	0	5	13	12	12	3	4	6	.464	.462	.467	10.80	7.20
Mahoney, Kolton	R-R	6-1	195	5-20-92	4	4	3.19	27	9	0	1	87	75	34	31	4	33	85	.231	.206	.249	8.76	3.40
Mateo, Alejandro	R-R	6-2	200	1-18-94	1	0	2.63	20	0	0	0	27	19	8	8	2	12	23	.196	.182	.208	7.57	3.95
Milbrath, Jordan	R-R	6-6	215	8-1-91	1	1	1.32	10	0	0	1	14	9	2	2	0	4	16	.192	.222	.172	10.54	2.63
Mills, McKenzie	L-L	6-4	205	11-19-95	1	8	5.36	28	9	0	2	84	90	54	50	14	32	74	.275	.269	.278	7.93	3.43
Poteet, Cody	R-R	6-1	190	7-30-94	5	3	2.25	13	13	0	0	84	63	23	21	3	19	58	.211	.181	.240	6.21	2.04
Roeder, Josh	R-R	6-0	175	12-2-92	1	4	3.33	16	6	0	0	49	40	21	18	5	22	40	.221	.309	.150	7.40	4.07
Rogers, Trevor	L-L	6-6	185	11-13-97	1	2	4.50	5	5	0	0	26	25	13	13	3	9	28	.250	.310	.225	9.69	3.12
Sanchez, Sixto	R-R	6-0	185	7-29-98	8	4	2.53	18	18	0	0	103	87	33	29	5	19	97	.225	.253	.196	8.48	1.66
Smith, Caleb	R-L	6-2	205	7-28-91	0	0	5.79	2	2	0	0	9	7	6	6	4	2	19	.200	.273	.167	18.32	1.93
Smith, Chad	R-R	6-4	200	6-8-95	2	1	4.42	14	0	0	0	18	19	10	9	3	9	23	.257	.292	.240	11.29	4.42
Stevens, Tyler	R-R	6-0	215	4-4-96	3	1	2.29	27	0	0	2	39	26	11	10	2	11	45	.188	.175	.198	10.30	2.52
Urena, Jose	R-R	6-2	200	9-12-91	0	0	0.00	2	1	0	0	3	1	0	0	0	1	1	.100	.000	.000	3.38	3.38
Vesia, Alex	L-L	6-2	195	4-11-96	2	0	0.00	9	0	0	1	16	8	0	0	0	1	25	.154	.118	.171	13.78	0.55
Yamamoto, Jordan	R-R	6-0	185	5-11-96	3	5	3.58	12	12	0	0	65	53	27	26	7	25	64	.223	.227	.220	8.82	3.44

Fielding

Catcher	PCT	G	PO	A	E	DP	PB
Chavez	.993	78	668	67	5	4	5
Lopez	.978	12	80	8	2	1	1
Nieto	1.000	17	164	6	0	0	1
Vigil	.990	38	288	20	3	4	2

First Base	PCT	G	PO	A	E	DP
Alonso	.964	7	52	1	2	5
Chavez	1.000	2	3	0	0	0
Diaz	.995	30	207	13	1	13
Fleming	.990	14	89	8	1	10
Guerrero	.941	3	15	1	1	0
Millan	.986	32	203	15	3	13
Prado	1.000	2	11	1	0	2
Silviano	.994	58	450	24	3	36

Second Base	PCT	G	PO	A	E	DP
Alvarez	1.000	1	3	1	0	1
Brigman	.987	46	69	84	2	21
Mahan	.973	48	71	107	5	25
Millan	.000	1	0	0	0	0
Twine	.995	49	69	113	1	16

Third Base	PCT	G	PO	A	E	DP
Dunand	.955	57	51	99	7	11
Millan	.947	41	36	54	5	5
Prado	1.000	1	0	2	0	0
Twine	.929	46	23	81	8	5

Shortstop	PCT	G	PO	A	E	DP
Brigman	.970	50	50	112	5	16
Chisholm	1.000	22	20	44	0	6
Dunand	.964	70	91	148	9	28

Outfield	PCT	G	PO	A	E	DP
Bird	.988	80	157	3	2	0
Garrett	.980	100	190	10	4	3
Guerrero	1.000	5	9	0	0	0
Mesa	1.000	26	76	3	0	2
Millan	1.000	4	3	0	0	0
Miller	.995	97	178	8	1	3
Seymour	.961	74	117	6	5	1
Sierra	.989	40	86	7	1	3
Twine	.000	1	0	0	0	0

JUPITER HAMMERHEADS   HIGH CLASS A
FLORIDA STATE LEAGUE

Batting	B-T	HT	WT	DOB	AVG	vLH	vRH	G	AB	R	H	2B	3B	HR	RBI	BB	HBP	SH	SF	SO	SB	CS	SLG	OBP
Alonso, Lazaro	L-R	6-3	220	12-17-94	.294	.238	.304	114	385	40	113	21	0	11	57	61	3	0	1	105	0	1	.434	.393
Alvarez, Eddy	B-R	5-9	180	1-30-90	.333	--	.333	3	9	3	3	0	0	0	1	1	0	1	0	0	0	0	.333	.400
Arcaya, Luis	R-R	6-1	170	2-26-99	.100	.000	.143	4	10	0	1	0	0	0	0	1	0	0	0	5	0	0	.100	.182
Baranek, Cameron	L-L	5-10	195	2-20-95	.168	.100	.180	38	131	11	22	6	0	0	10	8	2	0	0	44	6	1	.214	.227
Bird, Corey	L-L	6-1	185	8-11-95	.167	.000	.200	2	6	0	1	0	0	0	0	0	0	0	0	1	0	0	.167	.167
Bleday, JJ	L-L	6-3	205	11-10-97	.257	.192	.272	38	140	13	36	8	0	3	19	11	0	0	0	29	0	3	.379	.311
Brigman, Bryson	R-R	5-11	180	6-19-95	.267	.231	.274	20	75	11	20	3	0	0	4	8	2	1	1	11	2	0	.307	.349
Brown, Micah	R-R	6-2	200	5-9-96	.230	.243	.227	61	187	25	43	8	1	5	20	20	2	3	2	57	5	4	.364	.308
Castro, Samuel	B-R	5-10	160	10-16-97	.000	.000	.000	2	4	0	0	0	0	0	0	1	1	0	0	2	0	0	.000	.333
Cooper, Garrett	R-R	6-6	230	12-25-90	.539	.500	.546	5	13	1	7	2	0	1	3	0	0	0	0	6	0	0	.923	.625
Devers, Jose	L-R	6-0	155	12-7-99	.325	.222	.333	33	126	13	41	3	1	0	3	8	4	0	0	20	5	0	.365	.384
Dinicola, Harrison	L-R	6-0	195	4-28-97	.324	.833	.226	14	37	7	12	1	0	0	4	0	0	0	0	9	2	0	.351	.390
Donadio, Michael	L-R	6-0	195	4-23-95	.169	.154	.171	29	89	5	15	5	1	2	7	5	1	0	0	32	0	0	.315	.221
Encarnacion, Jerar	R-R	6-4	219	10-22-97	.253	.240	.256	67	253	27	64	10	1	6	28	17	0	0	2	71	3	2	.372	.298
Fortes, Nick	R-R	6-0	210	11-11-96	.217	.271	.205	76	263	22	57	11	2	3	29	25	5	0	4	49	1	1	.308	.293
Grant, Connor	R-R	6-3	195	11-15-96	.233	.269	.222	33	116	8	27	5	1	0	6	2	0	1	1	25	2	3	.293	.244
Harrison, Monte	R-R	6-3	220	8-10-95	.143	--	.143	2	7	2	1	0	0	0	0	0	0	0	0	1	3	0	.143	.143
Hernandez, Michael	R-R	5-10	195	5-24-95	.164	.125	.170	19	61	2	10	3	0	0	5	1	1	0	0	26	0	1	.213	.239
Lopez, B.J.	R-R	5-9	185	9-29-94	.161	.143	.164	28	87	3	14	1	0	0	4	1	1	1	1	19	1	0	.172	.204
Mahan, Riley	L-R	6-3	185	12-31-95	.279	.189	.298	60	215	25	60	9	1	5	19	25	5	2	1	72	3	1	.400	.366

	B-T	HT	WT	DOB	AVG	vLH	vRH	G	AB	R	H	2B	3B	HR	RBI	BB	HBP	SH	SF	SO	SB	CS	OBP	SLG
Mesa, Victor Victor	R-R	5-10	165	7-20-96	.252	.293	.244	89	357	37	90	5	3	0	26	19	5	4	5	48	15	2	.283	.295
Nelson, James	R-R	6-2	180	10-18-97	.228	.253	.223	121	429	36	98	13	2	4	36	30	3	1	7	89	5	3	.296	.279
Nieto, Adrian	B-R	5-10	205	11-12-89	.238	.000	.294	7	21	3	5	2	0	0	2	1	0	0	0	4	0	0	.333	.273
O'Brien, Peter	R-R	6-4	235	7-15-90	.250	--	.250	1	4	0	1	0	0	0	0	0	0	0	0	1	0	0	.250	.250
Pompey, Tristan	B-R	6-4	200	3-23-97	.194	.120	.210	42	144	19	28	7	2	0	13	20	1	0	1	58	4	0	.271	.295
Prado, Martin	R-R	6-0	215	10-27-83	.444	1.000	.375	3	9	1	4	1	0	0	1	0	0	0	0	0	0	0	.556	.500
Puello, Cesar	R-R	6-2	220	4-1-91	.667	--	.667	1	3	0	2	0	0	0	1	0	0	0	0	0	0	0	.667	.667
Reyes, Angel	R-R	6-0	175	5-6-95	.244	.300	.232	36	115	18	28	9	0	2	15	8	1	0	1	32	1	0	.374	.296
Riddle, JT	L-R	6-1	180	10-12-91	.200	.500	.000	2	5	1	1	0	0	0	1	0	0	0	0	3	0	0	.200	.200
Rojas, Miguel	R-R	5-11	195	2-24-89	.143	--	.143	2	7	1	1	1	0	0	0	0	0	0	0	0	0	0	.286	.143
Santos, Jhonny	R-R	6-0	160	10-2-96	.241	.226	.245	55	174	25	42	8	0	4	19	20	3	2	3	43	12	3	.356	.325
Schubert, Gunnar	R-R	5-11	205	5-19-96	.188	.182	.190	57	154	11	29	6	1	0	14	17	4	2	2	41	0	2	.240	.283
Scott, Connor	L-L	6-4	180	10-8-99	.235	.214	.238	27	98	12	23	4	1	1	5	11	0	0	2	26	2	1	.327	.306
Scott, Zach	L-R	6-0	185	4-27-95	.333	--	.333	5	12	1	4	1	0	0	4	1	0	0	1	2	0	0	.417	.357
Sims, Demetrius	R-R	6-2	200	7-14-95	.254	.268	.250	62	197	23	50	16	1	4	24	18	9	1	3	64	4	6	.406	.339
Soto, Isael	L-L	6-0	190	11-2-96	.161	.154	.162	60	217	20	35	7	2	5	20	15	0	1	0	92	0	0	.281	.216
Sthormes, Andres	R-R	5-10	195	8-7-96	.333	--	.333	1	3	0	1	0	0	0	0	0	0	0	0	2	0	0	.333	.333
Twine, Justin	R-R	5-11	205	10-7-95	.385	.000	.500	4	13	1	5	0	0	0	4	0	0	0	0	6	1	1	.385	.385
Walker, Neil	B-R	6-3	210	9-10-85	.222	.000	.250	3	9	2	2	2	0	0	2	0	0	0	0	2	0	0	.444	.364
Wallach, Chad	R-R	6-3	230	11-4-91	.000	.000	.000	2	5	0	0	0	0	0	0	0	0	0	0	2	0	0	.000	.000

Pitching

	B-T	HT	WT	DOB	W	L	ERA	G	GS	CG	SV	IP	H	R	ER	HR	BB	SO	AVG	vLH	vRH	K/9	BB/9
Aiello, Vincenzo	R-R	6-2	220	8-6-94	3	2	3.38	22	0	0	1	35	32	17	13	4	16	41	.244	.250	.240	10.64	4.15
Alcala, Elkin	R-R	5-11	175	8-2-97	0	0	7.36	4	0	0	0	7	9	6	6	0	1	6	.300	.417	.222	7.36	1.23
Andrews, Tanner	R-R	6-3	220	11-15-95	0	0	0.00	1	0	0	0	0	0	0	0	0	0	1	.000	.000	--	0.00	13.50
Baird, Cam	R-R	6-2	195	5-15-96	0	0	0.00	1	0	0	0	1	0	0	0	0	1	2	.000	.000	.000	18.00	9.00
Beggs, Dustin	R-R	6-3	180	6-14-93	2	1	3.51	5	5	0	0	26	33	11	10	0	4	24	.306	.333	.271	8.42	1.40
Braley, Taylor	R-R	5-11	220	1-13-96	3	6	3.38	25	11	0	0	101	103	46	38	8	15	65	.261	.276	.248	5.77	1.33
Brice, Austin	R-R	6-4	235	6-19-92	0	0	1.59	4	1	0	0	6	3	1	1	0	0	9	.158	.091	.250	14.29	0.00
Cabrera, Edward	R-R	6-4	175	4-13-98	5	3	2.02	11	11	1	0	58	37	16	13	1	18	73	.183	.228	.146	11.33	2.79
Carter, C.J.	R-R	6-0	165	5-27-97	1	0	0.41	11	0	0	2	22	18	3	1	0	7	20	.225	.258	.204	8.18	2.86
Castano, Daniel	L-L	6-4	230	9-17-94	0	2	3.82	12	0	0	0	33	33	18	14	2	7	31	.252	.316	.226	8.45	1.91
Farnworth, Steven	R-R	6-2	175	9-6-93	0	0	15.00	4	0	0	0	6	15	10	10	1	3	6	.469	.500	.444	9.00	4.50
Ferrell, Riley	R-R	6-2	200	10-18-93	0	0	0.00	1	0	0	0	1	0	0	0	0	0	1	.000	.000	.000	9.00	0.00
Garrett, Braxton	L-L	6-3	190	8-5-97	6	6	3.34	20	20	0	0	105	92	49	39	13	37	118	.230	.231	.230	10.11	3.17
Grant, Connor	R-R	6-3	195	11-15-96	0	0	0.00	1	0	0	0	1	1	0	0	0	0	1	.250	.000	.500	9.00	0.00
Guenther, Sean	L-L	5-11	194	12-29-95	3	1	2.55	23	2	0	1	42	31	14	12	4	6	44	.198	.175	.213	9.35	1.28
Guerrero, Tayron	R-R	6-8	210	1-9-91	1	0	0.00	4	0	0	0	4	0	0	0	0	1	1	.000	.000	.000	2.25	2.25
Gunkel, Joe	R-R	6-5	225	12-30-91	0	0	0.00	2	0	0	0	5	1	0	0	0	1	7	.059	.000	.083	12.60	1.80
Hock, Colton	R-R	6-4	220	3-15-96	3	4	3.16	36	0	0	5	51	49	23	18	1	20	47	.253	.305	.202	8.24	3.51
Holloway, Jordan	R-R	6-6	215	6-13-96	4	11	4.45	21	21	2	0	95	77	53	47	6	66	93	.220	.228	.213	8.81	6.25
Jones, Tyler	R-R	6-3	200	12-7-95	1	2	2.33	9	4	0	0	27	23	8	7	2	8	26	.232	.241	.222	8.67	2.67
Leach, Kale	R-R	6-4	240	6-8-97	0	0	0.00	1	0	0	1	2	2	0	0	0	1	2	.286	.250	.333	9.00	4.50
Lindgren, Jeff	R-R	6-1	200	9-17-96	1	1	1.48	14	0	0	0	24	20	4	4	0	6	23	.227	.297	.177	8.51	2.22
Mateo, Alejandro	R-R	6-2	200	1-18-94	1	7	4.31	22	0	0	4	31	34	20	15	5	13	42	.279	.264	.290	12.06	3.73
McKenna, Brian	R-R	6-0	202	11-19-92	0	0	0.96	6	0	0	0	9	4	1	1	0	1	12	.182	.117	.188	11.57	0.96
Mejia, Humberto	R-R	6-3	175	3-3-97	0	1	2.28	5	4	0	0	24	15	6	6	2	5	21	.177	.154	.196	7.99	1.90
Neidert, Nick	R-R	6-1	200	11-20-96	0	1	4.82	2	2	0	0	9	10	5	5	1	4	6	.270	.304	.214	5.79	3.86
Roeder, Josh	R-R	6-0	175	12-2-92	0	0	1.74	9	1	0	1	21	16	5	4	0	2	17	.208	.147	.256	7.40	0.87
Rogers, Trevor	L-L	6-6	185	11-13-97	5	8	2.53	18	18	0	0	110	97	45	31	7	24	122	.232	.231	.232	9.95	1.96
Sanchez, Sixto	R-R	6-0	185	7-29-98	2	2	4.91	2	2	0	0	11	14	6	6	1	2	6	.318	.381	.261	4.91	1.64
Schiraldi, Lukas	R-R	6-6	210	7-25-93	0	1	7.36	4	0	0	0	4	5	5	3	0	4	5	.294	.143	.400	12.27	9.82
Sherrod, Cason	R-R	6-4	215	6-25-96	0	3	3.38	17	0	0	2	21	16	8	8	2	8	20	.200	.205	.195	8.44	3.38
Smith, Chad	R-R	6-4	200	6-8-95	1	1	4.63	20	0	0	6	23	15	15	12	0	15	23	.185	.281	.122	8.87	5.79
Steckenrider, Drew	R-R	6-5	215	1-10-91	0	0	0.00	1	1	0	0	1	1	0	0	0	0	0	.250	.500	.000	0.00	0.00
Stevens, Tyler	R-R	6-0	215	4-4-96	1	0	1.80	3	0	0	0	5	2	1	1	0	1	6	.125	.111	.143	10.80	1.80
Stewart, Will	L-L	6-2	175	7-14-97	6	12	5.43	23	21	3	0	129	137	86	78	13	42	96	.275	.255	.283	6.68	2.92
Urena, Jose	R-R	6-2	200	9-12-91	0	0	9.00	1	1	0	0	1	1	1	1	0	0	0	.333	.500	.000	0.00	0.00
Vallimont, Chris	R-R	6-2	220	3-18-97	2	3	3.50	6	0	0	0	36	31	15	14	3	11	42	.228	.207	.244	10.50	2.75
2-team total (4 Fort Myers)					4	5	3.55	10	10	0	0	58	46	24	23	3	15	70	.212	.200	.221	10.80	2.31
Vesia, Alex	L-L	6-2	195	4-11-96	4	0	1.93	10	0	0	1	19	12	4	4	2	1	24	.179	.269	.122	11.57	0.48

Fielding

Catcher

	PCT	G	PO	A	E	DP	PB
Arcaya	1.000	4	23	3	0	0	1
Fortes	.991	75	610	44	6	1	4
Hernandez	.987	19	134	22	2	1	3
Lopez	.996	28	244	23	1	2	3
Nieto	.981	7	45	7	1	0	0
Sthormes	1.000	1	13	1	0	0	2
Wallach	1.000	2	6	2	0	0	0
Dinicola	1.000	14	90	4	0	12	
Encarnacion	1.000	3	9	1	0	1	
O'Brien	1.000	1	8	0	0	0	
Prado	1.000	2	10	1	0	0	
Reyes	1.000	4	20	0	0	1	
Walker	1.000	1	4	0	0	0	

First Base

	PCT	G	PO	A	E	DP
Alonso	.983	99	773	60	14	58
Brown	.990	14	96	8	1	6
Cooper	1.000	1	8	0	0	1

Second Base

	PCT	G	PO	A	E	DP
Alvarez	.667	1	1	1	1	0
Brigman	1.000	3	8	5	0	1
Brown	.975	33	41	76	3	17
Mahan	.977	56	78	135	5	20
Reyes	.500	1	1	0	1	0
Riddle	1.000	1	1	0	0	0
Schubert	.965	32	38	72	4	14
Scott	1.000	5	8	8	0	2
Sims	1.000	5	6	11	0	0
Twine	1.000	3	3	13	0	2

Third Base

	PCT	G	PO	A	E	DP
Brown	.818	4	1	8	2	0
Nelson	.886	119	65	207	35	12
Prado	1.000	1	1	7	0	0
Schubert	.895	8	3	14	2	1
Twine	.500	1	1	0	1	1
Walker	1.000	2	2	2	0	0

Shortstop	PCT	G	PO	A	E	DP
Alvarez	1.000	2	4	10	0	0
Brigman	.889	17	20	36	7	3
Brown	.896	10	13	30	5	6
Castro	.857	2	2	4	1	2
Devers	.937	32	38	66	7	12
Riddle	1.000	1	1	1	0	0
Rojas	1.000	2	2	4	0	1
Schubert	.969	16	25	38	2	10
Sims	.976	57	72	135	5	27

Outfield	PCT	G	PO	A	E	DP
Baranek	.981	29	49	2	1	0
Bird	1.000	2	6	0	0	0
Bleday	1.000	32	41	4	0	1
Brown	1.000	1	1	0	0	0
Cooper	.500	4	1	0	1	0
Donadio	1.000	18	30	0	0	0
Encarnacion	.973	55	102	5	3	2
Grant	1.000	32	58	7	0	1
Harrison	1.000	1	2	0	0	0
Mesa	1.000	76	152	8	0	1
Pompey	1.000	30	41	1	0	0
Puello	1.000	1	3	0	0	0
Reyes	1.000	12	19	1	0	0
Santos	.984	49	121	0	2	0
Scott	1.000	24	48	0	0	0
Soto	.933	42	68	2	5	1

CLINTON LUMBERKINGS   LOW CLASS A
MIDWEST LEAGUE

Batting	B-T	HT	WT	DOB	AVG	vLH	vRH	G	AB	R	H	2B	3B	HR	RBI	BB	HBP	SH	SF	SO	SB	CS	SLG	OBP
Banfield, Will	R-R	6-0	200	11-18-99	.199	.230	.194	101	397	44	79	13	2	9	55	25	5	0	6	121	0	0	.310	.252
Bradshaw, Davis	L-R	6-3	175	4-25-98	.258	.240	.260	63	225	27	58	7	2	0	16	8	7	6	0	44	6	3	.307	.304
Burdick, Peyton	R-R	6-0	210	2-26-97	.307	.250	.316	63	238	57	73	20	3	10	59	32	12	0	5	67	6	6	.542	.408
Castro, Samuel	B-R	5-10	160	10-16-97	.194	.222	.188	55	165	19	32	6	1	0	8	20	1	5	1	62	9	5	.242	.283
Cespedes, Ricardo	L-L	6-1	205	8-24-97	.204	.105	.223	33	113	10	23	3	2	1	10	7	0	2	0	34	5	1	.292	.250
Devers, Jose	L-R	6-0	155	12-7-99	.455	--	.455	3	11	5	5	2	0	0	2	2	0	0	0	2	0	0	.636	.539
Donadio, Michael	L-R	6-0	195	4-23-95	.316	--	.316	5	19	2	6	2	0	1	5	2	0	0	0	7	0	0	.579	.381
Edwards, Evan	L-L	6-0	200	6-21-97	.285	.162	.306	68	256	32	73	14	1	8	48	28	3	0	1	74	3	0	.441	.361
Encarnacion, Jerar	R-R	6-4	219	10-22-97	.298	.250	.305	68	255	34	76	16	0	10	43	23	3	0	0	69	3	1	.478	.363
Grant, Connor	R-R	6-3	195	11-15-96	.211	.000	.308	6	19	1	4	0	0	0	2	2	0	0	0	7	1	2	.211	.286
Hernandez, Brayan	R-R	6-2	175	9-11-97	.121	.200	.107	20	66	5	8	2	2	0	4	1	0	1	2	27	1	0	.212	.130
Hollins, Bubba	R-R	6-1	200	12-6-95	.269	.231	.276	95	349	36	94	23	0	2	33	26	7	1	3	64	0	2	.352	.330
Jones, Thomas	R-R	6-4	195	12-9-97	.239	.190	.248	114	385	46	92	19	3	10	54	31	24	5	3	135	19	9	.382	.332
Misner, Kameron	L-L	6-4	210	1-8-98	.276	.238	.283	34	134	25	37	7	0	2	20	21	2	0	1	35	8	0	.373	.380
Osborne, J.D.	R-R	6-1	215	7-13-95	.258	.348	.242	85	310	44	80	18	0	10	52	18	11	0	5	83	3	0	.413	.317
Reynolds, Sean	L-R	6-7	237	4-19-98	.173	.194	.170	68	231	28	40	12	1	9	32	33	0	0	2	145	7	4	.351	.274
Rivera, Marcos	R-R	6-1	160	5-13-97	.206	.348	.182	94	321	37	66	13	0	8	31	16	1	0	3	136	4	2	.321	.243
Scott, Connor	L-L	6-4	180	10-8-99	.251	.255	.251	95	378	56	95	24	4	4	36	31	2	1	0	91	21	9	.368	.311
Scott, Zach	L-R	6-0	185	4-27-95	.185	.074	.205	54	178	13	33	2	0	2	9	10	0	0	0	55	0	1	.230	.229
Sims, Demetrius	R-R	6-2	200	7-14-95	.297	.208	.314	43	145	27	43	6	2	3	12	20	7	1	1	49	9	4	.428	.405
Torres, Christopher	B-R	5-11	170	2-6-98	.234	.283	.227	112	432	82	101	14	5	4	32	75	0	1	1	141	25	6	.317	.347

Pitching	B-T	HT	WT	DOB	W	L	ERA	G	GS	CG	SV	IP	H	R	ER	HR	BB	SO	AVG	vLH	vRH	K/9	BB/9
Alcala, Elkin	R-R	5-11	175	8-2-97	3	3	4.09	26	0	0	4	44	43	21	20	1	12	30	.254	.211	.277	6.14	2.45
Alexander, Nathan	R-R	6-4	185	6-7-96	4	3	3.25	34	0	0	1	53	43	26	19	4	28	43	.219	.224	.217	7.35	4.78
Andrews, Tanner	R-R	6-3	220	11-15-95	8	5	3.52	22	18	0	2	128	100	55	50	7	38	110	.212	.175	.235	7.73	2.67
Baird, Cam	R-R	6-2	195	5-15-96	1	1	5.15	24	0	0	2	37	42	30	21	3	16	33	.290	.214	.337	8.10	3.93
Bautista, Nestor	L-L	6-3	200	5-13-92	0	1	5.40	1	0	0	0	2	2	1	1	0	1	1	.286	.500	.200	5.40	5.40
Brito, Raul	R-R	6-1	180	5-23-97	3	3	4.39	20	0	0	0	27	30	15	13	0	17	29	.275	.257	.284	9.79	5.74
Carter, C.J.	R-R	6-0	165	5-27-97	2	2	2.27	18	0	0	3	32	29	13	8	2	8	39	.244	.310	.180	11.08	2.27
Culbertson, Peyton	R-R	6-1	220	4-18-97	0	0	4.81	9	4	0	0	24	33	16	13	0	12	20	.337	.314	.362	7.40	4.44
Farnworth, Steven	R-R	6-2	175	9-6-93	0	0	0.00	3	0	0	2	3	1	1	0	0	0	1	.100	.000	.250	3.00	0.00
Guenther, Sean	L-L	5-11	194	12-29-95	2	2	1.24	12	1	0	0	29	25	6	4	1	10	28	.223	.227	.221	8.69	3.10
Guerrero, Alberto	R-R	6-3	192	12-13-97	9	6	3.13	26	24	0	1	132	127	57	46	5	53	104	.255	.242	.264	7.07	3.60
Howe, Bryce	R-R	6-2	250	11-27-95	0	0	27.00	2	0	0	0	2	6	5	5	0	1	1	.546	.500	.571	5.40	5.40
Jones, Tyler	R-R	6-3	200	12-7-95	3	4	1.87	19	4	0	1	53	49	13	11	2	18	59	.251	.274	.234	10.02	3.06
Kolek, Tyler	R-R	6-5	260	12-15-95	0	0	9.72	9	0	0	0	8	6	9	9	0	20	11	.194	.250	.174	11.88	21.60
Mejia, Humberto	R-R	6-3	175	3-3-97	5	1	2.03	13	10	1	1	67	42	17	15	4	19	68	.177	.226	.130	9.18	2.57
Mitzel, Tyler	R-R	6-4	210	5-10-96	5	3	2.53	24	1	0	4	46	30	19	13	5	19	61	.183	.159	.198	11.85	3.69
Ovalle, Jeremy	R-R	6-3	185	1-17-97	0	0	3.86	2	0	0	0	2	1	1	1	0	5	5	.143	.250	.000	19.29	19.29
Reed, Remey	R-R	6-5	230	5-5-95	4	3	3.28	9	9	0	0	49	49	21	18	2	10	43	.261	.235	.275	7.84	1.82
Roberson, Josh	R-R	6-3	175	5-12-96	4	4	2.25	11	11	0	0	56	48	19	14	3	18	54	.238	.177	.293	8.68	2.89
Rodriguez, Manuel	L-L	6-2	160	12-23-96	5	1	2.94	20	6	0	2	64	59	27	21	5	16	46	.239	.139	.275	6.44	2.24
Sherrod, Cason	R-R	6-4	215	6-25-96	0	0	0.00	1	0	0	1	4	2	0	0	0	2	.143	.000	.250	4.50	0.00
Soriano, George	R-R	6-2	170	3-24-99	4	7	3.91	23	20	2	1	120	108	62	52	8	50	99	.238	.249	.228	7.45	3.76
Vallimont, Chris	R-R	6-5	220	3-18-97	4	4	2.99	13	13	0	0	69	48	27	23	4	26	80	.198	.153	.240	10.38	3.38
Vesia, Alex	L-L	6-2	195	4-11-96	1	2	2.56	19	1	0	3	32	24	9	9	1	17	51	.207	.209	.206	14.49	4.83
Walters, Jake	R-R	6-0	190	3-11-96	7	4	2.35	19	17	0	1	92	69	29	24	4	29	87	.207	.197	.213	8.51	2.84
Wolf, Zach	R-R	5-8	175	11-15-97	4	2	3.07	34	0	0	15	44	39	19	15	0	15	50	.227	.200	.245	10.23	3.07

Fielding

Catcher	PCT	G	PO	A	E	DP	PB
Banfield	.984	93	788	83	14	2	4
Osborne	.982	46	361	25	7	2	4

First Base	PCT	G	PO	A	E	DP
Edwards	.987	67	529	20	7	45
Hollins	1.000	1	1	0	0	0
Osborne	1.000	12	76	8	0	4
Reynolds	.977	60	394	35	10	40

Second Base	PCT	G	PO	A	E	DP
Castro	.975	49	63	96	4	16
Devers	1.000	2	6	5	0	1
Hollins	.750	1	1	2	1	1
Rivera	.957	6	10	12	1	1
Scott	.976	52	83	120	5	29
Sims	.975	30	50	65	3	15
Torres	.900	7	10	17	3	3

Third Base	PCT	G	PO	A	E	DP
Hollins	.930	78	69	142	16	15
Osborne	1.000	1	1	0	0	0
Rivera	.900	63	52	74	14	5
Scott	1.000	2	0	2	0	0

Shortstop	PCT	G	PO	A	E	DP
Rivera	.964	23	36	45	3	6
Sims	.971	15	30	36	2	16
Torres	.912	103	143	229	36	43

Outfield	PCT	G	PO	A	E	DP
Bradshaw	.966	36	81	4	3	1
Burdick	.993	61	129	10	1	1
Castro	1.000	3	7	0	0	0

	PCT	G	PO	A	E	DP
Cespedes	.953	28	58	3	3	0
Donadio	1.000	1	1	0	0	0
Encarnacion	.907	63	104	13	12	0
Grant	1.000	4	6	1	0	0

	PCT	G	PO	A	E	DP
Hernandez	1.000	13	19	3	0	0
Jones	.976	99	192	8	5	2
Misner	.991	32	103	2	1	1
Scott	.980	86	197	3	4	1

BATAVIA MUCKDOGS
NEW YORK-PENN LEAGUE

SHORT SEASON

MIAMI MARLINS

Batting	B-T	HT	WT	DOB	AVG	vLH	vRH	G	AB	R	H	2B	3B	HR	RBI	BB	HBP	SH	SF	SO	SB	CS	SLG	OBP
Baez, Igor	R-R	6-1	214	6-6-95	.143	.000	.154	6	14	2	2	0	0	1	2	4	0	0	1	4	0	0	.357	.316
Burdick, Peyton	R-R	6-0	210	2-26-97	.318	.500	.250	6	22	3	7	0	1	1	5	2	1	0	0	5	1	1	.546	.400
Castro, Samuel	B-R	5-10	160	10-16-97	.200	.286	.125	5	15	0	3	0	0	0	1	2	0	0	0	4	1	0	.200	.294
Dinicola, Harrison	L-R	6-0	195	4-28-97	.246	.364	.217	34	114	11	28	6	0	0	12	12	2	0	1	31	2	1	.298	.326
Edwards, Evan	L-L	6-0	200	6-21-97	.222	.167	.250	5	18	1	4	1	0	1	2	2	0	0	0	9	1	0	.444	.300
Fish, Keegan	B-R	5-11	190	9-19-99	.250	.333	.231	7	16	6	4	1	0	0	0	8	0	0	0	6	0	0	.313	.500
Guaimaro, Albert	R-R	6-0	180	1-17-99	.238	.351	.202	40	151	16	36	3	2	3	16	3	2	0	0	24	4	3	.344	.263
Hampton, Lorenzo	R-R	6-5	225	8-8-97	.000	.000	.000	1	4	0	0	0	0	0	0	0	0	0	0	3	0	0	.000	.000
Hernandez, Brayan	R-R	6-2	175	9-11-97	.188	.160	.200	27	85	10	16	2	1	2	10	6	1	2	2	26	6	1	.306	.245
Hernandez, Michael	R-R	5-10	195	5-24-95	.182	.222	.171	30	88	5	16	5	0	3	7	3	1	0	0	40	0	0	.341	.217
Infante, Julian	R-R	6-3	210	9-24-96	.222	.500	.177	21	72	8	16	4	0	1	9	7	1	0	1	32	0	0	.319	.296
Johnston, Troy	L-L	5-11	205	6-22-97	.277	.261	.281	59	213	34	59	15	1	3	35	29	6	1	4	51	1	3	.399	.373
Nunez, Gerardo	R-R	6-1	180	2-6-98	.063	.000	.095	11	32	3	2	0	0	0	2	3	1	1	1	16	0	1	.063	.162
Nunez, Nasim	B-R	5-9	160	8-18-00	.000	.000	.000	3	10	1	0	0	0	0	0	1	0	1	0	5	0	0	.000	.091
Orr, J.D.	L-L	5-11	185	9-11-96	.352	.217	.389	64	213	57	75	9	3	0	18	44	3	2	0	30	29	17	.423	.469
Pollman, Gunner	R-R	6-2	210	2-3-95	.143	.500	.083	6	14	1	2	1	0	0	0	2	0	0	0	5	0	0	.214	.250
Ready, Nic	R-R	6-3	220	2-13-97	.263	.210	.280	67	262	30	69	30	2	10	47	20	1	0	6	82	1	1	.508	.311
Reynolds, Sean	L-R	6-7	237	4-19-98	.171	.235	.155	28	88	13	15	3	0	4	13	21	0	0	0	39	4	2	.341	.330
Reynoso, Ronal	L-R	6-1	165	5-23-98	.113	.177	.083	22	53	5	6	1	0	0	1	1	0	1	0	21	1	0	.132	.130
Rosario, Dalvy	R-R	6-0	160	7-22-00	.200	.236	.190	65	250	35	50	15	5	2	30	13	6	11	4	71	10	5	.324	.253
Schubert, Gunnar	R-R	5-11	205	5-19-96	.444	--	.444	3	9	0	4	0	1	0	2	1	0	0	0	2	0	0	.667	.500
Skelton, Dustin	R-R	6-0	202	7-31-97	.224	.177	.240	24	67	5	15	3	0	0	6	7	3	0	1	23	0	0	.269	.321
Smith II, Milton	L-L	5-10	165	9-25-97	.305	.412	.269	60	200	31	61	1	1	0	17	23	3	5	0	38	20	5	.320	.385
Sthormes, Andres	R-R	5-10	195	8-7-96	.217	.200	.229	21	60	8	13	2	1	1	6	11	3	1	0	15	0	1	.333	.365
Strunc, Jack	R-R	6-0	190	6-26-96	.224	.200	.231	48	165	15	37	7	0	1	17	10	4	1	1	38	1	4	.285	.283
Taylor, Kobie	R-R	6-0	183	8-13-98	.159	.238	.125	25	69	7	11	1	0	5	10	0	0	0	3	33	0	2	.203	.266
Turner, Andrew	R-R	6-2	190	9-26-95	.267	.216	.284	45	146	18	39	6	1	1	15	11	0	0	3	32	3	4	.322	.378

Pitching	B-T	HT	WT	DOB	W	L	ERA	G	GS	CG	SV	IP	H	R	ER	HR	BB	SO	AVG	vLH	vRH	K/9	BB/9
Bennett, Dakota	B-L	6-2	160	7-12-99	2	1	4.50	10	2	0	1	40	38	22	20	2	9	20	.257	.250	.260	4.50	2.03
Brabrand, Evan	R-R	6-3	205	11-23-95	4	1	1.29	20	0	0	13	21	15	4	3	0	10	25	.200	.233	.178	10.71	4.29
Brito, Raul	R-R	6-1	180	5-23-97	1	0	0.00	2	0	0	0	3	3	0	0	0	2	3	.300	.333	.286	9.00	6.00
Frias, Julio	L-L	6-2	160	6-1-98	5	4	2.83	14	14	0	0	70	62	30	22	1	23	73	.231	.181	.259	9.39	2.96
Galindez, Geremy	R-R	6-1	170	4-29-98	4	0	4.50	18	0	0	2	24	26	14	12	1	5	16	.286	.273	.293	6.00	1.88
Hoeing, Bryan	R-R	6-6	225	10-19-96	0	2	4.43	9	0	0	0	22	26	12	11	1	5	17	.296	.297	.294	6.85	2.01
Howe, Bryce	R-R	6-2	250	11-27-95	0	0	2.45	3	0	0	0	4	3	2	1	0	1	4	.200	.250	.143	9.82	2.45
Johnson, M.D.	R-R	6-6	185	7-7-97	1	0	4.26	15	0	0	0	19	21	14	9	1	11	22	.266	.222	.289	10.42	5.21
Kolek, Tyler	R-R	6-5	260	12-15-95	0	1	8.44	6	0	0	0	5	2	5	5	0	7	9	.118	.125	.111	15.19	11.81
Lindgren, Jeff	R-R	6-1	200	9-17-96	1	1	0.00	2	0	0	0	4	1	0	0	0	1	3	.077	.000	.100	6.75	2.25
Love, Brock	R-R	6-1	210	10-15-96	1	0	2.19	15	0	0	1	25	10	6	6	1	10	30	.118	.103	.130	10.95	3.65
Lucas, Easton	L-L	6-4	180	9-23-96	0	2	3.98	12	9	0	0	32	26	14	14	3	9	40	.222	.161	.244	11.37	2.56
Martinez, Edgar	R-R	6-1	170	7-13-97	4	4	2.50	15	13	1	0	72	53	26	20	6	22	62	.204	.220	.192	7.75	2.75
Miller, Andrew	L-L	6-3	195	12-15-96	3	5	3.76	15	15	0	0	67	79	35	28	3	22	49	.288	.267	.301	6.58	2.96
Nardi, Andrew	L-L	6-2	190	8-18-98	0	0	0.00	1	0	0	0	1	0	0	0	0	0	2	.000	.000	.000	18.00	0.00
Ovalle, Jeremy	R-R	6-3	185	1-17-97	0	0	3.86	4	0	0	0	5	4	3	2	0	2	8	.211	.571	.000	15.43	3.86
Reed, Remey	R-R	6-5	230	5-5-95	3	0	1.73	5	5	0	0	26	20	5	5	1	4	33	.204	.206	.206	11.42	1.38
Rose, Jackson	R-R	6-2	185	4-29-96	5	6	4.90	15	11	0	0	64	65	39	35	10	14	49	.259	.240	.271	6.85	1.96
Sherrod, Cason	R-R	6-4	215	6-25-96	1	0	6.00	3	0	0	1	3	3	3	2	0	2	3	.250	.167	.333	9.00	6.00
Simpson, Josh	L-L	6-2	190	8-19-97	1	0	2.35	15	0	0	2	23	20	8	6	0	6	25	.225	.258	.207	9.78	2.35
Steele, Joey	R-R	6-2	195	11-15-95	2	0	2.08	19	0	0	1	22	23	6	5	2	5	33	.277	.324	.239	13.71	2.08
Suriel, Edison	L-L	5-10	160	10-24-98	3	3	4.20	22	0	0	0	30	27	20	14	0	20	45	.235	.209	.250	13.50	6.00
Villalobos, Eli	R-R	6-4	195	6-26-97	0	3	6.08	14	7	0	2	47	54	34	32	5	16	48	.281	.253	.305	9.13	3.04
Villalobos, Jonaiker	L-L	6-0	160	7-11-99	1	1	5.46	18	0	0	0	28	30	19	17	1	14	35	.275	.156	.325	11.25	4.50

Fielding

C: Baez 6, Fish 4, Hernandez 30, Pollman 6, Skelton 20, Sthormes 20. **1B:** Dinicola 20, Edwards 4, Infante 14, Ready 18, Reynolds 22, Turner 3. **2B:** Castro 3, Nunez 11, Nunez 2, Reynoso 11, Schubert 2, Strunc 41, Turner 8. **3B:** Infante 4, Ready 47, Reynoso 3, Turner 26. **SS:** Castro 2, Nunez 1, Reynoso 3, Rosario 63, Strunc 7. **OF:** Burdick 4, Dinicola 1, Guaimaro 27, Hampton 1, Hernandez 19, Johnston 51, Orr 54, Smith II 58, Taylor 22.

GCL MARLINS
GULF COAST LEAGUE

ROOKIE

Batting	B-T	HT	WT	DOB	AVG	vLH	vRH	G	AB	R	H	2B	3B	HR	RBI	BB	HBP	SH	SF	SO	SB	CS	SLG	OBP
Arcaya, Luis	R-R	6-1	170	2-26-99	.216	.154	.257	17	51	6	11	4	0	1	12	3	2	0	0	11	0	0	.353	.286
Barstad, Cameron	L-R	6-0	160	11-29-00	.167	.143	.172	15	36	3	6	0	0	1	5	6	3	0	0	15	0	0	.250	.333
Cody, Javeon	R-R	6-3	205	7-29-99	.172	.200	.164	31	93	18	16	5	0	0	6	22	0	1	0	29	12	2	.226	.330
Combs, Casey	R-R	7-2	195	7-29-96	.222	.000	.231	13	27	5	6	0	0	0	2	4	2	2	0	4	1	0	.222	.364

Batting	B-T	HT	WT	DOB	AVG	vLH	vRH	G	AB	R	H	2B	3B	HR	RBI	BB	HBP	SH	SF	SO	SB	CS	SLG	OBP
Dean, Austin	R-R	6-1	190	10-14-93	.333	.000	.500	1	3	1	1	1	0	0	1	0	0	0	0	0	0	0	.667	.333
Devers, Jose	L-R	6-0	155	12-7-99	.275	.200	.300	11	40	7	11	3	1	0	2	4	2	0	0	4	3	1	.400	.370
Espinal, Walner	R-R	6-0	170	12-21-99	.191	.105	.208	38	115	10	22	6	0	3	17	7	0	1	1	37	1	0	.322	.236
Fish, Keegan	B-R	5-11	190	9-19-99	.167	.167	.167	5	12	1	2	1	0	0	1	5	1	0	0	5	0	0	.250	.444
Galloway, Isaac	R-R	6-2	205	10-10-89	.200	.200	.200	5	15	2	3	0	0	1	3	3	0	0	1	5	2	0	.400	.316
Hampton, Lorenzo	R-R	6-5	225	8-8-97	.280	.333	.268	45	161	26	45	7	0	2	31	24	6	0	3	30	5	2	.360	.387
Infante, Julian	R-R	6-3	210	9-24-96	.250	.286	.241	12	36	9	9	0	1	1	4	13	1	0	0	13	3	1	.389	.460
Lebron, Omar	L-L	6-0	175	4-11-99	.224	.231	.232	39	125	16	28	7	3	1	23	20	5	0	2	30	5	2	.352	.349
Lopez, B.J.	R-R	5-9	185	9-29-94	.000	.000	.000	1	3	0	0	0	0	0	0	0	0	0	0	1	0	0	.000	.000
Machado, Julio	R-R	6-0	185	9-12-00	.231	.333	.333	4	13	3	3	0	0	0	1	0	2	0	0	4	1	0	.231	.333
Marinez, Ynmanol	R-R	6-0	170	4-12-01	.304	.286	.313	7	23	2	7	2	0	0	7	0	0	0	1	8	0	0	.391	.292
Mercado, Jan	R-R	6-1	185	8-28-99	.233	.125	.273	10	30	4	7	1	0	1	4	3	1	0	0	6	1	0	.367	.324
Mesa Jr., Victor	L-L	5-11	175	9-8-01	.284	.351	.267	47	176	39	50	9	4	1	24	24	1	1	4	29	7	4	.398	.366
Misner, Kameron	L-L	6-4	219	1-8-98	.241	.286	.227	8	29	2	7	2	0	0	4	9	0	0	0	7	3	0	.310	.421
Mitchell, Tevin	R-R	6-1	170	5-2-97	.238	.214	.234	29	80	16	19	3	1	0	12	19	4	3	2	21	5	1	.300	.400
Montero, Alvaro	L-R	5-11	155	6-27-00	.200	.364	.157	22	65	7	13	1	0	1	3	11	0	0	0	23	1	2	.262	.316
Nunez, Nasim	B-R	5-9	160	8-18-00	.211	.152	.232	48	175	37	37	5	1	0	12	34	1	2	2	43	28	2	.251	.340
Owings, Zachary	L-R	6-1	195	12-17-97	.280	.259	.288	35	107	11	30	4	3	1	19	8	4	0	2	14	3	1	.402	.347
Paulino, Daniel	R-R	6-1	155	11-23-98	.218	.333	.209	21	55	7	12	3	1	0	1	1	1	0	0	16	2	0	.309	.246
Pompey, Tristan	R-R	6-4	200	3-23-97	.333	.000	.500	1	3	1	1	0	0	0	0	3	1	0	0	1	0	1	.333	.500
Reynoso, Ronal	L-R	6-1	165	5-23-98	.318	.200	.353	9	22	2	7	1	0	1	5	2	1	0	0	8	2	0	.500	.400
Rodriguez, Christopher	R-R	6-2	190	12-22-99	.280	.500	.250	14	50	2	14	4	0	1	4	4	1	0	0	18	1	0	.420	.346
Rodriguez, Cristhian	R-R	6-1	160	12-23-01	.231	.000	.375	3	13	1	3	1	0	0	0	0	0	0	0	1	0	0	.308	.231
Rowan, Thomas	R-R	6-1	200	11-8-95	.000	--	.000	3	5	0	0	0	0	0	0	1	0	1	0	1	0	0	.000	.167
Sims, Demetrius	R-R	6-2	200	7-14-95	.167	.000	.182	4	12	3	2	2	0	0	2	0	2	0	0	3	0	0	.333	.286
Snyder, Matt	L-R	6-5	230	6-17-90	.000	.000	.000	3	6	1	0	0	0	0	0	2	0	0	0	0	0	0	.000	.250
Vigil, Rodrigo	R-R	6-0	165	1-3-93	.438	.500	.400	5	16	3	7	1	0	0	2	1	1	0	1	0	0	1	.500	.474

Pitching	B-T	HT	WT	DOB	W	L	ERA	G	GS	CG	SV	IP	H	R	ER	HR	BB	SO	AVG	vLH	vRH	K/9	BB/9
Alegre, Delvis	R-R	6-2	180	2-2-01	0	0	0.00	1	0	0	0	1	0	0	0	0	0	1	.000	--	.000	9.00	0.00
Beggs, Dustin	R-R	6-3	180	6-14-93	0	0	6.00	1	1	0	0	3	5	2	2	0	0	5	.357	.571	.143	15.00	0.00
Culbertson, Peyton	R-R	6-2	220	4-18-97	1	0	2.84	4	1	0	0	6	9	2	2	0	1	3	.333	.143	.400	4.26	1.42
De Los Santos, Miguel	R-R	6-1	175	9-27-96	1	6	6.68	9	4	0	0	34	47	31	25	2	8	31	.326	.342	.320	8.29	2.14
Doble, Mario	R-R	6-1	195	11-1-00	1	0	0.00	1	0	0	0	1	0	0	0	0	0	1	.000	.000	.000	9.00	0.00
Fitterer, Evan	R-R	6-3	195	6-26-00	0	1	2.38	9	8	0	0	23	20	12	6	1	12	19	.233	.191	.246	7.54	4.76
Givin, Matt	R-R	6-3	180	6-17-99	5	1	2.74	10	5	0	1	46	36	18	14	2	15	35	.216	.262	.189	6.85	2.93
King, Zach	L-L	6-6	212	4-30-98	2	0	1.65	6	3	0	0	16	8	3	3	0	7	17	.151	.063	.189	9.37	3.86
Lara, Yeremin	R-R	6-1	160	11-6-98	1	3	4.54	10	6	0	2	36	33	25	18	4	18	33	.243	.208	.250	8.33	4.54
Leach, Kale	R-R	6-4	240	6-8-97	1	0	0.00	2	0	0	0	3	2	0	0	0	0	2	.182	.000	.200	6.00	0.00
Lopez, Giovanni	R-R	6-1	204	9-16-96	0	0	6.48	8	0	0	0	8	8	6	6	0	11	5	.250	.250	.250	5.40	11.88
Love, Brock	R-R	6-1	210	10-15-96	0	0	4.50	1	0	0	0	2	1	1	1	1	1	0	.143	--	.143	0.00	4.50
Lucas, Easton	L-L	6-4	180	9-23-96	1	0	0.00	1	0	0	0	3	3	0	0	0	0	1	.273	1.000	.200	3.00	0.00
Maldonado, Anthony	R-R	6-4	200	2-6-98	2	1	1.59	10	0	0	0	11	6	3	2	0	1	15	.150	.250	.125	11.91	0.79
Martinez, Leudy	R-R	6-2	180	6-9-00	3	0	4.89	12	4	0	0	35	31	23	19	3	29	37	.239	.256	.231	9.51	7.46
McKenna, Brian	R-R	6-0	202	11-19-92	0	0	0.00	1	0	0	0	2	1	0	0	0	2	3	.143	.333	.000	13.50	9.00
Mitzel, Tyler	R-R	6-4	210	5-10-96	1	1	12.00	2	0	0	0	3	6	4	4	0	2	3	.429	.400	.444	9.00	6.00
Mokma, Chris	R-R	6-4	190	2-11-01	0	1	2.19	5	5	0	0	12	12	3	3	0	2	12	.245	.294	.219	8.76	1.46
Nardi, Andrew	L-L	6-2	190	8-18-98	2	0	0.98	13	0	0	3	18	11	4	2	0	13	30	.159	.231	.143	14.73	6.38
Neidert, Nick	R-R	6-2	202	11-20-96	0	0	0.00	2	0	0	0	2	1	0	0	0	1	3	.154	.000	.167	7.36	2.45
Paiva, Codie	R-R	6-5	215	6-27-97	1	1	2.19	14	0	0	3	25	22	11	6	0	7	24	.227	.263	.218	8.76	2.55
Palacios, Luis	L-L	6-2	160	7-1-00	1	0	1.12	10	4	0	1	40	25	5	5	2	2	42	.180	.167	.182	9.37	0.45
Roberson, Josh	R-R	6-3	175	5-12-96	0	0	1.29	3	3	0	0	7	5	1	1	0	5	9	.200	.250	.177	11.57	6.43
Rodriguez, Eliezer	L-L	6-1	160	2-17-99	3	2	7.45	12	0	0	0	19	24	16	16	4	10	17	.304	.273	.309	7.91	4.66
Rodriguez, Manuel	L-L	6-2	160	12-23-96	0	1	1.93	2	0	0	0	5	4	1	1	1	1	5	.235	.000	.260	9.64	1.93
Sanchez, Edgar	R-R	6-1	190	8-2-00	2	3	3.13	10	2	0	0	32	18	14	11	2	33	31	.170	.171	.169	8.81	9.38
Sanchez, Jesus	R-R	5-11	150	4-8-99	0	2	3.75	14	0	0	3	24	16	12	10	1	10	28	.191	.179	.196	10.50	3.75
Simpson, Josh	L-L	6-2	190	8-19-97	0	0	0.00	1	0	0	0	1	0	0	0	0	0	1	.000	.000	.000	9.00	0.00
Vasquez, Jeremias	R-R	6-3	205	1-17-97	0	0	13.50	6	0	0	0	6	4	10	9	2	7	9	.182	.000	.235	13.50	10.50

Fielding

C: Arcaya 14, Barstad 13, Combs 13, Fish 5, Lopez 1, Mercado 10, Rowan 3, Vigil 4. **1B:** Arcaya 2, Infante 1, Lebron 25, Owings 25, Rodriguez 2, Snyder 2. **2B:** Espinal 26, Marinez 2, Mitchell 1, Montero 22, Reynoso 4, Sims 1. **3B:** Espinal 13, Infante 11, Machado 3, Marinez 3, Owings 10, Reynoso 4, Rodriguez 11, Rodriguez 3. **SS:** Devers 1, Espinal 1, Machado 1, Marinez 1, Nunez 48, Reynoso 1, Sims 1. **OF:** Cody 35, Dean 1, Galloway 3, Hampton 34, Lebron 4, Mesa Jr. 43, Misner 8, Mitchell 22, Paulino 20, Pompey 1, Rodriguez 1.

DSL MARLINS   ROOKIE
DOMINICAN SUMMER LEAGUE

Batting	B-T	HT	WT	DOB	AVG	vLH	vRH	G	AB	R	H	2B	3B	HR	RBI	BB	HBP	SH	SF	SO	SB	CS	SLG	OBP
Campos, Raul	R-R	5-10	175	11-10-01	.160	.222	.144	38	131	12	21	2	1	1	12	13	0	1	3	38	2	1	.214	.231
Chinchilla, Jonathan	R-R	5-11	160	11-18-00	.217	.000	.260	27	60	12	13	3	0	0	6	5	4	0	0	10	0	1	.267	.319
Cumana, Arquimedes	R-R	6-3	175	4-28-00	.300	.370	.282	60	220	28	66	15	1	1	36	23	14	0	3	44	3	4	.391	.396
De Leon, Isaac	R-R	6-2	170	11-7-01	.256	.250	.258	66	238	35	61	13	0	1	20	38	5	1	2	36	2	1	.324	.368
Felipe, Anthony	R-R	5-11	170	9-16-00	.215	.206	.217	48	163	18	35	5	2	1	18	26	4	0	1	67	7	4	.288	.335
Leon, Ene	R-R	5-10	170	11-3-01	.171	.000	.200	16	41	3	7	0	0	0	2	6	1	1	1	6	1	0	.171	.286
Machado, Julio	R-R	6-0	185	9-12-00	.308	.297	.311	44	172	25	53	8	2	1	23	14	12	1	0	24	7	3	.395	.399

	B-T	HT	WT	DOB	AVG	vLH	vRH	G	AB	R	H	2B	3B	HR	RBI	BB	HBP	SH	SF	SO	SB	CS	OBP	SLG
Melenciano, Jhonny	L-R	6-0	155	12-13-01	.204	.286	.180	50	157	23	32	4	1	0	8	31	2	0	1	35	17	5	.242	.340
Osorio, Jhonaiker	L-R	6-0	160	9-2-00	.221	.160	.241	40	104	8	23	5	1	0	13	3	1	0	1	19	3	1	.289	.248
Ozoria, Elvin	R-R	6-0	180	7-16-01	.191	.240	.179	44	131	23	25	9	2	1	15	26	2	0	1	61	9	3	.313	.331
Paulino, Jandel	R-R	6-1	175	11-3-00	.316	.263	.332	67	247	47	78	15	1	4	30	36	14	0	3	59	5	4	.433	.427
Rodriguez, Cristhian	R-R	6-1	160	12-23-01	.237	.182	.253	61	241	47	57	11	4	4	25	37	2	1	2	72	4	1	.365	.340
Roman, Richard	R-R	6-1	180	12-22-01	.298	.500	.243	28	94	12	28	6	0	2	16	11	1	0	3	25	4	0	.426	.367
Romero, Carlos	R-R	6-1	175	7-31-01	.083	.083	.083	18	48	1	4	0	0	0	1	2	0	1	0	30	0	0	.083	.120
Sanchez, Yoelvis	L-L	6-1	190	4-27-02	.224	.206	.228	57	192	19	43	6	3	2	18	20	4	3	1	59	10	3	.318	.309
Vegas, Derek	R-R	6-2	175	12-22-01	.159	.125	.170	30	69	6	11	0	0	0	4	9	5	0	2	18	0	0	.159	.294

Pitching	B-T	HT	WT	DOB	W	L	ERA	G	GS	CG	SV	IP	H	R	ER	HR	BB	SO	AVG	vLH	vRH	K/9	BB/9
Alegre, Delvis	R-R	6-2	180	2-2-01	3	4	2.62	14	8	0	1	58	45	23	17	1	17	40	.210	.225	.202	6.17	2.62
Bargallo, Sandro	L-L	6-1	185	12-29-01	2	0	3.66	17	0	0	1	20	13	11	8	0	18	33	.183	.300	.164	15.10	8.24
Carrasco, Erick	L-L	6-0	170	10-11-99	0	1	3.00	5	0	0	0	6	2	3	2	0	8	4	.095	.500	.053	6.00	12.00
De Los Santos, Miguel	R-R	6-1	175	9-27-96	0	1	0.00	1	0	0	0	1	0	1	0	0	1	1	.000	.000	--	9.00	9.00
Doble, Mario	R-R	6-1	195	11-1-00	3	3	3.24	13	7	0	1	50	49	25	18	2	18	55	.250	.232	.260	9.90	3.24
Encarnacion, Breidy	R-R	6-3	185	11-9-00	4	0	1.91	13	7	0	0	47	28	15	10	2	11	57	.170	.196	.158	10.91	2.11
Gonzalez, Luis	L-L	6-2	200	2-21-00	1	0	0.63	11	0	0	4	14	9	4	1	0	7	28	.184	.111	.200	17.58	4.40
Jimenez, Yeuris	R-R	6-3	185	3-23-01	2	2	8.22	13	4	0	0	31	48	33	28	0	24	32	.350	.362	.344	9.39	7.04
Leon, Maycold	L-L	6-1	160	4-29-02	1	0	3.94	14	6	0	3	46	44	23	20	0	13	50	.251	.120	.273	9.85	2.56
Lopez, Luis	R-R	6-3	185	10-8-01	1	2	3.61	12	6	0	0	42	44	21	17	2	5	26	.262	.275	.253	5.53	1.06
Medina, Manuel	L-L	5-10	140	3-25-02	0	0	1.17	6	0	0	0	8	8	1	1	0	2	10	.267	.333	.259	11.74	2.35
Mendez, Josan	R-R	6-2	180	7-10-00	1	3	2.68	14	6	0	3	50	48	17	15	2	11	42	.258	.266	.254	7.51	1.97
Moya, Wandy	R-R	6-1	160	10-29-97	1	1	8.44	6	0	0	1	5	4	7	5	0	8	3	.191	.000	.308	5.06	13.50
Perez, Ivan	L-L	6-6	200	8-30-01	0	0	2.25	4	0	0	1	4	2	1	1	0	4	2	.154	.000	.167	4.50	9.00
Puentes, Zaquiel	R-R	6-1	160	12-30-00	1	3	6.11	11	4	0	1	28	20	22	19	1	25	25	.206	.182	.219	8.04	8.04
Quinonez, Yoilan	R-R	6-4	200	8-11-99	6	4	3.24	15	9	0	0	58	51	29	21	2	16	57	.237	.279	.209	8.79	2.47
Ramirez, Guillermo	R-R	6-2	180	6-8-00	2	3	3.75	14	5	0	0	36	26	19	15	0	23	28	.208	.290	.172	7.00	5.75
Rosario, Jesus	R-R	6-1	180	10-25-99	1	1	7.20	10	0	0	0	10	16	10	8	1	4	7	.372	.235	.462	6.30	3.60
Tejeda, Luis	R-R	6-0	180	4-12-98	1	2	3.91	18	0	0	1	23	18	13	10	1	14	23	.231	.250	.222	9.00	5.48
Valencio, Henry	R-R	6-1	170	5-11-99	3	3	2.63	14	8	0	0	51	44	22	15	3	18	51	.233	.284	.205	8.94	3.16
Valera, Frank	R-R	6-3	210	10-2-99	1	3	4.50	16	0	0	4	18	11	15	9	0	8	12	.196	.111	.237	6.00	4.00
Vizcaino, Luis	R-R	6-3	195	7-9-01	0	0	1.93	4	0	0	0	5	2	1	1	0	5	5	.125	.000	.200	9.64	9.64

Fielding

C: Chinchilla 27, Cumana 12, Leon 6, Osorio 38, Vegas 23. **1B:** Cumana 48, Machado 18, Osorio 2, Ozoria 4. **2B:** Campos 28, Machado 15, Ozoria 31, Romero 1. **3B:** De Leon 29, Machado 10, Rodriguez 33. **SS:** De Leon 34, Machado 2, Rodriguez 28, Romero 11. **OF:** Campos 1, Felipe 48, Melenciano 48, Paulino 58, Roman 8, Romero 4, Sanchez 54.

MIAMI MARLINS

Milwaukee Brewers

MILWAUKEE BREWERS

SEASON IN A SENTENCE: The Brewers couldn't match the 96-win team they put together in 2018, but the club had its third straight winning season, finished second in the NL Central with an 89-73 record and squeaked into the NL wild card game with some late-season magic.

HIGH POINT: Many had the Brewers written off from postseason action when they entered September just three games above .500 and 6.5 games out of the division race. But Milwaukee rattled off its best month of the season, going 20-7 (with Christian Yelich playing in just nine of those games) to clinch the second wild card spot.

LOW POINT: The Brewers were just one game out of the division lead during the middle of August, but started to let things slip away by going 5-7 in the last 12 games of the month, including two series losses to the Cardinals. That stretch of games saw the team slide to six and a half games out of the division and would have prevented them from making the postseason if it weren't for a hot September.

NOTABLE ROOKIES: Second baseman Keston Hiura blitzed the Pacific Coast League for a month and a half before earning a brief 17-game callup in May. He was then called up full-time in late June and hit .303/.368/.570 with 19 home runs and 23 doubles in the middle of Milwaukee's lineup. Righthander Adrian Houser went 6-7, 3.72 while serving as a starter and reliever over 111.1 innings.

KEY TRANSACTIONS: The Brewers made one of the best free agent signings of the offseason by inking catcher Yasmani Grandal to a one-year $18.25 million deal. He was the second-best catcher in baseball according to Fangraphs.com WAR, hitting .246/.380/.468 with 28 home runs and serving as one of the best defensive backstops in baseball. Milwaukee also got 87.1 innings and 17 starts (3.50 ERA) out of lefthander Gio Gonzalez, who signed a one-year, $2 million deal.

DOWN ON THE FARM: Brice Turang, the club's 2018 first-round pick, had a strong season with low Class A Wisconsin (.287/.384/.760 with 21 stolen bases) before getting promoted to high Class A Carolina, where he struggled (.200/.338/.276) but ranked among the league's Top 20 prospects. After a strong 2018 season in Double-A, 2016 first round pick Corey Ray had a difficult, injury-hampered season. He hit just .218/.291/.363 across three different levels, with eight home runs and six stolen bases in 69 games.

OPENING DAY PAYROLL: $130,389,362 (14th).

PLAYERS OF THE YEAR

ALEX TRAUTWIG

SCOTT PAULUS

MAJOR LEAGUE	MINOR LEAGUE
Christian Yelich	**Trent Grisham**
OF	OF
.329/.429/.671	(Double-A/Triple-A)
Led MLB in SLG (.671)	.300/.407/.603
and OPS (1.100)	26 HR, 111 H

ORGANIZATION LEADERS

Batting		*Minimum 250 AB
MAJORS		
* AVG	Christian Yelich	.329
* OPS	Christian Yelich	1.100
HR	Christian Yelich	44
RBI	Christian Yelich	97
MINORS		
* AVG	David Freitas, San Antonio	.387
* OBP	David Freitas, San Antonio	.459
* SLG	Trent Grisham, Biloxi, San Antonio	.603
* OPS	David Freitas, San Antonio	1.030
* R	Nate Orf, San Antonio	85
H	Cory Spangenberg, San Antonio	131
TB	David Fry, Wisconsin	224
2B	David Fry, Wisconsin	41
3B	Yeison Coca, Wisconsin	8
HR	Trent Grisham, Biloxi, San Antonio	26
RBI	Mario Feliciano, Carolina, Biloxi	81
BB	Brice Turang, Wisconsin, Carolina	83
SO	Yeison Coca, Wisconsin	148
SB	Reidy Mercado, DSL Brewers, AZL Brewers Blue	43

Pitching		#Minimum 75 IP
MAJORS		
W	Brandon Woodruff	11
# ERA	Josh Hader	2.62
SO	Brandon Woodruff	143
SV	Josh Hader	37
MINORS		
W	Dylan File, Carolina, Biloxi	15
L	Matt Smith, Carolina	13
# ERA	Burch Smith, San Antonio	2.33
G	Angel Perdomo, Biloxi, San Antonio	47
GS	Bowden Francis, Carolina, Biloxi	27
GS	Trey Supak, Biloxi, San Antonio	27
SV	Nate Griep, Biloxi, San Antonio	22
IP	Trey Supak, Biloxi, San Antonio	153
BB	Zack Brown, San Antonio	64
SO	Bowden Francis, Carolina, Biloxi	165
# AVG	Burch Smith, San Antonio	.181

2019 PERFORMANCE

General Manager: David Stearns. **Farm Director:** Tom Flanagan. **Scouting Director:** Tod Johnson.

Class	Team	League	W	L	PCT	Finish	Manager
Majors	Milwaukee Brewers	National	89	73	.549	5th (15)	Craig Counsell
Triple-A	San Antonio Missions	Pacific Coast	80	60	.571	t-3rd (16)	Rick Sweet
Double-A	Biloxi Shuckers	Southern	82	57	.590	2nd (10)	Mike Guerrero
High A	Carolina Mudcats	Carolina	65	74	.468	7th (10)	Joe Ayrault
Low A	Wisconsin Timber Rattlers	Midwest	69	70	.496	9th (16)	Matt Erickson
Rookie	Rocky Mountain Vibes	Pioneer	32	43	.427	7th (8)	Nestor Corredor
Rookie	AZL Brewers Blue	Arizona	23	33	.411	16th (18)	Rafael Neda
Rookie	AZL Brewers Gold	Arizona	16	40	.286	21st (21)	Liu Rodriguez
Overall 2019 Minor League Record			367	377	.493	t-17th (30)	

ORGANIZATION STATISTICS

MILWAUKEE BREWERS
NATIONAL LEAGUE

Batting	B-T	HT	WT	DOB	AVG	vLH	vRH	G	AB	R	H	2B	3B	HR	RBI	BB	HBP	SH	SF	SO	SB	CS	SLG	OBP
Aguilar, Jesus	R-R	6-3	250	6-30-90	.225	.205	.237	94	222	26	50	9	0	8	34	31	2	0	4	59	0	0	.374	.321
Arcia, Orlando	R-R	6-0	165	8-4-94	.223	.240	.217	152	494	51	110	16	1	15	59	43	1	2	6	109	8	5	.350	.283
Austin, Tyler	R-R	6-2	220	9-6-91	.200	.333	.091	17	20	5	4	2	0	1	4	6	0	0	1	7	1	0	.450	.370
2-team total (70 San Francisco)					.187	.220	.136	87	150	29	28	4	1	9	24	23	0	0	1	64	2	0	.407	.293
Braun, Ryan	R-R	6-2	205	11-17-83	.285	.287	.285	144	459	70	131	31	2	22	75	34	8	0	3	105	11	1	.505	.343
Cain, Lorenzo	R-R	6-2	205	4-13-86	.260	.264	.258	148	562	75	146	30	0	11	48	50	6	4	106	18	8			.372	.325
Dubon, Mauricio	R-R	6-0	160	7-19-94	.000	.000	.000	2	2	0	0	0	0	0	0	0	0	0	0	1	0	0	.000	.000
2-team total (28 San Francisco)					.274	.267	.276	30	106	12	29	5	0	4	9	5	0	0	0	20	3	1	.434	.306
Freitas, David	R-R	6-3	225	3-18-89	.077	.000	.111	16	13	1	1	0	0	0	3	0	0	5	0	0	.077	.250
Gamel, Ben	L-L	5-11	185	5-17-92	.248	.354	.220	134	311	47	77	18	0	7	33	40	3	0	2	104	2	2	.373	.337
Grandal, Yasmani	B-R	6-1	235	11-8-88	.246	.258	.240	153	513	79	126	26	2	28	77	109	5	0	5	139	5	1	.468	.380
Grisham, Trent	L-L	6-0	205	11-1-96	.231	.219	.234	51	156	24	36	6	2	6	24	20	4	0	3	48	1	0	.410	.328
Hiura, Keston	R-R	5-11	190	8-2-96	.303	.240	.322	84	314	51	95	23	2	19	49	25	8	0	1	107	9	3	.570	.368
Moustakas, Mike	L-R	6-0	225	9-11-88	.254	.276	.244	143	523	80	133	30	1	35	87	53	6	0	2	98	3	0	.516	.329
Nottingham, Jacob	R-R	6-2	230	4-3-95	.333	.000	.400	9	6	1	2	0	0	1	4	0	1	0	0	2	0	0	.833	.429
Perez, Hernan	R-R	6-1	215	3-26-91	.228	.257	.202	91	232	29	53	11	0	8	18	11	0	2	1	66	5	1	.379	.262
Pina, Manny	R-R	6-0	215	6-5-87	.228	.319	.151	76	158	10	36	8	0	7	25	16	4	0	1	50	0	0	.411	.313
Saladino, Tyler	R-R	6-0	200	7-20-89	.123	.111	.128	28	65	7	8	0	0	2	8	5	1	0	0	26	2	0	.215	.197
Shaw, Travis	L-R	6-4	230	4-16-90	.157	.102	.171	86	230	22	36	5	1	7	16	36	4	0	0	89	0	0	.270	.282
Spangenberg, Cory	L-R	6-0	195	3-16-91	.232	.177	.244	32	95	11	22	2	2	1	6	6	0	1	0	36	3	0	.358	.277
Taylor, Tyrone	R-R	6-0	185	1-22-94	.400	.000	.444	15	10	1	4	2	0	0	1	1	1	0	0	1	0	0	.600	.500
Thames, Eric	L-R	6-0	210	11-10-86	.248	.200	.254	149	396	67	98	23	2	25	61	51	10	0	2	140	3	2	.505	.346
Yelich, Christian	L-R	6-3	195	12-5-91	.329	.278	.358	130	489	100	161	29	3	44	97	80	8	0	3	118	30	2	.671	.429

Pitching	B-T	HT	WT	DOB	W	L	ERA	G	GS	CG	SV	IP	H	R	ER	HR	BB	SO	AVG	vLH	vRH	K/9	BB/9
Albers, Matt	L-R	6-1	225	1-20-83	8	6	5.13	67	0	0	4	60	53	34	34	8	29	57	.239	.286	.220	8.60	4.37
Anderson, Chase	R-R	6-1	200	11-30-87	8	4	4.21	32	27	0	0	139	126	67	65	23	50	124	.240	.189	.280	8.03	3.24
Barnes, Jacob	R-R	6-2	220	4-14-90	1	1	6.86	18	1	0	0	20	22	17	15	3	11	22	.265	.222	.298	10.07	5.03
Black, Ray	R-R	6-5	225	6-26-90	0	1	5.14	15	0	0	0	14	10	8	8	4	8	13	.200	.167	.219	8.36	5.14
2-team total (2 San Francisco)					0	1	5.06	17	0	0	0	16	14	9	9	5	9	18	.233	.292	.194	10.13	5.06
Burnes, Corbin	R-R	6-3	205	10-22-94	1	5	8.82	32	4	0	1	49	70	52	48	17	20	70	.330	.398	.287	12.86	3.67
Chacin, Jhoulys	R-R	6-3	215	1-7-88	3	10	5.79	19	19	0	0	89	99	61	57	19	39	80	.282	.273	.289	8.12	3.96
Claudio, Alex	L-L	6-3	180	1-31-92	2	2	4.06	83	0	0	0	62	57	29	28	8	24	44	.246	.219	.274	6.39	3.48
Davies, Zach	R-R	6-0	155	2-7-93	10	7	3.55	31	31	0	0	160	155	73	63	20	51	102	.256	.254	.258	5.75	2.87
Faria, Jake	R-R	6-4	225	7-30-93	0	1	11.42	9	0	0	0	9	18	12	11	3	5	8	.439	.500	.368	8.31	5.19
Gonzalez, Gio	R-L	6-0	205	9-19-85	3	2	3.50	19	17	0	0	87	76	36	34	9	37	78	.234	.147	.257	8.04	3.81
Guerra, Deolis	R-R	6-5	245	4-17-89	0	0	54.00	1	0	0	0	1	4	4	4	1	0	0	.800	1.000	.500	0.00	0.00
Guerra, Junior	R-R	6-0	205	1-16-85	9	5	3.55	72	0	0	3	84	58	35	33	11	36	77	.194	.178	.206	8.28	3.87
Hader, Josh	L-L	6-3	185	4-7-94	3	5	2.62	61	0	0	37	76	41	24	22	15	20	138	.155	.143	.158	16.41	2.38
Hart, Donnie	L-L	5-11	180	9-6-90	0	0	0.00	4	0	0	0	7	4	0	0	0	4	3	.182	.214	.125	4.05	5.40
2-team total (1 New York)					0	0	0.00	5	0	0	0	8	4	0	0	0	4	3	.160	.214	.091	3.52	4.70
Houser, Adrian	R-R	6-4	235	2-2-93	6	7	3.72	35	18	0	0	111	101	49	46	14	37	117	.244	.277	.217	9.46	2.99
Jackson, Jay	R-R	6-1	195	10-27-87	1	0	4.45	28	0	0	0	30	22	15	15	6	18	47	.202	.250	.174	13.95	5.34
Jeffress, Jeremy	R-R	6-0	205	9-21-87	3	4	5.02	48	0	0	1	52	54	32	29	5	17	46	.269	.281	.259	7.96	2.94
Lyles, Jordan	R-R	6-5	230	10-19-90	7	1	2.45	11	11	0	0	59	43	19	16	9	22	56	.202	.214	.194	8.59	3.38
2-team total (17 Pittsburgh)					12	8	4.15	28	28	0	0	141	131	72	65	25	55	146	.244	.277	.220	9.32	3.51
Nelson, Jimmy	R-R	6-6	250	6-5-89	0	2	6.95	10	3	0	0	22	25	18	17	4	17	26	.291	.333	.250	10.64	6.95
Peralta, Freddy	R-R	5-11	175	6-4-96	7	3	5.29	39	8	0	1	85	87	58	50	15	37	115	.257	.219	.280	12.18	3.92
Perez, Hernan	R-R	6-1	215	3-26-91	0	0	3.00	3	0	0	0	3	2	1	1	1	2	1	.222	.000	.286	3.00	6.00
Petricka, Jake	R-R	6-5	220	6-5-88	0	0	3.38	6	0	0	0	6	3	3	0	6	3	.207	.250	.191	3.38	6.75
Pomeranz, Drew	R-L	6-6	240	11-22-88	0	1	2.39	25	1	0	2	26	16	7	7	4	8	45	.176	.182	.172	15.38	2.73
2-team total (21 San Francisco)					2	10	4.85	46	18	0	2	104	105	58	56	21	44	137	.261	.230	.274	11.86	3.81

MILWAUKEE BREWERS

	B-T	HT	WT	DOB	W	L	ERA	G	GS	CG	SV	IP	H	R	ER	HR	BB	SO	AVG	OBP	SLG	K/9	BB/9
Smith, Burch	R-R	6-4	225	4-12-90	0	1	7.82	7	0	0	0	13	16	11	11	3	10	14	.296	.318	.281	9.95	7.11
2-team total (10 San Francisco)					0	1	5.48	17	0	0	0	21	26	14	13	3	14	20	.289	.308	.275	8.44	5.91
Suter, Brent	L-L	6-5	195	8-29-89	4	0	0.49	9	0	0	0	18	10	1	1	1	1	15	.156	.235	.128	7.36	0.49
Wilkerson, Aaron	R-R	6-3	190	5-24-89	0	0	7.31	8	0	0	0	16	25	13	13	4	9	11	.357	.412	.306	6.19	5.06
Williams, Devin	R-R	6-3	165	9-21-94	0	0	3.95	13	0	0	0	14	18	9	6	2	6	14	.310	.269	.344	9.22	3.95
Williams, Taylor	B-R	5-11	195	7-21-91	1	1	9.82	10	0	0	0	15	22	17	16	1	7	15	.344	.385	.316	9.20	4.30
Wilson, Alex	R-R	6-0	220	11-3-86	1	1	9.53	13	0	0	1	11	15	12	12	3	9	13	.313	.357	.294	10.32	7.15
Woodruff, Brandon	L-R	6-4	215	2-10-93	11	3	3.62	22	22	0	0	122	109	49	49	12	30	143	.240	.265	.218	10.58	2.22

Fielding

Catcher	PCT	G	PO	A	E	DP	PB
Grandal	.993	137	1169	41	8	10	8
Nottingham	.929	6	13	0	1	0	0
Pina	.984	53	350	15	6	1	2

First Base	PCT	G	PO	A	E	DP
Aguilar	.991	60	405	35	4	38
Austin	.958	9	21	2	1	2
Grandal	.992	20	114	8	1	14
Nottingham	.000	1	0	0	0	0
Perez	1.000	5	7	0	0	1
Shaw	1.000	6	12	2	0	1
Thames	.996	105	639	45	3	63

Second Base	PCT	G	PO	A	E	DP
Hiura	.949	81	123	175	16	43
Moustakas	.993	47	64	86	1	25
Perez	.993	45	62	83	1	20
Saladino	1.000	3	3	6	0	0
Shaw	.000	2	0	0	0	0
Spangenberg	.983	22	24	35	1	8

Third Base	PCT	G	PO	A	E	DP
Aguilar	.000	2	0	0	0	0
Moustakas	.952	105	67	151	11	17
Perez	1.000	14	5	16	0	4
Pina	.000	1	0	0	0	0
Saladino	1.000	6	1	2	0	0
Shaw	.979	71	27	116	3	9
Spangenberg	1.000	6	3	12	0	2

Shortstop	PCT	G	PO	A	E	DP
Arcia	.976	150	208	350	14	79
Dubon	.000	1	0	0	0	0
Perez	.946	21	15	20	2	3
Saladino	.977	13	18	25	1	7
Spangenberg	1.000	4	2	4	0	0

Outfield	PCT	G	PO	A	E	DP
Braun	.970	112	155	6	5	0
Cain	.994	144	306	5	2	1
Gamel	.993	108	148	2	1	1
Grisham	1.000	42	69	1	0	0
Perez	1.000	10	11	0	0	0
Saladino	1.000	7	6	0	0	0
Spangenberg	1.000	3	6	1	0	0
Taylor	1.000	11	7	0	0	0
Thames	1.000	12	10	1	0	0
Yelich	.983	125	225	7	4	2

SAN ANTONIO MISSIONS   TRIPLE-A
PACIFIC COAST LEAGUE

Batting	B-T	HT	WT	DOB	AVG	vLH	vRH	G	AB	R	H	2B	3B	HR	RBI	BB	HBP	SH	SF	SO	SB	CS	SLG	OBP
Allemand, Blake	B-R	5-10	185	7-1-92	.219	.182	.235	50	73	12	16	3	1	4	15	12	0	0	0	12	0	1	.452	.329
Austin, Tyler	R-R	6-2	220	9-6-91	.333	.231	.366	15	54	15	18	3	0	4	10	8	0	0	1	17	3	1	.611	.413
Dubon, Mauricio	R-R	6-0	160	7-19-94	.297	.286	.301	98	404	59	120	22	1	16	47	18	4	1	0	59	9	6	.475	.333
2-team total (25 Sacramento)					.302	.317	.296	123	503	82	152	26	1	20	56	28	5	1	0	68	10	8	.477	.345
Erceg, Lucas	L-R	6-3	210	5-1-95	.219	.242	.211	116	357	55	78	17	1	15	52	44	2	0	3	102	2	2	.398	.305
Ewing, Skyler	R-R	6-1	225	8-22-92	.143	.200	.111	7	14	2	2	1	0	0	1	4	0	0	0	8	0	0	.214	.333
Freitas, David	R-R	6-3	225	3-18-89	.387	.490	.337	85	310	51	120	21	0	12	76	42	2	0	3	49	0	1	.571	.459
2-team total (6 Tacoma)					.381	.482	.329	91	328	55	125	23	0	12	81	47	4	0	3	55	0	1	.561	.461
Gamel, Ben	L-L	5-11	185	5-17-92	.286	.167	.375	4	14	7	4	0	0	1	2	4	1	0	0	3	1	0	.500	.474
Gosewisch, Tuffy	R-R	5-11	200	8-17-83	.205	.184	.215	48	117	9	24	3	0	3	9	11	5	0	1	34	0	1	.308	.299
Grisham, Trent	L-L	6-0	205	11-1-96	.381	.325	.404	34	134	37	51	8	3	13	30	23	0	1	0	22	6	1	.776	.471
Hager, Jake	R-R	6-1	170	3-4-93	.242	.270	.229	114	327	45	79	16	2	12	41	30	1	4	4	107	5	1	.413	.304
Hiura, Keston	R-R	5-11	190	8-2-96	.329	.290	.344	57	213	44	70	16	1	19	46	23	6	0	1	64	7	2	.681	.407
Nottingham, Jacob	R-R	6-2	230	4-3-95	.231	.256	.222	83	290	40	67	21	0	5	40	28	9	0	5	95	6	1	.355	.313
O'Neill, Michael	R-R	6-1	195	6-12-92	.229	.235	.226	17	48	8	11	3	0	0	6	4	0	0	0	15	0	0	.292	.289
Orf, Nate	R-R	5-9	180	2-1-90	.272	.307	.258	125	405	85	110	21	1	11	54	65	22	5	2	74	11	3	.410	.399
Perez, Hernan	R-R	6-1	215	3-26-91	.290	.364	.257	27	107	18	31	10	0	5	19	14	0	0	0	23	6	0	.523	.372
Ray, Corey	L-L	6-0	195	9-22-94	.188	.203	.182	53	207	23	39	8	0	7	21	20	1	0	2	89	3	1	.329	.261
Saladino, Tyler	R-R	6-0	200	7-20-89	.287	.351	.261	79	265	51	76	19	2	17	64	41	2	0	2	67	8	1	.566	.384
Shaw, Travis	L-R	6-4	230	4-16-90	.286	.293	.283	42	133	27	38	4	0	12	33	36	2	0	3	37	3	1	.587	.437
Spangenberg, Cory	L-R	6-0	195	3-16-91	.309	.264	.329	113	424	82	131	28	5	14	62	43	6	0	3	136	28	4	.498	.378
Stokes Jr., Troy	R-R	5-8	182	2-2-96	.233	.242	.229	95	322	50	75	22	0	9	40	47	8	0	4	87	14	3	.385	.341
Taylor, Tyrone	R-R	6-0	185	1-22-94	.270	.310	.252	92	334	44	90	20	1	14	59	28	7	1	5	85	5	0	.461	.334
Williams, Jess	L-R	5-11	185	5-31-99	.111	.200	.000	2	9	1	1	0	0	0	2	1	0	0	0	3	0	0	.111	.200
Wilson, Michael	L-R	6-0	200	3-29-98	.200	.250	.000	1	5	1	1	1	0	0	0	1	0	0	0	2	0	0	.400	.333

Pitching	B-T	HT	WT	DOB	W	L	ERA	G	GS	CG	SV	IP	H	R	ER	HR	BB	SO	AVG	vLH	vRH	K/9	BB/9
Anderson, Chase	R-R	6-1	200	11-30-87	0	0	4.50	1	1	0	0	4	3	2	2	1	0	6	.200	.250	.182	13.50	0.00
Archer, Tristan	R-R	6-2	200	10-18-90	0	1	4.32	10	1	0	0	17	18	10	8	1	6	14	.261	.370	.191	7.56	3.24
Barker, Luke	R-R	6-3	230	3-11-92	1	1	1.20	17	1	0	0	30	13	6	4	2	7	32	.130	.150	.150	9.60	2.10
Barnes, Jacob	R-R	6-2	220	4-14-90	2	0	4.50	14	0	0	1	14	14	7	7	3	2	15	.246	.222	.256	9.64	1.29
2-team total (3 Omaha)					2	0	4.32	17	0	0	1	17	18	8	8	3	2	21	.261	.250	.267	11.34	1.08
Belisario, Johan	R-R	5-11	165	8-13-93	0	2	21.60	2	2	0	0	5	15	15	12	2	6	3	.469	.588	.333	5.40	10.80
Black, Ray	R-R	6-5	225	6-26-90	0	0	1.50	6	0	0	1	6	1	2	1	0	2	9	.059	.100	.000	13.50	3.00
2-team total (23 Sacramento)					1	0	4.40	29	1	0	2	29	20	15	14	4	15	45	.200	.188	.212	14.13	4.71
Brown, Zack	R-R	6-1	180	12-15-94	3	7	5.79	25	23	0	0	117	138	86	75	16	64	98	.298	.312	.288	7.56	4.94
Burnes, Corbin	R-R	6-3	205	10-22-94	0	1	8.46	8	7	0	0	22	29	21	21	2	9	25	.312	.333	.289	10.07	3.63
Coulombe, Danny	L-L	5-10	190	10-26-89	1	0	4.15	14	0	0	0	13	13	7	6	4	2	18	.245	.191	.281	12.46	1.38
Derby, Bubba	L-R	5-11	185	2-24-94	7	8	4.99	27	18	0	1	115	117	68	64	21	49	104	.263	.288	.243	8.12	3.82
Faria, Jake	R-R	6-4	225	7-30-93	1	1	2.35	6	0	0	0	8	8	2	2	1	5	8	.276	.300	.263	9.39	5.87
Fields, Josh	R-R	6-0	191	8-19-85	1	0	8.22	8	0	0	3	8	7	8	7	2	4	5	.233	.222	.238	5.87	4.70
2-team total (17 Nashville)					2	1	6.57	25	0	0	6	25	26	21	18	9	10	24	.268	.250	.279	8.76	3.65

Gonzalez, Gio	R-L	6-0	205	9-19-85	0	0	1.93	1	1	0	0	5	5	1	1	1	0	4	.263	.333	.250	7.71	0.00
Gosewisch, Tuffy	R-R	5-11	200	8-17-83	0	1	0.00	1	0	0	0	3	1	1	0	0	1	0	.143	.000	.333	0.00	3.38
Griep, Nate	R-R	6-2	210	10-11-93	0	0	0.00	1	0	0	0	2	1	0	0	0	3	2	.167	.000	.333	10.80	16.20
Guerra, Deolis	R-R	6-5	245	4-17-89	4	0	1.89	45	1	0	0	67	43	19	14	5	16	88	.181	.156	.197	11.88	2.16
Hart, Donnie	L-L	5-11	180	9-6-90	4	3	4.10	40	0	0	3	37	43	21	17	3	13	30	.279	.246	.306	7.23	3.13
Houser, Adrian	R-R	6-4	235	2-2-93	2	0	1.27	4	4	0	0	21	13	4	3	2	4	23	.169	.267	.106	9.70	1.69
Jackson, Jay	R-R	6-1	195	10-27-87	5	2	1.33	34	0	0	8	41	28	10	6	1	10	54	.193	.122	.229	11.95	2.21
Jankins, Thomas	R-R	6-3	220	7-2-95	10	5	4.38	23	21	0	0	123	137	67	60	17	32	88	.282	.293	.275	6.42	2.34
Jeffress, Jeremy	R-R	6-0	205	9-21-87	0	0	14.54	4	0	0	0	4	9	7	7	3	0	5	.409	.400	.417	10.38	0.00
Kuntz, Brad	L-L	6-0	180	5-14-92	0	2	20.25	2	1	0	0	4	13	11	9	3	5	2	.565	.600	.556	4.50	11.25
Lindell, Karsen	R-R	6-3	190	6-2-96	0	0	13.50	1	0	0	0	2	4	3	3	2	1	2	.444	.333	.500	9.00	4.50
Luna, Carlos	R-R	6-1	175	9-25-96	0	0	1.80	1	1	0	0	5	4	1	1	0	1	5	.235	.333	.182	9.00	1.80
Miller, Shelby	R-R	6-3	225	10-10-90	1	2	4.79	5	5	0	0	21	17	13	11	1	16	20	.230	.200	.250	8.71	6.97
Nelson, Jimmy	R-R	6-6	250	6-5-89	3	2	4.69	16	4	0	0	40	33	24	21	4	24	57	.219	.234	.212	12.72	5.36
Olczak, Jon	R-R	6-0	180	11-14-93	1	3	4.95	24	0	0	1	36	41	24	20	5	8	35	.287	.400	.226	8.67	1.98
Peralta, Freddy	R-R	5-11	175	6-4-96	0	0	1.29	4	0	0	0	7	4	1	1	0	3	17	.160	.100	.200	21.86	3.86
Perdomo, Angel	L-L	6-6	198	5-7-94	3	2	5.17	40	0	0	1	54	47	33	31	8	38	86	.233	.227	.236	14.33	6.33
Petricka, Jake	R-R	6-5	220	6-5-88	1	1	1.89	16	0	0	3	19	14	5	4	0	4	22	.206	.200	.209	12.64	1.89
2-team total (24 Nashville)					2	2	3.74	40	0	0	7	46	43	21	19	3	15	51	.246	.275	.226	10.05	2.96
Sanchez, Miguel	R-R	6-3	190	12-31-93	4	5	4.35	40	5	0	1	60	56	32	29	5	23	62	.242	.270	.225	9.30	3.45
Smith, Burch	R-R	6-4	225	4-12-90	3	2	2.33	15	15	0	0	77	49	22	20	6	37	85	.181	.178	.183	9.89	4.31
2-team total (3 Sacramento)					7	4	2.63	18	17	0	0	92	65	34	27	7	46	103	.198	.199	.197	10.04	4.48
Smyly, Drew	L-L	6-3	190	6-13-89	1	0	4.97	3	3	0	0	13	10	7	7	2	3	18	.217	.125	.237	12.79	2.13
Supak, Trey	R-R	6-5	240	5-31-96	1	2	9.30	7	7	0	0	30	41	31	31	6	9	27	.325	.340	.317	8.10	2.70
Suter, Brent	L-L	6-5	195	8-29-89	0	0	0.00	4	2	0	0	12	4	0	0	0	2	18	.103	.100	.103	13.89	1.54
Tonkin, Michael	R-R	6-7	220	11-19-89	3	0	4.26	14	0	0	0	13	9	7	6	4	9	14	.200	.091	.235	9.95	6.39
2-team total (5 Reno)					3	0	5.73	19	0	0	0	22	21	17	14	6	14	25	.250	.294	.220	10.23	5.73
Wilkerson, Aaron	R-R	6-3	190	5-24-89	8	2	3.42	17	17	0	0	76	62	30	29	10	29	81	.221	.207	.229	9.55	3.42
Williams, Devin	R-R	6-3	165	9-21-94	0	0	0.00	3	0	0	0	4	2	0	0	1	6		.167	.000	.200	14.73	2.45
Williams, Taylor	B-R	5-11	195	7-21-91	3	3	2.83	46	0	0	6	54	40	24	17	8	21	57	.204	.233	.182	9.50	3.50
Wilson, Alex	R-R	6-0	220	11-3-86	4	1	2.13	29	0	0	2	38	33	11	9	8	7	31	.236	.200	.253	7.34	1.66
2-team total (10 Iowa)					5	3	2.86	39	0	0	3	50	45	18	16	10	9	42	.242	.235	.246	7.51	1.61

Fielding

Catcher	PCT	G	PO	A	E	DP	PB
Freitas	.991	47	417	14	4	1	3
Gosewisch	.993	34	253	16	2	1	4
Nottingham	.992	66	619	41	5	1	10

First Base	PCT	G	PO	A	E	DP
Austin	.963	13	95	8	4	7
Erceg	.993	18	118	15	1	10
Ewing	1.000	2	11	0	0	2
Freitas	.995	25	194	11	1	19
Gosewisch	1.000	1	5	1	0	1
Hager	1.000	47	284	32	0	29
Nottingham	1.000	8	49	4	0	5
Perez	.988	10	69	11	1	10
Saladino	1.000	15	102	7	0	17
Shaw	.973	10	63	8	2	8
Spangenberg	.974	11	67	9	2	12

Second Base	PCT	G	PO	A	E	DP
Allemand	.977	20	18	24	1	6
Dubon	.951	12	13	26	2	7
Hager	.957	13	22	22	2	8
Hiura	.971	46	93	111	6	30
Orf	.990	30	34	66	1	13
Perez	.972	9	16	19	1	5
Saladino	.955	11	18	24	2	7
Shaw	1.000	2	2	2	0	1
Spangenberg	.974	20	33	43	2	12

Third Base	PCT	G	PO	A	E	DP
Allemand	.500	4	0	1	1	0
Dubon	1.000	1	2	1	0	0
Erceg	.943	84	48	150	12	23
Hager	.960	16	4	20	1	1
Orf	.917	8	3	8	1	2
Perez	1.000	5	0	10	0	2
Saladino	.947	12	9	9	1	2
Shaw	.946	23	9	44	3	7
Spangenberg	.947	16	14	22	2	0
Williams	.800	1	1	3	1	0

Shortstop	PCT	G	PO	A	E	DP
Dubon	.964	83	100	219	12	51
Hager	.962	33	39	62	4	16
Orf	1.000	1	1	0	0	0
Perez	1.000	2	1	2	0	0
Saladino	.956	18	28	37	3	6
Spangenberg	.980	16	16	32	1	6

Outfield	PCT	G	PO	A	E	DP
Allemand	.000	4	0	0	0	0
Austin	.000	1	0	0	0	0
Gamel	1.000	3	7	0	0	0
Grisham	.972	33	68	1	2	1
Hager	1.000	6	2	0	0	0
O'Neill	1.000	15	18	0	0	0
Orf	.979	86	140	3	3	1
Perez	.000	2	0	0	0	0
Ray	.966	51	84	2	3	0
Saladino	.964	19	27	0	1	0
Spangenberg	.976	55	80	1	2	0
Stokes Jr.	.982	91	106	3	2	0
Taylor	.990	87	183	8	2	1
Williams	1.000	1	1	0	0	0
Wilson	1.000	1	7	0	0	0

BILOXI SHUCKERS

SOUTHERN LEAGUE

DOUBLE-A

Batting	B-T	HT	WT	DOB	AVG	vLH	vRH	G	AB	R	H	2B	3B	HR	RBI	BB	HBP	SH	SF	SO	SB	CS	SLG	OBP
Aguilar, Ryan	L-L	6-2	168	9-11-94	.236	.188	.250	24	72	12	17	2	0	3	8	8	0	1	0	24	2	2	.389	.313
Allemand, Blake	B-R	5-10	185	7-1-92	.234	.333	.154	18	47	4	11	3	0	2	6	2	4	0	0	15	0	0	.426	.321
Alvarez, Alexander	R-R	5-11	197	9-14-96	.245	.317	.214	45	139	13	34	8	0	1	14	15	1	1	1	46	0	0	.324	.321
Aviles Jr., Luis	R-R	6-1	170	3-16-95	.253	.267	.248	84	300	47	76	16	0	2	31	32	1	3	5	89	27	7	.327	.323
Caldwell, Bruce	L-R	5-11	175	11-27-91	.217	.157	.235	100	313	34	68	15	0	9	49	35	0	1	5	93	2	2	.351	.292
Ewing, Skyler	R-R	6-1	225	8-22-92	.130	.000	.158	10	23	0	3	2	0	0	3	1	0	0	0	9	0	0	.217	.167
Feliciano, Mario	R-R	6-1	195	11-20-98	.167	.143	.200	3	12	2	2	0	1	0	0	0	0	2	0	4	0	0	.333	.286
Gatewood, Jake	R-R	6-5	190	9-25-95	.187	.235	.167	94	353	49	66	10	1	13	45	26	2	0	4	140	3	0	.331	.244
Grisham, Trent	L-L	6-0	205	11-1-96	.254	.290	.240	63	236	34	60	14	3	13	41	44	1	0	2	50	6	4	.504	.371
Hairston, Devin	R-R	5-8	175	4-7-96	.091	.000	.143	6	11	1	1	1	0	0	3	2	0	1	0	3	0	0	.182	.231

MILWAUKEE BREWERS

	B-T	HT	WT	DOB	AVG	vLH	vRH	G	AB	R	H	2B	3B	HR	RBI	BB	HBP	SH	SF	SO	SB	CS	SLG	OBP
Hinojosa, C.J.	R-R	5-10	175	7-15-94	.280	.273	.283	120	415	51	116	24	1	8	45	39	0	2	4	61	3	5	.400	.338
Hummel, Cooper	B-R	5-10	198	11-28-94	.249	.272	.237	121	342	62	85	8	5	17	56	62	14	0	1	100	4	7	.450	.384
Leonard, Patrick	R-R	6-4	225	10-20-92	.301	.374	.270	99	355	54	107	22	2	10	45	42	2	0	4	109	9	1	.459	.375
McDowell, Max	R-R	6-1	208	1-12-94	.213	.217	.211	87	258	31	55	14	0	4	22	35	13	6	3	58	2	0	.314	.333
O'Neill, Michael	R-R	6-1	195	6-12-92	.286	.321	.273	57	206	27	59	5	1	4	19	16	2	0	0	62	15	3	.379	.344
2-team total (22 Chattanooga)					.291	.290	.292	79	292	42	85	7	1	5	23	22	3	2	0	82	15	3	.373	.347
Ray, Corey	L-L	6-0	195	9-22-94	.250	.400	.200	11	40	5	10	3	0	0	6	0	0	0	0	14	3	2	.325	.348
Rojas, Robie	R-R	5-7	179	12-3-94	.296	.167	.333	12	27	5	8	2	1	0	2	4	0	0	0	10	1	0	.444	.387
Segovia, Joantgel	R-R	6-1	194	11-8-96	.247	.341	.198	74	255	24	63	15	0	2	24	15	3	0	2	38	7	6	.329	.295
Thomas, Dillon	L-L	6-1	215	12-10-92	.265	.259	.267	131	449	62	119	25	6	13	71	41	11	0	3	132	22	11	.434	.339
Wilson, Weston	R-R	6-3	215	9-11-94	.232	.252	.222	127	445	70	103	19	3	19	58	58	4	0	3	111	12	3	.416	.324

Pitching	B-T	HT	WT	DOB	W	L	ERA	G	GS	CG	SV	IP	H	R	ER	HR	BB	SO	AVG	vLH	vRH	K/9	BB/9
Andrews, Clayton	L-L	5-6	160	1-4-97	3	0	2.59	17	0	0	0	31	19	9	9	3	15	33	.171	.152	.180	9.48	4.31
Barker, Luke	R-R	6-3	230	3-11-92	0	1	1.48	23	0	0	8	30	11	7	5	1	8	34	.113	.189	.067	10.09	2.37
Belisario, Johan	R-R	5-11	165	8-13-93	9	2	3.95	23	11	0	0	84	75	38	37	10	22	69	.241	.245	.238	7.36	2.35
Bender, Anthony	R-R	6-4	205	2-3-95	0	1	1.59	4	0	0	0	6	8	3	1	1	1	4	.364	.444	.308	6.35	1.59
Benoit, Rodrigo	R-R	6-2	200	2-23-94	1	5	5.19	7	0	0	0	9	8	6	5	1	3	11	.258	.200	.286	11.42	3.12
Bettinger, Alec	R-R	6-2	210	7-13-95	5	7	3.44	26	26	1	0	146	121	62	56	13	35	157	.223	.207	.236	9.66	2.15
Brown, Daniel	L-L	5-9	188	3-22-95	3	0	3.19	35	1	0	1	48	33	19	17	3	31	46	.194	.160	.221	8.63	5.81
Contreras, Luis	R-R	6-1	175	4-29-96	0	0	0.00	1	0	0	1	3	3	0	0	0	2	2	.273	.200	.333	6.00	6.00
Diplan, Marcos	R-R	6-0	170	9-18-96	3	4	4.99	30	5	0	3	58	47	34	32	6	37	63	.221	.206	.234	9.83	5.77
2-team total (8 Pensacola)					3	5	4.85	38	7	0	3	69	57	39	37	7	44	73	.225	.229	.222	9.57	5.77
Diplan, Nattino	R-R	6-3	180	12-30-93	1	1	4.44	21	0	0	0	26	33	21	13	2	20	23	.306	.287	.286	7.86	6.84
File, Dylan	R-R	6-1	205	6-4-96	9	2	2.79	14	14	0	0	81	74	27	25	5	15	73	.243	.282	.210	8.14	1.67
Francis, Bowden	R-R	6-5	225	4-22-96	7	8	3.99	25	24	0	0	129	111	61	57	14	49	145	.233	.304	.182	10.14	3.43
Griep, Nate	R-R	6-2	210	10-11-93	6	1	1.98	43	0	0	22	55	31	15	12	1	26	55	.169	.180	.160	9.05	4.28
Jankins, Thomas	R-R	6-3	220	7-2-95	1	0	2.25	2	2	1	0	12	8	4	3	0	2	11	.182	.280	.053	8.25	1.50
Kurcz, Aaron	R-R	6-0	175	8-8-90	2	1	2.08	26	0	0	1	30	23	10	7	4	6	33	.205	.204	.206	9.79	1.78
Olczak, Jon	R-R	6-0	180	11-14-93	0	0	1.54	11	0	0	0	12	14	4	2	0	6	13	.292	.462	.229	10.03	4.63
Peralta, Freddy	R-R	5-11	175	6-4-96	0	1	5.79	1	1	0	0	5	4	3	3	1	1	7	.235	.000	.267	13.50	1.93
Perdomo, Angel	L-L	6-6	198	5-7-94	2	0	1.17	7	0	0	0	15	6	2	2	0	8	21	.128	.105	.143	12.33	4.70
Ponce, Cody	R-R	6-5	240	4-25-94	1	3	3.29	27	0	0	1	38	33	17	14	1	12	44	.236	.234	.237	10.33	2.82
Rasmussen, Drew	R-R	6-1	225	7-27-95	1	3	3.54	22	18	0	0	61	49	26	24	4	29	77	.223	.253	.198	11.36	4.28
Roegner, Cameron	R-L	6-6	205	6-19-93	5	6	4.50	17	11	0	0	76	77	44	38	5	33	73	.258	.247	.263	8.64	3.91
Spurlin, Tyler	R-R	6-3	220	6-17-91	4	2	1.82	22	1	0	0	30	18	9	6	1	11	31	.177	.279	.102	9.40	3.34
Supak, Trey	R-R	6-5	240	5-31-96	11	4	2.20	20	20	1	0	123	84	33	30	6	23	91	.192	.196	.189	6.68	1.69
Suter, Brent	L-L	6-5	195	8-29-89	0	0	0.00	2	0	0	0	-	3	0	0	0	1	3	.000	.000	.000	9.00	3.00
Topa, Justin	R-R	6-4	200	3-7-91	0	3	2.63	18	0	0	0	24	22	9	7	0	8	22	.244	.216	.264	8.25	3.00
Webb, Braden	R-R	6-3	200	4-25-95	1	4	9.00	6	5	0	0	15	15	17	15	2	15	13	.259	.273	.250	7.80	9.00
Williams, Devin	R-R	6-3	165	9-21-94	7	2	2.36	31	0	0	4	53	34	16	14	3	29	76	.181	.178	.184	12.83	4.89

Fielding

Catcher	PCT	G	PO	A	E	DP	PB
Alvarez	.977	43	313	23	8	3	3
Ewing	.981	6	50	3	1	1	1
Feliciano	1.000	1	9	0	0	0	0
McDowell	.994	87	803	67	5	7	5
Rojas	1.000	5	42	4	0	0	0

First Base	PCT	G	PO	A	E	DP
Aguilar	.978	13	83	5	2	6
Caldwell	1.000	3	12	1	0	3
Leonard	.999	94	680	53	1	62
Wilson	.993	35	244	22	2	19

Second Base	PCT	G	PO	A	E	DP
Allemand	1.000	3	7	12	0	3
Caldwell	.979	32	35	58	2	15
Hairston	.800	1	2	2	1	0
Hinojosa	.981	100	176	229	8	45
Wilson	1.000	14	13	25	0	6

Third Base	PCT	G	PO	A	E	DP
Allemand	1.000	5	5	6	0	1
Caldwell	.938	7	5	10	1	0
Gatewood	.919	84	49	110	14	6
Hinojosa	1.000	2	2	6	0	1
Wilson	.923	45	22	74	8	7

Shortstop	PCT	G	PO	A	E	DP
Aviles Jr.	.928	77	106	164	21	37
Caldwell	.959	46	55	108	7	23
Hairston	1.000	2	2	4	0	0
Hinojosa	.974	11	15	22	1	6
Wilson	.973	9	18	18	1	4

Outfield	PCT	G	PO	A	E	DP
Aguilar	1.000	12	29	0	0	0
Allemand	1.000	2	1	0	0	0
Andrews	1.000	7	16	0	0	0
Caldwell	.000	1	0	0	0	0
Grisham	.993	59	139	2	1	1
Hummel	.973	78	137	9	4	2
Leonard	.000	1	0	0	0	0
O'Neill	.974	54	70	6	2	0
Ray	1.000	11	22	1	0	0
Rojas	1.000	1	1	0	0	0
Segovia	1.000	70	111	9	0	2
Thomas	.984	125	248	6	4	1
Wilson	1.000	22	27	1	0	0

CAROLINA MUDCATS

CAROLINA LEAGUE

HIGH CLASS A

Batting	B-T	HT	WT	DOB	AVG	vLH	vRH	G	AB	R	H	2B	3B	HR	RBI	BB	HBP	SH	SF	SO	SB	CS	SLG	OBP
Aguilar, Ryan	L-L	6-2	168	9-11-94	.272	.211	.300	105	357	71	97	22	0	9	47	70	10	1	2	118	10	1	.409	.403
Carroll, Dallas	R-R	6-0	205	5-18-94	.125	.125	.125	18	56	6	7	0	0	1	4	12	0	0	1	20	0	1	.179	.275
Castillo, Leugim	R-R	6-2	215	7-18-99	.204	.063	.273	13	49	4	10	1	0	2	3	0	0	0	0	19	0	0	.347	.204
Clark, Zach	R-R	6-2	198	12-5-95	.191	.136	.209	84	267	23	51	13	1	9	22	18	4	4	0	112	9	3	.247	.253
Feliciano, Mario	R-R	6-1	195	11-20-98	.273	.273	.273	116	440	62	120	25	4	19	81	29	7	0	6	139	2	1	.477	.324
Garcia, Julio	B-R	6-0	175	7-31-97	.143	.150	.140	53	154	12	22	5	0	0	7	6	3	2	1	58	0	2	.175	.189
Hairston, Devin	R-R	5-8	175	4-7-96	.193	.176	.201	111	352	38	68	13	2	1	28	29	3	5	2	108	2	4	.250	.259
Henry, Payton	R-R	6-1	215	6-24-97	.242	.207	.259	121	430	49	104	22	1	14	75	26	22	0	4	142	1	1	.395	.315

Name	B-T	HT	WT	DOB	AVG	vLH	vRH	G	AB	R	H	2B	3B	HR	RBI	BB	HBP	SH	SF	SO	SB	CS	SLG	OBP
Henry, Rob	R-R	6-1	195	5-19-95	.228	.208	.237	99	325	36	74	14	2	6	46	53	12	0	0	122	12	5	.339	.356
Kahle, Nick	R-R	5-10	210	2-28-98	.000	.000	.000	2	5	0	0	0	0	0	0	1	0	0	0	2	0	0	.000	.167
Lutz, Tristen	R-R	6-2	210	8-22-98	.255	.275	.246	112	420	62	107	24	3	13	54	46	7	0	4	137	3	2	.419	.335
McInerney, Pat	R-R	6-5	245	9-14-94	.234	.271	.217	83	269	29	63	18	1	10	34	35	6	0	2	90	2	2	.420	.333
Morrison, Trever	L-R	6-0	175	4-21-95	.142	.179	.129	34	113	9	16	5	1	0	5	8	3	0	2	44	2	1	.204	.214
Rodriguez, Nathan	R-R	5-10	210	9-30-95	.057	.286	.000	11	35	2	2	1	0	0	1	4	1	0	0	8	0	0	.086	.175
Rogers, Wes	R-R	6-4	180	3-7-94	.235	.234	.235	74	243	47	57	13	4	2	18	33	2	1	3	74	9	2	.346	.327
Roscetti, Nick	R-R	6-3	190	11-6-93	.169	.154	.172	23	71	7	12	1	0	0	2	3	2	1	0	32	2	1	.183	.224
Segovia, Joantgel	R-R	6-1	194	11-8-96	.302	.318	.296	43	169	28	51	9	0	5	22	22	2	0	0	35	8	2	.444	.389
Silva, Eddie	R-R	6-0	218	4-12-96	.211	.201	.215	129	456	45	96	23	2	9	48	27	18	0	4	95	2	4	.329	.278
Turang, Brice	L-R	6-0	173	11-21-99	.200	.200	.200	47	170	25	34	6	2	1	6	34	2	0	1	47	9	1	.277	.338
Urbaez, Jackie	B-R	5-8	185	8-29-97	.000	.000	.000	6	14	0	0	0	0	0	1	2	3	0	1	7	0	0	.000	.250

Pitching	B-T	HT	WT	DOB	W	L	ERA	G	GS	CG	SV	IP	H	R	ER	HR	BB	SO	AVG	vLH	vRH	K/9	BB/9
Andrews, Clayton	L-L	5-6	160	1-4-97	2	2	3.86	22	0	0	11	28	24	12	12	2	10	44	.240	.229	.246	14.14	3.21
Ashby, Aaron	R-L	6-2	181	5-24-98	2	6	3.46	13	13	0	0	65	54	31	25	1	32	55	.229	.167	.253	7.62	4.43
Beckman, Cody	R-L	6-2	205	11-1-94	3	4	4.28	41	0	0	0	61	66	35	29	3	28	61	.282	.230	.306	9.00	4.13
Bender, Anthony	R-R	6-4	205	2-3-95	2	1	1.59	15	0	0	4	17	13	7	3	1	6	16	.213	.318	.154	8.47	3.18
Benoit, Rodrigo	R-R	6-2	200	2-23-94	6	1	3.53	33	0	0	13	36	33	24	14	1	15	31	.248	.212	.272	7.82	3.79
Bickford, Phil	R-R	6-4	200	7-10-95	3	0	2.48	20	0	0	1	33	23	9	9	2	11	53	.197	.222	.181	14.60	3.03
Dula, Chris	R-R	6-2	215	8-6-92	0	0	25.83	10	0	0	0	8	11	22	22	2	7	7	.333	.250	.381	8.22	19.96
File, Dylan	R-R	6-1	205	6-4-96	6	4	3.80	12	12	1	0	66	71	30	28	4	7	63	.277	.245	.298	8.55	0.95
Francis, Bowden	R-R	6-5	225	4-22-96	1	1	3.86	3	3	0	0	14	13	6	6	1	6	20	.241	.217	.258	12.86	3.86
Friese, Gabe	L-R	6-4	203	5-5-95	0	0	--	1	0	0	0	0	0	0	0	0	1	0	--	--	--	--	--
Gonzalez, Gio	R-L	6-0	205	9-19-85	0	0	9.00	1	1	0	0	2	4	2	2	0	0	2	.400	.200	.600	9.00	0.00
Hardy, Matt	L-R	6-0	160	7-15-95	7	4	3.32	39	4	0	0	79	79	37	29	5	19	87	.261	.270	.254	9.95	2.17
Hernandez, Nelson	R-R	6-2	170	3-13-97	11	10	4.64	27	26	1	0	144	152	78	74	14	50	102	.272	.260	.282	6.39	3.13
Hintzen, J.T.	R-R	6-5	185	6-1-96	1	2	3.20	42	0	0	1	65	59	23	23	5	24	77	.241	.227	.250	10.72	3.34
Hitt, Robbie	R-R	6-2	205	6-21-96	0	0	2.93	12	0	0	0	15	18	5	5	1	11	16	.295	.391	.237	9.39	6.46
Meister, Christian	R-R	6-3	210	10-29-93	0	0	3.18	9	0	0	0	11	9	4	4	0	7	11	.237	.385	.168	8.74	5.56
Petersen, Michael	R-R	6-7	195	5-16-94	1	2	3.00	41	0	0	2	54	35	19	18	4	34	65	.186	.162	.202	10.83	5.67
Rasmussen, Drew	R-R	6-1	225	7-27-95	0	0	1.59	4	4	0	0	11	7	2	2	0	2	16	.184	.333	.087	12.71	1.59
Rodriguez, Wuilder	R-R	6-2	180	1-21-93	0	3	7.64	4	4	0	0	18	22	19	15	1	6	10	.290	.265	.310	5.09	3.06
Smith, Matt	R-R	6-3	215	8-27-93	4	13	3.67	28	22	0	0	115	117	54	47	17	32	91	.261	.269	.255	7.10	2.50
Strzelecki, Peter	R-R	6-2	195	10-24-94	2	0	2.51	8	0	0	0	14	11	4	4	0	1	19	.212	.188	.222	11.93	0.63
Sunitsch, Scott	L-L	6-1	205	6-16-96	2	0	0.93	4	3	0	0	19	13	2	2	0	5	23	.188	.095	.229	10.71	2.33
Taugner, Christian	R-R	6-3	215	5-14-95	5	10	5.06	26	17	1	0	110	130	72	62	7	35	73	.291	.249	.328	5.95	2.85
Topa, Justin	R-R	6-4	200	3-7-91	0	3	4.50	15	0	0	3	16	14	8	8	1	2	19	.226	.231	.222	10.69	1.13
Webb, Braden	R-R	6-3	200	4-25-95	1	2	3.44	8	8	0	0	37	23	16	14	2	25	31	.187	.175	.197	7.61	6.14
Whitmer, Chad	R-R	6-3	220	5-11-95	0	1	3.60	7	0	0	0	10	11	5	4	0	1	9	.275	.267	.280	8.10	0.90
Zavolas, Noah	R-R	6-1	190	5-11-96	6	5	2.98	22	22	1	0	133	128	52	44	8	23	102	.256	.282	.234	6.90	1.56

Fielding

Catcher	PCT	G	PO	A	E	DP	PB
Feliciano	.988	61	459	31	6	6	5
Henry	.992	67	558	63	5	4	9
Henry	.000	1	0	0	0	0	0
Kahle	1.000	2	11	1	0	0	1
Morrison	1.000	1	2	0	0	0	0
Rodriguez	.989	10	90	4	1	1	1

First Base	PCT	G	PO	A	E	DP
Aguilar	.993	89	690	41	5	52
Castillo	1.000	2	12	0	0	1
McInerney	.995	49	381	19	2	28

Second Base	PCT	G	PO	A	E	DP
Carroll	.971	12	13	21	1	2
Garcia	.968	29	25	65	3	14
Hairston	.986	37	66	78	2	15
Morrison	.949	17	34	41	4	9
Roscetti	.986	22	30	43	1	10
Silva	.987	26	31	45	1	11
Turang	1.000	5	8	7	0	1
Urbaez	.963	6	7	19	1	4

Third Base	PCT	G	PO	A	E	DP
Carroll	.929	6	7	6	1	2
Garcia	1.000	2	0	3	0	0
McInerney	.891	27	21	28	6	3
Morrison	1.000	7	4	10	0	3
Roscetti	.500	1	1	0	1	1
Silva	.920	108	75	143	19	11

Shortstop	PCT	G	PO	A	E	DP
Garcia	.922	22	21	62	7	7
Hairston	.974	74	100	202	8	33
Morrison	.857	10	10	14	4	2
Turang	.967	35	59	86	5	21

Outfield	PCT	G	PO	A	E	DP
Aguilar	.972	15	32	3	1	0
Andrews	1.000	9	25	1	0	0
Castillo	1.000	10	12	2	0	0
Clark	.994	80	155	7	1	3
Garcia	.000	1	0	0	0	0
Hairston	1.000	1	2	1	0	0
Henry	.989	95	173	13	2	3
Lutz	.973	107	208	5	6	1
Morrison	.000	1	0	0	0	0
Rogers	.981	67	98	7	2	3
Segovia	.964	42	78	2	3	1

WISCONSIN TIMBER RATTLERS   LOW CLASS A
MIDWEST LEAGUE

Batting	B-T	HT	WT	DOB	AVG	vLH	vRH	G	AB	R	H	2B	3B	HR	RBI	BB	HBP	SH	SF	SO	SB	CS	SLG	OBP
Abreu, Pablo	R-R	6-0	170	10-19-99	.186	.100	.196	27	102	13	19	4	1	0	11	9	0	0	2	35	3	0	.245	.248
Castillo, Leugim	R-R	6-2	215	7-18-99	.198	.308	.175	67	222	17	44	7	1	2	21	9	2	0	3	73	3	0	.266	.233
Coca, Yeison	B-R	5-10	155	5-22-99	.203	.102	.219	130	443	44	90	13	8	6	41	47	2	7	5	148	25	12	.309	.280
Diaz, Brent	R-R	6-3		3-22-96	.245	.350	.199	70	200	26	49	12	2	4	24	32	7	1	5	55	7	4	.385	.361
Dillard, Thomas	B-R	6-0	230	8-28-97	.246	.160	.260	51	171	27	42	6	0	6	24	43	1	0	1	50	7	0	.386	.398
Fry, David	R-R	6-2	215	11-20-95	.258	.284	.254	134	504	66	130	41	1	17	70	50	6	2	6	111	7	4	.444	.329
Garcia, Gabriel	R-R	6-3	212	12-16-97	.204	.237	.199	85	279	41	57	17	1	11	42	45	12	1	1	87	5	5	.391	.338
Howell, Korry	R-R	6-3	180	9-1-98	.236	.300	.222	91	293	35	69	12	3	2	22	37	4	1	0	94	19	8	.317	.329
Lujano, Jesus	L-L	5-10	160	2-18-99	.240	.103	.254	122	445	55	107	14	4	1	37	30	5	4	6	83	23	5	.297	.292
McClanahan, Chad	L-R	6-5	200	12-22-97	.194	.235	.188	113	386	35	75	13	1	3	44	57	6	0	1	110	9	5	.257	.307
McVey, Connor	R-R	5-11	190	4-10-95	.232	.286	.222	98	310	58	72	10	1	5	25	61	15	9	2	86	11	5	.319	.381

Batting	B-T	HT	WT	DOB	AVG	vLH	vRH	G	AB	R	H	2B	3B	HR	RBI	BB	HBP	SH	SF	SO	SB	CS	SLG	OBP
Pina, Manny	R-R	6-0	215	6-5-87	.231	.000	.273	4	13	1	3	0	0	0	2	1	1	0	0	4	0	0	.231	.333
Pinero, Antonio	R-R	6-1	152	3-15-99	.189	.217	.183	78	259	33	49	12	2	3	29	12	2	4	1	72	5	6	.286	.230
Rios, Kekai	R-R	5-11	196	6-6-97	.194	.188	.195	28	98	8	19	2	0	1	10	9	1	0	1	27	0	0	.245	.266
Turang, Brice	L-R	6-0	173	11-21-99	.287	.460	.263	82	303	57	87	13	4	2	31	49	1	0	4	54	21	4	.376	.384
Ward, Je'Von	L-R	6-5	190	10-25-99	.225	.220	.226	109	373	35	84	16	7	2	46	47	0	2	1	107	7	6	.322	.311

Pitching	B-T	HT	WT	DOB	W	L	ERA	G	GS	CG	SV	IP	H	R	ER	HR	BB	SO	AVG	vLH	vRH	K/9	BB/9
Adames, Freisis	R-R	6-3	175	11-18-96	3	2	3.59	18	9	0	2	73	60	30	29	9	30	73	.226	.239	.217	9.04	3.72
Ashby, Aaron	R-L	6-2	181	5-24-98	3	4	3.54	11	10	1	0	61	47	29	24	4	28	80	.216	.200	.222	11.80	4.13
Bender, Anthony	R-R	6-4	205	2-3-95	0	1	1.32	10	0	0	5	14	10	2	2	1	2	15	.227	.400	.138	9.88	1.32
Bennett, Nick	L-L	6-4	210	9-1-97	1	0	2.21	5	3	0	0	20	15	7	5	1	4	24	.192	.211	.186	10.62	1.77
Biasi, Sal	R-R	5-11	205	9-30-95	1	0	0.00	3	0	0	0	4	2	0	0	0	2	5	.167	.200	.143	11.25	4.50
Bullock, Justin	R-R	6-2	195	5-12-99	2	2	7.78	7	3	0	0	20	21	19	17	5	14	20	.266	.424	.152	9.15	6.41
Castaneda, Victor	R-R	6-1	185	8-27-98	4	2	4.50	32	1	0	6	44	44	22	22	4	14	53	.262	.164	.337	10.84	2.86
Contreras, Luis	R-R	6-1	175	4-29-96	2	3	3.96	6	4	0	0	25	20	11	11	3	11	32	.225	.128	.300	11.52	3.96
Cousins, Jake	R-R	6-4	185	7-14-94	1	0	1.26	7	0	0	2	14	6	2	2	0	2	18	.125	.250	.063	11.30	1.26
Gillaspie, Logan	R-R	6-2	220	4-17-97	3	7	3.96	31	16	0	2	109	106	54	48	9	30	92	.258	.244	.268	7.60	2.48
Gillies, Tyler	R-R	6-2	190	6-6-95	5	2	3.17	42	0	0	4	54	42	22	19	2	20	65	.215	.282	.171	10.83	3.33
Hill, Adam	R-R	6-6	225	3-24-97	7	9	3.92	26	23	0	0	122	113	61	53	12	55	109	.253	.225	.272	8.06	4.07
Hitt, Robbie	R-R	6-2	205	6-21-96	1	3	2.89	32	0	0	2	44	43	18	14	1	17	39	.261	.227	.283	8.04	3.50
Jarvis, Justin	R-R	6-2	168	2-22-00	4	1	3.50	18	11	0	0	75	52	34	29	6	36	52	.199	.213	.185	6.27	4.34
Kelly, Antoine	L-L	6-6	205	12-5-99	0	1	18.00	1	1	0	0	3	5	6	6	2	4	4	.417	.500	.400	12.00	12.00
Lazar, Max	R-R	6-3	185	6-3-99	7	3	2.39	19	10	0	1	79	67	22	21	5	15	109	.226	.289	.179	12.42	1.71
Matulovich, Joey	R-R	6-1	195	7-6-97	1	2	7.62	9	0	0	0	13	20	16	11	4	7	15	.333	.412	.302	10.38	4.85
Mediavilla, Michael	L-L	6-5	225	8-14-95	0	0	0.92	16	0	0	2	20	11	3	2	1	2	20	.157	.263	.118	9.15	0.92
Nelson, Jimmy	R-R	6-6	250	6-5-89	0	0	9.00	1	0	0	0	1	2	1	1	0	0	1	.400	.333	.500	9.00	0.00
Olson, Reese	R-R	6-1	160	7-31-99	4	7	4.66	27	14	0	0	95	104	56	49	8	47	84	.281	.267	.290	7.99	4.47
Perez, Yohandry	R-R	6-1	197	11-1-96	0	1	9.00	4	0	0	0	5	5	8	5	1	8	5	.227	.167	.250	9.00	14.40
Rasmussen, Drew	R-R	6-1	225	7-27-95	0	0	0.00	1	1	0	0	2	1	0	0	0	0	3	.167	.333	.000	13.50	0.00
Rios, Kekai	R-R	5-11	196	6-6-97	0	0	0.00	1	0	0	0	1	0	0	0	0	0	1	.000	.000	.000	9.00	0.00
Salaman, Wilfred	L-L	5-11	210	10-5-97	5	4	4.16	32	5	0	0	63	58	32	29	5	27	47	.251	.216	.268	6.75	3.88
Small, Ethan	L-L	6-3	214	2-14-97	0	2	1.00	5	5	0	0	18	11	5	2	0	4	31	.172	.091	.189	15.50	2.00
Strzelecki, Peter	R-R	6-2	195	10-24-94	0	1	3.22	31	0	0	3	45	44	18	16	4	13	47	.262	.293	.246	9.47	2.62
Sunitsch, Scott	L-L	6-1	205	6-16-96	9	11	4.62	24	23	0	0	117	128	65	60	8	38	123	.277	.203	.302	9.46	2.92
Whitmer, Chad	R-R	6-3	220	5-11-95	6	2	3.53	33	0	0	4	51	50	25	20	2	12	48	.253	.244	.258	8.47	2.12

Fielding

Catcher	PCT	G	PO	A	E	DP	PB
Diaz	.992	68	559	53	5	4	2
Dillard	1.000	1	3	0	0	0	0
Fry	.992	66	547	60	5	1	9
Pina	1.000	2	19	0	0	0	0
Rios	1.000	12	97	10	0	1	2

First Base	PCT	G	PO	A	E	DP
Dillard	.983	33	219	15	4	27
Fry	.987	28	207	17	3	28
Garcia	.983	15	105	11	2	13
McClanahan	.982	39	257	15	5	30
McVey	.984	32	235	17	4	24

Second Base	PCT	G	PO	A	E	DP
Coca	.989	70	113	154	3	48
Fry	.000	1	0	0	0	0
Howell	.968	14	30	31	2	8
McVey	1.000	25	37	62	0	19
Pinero	.957	6	11	11	1	2
Turang	.992	28	58	65	1	16

Third Base	PCT	G	PO	A	E	DP
Coca	.929	10	9	17	2	2
Fry	.917	21	16	28	4	6
Garcia	.910	68	49	113	16	12
McClanahan	1.000	1	1	0	0	0
McVey	.962	30	18	57	3	8
Pinero	.933	19	12	30	3	4

Shortstop	PCT	G	PO	A	E	DP
Coca	.943	46	63	102	10	18
Fry	.000	1	0	0	0	0
Pinero	.963	52	67	140	8	33
Turang	.949	43	67	101	9	28

Outfield	PCT	G	PO	A	E	DP
Abreu	.984	26	58	4	1	0
Castillo	.970	48	61	3	2	0
Dillard	1.000	9	12	3	0	0
Fry	1.000	5	4	0	0	0
Howell	.988	73	164	1	2	0
Lujano	.976	118	194	9	5	1
McClanahan	.965	62	105	4	4	2
Ward	.982	82	107	5	2	1

ROCKY MOUNTAIN VIBES   ROOKIE ADVANCED
PIONEER LEAGUE

Batting	B-T	HT	WT	DOB	AVG	vLH	vRH	G	AB	R	H	2B	3B	HR	RBI	BB	HBP	SH	SF	SO	SB	CS	SLG	OBP
Avalo, Luis	R-R	5-11	190	11-24-98	.236	.195	.250	48	157	16	37	11	0	4	21	3	4	0	0	47	1	1	.382	.268
Avila, Luis	R-R	5-11	150	3-5-99	.208	.200	.211	40	120	15	25	2	1	0	9	2	1	1	2	17	6	1	.242	.224
Bello, Micah	R-R	5-11	165	7-21-00	.232	.225	.234	50	177	30	41	9	3	6	20	18	2	0	1	47	5	4	.418	.308
Cipion, Arbert	R-R	6-2	186	5-9-00	.400	.333	.455	8	20	4	8	0	1	2	6	4	1	0	0	5	0	2	.800	.520
Devanney, Cam	R-R	6-1	195	4-13-97	.246	.257	.241	33	114	20	28	7	1	5	20	15	4	0	2	30	4	4	.456	.348
Egnatuk, Nick	R-R	6-2	185	12-21-98	.220	.239	.212	50	164	28	36	8	3	5	19	17	5	1	3	67	7	3	.396	.307
Gray, Joe	R-R	6-1	195	3-12-00	.164	.143	.171	31	110	19	18	4	1	3	9	13	5	0	1	36	3	2	.300	.279
Hall, Alex	B-R	5-8	161	6-8-99	.318	.333	.313	9	22	2	7	1	0	0	4	3	0	0	0	3	0	2	.364	.400
Holt, Gabe	L-R	5-11	175	1-7-98	.219	.125	.250	9	32	4	7	1	0	2	4	1	1	0	0	2	0	0	.438	.265
Kahle, Nick	R-R	5-10	210	2-28-98	.255	.361	.219	40	141	25	36	11	1	6	25	20	1	0	1	36	2	1	.475	.350
Martinez, Ernesto	L-L	6-6	229	6-20-99	.262	.302	.248	48	164	25	43	10	1	6	25	21	3	0	0	54	4	5	.445	.356
Pinero, Antonio	R-R	6-1	152	3-15-99	.317	.297	.322	37	158	21	50	16	1	1	26	6	0	1	0	29	5	3	.449	.342
Rodriguez, Carlos	L-L	5-10	150	12-7-00	.331	.214	.376	36	151	20	50	3	1	3	12	4	1	0	1	24	6	4	.424	.350
Sano, Edwin	B-R	5-9	160	12-12-98	.268	.283	.263	60	213	27	57	12	2	3	20	15	0	6	2	48	4	7	.385	.313
Sibrian, Jose	R-R	5-11	175	10-24-98	.274	.326	.252	47	157	23	43	11	0	3	20	10	3	2	2	38	1	1	.401	.326
Torres, Bryan	L-R	5-11	165	7-2-97	.283	.241	.297	67	233	37	66	13	2	0	27	30	5	0	3	30	21	6	.356	.373
Williams, Jess	L-R	5-11	183	5-31-99	.250	.106	.298	57	188	23	47	10	2	2	24	15	1	2	4	49	4	3	.356	.303
Wilson, Michael	L-R	6-0	200	3-29-98	.225	.231	.223	47	169	21	38	9	2	5	14	18	3	1	2	80	7	1	.391	.307

Pitching	B-T	HT	WT	DOB	W	L	ERA	G	GS	CG	SV	IP	H	R	ER	HR	BB	SO	AVG	vLH	vRH	K/9	BB/9
Alberro, Jose	L-L	6-1	168	2-2-98	1	2	6.92	10	0	0	0	13	7	14	10	1	20	16	.156	.077	.188	11.08	13.85
Avila, Luis	R-R	5-11	150	3-5-99	0	0	0.00	1	0	0	0	1	1	0	0	0	0	0	.250	.000	.500	0.00	0.00
Begue, Brock	R-L	6-3	210	4-1-99	1	5	6.16	13	10	0	0	38	46	26	26	7	8	33	.311	.276	.319	7.82	1.89
Bennett, Nick	L-L	6-4	210	9-1-97	0	0	1.42	6	3	0	0	13	13	4	2	0	6	19	.265	.182	.290	13.50	4.26
Chirino, Harold	R-R	6-2	173	1-12-98	0	0	0.00	3	0	0	0	6	2	1	0	0	3	6	.105	.000	.133	9.00	4.50
Floyd, Taylor	R-R	6-1	185	12-8-97	0	1	6.10	11	0	0	1	10	13	7	7	3	7	14	.296	.167	.344	12.19	6.10
Hernandez, Franklin	R-R	6-0	175	10-29-95	1	0	5.56	5	0	0	0	11	10	7	7	1	5	10	.238	.133	.296	7.94	3.97
Lillis, Blake	L-L	6-3	180	3-10-98	0	0	4.15	1	1	0	0	4	4	2	2	2	3	6	.235	.000	.286	12.46	6.23
Lindell, Karsen	R-R	6-3	190	6-2-96	2	2	3.12	17	6	0	0	49	33	21	17	4	28	67	.195	.179	.204	12.31	5.14
Luna, Carlos	R-R	6-1	175	9-25-96	3	4	3.58	14	14	0	0	70	70	33	28	9	10	70	.254	.185	.288	8.96	1.28
Milligan, Bryce	R-R	6-1	165	7-24-98	0	0	1.17	8	0	0	3	8	5	1	1	0	3	8	.185	.125	.211	9.39	3.52
Parra, Jose	R-R	6-3	180	3-18-97	0	0	6.00	3	0	0	1	6	7	4	4	2	1	11	.292	.125	.375	16.50	1.50
Pastora, Steve	R-R	5-11	185	9-3-94	1	1	2.37	14	0	0	0	19	18	14	5	3	10	19	.247	.048	.327	9.00	4.74
Pinto, Joel	R-R	6-3	180	9-25-96	1	1	4.37	24	0	0	4	35	35	23	17	3	23	28	.265	.342	.234	7.20	5.91
Prohoroff, Dylan	R-R	6-3	215	11-29-94	1	1	5.40	11	0	0	2	10	12	7	6	2	4	12	.308	.222	.333	10.80	3.60
Robinson, Cam	R-R	5-11	187	9-6-99	0	4	8.55	5	5	0	0	20	24	23	19	5	17	22	.304	.286	.314	9.90	7.65
Rodriguez, Wuilder	R-R	6-2	180	1-21-93	0	1	6.00	6	3	0	1	21	20	16	14	3	5	24	.250	.348	.211	10.29	2.14
Rubick, Austin	R-R	6-3	210	8-11-97	0	0	20.65	6	0	0	0	6	5	14	13	0	18	5	.263	.250	.273	7.94	28.59
Sabouri, Arman	R-L	5-10	200	6-28-98	2	3	4.62	21	1	0	1	37	44	21	19	1	7	37	.293	.256	.308	9.00	1.70
Schanuel, Brady	R-R	6-3	180	2-21-97	5	2	4.76	21	0	0	0	40	33	24	21	5	30	70	.232	.200	.245	15.08	6.81
Schultz, Paxton	L-R	6-3	205	1-5-98	1	3	3.86	9	1	0	0	23	26	10	10	2	7	22	.296	.191	.328	8.49	2.70
Sierra, Cristian	R-R	6-3	180	4-1-98	3	1	4.87	22	0	0	0	44	46	24	24	1	15	47	.281	.236	.303	9.54	3.05
Sigman, Jackson	R-R	6-2	200	6-13-95	0	2	7.13	23	0	0	2	24	26	21	19	5	18	29	.268	.351	.217	10.88	6.75
Torres-Costa, Quintin	L-L	5-11	190	9-11-94	0	0	0.00	4	1	0	0	4	3	0	0	0	3	5	.214	.333	.182	11.25	6.75
Uribe, Abner	R-R	6-2	200	6-20-00	2	1	9.00	4	0	0	0	7	11	7	7	1	7	7	.423	.556	.353	6.43	9.00
Vassalotti, Michele	R-R	6-2	180	8-2-00	5	6	6.09	15	15	0	0	65	75	50	44	12	31	60	.292	.359	.263	8.31	4.29
Walters, Nash	R-R	6-5	210	5-18-97	1	2	3.40	13	13	0	0	50	36	23	19	3	32	46	.203	.150	.231	8.23	5.72
Webb, Braden	R-R	6-3	200	4-25-95	0	1	5.79	2	2	0	0	5	5	4	3	1	3	4	.263	.250	.267	7.71	5.79
Williams, Jess	L-R	5-11	183	5-31-99	0	0	18.00	2	0	0	0	2	2	4	4	1	1	1	.222	.250	.200	4.50	4.50

Fielding

C: Avalo 31, Hall 2, Kahle 17, Sibrian 33. 1B: Avalo 7, Hall 5, Kahle 1, Martinez 46, Torres 18, Williams 7. 2B: Avila 21, Egnatuk 45, Holt 5, Kahle 1, Sano 3, Williams 6. 3B: Avalo 2, Avila 11, Sano 16, Torres 41, Williams 14. SS: Avila 7, Devanney 33, Pinero 37, Sano 1. OF: Avalo 3, Bello 49, Cipion 6, Gray 29, Rodriguez 36, Sano 39, Torres 2, Williams 29, Wilson 43.

AZL BREWERS BLUE

ROOKIE

ARIZONA LEAGUE

Batting	B-T	HT	WT	DOB	AVG	vLH	vRH	G	AB	R	H	2B	3B	HR	RBI	BB	HBP	SH	SF	SO	SB	CS	SLG	OBP
Casals, Danny	R-R	6-0	190	1-27-97	.333	.526	.289	29	102	15	34	8	0	3	16	12	0	0	1	24	6	3	.500	.400
Cipion, Arbert	R-R	6-2	186	5-9-00	.243	.275	.234	47	177	33	43	9	6	4	18	24	7	0	3	70	22	6	.429	.351
Devanney, Cam	R-R	6-1	195	4-13-97	.330	.500	.296	28	106	23	35	5	2	2	14	13	5	0	1	11	13	4	.472	.424
Dillard, Thomas	B-R	6-0	230	8-28-97	.278	.500	.250	4	18	2	5	3	0	1	4	1	0	0	0	3	1	0	.611	.316
Doston, Terence	L-R	5-10	160	9-22-00	.222	.250	.220	13	45	8	10	3	0	0	3	7	3	0	0	19	12	3	.289	.364
Hall, Alex	B-R	5-8	161	6-8-99	.275	.243	.284	41	171	25	47	7	4	1	22	9	1	0	2	42	4	2	.380	.312
Hardin, Kevin	L-L	6-5	245	5-24-99	.206	.083	.231	39	141	18	29	5	1	5	19	15	4	0	1	71	0	0	.362	.298
Kou, YongKang	L-R	6-2	170	1-29-01	.143	.000	.167	28	98	6	14	1	0	1	4	2	0	0	1	53	0	2	.184	.158
Marquez, Caleb	R-R	6-3	240	12-22-99	.216	.200	.220	14	51	9	11	3	0	1	11	5	2	1	1	31	3	2	.333	.305
Melendez, Anderson	R-R	6-2	165	5-31-00	.237	.333	.219	38	135	21	32	6	2	0	12	12	4	0	2	55	5	1	.311	.314
Mercado, Reidy	B-R	5-11	153	1-6-01	.235	.200	.244	23	98	18	23	0	4	0	5	8	1	0	0	20	11	3	.316	.299
Miller, Darrien	L-R	6-0	175	3-10-01	.175	.000	.203	23	80	7	14	3	0	0	4	9	7	0	0	16	3	2	.213	.313
Nnebe, Andre	R-R	6-6	230	11-14-97	.302	.290	.306	34	129	24	39	9	2	4	19	15	4	0	0	38	6	0	.496	.392
Saint, Orveo	R-R	6-2	190	11-10-99	.176	.240	.152	31	91	11	16	2	1	3	11	14	0	0	0	53	6	5	.319	.286
Silva, Luis	R-R	6-0	178	7-6-01	.295	.300	.293	43	163	17	48	4	2	0	21	9	3	0	2	32	6	2	.344	.339
Urbaez, Jackie	B-R	5-8	185	8-29-97	.209	.222	.206	51	182	24	38	8	0	2	22	31	10	0	3	58	18	9	.286	.350
Vargas, Victor	R-R	5-7	160	8-15-00	.162	.103	.183	31	111	12	18	2	2	0	5	7	2	0	1	33	4	2	.216	.223

Pitching	B-T	HT	WT	DOB	W	L	ERA	G	GS	CG	SV	IP	H	R	ER	HR	BB	SO	AVG	vLH	vRH	K/9	BB/9
Baez, Jeyner	R-R	6-1	175	7-25-95	1	3	4.32	18	0	0	2	33	34	21	16	2	12	36	.260	.289	.241	9.72	3.24
Belzer, Nick	R-R	6-2	185	8-1-95	3	1	3.70	10	6	0	0	49	42	22	20	3	14	41	.243	.162	.303	7.58	2.59
Chirino, Harold	R-R	6-2	173	1-12-98	2	0	3.74	19	0	0	0	34	32	15	14	0	15	41	.250	.220	.269	10.96	4.01
Colina, Leoner	R-R	5-11	165	11-1-00	0	0	0.00	2	0	0	0	2	4	1	0	0	0	3	.400	.667	.286	13.50	0.00
Cousins, Jake	R-R	6-4	185	7-14-94	2	0	2.57	7	0	0	1	14	10	4	4	0	0	21	.200	.333	.103	13.50	0.00
Cruz, Jhoan	R-R	5-9	147	5-31-00	1	6	6.97	10	5	0	0	41	58	43	32	7	10	40	.319	.381	.265	8.71	2.18
Dula, Chris	R-R	6-2	215	8-6-92	0	0	9.82	4	0	0	0	4	5	5	4	1	3	6	.333	.667	.250	14.73	7.36
Espiritu, Jose	R-R	6-4	172	11-20-98	0	0	0.00	1	0	0	0	1	0	0	0	0	1	1	.000	.000	.000	13.50	13.50
Exposito, Ian	L-L	6-1	185	6-28-96	2	1	2.78	5	4	0	0	23	25	7	7	0	8	22	.260	.350	.350	8.74	3.18
2-team total (5 Brewers Gold)					3	2	3.05	10	6	0	0	41	45	16	14	0	17	51	.290	.229	.308	11.10	3.70
Garabitos, Pablo	L-L	6-1	170	7-30-00	1	0	2.14	20	0	0	1	34	33	11	8	1	8	34	.250	.375	.210	9.09	2.14
Kelly, Antoine	L-L	6-6	205	12-5-99	0	0	1.26	9	9	0	0	29	21	4	4	0	5	41	.208	.250	.198	12.87	1.57
McCarville, Keegan	R-R	6-1	210	2-3-98	2	2	1.72	20	0	0	0	37	27	9	7	2	8	46	.200	.250	.165	11.29	1.96
Medina, Henry	R-R	6-0	175	9-5-97	2	2	5.24	11	5	0	0	34	39	22	20	3	8	26	.296	.205	.333	6.82	2.10
Miller,	R-R	6-2	225	10-10-90	0	0	6.00	1	1	0	0	3	4	3	2	1	2	2	.333	.333	.333	6.00	6.00
2-team total (2 Brewers Gold)					0	1	3.00	3	3	0	0	12	8	6	4	1	3	6	.186	.167	.194	12.00	2.25
Montero, Junior	R-R	6-3	175	9-20-98	0	1	2.25	4	0	0	0	10	5	2	0	3	6	.323	.500	.261	6.75	3.38

	B-T	HT	WT	DOB	W	L	ERA	G	GS	CG	SV	IP	H	R	ER	HR	BB	SO	AVG	vLH	vRH	K/9	BB/9
Morales, Karlos	L-L	6-3	170	8-10-99	0	2	10.64	7	4	0	0	11	13	14	13	2	8	8	.310	.143	.393	6.55	6.55
Prohoroff, Dylan	R-R	6-3	215	11-29-94	0	1	1.13	6	0	0	2	8	9	4	1	0	3	8	.243	.235	.250	9.00	3.38
Ramirez, Alexis	R-R	6-2	170	7-20-99	3	3	5.15	11	9	0	0	44	52	29	25	4	23	50	.297	.357	.269	10.31	4.74
Ruiz, Moises	R-R	6-2	170	10-3-98	1	3	5.02	12	9	0	0	52	63	32	29	5	24	30	.307	.288	.317	5.19	4.15
Silva, Luis	R-R	6-0	178	7-6-01	0	1	0.00	1	0	0	0	2	3	3	0	0	1	1	.333	.500	.286	4.50	4.50
Suter, Brent	L-L	6-5	195	8-29-89	0	0	0.00	1	1	0	0	1	0	0	0	0	0	1	.000	.000	.000	9.00	0.00
2-team total (1 Brewers Gold)					0	0	0.00	2	2	0	0	2	0	0	0	0	0	4	.000	.000	.000	18.00	0.00
Tavarez, Eddy	R-R	6-6	245	5-16-95	2	4	1.37	21	0	0	3	26	11	9	4	0	25	34	.128	.156	.111	11.62	8.54
Uribe, Abner	R-R	6-2	200	6-20-00	1	1	15.43	3	2	0	0	2	4	4	4	0	4	2	.444	1.000	.167	7.71	15.43
Vega, Ariel	R-R	6-2	190	4-4-01	0	1	45.00	2	1	0	0	1	5	5	5	0	3	0	.833	.667	1.000	0.00	27.00
Yi, Jian	R-R	5-11	170	2-9-01	0	1	7.20	8	0	0	0	10	15	11	8	0	7	7	.385	.500	.320	6.30	6.30
2-team total (7 Brewers Gold)					0	3	7.58	15	0	0	0	19	30	19	16	1	7	19	.366	.355	.373	9.00	3.32

Fielding

C: Hall 37, Marquez 4, Miller 15. **1B:** Hardin 33, Kou 19, Marquez 8. **2B:** Casals 15, Saint 24, Urbaez 7, Vargas 11. **3B:** Casals 5, Devanney 1, Kou 3, Silva 28, Urbaez 6, Vargas 15. **SS:** Casals 7, Devanney 26, Silva 8, Urbaez 15. **OF:** Cipion 45, Dillard 3, Doston 13, Kou 4, Melendez 35, Mercado 23, Nnebe 29, Silva 1, Urbaez 18.

AZL BREWERS GOLD — ROOKIE
ARIZONA LEAGUE

Batting	B-T	HT	WT	DOB	AVG	vLH	vRH	G	AB	R	H	2B	3B	HR	RBI	BB	HBP	SH	SF	SO	SB	CS	SLG	OBP
Abreu, Pablo	R-R	6-0	170	10-19-99	.226	.177	.250	14	53	7	12	4	1	1	10	6	1	0	2	21	0	0	.396	.307
Castillo, Daniel	R-R	5-11	150	1-25-01	.218	.222	.217	40	147	17	32	5	1	0	9	11	2	1	3	36	8	2	.265	.276
Chirinos, Jesus	R-R	6-0	165	7-27-01	.203	.130	.221	31	118	13	24	3	1	1	10	8	2	0	0	41	1	0	.271	.266
Ernesto, Larry	B-R	6-2	175	9-12-00	.172	.214	.160	32	122	15	21	3	0	2	9	7	2	0	0	59	5	1	.246	.229
Familia, Aaron	R-R	6-2	170	3-16-99	.262	.200	.280	39	130	14	34	6	3	3	20	22	1	0	0	49	0	0	.423	.373
Florentino, Francis	R-R	6-1	180	10-13-99	.272	.280	.271	43	158	15	43	7	3	3	21	10	4	0	2	41	10	2	.411	.328
Gonzalez, Abimael	R-R	6-0	175	5-23-01	.099	.154	.086	22	71	6	7	2	0	1	2	7	4	0	0	39	4	1	.169	.220
Holt, Gabe	L-R	5-11	175	1-7-98	.500	--	.500	2	6	0	3	0	0	0	1	1	0	0	0	0	0	0	.500	.571
Leones, Oswel	L-R	6-0	165	10-6-00	.204	.133	.223	40	142	19	29	6	1	0	9	21	0	0	1	34	10	7	.261	.305
Maria, Victor	R-R	6-2	160	9-22-99	.247	.556	.203	19	73	6	18	1	0	0	2	0	1	0	0	29	5	3	.260	.257
Martinez, Juan	R-R	6-0	210	12-5-95	.225	.417	.162	18	49	3	11	1	0	0	3	1	5	1	0	10	0	0	.245	.309
McGee, Ashton	L-R	6-1	215	11-19-98	.230	.100	.263	43	148	18	34	11	2	2	22	18	4	0	0	39	1	0	.372	.329
Melendez, Andres	R-R	5-10	150	5-21-01	.250	.269	.245	36	128	18	32	8	1	1	13	16	2	0	1	24	0	1	.352	.340
Mika, Matthew	R-R	5-10	180	7-3-96	.258	.286	.250	28	97	19	25	5	1	1	16	18	1	0	2	20	0	1	.361	.373
Molina, Roberto	R-R	5-9	160	12-7-99	.118	.056	.138	22	76	3	9	1	0	0	6	8	0	2	0	21	0	0	.132	.202
Pitre, Odrick	R-R	5-10	165	8-3-00	.067	.143	.049	23	75	8	5	1	0	0	2	16	0	0	4	43	2	1	.080	.231
Ray, Corey	L-L	6-0	195	9-22-94	.533	1.000	.500	5	15	5	8	3	0	1	4	1	0	0	0	3	0	0	.933	.563
Rodriguez, Carlos	L-L	5-10	150	12-7-00	.318	.667	.263	7	22	5	7	1	0	0	1	0	0	0	0	2	1	1	.364	.318
Taylor, Norris	R-R	6-0	185	1-22-94	.417	.333	.444	5	12	1	5	1	0	0	1	2	0	0	2	0	0	0	.500	.533
Valerio, Felix	R-R	5-7	165	12-26-00	.306	.194	.333	41	157	16	48	13	0	0	18	17	2	0	2	21	16	5	.389	.376
Zurbrugg, Zane	R-R	6-4	195	6-14-97	.263	.300	.253	29	95	12	25	3	0	0	6	6	4	0	0	37	9	3	.295	.333

Pitching	B-T	HT	WT	DOB	W	L	ERA	G	GS	CG	SV	IP	H	R	ER	HR	BB	SO	AVG	vLH	vRH	K/9	BB/9
Acosta, Daniel	R-R	6-1	185	2-27-97	0	0	1.08	7	0	0	1	8	2	1	1	0	11	8	.077	.000	.133	8.64	11.88
Beard, Seth	R-R	6-1	190	6-7-96	0	1	3.65	6	0	0	0	12	11	9	5	0	7	17	.239	.278	.214	12.41	5.11
Begue, Brock	R-L	6-3	210	4-1-99	0	0	13.50	1	0	0	0	1	1	1	1	0	2	1	.333	.000	.500	13.50	27.00
Bender, Kelvin	L-L	5-11	165	3-11-00	2	2	11.47	11	3	0	0	24	42	32	31	3	21	26	.382	.375	.385	9.62	7.77
Brink, Jordan	L-R	6-0	200	3-18-93	0	0	0.00	3	1	0	0	5	1	0	0	0	1	9	.059	.000	.077	15.19	1.69
Contreras, Luis	R-R	6-1	175	4-29-96	2	1	2.01	9	0	0	0	22	12	7	5	0	9	39	.160	.219	.116	15.72	3.63
Diaz, Wilber	R-R	6-3	170	8-7-00	0	1	27.00	1	1	0	0	1	2	4	4	0	4	0	.500	.000	.667	0.00	27.00
DiMeglio, Anthony	R-R	6-1	225	1-28-97	1	0	0.00	1	0	0	0	2	3	0	0	0	0	3	.333	.000	.375	13.50	0.00
Elizondo, Santiago	R-R	5-9	154	10-25-99	0	0	1.74	7	3	0	0	21	18	8	4	1	11	18	.228	.200	.245	7.84	4.79
Exposito, Ian	L-L	6-1	185	6-28-96	1	1	3.38	5	2	0	0	19	20	9	7	0	9	29	.286	.400	.267	13.98	4.34
2-team total (5 Brewers Blue)					3	2	3.05	10	6	0	0	41	45	16	14	0	17	51	.290	.229	.308	11.10	3.70
Hernandez, Franklin	R-R	6-0	170	10-29-95	1	0	0.00	1	0	0	0	2	1	0	0	0	2	4	.143	.000	.250	18.00	9.00
Herrera, Carlos	R-R	6-2	150	10-26-97	0	1	54.00	1	1	0	0	1	2	2	2	0	3	0	.500	.500	--	0.00	81.00
Lazar, Max	R-R	6-3	185	6-3-99	0	1	1.50	3	3	0	0	6	4	1	1	0	0	10	.191	.375	.077	15.00	0.00
Long, Peyton	R-R	6-4	210	10-28-97	2	4	4.19	12	4	0	0	43	50	22	20	2	15	38	.303	.348	.271	7.95	3.14
Matulovich, Joey	R-R	6-3	195	7-6-97	0	3	4.19	8	6	0	0	19	17	9	9	1	12	30	.257	.233	.273	13.97	5.59
Miller, Shelby	R-R	6-3	225	10-10-90	0	1	2.00	2	2	0	0	9	4	3	2	0	1	14	.129	.000	.160	14.00	1.00
2-team total (1 Brewers Blue)					0	1	3.00	3	3	0	0	12	8	6	4	1	3	16	.186	.167	.194	12.00	2.25
Nabholz, Eli	R-R	6-6	225	4-16-97	1	4	4.31	10	7	0	0	31	36	19	15	2	14	33	.293	.368	.227	9.48	4.02
Owenby, Drake	L-L	6-2	205	1-7-94	0	1	22.50	3	2	0	0	2	4	5	5	0	1	4	.400	1.000	.250	18.00	4.50
Parra, Jose	R-R	6-3	180	3-18-97	3	1	2.40	21	0	0	5	30	30	16	8	0	3	34	.256	.311	.222	10.20	0.90
Perez, Mario	R-R	5-11	148	4-18-02	1	3	6.50	12	5	0	0	36	53	36	26	4	25	34	.340	.380	.321	8.50	6.25
Perez, Yohandry	R-R	6-1	197	11-1-96	0	0	5.33	16	0	0	0	27	29	22	16	2	21	32	.286	.359	.214	10.67	7.00
Robinson, Cam	R-R	5-11	187	9-6-99	0	2	9.31	13	0	0	0	19	29	22	20	1	14	23	.341	.344	.340	10.71	6.52
Rodriguez, Wuilder	R-R	6-2	180	1-21-93	0	0	4.50	4	1	0	0	6	5	3	3	0	1	7	.217	.111	.286	10.50	1.50
Romero, Jose	R-R	6-1	170	11-1-97	0	1	6.46	10	0	0	0	15	14	13	11	3	14	14	.250	.364	.177	8.22	8.22
Salaya, Brayan	R-R	6-1	178	2-13-00	2	4	7.26	13	4	0	0	48	72	47	39	3	20	52	.348	.269	.386	9.68	3.72
Shapiro, Josh	L-L	6-0	175	5-16-97	0	2	4.76	12	3	0	0	34	50	21	18	1	5	38	.347	.267	.368	10.06	1.32
Small, Ethan	L-L	6-3	214	2-14-97	0	0	0.00	2	2	0	0	3	0	0	0	0	0	5	.000	.000	.000	15.00	0.00
Suter, Brent	L-L	6-5	195	8-29-89	0	0	0.00	1	1	0	0	1	0	0	0	0	0	3	.000	.000	.000	27.00	0.00
2-team total (1 Brewers Blue)					0	0	0.00	2	2	0	0	2	0	0	0	0	0	4	.000	.000	.000	18.00	0.00

Name	B-T	HT	WT	DOB	W	L	ERA	G	GS	CG	SV	IP	H	R	ER	HR	BB	SO	AVG	vLH	vRH	K/9	BB/9
Torres-Costa, Quintin	L-L	5-11	190	9-11-94	0	0	27.00	1	0	0	0	0	1	1	1	0	3	1	.500	.000	1.000	27.00	81.00
Vennaro, Zach	R-R	6-6	220	6-3-96	0	3	3.86	21	0	0	3	28	32	19	12	1	9	35	.274	.250	.284	11.25	2.89
Webb, Braden	R-R	6-3	200	4-25-95	0	1	2.25	5	5	0	0	8	1	2	2	0	5	13	.039	.000	.059	14.63	5.63
Yi, Jian	R-R	5-11	170	2-9-01	0	2	8.00	7	0	0	0	9	15	8	8	1	0	12	.349	.235	.423	12.00	0.00
2-team total (8 Brewers Blue)					0	3	7.58	15	0	0	0	19	30	19	16	1	7	19	.366	.355	.373	9.00	3.32
Zurbrugg, Zane	R-R	6-4	195	6-14-97	0	0	45.00	1	0	0	0	1	5	5	5	0	1	0	.625	.667	.600	0.00	9.00

Fielding

C: Chirinos 1, Martinez 13, Melendez 29, Molina 21. **1B:** Chirinos 27, Familia 14, McGee 18, Mika 1. **2B:** Holt 2, McGee 8, Mika 7, Pitre 9, Valerio 32. **3B:** Familia 21, Maria 14, Mika 17, Valerio 4. **SS:** Castillo 40, Pitre 13, Valerio 3. **OF:** Abreu 2, Ernesto 31, Familia 1, Florentino 37, Gonzalez 22, Leones 39, Maria 2, McGee 11, Ray 4, Rodriguez 7, Taylor 4, Zurbrugg 29.

DSL BREWERS   ROOKIE
DOMINICAN SUMMER LEAGUE

Batting	B-T	HT	WT	DOB	AVG	vLH	vRH	G	AB	R	H	2B	3B	HR	RBI	BB	HBP	SH	SF	SO	SB	CS	SLG	OBP
Bautista, Erys	B-R	6-1	220	11-9-01	.257	.172	.271	56	206	28	53	10	0	4	25	15	5	1	0	42	2	0	.364	.323
Burciaga, Sebastian	R-R	5-7	158	9-7-01	.261	.214	.267	57	215	41	56	10	2	0	21	13	10	1	4	33	16	3	.326	.326
Cabrera, Jhonnys	R-R	5-11	150	6-5-02	.274	.167	.290	53	179	37	49	12	1	3	20	29	8	0	1	63	3	2	.402	.396
Fernandez, Eduarqui	R-R	6-2	176	11-20-01	.214	.185	.218	72	266	48	57	9	0	11	31	29	5	0	2	98	15	5	.372	.301
Ferrer, Alberis	R-R	6-1	150	12-17-00	.268	.167	.286	25	82	18	22	3	0	4	13	7	3	0	0	24	9	2	.451	.348
2-team total (20 Indians/Brewers)					.241	.148	.263	45	141	25	34	5	1	5	18	14	3	0	0	44	12	4	.397	.323
Frias, Juan	R-R	6-0	175	11-7-00	.270	.250	.274	38	111	14	30	8	2	0	23	23	0	0	1	19	3	2	.378	.393
Garcia, Eduardo	R-R	6-2	160	7-10-02	.313	.000	.333	10	32	6	10	2	0	1	3	6	2	0	0	9	1	1	.469	.450
Garcia, Nader	L-R	5-9	160	5-14-02	.111	.000	.143	4	9	0	1	0	0	0	4	3	0	0	4	1	0	0	.111	.250
Jaraba, Branlyn	R-R	6-2	196	3-20-02	.247	.192	.253	69	247	41	61	12	1	4	31	20	10	0	3	75	5	5	.352	.325
Leon, Henry	R-R	5-9	175	1-30-02	.111	.000	.116	18	45	4	5	0	0	0	2	3	6	3	1	5	0	2	.111	.255
Manon, Farlyn	R-R	5-9	178	10-22-96	.243	.200	.250	39	107	16	26	7	1	3	25	19	6	0	2	13	1	3	.411	.381
Marte, Alejandro	R-R	6-2	180	5-23-00	.292	.191	.304	55	192	37	56	11	1	9	39	20	7	0	2	74	2	1	.500	.376
Martinez, Rafael	R-R	6-2	170	9-20-01	.247	.158	.260	43	146	23	36	4	4	1	22	13	0	1	3	42	12	2	.349	.303
Mercado, Reidy	B-R	5-11	153	1-6-01	.329	.563	.300	40	146	27	48	5	2	2	16	18	3	0	3	23	32	11	.432	.406
Moreno, Carlos	R-R	6-0	176	1-31-99	.077	.333	.000	7	13	1	1	0	0	0	0	3	1	0	0	6	0	0	.077	.294
Parra, Jesus	R-R	6-2	184	8-30-02	.247	.263	.245	65	227	39	56	15	2	6	37	26	15	0	1	71	9	2	.410	.361
Ponce de Leon, Joneiker	R-R	5-9	150	3-29-02	.273	.273	.273	45	183	25	50	3	0	0	20	7	2	1	1	21	12	4	.290	.306
Rodriguez, Randy	B-R	5-10	175	9-4-95	.222	.000	.286	5	18	3	4	0	1	0	3	2	0	0	0	8	1	1	.333	.300

Pitching	B-T	HT	WT	DOB	W	L	ERA	G	GS	CG	SV	IP	H	R	ER	HR	BB	SO	AVG	vLH	vRH	K/9	BB/9
Alcantara, Erovis	R-R	6-4	175	11-1-00	1	1	11.37	14	0	0	0	13	9	16	16	0	24	12	.205	.278	.154	8.53	17.05
Alfaro, Keiner	L-L	6-1	160	9-5-01	0	0	--	1	0	0	0	0	1	2	2	0	3	0	1.000	--	1.000	--	--
2-team total (6 Indians/Brewers)					0	0	5.25	7	2	0	0	12	14	8	7	0	12	12	.298	.154	.353	9.00	9.00
Atagua, Alis	R-R	6-1	160	3-14-01	2	2	6.08	24	0	0	1	37	38	26	25	3	25	26	.286	.290	.284	6.32	6.08
Bordones, Kleiber	R-R	6-3	175	12-10-00	4	1	3.45	13	11	0	0	60	56	34	23	2	28	56	.253	.266	.248	8.40	4.20
Caldera, Albert	L-L	6-1	170	11-30-01	1	0	3.38	4	1	0	0	5	5	4	2	0	9	6	.278	.000	.313	10.13	15.19
Camacho, Rafael	R-R	6-0	165	8-8-02	1	3	7.61	14	1	0	0	24	33	26	20	0	11	16	.330	.276	.352	6.08	4.18
Caridad, Raymer	R-R	6-4	200	4-3-00	3	4	5.56	20	0	0	4	34	40	23	21	1	19	23	.315	.333	.308	6.09	5.03
Carrasco, Ramon	R-R	6-0	167	8-9-02	0	0	4.70	7	0	0	3	8	11	4	4	0	1	4	.355	.429	.333	4.70	1.17
Castaneda, Oscar	R-R	5-11	205	5-9-01	6	2	2.85	12	12	0	0	60	55	25	19	2	22	44	.244	.230	.250	6.60	3.30
Chourio, Wilkerman	R-R	6-1	170	10-20-00	0	0	9.00	1	1	0	0	1	1	1	1	0	3	0	.250	.000	.333	0.00	27.00
Corniele, Alexander	R-R	6-2	180	8-22-01	0	0	2.25	3	0	0	0	4	2	1	1	0	4	4	.182	.200	.167	9.00	9.00
Cuevas, Nelson	R-R	6-2	145	4-20-01	1	0	8.64	13	0	0	1	17	12	16	16	2	23	10	.211	.143	.250	5.40	12.42
Encarnacion, Stanley	R-R	6-1	185	11-22-01	0	1	13.50	2	0	0	0	1	3	2	2	1	1	1	.500	.500	.500	6.75	6.75
Garcia, Rafael	R-R	6-1	158	4-28-01	2	7	4.13	13	12	0	0	52	45	30	24	3	25	49	.237	.189	.267	8.43	4.30
Gomez, Juan	L-R	6-3	185	5-1-97	3	1	2.67	13	10	0	0	61	50	25	18	0	23	42	.225	.179	.245	6.23	3.41
Manon, Farlyn	R-R	5-9	178	10-22-96	0	0	20.25	1	0	0	0	1	2	3	3	1	0	1	.333	.000	.400	6.75	0.00
Montero, Junior	R-R	6-3	170	9-20-98	2	3	2.88	18	0	0	4	25	19	11	8	0	27	25	.202	.300	.176	9.00	9.72
Morelo, Fray	R-R	6-2	178	5-23-02	0	1	6.86	14	0	0	1	21	19	19	16	3	21	18	.235	.238	.233	7.71	9.00
Nunez, Wellington	R-R	6-2	171	10-17-99	0	2	5.09	13	8	0	0	41	39	29	23	2	35	24	.262	.238	.271	5.31	7.75
Olguin, Fernando	R-R	5-9	155	3-4-01	2	0	1.88	16	4	0	2	43	39	16	9	0	15	53	.234	.327	.195	11.09	3.14
Ortiz, Robert	R-R	6-3	185	7-23-01	0	1	3.86	5	0	0	0	5	1	3	2	0	4	5	.067	.000	.125	9.64	7.71
Rodriguez, Brailin	R-R	6-2	185	8-10-02	3	6	5.72	12	11	0	0	50	49	36	32	0	30	36	.263	.312	.240	6.44	5.36
Tolentino, Joandris	L-L	6-1	201	11-21-99	2	1	4.50	17	0	0	2	28	44	20	14	2	13	37	.370	.440	.351	11.89	4.18
Vega, Ariel	R-R	6-2	190	4-4-01	0	3	3.34	14	1	0	1	32	30	18	12	1	14	22	.244	.216	.256	6.12	3.90

Fielding

C: Cabrera 44, Garcia 3, Leon 2, Manon 28. **1B:** Bautista 32, Cabrera 3, Frias 17, Leon 1, Manon 9, Parra 2, Ponce de Leon 15. **2B:** Burciaga 48, Manon 1, Martinez 3, Parra 24, Ponce de Leon 3. **3B:** Jaraba 46, Parra 30. **SS:** Burciaga 1, Ferrer 24, Garcia 10, Jaraba 14, Moreno 1, Ponce de Leon 26. **OF:** Bautista 17, Fernandez 71, Frias 21, Garcia 1, Jaraba 1, Leon 4, Manon 1, Marte 41, Martinez 36, Mercado 38, Moreno 5, Parra 2, Rodriguez 5.

DSL INDIANS/BREWERS

ROOKIE

DOMINICAN SUMMER LEAGUE

Batting	B-T	HT	WT	DOB	AVG	vLH	vRH	G	AB	R	H	2B	3B	HR	RBI	BB	HBP	SH	SF	SO	SB	CS	SLG	OBP
Bautista, Angel	R-R	5-8	160	4-10-02	.253	.361	.219	45	150	25	38	2	1	0	10	20	0	1	1	26	6	5	.280	.339
Cristian, Jeicor	L-L	6-3	175	5-31-01	.233	.234	.233	62	206	24	48	16	1	1	25	33	3	0	3	85	3	7	.335	.343
Curbata, Isaac	R-R	5-11	165	2-24-02	.172	.250	.147	34	99	7	17	3	2	1	5	11	4	0	0	35	7	5	.273	.281
Dimas, Bryan	B-R	6-1	165	2-4-00	.051	.083	.037	15	39	4	2	0	0	0	1	12	1	0	0	27	2	3	.051	.289
Ferrer, Alberis	R-R	6-1	150	12-17-00	.203	.133	.227	20	59	7	12	2	1	1	5	7	0	0	0	20	3	2	.322	.288
2-team total (25 Brewers)					.241	.148	.263	45	141	25	34	5	1	5	18	14	3	0	0	44	12	4	.397	.323
Gonzalez, Elian	R-R	6-2	175	4-15-00	.276	.227	.291	55	192	25	53	8	8	0	28	15	4	1	2	28	6	6	.401	.338
Gonzalez, Francisco	B-R	6-1	174	3-9-00	.287	.313	.282	52	174	22	50	6	6	3	22	16	5	0	1	16	6	4	.443	.362
Lugo, Eduin	R-R	5-11	170	7-14-01	.152	.150	.153	33	92	9	14	3	0	0	9	13	5	0	2	29	2	2	.185	.286
Nino, Bryan	R-R	6-0	169	4-22-02	.182	.158	.188	53	192	13	35	2	1	0	5	11	3	0	1	50	3	2	.203	.237
Roa, Carlos	R-R	5-11	165	9-4-01	.417	.667	.303	13	48	10	20	5	1	1	8	1	1	0	2	6	1	2	.625	.423
Valderrama, Luis	R-R	5-10	150	10-11-00	.214	.192	.221	36	112	6	24	4	1	0	12	8	3	0	0	16	1	2	.268	.285
Watanabe, Vitor	L-R	5-7	155	4-21-01	.197	.350	.143	26	76	7	15	1	1	0	4	16	3	0	0	30	4	2	.237	.358

Pitching	B-T	HT	WT	DOB	W	L	ERA	G	GS	CG	SV	IP	H	R	ER	HR	BB	SO	AVG	vLH	vRH	K/9	BB/9
Alfaro, Keiner	L-L	6-1	160	9-5-01	0	0	3.75	6	2	0	0	12	13	6	5	0	9	12	.283	.154	.333	9.00	6.75
2-team total (1 Brewers)					0	0	5.25	7	2	0	0	12	14	8	7	0	12	12	.298	.154	.353	9.00	9.00
Arias, Deybi	R-R	6-1	155	5-27-01	2	3	4.31	20	0	0	1	31	25	18	15	1	17	22	.223	.231	.219	6.32	4.88
Casado, Francis	R-R	5-11	170	10-30-00	1	1	7.02	15	0	0	0	17	19	14	13	3	7	11	.288	.250	.316	5.94	3.78
Chourio, Juan	R-R	6-2	185	4-22-02	0	0	16.88	4	0	0	0	3	6	6	5	1	4	3	.429	.500	.400	10.13	13.50
Javier, Starling	R-R	6-2	172	12-17-00	1	1	13.50	17	0	0	0	21	27	36	31	4	37	20	.329	.310	.340	8.71	16.11
Jimenez, Edwin	R-R	6-3	175	12-12-01	1	5	3.05	12	8	0	0	41	31	16	14	2	26	32	.204	.093	.248	6.97	5.66
Mejia, Edinson	R-R	6-1	163	8-9-01	0	2	5.00	4	4	0	0	9	9	6	5	0	7	13	.265	.308	.238	13.00	7.00
Rojas, Ronnald	R-R	5-9	170	4-1-02	0	1	20.39	17	0	0	0	16	19	42	37	3	34	9	.312	.227	.359	4.96	18.73
Rosario, Leony	R-R	6-1	198	10-21-00	0	5	4.89	10	9	0	0	46	55	32	25	4	21	35	.296	.206	.348	6.85	4.11
Villalobos, Yostin	R-R	6-0	155	10-17-00	3	4	3.64	13	8	0	0	47	44	21	19	3	15	24	.249	.253	.245	4.60	2.87
Watanabe, Vitor	L-R	5-7	155	4-21-01	0	0	0.00	1	0	0	0	1	0	0	0	0	0	1	.000	.000	.000	9.00	0.00

Fielding

C: Lugo 26, Valderrama 25. **1B:** Gonzalez 28, Gonzalez 31, Lugo 7, Valderrama 9. **2B:** Bautista 20, Ferrer 3, Gonzalez 8, Gonzalez 7, Roa 4. **3B:** Bautista 16, Ferrer 2, Gonzalez 7, Gonzalez 11, Roa 5. **SS:** Ferrer 10, Gonzalez 2, Gonzalez 4, Roa 3. **OF:** Cristian 53, Curbata 30, Gonzalez 4, Nino 49, Watanabe 25.

Minnesota Twins

SEASON IN A SENTENCE: After winning 78 games in 2018, the Twins jumped to 101 wins in 2019 to win the American League Central, but they were swiftly eliminated in the postseason, falling to the Yankees in a 3-0 sweep in the American League Division Series.

HIGH POINT: The Twins tore through May. They went 21-8 during the month, finishing the month with a 38-18 record and a 10.5-game lead in the AL Central. Minnesota also smashed the record for most home runs by one team in a single season, hitting 307 long balls, with eight different players hitting at least 20 homers.

LOW POINT: The playoffs were a mess for the Twins. They lost 10-4, 8-2 and then 5-1 to the Yankees, ending their season by losing three games in which they weren't competitive.

NOTABLE ROOKIES: Utilityman Luis Arraez never received a ton of attention as a prospect, but he always showed good bat control coming up through the minors. He made an immediate impact when he got to Minnesota, batting .334/.399/.439 in 92 games. Righthanders Randy Dobnak, Ryne Harper and Zack Littell all provided solid relief work for the Twins. The young trio covered nearly 120 innings for Minnesota, striking out more than 100 batters and posting a combined ERA below 3.00.

KEY TRANSACTIONS: The Twins didn't make any splashy in-season trades, instead making their most impactful moves in the offseason. They signed 38-year-old Nelson Cruz, who hit .311/.392/.639 with a team-high 41 home runs in 120 games. Utilityman Marwin Gonzalez was another free agent signing who helped Minnesota, batting .264/.322/.414 in 114 games.

DOWN ON THE FARM: Their No. 1 prospect, outfielder Alex Kirilloff, had a solid season in Double-A, while shortstop Royce Lewis, the No. 1 overall pick in 2017, struggled during the regular season. Lewis rebounded in the Arizona Fall League, however, winning the league's MVP award. Righthanders Brusdar Graterol, Jordan Balazovic and Jhoan Duran all raised their stocks with strong years, as did outfielders Trevor Larnach and Misael Urbina. In all, Twins affiliates combined to go 361-309 during the regular season, which was the fifth-best winning percentage (.539) among all major league organizations, trailing just the Rays (.573), Dodgers (562), Rangers (.559) and D-backs (.557)

OPENING DAY PAYROLL: $113,590,267 (16th).

PLAYERS OF THE YEAR

BILLIE WEISS

MAJOR LEAGUE	MINOR LEAGUE
Jorge Polanco	**Trevor Larnach**
SS	**OF**
.295/.356/.485	(High A/Double-A)
22 HR, 79 RBIs	.309/.384/.458
First-time all-star	13 HR, 30 2B

ORGANIZATION LEADERS

Batting		*Minimum 250 AB
MAJORS		
* AVG	Luis Arraez	.334
* OPS	Nelson Cruz	1.031
HR	Nelson Cruz	41
RBI	Eddie Rosario	109
MINORS		
* AVG	Tomas Telis, Rochester	.330
* OBP	Jaylin Davis, Pensacola, Rochester	.392
* SLG	Jaylin Davis, Pensacola, Rochester	.563
* OPS	Jaylin Davis, Pensacola, Rochester	.954
R	Zander Wiel, Rochester	86
H	Trevor Larnach, Fort Myers, Pensacola	147
TB	Zander Wiel, Rochester	241
2B	Zander Wiel, Rochester	40
3B	Rhodery Diaz, DSL Twins	6
3B	Gabriel Maciel, Cedar Rapids, Fort Myers	6
HR	Jaylin Davis, Pensacola, Rochester	25
RBI	Wilin Rosario, Rochester	91
BB	Drew Maggi, Pensacola, Rochester	64
SO	Zander Wiel, Rochester	158
SB	Aaron Whitefield, Fort Myers, Pensacola	30

Pitching		#Minimum 75 IP
MAJORS		
W	Jake Odorizzi	15
# ERA	Jake Odorizzi	3.51
SO	Jose Berrios	195
SV	Taylor Rogers	30
MINORS		
W	Randy Dobnak, Fort Myers, Pensacola, Rochester	12
L	Jhoan Duran, Fort Myers, Pensacola	12
# ERA	Bailey Ober, Fort Myers, GCL Twins, Pensacola	0.69
G	Sam Clay, Pensacola, Rochester	45
G	Jake Reed, Rochester	45
GS	Charlie Barnes, Fort Myers, Pensacola, Rochester	25
SV	Derek Molina, Cedar Rapids, Fort Myers	11
SV	Anthony Vizcaya, Fort Myers, Pensacola	11
IP	Randy Dobnak, Fort Myers, Pensacola, Rochester	135
BB	Charlie Barnes, Fort Myers, Pensacola, Rochester	55
SO	Jhoan Duran, Fort Myers, Pensacola	136
# AVG	Jordan Balazovic, Cedar Rapids, Fort Myers	.193

MINNESOTA TWINS

2019 PERFORMANCE

General Manager: Thad Levine. **Farm Director:** Jeremy Zoll. **Scouting Director:** Sean Johnson.

Class	Team	League	W	L	PCT	Finish	Manager
Majors	Minnesota Twins	American	101	61	.623	3rd (15)	Rocco Baldelli
Triple-A	Rochester Red Wings	International	70	70	.500	8th (14)	Joel Skinner
Double-A	Chattanooga Lookouts	Southern	76	63	.547	4th (10)	Ramon Borrego
High A	Fort Myers Miracle	Florida State	74	59	.556	3rd (12)	Toby Gardenhire
Low A	Cedar Rapids Kernels	Midwest	78	62	.557	6th (16)	Brian Dinkelman
Rookie	Elizabethton Twins	Appalachian	33	34	.493	7th (10)	Ray Smith
Rookie	GCL Twins	Gulf Coast	30	21	.588	4th (18)	Robbie Robinson
Overall 2019 Minor League Record			361	309	.539	5th (30)	

ORGANIZATION STATISTICS

MINNESOTA TWINS
AMERICAN LEAGUE

Batting	B-T	HT	WT	DOB	AVG	vLH	vRH	G	AB	R	H	2B	3B	HR	RBI	BB	HBP	SH	SF	SO	SB	CS	SLG	OBP
Adrianza, Ehire	B-R	6-1	195	8-21-89	.272	.269	.273	83	202	34	55	8	3	5	22	20	6	2	4	40	0	2	.416	.349
Arraez, Luis	L-R	5-10	177	4-9-97	.334	.274	.355	92	326	54	109	20	1	4	28	36	1	0	3	29	2	2	.439	.399
Astudillo, Willians	R-R	5-9	225	10-14-91	.268	.250	.275	58	190	28	51	9	0	4	21	5	5	0	4	8	0	0	.379	.299
Austin, Tyler	R-R	6-2	220	9-6-91	.250	1.000	.000	2	4	1	1	0	0	0	1	0	0	0	0	3	0	0	.500	.400
Buxton, Byron	R-R	6-2	190	12-18-93	.262	.318	.245	87	271	48	71	30	4	10	46	19	2	2	1	68	14	3	.513	.314
Castro, Jason	L-R	6-3	215	6-18-87	.232	.125	.254	79	237	39	55	9	0	13	30	33	3	1	1	88	0	0	.435	.332
Cave, Jake	L-L	6-0	200	12-4-92	.258	.283	.250	72	198	28	51	11	2	8	25	21	8	0	1	71	0	0	.455	.351
Cron, C.J.	R-R	6-4	235	1-5-90	.253	.326	.225	125	458	51	116	24	0	25	78	29	10	0	2	107	0	0	.469	.311
Cruz, Nelson	R-R	6-2	230	7-1-80	.311	.322	.307	120	454	81	141	26	0	41	108	56	7	0	3	131	0	1	.639	.392
Garver, Mitch	R-R	6-1	220	1-15-91	.273	.321	.249	93	311	70	85	16	1	31	67	41	5	0	2	87	0	0	.630	.365
Gonzalez, Marwin	B-R	6-1	205	3-14-89	.264	.300	.249	114	425	52	112	19	0	15	55	31	6	0	1	98	1	0	.414	.322
Kepler, Max	L-L	6-4	220	2-10-93	.252	.293	.236	134	524	98	132	32	0	36	90	60	8	0	4	99	1	5	.519	.336
LaMarre, Ryan	R-L	6-1	210	11-21-88	.217	.308	.100	14	23	3	5	0	0	2	3	3	0	0	5	1	1	.478	.308
Miller, Ian	L-R	6-0	175	2-21-92	.177	.000	.214	12	17	2	3	1	0	0	1	0	0	0	3	0	0	.235	.177
Polanco, Jorge	B-R	5-11	200	7-5-93	.295	.270	.306	153	631	107	186	40	7	22	79	60	4	2	7	116	4	3	.485	.356
Rosario, Eddie	L-R	6-1	180	9-28-91	.276	.281	.274	137	560	91	155	28	1	32	109	22	0	0	6	86	3	1	.500	.300
Sano, Miguel	R-R	6-4	272	5-11-93	.247	.284	.233	105	380	76	94	19	2	34	79	55	3	0	1	159	0	1	.576	.346
Schoop, Jonathan	R-R	6-1	225	10-16-91	.256	.277	.249	121	433	61	111	23	1	23	59	20	10	0	1	116	1	1	.473	.304
Torreyes, Ronald	R-R	5-8	151	9-2-92	.188	.000	.273	7	16	3	3	0	0	0	1	0	1	0	0	3	1	0	.188	.235
Wade Jr, LaMonte	L-L	6-1	205	1-1-94	.196	.000	.225	26	56	10	11	1	2	1	5	11	2	0	0	9	0	1	.375	.348

Pitching	B-T	HT	WT	DOB	W	L	ERA	G	GS	CG	SV	IP	H	R	ER	HR	BB	SO	AVG	vLH	vRH	K/9	BB/9
Adams, Austin	R-R	5-11	205	8-19-86	0	0	16.88	2	0	0	0	3	4	5	5	2	3	5	.333	.444	.000	16.88	10.13
2-team total (13 Detroit)					0	0	7.02	15	0	0	0	17	18	13	13	4	13	14	.273	.267		7.78	7.56	7.02
Adrianza, Ehire	B-R	6-1	195	8-21-89	0	0	27.00	1	0	0	0	1	5	3	3	0	0	1	.625	.333	.800	9.00	0.00
Alcala, Jorge	R-R	6-3	205	7-28-95	0	0	0.00	2	0	0	0	2	1	0	0	0	1	1	.167	1.000	.000	5.40	5.40
Berrios, Jose	R-R	6-0	205	5-27-94	14	8	3.68	32	32	1	0	200	194	94	82	26	51	195	.251	.247	.254	8.76	2.29
De Jong, Chase	L-R	6-4	205	12-29-93	0	0	36.00	1	0	0	0	1	3	4	4	1	3	0	.500	1.000	.400	0.00	27.00
Dobnak, Randy	R-R	6-1	230	1-17-95	2	1	1.59	9	5	0	1	28	27	9	5	1	5	23	.246	.175	.321	7.31	1.59
Duffey, Tyler	R-R	6-3	220	12-27-90	5	1	2.50	58	0	0	0	58	44	23	16	8	14	82	.201	.196		12.80	2.18
Dyson, Sam	R-R	6-1	212	5-7-88	1	0	7.15	12	0	0	0	11	14	9	9	3	6	8	.298	.211	.357	6.35	4.76
Eades, Ryan	R-R	6-2	210	12-15-91	0	0	0.00	1	0	0	0	4	4	0	0	0	2	5	.286	.400	.222	12.27	4.91
2-team total (6 Baltimore)					0	1	2.38	8	0	0	0	11	11	3	3	4	9	10	.256	.333	.226	7.94	4.76
Gibson, Kyle	R-R	6-6	215	10-23-87	13	7	4.84	34	29	0	0	160	175	99	86	23	56	160	.275	.288	.262	9.00	3.15
Graterol, Brusdar	R-R	6-1	265	8-26-98	1	1	4.66	10	0	0	0	10	10	5	5	1	2	10	.278	.214	.318	9.31	1.86
Harper, Ryne	R-R	6-3	215	3-27-89	4	2	3.81	61	0	0	1	54	54	25	23	7	10	50	.257	.265	.258	8.28	1.66
Hildenberger, Trevor	R-R	6-2	211	12-15-90	2	2	10.47	22	0	0	1	16	30	19	19	2	7	15	.395	.333	.423	8.27	3.86
Littell, Zack	R-R	6-4	220	10-5-95	6	0	2.68	29	0	0	0	37	34	12	11	4	9	32	.250	.255	.247	7.78	2.19
Magill, Matt	R-R	6-3	210	11-10-89	2	0	4.45	28	0	0	0	28	30	21	14	4	15	36	.263	.296	.243	11.44	4.76
2-team total (22 Seattle)					5	2	4.09	50	0	0	5	51	51	31	23	7	20	64	.251	.281	.231	11.37	3.55
May, Trevor	R-R	6-5	240	9-23-89	5	3	2.94	65	0	0	2	64	43	24	21	8	26	79	.184	.186	.182	11.05	3.64
Mejia, Adalberto	R-L	6-3	195	6-20-93	0	2	8.80	13	0	0	0	15	16	16	15	3	12	15	.276	.188	.310	8.80	7.04
2-team total (20 Los Angeles)					0	2	6.35	33	0	0	0	28	25	22	20	4	20	28	.234	.200	.254	8.89	6.35
Morin, Mike	R-R	6-4	220	5-3-91	0	0	3.18	23	0	0	1	23	20	11	8	3	2	11	.227	.191	.261	4.37	0.79
Odorizzi, Jake	R-R	6-2	190	3-27-90	15	7	3.51	30	30	0	0	159	139	65	62	16	53	178	.234	.227	.194	10.08	3.00
Parker, Blake	R-R	6-3	225	6-19-85	1	2	4.21	37	0	0	10	36	34	18	17	7	16	34	.246	.270	.227	8.42	3.96
Perez, Martin	L-R	6-0	200	4-4-91	10	7	5.12	32	29	0	0	165	184	104	94	23	67	135	.279	.228	.293	7.35	3.65
Pineda, Michael	R-R	6-7	280	1-18-89	11	5	4.01	26	26	0	0	146	141	68	65	23	28	140	.253	.260	.247	8.63	1.73
Poppen, Sean	R-R	6-3	205	3-15-94	0	0	7.56	4	0	0	0	8	10	7	7	1	5	9	.323	.111	.409	9.72	5.40
Rogers, Taylor	L-L	6-3	190	12-17-90	2	4	2.61	60	0	0	30	69	58	20	20	8	11	90	.225	.273	.208	11.74	1.43
Romero, Fernando	R-R	6-0	215	12-24-94	0	1	7.07	15	0	0	0	14	19	12	11	2	11	18	.317	.429	.256	11.57	7.07
Romo, Sergio	R-R	5-11	185	3-4-83	0	1	3.18	27	0	0	3	23	17	9	8	3	4	27	.198	.177	.212	10.72	1.59
Smeltzer, Devin	R-L	6-3	195	9-7-95	2	2	3.86	11	6	0	1	49	50	23	21	8	12	38	.265	.316	.252	6.98	2.20
Stashak, Cody	R-R	6-2	169	6-4-94	0	1	3.24	18	1	0	0	25	29	9	9	3	1	25	.287	.366	.233	9.00	0.36
Stewart, Kohl	R-R	6-3	195	10-7-94	2	2	6.39	9	2	0	0	25	29	18	18	5	8	10	.290	.242	.313	3.55	2.84
Thorpe, Lewis	R-L	6-1	218	11-23-95	3	2	6.18	12	2	0	0	28	38	19	19	3	10	31	.336	.364	.330	10.08	3.25
Vasquez, Andrew	L-L	6-6	228	9-14-93	0	0	--	1	0	0	0	0	3	3	0	2	0		--	--	--	--	--

MINNESOTA TWINS

Fielding

Catcher	PCT	G	PO	A	E	DP	PB
Astudillo	1.000	21	159	10	0	2	0
Castro	.999	78	637	29	1	2	7
Garver	.992	82	690	29	6	4	8

First Base	PCT	G	PO	A	E	DP
Adrianza	.990	20	92	8	1	11
Astudillo	1.000	15	88	6	0	5
Austin	1.000	2	14	0	0	0
Cron	.992	117	927	61	8	87
Garver	1.000	1	3	0	0	0
Gonzalez	.993	21	134	10	1	10
Sano	.956	9	40	3	2	5
Wade Jr	1.000	1	4	0	0	0

Second Base	PCT	G	PO	A	E	DP
Adrianza	1.000	7	9	21	0	8
Arraez	.974	49	59	88	4	22
Astudillo	1.000	2	3	6	0	3
Gonzalez	1.000	2	8	3	0	0
Schoop	.968	113	166	254	14	62
Torreyes	1.000	1	0	1	0	0

Third Base	PCT	G	PO	A	E	DP
Adrianza	.955	24	14	28	2	2
Arraez	1.000	17	6	20	0	4
Astudillo	.920	13	9	14	2	1
Gonzalez	.990	40	25	74	1	6
Sano	.926	91	52	161	17	14
Torreyes	1.000	1	0	1	0	0

Shortstop	PCT	G	PO	A	E	DP
Adrianza	.959	24	17	54	3	10
Arraez	.938	8	4	11	1	5
Gonzalez	1.000	1	0	5	0	0
Polanco	.957	142	141	343	22	57
Torreyes	.933	6	7	7	1	1

Outfield	PCT	G	PO	A	E	DP
Adrianza	.667	7	3	1	2	0
Arraez	1.000	21	32	0	0	0
Astudillo	.889	8	7	1	1	0
Buxton	.991	86	217	5	2	2
Cave	.977	68	125	3	3	1
Gonzalez	.980	59	88	8	2	0
Kepler	1.000	130	277	4	0	2
LaMarre	1.000	13	12	0	0	0
Miller	1.000	12	22	1	0	0
Rosario	.977	132	208	8	5	1
Torreyes	.000	1	0	0	0	0
Wade Jr	1.000	24	23	2	0	1

ROCHESTER RED WINGS

INTERNATIONAL LEAGUE

TRIPLE-A

Batting	B-T	HT	WT	DOB	AVG	vLH	vRH	G	AB	R	H	2B	3B	HR	RBI	BB	HBP	SH	SF	SO	SB	CS	SLG	OBP
Andreoli, John	R-R	6-1	215	6-9-90	.196	.304	.134	43	153	19	30	7	0	6	15	30	0	0	2	63	3	0	.360	.324
Arraez, Luis	L-R	5-10	177	4-9-97	.349	.250	.405	16	66	8	23	4	0	0	6	8	0	0	1	2	1	0	.409	.397
Astudillo, Williams	R-R	5-9	225	10-14-91	.423	.308	.481	18	78	18	33	1	0	5	19	2	2	0	1	2	1	1	.628	.446
Barnes, Brandon	R-R	6-2	210	5-15-86	.186	.214	.176	26	102	13	19	5	0	6	18	9	1	0	0	41	2	0	.412	.259
2-team total (94 Columbus)					.253	.225	.266	120	478	77	121	30	0	30	95	42	7	0	5	150	11	1	.504	.320
Cave, Jake	L-L	6-0	200	12-4-92	.352	.359	.349	48	196	37	69	18	4	7	39	15	0	0	3	50	5	0	.592	.393
Cesar, Randy	R-R	6-2	240	1-11-95	.262	.224	.282	45	168	22	44	12	0	4	31	20	1	0	0	56	0	0	.405	.344
Davis, Jaylin	R-R	6-1	190	7-1-94	.331	.265	.350	41	154	39	51	11	1	15	42	15	4	0	0	46	2	0	.708	.405
De Aza, Alejandro	L-L	6-0	195	4-11-84	.352	.286	.370	35	128	28	45	11	2	6	31	14	5	0	1	30	4	0	.609	.432
De Jesus Jr., Ivan	R-R	5-11	200	5-1-87	.250	.111	.296	9	36	5	9	2	0	2	2	2	0	0	0	12	0	0	.306	.290
2-team total (22 Charlotte)					.242	.174	.263	31	99	11	24	4	0	1	7	13	0	1	1	26	0	2	.313	.327
Encarnacion, Yeltsin	B-R	5-11	170	6-28-98	.455	1.000	.400	3	11	3	5	1	0	0	0	0	0	0	0	3	0	0	.546	.455
English, Tanner	R-R	5-10	160	3-11-93	.100	.143	.077	6	20	2	2	0	0	1	1	2	0	0	0	10	1	0	.250	.182
Flores, Ramon	L-L	5-10	190	3-26-92	.308	.318	.306	30	107	19	33	4	1	3	17	23	1	0	0	22	2	2	.449	.435
Gordon, Nick	L-R	6-0	160	10-24-95	.298	.273	.307	70	292	49	87	29	3	4	40	18	4	0	5	65	14	4	.459	.342
Hamilton, Caleb	R-R	6-0	185	2-5-95	.205	.273	.179	11	39	4	8	2	0	1	4	0	0	0	0	15	0	0	.333	.205
Hirabayashi, Jake	R-R	5-11	188	9-28-96	.000	--	.000	1	2	0	0	0	0	0	0	0	0	0	0	1	0	0	.000	.000
Kerrigan, Jimmy	R-R	6-1	215	3-16-94	.261	.353	.231	20	69	13	18	5	0	6	13	2	0	0	1	21	0	0	.594	.278
Maggi, Drew	R-R	6-0	192	5-16-89	.258	.271	.253	108	388	71	100	19	4	10	46	60	20	3	1	96	9	3	.405	.384
Miller, Ian	L-R	6-0	175	2-21-92	.233	.133	.267	15	60	8	14	3	1	0	4	6	2	0	1	8	6	2	.317	.319
Miller, Mike	R-R	5-9	190	9-27-89	.238	.200	.250	25	84	6	20	3	0	0	6	7	0	0	0	18	1	0	.274	.297
2-team total (53 Pawtucket)					.251	.215	.265	78	279	35	70	12	0	3	29	29	1	1	2	46	4	4	.326	.322
Raley, Luke	L-R	6-4	235	9-19-94	.302	.296	.305	33	126	28	38	6	0	7	21	7	5	0	0	42	4	0	.516	.362
Rooker, Brent	R-R	6-3	215	11-1-94	.281	.180	.317	65	228	41	64	16	0	14	47	35	10	0	1	95	2	0	.535	.398
Rosales, Adam	R-R	6-2	200	5-20-83	.194	.154	.217	20	72	5	14	2	0	0	7	7	0	0	1	22	0	0	.222	.263
2-team total (56 Columbus)					.210	.262	.186	76	272	34	57	10	0	7	26	19	3	0	1	84	1	0	.324	.268
Rosario, Wilin	R-R	5-11	225	2-23-89	.300	.311	.296	105	413	71	124	24	0	20	91	23	4	0	5	77	2	1	.504	.339
Sano, Miguel	R-R	6-4	272	5-11-93	.308	.429	.167	3	13	2	4	0	0	1	1	0	0	0	0	7	0	0	.462	.357
Sawyer, Wynston	R-R	6-3	215	11-14-91	.260	.435	.185	43	154	23	40	17	0	2	20	11	6	0	0	49	0	0	.409	.333
Schales, Brian	R-R	6-1	170	2-13-96	.153	.130	.167	17	59	3	9	2	0	2	6	2	1	0	2	29	0	0	.288	.188
Tademo, Victor	R-R	6-1	170	7-9-99	.000	.000	--	1	1	0	0	0	0	0	0	0	0	0	0	1	0	0	.000	.000
Telis, Tomas	B-R	5-8	220	6-18-91	.330	.313	.336	82	306	44	101	21	2	8	46	16	2	0	3	33	0	0	.490	.364
Torreyes, Ronald	R-R	5-8	151	9-2-92	.257	.174	.288	79	308	48	79	11	1	11	42	12	1	4	1	33	2	1	.406	.289
Valdespin, Jordany	L-R	6-0	205	12-23-87	.294	.340	.280	60	214	28	63	9	1	7	34	14	2	1	0	25	5	2	.444	.344
Wade Jr, LaMonte	L-L	6-1	205	1-1-94	.246	.253	.243	77	264	47	65	12	1	5	24	56	9	2	3	48	7	2	.356	.392
Wiel, Zander	R-R	6-3	220	1-11-93	.254	.292	.239	126	469	86	119	40	5	24	78	40	8	0	5	158	2	1	.524	.320

Pitching	B-T	HT	WT	DOB	W	L	ERA	G	GS	CG	SV	IP	H	R	ER	HR	BB	SO	AVG	vLH	vRH	K/9	BB/9
Adams, Austin	R-R	5-11	205	8-19-86	1	1	4.50	11	1	0	1	18	16	9	9	3	6	28	.229	.130	.277	14.00	3.00
2-team total (18 Toledo)					1	3	5.77	29	2	0	2	44	42	29	28	9	16	48	.246	.206	.276	9.89	3.30
Alcala, Jorge	R-R	6-3	205	7-28-95	1	0	0.00	5	0	0	0	8	4	0	0	0	2	11	.154	.188	.100	12.91	2.35
Allen, Cody	R-R	6-1	210	11-20-88	0	2	3.38	7	1	0	0	8	7	5	3	1	5	7	.250	.100	.333	7.88	5.63
Barnes, Charlie	L-L	6-2	190	10-1-95	1	2	6.75	4	4	0	0	19	29	15	14	1	11	16	.363	.438	.344	7.71	5.30
Baxendale, DJ	R-R	6-2	190	12-8-90	4	4	6.47	27	4	0	0	49	52	39	35	10	27	51	.271	.259	.279	9.43	4.99
Bentley, Denny	L-L	6-2	195	5-28-98	0	0	0.00	1	0	0	0	2	0	0	0	0	1	2	.000	.000	.000	9.00	4.50
Bleich, Jeremy	L-L	6-2	215	6-18-87	1	1	5.40	9	1	0	0	13	20	8	8	1	3	17	.351	.200	.383	11.48	2.03
2-team total (12 Pawtucket)					3	3	5.51	21	4	0	0	33	41	21	20	5	11	34	.306	.324	.300	9.37	3.03
Bray, Adam	R-R	6-3	210	4-14-93	1	1	2.77	8	5	0	0	26	20	9	8	4	7	17	.213	.259	.194	5.88	2.42
Camarena, Daniel	L-L	6-0	210	11-9-92	0	0	6.23	1	0	0	0	4	5	3	3	1	0	6	.278	.250	.286	12.46	0.00
2-team total (17 Scranton/Wilkes-Barre)					4	8	6.27	18	16	0	0	103	126	77	72	22	22	94	.301	.341	.284	8.19	1.92
Clay, Sam	L-L	6-2	190	6-21-93	1	1	4.37	14	0	0	2	23	26	12	11	0	10	26	.283	.217	.304	10.32	3.97
Colina, Edwar	R-R	5-11	240	5-3-97	0	0	17.36	1	0	0	0	5	8	9	9	1	2	4	.364	.583	.100	7.71	3.86
Cutura, Andro	R-R	6-0	195	8-22-93	0	0	9.00	1	1	0	0	4	7	4	4	1	2	0	.389	.714	.182	0.00	4.50
De Jong, Chase	L-R	6-4	205	12-29-93	0	5	9.73	13	10	0	0	45	72	53	49	16	26	30	.360	.411	.318	5.96	5.16

	B-T	HT	WT	DOB	W	L	ERA	G	GS	CG	SV	IP	H	R	ER	HR	BB	SO	AVG	vLH	vRH	K/9	BB/9
Dobnak, Randy	R-R	6-1	230	1-17-95	5	2	2.15	9	7	0	0	46	28	12	11	0	18	34	.175	.164	.183	6.65	3.52
Duffey, Tyler	R-R	6-3	220	12-27-90	0	0	1.32	7	0	0	1	14	8	2	2	0	5	22	.174	.167	.179	14.49	3.29
Eades, Ryan	R-R	6-2	210	12-15-91	4	3	5.51	29	2	0	3	51	59	32	31	7	16	63	.289	.281	.295	11.19	2.84
2-team total (2 Norfolk)					4	3	5.33	31	2	0	3	52	61	32	31	7	17	64	.291	.294	.294	11.01	2.92
Gonsalves, Stephen	L-L	6-5	220	7-8-94	0	1	4.50	1	1	0	0	2	1	1	1	0	5	2	.200	.000	.333	9.00	22.50
Graterol, Brusdar	R-R	6-1	265	8-26-98	1	0	5.06	4	0	0	0	5	4	3	3	1	2	7	.211	.200	.222	11.81	3.38
Guilmet, Preston	R-R	6-2	200	7-27-87	2	6	4.93	44	6	0	8	73	74	46	40	13	22	94	.262	.259	.264	11.59	2.71
Harper, Ryne	R-R	6-3	215	3-27-89	0	0	0.00	3	0	0	0	3	4	1	0	0	2	6	.286	.273	.333	18.00	6.00
Hildenberger, Trevor	R-R	6-2	211	12-15-90	1	0	4.74	14	0	0	2	19	19	11	10	2	4	15	.260	.293	.219	7.11	1.89
Hutchison, Drew	L-R	6-3	215	8-22-90	3	2	6.11	9	9	0	0	46	58	34	31	10	17	52	.305	.333	.288	10.25	3.35
2-team total (12 Scranton/Wilkes-Barre)					8	6	5.55	21	19	0	0	109	122	78	67	18	45	113	.282	.309	.265	9.36	3.73
Jax, Griffin	R-R	6-2	195	11-22-94	1	2	4.50	3	3	0	0	16	19	10	8	2	3	10	.292	.313	.273	5.63	1.69
Krol, Ian	L-L	6-1	210	5-9-91	0	1	5.23	18	0	0	8	21	27	13	12	1	10	30	.314	.154	.383	13.06	4.35
2-team total (28 Louisville)					1	4	5.28	46	0	0	9	46	54	29	27	3	22	58	.295	.257	.321	11.35	4.30
Littell, Zack	R-R	6-4	200	10-5-95	3	3	3.71	20	7	0	1	63	55	29	26	11	25	68	.234	.223	.241	9.71	3.57
Magill, Matt	R-R	6-3	210	11-10-89	0	1	1.69	5	1	0	1	5	2	1	1	0	1	8	.105	.000	.133	13.50	1.69
Morin, Mike	R-R	6-4	220	5-3-91	0	1	2.25	8	1	0	1	12	11	4	3	1	3	12	.234	.300	.185	9.00	2.25
Moya, Gabriel	L-L	6-0	225	1-9-95	1	3	7.63	26	6	0	0	31	41	26	26	7	18	35	.323	.188	.368	10.27	5.28
Nicolino, Justin	R-L	6-3	195	11-22-91	1	1	5.12	4	3	0	0	19	22	12	11	2	8	13	.297	.308	.295	6.05	3.72
2-team total (20 Charlotte)					8	7	6.12	24	22	1	0	135	156	102	92	36	41	97	.291	.324	.279	6.45	2.73
O'Rourke, Ryan	R-L	6-3	230	4-30-88	2	1	4.50	7	0	0	0	12	7	6	6	0	12	14	.167	.143	.171	10.50	9.00
2-team total (36 Syracuse)					4	4	3.54	43	2	0	2	56	46	27	22	4	35	61	.223	.178	.248	9.80	5.63
Poppen, Sean	R-R	6-3	205	3-15-94	5	1	3.84	12	9	0	0	61	53	29	26	4	27	68	.229	.242	.220	10.03	3.98
Reed, Addison	L-R	6-4	230	12-27-88	0	0	14.40	5	1	0	0	5	13	8	8	4	1	5	.500	.500	.500	9.00	1.80
Reed, Jake	R-R	6-2	195	9-29-92	5	3	5.76	45	1	0	0	75	75	49	48	7	35	92	.268	.327	.229	11.04	4.20
Romero, Fernando	R-R	6-0	215	12-24-94	2	4	4.37	35	1	0	4	58	53	36	28	7	29	63	.245	.292	.208	9.83	4.53
Schick, Alex	R-R	6-7	210	12-1-94	0	0	3.00	1	0	0	0	3	2	1	1	0	0		.182	.250	.000	0.00	0.00
Smeltzer, Devin	R-L	6-3	195	9-7-95	1	4	3.63	15	14	0	0	74	68	32	30	14	19	71	.241	.290	.225	8.60	2.30
Stashak, Cody	R-R	6-2	169	6-4-94	5	0	1.44	14	2	0	0	25	17	5	4	1	4	38	.185	.182	.186	12.24	1.44
Stewart, Kohl	R-R	6-3	195	10-7-94	8	6	5.14	20	19	0	0	91	90	67	52	10	44	80	.257	.311	.223	7.91	4.35
Thorpe, Lewis	R-L	6-1	218	11-23-95	5	4	4.58	20	19	0	0	96	91	51	49	13	25	119	.244	.244	.244	11.12	2.34
Torres, Carlos	R-R	6-1	180	10-22-82	4	1	4.15	8	0	0	0	17	19	8	8	1	8	16	.292	.292	.293	8.31	4.15
2-team total (5 Toledo)					4	1	3.13	13	0	0	0	23	24	8	8	1	8	19	.286	.303	.275	7.43	3.13
Vasquez, Andrew	L-L	6-6	228	9-14-93	1	2	6.00	15	1	0	0	18	17	13	12	1	18	27	.250	.177	.275	13.50	9.00
Weiss, Zack	R-R	6-3	210	6-16-92	0	1	9.28	6	0	0	0	11	19	11	11	2	3	10	.380	.286	.500	8.44	2.53

Fielding

Catcher	PCT	G	PO	A	E	DP	PB
Astudillo	1.000	8	86	5	0	0	1
Hamilton	1.000	4	31	0	0	0	1
Rosario	1.000	17	147	13	0	0	3
Sawyer	.988	34	312	10	4	4	2
Telis	.990	78	709	57	8	3	3

First Base	PCT	G	PO	A	E	DP
Astudillo	1.000	1	11	0	0	0
Cesar	.987	9	72	4	1	11
Hamilton	1.000	1	7	1	0	2
Rosario	.965	17	104	6	4	9
Sawyer	.977	6	39	4	1	3
Wiel	.997	108	826	62	3	78

Second Base	PCT	G	PO	A	E	DP
Arraez	1.000	6	4	15	0	5
De Jesus Jr.	1.000	5	8	6	0	1
Encarnacion	1.000	3	7	6	0	2
Gordon	.945	30	38	65	6	17
Hirabayashi	1.000	1	1	0	0	0
Maggi	.932	19	20	35	4	5
Miller	1.000	19	26	49	0	11

	PCT	G	PO	A	E	DP
Rosales	1.000	5	3	9	0	2
Tademo	1.000	1	1	2	0	1
Torreyes	1.000	1	1	2	0	0
Valdespin	.968	58	102	140	8	38

Third Base	PCT	G	PO	A	E	DP
Arraez	1.000	3	1	5	0	1
Astudillo	.857	5	0	6	1	1
Cesar	.808	20	10	32	10	4
De Jesus Jr.	.909	4	0	10	1	0
Hamilton	1.000	6	3	11	0	1
Maggi	.979	67	48	135	4	14
Miller	.000	1	0	0	0	0
Rosales	.960	14	8	16	1	3
Rosario	1.000	1	0	1	0	0
Sano	1.000	3	1	6	0	0
Schales	.945	17	15	37	3	3
Torreyes	1.000	6	3	9	0	1
Valdespin	.000	1	0	0	0	0

Shortstop	PCT	G	PO	A	E	DP
Arraez	1.000	8	7	20	0	7
Gordon	.944	40	48	86	8	20
Maggi	.957	23	16	51	3	10

	PCT	G	PO	A	E	DP
Miller	1.000	5	4	16	0	1
Rosales	.909	3	3	7	1	0
Torreyes	.983	64	77	150	4	34

Outfield	PCT	G	PO	A	E	DP
Andreoli	.989	41	86	1	1	0
Arraez	.000	1	0	0	0	0
Astudillo	1.000	5	4	0	0	0
Barnes	.962	26	48	2	2	1
Cave	1.000	44	78	0	0	0
Davis	.987	38	74	4	1	1
De Aza	.963	33	49	3	2	0
English	1.000	6	8	0	0	0
Flores	.977	29	41	1	1	0
Hamilton	1.000	1	0	0	0	0
Kerrigan	1.000	20	52	2	0	1
Maggi	1.000	2	4	0	0	0
Miller	1.000	15	31	0	0	0
Raley	1.000	26	48	3	0	0
Rooker	.987	56	71	3	1	1
Torreyes	1.000	9	15	1	0	0
Wade Jr	.962	72	98	3	4	0
Wiel	.900	6	9	0	1	0

PENSACOLA BLUE WAHOOS   DOUBLE-A
SOUTHERN LEAGUE

Batting	B-T	HT	WT	DOB	AVG	vLH	vRH	G	AB	R	H	2B	3B	HR	RBI	BB	HBP	SH	SF	SO	SB	CS	SLG	OBP
Arraez, Luis	L-R	5-10	177	4-9-97	.343	.353	.339	38	146	18	50	6	1	0	14	18	0	0	0	13	3	3	.397	.415
Astudillo, Willians	R-R	5-9	225	10-14-91	.353	.333	.364	5	17	5	6	1	0	2	4	1	1	0	0	0	1	0	.765	.421
Blankenhorn, Travis	L-R	6-2	228	8-3-96	.278	.263	.285	93	388	50	108	18	2	18	51	18	2	0	2	93	11	0	.474	.312
Cesar, Randy	R-R	6-2	240	1-11-95	.130	.167	.118	7	23	4	3	0	0	0	5	0	0	0	10	0	1		.130	.286
Contreras, Mark	R-R	6-0	195	1-24-95	.210	.141	.237	85	281	35	59	12	3	10	33	23	5	2	3	93	9	8	.381	.279
Costello, Ryan	L-R	6-2	215	6-13-96	.240	.297	.217	40	129	18	31	5	2	7	21	23	0	0	1	45	0	0	.473	.353
Cronin, Joe	R-R	5-10	185	5-15-94	.191	.224	.177	79	231	37	44	5	3	5	19	38	7	2	2	78	9	2	.303	.320
Davis, Jaylin	R-R	6-1	190	7-1-94	.274	.227	.286	58	212	34	58	9	0	10	25	36	2	0	1	64	7	3	.458	.383
Davis, Michael	L-R	6-0	200	1-22-96	.156	.133	.163	19	64	11	10	2	3	1	5	6	1	0	0	31	1	0	.328	.239
De Jesus Jr., Ivan	R-R	5-11	200	5-1-87	.224	.191	.239	21	67	7	15	2	0	2	8	12	1	0	0	11	0	0	.343	.350
De La Trinidad, Ernie	L-L	5-9	165	1-3-96	.205	.143	.223	40	122	9	25	2	1	2	17	13	1	3	2	32	0	4	.287	.310

Name	B-T	HT	WT	DOB	AVG	vLH	vRH	G	AB	R	H	2B	3B	HR	RBI	BB	HBP	SH	SF	SO	SB	CS	OBP	SLG
Diaz, Lewin	L-L	6-4	225	11-19-96	.302	.326	.288	33	126	12	38	16	1	6	26	8	1	0	3	23	0	0	.587	.341
2-team total (31 Jacksonville)					.253	.227	.268	64	241	28	61	22	1	14	40	19	3	0	4	51	0	1	.527	.311
English, Tanner	R-R	5-10	160	3-11-93	.174	.065	.208	40	132	19	23	2	1	2	15	9	4	0	1	51	7	1	.250	.247
Garver, Mitch	R-R	6-1	220	1-15-91	.111	.000	.167	3	9	1	1	0	0	0	0	0	0	0	0	3	0	0	.111	.111
Gore, Jordan	B-R	6-0	180	8-3-94	.204	.198	.206	93	304	31	62	11	0	3	27	26	3	3	2	81	2	3	.270	.272
Grzelakowski, Taylor	L-R	5-11	245	12-20-93	.184	.200	.179	59	196	22	36	9	1	1	24	25	2	0	3	51	1	0	.255	.279
Hamilton, Caleb	R-R	6-0	185	2-5-95	.226	.276	.206	88	296	41	67	15	2	6	38	40	3	0	2	82	7	6	.351	.323
Jeffers, Ryan	R-R	6-4	230	6-3-97	.287	.241	.310	24	87	13	25	5	0	4	9	9	3	0	0	19	0	0	.483	.374
Kerrigan, Jimmy	R-R	6-1	215	3-16-94	.209	.241	.196	78	278	40	58	11	0	9	31	15	10	3	3	77	15	6	.345	.271
Kirilloff, Alex	L-L	6-2	195	11-9-97	.283	.244	.302	94	375	47	106	18	2	9	43	29	6	0	1	76	7	6	.413	.343
Kranson, Mitchell	L-R	5-9	210	1-11-94	.217	.185	.226	35	120	15	26	2	0	4	16	10	2	2	0	19	0	0	.333	.288
Larnach, Trevor	L-R	6-4	223	2-26-97	.295	.289	.297	43	156	26	46	4	0	7	22	22	2	0	1	50	0	0	.455	.387
Lewis, Royce	R-R	6-2	200	6-5-99	.231	.308	.200	33	134	18	31	9	1	2	14	11	1	0	2	33	6	2	.358	.291
Maggi, Drew	R-R	6-0	192	5-16-89	.256	.308	.231	11	39	5	10	4	0	1	1	4	1	0	0	9	1	1	.436	.341
Miranda, Jose	R-R	6-2	190	6-29-98	.600	.667	.500	1	5	1	3	1	0	0	0	0	0	0	0	0	0	0	.800	.600
Navarreto, Brian	R-R	6-4	220	12-29-94	.177	.108	.204	40	130	8	23	5	0	5	16	6	3	6	1	28	0	0	.331	.229
Rortvedt, Ben	L-R	5-10	205	9-25-97	.239	.200	.250	55	197	19	47	8	0	5	19	23	5	0	1	51	0	0	.355	.332
Sano, Miguel	R-R	6-4	272	5-11-93	.200	.400	.133	5	20	1	4	2	0	1	5	1	0	0	2	7	0	0	.450	.217
Schales, Brian	R-R	6-1	170	2-13-96	.214	.077	.270	26	89	14	19	6	1	4	16	19	3	0	1	44	0	0	.438	.366
Wade Jr, LaMonte	L-L	6-1	205	1-1-94	.238	--	.238	6	21	3	5	3	0	0	3	3	0	0	0	3	0	0	.381	.333
Whitefield, Aaron	R-R	6-4	210	9-2-96	.137	.103	.159	31	102	9	14	2	1	0	8	4	1	1	2	37	5	0	.177	.174

Pitching

Pitching	B-T	HT	WT	DOB	W	L	ERA	G	GS	CG	SV	IP	H	R	ER	HR	BB	SO	AVG	vLH	vRH	K/9	BB/9
Acosta, Melvi	R-R	6-1	215	6-2-95	0	1	11.25	1	1	0	0	4	8	5	5	1	1	3	.400	.625	.250	6.75	2.25
Alcala, Jorge	R-R	6-3	205	7-28-95	5	7	5.87	26	16	0	0	103	114	68	67	12	37	105	.284	.286	.282	9.20	3.24
Ames, Jeff	R-R	6-4	220	1-31-91	1	3	4.57	25	1	0	0	41	38	24	21	4	29	60	.241	.242	.239	13.06	6.31
Barnes, Charlie	L-L	6-2	190	10-1-95	3	4	3.60	14	13	0	0	75	78	39	30	4	24	73	.275	.316	.260	8.76	2.88
Bray, Adam	R-R	6-3	210	4-14-93	3	3	2.55	27	4	0	1	67	56	21	19	1	19	66	.231	.204	.248	8.87	2.55
Cheshire, Jonathan	L-R	6-1	185	11-15-94	1	0	0.00	10	0	0	5	14	9	0	0	0	4	14	.184	.333	.118	9.22	2.63
Clay, Sam	L-L	6-2	190	6-21-93	3	3	2.70	31	1	0	8	47	44	18	14	0	18	46	.259	.314	.235	8.87	3.47
Colina, Edwar	R-R	5-11	240	5-3-97	4	0	2.03	7	4	1	0	31	21	8	7	0	15	37	.194	.213	.180	10.74	4.35
Cutura, Andro	R-R	6-0	195	8-22-93	2	4	4.70	14	9	0	0	46	55	30	24	2	12	35	.291	.337	.252	6.85	2.35
2-team total (30 Biloxi)					0	1	4.09	8	2	0	0	11	10	5	5	1	7	10	.250	.375	.167	8.18	5.73
Dobnak, Randy	R-R	6-1	230	1-17-95	4	2	2.57	11	10	1	0	67	58	23	19	6	6	61	.231	.220	.241	8.24	0.81
Duran, Jhoan	R-R	6-5	230	1-8-98	3	3	4.86	7	7	0	0	37	34	20	20	2	9	41	.243	.246	.240	9.97	2.19
Gonsalves, Stephen	L-L	6-5	220	7-8-94	0	0	13.50	2	0	0	0	2	4	3	1	2	3	2	.250	.333	.000	13.50	9.00
Gore, Jordan	B-R	6-0	180	8-3-94	0	0	0.00	2	0	0	0	1	3	0	0	0	0	0	.600	.750	.000	0.00	0.00
Graterol, Brusdar	R-R	6-1	265	8-26-98	6	0	1.71	12	9	0	1	53	32	10	10	2	21	50	.179	.270	.114	8.54	3.59
Hackimer, Tom	R-R	5-11	195	6-28-94	4	2	3.27	27	0	0	4	30	16	15	1	19	48	.204	.204	.204	10.45	4.14
Jax, Griffin	R-R	6-2	195	11-22-94	4	5	2.67	20	20	0	0	111	98	33	33	5	24	84	.235	.255	.218	6.79	1.94
Jay, Tyler	L-L	6-1	185	4-19-94	1	2	4.82	17	0	0	1	28	36	19	15	1	19	27	.308	.167	.370	8.68	6.11
2-team total (18 Chattanooga)					1	2	3.86	35	0	0	1	61	70	30	26	2	31	60	.294	.198	.354	8.90	4.60
Knight, Dusten	R-R	6-0	200	9-7-90	1	1	1.59	7	0	0	5	11	4	2	2	1	3	14	.108	.111	.105	11.12	2.38
Lujan, Hector	R-R	6-3	200	8-23-94	0	0	4.15	12	0	0	0	17	24	8	8	1	8	19	.329	.278	.378	9.87	4.15
Mason, Ryan	R-R	6-6	215	10-4-94	2	0	2.35	15	0	0	7	23	22	6	6	0	4	28	.247	.132	.333	10.96	1.57
Mejia, Adalberto	R-L	6-3	195	6-20-93	0	0	0.00	4	0	0	0	5	2	0	0	0	1	7	.111	.250	.000	12.60	1.80
Moran, Jovani	L-L	6-1	167	4-24-97	2	2	4.98	20	0	0	0	34	27	19	19	3	23	50	.220	.278	.195	13.11	6.03
Moya, Gabriel	L-L	6-0	225	1-9-95	0	1	1.23	8	1	0	0	15	10	2	2	1	3	20	.185	.250	.167	12.27	1.84
Ober, Bailey	R-R	6-9	260	7-12-95	3	0	0.38	4	0	0	0	24	10	2	1	1	2	34	.124	.103	.135	12.75	0.75
Palm, Tyler	R-R	6-9	226	12-10-94	1	1	3.00	2	0	0	0	3	2	3	1	0	2	1	.222	.500	.000	3.00	6.00
Phillips, Alex	R-R	6-4	220	12-16-94	2	1	4.36	22	1	0	5	33	30	17	16	4	13	30	.240	.269	.219	8.18	3.55
Poppen, Sean	R-R	6-3	205	3-15-94	2	3	4.40	8	7	0	0	39	30	16	14	0	17	39	.275	.208	.328	12.24	5.34
Ramirez, Williams	R-R	6-1	200	8-8-92	4	1	4.76	8	1	0	0	11	8	7	6	1	5	15	.191	.278	.125	11.91	3.97
Sammons, Bryan	L-L	6-4	235	4-27-95	5	6	4.24	17	16	1	0	81	67	39	38	11	36	85	.224	.310	.191	9.48	4.02
Sands, Cole	R-R	6-3	215	7-17-97	0	0	4.50	1	1	0	0	4	4	2	2	0	1	6	.267	.400	.200	13.50	2.25
Smeltzer, Devin	R-L	6-3	195	9-7-95	3	1	0.60	5	5	0	0	30	19	3	2	0	3	33	.183	.240	.165	9.90	0.90
Stashak, Cody	R-R	6-2	169	6-4-94	2	3	4.76	19	0	0	4	28	28	25	15	4	5	40	.250	.250	.250	12.71	1.59
Vasquez, Andrew	L-L	6-6	228	9-14-93	1	1	5.40	14	0	0	2	17	14	11	10	0	16	18	.222	.273	.195	9.72	8.64
Vizcaya, Anthony	R-R	6-0	220	10-24-93	2	2	0.78	26	0	0	4	46	32	5	4	2	20	48	.199	.156	.227	9.39	3.91
Weiss, Zack	R-R	6-3	210	6-16-92	1	2	5.94	10	0	0	0	18	13	11	3	12	20	.305	.357	.258	10.80	6.48

Fielding

Catcher	PCT	G	PO	A	E	DP	PB
Astudillo	1.000	3	17	1	0	0	0
Garver	1.000	2	15	2	0	0	0
Grzelakowski	1.000	5	25	2	0	0	1
Hamilton	.995	45	385	17	2	1	9
Jeffers	.994	17	173	5	1	0	0
Kranson	1.000	6	55	1	0	1	0
Navarreto	.985	31	308	27	5	3	6
Rortvedt	.994	37	323	26	2	5	5

First Base	PCT	G	PO	A	E	DP
Cesar	.970	4	30	2	1	4
Costello	1.000	20	129	8	0	11
Cronin	1.000	4	35	1	0	4
Diaz	1.000	31	276	18	0	25
Grzelakowski	.996	33	224	16	1	19
Hamilton	1.000	5	33	4	0	5
Kirilloff	.981	35	239	22	5	25
Kranson	1.000	5	47	2	0	4
Navarreto	.957	5	39	5	2	4

Second Base	PCT	G	PO	A	E	DP
Arraez	1.000	15	28	33	0	11
Blankenhorn	.973	67	117	171	8	43
Cronin	.984	37	48	76	2	14
Davis	1.000	5	6	8	0	2
De Jesus Jr.	.947	4	6	12	1	3
Gore	.969	7	13	18	1	5
Lewis	1.000	1	0	2	0	0
Maggi	1.000	5	5	9	0	4
Schales	1.000	2	5	4	0	2

Third Base	PCT	G	PO	A	E	DP
Arraez	.977	15	8	34	1	5
Cesar	.000	2	0	0	1	0
Costello	.964	22	16	38	2	3
Cronin	.915	26	10	33	4	5
Davis	.933	5	1	13	1	0
De Jesus Jr.	1.000	13	11	25	0	5
Hamilton	.907	35	26	52	8	5
Lewis	.000	1	0	0	0	0
Maggi	1.000	1	1	2	0	0
Sano	.909	4	2	8	1	0
Schales	.955	21	12	51	3	7

Shortstop	PCT	G	PO	A	E	DP
Arraez	1.000	5	4	12	0	1
Cronin	.977	11	14	28	1	4
Davis	.941	10	9	23	2	4
De Jesus Jr.	.833	1	2	3	1	1
Gore	.981	85	85	222	6	40
Lewis	.946	29	29	58	5	11
Miranda	1.000	1	1	0	0	0

Outfield	PCT	G	PO	A	E	DP
Arraez	1.000	1	2	0	0	0
Blankenhorn	1.000	18	23	3	0	0
Contreras	1.000	69	121	10	0	2
Davis	1.000	54	76	6	0	1
De La Trinidad	.964	32	49	4	2	1
English	.978	39	84	5	2	1
Grzelakowski	1.000	15	14	0	0	0

	PCT	G	PO	A	E	DP
Kerrigan	.994	75	162	5	1	0
Kirilloff	.973	49	67	5	2	1
Larnach	1.000	34	54	2	0	2
Lewis	1.000	1	4	1	0	1
Maggi	1.000	3	3	1	0	0
Wade Jr	1.000	5	13	1	0	0
Whitefield	1.000	31	64	1	0	0

FORT MYERS MIRACLE
FLORIDA STATE LEAGUE

HIGH CLASS A

Batting	B-T	HT	WT	DOB	AVG	vLH	vRH	G	AB	R	H	2B	3B	HR	RBI	BB	HBP	SH	SF	SO	SB	CS	SLG	OBP
Baddoo, Akil	L-L	6-1	210	8-16-98	.214	.154	.221	29	117	15	25	3	3	4	9	12	1	0	1	39	6	2	.393	.290
Banuelos, David	R-R	6-0	205	10-1-96	.163	.243	.138	45	153	7	25	4	1	0	11	3	4	0	0	62	1	0	.203	.290
Bechtold, Andrew	R-R	6-1	185	4-18-96	.274	.250	.279	59	190	18	52	8	1	2	26	23	0	0	2	52	2	0	.358	.349
Blankenhorn, Travis	L-R	6-2	228	8-3-96	.269	.111	.302	15	52	6	14	4	0	1	3	9	0	0	0	12	0	0	.404	.377
Cabbage, Trey	L-R	6-3	204	5-3-97	.222	.212	.223	81	284	41	63	19	3	9	37	21	3	0	1	97	5	1	.405	.282
Casanova, Trevor	L-R	6-0	200	6-22-96	.273	.333	.250	3	11	0	3	1	0	0	0	0	0	0	0	3	0	0	.364	.273
Celestino, Gilberto	R-L	6-0	170	2-13-99	.300	.600	.240	8	30	6	9	4	0	0	3	2	0	0	1	4	0	0	.433	.333
Contreras, Mark	L-R	6-0	195	1-24-95	.101	.000	.118	27	79	7	8	3	0	0	6	12	4	0	2	23	5	0	.139	.247
Costello, Ryan	L-R	6-2	215	6-13-96	.213	.188	.217	68	216	35	46	11	0	8	25	40	1	0	1	64	0	0	.375	.337
Cron, C.J.	R-R	6-4	235	1-5-90	.250	--	.250	1	4	1	1	0	0	0	1	1	0	0	0	0	0	0	1.000	.250
Cruz, Nelson	R-R	6-2	230	7-1-80	.286	.250	.333	2	7	0	2	0	0	0	0	0	0	0	0	3	0	0	.286	.286
Davis, Michael	L-R	6-0	200	1-22-96	.130	.000	.137	26	77	8	10	3	0	0	3	10	0	0	1	44	0	1	.169	.227
De La Trinidad, Ernie	L-L	5-9	165	1-3-96	.243	.233	.245	55	181	24	44	5	2	3	20	4	2	0	2	36	0	0	.343	.309
Diaz, Lewin	L-L	6-4	225	11-19-96	.290	.205	.309	57	214	34	62	11	1	13	36	14	2	0	4	40	0	0	.533	.333
Encarnacion, Yeltsin	B-R	5-11	170	6-28-98	.264	.364	.250	29	91	9	24	3	0	1	14	8	2	0	1	18	1	1	.330	.333
Grzelakowski, Taylor	R-R	5-11	245	12-20-93	.138	.333	.087	10	29	2	4	1	0	0	1	6	0	0	0	6	0	0	.172	.286
Helman, Michael	R-R	6-1	195	5-23-96	.197	.180	.202	82	284	26	56	13	1	3	25	17	1	1	3	40	3	3	.282	.243
Jeffers, Ryan	R-R	6-4	230	6-3-97	.256	.217	.267	79	281	35	72	11	0	10	40	28	4	0	2	64	0	0	.402	.330
Larnach, Trevor	L-R	6-4	223	2-26-97	.316	.284	.325	84	320	33	101	26	1	6	44	35	2	0	4	74	4	1	.459	.382
Lee, Hunter	L-R	5-9	180	1-17-96	.136	.000	.150	9	22	3	3	0	0	0	1	4	5	0	1	3	0	0	.136	.310
Lewis, Royce	R-R	6-2	200	6-5-99	.238	.318	.215	94	383	55	91	17	3	10	35	27	3	0	5	90	16	8	.376	.290
Maciel, Gabriel	B-R	5-10	170	1-10-99	.261	.342	.242	55	199	29	52	6	2	3	17	21	5	1	3	30	14	7	.357	.342
Miranda, Jose	R-R	6-2	210	6-29-98	.248	.291	.237	118	440	48	109	25	1	8	55	24	10	0	4	54	0	0	.364	.299
Pearson, Jacob	L-R	6-1	185	6-1-98	.262	.429	.241	35	122	12	32	9	2	1	9	10	0	0	2	22	7	0	.393	.313
Rortvedt, Ben	L-R	5-10	205	9-25-97	.238	.182	.246	24	80	13	19	8	1	2	10	12	1	0	1	16	0	0	.438	.340
Sano, Miguel	R-R	6-4	272	5-11-93	.800	1.000	.750	2	5	1	4	0	0	1	3	1	1	0	0	0	0	0	1.400	.857
Schales, Brian	R-R	6-1	170	2-13-96	.182	.429	.115	9	33	3	6	2	0	0	3	3	0	0	1	11	0	1	.242	.250
Torreyes, Ronald	R-R	5-8	151	9-2-92	.222	.250	.200	2	9	2	2	0	0	0	0	0	0	0	0	2	0	0	.222	.222
Weiss, Albee	R-R	6-1	225	9-20-95	.000	.000	.000	2	6	0	0	0	0	0	0	0	0	0	0	4	0	0	.000	.000
Whitefield, Aaron	R-R	6-4	190	9-16-96	.220	.254	.211	81	268	27	59	17	0	4	22	20	3	1	3	89	25	8	.328	.279
Williams, Chris	R-R	6-1	225	11-23-96	.073	.143	.059	15	41	3	3	0	0	1	2	6	1	0	0	18	0	0	.146	.235
Ziegler, Malique	R-R	6-2	190	9-8-96	.146	.050	.214	18	48	3	7	2	0	1	7	0	0	0	18	1	0	.188	.255

Pitching	B-T	HT	WT	DOB	W	L	ERA	G	GS	CG	SV	IP	H	R	ER	HR	BB	SO	AVG	vLH	vRH	K/9	BB/9
Acosta, Melvi	R-R	6-1	215	6-2-95	7	4	2.85	27	7	0	4	82	79	36	26	6	28	75	.255	.261	.250	8.23	3.07
Allen, Cody	R-R	6-1	210	11-20-88	0	0	0.00	4	1	0	0	4	3	0	0	0	0	4	.214	.500	.100	9.00	0.00
Balazovic, Jordan	R-R	6-5	215	9-17-98	6	4	2.84	15	14	0	0	73	52	25	23	3	21	96	.193	.165	.219	11.84	2.59
Barnes, Charlie	L-L	6-2	190	10-1-95	3	2	6.51	8	8	0	0	37	42	27	27	3	20	35	.288	.200	.321	8.44	4.82
Bechtold, Andrew	R-R	6-1	185	4-18-96	0	0	9.00	1	0	0	0	1	1	1	1	1	0	0	.250	.000	.333	0.00	0.00
Beck, Tyler	R-R	6-1	190	11-16-95	0	0	9.00	1	0	0	0	1	1	1	1	0	0	1	.250	--	.250	9.00	0.00
Blank, Jacob	R-R	6-4	215	2-16-96	0	0	0.00	2	0	0	0	1	0	0	0	0	2	3	.000	.000	.000	20.25	13.50
Cano, Yennier	R-R	6-4	185	3-9-94	0	0	2.77	8	0	0	2	13	9	4	4	2	10	13	.196	.091	.292	9.00	6.92
Chalmers, Dakota	R-R	6-3	175	10-8-96	1	1	3.38	5	5	0	0	21	12	10	8	0	15	29	.164	.156	.171	12.23	6.33
Colina, Edwar	R-R	5-11	240	5-3-97	4	2	2.34	10	10	0	0	62	53	20	16	3	15	61	.233	.256	.217	8.90	2.19
Costello, Ryan	L-R	6-2	215	6-13-96	0	0	0.00	1	0	0	0	1	0	0	0	0	0	0	.667	--	.667	0.00	0.00
Dobnak, Randy	R-R	6-1	230	1-17-95	3	0	0.40	4	4	0	0	22	18	1	1	0	4	14	.225	.180	.268	5.64	1.61
Duran, Jhoan	R-R	6-5	230	1-8-98	2	9	3.23	16	15	0	0	78	63	29	28	5	31	95	.224	.319	.158	10.96	3.58
Enlow, Blayne	R-R	6-3	170	3-21-99	4	4	3.38	13	12	0	0	69	61	31	26	4	23	51	.237	.256	.219	6.62	2.99
Faucher, Calvin	R-R	6-1	190	9-22-95	3	2	4.42	34	0	0	2	55	59	31	27	2	22	61	.280	.281	.279	9.98	3.60
Funderburk, Kody	L-L	6-4	230	11-27-96	0	0	0.00	1	0	0	0	3	2	0	0	0	1	2	.167	.200	.143	5.40	2.70
Gomez, Moises	R-R	6-1	215	2-8-97	0	2	3.00	13	0	0	4	21	11	9	7	3	9	30	.155	.133	.171	12.86	3.86
Hackimer, Tom	R-R	5-11	195	6-28-94	2	0	0.59	9	0	0	1	15	3	1	1	0	8	27	.064	.000	.097	15.85	4.70
Howell, Tanner	R-R	6-5	210	3-29-95	0	0	18.00	2	0	0	0	2	4	4	4	1	2	3	.400	.600	.200	13.50	9.00
Lujan, Hector	R-R	6-3	220	8-23-94	2	4	2.18	21	0	0	6	41	33	16	10	1	7	36	.220	.232	.213	7.84	1.52
Mejia, Adalberto	L-L	6-3	195	6-20-93	0	0	0.00	2	2	0	0	2	2	0	0	0	0	3	.250	.000	.286	13.50	0.00
Molina, Derek	L-R	6-3	206	7-27-97	0	0	3.18	7	0	0	2	11	11	5	4	1	2	15	.256	.250	.258	11.91	1.59
Neff, Zach	L-L	6-1	195	3-14-96	3	2	3.74	19	0	0	6	34	35	20	14	1	9	39	.267	.217	.294	10.43	2.41
Ober, Bailey	R-R	6-9	260	7-12-95	4	0	0.99	8	8	0	0	46	39	8	5	1	6	53	.231	.247	.213	10.45	1.18
Phillips, Alex	R-R	6-4	220	12-16-94	3	2	0.79	20	0	0	4	34	18	5	3	0	8	44	.162	.206	.143	11.65	2.12
Quezada, Johan	R-R	6-9	255	8-25-94	7	2	3.44	33	0	0	2	52	50	29	20	2	28	49	.250	.295	.221	8.43	4.82
Ramirez, Rickey	R-R	6-0	168	10-20-96	1	1	8.03	8	0	0	1	12	15	12	11	0	6	17	.300	.350	.267	12.41	4.38
Record, Joe	R-R	6-3	232	1-12-95	4	3	5.98	28	0	0	3	47	53	36	31	1	15	52	.275	.247	.295	10.03	2.89
Sammons, Bryan	L-L	6-4	235	4-27-95	4	0	0.94	8	8	0	0	38	32	8	4	1	13	46	.227	.208	.231	10.80	3.05
Sands, Cole	R-R	6-3	215	7-17-97	5	2	2.25	9	9	0	0	52	36	16	13	4	7	53	.199	.221	.183	9.17	1.21
Vallimont, Chris	R-R	6-5	220	3-18-97	2	2	3.63	4	4	0	0	22	15	9	9	1	4	28	.185	.189	.182	11.28	1.61

				4	5	3.55	10	10	0	0	58	46	24	23	3	15	70	.212	.200	.221	10.80	2.31
2-team total (6 Jupiter)				4	5	3.55	10	10	0	0	58	46	24	23	3	15	70	.212	.200	.221	10.80	2.31
Vizcaya, Anthony	R-R	6-0	220	10-24-93	1	1	2.22	15	0	0	7	28	19	10	7	1	10	35	.192	.143	.219	11.12	3.18
Watson, Tyler	R-L	6-6	240	5-22-97	1	5	3.62	23	18	0	1	112	105	50	45	6	31	88	.250	.222	.259	7.07	2.49
Wells, Lachlan	L-L	6-1	185	2-27-97	2	5	4.09	9	8	0	0	44	48	23	20	1	12	30	.293	.333	.279	6.14	2.45

Fielding

Catcher	PCT	G	PO	A	E	DP	PB
Banuelos	.990	45	361	27	4	2	7
Grzelakowski	1.000	1	11	4	0	0	0
Jeffers	.997	57	519	54	2	4	6
Rortvedt	.989	18	166	22	2	2	2
Williams	1.000	14	124	11	0	0	2

First Base	PCT	G	PO	A	E	DP
Bechtold	.984	24	176	8	3	15
Cabbage	.971	16	88	13	3	13
Costello	.986	38	263	16	4	17
Diaz	.991	52	414	36	4	43
Grzelakowski	.951	7	37	2	2	4
Williams	1.000	1	7	1	0	3

Second Base	PCT	G	PO	A	E	DP
Bechtold	.913	7	13	8	2	4
Blankenhorn	1.000	5	6	12	0	4
Davis	.970	8	16	16	1	4

	PCT	G	PO	A	E	DP
Encarnacion	.958	7	7	16	1	3
Helman	.974	65	115	145	7	32
Lee	.971	8	17	17	1	8
Miranda	.963	35	54	76	5	19
Torreyes	1.000	1	2	1	0	0

Third Base	PCT	G	PO	A	E	DP
Bechtold	.942	27	15	34	3	3
Blankenhorn	.833	2	2	3	1	1
Costello	.873	25	8	47	8	4
Davis	.500	3	1	0	1	0
Miranda	.958	71	38	121	7	10
Sano	1.000	2	0	1	0	0
Schales	.833	3	3	7	2	2

Shortstop	PCT	G	PO	A	E	DP
Bechtold	1.000	1	1	3	0	0
Davis	.976	12	16	25	1	5
Encarnacion	.921	22	24	46	6	13

	PCT	G	PO	A	E	DP
Helman	.923	9	10	14	2	2
Lewis	.954	84	98	216	15	51
Miranda	.960	6	12	12	1	2

Outfield	PCT	G	PO	A	E	DP
Baddoo	.958	27	45	1	2	0
Blankenhorn	1.000	6	5	0	0	0
Cabbage	.969	55	88	7	3	2
Casanova	1.000	3	6	1	0	0
Celestino	1.000	7	9	0	0	0
Contreras	1.000	25	48	3	0	1
Costello	1.000	2	2	0	0	0
De La Trinidad	.984	40	60	2	1	0
Larnach	.971	68	97	2	3	0
Maciel	.991	47	113	3	1	0
Pearson	1.000	29	38	0	0	0
Weiss	1.000	2	3	0	0	0
Whitefield	.989	80	176	7	2	3
Ziegler	.939	16	31	0	2	0

CEDAR RAPIDS KERNELS

MIDWEST LEAGUE

LOW CLASS A

Batting	B-T	HT	WT	DOB	AVG	vLH	vRH	G	AB	R	H	2B	3B	HR	RBI	BB	HBP	SH	SF	SO	SB	CS	SLG	OBP
Akins, Jared	L-R	6-3	220	12-12-96	.201	.125	.211	90	329	45	66	11	4	11	40	26	4	0	3	121	10	4	.359	.265
Arias, Jean Carlos	L-L	5-11	170	1-14-98	.128	.000	.146	15	47	4	6	1	0	2	10	2	0	1	3	14	0	0	.277	.154
Banuelos, David	R-R	6-0	205	10-1-96	.214	.091	.244	18	56	7	12	4	1	2	9	8	0	0	0	19	1	1	.429	.313
Bechtold, Andrew	R-R	6-1	185	4-18-96	.249	.214	.254	66	205	32	51	14	1	5	25	40	0	0	3	69	4	3	.400	.367
Buxton, Byron	R-R	6-2	190	12-18-93	.500	.500	--	1	2	1	1	0	0	0	1	0	0	0	1	0	0	1.000	.667
Cabbage, Trey	L-R	6-3	204	5-3-97	.313	.286	.317	18	67	16	21	1	1	6	16	9	1	0	0	20	2	0	.627	.403
Casanova, Trevor	L-R	6-0	200	6-22-96	.206	.172	.212	55	175	20	36	10	0	4	23	21	1	0	3	66	1	0	.331	.290
Celestino, Gilberto	R-L	6-0	170	2-13-99	.276	.299	.272	117	450	52	124	24	3	10	51	48	4	0	1	81	14	8	.409	.350
Cronin, Joe	R-R	5-10	185	5-15-94	.346	.500	.318	8	26	6	9	2	2	1	3	2	1	0	0	8	0	0	.692	.414
Davis, Michael	L-R	6-0	200	1-22-96	.266	.333	.259	21	64	8	17	6	1	0	8	11	0	0	1	19	2	0	.391	.368
De La Torre, Ricky	R-R	6-2	204	7-21-99	.173	.177	.172	33	104	10	18	2	1	2	10	10	3	0	1	38	0	0	.269	.263
Encarnacion, Yeltsin	B-R	5-11	170	6-28-98	.254	.278	.250	74	264	27	67	4	4	2	22	25	2	1	3	56	6	8	.322	.320
Gray, Seth	L-R	6-3	205	5-30-98	.313	.000	.333	4	16	0	5	0	0	1	0	1	0	0	0	7	0	0	.313	.353
Hirabayashi, Jake	R-R	5-11	188	9-28-96	.000	.000	.000	4	14	0	0	0	0	0	1	1	0	0	0	6	0	0	.000	.067
Isola, Alex	R-R	6-1	215	7-22-98	.268	.000	.319	18	56	7	15	3	0	2	9	5	0	0	1	9	0	0	.429	.323
Javier, Wander	R-R	6-1	165	12-29-98	.177	.212	.169	80	300	43	53	9	1	11	37	35	7	0	116		2	0	.323	.278
Keirsey, DaShawn	L-L	6-2	195	5-13-97	.137	.042	.160	36	124	9	17	1	1	0	11	18	0	0	1	40	2	1	.161	.245
Lee, Hunter	L-R	5-9	180	1-17-96	.121	.000	.127	20	58	7	7	0	0	2	4	9	1	1	1	15	0	0	.224	.246
Maciel, Gabriel	B-R	5-10	170	1-10-99	.309	.150	.331	45	162	28	50	3	4	0	17	23	0	1	0	31	8	2	.377	.395
Ozoria, Daniel	B-R	5-9	135	8-24-00	.190	.125	.201	58	163	21	31	2	0	1	6	15	3	1	1	45	15	1	.221	.269
Pearson, Jacob	L-R	6-1	185	6-1-98	.220	.158	.230	82	286	35	63	13	1	4	32	33	1	0	5	63	12	5	.315	.299
Prato, Anthony	R-R	5-10	186	5-11-98	.286	--	.286	2	7	0	2	0	0	0	1	0	0	0	2	0	0	.286	.375
Rodriguez, Ben	R-R	6-6	235	11-9-94	.208	.103	.225	55	202	20	42	9	0	5	19	12	3	0	0	54	0	0	.327	.263
Schmidt, Kyle	R-R	6-0	205	7-13-97	.053	.000	.067	11	38	0	2	1	0	0	1	3	0	0	1	13	0	1	.079	.119
Severino, Yunior	B-R	6-1	189	10-3-99	.244	.333	.227	22	78	7	19	7	0	0	8	7	0	0	1	27	0	0	.333	.302
Snyder, Gabe	L-L	6-5	235	3-4-95	.259	.193	.270	114	424	63	110	21	4	19	58	44	8	0	4	109	4	2	.462	.338
Steer, Spencer	R-R	5-11	185	12-7-97	.260	.242	.264	44	173	26	45	12	2	2	20	19	8	0	1	28	5	1	.387	.358
Urena, Estamy	R-R	6-0	175	5-29-97	.225	.227	.224	43	129	16	29	8	0	1	11	14	0	0	1	38	3	0	.310	.299
Wade Jr, LaMonte	L-L	6-1	205	1-1-94	.133	.000	.154	4	15	1	2	0	0	0	3	0	0	0	5	0	0	.133	.278
Wallner, Matt	L-R	6-5	220	12-12-97	.205	.125	.222	12	44	7	9	3	1	2	6	5	4	0	0	14	0	0	.455	.340
Webb, Tyler	R-R	6-0	175	4-15-96	.235	.241	.234	39	136	15	32	2	1	2	15	19	1	0	0	34	3	1	.309	.333
Weiss, Albee	R-R	6-1	225	9-20-95	.180	.158	.185	28	100	9	18	7	1	0	6	3	0	0	55		0	0	.340	.248
Williams, Chris	R-R	6-1	225	11-23-96	.218	.114	.242	59	188	33	41	12	3	10	30	42	0	0	3	57	0	0	.473	.356

Pitching	B-T	HT	WT	DOB	W	L	ERA	G	GS	CG	SV	IP	H	R	ER	HR	BB	SO	AVG	vLH	vRH	K/9	BB/9
Balan, Petru	L-L	6-0	185	2-22-96	0	0	0.00	1	0	0	0	1	1	3	0	0	2	2	.167	.000	.200	13.50	13.50
Balazovic, Jordan	R-R	6-5	215	9-17-98	2	1	2.18	4	4	0	0	21	15	7	5	1	4	33	.195	.262	.114	14.37	1.74
Bechtold, Andrew	R-R	6-1	185	4-18-96	0	0	0.00	1	0	0	0	1	0	0	0	0	1	0	.000	.000	.000	0.00	9.00
Blank, Jacob	R-R	6-4	215	2-16-96	2	0	0.00	2	0	0	0	3	1	0	0	0	4	3	.100	.000	.200	9.00	12.00
Cabezas, Andrew	R-R	5-10	175	12-5-96	5	7	3.54	23	22	1	0	114	95	51	45	11	40	90	.225	.224	.225	7.08	3.15
Canterino, Matt	R-R	6-2	222	12-14-97	1	1	1.35	5	5	0	0	20	6	5	3	0	7	25	.091	.136	.068	11.25	3.15
Casanova, Trevor	L-R	6-0	200	6-22-96	0	0	5.40	1	0	0	0	2	4	1	1	0	0	1	.444	.500	.400	5.40	0.00
Cha, Erik	L-L	6-2	190	6-19-97	0	0	0.00	2	0	0	1	5	2	0	0	0	4	4	.125	.000	.167	7.20	0.00
Cronin, Joe	R-R	5-10	185	5-15-94	0	0	0.00	1	0	0	0	1	0	0	0	0	0	0	.000	--	.000	0.00	0.00
Encarnacion, Yeltsin	B-R	5-11	170	6-28-98	0	0	0.00	1	0	0	0	1	0	0	0	0	0	0	.000	.000	.000	0.00	0.00
Enlow, Blayne	R-R	6-3	170	3-21-99	4	3	4.57	8	8	0	0	41	42	24	21	4	15	44	.250	.241	.258	9.58	3.27
Funderburk, Kody	L-L	6-4	230	11-27-96	1	3	4.68	12	10	0	0	50	46	30	26	1	25	55	.241	.283	.228	9.90	4.50
Gomez, Moises	R-R	6-1	215	2-8-97	1	2	2.84	19	0	0	6	32	17	12	10	2	12	48	.155	.154	.154	13.64	3.41

MINNESOTA TWINS

	B-T	HT	WT	DOB	W	L	ERA	G	GS	CG	SV	IP	H	R	ER	HR	BB	SO	AVG	vLH	vRH	K/9	BB/9
Hadley, Nate	R-R	5-11	182	12-7-95	2	1	2.10	15	0	0	2	26	17	7	6	2	12	30	.191	.129	.224	10.52	4.21
Howell, Tanner	R-R	6-5	210	3-29-95	0	1	3.18	5	0	0	2	6	3	3	2	0	7	1	.158	.250	.133	1.59	11.12
Laweryson, Cody	L-R	6-4	205	1-1-99	0	0	0.00	1	1	0	0	5	2	0	0	0	1	4	.118	.000	.167	7.20	1.80
Martinez, Jose	R-R	6-2	192	10-29-96	8	3	2.98	35	0	0	2	63	49	25	21	2	29	48	.215	.225	.208	6.82	4.12
Molina, Derek	L-R	6-3	206	7-27-97	2	1	2.12	19	0	0	9	30	20	8	7	1	9	46	.187	.200	.177	13.96	2.73
Neff, Zach	L-L	6-1	195	3-14-96	3	1	2.31	19	1	0	2	39	28	15	10	0	15	50	.192	.235	.168	11.54	3.46
Ozoria, Daniel	B-R	5-9	135	8-24-00	0	0	13.50	2	0	0	0	1	6	2	2	0	1	1	.600	.750	.500	6.75	6.75
Palm, Tyler	R-R	6-9	226	12-10-94	3	10	4.09	23	17	0	0	99	97	62	45	5	37	77	.253	.245	.259	7.00	3.36
Perez, J.T.	L-L	6-4	215	10-26-95	3	2	3.56	18	0	0	1	30	30	18	12	2	15	26	.261	.233	.271	7.71	4.45
Ramirez, Rickey	R-R	6-0	168	10-20-96	1	1	2.30	16	0	0	5	27	22	8	7	1	11	28	.216	.368	.125	9.22	3.62
Rapp, Brian	R-R	6-0	197	8-10-95	5	1	5.62	33	3	0	0	66	67	44	41	7	36	60	.266	.282	.255	8.22	4.93
Record, Joe	R-R	6-3	232	1-12-95	0	1	0.00	7	0	0	5	8	1	2	0	0	1	16	.036	.000	.111	17.28	1.08
Rijo, Luis	R-R	6-1	200	9-6-98	5	8	2.86	19	19	0	0	107	89	46	34	5	23	99	.225	.228	.223	8.33	1.93
Sands, Cole	R-R	6-3	215	7-17-97	2	1	3.05	8	8	0	0	41	41	14	14	0	11	49	.258	.291	.225	10.67	2.40
Schick, Alex	R-R	6-7	210	12-1-94	5	2	6.35	21	0	0	0	34	28	24	24	4	26	44	.226	.235	.219	11.65	6.88
Schulfer, Austin	R-R	6-2	175	12-22-95	7	6	3.96	30	13	0	1	98	73	48	43	9	47	124	.208	.189	.221	11.43	4.33
Suniaga, Carlos	R-R	6-2	187	5-26-97	3	2	5.18	28	0	0	2	42	46	28	24	8	12	51	.269	.221	.301	11.02	2.59
Teng, Kai-Wei	R-R	6-4	260	12-1-98	4	0	1.60	9	8	0	0	51	40	16	9	1	14	49	.212	.247	.188	8.70	2.49
Thomas, Dylan	R-R	6-4	205	4-14-97	2	1	2.00	11	0	0	0	18	18	6	4	1	7	12	.277	.160	.350	6.00	3.50
Torres, Frandy	R-R	5-10	160	8-4-95	0	1	9.00	1	0	0	0	1	1	1	1	0	2	1	.250	.500	.000	9.00	18.00
Winder, Josh	R-R	6-5	210	10-11-96	7	2	2.65	21	21	2	0	126	93	43	37	10	30	118	.205	.229	.188	8.45	2.15

Fielding

Catcher	PCT	G	PO	A	E	DP	PB
Banuelos	.987	17	130	18	2	0	2
Casanova	.988	29	223	26	3	2	4
Isola	.969	16	116	10	4	1	1
Rodriguez	.991	36	331	18	3	1	5
Schmidt	.990	11	97	6	1	0	1
Williams	.989	36	342	20	4	2	6

First Base	PCT	G	PO	A	E	DP
Bechtold	1.000	2	13	0	0	2
Casanova	.974	9	65	9	2	6
Davis	1.000	2	10	0	0	0
Rodriguez	.990	12	85	12	1	7
Snyder	.992	100	827	48	7	65
Weiss	.950	10	73	3	4	12
Williams	.981	7	50	2	1	6

Second Base	PCT	G	PO	A	E	DP
Bechtold	1.000	1	0	1	0	0
Casanova	1.000	1	1	0	0	0
Cronin	1.000	4	2	5	0	0
De La Torre	1.000	6	11	14	0	3
Encarnacion	.974	38	61	89	4	23

	PCT	G	PO	A	E	DP
Hirabayashi	.938	3	5	10	1	0
Lee	.948	20	29	63	5	8
Ozoria	.975	19	29	50	2	13
Prato	1.000	2	1	5	0	2
Severino	.955	20	17	46	3	8
Steer	.984	13	27	33	1	10
Urena	.967	21	36	51	3	14

Third Base	PCT	G	PO	A	E	DP
Bechtold	.947	60	46	80	7	10
Cabbage	.000	1	0	0	0	0
Casanova	.000	1	0	0	0	0
Cronin	1.000	3	3	3	0	0
Davis	1.000	3	4	8	0	2
De La Torre	.945	21	13	39	3	4
Gray	1.000	4	5	6	0	2
Hirabayashi	1.000	1	1	0	0	0
Ozoria	.914	11	10	22	3	2
Steer	.957	25	14	53	3	4
Urena	.909	15	7	23	3	4

Shortstop	PCT	G	PO	A	E	DP
Cronin	1.000	2	3	2	0	1
Davis	.968	16	27	34	2	8

	PCT	G	PO	A	E	DP
De La Torre	.889	2	1	7	1	0
Encarnacion	.902	36	35	76	12	13
Javier	.938	66	84	173	17	26
Ozoria	.969	17	17	46	2	3
Steer	.800	2	2	2	1	1
Urena	.857	3	6	6	2	1

Outfield	PCT	G	PO	A	E	DP
Akins	.982	73	109	3	2	1
Arias	.944	11	16	1	1	0
Cabbage	.947	14	18	0	1	0
Casanova	1.000	7	9	1	0	0
Celestino	.968	108	205	9	7	2
Encarnacion	1.000	1	4	0	0	0
Keirsey	.965	32	52	3	2	2
Maciel	.985	42	63	2	1	1
Ozoria	1.000	8	13	1	0	1
Pearson	1.000	70	121	2	0	0
Snyder	.000	1	0	0	0	0
Wade Jr	1.000	3	6	1	0	0
Wallner	.944	10	16	1	1	0
Webb	.984	37	58	2	1	0
Weiss	1.000	10	13	1	0	0
Williams	.000	1	0	0	0	0

ELIZABETHTON TWINS
APPALACHIAN LEAGUE
ROOKIE ADVANCED

Batting	B-T	HT	WT	DOB	AVG	vLH	vRH	G	AB	R	H	2B	3B	HR	RBI	BB	HBP	SH	SF	SO	SB	CS	SLG	OBP
De La Cruz, Yeremi	R-R	5-11	185	7-15-97	.222	.143	.250	8	27	0	6	2	0	0	6	5	0	0	0	8	0	0	.296	.344
De La Torre, Ricky	R-R	6-2	204	7-21-99	.156	.167	.154	10	32	0	5	1	0	0	0	6	2	0	0	15	0	1	.188	.325
Garry Jr., Willie Joe	L-L	6-1	170	5-29-00	.228	.189	.238	55	197	31	45	6	3	5	23	15	6	1	1	61	5	3	.366	.301
Gray, Seth	L-R	6-3	205	5-30-98	.225	.136	.247	57	218	34	49	15	0	11	36	30	7	1	1	53	4	1	.445	.336
Holland, Will	R-R	5-10	181	4-18-98	.192	.154	.202	36	125	22	24	2	0	7	16	14	5	1	0	44	8	1	.376	.299
Isola, Alex	R-R	6-1	215	7-22-98	.400	.500	.381	7	25	7	10	2	0	1	8	0	2	0	1	10	1	0	.600	.429
Jensen, Trevor	R-R	6-2	193	4-27-97	.246	.448	.183	38	122	17	30	4	2	1	12	16	3	0	4	29	2	2	.336	.338
Keirsey, DaShawn	L-L	6-2	195	5-13-97	.217	.400	.167	7	23	4	5	0	0	0	3	6	0	0	1	8	1	0	.217	.367
Mack, Charles	L-R	6-0	190	11-12-99	.234	.268	.226	53	205	33	48	8	1	8	28	21	3	0	1	60	0	2	.400	.313
Ozoria, Daniel	B-R	5-9	135	8-24-00	.000	.000	.000	2	5	1	0	0	0	0	1	3	0	0	0	2	0	0	.000	.375
Phillips, Parker	R-R	6-5	240	2-20-97	.231	.219	.235	39	147	21	34	7	0	5	18	18	10	0	0	49	0	1	.381	.354
Prato, Anthony	R-R	5-10	186	5-11-98	.267	.222	.280	45	161	20	43	7	1	2	17	19	10	0	3	24	3	2	.360	.373
Salva, Kidany	L-R	5-11	185	8-24-98	.253	.105	.292	27	91	10	23	2	0	3	12	8	4	0	1	25	0	0	.374	.337
Santana, Ruben	B-R	5-9	160	11-30-97	.276	.333	.259	40	145	25	40	7	2	1	12	18	4	1	0	31	2	1	.372	.371
Schmidt, Kyle	R-R	6-0	205	7-13-97	.333	.500	.286	5	18	1	6	1	0	0	4	1	0	0	0	4	0	0	.389	.368
Smith, Max	L-R	6-1	200	3-10-97	.286	.250	.296	55	213	37	61	12	1	7	28	22	2	0	4	58	4	3	.451	.353
Steer, Spencer	R-R	5-11	185	12-7-97	.325	.400	.298	20	77	14	25	6	1	2	13	15	2	0	1	5	0	1	.507	.442
Villalobos, Janison	R-R	5-9	195	5-10-97	.232	.316	.213	28	99	14	23	6	0	3	17	6	1	0	0	24	0	0	.384	.283
Wallner, Matt	L-R	6-5	220	12-12-97	.269	.273	.268	53	208	35	56	18	1	6	28	19	11	0	0	66	1	1	.452	.361
Webb, Tyler	R-R	6-0	175	4-15-96	.304	.091	.371	12	46	7	14	5	0	0	7	4	2	0	2	8	1	1	.413	.370
Weiss, Albee	R-R	6-1	225	9-20-95	.260	.227	.270	23	96	17	25	4	1	9	15	4	2	0	3	37	0	0	.604	.295

Pitching	B-T	HT	WT	DOB	W	L	ERA	G	GS	CG	SV	IP	H	R	ER	HR	BB	SO	AVG	vLH	vRH	K/9	BB/9
Baez, Yancarlos	B-R	6-2	165	9-21-95	0	1	9.00	4	0	0	0	4	3	4	4	1	2	6	.188	.222	.143	13.50	4.50
Beck, Tyler	R-R	6-1	190	11-16-95	1	0	1.23	8	0	0	1	15	14	2	2	2	4	19	.259	.294	.243	11.66	2.45
Benninghoff, Tyler	R-R	6-4	180	9-17-97	2	4	6.28	11	8	0	0	39	41	33	27	4	21	44	.272	.286	.259	10.24	4.89

Name	B-T	HT	WT	DOB	W	L	ERA	G	GS	CG	SV	IP	H	R	ER	HR	BB	SO	AVG	vLH	vRH	K/9	BB/9
Bentley, Denny	L-L	6-2	195	5-28-98	2	3	4.38	19	0	0	2	37	35	23	18	2	13	41	.241	.289	.220	9.97	3.16
Berroa, Prelander	R-R	5-11	170	4-18-00	2	1	4.55	7	7	0	0	32	29	19	16	4	16	37	.244	.275	.221	10.52	4.55
Cha, Erik	L-L	6-2	190	6-19-97	5	1	3.34	13	0	0	0	30	37	19	11	1	14	32	.301	.220	.342	9.71	4.25
Cruz, Steven	R-R	6-2	185	6-15-99	1	0	2.90	17	0	0	1	31	22	12	10	1	23	48	.198	.152	.231	13.94	6.68
Dum, Benjamin	L-R	6-0	215	9-30-96	4	2	3.21	8	0	0	0	14	14	7	5	1	0	20	.241	.235	.244	12.86	0.00
German, Osiris	R-R	6-1	170	11-2-98	3	1	3.11	16	0	0	0	38	30	14	13	3	10	47	.221	.250	.205	11.23	2.39
Gipson-Long, Sawyer	R-R	6-4	225	12-12-97	0	1	5.40	6	6	0	0	18	28	15	11	2	4	23	.337	.300	.359	11.29	1.96
Griffith, Owen	R-R	6-1	195	2-6-98	0	0	0.77	7	1	0	1	12	7	1	1	0	6	15	.184	.250	.136	11.57	4.63
Gross, Ben	R-L	6-1	210	10-5-96	3	3	4.30	11	11	0	0	52	56	30	25	3	14	49	.273	.290	.257	8.43	2.41
Hadley, Nate	R-R	5-11	182	12-7-95	1	0	1.13	6	0	0	1	8	4	1	1	0	1	13	.148	.100	.177	14.63	1.13
Headrick, Brent	L-L	6-6	227	12-17-97	0	0	0.00	3	2	0	0	4	2	2	0	0	5	2	.182	.250	.143	4.91	12.27
Laweryson, Cody	L-R	6-4	205	1-1-99	1	1	1.76	10	6	0	1	41	25	9	8	2	9	59	.174	.133	.217	12.95	1.98
Marin, Andriu	R-R	6-2	205	7-6-98	2	4	5.92	11	11	0	0	49	53	37	32	6	22	68	.265	.278	.255	12.58	4.07
Perez, J.T.	L-L	6-4	215	10-26-95	0	0	0.00	2	0	0	0	3	1	2	0	0	1	3	.100	.000	.125	10.13	3.38
Shreve, Ryan	R-R	6-6	215	6-23-98	2	2	3.40	14	2	0	3	45	55	21	17	3	7	58	.301	.286	.311	11.60	1.40
Smith, Max	L-R	6-1	200	3-10-97	0	0	0.00	1	0	0	0	1	0	0	0	0	0	0	.000	.000	--	0.00	0.00
Thomas, Dylan	R-R	6-4	205	4-14-97	1	1	1.69	11	0	0	4	16	19	7	3	0	4	21	.284	.240	.310	11.81	2.25
Torres, Frandy	R-R	5-10	160	8-4-95	1	1	4.57	19	0	0	2	41	42	26	21	7	10	56	.252	.267	.243	12.19	2.18
Varland, Louie	L-R	6-1	205	12-9-97	0	1	2.08	3	1	0	0	9	9	2	2	1	4	10	.257	.273	.250	10.38	4.15
Widell, Ryley	L-L	6-3	180	6-1-97	2	7	6.50	12	12	0	0	54	53	45	39	9	24	60	.257	.182	.285	10.00	4.00

Fielding

C: De La Cruz 7, Isola 5, Salva 25, Schmidt 5, Villalobos 28. **1B:** Jensen 18, Mack 1, Phillips 29, Weiss 19. **2B:** Mack 12, Prato 18, Santana 35, Steer 3. **3B:** De La Torre 1, Gray 34, Mack 19, Prato 12, Steer 1. **SS:** De La Torre 8, Gray 11, Holland 32, Ozoria 2, Prato 3, Steer 12. **OF:** Garry Jr. 55, Gray 10, Jensen 17, Keirsey 6, Phillips 2, Smith 54, Wallner 52, Webb 10.

GCL TWINS   ROOKIE
GULF COAST LEAGUE

Batting	B-T	HT	WT	DOB	AVG	vLH	vRH	G	AB	R	H	2B	3B	HR	RBI	BB	HBP	SH	SF	SO	SB	CS	SLG	OBP
Aguiar, Carlos	L-L	6-2	175	8-28-01	.056	.200	.000	7	18	2	1	1	0	0	0	1	0	0	0	11	0	0	.111	.105
Baez, Luis	R-R	5-11	170	11-23-00	.091	--	.091	5	11	1	1	0	0	0	0	0	0	0	0	5	1	0	.091	.091
Caceres, Jim	B-R	5-11	165	10-13-00	.172	.143	.178	31	87	9	15	2	0	0	7	11	3	2	1	22	4	1	.195	.284
Cavaco, Keoni	R-R	6-2	195	6-2-01	.172	.063	.197	25	87	9	15	4	0	1	6	4	1	0	0	35	1	1	.253	.217
Craig, Alec	L-R	5-9	160	8-26-00	.235	.200	.246	30	81	18	19	1	0	0	6	26	0	0	1	16	6	3	.247	.417
Cron, C.J.	R-R	6-4	235	1-5-90	.000	--	.000	1	4	0	0	0	0	0	0	0	0	0	0	0	0	0	.000	.000
Donaldson, Cole	R-R	6-0	180	12-24-95	.158	.500	.067	7	19	2	3	0	0	0	2	2	0	0	0	4	1	0	.158	.304
Feliz, Jesus	R-R	6-0	185	6-7-00	.228	.206	.235	42	149	19	34	9	3	4	18	8	4	0	0	33	2	2	.409	.286
Gandy, Bryson	L-L	5-11	185	11-8-98	.240	.294	.224	27	75	11	18	4	1	0	8	13	2	1	2	32	6	4	.320	.359
Grzelakowski, Taylor	L-R	5-11	245	12-20-93	.200	.000	.250	5	10	5	2	0	0	0	7	0	0	0	3	0	0	0	.200	.529
Guzman, Adrian	R-R	5-11	165	6-8-95	.111	--	.111	4	9	0	1	0	0	0	1	0	0	0	1	0	0	0	.111	.200
Heredia, Victor	R-R	6-2	230	6-10-00	.257	.333	.241	40	136	17	35	5	0	1	18	16	3	0	2	31	1	1	.316	.344
Hirabayashi, Jake	R-R	5-11	188	9-28-96	.231	.154	.246	29	78	15	18	2	1	2	17	18	6	0	1	24	7	2	.359	.408
Jones, Eric	R-R	6-0	193	3-20-96	.125	.000	.143	5	16	0	2	0	0	0	1	4	0	0	0	2	0	0	.125	.300
Martinez, Francisco	B-R	6-5	220	4-25-99	.200	.167	.207	43	155	20	27	7	3	5	20	16	1	0	0	57	3	0	.407	.290
Milla, Luis	L-R	6-0	175	9-5-98	.197	.063	.236	27	71	9	14	2	1	0	7	4	1	0	2	22	2	0	.254	.244
Morales, Jefferson	R-R	5-8	170	5-13-99	.236	.100	.267	36	110	24	26	7	3	3	16	20	4	0	0	18	0	1	.436	.373
Phillips, Parker	R-R	6-5	240	2-20-97	.351	.300	.362	15	57	8	20	2	1	1	8	4	2	0	2	13	1	0	.474	.400
Raley, Luke	L-R	6-4	235	9-19-94	.368	.400	.357	5	19	1	7	0	0	1	2	0	0	0	1	2	0	0	.526	.350
Rivera, Erick	L-L	6-0	183	11-11-00	.164	.167	.163	39	110	6	18	3	1	0	12	15	3	0	1	33	2	2	.209	.279
Rooker, Brent	R-R	6-3	215	11-1-94	.333	.667	.000	2	6	2	2	0	0	0	0	1	0	0	0	3	0	0	.333	.429
Schmidt, Kyle	R-R	6-0	205	7-13-97	.167	.000	.185	6	30	4	5	1	0	0	5	2	1	0	1	7	1	0	.200	.235
Severino, Yunior	B-R	6-1	189	10-3-99	.227	.000	.278	6	22	2	5	1	1	2	0	0	0	0	6	0	0	.500	.227
Smith, LaRon	B-R	6-2	200	9-16-00	.281	.500	.231	9	32	1	9	5	0	0	1	2	1	0	0	11	0	0	.438	.343
Toribio, Sergio	B-R	5-11	170	8-16-98	.161	.083	.182	23	56	6	9	2	1	0	7	7	0	1	1	24	0	1	.232	.250
Valdespin, Jordany	L-R	6-0	205	12-23-87	.125	.000	.167	2	8	1	1	1	0	0	0	0	0	0	0	0	0	0	.250	.125
Valdez, Wander	R-R	6-2	200	11-22-99	.323	.353	.316	29	93	15	30	6	0	4	13	9	0	0	2	29	1	1	.516	.382
Ziegler, Malique	R-R	6-2	200	9-8-96	.179	.000	.200	10	28	3	5	0	0	0	2	4	1	0	0	15	0	0	.179	.303

Pitching	B-T	HT	WT	DOB	W	L	ERA	G	GS	CG	SV	IP	H	R	ER	HR	BB	SO	AVG	vLH	vRH	K/9	BB/9
Balan, Petru	L-L	6-0	185	2-22-96	1	0	9.28	8	0	0	0	11	12	11	11	0	8	15	.286	.375	.265	12.66	6.75
Beck, Tyler	R-R	6-1	190	11-16-95	0	2	5.27	9	0	0	0	14	16	9	8	0	6	23	.276	.316	.256	15.15	3.95
Breek, Donny	R-R	6-2	205	11-8-99	1	2	0.74	10	7	0	0	36	21	10	3	0	19	38	.165	.180	.159	9.41	4.71
Cano, Yennier	R-R	6-4	185	3-9-94	0	0	13.50	2	0	0	0	2	1	4	3	0	4	2	.143	.000	.200	9.00	18.00
Canterino, Matt	R-R	6-2	222	12-14-97	0	0	1.80	2	2	0	0	5	2	1	1	0	1	6	.118	.143	.100	10.80	1.80
Chalmers, Dakota	R-R	6-3	175	10-8-96	1	0	4.05	4	4	0	0	13	8	7	6	0	8	19	.182	.231	.161	12.83	5.40
Escobar, Anthony	R-R	5-11	170	8-25-00	5	2	3.83	11	6	0	0	42	33	18	18	3	13	37	.222	.200	.229	7.87	2.76
Gillespie, Evan	L-L	5-9	190	10-15-94	3	1	2.16	12	1	0	2	17	14	5	4	2	4	18	.226	.222	.226	9.72	2.16
Gonsalves, Stephen	L-L	6-5	220	7-8-94	0	1	2.00	5	5	0	0	9	6	2	2	2	0	16	.182	.000	.214	16.00	0.00
Gore, Jordan	B-R	6-0	180	8-3-95	0	0	0.00	1	0	0	0	1	0	0	0	0	3	2	.000	.000	.000	27.00	40.50
Grace, Regi	L-R	6-1	215	12-10-99	1	2	5.14	6	5	0	0	21	23	14	12	1	9	24	.264	.250	.270	10.29	3.86
Graterol, Brusdar	R-R	6-1	265	8-26-98	0	0	0.00	2	0	0	0	3	1	0	0	0	0	4	.111	.250	.000	12.00	0.00
Guevara, Jose	R-R	6-3	180	10-24-95	1	1	2.79	13	0	0	2	19	17	7	6	0	6	14	.233	.200	.256	9.78	6.05
Hanner, Bradley	R-R	6-4	210	2-10-99	1	2	4.39	11	0	0	1	27	16	14	13	1	12	30	.180	.211	.157	10.13	4.05
Hildenberger, Trevor	R-R	6-2	211	12-15-90	0	0	2.25	3	0	0	0	4	4	1	1	0	0	4	.235	.250	.231	9.00	0.00
Moran, Jovani	L-L	6-1	167	4-24-97	0	0	0.00	3	0	0	0	3	2	0	0	0	2	5	.167	.333	.111	13.50	5.40
Moreno, Danny	R-R	6-1	180	10-10-99	1	0	0.00	2	0	0	0	2	2	0	0	0	1	9	.286	.000	.400	40.50	4.50
Navas, Junior	R-R	6-4	185	9-8-99	1	1	6.75	12	0	0	0	21	23	17	16	2	13	23	.284	.250	.302	9.70	5.48

	B-T	HT	WT	DOB	W	L	ERA	G	GS	CG	SV	IP	H	R	ER	HR	BB	SO	AVG	vLH	vRH	K/9	BB/9
Ober, Bailey	R-R	6-9	260	7-12-95	1	0	0.00	2	1	0	0	9	6	2	0	0	1	13	.177	.154	.191	13.00	1.00
Ramirez, Rickey	R-R	6-0	168	10-20-96	0	0	0.00	2	0	0	0	3	2	0	0	0	1	5	.182	.250	.143	15.00	3.00
Ramirez, Williams	R-R	6-1	200	8-8-92	0	0	0.00	4	0	0	0	5	1	0	0	1	8	.063	.167	.000	14.40	1.80
Reyes, Rogelio	R-R	6-2	175	1-6-98	1	0	7.11	4	0	0	0	6	8	7	5	0	5	9	.308	.100	.438	12.79	7.11
Rimmel, Niklas	R-R	6-3	200	7-5-99	3	1	2.15	9	7	0	0	38	30	11	9	1	8	34	.219	.226	.214	8.12	1.91
Rodriguez, Miguel	R-R	6-2	180	2-25-99	2	2	2.48	9	5	0	0	33	29	10	9	1	11	39	.236	.300	.205	10.74	3.03
Swain, Matthew	R-R	6-7	225	8-20-97	1	0	4.66	11	2	0	3	19	22	13	10	1	10	21	.290	.208	.327	9.78	4.66
Theetge, Steve	R-L	6-3	210	2-8-97	3	0	3.09	8	1	0	1	12	12	5	4	0	2	9	.273	.375	.250	6.94	1.54
Toledo, Jesus	L-L	5-11	180	8-25-99	2	1	4.18	10	2	0	0	24	22	14	11	1	12	27	.253	.381	.212	10.27	4.56
Vasquez, Andrew	L-L	6-6	228	9-14-93	0	0	0.00	1	0	0	0	2	0	0	0	0	1	6	.000	.000	.000	27.00	4.50
Wells, Lachlan	L-L	6-1	185	2-27-97	0	1	5.40	1	1	0	0	5	6	3	3	0	0	9	.273	.231	.333	16.20	0.00
Windeler, Niall	L-L	6-4	210	11-4-98	0	1	4.91	10	0	0	0	15	20	14	8	0	5	15	.318	.500	.275	9.20	3.07

Fielding

C: Donaldson 5, Heredia 5, Morales 20, Schmidt 7, Toribio 21. **1B:** Feliz 5, Grzelakowski 3, Heredia 34, Jones 3, Phillips 8, Schmidt 1, Valdez 3. **2B:** Caceres 11, Craig 22, Feliz 8, Guzman 1, Hirabayashi 11, Morales 1, Severino 5, Valdespin 2. **3B:** Caceres 8, Craig 2, Feliz 5, Hirabayashi 13, Phillips 5, Valdez 24. **SS:** Caceres 8, Cavaco 20, Craig 1, Feliz 26, Guzman 3, Hirabayashi 2, Valdez 1. **OF:** Aguiar 5, Baez 4, Caceres 1, Craig 4, Gandy 26, Grzelakowski 2, Hirabayashi 5, Jones 1, Martinez 38, Milla 27, Morales 5, Phillips 2, Raley 3, Rivera 37, Rooker 1, Ziegler 8.

DSL TWINS   ROOKIE
DOMINICAN SUMMER LEAGUE

Batting	B-T	HT	WT	DOB	AVG	vLH	vRH	G	AB	R	H	2B	3B	HR	RBI	BB	HBP	SH	SF	SO	SB	CS	SLG	OBP
Acevedo, Hector	R-R	5-9	160	11-20-97	.183	.235	.171	28	93	12	17	7	1	2	7	12	3	0	0	26	0	0	.344	.296
Andujar, Jose	R-R	6-2	185	11-20-00	.172	.217	.164	44	151	15	26	3	0	3	14	12	1	0	0	56	1	2	.252	.238
Baez, Luis	R-R	5-11	170	11-23-00	.307	.353	.300	40	127	35	39	5	4	5	14	24	5	0	1	27	16	3	.528	.433
Castro, Wilfri	R-R	5-11	165	3-21-01	.196	.125	.211	31	92	9	18	4	0	0	11	23	2	0	1	20	0	1	.239	.364
Cespedes, Rubel	L-R	6-2	180	8-29-00	.271	.281	.269	42	166	18	45	11	4	1	24	9	4	0	1	32	2	1	.404	.322
Diaz, Rhodery	B-R	5-11	170	9-12-01	.319	.143	.350	41	144	21	46	5	6	1	15	18	5	0	3	26	7	3	.458	.406
German, Ricardo	L-L	6-1	190	8-17-01	.208	.143	.220	15	48	4	10	2	0	0	6	5	0	0	1	22	2	1	.250	.278
Lopez, Jeury	R-R	5-11	170	11-3-01	.208	.235	.204	39	125	24	26	2	0	1	13	20	5	0	1	55	9	2	.248	.338
Mesa, Jorge	B-R	6-0	160	4-2-02	.196	.000	.229	17	56	5	11	2	3	1	10	5	0	0	0	20	1	0	.393	.262
Olivo, Anferny	R-R	5-9	180	1-12-02	.197	.067	.232	23	71	8	14	3	0	0	6	13	1	0	0	20	1	0	.239	.329
Pena, Alexander	B-R	6-2	175	4-12-02	.281	.267	.285	40	146	20	41	10	0	3	23	13	4	0	0	32	2	2	.411	.356
Pena, Yelinson	R-R	5-11	175	9-16-00	.244	.154	.267	39	131	17	32	5	0	2	15	14	13	0	1	25	7	4	.328	.371
Puente, Saul	R-R	5-11	160	7-21-02	.206	.071	.229	33	97	8	20	1	0	0	6	10	1	0	0	43	1	0	.217	.282
Roberto, Nelson	R-R	6-2	170	10-27-00	.216	.353	.192	30	111	19	24	5	0	6	16	9	3	0	0	43	4	3	.423	.293
Rodriguez, Jose	B-R	5-11	160	2-17-02	.221	.250	.214	40	145	21	32	5	2	2	13	12	1	1	0	22	6	3	.324	.285
Rosario, Jose	B-R	5-9	150	12-31-01	.248	.273	.242	42	113	23	28	2	1	0	12	33	1	0	0	21	15	2	.283	.422
Urbina, Misael	R-R	6-0	175	4-26-02	.279	.257	.284	50	183	34	51	14	5	2	26	23	9	0	2	14	19	8	.443	.383
Vallejo, Miguel Angel	R-R	6-1	190	8-21-01	.209	.296	.181	32	110	12	23	8	0	1	15	13	6	0	3	40	3	2	.309	.318

Pitching	B-T	HT	WT	DOB	W	L	ERA	G	GS	CG	SV	IP	H	R	ER	HR	BB	SO	AVG	vLH	vRH	K/9	BB/9
Aria, Develson	L-L	6-0	155	3-20-01	2	4	5.25	17	1	0	1	36	34	25	21	2	27	39	.248	.182	.269	9.75	6.75
Bonilla, Julio	R-R	6-3	180	11-15-00	3	2	3.20	11	2	0	1	25	18	13	9	1	12	25	.202	.156	.228	8.88	4.26
Castro, Wilfri	R-R	5-11	165	3-21-01	0	0	0.00	2	0	0	0	3	2	0	0	0	4	2	.222	.250	.200	6.75	13.50
Causado, Moises	R-R	6-1	170	1-7-01	1	2	5.91	20	4	0	1	32	39	25	21	1	19	37	.293	.326	.278	10.41	5.34
Corporan, Oscar	R-R	6-5	220	10-4-00	0	0	27.00	2	0	0	0	1	8	4	0	7	1	.375	1.000	.167	6.75	47.25
De La Cruz, Luciano	L-L	5-11	200	2-4-99	5	3	5.01	17	5	0	2	50	64	40	28	5	11	37	.294	.255	.305	6.62	1.97
Diaz, Rhodery	B-R	5-11	170	9-12-01	0	0	27.00	1	0	0	0	1	2	3	3	1	1	2	.400	.000	.500	18.00	9.00
Feliz, Rafael	R-R	6-0	160	11-20-00	1	4	6.35	16	2	0	0	28	37	25	20	0	12	19	.311	.333	.296	6.04	3.81
Garcia, Yeremi	R-R	6-2	185	11-16-99	0	2	5.79	13	5	0	1	33	33	22	21	6	16	27	.266	.280	.257	7.44	4.41
German, Giovahniey	R-R	6-2	165	10-8-00	0	6	5.53	16	8	0	0	42	37	31	26	3	24	32	.227	.143	.280	6.80	5.10
German, Steve	R-R	6-1	221	2-5-99	0	0	5.40	8	0	0	0	10	8	6	6	0	9	12	.211	.333	.154	10.80	8.10
Gutierrez, Carlos	R-R	6-3	180	1-16-00	2	1	5.73	15	4	0	0	44	49	36	28	5	11	43	.275	.183	.322	8.80	2.25
Mateo, Yordin	R-R	6-1	165	12-10-00	1	2	2.48	12	8	0	0	36	24	12	10	3	11	32	.185	.191	.182	7.93	2.72
Medina, Jesus	R-R	6-1	165	4-25-02	0	2	7.13	8	2	0	0	18	16	16	14	0	11	24	.229	.286	.204	12.23	5.60
Moreno, Erasmo	R-R	6-1	165	6-22-02	2	3	3.35	14	6	0	2	40	38	25	15	3	16	39	.241	.177	.271	8.70	3.57
Perez, Elpidio	L-L	6-3	248	11-11-98	1	1	4.38	6	0	0	0	12	11	10	6	0	7	16	.239	.182	.257	11.68	5.11
Pichardo, Juan	L-L	6-1	175	6-25-98	4	1	1.69	14	11	0	0	59	55	17	11	0	9	65	.248	.220	.256	9.97	1.38
Ponce, Leyner	R-R	6-1	190	12-22-02	0	3	4.11	20	0	0	2	31	30	27	14	2	13	34	.244	.213	.263	9.98	3.82
Puente, Saul	B-R	5-11	160	7-21-02	0	0	15.00	4	0	0	0	3	9	10	5	0	4	2	.500	.600	.462	6.00	12.00
Reyes, Wilker	L-L	6-0	170	2-25-02	1	4	5.67	16	5	0	0	33	33	28	21	2	21	33	.241	.222	.248	8.91	5.67
Rosario, Jose	B-R	5-9	150	12-31-01	0	0	6.75	2	0	0	0	3	4	2	2	0	2	1	.333	.000	.364	3.38	6.75
Sanchez, Fernando	R-R	5-9	155	2-20-00	1	0	1.80	8	1	0	2	10	7	2	2	1	3	6	.200	.133	.250	5.40	2.70

Fielding

C: Acevedo 23, Castro 30, Olivo 18. **1B:** Andujar 23, Cespedes 16, Pena 24, Pena 5. **2B:** Lopez 6, Mesa 2, Pena 12, Puente 7, Rodriguez 11, Rosario 34. **3B:** Cespedes 20, Mesa 2, Pena 12, Pena 17, Puente 16, Rodriguez 3. **SS:** Lopez 28, Mesa 13, Rodriguez 27. **OF:** Andujar 12, Baez 34, Diaz 39, German 14, Roberto 26, Rosario 7, Urbina 47, Vallejo 30.

New York Mets

SEASON IN A SENTENCE: Only the Astros and Cardinals won more games in the second half than the Mets, who stumbled out of the gate for a second straight season, costing manager Mickey Callaway his job after just two seasons.

HIGH POINT: The Mets improved to 67-60 and pulled to within 1.5 games of the second National League wild card after completing a sweep of the Indians at home on Aug. 22.

LOW POINT: After hitting high tide on Aug. 22, the Mets lost six straight games at home to the Braves and Cubs, dropping them to five games out in the wild card race.

NOTABLE ROOKIES: The Mets had only one notable rookie, but he cast a large shadow. Fresh off leading the minor leagues with 36 home runs and 119 RBIs in 2018, Pete Alonso cracked the Mets' Opening Day roster and mashed right out of the gate. The 24-year-old first baseman finished the year hitting .260/.358/.583 with a major league-leading 53 home runs. The BA Rookie of the Year broke Aaron Judge's two-year-old record for home runs by a rookie, while also cracking the all-time rookie leaderboards with 85 extra-base hits (fifth) and 120 RBIs (seventh).

KEY TRANSACTIONS: Incoming general manager Brodie Van Wagenen made his opening salvo in December 2018, when he traded prospects Jarred Kelenic and Justin Dunn to the Mariners for all-star closer Edwin Diaz and second baseman Robinson Cano. While neither Diaz (5.59 ERA, 7 losses) nor Cano (96 OPS+) played particularly well in 2019, a low-key trade paid off handsomely. New York added J.D. Davis in a January trade with the Astros, and Davis established himself as the Mets' regular left fielder in the second half. His 1.078 OPS at home set a franchise record. At the 2019 trade deadline, the Mets traded pitching prospects Anthony Kay and Simeon Woods Richardson to the Blue Jays for Marcus Stroman.

DOWN ON THE FARM: Short-season Brooklyn won the New York-Penn League title, but no other Mets affiliate qualified for the playoffs. Overall, the Mets' domestic farm clubs went 369-379 for a .493 winning percentage that ranked No. 17 in baseball. The Mets rewarded low Class A Columbia third baseman Mark Vientos (.255/.300/.411, 12 HR) and lefthander Kevin Smith, a 2018 seventh-round pick who finished the season at Double-A Binghamton, as the organization's minor league player and pitcher of the year.

OPENING DAY PAYROLL: $161,865,003 (8th).

PLAYERS OF THE YEAR

TONY FARRIOLO

MAJOR LEAGUE	MINOR LEAGUE
Jacob DeGrom	**Kevin Smith**
RHP	**LHP**
11-8, 2.43 in 32 GS	(High A/Double-A)
NL-best 255 SO	8-7, 3.15 in 117 IP
11.3 SO/9, 1.9 BB/9	130 SO, 39 BB, 6 HR

ORGANIZATION LEADERS

Batting		*Minimum 250 AB
MAJORS		
* AVG	Jeff McNeil	.318
* OPS	Pete Alonso	.941
HR	Pete Alonso	53
RBI	Pete Alonso	120
MINORS		
* AVG	Ruben Tejada, Binghamton, Syracuse	.333
* OBP	Ruben Tejada, Binghamton, Syracuse	.409
* SLG	Rene Rivera, Syracuse	.501
* OPS	Ruben Tejada, Binghamton, Syracuse	.889
R	Arismendy Alcantara, Binghamton, Syracuse	76
H	Jeremy Vasquez, St. Lucie, Binghamton	132
TB	Danny Espinosa, Syracuse	208
2B	Jason Krizan, Binghamton, Syracuse	31
3B	Arismendy Alcantara, Binghamton, Syracuse	6
3B	Omar De Los Santos, DSL Mets 1, DSL Mets 2	6
3B	Sam Haggerty, Binghamton, Brooklyn, Syracuse	6
HR	Rene Rivera, Syracuse	25
RBI	Danny Espinosa, Syracuse	84
BB	Travis Taijeron, Syracuse	64
SO	Brian Sharp, Columbia	168
SB	Andres Gimenez, Binghamton	28

Pitching		#Minimum 75 IP
MAJORS		
W	Jacob deGrom	11
W	Steven Matz	11
W	Zack Wheeler	11
# ERA	Jacob deGrom	2.43
SO	Jacob deGrom	255
SV	Edwin Diaz	26
MINORS		
W	Harol Gonzalez, Binghamton, Syracuse	12
L	Tony Dibrell, St. Lucie, Binghamton	12
# ERA	Drew Gagnon, Syracuse	2.33
G	Eric Hanhold, Syracuse, Binghamton	48
GS	Jose Butto, Columbia	25
SV	Allan Winans, Columbia	11
SV	Ezequiel Zabaleta, Columbia, St. Lucie	11
IP	Harol Gonzalez, Binghamton, Syracuse	138
BB	Tony Dibrell, St. Lucie, Binghamton	57
SO	Kevin Smith, St. Lucie, Binghamton	130
# AVG	Garrison Bryant, Columbia, Brooklyn	.182

General Manager: Sandy Alderson. **Farm Director:** Ian Levin. **Scouting Director:** Marc Tramuta.

Class	Team	League	W	L	PCT	Finish	Manager
Majors	New York Mets	National	86	76	.531	6th (15)	Mickey Callaway
Triple-A	Syracuse Mets	International	75	66	.532	6th (14)	Tony DeFrancesco
Double-A	Binghamton Rumble Ponies	Eastern	67	73	.479	8th (12)	Kevin Boles
High A	St. Lucie Mets	Florida State	68	66	.507	5th (12)	Chad Kreuter
Low A	Columbia Fireflies	South Atlantic	52	84	.382	14th (14)	Pedro Lopez
Short season	Brooklyn Cyclones	New York-Penn	43	32	.573	t-1st (14)	Edgardo Alfonzo
Rookie	Kingsport Mets	Appalachian	34	34	.500	t-5th (10)	Rich Donnelly
Rookie	GCL Mets	Gulf Coast	30	24	.556	6th (18)	David Davalillo
Overall 2019 Minor League Record			369	379	.493	t-17th (30)	

ORGANIZATION STATISTICS

NEW YORK METS
NATIONAL LEAGUE

Batting	B-T	HT	WT	DOB	AVG	vLH	vRH	G	AB	R	H	2B	3B	HR	RBI	BB	HBP	SH	SF	SO	SB	CS	SLG	OBP
Alonso, Pete	R-R	6-3	245	12-7-94	.260	.240	.266	161	597	103	155	30	2	53	120	72	21	0	3	183	1	0	.583	.358
Altherr, Aaron	R-R	6-5	215	1-14-91	.129	.222	.091	26	31	6	4	1	0	1	2	2	1	0	1	15	0	0	.258	.200
3-team total (22 Philadelphia, 1 San Francisco)					.082	.150	.049	49	61	8	5	2	0	1	3	3	1	0	1	25	0	0	.164	.136
Broxton, Keon	R-R	6-3	195	5-7-90	.143	.231	.111	34	49	5	7	1	0	0	2	4	0	0	0	22	4	1	.163	.208
Cano, Robinson	L-R	6-0	210	10-22-82	.256	.215	.272	107	390	46	100	28	0	13	39	25	5	0	3	69	0	0	.428	.307
Conforto, Michael	L-R	6-1	215	3-1-93	.257	.241	.264	151	549	90	141	29	1	33	92	84	10	0	5	149	7	2	.494	.363
d'Arnaud, Travis	R-R	6-2	210	2-10-89	.087	.500	.048	10	23	2	2	0	0	0	2	2	0	0	0	5	0	0	.087	.160
2-team total (1 Los Angeles)					.083	.333	.048	11	24	2	2	0	0	0	2	2	0	0	0	5	0	0	.083	.154
Davis, J.D.	R-R	6-3	225	4-27-93	.307	.312	.305	140	410	65	126	22	1	22	57	38	3	0	2	97	3	0	.527	.369
Davis, Rajai	R-R	5-10	195	10-19-80	.200	.267	.100	29	25	4	5	2	0	1	8	1	0	0	5	0	1	.400	.231
Frazier, Todd	R-R	6-2	220	2-12-86	.251	.294	.234	133	447	63	112	19	2	21	67	40	12	0	0	106	1	2	.443	.329
Gomez, Carlos	R-R	6-3	220	12-4-85	.198	.238	.185	34	86	10	17	3	0	3	10	7	3	2	1	30	4	1	.337	.278
Guillorme, Luis	L-R	5-10	195	9-27-94	.246	.333	.236	45	61	8	15	4	0	1	3	7	0	2	0	14	0	0	.361	.324
Haggerty, Sam	B-R	5-11	175	5-26-94	.000	--	.000	11	4	2	0	0	0	0	0	0	0	0	0	3	0	0	.000	.000
Hechavarria, Adeiny	R-R	6-0	195	4-15-89	.204	.222	.198	60	142	20	29	7	0	5	18	8	1	0	0	33	3	1	.359	.252
2-team total (24 Atlanta)					.241	.261	.236	84	203	34	49	12	1	9	33	14	3	0	1	48	3	1	.443	.299
Lagares, Juan	R-R	6-1	215	3-17-89	.213	.238	.202	133	258	38	55	12	1	5	27	22	2	2	1	75	4	1	.326	.279
Lowrie, Jed	B-R	6-0	180	4-17-84	.000	.000	.000	9	7	0	0	0	0	0	0	1	0	0	0	4	0	0	.000	.125
McNeil, Jeff	L-R	6-1	195	4-8-92	.318	.312	.320	133	510	83	162	38	1	23	75	35	21	0	1	75	5	6	.531	.385
Nido, Tomas	R-R	6-0	210	4-12-94	.191	.194	.190	50	136	9	26	5	0	4	14	7	0	1	0	37	0	0	.316	.231
Nimmo, Brandon	L-R	6-3	207	3-27-93	.221	.375	.182	69	199	34	44	11	1	8	29	46	5	1	3	71	3	0	.407	.376
Panik, Joe	L-R	6-1	200	10-30-90	.277	.444	.237	39	94	17	26	4	1	2	12	7	1	1	0	9	0	0	.404	.333
2-team total (103 San Francisco)					.244	.289	.232	142	438	50	107	21	2	5	39	43	4	2	4	47	4	2	.336	.315
Ramos, Wilson	R-R	6-1	245	8-10-87	.288	.346	.271	141	473	52	136	19	0	14	73	44	4	0	3	69	1	0	.417	.351
Rivera, Rene	R-R	5-10	215	7-31-83	.235	.000	.308	9	17	2	4	0	0	1	3	0	0	0	0	4	0	0	.412	.350
Rosario, Amed	R-R	6-2	189	11-20-95	.287	.311	.280	157	616	75	177	30	7	15	72	31	3	2	3	124	19	10	.432	.323
Smith, Dominic	L-L	6-0	239	6-15-95	.283	.303	.278	89	177	35	50	10	0	11	25	19	1	0	0	44	1	2	.525	.355
Tejada, Ruben	R-R	5-11	200	10-27-89	.000	.000	.000	6	9	1	0	0	0	0	0	0	0	0	0	3	0	0	.000	.000

Pitching	B-T	HT	WT	DOB	W	L	ERA	G	GS	CG	SV	IP	H	R	ER	HR	BB	SO	AVG	vLH	vRH	K/9	BB/9
Avilan, Luis	L-L	6-2	220	7-19-89	4	0	5.06	45	0	0	0	32	33	18	18	5	14	30	.266	.102	.373	8.44	3.94
Bashlor, Tyler	R-R	6-0	195	4-16-93	0	3	6.95	24	0	0	0	22	21	17	17	6	17	20	.250	.233	.259	8.18	6.95
Brach, Brad	R-R	6-6	215	4-12-86	1	1	3.68	16	0	0	0	15	15	6	6	1	3	15	.263	.381	.194	9.20	1.84
2-team total (42 Chicago)					5	4	5.47	58	0	0	0	54	57	33	33	4	31	60	.278	.403	.211	9.94	5.13
deGrom, Jacob	L-R	6-4	180	6-19-88	11	8	2.43	32	32	0	0	204	154	59	55	19	44	255	.207	.213	.202	11.25	1.94
Diaz, Edwin	R-R	6-3	165	3-22-94	2	7	5.59	66	0	0	26	58	58	36	36	15	22	99	.258	.193	.299	15.36	3.41
Familia, Jeurys	R-R	6-3	240	10-10-89	4	2	5.70	66	0	0	0	60	62	39	38	7	42	63	.274	.312	.248	9.45	6.30
Flexen, Chris	R-R	6-3	250	7-1-94	0	3	6.59	9	1	0	0	14	15	12	10	1	13	10	.268	.158	.324	6.59	8.56
Font, Wilmer	R-R	6-4	250	5-24-90	1	2	4.94	15	3	0	0	31	29	17	17	8	13	24	.244	.146	.295	6.97	3.77
Gagnon, Drew	R-R	6-4	215	6-26-90	3	1	8.37	18	0	0	0	24	34	26	22	11	7	17	.315	.432	.234	6.46	2.66
Gsellman, Robert	R-R	6-4	205	7-18-93	2	3	4.66	52	0	0	1	64	64	36	33	7	23	60	.261	.283	.248	8.48	3.25
Hart, Donnie	L-L	5-11	180	9-6-90	0	0	0.00	1	0	0	0	1	0	0	0	0	0	0	.000	--	.000	0.00	0.00
2-team total (4 Milwaukee)					0	0	0.00	5	0	0	0	8	4	0	0	0	4	3	.160	.214	.091	3.52	4.70
Lockett, Walker	R-R	6-5	225	5-3-94	1	1	8.34	9	4	0	0	23	33	21	21	6	6	16	.347	.429	.283	6.35	2.38
Lugo, Seth	R-R	6-4	225	11-17-89	7	4	2.70	61	0	0	6	80	56	28	24	8	16	104	.192	.167	.211	11.70	1.80
Matz, Steven	R-L	6-2	200	5-29-91	11	10	4.21	32	30	1	0	160	163	83	75	27	52	153	.260	.270	.258	8.59	2.92
Mazza, Chris	R-R	6-4	180	10-17-89	1	1	5.51	9	0	0	0	16	21	10	10	0	5	11	.328	.296	.351	6.06	2.76
Nogosek, Stephen	R-R	6-2	205	1-11-95	0	1	10.80	7	0	0	0	7	12	8	8	2	2	6	.387	.500	.316	8.10	2.70
O'Rourke, Ryan	R-L	6-3	230	4-30-88	0	0	0.00	2	0	0	0	1	0	0	0	0	3	1	.000	.000	.000	6.75	20.25
Oswalt, Corey	R-R	6-5	250	9-3-93	0	1	12.15	2	0	0	0	7	9	9	9	1	6	5	.321	.500	.188	6.75	8.10
Peterson, Tim	R-R	6-1	215	2-22-91	0	0	4.91	6	0	0	0	7	7	4	4	1	3	6	.259	.200	.294	3.68	8.59
Pounders, Brooks	R-R	6-5	265	9-26-90	1	0	6.14	7	0	0	0	7	9	5	5	1	2	5	.300	.222	.333	6.14	2.45
Rhame, Jacob	R-R	6-1	215	3-16-93	0	1	4.26	5	0	0	0	6	3	4	3	1	9	5	.150	.000	.273	7.11	12.79
Santiago, Hector	R-L	6-0	215	12-16-87	1	0	6.75	8	0	0	0	8	10	6	6	1	5	6	.303	.400	.261	6.75	5.63

Name	B-T	HT	WT	DOB	W	L	ERA	G	GS	CG	SV	IP	H	R	ER	HR	BB	SO	AVG	vLH	vRH	K/9	BB/9
Sewald, Paul	R-R	6-3	207	5-26-90	1	1	4.58	17	0	0	1	20	18	10	10	3	3	22	.243	.200	.259	10.07	1.37
Stroman, Marcus	R-R	5-7	180	5-1-91	4	2	3.77	11	11	0	0	60	65	27	25	8	23	60	.277	.326	.210	9.05	3.47
Syndergaard, Noah	L-R	6-6	240	8-29-92	10	8	4.28	32	32	1	0	198	194	101	94	24	50	202	.256	.265	.248	9.20	2.28
Vargas, Jason	L-L	6-0	215	2-2-83	6	5	4.01	19	18	1	0	94	81	45	42	14	39	81	.228	.247	.222	7.73	3.72
2-team total (11 Philadelphia)					7	9	4.51	30	29	1	0	150	141	84	75	21	63	124	.249	.254	.248	7.46	3.79
Wheeler, Zack	L-R	6-4	195	5-30-90	11	8	3.96	31	31	0	0	195	196	93	86	22	50	195	.258	.275	.246	8.98	2.30
Wilson, Justin	L-L	6-2	205	8-18-87	4	2	2.54	45	0	0	4	39	33	12	11	4	19	44	.228	.217	.232	10.15	4.38
Zamora, Daniel	L-L	6-3	195	4-15-93	0	1	5.19	17	0	0	0	9	10	5	5	1	5	8	.294	.294	.294	8.31	5.19

Fielding

Catcher	PCT	G	PO	A	E	DP	PB
d'Arnaud	.979	9	43	3	1	0	1
Nido	.992	48	376	13	3	2	2
Ramos	.994	124	1051	50	7	5	10
Rivera	1.000	8	65	1	0	0	1

First Base	PCT	G	PO	A	E	DP
Alonso	.990	156	1078	112	12	108
Frazier	1.000	3	17	0	0	0
Smith	1.000	36	95	9	0	12

Second Base	PCT	G	PO	A	E	DP
Cano	.986	99	164	189	5	51
Guillorme	.966	8	14	14	1	9
Haggerty	.000	1	0	0	0	0

Second Base (cont.)	PCT	G	PO	A	E	DP
Hechavarria	.979	26	42	52	2	14
McNeil	.981	37	52	50	2	16
Panik	.971	28	24	44	2	11
Tejada	1.000	2	2	0	0	0

Third Base	PCT	G	PO	A	E	DP
Davis	.931	31	12	55	5	5
Frazier	.964	120	89	229	12	24
Guillorme	1.000	5	0	2	0	1
Hechavarria	1.000	8	4	9	0	0
McNeil	.977	31	14	28	1	2
Tejada	1.000	2	1	4	0	0

Shortstop	PCT	G	PO	A	E	DP
Guillorme	1.000	8	5	12	0	2
Hechavarria	.923	15	10	26	3	6
Rosario	.969	152	161	370	17	72
Tejada	1.000	2	1	1	0	1

Outfield	PCT	G	PO	A	E	DP
Altherr	1.000	20	21	0	0	0
Broxton	1.000	28	37	0	0	0
Conforto	.990	149	297	8	3	1
Davis	.980	79	92	4	2	1
Davis	1.000	14	6	0	0	0
Gomez	.984	30	58	2	1	0
Haggerty	.000	1	0	0	0	0
Lagares	.983	125	169	1	3	1
McNeil	.965	93	104	5	4	0
Nimmo	.992	66	128	0	1	0
Rosario	1.000	1	1	0	0	0
Smith	.940	33	46	1	3	0

SYRACUSE METS   TRIPLE-A
INTERNATIONAL LEAGUE

Batting	B-T	HT	WT	DOB	AVG	vLH	vRH	G	AB	R	H	2B	3B	HR	RBI	BB	HBP	SH	SF	SO	SB	CS	SLG	OBP
Alcantara, Arismendy	B-R	5-10	170	10-29-91	.294	.278	.301	92	303	60	89	14	6	13	48	32	0	1	3	84	16	2	.508	.358
Altherr, Aaron	R-R	6-5	215	1-14-91	.270	.257	.282	28	74	9	20	5	1	4	13	10	3	0	1	16	3	2	.527	.375
Blanco, Gregor	L-L	5-10	187	12-24-83	.246	.276	.236	118	362	59	89	13	3	13	43	52	2	4	6	94	11	8	.406	.339
Cano, Robinson	L-R	6-0	210	10-22-82	.400	.667	.000	3	10	2	4	3	0	0	1	1	0	0	0	3	0	0	.700	.455
Cecchini, Gavin	R-R	6-2	200	12-22-93	.167	.000	.250	2	6	1	1	1	0	0	0	2	0	0	0	3	0	0	.333	.375
Davis, Rajai	R-R	5-10	195	10-19-80	.287	.330	.270	84	310	47	89	8	3	8	28	17	6	2	2	72	20	6	.410	.334
Espinosa, Danny	B-R	6-0	205	4-25-87	.256	.254	.257	129	473	75	121	27	0	20	84	51	10	3	5	132	17	4	.440	.338
Frazier, Todd	R-R	6-3	220	2-12-86	.400	--	.400	2	5	2	2	1	0	0	1	1	0	0	0	1	0	0	.600	.571
Gomez, Carlos	R-R	6-3	220	12-4-85	.270	.320	.257	35	126	16	34	9	1	6	22	8	4	0	2	29	5	5	.500	.329
Guillorme, Luis	L-R	5-10	195	9-27-94	.307	.322	.302	69	228	33	70	12	0	7	32	39	4	3	3	42	4	4	.452	.412
Haggerty, Sam	B-R	5-11	175	5-26-94	.310	.412	.240	12	42	9	13	4	1	1	9	4	1	2	0	10	4	0	.524	.383
Hechavarria, Adeiny	R-R	6-0	195	4-15-89	.348	.350	.347	25	92	15	32	9	0	0	17	6	1	0	3	14	2	1	.446	.382
Herrera, Dilson	R-R	5-10	210	3-3-94	.248	.289	.231	117	407	66	101	29	1	24	64	43	8	0	2	127	12	5	.501	.330
Kemp, Matt	R-R	6-4	225	9-23-84	.235	.333	.214	8	34	3	8	0	0	1	3	2	0	0	0	7	0	0	.324	.278
Krizan, Jason	L-R	6-0	185	6-28-89	.365	.261	.425	20	63	15	23	9	0	2	11	12	0	1	0	9	1	0	.603	.467
Lee, Braxton	L-R	5-10	185	8-23-93	.261	.276	.256	39	119	13	31	7	0	1	12	10	1	3	0	29	3	1	.345	.323
Liriano, Rymer	R-R	6-0	230	6-20-91	.209	.161	.230	82	201	38	42	9	0	10	29	41	2	1	2	90	7	2	.403	.346
Lowrie, Jed	B-R	6-0	180	4-17-84	.250	.200	.265	12	44	7	11	1	0	2	3	4	0	0	0	12	0	0	.409	.313
McNeil, Jeff	L-R	6-1	195	4-8-92	--	--	--	1	0	1	0	0	0	0	0	1	0	0	0	0	1	0	--	1.000
Nido, Tomas	R-R	6-0	210	4-12-94	.290	.222	.310	12	38	3	11	1	0	0	4	1	0	0	1	13	0	0	.316	.300
Nimmo, Brandon	L-R	6-3	207	3-27-93	.200	.143	.238	10	35	10	7	2	0	1	6	8	1	0	0	8	3	0	.343	.364
Plaia, Colton	R-R	6-2	219	9-25-90	.152	.171	.143	43	125	6	19	6	0	1	10	7	1	2	2	49	0	0	.224	.200
Rivera, Rene	R-R	5-10	215	7-31-83	.254	.305	.235	97	355	53	90	13	0	25	73	31	5	1	4	103	0	0	.501	.319
Sanchez, Ali	R-R	6-0	196	1-20-97	.179	.000	.244	21	56	5	10	4	0	0	3	5	3	0	1	11	0	1	.250	.277
Smith, Dominic	L-L	6-0	239	6-15-95	.222	.500	.143	2	9	1	2	1	0	0	1	0	0	0	0	3	0	0	.333	.222
Taijeron, Travis	R-R	6-2	224	1-20-89	.229	.256	.217	123	371	65	85	21	3	24	70	64	16	0	2	165	6	3	.496	.364
Tebow, Tim	L-L	6-3	245	8-14-87	.163	.208	.152	77	239	25	39	10	0	4	19	20	4	1	0	98	2	2	.255	.240
Tejada, Ruben	R-R	5-11	200	10-27-89	.324	.303	.333	73	276	54	90	20	1	6	42	30	7	0	1	53	3	3	.471	.405
Thompson, David	R-R	6-2	210	8-28-93	.189	.250	.166	41	127	19	24	10	0	3	22	11	2	0	4	40	3	0	.339	.257

Pitching	B-T	HT	WT	DOB	W	L	ERA	G	GS	CG	SV	IP	H	R	ER	HR	BB	SO	AVG	vLH	vRH	K/9	BB/9
Avilan, Luis	L-L	6-2	220	7-19-89	0	0	0.00	2	0	0	0	2	0	0	0	0	0	4	.000	.000	.000	15.43	0.00
Bashlor, Tyler	R-R	6-0	195	4-16-93	3	2	3.41	33	0	0	8	37	29	14	14	3	15	37	.218	.222	.215	9.00	3.65
Blackham, Matt	R-R	5-10	150	1-7-93	3	0	2.30	12	0	0	0	16	10	4	4	1	7	11	.175	.211	.158	6.32	4.02
Burnett, Sean	L-L	5-11	185	9-17-82	0	0	15.63	5	0	0	0	6	12	11	11	3	6	2	.387	.273	.450	2.84	8.53
Caminero, Arquimedes	R-R	6-4	245	6-16-87	0	2	5.09	17	0	0	8	18	18	11	10	4	10	15	.269	.259	.275	7.64	5.09
Church, Andrew	R-R	6-2	200	10-7-94	0	1	13.50	1	1	0	0	3	10	6	5	1	2	1	.556	.539	.600	2.70	5.40
Coleman, Casey	L-R	6-0	185	7-3-87	1	7	5.85	19	15	0	0	65	79	44	42	13	27	53	.305	.417	.225	7.38	3.76
Coleman, Louis	R-R	6-4	205	4-4-86	0	0	5.93	12	0	0	0	14	12	9	9	1	8	12	.231	.318	.167	7.90	5.27
Conlon, P.J.	L-L	5-11	192	11-11-93	0	1	9.00	6	0	0	0	8	9	9	8	2	8	8	.273	.000	.429	9.00	9.00
Familia, Jeurys	R-R	6-3	240	10-10-89	0	0	0.00	1	0	0	0	1	0	0	0	0	0	2	.000	.000	1.000	18.00	0.00
Flexen, Chris	R-R	6-3	250	7-1-94	5	3	4.46	26	14	0	0	79	94	41	39	11	21	92	.297	.250	.325	10.53	2.40
Gagnon, Drew	R-R	6-4	215	6-26-90	6	5	2.33	15	15	0	0	89	78	29	23	12	17	72	.230	.186	.257	7.31	1.73
Gilliam, Ryley	R-R	5-10	170	8-11-96	2	0	13.50	10	0	0	0	9	19	14	14	3	9	12	.432	.440	.421	11.57	8.68
Gonzalez, Harol	B-R	6-0	160	3-2-95	6	0	2.68	8	7	0	0	40	33	12	12	8	12	20	.223	.240	.214	5.13	2.23

Name	B-T	HT	WT	DOB	W	L	ERA	G	GS	CG	SV	IP	H	R	ER	HR	BB	SO	AVG	vLH	vRH	H9	BB9
Hanhold, Eric	R-R	6-5	220	11-1-93	3	4	4.62	39	0	0	0	49	59	27	25	5	21	36	.301	.333	.285	6.66	3.88
Hart, Donnie	L-L	5-11	180	9-6-90	0	0	6.14	8	0	0	0	7	11	5	5	2	1	3	.333	.286	.368	3.68	1.23
Jannis, Mickey	R-R	5-9	195	12-16-87	0	2	22.95	2	2	0	0	7	19	21	17	5	4	5	.475	.250	.571	6.75	5.40
Kay, Anthony	L-L	6-0	218	3-21-95	1	3	6.61	7	7	0	0	31	40	23	23	7	11	26	.325	.333	.323	7.47	3.16
2-team total (7 Buffalo)					3	5	4.41	14	14	0	0	67	73	44	33	10	33	65	.283	.218	.301	8.69	4.41
Lee, Zach	R-R	6-4	227	9-13-91	4	3	6.99	16	13	0	0	75	110	63	58	8	27	63	.345	.306	.373	7.59	3.25
Lockett, Walker	R-R	6-5	225	5-3-94	3	3	3.66	11	10	0	0	59	75	29	24	5	11	39	.305	.243	.353	5.95	1.68
Mazza, Chris	R-R	6-4	180	10-17-89	3	3	3.67	14	13	0	0	76	65	33	31	6	18	62	.236	.254	.222	7.34	2.13
Nogosek, Stephen	R-R	6-2	205	1-11-95	3	0	1.15	24	0	0	2	31	12	5	4	1	13	30	.118	.174	.071	8.62	3.73
O'Rourke, Ryan	R-L	6-3	230	4-30-88	2	3	3.27	36	2	0	2	44	39	21	16	4	23	47	.238	.182	.276	9.61	4.70
2-team total (7 Rochester)					4	4	3.54	43	2	0	2	56	46	27	22	4	35	61	.223	.178	.248	9.80	5.63
Oswalt, Corey	R-R	6-5	250	9-3-93	10	4	2.91	16	16	1	0	87	84	35	28	9	15	79	.252	.261	.245	8.20	1.56
Peterson, Tim	R-R	6-1	215	2-22-91	2	6	2.95	41	0	0	9	55	42	19	18	7	13	54	.208	.132	.254	8.84	2.13
Pounders, Brooks	R-R	6-2	265	9-26-90	1	2	7.59	19	1	0	0	21	29	19	18	4	9	20	.330	.448	.271	8.44	3.80
2-team total (24 Columbus)					3	3	4.31	43	1	0	1	56	48	28	27	8	20	66	.233	.307	.191	10.54	3.20
Rhame, Jacob	R-R	6-1	215	3-16-93	3	2	5.49	20	0	0	3	20	19	13	12	4	6	25	.253	.269	.245	11.44	2.75
Rivera, Rene	R-R	5-10	215	7-31-83	0	0	18.00	1	0	0	0	1	2	2	2	0	1	0	.500	1.000	.000	0.00	9.00
Roseboom, David	L-L	6-3	215	5-17-92	0	1	45.00	2	0	0	0	1	4	5	5	0	4	2	.500	.500	.500	18.00	36.00
Rumbelow, Nick	R-R	6-0	190	9-6-91	0	0	4.26	5	0	0	0	6	11	3	3	1	2	6	.379	.444	.350	8.53	2.84
Santana, Ervin	R-R	6-2	175	12-12-82	4	4	5.38	15	15	0	0	82	97	51	49	11	32	54	.294	.331	.272	5.93	3.51
Santiago, Hector	R-L	6-0	215	12-16-87	3	1	3.35	8	7	0	0	43	32	17	16	5	23	38	.204	.250	.190	7.95	4.81
2-team total (7 Charlotte)					4	5	4.50	15	14	0	0	80	77	42	40	14	32	71	.255	.244	.259	7.99	3.60
Sewald, Paul	R-R	6-3	207	5-26-90	3	3	3.35	41	0	0	3	51	56	23	19	6	15	52	.284	.288	.282	9.18	2.65
Shaw, Joseph	R-R	6-5	225	12-20-93	0	0	4.50	1	0	0	0	2	2	2	1	1	2	0	.222	.200	.250	0.00	9.00
Taylor, Blake	L-L	6-2	220	8-17-95	0	0	0.00	1	0	0	0	0	0	0	0	0	0	0	.000	.000	--	0.00	0.00
Taylor, Corey	R-R	6-1	240	1-8-93	2	0	2.37	10	1	0	0	19	20	5	5	0	7	15	.278	.304	.265	7.11	3.32
Uceta, Adonis	R-R	6-1	225	5-10-94	0	0	33.75	2	0	0	0	1	5	5	5	1	2	2	.556	.800	.250	13.50	13.50
Villines, Stephen	R-R	6-2	175	7-15-95	0	0	6.75	10	0	0	0	16	23	13	12	4	8	12	.333	.393	.293	6.75	4.50
Wilson, Justin	L-L	6-2	205	8-18-87	0	0	4.50	2	2	0	0	2	3	1	1	0	0	4	.333	.000	.500	18.00	0.00
Zamora, Daniel	L-L	6-3	195	4-15-93	2	1	4.20	29	0	0	4	30	26	14	14	1	7	36	.236	.225	.246	10.80	2.10
Zanghi, Joe	R-R	6-3	240	12-1-94	0	0	6.35	5	0	0	0	6	7	4	4	1	5	6	.304	.250	.364	9.53	7.94

Fielding

Catcher	PCT	G	PO	A	E	DP	PB
Nido	.979	11	88	4	2	1	1
Plaia	.997	38	287	16	1	1	4
Rivera	.998	80	596	51	1	8	9
Sanchez	.984	20	114	11	2	2	1

First Base	PCT	G	PO	A	E	DP
Frazier	1.000	1	4	0	0	1
Herrera	.996	35	217	17	1	24
Krizan	1.000	10	66	4	0	9
Rivera	1.000	2	9	1	0	1
Smith	1.000	2	15	2	0	0
Taijeron	.987	78	559	42	8	68
Thompson	.995	25	166	19	1	20

Second Base	PCT	G	PO	A	E	DP
Alcantara	.988	25	36	48	1	9
Cano	1.000	3	7	8	0	5
Cecchini	.889	2	2	6	1	0
Espinosa	.985	33	58	74	2	24
Guillorme	1.000	30	55	66	0	18
Haggerty	1.000	7	16	16	0	6
Hechavarria	1.000	2	1	3	0	1
Herrera	.976	36	52	70	3	22
Krizan	1.000	5	7	8	0	1
Lowrie	1.000	5	7	3	0	1
Tejada	.936	12	13	31	3	5
Guillorme	.990	26	36	63	1	19
Haggerty	1.000	2	0	1	0	1
Hechavarria	.965	14	16	39	2	9
Lowrie	1.000	1	0	1	0	0
Tejada	.986	18	32	38	1	12

Third Base	PCT	G	PO	A	E	DP
Alcantara	.886	28	15	47	8	5
Espinosa	1.000	2	5	3	0	0
Frazier	1.000	2	2	1	0	0
Guillorme	.939	13	5	26	2	3
Hechavarria	1.000	13	7	17	0	1
Herrera	.848	35	24	54	14	5
Lowrie	.778	5	4	3	2	1
Tejada	.982	44	35	72	2	10
Thompson	.892	13	8	25	4	5

Shortstop	PCT	G	PO	A	E	DP
Espinosa	.974	90	131	210	9	49
Frazier	.000	1	0	0	0	0

Outfield	PCT	G	PO	A	E	DP
Alcantara	.983	36	52	5	1	1
Altherr	.981	23	50	2	1	0
Blanco	.990	98	190	5	2	1
Davis	.987	73	146	6	2	0
Gomez	1.000	24	48	3	0	0
Haggerty	1.000	5	5	0	0	0
Herrera	.933	13	14	0	1	0
Kemp	1.000	3	2	0	0	0
Lee	1.000	36	81	3	0	1
Liriano	.968	72	117	5	4	0
McNeil	.000	1	0	0	0	0
Nimmo	1.000	8	21	0	0	0
Taijeron	.981	24	50	1	1	0
Tebow	.989	55	87	1	1	0

BINGHAMTON RUMBLE PONIES

DOUBLE-A

EASTERN LEAGUE

Batting	B-T	HT	WT	DOB	AVG	vLH	vRH	G	AB	R	H	2B	3B	HR	RBI	BB	HBP	SH	SF	SO	SB	CS	SLG	OBP
Alcantara, Arismendy	B-R	5-10	170	10-29-91	.263	.342	.213	27	99	16	26	7	0	2	10	11	1	0	0	27	5	1	.394	.342
Avant, Chandler	R-R	5-11	170	7-11-95	.000	.000	.000	2	6	0	0	0	0	0	0	0	0	0	0	2	0	0	.000	.000
Barnes, Barrett	R-R	5-11	209	7-29-91	.228	.250	.221	96	311	40	71	17	0	12	50	47	13	0	3	96	4	4	.399	.350
Bohanek, Cody	R-R	6-1	195	7-2-95	.182	.250	.143	8	22	4	4	0	0	0	2	4	0	0	0	5	0	2	.182	.217
Bossart, Austin	R-R	6-2	210	7-4-93	.200	.235	.186	19	60	4	12	6	0	0	4	7	2	0	1	16	0	0	.300	.300
2-team total (63 Reading)					.196	.237	.179	82	260	31	51	13	0	7	32	37	4	2	3	63	2	0	.327	.303
Brodey, Quinn	L-L	6-1	195	12-1-95	.251	.230	.258	77	247	22	62	16	0	5	24	22	2	2	3	61	5	2	.377	.314
Carpio, Luis	R-R	5-11	190	7-11-97	.263	.278	.257	82	243	28	64	15	0	3	22	28	3	2	0	49	2	6	.362	.347
Cecchini, Gavin	R-R	6-2	200	12-22-93	.245	.239	.247	43	139	13	34	3	0	3	21	12	0	0	5	32	3	1	.331	.295
Escalera, Alfredo	R-R	6-1	186	2-17-95	.125	.250	.063	7	24	0	3	0	0	0	1	1	0	0	0	11	0	1	.125	.160
Fermin, Edgardo	R-R	6-0	171	5-28-98	.314	.250	.333	14	35	5	11	3	1	0	3	2	1	1	0	2	1	1	.457	.390
Gimenez, Andres	L-R	6-0	161	9-4-98	.250	.320	.223	117	432	54	108	22	5	9	37	24	14	6	3	102	28	16	.387	.309
Haggerty, Sam	B-R	5-11	175	5-26-94	.259	.293	.244	68	247	39	64	8	5	2	13	40	4	0	1	78	19	4	.356	.370
Houle, Dustin	R-R	6-1	205	11-9-93	.205	.455	.121	15	44	3	9	3	0	1	5	1	0	0	0	12	0	0	.341	.222
Kaczmarski, Kevin	L-R	6-0	192	12-31-91	.241	.212	.259	45	137	13	33	6	0	2	17	20	1	1	1	39	4	3	.329	.340
Krizan, Jason	L-R	6-0	185	6-28-89	.257	.184	.289	97	323	36	83	22	1	12	54	38	1	3	2	36	0	0	.443	.335

Name	B-T	HT	WT	DOB	AVG	vLH	vRH	G	AB	R	H	2B	3B	HR	RBI	BB	HBP	SH	SF	SO	SB	CS	OBP	SLG
Lee, Braxton	L-R	5-10	185	8-23-93	.276	.253	.286	80	265	30	73	13	2	2	25	30	1	8	1	72	6	4	.362	.350
Mazeika, Patrick	L-R	6-3	208	10-14-93	.245	.263	.239	116	413	50	101	25	1	16	69	37	6	0	6	89	1	0	.426	.312
Paez, Michael	R-R	5-8	175	12-8-94	.219	.204	.226	99	311	30	68	13	1	3	31	29	6	7	1	58	0	2	.296	.297
Pizzano, Dario	L-R	5-11	200	4-25-91	.226	.188	.241	35	115	20	26	2	0	3	15	18	1	1	2	13	0	0	.322	.331
Sanchez, Ali	R-R	6-0	196	1-20-97	.278	.275	.279	71	270	28	75	13	0	1	30	23	1	0	0	52	1	0	.337	.337
Tejada, Ruben	R-R	5-11	200	10-27-89	.556	.750	.400	2	9	1	5	2	0	0	1	0	0	0	0	2	0	0	.778	.556
Thompson, David	R-R	6-2	210	8-28-93	.230	.220	.235	82	278	33	64	12	2	6	23	23	8	0	3	61	10	3	.353	.305
Toffey, Will	L-R	6-2	205	12-31-94	.219	.167	.237	91	269	42	59	18	1	5	27	50	3	0	1	90	5	3	.349	.347
Vasquez, Jeremy	L-L	6-1	205	7-17-96	.231	.455	.143	12	39	4	9	1	0	0	6	6	0	0	0	6	0	1	.256	.333
Zanon, Jacob	R-R	6-1	180	6-25-95	.188	.167	.194	16	48	5	9	3	0	0	3	3	0	1	1	14	0	0	.250	.231

Pitching	B-T	HT	WT	DOB	W	L	ERA	G	GS	CG	SV	IP	H	R	ER	HR	BB	SO	AVG	vLH	vRH	K/9	BB/9
Blackham, Matt	R-R	5-10	150	1-7-93	5	2	2.72	28	0	0	6	40	21	16	12	4	21	59	.156	.103	.195	13.39	4.76
Campos, Yeizo	R-R	5-11	175	4-29-96	0	3	5.52	8	1	0	0	15	15	9	9	3	3	12	.268	.333	.219	7.36	1.84
Church, Andrew	R-R	6-2	200	10-7-94	0	2	5.57	4	3	0	0	21	27	15	13	4	2	18	.314	.419	.255	7.71	0.86
Conlon, P.J.	L-L	5-11	192	11-11-93	1	0	0.00	1	0	0	0	1	0	0	0	0	0	2	.000	.000	.000	18.00	0.00
Dibrell, Tony	R-R	6-3	190	11-8-95	0	8	9.31	9	8	0	0	39	51	41	40	10	21	37	.321	.304	.338	8.61	4.89
Gibbons, Michael	R-R	6-4	205	4-24-93	3	5	5.06	8	8	0	0	37	38	24	21	7	18	40	.266	.253	.283	9.64	4.34
Gilliam, Ryley	R-R	5-10	170	8-11-96	3	0	4.34	12	0	0	1	19	15	9	9	1	7	28	.224	.270	.167	13.50	3.38
Gonzalez, Harol	B-R	6-0	160	3-2-95	6	4	3.14	17	16	0	0	97	83	37	34	12	23	89	.230	.234	.226	8.23	2.13
Hanhold, Eric	R-R	6-5	220	11-1-93	2	0	1.23	9	0	0	2	15	9	2	2	1	5	18	.177	.143	.217	11.05	3.07
Jannis, Mickey	R-R	5-9	195	12-16-87	7	5	3.10	20	18	1	0	119	123	48	41	2	31	103	.266	.252	.281	7.79	2.34
Jones, Zack	R-R	6-1	195	12-4-90	1	0	14.40	4	0	0	0	5	4	8	8	0	9	5	.211	.231	.167	9.00	16.20
Kay, Anthony	L-L	6-0	218	3-21-95	7	3	1.49	12	12	1	0	66	38	13	11	2	23	70	.165	.148	.176	9.50	3.12
Krizan, Jason	L-R	6-0	185	6-28-89	0	0	23.14	3	0	0	0	2	9	6	6	1	0	1	.563	.333	.857	3.86	0.00
Lee, Zach	R-R	6-4	227	9-13-91	5	1	2.09	8	8	0	0	47	37	13	11	3	6	37	.208	.255	.150	7.04	1.14
Mazza, Chris	R-R	6-4	180	10-17-89	0	2	3.42	4	4	0	0	24	26	10	9	0	8	21	.280	.284	.269	7.99	3.04
McGeorge, Austin	R-R	6-2	215	11-27-94	0	4	3.55	14	3	0	1	33	36	24	13	5	14	27	.255	.255	.290	7.36	3.82
McIlraith, Thomas	R-R	6-4	220	2-17-94	0	1	3.60	3	0	0	0	5	2	2	2	1	1	7	.125	.333	.000	12.60	1.80
Megill, Tylor	R-R	6-7	230	7-28-95	0	1	5.40	1	1	0	0	5	5	3	3	0	0	9	.250	.222	.273	16.20	0.00
Nogosek, Stephen	R-R	6-2	205	1-11-95	0	0	0.95	11	0	0	1	19	13	4	2	0	12	20	.203	.211	.192	9.47	5.68
Peterson, David	L-L	6-6	240	9-3-95	3	6	4.19	24	24	0	0	116	119	63	54	9	37	122	.263	.272	.258	9.47	2.87
Ramos, Darwin	R-R	6-2	210	11-23-95	0	0	9.00	1	0	0	0	2	4	2	2	0	1	0	.444	.800	.000	0.00	4.50
Rennie, Luc	R-R	6-2	215	4-26-94	0	2	5.01	4	4	0	0	23	17	15	13	5	8	23	.205	.263	.156	8.87	3.09
Renteria, Marcel	R-R	5-11	185	9-27-94	0	0	0.00	1	0	0	1	1	1	0	0	0	0	2	.250	.333	.000	18.00	0.00
Roseboom, David	L-L	6-3	215	5-17-92	1	1	8.76	8	0	0	1	12	16	13	12	3	9	11	.320	.304	.333	8.03	6.57
Ryan, Ryder	R-R	6-2	205	5-11-95	3	1	3.05	25	2	0	0	44	33	17	15	2	23	40	.210	.186	.239	8.12	4.67
Shaw, Joseph	R-R	6-5	225	12-20-93	1	4	3.83	20	3	0	1	40	39	21	17	3	17	45	.257	.290	.233	10.13	3.83
Simon, Jake	L-L	6-2	189	1-21-97	0	0	6.75	1	0	0	0	1	2	1	1	0	2	3	.400	.000	.500	20.25	13.50
Smith, Kevin	R-L	6-5	200	5-13-97	3	2	3.45	6	6	0	0	31	25	12	12	1	15	28	.227	.182	.247	8.04	4.31
Szapucki, Thomas	R-L	6-2	181	6-12-96	0	0	0.00	1	1	0	0	4	2	1	0	0	1	4	.133	.000	.182	9.00	2.25
Taylor, Blake	L-L	6-2	220	8-17-95	0	1	1.85	18	0	0	3	39	25	10	8	2	12	45	.179	.182	.177	10.38	2.77
Torres, Joshua	R-R	6-0	170	4-26-94	2	2	7.45	17	0	0	0	29	39	26	24	8	8	29	.310	.307	.314	9.00	2.48
Uceta, Adonis	R-R	6-1	225	5-10-94	5	3	1.44	36	1	0	7	56	41	11	9	3	17	55	.207	.272	.137	8.79	2.72
Vargas, Jason	L-L	6-0	215	2-2-83	0	0	2.25	1	1	0	0	4	2	1	1	1	3	5	.143	.125	.167	11.25	6.75
Vilera, Jaison	R-R	6-0	188	6-19-97	0	1	3.18	1	1	0	0	6	8	2	2	0	0	4	.320	.429	.182	6.35	0.00
Villines, Stephen	R-R	6-2	175	7-15-95	2	1	1.20	28	0	0	7	45	34	9	6	1	14	42	.209	.222	.195	8.40	2.80
Wilson, Tommy	R-R	6-4	220	5-26-96	4	5	4.96	13	13	1	0	69	65	41	38	11	18	60	.246	.242	.252	7.83	2.35
Zanghi, Joe	R-R	6-3	240	12-1-94	3	3	2.34	31	2	0	4	58	43	19	15	1	27	50	.212	.212	.212	7.80	4.21

Fielding

Catcher	PCT	G	PO	A	E	DP	PB
Bossart	.993	17	124	16	1	0	2
Houle	.983	7	55	2	1	1	0
Mazeika	.985	55	444	29	7	3	14
Sanchez	.992	65	554	45	5	3	12

First Base	PCT	G	PO	A	E	DP
Houle	1.000	1	3	0	0	0
Krizan	.991	35	214	19	2	22
Mazeika	.990	53	348	32	4	22
Pizzano	.979	7	44	3	1	1
Thompson	.994	50	327	26	2	31
Vasquez	1.000	9	60	7	0	7

Second Base	PCT	G	PO	A	E	DP
Alcantara	1.000	7	6	21	0	4
Bohanek	.833	3	5	0	1	0
Carpio	.993	46	51	87	1	15
Cecchini	.973	23	27	46	2	8

	PCT	G	PO	A	E	DP
Haggerty	.980	23	39	57	2	11
Krizan	1.000	3	5	8	0	4
Paez	.984	49	77	102	3	18

Third Base	PCT	G	PO	A	E	DP
Carpio	.950	8	5	14	1	1
Cecchini	.929	10	6	20	2	1
Haggerty	.800	4	3	5	2	0
Paez	.922	27	11	36	4	3
Thompson	.971	26	21	45	2	2
Toffey	.924	75	47	74	10	4

Shortstop	PCT	G	PO	A	E	DP
Alcantara	.947	6	6	12	1	5
Carpio	.976	20	25	56	2	13
Fermin	1.000	3	0	2	0	0
Gimenez	.973	112	147	255	11	44
Haggerty	1.000	2	5	4	0	3
Tejada	.750	2	1	5	2	0

Outfield	PCT	G	PO	A	E	DP
Alcantara	1.000	12	24	1	0	0
Avant	1.000	2	2	0	0	0
Barnes	1.000	74	126	4	0	1
Bohanek	1.000	6	2	0	0	0
Brodey	.968	77	176	5	6	1
Carpio	1.000	2	1	0	0	0
Escalera	.846	6	11	0	2	0
Fermin	1.000	9	19	0	0	0
Haggerty	.985	30	62	2	1	0
Kaczmarski	.957	43	65	2	3	0
Krizan	1.000	61	118	2	0	0
Lee	.981	74	150	6	3	2
Paez	1.000	8	14	0	0	0
Pizzano	1.000	22	31	1	0	0
Thompson	.857	3	6	0	1	0
Vasquez	1.000	3	3	0	0	0
Zanon	1.000	15	28	0	0	0

ST. LUCIE METS

HIGH CLASS A

FLORIDA STATE LEAGUE

Batting	B-T	HT	WT	DOB	AVG	vLH	vRH	G	AB	R	H	2B	3B	HR	RBI	BB	HBP	SH	SF	SO	SB	CS	SLG	OBP
Ashford, Zach	L-R	5-10	180	2-9-97	.353	--	.353	5	17	1	6	1	0	0	3	1	0	0	0	4	1	2	.412	.389
Bohanek, Cody	R-R	6-1	195	7-2-95	.229	.221	.231	99	306	41	70	17	1	5	22	39	19	1	4	110	12	9	.340	.348
Bohorquez, Anderson	R-R	5-11	180	10-3-97	.000	--	.000	1	3	0	0	0	0	0	0	0	0	0	0	1	0	0	.000	.000
Brodey, Quinn	L-L	6-1	195	12-1-95	.285	.308	.280	53	200	30	57	13	1	5	38	18	0	0	6	46	8	2	.435	.335
Carpio, Luis	R-R	5-11	190	7-11-97	.330	.407	.299	31	94	13	31	4	1	1	12	10	1	0	1	15	2	3	.426	.396
Cortes, Carlos	L-B	5-7	197	6-30-97	.256	.187	.273	127	458	64	117	26	3	11	68	52	7	2	7	77	6	5	.397	.336
d'Arnaud, Travis	R-R	6-2	210	2-10-89	.286	.500	.000	2	7	0	2	0	0	0	1	1	0	0	0	1	0	0	.286	.375
Escalera, Alfredo	R-R	6-1	186	2-17-95	.109	.067	.129	14	46	2	5	0	0	0	1	3	2	0	0	21	1	1	.109	.196
Fermin, Edgardo	R-R	6-0	171	5-28-98	.258	.294	.245	37	128	15	33	8	1	1	15	7	2	0	0	40	5	0	.359	.307
Frazier, Todd	R-R	6-3	220	2-12-86	.216	.000	.276	11	37	3	8	0	0	1	8	6	0	0	0	8	0	1	.297	.326
Ghelfi, Mitch	B-R	5-11	185	9-24-92	.240	.333	.228	57	183	24	44	3	2	1	21	19	0	2	3	50	6	0	.295	.307
Gladu, Raphael	L-R	6-2	195	6-23-95	.039	.000	.044	8	26	1	1	0	0	0	1	2	0	0	0	7	1	0	.039	.107
Houle, Dustin	R-T	6-1	205	11-9-93	.000	--	.000	1	1	0	0	0	0	0	0	0	0	0	0	0	0	0	.000	.667
Lagrange, Wagner	R-R	5-11	187	9-6-95	.293	.500	.248	36	133	21	39	8	1	2	17	13	2	1	1	24	2	0	.414	.362
Lindsay, Desmond	R-R	6-0	200	1-15-97	.196	.167	.205	15	51	8	10	2	0	1	5	7	1	0	0	25	1	0	.294	.305
Lowrie, Jed	B-R	6-0	180	4-17-84	.200	--	.200	6	20	0	4	1	0	0	1	0	0	0	0	2	0	0	.250	.238
Medina, Jose Miguel	R-R	6-3	180	10-21-96	.167	.250	.125	9	24	2	4	0	0	0	1	1	0	0	0	7	0	1	.167	.231
Meyer, Nick	R-R	6-1	200	2-18-97	.182	.104	.205	64	209	19	38	4	1	1	16	3	1	0	4	43	1	2	.225	.250
Moreno, Hansel	B-R	6-4	180	11-3-96	.216	.236	.210	77	236	31	51	4	3	3	22	19	1	7	3	62	13	9	.297	.274
Nimmo, Brandon	L-R	6-3	207	3-27-93	.214	.167	.250	5	14	1	3	0	1	0	0	3	0	0	0	2	0	1	.357	.353
Ortega, Jake	L-R	5-10	175	7-31-96	.267	.000	.286	5	15	5	4	0	0	0	0	2	1	1	0	3	1	1	.267	.389
Rizzie, Dan	R-R	6-2	200	11-26-93	.244	.263	.235	40	123	7	30	4	0	1	10	10	0	2	0	30	1	1	.301	.301
Rodriguez, Manny	R-R	5-10	166	7-4-96	.242	.284	.231	114	380	38	92	20	2	1	35	36	4	1	1	116	14	10	.313	.314
Romero, Yoel	R-R	6-0	180	4-10-98	.240	.143	.278	9	25	5	6	1	1	0	1	2	0	0	0	4	0	0	.280	.296
Tiberi, Blake	L-R	6-0	205	2-16-95	.252	.310	.239	120	448	72	113	29	0	3	35	52	3	3	3	87	16	5	.337	.332
Vasquez, Jeremy	L-L	6-1	205	7-17-96	.277	.280	.276	125	444	44	123	26	2	5	61	55	5	0	6	75	3	3	.378	.359
Winaker, Matt	L-L	6-1	195	11-29-95	.195	.290	.183	86	261	31	51	9	5	2	31	26	14	4	3	62	6	5	.291	.299
Zanon, Jacob	R-R	6-1	180	6-25-95	.248	.225	.257	97	355	42	88	13	2	7	48	32	2	6	8	83	18	7	.355	.307

Pitching	B-T	HT	WT	DOB	W	L	ERA	G	GS	CG	SV	IP	H	R	ER	HR	BB	SO	AVG	vLH	vRH	K/9	BB/9
Avilan, Luis	L-L	6-2	220	7-19-89	1	0	4.50	2	0	0	0	2	1	1	1	0	1	2	.125	.000	.167	9.00	4.50
Campos, Yeizo	R-R	5-11	175	4-29-96	1	0	1.10	19	1	0	4	33	25	6	4	2	8	39	.207	.157	.243	10.74	2.20
Campusano, Briam	R-R	6-2	172	3-26-96	1	1	3.24	19	1	0	1	33	28	14	12	4	9	24	.226	.237	.215	6.48	2.43
Cavallaro, Joe	R-R	6-4	190	7-19-95	6	5	3.54	32	8	0	3	81	74	36	32	6	34	74	.243	.268	.225	8.19	3.76
Dibrell, Tony	R-R	6-3	190	11-8-95	8	4	2.39	17	16	0	0	90	73	27	24	2	36	76	.225	.220	.230	7.57	3.59
Gilliam, Ryley	R-R	5-10	170	8-11-96	0	0	2.53	7	0	0	2	11	8	3	3	0	2	16	.200	.313	.125	13.50	1.69
Hernandez, Carlos	R-R	5-11	172	11-3-94	1	4	4.33	38	0	0	1	69	58	36	33	4	25	60	.233	.234	.232	7.86	3.28
Holderman, Colin	R-R	6-7	240	10-8-95	1	0	0.00	1	1	0	0	4	0	0	0	0	2	4	.174	.083	.273	5.68	2.84
Kisena, Alec	L-R	6-5	275	10-12-95	1	0	0.00	1	0	0	0	4	3	0	0	0	5	2	.214	.200	.222	10.38	0.00
Kuhns, Max	R-R	6-2	209	8-11-94	0	0	4.50	1	0	0	0	2	1	1	1	0	2	1	.143	.000	.500	4.50	9.00
Lockett, Walker	R-R	6-5	225	5-3-94	1	0	5.14	2	2	0	0	7	8	4	4	1	0	6	.276	.133	.429	7.71	0.00
McGeorge, Austin	R-R	6-2	215	11-27-94	0	0	0.90	2	2	0	0	10	11	3	1	1	1	13	.282	.231	.308	11.70	0.90
McIlraith, Thomas	R-R	6-4	220	2-17-94	4	5	2.79	20	0	0	1	39	29	19	12	3	18	35	.209	.279	.154	8.15	4.19
Megill, Tylor	R-R	6-7	230	7-28-95	3	4	4.04	7	7	0	0	36	36	20	16	1	10	42	.254	.250	.257	10.60	2.52
Mitchell, Andrew	L-L	6-1	200	10-23-94	1	0	3.14	18	1	0	1	29	23	10	10	2	10	30	.223	.200	.235	9.42	3.14
Nunez, Dedniel	R-R	6-2	180	6-5-96	2	3	4.53	12	12	0	0	58	59	31	29	3	20	61	.261	.250	.269	9.52	3.12
O'Neil, Conner	R-R	6-2	195	9-25-94	2	1	5.00	27	0	0	2	45	56	28	25	7	25	35	.308	.286	.321	7.00	5.00
Ramos, Darwin	R-R	6-2	210	11-23-95	4	2	1.43	23	1	0	0	38	37	14	6	1	14	31	.253	.296	.228	7.41	3.35
Rennie, Luc	R-R	6-2	215	4-26-94	7	8	3.83	22	22	0	0	108	106	54	46	14	32	67	.252	.281	.226	5.58	2.67
Renteria, Marcel	R-R	5-11	185	9-27-94	1	4	4.62	37	0	0	5	62	62	38	32	6	26	63	.253	.295	.218	9.10	3.75
Rhame, Jacob	R-R	6-1	215	3-16-93	0	0	0.00	1	0	0	0	1	0	0	0	0	0	0	.000	.000	.000	0.00	0.00
Santana, Ervin	R-R	6-2	175	12-12-82	1	1	4.85	3	3	0	0	13	15	9	7	2	3	11	.278	.269	.286	7.62	2.08
Shaw, Joseph	R-R	6-5	225	12-20-93	1	0	2.12	10	0	0	0	17	15	6	4	0	7	20	.231	.235	.226	10.59	3.71
Simon, Jake	L-L	6-2	189	1-21-97	0	0	4.70	5	1	0	0	8	5	4	4	0	7	7	.179	.300	.111	8.22	8.22
Smith, Kevin	R-L	6-5	200	5-13-97	5	5	3.05	17	17	0	0	86	83	30	29	5	24	102	.259	.277	.274	10.72	2.52
Szapucki, Thomas	R-L	6-2	181	6-12-96	1	3	3.25	9	9	0	0	36	33	16	13	1	15	42	.241	.344	.210	10.50	3.75
Taylor, Blake	L-L	6-2	220	8-17-95	2	2	2.63	21	0	0	7	24	15	8	1	12	29	.233	.303	.200	9.55	3.95
Vilera, Jaison	R-R	6-0	188	6-19-97	2	1	3.81	5	4	0	0	26	26	13	11	2	10	17	.265	.245	.289	5.88	3.46
Wilson, Kyle	R-R	6-1	185	9-27-96	4	8	3.80	21	20	0	0	90	106	48	38	4	41	54	.296	.291	.301	5.40	4.10
Wilson, Tommy	R-R	6-4	220	5-26-96	4	2	2.01	8	8	0	0	45	33	13	10	1	14	36	.203	.209	.194	7.25	2.82
Zabaleta, Ezequiel	R-R	6-0	175	8-20-95	3	3	4.14	26	0	0	8	37	26	18	17	3	14	38	.200	.232	.176	9.24	3.41

Fielding

Catcher	PCT	G	PO	A	E	DP	PB
d'Arnaud	1.000	2	19	0	0	0	0
Ghelfi	.994	40	299	35	2	3	8
Houle	1.000	1	6	2	0	2	0
Meyer	.981	64	458	65	10	13	9
Ortega	1.000	5	42	7	0	1	1
Rizzie	.996	31	228	18	1	1	4

First Base	PCT	G	PO	A	E	DP
Bohanek	1.000	1	8	0	0	1
Fermin	1.000	3	19	2	0	2
Frazier	1.000	5	16	0	0	1
Romero	1.000	2	14	1	0	0
Vasquez	.994	116	838	54	5	78
Winaker	.990	16	89	6	1	9

Second Base	PCT	G	PO	A	E	DP
Bohanek	1.000	4	1	9	0	0
Carpio	.985	17	22	43	1	7
Cortes	.942	76	106	172	17	29
Fermin	.980	12	16	32	1	9
Ghelfi	1.000	5	2	7	0	1
Lowrie	1.000	3	1	5	0	0
Moreno	1.000	3	10	7	0	2

	PCT	G	PO	A	E	DP
Rodriguez	.957	7	8	14	1	5
Romero	1.000	3	7	4	0	2
Tiberi	.952	18	22	37	3	11

Third Base	PCT	G	PO	A	E	DP
Bohanek	.946	72	53	140	11	15
Carpio	1.000	2	1	3	0	0
Fermin	.895	8	3	14	2	1
Frazier	1.000	10	4	5	0	1
Lowrie	1.000	1	0	2	0	0
Rodriguez	1.000	1	0	1	0	0
Romero	.714	3	2	3	2	1
Tiberi	.860	55	27	47	12	9

Shortstop	PCT	G	PO	A	E	DP
Bohanek	.966	25	31	54	3	14
Carpio	1.000	1	2	1	0	1
Fermin	.842	3	10	6	3	1
Frazier	1.000	3	5	3	0	2
Lowrie	1.000	2	0	5	0	0
Rodriguez	.944	111	173	245	25	46
Romero	1.000	1	2	2	0	0

Outfield	PCT	G	PO	A	E	DP
Ashford	1.000	4	11	0	0	0
Bohanek	1.000	5	7	0	0	0
Brodey	.969	53	118	8	4	4
Cortes	1.000	1	1	0	0	0
Escalera	.929	12	25	1	2	0
Fermin	1.000	12	20	2	0	0
Gladu	.917	7	11	0	1	0
Lagrange	.976	24	38	2	1	1
Lindsay	1.000	15	39	0	0	0
Medina	1.000	8	13	0	0	0
Moreno	.965	75	181	14	7	3
Nimmo	1.000	2	5	0	0	0
Tiberi	1.000	40	65	2	0	0
Vasquez	1.000	5	7	0	0	0
Winaker	.991	60	112	2	1	0
Zanon	.986	97	201	5	3	1

COLUMBIA FIREFLIES
SOUTH ATLANTIC LEAGUE

LOW CLASS A

NEW YORK METS

Batting	B-T	HT	WT	DOB	AVG	vLH	vRH	G	AB	R	H	2B	3B	HR	RBI	BB	HBP	SH	SF	SO	SB	CS	SLG	OBP
Adon, Ranfy	R-R	6-3	195	8-2-97	.000	--	.000	2	8	0	0	0	0	0	0	0	0	0	0	6	0	0	.000	.000
Avant, Chandler	R-R	5-11	170	7-11-95	.205	.197	.207	78	264	23	54	11	1	3	26	18	5	7	0	43	5	4	.288	.268
Capra, Phil	B-R	5-10	205	10-1-96	.098	.133	.077	14	41	5	4	0	0	0	3	8	0	0	1	18	0	0	.098	.240
Chambers, Chase	L-L	6-1	250	8-22-95	.246	.297	.230	106	382	42	94	15	2	5	41	26	13	0	7	95	0	1	.335	.311
Conti, Nick	R-R	5-9	160	2-14-97	.241	.294	.216	15	54	7	13	3	1	1	5	8	1	0	1	16	2	1	.389	.344
Dirocie, Anthony	R-R	5-11	175	4-24-97	.182	.357	.122	23	66	12	12	2	0	2	10	12	1	1	1	30	0	2	.303	.313
Granadillo, Guillermo	R-R	5-11	197	2-12-97	.198	.265	.167	36	106	8	21	4	2	0	8	2	1	2	3	20	0	0	.274	.214
Lagrange, Wagner	R-R	5-11	187	9-6-95	.282	.241	.289	71	252	28	71	18	3	4	31	16	1	1	3	47	0	1	.425	.324
Lane, Taylor	R-R	6-4	205	9-17-95	.148	.160	.138	19	54	8	8	2	0	0	1	7	1	0	0	15	0	0	.185	.258
Marquez, Bradley	R-R	6-1	185	12-14-92	.161	.083	.184	20	62	4	10	1	0	0	1	4	1	0	0	19	2	0	.177	.224
Mauricio, Ronny	B-R	6-3	166	4-4-01	.268	.232	.279	116	470	62	126	20	5	4	37	23	5	3	3	99	6	10	.357	.307
Medina, Jose Miguel	R-R	6-3	180	10-21-96	.244	.286	.229	59	197	24	48	9	0	5	21	23	2	0	3	41	8	5	.366	.324
Molina, Gerson	R-R	6-3	186	3-13-96	.231	.211	.238	93	290	44	67	19	2	4	24	28	6	2	0	106	6	5	.352	.312
Moreno, Hansel	B-R	6-4	180	11-3-96	.276	.321	.261	32	116	21	32	4	0	5	14	13	0	4	2	26	7	4	.440	.344
Newton, Shervyen	B-R	6-4	180	4-24-99	.209	.259	.195	109	382	35	80	15	2	9	32	37	2	0		139	1	4	.330	.283
Rasquin, Walter	R-R	5-9	200	3-21-96	.165	.153	.172	72	237	24	39	4	3	3	15	15	6	5	0	56	8	2	.245	.233
Rheams, Zach	L-L	6-0	225	7-5-96	.217	.214	.186	18	60	3	13	3	0	1	6	4	1	0	0	26	0	0	.317	.277
Romero, Yoel	R-R	6-0	180	4-10-98	.133	.250	.115	10	30	2	4	0	0	2	3	0	0	0		7	0	0	.133	.212
Sanchez, Carlos	R-R	6-0	203	6-6-96	.200	.000	.233	11	35	1	7	1	1	0	1	2	1	0	0	10	1	0	.286	.263
Senger, Hayden	R-R	6-1	210	4-3-97	.230	.238	.227	90	304	27	70	21	1	4	36	25	19	1	4	64	0	0	.345	.324
Sharp, Brian	L-R	6-2	205	2-18-97	.200	.214	.199	119	410	48	82	12	5	11	38	41	0	4	2	168	8	2	.334	.272
Uriarte, Juan	R-R	6-0	182	9-17-97	.200	.182	.206	50	175	18	35	8	0	3	16	5	4	0	1	50	0	0	.297	.238
Vientos, Mark	R-R	6-4	185	12-11-99	.255	.281	.246	111	416	48	106	27	1	12	62	22	8	0	8	110	1	4	.411	.300

Pitching	B-T	HT	WT	DOB	W	L	ERA	G	GS	CG	SV	IP	H	R	ER	HR	BB	SO	AVG	vLH	vRH	K/9	BB/9
Acosta, Daison	R-R	6-2	160	8-24-98	1	4	3.78	11	11	0	0	52	50	31	22	4	26	49	.244	.281	.220	8.43	4.47
Biddy, Jared	R-R	6-2	180	7-25-96	0	0	0.00	1	0	0	0	1	0	0	0	0	0	0	.000	.000	.000	0.00	0.00
Bryant, Garrison	L-R	6-3	189	12-3-98	0	0	21.60	1	0	0	0	2	4	4	1	1	1	2	.250	.000	.500	5.40	5.40
Butto, Jose	R-R	6-1	160	3-19-98	4	10	3.62	27	25	0	0	112	100	53	45	8	31	109	.234	.196	.268	8.76	2.49
Campusano, Briam	R-R	6-2	172	3-26-96	0	0	3.18	5	0	0	0	6	3	3	2	1	1	10	.143	.143	.143	15.88	1.59
Gordon, Cole	L-R	6-5	244	10-2-95	1	3	2.76	18	0	0	1	29	19	11	9	2	15	36	.183	.174	.190	11.05	4.60
Holderman, Colin	R-R	6-7	240	10-8-95	3	2	4.09	13	12	0	0	55	50	28	25	3	25	41	.244	.231	.254	6.71	4.09
Hrbek, Danny	L-R	5-11	195	12-27-94	4	0	3.12	20	0	0	0	40	38	14	14	4	11	50	.247	.269	.230	11.16	2.45
Hutchinson, Bryce	R-R	6-4	245	10-21-98	4	7	3.73	31	7	0	2	92	91	51	38	5	29	71	.263	.225	.296	6.97	2.85
James, Christian	R-R	6-3	210	5-24-98	3	11	5.07	24	21	0	0	114	132	78	64	6	46	76	.297	.340	.265	6.02	3.64
Kisena, Alec	L-R	6-5	275	10-12-95	4	2	3.50	24	4	0	2	69	64	28	27	2	29	70	.247	.308	.204	9.09	3.76
Lasko, Justin	R-R	6-4	210	3-16-97	4	4	2.57	11	1	0	0	21	17	8	6	1	6	19	.233	.229	.237	8.14	2.57
Leon, Nelson	R-R	6-1	154	3-1-95	0	1	9.49	8	0	0	1	12	18	14	13	1	6	14	.367	.500	.240	10.22	4.38
MacDonald, Nick	R-R	6-1	175	6-11-98	0	0	0.00	1	0	0	0	2	1	0	0	0	1	3	.143	--	.143	13.50	4.50
Megill, Tylor	R-R	6-7	230	7-28-95	3	2	2.61	14	3	0	2	31	23	11	9	1	15	41	.207	.225	.194	11.90	4.35
Mitchell, Andrew	L-L	6-0	200	10-23-94	2	0	0.92	15	0	0	2	20	16	6	2	0	6	32	.219	.136	.255	14.64	2.75
Moreno, Jose	R-R	6-4	165	7-31-96	3	5	2.28	37	0	0	3	43	36	22	11	1	25	52	.231	.219	.239	10.80	5.19
Nunez, Dedniel	R-R	6-2	180	6-5-96	3	1	4.03	4	3	0	0	22	14	10	10	2	3	33	.175	.250	.135	13.30	1.21
O'Neil, Conner	R-R	6-2	195	9-25-94	1	1	4.05	5	0	0	0	7	6	4	3	0	2	5	.240	.188	.333	6.75	2.70
Oxford, Billy	R-R	6-1	200	10-22-95	0	3	4.73	25	0	0	2	32	39	25	17	6	8	32	.291	.393	.206	8.91	2.23
Ramos, Darwin	R-R	6-2	210	11-23-95	0	0	2.81	18	0	0	1	26	20	11	8	2	8	30	.222	.194	.241	10.52	2.81
Sharp, Brian	L-R	6-2	205	2-18-97	0	0	4.50	2	0	0	0	2	3	1	1	0	2	2	.333	.333	.333	9.00	9.00
Simon, Jake	L-L	6-2	181	1-21-97	0	1	4.06	21	0	0	1	38	35	20	17	1	17	46	.248	.143	.293	10.99	4.06
Szapucki, Thomas	R-L	6-2	181	6-12-96	0	0	2.08	11	8	0	0	22	14	7	5	1	10	26	.182	.250	.158	10.80	4.15
Taveras, Willy	R-R	5-11	158	1-20-98	6	11	5.14	29	16	0	0	119	136	72	68	19	24	99	.288	.293	.284	7.49	1.82
Tripp, Christian	R-R	6-7	220	3-13-97	0	0	14.63	7	0	0	0	8	12	14	13	1	7	6	.343	.333	.353	6.75	7.88
Viall, Chris	R-R	6-9	253	9-28-95	0	1	9.55	19	0	0	2	22	28	24	23	2	14	24	.304	.375	.250	9.97	5.82
Vilera, Jaison	R-R	6-0	188	6-19-97	1	3	9.00	6	5	0	0	24	31	26	24	4	15	17	.320	.354	.286	6.38	5.63
Winans, Allan	R-R	6-2	165	8-10-95	1	3	2.74	30	0	0	11	43	30	16	13	2	16	40	.207	.258	.165	8.44	3.38
Wollersheim, Connor	L-L	6-2	205	5-18-97	0	0	1.50	3	0	0	0	6	7	3	1	0	4	6	.222	.000	.389	9.00	6.00
Woods Richardson, Simeon	R-R	6-3	210	9-27-00	3	8	4.25	20	20	0	0	78	78	44	37	5	17	97	.256	.287	.233	11.14	1.95
Zabaleta, Ezequiel	R-R	6-0	175	8-20-95	1	1	1.69	17	0	0	3	21	18	7	4	3	2	22	.220	.229	.213	9.28	0.84

Fielding

C: Capra 14, Chambers 1, Sanchez 11, Senger 69, Uriarte 46. **1B:** Chambers 75, Rheams 5, Sharp 65. **2B:** Avant 44, Conti 15, Newton 53, Rasquin 28, Romero 2. **3B:** Avant 3, Lane 2, Newton 27, Sharp 16, Vientos 100. **SS:** Avant 1, Mauricio 106, Newton 29. **OF:** Adon 2, Avant 32, Dirocie 23, Granadillo 36, Lagrange 46, Lane 15, Marquez 18, Medina 57, Molina 93, Moreno 32, Rasquin 28, Rheams 1, Romero 8, Sharp 39.

BROOKLYN CYCLONES
NEW YORK-PENN LEAGUE

SHORT SEASON

Batting	B-T	HT	WT	DOB	AVG	vLH	vRH	G	AB	R	H	2B	3B	HR	RBI	BB	HBP	SH	SF	SO	SB	CS	SLG	OBP
Adon, Ranfy	R-R	6-3	195	8-2-97	.270	.333	.261	41	137	22	37	4	1	2	13	10	0	0	1	41	11	3	.358	.318
Ashford, Zach	L-R	5-10	180	2-9-97	.136	.000	.157	16	59	7	8	1	1	1	4	5	1	1	0	17	2	1	.237	.215
Avant, Chandler	R-R	5-11	170	7-11-95	.231	.250	.227	8	26	6	6	1	0	0	2	2	0	0	0	3	1	0	.269	.286
Baty, Brett	L-R	6-3	210	11-13-99	.200	.000	.250	4	10	2	2	1	0	0	3	6	1	0	0	3	0	0	.300	.529
Beracierta, Raul	R-R	6-1	215	5-24-99	.188	.125	.203	31	80	11	15	2	0	0	6	9	2	2	0	26	2	2	.213	.286
Cano, Robinson	L-R	6-0	210	10-22-82	.286	.333	.250	2	7	1	2	1	0	0	2	0	0	0	0	1	0	0	.429	.286
Capra, Phil	B-R	5-10	205	10-1-96	.000	--	.000	1	4	0	0	0	0	0	0	0	0	0	0	3	0	0	.000	.000
Cecchini, Gavin	R-R	6-2	200	12-22-93	.333	.600	.143	3	12	1	4	2	0	0	1	1	0	0	0	6	0	1	.500	.385
Corona, Kenedy	R-R	5-11	185	3-21-00	.000	--	.000	4	3	1	0	0	0	0	1	3	0	0	0	2	0	0	.000	.500
Dirocie, Anthony	R-R	5-11	175	4-24-97	.140	.125	.152	20	57	3	8	0	0	1	6	6	0	0	1	25	2	0	.193	.219
Duplantis, Antoine	L-L	5-11	180	9-9-96	.237	.296	.228	52	194	25	46	5	3	0	20	12	3	3	4	31	5	4	.294	.286
Fryman, Branden	R-R	6-1	170	3-16-98	.356	.125	.405	13	45	4	16	2	0	0	4	3	0	0	0	7	4	2	.400	.396
Gaddis, Nic	R-R	5-11	170	10-12-96	.184	.286	.167	15	49	4	9	2	0	0	5	1	2	0	0	15	1	1	.225	.273
Garay, Gavin	R-R	6-2	205	6-18-97	.253	.177	.268	31	99	10	25	5	0	2	11	6	0	0	1	34	0	0	.364	.293
Genord, Joe	R-R	6-1	227	8-17-96	.204	.214	.207	64	216	30	44	13	0	9	44	15	8	0	6	65	2	0	.389	.274
Granadillo, Guillermo	R-R	5-11	197	2-12-97	.256	.286	.250	14	43	8	11	2	1	0	2	1	1	1	0	13	4	1	.349	.289
Haggerty, Sam	B-R	5-11	175	5-26-94	.333	.000	.333	6	21	5	7	3	0	0	4	4	0	0	0	8	0	0	.476	.440
Mangum, Jake	B-L	6-1	179	3-8-96	.247	.273	.242	53	182	29	45	5	2	0	18	15	10	2	1	26	17	5	.297	.337
Manzanarez, Angel	R-R	5-10	160	5-19-97	.304	.333	.300	15	23	4	7	1	0	0	0	3	1	0	0	4	1	0	.348	.407
McNeil, Jeff	L-R	6-1	195	4-8-92	.250	.000	.333	1	4	1	1	0	0	0	0	0	0	0	0	0	0	0	.250	.250
Medina, Jose Miguel	R-R	6-3	180	10-21-96	.160	.000	.125	7	25	1	4	2	0	0	4	0	0	0	0	8	1	0	.240	.160
Mena, Jose	R-R	6-0	208	12-22-96	.299	.467	.268	31	97	14	29	5	1	2	13	5	3	0	0	24	0	0	.433	.352
Ortega, Jake	L-R	5-10	175	7-31-96	.237	.182	.213	27	76	6	18	2	0	0	6	6	0	2	1	25	1	0	.263	.289
Peroza, Jose	R-R	6-1	214	6-15-00	.225	.136	.247	33	111	14	25	4	0	4	22	7	4	0	0	38	0	2	.369	.295
Reyes, Wilmer	R-R	6-0	161	12-22-97	.323	.268	.339	61	229	32	74	8	2	5	33	8	3	1	3	41	12	6	.441	.350
Rheams, Zach	L-L	6-0	225	7-5-96	.125	.000	.167	7	16	1	2	0	0	1	1	4	0	0	0	7	0	0	.313	.300
Ritter, Luke	R-R	5-11	187	2-15-97	.245	.367	.231	68	229	39	56	15	1	4	36	33	6	1	3	50	5	3	.371	.351
Romero, Yoel	R-R	6-0	180	4-10-98	.251	.185	.260	54	199	31	50	9	2	4	15	22	0	2	0	41	6	4	.377	.326
Taylor, Kennie	R-R	5-11	170	10-20-96	.195	.350	.140	22	77	10	15	3	2	2	8	5	0	0	0	19	4	1	.364	.244
Yera, Ariel	R-R	6-3	215	1-20-97	.221	.250	.212	23	68	2	15	1	0	0	4	6	0	1	0	27	1	1	.235	.284

Pitching	B-T	HT	WT	DOB	W	L	ERA	G	GS	CG	SV	IP	H	R	ER	HR	BB	SO	AVG	vLH	vRH	K/9	BB/9
Acosta, Daison	R-R	6-2	160	8-24-98	1	0	0.98	4	3	0	0	18	9	3	2	0	6	25	.150	.188	.136	12.27	2.95
Allan, Matthew	R-R	6-3	225	4-17-01	0	0	9.00	1	1	0	0	2	5	2	2	0	1	3	.500	.000	.556	13.50	4.50
Biddy, Jared	R-R	6-2	180	7-25-96	3	0	0.96	14	0	0	0	28	23	4	3	0	3	34	.226	.256	.206	10.93	0.96
Bryant, Garrison	L-R	6-3	189	12-3-98	5	1	2.39	14	12	0	0	75	49	21	20	3	14	75	.180	.167	.187	8.96	1.67
Campos, Yeizo	R-R	5-11	175	4-29-96	0	0	0.00	1	0	0	0	1	0	0	0	0	0	3	.000	--	.000	27.00	0.00
Cleveland, Matt	R-R	6-3	187	3-18-98	3	3	3.78	14	14	0	0	67	53	31	28	4	32	42	.215	.192	.231	5.67	4.32
Colon, Yeudy	R-R	6-1	230	6-9-95	1	0	6.75	6	0	0	1	8	7	7	6	0	9	10	.226	.167	.240	11.25	10.13
Conlon, P.J.	L-L	5-11	192	11-11-93	0	0	0.00	4	0	0	1	4	3	0	0	0	2	5	.200	.375	12.27	4.91	
Edwards, Andrew	L-L	6-2	210	5-12-97	3	2	3.30	16	0	0	3	30	23	12	11	2	14	35	.215	.258	.197	10.50	4.20
Familia, Jeurys	R-R	6-3	240	10-10-89	0	0	0.00	1	0	0	0	1	0	0	0	0	0	2	.000	.000	.000	13.50	0.00
Gaconi, Corey	R-R	6-4	215	1-22-97	4	1	4.54	12	0	0	0	34	37	17	17	3	2	25	.278	.309	.256	6.68	0.53
Gibbons, Michael	R-R	6-4	205	4-24-93	0	0	0.00	1	0	0	0	3	0	0	0	0	2	2	.000	.000	.000	6.00	6.00
Goggin, Dan	R-R	6-2	215	6-9-97	2	1	2.81	15	2	0	2	32	20	10	10	0	21	38	.175	.209	.136	10.69	5.91
Gordon, Cole	L-R	6-5	244	10-2-95	0	0	0.00	1	0	0	0	1	1	0	0	0	0	3	.250	.000	.333	27.00	0.00
Hejka, Josh	R-R	6-1	195	3-20-97	2	0	2.25	11	0	0	1	12	13	5	3	0	3	14	.260	.353	.212	10.50	2.25
Holderman, Colin	R-R	6-7	240	10-8-95	0	0	1.80	2	2	0	0	5	2	1	1	0	2	4	.133	.250	.000	7.20	3.60
Jones, Nathan	R-R	6-1	200	1-6-97	0	2	6.59	7	7	0	0	14	10	10	10	3	8	14	.204	.182	.222	9.22	5.27
Kisena, Alec	L-R	6-5	275	10-12-95	0	0	3.52	2	2	0	0	8	8	3	3	0	2	11	.258	.083	.368	12.91	2.35
Lasko, Justin	R-R	6-4	210	3-16-97	0	1	1.42	10	0	0	1	13	8	5	2	2	0	9	.170	.125	.194	6.39	0.00
Leon, Nelson	R-R	6-1	154	3-1-95	3	1	2.75	15	0	0	4	20	11	6	6	2	4	28	.162	.261	.111	12.81	1.83
MacDonald, Nick	R-R	6-1	175	6-11-98	0	0	0.00	2	0	0	0	2	2	0	0	0	0	3	.286	.500	.000	16.20	0.00
Medina, Jose Miguel	R-R	6-3	180	10-21-96	0	0	0.00	1	0	0	0	1	1	0	0	0	0	2	.333	--	.333	27.00	0.00
Mena, Malky	R-R	6-0	164	10-3-96	1	0	3.00	2	1	0	0	6	8	2	2	0	5	5	.348	.364	.333	7.50	0.00
Metoyer, Brian	R-R	6-4	160	11-13-96	2	2	5.65	16	0	0	2	29	15	20	18	3	22	40	.160	.143	.167	12.56	6.91
Mullenbach, Matt	R-R	6-4	195	10-6-96	1	5	2.84	19	0	0	5	25	14	12	8	2	13	26	.163	.241	.123	9.24	4.62
Oswalt, Corey	R-R	6-5	250	9-3-93	0	0	1.50	2	2	0	0	6	6	2	1	0	3	7	.240	.182	.286	10.50	4.50
Otanez, Michel	R-R	6-3	215	7-3-97	2	1	2.97	7	7	0	0	30	26	12	10	2	17	26	.232	.263	.216	7.71	5.04
Parsons, Hunter	R-R	6-3	200	6-24-97	1	1	2.89	11	0	0	0	19	18	6	6	0	9	21	.247	.167	.302	10.13	4.34
Ragan, Mitch	R-R	6-3	210	4-1-97	3	2	3.09	15	3	0	0	35	27	17	12	1	3	31	.208	.255	.181	7.97	0.77
Santos, Reyson	R-R	6-2	190	1-22-99	0	0	0.00	2	0	0	1	2	1	0	0	0	1	5	.143	.250	.000	22.50	4.50
Silva, Luis	R-R	6-0	200	11-17-96	1	2	6.60	14	0	0	3	15	14	12	11	1	13	14	.259	.333	.231	8.40	7.80
Syndergaard, Noah	L-R	6-6	240	8-29-92	1	0	5.40	1	1	0	0	5	5	3	3	1	0	9	.238	.500	.133	16.20	0.00
Tripp, Christian	R-R	6-7	220	3-13-97	0	0	0.00	1	0	0	2	1	0	0	0	0	2	1	.143	.250	.000	9.00	0.00
Valentino, Frank	R-R	6-3	205	3-15-95	2	4	3.41	12	11	0	0	58	52	26	22	3	13	63	.239	.202	.269	9.78	2.02

	B-T	HT	WT	DOB	W	L	ERA	G	GS	CG	SV	IP	H	R	ER	HR	BB	SO	AVG	vLH	vRH	K/9	BB/9
Vilera, Jaison	R-R	6-0	188	6-19-97	2	3	3.81	5	5	0	0	28	23	18	12	1	11	23	.221	.250	.208	7.31	3.49
Walker, Joshua	L-L	6-6	225	12-1-94	0	0	9.00	1	0	0	0	3	5	3	3	0	2	3	.357	.000	.455	9.00	6.00
Wilson, Justin	L-L	6-2	205	8-18-87	0	0	0.00	2	1	0	0	2	2	0	0	0	1	4	.250	.000	.286	18.00	4.50

Fielding

C: Capra 1, Mena 31, Ortega 25, Yera 23. **1B:** Garay 8, Genord 62, Reyes 8. **2B:** Avant 2, Cano 1, Cecchini 1, Haggerty 1, Manzanarez 6, Reyes 2, Ritter 60, Romero 7. **3B:** Avant 3, Baty 2, Cecchini 1, Gaddis 14, Haggerty 2, Manzanarez 3, McNeil 1, Peroza 26, Reyes 10, Romero 19. **SS:** Avant 1, Cecchini 1, Fryman 3, Haggerty 1, Manzanarez 4, Reyes 38, Romero 23. **OF:** Adon 39, Ashford 14, Avant 2, Beracierta 31, Corona 4, Dirocie 15, Duplantis 47, Granadillo 11, Haggerty 1, Mangum 51, McNeil 1, Medina 4, Rheams 1, Romero 1, Taylor 21.

KINGSPORT METS   ROOKIE ADVANCED
APPALACHIAN LEAGUE

Batting	B-T	HT	WT	DOB	AVG	vLH	vRH	G	AB	R	H	2B	3B	HR	RBI	BB	HBP	SH	SF	SO	SB	CS	SLG	OBP
Alvarez, Francisco	R-R	5-11	220	11-19-01	.282	.414	.245	35	131	24	37	6	0	5	16	17	3	0	0	33	1	1	.443	.378
Astudillo, Wilfred	B-R	5-11	209	3-14-00	.267	.320	.253	36	120	15	32	2	0	5	18	8	2	0	0	19	0	0	.408	.323
Baty, Brett	L-R	6-3	210	11-13-99	.222	.200	.229	42	158	30	35	12	2	6	22	24	4	0	0	56	0	0	.437	.339
Bohorquez, Anderson	R-R	5-11	180	10-3-97	.214	.000	.273	7	28	5	6	2	0	1	2	1	0	0	0	9	0	0	.393	.241
Dirocie, Anthony	R-R	5-11	175	4-24-97	.313	.500	.234	16	67	10	21	7	2	2	16	3	0	0	0	20	1	2	.567	.343
Espino, Sebastian	R-R	6-2	176	5-29-00	.251	.273	.245	52	187	26	47	7	1	2	12	12	2	1	0	61	3	2	.332	.304
Guerrero, Gregory	R-R	6-0	186	1-20-99	.222	.227	.221	53	189	31	42	7	2	6	23	26	2	1	0	55	2	0	.376	.323
Kleszcz, Cole	R-R	6-1	190	6-16-97	.254	.200	.271	44	173	26	44	9	4	3	26	9	5	0	2	56	0	1	.405	.307
Manzanarez, Angel	R-R	5-10	160	5-19-97	.250	.500	.200	3	12	0	3	0	0	0	0	0	0	0	0	2	1	0	.250	.250
Murphy, Tanner	R-R	6-4	195	5-1-98	.202	.243	.186	40	134	21	27	3	1	5	15	18	3	0	0	57	2	1	.351	.310
O'Neill, Matt	R-R	6-0	200	8-20-97	.231	.250	.222	8	26	3	6	0	1	0	2	2	1	0	0	7	0	0	.308	.310
Ota, Scott	L-L	5-11	195	8-16-97	.273	.333	.252	51	183	30	50	14	5	7	26	21	4	0	3	38	0	1	.519	.356
Palmer, Jaylen	R-R	6-3	195	7-31-00	.260	.185	.282	62	242	41	63	12	2	7	28	31	1	0	2	108	1	3	.413	.344
Pujols, Cristopher	R-R	6-2	180	8-19-97	.262	.220	.279	58	206	20	54	8	1	3	29	16	3	0	3	46	3	3	.354	.320
Regnault, Andres	R-R	6-0	251	12-21-98	.292	.333	.277	44	178	26	52	11	0	8	49	8	3	0	3	36	0	2	.489	.328
Saez, Jhoander	B-R	6-0	165	3-24-98	.269	.233	.282	30	108	14	29	6	1	0	8	9	0	1	0	26	6	4	.343	.325
Taylor, Kennie	R-R	5-11	170	10-20-96	.281	.346	.263	29	121	16	34	3	2	2	10	6	2	1	3	25	4	2	.388	.318
Whalin, Zak	R-R	6-1	225	4-14-95	.000	--	.000	2	1	0	0	0	0	0	0	1	0	0	0	0	0	0	.000	.500
Woodard, L.A.	B-R	5-11	165	6-3-97	.186	.133	.205	18	59	10	11	1	0	0	4	9	1	2	0	19	4	0	.203	.304

Pitching	B-T	HT	WT	DOB	W	L	ERA	G	GS	CG	SV	IP	H	R	ER	HR	BB	SO	vLH	vRH	K/9	BB/9
Biddy, Jared	R-R	6-2	180	7-25-96	1	0	0.00	3	0	0	0	2	1	0	0	0	1		.143	.250	.000	4.50	0.00
Colon, Yeudy	R-R	6-1	230	6-9-95	0	0	9.82	4	0	0	0	7	4	4	1	5			.389	.444	.333	7.36	12.27
De Jesus, Jender	R-R	6-2	165	1-3-98	4	1	3.41	17	0	0	1	29	29	14	11	3	14	21	.266	.196	.340	6.52	4.34
Dominguez, Christofer	L-L	6-2	222	1-3-98	3	3	5.24	14	8	0	1	45	49	30	26	1	15	39	.275	.279	.274	7.86	3.02
Escorcha, Jefferson	L-L	5-11	178	10-4-99	7	1	2.38	15	0	0	0	42	40	14	11	3	8	33	.252	.348	.212	7.13	1.73
Flores, Yadiel	R-R	6-2	165	7-31-99	1	1	4.37	17	0	0	1	23	25	19	11	1	16	21	.272	.298	.244	8.34	6.35
Gaconi, Corey	R-R	6-4	215	1-22-97	0	0	2.25	2	0	0	0	4	3	1	1	0	1	2	.200	.167	.222	4.50	2.25
Garcia, Benito	R-R	6-0	165	3-10-00	2	4	6.45	13	9	0	0	45	53	41	32	5	19	43	.293	.289	.296	8.66	3.83
German, Andres	R-R	6-1	150	5-16-97	3	1	3.55	11	6	0	0	38	42	21	15	6	7	29	.278	.148	.351	6.87	1.66
Guzman, Ramon	R-R	6-4	154	10-16-96	1	2	4.95	16	7	0	0	44	38	26	24	4	19	35	.239	.269	.210	7.21	3.92
Hardy, Brendan	R-R	6-4	170	12-15-99	2	1	6.83	16	0	0	0	28	19	24	21	3	25	29	.190	.174	.204	9.43	8.13
Hejka, Josh	R-R	6-1	175	3-20-97	0	0	0.00	11	0	0	3	8	4	0	0	0	2	10	.129	.071	.177	10.80	2.16
Loaiza, Cesar	L-L	6-3	165	7-10-98	1	4	5.71	13	12	0	0	41	45	34	26	3	26	41	.278	.225	.295	9.00	5.71
MacDonald, Nick	R-R	6-1	175	6-11-98	0	2	3.20	16	0	0	3	20	18	8	7	2	6	28	.254	.273	.237	12.81	2.75
Otanez, Michel	R-R	6-3	215	7-3-97	2	2	3.31	7	0	0	0	33	26	14	12	1	11	44	.219	.254	.179	12.12	3.03
Peden, Nate	R-R	6-4	170	10-16-98	1	4	8.58	12	3	0	0	36	51	38	34	6	14	31	.338	.306	.367	7.82	3.53
Planck, Cameron	R-R	6-4	218	3-5-98	0	0	0.00	1	0	0	0	1	0	0	0	0	0	0	.000	.000	.000	0.00	0.00
Rodriguez, Hector	L-L	6-2	166	12-27-97	3	2	6.07	22	0	0	0	30	29	25	20	2	21	40	.261	.333	.231	12.13	6.37
Santos, Junior	R-R	6-8	218	8-16-01	0	5	5.09	14	14	0	0	41	46	29	23	4	25	36	.277	.282	.273	7.97	5.53
Santos, Reyson	R-R	6-2	190	1-22-99	0	0	2.45	22	0	0	8	22	17	7	6	3	8	28	.205	.088	.286	11.45	3.27
Senger, Mitchell	L-L	6-7	240	1-13-98	0	0	54.00	2	0	0	0	0	4	2	0	0	0	0	.000	--	.000	0.00	216
Silva, Luis	R-R	6-0	200	11-17-96	0	0	9.95	5	0	0	0	6	11	12	7	2	3	8	.333	.333	.333	11.37	4.26
Silva, Nixon	L-L	5-10	165	8-20-99	0	2	4.50	16	0	0	1	22	26	14	11	1	8	20	.299	.304	.297	8.18	3.27
Tripp, Christian	R-R	6-2	220	3-13-97	0	0	4.32	10	0	0	0	8	10	5	4	1	3	8	.286	.167	.348	8.64	3.24
Ventura, Jordany	R-R	6-0	162	7-6-00	1	1	1.13	2	2	0	0	8	3	1	1	0	6	9	.120	.000	.150	10.13	6.75
Wollersheim, Connor	L-L	6-2	205	5-18-97	1	0	2.70	8	0	0	0	10	7	3	3	1	7	2	.194	.182	.200	1.80	6.30

Fielding

C: Alvarez 23, Astudillo 22, O'Neill 7, Regnault 21. **1B:** Astudillo 15, Bohorquez 5, Pujols 53. **2B:** Espino 14, Guerrero 53, Manzanarez 1. **3B:** Baty 30, Palmer 33, Pujols 7. **SS:** Espino 38, Manzanarez 2, Palmer 30. **OF:** Dirocie 15, Kleszcz 36, Murphy 36, Ota 47, Saez 27, Taylor 28, Woodard 16.

GCL METS   ROOKIE
GULF COAST LEAGUE

Batting	B-T	HT	WT	DOB	AVG	vLH	vRH	G	AB	R	H	2B	3B	HR	RBI	BB	HBP	SH	SF	SO	SB	CS	SLG	OBP
Alvarez, Francisco	R-R	5-11	220	11-19-01	.462	.429	.474	7	26	8	12	4	0	2	10	4	1	0	0	4	0	1	.846	.548
Ashford, Zach	L-R	5-10	180	2-9-97	.295	.182	.318	37	129	19	38	13	1	2	23	23	3	1	0	26	2	3	.457	.413
Baty, Brett	L-R	6-3	210	11-13-99	.350	.333	.353	5	20	5	7	3	0	1	8	5	0	0	0	6	0	0	.650	.480
Beracierta, Raul	R-R	6-1	215	5-24-99	.500	1.000	.444	2	10	1	5	1	0	0	5	0	0	0	0	2	0	0	.600	.500
Berbesi, Cesar	L-R	6-0	160	4-30-00	.173	.000	.205	17	52	6	9	2	1	0	6	7	2	3	1	17	1	3	.250	.290
Bohorquez, Anderson	R-R	5-11	180	10-3-97	.229	.154	.257	33	96	12	22	5	0	0	18	8	0	1	4	16	5	3	.281	.278
Capra, Phil	B-R	5-10	205	10-1-96	.500	--	.500	1	2	0	1	0	0	0	0	1	0	0	0	0	0	0	.500	.667

Name	B-T	HT	WT	DOB	AVG	vLH	vRH	G	AB	R	H	2B	3B	HR	RBI	BB	HBP	SH	SF	SO	SB	CS	SLG	OBP
Causa, Patrick	R-R	5-10	185	1-8-97	.200	.143	.217	31	60	10	12	3	1	0	4	12	1	0	1	21	0	1	.283	.338
Conti, Nick	R-R	5-9	160	2-14-97	.238	.191	.254	27	84	18	20	5	0	1	12	21	5	0	0	13	7	1	.333	.418
Corona, Kenedy	R-R	5-11	185	3-21-00	.311	.296	.315	42	151	35	47	9	1	5	21	17	7	4	2	25	11	2	.483	.401
Fryman, Branden	R-R	6-1	170	3-16-98	.357	.200	.444	4	14	4	5	2	0	0	6	1	1	0	1	2	0	0	.500	.412
Gaddis, Nic	R-R	5-11	171	10-12-96	.197	.200	.197	25	71	9	14	1	1	2	9	12	3	2	2	13	2	0	.324	.330
Ghelfi, Mitch	B-R	5-11	185	9-24-92	.222	.500	.000	3	9	1	2	0	0	0	2	0	0	0	2	3	0	0	.222	.182
Hernandez, Adrian	R-R	5-9	210	2-8-01	.286	.667	.182	4	14	3	4	2	0	1	1	1	1	0	0	4	2	1	.643	.375
Loyo, Juan	R-R	5-11	180	3-16-99	.210	.000	.266	30	81	10	17	3	1	1	8	10	5	1	0	20	0	0	.309	.333
Lugo, William	R-R	6-3	215	1-2-02	.158	.222	.143	43	146	14	23	6	0	1	14	21	5	1	3	46	1	4	.219	.280
McIntosh, Blaine	L-L	6-4	180	6-9-01	.228	.167	.243	24	92	13	21	0	0	0	4	11	0	0	0	22	5	3	.228	.311
Meyer, Nick	R-R	6-1	200	2-18-97	.000	.000	.000	4	12	0	0	0	0	0	1	2	0	1	0	4	0	0	.000	.143
O'Neill, Matt	R-R	6-0	200	8-20-97	.286	.429	.270	25	70	9	20	3	1	1	8	18	4	1	2	23	0	1	.400	.447
Peroza, Jose	R-R	6-1	214	6-15-00	.328	.000	.389	16	64	14	21	6	2	6	20	4	3	0	1	15	1	0	.766	.389
Polanco, Federico	L-R	5-10	155	3-20-01	.177	.286	.148	14	34	7	6	1	0	0	3	5	0	1	0	8	3	0	.206	.275
Rodriguez, Endy	B-R	6-0	170	5-26-00	.293	.313	.288	22	75	14	22	10	1	0	6	10	3	0	1	13	4	0	.453	.393
Salazar, Eduardo	R-R	6-3	167	12-15-00	.241	.154	.267	19	58	9	14	1	0	1	7	3	4	0	2	14	1	1	.310	.313
Saunders, Warren	R-R	6-3	188	12-15-98	.323	.200	.339	33	127	25	41	5	0	1	20	10	7	1	2	23	3	0	.386	.397
Shinn, Ryan	R-L	6-2	215	12-9-96	.242	.321	.223	46	149	24	36	8	0	3	20	24	12	1	2	48	6	4	.356	.385
Struble, LT	L-R	5-10	175	7-3-96	.231	.143	.244	18	52	14	12	1	0	0	5	11	0	2	0	20	4	0	.250	.365
Uriarte, Juan	R-R	6-0	182	9-17-97	.333	--	.333	3	6	3	2	0	0	0	0	1	0	0	0	0	0	0	.333	.429
Valdez, Freddy	R-R	6-3	212	12-6-01	.400	--	.400	3	10	4	4	1	0	1	3	0	0	0	3	0	0	1	.800	.539

Pitching	B-T	HT	WT	DOB	W	L	ERA	G	GS	CG	SV	IP	H	R	ER	HR	BB	SO	AVG	vLH	vRH	K/9	BB/9
Allan, Matthew	R-R	6-3	225	4-17-01	1	0	1.08	5	4	0	0	8	5	1	1	0	4	11	.167	.125	.182	11.88	4.32
Aybar, Adrian	R-R	6-4	180	3-8-98	1	3	4.61	12	2	0	1	27	29	16	14	1	17	25	.274	.314	.254	8.23	5.60
Beck, Jace	R-R	6-9	200	6-14-00	0	0	3.38	6	0	0	2	8	7	3	3	0	1	10	.219	.500	.154	11.25	1.13
Colina, Robert	R-R	5-11	175	4-24-01	4	4	3.57	11	4	0	1	40	42	22	16	0	13	35	.264	.289	.252	7.81	2.90
Colon, Jeffrey	R-R	6-1	170	11-9-99	4	3	4.94	19	0	0	3	27	28	21	15	1	17	22	.272	.143	.320	7.24	5.60
Conlon, P.J.	L-L	5-11	192	11-11-93	0	0	0.00	2	2	0	0	2	0	0	0	0	0	2	.000	.000	.000	9.00	0.00
Cornielly, Joshua	R-R	6-2	175	1-15-01	3	2	4.54	10	3	0	0	36	43	28	18	3	8	40	.299	.375	.260	10.09	2.02
Correa, Marcos	R-R	6-3	195	1-31-00	0	1	3.18	15	0	0	0	17	14	7	6	2	10	11	.226	.368	.163	5.82	5.29
Escalona, Jhonfran	R-R	5-10	159	4-8-99	2	2	3.48	11	1	0	1	41	33	20	16	1	10	35	.216	.220	.214	7.62	2.18
German, Andres	R-R	6-1	150	5-16-97	1	0	6.75	1	0	0	0	4	8	3	3	0	0	3	.421	1.000	.353	6.75	0.00
Gibbons, Michael	R-R	6-4	205	4-24-93	0	0	0.00	1	1	0	0	2	2	0	0	0	1	1	.250	.333	.200	4.50	4.50
Gonzalez, Brailin	L-L	6-2	180	9-23-99	2	0	3.68	13	0	0	1	22	18	13	9	1	14	24	.220	.150	.242	9.82	5.73
Hammer, Zachary	R-R	6-2	165	7-4-00	2	1	2.90	10	2	0	0	31	25	11	10	0	18	27	.225	.294	.195	7.84	5.23
Humphreys, Jordan	R-R	6-2	223	6-11-96	0	0	4.50	2	0	0	0	2	2	1	1	0	1	2	.286	--	.286	9.00	4.50
McCall, Liam	R-R	6-4	180	2-19-99	3	0	4.50	11	0	0	0	28	21	15	14	0	15	25	.280	.235	.194	8.04	4.82
Mitchell, Andrew	L-L	6-1	200	10-23-94	0	0	0.00	1	1	0	0	1	0	0	0	0	0	1	.000	.000	.000	9.00	0.00
Moreno, Jose	R-R	6-4	165	7-31-96	0	0	0.00	2	1	0	0	2	0	0	0	0	0	4	.286	.500	.200	18.00	4.50
Nunez, Noah	R-R	6-4	210	12-28-98	2	2	3.25	13	0	0	2	28	29	12	10	3	11	30	.269	.262	.273	9.76	3.58
Parra, Franklin	L-L	6-1	185	9-13-99	1	1	2.57	10	0	0	0	21	10	6	6	0	16	29	.141	.133	.143	12.43	6.86
Senger, Mitchell	L-L	6-7	240	1-13-98	1	0	10.80	11	0	0	0	8	14	11	10	1	10	4	.389	.500	.357	4.32	10.80
Suarez, Joander	R-R	6-3	181	2-27-00	1	0	1.79	11	8	0	0	40	27	8	8	1	16	47	.192	.196	.190	10.49	3.57
Taylor Jr., Ronnie	R-R	6-3	220	10-6-98	0	2	1.93	12	0	0	0	8	5	3	0	9	21	.167	.133	.182	13.50	5.79
Torres, Joshua	R-R	6-0	170	4-26-94	0	0	0.00	4	2	0	0	4	2	0	0	1	5	.143	.143	.143	11.25	2.25
Ventura, Jordany	R-R	6-0	162	7-6-00	2	1	4.36	9	7	0	0	33	27	16	16	2	8	34	.221	.200	.228	9.27	2.18
Walker, Joshua	L-L	6-6	225	12-1-94	0	1	6.00	1	1	0	0	3	3	2	2	0	0	2	.231	.167	.286	6.00	0.00
Wilson, Kyle	R-R	6-1	185	9-27-96	0	0	6.00	1	0	0	0	3	3	2	2	0	2	2	.182	.000	.222	9.00	6.00
Wolf, Josh	R-R	6-3	170	9-1-00	0	1	3.38	5	5	0	0	8	9	4	3	0	1	12	.281	.167	.350	13.50	1.13

Fielding

C: Alvarez 4, Gaddis 3, Ghelfi 2, Loyo 21, Meyer 3, O'Neill 22, Rodriguez 7, Uriarte 3. 1B: Bohorquez 23, Loyo 8, O'Neill 1, Peroza 3, Rodriguez 1, Salazar 1, Saunders 10, Shinn 12. 2B: Berbesi 4, Bohorquez 1, Causa 14, Conti 23, Gaddis 2, Loyo 1, Peroza 2, Polanco 10, Saunders 5, Struble 1. 3B: Baty 4, Berbesi 1, Gaddis 17, Lugo 8, Peroza 10, Polanco 1, Salazar 2, Saunders 13. SS: Berbesi 14, Causa 5, Conti 1, Fryman 2, Lugo 32, Polanco 2, Saunders 2. OF: Ashford 28, Beracierta 2, Bohorquez 3, Corona 39, Hernandez 4, McIntosh 24, Rodriguez 9, Salazar 14, Shinn 32, Struble 13, Valdez 2.

DSL METS   ROOKIE
DOMINICAN SUMMER LEAGUE

Batting	B-T	HT	WT	DOB	AVG	vLH	vRH	G	AB	R	H	2B	3B	HR	RBI	BB	HBP	SH	SF	SO	SB	CS	SLG	OBP
Arias, Eliam	B-R	5-11	165	3-6-01	.202	.130	.213	51	178	20	36	5	2	0	21	10	2	4	1	43	8	2	.253	.251
Aybar, Ronis	L-R	6-0	180	1-13-00	.255	.214	.262	26	98	17	25	7	1	0	6	11	7	0	0	36	3	3	.347	.371
Berbesi, Cesar	L-R	6-0	160	4-13-00	.324	.350	.321	44	176	34	57	13	2	0	22	25	4	1	1	23	5	4	.421	.418
Cabrera, Jan	R-R	6-1	170	9-11-00	.270	.375	.253	33	115	25	31	4	2	3	13	6	3	3	30	7	2	.417	.365
Campos, Dyron	R-R	5-10	155	12-26-00	.293	.353	.285	69	266	44	78	14	4	1	15	25	3	5	0	41	13	15	.387	.361
Castillo, Luis	L-R	6-1	180	11-13-01	.237	.200	.247	54	190	25	45	9	2	0	23	32	5	1	0	53	4	2	.305	.361
Castro, Wilmis	R-R	6-1	190	9-18-01	.249	.241	.250	50	177	23	44	10	2	0	24	21	5	1	0	42	3	2	.328	.321
Corona, Kenedy	R-R	5-11	185	3-21-00	.292	.111	.321	17	65	9	19	5	3	0	7	9	1	0	1	9	8	3	.462	.382
De Los Santos, Omar	R-R	6-1	172	8-8-99	.274	.290	.271	55	219	36	60	7	6	4	25	22	8	0	2	42	13	2	.416	.359
Dominguez, Carlos	R-R	6-1	190	4-28-01	.266	.357	.242	59	207	38	55	13	5	6	36	18	24	0	4	63	15	6	.464	.383
Encarnacion, Bradly	B-R	6-0	170	11-13-01	.199	.214	.196	50	161	31	32	7	0	0	16	27	18	1	1	37	13	3	.242	.372
Encarnacion, Darwyn	R-R	6-0	192	3-31-01	.248	.158	.266	35	113	17	28	4	0	1	8	15	1	0	0	54	10	2	.310	.341
Gonzalez, Moises	R-R	5-11	163	6-10-00	.291	.417	.279	41	148	24	43	7	4	1	21	13	5	2	1	41	7	3	.385	.365
Hernandez, Jose	R-R	5-11	190	5-13-02	.283	.316	.277	42	138	32	39	4	0	1	8	28	5	0	0	44	9	3	.333	.421
Linares, Franklin	R-R	6-0	165	11-5-00	.287	.261	.294	54	216	34	62	8	5	2	25	26	3	3	1	59	20	8	.398	.370

Name	B-T	HT	WT	DOB	AVG	vLH	vRH	G	AB	R	H	2B	3B	HR	RBI	BB	HBP	SH	SF	SO	SB	CS	OBP	SLG
Loyo, Juan	R-R	5-11	180	3-16-99	.261	.250	.263	5	23	3	6	3	0	0	2	0	1	0	0	6	0	1	.391	.292
Marte, Samuel	R-R	6-0	160	12-28-00	.208	.200	.209	62	221	30	46	8	4	4	27	32	1	2	2	63	8	4	.335	.309
Osorio, Jan Carlos	B-R	6-0	190	10-5-00	.141	.000	.158	20	64	5	9	4	0	1	12	6	1	0	4	15	1	0	.250	.213
Paiva, Mario	R-R	6-0	165	10-22-01	.210	.278	.200	50	148	16	31	2	1	2	9	28	1	1	0	47	5	5	.277	.339
Pascale, Domenico	R-R	5-10	196	1-6-00	.171	.318	.133	38	105	12	18	2	0	0	13	2	2	2	1	16	0	1	.191	.271
Pereira, Walter	R-R	5-10	165	11-2-99	.333	--	.333	4	12	4	4	2	0	0	3	2	0	0	0	2	0	0	.500	.429
Perez, Cristopher	L-R	6-0	175	10-5-00	.248	.267	.244	46	161	15	40	4	1	0	13	8	0	4	0	27	4	5	.286	.284
Polanco, Federico	L-R	5-10	155	3-20-01	.323	.400	.299	42	167	32	54	13	5	0	29	23	0	0	0	23	7	3	.461	.405
Rivera, Jose	R-R	5-9	190	9-7-99	.299	.500	.262	21	77	17	23	7	1	3	14	12	3	0	1	14	0	0	.533	.409
Rodriguez, Endy	B-R	6-0	170	5-26-00	.296	.333	.286	9	27	5	8	4	0	2	8	5	3	0	0	5	0	0	.667	.457
Rodriguez, Famin	L-R	5-10	180	3-5-02	.250	.333	.232	32	84	22	21	3	0	0	4	11	6	1	0	14	7	3	.286	.376
Torres, Kevin	R-R	6-0	169	5-4-99	.244	.240	.244	60	205	27	50	8	3	1	29	32	3	1	2	32	6		.327	.351
Troconiz, Derwis	R-R	6-0	180	11-18-99	.298	.375	.286	38	114	13	34	3	0	0	17	15	6	0	2	19	4	0	.325	.402
Valdez, Freddy	R-R	6-3	212	12-6-01	.268	.302	.260	57	220	36	59	15	3	5	36	28	5	0	4	46	6	1	.432	.358
Velasquez, Wilker	L-R	6-0	155	1-18-01	.239	.214	.243	57	197	15	47	4	3	0	21	14	2	0	3	45	3	4	.289	.292
Ventura, Jhonny	R-R	6-1	170	1-21-02	.224	.091	.240	44	107	17	24	9	0	0	13	16	1	0	3	23	5	3	.308	.323
Villalobos, Fernando	L-R	6-0	195	6-24-02	.195	.333	.164	30	82	10	16	3	0	0	6	22	4	0	2	33	5	2	.232	.382
Villaman, Ransel	L-R	6-0	155	1-10-02	.211	.500	.191	31	90	13	19	4	0	0	3	22	2	0	0	21	3	2	.256	.377

Pitching	B-T	HT	WT	DOB	W	L	ERA	G	GS	CG	SV	IP	H	R	ER	HR	BB	SO	AVG	vLH	vRH	K/9	BB/9
Abad, Yeremi	R-R	6-1	165	1-25-02	3	2	9.89	15	5	0	0	24	25	30	26	2	34	23	.291	.158	.328	8.75	12.93
Alfonseca, Miguel	R-R	6-0	190	2-13-00	0	2	11.57	4	4	0	0	14	14	19	18	0	14	5	.222	.400	.118	4.82	13.50
Almonte, Enmanuel	R-R	6-5	197	11-9-97	2	2	4.19	12	6	0	0	39	30	20	18	1	24	37	.221	.237	.214	8.61	5.59
Arias, Eliam	B-R	5-11	165	3-6-01	0	0	0.00	1	0	0	0	1	0	0	0	0	0	0	.000	.000	.000	0.00	0.00
Armado, Johan	L-L	6-0	175	5-4-01	0	0	3.00	2	0	0	0	3	2	2	1	0	2	1	.167	.500	.100	3.00	6.00
Arteaga, Melvin	R-R	6-1	200	12-7-00	2	2	5.75	19	0	0	3	41	39	28	26	2	26	38	.260	.321	.227	8.41	5.75
Atencio, Javier	L-L	6-0	160	11-26-01	0	1	4.75	12	8	0	0	36	42	22	19	2	16	25	.292	.257	.303	6.25	4.00
Castellanos, Carlos	L-L	6-3	170	1-27-01	1	1	4.50	16	0	0	1	24	28	18	12	0	18	22	.315	.389	.296	8.25	6.75
Castro, Carlos	R-R	5-11	155	10-8-98	0	0	1.80	3	3	0	0	10	4	2	2	0	11	9	.121	.100	.130	8.10	9.90
Colina, Robert	R-R	5-11	175	4-24-01	1	1	4.91	4	4	0	0	15	16	8	8	1	4	16	.271	.267	.273	9.82	2.45
Cornielly, Joshua	R-R	6-2	175	1-15-01	1	2	6.10	3	0	0	0	10	12	8	7	0	1	12	.279	.294	.269	10.45	0.87
Diaz, Edinson	R-R	6-0	170	12-25-99	0	1	1.61	7	0	0	0	22	19	8	4	0	4	8	.224	.250	.204	3.22	1.61
Encarnacion, Yeily	R-R	6-3	195	2-10-00	1	0	0.00	3	0	0	0	9	5	0	0	0	1	11	.156	.273	.095	11.00	1.00
Escalona, Jhonfran	R-R	5-10	159	4-8-99	1	0	5.00	5	0	0	0	8	8	0	0	0	0	3	.250	.182	.286	3.24	1.08
Feliz, Joon	R-R	6-1	198	7-11-00	2	1	2.29	10	5	0	0	20	15	7	5	0	10	24	.211	.348	.146	10.98	4.58
Figueroa, Alvaro	R-R	6-3	178	3-4-02	1	3	5.24	18	0	0	0	34	28	25	20	1	27	36	.224	.289	.188	9.44	7.08
Franco, Jhon	R-R	6-0	175	8-24-99	0	1	7.08	11	0	0	0	20	35	24	16	3	11	14	.402	.429	.390	6.20	4.87
Garcia, Benito	R-R	6-0	165	3-10-00	0	0	1.13	2	2	0	0	8	5	2	1	0	0	8	.172	.125	.191	9.00	0.00
Gonzalez, Moises	R-R	5-11	163	6-10-00	0	0	0.00	1	0	0	0	0	0	0	0	0	0	1	.000	.000	--	27.00	0.00
Hernandez, Kevin	L-L	6-1	170	4-23-01	3	1	3.64	19	6	0	0	47	43	25	19	0	27	46	.250	.367	.225	8.81	5.17
Huizi, Eiker	R-R	6-0	155	9-24-00	5	4	4.60	21	0	0	4	43	41	28	22	1	28	38	.265	.346	.223	7.95	5.86
Juarez, Daniel	L-L	5-11	155	9-28-00	0	1	3.74	16	1	0	1	34	31	16	14	3	17	53	.244	.435	.202	14.17	4.54
Lezama, Mauricio	L-L	6-0	160	4-2-01	2	1	5.68	9	0	0	0	13	9	11	8	1	11	15	.192	.333	.171	10.66	7.82
Lozano, Onil	R-R	6-3	165	8-3-01	2	0	6.98	15	0	0	0	19	23	16	15	3	18	17	.303	.242	.349	7.91	8.53
Marcano, David	R-R	6-3	180	8-28-01	1	2	3.07	11	11	0	0	41	31	20	14	1	23	32	.205	.222	.196	7.02	5.05
Marinez, Pablo	R-R	6-3	190	8-29-00	1	3	4.63	17	0	0	3	35	38	20	18	1	7	29	.286	.257	.296	7.46	1.80
Moreno, Luis	R-R	6-2	170	5-29-99	1	2	4.43	13	10	0	0	43	38	28	21	0	24	45	.239	.282	.225	9.49	5.06
Olivero, Cristian	R-R	6-5	170	3-7-00	2	2	3.86	10	2	0	1	23	11	14	10	0	18	20	.141	.053	.170	7.71	6.94
Ortega, Erickson	R-R	5-11	152	1-5-99	0	2	2.03	10	7	0	0	31	30	13	7	0	15	32	.242	.220	.253	9.29	4.35
Paniagua, Jaison	R-R	6-2	190	2-25-98	0	1	--	1	0	0	0	2	2	2	2	0	1	0	1.000	1.000	1.000		
Pereyra, Amaury	R-R	6-5	198	9-9-99	0	0	9.00	3	0	0	0	3	5	4	3	0	2	1	.357	.600	.222	3.00	6.00
Ramirez, Alan	L-L	5-10	205	7-20-99	2	4	3.67	14	11	0	1	56	39	28	23	2	27	69	.195	.118	.211	11.02	4.31
Rincones, Ronny	R-R	5-10	160	10-31-01	1	1	2.44	13	11	0	1	52	47	27	14	1	19	53	.234	.235	.233	9.23	3.31
Rivas, Jesus	R-R	6-1	175	11-10-00	2	0	10.13	8	0	0	0	11	10	12	12	0	15	12	.256	.263	.250	10.13	12.66
Rodriguez, Martin	R-R	6-1	195	1-13-00	5	2	5.49	17	0	0	1	39	51	33	24	5	11	33	.319	.269	.343	7.32	2.52
Rodriguez, Ricardo	R-R	5-10	177	8-11-99	2	2	6.10	7	5	0	0	21	26	18	14	1	12	18	.306	.379	.268	7.84	5.23
Sanchez, Brandon	L-L	5-11	165	12-20-00	1	4	4.97	11	5	0	1	29	33	19	16	1	17	16	.303	.227	.322	4.97	5.28
Silverio, Luis	R-R	6-6	178	10-6-00	1	3	12.56	11	4	0	0	14	11	25	20	0	29	7	.229	.250	.219	4.40	18.21
Sosa, Edward	R-R	5-11	165	5-26-00	0	2	4.17	19	0	0	1	41	37	29	19	1	22	27	.233	.200	.246	5.93	4.83
Valdez, Jose	R-R	6-5	185	9-5-00	3	0	3.38	19	3	0	0	40	30	18	15	1	28	56	.214	.135	.261	12.60	6.30
Valencia, Williams	R-R	6-0	167	7-21-00	2	4	4.69	20	0	0	0	48	49	29	25	0	25	37	.272	.222	.299	6.94	4.69
Valerio, Jose	R-R	6-1	180	8-17-00	7	2	3.38	23	0	0	8	35	29	23	13	1	14	38	.228	.234	.225	9.87	3.63
Vargas, Rolfy	R-R	6-3	160	8-25-00	4	5	3.62	18	3	0	0	50	51	25	20	1	17	55	.266	.259	.269	9.97	3.08
Velasquez, Wilker	L-R	6-0	155	1-18-01	0	0	0.00	1	0	0	0	1	1	0	0	0	0	0	.333	.000	1.000	0.00	0.00
Ventura, Jhonny	R-R	6-1	170	1-21-02	0	0	54.00	1	0	0	0	0	1	2	2	0	4	0	.500	1.000	.000	0.00	108.00
Ventura, Jordany	R-R	6-0	162	7-6-00	0	0	3.97	4	4	0	0	11	8	7	5	1	5	11	.211	.364	.148	8.74	3.97
Villalba, Antonio	R-R	6-3	175	7-10-99	2	2	2.22	21	0	0	4	45	26	16	11	3	24	46	.170	.283	.122	9.27	4.84
Villegas, Marco	R-R	6-0	168	4-17-01	1	1	5.34	18	0	0	0	30	29	22	18	0	24	30	.252	.257	.250	8.90	7.12

Fielding

C: Hernandez 5, Loyo 3, Osorio 4, Pascale 26, Rivera 6, Rodriguez 8, Torres 3, Troconiz 15, Villalobos 24. 1B: Castro 19, Gonzalez 10, Hernandez 27, Loyo 2, Osorio 1, Pascale 14, Perez 19, Rodriguez 1, Torres 7, Troconiz 10, Velasquez 22, Ventura 1. 2B: Arias 9, Berbesi 8, Campos 1, Castillo 11, Encarnacion 14, Pereira 2, Perez 9, Polanco 28, Rodriguez 8, Velasquez 30, Villaman 22. 3B: Arias 11, Berbesi 4, Castillo 8, Castro 28, Encarnacion 8, Marte 42, Pereira 1, Perez 16, Polanco 7, Rivera 12, Rodriguez 5, Velasquez 4. SS: Arias 31, Berbesi 27, Castillo 36, Encarnacion 25, Encarnacion 1, Marte 15, Perez 2, Polanco 3. OF: Aybar 24, Cabrera 28, Campos 60, Castro 2, Corona 16, De Los Santos 47, Dominguez 25, Encarnacion 18, Gonzalez 19, Linares 23, Paiva 24, Rodriguez 8, Valdez 48, Velasquez 1, Ventura 13, Villalba 1.

New York Yankees

SEASON IN A SENTENCE: Despite missing enormous stretches of time from some of their best players, the Yankees finished with the second-best record in the majors but fell to the Astros in the championship series.

HIGH POINT: The emergence of third baseman Gio Urshela and outfielder Mike Tauchman throughout the course of the season provided relief for the vacancies created by injuries to Miguel Andujar, Aaron Judge and Giancarlo Stanton. The duo combined for 34 homers and kept the team afloat while its stars got healthy.

LOW POINT: Jose Altuve's home run in the 10th inning of Game Six of the ALCS ended the Yankees' season in stunning, abrupt fashion.

NOTABLE ROOKIES: The Yankees got contributions from plenty of young players getting their first extended big league time, but most of them weren't true rookies. The only one who truly fits the bill is Mike Ford, a 27-year-old first baseman who hit 12 homers and produced a 137 OPS+ in 50 games. Righthander Jonathan Loaisiga provided 31.2 innings between injuries.

KEY TRANSACTIONS: The Yankees bolstered their pitching staff with the addition of lefthander James Paxton in a deal with the Mariners, and the free agent signings of J.A. Happ, Zack Britton and Adam Ottavino. They also dealt righthander Sonny Gray to the Reds in a three-way deal with the Mariners that netted the Yankees outfield prospect Josh Stowers. Bigger than any of those moves, though, was the signing of infielder D.J. LeMahieu to a two-year deal. In the first season, the 31-year-old led the team in bWAR, finished second in the race for the batting title and hit a career-best 26 homers. They also acquired slugging DH Edwin Encarnacion from the Mariners on June 15 but were quiet at the July 31 trading deadline otherwise.

DOWN ON THE FARM: The organization added its new No. 1 prospect in July when it signed Dominican outfielder Jasson Dominguez for $5.1 million, the team's largest-ever outlay for an international free agent. Among players who entered the year as Yankees, righthander Deivi Garcia was the clear highlight. The 20-year-old blitzed from high Class A to Triple-A with a Futures Game appearance in the middle and struck out a system-best 165 hitters. Righthander Clarke Schmidt rebounded as well, and a pack of pitchers at the lower levels took steps forward.

OPENING DAY PAYROLL: $206,407,750 (3rd).

PLAYERS OF THE YEAR

MAJOR LEAGUE	MINOR LEAGUE
DJ LeMahieu	**Deivi Garcia**
2B/3B	**RHP**
.327/.375/.518	(High A/AA/AAA)
26 HR, 33 2B, 102 RBIs	5-9, 4.28 in 111 IP
Career best 136 OPS+	13.3 SO/9, 4.4 BB/9

MIKE CARLSON

MIKE DILL/THUNDER

ORGANIZATION LEADERS

Batting		*Minimum 250 AB
MAJORS		
* AVG	DJ LeMahieu	.327
* OPS	Aaron Judge	.921
HR	Gleyber Torres	38
RBI	DJ LeMahieu	102
MINORS		
* AVG	Ryan McBroom, Scranton/Wilkes-Barre	.315
* AVG	Breyvic Valera, Scranton/Wilkes-Barre	.315
* OBP	Canaan Smith, Charleston	.405
* SLG	Mike Ford, Scranton/Wilkes-Barre	.605
* OPS	Mike Ford, Scranton/Wilkes-Barre	1.007
R	Ryan McBroom, Scranton/Wilkes-Barre	87
H	Canaan Smith, Charleston	138
TB	Ryan McBroom, Scranton/Wilkes-Barre	237
2B	Brandon Lockridge, Charleston	33
3B	Alexander Vargas, DSL Yankees, GCL Yankees East	7
HR	Ryan McBroom, Scranton/Wilkes-Barre	26
RBI	Chris Gittens, Trenton	77
BB	Canaan Smith, Charleston	74
SO	Isiah Gilliam, Tampa, Trenton	154
SB	Josh Stowers, Charleston	35

Pitching		#Minimum 75 IP
MAJORS		
W	Domingo German	18
# ERA	James Paxton	3.82
SO	James Paxton	186
SV	Aroldis Chapman	37
MINORS		
W	Roansy Contreras, Charleston	12
L	Rony Garcia, Tampa, Trenton	13
# ERA	Miguel Yajure, Tampa, Trenton	2.14
G	Daniel Alvarez, Trenton, Scranton/Wilkes-Barre	47
GS	Roansy Contreras, Charleston	24
GS	Rony Garcia, Tampa, Trenton	24
SV	Daniel Alvarez, Trenton, Scranton/Wilkes-Barre	21
IP	Miguel Yajure, Tampa, Trenton	139
IP	Brody Koerner, Trenton, Scranton/Wilkes-Barre	139
BB	Luis Medina, Charleston, Tampa	70
SO	Deivi Garcia, Tampa, Trenton, Scranton/W-B	165
# AVG	Luis Gil, Charleston, Tampa	.205

2019 PERFORMANCE

General Manager: Brian Cashman. **Farm Director:** Kevin Reese. **Scouting Director:** Damon Oppenheimer.

Class	Team	League	W	L	PCT	Finish	Manager
Majors	New York Yankees	American	103	59	.636	2nd (15)	Aaron Boone
Triple-A	Scranton/W-B RailRiders	International	76	65	.539	5th (14)	Jay Bell
Double-A	Trenton Thunder	Eastern	76	62	.551	3rd (12)	Pat Osborn
High A	Tampa Tarpons	Florida State	64	71	.474	9th (12)	Aaron Holbert
Low A	Charleston RiverDogs	South Atlantic	73	66	.525	5th (14)	Julio Mosquera
Short-season	Staten Island Yankees	New York-Penn	40	36	.526	t-6th (14)	David Adams
Rookie	Pulaski Yankees	Appalachian	42	26	.618	1st (10)	Luis Dorante
Rookie	GCL Yankees East	Gulf Coast	18	29	.383	15th (18)	Dan Fiorito
Rookie	GCL Yankees West	Gulf Coast	22	27	.449	12th (18)	Nick Ortiz
Overall 2019 Minor League Record			411	382	.518	9th (30)	

ORGANIZATION STATISTICS

NEW YORK YANKEES
AMERICAN LEAGUE

Batting	B-T	HT	WT	DOB	AVG	vLH	vRH	G	AB	R	H	2B	3B	HR	RBI	BB	HBP	SH	SF	SO	SB	CS	SLG	OBP
Andujar, Miguel	R-R	6-0	215	3-2-95	.128	.000	.167	12	47	1	6	0	0	0	1	1	0	0	1	11	0	0	.128	.143
Bird, Greg	L-R	6-4	220	11-9-92	.171	.250	.148	10	35	6	6	0	0	1	1	6	0	0	0	16	0	0	.257	.293
Encarnacion, Edwin	R-R	6-1	230	1-7-83	.249	.261	.244	44	177	33	44	11	0	13	37	17	3	0	0	48	0	0	.531	.325
2-team total (65 Seattle)					.244	.245	.244	109	418	81	102	18	0	34	86	58	7	0	3	103	0	1	.531	.344
Estrada, Thairo	R-R	5-10	190	2-22-96	.250	.154	.275	35	64	12	16	3	0	3	12	3	1	1	0	15	4	0	.438	.294
Ford, Mike	L-R	6-0	225	7-4-92	.259	.333	.236	50	143	30	37	7	0	12	25	17	3	0	0	28	0	0	.559	.350
Frazier, Clint	R-R	6-1	190	9-6-94	.267	.196	.290	69	225	31	60	14	0	12	38	16	2	0	3	70	1	2	.489	.317
Gardner, Brett	L-L	5-11	195	8-24-83	.251	.212	.265	141	491	86	123	26	7	28	74	52	4	0	3	108	10	2	.503	.326
Gregorius, Didi	L-R	6-3	205	2-18-90	.238	.216	.246	82	324	47	77	14	2	16	61	17	1	0	2	53	2	1	.441	.276
Hicks, Aaron	B-R	6-2	202	10-2-89	.235	.266	.218	59	221	41	52	10	0	12	36	31	0	0	3	72	1	2	.443	.326
Higashioka, Kyle	R-R	6-1	205	4-20-90	.214	.267	.195	18	56	8	12	5	0	3	11	0	0	0	1	26	0	0	.464	.211
Judge, Aaron	R-R	6-7	282	4-26-92	.273	.343	.247	102	378	75	103	18	1	27	55	64	3	0	1	141	3	2	.540	.381
LeMahieu, DJ	R-R	6-4	215	7-13-88	.327	.375	.310	145	602	109	197	33	2	26	102	46	2	1	4	90	5	2	.518	.375
Maybin, Cameron	R-R	6-3	215	4-4-87	.285	.231	.311	82	239	48	68	17	0	11	32	30	0	0	0	72	9	6	.494	.364
Morales, Kendrys	B-R	6-1	242	6-20-83	.177	.091	.196	19	62	7	11	1	0	1	5	12	1	0	0	6	0	0	.242	.320
2-team total (34 Oakland)					.194	.200	.193	53	170	16	33	2	1	2	12	26	4	0	1	26	0	0	.253	.313
Romine, Austin	R-R	6-1	220	11-22-88	.281	.309	.269	72	228	29	64	12	0	8	35	10	1	1	5	50	1	1	.439	.310
Sanchez, Gary	R-R	6-2	230	12-2-92	.232	.200	.243	106	396	62	92	12	1	34	77	40	9	0	1	125	0	1	.525	.316
Stanton, Giancarlo	R-R	6-6	245	11-8-89	.288	.286	.289	18	59	8	17	3	0	3	13	12	0	0	1	24	0	0	.492	.403
Tauchman, Mike	L-L	6-2	220	12-3-90	.277	.357	.247	87	260	46	72	18	1	13	47	34	1	0	1	71	6	0	.504	.362
Torres, Gleyber	R-R	6-1	200	12-13-96	.278	.286	.276	144	546	96	152	26	0	38	90	48	3	1	6	129	5	2	.535	.337
Tulowitzki, Troy	R-R	6-3	205	10-10-84	.182	.400	.000	5	11	1	2	1	0	1	1	2	0	0	0	4	0	0	.546	.308
Urshela, Gio	R-R	6-0	220	10-11-91	.315	.300	.320	132	442	73	139	34	0	21	74	25	5	0	4	87	1	1	.534	.355
Valera, Breyvic	B-R	5-11	160	1-8-92	.219	.333	.174	12	32	5	7	1	1	0	3	4	1	0	0	5	0	0	.313	.324
2-team total (5 Toronto)					.234	.267	.219	17	47	7	11	2	1	1	6	4	1	0	0	7	0	0	.383	.308
Voit, Luke	R-R	6-3	225	2-13-91	.263	.250	.268	118	429	72	113	21	1	21	62	71	9	0	1	142	0	0	.464	.378
Wade, Tyler	L-R	6-1	185	11-23-94	.245	.278	.237	43	94	16	23	3	1	2	11	11	1	2	0	28	7	0	.362	.330

Pitching	B-T	HT	WT	DOB	W	L	ERA	G	GS	CG	SV	IP	H	R	ER	HR	BB	SO	AVG	vLH	vRH	K/9	BB/9
Adams, Chance	R-R	6-1	225	8-10-94	1	1	8.53	13	0	0	1	25	39	25	24	7	11	23	.351	.319	.375	8.17	3.91
Barrett, Jake	R-R	6-2	240	7-22-91	0	0	14.73	2	0	0	0	4	6	6	6	2	2	4	.353	.250	.444	9.82	4.91
Betances, Dellin	R-R	6-8	265	3-23-88	0	0	0.00	1	0	0	0	1	0	0	0	0	0	2	.000	.000	.000	27.00	0.00
Britton, Zack	L-L	6-3	195	12-22-87	3	1	1.91	66	0	0	3	61	38	13	13	3	32	53	.182	.158	.191	7.78	4.70
Cessa, Luis	R-R	6-0	210	4-25-92	2	1	4.11	43	0	0	1	81	75	42	37	14	31	75	.246	.278	.224	8.33	3.44
Chapman, Aroldis	L-L	6-4	212	2-28-88	3	2	2.21	60	0	0	37	57	38	18	14	3	25	85	.185	.163	.192	13.42	3.95
Cortes Jr., Nestor	R-L	5-11	210	12-10-94	5	1	5.67	33	1	0	0	67	75	44	42	16	28	69	.281	.344	.249	9.32	3.78
Dull, Ryan	R-R	5-9	185	10-2-89	0	0	19.29	3	0	0	0	2	5	5	5	0	3	4	.417	.500	.400	15.43	11.57
3-team total (7 Oakland, 1 Toronto)					0	0	12.79	11	0	0	0	13	25	19	18	5	7	15	.410	.400	.417	10.66	4.97
Ford, Mike	L-R	6-0	225	7-4-92	0	0	22.50	1	0	0	0	2	6	5	5	2	0	1	.500	.571	.400	4.50	0.00
Gearrin, Cory	R-R	6-1	205	4-14-86	1	1	4.50	18	0	0	0	14	17	7	7	2	4	8	.298	.263	.316	5.14	2.57
2-team total (48 Seattle)					1	3	4.07	66	2	0	0	55	55	25	25	5	25	47	.261	.276	.252	7.64	4.07
German, Domingo	R-R	6-2	175	8-4-92	18	4	4.03	27	24	0	0	143	125	69	64	30	39	153	.228	.242	.210	9.63	2.45
Green, Chad	L-R	6-3	210	5-24-91	4	4	4.17	54	15	0	2	69	66	35	32	10	19	96	.247	.246	.248	12.78	2.48
Hale, David	R-R	6-2	210	9-27-87	3	0	3.11	20	0	0	2	38	39	13	13	2	7	23	.264	.274	.256	5.50	1.67
Happ, J.A.	L-L	6-5	205	10-19-82	12	8	4.91	31	30	0	0	161	160	88	88	34	49	140	.258	.228	.268	7.81	2.73
Harvey, Joe	R-R	6-2	235	1-9-92	1	0	4.50	9	0	0	0	10	11	6	5	1	7	11	.282	.077	.385	9.90	6.30
Heller, Ben	R-R	6-3	205	8-5-91	0	0	1.23	6	0	0	0	7	6	1	1	1	3	6	.250	.250	.250	11.05	3.68
Holder, Jonathan	R-R	6-2	235	6-9-93	5	2	6.31	34	1	0	0	41	43	32	29	8	11	46	.256	.262	.252	10.02	2.40
Kahnle, Tommy	R-R	6-1	235	8-7-89	3	2	3.67	72	0	0	0	61	45	27	25	9	20	88	.200	.209	.191	12.91	2.93
King, Michael	R-R	6-3	210	5-25-95	0	0	0.00	1	0	0	0	2	2	1	0	0	0	1	.222	.250	.200	4.50	0.00
Lail, Brady	R-R	6-2	205	8-9-93	0	0	10.13	1	0	0	0	3	2	3	3	1	1	2	.222	.167	.333	6.75	3.38
Loaisiga, Jonathan	R-R	5-11	165	11-2-94	2	2	4.55	15	4	0	0	32	31	16	16	6	16	37	.263	.321	.210	10.52	4.55

NEW YORK YANKEES

Name	B-T	HT	WT	DOB	W	L	ERA	G	GS	CG	SV	IP	H	R	ER	HR	BB	SO	AVG	vLH	vRH	K/9	BB/9
Lyons, Tyler	L-L	6-4	210	2-21-88	0	1	4.15	11	0	0	0	9	7	4	4	3	2	12	.226	.267	.188	12.46	2.08
Mantiply, Joe	R-L	6-4	215	3-1-91	1	0	9.00	1	0	0	0	3	3	3	3	1	2	2	.250	.000	.500	6.00	6.00
Montgomery, Jordan	L-L	6-6	225	12-27-92	0	0	6.75	2	1	0	0	4	7	3	3	1	0	5	.368	.250	.455	11.25	0.00
Ottavino, Adam	B-R	6-5	220	11-22-85	6	5	1.90	73	0	0	2	66	47	17	14	5	40	88	.198	.241	.177	11.94	5.43
Paxton, James	L-L	6-4	235	11-6-88	15	6	3.82	29	29	0	0	151	138	71	64	23	55	186	.242	.266	.234	11.11	3.29
Romine, Austin	R-R	6-1	220	11-22-88	0	0	27.00	1	0	0	0	1	4	3	3	2	0	0	.571	.500	.667	0.00	0.00
Rosa, Adonis	R-R	6-1	170	11-17-94	0	0	4.50	1	0	0	0	2	1	1	1	1	0	2	.143	.000	.333	9.00	0.00
Sabathia, CC	L-L	6-6	300	7-21-80	5	8	4.95	23	22	0	0	107	112	64	59	27	39	107	.265	.198	.284	8.97	3.27
Severino, Luis	R-R	6-2	215	2-20-94	1	1	1.50	3	3	0	0	12	6	2	2	0	6	17	.146	.148	.143	12.75	4.50
Tanaka, Masahiro	R-R	6-3	215	11-1-88	11	9	4.45	32	31	1	0	182	186	95	90	28	40	149	.261	.285	.237	7.37	1.98
Tarpley, Stephen	R-L	6-1	235	2-17-93	1	0	6.93	21	1	0	2	25	34	20	19	6	15	34	.330	.200	.413	12.41	5.47

Fielding

Catcher	PCT	G	PO	A	E	DP	PB
Higashioka	1.000	18	146	8	0	2	0
Romine	.997	70	610	26	2	4	6
Sanchez	.982	90	793	32	15	5	7

First Base	PCT	G	PO	A	E	DP
Bird	1.000	10	83	2	0	6
Encarnacion	1.000	12	88	2	0	6
Ford	.985	29	191	9	3	22
LeMahieu	.992	40	215	19	2	24
Morales	.983	7	56	1	1	4
Urshela	1.000	1	8	0	0	1
Voit	.989	83	575	28	7	60

Second Base	PCT	G	PO	A	E	DP
Estrada	1.000	17	24	18	0	6
LeMahieu	.993	75	118	155	2	32
Torres	.967	65	113	147	9	48
Valera	1.000	12	7	28	0	5
Wade	.985	18	24	40	1	10

Third Base	PCT	G	PO	A	E	DP
Andujar	.700	4	0	7	3	0
LeMahieu	.963	52	18	87	4	7
Urshela	.954	123	59	212	13	20
Wade	1.000	5	5	5	0	0

Shortstop	PCT	G	PO	A	E	DP
Estrada	.950	9	7	12	1	1
Gregorius	.979	80	93	181	6	48

	PCT	G	PO	A	E	DP
Torres	.961	77	91	180	11	40
Tulowitzki	1.000	4	3	7	0	0
Wade	1.000	4	0	2	0	0

Outfield	PCT	G	PO	A	E	DP
Estrada	1.000	4	2	0	0	0
Frazier	.963	53	71	6	3	1
Gardner	.996	140	280	3	1	0
Hicks	.991	58	115	0	1	0
Judge	1.000	92	177	7	0	0
Maybin	.984	77	121	2	2	0
Stanton	.938	13	15	0	1	0
Tauchman	.994	86	156	3	1	1
Urshela	1.000	1	2	0	0	0
Wade	1.000	18	18	1	0	0

SCRANTON/WILKES-BARRE RAILRIDERS

TRIPLE-A

INTERNATIONAL LEAGUE

Batting	B-T	HT	WT	DOB	AVG	vLH	vRH	G	AB	R	H	2B	3B	HR	RBI	BB	HBP	SH	SF	SO	SB	CS	SLG	OBP
Alvarez, Mandy	R-R	6-1	195	7-14-94	.277	.259	.288	66	238	31	66	18	0	6	44	18	1	0	3	39	1	2	.429	.327
Amburgey, Trey	R-R	6-2	210	10-24-94	.275	.320	.254	124	470	73	129	31	3	22	62	32	6	2	0	112	6	2	.494	.329
Arcia, Francisco	L-R	5-11	200	9-14-89	.289	.100	.343	14	45	5	13	3	0	1	6	3	0	0	1	11	0	0	.422	.327
Burns, Billy	B-R	5-9	170	8-30-89	.258	.338	.225	93	267	42	69	15	3	2	25	27	3	4	3	41	14	3	.360	.330
Carrizales, Omar	L-L	6-0	175	1-30-95	.167	.250	.125	5	12	0	2	0	0	0	0	3	0	0	0	4	0	0	.167	.333
Deglan, Kellin	L-R	6-2	220	5-3-92	.158	.250	.133	6	19	3	3	0	0	1	2	2	1	0	0	6	0	0	.316	.273
Encarnacion, Edwin	R-R	6-1	230	1-7-83	.125	.333	.000	2	8	2	1	0	0	0	1	0	1	0	0	2	0	0	.125	.222
Estrada, Thairo	R-R	5-10	190	2-22-96	.266	.294	.254	60	241	39	64	17	2	8	32	14	3	0	1	50	3	1	.452	.313
Fleming, Billy	R-R	6-1	210	9-20-92	.244	.200	.286	12	41	4	10	0	0	1	5	3	0	0	0	16	0	0	.317	.296
Ford, Mike	L-R	6-0	225	7-4-92	.303	.267	.317	79	294	59	89	20	0	23	60	46	5	0	4	55	0	1	.605	.401
Frazier, Clint	R-R	6-1	190	9-6-94	.247	.218	.260	61	247	35	61	20	1	8	26	17	4	0	1	56	1	2	.433	.305
Gore, Terrance	R-R	5-7	165	6-8-91	.164	.177	.158	21	55	8	9	3	1	0	1	12	1	1	0	17	3	0	.255	.324
Gregorius, Didi	L-R	6-3	205	2-18-90	.120	.273	.000	6	25	1	3	0	0	0	1	1	0	0	0	2	0	0	.120	.154
Hicks, Aaron	B-R	6-1	202	10-2-89	.429	.750	.000	2	7	4	3	2	0	1	1	1	0	0	0	1	1	0	1.143	.500
Higashioka, Kyle	R-R	6-1	205	4-20-90	.278	.312	.267	70	241	42	67	13	0	20	56	24	3	0	2	53	0	0	.581	.348
Judge, Aaron	R-R	6-7	282	4-26-92	.125	.000	.143	5	16	2	2	0	0	1	2	3	0	0	0	7	0	0	.313	.263
Katoh, Gosuke	L-R	6-2	195	10-8-94	.279	.299	.272	83	262	45	73	10	0	11	39	42	2	1	0	82	8	4	.443	.382
Kratz, Erik	R-R	6-4	250	6-15-80	.299	.196	.350	46	154	27	46	10	0	7	31	17	3	0	2	21	1	0	.500	.375
Lavarnway, Ryan	R-R	6-4	240	8-7-87	.213	.324	.155	35	108	13	23	2	0	9	17	11	3	0	1	26	0	0	.315	.333
3-team total (4 Columbus Clippers, 13 Louisville Bats)					.226	.275	.204	52	159	21	36	5	0	6	28	25	3	0	3	36	0	0	.371	.337
Lidge, Ryan	B-R	6-2	216	10-27-94	.182	.125	.333	3	11	1	2	1	0	0	0	0	0	0	0	5	0	0	.273	.182
Lipka, Matt	R-R	6-1	215	4-15-92	.281	.077	.333	18	64	7	18	5	0	2	11	8	0	0	0	16	4	1	.453	.361
Maybin, Cameron	R-R	6-3	215	4-4-87	.462	--	.462	3	13	4	6	2	0	1	2	1	0	0	0	0	0	0	.846	.500
2-team total (14 Columbus)					.266	.273	.264	17	64	8	17	5	0	1	7	14	2	0	1	22	1	2	.391	.407
McBroom, Ryan	R-L	6-3	235	4-9-92	.315	.328	.309	117	413	87	130	29	0	26	66	58	6	0	5	100	2	2	.574	.403
Miller, Brad	L-R	6-2	215	10-18-89	.294	.195	.337	41	136	31	40	9	1	10	29	24	1	0	2	40	1	3	.596	.399
Morrison, Logan	L-L	6-3	245	8-25-87	.290	.277	.295	43	152	29	44	11	0	15	37	8	4	0	0	38	0	1	.658	.342
2-team total (18 Lehigh Valley)					.308	.292	.315	61	211	36	65	16	0	18	49	15	6	0	1	38	0	1	.640	.369
Pennington, Cliff	B-R	5-10	200	6-15-84	.196	.172	.206	29	92	15	18	3	1	5	16	14	2	1	3	24	4	0	.413	.306
Rijo, Wendell	R-R	5-11	170	9-4-95	.270	.319	.244	43	137	18	37	10	0	7	17	8	3	0	0	35	1	0	.496	.324
Sanchez, Gary	R-R	6-2	230	12-2-92	.200	.000	.333	2	5	1	1	0	0	0	0	1	0	0	0	1	0	0	.200	.333
Stanton, Giancarlo	R-R	6-6	245	11-8-89	.091	.000	.111	3	11	1	1	0	0	0	3	0	0	0	0	7	0	0	.364	.091
Tauchman, Mike	L-L	6-2	210	12-3-90	.274	.091	.329	28	95	22	26	10	3	2	16	16	2	0	1	16	4	0	.505	.386
Urshela, Gio	R-R	6-0	220	10-11-91	.444	.667	.333	2	9	2	4	2	0	0	1	0	0	0	0	2	0	0	.667	.444
Valera, Breyvic	B-R	5-11	160	1-8-92	.315	.313	.315	83	305	44	96	18	2	13	49	34	3	5	1	34	8	6	.515	.388
Voit, Luke	R-R	6-3	225	2-13-91	.471	.400	.500	4	17	5	8	2	0	2	4	2	0	0	0	2	0	0	.941	.526
Wade, Tyler	L-R	6-1	185	11-23-94	.296	.278	.303	79	301	51	89	19	4	4	38	23	4	2	7	61	13	5	.425	.352
Wagner, Brandon	L-R	6-0	210	8-24-95	.333	.000	.400	2	6	1	2	0	0	0	2	0	0	0	0	2	0	0	.333	.333
Zehner, Zack	R-R	6-4	215	8-8-92	.266	.235	.277	55	192	32	51	11	1	9	37	18	0	0	4	63	2	2	.474	.322

Pitching

Pitching	B-T	HT	WT	DOB	W	L	ERA	G	GS	CG	SV	IP	H	R	ER	HR	BB	SO	AVG	vLH	vRH	K/9	BB/9
Acevedo, Domingo	R-R	6-7	250	3-6-94	1	0	5.40	10	0	0	0	17	19	10	10	4	4	21	.288	.318	.273	11.34	2.16
Adams, Chance	R-R	6-1	225	8-10-94	4	4	4.63	18	15	1	1	82	77	44	42	11	38	80	.242	.282	.207	8.82	4.19
Alvarez, Daniel	R-R	6-3	228	6-28-96	0	0	0.00	1	0	0	0	1	0	0	0	0	0	0	.000	--	.000	0.00	0.00
Barrett, Jake	R-R	6-2	240	7-22-91	0	1	1.17	10	0	0	1	15	10	2	2	0	4	20	.182	.261	.125	11.74	2.35
Bies, Daniel	R-R	6-9	245	4-9-96	0	0	3.00	1	0	0	0	3	2	2	1	0	3	3	.200	.000	.250	9.00	9.00
Brothers, Rex	L-L	6-0	205	12-18-87	0	3	4.93	34	0	0	0	46	37	25	25	6	36	81	.222	.275	.198	15.96	7.09
Camarena, Daniel	L-L	6-0	210	11-9-92	4	8	6.27	17	16	0	0	99	121	74	69	21	22	88	.303	.344	.284	8.00	2.00
2-team total (1 Rochester)					4	8	6.27	18	16	0	0	103	126	77	72	22	22	94	.301	.341	.284	8.19	1.92
Carter, Will	L-R	6-3	195	1-18-93	1	1	9.33	10	0	0	0	18	21	19	19	3	16	7	.284	.281	.286	3.44	7.85
Cortes Jr., Nestor	R-L	5-11	210	12-10-94	2	2	3.86	7	6	0	0	40	29	17	17	3	11	42	.203	.219	.198	9.53	2.50
Coshow, Cale	R-R	6-5	270	7-16-92	2	1	5.28	14	0	0	2	15	16	13	9	3	10	22	.262	.304	.237	12.91	5.87
Coulombe, Danny	L-L	5-10	190	10-26-89	3	2	5.01	17	0	0	1	23	26	13	13	5	15	43	.277	.222	.310	16.59	5.79
Delgado, Randall	R-R	6-4	220	2-9-90	2	5	6.49	10	10	0	0	51	62	41	37	9	16	44	.309	.275	.336	7.71	2.81
Dull, Ryan	R-R	5-9	185	10-2-89	1	0	2.70	4	0	0	0	7	3	3	2	1	1	4	.136	.200	.118	5.40	1.35
Espinal, Raynel	R-R	6-3	215	10-6-91	5	7	4.32	18	12	1	0	75	73	37	36	10	22	79	.259	.273	.247	9.48	2.64
Farquhar, Danny	R-R	5-9	185	2-17-87	0	0	21.00	2	0	0	0	3	6	7	7	3	2	4	.400	.571	.250	12.00	6.00
Feyereisen, J.P.	R-R	6-2	215	2-7-93	10	2	2.49	40	0	0	7	61	37	22	17	6	31	94	.173	.211	.143	13.79	4.55
Garcia, Deivi	R-R	5-9	163	5-19-99	1	3	5.40	11	6	0	0	40	39	25	24	8	20	45	.262	.232	.288	10.13	4.50
German, Domingo	R-R	6-2	175	8-4-92	0	0	9.00	1	1	0	0	4	4	4	4	2	5	5	.235	.333	.125	11.25	4.50
Gonzalez, Gio	R-L	6-0	205	9-19-85	2	1	6.00	3	3	0	0	15	19	10	10	1	6	19	.317	.438	.273	11.40	3.60
Green, Chad	L-R	6-3	210	5-24-91	0	0	2.45	3	3	0	0	7	5	2	2	0	2	14	.185	.000	.278	17.18	2.45
Hale, David	R-R	6-2	215	9-27-87	3	2	4.13	7	7	1	0	33	36	17	15	3	10	30	.277	.323	.235	8.27	2.76
Harvey, Joe	R-R	6-2	235	1-9-92	0	1	3.12	22	0	0	9	26	15	10	9	4	15	38	.161	.175	.151	13.15	5.19
Heller, Ben	R-R	6-3	205	8-5-91	0	0	0.82	9	4	0	1	11	5	1	1	0	3	13	.143	.143	.143	10.64	2.45
Hernandez, David	R-R	6-3	245	5-13-85	0	1	7.71	8	0	0	0	7	7	6	6	1	8	11	.200	.364	.071	14.14	10.29
Holder, Jonathan	R-R	6-2	235	6-9-93	1	1	2.92	9	0	0	2	12	13	5	4	1	2	15	.271	.273	.269	10.95	1.46
Hutchison, Drew	L-R	6-3	215	8-22-90	5	4	5.14	12	10	0	0	63	64	44	36	8	28	61	.265	.291	.245	8.71	4.00
2-team total (9 Rochester)					8	6	5.55	21	19	0	0	109	122	78	67	18	45	113	.282	.309	.265	9.36	3.73
Jennings, Dan	L-L	6-3	215	4-17-87	0	0	33.75	2	0	0	0	1	5	5	5	3	0	2	.556	.333	.667	13.50	0.00
Junk, Janson	R-R	6-1	177	1-15-96	0	0	11.57	1	1	0	0	2	5	4	3	1	0	2	.385	.667	.300	7.71	0.00
Keller, Brian	R-R	6-3	210	6-21-94	1	2	6.91	5	5	0	0	27	36	21	21	3	9	25	.321	.342	.311	8.23	2.96
King, Michael	R-R	6-3	210	5-25-95	3	1	4.18	4	3	0	0	24	20	12	11	3	6	28	.227	.216	.235	10.65	2.28
Koerner, Brody	R-R	6-2	220	10-17-93	4	6	5.63	21	16	0	0	112	135	80	70	17	37	89	.297	.294	.300	7.15	2.97
Lail, Brady	R-R	6-2	205	8-9-93	1	1	7.47	11	0	0	0	16	19	14	13	3	3	17	.297	.407	.216	9.77	1.72
Lane, Trevor	L-L	5-11	185	4-26-94	0	0	3.86	2	0	0	0	5	2	2	2	1	2	5	.125	.250	.083	9.64	3.86
Loaisiga, Jonathan	R-R	5-11	165	11-2-94	0	2	6.32	5	4	0	0	16	14	11	11	3	5	19	.230	.217	.237	10.91	2.87
Lyons, Tyler	L-L	6-4	210	2-21-88	0	0	1.93	3	0	0	0	5	5	1	1	0	3	5	.263	.000	.333	9.64	5.79
2-team total (35 Indianapolis)					4	3	3.22	38	0	0	3	50	39	21	18	4	19	60	.216	.116	.277	10.73	3.40
Maciejewski, Josh	R-L	6-3	175	8-14-95	0	1	5.25	3	2	0	0	12	13	8	7	4	9	11	.289	.333	.273	8.25	6.75
Mantiply, Joe	R-L	6-4	215	3-1-91	0	0	4.82	6	0	0	0	9	11	6	5	3	1	7	.282	.200	.310	6.75	0.96
2-team total (18 Louisville)					0	0	3.99	24	0	0	1	38	37	18	17	5	4	33	.252	.191	.276	7.75	0.94
Montgomery, Jordan	L-L	6-6	225	12-27-92	0	0	0.00	1	1	0	0	2	2	1	0	0	0	3	.250	.333	.200	16.20	0.00
Nelson, Nick	R-R	6-1	195	12-5-95	1	1	4.71	4	4	0	0	21	20	11	11	2	7	24	.247	.229	.261	10.29	3.00
Ort, Kaleb	R-R	6-4	240	2-5-92	4	0	4.05	24	0	0	2	33	29	17	15	2	24	51	.236	.241	.232	13.77	6.48
Rosa, Adonis	R-R	6-1	170	11-17-94	6	0	3.88	13	8	0	0	60	65	33	26	9	14	51	.270	.297	.246	7.61	2.09
Rosenthal, Trevor	R-R	6-2	230	5-29-90	0	0	108.00	1	0	0	0	0	0	4	4	0	3	0	.000	--	.000	0.00	81.00
2-team total (6 Toledo)					0	0	15.88	7	0	0	0	6	8	10	10	2	9	9	.320	.333	.313	14.29	14.29
Semple, Shawn	R-R	6-1	220	10-9-95	0	0	21.60	1	1	0	0	3	8	8	8	1	2	2	.471	.400	.571	5.40	8.10
Severino, Luis	R-R	6-2	215	2-20-94	0	0	18.00	1	1	0	0	1	3	2	2	1	0	2	.600	.667	.500	18.00	0.00
Sosebee, David	R-R	6-2	220	8-25-93	4	1	3.54	31	0	0	6	48	46	23	19	6	19	59	.246	.303	.207	10.99	3.54
Tarpley, Stephen	R-L	6-1	235	2-17-93	5	1	3.13	18	2	0	3	32	25	15	11	3	13	34	.212	.163	.240	9.66	3.69

Fielding

Catcher	PCT	G	PO	A	E	DP	PB
Arcia	.962	10	76	0	3	0	0
Deglan	1.000	6	65	4	0	0	0
Higashioka	.990	64	588	28	6	6	5
Kratz	.989	37	329	23	4	4	1
Lavarnway	.987	29	211	20	3	4	4
Lidge	1.000	3	34	2	0	0	0
Sanchez	.923	2	11	1	1	0	0

First Base	PCT	G	PO	A	E	DP
Encarnacion	.800	1	4	0	1	0
Ford	.991	44	298	22	3	22
Katoh	1.000	20	105	5	0	8
Kratz	1.000	2	16	1	0	2
Lavarnway	1.000	2	8	0	0	2
McBroom	.995	62	412	16	2	32
Miller	1.000	1	8	0	0	0
Morrison	.994	24	145	15	1	12
Voit	1.000	3	19	1	0	1

Second Base	PCT	G	PO	A	E	DP
Alvarez	1.000	3	10	9	0	4
Estrada	.988	24	30	50	1	18
Fleming	1.000	5	9	12	0	2
Katoh	.979	30	32	61	2	9
Miller	.946	13	13	22	2	4
Pennington	1.000	3	3	4	0	1
Rijo	.959	23	30	40	3	10
Valera	.977	22	25	60	2	8
Wade	.982	28	40	71	2	15

Third Base	PCT	G	PO	A	E	DP
Alvarez	.943	56	31	119	9	7
Arcia	.750	2	0	3	1	1
Estrada	1.000	2	0	4	0	0
Fleming	1.000	2	0	3	0	0
Ford	1.000	5	0	7	0	1
Katoh	.897	21	11	15	3	2
Miller	1.000	10	5	8	0	0
Pennington	1.000	4	2	7	0	1
Rijo	.917	14	6	16	2	1
Urshela	1.000	2	2	3	0	0

Shortstop	PCT	G	PO	A	E	DP
Alvarez	1.000	1	1	1	0	0
Estrada	.972	33	43	63	3	14
Gregorius	1.000	4	5	12	0	1
Katoh	.969	12	9	22	1	6
Miller	1.000	1	1	2	0	1
Pennington	.968	23	24	37	2	6
Valera	.989	30	31	59	1	14
Wade	.955	43	61	110	8	29

Outfield	PCT	G	PO	A	E	DP
Amburgey	.986	120	203	3	3	1
Burns	.975	83	151	4	4	0
Carrizales	1.000	5	8	0	0	0
Frazier	.957	58	88	2	4	0
Gore	1.000	20	38	0	0	1
Hicks	1.000	2	7	0	0	0
Judge	1.000	3	8	1	0	1

Valera	.985	28	26	38	1	4
Wade	1.000	4	2	7	0	0

Katoh	1.000	2	2	0	0	0
Lipka	.944	18	34	0	2	0
Maybin	.000	1	0	0	0	0
McBroom	.986	41	66	2	1	0

Miller	1.000	11	20	0	0	0
Stanton	1.000	2	0	1	0	0
Tauchman	1.000	28	68	0	0	0
Wade	1.000	4	5	0	0	0

Wagner	1.000	1	2	0	0	0
Zehner	.963	46	77	2	3	0

TRENTON THUNDER

EASTERN LEAGUE

DOUBLE-A

Batting	B-T	HT	WT	DOB	AVG	vLH	vRH	G	AB	R	H	2B	3B	HR	RBI	BB	HBP	SH	SF	SO	SB	CS	SLG	OBP
Aguilar, Angel	R-R	6-0	170	6-13-95	.217	.180	.237	40	143	17	31	9	1	3	21	6	2	1	2	47	2	1	.357	.255
Alvarez, Mandy	R-R	6-1	195	7-14-94	.262	.254	.266	58	210	21	55	13	1	5	32	17	2	0	1	35	3	2	.405	.322
Arcia, Francisco	L-R	5-11	200	9-14-89	.192	.143	.211	8	26	1	5	0	0	0	2	2	1	0	0	4	0	0	.192	.276
Burt, Max	R-R	6-2	185	8-28-96	.250	.211	.264	23	72	6	18	3	0	0	5	4	1	0	1	19	0	1	.292	.295
Carrizales, Omar	L-L	6-0	175	1-30-95	.156	.067	.235	9	32	2	5	1	1	0	3	2	0	0	0	6	0	0	.250	.206
Crawford, Rashad	L-R	6-3	185	10-15-93	.262	.219	.282	114	401	48	105	13	1	7	47	38	2	3	0	104	21	8	.352	.329
Deglan, Kellin	L-R	6-2	220	5-3-92	.265	.278	.261	65	230	30	61	13	1	8	30	17	7	0	1	73	1	0	.435	.333
Diaz, Francisco	B-R	5-11	185	3-21-90	.256	.250	.261	13	39	6	10	0	0	0	5	10	1	0	0	10	0	0	.256	.420
Frazier, Clint	R-R	6-1	190	9-6-94	.333	--	.333	1	3	1	1	0	0	0	1	0	0	0	0	1	0	0	.333	.500
Gilliam, Isiah	B-R	6-3	220	7-23-96	.180	.200	.170	47	161	13	29	5	1	9	23	13	2	0	1	61	0	2	.391	.249
Gittens, Chris	R-R	6-4	250	2-4-94	.281	.313	.265	115	398	58	112	16	1	23	77	71	5	0	4	139	0	0	.500	.393
Hendrix, Jeff	L-R	6-0	200	7-16-93	.200	.240	.182	26	80	8	16	2	0	0	6	8	2	0	0	29	2	0	.225	.256
Holder, Kyle	L-R	6-1	185	5-25-94	.265	.212	.291	112	412	48	109	25	3	9	40	41	4	14	1	65	7	1	.405	.336
Jackson, Jhalan	R-R	6-4	240	2-12-93	.200	.227	.174	12	45	6	9	3	1	2	4	2	0	0	0	16	0	1	.444	.234
Katoh, Gosuke	L-R	6-2	195	10-8-94	.237	.333	.194	30	97	11	23	3	1	0	7	10	0	0	1	28	3	1	.289	.306
Lidge, Ryan	B-R	6-2	216	10-27-94	.044	.143	.000	7	23	1	1	0	0	0	0	1	1	0	0	10	0	0	.044	.120
Lipka, Matt	R-R	6-1	215	4-15-92	.257	.264	.252	71	230	31	59	12	4	2	18	12	4	7	2	59	15	6	.370	.302
Mateo, Welfrin	R-R	5-10	170	9-8-95	.444	.400	.500	4	9	1	4	2	0	0	2	4	0	0	0	1	1	0	.667	.615
Metzgar, David	R-R	5-8	170	12-10-94	.111	.000	.167	3	9	0	1	0	0	0	0	1	0	1	0	1	0	0	.111	.200
Navarreto, Brian	R-R	6-4	220	12-29-94	.167	.222	.083	10	30	3	5	0	0	1	4	2	0	0	1	3	0	0	.267	.212
Navas, Eduardo	L-R	5-10	180	4-5-96	.400	1.000	.250	3	10	1	4	0	0	0	3	1	0	0	0	5	0	0	.400	.455
Palma, Alexander	R-R	6-0	201	10-18-95	.250	1.000	.143	2	8	0	2	0	0	0	1	0	0	0	0	0	0	0	.250	.333
Park, Hoy Jun	L-R	6-1	175	4-7-96	.272	.259	.279	113	416	60	113	20	6	3	41	57	4	6	2	91	20	10	.370	.363
Rijo, Wendell	R-R	5-11	170	9-4-95	.235	.269	.211	51	187	35	44	11	0	6	23	19	1	1	0	46	3	1	.390	.309
Ruta, Ben	L-R	6-3	195	6-8-94	.260	.197	.286	117	442	57	115	26	5	8	55	47	2	0	6	85	25	8	.396	.330
Saez, Jorge	R-R	5-10	200	8-28-90	.161	.173	.150	35	112	16	18	3	0	5	17	7	0	0	1	37	0	0	.321	.269
Wagner, Brandon	L-R	6-0	210	8-24-95	.177	.168	.181	117	390	43	69	12	2	8	37	48	15	0	3	147	1	0	.280	.290
Zehner, Zack	R-R	6-4	215	8-8-92	.181	.259	.142	50	171	19	31	3	3	3	14	22	1	0	1	50	1	2	.287	.277

Pitching	B-T	HT	WT	DOB	W	L	ERA	G	GS	CG	SV	IP	H	R	ER	HR	BB	SO	AVG	vLH	vRH	K/9	BB/9
Abreu, Albert	R-R	6-2	175	9-26-95	5	8	4.28	23	20	0	0	97	103	62	46	9	53	91	.276	.255	.299	8.47	4.93
Acevedo, Domingo	R-R	6-7	250	3-6-94	7	1	3.86	22	0	0	0	35	23	17	15	7	10	33	.183	.157	.214	8.49	2.57
Alvarez, Daniel	R-R	6-3	228	6-28-96	7	2	2.31	46	0	0	21	58	41	17	15	4	23	76	.195	.181	.210	11.73	3.55
Bellatti, Andrew	R-R	6-1	190	8-5-91	2	0	5.28	21	0	0	0	31	33	20	18	4	8	27	.280	.283	.277	7.92	2.35
Bristo, Braden	R-R	6-0	180	11-1-94	1	1	3.75	14	0	0	1	24	22	10	10	2	9	27	.247	.222	.273	10.13	3.38
Carter, Will	L-R	6-3	195	1-18-93	1	2	4.01	28	1	0	2	49	47	24	22	2	26	36	.245	.280	.207	6.57	4.74
Garcia, Deivi	R-R	5-9	163	5-19-99	4	4	3.86	11	11	0	0	54	43	23	23	2	26	87	.213	.231	.194	14.59	4.36
Garcia, Rony	R-R	6-3	200	12-19-97	4	11	4.44	20	20	0	0	105	94	56	52	14	38	104	.235	.274	.189	8.89	3.25
Green, Nick	R-R	6-1	175	3-25-95	3	4	7.08	15	3	0	0	69	87	59	54	3	34	51	.310	.291	.329	6.68	4.46
Junk, Janson	R-R	6-1	177	1-15-96	0	1	7.71	1	1	0	0	5	4	4	4	1	5	3	.267	.000	.364	5.79	9.64
Keller, Brian	R-R	6-3	210	6-21-94	3	1	2.32	7	7	1	0	43	30	14	11	1	10	33	.197	.187	.208	6.96	2.11
King, Michael	R-R	6-3	210	5-25-95	0	1	9.95	3	2	0	0	13	20	15	14	1	2	8	.351	.333	.364	5.68	1.42
Koerner, Brody	R-R	6-2	220	10-17-93	0	2	2.36	6	6	0	0	27	26	9	7	0	15	20	.253	.286	.209	6.75	5.06
Kriske, Brooks	R-R	6-3	190	2-3-94	2	2	2.59	36	0	0	11	49	30	14	14	3	23	64	.171	.228	.108	11.84	4.25
Lail, Brady	R-R	6-2	205	8-9-93	3	1	1.74	14	1	0	1	31	18	6	6	1	12	47	.167	.220	.121	13.65	3.48
Lane, Trevor	L-L	5-11	185	4-26-94	5	2	1.99	41	0	0	1	68	43	18	15	3	24	66	.177	.178	.177	8.74	3.18
Loaisiga, Jonathan	R-R	5-11	165	11-2-94	0	0	0.00	1	1	0	0	2	1	0	0	0	0	3	.167	.000	.333	13.50	0.00
Mesa Jr., Jose	R-R	6-4	215	8-13-93	0	1	7.71	7	1	0	0	12	15	13	10	0	14	11	.300	.214	.409	8.49	10.80
Nelson, Nick	R-R	6-1	195	12-5-95	7	2	2.35	13	12	1	0	65	48	18	17	4	35	83	.206	.239	.175	11.49	4.85
Ort, Kaleb	R-R	6-4	240	2-5-92	1	0	2.57	9	0	0	2	14	11	4	4	0	3	20	.220	.224	.227	12.86	1.93
Reeves, James	R-L	6-3	220	6-7-93	7	2	1.79	27	0	0	0	55	35	18	11	4	21	62	.182	.143	.218	10.08	3.42
Rosa, Adonis	R-R	6-1	170	11-17-94	3	1	4.60	12	5	0	0	43	41	22	22	3	19	37	.253	.263	.239	7.74	3.98
Schmidt, Clarke	R-R	6-1	200	2-20-96	2	0	2.37	3	3	0	0	19	14	5	5	1	9	20	.205	.167	.250	9.00	0.47
Semple, Shawn	R-R	6-1	220	10-9-95	0	3	5.00	7	6	1	0	36	37	21	20	6	19	34	.261	.243	.279	8.50	4.75
Sosebee, David	R-R	6-2	220	8-25-93	1	0	4.91	2	0	0	0	4	4	2	2	0	1	7	.286	.333	.200	17.18	2.45
Stephan, Trevor	R-R	6-5	225	11-25-95	2	4	5.24	12	12	0	0	46	51	29	27	3	24	57	.274	.310	.219	11.07	4.66
Weissert, Greg	R-R	6-2	215	2-4-95	1	2	1.88	14	0	0	1	24	10	5	5	0	13	28	.128	.174	.063	10.50	4.88
Whitlock, Garrett	R-R	6-5	190	6-11-96	3	3	3.07	14	14	0	0	70	73	34	24	4	18	57	.266	.258	.277	7.29	2.30
Wivinis, Matt	R-R	6-0	170	7-24-93	1	1	4.22	6	0	0	0	11	7	6	5	1	4	12	.184	.208	.143	10.13	3.38
Yajure, Miguel	R-R	6-1	175	5-1-98	1	0	0.82	2	2	0	0	11	9	1	1	0	2	11	.214	.233	.167	9.00	1.64

NEW YORK YANKEES

Fielding

Catcher	PCT	G	PO	A	E	DP	PB
Arcia	.978	8	82	6	2	0	0
Deglan	.990	63	564	37	6	3	7
Diaz	1.000	13	125	17	0	2	1
Lidge	1.000	7	64	7	0	2	2
Navarreto	1.000	10	77	4	0	1	1
Navas	1.000	3	24	2	0	0	0
Saez	.990	35	271	24	3	3	3

First Base	PCT	G	PO	A	E	DP
Gittens	.990	78	536	49	6	40
Katoh	1.000	1	8	0	0	1
Ruta	1.000	1	4	0	0	0
Wagner	.986	60	403	35	6	28

Second Base	PCT	G	PO	A	E	DP
Aguilar	1.000	12	11	28	0	5
Burt	1.000	4	5	7	0	2
Katoh	.975	18	41	36	2	9
Metzgar	1.000	1	3	2	0	0
Park	.977	77	103	152	6	25
Rijo	.957	18	24	42	3	9
Wagner	.885	11	9	14	3	2

Third Base	PCT	G	PO	A	E	DP
Aguilar	.947	19	14	22	2	4
Alvarez	.951	49	33	83	6	10
Burt	1.000	17	11	20	0	1
Katoh	.900	9	7	11	2	1
Mateo	.750	2	1	2	1	0
Metzgar	.833	2	0	5	1	1
Rijo	.958	20	16	30	2	1
Wagner	1.000	22	10	29	0	1

Shortstop	PCT	G	PO	A	E	DP
Aguilar	1.000	2	3	6	0	0
Holder	.973	107	118	241	10	40
Park	.973	30	41	69	3	10

Outfield	PCT	G	PO	A	E	DP
Carrizales	1.000	9	16	2	0	0
Crawford	.972	106	201	5	6	0
Frazier	1.000	1	2	0	0	0
Gilliam	.978	44	87	2	2	0
Hendrix	1.000	22	57	1	0	0
Jackson	.955	11	19	2	1	1
Lipka	.979	68	134	7	3	2
Palma	1.000	2	4	0	0	0
Ruta	.987	110	225	3	3	0
Zehner	1.000	44	85	1	0	0

TAMPA TARPONS　　　　HIGH CLASS A
FLORIDA STATE LEAGUE

Batting	B-T	HT	WT	DOB	AVG	vLH	vRH	G	AB	R	H	2B	3B	HR	RBI	BB	HBP	SH	SF	SO	SB	CS	SLG	OBP
Aguilar, Angel	R-R	6-0	170	6-13-95	.232	.333	.207	33	108	13	25	5	0	2	13	4	1	1	3	25	4	0	.333	.259
Andujar, Miguel	R-R	6-0	215	3-2-95	.300	--	.300	3	10	1	3	0	0	1	4	0	0	0	0	0	0	0	.600	.300
Burt, Max	R-R	6-2	185	8-28-96	.177	--	.177	12	34	4	6	0	0	1	6	2	1	0	0	13	0	0	.265	.243
Cabrera, Oswaldo	B-R	5-10	145	3-1-99	.260	.282	.255	120	450	55	117	29	0	8	56	33	2	2	6	105	10	8	.378	.310
Carrizales, Omar	L-L	6-0	175	1-30-95	.254	.350	.237	46	138	11	35	7	0	0	14	15	2	1	1	30	2	1	.304	.316
Castillo, Diego	R-R	6-0	170	10-28-97	.248	.217	.253	114	416	52	103	18	2	4	33	33	5	1	1	49	13	3	.329	.310
Crawford, Rashad	L-R	6-3	185	10-15-93	.000	--	.000	1	4	0	0	0	0	0	0	0	0	0	0	1	0	0	.000	.000
Florial, Estevan	L-R	6-1	185	11-25-97	.237	.200	.245	74	274	38	65	10	3	8	38	24	0	1	2	98	9	5	.383	.297
Garcia, Dermis	R-R	6-3	200	1-7-98	.247	.212	.256	75	271	35	67	15	0	17	54	19	2	0	5	105	4	2	.491	.296
Garcia, Wilkerman	B-R	6-0	176	4-1-98	.271	.105	.294	43	155	17	42	4	1	0	15	5	1	1	3	37	5	2	.310	.293
Gasper, Mickey	B-R	5-10	205	10-11-95	.321	.400	.309	23	78	10	25	5	0	2	11	7	3	0	1	16	2	0	.462	.393
Gilliam, Isiah	B-R	6-3	215	7-23-96	.269	.267	.270	70	249	36	67	15	0	8	28	29	3	0	0	93	13	6	.426	.352
Gray, Kyle	L-R	5-10	175	3-25-97	.217	.150	.234	31	97	7	21	5	0	0	8	11	1	0	0	21	2	0	.268	.303
Gregorius, Didi	L-R	6-3	205	2-18-90	.286	--	.286	2	7	1	2	0	0	1	1	0	0	0	0	2	0	0	.714	.375
Hess, Chris	R-R	6-2	195	12-3-94	.196	.111	.216	14	46	2	9	2	0	0	2	3	2	0	0	14	0	1	.239	.275
Hicks, Aaron	R-R	6-1	202	10-2-89	.000	--	.000	3	11	0	0	0	0	0	0	1	0	0	0	3	0	0	.000	.083
Hill, Tyler	R-R	6-0	195	3-4-96	.242	.280	.234	51	149	22	36	3	0	5	20	12	4	0	1	31	4	6	.362	.313
Lopez, Jason	R-R	5-10	160	3-16-98	.209	.177	.215	71	220	28	46	14	0	4	25	20	2	0	4	59	2	1	.327	.276
Martinez, Jose	R-R	6-0	198	1-28-99	.167	.000	.250	3	12	1	2	0	0	1	2	0	0	0	0	7	0	0	.167	.167
Mateo, Welfrin	R-R	5-10	170	9-8-95	.200	.333	.175	31	95	7	19	3	1	2	9	3	0	1	1	23	1	2	.316	.222
Metzgar, David	R-R	5-8	170	12-10-94	.230	.273	.224	27	87	8	20	2	0	1	5	4	0	1	0	11	0	0	.287	.261
Molina, Leonardo	R-R	6-2	180	7-31-97	.237	.278	.231	42	135	21	32	7	0	2	17	8	1	1	1	38	1	2	.333	.283
Mota, Sandy	R-R	6-0	170	9-25-96	.000	.000	.000	3	3	1	0	0	0	0	0	0	0	0	0	0	0	0	.000	.000
Munoz, Deivi	B-R	5-8	153	11-30-99	.172	.000	.238	12	29	4	5	0	0	0	0	2	0	0	0	5	0	1	.172	.226
Olivares, Pablo	R-R	6-0	160	1-27-98	.250	.207	.257	117	396	60	99	15	2	1	31	47	20	0	1	66	20	13	.306	.358
Palma, Alexander	R-R	6-0	201	10-18-95	.260	.500	.234	30	104	15	27	3	0	6	23	8	1	0	2	23	2	0	.462	.313
Pita, Matt	R-R	5-10	175	4-21-97	.163	.385	.123	25	86	7	14	5	1	0	4	2	2	1	0	21	3	1	.244	.200
Rijo, Wendell	R-R	5-11	170	9-4-95	.360	.000	.375	9	25	1	9	3	0	0	4	4	0	0	1	8	0	1	.480	.433
Rosario, Hemmanuel	R-R	6-2	200	8-21-00	.143	--	.143	2	7	1	1	0	0	0	0	0	0	0	0	3	0	0	.143	.143
Sands, Donny	R-R	6-2	190	5-16-96	.221	.200	.225	68	226	18	50	12	1	2	22	18	2	0	1	51	0	1	.310	.283
Sensley, Steven	L-L	6-1	220	9-6-95	.207	.135	.219	110	367	50	76	15	0	13	38	34	9	0	1	117	9	6	.354	.286
Stanton, Giancarlo	R-R	6-6	245	11-8-89	.500	.333	.571	3	10	4	5	0	0	4	5	0	0	0	3	0	0	1	1.500	.500
Tulowitzki, Troy	R-R	6-3	205	10-10-84	.500	--	.500	2	4	2	2	0	0	1	2	0	1	0	0	0	0	0	1.250	.600

Pitching	B-T	HT	WT	DOB	W	L	ERA	G	GS	CG	SV	IP	H	R	ER	HR	BB	SO	AVG	vLH	vRH	K/9	BB/9
Barclay, Edgar	L-L	5-10	200	5-25-98	0	0	3.86	2	0	0	0	5	3	2	2	0	3	5	.177	.143	.200	9.64	5.79
Barrios, Wilser	R-R	6-2	160	3-21-98	0	0	3.00	1	0	0	0	3	2	1	1	0	1	1	.182	.000	.500	3.00	3.00
Bellatti, Andrew	R-R	6-1	190	8-5-91	1	0	6.43	4	0	0	0	7	7	5	5	0	3	3	.259	.182	.313	10.29	3.86
Bies, Daniel	R-R	6-9	245	4-9-96	1	1	5.03	6	2	0	1	20	22	15	11	1	12	24	.282	.341	.206	10.98	5.49
Blanton, Bryan	R-R	6-0	190	12-19-95	0	0	3.24	4	0	0	1	8	5	3	3	0	4	8	.179	.143	.214	8.64	4.32
Bristo, Braden	R-R	6-0	180	11-1-94	3	1	1.94	24	0	0	1	42	28	11	9	3	11	57	.199	.206	.192	12.31	2.38
Cordero, Diego	R-R	5-11	216	10-21-99	1	0	0.00	1	0	0	0	3	0	0	0	0	0	3	.000	.000	.000	9.00	0.00
Diaz, Deivi	L-L	5-10	197	6-9-99	0	0	0.00	1	0	0	0	4	3	1	0	0	2	6	.214	.286	.143	12.46	4.15
Diaz, Wellington	R-R	6-4	190	4-25-97	0	0	2.35	2	0	0	0	8	4	2	2	0	5	4	.167	.222	.133	4.70	5.87
Frawley, Matt	R-R	6-1	195	8-8-95	1	0	5.40	3	0	0	1	5	3	3	3	0	1	4	.167	.000	.429	7.20	1.80
Garcia, Deivi	R-R	5-9	163	5-19-99	0	2	3.06	4	4	0	0	18	14	10	6	0	8	33	.215	.115	.282	16.81	4.08
Garcia, Rony	R-R	6-3	200	12-19-97	0	2	2.16	5	4	0	0	25	21	7	6	2	7	25	.231	.233	.229	9.00	2.52
Gasper, Mickey	B-R	5-10	205	10-11-95	0	0	0.00	2	0	0	0	2	0	0	0	0	3	0	.000	.000	.333	0.00	13.50
German, Frank	R-R	6-2	190	9-22-97	4	4	3.79	16	15	0	0	76	70	35	32	9	30	82	.248	.200	.293	9.71	4.14
Gil, Luis	R-R	6-3	176	6-3-98	1	0	4.85	3	3	0	0	13	11	7	7	0	8	11	.234	.200	.250	7.62	5.54
Gomez, Carlos	R-R	6-1	175	6-14-98	0	0	4.50	1	1	0	0	4	4	5	2	0	3	3	.286	.286	.286	6.75	6.75

NEW YORK YANKEES

Name	B-T	HT	WT	DOB	W	L	ERA	G	GS	CG	SV	IP	H	R	ER	HR	BB	SO	AVG	vLH	vRH	K/9	BB/9
Harris, Hobie	R-R	6-3	200	6-23-93	3	4	4.62	29	0	0	1	49	35	31	25	5	29	59	.198	.241	.160	10.91	5.36
Heller, Ben	R-R	6-3	205	8-5-91	0	0	0.00	2	2	0	0	3	3	0	0	0	1	2	.273	.167	.400	6.75	3.38
Jennings, Dan	L-L	6-3	215	4-17-87	0	0	1.80	2	2	0	0	5	3	1	1	0	0	6	.167	.000	.231	10.80	0.00
Junk, Janson	R-R	6-1	177	1-15-96	4	6	5.24	20	12	1	0	81	94	53	47	8	37	76	.282	.267	.294	8.48	4.13
Kriske, Brooks	R-R	6-3	190	2-3-94	1	1	0.00	7	0	0	1	12	4	1	0	0	5	16	.111	.067	.143	12.00	3.75
Lail, Brady	R-R	6-2	205	8-9-93	0	0	6.75	1	0	0	0	3	5	3	2	1	0	3	.357	.250	.400	10.13	0.00
Lane, Trevor	L-L	5-11	185	4-26-94	1	0	0.00	1	0	0	0	2	0	0	0	0	0	3	.000	.000	.000	13.50	0.00
Lehnen, Dalton	L-L	6-3	222	5-16-96	2	4	4.98	11	0	0	0	34	33	21	19	1	20	26	.252	.216	.266	6.82	5.24
Maciejewski, Josh	R-L	6-3	175	8-14-95	0	1	1.80	2	2	0	0	10	6	5	2	0	3	11	.162	.167	.160	9.90	2.70
McGarity, Aaron	R-R	6-3	185	1-31-95	0	1	5.40	4	0	0	0	5	9	3	3	1	2	8	.391	.500	.308	14.40	3.50
Medina, Luis	R-R	6-1	175	5-3-99	0	0	0.84	2	2	0	0	11	7	5	1	0	3	12	.175	.182	.167	10.13	2.53
Montgomery, Jordan	L-L	6-6	225	12-27-92	0	0	0.00	1	1	0	0	2	0	0	0	0	0	2	.000	.000	.000	9.00	0.00
Nelson, Nick	R-R	6-1	195	12-5-95	0	0	0.00	1	1	0	0	4	4	0	0	0	1	7	.286	.400	.222	17.18	2.45
Orozco, Jio	R-R	6-1	210	8-15-97	3	2	3.45	9	9	0	0	44	50	22	17	2	16	42	.283	.267	.294	8.53	3.25
Otto, Glenn	R-R	6-3	240	3-11-96	3	3	3.20	14	12	0	0	56	54	24	20	1	33	68	.258	.245	.270	10.86	5.27
Reeves, James	R-L	6-3	220	6-7-93	0	0	2.25	6	0	0	0	12	6	3	3	0	5	21	.150	.067	.205	10.13	3.75
Sabathia, CC	L-L	6-6	300	7-21-80	0	0	1.93	1	1	0	0	5	1	1	1	0	1	6	.067	.167	.000	11.57	1.93
Schmidt, Clarke	R-R	6-1	200	2-20-96	4	5	3.84	13	12	0	0	63	59	35	27	2	24	69	.247	.244	.250	9.81	3.41
Sears, JP	R-L	5-11	180	2-19-96	4	4	4.07	13	6	0	1	49	41	23	22	3	16	45	.233	.302	.203	8.32	2.96
Semple, Shawn	R-R	6-1	220	10-9-95	1	4	4.32	13	13	0	0	67	74	38	32	5	21	53	.282	.303	.262	7.16	2.84
Severino, Anderson	L-L	5-10	165	9-17-94	3	3	4.94	15	0	0	0	27	28	22	15	3	19	30	.250	.188	.275	9.88	6.26
Stephan, Trevor	R-R	6-5	225	11-25-95	2	3	4.01	8	7	1	0	34	35	17	15	2	5	34	.271	.333	.235	9.09	1.34
Valdez, Jefry	R-R	6-1	175	8-20-95	2	3	6.98	13	1	0	1	30	40	24	23	1	14	22	.333	.333	.333	6.67	4.25
Vizcaino, Alexander	R-R	6-2	160	5-22-97	1	1	4.28	5	5	0	0	27	33	14	13	2	11	27	.320	.406	.282	8.89	3.62
Weissert, Greg	R-R	6-2	215	2-4-95	2	2	5.27	25	0	0	3	41	36	29	24	3	22	49	.234	.176	.288	10.76	4.83
Wivinis, Matt	R-R	6-0	170	7-24-93	2	4	2.50	31	0	0	9	40	30	20	11	2	18	43	.206	.164	.247	9.76	4.08
Yajure, Miguel	R-R	6-1	175	5-1-98	8	6	2.26	22	18	1	0	128	110	47	32	5	28	122	.233	.254	.216	8.60	1.97
Zurak, Kyle	R-R	6-1	208	11-28-94	6	4	2.93	41	0	0	8	61	49	27	20	2	24	50	.221	.229	.214	7.34	3.52

Fielding

Catcher	PCT	G	PO	A	E	DP	PB
Gasper	.909	2	10	0	1	0	0
Lopez	.982	71	547	58	11	6	6
Rosario	1.000	2	18	0	0	0	0
Sands	.986	67	598	58	9	6	9

First Base	PCT	G	PO	A	E	DP
Aguilar	1.000	1	4	0	0	0
Burt	1.000	1	5	0	0	1
Garcia	.993	54	392	27	3	34
Gasper	.974	12	69	6	2	12
Gray	.989	11	82	5	1	9
Hess	1.000	1	8	0	0	0
Martinez	1.000	1	1	0	0	0
Metzgar	.875	7	7	0	1	0
Mota	1.000	1	5	1	0	0
Sands	1.000	1	7	0	0	4
Sensley	.988	59	378	36	5	44

Second Base	PCT	G	PO	A	E	DP
Cabrera	.968	50	76	135	7	33
Castillo	.938	18	27	48	5	12
Garcia	.980	11	19	30	1	6

	PCT	G	PO	A	E	DP
Gray	.979	12	21	26	1	10
Hess	1.000	5	8	9	0	0
Mateo	.963	9	20	32	2	9
Metzgar	.984	18	26	34	1	9
Munoz	1.000	6	3	15	0	1
Pita	1.000	4	8	8	0	4
Rijo	.952	5	9	11	1	2

Third Base	PCT	G	PO	A	E	DP
Aguilar	.886	24	12	27	5	3
Andujar	.600	2	1	2	2	0
Burt	1.000	9	5	13	0	2
Cabrera	.911	43	33	69	10	10
Garcia	.953	21	12	29	2	3
Gray	.846	9	3	8	2	1
Hess	.950	7	3	16	1	1
Martinez	1.000	3	1	2	0	0
Mateo	.971	16	16	18	1	1
Metzgar	.875	7	3	11	2	0
Munoz	1.000	3	1	1	0	0
Rijo	.625	2	2	3	3	0

Shortstop	PCT	G	PO	A	E	DP
Aguilar	1.000	8	7	0	1	

	PCT	G	PO	A	E	DP
Burt	1.000	2	4	7	0	2
Cabrera	.915	21	36	50	8	13
Castillo	.941	94	130	223	22	54
Garcia	.889	9	14	18	4	5
Gregorius	1.000	1	1	5	0	3
Mateo	1.000	3	9	8	0	3
Munoz	1.000	3	0	5	0	0
Tulowitzki	.000	1	0	0	0	0

Outfield	PCT	G	PO	A	E	DP
Burt	1.000	1	3	0	0	0
Carrizales	.974	42	74	2	2	1
Crawford	1.000	1	4	0	0	0
Florial	.973	64	138	4	4	3
Gilliam	.964	57	98	8	4	4
Hicks	1.000	2	1	0	0	0
Hill	.952	42	56	3	3	0
Mateo	1.000	2	1	0	0	0
Molina	1.000	38	62	2	0	1
Olivares	.981	108	202	9	4	4
Palma	1.000	13	18	0	0	0
Pita	1.000	20	28	2	0	0
Sensley	.956	27	42	1	2	0
Stanton	.000	2	0	0	0	0

CHARLESTON RIVERDOGS

LOW CLASS A

SOUTH ATLANTIC LEAGUE

Batting	B-T	HT	WT	DOB	AVG	vLH	vRH	G	AB	R	H	2B	3B	HR	RBI	BB	HBP	SH	SF	SO	SB	CS	SLG	OBP
Breaux, Josh	R-R	6-1	220	10-7-97	.271	.250	.279	51	199	28	54	10	0	13	49	15	1	0	1	59	0	0	.518	.324
Burt, Max	R-R	6-2	185	8-28-96	.220	.227	.217	70	255	32	56	4	1	7	27	9	10	1	4	72	5	4	.326	.270
Carrizales, Omar	L-L	6-0	175	1-30-95	.180	.182	.179	11	39	1	7	1	1	0	4	2	0	0		12	1	0	.256	.200
Cuevas, Frederick	L-L	5-11	185	10-27-97	.226	.154	.251	72	252	28	57	19	1	1	24	18	1	8	2	64	3	2	.321	.278
Dunn, Oliver	L-R	5-10	185	9-2-97	.220	.217	.221	37	118	13	26	5	0	1	11	19	1	1	1	35	3	5	.288	.331
Garcia, Wilkerman	B-R	6-0	176	4-1-98	.268	.294	.262	19	82	13	22	6	0	3	13	2	1	0	1	20	3	1	.451	.291
Gasper, Mickey	B-R	5-10	205	10-11-95	.233	.163	.260	84	288	34	67	17	0	8	42	44	8	0	3	63	1	0	.375	.347
Gomez, Nelson	R-R	6-1	220	10-8-97	.200	.286	.176	29	95	13	19	4	0	3	13	13	2	0	1	37	1	1	.337	.306
Gray, Kyle	L-R	5-10	175	3-25-97	.237	.158	.264	82	296	47	70	15	6	5	38	37	3	2	2	99	9	5	.378	.325
Lidge, Ryan	B-R	6-2	216	10-27-96	.310	.250	.320	17	58	7	18	3	0	1	6	9	0	0	0	19	0	2	.414	.403
Lockridge, Brandon	R-R	6-1	185	3-14-97	.251	.202	.266	121	498	69	125	33	5	12	56	45	7	2	4	140	22	8	.410	.320
Mateo, Welfrin	R-R	5-10	170	9-8-95	.263	.136	.304	57	179	27	47	16	0	3	18	19	3	0	2	37	4	0	.402	.340
Mota, Sandy	R-R	6-0	170	9-25-96	.263	.286	.250	5	19	3	5	2	0	0	4	0	0	0		8	0	0	.368	.263
Navas, Eduardo	L-R	5-10	180	4-5-96	.160	.148	.164	64	188	21	30	4	0	2	16	19	7	1		65	0	0	.213	.261
Pasteur, Isaiah	R-R	6-2	182	6-19-96	.152	.091	.171	13	46	8	7	0	1	1	4	4	2	0	0	24	5	2	.261	.250
Peraza, Oswald	R-R	6-0	176	6-15-00	.273	.217	.292	46	183	31	50	5	0	2	13	16	6	1	2	28	18	5	.333	.348

Name	B-T	HT	WT	DOB	AVG	vLH	vRH	G	AB	R	H	2B	3B	HR	RBI	BB	HBP	SH	SF	SO	SB	CS	OBP	SLG
Pita, Matt	R-R	5-10	175	4-21-97	.210	.200	.216	26	81	10	17	6	1	0	8	4	5	0	1	20	2	2	.309	.286
Robinson, Mitchell	R-R	6-3	200	3-17-96	.155	.143	.157	16	58	8	9	1	0	1	3	7	0	0	0	24	0	1	.224	.246
Sanchez, Gary	R-R	6-2	230	12-2-92	.000	--	.000	1	3	0	0	0	0	0	0	0	0	0	0	0	0	0	.000	.000
Seigler, Anthony	B-B	6-0	200	6-20-99	.175	.130	.189	30	97	10	17	3	0	0	6	20	2	1	0	28	1	0	.206	.328
Smith, Canaan	L-R	6-0	215	4-30-99	.307	.241	.329	124	449	67	138	32	3	11	74	74	2	0	3	108	16	4	.466	.405
Soto, Junior	R-R	6-3	175	1-21-97	.083	.100	.077	11	36	1	3	0	0	1	3	0	0	0	1	15	0	0	.167	.081
Stowers, Josh	R-R	6-0	200	2-25-97	.273	.217	.288	105	385	61	105	24	2	7	40	64	8	2	1	123	35	16	.400	.387
Surum, Ricky	R-R	5-10	170	12-7-94	.220	.429	.177	15	41	5	9	3	0	0	6	5	0	0	2	19	2	1	.293	.292
Torrealba, Eduardo	R-R	5-8	140	3-26-99	.241	.254	.237	97	324	47	78	14	0	1	27	28	9	6	3	75	3	4	.293	.316
Wagaman, Eric	R-R	6-4	210	8-14-97	.234	.203	.243	82	304	22	71	13	0	7	38	26	0	0	2	87	4	6	.345	.292

Pitching

Name	B-T	HT	WT	DOB	W	L	ERA	G	GS	CG	SV	IP	H	R	ER	HR	BB	SO	AVG	vLH	vRH	K/9	BB/9
Bies, Daniel	R-R	6-9	245	4-9-96	2	2	2.86	17	6	0	4	69	58	26	22	2	18	78	.225	.266	.193	10.13	2.34
Blanton, Bryan	R-R	6-0	190	12-19-95	1	1	7.11	3	0	0	1	6	7	6	5	0	1	8	.259	.333	.200	11.37	1.42
Brito, Jhony	R-R	6-2	160	2-17-98	6	4	3.58	22	9	0	2	101	91	50	40	5	14	79	.240	.281	.212	7.06	1.25
Burt, Max	R-R	6-2	185	8-28-96	0	0	6.75	1	0	0	0	1	2	1	1	0	0	0	.333	.333	.333	0.00	0.00
Contreras, Roansy	R-R	6-0	175	11-7-99	12	5	3.33	24	24	0	0	132	105	55	49	10	36	113	.215	.205	.223	7.69	2.45
Cordero, Diego	R-R	5-11	216	10-21-99	1	0	5.40	1	1	0	0	5	5	5	3	0	1	3	.294	.200	.333	5.40	1.80
Cortijo, Harold	R-R	6-2	180	9-29-98	5	4	3.45	14	14	0	0	73	67	33	28	9	30	57	.239	.216	.256	7.03	3.70
Curtis, Keegan	R-R	6-0	175	9-30-95	3	1	1.56	8	0	0	2	17	11	4	3	0	7	17	.175	.077	.243	8.83	3.63
De La Cruz, Adonis	R-R	6-2	170	12-20-94	1	0	0.00	3	0	0	0	3	1	0	0	0	0	4	.091	.125	.000	10.80	0.00
Diaz, Wellington	R-R	6-4	190	4-25-97	3	1	4.35	7	0	0	0	21	23	12	10	3	12	19	.284	.243	.318	8.27	5.23
Espinal, Carlos	R-R	5-11	175	10-21-96	1	2	2.41	29	0	0	5	60	45	21	16	2	16	75	.205	.206	.203	11.31	2.41
Espinola, Pedro	R-R	6-4	207	2-1-96	0	0	0.00	1	0	0	0	3	0	0	0	0	0	4	.000	.000	.000	12.00	0.00
Gil, Luis	R-R	6-3	176	6-3-98	4	5	2.39	17	17	0	0	83	60	29	22	1	39	112	.205	.215	.186	12.14	4.23
Gomez, Yoendrys	R-R	6-3	175	10-15-99	0	3	6.08	6	6	0	0	27	28	19	18	2	9	25	.272	.250	.282	8.44	3.04
Hardy, Tim	L-L	6-7	250	3-1-96	2	0	3.24	9	0	0	2	25	17	10	9	2	9	26	.198	.200	.197	9.36	3.24
Higgins, Dalton	R-R	6-1	185	8-8-95	1	0	1.59	9	0	0	0	17	14	3	3	0	0	23	.230	.269	.200	12.18	0.00
Hutchison, Rodney	R-R	6-5	225	8-9-96	0	1	11.81	5	0	0	1	16	17	22	21	3	15	14	.274	.200	.324	7.88	8.44
Lehnen, Dalton	L-L	6-3	222	5-16-96	4	3	2.87	15	0	0	3	38	24	13	12	5	18	44	.181	.219	.168	10.51	4.30
Maciejewski, Josh	R-L	6-3	175	8-14-95	2	1	1.35	3	3	0	0	20	11	3	3	0	5	9	.175	.167	.178	4.05	2.25
Marinaccio, Ron	R-R	6-2	205	7-1-95	0	0	4.18	18	0	0	4	32	23	18	15	0	18	40	.200	.226	.177	11.13	5.01
Martinez, Nolan	R-R	6-2	165	6-30-98	1	2	3.86	7	6	0	1	33	27	17	14	1	9	21	.235	.254	.214	5.79	2.48
Mauricio, Alex	R-R	6-0	180	9-24-96	0	1	47.25	1	0	0	0	1	5	7	7	2	2	2	.556	.600	.500	13.50	13.50
McGarity, Aaron	R-R	6-3	185	1-31-95	2	5	3.19	19	0	0	2	31	28	15	11	1	9	34	.246	.294	.206	9.87	2.61
Medina, Luis	R-R	6-1	175	5-3-99	1	8	6.00	20	20	0	0	93	86	65	62	9	67	115	.248	.199	.284	11.13	6.48
Munoz, Anderson	R-R	5-8	158	8-4-98	1	1	6.14	6	0	0	0	22	20	17	15	2	14	31	.235	.227	.244	12.68	5.73
Myatt, Tanner	R-R	6-7	220	5-24-98	3	3	4.24	19	3	0	3	40	21	20	19	0	45	40	.157	.170	.147	8.93	10.04
Orozco, Jio	R-R	6-1	210	8-15-97	4	2	2.81	9	7	0	0	51	40	18	16	3	12	38	.217	.185	.243	6.66	2.10
Ramos, Daniel	R-R	5-10	169	3-6-95	1	0	0.90	6	0	0	0	10	6	1	1	1	2	7	.167	.177	.158	6.30	1.80
Ruegger, Charlie	R-R	6-6	218	7-14-97	3	3	7.86	11	5	0	1	45	58	44	39	6	14	30	.310	.269	.333	6.04	2.82
Sauer, Matt	R-R	6-4	195	1-21-99	0	1	2.08	2	2	0	0	9	6	3	2	0	6	8	.188	.417	.050	8.31	6.23
Semple, Shawn	R-R	6-1	220	10-9-95	2	0	1.71	5	0	0	3	21	9	4	4	1	2	32	.127	.120	.130	13.71	0.86
Valdez, Jefry	R-R	6-1	165	8-20-95	2	2	2.81	16	0	0	2	32	22	14	10	0	8	30	.202	.240	.170	8.44	2.25
Vizcaino, Alexander	R-R	6-2	160	5-22-97	5	5	4.41	16	16	1	0	88	80	47	43	6	27	101	.242	.278	.207	10.37	2.77

Fielding

Catcher	PCT	G	PO	A	E	DP	PB
Breaux	.995	22	208	12	1		2
Gasper	.980	27	224	21	5	1	8
Lidge	.994	16	137	17	1	0	4
Navas	.991	61	506	52	5	7	6
Sanchez	1.000	5	1	0	0		2
Seigler	.984	23	161	19	3	1	3

First Base	PCT	G	PO	A	E	DP
Burt	1.000	16	107	9	0	9
Gasper	.975	36	286	31	8	28
Mota	1.000	1	7	0	0	0
Navas	1.000	2	11	1	0	0
Robinson	.986	16	138	7	2	6
Wagaman	.989	72	574	38	7	35

Second Base	PCT	G	PO	A	E	DP
Burt	1.000	2	3	4	0	0
Dunn	.956	17	21	44	3	7
Garcia	.857	3	3	3	1	0
Gray	.977	75	81	169	6	32
Mateo	1.000	4	11	9	0	5
Pita	.875	4	4	10	2	1
Surum	1.000	4	7	10	0	0
Torrealba	.984	32	46	79	2	10

Third Base	PCT	G	PO	A	E	DP
Burt	.942	40	25	73	6	11
Dunn	.911	16	4	37	4	1
Garcia	.870	8	3	17	3	0
Gomez	.791	26	15	38	14	2
Gray	.889	2	2	6	1	0
Mateo	.954	36	26	77	5	3
Mota	.800	4	4	8	3	0
Pita	.800	5	6	6	3	0
Surum	.833	9	6	19	5	1

Shortstop	PCT	G	PO	A	E	DP
Burt	.954	15	23	39	3	9
Dunn	1.000	1	0	3	0	0
Garcia	.889	7	8	16	3	3
Mateo	.955	6	7	14	1	5
Peraza	.973	44	71	112	5	13
Surum	.900	3	1	8	1	2
Torrealba	.971	65	99	138	7	29

Outfield	PCT	G	PO	A	E	DP
Carrizales	1.000	8	9	0	0	0
Cuevas	.976	60	79	4	2	1
Gray	1.000	4	5	0	0	0
Lockridge	.989	118	254	11	3	4
Mateo	.000	2	0	0	0	0
Pasteur	.933	11	14	0	1	0
Pita	.952	13	19	1	1	0
Smith	.972	100	164	8	5	2
Soto	1.000	11	20	4	0	0
Stowers	.990	97	192	2	2	1

Batting	B-T	HT	WT	DOB	AVG	vLH	vRH	G	AB	R	H	2B	3B	HR	RBI	BB	HBP	SH	SF	SO	SB	CS	SLG	OBP
Alexander, Evan	L-L	6-2	175	2-26-98	.193	.308	.165	48	135	20	26	4	2	0	9	22	1	0	1	50	4	5	.252	.308
Alvarez, Nelson B	L-L	6-3	210	3-10-96	.149	.111	.154	26	74	7	11	3	0	2	7	12	1	0	1	33	1	1	.270	.273
Bastidas, Jesus	R-R	5-10	145	9-14-98	.188	.250	.167	5	16	2	3	0	0	0	2	2	0	0	0	0	0	0	.188	.278
Chaparro, Andres	R-R	6-1	200	5-4-99	.246	.180	.264	57	187	22	46	7	0	3	22	29	8	0	3	39	0	0	.332	.366
De Leon, Juan	R-R	6-2	185	9-13-97	.213	.121	.235	51	169	16	36	8	0	5	14	18	6	0	1	78	2	2	.349	.309
DeMarco, Pat	R-R	5-9	192	3-10-98	.120	.091	.124	28	100	12	12	3	0	3	12	6	1	0	2	40	2	1	.240	.174
Duran, Ezequiel	R-R	5-11	185	5-22-99	.256	.273	.253	66	246	49	63	12	4	13	37	25	3	0	3	77	11	4	.496	.329
Flames, Miguel	R-R	6-2	210	9-14-97	.177	.000	.188	5	17	2	3	0	0	1	5	2	0	0	0	4	0	0	.353	.263
Gallardo, Carlos	R-R	5-10	160	1-26-97	.167	.273	.143	24	60	6	10	3	0	0	4	9	0	0	0	25	0	0	.217	.275
Henson, Spencer	R-R	6-2	235	11-3-97	.222	.333	.182	14	45	7	10	3	0	2	8	9	1	0	0	12	0	0	.422	.364
Illig, Chase	B-R	6-0	210	9-14-96	.241	.250	.240	10	29	1	7	3	0	0	1	6	0	0	1	12	0	1	.345	.361
Junior, Alex	L-L	5-10	188	5-28-96	.250	.200	.269	14	36	4	9	1	0	1	3	4	0	0	1	15	1	0	.361	.317
Lidge, Ryan	B-R	6-2	216	10-27-94	.300	.000	.429	3	10	1	3	0	0	0	1	1	0	0	0	0	0	0	.300	.364
Mendez, Borinquen	B-R	5-11	165	2-1-98	.154	.500	.000	5	13	1	2	0	1	0	3	0	0	1	0	5	0	0	.308	.154
Metzgar, David	R-R	5-8	170	12-10-94	.357	.524	.312	29	98	16	35	4	1	0	8	13	0	0	2	21	2	0	.418	.432
Molina, Leonardo	R-R	6-2	180	7-31-97	.140	.125	.143	12	43	3	6	2	1	0	8	6	0	0	0	13	0	1	.233	.245
Narvaez, Carlos	R-R	6-0	190	11-26-98	.265	.385	.240	43	147	17	39	6	0	1	13	17	3	1	2	21	1	0	.327	.349
Pasteur, Isaiah	R-R	6-2	182	6-19-96	.198	.200	.197	37	81	19	16	5	1	2	14	17	2	0	2	42	10	0	.358	.343
Peraza, Oswald	R-R	6-0	176	6-15-00	.241	.143	.276	19	79	7	19	1	1	2	7	5	1	0	0	9	5	2	.354	.294
Pereira, Everson	R-R	6-0	191	4-10-01	.171	.063	.204	18	70	9	12	3	0	1	3	4	0	0	0	26	3	0	.257	.216
Pita, Matt	R-R	5-10	175	4-21-97	.232	.316	.213	35	99	13	23	3	0	3	16	14	2	0	0	23	2	0	.354	.339
Robinson, Mitchell	R-R	6-3	200	3-17-96	.162	.136	.169	30	99	11	16	5	0	2	13	15	0	0	0	38	0	0	.273	.272
Saez, Jorge	R-R	5-10	200	8-28-90	.214	.000	.273	4	14	0	3	0	0	0	1	1	0	0	0	2	0	0	.214	.267
Sanford, Jacob	L-R	6-2	215	10-24-97	.238	.204	.247	60	231	27	55	13	3	7	27	14	3	0	1	81	3	3	.411	.289
Santos, Luis	R-R	5-8	160	1-4-00	.221	.261	.206	30	86	12	19	0	1	1	5	11	2	0	0	19	5	4	.279	.323
Seitz, Jerry	R-R	5-10	180	9-27-94	.214	.333	.188	28	84	3	18	4	0	0	9	4	0	1	1	17	0	0	.262	.247
Smith, Josh	L-R	5-10	172	8-7-97	.324	.235	.340	33	111	17	36	6	1	3	15	25	2	1	2	17	6	3	.478	.450
Surum, Ricky	R-R	5-10	170	12-7-94	.056	.000	.063	7	18	4	1	0	0	0	3	2	0	2	2	7	1	0	.056	.136
Villa, Jose	R-R	6-1	170	11-16-98	.191	.125	.231	6	21	0	4	0	0	0	1	0	0	0	0	6	0	0	.191	.191

Pitching	B-T	HT	WT	DOB	W	L	ERA	G	GS	CG	SV	IP	H	R	ER	HR	BB	SO	AVG	vLH	vRH	K/9	BB/9
Agnos, Jake	L-L	5-11	207	5-23-98	1	1	4.50	4	3	0	0	10	12	5	5	0	3	9	.279	.231	.300	8.10	2.70
Bertsch, Jackson	L-R	6-3	225	2-14-95	0	0	2.00	5	0	0	0	9	6	2	2	1	3	11	.188	.250	.125	11.00	3.00
Blanton, Bryan	R-R	6-0	190	12-19-95	1	1	1.99	19	0	0	0	32	16	7	7	3	15	51	.148	.125	.158	14.49	4.26
Boyle, Sean	R-R	6-1	205	10-29-96	0	0	6.97	5	0	0	1	10	12	9	8	2	0	11	.286	.357	.250	9.58	0.00
Brothers, Rex	L-L	6-0	205	12-18-87	0	0	0.00	2	2	0	0	3	1	0	0	0	1	7	.091	.000	.125	21.00	3.00
Brown, Blakely	R-R	6-0	165	8-20-96	3	2	2.98	11	9	0	0	51	33	20	17	3	22	55	.185	.192	.181	9.64	3.86
Correa, Nelvin	R-R	6-1	170	1-25-97	2	2	1.91	5	5	1	0	28	23	8	6	0	8	26	.215	.240	.193	8.26	2.54
Craft, Derek	R-R	6-8	220	7-11-96	1	1	4.26	13	0	0	1	19	16	10	9	2	7	23	.235	.296	.195	10.89	3.32
Curtis, Keegan	R-R	6-0	175	9-30-95	0	0	1.20	8	0	0	2	15	7	2	2	0	3	20	.146	.077	.171	12.00	1.80
Diaz, Wellington	R-R	6-4	190	4-25-97	3	5	6.17	12	7	0	0	42	44	33	29	5	24	46	.270	.242	.287	9.78	5.10
Ernst, Nick	R-R	6-3	195	8-27-96	0	3	5.70	13	5	0	0	30	32	20	19	1	6	32	.271	.417	.207	9.60	1.80
Evey, Marcus	R-R	5-10	175	8-4-97	2	2	4.99	18	0	0	2	31	35	18	17	2	16	28	.287	.289	.286	8.22	4.70
Garcia, Alfredo	L-L	6-2	225	7-22-99	2	2	2.49	5	5	0	0	25	19	10	7	1	7	28	.218	.208	.222	9.95	2.49
Gardner, Austin	R-R	6-2	215	12-2-94	0	3	7.77	11	1	0	0	22	32	22	19	2	6	34	.327	.452	.269	13.91	2.45
Green, Nick	R-R	6-1	175	3-25-95	0	2	4.61	3	3	0	0	14	16	10	7	0	3	12	.286	.222	.316	7.90	1.98
Greene, Zach	R-R	6-1	215	8-29-96	0	0	0.00	2	0	0	0	2	0	0	0	0	0	2	.000	.000	.000	9.00	0.00
Hardy, Tim	L-L	6-7	250	3-1-96	1	0	0.00	7	0	0	1	12	2	0	0	0	0	20	.054	.125	.035	15.00	0.00
Hutchison, Rodney	R-R	6-5	225	8-9-96	0	1	29.25	6	0	0	0	4	7	18	13	1	4	1	.333	.444	.250	2.25	9.00
Keller, Brian	R-R	6-3	210	6-21-94	0	0	0.00	1	1	0	0	6	3	0	0	0	0	4	.143	.143	.143	6.00	0.00
King, Michael	R-R	6-3	210	5-25-95	0	0	0.00	1	1	0	0	4	4	0	0	0	0	4	.308	.600	.125	0.00	0.00
Loseke, Barrett	R-R	6-0	180	11-12-96	3	1	2.96	18	0	0	4	27	19	12	9	2	7	32	.186	.180	.191	10.54	2.30
Maciejewski, Josh	R-L	6-3	175	8-14-95	2	2	2.01	6	5	0	0	31	17	10	7	3	7	23	.159	.133	.169	6.61	2.01
McGarity, Aaron	R-R	6-3	185	1-31-95	4	0	0.83	12	0	0	1	22	10	2	2	0	1	27	.133	.138	.130	11.22	0.42
Mejias, Alex	R-R	5-11	185	11-26-96	2	1	4.63	7	5	0	0	23	24	12	12	2	11	20	.261	.342	.204	7.71	4.24
Munoz, Anderson	R-R	5-8	158	8-4-98	7	2	2.60	13	10	0	0	62	46	21	18	1	23	63	.204	.227	.190	9.10	3.32
Ort, Kaleb	R-R	6-4	240	2-5-92	1	0	0.00	2	0	0	0	3	0	0	0	0	1	7	.000	.000	.000	21.00	3.00
Ramos, Daniel	R-R	5-10	169	3-6-95	0	0	1.77	14	0	0	5	20	13	4	4	2	4	21	.176	.182	.171	9.30	1.77
Ruegger, Charlie	R-R	6-6	218	7-14-97	1	0	1.80	3	2	0	0	15	9	4	3	1	1	12	.167	.000	.196	7.20	0.60
Sikkema, T.J.	L-L	6-0	221	7-25-98	0	0	0.84	4	4	0	0	11	6	1	1	0	1	13	.158	.000	.180	10.97	0.84
Villaman, Abismael	L-L	6-2	195	9-27-95	2	2	3.56	12	8	0	0	43	50	25	17	1	13	41	.279	.275	.281	8.58	2.72
Wilson, Justin	R-R	6-0	180	9-9-96	2	3	1.46	17	0	0	2	25	13	6	4	1	12	34	.153	.250	.105	12.41	4.38

Fielding

C: Gallardo 16, Illig 5, Lidge 3, Narvaez 38, Saez 3, Seitz 17. **1B:** Alvarez 25, Chaparro 5, Flames 5, Gallardo 6, Henson 11, Robinson 23, Seitz 6, Villa 5. **2B:** Bastidas 3, Duran 57, Mendez 2, Metzgar 8, Pita 6, Santos 3, Surum 1. **3B:** Chaparro 46, Henson 1, Metzgar 10, Pita 4, Robinson 7, Santos 6, Surum 6, Villa 1. **SS:** Bastidas 2, Mendez 2, Metzgar 9, Peraza 18, Santos 21, Smith 25. **OF:** Alexander 41, De Leon 41, DeMarco 25, Junior 11, Molina 8, Pasteur 25, Pereira 16, Pita 22, Sanford 53.

PULASKI YANKEES
APPALACHIAN LEAGUE
ROOKIE ADVANCED

Batting	B-T	HT	WT	DOB	AVG	vLH	vRH	G	AB	R	H	2B	3B	HR	RBI	BB	HBP	SH	SF	SO	SB	CS	SLG	OBP
Alvarez, Nelson B	L-L	6-3	210	3-10-96	.232	.000	.317	18	56	13	13	1	1	5	12	9	1	0	1	22	1	0	.554	.343
Bastidas, Jesus	R-R	5-10	145	9-14-98	.200	.000	.250	3	10	1	2	1	0	0	0	2	0	0	0	2	0	0	.300	.333
Bell, Chad	L-R	6-3	210	3-4-97	.251	.194	.265	55	191	28	48	5	0	9	41	21	0	1	4	74	1	1	.419	.319
Cabello, Antonio	R-R	5-10	160	11-1-00	.212	.205	.213	56	227	31	48	10	4	3	19	19	3	1	1	77	5	4	.330	.280
Campero, Gustavo	B-R	5-6	182	9-20-97	.293	.211	.309	36	116	14	34	6	1	2	12	13	2	0	0	16	10	2	.414	.374
Chirinos, Roberto	R-R	5-11	172	9-8-00	.256	.293	.247	50	203	37	52	12	0	6	27	8	6	0	0	47	4	2	.404	.304
Dunn, Oliver	L-R	5-10	185	9-2-97	.240	.250	.237	14	50	9	12	2	0	2	11	7	0	0	0	11	3	1	.400	.333
Farrell, Jake	L-R	6-4	215	5-10-96	.209	.286	.195	28	91	19	19	4	0	2	14	11	1	0	2	17	1	3	.319	.295
Garcia, Anthony	B-R	6-5	204	9-5-00	.294	.000	.313	6	17	4	5	2	1	1	8	5	0	0	2	9	0	0	.706	.417
Green, Ryder	R-R	6-0	200	5-5-00	.262	.350	.243	61	225	45	59	15	1	8	28	25	3	0	1	67	10	3	.444	.343
Henson, Spencer	R-R	6-2	235	11-3-97	.297	.200	.333	10	37	6	11	3	1	4	9	6	0	0	0	11	1	0	.757	.395
Javier, Robert	R-R	5-8	173	2-1-99	.177	.067	.203	28	79	13	14	3	2	1	9	10	1	0	1	28	5	0	.304	.275
Martinez, Jose	R-R	6-0	198	1-28-99	.145	.091	.155	20	69	6	10	1	0	3	4	4	2	0	1	30	0	0	.290	.211
McGarry, Matt	R-R	5-10	175	3-24-96	.000	--	.000	2	1	0	0	0	0	0	0	1	0	0	0	1	0	0	.000	.500
Mendez, Borinquen	B-R	5-11	165	2-1-98	.262	.233	.271	40	126	23	33	6	2	0	10	12	0	3	0	22	8	2	.341	.326
Mora, Gabriel	R-R	5-11	155	6-1-00	.135	.111	.143	14	37	0	5	3	0	0	1	2	0	0	1	12	0	0	.216	.175
Munoz, Deivi	B-R	5-8	153	11-30-99	.364	1.000	.222	4	11	3	4	1	1	0	1	1	0	0	0	2	1	0	.636	.417
Pries, Jake	R-R	6-4	226	10-11-96	.205	.258	.188	38	127	14	26	7	0	6	15	9	5	0	0	36	2	1	.402	.284
Santos, Luis	R-R	5-8	160	1-4-00	.229	.111	.256	16	48	10	11	1	0	1	5	3	0	0	1	16	1	3	.313	.269
Santos, Madison	L-R	5-10	165	9-6-99	.203	.067	.226	57	207	29	42	7	3	8	27	20	1	1	0	63	7	3	.382	.276
Tatis, Carlos	R-R	6-5	211	12-19-96	.200	--	.200	2	5	2	1	0	0	0	1	0	0	0	1	0	0	.200	.333
Torres, Saul	R-R	6-2	190	2-19-99	.218	.177	.229	48	165	18	36	9	0	8	32	22	2	0	0	70	1	0	.418	.318
Volpe, Anthony	R-R	5-11	180	4-28-01	.215	.136	.232	34	121	19	26	7	2	2	11	23	3	1	2	38	6	1	.355	.349

Pitching	B-T	HT	WT	DOB	W	L	ERA	G	GS	CG	SV	IP	H	R	ER	HR	BB	SO	AVG	vLH	vRH	K/9	BB/9
Alvarez, Nelson L	R-R	6-4	220	6-11-98	2	1	8.84	13	0	0	1	19	26	20	19	4	9	23	.351	.353	.350	10.71	4.19
Anderson, Reid	R-R	6-0	200	9-6-95	6	1	3.09	11	6	0	0	47	36	17	16	1	17	51	.214	.241	.188	9.84	3.28
Anderson, Ryan	L-L	6-6	205	9-9-98	0	1	4.78	11	8	0	0	32	30	19	17	4	16	43	.248	.222	.263	12.09	4.50
Barrios, Wilser	R-R	6-2	160	3-21-98	0	0	0.00	2	0	0	0	1	1	0	0	0	1	2	.167	.500	.000	13.50	6.75
Bertsch, Jackson	L-R	6-3	225	2-14-95	2	0	4.66	13	0	0	1	19	15	11	10	2	10	28	.200	.267	.156	13.03	4.66
Boyle, Sean	R-R	6-2	205	10-29-96	2	1	1.88	11	0	0	0	29	15	6	6	1	5	32	.153	.234	.078	10.05	1.57
Correa, Nelvin	R-R	6-1	170	1-25-97	5	0	4.04	7	3	0	0	36	32	16	16	6	2	27	.234	.266	.206	6.81	0.50
Craft, Derek	R-R	6-8	220	7-11-96	0	0	0.00	8	0	0	3	11	3	0	0	0	3	16	.083	.067	.095	13.09	2.45
Gomez, Yoendrys	R-R	6-3	175	10-15-99	4	2	2.12	6	6	0	0	30	26	11	7	1	10	28	.243	.195	.273	8.49	3.03
Johnson, Tyler	R-R	6-0	195	7-12-96	3	0	1.04	16	0	0	3	26	15	4	3	1	8	34	.163	.171	.158	11.77	2.77
Mejia, Renso	R-R	5-11	165	3-6-00	0	2	5.14	2	1	0	0	7	8	4	4	0	2	4	.296	.357	.231	5.14	2.57
Mejias, Alex	R-R	5-11	185	11-26-96	0	0	2.51	6	0	0	0	14	14	4	4	0	3	12	.246	.273	.229	7.53	1.88
Milam, Kevin	R-R	6-0	200	2-13-98	1	0	2.57	5	0	0	0	7	7	2	2	0	7	7	.259	.357	.154	9.00	9.00
Montas, Kenlly	R-R	6-0	187	5-31-96	1	1	3.80	9	0	0	0	24	15	11	10	1	17	20	.188	.186	.189	7.61	6.46
Munoz, Jhonatan	R-R	5-10	200	8-10-99	5	3	4.13	11	11	0	0	57	52	34	26	8	18	68	.239	.322	.183	10.80	2.86
Ojeda, Luis	R-R	5-11	180	1-10-97	0	0	8.71	6	0	0	0	10	18	11	10	1	5	9	.409	.400	.417	7.84	4.35
Peguero, Elvis	R-R	6-5	208	3-20-97	2	2	4.19	15	1	0	0	34	39	20	16	4	11	29	.293	.345	.253	7.60	2.88
Pestana, Leonardo	R-R	6-4	198	7-30-98	1	4	7.32	11	11	0	0	39	31	33	32	6	32	52	.214	.215	.213	11.90	7.32
Rodriguez, Carlos D.	R-R	5-10	155	12-13-98	1	0	0.00	1	0	0	0	1	1	0	0	0	1	2	.250	.000	1.000	18.00	9.00
Spence, Mitch	R-R	6-1	185	5-6-98	2	3	3.54	16	0	0	4	28	16	13	11	1	4	29	.163	.140	.182	9.32	1.29
Vasquez, Randy	R-R	6-0	165	11-3-98	4	1	3.29	11	11	0	0	55	36	23	20	6	28	53	.188	.178	.196	8.73	4.61
Voliva, Evan	R-R	5-10	205	6-10-96	0	1	0.96	6	0	0	0	9	3	2	1	0	3	15	.107	.077	.133	14.46	2.89
Waldichuk, Ken	L-L	6-4	220	1-8-98	0	2	3.68	10	10	0	0	29	19	12	12	2	7	49	.181	.148	.192	15.03	2.15
Wesneski, Hayden	R-R	6-3	210	12-5-97	1	1	4.76	18	0	0	3	28	32	21	15	1	6	30	.271	.288	.254	9.53	1.91

Fielding

C: Campero 26, Mora 14, Torres 36. **1B:** Alvarez 17, Farrell 26, Henson 10, Martinez 14, Tatis 2. **2B:** Chirinos 18, Dunn 10, Martinez 1, McGarry 2, Mendez 36, Munoz 4, Santos 3. **3B:** Bell 48, Chirinos 10, Martinez 6, Mendez 2, Santos 3. **SS:** Bastidas 3, Chirinos 24, Dunn 1, Mendez 3, Santos 9, Volpe 33. **OF:** Cabello 43, Farrell 2, Garcia 4, Green 47, Javier 28, Pries 36, Santos 51.

GCL YANKEES EAST
GULF COAST LEAGUE
ROOKIE

Batting	B-T	HT	WT	DOB	AVG	vLH	vRH	G	AB	R	H	2B	3B	HR	RBI	BB	HBP	SH	SF	SO	SB	CS	SLG	OBP
Alcantara, Kevin	R-R	6-6	188	7-12-02	.260	.200	.276	32	123	19	32	5	2	1	13	3	2	0	0	27	3	3	.358	.289
Alvarez, Asdrubal	R-R	6-0	160	10-10-99	.136	.111	.140	22	59	9	8	2	0	0	5	11	2	0	0	14	4	1	.170	.292
Farrell, Jake	L-R	6-4	215	5-10-96	.286	.167	.318	8	28	4	8	2	0	1	4	2	0	0	1	7	0	1	.464	.323
Garcia, Wilkerman	B-R	6-0	176	4-1-98	.500	1.000	.333	2	4	0	2	0	0	0	0	0	0	0	0	0	0	0	.500	.500
2-team total (3 Yankees West)					.357	.286	.429	5	14	3	5	0	0	1	4	2	0	0	1	0	0	0	.571	.438
Gomez, Antonio	R-R	6-2	210	11-13-01	.255	.308	.235	14	47	9	12	4	0	1	7	3	1	0	0	7	0	0	.404	.314
Guerrero, Alex	L-R	6-0	185	3-10-00	.172	.143	.182	27	58	4	10	0	0	0	4	4	2	0	0	21	0	0	.172	.250
Hernandez, Leonel	L-L	5-9	163	2-24-98	.205	.188	.208	33	88	15	18	4	1	1	11	11	3	0	1	20	6	1	.307	.311
Illig, Chase	R-R	6-0	210	9-14-96	.250	.000	.290	14	36	6	9	2	0	1	6	3	0	0	1	10	0	0	.389	.300
Knowles, D'Vaughn	R-R	5-10	161	1-16-01	.179	.200	.172	27	84	10	15	4	0	0	12	6	2	1	1	22	1	0	.226	.247
Marte, Miguel	R-R	5-11	165	5-26-01	.185	.200	.182	20	65	9	12	2	1	0	5	7	0	0	1	14	2	0	.246	.260
Moreno, Raymundo	R-R	6-1	185	3-9-98	.300	.231	.319	25	60	9	18	4	1	0	7	9	1	0	1	12	0	0	.400	.394
Mota, Sandy	R-R	6-0	170	9-25-96	.247	.240	.250	31	89	14	22	3	2	3	12	11	1	0	1	29	6	1	.427	.333

Player	B-T	HT	WT	DOB	AVG	vLH	vRH	G	AB	R	H	2B	3B	HR	RBI	BB	HBP	SH	SF	SO	SB	CS	SLG	OBP
2-team total (1 Yankees West)					.247	.240	.250	32	93	14	23	3	2	3	12	11	1	0	1	29	6	1	.419	.330
Munoz, Deivi	B-R	5-8	153	11-30-99	.667	--	.667	1	3	1	2	0	0	0	0	0	0	0	0	0	1	0	.667	.667
Negueis, Felix	R-R	6-0	200	12-29-00	.143	.000	.167	6	14	0	2	0	0	0	1	3	1	0	0	5	1	0	.143	.333
Palma, Alexander	R-R	6-0	201	10-18-95	.382	.250	.423	10	34	3	13	6	0	0	5	2	0	0	0	5	0	0	.559	.417
2-team total (5 Yankees West)					.431	.500	.410	15	51	8	22	7	0	4	12	2	0	0	0	9	1	0	.804	.453
Paulino, Starlin	R-R	6-1	170	2-24-00	.256	.400	.222	29	78	10	20	6	0	1	13	12	3	0	3	13	2	0	.372	.365
Reynoso, Javier	R-R	6-2	190	7-27-00	.214	.174	.223	38	126	14	27	3	0	1	14	14	5	0	3	48	0	1	.262	.311
Rodriguez, Jhoiner	R-R	5-11	180	9-12-99	.150	.214	.115	19	40	2	6	1	0	0	2	5	0	0	1	12	0	0	.175	.239
Rodriguez, Meure	R-R	6-0	200	5-20-99	.214	.000	.250	11	14	4	3	0	0	1	1	7	0	0	0	5	0	0	.429	.476
Rojas, Angel	R-R	6-0	160	11-26-00	.281	.318	.262	18	64	5	18	3	3	0	6	3	1	0	1	16	1	1	.422	.319
2-team total (23 Yankees West)					.241	.273	.226	41	137	17	33	8	3	0	10	9	3	0	2	42	6	1	.343	.298
Rojas, Ronny	R-R	6-1	180	8-23-01	.000	--	.000	1	4	0	0	0	0	0	0	0	0	0	0	4	0	0	.000	.000
2-team total (43 Yankees West)					.128	.154	.117	44	133	17	17	7	0	4	18	36	1	0	1	69	2	2	.271	.316
Rosario, Hemmanuel	R-R	6-2	200	8-21-00	.151	.118	.158	29	93	6	14	5	0	1	10	5	2	0	1	30	0	0	.237	.208
Smith, Sincere	R-R	5-11	170	3-13-00	.375	.000	.429	3	8	3	3	0	0	0	0	2	0	0	1	1	1	1	.375	.500
2-team total (26 Yankees West)					.270	.160	.327	29	74	16	20	3	1	1	8	8	1	0	1	16	7	3	.378	.345
Torres, Miguel	R-R	6-0	170	3-3-00	.462	.167	.714	5	13	2	6	2	0	0	2	0	0	0	0	4	0	0	.615	.462
2-team total (20 Yankees West)					.250	.143	.300	25	44	4	11	3	0	0	5	6	1	0	1	13	0	0	.318	.346
Vallejo, Dionys	R-R	6-2	159	5-25-00	.184	.286	.167	18	49	10	9	3	1	2	5	12	2	1	1	16	2	0	.408	.359
2-team total (18 Yankees West)					.162	.211	.151	36	105	19	17	5	2	2	11	22	3	1	1	34	3	1	.305	.321
Vargas, Alexander	B-R	5-11	148	10-29-01	.219	.219	.220	40	155	23	34	5	5	1	16	14	4	0	0	22	13	0	.336	.301
Villa, Jose	R-R	6-1	170	11-16-98	.000	.000	--	1	1	0	0	0	0	0	0	0	0	0	0	0	0	0	.000	.000
2-team total (3 Yankees West)					.333	.250	.375	4	12	2	4	0	0	0	2	0	0	0	2	0	0	0	.333	.333
Wagaman, Eric	R-R	6-4	210	8-14-97	.182	.000	.222	4	11	1	2	0	0	0	1	2	0	0	0	5	0	0	.182	.308
2-team total (2 Yankees West)					.222	.200	.231	6	18	3	4	1	0	0	3	2	0	0	0	7	0	0	.278	.300

Pitching

Pitching	B-T	HT	WT	DOB	W	L	ERA	G	GS	CG	SV	IP	H	R	ER	HR	BB	SO	AVG	vLH	vRH	K/9	BB/9
Nova, Luis	R-R	6-0	174	4-24-83	1	0	5.40	1	0	0	0	3	4	2	2	0	1	3	.308	.000	.444	8.10	2.70
Abreu, Joensy	R-R	6-1	190	12-29-97	0	0	6.75	10	0	0	0	16	22	18	12	1	14	10	.333	.286	.356	5.63	7.88
Alvarez, Nelson L	R-R	6-4	220	6-11-98	0	1	27.00	1	0	0	0	1	1	2	2	0	2	1	.500	.500	--	13.50	27.00
2-team total (2 Yankees West)					1	1	6.75	3	0	0	0	3	2	2	2	0	3	2	.222	.200	.250	6.75	10.13
Barclay, Edgar	L-L	5-10	200	5-25-98	2	0	1.69	10	0	0	1	21	20	5	4	0	5	24	.241	.286	.226	10.13	2.11
Barrios, Wilser	R-R	6-2	160	3-21-98	0	0	0.00	1	0	0	0	2	0	0	0	0	2	2	.125	.000	.000	6.75	6.75
2-team total (9 Yankees West)					3	1	3.22	10	0	0	0	22	20	9	8	1	8	23	.235	.276	.214	9.27	3.22
Carela, Juan	R-R	6-3	186	12-15-01	0	7	7.11	10	6	0	0	25	24	29	20	1	24	25	.250	.310	.204	8.88	8.53
Castro, Yon	R-R	5-10	203	5-23-99	1	2	5.66	10	0	0	0	21	21	13	13	3	14	17	.276	.306	.250	7.40	6.10
Diaz, Deivi	L-L	5-10	197	6-9-99	4	4	3.95	10	7	1	0	41	49	27	18	1	17	37	.295	.326	.285	8.12	3.73
Diaz, Yoljeldriz	R-R	5-11	165	7-14-01	0	0	9.00	1	0	0	0	3	4	3	3	1	3	2	.364	.333	.375	6.00	9.00
German, Frank	R-R	6-2	195	9-22-97	0	1	6.75	2	2	0	0	4	3	3	3	1	1	5	.214	.167	.250	11.25	2.25
2-team total (1 Yankees West)					0	1	9.00	3	3	0	0	5	5	5	5	1	3	5	.278	.167	.333	9.00	5.40
Gomez, Carlos	R-R	6-1	175	6-14-98	1	0	3.86	9	3	0	0	21	11	9	9	2	10	18	.155	.235	.081	7.71	4.29
Gomez, Ismael	R-R	5-8	186	12-9-99	1	1	5.96	11	1	0	0	23	26	15	15	2	7	16	.283	.273	.288	6.35	2.78
Greene, Zach	R-R	6-1	215	8-29-96	1	1	1.69	12	0	0	5	16	11	5	3	0	4	22	.190	.261	.143	12.38	2.25
Kohn, Zach	R-R	6-4	190	9-30-97	1	1	2.61	6	0	0	0	10	7	4	3	0	3	15	.184	.083	.231	13.06	2.61
Larrondo, Denny	R-R	6-2	180	5-31-02	0	0	0.00	1	1	0	0	2	0	0	0	0	2	1	.000	.000	.000	5.40	10.80
2-team total (11 Yankees West)					2	5	5.01	12	9	0	0	32	18	19	18	0	21	24	.171	.156	.183	6.68	5.85
Marten, Daniel	R-R	6-0	179	5-7-97	0	1	1.54	4	1	0	0	12	10	2	2	2	3	8	.238	.111	.273	6.17	2.31
Mejia, Renso	R-R	5-11	165	3-6-00	2	1	1.50	5	2	0	0	18	15	9	3	1	2	15	.214	.318	.167	7.50	1.00
Mendez, Erick	R-R	6-0	185	4-7-96	0	0	8.44	4	0	0	0	5	6	5	5	0	3	8	.273	.400	.235	13.50	5.06
2-team total (6 Yankees West)					0	0	6.75	10	0	0	0	15	14	11	11	0	13	15	.246	.222	.256	9.20	7.98
Minnick, Matt	R-L	6-2	210	3-11-96	1	0	3.18	9	1	0	0	17	15	6	6	2	8	18	.246	.235	.250	9.53	4.24
Nova, Luis	R-R	5-11	196	9-5-97	1	0	5.40	1	0	0	0	3	4	2	2	0	1	3	.308	.000	.444	8.10	2.70
2-team total (7 Yankees West)					1	1	6.89	8	0	0	0	16	24	18	12	1	9	18	.348	.364	.348	10.34	5.17
Ojeda, Luis	R-R	5-11	180	1-10-97	1	1	5.14	4	3	0	0	14	12	8	8	1	6	12	.240	.333	.172	7.71	3.86
Otto, Glenn	R-R	6-3	240	3-11-96	0	0	9.00	1	1	0	0	1	1	1	1	0	0	1	.250	.000	.500	9.00	0.00
2-team total (2 Yankees West)					0	0	3.60	3	2	0	0	5	2	2	2	0	3	6	.118	.167	.091	10.80	5.40
Panacual, Josue	R-R	5-10	158	1-13-02	0	0	9.00	1	1	0	0	3	3	3	3	1	1	1	.273	.400	.167	3.00	9.00
Paredes, Edward	R-R	5-11	170	1-7-99	0	0	0.00	1	1	0	0	5	2	0	0	0	2	3	.125	.000	.182	5.40	3.60
2-team total (9 Yankees West)					3	4	2.74	10	7	0	0	43	42	22	13	3	13	33	.256	.304	.232	6.96	2.74
Peguero, Geremias	L-L	6-1	198	2-7-00	0	3	7.24	5	4	0	0	14	11	12	11	0	12	9	.229	.333	.214	5.93	7.90
Peguero, Jose	R-R	6-1	177	8-8-98	0	1	3.38	9	0	0	0	16	17	17	6	2	11	18	.254	.333	.209	10.13	6.19
Rodriguez, Carlos D.	R-R	5-10	155	12-13-98	0	0	18.00	1	0	0	0	1	2	2	2	0	2	1	.400	.000	.667	9.00	18.00
Rodriguez, Nicio	R-R	6-3	175	9-3-99	0	0	6.10	3	3	0	0	10	11	7	7	1	7	15	.268	.357	.222	13.06	6.10
Rojas, Adonny	R-R	6-0	170	1-3-96	0	1	2.70	8	0	0	1	13	10	6	4	2	7	8	.192	.263	.152	5.40	4.73
2-team total (3 Yankees West)					0	1	2.95	11	0	0	0	18	15	8	6	2	12	11	.214	.250	.196	5.40	5.89
Sanchez, Brandom	L-L	6-2	207	2-17-00	1	2	1.69	5	5	0	0	16	12	11	3	0	10	18	.203	.375	.177	10.13	5.63
Schmidt, Clarke	R-R	6-1	200	2-20-96	0	0	3.24	3	3	0	0	8	6	3	3	1	3	14	.200	.231	.177	15.12	3.24
Semmel, Montana	R-R	6-4	225	1-1-02	0	1	2.89	6	0	0	0	9	8	4	3	0	4	8	.235	.067	.368	3.86	3.86
Severino, Anderson	L-L	5-10	165	9-17-94	0	0	0.00	1	0	0	0	1	2	0	0	0	0	1	.400	1.000	.250	6.75	0.00
Vorhof, Mick	R-R	6-1	200	9-7-95	0	0	0.00	2	2	0	0	3	0	0	0	0	0	5	.000	.000	.000	15.00	0.00
2-team total (1 Yankees West)					0	0	0.00	3	3	0	0	5	0	0	0	0	1	7	.000	.000	.000	13.50	1.93

Fielding

C: Gomez 8, Guerrero 21, Illig 11, Rodriguez 6, Rodriguez 9, Rosario 18, Torres 3. 1B: Alvarez 3, Farrell 4, Mota 2, Paulino 25, Rodriguez 10, Rodriguez 5, Torres 1, Villa 1, Wagaman 3. 2B: Alvarez 12, Marte 15, Munoz 1, Reynoso 5, Rojas 14, Smith 1, Vallejo 6. 3B: Alvarez 5, Marte 2, Mota 1, Paulino 3, Reynoso 31, Rojas 1, Vallejo 8. SS: Garcia 1, Marte 4, Rojas 5, Vallejo 4, Vargas 37. OF: Alcantara 27, Alvarez 3, Farrell 5, Hernandez 33, Knowles 26, Moreno 24, Mota 27, Negueis 6, Palma 7, Smith 2.

GCL YANKEES WEST
GULF COAST LEAGUE

ROOKIE

Batting	B-T	HT	WT	DOB	AVG	vLH	vRH	G	AB	R	H	2B	3B	HR	RBI	BB	HBP	SH	SF	SO	SB	CS	SLG	OBP
Ascanio, Enyerberth	R-R	5-10	170	12-3-00	.167	.250	.158	17	42	8	7	0	1	0	0	12	3	1	0	14	2	1	.214	.386
Bastidas, Jesus	R-R	5-10	145	9-14-98	.167	.000	.200	2	6	1	1	0	0	0	0	0	0	0	0	0	0	0	.167	.167
Colmenares, Jose	R-R	5-11	173	4-3-02	.212	.167	.232	40	137	20	29	4	1	3	16	19	3	1	1	28	6	3	.321	.319
Crisp, Juan	R-R	6-1	170	5-23-00	.196	.133	.221	36	107	17	21	6	1	1	18	27	6	0	0	30	5	2	.299	.386
Diaz, Pedro	R-R	6-2	202	11-6-97	.258	.350	.217	30	66	6	17	3	0	0	7	19	0	0	2	30	2	0	.303	.414
Ferreira, Ricardo	B-R	5-11	175	2-3-95	.333	.333	.333	5	9	3	3	0	0	0	0	2	0	0	0	2	0	0	.333	.455
Garcia, Wilkerman	B-R	6-0	176	4-1-98	.300	.167	.500	3	10	3	3	0	0	1	4	2	0	0	0	1	0	0	.600	.417
2-team total (2 Yankees East)					.357	.286	.429	5	14	3	5	0	0	1	4	2	0	0	0	1	0	0	.571	.438
MacDonald, Kyle	L-R	6-3	240	6-17-96	.354	.417	.333	15	48	5	17	4	1	2	11	8	1	0	1	7	0	0	.604	.448
Martinez, Jose	R-R	6-0	198	1-28-99	.328	.381	.297	19	58	8	19	7	2	4	14	8	4	0	0	13	1	1	.724	.443
Martinez, Omar	L-R	5-11	192	7-5-01	.237	.233	.238	34	93	8	22	4	0	1	15	18	0	0	3	21	0	0	.312	.351
Medina, Nelson	R-R	6-2	175	9-14-00	.197	.208	.189	39	122	15	24	5	3	1	6	15	3	0	1	32	5	2	.344	.298
Mejia, Alan	R-R	6-0	165	7-20-01	.177	.171	.179	37	130	19	23	3	2	3	13	20	3	0	3	40	6	3	.300	.295
Mota, Sandy	R-R	6-0	170	9-25-96	.250	--	.250	1	4	0	1	0	0	0	0	0	0	0	0	0	0	0	.250	.250
2-team total (31 Yankees East)					.247	.240	.250	32	93	14	23	3	2	3	12	11	1	0	1	29	6	1	.419	.330
Palma, Alexander	R-R	6-0	201	10-18-95	.529	1.000	.385	5	17	5	9	1	0	4	7	0	0	0	0	4	1	0	1.294	.529
2-team total (10 Yankees East)					.431	.500	.410	15	51	8	22	7	0	4	12	2	0	0	0	9	1	0	.804	.453
Rojas, Angel	R-R	6-0	160	11-26-00	.206	.227	.196	23	73	12	15	5	0	0	4	6	2	0	1	26	5	0	.274	.281
2-team total (18 Yankees East)					.241	.273	.226	41	137	17	33	8	3	0	10	9	3	0	2	42	6	1	.343	.298
Rojas, Ronny	B-R	6-1	180	8-23-01	.132	.154	.122	43	129	17	17	7	0	4	18	36	1	0	1	65	2	2	.279	.323
2-team total (1 Yankees East)					.128	.154	.117	44	133	17	17	7	0	4	18	36	1	0	1	69	2	2	.271	.316
Rosario, Stanley	L-R	6-2	195	12-1-00	.202	.086	.257	37	109	16	22	4	0	2	16	21	1	0	0	46	2	0	.294	.336
Salinas, Raimfer	R-R	6-0	175	12-31-00	.270	.250	.277	42	159	25	43	10	2	3	15	7	7	0	0	45	11	5	.415	.330
Severino, Jesus	R-R	6-0	186	6-7-00	.053	.000	.000	7	19	3	1	0	0	0	1	4	1	0	0	7	0	0	.053	.250
Smith, Sincere	R-R	5-11	170	3-13-00	.258	.167	.310	26	66	13	17	3	1	1	8	6	1	0	1	15	6	2	.379	.324
2-team total (3 Yankees East)					.270	.160	.327	29	74	16	20	3	1	1	8	8	1	0	1	16	7	3	.378	.345
Torres, Miguel	R-R	6-0	170	3-3-00	.161	.125	.174	20	31	2	5	1	0	0	3	6	1	0	1	9	0	0	.194	.308
2-team total (5 Yankees East)					.250	.143	.300	25	44	4	11	3	0	0	5	6	1	0	1	13	0	0	.318	.346
Vallejo, Dionys	R-R	6-2	159	5-25-00	.143	.167	.136	18	56	9	8	2	1	0	6	10	1	0	0	18	1	1	.214	.284
2-team total (18 Yankees East)					.162	.211	.151	36	105	19	17	5	2	1	11	22	3	1	1	34	3	1	.305	.321
Villa, Jose	R-R	6-1	170	11-16-98	.364	.333	.375	3	11	2	4	0	0	0	2	0	0	0	0	2	0	0	.364	.364
2-team total (1 Yankees East)					.333	.250	.375	4	12	2	4	0	0	0	2	0	0	0	0	2	0	0	.333	.333
Wagaman, Eric	R-R	6-4	210	8-14-97	.286	.333	.250	2	7	2	2	1	0	0	2	0	0	0	0	2	0	0	.429	.286
2-team total (4 Yankees East)					.222	.200	.231	3	18	3	4	1	0	0	3	2	0	0	0	7	0	0	.278	.300

Pitching	B-T	HT	WT	DOB	W	L	ERA	G	GS	CG	SV	IP	H	R	ER	HR	BB	SO	AVG	vLH	vRH	K/9	BB/9
Agnos, Jake	L-L	5-11	207	5-23-98	0	1	9.00	1	1	0	0	2	2	4	2	0	1	6	.000	.000	.222	27.00	4.50
Alonzo, Felix	R-R	6-1	212	6-3-99	0	0	9.00	4	0	0	1	5	7	5	5	1	4	2	.318	.200	.417	3.60	7.20
Alvarez, Nelson L	R-R	6-4	220	6-11-98	1	0	0.00	2	0	0	0	2	1	0	0	1	1	.143	.000	.250	4.50	4.50	
2-team total (1 Yankees East)					1	1	6.75	3	0	0	0	3	2	2	2	0	3	2	.222	.200	.250	6.75	10.13
Barrios, Pedro	R-R	6-1	199	3-27-99	0	0	1.80	2	2	0	0	5	2	1	1	0	2	6	.118	.000	.182	10.80	3.60
Barrios, Wilser	R-R	6-2	160	3-21-98	3	1	3.66	9	0	0	0	20	19	9	8	1	6	21	.247	.308	.216	9.61	2.75
2-team total (1 Yankees East)					3	1	3.22	10	0	0	0	22	20	9	8	1	8	23	.235	.276	.214	9.27	3.22
Castano, Blas	R-R	5-10	162	9-8-98	2	5	4.67	11	7	0	0	52	67	31	27	6	11	30	.312	.329	.302	5.19	1.90
Chambuco, Jose	R-R	5-9	188	6-28-02	4	1	4.67	7	5	0	0	27	26	18	14	4	5	30	.233	.268	.210	10.00	1.67
Cordero, Diego	R-R	5-11	216	10-21-99	1	2	3.21	10	2	0	0	28	22	11	10	2	5	18	.208	.389	.114	5.79	1.61
Feliz, Maiker	R-R	6-0	195	8-17-97	0	0	3.00	3	0	0	0	3	2	1	1	0	2	2	.182	.000	.222	6.00	6.00
German, Frank	R-R	6-2	195	9-22-97	0	0	18.00	1	1	0	0	1	2	2	2	0	2	0	.500	--	.500	0.00	18.00
2-team total (2 Yankees East)					0	1	9.00	3	3	0	0	5	5	5	5	1	3	5	.278	.167	.333	9.00	5.40
Herrera, Argelis	L-L	6-5	165	10-17-98	0	0	13.50	6	0	0	0	6	8	10	9	1	10	4	.308	.000	.333	6.00	15.00
King, Michael	R-R	6-3	210	5-25-95	0	0	4.76	3	2	0	0	6	3	3	3	0	2	8	.150	.167	.143	12.71	3.18
Larrondo, Denny	R-R	6-2	180	5-31-02	2	5	5.28	11	8	0	0	31	18	19	18	0	19	23	.178	.163	.190	6.75	5.58
2-team total (1 Yankees East)					2	5	5.01	12	9	0	0	32	18	19	18	0	21	24	.171	.156	.183	6.68	5.85
Luna, Anyelo	R-R	6-3	184	12-16-97	1	2	6.27	12	1	0	0	19	21	16	13	0	9	16	.280	.360	.240	7.71	4.34
Marte, Deurys	R-R	6-5	193	6-25-99	1	0	6.98	7	6	0	0	19	21	18	15	2	13	13	.269	.290	.255	6.05	6.05
McNeely, Shaine	L-R	6-4	210	5-10-98	2	0	1.20	9	0	0	1	15	8	2	2	1	6	14	.157	.100	.194	8.40	3.60
Mendez, Erick	R-R	6-0	185	4-7-96	0	0	5.79	6	0	0	0	9	9	6	6	0	10	7	.229	.154	.273	6.75	9.64
2-team total (4 Yankees East)					0	0	6.75	10	0	0	0	15	14	11	11	0	13	15	.246	.222	.256	9.20	7.98
Milam, Kevin	R-R	6-0	200	2-13-98	1	0	0.66	13	0	0	0	14	3	2	1	0	6	18	.067	.063	.069	11.85	3.95
Nova, Luis	R-R	5-11	196	9-5-97	0	1	7.30	7	0	0	0	12	20	16	10	1	8	15	.357	.421	.324	10.95	5.84
2-team total (1 Yankees East)					1	1	6.89	8	0	0	0	16	24	18	12	1	9	18	.348	.364	.348	10.34	5.17
Otto, Glenn	R-R	6-3	240	3-11-96	0	0	2.25	2	1	0	0	4	1	1	1	0	3	5	.077	.250	.000	11.25	6.75
2-team total (1 Yankees East)					0	0	3.60	3	2	0	0	5	2	2	2	0	3	6	.118	.167	.091	10.80	5.40
Paciorek, Nick	R-R	6-2	195	6-1-98	2	0	2.57	7	0	0	0	14	9	5	4	0	9	13	.184	.143	.214	8.36	5.79
Paredes, Edward	R-R	5-11	170	1-7-99	2	4	3.11	9	6	0	0	38	40	22	13	3	11	30	.270	.333	.237	7.17	2.63
2-team total (1 Yankees East)					3	4	2.74	10	7	0	0	43	42	22	13	3	13	33	.256	.304	.232	6.96	2.74
Perez, Starling	R-R	6-3	182	9-2-00	1	0	4.34	11	1	0	1	19	19	10	9	2	10	12	.284	.259	.300	5.79	4.82
Reynoso, Anderson	R-R	6-2	180	11-25-97	0	1	10.45	5	0	0	0	10	17	13	12	3	6	5	.386	.389	.385	4.35	5.23
Rojas, Adonny	R-R	6-0	170	1-3-96	0	0	3.60	3	0	0	0	5	5	2	2	0	5	9	.278	.200	.308	5.40	9.00
2-team total (8 Yankees East)					0	1	2.95	11	0	0	1	18	15	8	6	2	12	11	.214	.250	.196	5.40	5.89
Sumoza, Christian	R-R	5-10	164	11-18-00	0	1	6.75	1	1	0	0	4	3	3	3	1	2	5	.188	.100	.333	11.25	4.50
Vega, Alfred	R-R	6-1	169	1-19-01	0	1	4.42	6	3	0	0	18	26	13	9	2	5	15	.325	.353	.304	7.36	2.45

NEW YORK YANKEES

	B-T	HT	WT	DOB	W	L	ERA	G	GS	CG	SV	IP	H	R	ER	HR	BB	SO	AVG	vLH	vRH	K/9	BB/9
Voliva, Evan	R-R	5-10	205	6-10-96	0	1	2.55	10	0	0	2	18	13	7	5	1	7	19	.213	.191	.225	9.68	3.57
Vorhof, Mick	R-R	6-1	200	9-7-95	0	0	0.00	1	1	0	0	2	0	0	0	0	1	2	.000	.000	.000	10.80	5.40
2-team total (2 Yankees East)					0	0	0.00	3	3	0	0	5	0	0	0	0	1	7	.000	.000	.000	13.50	1.93
Wilson, Justin	R-R	6-0	180	9-9-96	0	0	0.00	1	1	0	0	1	2	1	0	0	1	3	.333	.000	.500	27.00	9.00

Fielding

C: Ascanio 14, Crisp 19, Diaz 9, Martinez 14, Torres 17. 1B: Diaz 14, MacDonald 13, Martinez 10, Martinez 15, Torres 1, Villa 3, Wagaman 1. 2B: Bastidas 1, Colmenares 25, Mota 1, Rojas 7, Rojas 4, Smith 21. 3B: MacDonald 2, Martinez 10, Rojas 37, Smith 1, Vallejo 6, Villa 1. SS: Bastidas 2, Colmenares 18, Garcia 2, Rojas 19, Smith 3, Vallejo 15. OF: Ferreira 5, Medina 39, Mejia 37, Palma 3, Rosario 29, Salinas 40, Severino 5, Smith 3.

DSL YANKEES — ROOKIE
DOMINICAN SUMMER LEAGUE

Batting	B-T	HT	WT	DOB	AVG	vLH	vRH	G	AB	R	H	2B	3B	HR	RBI	BB	HBP	SH	SF	SO	SB	CS	SLG	OBP
Alcantara, Kevin	R-R	6-6	188	7-12-02	.237	.200	.250	9	38	7	9	3	1	0	6	5	2	0	1	9	0	0	.368	.348
Alvarez, Asdrubal	R-R	6-0	160	10-10-99	.243	.273	.231	13	37	4	9	4	0	1	8	2	1	0	0	8	0	0	.432	.300
Bonifacio, Mauro	R-R	6-7	226	8-31-01	.196	.235	.185	42	153	28	30	9	2	4	19	22	6	0	1	73	3	1	.360	.319
Cabrera, Marcos	R-R	6-3	189	10-10-01	.269	.271	.269	48	182	43	49	11	6	3	31	31	2	0	1	43	10	1	.445	.380
Cairo, Jose	R-R	6-2	180	3-27-01	.250	--	.250	1	4	1	1	0	0	0	0	1	0	0	0	1	0	0	.250	.400
Camacho, Kevyn	L-R	5-9	140	3-9-02	.345	.400	.333	10	29	13	10	1	0	0	10	8	1	0	0	5	0	0	.379	.500
Colmenares, Jose	R-R	5-11	173	4-3-02	.182	.143	.200	6	22	3	4	1	0	0	3	2	0	0	2	3	0	0	.227	.231
Escotto, Maikol	R-R	5-11	180	6-4-02	.315	.237	.336	45	181	47	57	11	4	8	26	32	4	1	0	57	13	3	.553	.429
Espino, Kelvin	L-R	6-1	193	12-8-01	.208	.167	.217	38	130	19	27	3	5	1	17	25	1	0	3	54	1	2	.331	.333
Familia, Christopher	L-L	5-11	170	6-10-00	.275	.273	.276	12	40	7	11	4	1	1	9	5	2	0	2	9	1	0	.500	.367
Favelo, Wilfre	R-R	6-0	173	4-1-01	.226	.115	.255	36	124	29	28	6	3	2	16	18	1	0	0	39	6	2	.371	.329
Garcia, Alex	B-R	5-10	155	12-8-01	.254	.222	.262	36	130	29	33	4	3	1	19	18	3	0	0	28	16	6	.354	.358
Garcia, Nicolas	R-R	5-11	200	6-15-01	.258	.160	.294	30	93	14	24	7	0	0	10	9	3	1	1	30	6	3	.333	.340
Gomez, Antonio	R-R	6-2	210	11-13-01	.600	.667	.500	1	5	2	3	1	0	0	1	0	0	0	0	2	0	0	.800	.667
Jimenez, Brayan	R-R	6-0	140	5-31-99	.253	.059	.297	25	91	19	23	8	1	1	18	9	1	0	0	17	3	0	.396	.327
Martinez, Omar	L-R	5-11	192	7-5-01	.200	.333	.167	6	15	3	3	0	0	1	3	6	1	0	0	6	0	0	.400	.455
Mejia, Alan	R-R	6-0	165	7-20-01	.275	.375	.208	12	40	11	11	1	0	0	5	9	0	1	0	10	2	2	.300	.408
Naranjo, Marco	R-R	5-11	155	3-26-01	.150	.250	.125	17	40	9	6	0	1	1	4	8	2	0	0	15	1	3	.275	.320
Negueis, Felix	R-R	6-0	200	12-29-00	.526	.400	.571	5	19	4	10	1	0	1	8	1	0	0	0	6	1	1	.737	.550
Perez, Dayro	R-R	6-2	180	1-31-02	.226	.226	.225	47	204	32	46	8	4	1	21	11	2	0	3	62	21	9	.319	.268
Ramirez, Agustin	R-R	6-0	210	9-10-01	.239	.250	.236	41	163	21	39	10	4	6	26	12	3	0	2	34	1	1	.374	.300
Rodriguez, Jesus	R-R	5-10	182	4-23-02	.310	.353	.293	18	58	14	18	4	2	2	12	11	0	0	3	10	3	2	.552	.403
Tordecilla, Edwin	R-R	5-10	165	5-24-99	.180	.071	.213	19	61	7	11	4	0	0	7	8	1	0	2	8	0	0	.246	.278
Valenzuela, Anthony	R-R	5-11	180	6-16-01	.224	.229	.222	32	125	18	28	2	0	5	18	14	2	0	0	45	8	1	.360	.312
Vallejo, Dionys	R-R	6-2	159	5-25-00	.167	.000	.250	4	6	1	1	0	1	0	5	1	0	0	0	0	0	0	.500	.583
Vargas, Alexander	R-R	5-11	148	10-29-01	.290	.250	.308	8	38	6	11	5	2	0	2	4	1	0	1	6	2	3	.526	.364
Vargas, Sergio	R-R	6-1	170	6-16-02	.191	.188	.192	20	63	19	12	5	0	1	12	18	1	0	2	28	2	2	.318	.369
Verdecia, Carlos	B-R	5-11	170	3-16-02	.280	.261	.286	28	100	18	28	9	4	0	15	22	1	0	0	19	12	5	.450	.415

Pitching	B-T	HT	WT	DOB	W	L	ERA	G	GS	CG	SV	IP	H	R	ER	HR	BB	SO	AVG	vLH	vRH	K/9	BB/9
Alonzo, Felix	R-R	6-1	212	6-3-99	3	0	1.13	16	0	0	2	32	18	6	4	2	5	41	.165	.122	.191	11.53	1.41
Calderon, Yorlin	R-R	6-3	155	8-17-01	2	1	6.61	8	2	0	0	16	16	14	12	2	5	17	.258	.217	.282	9.37	2.76
Carela, Juan	R-R	6-3	186	12-15-01	0	1	9.45	2	2	0	0	7	11	9	7	0	5	5	.407	.533	.250	6.75	6.75
Carrizo, Albert	R-R	6-4	165	11-11-99	1	1	3.86	8	0	0	2	14	15	8	6	1	4	11	.259	.263	.256	7.07	2.57
Castano, Blas	R-R	5-10	162	9-8-98	0	0	1.84	3	3	0	0	15	13	6	3	1	3	11	.236	.313	.205	6.75	1.84
Castro, Yon	R-R	6-0	203	5-23-99	2	0	4.35	5	0	0	0	10	7	5	5	0	2	14	.180	.250	.130	12.19	1.74
Chambuco, Jose	R-R	5-9	188	6-28-02	2	2	4.56	6	3	0	0	24	29	18	12	0	3	36	.290	.200	.350	13.69	1.14
Cordero, Diego	R-R	5-11	216	10-21-99	0	0	2.70	3	0	0	2	3	3	2	1	0	0	4	.231	.400	.125	10.80	0.00
Diaz, Yoljeldriz	R-R	5-11	165	7-14-01	1	1	3.22	8	3	0	0	22	18	8	8	0	13	16	.225	.179	.250	6.45	5.24
Estevez, Abel	R-R	5-11	170	1-17-00	2	1	4.45	17	0	0	4	28	31	17	14	0	12	19	.287	.385	.232	6.04	3.81
Gomez, Ismael	R-R	5-8	186	12-9-99	0	1	5.23	6	0	0	0	10	13	13	6	1	2	10	.283	.304	.261	8.71	1.74
Henriquez, Nolberto	R-R	6-4	170	10-16-99	1	0	5.40	6	0	0	0	8	11	13	5	2	7	9	.306	.333	.286	9.72	7.56
Hernandez, Franyer	R-R	5-11	204	2-1-01	3	0	4.62	13	2	0	0	51	56	34	26	1	11	33	.269	.265	.272	5.86	1.95
Lezcano, Oliver	R-R	6-0	175	10-30-99	0	3	4.50	9	3	0	0	26	30	21	13	0	8	23	.286	.361	.246	7.96	2.77
Marte, Deurys	R-R	6-5	193	6-25-99	0	1	2.70	3	3	0	0	10	10	6	3	2	14	.270	.235	.300	12.60	1.80
Martinez, Thowar	R-R	6-1	173	3-29-98	6	3	5.67	18	0	0	1	33	34	30	21	5	17	37	.274	.207	.333	9.99	4.59
Mejia, Renso	R-R	5-11	165	3-6-00	0	0	0.00	2	0	0	0	7	2	0	0	3	5	.091	.000	.200	6.43	3.86
Nova, Luis	R-R	5-11	196	9-5-97	0	1	3.86	7	0	0	1	7	6	5	3	0	5	10	.214	.091	.294	12.86	6.43
Obando, Angel	R-R	5-11	178	1-19-99	0	0	27.00	1	0	0	0	1	1	3	3	0	1	1	.250	.000	.333	9.00	9.00
Panacual, Josue	R-R	5-10	158	1-13-02	3	1	4.43	10	9	0	0	43	42	33	21	2	24	31	.261	.206	.301	6.54	5.06
Peguero, Geremias	L-L	6-1	198	2-7-00	1	1	12.60	3	0	0	0	5	6	9	7	1	7	3	.300	.444	.182	5.40	12.60
Perez, Starling	R-R	6-3	182	9-2-00	1	0	0.00	5	0	0	0	5	3	0	0	0	1	.177	.167	.182	1.80	0.00
Radney, Ignacio	R-R	6-3	165	10-4-01	2	0	6.10	9	0	0	1	10	9	8	7	1	9	13	.200	.250	.150	11.32	7.84
Rodriguez, Nicio	R-R	6-3	175	9-3-99	0	2	8.53	5	3	0	0	13	14	16	12	0	7	15	.259	.235	.270	10.66	4.97
Rodriguez, Osiel	R-R	6-2	210	11-22-01	0	1	5.59	5	4	0	0	10	12	11	6	1	4	9	.293	.400	.231	8.38	3.72
Sanchez, Brandom	L-L	6-2	207	2-17-00	0	1	8.53	2	2	0	0	6	9	7	6	1	1	8	.346	.500	.300	11.37	1.42
Sosa, Yordanny	R-R	6-2	139	10-12-01	1	0	2.21	12	1	0	0	20	9	8	5	0	12	9	.125	.083	.146	3.98	5.31
Sumoza, Christian	R-R	5-10	164	11-18-00	0	1	3.79	6	6	0	0	19	17	8	8	1	0	9	.224	.219	.227	4.26	0.00
Vargas, Miguel	L-L	5-10	180	2-22-01	1	2	5.79	12	7	0	0	47	53	37	30	2	21	48	.279	.283	.278	9.26	4.05
Vega, Alfred	R-R	6-1	169	1-19-01	0	1	3.72	2	2	0	0	10	8	4	4	0	2	12	.211	.053	.368	11.17	1.86
Velasquez, Luis	R-R	5-10	155	7-1-01	3	1	3.38	11	0	0	3	35	40	23	13	1	14	39	.284	.289	.281	10.13	3.63
Yulie, Tyrone	R-R	6-4	180	8-4-01	0	4	6.46	9	9	0	0	24	31	21	17	2	10	18	.320	.263	.356	6.85	3.80

Fielding

C: Camacho 8, Garcia 11, Gomez 1, Martinez 3, Ramirez 28, Rodriguez 12, Tordecilla 11. 1B: Alvarez 6, Garcia 17, Jimenez 18, Martinez 3, Tordecilla 9, Vallejo 2, Vargas 12. 2B: Alvarez 2, Colmenares 4, Escotto 23, Garcia 12, Jimenez 3, Perez 2, Verdecia 23. 3B: Alvarez 1, Cabrera 43, Colmenares 2, Escotto 8, Jimenez 5, Vallejo 1, Vargas 7. SS: Alvarez 3, Escotto 8, Garcia 5, Jimenez 1, Perez 38, Vargas 8, Verdecia 2. OF: Alcantara 8, Bonifacio 39, Cairo 1, Espino 31, Familia 9, Favelo 35, Garcia 16, Mejia 11, Naranjo 16, Negueis 4, Valenzuela 31.

Oakland Athletics

SEASON IN A SENTENCE: A well-rounded Athletics club won 97 games and an American League wild card for a second straight season.

HIGH POINT: Oakland saved its best work for the later stages of the season, going 35-17 (.673) in August and September to sew up the top wild card.

LOW POINT: For a second straight year, a successful regular season gave way to disappointment in the AL Wild Card game. This time, Oakland lost 5-1 to the Rays at home in a matchup of bullpen games. A second candidate for lowest point of the season occurred right before spring training, when outfielder Kyler Murray, the ninth overall pick in 2018, announced he was dropping baseball to pursue a pro football career. In April he was the No. 1 overall pick in the NFL draft.

NOTABLE ROOKIES: The organization's top three preseason prospects made their big league debuts in the second half and offer hope for the future. All three retain their rookie eligibility for 2020. Sean Murphy will look to fill a void at catcher after putting up a 137 OPS+ in 20 games. Lefthanders Jesus Luzardo and A.J. Puk both debuted as relievers and showed electric stuff. Luzardo struck out 16 and walked three in 12 innings and even pitched in the Wild Card game. He would have contributed more but missed about half of the season with a lat injury. Puk, in his first season back from Tommy John surgery, made 10 relief appearances and struck out 13 in 11 innings. A 26-year-old Seth Brown burst on the scene with 37 home runs at Triple-A Las Vegas before reaching Oakland in late August and batting .293/.361/.451 (120 OPS+) in 26 games. The lefthanded-hitting left fielder/first baseman was a 19th-round pick in 2015 out of Lewis-Clark State.

KEY TRANSACTIONS: Oakland's offseason trade for second baseman Jurickson Profar largely fizzled—and cost the A's Emilio Pagan, who would ascend to the role of closer with the Rays—but the club's in-season trades adeptly addressed a lack of pitching depth. The A's added starters Homer Bailey and Tanner Roark and lefty reliever Jake Diekman for a bundle of prospects headlined by shortstop Kevin Merrell and outfielders Jameson Hannah and Dairon Blanco.

DOWN ON THE FARM: Athletics affiliates went 354-388 (.477) to rank 22nd in baseball. Three clubs made the playoffs—Triple-A Las Vegas, Double-A Midland and the Rookie-level Athletics Gold—but none played for a championship.

OPENING DAY PAYROLL: $96,825,833 (21st).

PLAYERS OF THE YEAR

MAJOR LEAGUE	MINOR LEAGUE
Marcus Semien	**Sheldon Neuse**
SS	**3B**
.285/.369/.522	(Triple-A)
33 HR, 123 R, 92 RBIs	.317/.389/.550
8.1 WAR 4th in MLB	27 HR, 102 RBIs, 99 R

ORGANIZATION LEADERS

Batting		*Minimum 250 AB
MAJORS		
* AVG	Ramon Laureano	.288
* OPS	Mark Canha	.914
HR	Matt Chapman	36
HR	Matt Olson	36
RBI	Marcus Semien	92
MINORS		
* AVG	Corban Joseph, Las Vegas	.371
* OBP	Nick Martini, Las Vegas	.432
* SLG	Mark Payton, Las Vegas	.653
* OPS	Mark Payton, Las Vegas	1.053
R	Seth Brown, Las Vegas	101
H	Sheldon Neuse, Las Vegas	158
TB	Seth Brown, Las Vegas	286
2B	Edwin Diaz, Midland, Las Vegas	36
3B	Jorge Mateo, Las Vegas	14
HR	Seth Brown, Las Vegas	37
RBI	Seth Brown, Las Vegas	104
BB	Chase Calabuig, Beloit, Midland	75
SO	Lazaro Armenteros, Stockton	227
SB	Dairon Blanco, Midland	27

Pitching		#Minimum 75 IP
MAJORS		
W	Mike Fiers	15
# ERA	Liam Hendriks	1.80
SO	Chris Bassitt	141
SV	Liam Hendriks	25
MINORS		
W	Paul Blackburn, Las Vegas	11
L	Xavier Altamirano, Stockton	13
# ERA	Ben Bracewell, Midland, Las Vegas	2.96
G	Eric Marinez, Beloit, Stockton	45
G	Trey McNutt, Midland, Las Vegas	45
G	Miguel Romero, Las Vegas	45
GS	Brian Howard, Midland, Las Vegas	27
SV	Kyle Finnegan, Midland	14
IP	Matt Milburn, Midland	151
BB	Aiden McIntyre, Beloit	76
SO	Aiden McIntyre, Beloit	150
# AVG	Bryce Conley, Beloit, Stockton	.197

2019 PERFORMANCE

General Manager: David Forst. **Farm Director:** Keith Lieppman. **Scouting Director:** Eric Kubota.

Class	Team	League	W	L	PCT	Finish	Manager
Majors	Oakland Athletics	American	97	65	.599	4th (15)	Bob Melvin
Triple-A	Las Vegas Aviators	Pacific Coast	83	57	.593	2nd (16)	Fran Riordan
Double-A	Midland RockHounds	Texas	73	66	.525	3rd (8)	Scott Steinmann
High A	Stockton Ports	California	60	78	.435	7th (8)	Webster Garrison
Low A	Beloit Snappers	Midwest	54	84	.391	14th (16)	Lloyd Turner
Short season	Vermont Lake Monsters	New York-Penn	33	42	.440	11th (14)	Aaron Nieckula
Rookie	AZL Athletics Gold	Arizona	31	25	.554	t-8th (21)	Hiram Bocachica
Rookie	AZL Athletics Green	Arizona	20	36	.357	19th (21)	Eddie Menchaca
Overall 2019 Minor League Record			354	388	.477	22nd (30)	

ORGANIZATION STATISTICS

OAKLAND ATHLETICS
AMERICAN LEAGUE

Batting	B-T	HT	WT	DOB	AVG	vLH	vRH	G	AB	R	H	2B	3B	HR	RBI	BB	HBP	SH	SF	SO	SB	CS	SLG	OBP
Barreto, Franklin	R-R	5-10	200	2-27-96	.123	.148	.100	23	57	6	7	2	0	2	5	1	0	0	0	23	1	0	.263	.138
Bolt, Skye	B-R	6-2	187	1-15-94	.100	.000	.125	5	10	1	1	1	0	0	0	1	0	0	0	3	0	0	.200	.182
Brown, Seth	L-L	6-3	220	7-13-92	.293	.214	.312	26	75	11	22	8	2	0	13	7	1	0	0	23	1	0	.453	.361
Canha, Mark	R-R	6-2	212	2-15-89	.273	.221	.298	126	410	80	112	16	3	26	58	67	18	0	2	107	3	2	.517	.396
Chapman, Matt	R-R	6-0	220	4-28-93	.249	.234	.254	156	583	102	145	36	3	36	91	73	11	0	3	147	1	1	.506	.342
Davis, Khris	R-R	5-11	203	12-21-87	.220	.285	.197	133	481	61	106	11	0	23	73	47	3	0	2	146	0	0	.387	.293
Garneau, Dustin	R-R	6-2	205	8-13-87	.294	.250	.400	7	17	3	5	2	0	1	7	2	0	0	0	4	0	0	.588	.368
2-team total (28 Los Angeles)					.244	.300	.214	35	86	14	21	5	0	3	14	10	4	0	0	22	0	0	.407	.350
Grossman, Robbie	B-L	6-0	215	9-16-89	.241	.173	.250	138	420	57	101	21	3	6	38	59	1	0	2	86	9	4	.348	.334
Herrmann, Chris	L-R	6-0	200	11-24-87	.202	.200	.203	30	84	9	17	3	0	1	8	9	0	1	0	29	0	0	.274	.280
Hundley, Nick	R-R	6-0	203	9-8-83	.200	.118	.226	31	70	5	14	3	1	2	5	2	1	0	0	18	0	1	.357	.233
Joseph, Corban	L-R	6-0	185	10-28-88	.189	1.000	.167	11	37	4	7	2	0	1	5	2	0	0	1	5	0	0	.324	.225
Laureano, Ramon	R-R	5-11	200	7-15-94	.288	.296	.285	123	434	79	125	29	0	24	67	27	11	1	8	123	13	2	.521	.340
Martini, Nick	L-L	5-11	205	6-27-90	.091	--	.091	6	11	1	1	0	0	1	2	2	0	0	0	5	0	0	.364	.231
Morales, Kendrys	B-R	6-1	242	6-20-83	.204	.286	.192	34	108	9	22	1	1	1	7	14	3	0	1	20	0	0	.259	.310
2-team total (19 New York)					.194	.200	.193	53	170	16	33	2	1	2	12	26	4	0	1	26	0	0	.253	.313
Murphy, Sean	R-R	6-3	232	10-4-94	.245	.278	.229	20	53	14	13	5	0	4	8	6	1	0	0	16	0	0	.566	.333
Neuse, Sheldon	R-R	6-0	218	12-10-94	.250	.212	.304	25	56	3	14	3	0	0	7	4	0	0	1	19	0	0	.304	.295
Olson, Matt	L-R	6-5	230	3-29-94	.267	.223	.288	127	483	73	129	26	0	36	91	51	12	0	1	138	0	0	.545	.351
Phegley, Josh	R-R	5-10	225	2-12-88	.239	.284	.219	106	314	44	75	18	0	12	62	15	6	2	5	63	0	1	.411	.282
Pinder, Chad	R-R	6-2	207	3-29-92	.241	.252	.230	124	341	45	82	21	0	13	47	20	5	1	3	88	0	1	.416	.290
Piscotty, Stephen	R-R	6-4	205	1-14-91	.249	.361	.214	93	357	46	89	17	1	13	44	29	3	1	3	84	2	0	.412	.309
Profar, Jurickson	B-R	6-0	190	2-20-93	.218	.305	.192	139	459	65	100	24	2	20	67	48	8	0	3	75	9	1	.410	.301
Semien, Marcus	R-R	6-0	195	9-17-90	.285	.309	.276	162	657	123	187	43	7	33	92	87	2	0	1	102	10	8	.522	.370
Taylor, Beau	L-R	5-11	205	2-13-90	.174	.000	.191	10	23	3	4	0	0	2	2	4	1	0	0	6	0	0	.435	.321
2-team total (1 Toronto)					.160	.000	.174	11	25	3	4	0	0	2	2	4	1	0	0	7	0	0	.400	.300

Pitching	B-T	HT	WT	DOB	W	L	ERA	G	GS	CG	SV	IP	H	R	ER	HR	BB	SO	AVG	vLH	vRH	K/9	BB/9
Anderson, Brett	L-L	6-4	230	2-1-88	13	9	3.89	31	31	0	0	176	181	80	76	20	49	90	.265	.221	.280	4.60	2.51
Anderson, Tanner	R-R	6-2	203	5-27-93	0	3	6.04	5	5	0	0	22	30	16	15	4	7	18	.309	.360	.255	7.25	2.82
Bailey, Homer	R-R	6-4	223	5-3-86	6	3	4.30	13	13	0	0	73	73	35	35	9	15	68	.254	.197	.314	8.35	1.84
2-team total (18 Kansas City)					13	9	4.57	31	31	0	0	163	162	84	83	21	53	149	.256	.217	.299	8.21	2.92
Bassitt, Chris	R-R	6-5	220	2-22-89	10	5	3.81	28	25	0	0	144	125	66	61	21	47	141	.229	.209	.251	8.81	2.94
Blackburn, Paul	R-R	6-1	200	12-4-93	0	2	10.64	4	1	0	0	11	19	14	13	3	4	8	.380	.423	.333	6.55	3.27
Brooks, Aaron	R-R	6-4	230	4-27-90	2	3	5.01	15	6	0	0	50	49	29	28	12	14	43	.249	.265	.232	7.69	2.50
2-team total (14 Baltimore)					6	8	5.65	29	18	0	0	110	118	72	69	21	34	82	.271	.283	.258	6.71	2.78
Buchter, Ryan	L-L	6-4	232	2-13-87	1	1	2.98	64	0	0	0	45	42	16	15	8	23	50	.252	.238	.274	9.93	4.57
Diekman, Jake	L-L	6-4	200	1-21-87	1	1	4.43	28	0	0	0	20	16	11	10	0	16	21	.222	.237	.206	9.30	7.08
2-team total (48 Kansas City)					1	7	4.65	76	0	0	0	62	49	34	32	3	39	84	.215	.224	.210	12.19	5.66
Dull, Ryan	R-R	5-9	185	10-2-89	0	0	12.00	7	0	0	0	9	19	13	12	4	4	8	.432	.381	.478	8.00	4.00
3-team total (3 New York, 1 Toronto)					0	0	12.79	11	0	0	0	13	25	19	18	5	7	15	.410	.400	.417	10.66	4.97
Estrada, Marco	R-R	6-0	180	7-5-83	0	2	6.85	5	5	0	0	24	23	19	18	7	8	11	.242	.146	.315	4.18	3.04
Fiers, Mike	R-R	6-2	202	6-15-85	15	4	3.90	33	33	1	0	185	166	82	80	30	53	126	.243	.248	.239	6.14	2.58
Hendriks, Liam	R-R	6-0	225	2-10-89	4	4	1.80	75	2	0	25	85	61	18	17	5	21	124	.201	.257	.145	13.13	2.22
Luzardo, Jesus	L-L	6-0	209	9-30-97	0	0	1.50	6	0	0	2	12	5	2	2	1	3	16	.119	.071	.143	12.00	2.25
Manaea, Sean	R-L	6-5	245	2-1-92	4	0	1.21	5	5	0	0	30	16	4	4	3	7	30	.160	.211	.129	9.10	2.12
Martini, Nick	L-L	5-11	205	6-27-90	0	0	0.00	1	0	0	0	1	0	0	0	0	2	1	.000	.000	.000	9.00	18.00
Mengden, Daniel	R-R	6-1	225	2-19-93	5	2	4.83	13	9	0	1	60	59	32	32	7	27	42	.254	.260	.173	6.34	4.07
Montas, Frankie	R-R	6-2	245	3-21-93	9	2	2.63	16	16	0	0	96	84	35	28	8	23	103	.230	.231	.229	9.66	2.16
Morales, Kendrys	B-R	6-1	242	6-20-83	0	0	9.00	1	0	0	0	1	1	1	1	0	2	0	.333	.333	--	0.00	18.00
Petit, Yusmeiro	R-R	6-1	255	11-22-84	5	3	2.71	80	0	0	0	83	57	25	25	11	10	71	.194	.218	.177	7.70	1.08
Puk, A.J.	L-L	6-7	238	4-25-95	2	0	3.18	10	0	0	0	11	10	4	4	1	5	13	.238	.385	.172	10.32	3.97
Roark, Tanner	R-R	6-2	240	10-5-86	4	3	4.58	10	10	0	0	55	61	29	28	14	13	50	.279	.229	.327	8.18	2.13

Name	B-T	HT	WT	DOB	W	L	ERA	G	GS	CG	SV	IP	H	R	ER	HR	BB	SO	AVG	vLH	vRH	K/9	BB/9
Rodney, Fernando	R-R	5-11	240	3-18-77	0	2	9.42	17	0	0	0	14	20	15	15	2	12	14	.345	.400	.286	8.79	7.53
Schlitter, Brian	R-R	6-3	238	12-21-85	0	0	3.72	6	0	0	0	10	12	4	4	0	4	6	.324	.308	.333	5.59	3.72
Soria, Joakim	R-R	6-3	200	5-18-84	2	4	4.30	71	1	0	1	69	51	33	33	9	20	79	.202	.230	.175	10.30	2.61
Treinen, Blake	R-R	6-5	225	6-30-88	6	5	4.91	57	0	0	16	59	58	33	32	9	37	59	.257	.254	.259	9.05	5.68
Trivino, Lou	R-R	6-5	240	10-1-91	4	6	5.25	61	0	0	0	60	61	40	35	7	31	57	.265	.267	.263	8.55	4.65
Wang, Wei-Chung	L-L	6-1	160	4-25-92	1	0	3.33	20	0	0	0	27	22	10	10	4	11	16	.227	.186	.259	5.33	3.67
Wendelken, J.B.	R-R	6-1	240	3-24-93	3	1	3.58	27	0	0	0	33	21	14	13	2	9	34	.178	.160	.191	9.37	2.48

Fielding

Catcher	PCT	G	PO	A	E	DP	PB
Garneau	1.000	7	33	4	0	0	0
Herrmann	.990	25	187	4	2	0	1
Hundley	1.000	30	167	12	0	0	0
Murphy	.994	18	151	4	1	0	2
Phegley	.997	106	704	46	2	3	15
Taylor	1.000	9	62	3	0	0	1

First Base	PCT	G	PO	A	E	DP
Brown	1.000	4	21	2	0	4
Canha	1.000	15	81	4	0	6
Morales	.989	26	165	13	2	10
Olson	.993	127	1023	90	8	95
Pinder	1.000	2	13	0	0	2
Profar	1.000	1	6	1	0	2

Second Base	PCT	G	PO	A	E	DP
Barreto	.935	17	18	40	4	5
Joseph	.966	9	12	16	1	5
Neuse	1.000	20	22	20	0	7
Pinder	.963	21	24	28	2	5
Profar	.973	124	221	245	13	63

Third Base	PCT	G	PO	A	E	DP
Chapman	.981	156	146	311	9	27
Joseph	.000	1	0	0	0	0
Neuse	.938	5	4	11	1	1
Pinder	.938	17	10	20	2	3

Shortstop	PCT	G	PO	A	E	DP
Barreto	.889	5	2	6	1	3

	PCT	G	PO	A	E	DP
Pinder	1.000	3	1	2	0	0
Semien	.981	161	186	436	12	85

Outfield	PCT	G	PO	A	E	DP
Bolt	1.000	4	10	0	0	0
Brown	1.000	23	23	2	0	0
Canha	.990	90	199	1	2	0
Davis	1.000	4	3	0	0	0
Grossman	1.000	129	226	2	0	0
Herrmann	.000	3	0	0	0	0
Laureano	.977	122	285	10	7	2
Martini	1.000	3	5	0	0	0
Pinder	.992	77	128	4	1	1
Piscotty	1.000	90	168	2	0	0
Profar	1.000	8	8	0	0	0

LAS VEGAS AVIATORS

PACIFIC COAST LEAGUE

TRIPLE-A

Batting	B-T	HT	WT	DOB	AVG	vLH	vRH	G	AB	R	H	2B	3B	HR	RBI	BB	HBP	SH	SF	SO	SB	CS	SLG	OBP
Barreto, Franklin	R-R	5-10	200	2-27-96	.295	.330	.282	98	373	88	110	29	5	19	65	42	6	1	2	113	15	1	.552	.374
Bolt, Skye	B-R	6-2	187	1-15-94	.269	.261	.272	89	305	57	82	19	3	11	61	37	2	1	2	94	7	5	.459	.350
Brown, Seth	L-L	6-3	220	7-13-92	.297	.262	.308	112	451	101	134	29	6	37	104	38	4	0	7	127	8	1	.634	.352
Campbell, Eric	R-R	6-3	215	4-9-87	.276	.337	.251	94	333	64	92	24	0	16	65	54	4	1	2	68	6	3	.493	.382
Canha, Mark	R-R	6-2	212	2-15-89	.125	.167	.000	2	8	0	1	1	0	0	1	0	0	0	1	3	0	0	.250	.111
Devencenzi, Jordan	R-R	5-11	203	6-26-93	1.000	--	1.000	1	1	0	1	0	0	0	0	0	0	0	0	0	0	0	1.000	1.000
Diaz, Edwin	R-R	6-2	223	8-25-95	.000	.000	.000	4	13	0	0	0	0	0	0	1	0	0	3	0	0	.000	.071
Fowler, Dustin	L-L	6-0	190	12-29-94	.277	.248	.288	130	556	98	154	22	7	25	89	42	6	0	2	145	12	4	.477	.333
Garneau, Dustin	R-R	6-2	205	8-13-87	.308	.444	.235	8	26	2	8	2	1	1	3	3	1	0	1	9	0	0	.577	.387
2-team total (26 Salt Lake)					.248	.258	.244	34	109	18	27	10	1	7	16	14	5	0	1	37	0	0	.551	.357
Heim, Jonah	B-R	6-4	220	6-27-95	.359	.278	.375	35	106	22	38	9	0	4	19	11	0	0	2	18	0	0	.557	.412
Herrmann, Chris	L-R	6-0	200	11-24-87	.333	.316	.344	13	51	14	17	3	1	4	6	0	0	1	18	0	0	.667	.397
Joseph, Corban	L-R	6-0	185	10-28-88	.371	.327	.386	97	383	63	142	35	4	13	73	33	4	0	5	46	0	0	.585	.421
Loehr, Trace	L-R	5-10	185	5-23-95	.333	.333	.333	15	36	11	12	2	0	2	5	2	0	0	0	7	0	0	.556	.368
Martini, Nick	L-L	5-11	205	6-27-90	.329	.321	.332	70	274	57	90	18	0	8	42	49	3	0	3	51	0	0	.482	.432
Mateo, Jorge	R-R	6-0	192	6-23-95	.290	.303	.285	119	532	95	154	29	14	19	78	29	4	0	1	145	24	11	.504	.330
Murphy, Sean	R-R	6-3	232	10-4-94	.308	.188	.352	31	120	25	37	6	1	10	30	15	2	0	3	31	0	1	.625	.386
Neuse, Sheldon	R-R	6-0	218	12-10-94	.317	.391	.290	126	498	99	158	31	2	27	102	56	4	0	2	132	3	3	.550	.389
Olson, Matt	L-R	6-5	230	3-29-94	.182	1.000	.143	5	22	3	4	0	0	1	2	1	0	0	3	0	0	.318	.250
Payton, Mark	L-L	5-8	190	12-7-91	.334	.263	.357	118	395	80	132	30	3	30	97	45	1	2	4	76	7	4	.653	.400
Phegley, Josh	R-R	5-10	225	2-12-88	.167	.333	.000	2	6	2	1	0	0	0	0	2	1	0	0	1	0	0	.167	.444
Piscotty, Stephen	R-R	6-4	205	1-14-91	.304	.143	.375	5	23	4	7	0	0	1	3	2	0	0	0	4	0	0	.435	.360
Ramirez, Tyler	L-L	5-9	185	2-21-95	.188	.257	.159	38	117	18	22	4	1	3	18	21	1	0	0	38	0	0	.316	.317
Rivas, Alfonso	L-L	6-0	188	9-13-96	.406	.400	.409	8	32	2	13	2	1	1	5	2	0	0	0	7	0	0	.625	.441
Rupp, Cameron	R-R	6-2	260	9-28-88	.209	.250	.193	37	115	13	24	5	0	9	17	16	4	0	1	43	0	0	.487	.324
Taylor, Beau	L-R	5-11	205	2-13-90	.257	.184	.282	62	191	38	49	13	1	8	32	47	2	0	0	70	0	0	.461	.408
Theroux, Collin	R-R	6-2	220	3-10-94	.167	.167	.167	5	18	1	3	1	0	0	0	0	0	0	0	12	0	0	.222	.167
White, Mikey	R-R	6-1	200	9-3-93	.250	.500	.167	3	8	2	2	0	0	1	2	0	0	0	0	3	0	0	.625	.250

Pitching	B-T	HT	WT	DOB	W	L	ERA	G	GS	CG	SV	IP	H	R	ER	HR	BB	SO	AVG	vLH	vRH	K/9	BB/9
Alexander, Tyler	L-L	6-1	180	9-22-91	5	5	6.72	21	18	0	0	86	95	68	64	25	37	96	.277	.297	.271	10.09	3.89
Anderson, Tanner	R-R	6-2	203	5-27-93	9	5	6.00	21	16	1	0	96	121	68	64	21	41	59	.307	.321	.297	5.53	3.84
Bassitt, Chris	R-R	6-5	200	2-22-89	0	0	4.50	2	2	0	0	8	8	4	4	2	2	9	.242	.385	.150	10.13	2.25
Blackburn, Paul	R-R	6-1	200	12-4-93	11	3	4.34	24	22	0	0	133	133	70	64	18	34	92	.266	.265	.266	6.24	2.31
Blevins, Jerry	L-L	6-6	190	9-6-83	0	0	1.69	7	0	0	0	11	9	2	2	2	4	16	.225	.250	.208	13.50	3.38
Bracewell, Ben	R-R	6-0	195	9-19-90	1	3	3.13	41	1	0	2	72	69	40	25	4	38	70	.250	.236	.259	8.75	4.75
Buchanan, Jake	R-R	6-0	232	9-24-89	3	6	6.16	20	20	0	0	99	125	75	68	24	34	71	.313	.291	.329	6.43	3.08
2-team total (4 Fresno)					3	6	6.32	24	20	0	0	104	133	80	73	24	36	74	.317	.287	.339	6.40	3.12
Buchter, Ryan	L-L	6-4	232	2-13-87	0	0	0.00	1	0	0	0	1	0	0	0	0	0	0	.000	.000	.000	0.00	0.00
Campbell, Eric	R-R	6-3	215	4-9-87	0	0	13.50	2	0	0	0	3	7	5	4	1	2	0	.467	.200	.600	0.00	6.75
Cotton, Jharel	R-R	5-11	200	1-19-92	0	2	7.71	14	1	0	0	19	23	17	16	5	10	24	.303	.333	.270	11.57	4.82
Dull, Ryan	R-R	5-9	185	10-2-89	1	4	5.45	30	0	0	4	40	43	28	24	6	13	50	.272	.362	.220	11.34	2.95
2-team total (2 Sacramento)					1	4	5.70	32	0	0	4	43	45	31	27	8	14	53	.266	.356	.218	11.18	2.95
Dunshee, Parker	R-R	6-0	215	2-12-95	4	5	5.38	20	19	0	1	92	86	62	55	21	37	90	.245	.276	.223	8.80	3.62
Estrada, Marco	R-R	6-0	180	7-5-83	0	0	12.00	1	1	0	0	3	4	4	4	1	3	3	.308	.600	.125	9.00	9.00
Finnegan, Kyle	R-R	6-2	196	9-4-91	3	1	2.89	21	0	0	5	28	23	10	9	3	12	36	.228	.209	.241	11.57	3.86

OAKLAND ATHLETICS

OAKLAND ATHLETICS

Pitching	B-T	HT	WT	DOB	W	L	ERA	G	GS	CG	SV	IP	H	R	ER	HR	BB	SO	AVG	vLH	vRH	K/9	BB/9
Harvey, Matt	R-R	6-4	220	3-27-89	1	0	3.18	5	3	0	0	17	13	6	6	2	5	21	.210	.182	.225	11.12	2.65
2-team total (2 Salt Lake)					1	2	6.65	7	5	0	0	23	26	17	17	3	8	31	.280	.194	.323	12.13	3.13
Holmes, Grant	L-R	6-0	224	3-22-96	0	0	1.93	1	1	0	0	5	6	1	1	1	1	5	.353	.286	.400	9.64	1.93
Howard, Brian	R-R	6-9	185	4-25-95	0	1	13.81	4	4	0	0	14	28	23	22	4	8	16	.412	.444	.375	10.05	5.02
Jackson, Edwin	R-R	6-2	215	9-9-83	0	0	8.38	2	2	0	0	10	9	9	9	3	7	10	.237	.250	.222	9.31	6.52
Joseph, Corban	R-R	6-0	185	10-28-88	0	0	27.00	1	0	0	0	1	2	3	3	2	1	0	.400	.000	.500	9.00	9.00
Kaprielian, James	R-R	6-3	210	3-2-94	0	0	2.25	1	1	0	0	4	6	1	1	0	0	6	.333	.375	.300	13.50	0.00
Kiekhefer, Dean	L-L	6-0	175	6-7-89	0	1	54.00	2	0	0	0	1	4	4	4	1	1	0	.667	.667	.667	0.00	13.50
Lobstein, Kyle	L-L	6-3	220	8-12-89	6	4	4.75	43	1	0	2	66	67	39	35	6	32	66	.264	.266	.263	8.95	4.34
Luzardo, Jesus	L-L	6-0	209	9-30-97	1	1	3.19	7	7	0	0	31	29	12	11	3	8	34	.240	.167	.264	9.87	2.32
Manaea, Sean	R-L	6-5	245	2-1-92	3	1	3.21	5	5	0	0	28	16	11	10	5	6	43	.165	.219	.139	13.82	1.93
McNutt, Trey	R-R	6-4	220	8-2-89	5	2	4.99	30	0	0	2	40	41	22	22	5	18	45	.268	.250	.277	10.21	4.08
Mengden, Daniel	R-R	6-1	225	2-19-93	4	3	4.22	13	10	0	0	64	56	37	30	8	20	61	.228	.227	.228	8.58	2.81
Naile, James	R-R	6-4	185	2-8-93	2	0	4.41	3	3	0	0	16	18	8	8	4	6	10	.281	.344	.219	5.51	3.31
Puk, A.J.	L-L	6-7	238	4-25-95	4	1	4.91	9	0	0	0	11	7	7	6	3	3	16	.175	.133	.200	13.09	2.45
Romero, Miguel	R-R	6-0	202	4-23-94	4	1	3.96	45	1	0	3	73	65	34	32	11	36	81	.234	.279	.204	10.03	4.46
Ruiz, Norge	R-R	5-10	180	3-15-94	2	3	9.08	19	0	0	2	36	62	39	36	10	14	24	.383	.403	.370	6.06	3.53
Rupp, Cameron	R-R	6-2	260	9-28-88	0	0	18.00	1	0	0	0	1	1	2	2	1	2	0	.250	.000	.333	0.00	18.00
Schlitter, Brian	R-R	6-3	238	12-21-85	4	1	4.64	35	1	0	11	43	51	25	22	6	11	31	.300	.270	.318	6.54	2.32
Seddon, Joel	R-R	6-1	165	7-13-92	1	0	3.00	1	0	0	0	3	3	1	1	0	1	2	.250	.167	.333	6.00	3.00
Stull, Cody	L-L	6-2	160	3-23-92	0	0	3.68	5	0	0	0	7	8	3	3	0	4	5	.296	.444	.222	6.14	4.91
Taylor, Beau	L-R	5-11	205	2-13-90	0	0	18.00	1	0	0	0	1	2	2	2	1	0	0	.500	.667	.000	0.00	0.00
Treinen, Blake	R-R	6-5	225	6-30-88	1	0	27.00	1	0	0	0	1	4	3	3	2	0	0	.667	.000	1.000	0.00	0.00
Triggs, Andrew	R-R	6-4	223	3-16-89	1	0	6.75	3	0	0	0	3	3	2	2	0	4	3	.273	.250	.286	10.13	13.50
Wang, Wei-Chung	L-L	6-1	160	4-25-92	1	1	4.78	19	0	0	1	26	29	14	14	5	8	24	.276	.186	.339	8.20	2.73
Wendelken, J.B.	R-R	6-1	240	3-24-93	6	3	5.59	30	1	0	3	39	47	26	24	8	19	43	.298	.322	.283	10.01	4.42

Fielding

Catcher	PCT	G	PO	A	E	DP	PB
Devencenzi	1.000	1	5	0	0	0	
Garneau	1.000	7	75	3	0	0	
Heim	.990	28	183	14	2	4	1
Herrmann	1.000	8	56	1	0	0	1
Murphy	.988	27	235	9	3	1	1
Phegley	1.000	2	12	2	0	0	1
Rupp	1.000	27	176	6	0	1	2
Taylor	.988	54	401	23	5	2	6
Theroux	1.000	4	32	1	0	0	

First Base	PCT	G	PO	A	E	DP
Brown	.987	64	507	41	7	49
Campbell	.993	51	391	33	3	40
Canha	1.000	1	9	1	0	0
Garneau	1.000	1	8	1	0	2
Joseph	1.000	21	143	13	0	19
Olson	1.000	3	29	0	0	3
Rivas	1.000	7	59	4	0	6

	PCT	G	PO	A	E	DP
Rupp	1.000	1	1	0	0	0
Taylor	1.000	1	1	0	0	0
White	1.000	1	10	0	0	1

Second Base	PCT	G	PO	A	E	DP
Barreto	.980	47	86	108	4	33
Campbell	.917	7	4	18	2	1
Joseph	.987	56	77	144	3	36
Loehr	1.000	4	13	0	0	3
Mateo	.984	14	27	35	1	8
Neuse	.984	16	24	39	1	8
White	1.000	1	1	0	0	0

Third Base	PCT	G	PO	A	E	DP
Barreto	.920	9	6	17	2	3
Campbell	.986	35	18	53	1	3
Diaz	1.000	4	3	8	0	0
Loehr	1.000	1	1	2	0	0
Neuse	.965	96	76	198	10	20

Shortstop	PCT	G	PO	A	E	DP
Barreto	.947	31	33	75	6	11
Loehr	1.000	4	6	11	0	4
Mateo	.957	100	140	304	20	76
Neuse	.927	9	13	25	3	6

Outfield	PCT	G	PO	A	E	DP
Barreto	.955	11	21	0	1	0
Bolt	.984	83	178	4	3	1
Brown	.974	26	37	1	1	1
Canha	1.000	1	1	0	0	0
Fowler	.988	124	231	6	3	4
Martini	.982	51	53	1	1	0
Neuse	1.000	3	3	0	0	0
Payton	.995	106	173	12	1	1
Piscotty	1.000	3	5	0	0	0
Ramirez	1.000	34	42	2	0	0
Rivas	1.000	1	3	0	0	0

MIDLAND ROCKHOUNDS   DOUBLE-A
TEXAS LEAGUE

Batting	B-T	HT	WT	DOB	AVG	vLH	vRH	G	AB	R	H	2B	3B	HR	RBI	BB	HBP	SH	SF	SO	SB	CS	SLG	OBP
Barrera, Luis	L-L	6-0	205	11-15-95	.321	.314	.324	54	224	35	72	9	11	4	24	12	1	2	1	48	9	7	.513	.357
Blanco, Dairon	R-R	6-0	170	4-26-93	.276	.273	.276	78	301	57	83	13	12	7	44	29	2	1	1	95	27	7	.468	.342
2-team total (32 Northwest Arkansas)					.262	.261	.263	110	427	67	112	20	13	7	49	37	3	1	1	137	33	13	.419	.325
Bride, Jonah	R-R	5-10	200	12-27-95	.222	.000	.333	2	9	2	2	0	0	0	0	0	0	0	1	0	0	.222	.222
Calabuig, Chase	L-L	5-11	185	12-10-95	.280	.241	.291	109	403	57	113	14	3	4	50	63	5	0	5	101	7	4	.360	.380
Deichmann, Greg	L-R	6-2	190	5-31-95	.219	.170	.228	80	301	42	66	10	2	11	36	34	2	0	3	103	19	5	.375	.300
Diaz, Edwin	R-R	6-2	223	8-25-95	.238	.235	.239	127	458	63	109	36	7	14	72	48	9	2	3	153	3	1	.439	.321
Gamache, Dan	L-R	5-11	205	11-20-90	.194	.200	.193	39	144	12	28	6	0	0	14	22	3	0	0	34	0	0	.236	.314
Goldby, Cooper	R-R	5-10	190	1-18-95	.115	.000	.159	22	61	3	7	0	0	0	9	1	0	0	30	0	0	.115	.239
Heim, Jonah	B-R	6-4	220	6-27-95	.282	.216	.299	50	181	20	51	12	0	5	34	24	2	0	1	27	0	1	.431	.370
McDonald, Mickey	B-R	6-2	175	6-2-95	.244	.229	.248	44	156	14	38	6	0	0	11	14	1	2	1	48	4	2	.282	.308
Merrell, Kevin	L-R	5-11	185	12-14-95	.246	.273	.239	82	289	37	71	13	4	2	34	18	3	3	5	67	13	4	.339	.292
2-team total (42 Northwest Arkansas)					.242	.247	.241	124	455	51	110	18	8	2	47	27	4	3	5	105	22	6	.330	.287
Miller, Anthony	L-R	6-4	240	10-4-94	.188	.167	.189	25	80	7	15	3	0	0	5	13	0	0	0	40	0	0	.225	.301
Mondou, Nate	L-R	5-10	185	3-24-95	.248	.270	.244	122	427	54	106	15	3	5	45	58	8	3	7	94	7	8	.333	.344
Motter, Taylor	R-R	6-1	195	9-18-89	.213	.351	.185	60	221	30	47	8	0	8	26	26	2	0	1	58	3	2	.358	.300
Mullen, Robert	R-R	5-11	225	5-23-96	.200	.000	.250	2	5	1	1	0	0	1	2	0	0	0	0	0	0	.800	.200
Perez, Brallan	R-R	5-10	165	1-27-96	.254	.234	.260	74	268	30	68	7	1	1	26	6	3	2	48	5	7	.299	.331
Persico, Chris	R-R	6-2	190	4-5-94	.257	.314	.238	37	136	21	35	6	2	2	13	13	1	1	38	1	0	.375	.325
Ramirez, Tyler	L-L	5-9	185	2-21-95	.240	.245	.239	79	279	35	67	14	2	5	42	47	7	0	3	89	5	2	.358	.360
Theroux, Collin	R-R	6-2	220	3-10-94	.180	.140	.186	93	306	42	55	13	0	12	36	49	4	1	4	178	0	0	.340	.298
White, Mikey	R-R	6-1	200	9-3-93	.261	.284	.256	97	391	59	102	26	0	10	61	40	7	1	2	102	2	3	.404	.339

Pitching	B-T	HT	WT	DOB	W	L	ERA	G	GS	CG	SV	IP	H	R	ER	HR	BB	SO	AVG	vLH	vRH	K/9	BB/9
Alexander, Tyler	L-L	6-1	180	9-22-91	1	1	0.56	8	0	0	0	16	7	1	1	0	5	14	.137	.273	.100	7.88	2.81
Bracewell, Ben	R-R	6-0	195	9-19-90	0	0	0.00	2	0	0	0	4	1	0	0	0	3	4	.083	.000	.111	9.00	6.75
Charles, Wandisson	R-R	6-6	220	9-7-96	1	0	1.88	9	0	0	0	14	9	4	3	1	5	17	.173	.188	.167	10.67	3.14
Cochran-Gill, Trey	R-R	5-9	195	12-10-92	3	4	5.36	35	2	0	2	49	49	31	29	6	28	38	.269	.296	.252	7.03	5.18
Duno, Angel	R-R	6-0	180	1-10-94	4	3	6.26	29	0	0	1	46	51	34	32	7	8	44	.276	.295	.262	8.61	1.57
Dunshee, Parker	R-R	6-0	215	2-12-95	2	2	1.89	6	6	0	0	38	26	11	8	1	11	34	.196	.207	.187	8.05	2.61
Erwin, Zack	L-L	6-5	195	1-24-94	6	3	3.22	39	0	0	7	59	71	28	21	6	15	68	.306	.282	.317	10.43	2.30
Finnegan, Kyle	R-R	6-2	196	9-4-91	0	1	1.59	21	0	0	9	23	16	5	4	0	7	36	.191	.226	.170	14.29	2.78
Friedrichs, Kyle	R-R	6-1	195	1-22-92	6	7	3.43	20	19	0	0	113	121	45	43	5	31	81	.281	.282	.281	6.47	2.48
Goldby, Cooper	R-R	5-10	190	1-18-95	0	0	108.00	1	0	0	0	1	5	8	8	1	2	0	.714	.667	.750	0.00	27.00
Gorman, John	R-R	6-1	230	2-19-92	4	5	4.76	43	1	0	0	57	63	35	30	7	19	72	.283	.266	.292	11.44	3.02
Hall, Charles	R-R	5-10	170	9-6-94	0	0	27.00	1	0	0	0	1	2	4	4	1	1	2	.333	.000	.500	13.50	6.75
Holmes, Grant	L-R	6-0	224	3-22-96	6	5	3.31	22	16	0	0	82	71	34	30	9	27	76	.235	.272	.205	8.38	2.98
Howard, Brian	R-R	6-9	185	4-25-95	8	8	3.25	23	23	0	0	130	137	54	47	7	39	118	.277	.279	.277	8.17	2.70
Hurtado, Jhenderson	L-L	5-11	205	3-28-96	0	0	0.00	1	1	0	0	4	2	0	0	0	2	4	.154	.000	.200	9.00	4.50
Jefferies, Daulton	L-R	6-0	182	8-2-95	1	2	3.66	21	12	0	0	64	63	30	26	7	7	72	.255	.213	.296	10.13	0.98
Jordan, Mitchell	R-R	6-1	210	4-10-95	0	0	6.75	1	1	0	0	4	3	3	3	1	4	4	.240	.000	.231	9.00	9.00
Kaprielian, James	R-R	6-3	210	3-2-94	2	1	1.63	7	5	0	0	28	18	5	5	2	8	26	.186	.150	.211	8.46	2.60
Martinez, Seth	R-R	6-2	200	8-29-94	4	1	1.26	16	0	0	0	29	21	5	4	0	9	33	.206	.389	.106	10.36	2.83
McNutt, Trey	R-R	6-4	220	8-2-89	2	3	5.33	15	0	0	0	25	29	15	15	2	4	35	.287	.222	.339	12.43	1.42
Milburn, Matt	R-R	6-3	210	7-29-93	8	9	4.90	26	25	1	0	151	179	89	82	18	37	86	.302	.332	.281	5.14	2.21
Mondou, Nate	L-R	5-10	205	3-24-95	0	0	0.00	1	0	0	0	0	1	0	0	0	0	0	.500	.500	--	0.00	0.00
Naile, James	R-R	6-4	185	2-8-93	8	7	5.54	24	21	0	1	125	155	83	77	12	44	82	.306	.337	.285	5.90	3.17
Puk, A.J.	L-L	6-7	238	4-25-95	0	0	4.32	6	1	0	0	8	9	4	4	2	3	13	.281	.444	.217	14.04	3.24
Ruiz, Norge	R-R	5-10	180	3-15-94	0	2	3.74	19	0	0	1	34	37	17	14	4	9	30	.282	.314	.263	8.02	2.41
Seddon, Joel	R-R	6-1	165	7-13-92	0	0	16.43	4	1	0	0	8	19	14	14	3	4	4	.500	.615	.440	4.70	4.70
Stull, Cody	L-L	6-2	160	3-23-92	2	2	2.87	29	0	0	0	38	32	13	12	1	13	34	.227	.196	.242	8.12	3.11
Verrett, Logan	R-R	6-2	190	6-19-90	1	0	3.93	7	4	0	0	34	30	15	15	4	4	33	.234	.273	.206	8.65	1.05
Zambrano, Jesus	R-R	5-10	204	8-23-96	4	0	1.21	28	1	0	7	45	41	9	6	1	13	32	.246	.212	.267	6.45	2.62

Fielding

Catcher	PCT	G	PO	A	E	DP	PB
Goldby	.983	18	105	14	2	0	0
Heim	.994	43	322	29	2	3	3
Mullen	1.000	2	11	0	0	0	0
Theroux	.989	82	663	60	8	3	9

First Base	PCT	G	PO	A	E	DP
Calabuig	.994	36	309	19	2	33
Diaz	1.000	1	4	0	0	0
Gamache	.990	24	181	15	2	20
Goldby	.000	1	0	0	0	0
Miller	.992	17	118	7	1	13
Motter	1.000	5	40	2	0	4
Persico	.992	17	118	4	1	16
Theroux	1.000	1	3	0	0	0
White	.986	44	337	24	5	38

Second Base	PCT	G	PO	A	E	DP
Diaz	1.000	1	1	1	0	0
Merrell	1.000	2	1	5	0	2
Mondou	.990	103	193	298	5	68
Motter	1.000	2	0	5	0	0
Perez	.967	27	55	90	5	25
White	.962	8	12	13	1	2

Third Base	PCT	G	PO	A	E	DP
Bride	1.000	2	1	2	0	0
Diaz	.976	73	61	141	5	20
Gamache	1.000	5	2	5	0	0
Mondou	1.000	10	4	13	0	2
Motter	.951	20	8	31	2	5
Perez	1.000	1	0	1	0	0
White	.913	30	19	44	6	4

Shortstop	PCT	G	PO	A	E	DP
Diaz	.970	53	81	174	8	41
Merrell	.970	80	121	197	10	53
Motter	1.000	3	3	10	0	2
White	.960	4	9	15	1	2

Outfield	PCT	G	PO	A	E	DP
Barrera	.983	50	109	5	2	0
Blanco	.987	71	144	6	2	0
Calabuig	.991	58	104	3	1	1
Deichmann	.973	72	139	7	4	1
Goldby	.500	1	1	0	1	0
McDonald	1.000	44	117	3	0	1
Motter	.941	23	46	2	3	0
Perez	.973	41	69	3	2	0
Persico	.953	20	39	2	2	0
Ramirez	.987	44	73	4	1	1
White	.000	1	0	0	0	0

STOCKTON PORTS   HIGH CLASS A
CALIFORNIA LEAGUE

Batting	B-T	HT	WT	DOB	AVG	vLH	vRH	G	AB	R	H	2B	3B	HR	RBI	BB	HBP	SH	SF	SO	SB	CS	SLG	OBP
Allen, Nick	R-R	5-9	166	10-8-98	.292	.397	.265	72	288	45	84	22	5	3	25	28	4	8	0	52	13	5	.434	.363
Armenteros, Lazaro	R-R	6-0	182	5-22-99	.222	.274	.209	126	459	65	102	22	5	17	61	73	6	0	0	227	22	6	.403	.336
Beck, Austin	R-R	6-1	200	11-21-98	.252	.254	.251	85	338	40	85	22	4	8	49	24	2	0	3	126	2	2	.411	.303
Bride, Jonah	R-R	5-10	200	12-27-95	.279	.250	.287	115	402	54	112	18	4	10	58	44	17	0	3	97	2	0	.418	.371
Cross, Matt	R-R	6-1	205	7-28-98	.091	.000	.100	3	11	1	1	0	0	0	1	1	1	0	0	6	0	0	.364	.231
Devencenzi, Jordan	R-R	5-11	203	6-26-93	.251	.324	.237	73	227	17	57	6	0	1	20	15	7	3	3	59	0	0	.291	.314
Eierman, Jeremy	R-R	6-0	205	9-10-96	.208	.206	.208	131	501	57	104	22	7	13	64	39	5	3	4	177	11	3	.357	.270
Giarratano, Nico	B-R	5-11	172	12-15-94	.193	.111	.214	28	88	13	17	3	0	1	7	9	2	0	1	36	1	0	.261	.280
Gonzalez, Yhoelnys	R-R	6-0	170	10-30-96	.133	.091	.147	14	45	6	6	1	0	0	2	4	1	0	0	25	2	0	.156	.220
Gridley, Ryan	R-R	5-8	180	5-4-95	.274	.208	.294	59	237	27	65	15	0	3	20	17	3	2	2	43	4	2	.376	.328
Hannah, Jameson	L-L	5-9	185	8-10-97	.283	.305	.277	92	375	48	106	25	3	2	31	29	6	0	3	88	6	7	.381	.341
Hargrove, Hunter	R-R	5-10	200	9-9-94	.209	.279	.187	48	182	13	38	8	1	3	21	13	1	0	0	43	0	1	.313	.265
Hundley, Nick	R-R	6-0	203	9-8-83	.191	.000	.267	5	21	3	4	1	0	0	1	2	0	0	0	7	0	0	.238	.261
Loehr, Trace	L-R	5-10	185	5-23-95	.291	.315	.285	93	350	54	102	20	3	3	40	30	3	0	2	71	10	7	.391	.351
McDonald, Mickey	B-R	6-2	175	6-25-95	.229	.289	.213	66	214	28	49	9	2	4	25	16	6	2	4	66	12	6	.294	.324
Mullen, Robert	R-R	5-11	225	5-23-96	.280	.314	.271	70	250	31	70	15	0	10	36	13	7	0	4	65	0	0	.460	.329
Perez, Brallan	R-R	5-10	165	1-27-96	.192	.000	.208	10	26	2	5	2	0	0	1	2	0	0	0	7	1	0	.269	.250
Phegley, Josh	R-R	5-10	225	2-12-88	.400	--	.400	1	5	2	2	0	0	0	1	0	0	0	0	2	0	0	.400	.400
Rincones, Rafael	R-R	6-0	159	7-1-99	.091	.000	.100	4	11	0	1	0	0	0	0	3	1	0	0	6	0	0	.091	.333
Rivas, Alfonso	L-L	6-0	188	9-13-96	.283	.245	.294	114	431	60	122	24	3	8	55	66	7	0	5	113	2	2	.408	.383

Name	B-T	HT	WT	DOB	AVG	vLH	vRH	G	AB	R	H	2B	3B	HR	RBI	BB	HBP	SH	SF	SO	SB	CS	OBP	SLG
Schwarz, JJ	R-R	6-1	205	3-28-96	.109	.053	.133	20	64	2	7	1	0	0	3	7	0	0	0	19	0	0	.125	.197
Squier, Payton	L-R	6-0	220	10-29-95	.176	.067	.203	21	74	10	13	5	0	0	3	4	1	0	0	11	1	0	.243	.228
Watson, Josh	B-R	5-11	205	9-10-96	.109	.182	.091	20	55	9	6	1	1	1	7	11	1	0	2	19	2	0	.218	.261

Pitching

Name	B-T	HT	WT	DOB	W	L	ERA	G	GS	CG	SV	IP	H	R	ER	HR	BB	SO	AVG	vLH	vRH	K/9	BB/9
Altamirano, Xavier	R-R	6-1	208	7-20-94	5	13	5.61	28	26	0	0	130	156	90	81	23	39	104	.293	.286	.297	7.20	2.70
Bassitt, Chris	R-R	6-5	220	2-22-89	0	0	0.00	1	1	0	0	3	0	0	0	0	0	7	.000	.000	.000	21.00	0.00
Bayer, Peter	R-R	6-4	195	3-6-94	1	1	3.38	37	0	0	4	51	38	21	19	3	38	60	.205	.264	.168	10.66	6.75
Bray, Jake	R-R	6-0	190	12-8-92	2	3	5.34	35	1	0	4	61	63	37	36	12	32	74	.266	.316	.232	10.98	4.75
Charles, Wandisson	R-R	6-6	220	9-7-96	2	0	3.16	18	0	0	2	26	14	15	9	1	18	39	.161	.100	.193	13.68	6.31
Cochran-Gill, Trey	R-R	5-9	195	12-10-92	0	2	5.06	9	0	0	2	11	12	6	6	3	8	7	.300	.455	.241	5.91	6.75
Conley, Bryce	R-R	6-3	200	8-22-94	3	1	2.78	9	7	0	0	32	20	11	10	4	21	29	.184	.231	.157	8.07	5.85
Cotton, Jharel	R-R	5-11	200	1-19-92	1	1	6.00	4	2	0	0	9	7	6	6	3	2	9	.200	.250		9.00	2.00
Damron, Ty	L-L	6-2	200	7-28-94	1	0	2.03	17	0	0	0	27	13	6	6	2	9	31	.155	.039	.207	10.46	3.04
Danielak, Michael	R-R	6-4	215	3-16-94	3	0	3.41	16	0	0	0	29	27	15	11	3	8	40	.246	.255	.238	12.41	2.48
Duno, Angel	R-R	6-0	180	1-10-94	0	2	4.08	11	0	0	0	18	17	9	8	2		15	.254	.200	.286	7.64	1.02
Estrada, Marco	R-R	6-0	180	7-5-83	0	1	8.10	3	3	0	0	7	9	7	6	3	1	8	.300	.154	.412	10.80	1.35
Feigl, Brady	R-R	6-4	235	11-27-95	5	11	4.42	27	25	0	0	134	148	83	66	12	35	119	.282	.261	.298	7.97	2.34
Friedrichs, Kyle	R-R	6-1	195	1-22-92	0	0	3.38	3	3	0	0	11	9	4	4	1	3	8	.237	.375	.136	6.75	2.53
Giarratano, Nico	B-R	5-11	172	12-15-94	0	0	6.75	3	0	0	0	3	2	2	2	1	1	1	.200	.000	.286	3.38	3.38
Gilbert, Will	L-L	5-11	174	2-9-94	5	1	4.30	35	0	0	0	59	56	36	28	7	23	66	.246	.232	.250	10.13	3.53
Hargrove, Hunter	R-R	5-10	208	9-9-94	0	0	6.00	3	0	0	0	3	5	2	2	0	2	4	.357	.250	.400	12.00	6.00
Harris, Hogan	R-L	6-3	230	12-26-96	0	2	2.51	7	7	0	0	29	18	8	8	2	10	29	.184	.276	.145	9.10	3.14
Highberger, Nick	R-R	5-11	200	11-4-93	5	4	4.38	44	0	0	6	64	61	40	31	5	36	46	.255	.232	.271	6.50	5.09
Hurtado, Jhenderson	L-L	5-11	205	3-28-96	0	1	36.00	1	1	0	0	1	3	4	4	0	2	1	.500	1.000	.400	9.00	18.00
Jackson, Edwin	R-R	6-2	215	9-9-83	1	0	3.60	1	1	0	0	5	5	2	2	1	0	9	.263	.308	.167	16.20	0.00
Jefferies, Daulton	L-R	6-0	182	8-2-95	1	0	2.40	5	3	0	0	15	10	4	4	1	2	21	.182	.217	.156	12.60	1.20
Jordan, Mitchell	R-R	6-1	210	4-10-95	10	7	4.41	27	22	0	0	141	141	75	69	24	39	131	.258	.271	.248	8.38	2.50
Kaprielian, James	R-R	6-3	210	3-2-94	2	2	4.46	11	10	0	0	36	35	19	18	6	8	43	.250	.203	.284	10.65	1.98
Kelly, Rafael	R-R	6-2	190	6-9-97	0	1	4.15	6	5	0	0	26	27	15	12	3	9	20	.257	.259	.256	6.92	3.12
Krall, Pat	L-L	6-2	225	8-27-94	2	3	5.12	23	1	0	1	32	41	18	18	2	11	23	.318	.244	.352	6.54	3.13
Leal, David	L-L	6-5	250	4-22-97	0	0	4.50	1	1	0	0	4	4	2	2	0	1	2	.250	.000	.333	4.50	2.25
Loehr, Trace	L-R	5-10	185	5-23-95	0	0	0.00	1	0	0	0	0	1	0	0	0	0	1	.500	1.000	.000	27.00	0.00
Luzardo, Jesus	L-L	6-0	209	9-30-97	1	0	0.90	3	1	0	0	10	6	1	1	1	0	18	.171	.000	.222	16.20	0.00
Manaea, Sean	R-L	6-5	245	2-1-92	0	2	9.72	3	3	0	0	8	14	11	9	1	4	10	.368	.200	.429	10.80	4.32
Marinez, Eric	B-R	6-1	160	9-12-95	1	0	5.40	20	0	0	1	30	26	18	18	2	17	41	.222	.260	.194	12.30	5.10
Marks, Wyatt	R-R	6-2	215	6-28-95	2	2	5.40	4	4	0	0	18	15	11	11	2	14	10	.224	.080	.310	4.91	6.87
Martinez, Seth	R-R	6-2	200	8-29-94	3	3	3.35	26	0	0	2	43	29	16	16	3	9	41	.193	.183	.200	8.58	1.88
McDonald, Mickey	B-R	6-2	175	6-2-95	0	0	0.00	1	0	0	0	1	0	0	0	0	1	0	.000	.000		9.00	0.00
Nambiar, Kumar	L-L	5-11	188	4-17-98	1	0	6.00	1	0	0	0	3	3	3	2	0	3	2	.273	.333	.250	6.00	9.00
Perez, Brallan	R-R	5-10	165	1-27-96	0	0	0.00	1	0	0	0	2	0	0	0	0	1	0	.400	.500	.333	9.00	0.00
Pineda, Leudeny	R-R	6-1	205	1-29-96	0	1	11.25	1	1	0	0	4	7	5	5	1	2	3	.389	.182	.714	6.75	4.50
Poche', Jared	R-L	6-0	217	11-21-94	0	6	8.53	8	1	0	0	25	26	25	24	4	16	21	.268	.385	.225	7.46	5.68
Puk, A.J.	L-L	6-7	238	4-25-95	0	0	6.00	3	3	0	0	6	5	5	4	2	4	9	.238	.000	.278	13.50	6.00
Seddon, Joel	R-R	6-1	165	7-13-92	0	2	6.59	5	2	0	0	14	18	10	10	2	6	15	.321	.414	.222	9.88	3.95
Sheehan, Sam	R-R	6-2	200	8-8-93	0	4	7.48	22	0	0	0	28	31	29	23	1	37	43	.282	.325	.257	13.99	12.04
Varland, Gus	L-R	6-1	205	11-6-96	2	1	2.39	5	4	0	0	26	23	8	7	3	8	27	.235	.268	.211	9.23	2.73
Zambrano, Jesus	R-R	5-10	204	8-23-96	1	1	1.88	15	0	0	2	29	19	7	6	2	8	31	.186	.200	.177	9.73	2.51

Fielding

Catcher	PCT	G	PO	A	E	DP	PB
Cross	.889	1	8	0	1	0	0
Devencenzi	.997	69	595	53	2	4	9
Hundley	1.000	3	36	2	0	0	1
Mullen	.985	52	408	42	7	3	14
Phegley	1.000	1	7	0	0	0	0
Schwarz	.994	20	154	10	1	0	7

First Base	PCT	G	PO	A	E	DP
Bride	.983	9	54	4	1	6
Hargrove	.990	23	181	13	2	14
Rivas	.995	98	724	35	4	70
Squier	.975	10	75	3	2	9

Second Base	PCT	G	PO	A	E	DP
Allen	.982	24	49	58	2	14
Eierman	.957	33	51	83	6	21
Gridley	.981	37	67	88	3	19
Loehr	.981	43	59	93	3	19
Perez	1.000	1	5	4	0	1

Third Base	PCT	G	PO	A	E	DP
Bride	.969	93	69	151	7	14
Eierman	1.000	4	2	9	0	0
Giarratano	1.000	5	3	6	0	1
Gridley	.857	3	1	5	1	0
Loehr	.892	32	12	54	8	6
McDonald	1.000	1	0	3	0	1

Shortstop	PCT	G	PO	A	E	DP
Allen	.979	45	56	129	4	27
Eierman	.975	91	133	220	9	47
Gridley	.923	2	8	4	1	2

Outfield	PCT	G	PO	A	E	DP
Armenteros	.983	119	221	4	4	0
Beck	.979	79	175	8	4	2
Giarratano	.972	21	33	2	1	0
Gonzalez	1.000	14	29	0	0	0
Hannah	.984	89	177	8	3	0
McDonald	.984	63	123	2	2	1
Perez	.917	7	11	0	1	0
Rincones	.667	3	3	1	2	0
Rivas	.947	10	17	1	1	0
Squier	1.000	6	9	0	0	0
Watson	.971	19	32	2	1	0

Batting	B-T	HT	WT	DOB	AVG	vLH	vRH	G	AB	R	H	2B	3B	HR	RBI	BB	HBP	SH	SF	SO	SB	CS	SLG	OBP
Brito, Marcos	B-R	6-0	165	3-6-00	.181	.195	.178	62	204	21	37	8	0	2	13	22	0	1	1	67	3	4	.250	.260
Calabuig, Chase	L-L	5-11	185	12-10-95	.304	.429	.200	13	46	4	14	2	0	1	5	12	0	0	0	10	1	2	.413	.448
Churlin, Anthony	R-R	6-1	205	5-27-97	.259	.235	.265	91	328	31	85	16	0	4	39	31	6	2	3	98	8	6	.345	.332
Farrar, Logan	L-R	5-10	180	4-16-95	.221	.125	.245	72	244	34	54	8	0	2	27	34	3	1	3	70	5	2	.279	.320
Foyle, Devin	B-L	6-3	190	11-18-96	.236	.146	.254	95	327	49	77	15	3	6	43	52	6	2	4	98	16	8	.355	.347
Goldby, Cooper	R-R	5-10	190	1-18-95	.172	.500	.087	10	29	1	5	1	0	0	2	4	0	0	0	7	1	0	.207	.273
Gridley, Ryan	R-R	5-8	180	5-4-95	.259	.342	.237	53	189	27	49	14	1	3	20	16	5	2	1	32	6	2	.392	.332
Jones, John	B-R	5-10	190	10-9-95	.238	.182	.248	86	298	36	71	9	0	6	42	52	4	0	3	86	2	2	.329	.356
Madden, Lester	R-R	6-2	190	1-19-99	.212	.243	.205	105	391	43	83	19	4	2	38	22	5	1	1	118	5	6	.297	.263
Osborne, Nick	R-R	6-2	205	2-20-97	.240	.208	.249	67	246	26	59	19	1	7	38	23	1	0	5	87	6	5	.411	.332
Pena, Joseph	B-R	5-9	175	10-27-95	.241	.191	.253	96	336	54	81	9	3	1	28	61	7	4	5	65	9	4	.295	.364
Perez, Brallan	R-R	5-10	165	1-27-96	.222	1.000	.125	3	9	1	2	0	0	0	0	1	2	0	0	2	1	1	.222	.417
Sanchez, Santis	R-R	6-1	199	8-21-98	.168	.313	.132	46	161	10	27	8	0	2	14	12	3	0	2	52	0	0	.255	.236
Schuemann, Max	R-R	6-1	186	6-11-97	.256	.295	.247	94	340	57	87	29	1	3	35	30	14	2	2	75	25	11	.374	.339
Schwarz, JJ	R-R	6-1	205	3-28-96	.180	.177	.180	24	78	6	14	1	0	3	11	10	1	0	3	21	0	0	.308	.272
Squier, Payton	L-R	6-0	220	10-29-95	.315	.231	.337	36	127	18	40	8	1	0	13	15	2	0	1	30	8	1	.394	.393
Vance, Cobie	R-R	5-8	185	8-24-97	.232	.290	.217	85	293	39	68	18	0	1	28	39	6	0	7	59	4	1	.304	.328
Vaughan, Noah	L-L	6-0	200	6-6-97	.170	.273	.139	15	47	4	8	1	2	1	4	1	0	0	0	25	0	0	.340	.188
Ward, Nick	L-R	5-10	180	10-19-95	.232	.345	.204	85	293	35	68	10	3	4	35	40	6	2	2	91	6	1	.328	.334
Weber, Skyler	L-R	5-10	176	6-6-95	.195	.159	.204	101	343	41	67	19	0	4	34	35	5	2	2	87	11	3	.286	.278
Woodworth, Michael	R-R	5-9	175	8-5-97	.217	.308	.200	26	83	10	18	5	0	0	3	7	2	3	1	18	4	1	.229	.333

Pitching	B-T	HT	WT	DOB	W	L	ERA	G	GS	CG	SV	IP	H	R	ER	HR	BB	SO	AVG	vLH	vRH	K/9	BB/9
Birlingmair, Reid	L-R	5-10	210	11-13-96	6	6	4.02	24	21	0	0	123	108	62	55	12	50	120	.235	.241	.231	8.78	3.66
Cerny, Charlie	R-R	6-5	230	9-23-96	2	5	3.57	38	0	0	8	53	45	29	21	1	37	42	.236	.200	.256	7.13	6.28
Charles, Wandisson	R-R	6-6	220	9-7-96	1	0	3.22	13	0	0	0	22	12	9	8	1	20	37	.158	.111	.184	14.91	8.06
Cohen, Chase	L-R	6-1	183	4-26-97	5	10	4.64	27	18	0	2	114	113	68	59	9	56	106	.260	.261	.259	8.34	4.41
Coker, Calvin	R-R	6-3	174	3-6-96	1	3	4.82	24	0	0	3	37	33	21	20	4	7	33	.234	.304	.167	7.96	1.69
Conley, Bryce	R-R	6-3	200	8-22-94	3	4	3.73	16	12	0	1	70	51	31	29	7	38	69	.202	.250	.164	8.87	4.89
Damron, Ty	L-L	6-2	200	7-28-94	0	0	1.50	9	0	0	1	18	6	3	3	0	9	25	.105	.111	.103	12.50	4.50
Danielak, Michael	R-R	6-4	215	3-16-94	3	1	2.05	19	0	0	1	31	28	8	7	3	6	38	.237	.170	.282	11.15	1.76
DeMers, Joe	R-R	6-1	240	11-9-96	5	4	5.49	23	13	0	2	95	111	59	58	11	17	75	.294	.311	.283	7.11	1.61
Goldby, Cooper	R-R	5-10	190	1-18-95	0	0	0.00	2	0	0	0	1	0	0	0	0	0	0	.000	.000	.000	0.00	0.00
Guasch, Richard	R-R	6-4	205	4-10-98	0	4	4.53	18	10	0	2	60	52	31	30	1	37	77	.236	.238	.235	11.61	5.58
Hurtado, Jhenderson	L-L	5-11	205	3-28-96	1	1	2.61	7	5	0	1	31	22	13	9	1	13	38	.190	.121	.217	11.03	3.77
Infante, Angello	R-R	6-1	180	4-16-99	3	6	2.83	13	8	0	1	60	51	26	19	3	13	37	.228	.253	.213	5.52	1.94
Kelly, Rafael	R-R	6-2	190	6-9-97	5	4	2.81	13	8	0	1	58	48	26	18	6	11	50	.219	.202	.230	7.80	1.72
Lebron, Jaimito	R-R	6-2	195	10-20-96	2	1	3.86	35	1	0	0	51	50	27	22	2	24	50	.263	.259	.266	8.77	4.21
Marinez, Eric	B-R	6-1	160	9-12-95	4	2	2.87	25	0	0	10	31	19	12	10	0	18	44	.173	.149	.191	12.64	5.17
Martinez, Daniel	L-R	5-11	190	7-28-98	1	1	2.35	4	3	0	0	15	12	9	4	1	6	14	.211	.036	.379	8.22	3.52
McIntyre, Aiden	R-R	6-5	220	8-27-95	3	10	4.15	27	22	0	1	113	99	68	52	5	76	150	.228	.194	.254	11.98	6.07
Mejia, Jeferson	R-R	6-7	255	8-2-94	0	0	90.00	3	0	0	0	1	5	10	10	0	8	1	.714	.667	.750	9.00	72.00
Murray, Michael	R-R	6-3	215	9-26-93	0	4	10.13	5	3	0	0	13	18	16	15	1	7	14	.333	.346	.321	9.45	4.73
Nightengale, Bryce	R-R	6-5	215	8-16-96	1	6	5.29	16	9	0	0	49	44	35	29	3	35	40	.239	.208	.259	7.30	6.39
Pena, Joseph	B-R	5-9	175	10-27-95	0	0	0.00	1	0	0	0	1	1	0	0	0	1	0	.333	1.000	.000	0.00	9.00
Reagan, Josh	B-L	6-1	185	10-2-94	4	2	2.20	16	0	0	0	33	27	16	8	3	12	31	.221	.234	.213	8.54	3.31
Reuss, Adam	R-R	6-4	220	3-14-95	0	5	4.89	9	5	0	0	39	42	31	21	3	20	30	.273	.286	.264	6.98	4.66
Ward, Nick	L-R	5-10	180	10-19-95	1	0	0.00	4	0	0	0	4	5	1	0	0	1	0	.313	.500	.200	0.00	2.45
Withers, Brandon	R-R	6-0	200	7-4-94	3	5	4.87	41	0	0	2	61	78	41	33	3	22	60	.308	.326	.298	8.85	3.25

Fielding

Catcher	PCT	G	PO	A	E	DP	PB
Goldby	.962	6	47	3	2	0	2
Jones	.986	48	374	37	6	2	4
Sanchez	1.000	1	8	0	0	0	1
Weber	.985	83	744	67	12	2	18

First Base	PCT	G	PO	A	E	DP
Goldby	1.000	3	13	1	0	1
Jones	.933	2	12	2	1	0
Sanchez	.975	38	295	16	8	29
Schuemann	1.000	14	113	1	0	10
Schwarz	.981	19	142	11	3	17
Squier	.983	17	111	6	2	14
Vaughan	.961	8	69	4	3	5
Ward	.985	44	311	19	5	20
Weber	1.000	3	6	0	0	2

Second Base	PCT	G	PO	A	E	DP
Gridley	.978	25	40	50	2	13
Pena	.969	94	167	234	13	47
Schuemann	1.000	2	3	0	0	0
Vance	.000	1	0	0	0	0
Ward	.963	18	27	52	3	15
Woodworth	1.000	2	4	4	0	1

Third Base	PCT	G	PO	A	E	DP
Jones	1.000	1	1	0	0	0
Schuemann	.934	24	13	44	4	8
Vance	.948	83	79	141	12	12
Ward	.898	20	14	30	5	4
Weber	.000	1	0	0	0	0
Woodworth	.975	16	14	25	1	3

Shortstop	PCT	G	PO	A	E	DP
Brito	.938	60	69	114	12	24
Gridley	.970	27	41	88	4	17
Perez	1.000	1	2	1	0	0

Schuemann	.954	51	68	138	10	27
Vance	1.000	2	2	4	0	0
Woodworth	1.000	1	1	3	0	1

Outfield	PCT	G	PO	A	E	DP
Calabuig	.964	12	26	1	1	1
Churlin	.958	78	110	5	5	0
Farrar	.938	50	72	4	5	0
Foyle	.989	93	182	4	2	2
Madden	.952	98	166	11	9	0
Osborne	.953	54	94	7	5	1
Perez	1.000	2	1	0	0	0
Schuemann	1.000	3	2	1	0	0
Squier	1.000	11	15	0	0	0
Vaughan	1.000	6	7	0	0	0
Weber	1.000	5	12	1	0	0
Woodworth	1.000	8	19	1	0	1

OAKLAND ATHLETICS

VERMONT LAKE MONSTERS
SHORT SEASON

NEW YORK-PENN LEAGUE

Batting	B-T	HT	WT	DOB	AVG	vLH	vRH	G	AB	R	H	2B	3B	HR	RBI	BB	HBP	SH	SF	SO	SB	CS	SLG	OBP
Bautista, Danny	R-R	6-2	185	9-20-00	.276	.250	.286	15	58	7	16	2	1	0	3	4	0	0	1	16	0	3	.345	.318
Bechina, Marty	R-R	6-0	200	10-31-96	.235	.286	.222	47	179	18	42	10	1	3	17	13	2	1	1	53	1	1	.352	.292
Butler, Lawrence	L-R	6-4	185	7-10-00	.177	.171	.179	55	192	20	34	5	2	4	22	26	1	0	2	90	1	0	.287	.276
Cross, Matt	R-R	6-1	205	7-28-98	.000	.000	.000	5	14	0	0	0	0	0	0	2	1	0	0	3	0	0	.000	.177
Davidson, Logan	B-R	6-3	185	12-26-97	.239	.200	.249	54	205	42	49	7	0	4	12	31	2	0	0	55	5	0	.332	.345
Diaz, Jordan	R-R	5-10	175	8-13-00	.264	.235	.273	70	277	31	73	17	1	9	47	18	1	0	4	46	2	2	.430	.307
Gordon, Jorge	R-R	5-10	175	10-28-97	.140	.167	.133	19	57	3	8	1	0	0	3	3	1	1	1	27	0	0	.158	.194
Harris, Dustin	L-R	6-2	185	7-8-99	.321	.462	.296	23	84	10	27	2	0	0	10	11	2	0	1	19	0	3	.345	.408
McCann, Kyle	L-R	6-2	217	12-2-97	.192	.132	.206	55	198	23	38	7	1	7	25	25	2	0	0	81	0	0	.343	.289
Osborne, Nick	R-R	6-2	205	2-20-97	.181	.091	.220	22	72	5	13	4	0	0	4	5	1	1	1	15	1	0	.236	.241
Quintin, Christopher	R-R	6-0	135	6-7-99	.194	.111	.227	10	31	1	6	1	0	0	1	3	0	0	0	16	0	1	.226	.265
Richards, Kevin	R-R	6-2	160	1-8-00	.228	.193	.239	68	254	20	58	11	1	4	37	12	2	2	6	76	1	1	.350	.263
Rivas, Jose	R-R	5-11	220	8-5-98	.204	.195	.207	57	191	22	39	7	3	1	14	19	8	0	0	42	2	2	.288	.303
Selman, Shane	R-L	5-11	198	8-30-96	.140	.222	.113	36	107	10	15	6	1	0	6	13	2	0	1	30	0	0	.215	.244
Vargas, Yerdel	R-R	6-0	170	2-17-00	.158	.250	.132	60	196	20	31	5	0	4	20	19	2	1	0	73	1	1	.245	.240
Vaughan, Noah	L-L	6-3	200	6-6-97	.122	.091	.127	31	90	10	11	1	0	2	7	6	4	1	0	38	2	3	.200	.210
Ward, Nick	L-R	5-10	180	9-19-95	.267	.333	.250	13	45	13	12	2	0	2	5	11	3	0	1	6	0	1	.444	.433
Watson, Josh	B-R	5-11	205	9-10-96	.218	.313	.194	23	78	8	17	3	0	1	6	15	3	1	0	25	0	0	.295	.365
Woodworth, Michael	R-R	5-9	175	8-5-97	.221	.281	.198	33	113	12	25	3	0	0	10	12	7	1	2	18	4	2	.248	.328

Pitching	B-T	HT	WT	DOB	W	L	ERA	G	GS	CG	SV	IP	H	R	ER	HR	BB	SO	AVG	vLH	vRH	K/9	BB/9
Baum, Tyler	R-R	6-2	195	1-14-98	0	3	4.70	11	11	0	0	31	29	18	16	4	7	34	.246	.265	.232	9.98	2.05
Berrios, Osvaldo	R-R	6-2	200	11-29-99	0	4	5.79	11	6	0	0	37	44	28	24	5	11	29	.295	.241	.326	6.99	2.65
Briggs, Austin	R-L	6-1	205	10-11-95	1	1	4.71	19	0	0	0	29	32	24	15	2	22	22	.278	.148	.318	6.91	6.91
Coker, Calvin	R-R	6-3	174	3-6-96	0	0	4.91	6	0	0	1	4	4	3	2	0	4	2	.267	.000	.308	4.91	9.82
Coletti, Vince	R-R	6-2	210	11-3-96	1	1	5.40	14	0	0	0	23	31	16	14	0	8	20	.313	.382	.277	7.71	3.09
Cota, Clark	R-R	6-2	230	10-6-96	2	3	5.06	19	0	0	0	32	26	22	18	1	24	37	.219	.147	.247	10.41	6.75
Cushing, Jack	R-R	6-3	195	12-3-96	2	6	5.59	11	6	0	0	37	40	27	23	5	20	21	.274	.264	.280	5.11	4.86
Guasch, Richard	R-R	6-4	205	4-10-98	0	0	0.00	1	1	0	0	4	1	0	0	0	1	5	.077	.143	.000	11.25	2.25
Harris, Hogan	R-L	6-3	230	12-26-96	1	3	3.12	8	6	0	0	26	14	11	9	2	9	36	.154	.158	.153	12.46	3.12
Hurtado, Jhenderson	L-L	5-11	205	3-28-96	3	0	0.77	7	0	0	1	23	12	2	2	1	10	34	.156	.222	.098	13.11	3.86
Infante, Angello	R-R	6-1	180	4-16-99	0	3	3.86	4	3	0	0	14	14	9	6	2	3	12	.250	.200	.290	7.71	1.93
Kelly, Rafael	R-R	6-2	190	6-9-97	1	0	5.40	1	1	0	0	5	5	3	3	0	1	6	.263	.571	.083	10.80	1.80
Martinez, Jorge	L-L	5-11	170	1-6-99	5	2	3.67	17	0	0	1	34	31	17	14	2	15	47	.231	.192	.241	12.32	3.93
Mejia, Jeferson	R-R	6-7	255	8-2-94	1	2	4.76	18	0	0	5	28	30	17	15	5	8	42	.275	.400	.203	13.34	2.54
Mora, Jose	R-R	6-3	200	10-1-97	2	0	2.30	20	0	0	11	27	8	7	7	0	15	47	.093	.167	.054	15.48	4.94
Morban, Richard	R-R	6-2	162	12-24-97	2	1	2.67	15	9	0	0	71	63	24	21	5	26	69	.244	.273	.232	8.79	3.31
Murray, Michael	R-R	6-3	215	9-26-93	3	1	2.47	12	11	0	0	47	42	13	13	2	9	45	.244	.262	.234	8.56	1.71
Noa, Yorlenis	L-L	6-3	185	4-12-96	1	6	5.36	14	6	0	1	47	43	30	28	1	20	40	.247	.195	.263	7.66	3.83
Pantuso, Alexander	L-R	6-6	235	10-14-95	0	0	4.50	2	0	0	0	4	4	3	2	0	0	8	.250	.200	.273	18.00	0.00
Peluse, Colin	R-R	6-3	230	6-11-98	2	1	2.25	8	5	0	0	24	21	8	6	1	6	26	.226	.250	.215	9.75	2.25
Pineda, Leudeny	R-R	6-1	205	1-29-96	2	1	7.36	7	2	0	0	22	34	21	18	2	12	19	.358	.421	.316	7.77	4.91
Reagan, Josh	B-L	6-1	185	10-2-94	0	0	0.90	4	0	0	1	10	8	2	1	1	1	18	.211	.250	.192	16.20	0.90
Sanchez, Carlos	R-R	5-11	150	12-26-97	4	0	2.88	18	0	0	1	41	27	16	13	3	16	38	.181	.216	.163	8.41	3.54
Selman, Shane	R-L	5-11	198	8-30-96	0	0	0.00	1	0	0	0	1	0	0	0	0	2	2	.000	.000	.000	18.00	18.00
Shuman, Seth	R-R	6-1	195	12-1-97	0	3	2.39	11	8	0	0	38	34	14	10	2	9	21	.246	.196	.272	5.02	2.15
Ward, Nick	L-R	5-10	180	10-19-95	0	1	--	1	0	0	0	0	1	1	0	0	1	0	1.000	--1.000	--	--	--

Fielding

C: Cross 3, Gordon 16, McCann 18, Rivas 42. **1B:** Butler 36, Harris 13, McCann 20, Quintin 4, Rivas 3. **2B:** Bechina 11, Quintin 2, Vargas 35, Ward 13, Woodworth 16. **3B:** Bechina 10, Diaz 61, Harris 1, Quintin 1, Woodworth 2. **SS:** Davidson 50, Quintin 1, Vargas 25. **OF:** Bautista 15, Bechina 22, Butler 14, Osborne 16, Quintin 2, Richards 66, Selman 35, Vaughan 24, Watson 23, Woodworth 14.

AZL ATHLETICS GOLD
ROOKIE

ARIZONA LEAGUE

Batting	B-T	HT	WT	DOB	AVG	vLH	vRH	G	AB	R	H	2B	3B	HR	RBI	BB	HBP	SH	SF	SO	SB	CS	SLG	OBP
Alvarez, Wilson	R-R	5-10	155	5-19-98	.248	.313	.237	27	109	23	27	4	1	0	8	12	1	1	0	18	4	0	.303	.328
2-team total (27 Athletics Green)					.286	.349	.271	54	220	40	63	9	2	0	18	25	3	2	2	49	7	1	.346	.364
Astorri, Cesarre	R-R	6-0	188	6-7-96	.161	.188	.155	29	87	10	14	4	2	0	11	11	7	0	2	30	1	0	.253	.299
Bechina, Marty	R-R	6-0	200	10-31-96	.302	.500	.244	14	53	13	16	9	0	1	15	14	1	0	1	12	0	2	.528	.449
Betancourt, Marcos	R-R	6-0	165	1-17-01	.286	.000	.400	5	14	3	4	0	0	0	1	2	1	0	0	3	0	0	.286	.412
2-team total (23 Athletics Green)					.179	.107	.209	28	95	7	17	3	0	0	13	11	4	0	0	25	1	0	.211	.291
Cross, Matt	R-R	6-1	205	7-28-98	.235	.267	.229	33	98	17	23	3	2	3	16	19	1	0	2	25	0	1	.398	.358
Dingcong, Gio	R-R	6-3	245	5-23-95	.157	.177	.153	38	115	20	18	3	0	3	15	18	2	0	2	43	1	1	.261	.277
2-team total (4 Athletics Green)					.169	.191	.165	42	130	23	22	3	0	3	15	19	2	0	2	49	1	1	.262	.281
Gonzalez, Yhoelnys	R-R	6-0	170	10-30-96	.317	.222	.333	30	123	26	39	3	2	1	15	11	1	2	0	39	8	3	.398	.378
Gordon, Jorge	R-R	5-10	175	10-28-97	.250	--	.250	2	8	0	2	0	0	0	2	0	0	0	0	0	0	0	.250	.250
Hundley, Nick	R-R	6-0	203	9-8-83	.250	--	.250	2	4	2	1	0	0	1	3	4	1	0	0	1	0	0	1.000	.667
Jones, Alonzo	B-R	5-9	197	2-24-97	.217	.000	.278	8	23	5	5	0	0	0	8	0	0	0	0	11	1	1	.217	.419
2-team total (4 Athletics Green)					.200	.000	.241	12	35	4	7	0	0	0	8	0	0	0	0	15	1	1	.200	.349
Martinez, Ramon	R-R	6-0	170	11-17-01	.236	.267	.231	38	106	14	25	5	0	1	11	13	0	0	1	36	5	1	.311	.317

Batting	B-T	HT	WT	DOB	AVG	vLH	vRH	G	AB	R	H	2B	3B	HR	RBI	BB	HBP	SH	SF	SO	SB	CS	SLG	OBP
McCann, Kyle	L-R	6-2	217	12-2-97	.400	.429	.385	5	20	10	8	2	2	2	7	5	0	0	0	6	0	0	1.000	.520
McGarry, Matt	R-R	5-10	175	3-24-96	.280	.235	.290	34	93	17	26	6	1	0	12	20	2	0	0	24	3	2	.366	.417
Murphy, Sean	R-R	6-3	232	10-4-94	.214	.333	.182	9	28	8	6	2	0	1	1	4	0	0	0	4	0	0	.393	.313
2-team total (1 Athletics Green)					.233	.286	.217	10	30	9	7	2	0	1	1	7	0	0	0	5	0	0	.400	.378
Pantoja, Enrry	R-R	5-11	215	9-27-96	.412	.385	.421	15	51	8	21	2	0	0	11	7	2	0	2	6	3	2	.451	.484
Peralta, Elvis	L-R	5-9	160	12-7-96	.283	.333	.273	48	177	41	50	9	1	2	20	30	4	3	0	47	10	6	.379	.398
Quintin, Christopher	R-R	6-0	135	6-7-99	.273	.267	.274	31	99	17	27	4	1	0	14	7	2	1	0	29	2	0	.333	.333
Rincones, Rafael	R-R	6-0	159	7-1-99	.276	.355	.259	46	174	25	48	5	2	2	39	24	5	0	4	47	3	1	.362	.372
Sanchez, Santis	R-R	6-1	199	8-21-98	.318	.571	.200	5	22	5	7	0	0	3	8	4	0	0	1	5	0	0	.727	.407
Schofield-Sam, T.J.	L-R	6-1	185	6-20-01	.071	--	.071	6	14	1	1	0	0	0	1	2	0	0	0	4	0	0	.071	.188
2-team total (16 Athletics Green)					.203	.333	.177	22	74	10	15	2	0	0	6	11	0	0	0	18	1	0	.230	.306
Selman, Shane	R-L	5-11	198	8-30-96	.351	.600	.313	10	37	10	13	1	0	0	9	7	1	0	4	2	0	1	.378	.429
Serrano, Iraj	L-L	5-11	165	2-19-99	.252	.300	.242	38	111	19	28	4	0	0	15	18	3	0	0	27	1	1	.288	.371
2-team total (7 Athletics Green)					.242	.240	.243	45	128	22	31	4	0	0	16	24	5	0	0	34	3	1	.273	.382
Smith, Marcus	L-L	5-11	190	9-11-00	.361	.539	.333	29	97	21	35	6	1	0	14	20	0	1	1	29	1	1	.443	.466
Spitznagel, Ben	L-R	5-11	170	8-30-94	.154	.500	.091	5	13	3	2	0	0	0	0	5	1	0	0	2	2	1	.154	.421
Squier, Payton	L-R	6-0	220	10-29-95	.240	.000	.273	7	25	2	6	1	0	0	3	1	0	0	1	3	4	0	.280	.259
Woodworth, Michael	R-R	5-9	175	8-5-97	.276	.333	.250	7	29	11	8	3	1	2	10	4	4	0	1	4	0	0	.655	.421
Wright, Joshwan	R-R	5-8	170	11-9-00	.330	.243	.351	50	191	37	63	9	4	0	37	17	3	0	4	25	4	2	.419	.386

Pitching	B-T	HT	WT	DOB	W	L	ERA	G	GS	CG	SV	IP	H	R	ER	HR	BB	SO	AVG	vLH	vRH	K/9	BB/9
Alvarez, Wilson	R-R	5-10	155	5-19-98	0	0	0.00	1	0	0	0	0	0	0	0	0	2	0	.000	.000	--	0.00	54.00
2-team total (2 Athletics Green)					0	0	0.00	3	0	0	0	2	1	0	0	0	3	1	.200	.500	.000	5.40	16.20
Basso, Brady	R-L	6-2	213	10-8-97	0	0	1.75	15	1	0	0	26	20	9	5	0	8	38	.211	.250	.194	13.32	2.81
Berrios, Osvaldo	R-R	6-2	200	11-29-99	2	1	3.60	4	2	0	1	15	14	6	6	1	0	17	.241	.177	.268	10.20	0.00
Carrasco, Luis	R-R	6-1	180	12-19-01	0	0	6.91	6	4	0	0	14	19	11	11	0	4	12	.322	.375	.286	7.53	2.51
Coletti, Vince	R-R	6-2	210	11-3-96	0	0	2.25	2	0	0	0	4	2	1	1	1	0	2	.133	.200	.100	4.50	0.00
Cushing, Jack	R-R	6-3	195	12-3-96	1	0	9.00	2	1	0	0	5	11	5	5	1	2	4	.458	.222	.600	7.20	3.60
Dicochea, Jose	R-R	6-3	180	3-21-01	0	1	19.06	4	4	0	0	6	10	13	12	0	6	5	.400	.455	.357	7.94	9.53
2-team total (6 Athletics Green)					0	3	10.38	10	9	0	0	22	28	27	25	3	14	14	.322	.387	.286	5.82	5.82
Estrada, Marco	R-R	6-0	180	7-5-83	0	0	0.00	1	1	0	0	1	0	0	0	0	0	2	.000	.000		18.00	0.00
Garcia, Gerald	L-L	6-2	200	10-21-01	0	2	5.32	14	12	0	0	46	55	33	27	3	12	57	.297	.304	.295	11.23	2.36
Gonzalez, Yhoelnys	R-R	6-0	170	10-30-96	1	0	16.20	3	0	0	0	2	4	4	3	0	2	1	.500	.000		5.40	10.80
Hall, Charles	R-R	5-10	170	9-6-94	3	1	3.55	12	4	0	0	33	24	15	13	0	9	40	.202	.244	.180	10.91	2.45
Jones, Malik	R-R	6-1	185	3-14-96	1	2	11.12	6	2	0	0	11	16	17	14	0	15	13	.348	.333	.357	10.32	11.91
2-team total (9 Athletics Green)					2	2	9.59	15	3	0	0	25	34	34	27	0	27	25	.337	.344	.333	8.88	9.59
Kiekhefer, Dean	L-L	6-0	175	6-7-89	0	1	7.94	4	2	0	0	6	8	6	5	0	1	6	.348	.200	.389	9.53	1.59
Kubo, Trayson	R-R	6-0	180	9-26-97	0	1	8.31	2	2	0	0	4	5	4	4	2	2	8	.294	.250	.308	16.62	4.15
2-team total (9 AZL Athletics Green)					0	2	8.84	11	5	0	1	18	27	23	18	2	12	28	.325	.333	.320	13.75	5.89
Lage, Jesus	R-R	6-1	155	12-1-97	4	0	5.61	18	1	0	0	26	26	18	16	1	15	27	.257	.235	.269	9.47	5.26
Leal, David	L-L	6-5	250	4-22-97	0	0	1.43	15	0	0	0	38	21	9	6	0	3	50	.162	.075	.200	11.95	0.72
Munoz, Keiro	R-R	6-3	195	9-23-98	0	2	4.42	11	0	0	0	18	15	9	9	2	7	18	.227	.280	.195	8.84	3.44
2-team total (7 Athletics Green)					0	3	5.08	18	0	0	0	28	24	16	16	2	14	29	.233	.306	.194	9.21	4.45
Pantuso, Alexander	L-R	6-6	235	10-14-95	1	2	2.33	14	0	0	3	19	11	6	5	0	12	33	.167	.280	.098	15.36	5.59
Patterson, Nathan	R-R	6-0	180	2-5-96	0	1	4.76	3	3	0	0	6	3	3	3	1	1	8	.150	.222	.091	12.71	1.59
Rafuse, Zach	R-R	6-0	185	12-3-96	3	1	2.45	14	0	0	0	33	27	9	9	0	8	32	.229	.313	.171	8.73	2.18
Santos, Pedro	R-R	6-4	205	1-7-00	2	2	2.73	9	6	0	0	30	26	13	9	0	16	50	.230	.172	.291	11.53	4.85
2-team total (6 Athletics Green)					2	3	4.60	15	11	0	0	43	45	27	22	0	34	49	.270	.227	.304	10.26	7.12
Serrano, Iraj	L-L	5-11	165	2-19-99	0	0	5.79	4	0	0	0	5	6	5	3	1	3	0	.300	.000	.429	5.79	5.79
2-team total (2 Athletics Green)					0	0	9.45	6	0	0	0	7	13	9	7	2	3	1	.406	.200	.500	1.35	4.05
Stull, Cody	L-L	6-2	160	3-23-92	0	1	1.93	3	0	0	1	5	4	1	1	0	1	8	.222	.667	.133	15.43	1.93
Vazquez, Robin	R-R	6-2	187	4-15-98	1	1	5.66	14	10	0	0	49	58	40	31	6	18	62	.293	.320	.276	11.31	3.28
Wahl, Austin	R-R	6-4	195	5-16-95	2	0	10.80	18	0	0	0	22	30	28	26	1	21	27	.337	.314	.352	11.22	8.72
Weisenburger, Jack	R-R	6-3	220	10-8-96	0	1	3.00	11	1	0	4	15	7	6	5	0	10	28	.140	.235	.091	16.80	6.00
Wheatcroft, Chase	R-R	6-6	180	12-17-96	0	1	6.00	16	0	0	1	27	39	22	18	2	7	29	.339	.349	.333	9.67	2.33
Whittlesey, Brock	R-R	6-3	210	2-27-97	5	3	4.50	18	0	0	1	28	35	21	14	0	4	29	.321	.316	.324	9.32	1.29
Woolfolk, Dallas	R-R	6-2	225	10-30-96	0	0	2.25	3	0	0	0	4	1	1	1	0	2	4	.071	.000	.167	9.00	4.50

Fielding

C: Astorri 24, Betancourt 5, Cross 23, Gordon 2, McCann 3, Murphy 8, Wright 1. **1B:** Astorri 1, Bechina 1, Cross 3, Dingcong 26, McCann 1, Quintin 9, Sanchez 4, Schofield-Sam 1, Serrano 19, Squier 6. **2B:** Alvarez 24, Bechina 1, McGarry 17, Peralta 2, Quintin 4, Woodworth 7, Wright 6. **3B:** Bechina 9, Cross 1, McGarry 4, Quintin 2, Schofield-Sam 4, Wright 41. **SS:** Bechina 3, McGarry 11, Peralta 43. **OF:** Dingcong 2, Gonzalez 29, Jones 6, Martinez 37, McGarry 1, Pantoja 13, Quintin 10, Rincones 39, Selman 7, Serrano 16, Smith 29, Spitznagel 5.

AZL ATHLETICS GREEN   *ROOKIE*
ARIZONA LEAGUE

Batting	B-T	HT	WT	DOB	AVG	vLH	vRH	G	AB	R	H	2B	3B	HR	RBI	BB	HBP	SH	SF	SO	SB	CS	SLG	OBP
Alvarez, Wilson	R-R	5-10	155	5-19-98	.324	.370	.310	27	111	17	36	5	1	0	10	13	2	1	2	31	3	1	.387	.398
2-team total (27 Athletics Gold)					.286	.349	.271	54	220	40	63	9	2	0	18	25	3	2	2	49	7	1	.346	.364
Basilia, Givaine	R-R	6-1	160	6-22-00	.237	.242	.235	42	131	23	31	3	2	1	10	12	3	0	0	45	8	3	.313	.315
Betancourt, Marcos	R-R	6-0	165	1-17-01	.161	.125	.175	23	81	4	13	3	0	0	12	9	3	0	0	22	1	0	.198	.269
2-team total (5 Athletics Gold)					.179	.107	.209	28	95	7	17	3	0	0	13	11	4	0	0	25	1	0	.211	.291
Bonilla, Jose	R-R	6-3	180	2-20-01	.195	.135	.213	48	164	17	32	5	1	1	24	25	1	0	1	71	1	3	.262	.305
Buelvas, Brayan	R-R	5-11	155	6-8-02	.300	.342	.286	44	160	26	48	10	7	3	27	22	3	0	1	46	12	5	.506	.393
Davila, Geykler	R-R	5-11	180	10-19-00	.182	.375	.071	9	22	2	4	1	0	0	2	3	0	0	0	6	1	0	.227	.280

OAKLAND ATHLETICS

	B-T	HT	WT	DOB	AVG	vLH	vRH	G	AB	R	H	2B	3B	HR	RBI	BB	HBP	SH	SF	SO	SB	CS	SLG	OBP
Dingcong, Gio	R-R	6-3	245	5-23-95	.267	.250	.273	4	15	3	4	0	0	0	0	1	0	0	0	6	0	0	.267	.313
2-team total (38 Athletics Gold)					.169	.191	.165	42	130	23	22	3	0	3	15	19	2	0	2	49	1	1	.262	.281
Giarratano, Nico	B-R	5-11	172	12-15-94	.533	.333	.583	6	15	8	8	1	0	0	1	6	0	0	1	1	0	2	.600	.636
Greer, Jalen	R-R	6-3	185	7-19-01	.165	.179	.161	42	121	10	20	1	1	0	10	21	2	0	2	69	4	1	.190	.295
Harris, Dustin	L-R	6-2	185	7-8-99	.328	.268	.357	35	125	23	41	10	1	1	16	14	1	0	0	20	9	4	.448	.400
Jones, Alonzo	B-R	5-9	197	2-24-97	.167	.000	.182	4	12	1	2	0	0	0	0	0	0	0	0	4	0	0	.167	.167
2-team total (8 Athletics Gold)					.200	.000	.241	12	35	4	7	0	0	0	0	8	0	0	0	15	1	1	.200	.349
Jones, Gavin	R-R	6-2	210	7-19-98	.208	.294	.177	52	192	28	40	6	0	1	20	20	3	0	2	75	3	3	.255	.290
Koehler, Matthew	L-R	6-2	205	3-6-96	.249	.220	.258	45	169	20	42	12	2	1	22	22	2	3	0	44	9	0	.361	.342
Lopez, Hansen	R-R	5-9	170	7-3-00	.236	.364	.205	32	110	11	26	4	3	1	16	7	0	0	2	49	1	0	.355	.277
Mackey, Davonn	R-R	6-2	170	10-10-00	.162	.167	.160	13	37	3	6	1	0	0	3	4	0	0	0	16	0	0	.189	.244
Murphy, Sean	R-R	6-3	232	10-4-94	.500	.000	1.000	1	2	1	1	0	0	0	1	0	0	0	0	0	0	0	.500	.800
2-team total (9 Athletics Gold)					.233	.286	.217	10	30	9	7	2	0	1	1	7	0	0	0	5	0	0	.400	.378
Paulino, Jhoan	R-R	6-1	176	6-11-01	.239	.245	.237	50	197	26	47	17	3	2	25	13	1	1	2	61	2	6	.386	.286
Romero, Jorge	R-R	6-2	185	5-30-00	.273	.214	.316	12	33	5	9	0	1	1	4	4	3	0	0	15	2	0	.424	.400
Schofield-Sam, T.J.	L-R	6-1	185	6-20-01	.233	.333	.208	16	60	7	14	2	0	0	5	9	0	0	0	14	1	0	.267	.333
2-team total (6 Athletics Gold)					.203	.333	.177	22	74	10	15	2	0	0	6	11	0	0	0	18	1	0	.230	.306
Serrano, Iraj	L-L	5-11	165	2-19-99	.177	.000	.250	7	17	3	3	0	0	0	1	6	2	0	0	7	2	0	.177	.440
2-team total (38 Athletics Gold)					.242	.240	.243	45	128	22	31	4	0	0	16	24	5	0	0	34	3	1	.273	.382
Vaughan, Noah	L-L	6-3	200	6-6-97	.230	.389	.179	17	74	16	17	6	1	2	12	5	0	0	1	18	1	1	.419	.275
Watson, Josh	B-R	5-11	205	9-10-96	.227	.333	.154	7	22	3	5	0	0	0	1	4	3	0	0	5	3	0	.227	.414

Pitching	B-T	HT	WT	DOB	W	L	ERA	G	GS	CG	SV	IP	H	R	ER	HR	BB	SO	AVG	vLH	vRH	K/9	BB/9
Alvarez, Wilson	R-R	5-10	155	5-19-98	0	0	0.00	2	0	0	0	1	1	0	0	0	1	1	.250	1.000	.000	6.75	6.75
2-team total (1 Athletics Gold)					0	0	0.00	3	0	0	0	2	1	0	0	0	3	1	.200	.500	.000	5.40	16.20
Aquino, Ismael	R-R	6-2	170	9-2-98	1	1	4.58	10	1	0	0	18	15	15	9	0	11	20	.227	.261	.209	10.19	5.60
2-team total (8 Royals)					2	2	7.22	18	1	0	1	29	31	29	23	2	18	34	.272	.258	.277	10.67	5.65
Baram, Edward	R-R	6-3	205	6-2-97	0	0	6.57	16	0	0	1	25	24	21	18	1	22	33	.255	.212	.279	12.04	8.03
Basilia, Givaine	R-R	6-1	160	6-22-00	0	0	5.40	2	0	0	0	2	3	3	1	0	0	0	.333	1.000	.250	0.00	0.00
Dicochea, Jose	R-R	6-3	180	3-21-01	0	2	7.31	6	5	0	0	16	18	14	13	3	8	9	.290	.350	.262	5.06	4.50
2-team total (4 Athletics Gold)					0	3	10.38	10	9	0	0	22	28	27	25	3	14	14	.322	.387	.286	5.82	5.82
Dingcong, Gio	R-R	6-3	245	5-23-95	0	0	27.00	1	0	0	0	0	0	1	1	0	3	0	.000	.000	--	0.00	81.00
Gray, Cole	R-R	6-3	230	1-17-97	0	1	4.50	2	1	0	0	2	1	1	1	0	2		.143	.000	.200	9.00	0.00
Herrera, Dennis	L-L	6-0	165	9-28-98	0	4	3.61	14	13	0	0	47	37	27	19	3	27	46	.208	.154	.223	8.75	5.13
Jones, Gavin	R-R	6-2	210	7-19-98	0	0	0.00	1	0	0	0	1	0	0	0	0	0	0	.000	.000	.000	0.00	0.00
Jones, Malik	R-R	6-1	185	3-14-96	1	0	8.36	9	1	0	0	14	18	17	13	0	12	12	.327	.357	.317	7.71	7.71
2-team total (6 Athletics Gold)					2	2	9.59	15	3	0	0	25	34	34	27	0	27	25	.337	.344	.333	8.88	9.59
Juan, Jorge	R-R	6-8	200	3-6-99	1	5	7.29	13	6	0	0	33	32	34	27	1	33	36	.258	.212	.292	9.72	8.91
Kubo, Trayson	R-R	6-0	180	9-26-97	0	1	9.00	9	3	0	1	14	22	19	14	0	10	20	.333	.345	.324	12.86	6.43
2-team total (2 Athletics Gold)					0	2	8.84	11	5	0	1	18	27	23	18	2	12	28	.325	.333	.320	13.75	5.89
Lopez, Hansen	R-R	5-9	170	7-3-00	1	0	0.00	1	0	0	0	2	1	0	0	0	0	0	.200	--	.200	0.00	0.00
Luzardo, Jesus	L-L	6-0	209	9-30-97	0	0	0.00	1	0	0	0	2	1	0	0	0	0	5	.143	--	.143	22.50	0.00
Manzanillo, Manuel	R-R	5-11	185	3-21-98	1	4	7.11	17	0	0	0	25	37	28	20	2	17	27	.356	.351	.358	9.59	6.04
Martinez, Luis	R-R	6-2	170	3-30-01	4	1	3.02	15	4	0	0	42	48	19	14	3	5	38	.279	.271	.284	8.21	1.08
Monserratt, Jesus	R-R	6-0	180	1-3-97	1	1	6.11	17	0	0	0	28	38	25	19	5	9	32	.312	.404	.253	10.29	2.89
Munoz, Keiro	R-R	6-3	195	9-23-98	0	1	6.30	7	0	0	0	10	9	7	7	0	7	11	.243	.364	.192	9.90	6.30
2-team total (11 Athletics Gold)					0	3	5.08	18	0	0	0	28	24	16	16	2	14	29	.233	.306	.194	9.21	4.45
Nambiar, Kumar	L-L	5-11	188	4-17-98	1	4	5.25	15	5	0	0	36	37	22	21	0	17	47	.270	.229	.284	11.75	4.25
Nightengale, Bryce	R-R	6-5	215	8-16-96	0	0	4.50	1	1	0	0	2	1	1	1	0	1	1	.167	.000	.200	4.50	4.50
Pineda, Leudeny	R-R	6-1	205	1-29-96	0	2	4.05	6	6	0	0	27	27	19	12	1	5	28	.257	.250	.262	9.45	1.69
Romero, Sam	R-R	6-2	180	1-1-97	2	1	4.97	16	0	0	3	29	32	18	16	0	10	35	.281	.378	.234	10.86	3.10
Sanchez, Livan	L-L	6-0	165	10-21-97	1	5	6.15	14	4	0	0	45	52	41	31	1	27	44	.289	.275	.293	8.74	5.36
Santos, Pedro	R-R	6-4	205	1-7-00	0	1	8.78	6	5	0	0	13	19	14	13	0	18	11	.352	.412	.324	7.43	12.15
2-team total (9 Athletics Gold)					2	3	4.60	15	11	0	0	43	45	27	22	0	34	49	.270	.227	.304	10.26	7.12
Serrano, Iraj	L-L	5-11	165	2-19-99	0	0	18.00	2	0	0	0	2	7	4	4	1	0	1	.583	.500	.625	4.50	0.00
2-team total (4 Athletics Gold)					0	0	9.45	4	0	0	0	7	13	9	7	2	3	1	.406	.200	.500	1.35	4.05
Vaughan, Noah	L-L	6-3	200	6-6-97	1	0	0.00	1	0	0	0	1	1	1	0	0	1	0	.500	--	.500	0.00	13.50
Walkinshaw, Jake	R-R	6-3	200	7-7-96	3	0	3.28	18	0	0	1	25	26	11	9	1	4	29	.265	.200	.302	10.58	1.46
Yearego, Dominic	L-R	6-4	225	3-10-96	2	2	2.16	15	0	0	0	25	20	13	6	1	12	38	.208	.229	.197	13.68	4.32

Fielding

C: Betancourt 23, Davila 4, Lopez 31. **1B:** Davila 5, Dingcong 3, Harris 22, Jones 24, Serrano 5. **2B:** Alvarez 15, Basilia 28, Giarratano 3, Greer 15, Jones 1. **3B:** Alvarez 13, Basilia 3, Harris 4, Jones 26, Paulino 2, Schofield-Sam 14. **SS:** Giarratano 1, Greer 18, Paulino 40. **OF:** Basilia 8, Bonilla 47, Buelvas 40, Giarratano 2, Jones 3, Koehler 39, Mackey 9, Romero 8, Serrano 1, Vaughan 17, Watson 7.

DSL ATHLETICS   ROOKIE
DOMINICAN SUMMER LEAGUE

Batting	B-T	HT	WT	DOB	AVG	vLH	vRH	G	AB	R	H	2B	3B	HR	RBI	BB	HBP	SH	SF	SO	SB	CS	SLG	OBP
Avila, Albert	L-L	6-2	160	9-26-00	.162	.167	.161	49	148	21	24	4	2	0	9	29	2	0	5	40	3	3	.216	.299
Beltran, Nelson	R-R	5-10	180	12-28-01	.167	.182	.164	43	126	22	21	1	0	0	8	13	6	1	1	38	10	1	.175	.274
Buelvas, Brayan	R-R	5-11	155	6-8-02	.244	.333	.227	23	78	4	19	5	1	0	14	8	2	0	0	14	4	4	.333	.330
Cruz, Cristopher	R-R	6-0	180	3-28-02	.184	.032	.212	63	196	24	36	7	0	2	15	36	6	2	5	76	3	3	.250	.321
Davila, Geykler	R-R	5-11	180	10-19-00	.143	--	.143	5	7	3	1	1	0	0	4	1	0	0	0	4	0	0	.286	.500
Escorche, Jose	R-R	5-10	145	4-29-02	.217	.188	.224	54	166	18	36	1	3	1	18	14	7	3	3	55	16	4	.277	.300
Garcia, Kelvin	R-R	6-3	194	10-14-00	.138	.267	.114	36	94	6	13	2	0	1	10	10	4	0	2	47	0	0	.192	.246

Name	B-T	HT	WT	DOB	AVG	vLH	vRH	G	AB	R	H	2B	3B	HR	RBI	BB	HBP	SH	SF	SO	SB	CS	OBP	SLG
Hipolito, Cesar	R-R	5-9	160	6-3-02	.170	.000	.204	35	112	14	19	4	0	0	3	22	6	1	1	36	9	2	.205	.333
Lelis, Matheus	R-R	5-9	160	6-12-02	.203	.071	.233	29	74	9	15	2	0	0	6	10	1	0	1	16	0	3	.230	.302
Martinez, Ramon	R-R	6-0	170	11-17-01	.230	.100	.255	19	61	7	14	2	0	2	5	6	0	1	0	21	4	2	.361	.299
Montero, Darlyn	B-R	6-2	170	5-11-02	.213	.278	.197	55	188	20	40	6	3	0	17	23	1	0	5	58	8	3	.277	.295
Mujica, Jose	R-R	6-0	164	3-28-01	.262	.280	.259	51	164	21	43	3	0	0	16	19	5	2	1	32	10	0	.281	.355
Pastrano, Jose	B-R	5-10	150	11-25-00	.190	.200	.187	46	121	15	23	6	1	0	12	14	3	4	1	30	12	2	.256	.288
Salom, Dereck	R-R	5-10	135	2-22-01	.198	.348	.165	41	126	17	25	5	0	0	5	23	1	3	1	25	5	2	.238	.325
Sanchez, Saul	B-R	5-11	160	1-5-01	.195	.136	.209	42	113	14	22	7	0	0	11	24	5	1	1	29	8	0	.257	.357
Santana, Juan	L-L	6-2	180	7-17-01	.200	.053	.229	42	115	15	23	3	0	0	18	21	4	1	0	28	0	2	.226	.343
Santana, Ronny	B-R	6-1	155	12-30-01	.118	.000	.143	27	68	3	8	1	0	0	3	8	2	1	0	14	0	0	.132	.231
Vallejo, Otoniel	R-L	6-2	180	7-16-01	.167	.069	.183	56	198	18	33	1	2	0	15	19	1	0	1	63	7	2	.192	.242

Pitching	B-T	HT	WT	DOB	W	L	ERA	G	GS	CG	SV	IP	H	R	ER	HR	BB	SO	AVG	vLH	vRH	K/9	BB/9
Cantillo, Marshall	R-R	6-1	183	3-28-01	3	1	8.69	17	0	0	0	20	22	22	19	0	23	26	.286	.300	.281	11.90	10.53
Cedano, Alexis	L-R	6-0	180	11-12-97	3	0	3.55	17	0	0	0	25	25	14	10	1	13	30	.248	.229	.258	10.66	4.62
De Paula, Willy	R-R	6-2	180	4-1-02	0	0	17.18	4	1	0	0	4	6	7	7	1	6	6	.353	.400	.333	14.73	14.73
Delgado, Gabriel	R-R	6-0	175	11-1-00	1	0	2.86	15	0	0	3	22	14	12	7	0	7	18	.173	.208	.158	7.36	2.86
Florentino, Luis	R-R	6-2	190	3-13-00	3	1	1.99	14	7	0	2	50	38	17	11	2	14	43	.209	.233	.197	7.79	2.54
Garza, Roberto	R-R	6-2	175	6-22-02	3	4	3.74	13	5	0	0	43	38	19	18	1	13	33	.238	.211	.252	6.85	2.70
Gimenez, Dheygler	R-R	6-2	170	12-3-01	0	0	4.50	2	1	0	0	2	2	1	1	0	2	1	.250	.000	.286	4.50	9.00
Gonzalez, Adriel	R-R	6-2	145	4-28-02	4	2	3.22	13	6	0	0	45	36	19	16	0	14	23	.221	.273	.194	4.63	2.82
Gonzalez, Dangiover	R-R	6-0	149	2-26-02	2	3	6.03	14	6	0	0	37	29	29	25	1	24	23	.213	.300	.177	5.54	5.79
Gonzalez, James	L-L	6-2	230	9-15-00	2	3	4.82	7	4	0	0	19	18	13	10	1	5	22	.250	.118	.291	10.61	2.41
Gonzalez, Jose	R-R	6-0	160	1-5-02	1	0	3.04	15	0	0	0	27	26	17	9	0	8	24	.245	.342	.185	8.10	2.70
Guante, Wander	R-R	6-1	180	6-15-00	2	3	3.77	12	5	0	0	45	47	24	19	2	10	29	.266	.226	.282	5.76	1.99
Hernandez, Marcelo	R-R	6-1	170	1-23-99	3	3	2.25	16	0	0	1	32	33	14	8	0	7	42	.254	.286	.242	11.81	1.97
Leandro, Carlos	L-L	6-1	170	1-1-01	0	8	8.84	14	8	0	0	39	35	46	38	1	42	34	.248	.211	.254	7.91	9.78
Medina, Alonzo	R-R	6-2	190	2-2-99	0	1	3.05	17	0	0	5	21	10	8	7	0	18	21	.147	.200	.125	9.15	7.84
Montilla, Stiven	R-R	6-2	197	11-21-99	0	5	3.54	13	8	0	1	48	39	24	19	1	40	35	.235	.192	.252	6.52	7.45
Rodriguez, Roger	R-R	6-1	145	9-11-01	2	3	2.70	14	5	0	1	50	44	20	15	2	9	39	.240	.250	.234	7.02	1.62
Rojas, Edwin	R-R	6-1	160	11-1-00	0	4	4.60	13	10	0	0	47	59	29	24	2	30	32	.317	.351	.302	6.13	5.74
Sanchez, Yehizon	R-R	6-2	170	11-16-00	0	0	0.43	7	4	0	0	21	11	3	1	0	7	15	.151	.207	.114	6.43	3.00

Fielding

C: Davila 5, Lelis 29, Mujica 49. **1B:** Cruz 46, Montero 24, Mujica 2, Santana 1. **2B:** Beltran 9, Escorche 7, Hipolito 35, Pastrano 11, Salom 12, Santana 4. **3B:** Beltran 29, Cruz 6, Escorche 1, Montero 18, Salom 2, Sanchez 17, Santana 7. **SS:** Escorche 45, Montero 2, Salom 24, Sanchez 1, Santana 6. **OF:** Avila 28, Buelvas 22, Garcia 19, Martinez 19, Pastrano 33, Sanchez 24, Santana 34, Vallejo 55.

Philadelphia Phillies

SEASON IN A SENTENCE: A big offseason got the city of Philadelphia excited, but a disappointing 81-81 record (on the heels of last year's 80-82 record) led to manager Gabe Kapler being fired.

HIGH POINT: Free agent signings Bryce Harper and Andrew McCutchen both homered in an 11-4 win over St. Louis on May 29 which pushed the Phillies to a 3.5 game lead in the division.

LOW POINT: Spot starter Enyel de los Santos was knocked out quickly and Edgar Garcia was no more effective as the Phillies lost 6-4 to the Marlins on June 23. That completed a three-game Marlins sweep on the heels of a Nationals sweep of the Phillies and a series loss to the Braves. Four straight series losses turned a tenuous division lead into a 6.5 deficit. The Phillies never challenged for the division title again and went from a team that had been 10 games above .500 to one that hovered around even for the rest of the season.

NOTABLE ROOKIES: Outfielder Adam Haseley was brought up as a fill-in in June, then arrived for good in July. He played all three outfield spots while hitting .266/.324/.396 in a middling rookie season. Lefthander Ranger Suarez served as an effective middle-inning reliever for the final four months of the season.

KEY TRANSACTIONS: The Phillies signed outfielders Bryce Harper and Andrew McCutchen and traded for catcher J.T. Realmuto, giving the club a very productive offseason. Harper had a solid first season in Philly (.260/.372/.510) and Realmuto remained the best catcher in the National League, being the rare catcher who can hit and provide outstanding defense. That helped the club draw more than a half-million additional fans. But injuries crushed the Phillies. Philadelphia placed 10 players on the 60-day injured list, including Jake Arrieta, McCutchen, Tommy Hunter, David Robertson and Pat Neshek.

DOWN ON THE FARM: The J.T. Realmuto trade cost the Phillies top prospect Sixto Sanchez as well as Will Stewart. After graduating Haseley on the heels of Scott Kingery (and the since-traded J.P. Crawford) the Phillies system is thinner than it has been in recent years, but righthander Spencer Howard and third baseman Alec Bohm both took significant steps forward in their development. The story wasn't as encouraging at low Class A Lakewood, where shortstop Luis Garcia struggled to follow up his impressive 2018 in the Gulf Coast League.

OPENING DAY PAYROLL: $172,374,872 (6th).

PLAYERS OF THE YEAR

MIKE CARLSON

MAJOR LEAGUE	MINOR LEAGUE
J.T. Realmuto	**Alec Bohm**
C	3B
.275/.328/.493	(Low A/High A/AA)
25 HR, 36 2B	.305/.378/.518
83 RBIs, 92 R	21 HR, 80 RBIs

ORGANIZATION LEADERS

Batting		*Minimum 250 AB
MAJORS		
* AVG	Jean Segura	.280
* OPS	Bryce Harper	.882
HR	Bryce Harper	35
RBI	Bryce Harper	114
MINORS		
* AVG	Ali Castro, Reading, Lehigh Valley	.322
* OBP	Phil Gosselin, Lehigh Valley	.405
* SLG	Alec Bohm, Lakewood, Clearwater, Reading	.518
* OPS	Phil Gosselin, Lehigh Valley	.901
R	Luke Williams, Reading	77
H	Ali Castillo, Reading, Lehigh Valley	150
TB	Alec Bohm, Lakewood, Clearwater, Reading	246
2B	Darick Hall, Reading	38
3B	Mickey Moniak, Reading	13
HR	Alec Bohm, Lakewood, Clearwater, Reading	21
HR	Deivy Grullon, Lehigh Valley	21
RBI	Austin Listi, Reading, Lehigh Valley	83
BB	Mitch Walding, Lehigh Valley	62
SO	Carlos De La Cruz, Lakewood	159
SB	Jonathan Guzman, Lakewood	31

Pitching		#Minimum 75 IP
MAJORS		
W	Aaron Nola	12
# ERA	Aaron Nola	3.87
SO	Aaron Nola	229
SV	Hector Neris	28
MINORS		
W	David Parkinson, Reading	10
L	Victor Santos, Lakewood	10
L	Alejandro Requena, Clearwater, Reading	10
# ERA	Kyle Glogoski, Lakewood, Clearwater	1.68
G	Addison Russ, Reading	55
GS	JoJo Romero, Lehigh Valley, Reading	24
GS	Ramon Rosso, Reading, Lehigh Valley	24
SV	Addison Russ, Reading	22
IP	Colton Eastman, Lakewood, Clearwater, Reading	129
BB	Jhordany Mezquita, Lakewood	59
BB	Damon Jones, Clearwater, Reading, Lehigh Valley	59
BB	Kyle Dohy, Reading, Lehigh Valley	59
SO	Damon Jones, Clearwater, Reading, Lehigh Valley	152
# AVG	Connor Brogdon, Clewater, Reading, Lehigh Valley	.173

General Manager: Matt Klentak. **Farm Director:** Josh Bonifay. **Scouting Director:** Johnny Almaraz.

Class	Team	League	W	L	PCT	Finish	Manager
Majors	Philadelphia Phillies	National	81	81	.500	9th (15)	Gabe Kapler
Triple-A	Lehigh Valley IronPigs	International	66	74	.471	t-9th (14)	Gary Jones
Double-A	Reading Fightin Phils	Eastern	80	59	.576	1st (12)	Shawn Williams
High A	Clearwater Threshers	Florida State	68	68	.500	6th (12)	Marty Malloy
Low A	Lakewood BlueClaws	South Atlantic	58	80	.420	12th (14)	Mike Micucci
Short season	Williamsport Crosscutters	New York-Penn	32	43	.427	13th (14)	Pat Borders
Rookie	GCL Phillies East	Gulf Coast	21	27	.438	13th (18)	Roly de Armas
Rookie	GCL Phillies West	Gulf Coast	33	15	.688	2nd (18)	Milver Reyes
Overall 2019 Minor League Record			358	366	.494	16th (30)	

ORGANIZATION STATISTICS

PHILADELPHIA PHILLIES
NATIONAL LEAGUE

Batting	B-T	HT	WT	DOB	AVG	vLH	vRH	G	AB	R	H	2B	3B	HR	RBI	BB	HBP	SH	SF	SO	SB	CS	SLG	OBP
Altherr, Aaron	R-R	6-5	215	1-14-91	.035	.091	.000	22	29	2	1	1	0	0	1	1	0	0	0	9	0	0	.069	.067
3-team total (26 New York, 1 San Francisco)					.082	.150	.049	49	61	8	5	2	0	1	3	3	1	0	1	25	0	0	.164	.136
Brantly, Rob	L-R	6-1	195	7-14-89	.000	.000	--	1	1	0	0	0	0	0	0	0	0	0	0	1	0	0	.000	.000
Bruce, Jay	L-L	6-3	225	4-3-87	.221	.212	.223	51	145	16	32	6	0	12	31	3	0	0	1	29	0	0	.510	.235
Cozens, Dylan	L-L	6-6	235	5-31-94	.000	--	.000	1	1	0	0	0	0	0	0	0	0	0	0	0	0	0	.000	.000
Dickerson, Corey	L-R	6-1	210	5-22-89	.293	.293	.294	34	133	13	39	10	2	8	34	3	0	0	1	33	0	0	.579	.307
2-team total (44 Pittsburgh)					.304	.271	.313	78	260	33	79	28	2	12	59	16	0	0	3	56	1	0	.565	.341
Franco, Maikel	R-R	6-1	215	8-26-92	.234	.245	.230	123	389	48	91	17	0	17	56	36	0	0	3	61	0	0	.409	.297
Gosselin, Phil	R-R	6-1	200	10-3-88	.262	.296	.237	44	65	5	17	3	0	0	7	3	0	0	0	16	0	0	.308	.294
Grullon, Deivy	R-R	6-1	180	2-17-96	.111	.333	.000	4	9	0	1	0	0	0	1	0	0	0	0	2	0	0	.222	.111
Harper, Bryce	L-R	6-3	220	10-16-92	.260	.283	.249	157	573	98	149	36	1	35	114	99	6	0	4	178	15	3	.510	.372
Haseley, Adam	L-L	6-1	195	4-12-96	.266	.212	.282	67	222	30	59	14	0	5	26	14	5	1	0	60	4	0	.396	.324
Hernandez, Cesar	B-R	5-10	160	5-23-90	.279	.263	.286	161	612	77	171	31	3	14	71	45	6	4	10	100	9	2	.409	.333
Herrera, Odubel	L-R	5-11	205	12-29-91	.222	.280	.208	39	126	12	28	10	1	1	16	11	1	0	1	33	2	1	.341	.288
Hoskins, Rhys	R-R	6-4	225	3-17-93	.226	.261	.215	160	570	86	129	33	5	29	85	116	11	0	6	173	2	2	.454	.364
Kingery, Scott	R-R	5-10	180	4-29-94	.258	.293	.245	126	458	64	118	34	4	19	55	34	5	1	2	147	15	4	.474	.315
Knapp, Andrew	B-R	6-1	195	11-9-91	.213	.250	.202	74	136	12	29	9	0	2	8	18	3	3	0	51	0	0	.324	.319
McCutchen, Andrew	R-R	5-11	195	10-10-86	.256	.294	.244	59	219	45	56	12	1	10	29	43	0	0	0	55	2	1	.457	.378
Miller, Brad	L-R	6-2	215	10-18-89	.263	.143	.279	66	118	22	31	3	1	12	21	11	1	0	0	35	1	0	.610	.331
Morrison, Logan	L-L	6-3	245	8-25-87	.200	.000	.233	29	35	5	7	1	0	2	3	3	0	0	0	10	0	0	.400	.263
Pirela, Jose	R-R	6-0	220	11-21-89	.235	.364	.000	12	17	1	4	1	0	1	2	2	0	0	0	4	0	0	.471	.316
2-team total (2 San Diego)					.182	.333	.000	14	22	1	4	1	0	1	2	2	0	0	0	7	0	0	.364	.250
Quinn, Roman	B-R	5-10	170	5-14-93	.213	.192	.230	44	108	18	23	3	1	4	11	12	1	1	0	34	8	3	.370	.298
Realmuto, J.T.	R-R	6-1	210	3-18-91	.275	.276	.275	145	538	92	148	36	3	25	83	41	5	0	8	123	9	1	.493	.328
Rodriguez, Sean	R-R	6-0	200	4-26-85	.223	.227	.217	76	112	24	25	5	0	4	12	19	3	4	1	41	1	1	.375	.348
Segura, Jean	R-R	5-10	205	3-17-90	.280	.289	.277	144	576	79	161	37	4	12	60	30	8	1	3	73	10	2	.420	.323
Walding, Mitch	L-R	6-3	190	9-10-92	.000	--	.000	2	2	0	0	0	0	0	0	0	0	0	0	2	0	0	.000	.000
Williams, Nick	L-L	6-3	195	9-8-93	.151	.118	.157	67	106	9	16	4	0	2	5	4	2	0	0	43	0	0	.245	.196

Pitching	B-T	HT	WT	DOB	W	L	ERA	G	GS	CG	SV	IP	H	R	ER	HR	BB	SO	AVG	vLH	vRH	K/9	BB/9
Altherr, Aaron	R-R	6-5	215	1-14-91	0	0	9.00	1	0	0	0	1	2	1	1	0	0	2	.400	.500	.333	18.00	0.00
Alvarez, Jose	L-L	5-11	180	5-6-89	3	4	3.36	67	0	0	1	59	66	25	22	8	18	51	.285	.236	.328	7.78	2.75
Anderson, Drew	R-R	6-3	185	3-22-94	0	0	7.50	2	0	0	0	6	6	5	5	1	6	6	.250	.300	.214	9.00	9.00
Arano, Victor	R-R	6-2	200	2-7-95	1	0	3.86	3	0	0	0	5	2	2	2	1	2	7	.154	.167	.143	13.50	3.86
Arrieta, Jake	R-R	6-4	225	3-6-86	8	8	4.64	24	24	0	0	136	149	76	70	21	51	110	.283	.317	.252	7.30	3.38
Davis, Austin	L-L	6-4	245	2-3-93	0	0	6.53	14	0	0	0	21	22	15	15	6	14	24	.272	.269	.273	10.45	6.10
De Los Santos, Enyel	R-R	6-3	170	12-25-95	0	1	7.36	5	1	0	0	11	13	9	9	4	5	9	.317	.500	.273	7.36	4.09
Dominguez, Seranthony	R-R	6-1	185	11-25-94	3	0	4.01	27	0	0	0	25	24	13	11	3	12	29	.250	.372	.150	10.58	4.38
Eflin, Zach	R-R	6-6	215	4-8-94	10	13	4.13	32	28	2	0	163	172	88	75	28	48	129	.268	.268	.268	7.11	2.64
Eickhoff, Jerad	R-R	6-4	245	7-2-90	3	4	5.71	12	10	0	1	58	58	37	37	18	18	51	.261	.308	.236	7.87	2.78
Garcia, Edgar	R-R	6-1	180	10-4-96	2	0	5.77	37	0	0	0	39	38	25	25	11	26	45	.266	.313	.242	10.38	6.00
Hammer, JD	R-R	6-3	215	7-12-94	1	0	3.79	20	0	0	0	19	15	8	8	2	12	13	.217	.208	.222	6.16	5.68
Hughes, Jared	R-R	6-7	240	7-4-85	2	1	3.91	25	0	0	0	23	16	10	10	7	8	20	.198	.125	.228	7.83	3.13
2-team total (47 Cincinnati)					5	5	4.04	72	0	0	1	71	57	37	32	13	27	54	.224	.193	.228	6.81	3.41
Hunter, Tommy	R-R	6-3	250	7-3-86	0	0	0.00	5	0	0	0	5	2	0	0	0	5	5	.111	.000	.182	8.44	0.00
Irvin, Cole	L-L	6-4	180	1-31-94	2	1	5.83	16	3	0	1	42	45	28	27	7	13	31	.278	.365	.236	6.70	2.81
Morgan, Adam	L-L	6-1	200	2-27-90	3	3	3.94	40	0	0	0	30	20	14	13	4	10	29	.187	.143	.224	8.80	3.03
Morin, Mike	R-R	6-4	200	5-3-91	1	2	5.79	29	0	0	0	28	26	18	18	3	8	15	.248	.263	.239	4.82	2.57
Neris, Hector	R-R	6-2	215	6-14-89	3	6	2.93	68	0	0	28	68	45	24	22	10	24	89	.186	.167	.202	11.84	3.19
Neshek, Pat	R-R	6-3	220	9-4-80	0	1	5.00	20	0	0	3	18	23	11	10	5	2	9	.303	.308	.300	4.50	1.00
Nicasio, Juan	R-R	6-4	252	8-31-86	2	3	4.75	47	0	0	1	47	57	27	25	4	21	65	.296	.279	.309	8.56	3.99
Nola, Aaron	R-R	6-2	195	6-4-93	12	7	3.87	34	34	0	0	202	176	91	87	27	80	229	.233	.240	.228	10.19	3.56
Parker, Blake	R-R	6-3	225	6-19-85	2	1	5.04	23	2	0	0	25	19	14	14	6	6	31	.216	.242	.200	11.16	2.16
Pivetta, Nick	R-R	6-5	220	2-14-93	4	6	5.38	30	13	1	1	94	103	64	56	20	39	89	.278	.261	.294	8.55	3.75
Quinn, Roman	B-R	5-10	170	5-14-93	0	1	8.10	2	0	0	0	3	7	3	3	0	3	1	.438	.667	.300	2.70	8.10

	B-T	HT	WT	DOB	W	L	ERA	G	GS	CG	SV	IP	H	R	ER	HR	BB	SO	AVG	vLH	vRH	K/9	BB/9
Ramos, Edubray	R-R	6-0	160	12-19-92	1	0	5.40	20	0	0	0	15	19	10	9	5	7	11	.312	.368	.286	6.60	4.20
Rios, Yacksel	R-R	6-3	185	6-27-93	0	0	13.50	4	0	0	0	3	6	7	4	2	3	2	.462	.500	.333	6.75	10.13
2-team total (10 Pittsburgh)					1	0	6.92	14	0	0	0	13	16	13	10	4	8	12	.314	.364	.276	8.31	5.54
Robertson, David	R-R	5-11	195	4-9-85	0	1	5.40	7	0	0	0	7	8	4	4	1	6	6	.296	.235	.400	8.10	8.10
Rodriguez, Sean	R-R	6-0	200	4-26-85	0	0	0.00	2	0	0	0	1	0	0	0	0	0	1	.000	.000	.000	6.75	0.00
Salas, Fernando	R-R	6-2	200	5-30-85	0	0	6.75	3	0	0	0	3	8	2	2	1	0	3	.533	.833	.333	10.13	0.00
Smyly, Drew	L-L	6-3	190	6-13-89	3	2	4.45	12	12	0	0	63	62	34	31	13	21	68	.259	.250	.262	9.77	3.02
Suarez, Ranger	L-L	6-1	180	8-26-95	6	1	3.14	37	0	0	0	49	52	18	17	6	12	42	.278	.213	.310	7.77	2.22
Vargas, Jason	L-L	6-0	215	2-2-83	1	4	5.37	11	11	0	0	55	60	39	33	7	24	43	.284	.268	.288	6.99	3.90
2-team total (19 New York)					7	9	4.51	30	29	1	0	150	141	84	75	21	63	124	.249	.254	.248	7.46	3.79
Velasquez, Vince	R-R	6-3	205	6-7-92	7	8	4.91	33	23	0	0	117	120	69	64	26	43	130	.262	.266	.259	9.97	3.30
Vincent, Nick	R-R	6-0	185	7-12-86	1	2	1.93	14	0	0	0	14	11	3	3	1	4	17	.220	.118	.273	10.93	2.57
2-team total (18 San Francisco)					1	4	4.43	32	1	0	0	45	47	23	22	8	12	47	.267	.250	.276	9.47	2.42

Fielding

Catcher	PCT	G	PO	A	E	DP	PB
Grullon	1.000	2	21	0	0	0	0
Knapp	.991	43	311	27	3	3	3
Realmuto	.992	133	1098	67	9	14	8

First Base	PCT	G	PO	A	E	DP
Franco	1.000	2	1	0	0	1
Hoskins	.993	158	1193	122	9	111
Knapp	1.000	1	8	0	0	1
Morrison	1.000	3	14	0	0	2
Realmuto	1.000	4	17	2	0	2
Rodriguez	1.000	1	1	0	0	0

Second Base	PCT	G	PO	A	E	DP
Hernandez	.981	157	271	354	12	96
Kingery	1.000	10	18	20	0	6

	PCT	G	PO	A	E	DP
Rodriguez	1.000	3	3	2	0	1

Third Base	PCT	G	PO	A	E	DP
Franco	.970	110	62	195	8	10
Gosselin	1.000	1	0	1	0	0
Kingery	.962	41	26	76	4	11
Miller	.941	19	5	27	2	1
Rodriguez	1.000	24	11	25	0	3

Shortstop	PCT	G	PO	A	E	DP
Gosselin	.933	5	6	8	1	2
Kingery	.967	18	17	41	2	11
Miller	1.000	1	0	1	0	0
Rodriguez	1.000	11	11	26	0	4
Segura	.963	142	175	351	20	83

Outfield	PCT	G	PO	A	E	DP
Altherr	.938	11	15	0	1	0
Bruce	1.000	31	55	4	0	1
Dickerson	1.000	32	53	0	0	0
Gosselin	1.000	6	5	0	0	0
Harper	.983	152	284	13	5	1
Haseley	.992	65	126	4	1	2
Herrera	1.000	37	75	0	0	0
Kingery	.979	69	139	1	3	1
McCutchen	.982	58	106	2	2	0
Miller	1.000	17	20	2	0	0
Pirela	1.000	5	4	0	0	0
Quinn	.984	34	58	4	1	1
Rodriguez	1.000	14	14	1	0	0
Velasquez	1.000	1	1	0	0	0
Williams	1.000	28	31	1	0	0

LEHIGH VALLEY IRONPIGS   TRIPLE-A
INTERNATIONAL LEAGUE

Batting	B-T	HT	WT	DOB	AVG	vLH	vRH	G	AB	R	H	2B	3B	HR	RBI	BB	HBP	SH	SF	SO	SB	CS	SLG	OBP
Adams, Lane	R-R	6-4	220	11-13-89	.255	.281	.246	72	271	41	69	17	2	12	29	30	5	0	0	103	8	2	.465	.340
Antequera, Jose	R-R	5-10	160	8-1-95	.211	.375	.091	6	19	0	4	0	0	0	2	1	0	0	0	4	0	0	.211	.250
Brantly, Rob	L-R	6-1	195	7-14-89	.314	.286	.322	82	236	32	74	13	2	6	28	32	4	0	0	29	0	0	.462	.404
Canelo, Malquin	R-R	5-10	156	9-5-94	.262	.258	.264	128	423	57	111	27	2	2	35	32	5	10	3	137	8	10	.350	.320
Castillo, Ali	R-R	5-9	180	6-19-89	.316	.298	.322	113	415	60	131	22	4	7	58	27	1	4	7	55	4	4	.439	.353
Cozens, Dylan	L-L	6-6	235	5-31-94	.167	.143	.175	23	78	20	13	1	2	6	15	20	0	0	1	42	5	2	.462	.333
2-team total (2 Durham)					.177	.174	.177	25	85	22	15	2	2	7	16	22	0	0	1	43	5	2	.494	.343
Cumana, Grenny	R-R	5-5	145	11-10-95	.192	.000	.217	11	26	2	5	1	0	0	2	0	0	1	0	4	0	0	.231	.192
Franco, Maikel	R-R	6-1	215	8-26-92	.175	.300	.133	12	40	5	7	2	1	2	6	5	1	0	0	7	0	0	.425	.283
Gosselin, Phil	R-R	6-1	200	10-3-88	.314	.295	.321	78	296	54	93	20	5	8	47	46	3	2	6	61	3	2	.497	.405
Grullon, Deivy	R-R	6-1	180	2-17-96	.283	.278	.284	108	407	55	115	24	0	21	77	45	2	0	3	133	1	0	.496	.355
Haseley, Adam	L-L	6-1	195	4-12-96	.294	.273	.304	18	68	8	20	6	0	2	9	8	1	1	0	14	1	1	.471	.377
Hernandez, Jan	R-R	6-1	195	1-3-95	.250	.286	.239	61	232	38	58	13	1	12	44	25	4	0	2	101	2	3	.470	.331
Hundley, Nick	R-R	6-0	203	9-8-83	.125	.000	.133	12	32	2	4	1	0	1	3	2	0	0	2	17	0	0	.250	.167
Listi, Austin	R-R	6-0	218	11-5-93	.278	.300	.271	71	259	38	72	17	1	12	50	21	9	1	4	62	0	2	.490	.348
Matera, Nick	R-R	6-2	215	8-29-96	.250	--	.250	1	4	1	1	0	0	0	1	0	0	0	0	0	0	0	.250	.400
McBride, Matt	R-R	6-2	215	5-23-85	.225	.143	.274	48	151	20	34	6	0	9	28	8	2	0	1	37	0	1	.444	.272
Morrison, Logan	L-L	6-3	245	8-25-87	.356	.333	.366	18	59	7	21	5	0	3	12	7	2	0	1	12	0	0	.593	.435
2-team total (43 Scranton/Wilkes-Barre)					.308	.292	.315	61	211	36	65	16	0	18	49	15	6	0	1	38	0	1	.640	.369
Ngoepe, Gift	R-R	5-8	200	1-18-90	.221	.160	.237	41	122	17	27	8	0	5	21	12	1	0	0	56	1	0	.410	.296
Pirela, Jose	R-R	6-0	220	11-21-89	.281	.304	.276	33	121	19	34	9	0	4	14	8	1	0	2	25	5	0	.455	.331
Quinn, Roman	B-R	5-10	170	5-14-93	.333	.167	.417	4	18	6	6	0	1	0	2	2	0	2	0	8	1	1	.444	.400
Rivas, Raul	B-R	5-10	160	10-27-96	.375	.333	.400	2	8	3	3	0	0	1	1	0	0	0	0	2	0	2	.375	.444
Robinson, Shane	R-R	5-9	170	10-30-84	.288	.283	.289	89	306	51	88	10	0	7	31	39	3	2	6	34	8	3	.389	.367
Rodriguez, Sean	R-R	6-0	200	4-26-85	.267	.286	.263	12	45	7	12	2	1	4	12	3	1	0	0	19	0	0	.622	.327
Romine, Andrew	B-R	6-1	200	12-24-85	.290	.284	.291	106	380	57	110	15	3	8	53	27	5	2	3	67	21	4	.408	.342
Tomscha, Damek	R-R	6-2	200	8-27-91	.219	.250	.207	53	183	23	40	9	0	3	19	16	6	0	1	55	0	2	.399	.301
2-team total (2 Charlotte)					.216	.235	.209	55	190	23	41	9	0	8	19	16	6	0	1	57	0	2	.390	.296
Walding, Mitch	L-R	6-3	190	9-10-92	.206	.250	.193	90	282	46	58	11	1	11	40	62	3	0	3	133	2	1	.369	.351
Williams, Nick	L-L	6-3	195	9-8-93	.316	.276	.323	48	190	33	60	15	2	10	25	14	6	0	0	52	1	0	.574	.381

Pitching	B-T	HT	WT	DOB	W	L	ERA	G	GS	CG	SV	IP	H	R	ER	HR	BB	SO	AVG	vLH	vRH	K/9	BB/9
Anderson, Drew	R-R	6-3	185	3-22-94	0	6	5.77	11	11	0	0	48	48	35	31	9	27	40	.257	.277	.237	7.45	5.03
Antequera, Jose	R-R	5-10	160	8-1-95	0	0	9.00	2	0	0	0	2	4	2	2	0	0	1	.444	.250	.600	4.50	0.00
Arano, Victor	R-R	6-2	200	2-7-95	2	0	0.00	3	0	0	0	4	0	0	0	0	1	7	.000	.000	.000	15.75	2.25
Aris, Abdallah	R-L	5-11	155	10-8-96	0	0	27.00	1	0	0	0	1	4	3	3	1	1	2	.571	.500	.667	18.00	9.00
Arjona, Kyle	R-R	5-10	195	1-17-97	0	0	4.50	1	0	0	0	2	2	1	1	0	2	1	.286	.000	.400	4.50	9.00
Brogdon, Connor	R-R	6-6	192		3	1	3.06	26	0	0	2	32	23	12	11	4	12	44	.193	.199	.192	12.25	3.34
Castillo, Ali	R-R	5-9	180	6-19-89	0	0	13.50	2	0	0	0	2	3	3	3	1	1	0	.333	.500	.286	0.00	4.50
Curtiss, John	R-R	6-5	220	4-5-93	0	1	10.95	9	1	0	0	12	20	15	15	5	9	15	.351	.435	.294	10.95	6.57
Davis, Austin	L-L	6-4	245	2-3-93	4	1	2.75	37	0	0	5	52	43	17	16	2	24	64	.224	.344	.168	11.01	4.13
De Los Santos, Enyel	R-R	6-3	170	12-25-95	5	7	4.40	19	19	0	0	94	81	52	46	16	35	83	.232	.245	.222	7.95	3.35

Name	B-T	HT	WT	DOB	W	L	ERA	G	GS	CG	SV	IP	H	R	ER	HR	BB	SO	AVG	vLH	vRH	SO/9	BB/9
Dohy, Kyle	L-L	6-2	188	9-17-96	6	5	6.19	41	0	0	1	57	57	48	39	4	54	83	.253	.318	.226	13.18	8.58
Eickhoff, Jerad	R-R	6-4	245	7-2-90	3	1	4.67	4	4	0	0	17	13	10	9	3	8	16	.206	.250	.192	8.31	4.15
Eshelman, Tom	R-R	6-3	210	6-20-94	1	1	2.77	4	4	1	0	26	23	8	8	3	5	23	.237	.226	.257	7.96	1.73
2-team total (7 Norfolk)					3	2	3.92	11	10	1	0	64	66	29	28	9	12	51	.261	.237	.287	7.13	1.68
Garcia, Edgar	R-R	6-1	180	10-4-96	2	1	2.48	25	0	0	8	29	15	8	8	4	8	38	.152	.138	.157	11.79	2.48
Gilbert, Tyler	L-L	6-3	190	12-22-93	2	4	2.83	36	0	0	2	48	39	18	15	4	14	46	.224	.220	.226	8.69	2.64
Hammer, JD	R-R	6-3	215	7-12-94	2	2	12.64	17	0	0	0	16	20	22	22	4	15	16	.313	.393	.250	9.19	8.62
Irvin, Cole	L-L	6-4	180	1-31-94	6	1	3.94	17	16	0	0	94	113	46	41	13	14	65	.297	.339	.289	6.25	1.35
Jones, Damon	L-L	6-5	225	9-30-94	0	1	6.62	8	8	0	0	34	27	25	25	4	26	33	.214	.200	.219	8.74	6.88
Leftwich, Luke	L-R	6-3	205	6-9-94	0	1	8.28	16	1	0	0	25	33	24	23	8	12	32	.314	.333	.303	11.52	4.32
Martin, Josh	R-R	6-5	230	12-30-89	1	2	6.09	30	0	0	2	34	26	24	23	6	35	37	.210	.133	.253	9.79	9.26
McBride, Matt	R-R	6-2	215	5-23-85	0	0	0.00	1	0	0	0	1	4	6	0	0	0	1	.444	.250	.600	9.00	0.00
McGarry, Seth	R-R	6-0	180	1-5-94	0	2	6.15	20	4	0	1	45	60	38	31	8	19	40	.316	.342	.296	7.94	3.77
Pazos, James	R-L	6-2	235	5-5-91	0	1	6.14	7	0	0	2	7	8	6	5	0	7	4	.267	.333	.238	4.91	8.59
Pivetta, Nick	R-R	6-5	220	2-14-93	5	1	3.07	9	6	0	0	41	23	14	14	2	22	58	.164	.190	.146	12.73	4.83
Ramos, Edubray	R-R	6-0	160	12-19-92	2	0	1.80	10	0	0	6	10	6	3	2	1	4	8	.182	.231	.150	7.20	3.60
Rios, Yacksel	R-R	6-3	185	6-27-93	1	3	7.41	31	0	0	7	34	38	31	28	4	22	37	.284	.275	.289	9.79	5.82
2-team total (9 Indianapolis)					1	3	5.84	40	0	0	8	49	57	35	32	6	26	49	.291	.274	.301	8.94	4.74
Rivero, Alexis	R-R	6-0	180	10-18-94	2	3	5.92	12	4	0	0	24	26	16	16	5	12	16	.286	.189	.352	5.92	4.44
Romero, JoJo	L-L	5-11	190	9-9-96	3	3	6.88	13	13	0	0	54	68	47	41	8	35	40	.312	.268	.327	6.11	5.87
Romine, Andrew	B-R	6-1	200	12-24-85	0	0	0.00	2	0	0	0	2	1	0	0	0	2	0	.250	.000	.333	0.00	10.80
Rosso, Robert	R-R	6-4	215	6-9-96	2	4	5.50	14	14	0	0	69	67	43	42	13	31	64	.252	.266	.242	8.39	4.06
Salas, Fernando	R-R	6-2	200	5-30-85	1	1	4.24	18	0	0	1	23	24	12	11	3	7	21	.276	.308	.250	8.10	2.70
Straily, Dan	R-R	6-2	220	12-1-88	1	4	5.18	6	6	0	0	33	33	22	19	5	9	30	.254	.265	.247	8.18	2.45
2-team total (6 Norfolk)					5	4	3.76	12	12	0	0	67	57	31	28	9	17	68	.225	.253	.211	9.13	2.28
Suarez, Ranger	L-L	6-1	180	8-26-95	2	2	5.68	7	7	0	0	38	41	26	24	8	10	32	.281	.178	.327	7.58	2.37
Taveras, Jose	R-R	6-4	210	11-6-93	1	2	7.31	16	0	0	0	28	33	23	23	6	13	20	.287	.233	.319	6.35	4.13
Tols, Josh	L-L	5-7	185	10-6-89	1	1	5.73	24	0	0	0	33	33	29	21	5	25	35	.252	.191	.281	9.55	6.82
Vincent, Nick	R-R	6-0	185	7-12-86	0	0	1.46	10	0	0	0	12	9	2	2	1	1	13	.192	.214	.182	9.49	0.73
Viza, Tyler	R-R	6-3	170	10-21-94	1	8	7.23	19	16	0	0	71	100	69	57	17	23	67	.321	.344	.304	8.49	2.92
Windle, Tom	L-L	6-4	215	3-10-92	7	2	4.26	42	0	0	0	51	42	30	24	2	32	51	.228	.289	.205	9.06	5.68

Fielding

Catcher	PCT	G	PO	A	E	DP	PB
Brantly	.997	47	335	19	1	2	7
Grullon	.992	86	716	38	6	5	12
Hundley	.985	8	67	0	1	0	0
McBride	.986	9	67	5	1	0	0

First Base	PCT	G	PO	A	E	DP
Adams	.947	3	16	2	1	0
Brantly	1.000	2	4	0	0	0
Cozens	1.000	1	7	0	0	0
Gosselin	.978	7	40	5	1	5
Grullon	.875	7	20	1	3	3
Listi	.989	51	339	16	4	34
McBride	1.000	25	175	17	0	18
Morrison	1.000	10	80	3	0	12
Rodriguez	1.000	5	24	3	0	1
Romine	.981	7	51	2	1	5
Tomscha	1.000	31	211	16	0	22
Walding	.971	9	65	3	2	10

Second Base	PCT	G	PO	A	E	DP
Antequera	.944	4	7	10	1	3
Canelo	.935	12	21	22	3	6
Castillo	.950	36	58	74	7	24
Gosselin	.983	58	106	131	4	38
Ngoepe	.991	28	44	66	1	15
Rivas	1.000	2	4	7	0	1
Rodriguez	.818	3	3	6	2	1
Romine	1.000	5	6	5	0	1

Third Base	PCT	G	PO	A	E	DP
Castillo	.867	10	4	9	2	0
Franco	.947	11	11	25	2	2
Gosselin	.875	6	3	11	2	0
Listi	.922	16	11	36	4	5
Ngoepe	.923	5	3	9	1	0
Rodriguez	.917	3	1	10	1	2
Romine	.927	17	9	29	3	3
Tomscha	.840	8	1	20	4	5
Walding	.945	79	44	144	11	16

Shortstop	PCT	G	PO	A	E	DP
Canelo	.956	94	118	210	15	42
Castillo	1.000	2	1	4	0	0
Gosselin	1.000	3	5	3	0	2
Ngoepe	.875	3	3	4	1	1
Rodriguez	1.000	2	3	3	0	1
Romine	.976	45	53	112	4	30
Walding	.000	1	0	0	0	0

Outfield	PCT	G	PO	A	E	DP
Adams	.971	55	98	2	3	0
Canelo	.973	20	35	1	1	0
Castillo	1.000	60	87	3	0	0
Cozens	1.000	17	32	3	0	2
Cumana	.929	8	12	1	1	1
Haseley	1.000	18	35	1	0	0
Hernandez	1.000	56	111	2	0	0
Listi	1.000	7	8	0	0	0
McBride	1.000	2	1	0	0	0
Pirela	.986	33	67	1	1	0
Quinn	1.000	4	12	1	0	1
Robinson	.982	82	159	6	3	1
Rodriguez	1.000	2	1	0	0	0
Romine	.962	20	49	1	2	0
Tomscha	1.000	12	23	0	0	0
Williams	.990	45	94	4	1	2

READING FIGHTIN PHILS
EASTERN LEAGUE

DOUBLE-A

Batting	B-T	HT	WT	DOB	AVG	vLH	vRH	G	AB	R	H	2B	3B	HR	RBI	BB	HBP	SH	SF	SO	SB	CS	SLG	OBP
Antequera, Jose	R-R	5-10	160	8-1-95	.247	.200	.262	30	81	7	20	2	0	4	6	2	2	0		17	1	1	.272	.315
Bohm, Alec	R-R	6-5	225	8-3-96	.269	.218	.284	63	238	38	64	11	1	14	42	28	1	0	3	38	2	2	.500	.344
Bossart, Austin	R-R	6-2	210	7-4-93	.195	.237	.177	63	200	27	39	7	0	7	28	30	2	2	2	47	2	0	.335	.303
2-team total (19 Binghamton)					.196	.237	.179	82	260	31	51	13	0	7	32	37	4	2	3	63	2	0	.327	.303
Bruce, Jay	L-L	6-3	225	4-3-87	.000	.000	.000	2	8	0	0	0	0	0	0	0	0	0	0	4	0	0	.000	.000
Castillo, Ali	R-R	5-9	180	6-19-89	.373	.462	.342	16	51	7	19	5	1	1	8	7	0	2	0	10	2	2	.569	.448
Conley, Jack	R-R	6-1	190	1-16-97	.273	.000	.316	8	22	5	6	1	0	1	1	6	0	0		7	1	0	.455	.429
Cumana, Grenny	R-R	5-5	145	11-10-95	.319	.400	.270	49	160	20	51	6	3	2	22	6	2	1	0	18	1	5	.431	.351
Gamboa, Arquimedes	B-R	6-0	175	9-23-97	.188	.198	.185	113	356	35	67	10	5	3	28	59	1	4	1	112	21	8	.270	.305
Gomez, Jose	R-R	5-11	175	12-10-96	.253	.263	.250	91	292	31	74	10	3	3	30	20	5	1	4	73	5	6	.339	.308
Hall, Darick	L-R	6-4	236	7-25-95	.235	.262	.229	132	456	69	107	38	1	20	67	60	17	0	2	134	5	1	.454	.344
Haseley, Adam	L-L	6-1	195	4-12-96	.267	.316	.241	44	165	30	44	8	2	8	21	21	2	0	2	35	4	2	.485	.353
Kingery, Scott	R-R	5-10	180	4-29-94	.091	.100	.000	3	11	1	1	0	0	0	2	0	0	0	1	3	1	0	.091	.083
Lartigue, Henri	B-R	6-0	205	2-24-95	.136	.153	.131	77	242	24	33	4	1	7	26	39	2	1	3	88	3	2	.248	.259
Listi, Austin	R-R	6-0	218	11-5-93	.220	.219	.221	62	209	29	46	7	1	7	33	36	3	0	3	44	1	2	.364	.339
Maton, Nick	L-R	6-1	165	2-18-97	.210	.125	.222	21	62	6	13	3	0	2	6	9	0	0	1	14	1	1	.355	.306

	B-T	HT	WT	DOB	AVG	vLH	vRH	G	AB	R	H	2B	3B	HR	RBI	BB	HBP	SH	SF	SO	SB	CS	SLG	OBP
Mayer, Danny	R-R	6-5	245	6-25-95	.182	.250	.143	7	11	2	2	0	0	0	0	3	2	0	0	6	1	0	.182	.438
Moniak, Mickey	L-R	6-2	185	5-13-98	.252	.252	.252	119	465	63	117	28	13	11	67	33	2	1	2	111	15	3	.439	.303
Quinn, Roman	B-R	5-10	170	5-14-93	.125	.000	.167	2	8	0	1	0	0	0	0	1	0	1	0	0	2	0	0	.125	.222
Randolph, Cornelius	L-R	5-11	205	6-2-97	.247	.187	.269	102	348	42	86	15	4	10	44	37	3	0	1	102	9	5	.399	.324
Rivas, Raul	B-R	5-10	160	10-27-96	.204	.250	.185	57	147	15	30	5	3	0	10	10	3	3	1	41	3	1	.279	.267
Stephen, Josh	L-L	6-0	185	9-22-97	.271	.189	.292	113	362	48	98	29	6	12	47	39	1	0	1	110	7	6	.483	.342
Williams, Luke	R-R	6-1	180	8-9-96	.238	.232	.241	125	441	77	105	30	3	11	51	49	6	3	5	113	30	9	.395	.319

Pitching	B-T	HT	WT	DOB	W	L	ERA	G	GS	CG	SV	IP	H	R	ER	HR	BB	SO	AVG	vLH	vRH	K/9	BB/9
Armas, Gustavo	R-R	6-1	195	1-15-96	0	1	10.29	2	2	0	0	7	9	8	8	1	5	4	.300	.400	.200	5.14	6.43
Bettencourt, Trevor	R-R	6-0	195	7-21-94	0	0	3.38	2	0	0	0	3	3	1	1	0	2	5	.273	.000	.500	16.88	6.75
Brogdon, Connor	R-R	6-6	192	1-29-95	1	1	2.66	15	0	0	2	24	12	8	7	4	7	39	.150	.093	.216	14.83	2.66
Brown, Aaron	L-L	6-2	223	6-20-92	5	4	3.82	45	0	0	2	66	58	35	28	6	35	81	.239	.301	.200	11.05	4.77
Carr, Tyler	R-R	5-10	175	5-1-96	0	0	0.00	1	0	0	0	3	1	0	0	0	0	6	.111	.143	.000	20.25	0.00
Carrasco, Luis	R-R	6-3	181	9-11-96	0	0	54.00	3	0	0	0	1	5	8	8	0	6	1	.625	.500	.667	6.75	40.50
Cedeno, Luis	R-R	5-11	154	7-14-94	0	0	5.40	1	0	0	0	2	2	1	1	0	2	3	.333	.333	.333	16.20	10.80
Cleavinger, Garrett	R-L	6-1	210	4-23-94	3	2	3.66	34	0	0	0	52	32	25	21	2	34	83	.172	.155	.183	14.46	5.92
Dohy, Kyle	L-L	6-2	188	9-17-96	1	0	0.82	6	0	0	2	11	2	1	1	0	5	22	.059	.000	.087	18.00	4.09
Dyer, Grant	R-R	6-1	195	7-31-95	1	0	4.39	19	0	0	1	27	26	17	13	3	10	28	.252	.300	.208	9.45	3.38
Eastman, Colton	R-R	6-3	185	8-22-96	1	1	3.03	6	4	0	0	33	25	14	11	3	12	30	.216	.182	.260	8.27	3.31
Eickhoff, Jerad	R-R	6-4	245	7-2-90	0	1	9.82	2	2	0	0	7	8	8	8	2	3	6	.286	.313	.250	7.36	3.68
Eshelman, Tom	R-R	6-3	210	6-20-94	0	3	6.28	6	6	0	0	29	43	22	20	4	6	26	.341	.337	.351	8.16	1.88
Falter, Bailey	R-L	6-4	175	4-24-97	6	5	3.84	14	14	0	0	77	82	37	33	9	15	62	.272	.276	.269	7.22	1.75
Garcia, Julian	L-R	6-3	206	5-13-95	2	2	6.28	6	6	0	0	29	37	21	20	2	10	26	.308	.338	.269	8.16	3.14
Hammer, JD	R-R	6-3	215	7-12-94	1	0	1.77	13	0	0	2	20	17	7	4	1	4	26	.221	.200	.250	11.51	1.77
Hennigan, Jonathan	L-L	6-4	193	8-27-94	3	4	4.47	31	0	0	2	46	50	27	23	2	28	41	.275	.258	.283	7.96	5.44
Hernandez, Jakob	L-L	6-4	260	5-19-96	5	1	1.68	47	0	1	5	70	43	14	13	4	27	73	.178	.178	.177	9.43	3.49
Howard, Spencer	R-R	6-2	205	7-28-96	1	0	2.35	6	6	0	0	31	20	9	8	2	9	38	.180	.222	.125	11.15	2.64
Hunter, Tommy	R-R	6-3	250	7-3-86	0	0	0.00	1	1	0	0	2	2	0	0	0	0	2	.333	.250	.500	9.00	0.00
Jones, Damon	L-L	6-5	225	9-30-94	1	0	0.82	4	4	0	0	22	9	2	2	0	9	31	.129	.177	.113	12.68	3.68
Lartigue, Henri	B-R	6-0	205	2-24-95	0	0	22.50	2	0	0	0	2	6	5	5	0	1	0	.546	.375	1.000	0.00	4.50
Leftwich, Luke	L-R	6-3	205	6-9-94	2	0	1.02	12	0	0	0	18	4	3	2	0	8	28	.073	.061	.091	14.26	4.08
Llovera, Mauricio	R-R	5-11	200	4-17-96	3	4	4.55	14	12	0	0	65	60	35	33	7	28	72	.243	.248	.235	9.92	3.86
McGarry, Seth	R-R	6-0	180	1-5-94	2	0	1.13	4	2	0	0	16	7	2	2	1	8	16	.140	.129	.158	9.00	4.50
Medina, Adonis	R-R	6-1	185	12-18-96	7	7	4.94	22	21	0	0	106	103	69	58	11	41	82	.254	.302	.196	6.98	3.49
Morgan, Adam	L-L	6-1	200	2-27-90	0	0	0.00	1	1	0	0	1	0	0	0	0	1	0	.000	.000	.000	9.00	9.00
Parkinson, David	R-L	6-2	210	12-14-95	10	9	4.08	22	22	0	0	119	107	56	54	10	39	118	.247	.271	.237	8.92	2.95
Ramirez, Luis	R-R	5-11	175	9-5-94	0	0	9.00	1	0	0	0	2	3	2	2	0	2	0	.333	.286	.500	0.00	9.00
Ramos, Edubray	R-R	6-0	160	12-19-92	0	0	18.00	1	0	0	0	1	2	2	2	0	2	0	.400	.333	.500	0.00	9.00
Requena, Alejandro	R-R	6-2	200	11-29-96	0	0	0.00	1	1	0	0	1	0	0	0	0	0	1	.000	.000	.000	9.00	0.00
Rivero, Alexis	R-R	6-0	180	10-18-94	0	0	4.91	3	0	0	1	4	3	2	2	1	3	3	.231	.300	.000	7.36	2.45
Romero, JoJo	L-L	5-11	190	9-9-96	4	4	4.84	11	11	0	0	58	58	33	31	4	12	52	.261	.250	.267	8.12	1.87
Rosso, Ramon	R-R	6-4	215	6-9-96	3	2	3.15	10	10	0	0	54	46	19	19	8	15	52	.235	.231	.239	8.61	2.48
Russ, Addison	R-R	6-1	190	10-29-94	5	6	2.54	55	0	0	22	57	47	28	16	5	20	81	.223	.225	.220	12.86	3.18
Seabold, Connor	R-R	6-2	190	1-24-96	3	1	2.67	7	7	0	0	40	35	12	10	2	10	36	.240	.239	.240	8.10	2.25
Singer, Jeff	L-L	6-0	200	9-13-93	7	0	2.34	42	0	0	3	62	39	21	16	3	22	74	.180	.169	.188	10.80	3.21
Taveras, Jose	R-R	6-4	210	11-6-93	3	1	3.41	7	5	0	0	29	29	13	11	2	5	16	.279	.250	.300	4.97	1.55
Tols, Josh	L-L	5-7	185	10-6-89	0	0	0.00	2	0	0	0	4	3	0	0	1	0	4	.200	.333	.167	9.00	2.25
Viza, Tyler	R-R	6-3	170	10-21-94	0	0	9.00	1	1	0	0	5	11	6	5	1	0	2	.423	.556	.353	3.60	0.00

Fielding

Catcher	PCT	G	PO	A	E	DP	PB
Bossart	.990	61	559	49	6	1	6
Conley	.986	8	60	11	1	0	1
Lartigue	.990	72	639	45	7	3	13

First Base	PCT	G	PO	A	E	DP
Bohm	.986	12	68	4	1	6
Hall	.996	120	846	62	4	84
Listi	1.000	10	71	6	0	4
Williams	1.000	1	4	2	0	1

Second Base	PCT	G	PO	A	E	DP
Antequera	.986	22	32	38	1	9
Castillo	.968	8	11	19	1	5
Gamboa	1.000	2	2	2	0	1
Gomez	.980	41	56	91	3	21
Kingery	1.000	1	2	1	0	1
Maton	1.000	11	22	23	0	4
Rivas	.961	24	40	59	4	13
Williams	1.000	40	47	78	0	18

Third Base	PCT	G	PO	A	E	DP
Antequera	1.000	1	0	4	0	0
Bohm	.920	44	30	62	8	10
Castillo	1.000	4	3	5	0	0
Gamboa	.800	3	2	2	1	0
Gomez	.925	20	17	32	4	8
Kingery	1.000	1	2	2	0	1
Listi	.941	44	34	62	6	7
Rivas	1.000	1	0	3	0	0
Williams	.924	31	16	45	5	3

Shortstop	PCT	G	PO	A	E	DP
Castillo	1.000	1	1	1	0	0
Gamboa	.980	102	165	219	8	52
Gomez	.949	30	37	56	5	9
Maton	.895	8	5	12	2	1
Rivas	1.000	1	1	1	0	0
Williams	.892	10	12	21	4	5

Outfield	PCT	G	PO	A	E	DP
Cumana	.971	36	64	2	2	0
Gamboa	1.000	1	2	0	0	0
Haseley	1.000	44	90	2	0	0
Kingery	1.000	1	1	0	0	0
Listi	1.000	3	5	1	0	0
Mayer	1.000	3	3	0	0	0
Moniak	.985	117	250	8	4	4
Quinn	1.000	2	4	0	0	0
Randolph	.985	88	132	3	2	0
Rivas	1.000	20	41	2	0	1
Stephen	.978	69	88	2	2	0
Williams	.990	50	94	1	1	0

CLEARWATER THRESHERS   HIGH CLASS A
FLORIDA STATE LEAGUE

Batting	B-T	HT	WT	DOB	AVG	vLH	vRH	G	AB	R	H	2B	3B	HR	RBI	BB	HBP	SH	SF	SO	SB	CS	SLG	OBP
Aklinski, Ben	R-R	5-11	210	6-3-96	.196	.135	.215	51	158	17	31	9	0	2	16	10	6	3	1	52	2	3	.291	.269
Alastre, Jesus	R-R	6-1	155	11-25-96	.000	.000	.000	2	7	0	0	0	0	0	0	1	0	0	0	4	0	0	.000	.125
Bohm, Alec	R-R	6-5	225	8-3-96	.329	.294	.339	40	158	25	52	10	3	4	27	17	1	0	1	21	1	2	.506	.396
Brito, Daniel	L-R	6-1	170	1-23-98	.243	.151	.260	103	342	37	83	14	1	4	32	22	6	4	5	73	6	10	.325	.296

Batting	B-T	HT	WT	DOB	AVG	vLH	vRH	G	AB	R	H	2B	3B	HR	RBI	BB	HBP	SH	SF	SO	SB	CS	OBP	SLG
Cabral, Edgar	R-R	5-11	210	9-12-95	.197	.188	.200	21	71	6	14	5	0	4	11	6	0	0	2	19	0	0	.437	.253
Conley, Jack	R-R	6-1	190	1-16-97	.167	.167	.167	9	30	1	5	1	0	0	3	0	2	2	0	8	0	0	.200	.219
Duran, Rodolfo	R-R	5-9	181	2-19-98	.240	.243	.240	66	233	25	56	10	1	6	23	10	1	0	1	53	0	0	.369	.274
Fitch, Colby	L-R	5-11	215	7-27-95	.224	.286	.203	27	85	15	19	4	1	0	9	15	4	0	2	20	3	0	.294	.359
Gomez, Jose	R-R	5-11	175	12-10-96	.348	.182	.400	14	46	4	16	4	0	0	6	5	0	1	0	14	0	1	.435	.412
Guthrie, Dalton	R-R	5-11	160	12-23-95	.243	.210	.251	88	301	39	73	16	4	4	22	13	5	4	2	51	6	2	.362	.284
Kroon, Matt	R-R	6-1	195	12-5-96	.225	.238	.222	69	222	29	50	8	6	4	24	18	1	2	68	10	4		.369	.304
Marchan, Rafael	B-R	5-9	170	2-25-99	.231	.000	.257	22	78	6	18	4	0	0	3	6	1	0	1	8	1	2	.282	.291
Matera, Nick	R-R	6-2	215	8-29-96	.128	.000	.156	14	39	3	5	1	0	1	6	5	0	0	1	15	0	0	.231	.222
Maton, Nick	L-R	6-1	165	2-18-97	.276	.270	.277	93	337	35	93	14	3	5	45	41	3	1	2	71	11	8	.380	.358
Mayer, Danny	R-R	6-5	245	6-25-95	.199	.071	.225	49	166	21	33	7	1	9	18	14	3	0	0	48	1	1	.416	.273
Miller, Luke	R-R	6-2	192	7-17-96	.256	.357	.235	49	164	15	42	8	1	7	20	12	1	0	2	55	0	0	.445	.307
Muzziotti, Simon	L-L	6-1	175	12-27-98	.287	.173	.314	110	425	52	122	21	3	3	28	32	1	5	2	60	21	12	.372	.337
Ortiz, Jhailyn	R-R	6-3	215	11-18-98	.200	.209	.198	115	430	57	86	15	3	19	65	36	8	0	4	149	2	3	.381	.272
Quinn, Roman	B-R	5-10	170	5-14-93	.500	1.000	.444	6	20	6	10	3	0	1	1	3	0	2	0	6	2	0	.800	.565
Rivas, Raul	B-R	5-10	160	10-27-96	.250	.375	.229	16	56	7	14	1	1	0	5	5	1	4	0	9	1	1	.304	.323
Scheiner, Jake	R-R	6-1	200	8-13-95	.256	.212	.268	45	160	19	41	8	1	2	20	16	2	1	4	28	3	2	.356	.324
Stokes, Madison	R-R	6-2	200	4-25-96	.242	.290	.226	110	418	38	101	21	2	10	42	21	6	1	2	108	0	4	.373	.286
Vierling, Matt	R-R	6-3	205	9-16-96	.232	.183	.246	118	431	41	100	23	2	5	41	34	9	1	8	94	22	5	.330	.297

Pitching	B-T	HT	WT	DOB	W	L	ERA	G	GS	CG	SV	IP	H	R	ER	HR	BB	SO	AVG	vLH	vRH	K/9	BB/9
Arjona, Kyle	R-R	5-10	195	1-17-97	1	2	4.25	23	1	0	0	42	44	24	20	5	17	30	.268	.260	.275	6.38	3.61
Armas, Gustavo	R-R	6-1	195	1-15-96	2	1	10.00	11	0	0	0	18	35	21	20	4	5	16	.412	.425	.400	8.00	2.50
Brogdon, Connor	R-R	6-6	192	1-29-95	2	0	1.80	10	0	0	0	26	11	6	4	1	5	23	.164	.133	.189	10.35	2.25
Brown, Andrew	R-R	6-1	180	10-24-97	5	7	6.17	24	20	0	0	101	128	74	69	8	37	66	.315	.340	.291	5.90	3.31
Cabrera, Ismael	R-R	6-1	185	6-19-94	0	1	2.79	6	0	0	0	10	5	3	3	1	6	6	.156	.231	.105	5.59	5.59
Carr, Tyler	R-R	5-10	175	5-1-96	3	3	1.64	27	1	0	5	49	29	10	9	1	17	50	.174	.162	.183	9.12	3.10
Carrasco, Luis	R-R	6-3	181	9-11-94	1	2	7.56	13	0	0	0	17	14	14	14	1	16	14	.246	.160	.313	7.56	8.64
Cedeno, Luis	R-R	5-11	154	7-14-94	0	1	3.86	4	0	0	0	7	6	3	3	1	9	7	.214	.200	.222	9.00	11.57
Dyer, Grant	R-R	6-1	195	7-31-95	1	2	0.54	23	0	0	6	33	15	7	2	0	6	34	.133	.118	.145	9.18	1.62
Eastman, Colton	R-R	6-3	185	8-22-96	5	5	3.36	13	12	1	0	75	74	30	28	9	22	79	.258	.234	.277	9.48	2.64
Eickhoff, Jerad	R-R	6-4	245	7-2-90	0	0	3.38	2	2	0	0	3	3	1	1	0	1	2	.300	.333	.250	6.75	3.38
Evanko, Ethan	L-L	6-4	185	6-7-95	5	2	1.49	10	9	0	0	54	42	13	9	5	13	45	.211	.183	.223	7.45	2.15
Garcia, Julian	L-R	6-3	206	5-13-95	7	6	2.78	17	16	0	0	97	82	37	30	12	27	94	.229	.249	.212	8.72	2.51
Glogoski, Kyle	R-R	6-2	183	1-6-99	2	2	1.88	11	11	0	0	53	37	13	11	2	20	45	.197	.167	.228	7.69	3.42
Gomez, Michael	R-R	6-3	210	8-15-96	1	0	1.47	10	0	0	1	18	14	3	3	1	6	22	.206	.189	.226	10.80	2.95
Hennigan, Jonathan	L-L	6-4	193	8-27-94	0	1	2.25	14	0	0	7	20	13	5	5	0	6	29	.178	.161	.191	13.05	2.70
Howard, Spencer	R-R	6-2	205	7-28-96	2	1	1.29	7	7	0	0	35	19	5	5	1	5	48	.162	.194	.127	12.34	1.29
Hunter, Tommy	R-R	6-3	250	7-3-86	0	0	3.00	3	2	0	0	3	1	1	1	0	0	4	.100	.167	.000	12.00	0.00
Jones, Damon	L-L	6-5	225	9-30-94	4	3	1.54	11	11	0	0	58	38	14	10	3	24	88	.188	.164	.199	13.58	3.70
Killgore, Keylan	L-L	6-3	185	9-30-96	1	3	3.57	36	0	0	11	53	46	22	21	4	25	61	.234	.235	.233	10.36	4.25
Kinney, Jake	R-R	6-7	22	1-14-97	0	0	21.60	1	0	0	0	2	3	4	4	1	3	4	.429	.667	.250	16.20	5.40
Lin, Hsin-Chieh	R-R	6-2	198	3-18-99	0	0	0.00	1	0	0	0	2	0	0	0	0	0	1	.000	.000	.000	4.50	0.00
Lindow, Ethan	R-L	6-3	180	10-15-98	0	2	1.69	3	3	0	0	16	17	8	3	0	2	16	.274	.222	.296	9.00	1.13
Maldonado, Omar	R-R	6-5	240	7-22-95	0	0	4.50	1	0	0	0	2	3	1	1	0	0	4	.333	.400	.250	18.00	0.00
Marcelino, Oscar	R-R	6-3	166	6-8-97	2	1	7.84	14	0	0	0	21	27	24	18	2	18	16	.318	.361	.286	6.97	7.84
McArthur, James	R-R	6-2	230	12-11-96	3	1	3.03	7	7	0	0	30	26	10	10	3	16	30	.239	.304	.170	9.10	4.85
McGarry, Seth	R-R	6-0	180	1-5-94	1	1	2.00	7	1	0	1	18	17	4	4	0	4	15	.254	.286	.231	7.50	2.00
Perkins, Jack	R-R	6-4	200	8-6-97	0	4	5.85	5	4	0	0	20	22	13	13	2	4	15	.282	.250	.324	6.75	1.80
Ramirez, Luis	R-R	5-11	175	9-14-97	2	0	4.32	8	1	0	0	17	18	8	8	2	8	15	.281	.219	.344	8.10	4.32
Ramos, Edubray	R-R	6-0	160	12-19-92	0	0	3.00	3	2	0	0	3	1	1	1	0	1	5	.100	.000	.000	15.00	3.00
Requena, Alejandro	R-R	6-2	200	11-29-96	9	10	4.90	22	20	1	0	112	116	67	61	12	38	105	.270	.258	.281	8.44	3.05
Ross, Austin	R-R	6-1	185	8-16-94	5	1	3.66	38	0	0	4	66	55	29	27	7	24	74	.226	.236	.218	10.04	3.26
Seabold, Connor	R-R	6-2	190	1-24-96	1	0	1.00	2	1	0	0	9	4	1	1	1	1	10	.133	.000	.267	10.00	1.00
Taveras, Jose	R-R	6-4	210	11-6-93	1	0	1.29	1	1	0	0	7	6	1	1	1	1	1	.250	.200	.286	3.86	1.29
Warren, Zach	L-L	6-5	200	6-9-96	1	3	3.30	40	0	0	7	60	43	25	22	2	38	80	.199	.208	.194	12.00	5.70
Young, Kyle	L-L	6-10	205	12-2-97	1	3	4.29	4	4	0	0	21	21	11	10	2	1	25	.256	.111	.297	10.71	0.43

Fielding

Catcher	PCT	G	PO	A	E	DP	PB
Cabral	.976	15	149	15	4	0	1
Conley	.989	9	82	7	1	1	1
Duran	1.000	64	544	65	0	5	10
Fitch	.994	17	136	24	1	1	3
Marchan	.977	22	152	21	4	1	1
Matera	.977	14	82	4	2	0	3

First Base	PCT	G	PO	A	E	DP
Bohm	1.000	7	67	3	0	4
Kroon	.987	36	285	13	4	22
Mayer	1.000	6	48	4	0	2
Miller	1.000	22	163	10	0	13
Scheiner	.974	12	75	1	2	8
Stokes	.988	54	454	21	6	38

Second Base	PCT	G	PO	A	E	DP
Brito	.993	65	95	177	2	36
Gomez	1.000	9	15	22	0	5

	PCT	G	PO	A	E	DP
Guthrie	.987	35	53	95	2	17
Maton	1.000	15	20	31	0	7
Rivas	1.000	6	12	6	0	3
Stokes	1.000	6	12	16	0	3

Third Base	PCT	G	PO	A	E	DP
Bohm	.967	25	20	39	2	4
Brito	.941	7	4	12	1	0
Gomez	1.000	3	1	6	0	1
Guthrie	.900	11	4	23	3	2
Kroon	.880	8	4	18	3	2
Maton	.944	8	5	12	1	1
Miller	.818	9	6	12	4	0
Rivas	.957	9	8	14	1	1
Scheiner	.949	18	11	26	2	4
Stokes	.961	39	35	64	4	12

Shortstop	PCT	G	PO	A	E	DP
Brito	.966	29	29	85	4	12

	PCT	G	PO	A	E	DP
Gomez	1.000	2	3	3	0	2
Guthrie	.977	40	56	112	4	27
Maton	.964	65	96	145	9	23

Outfield	PCT	G	PO	A	E	DP
Aklinski	.990	44	93	5	1	1
Alastre	1.000	2	4	0	0	0
Kroon	1.000	19	27	0	0	0
Mayer	.979	32	46	0	1	0
Miller	1.000	5	8	1	0	1
Muzziotti	.991	102	211	6	2	3
Ortiz	1.000	89	166	14	0	3
Quinn	1.000	5	13	0	0	0
Rivas	1.000	1	2	0	0	0
Scheiner	1.000	8	10	0	0	0
Stokes	1.000	4	5	0	0	0
Vierling	.988	99	160	9	2	3

PHILADELPHIA PHILLIES

Batting	B-T	HT	WT	DOB	AVG	vLH	vRH	G	AB	R	H	2B	3B	HR	RBI	BB	HBP	SH	SF	SO	SB	CS	SLG	OBP
Aparicio, Juan	R-R	5-11	175	5-26-00	.191	.286	.167	20	68	8	13	3	0	1	10	3	1	0	2	19	0	0	.279	.230
Bohm, Alec	R-R	6-5	225	8-3-96	.367	.450	.339	22	79	13	29	9	0	3	11	12	0	0	2	14	3	0	.595	.441
Conley, Jack	R-R	6-1	190	1-16-97	.190	.167	.196	19	58	5	11	3	0	0	2	6	1	0	0	14	0	0	.241	.277
De La Cruz, Carlos	R-R	6-8	210	10-6-99	.220	.210	.223	117	428	38	94	17	4	7	50	27	4	0	2	159	7	7	.327	.271
Garcia, Luis	B-R	5-11	170	10-1-00	.186	.232	.170	127	467	36	87	14	3	4	36	44	5	3	5	132	9	8	.255	.261
Gutierrez, Abrahan	R-R	6-2	214	10-31-99	.246	.338	.211	83	289	23	71	9	0	4	27	28	2	0	3	62	3	1	.318	.314
Guzman, Jonathan	R-R	6-0	156	8-17-99	.251	.272	.244	123	475	55	119	18	2	3	40	32	1	4	2	97	31	11	.316	.298
Holmes, Jake	R-R	6-4	198	7-2-98	.154	.167	.150	55	175	13	27	5	1	1	16	13	0	4	3	62	7	1	.211	.209
Kingery, Scott	R-R	5-10	180	4-29-94	.333	--	.333	1	3	0	1	0	0	0	0	0	0	0	0	0	0	0	.333	.333
Kroon, Matt	R-R	6-1	195	12-5-96	.268	.414	.229	37	138	19	37	6	1	1	12	12	1	0	1	46	8	4	.348	.329
Lancaster, Seth	L-R	6-2	208	6-21-96	.199	.143	.209	41	136	19	27	10	1	3	13	20	1	0	1	45	11	4	.353	.304
Marchan, Rafael	B-R	5-9	170	2-25-99	.271	.219	.291	63	236	21	64	16	0	0	20	24	4	0	1	31	1	3	.339	.347
Matera, Nick	R-R	6-2	215	8-29-96	.300	--	.300	3	10	3	3	0	0	2	4	0	0	0	0	3	0	0	.900	.300
Matos, Malvin	R-R	6-3	170	8-19-96	.248	.276	.238	116	391	57	97	17	1	10	39	47	9	7	1	105	18	8	.373	.342
Miller, Luke	R-R	6-2	192	7-17-96	.260	.217	.280	21	73	13	19	2	0	3	12	12	1	0	0	20	1	2	.411	.372
Pelletier, Ben	R-R	6-2	190	8-22-98	.197	.157	.212	107	371	43	73	16	1	13	40	31	9	0	0	130	2	1	.350	.275
Smith, Jimmy	R-R	6-1	210	8-27-95	.194	.158	.208	21	72	7	14	1	0	1	5	1	1	0	1	24	0	1	.250	.213
Stobbe, Cole	R-R	6-2	194	8-30-97	.213	.194	.220	108	352	50	75	19	3	15	34	38	5	2	0	158	10	7	.412	.299
Stovall, Hunter	R-R	5-8	170	9-5-96	.233	.276	.218	71	228	24	53	8	3	1	23	22	4	2	4	32	7	4	.307	.306
2-team total (18 Asheville)					.242	.279	.230	89	285	33	69	15	4	1	25	34	5	2	4	44	8	7	.333	.329
Tatum, McCarthy	R-R	6-6	210	5-15-96	.233	.191	.248	43	159	15	37	10	1	2	15	16	0	0	1	52	3	2	.346	.301
Trejo, Yerwin	R-R	6-0	170	1-3-97	.252	.324	.221	73	222	27	56	5	1	1	13	14	0	0	2	58	25	5	.297	.297

Pitching	B-T	HT	WT	DOB	W	L	ERA	G	GS	CG	SV	IP	H	R	ER	HR	BB	SO	AVG	vLH	vRH	K/9	BB/9
Aris, Abdallah	R-L	5-11	155	10-8-96	0	0	11.57	2	0	0	0	2	2	3	3	1	3	5	.200	.000	.250	19.29	11.57
Barber, Albertus	R-R	6-2	175	2-18-96	4	0	0.00	11	0	0	0	12	9	0	0	0	2	10	.220	.177	.250	7.30	1.46
Bennett, Blake	R-R	6-2	195	3-7-96	0	1	19.29	4	0	0	0	5	9	10	10	4	1	5	.409	.500	.375	9.64	1.93
Brown, Ben	R-R	6-6	210	9-9-99	0	0	0.00	4	1	0	0	14	11	0	0	0	3	20	.216	.136	.276	13.17	1.98
Cabrera, Ismael	R-R	6-1	185	6-19-94	3	0	0.00	9	0	0	1	10	5	1	0	0	4	11	.147	.000	.200	9.58	3.48
Carr, Tyler	R-R	5-10	175	5-1-96	2	1	0.51	11	0	0	1	18	13	6	1	0	9	20	.206	.227	.195	10.19	4.58
Carrasco, Luis	R-R	6-3	181	9-11-94	0	0	1.69	8	0	0	2	11	3	2	2	0	7	12	.100	.100	.100	10.13	5.91
Eastman, Colton	R-R	6-3	185	8-22-96	1	2	6.00	5	3	0	1	21	21	15	14	2	3	25	.244	.192	.267	10.71	1.29
Evanko, Ethan	L-L	6-4	185	6-7-95	2	0	2.13	9	0	0	0	13	6	3	3	1	4	13	.143	.154	.138	9.24	2.84
Glogoski, Kyle	R-R	6-2	183	1-6-99	3	1	1.80	8	3	0	0	28	14	6	4	1	8	45	.144	.086	.177	14.64	2.60
Gomez, Michael	R-R	6-3	210	8-15-96	1	0	0.00	5	0	0	1	8	2	0	0	0	1	6	.083	.111	.067	6.48	1.08
Gonell, Rafi	R-R	6-2	190	2-26-97	4	3	5.10	19	5	0	2	55	51	34	31	5	19	50	.243	.284	.209	8.23	3.13
Gowdy, Kevin	R-R	6-4	170	11-16-97	0	6	4.68	24	16	0	0	77	83	46	40	4	51	53	.281	.304	.268	6.19	5.96
Hendrickson, Josh	L-L	6-4	215	9-18-97	1	1	0.47	5	2	0	0	19	11	5	1	1	5	22	.175	.200	.163	10.42	2.37
Lehman, Taylor	L-L	6-8	240	12-30-95	2	2	2.78	9	4	0	2	32	24	11	10	0	15	21	.214	.209	.217	5.85	4.18
Lindow, Ethan	R-L	6-3	180	10-15-98	5	2	2.66	23	13	0	2	95	73	35	28	4	20	103	.208	.227	.201	9.79	1.90
Maldonado, Omar	R-R	6-5	240	7-22-95	0	0	2.25	6	0	0	0	8	8	3	2	0	6	7	.286	.400	.222	7.88	6.75
Marcelino, Oscar	R-R	6-3	166	6-8-97	1	1	3.86	18	0	0	2	21	19	10	9	0	13	22	.238	.194	.265	9.43	5.57
Martinez, Robinson	R-R	6-0	190	3-20-98	0	3	10.05	15	0	0	2	14	14	16	16	2	13	24	.255	.200	.286	15.07	8.16
McArthur, James	R-R	6-7	230	12-11-96	0	6	6.00	18	6	0	0	54	47	39	36	4	32	61	.237	.218	.250	10.17	5.33
McKay, Tyler	R-R	6-6	180	8-18-97	3	5	5.05	18	12	0	0	66	57	41	37	7	24	57	.234	.206	.254	7.77	3.27
Mezquita, Jhordany	L-L	6-1	185	1-30-98	4	7	3.97	27	14	0	0	95	87	54	42	9	59	92	.244	.262	.236	8.69	5.57
Miller, Erik	L-L	6-5	240	2-13-98	1	0	2.08	3	2	0	0	13	10	3	3	0	6	13	.208	.211	.207	11.77	4.15
Morales, Francisco	R-R	6-4	185	10-27-99	1	8	3.82	27	15	0	1	97	82	47	41	8	46	129	.226	.196	.248	12.01	4.28
Perkins, Jack	R-R	6-4	200	8-6-97	0	1	2.53	3	2	0	0	11	12	4	3	0	7	16	.293	.188	.360	13.50	5.91
Pipkin, Dominic	R-R	6-4	160	11-5-99	3	4	5.15	24	12	0	1	72	71	51	41	4	45	44	.261	.309	.234	5.53	5.65
Potter, Mark	R-R	6-6	284	11-12-97	0	4	2.50	27	0	0	9	36	25	13	10	3	14	33	.194	.289	.143	8.25	3.50
Ramirez, Luis	R-R	5-11	175	9-14-97	0	1	16.20	3	0	0	0	2	4	3	3	1	0	1	.444	.333	.500	5.40	0.00
Santos, Victor	R-R	6-1	191	7-12-00	5	10	4.02	27	13	0	0	105	106	54	47	11	18	89	.264	.252	.273	7.60	1.54
Schultz, Andrew	R-R	6-4	195	7-31-97	0	2	7.20	11	0	0	0	10	11	11	8	1	9	15	.262	.211	.304	13.50	8.10
Silva, Manuel	L-L	6-2	145	12-18-98	6	6	3.61	23	12	0	1	90	65	39	36	3	35	79	.206	.208	.205	7.93	3.51
Sutera, Tom	R-R	6-5	190	5-29-97	1	3	4.26	7	3	0	0	25	25	13	12	0	9	24	.266	.214	.308	8.53	3.20
Troya, Gilmael	R-R	6-0	196	4-4-97	5	0	2.56	37	0	0	2	53	37	16	15	3	25	52	.199	.247	.168	8.89	4.27

Fielding

Catcher	PCT	G	PO	A	E	DP	PB
Aparicio	1.000	14	111	8	0	2	7
Conley	.974	15	141	9	4	1	3
Gutierrez	.986	64	519	46	8	8	9
Marchan	.992	48	417	51	4	5	7
Matera	.920	3	19	4	2	1	0

First Base	PCT	G	PO	A	E	DP
Aparicio	1.000	1	3	1	0	0
Bohm	.968	5	24	6	1	3
Holmes	.988	30	227	17	3	33
Kroon	.974	21	135	12	4	11
Lancaster	.972	14	98	7	3	13
Miller	.971	10	66	2	2	2
Stobbe	.984	43	305	12	5	32

	PCT	G	PO	A	E	DP
Tatum	.979	18	134	7	3	11

Second Base	PCT	G	PO	A	E	DP
Garcia	.944	55	82	105	11	31
Guzman	.983	54	101	125	4	36
Stobbe	.919	20	30	38	6	9
Stovall	.982	14	26	28	1	11

Third Base	PCT	G	PO	A	E	DP
Bohm	.941	14	10	22	2	3
Holmes	.977	21	16	27	1	1
Kroon	1.000	5	1	5	0	1
Lancaster	.975	15	16	23	1	1
Miller	1.000	5	1	6	0	2
Stobbe	.871	24	13	41	8	5

	PCT	G	PO	A	E	DP
Stovall	.978	37	23	64	2	6
Tatum	.963	20	15	37	2	4

Shortstop	PCT	G	PO	A	E	DP
Garcia	.948	72	85	154	13	39
Guzman	.963	68	91	171	10	42
Kingery	.667	1	1	1	1	0
Lancaster	1.000	1	0	3	0	0

Outfield	PCT	G	PO	A	E	DP
De La Cruz	.972	104	201	8	6	2
Holmes	.000	1	0	0	0	0
Lancaster	.923	5	12	0	1	0
Matos	.985	104	195	7	3	3

Miller	1.000	2	3	0	0	0		Smith	1.000	17	26	1	0	1		Stovall	1.000	12	17	0	0	0
Pelletier	.964	92	174	14	7	4		Stobbe	.944	18	17	0	1	0		Trejo	.988	65	157	5	2	1

WILLIAMSPORT CROSSCUTTERS   SHORT SEASON
NEW YORK-PENN LEAGUE

PHILADELPHIA PHILLIES

Batting	B-T	HT	WT	DOB	AVG	vLH	vRH	G	AB	R	H	2B	3B	HR	RBI	BB	HBP	SH	SF	SO	SB	CS	SLG	OBP
Aparicio, Juan	R-R	5-11	175	5-26-00	.374	.440	.354	32	107	14	40	10	4	1	15	9	5	0	0	22	3	2	.570	.446
Bocio, Keudy	R-R	5-10	161	11-15-98	.167	1.000	.000	2	6	0	1	0	0	0	0	0	0	0	0	0	0	0	.333	.167
Edwards, Mitchell	B-R	5-11	200	8-1-99	.158	.154	.159	17	57	5	9	1	0	0	1	6	0	0	18	0	0		.175	.238
Fassnacht, Nate	R-R	5-11	180	1-5-98	.227	.205	.234	45	150	22	34	8	1	2	17	18	3	0	0	42	6	2	.333	.322
Francisco, Julio	L-L	6-1	140	3-19-98	.286	.000	.400	7	21	2	6	2	0	0	2	4	0	0	0	3	2	1	.381	.400
Gonzalez, Brayan	B-R	5-11	172	1-14-00	.083	.091	.081	13	48	2	4	2	0	0	1	4	0	0	0	26	3	0	.125	.154
Hearn, Hunter	R-R	6-2	205	10-30-96	.180	.125	.196	52	178	12	32	8	0	5	19	12	5	0	0	55	1	7	.309	.251
Holmes, Jake	R-R	6-4	198	7-2-98	.247	.250	.246	44	146	14	36	3	0	0	21	19	1	1	3	36	11	4	.267	.331
Iser, Herbert	L-R	6-3	210	12-14-97	.179	.042	.220	32	106	12	19	4	1	2	6	6	1	0	3	38	2	0	.293	.224
Lancaster, Seth	L-R	6-2	208	6-21-96	.833	1.000	.800	2	6	2	5	1	0	0	1	1	0	0	0	1	2	0	1.000	.857
Litton, Connor	R-R	6-3	220	1-14-97	.375	.333	.400	4	8	0	3	0	0	0	1	4	1	0	0	1	2	2	.375	.615
Made, Edgar	B-R	5-10	145	12-15-99	.174	.200	.167	6	23	1	4	0	0	1	2	0	0	0	0	6	1	1	.304	.174
Markwardt, Hunter	L-L	6-1	185	8-22-97	.307	.231	.327	18	62	7	19	1	1	0	8	2	1	0	3	14	6	1	.355	.324
Matera, Nick	R-R	6-2	215	8-29-96	.269	.143	.316	8	26	2	7	3	0	1	3	3	0	0	0	4	0	0	.500	.345
Maxwell, Tucker	L-L	6-0	171	9-29-96	.044	.000	.054	14	45	2	2	1	0	0	1	5	0	0	1	20	1	0	.067	.137
O'Hoppe, Logan	R-R	6-2	185	2-9-00	.216	.231	.211	45	162	20	35	12	2	5	26	12	0	0	3	49	3	0	.407	.266
Rojas, Johan	R-R	6-1	165	8-14-00	.244	.231	.248	42	164	17	40	5	6	2	11	5	2	0	1	29	11	4	.384	.273
Rott, Rudy	L-R	6-0	212	9-7-96	.233	.235	.232	46	159	11	37	5	1	1	13	13	5	1	1	25	2	2	.296	.309
Simmons, Kendall	R-R	6-2	180	4-11-00	.234	.222	.238	51	171	31	40	7	3	12	34	20	8	1	5	54	5	6	.521	.333
Smith, Juan Carlos	R-R	6-1	190	8-22-97	.111	.400	.000	5	18	0	2	0	0	0	0	0	0	0	0	7	1	2	.111	.111
Stewart, D.J.	R-R	6-2	205	2-2-99	.264	.290	.255	39	125	11	33	11	1	0	11	10	2	0	3	31	3	4	.368	.321
Stott, Bryson	L-R	6-3	200	10-6-97	.274	.206	.293	44	157	27	43	8	2	5	24	22	2	1	0	39	5	3	.446	.370
Tatum, Nicolas	R-R	6-6	210	5-15-96	.326	.231	.364	14	46	6	15	3	1	0	5	5	2	0	0	12	3	3	.435	.415
Torres, Nicolas	R-R	5-10	155	9-23-99	.260	.182	.282	47	150	21	39	4	0	0	10	13	1	2	0	36	8	2	.287	.323
Valerio, Christian	R-R	6-1	155	2-27-00	.182	.333	.125	8	22	1	4	2	0	0	1	0	0	0	1	6	0	1	.273	.174
Williams, Corbin	R-R	6-2	170	1-19-98	.220	.196	.227	58	200	28	44	4	1	0	8	21	3	7	1	74	30	6	.250	.302

Pitching	B-T	HT	WT	DOB	W	L	ERA	G	GS	CG	SV	IP	H	R	ER	HR	BB	SO	AVG	vLH	vRH	K/9	BB/9
Aponte, Leonel	R-R	6-4	144	7-2-99	3	1	3.30	14	9	0	0	46	35	17	17	2	13	36	.206	.243	.180	6.99	2.53
Aris, Abdallah	R-L	5-11	155	10-8-96	0	0	0.00	4	0	0	0	4	2	0	0	0	2	6	.154	.000		13.50	4.50
Armas, Gustavo	R-R	6-1	195	1-15-96	0	2	5.84	4	2	0	0	12	19	10	8	1	4	11	.328	.400	.290	8.03	2.92
Barber, Albertus	R-R	6-2	175	2-18-96	0	0	1.69	4	0	0	1	5	5	1	1	0	1	9	.250	.333	.182	15.19	1.69
Bennett, Blake	R-R	6-2	195	3-7-96	0	2	0.00	4	0	0	1	3	3	4	0	1	0	3	.231	.250	.222	8.10	0.00
Burch, Tyler	R-R	6-2	190	9-2-97	4	1	1.56	11	4	0	1	35	29	8	6	2	6	32	.230	.231	.230	8.31	1.56
Carvajal, Rafael	R-R	6-0	170	11-13-96	3	3	2.65	17	2	0	4	37	26	11	11	0	5	39	.194	.261	.159	9.40	1.21
Cedeno, Luis	R-R	5-11	154	7-14-94	0	0	1.80	3	1	0	0	4	2	2	0		2	8	.129	.100	.143	7.20	1.80
Conopoima, Jose	R-R	6-0	157	3-1-00	1	3	2.83	14	7	0	0	48	46	22	15	3	11	43	.258	.169	.327	8.12	2.08
Cox, Adam	R-R	6-3	187	8-31-95	1	2	5.40	9	0	0	0	12	6	7	7	0	9	13	.154	.111	.191	10.03	6.94
Francisco, Carlos	R-R	6-2	179	3-28-98	0	2	6.94	9	5	0	0	23	34	21	18	2	12	18	.337	.366	.317	6.94	4.63
Gomez, Michael	R-R	6-3	210	8-15-96	0	0	1.93	3	0	0	0	5	3	1	1	0	1	6	.177	.333	.091	11.57	1.93
Gonell, Rafi	R-R	6-2	190	2-26-97	0	0	5.40	1	0	0	0	2	5	1	1	0	0	1	.500	.250	.667	5.40	0.00
Kinney, Jake	R-R	6-7	22	1-14-97	2	1	4.43	16	0	0	0	22	19	15	11	0	24	30	.229	.310	.185	12.09	9.67
Kuznetsov, Anton	R-L	6-1	185	5-26-98	3	1	1.91	17	0	0	0	33	28	13	7	0	6	30	.231	.175	.247	8.18	1.64
Lehman, Taylor	L-L	6-8	240	12-30-95	0	1	2.12	5	4	0	0	17	17	4	4	0	7	16	.270	.316	.250	8.47	3.71
Leverett, Adam	L-R	6-4	190	9-19-98	1	2	4.45	9	5	0	0	28	31	16	14	3	13	22	.279	.234	.313	6.99	4.13
Lin, Hsin-Chieh	R-R	6-2	198	3-18-99	1	0	2.36	10	6	0	0	34	28	11	9	3	17	37	.224	.262	.205	9.70	4.46
Made, Alejandro	R-R	6-4	190	12-29-97	1	4	3.10	18	0	0	4	29	27	20	10	1	12	35	.235	.191	.260	10.86	3.72
Maldonado, Omar	R-R	6-5	240	7-22-95	2	0	0.73	8	0	0	2	12	6	1	1	1	3	15	.146	.050	.238	10.95	2.19
Marconi, Brian	R-L	6-3	175	5-9-97	1	4	4.56	14	0	0	1	24	27	15	12	0	11	25	.294	.265	.310	9.51	4.18
Micheles, Chris	L-L	6-1	175	6-5-97	0	3	5.40	7	4	0	1	17	23	16	10	0	8	24	.319	.286	.341	12.96	4.32
Miller, Erik	L-L	6-5	240	2-13-98	0	0	0.90	6	4	0	0	20	13	5	2	0	7	29	.176	.148	.192	13.05	3.15
Ramirez, Luis	R-R	5-11	175	9-14-97	0	1	2.84	4	2	0	0	13	10	5	4	0	7	14	.213	.200	.222	9.95	4.97
Schulze, Brett	R-R	6-2	180	11-24-97	0	0	0.38	10	5	0	1	24	21	7	1	1	16	34	.241	.286	.212	12.93	6.08
Sutera, Tom	R-R	6-5	190	5-29-97	1	3	1.90	7	3	0	0	24	22	8	5	1	1	30	.244	.237	.250	11.41	0.38
Tejada, Junior	L-L	6-1	170	5-23-97	2	2	4.30	14	7	0	0	44	43	22	21	5	15	49	.249	.259	.244	10.02	3.07
Van Scoyoc, Spencer	L-L	6-4	200	10-4-97	4	4	6.30	10	3	0	0	20	19	21	14	0	21	19	.253	.261	.250	8.55	9.45
Vargas, Victor	R-R	6-1	175	9-3-00	2	0	1.84	4	2	0	0	15	15	3	3	0	8	11	.289	.267	.297	6.75	4.91
Yanez, Gabriel	L-L	6-3	168	7-22-99	0	1	3.32	5	1	0	1	19	15	7	7	1	5	16	.211	.174	.229	7.58	2.37

Fielding

C: Aparicio 17, Edwards 11, Iser 5, Matera 1, O'Hoppe 34. **1B:** Aparicio 9, Iser 6, Litton 3, Matera 4, Rott 43, Stewart 12. **2B:** Fassnacht 16, Gonzalez 6, Lancaster 1, Made 3, Simmons 23, Stott 2, Torres 24, Valerio 1. **3B:** Fassnacht 9, Gonzalez 1, Holmes 25, Made 3, Simmons 16, Stewart 10, Stott 2, Tatum 10, Torres 2, Valerio 1. **SS:** Fassnacht 12, Gonzalez 5, Simmons 8, Stott 34, Torres 15, Valerio 3. **OF:** Bocio 2, Francisco 7, Hearn 51, Holmes 16, Litton 1, Markwardt 18, Maxwell 14, Rojas 41, Smith 5, Stewart 16, Torres 1, Valerio 1, Williams 58.

GCL PHILLIES EAST
GULF COAST LEAGUE

ROOKIE

Batting	B-T	HT	WT	DOB	AVG	vLH	vRH	G	AB	R	H	2B	3B	HR	RBI	BB	HBP	SH	SF	SO	SB	CS	SLG	OBP
Aklinski, Ben	R-R	5-11	210	6-3-96	.500	--	.500	1	2	1	1	0	0	1	1	0	0	0	0	1	0	0	2.000	.500
2-team total (4 Phillies West)					.250	.000	.273	5	12	2	3	1	0	1	2	2	1	0	0	5	0	0	.583	.400
Cedeno, Jose	L-L	6-2	168	3-19-01	.181	.250	.155	37	116	15	21	1	0	0	6	12	1	0	1	37	7	2	.190	.262
Dipre, Guarner	R-R	6-0	160	10-26-00	.301	.200	.325	31	103	15	31	7	1	1	12	9	2	2	1	22	6	1	.418	.365
Edwards, Mitchell	B-R	5-11	200	8-1-99	.226	.200	.238	13	31	3	7	1	0	1	7	5	0	0	1	10	0	0	.355	.324
2-team total (6 Phillies West)					.227	.188	.250	19	44	5	10	1	1	1	7	6	0	0	1	13	0	0	.364	.314
Escalante, Kevin	R-R	6-1	190	12-15-99	.300	.000	.333	5	10	0	3	1	0	0	1	1	0	0	1	3	0	0	.400	.333
2-team total (15 Phillies West)					.132	.000	.152	20	38	3	5	1	0	0	2	2	5	0	1	17	0	0	.158	.261
Flores, Wilfredo	L-R	5-10	170	5-14-00	.342	.516	.281	32	120	20	41	6	2	0	11	4	1	4	1	16	9	4	.425	.365
Friscia, Vito	R-R	6-3	225	12-19-96	.275	.300	.268	43	142	19	39	9	1	3	18	19	1	0	3	33	1	0	.416	.358
Gonzalez, Brayan	B-R	5-11	172	1-14-00	.213	.200	.217	24	75	4	16	4	0	0	4	12	1	1	0	20	2	1	.267	.330
Hernandez, Jevi	R-R	6-0	140	3-2-99	.240	.269	.232	37	125	18	30	4	2	0	7	12	4	1	0	34	12	3	.304	.326
Lee Sang, Marcus	L-L	6-0	200	1-2-01	.224	.200	.232	36	125	8	28	2	2	2	16	11	0	0	2	42	6	4	.320	.283
Matos, Luis	B-R	6-0	175	12-17-99	.260	.286	.250	35	131	21	34	5	4	0	12	9	1	0	0	36	6	3	.359	.312
Mead, Curtis	R-R	6-2	171	10-26-00	.285	.324	.274	44	158	26	45	12	2	4	19	13	3	1	0	23	4	3	.462	.351
Mercado, Jose	R-R	6-1	170	1-4-00	.168	.136	.177	30	101	10	17	3	1	0	8	3	2	1	0	23	3	2	.218	.208
Pujols, Jose	R-R	6-3	175	9-29-95	.000	--	.000	1	2	0	0	0	0	0	0	0	0	0	0	0	0	0	.000	.000
2-team total (2 Phillies West)					.000	.000	.000	3	5	0	0	0	0	0	0	0	0	0	0	0	0	0	.000	.000
Rodriguez, Cesar	B-R	5-10	160	12-26-00	.172	.191	.167	30	87	10	15	4	0	1	10	10	0	0	2	11	0	0	.253	.253
Stott, Bryson	L-R	6-3	200	10-6-97	.667	1.000	.625	4	9	3	6	1	1	1	3	2	0	0	0	0	0	0	1.333	.727
Tortolero, Jose	R-R	5-11	154	12-31-99	.214	.273	.198	30	103	16	22	3	1	2	15	4	1	1	4	20	3	1	.320	.241
Yonamine, Micah	R-R	6-4	210	10-10-00	.159	.231	.143	29	69	8	11	2	0	0	9	8	0	0	1	22	1	1	.188	.247

Pitching	B-T	HT	WT	DOB	W	L	ERA	G	GS	CG	SV	IP	H	R	ER	HR	BB	SO	AVG	vLH	vRH	K/9	BB/9
Adams, Tyler	L-L	6-1	203	3-17-98	3	1	6.06	13	0	0	0	16	19	19	11	0	14	13	.292	.412	.250	7.16	7.71
Barber, Albertus	R-R	6-2	175	2-18-96	0	0	3.00	2	0	0	0	3	2	1	1	0	2	4	.182	.500	.111	12.00	6.00
Beauchamp, Cam	L-L	6-2	221	3-13-98	0	0	1.23	5	0	0	0	7	1	1	1	0	2	5	.192	.250	.182	6.14	2.45
Bell, Brendan	R-R	5-11	175	3-11-00	1	1	6.62	14	0	0	0	18	20	15	13	1	10	10	.294	.227	.326	5.09	5.09
Betancourt, Carlos	R-R	6-1	160	3-27-01	0	3	4.06	10	9	0	0	31	29	18	14	2	14	32	.236	.182	.266	9.29	4.06
Castillo, Starlyn	R-R	6-0	210	2-24-02	0	2	7.71	5	4	0	0	9	9	8	8	0	8	10	.257	.250	.261	9.64	7.71
Cotto, Gabriel	L-L	6-5	175	5-15-00	0	0	7.91	11	2	0	0	19	23	20	17	2	15	17	.274	.313	.265	7.91	6.98
De La Cruz, Jonas	R-R	6-3	175	1-1-98	0	0	0.00	6	6	0	0	10	2	0	0	0	4	14	.067	.000	.100	13.03	3.72
2-team total (2 Phillies West)					0	1	2.77	8	8	0	0	13	9	4	4	2	4	23	.192	.235	.167	15.92	2.77
Escalante, Kevin	R-R	6-1	190	12-15-99	0	0	0.00	1	0	0	0	1	1	0	0	0	1	0	.333	--	.333	0.00	9.00
Estevez, Engel	R-R	6-1	180	2-8-00	1	2	4.73	5	1	0	0	13	8	10	7	0	6	6	.167	.067	.212	4.05	4.05
Francisco, Carlos	R-R	6-4	220	7-2-99	3	2	3.68	14	0	0	0	22	24	11	9	0	3	19	.276	.407	.217	7.77	1.23
Garrido, Maikel	L-L	6-4	175	1-24-00	2	1	7.31	15	0	0	0	16	11	14	13	1	26	19	.193	.077	.227	10.69	14.63
Geraldo, Juan	R-R	6-0	175	8-6-01	2	0	3.96	12	2	0	0	25	21	11	11	1	7	33	.223	.156	.258	11.88	2.52
Howard, Spencer	R-R	6-2	205	7-28-96	0	0	11.57	1	1	0	0	2	3	3	3	1	1	3	.300	.000	.429	11.57	3.86
2-team total (1 Phillies West)					0	0	5.06	2	2	0	0	5	4	3	3	1	2	8	.200	.167	.214	13.50	3.38
Hsu, Chi-Ling	R-R	6-2	202	8-9-99	0	1	40.50	1	1	0	0	1	1	3	3	1	3	0	.333	.000	.500	0.00	40.50
Jefferson, DJ	R-R	6-5	185	1-9-01	0	1	1.69	5	1	0	0	11	7	2	2	1	4	7	.189	.231	.167	5.91	3.38
Kudlinski, Brenden	L-L	6-2	215	7-15-98	1	0	3.21	11	0	0	0	14	3	5	5	0	16	7	.071	.111	.061	4.50	10.29
Lackney, Nick	L-L	6-4	210	6-5-97	0	0	4.70	7	0	0	0	8	8	4	4	0	7	4	.267	.200	.280	4.70	8.22
Leftwich, Luke	L-R	6-3	205	6-9-94	0	0	0.00	1	1	0	0	1	0	0	0	0	0	2	.000	.000	.000	18.00	0.00
Leverett, Adam	L-R	6-4	190	9-19-98	0	0	2.45	2	1	0	0	4	4	1	1	0	0	6	.267	.444	.000	14.73	0.00
Marcano, Rafael	L-L	6-1	170	4-20-00	0	2	4.24	9	4	0	1	23	22	12	11	1	7	24	.242	.333	.219	9.26	2.70
Martinez, Jordi	L-L	6-2	185	7-18-00	1	0	3.00	5	1	0	0	12	9	4	4	1	5	13	.205	.333	.138	9.75	3.75
Micheles, Chris	L-L	6-1	175	6-5-97	1	0	2.35	5	0	0	0	8	6	5	2	0	2	9	.200	.167	.208	10.57	2.35
Milam, Hunter	L-L	6-1	200	5-26-00	2	3	4.30	9	4	0	0	23	14	11	11	2	14	30	.167	.130	.180	11.74	5.48
Reyes, Andy	R-R	6-0	160	3-11-00	1	0	3.66	14	0	0	0	20	20	12	8	1	15	18	.274	.286	.269	8.24	6.86
Richardson, Waylon	R-R	6-5	235	3-1-97	0	0	0.00	2	0	0	0	2	0	0	0	0	0	0	.000	.000	.000	0.00	0.00
2-team total (1 Phillies West)					1	0	0.00	3	0	0	0	3	0	0	0	0	0	0	.000	.000	.000	0.00	0.00
Sara, Jamie	R-R	6-3	200	4-17-98	0	1	27.00	4	0	0	0	2	6	6	6	0	4	3	.500	.600	.429	13.50	18.00
Schultz, Andrew	R-R	6-4	195	7-31-97	0	0	0.00	1	0	0	0	1	1	0	0	0	0	0	.333	1.000	.000	0.00	0.00
Seabold, Connor	R-R	6-2	190	1-24-96	0	1	11.57	1	1	0	0	2	6	3	3	0	0	2	.462	.000	.625	7.71	0.00
2-team total (2 Phillies West)					0	1	3.68	3	3	0	0	7	7	3	3	0	0	12	.241	.077	.375	14.73	0.00
Ulloa, Jose	R-R	6-2	200	5-6-99	2	1	5.09	12	0	0	0	18	14	12	10	3	13	14	.212	.200	.220	7.13	6.62
Van Scoyoc, Spencer	L-L	6-4	200	10-4-97	0	0	4.50	2	0	0	0	2	2	1	1	0	3	2	.250	.250	.250	9.00	13.50
Vargas, Victor	R-R	6-1	175	9-3-00	1	1	1.44	7	6	0	0	25	26	4	4	1	4	15	.274	.225	.309	5.40	1.44
Vilchez, Daniel	R-R	6-1	192	10-4-00	0	0	2.25	1	0	0	0	4	2	1	1	0	0	1	.143	.000	.200	2.25	0.00
2-team total (8 Phillies West)					1	1	2.88	9	6	0	0	34	27	12	11	2	5	23	.221	.313	.189	6.03	1.31
Yanez, Gabriel	L-L	6-3	168	7-22-99	0	0	1.33	7	3	0	0	20	17	4	3	0	3	14	.227	.333	.206	6.20	1.33

Fielding

C: Edwards 10, Escalante 3, Friscia 17, Rodriguez 22, Yonamine 15. **1B:** Friscia 25, Hernandez 4, Rodriguez 7, Yonamine 12. **2B:** Dipre 10, Flores 9, Gonzalez 6, Mead 7, Mercado 5, Tortolero 11. **3B:** Dipre 7, Flores 7, Gonzalez 5, Mead 13, Mercado 9, Tortolero 7. **SS:** Dipre 12, Flores 1, Gonzalez 7, Mead 7, Mercado 14, Stott 4, Tortolero 8. **OF:** Aklinski 1, Cedeno 36, Flores 12, Hernandez 33, Lee Sang 31, Matos 34, Pujols 1.

GCL PHILLIES WEST
GULF COAST LEAGUE

ROOKIE

BaseballAmerica.com

Batting

Batting	B-T	HT	WT	DOB	AVG	vLH	vRH	G	AB	R	H	2B	3B	HR	RBI	BB	HBP	SH	SF	SO	SB	CS	SLG	OBP
Aklinski, Ben	R-R	5-11	210	6-3-96	.200	.000	.222	4	10	1	2	1	0	0	1	2	1	0	0	4	0	0	.300	.385
2-team total (1 Phillies East)					.250	.000	.273	5	12	2	3	1	0	1	2	2	1	0	0	5	0	0	.583	.400
Baylor, Jamari	R-R	5-11	190	8-25-00	.273	.500	.222	4	11	4	3	2	0	0	1	0	0	0	0	2	0	0	.455	.333
Cornelius, Chris	R-R	6-0	186	9-4-97	.167	.333	.000	3	6	0	1	0	0	0	1	1	0	0	0	1	0	0	.167	.375
Edwards, Mitchell	B-R	5-11	200	8-1-99	.231	.167	.286	6	13	2	3	0	1	0	1	0	0	0	0	3	0	0	.385	.286
2-team total (13 Phillies East)					.227	.188	.250	19	44	5	10	1	1	1	7	6	0	0	1	13	0	0	.364	.314
Escalante, Kevin	R-R	6-1	190	12-15-99	.071	.000	.083	15	28	3	2	0	0	0	1	1	5	0	0	14	0	0	.071	.235
2-team total (5 Phillies East)					.132	.000	.152	20	38	3	5	1	0	0	2	2	5	0	1	17	0	0	.158	.261
Francisco, Freddy	R-R	5-11	180	2-7-01	.276	.273	.278	13	29	6	8	4	0	1	5	2	0	0	0	5	0	0	.517	.323
Gozzo, Sal	B-R	6-0	196	3-29-98	.186	.242	.167	39	129	19	24	5	2	1	14	22	1	0	0	29	5	0	.279	.309
Greenwalt, Keaton	R-R	6-3	175	11-23-97	.260	.265	.258	45	169	23	44	13	1	5	22	8	1	0	2	26	4	2	.438	.294
Iser, Herbert	L-R	6-3	210	12-14-97	.500	.667	.400	5	16	5	8	2	2	0	3	3	1	0	0	2	0	1	.875	.600
Made, Edgar	B-R	5-10	145	12-15-99	.333	.333	.333	42	165	31	55	12	4	3	34	13	4	0	2	26	5	5	.509	.391
Maxwell, Tucker	L-L	6-0	171	9-29-96	.246	.000	.349	20	61	9	15	1	0	2	5	13	1	0	0	32	3	0	.361	.387
Nava, Andrick	B-R	5-11	175	10-6-01	.314	.278	.325	44	156	25	49	6	0	1	20	8	1	0	1	20	1	1	.372	.349
Pujols, Jose	R-R	6-3	175	9-29-95	.000	.000	.000	2	3	0	0	0	0	0	0	0	0	0	0	0	0	0	.000	.000
2-team total (1 Phillies East)					.000	.000	.000	3	5	0	0	0	0	0	0	0	0	0	0	0	0	0	.000	.000
Rivera, Jose	R-R	5-10	165	5-26-99	.198	.217	.190	31	81	14	16	5	0	1	15	20	1	0	2	25	7	2	.296	.356
Rojas, Johan	R-R	6-1	165	8-14-00	.311	.261	.333	18	74	13	23	6	5	0	4	9	1	0	0	12	3	2	.527	.393
Rojas, Luis	R-R	5-9	150	4-19-00	.238	.143	.286	34	105	17	25	1	0	2	13	9	1	1	3	16	4	5	.305	.297
Sanchez, Jadiel	R-R	6-2	185	5-10-01	.167	.182	.160	10	36	3	6	0	0	1	4	2	0	0	0	9	0	1	.250	.211
Smith, Juan Carlos	R-R	6-1	190	8-22-97	.282	.290	.279	42	149	25	42	9	2	2	16	11	2	0	1	38	7	1	.409	.337
Valerio, Christian	R-R	6-1	155	2-27-00	.194	.182	.197	28	93	12	18	3	0	1	11	11	0	2	1	23	2	3	.258	.276
Wang, Bruce	L-R	5-8	161	9-6-99	.196	.133	.222	23	51	6	10	2	0	0	7	8	0	1	2	13	0	0	.235	.295
Wingrove, Rixon	L-R	6-5	260	5-23-00	.298	.205	.328	48	178	28	53	17	2	5	37	22	1	0	2	38	0	2	.500	.374

Pitching

Pitching	B-T	HT	WT	DOB	W	L	ERA	G	GS	CG	SV	IP	H	R	ER	HR	BB	SO	AVG	vLH	vRH	K/9	BB/9
Anderson, Aidan	R-R	6-1	195	6-21-97	3	0	3.86	15	0	0	2	26	20	15	11	1	13	19	.204	.294	.156	6.66	4.56
Burch, Tyler	R-R	6-2	190	9-2-97	0	0	0.00	1	0	0	0	1	0	0	0	0	0	2	.000	.000	.000	18.00	0.00
Castaneda, Dylan	R-R	6-2	190	7-16-01	1	0	2.70	5	2	0	0	10	6	6	3	1	9	12	.162	.143	.174	10.80	8.10
Crowson, Austin	B-L	6-5	210	9-6-96	5	1	2.82	13	0	0	0	22	14	9	7	1	12	17	.192	.071	.220	6.85	4.84
De La Cruz, Jonas	R-R	6-3	175	1-1-98	0	1	10.80	2	2	0	0	3	7	4	4	2	0	9	.412	.571	.300	24.30	0.00
2-team total (6 Phillies East)					0	1	2.77	8	8	0	0	13	9	4	4	2	4	23	.192	.235	.167	15.92	2.77
Gessner, Josh	R-R	6-1	205	6-25-00	1	0	2.84	6	3	0	0	13	7	4	4	0	7	17	.152	.083	.177	12.08	4.97
Hendrickson, Josh	L-L	6-4	215	9-18-97	2	1	3.50	11	2	0	1	18	14	7	7	2	3	22	.212	.214	.212	11.00	1.50
Hinchliffe, Connor	R-R	6-2	195	8-21-96	1	1	1.82	16	1	0	1	25	14	10	5	0	17	17	.163	.150	.167	6.20	6.20
Howard, Spencer	R-R	6-2	205	7-28-96	0	0	0.00	1	1	0	0	3	1	0	0	0	1	5	.100	.333	.000	15.00	3.00
2-team total (1 Phillies East)					0	0	5.06	2	2	0	0	5	6	3	3	1	2	8	.200	.167	.214	13.50	3.38
Lin, Hsin-Chieh	R-R	6-2	198	3-18-99	1	0	0.00	1	0	0	0	4	0	0	0	0	1	6	.000	.000	.000	14.73	2.45
Lozano, Fernando	R-R	6-2	186	1-11-00	5	0	1.99	17	0	0	2	32	24	8	7	1	6	31	.211	.132	.250	8.81	1.71
Marconi, Brian	R-L	6-3	175	5-9-97	0	0	0.00	3	0	0	0	2	1	0	0	0	3	3	.125	.000	.200	11.57	11.57
Martinez, Robinson	R-R	6-0	190	3-20-98	0	0	0.00	1	0	0	0	1	1	0	0	0	0	1	.250	.000	.333	9.00	0.00
Mayer, Gunner	R-R	6-6	190	7-27-00	0	0	5.40	4	2	0	0	8	8	5	5	0	3	10	.250	.286	.240	10.80	3.24
Miller, Erik	L-L	6-5	240	2-13-98	0	0	3.00	2	1	0	0	3	2	1	1	0	2	6	.182	.000	.222	18.00	6.00
Miranda, Juan	L-L	5-11	165	2-27-99	3	1	3.67	15	0	0	1	27	21	12	11	0	10	28	.221	.182	.233	9.33	3.33
Pacheco, Luis	R-R	6-2	185	4-22-99	2	1	4.45	11	6	0	0	32	37	19	16	1	16	33	.282	.383	.226	9.19	4.45
Perkins, Jack	R-R	6-4	200	8-6-99	0	0	2.08	3	3	0	0	9	7	2	2	0	3	14	.226	.375	.174	14.54	3.12
Pina, Nicoly	R-R	6-3	203	10-8-99	2	1	3.57	15	0	0	3	18	9	7	7	0	14	28	.153	.222	.122	14.26	7.13
Ramey, Brandon	R-R	6-3	170	8-31-00	0	2	2.78	7	7	0	0	23	11	7	7	1	6	30	.143	.222	.100	11.91	2.38
Richardson, Waylon	R-R	6-5	235	3-1-97	0	0	0.00	1	0	0	0	1	0	0	0	0	0	0	.000	.000	.000	0.00	0.00
2-team total (2 Phillies East)					1	0	0.00	3	0	0	0	3	0	0	0	0	0	0	.000	.000	.000	0.00	0.00
Rosario, Dalvin	R-R	6-1	167	6-15-00	2	1	7.13	12	0	0	0	18	19	15	14	0	16	14	.275	.296	.262	7.13	8.15
Schulze, Brett	R-R	6-2	180	11-24-97	1	0	0.00	2	0	0	0	3	1	0	0	0	1	3	.100	.500	.000	9.00	3.00
Seabold, Connor	R-R	6-2	190	1-24-96	0	0	0.00	2	2	0	0	5	1	0	0	0	0	10	.063	.000	.125	18.00	0.00
2-team total (1 Phillies East)					0	1	3.68	3	3	0	0	7	7	3	3	0	0	12	.241	.077	.375	14.73	0.00
Segovia, Eduar	R-R	6-0	180	1-10-01	1	2	2.43	10	9	0	0	30	15	11	8	0	10	39	.150	.263	.081	11.83	3.03
Smith, Jaylen	L-L	5-11	170	11-5-99	1	1	3.38	15	1	0	1	19	10	10	7	1	17	14	.161	.071	.188	6.75	8.20
Vilchez, Daniel	R-R	6-1	192	10-4-00	1	1	2.97	8	6	0	0	30	25	11	10	2	5	22	.232	.357	.188	6.53	1.48
2-team total (1 Phillies East)					1	1	2.88	9	6	0	0	34	27	12	11	2	5	23	.221	.313	.189	6.03	1.31
Wilson, Riley	L-L	6-0	180	8-2-96	0	1	2.91	14	0	0	2	22	16	10	7	0	5	21	.203	.125	.222	8.72	2.08

Fielding

C: Edwards 6, Escalante 15, Francisco 11, Iser 4, Nava 17, Wang 20. **1B:** Iser 1, Rivera 1, Wingrove 47. **2B:** Gozzo 8, Made 15, Rivera 3, Rojas 6, Valerio 18. **3B:** Gozzo 3, Made 23, Rivera 21, Rojas 1. **SS:** Baylor 3, Cornelius 2, Gozzo 26, Rojas 12, Valerio 9. **OF:** Aklinski 4, Greenwalt 45, Maxwell 18, Pujols 2, Rivera 1, Rojas 18, Rojas 14, Sanchez 9, Smith 40, Wingrove 1.

DSL PHILLIES ROOKIE

DOMINICAN SUMMER LEAGUE

Batting	B-T	HT	WT	DOB	AVG	vLH	vRH	G	AB	R	H	2B	3B	HR	RBI	BB	HBP	SH	SF	SO	SB	CS	SLG	OBP
Azuaje, Alexeis	R-R	5-10	155	4-24-02	.281	.231	.295	49	185	41	52	14	3	5	19	4	6	0	3	41	13	3	.470	.313
Barboza, Edward	R-R	5-11	175	4-2-01	.302	.381	.286	42	126	21	38	7	1	2	21	17	6	1	2	21	6	2	.421	.404
Barreto, Freddy	R-R	6-0	155	9-27-99	.286	.500	.227	10	28	2	8	3	0	0	6	3	1	0	2	5	0	1	.393	.353
Blanc, Raulyn	B-R	5-10	168	7-10-01	.234	.147	.251	66	209	29	49	10	3	0	25	39	3	4	2	64	17	7	.311	.360
Boekhoudt, Siamani	R-L	6-0	165	9-20-99	.120	.250	.095	8	25	3	3	2	0	0	4	3	1	0	0	13	1	0	.200	.241
Brito, Erick	R-R	5-10	134	5-25-02	.269	.308	.256	21	52	7	14	3	0	0	5	15	3	1	1	9	1	4	.327	.451
Cairo, Victor	R-R	5-10	174	4-17-01	.125	--	.125	4	8	1	1	0	0	0	0	0	0	0	0	3	0	0	.125	.222

Name	B-T	HT	WT	DOB	AVG	vLH	vRH	G	AB	R	H	2B	3B	HR	RBI	BB	HBP	SH	SF	SO	SB	CS	OBP	SLG
Corona, Jeury	R-R	5-11	140	9-7-01	.235	.357	.224	43	166	32	39	4	0	0	5	16	3	3	0	25	17	12	.259	.314
Diaz, Victor	R-R	5-10	175	11-25-01	.289	.273	.292	61	232	39	67	16	3	2	36	17	3	0	5	45	6	5	.410	.339
Duran, Christopher	R-R	5-10	165	11-2-00	.211	.600	.071	8	19	2	4	2	0	0	1	3	0	0	0	8	0	2	.316	.318
Encarnacion, Jefferson	L-L	6-2	185	8-28-01	.250	.158	.269	60	220	31	55	7	6	1	26	27	1	0	2	46	8	5	.350	.332
Escalante, Kevin	R-R	6-1	190	12-15-99	.211	.500	.177	7	19	3	4	2	0	0	2	6	3	0	0	7	2	0	.316	.464
Escobar, Derek	L-R	5-11	170	1-28-02	.270	.407	.226	33	111	20	30	4	1	1	9	19	8	2	1	27	12	11	.351	.410
Garcia, Wilbert	R-R	5-11	179	1-20-00	.255	.371	.223	54	165	28	42	7	3	1	22	15	7	1	3	43	26	9	.352	.337
Gil, Reiberth	R-R	6-0	165	4-9-02	.193	.300	.178	28	83	6	16	1	0	0	3	9	1	2	1	28	5	2	.205	.277
Gonzalez, Brayan	B-R	5-11	172	1-14-00	.444	.000	.571	3	9	3	4	0	0	0	1	0	1	0	0	2	0	0	.444	.500
Gonzalez, Oscar	R-R	6-0	184	11-21-00	.263	.333	.247	59	209	24	55	5	2	1	29	23	5	1	3	36	5	4	.321	.346
Hernandez, Carlos	L-R	5-10	168	5-1-01	.200	.000	.225	16	45	5	9	5	0	0	7	7	1	1	0	14	1	0	.311	.321
Herrera, Juan	R-R	6-3	165	12-14-99	.275	.227	.285	68	258	50	71	14	3	7	48	26	5	1	3	54	13	4	.434	.349
Jerez, Albert	R-R	6-2	165	5-18-01	.263	.258	.264	63	213	24	56	9	3	3	32	16	10	3	0	47	11	9	.356	.343
Mejia, Adony	R-R	5-11	170	6-9-01	.162	.226	.147	51	167	27	27	3	1	0	9	22	10	0	1	43	4	2	.192	.295
Mendez, Juan	L-R	5-10	165	2-27-99	.276	.118	.302	37	123	23	34	8	2	4	26	29	3	0	3	19	2	1	.472	.418
Mendoza, Carlos	L-L	5-9	139	2-18-01	.235	.400	.167	8	17	5	4	2	0	0	2	3	0	0	1	4	1	1	.353	.333
Mora, Raymond	R-R	6-0	155	7-29-00	.289	.200	.305	63	194	38	56	12	3	0	22	53	7	5	2	39	12	8	.381	.453
Mujica, Luiggi	B-R	5-10	155	11-25-99	.313	.000	.333	7	16	4	5	0	0	0	0	6	0	0	0	7	0	1	.313	.500
Ortega, Junior	R-R	5-11	175	9-30-99	.254	.361	.231	57	209	40	53	14	7	5	35	17	6	0	4	43	15	4	.459	.322
Peguero, Giuseppe	R-R	6-0	175	6-30-00	.187	.241	.178	62	198	34	37	13	2	4	18	33	15	3	2	74	19	11	.333	.343
Pichardo, Kervin	R-R	6-0	180	10-15-01	.214	.346	.184	39	140	16	30	4	0	0	14	17	5	2	0	20	5	2	.243	.321
Pineda, Leandro	L-L	6-1	165	6-4-02	.184	.375	.157	61	190	22	35	4	0	1	19	22	6	3	2	40	4	4	.221	.286
Rodriguez, Jonathan	R-R	5-10	165	5-17-02	.214	.000	.375	6	14	1	3	1	0	0	0	1	0	0	0	6	1	0	.286	.267
Rondon, Carlos	B-R	5-10	155	4-18-02	.233	.211	.236	51	163	23	38	5	1	0	17	28	1	3	1	17	5	3	.276	.347
Rondon, Ellian	L-R	5-11	166	6-24-00	.165	.200	.159	37	97	14	16	2	1	0	5	21	7	1	0	39	6	6	.206	.352
Tejeda, Miguel	R-R	6-1	190	12-17-01	.156	.125	.165	46	141	13	22	8	1	1	11	14	6	1	0	43	5	4	.248	.261
Valdez, Wilson	R-R	6-2	185	10-25-99	.296	.256	.304	57	220	31	65	9	3	3	31	17	2	0	5	32	3	4	.405	.344
Viloria, Uziel	B-R	5-9	155	10-6-01	.236	.250	.232	28	106	10	25	2	2	1	12	8	0	1	2	30	6	4	.321	.285

Pitching	B-T	HT	WT	DOB	W	L	ERA	G	GS	CG	SV	IP	H	R	ER	HR	BB	SO	AVG	vLH	vRH	K/9	BB/9
Adames, Cristofer	R-R	6-1	163	8-31-99	5	0	3.79	19	1	0	0	40	34	22	17	2	19	37	.219	.235	.212	8.26	4.24
Alcala, Saul	R-R	6-1	158	11-7-00	0	0	15.43	2	0	0	0	2	1	4	4	0	3	6	.111	.500	.000	23.14	11.57
Aleman, Edinso	L-L	5-11	178	10-6-00	2	3	3.04	15	8	0	0	53	51	22	18	1	15	38	.256	.333	.241	6.41	2.53
Anciani, Norman	R-R	6-2	165	4-23-02	0	0	10.80	2	0	0	0	2	1	2	2	0	2	1	.167	.000	.333	5.40	10.80
Angulo, Joalbert	L-L	6-5	165	10-30-01	2	0	8.87	15	3	0	0	22	16	29	22	0	38	18	.208	.278	.186	7.25	15.31
Aponte, Ruben	R-R	6-0	180	5-18-97	0	0	12.00	3	0	0	0	3	4	5	4	0	4	0	.333	.375	.250	0.00	12.00
Araujo, Alexis	R-R	6-5	200	1-7-99	4	2	2.21	19	4	0	0	41	34	14	10	3	22	26	.235	.259	.220	5.75	4.87
Astudillo, Hermes	R-R	5-11	160	3-2-02	0	0	9.00	2	0	0	0	2	3	3	2	0	1	0	.333	.333	.333	0.00	4.50
Brazoban, Camilo	R-R	6-1	190	10-15-98	0	0	3.68	6	0	0	0	7	7	6	3	1	8	7	.241	.167	.261	8.59	9.82
Brazon, Emiliano	R-R	6-2	170	2-2-00	0	0	6.75	4	0	0	0	4	4	3	3	1	2	2	.250	.167	.300	4.50	4.50
Candelo, Luis	R-R	5-11	190	6-27-97	3	3	3.07	22	0	0	5	41	41	23	14	1	11	35	.253	.267	.245	7.68	2.41
Cruz, Cristofer	R-R	6-0	155	4-5-99	2	0	4.00	7	0	0	2	9	7	5	4	0	8	8	.200	.250	.185	8.00	8.00
Gherbaz, Wilson	R-R	6-2	145	9-30-00	1	3	4.10	14	14	0	0	48	44	28	22	3	32	44	.240	.279	.217	8.19	5.96
Gomez, Luis	R-R	6-1	174	5-14-01	4	0	2.31	8	0	0	1	23	17	6	6	0	7	12	.207	.185	.218	4.63	2.70
Guzman, Michael	L-L	6-0	175	7-31-00	3	1	4.24	10	0	0	0	17	11	8	8	1	12	14	.186	.000	.212	7.41	6.35
Hinestroza, Camilo	L-L	5-11	200	9-30-01	1	0	6.97	9	0	0	0	10	9	9	8	0	13	10	.237	.500	.222	8.71	11.32
Ibarra, Neyker	L-L	5-11	165	3-30-02	2	5	2.89	13	12	0	0	53	50	26	17	3	11	48	.244	.229	.248	8.15	1.87
Liendo, Wilberson	R-R	6-3	160	9-13-99	5	1	1.86	16	8	0	1	58	44	16	12	1	22	59	.213	.205	.217	9.16	3.41
Lima, Cristian	R-R	6-2	190	1-20-00	3	0	4.31	16	0	0	1	31	34	19	15	2	14	35	.281	.329	.315	10.05	4.02
Lopez, Victor	R-R	6-4	192	9-2-99	1	3	2.29	14	14	0	0	51	46	19	13	1	25	46	.241	.241	.241	8.12	4.41
Malaver, Jhongel	R-R	5-11	160	1-27-01	2	2	7.52	17	0	0	0	26	27	32	22	1	35	17	.278	.290	.273	5.81	11.96
Mejia, Hernando	R-R	6-3	230	6-8-00	3	3	5.80	21	0	0	3	36	27	24	23	5	30	20	.216	.270	.193	5.05	7.57
Mendoza, Raul	R-R	5-11	168	12-9-00	0	1	4.66	5	1	0	1	10	7	6	5	0	7	10	.206	.222	.200	9.31	6.52
Mijares, Douglas	R-R	6-3	165	4-27-00	0	0	9.00	3	0	0	0	3	2	3	3	0	3	1	.182	.200	.167	9.00	9.00
Moreno, Noelis	R-R	6-2	207	1-23-99	1	1	0.00	2	0	0	0	2	2	1	0	0	1	4	.222	.250	.200	15.43	3.86
Naranjo, Yosmel	L-L	6-4	205	3-8-00	3	1	1.77	22	0	0	3	46	33	12	9	2	11	47	.204	.184	.210	9.26	2.17
Ortega, Fernando	R-R	6-4	160	10-10-01	1	3	3.68	15	15	0	0	51	40	26	21	0	37	37	.222	.242	.212	6.49	6.49
Palacio, Jose	B-L	6-0	165	2-7-00	2	2	4.15	14	1	0	0	26	23	14	12	1	13	20	.237	.391	.189	6.92	4.50
Pediet, Fausto	R-R	5-11	175	12-4-00	5	2	6.06	19	0	0	2	49	47	35	33	1	19	27	.253	.157	.289	4.96	3.49
Puello, Israel	R-R	6-3	200	10-10-00	2	1	1.92	15	15	0	0	66	44	16	14	2	19	83	.190	.213	.178	11.38	2.60
Reyes, Carlo	R-R	6-0	212	7-4-98	4	2	2.45	14	14	0	0	62	50	20	17	2	13	72	.217	.262	.200	10.40	1.88
Rivas, Aldemar	R-R	6-1	170	1-21-99	3	4	4.54	22	0	0	2	38	37	26	19	1	21	36	.245	.318	.215	8.60	5.02
Rivas, Jonathan	R-R	5-11	160	9-1-01	2	0	3.38	21	0	0	5	40	37	19	15	2	20	34	.245	.300	.218	7.65	4.50
Sanchez, Sergio	L-L	5-11	160	1-27-02	1	1	3.25	14	0	0	3	28	18	10	10	0	13	31	.180	.185	.178	10.08	4.23
Sanchez, Yeison	R-R	6-0	170	11-13-97	4	0	2.35	20	0	0	6	31	27	10	8	1	6	44	.229	.237	.225	12.91	1.76
Soriano, Christopher	L-L	6-1	160	9-17-01	1	2	3.50	13	12	0	0	46	43	26	18	2	27	34	.253	.200	.269	6.60	5.24
Torres, Alberto	L-L	6-0	155	4-28-01	0	0	12.00	3	0	0	0	3	2	5	4	0	6	5	.167	.000	.182	15.00	18.00
Urias, Manuel	R-R	6-6	200	3-8-01	3	1	1.48	13	13	0	0	61	38	13	10	3	8	55	.175	.173	.177	8.11	1.18
Valdez, Joel	L-L	6-4	171	4-28-00	1	1	5.31	11	4	0	1	20	25	17	12	0	16	16	.291	.231	.301	7.08	7.08
Vegas, Luis	R-R	5-10	160	8-5-01	4	3	4.59	18	0	0	1	33	29	18	17	0	21	18	.236	.281	.220	4.86	5.67
Ventura, Ezequiel	R-R	6-1	151	6-20-02	0	1	9.00	2	0	0	0	3	5	3	3	1	0	2	.385	.143	.667	6.00	0.00

Fielding

C: Baez 21, Ceballo 2, Escalante 22, Hernandez 20, Hernandez 28, Mena 8, Planchart 27, Polanco 39, Urbina 1. **1B:** Apostel 24, Arroyo 1, Baez 33, Carrasco 17, Escalante 14, Hernandez 22, Lopez 7, Mateo 23, Matos 6, Mena 17, Mojica 2, Ramirez 5, Tello 2. **2B:** Arroyo 33, Escalante 1, Hernandez 1, Jerez 31, Matos 22, Montero 10, Nadal 17, Quintero 10, Romero 15, Susana 4, Tejeda 6, Urbina 3. **3B:** Arroyo 12, Carrasco 14, Chivilli 2, Escalante 1, Lopez 3, Matos 7, Mojica 36, Montero 22, Quintero 11, Romero 6, Sanchez 22, Tejeda 1, Urbina 17. **SS:** Arroyo 1, Jerez 16, Lopez 32, Matos 8, Montero 8, Nadal 33, Quintero 1, Romero 2, Susana 8, Tejeda 10. **OF:** Arroyo 7, Bastardo 27, Berroa 27, Campana 43, Carrasco 1, Custodio 53, Gavilan 34, Jerez 24, Mateo 29, Matos 2, Mena 1, Montero 10, Nolasco 38, Nova 34, Romero 60, Romero 8, Sanchez 7, Susana 1, Tello 50, Valerio 2.

Pittsburgh Pirates

SEASON IN A SENTENCE: The Pirates finished last in the National League Central with a 69-93 record, their third losing campaign within their last four seasons, and fired manager Clint Hurdle before the final game of the season.

HIGH POINTS: The Pirates went on a five-game winning streak in mid-April, which was their longest of the season. They also had three, three-game winning streaks during the month of May, which was their only month in which they finished with a winning record.

LOW POINT: July was a tough month for the Pirates, who they went on a nine-game losing skid. Pittsburgh managed to match that lowly mark in late September, allowing double-digit runs in five of the nine losses. Playing on the road was particularly difficult at times, with Pittsburgh winning just two of its 12 games away from PNC Park in July.

NOTABLE ROOKIES: Outfielder Bryan Reynolds burst onto the scene and hit .314/.377/.503 with 16 home runs and 37 doubles in 134 games for the Pirates. He led all rookies in both batting average and doubles, and he was nearly the first rookie in National League history to win the batting title before ultimately falling just short. On the infield, Kevin Newman has always carried a reputation as being a defense-first player, but he hit .308/.353/.446 with 12 home runs and 16 stolen bases in 2019 after a lackluster 31-game major league debut in the previous season.

KEY TRANSACTIONS: Outfielder Melky Cabrera inked a one-year deal in February and proved to be a solid player for Pittsburgh. The Pirates also brought in lefthander Francisco Liriano, who pitched to a 3.47 ERA in 69 appearances out of the bullpen. While their trade deadline was relatively quiet, Pittsburgh did send outfielder Corey Dickerson to Philadelphia in exchange for international bonus pool money and a player to be named later. The team also sent righthander Jordan Lyles to Milwaukee in exchange for minor league pitcher Cody Ponce.

DOWN ON THE FARM: DSL Pirates 2 posted an impressive .778 winning percentage, which was by far the highest of any Pirates affiliate. Low Class A Greensboro finished 20 games above .500 but failed to qualify for the South Atlantic League playoffs while short-season Bristol made it to the Appalachian League playoffs but lost in the semifinals.

OPENING DAY PAYROLL: $65,918,500 (29th).

PLAYERS OF THE YEAR

MAJOR LEAGUE	MINOR LEAGUE
Bryan Reynolds	**Mason Martin**
OF	1B
.314/.377/.503	(Low A/High A)
16 HR, 37 2B	.254/.351/.558
Led rookies in AVG, 2B	35 HR, 129 RBIs

ORGANIZATION LEADERS

Batting · *Minimum 250 AB

MAJORS

* AVG	Bryan Reynolds	.314
* OPS	Josh Bell	.936
HR	Josh Bell	37
RBI	Josh Bell	116

MINORS

* AVG	Ji-Hwan Bae, Greensboro	.323
* OBP	Ji-Hwan Bae, Greensboro	.403
* SLG	Mason Martin, Greensboro, Bradenton	.558
* OPS	Mason Martin, Greensboro, Bradenton	.908
R	Mason Martin, Greensboro, Bradenton	90
H	Fabricio Macias, Greensboro	132
TB	Mason Martin, Greensboro, Bradenton	266
2B	Mason Martin, Greensboro, Bradenton	32
3B	Lolo Sanchez, Greensboro, Bradenton	9
HR	Mason Martin, Greensboro, Bradenton	35
RBI	Mason Martin, Greensboro, Bradenton	129
BB	Mason Martin, Greensboro, Bradenton	68
SO	Mason Martin, Greensboro, Bradenton	168
SB	Jared Oliva, Altoona	36
SB	Randy Romero, DSL Pirates 2	36

Pitching · #Minimum 75 IP

MAJORS

W	Joe Musgrove	11
# ERA	Joe Musgrove	4.44
SO	Joe Musgrove	157
SV	Felipe Vazquez	28

MINORS

W	James Marvel, Altoona, Indianapolis	16
L	Steven Jennings, Greensboro	12
# ERA	Beau Sulser, Altoona	2.72
G	Matt Eckelman, Altoona, Indianapolis	48
GS	Domingo Robles, Bradenton, Altoona	28
GS	James Marvel, Altoona, Indianapolis	28
SV	Matt Eckelman, Altoona, Indianapolis	23
IP	Domingo Robles, Bradenton, Altoona	165
BB	Cam Vieaux, Altoona, Indianapolis	58
SO	James Marvel, Altoona, Indianapolis	136
# AVG	Cody Bolton, Bradenton, Altoona	.204

2019 PERFORMANCE

General Manager: Neal Huntington. **Farm Director:** Larry Broadway. **Scouting Director:** Joe Delli Carri.

Class	Team	League	W	L	PCT	Finish	Manager
Majors	Pittsburgh Pirates	National	69	93	.426	14th (15)	Clint Hurdle
Triple-A	Indianapolis Indians	International	66	74	.471	t-9th (14)	Brian Esposito
Double-A	Altoona Curve	Eastern	69	71	.493	7th (12)	Michael Ryan
High A	Bradenton Marauders	Florida State	73	62	.541	4th (12)	Wyatt Toregas
Low A	Greensboro Grasshoppers	South Atlantic	79	59	.572	3rd (14)	Miguel Perez
Short season	West Virginia Black Bears	New York-Penn	40	36	.526	t-6th (14)	Drew Saylor
Rookie	Bristol Pirates	Appalachian	34	33	.507	4th (10)	Kieran Mattison
Rookie	GCL Pirates	Gulf Coast	18	36	.333	18th (18)	Gera Alvarez
Overall 2019 Minor League Record			379	371	.505	13th (30)	

ORGANIZATION STATISTICS

PITTSBURGH PIRATES
NATIONAL LEAGUE

Batting	B-T	HT	WT	DOB	AVG	vLH	vRH	G	AB	R	H	2B	3B	HR	RBI	BB	HBP	SH	SF	SO	SB	CS	SLG	OBP
Baron, Steven	R-R	6-0	205	12-7-90	.200	.250	.167	7	10	0	2	1	0	0	1	0	0	0	0	6	0	0	.300	.200
Bell, Josh	B-R	6-4	240	8-14-92	.277	.224	.297	143	527	94	146	37	3	37	116	74	5	0	7	118	0	1	.569	.367
Cabrera, Melky	B-L	5-10	210	8-11-84	.280	.270	.286	133	378	43	106	22	1	7	47	17	1	1	0	41	2	0	.400	.313
Cervelli, Francisco	R-R	6-1	210	3-6-86	.193	.160	.202	34	109	11	21	3	0	1	5	9	4	1	0	31	1	0	.248	.279
2-team total (14 Atlanta)					.213	.156	.229	48	141	15	30	8	1	3	12	13	5	1	0	41	1	0	.348	.302
Diaz, Elias	R-R	6-1	220	11-17-90	.241	.268	.231	101	303	31	73	14	0	2	28	23	2	1	3	56	0	0	.307	.296
Dickerson, Corey	L-R	6-1	210	5-22-89	.315	.222	.330	44	127	20	40	18	0	4	25	13	0	0	2	23	1	0	.551	.373
2-team total (34 Philadelphia)					.304	.271	.313	78	260	33	79	28	2	12	59	16	0	0	3	56	1	0	.565	.341
Elmore, Jake	R-R	5-10	180	6-15-87	.213	.150	.259	20	47	3	10	1	0	0	4	2	0	0	0	8	0	1	.234	.245
Frazier, Adam	L-R	5-10	180	12-14-91	.278	.259	.285	152	554	80	154	33	7	10	50	40	9	4	1	75	5	5	.417	.336
Gonzalez, Erik	R-R	6-3	205	8-31-91	.254	.333	.213	53	142	15	36	4	1	6	9	1	3	1	37	4	1	.317	.301
Joseph, Corban	L-R	6-0	185	10-28-88	.182	--	.182	9	11	1	2	1	0	0	6	0	0	0	0	1	0	0	.273	.182
2-team total (8 San Francisco)					.111	.000	.115	17	27	1	3	1	0	0	2	1	0	0	0	7	0	0	.148	.143
Kang, Jung Ho	R-R	6-0	210	4-5-87	.169	.160	.175	65	172	15	29	7	1	10	24	11	1	0	1	60	0	0	.395	.222
Kramer, Kevin	L-R	6-0	200	10-3-93	.167	.100	.188	22	42	5	7	1	0	0	5	6	0	0	2	17	0	1	.191	.260
Marte, Starling	R-R	6-1	190	10-9-88	.295	.269	.304	132	539	97	159	31	6	23	82	25	16	2	4	94	25	6	.503	.343
Martin, Jason	L-R	5-9	185	9-5-95	.250	.400	.226	20	36	5	9	0	2	0	4	4	0	0	0	10	2	0	.306	.325
Moran, Colin	L-R	6-4	205	10-1-92	.277	.273	.278	149	466	46	129	30	1	13	80	30	3	0	4	117	0	1	.429	.322
Newman, Kevin	R-R	6-0	195	8-4-93	.308	.286	.316	130	493	61	152	20	6	12	64	28	7	2	1	62	16	8	.446	.354
Osuna, Jose	R-R	6-2	240	12-12-92	.264	.228	.284	95	261	41	69	20	0	10	36	18	1	0	4	48	0	0	.456	.310
Polanco, Gregory	L-L	6-5	235	9-14-91	.242	.229	.246	42	153	23	37	8	1	6	17	12	1	0	0	49	3	1	.425	.301
Reyes, Pablo	R-R	5-8	175	9-5-93	.203	.259	.165	71	143	18	29	7	2	2	19	13	1	0	0	36	1	1	.322	.274
Reynolds, Bryan	B-R	6-3	205	1-27-95	.314	.264	.334	134	491	83	154	37	4	16	68	46	6	0	3	121	3	2	.503	.377
Shuck, JB	L-L	5-11	195	6-18-87	.213	.267	.188	27	47	4	10	1	0	2	8	1	1	0	10	1	1	.255	.339
Stallings, Jacob	R-R	6-4	220	12-22-89	.262	.340	.236	71	191	26	50	5	0	6	13	16	2	1	0	40	0	0	.382	.325
Tucker, Cole	B-R	6-3	205	7-3-96	.211	.192	.220	56	147	16	31	10	3	2	13	10	1	1	0	40	0	0	.361	.266

Pitching	B-T	HT	WT	DOB	W	L	ERA	G	GS	CG	SV	IP	H	R	ER	HR	BB	SO	AVG	vLH	vRH	K/9	BB/9
Agrazal, Dario	R-R	6-2	240	12-28-94	4	5	4.91	15	14	0	0	73	82	43	40	15	18	41	.283	.238	.329	5.03	2.21
Archer, Chris	R-R	6-2	195	9-26-88	3	9	5.19	23	23	0	0	120	114	73	69	25	55	143	.249	.235	.260	10.75	4.14
Brault, Steven	L-L	6-0	195	4-29-92	4	6	5.16	25	19	0	0	113	117	69	65	15	53	100	.265	.250	.270	7.94	4.21
Burdi, Nick	R-R	6-3	225	1-19-93	2	1	9.35	11	0	0	0	9	11	9	9	1	3	17	.297	.188	.381	17.65	3.12
Crick, Kyle	L-R	6-4	220	11-30-92	3	7	4.96	52	0	0	0	49	41	30	27	10	35	61	.224	.210	.235	11.20	6.43
Davis, Rookie	R-R	6-5	255	4-29-93	0	1	6.75	5	1	0	0	11	12	8	8	3	8	10	.300	.300	.300	8.44	6.75
DuRapau, Montana	R-R	5-11	175	3-27-92	0	1	9.35	14	2	0	0	17	27	24	18	4	9	22	.342	.400	.296	11.42	4.67
Escobar, Luis	R-R	6-1	205	5-30-96	0	0	7.94	4	0	0	0	6	10	5	5	1	4	2	.455	.556	.385	3.18	6.35
Feliz, Michael	R-R	6-4	240	6-28-93	4	4	3.99	58	1	0	0	56	44	27	25	11	27	73	.214	.194	.227	11.66	4.31
Hartlieb, Geoff	R-R	6-5	235	12-9-93	0	1	9.00	29	0	0	0	35	52	35	35	8	18	38	.351	.394	.312	9.77	4.63
Holmes, Clay	R-R	6-5	225	3-27-93	1	2	5.58	35	0	0	0	50	45	36	31	5	36	56	.232	.266	.209	10.08	6.48
Jerez, Williams	L-L	6-4	205	5-16-92	0	0	7.36	6	0	0	0	4	5	3	3	1	3	5	.313	.571	.111	12.27	7.36
2-team total (6 San Francisco)					1	0	4.35	12	0	0	0	10	12	5	5	2	9	9	.308	.375	.261	7.84	7.84
Kela, Keone	R-R	6-1	210	4-16-93	2	0	2.12	32	0	0	1	30	19	7	7	5	3	11	33	.178	.200	.164	10.01	3.34
Keller, Mitch	R-R	6-2	210	4-4-96	1	5	7.13	11	11	0	0	48	72	41	38	6	16	65	.348	.380	.322	12.19	3.00
Kingham, Nick	R-R	6-5	235	11-8-91	1	1	9.87	14	4	0	1	35	54	38	38	7	17	32	.365	.389	.342	8.31	4.41
Liriano, Francisco	L-L	6-3	218	10-26-83	5	3	3.47	69	0	0	0	70	60	32	27	8	35	63	.232	.194	.246	8.10	4.50
Lyles, Jordan	R-R	6-5	230	10-19-90	5	7	5.36	17	17	0	0	82	88	53	49	16	33	90	.271	.321	.237	9.84	3.61
2-team total (11 Milwaukee)					12	8	4.15	28	28	0	0	141	131	72	65	25	55	146	.244	.277	.220	9.32	3.51
Lyons, Tyler	L-L	6-4	210	2-21-88	1	1	11.25	3	0	0	0	4	6	5	5	1	3	5	.353	.333	.364	11.25	6.75
Markel, Parker	R-R	6-5	240	9-15-90	0	1	5.71	15	0	0	0	17	16	12	11	3	13	21	.239	.226	.250	10.90	6.75
Marvel, James	R-R	6-2	205	9-17-93	0	3	8.31	4	4	0	0	17	25	16	16	4	6	9	.338	.250	.405	4.67	3.12
McRae, Alex	R-R	6-2	220	4-6-93	0	4	8.78	11	2	0	0	27	36	30	26	9	16	19	.339	.350	.283	6.41	5.40
Musgrove, Joe	R-R	6-5	230	12-4-92	11	12	4.44	32	31	0	0	170	168	98	84	21	39	157	.254	.270	.239	8.30	2.06
Neverauskas, Dovydas	R-R	6-3	225	1-14-93	0	0	10.61	10	0	0	0	9	15	11	11	2	7	10	.349	.158	.500	9.64	6.75

	B-T	HT	WT	DOB	W	L	ERA	G	GS	CG	SV	IP	H	R	ER	HR	BB	SO	AVG	vLH	vRH	K/9	BB/9
Osuna, Jose	R-R	6-2	240	12-12-92	0	0	3.86	2	0	0	0	2	3	1	1	1	0	0	.333	.000	.500	0.00	0.00
Ramirez, Yefry	R-R	6-2	215	11-28-93	0	0	7.71	9	0	0	0	14	19	15	12	2	7	16	.312	.375	.270	10.29	4.50
Rios, Yacksel	R-R	6-3	185	6-27-93	1	0	5.23	10	0	0	0	10	10	6	6	2	5	10	.263	.250	.269	8.71	4.35
2-team total (4 Philadelphia)					1	0	6.92	14	0	0	0	13	16	13	10	4	8	12	.314	.364	.276	8.31	5.54
Rodriguez, Richard	R-R	6-4	230	3-4-90	4	5	3.72	72	0	0	1	65	65	30	27	14	23	63	.252	.294	.222	8.68	3.17
Shuck, JB	L-L	5-11	195	6-18-87	0	0	0.00	1	0	0	0	1	1	0	0	0	1	0	.250	1.000	.000	0.00	9.00
Stallings, Jacob	R-R	6-4	220	12-22-89	0	0	0.00	1	0	0	0	1	0	0	0	0	0	0	.000	.000	.000	0.00	0.00
Stratton, Chris	R-R	6-2	211	8-22-90	1	1	3.66	28	0	0	0	47	50	22	19	7	15	47	.270	.253	.283	9.06	2.89
Taillon, Jameson	R-R	6-5	230	11-18-91	2	3	4.10	7	7	1	0	37	34	24	17	4	8	30	.231	.216	.247	7.23	1.93
Vazquez, Felipe	L-L	6-2	225	7-5-91	5	1	1.65	56	0	0	28	60	43	12	11	5	13	90	.197	.192	.199	13.50	1.95
Wang, Wei-Chung	L-L	6-1	160	4-25-92	2	0	6.75	5	0	0	0	4	3	3	3	0	3	2	.313	.429	.222	4.50	6.75
Williams, Trevor	R-R	6-3	230	4-25-92	7	9	5.38	26	26	0	0	146	162	93	87	27	44	113	.284	.335	.247	6.98	2.72

Fielding

Catcher	PCT	G	PO	A	E	DP	PB
Baron	.857	5	12	0	2	0	0
Cervelli	.993	32	259	17	2	3	5
Diaz	.984	96	694	47	12	5	8
Stallings	.991	61	510	24	5	1	4

First Base	PCT	G	PO	A	E	DP
Bell	.988	134	981	96	13	91
Cervelli	.000	1	0	0	0	0
Moran	1.000	8	36	3	0	5
Osuna	.987	31	206	15	3	24

Second Base	PCT	G	PO	A	E	DP
Elmore	.000	1	0	0	0	0
Frazier	.989	142	222	327	6	78
Joseph	.000	1	0	0	0	0
Kramer	1.000	3	0	2	0	1
Moran	1.000	11	6	19	0	2

	PCT	G	PO	A	E	DP
Newman	1.000	23	30	46	0	10
Reyes	.875	7	0	7	1	1

Third Base	PCT	G	PO	A	E	DP
Elmore	.750	4	1	2	1	0
Gonzalez	.927	16	4	34	3	3
Kang	.920	44	20	60	7	9
Moran	.938	121	62	151	14	19
Newman	.867	6	5	8	2	2
Osuna	1.000	19	11	20	0	2
Reyes	.857	2	1	5	1	0

Shortstop	PCT	G	PO	A	E	DP
Gonzalez	.966	26	22	63	3	16
Kang	.952	15	16	24	2	4
Newman	.973	104	124	235	10	43
Reyes	1.000	2	0	3	0	0
Tucker	.986	45	45	92	2	20

Outfield	PCT	G	PO	A	E	DP
Cabrera	.992	97	113	5	1	1
Dickerson	.966	33	57	0	2	0
Elmore	1.000	7	11	1	0	0
Gonzalez	1.000	5	4	0	0	0
Joseph	1.000	1	2	0	0	0
Kramer	1.000	14	13	0	0	0
Marte	.984	130	297	8	5	2
Martin	.960	15	24	0	1	0
Moran	1.000	2	2	0	0	0
Newman	1.000	2	2	0	0	0
Osuna	.957	25	45	0	2	0
Polanco	.987	36	74	0	1	0
Reyes	1.000	45	43	2	0	0
Reynolds	.984	129	237	4	4	0
Shuck	1.000	18	24	0	0	0

INDIANAPOLIS INDIANS
INTERNATIONAL LEAGUE
TRIPLE-A

Batting	B-T	HT	WT	DOB	AVG	vLH	vRH	G	AB	R	H	2B	3B	HR	RBI	BB	HBP	SH	SF	SO	SB	CS	SLG	OBP
Baron, Steven	R-R	6-0	205	12-7-90	.181	.100	.204	45	133	17	24	3	0	2	8	13	2	1	0	38	0	0	.248	.264
Cervelli, Francisco	R-R	6-1	210	3-6-86	.438	.250	.625	5	16	3	7	1	0	1	3	2	2	0	0	5	0	0	.688	.550
Chisenhall, Lonnie	L-R	6-2	190	10-4-88	.208	.000	.313	7	24	2	5	1	0	0	0	0	0	0	0	8	0	0	.250	.208
Craig, Will	R-R	6-3	212	11-16-94	.249	.234	.255	131	494	69	123	23	0	23	78	44	14	0	4	146	2	3	.435	.326
Diaz, Elias	R-R	6-2	220	11-17-90	.414	.375	.429	7	29	5	12	3	0	0	4	1	0	0	0	5	0	0	.517	.433
Dickerson, Corey	L-R	6-1	210	5-22-89	.182	.000	.214	9	33	4	6	1	0	0	4	3	0	0	2	8	0	0	.212	.237
Elmore, Jake	R-R	5-10	180	6-15-87	.322	.333	.317	109	367	56	118	31	0	6	35	37	5	1	4	55	3	8	.455	.387
Franklin, Nick	B-R	6-1	195	3-2-91	.193	.263	.158	44	114	15	22	5	0	3	12	15	2	1	4	31	2	2	.316	.289
Gonzalez, Erik	R-R	6-3	205	8-31-91	.192	.111	.217	20	78	6	15	3	1	1	10	3	0	0	0	29	1	1	.295	.222
Hayes, Ke'Bryan	R-R	6-1	210	1-28-97	.265	.241	.273	110	427	64	113	30	2	10	53	43	5	1	4	90	12	1	.415	.336
Hill, Logan	R-R	6-3	226	5-26-93	.184	.200	.177	14	49	7	9	4	0	2	3	2	3	0	0	12	0	0	.388	.259
Kang, Jung Ho	R-R	6-0	210	4-5-87	.444	.571	.400	8	27	4	12	3	0	1	6	4	0	0	0	8	0	0	.667	.516
Kelley, Christian	R-R	5-10	190	9-23-93	.179	.182	.177	80	252	24	45	9	1	5	21	21	4	2	2	79	0	0	.282	.251
Kivlehan, Patrick	R-R	6-2	223	12-22-89	.212	.273	.191	24	85	11	18	5	0	4	9	8	1	1	0	27	0	0	.412	.287
2-team total (90 Buffalo)					.240	.230	.243	114	413	59	99	18	3	29	75	45	9	1	2	132	0	1	.509	.326
Kramer, Kevin	L-R	6-0	200	10-3-93	.260	.286	.251	113	393	49	102	30	1	10	54	43	5	0	7	116	4	5	.417	.335
Martin, Jason	L-R	5-9	185	9-5-95	.260	.258	.260	101	370	47	96	25	5	8	50	29	1	2	4	79	9	6	.419	.312
Newman, Kevin	R-R	6-0	195	8-4-93	.233	.286	.217	8	30	5	7	2	0	0	1	5	0	0	0	7	0	1	.300	.343
Osuna, Jose	R-R	6-2	240	12-12-92	.268	.313	.255	19	71	13	19	7	1	2	9	2	0	1	2	22	0	0	.479	.361
Owen, Hunter	R-R	5-11	197	9-22-93	.192	.177	.198	42	120	12	23	4	0	4	9	10	8	0	0	45	0	0	.325	.297
Polanco, Gregory	L-L	6-5	235	9-14-91	.267	.333	.250	13	45	5	12	4	0	1	11	9	0	0	0	16	2	0	.422	.389
Reyes, Alfredo	R-R	6-2	179	10-4-93	.278	.429	.182	8	18	2	5	3	0	0	2	0	0	0	0	8	0	0	.389	.278
Reyes, Pablo	R-R	5-8	175	9-5-93	.286	.225	.304	51	175	22	50	15	0	10	30	13	2	1	0	37	5	3	.543	.342
Reynolds, Bryan	B-R	6-3	205	1-27-95	.367	.500	.290	13	49	10	18	1	1	5	11	7	0	0	0	11	3	2	.735	.446
Robinson, Trayvon	B-R	5-10	200	9-1-87	.297	.348	.278	92	263	31	78	10	5	7	36	36	1	0	2	67	6	2	.453	.381
Shuck, JB	L-L	5-11	195	6-18-87	.268	.292	.263	53	142	17	38	12	2	3	14	16	0	0	0	17	3	1	.444	.342
Stallings, Jacob	R-R	6-4	220	12-22-89	.275	.500	.220	15	51	11	14	9	0	2	7	4	4	0	2	9	0	0	.569	.361
Sweeney, Darnell	B-R	6-1	205	2-1-91	.200	.290	.190	29	89	10	20	4	1	2	13	5	2	2	0	35	2	1	.360	.281
Tolman, Mitchell	L-R	5-10	195	6-8-94	.273	.231	.300	12	33	7	9	2	1	2	4	5	0	0	0	7	0	0	.576	.368
Tucker, Cole	B-R	6-3	205	7-3-96	.261	.267	.260	77	310	51	81	15	4	8	28	38	2	3	0	73	11	3	.413	.346
Weiss, Erich	L-R	6-2	200	9-11-91	.206	.100	.250	14	34	3	7	1	1	2	4	4	0	0	0	10	1	0	.471	.290
Wood, Eric	R-R	6-1	210	11-22-92	.247	.221	.262	78	227	30	56	11	0	9	32	22	2	0	3	68	1	2	.414	.319

Pitching	B-T	HT	WT	DOB	W	L	ERA	G	GS	CG	SV	IP	H	R	ER	HR	BB	SO	AVG	vLH	vRH	K/9	BB/9
Agrazal, Dario	R-R	6-2	240	12-28-94	4	4	4.78	12	12	0	0	64	62	36	34	8	12	55	.258	.281	.243	7.73	1.69
Brault, Steven	L-L	6-0	195	4-29-92	0	0	4.50	1	1	0	0	4	3	2	2	0	5	2	.214	.500	.167	4.50	11.25
Brentz, Jake	L-L	6-1	195	9-14-94	1	0	5.55	27	0	0	8	36	42	24	22	4	23	41	.296	.267	.309	10.35	5.80
Brubaker, JT	R-R	6-3	185	11-17-93	2	1	2.57	4	4	0	0	21	19	6	6	2	4	20	.241	.167	.286	8.57	1.71
Cederlind, Blake	R-R	6-3	190	1-4-96	0	1	7.50	3	0	0	0	6	11	5	5	1	2	5	.393	.539	.267	7.50	3.00

PITTSBURGH PIRATES

Player	B-T	HT	WT	DOB	W	L	ERA	G	GS	CG	SV	IP	H	R	ER	HR	BB	SO	AVG	vLH	vRH	K/9	BB/9
Davis, Rookie	R-R	6-5	255	4-29-93	1	6	5.64	13	9	0	0	53	61	33	33	9	22	40	.295	.276	.308	6.84	3.76
DuRapau, Montana	R-R	5-11	175	3-27-92	2	1	2.14	37	0	0	10	46	21	13	11	3	14	57	.135	.211	.091	11.07	2.72
Eckelman, Matt	R-R	6-3	281	10-6-93	0	0	15.43	3	0	0	0	2	10	5	4	0	0	2	.625	.625	.625	7.71	0.00
Escobar, Elvis	L-L	5-8	181	9-6-94	0	0	0.00	1	0	0	0	2	1	0	0	0	2	2	.143	.000	.250	9.00	9.00
Escobar, Luis	R-R	6-1	205	5-30-96	2	1	4.09	24	5	0	1	55	54	27	25	7	32	57	.263	.216	.299	9.33	5.24
Feliz, Michael	R-R	6-4	240	6-28-93	0	0	1.20	10	0	0	2	15	13	2	2	1	7	22	.236	.217	.250	13.20	4.20
Hartlieb, Geoff	R-R	6-5	235	12-9-93	4	1	2.50	26	0	0	3	40	31	11	11	0	15	50	.212	.275	.179	11.34	3.40
Holmes, Clay	R-R	6-5	225	3-27-93	2	1	6.32	10	0	0	1	16	17	15	11	1	15	13	.279	.304	.263	7.47	8.62
Kela, Keone	R-R	6-1	210	4-16-93	0	0	13.50	4	1	0	0	3	5	5	5	2	1	7	.333	.167	.444	18.90	2.70
Keller, Mitch	R-R	6-2	210	4-4-96	7	5	3.56	19	19	0	0	104	94	44	41	9	35	123	.243	.238	.247	10.68	3.04
Keselica, Sean	L-L	6-2	210	6-14-93	1	6	4.33	29	0	0	1	52	52	28	25	4	33	49	.264	.133	.321	8.48	5.71
Liranzo, Jesus	R-R	6-2	225	3-7-95	0	3	8.13	22	0	0	1	31	36	30	28	7	21	30	.298	.286	.306	8.71	6.10
Lyles, Jordan	R-R	6-5	230	10-19-90	0	0	1.69	1	1	0	0	5	2	1	1	1	3	7	.111	.000	.167	11.81	5.06
Lyons, Tyler	L-L	6-4	210	2-21-88	4	3	3.35	35	0	0	3	46	34	20	17	4	16	55	.210	.123	.268	10.84	3.15
2-team total (3 Scranton/Wilkes-Barre)					4	3	3.22	38	0	0	3	50	39	21	18	4	19	60	.216	.116	.277	10.73	3.40
Markel, Parker	R-R	6-5	240	9-15-90	1	0	0.00	4	0	0	0	4	0	0	0	0	3	13	.000	.000	.000	19.50	4.50
Marvel, James	R-R	6-4	205	9-17-93	0	2	2.67	11	11	1	0	61	46	19	18	4	22	53	.214	.148	.254	7.86	3.26
Maurer, Brandon	R-R	6-5	225	7-3-90	2	0	4.26	6	0	0	0	6	5	3	3	0	4	7	.208	.143	.235	9.95	5.68
McRae, Alex	R-R	6-2	220	4-6-93	7	8	5.20	22	22	0	0	114	128	70	66	20	43	101	.286	.315	.265	7.95	3.38
Neverauskas, Dovydas	R-R	6-3	225	1-14-93	3	4	5.02	36	0	0	0	52	51	30	29	8	22	73	.256	.263	.252	12.63	3.81
Ponce, Cody	R-R	6-5	240	4-25-94	1	3	5.30	4	4	0	0	19	18	14	11	4	7	20	.250	.225	.281	9.64	3.38
Ramirez, Yefry	R-R	6-2	215	11-28-93	1	4	5.20	15	5	0	0	45	42	28	26	5	29	58	.247	.224	.262	11.60	5.80
2-team total (4 Norfolk)					2	5	4.14	19	9	0	0	63	53	32	29	7	38	82	.228	.208	.244	11.71	5.43
Rios, Yacksel	R-R	6-3	185	6-27-93	0	0	2.35	9	0	0	1	15	19	4	4	2	4	12	.307	.273	.325	7.04	2.35
2-team total (31 Lehigh Valley)					1	3	5.84	40	0	0	8	49	57	35	32	6	26	49	.291	.274	.301	8.94	4.74
Rodriguez, Richard	R-R	6-4	230	3-4-90	1	0	3.00	2	0	0	1	3	2	1	1	1	0	3	.182	.200	.167	9.00	0.00
Shuck, JB	L-L	5-11	195	6-18-87	0	0	3.79	14	2	0	0	19	15	8	8	3	17	23	.214	.083	.241	10.89	8.05
Stratton, Chris	R-R	6-2	211	8-22-90	0	1	4.50	2	0	0	0	4	7	4	2	1	1	4	.368	.182	.625	9.00	2.25
Sweeney, Darnell	B-R	6-1	205	2-1-91	0	0	3.38	2	0	0	0	3	4	1	1	0	3	2	.333	.400	.286	6.75	10.13
Vasquez, Pedro	R-R	6-4	190	9-23-95	1	1	7.71	2	1	0	0	9	7	8	8	1	4	10	.206	.231	.191	9.64	3.86
Vera, Eduardo	R-R	6-2	195	7-3-94	5	9	6.75	23	22	0	0	119	145	92	89	17	33	83	.308	.330	.293	6.29	2.50
Vieaux, Cam	L-L	6-3	200	12-5-93	4	2	5.05	13	13	0	0	62	63	35	35	15	29	61	.260	.296	.250	8.81	4.19
Waddell, Brandon	L-L	6-3	180	6-3-94	3	7	8.70	29	7	0	1	61	78	62	59	11	40	69	.302	.260	.320	10.18	5.90
Weiman, Blake	R-L	6-4	208	11-5-95	0	1	4.63	8	0	0	1	12	12	7	6	3	4	10	.267	.214	.290	7.71	3.09
Williams, Trevor	R-R	6-3	230	4-25-92	1	0	6.00	1	1	0	0	3	4	2	2	0	1	5	.308	.500	.143	15.00	3.00

Fielding

Catcher	PCT	G	PO	A	E	DP	PB
Baron	.990	45	350	30	4	2	1
Cervelli	1.000	5	42	3	0	0	1
Diaz	1.000	6	46	9	0	0	0
Kelley	.992	79	678	41	6	5	3
Stallings	.993	15	137	7	1	0	0

First Base	PCT	G	PO	A	E	DP
Chisenhall	1.000	1	10	0	0	0
Craig	.999	111	828	57	1	92
Kivlehan	1.000	4	28	2	0	4
Kramer	1.000	1	6	0	0	1
Osuna	1.000	1	3	0	0	0
Owen	.982	17	99	9	2	15
Weiss	1.000	2	10	0	0	2
Wood	.983	7	56	1	1	3

Second Base	PCT	G	PO	A	E	DP
Elmore	.988	44	71	91	2	23
Franklin	.982	15	27	27	1	5
Gonzalez	.973	8	18	18	1	7
Kramer	.981	50	87	122	4	30
Reyes	.921	7	16	19	3	4
Sweeney	1.000	5	7	10	0	2

(Second Base cont.)	PCT	G	PO	A	E	DP
Tolman	.909	11	13	27	4	8
Tucker	1.000	6	9	17	0	7
Weiss	1.000	4	7	11	0	3

Third Base	PCT	G	PO	A	E	DP
Elmore	.905	9	9	10	2	2
Franklin	1.000	3	0	3	0	0
Hayes	.989	104	65	208	3	23
Kang	1.000	3	3	5	0	0
Kramer	.905	15	12	26	4	3
Osuna	1.000	1	0	2	0	0
Owen	1.000	7	2	14	0	0
Wood	.833	4	2	3	1	1

Shortstop	PCT	G	PO	A	E	DP
Elmore	.981	29	41	61	2	16
Franklin	.897	12	9	26	4	8
Gonzalez	1.000	9	11	15	0	3
Kang	.900	3	2	7	1	1
Kramer	.941	5	7	9	1	2
Newman	1.000	4	5	6	0	1
Reyes	1.000	1	2	1	0	0
Reyes	.959	15	16	31	2	6
Sweeney	1.000	1	2	1	0	1

(Catcher cont.)	PCT	G	PO	A	E	PB
Tucker	.959	70	95	160	11	39

Outfield	PCT	G	PO	A	E	DP
Chisenhall	1.000	4	7	0	0	0
Craig	.909	13	19	1	2	0
Dickerson	1.000	7	12	0	0	0
Elmore	1.000	28	49	3	0	0
Franklin	1.000	10	11	0	0	0
Hill	1.000	12	20	1	0	0
Kivlehan	.906	17	29	0	3	0
Kramer	.972	30	33	2	1	1
Martin	.985	96	201	0	3	0
Newman	1.000	4	9	0	0	0
Osuna	1.000	15	16	0	0	0
Owen	1.000	15	24	0	0	0
Polanco	1.000	8	11	1	0	0
Reyes	1.000	6	14	0	0	0
Reyes	.981	27	51	1	1	0
Reynolds	1.000	13	25	0	0	0
Robinson	.978	67	84	3	2	0
Shuck	.989	41	86	6	1	1
Sweeney	.950	17	19	0	1	0
Wood	.978	32	44	1	1	0

ALTOONA CURVE — DOUBLE-A
EASTERN LEAGUE

Batting	B-T	HT	WT	DOB	AVG	vLH	vRH	G	AB	R	H	2B	3B	HR	RBI	BB	HBP	SH	SF	SO	SB	CS	SLG	OBP
Alemais, Stephen	R-R	5-11	190	4-12-95	.267	.250	.273	12	45	4	12	0	0	0	2	1	0	0	0	9	2	0	.267	.283
Cervelli, Francisco	R-R	6-1	210	3-6-86	.333	--	.333	1	3	0	1	1	0	0	0	1	0	0	0	0	0	0	.667	.500
Cruz, Oneil	L-R	6-7	175	10-4-98	.269	.200	.292	35	119	14	32	8	3	1	17	15	0	0	2	35	3	1	.412	.346
Delay, Jason	R-R	6-0	200	3-7-95	.234	.197	.249	67	231	22	54	12	1	8	37	13	5	0	3	63	1	0	.398	.286
Glendinning, Robbie	R-R	6-2	196	10-6-95	.261	.294	.248	58	184	21	48	7	1	5	31	24	1	2	2	65	2	1	.391	.346
Hill, Logan	R-R	6-3	226	5-26-93	.258	.276	.252	113	407	53	105	27	3	12	69	42	5	0	4	120	1	2	.428	.332
Jackson, Bralin	R-L	5-11	212	12-2-93	.257	.236	.268	95	272	32	70	13	2	0	20	16	1	1	2	71	7	2	.320	.299
Madris, Bligh	L-R	6-0	208	2-29-96	.260	.277	.255	132	457	50	119	26	2	8	55	43	2	4	4	99	3	4	.379	.324
Medrano, Jesse	R-R	5-11	190	3-27-95	.056	.111	.000	7	18	1	1	0	0	0	0	1	2	0	1	2	0	3	.056	.150

PITTSBURGH PIRATES

Ngoepe, Gift	R-R	5-8	200	1-18-90	.100	.000	.150	14	30	5	3	0	0	0	0	8	0	0	14	2	1	.100	.290
Oliva, Jared	R-R	6-3	203	11-27-95	.277	.254	.286	123	447	70	124	24	6	6	42	42	11	4	3	104	36	10	.398	.352
Owen, Hunter	R-R	5-11	197	9-22-93	.295	.245	.310	68	237	45	70	15	2	15	44	17	12	0	2	75	1	3	.565	.369
Pabst, Arden	R-R	6-1	210	3-14-95	.192	.138	.208	73	250	18	48	11	3	4	23	11	3	3	3	73	0	3	.308	.232
Peurifoy, Ryan	R-R	6-2	196	3-26-95	.106	.222	.079	26	47	6	5	0	0	1	1	6	0	0	0	19	0	1	.170	.208
Pope, Brett	L-R	6-0	180	5-28-96	.252	.244	.253	100	282	30	71	15	1	2	22	26	5	3	1	58	7	3	.333	.325
Reyes, Alfredo	R-R	6-2	179	10-4-93	.176	.208	.158	54	148	11	26	6	1	1	9	20	3	1	0	56	7	5	.250	.287
Sharpe, Chris	R-R	6-1	195	6-6-96	.217	.303	.182	68	231	44	50	14	1	11	38	17	4	2	3	67	2	3	.429	.278
Suiter, Jerrick	R-R	6-2	253	3-4-93	.235	.263	.224	121	408	39	96	14	0	4	39	22	4	0	7	77	2	2	.299	.277
Sweeney, Darnell	B-R	6-1	205	2-1-91	.196	.250	.171	15	51	5	10	3	0	2	5	4	0	0	0	22	0	2	.373	.255
Tolman, Mitchell	L-R	5-10	195	6-8-94	.254	.241	.259	116	401	56	102	18	3	4	32	47	6	4	2	100	10	5	.344	.340
Valerio, Adrian	B-R	5-11	150	3-13-97	.198	.211	.191	33	106	12	21	2	2	0	10	6	1	0	0	29	1	0	.255	.248

Pitching	B-T	HT	WT	DOB	W	L	ERA	G	GS	CG	SV	IP	H	R	ER	HR	BB	SO	AVG	vLH	vRH	K/9	BB/9
Agrazal, Dario	R-R	6-2	240	12-28-94	1	1	3.60	4	4	0	0	25	29	10	10	3	0	19	.305	.373	.194	6.84	0.00
Bolton, Cody	R-R	6-3	185	6-19-98	2	3	5.85	9	9	0	0	40	37	26	26	6	16	33	.248	.262	.238	7.43	3.60
Brady, Sean	L-L	6-1	210	6-9-94	5	11	3.65	22	22	1	0	138	135	67	56	15	36	82	.258	.225	.274	5.35	2.35
2-team total (3 Akron)					5	13	4.20	25	25	1	0	152	155	83	71	15	45	90	.265	.233	.281	5.33	2.66
Brentz, Jake	L-L	6-1	195	9-14-94	1	0	0.77	9	0	0	0	12	6	1	1	0	3	13	.146	.118	.167	10.03	2.31
Campos, Vicente	R-R	6-3	230	7-27-92	2	2	4.85	20	0	0	1	26	29	17	14	5	13	23	.287	.320	.255	7.96	4.50
Cederlind, Blake	R-R	6-3	190	1-4-96	5	1	1.77	31	0	0	2	46	31	10	9	1	16	42	.191	.235	.143	8.28	3.15
Cesar, Joel	R-R	5-11	191	1-26-96	3	4	3.76	28	1	0	1	38	38	18	16	5	12	36	.260	.232	.297	8.45	2.82
Coley, Austin	R-R	6-2	203	7-14-92	2	2	4.07	16	4	0	0	24	35	17	11	1	9	18	.350	.273	.444	6.66	3.33
Eckelman, Matt	R-R	6-3	281	10-6-93	1	5	3.33	45	1	0	23	49	43	21	18	3	25	45	.240	.310	.152	8.32	4.62
Economos, Nicholas	R-R	6-6	215	6-27-95	0	3	8.83	4	3	0	0	17	24	18	17	4	7	17	.324	.375	.286	8.83	3.63
Escobar, Elvis	L-L	5-8	181	9-6-94	1	0	1.80	3	0	0	0	5	4	1	1	0	1	6	.222	.250	.214	10.80	1.80
Garcia, Yeudy	R-R	6-2	220	10-6-92	1	2	6.10	33	2	0	1	62	76	45	42	4	34	53	.312	.290	.336	7.69	4.94
German, Angel	R-R	6-4	241	5-25-96	3	3	4.33	39	0	0	2	52	33	25	25	8	31	48	.182	.221	.140	8.31	5.37
Hightower, Scooter	R-R	6-3	220	10-15-93	2	5	6.02	10	9	0	0	43	51	32	29	8	12	21	.298	.311	.284	4.36	2.49
Holmes, Clay	R-R	6-5	225	3-27-93	1	0	6.75	2	0	0	0	4	5	3	3	0	1	3	.333	.400	.300	6.75	2.25
Jacques, Joe	L-L	6-4	210	3-11-95	0	0	0.00	1	0	0	0	1	1	0	0	0	2	0	.333	.000	1.000	0.00	18.00
Keselica, Sean	L-L	6-2	210	6-14-93	0	0	0.00	7	0	0	0	9	6	5	0	0	6	8	.182	.143	.211	8.00	6.00
Koehler, Tom	R-R	6-3	235	6-29-86	0	0	54.00	1	0	0	0	0	2	2	2	1	1	1	.667	1.000	.500	27.00	27.00
Liranzo, Jesus	R-R	6-2	225	3-7-95	2	1	1.61	20	0	0	1	28	14	7	5	0	13	24	.146	.114	.173	7.71	4.18
Marvel, James	R-R	6-4	205	9-17-93	9	5	3.10	17	17	1	0	102	85	36	35	6	24	83	.229	.217	.242	7.35	2.12
Mears, Nick	R-R	6-3	185	10-7-96	0	0	1.80	4	0	0	0	5	4	3	1	0	2	7	.211	.200	.222	12.60	3.60
Medrano, Jesse	R-R	5-11	200	3-27-95	0	0	18.00	1	0	0	0	1	2	2	2	0	0	0	.500	.500	--	0.00	0.00
Murray, Shea	R-R	6-6	215	11-5-93	0	0	162.00	1	0	0	0	0	5	6	6	0	1	0	1.000	1.000	1.000	0.00	27.00
O'Reilly, John	R-R	6-5	195	10-4-95	0	0	0.00	1	0	0	0	1	1	0	0	0	1	1	.333	--	.333	9.00	9.00
Ponce, Cody	R-R	6-5	240	4-25-94	0	0	6.00	3	1	0	1	6	3	4	4	1	1	6	.143	.091	.200	9.00	1.50
Reyes, Alfredo	R-R	6-2	179	10-4-93	0	0	0.00	1	0	0	0	1	0	0	0	0	1	0	.000	.000	.000	9.00	9.00
Robles, Domingo	L-L	6-2	170	4-29-98	4	6	4.02	18	18	3	0	103	113	51	46	13	21	77	.279	.256	.291	6.73	1.83
Scioneaux, Tate	R-R	6-0	219	12-14-92	1	1	12.75	13	0	0	1	12	20	17	17	5	6	16	.370	.452	.261	12.00	4.50
2-team total (20 Hartford)					5	2	6.25	33	0	0	1	40	46	29	28	8	11	54	.288	.367	.210	12.05	2.45
Suiter, Jerrick	R-R	6-2	253	3-4-93	0	0	0.00	2	0	0	0	2	1	0	0	0	1	0	.167	.333	.000	5.40	0.00
Sulser, Beau	R-R	6-2	195	5-5-94	8	3	2.72	33	6	0	2	96	88	35	29	4	31	63	.241	.237	.246	5.91	2.91
Valdes, Ryan	R-R	5-11	185	8-22-93	0	0	9.00	1	0	0	0	2	4	2	2	0	2	2	.364	.375	.333	9.00	9.00
Vasquez, Pedro	R-R	6-4	190	9-3-95	8	5	2.71	24	23	1	0	123	107	46	37	8	29	91	.233	.269	.198	6.66	2.12
Vieaux, Cam	L-L	6-3	200	12-5-93	4	4	2.23	13	13	0	0	77	54	20	19	6	29	59	.201	.161	.220	6.93	3.40
Waddell, Brandon	L-L	6-3	180	6-3-94	3	1	2.23	7	7	0	0	36	29	10	9	0	9	42	.216	.270	.196	10.40	2.23
Weiman, Blake	R-L	6-4	208	11-5-95	1	2	1.86	16	0	0	2	19	11	6	4	1	4	24	.164	.185	.150	11.17	1.86

Fielding

Catcher	PCT	G	PO	A	E	DP	PB
Cervelli	1.000	1	7	0	0	0	0
Delay	.993	67	407	45	3	1	8
Pabst	.998	73	558	45	1	3	7

First Base	PCT	G	PO	A	E	DP
Hill	.988	29	226	11	3	25
Owen	1.000	2	2	0	0	0
Reyes	1.000	7	33	4	0	0
Suiter	.993	113	871	67	7	97

Second Base	PCT	G	PO	A	E	DP
Glendinning	1.000	1	2	1	0	0
Pope	.986	17	21	47	1	14
Reyes	.972	10	14	21	1	4
Sweeney	.000	1	0	0	1	0

Tolman	.974	102	173	285	12	67
Valerio	.966	15	21	35	2	10

Third Base	PCT	G	PO	A	E	DP
Glendinning	.924	31	14	47	5	5
Medrano	1.000	6	0	6	0	1
Owen	.970	65	52	109	5	16
Pope	.971	34	14	53	2	6
Reyes	.947	8	8	10	1	0
Sweeney	1.000	5	5	12	0	1
Tolman	1.000	3	1	2	0	0

Shortstop	PCT	G	PO	A	E	DP
Alemais	1.000	12	12	22	0	1
Cruz	.944	35	56	95	9	19
Glendinning	.951	21	29	49	4	14
Ngoepe	.940	14	12	35	3	6

Pope	.965	39	45	93	5	23
Reyes	.968	16	20	41	2	14
Valerio	.985	18	20	44	1	12

Outfield	PCT	G	PO	A	E	DP
Hill	.974	42	75	1	2	0
Jackson	1.000	67	143	6	0	4
Madris	.988	118	248	5	3	0
Medrano	.000	1	0	0	0	0
Oliva	1.000	114	288	3	0	0
Owen	1.000	1	2	0	0	0
Peurifoy	1.000	14	38	1	0	0
Reyes	.957	11	21	1	1	0
Sharpe	.976	59	111	9	3	2
Suiter	1.000	1	1	0	0	0
Sweeney	1.000	10	13	2	0	0

FLORIDA STATE LEAGUE

Batting	B-T	HT	WT	DOB	AVG	vLH	vRH	G	AB	R	H	2B	3B	HR	RBI	BB	HBP	SH	SF	SO	SB	CS	SLG	OBP
Amaral, Daniel	R-R	5-11	180	3-7-97	.278	.346	.259	69	245	37	68	14	1	1	24	22	8	5	2	53	15	2	.355	.354
Bormann, John	R-R	6-0	205	4-4-93	.000	.000	.000	5	13	0	0	0	0	0	0	1	0	0	0	4	0	0	.000	.071
Busby, Dylan	R-R	6-2	196	11-28-95	.213	.218	.212	114	375	50	80	16	4	22	63	47	10	0	2	158	2	1	.453	.316
Castro, Rodolfo	B-R	6-0	200	5-21-99	.243	.283	.228	57	202	26	49	13	1	5	27	13	0	0	0	54	1	0	.391	.288
Cruz, Oneil	L-R	6-7	175	10-4-98	.302	.321	.296	35	136	21	41	6	1	7	16	8	1	0	0	38	7	3	.515	.345
Diaz, Elias	R-R	6-1	220	11-17-90	.400	.000	.667	2	5	1	2	2	0	0	2	2	0	0	0	1	1	0	.800	.571
Franklin, Nick	R-R	6-1	190	3-2-91	.000	.000	.000	4	16	1	0	0	0	0	0	0	0	0	0	8	0	0	.000	.000
Gassaway, Randolph	R-R	6-4	210	5-23-95	.149	.077	.177	14	47	4	7	1	0	0	2	4	0	2	0	16	0	1	.170	.216
Glendinning, Robbie	R-R	6-2	196	10-6-95	.340	.385	.325	43	162	22	55	16	1	8	26	14	1	0	1	50	6	2	.599	.393
Gretler, Michael	R-R	6-2	180	1-11-96	.189	.333	.159	15	53	2	10	1	0	0	3	2	0	1	0	13	0	0	.208	.218
Hernandez, Raul	R-R	6-0	182	12-20-95	.247	.268	.241	76	255	26	63	14	0	0	19	14	4	1	1	51	1	1	.302	.296
Lambert, Chase	R-R	5-11	175	6-28-96	.197	.095	.218	41	122	12	24	5	0	1	8	18	2	3	2	32	1	2	.262	.306
Lockery, Dean	L-R	5-11	185	5-28-96	.182	1.000	.100	3	11	0	2	0	0	0	1	1	0	0	0	5	0	0	.182	.250
Martin, Mason	L-R	6-0	201	6-2-99	.239	.156	.257	49	176	32	42	13	1	12	46	22	3	0	0	65	0	1	.528	.333
Medrano, Jesse	R-R	5-11	200	3-27-95	.192	.163	.200	73	224	24	43	9	1	3	16	10	9	3	1	71	4	4	.281	.254
Mitchell, Cal	L-L	6-0	209	3-8-99	.251	.218	.258	118	451	54	113	21	2	15	64	32	5	0	5	142	1	1	.406	.304
Morrow, Matt	L-R	5-10	180	1-9-96	.000	--	.000	1	1	0	0	0	0	0	0	0	0	0	0	0	0	0	.000	.000
Osuna, Jose	R-R	6-2	240	12-12-92	.200	.429	.077	5	20	3	4	1	0	0	2	2	0	0	0	3	0	0	.250	.273
Peurifoy, Ryan	R-R	6-2	206	3-26-95	.154	.167	.143	4	13	2	2	0	0	1	1	1	1	0	0	6	0	0	.385	.267
Polanco, Gregory	L-L	6-5	235	9-14-91	.154	1.000	.083	4	13	2	2	0	0	0	1	4	0	0	0	2	0	0	.154	.353
Sanchez, Lolo	R-R	5-11	168	4-23-99	.196	.093	.233	52	163	21	32	3	1	1	9	18	7	5	2	31	13	5	.270	.300
Sharpe, Chris	R-R	6-1	195	6-6-96	.292	.229	.309	64	226	36	66	17	2	5	30	28	8	1	3	52	15	7	.451	.385
Siri, Raul	R-R	5-9	175	10-21-94	.170	.250	.149	19	59	7	10	2	0	0	4	8	2	0	0	23	3	0	.203	.290
Stafford, Deon	R-R	5-11	211	3-17-96	.229	.250	.221	79	275	30	63	9	2	6	32	35	2	2	2	86	1	1	.342	.319
Swaggerty, Travis	L-L	5-11	180	8-19-97	.265	.333	.248	121	457	79	121	20	3	9	40	57	2	5	3	116	23	8	.381	.347
Tancas, Lucas	R-R	6-2	220	11-12-93	.280	.298	.275	106	389	47	109	28	1	9	58	29	8	1	1	142	3	4	.427	.342
Valerio, Adrian	B-R	5-11	150	3-13-97	.247	.232	.251	69	231	20	57	8	1	2	18	9	3	1	1	54	12	4	.316	.283

Pitching	B-T	HT	WT	DOB	W	L	ERA	G	GS	CG	SV	IP	H	R	ER	HR	BB	SO	AVG	vLH	vRH	K/9	BB/9
Bido, Osvaldo	R-R	6-3	175	10-18-95	1	3	2.25	5	5	0	0	24	18	10	6	1	9	17	.205	.167	.231	6.38	3.38
Bolton, Cody	R-R	6-3	185	6-19-98	6	3	1.61	12	12	0	0	62	39	14	11	1	14	69	.174	.174	.174	10.07	2.04
Case, Brad	R-R	6-6	220	9-13-96	5	5	4.29	13	13	0	0	71	74	37	34	11	22	58	.264	.263	.265	7.32	2.78
Cederlund, Blake	R-R	6-3	190	1-4-96	0	0	1.17	7	0	0	2	8	4	1	1	0	6	8	.143	.077	.200	9.39	7.04
Cesar, Joel	R-R	5-11	191	1-26-96	2	0	0.73	9	0	0	5	12	4	1	1	1	5	16	.100	.222	.000	11.68	3.65
Coley, Austin	R-R	6-2	203	7-14-92	0	0	0.00	2	0	0	0	3	2	0	0	0	1	4	.182	.250	.143	12.00	3.00
Eardensohn, Matt	R-R	6-3	190	5-13-96	1	0	0.00	3	0	0	0	3	3	1	0	0	1	1	.273	.286	.250	3.00	3.00
Economos, Nicholas	R-R	6-6	215	6-27-95	6	4	2.67	14	14	0	0	84	62	29	25	7	24	63	.199	.225	.178	6.72	2.56
Escobar, Luis	R-R	6-1	205	5-30-96	0	0	0.00	10	0	0	3	13	6	0	0	0	6	15	.133	.167	.111	10.13	4.05
Fischer, Drew	R-R	6-3	205	6-3-96	0	1	2.89	8	0	0	2	9	8	3	3	0	3	6	.242	.278	.200	5.79	2.89
Jacques, Joe	L-L	6-4	210	11-15-95	4	3	2.41	20	2	0	1	41	32	13	11	1	16	30	.213	.180	.225	8.56	3.51
Kranick, Max	R-R	6-3	175	7-21-97	6	7	3.79	20	20	1	0	109	100	49	46	11	30	78	.246	.237	.254	6.42	2.47
Loeprich, Conner	R-R	6-3	215	9-13-97	2	1	3.38	8	5	0	0	37	44	18	14	1	7	28	.286	.323	.258	6.75	1.69
Mears, Nick	R-R	6-3	185	10-7-96	4	2	3.60	23	0	0	5	30	22	14	12	3	9	43	.202	.308	.105	12.90	2.70
Montgomery, Allen	R-R	6-3	190	8-15-96	0	0	1.50	4	0	0	0	6	3	1	1	0	9	2	.150	.182	.111	3.00	13.50
Murray, Shea	R-R	6-6	215	11-5-93	1	0	4.86	26	0	0	6	33	23	19	18	1	26	54	.189	.125	.230	14.58	7.02
Neverauskas, Dovydas	R-R	6-3	225	1-14-93	0	0	0.00	2	0	0	0	2	0	0	0	0	2	2	.000	.000	.000	9.00	9.00
Nova, Luis	R-R	5-11	190	6-10-98	0	0	10.80	2	0	0	0	5	8	6	6	1	6	6	.381	.500	.143	10.80	9.00
Nunez, Oddy	L-L	6-8	230	12-20-96	1	1	4.67	8	0	0	0	35	32	22	18	3	21	20	.258	.250	.260	5.19	5.45
O'Reilly, John	R-R	6-5	195	10-4-95	1	0	0.47	9	0	0	2	19	15	3	1	0	5	13	.208	.265	.158	6.16	2.37
Ogle, Braeden	L-L	6-2	170	7-30-97	2	1	3.18	7	0	0	0	11	8	5	4	1	3	10	.200	.083	.250	7.94	2.38
Reyes, Samuel	R-R	5-11	180	3-13-96	1	4	2.87	25	3	0	3	53	48	18	17	4	15	50	.229	.183	.265	8.44	2.53
Robles, Domingo	L-L	6-2	170	4-29-98	5	5	2.61	10	10	0	0	62	47	22	18	5	15	47	.204	.212	.200	6.82	2.18
Schlabach, Ike	R-L	6-5	185	12-27-96	4	1	2.50	25	3	0	1	50	46	14	14	2	9	37	.238	.210	.252	6.62	1.61
Shortridge, Aaron	R-R	6-3	196	5-29-97	9	5	3.21	24	24	1	0	136	129	50	49	13	25	104	.252	.288	.226	6.90	1.66
Stoelke, Logan	R-R	6-3	185	8-26-95	0	2	10.31	13	0	0	3	18	23	21	21	6	13	12	.315	.345	.296	5.89	6.38
Stratton, Hunter	R-R	6-4	225	11-17-96	5	4	4.25	33	3	0	0	72	56	37	34	4	42	64	.209	.243	.185	8.00	5.25
Valdes, Ryan	R-R	5-11	185	8-22-93	2	2	6.83	23	0	0	2	28	31	25	21	5	20	24	.279	.269	.288	7.81	6.51
Wallace, Gavin	R-R	6-5	210	11-14-95	5	8	4.13	30	13	2	0	109	124	58	50	15	22	90	.281	.229	.329	7.43	1.82

Fielding

Catcher	PCT	G	PO	A	E	DP	PB
Bormann	1.000	5	34	6	0	0	1
Diaz	1.000	2	7	0	0	0	0
Gretler	1.000	1	8	0	0	0	0
Hernandez	.985	60	407	50	7	1	15
Stafford	.988	71	517	39	7	2	6

First Base	PCT	G	PO	A	E	DP
Busby	1.000	7	28	1	0	3
Gassaway	1.000	4	31	4	0	4
Gretler	.981	5	47	5	1	2

	PCT	G	PO	A	E	DP
Hernandez	.930	6	37	3	3	1
Martin	.984	47	348	29	6	25
Osuna	1.000	1	12	0	0	1
Tancas	.993	69	560	31	4	39

Second Base	PCT	G	PO	A	E	DP
Castro	.973	37	54	89	4	15
Franklin	1.000	2	4	2	0	0
Glendinning	1.000	4	6	9	0	2
Gretler	.714	2	3	2	2	0
Lambert	.992	35	44	74	1	9

	PCT	G	PO	A	E	DP
Lockery	.938	3	6	9	1	3
Medrano	1.000	29	54	60	0	17
Siri	1.000	2	2	1	0	0
Valerio	.982	29	36	76	2	14

Third Base	PCT	G	PO	A	E	DP
Busby	.937	99	60	179	16	13
Castro	.824	4	4	10	3	2
Glendinning	1.000	1	1	0	0	0
Gretler	.900	3	4	5	1	1
Medrano	1.000	32	23	41	0	2

	PCT	G	PO	A	E	DP
Morrow	1.000	1	0	1	0	0
Osuna	1.000	1	0	1	0	0
Siri	1.000	5	3	4	0	0

Shortstop	PCT	G	PO	A	E	DP
Castro	.964	16	20	34	2	6
Cruz	.957	35	60	94	7	21
Franklin	.857	2	1	5	1	0

	PCT	G	PO	A	E	DP
Glendinning	.943	39	51	99	9	14
Lambert	.947	7	7	11	1	1
Valerio	.971	41	41	94	4	12

Outfield	PCT	G	PO	A	E	DP
Amaral	.989	40	89	1	1	0
Gassaway	1.000	2	5	0	0	0
Mitchell	.977	111	206	10	5	2

	PCT	G	PO	A	E	DP
Osuna	1.000	2	2	0	0	0
Peurifoy	1.000	3	12	0	0	0
Polanco	1.000	2	3	0	0	0
Sanchez	1.000	48	81	2	0	0
Sharpe	.970	62	126	4	4	1
Swaggerty	.991	121	312	7	3	1
Tancas	1.000	20	26	0	0	0

GREENSBORO GRASSHOPPERS

SOUTH ATLANTIC LEAGUE

LOW CLASS A

Batting	B-T	HT	WT	DOB	AVG	vLH	vRH	G	AB	R	H	2B	3B	HR	RBI	BB	HBP	SH	SF	SO	SB	CS	SLG	OBP
Alvarez, Andres	R-R	5-10	175	3-29-97	.143	.000	.167	5	14	2	2	0	0	0	2	0	0	0	0	4	0	0	.143	.250
Bae, Ji-Hwan	L-R	6-1	170	7-26-99	.323	.299	.331	86	328	69	106	25	5	0	38	33	3	3	3	77	31	11	.430	.403
Castro, Rodolfo	B-R	6-0	200	5-21-99	.242	.298	.226	61	215	33	52	13	2	14	46	18	5	1	7	68	6	5	.516	.306
Davis, Jonah	L-R	5-10	181	7-2-97	.249	.247	.250	80	317	49	79	15	2	19	52	33	5	1	3	130	5	9	.489	.327
Dorrian, Patrick	L-R	6-2	188	6-26-96	.256	.234	.262	64	219	39	56	17	3	6	31	28	4	1	3	64	8	2	.443	.347
Gretler, Michael	R-R	6-2	180	1-1-96	.214	.242	.205	79	276	30	59	17	1	2	34	32	3	2	3	81	3	0	.304	.299
Harrer, Justin	R-R	6-2	195	3-2-97	.231	.158	.256	71	229	36	53	14	1	6	21	25	7	1	0	67	7	1	.380	.326
Haug, Ryan	R-R	6-0	165	12-29-94	.250	.000	.333	2	4	0	1	0	0	0	0	0	0	0	0	0	0	0	.250	.250
Herman, Jack	R-R	6-0	190	9-30-99	.257	.231	.265	75	265	47	68	12	2	13	34	28	6	0	1	88	6	6	.464	.340
Kaiser, Connor	R-R	6-4	195	11-20-96	.200	.228	.189	79	280	44	56	12	1	7	36	51	5	5	2	77	4	2	.325	.331
Kinneman, Brett	L-L	6-1	195	8-28-96	.160	.214	.148	44	156	14	25	6	1	5	26	17	2	0	4	63	3	0	.308	.246
Koch, Grant	R-R	6-0	190	2-5-97	.202	.230	.194	94	337	39	68	15	0	8	34	32	2	1	2	60	1	1	.318	.274
Kone, Zack	R-R	6-3	202	11-5-96	.186	.203	.181	76	269	28	50	9	1	2	15	30	2	0	2	94	5	2	.249	.271
Lambert, Chase	R-R	5-11	175	6-28-96	.355	.500	.333	11	31	8	11	1	1	1	3	8	1	0	0	6	3	1	.548	.500
Macias, Fabricio	R-R	6-0	188	3-11-98	.280	.291	.276	122	472	72	132	25	3	8	79	28	10	0	5	90	18	11	.396	.330
Mangieri, Luke	L-R	6-3	215	10-15-96	.231	.256	.222	47	169	19	39	4	1	5	25	21	1	2	2	27	2	5	.355	.316
Martin, Mason	L-R	6-0	201	6-2-99	.263	.254	.265	82	301	58	79	19	3	23	83	46	3	0	5	103	8	2	.575	.361
Mottice, Kyle	L-R	5-11	185	1-18-96	.316	.324	.314	53	171	39	54	8	0	0	19	26	22	3	0	25	18	7	.363	.466
Ngoepe, Victor	R-R	5-8	150	2-9-98	.100	.000	.154	6	20	1	2	0	0	0	0	0	0	0	0	8	0	0	.100	.100
Sanchez, Lolo	R-R	5-11	168	4-23-99	.301	.222	.320	61	226	43	68	10	6	4	26	17	12	6	2	28	20	10	.451	.377
Siri, Raul	R-R	5-9	175	10-21-94	.265	.333	.240	11	34	7	9	6	0	1	6	4	1	0	1	14	1	2	.529	.350
Susi, Zac	L-R	6-1	200	10-30-96	.189	.177	.192	52	159	23	30	7	0	3	18	18	3	1	2	32	1	3	.289	.280

Pitching	B-T	HT	WT	DOB	W	L	ERA	G	GS	CG	SV	IP	H	R	ER	HR	BB	SO	AVG	vLH	vRH	K/9	BB/9
Alldred, Cam	L-L	6-3	205	7-25-96	4	1	4.20	39	0	0	3	60	59	28	28	6	24	63	.263	.253	.269	9.45	3.60
Bido, Osvaldo	R-R	6-3	175	10-18-95	11	5	3.55	20	20	0	0	112	94	46	44	9	29	90	.228	.230	.226	7.25	2.34
Case, Brad	R-R	6-6	220	9-13-96	7	1	2.45	11	11	0	0	66	48	20	18	6	3	50	.195	.174	.210	6.82	0.41
De Los Santos, Yerry	R-R	6-2	160	12-12-97	4	2	1.44	37	0	0	13	50	32	9	8	3	12	73	.183	.206	.170	13.14	2.16
Economos, Nicholas	R-R	6-6	215	6-27-95	4	2	2.48	8	5	0	0	33	24	11	9	2	13	50	.200	.159	.224	13.78	3.58
Garcia, Oliver	R-R	6-3	213	1-8-98	1	0	3.38	6	0	0	1	8	4	3	3	0	4	6	.154	.222	.118	6.75	4.50
Gardner, Will	R-R	6-2	200	5-8-96	3	1	3.00	30	0	0	4	48	31	18	16	1	29	58	.191	.167	.202	10.88	5.44
Harrer, Justin	R-R	6-2	195	3-2-97	0	0	0.00	1	0	0	0	1	0	0	0	0	0	0	.500	--	.500	0.00	0.00
Jacques, Joe	L-L	6-4	210	3-11-95	0	1	2.96	14	0	0	0	24	15	9	8	2	15	20	.177	.208	.164	7.40	5.55
Jennings, Steven	R-R	6-2	175	11-13-98	7	12	4.71	27	27	0	0	130	134	83	68	15	39	115	.269	.307	.247	7.96	2.70
Kobos, Will	R-R	6-2	180	8-3-97	2	3	2.12	7	7	0	0	34	17	10	8	0	18	41	.144	.070	.187	10.85	4.76
Loeprich, Conner	R-R	6-3	215	9-13-97	3	3	4.30	25	3	0	1	59	68	33	28	5	18	67	.286	.275	.290	10.28	2.76
LoPresti, Mike	R-R	6-4	220	10-22-96	1	0	9.56	15	0	0	1	16	30	22	17	0	9	12	.405	.458	.380	6.75	5.06
Manasa, Alex	L-R	6-4	195	1-6-98	9	5	3.48	25	25	1	0	140	134	57	54	15	32	120	.253	.256	.251	7.73	2.06
Mears, Nick	R-R	6-3	185	10-7-96	1	1	3.09	7	0	0	0	12	5	4	4	2	7	19	.128	.200	.103	14.66	5.40
Melendez, Cristofer	R-R	6-3	170	9-16-97	2	3	5.13	28	0	0	1	47	35	29	27	4	26	76	.204	.260	.180	14.45	4.94
Montgomery, Allen	R-R	6-3	190	8-15-96	0	0	7.91	12	0	0	0	19	21	18	17	1	13	15	.276	.308	.260	6.98	6.05
Murray, Shea	R-R	6-6	215	11-5-93	0	0	2.57	8	0	0	0	7	4	2	2	0	5	10	.182	.143	.200	12.86	6.43
Nicacio, Winston	R-R	6-2	180	12-29-96	2	3	2.70	8	5	0	1	37	30	12	11	0	3	33	.224	.260	.202	8.10	0.74
Nova, Luis	R-R	5-11	190	6-10-98	4	2	4.39	9	9	0	0	41	44	28	20	6	9	37	.267	.279	.260	8.12	1.98
O'Reilly, John	R-R	6-5	195	10-4-95	1	2	2.15	20	0	0	3	29	35	16	7	4	10	17	.297	.351	.272	5.22	3.07
Ogle, Braeden	L-L	6-2	170	7-30-97	1	2	3.69	20	2	0	4	32	28	18	13	6	10	34	.237	.250	.234	9.66	2.84
Reyes, Alfredo	R-R	6-2	179	10-4-93	0	1	10.32	10	0	0	0	11	18	13	13	3	5	15	.353	.467	.306	11.91	3.97
Reyes, Samuel	R-R	5-11	180	3-13-96	1	0	0.52	10	0	0	3	17	4	1	1	0	8	23	.073	.000	.108	11.94	4.15
Selby, Colin	R-R	6-1	218	10-24-97	6	3	2.97	17	17	0	0	88	71	39	29	8	27	86	.215	.213	.216	8.80	2.76
Smith, Cody	R-R	6-0	202	9-12-95	2	1	2.84	18	0	0	2	32	27	13	10	3	8	40	.227	.308	.188	11.37	2.27
Stoelke, Logan	R-R	6-3	185	8-26-95	2	5	5.25	11	0	0	4	12	8	8	7	3	4	13	.191	.125	.231	9.75	3.00
Susi, Zac	L-R	6-1	200	10-30-96	0	1	27.00	1	0	0	0	0	2	2	1	0	0	0	.667	1.000	.500	0.00	0.00
Toribio, Noe	R-R	6-2	194	8-25-99	2	3	3.79	7	7	0	0	38	31	16	16	3	12	35	.223	.320	.169	8.29	2.84

Fielding

Catcher	PCT	G	PO	A	E	DP	PB
Haug	.900	1	8	1	1	0	0
Koch	.988	90	802	57	10	3	14
Susi	.979	49	390	38	9	2	11

First Base	PCT	G	PO	A	E	DP
Dorrian	1.000	1	7	0	0	0
Gretler	.992	13	112	6	1	11

	PCT	G	PO	A	E	DP
Koch	1.000	1	5	0	0	0
Mangieri	.989	47	348	18	4	29
Martin	.988	77	605	42	8	61

Second Base	PCT	G	PO	A	E	DP
Bae	.994	44	77	90	1	19
Castro	.955	34	77	73	7	22
Dorrian	1.000	1	1	5	0	1

	PCT	G	PO	A	E	DP
Kaiser	1.000	3	8	13	0	5
Kone	1.000	8	11	20	0	3
Lambert	.964	8	10	17	1	5
Mottice	.993	34	53	80	1	22
Ngoepe	.938	5	5	10	1	1
Siri	.952	5	11	9	1	3

Third Base	PCT	G	PO	A	E	DP
Castro	.840	7	10	11	4	1
Dorrian	.968	35	22	69	3	8
Gretler	.985	51	39	92	2	4
Kaiser	1.000	3	2	11	0	0
Kone	.948	39	19	73	5	6
Lambert	1.000	1	1	3	0	0
Mangieri	1.000	1	0	2	0	0
Siri	.727	4	3	5	3	1

Shortstop	PCT	G	PO	A	E	DP
Alvarez	1.000	4	3	8	0	1
Bae	.903	33	36	66	11	10
Castro	.947	17	28	44	4	15
Dorrian	.900	3	4	5	1	1
Kaiser	.978	74	100	209	7	40
Kone	.933	4	3	11	1	4
Lambert	1.000	1	0	1	0	0
Mottice	1.000	3	4	10	0	3
Ngoepe	.750	1	0	3	1	0

Outfield	PCT	G	PO	A	E	DP
Davis	1.000	75	135	1	0	0
Harrer	.967	56	83	4	3	0
Haug	1.000	1	7	0	0	0
Herman	.972	70	130	11	4	3
Kinneman	.986	40	68	3	1	0
Macias	.978	115	213	6	5	1
Mottice	.000	1	0	0	0	0
Sanchez	.991	60	101	8	1	1

WEST VIRGINIA BLACK BEARS SHORT SEASON
NEW YORK-PENN LEAGUE

PITTSBURGH PIRATES

Batting	B-T	HT	WT	DOB	AVG	vLH	vRH	G	AB	R	H	2B	3B	HR	RBI	BB	HBP	SH	SF	SO	SB	CS	SLG	OBP
Basabe, Angel	L-L	6-0	153	12-12-00	.000	.000	.000	2	5	0	0	0	0	0	0	1	0	0	0	0	0	0	.000	.167
Citta, Brendt	R-R	6-2	180	7-12-96	.294	.120	.345	32	109	15	32	8	2	1	16	8	4	0	1	22	1	1	.431	.361
Davis, Jonah	L-R	5-10	181	7-2-97	.000	.000	.000	5	13	3	0	0	0	0	0	5	0	0	0	7	0	0	.000	.278
Escobar, Elys	R-R	6-0	190	9-21-96	.188	.188	.189	24	69	7	13	5	0	1	8	9	1	0	0	24	0	1	.304	.291
Fajardo, Yoyner	L-R	6-0	179	4-6-99	.000	.000	.000	1	2	0	0	0	0	0	0	0	0	0	0	0	0	0	.000	.000
Fraizer, Matthew	L-R	6-3	205	1-12-98	.221	.140	.252	43	154	20	34	5	1	0	15	14	1	0	2	38	5	3	.266	.287
Gorski, Matt	R-R	6-4	198	12-22-97	.224	.311	.194	49	179	32	40	9	2	3	22	19	1	0	3	48	11	3	.346	.297
Haug, Ryan	R-R	6-0	165	12-29-94	.275	.267	.278	17	51	7	14	4	0	0	5	4	5	0	1	14	3	2	.353	.377
Hayes, Ke'Bryan	R-R	6-1	210	1-28-97	.111	.000	.125	3	9	1	1	1	0	0	2	2	0	0	1	2	1	0	.222	.250
Kinneman, Brett	L-L	6-1	195	8-26-96	.183	.120	.206	57	191	28	35	10	1	2	26	29	5	0	2	76	6	2	.278	.304
Kone, Zack	R-R	6-3	202	11-5-96	.194	.167	.200	9	31	1	6	0	0	0	1	4	0	0	0	16	1	0	.194	.286
Lockery, Dean	L-R	5-11	185	5-28-96	.241	.250	.239	42	137	13	33	5	2	0	13	18	0	0	1	29	2	0	.307	.327
Mangieri, Luke	L-R	6-3	215	10-15-96	.328	.313	.333	17	58	14	19	5	0	2	7	7	2	0	0	8	0	0	.517	.418
Matthiessen, Will	R-R	6-7	220	1-9-98	.220	.342	.182	45	159	21	35	5	1	4	19	18	1	1	0	46	2	0	.340	.303
Mottice, Kyle	L-R	5-11	185	1-18-96	.400	1.000	.333	5	20	5	8	2	0	0	3	2	1	0	0	3	3	1	.500	.478
Ngoepe, Victor	R-R	5-8	150	2-9-98	.242	.316	.222	28	91	11	22	4	1	0	9	9	2	0	1	22	2	0	.308	.320
Patten, Nick	R-R	6-4	205	9-12-96	.189	.182	.192	40	132	18	25	6	1	3	11	17	3	0	1	54	1	2	.318	.294
Paul, Ethan	L-R	5-10	180	8-27-96	.232	.257	.222	33	125	14	29	8	0	1	8	17	4	0	1	35	2	1	.320	.340
Pie, Juan	L-L	6-2	170	4-1-01	.357	.333	.364	4	14	3	5	3	0	0	5	2	0	0	0	5	1	1	.571	.438
Reyes, Pablo	R-R	5-8	175	9-5-93	.300	.000	.375	3	10	1	3	1	0	0	1	1	0	0	0	1	1	0	.400	.417
Rosado, Emilson	R-R	6-3	229	2-11-01	.000	.000	.000	2	6	0	0	0	0	0	0	1	0	0	0	1	0	0	.000	.143
Sabol, Blake	L-R	6-4	215	1-7-98	.245	.179	.270	57	208	26	51	8	4	2	22	34	1	0	3	61	5	4	.351	.350
Triolo, Jared	R-R	6-3	212	2-8-98	.239	.307	.215	60	234	30	56	19	5	2	34	27	0	0	3	49	3	1	.389	.314
Villegas, Fernando	R-R	5-10	176	6-28-98	.219	.214	.220	21	73	9	16	5	1	1	15	8	1	0	0	15	0	0	.356	.305
Wilkie, Kyle	R-R	5-11	205	10-20-97	.243	.319	.217	50	185	20	45	7	0	0	20	17	1	0	1	20	1	2	.281	.309
Wood, Cory	L-R	5-9	180	6-26-97	.234	.185	.252	56	201	30	47	8	3	2	24	26	4	0	0	50	4	0	.333	.333

Pitching	B-T	HT	WT	DOB	W	L	ERA	G	GS	CG	SV	IP	H	R	ER	HR	BB	SO	AVG	vLH	vRH	K/9	BB/9
Ashcraft, Braxton	L-R	6-5	195	10-5-99	1	9	5.77	11	11	0	0	53	49	40	34	4	22	39	.239	.325	.180	6.62	3.74
Bellomy, Bear	R-R	6-4	205	11-29-96	1	1	3.86	9	5	0	2	30	30	14	13	3	10	23	.268	.293	.254	6.82	2.97
Brubaker, JT	R-R	6-3	185	11-17-93	0	0	1.35	2	2	0	0	7	5	2	1	0	4	4	.217	.286	.188	5.40	5.40
Burrows, Michael	R-R	6-2	183	11-8-99	2	3	4.33	11	11	0	0	44	44	27	21	2	20	43	.262	.200	.292	8.86	4.12
Concepcion, Xavier	R-R	6-2	175	1-22-98	3	0	2.64	18	0	0	0	31	22	13	9	0	22	30	.193	.178	.203	8.80	6.46
Del Orbe, Francis	R-R	6-4	173	10-9-98	3	1	3.43	17	1	0	0	42	35	19	16	3	16	48	.231	.182	.245	10.29	3.43
Eardensohn, Matt	R-R	6-3	190	5-13-96	1	0	1.80	2	0	0	0	5	3	1	1	0	0	6	.200	.250	.182	10.80	0.00
Escobar, Elvis	L-L	5-8	181	9-6-94	1	0	1.80	5	0	0	0	5	6	1	1	0	1	4	.316	.625	.091	7.20	1.80
Flowers, J.C.	R-R	6-3	190	5-19-98	0	2	4.30	9	8	0	0	29	33	18	14	5	11	24	.282	.286	.280	7.36	3.38
Flynn, Michael	R-R	6-4	185	8-7-96	0	0	108.00	1	0	0	0	0	1	4	4	0	3	0	.500	--	.500	0.00	81.00
Ford, Grant	R-R	6-1	175	3-11-98	3	1	2.97	11	8	0	0	36	32	14	12	2	17	35	.241	.216	.256	8.67	4.21
Garcia, Oliver	R-R	6-3	213	1-8-98	0	0	0.00	5	0	0	2	6	0	0	0	0	2	7	.000	.000	.000	10.50	3.00
Gong, Hai-Cheng	R-R	6-2	168	12-28-98	0	0	0.00	2	0	0	0	1	1	0	0	0	0	2	.200	.333	.000	0.00	0.00
Gonzalez, Domingo	R-R	6-0	185	9-27-99	1	0	0.00	1	1	0	0	6	3	0	0	0	1	8	.150	.429	.000	12.00	1.50
Junker, Cameron	R-R	6-5	220	9-3-97	5	0	1.29	19	0	0	5	28	13	4	4	0	11	45	.143	.233	.098	14.46	3.54
Kobos, Will	R-R	6-2	180	8-3-97	1	3	6.05	5	5	0	0	19	23	14	13	2	7	17	.311	.345	.289	7.91	3.26
Koehler, Tom	R-R	6-3	235	6-29-86	1	0	6.00	2	0	0	0	3	2	2	2	0	1	3	.182	.333	.125	9.00	3.00
Leonard, Garrett	R-R	6-3	190	9-25-96	2	2	4.60	20	0	0	4	29	30	19	15	2	15	29	.263	.239	.279	8.90	4.60
LoPresti, Mike	R-R	6-4	220	10-22-96	0	1	1.32	8	0	0	2	14	10	4	2	1	5	14	.208	.125	.250	9.22	3.29
Maurer, Brandon	R-R	6-5	225	7-3-90	1	0	0.00	2	0	0	0	3	0	0	0	0	0	6	.000	.000	.000	18.00	0.00
McGough, Trey	L-L	6-3	195	3-29-98	1	1	7.04	9	0	0	0	15	18	13	12	2	4	15	.286	.217	.325	8.80	2.35
Nicacio, Winston	R-R	6-2	180	12-29-96	2	1	2.96	8	2	0	0	24	20	8	8	2	11	22	.227	.133	.276	8.14	4.07
Priester, Quinn	R-R	6-1	195	9-15-00	0	0	4.50	1	1	0	0	4	3	2	2	0	2	4	.214	.286	.143	9.00	9.00
Rennard, Alec	R-R	6-3	210	5-6-95	0	4	5.92	17	0	0	1	24	42	23	16	1	9	21	.378	.237	.452	7.77	3.33
Roberts, Austin	R-R	6-0	219	7-27-98	2	1	2.70	15	5	0	1	40	31	13	12	3	11	38	.214	.241	.195	8.55	2.48
Roman, Denny	L-R	5-9	180	9-30-98	2	2	4.19	17	0	0	0	39	39	18	18	2	8	39	.262	.289	.250	9.08	1.86
Smith, Cody	R-R	6-0	202	9-12-95	0	0	2.25	2	0	0	1	4	1	1	1	0	1	5	.083	.000	.111	11.25	2.25
Toribio, Noe	R-R	6-2	194	8-25-99	2	1	2.40	7	4	0	1	30	20	10	8	2	8	31	.185	.258	.156	9.30	2.40
Valles, Jesus	R-R	6-3	178	12-15-97	3	2	3.55	14	12	0	0	66	65	34	26	8	16	36	.256	.306	.224	4.91	2.18
Vega, Yandy	R-R	6-0	160	12-2-98	0	0	9.00	2	0	0	0	2	4	2	2	0	1	1	.500	1.000	.333	4.50	4.50
Webb, Jacob	R-R	6-4	200	6-5-99	2	1	2.76	13	0	0	1	16	16	10	5	0	12	15	.258	.286	.244	8.27	6.61

Fielding

C: Escobar 24, Haug 16, Wilkie 40. **1B:** Citta 12, Mangieri 7, Matthiessen 20, Patten 38. **2B:** Fajardo 1, Lockery 12, Mottice 5, Ngoepe 12, Paul 1, Reyes 1, Wood 44. **3B:** Hayes 3, Kone 7, Lockery 26, Triolo 41. **SS:** Kone 1, Lockery 3, Ngoepe 15, Paul 32, Triolo 17, Wood 9. **OF:** Basabe 2, Citta 9, Davis 5, Fraizer 35, Gorski 44, Kinneman 55, Mangieri 5, Matthiessen 17, Pie 4, Reyes 1, Sabol 40, Villegas 18.

BRISTOL PIRATES
APPALACHIAN LEAGUE

Batting	B-T	HT	WT	DOB	AVG	vLH	vRH	G	AB	R	H	2B	3B	HR	RBI	BB	HBP	SH	SF	SO	SB	CS	SLG	OBP
Acuna, Francisco	R-R	5-7	150	1-12-00	.293	.413	.252	53	181	31	53	20	1	1	30	13	9	4	4	34	9	5	.431	.362
Bissonette, Josh	R-R	6-0	185	11-1-96	.266	.302	.255	50	188	26	50	13	2	0	25	20	3	3	2	28	6	2	.356	.343
Citta, Brendt	R-R	6-2	180	7-12-96	.262	.263	.261	18	65	14	17	4	1	2	15	11	2	0	0	16	2	1	.446	.385
Dotel, Mariano	B-R	5-10	155	1-4-00	.167	.250	.125	5	12	1	2	1	0	0	1	0	0	0	0	5	0	0	.250	.167
Eusebio, Jean	L-R	6-1	170	8-22-00	.226	.087	.266	35	102	15	23	3	1	2	17	18	1	2	1	25	4	5	.333	.344
Fajardo, Yoyner	L-R	6-0	179	4-6-99	.348	.500	.316	12	46	7	16	1	0	0	7	1	2	0	1	7	2	0	.370	.380
Fishback, Mason	R-R	6-1	190	9-19-94	.125	.000	.250	2	8	0	1	0	0	0	0	0	0	0	0	5	0	0	.125	.125
Gilbert, Marshall	R-R	6-0	203	2-21-97	.226	.143	.239	16	53	6	12	0	1	0	4	4	0	1	0	21	0	0	.264	.281
Goforth, Ethan	R-R	5-10	190	6-25-97	.226	.000	.275	20	62	5	14	3	0	2	6	1	5	0	0	19	0	2	.371	.294
Inoa, Samuel	R-R	5-10	211	10-6-98	.289	.350	.270	27	83	12	24	2	0	3	10	7	2	0	0	29	3	3	.422	.359
Medina, Joseivin	L-L	6-4	222	2-2-00	.290	.111	.345	13	38	2	11	0	1	0	4	1	0	0	1	14	0	0	.342	.300
Morrow, Matt	L-R	5-10	180	1-9-96	.295	.222	.311	41	146	24	43	9	0	0	18	13	2	0	1	18	5	1	.356	.358
Murray, Chase	L-R	6-0	188	6-3-98	.221	.290	.200	35	136	16	30	4	0	2	20	7	1	1	1	34	6	3	.294	.262
Ordonez, Ernny	R-R	6-2	210	1-17-99	.230	.206	.238	37	139	22	32	8	0	1	17	14	2	1	1	39	2	1	.309	.308
Rivero, Daniel	R-R	6-1	191	1-22-01	.270	.265	.272	47	159	19	43	5	0	1	24	13	2	5	0	29	4	9	.321	.333
Shackelford, Aaron	L-R	5-10	205	10-16-96	.274	.245	.282	53	212	32	58	18	2	8	36	20	1	1	0	54	1	3	.491	.339
Snider, Jake	L-R	6-1	190	5-19-98	.300	.417	.279	21	80	17	24	1	1	1	7	17	1	0	0	18	3	1	.375	.429
Valdez, Jesus	R-R	6-0	175	12-29-97	.292	.250	.304	55	209	38	61	12	1	5	34	21	8	0	1	42	7	4	.431	.377
Villegas, Fernando	R-R	5-10	176	6-28-98	.319	.313	.321	18	72	16	23	8	0	1	9	5	1	0	0	10	1	0	.472	.372
Wilson, Eli	R-R	6-2	190	7-6-98	.235	.293	.212	44	145	31	34	7	0	4	20	23	6	1	3	30	1	0	.366	.356
Wright, Jake	L-L	5-9	195	9-5-97	.241	.188	.254	27	87	17	21	6	0	0	12	.12	8	0	3	25	4	1	.310	.373

Pitching	B-T	HT	WT	DOB	W	L	ERA	G	GS	CG	SV	IP	H	R	ER	HR	BB	SO	AVG	vLH	vRH	K/9	BB/9
Abernathy, Samson	R-R	6-0	195	4-19-96	1	3	2.52	17	0	0	8	25	15	10	7	1	12	33	.171	.162	.177	11.88	4.32
Arrieta, Luis	R-R	6-2	180	6-21-99	3	1	5.73	13	0	0	1	22	21	20	14	2	20	18	.259	.184	.326	7.36	8.18
Bellomy, Bear	R-R	6-4	205	11-29-96	0	0	0.00	7	0	0	2	11	11	1	0	0	1	17	.256	.227	.286	13.91	0.82
Camacho, Wilger	R-R	6-4	185	10-16-97	0	1	9.00	2	0	0	0	1	2	1	1	0	2	1	.400	.250	1.000	9.00	18.00
Dandeneau, C.J.	R-R	6-0	215	5-7-96	1	2	2.83	14	0	0	0	29	25	9	9	1	5	31	.227	.283	.188	9.73	1.57
De La Cruz, Saul	R-R	6-4	174	10-26-97	2	0	1.88	8	0	0	0	14	8	5	3	2	5	20	.163	.125	.200	12.56	3.14
Dicent, Lizardy	R-R	6-3	178	2-11-97	1	0	9.00	4	0	0	0	6	6	6	6	1	5	5	.250	.214	.300	7.50	7.50
Eardensohn, Matt	R-R	6-3	190	5-13-96	1	2	3.63	7	0	0	1	17	20	9	7	1	2	16	.299	.286	.313	8.31	1.04
Florencio, Adrian	R-R	6-6	205	10-11-98	2	1	4.75	11	11	0	0	47	51	28	25	7	24	38	.282	.264	.298	7.23	4.56
Florez, Santiago	R-R	6-5	222	5-9-00	2	2	3.46	10	10	1	0	42	35	19	16	4	21	36	.226	.225	.226	7.78	4.54
Garcia, Oliver	R-R	6-3	213	1-8-98	0	1	2.57	9	0	0	2	14	16	5	4	0	4	20	.281	.310	.250	12.86	2.57
Gong, Hai-Cheng	R-R	6-2	168	12-28-98	0	0	27.00	1	0	0	0	1	3	3	3	0	2	1	.500	.500	.500	9.00	18.00
Maldonado, Jose	R-R	6-2	198	1-17-99	4	6	4.34	11	11	0	0	46	39	24	22	3	26	40	.238	.229	.245	7.88	5.12
Mateo, Oliver	R-R	6-2	170	11-7-97	0	0	54.00	1	0	0	0	0	0	2	2	0	2	1	.000	--	.000	27.00	54.00
McGough, Trey	L-L	6-3	195	3-29-98	2	0	1.04	9	0	0	1	17	13	3	2	0	5	26	.197	.143	.222	13.50	2.60
Medina, Joseivin	L-L	6-4	222	2-2-00	0	0	18.00	1	0	0	0	1	2	2	2	0	2	2	.400	.333	.500	18.00	0.00
Mendoza, Dante	R-R	6-5	186	12-16-98	0	2	5.82	11	11	0	0	43	38	30	28	6	28	39	.230	.222	.240	8.10	5.82
Ortiz, Luis	R-R	6-2	163	1-27-99	2	2	4.09	11	11	0	0	51	48	31	23	4	24	37	.246	.242	.250	6.57	4.26
Reyes, Yoelvis	L-L	6-2	192	12-10-99	4	1	5.28	16	1	0	2	46	47	31	27	5	15	40	.266	.250	.273	7.83	2.93
Rosario, Yordi	R-R	6-2	185	1-30-99	3	0	2.87	19	0	0	1	31	27	10	10	3	4	33	.227	.269	.194	9.48	1.15
Roth, Alex	R-R	6-5	220	12-9-97	1	2	3.32	13	0	0	4	19	16	9	7	0	7	24	.225	.172	.262	11.37	3.32
Santana, Enrique	R-R	5-11	190	9-23-97	2	1	4.44	16	0	0	0	24	28	14	12	2	11	35	.292	.392	.178	12.95	4.07
Thomas, Tahnaj	R-R	6-4	190	6-16-99	2	3	3.17	12	12	0	0	48	40	22	17	5	14	59	.217	.171	.250	10.99	2.61
Troutman, Ryan	R-R	6-1	205	12-25-96	1	3	5.87	14	0	0	2	23	27	16	15	4	12	26	.278	.217	.333	10.17	4.70
Vega, Yandy	R-R	6-0	160	12-2-98	0	0	10.80	1	0	0	0	2	2	2	2	0	2	1	.333	.000	.400	5.40	10.80

Fielding

C: Fishback 1, Gilbert 8, Goforth 19, Wilson 42. **1B:** Citta 3, Gilbert 5, Inoa 15, Morrow 13, Ordonez 37. **2B:** Acuna 4, Bissonette 46, Dotel 2, Fajardo 4, Morrow 1, Shackelford 6, Valdez 7. **3B:** Acuna 1, Gilbert 2, Morrow 19, Shackelford 35, Valdez 11. **SS:** Acuna 43, Bissonette 4, Dotel 2, Valdez 19. **OF:** Acuna 4, Citta 16, Dotel 1, Eusebio 34, Fajardo 4, Medina 13, Morrow 1, Murray 31, Rivero 47, Shackelford 1, Snider 18, Villegas 16, Wright 25.

GCL PIRATES
GULF COAST LEAGUE

Batting	B-T	HT	WT	DOB	AVG	vLH	vRH	G	AB	R	H	2B	3B	HR	RBI	BB	HBP	SH	SF	SO	SB	CS	SLG	OBP
Alvarez, Andres	R-R	5-10	175	3-29-97	.235	.364	.192	38	132	15	31	5	2	1	21	15	5	1	0	29	3	2	.326	.336
Amaral, Daniel	R-R	5-11	180	3-7-97	.286	.333	.250	2	7	2	2	0	0	0	0	1	1	0	0	1	2	0	.286	.444
Angulo, Daniel	L-R	5-10	164	8-10-98	.230	.143	.264	27	74	8	17	3	0	0	5	8	2	1	0	11	1	3	.270	.321
Barrios, Edgar	R-R	5-9	145	7-20-00	.186	.250	.135	19	41	5	6	0	0	0	5	5	0	1	1	13	1	1	.146	.234
Basabe, Angel	L-L	6-0	153	12-12-00	.210	.050	.242	36	119	9	25	5	3	0	11	9	3	1	2	30	4	2	.303	.278
Bowen, Jase	R-R	6-1	190	9-2-00	.223	.258	.212	36	130	15	29	4	4	0	7	14	1	1	1	35	5	2	.315	.301
Canache, Carlos	R-R	6-1	170	11-4-00	.209	.167	.224	34	91	8	19	3	1	1	3	12	2	2	1	22	3	4	.297	.311
Cruz, Oneil	L-R	6-7	175	10-4-98	.600	.600	.600	3	10	0	6	1	0	0	1	1	0	0	0	1	1	0	.700	.636
Dixon, Jasiah	R-R	6-0	180	8-31-01	.329	.333	.328	22	73	12	24	5	1	0	7	10	1	0	0	11	8	3	.425	.417

PITTSBURGH PIRATES

	B-T	HT	WT	DOB	AVG	vLH	vRH	G	AB	R	H	2B	3B	HR	RBI	BB	HBP	SH	SF	SO	SB	CS	SLG	OBP
Dotel, Mariano	R-R	5-10	155	1-4-00	.103	.000	.136	10	29	3	3	0	0	0	0	2	0	0	0	8	1	0	.103	.161
Fajardo, Yoyner	L-R	6-0	179	4-6-99	.337	.429	.303	28	104	14	35	3	0	0	10	9	3	0	3	11	16	4	.365	.395
Foster, Kaleb	L-R	5-11	210	10-24-96	.182	.250	.167	32	88	8	16	6	0	1	8	17	12	1	1	34	1	0	.284	.381
Garland, Nick	R-R	6-1	200	11-3-95	.063	.000	.083	6	16	0	1	0	0	0	0	2	3	3	1	0	3	0	0	.063	.318
Marcos, Norkis	R-R	6-0	170	5-26-01	.239	.225	.245	43	142	22	34	3	2	2	11	11	1	2	0	50	12	4	.331	.299
Melendez, Jose	R-R	5-10	196	9-29-99	.273	.333	.250	6	11	2	3	1	0	0	0	0	1	0	0	4	0	0	.364	.333
Melfor, Tilsaimy	R-R	6-0	183	2-14-01	.237	.125	.279	28	59	7	14	0	0	0	3	4	3	0	1	20	1	0	.237	.313
Pie, Juan	L-L	6-2	170	4-1-01	.231	.350	.208	38	121	14	28	2	3	2	16	13	2	2	1	27	6	5	.347	.314
Rosado, Emilson	R-R	6-3	229	2-11-01	.227	.175	.250	38	128	11	29	7	2	2	13	14	1	0	1	43	0	1	.359	.306
Shockley, Dylan	R-R	5-11	195	4-10-97	.183	.118	.200	26	82	5	15	2	0	0	10	6	3	1	4	28	1	0	.207	.253
Siani, Sammy	L-L	6-0	195	12-14-00	.241	.212	.250	39	133	21	32	3	3	0	9	26	3	0	2	41	5	0	.308	.372
Villegas, Fernando	R-R	5-10	176	6-28-98	.000	.000	.000	4	9	4	0	0	0	0	1	4	0	0	1	6	0	0	.000	.286
Walker, Deion	R-R	6-4	180	8-20-01	.270	.294	.263	22	74	5	20	5	3	1	9	5	2	1	1	18	0	1	.460	.329

Pitching	B-T	HT	WT	DOB	W	L	ERA	G	GS	CG	SV	IP	H	R	ER	HR	BB	SO	AVG	vLH	vRH	K/9	BB/9
Basil, Willy	R-R	6-4	189	4-27-97	2	2	3.97	16	0	0	1	23	17	11	10	1	19	28	.205	.115	.246	11.12	7.54
Camacho, Wilger	R-R	6-5	185	10-16-97	1	1	5.54	11	0	0	3	13	9	11	8	1	13	9	.209	.267	.179	6.23	9.00
Dandeneau, C.J.	R-R	6-0	215	5-7-96	0	1	0.00	2	0	0	0	3	1	3	0	0	1	3	.091	.250	.000	9.00	3.00
De Dios, Arlinthon	R-R	6-2	183	1-24-00	2	4	3.54	10	10	0	0	41	47	22	16	4	17	35	.294	.250	.315	7.75	3.76
De La Cruz, Saul	R-R	6-4	174	10-26-97	0	1	0.00	7	0	0	0	10	5	2	0	0	1	11	.147	.167	.136	9.90	0.90
De Los Santos, Enmanuel	R-R	6-4	163	10-14-00	1	0	2.51	4	4	0	0	14	12	4	4	0	8	15	.231	.500	.150	9.42	5.02
Dicent, Lizardy	R-R	6-3	178	2-11-97	0	0	3.38	3	0	0	0	3	4	1	1	1	2	4	.364	.667	.250	13.50	6.75
Eardensohn, Matt	R-R	6-3	190	5-13-96	1	0	0.00	4	0	0	0	5	4	0	0	0	1	3	.211	.143	.250	5.06	1.69
Escobar, Elvis	L-L	5-8	181	9-6-94	0	0	5.40	2	0	0	0	2	2	1	1	0	2	2	.286	--	.286	10.80	10.80
Flynn, Michael	R-R	6-4	185	8-7-96	0	0	2.25	3	0	0	0	4	4	1	1	0	0	4	.250	.667	.154	9.00	0.00
Garcia, Mario	R-R	6-1	183	12-27-98	0	1	6.00	11	5	0	1	27	29	18	18	2	22	23	.266	.345	.238	7.67	7.33
Gong, Hai-Cheng	R-R	6-2	168	12-28-98	0	2	6.14	11	0	0	0	22	33	16	15	1	6	16	.333	.148	.403	6.55	2.45
Gonzalez, Domingo	R-R	6-0	185	9-27-99	1	3	3.58	9	8	0	0	38	30	19	15	1	14	43	.211	.233	.202	10.27	3.35
Harbin, Ryan	R-R	6-4	195	8-6-01	0	3	9.31	4	3	0	0	10	11	10	10	1	8	7	.282	.000	.314	6.52	7.45
Josephina, Orsen	R-R	6-2	190	9-8-95	3	1	3.00	12	0	0	1	15	11	6	5	1	2	20	.193	.083	.222	12.00	1.20
Koehler, Tom	R-R	6-3	235	6-29-86	0	1	27.00	1	1	0	0	1	2	2	2	0	0	1	.500	.000	1.000	13.50	0.00
Ortiz, Estalin	L-L	6-4	213	11-20-98	2	2	5.93	11	0	0	0	27	25	21	18	2	21	27	.229	.278	.220	8.89	6.91
Priester, Quinn	R-R	6-3	195	9-15-00	1	1	3.03	8	7	0	0	33	29	15	11	1	10	37	.238	.333	.169	10.19	2.76
Ramos, Wilkin	R-R	6-5	165	10-31-00	0	2	6.39	4	4	0	0	13	14	10	9	1	10	8	.292	.333	.278	5.68	7.11
Reynoso, Starlyn	L-L	6-0	168	7-29-97	0	2	6.85	13	1	0	0	24	28	19	18	1	22	15	.308	.423	.262	5.70	8.37
Rosario, Julio	R-R	6-2	200	6-5-99	0	0	6.04	13	0	0	0	22	22	20	15	2	16	15	.256	.231	.267	6.04	6.45
Ross, Daniel	R-R	6-5	220	1-5-96	2	2	5.79	13	0	0	0	14	14	12	9	0	14	15	.250	.188	.275	9.64	9.00
Suero, Angel	R-R	6-4	202	8-27-99	1	1	5.02	16	0	0	3	14	12	10	8	1	16	20	.222	.000	.279	12.56	10.05
Sweeney, Jake	R-L	6-7	240	6-14-00	0	2	3.45	13	0	0	0	16	8	6	6	0	15	12	.148	.091	.163	6.89	8.62
Torres, Bryan	R-R	6-2	211	4-12-01	0	3	6.75	14	3	0	0	36	47	28	27	7	10	28	.315	.356	.298	7.00	2.50
Vega, Yandy	R-R	6-0	160	12-2-98	1	1	7.65	14	0	0	0	20	25	17	17	3	10	18	.321	.345	.306	8.10	4.50

Fielding

C: Angulo 26, Foster 5, Melendez 5, Shockley 25. **1B:** Canache 7, Foster 28, Garland 6, Melfor 1, Rosado 13, Shockley 3. **2B:** Alvarez 4, Barrios 10, Bowen 12, Canache 2, Dotel 3, Fajardo 18, Marcos 8, Melfor 1. **3B:** Alvarez 16, Barrios 7, Dotel 6, Fajardo 1, Melfor 13, Rosado 19. **SS:** Alvarez 19, Barrios 2, Cruz 3, Dotel 2, Marcos 33, Melfor 1. **OF:** Amaral 2, Angulo 1, Basabe 26, Bowen 21, Canache 22, Dixon 21, Fajardo 5, Melfor 1, Pie 14, Siani 37, Villegas 4, Walker 17.

DSL PIRATES · ROOKIE
DOMINICAN SUMMER LEAGUE

Batting	B-T	HT	WT	DOB	AVG	vLH	vRH	G	AB	R	H	2B	3B	HR	RBI	BB	HBP	SH	SF	SO	SB	CS	SLG	OBP
Apostel, Shendrik	R-R	6-5	245	4-24-00	.256	.385	.232	27	82	16	21	1	0	5	16	21	3	0	1	18	0	0	.451	.421
Arroyo, Carlos	R-R	5-9	170	7-11-01	.303	.308	.301	44	162	38	49	11	1	1	29	10	5	2	4	10	16	7	.401	.354
Baez, Darwin	R-R	6-0	186	11-6-00	.263	.158	.283	59	236	24	62	16	1	5	44	15	4	6	2	40	20	6	.403	.313
Bastardo, Franrielis	R-R	6-2	196	7-19-02	.204	.083	.236	33	113	21	23	6	0	4	15	14	5	0	2	23	0	2	.363	.313
Berroa, Jose	B-R	6-0	165	9-8-01	.254	.242	.256	56	189	37	48	6	3	0	21	27	5	4	1	39	11	2	.318	.360
Campana, Sergio	R-R	6-1	160	3-29-02	.281	.276	.282	45	171	32	48	4	0	0	18	15	8	1	2	44	24	5	.374	.362
Carrasco, Eudys	R-R	6-1	180	10-4-01	.191	.233	.173	37	105	14	20	7	0	2	15	11	2	1	2	42	0	1	.314	.275
Ceballo, Yeison	R-R	5-11	175	2-20-01	.379	.333	.391	10	29	6	11	0	1	0	6	2	0	0	0	6	0	0	.448	.419
Chivilli, Orlando	R-R	6-0	175	5-4-02	.242	.192	.255	39	132	19	32	4	2	3	15	18	7	0	1	53	0	1	.371	.361
Custodio, Jauri	R-R	5-10	162	9-21-01	.324	.323	.324	53	210	39	68	8	3	4	34	10	3	1	3	18	15	4	.448	.358
Escalante, Rafael	R-R	5-11	160	9-13-01	.207	.231	.203	33	87	19	18	5	2	3	12	15	9	0	1	13	2	4	.414	.375
Gavilan, Osvaldo	L-L	5-11	150	10-10-01	.200	.138	.214	37	155	23	31	2	5	2	26	9	5	0	1	27	3	1	.316	.265
Hernandez, Jommer	R-R	5-11	181	10-20-01	.317	.269	.328	46	142	28	45	5	5	0	22	19	3	1	1	25	3	2	.423	.406
Hernandez, Luis	R-R	5-9	150	9-6-00	.232	.111	.266	29	82	11	19	1	0	0	10	6	5	1	2	19	3	0	.244	.316
Jerez, Juan	R-R	6-0	160	11-28-01	.272	.233	.278	60	228	31	62	12	6	7	49	14	6	1	5	48	6	6	.469	.324
Jerez, Mario	R-R	6-3	185	9-19-01	.305	.333	.300	27	82	18	25	2	2	0	13	10	4	1	2	24	3	0	.378	.398
Lopez, Dariel	R-R	6-1	183	2-7-02	.341	.464	.317	47	167	41	57	10	4	2	33	14	5	0	2	30	5	2	.485	.404
Mateo, Bryan	L-L	6-2	180	10-20-98	.283	.280	.283	48	138	29	39	3	2	2	22	16	4	3	3	34	5	3	.377	.367
Matos, Omar	B-R	6-0	170	5-27-00	.233	.214	.236	44	103	19	24	3	2	0	10	24	0	1	0	30	13	1	.301	.378
Mena, Juan	R-R	5-11	176	8-3-00	.292	.095	.353	30	89	14	26	3	1	1	14	10	2	1	0	14	0	2	.382	.376
Mojica, Alexander	R-R	6-1	195	8-2-02	.351	.290	.364	55	174	37	61	14	1	8	46	37	4	0	3	34	2	1	.581	.468
Montero, Eliazer	R-R	5-10	157	9-15-00	.259	.286	.254	51	147	28	38	8	5	0	16	4	1	1		35	14	4	.381	.345
Nadal, Deivis	B-R	5-11	150	2-8-02	.294	.275	.299	54	194	41	57	7	2	3	29	26	8	5	3	41	10	6	.397	.394
Nolasco, Rodolfo	R-R	6-1	175	9-23-01	.302	.289	.305	54	199	43	60	13	3	5	34	16	8	0	2	26	3	4	.472	.373

	B-T	HT	WT	DOB	AVG	vLH	vRH	G	AB	R	H	2B	3B	HR	RBI	BB	HBP	SH	SF	SO	SB	CS	OBP	SLG
Nova, Fleury	R-R	5-11	160	1-17-01	.328	.304	.333	37	131	26	43	5	1	0	11	11	1	1	0	28	12	2	.382	.385
Planchart, Geovanny	R-R	6-0	176	9-17-01	.368	.250	.389	32	106	21	39	0	2	0	18	12	1	1	1	9	0	2	.406	.433
Polanco, Jhan	B-R	5-11	175	11-4-00	.252	.154	.274	43	139	25	35	10	0	2	11	30	1	1	1	16	1	0	.367	.386
Quintero, Francisco	R-R	5-10	167	9-19-00	.289	.273	.293	20	52	7	15	3	2	0	4	8	0	1	1	9	4	2	.423	.377
Ramirez, Eduar	R-R	5-11	200	6-4-01	.279	.200	.293	24	68	16	19	4	0	1	13	19	2	0	0	13	2	1	.382	.449
Romero, Randy	R-R	5-11	155	8-10-99	.376	.468	.351	62	218	52	82	13	5	1	35	17	3	1	6	15	36	1	.495	.418
Romero, Rayber	B-R	5-10	155	5-28-02	.314	.333	.309	31	105	29	33	3	0	2	22	19	5	3	1	16	14	4	.400	.439
Sanchez, Ronny	R-R	5-11	191	7-22-02	.236	.231	.237	38	127	22	30	6	0	1	9	10	9	0	0	30	3	2	.307	.336
Susana, Bladimir	B-R	5-9	154	5-20-00	.248	.227	.253	44	117	18	29	0	0	0	13	8	3	2	0	18	6	3	.248	.313
Tejeda, Luis	R-R	5-11	170	8-26-02	.250	.293	.238	49	192	21	48	8	2	1	14	11	5	2	1	45	5	5	.328	.306
Tello, Luis	R-R	6-0	160	6-22-01	.273	.250	.277	54	176	33	48	5	1	1	17	15	10	1	4	24	8	2	.330	.356
Urbina, Fabian	L-R	5-8	175	10-25-01	.296	.364	.279	20	54	10	16	3	2	0	9	0	0	0	0	11	3	1	.426	.397
Valerio, Stiwatt	R-R	6-2	186	9-9-00	.000	.000	.000	2	4	0	0	0	0	0	0	0	0	0	0	2	0	0	.000	.000

Pitching	B-T	HT	WT	DOB	W	L	ERA	G	GS	CG	SV	IP	H	R	ER	HR	BB	SO	AVG	vLH	vRH	K/9	BB/9
Amaya, Jose	L-L	6-1	169	2-28-00	10	1	2.97	18	0	0	0	39	26	14	13	1	27	35	.186	.105	.198	8.01	6.18
Blanco, Joel	R-R	6-5	200	1-14-02	0	0	1.93	6	0	0	1	9	9	3	2	1	4	12	.257	.200	.280	11.57	3.86
Campos, Carlos	R-R	6-1	169	5-10-01	5	2	4.57	19	0	0	1	43	39	29	22	5	15	32	.227	.246	.215	6.65	3.12
Del Rosario, Joelvis	R-R	5-11	170	4-16-01	1	1	3.40	12	11	0	0	50	47	25	19	0	16	43	.240	.232	.246	7.69	2.86
Diaz, Miguel	R-R	6-0	160	8-19-01	3	3	3.24	17	0	0	1	33	21	20	12	2	22	38	.174	.211	.167	10.26	5.94
Disla, Kelvin	R-R	6-0	170	7-5-01	2	1	1.57	12	0	0	1	23	20	10	4	0	4	27	.217	.286	.175	10.57	1.57
Dominguez, Argenys	R-R	6-3	170	5-10-01	0	0	19.58	14	0	0	0	13	24	32	29	0	26	18	.400	.471	.308	12.15	17.55
Echarry, Oscar	R-R	6-3	175	1-6-99	0	1	8.53	7	0	0	0	6	7	9	6	0	5	5	.269	.250	.286	7.11	7.11
Garcia, Darvin	R-R	6-3	170	4-25-99	1	0	3.97	6	0	0	1	11	12	7	5	0	5	15	.261	.364	.229	11.91	3.97
Garcia, Mario	R-R	6-1	183	12-27-98	4	0	2.38	6	0	0	0	23	22	6	6	0	6	31	.253	.238	.267	12.31	2.38
Gonzalez, Antonio	R-R	6-3	190	1-14-00	2	3	2.11	15	0	0	1	38	30	18	9	1	27	42	.221	.233	.211	9.86	6.34
Gonzalez, Domingo	R-R	6-0	185	9-27-99	5	0	0.36	7	0	0	1	25	12	1	1	0	3	33	.146	.318	.083	11.72	1.07
Gonzalez, Luis	R-R	6-2	191	9-6-98	2	0	5.22	19	0	0	4	29	26	19	17	1	31	41	.243	.226	.250	12.58	9.51
Hernandez, Luis	R-R	5-9	150	9-6-00	0	0	0.00	1	0	0	1	1	0	0	0	0	0	1	.000	.000	.000	9.00	0.00
Hodge, Francisco	L-L	6-3	209	5-23-00	6	0	1.64	16	3	0	1	49	43	17	9	0	24	44	.232	.296	.222	8.03	4.38
Jimenez, Carlos	R-R	6-2	140	7-14-02	1	0	2.54	10	0	0	0	39	36	13	11	2	17	45	.247	.206	.259	10.38	3.92
Linarez, Valentin	R-R	6-5	226	2-14-00	5	3	2.28	12	12	0	0	55	43	17	14	0	14	55	.214	.224	.207	8.95	2.28
Maldonado, Andy	R-R	6-4	196	7-21-02	0	3	8.62	12	12	0	0	31	30	34	30	1	37	18	.248	.231	.261	5.17	10.63
Martinez, Wilbur	R-R	6-2	162	8-3-01	0	0	8.86	17	0	0	1	21	28	26	21	1	16	19	.329	.448	.268	8.02	6.75
Matos, Omar	B-R	6-0	170	5-27-00	0	0	0.00	1	0	0	0	1	0	0	0	0	2	1	.000	.000	.000	9.00	18.00
Mejia, Enmanuel	R-R	5-11	185	12-22-98	2	1	1.74	18	0	0	7	21	10	6	4	0	7	37	.137	.182	.118	16.11	3.05
Mendez, Adrian	L-L	6-1	160	3-7-02	0	3	7.01	13	13	0	0	44	49	42	34	1	33	32	.290	.167	.310	6.60	6.80
Mezquita, Felipe	R-R	6-4	174	10-4-01	0	1	3.83	14	14	0	0	49	40	26	21	0	40	45	.229	.198	.195	8.21	7.30
Montero, Johan	R-R	6-3	187	8-26-99	6	0	2.57	17	0	0	2	42	38	14	12	3	19	35	.252	.180	.277	7.50	4.07
Montout, Wandi	R-R	6-5	190	3-21-97	2	1	3.03	10	4	0	3	30	25	12	10	0	11	29	.234	.227	.238	8.80	3.34
Mora, Raul	L-L	6-3	145	12-9-99	2	1	2.19	12	0	0	0	25	14	10	6	0	17	21	.177	.214	.169	7.66	6.20
Ortega, Jordy	R-R	6-2	184	10-17-99	0	2	3.86	19	0	0	1	28	23	18	12	1	13	23	.215	.256	.191	7.39	4.18
Peralta, Luis	L-L	5-11	170	1-6-01	2	2	2.01	14	6	0	1	40	35	13	9	3	16	34	.241	.290	.228	7.59	3.57
Peralta, Miguel	R-R	6-2	212	4-20-99	0	1	10.97	9	0	0	0	11	10	22	13	0	23	11	.233	.235	.231	9.28	19.41
Polonia, Eddison	R-R	6-5	198	10-10-98	1	1	3.38	6	0	0	0	11	5	4	4	0	6	11	.293	.364	.267	9.28	5.06
Ramos, Jorge	R-R	6-0	150	6-5-02	3	1	3.04	12	12	0	0	53	49	24	18	1	22	46	.246	.220	.257	7.76	3.71
Rosario, Axel	R-R	6-5	192	5-22-00	0	2	7.56	13	0	0	0	17	15	17	14	0	25	23	.254	.267	.250	12.42	13.50
Rosario, Braham	L-L	6-1	198	2-18-00	1	1	2.59	13	12	0	0	59	51	20	17	0	20	61	.225	.212	.229	9.31	3.05
Santos, Yeison	L-L	6-2	170	4-16-01	1	6	3.09	19	0	0	0	44	42	20	15	2	13	44	.243	.147	.266	9.07	2.68
Sosa, Listher	R-R	6-4	208	9-6-01	3	2	2.72	11	11	0	0	53	40	21	16	3	15	51	.207	.247	.183	8.66	2.55
Susana, Bladimir	B-R	5-9	154	5-20-00	0	0	0.00	3	0	0	0	3	2	0	0	0	1	1	.200	.500	.125	3.38	3.38
Toribio, Miguel	R-R	6-1	165	12-8-01	6	1	1.59	14	3	0	1	40	34	16	7	0	18	34	.235	.220	.240	7.71	4.08
Umana, Sergio	R-R	6-0	175	5-21-00	9	1	2.39	13	13	0	0	64	63	22	17	2	8	59	.259	.262	.258	8.30	1.13
Valdez, Wilkin	R-R	6-5	210	7-14-01	2	1	5.74	17	0	0	0	27	23	20	17	1	32	18	.232	.234	.231	6.08	10.80
Velette, Raydel	R-R	6-6	196	6-20-01	3	2	3.22	12	7	0	0	36	30	17	13	4	30	30	.240	.200	.267	7.43	7.43
Yes, Jarlin	R-R	6-4	210	3-7-00	0	4	6.43	9	0	0	2	14	18	18	10	0	9	12	.340	.208	.448	7.71	5.79

Fielding

C: Baez 21, Ceballo 2, Escalante 22, Hernandez 20, Hernandez 28, Mena 8, Planchart 27, Polanco 39, Urbina 1. **1B:** Apostel 24, Arroyo 1, Baez 33, Carrasco 17, Escalante 14, Hernandez 22, Lopez 7, Mateo 23, Matos 6, Mena 17, Mojica 2, Ramirez 5, Tello 2. **2B:** Arroyo 33, Escalante 1, Hernandez 1, Jerez 31, Matos 22, Montero 10, Nadal 17, Quintero 10, Romero 15, Susana 4, Tejeda 6, Urbina 3. **3B:** Arroyo 12, Carrasco 14, Chivilli 22, Escalante 1, Lopez 3, Matos 7, Mojica 36, Montero 22, Quintero 11, Romero 6, Sanchez 22, Tejeda 1, Urbina 17. **SS:** Arroyo 1, Jerez 16, Lopez 32, Matos 8, Montero 8, Nadal 33, Quintero 1, Romero 2, Susana 8, Tejeda 40. **OF:** Arroyo 7, Bastardo 27, Berroa 27, Campana 43, Carrasco 1, Custodio 53, Gavilan 34, Jerez 24, Mateo 29, Matos 2, Mena 1, Montero 10, Nolasco 38, Nova 34, Romero 60, Romero 8, Sanchez 7, Susana 1, Tello 50, Valerio 2.

St. Louis Cardinals

SEASON IN A SENTENCE: After a three-year postseason hiatus, the Cardinals returned to the top of the National League Central powered by offseason acquisition Paul Goldschmidt and the continued growth of burgeoning ace Jack Flaherty.

HIGH POINT: Needing a win on the season's final day to clinch the division title, Flaherty pitched seven scoreless innings to lead the Cardinals to a 9-0 romp over the rival Cubs, securing the Cardinals' first division title since 2015.

LOW POINT: The Cardinals mustered just six runs in the National League Championship Series and were swept out of the playoffs by the Nationals. The capper came in a miserable Game 4 in which they trailed 7-0 after the first inning.

NOTABLE ROOKIES: Righthander Dakota Hudson won a rotation spot out of spring training and ranked second among Cardinals starters—behind only Flaherty—with a 3.35 ERA. Infielder Tommy Edman provided an injection of energy as he took over the Cardinals' starting third base job and hit .304 while primarily batting first or second in the lineup. Ryan Helsley emerged as one of the Cardinals' most reliable relievers with a 2.95 ERA and a fastball that reached 102 mph, and outfielder Lane Thomas provided power and stellar defense off the bench before going down with a season-ending wrist fracture. Outfielder Randy Arozarena and lefthander Genesis Cabrera made their major league debuts and showed enough in limited time to earn spots on the Cardinals' postseason roster.

KEY TRANSACTIONS: The Cardinals made waves before the season when they acquired Goldschmidt for righthander Luke Weaver, catcher Carson Kelly, infield prospect Andy Young and a compensatory draft pick. Goldschmidt struggled early but still hit .260 and with a team-leading 34 home runs and .821 OPS. They also signed lefthander Andrew Miller to a two-year contract before the season, but he battled his control and posted a 4.45 ERA, his highest since 2011.

DOWN ON THE FARM: Outfielder Dylan Carlson won MVP of the Double-A Texas League and finished the year at Triple-A in a breakout season. He hit 26 home runs and stole 20 bases, becoming one of only 10 players to go 20-20 in the minors in 2019. Rookie-level Johnson City won the Appalachian League championship, with outfielder William Jimenez hitting the tie-breaking, two-run double in the seventh inning of the deciding Game 3.

OPENING DAY PAYROLL: $150,367,083 (10th).

ORGANIZATION LEADERS

Batting		*Minimum 250 AB
MAJORS		
* AVG	Tommy Edman	.304
* OPS	Tommy Edman	.850
HR	Paul Goldschmidt	34
RBI	Paul Goldschmidt	97
MINORS		
* AVG	Randy Arozarena, Springfield, Memphis	.344
* OBP	Randy Arozarena, Springfield, Memphis	.431
* SLG	Randy Arozarena, Springfield, Memphis	.571
* OPS	Randy Arozarena, Springfield, Memphis	1.003
R	Adolis Garcia, Memphis	96
H	Dylan Carlson, Springfield, Memphis	143
TB	Dylan Carlson, Springfield, Memphis	265
2B	Luken Baker, Palm Beach	32
3B	Dylan Carlson, Springfield, Memphis	8
HR	Adolis Garcia, Memphis	32
RBI	Adolis Garcia, Memphis	96
BB	John Nogowski, Memphis	69
SO	Adolis Garcia, Memphis	159
SB	John Nogowski, Memphis	33

Pitching		#Minimum 75 IP
MAJORS		
W	Dakota Hudson	16
# ERA	Jack Flaherty	2.75
SO	Jack Flaherty	231
SV	Carlos Martinez	24
MINORS		
W	Johan Oviedo, Palm Beach, Springfield	12
L	Edgar Gonzalez, Palm Beach, Memphis	15
# ERA	Alvaro Seijas, Peoria, Palm Beach	2.81
G	Jesus Cruz, Springfield, Memphis	52
GS	Johan Oviedo, Palm Beach, Springfield	28
GS	Angel Rondon, Palm Beach, Springfield	28
SV	Junior Fernandez, Palm Beach, Springfield, Memphis	11
IP	Tommy Parsons, Peoria, Palm Beach, Springfield, Memphis	166
BB	Johan Oviedo, Palm Beach, Springfield	76
SO	Johan Oviedo, Palm Beach, Springfield	163
# AVG	Daniel Ponce de Leon, Memphis	.203

2019 PERFORMANCE

General Manager: Mike Girsch. **Farm Director:** Gary LaRocque. **Scouting Director:** Randy Flores.

Class	Team	League	W	L	PCT	Finish	Manager
Majors	St. Louis Cardinals	National	91	71	.562	4th (15)	Mike Shildt
Triple-A	Memphis Redbirds	Pacific Coast	69	71	.493	8th (16)	Ben Johnson
Double-A	Springfield Cardinals	Texas	60	80	.429	7th (8)	Joe Kruzel
High A	Palm Beach Cardinals	Florida State	57	73	.438	10th (12)	Dann Bilardello
Low A	Peoria Chiefs	Midwest	54	85	.388	15th (16)	Erick Almonte
Short season	State College Spikes	New York-Penn	39	36	.520	8th (14)	Jose Leon
Rookie	Johnson City Cardinals	Appalachian	35	33	.515	3rd (10)	Roberto Espinoza
Rookie	GCL Cardinals	Gulf Coast	20	34	.370	16th (18)	Josh Lopez
Overall 2019 Minor League Record			334	412	.448	29th (30)	

ORGANIZATION STATISTICS

ST. LOUIS CARDINALS
NATIONAL LEAGUE

Batting	B-T	HT	WT	DOB	AVG	vLH	vRH	G	AB	R	H	2B	3B	HR	RBI	BB	HBP	SH	SF	SO	SB	CS	SLG	OBP
Arozarena, Randy	R-R	5-11	170	2-28-95	.300	.333	.294	19	20	4	6	1	0	1	2	2	1	0	0	4	2	1	.500	.391
Bader, Harrison	R-R	6-0	195	6-3-94	.205	.177	.215	128	347	54	71	14	3	12	39	46	10	1	2	117	11	3	.366	.314
Carpenter, Matt	L-R	6-3	205	11-26-85	.226	.217	.228	129	416	59	94	20	2	15	46	63	7	1	5	129	6	1	.392	.334
DeJong, Paul	R-R	6-0	200	8-2-93	.233	.221	.236	159	583	97	136	31	1	30	78	62	13	0	6	149	9	5	.444	.318
Edman, Tommy	B-R	5-10	180	5-9-95	.304	.321	.298	92	326	59	99	17	7	11	36	16	7	0	0	61	15	1	.500	.350
Fowler, Dexter	B-R	6-5	195	3-22-86	.238	.213	.245	150	487	69	116	24	1	19	67	74	8	1	4	142	8	5	.409	.346
Goldschmidt, Paul	R-R	6-3	225	9-10-87	.260	.269	.258	161	597	97	155	25	1	34	97	78	2	0	3	166	3	1	.476	.346
Gyorko, Jedd	R-R	5-10	215	9-23-88	.196	.133	.220	38	56	5	11	0	0	2	7	6	0	0	0	14	2	0	.304	.274
2-team total (24 Los Angeles)					.174	.135	.200	62	92	6	16	1	0	2	9	9	0	0	0	24	2	0	.250	.248
Hudson, Joe	R-R	6-0	210	5-21-91	.000	--	.000	1	1	0	0	0	0	0	0	0	0	0	0	1	0	0	.000	.000
Knizner, Andrew	R-R	6-1	200	2-3-95	.226	.200	.233	18	53	7	12	2	0	2	7	4	1	0	0	14	2	0	.377	.293
Martinez, Jose	R-R	6-6	215	7-25-88	.270	.329	.254	128	334	45	90	13	2	10	42	35	2	0	2	82	3	0	.410	.341
Molina, Yadier	R-R	5-11	205	7-13-82	.270	.320	.259	113	419	45	113	24	0	10	57	23	5	0	5	58	6	0	.399	.312
Munoz, Yairo	R-R	6-1	201	1-23-95	.267	.282	.263	88	172	20	46	7	1	2	13	7	1	0	1	37	8	3	.355	.298
O'Neill, Tyler	R-R	5-11	210	6-22-95	.262	.269	.261	60	141	18	37	6	0	5	16	10	0	0	0	53	1	0	.411	.311
Ozuna, Marcell	R-R	6-1	225	11-12-90	.241	.217	.246	130	485	80	117	23	1	29	89	62	1	0	1	114	12	2	.472	.328
Ravelo, Rangel	R-R	6-1	225	4-24-92	.205	.167	.212	29	39	4	8	2	0	2	7	3	0	0	1	12	0	0	.410	.256
Robinson, Drew	L-R	6-1	200	4-20-92	.143	--	.143	5	7	1	1	0	0	0	0	0	0	0	0	3	0	0	.143	.143
Sosa, Edmundo	R-R	5-11	170	3-6-96	.250	.000	.286	8	8	2	2	0	0	0	1	1	0	0	0	2	1	0	.250	.400
Thomas, Lane	R-R	6-1	210	8-23-95	.316	.364	.296	34	38	6	12	0	1	4	12	4	2	0	0	8	1	1	.684	.409
Wieters, Matt	B-R	6-5	235	5-21-86	.214	.195	.221	67	168	15	36	4	0	11	27	12	1	0	2	47	1	1	.435	.268
Wong, Kolten	L-R	5-9	185	10-10-90	.285	.288	.283	148	478	61	136	25	4	11	59	47	13	6	5	83	24	4	.423	.361

Pitching	B-T	HT	WT	DOB	W	L	ERA	G	GS	CG	SV	IP	H	R	ER	HR	BB	SO	AVG	vLH	vRH	K/9	BB/9
Brebbia, John	L-R	6-1	185	5-30-90	3	4	3.59	66	0	0	0	73	59	31	29	6	27	87	.216	.225	.212	10.78	3.34
Cabrera, Genesis	L-L	6-2	190	10-10-96	0	2	4.87	13	2	0	1	20	23	16	11	2	11	19	.274	.500	.203	8.41	4.87
Fernandez, Junior	R-R	6-1	180	3-2-97	0	1	5.40	13	0	0	0	12	9	7	7	2	6	16	.205	.100	.235	12.34	4.63
Flaherty, Jack	R-R	6-4	205	10-15-95	11	8	2.75	33	33	0	0	196	135	62	60	25	55	231	.192	.202	.182	10.59	2.52
Gallegos, Giovanny	R-R	6-2	210	8-14-91	3	2	2.31	66	0	0	1	74	44	19	19	9	16	93	.170	.149	.186	11.31	1.95
Gant, John	R-R	6-3	200	8-6-92	11	1	3.66	64	0	0	3	66	51	29	27	4	34	60	.217	.221	.215	8.14	4.61
Gregerson, Luke	L-R	6-3	205	5-14-84	0	0	7.94	6	0	0	0	6	11	5	5	0	1	2	.423	.364	.467	3.18	1.59
Gyorko, Jedd	R-R	5-10	215	9-23-88	0	0	0.00	1	0	0	0	0	0	0	0	0	0	1	.000	--	.000	27.00	0.00
Helsley, Ryan	R-R	6-1	195	7-18-94	2	0	2.95	24	0	0	0	37	34	13	12	5	12	32	.245	.231	.257	7.85	2.95
Hicks, Jordan	R-R	6-2	185	9-6-96	2	2	3.14	29	0	0	14	29	16	10	10	2	11	31	.163	.250	.113	9.73	3.45
Hudson, Dakota	R-R	6-5	215	9-15-94	16	7	3.35	33	32	0	1	175	160	80	65	22	86	136	.245	.260	.232	7.01	4.43
Leone, Dominic	R-R	5-11	210	10-26-91	1	0	5.53	40	0	0	1	41	39	28	25	9	22	46	.250	.243	.256	10.18	4.87
Martinez, Carlos	R-R	6-0	190	9-21-91	4	2	3.17	48	0	0	24	48	39	18	17	2	18	53	.220	.237	.208	9.87	3.35
Mayers, Mike	R-R	6-3	200	12-6-91	0	1	6.63	16	0	0	0	19	21	14	14	3	11	16	.276	.333	.239	7.58	5.21
Mejia, Adalberto	R-L	6-3	195	6-20-93	0	0	9.00	2	0	0	0	3	8	3	3	0	1	2	.500	.667	.400	6.00	3.00
Mikolas, Miles	R-R	6-5	220	8-23-88	9	14	4.16	32	32	1	0	184	193	90	85	27	32	144	.272	.284	.261	7.04	1.57
Miller, Andrew	L-L	6-7	205	5-21-85	5	6	4.45	73	0	0	6	55	45	32	27	11	27	70	.225	.211	.238	11.52	4.45
Ponce de Leon, Daniel	R-R	6-3	200	1-16-92	1	2	3.70	13	8	0	0	49	36	21	20	6	26	52	.207	.164	.234	9.62	4.81
Reyes, Alex	R-R	6-3	175	8-29-94	0	1	15.00	4	0	0	0	3	2	5	5	1	6	1	.200	.000	.333	3.00	18.00
Shreve, Chasen	L-L	6-4	195	7-12-90	1	0	9.00	3	0	0	0	2	2	2	2	0	1	2	.250	.000	.333	9.00	4.50
Wacha, Michael	R-R	6-6	215	7-1-91	6	7	4.76	29	24	0	0	127	143	71	67	26	55	104	.290	.259	.309	7.39	3.91
Wainwright, Adam	R-R	6-7	235	8-30-81	14	10	4.19	31	31	0	0	172	181	83	80	22	64	153	.273	.288	.262	8.02	3.36
Webb, Tyler	L-L	6-5	230	7-20-90	2	1	3.76	65	0	0	1	55	33	23	23	7	23	48	.172	.157	.189	7.85	3.76

Fielding

Catcher	PCT	G	PO	A	E	DP	PB
Knizner	.992	16	121	6	1	3	0
Molina	.999	111	916	30	1	5	4
Wieters	.995	54	379	15	2	5	2

First Base	PCT	G	PO	A	E	DP
Carpenter	1.000	4	14	0	0	1
Goldschmidt	.996	159	1256	111	5	145
Gyorko	1.000	1	2	0	0	0
Knizner	1.000	1	3	0	0	0
Molina	1.000	4	6	0	0	1
Ravelo	1.000	9	35	1	0	2

Second Base	PCT	G	PO	A	E	DP
Edman	.991	29	39	67	1	21
Gyorko	1.000	2	0	4	0	0
Munoz	1.000	4	7	6	0	1
Sosa	1.000	4	1	1	0	0
Wong	.987	147	250	412	9	103

Third Base	PCT	G	PO	A	E	DP
Carpenter	.964	107	55	162	8	16
Edman	.972	55	28	78	3	7
Gyorko	.926	12	6	19	2	1

	PCT	G	PO	A	E	DP
Molina	.000	1	0	0	0	0
Munoz	1.000	21	5	15	0	1

Shortstop	PCT	G	PO	A	E	DP
DeJong	.989	157	211	435	7	119
Munoz	.977	17	12	30	1	7

Outfield	PCT	G	PO	A	E	DP
Arozarena	1.000	11	11	1	0	0

	PCT	G	PO	A	E	DP
Bader	.984	122	239	8	4	4
Edman	.950	13	18	1	1	0
Fowler	.980	140	238	8	5	3
Martinez	.975	79	112	3	3	0
Munoz	1.000	28	22	0	0	0
O'Neill	.930	43	40	0	3	0
Ozuna	.979	129	181	4	4	0
Robinson	1.000	2	2	0	0	0
Thomas	1.000	25	22	1	0	1

MEMPHIS REDBIRDS · TRIPLE-A
PACIFIC COAST LEAGUE

Batting	B-T	HT	WT	DOB	AVG	vLH	vRH	G	AB	R	H	2B	3B	HR	RBI	BB	HBP	SH	SF	SO	SB	CS	SLG	OBP
Arozarena, Randy	R-R	5-11	170	2-28-95	.358	.360	.357	64	246	51	88	18	2	12	38	24	11	0	2	48	9	7	.594	.435
Bader, Harrison	R-R	6-0	195	6-3-94	.318	.300	.326	16	63	23	20	3	0	7	15	8	4	0	0	16	3	0	.698	.427
Capel, Conner	L-L	6-1	185	5-19-97	.433	.600	.400	8	30	5	13	5	0	2	7	1	0	0	0	6	1	0	.800	.452
Carlson, Dylan	B-L	6-3	205	10-23-98	.361	.385	.348	18	72	14	26	4	2	5	9	6	1	0	0	18	1	1	.681	.418
Carpenter, Matt	L-R	6-3	205	11-26-85	.182	.333	.125	4	11	2	2	1	0	0	3	3	0	0	0	4	0	0	.273	.357
Chinea, Chris	R-R	5-11	220	5-3-94	.250	.000	.333	6	8	1	2	1	0	0	0	0	0	0	0	0	0	0	.375	.250
Donovan, Brendan	L-R	6-1	195	1-16-97	1.000	1.000	--	1	1	0	1	1	0	0	1	0	0	0	0	0	0	0	2.000	1.000
Edman, Tommy	B-R	5-10	180	5-9-95	.305	.349	.292	49	197	39	60	12	4	7	29	15	2	2	2	33	9	0	.513	.357
Garcia, Adolis	R-R	6-1	180	3-2-93	.253	.266	.249	132	491	96	124	22	6	32	96	22	13	1	2	159	14	10	.517	.301
Godoy, Jose	L-R	5-11	180	10-13-94	.317	.375	.302	27	79	10	25	6	0	2	9	7	0	0	1	16	0	0	.468	.368
Gonzalez, Yariel	B-R	6-1	190	6-1-94	.136	.143	.133	7	22	3	3	0	0	3	6	3	0	1	0	6	0	0	.546	.240
Hudson, Joe	R-R	6-0	210	5-21-91	.223	.214	.227	60	197	24	44	5	1	10	30	20	1	0	4	69	0	0	.411	.293
Knizner, Andrew	R-R	6-1	200	2-3-95	.276	.182	.297	66	246	41	68	10	0	12	34	24	8	0	2	37	2	0	.463	.357
Lopez, Irving	L-R	5-10	170	6-30-95	.300	.429	.283	21	60	13	18	3	2	1	5	9	0	0	1	14	0	1	.467	.386
Martinez, Jose	B-R	5-10	185	8-15-96	.278	.179	.323	42	90	16	25	6	0	3	11	12	1	0	0	20	1	0	.444	.369
Mendoza, Evan	R-R	6-2	200	6-28-96	.313	.000	.357	6	16	3	5	1	0	0	1	3	0	0	0	2	0	0	.375	.421
Mieses, Johan	R-R	6-2	185	7-13-95	.339	.273	.375	22	62	12	21	1	1	6	17	8	0	0	0	11	0	1	.677	.414
Molina, Yadier	R-R	5-11	205	7-13-82	.250	.333	.000	4	8	2	2	0	0	1	5	0	0	2	0	4	0	0	.625	.250
Munoz, Yairo	R-R	6-1	201	1-23-95	.231	--	.231	3	13	1	3	0	0	1	2	1	0	0	0	4	0	0	.462	.286
Nogowski, John	R-L	6-2	210	1-5-93	.295	.288	.297	117	380	77	112	22	1	15	75	69	10	0	4	54	1	2	.476	.413
O'Neill, Tyler	R-R	5-11	210	6-22-95	.265	.421	.212	41	151	26	40	5	0	11	26	14	0	0	1	51	3	0	.517	.325
Ozuna, Marcell	R-R	6-1	225	11-12-90	.444	1.000	.375	3	9	3	4	1	0	1	6	2	1	0	0	0	0	0	.889	.583
Pena, Francisco	R-R	6-2	230	12-18-89	.333	.000	.429	6	18	3	6	2	0	1	4	3	0	0	0	3	0	0	.611	.429
2-team total (68 Sacramento)					.290	.247	.312	74	276	37	80	20	0	17	50	16	1	0	4	46	1	0	.547	.327
Ravelo, Rangel	R-R	6-1	225	4-24-92	.299	.342	.286	95	334	50	100	20	1	12	56	37	9	0	1	61	0	1	.473	.383
Robertson, Kramer	R-R	5-10	166	9-20-94	.235	.256	.229	66	179	28	42	10	0	5	24	27	3	0	0	42	2	4	.374	.345
Robinson, Drew	L-R	6-1	200	4-20-92	.265	.255	.268	55	189	28	50	8	2	6	28	36	3	3	3	71	10	3	.423	.385
Schrock, Max	L-R	5-9	195	10-12-94	.276	.175	.303	85	265	42	73	20	1	2	31	37	1	0	0	49	12	2	.381	.366
Sosa, Edmundo	R-R	5-11	170	3-6-96	.291	.352	.276	118	433	70	132	18	5	17	62	17	16	4	6	96	2	3	.466	.335
Thomas, Lane	R-R	6-1	210	8-23-95	.268	.300	.261	75	265	42	71	17	2	10	44	32	4	0	3	80	11	6	.460	.352
Urias, Ramon	R-R	5-10	150	6-3-94	.263	.319	.246	96	316	51	83	24	0	9	52	44	11	1	3	71	4	1	.424	.369
Williams, Justin	L-R	6-2	215	8-20-95	.353	.379	.343	36	102	20	36	5	0	7	26	16	0	1	0	30	0	0	.608	.437

Pitching	B-T	HT	WT	DOB	W	L	ERA	G	GS	CG	SV	IP	H	R	ER	HR	BB	SO	AVG	vLH	vRH	K/9	BB/9
Arauz, Harold	R-R	6-2	185	5-29-95	7	2	5.93	13	0	0	0	58	67	40	38	12	22	31	.300	.299	.302	4.84	3.43
Beck, Chris	R-R	6-3	230	9-4-90	0	7	6.10	37	0	0	6	41	50	31	28	8	18	39	.294	.328	.275	8.49	3.92
Cabrera, Genesis	L-L	6-2	190	10-10-96	5	6	5.91	20	18	0	0	99	107	68	65	20	39	106	.277	.313	.266	9.64	3.55
Cervenka, Hunter	L-L	6-1	250	1-3-90	1	2	2.95	36	0	0	4	43	31	16	14	2	23	50	.211	.245	.194	10.55	4.85
Cruz, Jesus	R-R	6-1	225	4-15-95	6	6	6.24	50	0	0	0	58	51	44	40	8	41	79	.239	.333	.194	12.33	6.40
Dobzanski, Bryan	R-R	6-4	220	8-31-95	0	1	7.36	3	0	0	0	4	2	3	3	0	5	4	.154	.200	.125	9.82	12.27
Elledge, Seth	R-R	6-3	240	5-20-96	3	1	4.72	21	3	0	0	34	28	18	18	3	19	32	.233	.192	.265	8.39	4.98
Ellis, Chris	L-R	6-5	205	9-22-92	5	5	7.18	40	7	0	1	79	98	65	63	13	47	82	.299	.346	.275	9.34	5.35
Fasola, John	R-R	6-2	195	12-12-91	0	2	8.71	8	0	0	2	10	12	10	10	1	6	6	.293	.100	.355	5.23	5.23
Fernandez, Junior	R-R	6-1	180	3-2-97	2	1	1.48	18	0	0	2	24	17	6	4	0	11	27	.191	.222	.177	9.99	4.07
Gallegos, Giovanny	R-R	6-2	210	8-14-91	0	0	0.00	1	0	0	0	1	0	0	0	0	0	1	.000	.000	.000	9.00	0.00
Gomber, Austin	L-L	6-5	230	11-23-93	4	0	2.98	8	8	1	0	45	42	17	15	5	16	52	.250	.243	.252	10.32	3.18
Gonzalez, Edgar	R-R	6-1	200	12-22-96	0	0	0.00	1	0	0	0	1	0	0	0	0	0	0	.200	.250	.000	0.00	5.40
Gregerson, Luke	L-R	6-3	205	5-14-84	0	0	0.00	2	0	0	0	2	2	0	0	0	1	1	.333	.333	.333	4.50	0.00
Hauschild, Mike	R-R	6-3	210	1-22-90	1	3	7.96	10	9	0	0	37	45	34	33	5	25	23	.306	.275	.333	5.54	6.03
Helsley, Ryan	R-R	6-1	195	7-18-94	2	3	4.58	17	7	0	1	37	29	20	19	3	20	41	.218	.275	.194	9.88	4.82
Jones, Connor	R-R	6-3	220	10-10-94	0	0	0.00	1	0	0	0	1	0	0	0	0	1	0	.000	.000	.000	4.50	0.00
Kruczynski, Evan	L-L	6-5	215	3-31-95	1	2	8.01	7	6	0	0	30	44	27	27	3	17	28	.347	.205	.409	8.31	5.04
Layne, Tommy	L-L	6-2	195	11-2-84	3	1	6.45	34	0	0	0	38	44	31	27	8	18	37	.291	.302	.286	8.84	4.30
Leone, Dominic	R-R	5-11	180	10-26-91	1	0	2.84	23	0	0	0	32	20	10	10	3	14	42	.175	.200	.156	11.94	3.98
Martinez, Carlos	R-R	6-0	190	9-21-91	0	0	0.00	3	0	0	0	4	1	0	0	0	4	6	.083	.250	.000	14.73	9.82
Mayers, Mike	R-R	6-3	200	12-6-91	0	1	3.15	20	0	0	1	20	21	10	7	4	7	24	.266	.407	.192	10.80	3.15
Meisinger, Ryan	R-R	6-4	235	5-4-94	0	3	3.09	21	3	0	0	35	36	18	12	5	10	42	.257	.338	.214	10.80	2.57
Nogowski, John	R-L	6-2	210	1-5-93	0	0	0.00	3	0	0	0	3	4	0	0	0	2	1	.308	.333	.300	3.00	6.00
Parsons, Tommy	R-R	6-4	185	9-1-95	0	1	9.00	1	0	0	0	7	8	7	7	3	5	2	.318	.444	.231	10.80	3.60
Ponce de Leon, Daniel	R-R	6-3	200	1-16-92	8	4	2.88	16	16	0	0	84	62	30	27	7	43	86	.203	.128	.240	9.18	4.59
Ramirez, Roel	R-R	6-1	210	5-26-95	1	0	0.00	2	0	0	0	3	0	0	0	0	1	5	.000	.000	.000	15.00	3.00
Reyes, Alex	R-R	6-3	175	8-29-94	1	3	7.39	10	7	0	0	28	27	24	23	5	24	38	.265	.347	.189	12.21	7.71
Rosscup, Zac	L-L	6-2	220	6-9-88	0	0	4.50	8	0	0	0	8	7	4	4	0	15	9	.233	.200	.250	10.13	16.88
2-team total (9 Oklahoma City)					0	1	5.40	17	0	0	1	17	15	10	10	1	18	23	.246	.222	.256	12.42	9.72

Shew, Anthony	R-R	6-2	205	11-3-93	1	3	5.58	10	8	0	0	40	47	28	25	7	20	43	.283	.307	.269	9.60	4.46
Shreve, Chasen	L-L	6-4	195	7-12-90	2	2	3.45	51	0	0	3	60	45	25	23	6	26	68	.208	.177	.223	10.20	3.90
Warner, Austin	L-L	5-11	185	6-27-94	4	2	5.70	11	11	0	0	60	71	40	38	15	30	55	.296	.207	.324	8.25	4.50
Webb, Tyler	L-L	6-5	230	7-20-90	0	1	2.70	5	0	0	0	7	7	3	2	0	2	5	.280	.200	.333	6.75	2.70
Whitley, Kodi	R-R	6-4	220	2-21-95	2	0	1.52	16	0	0	2	24	21	5	4	0	4	27	.233	.250	.222	10.27	1.52
Woodford, Jake	R-R	6-4	220	10-28-96	9	8	4.15	26	26	0	0	152	124	75	70	22	75	131	.223	.251	.204	7.77	4.45

Fielding

Catcher	PCT	G	PO	A	E	DP	PB
Chinea	.000	1	0	0	0	0	0
Godoy	.995	22	196	7	1	1	1
Hudson	.998	53	507	31	1	5	0
Knizner	.990	61	487	32	5	5	3
Molina	1.000	4	28	0	0	0	0
Pena	1.000	4	29	2	0	0	0

First Base	PCT	G	PO	A	E	DP
Chinea	1.000	1	2	0	0	0
Mendoza	1.000	1	6	1	0	0
Nogowski	.997	107	682	69	2	72
Ravelo	.992	43	242	9	2	27
Urias	1.000	3	14	1	0	0

Second Base	PCT	G	PO	A	E	DP
Edman	1.000	25	46	58	0	24
Lopez	.983	17	33	25	1	8
Martinez	1.000	4	1	2	0	1
Munoz	.000	1	0	0	0	0
Robertson	.976	12	20	20	1	4
Robinson	.929	5	6	7	1	0
Schrock	.953	10	17	24	2	7

Third Base	PCT	G	PO	A	E	DP
Carpenter	.833	4	1	4	1	0
Donovan	1.000	1	0	1	0	0
Edman	1.000	9	6	18	0	5
Gonzalez	1.000	7	3	9	0	0
Hudson	.500	1	1	0	1	0
Martinez	.953	27	8	33	2	3
Mendoza	.750	4	1	5	2	0
Ravelo	.800	5	1	3	1	0
Robertson	.871	11	10	17	4	4
Robinson	.917	7	3	8	1	0
Schrock	.960	56	20	76	4	7
Sosa	.960	15	7	17	1	2
Urias	.929	20	14	25	3	6

Shortstop	PCT	G	PO	A	E	DP
Edman	.964	10	10	17	1	4
Martinez	.933	7	4	10	1	0
Munoz	1.000	1	1	2	0	1
Robertson	.936	31	41	61	7	15

	PCT	G	PO	A	E	DP
Sosa	.962	17	19	32	2	6
Urias	.981	64	83	128	4	33

Robinson	.919	14	22	35	5	12
Sosa	.968	84	106	193	10	35
Urias	1.000	5	6	13	0	2

Outfield	PCT	G	PO	A	E	DP
Arozarena	1.000	59	121	2	0	1
Bader	.977	16	40	2	1	0
Capel	1.000	7	16	1	0	0
Carlson	.968	18	30	0	1	0
Edman	1.000	2	5	0	0	0
Garcia	.989	117	257	17	3	1
Hudson	.000	1	0	0	0	0
Mieses	1.000	19	28	1	0	0
Munoz	1.000	2	8	0	0	0
O'Neill	1.000	35	59	1	0	0
Ozuna	.000	3	0	0	0	0
Ravelo	.969	38	59	3	2	0
Robertson	.000	1	0	0	0	0
Robinson	.984	32	61	2	1	0
Schrock	1.000	7	6	0	0	0
Thomas	.993	72	130	6	1	1
Williams	1.000	25	57	2	0	1

SPRINGFIELD CARDINALS — DOUBLE-A

TEXAS LEAGUE

Batting	B-T	HT	WT	DOB	AVG	vLH	vRH	G	AB	R	H	2B	3B	HR	RBI	BB	HBP	SH	SF	SO	SB	CS	SLG	OBP
Arozarena, Randy	R-R	5-11	170	2-28-95	.309	.529	.263	28	97	14	30	7	2	3	15	13	6	0	0	23	8	5	.516	.422
Ascanio, Rayder	R-R	5-11	155	3-17-96	.270	.298	.264	76	267	35	72	17	0	6	40	19	5	0	1	54	3	2	.401	.329
Billings, Shane	R-L	5-11	190	12-14-94	.370	.364	.375	13	27	5	10	1	0	2	7	1	0	0	0	3	0	0	.630	.393
Capel, Conner	L-R	6-1	185	5-19-97	.232	.210	.237	98	341	39	79	12	1	9	40	23	2	0	2	84	9	4	.352	.283
Carlson, Dylan	B-L	6-3	205	10-23-98	.281	.245	.292	108	417	81	117	24	6	21	59	52	7	0	7	98	18	7	.518	.364
Carpenter, Matt	L-R	6-3	205	11-26-85	.000	.000	.000	5	15	0	0	0	0	0	0	4	0	0	0	4	0	0	.000	.211
Chinea, Chris	R-R	5-11	220	5-3-94	.280	.313	.270	83	286	28	80	14	1	10	32	16	3	1	0	83	0	0	.441	.324
Godoy, Jose	L-R	5-11	180	10-13-94	.256	.111	.286	47	160	22	41	10	0	5	33	18	6	1	3	30	0	1	.413	.348
Gonzalez, Yariel	B-R	6-1	190	6-1-94	.274	.319	.262	56	215	30	59	10	0	11	45	17	1	0	1	34	3	4	.474	.329
Hurst, Scott	L-R	5-11	175	3-25-96	.192	.074	.219	45	141	18	27	9	0	1	13	17	0	3	0	46	1	0	.277	.279
Kirtley, Zach	R-R	6-1	190	10-1-96	.230	.200	.239	63	187	27	43	13	0	5	19	21	4	4	1	56	2	0	.380	.319
Lopez, Irving	L-R	5-10	170	6-30-95	.255	.258	.254	84	302	50	77	15	4	10	30	20	14	2	0	63	1	1	.431	.330
Martinez, Jose	R-R	6-6	215	7-25-88	.500	.200	.266	5	16	0	8	1	0	0	4	3	0	0	0	1	1	0	.563	.579
Martinez, Jose	B-R	5-10	185	8-15-96	.253	.200	.266	23	79	7	20	3	0	1	5	11	0	0	1	18	1	0	.329	.341
Mendoza, Evan	R-R	6-2	200	6-28-96	.248	.244	.249	54	206	20	51	8	1	1	20	14	0	0	2	44	5	1	.311	.293
Mieses, Johan	R-R	6-2	185	7-13-95	.213	.262	.202	96	324	41	69	11	0	16	49	30	11	1	1	86	6	0	.395	.301
Molina, Yadier	R-R	5-11	205	7-13-82	.083	.167	.000	4	12	0	1	0	0	0	1	0	1	0	1	8	1	0	.083	.143
Montero, Elehuris	R-R	6-3	215	8-17-98	.188	.229	.176	59	224	23	42	8	0	7	18	14	0	0	0	74	0	1	.317	.235
Nootbaar, Lars	L-R	6-3	210	9-8-97	.269	.286	.264	33	93	12	25	2	1	0	3	16	0	0	1	22	1	1	.312	.373
O'Keefe, Brian	R-R	6-1	215	7-15-93	.229	.254	.223	88	301	36	69	9	0	13	40	37	4	1	3	71	1	1	.389	.319
O'Neill, Tyler	R-R	5-11	210	6-22-95	.167	.333	.143	6	24	4	4	1	0	2	2	0	0	0	0	9	0	0	.458	.167
Perri, Michael	R-R	6-3	195	9-5-95	.156	.000	.180	12	45	3	7	0	0	0	1	2	0	0	0	7	0	0	.156	.192
Pinder, Chase	R-R	5-10	190	3-16-96	.160	.000	.167	14	50	4	8	0	0	0	1	5	0	1	0	19	0	0	.160	.236
Robertson, Kramer	R-R	5-10	166	9-20-94	.227	.250	.220	57	194	40	44	5	1	6	27	39	8	2	3	43	12	6	.356	.373
Rodriguez, Julio	R-R	6-0	197	6-11-97	.222	.222	.222	14	45	2	10	1	0	1	7	2	0	0	0	15	0	0	.311	.255
Toerner, Justin	L-L	5-10	165	8-11-96	.211	.035	.248	49	166	30	35	5	0	7	18	28	4	1	0	55	10	3	.368	.338
Triunfel, Alberto	R-R	5-11	160	2-1-94	.189	.149	.200	67	212	22	40	12	0	0	11	16	1	4	1	61	1	4	.245	.248
Trosclair, Stefan	R-R	6-2	195	7-23-94	.000	.000	.000	2	7	0	0	0	0	0	0	0	0	0	0	5	0	0	.000	.000
Urias, Ramon	R-R	5-10	150	6-3-94	.375	.286	1.000	2	8	1	3	0	0	0	1	0	0	0	0	2	0	0	.375	.375
Williams, Justin	L-R	6-2	215	8-20-95	.193	.000	.213	17	57	7	11	1	0	1	3	4	0	0	0	17	1	0	.263	.246
Yepez, Juan	R-R	6-1	200	2-19-98	.231	.000	.273	17	52	8	12	2	0	2	10	5	0	0	2	14	0	0	.385	.288

Pitching	B-T	HT	WT	DOB	W	L	ERA	G	GS	CG	SV	IP	H	R	ER	HR	BB	SO	AVG	vLH	vRH	K/9	BB/9
Arauz, Harold	R-R	6-2	185	5-29-95	0	4	7.71	6	6	0	0	28	46	26	24	5	14	20	.357	.275	.450	6.43	4.50
Baird, Michael	R-R	6-5	210	7-9-95	0	0	21.60	1	0	0	0	2	5	4	4	1	0	2	.556	.600	.500	5.40	0.00
Cruz, Jesus	R-R	6-1	225	4-15-95	0	0	2.45	2	0	0	0	4	1	1	1	0	5	10	.083	.125	.000	24.55	12.27
Dayton, Patrick	L-L	6-0	170	7-20-95	0	0	6.75	1	0	0	0	4	3	3	3	0	1	1	.267	.000	.444	2.25	2.25
Dobzanski, Bryan	R-R	6-4	220	8-31-95	2	1	3.55	24	1	0	2	33	35	15	13	6	15	39	.280	.271	.339	10.64	4.09
Elledge, Seth	R-R	6-3	240	5-20-96	3	3	3.78	26	0	0	3	33	34	15	14	3	13	43	.276	.172	.369	11.61	3.51
Fagalde, Alex	R-R	6-3	225	4-29-94	4	5	4.43	12	11	0	0	67	62	34	33	11	23	51	.250	.236	.264	6.85	3.09
Fasola, John	R-R	6-2	195	12-12-91	0	1	4.15	5	0	0	1	4	4	2	2	1	3	5	.250	.333	.200	10.38	6.23
Fernandez, Junior	R-R	6-1	180	3-2-97	1	1	1.55	18	0	0	9	29	18	6	5	0	11	42	.177	.200	.149	13.03	3.41

Name	B-T	HT	WT	DOB	W	L	ERA	G	GS	CG	SV	IP	H	R	ER	HR	BB	SO	AVG	vLH	vRH	SO/9	BB/9
Godoy, Jose	L-R	5-11	180	10-13-94	0	0	0.00	2	0	0	0	1	0	0	0	0	1	1	.000	.000	.000	6.75	6.75
Gomber, Austin	L-L	6-5	230	11-23-93	0	0	0.00	3	2	0	0	4	1	0	0	0	1	2	.083	--	.083	4.50	2.25
Gonzalez, Merandy	R-R	6-0	216	10-9-95	2	3	6.64	34	1	0	4	41	54	33	30	5	31	39	.318	.354	.284	8.63	6.86
Gregerson, Luke	L-R	6-3	205	5-14-84	0	0	1.50	6	0	0	0	6	3	1	1	0	0	7	.143	.000	.214	10.50	0.00
Jones, Connor	R-R	6-3	220	10-10-94	1	1	4.66	42	0	0	9	48	54	29	25	5	35	49	.284	.333	.243	9.12	6.52
Kruczynski, Evan	L-L	6-5	215	3-31-95	3	8	5.60	21	20	0	0	117	123	77	73	18	50	118	.269	.298	.258	9.05	3.84
Latcham, Will	R-R	6-2	200	1-26-96	0	2	7.08	31	0	0	0	41	56	32	32	9	20	31	.348	.343	.352	6.86	4.43
Leahy, Kyle	B-R	6-5	200	6-4-97	0	0	0.00	1	0	0	0	3	1	0	0	0	0	2	.091	.000	.200	6.00	0.00
Lopez, Irving	L-R	5-10	170	6-30-95	0	0	27.00	1	0	0	0	0	2	1	1	0	1	0	.667	.000	1.000	0.00	27.00
Martinez, Carlos	R-R	6-0	190	9-21-91	0	0	4.50	1	0	0	0	2	4	1	1	0	0	0	.500	.600	.333	0.00	0.00
Meisner, Casey	R-R	6-7	190	5-22-95	0	2	9.78	6	4	0	0	19	33	24	21	10	6	20	.367	.375	.357	9.31	2.79
Mendoza, Hector	R-R	6-2	176	3-5-94	0	1	2.00	6	0	0	0	9	5	2	2	1	6	8	.161	.118	.214	8.00	6.00
O'Reilly, Mike	R-R	5-11	180	9-3-94	0	1	7.94	5	0	0	0	11	12	10	10	0	5	8	.267	.238	.292	6.35	3.97
Osnowitz, Mitchell	R-R	6-5	245	7-2-91	2	1	4.62	20	0	0	1	26	24	13	13	4	9	25	.240	.255	.225	8.88	3.20
Oviedo, Johan	R-R	6-6	210	3-2-98	7	8	5.65	23	23	0	0	113	120	72	71	9	64	128	.273	.287	.259	10.19	5.10
Parsons, Tommy	R-R	6-4	185	9-1-95	4	6	5.29	14	14	0	0	83	91	50	49	26	13	77	.276	.275	.276	8.32	1.40
Patterson, Jacob	R-L	6-2	200	10-30-95	6	5	5.55	51	1	0	1	58	66	42	36	13	18	78	.279	.284	.273	12.03	2.78
Perez, Williams	R-R	6-0	240	5-21-91	6	3	5.61	13	13	0	0	67	77	43	42	10	28	70	.292	.341	.240	9.36	3.74
Ramirez, Roel	R-R	6-1	210	5-26-95	5	3	4.98	41	5	0	1	72	76	45	40	6	29	80	.276	.266	.288	9.95	3.61
Rondon, Angel	R-R	6-2	185	12-1-97	6	6	3.21	20	20	0	0	115	99	45	41	11	42	112	.230	.215	.248	8.77	3.29
Shew, Anthony	R-R	6-2	205	11-3-93	1	2	1.93	5	5	0	0	28	27	8	6	1	6	27	.255	.236	.275	8.68	1.93
Warner, Austin	L-L	5-11	185	6-27-94	4	6	3.83	15	14	0	0	82	83	41	35	10	25	88	.261	.307	.235	9.62	2.73
Whitley, Kodi	R-R	6-4	220	2-21-95	1	4	1.83	31	0	0	7	39	31	14	8	3	13	46	.208	.253	.162	10.53	2.97
Williams, Ronnie	R-R	6-0	170	1-6-96	2	3	4.24	25	0	0	1	34	32	16	16	6	21	36	.244	.221	.270	9.53	5.56

Fielding

Catcher	PCT	G	PO	A	E	DP	PB
Chinea	1.000	10	62	3	0	1	1
Godoy	.995	40	380	22	2	0	6
Molina	1.000	3	23	2	0	0	6
O'Keefe	.996	78	714	41	3	8	3
Rodriguez	1.000	13	115	8	0	1	2

First Base	PCT	G	PO	A	E	DP
Chinea	.995	55	375	23	2	45
Gonzalez	1.000	13	62	10	0	1
Kirtley	.983	54	325	20	6	37
Mendoza	1.000	21	131	16	0	10
Trosclair	.941	2	15	1	1	1
Yepez	1.000	5	38	2	0	3

Second Base	PCT	G	PO	A	E	DP
Gonzalez	1.000	3	3	8	0	1
Kirtley	.000	1	0	0	0	0
Lopez	.992	82	147	204	3	49
Martinez	1.000	8	19	27	0	6
Perri	1.000	9	10	18	0	4

	PCT	G	PO	A	E	DP
Robertson	1.000	15	33	38	0	7
Triunfel	.991	25	51	60	1	9
Urias	1.000	2	2	2	0	0

Third Base	PCT	G	PO	A	E	DP
Ascanio	1.000	1	1	1	0	0
Carpenter	1.000	4	1	6	0	0
Gonzalez	.955	34	24	40	3	4
Kirtley	1.000	3	6	3	0	0
Martinez	1.000	2	2	2	0	1
Mendoza	.966	31	19	67	3	9
Montero	.930	52	36	57	7	7
Robertson	1.000	1	1	1	0	0
Triunfel	.927	18	7	31	3	1
Yepez	1.000	1	2	1	0	0

Shortstop	PCT	G	PO	A	E	DP
Ascanio	.984	70	83	169	4	41
Gonzalez	1.000	4	5	7	0	2
Martinez	.955	12	17	25	2	8
Perri	1.000	1	2	2	0	0

	PCT	G	PO	A	E	DP
Robertson	.961	37	52	70	5	14
Triunfel	.983	18	30	29	1	6

Outfield	PCT	G	PO	A	E	DP
Arozarena	.981	23	53	0	1	0
Billings	1.000	6	3	1	0	0
Capel	.983	85	162	15	3	3
Carlson	.995	100	198	5	1	2
Gonzalez	1.000	4	12	0	0	0
Hurst	.977	35	80	5	2	2
Kirtley	.000	1	0	0	0	0
Lopez	.000	1	0	0	0	0
Martinez	1.000	2	2	0	0	0
Mieses	.935	74	135	8	10	2
Nootbaar	.976	26	36	4	1	0
O'Neill	1.000	6	12	0	0	0
Pinder	.889	9	15	1	2	0
Toerner	1.000	47	100	4	0	0
Triunfel	.000	3	0	0	0	0
Williams	1.000	14	18	0	0	0
Yepez	1.000	12	16	1	0	0

PALM BEACH CARDINALS   HIGH CLASS A
FLORIDA STATE LEAGUE

Batting	B-T	HT	WT	DOB	AVG	vLH	vRH	G	AB	R	H	2B	3B	HR	RBI	BB	HBP	SH	SF	SO	SB	CS	SLG	OBP
Ascanio, Rayder	R-R	5-11	155	3-17-96	.259	.300	.246	31	85	11	22	4	0	0	9	12	0	4	1	21	0	0	.306	.347
Baker, Luken	R-R	6-4	265	3-10-97	.244	.235	.247	122	439	47	107	32	1	10	53	52	3	0	2	112	1	1	.390	.327
Castillo, Moises	R-R	6-1	170	7-14-99	.250	--	.250	2	4	1	1	0	0	1	2	0	0	0	0	2	0	0	1.000	.250
Denton, Bryce	R-R	6-0	190	8-1-97	.202	.289	.165	52	173	13	35	7	0	1	15	14	1	0	1	60	0	0	.260	.265
Diaz, Imeldo	R-R	6-0	175	11-2-97	.346	.370	.333	24	78	12	27	5	0	0	9	5	0	0	0	15	1	3	.410	.386
Dunn, Nick	L-R	5-10	175	1-29-97	.247	.230	.253	104	380	35	94	19	3	3	38	24	2	0	5	58	2	1	.337	.292
Figuera, Edwin	R-R	5-10	160	9-2-97	.000	.000	.000	2	4	0	0	0	0	0	0	0	0	0	0	3	0	0	.000	.000
Gahagan, Zack	R-R	6-1	195	8-3-95	.206	.214	.202	41	126	12	26	5	3	1	9	13	0	0	1	40	0	0	.318	.279
Gil, Mateo	R-R	6-1	180	7-24-00	.000	.000	.000	2	6	0	0	0	0	0	0	0	0	0	0	2	0	0	.000	.000
Gonzalez, Yariel	B-R	6-1	190	6-1-94	.261	.260	.261	57	215	17	56	10	0	1	21	17	0	0	2	30	2	1	.321	.312
Gorman, Nolan	L-R	6-1	210	5-10-00	.256	.326	.237	58	215	24	55	16	3	5	21	13	2	0	0	73	0	1	.428	.304
Hernandez, Francisco	R-R	5-11	190	10-8-99	.167	.000	.500	2	6	1	1	1	0	0	0	0	0	0	0	3	0	0	.333	.167
Herrera, Ivan	R-R	6-0	180	6-1-00	.276	.250	.280	18	58	7	16	0	0	1	5	5	1	0	1	16	0	0	.328	.339
Hurst, Scott	L-R	5-10	175	3-25-96	.233	.239	.232	63	223	23	52	4	1	4	20	18	1	1	1	61	1	3	.314	.292
Kirtley, Zach	R-R	6-1	190	10-1-96	.253	.192	.280	45	170	23	43	11	0	4	21	19	3	3	0	46	0	1	.388	.339
Kreuter, Cole	R-R	6-0	190	11-29-95	.178	.083	.212	18	45	6	8	1	0	1	6	2	1	1	0	20	0	0	.267	.225
Luna, Andres	R-R	5-10	175	7-17-97	.353	.333	.364	6	17	4	6	2	0	2	8	0	2	0	0	4	0	0	.824	.421
Martinez, Jose	B-R	5-10	185	8-15-96	.209	.290	.178	41	139	14	29	2	2	0	7	10	0	1	2	19	5	0	.252	.258
Montano, Luis	L-R	6-2	170	4-10-00	.125	.000	.133	5	16	0	2	1	0	0	2	1	0	0	1	6	0	0	.188	.167
Nootbaar, Lars	L-R	6-3	210	9-8-97	.275	.300	.265	39	142	10	39	3	0	2	17	13	0	0	0	20	1	2	.338	.336
Ortega, Dennis	R-R	6-2	180	6-11-97	.205	.231	.193	58	200	15	41	6	1	0	19	5	2	1	0	39	0	0	.250	.257
Perri, Michael	R-R	6-3	195	9-5-95	.235	.313	.215	67	234	26	55	8	0	3	18	11	5	2	0	32	1	0	.308	.304
Pinder, Chase	R-R	6-1	190	3-16-96	.203	.233	.192	73	242	31	49	7	0	4	21	32	8	4	3	72	1	3	.281	.312
Plummer, Nick	L-L	5-10	200	7-31-96	.177	.196	.172	96	289	35	51	15	2	5	29	47	12	3	5	119	3	3	.294	.312
Reichenborn, Tyler	R-R	5-11	180	7-23-98	.400	.000	.444	3	10	2	4	1	0	1	3	1	0	0	0	1	0	0	.800	.455

Name	B-T	HT	WT	DOB	AVG	vLH	vRH	G	AB	R	H	2B	3B	HR	RBI	BB	HBP	SH	SF	SO	SB	CS	SLG	OBP
Rodriguez, Julio	R-R	6-0	197	6-11-97	.276	.296	.269	71	268	28	74	14	0	7	31	16	2	0	1	53	0	0	.407	.321
Soto, Franklin	R-R	5-11	168	9-23-99	.167	.000	.250	2	6	1	1	1	0	0	0	0	0	0	0	4	0	0	.333	.167
Toerner, Justin	L-L	5-10	165	8-11-96	.290	.286	.291	54	193	39	56	5	1	4	29	33	5	2	2	50	4	5	.389	.403
Urias, Ramon	R-R	5-10	150	6-3-94	.200	.000	.222	5	20	5	4	0	0	1	2	1	0	0	0	8	0	0	.350	.238
Wilson, Alexis	R-R	5-10	168	8-13-96	.409	.500	.389	6	22	2	9	0	0	1	2	2	0	1	0	4	0	0	.546	.458
Yepez, Juan	R-R	6-1	200	2-19-98	.275	.233	.292	29	102	16	28	4	0	4	20	10	2	1	0	21	1	0	.431	.351
Ynfante, Wadye	R-R	6-0	160	8-15-97	.100	.222	.048	11	30	4	3	0	0	0	3	1	0	0	0	7	0	0	.100	.206

Pitching	B-T	HT	WT	DOB	W	L	ERA	G	GS	CG	SV	IP	H	R	ER	HR	BB	SO	AVG	vLH	vRH	K/9	BB/9
Aker, Cole	R-R	6-2	205	9-18-96	1	1	2.91	19	0	0	1	22	15	10	7	1	7	18	.197	.133	.239	7.48	2.91
Baird, Michael	R-R	6-5	210	7-9-95	1	3	2.42	9	4	0	0	26	17	10	7	1	8	29	.181	.159	.200	10.04	2.77
Cordero, Diego	L-L	6-3	175	9-8-97	2	6	3.39	11	11	0	0	58	76	33	22	4	16	34	.317	.393	.291	5.25	2.47
Dayton, Patrick	L-L	6-0	170	7-20-95	3	2	3.64	42	0	0	4	59	58	28	24	4	17	60	.259	.233	.275	9.10	2.58
DellaValle, Perry	R-R	6-0	185	1-23-96	5	6	3.22	20	19	0	0	106	98	42	38	7	23	87	.250	.239	.259	7.36	1.95
Dobzanski, Bryan	R-R	6-4	220	8-31-95	1	1	0.89	19	0	0	6	20	9	3	2	0	10	23	.132	.118	.147	10.18	4.43
Escobar, Edgar	R-R	6-1	220	1-20-97	1	1	4.10	16	0	0	1	26	21	12	12	1	8	33	.212	.146	.259	11.28	2.73
Fagalde, Alex	R-R	6-3	225	4-29-94	6	3	1.99	13	13	0	0	72	48	18	16	6	16	62	.188	.190	.187	7.71	1.99
Fernandez, Junior	R-R	6-1	180	3-2-97	0	0	1.54	9	0	0	4	12	8	2	2	0	8	11	.191	.136	.250	8.49	6.17
Gahagan, Zack	R-R	6-1	195	8-3-95	0	0	0.00	3	0	0	0	2	3	0	0	0	0	1	.333	1.000	.000	3.86	0.00
Gomber, Austin	L-L	6-5	230	11-23-93	0	1	81.00	1	1	0	0	0	2	3	3	0	2	0	.667	.000	1.000	0.00	54.00
Gonzalez, Edgar	R-R	6-1	200	12-22-96	6	15	5.23	25	24	0	1	115	134	80	67	6	65	110	.294	.278	.308	8.58	5.07
Gonzalez, Merandy	R-R	6-0	216	10-9-95	1	0	0.00	2	0	0	0	2	1	0	0	0	1	2	.143	.333	.000	9.00	4.50
Gregerson, Luke	L-R	6-3	205	5-14-84	0	0	3.00	3	1	0	0	3	2	1	1	0	0	2	.167	.250	.000	6.00	0.00
Jimenez, Ludwin	R-R	6-2	165	8-9-01	0	0	7.71	1	0	0	0	2	3	2	2	0	1	2	.300	.200	.400	7.71	3.86
Kraus, Eli	L-L	6-1	190	2-3-96	0	0	0.00	3	0	0	0	4	3	0	0	0	0	4	.200	.000	.375	9.00	0.00
Leahy, Kyle	B-R	6-5	200	6-4-97	1	5	6.30	6	6	0	0	30	43	27	21	3	12	19	.336	.356	.325	5.70	3.60
Osnowitz, Mitchell	R-R	6-5	245	7-2-91	1	3	5.29	15	0	0	1	17	15	11	10	3	10	20	.231	.429	.136	10.59	5.29
Oviedo, Johan	R-R	6-6	210	3-2-98	5	0	1.60	6	5	0	0	34	29	7	6	1	12	35	.230	.247	.204	9.36	3.21
Parsons, Tommy	R-R	6-4	185	9-1-95	3	2	2.13	7	7	1	0	42	41	14	10	1	7	39	.246	.161	.295	8.29	1.49
Perez, Williams	R-R	6-0	240	5-21-91	0	0	0.00	2	0	0	0	4	1	0	0	0	0	6	.077	.200	.000	13.50	0.00
Prendergast, Zach	R-R	6-2	175	5-6-95	3	5	5.24	32	3	0	0	67	77	43	39	5	21	76	.290	.302	.280	10.21	2.82
Reyes, Alex	R-R	6-3	175	8-29-94	0	1	1.93	2	2	0	0	9	9	4	2	0	3	11	.250	.350	.125	10.61	2.89
Roberts, Griffin	R-R	6-3	205	6-13-96	1	7	6.44	15	13	0	0	66	79	53	47	3	35	36	.305	.396	.237	4.93	4.80
Rondon, Angel	R-R	6-2	185	12-1-97	5	1	2.20	8	8	0	0	45	26	11	11	3	17	47	.165	.128	.200	9.40	3.40
Santos, Ramon	R-R	6-2	160	9-20-94	1	1	3.00	34	2	0	2	57	51	21	19	3	24	65	.245	.244	.246	10.26	3.79
Saylor, C.J.	R-R	5-11	195	10-14-93	2	3	5.25	28	0	0	1	36	37	22	21	3	18	39	.274	.308	.243	9.75	4.50
Seijas, Alvaro	R-R	6-1	175	10-10-98	4	1	2.65	10	10	0	0	54	54	21	16	2	26	43	.262	.275	.252	7.12	4.31
Solano, Enmanuel	R-R	6-1	160	9-23-98	0	0	0.00	1	0	0	0	2	2	0	0	0	0	2	.250	.000	.333	9.00	0.00
Soto, Hector	R-R	6-1	175	3-2-99	0	0	9.00	2	0	0	0	5	6	5	5	2	2	4	.273	.500	.188	7.20	3.60
Taveras, Leonardo	R-R	6-5	190	9-7-98	0	0	7.71	6	0	0	0	7	7	6	6	0	13	13	.250	.154	.333	16.71	16.71
Thompson, Zack	L-L	6-2	225	10-28-97	0	0	4.05	11	0	0	0	13	16	6	6	0	4	19	.302	.250	.333	12.83	2.70
Whitley, Kodi	R-R	6-4	220	2-21-95	0	0	0.00	3	0	0	0	4	1	0	0	0	2	5	.077	.000	.167	10.38	4.15
Williams, Ronnie	R-R	6-0	170	1-6-96	3	2	3.70	19	0	0	1	24	24	11	10	3	8	22	.250	.293	.218	8.14	2.96
Yepez, Juan	R-R	6-1	200	2-19-98	0	0	0.00	1	0	0	0	1	1	0	0	0	1	1	.250	.333	.000	9.00	9.00
Yokley, Ben	R-R	6-1	190	9-1-92	1	3	3.26	31	0	0	4	47	42	22	17	5	20	41	.235	.264	.215	7.85	3.83

Fielding

Catcher	PCT	G	PO	A	E	DP	PB
Herrera	.994	18	145	16	1	3	3
Ortega	.993	39	278	25	2	1	1
Rodriguez	.983	67	545	47	10	3	5
Wilson	1.000	6	54	5	0	0	0

First Base	PCT	G	PO	A	E	DP
Baker	.987	97	704	44	10	71
Gahagan	.978	5	45	0	1	5
Kirtley	.981	27	191	15	4	15
Yepez	1.000	4	25	1	0	8

Second Base	PCT	G	PO	A	E	DP
Ascanio	.978	11	14	31	1	4
Dunn	.970	97	136	224	11	48
Figuera	1.000	1	2	0	0	0
Gahagan	1.000	12	16	23	0	9
Kirtley	.857	4	9	9	3	1
Martinez	.800	2	3	1	1	0
Perri	.978	10	17	28	1	8

Third Base	PCT	G	PO	A	E	DP
Ascanio	.950	10	4	15	1	1
Gahagan	.958	14	9	14	1	3
Gonzalez	.972	46	34	72	3	9
Gorman	.897	49	45	60	12	12
Hernandez	.833	2	3	2	1	0
Kirtley	.667	3	1	1	1	0
Martinez	1.000	2	1	4	0	0
Perri	.800	3	2	2	1	1
Yepez	.909	5	1	9	1	2

Shortstop	PCT	G	PO	A	E	DP
Ascanio	.920	6	8	15	2	3
Castillo	1.000	1	1	2	0	0
Diaz	.925	24	33	66	8	13
Gahagan	1.000	4	5	11	0	3
Gil	1.000	2	1	2	0	0
Martinez	.956	38	57	95	7	25
Perri	.940	54	65	137	13	24
Soto	1.000	2	1	5	0	1
Urias	1.000	3	1	10	0	2

Outfield	PCT	G	PO	A	E	DP
Ascanio	1.000	4	7	0	0	0
Denton	.963	40	52	0	2	0
Gahagan	1.000	3	4	0	0	0
Hurst	.993	60	140	8	1	3
Kirtley	.800	4	4	0	1	0
Kreuter	.957	11	20	2	1	0
Luna	1.000	6	7	0	0	0
Montano	1.000	2	6	0	0	0
Nootbaar	1.000	39	75	10	0	4
Pinder	.988	70	163	5	2	0
Plummer	.993	79	145	5	1	0
Reichenborn	1.000	3	4	1	0	0
Toerner	.991	52	101	5	1	1
Yepez	.952	22	38	2	2	0
Ynfante	.967	11	27	2	1	0

PEORIA CHIEFS
LOW CLASS A
MIDWEST LEAGUE

Batting	B-T	HT	WT	DOB	AVG	vLH	vRH	G	AB	R	H	2B	3B	HR	RBI	BB	HBP	SH	SF	SO	SB	CS	SLG	OBP
Benson, Brandon	R-R	6-1	195	6-13-96	.150	.160	.148	38	133	12	20	3	0	4	12	9	1	0	1	49	0	1	.263	.208
Cedeno, Leandro	R-R	6-2	195	8-22-98	.271	.283	.269	100	366	35	99	24	2	6	44	18	6	0	6	101	4	1	.396	.311
Denton, Bryce	R-R	6-0	190	8-1-97	.189	.222	.185	25	90	8	17	4	1	2	11	5	2	0	0	25	1	0	.322	.247
Diaz, Imeldo	R-R	6-0	175	11-2-97	.316	.300	.318	35	136	11	43	14	0	2	23	4	2	1	2	22	0	2	.463	.340
Donovan, Brendan	L-R	6-1	195	1-16-97	.266	.299	.260	113	402	70	107	26	3	8	53	63	11	0	4	91	4	2	.406	.377
Figuera, Edwin	R-R	5-10	160	9-2-97	.222	.310	.209	67	225	28	50	9	1	0	18	9	1	2	5	23	3	3	.271	.278

Batting	B-T	HT	WT	DOB	AVG	vLH	vRH	G	AB	R	H	2B	3B	HR	RBI	BB	HBP	SH	SF	SO	SB	CS	SLG	OBP
Gorman, Nolan	L-R	6-1	210	5-10-00	.241	.139	.259	67	241	41	58	14	3	10	41	32	7	0	2	79	2	0	.448	.344
Herrera, Ivan	R-R	6-0	180	6-1-00	.286	.279	.288	69	248	41	71	10	0	8	42	35	5	0	3	56	1	1	.423	.381
Jackson, Zach	L-R	6-3	215	5-24-98	.154	.250	.136	7	26	3	4	1	0	2	2	0	0	0	0	11	0	0	.423	.154
Luna, Andres	R-R	5-10	175	7-17-97	.267	.000	.308	5	15	2	4	1	0	0	4	0	0	0	0	4	0	0	.333	.267
Machado, Jonatan	L-L	5-9	155	1-21-99	.272	.192	.286	40	173	19	47	9	0	0	11	8	1	0	1	39	1	3	.324	.306
Nootbaar, Lars	L-R	6-3	210	9-8-97	.245	.267	.242	29	106	17	26	4	1	5	18	16	0	0	0	13	2	1	.443	.344
Nunez, Malcom	R-R	5-11	205	3-9-01	.183	.100	.197	21	71	5	13	1	0	0	5	5	1	0	0	15	0	0	.197	.247
Perez, Delvin	R-R	6-3	175	11-24-98	.269	.350	.256	118	458	64	123	17	3	1	30	27	14	7	0	117	22	9	.325	.329
Riley, Brandon	L-R	6-0	170	12-13-96	.234	.246	.232	118	411	43	96	20	3	1	35	50	0	0	1	104	14	4	.304	.316
Shaw, John	R-R	6-1	195	11-30-96	.230	.175	.239	83	274	32	63	13	0	0	19	20	5	0	0	39	1	5	.277	.294
Soto, Carlos	L-R	6-2	220	4-27-99	.203	.364	.172	20	69	6	14	1	0	1	7	6	2	0	1	18	0	0	.261	.282
Torres, Jhon	R-R	6-4	199	3-29-00	.167	.000	.186	21	66	4	11	3	0	0	8	7	0	0	2	29	0	1	.212	.240
Whalen, Brady	B-R	6-4	180	1-15-98	.248	.191	.259	121	435	57	108	30	1	7	81	56	6	0	11	101	0	5	.370	.335
Wilson, Alexis	R-R	5-10	168	8-13-96	.265	.200	.271	53	181	15	48	8	0	4	15	14	3	0	2	32	1	1	.376	.325
Yepez, Juan	R-R	6-1	200	2-19-98	.284	.000	.309	25	88	14	25	7	0	4	13	11	1	0	1	24	2	1	.500	.366
Ynfante, Wadye	R-R	6-0	160	8-15-97	.219	.257	.214	91	301	36	66	7	1	3	19	21	8	0	2	94	12	5	.279	.286

Pitching	B-T	HT	WT	DOB	W	L	ERA	G	GS	CG	SV	IP	H	R	ER	HR	BB	SO	AVG	vLH	vRH	K/9	BB/9
Aker, Cole	R-R	6-2	205	9-18-96	0	3	6.17	20	8	0	3	47	31	37	32	6	46	61	.190	.193	.188	11.76	8.87
Avelino, Rodard	R-R	6-1	170	6-3-99	0	3	22.09	9	0	0	0	7	7	22	18	0	25	8	.269	.111	.353	9.82	30.68
Baird, Michael	R-R	6-5	210	7-9-95	0	1	1.54	4	3	0	0	12	11	2	2	0	3	14	.239	.095	.360	10.80	2.31
Blanco, Fabian	L-L	6-0	205	12-22-97	2	1	7.65	17	0	0	0	20	23	17	17	1	19	22	.295	.241	.327	9.90	8.55
Brettell, Michael	R-R	6-3	195	7-13-97	5	10	5.76	26	21	0	0	120	151	89	77	13	47	79	.311	.330	.297	5.91	3.52
Casadilla, Franyel	R-R	6-3	240	4-5-97	6	4	5.21	27	8	0	0	76	94	50	44	11	24	61	.308	.276	.333	7.22	2.84
Cordero, Diego	L-L	6-3	175	9-8-97	2	6	3.45	12	12	0	0	70	72	32	27	4	22	49	.263	.260	.264	6.27	2.82
Coward, Connor	R-R	6-0	200	5-31-96	1	0	3.48	7	0	0	1	10	10	4	4	2	6	14	.250	.154	.296	12.19	5.23
De Jesus, Noel	R-R	6-3	181	1-8-97	0	0	4.15	5	0	0	0	9	9	5	4	2	3	8	.290	.177	.429	8.31	3.12
Escobar, Edgar	R-R	6-1	220	1-20-97	1	2	1.36	24	0	0	5	33	19	10	5	0	14	39	.164	.182	.148	10.64	3.82
Figuera, Edwin	R-R	5-10	160	9-2-97	0	0	18.00	1	0	0	0	1	3	2	2	0	2	0	.500	1.000	.400	0.00	18.00
Gragg, Logan	R-R	6-5	200	8-8-98	0	3	3.38	9	8	0	0	35	37	17	13	3	12	35	.270	.293	.253	9.09	3.12
Hunt, Chris	R-R	6-3	210	1-16-95	0	0	8.53	3	0	0	0	6	9	7	6	1	2	4	.333	.385	.286	5.68	2.84
Kelly, Parker	R-R	6-1	235	4-1-97	3	6	4.08	21	9	0	0	75	72	41	34	6	19	62	.254	.266	.247	7.44	2.28
Kraus, Eli	L-L	6-1	190	2-3-96	1	2	5.79	10	0	0	0	14	15	9	9	2	5	13	.273	.444	.239	8.36	3.21
Leahy, Kyle	B-R	6-5	200	6-4-97	4	8	3.00	16	16	1	0	90	78	33	30	4	22	81	.232	.247	.219	8.10	2.20
Locey, Tony	R-R	6-3	239	7-29-98	1	2	6.00	10	0	0	0	15	15	12	10	1	10	28	.259	.227	.278	16.80	6.00
Martinez, Carlos	R-R	6-0	190	9-21-91	0	0	0.00	1	0	0	0	1	0	0	0	0	0	0	.000	.000	.000	0.00	0.00
Pacheco, Freddy	R-R	5-11	203	4-17-98	1	4	4.12	41	0	0	3	55	38	29	25	0	56	90	.192	.205	.182	14.82	9.22
Parsons, Tommy	R-R	6-4	185	9-1-95	4	0	0.26	5	5	1	0	35	14	1	1	1	5	26	.120	.106	.129	6.69	1.29
Pereira, Wilfredo	R-R	5-11	197	4-26-99	1	0	2.45	7	0	0	0	26	21	7	7	0	6	28	.223	.171	.264	9.82	2.10
Roach, Dalton	R-R	6-2	210	4-8-96	1	1	3.71	6	6	0	0	34	30	16	14	0	15	34	.240	.225	.250	9.00	3.97
Schlesener, Jacob	L-L	6-3	175	10-8-96	0	4	12.42	8	5	0	0	17	16	26	23	1	35	22	.246	.235	.250	11.88	18.90
Schmid, Colin	L-L	6-1	195	8-13-97	6	7	4.58	20	20	0	0	106	119	63	54	8	42	97	.285	.273	.287	8.24	3.57
Seijas, Alvaro	R-R	6-1	175	10-10-98	4	5	2.93	14	14	1	0	80	73	30	26	6	28	71	.246	.241	.252	7.99	3.15
Shaw, Josh	R-R	6-1	195	11-30-96	0	0	81.00	1	0	0	0	0	3	3	3	2	0	1	.750	--	.750	27.00	0.00
Sisk, Evan	L-L	6-2	209	4-23-97	3	6	3.25	41	0	0	5	61	59	27	22	3	26	56	.260	.214	.280	8.26	3.84
St. Clair, Thomas	R-R	6-1	186	5-16-94	2	0	9.00	24	0	0	1	34	37	34	34	3	38	35	.285	.307	.265	9.26	10.06
Tabata, Sebastian	R-R	6-5	210	2-27-98	3	4	9.30	40	0	0	5	49	50	57	51	6	55	49	.269	.325	.226	8.94	10.03
Taveras, Leonardo	R-R	6-5	190	9-7-98	1	0	4.50	6	0	0	3	8	9	4	4	0	7	13	.273	.182	.318	14.63	7.88
Thomas, Connor	L-L	5-11	173	5-29-98	2	1	3.62	10	2	0	1	27	25	12	11	2	9	19	.248	.231	.253	6.26	2.96
Voyles, Jim	R-R	6-7	205	3-20-95	0	0	5.40	2	0	0	0	5	7	3	3	1	2	4	.333	.600	.091	7.20	3.60
Zamora, Dionis	R-R	6-2	193	8-2-96	0	2	15.43	2	2	0	0	7	14	12	12	1	5	13	.400	.333	.450	16.71	6.43

Fielding

Catcher	PCT	G	PO	A	E	DP	PB
Herrera	.984	64	561	38	10	6	10
Jackson	.986	7	67	6	1	0	0
Soto	.993	17	131	12	1	1	1
Wilson	.985	52	405	46	7	3	4

First Base	PCT	G	PO	A	E	DP
Cedeno	.977	20	153	14	4	22
Shaw	.993	16	128	10	1	11
Whalen	.991	99	697	50	7	60
Yepez	.982	6	50	6	1	5

Second Base	PCT	G	PO	A	E	DP
Donovan	.977	101	161	225	9	52

	PCT	G	PO	A	E	DP
Figuera	.964	24	35	45	3	9
Shaw	1.000	15	19	32	0	5

Third Base	PCT	G	PO	A	E	DP
Diaz	.943	27	22	44	4	3
Figuera	.940	18	19	28	3	6
Gorman	.940	51	43	97	9	10
Nunez	.750	8	4	8	4	0
Shaw	.912	24	17	45	6	5
Yepez	1.000	11	7	22	0	1

Shortstop	PCT	G	PO	A	E	DP
Diaz	1.000	2	0	1	0	0
Figuera	.949	16	19	37	3	7
Perez	.947	112	167	265	24	59

	PCT	G	PO	A	E	DP
Shaw	.967	10	14	15	1	4

Outfield	PCT	G	PO	A	E	DP
Benson	.976	36	78	3	2	0
Cedeno	.969	64	115	10	4	1
Denton	.946	22	35	0	2	0
Figuera	.000	1	0	0	0	0
Luna	1.000	4	6	0	0	0
Machado	.945	38	67	2	4	0
Nootbaar	.980	27	46	2	1	0
Riley	.986	115	200	9	3	1
Shaw	1.000	2	1	0	0	0
Torres	.979	20	44	3	1	1
Yepez	1.000	3	7	0	0	0
Ynfante	.981	89	195	13	4	2

STATE COLLEGE SPIKES

SHORT SEASON

NEW YORK-PENN LEAGUE

Batting	B-T	HT	WT	DOB	AVG	vLH	vRH	G	AB	R	H	2B	3B	HR	RBI	BB	HBP	SH	SF	SO	SB	CS	SLG	OBP
Benes, Shane	R-R	6-2	195	2-16-96	.126	.191	.108	27	95	7	12	6	0	1	3	1	0	0	43	0	0	.221	.162
Castillo, Moises	R-R	6-1	170	7-14-99	.249	.286	.240	56	221	35	55	9	0	1	16	23	5	3	1	44	8	2	.303	.332
Diaz, Imeldo	R-R	6-0	175	11-2-97	.154	.200	.125	3	13	3	2	0	0	0	0	0	0	0	3	0	0	.154	.154
Duce, Matt	L-R	5-11	190	11-22-95	.308	.333	.300	35	133	19	41	10	0	3	18	14	0	0	0	30	0	0	.451	.374
Espinal, Stanley	R-R	6-2	190	11-15-96	.267	.280	.263	58	210	29	56	14	3	3	34	20	2	0	5	39	2	3	.405	.329

Name	B-T	HT	WT	DOB	AVG	vLH	vRH	G	AB	R	H	2B	3B	HR	RBI	BB	HBP	SH	SF	SO	SB	CS	SLG	OBP
Figuera, Edwin	R-R	5-10	160	9-2-97	.167	.000	.211	8	24	5	4	1	0	0	0	1	4	0	0	8	1	0	.208	.310
Figueroa, Martin	B-R	5-11	200	12-14-95	.282	.233	.298	35	124	18	35	4	3	4	27	14	1	0	0	24	3	1	.460	.360
Flores, Luis	B-R	6-0	190	10-22-96	.167	.139	.180	39	114	11	19	2	1	2	15	12	0	1	2	29	3	3	.254	.242
Fuller, Terry	L-R	6-4	210	12-5-98	.223	.205	.229	42	157	24	35	5	1	1	19	23	0	0	1	54	1	0	.357	.320
Gomez, Dariel	L-R	6-4	190	7-15-96	.262	.231	.272	63	221	30	58	14	1	6	27	28	0	0	1	51	0	1	.416	.344
Knight, Cameron	R-R	6-0	205	11-15-94	.148	.154	.146	18	54	2	8	2	0	0	3	3	0	0	0	17	0	0	.185	.193
Luna, Andres	R-R	5-10	175	7-17-97	.255	.400	.216	13	47	9	12	5	0	0	7	8	1	0	0	10	1	1	.362	.375
Machado, Jonatan	L-L	5-9	155	1-21-99	.324	.191	.377	17	74	14	24	3	1	1	12	9	0	0	1	9	4	2	.432	.393
Pages, Pedro	R-R	6-1	234	9-17-98	.291	.308	.286	50	179	29	52	17	1	2	21	28	4	0	3	39	1	0	.430	.393
Purcell, Brandon	R-R	6-1	205	7-2-94	.400	1.000	.357	5	15	2	6	1	0	0	5	2	1	0	0	3	0	0	.467	.500
Sabino, Liam	R-R	6-0	205	5-1-96	.286	.000	.333	4	14	4	4	0	0	0	1	2	1	0	0	2	0	0	.286	.412
Soto, Carlos	L-R	6-2	220	4-27-99	.250	.241	.253	30	116	15	29	6	1	4	23	14	1	0	4	35	0	0	.422	.326
Vinsky, David	R-L	6-0	198	7-9-98	.284	.321	.273	56	236	34	67	14	2	1	19	19	2	0	2	44	9	3	.373	.340
Ware, Brylie	R-R	6-0	220	7-17-96	.197	.152	.207	51	173	15	34	7	1	1	24	22	4	1	2	33	0	1	.266	.299
Warner, Andrew	R-R	6-2	225	12-4-95	.248	.231	.254	46	153	26	38	8	1	7	28	22	7	0	0	65	1	2	.451	.368
Williams, Donivan	R-R	6-0	190	7-25-99	.218	.143	.240	46	156	21	34	5	1	1	11	26	4	0	2	53	4	2	.282	.340
Woodall, Kevin	R-R	6-6	240	3-20-96	.250	.500	.000	1	4	1	1	0	0	1	0	0	1	0	0	0	2	0	1.000	.250

Pitching	B-T	HT	WT	DOB	W	L	ERA	G	GS	CG	SV	IP	H	R	ER	HR	BB	SO	AVG	vLH	vRH	K/9	BB/9
Avelino, Rodard	R-R	6-1	170	6-3-99	0	0	8.31	5	0	0	0	4	3	5	4	0	10	7	.188	.200	.182	14.54	20.77
Baird, Michael	R-R	6-5	210	7-9-95	2	0	0.00	3	1	0	0	10	4	1	0	0	3	13	.111	.333	.037	11.32	2.61
Blanco, Fabian	L-L	6-0	205	12-22-97	3	1	2.48	22	0	0	3	33	27	10	9	1	10	40	.227	.293	.192	11.02	2.76
Cordova, Martin	R-R	6-0	175	6-28-99	1	0	0.00	2	0	0	0	4	2	0	0	0	1	2	.143	.000	.182	4.15	2.08
Dulle, Cameron	R-R	6-3	202	6-14-95	2	1	2.50	11	0	0	1	18	18	5	5	1	3	22	.247	.167	.302	11.00	1.50
Gonzalez, Junior	R-R	6-3	175	11-7-96	3	6	6.50	18	7	0	1	54	72	46	39	6	21	37	.316	.348	.294	6.17	3.50
Gragg, Logan	R-R	6-5	200	8-8-98	0	0	2.45	8	0	0	2	11	8	5	3	1	3	15	.186	.071	.241	12.27	2.45
Heredia, Nathanael	L-L	6-3	190	9-10-00	0	0	27.00	1	1	0	0	1	2	5	2	1	3	1	.500	1.000	.000	13.50	40.50
Kraus, Eli	L-L	6-1	190	2-3-96	1	2	3.86	4	0	0	0	7	7	5	3	0	3	7	.259	.300	.235	9.00	3.86
Lex, Eric	R-R	6-2	205	11-1-95	0	3	3.55	19	0	0	4	25	22	11	10	1	6	25	.222	.229	.219	8.88	2.13
Lunn, Connor	R-R	6-3	215	7-8-98	0	0	1.96	12	0	0	0	18	13	5	4	0	6	20	.191	.214	.175	9.82	2.95
Mardueno, Adrian	R-R	5-10	180	2-3-98	3	2	3.59	13	11	0	0	53	51	23	21	5	20	38	.258	.305	.224	6.49	3.42
Pallante, Andre	R-R	6-0	203	9-18-98	1	0	2.78	11	9	0	0	36	27	11	11	2	11	38	.211	.208	.213	9.59	2.78
Paniagua, Inohan	R-R	6-1	148	2-6-00	0	0	10.13	2	2	0	0	5	7	6	6	0	6	1	.389	.333	.400	1.69	10.13
Politz, Scott	R-R	6-2	205	8-22-96	4	3	4.63	14	13	0	0	70	71	40	36	4	22	49	.260	.283	.246	6.30	2.83
Ralston, Jack	R-R	6-6	231	8-13-97	1	0	1.07	17	0	0	5	25	12	4	3	0	7	26	.135	.121	.143	9.24	2.49
Randolph, Jeremy	R-R	5-11	210	10-2-95	3	2	4.04	16	3	0	0	42	44	27	19	4	20	49	.259	.243	.270	10.42	4.25
Roach, Dalton	R-R	6-2	210	4-8-96	1	0	2.45	2	2	0	0	11	8	4	3	2	4	16	.195	.300	.095	13.09	3.27
Schlesener, Jacob	L-L	6-3	175	10-8-96	2	6	4.37	18	6	0	0	58	46	43	28	3	35	81	.215	.281	.187	12.64	5.46
Solano, Enmanuel	R-R	6-1	160	9-23-98	4	7	3.39	14	13	1	0	82	75	38	31	4	26	58	.246	.276	.228	6.34	2.84
Soto, Hector	R-R	6-1	175	3-2-99	0	0	0.00	1	1	0	0	4	3	0	0	0	1	4	.200	.200	.200	9.00	2.25
Taveras, Leonardo	R-R	6-5	190	9-7-98	1	1	3.68	6	0	0	1	7	3	5	3	0	4	10	.125	.143	.118	12.27	4.91
Thomas, Connor	L-L	5-11	173	5-29-98	2	0	4.02	5	2	0	0	16	17	9	7	0	1	17	.266	.143	.326	9.77	0.57
Ventura, Francis	R-R	6-2	195	7-22-99	0	0	5.73	2	2	0	0	11	13	7	7	1	4	4	.317	.471	.208	3.27	3.27
Villalobos, Hector	L-L	5-11	182	8-19-96	4	1	2.88	20	0	0	0	41	32	16	13	2	13	44	.212	.111	.255	9.74	2.85
YaSenka, Michael	R-R	6-1	195	5-26-98	1	1	2.45	3	0	0	0	15	9	5	4	0	7	12	.170	.211	.147	7.36	4.30

Fielding

C: Duce 15, Knight 13, Pages 27, Purcell 4, Soto 19. 1B: Benes 8, Gomez 51, Soto 7, Ware 11. 2B: Figueroa 27, Sabino 3, Ware 1, Williams 46. 3B: Benes 17, Diaz 2, Figuera 5, Flores 13, Ware 41. SS: Castillo 56, Diaz 1, Figuera 2, Flores 20. OF: Espinal 58, Flores 4, Fuller 40, Gomez 8, Luna 12, Machado 17, Vinsky 56, Warner 38, Woodall 1.

JOHNSON CITY CARDINALS   ROOKIE ADVANCED
APPALACHIAN LEAGUE

Batting	B-T	HT	WT	DOB	AVG	vLH	vRH	G	AB	R	H	2B	3B	HR	RBI	BB	HBP	SH	SF	SO	SB	CS	SLG	OBP
Antonini, Aaron	L-R	6-0	200	7-27-98	.219	.333	.197	25	73	18	16	4	1	5	14	18	2	1	0	8	2	0	.507	.387
Baird, Ben	R-R	6-3	190	1-7-98	.091	.071	.100	16	44	6	4	0	0	0	1	4	1	1	0	22	1	0	.091	.184
Del Rio, Diomedes	L-L	5-10	160	9-15-97	.216	.348	.186	45	125	21	27	5	2	2	19	13	1	0	0	47	4	1	.336	.295
Fletcher, Trejyn	R-R	6-2	200	4-30-01	.228	.225	.229	34	123	9	28	4	1	2	18	7	1	0	2	59	7	1	.325	.271
Fuller, Terry	L-R	6-4	210	12-5-98	.247	.400	.222	21	73	13	18	5	1	1	9	15	2	0	0	26	3	4	.384	.389
Garcia, Victor	R-R	6-3	235	9-16-99	.254	.367	.236	36	118	13	30	3	0	3	13	6	2	0	1	32	0	0	.356	.299
Gil, Mateo	R-R	6-1	180	7-24-00	.270	.278	.268	51	204	42	55	8	2	7	30	17	1	0	3	56	1	3	.431	.324
Jackson, Zach	L-R	6-3	215	5-24-98	.171	.171	.171	44	158	27	27	6	1	5	29	25	2	0	2	58	1	0	.317	.289
Jimenez, William	R-R	5-10	171	1-23-96	.218	.200	.225	18	55	10	12	2	0	1	4	14	2	0	0	16	3	1	.309	.394
Lott, Todd	R-R	6-4	235	8-22-97	.250	.232	.256	57	212	28	53	15	2	4	25	12	2	0	3	53	6	0	.396	.293
Nunez, Malcom	R-R	5-11	205	3-9-01	.254	.282	.242	37	130	14	33	11	0	2	13	13	3	0	0	32	3	2	.385	.336
Ozuna, Raffy	R-R	6-3	196	9-6-98	.169	.306	.105	30	77	7	13	3	0	2	9	10	0	0	2	33	0	1	.286	.258
Purcell, Brandon	R-R	6-1	205	7-2-94	.381	.000	.421	7	21	5	8	3	0	1	6	5	0	0	1	4	1	0	.667	.482
Redmond, Chandler	L-R	6-1	231	1-9-97	.287	.257	.295	54	181	37	52	12	0	12	40	25	4	0	2	55	4	2	.553	.382
Sabino, Liam	R-R	6-0	205	5-1-96	.282	.303	.277	51	174	30	49	11	2	6	33	25	5	0	1	53	4	3	.471	.385
Skeels, Kyle	R-R	6-2	250	9-9-96	.250	.250	.250	27	88	13	22	5	0	2	9	8	5	1	1	28	0	1	.375	.343
Soler, Carlos	L-R	6-2	163	10-29-99	.224	.241	.219	48	143	22	32	7	0	1	12	16	0	1	0	50	6	2	.294	.302
Torres, Jhon	R-R	6-4	199	3-29-00	.286	.375	.271	33	112	24	32	9	0	6	17	19	1	0	1	36	0	2	.527	.391
Vargas, Kevin	R-R	6-1	175	2-14-00	.238	.294	.222	28	80	11	19	3	0	0	6	9	3	2	1	21	8	1	.275	.333
Vinsky, David	R-L	6-0	198	7-9-98	.211	.250	.200	5	19	3	4	0	0	1	4	2	1	0	0	7	0	1	.368	.318

Pitching	B-T	HT	WT	DOB	W	L	ERA	G	GS	CG	SV	IP	H	R	ER	HR	BB	SO	AVG	vLH	vRH	K/9	BB/9
Drake, Blake	R-R	6-1	190	7-11-93	0	1	8.22	6	0	0	0	8	11	11	7	1	6	8	.344	.188	.500	9.39	7.04
Dulle, Cameron	R-R	6-3	202	6-14-95	2	1	5.19	8	0	0	1	9	7	5	5	0	4	5	.219	.222	.214	5.19	4.15
Gallegos, Alex	R-R	6-3	174	5-14-98	0	1	11.90	17	0	0	0	20	36	27	26	3	15	10	.396	.410	.385	4.58	6.86

ST. LOUIS CARDINALS

Name	B-T	HT	WT	DOB	W	L	ERA	G	GS	CG	SV	IP	H	R	ER	HR	BB	SO	AVG	vLH	vRH	K/9	BB/9
Guay, Will	R-R	6-3	216	5-30-97	1	1	2.35	16	3	0	4	31	26	12	8	3	14	42	.222	.200	.239	12.33	4.11
Justo, Francisco	R-R	6-4	217	10-12-98	3	2	3.83	12	8	0	0	54	45	28	23	4	12	43	.226	.257	.194	7.17	2.00
Moreno, Jose	R-R	6-0	197	8-20-00	3	5	8.33	13	13	0	0	54	93	60	50	8	29	41	.391	.417	.369	6.83	4.83
Ortiz, Luis	R-R	6-3	170	7-23-00	0	4	10.73	7	6	0	0	24	46	34	29	4	13	16	.393	.346	.431	5.92	4.81
Pearce, Dylan	L-R	5-9	175	5-1-97	1	2	4.35	14	0	0	2	21	24	14	10	3	10	29	.289	.394	.220	12.63	4.35
Peck, Tyler	R-R	6-1	221	10-2-97	2	3	4.84	14	0	0	1	22	25	14	12	2	11	23	.294	.167	.516	9.27	4.43
Pereira, Wilfredo	R-R	5-11	197	4-26-99	2	1	2.42	11	1	0	2	26	21	9	7	5	7	21	.217	.333	.156	7.27	2.42
Perez, Enrique	L-L	6-2	180	8-10-97	2	3	5.01	19	0	0	1	23	23	17	13	1	17	29	.245	.282	.218	11.19	6.56
Puello, Julio	R-R	6-4	185	1-7-99	5	4	5.40	13	13	0	0	72	77	45	43	8	18	68	.274	.264	.285	8.54	2.26
Rivera, Wilberto	R-R	6-3	207	4-26-99	1	0	5.33	15	0	0	1	25	28	19	15	3	9	27	.286	.326	.250	9.59	3.20
Roach, Dalton	R-R	6-2	210	4-8-96	1	0	5.64	4	4	0	0	22	21	15	14	4	3	21	.247	.263	.234	8.46	1.21
Robbins, Walker	L-L	6-3	215	11-18-97	3	0	2.52	17	0	0	2	25	22	11	7	0	10	31	.227	.212	.234	11.16	3.60
Santana, Saniel	R-R	6-1	213	8-12-99	0	0	0.00	2	0	0	0	4	4	0	0	0	0	3	.267	.300	.200	7.36	0.00
Sommers, Jake	R-R	6-2	190	5-5-97	2	3	4.18	12	10	0	0	52	51	27	24	7	19	55	.256	.284	.231	9.58	3.31
Soto, Hector	R-R	6-1	175	3-2-99	1	1	2.56	9	5	0	1	32	26	15	9	3	6	35	.213	.196	.227	9.95	1.71
Taveras, Leonardo	R-R	6-5	190	9-7-98	0	0	0.00	3	0	0	0	3	0	0	0	0	0	7	.000	.000	.000	21.00	0.00
Witkowski, John	B-R	6-5	210	3-14-96	4	0	2.81	15	0	0	4	26	21	9	8	3	4	27	.208	.255	.160	9.47	1.40
YaSenka, Michael	R-R	6-1	195	5-26-98	2	1	0.56	7	5	1	0	32	21	7	2	1	6	37	.184	.188	.182	10.30	1.67

Fielding
C: Antonini 24, Jackson 30, Purcell 7, Skeels 9. 1B: Lott 41, Ozuna 9, Redmond 13, Sabino 6, Skeels 5. 2B: Baird 9, Ozuna 4, Redmond 13, Sabino 29, Vargas 20. 3B: Nunez 32, Ozuna 9, Redmond 19, Sabino 13. SS: Baird 7, Gil 51, Ozuna 6, Vargas 10. OF: Del Rio 44, Fletcher 32, Fuller 17, Garcia 27, Jimenez 18, Soler 46, Torres 30, Vinsky 5, Witkowski 1.

GCL CARDINALS   ROOKIE
GULF COAST LEAGUE

Batting	B-T	HT	WT	DOB	AVG	vLH	vRH	G	AB	R	H	2B	3B	HR	RBI	BB	HBP	SH	SF	SO	SB	CS	SLG	OBP
Burgos, Diowill	L-R	6-1	190	1-29-01	.205	.250	.194	22	78	11	16	4	0	2	8	11	1	0	0	27	2	2	.333	.311
Cruz, Adanson	R-R	6-2	175	10-6-00	.000	.000	.000	3	11	0	0	0	0	0	0	0	0	0	0	2	0	0	.000	.000
De Jesus, Freddy	R-R	6-1	200	10-15-99	.180	.211	.175	38	122	15	22	4	0	3	10	16	5	0	1	37	0	0	.287	.299
De Los Santos, Joerlin	R-R	5-11	175	9-16-00	.167	.077	.196	30	72	9	12	0	0	0	2	9	1	1	1	11	2	0	.167	.265
Fletcher, Trejyn	R-R	6-2	200	4-30-01	.297	.286	.300	9	37	6	11	3	0	2	8	4	0	0	1	17	0	0	.541	.357
Garcia, Joyser	R-R	5-10	165	10-14-99	.241	.400	.208	21	58	6	14	3	0	0	6	6	0	0	1	16	0	0	.293	.308
Gomez, Pablo	R-R	5-11	170	9-4-99	.210	.207	.198	44	124	15	26	6	1	3	16	21	5	1	3	30	0	3	.347	.340
Hernandez, Francisco	R-R	5-11	190	10-8-99	.226	.207	.239	40	146	20	33	8	0	7	21	14	4	0	1	31	4	2	.425	.309
Jimenez, William	R-R	5-10	171	1-23-96	.343	.111	.377	21	73	14	25	3	1	3	17	10	1	0	2	17	5	2	.534	.419
Kreuter, Cole	R-R	6-0	190	11-29-95	.222	.667	.133	7	18	5	4	3	0	0	2	1	1	0	0	3	0	0	.389	.333
Longa, Cristhian	R-R	5-11	180	4-28-00	.226	.125	.244	28	102	7	23	7	0	0	8	4	4	0	0	28	2	2	.294	.282
Mendoza, Ramon	R-R	5-11	174	8-31-00	.284	.261	.291	33	102	19	29	9	0	1	9	14	4	2	1	27	0	4	.402	.388
Montano, Luis	L-R	6-2	170	4-10-00	.192	.069	.223	40	141	17	27	11	3	0	19	13	3	0	1	60	1	2	.312	.272
Montero, Elehuris	R-R	6-3	215	8-17-98	.308	.333	.300	4	13	1	4	0	0	0	1	1	0	0	0	2	0	0	.308	.400
Reichenborn, Tyler	R-R	5-11	180	7-23-98	.250	.444	.220	21	68	9	17	2	3	3	8	10	0	3	15	1	5	.500	.357
Richardson, Zade	R-R	6-1	200	5-10-00	.191	.167	.200	22	68	8	13	4	0	1	4	12	2	0	0	27	1	1	.294	.329
Romeri, Patrick	R-R	6-3	195	6-29-01	.246	.222	.252	41	138	23	34	6	3	6	20	19	3	0	2	46	4	0	.464	.346
Rosario, Yowelfy	R-R	6-3	165	6-9-00	.207	.222	.209	40	140	7	29	5	2	1	18	13	2	1	1	50	3	4	.293	.282
Selmo, Jean	R-R	6-2	190	4-25-00	.182	.300	.161	23	66	5	12	3	0	1	9	4	0	0	1	31	1	0	.273	.247
Soto, Franklin	R-R	5-11	168	9-23-99	.226	.231	.233	41	146	24	33	9	2	2	12	20	5	0	3	33	6	4	.356	.339

Pitching	B-T	HT	WT	DOB	W	L	ERA	G	GS	CG	SV	IP	H	R	ER	HR	BB	SO	AVG	vLH	vRH	K/9	BB/9
Cordova, Martin	R-R	6-0	175	6-28-99	0	1	6.31	16	2	0	1	36	42	28	25	5	18	17	.292	.281	.300	4.29	4.54
Coward, Connor	R-R	6-0	200	5-31-96	1	0	0.00	9	0	0	3	12	4	0	0	0	3	9	.050	.000	.074	6.75	2.25
Drake, Blake	R-R	6-1	190	7-11-93	0	0	15.00	4	3	0	0	3	3	5	5	0	4	2	.273	.000	.375	6.00	12.00
Garcia, Roy	R-R	6-0	190	8-28-00	2	5	8.65	14	2	0	3	26	32	28	25	2	24	28	.305	.321	.299	9.69	8.31
Gingery, Steven	R-L	6-1	210	9-23-97	0	1	13.50	1	1	0	0	1	1	1	1	0	1	1	.333	--	.333	13.50	13.50
Gonzalez, Merandy	R-R	6-0	216	10-9-95	0	0	0.00	5	2	0	0	6	4	0	0	0	2	10	.211	.167	.231	15.00	3.00
Green, Anthony	R-R	6-4	210	10-15-97	1	2	5.04	10	4	0	0	30	39	20	17	2	14	28	.310	.326	.300	8.31	4.15
Hart, Thomas	R-R	6-2	155	12-5-00	2	2	7.59	12	1	0	0	21	18	19	18	4	34	11	.240	.278	.205	4.64	14.34
Heredia, Nathanael	L-L	6-3	190	9-10-00	5	4	3.83	12	7	0	0	49	43	27	21	2	35	48	.234	.213	.241	8.76	6.39
Herget, Kevin	L-R	5-10	185	4-3-91	0	0	6.00	2	1	0	0	3	3	2	2	1	0	4	.250	.500	.200	12.00	0.00
Jimenez, Ludwin	R-R	6-2	165	8-9-01	2	4	4.59	10	7	0	0	51	48	29	26	6	24	51	.246	.257	.240	9.00	4.24
Locey, Tony	R-R	6-3	239	7-29-98	0	0	0.00	2	0	0	0	1	0	0	0	0	2	3	.143	.250	.000	13.50	9.00
Madera, Wilman	R-R	6-2	200	3-10-99	1	1	5.20	14	0	0	0	28	26	19	16	3	7	30	.239	.257	.230	9.76	2.28
Ortiz, Luis	R-R	6-3	170	7-23-00	1	3	3.43	5	3	0	1	21	26	18	8	3	9	15	.292	.216	.346	6.43	3.86
Paniagua, Inohan	R-R	6-1	148	2-6-00	2	5	5.98	11	9	0	0	50	59	40	33	3	16	47	.295	.284	.301	8.52	2.90
Perez, Williams	R-R	6-0	240	5-21-91	0	0	0.00	3	3	0	0	4	3	1	0	0	2	5	.200	.222	.167	11.25	4.50
Santana, Saniel	R-R	6-1	213	8-12-99	0	0	7.94	6	0	0	0	6	6	6	5	1	9	4	.286	.400	.250	6.35	14.29
Soto, Hector	R-R	6-1	175	3-2-99	0	0	5.91	4	0	0	1	11	7	7	7	1	3	14	.175	.182	.172	11.81	2.53
Statler, Tyler	R-R	6-6	230	7-1-01	0	2	5.91	10	1	0	0	11	13	9	7	0	10	12	.296	.353	.259	10.13	8.44
Tena, Luis	R-R	5-11	172	10-21-99	1	0	5.03	10	0	0	0	20	24	11	11	0	7	20	.308	.286	.320	9.15	3.20
Thompson, Zack	L-L	6-2	225	10-28-97	0	0	0.00	2	2	0	0	3	1	0	0	0	4	4	.300	.500	.250	18.00	0.00
Trompiz, Anthony	R-R	6-3	214	11-20-97	1	2	4.74	14	0	0	3	25	27	14	13	2	9	18	.294	.282	.302	6.57	3.28
Ventura, Francis	R-R	6-2	195	7-22-99	1	2	5.18	11	5	0	0	49	65	36	28	2	19	31	.330	.359	.311	5.73	3.51
Walsh, Jake	R-R	6-1	192	7-20-95	0	0	10.80	2	1	0	0	2	2	2	2	0	1	4	.286	.500	.200	21.60	5.40

Fielding
C: Garcia 19, Kreuter 3, Longa 25, Richardson 15. 1B: De Jesus 32, Gomez 25, Hernandez 1, Kreuter 2, Longa 1. 2B: Gomez 15, Kreuter 1, Mendoza 32, Rosario 6. 3B: Gomez 5, Hernandez 37, Montero 2, Rosario 13. SS: Rosario 18, Soto 39. OF: Burgos 16, Cruz 1, De Los Santos 26, Fletcher 7, Jimenez 19, Montano 37, Reichenborn 19, Romeri 38, Selmo 15.

DOMINICAN SUMMER LEAGUE

Batting	B-T	HT	WT	DOB	AVG	vLH	vRH	G	AB	R	H	2B	3B	HR	RBI	BB	HBP	SH	SF	SO	SB	CS	SLG	OBP
Andujar, Luis	R-R	6-1	165	1-19-00	.321	.280	.326	60	215	37	69	15	3	1	47	33	4	1	6	47	12	6	.433	.411
Arcia, Carlos	B-R	5-8	140	5-4-02	.226	.240	.222	36	115	26	26	2	0	1	13	25	3	1	1	35	7	2	.270	.375
Brazoban, Fernando	R-R	6-0	170	4-11-02	.217	.296	.203	55	180	30	39	7	4	3	37	31	9	2	3	46	8	0	.350	.354
Burgos, Diowill	L-R	6-1	190	1-29-01	.382	.360	.387	36	131	30	50	12	3	9	42	27	0	1	2	24	5	2	.725	.481
De Jesus, Elvin	B-R	5-11	160	8-29-01	.272	.360	.243	49	202	36	55	9	6	3	28	29	5	1	1	60	19	2	.421	.376
Del Villar, Darlyn	R-R	6-0	176	11-8-00	.219	.183	.233	55	219	40	48	8	3	1	34	34	3	1	2	49	9	3	.297	.330
Diaz, Fernando	L-R	6-4	185	1-12-02	.270	.306	.258	54	200	31	54	12	0	6	30	23	13	0	2	72	1	2	.420	.378
Heredia, Roblin	L-R	6-0	200	7-22-02	.231	.357	.218	41	147	24	34	4	4	1	27	28	3	1	2	46	5	1	.333	.361
Hernandez, Brandon	L-R	6-0	190	8-21-01	.271	.281	.269	38	140	19	38	9	2	1	20	21	6	0	0	41	2	2	.386	.389
Inoa, Albert	R-R	5-11	170	12-4-01	.306	.231	.316	59	216	54	66	10	2	1	25	52	8	2	1	47	14	5	.384	.455
Marcos, Miguel	R-R	6-0	150	12-26-01	.218	.333	.198	34	101	10	22	3	0	2	16	12	1	1	2	36	5	1	.307	.302
Matute, Bryan	R-R	5-11	165	3-25-02	.214	.130	.228	53	168	30	36	10	0	0	14	41	2	0	0	51	9	2	.274	.374
Moquete, Darlin	R-R	5-11	175	9-19-99	.390	.286	.420	43	154	43	60	5	4	5	33	17	6	0	4	16	23	4	.571	.459
Mora, Sander	R-R	5-9	155	2-23-01	.266	.171	.281	65	256	63	68	13	2	0	26	49	4	1	2	54	33	8	.332	.389
Orecchia, Jesus	R-R	6-1	175	4-22-01	.192	.174	.195	44	146	19	28	5	1	1	18	20	1	1	1	25	1	0	.260	.292
Otamendi, Hansel	R-R	5-9	180	2-15-02	.237	.225	.241	57	194	39	46	7	2	0	43	7	1	5	23	10	2	.294	.386
Pena, Erik	B-R	5-8	140	1-6-00	.252	.333	.225	43	107	27	27	4	0	0	8	20	9	3	0	24	9	2	.290	.412
Pena, Leudy	L-R	6-3	197	11-17-00	.215	.139	.234	51	177	32	38	9	0	4	29	35	5	0	1	65	0	1	.333	.358
Ramirez, Claudio	R-R	6-1	185	11-3-00	.264	.290	.259	56	201	32	53	10	1	2	32	40	1	1	3	70	3	1	.353	.384
Rodriguez, Gustavo A.	R-R	6-2	185	1-24-00	.266	.393	.216	56	207	37	55	15	3	1	41	31	1	0	10	76	5	1	.382	.349
Rodriguez, Jose	R-R	6-3	200	8-4-02	.200	.125	.227	17	60	8	12	3	0	1	9	7	2	0	0	25	0	0	.300	.304
Rodriguez, Luis	R-R	6-0	175	2-26-00	.265	.256	.269	43	151	21	40	6	1	1	24	11	4	0	1	33	1	3	.338	.329
Salas, Endri	R-R	6-5	165	7-10-01	.279	.364	.267	23	86	15	24	4	2	0	10	10	5	0	0	17	2	1	.372	.386
Samuel, Alexander	R-R	6-3	190	3-24-00	.194	.077	.213	27	93	20	18	4	0	0	7	19	5	1	0	39	3	2	.237	.359
Sanchez, Juan	R-R	5-11	170	10-15-01	.193	.188	.194	28	88	11	17	4	0	0	12	10	2	0	1	30	1	0	.239	.287
Thomas, Erick	R-R	5-10	175	12-9-99	.226	.125	.244	33	106	16	24	4	1	2	15	12	4	0	0	34	2	5	.340	.328
Vargas, Smith	R-R	5-10	160	8-30-01	.249	.136	.261	59	225	42	56	9	5	0	20	31	3	3	1	63	28	4	.333	.346
Velasquez, Diego	R-R	5-10	175	3-25-02	.227	.125	.247	28	97	10	22	3	0	1	8	10	5	0	1	39	1	2	.289	.327
Zapata, Jose	R-R	5-11	195	2-14-01	.243	.222	.252	42	148	26	36	11	1	1	16	20	7	1	2	40	1	3	.351	.356

Pitching	B-T	HT	WT	DOB	W	L	ERA	G	GS	CG	SV	IP	H	R	ER	HR	BB	SO	AVG	vLH	vRH	K/9	BB/9
Arias, Benjamin	R-R	6-5	195	11-5-01	1	2	8.39	18	0	0	0	25	38	30	23	1	19	22	.328	.282	.351	8.03	6.93
Benitez, Allinson	R-R	6-4	200	11-4-99	2	0	1.64	8	0	0	0	11	9	2	2	0	10	11	.220	.313	.160	9.00	8.18
Calderon, Augusto	R-R	6-0	190	10-6-00	4	4	5.54	18	0	0	1	26	24	21	16	1	19	34	.242	.243	.242	11.77	6.58
Cordero, Hemerson	L-L	6-0	170	5-10-02	2	1	5.12	18	0	0	0	32	34	22	18	5	20	26	.272	.286	.269	7.39	5.68
Cuenca, Angel	R-R	6-1	160	7-10-01	5	1	2.00	12	12	0	0	63	40	21	14	3	18	60	.185	.181	.188	8.57	2.57
De Los Santos, Hector	R-R	6-0	170	9-18-98	1	3	4.25	18	0	0	3	30	25	19	14	2	26	42	.234	.194	.254	12.74	7.89
Dominguez, Yonael	R-R	6-2	175	10-24-01	2	1	4.46	12	7	0	0	40	38	21	20	2	28	38	.253	.326	.221	8.48	6.25
Fernandez, Ramon	R-R	6-2	180	10-26-98	3	3	6.07	19	0	0	1	30	31	28	20	2	21	25	.272	.250	.281	7.58	6.37
Garcia, Luis	R-R	6-2	185	2-13-01	2	0	3.23	22	1	0	3	39	40	19	14	4	17	31	.261	.263	.260	7.15	3.92
Gomez, Henry	R-R	6-1	163	10-17-01	1	1	4.14	11	10	0	0	46	52	26	21	2	12	29	.286	.364	.252	5.72	2.36
Guerrero, Diorys	L-L	6-0	170	2-1-01	0	3	6.51	11	11	0	0	37	40	32	27	0	21	36	.267	.148	.293	8.68	5.06
Jaquez, Jesus	R-R	6-3	195	12-26-01	0	0	8.84	12	0	0	0	18	24	22	18	3	11	11	.308	.286	.320	5.40	5.40
Jimenez, Ludwin	R-R	6-2	165	8-9-01	2	1	3.15	4	4	0	0	20	21	7	7	1	7	13	.296	.318	.286	5.85	3.15
Lopez, Oliver	R-R	6-2	165	4-1-02	2	2	5.46	18	0	0	0	28	30	27	17	3	25	13	.294	.333	.273	4.18	8.04
Lugo, Americo	R-R	6-1	192	8-27-00	0	1	4.38	9	0	0	1	12	16	7	6	0	2	14	.308	.286	.316	10.22	1.46
Maiz, Miguel	R-R	6-1	198	6-27-01	1	2	5.40	10	0	0	0	15	16	9	9	1	8	13	.276	.267	.279	7.80	4.80
Manzo, Edgar	R-R	5-11	181	10-24-00	2	4	3.68	12	12	0	0	59	62	36	24	5	23	56	.296	.292	.268	8.59	3.53
Marcelino, Hansel	R-R	6-1	165	6-16-02	0	0	5.25	10	0	0	0	12	12	8	7	1	13	11	.255	.286	.242	8.25	9.75
Martinez, Engels	R-R	5-11	165	5-13-02	2	3	4.39	12	11	0	0	55	50	38	27	5	16	40	.236	.198	.260	6.51	2.60
Miranda, William	R-R	6-1	170	2-14-01	4	0	1.74	22	1	0	0	41	39	8	8	0	21	41	.262	.378	.212	8.93	4.57
Ortega, Wilmer	R-R	6-1	169	4-4-01	5	0	2.77	12	12	0	0	55	49	23	17	1	17	39	.239	.349	.190	6.34	2.77
Ortiz, Luis	R-R	6-3	170	7-23-00	0	1	1.74	3	2	0	0	10	11	6	2	0	2	10	.268	.273	.267	8.71	1.74
Peralta, Juan	R-R	6-2	175	8-9-02	1	1	5.85	12	1	0	1	20	30	18	13	2	4	11	.349	.294	.385	4.95	1.80
Pimentel, Eduar	R-R	6-2	170	2-23-01	0	2	6.05	11	4	0	0	19	23	17	13	1	8	17	.284	.179	.340	7.91	3.72
Portillo, Reinys	R-R	6-2	165	1-14-01	2	4	2.87	12	12	0	0	60	49	23	19	3	20	56	.219	.203	.228	8.45	3.02
Prada, Nelson	L-L	6-2	170	5-6-00	5	2	3.33	18	0	0	0	27	31	12	10	0	7	23	.307	.318	.304	7.67	2.33
Ramirez, Brayan	R-R	6-4	200	9-29-01	1	1	3.31	10	1	0	0	16	13	16	6	1	21	17	.217	.118	.256	9.37	11.57
Ramirez, Josue	R-R	6-1	185	6-1-00	0	0	40.50	1	0	0	0	1	2	3	3	2	3	2	.500		.500	27.00	40.50
Richard, Yordy	R-R	6-1	195	8-27-02	4	0	4.31	12	8	0	0	48	46	26	23	1	21	43	.251	.281	.238	8.06	3.94
Rincon, Hancel	R-R	6-2	160	4-28-02	1	5	3.75	15	9	0	0	50	47	27	21	2	19	41	.242	.254	.237	7.33	3.40
Rodriguez, Dionys	L-R	6-0	188	9-3-00	2	1	5.88	17	0	0	2	26	18	20	17	1	19	32	.188	.214	.177	11.08	6.58
Rodriguez, Gustavo J.	R-R	6-3	160	1-8-01	4	1	2.04	12	12	0	0	57	51	22	13	1	11	53	.238	.236	.239	8.32	1.73
Soriano, Larimel	R-R	5-11	160	1-28-00	1	2	3.03	20	0	0	0	30	34	19	10	0	20	35	.283	.265	.296	10.62	6.07
Suarez, Ronald	R-R	6-4	215	3-5-00	1	2	6.75	16	0	0	0	21	18	17	16	1	26	22	.243	.364	.192	9.28	10.97
Tena, Luis	R-R	5-11	172	10-21-99	3	1	2.52	14	1	0	0	25	23	8	7	2	9	31	.247	.345	.203	11.16	3.24
Villanueva, Victor	R-R	6-1	170	3-26-01	3	3	1.64	12	0	0	3	33	28	14	6	0	6	16	.237	.237	.238	4.36	1.64
Yedis, Miguel	R-R	6-5	165	12-18-00	2	3	6.00	13	4	0	0	33	37	29	22	1	18	18	.294	.349	.265	4.91	4.91
Zapata, Cristoffer	L-L	6-1	150	10-30-98	2	1	3.57	18	0	0	6	18	7	7	7	1	14	18	.127	.091	.136	9.17	7.13

Fielding

C: Heredia 23, Orecchia 34, Rodriguez 23, Sanchez 12, Velasquez 7, Zapata 31. **1B:** Andujar 25, Diaz 45, Heredia 14, Orecchia 8, Rodriguez 21, Samuel 27, Thomas 1. **2B:** Arcia 11, De Jesus 46, Inoa 50, Matute 7, Mora 15, Pena 10, Thomas 1. **3B:** Andujar 33, Arcia 8, Hernandez 36, Inoa 4, Matute 9, Mora 7, Orecchia 1, Pena 23, Thomas 18. **SS:** Arcia 18, Del Villar 49, Matute 36, Mora 35, Pena 1. **OF:** Brazoban 55, Burgos 29, Marcos 27, Moquete 39, Otamendi 56, Pena 43, Ramirez 42, Rodriguez 16, Rodriguez 47, Salas 17, Thomas 4, Vargas 54.

ST. LOUIS CARDINALS

San Diego Padres

SEASON IN A SENTENCE: Fernando Tatis Jr. and Chris Paddack provided an early injection of energy with their debuts, but the Padres fell flat in the second half and tumbled to a 70-92 record and a last-place finish in the National League West, costing manager Andy Green his job.

HIGH POINT: After staying competitive most of the first half, the Padres finished with an exclamation point. They went up to Los Angeles and took three of four from the rival Dodgers in the final series of the first half, securing a .500 record (45-45) heading into the All-Star break.

LOW POINT: Losing records in July and August extinguished the Padres' early momentum, but they still had a chance to avoid last place. Instead, they lost 15 of their final 17 games, including a walk-off loss to the D-backs on the final day of the season to drop into the cellar.

NOTABLE ROOKIES: Tatis Jr. electrified baseball with his power, speed and finesse and nearly went 20-20 (22 home runs, 16 stolen bases) despite playing just 86 games because of back and hamstring injuries. Paddack's 3.33 ERA was second-lowest among rookie starters, and Francisco Mejia supplanted Austin Hedges as the Padres' everyday catcher by July. Michel Baez (3.03 ERA) and Andres Munoz (3.91) proved a boon to the relief corps, but the rest of the rookie class was less convincing. Luis Urias, Josh Naylor, Cal Quantrill, Trey Wingenter, Ty France and Nick Margevicius all showed flashes but largely struggled.

KEY TRANSACTIONS: The Padres signed Manny Machado to a 10-year, $300 million contract before the season, the largest contract in baseball history when it was signed. (Bryce Harper and Mike Trout would break the record later in the offseason.) The Padres took part in the biggest deal of the trade deadline, trading outfielder Franmil Reyes and pitching prospect Logan Allen to the Indians and receiving outfield prospect Taylor Trammell from the Reds in a three-team deal.

DOWN ON THE FARM: Double-A Amarillo won the Texas League championship in its inaugural season while high Class A Lake Elsinore and short-season Tri-City each reached their league championship series. Infielder Ivan Castillo (Texas League), catcher Luis Campusano (California League) and infielder C.J. Abrams (Arizona League) all won batting titles. France hit .399 in the Triple-A Pacific Coast League but was promoted before he could qualify for the batting title.

OPENING DAY PAYROLL: $94,429,433 (24th).

PLAYERS OF THE YEAR

JENNIFER STEWART

MAJOR LEAGUE	MINOR LEAGUE
Fernando Tatis Jr. SS	**MacKenzie Gore** LHP
.317/.379/.590	(High A/Double-A)
22 HR, 53 RBIs	9-2, 1.69 in 20 GS
16-for-22 SB	135 SO, 101 IP

ORGANIZATION LEADERS

Batting		*Minimum 250 AB
MAJORS		
* AVG	Fernando Tatis Jr.	.317
* OPS	Fernando Tatis Jr.	.969
HR	Hunter Renfroe	33
RBI	Eric Hosmer	99
MINORS		
* AVG	Ty France, El Paso	.399
* OBP	Ty France, El Paso	.477
* SLG	Ty France, El Paso	.770
* OPS	Ty France, El Paso	1.247
R	Michael Gettys, El Paso	97
H	Xavier Edwards, Fort Wayne, Lake Elsinore	162
TB	Michael Gettys, El Paso	262
2B	Luis Campusano, Lake Elsinore	31
3B	CJ Abrams, AZL Padres 1, Fort Wayne	8
3B	Xavier Edwards, Fort Wayne, Lake Elsinore	8
3B	Eguy Rosario, Lake Elsinore	8
HR	Michael Gettys, El Paso	31
RBI	Michael Gettys, El Paso	91
BB	Jeisson Rosario, Lake Elsinore	87
SO	Michael Gettys, El Paso	168
SB	Edward Olivares, Amarillo	35

Pitching		#Minimum 75 IP
MAJORS		
W	Joey Lucchesi	10
# ERA	Craig Stammen	3.29
SO	Joey Lucchesi	158
SV	Kirby Yates	41
MINORS		
W	Ronald Bolanos, Lake Elsinore, Amarillo	13
L	Angel Acevedo, Fort Wayne, Tri-City, Lake Elsinore	12
# ERA	MacKenzie Gore, Lake Elsinore	1.69
G	Blake Rogers, Amarillo, Lake Elsinore	51
GS	Jerry Keel, El Paso	26
SV	Evan Miller, Lake Elsinore, Amarillo, El Paso	15
IP	Jerry Keel, El Paso	151
BB	Lake Bachar, Amarillo, Lake Elsinore	60
BB	Jerry Keel, El Paso	60
SO	Joey Cantillo, Fort Wayne, Lake Elsinore	144
# AVG	MacKenzie Gore, Lake Elsinore, Amarillo	.164

2019 PERFORMANCE

General Manager: A.J. Preller. **Farm Director:** Sam Geaney. **Scouting Director:** Mark Conner.

Class	Team	League	W	L	PCT	Finish	Manager
Majors	San Diego Padres	National	70	92	.432	13th (15)	A. Green/R. Barajas
Triple-A	El Paso Chihuahuas	Pacific Coast	80	60	.571	t-3rd (16)	Edwin Rodriguez
Double-A	Amarillo Sod Poodles	Texas	72	66	.522	4th (8)	Phillip Wellman
High A	Lake Elsinore Storm	California	73	65	.529	3rd (8)	Tony Tarasco
Low A	Fort Wayne TinCaps	Midwest	62	76	.449	12th (16)	Anthony Contreras
Short season	Tri-City Dust Devils	Northwest	38	38	.500	4th (8)	Mike McCoy
Rookie	AZL Padres 1	Arizona	32	23	.582	7th (21)	Vinny Lopez
Rookie	AZL Padres 2	Arizona	39	17	.696	2nd (21)	Aaron Levin
Overall 2019 Minor League Record			396	345	.534	6th (30)	

ORGANIZATION STATISTICS

SAN DIEGO PADRES
NATIONAL LEAGUE

Batting	B-T	HT	WT	DOB	AVG	vLH	vRH	G	AB	R	H	2B	3B	HR	RBI	BB	HBP	SH	SF	SO	SB	CS	SLG	OBP
Allen, Austin	L-R	6-2	220	1-16-94	.215	.100	.236	34	65	4	14	4	0	0	3	6	0	0	0	21	0	0	.277	.282
Cordero, Franchy	L-R	6-3	175	9-2-94	.333	--	.333	9	15	2	5	1	0	0	1	4	0	0	1	7	1	0	.400	.450
Dickerson, Alex	L-L	6-3	235	5-26-90	.158	.000	.200	12	19	1	3	0	0	0	2	0	0	0	0	7	0	0	.158	.158
2-team total (56 San Francisco)					.276	.191	.288	68	174	29	48	13	3	6	28	13	2	0	1	42	1	1	.489	.332
France, Ty	R-R	6-0	205	7-13-94	.234	.236	.233	69	184	20	43	8	1	7	24	9	7	0	1	49	0	2	.402	.294
Garcia, Greg	L-R	6-0	190	8-8-89	.248	.200	.254	134	311	52	77	13	4	4	31	53	5	1	2	83	0	2	.354	.364
Hedges, Austin	R-R	6-1	206	8-18-92	.176	.143	.186	102	312	28	55	9	0	11	36	27	5	2	1	109	1	0	.311	.252
Hosmer, Eric	L-L	6-4	225	10-24-89	.265	.231	.277	160	619	72	164	29	2	22	99	40	3	0	5	163	0	3	.425	.310
Jankowski, Travis	L-R	6-2	185	6-15-91	.182	.000	.200	25	22	4	4	0	0	0	2	0	0	0	4	2	2	.182	.250
Kinsler, Ian	R-R	6-0	200	6-22-82	.217	.206	.221	87	258	28	56	12	0	9	22	19	3	0	1	54	2	4	.368	.278
Machado, Manny	R-R	6-3	215	7-6-92	.256	.315	.239	156	587	81	150	21	2	32	85	65	6	0	3	128	5	3	.462	.334
Margot, Manuel	R-R	5-11	180	9-28-94	.234	.330	.200	151	398	59	93	19	3	12	37	38	2	3	0	88	20	4	.387	.304
Martini, Nick	L-L	5-11	205	6-27-90	.244	.000	.313	26	82	7	20	4	1	0	5	12	1	0	1	21	0	0	.317	.344
Mejia, Francisco	B-R	5-10	180	10-27-95	.266	.279	.261	79	226	27	60	11	2	8	22	13	4	0	1	56	1	1	.438	.316
Mejias-Brean, Seth	R-R	6-2	216	4-5-91	.233	.222	.238	14	30	3	7	2	0	2	5	3	0	0	0	9	0	0	.500	.303
Myers, Wil	R-R	6-3	205	12-10-90	.239	.233	.241	155	435	58	104	22	1	18	53	51	2	1	1	168	16	7	.418	.321
Naylor, Josh	L-L	5-11	250	6-22-97	.249	.292	.239	94	253	29	63	15	0	8	32	25	0	0	1	64	1	1	.403	.315
Pirela, Jose	R-R	6-0	220	11-21-89	.000	.000	.000	2	5	0	0	0	0	0	0	0	0	0	0	3	0	0	.000	.000
2-team total (12 Philadelphia)					.182	.333	.000	14	22	1	4	1	0	1	2	2	0	0	0	7	0	0	.364	.250
Renfroe, Hunter	R-R	6-1	220	1-28-92	.216	.239	.208	140	440	64	95	19	1	33	64	46	2	0	6	154	5	0	.489	.290
Reyes, Franmil	R-R	6-5	275	7-7-95	.256	.258	.255	99	321	43	82	9	0	27	46	29	0	0	4	93	0	0	.536	.314
Tatis Jr., Fernando	R-R	6-3	185	1-2-99	.317	.419	.294	84	334	61	106	13	6	22	53	30	5	0	3	110	16	6	.590	.379
Torrens, Luis	R-R	6-0	175	5-2-96	.214	.167	.250	7	14	2	3	1	0	0	2	0	0	0	6	0	0	.286	.313
Urias, Luis	R-R	5-9	185	6-3-97	.223	.351	.177	71	215	27	48	8	1	4	24	25	9	0	0	56	0	1	.326	.329

Pitching	B-T	HT	WT	DOB	W	L	ERA	G	GS	CG	SV	IP	H	R	ER	HR	BB	SO	AVG	vLH	vRH	K/9	BB/9
Allen, Logan	R-L	6-3	200	5-23-97	2	3	6.75	8	4	0	0	25	33	20	19	4	13	14	.330	.333	.329	4.97	4.62
Avila, Pedro	R-R	5-11	190	1-14-97	0	0	1.69	1	1	0	0	5	4	1	1	0	2	5	.200	.222	.182	8.44	3.38
Baez, Michel	R-R	6-8	220	1-21-96	1	1	3.03	24	1	0	0	30	25	10	10	3	14	28	.223	.212	.233	8.49	4.25
Bednar, David	L-R	6-1	220	10-10-94	0	2	6.55	13	0	0	0	11	10	8	8	3	5	14	.250	.261	.235	11.45	4.09
Bolanos, Ronald	R-R	6-3	220	8-23-96	0	2	5.95	5	3	0	0	20	17	13	13	3	12	19	.230	.250	.206	8.69	5.49
Castillo, Jose	L-L	6-5	246	1-10-96	0	0	0.00	1	0	0	0	1	0	0	0	0	1	2	.000	.000	.000	27.00	13.50
Diaz, Miguel	R-R	6-0	214	11-28-94	0	0	7.11	5	0	0	0	6	9	5	5	1	1	4	.346	.625	.222	5.68	1.42
Edwards Jr., Carl	R-R	6-3	170	9-3-91	0	0	32.40	2	0	0	0	2	4	6	6	0	4	2	.400	.333	.429	10.80	21.60
2-team total (20 Chicago)					1	1	8.47	22	0	0	0	17	12	17	16	3	13	19	.191	.222	.178	10.06	6.88
Erlin, Robbie	R-L	6-0	190	10-8-90	0	1	5.37	37	1	0	0	55	72	36	33	6	15	52	.332	.333	.296	8.46	2.44
France, Ty	R-R	6-0	205	7-13-94	0	0	4.50	2	0	0	0	2	2	1	1	1	0	0	.250	.000	.333	0.00	0.00
Guerra, Javy	L-R	5-11	155	9-25-95	0	0	5.19	8	0	0	0	9	7	5	5	3	3	6	.219	.211	.231	6.23	3.12
Kinsler, Ian	R-R	6-0	200	6-22-82	0	0	0.00	1	0	0	0	1	1	0	0	0	2	0	.333	1.000	.000	0.00	18.00
Lamet, Dinelson	R-R	6-4	187	7-18-92	3	5	4.07	14	14	0	0	73	62	38	33	12	30	105	.226	.242	.208	12.95	3.70
Lauer, Eric	R-L	6-3	205	6-3-95	8	10	4.45	30	29	0	0	150	158	82	74	20	51	138	.268	.331	.247	8.30	3.07
Loup, Aaron	L-L	5-11	210	12-19-87	0	0	0.00	4	0	0	0	3	2	0	0	0	1	5	.182	.500	.000	13.50	2.70
Lucchesi, Joey	L-L	6-5	204	6-6-93	10	10	4.18	30	30	0	0	164	144	78	76	23	56	158	.233	.221	.236	8.69	3.08
Margevicius, Nick	L-L	6-5	220	6-18-96	2	6	6.79	17	12	0	0	57	73	46	43	12	19	42	.307	.390	.263	6.63	3.00
Maton, Phil	R-R	6-3	220	3-25-93	0	0	7.77	21	0	0	0	24	34	22	21	6	6	20	.321	.390	.277	7.40	2.22
Morejon, Adrian	L-L	6-0	175	2-27-99	0	0	10.13	5	2	0	0	8	15	9	9	1	3	9	.385	.412	.364	10.13	3.38
Munoz, Andres	R-R	6-2	165	1-16-99	1	1	3.91	22	0	0	1	23	16	10	10	2	11	30	.188	.220	.159	11.74	4.30
Paddack, Chris	R-R	6-4	195	1-8-96	9	7	3.33	26	26	0	0	141	107	58	52	23	31	153	.204	.211	.198	9.79	1.98
Perdomo, Luis	R-R	6-2	185	5-9-93	2	4	4.00	47	1	0	0	72	69	34	32	6	18	55	.252	.289	.229	6.88	2.25
Quantrill, Cal	L-R	6-3	220	2-10-95	6	8	5.16	23	18	0	0	103	106	61	59	15	28	89	.260	.291	.217	7.78	2.45
Reyes, Gerardo	R-R	5-11	160	5-13-93	4	0	7.62	27	0	0	0	26	24	22	22	3	11	38	.240	.250	.229	13.15	3.81
Richards, Garrett	R-R	6-3	210	5-27-88	0	1	8.31	3	3	0	0	9	10	8	8	2	6	11	.294	.191	.462	11.42	6.23
Stammen, Craig	R-R	6-4	230	3-9-84	8	7	3.29	76	0	0	4	82	80	36	30	13	15	73	.251	.203	.290	8.01	1.65

Name	B-T	HT	WT	DOB	W	L	ERA	G	GS	CG	SV	IP	H	R	ER	HR	BB	SO	AVG	vLH	vRH	K/9	BB/9
Stock, Robert	L-R	6-1	214	11-21-89	1	0	10.13	10	0	0	0	11	14	14	12	2	8	15	.298	.381	.231	12.66	6.75
Strahm, Matt	R-L	6-3	185	11-12-91	6	11	4.71	46	16	0	0	115	121	61	60	22	22	118	.267	.274	.264	9.26	1.73
Warren, Adam	R-R	6-1	224	8-25-87	4	1	5.34	25	0	0	0	29	28	18	17	9	12	25	.257	.163	.318	7.85	3.77
Wieck, Brad	L-L	6-9	255	10-14-91	0	1	6.57	30	0	0	0	25	26	19	18	7	9	31	.263	.293	.241	11.31	3.28
2-team total (14 Chicago)					2	2	5.71	44	0	0	0	35	28	23	22	8	13	49	.214	.265	.183	12.72	3.38
Wingenter, Trey	R-R	6-7	200	4-15-94	1	3	5.65	51	1	0	1	51	34	32	32	5	28	72	.187	.140	.236	12.71	4.94
Wisler, Matt	R-R	6-3	215	9-12-92	2	2	5.28	21	0	0	0	29	34	17	17	5	10	34	.291	.279	.297	10.55	3.10
Yardley, Eric	R-R	6-0	165	8-18-90	0	1	2.31	10	0	0	0	12	12	5	3	1	3	7	.261	.188	.300	5.40	2.31
Yates, Kirby	L-R	5-10	210	3-25-87	0	5	1.19	60	0	0	41	61	41	14	8	2	13	101	.186	.197	.172	14.98	1.93

Fielding

Catcher	PCT	G	PO	A	E	DP	PB
Allen	.993	19	126	10	1	0	3
Hedges	.988	95	858	35	11	3	2
Mejia	.996	60	459	24	2	1	1
Torrens	1.000	4	32	1	0	0	0

First Base	PCT	G	PO	A	E	DP
Allen	1.000	2	5	1	0	3
France	1.000	1	1	0	0	1
Garcia	1.000	1	1	0	0	0
Hosmer	.989	157	1128	106	14	82
Mejias-Brean	1.000	5	17	0	0	1
Myers	1.000	7	41	1	0	3

Second Base	PCT	G	PO	A	E	DP
France	1.000	21	15	41	0	5

	PCT	G	PO	A	E	DP
Garcia	.987	74	98	131	3	30
Kinsler	.980	72	96	155	5	36
Urias	.989	26	40	52	1	12

Third Base	PCT	G	PO	A	E	DP
France	.970	36	7	57	2	2
Garcia	.967	13	9	20	1	2
Hedges	.000	2	0	0	0	0
Machado	.960	119	79	187	11	18
Mejias-Brean	1.000	2	0	6	0	0
Myers	.000	2	0	0	0	0
Urias	1.000	1	0	2	0	0

Shortstop	PCT	G	PO	A	E	DP
Garcia	.952	9	7	13	1	2
Machado	.973	37	40	67	3	11
Mejias-Brean	.875	3	3	4	1	2

	PCT	G	PO	A	E	DP
Tatis Jr.	.944	83	90	215	18	36
Urias	.927	41	37	77	9	10

Outfield	PCT	G	PO	A	E	DP
Cordero	1.000	7	8	0	0	0
Dickerson	1.000	6	8	0	0	0
Garcia	.000	1	0	0	0	0
Jankowski	1.000	11	8	1	0	0
Margot	.992	135	249	2	2	0
Martini	1.000	23	42	1	0	1
Mejia	1.000	4	3	0	0	0
Myers	.979	134	228	4	5	1
Naylor	.936	62	84	4	6	1
Pirela	1.000	1	1	0	0	0
Renfroe	.992	127	221	13	2	3
Reyes	.970	83	160	3	5	1

EL PASO CHIHUAHUAS   TRIPLE-A
PACIFIC COAST LEAGUE

Batting	B-T	HT	WT	DOB	AVG	vLH	vRH	G	AB	R	H	2B	3B	HR	RBI	BB	HBP	SH	SF	SO	SB	CS	SLG	OBP
Allen, Austin	L-R	6-2	220	1-16-94	.330	.268	.356	67	270	52	89	27	0	21	67	22	2	0	4	56	0	0	.663	.379
Batten, Matthew	R-R	5-11	180	6-22-95	.299	.314	.293	109	354	59	106	20	3	6	48	28	3	3	5	86	7	8	.424	.351
Cantu, Michael	R-R	6-3	225	8-28-95	.286	.444	.167	6	21	4	6	0	0	3	5	0	0	0	0	9	0	0	.714	.286
Cordero, Franchy	L-R	6-3	175	9-2-94	.217	.200	.222	11	46	7	10	2	1	3	8	4	1	0	0	19	0	0	.500	.294
Dickerson, Alex	L-L	6-3	235	5-26-90	.372	.412	.350	26	94	17	35	5	1	5	20	14	4	0	1	18	0	0	.606	.469
2-team total (7 Sacramento)					.333	.389	.308	33	114	19	38	5	1	5	21	17	5	0	1	20	0	0	.526	.438
France, Ty	R-R	6-0	205	7-13-94	.399	.423	.390	76	296	83	118	27	1	27	89	30	18	0	4	51	1	0	.770	.477
Gettys, Michael	R-R	6-1	203	10-22-95	.256	.260	.255	128	507	97	130	29	5	31	91	33	5	0	6	168	14	6	.517	.305
Jankowski, Travis	L-R	6-2	185	6-15-91	.313	.368	.295	39	160	27	50	6	0	0	12	21	1	0	1	32	7	2	.350	.393
Kennedy, A.J.	R-R	6-0	190	1-23-94	.152	.200	.130	9	33	5	5	1	0	3	5	1	0	0	0	14	0	0	.455	.177
Kohlwey, Taylor	L-L	6-3	200	7-20-94	.304	.429	.250	11	23	4	7	2	0	0	9	3	1	0	1	4	1	0	.391	.393
Mejia, Francisco	B-R	5-10	180	10-27-95	.365	.625	.327	18	63	14	23	8	2	4	12	5	2	0	3	10	0	0	.746	.411
Mejias-Brean, Seth	R-R	6-2	216	4-5-91	.316	.307	.320	117	411	69	130	18	3	11	66	33	3	0	1	79	4	2	.455	.371
Naylor, Josh	L-L	5-11	250	6-22-97	.314	.352	.296	54	223	51	70	20	1	10	42	28	0	0	1	30	1	0	.547	.389
Orozco, Rodrigo	B-R	5-11	155	4-2-95	.305	.250	.324	26	95	20	29	5	3	2	16	11	2	0	2	19	2	2	.484	.382
Panas, Connor	L-R	6-0	218	2-11-93	.267	.250	.273	12	30	6	8	2	0	3	7	3	0	0	0	7	0	0	.633	.333
Pirela, Jose	R-R	6-0	220	11-21-89	.353	.333	.362	55	221	50	78	13	2	18	59	17	2	0	2	51	0	1	.674	.401
Powell, Boog	L-L	5-10	185	1-14-93	.288	.306	.282	105	340	66	98	25	1	8	37	59	0	1	3	94	14	0	.438	.391
Quiroz, Esteban	L-R	5-7	175	2-17-92	.271	.312	.258	96	306	64	83	25	0	19	66	52	5	1	2	82	3	1	.539	.384
Rivas, Webster	R-R	6-2	218	8-8-90	.296	.200	.333	39	125	26	37	9	0	5	22	22	1	1	0	23	0	0	.488	.405
Rodriguez, Aderlin	R-R	6-3	210	11-18-91	.321	.309	.326	75	265	54	85	26	0	19	64	14	6	0	4	46	0	0	.634	.363
Scavuzzo, Jacob	R-R	6-4	185	1-15-94	.259	.306	.237	35	112	22	29	2	1	15	34	5	2	0	1	40	1	0	.696	.300
Stewart, Chris	R-R	6-4	215	2-19-82	.277	.280	.275	19	65	9	18	2	0	1	8	5	1	1	1	10	0	0	.354	.333
Urias, Luis	R-R	5-9	185	6-3-97	.315	.265	.330	73	295	62	93	19	4	19	50	36	6	0	2	62	7	2	.600	.398
Van Gansen, Peter	L-R	5-9	175	3-4-94	.223	.160	.241	47	112	15	25	5	1	5	15	9	0	1	1	28	0	0	.420	.279
Vosler, Jason	L-R	6-2	205	9-6-93	.291	.253	.300	116	375	73	109	19	4	20	63	45	2	0	3	102	0	1	.523	.367

Pitching	B-T	HT	WT	DOB	W	L	ERA	G	GS	CG	SV	IP	H	R	ER	HR	BB	SO	AVG	vLH	vRH	K/9	BB/9
Allen, Logan	R-L	6-3	200	5-23-97	4	3	5.15	13	13	0	0	58	61	39	33	8	22	63	.269	.230	.283	9.83	3.43
Batten, Matthew	R-R	5-11	180	6-22-95	1	0	2.57	7	0	0	0	7	5	2	2	2	2	1	.192	.214	.167	1.29	2.57
Castillo, Jose	L-L	6-5	246	1-10-96	0	0	6.75	2	0	0	0	1	1	1	1	1	1	2	.200	.500	.000	20.25	6.75
Colletti, Tom	R-R	6-3	220	6-22-95	0	0	15.00	2	0	0	0	3	5	5	5	3	1	5	.385	.250	.600	15.00	3.00
Dallas, Dan	L-L	6-2	235	12-24-97	0	0	--	1	0	0	0	0	1	4	4	1	2	0	1.000	1.000	--	--	--
Diaz, Miguel	R-R	6-0	214	11-28-94	0	1	2.35	4	4	0	0	8	8	2	2	1	2	7	.286	.143	.429	8.22	2.35
Edwards Jr., Carl	R-R	6-3	170	9-3-91	0	1	9.00	3	0	0	0	3	4	3	3	0	1	4	.308	.333	.300	12.00	3.00
2-team total (14 Iowa)					2	1	4.08	17	0	0	0	18	16	9	8	2	7	18	.232	.421	.160	9.17	3.57
Enns, Dietrich	L-L	6-1	210	5-16-91	11	11	6.70	28	25	0	0	137	182	108	102	37	56	105	.319	.264	.344	6.90	3.68
Erlin, Robbie	R-L	6-0	190	10-8-90	0	1	8.80	10	0	0	1	15	26	15	15	2	2	14	.388	.375	.395	8.22	1.17
Higgins, Tyler	R-R	6-3	215	4-22-91	4	1	5.52	33	2	0	4	46	43	30	28	13	13	50	.240	.256	.225	9.85	2.56
Keel, Jerry	L-L	6-6	240	9-26-93	10	7	6.78	29	26	0	0	151	207	127	114	28	60	114	.329	.324	.331	6.78	3.57
Lamet, Dinelson	R-R	6-4	187	7-18-92	1	0	4.80	3	3	0	0	15	8	8	8	4	9	19	.185	.125	.233	11.40	2.40
Lloyd, Kyle	R-R	6-4	220	10-16-90	0	0	0.00	2	0	0	0	4	3	0	0	0	0	2	.214	.500	.000	4.91	0.00
Makita, Kazuhisa	R-R	5-10	181	11-10-84	3	1	3.86	8	0	0	0	16	14	7	7	0	4	20	.222	.269	.189	11.02	2.20

Name	B-T	HT	WT	DOB	W	L	ERA	G	GS	CG	SV	IP	H	R	ER	HR	BB	SO	AVG	vLH	vRH	SO/9	BB/9
Maton, Phil	R-R	6-3	220	3-25-93	2	1	2.89	13	0	0	2	19	17	6	6	2	6	30	.250	.194	.297	14.46	2.89
McGrath, Kyle	L-L	6-2	185	7-31-92	3	3	8.78	22	7	0	0	55	79	59	54	17	19	38	.332	.352	.323	6.18	3.09
Megill, Trevor	L-R	6-8	235	12-5-93	2	2	4.47	32	0	0	6	50	56	28	25	5	19	71	.284	.320	.262	12.70	3.40
Miller, Evan	R-R	6-2	200	5-23-95	0	0	14.54	4	0	0	0	4	9	7	7	1	6	4	.429	.462	.375	8.31	12.46
Mitchell, Bryan	L-R	6-3	210	4-19-91	0	3	9.41	13	11	0	0	44	66	47	46	9	28	34	.349	.340	.359	6.95	5.73
Munoz, Andres	R-R	6-2	165	1-16-99	3	2	3.79	19	0	0	2	19	16	8	8	3	7	24	.235	.129	.324	11.37	3.32
Nix, Jacob	R-R	6-4	220	1-9-96	1	0	0.82	2	2	0	0	11	7	1	1	1	1	12	.189	.143	.217	9.82	0.82
Overton, Dillon	L-L	6-2	175	8-17-91	10	5	5.46	25	22	0	0	115	141	76	70	25	31	103	.300	.285	.306	8.04	2.42
Perdomo, Luis	R-R	6-2	185	5-9-93	2	1	3.60	11	0	0	1	15	21	9	6	3	4	17	.339	.321	.353	10.20	2.40
Powell, Boog	L-L	5-10	185	1-14-93	0	0	4.50	2	0	0	0	2	3	1	1	0	1	0	.333	.250	.400	0.00	4.50
Quantrill, Cal	L-R	6-3	208	2-10-95	4	2	4.54	7	7	0	0	36	38	21	18	3	12	33	.270	.343	.203	8.33	3.03
Radke, Travis	L-L	6-4	237	3-6-93	1	0	2.97	24	0	0	0	30	36	17	10	1	12	28	.290	.293	.289	8.31	3.56
Ramirez, Emmanuel	R-R	6-2	190	7-15-94	2	3	10.07	10	9	0	0	45	69	51	50	19	24	37	.356	.296	.406	7.46	4.84
Reyes, Gerardo	R-R	5-11	160	5-13-93	4	2	3.57	34	0	0	3	45	39	22	18	8	20	61	.232	.281	.186	12.11	3.97
Rodriguez Jr., Fernando	R-R	6-3	235	6-18-84	2	1	5.91	18	3	0	4	32	31	21	21	6	16	40	.254	.239	.263	11.25	4.50
Rodriguez, Paco	L-L	6-3	220	4-16-91	3	1	4.19	21	1	0	0	34	40	18	16	4	6	31	.284	.178	.333	8.13	1.57
Rowley, Chris	R-R	6-2	195	8-14-90	0	0	11.02	5	2	0	0	16	27	20	20	5	9	11	.370	.333	.412	6.06	4.96
Solis, Sammy	R-L	6-5	251	8-10-88	1	1	3.57	19	0	0	1	23	19	10	9	3	8	28	.226	.344	.154	11.12	3.18
Stock, Robert	L-R	6-1	214	11-21-89	3	0	4.13	25	3	0	0	28	36	14	13	6	19	40	.308	.264	.344	12.71	6.04
Torres, Carlos	R-R	6-1	180	10-22-82	1	1	2.49	15	0	0	1	25	21	7	7	2	10	23	.226	.180	.279	8.17	3.55
2-team total (4 Sacramento)					1	2	5.03	19	3	0	1	39	40	22	22	6	15	35	.265	.254	.274	8.01	3.43
Tyler, Cody	R-L	6-0	190	10-26-94	0	0	7.36	2	0	0	0	4	9	3	3	0	1	3	.474	1.000	.444	7.36	2.45
Van Gansen, Peter	L-R	5-9	175	3-4-94	0	0	0.00	3	0	0	0	2	0	0	0	0	0	1	.000	.000	.000	3.86	0.00
Wieck, Brad	L-L	6-9	255	10-14-91	1	1	6.11	14	0	0	2	18	16	12	12	5	6	34	.235	.250	.225	17.32	3.06
2-team total (6 Iowa)					2	1	5.01	20	0	0	2	23	20	13	13	5	9	45	.227	.211	.240	17.36	3.47
Wilson, Steven	R-R	6-3	185	8-24-94	1	3	4.11	25	0	0	0	35	26	19	16	5	22	42	.213	.151	.261	10.80	5.66
Wingenter, Trey	R-R	6-7	200	4-15-94	0	0	0.00	3	0	0	1	3	1	0	0	0	0	7	.091	.143	.000	18.90	0.00
Yardley, Eric	R-R	6-0	165	8-18-90	0	2	2.83	43	0	0	7	64	60	27	20	3	14	52	.247	.316	.203	7.35	1.98

Fielding

Catcher	PCT	G	PO	A	E	DP	PB
Allen	.995	61	526	41	3	5	6
Cantu	.976	5	41	0	1	0	0
Kennedy	1.000	9	70	5	0	0	0
Mejia	.993	16	124	10	1	2	5
Rivas	.994	37	298	25	2	1	4
Stewart	.994	19	154	9	1	1	3

First Base	PCT	G	PO	A	E	DP
Allen	1.000	2	6	0	0	1
Batten	.992	15	114	4	1	7
Dickerson	1.000	6	42	3	0	5
France	.996	29	214	16	1	26
Kohlwey	1.000	1	1	0	0	0
Panas	1.000	3	25	0	0	7
Rivas	1.000	1	0	1	0	0
Rodriguez	.993	54	426	19	3	36
Vosler	.995	47	358	27	2	37

Second Base	PCT	G	PO	A	E	DP
Batten	.980	27	37	60	2	14
France	1.000	15	26	27	0	9
Orozco	1.000	1	1	0	0	0
Pirela	.000	1	0	0	0	0
Quiroz	.983	77	108	183	5	49
Urias	.989	21	27	59	1	13
Van Gansen	.962	16	19	31	2	8

Third Base	PCT	G	PO	A	E	DP
Batten	.957	24	8	37	2	6
France	.924	32	14	47	5	3
Mejias-Brean	.927	56	34	81	9	5
Quiroz	.500	1	0	1	1	0
Rodriguez	.000	1	0	0	0	0
Van Gansen	1.000	1	0	2	0	0
Vosler	.933	49	22	76	7	9

Shortstop	PCT	G	PO	A	E	DP
Batten	.978	24	25	63	2	8
Mejias-Brean	.980	56	54	144	4	28
Quiroz	.857	5	3	3	1	1
Urias	.972	53	72	169	7	34
Van Gansen	.979	17	13	34	1	10

Outfield	PCT	G	PO	A	E	DP
Batten	1.000	9	15	1	0	0
Cordero	.920	9	22	1	2	0
Dickerson	1.000	9	20	0	0	0
Gettys	.960	118	233	12	10	2
Jankowski	.975	37	76	2	2	0
Kohlwey	.800	6	4	0	1	0
Naylor	.978	51	83	5	2	1
Orozco	.974	23	35	3	1	0
Panas	1.000	4	10	0	0	0
Pirela	.978	52	87	2	2	0
Powell	.989	92	172	5	2	0
Rowley	.000	1	0	0	0	0
Scavuzzo	.953	23	40	1	2	1

AMARILLO SOD POODLES · DOUBLE-A
TEXAS LEAGUE

Batting	B-T	HT	WT	DOB	AVG	vLH	vRH	G	AB	R	H	2B	3B	HR	RBI	BB	HBP	SH	SF	SO	SB	CS	SLG	OBP
Baker, Chris	R-R	6-1	180	11-29-94	.192	.182	.195	36	104	17	20	2	0	2	8	14	0	0	2	37	1	1	.269	.283
Batten, Matthew	R-R	5-11	180	6-22-95	.200	.000	.333	2	5	1	1	0	1	0	0	2	0	0	0	1	1	0	.600	.429
Benson, Tyler	L-R	5-11	196	6-17-96	.417	.333	.429	11	24	5	10	0	0	2	4	2	0	0	0	6	2	0	.667	.462
Castillo, Ivan	B-R	5-9	173	5-30-95	.313	.359	.298	104	432	62	135	30	5	8	57	20	6	2	6	59	15	4	.461	.347
Easley, Nate	R-R	5-10	170	1-11-96	.135	.167	.130	19	52	7	7	1	0	0	0	5	0	0	0	29	3	0	.154	.211
Giron, Ruddy	R-R	6-0	205	1-4-97	.197	.125	.222	23	61	6	12	2	1	2	7	2	1	0	0	13	0	0	.361	.234
Kennedy, A.J.	R-R	6-0	190	1-23-94	.164	.182	.160	19	61	4	10	3	0	2	6	5	0	1	0	25	0	0	.312	.227
Kohlwey, Taylor	L-L	6-3	200	7-20-94	.276	.233	.283	65	203	46	56	10	1	4	22	29	6	1	0	54	6	3	.394	.382
Miller, Owen	R-R	6-0	190	11-15-96	.290	.347	.276	130	507	76	147	28	2	13	68	46	6	0	1	86	5	5	.430	.355
Olivares, Edward	R-R	6-2	186	3-6-96	.283	.269	.287	127	488	85	138	25	2	18	77	43	10	3	7	98	35	10	.453	.349
Ona, Jorge	R-R	6-0	220	12-31-96	.348	.250	.364	25	89	11	31	2	0	5	18	11	1	0	2	26	2	1	.539	.418
Orozco, Rodrigo	B-R	5-11	155	4-2-95	.263	.246	.268	66	274	45	72	12	0	2	24	32	0	1	0	54	15	7	.329	.339
Overstreet, Kyle	R-R	5-11	205	9-4-93	.259	.234	.266	102	367	38	95	12	1	7	44	31	4	0	4	81	1	0	.354	.320
Potts, Hudson	R-R	6-3	205	10-28-98	.227	.233	.226	107	409	56	93	23	1	16	59	52	5	0	2	128	3	1	.406	.290
Reed, Buddy	B-R	6-4	210	4-27-95	.228	.246	.225	121	381	49	87	15	2	14	50	42	6	4	7	126	23	8	.389	.310
Rivas, Webster	R-R	6-2	218	8-8-90	.264	.273	.262	30	106	14	28	3	1	1	14	8	3	0	2	23	1	0	.340	.328
Tatis Jr., Fernando	R-R	6-3	185	1-2-99	.400	.500	.333	2	5	2	2	0	0	0	0	3	0	0	0	1	1	0	.400	.625
Torrens, Luis	R-R	6-0	175	5-2-96	.300	.429	.268	97	350	50	105	23	1	15	62	42	1	0	4	67	1	2	.500	.373
Trammell, Taylor	L-L	6-2	215	9-13-97	.229	.280	.215	32	118	14	27	4	1	4	10	13	2	0	0	36	3	4	.381	.316
Van Gansen, Peter	L-R	5-9	175	3-4-94	.268	.276	.266	49	168	25	45	7	1	8	23	15	0	3	1	40	0	0	.464	.326
Zunica, Brad	L-R	6-6	254	10-21-95	.230	.241	.227	113	383	45	88	25	2	16	53	42	5	0	1	115	1	2	.431	.313

Pitching

Pitching	B-T	HT	WT	DOB	W	L	ERA	G	GS	CG	SV	IP	H	R	ER	HR	BB	SO	AVG	vLH	vRH	K/9	BB/9
Ashbeck, Elliot	L-R	6-3	220	11-16-93	0	0	0.00	1	0	0	0	1	2	0	0	0	0	1	.500	.500	.500	13.50	0.00
Avila, Pedro	R-R	5-11	190	1-14-97	0	2	8.25	3	3	0	0	12	14	12	11	4	6	13	.286	.304	.269	9.75	4.50
Bachar, Lake	R-R	6-3	215	6-3-95	8	4	3.98	24	19	0	0	127	121	62	56	18	58	126	.259	.298	.224	8.95	4.12
Baez, Michel	R-R	6-8	220	1-21-96	3	2	2.00	15	0	0	1	27	22	9	6	1	11	38	.216	.119	.283	12.67	3.67
Baker, Chris	R-R	6-1	180	11-29-94	0	0	0.00	1	0	0	0	1	0	0	0	0	0	1	.000	.000	.000	0.00	9.00
Bednar, David	L-R	6-1	220	10-10-94	2	5	2.95	44	0	0	14	58	49	24	19	4	18	86	.226	.240	.212	13.34	2.79
Belen, Carlos	R-R	6-1	250	2-28-96	2	0	4.68	15	0	0	1	25	27	13	13	3	7	28	.267	.280	.255	10.08	2.52
Bolanos, Ronald	R-R	6-3	220	8-23-96	8	5	4.23	15	13	0	0	77	71	39	36	7	30	88	.249	.265	.235	10.33	3.52
Colletti, Tom	R-R	6-3	220	6-22-95	0	1	11.81	3	0	0	1	5	11	7	7	2	2	3	.458	.417	.500	5.06	3.38
Cosme, Jean	R-R	6-2	155	5-24-96	1	1	6.94	15	0	0	2	23	30	20	18	3	11	22	.319	.293	.340	8.49	4.24
Diaz, Miguel	R-R	6-0	214	11-28-94	2	1	4.37	6	4	0	0	23	21	11	11	9	8	33	.236	.278	.208	13.10	3.18
Giron, Ruddy	R-R	6-0	205	1-4-97	0	0	0.00	3	0	0	0	3	2	0	0	0	2	2	.222	.333	.000	6.00	6.00
Gore, MacKenzie	L-L	6-3	195	2-24-99	2	1	4.15	5	5	0	0	22	20	10	10	3	8	25	.250	.389	.210	10.38	3.32
Guerra, Javy	L-R	5-11	155	9-25-95	0	0	2.08	4	0	0	0	4	2	1	1	1	5	7	.133	.000	.250	14.54	10.38
Guerrero, Jordan	R-R	6-5	296	8-1-96	0	0	54.00	1	0	0	0	0	2	2	2	0	1	0	1.000	1.000	1.000	0.00	27.00
Higgins, Tyler	R-R	6-3	215	4-22-91	1	0	1.08	5	0	0	0	8	5	1	1	0	0	13	.172	.071	.267	14.04	0.00
Kennedy, A.J.	R-R	6-0	190	1-23-94	0	0	0.00	1	0	0	0	1	0	0	0	0	0	1	.000	.000	.000	9.00	0.00
Kuzia, Nick	R-R	6-4	190	2-7-96	2	2	11.20	9	0	0	0	14	20	20	17	6	8	8	.345	.313	.385	5.27	5.27
Lawson, Reggie	R-R	6-4	205	8-2-97	3	1	5.20	6	6	0	0	28	28	16	16	4	13	36	.262	.351	.160	11.71	4.23
Leasher, Aaron	L-L	6-3	208	4-28-96	0	0	27.00	1	0	0	0	2	4	7	7	1	4	1	.400	.400	.400	3.86	15.43
Lloyd, Kyle	R-R	6-4	220	10-16-90	8	7	4.34	26	14	0	3	110	119	60	53	20	35	100	.277	.261	.293	8.18	2.86
Makita, Kazuhisa	R-R	5-10	181	11-10-84	3	2	3.17	35	0	0	3	54	53	28	19	5	7	47	.257	.245	.268	7.83	1.17
Margevicius, Nick	L-L	6-5	220	6-18-96	4	4	4.30	12	12	0	0	69	75	35	33	14	13	53	.276	.221	.297	6.91	1.70
McGrath, Kyle	L-L	6-2	185	7-31-92	1	0	0.00	4	0	0	0	7	4	0	0	0	1	5	.154	.100	.188	6.14	1.23
Megill, Trevor	L-R	6-8	235	12-5-93	0	0	1.42	4	0	0	0	6	5	1	1	0	2	8	.227	.091	.364	11.37	2.84
Miller, Evan	R-R	6-2	200	5-23-95	1	2	4.39	19	0	0	5	27	26	14	13	3	8	31	.255	.268	.240	10.46	2.70
Morejon, Adrian	L-L	6-0	175	2-27-99	0	4	4.25	16	16	0	0	36	29	20	17	3	15	44	.215	.195	.223	11.00	3.75
Munoz, Andres	R-R	6-2	165	1-16-99	0	2	2.16	16	0	0	4	17	9	10	4	1	11	34	.153	.100	.207	18.36	5.94
Patino, Luis	R-R	6-0	192	10-26-99	0	0	1.17	2	2	0	0	8	4	1	1	0	4	10	.258	.353	.143	11.74	4.70
Radke, Travis	L-L	6-4	237	3-6-93	3	1	2.79	21	0	0	0	29	31	11	9	1	9	37	.274	.283	.269	11.48	2.79
Ramirez, Emmanuel	R-R	6-2	190	7-15-94	6	5	4.15	17	12	0	1	85	74	44	39	10	26	79	.230	.205	.247	8.40	2.76
Rodriguez, Paco	L-L	6-3	220	4-16-91	1	0	1.29	7	0	0	0	14	8	2	2	1	3	12	.160	.000	.276	7.71	1.93
Rogers, Blake	R-R	6-2	200	2-23-94	2	2	5.60	40	2	0	2	64	76	42	40	6	27	65	.299	.301	.298	9.09	3.78
Scholtens, Jesse	R-R	6-4	230	4-6-94	5	7	5.40	24	20	0	0	125	145	81	75	15	40	129	.294	.293	.294	9.29	2.88
Valdez, Dauris	R-R	6-8	221	10-22-95	2	0	4.23	43	0	0	1	55	51	33	26	11	28	68	.238	.225	.252	11.06	4.55
Van Gansen, Peter	L-R	5-9	175	3-4-94	0	0	0.00	1	0	0	0	1	0	0	0	0	2	0	.000	.000	.000	0.00	18.00
Weir, T.J.	R-R	6-0	212	9-15-91	2	4	6.10	9	9	0	0	41	61	36	28	1	25	44	.355	.384	.326	9.58	5.44
Williams, Sam	L-L	6-3	195	6-26-96	0	0	9.53	3	1	0	0	6	8	6	6	1	2	10	.320	.313	.333	15.88	3.18
Wingenter, Trey	R-R	6-7	200	4-15-94	0	1	54.00	1	0	0	0	1	2	4	4	1	1	1	.500	.500	.500	13.50	13.50
Zunica, Brad	L-R	6-6	254	10-21-95	0	0	0.00	1	0	0	0	1	0	0	0	0	0	0	.250	.333	.000	0.00	0.00

Fielding

Catcher	PCT	G	PO	A	E	DP	PB
Kennedy	.982	18	155	11	3	2	3
Overstreet	.994	15	150	6	1	0	2
Rivas	1.000	22	225	25	0	1	0
Torrens	.992	85	757	90	7	5	7

First Base	PCT	G	PO	A	E	DP
Baker	1.000	3	8	0	0	0
Giron	1.000	1	6	3	0	1
Kohlwey	1.000	8	29	3	0	1
Overstreet	.997	43	326	13	1	28
Rivas	.800	1	3	1	1	0
Torrens	1.000	1	4	0	0	0
Van Gansen	.984	8	58	3	1	5
Zunica	.987	87	630	35	9	52

Second Base	PCT	G	PO	A	E	DP
Baker	1.000	9	12	18	0	2
Batten	1.000	2	0	2	0	0
Castillo	.992	51	97	142	2	31
Easley	.833	1	3	2	1	0
Miller	.980	48	83	117	4	26
Potts	.975	19	32	45	2	7
Van Gansen	1.000	12	11	36	0	4

Third Base	PCT	G	PO	A	E	DP
Baker	.885	15	9	14	3	0
Castillo	.950	7	7	12	1	3
Giron	1.000	7	4	16	0	4
Miller	1.000	6	4	7	0	0
Overstreet	1.000	8	5	8	0	1
Potts	.966	86	52	116	6	8
Van Gansen	1.000	12	9	12	0	0

Shortstop	PCT	G	PO	A	E	DP
Baker	.917	8	5	17	2	2
Castillo	.986	38	51	86	2	14
Giron	1.000	6	6	7	0	1
Miller	.980	71	79	172	5	35
Tatis Jr.	.857	2	2	4	1	1
Van Gansen	.974	16	23	53	2	15

Outfield	PCT	G	PO	A	E	DP
Benson	1.000	8	12	0	0	0
Castillo	1.000	8	13	1	0	0
Easley	1.000	14	24	0	0	0
Kohlwey	.988	52	79	2	1	1
Olivares	.975	121	225	9	6	3
Ona	.857	15	17	1	3	0
Orozco	.989	62	87	5	1	0
Reed	.977	115	233	18	6	2
Trammell	.972	31	69	1	2	0

LAKE ELSINORE STORM
CALIFORNIA LEAGUE

HIGH CLASS A

Batting	B-T	HT	WT	DOB	AVG	vLH	vRH	G	AB	R	H	2B	3B	HR	RBI	BB	HBP	SH	SF	SO	SB	CS	SLG	OBP
Arias, Gabriel	R-R	6-1	201	2-27-00	.302	.353	.288	120	477	62	144	21	4	17	75	25	4	1	4	128	8	4	.470	.339
Basabe, Olivier	R-R	5-11	190	7-15-97	.233	.222	.236	116	421	40	98	17	3	7	51	41	9	1	3	87	6	0	.337	.312
Benson, Tyler	L-R	5-11	180	6-17-96	.214	.500	.167	5	14	0	3	1	0	0	2	0	0	0	0	7	0	0	.286	.214
Burgos, Aldemar	R-R	6-0	165	1-23-97	.188	.231	.158	19	64	10	12	2	0	3	10	3	0	0	0	20	0	0	.359	.224
Campusano, Luis	R-R	6-0	215	9-29-98	.325	.330	.323	110	422	63	137	31	1	15	81	52	4	0	9	57	0	0	.510	.396
Cantu, Michael	R-R	6-3	225	8-28-95	.056	.000	.067	6	18	0	1	0	0	0	2	2	0	0	0	8	0	0	.056	.150
Cordero, Franchy	L-R	6-3	175	9-2-94	.125	.250	.000	2	8	0	1	0	1	0	2	0	0	0	0	4	0	0	.375	.125
Cordoba, Allen	R-R	6-1	175	12-6-95	.301	.316	.297	105	422	68	127	20	6	5	43	31	14	1	2	77	32	11	.412	.367
Easley, Nate	R-R	5-10	170	1-11-96	.158	.400	.121	11	38	4	6	1	0	1	4	0	0	0	12	0	1	.237	.238

Name	B-T	HT	WT	DOB	AVG	vLH	vRH	G	AB	R	H	2B	3B	HR	RBI	BB	HBP	SH	SF	SO	SB	CS	OBP	SLG
Edwards, Xavier	B-R	5-10	175	8-9-99	.301	.304	.300	46	196	32	59	5	4	0	13	14	1	5	1	19	14	2	.367	.349
Giron, Ruddy	R-R	6-0	205	1-4-97	.217	.000	.238	6	23	1	5	0	0	0	2	1	0	0	0	10	0	0	.217	.250
Jankowski, Travis	L-R	6-2	185	6-15-91	.143	.000	.333	2	7	0	1	0	0	0	0	2	0	0	0	1	1	2	.143	.333
Kennedy, A.J.	R-R	6-0	190	1-23-94	.143	--	.143	2	7	0	1	0	0	0	0	0	0	0	0	0	0	0	.143	.143
Kohlwey, Taylor	L-L	6-3	200	7-20-94	.387	.273	.412	19	62	8	24	2	2	1	10	7	1	0	2	15	2	0	.532	.444
Melean, Kelvin	R-R	6-0	195	9-5-98	.196	.167	.200	13	46	1	9	2	0	1	7	2	0	0	1	11	1	1	.304	.225
Ornelas, Tirso	L-R	6-3	200	3-11-00	.220	.202	.226	89	332	41	73	11	5	1	30	44	0	0	3	91	3	1	.292	.309
Panas, Connor	L-R	6-0	218	2-11-93	.208	.111	.237	21	77	12	16	3	2	1	7	10	5	0	0	17	2	0	.338	.337
Podorsky, Robbie	R-R	5-8	170	1-27-95	.289	.435	.261	40	142	21	41	4	2	1	12	15	1	4	2	19	12	3	.366	.356
Quintero, Alison	R-R	5-11	175	4-24-00	.125	.000	.143	3	8	0	1	1	0	0	3	0	0	0	1	4	0	0	.250	.111
Rosario, Eguy	R-R	5-9	150	8-25-99	.278	.286	.276	122	464	60	129	25	8	7	72	37	3	1	7	103	21	9	.412	.331
Rosario, Jeisson	L-L	6-1	191	10-22-99	.242	.262	.237	120	430	67	104	14	4	3	35	87	3	4	1	114	11	4	.314	.372
Ruiz, Esteury	R-R	6-0	169	2-15-99	.239	.154	.259	98	339	45	81	18	2	6	36	26	5	7	3	101	34	11	.357	.300
Solomon, Lee	R-R	5-10	200	8-6-96	.237	.267	.217	12	38	10	9	2	0	1	6	5	0	1	0	8	1	1	.368	.326
Suwinski, Jack	L-R	6-2	206	7-29-98	.208	.202	.210	116	408	56	85	16	3	12	51	56	1	2	4	141	2	1	.351	.303
Washington, Jalen	R-R	5-11	190	2-28-95	.215	.193	.223	63	205	27	44	7	3	4	28	20	7	3	4	46	5	1	.337	.301

Pitching	B-T	HT	WT	DOB	W	L	ERA	G	GS	CG	SV	IP	H	R	ER	HR	BB	SO	AVG	vLH	vRH	K/9	BB/9
Acevedo, Angel	R-R	6-1	205	9-19-98	0	0	5.19	2	0	0	0	9	10	6	5	2	3	5	.286	.125	.333	5.19	3.12
Ashbeck, Elliot	L-R	6-3	220	11-16-93	6	3	2.95	33	8	0	0	104	86	37	34	9	24	102	.221	.148	.259	8.86	2.08
Bachar, Lake	R-R	6-3	215	6-3-95	0	0	3.00	1	1	0	0	6	6	4	2	0	2	7	.273	.250	.300	10.50	3.00
Bencomo, Edwuin	R-R	6-2	200	4-14-99	1	0	5.40	1	1	0	0	5	4	3	3	1	3	5	.211	.167	.231	9.00	5.40
Blair, Seth	R-R	6-2	185	3-3-89	2	3	4.11	17	2	0	0	35	31	20	16	5	14	47	.246	.237	.250	12.09	3.60
Bolanos, Ronald	R-R	6-3	200	8-23-96	5	2	2.85	10	10	0	0	54	37	24	17	4	23	54	.193	.300	.155	9.06	3.86
Boushley, Caleb	R-R	6-3	190	10-1-93	5	4	3.61	26	10	0	1	102	112	48	41	7	16	104	.275	.215	.304	9.15	1.41
Cantillo, Joey	L-L	6-4	220	12-18-99	1	1	4.61	3	3	0	0	14	12	9	7	2	7	16	.222	.273	.209	10.54	4.61
Castillo, Jose	L-L	6-5	246	1-10-96	0	1	3.18	6	1	0	0	6	2	2	2	1	1	12	.105	.200	.071	19.06	1.59
Coleman, Dylan	R-R	6-5	230	9-16-96	0	1	15.43	2	0	0	0	2	4	6	4	0	3	1	.333	.200	.429	3.86	11.57
Colletti, Tom	R-R	6-3	220	6-22-95	0	0	3.00	1	0	0	0	3	4	3	1	0	0	2	.308	.400	.250	6.00	0.00
Cosgrove, Tom	L-L	6-2	190	6-14-96	1	4	6.21	6	6	0	0	29	40	25	20	5	12	26	.331	.160	.375	8.07	3.72
Cosme, Jean	R-R	6-2	155	5-24-96	3	0	1.48	17	1	0	1	24	18	5	4	0	9	31	.200	.154	.219	11.47	3.33
Erlin, Robbie	R-L	6-0	190	10-8-90	0	0	4.91	3	0	0	0	4	6	2	2	1	1	6	.375	.000	.500	14.73	2.45
Fox, Mason	R-R	6-2	170	1-7-97	2	0	0.00	5	0	0	1	6	2	1	0	0	6	8	.100	.000	.125	12.71	9.53
Giron, Ruddy	R-R	6-0	205	1-4-97	1	0	0.00	1	0	0	0	1	1	0	0	0	1	1	.333	.000	.500	9.00	0.00
Gore, MacKenzie	L-L	6-3	195	2-24-99	7	1	1.02	15	15	0	0	79	36	9	9	4	20	110	.137	.122	.141	12.48	2.27
Guerra, Javy	L-R	5-11	155	9-25-95	0	0	3.71	17	0	0	1	17	13	7	7	2	5	23	.213	.158	.238	12.18	2.65
Guerrero, Jordan	R-R	6-5	296	8-1-96	2	3	2.05	35	0	0	0	53	38	18	12	4	19	57	.202	.270	.168	9.74	3.25
Headean, Will	R-L	6-4	230	10-11-93	0	2	5.84	12	0	0	0	12	12	14	8	1	17	16	.267	.182	.294	11.68	12.41
Hernandez, Osvaldo	L-L	6-0	181	5-15-98	0	2	3.90	12	10	0	0	32	30	14	14	2	9	22	.248	.243	.250	6.12	2.51
Higgins, Tyler	R-R	6-3	215	4-22-91	0	0	0.00	1	0	0	0	1	0	0	0	0	0	2	.000	--	.000	18.00	0.00
Knehr, Reiss	L-R	6-2	205	11-3-96	3	5	5.43	17	12	0	1	66	71	43	40	11	28	83	.267	.323	.235	11.26	3.80
Kuzia, Nick	R-R	6-4	190	2-7-96	1	0	2.20	19	0	0	0	33	24	11	8	2	11	38	.203	.294	.167	10.47	3.03
Lamet, Dinelson	R-R	6-4	187	7-18-92	0	2	8.00	3	3	0	0	9	11	8	8	1	5	14	.306	.154	.391	14.00	5.00
Leasher, Aaron	L-L	6-3	208	4-28-96	10	7	3.15	22	19	0	0	120	113	44	42	11	34	113	.247	.261	.243	8.48	2.55
Martinez, Adrian	R-R	6-2	215	12-10-96	1	0	1.50	1	1	0	0	6	6	1	1	0	0	7	.261	.429	.188	10.50	0.00
Megill, Trevor	L-R	6-8	235	12-5-93	0	0	0.00	3	0	0	0	4	2	0	0	0	1	8	.143	.500	.083	18.00	2.25
Mendez, Deivy	R-R	6-2	190	10-27-95	1	0	3.97	7	0	0	0	11	12	6	5	0	4	11	.267	.125	.297	8.74	3.18
Miller, Evan	R-R	6-2	200	5-23-95	2	1	1.15	23	0	0	10	31	13	5	4	1	9	34	.122	.067	.143	9.77	2.59
Minjarez, Felix	R-R	6-3	205	9-13-96	1	1	4.00	3	1	0	0	9	11	4	4	1	5	8	.306	.222	.333	8.00	5.00
Mosser, Gabe	R-R	6-4	185	6-8-96	3	0	4.00	8	5	0	0	36	40	20	16	5	13	34	.286	.293	.283	8.50	3.25
Nix, Jacob	R-R	6-4	220	1-9-96	0	2	3.12	2	2	0	0	9	10	10	3	1	3	11	.278	.500	.214	11.42	3.12
Patino, Luis	R-R	6-0	192	10-26-99	6	8	2.69	18	17	0	0	87	61	30	26	4	34	113	.192	.248	.146	11.69	3.52
Radke, Travis	L-L	6-4	237	3-6-93	0	1	1.46	4	0	0	0	12	10	2	2	0	3	11	.200	.077	.243	8.03	2.19
Richards, Garrett	R-R	6-3	210	5-27-88	0	1	8.10	3	3	0	0	7	8	7	6	1	8	8	.296	.375	.263	10.80	10.80
Rodriguez, Hansel	R-R	6-2	170	2-27-97	3	1	2.92	19	0	0	0	25	19	12	8	0	7	32	.211	.192	.219	11.68	2.55
Rogers, Blake	R-R	6-2	200	2-23-94	0	0	3.86	11	0	0	1	19	23	13	8	0	7	21	.281	.280	.296	10.13	3.38
Schlichtholz, Fred	R-L	6-3	215	9-18-95	1	0	3.97	32	1	0	1	48	50	27	21	4	24	63	.265	.279	.260	11.90	4.53
Thompson, Mason	R-R	6-7	223	2-20-98	0	5	7.66	7	6	0	0	22	22	21	19	3	19	22	.253	.259	.250	8.87	7.66
Tyler, Cody	R-R	6-0	190	10-26-94	0	0	3.09	6	0	0	2	12	14	5	4	1	1	16	.292	.556	.231	12.34	0.77
Van Gurp, Franklin	R-R	6-1	225	10-26-95	1	3	6.38	14	0	0	0	18	26	16	13	0	15	19	.342	.462	.280	9.33	7.36
Williams, Sam	L-L	6-3	195	6-26-96	1	0	4.50	4	0	0	0	6			3	0	2	6	.238	.200	.250	9.00	3.00
Wilson, Steven	R-R	6-3	185	8-24-94	2	0	0.93	17	0	0	0	29	19	3	3	2	4	43	.185	.182	.186	13.34	1.24

Fielding

Catcher	PCT	G	PO	A	E	DP	PB
Campusano	.989	77	786	40	9	4	4
Cantu	.978	5	41	4	1	0	0
Kennedy	1.000	2	24	0	0	0	0
Quintero	1.000	2	15	2	0	0	0
Washington	.988	56	528	46	7	5	10
Panas	1.000	8	43	1	0		3
Rosario	.988	12	78	5	1		3
Solomon	1.000	6	32	1	0		5
Washington	.938	2	14	1	1		2

First Base	PCT	G	PO	A	E	DP
Basabe	.989	98	677	38	8	53
Campusano	1.000	2	10	1	0	1
Kohlwey	.989	13	90	1	1	7

Second Base	PCT	G	PO	A	E	DP
Arias	1.000	2	2	0	0	1
Basabe	1.000	3	8	6	0	4
Edwards	.985	36	48	85	2	17
Giron	1.000	4	6	11	0	1
Melean	1.000	2	2	5	0	1
Rosario	1.000	15	35	28	0	6
Ruiz	.926	75	92	108	16	21
Solomon	.923	5	11	13	2	4

Third Base	PCT	G	PO	A	E	DP
Arias	.967	10	9	20	1	1
Basabe	.917	10	6	16	2	0
Cordoba	.944	40	23	78	6	5
Giron	1.000	1	1	1	0	0
Melean	.813	9	4	9	3	1
Rosario	.904	69	46	114	17	9

	PCT	G	PO	A	E	DP
Ruiz	1.000	1	0	1	0	0

Shortstop	PCT	G	PO	A	E	DP
Arias	.935	104	129	248	26	43
Basabe	.875	2	2	5	1	0
Cordoba	1.000	5	7	6	0	2
Edwards	.962	9	8	17	1	2
Melean	1.000	2	3	4	0	0
Rosario	.948	20	21	34	3	6

Outfield	PCT	G	PO	A	E	DP
Basabe	1.000	3	2	0	0	0
Benson	1.000	3	1	0	0	0
Burgos	1.000	15	21	1	0	0
Cordero	1.000	1	5	0	0	0
Cordoba	.962	53	95	7	4	1
Easley	1.000	10	20	0	0	0
Jankowski	1.000	1	3	0	0	0

	PCT	G	PO	A	E	DP
Kohlwey	.667	2	2	0	1	0
Ornelas	.957	78	152	3	7	0
Panas	1.000	1	4	0	0	0
Podorsky	1.000	20	36	0	0	0
Rosario	.955	118	263	15	13	6
Ruiz	.926	12	25	0	2	0
Suwinski	.984	104	173	10	3	4
Washington	1.000	1	1	0	0	0

FORT WAYNE TINCAPS

LOW CLASS A

MIDWEST LEAGUE

Batting	B-T	HT	WT	DOB	AVG	vLH	vRH	G	AB	R	H	2B	3B	HR	RBI	BB	HBP	SH	SF	SO	SB	CS	SLG	OBP
Abrams, CJ	L-R	6-2	185	10-3-00	.250	--	.250	2	8	1	2	1	0	0	1	0	0	0	0	1	0	.375	.333
Alarcon, Kelvin	B-R	6-1	155	3-6-99	.191	.000	.235	12	42	1	8	2	0	0	1	3	1	0	0	14	0	0	.238	.261
Almanzar, Luis	R-R	6-0	205	11-1-99	.183	.167	.188	53	175	13	32	3	1	3	20	23	0	2	2	64	2	1	.263	.275
Becker, Luke	B-R	5-11	190	4-8-96	.147	.182	.140	20	68	13	10	2	0	1	6	11	1	1	0	14	1	1	.221	.275
Benson, Tyler	L-R	5-11	180	6-17-96	.279	.000	.302	20	68	16	19	4	2	0	7	9	0	0	0	13	7	0	.397	.364
Burgos, Aldemar	R-R	6-0	165	1-23-97	.231	.500	.208	9	26	6	6	3	0	0	1	4	0	0	0	5	0	0	.346	.333
Curry, Michael	R-R	6-1	212	7-4-97	.285	.246	.296	83	284	45	81	19	0	8	45	41	3	0	2	70	1	0	.437	.379
Edwards, Xavier	B-R	5-10	175	8-9-99	.336	.276	.355	77	307	44	103	13	4	1	30	30	1	2	4	35	20	9	.414	.392
Feight, Nick	R-R	5-11	200	11-4-95	.119	.222	.091	13	42	4	5	1	0	0	2	4	2	0	1	8	0	1	.143	.225
Fernandez, Juan	R-R	5-11	205	3-7-99	.274	.265	.276	53	179	22	49	9	2	2	26	17	4	0	1	31	2	0	.380	.348
Gatewood, Nick	L-R	6-1	205	7-17-97	.146	.111	.154	13	48	5	7	5	0	0	4	3	0	0	0	19	0	0	.250	.196
Givin, Chris	R-R	6-2	185	3-21-97	.167	.600	.108	13	42	3	7	3	0	0	5	4	2	0	1	9	1	0	.238	.265
Harris, Jawuan	R-R	5-9	190	11-3-96	.212	.279	.199	113	358	62	76	16	5	8	37	63	11	5	1	141	29	6	.352	.346
Hunt, Blake	R-R	6-3	215	11-10-98	.255	.329	.236	89	333	40	85	21	3	5	39	35	4	1	3	67	4	1	.381	.331
Lezama, Jose	B-R	5-10	195	2-19-98	.200	.000	.231	5	15	1	3	1	0	0	2	2	0	0	3	0	0	.267	.294
Little, Grant	R-R	6-1	185	7-8-97	.256	.238	.262	70	254	26	65	15	0	0	21	29	3	3	1	44	6	0	.315	.338
Lopez, Justin	B-R	6-2	195	5-9-00	.228	.226	.229	114	443	65	101	17	3	13	57	28	3	3	1	119	0	1	.368	.278
Marcano, Tucupita	L-R	6-0	170	9-16-99	.270	.303	.262	111	460	55	124	19	3	2	45	35	3	3	3	45	15	16	.337	.323
Melean, Kelvin	R-R	6-0	195	9-5-98	.159	.200	.151	19	63	3	10	4	0	0	3	4	0	0	0	18	3	0	.222	.209
Reyes, Ripken	B-R	5-10	180	4-1-97	.286	.286	.286	16	49	5	14	2	1	1	4	5	4	0	1	5	0	0	.429	.390
Roman, Luis	L-R	6-0	215	12-19-94	.294	.333	.282	14	51	5	15	1	0	2	5	2	0	0	0	8	0	0	.431	.321
Ruiz, Agustin	L-R	6-2	215	9-23-99	.239	.245	.238	120	443	49	106	26	2	4	55	51	6	1	9	127	2	1	.334	.320
Seagle, Chandler	R-R	6-0	190	5-23-96	.227	.000	.278	6	22	4	5	2	0	0	2	0	0	0	1	5	0	0	.318	.217
Skender, Ethan	R-R	5-11	185	12-22-96	.275	.333	.264	41	153	23	42	6	1	2	25	12	5	0	0	30	4	1	.366	.347
Solomon, Lee	R-R	5-10	200	8-6-96	.223	.196	.228	95	310	31	69	22	1	3	32	38	8	4	2	83	3	4	.329	.321
Williams-Sutton, Dwanya	R-R	6-2	225	10-7-98	.236	.286	.221	95	305	58	72	11	1	9	52	60	32	0	2	99	12	2	.367	.411

Pitching	B-T	HT	WT	DOB	W	L	ERA	G	GS	CG	SV	IP	H	R	ER	HR	BB	SO	AVG	vLH	vRH	K/9	BB/9
Acevedo, Angel	R-R	6-1	205	9-19-98	0	7	6.53	17	6	0	0	51	60	46	37	5	24	55	.284	.317	.264	9.71	4.24
Alarcon, Kelvin	B-R	6-1	155	3-6-99	0	0	0.00	2	0	0	0	2	0	0	0	0	0	0	.000	.000	.000	0.00	0.00
Anderson, Korey	R-R	6-2	205	9-11-94	0	0	8.10	4	0	0	0	7	10	7	6	0	6	8	.323	.357	.294	10.80	8.10
Belen, Carlos	R-R	6-1	250	2-28-96	0	3	3.80	34	0	0	4	43	40	24	18	3	11	45	.240	.262	.226	9.49	2.32
Bencomo, Edwuin	R-R	6-2	200	4-14-99	1	1	3.69	12	3	0	0	32	41	17	13	3	12	30	.311	.242	.371	8.53	3.41
Benson, Tyler	L-R	5-11	180	6-17-96	0	0	67.50	1	0	0	0	1	4	5	5	1	2	0	.667	.667	.667	0.00	13.50
Brash, Matt	R-R	6-1	170	5-12-98	0	0	2.08	4	0	0	0	4	3	1	1	0	0	6	.188	.143	.222	12.46	0.00
Cantillo, Joey	L-L	6-4	220	12-18-99	9	3	1.93	19	19	1	0	98	58	24	21	3	27	128	.173	.165	.176	11.76	2.48
Coleman, Dylan	R-R	6-5	230	9-16-96	2	1	2.13	9	0	0	0	13	13	7	3	0	8	12	.265	.227	.296	8.53	5.68
Colletti, Tom	R-R	6-3	220	6-22-95	1	1	6.75	7	0	0	0	16	20	13	12	1	5	14	.308	.280	.325	7.88	2.81
Contreras, Efrain	R-R	5-10	210	1-2-00	6	6	3.61	25	23	0	0	110	97	49	44	12	32	121	.236	.214	.252	9.93	2.63
Cruz, Omar	L-L	6-0	200	1-26-99	2	2	2.76	10	10	0	0	49	42	18	15	1	13	62	.236	.250	.228	11.39	2.39
Dallas, Dan	L-L	6-2	235	12-24-97	1	2	5.74	10	0	0	0	16	19	12	10	3	8	13	.288	.455	.255	7.47	4.60
Dana, Cullen	B-L	6-5	240	8-7-97	2	4	7.36	7	7	0	0	29	37	26	24	3	14	13	.336	.357	.329	3.99	4.30
Dean, Andrew	R-L	6-1	185	7-17-96	1	0	9.00	3	0	0	0	6	9	6	6	0	2	3	.360	.750	.286	4.50	3.00
Feight, Nick	R-R	5-11	200	11-4-95	0	0	0.00	1	0	0	0	2	0	0	0	0	0	0	.667	1.000	.500	0.00	0.00
Fernandez, Juan	R-R	5-11	205	3-7-99	0	0	4.50	1	0	0	0	2	2	1	1	1	2	0	.250	.000	.333	0.00	9.00
Fox, Mason	R-R	6-2	170	1-7-97	1	0	0.00	6	0	0	2	8	3	0	0	0	0	16	.115	.071	.167	18.00	0.00
Gonzalez, Jesus	L-L	5-10	160	6-12-01	0	1	1.80	1	1	0	0	5	2	1	1	0	1	2	.125	.000	.182	3.60	1.80
Guarate, Carlos	R-R	6-2	178	3-30-01	0	0	2.25	1	1	0	0	4	5	1	1	0	1	5	.313	.000	.313	11.25	2.25
Guzman, Jonathan	R-R	5-10	205	2-8-95	0	0	5.40	4	0	0	0	5	3	3	3	0	5	7	.177	.250	.111	12.60	9.00
Henry, Henry	R-R	6-4	215	12-17-98	7	5	3.32	43	0	0	10	81	73	35	30	3	16	80	.233	.244	.224	8.85	1.77
Keating, Sam	R-R	6-3	190	8-31-98	3	8	7.50	14	13	0	0	60	80	59	50	7	22	35	.327	.344	.309	5.25	3.30
Komar, Brandon	R-R	6-0	195	5-8-99	0	1	9.00	4	2	0	0	16	17	16	16	3	9	17	.270	.200	.333	9.56	5.06
Kuzia, Nick	R-R	6-4	190	2-7-96	0	1	3.95	9	0	0	0	14	15	11	6	3	7	16	.273	.393	.148	10.54	4.61
Lugo, Moises	R-R	6-1	185	1-20-99	0	1	16.20	3	2	0	0	5	8	9	9	2	3	3	.381	.375	.385	5.40	5.40
Martinez, Adrian	R-R	6-2	215	12-10-96	6	4	3.36	32	5	0	1	75	68	31	28	7	22	69	.245	.268	.226	8.28	2.64
Melean, Kelvin	R-R	6-0	195	9-5-98	0	0	0.00	1	0	0	0	1	0	0	0	0	1	0	.000	.000	.000	9.00	0.00
Mosser, Gabe	R-R	6-4	185	6-8-96	4	5	4.25	14	14	0	0	72	80	42	34	4	12	72	.275	.280	.270	9.50	1.50
Perez, Ramon	L-L	6-1	225	7-2-99	1	5	6.07	16	10	0	0	56	59	42	38	3	28	51	.271	.229	.293	8.15	4.47
Quezada, Jose	R-S	5-9	165	9-7-95	6	4	4.09	48	0	0	1	70	73	37	32	4	37	89	.267	.239	.287	11.39	4.73
Quijada, Hazahel	L-L	6-2	185	9-18-97	0	0	3.38	3	0	0	0	3	2	1	1	0	1	5	.200	.000	.250	16.88	3.38
Shelton, Trent	L-L	6-4	205	6-24-94	0	1	1.80	2	0	0	1	5	3	1	1	0	2	4	.177	.000	.188	7.20	3.60
Smith, Austin	R-R	6-4	250	7-9-96	2	1	3.51	35	0	0	5	67	68	36	26	3	20	62	.256	.265	.250	8.37	2.70

	B-T	HT	WT	DOB	W	L	ERA	G	GS	CG	SV	IP	H	R	ER	HR	BB	SO	AVG	vLH	vRH	K/9	BB/9
Solomon, Lee	R-R	5-10	200	8-6-96	0	0	9.00	3	0	0	0	3	6	4	3	1	2	0	.429	.455	.333	0.00	6.00
Tyler, Cody	R-L	6-0	190	10-26-94	3	2	3.27	29	0	0	3	52	49	24	19	5	11	52	.244	.194	.271	8.94	1.89
Van Gurp, Franklin	R-R	6-1	225	10-26-95	0	1	2.87	9	0	0	1	16	16	6	5	0	5	16	.271	.385	.182	9.19	2.87
Weathers, Ryan	R-L	6-1	230	12-17-99	3	7	3.84	22	22	0	0	96	101	45	41	6	18	90	.275	.259	.282	8.44	1.69

Fielding

Catcher	PCT	G	PO	A	E	DP	PB
Fernandez	.991	49	370	65	4	2	2
Gatewood	1.000	2	18	2	0	0	1
Hunt	.990	77	699	61	8	4	5
Lezama	1.000	5	36	6	0	1	0
Seagle	1.000	6	57	4	0	0	0
Solomon	.982	77	606	46	12	66	
Skender	.925	32	18	56	6	10	

First Base	PCT	G	PO	A	E	DP
Alarcon	1.000	9	57	8	0	6
Almanzar	1.000	6	44	3	0	3
Becker	.966	11	75	11	3	9
Curry	1.000	6	20	1	0	4
Feight	1.000	7	50	2	0	1
Fernandez	.909	2	10	0	1	3
Gatewood	1.000	3	20	0	0	1
Givin	.987	12	72	4	1	9
Hunt	1.000	9	54	3	0	1
Roman	1.000	5	49	1	0	4
Skender	1.000	1	4	1	0	0

Second Base	PCT	G	PO	A	E	DP
Edwards	.973	51	82	132	6	29
Fernandez	1.000	1	0	1	0	0
Little	.000	1	0	0	1	0
Lopez	.962	28	41	61	4	15
Marcano	.955	32	45	82	6	21
Reyes	.984	15	26	34	1	10
Solomon	.941	17	28	36	4	12

Third Base	PCT	G	PO	A	E	DP
Almanzar	.840	36	33	35	13	3
Becker	1.000	9	4	10	0	3
Givin	.400	1	1	1	3	0
Lopez	.923	5	0	12	1	0
Marcano	.905	42	35	60	10	7
Melean	.946	16	11	24	2	3
Roman	.000	1	0	0	1	0

Shortstop	PCT	G	PO	A	E	DP
Abrams	.800	1	2	2	1	1
Edwards	.938	22	23	52	5	12
Givin	1.000	1	4	0	0	0
Lopez	.958	80	106	214	14	46
Marcano	.929	40	58	86	11	22
Melean	1.000	1	2	4	0	1

Outfield	PCT	G	PO	A	E	DP
Becker	.000	1	0	0	0	0
Benson	1.000	15	32	0	0	0
Burgos	1.000	8	12	2	0	1
Curry	.969	36	60	2	2	0
Harris	.979	111	228	5	5	0
Little	.969	68	121	4	4	0
Ruiz	.984	102	175	5	3	1
Williams-Sutton	.961	87	141	5	6	1

TRI-CITY DUST DEVILS
NORTHWEST LEAGUE

SHORT SEASON

Batting

	B-T	HT	WT	DOB	AVG	vLH	vRH	G	AB	R	H	2B	3B	HR	RBI	BB	HBP	SH	SF	SO	SB	CS	SLG	OBP
Acosta, Matthew	L-L	5-11	185	4-1-98	.264	.350	.246	62	231	34	61	10	2	2	24	30	2	2	3	37	5	1	.351	.350
Alarcon, Kelvin	B-R	6-1	155	3-6-99	.256	.000	.286	12	39	5	10	1	1	1	3	5	0	0	0	5	2	1	.410	.341
Barley, Jordy	R-R	6-0	175	12-3-99	.255	.170	.272	66	279	45	71	11	6	8	30	22	1	1	1	98	14	8	.423	.310
Becker, Luke	B-R	5-11	190	4-8-96	.222	.150	.241	31	99	17	22	4	2	0	12	21	1	1	0	18	3	0	.303	.364
Benson, Tyler	L-R	5-11	180	6-17-96	.250	.333	.227	10	28	5	7	1	0	0	2	8	0	0	0	9	4	0	.286	.417
Carter, Tre	L-R	6-2	181	3-22-97	.208	.200	.209	51	159	16	33	4	4	2	12	17	0	2	3	52	4	1	.321	.279
Driscoll, Logan	L-R	6-1	195	11-3-97	.268	.227	.275	39	142	20	38	14	2	3	20	15	2	0	3	23	0	1	.458	.340
Gatewood, Nick	L-R	6-1	205	7-17-97	.255	.250	.256	41	153	17	39	5	1	5	33	16	1	0	2	42	1	0	.399	.326
Guilbe, Sean	R-R	6-1	190	12-13-99	.233	.067	.264	53	189	33	44	14	3	6	17	21	3	0	1	67	3	1	.434	.318
Homza, Jonny	R-R	6-0	185	6-13-99	.216	.200	.219	53	185	18	40	14	1	0	13	21	5	0	0	62	2	0	.303	.313
House, Mason	L-L	6-3	190	9-10-98	.147	.222	.136	23	75	5	11	1	0	2	11	5	3	0	0	43	0	0	.240	.229
Ilarraza, Reinaldo	B-R	5-10	150	1-12-99	.222	.191	.229	68	234	45	52	4	3	6	28	49	0	2	1	60	26	5	.342	.356
Luis, Carlos	L-R	6-2	160	9-4-99	.254	.111	.277	35	130	10	33	7	1	1	12	12	0	1	0	28	2	0	.346	.315
Melean, Kelvin	R-R	6-0	195	9-5-98	.308	.273	.316	50	185	21	57	14	0	1	27	22	9	0	4	37	5	4	.400	.400
Pineda, Jason	R-R	6-2	202	11-22-99	.224	.250	.219	44	152	12	34	11	1	1	16	16	2	0	1	60	2	1	.329	.304
Quintero, Alison	R-R	5-11	175	4-24-00	.144	.063	.156	34	125	7	18	4	0	0	8	6	0	0	0	36	0	1	.176	.183
Stronach, Jack	L-R	6-3	195	8-2-97	.236	.476	.195	44	144	20	34	9	0	2	16	13	5	0	1	36	2	2	.340	.319

Pitching

	B-T	HT	WT	DOB	W	L	ERA	G	GS	CG	SV	IP	H	R	ER	HR	BB	SO	AVG	vLH	vRH	K/9	BB/9
Acevedo, Angel	R-R	6-1	205	9-19-98	1	5	6.54	9	8	0	0	32	42	31	23	2	8	32	.309	.396	.253	9.09	2.27
Alarcon, Kelvin	B-R	6-1	155	3-6-99	0	0	0.00	2	0	0	0	2	1	1	0	0	0	0	.125	.000	.143	0.00	0.00
Arias, Luarbert	R-R	6-2	176	12-12-00	1	0	1.80	1	1	0	0	5	3	1	1	0	1	4	.177	.000	.273	7.20	1.80
Becker, Luke	B-R	5-11	190	4-8-96	0	0	18.00	1	0	0	0	1	2	3		1		3	.400	.000	.500	9.00	27.00
Blanchard, Jason	R-L	6-0	185	6-25-97	1	3	3.38	13	10	0	0	32	23	17	12	0	12	41	.187	.273	.168	11.53	3.38
Carrasco, Martin	R-R	6-0	165	11-22-99	0	0	0.00	2	0	0	0	5	4	2	0	0	2	7	.235	.600	.083	13.50	3.86
Colletti, Tom	R-R	6-3	220	6-22-95	3	4	1.98	16	0	0	3	27	21	14	6	2	12	41	.210	.179	.222	13.50	3.95
Cordero, Starlin	R-R	6-7	220	7-21-98	2	0	4.54	21	0	0	0	34	30	19	17	1	23	50	.246	.289	.221	13.37	6.15
Cruz, Omar	L-L	6-0	200	1-26-99	0	1	2.57	2	2	0	0	7	4	3	2	0	6	14	.167	.250	.150	18.00	7.71
Dallas, Dan	L-L	6-2	235	12-24-97	1	0	1.41	21	1	0	2	32	27	6	5	1	17	45	.229	.333	.193	12.66	4.78
Dana, Cullen	B-L	6-5	240	8-7-97	1	0	0.00	6	2	0	0	15	12	1	0	0	1	16	.214	.167	.220	9.60	0.60
DiSabatino, Dominic	R-R	6-5	190	3-21-96	4	0	8.03	20	0	0	1	25	21	24	22	0	23	13	.239	.174	.262	4.74	8.39
Elliott, Ethan	L-L	6-3	180	4-28-97	0	1	1.77	12	12	0	0	36	27	8	7	3	4	38	.205	.118	.235	9.59	1.01
Feliz, Ignacio	R-R	6-1	180	10-23-99	2	4	4.40	13	12	0	0	57	57	38	28	7	27	55	.256	.243	.262	8.63	4.24
Fox, Mason	R-R	6-2	170	1-7-97	0	0	0.95	13	0	0	1	19	11	2	2	0	10	32	.164	.136	.178	15.16	4.74
Garcia, Jeferson	R-R	6-0	165	2-4-00	0	0	4.91	1	0	0	0	4	3	2	2	0	2	4	.231	.200	.250	9.82	4.91
Keating, Sam	R-R	6-3	190	8-31-98	0	0	9.64	7	0	0	1	9	8	10	10	0	7	5	.250	.091	.333	4.82	6.75
Lehmann, Connor	R-R	6-7	210	8-15-96	1	1	3.03	12	6	0	0	30	22	11	10	2	16	26	.202	.180	.214	7.89	4.85
Lincoln, Chris	R-R	6-4	175	1-2-98	2	0	0.00	4	0	0	0	8	2	1	0	0	2	11	.080	.250	.048	12.38	2.25
Mayberry, Seth	R-R	6-3	200	6-22-00	0	0	6.75	2	0	0	0	3	3	2	2	0	5	3	.273	.000	.375	16.88	16.88
Medders, Deacon	R-R	6-4	200	9-2-96	1	5	4.84	24	0	0	4	35	34	21	19	4	18	43	.254	.128	.305	10.95	4.58
Mendez, Deivy	R-R	6-2	190	10-27-95	1	1	4.34	18	0	0	6	19	20	13	9	0	10	22	.267	.350	.236	10.61	4.82
Minjarez, Felix	R-R	6-3	205	9-13-96	1	2	2.23	19	2	0	1	44	38	21	11	3	11	46	.224	.217	.227	9.34	2.23
Morales, Gabriel	L-L	6-3	175	4-14-99	0	1	15.43	1	1	0	0	2	3	4	4	0	3	2	.333	.000	.375	7.71	11.57
Perez, Ramon	L-L	6-1	225	7-2-99	2	2	3.82	15	0	0	1	38	30	17	16	2	22	52	.217	.177	.231	12.42	5.26
Reynolds, Jason	R-R	6-3	200	9-25-98	2	4	8.64	12	6	0	0	25	25	29	24	3	20	28	.255	.237	.267	10.08	7.20

	B-T	HT	WT	DOB	W	L	ERA	G	GS	CG	SV	IP	H	R	ER	HR	BB	SO	AVG	vLH	vRH	K/9	BB/9
Sims, Jake	L-R	6-2	215	3-8-97	3	2	5.40	22	0	0	0	30	30	26	18	4	28	50	.250	.256	.247	15.00	8.40
Sung, Wen-Hua	R-R	6-1	198	9-2-96	4	1	3.05	21	0	0	0	41	32	17	14	3	14	59	.212	.188	.223	12.85	3.05
Thwaits, Nick	R-R	6-2	195	6-27-99	4	3	4.66	13	13	0	0	58	70	32	30	5	18	47	.298	.315	.290	7.29	2.79

Fielding

C: Driscoll 11, Gatewood 1, Homza 35, Quintero 34. **1B:** Alarcon 2, Becker 10, Gatewood 18, Luis 17, Pineda 36. **2B:** Alarcon 9, Barley 6, Becker 7, Homza 1, Ilarraza 36, Melean 20. **3B:** Alarcon 2, Becker 9, Guilbe 23, Homza 20, Ilarraza 1, Luis 8, Melean 17. **SS:** Barley 56, Ilarraza 7, Melean 15. **OF:** Acosta 59, Becker 5, Benson 9, Carter 51, Driscoll 19, Guilbe 22, House 12, Ilarraza 26, Stronach 43.

AZL PADRES 1   ROOKIE
ARIZONA LEAGUE

Batting	B-T	HT	WT	DOB	AVG	vLH	vRH	G	AB	R	H	2B	3B	HR	RBI	BB	HBP	SH	SF	SO	SB	CS	SLG	OBP
Abrams, CJ	L-R	6-2	185	10-3-00	.401	.387	.405	32	142	40	57	12	8	3	22	10	2	0	2	14	14	6	.662	.442
Aquino, Charlis	R-R	6-2	165	11-18-01	.294	.250	.308	4	17	2	5	1	0	0	2	1	0	0	0	6	1	0	.353	.333
Cordero, Franchy	L-R	6-3	175	9-2-94	.200	.000	.250	2	5	1	1	0	0	0	1	1	0	0	0	2	0	0	.200	.333
Francisco, Yordi	L-R	6-1	175	3-14-97	.251	.191	.268	49	195	29	49	9	5	5	23	18	5	1	4	57	16	5	.426	.324
Garcia, Juan	R-R	6-0	170	3-16-01	.125	.000	.143	6	16	2	2	1	0	0	2	1	0	0	1	7	1	0	.188	.167
2-team total (4 Padres 2)					.158	.000	.188	10	19	2	3	1	0	0	2	1	1	0	1	8	1	0	.211	.227
Givin, Chris	R-R	6-2	185	3-21-97	.356	.333	.362	31	118	23	42	9	3	1	25	12	2	0	2	19	5	0	.509	.418
Head, Hudson	L-L	6-1	180	4-8-01	.283	.357	.261	32	120	19	34	7	3	1	12	15	5	0	1	29	3	3	.417	.383
Landinez, Yerry	B-R	6-1	170	1-20-01	.196	.268	.172	45	163	24	32	7	1	3	14	24	2	0	0	75	1	1	.307	.307
Malone, Tyler	L-R	5-11	190	11-4-97	.258	.235	.265	19	66	9	17	5	1	0	9	15	1	0	1	19	1	2	.364	.398
Mears, Joshua	R-R	6-3	230	2-21-01	.253	.294	.242	43	166	30	42	4	3	7	24	23	4	0	2	59	9	1	.440	.354
Nova, Victor	L-R	5-9	160	1-6-00	.330	.278	.343	26	91	22	30	2	3	1	17	15	0	2	1	22	7	2	.451	.421
2-team total (16 Indians Blue)					.297	.242	.313	42	148	37	44	3	3	1	20	26	2	3	2	37	9	2	.378	.405
Ornelas, Tirso	L-R	6-3	200	3-11-00	.205	.174	.215	21	88	6	18	2	0	0	11	9	0	0	0	22	4	0	.227	.278
Paez, Luis	L-R	5-10	160	9-3-00	.285	.385	.256	36	116	21	33	3	0	0	12	10	1	1	1	36	1	2	.310	.344
Polanco, Matias	L-R	5-11	175	9-18-00	.147	.182	.130	13	34	2	5	2	0	0	6	3	0	0	0	9	0	0	.206	.216
Potts, Hudson	R-R	6-3	205	10-28-98	.667	.500	.833	4	12	3	8	1	0	1	6	0	1	0	0	3	0	0	1.000	.692
Quintero, Alison	R-R	5-11	175	4-24-00	.000	--	.000	1	1	0	0	0	0	0	0	0	0	0	0	0	0	0	.000	.000
Rodriguez, Emmanuel	R-R	6-4	200	11-17-01	.091	.000	.095	7	22	3	2	1	0	0	2	1	0	0	0	12	0	0	.136	.130
Seagle, Chandler	R-R	6-0	190	5-23-96	.223	.222	.224	27	94	14	21	9	0	1	11	12	2	0	1	29	1	0	.351	.321
Smith, Payton	R-R	6-5	225	5-22-00	.245	.238	.247	32	106	19	26	4	0	3	10	10	2	0	0	35	1	0	.368	.322
Suarez, Michael	L-L	6-2	205	5-21-00	.303	.292	.308	21	76	9	23	3	1	1	10	6	0	0	0	21	1	0	.408	.379
Torres, Bryan	R-R	5-9	165	12-11-99	.259	.360	.229	33	108	14	28	4	2	0	13	17	2	0	3	22	2	1	.333	.362
Valenzuela, Brandon	R-R	6-0	170	10-2-00	.248	.424	.196	42	145	21	36	4	1	0	20	34	3	0	1	32	0	0	.290	.399

Pitching	B-T	HT	WT	DOB	W	L	ERA	G	GS	CG	SV	IP	H	R	ER	HR	BB	SO	AVG	vLH	vRH	K/9	BB/9
Arias, Luarbert	R-R	6-2	176	12-12-00	4	1	3.68	12	8	0	0	51	42	22	21	1	9	60	.221	.203	.229	10.52	1.58
Avila, Pedro	R-R	5-11	190	1-14-97	0	1	0.90	3	1	0	0	10	5	1	1	0	2	15	.143	.200	.100	13.50	1.80
2-team total (1 Padres 2)					0	1	2.25	4	3	0	0	12	7	3	3	1	3	18	.163	.188	.148	13.50	2.25
Ballard, Sam	L-L	6-0	200	1-16-98	1	1	5.09	10	0	0	0	18	12	11	10	2	14	17	.200	.231	.192	8.66	7.13
2-team total (5 Padres 2)					1	1	4.13	15	0	0	0	24	18	16	11	3	16	25	.209	.211	.209	9.38	6.00
Bencomo, Edwuin	R-R	6-2	200	4-14-99	0	0	5.63	4	0	0	1	8	10	8	5	0	0	13	.278	.308	.261	14.63	0.00
Brash, Matt	R-R	6-1	170	5-12-98	0	0	0.00	1	1	0	0	1	1	0	0	0	0	2	.250	.000	1.000	18.00	0.00
Carrasco, Martin	R-R	6-0	165	11-22-99	4	0	1.46	17	0	0	2	25	20	11	4	0	4	41	.200	.139	.234	14.96	1.46
Castillo, Jose	L-L	6-5	246	1-10-96	0	0	9.00	1	1	0	0	1	2	1	1	0	3	4	.400	.000	.667	27.00	0.00
Coleman, Dylan	R-R	6-5	230	9-16-96	2	1	2.37	16	2	0	1	19	15	8	5	2	6	26	.214	.148	.256	12.32	2.84
Cosgrove, Tom	L-L	6-2	190	6-14-96	0	0	0.00	2	2	0	0	3	1	0	0	0	1	4	.100	.000	.125	12.00	3.00
2-team total (1 Padres 2)					0	0	0.00	3	3	0	0	4	2	0	0	0	1	7	.143	.333	.091	15.75	2.25
Dean, Andrew	R-L	6-1	185	7-17-96	2	0	1.80	11	2	0	0	25	16	6	5	2	6	27	.180	.120	.203	9.72	2.16
Eusebio, Luis	R-R	6-0	180	3-15-96	0	0	5.40	4	0	0	1	7	8	5	4	1	2	8	.286	.385	.200	10.80	2.70
2-team total (12 AZL Padres 2)					2	2	4.41	16	0	0	4	35	32	22	17	4	15	41	.241	.259	.227	10.64	3.89
Fallon, Koty	R-R	6-3	210	7-10-96	1	0	4.11	13	0	0	1	15	10	10	7	1	10	21	.211	.241	.179	12.33	5.87
2-team total (1 Padres 2)					1	0	3.86	14	0	0	2	16	12	10	7	1	12	22	.203	.233	.172	12.12	6.61
Gonzalez, Jesus	L-L	5-10	160	6-12-01	3	3	5.20	11	5	0	0	45	53	31	26	1	13	46	.298	.300	.297	9.20	2.60
Guzman, Manny	R-R	6-4	180	11-1-99	0	0	0.00	2	0	0	0	3	2	0	0	0	2	1	.182	.000	.250	3.00	6.00
Guzman, Oliber	R-R	5-11	180	3-15-97	0	1	8.44	6	0	0	0	5	9	6	5	1	1	6	.409	.750	.333	10.13	1.69
2-team total (11 Padres 2)					3	2	5.68	17	0	0	0	25	27	23	16	4	14	21	.276	.219	.303	7.46	4.97
Hernandez, Osvaldo	L-L	6-0	181	5-15-98	0	0	0.00	2	2	0	0	5	3	1	0	0	2	6	.188	.000	.214	10.80	3.60
Hoffman, Dylan	R-L	6-1	185	2-28-95	0	1	6.00	6	0	0	0	6	9	4	4	1	1	5	.321	.250	.333	7.50	1.50
Komar, Brandon	R-R	6-0	195	5-8-99	1	0	3.93	8	0	0	1	18	19	14	8	1	6	22	.257	.367	.182	10.80	2.95
Lincoln, Chris	R-R	6-4	175	1-2-98	0	0	2.87	13	4	0	2	16	13	5	5	0	4	12	.232	.087	.333	6.89	2.30
Lopez, Frank	R-R	6-1	170	4-23-01	0	4	3.30	11	5	0	0	44	46	30	16	0	19	49	.269	.230	.291	10.10	3.92
Lugo, Moises	R-R	6-1	185	1-20-99	4	1	1.93	9	0	0	0	28	28	13	6	1	2	28	.269	.333	.239	9.00	0.64
2-team total (2 Padres 2)					5	1	2.06	11	0	0	0	35	34	15	8	1	5	38	.262	.357	.216	9.77	1.29
Martinez, Edgar	R-R	5-10	155	2-26-01	3	3	4.40	11	7	0	1	43	53	30	21	2	10	54	.291	.301	.284	11.30	2.09
Mayberry, Seth	R-R	6-3	200	6-22-00	3	1	2.10	18	0	0	3	26	18	6	6	1	12	28	.198	.387	.100	9.82	4.21
Mitchell, Bryan	L-R	6-3	210	4-19-91	0	0	9.00	1	1	0	0	4	5	4	4	3	1	2	.294	.375	.222	4.50	2.25
2-team total (3 Padres 2)					0	0	6.23	4	4	0	0	13	14	9	9	3	6	13	.264	.259	.269	9.00	4.15
Nix, Jacob	R-R	6-4	220	1-9-96	0	0	1.93	2	2	0	0	5	6	2	1	0	2	6	.333	.429	.273	11.57	3.86
Richards, Garrett	R-R	6-3	210	5-27-88	0	0	4.50	1	1	0	0	2	2	1	1	0	0	3	.250	.000	.286	13.50	0.00
2-team total (1 Padres 2)					0	0	16.88	2	2	0	0	3	4	5	5	0	3	5	.333	.333	.333	16.88	10.13
Rodriguez, Hansel	R-R	6-2	170	2-27-97	1	0	0.00	3	0	0	0	4	2	0	0	0	4	.143	.000	.167	9.00	0.00
2-team total (2 Padres 2)					2	0	0.00	5	0	0	0	6	3	1	0	0	8	.136	.000	.167	12.00	0.00

Player	B-T	HT	WT	DOB	W	L	ERA	G	GS	CG	SV	IP	H	R	ER	HR	BB	SO	AVG	vLH	vRH	K/9	BB/9
Rondon, Miguel	R-R	5-11	150	1-26-01	3	2	3.79	11	6	0	1	40	43	23	17	4	13	48	.274	.307	.253	10.71	2.90
Smith, Payton	R-R	6-5	225	5-22-00	0	0	0.00	1	0	0	0	0	0	0	0	0	1	1	.000	.000	--	27.00	27.00
Thompson, Mason	R-R	6-7	223	2-20-98	0	0	0.00	1	0	0	0	1	0	0	0	0	0	0	.000	.000	.000	0.00	0.00
2-team total (2 Padres 2)					0	0	5.40	3	2	0	0	5	6	4	3	1	3	3	.300	.400	.267	5.40	5.40
Vela, Noel	L-L	6-1	165	12-21-98	0	3	10.45	7	4	0	0	10	18	14	12	0	11	12	.391	.500	.368	10.45	9.58

Fielding

C: Malone 1, Polanco 8, Quintero 1, Seagle 26, Valenzuela 26. 1B: Givin 2, Landinez 13, Malone 10, Suarez 20, Valenzuela 13. 2B: Garcia 5, Givin 10, Nova 1, Paez 31, Torres 13. 3B: Givin 7, Landinez 29, Nova 12, Paez 3, Potts 2, Torres 6. SS: Abrams 28, Aquino 4, Givin 9, Landinez 1, Torres 15. OF: Francisco 38, Head 26, Malone 8, Mears 38, Nova 4, Ornelas 20, Rodriguez 4, Smith 32.

AZL PADRES 2 — ROOKIE
ARIZONA LEAGUE

Batting	B-T	HT	WT	DOB	AVG	vLH	vRH	G	AB	R	H	2B	3B	HR	RBI	BB	HBP	SH	SF	SO	SB	CS	SLG	OBP
Alarcon, Kelvin	B-R	6-1	155	3-6-99	.457	.250	.529	12	46	12	21	2	1	0	8	8	0	0	0	8	6	0	.544	.537
Almanzar, Luis	R-R	6-0	205	11-1-99	.296	.177	.324	25	88	20	26	8	1	1	19	24	0	1	3	25	4	5	.443	.435
Alvarez-Lopez, Jared	R-R	6-2	200	1-18-01	.222	.267	.208	17	63	12	14	0	0	1	12	10	0	1	1	24	1	0	.270	.324
Cantu, Michael	R-R	6-3	225	8-28-95	.326	.143	.359	13	46	6	15	4	0	0	7	7	1	0	1	10	0	0	.413	.418
Dale, Jarryd	R-R	6-1	176	9-11-00	.301	.300	.301	31	113	16	34	5	0	0	16	8	2	0	0	36	6	1	.345	.358
Echavarria, Vladimir	R-R	5-11	160	4-12-00	.276	.250	.279	31	98	15	27	6	0	0	10	21	1	0	1	34	11	4	.337	.405
Garcia, Juan	R-R	6-0	170	3-16-01	.333	.000	.500	4	3	0	1	0	0	0	0	0	1	0	0	1	0	0	.333	.500
2-team total (6 Padres 1)					.158	.000	.188	10	19	2	3	1	0	0	2	1	1	0	1	8	1	0	.211	.227
Guerra, Emmanuel	R-R	6-3	185	11-16-00	.265	.067	.294	36	117	17	31	5	3	3	11	11	0	0	0	55	2	1	.436	.328
Heredia, Cristian	R-R	6-3	175	4-12-01	.265	.385	.243	43	166	21	44	10	0	5	35	20	2	0	1	42	0	0	.416	.349
Jones, Taylor	R-R	6-5	215	6-15-01	.136	.063	.160	22	66	14	9	2	0	0	5	7	1	0	0	33	3	1	.167	.230
Lomack, Taylor	R-R	5-11	185	8-22-99	.343	.294	.350	39	137	30	47	3	3	0	14	15	0	0	1	30	11	1	.409	.405
Nunez, Anthony	B-R	6-1	190	7-10-01	.222	.118	.240	38	117	13	26	4	1	0	11	26	0	0	0	41	3	1	.274	.364
Perez, Junior	R-R	6-1	165	7-4-01	.268	.368	.246	51	209	44	56	14	2	11	39	24	3	0	2	59	11	2	.512	.349
Reyes, Ripken	B-R	5-10	180	4-1-97	.315	.278	.326	42	165	39	52	10	3	1	20	16	15	2	2	15	3		.430	.419
Santana, Yeison	R-R	5-11	170	12-7-00	.346	.393	.336	41	162	38	56	5	5	3	30	23	3	1	3	38	4	5	.494	.429
Skender, Ethan	R-R	5-11	185	12-22-96	.385	.333	.395	14	52	15	20	2	2	3	15	5	1	0	1	9	3	3	.673	.441
Solarte, Angel	R-R	5-11	155	3-29-01	.248	.290	.239	53	214	37	53	9	3	4	41	18	3	0	6	45	5	2	.374	.307
Vizcarra, Gilberto	R-R	5-10	180	3-1-99	.302	.191	.326	33	116	20	35	6	1	1	18	13	0	3	2	17	2	0	.371	.381

Pitching	B-T	HT	WT	DOB	W	L	ERA	G	GS	CG	SV	IP	H	R	ER	HR	BB	SO	AVG	vLH	vRH	K/9	BB/9
Alarcon, Kelvin	B-R	6-1	155	3-6-99	0	0	0.00	1	0	0	0	1	0	0	0	0	0	1	.000	.000	.000	9.00	0.00
Asencio, Eudi	R-R	6-1	170	6-18-99	2	1	7.23	8	3	0	0	19	12	16	15	4	19	12	.194	.136	.225	5.79	9.16
Avila, Pedro	R-R	5-11	190	1-14-97	0	0	9.00	1	1	0	0	2	2	2	2	1	1	3	.250	.000	.286	13.50	4.50
2-team total (3 Padres 1)					0	1	2.25	4	3	0	0	12	7	3	3	1	3	18	.163	.188	.148	13.50	2.25
Baker, Blake	R-R	6-3	195	1-10-99	1	1	2.35	18	0	0	8	23	15	10	6	1	13	34	.188	.188	.188	13.30	5.09
Ballard, Sam	L-L	6-0	200	1-16-98	0	0	1.42	5	0	0	0	6	6	5	1	1	2	8	.231	.167	.250	11.37	2.84
2-team total (10 Padres 1)					1	1	4.13	15	0	0	0	24	18	16	11	3	16	25	.209	.211	.209	9.38	6.00
Briley, Robert	R-R	6-5	225	9-15-99	0	1	7.90	9	5	0	0	14	13	18	12	1	17	7	.250	.200	.318	4.61	11.20
Collett, Keegan	R-R	6-3	215	7-27-98	2	0	4.56	10	2	0	0	24	18	15	12	1	22	36	.205	.262	.152	13.69	8.37
Cosgrove, Tom	L-L	6-2	190	6-14-96	0	0	0.00	1	1	0	0	1	0	0	0	0	0	3	.250	1.000	.000	27.00	0.00
2-team total (2 Padres 1)					0	0	0.00	3	3	0	0	4	2	0	0	0	1	6	.143	.333	.091	15.75	2.25
Eusebio, Luis	R-R	6-0	180	3-15-96	2	2	4.18	12	0	0	3	28	24	17	13	3	13	33	.229	.222	.233	10.61	4.18
2-team total (4 Padres 1)					2	2	4.41	16	0	0	4	35	32	22	17	4	15	41	.241	.259	.227	10.64	3.89
Fallon, Koty	R-R	6-3	210	7-10-96	0	0	0.00	1	0	0	1	1	0	0	0	0	2	1	.000	.000	.000	9.00	18.00
2-team total (13 Padres 1)					1	0	3.86	14	0	0	2	16	12	10	7	1	12	22	.203	.233	.172	12.12	6.61
Garcia, Jefferson	R-R	6-0	165	2-4-00	3	3	5.76	11	9	0	0	45	47	32	29	5	17	58	.267	.195	.330	11.51	3.38
Garcia, Jose	L-L	5-11	169	2-19-96	5	2	3.40	13	0	0	0	45	51	20	17	3	11	43	.288	.150	.329	8.60	2.20
Garcia, Juan	R-R	6-0	170	3-16-01	0	1	--	1	0	0	0	0	0	3	2	0	1	0	--	--	--	--	--
Geraldo, Jose	R-R	6-3	200	1-30-99	0	1	3.09	17	0	0	2	23	22	8	8	1	8	27	.237	.293	.192	10.41	3.09
Guarate, Carlos	R-R	6-2	178	3-30-01	6	1	2.22	11	9	0	0	45	41	17	11	0	12	38	.246	.123	.309	7.66	2.42
Guerra, Emmanuel	R-R	6-3	185	11-16-00	0	0	0.00	1	0	0	0	0	0	0	0	0	2	1	.000	.000	--	27.00	54.00
Guzman, Oliber	R-R	5-11	180	5-15-97	3	1	4.95	11	0	0	0	20	18	17	11	3	13	15	.237	.143	.292	6.75	5.85
2-team total (6 Padres 1)					3	2	5.68	17	0	0	0	25	27	23	16	4	14	21	.276	.219	.303	7.46	4.97
Kennedy, Brett	R-R	6-0	200	8-4-94	0	0	0.00	1	1	0	0	1	2	1	1	0	1	1	.400	.000	.500	9.00	9.00
Lugo, Moises	R-R	6-1	185	1-20-99	1	0	2.57	2	0	0	0	7	6	2	2	0	3	10	.231	.444	.118	12.86	3.86
2-team total (9 Padres 1)					5	1	2.06	11	0	0	0	35	34	15	8	1	5	38	.262	.357	.216	9.77	1.29
Miliano, Michell	R-R	6-3	185	12-22-99	2	0	5.14	18	0	0	0	14	13	12	8	3	26	35	.195	.192	.196	15.00	11.14
Mitchell, Bryan	R-R	6-3	210	4-19-91	0	0	5.00	3	3	0	0	9	9	5	5	0	5	11	.250	.211	.294	11.00	5.00
2-team total (1 Padres 1)					0	0	6.23	4	4	0	0	13	14	9	9	3	6	13	.264	.259	.269	9.00	4.15
Morales, Gabriel	L-L	6-3	175	4-14-99	4	0	1.66	11	6	0	0	49	32	10	9	1	14	58	.184	.214	.170	10.73	2.59
Ochoa, Duilio	R-R	6-0	180	8-7-01	1	1	3.00	3	0	0	0	3	3	1	1	0	1	2	.300	1.000	.222	6.00	3.00
Polanco, Anderson	L-L	6-3	175	2-5-98	1	1	5.73	17	0	0	0	22	24	16	14	2	12	24	.279	.208	.307	9.82	4.91
Rascon, Bodi	L-L	6-5	205	2-3-01	0	0	0.00	3	0	0	0	6	3	1	0	0	2	6	.143	.000	.167	9.00	3.00
Reyes, Ripken	B-R	5-10	180	4-1-97	0	0	0.00	2	1	0	0	6	5	1	0	0	2	1	.714	.667	.750	6.00	9.00
Richards, Garrett	R-R	6-2	210	5-27-88	0	0	54.00	1	1	0	0	1	4	5	5	0	3	3	.500	.500	.500	27.00	40.50
2-team total (1 Padres 1)					0	0	16.88	2	2	0	0	4	5	4	5	0	3	5	.333	.333	.333	16.88	10.13
Rodriguez, Hansel	R-R	6-2	170	2-27-97	1	0	0.00	1	1	0	0	4	2	1	0	0	0	4	.125	.000	.167	18.00	0.00
2-team total (2 Padres 1)					2	0	0.00	5	5	0	0	6	3	1	0	0	0	8	.136	.000	.167	12.00	0.00
Sanchez, Fernando	L-L	6-0	198	9-13-00	3	0	4.64	13	1	0	2	36	24	23	17	0	22	36	.203	.208	.202	11.18	6.00
Stock, Robert	L-R	6-1	214	11-21-89	0	0	0.00	2	2	0	0	2	0	0	0	0	0	5	.000	.000	.000	22.50	0.00

SAN DIEGO PADRES

	B-T	HT	WT	DOB	W	L	ERA	G	GS	CG	SV	IP	H	R	ER	HR	BB	SO	AVG	vLH	vRH	K/9	BB/9
Thompson, Mason	R-R	6-7	223	2-20-98	0	0	6.75	2	2	0	0	4	6	4	3	1	3	3	.353	.500	.308	6.75	6.75
2-team total (1 Padres 1)					0	0	5.40	3	2	0	0	5	6	4	3	1	3	3	.300	.400	.267	5.40	5.40
Vega, Alexuan	L-L	6-2	160	6-22-99	1	1	6.26	9	6	0	0	27	37	27	19	1	24	29	.322	.423	.292	9.55	7.90
Williams, Sam	L-L	6-3	195	6-26-96	1	0	3.38	11	0	0	0	21	20	9	8	1	3	18	.238	.053	.292	7.59	1.27
Zimmerman, Mark	L-R	6-0	195	3-29-94	0	0	0.00	1	1	0	0	1	1	0	0	0	2	1	.500	.500	--	9.00	18.00

Fielding

C: Alvarez-Lopez 16, Cantu 11, Vizcarra 33. **1B:** Alarcon 11, Almanzar 11, Cantu 3, Guerra 34, Nunez 9. **2B:** Alarcon 2, Echavarria 16, Garcia 3, Nunez 4, Reyes 37. **3B:** Alarcon 1, Dale 27, Echavarria 8, Nunez 19, Skender 9. **SS:** Almanzar 6, Echavarria 4, Garcia 1, Nunez 7, Reyes 5, Santana 37. **OF:** Almanzar 5, Heredia 20, Jones 15, Lomack 33, Perez 49, Solarte 50.

DSL PADRES ROOKIE
DOMINICAN SUMMER LEAGUE

Batting	B-T	HT	WT	DOB	AVG	vLH	vRH	G	AB	R	H	2B	3B	HR	RBI	BB	HBP	SH	SF	SO	SB	CS	SLG	OBP
Angeles, Euribiel	R-R	5-11	175	5-11-02	.301	.333	.292	44	173	28	52	9	2	0	26	15	4	0	6	19	17	9	.376	.359
Antunez, Neifi	R-R	5-10	160	4-21-02	.274	.310	.260	29	106	21	29	5	1	0	13	18	4	0	0	34	6	2	.340	.398
Aquino, Charlis	R-R	6-2	165	11-18-01	.251	.200	.269	44	175	35	44	10	2	0	23	18	5	0	1	33	7	4	.331	.337
Arias, Andelson	B-R	6-1	170	6-14-00	.167	.111	.185	14	36	6	6	1	0	1	4	3	4	0	0	13	2	0	.278	.302
Cedeno, Nerwilian	B-R	5-11	175	3-16-02	.193	.261	.167	47	166	26	32	6	1	0	21	40	2	0	2	43	4	1	.241	.352
Diaz, Josttin	B-R	6-0	170	5-18-02	.153	.238	.130	37	98	17	15	3	2	1	15	22	3	0	2	43	5	2	.255	.320
Dowston, Reginald	R-R	5-11	170	6-28-02	.231	.234	.229	45	156	27	36	9	2	6	27	16	7	1	1	67	10	5	.430	.328
Duarte, Victor	R-R	5-11	170	2-23-01	.173	.097	.196	40	133	20	23	6	1	1	19	15	10	1	4	17	6	3	.256	.296
Fabian, Albert	L-L	6-0	215	12-21-01	.245	.293	.225	41	139	16	34	11	1	2	20	23	3	0	1	34	3	2	.381	.361
Garcia, Juan	R-R	6-0	170	3-16-01	.200	--	.200	1	5	1	1	0	0	0	0	0	0	0	0	2	0	0	.200	.200
Hidalgo, Eduard	L-L	5-10	150	5-25-02	.252	.229	.262	38	119	25	30	5	0	1	11	30	4	0	0	31	9	4	.319	.418
Moreno, Eddyson	L-L	5-9	175	6-23-01	.181	.191	.179	33	105	11	19	5	1	2	4	13	1	0	1	42	1	5	.305	.275
Paula, Willmert	L-R	6-1	165	9-30-01	.230	.191	.243	49	178	25	41	7	4	3	21	24	2	0	0	62	10	1	.365	.328
Peralta, Axcel	L-L	6-4	190	10-24-01	.224	.225	.223	48	179	25	40	11	2	2	26	23	1	0	1	56	2	2	.341	.314
Ramirez, Alex	R-R	5-9	170	11-16-02	.260	.366	.220	41	150	23	39	11	1	4	21	12	5	0	1	40	3	0	.427	.333
Rojas, Edwin	R-R	6-2	170	11-12-01	.279	.344	.259	42	140	28	39	10	3	1	29	29	8	0	4	30	9	5	.414	.420
Tovar, Wilfredo	R-R	6-0	174	11-13-01	.369	.348	.381	19	65	10	24	4	0	0	7	8	4	0	1	15	1	2	.431	.462
Velez, Jose	R-R	5-11	170	10-21-01	.193	.071	.217	26	83	13	16	5	1	1	9	15	3	0	0	32	5	1	.313	.337
Vergara, Carlos	R-R	6-3	170	1-7-02	.168	.136	.176	35	113	19	19	7	1	0	18	6	0	2	46	3	0	.248	.309

Pitching	B-T	HT	WT	DOB	W	L	ERA	G	GS	CG	SV	IP	H	R	ER	HR	BB	SO	AVG	vLH	vRH	K/9	BB/9
Alcantara, Jonathan	R-R	6-4	175	9-16-01	0	1	10.93	14	0	0	0	14	13	19	17	0	29	14	.265	.231	.278	9.00	18.64
Arias, Andelson	B-R	6-1	170	6-14-00	0	0	0.00	1	0	0	0	0	0	0	0	0	0	0	.000	.000	--	0.00	0.00
Avila, Manuel	R-R	5-11	160	1-27-01	4	2	6.00	15	7	0	1	48	57	38	32	3	15	27	.294	.212	.311	5.06	2.81
Batista, Elias	R-R	6-2	180	5-20-99	1	2	8.77	15	0	0	1	26	40	32	25	2	14	23	.351	.417	.333	8.06	4.91
Batista, Ramiro	R-R	6-7	191	10-5-98	0	1	6.94	15	0	0	0	23	23	23	18	0	22	20	.267	.280	.262	7.71	8.49
Castaneda, Alfredo	R-R	6-2	175	7-10-00	1	1	4.50	18	0	0	0	24	29	18	12	2	10	23	.293	.333	.275	8.63	3.75
Cisneros, Jesus	R-R	6-0	155	12-7-00	1	1	5.00	4	4	0	0	18	18	11	10	3	4	15	.273	.091	.309	7.50	2.00
Crisostomo, Luis	R-R	6-2	175	8-18-00	2	2	4.96	11	8	0	0	45	46	31	25	3	14	29	.261	.120	.285	5.76	2.78
Diaz, Jonfy	L-L	6-5	175	10-20-96	1	4	1.89	16	0	0	0	38	30	21	8	1	20	32	.207	.214	.206	7.58	4.74
Garcia, Jose	L-L	5-11	169	2-19-98	0	1	3.46	3	3	0	0	13	15	5	5	0	1	12	.294	.143	.318	8.31	0.69
Iriarte, Jairo	R-R	6-2	160	12-15-01	1	2	3.31	12	5	0	0	35	35	18	13	4	14	21	.259	.238	.263	5.35	3.57
Lopez, Frank	R-R	6-1	170	4-23-01	1	1	4.15	3	3	0	0	13	11	6	6	1	3	17	.234	.158	.286	11.77	2.08
Lugo, Alejandro	R-R	6-0	165	8-20-02	0	5	5.24	19	0	0	3	22	21	20	13	0	15	24	.263	.300	.250	9.67	6.04
Lugo, Jesus	R-R	5-11	170	1-27-98	7	1	2.12	14	11	0	0	68	46	28	16	4	17	69	.189	.229	.156	9.13	2.25
Matos, Dwayne	R-R	6-1	154	11-7-00	2	3	3.74	18	7	0	3	46	47	23	19	2	6	31	.260	.280	.256	6.11	1.18
Paulino, Abismael	R-R	6-7	195	6-3-97	2	4	3.65	14	11	0	0	67	62	31	27	3	17	37	.247	.281	.231	5.00	2.30
Rios, Nick	L-L	6-0	170	6-24-00	0	3	2.41	14	0	0	2	19	23	10	5	1	4	9	.311	.250	.318	4.34	1.93
Rodriguez, Mauricio	R-R	6-0	155	2-14-01	2	2	9.82	6	6	0	0	22	34	24	24	1	5	22	.362	.286	.375	9.00	2.05
Sosa, Gilberto	R-R	6-7	190	10-14-99	3	4	4.50	16	6	0	1	46	42	29	23	3	19	29	.243	.207	.250	5.67	3.72
Soto, Jessel	R-R	6-4	186	1-20-02	2	1	2.12	19	0	0	1	30	29	10	7	1	14	14	.261	.280	.256	4.25	4.25
Urosa, Alfonzo	R-R	6-2	185	1-17-01	0	0	16.62	3	0	0	0	4	8	10	8	0	4	2	.381	.286	.429	4.15	8.31

Fielding

C: Arias 14, Duarte 22, Ramirez 29, Tovar 12. **1B:** Diaz 4, Duarte 11, Fabian 15, Peralta 43. **2B:** Angeles 6, Antunez 20, Aquino 15, Cedeno 17, Diaz 14, Garcia 1, Paula 4, Rojas 1. **3B:** Angeles 19, Antunez 4, Cedeno 7, Diaz 15, Paula 30. **SS:** Angeles 17, Aquino 26, Cedeno 19, Diaz 3, Paula 11. **OF:** Antunez 4, Dowston 43, Fabian 7, Hidalgo 38, Moreno 31, Paula 1, Peralta 1, Rojas 41, Velez 22, Vergara 33.

San Francisco Giants

SEASON IN A SENTENCE: Despite an extended stretch of great play during July and contributions from unlikely sources throughout, the Giants finished below .500 and missed the playoffs for the third straight season—the franchise's longest playoff drought since a six-year stretch from 2004-09.

HIGH POINT: The Giants won 17 of 20 from June 30 to July 23, including four walk-off wins in six days from July 18-23. This prolonged stretch of winning, which wrapped around the All-Star break, pulled the Giants to within two games of an NL Wild Card spot and put them into the thick of the playoff race at the July 31 trade deadline.

LOW POINT: Standing at 65-65 heading into a six-game homestand against the D-backs and Padres on Aug. 26, the Giants lost eight of 10 against their two NL West rivals and the eventual NL Central-winning Cardinals over the next 11 days. After spending all summer crawling back into playoff contention, San Francisco remained below .500 for season's the final month.

NOTABLE ROOKIES: The grandson of Hall of Famer and Triple Crown winner Carl Yastrzemski, Mike Yastrzemski was acquired from the Orioles in March and made his major league debut in May. On Aug. 16, Yastrzemski hit three home runs against the D-backs, and he finished tied for the team lead in home runs (21) despite playing in just 107 games. A 2014 first-round pick, righthander Tyler Beede went 5-10, 5.08 in 24 appearances, while fellow righthander Shaun Anderson posted a 3-5, 5.44 record in 28 appearances.

KEY TRANSACTIONS: The Giants' biggest acquisition came just after the season began, when the team acquired Kevin Pillar from the Blue Jays. Pillar was arguably the Giants' best offensive player in 2019, leading the team in average (.264), slugging percentage (.442), hits (157), doubles (37), stolen bases (14) and runs (82). After deciding to hold on to their two biggest pieces (Madison Bumgarner and Will Smith) at the trade deadline, the Giants dealt Drew Pomeranz and Ray Black to the Brewers for shortstop prospect Mauricio Dubon, now one of the Giants' Top 10 Prospects.

DOWN ON THE FARM: Triple-A Sacramento won the Pacific Coast League championship and then went on to win the Triple-A National Championship Game with a 5-0 win over Columbus (Indians). The Giants finished tied with the Dodgers for having the most domestic affiliates qualify for the minor league playoffs with five.

OPENING DAY PAYROLL: $138,030,231 (12th).

PLAYERS OF THE YEAR

MAJOR LEAGUE	**MINOR LEAGUE**
Madison Bumgarner	**Seth Corry**
LHP	**LHP**
9-9, 3.90 in 34 GS	(Low Class A)
Led Giants in SO	9-3, 1.76 in 123 IP
(203) and IP (208)	12.6 SO/9

ORGANIZATION LEADERS

Batting *Minimum 250 AB

MAJORS

* AVG	Mike Yastrzemski	.272
* OPS	Mike Yastrzemski	.852
HR	Kevin Pillar	21
HR	Mike Yastrzemski	21
RBI	Kevin Pillar	87

MINORS

* AVG	Luis Matos, DSL Giants, AZL Giants	.367
* OBP	Luis Matos, DSL Giants, AZL Giants	.438
* SLG	Zach Green, Sacramento	.659
* OPS	Zach Green, Sacramento	1.039
R	Mike Gerber, Sacramento	95
H	Mike Gerber, Sacramento	143
TB	Mike Gerber, Sacramento	264
2B	Mike Gerber, Sacramento	41
3B	Manuel Geraldo, San Jose	9
HR	Chris Shaw, Richmond, Sacramento	28
RBI	Chris Shaw, Richmond, Sacramento	94
BB	Jacob Heyward, Richmond, Sacramento	83
SO	Jacob Heyward, Richmond, Sacramento	149
SB	Johneshwy Fargas, Richmond	50

Pitching #Minimum 75 IP

MAJORS

W	Jeff Samardzija	11
# ERA	Jeff Samardzija	3.52
SO	Madison Bumgarner	203
SV	Will Smith	34

MINORS

W	Seth Corry, Augusta	9
W	Matt Frisbee, Augusta, San Jose	9
W	Aaron Phillips, San Jose, Sacramento	9
W	Jasier Herrera, AZL Giants Black, Salem-Keizer	9
W	Alfred Gutierrez, Richmond	9
L	Matt Frisbee, Augusta	9
L	Sean Hjelle, Augusta, San Jose, Richmond	9
L	Jose Marte, San Jose	9
L	Brandon Lawson, Richmond	9
# ERA	Seth Corry, Augusta	1.76
G	Steven Okert, Sacramento	50
GS	Sean Hjelle, Augusuta, San Jose, Richmond	28
SV	Jesus Tona, Augusta, San Jose	16
IP	Sean Hjelle, Augusta, San Jose, Richmond	144
BB	Garrett Williams, Richmond	61
SO	Seth Corry, Augusta	172
# AVG	Seth Corry, Augusta	.171

General Manager: Farhan Zaidi. **Farm Director:** Kyle Haines. **Scouting Director:** Michael Holmes.

Class	Team	League	W	L	PCT	Finish	Manager
Majors	San Francisco Giants	National	77	85	.475	10th (15)	Bruce Bochy
Triple-A	Sacramento River Cats	Pacific Coast	73	67	.521	7th (16)	Dave Brundage
Double-A	Richmond Flying Squirrels	Eastern	55	84	.396	12th (12)	Willie Harris
High A	San Jose Giants	California	66	73	.475	5th (8)	B. Hayes/H. Borg
Low A	Augusta GreenJackets	South Atlantic	77	61	.558	4th (14)	Carlos Valderrama
Short season	Salem-Keizer Volcanoes	Northwest	46	30	.605	2nd (8)	Mark Hallberg
Rookie	AZL Giants Black	Arizona	24	32	.429	15th (21)	Michael Johnson
Rookie	AZL Giants Orange	Arizona	43	13	.768	1st (21)	Alvaro Espinoza
Overall 2019 Minor League Record			384	360	.516	10th (30)	

ORGANIZATION STATISTICS

SAN FRANCISCO GIANTS
NATIONAL LEAGUE

Batting	B-T	HT	WT	DOB	AVG	vLH	vRH	G	AB	R	H	2B	3B	HR	RBI	BB	HBP	SH	SF	SO	SB	CS	SLG	OBP
Adames, Cristhian	B-R	6-0	185	7-26-91	.318	.222	.385	10	22	1	7	1	0	0	2	2	0	0	0	8	0	0	.364	.375
Altherr, Aaron	R-R	6-5	215	1-14-91	.000	--	.000	1	1	0	0	0	0	0	0	0	0	0	0	1	0	0	.000	.000
3-team total (26 New York, 22 Philadelphia)					.082	.150	.049	49	61	8	5	2	0	1	3	3	1	0	1	25	0	0	.164	.136
Austin, Tyler	R-R	6-2	220	9-6-91	.185	.207	.146	70	130	24	24	2	1	8	20	17	0	0	0	57	1	0	.400	.279
2-team total (17 Milwaukee)					.187	.220	.136	87	150	29	28	4	1	9	24	23	0	0	1	64	2	0	.407	.293
Avelino, Abiatal	R-R	5-11	195	2-14-95	.286	.333	.000	4	7	0	2	0	0	0	1	1	0	0	0	3	0	0	.286	.375
Belt, Brandon	L-L	6-4	235	4-20-88	.234	.211	.242	156	526	76	123	32	3	17	57	83	3	0	4	127	4	3	.403	.339
Crawford, Brandon	L-R	6-2	227	1-21-87	.228	.236	.225	147	500	58	114	24	2	11	59	53	3	0	4	117	3	2	.350	.304
Davis, Jaylin	R-R	6-1	190	7-1-94	.167	.154	.172	17	42	2	7	0	0	1	3	3	2	0	0	11	1	2	.238	.255
Dickerson, Alex	L-L	6-3	235	5-26-90	.290	.235	.297	56	155	28	45	13	3	6	26	13	2	0	1	35	1	1	.529	.351
2-team total (12 San Diego)					.276	.191	.288	68	174	29	48	13	3	6	28	13	2	0	1	42	1	1	.489	.332
Dubon, Mauricio	R-R	6-0	160	7-19-94	.279	.276	.280	28	104	12	29	5	0	4	9	5	0	0	0	19	3	1	.442	.312
2-team total (2 Milwaukee)					.274	.267	.276	30	106	12	29	5	0	4	9	5	0	0	0	20	3	1	.434	.306
Duggar, Steven	L-R	6-2	189	11-4-93	.234	.207	.247	73	261	26	61	12	2	4	28	16	1	0	3	78	1	4	.341	.278
Garcia, Aramis	R-R	6-2	220	1-12-93	.143	.120	.177	18	42	5	6	1	0	2	5	4	0	0	0	21	0	0	.310	.217
Gennett, Scooter	L-R	5-10	185	5-1-90	.234	.188	.250	21	64	11	15	4	0	2	6	1	1	0	1	21	0	0	.391	.254
2-team total (21 Cincinnati)					.226	.172	.240	42	133	15	30	7	0	2	11	2	2	0	2	41	0	0	.323	.245
Gerber, Mike	L-R	6-0	190	7-8-92	.042	.000	.056	12	24	0	1	1	0	0	0	2	0	0	0	15	0	0	.083	.115
Green, Zach	R-R	6-3	210	3-7-94	.143	.200	.000	8	14	1	2	1	0	0	1	2	0	0	0	6	0	0	.214	.250
Joe, Connor	R-R	6-0	205	8-16-92	.067	.077	.000	8	15	1	1	0	0	0	0	1	0	0	0	5	0	0	.067	.125
Joseph, Corban	L-R	6-0	185	10-28-88	.063	.000	.067	8	16	0	1	0	0	0	2	1	0	0	0	6	0	0	.063	.118
2-team total (9 Pittsburgh)					.111	.000	.115	17	27	1	3	1	0	0	2	1	0	0	0	7	0	0	.148	.143
Kratz, Erik	R-R	6-4	250	6-15-80	.125	.250	.083	15	32	1	4	2	0	1	3	2	2	0	0	6	0	0	.281	.222
Longoria, Evan	R-R	6-1	215	10-7-85	.254	.286	.240	129	453	59	115	19	2	20	69	43	7	0	5	112	3	1	.437	.325
Panik, Joe	L-R	6-1	200	10-30-90	.236	.253	.230	103	344	33	81	17	1	3	27	36	3	1	4	38	4	2	.317	.310
2-team total (39 New York)					.244	.289	.232	142	438	50	107	21	2	5	39	43	4	2	4	47	4	2	.336	.315
Parra, Gerardo	L-L	5-11	210	5-6-87	.198	.304	.159	30	86	8	17	3	0	1	6	8	2	0	1	18	2	1	.267	.278
2-team total (89 Washington)					.234	.226	.236	119	274	38	64	14	1	9	48	19	5	1	2	59	8	3	.391	.293
Pillar, Kevin	R-R	6-0	210	1-4-89	.264	.289	.255	156	595	82	157	37	3	21	87	18	9	0	6	86	14	5	.442	.293
Posey, Buster	R-R	6-1	210	3-27-87	.257	.230	.269	114	405	43	104	24	0	7	38	34	4	1	1	71	0	0	.368	.320
Reed, Michael	R-R	6-0	215	11-18-92	.000	.000	.000	4	8	0	0	0	0	0	0	0	0	0	0	6	0	0	.000	.000
Rickard, Joey	R-L	6-1	185	5-21-91	.280	.353	.125	26	50	4	14	2	0	1	4	4	0	0	0	17	1	0	.380	.333
Sandoval, Pablo	B-R	5-11	268	8-11-86	.268	.313	.259	108	272	42	73	23	0	14	41	18	1	2	3	67	1	0	.507	.313
Shaw, Chris	L-R	6-3	226	10-20-93	.056	.500	.000	16	18	0	1	0	0	0	0	2	0	0	0	8	0	0	.056	.150
Slater, Austin	R-R	6-2	197	12-13-92	.238	.275	.205	68	168	20	40	9	3	5	21	22	2	0	0	59	1	0	.417	.333
Solano, Donovan	R-R	5-10	205	12-17-87	.330	.339	.320	81	215	27	71	13	1	4	23	10	1	0	2	49	0	1	.456	.360
Solarte, Yangervis	B-R	5-11	205	7-3-87	.206	.177	.231	28	73	9	15	5	0	1	7	4	0	1	0	16	0	0	.315	.247
Vogt, Stephen	L-R	6-0	225	11-1-84	.263	.222	.271	99	255	30	67	24	2	10	40	20	1	0	4	66	3	1	.490	.314
Williamson, Mac	R-R	6-4	237	7-15-90	.118	.111	.119	15	51	3	6	1	0	1	5	1	0	0	18	2	0	.196	.211
Yastrzemski, Mike	L-L	5-11	180	8-23-90	.272	.329	.256	107	371	64	101	22	3	21	55	32	4	1	3	107	2	4	.518	.334

Pitching	B-T	HT	WT	DOB	W	L	ERA	G	GS	CG	SV	IP	H	R	ER	HR	BB	SO	AVG	vLH	vRH	K/9	BB/9
Abad, Fernando	L-L	6-1	220	12-17-85	0	2	4.15	21	0	0	0	13	9	6	6	2	3	9	.196	.172	.235	6.23	2.08
Anderson, Shaun	R-R	6-4	225	10-29-94	3	5	5.44	28	16	0	2	96	111	61	58	13	38	70	.291	.292	.289	6.56	3.56
Barraclough, Kyle	R-R	6-3	225	5-23-90	0	0	2.25	10	0	0	0	8	5	3	2	1	9	10	.167	.188	.143	11.25	10.13
2-team total (33 Washington)					1	2	5.61	43	0	0	0	34	38	24	21	9	21	40	.273	.235	.296	10.69	5.61
Beede, Tyler	R-R	6-3	211	5-23-93	5	10	5.08	24	22	0	0	117	127	70	66	22	46	113	.271	.272	.271	8.69	3.54
Bergen, Travis	L-L	6-1	205	10-8-93	2	0	5.49	21	0	0	0	20	18	12	12	4	9	18	.240	.192	.265	8.24	4.12
Blach, Ty	R-L	6-1	213	10-20-90	0	0	14.21	2	0	0	0	6	14	10	10	2	4	3	.438	.417	.450	4.26	5.68
Black, Ray	R-R	6-5	225	6-26-90	0	0	4.50	2	0	0	0	2	4	1	1	1	5	.400	.667	.200	22.50	4.50
2-team total (15 Milwaukee)					0	1	5.06	17	0	0	0	16	14	9	9	5	9	18	.233	.292	.194	10.13	5.06
Bumgarner, Madison	R-L	6-4	242	8-1-89	9	9	3.90	34	34	0	0	208	191	99	90	30	43	203	.245	.200	.258	8.80	1.86

	B-T	HT	WT	DOB	W	L	ERA	G	GS	CG	SV	IP	H	R	ER	HR	BB	SO	AVG	vLH	vRH	SO/9	BB/9
Coonrod, Sam	R-R	6-2	225	9-22-92	5	1	3.58	33	0	0	0	28	19	11	11	3	15	20	.202	.207	.200	6.51	4.88
Cueto, Johnny	R-R	5-11	229	2-15-86	1	2	5.06	4	4	0	0	16	11	9	9	3	9	13	.196	.280	.129	7.31	5.06
Dyson, Sam	R-R	6-1	212	5-7-88	4	1	2.47	49	0	0	2	51	39	17	14	3	7	47	.213	.229	.204	8.29	1.24
Franco, Enderson	R-R	6-2	180	12-29-92	0	0	3.38	5	0	0	0	5	4	2	2	1	1	4	.211	.200	.222	6.75	1.69
Gott, Trevor	R-R	6-0	185	8-26-92	7	0	4.44	50	0	0	1	53	41	26	26	4	17	57	.216	.208	.220	9.74	2.91
Gustave, Jandel	R-R	6-2	210	10-12-92	0	0	2.96	23	0	0	1	24	18	11	8	1	9	14	.209	.242	.189	5.18	3.33
Holland, Derek	B-L	6-2	213	10-9-86	2	4	5.90	31	7	1	0	69	68	49	45	17	35	71	.261	.182	.294	9.31	4.59
2-team total (20 Chicago)					2	5	6.08	51	8	1	0	84	82	61	57	20	45	82	.258	.192	.288	8.75	4.80
Jerez, Williams	L-L	6-4	205	5-16-92	1	0	2.70	6	0	0	0	7	7	2	2	1	6	4	.304	.222	.357	5.40	8.10
2-team total (6 Pittsburgh)					1	0	4.35	12	0	0	0	10	12	5	5	2	9	9	.308	.375	.261	7.84	7.84
Melancon, Mark	R-R	6-2	215	3-28-85	4	2	3.50	43	0	0	1	46	49	19	18	3	16	44	.278	.292	.270	8.55	3.11
2-team total (23 Atlanta)					5	2	3.61	66	0	0	12	67	71	28	27	4	18	68	.270	.278	.265	9.09	2.41
Menez, Conner	L-L	6-3	205	5-29-95	0	1	5.29	8	3	0	0	17	13	10	10	4	12	22	.220	.182	.243	11.65	6.35
Moronta, Reyes	R-R	5-11	241	1-6-93	3	7	2.86	56	0	0	0	57	41	19	18	4	33	70	.197	.227	.181	11.12	5.24
Peralta, Wandy	L-L	6-0	220	7-27-91	0	0	3.18	8	0	0	0	6	4	2	2	1	1	5	.200	.083	.375	7.94	1.59
2-team total (39 Cincinnati)					1	1	5.67	47	0	0	0	40	40	25	25	11	16	32	.265	.237	.293	7.26	3.63
Pomeranz, Drew	R-L	6-6	240	11-22-88	2	9	5.68	21	17	0	0	78	89	51	49	17	36	92	.285	.247	.300	10.66	4.17
2-team total (25 Milwaukee)					2	10	4.85	46	18	0	2	104	105	58	56	21	44	137	.261	.230	.274	11.86	3.81
Rodriguez, Dereck	R-R	6-1	215	6-5-92	6	11	5.64	28	16	0	0	99	108	74	62	21	36	71	.271	.250	.288	6.45	3.27
Rogers, Tyler	R-R	6-5	187	12-17-90	2	0	1.02	17	0	0	0	18	12	3	2	0	3	16	.185	.136	.209	8.15	1.53
Samardzija, Jeff	R-R	6-5	240	1-23-85	11	12	3.52	32	32	0	0	181	152	78	71	28	49	140	.225	.233	.216	6.95	2.43
Sandoval, Pablo	B-R	5-11	268	8-11-86	0	0	0.00	1	0	0	0	1	0	0	0	0	0	0	.000	.000	.000	0.00	0.00
Selman, Sam	R-L	6-3	190	11-14-90	0	0	4.35	10	0	0	0	10	6	5	5	2	6	10	.171	.150	.200	8.71	5.23
Smith, Burch	R-R	6-4	225	4-12-90	0	0	2.08	10	0	0	0	9	10	3	2	0	4	6	.278	.294	.263	6.23	4.15
2-team total (7 Milwaukee)					0	1	5.48	17	0	0	0	21	26	14	13	3	14	20	.289	.308	.275	8.44	5.91
Smith, Will	R-L	6-5	248	7-10-89	6	0	2.76	63	0	0	34	65	46	20	20	10	21	96	.196	.157	.212	13.22	2.89
Suarez, Andrew	L-L	6-0	187	9-11-92	0	2	5.79	21	2	0	0	33	39	23	21	7	14	25	.302	.259	.333	6.89	3.86
Venditte, Pat	L-B	6-1	185	6-30-85	0	0	16.20	2	0	0	0	3	4	6	6	1	2	2	.286	.000	.400	5.40	5.40
Vincent, Nick	R-R	6-0	185	7-12-86	0	2	5.58	18	1	0	0	31	36	20	19	7	8	30	.286	.302	.277	8.80	2.35
2-team total (14 Philadelphia)					1	4	4.43	32	1	0	0	45	47	23	22	8	12	47	.267	.250	.276	9.47	2.42
Watson, Tony	L-L	6-3	218	5-30-85	2	2	4.17	60	0	0	0	54	56	26	25	9	12	41	.264	.359	.223	6.83	2.00
Webb, Logan	R-R	6-2	220	11-18-96	2	3	5.22	8	8	0	0	40	44	25	23	5	14	37	.279	.247	.319	8.39	3.18

Fielding

Catcher	PCT	G	PO	A	E	DP	PB
Garcia	1.000	11	90	6	0	2	0
Kratz	.964	11	101	7	4	0	2
Posey	.998	101	771	46	2	1	1
Vogt	.998	60	415	24	1	0	4

First Base	PCT	G	PO	A	E	DP
Austin	1.000	12	53	4	0	3
Belt	.995	144	1017	99	6	108
Garcia	1.000	5	23	0	0	3
Posey	1.000	4	22	1	0	2
Sandoval	.991	23	106	8	1	16
Shaw	1.000	4	4	1	0	0
Slater	1.000	8	34	3	0	3
Vogt	1.000	1	5	0	0	0

Second Base	PCT	G	PO	A	E	DP
Adames	1.000	4	4	2	0	0
Dubon	.973	22	44	63	3	17
Gennett	.986	17	31	38	1	11

	PCT	G	PO	A	E	DP	PB
Joseph	.857	3	2	4	1	1	
Panik	.992	90	155	217	3	48	
Slater	1.000	1	1	1	0	1	
Solano	1.000	36	66	64	0	20	
Solarte	1.000	10	21	19	0	10	

Third Base	PCT	G	PO	A	E	DP
Adames	1.000	3	3	6	0	2
Green	1.000	5	2	4	0	2
Joseph	1.000	2	2	5	0	0
Longoria	.953	119	69	233	15	27
Sandoval	.953	45	39	62	5	7
Solano	1.000	2	0	3	0	0
Solarte	1.000	2	0	1	0	0

Shortstop	PCT	G	PO	A	E	DP
Avelino	1.000	1	2	3	0	1
Crawford	.972	142	190	366	16	81
Dubon	.963	9	7	19	1	1
Solano	.970	19	18	46	2	7

	PCT	G	PO	A	E	DP
Solarte	.900	4	4	5	1	2

Outfield	PCT	G	PO	A	E	DP
Austin	.967	25	26	3	1	1
Avelino	1.000	1	1	0	0	0
Belt	.944	15	15	2	1	0
Davis	1.000	15	24	0	0	0
Dickerson	1.000	45	58	0	0	0
Duggar	.981	72	155	3	3	2
Gerber	1.000	10	5	1	0	0
Joe	1.000	5	7	1	0	1
Parra	.983	29	53	4	1	1
Pillar	.986	152	343	6	5	2
Reed	1.000	4	2	1	0	0
Rickard	1.000	21	25	0	0	0
Slater	.977	48	82	3	2	0
Solarte	1.000	9	13	0	0	0
Vogt	1.000	7	10	0	0	0
Williamson	.962	14	23	2	1	0
Yastrzemski	.979	102	189	2	4	0

SACRAMENTO RIVER CATS TRIPLE-A
PACIFIC COAST LEAGUE

Batting	B-T	HT	WT	DOB	AVG	vLH	vRH	G	AB	R	H	2B	3B	HR	RBI	BB	HBP	SH	SF	SO	SB	CS	SLG	OBP
Adames, Cristhian	B-R	6-0	185	7-26-91	.283	.200	.314	43	145	23	41	12	2	6	25	19	0	0	1	32	1	1	.517	.364
2-team total (12 Iowa)					.277	.184	.311	55	184	32	51	14	2	8	31	27	0	0	2	39	2	1	.505	.366
Avelino, Abiatal	R-R	5-11	195	2-14-95	.283	.350	.260	121	473	70	134	24	8	12	62	23	0	3	3	84	17	5	.444	.315
Brusa, Gio	B-R	6-3	235	7-26-93	.000	--	.000	1	1	0	0	0	0	0	0	0	0	0	0	1	0	0	.000	.000
Combs, Dalton	L-L	6-3	200	10-29-94	.000	--	.000	1	3	0	0	0	0	0	0	0	0	0	0	2	0	0	.000	.000
Davis, Jaylin	R-R	6-1	190	7-1-94	.333	.205	.413	27	102	21	34	6	0	10	27	14	1	0	0	28	1	1	.686	.419
Dickerson, Alex	L-L	6-3	235	5-26-90	.150	.000	.167	7	20	2	3	0	0	0	1	3	1	0	0	2	0	0	.150	.292
2-team total (26 El Paso)					.333	.389	.308	33	114	19	38	5	1	5	21	17	5	0	1	20	0	0	.526	.438
Dubon, Mauricio	R-R	6-0	160	7-19-94	.323	.424	.273	25	99	23	32	4	0	4	9	10	1	0	0	9	1	2	.485	.391
2-team total (98 San Antonio)					.302	.317	.296	123	503	82	152	26	1	20	56	28	5	1	0	68	10	8	.477	.345
Duggar, Steven	L-R	6-2	189	11-4-93	.337	.286	.355	23	83	24	28	6	1	3	13	18	1	0	0	21	2	3	.542	.461
Flores, Tyler	L-L	6-2	185	1-24-96	--	--	--	1	0	1	0	0	0	0	0	0	1	0	0	0	0	0	--	1.000
Freeman, Ronnie	R-R	6-1	190	1-8-91	.295	.333	.281	45	122	18	36	3	1	5	19	14	1	0	1	29	0	0	.459	.370
Garcia, Anthony	R-R	6-0	180	1-4-92	.284	.254	.298	55	183	25	52	8	0	6	25	25	2	0	3	46	1	2	.426	.371
Garcia, Aramis	R-R	6-2	220	1-12-93	.271	.377	.235	89	332	52	90	20	2	16	55	34	3	1	1	114	0	2	.488	.343
Gerber, Mike	L-R	6-0	190	7-8-92	.308	.327	.303	119	464	95	143	41	1	26	83	39	7	0	3	140	5	4	.569	.368

SAN FRANCISCO GIANTS

Green, Zach	R-R	6-3	210	3-7-94	.282	.284	.281	72	252	43	71	18	1	25	64	39	3	0	3	99	1	0	.659	.381
Heyward, Jacob	R-R	6-1	215	8-1-95	.400	.500	.000	2	5	4	2	0	0	1	1	3	0	0	0	2	0	0	1.000	.625
Houchins, Zach	R-R	6-2	210	9-16-92	.500	.500	.500	1	4	2	2	0	0	1	1	0	0	0	1	0	0	1.250	.500
Howard, Ryan	R-R	6-2	195	7-25-94	.235	.205	.248	42	153	18	36	6	0	4	23	11	0	1	2	36	2	0	.353	.283
Jones, Ryder	L-R	6-2	221	6-7-94	.000	--	.000	1	1	0	0	0	0	0	0	0	0	0	0	0	0	0	.000	.000
Malkin, Matt	R-R	6-3	220	10-8-95	.250	.333	.000	4	4	0	1	0	0	0	0	0	0	0	0	2	0	0	.250	.250
Maris, Peter	L-R	5-10	175	9-16-93	.057	.000	.063	12	35	2	2	0	0	0	2	0	0	0	11	0	0	.057	.108
McCarthy, Joe	L-L	6-3	220	2-23-94	.165	.263	.133	24	79	10	13	3	0	1	4	8	1	0	1	30	0	0	.241	.247
Medina, Francisco	R-R	6-1	165	3-20-98	.000	.000	--	2	1	0	0	0	0	0	0	1	0	0	0	0	0	0	.000	.500
Michael, Levi	R-R	5-10	180	2-9-91	.248	.310	.225	94	302	49	75	11	4	10	47	24	12	6	2	86	5	1	.411	.327
Pena, Francisco	R-R	6-2	230	10-12-89	.287	.258	.302	68	258	34	74	18	0	16	46	13	1	0	4	43	1	0	.543	.319
2-team total (6 Memphis)					.290	.247	.312	74	276	37	80	20	0	17	50	16	1	0	4	46	1	0	.547	.327
Ramos, Henry	B-R	6-2	220	4-15-92	.269	.235	.283	96	335	50	90	21	0	12	40	24	2	2	3	74	3	2	.439	.319
Reed, Michael	R-R	6-0	215	11-18-92	.226	.353	.167	15	53	8	12	4	0	1	9	7	0	0	0	21	2	0	.359	.317
Rickard, Joey	R-L	6-1	185	5-21-91	.372	.361	.378	46	172	45	64	15	2	6	23	18	2	0	3	27	0	2	.587	.431
Shaw, Chris	L-R	6-3	226	10-20-93	.298	.281	.303	75	282	52	84	18	1	21	70	20	6	0	2	78	0	0	.592	.355
Slater, Austin	R-R	6-1	197	12-13-92	.308	.339	.298	70	240	47	74	17	0	12	45	46	9	0	1	69	6	2	.529	.436
Solano, Donovan	R-R	5-10	205	12-17-87	.322	.500	.254	24	87	12	28	4	0	2	16	9	1	0	0	11	0	0	.437	.392
Stassi, Brock	L-L	6-2	190	8-7-89	.231	.333	.143	3	13	1	3	1	0	0	1	0	0	0	0	4	0	0	.308	.231
Valera, Breyvic	B-R	5-11	160	1-8-92	.257	.231	.262	24	74	10	19	3	0	1	7	16	1	1	0	10	2	1	.338	.396
Van Horn, Brandon	R-R	6-2	180	12-18-93	.400	.500	.300	8	20	2	8	1	0	1	2	0	0	0	0	8	0	0	.600	.400
Vogt, Stephen	L-R	6-0	225	11-1-84	.241	.214	.250	17	58	9	14	3	0	4	7	14	0	0	0	11	0	0	.500	.389
Williamson, Mac	R-R	6-4	237	7-15-90	.378	.565	.305	23	82	23	31	4	0	9	22	13	1	0	2	25	1	0	.756	.459
2-team total (2 Tacoma)					.367	.542	.303	25	90	23	33	5	0	9	23	13	1	0	2	27	1	0	.722	.443
Yastrzemski, Mike	L-L	5-11	180	8-23-90	.316	.267	.330	40	136	38	43	11	1	12	25	22	1	1	4	36	2	2	.657	.414

Pitching	B-T	HT	WT	DOB	W	L	ERA	G	GS	CG	SV	IP	H	R	ER	HR	BB	SO	AVG	vLH	vRH	K/9	BB/9
Abad, Fernando	L-L	6-1	220	12-17-85	2	3	3.07	38	0	0	13	44	49	17	15	3	4	49	.277	.148	.345	10.02	0.82
Adon, Melvin	L-R	6-3	235	6-9-94	0	1	13.94	12	0	0	0	10	16	17	16	1	8	18	.340	.385	.324	15.68	6.97
Anderson, Shaun	R-R	6-4	225	10-29-94	2	1	3.76	8	8	0	0	38	36	18	16	3	13	41	.245	.239	.250	9.63	3.05
Baragar, Caleb	R-L	6-3	215	4-9-94	0	0	10.38	1	1	0	0	4	6	5	5	1	2	6	.333	.167	.417	12.46	4.15
Barraclough, Kyle	R-R	6-3	225	5-23-90	0	0	11.12	7	0	0	0	6	6	9	7	0	6	9	.273	.143	.333	14.29	9.53
Beachy, Brandon	R-R	6-2	220	9-3-86	0	1	10.13	1	1	0	0	5	7	7	6	3	1	4	.280	.300	.200	6.75	1.69
Beede, Tyler	R-R	6-3	211	5-23-93	2	2	2.34	7	7	0	0	35	24	10	9	3	14	49	.197	.207	.188	12.72	3.63
Bergen, Travis	L-L	6-1	205	10-8-93	0	0	3.78	15	0	0	1	17	13	9	7	2	10	15	.206	.208	.205	8.10	5.40
Blach, Ty	R-L	6-1	213	10-20-90	3	4	5.93	17	15	0	0	91	121	65	60	14	25	65	.314	.318	.313	6.43	2.47
Black, Ray	R-R	6-5	225	6-26-90	1	0	5.16	23	1	0	1	23	19	13	13	4	13	36	.229	.211	.244	14.29	5.16
2-team total (6 San Antonio)					1	0	4.40	29	1	0	2	29	20	15	14	4	15	45	.200	.188	.212	14.13	4.71
Callahan, Jamie	R-R	6-2	230	8-24-94	0	0	14.29	5	0	0	0	6	14	9	9	0	3	4	.483	.143	.591	6.35	4.76
Coonrod, Sam	R-R	6-2	225	9-22-92	2	4	6.96	33	1	0	3	32	41	27	25	4	18	43	.304	.269	.325	11.97	5.01
Cueto, Johnny	R-R	5-11	229	2-15-86	0	1	2.61	2	2	0	0	10	10	4	3	2	0	9	.256	.167	.333	7.84	0.00
Cyr, Tyler	R-R	6-2	211	5-5-93	0	0	0.00	1	0	0	0	2	0	0	0	1	2	0	.000	.000	.000	9.00	4.50
Dull, Ryan	R-R	5-9	185	10-2-89	0	0	9.00	2	0	0	0	3	2	3	3	2	1	3	.182	.000	.200	9.00	3.00
2-team total (30 Las Vegas)					1	4	5.70	32	0	0	4	43	45	31	27	8	14	53	.266	.356	.218	11.18	2.95
Franco, Enderson	R-R	6-2	180	12-29-92	6	5	5.97	26	22	0	0	113	139	80	75	24	36	98	.302	.294	.307	7.81	2.87
Freeman, Ronnie	R-R	6-1	190	1-8-91	0	0	13.50	2	0	0	0	1	2	2	2	1	0	0	.333	--	.333	0.00	0.00
Gustave, Jandel	R-R	6-2	210	10-12-92	2	2	6.15	29	1	0	7	26	28	19	18	5	12	25	.269	.227	.300	8.54	4.10
Haley, Justin	L-R	6-5	230	6-16-91	2	2	5.32	4	4	0	0	22	22	13	13	6	6	19	.256	.257	.255	7.77	2.45
Halstead, Ryan	L-R	6-5	205	5-13-92	0	0	0.00	1	0	0	0	5	3	3	0	1	1	2	.177	.400	.083	3.86	1.93
Jerez, Williams	L-L	6-4	205	5-16-92	4	4	3.86	47	0	0	2	56	46	33	24	6	16	61	.215	.169	.241	9.80	2.57
Johnson, Chase	R-R	6-4	192	1-9-92	1	2	7.64	7	3	0	0	18	22	18	15	3	15	20	.310	.177	.432	10.19	7.64
Martinez, Rodolfo	R-R	6-2	200	4-4-94	0	0	36.00	1	0	0	0	1	3	4	4	0	2	1	.600	.667	.500	9.00	18.00
McNamara, Dillon	R-R	6-5	230	10-6-91	0	1	4.13	22	0	0	0	24	24	11	11	3	17	20	.253	.211	.281	7.50	6.38
Meisner, Casey	R-R	6-7	190	5-22-95	2	1	4.57	4	3	0	0	22	19	11	11	2	7	6	.238	.214	.250	2.49	2.91
Menez, Conner	L-L	6-3	205	5-29-95	3	1	4.84	12	11	0	0	61	60	33	33	12	30	84	.256	.200	.276	12.33	4.40
Moll, Sam	L-L	5-10	185	1-3-92	1	0	1.69	6	0	0	0	11	11	3	2	1	3	12	.268	.316	.227	10.13	2.53
Myers, DJ	L-R	6-5	265	12-24-94	0	0	0.00	1	0	0	0	3	0	0	0	0	0	4	.000	.000	.000	12.00	0.00
Navas, Carlos	R-R	6-1	170	8-13-92	0	5	5.08	15	6	0	0	44	42	26	25	8	11	43	.250	.228	.270	8.73	2.23
Okert, Steven	L-L	6-2	202	7-9-91	3	2	5.31	50	4	0	0	58	64	44	34	14	18	75	.272	.224	.300	11.71	2.81
Parra, Olbis	R-R	6-2	180	10-1-94	1	0	0.00	3	0	0	0	3	0	0	0	0	5	7	.235	.500	.000	14.54	10.38
Phillips, Aaron	R-R	6-5	225	10-11-96	1	0	1.50	1	0	0	0	6	3	1	1	0	1	7	.143	.100	.182	10.50	1.50
Quiala, Yoanys	R-R	6-2	235	1-15-94	6	8	6.68	19	19	0	0	97	123	77	72	22	36	91	.311	.292	.326	8.44	3.34
Rodriguez, Dereck	R-R	6-1	215	6-5-92	3	0	3.64	6	6	0	0	30	26	18	12	6	8	28	.236	.225	.243	8.49	3.03
Rogers, Tyler	R-R	6-5	187	12-17-90	4	2	4.21	49	1	0	5	62	59	31	29	6	28	55	.250	.269	.241	7.98	4.06
Sano, Carlos	R-R	6-2	205	2-24-93	0	0	54.00	1	0	0	0	1	4	4	0	2	1	.667	1.000	.500	13.50	27.00
Santa Cruz, JJ	L-L	6-7	220	1-15-96	0	0	9.00	2	0	0	0	2	2	2	3	0	3	.000	.000	.333	13.50	13.50
Selman, Sam	R-L	6-3	190	11-14-90	3	2	2.06	39	1	0	0	48	25	13	11	4	16	81	.151	.093	.179	15.19	3.00
Smith, Burch	R-R	6-2	225	4-12-90	1	1	4.20	3	2	0	0	15	16	12	7	1	9	18	.276	.276	.276	10.80	5.40
2-team total (15 San Antonio)					7	4	2.63	18	17	0	0	95	65	34	27	7	46	103	.198	.199	.197	10.04	4.48
Suarez, Andrew	L-L	6-0	187	9-11-92	7	6	5.73	18	15	0	0	88	112	57	56	11	32	57	.316	.291	.327	5.83	3.27
Taylor, Cory	R-R	6-2	255	12-14-93	0	0	18.00	1	0	0	0	1	2	2	2	0	0	.400	.333	.500	0.00	0.00
Torres, Carlos	R-R	6-1	180	10-22-82	0	1	9.64	4	3	0	0	19	15	15	4	5	12	.328	.471	.268	7.71	3.21
2-team total (15 El Paso)					1	2	5.03	19	3	0	0	39	40	22	22	6	15	35	.265	.254	.274	8.01	3.43
Venditte, Pat	L-B	6-1	185	6-30-85	6	2	2.85	25	1	0	0	47	31	19	15	5	17	59	.181	.200	.167	11.22	3.23
Vincent, Nick	R-R	6-0	185	7-12-86	0	0	0.00	3	0	0	0	4	3	0	0	0	5	.200	.143	.250	11.25	0.00

	B-T	HT	WT	DOB	W	L	ERA	G	GS	CG	SV	IP	H	R	ER	HR	BB	SO	AVG	vLH	vRH	K/9	BB/9
Webb, Logan	R-R	6-2	220	11-18-96	0	0	1.29	1	1	0	0	7	7	1	1	0	0	7	.269	.500	.200	9.00	0.00
Winkler, Dan	R-R	6-3	205	2-2-90	0	1	0.64	12	0	0	0	14	6	1	1	1	5	9	.130	.000	.200	5.79	3.21
Wolff, Sam	R-R	6-1	204	4-14-91	0	1	6.00	5	0	0	1	6	7	4	4	1	3	7	.318	.286	.375	10.50	4.50

Fielding

Catcher	PCT	G	PO	A	E	DP	PB
Freeman	1.000	29	242	15	0	0	6
Garcia	.991	60	541	42	5	5	8
Pena	.998	45	393	28	1	3	4
Vogt	.989	9	84	5	1	0	1

First Base	PCT	G	PO	A	E	DP
Adames	1.000	3	20	2	0	3
Flores	1.000	1	1	1	0	0
Garcia	.846	3	11	0	2	3
Garcia	.995	24	171	10	1	23
Green	.957	16	104	8	5	5
Houchins	1.000	1	5	1	0	1
Pena	.991	15	105	5	1	13
Shaw	.982	43	317	13	6	29
Slater	.993	38	262	25	2	25
Stassi	1.000	3	22	1	0	3
Van Horn	1.000	1	1	0	0	0
Vogt	.983	6	55	3	1	7

Second Base	PCT	G	PO	A	E	DP
Adames	1.000	16	19	47	0	12
Avelino	.945	11	23	29	3	13
Dubon	.951	7	15	24	2	5
Howard	.935	15	17	26	3	4
Maris	1.000	6	7	8	0	2
Michael	.980	58	114	127	5	39
Ramos	1.000	2	4	2	0	3
Slater	.900	7	6	12	2	2
Solano	.962	14	21	29	2	3
Valera	.915	16	21	44	6	10

Third Base	PCT	G	PO	A	E	DP
Adames	.957	21	8	36	2	4
Avelino	.931	11	8	21	2	6
Green	.929	57	22	95	9	7
Houchins	1.000	1	0	1	0	0
Howard	.900	17	11	16	3	1
Jones	1.000	1	1	2	0	1
Maris	.833	3	2	3	1	0
Michael	.947	19	9	27	2	5
Slater	.944	11	4	13	1	0
Solano	1.000	10	1	13	0	3
Valera	1.000	1	0	2	0	0
Van Horn	.857	5	2	4	1	1

Shortstop	PCT	G	PO	A	E	DP
Adames	1.000	1	2	3	0	2
Avelino	.967	97	142	243	13	56
Dubon	.988	17	26	53	1	11
Howard	.943	11	16	17	2	4
Michael	.976	10	14	27	1	6
Solano	1.000	1	1	4	0	0
Valera	.939	8	11	20	2	4
Van Horn	.800	1	2	2	1	1

Outfield	PCT	G	PO	A	E	DP
Avelino	1.000	1	0	1	0	0
Combs	1.000	1	1	0	0	0
Davis	.972	27	69	1	2	0
Dickerson	1.000	3	5	0	0	0
Duggar	1.000	19	46	0	0	0
Garcia	.981	34	50	2	1	0
Garcia	1.000	5	9	0	0	0
Gerber	.977	107	167	5	4	0
Heyward	1.000	2	4	0	0	0
McCarthy	.976	20	39	2	1	0
Michael	1.000	7	13	0	0	0
Ramos	.977	75	124	4	3	0
Reed	.962	11	25	0	1	0
Rickard	.976	41	79	3	2	0
Shaw	.919	20	32	2	3	0
Slater	.929	17	26	0	2	0
Vogt	.000	1	0	0	0	0
Williamson	.967	18	27	2	1	1
Yastrzemski	1.000	36	71	0	0	0

RICHMOND FLYING SQUIRRELS
DOUBLE-A
EASTERN LEAGUE

Batting	B-T	HT	WT	DOB	AVG	vLH	vRH	G	AB	R	H	2B	3B	HR	RBI	BB	HBP	SH	SF	SO	SB	CS	SLG	OBP
Arenado, Jonah	R-R	6-4	240	2-3-95	.243	.289	.220	112	378	32	92	16	2	4	36	26	3	0	2	80	2	4	.328	.296
Austin, Brett	B-R	6-1	210	11-24-92	.101	.167	.078	25	69	4	7	1	0	0	2	12	1	1	1	35	0	0	.116	.241
Bart, Joey	R-R	6-3	235	12-15-96	.317	.393	.275	22	79	9	25	4	1	4	11	7	0	0	1	21	0	2	.544	.368
Brusa, Gio	B-R	6-3	235	7-26-93	.223	.118	.265	101	300	35	67	18	1	12	38	34	2	0	1	104	4	2	.410	.306
Fargas, Johneshwy	R-R	6-1	180	12-15-94	.249	.250	.249	127	413	55	103	10	5	5	33	33	14	5	1	94	50	23	.334	.325
Heyward, Jacob	R-R	6-1	215	8-1-95	.209	.194	.216	125	383	46	80	20	0	10	46	80	10	0	3	147	10	7	.339	.357
Houchins, Zach	R-R	6-2	210	9-16-92	.236	.208	.251	96	331	38	78	18	2	10	44	18	2	0	5	86	2	3	.393	.275
Howard, Ryan	R-R	6-2	195	7-25-94	.223	.242	.214	91	309	26	69	10	2	3	22	22	1	2	3	48	5	2	.298	.275
Jhang, Jin-De	L-R	5-9	225	5-17-93	.138	.125	.143	33	94	1	13	1	0	1	7	6	0	0	0	15	0	0	.181	.190
Johnson, Bryce	B-R	6-1	195	10-27-95	.243	.304	.221	60	210	29	51	14	1	3	18	24	1	0	1	55	8	7	.362	.322
Jones, Ryder	L-R	6-2	221	6-7-94	.300	.250	.333	3	10	2	3	1	0	0	2	0	0	0	2	0	0	.400	.417
Layer, Jose	R-R	6-0	160	5-28-97	.143	.200	.000	2	7	1	1	0	0	1	1	0	0	0	3	0	0	.571	.143
Maddox, Will	L-R	5-10	180	6-11-92	.202	.091	.215	36	104	10	21	3	1	1	6	7	0	0	0	20	4	2	.279	.252
2-team total (9 Erie)					.192	.063	.211	45	130	14	25	3	1	1	8	9	0	0	1	24	4	4	.254	.243
Maris, Peter	L-R	5-10	175	9-16-93	.222	.240	.218	43	135	14	30	7	2	1	13	8	2	0	1	27	3	1	.326	.274
Marte, Hamlet	R-R	5-10	180	3-24-94	.187	.200	.180	60	187	11	35	5	1	2	19	16	2	1	3	66	2	3	.257	.255
McElroy, C.J.	R-R	5-10	180	5-29-93	.189	.227	.161	14	53	6	10	1	1	0	2	6	0	0	0	14	6	1	.245	.271
Michael, Levi	R-R	5-10	180	2-9-91	.205	.207	.204	23	78	6	16	4	1	0	5	6	3	1	1	17	3	0	.282	.284
Miller, Jalen	R-R	6-0	190	12-19-96	.216	.186	.232	135	491	55	106	18	3	11	48	49	2	3	5	106	27	13	.332	.287
Quinn, Heath	R-R	6-3	220	6-7-95	.206	.138	.235	32	97	6	20	4	1	2	9	14	0	0	2	35	0	0	.330	.301
Ramos, Heliot	R-R	6-0	188	9-7-99	.242	.265	.230	25	95	13	23	6	1	3	15	10	1	0	0	33	2	3	.421	.321
Riley, John	R-R	6-0	205	2-14-94	.000	.000	.000	9	16	1	0	0	0	0	0	2	1	0	0	9	0	0	.000	.158
Shaw, Chris	L-R	6-3	226	10-20-93	.288	.359	.252	45	160	25	46	9	2	7	24	19	2	0	1	33	2	2	.500	.368
Sivira, Anyesber	R-R	5-9	155	1-9-00	.000	.000	--	2	5	1	0	0	0	0	0	0	2	0	0	4	0	0	.000	.286
Stassi, Brock	L-L	6-2	190	8-7-89	.315	.200	.359	25	73	8	23	4	0	2	10	12	0	0	1	13	0	1	.452	.412
Van Horn, Brandon	R-R	6-2	180	12-18-93	.185	.224	.153	47	130	7	24	3	1	1	11	7	3	4	3	39	0	0	.246	.238
Winn, Matt	R-R	6-1	210	8-5-92	.122	.158	.096	35	90	9	11	3	1	1	5	16	0	0	0	36	0	0	.211	.255

Pitching	B-T	HT	WT	DOB	W	L	ERA	G	GS	CG	SV	IP	H	R	ER	HR	BB	SO	AVG	vLH	vRH	K/9	BB/9
Abad, Fernando	L-L	6-1	220	12-17-85	1	0	0.00	3	0	0	0	6	3	0	0	0	1	6	.143	.000	.231	9.00	1.50
Adon, Melvin	L-R	6-3	235	6-9-94	2	6	2.60	36	0	0	14	45	38	20	13	2	26	59	.238	.257	.222	11.80	5.20
Baragar, Caleb	R-L	6-3	215	4-9-94	5	5	3.45	22	21	1	0	120	83	52	46	12	43	107	.192	.208	.184	8.03	3.23
Beachy, Brandon	R-R	6-2	220	9-3-86	3	6	5.80	11	10	0	0	50	51	33	32	4	19	47	.270	.255	.289	8.52	3.44
Cabrera, Sandro	L-L	6-2	195	6-22-95	0	1	8.59	5	1	0	0	7	9	7	7	2	3	11	.281	.083	.400	13.50	3.68
Callahan, Jamie	R-R	6-2	230	8-24-94	1	0	4.50	4	0	0	1	4	5	3	2	0	2	2	.313	.500	.200	4.50	4.50
Casad, Cooper	R-R	6-0	185	5-14-96	0	0	0.00	1	0	0	0	1	0	0	0	0	0	3	.000	.000	.000	4.50	0.00
Cyr, Tyler	R-R	6-2	211	5-5-93	0	0	2.05	37	0	0	5	48	34	18	11	1	22	57	.195	.193	.198	10.61	4.10
Davis, Dylan	R-R	6-0	205	7-20-93	0	0	0.00	1	0	0	0	2	0	0	0	0	0	1	.000	.000	.000	4.50	0.00
Gutierrez, Alfred	R-R	6-1	200	6-12-95	9	5	4.09	27	26	0	1	123	119	62	56	9	60	120	.257	.245	.270	8.76	4.38
Halstead, Ryan	L-R	6-5	220	5-13-92	3	6	3.53	33	6	0	0	64	54	30	25	2	19	53	.230	.270	.192	7.49	2.69

SAN FRANCISCO GIANTS

	B-T	HT	WT	DOB	W	L	ERA	G	GS	CG	SV	IP	H	R	ER	HR	BB	SO	AVG	vLH	vRH	K/9	BB/9
Hjelle, Sean	R-R	6-11	225	5-7-97	1	2	6.04	5	5	0	0	25	38	19	17	1	9	21	.355	.339	.381	7.46	3.20
Johnson, Chase	R-R	6-4	192	1-9-92	0	5	4.05	29	2	0	2	60	64	33	27	2	26	50	.272	.276	.269	7.50	3.90
Lawson, Brandon	L-R	6-3	205	12-13-94	5	9	3.70	24	24	0	0	129	137	70	53	8	47	83	.272	.288	.253	5.79	3.28
Lovegrove, Kieran	R-R	6-4	185	7-28-94	2	2	8.69	15	0	0	1	20	17	20	19	3	14	18	.230	.162	.297	8.24	6.41
Martinez, Rodolfo	R-R	6-2	200	4-4-94	0	2	5.94	14	0	0	2	17	26	14	11	1	14	16	.361	.400	.324	8.64	7.56
McNamara, Dillon	R-R	6-5	230	10-6-91	1	1	1.59	6	0	0	0	6	4	2	1	0	2	8	.200	.200	.200	12.71	3.18
Menez, Conner	L-L	6-3	205	5-29-95	3	3	2.72	11	11	0	0	60	37	22	18	5	20	70	.179	.197	.170	10.56	3.02
Moll, Sam	L-L	5-10	185	1-3-92	1	2	2.58	35	0	0	2	38	32	18	11	0	20	42	.234	.276	.180	9.86	4.70
Moore, Andrew	R-R	6-0	195	6-2-94	0	1	27.00	1	1	0	0	2	5	5	5	1	1	2	.500	.286	1.000	10.80	5.40
Navas, Carlos	R-R	6-1	170	8-13-92	2	2	1.56	20	1	0	0	40	29	10	7	2	11	40	.203	.246	.162	8.93	2.45
Overton, Connor	L-R	6-0	190	7-24-93	3	0	3.62	14	0	0	0	27	33	16	11	3	11	25	.317	.306	.327	8.23	3.62
Quiala, Yoanys	R-R	6-3	235	1-15-94	0	1	1.13	2	1	0	0	8	5	1	1	0	3	7	.172	.111	.200	7.88	3.38
Riggs, Nolan	R-R	6-8	255	5-22-93	0	0	0.00	3	0	0	0	5	3	0	0	0	0	6	.158	.250	.000	10.13	0.00
Rubio, Frank	R-R	6-0	220	4-23-95	1	2	7.11	11	0	0	0	13	20	12	10	0	4	7	.351	.300	.378	4.97	2.84
Sampson, Keyvius	R-R	6-2	225	1-6-91	0	2	8.10	2	2	0	0	7	8	7	6	1	4	3	.296	.250	.333	4.05	5.40
Sano, Carlos	R-R	6-4	205	2-24-93	0	0	0.00	1	1	0	0	2	1	0	0	0	0	0	.167	.000	.333	0.00	0.00
Selman, Sam	R-L	6-3	190	11-14-90	0	0	0.00	4	0	0	1	7	3	1	0	0	1	13	.125	.091	.154	16.71	1.29
Simpson, Caleb	R-R	6-3	230	9-15-91	1	3	2.45	23	0	0	0	29	14	10	8	1	18	41	.140	.191	.103	12.58	5.52
Van Gurp, Franklin	R-R	6-1	225	10-26-95	0	1	9.00	2	0	0	0	5	5	5	5	0	2	9	.250	.286	.231	16.20	3.60
Vizcaino, Raffi	R-R	6-2	235	12-2-95	0	5	3.66	32	0	0	4	47	40	23	19	3	27	44	.235	.237	.234	8.49	5.21
Webb, Logan	R-R	6-2	220	11-18-96	1	4	2.18	8	7	0	0	41	41	21	10	2	12	47	.246	.247	.244	10.23	2.61
Williams, Garrett	L-L	6-1	200	9-15-94	7	8	3.60	29	20	0	0	110	88	50	44	6	61	108	.219	.234	.210	8.84	4.99
Winn, Matt	R-R	6-1	210	8-5-92	1	1	2.25	3	0	0	0	4	2	3	1	1	0	0	.143	.091	.333	0.00	0.00
Wolff, Sam	R-R	6-1	204	4-14-91	2	0	1.78	25	0	0	3	35	25	7	7	1	11	42	.200	.215	.183	10.70	2.80

Fielding

Catcher	PCT	G	PO	A	E	DP	PB
Austin	.994	24	160	14	1	4	1
Bart	.993	15	135	4	1	1	1
Jhang	.983	26	203	23	4	1	2
Marte	.989	51	411	43	5	5	10
Riley	1.000	2	13	7	0	0	0
Winn	.984	32	235	19	4	3	4

First Base	PCT	G	PO	A	E	DP
Arenado	.994	26	149	12	1	6
Brusa	.981	44	287	19	6	30
Houchins	.990	65	458	40	5	46
Jones	.900	1	9	0	1	0
Marte	.944	4	16	1	1	1
Riley	1.000	3	14	0	0	2
Shaw	1.000	1	3	0	0	0
Stassi	.993	20	129	9	1	19
Winn	1.000	1	4	2	0	0

Second Base	PCT	G	PO	A	E	DP
Howard	1.000	2	4	2	0	1
Maddox	.923	6	2	10	1	1
Maris	1.000	7	13	13	0	5
Miller	.975	128	194	321	13	69

Third Base	PCT	G	PO	A	E	DP
Arenado	.938	76	49	134	12	9
Houchins	.921	18	8	27	3	4
Howard	.933	17	14	28	3	5
Jones	1.000	1	1	2	0	0
Maddox	.914	20	16	16	3	0
Maris	.927	25	12	26	3	2
Michael	.926	10	6	19	2	1
Van Horn	.800	2	2	2	1	1

Shortstop	PCT	G	PO	A	E	DP
Arenado	.951	24	29	48	4	12
Howard	.936	69	95	139	16	29

	PCT	G	PO	A	E	DP
Maris	1.000	10	9	14	0	0
Michael	.941	10	16	16	2	5
Sivira	1.000	2	5	6	0	3
Van Horn	.948	44	70	94	9	31

Outfield	PCT	G	PO	A	E	DP
Arenado	1.000	1	1	0	0	0
Brusa	.976	36	39	2	1	0
Davis	1.000	9	15	0	0	0
Fargas	.993	123	259	14	2	3
Heyward	.978	101	177	5	4	0
Houchins	.975	20	38	1	1	0
Johnson	.983	56	112	4	2	2
Layer	1.000	4	4	0	0	0
McElroy	1.000	14	24	2	0	1
Michael	1.000	4	8	0	0	0
Quinn	.973	28	35	1	1	0
Ramos	1.000	19	42	1	0	0
Shaw	.959	36	45	2	2	0

SAN JOSE GIANTS — HIGH CLASS A
CALIFORNIA LEAGUE

Batting	B-T	HT	WT	DOB	AVG	vLH	vRH	G	AB	R	H	2B	3B	HR	RBI	BB	HBP	SH	SF	SO	SB	CS	SLG	OBP
Angomas, Jean	L-R	6-0	170	6-5-95	.228	.227	.229	45	162	17	37	2	0	2	19	9	0	0	4	24	5	1	.278	.263
Baldwin, Logan	L-R	6-0	190	4-9-96	.204	.281	.189	58	201	21	41	6	3	3	20	9	2	3	2	85	6	4	.309	.243
Bart, Joey	R-R	6-3	235	12-15-96	.265	.279	.262	57	234	37	62	10	2	12	37	14	3	0	0	50	5	2	.479	.315
Bond, Aaron	L-R	6-5	195	2-16-97	.231	.000	.273	4	13	1	3	1	0	0	4	1	0	0	2	5	0	1	.308	.250
Brusa, Gio	B-R	6-3	235	7-26-93	.115	.182	.100	19	61	11	7	1	0	3	3	14	1	0	0	31	4	0	.279	.290
Clarke, Zander	R-R	6-5	225	1-19-96	.200	.136	.217	31	105	9	21	5	0	1	15	7	1	1	1	31	1	1	.276	.254
Combs, Dalton	L-L	6-3	200	10-29-94	.262	.275	.259	60	210	25	55	8	0	2	27	24	10	0	3	49	3	2	.329	.360
Corbett, Chris	R-R	6-1	195	7-7-94	.229	.000	.258	13	35	4	8	2	0	0	2	4	0	0	0	15	0	0	.286	.308
Fabian, Sandro	R-R	6-1	180	3-6-98	.287	.283	.289	44	167	20	48	4	1	5	33	14	4	0	2	33	3	1	.413	.353
Freeman, Ronnie	R-R	6-1	190	1-8-91	.222	.333	.200	5	18	3	4	1	0	2	3	0	0	0	0	8	0	0	.611	.222
Garcia, Orlando	R-R	6-1	200	12-31-95	.209	.250	.197	29	91	8	19	3	0	1	11	10	5	1	1	32	3	0	.275	.318
Geraldo, Manuel	B-R	6-1	170	9-23-96	.255	.186	.274	121	475	61	121	22	9	5	53	28	2	6	1	136	18	2	.371	.298
Hawkins, Courtney	R-R	6-3	245	11-12-93	.256	.266	.253	88	348	60	89	21	0	21	59	29	2	1	3	91	2	5	.497	.314
Johnson, Bryce	B-R	6-1	195	10-27-95	.265	.193	.286	68	260	39	69	9	6	2	26	39	3	0	2	71	18	8	.369	.365
Jones, Ryder	L-R	6-2	221	6-7-94	.500	.333	1.000	2	4	0	2	0	0	0	0	0	0	0	0	1	0	0	.500	.500
Kirby, Ryan	L-R	6-2	210	1-25-95	.149	.133	.151	20	101	10	15	3	0	4	16	8	1	0	1	48	2	0	.297	.216
Malkin, Matt	R-R	6-3	220	10-8-95	.000	--	.000	1	3	0	0	0	0	0	0	0	0	0	0	1	0	0	.000	.000
Manning, Jett	B-R	6-1	180	5-13-97	.253	.172	.304	27	75	9	19	3	0	1	4	8	2	0	0	29	3	0	.333	.341
Maris, Peter	L-R	5-10	175	9-16-93	.296	.200	.313	29	98	16	29	4	2	4	16	22	0	3	2	20	3	0	.500	.405
Marte, Hamlet	R-R	5-10	180	2-3-94	.245	.364	.214	16	53	6	13	3	0	0	7	9	0	0	1	16	0	0	.302	.349
Matheny, Shane	L-R	6-1	205	4-24-96	.316	.333	.311	14	57	10	18	3	0	1	9	4	0	0	0	14	0	0	.526	.361
McPherson, Kyle	R-R	5-11	180	2-9-96	.254	.250	.256	113	397	47	101	21	2	2	20	38	6	10	1	93	13	8	.333	.328
Norris, Randy	R-R	6-1	190	8-8-97	.247	.115	.296	29	97	12	24	4	1	0	10	2	0	0	2	36	2	2	.309	.303
Pena, Fabian	R-R	5-11	205	10-18-96	.222	.206	.227	40	144	15	32	13	0	4	16	9	1	1	2	31	2	1	.396	.269
Quinn, Heath	R-R	6-3	220	6-7-95	.290	.420	.243	52	190	17	55	14	2	5	30	22	2	0	1	59	1	1	.463	.367

Player	B-T	HT	WT	DOB	AVG	vLH	vRH	G	AB	R	H	2B	3B	HR	RBI	BB	HBP	SH	SF	SO	SB	CS	SLG	OBP
Ramos, Heliot	R-R	6-0	188	9-7-99	.306	.296	.309	77	294	51	90	18	0	13	40	32	8	0	4	85	6	7	.500	.385
Riley, John	R-R	6-0	205	2-14-94	.212	.333	.167	40	132	18	28	6	0	4	7	13	2	2	0	55	3	0	.349	.293
Rincones, Diego	R-R	6-0	175	6-14-99	.247	.188	.263	19	73	14	18	4	0	2	8	11	4	0	0	8	0	0	.384	.375
Van Horn, Brandon	R-R	6-2	180	12-18-93	.198	.205	.196	45	177	19	35	8	1	1	21	12	2	0	1	67	2	1	.271	.255
Villar, David	R-R	6-1	215	1-27-97	.262	.229	.272	113	423	68	111	24	2	13	57	40	9	0	7	144	4	1	.421	.334
Ziegler, Malique	R-R	6-2	190	9-8-96	.250	.000	.286	2	8	0	2	0	0	0	0	0	0	0	0	3	0	0	.250	.250

Pitching	B-T	HT	WT	DOB	W	L	ERA	G	GS	CG	SV	IP	H	R	ER	HR	BB	SO	AVG	vLH	vRH	K/9	BB/9
Amaya, Luis	L-L	5-11	160	8-26-98	1	0	1.26	8	0	0	1	14	10	2	2	0	3	16	.196	.125	.229	10.05	1.88
Baragar, Caleb	R-L	6-3	215	4-9-94	0	1	2.70	5	4	0	0	17	15	5	5	2	8	22	.238	.080	.342	11.88	4.32
Bates, Solomon	R-R	6-2	210	3-16-97	1	0	4.41	9	0	0	0	16	16	9	8	1	7	17	.250	.333	.189	9.37	3.86
Beck, Tristan	R-R	6-4	165	6-24-96	3	2	2.27	6	6	0	0	36	33	9	9	1	13	37	.250	.273	.239	9.34	3.28
Bergen, Travis	L-L	6-1	205	10-8-93	0	0	0.00	2	0	0	0	2	2	0	0	0	1	3	.286	.000	.400	16.20	5.40
Cabrera, Sandro	L-L	6-2	195	6-22-95	1	0	0.00	1	0	0	0	2	0	0	0	0	0	4	.000	--		18.00	0.00
Callahan, Jamie	R-R	6-2	230	8-24-94	0	0	1.80	5	0	0	1	5	4	1	1	0	0	11	.222	.143	.273	19.80	0.00
Casad, Cooper	R-R	6-0	185	5-14-96	1	0	0.00	2	0	0	0	3	3	0	0	0	1	5	.231	.250	.222	13.50	2.70
Cave, Garrett	R-R	6-4	200	7-18-96	0	5	4.95	26	5	0	2	40	28	26	22	0	48	47	.199	.250	.165	10.58	10.80
Cruz, Israel	R-R	6-1	170	6-1-97	0	0	0.00	2	0	0	1	3	2	0	0	0	2	0	.222	.500	.143	0.00	6.00
Cueto, Johnny	R-R	5-11	229	2-15-86	0	1	6.43	2	2	0	0	7	8	6	5	1	1	5	.320	.400	.267	6.43	1.29
Doval, Camilo	R-R	6-2	180	7-4-97	3	5	3.83	45	0	0	0	56	41	26	24	2	34	80	.200	.313	.149	12.78	5.43
Freeman, Ronnie	R-R	6-1	190	1-8-91	0	0	0.00	1	0	0	0	0	0	0	0	0	0	0	.000	.000		0.00	0.00
Frisbee, Matt	R-R	6-5	215	11-18-96	9	8	3.17	22	20	1	0	116	102	47	41	12	22	131	.231	.269	.211	10.13	1.70
Gavin, John	R-L	6-6	250	10-10-95	2	8	5.38	34	8	0	1	82	92	55	49	6	45	87	.282	.289	.280	9.55	4.94
Gustave, Jandel	R-R	6-2	210	10-12-92	0	0	0.00	3	0	0	0	3	0	0	0	0	0	4	.000	.000		12.00	0.00
Helvey, Clay	R-R	6-3	195	2-14-97	1	0	2.25	2	0	0	0	4	5	1	1	0	3	2	.333	.400	.300	4.50	6.75
Hjelle, Sean	R-R	6-11	225	5-7-97	5	5	2.78	14	14	0	0	78	73	31	24	2	19	74	.251	.223	.271	8.58	2.20
Horn, Trevor	R-R	6-1	200	12-25-95	1	1	5.02	10	0	0	0	14	15	8	8	0	10	15	.278	.444	.194	9.42	6.28
Johnson, Chase	R-R	6-4	192	1-9-92	0	0	0.00	1	0	0	0	3	0	0	0	0	1	5	.000	.000		15.00	3.00
Lannoo, Peter	R-R	6-6	220	11-13-94	0	1	4.89	21	0	0	0	35	38	20	19	5	15	33	.279	.268	.284	8.49	3.86
Marciano, Joey	L-L	6-5	250	1-11-95	2	1	4.75	27	0	0	1	42	40	28	22	4	23	46	.248	.321	.213	9.94	4.97
Marshall, Mac	R-L	6-1	205	1-27-96	2	0	2.25	4	0	0	0	8	5	2	2	0	5	7	.185	.100	.235	7.88	5.63
Marte, Jose	R-R	6-3	180	6-14-96	3	9	5.59	18	17	0	0	74	70	51	46	7	44	80	.255	.298	.232	9.73	5.35
Martinez, Rodolfo	R-R	6-2	200	4-4-94	0	2	3.57	13	0	0	2	23	17	9	9	0	9	23	.215	.154	.245	9.13	3.57
Meisner, Casey	R-R	6-7	190	5-22-95	4	3	4.17	16	11	0	1	69	68	35	32	8	32	57	.259	.260	.258	7.43	4.17
Myers, DJ	L-R	6-5	265	12-24-94	1	2	5.63	8	6	0	0	24	26	17	15	2	13	33	.277	.259	.284	12.38	4.88
Parra, Olbis	R-R	6-2	180	10-1-94	6	2	2.12	36	0	0	3	51	46	21	12	3	19	54	.238	.254	.230	9.53	3.35
Phillips, Aaron	R-R	6-5	225	10-11-96	8	7	4.62	25	21	1	0	115	119	66	59	15	43	101	.267	.280	.260	7.90	3.37
Rodriguez, Dereck	R-R	6-1	215	6-5-92	0	0	3.86	1	1	0	0	5	4	2	2	1	2	9	.222	.200	.231	17.36	1.93
Rubio, Frank	R-R	6-0	220	4-23-95	2	1	1.89	32	0	0	7	48	34	13	10	2	17	51	.204	.246	.182	9.63	3.21
Ruotolo, Patrick	R-R	5-10	220	1-16-95	0	0	1.80	6	0	0	2	10	8	2	2	0	8	12	.235	.231	.238	10.80	7.20
Russell, John	R-R	6-3	195	10-17-95	1	0	5.73	9	0	0	0	11	11	8	7	1	6	18	.256	.067	.357	14.73	4.91
Sano, Carlos	R-R	6-4	205	2-24-93	1	1	6.00	11	0	0	1	18	15	14	12	7	9	21	.214	.167	.239	10.50	4.50
Santa Cruz, JJ	L-L	6-7	220	1-15-96	0	1	3.32	10	0	0	0	19	16	7	7	2	8	14	.235	.263	.225	6.63	3.79
Schimpf, Tyler	R-R	6-4	210	8-7-95	0	0	0.00	1	0	0	1	2	0	0	0	0	2	4	.000	.000	.000	18.00	9.00
Simpson, Caleb	R-R	6-3	230	9-15-91	1	2	4.26	11	0	0	1	13	6	7	6	1	12	15	.140	.000	.188	10.60	8.53
Tona, Jesus	R-R	5-10	170	3-30-96	1	1	5.71	14	0	0	0	17	16	14	11	2	14	14	.250	.200	.273	7.27	7.27
Toplikar, Trenton	R-R	6-4	215	5-21-96	3	1	3.98	15	8	0	2	54	45	31	24	3	24	50	.218	.213	.221	8.28	3.98
Vincent, Nick	R-R	6-0	185	7-14-86	0	0	0.00	2	1	0	0	2	3	0	0	0	0	3	.375	.000	.429	21.60	0.00
Vizcaino, Raffi	R-R	6-2	235	12-2-95	1	0	1.69	11	0	0	3	16	3	3	3	0	8	30	.058	.000	.100	16.88	4.50
Wong, Jake	R-R	6-2	215	9-3-96	3	2	4.98	15	15	0	0	72	76	45	40	6	24	67	.275	.290	.265	8.34	2.99

Fielding

Catcher	PCT	G	PO	A	E	DP	PB
Bart	.992	50	465	36	4	5	9
Corbett	.981	12	98	7	2	0	0
Freeman	.980	5	47	2	1	1	0
Marte	.993	16	145	5	1	0	4
Pena	.987	37	341	26	5	1	13
Riley	.974	24	218	9	6	0	8

First Base	PCT	G	PO	A	E	DP
Brusa	.935	5	28	1	2	4
Clarke	.990	26	189	10	2	23
Combs	.987	50	369	12	5	43
Garcia	1.000	2	11	1	0	1
Kirby	.983	26	167	5	3	12
Manning	.000	1	0	0	0	0
Matheny	.974	5	30	8	1	6
Riley	1.000	12	78	9	0	6
Van Horn	1.000	4	29	0	0	3
Villar	.988	12	78	5	1	6

Second Base	PCT	G	PO	A	E	DP
Garcia	1.000	8	15	12	0	7
Manning	1.000	7	15		0	1
Maris	1.000	5	8	14	0	1
McPherson	.978	105	183	216	9	58
Van Horn	.984	17	26	34	1	8

Third Base	PCT	G	PO	A	E	DP
Garcia	.913	18	11	31	4	3
Jones	1.000	1	1	3	0	0
Manning	1.000	4	0	2	0	0
Maris	1.000	1	1	2	0	0
Matheny	1.000	8	4	12	0	1
Riley	.500	2	1	0	1	0
Van Horn	.978	14	10	34	1	5
Villar	.962	97	63	167	9	20

Shortstop	PCT	G	PO	A	E	DP
Garcia	1.000	3	1	10	0	1
Geraldo	.964	117	140	256	15	59
Manning	1.000	11	8	17	0	3
Van Horn	.925	9	11	26	3	5

Outfield	PCT	G	PO	A	E	DP
Angomas	1.000	34	61	1	0	0
Baldwin	.992	56	115	4	1	1
Bond	1.000	4	10	0	0	0
Brusa	1.000	4	4	0	0	0
Clarke	.909	5	10	0	1	0
Combs	.833	2	5	0	1	0
Fabian	1.000	37	83	3	0	2
Hawkins	.981	79	153	4	3	0
Johnson	.993	64	144	2	1	1
Norris	.935	25	41	2	3	0
Quinn	.955	34	60	4	3	0
Ramos	.987	71	143	5	2	2
Rincones	.964	15	25	2	1	1
Ziegler	1.000	2	3	0	0	0

AUGUSTA GREENJACKETS
SOUTH ATLANTIC LEAGUE

LOW CLASS A

Batting

Batting	B-T	HT	WT	DOB	AVG	vLH	vRH	G	AB	R	H	2B	3B	HR	RBI	BB	HBP	SH	SF	SO	SB	CS	SLG	OBP
Angulo, Andres	R-R	5-10	181	9-5-97	.210	.278	.192	73	252	22	53	10	1	3	20	14	3	3	6	67	1	1	.294	.260
Bond, Aaron	L-R	6-5	195	2-16-97	.179	.000	.219	42	140	27	25	6	2	7	20	18	4	0	1	67	8	1	.400	.288
Clarke, Zander	R-R	6-5	225	1-19-96	.200	.200	.200	21	75	5	15	6	0	1	17	9	0	0	2	29	0	0	.320	.279
Combs, Dalton	L-L	6-3	200	10-29-94	.344	.273	.381	11	32	6	11	0	0	1	11	6	1	1	0	8	0	0	.438	.462
Edie, Mikey	R-R	5-11	175	7-3-97	.244	.213	.255	86	271	38	66	10	3	2	21	15	12	4	0	63	6	4	.325	.312
Fitzgerald, Tyler	R-R	6-3	205	9-15-97	.264	.389	.222	19	72	11	19	3	0	0	9	8	0	2	1	17	4	0	.306	.333
Flores, Tyler	L-L	6-2	185	1-24-96	.177	.200	.172	12	34	7	6	1	0	0	3	6	0	1	0	10	0	0	.206	.300
Franco, Wander	B-R	6-1	189	10-11-96	.179	.286	.143	26	84	12	15	3	0	5	16	14	0	0	0	33	0	0	.393	.296
Garcia, Orlando	R-R	6-1	200	12-31-95	.161	.077	.175	28	93	9	15	2	0	1	4	9	5	1	0	33	0	0	.215	.271
Genoves, Ricardo	R-R	6-2	190	5-14-99	.292	.250	.302	19	65	9	19	4	0	2	14	6	1	0	0	17	0	0	.446	.361
Giarratano, Nico	B-R	5-11	172	12-15-94	.180	.132	.199	65	194	19	35	8	0	0	14	20	3	3	1	72	0	2	.222	.266
Gonzalez, Jacob	R-R	6-3	190	6-26-98	.241	.270	.231	125	449	54	108	25	1	10	57	39	10	0	6	80	0	0	.368	.312
Labour, Franklin	R-R	6-1	190	5-11-98	.215	.179	.228	31	107	16	23	6	0	1	11	8	2	0	0	40	0	0	.299	.282
Layer, Jose	R-R	6-0	160	5-28-97	.213	.230	.208	92	319	27	68	7	1	4	30	15	3	3	0	84	6	3	.279	.255
Manning, Jett	B-R	6-1	180	5-13-97	.184	.000	.233	11	38	3	7	3	0	0	1	2	1	0	0	15	1	1	.263	.244
Matheny, Shane	L-R	6-1	205	6-5-96	.212	.159	.230	92	339	44	72	16	2	7	43	42	4	1	4	112	1	1	.333	.303
Munguia, Ismael	L-L	5-10	158	10-19-98	.286	.282	.287	100	388	67	111	22	5	1	39	24	10	4	1	41	13	5	.376	.343
Norris, Randy	R-R	6-1	190	8-8-97	.185	.571	.050	10	27	2	5	1	0	0	2	0	1	0	0	12	0	0	.222	.241
Parra, Jeffry	R-R	6-0	195	1-24-98	.161	.244	.134	50	168	15	27	8	0	5	17	20	5	1	0	55	0	0	.298	.269
Rincones, Diego	R-R	6-0	175	6-14-99	.295	.253	.307	105	400	48	118	25	4	5	57	27	8	0	7	56	0	0	.415	.346
Roby, Sean	R-R	6-2	215	7-8-98	.187	.111	.211	19	75	11	14	5	1	3	13	4	0	0	0	30	0	0	.400	.228
Sivira, Anyesber	R-R	5-9	155	1-9-00	.229	.264	.219	76	245	43	56	9	1	2	19	25	16	1	2	55	5	3	.298	.337
Tostado, Frankie	L-L	6-2	205	3-31-98	.259	.240	.265	128	494	71	128	17	6	18	85	36	5	1	5	113	0	0	.427	.313
Whiteman, Simon	R-R	5-10	165	1-28-97	.269	.214	.284	36	130	25	35	1	0	0	7	20	1	1	0	36	16	3	.277	.371
Wyatt, Logan	L-R	6-4	230	11-15-97	.233	.235	.233	19	60	9	14	3	0	1	9	12	2	0	2	14	0	0	.333	.368

Pitching

Pitching	B-T	HT	WT	DOB	W	L	ERA	G	GS	CG	SV	IP	H	R	ER	HR	BB	SO	AVG	vLH	vRH	K/9	BB/9
Amaya, Luis	L-L	5-11	160	8-26-98	4	1	1.95	19	0	0	0	32	21	9	7	0	13	35	.184	.200	.179	9.74	3.62
Bates, Solomon	R-R	6-2	210	3-16-97	4	3	3.81	13	0	0	0	26	29	12	11	4	3	41	.279	.261	.293	14.19	1.04
Cabrera, Sandro	L-L	6-2	195	6-22-95	3	1	2.06	25	0	0	8	44	33	13	10	1	27	63	.208	.200	.211	12.98	5.56
Casad, Cooper	R-R	6-0	185	5-14-96	0	0	2.45	1	0	0	0	4	1	1	1	0	1	1	.091	.000	.143	2.45	2.45
Corry, Seth	L-L	6-2	195	11-3-98	9	3	1.76	27	26	0	0	123	73	35	24	4	58	172	.171	.181	.168	12.62	4.26
Davis, Dylan	R-R	6-0	205	7-20-93	0	0	7.15	9	0	0	2	11	15	14	9	1	9	5	.300	.278	.313	3.97	7.15
Frisbee, Matt	R-R	6-5	215	11-18-96	0	1	2.81	4	2	0	0	16	11	5	5	3	6	23	.196	.191	.200	12.94	3.38
Giarratano, Nico	B-R	5-11	172	12-15-94	0	0	36.00	1	0	0	0	1	6	4	4	0	0	1	.667	.500	.800	9.00	0.00
Gudino, Norwith	R-R	6-2	200	11-22-95	2	0	0.60	5	1	0	0	15	8	3	1	1	3	25	.154	.156	.150	15.00	1.80
Hjelle, Sean	R-R	6-11	225	5-7-97	1	2	2.66	9	9	0	0	41	41	16	12	3	9	44	.256	.260	.253	9.74	1.99
Lannoo, Peter	R-R	6-6	220	11-13-94	1	1	2.25	6	0	0	1	12	10	4	3	1	4	17	.217	.200	.231	12.75	3.00
Madison, Ben	R-R	6-3	205	9-15-97	4	0	4.58	20	0	0	0	20	16	11	10	1	7	19	.219	.243	.194	8.69	3.20
Oller, Adam	R-R	6-4	205	10-17-94	5	6	4.02	17	17	0	0	87	94	49	39	5	26	93	.284	.259	.303	9.58	2.68
Ozoria, Jesus	R-R	6-2	195	6-1-98	1	3	5.17	10	5	0	1	31	31	19	18	3	20	20	.263	.200	.295	6.89	5.74
Rivera, Blake	R-R	6-4	225	1-9-98	4	6	3.95	16	15	0	0	73	59	38	32	3	39	87	.215	.190	.234	10.73	4.81
Santa Cruz, JJ	L-L	6-7	220	1-15-96	6	1	2.74	28	0	0	2	49	40	18	15	2	14	69	.211	.155	.235	12.59	2.55
Santos, Gregory	R-R	6-2	190	8-28-99	1	5	2.86	8	8	0	0	35	34	16	11	4	9	26	.256	.346	.198	6.75	2.34
Schimpf, Tyler	R-R	6-4	210	8-7-95	3	1	5.34	18	1	0	1	30	23	18	18	2	19	44	.209	.180	.233	13.05	5.64
Seelinger, Matt	R-R	6-0	205	4-19-95	1	4	4.97	24	0	0	2	42	37	30	23	3	16	69	.227	.254	.208	14.90	3.46
Teng, Kai-Wei	R-R	6-4	260	12-1-98	3	0	1.55	5	5	0	0	29	16	8	5	0	7	39	.160	.225	.117	12.10	2.17
Tona, Jesus	R-R	5-10	170	3-30-96	2	2	1.50	27	0	0	16	42	24	7	7	2	17	60	.164	.098	.212	12.86	3.64
Toplikar, Trenton	R-R	6-4	215	5-21-96	5	2	3.62	10	10	0	0	55	43	25	22	5	19	40	.218	.237	.200	6.59	3.13
Tucker, Bryce	L-L	6-3	205	12-10-96	0	1	1.17	5	0	0	1	8	1	2	1	0	2	11	.042	.000	.059	12.91	2.35
Van Gurp, Franklin	R-R	6-1	225	10-26-95	2	0	3.77	16	0	0	4	29	21	13	12	4	9	40	.198	.234	.170	12.56	2.83
Walker, Ryan	R-R	6-2	200	11-26-95	2	3	3.36	37	0	0	7	59	58	28	22	1	18	61	.264	.253	.273	9.31	2.75
Webb, Logan	R-R	6-2	220	11-18-96	1	0	0.90	2	1	0	0	10	4	1	1	0	3	9	.125	.071	.167	8.10	2.70
Weisenberg, Keith	R-R	6-5	195	12-6-95	1	3	4.88	17	9	0	2	59	49	33	32	2	49	58	.237	.242	.233	8.85	7.47
White, Preston	R-R	6-6	215	7-29-96	3	4	3.47	34	1	0	0	62	63	30	24	5	18	49	.259	.273	.250	7.07	2.60
Winn, Keaton	R-R	6-4	205	2-20-98	7	7	3.32	26	20	0	0	127	123	54	47	9	26	99	.255	.294	.221	7.00	1.84
Wong, Jake	R-R	6-2	215	9-3-96	2	1	1.99	8	8	0	0	41	31	11	9	2	11	34	.186	.161	.202	7.52	2.43

Fielding

Catcher	PCT	G	PO	A	E	DP	PB
Angulo	.986	72	704	84	11	6	17
Genoves	.989	19	163	21	2	1	3
Parra	.994	50	448	71	3	4	14

First Base	PCT	G	PO	A	E	DP
Angulo	1.000	1	1	0	0	0
Combs	1.000	1	3	0	0	0
Flores	.950	3	16	3	1	3
Franco	1.000	5	41	6	0	3
Garcia	.889	1	8	0	1	1
Gonzalez	.979	18	136	5	3	10
Tostado	.989	99	756	55	9	60
Wyatt	.991	14	108	6	1	13

Second Base	PCT	G	PO	A	E	DP
Franco	.925	12	17	20	3	2
Garcia	1.000	7	9	19	0	1
Giarratano	1.000	17	14	34	0	4
Layer	1.000	1	0	1	0	0
Manning	.964	6	11	16	1	2
Matheny	.967	35	55	91	5	18
Sivira	.991	50	85	132	2	34
Whiteman	.986	17	23	50	1	11

Third Base	PCT	G	PO	A	E	DP
Franco	.750	7	4	5	3	0
Garcia	.800	3	2	2	1	0
Giarratano	.000	1	0	0	0	0
Gonzalez	.855	66	36	88	21	5

Manning	.769	4	4	6	3	0
Matheny	.940	40	27	67	6	3
Roby	.919	14	13	21	3	5
Sivira	1.000	8	1	5	0	0

Shortstop	PCT	G	PO	A	E	DP
Fitzgerald	.972	19	30	40	2	11
Garcia	.919	17	24	44	6	17
Giarratano	.958	47	59	100	7	24
Manning	1.000	1	1	2	0	0
Matheny	.929	19	22	43	5	3
Sivira	.951	18	30	48	4	11
Whiteman	.910	18	22	49	7	10

Outfield	PCT	G	PO	A	E	DP

Bond	.968	37	55	5	2	1	Flores	1.000	6	8	1	0	1	
Clarke	.875	7	7	0	1	0	Gonzalez	1.000	8	13	0	0	0	
Combs	.875	5	7	0	1	0	Labour	.971	28	33	0	1	0	
Edie	1.000	75	124	5	0	0	Layer	.988	86	164	5	2	1	

Munguia	.974	81	149	2	4	0
Norris	1.000	7	11	0	0	0
Rincones	.992	84	108	9	1	0
Tostado	.941	13	16	0	1	0

SALEM-KEIZER VOLCANOES SHORT SEASON
NORTHWEST LEAGUE

SAN FRANCISCO GIANTS

Batting	B-T	HT	WT	DOB	AVG	vLH	vRH	G	AB	R	H	2B	3B	HR	RBI	BB	HBP	SH	SF	SO	SB	CS	SLG	OBP
Adkins, Kwan	L-L	6-2	195	10-2-96	.269	.250	.273	45	160	30	43	7	2	4	19	17	2	4	0	51	10	6	.413	.346
Aldrete, Carter	R-R	6-2	205	10-12-97	.257	.235	.262	28	101	12	26	5	1	3	16	14	1	0	2	29	1	0	.416	.348
Bell, George	R-R	6-4	215	5-8-98	.149	.000	.184	11	47	3	7	3	0	0	2	3	0	0	0	13	1	3	.213	.200
Bishop, Hunter	L-R	6-5	210	6-25-98	.224	.286	.203	25	85	21	19	1	1	4	9	29	2	0	1	28	6	2	.400	.427
Campos, Marcos	R-R	5-11	205	10-26-96	.100	.000	.105	6	20	2	2	0	0	0	2	1	0	2	0	4	1	0	.100	.143
Canario, Alexander	R-R	6-1	165	5-7-00	.301	.263	.310	49	193	38	58	17	1	9	40	18	4	0	4	71	3	1	.539	.365
Cannon, Connor	R-R	6-5	240	5-16-98	.286	--	.286	2	7	0	2	0	0	0	1	0	0	0	0	1	0	0	.286	.286
Corbett, Chris	R-R	6-1	195	7-7-94	.125	.333	.077	15	48	3	6	2	0	0	2	7	1	0	0	16	0	0	.167	.250
Fitzgerald, Tyler	R-R	6-3	205	9-15-97	.284	.250	.297	26	102	20	29	11	2	0	16	15	1	0	0	24	2	1	.431	.381
Flores, Tyler	L-L	6-2	185	1-24-96	.261	.160	.287	31	119	13	31	4	1	7	23	13	1	0	3	20	1	1	.487	.331
Freed, Harrison	R-R	5-11	205	5-13-98	.236	.257	.231	42	165	22	39	12	0	6	19	12	2	0	0	53	1	0	.418	.296
Genoves, Ricardo	R-R	6-2	190	5-14-99	.252	.226	.260	32	131	19	33	7	1	7	31	11	3	0	1	24	1	0	.481	.322
Houghtby, Jeff	L-R	5-11	175	5-13-97	.235	.189	.246	56	204	31	48	16	1	4	21	28	6	0	1	50	2	4	.382	.343
Labour, Franklin	R-R	6-1	190	5-11-98	.307	.342	.297	41	166	37	51	9	2	14	34	18	5	0	0	43	2	1	.639	.392
Layer, Abdiel	B-R	6-2	170	8-9-98	.182	--	.182	3	11	2	2	1	0	0	1	1	0	0	0	2	0	0	.273	.250
Luciano, Marco	R-R	6-2	170	9-10-01	.212	.500	.172	9	33	6	7	4	0	0	4	5	0	0	0	6	1	0	.333	.316
Malkin, Matt	R-R	6-3	220	10-8-95	.308	.000	.444	4	13	0	4	1	0	0	1	4	0	0	0	5	0	0	.385	.471
Martorano, Brandon	R-R	6-2	198	1-6-98	.260	.250	.263	29	96	13	25	3	0	3	22	17	0	1	2	36	1	0	.385	.365
Mejias, Keyberth	R-R	6-0	170	9-24-99	.160	.000	.191	7	25	6	4	1	0	0	4	4	0	0	1	5	0	0	.200	.267
Mendoza, Beicker	R-R	6-2	185	2-14-98	.261	.423	.215	33	119	13	31	8	0	3	15	6	2	0	0	32	0	1	.403	.307
Pomares, Jairo	L-R	6-1	185	8-4-00	.207	.333	.200	14	58	7	12	3	0	0	4	1	3	0	0	17	0	0	.259	.258
Roby, Sean	R-R	6-2	215	7-8-98	.338	.300	.347	37	151	31	51	7	2	2	34	25	0	1	4	40	1	0	.450	.429
Rodriguez, Yorlis	R-R	6-0	187	7-20-99	.256	.348	.228	51	195	31	50	9	1	1	14	9	5	1	1	34	1	1	.333	.305
Smith, Armani	R-R	6-4	215	7-19-98	.307	.282	.315	43	163	20	50	6	3	4	25	18	0	0	2	55	2	2	.454	.372
Toribio, Luis	R-R	6-1	165	9-28-00	.273	--	.273	3	11	2	3	1	0	0	0	2	0	0	0	5	0	0	.364	.385
Whiteman, Simon	R-R	5-10	165	1-28-97	.279	.276	.280	33	129	28	36	7	1	0	14	25	2	1	1	23	15	8	.349	.401
Wyatt, Logan	L-R	6-4	230	11-15-97	.284	.294	.280	18	67	10	19	2	0	2	12	10	1	0	0	9	0	1	.403	.385
Wyatt, Tyler	R-R	5-11	185	12-9-96	.280	.500	.211	7	25	5	7	0	0	0	1	4	0	0	0	7	0	0	.280	.379

Pitching	B-T	HT	WT	DOB	W	L	ERA	G	GS	CG	SV	IP	H	R	ER	HR	BB	SO	AVG	vLH	vRH	K/9	BB/9
Adames, Abel	R-R	6-5	190	12-8-95	2	0	6.55	16	0	0	0	22	25	20	16	0	12	22	.281	.310	.267	9.00	4.91
Avila, Nick	R-R	6-4	195	7-25-97	0	0	0.00	1	1	0	0	4	2	0	0	0	2	3	.143	.000	.182	6.75	4.50
Berroa, Prelander	R-R	5-11	170	4-18-00	0	1	9.56	4	4	0	0	16	17	18	17	2	9	11	.274	.273	.276	6.19	5.06
Bolivar, Deiyerbert	L-L	5-11	155	4-3-96	3	0	0.87	17	0	0	3	21	15	4	2	0	13	23	.195	.125	.213	10.02	5.66
Casad, Cooper	R-R	6-0	185	5-14-96	1	1	3.86	15	0	0	1	28	27	16	12	0	6	21	.243	.283	.215	6.75	1.93
Castro, Kervin	R-R	6-2	185	2-7-99	5	3	2.66	14	14	0	0	68	52	24	20	2	13	61	.211	.236	.196	8.11	1.73
Cruz, Israel	R-R	6-1	170	6-1-97	2	1	4.62	19	0	0	5	25	22	16	13	0	13	33	.229	.225	.232	11.72	4.62
DuBord, Alex	R-R	6-5	225	12-4-96	0	2	11.21	7	5	0	0	18	29	26	22	1	10	16	.372	.250	.414	8.15	5.09
Fehmel, Bryce	R-R	6-2	205	12-16-96	0	0	9.00	1	0	0	0	2	4	2	2	1	1	2	.400	.333	.429	9.00	4.50
Figueroa, Miguel	R-R	6-2	165	8-9-97	0	0	2.08	9	0	0	2	17	12	7	4	0	10	17	.185	.174	.191	8.83	5.19
Gudino, Norwith	R-R	6-2	200	11-22-95	1	0	0.77	4	1	0	0	12	9	1	1	0	5	12	.220	.261	.167	9.26	3.86
Helvey, Clay	R-R	6-3	195	2-14-97	1	2	4.84	14	1	0	4	35	35	25	19	1	25	41	.265	.188	.310	10.46	6.37
Herrera, Jasier	R-R	6-5	190	1-1-98	3	1	4.00	5	5	0	0	27	26	12	12	1	10	17	.257	.265	.250	5.67	3.33
Horn, Trevor	R-R	6-1	200	12-25-95	2	3	8.59	10	1	0	0	22	34	22	21	4	10	11	.370	.414	.349	4.50	4.09
Kilian, Caleb	R-R	6-4	180	6-2-97	0	0	0.00	1	1	0	0	4	1	0	0	0	0	6	.077	.143	.000	13.50	0.00
Labrador, Jorge	R-R	6-1	180	3-9-99	0	1	4.38	8	0	0	1	12	12	7	6	0	4	16	.240	.333	.154	11.68	2.92
Lopez, Jacob	L-L	6-4	220	3-11-98	2	3	3.02	9	9	0	0	42	41	17	14	2	7	39	.256	.172	.275	8.42	1.51
Madison, Ben	R-R	6-3	205	9-15-97	2	0	1.95	15	0	0	1	28	18	8	6	0	16	33	.194	.171	.212	10.73	5.20
Meyer, Mack	R-R	6-0	190	10-31-96	0	0	20.25	2	0	0	0	1	2	3	3	0	3	1	.333	.500	.250	9.00	20.25
Moreno, Luis	R-R	6-2	174	8-3-98	2	1	10.61	7	7	0	0	28	45	35	33	7	7	18	.363	.457	.326	5.79	2.25
Nurse, Conner	R-R	6-6	210	7-31-99	2	4	5.26	9	8	0	0	39	41	26	23	6	16	32	.270	.259	.277	7.32	3.66
Ozoria, Jasmin	R-R	6-2	195	6-14-98	4	3	4.32	9	9	0	0	42	40	24	20	1	10	24	.250	.260	.246	5.18	2.16
Perry, Travis	R-R	6-4	190	3-8-97	5	2	3.82	14	9	0	0	64	56	31	27	2	25	47	.234	.312	.198	6.64	3.53
Rashi, Taylor	R-R	6-4	220	1-15-96	0	0	0.00	1	0	0	0	2	2	0	0	0	2	2	.000	.000	.000	9.00	9.00
Roberts, Chris	R-R	6-0	210	7-3-97	1	0	2.38	9	0	0	0	11	14	4	3	2	8	9	.318	.455	.273	7.15	6.35
Rohloff, Andy	R-R	6-2	180	7-17-96	0	1	5.95	17	0	0	0	20	15	14	13	0	12	22	.203	.231	.188	10.07	5.49
Schimpf, Tyler	R-R	6-4	210	8-7-95	3	0	1.07	13	0	0	2	25	13	3	3	1	13	33	.151	.192	.133	11.72	4.62
Scott, Jordan	R-R	6-3	190	4-3-95	3	1	3.79	10	1	0	1	19	16	9	8	3	6	17	.216	.160	.245	8.05	2.84
Strahm, Ben	R-R	6-5	210	12-16-96	0	0	9.00	3	0	0	0	4	4	4	4	1	3	5	.250	.000	.364	11.25	6.75
Tucker, Bryce	L-L	6-3	205	12-10-96	1	0	1.35	13	0	0	4	13	7	3	2	1	6	22	.149	.167	.143	14.85	4.05
Veras, Yoel	R-R	6-0	175	10-2-96	1	0	6.23	7	0	0	0	9	11	7	6	1	6	6	.297	.385	.250	6.23	6.23

Fielding

C: Corbett 14, Genoves 28, Malkin 1, Martorano 28, Mejias 7. **1B:** Aldrete 7, Cannon 1, Corbett 1, Flores 24, Houghtby 1, Malkin 2, Mendoza 22, Roby 3, Wyatt 17. **2B:** Aldrete 5, Campos 5, Houghtby 24, Rodriguez 36, Whiteman 8, Wyatt 1. **3B:** Aldrete 15, Houghtby 16, Mendoza 5, Roby 23, Rodriguez 12, Toribio 1, Wyatt 6. **SS:** Aldrete 1, Campos 1, Fitzgerald 26, Houghtby 15, Layer 3, Luciano 9, Whiteman 22. **OF:** Adkins 43, Bell 11, Bishop 22, Canario 42, Flores 3, Freed 28, Labour 37, Mendoza 1, Pomares 12, Smith 30.

ARIZONA LEAGUE

SAN FRANCISCO GIANTS

Batting	B-T	HT	WT	DOB	AVG	vLH	vRH	G	AB	R	H	2B	3B	HR	RBI	BB	HBP	SH	SF	SO	SB	CS	SLG	OBP
Aldrete, Carter	R-R	6-2	205	10-12-97	.258	.231	.264	19	66	8	17	3	0	1	7	13	1	0	2	14	1	1	.349	.378
Bell, George	R-R	6-4	215	5-8-98	.234	.111	.284	28	94	14	22	4	1	3	17	11	3	0	0	19	2	0	.394	.333
Caraballo, Andrew	R-R	6-0	175	4-29-00	.200	.231	.189	15	50	2	10	3	1	1	2	6	0	0	0	23	2	2	.360	.286
2-team total (14 Giants Orange)					.204	.241	.188	29	98	5	20	4	1	2	14	8	0	0	0	37	6	3	.327	.264
Dempsey, Nolan	R-R	6-0	175	9-9-96	.257	.286	.250	24	70	13	18	5	1	0	5	8	9	0	1	14	1	2	.357	.398
Fabian, Sandro	R-R	6-1	180	3-6-98	.219	.500	.154	10	32	4	7	3	0	2	8	5	3	0	1	13	0	0	.500	.366
Fitzgerald, Tyler	R-R	6-3	205	9-15-97	.273	.000	.333	3	11	2	3	1	0	1	5	1	0	0	1	0	0	0	.636	.308
Frechette, Garrett	L-L	6-3	200	12-31-00	.290	.303	.286	39	145	23	42	7	2	0	20	11	7	0	2	35	1	0	.366	.364
Freed, Harrison	R-R	5-11	205	5-13-98	.440	.600	.400	6	25	6	11	3	0	1	7	3	1	0	1	4	1	0	.680	.500
Gonzalez, Cesar	R-R	5-11	206	5-8-01	.200	.105	.244	17	60	4	12	2	0	0	7	4	0	0	0	19	0	0	.233	.250
Hernandez, Bryan	R-R	6-2	178	12-24-99	.143	.077	.172	29	84	16	12	3	1	1	5	14	2	0	0	45	4	1	.238	.280
Jhang, Jin-De	L-R	5-9	225	5-17-93	.256	.231	.267	12	43	5	11	1	1	1	7	6	0	0	1	4	1	0	.395	.340
Jones, Ryder	L-R	6-2	221	6-7-94	.091	.250	.056	6	22	1	2	1	0	0	1	3	0	0	0	8	0	0	.136	.200
Juliana, Richgelon	R-R	6-0	170	5-30-00	.217	.231	.212	30	92	12	20	3	1	0	8	22	0	0	1	35	3	3	.272	.365
Malkin, Matt	R-R	6-3	220	10-8-95	.322	.529	.274	25	90	10	29	8	1	0	12	2	0	1	2	15	0	0	.433	.330
Martorano, Brandon	R-R	6-2	198	1-6-98	.238	.167	.267	5	21	4	5	1	1	1	3	0	0	0	0	10	0	0	.524	.238
McCray, Grant	L-R	6-2	170	12-7-00	.270	.289	.263	48	185	43	50	5	2	1	11	30	3	1	1	54	17	13	.335	.379
Medina, Francisco	R-R	6-1	165	3-20-98	.196	.111	.216	16	46	6	9	3	1	0	2	3	1	0	0	24	0	0	.304	.260
Mejias, Keyberth	R-R	6-0	170	9-24-99	.162	.200	.148	10	37	1	6	0	0	0	1	0	0	1	0	11	1	0	.162	.184
Pena, Jean	R-R	6-1	175	12-22-00	.186	.154	.198	42	145	14	27	2	3	1	13	9	2	0	4	74	3	1	.262	.238
Pomares, Jairo	L-R	6-1	185	8-4-00	.368	.412	.355	37	155	17	57	10	4	3	33	10	0	0	2	26	5	3	.542	.401
Rivero, Jose	L-R	5-11	158	4-30-98	.227	.000	.250	8	22	2	5	0	0	1	2	4	0	1	1	8	1	1	.364	.333
Rodriguez, Yorlis	R-R	6-0	187	7-20-99	.250	.500	.000	1	4	1	1	0	0	0	0	0	0	0	0	1	0	0	.250	.250
Rosario, Dilan	R-R	6-0	175	6-16-01	.214	.265	.196	47	187	22	40	9	2	5	30	11	0	0	3	72	9	3	.364	.254
Santos, Ghordy	B-R	6-1	177	9-2-99	.314	.238	.339	21	86	21	27	5	1	1	8	12	0	0	0	24	10	0	.430	.398
Smith, Armani	R-R	6-4	215	7-19-98	.211	.400	.143	5	19	2	4	0	1	0	3	3	0	0	0	7	1	0	.316	.318
Wyatt, Logan	L-R	6-4	230	11-15-97	.375	.500	.333	7	24	7	9	1	0	0	9	4	0	0	1	6	0	1	.417	.448
Wyatt, Tyler	R-R	5-11	185	12-9-96	.241	.333	.209	17	58	7	14	7	0	0	4	9	4	0	2	14	3	3	.362	.370
2-team total (27 Giants Orange)					.237	.265	.228	44	135	22	32	15	0	0	15	34	8	0	3	30	5	5	.348	.411

Pitching	B-T	HT	WT	DOB	W	L	ERA	G	GS	CG	SV	IP	H	R	ER	HR	BB	SO	AVG	vLH	vRH	K/9	BB/9
Armstrong, Ivan	R-R	6-5	247	7-27-00	1	3	6.43	12	6	0	0	35	42	29	25	3	22	31	.300	.286	.312	7.97	5.66
Bolivar, Deiyerbert	L-L	5-11	155	4-3-96	0	1	3.00	2	0	0	0	3	4	2	1	0	0	3	.286	.000	.400	9.00	0.00
Crawford, Brooks	R-R	6-4	215	8-19-96	0	1	6.14	12	0	0	3	15	12	14	10	1	7	14	.226	.368	.147	8.59	4.30
Cruz, Jose	R-R	6-1	178	5-18-00	2	3	4.50	14	3	0	1	46	41	25	23	1	29	45	.237	.232	.240	8.80	5.67
Cueto, Johnny	R-R	5-11	229	2-15-86	0	0	0.00	1	1	0	0	2	0	0	0	0	0	5	.000	.000	.000	22.50	0.00
2-team total (1 Giants Orange)					0	0	0.00	2	2	0	0	4	2	0	0	0	0	7	.143	.200	.111	15.75	0.00
Davis, Dylan	R-R	6-0	205	7-20-93	0	0	3.12	7	0	0	0	9	4	3	3	0	5	8	.138	.000	.160	8.31	5.19
Fehmel, Bryce	R-R	6-2	205	12-16-96	0	1	1.29	7	7	0	0	14	11	4	2	0	0	13	.200	.240	.167	8.36	0.00
Herrera, Jasier	R-R	6-5	190	1-1-98	6	1	1.99	10	7	0	0	54	53	18	12	1	8	48	.244	.286	.225	7.95	1.33
Horn, Trevor	R-R	6-1	200	12-25-95	1	0	2.00	3	1	0	0	9	5	2	2	1	2	7	.156	.154	.158	7.00	2.00
Lumbert, Evan	L-R	6-0	175	5-10-96	0	0	0.00	3	0	0	0	2	0	0	0	0	0	6	.286	.167	1.000	10.00	0.00
2-team total (7 Giants Orange)					3	0	1.50	8	0	0	1	12	9	3	2	0	8	7	.225	.182	.278	5.25	6.00
Marshall, Mac	R-L	6-1	205	1-27-96	1	0	1.50	5	0	0	0	6	6	1	1	0	3	7	.250	.250	.250	10.50	4.50
McDonald, Trevor	R-R	6-2	180	2-26-01	0	0	2.25	3	3	0	0	4	2	1	1	0	2	8	.143	.000	.222	18.00	4.50
Medina, Francisco	R-R	6-1	165	3-20-98	0	0	0.00	1	0	0	0	1	2	0	0	0	0	4	.400	.333	.500	0.00	0.00
Moronta, Yovanny	R-R	6-1	175	5-22-96	0	0	6.23	8	0	0	0	9	9	6	6	0	11	10	.300	.357	.250	10.38	11.42
Paulino, Freddery	R-R	6-2	181	9-12-00	2	3	4.12	14	6	0	0	55	59	31	25	0	19	42	.274	.294	.257	6.91	3.13
Pena, Francis	R-R	6-3	175	6-2-97	0	4	5.61	17	0	0	1	26	34	19	16	1	3	16	.327	.311	.339	5.61	1.05
Reich, Austin	R-R	6-3	210	4-15-97	0	0	9.24	11	0	0	0	13	20	13	13	0	11	17	.370	.280	.448	12.08	7.82
Reyes, Jesus	R-R	6-4	180	7-31-96	1	1	7.65	14	0	0	0	20	22	22	17	3	14	20	.282	.241	.306	9.00	6.30
Riggs, Nolan	R-R	6-8	255	5-22-93	0	0	1.93	4	0	0	0	5	3	2	1	0	3	8	.177	.375	.000	15.43	5.79
Rodriguez, Randy	R-R	6-0	166	9-5-99	2	6	5.40	16	0	0	0	25	26	17	15	1	16	29	.274	.290	.263	10.44	5.76
Ruotolo, Patrick	R-R	5-10	220	1-16-95	1	0	0.00	7	0	0	0	9	4	0	0	0	1	12	.129	.000	.200	12.00	1.00
Sampson, Keyvius	R-R	6-2	225	1-6-91	1	1	3.27	4	3	0	0	11	10	4	4	0	2	15	.238	.294	.200	12.27	1.64
Severino, Jerson	R-R	6-3	191	7-30-98	0	1	14.90	10	0	0	0	10	20	17	16	1	12	11	.417	.389	.433	10.24	11.17
Strahm, Ben	R-T	6-5	210	12-16-96	3	1	6.86	14	0	0	2	20	22	19	15	0	11	25	.272	.233	.294	11.44	5.03
Vargas, Sonny	L-L	6-2	180	11-8-00	2	4	5.03	13	5	0	1	54	65	46	30	4	20	57	.289	.373	.264	9.56	3.35
Vincent, Nick	R-R	6-0	185	7-12-86	0	0	0.00	2	0	0	0	2	1	0	0	0	0	3	.143	.000	.250	13.50	0.00
Waites, Cole	R-R	6-3	180	6-10-98	1	1	6.23	9	7	0	0	17	17	14	12	1	13	28	.254	.238	.261	14.54	6.75
Wright, Chris	L-L	6-1	205	10-14-98	0	0	2.03	8	5	0	0	13	15	4	3	0	8	8	.294	.333	.282	5.40	5.40

Fielding

C: Gonzalez 17, Jhang 7, Malkin 23, Martorano 2, Mejias 10. **1B:** Aldrete 8, Frechette 34, Medina 7, Wyatt 5, Wyatt 6. **2B:** Aldrete 3, Caraballo 11, Dempsey 18, Rivero 4, Rodriguez 1, Santos 19, Wyatt 3. **3B:** Aldrete 5, Dempsey 1, Jones 6, Medina 4, Pena 35, Rivero 2, Wyatt 8. **SS:** Caraballo 2, Dempsey 1, Fitzgerald 3, Pena 3, Rivero 2, Rosario 44, Santos 3. **OF:** Bell 26, Fabian 4, Freed 6, Hernandez 22, Juliana 29, McCray 48, Medina 1, Pomares 34, Smith 5.

ARIZONA LEAGUE

Batting	B-T	HT	WT	DOB	AVG	vLH	vRH	G	AB	R	H	2B	3B	HR	RBI	BB	HBP	SH	SF	SO	SB	CS	SLG	OBP
Alcantara, Ismael	L-R	6-3	190	4-15-00	.145	.000	.173	21	62	12	9	1	1	0	2	15	2	0	0	33	4	0	.194	.329
Baldwin, Logan	L-L	6-0	190	4-9-96	.000	.000	.000	1	3	0	0	0	0	0	0	1	0	0	0	1	0	0	.000	.250
Bericoto, Victor	R-R	6-1	155	12-3-01	.273	.286	.267	5	22	3	6	1	0	0	4	0	0	0	0	6	3	0	.318	.273
Bishop, Hunter	L-R	6-5	210	6-25-98	.250	.000	.313	7	20	4	5	3	0	1	3	9	0	0	0	11	2	0	.550	.483
Bond, Aaron	L-R	6-5	195	2-16-97	.191	.250	.182	19	63	9	12	4	2	0	11	11	2	0	0	25	4	4	.318	.329
Bone, Rodolfo	R-R	5-11	170	3-22-00	.240	.136	.269	28	100	12	24	5	1	1	9	8	1	1	1	23	2	0	.340	.300
Canario, Alexander	R-R	6-1	165	5-7-00	.395	.333	.405	10	43	13	17	3	1	7	14	2	1	0	0	9	1	0	1.000	.435
Cannon, Connor	R-R	6-5	240	5-16-98	.326	.321	.327	35	132	32	43	7	1	13	38	11	5	0	0	37	0	0	.689	.399
Caraballo, Andrew	R-R	6-0	175	4-29-00	.208	.250	.188	14	48	3	10	1	0	1	12	2	0	0	0	14	4	1	.292	.240
2-team total (15 Giants total)					.204	.241	.188	29	98	5	20	4	1	2	14	8	0	0	0	37	6	3	.327	.264
Gaskins, Najee	R-R	6-0	185	9-7-97	.340	.261	.361	36	106	27	36	8	2	0	7	20	7	1	0	19	19	2	.453	.474
Gutierrez, Raiber	R-R	5-10	165	12-10-99	.219	.200	.222	15	32	3	7	0	0	0	6	3	0	0	1	12	1	0	.219	.278
Guzman, Angel	R-R	6-0	155	5-17-00	.081	.091	.077	14	37	4	3	2	0	0	3	8	1	0	1	17	1	1	.135	.255
Hilson, P.J.	R-R	5-11	175	8-25-00	.221	.179	.232	35	127	23	28	6	2	2	15	12	5	0	1	53	13	2	.347	.310
Layer, Abdiel	B-R	6-2	170	8-9-98	.292	.370	.276	40	154	24	45	10	4	5	30	12	0	1	2	48	9	3	.507	.339
Luciano, Marco	R-R	6-2	178	9-10-01	.322	.179	.356	38	146	46	47	9	2	10	38	27	4	0	1	39	8	6	.616	.438
Matos, Luis	R-R	5-11	160	1-28-02	.438	.375	.500	5	16	5	7	1	0	0	1	1	3	0	0	1	1	1	.500	.550
Medina, Omar	B-R	5-11	170	12-20-99	.169	.083	.186	22	71	10	12	1	0	0	11	11	4	0	1	18	3	3	.183	.310
Mora, Edison	R-R	6-2	165	8-13-00	.250	.286	.243	37	132	24	33	5	1	0	12	15	1	0	3	37	11	2	.303	.325
Norris, Randy	R-R	6-1	190	8-8-97	.260	.375	.238	14	50	9	13	1	0	1	7	8	2	1	0	17	5	1	.340	.383
Quinn, Heath	R-R	6-3	220	6-7-95	.280	.429	.232	7	25	5	7	3	0	2	7	3	3	0	0	5	0	0	.640	.419
Toribio, Luis	L-R	6-1	165	9-28-00	.297	.133	.329	51	185	45	55	15	3	3	33	45	2	0	2	54	4	5	.460	.436
Watts, Enoc	B-R	6-0	160	12-2-99	.245	.100	.282	19	49	6	12	1	0	0	5	4	1	1	1	15	4	1	.265	.309
Williams, Javeyan	L-L	5-9	160	6-27-97	.286	.226	.302	39	147	28	42	7	0	0	12	15	5	2	1	36	18	2	.333	.369
Wyatt, Tyler	R-R	5-11	185	12-9-96	.234	.211	.241	27	77	15	18	8	0	0	11	25	4	0	1	16	2	2	.338	.439
2-team total (17 Giants Black)					.237	.265	.228	44	135	22	32	15	0	0	15	34	8	0	3	30	5	5	.348	.411

Pitching	B-T	HT	WT	DOB	W	L	ERA	G	GS	CG	SV	IP	H	R	ER	HR	BB	SO	AVG	vLH	vRH	K/9	BB/9
Avila, Nick	R-R	6-4	195	7-25-97	0	2	1.11	9	8	0	0	24	19	8	3	1	6	11	.216	.233	.207	4.07	2.22
Bates, Solomon	R-R	6-2	210	3-16-97	0	0	0.00	1	0	0	0	1	0	0	0	0	0	2	.000	--	.000	18.00	0.00
Berroa, Prelander	R-R	5-11	170	4-18-00	1	0	0.00	1	0	0	0	3	1	0	0	0	1	7	.111	.000	.125	21.00	3.00
Callahan, Jamie	R-R	6-2	230	8-24-94	1	0	1.04	8	0	0	2	9	7	1	1	0	2	13	.241	.167	.261	13.50	2.08
Castillo, Wilkelma	R-R	6-0	170	1-6-00	3	1	5.26	13	5	0	1	39	41	25	23	1	21	48	.261	.310	.221	10.98	4.81
Cueto, Johnny	R-R	5-11	229	2-15-86	0	0	0.00	1	1	0	0	2	2	0	0	0	0	2	.286	.333	.250	9.00	0.00
2-team total (1 Giants Black)					0	0	0.00	2	2	0	0	4	2	0	0	0	0	7	.143	.200	.111	15.75	0.00
DuBord, Alex	R-R	6-5	225	12-4-96	2	0	0.00	7	0	0	2	9	4	0	0	0	7	16	.148	.167	.143	16.62	7.27
Figueroa, Miguel	R-R	6-2	165	8-9-97	1	0	3.86	6	0	0	1	19	13	9	8	0	5	28	.191	.167	.211	13.50	2.41
Gomez, Jesus	L-L	6-2	180	4-1-01	4	1	3.83	13	12	0	0	54	42	24	23	6	22	63	.215	.216	.215	10.50	3.67
Gonzalez, Marco	L-L	6-1	180	12-8-97	2	2	3.46	12	0	0	1	26	20	12	10	1	9	29	.211	.238	.203	10.04	3.12
Greenwalt, Jake	R-R	6-1	175	4-30-98	0	1	6.75	12	0	0	1	12	17	18	9	0	12	12	.327	.290	.381	9.00	9.00
Gudino, Norwith	R-R	6-2	200	11-22-95	0	0	0.00	2	1	0	0	7	2	0	0	0	1	13	.087	.000	.118	16.71	1.29
Harasta, Logan	R-R	6-6	235	8-29-96	1	0	2.89	9	0	0	1	9	7	7	3	1	5	12	.200	.118	.278	11.57	4.82
Kilian, Caleb	R-R	6-4	180	6-2-97	0	0	0.00	6	5	0	0	12	6	1	0	0	2	11	.154	.200	.125	8.25	1.50
Labrador, Jorge	R-R	6-1	180	3-9-99	3	0	2.38	10	0	0	3	23	21	7	6	0	6	30	.241	.231	.250	11.91	2.38
Lumbert, Evan	L-R	6-0	175	5-10-96	3	0	1.80	7	0	0	1	10	7	3	2	0	8	7	.212	.188	.235	6.30	7.20
2-team total (1 Giants Black)					3	0	1.50	8	0	0	1	12	9	3	2	0	8	7	.225	.182	.278	5.25	6.00
Martinez, Rodolfo	R-R	6-2	200	4-4-94	0	0	0.00	6	0	0	0	7	5	3	0	0	2	12	.185	.308	.071	15.43	2.57
Moreno, Luis	R-R	6-2	174	8-3-98	3	2	3.33	7	0	0	0	27	33	12	10	0	8	18	.317	.243	.358	6.00	2.67
Morreale, Nick	R-R	6-5	220	7-27-97	0	0	1.52	9	7	0	0	24	13	4	4	0	8	24	.165	.135	.191	9.13	3.04
Nurse, Conner	R-R	6-6	210	7-31-99	3	0	1.26	6	6	0	0	29	23	8	4	0	10	27	.215	.226	.204	8.48	3.14
Pagan, Kanoa	R-R	6-2	190	9-29-98	0	1	6.14	10	0	0	2	15	15	13	10	0	11	21	.263	.348	.206	12.89	6.75
Rashi, Taylor	R-R	6-4	220	1-15-96	2	0	1.32	9	0	0	0	14	11	3	2	1	4	20	.212	.227	.200	13.17	2.63
Rivera, Blake	R-R	6-4	225	1-9-98	0	1	18.00	2	2	0	0	2	4	4	4	0	2	0	.500	.333	.600	0.00	9.00
Rodriguez, Julio	R-R	6-3	180	2-10-00	1	0	4.63	9	0	0	1	12	10	6	6	0	6	13	.217	.188	.233	10.13	4.63
Sanchez, Juan	L-L	6-2	165	11-12-00	7	1	3.77	14	8	0	0	57	60	29	24	3	27	53	.272	.315	.250	8.32	4.24
Sano, Carlos	R-R	6-4	205	2-24-93	1	0	7.36	4	0	0	0	4	4	3	3	0	3	5	.267	.200	.300	12.27	7.36
Scott, Jordan	B-R	6-3	190	4-3-95	4	0	1.42	7	0	0	0	19	13	4	3	1	5	25	.200	.056	.255	11.84	2.37
Taylor, Cory	R-R	6-2	255	12-14-93	1	0	3.38	8	0	0	1	11	12	4	4	0	1	7	.286	.231	.310	5.91	0.84
Veras, Yoel	R-R	6-0	175	10-2-96	0	0	4.50	5	0	0	1	4	9	2	2	0	4	4	.474	.429	.500	9.00	0.00
Warren, Brac	R-R	6-4	220	2-14-96	0	0	10.13	4	0	0	0	3	3	3	3	0	5	1	.300	.400	.200	3.38	16.88
Watts, Enoc	B-R	6-0	160	12-2-99	0	0	0.00	1	0	0	0	1	0	0	0	0	0	0	.000	.000	.000	0.00	0.00
Webb, Logan	R-R	6-2	220	11-18-96	0	0	1.80	1	1	0	0	5	6	1	1	0	0	6	.333	.500	.200	10.80	0.00
Wolff, Sam	R-R	6-1	204	4-14-91	0	1	6.35	5	0	0	0	6	7	4	4	0	1	7	.280	.400	.200	11.12	1.59

Fielding
C: Bone 28, Guzman 14, Medina 17. **1B:** Alcantara 12, Bericoto 5, Cannon 28, Medina 4, Wyatt 8. **2B:** Caraballo 8, Layer 24, Mora 19, Watts 9. **3B:** Caraballo 1, Layer 13, Medina 1, Toribio 41, Wyatt 2. **SS:** Layer 1, Luciano 31, Mora 19, Watts 8. **OF:** Alcantara 7, Baldwin 1, Bishop 4, Bond 10, Canario 8, Gaskins 34, Gutierrez 15, Hilson 35, Matos 5, Norris 11, Quinn 4, Williams 37, Wyatt 17.

SAN FRANCISCO GIANTS

DSL GIANTS

DOMINICAN SUMMER LEAGUE

SAN FRANCISCO GIANTS

ROOKIE

Batting	B-T	HT	WT	DOB	AVG	vLH	vRH	G	AB	R	H	2B	3B	HR	RBI	BB	HBP	SH	SF	SO	SB	CS	SLG	OBP
Bericoto, Victor	R-R	6-1	155	12-3-01	.344	.380	.333	60	227	58	78	15	1	5	41	53	3	0	1	56	10	2	.485	.472
Cuevas, Carlos	R-R	5-11	187	9-16-01	.153	.226	.126	37	118	23	18	3	1	3	9	34	4	0	0	51	12	1	.271	.359
Flores, Ronaldo	R-R	6-0	175	5-17-02	.325	.432	.293	51	191	34	62	7	0	3	35	9	7	0	4	29	1	1	.408	.370
Gomez, Robert	R-R	6-1	170	12-4-00	.222	.205	.229	44	149	24	33	10	0	3	18	32	7	0	0	65	3	5	.349	.383
Hernandez, Jose	R-R	5-11	160	9-15-99	.272	.364	.243	30	92	23	25	4	1	0	12	17	13	0	0	16	5	4	.337	.451
Jaramillo, Eduardo	R-R	5-11	160	3-26-02	.177	.286	.141	25	85	6	15	4	0	1	14	1	1	0	3	21	0	3	.259	.189
Jorge, Samuel	R-R	6-2	190	9-9-99	.224	.178	.240	46	174	26	39	6	2	3	24	16	10	1	2	45	1	2	.333	.322
Liscano, Jesus	L-L	5-11	175	12-30-00	.182	.067	.210	23	77	9	14	2	1	1	8	15	2	0	2	27	0	2	.273	.323
Marin, Nelson	R-R	6-0	165	10-11-01	.183	.174	.186	28	82	10	15	0	0	1	8	10	5	1	0	22	3	1	.220	.309
Matos, Luis	R-R	5-11	160	1-28-02	.362	.388	.355	55	235	60	85	24	2	7	47	19	12	0	4	30	20	2	.570	.430
Medina, Omar	B-R	5-11	170	12-20-99	.317	.231	.357	13	41	12	13	3	0	1	6	9	2	0	0	5	3	0	.463	.462
Monegro, Roberto	R-R	5-10	145	11-15-01	.239	.204	.252	51	184	33	44	6	3	0	17	26	4	0	0	57	3	1	.304	.346
Peralta, Jose	B-R	5-11	160	7-4-01	.290	.322	.279	64	238	40	69	10	5	1	34	45	4	0	1	65	10	8	.387	.410
Polanco, Yohan	R-R	6-3	200	4-1-01	.185	.167	.194	19	54	5	10	1	1	0	4	7	1	0	0	29	0	0	.241	.290
Santana, Rayner	R-R	6-2	180	8-15-02	.294	.233	.315	48	170	31	50	14	0	10	36	37	7	0	0	58	2	3	.553	.439
Suarez, Alexander	R-R	6-2	160	12-20-01	.308	.222	.333	12	39	15	12	4	0	1	6	10	3	0	1	12	2	3	.487	.472
Valdez, Adolfo	L-R	5-10	170	8-29-99	.215	.279	.191	47	158	32	34	5	3	5	25	24	9	0	1	42	17	6	.380	.349
Verbel, Diego	R-R	6-0	162	7-24-02	.253	.267	.250	46	150	30	38	6	0	1	15	31	5	0	2	53	4	2	.313	.394

Pitching	B-T	HT	WT	DOB	W	L	ERA	G	GS	CG	SV	IP	H	R	ER	HR	BB	SO	AVG	vLH	vRH	K/9	BB/9
Acosta, Cristian	R-R	6-0	170	9-19-99	3	4	3.69	25	0	0	0	39	43	23	16	3	8	39	.274	.192	.309	9.00	1.85
Bonilla, Jason	R-R	6-0	165	8-30-98	1	4	3.21	14	14	0	0	56	55	29	20	1	25	50	.257	.228	.268	8.04	4.02
Brown, Marvin	L-L	6-1	177	5-21-01	1	4	5.10	16	9	0	0	48	51	37	27	5	20	46	.283	.256	.291	8.69	3.78
Castillo, Luis	L-L	5-11	170	8-24-02	1	5	5.06	14	14	0	0	53	57	38	30	6	28	52	.273	.238	.281	8.78	4.73
Chango, Albenis	R-R	6-5	175	2-17-00	0	1	20.65	12	0	0	0	11	16	28	26	0	34	10	.356	.250	.394	7.94	27.00
Civada, Odue	R-R	6-1	165	4-5-02	1	4	8.20	14	3	0	0	26	33	32	24	1	25	16	.324	.394	.290	5.47	8.54
Encarnacion, Estiven	R-R	6-4	196	9-27-01	1	0	6.49	17	0	0	1	26	23	21	19	2	28	19	.245	.286	.227	6.49	9.57
Escobar, Robinson	R-R	5-11	200	7-4-98	2	3	5.74	21	0	0	2	31	33	24	20	1	20	34	.260	.297	.244	9.77	5.74
Garcia, Jorge	R-R	6-0	185	5-21-02	4	0	3.46	13	10	0	0	52	57	27	20	3	7	41	.273	.215	.299	7.10	1.21
Marcano, Josdeiker	R-R	6-2	170	8-20-99	0	0	27.00	1	0	0	0	0	1	1	1	0	1	0	.500	--	.500	0.00	27.00
Marte, Melvin	R-R	6-0	165	7-15-00	2	3	3.08	23	0	0	2	38	36	19	13	0	17	35	.240	.350	.200	8.29	4.03
Martinez, Rafael	R-R	6-0	160	4-18-00	2	3	4.06	14	7	0	0	38	36	24	17	1	14	32	.254	.147	.287	7.65	3.35
Montero, Luis	R-R	5-11	198	3-29-98	0	0	27.00	4	0	0	0	3	8	9	9	1	6	2	.533	.000	.667	6.00	18.00
Mullings, Jose	R-R	6-3	170	12-22-99	2	2	4.56	14	14	0	0	53	56	35	27	3	17	66	.264	.263	.265	11.14	2.87
Peniche, Aaron	L-L	6-1	166	8-30-99	0	1	10.73	18	0	0	0	24	30	44	29	2	35	27	.291	.353	.279	9.99	12.95
Perez, Jose	R-R	6-1	175	3-1-01	1	0	7.36	8	0	0	0	11	11	10	9	1	9	14	.275	.273	.276	11.45	7.36
Quintana, Samuel	L-L	6-5	215	11-29-00	2	0	1.64	7	0	0	0	11	6	3	2	0	8	16	.158	.000	.182	13.09	6.55
Ramirez, Yoniel	R-R	6-0	180	5-27-01	6	3	4.28	19	0	0	1	34	34	21	16	1	14	33	.260	.275	.253	8.82	3.74
Suarez, Willian	R-R	6-3	175	3-21-98	2	2	6.68	22	1	0	2	34	42	30	25	1	23	39	.304	.311	.301	10.43	6.15
Torres, Anthony	L-L	6-1	165	11-25-01	0	2	6.75	22	0	0	0	33	37	33	25	2	30	31	.287	.250	.292	8.37	8.10

Fielding

C: Flores 27, Jaramillo 18, Medina 2, Santana 37, Valdez 1. **1B:** Bericoto 30, Flores 22, Jorge 10, Liscano 12, Medina 1, Santana 1. **2B:** Marin 9, Peralta 22, Verbel 45. **3B:** Jorge 32, Marin 8, Medina 10, Monegro 1, Peralta 26, Verbel 1. **SS:** Marin 9, Monegro 50, Peralta 18. **OF:** Bericoto 18, Cuevas 37, Gomez 39, Hernandez 29, Liscano 7, Matos 52, Polanco 14, Suarez 12, Valdez 28.

Seattle Mariners

SEASON IN A SENTENCE: The Mariners launched into a rebuilding effort in the offseason but then teased its fans with a strong start before ultimately finishing 68-94 and missing the playoffs for a major league-worst 18th consecutive season.

HIGH POINT: The Mariners raced to a 13-2 start, with the first two wins coming in Japan against the Athletics. The late March trip to Japan was especially significant because longtime veteran Ichiro Suzuki played his final major league games in front of a sold-out Tokyo Dome.

LOW POINT: The euphoria of the blazing start came crashing down in mid-April, when the Mariners lost six straight games. The Mariners proceeded to win just seven of 28 games in May.

NOTABLE ROOKIES: Preseason No. 1 prospect Justus Sheffield started seven games for the Mariners, posting a 5.50 ERA while striking out more than one batter per inning. Dan Vogelbach spent the year as the Mariners' designated hitter, leading the team with 30 home runs and 76 RBIs. Japanese free agent Yusei Kikuchi was a regular starter in Seattle's rotation in his first season stateside, but the 28-year-old southpaw struggled with a record of 6-11, 5.46.

KEY TRANSACTIONS: GM Jerry Dipoto made a sharp turn in the direction of the franchise in the offseason by trading valuable veterans for prospects. The biggest blockbuster deal involved trading second baseman Robinson Cano and closer Edwin Diaz to the Mets for Jay Bruce, Anthony Swarzak, Gerson Bautista, outfielder Jarred Kelenic and righthander Justin Dunn. Ace starter James Paxton went to the Yankees in exchange for Justus Sheffield, righthander Erik Swanson and outfielder Dom Thompson-Williams. Shortstop J.P. Crawford was acquired from Philadelphia in exchange for 2018 All-Star Jean Segura.

DOWN ON THE FARM: For the second straight year, Double-A Arkansas was the only one of the Mariners' six domestic affiliates to post a final regular-season record above .500, finishing at 81-57 in the Texas League. In terms of prospects, the most positive note for the Mariners' system was the development of outfielders Jarred Kelenic and Julio Rodriguez, both of whom now rank among the best prospects in the minors. Righthander Logan Gilbert, the Mariners' first-round pick in 2018, made his pro debut by pitching well across three levels, posting a combined 10-5, 2.13 record at low Class A, high Class A and Double-A.

OPENING DAY PAYROLL: $135,802,314 (13th).

PLAYERS OF THE YEAR

ALEX TRAUTWIG / SAM SANTILLI

MAJOR LEAGUE	MINOR LEAGUE
Marco Gonzales	**Jarred Kelenic**
LHP	**OF**
16-13, 3.99 in 34 GS	(Low A/High A/AA)
Led team in W, ERA,	.291/.364/.540
SO (147), WHIP (1.31)	23 HR, 20 SB

ORGANIZATION LEADERS

Batting		*Minimum 250 AB
MAJORS		
* AVG	Omar Narvaez	.278
* OPS	Tom Murphy	.859
HR	Daniel Vogelbach	30
RBI	Daniel Vogelbach	76
MINORS		
* AVG	Julio Rodriguez, West Virginia, Modesto	.326
* OBP	John Andreoli, Tacoma	.426
* SLG	Jaycob Brugman, Tacoma	.601
* OPS	Jaycob Brugman, Tacoma	.963
R	Jarred Kelenic, West Virginia, Modesto, Arkansas	80
H	Joe Rizzo, Modesto	153
TB	Jarred Kelenic, West Virginia, Modesto, Arkansas	239
2B	Jarred Kelenic, West Virginia, Modesto, Arkansas	31
2B	Tim Lopes, Tacoma	31
3B	Jonatan Clase, DSL Mariners	7
HR	Cal Raleigh, Modesto, Arkansas	29
RBI	Cal Raleigh, Modesto, Arkansas	82
BB	Jack Larsen, Modesto	65
BB	Ryan Ramiz, West Virginia	65
SO	Onil Pena, West Virginia	159
SB	Jonatan Clase, DSL Mariners	31

Pitching		#Minimum 75 IP
MAJORS		
W	Marco Gonzales	16
# ERA	Marco Gonzales	3.99
SO	Marco Gonzales	147
SV	Roenis Elias	14
MINORS		
W	Ian McKinney, Modesto, Arkansas	13
L	Austin Hutchison, Modesto	12
L	Ricardo Sanchez, Arkansas	12
# ERA	Logan Gilbert, West Virginia, Modesto, Arkansas	2.13
G	Collin Kober, Modesto, Tacoma	48
GS	Clay Chandler, West Virginia, Modesto	28
GS	Ian McKinney, Modesto, Arkansas	28
GS	Ljay Newsome, Modesto, Tacoma, Arkansas	28
SV	Art Warren, Arkansas	15
IP	Steven Moyers, West Virginia, Modesto	164
BB	Ian McKinney, Modesto, Arkansas	59
BB	Justus Sheffield, Tacoma, Arkansas	59
SO	Ljay Newsome, Modesto, Tacoma, Arkansas	169
# AVG	Logan Gilbert, West Virginia, Modesto, Arkansas	.198

2019 PERFORMANCE

General Manager: Jerry Dipoto. **Farm Director:** Andy McKay. **Scouting Director:** Scott Hunter.

Class	Team	League	W	L	PCT	Finish	Manager
Majors	Seattle Mariners	American	68	94	.420	11th (15)	Scott Servais
Triple-A	Tacoma Rainiers	Pacific Coast	61	78	.439	13th (16)	Daren Brown
Double-A	Arkansas Travelers	Texas	81	57	.587	1st (8)	M. Canham/C. Nicolas
High A	Modesto Nuts	California	65	75	.464	6th (8)	Denny Hocking
Low A	West Virginia Power	South Atlantic	69	70	.496	6th (14)	Dave Berg
Short season	Everett Aquasox	Northwest	37	39	.487	5th (8)	J. Moreno/L. Boyd
Rookie	AZL Mariners	Arizona	22	34	.393	t-17th (21)	Zac Livingston
Overall 2019 Minor League Record			335	353	.487	21st (30)	

ORGANIZATION STATISTICS

SEATTLE MARINERS
AMERICAN LEAGUE

Batting	B-T	HT	WT	DOB	AVG	vLH	vRH	G	AB	R	H	2B	3B	HR	RBI	BB	HBP	SH	SF	SO	SB	CS	SLG	OBP
Beckham, Tim	R-R	6-1	205	1-27-90	.237	.280	.218	88	304	39	72	21	1	15	47	21	3	0	0	102	1	3	.461	.293
Bishop, Braden	R-R	6-1	190	8-22-93	.107	.083	.125	27	56	3	6	0	0	0	4	3	0	1	0	21	0	0	.107	.153
Broxton, Keon	R-R	6-3	195	5-7-90	.115	.100	.125	29	52	5	6	0	0	2	5	8	1	0	2	33	2	4	.231	.238
2-team total (37 Baltimore)					.174	.187	.163	66	155	19	27	3	0	6	14	16	1	1	2	82	6	5	.310	.253
Bruce, Jay	L-L	6-3	225	4-3-87	.212	.211	.213	47	165	27	35	11	0	14	28	16	1	0	2	53	1	0	.533	.283
Court, Ryan	R-R	6-2	210	5-28-88	.208	.267	.111	12	24	1	5	1	0	1	5	1	0	0	0	13	0	0	.375	.240
Crawford, J.P.	L-R	6-2	180	1-11-95	.226	.160	.255	93	345	43	78	21	4	7	46	43	2	3	3	83	5	3	.371	.313
Encarnacion, Edwin	R-R	6-1	230	1-7-83	.241	.233	.243	65	241	48	58	7	0	21	49	41	4	0	3	55	0	1	.531	.356
2-team total (44 New York)					.244	.245	.244	109	418	81	102	18	0	34	86	58	7	0	3	103	0	1	.531	.344
Fraley, Jake	L-L	6-0	195	5-25-95	.150	.111	.161	12	40	3	6	2	0	0	1	0	1	0	0	14	0	0	.200	.171
Freitas, David	R-R	6-3	225	3-18-89	.000	--	.000	1	2	1	0	0	0	0	1	0	0	1	0	0	0	0	.000	.250
Gordon, Dee	L-R	5-11	170	4-22-88	.275	.326	.259	117	393	36	108	12	6	3	34	18	1	3	6	61	22	5	.359	.304
Haniger, Mitch	R-R	6-2	215	12-23-90	.220	.263	.206	63	246	46	54	13	1	15	32	30	5	0	2	81	4	0	.463	.315
Healy, Ryon	R-R	6-5	225	1-10-92	.237	.200	.250	47	169	24	40	16	0	7	26	13	1	0	4	40	0	0	.456	.289
Lewis, Kyle	R-R	6-4	210	7-13-95	.268	.158	.308	18	71	10	19	5	0	6	13	3	0	0	1	29	0	0	.592	.293
Long, Shed	L-R	5-8	184	8-22-95	.263	.333	.241	42	152	21	40	12	1	5	15	16	0	0	0	40	3	3	.454	.333
Lopes, Tim	R-R	5-11	180	6-24-94	.270	.319	.234	41	111	11	30	7	0	1	12	15	1	0	1	29	6	3	.360	.359
Moore, Dylan	R-R	6-0	200	8-2-92	.207	.224	.199	113	247	31	51	14	2	9	28	25	9	1	0	93	11	9	.389	.303
Murphy, Tom	R-R	6-1	218	4-3-91	.273	.348	.211	75	260	32	71	12	1	18	40	19	1	0	1	87	2	0	.535	.324
Narvaez, Omar	L-R	5-11	220	2-10-92	.278	.227	.289	132	428	63	119	12	0	22	55	47	4	0	3	92	0	0	.460	.353
Negron, Kristopher	R-R	6-0	190	2-11-86	.217	.125	.267	10	23	3	5	0	0	1	2	0	0	0	0	9	1	0	.217	.280
Nola, Austin	R-R	6-0	195	12-28-89	.269	.256	.275	79	238	37	64	12	1	10	31	23	4	1	1	63	1	0	.454	.342
Santana, Domingo	R-R	6-5	220	8-5-92	.253	.238	.258	121	451	63	114	20	1	21	69	50	2	0	2	164	8	3	.441	.329
Seager, Kyle	L-R	6-0	210	11-3-87	.239	.285	.217	106	393	55	94	19	1	23	63	44	4	0	2	86	2	2	.468	.321
Smith, Mallex	R-R	5-10	180	5-6-93	.228	.264	.213	134	510	70	116	19	6	3	47	42	1	2	1	141	46	9	.335	.300
Suzuki, Ichiro	L-R	5-11	175	10-22-73	.000	--	.000	2	5	0	0	0	0	0	0	1	0	0	0	1	0	0	.000	.167
Vogelbach, Daniel	L-R	6-0	250	12-17-92	.208	.161	.225	144	462	73	96	17	0	30	76	92	2	0	2	149	0	0	.439	.341
Walton, Donnie	L-R	5-10	184	5-25-94	.188	.000	.200	7	16	2	3	0	0	0	2	3	0	0	0	5	0	1	.188	.316
Williamson, Mac	R-R	6-4	237	7-15-90	.182	.143	.196	25	77	10	14	0	0	3	10	9	1	0	0	26	0	1	.299	.276

Pitching	B-T	HT	WT	DOB	W	L	ERA	G	GS	CG	SV	IP	H	R	ER	HR	BB	SO	AVG	vLH	vRH	K/9	BB/9
Adams, Austin	R-R	6-3	225	5-5-91	2	2	3.77	29	2	0	0	31	20	13	13	4	14	51	.184	.152	.206	14.81	4.06
Alaniz, R.J.	R-R	6-4	219	6-14-91	0	0	20.25	4	0	0	0	4	11	10	9	3	3	6	.500	.500	.500	13.50	6.75
Altavilla, Dan	R-R	5-11	200	9-8-92	2	1	5.52	17	0	0	0	15	9	9	9	1	12	18	.180	.188	.177	11.05	7.36
Armstrong, Shawn	R-R	6-2	225	9-11-90	0	1	14.73	4	0	0	0	4	8	6	6	1	3	3	.444	.286	.546	7.36	7.36
2-team total (51 Baltimore)					1	1	5.74	55	0	0	4	58	66	38	37	8	29	63	.282	.209	.324	9.78	4.50
Bass, Anthony	R-R	6-2	200	11-1-87	2	4	3.56	44	0	0	5	48	30	20	19	5	17	43	.179	.165	.191	8.06	3.19
Bautista, Gerson	R-R	6-3	195	5-31-95	0	1	11.00	8	2	0	0	9	13	11	11	2	9	7	.333	.167	.476	7.00	9.00
Biddle, Jesse	L-L	6-5	220	10-22-91	0	0	9.82	11	0	0	0	11	20	14	12	2	7	8	.400	.381	.414	6.55	5.73
2-team total (4 Texas)					0	0	10.47	15	0	0	0	16	24	22	19	4	12	15	.343	.385	.318	8.27	6.61
Bradford, Chasen	R-R	6-1	229	8-5-89	0	0	4.86	12	0	0	1	17	17	9	9	6	4	11	.266	.280	.256	5.94	2.16
Brennan, Brandon	R-R	6-4	220	7-26-91	3	6	4.56	44	0	0	0	47	34	25	24	6	24	47	.201	.242	.175	8.94	4.56
Carasiti, Matt	R-R	6-3	210	7-23-91	0	1	4.66	11	5	0	0	10	11	6	5	2	5	10	.297	.200	.333	9.31	4.66
Dunn, Justin	R-R	6-2	185	9-22-95	0	0	2.70	4	4	0	0	7	2	2	2	0	9	5	.105	.000	.133	6.75	12.15
Elias, Roenis	L-L	6-1	205	8-1-88	4	2	3.64	44	0	0	14	47	41	18	19	8	17	45	.224	.353	.174	8.62	3.26
Festa, Matt	R-R	6-2	195	3-11-93	0	2	5.64	20	0	0	0	22	20	15	14	5	12	21	.241	.214	.255	8.46	4.84
Garton, Ryan	R-R	5-10	190	12-5-89	0	0	12.00	2	0	0	0	3	4	4	4	2	1	1	.308	.250	.400	3.00	3.00
Gearrin, Cory	R-R	6-1	205	4-14-86	0	2	3.92	48	2	0	0	41	38	18	18	3	21	39	.247	.281	.227	8.49	4.57
2-team total (18 New York)					1	3	4.07	66	2	0	0	55	55	25	25	5	26	47	.261	.276	.252	7.64	4.07
Gonzales, Marco	L-L	6-1	195	2-16-92	16	13	3.99	34	34	0	0	203	210	106	90	23	56	147	.265	.302	.251	6.52	2.48
Grotz, Zac	R-R	6-2	195	2-17-93	1	0	4.15	14	0	0	0	17	14	9	8	0	8	18	.222	.154	.270	9.35	4.15
Guilbeau, Taylor	L-L	6-4	180	5-12-93	0	0	3.65	17	0	0	0	12	10	6	5	2	3	7	.213	.227	.200	5.11	2.19
Hernandez, Felix	R-R	6-3	225	4-8-86	1	8	6.40	15	15	0	0	72	85	58	51	17	25	57	.291	.294	.289	7.16	3.14

Kikuchi, Yusei	L-L	6-0	194	6-17-91	6	11	5.46	32	32	1	0	162	195	109	98	36	50	116	.296	.263	.304	6.46	2.78
Leake, Mike	R-R	5-10	170	11-12-87	9	8	4.27	22	22	2	0	137	153	78	65	26	19	100	.278	.278	.277	6.57	1.25
LeBlanc, Wade	L-L	6-3	205	8-7-84	6	7	5.71	26	8	0	0	121	145	80	77	28	31	92	.291	.276	.296	6.82	2.30
Magill, Matt	R-R	6-3	210	11-10-89	3	2	3.63	22	0	0	5	22	21	10	9	3	5	28	.236	.263	.216	11.28	2.01
2-team total (28 Minnesota)					5	2	4.09	50	0	0	5	51	51	31	23	7	20	64	.251	.281	.231	11.37	3.55
Markel, Parker	R-R	6-5	240	9-15-90	0	0	15.43	5	0	0	0	5	10	9	8	3	4	3	.435	.417	.455	5.79	7.71
McClain, Reggie	R-R	6-2	180	11-16-92	1	1	6.00	14	2	0	0	21	22	14	14	2	13	11	.268	.273	.265	4.71	5.57
McKay, David	R-R	6-3	205	3-31-95	0	0	5.14	7	0	0	0	7	5	5	4	1	8	5	.192	.143	.250	6.43	10.29
2-team total (18 Detroit)					0	0	5.47	25	0	0	0	26	20	17	16	3	17	34	.206	.244	.173	11.62	5.81
Milone, Tommy	L-L	6-0	215	2-16-87	4	10	4.76	23	6	0	0	112	102	61	59	24	23	94	.241	.248	.238	7.58	1.85
Moore, Andrew	R-R	6-0	195	6-2-94	0	0	7.71	1	1	0	0	5	6	4	4	2	1	2	.316	.375	.273	3.86	1.93
Moore, Dylan	R-R	6-0	200	8-2-92	0	0	36.00	1	0	0	0	1	5	4	4	0	2	0	.625	.600	.667	0.00	18.00
Murphy, Tom	R-R	6-1	218	4-3-91	0	0	6.00	3	0	0	0	3	1	2	2	0	1	2	.125	.000	.250	6.00	3.00
Rosscup, Zac	R-L	6-2	220	6-9-88	2	3	3.21	19	0	0	0	14	13	8	5	1	14	20	.236	.087	.344	12.86	9.00
2-team total (2 Toronto)					2	0	4.80	21	0	0	0	15	16	12	8	1	16	22	.262	.154	.343	13.20	9.60
Rumbelow, Nick	R-R	6-0	190	9-6-91	0	0	27.00	3	0	0	1	1	3	4	4	2	1	2	.375	.500	.333	13.50	6.75
Sadzeck, Connor	R-R	6-7	240	10-1-91	0	1	2.66	20	0	0	1	24	18	10	7	3	15	27	.200	.135	.245	10.27	5.70
Scott, Tayler	R-R	6-3	185	6-1-92	0	0	9.39	5	2	0	0	8	11	10	8	1	6	7	.333	.313	.353	8.22	7.04
2-team total (8 Baltimore)					0	0	14.33	13	2	0	0	16	31	28	26	6	11	14	.397	.371	.419	7.71	6.06
Sheffield, Justus	L-L	6-0	200	5-13-96	0	1	5.50	8	7	0	0	36	44	22	22	5	18	37	.303	.207	.328	9.25	4.50
Strickland, Hunter	R-R	6-3	225	9-24-88	0	1	8.10	4	0	0	2	3	2	3	3	1	0	4	.167	.400	.000	8.10	0.00
Swanson, Erik	R-R	6-3	235	9-4-93	1	5	5.74	27	8	0	2	58	56	41	37	17	12	52	.244	.267	.224	8.07	1.86
Swarzak, Anthony	R-R	6-4	215	9-10-85	2	2	5.27	15	0	0	3	14	14	11	8	6	8	17	.250	.227	.265	11.20	5.27
Tuivailala, Sam	R-R	6-3	225	10-19-92	1	0	2.35	23	2	0	0	15	13	6	6	1	11	27	.163	.185	.151	10.57	4.30
Warren, Art	R-R	6-3	230	3-23-93	1	0	0.00	6	0	0	0	5	2	0	0	0	2	5	.105	.286	.000	8.44	3.38
Wisler, Matt	R-R	6-3	215	9-12-92	1	2	6.04	23	8	0	0	22	22	17	15	5	6	29	.247	.222	.258	11.69	2.42
Wright, Mike	R-R	6-6	215	1-3-90	0	0	6.75	9	0	0	0	16	24	16	12	1	5	16	.324	.290	.349	9.00	2.81
2-team total (10 Baltimore)					0	1	7.98	19	0	0	1	29	44	30	26	6	12	30	.336	.319	.345	9.20	3.68

Fielding

Catcher	PCT	G	PO	A	E	DP	PB
Freitas	1.000	1	8	0	0	0	0
Murphy	.992	67	499	23	4	3	3
Narvaez	.992	98	712	34	6	3	3
Nola	1.000	7	34	2	0	0	1

First Base	PCT	G	PO	A	E	DP
Beckham	1.000	5	35	0	0	2
Bruce	.982	16	101	8	2	11
Court	1.000	7	17	1	0	3
Encarnacion	.995	45	347	22	2	32
Healy	1.000	11	30	3	0	4
Moore	1.000	5	13	0	0	2
Nola	1.000	59	377	20	0	38
Vogelbach	.995	57	394	22	2	45

Second Base	PCT	G	PO	A	E	DP
Beckham	.943	8	15	18	2	3
Encarnacion	.000	1	0	0	0	0
Gordon	.980	111	190	242	9	63
Long	.981	24	41	65	2	21
Lopes	.800	3	1	3	1	1
Moore	1.000	18	19	39	0	10
Narvaez	1.000	1	1	0	0	0
Nola	.984	15	25	36	1	11
Walton	1.000	2	4	3	0	1

Third Base	PCT	G	PO	A	E	DP
Beckham	1.000	10	7	15	0	2
Healy	.919	44	24	78	9	6
Long	.667	1	1	1	1	0
Moore	.857	14	7	11	3	3
Negron	.000	1	0	0	0	0
Nola	1.000	4	1	4	0	0
Seager	.962	104	64	218	11	23

Shortstop	PCT	G	PO	A	E	DP
Beckham	.932	41	60	104	12	25
Crawford	.970	93	110	273	12	46
Gordon	.900	2	5	4	1	0
Moore	.967	31	34	83	4	20
Walton	1.000	5	4	4	0	0

Outfield	PCT	G	PO	A	E	DP
Beckham	1.000	13	10	2	0	1
Bishop	1.000	24	41	1	0	0
Broxton	.974	25	36	1	1	0
Bruce	.964	28	50	4	2	1
Court	.909	5	9	1	1	1
Fraley	.950	12	19	0	1	0
Haniger	.994	62	165	0	1	0
Lewis	.977	18	43	0	1	0
Long	1.000	16	22	2	0	0
Lopes	.980	35	49	0	1	0
Moore	.969	45	63	0	2	0
Murphy	1.000	1	1	0	0	0
Negron	1.000	9	14	0	0	0
Nola	.000	2	0	0	0	0
Santana	.940	100	184	4	12	1
Smith	.984	132	312	2	5	2
Suzuki	1.000	2	3	0	0	0
Williamson	.980	24	46	2	1	0

TACOMA RAINIERS   TRIPLE-A
PACIFIC COAST LEAGUE

Batting	B-T	HT	WT	DOB	AVG	vLH	vRH	G	AB	R	H	2B	3B	HR	RBI	BB	HBP	SH	SF	SO	SB	CS	SLG	OBP
Andreoli, John	R-R	6-1	215	6-9-90	.290	.246	.307	73	255	49	74	18	3	10	32	60	3	0	4	78	9	1	.502	.426
Bishop, Braden	R-R	6-1	190	8-22-93	.276	.340	.250	43	185	29	51	15	0	8	31	23	2	0	1	44	2	2	.487	.360
Brugman, Jaycob	L-L	6-0	195	1-18-92	.283	.259	.293	78	293	43	83	22	1	23	65	35	2	0	1	86	0	0	.601	.363
Calixte, Orlando	R-R	6-0	183	2-3-92	.278	.292	.274	25	97	13	27	2	0	2	10	7	0	0	0	24	3	2	.361	.327
Castro, Daniel	R-R	5-11	201	11-14-92	.214	.130	.236	29	112	8	24	3	0	2	7	4	3	1	0	14	0	0	.295	.261
2-team total (46 Oklahoma City)					.232	.169	.254	75	280	26	65	9	0	3	18	17	6	2	2	29	3	0	.296	.289
Cooke, Billy	R-R	5-10	175	9-26-95	.275	.333	.250	17	51	8	14	2	1	0	5	6	2	1	1	11	5	2	.353	.367
Court, Ryan	R-R	6-2	210	5-28-88	.258	.290	.252	54	190	40	49	10	2	11	48	32	2	0	4	63	2	0	.505	.364
Crawford, J.P.	L-R	6-2	180	1-11-95	.319	.429	.257	31	116	20	37	7	0	3	15	19	2	0	1	25	3	0	.457	.420
Curletta, Joey	R-R	6-4	245	3-8-94	.246	.212	.260	27	110	16	27	2	0	5	11	9	0	0	0	39	1	0	.400	.303
Davis, J.R.	R-R	5-10	190	8-10-94	.250	1.000	.000	1	4	1	1	0	0	0	0	0	0	0	0	0	0	0	.250	.250
Filia, Eric	L-R	6-0	189	7-6-92	.331	.432	.286	35	121	24	40	13	0	2	13	25	3	0	2	15	0	0	.488	.450
Fraley, Jake	L-L	6-0	195	5-25-95	.276	.289	.271	38	152	28	42	12	3	8	33	11	3	0	2	34	6	2	.553	.333
Freitas, David	R-R	6-3	225	3-18-89	.278	.400	.125	6	18	4	5	2	0	0	5	2	0	0	0	6	0	0	.389	.480
2-team total (85 San Antonio)					.381	.482	.329	91	328	55	125	23	0	12	81	47	4	0	3	55	0	1	.561	.461
Gordon, Dee	L-R	5-11	170	4-22-88	.214	.333	.182	3	14	0	3	0	0	0	0	0	0	0	0	2	0	1	.214	.214
Haniger, Mitch	R-R	6-2	215	12-23-90	.250	--	.250	1	4	0	1	0	1	0	0	0	0	0	0	3	0	0	.750	.400
Hoover, Connor	L-R	5-10	185	7-18-96	.250	.333	.200	2	8	3	2	0	0	2	2	0	0	0	1	0	0	0	1.000	.250
Kaleiwahea, Brennon	R-R	6-0	200	5-28-96	.000	.000	.000	2	7	1	0	0	0	0	0	1	0	0	5	0	0	.000	.125

SEATTLE MARINERS

Batting	B-T	HT	WT	DOB	AVG	vLH	vRH	G	AB	R	H	2B	3B	HR	RBI	BB	HBP	SH	SF	SO	SB	CS	SLG	OBP
Knapp, Aaron	L-R	5-10	175	11-4-94	.122	.000	.132	12	41	2	5	0	0	0	5	6	0	0	0	18	0	0	.122	.234
Kopach, Connor	R-R	6-0	170	8-4-94	.286	.267	.293	15	56	8	16	1	0	2	7	4	0	0	0	23	2	0	.411	.333
Liberato, Luis	L-L	6-1	175	12-18-95	.500	.000	.667	1	4	3	2	0	0	0	0	0	0	0	0	0	0	0	.500	.500
Lobaton, Jose	B-R	6-1	205	10-21-84	.236	.302	.208	75	288	34	68	18	0	13	38	27	2	0	1	83	1	0	.434	.305
2-team total (15 Oklahoma City)					.236	.298	.212	90	335	39	79	22	0	14	43	35	2	0	2	98	1	0	.427	.310
Long, Shed	L-R	5-8	184	8-22-95	.274	.328	.252	56	226	38	62	7	4	9	36	20	1	2	1	65	1	3	.460	.335
Lopes, Tim	R-R	5-11	180	6-24-94	.302	.289	.307	95	374	59	113	31	2	10	60	36	3	0	7	72	26	9	.476	.362
Mariscal, Chris	R-R	5-10	170	4-26-93	.209	.250	.197	74	258	38	54	10	0	10	29	26	3	3	2	70	0	1	.364	.287
Miller, Ian	L-R	6-0	175	2-21-92	.269	.321	.248	106	390	64	105	27	5	11	54	45	6	0	4	81	29	5	.449	.351
Moore, Dylan	R-R	6-0	200	8-2-92	.172	.000	.278	7	29	3	5	0	0	0	7	3	2	1	0	3	2	1	.172	.294
Negron, Kristopher	R-R	6-0	190	2-1-86	.311	.349	.296	82	306	62	95	15	4	12	61	41	5	0	4	91	11	3	.503	.396
Nola, Austin	R-R	6-0	195	12-28-89	.327	.400	.301	55	196	36	64	15	1	7	37	29	2	0	2	40	4	1	.520	.415
Odom, Joseph	R-R	6-2	225	1-9-92	.307	.000	.373	17	62	5	19	5	0	2	10	7	0	0	0	19	0	0	.484	.377
Pacheco, Jordan	R-R	6-1	200	1-30-86	.263	.395	.219	46	171	14	45	10	0	1	16	9	5	0	2	35	1	0	.339	.316
Perez, Robert	R-R	6-1	170	6-26-00	.250	.333	.209	19	64	9	16	3	1	3	8	4	1	0	0	24	0	0	.469	.304
Polo, Tito	R-R	5-10	195	8-23-94	.263	.133	.348	10	38	4	10	4	0	0	3	2	0	0	0	4	1	2	.368	.300
Santa, Kevin	L-R	5-11	175	3-9-95	.138	.000	.160	9	29	2	4	1	0	0	1	2	1	0	0	6	0	0	.172	.219
Seager, Kyle	L-R	6-0	210	11-3-87	.256	.333	.242	9	39	5	10	2	0	2	7	3	0	0	0	7	0	0	.308	.310
Sheaffer, David	R-R	6-2	170	5-9-95	.278	.167	.333	7	18	3	5	1	0	1	3	0	0	0	0	7	0	0	.500	.278
Slater, Johnny	L-L	6-1	190	8-9-95	.154	.000	.167	4	13	0	2	0	0	0	1	0	0	0	0	6	2	0	.154	.154
Smith, Mallex	L-R	5-10	180	5-6-93	.333	.273	.353	10	45	8	15	3	0	1	6	3	0	0	0	4	0	0	.467	.375
Tomlinson, Kelby	R-R	6-2	175	6-16-90	.250	.282	.237	69	248	30	62	13	1	0	11	15	1	3	2	54	2	1	.311	.293
2-team total (30 Reno)					.242	.306	.215	99	335	45	81	16	2	0	16	27	2	3	2	79	4	3	.302	.301
Williamson, Mac	R-R	6-4	237	7-15-90	.250	.000	.286	2	8	0	2	1	0	0	1	0	0	0	0	2	0	0	.375	.250
2-team total (23 Sacramento)					.367	.542	.303	25	90	23	33	5	0	9	23	13	1	0	2	27	1	0	.722	.443
Young Jr., Eric	B-R	5-10	195	5-25-85	.236	.429	.163	33	127	16	30	4	3	2	11	10	2	0	3	26	3	2	.362	.296

Pitching	B-T	HT	WT	DOB	W	L	ERA	G	GS	CG	SV	IP	H	R	ER	HR	BB	SO	AVG	vLH	vRH	K/9	BB/9
Adams, Austin	R-R	6-3	225	5-5-91	0	0	0.00	4	0	0	0	4	1	0	0	0	0	7	.071	.000	.143	14.54	0.00
2-team total (8 Fresno)					0	1	1.88	12	0	0	1	14	8	4	3	0	3	27	.157	.138	.182	16.95	1.88
Alaniz, R.J.	R-R	6-4	219	6-14-91	2	1	6.39	10	0	0	2	13	18	10	9	3	7	23	.327	.310	.346	16.34	4.97
Altavilla, Dan	R-R	5-11	200	9-8-92	1	1	8.36	14	0	0	0	14	11	13	13	0	11	25	.212	.217	.207	16.07	7.07
Armstrong, Shawn	R-R	6-2	225	9-11-90	0	0	0.00	2	1	0	0	2	2	0	0	0	0	3	.250	.500	.000	13.50	0.00
Bautista, Gerson	R-R	6-3	195	5-31-95	0	0	8.75	21	0	0	1	24	29	23	23	7	18	31	.293	.304	.283	11.79	6.85
Bergman, Christian	R-R	6-1	195	5-4-88	2	3	9.57	8	6	0	0	26	40	31	28	10	8	19	.339	.377	.298	6.49	2.73
Boches, Scott	R-R	6-5	205	10-17-94	1	0	9.00	1	0	0	0	2	4	3	2	0	0	2	.400	.333	.500	9.00	0.00
Bradford, Chasen	R-R	6-1	229	8-5-89	0	0	6.75	5	0	0	1	5	5	5	4	2	3	2	.227	.231	.222	3.38	5.06
Brennan, Brandon	R-R	6-4	220	7-26-91	1	0	1.04	9	0	0	0	9	5	1	1	1	4	10	.185	.333	.111	10.38	4.15
Carasiti, Matt	R-R	6-3	210	7-23-91	1	0	4.96	15	0	0	4	16	19	11	9	3	7	17	.279	.304	.267	9.37	3.86
2-team total (16 Iowa)					2	1	3.53	31	0	0	5	43	39	22	17	4	18	40	.235	.241	.232	8.31	3.74
Cloyd, Tyler	R-R	6-3	210	5-16-87	2	8	7.43	15	13	0	0	67	95	56	55	14	29	54	.333	.383	.291	9.32	3.92
Crismatt, Nabil	R-R	6-1	215	12-25-94	0	5	9.06	13	8	0	0	47	67	51	47	15	21	68	.324	.386	.264	13.11	4.05
Danish, Tyler	R-R	6-0	200	9-12-94	0	4	21.26	6	4	0	0	16	44	41	37	9	9	10	.506	.474	.531	5.74	5.17
Ellington, Brian	R-R	6-3	215	8-4-90	0	1	7.20	10	0	0	0	10	9	8	8	3	2	12	.302	.444	.200	10.80	4.11
Festa, Matt	R-R	6-2	195	3-11-93	1	1	2.64	23	0	0	5	31	23	11	9	3	14	33	.204	.185	.220	9.68	4.11
Florido, Deivy	R-R	6-2	165	9-17-00	0	0	0.00	1	0	0	0	2	3	0	0	0	1	1	.333	.000	.500	4.50	4.50
Garton, Ryan	R-R	5-10	190	12-5-89	4	2	3.99	39	1	0	1	65	57	33	29	9	30	77	.233	.219	.246	10.61	4.13
Gillies, Darin	R-R	6-4	220	11-6-92	1	2	8.55	24	0	0	1	34	47	32	32	9	14	43	.326	.382	.265	11.50	3.74
Grotz, Zac	R-R	6-2	195	2-17-93	1	0	0.00	2	0	0	0	3	2	0	0	0	1	3	.182	.333	.000	9.00	3.00
Guilbeau, Taylor	L-L	6-4	180	5-12-93	0	0	1.80	5	0	0	0	5	3	1	1	0	2	5	.177	.286	.100	9.00	3.60
2-team total (7 Fresno)					2	0	3.95	12	0	0	0	14	13	6	6	0	7	11	.260	.294	.242	7.24	4.61
Haberer, Jake	R-R	6-2	225	2-9-95	0	0	13.50	3	0	0	0	4	8	7	6	2	2	2	.381	.500	.333	4.50	4.50
Hernandez, Carlos	R-R	6-3	195	2-8-96	0	0	0.00	1	0	0	0	1	1	0	0	0	0	1	.333	.000	.500	13.50	0.00
Hernandez, Felix	R-R	6-3	225	4-8-86	0	1	5.06	2	0	0	0	5	6	3	3	0	4	7	.300	.444	.182	11.81	6.75
Kerr, Raymond	L-L	6-3	185	9-10-94	1	0	0.00	1	0	0	0	2	0	0	0	0	0	2	.000	.000	.000	7.71	0.00
Kober, Collin	R-R	6-1	185	9-8-94	0	0	4.50	1	0	0	0	2	3	1	1	1	3	0	.429	.500	.333	0.00	13.50
LeBlanc, Wade	L-L	6-3	205	8-7-84	0	0	2.08	1	1	0	0	4	3	1	1	0	2	2	.214	.286	.143	4.15	4.15
Leyer, Robinson	R-R	6-2	175	3-13-93	1	1	4.58	13	0	0	0	20	20	11	10	3	11	27	.263	.290	.237	12.36	5.03
Markel, Parker	R-R	6-5	240	9-15-90	2	0	2.60	22	0	0	8	28	13	9	8	3	21	44	.138	.154	.127	14.31	6.83
McCaughan, Darren	R-R	6-1	195	3-18-96	0	6	8.06	9	9	1	0	41	55	40	37	11	11	36	.313	.310	.315	7.84	2.40
McClain, Reggie	R-R	6-2	180	11-16-92	3	4	3.29	17	1	0	2	41	29	20	15	3	18	34	.203	.207	.200	7.46	3.95
McKay, David	R-R	6-3	205	3-31-95	3	1	5.15	30	0	0	1	44	31	26	25	4	31	71	.199	.169	.220	14.63	6.39
Milone, Tommy	L-L	6-0	215	2-16-87	4	2	3.83	9	8	1	0	49	49	26	21	7	12	43	.250	.132	.294	7.84	2.19
Misiewicz, Anthony	R-L	6-1	190	11-1-94	8	6	5.36	19	17	0	0	96	95	60	57	17	28	89	.256	.255	.257	8.37	2.63
Moore, Andrew	R-R	6-0	195	6-2-94	0	5	8.00	13	8	0	0	54	71	52	48	14	17	36	.309	.250	.368	6.00	2.83
Murfee, Penn	R-R	6-2	195	5-2-94	0	0	10.38	5	0	0	0	9	13	10	10	3	7	12	.342	.333	.364	12.46	7.27
Negron, Kristopher	R-R	6-0	190	2-1-86	0	0	18.00	2	0	0	0	1	3	2	2	1	0	0	.500	1.000	.400	0.00	0.00
Newsome, Ljay	R-R	5-11	210	11-8-96	0	0	6.35	1	1	0	0	6	5	4	4	1	1	10	.227	.333	.188	15.88	1.59
Niese, Jonathon	L-L	6-3	215	10-27-86	4	2	5.12	14	13	0	0	70	82	45	40	13	23	30	.288	.308	.266	3.86	4.86
Nolin, Sean	L-L	6-4	250	12-26-89	6	4	4.76	15	14	0	0	79	78	43	42	13	26	74	.259	.235	.266	8.39	2.95
Northcraft, Aaron	R-R	6-4	230	5-28-90	0	2	1.87	27	0	0	4	34	18	7	7	2	13	35	.161	.189	.136	9.36	3.48
Pedrol, Christian	R-R	5-11	190	6-15-00	0	0	40.50	1	0	0	0	1	6	6	6	4	2	0	.600	.000	.857	0.00	13.50
Rumbelow, Nick	R-R	6-0	190	9-6-91	3	2	8.17	19	0	0	0	25	37	26	23	5	15	22	.339	.400	.297	7.82	5.33
Scott, Tayler	R-R	6-3	185	6-1-92	3	2	6.43	20	0	0	1	35	32	25	25	4	19	47	.246	.268	.230	12.09	4.89
Sheaffer, David	R-R	6-2	170	5-9-95	0	0	63.00	2	0	0	0	1	8	8	7	2	0	0	.667	.600	.714	0.00	0.00

Pitcher	B-T	HT	WT	DOB	W	L	ERA	G	GS	CG	SV	IP	H	R	ER	HR	BB	SO	AVG	vLH	vRH	K/9	BB/9
Sheffield, Justus	L-L	6-0	200	5-13-96	2	6	6.87	13	12	0	0	55	59	47	42	12	41	48	.268	.263	.270	7.85	6.71
Strickland, Hunter	R-R	6-3	225	9-24-88	0	0	3.00	3	0	0	0	3	2	1	1	1	1	4	.182	.250	.143	12.00	3.00
Swanson, Erik	R-R	6-3	235	9-4-93	0	1	5.55	10	6	0	0	24	28	16	15	5	12	28	.283	.292	.275	10.36	4.44
Tenuta, Matt	L-L	6-4	225	12-16-93	0	0	8.76	9	2	0	0	12	19	13	12	2	8	10	.373	.167	.485	7.30	5.84
Tuivailala, Sam	R-R	6-3	225	10-19-92	1	0	4.76	6	0	0	0	6	5	3	3	1	1	5	.227	.200	.250	7.94	1.59
Wright, Mike	R-R	6-6	215	1-3-90	2	5	5.28	15	12	0	0	58	61	35	34	4	17	56	.269	.302	.240	8.69	2.64

Fielding

Catcher	PCT	G	PO	A	E	DP	PB
Freitas	1.000	3	30	1	0	0	2
Kaleiwahea	.947	2	17	1	1	0	0
Lobaton	.991	66	596	40	6	5	0
Nola	1.000	28	230	16	0	4	4
Odom	1.000	15	144	3	0	0	1
Pacheco	1.000	27	238	5	0	0	2

First Base	PCT	G	PO	A	E	DP
Court	.997	36	268	19	1	24
Curletta	.983	22	160	14	3	17
Filia	1.000	14	91	3	0	10
Negron	.994	25	165	14	1	16
Nola	1.000	24	170	10	0	17
Odom	1.000	1	8	1	0	0
Pacheco	1.000	19	142	9	0	12
Perez	.800	7	4	0	1	0
Sheaffer	1.000	2	2	0	0	0

Second Base	PCT	G	PO	A	E	DP
Castro	.971	8	12	21	1	5
Davis	1.000	1	0	2	0	0
Gordon	1.000	2	6	4	0	2
Hoover	1.000	2	3	3	0	1
Kopach	.985	15	23	44	1	9

(Second Base cont.)	PCT	G	PO	A	E	DP
Long	.965	21	34	49	3	14
Lopes	.978	63	94	130	5	27
Mariscal	.933	15	20	36	4	6
Moore	1.000	2	2	7	0	2
Negron	.923	2	7	5	1	5
Santa	1.000	9	21	17	0	4
Tomlinson	1.000	2	5	2	0	0

Third Base	PCT	G	PO	A	E	DP
Calixte	1.000	8	4	12	0	2
Castro	.971	17	6	27	1	4
Court	1.000	15	3	18	0	0
Long	.900	21	9	36	5	4
Lopes	.842	21	10	38	9	3
Mariscal	.923	39	20	52	6	6
Moore	1.000	1	0	2	0	0
Negron	.947	16	10	26	2	3
Nola	1.000	3	2	7	0	0
Seager	.917	5	2	9	1	1

Shortstop	PCT	G	PO	A	E	DP
Calixte	.917	3	6	5	1	3
Castro	1.000	4	5	12	0	2
Crawford	.964	31	28	78	4	15
Mariscal	1.000	14	16	37	0	8
Moore	.917	3	3	8	1	1

(Shortstop cont.)	PCT	G	PO	A	E	DP
Negron	.938	18	23	37	4	7
Tomlinson	.980	67	75	173	5	32

Outfield	PCT	G	PO	A	E	DP
Andreoli	.983	64	109	4	2	1
Bishop	.970	41	95	3	3	0
Brugman	.986	40	66	4	1	1
Calixte	1.000	6	11	0	0	0
Cooke	.974	17	37	1	1	1
Court	1.000	4	11	0	0	0
Filia	1.000	16	26	0	0	0
Fraley	.977	37	85	1	2	0
Knapp	1.000	12	30	0	0	0
Liberato	1.000	1	1	0	0	0
Long	1.000	12	20	1	0	0
Mariscal	1.000	4	3	0	0	0
Miller	.973	97	211	2	6	0
Negron	1.000	23	48	4	0	2
Perez	1.000	2	3	0	0	0
Polo	.947	10	18	0	1	0
Sheaffer	1.000	3	3	0	0	0
Slater	1.000	4	11	0	0	0
Smith	.920	10	12	1	2	1
Williamson	1.000	1	2	0	0	0
Young Jr.	1.000	22	35	1	0	0

ARKANSAS TRAVELERS   DOUBLE-A
TEXAS LEAGUE

Batting	B-T	HT	WT	DOB	AVG	vLH	vRH	G	AB	R	H	2B	3B	HR	RBI	BB	HBP	SH	SF	SO	SB	CS	SLG	OBP
Ahmed, Mike	R-R	6-2	195	1-20-92	.233	.200	.239	62	215	18	50	11	2	4	20	18	3	1	1	76	6	1	.358	.300
Cowan, Jordan	L-R	6-0	160	4-13-95	.264	.254	.266	124	440	49	116	13	0	2	33	53	4	3	4	85	17	4	.307	.345
DeCarlo, Joe	R-R	5-10	210	9-13-93	.170	.065	.193	52	171	17	29	4	0	1	14	21	4	0	2	65	0	0	.211	.273
Fraley, Jake	L-L	6-0	195	5-25-95	.313	.231	.330	61	230	40	72	15	2	11	47	23	5	0	1	55	16	5	.539	.386
Hoover, Connor	L-R	5-10	185	7-18-96	.000	.000	.000	3	7	1	0	0	0	0	0	0	0	0	0	4	0	0	.000	.000
Jones, Utah	B-R	6-0	165	5-28-96	.400	.429	.333	5	10	1	4	1	0	0	1	2	0	0	0	2	0	0	.500	.400
Kaleiwahea, Brennon	R-R	6-0	200	5-28-96	.250	.000	1.000	1	4	1	1	0	0	1	2	0	0	0	1	0	0	1.000	.250
Kelenic, Jarred	L-L	6-0	196	7-16-99	.253	.333	.239	21	83	11	21	4	1	6	17	8	0	1	17	3	0	.542	.315
Knapp, Aaron	L-R	5-10	175	11-4-94	.216	.173	.226	86	264	43	57	6	3	3	20	37	1	4	4	88	15	6	.296	.311
Lewis, Kyle	R-R	6-4	210	7-13-95	.263	.216	.272	122	457	61	120	25	2	11	62	56	1	0	3	152	3	2	.398	.342
Liberato, Luis	L-L	6-1	175	12-18-95	.237	.343	.214	52	194	25	46	10	1	2	18	15	0	2	0	49	4	1	.330	.292
Mariscal, Chris	R-R	5-10	170	4-26-93	.308	.286	.314	17	65	12	20	1	0	3	11	6	2	0	0	18	2	0	.462	.384
Odom, Joseph	R-R	6-2	225	1-29-92	.219	.293	.200	81	283	21	62	13	0	4	24	24	2	1	0	89	1	1	.307	.285
Raleigh, Cal	B-R	6-3	215	11-26-96	.228	.231	.227	39	145	16	33	6	0	7	16	14	0	0	0	47	0	0	.414	.296
Sheaffer, David	R-R	6-2	170	5-9-95	.188	.000	.250	6	16	5	3	0	0	1	2	3	0	0	0	3	0	0	.375	.316
Taylor, Logan	L-R	6-1	200	9-22-93	.212	.231	.208	107	387	36	82	14	1	7	44	26	5	0	5	132	4	3	.308	.267
Thompson-Williams, Dom	L-L	6-0	190	4-21-95	.234	.188	.242	115	432	46	101	24	4	12	41	35	6	0	4	152	15	2	.391	.298
Thurman, Nick	L-R	6-2	210	9-9-93	.032	.000	.039	9	31	2	1	0	0	1	1	2	0	1	0	22	0	0	.129	.091
Walton, Donnie	L-R	5-10	184	5-9-94	.300	.286	.303	124	480	72	144	22	3	11	50	63	10	2	3	72	10	13	.427	.390
White, Evan	R-L	6-3	205	4-26-96	.293	.318	.288	92	365	61	107	13	2	18	55	29	4	0	2	92	2	0	.488	.350
Zammarelli III, Nick	L-R	6-1	195	7-30-94	.231	.178	.245	101	347	35	80	13	3	9	42	30	6	1	3	109	2	2	.363	.301

Pitching	B-T	HT	WT	DOB	W	L	ERA	G	GS	CG	SV	IP	H	R	ER	HR	BB	SO	AVG	vLH	vRH	K/9	BB/9
Adams, Austin	R-R	6-3	225	5-5-91	1	0	0.00	2	0	0	0	2	0	0	0	0	2	5	.000	.000	.000	22.50	9.00
Altavilla, Dan	R-R	5-11	200	9-8-92	3	0	1.10	14	0	0	4	16	7	3	2	1	3	25	.125	.138	.111	13.78	1.65
Anderson, Jack	R-R	6-3	210	1-10-94	4	2	1.50	41	0	0	0	54	52	12	9	1	16	51	.259	.239	.275	8.50	2.67
Boches, Scott	R-R	6-5	205	10-17-94	0	1	6.75	2	1	0	0	7	10	5	5	2	2	4	.357	.429	.286	5.40	2.70
Bonnell, Bryan	L-R	6-5	240	9-28-93	1	0	4.26	10	0	0	0	19	18	9	9	2	4	19	.243	.308	.171	9.00	1.89
Cavanerio, Jorgan	R-R	6-1	155	8-18-94	2	0	7.88	7	1	0	1	16	29	18	14	1	0	13	.372	.348	.406	7.31	0.00
Cordero, Jimmy	R-R	6-4	222	10-19-91	0	0	0.00	1	0	0	0	1	1	0	0	0	1	2	.333	.000	.500	13.50	54.00
Crismatt, Nabil	R-R	6-1	215	12-25-94	4	5	1.94	14	13	2	0	84	57	22	18	6	11	89	.186	.209	.161	9.57	1.18
Delaplane, Sam	R-R	5-11	175	3-27-95	3	1	0.49	25	0	0	5	37	13	4	2	2	9	58	.107	.221	.000	14.11	2.19
Dunn, Justin	R-R	6-2	185	9-22-95	9	5	3.55	25	25	0	0	132	118	62	52	13	39	158	.236	.277	.200	10.80	2.67
Fletcher, Aaron	L-L	6-0	220	2-25-96	0	0	3.46	9	0	0	0	13	14	5	5	0	3	15	.275	.000	.359	10.38	2.08
Gerber, Joey	R-R	6-4	215	5-3-97	1	2	1.59	19	0	0	0	23	21	8	4	2	7	30	.247	.188	.283	11.91	2.78
Gilbert, Logan	R-R	6-6	225	5-5-97	4	2	2.88	9	9	0	0	50	34	16	16	2	15	56	.194	.180	.206	10.08	2.70
Gillies, Darin	R-R	6-4	220	11-6-92	2	1	3.62	16	1	0	4	27	24	13	11	3	9	22	.240	.259	.221	7.29	2.96

Pitcher	B-T	HT	WT	DOB	W	L	ERA	G	GS	CG	SV	IP	H	R	ER	HR	BB	SO	AVG	vLH	vRH	K/9	BB/9
Grotz, Zac	R-R	6-2	195	2-17-93	4	4	2.51	26	6	0	1	57	47	18	16	4	11	69	.225	.234	.216	10.83	1.73
Haberer, Jake	R-R	6-2	225	2-9-95	1	2	4.56	19	0	0	0	24	15	13	12	1	19	32	.183	.273	.122	12.17	7.23
Hernandez, Carlos	R-R	6-3	195	2-8-96	0	0	3.00	1	0	0	0	3	2	1	1	0	2	3	.200	.200	.200	9.00	6.00
Jaskie, Oliver	L-L	6-3	210	11-17-95	0	0	—	1	0	0	0	0	3	3	3	0	5	0	—	—	—	—	—
Knapp, Aaron	L-R	5-10	175	11-4-94	0	0	0.00	1	0	0	0	1	0	0	0	0	0	0	.000	.000	.000	0.00	0.00
Leyer, Robinson	R-R	6-2	175	3-13-93	1	0	8.71	9	0	0	1	10	19	11	10	0	7	11	.388	.350	.414	9.58	6.10
Markel, Parker	R-R	6-5	240	9-15-90	2	0	0.00	5	0	0	1	8	2	0	0	0	2	18	.080	.000	.182	21.13	2.35
Martinez, Bernie	R-R	6-0	195	12-24-96	0	0	9.00	2	0	0	0	5	6	5	5	3	0	4	.286	.625	.077	7.20	0.00
McCaughan, Darren	R-R	6-1	195	3-18-96	7	5	2.89	17	17	0	0	103	103	35	33	13	10	89	.258	.270	.246	7.80	0.88
McClain, Reggie	R-R	6-2	180	11-16-92	0	0	1.15	6	2	0	0	16	6	2	2	0	4	20	.122	.111	.136	11.49	2.30
McKinney, Ian	L-L	5-11	185	11-18-94	1	0	4.80	3	3	0	0	15	13	8	8	5	5	20	.232	.375	.208	12.00	3.00
Mills, Wyatt	R-R	6-3	175	1-25-95	4	2	4.27	41	0	0	8	53	43	26	25	2	17	66	.222	.216	.225	11.28	2.91
Misiewicz, Anthony	R-L	6-1	190	11-1-94	1	2	2.52	7	7	1	0	36	36	10	10	0	7	36	.269	.214	.294	9.08	1.77
Moore, Andrew	R-R	6-0	195	6-2-94	2	1	3.86	5	5	0	0	28	24	12	12	1	4	29	.233	.185	.286	9.32	1.29
Murfee, Penn	R-R	6-2	195	5-2-94	1	0	0.00	1	0	0	0	2	0	0	0	0	1	2	.000	.000	.000	9.00	4.50
Newsome, Ljay	R-R	5-11	210	11-8-96	3	4	2.77	9	9	0	0	49	41	15	15	4	7	35	.229	.260	.208	6.47	1.29
Northcraft, Aaron	R-R	6-4	230	5-28-90	0	0	1.69	3	0	0	0	5	4	1	1	0	0	3	.211	.111	.300	5.06	0.00
Sanchez, Ricardo	L-L	5-11	215	4-11-97	8	12	4.44	27	27	0	0	146	157	77	72	10	38	135	.279	.291	.274	8.32	2.34
Sheaffer, David	R-R	6-2	170	5-9-95	0	0	0.00	1	0	0	0	1	1	0	0	0	0	0	.250	1.000	.000	0.00	0.00
Sheffield, Justus	L-L	6-0	200	5-13-96	5	3	2.19	12	12	0	0	78	62	20	19	4	18	85	.218	.155	.239	9.81	2.08
Tenuta, Matt	L-L	6-4	225	12-16-93	3	2	2.56	33	0	0	1	46	34	14	13	6	11	48	.205	.129	.260	9.46	2.17
Tuivailala, Sam	R-R	6-3	225	10-19-92	0	0	0.00	5	0	0	0	5	1	0	0	0	2	6	.067	.000	.111	10.80	3.60
Walker, Matt	R-R	6-6	201	9-28-94	0	0	13.50	2	0	0	0	1	3	2	2	0	3	0	.429	.250	.667	0.00	20.25
Warren, Art	R-R	6-3	230	3-23-93	2	1	1.71	29	0	0	15	32	23	9	6	1	13	41	.202	.255	.153	11.65	3.69
Wilcox, Kyle	R-R	6-3	195	6-14-94	1	0	0.00	7	0	0	0	2	0	0	0	0	4	13	.069	.083	.059	13.00	4.00
Willrodt, Matthew	R-R	6-4	220	10-19-97	1	0	5.40	2	0	0	0	5	6	3	3	0	3	3	.333	.222	.444	5.40	5.40
Zammarelli III, Nick	L-R	6-1	195	7-30-94	0	0	36.00	1	0	0	0	1	3	4	4	1	1	1	.600	1.000	.500	9.00	9.00

Fielding

Catcher

Catcher	PCT	G	PO	A	E	DP	PB
DeCarlo	.987	37	290	24	4	0	9
Odom	.992	72	721	33	6	9	4
Raleigh	.988	26	228	14	3	2	2
Thurman	1.000	9	90	7	0	1	2

First Base

First Base	PCT	G	PO	A	E	DP
Ahmed	.982	7	52	4	1	2
DeCarlo	.981	8	49	2	1	5
Mariscal	1.000	1	4	1	0	1
Odom	1.000	7	60	4	0	9
White	.993	88	644	30	5	57
Zammarelli III	.981	30	242	11	5	18

Second Base

Second Base	PCT	G	PO	A	E	DP
Ahmed	1.000	3	5	3	0	1
Cowan	.995	113	178	251	2	64
Jones	1.000	1	1	1	0	1
Mariscal	1.000	2	0	11	0	0
Taylor	.938	3	6	9	1	3
Walton	.973	19	21	52	2	10

Third Base

Third Base	PCT	G	PO	A	E	DP
Ahmed	.985	28	20	45	1	4
Cowan	1.000	8	3	6	0	0
DeCarlo	1.000	10	6	11	0	0
Hoover	1.000	2	0	4	0	0
Jones	1.000	2	0	2	0	1
Mariscal	.800	5	3	5	2	0
Taylor	.944	91	46	123	10	7
Zammarelli III	.750	2	1	2	1	0

Shortstop

Shortstop	PCT	G	PO	A	E	DP
Ahmed	.952	25	30	70	5	10
Cowan	1.000	1	0	3	0	2
Hoover	1.000	1	0	3	0	1
Jones	1.000	1	0	2	0	1
Mariscal	1.000	10	10	26	0	5
Walton	.990	103	104	273	4	44

Outfield

Outfield	PCT	G	PO	A	E	DP
Fraley	.963	45	78	1	3	0
Kelenic	1.000	20	32	4	0	1
Knapp	.979	78	135	4	3	0
Lewis	.979	99	180	3	4	1
Liberato	.983	49	112	5	2	3
Sheaffer	1.000	3	1	0	0	0
Taylor	1.000	8	10	1	0	0
Thompson-Williams	.990	98	204	2	2	0
Zammarelli III	1.000	27	40	0	0	0

MODESTO NUTS

HIGH CLASS A

CALIFORNIA LEAGUE

Batting	B-T	HT	WT	DOB	AVG	vLH	vRH	G	AB	R	H	2B	3B	HR	RBI	BB	HBP	SH	SF	SO	SB	CS	SLG	OBP
Adams, Johnny	R-R	6-0	200	9-2-94	.201	.194	.202	117	394	43	79	11	3	6	35	35	5	7	1	122	6	3	.289	.274
Anchia, Jake	R-R	6-1	210	3-5-97	.105	.083	.115	11	38	2	4	0	0	0	0	5	0	0	0	15	0	0	.105	.209
Bishop, Braden	R-R	6-1	190	8-22-93	.240	.000	.333	7	25	7	6	1	1	0	3	2	2	0	0	9	0	0	.360	.345
Caballero, Jose	R-R	5-10	185	8-30-96	.256	.111	.292	23	90	16	23	5	1	0	10	12	2	0	5	15	4	5	.333	.339
2-team total (43 Visalia)					.264	.232	.273	66	254	52	67	17	1	3	22	36	10	2	5	55	32	12	.374	.371
Camacho, Juan	R-R	6-3	215	4-19-96	.000	—	.000	1	3	0	0	0	0	0	1	0	0	0	1	0	0	0	.000	.000
Cooke, Billy	R-R	5-10	175	9-26-95	.286	.500	.250	5	7	1	2	0	0	0	0	2	1	0	0	2	1	0	.286	.500
Crawford, J.P.	L-R	6-2	180	1-11-95	.100	—	.100	3	10	2	1	0	0	1	3	2	0	0	0	5	0	0	.400	.250
Haniger, Mitch	R-R	6-2	215	12-23-90	.167	.000	.333	2	6	2	1	1	0	0	1	1	1	0	0	2	0	0	.333	.375
Helder, Eugene	R-R	5-11	165	2-26-96	.234	.207	.239	94	359	36	84	14	1	6	36	31	0	1	1	86	1	4	.329	.294
Hoover, Connor	L-R	5-10	185	7-18-96	.000	—	.000	4	10	0	0	0	0	0	0	0	0	0	0	5	0	0	.000	.000
Jimenez, Anthony	R-R	5-11	165	10-21-95	.223	.242	.219	51	188	22	42	9	4	2	12	15	8	0	0	53	10	6	.346	.308
Kelenic, Jarred	L-L	6-0	196	7-16-99	.290	.269	.294	46	169	36	49	13	1	6	22	17	1	0	3	49	10	3	.485	.353
Kopach, Connor	R-R	6-0	170	8-4-94	.224	.243	.220	99	375	55	84	23	5	8	45	41	9	4	6	116	25	5	.376	.311
Larsen, Jack	L-R	6-1	195	6-13-95	.237	.225	.239	118	443	59	105	25	6	12	63	65	1	3	2	157	5	1	.402	.335
Lepre, Anthony	R-R	5-10	195	5-29-97	—	—	—	1	0	0	0	0	0	0	0	1	0	0	0	0	0	0	—	1.000
Liberato, Luis	L-L	6-1	175	12-18-95	.283	.265	.288	44	166	25	47	5	0	7	29	20	1	3	2	41	4	2	.440	.360
McGovern, Keegan	R-R	6-3	200	9-13-95	.210	.184	.217	65	224	34	47	9	1	10	28	30	14	0	1	89	0	0	.393	.338
Morgan, Gareth	R-R	6-4	265	4-12-96	.074	.000	.083	8	27	2	2	0	0	1	3	6	0	0	0	20	1	0	.185	.219
2-team total (44 Inland Empire)					.262	.327	.242	52	210	34	55	5	0	21	52	14	2	0	2	115	1	1	.586	.311
Pazos, Manny	R-R	5-11	190	1-23-95	.236	.333	.200	21	55	10	13	3	1	0	5	12	0	1	0	23	1	0	.327	.373
Raleigh, Cal	S-R	6-3	215	11-26-96	.261	.222	.270	82	310	48	81	19	0	22	66	33	3	0	2	69	4	0	.536	.336
Rivera, Jansiel	L-L	6-1	205	8-28-98	.182	1.000	.100	4	11	1	2	0	0	0	0	0	0	0	0	5	0	1	.182	.182
Rizzo, Joe	L-R	5-10	194	3-31-98	.295	.321	.290	129	518	77	153	30	3	10	63	45	4	0	3	94	0	3	.423	.354

	B-T	HT	WT	DOB	AVG	vLH	vRH	G	AB	R	H	2B	3B	HR	RBI	BB	HBP	SH	SF	SO	SB	CS	SLG	OBP
Rodriguez, Julio	R-R	6-4	225	12-29-00	.462	.429	.466	17	65	13	30	6	3	2	19	5	2	0	0	10	0	0	.739	.514
Rosa, Joseph	B-R	5-10	165	3-6-97	.277	.241	.287	38	130	21	36	11	2	1	14	17	3	2	2	34	1	2	.415	.368
Sanders, Matt	R-R	5-8	175	6-7-96	.232	.180	.242	68	237	17	55	8	0	1	20	17	2	1	4	41	3	3	.279	.285
Sandoval, Ariel	R-R	6-2	180	11-6-95	.239	.210	.246	99	355	48	85	26	3	6	37	24	3	1	1	108	11	3	.380	.292
Santa, Kevin	L-R	5-11	175	3-9-95	.353	.000	.429	4	17	2	6	0	0	0	3	2	0	0	0	2	2	0	.353	.421
Scheiner, Jake	R-R	6-1	200	8-13-95	.271	.283	.268	74	288	53	78	15	5	14	63	20	5	1	4	79	2	4	.504	.325
Sheaffer, David	R-R	6-2	170	5-9-95	.247	.133	.274	22	77	9	19	3	0	4	9	7	0	0	2	19	1	0	.442	.302
Thurman, Nick	L-R	6-2	210	9-9-93	.174	.031	.204	57	184	16	32	8	0	3	9	16	3	5	0	81	4	1	.266	.251

Pitching	B-T	HT	WT	DOB	W	L	ERA	G	GS	CG	SV	IP	H	R	ER	HR	BB	SO	AVG	vLH	vRH	K/9	BB/9
Adams, Johnny	R-R	6-0	200	9-2-94	0	1	4.50	5	0	0	1	4	7	3	2	0	3	3	.368	.300	.444	6.75	6.75
Arias, Dayeison	R-R	6-1	160	1-7-97	2	0	0.00	5	0	0	0	7	3	1	0	0	2	10	.125	.250	.063	12.27	2.45
Bautista, Gerson	R-R	6-3	195	5-31-95	0	0	3.60	5	0	0	0	5	1	2	2	0	4	9	.067	.111	.000	16.20	7.20
Boches, Scott	R-R	6-5	205	10-17-94	2	7	3.65	41	1	0	1	74	61	38	30	2	30	98	.224	.219	.228	11.92	3.65
Casetta-Stubbs, Damon	R-R	6-4	225	7-22-99	0	0	0.00	1	0	0	0	2	2	4	0	0	2	3	.182	.250	.143	11.57	7.71
Chandler, Clay	R-R	6-3	180	4-27-94	2	2	4.96	9	9	0	0	45	50	29	25	6	11	38	.269	.258	.274	7.54	2.18
Delaplane, Sam	R-R	5-11	175	3-27-95	3	2	4.26	21	0	0	2	32	22	16	15	2	14	62	.200	.229	.187	17.62	3.98
Duron, Nick	R-R	6-4	190	1-30-96	3	1	2.23	25	0	0	2	36	31	13	9	1	17	51	.228	.130	.293	12.63	4.21
Ellingson, David	R-R	6-2	200	1-23-95	0	1	2.61	11	0	0	1	21	23	11	6	1	7	22	.277	.375	.237	9.58	3.05
Garcia, Danny	L-L	6-1	195	2-21-94	0	0	3.60	6	0	0	0	10	7	4	4	0	7	11	.206	.200	.208	9.90	6.30
Gerber, Joey	R-R	6-4	215	5-3-97	0	2	3.46	25	0	0	8	26	17	10	10	0	12	39	.185	.259	.154	13.50	4.15
Gilbert, Logan	R-R	6-6	225	5-5-97	5	3	1.73	12	12	0	0	62	52	16	12	3	12	73	.228	.226	.229	10.54	1.73
Haberer, Jake	R-R	6-2	225	2-9-95	3	1	3.74	16	0	0	1	22	13	12	9	0	11	34	.169	.035	.250	14.12	4.57
Hernandez, Carlos	R-R	6-3	195	2-8-96	0	0	0.00	1	0	0	0	4	3	2	0	0	2	3	.214	.000	.273	6.23	4.15
Hernandez, Felix	R-R	6-3	225	4-8-86	0	0	9.00	1	1	0	0	2	3	2	2	0	0	3	.333	.500	.200	13.50	0.00
Hutchison, Austin	R-R	6-1	205	4-9-95	5	12	4.64	26	24	0	0	130	144	79	67	15	53	136	.282	.308	.267	9.42	3.67
Johnson, Evan	R-R	5-11	190	1-17-97	0	0	12.00	1	1	0	0	3	4	4	4	0	2	5	.333	.167	.500	15.00	6.00
Kerr, Raymond	L-L	6-3	185	9-10-94	3	7	3.91	35	10	0	4	90	85	54	39	1	51	93	.252	.244	.255	9.33	5.12
Kober, Collin	R-R	6-1	185	9-8-94	4	2	3.42	47	0	0	2	68	71	30	26	4	20	91	.264	.280	.256	11.99	2.63
Martinez, Bernie	R-R	6-0	195	12-24-96	0	1	31.50	2	0	0	0	2	6	7	7	1	4	1	.500	.571	.400	4.50	18.00
McClain, Reggie	R-R	6-2	180	11-16-92	0	0	0.56	6	0	0	0	16	9	1	1	0	1	8	.155	.118	.171	10.13	0.00
McKinney, Ian	L-L	5-11	185	11-18-94	12	5	2.84	25	25	1	0	136	108	53	43	6	54	148	.218	.245	.211	9.77	3.56
Mercedes, Juan	R-R	6-2	190	4-3-00	0	1	2.25	2	0	0	0	4	3	1	1	0	0	2	.214	.250	.200	4.50	0.00
Morgan, Reid	R-R	6-0	187	3-24-97	0	1	0.00	2	0	0	0	2	1	0	0	1	1	2	.300	.500	.167	7.71	3.86
Moyers, Steven	R-L	6-0	190	9-27-93	3	3	5.16	9	8	0	0	52	65	36	30	3	10	44	.304	.283	.310	7.57	1.72
Murfee, Penn	R-R	6-2	195	5-2-94	5	5	3.07	26	20	0	0	103	95	40	35	3	23	122	.245	.299	.212	10.69	2.02
Newsome, Ljay	R-R	5-11	210	11-8-96	6	6	3.75	18	18	1	0	101	105	44	42	11	9	124	.266	.297	.246	11.09	0.80
Nunez, Kelvin	R-R	6-1	170	12-10-99	0	0	5.40	1	0	0	0	2	3	1	1	0	1	3	.375	1.000	.167	16.20	5.40
Pazos, Manny	R-R	5-11	190	1-23-95	0	1	36.00	1	0	0	0	1	3	5	4	0	2	0	.600	1.000	.333	0.00	18.00
Salter, J.T.	R-R	6-8	295	6-10-96	1	2	5.14	28	0	0	0	42	34	27	24	2	33	46	.222	.210	.231	9.86	7.07
Stryffeler, Michael	R-R	6-2	210	5-22-96	0	0	6.75	2	0	0	0	1	3	2	1	0	0	3	.429	.500	.400	20.25	0.00
Sweet, Devin	B-R	5-11	183	9-6-96	1	0	0.96	3	3	0	0	19	12	3	2	1	4	21	.182	.214	.158	10.13	1.93
Thurman, Nick	L-R	6-2	210	9-9-93	0	0	0.00	2	0	0	0	2	1	0	0	0	1	1	.143	.250	.000	4.50	4.50
Tuivailala, Sam	R-R	6-3	225	10-19-92	0	1	1.50	6	0	0	0	6	1	1	1	2	6		.053	.000	.091	9.00	3.00
Walker, Matt	R-R	6-6	201	9-28-94	0	0	8.49	13	3	0	0	12	13	12	11	2	14	19	.277	.200	.313	14.66	10.80
Wells, Nick	L-L	6-5	185	2-21-96	1	2	7.91	5	5	0	0	19	23	20	17	2	7	21	.303	.154	.333	9.78	3.26
Wilcox, Kyle	R-R	6-3	195	6-14-94	2	5	3.76	39	0	0	2	53	39	26	22	4	45	78	.204	.254	.175	13.33	7.69
Willrodt, Matthew	R-R	6-4	220	10-19-97	2	1	2.53	19	0	0	2	43	36	13	12	2	8	36	.229	.177	.263	7.59	1.69

Fielding

Catcher	PCT	G	PO	A	E	DP	PB
Anchia	1.000	11	96	13	0	3	2
Camacho	1.000	1	10	1	0	0	0
Lepre	.000	1	0	0	0	0	0
Pazos	1.000	3	31	3	0	1	2
Raleigh	.984	55	575	57	10	3	8
Sheaffer	.985	21	177	16	3	0	3
Thurman	.986	55	568	59	9	5	12

First Base	PCT	G	PO	A	E	DP
Helder	.989	83	572	43	7	49
Larsen	1.000	1	1	0	0	0
Rizzo	.995	31	199	14	1	14
Scheiner	.991	28	205	10	2	21
Sheaffer	1.000	1	4	0	0	0

Second Base	PCT	G	PO	A	E	DP
Caballero	1.000	6	6	11	0	5
Hoover	1.000	3	10	5	0	3
Kopach	.987	42	75	76	2	14
Pazos	.895	10	5	12	2	2
Rizzo	.941	8	4	12	1	2
Rosa	.966	33	67	76	5	26
Sanders	.989	49	75	104	2	25

Third Base	PCT	G	PO	A	E	DP
Adams	.800	8	5	7	3	2
Helder	.857	8	2	10	2	0
Kopach	.905	9	5	14	2	0
Rizzo	.916	85	37	126	15	12
Sanders	.955	15	4	17	1	0
Santa	1.000	3	0	6	0	0
Scheiner	.846	19	10	23	6	4
Sheaffer	1.000	1	0	1	0	0

Shortstop	PCT	G	PO	A	E	DP
Adams	.961	105	147	224	15	45
Caballero	.943	19	29	54	5	11
Crawford	1.000	3	3	7	0	1
Kopach	.931	16	21	33	4	10
Rosa	1.000	2	2	3	0	0
Sanders	1.000	1	0	2	0	0
Santa	.750	1	2	1	1	0

Outfield	PCT	G	PO	A	E	DP
Bishop	1.000	3	10	1	0	0
Cooke	1.000	5	3	0	0	0
Haniger	1.000	1	2	0	0	0
Jimenez	.910	40	60	1	6	0
Kelenic	.920	42	79	1	7	1
Kopach	.958	37	63	6	3	1
Larsen	.969	115	217	3	7	0
Liberato	1.000	41	92	3	0	1
McGovern	.984	37	59	2	1	1
Morgan	.000	1	0	0	0	0
Pazos	1.000	2	3	0	0	0
Rivera	1.000	4	4	0	0	0
Rodriguez	.950	16	19	0	1	0
Sandoval	.980	75	144	4	3	1
Scheiner	.963	22	25	1	1	0

WEST VIRGINIA POWER

LOW CLASS A

SOUTH ATLANTIC LEAGUE

Batting	B-T	HT	WT	DOB	AVG	vLH	vRH	G	AB	R	H	2B	3B	HR	RBI	BB	HBP	SH	SF	SO	SB	CS	SLG	OBP

Anchia, Jake	R-R	6-1	210	3-5-97	.213	.123	.240	81	286	39	61	10	0	12	43	25	6	0	2	107	0	0	.374	.288
Cooke, Billy	R-R	5-10	175	9-26-95	.231	.400	.172	12	39	4	9	3	0	0	2	2	3	1	0	13	2	2	.308	.318
Davis, J.R.	R-R	5-10	190	8-10-94	.239	.178	.259	47	180	24	43	6	0	2	14	15	5	0	0	35	2	0	.306	.315
Honeyman, Bobby	L-R	6-1	185	5-25-96	.280	.237	.292	122	460	63	129	20	0	7	57	36	7	1	5	65	2	2	.370	.339
Hoover, Connor	L-R	5-10	185	7-18-96	.188	.250	.167	6	16	1	3	1	0	0	2	1	0	0	0	10	1	0	.250	.316
Izturis Jr., Cesar	B-R	5-11	145	11-11-99	.215	.156	.235	38	130	15	28	3	0	0	10	5	3	1	2	35	3	1	.239	.257
Jones, Utah	B-R	6-0	165	5-28-96	.159	.177	.148	12	44	3	7	3	0	0	2	4	0	0	0	13	0	0	.227	.229
Kelenic, Jarred	L-L	6-0	196	7-16-99	.309	.240	.333	50	191	33	59	14	3	11	29	25	2	0	0	45	7	4	.586	.395
Lepre, Anthony	R-R	5-10	195	5-29-97	.063	.000	.077	5	16	0	1	0	0	0	0	1	0	0	0	8	0	0	.063	.118
McConnell, Charlie	L-R	6-2	195	1-7-96	.200	.163	.211	113	395	43	79	18	3	3	38	31	2	3	3	127	11	0	.284	.260
McGovern, Keegan	L-R	6-3	200	9-13-95	.263	.333	.250	10	38	5	10	3	1	2	5	4	1	0	0	9	0	0	.553	.349
Moses, DeAires	L-L	5-9	170	11-30-95	.150	.000	.182	13	40	0	6	0	2	0	3	1	0	0	1	21	0	0	.250	.167
Nevarez, Dean	R-R	6-0	220	1-4-97	.227	.133	.263	47	163	20	37	8	0	7	28	13	2	0	0	55	0	0	.405	.292
Ogren, Ryne	R-R	6-0	180	4-11-97	.174	.000	.235	13	46	5	8	1	0	2	5	4	0	0	0	11	0	0	.326	.240
2-team total (92 Delmarva)					.243	.169	.264	105	354	42	86	14	2	3	36	37	10	1	2	86	5	1	.319	.330
Pazos, Manny	R-R	5-11	190	1-23-95	.155	.189	.139	50	161	20	25	5	1	1	9	22	1	0	2	49	0	0	.217	.258
Pena, Onil	R-R	6-0	180	11-6-96	.208	.219	.205	117	413	54	86	25	2	15	60	53	14	0	4	159	0	2	.387	.316
Ramiz, Ryan	L-L	6-1	185	1-13-96	.230	.144	.253	119	453	61	104	23	3	7	42	65	1	1	1	140	4	2	.340	.327
Ricca, Caleb	R-R	5-8	165	10-21-97	.114	.111	.115	10	35	3	4	0	0	1	2	0	0	0	0	17	1	0	.200	.162
Rodriguez, Julio	R-R	6-4	225	12-29-00	.293	.295	.292	67	263	50	77	20	1	10	50	20	9	0	3	66	1	3	.491	.359
Rodriguez, Nick	R-R	6-2	170	6-28-96	.186	.216	.175	79	263	17	49	15	0	4	29	17	4	0	2	73	0	1	.289	.245
Rosa, Joseph	B-R	5-10	165	3-6-97	.268	.227	.282	80	272	39	73	15	2	3	33	33	10	0	3	64	6	4	.371	.365
Salvatore, Mike	R-R	6-0	186	12-27-96	.175	.133	.185	42	149	15	26	5	0	1	10	12	1	0	4	29	1	0	.228	.235
Sanders, Matt	R-R	5-8	175	6-7-96	.300	.375	.277	43	170	31	51	10	0	5	20	11	1	1	2	20	0	1	.447	.342
Sheaffer, David	R-R	6-2	170	5-9-95	.314	.409	.281	22	86	11	27	10	0	1	12	6	2	0	1	26	0	0	.465	.368
Shenton, Austin	L-R	6-0	195	1-22-98	.252	.231	.258	32	119	13	30	7	1	5	20	11	3	0	1	29	0	0	.454	.328
Slater, Johnny	L-L	6-1	190	8-9-95	.148	.056	.175	26	81	9	12	5	2	1	5	10	3	1	0	38	2	2	.296	.266
Trejo, Cesar	R-R	6-2	200	5-15-97	.180	.063	.210	24	78	11	14	2	1	3	13	10	1	0	1	35	3	1	.346	.278

Pitching	B-T	HT	WT	DOB	W	L	ERA	G	GS	CG	SV	IP	H	R	ER	HR	BB	SO	AVG	vLH	vRH	K/9	BB/9
Alvarado, Elvis	R-R	6-4	183	2-23-99	0	0	5.40	1	0	0	0	2	1	1	1	1	0	2	.167	.000	.250	10.80	0.00
Arias, Dayeison	R-R	6-1	160	1-7-97	2	1	1.32	39	0	0	13	48	25	11	7	3	13	70	.149	.164	.140	13.22	2.45
Biasi, Sal	R-R	5-11	205	9-30-95	6	4	5.36	31	0	0	0	49	43	31	29	6	30	58	.239	.246	.235	10.73	5.55
Casetta-Stubbs, Damon	R-R	6-4	225	7-22-99	3	5	7.11	10	10	0	0	44	61	35	35	4	13	37	.337	.379	.313	7.51	2.64
Chandler, Clay	R-R	6-3	180	4-27-94	8	5	3.89	19	19	1	0	111	111	52	48	12	18	104	.261	.286	.237	8.43	1.46
De Los Santos, Josias	R-R	6-2	174	7-29-99	4	8	4.97	22	17	0	1	101	101	62	56	13	39	83	.259	.244	.270	7.37	3.46
Driver, Tyler	R-R	6-2	185	2-4-01	0	0	0.00	1	0	0	0	3	1	0	0	0	1	3	.100	.000	.167	9.00	3.00
Ellingson, David	R-R	6-2	200	1-23-95	3	3	2.95	21	0	0	4	37	35	14	12	1	14	37	.252	.207	.284	9.08	3.44
Espino, Elias	R-R	6-2	195	4-19-97	2	3	4.18	29	1	0	2	56	45	33	26	8	29	57	.220	.215	.223	9.16	4.66
Fisher, Nate	L-L	6-1	205	5-28-96	0	1	5.33	5	5	0	0	25	35	16	15	3	5	17	.330	.276	.351	6.04	1.78
Florido, Deivy	R-R	6-2	165	9-17-00	2	3	4.95	10	6	0	0	40	51	29	22	6	7	27	.311	.315	.308	6.08	1.53
Gilbert, Logan	R-R	6-6	225	5-5-97	1	0	1.59	5	5	0	0	23	9	4	4	2	6	36	.118	.097	.133	14.29	2.38
Hill, Kyle	R-R	5-11	200	5-12-97	1	2	6.05	14	0	0	0	19	24	18	13	4	7	21	.304	.480	.222	9.78	3.26
Hoffman, Nolan	R-R	6-4	190	8-9-97	0	1	1.08	9	0	0	4	8	4	2	1	0	4	7	.138	.273	.056	7.56	4.32
Inman, Ryne	R-R	6-5	215	5-13-96	8	7	4.42	26	26	2	0	126	106	77	62	14	53	146	.224	.266	.191	10.40	3.78
Jaskie, Oliver	L-L	6-3	210	11-17-95	0	0	9.82	3	2	0	0	7	10	8	8	1	14	9	.345	.375	.333	11.05	17.18
Johnson, Evan	R-R	5-11	190	1-17-97	2	4	4.70	9	9	0	0	38	35	26	20	2	21	36	.235	.238	.233	8.45	4.93
Kuhn, Travis	R-R	5-10	195	5-20-98	0	0	9.00	2	0	0	0	4	4	2	2	0	3	4	.400	.333	.429	18.00	13.50
Martin, Matt	R-R	6-1	190	7-8-96	1	1	2.65	3	3	0	0	17	11	5	5	2	3	11	.180	.160	.194	5.82	1.59
Martin, Reeves	R-R	5-8	180	12-25-96	3	0	3.09	16	0	0	0	23	27	8	8	3	5	24	.281	.325	.250	9.26	1.93
Martinez, Bernie	R-R	6-2	195	12-24-96	1	1	1.50	1	1	0	0	6	4	1	1	0	0	5	.182	.143	.250	7.50	0.00
McGuigan, Brendan	R-R	6-2	210	10-9-95	1	1	1.59	5	0	0	0	11	9	10	2	0	4	12	.192	.263	.143	9.53	3.18
Morgan, Reid	R-R	6-0	187	3-24-97	1	1	6.91	7	0	0	0	14	21	14	11	4	2	12	.333	.438	.298	7.53	1.26
Moyers, Steven	R-L	6-0	190	9-27-93	7	4	3.86	19	18	0	0	112	123	54	48	9	17	110	.280	.353	.253	8.84	1.37
Nevarez, Dean	R-R	6-0	220	1-4-97	0	0	13.50	1	0	0	0	1	1	1	1	0	0	0	.333	1.000	.000	0.00	0.00
Onyshko, Benjamin	R-L	6-2	205	10-18-96	3	4	3.99	38	1	0	2	70	77	43	31	4	24	82	.277	.256	.286	10.54	3.09
Pall, Bryan	R-R	6-1	215	10-28-95	1	0	2.04	29	0	0	6	35	22	9	8	0	14	45	.175	.218	.141	11.46	3.57
Pedrol, Christian	R-R	5-11	190	6-15-00	0	1	4.50	1	0	0	0	6	5	3	3	2	2	9	.227	.250	.214	13.50	3.00
Rinehart, Logan	R-R	6-3	185	9-21-97	0	1	3.52	10	0	0	1	23	23	10	9	0	3	19	.264	.184	.327	7.43	1.17
Rodriguez, Nick	R-R	6-2	170	6-28-96	0	0	22.50	2	0	0	0	2	7	5	5	1	1	1	.539	.800	.375	4.50	4.50
Slater, Johnny	L-L	6-1	190	8-9-95	1	0	0.00	1	0	0	0	1	0	0	0	0	0	0	.000	.000	.000	0.00	0.00
Sweet, Devin	B-R	5-11	183	9-6-96	7	5	3.06	31	12	1	0	109	100	41	37	8	23	131	.244	.224	.257	10.85	1.90
Then, Juan	R-R	6-1	155	2-7-00	1	2	2.25	3	3	0	0	16	7	4	4	1	4	14	.127	.154	.103	7.88	2.25
Wade, Jamal	R-R	6-0	205	2-8-96	1	1	3.86	2	0	0	0	5	4	2	2	0	4	10	.235	.273	.167	19.29	7.71
Willrodt, Matthew	R-R	6-4	220	10-19-97	0	2	8.44	12	0	0	0	21	25	23	20	3	15	25	.294	.286	.302	10.55	6.33
Winslow, Robert	R-R	6-5	215	8-19-97	0	0	1.50	4	0	0	1	6	4	1	1	0	3	6	.191	.125	.231	9.00	4.50

Fielding

Catcher	PCT	G	PO	A	E	DP	PB
Anchia	.987	68	628	64	9	4	15
Lepre	1.000	4	41	5	0	0	0
Nevarez	.990	34	274	28	3	4	3
Pazos	.987	33	266	31	4	0	9
Sheaffer	1.000	4	36	6	0	0	0

First Base	PCT	G	PO	A	E	DP
Honeyman	1.000	3	17	2	0	3
Pazos	.964	6	23	4	1	3
Pena	.985	111	740	42	12	55
Rodriguez	.984	16	119	6	2	6
Sheaffer	.972	3	32	3	1	4

Second Base	PCT	G	PO	A	E	DP
Davis	.980	15	22	27	1	4
Hoover	.938	3	8	7	1	3
Izturis Jr.	.936	13	28	16	3	5
Ogren	1.000	1	2	4	0	1
Pazos	.750	2	4	2	2	0
Rodriguez	.947	35	61	65	7	11

	PCT	G	PO	A	E	DP
Rosa	.965	41	70	96	6	18
Sanders	.969	26	36	57	3	9
Shenton	.926	8	11	14	2	2

Third Base	PCT	G	PO	A	E	DP
Honeyman	.955	110	79	154	11	8
Hoover	1.000	1	0	1	0	0
Ogren	1.000	3	4	2	0	0
Ricca	.667	1	2	0	1	0
Rodriguez	.778	10	7	7	4	0
Rosa	.800	1	0	4	1	0
Sanders	.882	7	6	9	2	1
Shenton	.813	7	2	11	3	2

Shortstop	PCT	G	PO	A	E	DP
Honeyman	1.000	1	1	3	0	0
Hoover	1.000	1	0	1	0	0
Izturis Jr.	.977	25	24	60	2	10
Jones	.933	12	13	29	3	7
Ogren	.939	9	17	14	2	5
Ricca	.885	8	14	9	3	2
Rosa	.968	37	41	81	4	11
Salvatore	.973	42	55	87	4	19
Sanders	.962	8	12	13	1	1

Outfield	PCT	G	PO	A	E	DP
Cooke	1.000	12	35	0	0	0

	PCT	G	PO	A	E	DP
Davis	.972	16	35	0	1	0
Honeyman	1.000	4	9	0	0	0
Kelenic	.953	44	78	4	4	1
McConnell	.993	109	264	9	2	2
Moses	.963	13	26	0	1	0
Pazos	1.000	7	15	1	0	0
Ramiz	.969	102	185	2	6	0
Ricca	1.000	1	1	0	0	0
Rodriguez	.987	61	141	7	2	2
Rodriguez	1.000	7	14	0	0	0
Sheaffer	1.000	11	16	0	0	0
Shenton	1.000	6	11	0	0	0
Slater	.965	26	51	4	2	3
Trejo	1.000	12	21	1	0	0

EVERETT AQUASOX
NORTHWEST LEAGUE

SHORT SEASON

Batting	B-T	HT	WT	DOB	AVG	vLH	vRH	G	AB	R	H	2B	3B	HR	RBI	BB	HBP	SH	SF	SO	SB	CS	SLG	OBP
Bins, Carter	R-R	6-0	200	10-7-98	.208	.174	.222	49	154	31	32	2	0	7	26	33	14	0	1	56	5	2	.357	.391
Camacho, Juan	R-R	6-3	215	4-19-96	.188	.184	.190	36	117	8	22	2	0	2	9	5	1	0	1	32	0	0	.256	.256
Cooke, Billy	R-R	5-10	175	9-26-95	.304	.500	.235	22	69	14	21	2	3	2	8	7	5	2	0	19	7	2	.507	.407
Court, Ryan	R-R	6-2	210	5-28-88	.400	1.000	.333	4	10	5	4	0	0	1	3	4	1	0	0	4	0	0	.700	.600
Frick, Patrick	R-R	6-2	200	2-14-97	.302	.241	.323	60	215	46	65	12	0	0	21	41	9	0	2	40	7	6	.358	.431
Gladfelter, Cash	L-R	6-4	200	11-9-96	.188	.154	.200	46	154	20	29	8	1	4	26	16	0	0	1	75	2	1	.331	.263
Hoover, Connor	L-R	5-10	185	7-18-96	.226	.357	.184	34	115	21	26	7	3	5	24	25	2	1	3	38	9	1	.470	.366
Izturis Jr., Cesar	B-R	5-11	145	11-11-99	.285	.255	.299	60	214	29	61	10	1	0	32	23	4	3	2	41	11	3	.341	.362
Jones, Utah	B-R	6-0	165	5-28-96	.233	.161	.255	34	133	34	31	2	1	3	16	17	6	0	1	24	4	1	.331	.344
Joseph, Luis	R-R	5-9	160	9-20-96	.211	.231	.204	47	142	17	30	12	2	1	14	6	0	0	3	35	0	1	.345	.238
Kaleiwahea, Brennon	R-R	6-0	200	5-28-96	.226	.125	.244	17	53	7	12	2	1	2	3	7	3	1	0	20	0	0	.415	.349
Marlowe, Cade	L-R	6-2	200	6-24-97	.301	.392	.274	62	219	29	66	15	3	3	30	26	1	1	4	62	10	5	.438	.372
Moses, DeAires	L-L	5-9	170	11-30-95	.192	.292	.160	36	99	21	19	2	3	3	11	19	3	2	2	42	15	6	.364	.333
Nevarez, Dean	R-R	6-0	220	1-4-97	.200	.182	.206	12	45	2	9	4	0	0	1	4	0	0	1	12	0	2	.289	.260
Perez, Miguel	R-R	6-2	170	8-21-00	.179	.216	.169	67	223	19	40	11	3	5	25	29	2	2	2	103	5	5	.323	.277
Perez, Robert	R-R	6-1	170	6-26-00	.233	.220	.238	54	206	31	48	9	0	7	36	23	7	0	4	68	1	1	.379	.325
Santa, Kevin	L-R	5-11	175	3-9-95	.191	.000	.200	6	21	2	4	0	0	1	3	0	0	0	1	1	0	.191	.292
Shenton, Austin	L-R	6-0	195	1-22-98	.367	.400	.356	21	79	16	29	10	1	2	16	8	4	0	1	15	0	0	.595	.446
Tingelstad, Trent	L-R	5-10	215	6-14-98	.240	.222	.246	67	242	33	58	11	1	5	41	51	1	1	3	64	2	2	.355	.370

Pitching	B-T	HT	WT	DOB	W	L	ERA	G	GS	CG	SV	IP	H	R	ER	HR	BB	SO	AVG	vLH	vRH	K/9	BB/9
Altavilla, Dan	R-R	5-11	200	9-8-92	0	0	0.00	1	0	0	0	0	0	0	0	0	2	.000	.000	.000	18.00	0.00
Bayless, Jarod	R-R	6-4	225	12-29-96	0	0	5.63	5	0	0	1	8	13	5	5	1	0	12	.394	.417	.381	13.50	0.00
Benitez, Jorge	L-L	6-2	155	6-1-99	2	3	4.91	15	3	0	0	55	48	36	30	2	38	55	.235	.277	.223	9.00	6.22
Bins, Carter	R-R	6-0	200	10-7-98	0	0	0.00	1	0	0	0	1	0	0	0	0	1	.500	1.000	.000	0.00	0.00
Camacho, Juan	R-R	6-3	215	4-19-96	0	0	33.75	1	0	0	0	1	7	5	5	2	0	0	.636	.600	.667	0.00	0.00
Casetta-Stubbs, Damon	R-R	6-4	225	7-22-99	3	3	4.11	15	15	0	0	70	52	37	32	7	27	67	.206	.147	.227	8.61	3.47
Curvelo, Luis	R-R	6-1	170	10-21-00	1	1	9.00	4	0	0	0	18	14	14	3	5	5	.316	.391	.265	3.21	3.21
Elliott, Tim	R-R	6-1	200	10-11-97	1	3	3.86	14	11	0	0	30	29	17	13	1	13	35	.250	.182	.292	10.38	3.86
Fisher, Nate	L-L	6-1	205	5-28-96	0	1	2.20	7	1	0	1	16	16	5	4	0	2	23	.250	.250	.250	12.67	1.10
Florido, Deivy	R-R	6-2	165	9-17-00	4	1	4.76	10	3	0	0	51	53	30	27	9	11	34	.261	.228	.288	6.00	1.94
Fortunato, Ivan	R-R	6-1	170	12-1-98	0	0	3.20	17	0	0	0	25	26	14	9	1	13	30	.252	.294	.232	10.66	4.62
Gladfelter, Cash	L-R	6-4	200	11-9-96	0	1	7.71	2	0	0	0	2	5	2	2	1	0	1	.500	.750	.333	3.86	0.00
Hernandez, Felix	R-R	6-3	225	4-8-86	0	0	0.00	2	2	0	0	6	1	0	0	0	10	.053	.000	.125	15.00	0.00
Johnson, Evan	R-R	5-11	190	1-17-97	0	1	3.07	5	2	0	1	15	6	5	5	1	10	14	.125	.154	.114	8.59	6.14
Joseph, Luis	R-R	5-9	160	9-20-96	0	0	27.00	2	0	0	0	2	4	6	6	0	4	0	.444	.333	.500	0.00	18.00
Kirby, George	R-R	6-4	201	2-4-98	0	0	2.35	9	8	0	0	23	24	6	6	1	0	25	.270	.263	.275	9.78	0.00
Kuhn, Travis	R-R	5-10	195	5-20-98	5	3	6.95	18	0	0	4	22	20	19	17	3	11	25	.238	.290	.208	10.23	4.50
Macko, Adam	L-L	6-0	170	12-30-00	0	0	0.00	1	0	0	0	2	0	0	0	0	1	1	1.000	.000	.000	4.50	4.50
Marte, Cristhopher	R-R	6-2	170	4-2-99	0	1	9.00	1	0	0	0	2	4	2	2	0	0	.444	.250	.600	0.00	0.00
Martin, Matt	R-R	6-1	190	7-8-96	4	2	4.28	11	0	0	2	40	38	25	19	4	15	35	.239	.273	.226	7.88	3.38
Martin, Reeves	R-R	5-8	180	12-25-96	0	0	6.23	4	0	0	0	4	5	3	3	0	4	4	.278	.400	.231	8.31	8.31
Martinez, Bernie	R-R	6-0	195	12-24-96	0	0	0.00	4	0	0	0	7	1	0	0	0	1	6	.048	.000	.077	7.71	1.29
Mercedes, Juan	R-R	6-2	190	4-3-00	3	3	5.40	9	4	0	0	42	49	30	25	8	5	29	.288	.286	.290	6.26	1.08
Minich, Brock	R-R	6-6	220	9-29-96	0	5	6.00	17	0	0	0	21	18	18	14	3	16	20	.231	.348	.182	8.57	6.86
Morgan, Reid	R-R	6-0	187	3-24-97	0	0	1.17	6	0	0	2	8	6	2	1	0	2	5	.200	.077	.294	5.87	2.35
Northcraft, Aaron	R-R	6-4	230	5-28-90	1	0	9.00	1	0	0	0	1	2	1	1	0	0	1	.400	.000	.667	9.00	0.00
Nunez, Kelvin	R-R	6-1	170	12-10-99	2	2	4.50	12	9	0	0	48	50	26	24	6	14	35	.272	.314	.246	6.56	2.63
Perez, Brayan	L-L	6-0	170	9-5-00	4	1	3.23	7	1	0	0	31	39	13	11	2	9	29	.317	.290	.326	8.51	2.64
Rinehart, Logan	R-R	6-3	185	9-21-97	1	0	3.09	8	0	0	1	12	12	6	4	1	4	7	.250	.278	.233	5.40	3.09
Rollings, Kipp	R-R	6-2	188	9-13-96	1	2	4.85	20	0	0	0	30	40	20	16	4	14	24	.325	.268	.354	7.28	4.25
Then, Juan	R-R	6-1	155	2-7-00	0	3	3.56	7	6	0	0	30	24	12	12	1	9	32	.222	.200	.233	9.49	2.67
Tuivailala, Sam	R-R	6-3	225	10-19-92	0	1	21.60	2	2	0	0	2	5	5	4	1	0	3	.500	.667	.429	16.20	0.00
Villarreal, Fred	R-R	5-11	187	4-7-98	1	1	5.68	12	0	0	3	13	12	9	8	1	7	11	.231	.118	.286	7.82	4.97
Westberg, Garrett	R-R	6-2	210	2-24-97	4	1	6.95	19	0	0	0	22	27	20	17	5	11	24	.290	.357	.262	9.82	4.50
Williamson, Brandon	L-L	6-6	210	4-2-98	0	0	2.35	10	9	0	0	15	9	6	4	0	5	25	.167	.214	.150	14.67	2.93

Fielding

C: Bins 47, Camacho 15, Kaleiwahea 11, Nevarez 9. **1B:** Camacho 9, Court 1, Gladfelter 27, Hoover 1, Nevarez 1, Perez 42. **2B:** Frick 7, Hoover 22, Izturis Jr. 23, Jones 19, Joseph 4, Santa 2, Shenton 1. **3B:** Court 2, Frick 21, Hoover 5, Izturis Jr. 1, Jones 3, Joseph 33, Perez 1, Santa 2, Shenton 14. **SS:** Frick 31, Hoover 1, Izturis Jr. 36, Jones 9. **OF:** Cooke 19, Gladfelter 10, Hoover 1, Joseph 8, Marlowe 49, Moses 32, Perez 66, Perez 1, Shenton 1, Tingelstad 56.

AZL MARINERS   ROOKIE
ARIZONA LEAGUE

Batting	B-T	HT	WT	DOB	AVG	vLH	vRH	G	AB	R	H	2B	3B	HR	RBI	BB	HBP	SH	SF	SO	SB	CS	SLG	OBP
Batista, Freuddy	R-R	6-0	182	12-12-99	.203	.059	.242	22	79	13	16	3	1	1	4	3	1	0	1	27	0	0	.304	.238
Caballero, Jose	R-R	5-10	185	8-30-96	.455	.000	.500	3	11	5	5	2	0	0	1	0	1	0	0	1	1	0	.636	.500
Castillo, Osiris	R-R	5-11	170	9-5-00	.208	.238	.203	41	144	10	30	3	1	0	11	11	2	0	0	29	2	1	.243	.274
DeCarlo, Joe	R-R	5-10	210	9-13-93	.125	.500	.000	2	8	0	1	0	0	0	0	0	0	0	0	2	0	0	.125	.125
Garcia, Jepherson	R-R	6-2	185	4-19-99	.167	.111	.179	30	102	7	17	4	1	0	6	9	1	0	0	40	1	0	.226	.241
Gil, Edwin	R-R	6-0	194	7-22-99	.204	.297	.181	51	186	23	38	6	1	8	22	11	2	0	1	83	4	1	.376	.255
Grosse, Cody	L-R	5-8	165	12-30-96	.293	.158	.316	40	133	22	39	5	5	0	17	22	3	1	4	32	7	3	.406	.395
Hoover, Connor	R-R	5-10	185	7-18-96	.333	.318	.339	23	87	18	29	7	1	2	15	18	0	0	0	23	6	1	.506	.448
Kaleiwahea, Brennon	R-R	6-0	200	5-28-96	.000	--	.000	1	3	0	0	0	0	0	0	0	0	0	0	1	0	0	.000	.000
Lepre, Anthony	R-R	5-10	195	5-29-97	.156	.107	.170	36	122	13	19	6	0	5	15	18	0	0	1	40	1	1	.328	.262
Mistico, Antoine	L-R	6-0	180	6-30-98	.250	.333	.229	22	60	6	15	2	0	1	9	12	2	1	1	15	5	0	.333	.387
Ochoa, Sebastian	R-R	6-1	180	5-8-98	.250	.270	.245	51	192	18	48	7	1	0	14	14	2	0	2	52	3	5	.297	.305
Perez, Nolan	B-R	6-1	190	5-9-99	.283	.189	.309	46	173	16	49	9	3	3	33	6	2	0	3	56	1	4	.422	.310
Perez, Robert	R-R	6-1	170	6-26-00	.182	--	.182	3	11	2	2	1	0	0	2	0	0	0	0	5	0	0	.273	.182
Querecuto, Juan	R-R	6-2	175	9-21-00	.203	.286	.185	23	79	10	16	3	0	0	8	12	1	1	0	35	2	1	.241	.315
Ricca, Caleb	R-R	5-8	165	10-21-97	.214	.273	.200	17	56	8	12	3	1	1	8	2	0	0	24	5	0	.357	.333
Santa, Kevin	L-R	5-11	175	3-9-95	.467	.200	.520	7	30	8	14	4	0	1	8	3	0	0	4	1	0	.700	.515
Santos, Daniel	R-R	6-2	175	1-25-99	.209	.167	.219	28	91	14	19	3	2	0	9	9	4	0	1	27	2	0	.286	.305
Slater, Johnny	L-L	6-1	190	8-9-95	.190	.273	.170	17	58	6	11	3	1	2	7	6	3	1	0	19	1	0	.379	.299
Trejo, Cesar	R-R	6-2	200	5-15-97	.217	.258	.207	45	152	25	33	4	3	5	15	16	4	0	0	56	9	2	.382	.308
Veloz, Luis	R-R	6-4	180	12-15-99	.219	.087	.260	36	96	15	21	4	2	0	3	9	1	0	1	32	3	0	.302	.290
Young Jr., Eric	B-R	5-10	195	5-25-85	.333	.500	.250	2	6	3	2	0	0	0	1	3	0	0	0	1	1	0	.333	.556

Pitching	B-T	HT	WT	DOB	W	L	ERA	G	GS	CG	SV	IP	H	R	ER	HR	BB	SO	vLH	vRH	K/9	BB/9
Alcantara, Raul	L-L	6-0	167	1-22-01	0	2	9.00	5	1	0	0	9	18	11	9	0	6	4	.439	.455	4.33	4.00	6.00
Alvarado, Elvis	R-R	6-4	183	2-23-99	0	1	2.25	5	1	0	0	12	10	4	3	0	3	13	.233	.308	.200	9.75	2.25
Bayless, Jarod	R-R	6-4	225	12-29-96	2	0	0.57	8	0	0	1	16	8	1	1	0	1	21	.143	.115	.167	12.06	0.57
Brennan, Brandon	R-R	6-4	220	7-26-91	0	1	0.00	1	1	0	0	1	1	0	0	1	3	.200	.500	.000	27.00	9.00
Chang, Danny	L-L	6-3	176	2-11-00	0	3	5.31	14	6	0	0	41	44	31	24	5	22	50	.272	.255	.278	11.07	4.87
Curvelo, Luis	R-R	6-1	170	10-21-00	1	1	2.31	12	0	0	1	23	13	8	6	1	3	32	.157	.138	.167	12.34	1.16
Driver, Tyler	R-R	6-2	185	2-4-01	0	6	5.67	13	10	0	0	46	44	30	29	6	13	41	.249	.215	.268	8.02	2.54
Florido, Deivy	R-R	6-2	165	9-17-00	0	1	9.45	2	0	0	1	7	8	7	7	0	1	6	.286	.400	.222	8.10	1.35
Landis, Dutch	R-R	6-2	185	6-23-01	0	1	4.91	6	5	0	0	11	14	8	6	0	6	9	.311	.364	.261	7.36	4.91
Laws, Holden	L-L	6-2	166	12-8-99	1	1	5.54	11	6	0	0	26	33	20	16	1	5	30	.311	.361	.286	10.38	1.73
Macko, Adam	L-L	6-0	170	12-30-00	0	3	3.38	8	2	0	0	21	19	10	8	1	11	31	.241	.238	.241	13.08	4.64
Marte, Cristhopher	R-R	6-2	170	4-2-99	1	1	1.99	16	0	0	2	23	18	7	5	1	12	15	.228	.267	.177	5.96	4.76
Martinez, Bernie	R-R	6-0	195	12-24-96	2	0	0.77	9	0	0	1	23	14	4	2	0	1	33	.171	.152	.194	12.73	0.39
Mercedes, Anderson	L-L	6-0	178	12-23-98	2	1	7.45	11	3	0	0	29	42	27	24	2	18	30	.342	.278	.368	9.31	5.59
Mogollon, Matt	R-R	6-0	185	8-13-96	0	0	0.00	4	0	0	0	5	1	0	0	0	2	6	.059	.000	.100	10.13	3.38
Nunez, Kelvin	R-R	6-1	170	12-10-99	1	0	3.60	1	0	0	0	5	4	2	2	1	0	4	.222	.375	.100	7.20	0.00
Pedrol, Christian	R-R	5-11	190	6-15-00	4	4	4.13	14	7	0	0	52	44	27	24	4	18	41	.229	.189	.254	7.05	3.10
Perez, Brayan	L-L	6-0	170	9-5-00	4	1	3.44	8	3	0	0	37	32	18	14	2	8	33	.239	.086	.293	8.10	1.96
Rodriguez, Leo	R-R	6-2	205	12-20-95	0	0	13.50	1	0	0	0	1	2	1	1	0	0	1	.500	1.000	.333	13.50	0.00
Stryffeler, Michael	R-R	6-2	210	5-22-96	0	0	1.38	10	0	0	3	13	10	2	2	0	5	20	.213	.286	.182	13.85	3.46
Suellentrop, Tyler	R-R	6-3	217	1-22-97	2	0	3.15	15	0	0	1	20	15	8	7	0	13	17	.208	.171	.243	7.65	5.85
Tatiz, Yeury	R-R	6-3	175	4-18-00	1	2	5.70	8	2	0	0	24	29	17	15	1	13	19	.302	.308	.296	7.23	4.94
Then, Juan	R-R	6-1	155	2-7-00	0	0	0.00	1	0	0	0	2	2	0	0	0	0	2	.286	.333	.000	9.00	0.00
Tomczak, Anthony	R-R	6-2	200	10-17-00	0	2	7.88	5	5	0	0	8	11	7	7	2	5	6	.333	.400	.321	6.75	5.63
Townsend, Blake	L-L	6-4	220	4-5-01	0	1	6.75	2	2	0	0	5	8	5	4	1	0	8	.333	.667	.286	13.50	0.00
Villarreal, Fred	R-R	5-11	187	4-7-98	0	0	0.00	1	0	0	0	1	0	0	0	0	1	.286	.000	.500	6.75	0.00
Walker, Matt	R-R	6-6	201	9-28-94	0	0	0.00	1	1	0	0	1	1	0	0	0	0	2	.250	.000	.333	18.00	0.00
Winslow, Robert	R-R	6-5	215	8-19-97	1	2	0.90	13	1	0	1	30	22	13	3	0	13	43	.200	.192	.206	12.90	3.90

Fielding

C: Batista 15, DeCarlo 1, Kaleiwahea 1, Lepre 29, Santos 15. **1B:** Garcia 3, Gil 42, Hoover 1, Perez 2, Perez 4, Querecuto 2, Santos 4. **2B:** Castillo 13, Grosse 36, Hoover 5, Perez 5, Querecuto 3, Ricca 3, Trejo 3. **3B:** Castillo 3, DeCarlo 1, Gil 8, Hoover 4, Perez 38, Ricca 8. **SS:** Caballero 2, Castillo 14, Gil 4, Grosse 6, Hoover 9, Querecuto 18, Ricca 7, Santa 6. **OF:** Garcia 18, Hoover 4, Mistico 20, Ochoa 49, Slater 16, Trejo 42, Veloz 35, Young Jr. 1.

DSL MARINERS   ROOKIE
DOMINICAN SUMMER LEAGUE

Batting	B-T	HT	WT	DOB	AVG	vLH	vRH	G	AB	R	H	2B	3B	HR	RBI	BB	HBP	SH	SF	SO	SB	CS	SLG	OBP
Bueno, Asdrubal	R-R	5-11	170	11-25-01	.250	.333	.226	21	68	13	17	5	0	2	7	9	0	0	0	12	1	2	.412	.338
Caguana, Jose	R-R	5-10	175	4-5-02	.247	.229	.252	47	170	28	42	10	2	4	23	15	3	0	1	54	6	2	.400	.318
Casilla, Yeral	R-R	6-2	175	11-9-00	.155	.194	.143	41	129	13	20	4	0	3	10	21	5	0	1	45	0	1	.256	.295
Chevalier, Luis	R-R	5-11	160	1-18-02	.139	.077	.174	11	36	4	5	1	0	0	1	6	1	1	0	14	1	1	.167	.279
Clase, Jonatan	L-R	5-8	150	5-23-02	.300	.216	.326	63	223	64	67	12	7	2	26	51	4	5	3	56	31	10	.444	.434

	B-T	HT	WT	DOB	AVG	vLH	vRH	G	AB	R	H	2B	3B	HR	RBI	BB	HBP	SH	SF	SO	SB	CS	SLG	OBP
De La Cruz, Julio	R-R	6-3	170	1-29-01	.285	.240	.294	43	144	22	41	7	3	3	27	31	2	0	0	47	5	1	.438	.418
Fernandez, Carlos	R-R	6-0	160	9-18-01	.248	.346	.225	44	137	24	34	2	0	0	11	19	1	3	0	31	4	2	.263	.344
Franco, Francis	R-R	6-1	160	3-27-00	.200	.235	.189	43	145	23	29	5	4	0	10	22	7	1	0	45	0	2	.290	.333
Gil, Edwin	R-R	6-0	194	7-22-99	.250	.429	.177	6	24	5	6	3	1	0	5	1	0	1	0	7	0	0	.458	.280
Gonzalez, Junior	R-R	5-11	186	5-10-00	.198	.231	.188	56	212	31	42	7	1	2	36	23	3	0	6	48	1	2	.269	.279
Guerrero, Arturo	R-R	6-3	165	9-21-00	.238	.286	.226	53	181	32	43	5	1	6	27	22	26	3	0	63	11	0	.376	.397
Hernandez, Jery	R-R	6-2	160	4-22-01	.199	.240	.185	57	196	24	39	8	2	1	15	18	3	7	2	67	2	3	.276	.274
Marte, Noelvi	R-R	6-1	181	10-16-01	.309	.377	.289	65	262	56	81	18	4	9	54	29	1	0	7	55	17	7	.512	.371
Moncada, Gabe	L-L	6-2	175	12-17-01	.239	.405	.178	37	138	14	33	6	0	0	16	13	1	0	1	29	1	2	.283	.307
Perez, Milkar	R-R	5-11	173	10-16-01	.274	.226	.288	64	237	38	65	11	2	4	44	37	5	0	2	55	8	6	.388	.381
Pieternella, Ortwin	R-R	6-0	184	5-19-99	.327	.357	.315	32	101	19	33	7	2	1	13	18	1	0	1	33	7	1	.465	.430

Pitching	B-T	HT	WT	DOB	W	L	ERA	G	GS	CG	SV	IP	H	R	ER	HR	BB	SO	AVG	vLH	vRH	K/9	BB/9
Afanador, Elbis	R-R	6-2	175	10-30-99	5	1	2.05	13	2	0	1	48	47	19	11	2	15	28	.264	.309	.244	5.21	2.79
Alcantara, Luis	R-R	6-0	180	9-30-99	1	1	6.92	14	0	0	6	13	22	13	10	1	6	21	.373	.333	.390	14.54	4.15
Alcantara, Raul	L-L	6-0	167	1-22-01	3	3	4.54	10	7	0	0	42	52	31	21	1	9	21	.311	.296	.314	4.54	1.94
Aquino, Jose	L-L	6-3	175	6-27-02	1	1	2.45	9	8	0	0	29	21	12	8	1	16	27	.214	.125	.222	8.28	4.91
Baez, Luis	R-R	6-3	165	2-6-01	1	4	6.40	11	7	0	0	32	45	35	23	1	21	17	.338	.409	.303	4.73	5.85
Brito, Lisander	R-R	6-3	175	7-9-02	1	3	7.86	12	8	0	0	26	29	27	23	1	28	22	.284	.424	.217	7.52	9.57
Burgos, Juan	R-R	6-0	155	12-22-99	2	3	3.19	17	4	0	0	42	38	21	15	3	20	42	.245	.275	.231	8.93	4.25
Casilla, Yeral	R-R	6-2	175	11-9-00	0	0	6.23	4	0	0	0	4	10	3	3	0	2	4	.435	.500	.421	8.31	4.15
Franco, Francis	R-R	6-1	160	3-27-00	0	0	0.00	1	0	0	0	1	1	0	0	0	0	0	.250	.000	.500	0.00	0.00
Garabitos, Natanael	R-R	6-0	185	8-4-00	2	0	3.10	14	0	0	3	20	17	7	7	1	17	18	.236	.167	.259	7.97	7.52
German, Carlos	R-R	6-3	180	12-30-00	0	0	12.56	13	0	0	0	14	14	25	20	4	30	19	.259	.167	.286	11.93	18.84
Gonzalez, Junior	R-R	5-11	186	5-10-00	0	0	108.00	1	0	0	0	0	2	4	4	1	1	0	.667	--	.667	0.00	27.00
Hernandez, Joseph	R-R	5-11	150	6-15-00	0	1	6.00	4	0	0	0	6	8	8	4	0	6	5	.348	.429	.313	7.50	9.00
Januario, Igor	L-R	6-2	260	1-20-98	2	1	2.79	12	0	0	5	19	16	11	6	1	7	16	.216	.107	.283	7.45	3.26
Lopez, Abrahan	R-R	5-10	160	9-27-99	0	1	4.86	11	0	0	0	17	21	12	9	2	9	12	.328	.409	.286	6.48	4.86
Medina, Abdiel	R-R	5-11	155	1-20-02	3	3	4.25	15	6	0	1	49	46	32	23	2	17	51	.243	.233	.248	9.43	3.14
Mejia, Eliezer	L-L	6-2	160	9-13-00	0	2	13.50	11	0	0	0	16	23	27	24	3	17	18	.315	.429	.303	10.13	9.56
Melenge, Harold	L-L	5-10	170	1-15-02	1	3	6.35	15	2	0	0	40	59	34	28	5	16	31	.341	.261	.353	7.03	3.63
Mercedes, Anderson	L-L	6-0	178	12-23-98	2	2	2.95	5	3	0	0	18	17	19	6	3	5	28	.218	.364	.194	13.75	2.45
Morillo, David	R-R	6-2	168	9-26-01	3	1	1.62	14	5	0	0	39	31	16	7	1	14	41	.212	.237	.195	9.46	3.23
Perez, Wilton	R-R	6-3	171	3-7-02	4	2	2.44	15	13	0	0	55	49	26	15	3	18	38	.241	.286	.230	6.18	2.93
Santana, Pablo	R-R	6-1	186	2-28-99	1	0	5.84	11	0	0	1	25	30	21	16	2	12	25	.291	.237	.323	9.12	4.38
Sosa, Gabriel	R-R	6-2	182	4-17-01	0	2	4.58	6	2	0	1	18	19	13	9	1	4	12	.268	.250	.279	6.11	2.04
Tatiz, Yeury	R-R	6-3	175	11-22-00	1	1	2.14	5	5	0	0	21	15	9	5	0	6	25	.195	.214	.184	10.71	2.57
Volquez, Ricardo	R-R	6-1	160	3-9-98	1	1	6.91	12	0	0	0	27	30	26	21	5	20	34	.268	.273	.266	11.20	6.59

Fielding

C: Caguana 25, Gonzalez 35, Pieternella 17. **1B:** Bueno 1, Caguana 2, Casilla 6, De La Cruz 35, Fernandez 2, Franco 1, Gil 5, Hernandez 1, Moncada 27. **2B:** Bueno 20, Chevalier 7, De La Cruz 1, Fernandez 24, Franco 18, Guerrero 1, Hernandez 10. **3B:** Fernandez 5, Franco 7, Perez 64. **SS:** Chevalier 4, Fernandez 4, Franco 3, Marte 63. **OF:** Caguana 4, Casilla 28, Clase 63, Fernandez 15, Franco 10, Gonzalez 2, Guerrero 51, Hernandez 46, Januario 1, Lopez 1, Moncada 6, Pieternella 7.

Tampa Bay Rays

SEASON IN A SENTENCE: Baseball's innovators in 2018, the Rays dumped high-priced veterans in the offseason, endured a series of costly injuries and still surprised everyone by winning 90 games.

SEASON IN A SENTENCE: The Rays returned to the playoffs for the first time in six years and won 96 games (tied for second-most in franchise history), but it feels more like foreshadowing than a finish line.

HIGH POINT: Yandy Diaz homered twice in the first three innings as Tampa Bay jumped out to a quick lead on Oakland in the American League Wild Card game. Charlie Morton and three relievers ensured that the game never was in doubt after that as the Rays held on for a 5-1 win. That was the Rays' first playoff win since 2013, when the Rays beat the Indians in the wild card game before losing to the Red Sox in four games in the AL Division Series.

LOW POINT: The Rays pushed the eventual AL champion Houston Astros to five games in the ALDS and threw nine different pitchers at the Astros in the deciding Game 5, but Gerrit Cole was simply dominating in a 6-1 Houston win.

NOTABLE ROOKIES: Lefty Brendan McKay made 11 starts in the second half of the season while also getting a chance to serve as a pinch-hitter. Lefthander Colin Poche made 51 appearances out of the bullpen.

KEY TRANSACTIONS: The Rays acquired righthander Nick Anderson at the trade deadline and quickly saw him turn into the club's best reliever. Anderson had a 41-2 strikeout-to-walk ratio over 23 appearances and 21 innings with the club. The Rays acquired Travis D'Arnaud from the Dodgers for cash in April in what appeared to be a modest move to add depth when Mike Zunino went down with a quad strain. D'Arnaud ended up being a useful part-time catcher who split the job with Zunino. He hit .263/.323/.459 and played regularly in the playoffs.

DOWN ON THE FARM: The Rays had to make a number of moves during the season to clear spots on a crowded 40-man roster, but despite that they finished the season with one of the best farm systems in baseball. Shortstop Wander Franco ended the year as the No. 1 prospect in baseball, and the team's pitching depth is formidable thanks to arms like Brendan McKay, Matthew Liberatore, Shane Baz and Shane McClanahan. The Rays added SS Greg Jones and RHP J.J. Goss in the draft.

OPENING DAY PAYROLL: $68,976,867 (26th).

PLAYERS OF THE YEAR

MAJOR LEAGUE	MINOR LEAGUE
Charlie Morton	**Wander Franco**
RHP	**SS**
16-6, 3.05 in 33 GS	(Low A/High A)
240 SO in 195 IP	.327/.398/.487
AL-best 0.7 HR/9	43 XBH, 56 BB, 35 SO

MARY DeCICCO

BG HOT RODS

ORGANIZATION LEADERS

Batting		*Minimum 250 AB
MAJORS		
* AVG	Austin Meadows	.291
* OPS	Austin Meadows	.922
HR	Austin Meadows	33
RBI	Austin Meadows	89
MINORS		
* AVG	Jake Cronenworth, Durham, GCL Rays	.329
* OBP	Jake Cronenworth, Durham, GCL Rays	.422
* SLG	Michael Brosseau, Durham	.567
* OPS	Michael Brosseau, Durham	.960
R	Wander Franco, Bowling Green, Charlotte	82
H	Wander Franco, Bowling Green, Charlotte	139
H	Kean Wong, Durham	139
TB	Kean Wong, Durham	210
2B	Kevin Padlo, Montgomery, Durham	31
3B	Thomas Milone, Montgomery, Charlotte	10
HR	Kevin Padlo, Montgomery, Durham	21
RBI	Jim Haley, Charlotte, Montgomery	81
BB	Nate Lowe, Durham	72
SO	Moises Gomez, Charlotte	164
SB	Vidal Brujan, Charlotte, Montgomery	48

Pitching		#Minimum 75 IP
MAJORS		
W	Charlie Morton	16
# ERA	Charlie Morton	3.05
SO	Charlie Morton	240
SV	Charlie Morton	20
MINORS		
W	Paul Campbell, Charlotte, Montgomery	13
W	Tommy Romero, Charlotte, Montgomery	13
L	Sam McWilliams, Montgomery, Durham	9
# ERA	Stephen Woods Jr., Charlotte	1.88
G	Hoby Milner, Durham	50
GS	Michael Plassmeyer, Bowling Green, Charlotte, Durham	23
GS	Arturo Reyes, Montgomery, Durham	23
SV	Joel Peguero, Bowling Green	16
IP	Josh Fleming, Montgomery, Durham	149
BB	Kenny Rosenberg, Montgomery, Durham	59
SO	Joe Ryan, Bowling Green, Charlotte, Montgomery	183
# AVG	Joe Ryan, Bowling Green, Charlotte, Montgomery	.173

2019 PERFORMANCE

General Manager: Erik Neander. **Farm Director:** Mitch Lukevics. **Scouting Director:** Rob Metzler.

Class	Team	League	W	L	PCT	Finish	Manager
Majors	Tampa Bay Rays	American	96	66	.593	5th (15)	Kevin Cash
Triple-A	Durham Bulls	International	75	64	.540	t-3rd (14)	Brady Williams
Double-A	Montgomery Biscuits	Southern	88	50	.638	1st (10)	Morgan Ensberg
High A	Charlotte Stone Crabs	Florida State	82	53	.607	1st (12)	Jeff Smith
Low A	Bowling Green Hot Rods	Midwest	81	58	.583	t-2nd (16)	Reinaldo Ruiz
Short season	Hudson Valley Renegades	New York-Penn	43	32	.573	t-1st (14)	Blake Butera
Rookie	Princeton Rays	Appalachian	34	34	.500	t-5th (10)	Danny Sheaffer
Rookie	GCL Rays	Gulf Coast	25	28	.472	11th (18)	Rafael Valenzuela
Overall 2019 Minor League Record			428	319	.573	1st (30)	

ORGANIZATION STATISTICS

TAMPA BAY RAYS
AMERICAN LEAGUE

Batting	B-T	HT	WT	DOB	AVG	vLH	vRH	G	AB	R	H	2B	3B	HR	RBI	BB	HBP	SH	SF	SO	SB	CS	SLG	OBP
Adames, Willy	R-R	6-0	205	9-2-95	.254	.181	.292	152	531	69	135	25	1	20	52	46	3	1	153	4	2	.418	.317
Aguilar, Jesus	R-R	6-3	250	6-30-90	.261	.300	.231	37	92	13	24	3	0	4	16	12	0	0	3	22	0	0	.424	.336
Arroyo, Christian	R-R	6-1	220	5-30-95	.220	.240	.200	16	50	8	11	2	0	2	7	5	1	1	0	18	0	0	.380	.304
Bemboom, Anthony	L-R	6-2	200	1-18-90	.400	--	.400	3	5	0	2	1	0	0	1	0	0	0	0	2	0	0	.600	.400
2-team total (22 Los Angeles)					.130	.200	.122	25	54	2	7	1	0	1	4	1	0	1	0	21	0	0	.204	.146
Brosseau, Michael	R-R	5-10	215	3-15-94	.273	.300	.242	50	132	17	36	7	0	6	16	7	2	1	0	39	1	0	.462	.319
Choi, Ji-Man	L-R	6-1	250	5-19-91	.261	.210	.274	127	410	54	107	20	2	19	63	64	6	0	7	108	2	3	.459	.363
Ciuffo, Nick	L-R	6-0	200	3-7-95	.167	--	.167	3	6	0	1	0	0	0	0	0	0	0	0	3	0	0	.167	.167
d'Arnaud, Travis	R-R	6-2	210	2-10-89	.263	.275	.255	92	327	50	86	16	0	16	67	30	2	0	6	80	0	1	.459	.323
Davis, Johnny	B-R	5-10	180	4-26-90	.250	--	.250	8	4	5	1	0	1	0	0	0	0	0	0	2	0	0	.750	.250
Diaz, Yandy	R-R	6-2	215	8-8-91	.267	.311	.245	79	307	53	82	20	1	14	38	35	1	0	4	61	2	2	.476	.340
Duffy, Matt	R-R	6-2	190	1-15-91	.252	.164	.304	46	147	12	37	8	0	1	12	19	2	0	1	29	0	1	.327	.343
Garcia, Avisail	R-R	6-4	250	6-12-91	.282	.265	.291	125	489	61	138	25	2	20	72	31	7	0	3	125	10	4	.464	.332
Heredia, Guillermo	R-L	5-10	195	1-31-91	.226	.281	.156	89	204	31	46	13	0	5	20	18	6	2	1	60	2	2	.363	.306
Kiermaier, Kevin	L-R	6-1	210	4-22-90	.228	.312	.197	129	447	60	102	20	7	14	55	26	5	1	1	104	19	5	.398	.278
Kratz, Erik	R-R	6-4	250	6-15-80	.059	.000	.067	6	17	0	1	0	0	0	0	0	0	0	0	8	0	0	.059	.059
Lowe, Brandon	L-R	5-10	185	7-6-94	.270	.242	.278	82	296	42	80	17	2	17	51	25	5	0	1	113	5	0	.514	.336
Lowe, Nate	L-R	6-4	245	7-7-95	.263	.292	.258	50	152	24	40	8	0	7	19	13	2	0	2	50	0	0	.454	.325
Meadows, Austin	L-L	6-3	220	5-3-95	.291	.275	.298	138	530	83	154	29	7	33	89	54	7	0	0	131	12	7	.559	.364
Perez, Michael	L-R	5-10	195	8-7-92	.217	.273	.200	22	46	6	10	5	0	0	2	8	1	0	0	19	0	0	.326	.346
Pham, Tommy	R-R	6-1	215	3-8-88	.273	.340	.248	145	567	77	155	33	2	21	68	81	5	0	1	123	25	4	.450	.369
Robertson, Daniel	R-R	5-11	200	3-22-94	.213	.250	.187	74	207	23	44	9	1	2	19	24	6	0	0	59	2	2	.295	.312
Sogard, Eric	L-R	5-10	185	5-22-86	.266	.235	.272	37	109	14	29	6	0	3	10	9	1	0	0	16	2	0	.404	.328
2-team total (73 Toronto)					.290	.279	.295	110	396	59	115	23	2	13	40	38	2	3	3	63	8	0	.457	.353
Velazquez, Andrew	B-R	5-8	170	7-14-94	.083	.000	.111	10	12	2	1	1	0	0	0	0	0	0	0	6	0	0	.167	.083
2-team total (5 Cleveland)					.087	.143	.063	15	23	3	2	2	0	0	1	0	0	0	0	13	1	0	.174	.125
Wendle, Joey	L-R	6-1	200	4-26-90	.231	.130	.261	75	238	32	55	13	2	3	19	14	8	0	3	47	8	3	.340	.293
Wong, Kean	L-R	5-11	185	4-17-95	.214	.500	.167	6	14	1	3	0	0	0	0	0	0	0	0	5	0	1	.214	.214
2-team total (1 Los Angeles)					.167	.333	.133	7	18	2	3	0	0	0	0	0	0	0	0	6	0	1	.167	.167
Zunino, Mike	R-R	6-2	235	3-25-91	.165	.154	.171	90	266	30	44	10	1	9	32	20	3	0	0	98	0	0	.312	.232

Pitching	B-T	HT	WT	DOB	W	L	ERA	G	GS	CG	SV	IP	H	R	ER	HR	BB	SO	AVG	vLH	vRH	K/9	BB/9
Alvarado, Jose	L-L	6-2	245	5-21-95	1	6	4.80	35	1	0	7	30	29	18	16	2	27	39	.254	.194	.282	11.70	8.10
Anderson, Nick	R-R	6-5	195	7-5-90	3	0	2.11	23	0	0	0	21	12	5	5	3	2	41	.160	.243	.079	17.30	0.84
Banda, Anthony	L-L	6-2	225	8-10-93	0	0	6.75	3	0	0	0	4	6	3	3	0	2	3	.333	.400	.308	6.75	4.50
Beeks, Jalen	L-L	5-11	200	7-10-93	6	3	4.31	33	3	0	1	104	115	56	50	12	40	89	.281	.318	.268	7.68	3.45
Brosseau, Michael	R-R	5-10	215	3-15-94	0	0	4.50	3	0	0	0	4	5	2	2	1	0	0	.294	.286	.300	0.00	0.00
Castillo, Diego	R-R	6-3	250	1-18-94	5	8	3.41	65	6	0	8	69	59	32	26	8	26	81	.230	.271	.205	10.62	3.41
Chirinos, Yonny	R-R	6-2	240	12-26-93	9	5	3.85	26	18	0	0	133	112	61	57	23	28	114	.225	.189	.255	7.70	1.89
De Leon, Jose	R-R	6-1	220	8-7-92	1	0	2.25	3	0	0	0	4	3	2	1	0	3	7	.188	.143	.222	15.75	6.75
Drake, Oliver	R-R	6-4	215	1-13-87	5	2	3.21	50	0	0	0	56	36	20	20	9	19	70	.181	.147	.217	11.25	3.05
Fairbanks, Peter	R-R	6-6	219	12-16-93	2	1	5.11	13	0	0	2	12	17	10	7	1	3	13	.309	.267	.360	9.49	2.19
2-team total (8 Texas)					2	3	6.86	21	0	0	2	21	25	20	16	5	10	28	.281	.182	.378	12.00	4.29
Faria, Jake	R-R	6-4	225	7-30-93	0	0	2.70	7	0	0	0	10	10	3	3	2	7	11	.250	.095	.421	9.90	6.30
Font, Wilmer	R-R	6-4	250	5-24-90	1	0	5.79	10	0	0	0	14	15	9	9	2	5	18	.273	.375	.194	11.57	3.21
2-team total (23 Toronto)					3	3	4.22	33	14	0	0	53	49	25	25	9	16	71	.241	.296	.200	11.98	2.70
Gibaut, Ian	R-R	6-3	250	11-19-93	0	0	9.00	1	0	0	0	2	1	2	2	0	2	2	.167	.000	.333	9.00	9.00
2-team total (9 Texas)					1	1	5.65	10	0	0	0	14	12	9	9	1	10	16	.235	.185	.292	10.05	6.28
Glasnow, Tyler	L-R	6-8	230	8-23-93	6	1	1.78	12	12	0	0	61	40	13	12	4	14	76	.186	.155	.212	11.27	2.08
Kittredge, Andrew	R-R	6-1	235	3-17-90	1	0	4.17	37	7	0	0	50	51	25	23	7	12	58	.263	.318	.237	10.51	2.17
Kolarek, Adam	L-L	6-3	215	1-14-89	4	3	3.95	54	0	0	1	43	39	19	19	6	14	36	.234	.187	.272	7.48	2.91
McKay, Brendan	L-L	6-2	212	12-18-95	2	4	5.14	13	11	0	0	49	53	32	28	8	16	56	.268	.220	.284	10.29	2.94
Milner, Hoby	L-L	6-3	175	1-13-91	0	0	7.36	4	0	0	0	4	4	3	3	0	1	3	.267	.286	.250	7.36	2.45

Morton, Charlie	R-R	6-5	215	11-12-83	16	6	3.05	33	33	0	0	195	154	71	66	15	57	240	.215	.227	.202	11.10	2.64
Pagan, Emilio	L-R	6-3	205	5-7-91	4	2	2.31	66	0	0	20	70	45	19	18	12	13	96	.179	.179	.179	12.34	1.67
Pinto, Ricardo	R-R	6-0	195	1-20-94	0	0	15.43	2	0	0	0	2	4	4	4	1	2	0	.364	.400	.333	0.00	7.71
Poche, Colin	L-L	6-3	235	1-17-94	5	5	4.70	51	0	0	2	52	33	27	27	9	19	72	.181	.167	.190	12.54	3.31
Pruitt, Austin	R-R	5-10	185	8-31-89	3	0	4.40	14	2	0	0	47	47	23	23	7	12	39	.266	.209	.326	7.47	2.30
Richards, Trevor	R-R	6-2	190	5-15-93	3	0	1.93	7	3	0	0	23	23	7	5	3	5	24	.253	.171	.320	9.26	1.93
Robertson, Daniel	R-R	5-11	200	3-22-94	0	0	0.00	1	0	0	0	1	0	0	0	0	0	0	.333	--	.333	0.00	0.00
Roe, Chaz	R-R	6-5	190	10-9-86	1	3	4.06	71	0	0	1	51	49	27	23	3	31	65	.251	.227	.258	11.47	5.47
Sadler, Casey	R-R	6-3	205	7-13-90	0	0	1.86	9	0	0	0	19	16	5	4	2	5	11	.219	.250	.189	5.12	2.33
Slegers, Aaron	R-R	6-10	245	9-4-92	0	0	3.00	1	0	0	1	3	3	1	1	1	0	0	.273	.333	.200	0.00	0.00
Snell, Blake	L-L	6-4	215	12-4-92	6	8	4.29	23	23	0	0	107	96	53	51	14	40	147	.241	.329	.222	12.36	3.36
Stanek, Ryne	R-R	6-4	225	7-26-91	0	2	3.40	41	27	0	0	56	44	24	21	7	20	61	.214	.209	.217	9.86	3.23
Sulser, Cole	R-R	6-1	190	3-12-90	0	0	0.00	7	0	0	0	7	5	0	0	0	3	9	.192	.125	.222	11.05	3.68
Wood, Hunter	R-R	6-1	175	8-12-93	1	1	2.48	19	2	0	1	29	26	11	8	4	7	24	.236	.214	.250	7.45	2.17
2-team total (17 Cleveland)					1	1	2.98	36	2	0	1	45	46	20	15	7	12	39	.256	.257	.255	7.74	2.38
Yarbrough, Ryan	R-L	6-5	210	12-31-91	11	6	4.13	28	14	0	0	142	121	69	65	15	20	117	.228	.231	.228	7.43	1.27

Fielding

Catcher	PCT	G	PO	A	E	DP	PB
Bemboom	1.000	3	26	0	0	0	2
Ciuffo	1.000	3	21	2	0	0	2
d'Arnaud	.997	76	659	23	2	4	6
Kratz	1.000	6	40	5	0	1	0
Perez	.993	20	130	12	1	3	0
Zunino	.993	89	764	37	6	7	4

First Base	PCT	G	PO	A	E	DP
Aguilar	1.000	15	99	7	0	11
Brosseau	1.000	1	1	0	0	0
Choi	.992	103	748	36	6	66
d'Arnaud	1.000	21	103	5	0	6
Diaz	.993	22	136	5	1	17
Kolarek	.000	2	0	0	0	0
Lowe	1.000	5	38	3	0	4
Lowe	.994	21	158	5	1	11
Perez	1.000	2	4	0	0	0

Second Base	PCT	G	PO	A	E	DP
Arroyo	1.000	1	0	2	0	0
Brosseau	1.000	26	25	39	0	8
Lowe	.989	69	107	161	3	49
Robertson	.975	26	34	43	2	16
Sogard	.964	31	50	58	4	7
Velazquez	1.000	2	5	4	0	0
Wendle	1.000	48	59	96	0	21
Wong	1.000	2	2	3	0	1

Third Base	PCT	G	PO	A	E	DP
Arroyo	.938	13	8	22	2	3
Brosseau	.968	18	12	18	1	2
Diaz	.962	50	21	79	4	7
Duffy	.933	46	24	73	7	11
Lowe	1.000	4	1	0	0	0
Robertson	.976	43	21	62	2	8
Velazquez	.833	4	2	3	1	0
Wendle	.945	27	17	35	3	2

Shortstop	PCT	G	PO	A	E	DP
Adames	.970	152	157	388	17	68
Duffy	.000	1	0	0	0	0
Robertson	.943	16	7	26	2	4
Wendle	1.000	10	8	18	0	6

Outfield	PCT	G	PO	A	E	DP
Brosseau	1.000	11	7	0	0	0
Davis	1.000	3	2	0	0	0
Garcia	.972	100	170	6	5	1
Heredia	.979	79	137	1	3	0
Kiermaier	.985	125	250	6	4	1
Lowe	1.000	7	5	0	0	0
Meadows	.987	88	152	2	2	1
Pham	1.000	123	158	8	0	0
Velazquez	.000	1	0	0	0	0
Wendle	.000	1	0	0	0	0
Wong	1.000	2	1	0	0	0

DURHAM BULLS
INTERNATIONAL LEAGUE
TRIPLE-A

Batting	B-T	HT	WT	DOB	AVG	vLH	vRH	G	AB	R	H	2B	3B	HR	RBI	BB	HBP	SH	SF	SO	SB	CS	SLG	OBP
Arroyo, Christian	R-R	6-1	220	5-30-95	.314	.325	.309	33	121	21	38	9	1	8	29	12	1	0	0	26	1	0	.603	.381
Bemboom, Anthony	L-R	6-2	200	1-18-90	.213	.083	.257	14	47	7	10	3	0	1	6	2	0	0	1	10	0	1	.340	.240
Bonifacio, Emilio	B-R	5-10	200	4-23-85	.286	.356	.262	76	259	48	74	19	3	8	36	25	2	2	0	63	15	6	.475	.353
Brosseau, Michael	R-R	5-10	215	3-15-94	.304	.378	.262	73	270	53	82	21	1	16	60	34	8	0	3	58	2	3	.567	.394
Ciuffo, Nick	L-R	6-0	200	3-7-95	.228	.173	.268	34	123	14	28	7	1	2	16	9	0	0	2	37	1	1	.350	.276
2-team total (7 Louisville)					.231	.170	.274	41	143	18	33	10	1	3	19	14	0	0	2	43	1	1	.378	.296
Coats, Jason	R-R	6-2	200	2-24-90	.250	.252	.249	92	336	46	84	17	0	18	50	20	2	1	4	97	6	3	.461	.293
Cozens, Dylan	L-L	6-6	235	5-31-94	.286	.500	.200	2	7	2	2	1	0	1	1	2	0	0	1	0	0		.857	.444
2-team total (23 Lehigh Valley)					.177	.174	.177	25	85	22	15	2	2	7	16	22	0	0	1	43	5	2	.494	.343
Cronenworth, Jake	L-R	6-1	185	1-21-94	.334	.357	.321	88	344	75	115	26	4	10	45	49	10	0	3	62	12	5	.520	.429
Duffy, Matt	R-R	6-2	190	1-15-91	.273	.250	.280	9	33	4	9	1	0	1	9	1	1	0	1	5	0	0	.394	.306
Fox, Lucius	B-R	6-1	180	7-2-97	.143	.071	.179	15	42	6	6	0	1	0	1	6	0	1	0	15	2	0	.191	.250
Gale, Rocky	R-R	6-1	185	2-22-88	.323	.389	.296	17	62	6	20	2	0	0	2	0	0	0	0	9	0	0	.355	.344
Garcia, Avisail	R-R	6-4	250	6-12-91	.667	--	.667	1	3	0	2	0	0	0	0	0	0	0	0	1	0	0	.667	.667
Heredia, Guillermo	R-L	5-10	195	1-31-91	.214	.273	.177	8	28	3	6	1	0	1	4	1	1	0	0	10	0	1	.357	.267
James, Mac	R-R	6-1	215	6-2-93	.222	.253	.202	69	203	24	45	5	0	4	19	30	1	0	2	53	1	1	.305	.322
Kelly, Dalton	L-L	6-3	200	8-4-94	.283	.234	.304	73	258	43	73	13	1	7	29	33	4	0	3	75	5	1	.423	.369
Ladendorf, Tyler	R-R	5-11	195	3-7-88	.074	.000	.125	9	27	2	2	0	0	0	3	1	0	0	1	12	0	0	.074	.103
Lowe, Brandon	L-R	5-10	185	7-6-94	.143	.000	.333	2	7	0	1	0	0	0	0	0	0	0	0	2	0	0	.143	.143
Lowe, Nate	L-R	6-4	245	7-7-95	.289	.285	.291	93	329	63	95	24	0	16	63	72	4	0	1	82	1	0	.508	.421
Lukes, Nathan	L-R	5-11	185	7-12-94	.289	.191	.229	91	260	26	57	8	3	4	31	26	3	2	4	56	7	3	.319	.294
Mastrobuoni, Miles	L-R	5-11	175	10-31-95	.091	.000	.100	4	11	0	1	0	0	0	1	0	0	0	0	4	0	0	.091	.167
McCarthy, Joe	L-L	6-3	220	2-23-94	.196	.163	.210	41	148	24	29	6	2	6	23	29	3	0	2	54	1	0	.385	.335
Padlo, Kevin	R-R	6-2	205	7-15-96	.290	.463	.241	40	131	25	38	11	1	9	27	21	3	0	0	46	1	0	.595	.400
Perez, Michael	L-R	5-10	195	8-7-92	.245	.167	.272	54	184	23	45	7	0	13	42	28	0	0	4	51	0	2	.495	.338
Ricardo, Dashenko	R-R	6-0	205	3-1-90	.171	.200	.160	16	35	7	6	2	0	1	5	2	0	0	1	10	0	1	.314	.211
Robertson, Daniel	R-R	5-11	200	3-22-94	.260	.294	.243	28	104	11	27	1	0	2	9	16	3	0	0	25	1	0	.327	.374
Sanchez, Jesus	L-R	6-3	230	10-7-97	.206	.191	.214	18	63	6	13	2	1	1	5	6	1	0	1	20	0	0	.318	.282
Smolinski, Jake	R-R	5-11	210	2-9-89	.270	.293	.255	67	248	38	67	18	2	12	46	29	7	0	2	58	9	2	.504	.360
Solak, Nick	R-R	5-11	190	1-11-95	.266	.281	.256	85	301	56	80	13	1	17	47	39	4	0	4	80	3	2	.485	.353
Velazquez, Andrew	B-R	5-8	170	7-14-94	.271	.244	.286	34	129	20	35	9	1	4	16	10	1	1	0	30	2	4	.450	.329
2-team total (12 Columbus)					.264	.273	.261	46	174	25	46	13	2	4	21	10	2	1	0	39	3	5	.431	.312
Wendle, Joey	L-R	6-1	200	4-26-90	.263	.167	.429	5	19	3	5	2	0	0	2	0	0	0	0	4	1	0	.368	.333

Wong, Kean	L-R	5-11	185	4-17-95	.307	.262	.328	113	453	71	139	29	6	10	63	42	8	2	1	112	6	3	.464	.375

Pitching	B-T	HT	WT	DOB	W	L	ERA	G	GS	CG	SV	IP	H	R	ER	HR	BB	SO	AVG	vLH	vRH	K/9	BB/9
Alvarado, Jose	L-L	6-2	245	5-21-95	0	0	3.38	4	0	0	0	3	2	1	1	1	2	3	.200	.333	.143	10.13	6.75
Banda, Anthony	L-L	6-2	225	8-10-93	2	3	6.04	9	4	0	0	28	28	19	19	7	11	27	.262	.240	.268	8.58	3.49
Beeks, Jalen	L-L	5-11	200	7-10-93	0	1	4.22	3	3	0	0	11	8	5	5	2	4	10	.211	.125	.233	8.44	3.38
Cronenworth, Jake	L-R	6-1	185	1-21-94	0	0	0.00	7	6	0	0	7	4	2	0	0	8	9	.160	.200	.133	11.05	9.82
De Leon, Jose	R-R	6-1	220	8-7-92	2	1	3.51	17	13	0	1	51	41	20	20	4	27	73	.219	.238	.206	12.80	4.73
Drake, Oliver	R-R	6-4	215	1-13-87	1	2	4.94	19	2	0	6	24	20	13	13	2	7	40	.233	.235	.231	15.21	2.66
Fairbanks, Peter	R-R	6-6	219	12-16-93	1	2	5.09	16	1	0	0	18	15	11	10	3	6	30	.221	.400	.079	15.28	3.06
Faria, Jake	R-R	6-4	225	7-30-93	6	2	4.07	23	7	0	1	60	55	29	27	8	26	74	.246	.228	.258	11.16	3.92
Fleming, Josh	R-L	6-2	210	5-18-96	1	3	5.14	4	3	0	0	21	24	13	12	6	8	16	.286	.056	.349	6.86	3.43
Franco, Mike	R-R	5-11	220	11-30-91	5	0	4.11	22	0	0	1	35	30	16	16	5	17	34	.234	.292	.200	8.74	4.37
Gale, Rocky	R-R	6-1	185	2-22-88	0	0	18.00	1	0	0	0	1	3	2	2	0	0	0	.500	.667	.333	0.00	0.00
Gibaut, Ian	R-R	6-3	250	11-19-93	1	0	3.48	11	1	0	4	10	7	4	4	0	10	16	.189	.188	.191	13.94	8.71
Glasnow, Tyler	L-R	6-8	230	8-23-93	0	0	0.00	2	2	0	0	2	2	0	0	0	3	3	.250	.000	.286	11.57	11.57
James, Mac	R-R	6-1	215	6-2-93	0	0	40.50	1	0	0	0	1	3	3	3	0	1	0	.600	.500	.667	0.00	13.50
Kittredge, Andrew	R-R	6-1	235	3-17-90	2	1	1.93	27	1	0	6	37	24	9	8	3	6	55	.182	.250	.143	13.26	1.45
McKay, Brendan	L-L	6-2	212	12-18-95	3	0	0.84	7	6	0	0	32	17	4	3	1	9	40	.156	.238	.136	11.25	2.53
McWilliams, Sam	R-R	6-7	190	9-4-95	1	6	8.18	11	8	0	0	44	72	44	40	7	17	43	.369	.346	.386	8.83	3.48
Merritt, Ryan	L-L	6-0	170	2-21-92	4	4	7.04	27	11	0	0	78	115	66	61	19	23	64	.337	.431	.297	7.38	2.65
Milner, Hoby	L-L	6-3	175	1-13-91	3	3	3.06	50	0	0	12	62	47	25	21	7	13	89	.209	.241	.190	12.99	1.90
Moore, Andrew	R-R	6-0	195	6-2-94	0	2	12.98	5	4	0	0	17	29	26	25	9	10	10	.367	.290	.439	5.19	5.19
Nuno III, Vidal	L-L	5-11	210	7-26-87	1	2	7.58	27	2	0	0	30	44	29	25	4	12	33	.339	.325	.344	10.01	3.64
Pagan, Emilio	L-R	6-3	205	5-7-91	0	0	0.00	4	1	0	2	6	2	1	0	0	4	10	.095	.000	.154	15.00	6.00
Pinto, Ricardo	R-R	6-0	195	1-20-94	10	5	4.13	24	4	0	0	105	96	49	48	18	46	96	.249	.252	.247	8.25	3.96
Plassmeyer, Michael	L-L	6-2	197	11-5-96	0	0	0.00	1	0	0	0	0	0	0	0	0	1	0	.000	--	.000	9.00	0.00
Poche, Colin	L-L	6-3	235	1-17-94	2	2	6.26	20	2	0	0	27	32	20	19	4	9	48	.286	.263	.297	15.80	2.96
Pruitt, Austin	R-R	5-10	185	8-31-89	3	3	5.40	18	6	0	0	48	61	31	29	9	12	51	.305	.340	.274	9.50	2.23
Reyes, Arturo	R-R	5-11	185	4-6-92	7	6	4.82	23	19	0	0	106	112	71	57	19	43	89	.266	.299	.246	7.53	3.64
Richards, Trevor	R-R	6-2	190	5-15-93	0	0	1.69	3	3	0	0	5	4	1	1	0	4	8	.200	.182	.222	13.50	6.75
Rosenberg, Kenny	L-L	6-1	195	7-9-95	1	1	7.20	1	1	0	0	5	5	4	4	1	4	6	.278	.333	.267	10.80	7.20
Sadler, Casey	R-R	6-3	205	7-13-90	1	1	2.76	11	3	0	1	33	30	13	10	5	5	44	.233	.273	.212	12.12	1.38
Sanchez, Cristopher	L-L	6-5	165	12-12-96	0	0	20.25	1	0	0	0	1	2	3	3	0	2	0	.400	--	.400	0.00	13.50
Sanders, Phoenix	R-R	5-10	184	6-5-95	1	0	2.38	8	0	0	0	11	9	3	3	2	3	11	.220	.150	.286	8.74	2.38
Santos, Luis	R-R	6-0	225	2-11-91	3	2	4.90	32	3	0	1	64	64	38	35	10	28	74	.257	.263	.253	10.35	3.92
Slegers, Aaron	R-R	6-10	245	9-4-92	6	7	5.05	26	15	1	0	112	130	72	63	22	28	80	.290	.310	.273	6.41	2.24
Sulser, Cole	R-R	6-1	190	3-12-90	6	3	3.27	49	4	0	2	66	51	24	24	4	24	89	.208	.265	.170	12.14	3.27
Wood, Hunter	R-R	6-1	175	8-12-93	1	0	7.59	8	0	0	1	11	16	11	9	3	5	14	.333	.350	.321	11.81	4.22
2-team total (1 Columbus)					1	0	7.50	9	0	0	1	12	17	12	10	4	5	17	.321	.333	.313	12.75	3.75
Yarbrough, Ryan	R-L	6-5	210	12-31-91	2	1	3.81	5	4	0	0	26	24	11	11	2	3	35	.238	.200	.250	12.12	1.04
Zombro, Tyler	R-R	6-0	200	9-2-94	0	1	6.75	4	0	0	0	5	6	5	4	1	3	4	.286	.333	.267	6.75	5.06

Fielding

Catcher	PCT	G	PO	A	E	DP	PB
Bemboom	1.000	8	64	2	0	0	2
Ciuffo	.993	29	279	20	2	1	2
Gale	.969	7	62	1	2	0	0
James	.996	54	476	36	2	6	8
Perez	.995	44	371	31	2	1	2
Ricardo	1.000	11	53	8	0	1	1

First Base	PCT	G	PO	A	E	DP
Brosseau	.974	17	107	6	3	5
James	.983	9	53	5	1	3
Kelly	1.000	44	320	16	0	32
Lowe	.996	72	504	26	2	48
Padlo	.939	3	28	3	2	2

Second Base	PCT	G	PO	A	E	DP
Arroyo	1.000	1	3	3	0	0
Bonifacio	.000	2	0	0	0	0
Brosseau	1.000	7	15	16	0	6
Cronenworth	1.000	11	21	28	0	6
Fox	1.000	1	6	5	0	3
Ladendorf	1.000	1	6	8	0	2
Lowe	1.000	2	2	5	0	1
Mastrobuoni	1.000	1	0	2	0	0
Padlo	1.000	3	8	6	0	2
Robertson	.913	4	5	16	2	3
Solak	.964	61	87	101	7	21
Velazquez	1.000	1	2	1	0	0

Wendle	1.000	2	3	3	0	2
Wong	.971	48	73	95	5	24

Third Base	PCT	G	PO	A	E	DP
Arroyo	.918	20	17	28	4	4
Bonifacio	.958	7	6	17	1	1
Brosseau	.924	32	18	43	5	5
Cronenworth	1.000	3	2	5	0	0
Duffy	1.000	5	3	10	0	1
James	1.000	5	2	5	0	1
Lowe	.889	5	4	4	1	1
Mastrobuoni	1.000	3	0	3	0	0
Padlo	.967	31	25	63	3	8
Robertson	1.000	2	2	1	0	0
Solak	1.000	1	0	1	0	0
Velazquez	1.000	1	1	3	0	0
Wendle	1.000	1	1	1	0	0
Wong	.944	38	18	50	4	4

Shortstop	PCT	G	PO	A	E	DP
Arroyo	.968	9	12	18	1	1
Bonifacio	.969	12	10	21	1	2
Brosseau	1.000	7	7	19	0	6
Cronenworth	.960	64	62	152	9	27
Duffy	1.000	1	0	4	0	2
Fox	1.000	12	15	31	0	9
Ladendorf	.667	2	1	3	2	0
Robertson	.987	22	22	54	1	11

Velazquez	.935	10	12	17	2	2
Wendle	1.000	2	2	4	0	1
Wong	.875	6	9	5	2	0

Outfield	PCT	G	PO	A	E	DP
Bonifacio	.989	55	84	5	1	1
Brosseau	1.000	4	9	2	0	0
Coats	.972	83	132	6	4	0
Cozens	1.000	2	1	0	0	0
Duffy	1.000	2	1	0	0	0
Garcia	1.000	1	2	0	0	0
Heredia	1.000	8	11	1	0	0
Kelly	1.000	27	42	1	0	0
Ladendorf	1.000	4	6	0	0	0
Lukes	.976	86	163	3	4	1
Mastrobuoni	1.000	1	1	0	0	0
McCarthy	.985	36	65	0	1	0
Merritt	.000	1	0	0	0	0
Sanchez	1.000	15	35	0	0	0
Smolinski	.973	58	107	1	3	0
Solak	1.000	18	25	2	0	1
Velazquez	.981	22	49	2	1	0
Wong	1.000	21	38	4	0	0

Batting	B-T	HT	WT	DOB	AVG	vLH	vRH	G	AB	R	H	2B	3B	HR	RBI	BB	HBP	SH	SF	SO	SB	CS	SLG	OBP
Brujan, Vidal	B-R	5-9	155	2-9-98	.266	.193	.293	55	207	28	55	9	4	3	25	20	3	1	2	35	24	8	.391	.336
Chester, Carl	R-R	6-0	200	12-12-95	.265	.282	.256	31	121	14	32	7	2	2	14	6	0	0	0	31	5	2	.405	.299
Davis, Johnny	B-R	5-10	180	4-26-90	.000	.000	.000	5	2	1	0	0	0	0	0	0	0	0	0	1	3	1	.000	.000
Fox, Lucius	B-R	6-1	180	7-2-97	.230	.299	.205	104	365	60	84	16	8	3	33	53	9	1	3	89	37	11	.343	.340
Gray, Tristan	L-R	6-3	185	3-22-96	.225	.212	.230	122	418	59	94	16	5	17	64	61	9	1	6	92	2	10	.409	.332
Haley, Jim	R-R	6-1	195	2-23-95	.286	.325	.269	37	133	27	38	6	2	8	34	6	1	0	2	23	9	2	.541	.317
Kay, Grant	R-R	6-0	185	5-29-93	.250	.182	.286	11	32	5	8	1	0	2	5	2	0	0	0	13	2	1	.469	.294
Kelly, Dalton	L-L	6-3	180	8-4-94	.278	.206	.297	49	162	27	45	7	0	3	17	36	7	0	0	43	7	5	.377	.429
Lowe, Josh	L-R	6-4	205	2-2-98	.252	.264	.248	121	448	70	113	23	4	18	62	59	3	6	3	132	30	9	.442	.341
Mastrobuoni, Miles	L-R	5-11	175	10-31-95	.299	.324	.289	107	381	57	114	10	6	4	34	42	0	5	2	82	15	13	.389	.367
Milone, Thomas	L-L	5-11	190	1-26-95	.214	.200	.219	28	84	10	18	3	0	1	7	12	0	0	0	19	6	1	.286	.313
Padlo, Kevin	R-R	6-2	205	7-15-96	.250	.283	.241	70	220	39	55	20	0	12	35	47	4	0	6	70	11	4	.505	.383
Palacios, Jermaine	R-R	6-0	145	7-19-96	.195	.270	.163	42	123	18	24	3	1	2	17	14	0	1	2	27	8	5	.285	.273
Pinto, Rene	R-R	5-11	195	11-2-96	.235	.194	.248	77	260	23	61	16	0	5	30	22	4	0	1	68	1	2	.354	.303
Rodriguez, David	R-R	6-1	215	2-25-96	.225	.200	.233	78	262	34	59	10	3	7	36	29	1	1	2	68	4	1	.366	.303
Sanchez, Jesus	L-R	6-3	230	10-7-97	.275	.277	.275	78	287	32	79	11	1	8	49	24	2	0	3	65	5	4	.404	.332
Sullivan, Brett	L-R	6-1	195	2-22-94	.280	.272	.284	102	364	53	102	25	5	10	51	32	0	1	6	48	21	5	.459	.333
Tenerowicz, Robbie	R-R	6-1	185	1-6-95	.216	.312	.186	77	255	32	55	10	0	4	27	24	7	3	1	62	8	6	.302	.300
Walls, Taylor	B-R	5-10	180	7-10-96	.270	.179	.303	55	211	42	57	16	5	6	20	26	1	0	5	51	15	9	.479	.346

Pitching	B-T	HT	WT	DOB	W	L	ERA	G	GS	CG	SV	IP	H	R	ER	HR	BB	SO	AVG	vLH	vRH	K/9	BB/9
Bivens, Blake	R-R	6-2	205	8-11-95	4	0	3.95	27	3	0	1	57	54	29	25	5	39	33	.256	.260	.254	5.21	6.16
Campbell, Paul	L-R	6-0	190	7-26-95	8	4	3.36	16	11	0	0	86	74	33	32	6	20	63	.236	.298	.196	6.62	2.10
Charpie, Trevor	R-R	6-1	195	12-30-93	0	0	0.00	1	0	0	0	1	1	0	0	0	1	0	.200	.000	.250	6.75	6.75
Disla, Jose	R-R	6-2	165	3-11-96	0	2	3.38	6	1	0	0	8	3	3	3	1	5	3	.125	.091	.154	3.38	5.63
Fleming, Josh	R-L	6-2	210	5-18-96	11	4	3.31	21	17	3	0	128	127	57	47	9	19	92	.259	.178	.294	6.49	1.34
Garcia, Jason	R-R	6-0	185	11-21-92	7	1	5.07	10	8	0	0	50	60	31	28	3	21	35	.303	.348	.266	6.34	3.81
Gardeck, Ian	R-R	6-2	230	11-21-90	1	1	2.41	17	0	0	3	19	9	5	5	1	9	22	.148	.154	.143	10.61	4.34
Krook, Matt	L-L	6-4	225	10-21-94	2	3	4.50	32	18	0	0	50	46	28	25	3	32	52	.245	.180	.276	9.36	5.76
McClanahan, Shane	L-L	6-1	200	4-28-97	1	1	8.35	4	4	0	0	18	30	18	17	3	6	21	.366	.516	.275	10.31	2.95
McKay, Brendan	L-L	6-2	212	12-18-95	3	0	1.30	8	7	0	0	42	25	6	6	2	9	62	.172	.184	.168	13.39	1.94
McWilliams, Sam	R-R	6-7	190	9-4-95	6	3	2.05	15	11	0	0	88	80	22	20	3	30	66	.250	.291	.218	6.78	3.08
Moats, Dalton	L-L	6-3	210	5-24-95	2	3	3.17	42	2	0	6	65	60	30	23	8	24	62	.244	.163	.292	8.54	3.31
Moss, Benton	R-R	6-2	193	2-21-93	2	0	0.90	4	0	0	2	14	5	1	0	2	12	.182	.083	.238	10.80	1.80
O'Brien, Riley	R-R	6-4	170	2-6-95	5	6	3.93	14	11	1	0	69	56	33	30	4	29	72	.215	.209	.220	9.44	3.80
Pelaez, Ivan	L-L	5-11	155	2-1-94	3	3	4.31	36	3	0	2	56	62	31	27	7	10	33	.278	.288	.273	5.27	1.60
Pinto, Ricardo	R-R	6-0	195	1-20-94	2	1	4.82	4	2	0	0	19	20	10	10	2	8	15	.282	.269	.289	7.23	3.86
Raiden, Chandler	R-R	6-1	170	6-7-96	1	1	12.79	5	0	0	0	6	15	10	9	1	2	5	.429	.464	.411	7.11	2.84
Reyes, Arturo	R-R	5-11	185	4-6-92	4	1	3.00	5	4	0	0	30	20	10	10	2	4	23	.184	.143	.217	6.90	1.20
Romero, Tommy	L-R	6-2	225	7-8-97	1	0	7.50	1	1	0	0	6	7	5	5	1	2	1	.304	.500	.154	1.50	3.00
Rosenberg, Kenny	L-L	6-1	195	7-9-95	11	4	3.29	25	16	0	0	134	118	52	49	10	55	108	.240	.224	.247	7.25	3.69
Ryan, Joe	R-R	6-1	185	6-5-96	0	0	3.38	3	3	0	0	13	11	5	5	2	4	24	.220	.185	.261	16.20	2.70
Salinas, Jhonleider	R-R	6-7	215	9-25-95	4	2	2.70	23	3	0	1	30	25	10	9	2	17	39	.227	.220	.232	11.70	5.10
Sanders, Phoenix	R-R	5-10	184	6-5-95	3	3	1.81	37	1	0	15	50	35	17	10	3	23	57	.197	.220	.185	10.33	4.17
Shaffer, Brian	R-R	6-5	200	8-12-96	4	3	2.38	25	3	0	1	72	55	19	19	0	21	70	.211	.217	.207	8.75	2.63
Sullivan, Brett	L-R	6-1	195	2-22-94	0	0	4.50	2	0	0	0	2	1	1	1	0	0	0	.200	.000	.333	0.00	0.00
Taylor, Curtis	R-R	6-6	230	7-25-95	0	3	3.06	15	1	0	7	18	14	9	6	0	5	16	.206	.044	.289	8.15	2.55
Thompson, Ryan	R-R	6-6	221	6-26-92	1	1	3.10	14	5	0	0	20	24	8	7	1	6	20	.289	.387	.231	8.85	2.66
Zombro, Tyler	R-R	6-0	200	9-2-94	2	0	1.87	37	3	0	11	58	44	14	12	1	7	53	.216	.231	.206	8.27	1.09

Fielding

Catcher	PCT	G	PO	A	E	DP	PB
Pinto	.991	67	514	62	5	4	5
Rodriguez	.990	61	463	32	5	3	2
Sullivan	1.000	14	87	8	0	1	1

First Base	PCT	G	PO	A	E	DP
Gray	.988	47	377	19	5	32
Haley	1.000	5	43	1	0	4
Kay	1.000	8	51	2	0	8
Kelly	.997	47	345	23	1	31
Padlo	.967	6	56	3	2	4
Pinto	.000	1	0	0	0	0
Rodriguez	1.000	2	5	0	0	0
Tenerowicz	.988	28	237	19	3	29

Second Base	PCT	G	PO	A	E	DP
Brujan	.994	33	64	94	1	21
Fox	1.000	12	22	34	0	10

	PCT	G	PO	A	E	DP
Gray	.972	30	51	54	3	17
Mastrobuoni	.972	26	47	59	3	14
Palacios	.983	24	43	74	2	14
Tenerowicz	.973	8	15	21	1	4
Walls	.957	9	14	30	2	7

Third Base	PCT	G	PO	A	E	DP
Fox	.917	9	8	14	2	1
Gray	.906	30	19	39	6	6
Haley	.945	26	13	39	3	7
Mastrobuoni	.778	4	3	4	2	0
Padlo	.951	57	52	121	9	8
Palacios	.905	10	8	11	2	2
Tenerowicz	.667	2	0	2	1	0
Walls	1.000	6	3	13	0	2

Shortstop	PCT	G	PO	A	E	DP
Brujan	.913	15	19	44	6	9
Fox	.945	79	83	177	15	36
Gray	.952	10	11	29	2	5
Palacios	1.000	2	1	8	0	0
Walls	.966	35	50	93	5	19

Outfield	PCT	G	PO	A	E	DP
Chester	.971	29	64	3	2	0
Davis	1.000	2	1	0	0	0
Haley	1.000	6	9	0	0	0
Kelly	1.000	3	9	0	0	0
Lowe	.993	120	275	11	2	3
Mastrobuoni	.994	78	147	7	1	1
Milone	1.000	28	55	2	0	1
Sanchez	.986	72	132	6	2	1
Sullivan	.984	61	109	11	2	1
Tenerowicz	1.000	28	52	4	0	1

CHARLOTTE STONE CRABS

FLORIDA STATE LEAGUE

Batting	B-T	HT	WT	DOB	AVG	vLH	vRH	G	AB	R	H	2B	3B	HR	RBI	BB	HBP	SH	SF	SO	SB	CS	SLG	OBP
Aranda, Jonathan	L-R	5-10	173	5-23-98	.235	.250	.231	5	17	3	4	0	0	0	0	2	0	0	0	1	0	0	.235	.316
Bemboom, Anthony	L-R	6-2	200	1-18-90	.133	.000	.167	4	15	1	2	0	0	0	0	1	0	0	0	6	0	0	.133	.188
Brujan, Vidal	B-R	5-9	155	2-9-98	.290	.216	.309	44	176	28	51	8	3	1	15	17	2	0	1	26	24	5	.386	.357
Chester, Carl	R-R	6-0	200	12-12-95	.254	.232	.260	88	323	34	82	12	2	4	32	25	4	1	1	82	17	5	.341	.314
Dodson, Tanner	B-R	6-1	160	5-9-97	.250	.200	.267	15	60	9	15	4	1	0	8	3	0	0	0	10	3	1	.350	.286
Duffy, Matt	R-R	6-2	190	1-15-91	.250	.286	.222	7	16	4	4	0	1	1	1	5	2	0	0	1	0	0	.563	.478
Franco, Wander	B-R	5-10	189	3-1-01	.339	.375	.331	52	192	40	65	11	2	3	24	26	0	0	5	15	4	5	.464	.408
Frank, Tyler	R-R	6-0	185	1-15-97	.154	.188	.139	16	52	8	8	1	0	0	4	9	1	0	1	13	3	0	.173	.286
Gomez, Moises	R-R	5-11	200	8-27-98	.220	.266	.209	119	428	55	94	26	2	16	66	48	3	0	10	164	3	3	.402	.297
Haley, Jim	R-R	6-1	195	2-23-95	.280	.250	.287	85	318	46	89	13	1	8	47	19	7	0	1	85	18	3	.403	.333
Hernandez, Ronaldo	R-R	6-1	185	11-11-97	.265	.254	.267	103	393	43	104	19	3	9	60	17	6	0	9	65	7	0	.397	.299
Hollis, Connor	R-R	5-10	170	11-18-94	.226	.143	.250	12	31	7	7	1	0	0	3	7	2	0	0	7	1	1	.258	.400
Hulsizer, Niko	R-R	6-2	225	2-1-97	.235	.167	.250	9	34	4	8	2	0	1	4	4	0	0	1	11	0	1	.382	.308
Johnson, Kaleo	R-R	6-3	220	8-26-96	.231	.441	.193	61	221	17	51	13	0	4	24	10	8	0	2	66	1	0	.344	.286
Kiermaier, Kevin	L-R	6-1	210	4-22-90	.125	.500	.000	2	8	1	1	1	0	0	3	1	0	0	0	3	0	0	.250	.222
Law, Zacrey	R-R	6-0	190	7-8-96	.208	.316	.170	22	72	9	15	4	0	0	6	7	4	0	1	20	1	0	.264	.310
Lowe, Brandon	L-R	5-10	185	7-6-94	.167	--	.167	2	6	2	1	1	0	0	2	1	1	0	0	0	0	0	.333	.375
McCarthy, Joe	L-L	6-3	220	2-23-94	.125	.333	.000	2	8	0	1	0	0	0	0	0	0	0	0	4	0	0	.125	.125
Milone, Thomas	L-L	5-11	190	1-26-95	.309	.250	.317	55	204	38	63	7	10	3	28	20	2	3	4	42	12	2	.485	.370
Olive, Russ	L-L	6-3	205	6-3-96	.151	.200	.146	32	93	4	16	3	0	0	7	4	1	0	2	31	0	1	.179	.186
Palacios, Jermaine	R-R	6-0	145	7-19-96	.231	.188	.240	32	91	9	21	1	0	0	9	5	1	0	0	25	1	2	.242	.278
Palomaki, Jake	B-R	5-10	175	7-17-95	.253	.179	.264	70	225	35	57	8	0	0	17	24	5	0	2	28	11	4	.289	.336
Perez, Michael	L-R	5-10	195	8-7-92	.556	--	.556	3	9	1	5	0	0	0	1	0	0	0	0	1	0	0	.556	.556
Roach, Joey	L-R	6-0	205	8-27-93	.248	.364	.221	43	117	14	29	6	2	1	13	12	5	1	0	17	1	1	.359	.343
Robertson, Daniel	R-R	5-11	200	3-22-94	.222	.000	.333	3	9	0	2	1	0	0	2	1	1	0	0	3	0	0	.333	.364
Rutherford, Zach	R-R	6-2	180	3-13-96	.224	.172	.235	109	349	39	78	9	0	2	28	37	8	5	6	92	9	4	.267	.308
Seibert, Mac	R-R	6-0	195	11-17-93	.267	.000	.333	16	45	3	12	0	0	0	4	4	0	0	1	15	0	1	.267	.320
Smith, Michael	L-L	5-11	165	5-30-97	.263	.222	.267	50	179	26	47	10	1	2	20	15	6	4	2	51	11	5	.363	.337
Walls, Taylor	B-R	5-10	180	7-10-96	.269	.263	.271	41	156	22	42	7	2	4	26	19	0	0	5	28	13	6	.417	.339
Wendle, Joey	L-R	6-1	200	4-26-90	.364	.000	.400	3	11	3	4	1	0	1	3	2	0	0	0	1	1	0	.727	.462
Whalen, Seaver	R-R	6-2	185	2-5-95	.188	.208	.180	30	85	7	16	4	1	1	8	6	5	3	0	31	0	0	.294	.281
Whitley, Garrett	R-R	6-1	195	3-13-97	.226	.206	.231	114	371	51	84	25	7	10	40	62	2	2	2	163	16	12	.412	.339
Wilson, Izzy	L-R	6-3	185	3-6-98	.270	.091	.308	20	63	7	17	5	1	1	8	11	0	0	0	19	3	2	.429	.378
2-team total (45 Florida)					.209	.125	.221	65	187	27	39	10	3	3	14	29	1	0	0	73	10	3	.342	.318
Zunino, Mike	R-R	6-2	235	3-25-91	.500	--	.500	2	6	3	3	1	0	0	1	2	0	0	0	3	0	0	.667	.625

Pitching	B-T	HT	WT	DOB	W	L	ERA	G	GS	CG	SV	IP	H	R	ER	HR	BB	SO	AVG	vLH	vRH	K/9	BB/9
Alvarado, Jose	L-L	6-2	245	5-21-95	0	0	0.00	1	1	0	0	1	0	0	0	0	0	0	.000	.000	.000	0.00	0.00
Banda, Anthony	L-L	6-2	225	8-10-93	0	0	0.00	2	2	0	0	3	1	0	0	0	0	2	.111	.167	.000	6.75	0.00
Campbell, Paul	L-R	6-0	190	7-26-95	5	4	4.12	11	9	0	0	59	52	29	27	3	17	49	.240	.255	.226	7.47	2.59
Cumbie, Trey	L-L	6-2	200	7-12-96	1	0	1.91	16	1	0	2	28	23	7	6	0	11	28	.223	.125	.286	8.89	3.49
De Leon, Jose	R-R	6-2	220	8-7-92	0	0	3.86	2	2	0	0	5	4	3	2	1	3	1	.250	.300	.167	1.93	5.79
Dodson, Tanner	B-R	6-1	160	5-9-97	0	1	5.29	8	3	0	0	17	28	11	10	2	9	15	.378	.460	.297	7.94	4.76
Franco, Mike	R-R	5-11	220	11-30-91	0	0	9.00	2	0	0	0	3	3	3	3	0	2	7	.273	.250	.286	21.00	6.00
Garcia, Carlos	R-R	6-3	185	11-28-94	0	0	0.00	2	0	0	0	4	1	0	0	0	0	6	.071	.200	.000	12.46	2.08
Gardeck, Ian	R-R	6-2	230	11-21-90	0	0	0.00	1	0	0	0	1	0	0	0	0	0	0	.000	.000	.000	0.00	0.00
Gibaut, Ian	R-R	6-3	250	11-19-93	0	1	0.00	2	0	0	0	2	5	6	0	1	1	1	.417	.571	.200	4.50	4.50
Hogan, Miller	R-R	6-2	200	7-18-96	0	0	0.00	1	0	0	0	2	0	0	0	0	2	1	.000	.000	.000	4.50	9.00
Jackson, Ryan	R-R	5-10	190	3-5-96	0	0	0.00	3	0	0	0	3	1	0	0	0	1	0	.111	.000	.167	3.00	0.00
Labosky, Jack	R-R	6-3	235	7-19-96	3	6	2.62	33	1	0	5	65	62	24	19	3	7	50	.246	.203	.287	6.89	0.96
Linares, Resly	L-L	6-2	170	12-11-97	0	0	5.79	2	2	0	0	5	6	3	3	0	6	2	.316	.429	.250	3.86	11.57
Marsden, Justin	R-R	6-4	175	1-27-97	1	4	6.82	18	1	0	3	33	40	28	25	2	17	33	.310	.421	.222	9.00	4.64
McClanahan, Shane	L-L	6-1	200	4-28-97	6	1	1.46	9	8	0	0	49	33	11	8	1	8	59	.183	.196	.178	10.76	1.46
Moss, Benton	R-R	6-2	193	2-21-93	1	0	2.25	2	0	0	0	4	6	2	1	0	0	1	.353	.375	.333	2.25	0.00
Myers, Tobias	R-R	6-0	193	8-5-98	8	1	2.31	18	13	0	0	78	72	22	20	4	25	53	.253	.250	.255	6.12	2.88
O'Brien, Riley	R-R	6-4	170	2-6-95	2	0	1.59	6	0	0	0	34	20	8	6	2	15	35	.172	.226	.127	9.26	3.97
Ogando, Cristofer	R-R	6-3	195	10-23-93	0	0	2.70	7	0	0	2	10	5	3	3	1	2	5	.152	.125	.177	4.50	1.80
Palacios, Jermaine	R-R	6-0	145	7-19-96	0	0	0.00	1	0	0	0	1	1	0	0	0	0	0	.250	.333	.000	0.00	0.00
Plassmeyer, Michael	L-L	6-2	197	11-5-96	7	2	2.12	19	18	1	0	102	89	34	24	5	16	76	.235	.188	.253	6.73	1.42
Raiden, Chandler	R-R	6-1	170	6-7-96	6	4	2.93	37	1	0	9	55	47	24	18	3	17	44	.232	.227	.235	7.16	2.77
Romero, Orlando	R-R	6-0	211	9-26-96	0	0	6.14	8	0	0	0	15	19	10	10	2	7	15	.317	.370	.273	9.20	4.30
Romero, Tommy	R-R	6-2	225	7-8-97	12	4	1.89	23	18	1	0	119	86	28	25	4	36	103	.205	.241	.175	7.77	2.72
Rosenblum-Larson, Simon	R-R	6-3	202	2-11-97	2	3	3.13	37	2	0	8	60	44	28	21	4	34	74	.202	.180	.220	11.04	5.07
Ryan, Joe	R-R	6-1	185	6-5-96	7	2	1.42	15	13	0	0	83	47	16	13	3	12	112	.161	.165	.157	12.19	1.31
Salinas, Jhonleider	R-R	6-7	215	9-25-95	3	3	3.75	19	5	0	3	36	36	18	15	3	16	29	.263	.317	.221	7.25	4.00
Sanchez, Cristopher	L-L	6-5	165	12-12-96	1	0	1.85	12	6	0	0	34	28	9	7	0	13	36	.231	.326	.180	9.53	3.44
Seelinger, Matt	R-R	6-0	205	4-19-95	2	0	10.00	6	0	0	0	9	10	10	10	1	4	7	.278	.313	.250	7.00	4.00
Shaffer, Brian	R-R	6-5	200	8-12-96	0	0	2.40	8	3	0	0	30	24	12	8	3	5	24	.212	.140	.286	7.20	1.50
Sherriff, Ryan	L-L	6-1	185	5-25-90	0	1	3.00	2	0	0	1	3	5	1	1	0	0	0	.385	.750	.222	0.00	0.00
Strotman, Drew	R-R	6-3	195	9-3-96	0	2	5.06	5	5	0	0	16	20	10	9	3	9	13	.318	.333	.300	7.31	5.06
Thompson, Ryan	R-R	6-6	221	6-26-92	0	0	0.00	2	0	0	1	3	2	0	0	0	0	5	.286	.000		15.00	0.00

Pitching	B-T	HT	WT	DOB	W	L	ERA	G	GS	CG	SV	IP	H	R	ER	HR	BB	SO	AVG	vLH	vRH	K/9	BB/9
Valverde, Alex	R-R	6-2	185	9-26-96	4	6	4.29	34	0	0	3	65	63	35	31	11	22	65	.249	.264	.238	9.00	3.05
Wood, Hunter	R-R	6-1	175	8-12-93	0	0	0.00	2	1	0	0	3	0	0	0	0	1	4	.000	.000	.000	12.00	3.00
Woods Jr., Stephen	R-R	6-2	200	6-10-95	9	3	1.88	18	12	0	0	86	71	25	18	2	33	79	.225	.275	.166	8.24	3.44
York, Mikey	R-R	6-2	190	2-24-96	1	5	3.56	28	2	0	7	43	43	20	17	3	19	46	.259	.236	.277	9.63	3.98

Fielding

Catcher	PCT	G	PO	A	E	DP	PB
Bemboom	1.000	4	32	3	0	0	2
Hernandez	.990	81	634	47	7	2	13
Law	.984	15	111	9	2	1	2
Perez	1.000	2	18	0	0	0	0
Roach	.996	33	236	14	1	1	4
Seibert	.964	8	49	4	2	0	1
Zunino	1.000	2	13	2	0	0	0

First Base	PCT	G	PO	A	E	DP
Haley	.976	27	190	15	5	17
Hollis	1.000	2	10	0	0	1
Johnson	.972	47	324	23	10	31
Olive	.986	28	203	15	3	29
Roach	.950	8	52	5	3	7
Rutherford	.971	10	64	4	2	11
Seibert	1.000	2	5	1	0	1
Whalen	1.000	24	159	19	0	22

Second Base	PCT	G	PO	A	E	DP
Aranda	.962	5	11	14	1	5
Brujan	.967	29	47	70	4	19
Frank	.957	5	9	13	1	3
Haley	.958	5	9	14	1	4
Hollis	.952	5	10	10	1	4
Lowe	1.000	1	2	3	0	0
Palacios	1.000	6	8	10	0	2
Palomaki	.991	55	89	125	2	44
Robertson	.000	1	0	0	0	0
Rutherford	.981	31	48	54	2	15
Walls	1.000	1	1	3	0	0
Wendle	1.000	2	1	3	0	2

Third Base	PCT	G	PO	A	E	DP
Duffy	1.000	4	1	5	0	0
Frank	1.000	4	3	3	0	1
Haley	.929	41	29	49	6	5
Hollis	1.000	5	0	9	0	0
Johnson	.833	9	7	8	3	1
Palacios	1.000	14	7	13	0	1
Palomaki	.944	14	4	30	2	3
Robertson	1.000	1	1	1	0	0
Rutherford	.979	47	37	57	2	8
Wendle	1.000	1	0	3	0	0
Whalen	1.000	5	2	2	0	0
Wilson	.000	1	0	0	0	0

Shortstop	PCT	G	PO	A	E	DP
Brujan	.900	14	18	36	6	10
Duffy	1.000	1	0	4	0	1
Franco	.967	45	69	133	7	29
Frank	.950	6	11	8	1	5
Palacios	.974	10	12	25	1	5
Palomaki	.000	1	0	0	0	0
Rutherford	.927	25	16	53	7	7
Walls	.979	36	38	99	3	24

Outfield	PCT	G	PO	A	E	DP
Chester	.982	74	163	3	3	2
Dodson	1.000	11	30	1	0	0
Gomez	.986	98	197	9	3	2
Haley	1.000	7	9	2	0	0
Hulsizer	1.000	8	19	0	0	0
Kiermaier	1.000	1	3	0	0	0
McCarthy	1.000	2	4	0	0	0
Milone	.990	46	96	5	1	1
Smith	.989	46	92	2	1	0
Whitley	.995	101	193	4	1	0
Wilson	.968	15	30	0	1	0

BOWLING GREEN HOT RODS

MIDWEST LEAGUE

LOW CLASS A

Batting	B-T	HT	WT	DOB	AVG	vLH	vRH	G	AB	R	H	2B	3B	HR	RBI	BB	HBP	SH	SF	SO	SB	CS	SLG	OBP
Alvarez, Roberto	R-R	5-11	151	7-28-99	.249	.245	.251	102	377	30	94	13	3	3	42	17	7	1	4	70	2	0	.324	.291
Aranda, Jonathan	L-R	5-10	173	5-23-98	.275	.273	.276	59	211	28	58	13	2	3	35	30	0	0	4	43	1	1	.398	.359
Betts, Chris	L-R	6-2	215	3-10-97	.210	.162	.226	110	395	60	83	14	2	19	73	67	7	0	3	136	3	0	.400	.333
Brown, Bryce	R-R	6-1	185	7-23-96	.200	.294	.143	13	45	10	9	1	1	1	6	7	1	0	1	18	3	2	.333	.315
Brundage, Beau	L-R	6-3	170	4-29-97	.181	.120	.194	44	133	16	24	5	2	1	16	26	5	0	0	44	5	3	.271	.335
Cardenas, Ruben	R-R	6-2	185	10-10-97	.234	.250	.228	30	111	14	26	5	1	3	16	13	2	0	1	21	2	3	.378	.323
2-team total (84 Lake County)					.272	.309	.261	114	431	58	117	24	7	13	70	40	5	1	4	90	11	10	.450	.338
Franco, Wander	B-R	5-10	189	3-1-01	.318	.250	.341	62	233	42	74	16	5	6	29	30	2	0	7	20	14	9	.506	.390
Gregorio, Osmy	R-R	6-2	175	5-27-98	.201	.185	.207	115	408	58	82	14	2	7	37	36	5	1	4	111	19	4	.297	.272
Hollis, Connor	R-R	5-10	170	11-18-94	.281	.317	.268	41	153	28	43	13	2	4	18	13	7	0	2	33	4	1	.471	.360
Johnson, Kaleo	R-R	6-3	220	8-26-96	.286	.269	.290	60	238	26	68	13	1	7	37	14	5	0	1	59	4	1	.437	.337
Olive, Russ	L-L	6-5	205	6-3-96	.154	.188	.143	21	65	5	10	2	0	1	6	3	0	0	1	15	0	0	.231	.188
Ostberg, Erik	L-R	5-10	225	10-12-95	.247	.313	.215	29	97	12	24	3	0	1	7	10	2	0	0	30	0	0	.309	.330
Palomaki, Jake	B-R	5-10	175	7-17-95	.250	.226	.260	33	108	17	27	4	2	1	18	16	1	1	2	22	4	1	.352	.347
Pena, Tony	R-R	5-11	180	9-24-97	.235	.233	.235	76	264	26	62	8	1	1	18	21	2	1	0	67	7	4	.284	.296
Proctor, Ford	L-R	6-1	195	12-4-96	.290	.283	.293	121	458	76	133	29	2	6	53	69	3	1	5	90	11	8	.402	.383
Qsar, Jordan	L-R	6-3	195	12-2-95	.209	.170	.224	59	196	32	41	8	3	9	28	36	1	0	0	93	5	2	.418	.335
Santiago, Kevin	R-R	6-0	170	9-28-97	.164	.375	.128	18	55	9	9	2	1	2	9	6	5	1	1	21	0	1	.346	.299
Schnell, Nick	L-R	6-3	180	4-25-00	.236	.211	.250	14	55	7	13	3	1	0	3	2	1	1	1	24	0	1	.327	.271
Smith, Michael	L-L	5-11	165	5-30-97	.270	.311	.254	48	167	18	45	3	3	0	20	24	3	3	1	30	8	4	.323	.369
Soria, Nate	R-R	5-10	175	11-24-95	.111	--	.111	3	9	2	1	0	1	0	1	2	0	0	0	5	0	0	.333	.273
Whalen, Seaver	R-R	6-2	185	2-5-95	.237	.254	.231	70	241	27	57	12	0	6	30	20	14	1	3	43	4	1	.361	.327
Wilson, Izzy	L-R	6-3	185	3-6-98	.235	.222	.239	25	85	11	20	1	1	3	13	11	2	0	0	28	7	2	.377	.337
Witherspoon, Grant	L-L	6-3	200	9-27-96	.248	.269	.241	119	440	71	109	24	5	10	54	44	2	0	4	101	22	6	.393	.316

Pitching	B-T	HT	WT	DOB	W	L	ERA	G	GS	CG	SV	IP	H	R	ER	HR	BB	SO	AVG	vLH	vRH	K/9	BB/9
Baz, Shane	R-R	6-2	190	6-17-99	3	2	2.99	17	17	0	0	81	63	30	27	5	37	87	.213	.215	.211	9.63	4.09
Costanzo, Michael	L-L	6-1	190	11-14-95	1	3	3.73	16	1	0	3	31	33	14	13	2	8	29	.271	.162	.318	8.33	2.30
Cumbie, Trey	L-L	6-2	200	7-12-96	2	1	3.06	17	0	0	4	32	28	14	11	3	18	50	.230	.324	.188	13.92	5.01
Figueroa, Hector	R-R	6-3	190	11-30-94	1	1	0.84	6	0	0	0	11	9	4	1	0	3	8	.225	.381	.053	6.75	2.53
Gau, Christopher	R-R	6-2	205	2-3-97	0	1	36.00	2	0	0	0	1	3	4	4	0	2	2	.500	.000	.600	18.00	18.00
Hogan, Miller	R-R	6-2	200	7-18-96	7	3	3.08	20	9	0	1	79	73	29	27	8	9	79	.241	.248	.235	9.00	1.03
Hollis, Connor	R-R	5-10	170	11-18-94	0	0	20.25	1	0	0	0	1	3	3	2	0	1	0	.429	.500	.333	6.75	0.00
Lara, Miguel	R-R	6-1	165	7-17-97	0	1	11.81	8	1	0	0	11	14	14	14	1	14	15	.306	.455	.240	12.66	11.81
Liberatore, Matthew	L-L	6-5	200	11-6-99	6	2	3.10	16	15	1	0	78	70	33	27	2	31	76	.237	.290	.213	8.73	3.56
Marsden, Justin	R-R	6-4	175	1-27-97	2	1	3.29	7	0	0	0	14	12	10	5	2	8	15	.235	.375	.171	9.88	5.27
McClanahan, Shane	L-L	6-1	200	4-28-97	4	4	3.40	11	10	0	0	53	38	22	20	3	24	75	.199	.068	.238	12.57	5.26
McGee, Easton	R-R	6-6	205	12-26-97	7	5	3.67	24	22	0	0	125	129	57	51	13	25	95	.265	.242	.280	6.84	1.80
Moore, Steffon	L-L	6-3	185	6-25-97	0	1	11.05	5	1	0	0	7	17	15	9	2	9	12	.425	.222	.484	14.73	11.05
Muller, Chris	R-R	6-5	210	4-22-96	2	5	2.88	31	1	0	4	56	39	26	18	4	26	87	.188	.184	.191	13.90	4.15
Ogando, Cristofer	R-R	6-3	195	10-23-93	2	2	2.61	31	0	0	6	52	35	19	15	5	32	65	.189	.144	.240	11.32	5.57
Padilla, Nicholas	R-R	6-2	220	12-24-96	7	2	3.48	32	0	0	2	62	61	26	24	4	29	76	.260	.263	.257	11.03	4.21
Palomaki, Jake	B-R	5-10	175	7-17-95	0	0	0.00	1	0	0	0	2	0	0	0	0	0	0	.000	.000	.000	0.00	0.00
Peguero, Joel	R-R	5-11	160	5-5-97	3	4	2.85	31	0	0	16	47	42	19	15	1	11	44	.240	.275	.217	8.37	2.09

Pitching	B-T	HT	WT	DOB	W	L	ERA	G	GS	CG	SV	IP	H	R	ER	HR	BB	SO	AVG	vLH	vRH	K/9	BB/9
Plassmeyer, Michael	L-L	6-2	197	11-5-96	2	1	1.23	5	5	0	0	29	21	4	4	3	7	32	.208	.125	.234	9.82	2.15
Ryan, Joe	R-R	6-1	185	6-5-96	2	2	2.93	6	6	0	0	28	19	13	9	2	11	47	.185	.178	.190	15.29	3.58
Sampen, Caleb	R-R	6-2	185	7-23-96	9	4	2.68	22	21	0	0	121	91	39	36	3	32	104	.206	.188	.217	7.74	2.38
Sanchez, Cristopher	L-L	6-5	165	12-12-96	3	1	2.01	11	4	0	2	40	28	11	9	3	11	37	.191	.189	.192	8.26	2.45
Sprengel, Nick	L-L	6-2	220	6-4-97	1	5	3.82	35	0	0	1	66	63	38	28	2	20	63	.252	.261	.247	8.59	2.73
Strong, Alan	R-R	6-3	200	10-22-96	10	4	2.85	22	18	0	0	126	114	46	40	12	24	109	.238	.254	.227	7.77	1.71
Trageton, Zack	R-R	6-1	225	9-2-98	5	0	2.31	7	6	0	0	35	35	10	9	2	8	34	.256	.172	.317	8.74	2.06
Witt, Nathan	R-R	6-4	210	4-19-96	1	3	2.92	15	2	0	1	25	23	15	8	0	13	21	.235	.268	.211	7.66	4.74
2-team total (22 Great Lakes)					2	5	4.10	37	2	0	6	48	50	31	22	2	20	52	.255	.284	.235	9.68	3.72

Fielding

Catcher	PCT	G	PO	A	E	DP	PB
Alvarez	.979	65	538	57	13	3	6
Betts	.994	68	638	62	4	8	8
Ostberg	1.000	5	28	6	0	0	0
Soria	1.000	3	26	1	0	0	2

First Base	PCT	G	PO	A	E	DP
Aranda	1.000	10	68	2	0	9
Hollis	.992	15	111	9	1	8
Johnson	.987	54	426	26	6	40
Olive	.985	21	126	5	2	8
Ostberg	.992	17	114	10	1	9
Whalen	.985	31	243	21	4	21

Second Base	PCT	G	PO	A	E	DP
Aranda	.956	44	66	108	8	26
Gregorio	.949	18	35	40	4	9

	PCT	G	PO	A	E	DP
Hollis	.889	5	10	6	2	2
Palomaki	1.000	10	12	21	0	3
Proctor	1.000	47	80	122	0	26
Santiago	.960	18	27	45	3	8

Third Base	PCT	G	PO	A	E	DP
Aranda	.778	3	3	4	2	1
Gregorio	.887	64	36	98	17	6
Hollis	.979	20	13	34	1	4
Johnson	1.000	2	0	3	0	0
Palomaki	.846	16	7	15	4	2
Proctor	.889	12	12	20	4	1
Whalen	.965	32	22	60	3	1

Shortstop	PCT	G	PO	A	E	DP
Franco	.969	53	68	122	6	27
Gregorio	.887	32	37	57	12	14
Proctor	.947	57	74	139	12	29

Outfield	PCT	G	PO	A	E	DP
Brown	1.000	13	24	1	0	0
Brundage	.988	44	78	1	1	0
Cardenas	1.000	28	52	2	0	0
Palomaki	.900	9	8	1	1	1
Pena	.938	76	116	6	8	0
Qsar	.977	50	79	7	2	1
Schnell	1.000	12	32	1	0	1
Smith	1.000	48	100	7	0	2
Whalen	.933	10	13	1	1	0
Wilson	.948	25	52	3	3	0
Witherspoon	.986	109	212	6	3	3

HUDSON VALLEY RENEGADES
NEW YORK-PENN LEAGUE

SHORT SEASON

Batting	B-T	HT	WT	DOB	AVG	vLH	vRH	G	AB	R	H	2B	3B	HR	RBI	BB	HBP	SH	SF	SO	SB	CS	SLG	OBP
Alexander, Hill	R-R	6-2	200	6-13-96	.264	.279	.261	64	231	43	61	10	3	4	41	26	8	0	3	69	8	2	.385	.355
Arcendo, Luis	B-R	6-1	160	11-1-99	.256	.167	.271	26	82	10	21	2	2	0	6	10	0	3	0	17	5	4	.329	.337
Brito, Raider	R-R	6-1	164	5-17-99	.125	.000	.143	2	8	0	1	0	0	0	2	0	0	0	0	5	0	0	.125	.125
Brundage, Beau	L-R	6-3	170	4-29-97	.259	.292	.250	33	116	16	30	5	2	1	11	17	3	1	2	46	4	5	.362	.365
Diaz, Pedro	R-R	6-3	210	1-9-99	.220	.227	.219	34	118	17	26	6	1	1	17	3	6	0	0	40	4	0	.314	.276
Edwards, K.V.	R-R	6-1	175	3-5-98	.213	.325	.187	62	211	35	45	6	4	4	12	18	2	2	1	71	19	7	.337	.280
Embry, Jonathan	L-R	5-11	180	11-26-96	.185	.167	.191	37	119	13	22	5	2	0	11	24	2	0	1	32	3	1	.261	.329
Hiott, Garrett	R-R	5-11	175	7-7-97	.271	.250	.275	56	203	37	55	4	5	1	28	32	4	0	2	46	20	5	.355	.378
Jones, Greg	B-R	6-2	175	3-7-98	.335	.303	.342	48	191	39	64	13	4	1	24	22	4	0	1	56	19	8	.461	.413
Kinamon, Duke	R-R	5-11	185	9-4-96	.000	--	.000	1	2	1	0	0	0	0	1	0	0	1	0	1	0	0	.000	.333
Leon, Luis	B-R	6-0	175	9-10-98	.125	--	.125	3	8	0	1	1	0	0	1	0	0	0	0	1	0	0	.250	.222
Mallard, Mason	R-R	5-10	185	2-22-96	.277	.177	.299	29	94	11	26	3	2	0	11	7	1	0	1	20	3	1	.351	.330
McGowan, Jacson	R-R	6-3	212	6-14-96	.244	.283	.234	67	238	23	58	17	1	2	43	39	1	0	5	77	6	1	.349	.346
Muffley, Jordyn	R-R	6-1	195	4-14-97	.175	.160	.179	38	137	13	24	1	0	2	13	3	2	0	2	26	4	0	.226	.201
Pedroza, Cristhian	R-R	5-10	173	2-14-99	.181	.188	.180	47	149	23	27	5	0	2	15	15	6	3	3	52	2	1	.255	.278
Santiago, Kevin	R-R	6-0	170	9-28-97	.059	.200	.035	16	34	5	2	1	0	0	7	3	0	0	0	18	0	0	.088	.273
Sogard, Nick	B-R	6-1	180	9-9-97	.290	.267	.296	63	214	36	62	5	0	0	21	39	5	0	4	43	20	6	.313	.405
Trevino, Luis	R-R	5-11	200	3-23-96	.272	.150	.298	34	114	10	31	7	0	1	19	7	6	0	1	16	0	1	.360	.344
Troike, Ben	R-R	5-10	170	2-5-98	.168	.000	.205	30	95	9	16	2	0	0	9	3	3	1	2	23	0	1	.190	.259
Vargas, Carlos	R-R	6-1	200	3-18-99	.204	.222	.200	16	54	6	11	5	1	1	3	4	0	0	0	13	1	0	.389	.259

Pitching	B-T	HT	WT	DOB	W	L	ERA	G	GS	CG	SV	IP	H	R	ER	HR	BB	SO	AVG	vLH	vRH	K/9	BB/9
Arcendo, Luis	B-R	6-1	160	11-1-99	0	0	0.00	1	0	0	0	0	0	0	0	0	0	0	.000	--	.000	0.00	0.00
Brecht, Ben	L-L	6-7	215	1-7-98	2	0	2.19	10	6	0	0	25	18	7	6	0	4	23	.200	.304	.164	8.39	1.46
Cabrera, Eleardo	L-R	5-11	195	11-8-95	2	1	3.18	7	0	0	2	11	5	4	4	0	5	12	.132	.167	.115	9.53	3.97
Costanzo, Michael	L-L	6-1	190	11-14-95	0	0	5.40	3	0	0	0	7	8	4	4	2	0	7	.296	.167	.333	9.45	0.00
Doxakis, John	B-L	6-4	215	8-20-98	0	0	1.93	12	10	0	0	33	20	8	7	0	11	31	.174	.161	.179	8.54	3.03
Figueroa, Hector	R-R	6-3	190	11-30-94	0	2	2.10	14	0	0	5	26	24	10	6	1	9	23	.242	.256	.233	8.06	3.16
Gau, Christopher	R-R	6-2	205	2-3-97	3	6	4.01	15	3	0	0	49	34	27	22	4	18	52	.194	.188	.198	9.49	3.28
Gonzalez, Edisson	R-R	5-10	160	10-2-99	4	2	2.45	13	11	0	0	62	55	19	17	6	13	77	.228	.186	.246	11.12	1.88
Gross, Andrew	R-R	6-4	195	9-19-96	1	4	3.41	20	0	0	7	29	28	17	11	0	11	31	.246	.343	.203	9.62	3.41
Jackson, Ryan	R-R	5-10	190	3-5-94	0	0	0.00	2	0	0	2	3	3	0	0	0	0	5	.143	.250	.118	7.50	0.00
LaSorsa, Joe	L-L	6-5	215	4-29-98	5	3	2.23	17	0	0	1	36	29	13	9	2	9	30	.221	.273	.204	7.43	2.23
Lopez, Jacob	L-L	6-4	220	3-11-98	2	0	2.40	3	3	0	0	15	8	4	4	2	4	18	.157	.182	.150	10.80	2.40
Lugo, Audry	R-R	5-11	160	10-29-99	0	0	0.00	1	0	0	0	2	2	0	0	0	1	2	.250	--	.250	9.00	4.50
McKendry, Evan	R-R	6-3	200	2-6-98	4	1	1.60	9	7	0	0	39	38	10	7	1	4	43	.255	.200	.289	9.84	0.92
Montgomery, Justin	R-R	6-5	200	9-10-96	0	0	19.06	4	0	0	0	6	13	13	12	1	5	8	.433	.300	.500	12.71	7.94
Moore, Steffon	L-L	6-3	185	6-25-97	2	1	5.68	17	0	0	2	38	28	21	20	1	25	41	.231	.129	.267	11.65	7.11
Murray, Jayden	R-R	6-1	190	4-11-97	1	0	0.00	1	1	0	0	6	1	0	0	0	0	10	.056	.167	.000	15.00	0.00
Pflughaupt, Blake	L-L	6-0	210	9-4-96	0	1	18.00	4	0	0	0	5	12	11	10	0	4	4	.444	.500	.435	7.20	7.20
Roca, Jose	R-R	6-0	195	8-27-96	3	3	3.58	18	0	0	2	38	41	20	15	1	13	25	.275	.335	.228	5.97	3.10
Sanchez, Rodolfo	R-R	5-10	165	1-12-00	3	2	3.41	13	13	0	0	63	55	24	24	4	20	57	.230	.226	.232	8.10	2.84
Smiddy, Shay	R-R	6-5	215	12-19-97	2	1	1.13	12	1	0	2	24	20	4	3	1	9	23	.230	.303	.185	8.63	3.38
Trageton, Zack	R-R	6-1	225	9-2-98	5	2	2.11	7	5	0	0	38	30	9	9	1	9	39	.210	.283	.167	9.16	0.00
White, Colby	R-R	6-0	190	7-4-98	1	0	2.79	15	0	0	1	19	8	6	6	3	16	29	.119	.091	.133	13.50	7.45

	B-T	HT	WT	DOB	W	L	ERA	G	GS	CG	SV	IP	H	R	ER	HR	BB	SO	AVG	vLH	vRH	K/9	BB/9
Whittle, Daiveyon	R-R	6-1	236	11-11-99	0	3	0.95	11	8	0	0	47	38	12	5	0	11	43	.208	.197	.214	8.18	2.09
Wiles, Nathan	R-R	6-4	228	7-2-98	3	0	3.06	14	7	0	0	35	40	13	12	4	2	39	.282	.326	.263	9.93	0.51

Fielding

C: Embry 33, Leon 2, Muffley 33, Trevino 10. **1B:** Mallard 8, McGowan 66, Vargas 4. **2B:** Arcendo 4, Kinamon 1, Pedroza 45, Santiago 9, Sogard 3, Troike 17. **3B:** Arcendo 16, Edwards 3, Mallard 18, Pedroza 1, Santiago 5, Sogard 21, Troike 2, Vargas 13. **SS:** Arcendo 7, Jones 21, Santiago 1, Sogard 38, Troike 10. **OF:** Alexander 57, Brito 2, Brundage 32, Diaz 25, Edwards 56, Hiott 56.

PRINCETON RAYS
APPALACHIAN LEAGUE

ROOKIE ADVANCED

Batting	B-T	HT	WT	DOB	AVG	vLH	vRH	G	AB	R	H	2B	3B	HR	RBI	BB	HBP	SH	SF	SO	SB	CS	SLG	OBP
Allen, Logan	R-R	5-10	180	8-13-98	.300	.167	.500	3	10	2	3	0	0	0	0	2	0	0	0	2	0	1	.300	.417
Armenta, Angelo	B-R	5-11	190	5-30-96	.239	.177	.256	48	159	27	38	6	1	2	19	22	2	0	2	33	1	3	.327	.335
Castellanos, Daiwer	L-R	5-11	155	8-16-00	.275	.250	.278	10	40	7	11	2	0	1	4	3	1	0	0	11	2	0	.400	.341
Dimon, Dawson	R-R	6-1	185	5-17-99	.226	.300	.191	9	31	5	7	4	0	0	3	3	0	0	0	16	0	0	.355	.294
Guenther, Jake	L-L	6-4	230	5-16-97	.320	.241	.336	48	175	29	56	10	1	2	30	23	11	0	0	26	2	0	.423	.431
Infante, Diego	R-R	6-2	178	10-22-99	.288	.268	.294	61	240	37	69	14	1	12	52	16	5	0	1	71	4	1	.504	.344
Leon, Luis	B-R	6-0	175	9-10-98	.341	.320	.350	43	173	29	59	12	1	5	30	11	1	0	1	40	0	0	.509	.382
Mallard, Mason	R-R	5-10	185	2-22-96	.304	.211	.370	14	46	4	14	2	0	0	1	8	2	0	0	10	3	3	.348	.429
Marte, Jelfry	B-R	5-10	130	3-27-01	.188	.229	.172	45	176	24	33	4	1	0	16	6	3	1	54	2	5	.222	.276
Martinez, Yunior	B-R	6-1	166	12-24-98	.265	.350	.234	41	151	23	40	5	3	5	22	4	1	0	1	44	10	5	.437	.287
Melendez, Kevin	R-R	6-1	185	3-15-00	.215	.297	.187	39	144	15	31	7	0	5	25	7	1	0	0	48	2	0	.368	.257
Ramirez, Abiezel	B-R	5-11	160	1-26-00	.156	.000	.286	10	39	8	10	0	0	1	3	4	3	1	0	14	2	0	.333	.356
Sanchez, Aldenis	R-R	6-2	165	9-26-98	.255	.255	.256	52	184	39	47	6	4	0	12	28	4	2	0	34	21	5	.332	.366
Schnell, Nick	L-R	6-3	180	3-27-00	.286	.235	.301	37	147	28	42	11	3	5	27	18	0	0	1	51	5	2	.503	.361
Soria, Nate	R-R	5-10	175	11-24-95	.233	.333	.216	13	43	6	10	2	0	1	3	2	3	2	0	15	0	0	.349	.313
Turner, Gionti	R-R	6-2	178	8-17-00	.265	.319	.250	60	219	32	58	12	1	3	37	13	4	2	1	54	7	6	.370	.317
Vargas, Jhosner	B-R	5-11	158	1-24-99	.284	.281	.285	45	162	23	46	5	0	0	21	10	2	1	2	26	7	1	.315	.330
Wisely, Brett	L-R	5-10	180	5-8-99	.274	.200	.302	47	179	30	49	9	3	5	25	17	2	5	2	29	3	2	.441	.335

Pitching	B-T	HT	WT	DOB	W	L	ERA	G	GS	CG	SV	IP	H	R	ER	HR	BB	SO	AVG	vLH	vRH	K/9	BB/9
Allain, Ryan	R-R	5-10	225	3-24-97	0	3	7.04	12	0	0	1	15	16	15	12	1	14	18	.271	.308	.242	10.57	8.22
Bach, Carter	R-L	6-7	230	2-14-98	0	0	5.18	16	1	0	2	33	42	25	19	3	20	25	.311	.265	.337	6.82	5.45
Bradley, Taj	R-R	6-2	190	3-20-01	2	5	3.18	12	11	0	0	51	42	29	18	4	19	57	.219	.165	.262	10.06	3.35
Brigden, Trevor	L-R	6-3	210	9-20-95	3	1	2.45	10	1	0	1	18	14	7	5	1	1	23	.200	.147	.250	11.29	0.49
Byrd, Vincent	L-R	6-7	240	10-8-97	1	1	2.89	5	0	0	0	9	4	5	3	1	1	10	.125	.071	.167	9.64	0.96
Cabrera, Eleardo	R-R	5-11	195	11-8-95	0	1	3.13	9	0	0	1	23	20	12	8	1	10	19	.238	.257	.225	7.43	3.91
Dimon, Dawson	R-R	6-1	185	5-17-99	0	0	0.00	1	0	0	0	1	0	0	0	0	0	0	.000	.000	.000	0.00	0.00
Felipe, Angel	R-R	6-5	190	8-30-97	3	4	4.45	15	0	0	0	30	23	23	15	0	24	36	.198	.174	.214	10.68	7.12
Fernandez, Christian	R-R	6-2	170	8-11-99	2	2	6.00	12	11	0	0	51	53	36	34	9	19	51	.266	.220	.299	9.00	3.35
Herrera, Bryan	R-R	6-2	175	4-22-98	1	3	2.70	18	0	0	0	37	24	12	11	2	10	38	.182	.200	.164	9.33	2.45
Jackson, Ryan	R-R	5-10	190	3-5-96	0	0	2.16	4	0	0	0	8	7	3	2	2	1	12	.219	.250	.188	12.96	1.08
Johnson, Seth	R-R	6-1	200	9-19-98	0	1	5.14	4	4	0	0	7	10	5	4	0	1	9	.345	.333	.357	11.57	1.29
Lopez, Jose	L-L	6-1	200	2-15-99	4	3	2.54	12	12	0	0	50	42	23	14	3	23	55	.225	.220	.227	9.97	4.17
Moss, Addison	R-R	6-1	190	9-10-97	0	0	5.68	5	0	0	2	6	5	4	4	2	2	11	.208	.444	.067	15.63	2.84
Murray, Jayden	R-R	6-1	190	4-11-97	0	2	2.88	11	8	0	1	34	30	11	11	4	8	37	.234	.200	.265	9.70	2.10
Peguero, Matthew	R-R	6-2	200	1-12-00	3	2	5.35	10	0	0	0	37	48	24	22	5	15	23	.312	.397	.224	5.59	3.65
Ramirez, Wikelman	R-R	6-0	183	8-9-00	2	1	11.22	10	1	0	0	22	33	27	27	6	19	18	.340	.327	.356	7.89	2.49
Rodriguez, Aldor	R-R	6-1	182	7-4-97	0	4	5.40	15	6	0	2	45	47	29	27	8	11	47	.263	.236	.280	9.40	2.20
Sabino, Stanly	L-L	6-0	150	9-6-99	6	0	3.19	16	3	0	0	42	41	25	15	5	17	57	.243	.315	.209	12.12	3.61
Sanchez, Francisco	L-L	6-1	180	4-24-98	1	0	10.38	5	0	0	0	9	12	11	10	2	11	8	.353	.364	.348	8.31	11.42
Soria, Nate	R-R	5-10	175	11-24-95	0	0	0.00	2	0	0	0	1	1	0	0	0	2	0	.200	.333	.000	13.50	0.00
Theriot, Brayden	R-R	6-2	195	12-19-96	5	1	2.45	13	0	0	1	26	29	11	7	1	2	30	.274	.311	.246	10.52	0.70
Walters, Mitchell	R-R	6-1	210	2-19-98	1	0	3.68	18	0	0	2	29	25	14	12	4	11	28	.227	.192	.254	8.59	3.38

Fielding

C: Dimon 5, Leon 32, Melendez 26, Soria 8. **1B:** Guenther 46, Mallard 12, Vargas 11. **2B:** Armenta 22, Turner 3, Vargas 2, Wisely 43. **3B:** Armenta 11, Turner 25, Vargas 31, Wisely 2. **SS:** Armenta 15, Marte 45, Ramirez 10. **OF:** Allen 2, Castellanos 9, Infante 47, Mallard 1, Martinez 35, Sanchez 51, Schnell 32, Turner 28.

GCL RAYS
GULF COAST LEAGUE

ROOKIE

Batting	B-T	HT	WT	DOB	AVG	vLH	vRH	G	AB	R	H	2B	3B	HR	RBI	BB	HBP	SH	SF	SO	SB	CS	SLG	OBP
Aranda, Jonathan	L-R	5-10	173	5-23-98	.286	.000	.400	2	7	1	2	0	0	0	1	1	0	0	1	0	0	.286	.444
Arcendo, Luis	B-R	6-0	160	11-1-99	.360	.750	.177	12	25	5	9	1	0	0	2	2	0	1	0	7	3	0	.400	.407
Arias, Amador	R-R	5-11	143	8-25-00	.227	.462	.129	13	44	6	10	1	0	1	4	3	1	1	1	11	0	0	.318	.286
Arrendoll, Johampher	L-R	6-2	165	10-15-98	.196	.167	.206	32	92	9	18	1	1	4	11	4	0	0	35	1	1	.261	.308
Bemboom, Anthony	L-R	6-2	200	1-18-90	.400	.000	.500	2	5	1	2	1	0	0	1	2	0	0	0	2	0	0	.600	.571
Castellanos, Daiwer	L-R	5-11	155	8-16-00	.273	.188	.302	35	128	19	35	1	3	1	0	11	11	2	0	1	12	4	3	.297	.338
Chevez, Freddvil	R-R	6-4	200	3-13-00	.245	.296	.225	26	98	9	24	2	1	0	8	2	1	0	1	19	0	0	.286	.265
Cozens, Dylan	L-L	6-6	235	5-31-94	.250	.000	.400	4	8	2	2	1	0	1	2	3	0	0	1	3	1	1	.750	.417
Cronenworth, Jake	L-R	6-1	185	1-21-94	.167	.167	.167	3	12	2	2	1	0	0	1	0	0	0	0	2	0	0	.250	.231
Dimon, Dawson	R-R	6-1	185	5-17-99	.138	.000	.182	11	29	0	4	1	0	0	2	0	0	0	0	10	1	0	.172	.138
Duffy, Matt	R-R	6-2	190	1-15-91	.250	.500	.000	3	8	1	2	1	0	0	1	1	0	0	0	5	0	0	.375	.250
Ezell, Trevor	B-R	5-8	200	4-3-96	.308	.333	.300	5	13	2	4	0	1	0	2	4	1	0	1	2	0	0	.462	.474
Figueroa, Alberto	B-R	5-8	145	4-24-00	.267	.212	.292	36	105	12	28	3	1	0	3	8	2	2	0	21	4	2	.314	.330
Fineman, Ryan	R-R	6-0	227	11-17-96	.158	.167	.156	17	38	4	6	3	0	0	5	3	2	0	0	10	0	0	.237	.256

Batting	B-T	HT	WT	DOB	AVG	vLH	vRH	G	AB	R	H	2B	3B	HR	RBI	BB	HBP	SH	SF	SO	SB	CS	SLG	OBP
Fortuna, Saul	R-R	6-3	185	8-3-00	.205	.308	.161	11	44	7	9	2	1	1	6	1	0	0	1	13	0	0	.364	.217
Garcia, Juan	R-R	6-0	191	1-6-99	.182	.333	.125	26	77	6	14	3	0	0	7	9	1	2	1	18	4	0	.221	.273
Hollis, Connor	R-R	5-10	170	11-18-94	.000	.000	.000	2	4	1	0	0	0	0	0	2	0	0	0	0	1	0	.000	.333
Huffins, Zach	R-R	6-1	185	6-16-99	.272	.375	.235	28	92	15	25	3	3	0	7	6	0	0	0	24	7	1	.370	.316
Hulsizer, Niko	R-R	6-2	225	2-1-97	.111	.000	.143	4	9	0	1	0	0	0	1	2	0	0	0	4	0	1	.111	.273
Johnson, Christian	R-R	5-11	180	6-4-01	.169	.167	.170	23	65	3	11	1	0	0	4	1	1	1	1	18	2	3	.185	.191
Kay, Grant	R-R	6-0	185	5-29-93	.125	.000	.143	6	16	0	2	1	0	0	1	2	0	0	0	6	0	0	.188	.222
Kinamon, Duke	R-R	5-11	185	9-4-96	.130	.000	.158	9	23	3	3	0	0	0	2	2	1	0	0	8	0	1	.130	.231
Law, Zacrey	R-R	6-0	190	7-8-96	.217	.333	.177	7	23	5	5	1	0	0	3	2	0	0	0	3	0	0	.261	.280
Lopez, Johan	R-R	5-10	167	7-28-00	.279	.267	.284	34	111	20	31	6	2	1	12	12	2	3	2	8	2	1	.396	.354
Lowe, Brandon	L-R	5-10	185	7-6-94	.000	.000	.000	2	4	0	0	0	0	0	0	0	0	0	0	2	0	0	.000	.000
Manzueta, Oneill	R-R	6-0	190	2-7-01	.202	.100	.246	31	99	13	20	8	2	0	8	7	2	0	1	26	2	1	.323	.266
Marte, Jelfry	B-R	5-10	130	3-27-01	.316	.125	.455	6	19	2	6	0	3	0	7	2	0	0	0	7	0	0	.632	.381
Meza, Julio	R-R	6-0	185	4-9-98	.237	.342	.194	39	139	11	33	4	1	0	16	5	5	1	4	28	0	0	.281	.281
Ostberg, Erik	L-R	5-10	225	10-12-95	.000	--	.000	3	5	0	0	0	0	0	0	4	0	0	0	2	0	0	.000	.444
Perez, Luis	R-R	6-0	241	6-16-97	.170	.167	.171	18	47	4	8	1	0	0	4	2	0	0	0	16	0	0	.192	.264
Ramirez, Abiezel	R-R	5-11	160	1-26-00	.289	.226	.308	37	135	19	39	8	2	2	24	13	0	2	0	38	7	0	.422	.351
Rodriguez, Edgardo	R-R	6-0	207	11-29-00	.400	.308	.500	10	25	3	10	1	1	0	6	1	1	0	1	6	0	0	.520	.429
Sasaki, Shane	R-R	6-0	165	7-1-00	.182	.200	.177	13	44	6	8	2	0	0	1	3	0	0	0	18	1	0	.227	.234
Schnell, Nick	L-R	6-3	180	3-27-00	.191	.167	.200	4	21	4	4	0	2	0	1	0	0	0	0	9	0	0	.381	.191
Troike, Ben	R-R	5-10	187	2-5-98	.250	.333	.200	5	16	3	4	1	0	0	3	0	0	0	0	2	1	0	.313	.368
Wendle, Joey	L-R	6-1	200	4-26-90	.000	--	.000	1	3	0	0	0	0	0	0	0	0	0	0	0	0	0	.000	.000

Pitching	B-T	HT	WT	DOB	W	L	ERA	G	GS	CG	SV	IP	H	R	ER	HR	BB	SO	AVG	vLH	vRH	K/9	BB/9
Alfonzo, Emilio	R-R	6-6	170	8-2-00	3	2	4.11	11	5	0	0	35	25	16	16	1	31	32	.217	.298	.162	8.23	7.97
Banda, Anthony	L-L	6-2	225	8-10-93	0	1	7.71	2	2	0	0	2	6	3	2	0	3	4	.462	.600	.375	15.43	11.57
Byrd, Vincent	L-R	6-7	240	10-8-97	1	1	3.38	9	0	0	2	16	9	9	6	0	6	21	.161	.150	.167	11.81	3.38
Castillo, Diego	R-R	6-3	250	1-18-94	0	0	0.00	1	0	0	0	1	0	0	0	0	1	1	.000	.000	.000	9.00	9.00
Catalina, Neraldo	R-R	6-6	202	6-21-00	3	3	2.14	11	1	0	0	21	20	12	5	0	9	23	.256	.185	.294	9.86	3.86
Cordero, Dauris	R-R	6-3	185	7-18-99	2	1	2.45	10	0	0	0	29	21	9	8	1	12	33	.198	.286	.155	10.13	3.68
Cortorreal, Aneudy	R-R	6-3	200	12-13-99	0	1	3.86	3	0	0	0	5	6	3	2	0	3	7	.316	.444	.200	13.50	5.79
Dacosta, Franklin	L-L	5-11	162	2-27-00	3	2	2.09	10	5	0	0	39	31	11	9	2	10	36	.218	.156	.236	8.38	2.33
Fineman, Ryan	R-R	6-0	227	11-17-96	0	0	0.00	1	0	0	0	1	2	0	0	0	1	0	.400	.000	.500	9.00	9.00
Garcia, Carlos	R-R	6-3	185	11-28-98	1	0	1.29	11	0	0	0	21	20	4	3	0	11	25	.263	.290	.244	10.71	4.71
Garcia, Juan	R-R	6-0	191	1-6-99	0	0	0.00	1	0	0	0	0	0	0	0	0	0	1	.000	--	.000	27.00	0.00
Gardeck, Ian	R-R	6-2	230	11-1-91	0	0	0.00	3	0	0	0	1	0	0	0	0	1	5	.000	.000	.000	13.50	2.70
Gaston, Sandy	R-R	6-3	200	12-16-01	1	2	6.00	11	6	0	0	27	23	20	18	1	27	31	.232	.235	.231	10.33	9.00
Gobillot, Joe	L-L	6-6	228	6-3-98	2	1	4.05	4	1	0	0	7	2	5	3	0	11	10	.100	.200	.067	13.50	14.85
Goss, JJ	R-R	6-3	185	12-25-00	1	3	5.82	9	8	0	0	17	19	11	11	1	2	16	.279	.364	.239	8.47	1.06
Harris, Greg	R-R	6-2	170	8-17-94	0	0	6.75	3	0	0	0	3	5	2	2	0	1	2	.455	.429	.500	6.75	3.38
Jackson, Ryan	R-R	5-10	190	3-5-96	0	0	0.00	7	0	0	2	11	6	0	0	0	2	16	.154	.182	.143	13.50	1.69
Johnson, Seth	R-R	6-1	200	9-19-98	0	0	0.00	5	5	0	0	10	7	0	0	0	2	7	.189	.286	.130	6.30	1.80
Lugo, Audry	R-R	5-11	160	10-29-98	1	0	2.59	12	0	0	2	24	19	9	7	2	10	29	.226	.241	.218	10.73	3.70
McKendry, Evan	R-R	6-3	200	2-6-98	0	0	0.00	2	2	0	0	4	1	0	0	0	0	2	.083	.143	.000	4.50	0.00
Melo, Fernando	L-L	6-6	200	12-31-99	1	2	4.29	11	0	0	0	21	14	12	10	0	16	18	.184	.192	.180	7.71	6.86
Montgomery, Justin	R-R	6-5	200	9-10-96	1	0	2.66	11	0	0	1	20	12	11	6	1	22	22	.177	.107	.225	9.74	9.74
Moss, Addison	R-R	6-1	190	9-10-97	0	0	0.00	1	0	0	0	1	1	0	0	0	0	3	.200	.500	.000	20.25	0.00
Munoz, Victor	R-R	6-3	160	12-25-00	1	3	3.57	7	4	0	0	23	21	14	9	2	13	21	.250	.233	.268	8.34	5.16
Myers, Tobias	R-R	6-0	193	8-5-98	1	0	0.00	3	1	0	0	7	1	0	0	0	3	6	.000	.167	.000	8.10	4.05
Peoples, Ben	L-R	6-1	175	5-1-01	0	1	5.91	5	2	0	0	11	6	8	7	1	11	16	.162	.091	.192	13.50	9.28
Pflughaupt, Blake	L-L	6-0	210	9-4-96	0	0	3.00	3	2	0	0	6	6	2	2	0	1	10	.273	.429	.200	15.00	1.50
Ramirez, Wikelman	R-R	6-0	183	8-9-00	1	0	0.00	5	0	0	2	15	2	0	0	0	4	18	.043	.042	.044	10.80	2.40
Santana, Daniel	R-R	6-2	193	4-16-98	1	1	1.64	4	1	0	0	11	8	3	2	1	2	9	.200	.286	.154	7.36	1.64
Sherriff, Ryan	L-L	6-1	185	5-25-90	0	0	0.00	4	2	0	0	4	5	2	0	0	0	3	.250	.000	.333	6.75	0.00
Stinson, Graeme	L-L	6-5	250	8-6-97	0	1	13.50	1	1	0	0	1	2	1	1	0	0	1	.500	.000	.667	13.50	0.00
Strotman, Drew	R-R	6-3	195	9-3-96	0	1	3.38	4	4	0	0	8	9	5	3	0	3	11	.265	.294	.235	12.38	3.38
Urena, Wilfry	R-R	6-1	160	1-20-99	1	2	9.82	11	1	0	0	26	36	30	28	3	16	31	.330	.273	.355	10.87	5.61

Fielding

C: Bemboom 1, Dimon 7, Fineman 11, Law 7, Meza 29, Ostberg 3, Rodriguez 6. **1B:** Aranda 1, Chevez 25, Dimon 4, Ezell 5, Fineman 1, Garcia 5, Kay 1, Perez 16. **2B:** Aranda 1, Arcendo 4, Arias 1, Figuereo 30, Garcia 2, Kay 3, Kinamon 4, Lowe 1, Ramirez 6, Troike 4. **3B:** Arcendo 7, Arias 6, Duffy 3, Figuereo 7, Garcia 21, Hollis 1, Kay 1, Kinamon 4, Lopez 10, Wendle 1. **SS:** Arias 2, Cronenworth 3, Lopez 18, Marte 3, Ramirez 27, Troike 1. **OF:** Arrendoll 32, Castellanos 33, Cozens 4, Fortuna 11, Huffins 26, Hulsizer 3, Johnson 18, Manzueta 29, Sasaki 9, Schnell 4.

DSL RAYS   ROOKIE
DOMINICAN SUMMER LEAGUE

Batting	B-T	HT	WT	DOB	AVG	vLH	vRH	G	AB	R	H	2B	3B	HR	RBI	BB	HBP	SH	SF	SO	SB	CS	SLG	OBP
Aguilar, Ismael	R-R	6-0	150	8-25-01	.197	.162	.211	38	132	21	26	5	0	1	13	5	4	0	4	32	9	2	.258	.241
Aponte, Cesar	R-R	6-3	160	7-16-02	.228	.205	.235	55	189	27	43	9	0	0	19	22	8	0	3	29	8	8	.275	.329
Arrendoll, Johampher	L-R	6-2	165	10-15-98	.193	.111	.208	16	57	14	11	2	0	2	12	3	1	0	1	18	5	1	.333	.361
Balbuena, Alfredo	R-R	5-9	178	11-25-98	.313	.370	.298	62	214	45	67	14	4	7	42	30	3	0	5	30	14	6	.514	.397
Barete, Cristopher	L-L	5-9	155	12-10-01	.200	.244	.186	53	190	38	38	7	0	1	12	20	3	3	0	32	14	7	.253	.286
Bolivar, Roimer	R-R	6-0	175	12-10-99	.323	.333	.319	47	155	43	50	12	1	1	24	39	7	0	3	30	15	5	.432	.471
Calmes, Nigel	R-R	6-1	175	9-21-99	.230	.241	.227	43	139	20	32	7	0	0	8	21	3	0	2	19	4	0	.281	.339
Candelario, Stir	R-R	6-0	185	9-3-00	.183	.238	.163	65	241	33	44	8	2	4	20	29	6	1	2	71	12	2	.282	.284
Castillo, Estanli	R-R	6-3	195	10-7-01	.272	.217	.291	61	232	20	63	8	0	2	27	13	1	0	3	61	7	1	.332	.309
Chevez, Freddvil	R-R	6-4	200	3-13-00	.331	.385	.320	37	148	31	49	8	0	4	32	11	10	0	1	11	0	1	.466	.412

	B-T	HT	WT	DOB	AVG	vLH	vRH	G	AB	R	H	2B	3B	HR	RBI	BB	HBP	SH	SF	SO	SB	CS	OBP	SLG
Del Rosario, Daury	B-R	6-0	175	2-14-02	.193	.171	.198	60	207	29	40	8	1	1	26	36	5	1	4	61	5	7	.256	.321
Feliz, Luis	B-R	5-10	155	5-8-02	.265	.211	.286	23	68	15	18	5	3	0	3	14	0	0	0	18	6	2	.427	.390
Fernandez, Mario	R-R	5-11	172	9-28-00	.118	.111	.120	12	34	2	4	1	0	0	3	2	6	0	0	5	2	1	.147	.286
Galarraga, Angel	L-R	6-1	178	8-1-02	.200	.333	.167	6	15	0	3	0	0	0	2	1	0	0	0	3	1	1	.200	.250
Johnson, Dahiandy	L-R	6-3	200	9-25-99	.268	.167	.294	62	235	39	63	10	2	6	51	32	4	0	3	42	5	3	.404	.361
Lantigua, Albert	L-R	5-9	160	10-9-99	.079	.000	.103	14	38	5	3	1	0	0	1	4	0	0	1	14	1	1	.105	.167
Lopez, Angel	R-R	5-11	160	11-14-99	.253	.333	.227	59	202	43	51	10	2	4	39	31	9	1	4	44	14	2	.381	.370
Lopez, Jerry	R-R	6-1	176	7-13-02	.149	.091	.157	29	94	8	14	0	0	0	6	4	2	0	2	20	0	2	.149	.180
Lopez, Johan	R-R	5-10	167	7-28-00	.357	.200	.387	30	126	39	45	7	7	1	28	16	4	1	0	12	24	4	.548	.445
Manzueta, Oneill	R-R	6-0	190	2-7-01	.296	.350	.284	31	115	29	34	11	3	3	20	17	4	0	2	31	5	2	.522	.399
Mata, Juan	R-R	6-0	165	8-1-01	.234	.172	.250	38	137	14	32	3	1	1	14	12	2	4	0	16	9	3	.292	.300
Merino, Patrick	R-R	6-2	220	8-13-98	.255	.191	.273	29	98	30	25	6	0	8	17	23	7	0	1	28	2	1	.561	.426
Pereira, Jose	R-R	5-11	153	3-3-99	.299	.250	.313	38	127	15	38	4	0	0	10	17	0	1	1	21	6	3	.331	.379
Petiyan, Elias	B-R	5-11	160	12-3-01	.211	.111	.241	13	38	4	8	1	0	0	3	8	1	1	0	10	4	0	.237	.362
Pie, Alejandro	R-R	6-4	175	1-31-02	.289	.275	.293	57	225	29	65	10	1	0	19	11	15	1	1	46	24	8	.342	.361
Pierre, Yonathan	R-R	6-1	170	6-4-99	.323	.241	.341	47	158	32	51	13	3	4	30	22	4	0	1	40	13	2	.519	.416
Polonius, Rainer	L-R	5-11	147	9-24-01	.269	.316	.247	37	119	18	32	4	1	1	18	26	1	4	3	24	10	7	.345	.396
Polonius, Ryson	L-R	5-11	147	9-24-01	.137	.167	.130	38	124	13	17	2	3	2	14	20	0	1	3	40	4	1	.250	.252
Salazar, Ricardo	B-R	5-11	170	5-30-02	.194	.182	.196	39	124	18	24	4	0	0	9	23	2	1	0	22	7	2	.226	.329
Salguera, Felix	R-R	6-0	171	3-1-02	.236	.194	.250	35	127	25	30	4	2	0	16	19	3	1	1	23	3	1	.299	.347
Sangrona, Isaias	R-R	6-2	180	4-19-01	.178	.175	.179	43	135	16	24	9	0	1	12	18	6	1	1	43	5	2	.267	.300
Santos, Bryan	L-L	6-0	165	5-4-99	.274	.298	.267	66	237	26	65	12	4	1	32	30	2	0	3	40	4	8	.371	.357
Tejeda, Gioser	R-R	5-11	204	9-23-97	.126	.111	.130	30	87	9	11	3	0	1	8	12	1	0	1	18	0	0	.195	.238
Vasquez, Willy	R-R	6-0	191	9-6-01	.364	.500	.324	11	44	6	16	2	1	0	5	1	0	0	1	4	2	1	.455	.370

Pitching	B-T	HT	WT	DOB	W	L	ERA	G	GS	CG	SV	IP	H	R	ER	HR	BB	SO	AVG	vLH	vRH	K/9	BB/9
Andujar, Gustavo	R-R	5-11	164	4-6-00	0	3	4.28	14	14	0	0	61	58	31	29	5	23	55	.250	.200	.272	8.11	3.39
Barrios, Orlando	R-R	6-6	180	8-27-01	1	1	6.46	14	1	0	0	24	33	20	17	0	19	26	.330	.345	.324	9.89	7.23
Caro, Christopher	R-R	6-0	175	12-14-98	1	0	3.48	9	1	0	0	8	8	4	3	0	8	6	.200	.158	.238	6.97	9.58
Cerda, Jose	R-R	6-0	180	10-18-99	1	1	3.79	9	1	0	0	19	18	10	8	2	7	26	.247	.292	.225	12.32	3.32
Colina, Jhoan	R-R	6-0	165	1-1-99	1	1	1.82	12	2	0	0	25	22	11	5	2	13	23	.234	.345	.185	8.39	4.74
Cortorreal, Aneudy	R-R	6-3	200	12-13-99	5	0	2.03	16	1	0	2	31	20	8	7	1	21	44	.184	.175	.188	12.77	6.10
Cruz, Samuel	R-R	6-3	160	1-9-02	0	0	12.42	15	0	0	0	17	19	29	23	1	32	16	.275	.208	.311	8.64	17.28
Cuevas, Johan	R-R	6-2	180	5-8-00	3	0	4.29	15	0	0	1	21	19	12	10	0	15	18	.250	.303	.209	7.71	6.43
Curbata, Yosmer	R-R	6-3	170	7-19-00	1	0	0.00	3	0	0	0	8	7	1	0	0	3	9	.219	.400	.185	10.57	3.52
De Los Santos, Jose	R-R	6-0	175	9-19-99	1	2	4.66	18	1	0	1	29	37	28	15	0	14	26	.298	.300	.297	8.07	4.34
Dominguez, Justino	R-R	5-11	178	9-26-01	0	6	8.71	9	7	0	0	21	25	24	20	2	23	15	.317	.261	.339	6.53	10.02
Dum, Bryan	L-L	5-11	170	10-26-01	0	0	13.50	1	1	0	0	1	2	2	1	0	2	0	.667	.000	1.000	0.00	27.00
Galue, Over	R-R	6-2	188	7-31-01	1	1	3.12	4	3	0	0	9	6	3	3	1	3	1	.182	.250	.143	1.04	3.12
Garcia, Yeury	R-R	6-4	190	1-18-00	1	1	4.71	14	0	0	1	21	18	13	11	0	23	26	.231	.290	.192	11.14	9.86
Gomez, Yonathan	R-R	6-2	154	8-17-01	2	0	3.58	18	0	0	4	33	28	18	13	0	15	26	.222	.269	.189	7.16	4.13
Gonzalez, Daniel	L-L	6-2	180	11-20-01	3	1	2.25	14	0	0	0	48	30	17	12	3	27	54	.182	.177	.182	10.13	5.06
Gonzalez, Jose	R-R	6-3	175	4-1-02	1	6	4.57	17	6	1	0	43	48	30	22	2	19	35	.273	.317	.250	7.27	3.95
Hernandez, Jesus	R-R	6-4	167	7-10-01	0	3	10.38	11	0	0	0	13	12	20	15	3	24	11	.255	.200	.281	7.62	16.62
Jimenez, Antonio	L-L	5-11	145	5-6-01	2	2	2.90	14	13	0	0	62	44	28	20	0	30	68	.202	.237	.194	9.87	4.35
Kimura, Igor	R-R	6-1	207	4-14-99	3	2	3.29	16	8	0	0	55	47	21	20	0	18	47	.232	.250	.219	7.74	3.13
King, Pedro	R-R	6-0	180	10-10-99	3	2	2.54	15	9	0	0	50	41	19	14	2	26	40	.218	.256	.184	7.25	4.71
Leon, Maicor	L-L	5-7	165	3-6-01	0	1	1.59	7	7	0	0	17	13	4	3	1	4	12	.213	.333	.207	6.35	2.12
Liriano, Argenis	R-R	6-0	185	9-30-96	6	1	1.93	21	0	0	5	37	22	10	8	1	13	43	.173	.205	.159	10.37	3.13
Lopez, Dauris	R-R	6-3	185	10-20-98	3	1	4.25	16	0	0	0	30	28	18	14	2	21	22	.255	.217	.281	6.67	6.37
Lopez, Janick	R-R	6-3	187	4-24-99	2	2	10.67	9	1	0	0	14	21	20	17	1	13	17	.323	.348	.310	10.67	8.16
Lopez, Victor	R-R	6-0	172	1-11-02	4	1	4.60	21	0	0	3	31	37	20	16	3	5	27	.278	.264	.288	7.76	1.44
Lugo, Audry	R-R	5-11	160	10-29-98	0	0	1.54	6	0	0	2	12	5	3	2	0	3	10	.132	.071	.167	7.71	2.31
Manrique, Endry	R-R	6-0	150	11-3-00	2	2	3.57	12	8	0	0	40	36	21	16	1	21	28	.240	.230	.247	6.25	4.69
Molina, Anthony	R-R	6-1	170	1-12-02	2	3	3.23	14	8	0	0	53	66	30	19	1	9	31	.300	.284	.308	5.26	1.53
Munoz, Victor	R-R	6-3	160	12-25-00	1	0	1.45	4	4	0	0	19	14	6	3	0	5	17	.197	.200	.196	8.20	2.41
Nunez, Cristhian	R-R	6-3	185	12-15-00	3	1	2.23	14	5	0	0	32	20	11	8	0	18	23	.180	.244	.136	6.40	5.01
Nunez, Rafael	L-L	5-7	160	12-9-00	0	2	5.74	10	3	0	0	15	17	13	10	1	7	17	.266	.167	.276	9.76	4.02
Ortiz, Julio	R-R	6-3	165	12-30-00	0	3	6.75	4	1	0	0	5	5	8	4	0	7	8	.278	.000	.455	13.50	11.81
Pichardo, Alexis	R-R	6-0	180	8-20-02	1	0	11.57	9	1	0	1	9	9	13	12	0	18	8	.265	.286	.250	7.71	17.36
Prensa, Rafael	R-R	6-4	190	2-15-98	1	6	5.31	16	7	0	0	39	43	26	23	4	11	35	.285	.380	.238	8.08	2.54
Rivera, Juan	R-R	6-3	220	6-4-98	2	1	6.95	17	0	0	0	22	10	27	17	1	43	36	.133	.053	.161	14.73	17.59
Rojas, Nomar	R-R	6-4	168	3-30-01	3	2	2.88	14	13	0	0	56	49	23	18	2	25	38	.244	.271	.229	6.07	3.99
Ruiz, Raynalf	R-R	6-3	175	4-27-01	3	1	3.33	14	8	0	0	46	46	25	17	1	21	39	.254	.232	.268	5.67	4.11
Santana, Daniel	R-R	6-2	193	4-16-98	0	1	4.11	4	4	0	0	15	18	8	7	1	9	16	.220	.231	.217	9.39	5.28
Santodomingo, Roybell	R-R	6-2	170	5-6-01	2	0	3.99	15	0	0	0	29	21	19	13	0	23	26	.194	.077	.232	7.98	7.06
Tejeda, Gioser	R-R	5-11	204	9-23-97	0	0	0.00	1	0	0	0	0	0	0	0	0	3	1	.000	--	.000	27.00	81.00
Torres, Henry	R-R	6-2	175	3-24-98	1	1	5.86	15	0	0	0	28	27	12	18	0	25	29	.250	.281	.237	9.43	8.13
Trinidad, Luis	R-R	6-0	165	5-16-98	3	5	3.93	17	0	0	4	37	31	26	16	1	20	41	.230	.250	.220	10.06	4.91
Urena, Wilfry	R-R	6-0	160	1-20-99	0	0	6.75	4	0	0	1	7	3	7	5	0	6	7	.130	.111	.143	9.45	8.10
Valeriano, Shuruendy	R-R	6-0	160	2-26-98	4	2	3.27	20	0	0	4	33	21	19	12	1	23	44	.177	.180	.175	12.00	6.27

Fielding

C: Calmes 20, Fernandez 8, Galarraga 6, Lantigua 1, Lopez 14, Merino 0, Salguera 24, Sangrona 33, Tejeda 18. **1B:** Balbuena 5, Chevez 34, Lopez 4, Pereira 3, Santos 66, Tejeda 12. **2B:** Aponte 6, Balbuena 11, Del Rosario 53, Lopez 8, Petiyan 11, Polonius 32, Polonius 9, Salazar 10. **3B:** Aponte 12, Balbuena 21, Lopez 9, Pereira 10, Polonius 3, Polonius 13, Salazar 9, Vasquez 9. **SS:** Aponte 9, Del Rosario 1, Lopez 2, Lopez 30, Petiyan 2, Pie 55, Polonius 11, Salazar 1. **OF:** Aguilar 35, Arrendoll 16, Balbuena 1, Barete 51, Bolivar 44, Candelario 51, Castillo 45, Feliz 21, Johnson 49, Manzueta 24, Mata 36, Merino 21, Pierre 44.

Texas Rangers

SEASON IN A SENTENCE: The Rangers stayed competitive longer than expected into the end of June, but they eventually slid back to mediocrity, and finished under .500 for the third straight year.

HIGH POINT: The Rangers went 18-11 in June, ripping off a six-game winning streak that ended on June 29, when the team was just 4.5 games back in the American League West and holding on to the top spot in the AL Wild Card race.

LOW POINT: Texas followed its best month of the season with its worst, going 8-16 in July and dropping a distant 14.5 games behind the Astros in the AL West. The Rangers posted losing records in both August and September, as well, eventually ending the season 18 games out of a playoff spot.

NOTABLE ROOKIES: One of the reasons for the Rangers' struggles in 2019 was the lack of help they received from their farm system. Infielder Nick Solak, acquired from the Rays in a mid-July trade for righthander Peter Fairbanks, arrived in Texas at the end of August and hit .293/.393/.491 in 33 games. Lefthander Brett Martin posted quality peripheral numbers with a 62-to-18 strikeout-to-walk ratio in 62.1 innings, but he posted a pedestrian 4.92 ERA. Still, that was a marked improvement from the 7.28 ERA he recorded at Double-A Frisco in 2018.

KEY TRANSACTIONS: For a team that was clearly sellers by the end of July, the Rangers didn't make many moves. The deal for Solak provided promising early returns, and they also dealt reliever Chris Martin to the Braves at the trade deadline for lefthanded pitching prospect Kolby Allard. A first-round pick by the Braves in 2015 and former Top 100 Prospect, Allard made nine starts for the Rangers this season, posting a 4-2, 4.96 record with 33 strikeouts and 19 walks in 45.1 innings.

DOWN ON THE FARM: Injuries ravaged the Rangers' farm system in 2019. Lefthander Cole Ragans, who missed the 2018 season due to Tommy John surgery, had a second TJ operation that cost him the 2019 season as well. Two of the organization's top 2018 draft picks—righthanders Owen White (2nd round) and Mason Englert (4th round)—also needed Tommy John surgery. Among the brighter spots were a breakout season from catcher Sam Huff, the rise of 18-year-old righthander Ronny Henriquez and the emergence of catcher/outfielder Heriberto Hernandez and shortstop Luisangel Acuña, the younger brother of Braves outfielder Ronald Acuña Jr.

OPENING DAY PAYROLL: $102,462,762 (20th).

PLAYERS OF THE YEAR

BEN VANHOUTEN

MAJOR LEAGUE	MINOR LEAGUE
Mike Minor	**Sam Huff**
LHP	**C**
14-10, 3.59 in 32 GS	(Low A/High A)
Led Rangers in ERA,	.278/.335/.509, 28 HR
IP (208.1) and CG (2)	Futures Game MVP

ORGANIZATION LEADERS

Batting		*Minimum 250 AB
MAJORS		
* AVG	Hunter Pence	.297
* OPS	Hunter Pence	.910
HR	Rougned Odor	30
RBI	Rougned Odor	93
MINORS		
* AVG	Andy Ibanez, Nashville	.300
* OBP	Yonny Hernandez, Down East, Frisco	.413
* SLG	Curtis Terry, Hickory, Down East	.537
* OPS	Curtis Terry, Hickory, Down East	.899
R	Andy Ibanez, Nashville	91
H	Zack Granite, Nashville	146
TB	Curtis Terry, Hickory, Down East	253
2B	Curtis Terry, Hickory, Down East	36
3B	Miguel Aparicio, Hickory	8
3B	Zack Granite, Nashville	8
3B	Leody Taveras, Down East, Frisco	8
HR	Matt Davidson, Nashville	33
RBI	Matt Davidson, Nashville	101
BB	Yonny Hernandez, Down East, Frisco	78
SO	Julio Pablo Martinez, Hickory, Down East	156
SB	Yonny Hernandez, Down East, Frisco	33

Pitching		#Minimum 75 IP
MAJORS		
W	Lance Lynn	16
# ERA	Mike Minor	3.59
SO	Lance Lynn	246
SV	Jose Leclerc	14
MINORS		
W	Tim Brennan, Hickory, Down East	11
L	Tyler Phillips, Down East, Frisco	11
# ERA	Sal Mendez, Down East	2.37
G	Joe Barlow, Down East, Frisco, Nashville	49
GS	Wes Benjamin, Nashville	25
SV	David Carpenter, Nashville	21
IP	Tim Dillard, Nashville	153
BB	Reid Anderson, Down East	64
SO	Jason Bahr, Down East, Frisco	126
# AVG	Jason Bahr, Down East, Frisco	.189

2019 PERFORMANCE

General Manager: Jon Daniels. **Farm Director:** Jayce Tingler. **Scouting Director:** Kip Fagg.

Class	Team	League	W	L	PCT	Finish	Manager
Majors	Texas Rangers	American	78	84	.481	8th (15)	Chris Woodward
Triple-A	Nashville Sounds	Pacific Coast	66	72	.478	9th (16)	Jason Wood
Double-A	Frisco RoughRiders	Texas	68	71	.489	5th (8)	Joe Mikulik
High A	Down East Wood Ducks	Carolina	87	52	.626	1st (10)	Corey Ragsdale
Low A	Hickory Crawdads	South Atlantic	83	52	.615	2nd (14)	Matt Hagen
Short season	Spokane Indians	Northwest	45	31	.592	3rd (8)	Kenny Hook
Rookie	AZL Rangers	Arizona	33	23	.589	t-4th (21)	Carlos Cardoza
Overall 2019 Minor League Record			382	301	.559	3rd (30)	

ORGANIZATION STATISTICS

TEXAS RANGERS
AMERICAN LEAGUE

Batting	B-T	HT	WT	DOB	AVG	vLH	vRH	G	AB	R	H	2B	3B	HR	RBI	BB	HBP	SH	SF	SO	SB	CS	SLG	OBP
Andrus, Elvis	R-R	6-0	200	8-26-88	.275	.275	.275	147	600	81	165	27	4	12	72	34	4	0	10	96	31	8	.393	.313
Cabrera, Asdrubal	B-R	6-0	205	11-13-85	.235	.222	.240	93	323	45	76	15	0	12	51	38	3	0	4	85	4	0	.393	.318
Calhoun, Willie	L-R	5-8	187	11-4-94	.269	.226	.290	83	309	51	83	14	1	21	48	23	3	0	2	53	0	0	.524	.323
Choo, Shin-Soo	L-L	5-11	210	7-13-82	.265	.229	.280	151	563	93	149	31	2	24	61	78	18	0	1	165	15	1	.455	.371
DeShields, Delino	R-R	5-9	200	8-16-92	.249	.274	.236	118	357	42	89	15	4	4	32	38	3	8	2	100	24	6	.347	.325
Federowicz, Tim	R-R	5-10	215	8-5-87	.160	.200	.140	29	75	6	12	2	0	4	7	5	0	3	0	31	1	0	.347	.213
Forsythe, Logan	R-R	6-1	205	1-14-87	.227	.184	.251	101	317	38	72	17	1	7	39	44	3	0	2	100	1	0	.353	.325
Gallo, Joey	L-R	6-5	235	11-19-93	.253	.333	.217	70	241	54	61	15	1	22	49	52	2	1	1	114	4	2	.598	.389
Guzman, Ronald	L-L	6-5	225	10-20-94	.219	.134	.249	87	256	34	56	20	0	10	36	32	3	0	4	87	1	2	.414	.309
Heineman, Scott	R-R	6-1	215	12-4-92	.213	.200	.222	25	75	8	16	6	0	2	7	9	1	0	0	20	1	2	.373	.306
Kiner-Falefa, Isiah	R-R	5-10	176	3-23-95	.238	.209	.252	65	202	23	48	12	1	1	21	14	4	1	1	49	3	0	.322	.299
Mathis, Jeff	R-R	6-0	205	3-31-83	.158	.149	.162	86	228	17	36	9	0	2	12	15	0	0	1	87	1	0	.224	.209
Mazara, Nomar	L-L	6-4	215	4-26-95	.268	.221	.288	116	429	69	115	27	1	19	66	28	6	0	6	108	4	1	.469	.318
Odor, Rougned	L-R	5-11	195	2-3-94	.205	.236	.191	145	522	77	107	30	1	30	93	52	5	1	1	178	11	9	.439	.283
Pence, Hunter	R-R	6-4	220	4-13-83	.297	.327	.278	83	286	53	85	17	1	18	59	26	2	0	2	69	6	1	.552	.358
Santana, Danny	B-R	5-11	185	11-7-90	.283	.276	.286	130	474	81	134	23	6	28	81	25	6	0	5	151	21	6	.534	.324
Solak, Nick	R-R	5-11	190	1-11-95	.293	.319	.275	33	116	19	34	6	1	5	17	15	4	0	0	29	2	0	.491	.393
Trevino, Jose	R-R	5-11	211	11-28-92	.258	.333	.222	40	120	18	31	9	0	2	13	3	0	1	2	27	0	0	.383	.272
Wisdom, Patrick	R-R	6-2	220	8-27-91	.154	.125	.167	9	26	1	4	1	0	0	1	1	0	1	0	15	0	0	.192	.185

Pitching	B-T	HT	WT	DOB	W	L	ERA	G	GS	CG	SV	IP	H	R	ER	HR	BB	SO	AVG	vLH	vRH	K/9	BB/9
Allard, Kolby	L-L	6-1	190	8-13-97	4	2	4.96	9	9	0	0	45	52	26	25	3	19	33	.281	.296	.275	6.55	3.77
Biddle, Jesse	L-L	6-5	220	10-22-91	0	0	11.81	4	0	0	0	5	4	8	7	2	5	7	.200	.400	.133	11.81	8.44
2-team total (11 Seattle)					0	0	10.47	15	0	0	0	16	24	22	19	4	12	15	.343	.385	.318	8.27	6.61
Bird, Kyle	L-L	6-2	175	4-12-93	0	0	7.82	12	0	0	1	13	11	11	11	5	15	10	.229	.227	.231	7.11	10.66
Burke, Brock	L-L	6-4	180	8-4-96	0	2	7.43	6	6	0	0	27	30	22	22	6	11	14	.286	.391	.256	4.73	3.71
Carpenter, David	R-R	6-3	250	7-15-85	0	0	5.40	4	0	0	0	3	4	4	2	0	4	2	.267	.364	.000	5.40	10.80
Chavez, Jesse	R-R	6-2	175	8-21-83	3	5	4.85	48	9	0	1	78	82	48	42	12	22	72	.267	.248	.281	8.31	2.54
Clase, Emmanuel	R-R	6-2	206	3-18-98	2	3	2.31	21	1	0	1	23	20	8	6	2	6	21	.230	.227	.233	8.10	2.31
Dowdy, Kyle	R-R	6-1	195	2-3-93	2	1	7.25	13	1	0	0	22	26	20	18	4	18	17	.296	.214	.333	6.85	7.25
Fairbanks, Peter	R-R	6-6	219	12-16-93	0	2	9.35	8	0	0	0	9	8	10	9	4	7	15	.235	.000	.400	15.58	7.27
2-team total (13 Tampa Bay)					2	3	6.86	21	0	0	2	21	25	20	16	5	10	28	.281	.182	.378	12.00	4.29
Farrell, Luke	L-R	6-6	210	6-7-91	1	0	2.70	9	1	0	0	13	6	4	4	3	3	12	.136	.167	.115	8.10	2.03
Federowicz, Tim	R-R	5-10	215	8-5-87	0	0	9.00	1	0	0	0	1	3	1	1	0	0	0	.500	1.000	.400	0.00	0.00
Gibaut, Ian	R-R	6-3	250	11-19-93	1	1	5.11	9	0	0	0	12	11	7	7	1	8	14	.244	.208	.286	10.22	5.84
2-team total (1 Tampa Bay)					1	1	5.65	10	0	0	0	14	12	9	9	1	10	16	.235	.185	.292	10.05	6.28
Gomez, Jeanmar	R-R	6-3	215	2-10-88	1	0	8.22	16	0	0	0	15	23	15	14	2	6	10	.359	.154	.412	5.87	3.52
Guerrieri, Taylor	R-R	6-2	210	12-1-92	0	0	5.81	20	0	0	0	26	26	19	17	3	22	27	.263	.304	.226	9.23	7.52
Hearn, Taylor	L-L	6-5	210	8-30-94	0	1	108.00	1	1	0	0	0	3	5	4	0	4	0	.750	.000	1.000	0.00	108.00
Hernandez, Jonathan	R-R	6-2	175	7-6-96	2	1	4.32	9	2	0	0	17	14	10	8	3	13	19	.219	.241	.200	10.26	7.02
Huang, Wei-Chieh	R-R	6-1	170	9-26-93	0	0	3.18	4	0	0	0	6	8	5	2	0	5	2	.308	.167	.429	3.18	7.94
Jurado, Ariel	R-R	6-1	180	1-30-96	7	11	5.81	32	18	1	0	122	148	94	79	21	36	81	.304	.281	.324	5.96	2.65
Kelley, Shawn	R-R	6-2	210	4-26-84	5	2	4.94	50	0	0	11	47	55	27	26	12	11	43	.291	.374	.214	8.18	2.09
Leclerc, Jose	R-R	6-0	190	12-19-93	2	4	4.33	70	3	0	14	69	52	34	33	7	39	100	.209	.267	.158	13.11	5.11
Lynn, Lance	B-R	6-5	280	5-12-87	16	11	3.67	33	33	0	0	208	195	89	85	21	59	246	.243	.267	.219	10.63	2.55
Martin, Brett	L-L	6-4	190	4-28-95	2	3	4.76	51	2	0	0	62	72	38	33	7	18	62	.280	.269	.288	8.95	2.60
Martin, Chris	R-R	6-8	215	6-2-86	0	2	3.08	38	0	0	4	38	35	13	13	8	4	43	.247	.206	.284	10.18	0.95
Mathis, Jeff	R-R	6-0	205	3-31-83	0	0	9.00	2	0	0	0	2	3	2	2	1	0	1	.333	.500	.200	4.50	0.00
Mendez, Yohander	L-L	6-5	200	1-17-95	1	0	5.79	3	0	0	0	5	4	3	3	2	5	8	.250	.333	.143	15.43	9.64
Miller, Shelby	R-R	6-3	225	10-10-90	1	3	8.59	19	8	0	0	44	58	46	42	8	29	30	.317	.256	.362	6.14	5.93
Minor, Mike	R-L	6-4	210	12-26-87	14	10	3.59	32	32	2	0	208	190	86	83	30	68	200	.244	.249	.242	8.64	2.94
Montero, Rafael	R-R	6-0	185	10-17-90	2	0	2.48	22	0	0	0	29	23	8	8	5	5	34	.217	.111	.327	10.55	1.55
Palumbo, Joe	L-L	6-1	168	10-26-94	0	3	9.18	7	4	0	0	17	21	17	17	7	8	21	.300	.267	.309	11.34	4.32
Payano, Pedro	R-R	6-2	170	9-27-94	1	2	5.73	6	4	0	0	22	26	17	14	3	15	17	.302	.255	.359	6.95	6.14
Sampson, Adrian	R-R	6-2	210	10-7-91	6	8	5.89	35	15	1	0	125	156	86	82	29	36	101	.302	.274	.324	7.25	2.59

Name	B-T	HT	WT	DOB	W	L	ERA	G	GS	CG	SV	IP	H	R	ER	HR	BB	SO	AVG	vLH	vRH	K/9	BB/9
Smyly, Drew	L-L	6-3	190	6-13-89	1	5	8.42	13	9	0	1	51	64	49	48	19	34	52	.299	.327	.291	9.12	5.96
Springs, Jeffrey	L-L	6-3	180	9-20-92	4	1	6.40	25	0	0	0	32	38	23	23	4	23	32	.295	.356	.262	8.91	6.40
St. John, Locke	L-L	6-3	180	1-31-93	0	0	5.40	7	0	0	0	7	7	4	4	0	4	5	.241	.375	.191	6.75	5.40
Valdez, Phillips	R-R	6-2	160	11-16-91	0	0	3.94	11	0	0	0	16	17	7	7	3	9	18	.270	.292	.256	10.13	5.06
Volquez, Edinson	R-R	6-0	220	7-3-83	0	1	6.75	11	4	0	0	16	20	12	12	3	12	10	.318	.222	.389	5.63	6.75

Fielding

Catcher	PCT	G	PO	A	E	DP	PB
Federowicz	.981	29	203	4	4	0	1
Kiner-Falefa	.996	38	243	11	1	0	4
Mathis	.992	86	686	30	6	2	5
Trevino	.996	40	259	13	1	1	1

Second Base	PCT	G	PO	A	E	DP
Forsythe	1.000	8	8	20	0	5
Odor	.973	137	246	294	15	85
Santana	.955	17	24	40	3	12
Solak	1.000	5	6	9	0	3

Shortstop	PCT	G	PO	A	E	DP
Andrus	.978	146	205	379	13	80
Forsythe	.952	15	10	30	2	10
Santana	.917	9	8	14	2	5

First Base	PCT	G	PO	A	E	DP
Forsythe	.994	46	296	20	2	39
Guzman	.991	81	544	33	5	61
Heineman	1.000	4	38	3	0	3
Santana	.985	44	298	21	5	29
Wisdom	.962	5	23	2	1	3

Third Base	PCT	G	PO	A	E	DP
Cabrera	.972	93	66	173	7	25
Forsythe	.930	33	19	61	6	5
Kiner-Falefa	.973	25	18	53	2	5
Santana	.913	8	5	16	2	2
Solak	.889	11	9	15	3	1
Wisdom	1.000	4	2	4	0	2

Outfield	PCT	G	PO	A	E	DP
Calhoun	.991	71	113	2	1	0
Choo	.975	81	153	0	4	0
DeShields	.981	112	261	2	5	1
Gallo	.974	63	142	8	4	1
Heineman	1.000	21	32	0	0	0
Mazara	.995	101	192	4	1	0
Pence	1.000	23	49	0	0	0
Santana	.969	51	92	2	3	0

NASHVILLE SOUNDS
PACIFIC COAST LEAGUE

TRIPLE-A

Batting

Name	B-T	HT	WT	DOB	AVG	vLH	vRH	G	AB	R	H	2B	3B	HR	RBI	BB	HBP	SH	SF	SO	SB	CS	SLG	OBP
Bandy, Jett	R-R	6-4	235	3-26-90	.231	.344	.193	71	242	34	56	9	0	13	33	16	9	1	0	70	0	2	.430	.303
Beck, Preston	L-R	6-2	190	10-26-90	.340	.385	.324	14	50	6	17	3	1	0	9	7	0	0	1	8	0	0	.440	.414
Calhoun, Willie	L-R	5-8	187	11-4-94	.297	.367	.278	41	138	23	41	8	0	8	28	32	1	1	0	24	1	1	.529	.433
Cole, Hunter	R-R	6-1	190	10-3-92	.308	.321	.303	34	104	18	32	6	1	5	18	12	0	0	0	33	0	1	.529	.379
d'Arnaud, Chase	R-R	6-1	197	1-21-87	.165	.256	.128	46	152	20	25	5	0	6	18	21	4	0	2	54	4	2	.316	.279
2-team total (47 Omaha)					.218	.282	.195	93	321	45	70	10	3	10	35	35	8	0	4	102	11	3	.361	.307
Davidson, Matt	R-R	6-3	230	3-26-91	.264	.322	.245	124	469	74	124	24	0	33	101	42	13	0	4	151	1	0	.527	.339
Depreta-Johnson, Tyler	R-R	5-9	180	5-10-96	.111	.333	.000	3	9	1	1	0	0	0	1	1	0	0	0	5	0	0	.222	.200
DeShields, Delino	R-R	5-9	200	8-16-92	.258	.200	.283	15	66	10	17	3	0	3	11	8	0	1	0	17	8	0	.439	.338
Federowicz, Tim	R-R	5-10	215	8-5-87	.140	.200	.128	16	57	5	8	0	0	1	8	4	0	0	2	16	0	0	.193	.191
Fontana, Nolan	L-R	5-11	195	6-6-91	.167	.250	.143	34	108	14	18	4	0	3	10	21	2	0	1	40	0	0	.287	.311
Granite, Zack	L-L	6-1	175	9-17-92	.290	.306	.284	119	504	66	146	18	8	3	37	31	2	0	4	45	25	13	.375	.331
Guzman, Ronald	L-L	6-5	225	10-20-94	.308	.279	.324	30	117	22	36	8	0	5	16	17	1	0	0	31	0	0	.504	.400
Heineman, Scott	R-R	6-1	215	12-4-92	.340	.354	.333	42	159	34	54	6	2	8	25	17	4	0	2	45	4	3	.554	.412
Ibanez, Andy	R-R	5-10	170	4-3-93	.300	.293	.302	121	467	91	140	30	1	20	65	53	4	3	2	91	7	7	.497	.375
Kapers, Scott	R-R	5-11	175	11-27-96	.000	.000	.000	1	3	0	0	0	0	0	0	1	0	0	0	1	0	0	.000	.250
Kiner-Falefa, Isiah	R-R	5-10	176	3-23-95	.147	.000	.172	9	34	3	5	3	0	0	2	1	2	0	0	6	1	0	.235	.216
Lopes, Christian	R-R	6-0	185	10-1-92	.272	.298	.264	54	195	24	53	15	0	5	33	24	5	3	1	45	4	4	.426	.364
Mendoza, Kevin	B-R	5-10	155	8-16-95	.182	.143	.200	8	22	3	4	0	0	1	1	0	0	1	0	7	0	0	.182	.217
Moore, Adam	R-R	6-3	220	5-8-84	.255	.214	.269	31	106	13	27	2	1	2	19	17	1	0	0	45	0	0	.349	.363
2-team total (12 Omaha)					.233	.186	.252	43	146	18	34	3	1	4	21	20	1	0	0	54	0	0	.349	.329
Moorman, Chuck	R-R	5-11	200	1-9-94	.500	.500	.500	1	4	0	2	1	0	0	0	0	0	0	0	0	0	0	.750	.500
Odor, Rougned	L-R	5-11	195	2-3-94	.286	--	.286	2	7	1	2	1	0	1	2	0	0	0	0	3	0	0	.857	.286
Pill, Tyler	L-R	6-1	195	5-29-90	.233	.129	.278	31	103	13	24	3	0	2	11	12	3	0	3	21	0	0	.320	.322
Profar, Juremi	R-R	6-1	185	1-30-96	.163	.125	.177	23	86	10	14	2	0	0	7	7	1	0	1	8	0	0	.186	.232
Rollin, Franklin	R-R	5-11	165	8-26-95	.100	.000	.125	8	20	3	2	0	0	0	1	0	1	0	0	8	1	0	.100	.143
Santana, Danny	B-R	5-11	185	11-7-90	.343	.667	.276	9	35	4	12	4	1	0	6	4	1	0	0	10	1	1	.514	.425
Solak, Nick	R-R	5-11	190	1-11-95	.348	.393	.333	30	118	23	41	6	0	10	27	6	2	1	1	25	2	0	.653	.386
Tocci, Carlos	R-R	6-2	160	8-23-95	.244	.216	.254	89	328	45	80	9	0	4	31	30	5	0	4	64	4	6	.308	.313
Trevino, Jose	R-R	5-11	211	11-28-92	.226	.237	.222	40	146	16	33	10	0	2	22	8	0	0	2	28	2	0	.336	.263
Viera, Hasuan	L-L	6-0	195	1-30-96	.308	.000	.333	4	13	1	4	0	0	0	4	1	0	0	0	1	0	0	.308	.471
White, Eli	R-R	6-2	175	6-26-94	.253	.281	.244	116	438	63	111	20	5	14	43	43	14	1	3	138	14	5	.418	.337
Wisdom, Patrick	R-R	6-2	220	8-27-91	.240	.215	.249	107	396	68	95	15	0	31	74	53	2	1	1	125	8	2	.513	.332

Pitching

Name	B-T	HT	WT	DOB	W	L	ERA	G	GS	CG	SV	IP	H	R	ER	HR	BB	SO	AVG	vLH	vRH	K/9	BB/9
Allard, Kolby	L-L	6-1	190	8-13-97	0	0	0.00	1	1	0	0	5	4	0	0	0	2	8	.235	.000	.333	14.40	3.60
Bandy, Jett	R-R	6-4	235	3-26-90	0	0	3.86	3	0	0	0	2	3	1	1	0	2	1	.333	1.000	.143	3.86	7.71
Barlow, Joe	R-R	6-3	195	9-28-95	1	1	8.83	19	0	0	0	17	23	17	17	1	21	22	.319	.385	.283	11.42	10.90
Benjamin, Wes	R-L	6-3	205	7-26-93	7	6	5.52	27	25	0	1	135	154	96	83	24	53	114	.284	.323	.268	7.58	3.52
Bibens-Dirkx, Austin	R-R	6-1	210	4-29-85	2	3	7.98	8	0	0	0	38	49	35	34	11	15	33	.304	.342	.268	7.75	3.52
Bird, Kyle	L-L	6-2	175	4-12-93	5	1	2.86	29	0	0	2	35	35	11	11	4	15	39	.263	.256	.266	10.13	3.89
Burke, Brock	L-L	6-4	180	8-4-96	0	0	7.88	2	2	0	0	8	12	7	7	1	6	11	.343	.417	.304	12.38	6.75
Carle, Shane	R-R	6-4	210	8-30-91	1	0	8.10	7	0	0	0	7	13	7	6	0	3	6	.394	.500	.316	5.40	4.05
Carpenter, David	R-R	6-3	250	7-15-85	2	0	1.63	39	0	0	21	39	30	8	7	3	13	42	.219	.292	.180	9.78	3.03
Curtis, Zac	L-L	5-9	190	7-4-92	1	1	8.90	22	0	0	1	30	36	33	30	10	25	40	.286	.206	.315	11.87	7.42
Davidson, Matt	R-R	6-3	230	3-26-91	0	0	0.00	1	0	0	0	1	0	0	0	0	0	0	.333	.333	.333	0.00	0.00
Del Pozo, Miguel	L-L	6-1	180	10-14-92	2	3	5.12	38	0	0	1	46	53	27	26	5	21	65	.294	.407	.240	12.81	4.14
2-team total (2 Salt Lake)					2	3	4.99	40	0	0	2	49	54	28	27	6	21	68	.284	.387	.234	12.58	3.88
Depreta-Johnson, Tyler	R-R	5-9	180	5-10-96	0	1	9.00	1	0	0	0	2	3	4	2	1	0	1	.375	.250	.500	4.50	0.00
Dillard, Tim	R-R	6-4	220	7-19-83	9	9	4.75	33	21	1	0	153	169	93	81	16	37	103	.280	.356	.232	6.05	2.17
Dowdy, Kyle	R-R	6-1	195	2-3-93	1	1	6.57	8	1	0	0	12	13	12	9	0	10	11	.277	.250	.296	8.03	7.30
Espinal, Yoel	R-R	6-2	200	11-7-92	0	0	5.40	4	0	0	0	5	2	3	3	1	8	5	.125	.000	.154	9.00	14.40

Fairbanks, Peter	R-R	6-6	219	12-16-93	0	0	11.37	7	0	0	0	6	10	8	8	1	2	11	.370	.333	.389	15.63	2.84
Feigl, Brady	R-L	6-4	195	12-27-90	2	0	3.43	14	0	0	0	21	19	9	8	3	3	24	.247	.250	.246	10.29	1.29
Fields, Josh	R-R	6-0	191	8-19-85	1	1	5.82	17	0	0	3	17	19	13	11	7	6	19	.284	.259	.300	10.06	3.18
2-team total (8 San Antonio)					2	1	6.57	25	0	0	6	25	26	21	18	9	10	24	.268	.250	.279	8.76	3.65
Gardewine, Nick	R-R	6-1	179	8-15-93	0	0	0.00	4	0	0	1	4	3	0	0	0	2	8	.177	.286	.100	16.62	4.15
Garrett, Reed	R-R	6-2	210	1-2-93	1	3	4.91	34	0	0	2	40	48	23	22	4	19	40	.300	.299	.301	8.93	4.24
Gibaut, Ian	R-R	6-3	250	11-19-93	0	1	7.94	6	0	0	0	6	8	5	5	0	4	6	.333	.571	.235	9.53	6.35
Guerrieri, Taylor	R-R	6-2	210	12-1-92	1	3	3.47	23	2	0	0	36	36	15	14	1	15	39	.265	.220	.291	9.63	3.72
Hearn, Taylor	L-L	6-5	210	8-30-94	1	3	4.05	4	4	0	0	20	14	9	9	3	16	26	.200	.273	.167	11.70	4.50
Hernandez, Ariel	R-R	6-4	230	3-2-92	0	0	2.08	4	0	0	0	4	1	1	1	1	0	2	.071	.143	.000	4.15	0.00
Herrera, Ronald	R-R	5-11	185	5-3-95	1	4	13.02	8	5	0	0	19	29	29	27	9	10	17	.345	.406	.308	8.20	4.82
Huang, Wei-Chieh	R-R	6-1	170	9-26-93	1	2	6.10	18	3	0	0	31	24	23	21	5	25	42	.214	.244	.194	12.19	7.26
Jones, James	L-L	6-4	200	9-24-88	1	0	3.52	5	0	0	0	8	6	3	3	0	1	7	.231	.111	.294	8.22	1.17
Jurado, Ariel	R-R	6-1	180	1-30-96	3	0	3.57	4	4	0	0	23	29	9	9	1	2	22	.315	.235	.362	8.74	0.79
Kuzia, Joe	R-R	6-5	190	10-3-93	0	0	3.86	2	0	0	0	2	2	1	1	0	1	3	.222	.500	.143	11.57	3.86
Leal, Werner	R-R	6-1	160	7-8-95	0	0	0.00	1	0	0	0	2	3	1	0	0	1	0	.375	.000	.600	0.00	5.40
Lemoine, Jacob	R-R	6-5	220	11-28-93	0	2	9.82	18	0	0	1	22	40	24	24	3	11	23	.381	.441	.352	9.41	4.50
Maness, Seth	R-R	6-0	190	10-14-88	8	4	5.38	21	21	0	0	117	155	74	70	19	16	69	.317	.343	.299	5.31	1.23
Martin, Brett	L-L	6-4	190	4-28-95	0	0	0.71	10	0	0	1	13	10	1	1	0	4	19	.213	.200	.222	13.50	2.84
Martin, Jarret	L-L	6-3	230	8-14-89	0	0	17.47	4	0	0	0	6	10	12	11	0	9	6	.400	.375	.412	9.53	14.29
Mendez, Yohander	L-L	6-5	200	1-17-95	0	1	4.91	5	0	0	0	7	3	4	4	1	2	15	.125	.000	.158	18.41	2.45
Montero, Rafael	R-R	6-0	185	10-17-90	1	0	0.00	1	0	0	0	2	0	0	0	0	0	4	.000	.000	.000	15.43	0.00
Palumbo, Joe	L-L	6-1	168	10-26-94	3	0	2.67	6	6	0	0	27	13	9	8	4	10	39	.143	.167	.131	13.00	3.33
Payano, Pedro	R-R	6-2	170	9-27-94	2	3	5.44	11	10	0	0	41	42	33	25	8	28	44	.259	.400	.165	9.58	6.10
Pelham, CD	L-L	6-6	235	2-21-95	0	1	11.81	13	0	0	0	11	16	15	14	2	11	7	.340	.500	.273	5.91	9.28
Pena, Richelson	R-R	6-1	170	9-29-93	1	5	7.82	7	7	0	0	36	41	35	31	8	11	27	.289	.180	.348	6.81	2.78
Petricka, Jake	R-R	6-5	220	6-5-88	1	1	5.06	24	0	0	4	27	29	16	15	3	11	29	.271	.318	.238	9.79	3.71
2-team total (16 San Antonio)					2	2	3.74	40	0	0	7	46	43	21	19	3	15	51	.246	.275	.226	10.05	2.96
Pill, Tyler	L-R	6-1	199	5-29-90	0	0	0.00	1	0	0	0	1	1	0	0	0	0	1	.250	.500	.000	9.00	0.00
Springs, Jeffrey	L-L	6-3	180	9-20-92	3	0	3.86	6	0	0	0	7	6	4	3	1	0	12	.240	.200	.250	15.43	0.00
St. John, Locke	L-L	6-3	180	1-31-93	2	2	8.69	17	0	0	0	20	19	19	19	4	11	23	.257	.194	.302	10.53	5.03
Valdez, Phillips	R-R	6-2	160	11-16-91	1	7	4.92	26	14	0	1	79	87	53	43	10	36	65	.274	.266	.278	7.44	4.12
Vasquez, Esmerling	R-R	6-1	200	11-7-83	1	2	5.60	7	4	0	0	18	15	12	11	0	11	10	.234	.172	.286	5.09	5.60

Fielding

Catcher	PCT	G	PO	A	E	DP	PB
Bandy	.990	56	459	29	5	4	1
Federowicz	1.000	15	124	8	0	0	0
Kapers	1.000	1	6	2	0	0	0
Kiner-Falefa	1.000	2	11	1	0	0	0
Mendoza	1.000	4	15	0	0	0	0
Moore	.992	26	219	20	2	2	1
Moorman	1.000	1	7	1	0	1	0
Trevino	1.000	40	324	21	0	3	1

First Base	PCT	G	PO	A	E	DP
Bandy	1.000	3	22	0	0	1
Cole	1.000	4	26	5	0	5
d'Arnaud	.933	2	14	0	1	0
Davidson	.991	70	548	28	5	56
Guzman	.995	23	192	12	1	23
Heineman	.974	9	73	1	2	6
Profar	.991	14	105	7	1	8
Wisdom	1.000	14	102	4	0	9

Second Base	PCT	G	PO	A	E	DP
Calhoun	1.000	3	4	4	0	1

	PCT	G	PO	A	E	DP
d'Arnaud	.971	18	27	40	2	7
Depreta-Johnson	1.000	2	3	5	0	1
Fontana	.973	30	36	71	3	13
Ibanez	.979	35	63	78	3	18
Lopes	.988	21	34	51	1	12
Mendoza	1.000	4	8	11	0	2
Odor	1.000	2	5	6	0	2
Profar	1.000	2	3	5	0	1
Santana	1.000	1	2	6	0	2
Solak	1.000	22	41	61	0	20
White	1.000	2	2	3	0	0

Third Base	PCT	G	PO	A	E	DP
d'Arnaud	1.000	5	3	16	0	1
Davidson	.975	27	19	60	2	7
Ibanez	.946	48	25	80	6	8
Profar	1.000	3	0	5	0	0
Wisdom	.916	56	51	113	15	10

Shortstop	PCT	G	PO	A	E	DP
d'Arnaud	.913	4	7	14	2	3
Depreta-Johnson	1.000	1	1	1	0	0
Ibanez	.948	26	27	65	5	15

	PCT	G	PO	A	E	DP
Kiner-Falefa	1.000	4	7	12	0	2
Lopes	.956	12	20	23	2	4
Santana	.944	3	8	9	1	4
White	.964	92	121	223	13	55

Outfield	PCT	G	PO	A	E	DP
Beck	.923	14	24	0	2	0
Calhoun	.925	33	37	0	3	0
Cole	.974	20	33	4	1	0
d'Arnaud	1.000	7	12	0	0	0
DeShields	1.000	14	40	2	0	0
Granite	.981	107	197	11	4	0
Heineman	.985	32	60	4	1	1
Lopes	1.000	21	33	0	0	0
Maness	1.000	1	3	0	0	0
Pill	.957	20	43	1	2	1
Rollin	.929	8	12	1	1	0
Santana	1.000	4	4	0	0	0
Solak	.938	7	15	0	1	0
Tocci	1.000	87	204	6	0	1
Viera	1.000	4	12	0	0	0
White	.962	22	50	1	2	0
Wisdom	.955	25	38	4	2	0

FRISCO ROUGHRIDERS

DOUBLE-A

TEXAS LEAGUE

Batting	B-T	HT	WT	DOB	AVG	vLH	vRH	G	AB	R	H	2B	3B	HR	RBI	BB	HBP	SH	SF	SO	SB	CS	SLG	OBP
Altmann, Josh	R-R	6-3	190	7-6-94	.222	.125	.233	54	162	21	36	13	0	4	25	10	9	0	3	44	1	1	.377	.299
Alvarez, Eliezer	L-R	5-11	165	10-15-94	.230	.237	.229	98	352	48	81	14	2	9	44	49	0	1	1	123	12	8	.358	.323
Andrus, Elvis	R-R	6-0	200	8-26-88	.167	--	.167	2	6	1	1	0	0	1	0	0	0	0	1	0	0	.667	.167
Beck, Preston	L-R	6-2	190	10-26-90	.247	.205	.253	99	372	51	92	21	3	11	46	45	3	0	1	87	3	1	.409	.333
Clark, LeDarious	R-R	5-10	185	12-17-93	.200	.231	.196	38	110	17	22	3	0	5	11	6	4	2	2	37	2	3	.364	.262
Cordero, Andretty	R-R	6-1	170	5-3-97	.270	.306	.263	127	500	60	135	21	0	16	82	28	4	0	2	98	2	1	.408	.313
Davis, Brendon	R-R	6-4	185	7-28-97	.202	.250	.194	109	346	38	70	13	1	3	35	42	7	0	5	113	0	3	.272	.298
De Leon, Michael	B-R	6-1	160	1-14-97	.260	.307	.251	127	477	51	124	17	0	3	40	30	5	1	3	62	3	3	.315	.309
Dorow, Ryan	R-R	6-0	195	8-21-95	.213	.296	.187	54	183	23	39	3	3	4	18	20	7	0	1	66	3	1	.328	.313
Guzman, Ronald	L-L	6-5	230	10-20-94	.222	.000	.286	4	18	2	4	1	0	1	2	0	0	0	0	4	0	0	.444	.222
Hernandez, Yonny	B-R	5-9	140	5-4-98	.277	.310	.270	50	170	28	47	5	2	0	16	30	3	3	0	25	16	4	.329	.394
Kiner-Falefa, Isiah	R-R	5-10	176	3-23-95	.283	.200	.325	17	60	7	17	4	0	2	11	8	2	0	1	9	1	0	.450	.380
Kowalczyk, Alex	R-R	6-3	205	10-17-93	.250	.143	.265	53	176	19	44	4	0	3	16	8	2	0	1	59	1	1	.324	.289
Leblanc, Charles	R-R	6-3	195	6-3-96	.265	.215	.275	124	479	73	127	14	4	7	54	46	1	0	3	114	3	3	.355	.329

Batting	B-T	HT	WT	DOB	AVG	vLH	vRH	G	AB	R	H	2B	3B	HR	RBI	BB	HBP	SH	SF	SO	SB	CS	SLG	OBP
Lopes, Christian	R-R	6-0	185	10-1-92	.259	.194	.268	67	251	46	65	14	1	8	32	39	6	1	4	59	10	2	.418	.367
Moorman, Chuck	R-R	5-11	200	1-9-94	.203	.143	.212	20	59	5	12	1	0	3	4	6	2	1	1	19	0	0	.373	.294
Morgan, Josh	R-R	5-11	185	11-16-95	.000	--	.000	1	3	0	0	0	0	0	0	0	1	0	0	0	0	0	.000	.250
Pence, Hunter	R-R	6-4	230	4-13-83	.167	.000	.231	5	18	1	3	0	0	0	1	0	0	0	0	6	0	0	.167	.211
Profar, Juremi	R-R	6-1	185	1-30-96	.290	.321	.285	90	348	46	101	24	0	10	53	31	1	0	3	53	0	1	.445	.347
Rollin, Franklin	R-R	5-11	165	8-26-95	.211	.600	.152	11	38	6	8	1	0	1	7	4	3	2	0	7	2	1	.316	.333
Sanchez, Tony	R-R	5-11	220	5-20-88	.246	.297	.236	64	228	25	56	11	0	4	31	16	9	0	3	55	0	0	.347	.316
Taveras, Leody	B-R	6-1	171	9-8-98	.265	.288	.259	65	264	32	70	12	4	3	31	23	0	2	4	60	11	8	.375	.320

Pitching	B-T	HT	WT	DOB	W	L	ERA	G	GS	CG	SV	IP	H	R	ER	HR	BB	SO	AVG	vLH	vRH	K/9	BB/9
Altmann, Josh	R-R	6-3	190	7-6-94	0	0	0.00	3	0	0	0	2	1	0	0	0	1	0	.143	.000	.333	0.00	4.50
Arredondo, Edgar	R-R	6-3	230	5-16-97	7	3	4.17	20	19	0	0	101	117	48	47	11	28	75	.296	.298	.293	6.66	2.49
Bahr, Jason	R-R	6-5	190	2-15-95	4	3	3.23	12	12	0	0	64	43	25	23	2	25	68	.198	.155	.233	9.56	3.52
Barlow, Joe	R-R	6-3	195	9-28-95	1	1	1.13	13	0	0	0	16	6	2	2	1	6	27	.118	.130	.107	15.19	3.38
Bass, Blake	R-R	6-7	265	6-3-93	8	5	4.63	34	2	0	2	72	65	41	37	3	29	72	.240	.209	.263	9.00	3.63
Beck, Preston	L-R	6-2	190	10-26-90	0	0	18.00	1	0	0	0	1	4	2	2	1	0	0	.667	.500	.750	0.00	0.00
Beras, Jairo	R-R	6-6	195	12-25-94	1	2	10.50	20	0	0	2	18	26	22	21	3	18	20	.338	.375	.297	10.00	9.00
Burke, Brock	L-L	6-4	180	8-4-96	3	5	3.18	9	9	0	0	45	34	19	16	2	12	49	.205	.233	.189	9.73	2.38
Bush, Matt	R-R	5-9	180	2-8-86	0	0	1.04	9	0	0	0	9	3	1	1	1	2	7	.103	.167	.059	7.27	2.08
Clase, Emmanuel	R-R	6-2	206	3-18-98	1	2	3.35	33	1	0	11	38	34	15	14	1	8	39	.236	.209	.260	9.32	1.91
Dorow, Ryan	R-R	6-0	195	8-21-95	0	0	15.00	2	0	0	0	3	6	5	5	2	0	0	.429	.000	.556	0.00	0.00
Dowdy, Kyle	R-R	6-1	195	2-3-93	0	0	0.00	1	0	0	0	1	0	0	0	0	0	1	.250	.000	.500	9.00	0.00
Espinal, Yoel	R-R	6-2	200	11-7-92	3	4	5.84	28	0	0	0	45	37	33	29	5	29	49	.219	.240	.202	9.87	5.84
Evans, Demarcus	R-R	6-4	270	10-22-96	2	0	0.96	30	0	0	6	38	14	4	4	2	22	60	.114	.093	.130	14.34	5.26
Fairbanks, Peter	R-R	6-6	219	12-16-93	1	0	0.00	6	0	0	0	7	2	0	0	0	0	14	.083	.167	.000	17.18	0.00
Farrell, Luke	L-R	6-6	210	6-7-91	0	0	1.04	5	0	0	0	9	2	2	1	0	4	12	.077	.333	.000	12.46	4.15
Hernandez, Jonathan	R-R	6-2	175	7-6-96	5	9	5.16	22	16	0	0	96	100	58	55	11	38	95	.267	.290	.243	8.91	3.56
Herrera, Ronald	R-R	5-11	185	5-3-95	2	6	6.13	13	12	0	0	62	79	45	42	12	11	44	.306	.333	.276	6.42	1.61
Huang, Wei-Chieh	R-R	6-1	170	9-26-93	1	0	1.86	6	1	0	0	10	7	2	2	2	2	14	.200	.231	.182	13.03	1.86
Jones, James	L-L	6-4	200	9-24-88	1	1	2.56	40	0	0	2	56	38	22	16	6	29	64	.191	.166	.207	10.22	4.63
Lemoine, Jacob	R-R	6-5	220	11-28-93	2	0	0.83	26	0	0	4	33	23	5	3	2	10	28	.202	.200	.203	7.71	2.76
Martinez, Emerson	R-R	6-0	190	1-11-95	3	2	4.37	15	8	0	0	58	67	29	28	5	20	45	.298	.298	.297	7.02	3.12
Medina, Jefferson	R-R	6-2	184	5-31-94	0	1	6.64	12	1	0	0	20	25	15	15	3	9	17	.305	.318	.290	7.52	3.98
Mendez, Yohander	L-L	6-5	200	1-17-95	0	0	1.23	4	0	0	1	7	5	1	1	1	6	6	.172	.200	.158	7.36	7.36
Montero, Rafael	R-R	6-0	185	10-17-90	0	0	7.00	5	2	0	0	9	15	7	7	0	2	15	.366	.300	.429	15.00	2.00
Moorman, Chuck	R-R	5-11	200	1-9-94	0	0	0.00	1	0	0	0	1	0	0	0	0	1	0	.000	--	.000	9.00	9.00
Palumbo, Joe	L-L	6-1	168	10-26-94	0	0	3.19	11	10	0	0	54	43	21	19	5	25	69	.221	.150	.252	11.57	4.19
Payano, Pedro	R-R	6-2	170	9-27-94	3	1	4.43	8	8	0	0	43	30	21	21	3	18	49	.199	.257	.143	10.34	3.80
Pelham, CD	L-L	6-6	235	2-21-95	1	3	12.05	29	0	0	2	22	32	31	29	4	29	30	.337	.344	.333	12.46	12.05
Pena, Richelson	R-R	6-1	170	9-29-93	1	4	4.41	13	6	0	0	35	33	18	17	1	5	33	.246	.254	.239	8.57	1.30
Phillips, Tyler	R-R	6-5	191	10-27-97	7	9	4.73	18	16	0	0	93	95	56	49	15	20	74	.263	.260	.265	7.14	1.93
St. John, Locke	L-L	6-3	180	1-31-93	3	2	1.52	22	0	0	4	30	21	8	5	2	13	42	.202	.128	.246	12.74	3.94
Vasquez, Esmerling	R-R	6-1	200	11-7-83	1	2	6.11	5	4	0	0	18	16	13	12	2	15	7	.254	.241	.265	3.57	7.64
Volquez, Edinson	R-R	6-0	220	7-3-83	0	1	2.25	4	4	0	0	4	3	1	1	0	1	5	.200	.000	.300	11.25	2.25
Weickel, Walker	R-R	6-6	195	11-14-93	7	2	3.63	43	1	0	3	72	57	31	29	6	29	62	.214	.208	.221	7.75	3.63
Wiles, Collin	R-R	6-4	222	5-30-94	0	3	5.52	9	7	0	0	31	31	19	19	5	9	22	.263	.245	.276	6.39	2.61

Fielding

Catcher	PCT	G	PO	A	E	DP	PB
Kiner-Falefa	1.000	9	77	5	0	1	2
Kowalczyk	.995	51	394	17	2	2	6
Moorman	.983	20	162	13	3	0	4
Morgan	1.000	1	8	0	0	0	0
Sanchez	.990	64	574	45	6	9	3

	PCT	G	PO	A	E	DP
De Leon	.990	20	35	67	1	16
Dorow	.978	23	48	43	2	18
Hernandez	.987	33	56	93	2	17
Leblanc	.987	20	33	41	1	10
Lopes	.955	40	68	100	8	22
Profar	1.000	2	5	2	0	0

	PCT	G	PO	A	E	DP
Davis	1.000	7	9	20	0	4
De Leon	.978	99	151	243	9	62
Hernandez	.914	16	24	40	6	9
Kiner-Falefa	1.000	1	1	2	0	0
Leblanc	.833	2	0	5	1	1
Lopes	.976	14	14	26	1	7

First Base	PCT	G	PO	A	E	DP
Beck	1.000	6	23	1	0	2
Cordero	.976	43	313	12	8	36
De Leon	1.000	5	43	1	0	3
Guzman	1.000	2	21	1	0	0
Leblanc	.988	30	222	17	3	21
Profar	.996	58	425	29	2	50

Second Base	PCT	G	PO	A	E	DP
Cordero	1.000	4	5	10	0	3

Third Base	PCT	G	PO	A	E	DP
Cordero	.966	37	18	67	3	8
Davis	.875	4	1	6	1	0
De Leon	1.000	1	3	4	0	1
Dorow	.986	28	22	50	1	6
Kiner-Falefa	1.000	4	2	12	0	2
Leblanc	.956	53	41	89	6	8
Profar	.938	13	5	25	2	4

Shortstop	PCT	G	PO	A	E	DP

Outfield	PCT	G	PO	A	E	DP
Altmann	1.000	51	99	2	0	1
Alvarez	.989	96	176	12	2	3
Beck	.982	70	103	8	2	1
Clark	.974	36	75	1	2	0
Davis	.963	90	142	14	6	4
Hernandez	1.000	1	1	0	0	0
Leblanc	1.000	7	9	1	0	0
Rollin	1.000	10	27	0	0	0
Taveras	.989	65	173	4	2	2

DOWN EAST WOOD DUCKS
HIGH CLASS A

CAROLINA LEAGUE

Batting	B-T	HT	WT	DOB	AVG	vLH	vRH	G	AB	R	H	2B	3B	HR	RBI	BB	HBP	SH	SF	SO	SB	CS	SLG	OBP
Altmann, Josh	R-R	6-3	190	7-6-94	.195	.225	.180	53	149	17	29	5	0	3	14	35	7	1	2	40	8	3	.289	.368
Apostel, Sherten	R-R	6-4	200	3-11-99	.237	.262	.226	41	135	18	32	5	1	4	16	23	1	0	0	49	0	0	.378	.352
Arias, Diosbel	R-R	6-2	190	7-21-96	.270	.270	.270	134	485	60	131	24	4	6	56	55	4	0	5	124	4	5	.361	.346
Depreta-Johnson, Tyler	R-R	5-9	180	5-10-95	.189	.125	.216	53	159	13	30	6	0	0	13	14	2	1	0	35	1	1	.226	.263
Dorow, Ryan	R-R	6-0	195	8-21-95	.265	.267	.264	70	249	45	66	9	0	8	43	42	5	1	3	69	11	2	.398	.378
Hernandez, Yonny	B-R	5-9	140	5-4-98	.298	.315	.291	72	245	42	73	6	1	0	34	48	9	4	3	47	17	14	.331	.426
Huff, Sam	R-R	6-4	230	1-14-98	.262	.294	.249	97	367	49	96	17	2	13	43	27	9	0	2	117	2	5	.425	.326
Jenkins, Eric	L-R	6-1	170	1-30-97	.177	.200	.169	87	255	30	45	4	5	4	17	30	3	6	1	95	21	7	.278	.270

Batting	B-T	HT	WT	DOB	AVG	vLH	vRH	G	AB	R	H	2B	3B	HR	RBI	BB	HBP	SH	SF	SO	SB	CS	SLG	OBP
Martinez, Julio Pablo	L-L	5-9	174	3-21-96	.248	.270	.240	113	407	59	101	21	4	14	58	39	5	1	4	144	28	12	.423	.319
Middleton, Clayton	R-R	6-0	205	10-8-93	.160	.184	.135	25	75	4	12	2	0	1	4	5	1	1	0	31	1	1	.227	.222
Novoa, Melvin	R-R	5-11	215	6-17-96	.143	.158	.136	17	63	3	9	2	0	0	7	2	2	0	0	11	0	0	.175	.194
Perez, Yanio	R-R	6-2	205	8-10-95	.260	.315	.239	110	384	38	100	17	2	7	44	29	5	0	3	88	9	8	.370	.318
Pozo, Yohel	R-R	6-0	201	6-14-97	.246	.314	.221	107	395	43	97	17	0	9	43	15	3	0	6	38	6	2	.357	.275
Quiroz, Isaias	R-R	5-10	234	10-22-96	.000	--	.000	1	2	0	0	0	0	0	0	0	0	1	0	0	2	0	0	.000	.333
Reed, Tyreque	R-R	6-1	250	6-6-97	.216	.226	.213	32	111	13	24	6	0	4	17	8	5	0	2	36	0	2	.378	.294
Rollin, Franklin	R-R	5-11	165	8-26-95	.177	.147	.206	23	68	3	12	0	1	0	4	3	0	1	1	16	1	5	.206	.208
Taveras, Leody	B-R	6-1	171	9-8-98	.294	.254	.309	66	255	44	75	7	4	2	25	31	0	2	2	62	21	5	.377	.368
Tejeda, Anderson	B-R	5-11	160	5-1-98	.234	.260	.222	43	158	22	37	10	1	4	24	17	3	0	3	58	9	4	.386	.315
Terry, Curtis	R-R	6-3	264	10-6-96	.322	.282	.339	67	239	35	77	12	2	10	33	23	7	0	2	50	0	1	.515	.395
Thompson, Bubba	R-R	6-1	180	6-9-98	.178	.109	.204	57	202	24	36	8	2	5	21	21	2	2	1	72	12	3	.312	.261
Viera, Hasuan	L-L	6-0	195	1-30-96	.211	.000	.281	27	76	14	16	1	1	1	4	14	0	0	0	25	5	0	.290	.333

Pitching	B-T	HT	WT	DOB	W	L	ERA	G	GS	CG	SV	IP	H	R	ER	HR	BB	SO	AVG	vLH	vRH	K/9	BB/9
Advocate, Josh	R-R	6-0	195	1-18-94	5	2	2.64	35	4	0	0	75	55	23	22	5	26	77	.212	.168	.239	9.24	3.12
Alexy, A.J.	R-R	6-4	195	4-21-98	0	3	5.12	5	5	0	0	19	14	12	11	1	13	23	.206	.206	.206	10.71	6.05
Anderson, Reid	R-R	6-3	185	8-22-95	6	8	3.92	24	24	1	0	126	120	61	55	9	64	109	.255	.226	.276	7.77	4.56
Bahr, Jason	R-R	6-5	190	2-15-95	6	1	1.71	11	11	0	0	58	37	13	11	2	26	58	.179	.147	.210	9.00	4.03
Barlow, Joe	R-R	6-3	195	9-28-95	4	0	0.38	17	0	0	0	24	10	2	1	1	15	44	.132	.161	.111	16.73	5.70
Beras, Jairo	R-R	6-6	195	12-25-94	3	1	5.55	16	0	0	0	24	18	16	15	1	21	20	.202	.189	.212	7.40	7.77
Bremer, Noah	R-R	6-5	200	5-13-96	3	0	2.97	14	14	0	0	76	53	26	25	2	24	68	.204	.171	.234	8.09	2.85
Brennan, Tim	L-R	6-4	200	12-18-96	4	3	4.27	8	8	1	0	46	52	24	22	1	5	25	.286	.338	.245	4.86	0.97
Clase, Emmanuel	R-R	6-2	206	3-18-98	2	0	0.00	6	0	0	1	7	4	0	0	0	1	11	.167	.111	.200	14.14	1.29
Depreta-Johnson, Tyler	R-R	5-9	180	5-10-96	0	1	5.40	2	0	0	0	2	5	2	1	0	1	0	.556	.667	.500	0.00	5.40
Engler, Scott	R-R	6-4	220	12-12-96	3	1	1.91	21	3	0	0	42	33	12	9	2	22	58	.212	.177	.239	12.33	4.68
Eubanks, Alex	R-R	6-2	180	9-13-95	9	5	3.44	29	13	0	2	107	105	46	41	5	31	64	.261	.301	.219	5.37	2.60
Evans, Demarcus	R-R	6-4	270	10-22-96	4	0	0.81	17	0	0	0	22	9	3	2	0	17	40	.127	.152	.105	16.12	6.85
Fairbanks, Peter	R-R	6-6	219	12-16-93	1	0	2.92	11	0	0	2	12	10	4	4	0	4	15	.213	.158	.250	10.95	2.92
Fontenot, Kaleb	R-R	6-1	180	6-23-93	1	0	8.10	3	0	0	0	3	6	3	3	0	1	3	.375	.250	.417	2.70	2.70
Hellinger, Sam	R-R	6-1	195	9-6-94	1	1	11.12	3	0	0	0	6	6	7	7	3	7	4	.273	.286	.250	6.35	11.12
King, John	L-L	6-2	215	9-14-94	2	4	2.03	14	14	1	0	71	59	20	16	4	11	62	.228	.209	.237	7.86	1.39
Kuzia, Joe	R-R	6-5	190	10-3-93	4	2	1.51	37	0	0	18	48	40	11	8	2	15	50	.231	.149	.283	9.44	2.83
Latz, Jake	R-L	6-2	185	4-8-96	5	1	1.76	11	11	0	0	51	28	14	10	2	22	60	.160	.157	.161	10.59	3.88
Matuella, Michael	R-R	6-6	220	6-3-94	5	2	4.04	39	0	0	0	42	42	22	19	0	31	52	.261	.254	.265	11.06	6.59
Medina, Jefferson	R-R	6-2	184	5-31-94	3	2	2.77	20	0	0	6	39	28	12	12	2	22	35	.201	.186	.217	8.08	5.08
Mendez, Sal	R-L	6-4	185	2-25-95	7	2	2.37	26	16	0	1	118	107	38	31	4	37	89	.244	.268	.233	6.81	2.83
Phillips, Tyler	R-R	6-5	191	10-27-97	2	2	1.19	6	6	0	0	38	28	6	5	1	6	28	.212	.193	.227	6.69	1.43
Robertson, Wes	R-R	6-2	190	3-11-96	1	0	7.07	8	0	0	0	14	15	12	11	4	7	6	.273	.286	.265	3.86	4.50
Santiago, Manuel	L-L	6-0	175	10-15-99	0	1	10.80	1	1	0	0	2	2	2	2	1	3	0	.286	.000	.667	0.00	16.20
Thomas, Tyler	R-L	6-1	175	12-22-95	0	2	5.19	2	2	0	0	9	10	5	5	1	5	7	.323	.250	.348	7.27	5.19
Uvila, Cole	R-R	6-3	206	1-30-94	5	3	2.50	35	0	0	5	58	31	20	16	2	33	85	.163	.073	.232	13.27	5.15
Villegas, Francisco	L-L	6-2	175	8-31-97	0	3	4.88	35	4	0	2	59	42	32	32	10	32	58	.169	.250	.169	8.85	4.88
Wiles, Collin	R-R	6-4	222	5-30-94	1	1	3.77	3	3	0	0	14	13	6	6	0	5	14	.255	.250	.257	8.79	3.14
Williams, Scott	R-R	6-2	200	11-17-93	0	1	9.00	3	0	0	0	3	5	3	3	0	0	1	.385	.167	.571	3.00	0.00

Fielding

Catcher	PCT	G	PO	A	E	DP	PB
Huff	.988	51	449	39	6	4	6
Middleton	1.000	7	43	2	0	0	0
Novoa	.993	14	138	13	1	2	1
Pozo	.987	70	525	76	8	3	4
Quiroz	1.000	1	10	1	0	0	0

First Base	PCT	G	PO	A	E	DP
Arias	1.000	12	65	11	0	3
Huff	1.000	4	26	1	0	4
Middleton	.988	13	80	3	1	4
Perez	.986	21	131	6	2	12
Pozo	.978	7	42	1	2	7
Reed	.995	25	208	11	1	20
Terry	.998	58	438	36	1	53
Viera	.989	13	89	5	1	9

Second Base	PCT	G	PO	A	E	DP
Altmann	.989	48	77	111	2	30
Arias	.983	45	78	95	3	16
Depreta-Johnson	1.000	13	19	31	0	10
Dorow	1.000	2	2	4	0	2
Hernandez	.988	34	67	96	2	28
Rollin	.000	1	0	0	0	0

Third Base	PCT	G	PO	A	E	DP
Altmann	.889	3	3	5	1	2
Apostel	.942	41	27	71	6	9
Arias	.957	35	20	46	3	10
Dorow	.979	55	39	103	3	7
Perez	.947	7	6	12	1	0

Shortstop	PCT	G	PO	A	E	DP
Arias	.975	31	40	78	3	15
Depreta-Johnson	.959	39	52	110	7	28
Dorow	.953	10	16	25	2	6
Hernandez	.982	25	46	64	2	13
Tejeda	.963	39	58	100	6	25

Outfield	PCT	G	PO	A	E	DP
Altmann	1.000	2	4	0	0	0
Hernandez	.875	7	6	1	1	0
Jenkins	.973	82	138	4	4	0
Martinez	.986	109	210	2	3	0
Middleton	1.000	3	1	0	0	0
Perez	.983	77	161	13	3	3
Pozo	1.000	1	1	0	0	0
Rollin	1.000	21	28	1	0	0
Taveras	.985	63	124	8	2	2
Thompson	.971	56	98	1	3	0
Viera	1.000	13	18	1	0	0

HICKORY CRAWDADS   LOW CLASS A
SOUTH ATLANTIC LEAGUE

Batting	B-T	HT	WT	DOB	AVG	vLH	vRH	G	AB	R	H	2B	3B	HR	RBI	BB	HBP	SH	SF	SO	SB	CS	SLG	OBP
Almonte, Jose	R-R	6-3	205	9-9-96	.160	.088	.194	57	194	22	31	12	1	3	22	10	3	1	2	70	1	0	.278	.211
Anderson, Ryan	R-R	6-1	205	8-30-95	.271	.333	.248	51	170	29	46	14	1	5	22	15	2	0	1	23	11	1	.453	.335
Aparicio, Miguel	L-L	6-0	188	3-17-99	.251	.256	.250	112	406	55	102	21	8	12	49	21	7	7	4	87	12	4	.431	.297
Apostel, Sherten	R-R	6-4	200	3-11-99	.258	.310	.243	80	283	38	73	13	1	15	43	28	5	0	3	71	2	1	.470	.332
Biggers, Jax	L-R	5-11	175	4-7-97	.282	.261	.287	76	255	42	72	8	2	2	24	34	3	5	3	39	12	6	.353	.370
Chavez, Frainyer	R-R	5-10	170	5-24-99	.255	.255	.255	115	365	54	93	15	2	1	36	41	2	5	2	76	17	8	.315	.332
Depreta-Johnson, Tyler	R-R	5-9	180	5-10-96	.232	.214	.238	17	56	4	13	1	0	0	5	9	1	0	0	7	0	0	.250	.349
Enright, Kole	B-R	6-1	175	1-21-98	.258	.213	.271	62	217	33	56	15	1	10	35	22	4	4	3	62	0	1	.475	.333
Gardner, Tanner	L-R	6-0	210	9-28-95	.214	.267	.185	13	42	11	9	1	3	2	7	5	0	0	1	11	0	2	.524	.292

Name	B-T	HT	WT	DOB	AVG	vLH	vRH	G	AB	R	H	2B	3B	HR	RBI	BB	HBP	SH	SF	SO	SB	CS	SLG	OBP
Gonzalez, Pedro	R-R	6-5	190	10-27-97	.248	.356	.213	119	412	69	102	13	5	23	67	39	4	1	3	129	14	6	.471	.317
Huff, Sam	R-R	6-4	230	1-14-98	.333	.290	.324	30	108	22	36	5	0	15	29	6	0	0	0	37	4	1	.796	.368
Jung, Josh	R-R	6-2	215	2-12-98	.287	.167	.315	40	157	18	45	13	0	1	23	16	4	0	2	29	4	1	.389	.363
Martinez, Julio Pablo	L-L	5-9	174	3-21-96	.250	.211	.286	10	40	7	10	1	1	1	5	3	0	0	1	12	4	1	.400	.296
Novoa, Melvin	R-R	5-11	215	6-17-96	.246	.225	.252	85	305	40	75	23	0	12	46	22	7	0	6	67	1	2	.439	.306
Ornelas, Jonathan	R-R	6-1	178	5-26-00	.257	.279	.248	113	413	61	106	24	3	6	38	42	9	1	7	103	13	4	.373	.333
Quiroz, Isaias	R-R	5-10	234	10-22-96	.111	.111	.111	22	63	1	7	2	0	0	2	8	2	1	0	30	0	0	.143	.233
Reed, Tyreque	R-R	6-1	250	6-6-97	.282	.281	.282	64	238	37	67	17	0	13	48	34	4	0	4	60	4	2	.517	.375
Seise, Chris	R-R	6-2	175	1-6-99	.241	.174	.250	21	87	12	21	4	3	0	6	3	1	0	1	33	6	5	.356	.272
Smith, Chad	L-L	6-2	200	9-30-97	.150	.000	.214	7	20	2	3	0	0	2	4	2	0	1	0	8	0	1	.450	.227
Terry, Curtis	R-R	6-3	264	10-6-96	.263	.237	.278	62	232	39	61	24	0	15	47	14	10	0	3	67	0	1	.560	.328
Whatley, Matt	R-R	5-9	200	1-7-96	.234	.186	.251	117	380	56	89	17	2	4	49	62	8	9	6	84	29	7	.321	.349

Pitching	B-T	HT	WT	DOB	W	L	ERA	G	GS	CG	SV	IP	H	R	ER	HR	BB	SO	AVG	vLH	vRH	K/9	BB/9
Anderson, Grant	R-R	6-0	180	6-21-97	7	4	3.22	37	0	0	8	64	56	29	23	1	24	50	.239	.235	.242	6.99	3.36
Bice, Dylan	L-R	6-4	220	8-17-97	0	0	2.53	7	0	0	0	11	9	3	3	1	3	16	.225	.111	.258	13.50	2.53
Brennan, Tim	L-R	6-4	200	12-18-96	7	3	3.58	13	13	1	0	78	66	35	31	4	9	57	.228	.276	.193	6.58	1.04
Bueno, Hever	R-R	6-2	179	11-23-94	4	1	2.14	25	0	0	0	42	25	11	10	2	22	54	.172	.169	.175	11.57	4.71
Burke, Brock	L-L	6-4	180	8-4-96	0	0	7.20	1	1	0	0	5	9	4	4	0	0	1	.429	.556	.333	1.80	0.00
Casanova, Jean	R-R	6-3	181	3-4-97	0	0	4.41	4	0	0	0	16	20	8	8	1	5	15	.303	.278	.313	8.27	2.76
Chandler, Sean	R-R	6-5	200	1-24-97	0	1	5.91	11	0	0	0	11	9	9	7	1	10	17	.214	.077	.276	14.34	8.44
Crouse, Hans	L-R	6-4	180	9-15-98	6	1	4.41	19	19	0	0	88	86	49	43	12	19	76	.256	.290	.224	7.80	1.95
Depreta-Johnson, Tyler	R-R	5-9	180	5-10-96	1	0	0.00	2	0	0	1	3	2	2	0	0	2	2	.222	.200	.250	6.00	0.00
Engler, Scott	R-R	6-4	220	12-12-96	2	1	2.67	14	0	0	4	30	19	9	9	2	6	45	.181	.122	.232	13.35	1.78
Gardner, Tanner	L-R	6-0	210	9-28-95	0	0	0.00	1	0	0	0	1	0	0	0	0	0	0	.000	---	.000	0.00	0.00
Gonzalez, Kelvin	R-R	6-0	170	12-24-97	6	2	1.99	28	0	0	5	45	28	13	10	4	15	58	.177	.211	.146	11.51	2.98
Hellinger, Sam	R-R	6-1	195	9-6-94	0	1	1.53	8	0	0	1	18	11	4	3	2	10	26	.180	.226	.133	13.25	5.09
Henriquez, Ronny	R-R	5-10	155	6-20-00	6	6	4.50	21	19	0	0	82	91	50	41	6	27	99	.284	.260	.309	10.87	2.96
Jacobsen, Lucas	L-L	6-5	190	7-1-95	1	4	3.90	20	0	0	2	30	25	14	13	3	11	48	.219	.149	.269	14.40	3.30
King, John	L-L	6-2	215	9-14-94	1	2	3.42	5	5	0	0	26	31	13	10	1	2	29	.287	.182	.299	9.91	0.68
Latz, Jake	R-L	6-2	185	4-8-96	2	0	0.90	2	2	0	0	10	5	2	1	0	3	14	.152	.500	.129	12.60	2.70
Linarez, Jesus	R-R	6-4	216	1-10-97	1	1	2.35	22	2	0	2	61	51	16	16	1	20	60	.223	.283	.183	8.80	2.93
Mendoza, Abdiel	R-R	5-10	160	9-19-98	2	2	3.15	25	8	0	3	86	65	31	30	8	25	75	.215	.222	.208	7.88	2.63
Pacheco, Sergio	R-R	6-1	170	8-17-99	1	0	0.00	1	0	0	0	6	2	1	0	0	2	6	.100	.083	.125	9.00	3.00
Robert, Daniel	L-R	6-4	210	8-30-94	0	1	3.12	4	0	0	1	9	5	3	3	1	3	13	.167	.267	.067	13.50	3.12
Robertson, Wes	R-R	6-2	190	3-11-96	2	0	1.38	6	0	0	1	13	6	2	2	1	5	10	.140	.000	.207	6.92	3.46
Rodriguez, Yerry	R-R	6-2	198	10-15-97	7	3	2.08	13	13	0	0	74	45	20	17	5	21	85	.177	.197	.158	10.38	2.57
Snyder, Nick	R-R	6-4	190	10-10-95	5	3	3.06	33	0	0	6	53	46	18	18	3	18	60	.237	.282	.207	10.19	3.06
Starr, Nick	R-R	6-3	225	12-3-96	1	0	11.91	8	0	0	0	11	19	16	15	2	8	13	.388	.400	.375	10.32	6.35
Thompson, Tyree	R-R	6-4	165	6-12-97	6	7	3.30	18	18	0	0	93	75	37	34	8	44	60	.225	.179	.261	5.83	4.27
Tiedemann, Tai	R-R	6-6	195	5-31-96	4	2	2.99	27	2	0	1	72	66	24	24	5	26	71	.245	.258	.238	8.83	3.24
Uvila, Cole	R-R	6-2	206	1-30-94	2	0	0.00	3	0	0	1	7	3	1	0	0	1	10	.136	.167	.125	12.86	1.29
Vanasco, Ricky	R-R	6-3	180	10-13-98	0	0	1.69	2	2	0	0	11	5	3	2	0	3	16	.143	.091	.167	13.50	2.53
Winn, Cole	R-R	6-2	190	11-25-99	4	4	4.46	18	18	0	0	69	59	36	34	5	39	65	.233	.200	.263	8.52	5.11
Wolfram, Grant	L-L	6-6	210	12-12-96	5	3	4.28	25	9	0	0	69	72	38	33	3	30	73	.265	.290	.257	9.48	3.89

Fielding

Catcher	PCT	G	PO	A	E	DP	PB
Huff	1.000	14	141	12	0	2	1
Novoa	.980	31	218	28	5	0	7
Quiroz	.990	12	100	3	1	0	1
Whatley	.987	87	723	99	11	4	4

First Base	PCT	G	PO	A	E	DP
Almonte	1.000	5	22	2	0	2
Anderson	1.000	2	5	0	0	0
Apostel	.988	12	72	7	1	10
Enright	1.000	13	63	6	0	2
Gardner	1.000	1	15	0	0	1
Quiroz	1.000	1	2	0	0	2
Reed	.991	54	427	23	4	35
Terry	.989	58	429	34	5	40

Second Base	PCT	G	PO	A	E	DP
Anderson	1.000	1	1	0	0	0
Biggers	.992	55	90	145	2	39
Chavez	1.000	37	51	79	0	12
Depreta-Johnson	.986	17	27	44	1	13
Ornelas	.974	34	71	81	4	18

Third Base	PCT	G	PO	A	E	DP
Almonte	1.000	2	1	1	0	0
Apostel	.931	70	44	118	12	11
Chavez	.968	34	18	43	2	4
Jung	.989	35	21	72	1	2
Ornelas	.875	4	5	2	1	0

Shortstop	PCT	G	PO	A	E	DP
Biggers	.958	10	20	26	2	5
Chavez	.954	48	61	105	8	30
Ornelas	.951	63	85	130	11	29
Seise	.946	18	26	44	4	10

Outfield	PCT	G	PO	A	E	DP
Almonte	.978	50	86	4	2	0
Anderson	.976	45	81	1	2	0
Aparicio	.996	110	244	9	1	4
Biggers	1.000	12	21	0	0	0
Enright	.978	52	88	1	2	0
Gardner	1.000	11	13	0	0	0
Gonzalez	.964	112	206	11	8	0
Martinez	1.000	10	18	0	0	0
Ornelas	.944	11	16	1	1	0
Smith	.900	7	9	0	1	0

SPOKANE INDIANS   SHORT SEASON
NORTHWEST LEAGUE

Batting	B-T	HT	WT	DOB	AVG	vLH	vRH	G	AB	R	H	2B	3B	HR	RBI	BB	HBP	SH	SF	SO	SB	CS	SLG	OBP
Anderson, Ryan	R-R	6-1	205	8-30-95	.265	.286	.262	14	49	6	13	2	0	0	6	9	1	0	0	8	0	1	.306	.390
Asuncion, Luis	R-R	6-4	205	2-27-97	.241	.275	.231	59	220	27	53	9	2	4	32	20	5	0	2	66	4	3	.355	.316
Barreto, Derwin	B-R	5-9	155	9-1-00	.234	.240	.232	30	107	19	25	2	0	2	13	17	0	2	3	19	3	3	.308	.331
Basabe, Osleivis	R-R	6-1	165	9-13-00	.300	.500	.250	2	10	0	3	0	0	0	1	0	0	0	0	1	0	0	.300	.300
Crim, Blaine	R-R	5-11	200	6-17-97	.335	.315	.342	53	212	34	71	15	1	8	45	19	4	0	1	28	1	0	.528	.398
Easley, Jayce	B-R	5-8	145	8-2-99	.000	.000	.000	4	10	1	0	0	0	0	0	7	0	0	0	6	0	1	.000	.412
Florentino, Randy	L-R	5-11	175	7-5-00	.250	---	.250	1	4	0	1	0	0	0	0	0	0	0	0	2	0	0	.250	.250
Garcia, David	B-R	5-11	170	2-6-00	.277	.205	.297	48	184	33	51	14	0	5	29	21	1	0	2	42	1	1	.435	.351
Gardner, Tanner	L-R	6-0	210	9-28-95	.178	.133	.190	23	73	10	13	3	2	1	8	11	1	0	0	29	2	0	.315	.294
Hernandez, Heriberto	R-R	6-1	180	12-16-99	.375	1.000	.167	3	8	4	3	0	0	0	1	2	0	0	0	3	3	0	.375	.500
Hoover, Jake	R-R	6-0	180	7-11-97	.239	.361	.202	51	155	36	37	11	3	0	13	26	4	1	1	51	11	2	.348	.360

Batting	B-T	HT	WT	DOB	AVG	vLH	vRH	G	AB	R	H	2B	3B	HR	RBI	BB	HBP	SH	SF	SO	SB	CS	SLG	OBP
Inoa, Cristian	R-R	5-10	165	7-4-99	.199	.067	.236	58	206	28	41	13	0	2	19	23	2	0	2	60	5	4	.291	.283
Irizarry, Kenen	L-R	6-0	150	5-6-00	.253	.257	.252	49	174	23	44	10	1	4	22	22	2	3	1	51	2	3	.391	.342
Joseph, Starling	R-R	6-3	209	8-1-98	.169	.161	.171	50	148	21	25	5	1	2	17	13	6	2	1	69	7	1	.257	.262
Kapers, Scott	R-R	5-11	175	11-27-96	.193	.200	.191	28	88	17	17	4	0	1	12	9	14	1	0	22	1	0	.273	.360
Martinez, Stanley	R-R	6-0	176	1-5-97	.147	.177	.138	23	75	9	11	4	0	0	4	8	2	1	0	32	1	1	.200	.247
McReynolds, Jonah	R-R	5-11	165	12-16-95	.239	.196	.255	56	197	27	47	10	1	6	32	16	10	0	0	79	2	3	.391	.327
Morales, Maxwell	R-R	6-0	190	9-28-97	.188	.133	.212	16	48	4	9	1	0	2	9	4	2	0	0	16	0	0	.333	.278
Ovalles, Alexander	L-L	6-0	180	10-6-00	.187	.222	.178	24	91	13	17	6	0	2	15	8	0	0	1	24	3	1	.319	.250
Ricumstrict, Obie	R-R	6-2	175	7-20-98	.208	.154	.226	60	216	27	45	10	1	6	29	15	4	1	2	89	7	3	.347	.270
Strahm, Kellen	R-R	6-1	215	4-25-97	.278	.196	.304	50	194	40	54	5	1	5	24	32	3	1	1	46	12	1	.392	.387
Ventura, Francisco	R-R	5-9	206	11-19-98	.243	.143	.267	23	74	5	18	2	0	0	2	9	2	0	0	13	0	1	.270	.341
Wendzel, Davis	R-R	6-0	205	5-23-97	.200	.000	.222	3	10	4	2	0	0	0	3	0	0	0	3	2	1		.200	.385

Pitching	B-T	HT	WT	DOB	W	L	ERA	G	GS	CG	SV	IP	H	R	ER	HR	BB	SO	AVG	vLH	vRH	K/9	BB/9
Anderson, Ben	R-R	6-4	200	5-2-98	0	0	3.86	2	1	0	0	2	3	1	1	0	2	3	.300	.500	.000	11.57	7.71
Bice, Dylan	L-R	6-4	220	8-17-97	0	0	0.00	3	0	0	1	6	3	0	0	0	3	5	.150	.083	.250	7.50	4.50
Castillo, Juan	R-R	6-3	166	9-18-95	1	0	8.46	18	0	0	0	28	31	30	26	4	32	20	.282	.227	.318	6.51	10.41
Corbett, Joe	R-R	6-5	230	10-12-96	3	0	1.61	17	0	0	3	22	7	7	4	0	11	27	.096	.100	.093	10.88	4.43
Garcia, Ryan	R-R	6-0	180	1-24-98	0	0	2.25	2	2	0	0	4	2	1	1	0	1	6	.154	.286	.000	13.50	2.25
Hellinger, Sam	R-R	6-1	195	9-6-94	2	1	3.00	6	0	0	1	12	7	4	4	0	5	18	.175	.143	.182	13.50	3.75
Hunter, Leon	R-R	6-3	230	3-17-97	0	0	0.00	1	0	0	0	2	2	0	0	0	2	3	.286	.500	.000	16.20	10.80
Javier, Joshua	L-L	6-3	195	12-16-98	0	1	3.35	11	11	0	0	38	26	16	14	2	28	43	.190	.243	.170	10.27	6.69
Kent, Zak	R-R	6-3	205	2-24-98	0	1	5.40	10	7	0	0	18	25	11	11	2	7	16	.321	.343	.302	7.85	3.44
Laio, Nic	R-R	6-5	205	7-28-97	4	1	3.74	22	0	0	2	46	50	21	19	5	10	58	.275	.275	.274	11.43	1.97
Layne Jr., Billy	R-R	6-4	185	12-19-96	2	1	4.83	13	4	0	0	32	27	19	17	1	10	35	.229	.211	.246	9.95	2.84
Leal, Werner	R-R	6-1	160	7-8-95	3	1	0.97	23	0	0	4	46	26	6	5	1	10	56	.166	.167	.165	10.88	1.94
Martinez, Stanley	R-R	6-0	176	1-5-97	0	0	0.00	1	0	0	0	0	0	0	0	0	0	0	.000	--	.000	0.00	0.00
Matthews, John	R-R	6-1	190	1-21-98	0	2	5.63	5	3	0	0	8	8	5	5	1	3	11	.250	.231	.263	12.38	3.38
McDowell, Theo	R-R	6-4	175	12-2-98	1	5	6.55	12	7	0	0	33	36	30	24	5	26	37	.286	.283	.288	10.09	7.09
McReynolds, Jonah	R-R	5-11	165	12-16-95	0	0	0.00	1	0	0	0	0	0	0	0	0	0	0	.000	.000	--	0.00	0.00
Mejia, Juan	L-L	5-11	160	1-9-99	4	1	2.88	14	0	0	0	34	31	15	11	0	11	28	.230	.167	.258	7.34	2.88
Mraz, Spencer	R-R	6-10	245	5-5-98	1	1	13.50	3	2	0	0	4	7	6	6	0	3	5	.350	.455	.222	11.25	6.75
Nunez, Jeifry	R-R	5-11	160	4-1-98	5	0	3.06	18	1	0	2	53	39	20	18	3	11	55	.205	.179	.226	9.34	1.87
Ortega, Teodoro	R-R	6-0	145	3-12-00	2	2	2.89	12	6	0	0	44	37	14	14	6	14	37	.227	.209	.240	7.63	2.89
Polley, Triston	L-L	6-0	190	12-20-96	2	0	2.49	16	0	0	2	22	18	9	6	2	2	32	.214	.154	.241	13.29	0.83
Richardson, Glen	R-R	6-1	210	7-30-98	1	0	2.45	4	0	0	0	7	4	2	2	0	4	10	.250	.500	.182	12.27	4.91
Robert, Daniel	L-R	6-4	210	8-30-94	2	0	0.33	16	0	0	3	28	12	2	1	0	5	37	.129	.143	.121	12.04	1.63
Rosario, Luis	R-R	5-11	165	2-8-97	5	1	2.76	12	1	0	0	49	46	19	15	3	10	40	.245	.244	.246	7.35	1.84
Serrano, Florencio	R-R	6-0	175	2-23-00	0	2	12.91	3	3	0	0	14	14	13	11	3	7	9	.378	.533	.273	10.57	8.22
Slaten, Justin	R-R	6-4	197	9-15-97	0	2	6.46	10	10	0	0	15	21	13	11	2	7	21	.313	.370	.275	12.33	4.11
Smith, Josh	L-L	6-5	205	2-5-97	2	1	2.84	12	0	0	0	19	21	7	6	1	10	12	.288	.217	.320	5.68	6.16
Sparks, Wyatt	R-R	6-2	185	9-27-99	0	1	5.40	1	1	0	0	3	5	2	2	0	2	2	.294	.500	.267	5.40	5.40
Starr, Nick	R-R	6-3	225	12-3-96	1	3	2.70	15	0	0	1	27	17	12	8	0	14	31	.179	.105	.228	10.46	4.73
Tejada, Leury	R-R	6-1	160	12-24-99	1	2	3.16	8	7	0	0	26	17	13	9	0	16	24	.202	.188	.212	8.42	5.61
Tseng, Jen-Ho	L-R	6-1	210	10-3-94	1	1	54.00	1	1	0	0	0	2	2	2	0	1	0	.000	--	.000	0.00	27.00
Vanasco, Ricky	R-R	6-3	180	10-13-98	3	1	1.85	9	9	0	0	39	23	10	8	2	22	59	.173	.205	.157	13.62	5.08
Williams, Scott	R-R	6-2	200	11-17-93	0	0	0.00	3	0	0	0	3	0	0	0		2	5	.000	.000	.000	13.50	5.40

Fielding

C: Garcia 38, Kapers 21, Ventura 19. **1B:** Asuncion 2, Crim 43, Florentino 1, Gardner 5, Irizarry 3, Kapers 2, Martinez 2, McReynolds 14, Morales 7, Ovalles 4. **2B:** Barreto 5, Basabe 2, Easley 4, Hoover 29, Inoa 6, Irizarry 26, Martinez 10. **3B:** Barreto 1, Crim 1, Hoover 1, Inoa 16, Irizarry 2, Martinez 12, McReynolds 43, Wendzel 3. **SS:** Barreto 22, Hoover 18, Inoa 36. **OF:** Anderson 9, Asuncion 36, Gardner 14, Hernandez 1, Irizarry 7, Joseph 45, McReynolds 2, Ovalles 20, Ricumstrict 56, Strahm 50.

AZL RANGERS   ROOKIE
ARIZONA LEAGUE

Batting	B-T	HT	WT	DOB	AVG	vLH	vRH	G	AB	R	H	2B	3B	HR	RBI	BB	HBP	SH	SF	SO	SB	CS	SLG	OBP
Aponte, Angel	R-R	6-0	170	2-3-00	.304	.361	.290	47	191	38	58	13	3	3	23	22	1	1	3	47	17	4	.450	.373
Bannister, Zion	B-R	6-3	187	9-9-01	.250	.000	.429	4	12	1	3	1	0	0	1	2	0	0	0	8	0	0	.333	.357
Barete, Rafy	B-R	5-11	160	1-15-99	.205	.214	.202	36	117	21	24	4	2	1	9	16	1	2	0	35	11	1	.299	.306
Barreto, Derwin	R-S	5-9	155	9-1-00	.281	.214	.300	18	64	15	18	1	3	2	13	10	0	1	0	16	4	1	.484	.373
Basabe, Osleivis	R-R	6-1	165	9-13-00	.325	.375	.315	35	151	29	49	2	5	0	31	8	2	0	5	20	7	2	.404	.355
Crim, Blaine	R-R	5-11	200	6-17-97	.667	1.000	.625	2	9	2	6	2	0	0	3	1	0	0	0	0	0	0	.889	.700
Florentino, Randy	L-R	5-11	175	7-5-00	.243	.250	.241	39	140	18	34	4	1	2	19	25	1	0	4	39	0	3	.329	.353
Freeman, Cody	R-R	5-10	165	1-5-01	.233	.261	.227	34	120	25	28	4	1	0	10	26	4	0	1	23	8	3	.283	.384
Gallo, Joey	L-R	6-5	235	11-19-93	.273	.333	.250	4	11	3	3	1	0	2	3	5	0	0	0	3	0	0	.909	.500
Guzman, Yaniery	B-R	5-11	185	5-30-98	.244	.286	.230	25	82	10	20	3	3	1	13	6	0	0	0	27	1	0	.390	.296
Heineman, Scott	R-R	6-1	215	12-4-92	.412	.200	.500	4	17	6	7	3	0	2	6	1	0	0	0	2	1	0	.941	.444
Hoover, Jake	R-R	6-0	180	7-11-97	.250	--	.250	2	4	1	1	1	0	0	3	0	0	0		1	0		.500	.571
Jeffry, William	R-R	5-11	170	5-11-99	.200	.111	.214	23	65	6	13	2	1	1	9	6	1	0	0	28	1	1	.308	.278
Jung, Josh	R-R	6-2	215	2-12-98	.588	.000	.625	4	17	5	10	1	1	1	5	2	0	0	0	4	0	0	.941	.632
Martinez, Stanley	R-R	6-0	176	1-5-97	.444	.286	.474	15	45	11	20	3	1	3	14	6	1	0	0	11	2	0	.756	.519
Mejia, Leuri	B-R	6-0	150	8-30-00	.274	.292	.270	37	113	22	31	4	2	1	11	13	2	1	1	51	11	1	.372	.357
Moss, Keithron	B-R	5-11	165	8-20-01	.308	.321	.304	34	120	37	37	4	3	2	14	21	4	1	1	40	8	2	.442	.425
Ovalles, Alexander	L-L	6-0	180	10-6-00	.377	.474	.358	25	114	33	43	8	7	2	18	10	2	0	0	18	2	1	.623	.437
Pena, Yenci	R-R	6-2	193	7-13-00	.244	.304	.230	33	123	24	30	3	2	3	22	19	2	0	1	31	2	2	.374	.352

Name	B-T	HT	WT	DOB	AVG	vLH	vRH	G	AB	R	H	2B	3B	HR	RBI	BB	HBP	SH	SF	SO	SB	CS	SLG	OBP
Pichardo, Reynaldo	R-R	5-10	190	12-29-98	.276	.400	.250	18	58	8	16	1	0	2	10	4	0	0	18	0	1		.397	.323
Reed, Tyreque	R-R	6-1	250	6-6-97	.600	.500	.625	4	10	7	6	1	0	1	2	6	0	0	1	0	0		1.000	.750
Rodriguez, Josue	R-R	5-10	160	12-27-99	.571	--	.571	2	7	1	4	0	0	0	1	0	0	0	1	0	0		.571	.625
Rodriguez, Keyber	B-R	5-9	160	10-24-00	.262	.370	.238	39	149	27	39	5	4	6	22	14	1	0	2	39	5	1	.470	.325
Strahm, Kellen	R-R	6-1	215	4-25-97	.750	1.000	.667	1	4	2	3	0	0	0	4	1	0	0	0	1	0		.750	.800
Trevino, Jose	R-R	5-11	211	11-28-92	.167	.250	.125	11	36	3	6	1	0	1	6	2	0	0	0	2	0	0	.278	.211
Valdez, Fernando	B-R	6-0	175	11-14-98	.125	.000	.143	6	16	0	2	1	0	0	2	1	0	0	8	0	0		.188	.177
Wendzel, Davis	R-R	6-0	205	5-23-97	.444	1.000	.286	4	9	4	4	1	0	1	2	2	0	0	3	0	0		.889	.546

Pitching	B-T	HT	WT	DOB	W	L	ERA	G	GS	CG	SV	IP	H	R	ER	HR	BB	SO	AVG	vLH	vRH	K/9	BB/9
Anderson, Ben	R-R	6-4	200	5-2-98	0	0	4.50	5	1	0	0	4	3	2	2	1	2	4	.188	.111	.286	9.00	4.50
Barete, Rafy	B-R	5-11	160	1-15-99	0	1	0.00	1	0	0	0	0	0	1	0	0	3	1	.000	--	.000	27.00	81.00
Barreto, Derwin	B-R	5-9	155	9-1-00	0	0	13.50	1	0	0	0	1	2	1	1	0	0	2	.500	--	.500	27.00	0.00
Bautista, Kelvin	L-L	5-11	155	7-7-99	0	0	6.00	3	0	0	0	6	6	4	4	0	4	9	.261	.000	.353	13.50	6.00
Bice, Dylan	L-R	6-4	220	8-17-97	0	0	0.00	3	1	0	0	4	2	2	0	0	2	8	.143	.250	.000	18.00	4.50
Bremer, Noah	R-R	6-5	200	5-13-96	1	0	0.00	1	0	0	0	3	4	1	0	0	0	6	.333	.400	.286	18.00	0.00
Burke, Brock	L-L	6-4	180	8-4-96	0	0	0.00	1	1	0	0	4	2	0	0	0	0	3	.154	.000	.167	6.75	0.00
Carrillo, Alex	R-R	6-2	220	6-6-97	0	0	0.00	3	0	0	0	4	2	0	0	0	2	6	.133	.143	.125	12.46	4.15
Collyer, Gavin	R-R	6-1	150	5-12-01	1	1	10.80	1	0	0	0	5	5	6	6	1	6	7	.278	.333	.250	12.60	10.80
Corbett, Joe	R-R	6-5	230	10-12-96	0	0	0.00	2	0	0	1	2	1	0	0	0	0	3	.143	.333	.000	13.50	0.00
Dotson, Destin	L-L	6-6	235	11-17-99	2	3	2.29	10	5	0	1	35	33	12	9	0	13	41	.250	.242	.253	10.44	3.31
Dowdy, Kyle	R-R	6-1	195	2-3-93	0	0	0.00	1	1	0	0	1	1	0	0	0	0	0	.333	.000	.500	0.00	0.00
Farrell, Luke	L-R	6-4	210	6-7-91	0	0	8.44	4	0	0	0	5	8	6	5	0	1	10	.296	.333	.278	16.88	1.69
Feigl, Brady	R-L	6-4	195	12-27-90	0	0	0.00	2	2	0	0	2	1	0	0	0	1	3	.143	.500	.000	13.50	4.50
Garcia, Jesus Rodolfo	R-R	6-2	155	7-3-99	0	0	7.63	7	2	0	0	15	17	13	13	3	8	16	.274	.250	.286	9.39	4.70
Garcia, Ryan	R-R	6-0	180	1-24-98	0	0	9.00	1	1	0	0	1	1	1	1	0	1	2	.250	.000	.500	18.00	9.00
Guzman, Yaniery	B-R	5-11	185	5-30-98	0	0	0.00	1	0	0	0	0	0	0	0	0	1	1	.000	--	.000	27.00	27.00
Hehnke, Cal	L-R	6-3	215	9-18-96	1	0	0.00	2	0	0	0	5	2	0	0	0	2	6	.133	.167	.111	10.80	3.60
Huang, Wei-Chieh	R-R	6-1	170	9-26-93	0	0	0.00	2	2	0	0	3	3	0	0	0	1	5	.250	.250	.250	15.00	3.00
Hunter, Leon	R-R	6-3	230	3-17-97	2	1	1.48	17	0	0	8	24	15	6	4	0	3	27	.169	.135	.192	9.99	1.11
Inojosa, Rosmer	R-R	6-3	165	8-10-99	3	4	9.17	10	6	0	0	36	60	39	37	8	16	46	.364	.382	.355	11.39	3.96
Janca, George	R-R	6-2	190	5-8-97	0	0	2.57	6	0	0	0	7	5	3	2	0	5	12	.200	.250	.111	15.43	6.43
Jarneski, Joseph	R-R	6-0	170	10-28-99	2	0	1.62	10	0	0	0	17	8	3	3	0	11	16	.151	.185	.115	8.64	5.94
2-team total (8 White Sox)					2	0	3.76	18	0	0	0	26	17	13	11	1	21	22	.189	.178	.200	7.52	7.18
Kent, Zak	R-R	6-3	205	2-24-98	0	0	0.00	1	0	0	0	1	0	0	0	0	0	2	.000	.000	--	18.00	0.00
Lang, Jamarcus	R-R	6-2	170	10-19-98	0	1	6.92	10	0	0	0	13	16	13	10	0	9	18	.302	.353	.278	12.46	6.23
Layne Jr., Billy	R-R	6-4	185	12-19-96	1	0	0.00	1	0	0	0	1	2	1	0	0	0	1	.400	.000	.500	9.00	0.00
Lockhart, Nick	R-R	6-6	210	2-12-01	0	0	4.50	6	0	0	0	6	6	4	3	0	4	9	.273	.143	.333	13.50	6.00
Martinez, Emerson	R-R	6-0	190	1-11-95	0	1	8.71	6	2	0	0	10	12	14	10	2	2	14	.273	.375	.214	12.19	1.74
Matthews, John	R-R	6-1	190	1-21-98	1	0	5.00	5	0	0	0	9	6	5	5	0	6	12	.194	.167	.211	12.00	6.00
Mejia, Juan	L-L	5-11	160	1-9-99	0	0	4.91	4	0	0	0	7	13	4	4	1	0	12	.371	.400	.360	14.73	0.00
Mejia, Leuri	B-R	6-0	150	8-30-00	0	0	9.00	1	0	0	0	1	1	1	1	0	0	1	.333	1.000	.000	9.00	0.00
Mendez, Yohander	L-L	6-5	200	1-17-95	0	0	12.27	3	0	0	0	4	6	5	5	2	1	6	.353	.333	.357	14.73	2.45
Mendoza, Damian	R-R	6-1	175	1-25-01	2	2	4.95	12	2	0	2	36	35	22	20	5	9	32	.259	.293	.234	7.93	2.23
Montero, Rafael	R-R	6-0	185	10-17-90	0	0	0.00	5	3	0	0	7	2	0	0	0	0	12	.087	.143	.063	15.43	0.00
Mraz, Spencer	R-R	6-10	245	5-5-98	1	1	1.52	14	0	0	0	24	12	5	4	1	10	32	.138	.139	.137	12.17	3.80
Pacheco, Sergio	R-R	6-1	170	8-17-99	1	0	2.63	10	6	0	0	38	35	13	11	1	11	27	.254	.246	.260	6.45	2.63
Polley, Triston	L-L	6-0	190	12-20-96	1	0	7.71	2	0	0	0	2	4	2	2	0	1	2	.500	--	.500	7.71	3.86
Richardson, Glen	R-R	6-1	210	7-30-98	1	1	2.93	15	0	0	1	28	18	11	9	1	15	36	.188	.177	.194	11.71	4.88
Santiago, Manuel	L-L	6-0	175	10-15-99	3	0	3.57	7	2	0	0	23	20	11	9	3	7	17	.233	.278	.221	6.75	2.78
Schiltz, Luke	R-R	6-5	200	7-2-00	1	0	4.30	11	0	0	0	15	11	7	7	1	6	9	.216	.091	.310	5.52	3.68
Serrano, Florencio	R-R	6-0	175	2-23-00	3	1	4.67	7	3	0	0	27	26	18	14	5	12	24	.245	.340	.170	8.00	4.00
Slaten, Justin	R-R	6-4	197	9-15-97	0	0	0.00	1	0	0	0	1	0	0	0	0	0	1	.000	.000	.000	9.00	0.00
Smith, Josh	L-L	6-5	205	2-5-97	1	1	3.00	8	0	0	1	15	15	8	5	1	3	19	.259	.250	.262	11.40	1.80
Speas, Alex	R-R	6-4	180	3-4-98	0	0	0.00	2	2	0	0	1	1	0	0	0	2	2	.250	.250	--	18.00	18.00
Springs, Jeffrey	L-L	6-3	180	9-20-92	0	0	0.00	2	2	0	0	2	0	0	0	0	0	3	.000	.000	.000	13.50	0.00
Stone, Corey	L-L	6-2	195	12-27-98	1	3	8.44	15	3	0	0	21	33	25	20	3	13	22	.375	.346	.387	9.28	5.48
Tejada, Leury	R-R	6-0	160	12-24-99	1	1	7.04	4	0	0	0	8	10	6	6	0	3	7	.294	.286	.300	8.22	3.52
Tseng, Jen-Ho	L-R	6-1	210	10-3-94	0	0	--	1	0	0	0	0	1	3	3	0	2	0	1.000	1.000	--	--	--
Volquez, Edinson	R-R	6-0	220	7-3-83	0	0	0.00	4	4	0	0	4	3	1	0	0	1	1	.214	.286	.143	2.25	2.25
Wiles, Collin	R-R	6-4	222	5-30-94	0	1	10.80	1	1	0	0	3	5	5	4	1	1	5	.333	.250	.364	13.50	2.70
Williams, Scott	R-R	6-2	200	11-17-93	0	0	0.00	1	0	0	0	1	1	0	0	0	0	1	.250	.000	.333	9.00	9.00
Yoder, Nick	R-R	6-6	190	3-3-99	0	0	2.25	3	0	0	0	4	2	1	1	0	3	4	.167	.000	.200	9.00	6.75

Fielding

C: Florentino 29, Hernandez 11, Pichardo 17, Rodriguez 1, Trevino 8. **1B:** Crim 1, Florentino 8, Guzman 16, Hernandez 13, Martinez 9, Ovalles 5, Pena 5, Pichardo 1, Reed 3, Valdez 3. **2B:** Barreto 6, Basabe 4, Freeman 21, Hoover 1, Martinez 3, Moss 17, Rodriguez 6. **3B:** Barreto 2, Basabe 6, Guzman 2, Jung 3, Martinez 2, Moss 11, Pena 18, Rodriguez 14, Valdez 1, Wendzel 2. **SS:** Barreto 8, Basabe 20, Freeman 14, Pena 2, Rodriguez 16. **OF:** Aponte 47, Bannister 4, Barete 29, Gallo 3, Heineman 4, Hernandez 18, Jeffry 23, Mejia 37, Moss 1, Ovalles 21, Pena 1, Strahm 1, Valdez 2.

DSL RANGERS
DOMINICAN SUMMER LEAGUE
ROOKIE

Batting	B-T	HT	WT	DOB	AVG	vLH	vRH	G	AB	R	H	2B	3B	HR	RBI	BB	HBP	SH	SF	SO	SB	CS	SLG	OBP
Acuna, Luisangel	R-R	5-10	155	3-12-02	.342	.386	.329	51	202	61	69	11	3	2	29	34	2	0	2	26	17	6	.455	.438
Almonte, Jeremia	B-R	5-11	170	7-5-00	.248	.233	.250	56	198	25	49	6	1	2	25	30	3	0	5	49	7	2	.318	.348
Bannister, Zion	B-B	6-3	187	9-9-01	.300	--	.300	2	10	2	3	0	0	0	0	0	0	0	0	1	0	0	.300	.300
Baptista, Angel	R-R	5-8	150	3-21-01	.257	.231	.263	42	140	35	36	7	3	0	18	30	4	1	0	25	12	2	.350	.402

TEXAS RANGERS

Batting	B-T	HT	WT	DOB	AVG	vLH	vRH	G	AB	R	H	2B	3B	HR	RBI	BB	HP	SH	SF	SO	SB	CS	OBP	SLG
Bermudez, Reyber	R-R	5-10	155	4-14-02	.136	.077	.152	20	59	7	8	2	1	0	4	15	4	2	0	15	1	0	.203	.346
Bidau, Juan	R-R	5-9	155	12-29-99	.247	.444	.221	46	154	22	38	4	4	2	16	25	3	1	3	21	5	1	.364	.357
Chirinos, Michael	B-R	5-10	155	10-11-99	.289	.273	.293	53	194	38	56	7	1	3	45	25	2	0	12	11	19	4	.381	.356
De La Rosa, Darlin	R-R	6-1	195	1-2-01	.159	.143	.161	23	69	12	11	2	1	2	11	9	0	2	31	1	0		.304	.341
Del Orbe, Alisson	B-R	6-3	185	9-6-01	.296	.077	.319	41	132	26	39	12	4	4	23	24	4	1	3	36	2	1	.538	.411
Drullard, Danny	L-L	6-1	175	5-8-00	.267	.129	.289	59	232	48	62	8	6	7	30	33	1	1	0	63	8	2	.444	.361
Feliz, Luis	R-R	6-2	180	3-8-01	.235	.231	.235	43	162	19	38	8	4	2	12	13	4	1	1	53	4	1	.370	.306
Gonzalez, Leandro	R-R	5-11	154	9-30-01	.067	.000	.091	6	15	1	1	0	0	0	1	2	1	0	0	9	1	0	.067	.222
Gonzalez, Robert	R-R	6-0	175	6-19-01	.278	.235	.289	52	162	45	45	14	4	3	26	43	7	0	2	49	8	0	.469	.444
Guacare, Joiquer	R-R	5-10	150	1-7-02	.270	.188	.288	24	89	12	24	0	4	0	10	15	2	0	0	17	1	3	.360	.387
Guardo, Jose	R-R	6-0	180	2-6-99	.187	.182	.188	26	75	9	14	3	0	0	9	10	10	1	1	22	1	2	.227	.354
Gutierrez, Jember	R-R	5-11	160	9-8-99	.273	.286	.270	61	227	27	62	14	1	1	33	32	8	0	7	21	22	2	.357	.372
Hurtado, Frankely	R-R	5-10	165	10-11-01	.149	.278	.125	41	114	27	17	0	0	1	9	23	6	1	1	52	5	1	.175	.319
Lascarro, Ronier	L-L	5-10	155	1-31-01	.281	.177	.303	58	199	49	56	6	2	2	32	51	4	0	3	39	4	4	.402	.437
Linares, Brandon	R-R	6-0	165	8-14-00	.228	.205	.234	52	180	26	41	8	2	2	28	24	4	1	4	44	2	1	.328	.326
Lopez, Johan	R-R	6-1	175	9-27-01	.228	.306	.212	59	206	35	47	11	2	3	19	31	12	4	1	55	16	6	.345	.360
Mateo, Daniel	R-R	6-1	165	7-3-01	.294	.324	.284	41	143	25	42	6	3	0	24	13	0	3	28	14	5		.378	.358
Mejia, John	R-R	5-10	163	1-12-01	.204	.267	.192	50	181	23	37	8	0	1	22	30	4	1	4	45	7	1	.265	.324
Mendoza, Edilberto	L-R	6-0	180	7-2-99	.234	.333	.214	44	141	37	33	9	2	2	20	43	5	0	3	29	2	1	.369	.422
Moreno, Jesus	R-R	5-11	170	4-16-01	.292	.292	.292	33	120	17	35	10	0	1	20	13	3	0	1	24	0	0	.400	.372
Narvaez, Efrenyer	R-R	5-11	155	7-25-02	.226	.167	.244	33	102	20	23	4	1	0	16	25	3	1	2	20	0	1	.284	.386
Noguera, Abel	R-R	6-1	185	2-22-02	.167	.192	.160	35	126	9	21	6	0	0	16	9	2	1	0	50	0	1	.214	.284
Ortega, Cesar	L-R	5-11	180	10-16-00	.311	.000	.342	13	45	11	14	1	0	0	12	7	3	1	0	7	2	0	.333	.436
Paniagua, Junior	R-R	5-10	160	10-8-01	.251	.250	.252	46	179	29	45	4	2	2	26	26	3	1	4	27	4	1	.330	.349
Perozo, Rehybell	B-R	6-3	180	11-6-99	.253	.171	.277	50	182	38	46	6	5	2	29	34	0	2	3	41	6	1	.374	.365
Puerta, Freddy	R-R	5-11	165	1-17-01	.114	.000	.138	12	35	5	4	1	0	0	4	8	2	0	0	12	3	0	.143	.311
Reinoso, Roldany	R-R	6-0	175	12-24-01	.183	.158	.188	35	120	8	22	5	0	0	7	10	1	0	0	17	1	1	.225	.252
Rodriguez, Jose	R-R	6-0	185	10-5-01	.245	.222	.252	57	212	37	52	9	1	3	43	39	3	0	8	34	0	0	.340	.359
Rodriguez, Josue	R-R	5-10	160	12-27-99	.000	.000	.000	2	4	1	0	0	0	0	0	0	0	0	0	0	0	0	.000	.429
Zambrano, Abraham	B-R	5-9	160	1-2-01	.203	.667	.133	24	69	12	14	0	0	1	9	13	1	1	1	20	1	1	.246	.333
Zambrano, Luis	R-R		165	10-30-01	.222	.200	.227	43	153	29	34	4	2	0	11	22	4	0	4				.275	.335

Pitching	B-T	HT	WT	DOB	W	L	ERA	G	GS	CG	SV	IP	H	R	ER	HR	BB	SO	AVG	vLH	vRH	K/9	BB/9
Abreu, Oscar	R-R	6-1	175	12-11-99	2	1	2.97	14	4	0	3	39	32	15	13	1	12	39	.224	.250	.214	8.92	2.75
Ayola, Julio	R-R	6-3	173	4-8-02	2	0	4.74	11	0	0	0	25	33	16	13	1	6	17	.327	.200	.358	6.20	2.19
Bautista, Kelvin	L-L	5-11	155	7-7-99	1	0	1.57	11	0	0	3	23	14	4	4	1	9	37	.184	.200	.180	14.48	3.52
Buitimea, Martin	R-R	6-1	155	4-14-98	5	3	1.89	12	12	0	0	62	44	13	13	0	16	59	.202	.246	.183	8.56	2.32
Burgos, Samuel	R-R	6-3	205	6-7-99	2	1	3.21	14	0	0	2	28	25	13	10	2	8	19	.240	.273	.225	6.11	2.57
Castillo, Wilson	R-R	6-4	210	6-13-01	2	3	4.00	12	12	0	0	54	58	34	24	5	15	58	.274	.324	.248	9.67	2.50
Castro, Ray	R-R	6-3	165	5-9-97	4	0	2.02	9	7	0	0	36	23	9	8	0	15	28	.177	.170	.182	7.07	3.79
2-team total (3 White Sox)					5	1	2.01	12	9	0	0	45	30	11	10	0	17	41	.183	.169	.194	8.26	3.43
De La Cruz, Yangely	R-R	6-1	175	9-14-99	3	0	5.40	14	0	0	3	25	22	17	15	1	15	20	.229	.156	.266	7.20	5.40
De Leon, Daniel	R-R	6-4	195	5-9-01	3	1	6.83	15	0	0	0	29	43	29	22	0	23	30	.336	.424	.305	7.14	6.21
Duran, Jhonny	R-R	6-1	150	5-27-00	2	6	4.15	13	7	0	0	48	49	27	22	4	12	36	.271	.255	.278	6.80	2.27
Ferreira, Elian	R-R	6-4	175	4-12-00	4	3	3.93	12	12	0	0	55	64	30	24	1	19	52	.296	.337	.269	8.51	3.11
Frias, Ricardo	L-L	5-10	160	9-7-00	1	0	0.77	8	0	0	3	23	18	2	2	0	5	15	.217	.353	.182	5.79	1.93
Gil, Orlando	R-R	6-3	165	9-10-01	1	3	6.26	9	8	0	0	27	31	22	19	1	16	22	.293	.375	.257	7.24	5.27
Gomez, Orceli	R-R	6-5	175	11-23-00	5	3	2.50	11	11	0	0	50	50	19	14	0	11	36	.262	.296	.242	6.44	1.97
Guzman, Stanley	R-R	6-3	170	12-28-99	2	3	6.75	15	0	0	1	27	34	23	20	1	11	26	.312	.333	.301	8.78	3.71
Hernandez, Nyan	R-L	6-2	198	7-11-01	1	3	3.13	14	1	0	2	32	30	23	11	4	11	23	.234	.192	.245	6.54	3.13
Hernandez, Wuilliam	R-R	6-0	160	2-21-02	3	6	2.89	12	12	0	0	56	43	26	18	3	25	46	.210	.191	.219	7.39	4.02
Herrera, Jeremis	R-R	6-1	175	7-3-99	4	0	2.11	14	0	0	3	38	28	9	9	1	9	46	.197	.231	.178	10.80	2.11
Leon, Isaias	R-R	6-2	182	8-23-99	0	0	2.61	8	0	0	0	10	14	4	3	1	8	10	.333	.385	.310	8.71	6.97
Manon, Eudrys	R-R	6-1	160	1-16-98	2	0	3.97	13	0	0	2	23	24	12	10	0	12	32	.270	.233	.288	12.71	4.76
Marine, Luis	R-R	6-4	210	2-12-01	3	2	1.95	15	0	0	1	32	26	12	7	2	11	23	.226	.273	.207	6.40	3.06
Medina, Rafmar	R-R	6-5	190	9-9-99	1	3	2.87	12	12	0	0	53	48	23	17	0	25	56	.240	.283	.221	9.45	4.22
Mena, Peniel	R-R	6-1	160	11-28-00	0	3	5.12	16	1	0	3	32	35	22	18	1	10	24	.285	.317	.268	6.82	2.84
Morel, Emmy	L-L	6-4	178	9-18-99	7	1	2.20	9	9	0	0	49	48	15	12	2	6	44	.255	.225	.264	8.08	1.10
Naveda, Carlos	R-R	6-2	190	7-5-99	0	2	8.00	3	2	0	0	9	12	11	8	1	3	10	.316	.111	.379	10.00	3.00
Parra, Deretd	R-R	6-0	160	6-18-00	1	1	4.32	6	3	0	0	17	15	9	8	2	6	17	.238	.200	.250	9.18	3.24
Paulino, Luis	L-L	5-10	135	5-2-98	4	0	1.33	14	0	0	4	27	19	4	4	1	10	20	.207	.192	.212	10.00	3.33
Ramirez, Bladimir	R-R	6-2	190	5-20-02	2	0	3.07	13	0	0	0	29	23	15	10	3	16	23	.209	.188	.218	7.06	4.91
Ramon, Jhon	L-L	5-10	180	1-10-02	0	0	1.84	11	0	0	0	15	13	4	3	1	7	14	.236	.167	.245	8.59	4.30
Ramos, Adrian	L-L	6-2	170	7-16-01	0	3	7.27	14	0	0	1	26	29	26	21	1	19	34	.284	.350	.268	11.77	6.58
Rodriguez, Moises	R-R	6-2	186	8-22-99	1	3	3.73	11	7	0	0	31	25	14	13	1	20	34	.227	.229	.227	9.77	5.74
Rovain, Hector	R-R	6-1	165	5-5-98	1	0	12.19	10	0	0	0	10	14	14	11	2	7	22	.263	.235	.286	6.10	19.16
Sabino, Arthur	R-R	6-2	190	3-26-02	3	0	6.43	16	0	0	0	28	29	22	20	1	23	29	.269	.188	.303	9.32	7.39
Sanchez, Yosber	R-R	6-1	170	5-22-01	0	1	4.58	7	4	0	0	18	19	13	9	2	10	18	.268	.286	.260	9.17	5.09
Sandobal, Darlwin	R-R	6-2	200	5-8-00	1	2	10.61	8	0	0	0	9	13	12	11	0	8	10	.333	.222	.367	9.64	7.71
Santiago, Manuel	L-L	6-0	175	10-15-99	4	0	1.93	6	0	0	0	33	25	10	7	1	3	38	.202	.222	.198	10.47	0.83
Simeon, Victor	R-R	6-2	160	12-4-00	0	0	15.00	5	0	0	0	6	7	10	10	0	11	4	.333	.333	.333	6.00	16.50
Torres, Darel	R-R	5-11	160	1-5-99	0	0	0.81	8	0	0	2	22	11	2	2	0	10	29	.143	.111	.171	11.69	4.03
Viola, Jose	R-R	6-0	175	4-25-01	0	0	3.00	6	0	0	0	15	11	5	5	0	7	19	.204	.217	.194	11.40	4.20
Zambrano, Jhan	R-R	6-3	165	12-21-01	5	2	2.55	12	11	0	0	60	49	18	17	3	16	52	.226	.204	.242	7.80	2.40

Fielding

C: Guardo 4, Mendoza 26, Moreno 21, Narvaez 32, Noguera 15, Puerta 11, Reinoso 23, Rodriguez 1. 1B: Almonte 34, Bidau 1, Chirinos 24, Guardo 2, Gutierrez 26, Mendoza 10, Noguera 3, Perozo 3, Puerta 1, Reinoso 5, Rodriguez 30, Rodriguez 1. 2B: Acuna 18, Almonte 1, Baptista 3, Bermudez 10, Bidau 5, Guacare 3, Gutierrez 2, Mejia 37, Paniagua 26, Zambrano 15. 3B: Almonte 13, Baptista 9, Bermudez 5, Bidau 6, Chirinos 17, Del Orbe 32, Guacare 1, Gutierrez 12, Mejia 5, Perozo 42. SS: Acuna 30, Almonte 2, Baptista 23, Bermudez 4, Bidau 20, Chirinos 1, Del Orbe 3, Mejia 3, Paniagua 20, Perozo 1, Zambrano 41. OF: Bannister 2, Bidau 7, Chirinos 4, De La Rosa 6, Drullard 5, Feliz 40, Gonzalez 5, Gonzalez 11, Gutierrez 1, Hurtado 38, Lascarro 55, Linares 50, Lopez 59, Mateo 39, Ortega 13, Rodriguez 11.

Toronto Blue Jays

SEASON IN A SENTENCE: The Blue Jays were as bad as expected in 2019, but by the end of the season fans got a glimpse of the young nucleus that could carry their future lineup.

HIGH POINT: The Blue Jays won five games in a row in September—their longest winning streak of the season—against the Yankees and Orioles, with a top of the lineup that included Bo Bichette, Cavan Biggio, Lourdes Gurriel Jr. and Vladimir Guerrero Jr. and showed signs of hope for the future.

LOW POINT: The Blue Jays didn't have a winning record in any month, but May was particularly bad. Toronto went 7-21 for a .250 winning percentage in May, never winning back-to-back games and finishing the month at 21-36 to fall 16.5 games back in the AL East.

NOTABLE ROOKIES: Rookies were the highlight of the season for the Blue Jays, with lots of family ties and big league bloodlines. Guerrero Jr. graduated from becoming the No. 1 prospect in baseball to make his major league debut as a 20-year-old. Biggio arrived in late May and made an impact with his combination of patience and power. Bichette spent the least amount of time in Toronto, arriving just before the trade deadline, but he was the top performer on a rate basis, hitting .311/.358/.571 in 46 games.

KEY TRANSACTIONS: Marcus Stroman's time with the Blue Jays ended on July 28, when the Blue Jays traded the righthander to the Mets in exchange for two pitching prospects in righthander Simeon Woods Richardson and lefthander Anthony Kay. While Kay made his major league debut in September, Woods Richardson was the prize of the deal with more upside. Shortly after the Stroman trade, Toronto sent righthanders Aaron Sanchez and Joe Biagini, along with high Class A outfielder Cal Stevens, to the Astros to acquire outfielder Derek Fisher.

DOWN ON THE FARM: For a team that just graduated two of the top 10 prospects in baseball in Guerrero and Bichette, the Blue Jays' farm system remains strong. After missing nearly the entire 2018 season, righthander Nate Pearson rose three levels to Triple-A and made a case for himself as the best pitching prospect in baseball. Catchers Alejandro Kirk and Gabriel Moreno both performed well at the Class A level, while righthander Adam Kloffenstein and shortstop Orelvis Martinez ranked as top prospects in short-season leagues.

OPENING DAY PAYROLL: $66,626,457 (28th).

PLAYERS OF THE YEAR

MIKE CARLSON

MAJOR LEAGUE	MINOR LEAGUE
Ken Giles RHP	**Nate Pearson** RHP
1.87 ERA, 23 SV	(High A/AA/AAA)
Led AL closers	5-4, 2.30 in 25 GS
with 14.1 SO/9	119 SO, 101.2 IP

ORGANIZATION LEADERS

Batting		*Minimum 250 AB
MAJORS		
* AVG	Eric Sogard	.300
* OPS	Lourdes Gurriel Jr.	.869
HR	Randal Grichuk	31
RBI	Randal Grichuk	80
MINORS		
* AVG	Yorman Rodriguez, Vancouver, Lansing	.360
* OBP	Alejandro Kirk, Lansing, Dunedin	.403
* SLG	Griffin Conine, Lansing	.576
* OPS	Griffin Conine, Lansing	.946
R	Forrest Wall, New Hampshire, Buffalo	79
H	Otto Lopez, Lansing	145
TB	Patrick Kivlehan, Buffalo, New Hampshire	205
2B	Alejandro Kirk, Lansing	31
3B	Reggie Pruitt, Lansing	10
HR	Patrick Kivlehan, Buffalo, New Hampshire	28
RBI	Patrick Kivlehan, Buffalo, New Hampshire	75
BB	Ryan Noda, Dunedin	74
SO	Christian Williams, Dunedin, New Hampshire	157
SB	Reggie Pruitt, Lansing, Dunedin	48

Pitching		#Minimum 75 IP
MAJORS		
W	Daniel Hudson	6
W	Marcus Stroman	6
W	Trent Thornton	6
# ERA	Marcus Stroman	2.96
SO	Trent Thornton	149
SV	Ken Giles	23
MINORS		
W	Maximo Castillo, Dunedin	11
W	Yennsy Diaz, New Hampshire	11
L	Sean Wymer, Lansing	11
# ERA	Nate Pearson, Dunedin, New Hampshire, Buffalo	2.30
G	Kirby Snead, New Hampshire, Buffalo	50
GS	Sean Wymer, Lansing	26
SV	Cre Finfrock, Lansing	18
IP	Yennsy Diaz, New Hampshire	144
BB	Hector Perez, New Hampshire	67
SO	Joey Murray, Lansing, Dunedin, New Hampshire	169
# AVG	Nate Pearson, Dunedin, New Hampshire, Buffalo	.176

2019 PERFORMANCE

General Manager: Ross Atkins. **Farm Director:** Gil Kim. **Scouting Director:** Steve Sanders.

Class	Team	League	W	L	PCT	Finish	Manager
Majors	Toronto Blue Jays	American	67	95	.414	12th (15)	Charlie Montoyo
Triple-A	Buffalo Bisons	International	71	69	.507	7th (14)	Bobby Meacham
Double-A	N. Hampshire Fisher Cats	Eastern	63	76	.453	9th (12)	Mike Mordecai
High A	Dunedin Blue Jays	Florida State	80	55	.593	2nd (12)	Cesar Martin
Low A	Lansing Lugnuts	Midwest	68	71	.489	10th (16)	Dallas McPherson
Short season	Vancouver Canadians	Northwest	30	46	.395	7th (8)	Casey Candaele
Rookie	Bluefield Blue Jays	Appalachian	31	36	.463	8th (10)	Luis Hurtado
Rookie	GCL Blue Jays	Gulf Coast	27	23	.540	7th (18)	Dennis Holmberg
Overall 2019 Minor League Record			370	376	.496	14th (30)	

ORGANIZATION STATISTICS

TORONTO BLUE JAYS
AMERICAN LEAGUE

Batting	B-T	HT	WT	DOB	AVG	vLH	vRH	G	AB	R	H	2B	3B	HR	RBI	BB	HBP	SH	SF	SO	SB	CS	SLG	OBP
Alford, Anthony	R-R	6-1	215	7-20-94	.179	.000	.333	16	28	3	5	0	0	1	1	1	1	0	0	11	2	0	.286	.233
Bichette, Bo	R-R	6-0	185	3-5-98	.311	.368	.288	46	196	32	61	18	0	11	21	14	1	0	1	50	4	4	.571	.359
Biggio, Cavan	L-R	6-2	200	4-11-95	.235	.237	.233	100	354	66	83	17	2	16	48	71	2	0	2	123	14	0	.429	.364
Brito, Socrates	L-L	6-2	205	9-6-92	.077	.000	.081	17	39	5	3	0	1	0	2	4	0	0	0	17	0	0	.128	.163
Davis, Jonathan	R-R	5-8	190	5-12-92	.181	.273	.148	37	83	8	15	1	0	2	6	5	5	1	1	24	3	1	.265	.266
Drury, Brandon	R-R	6-2	215	8-21-92	.218	.231	.211	120	418	43	91	21	1	15	41	25	1	0	3	113	0	1	.380	.262
Fisher, Derek	L-R	6-3	205	8-21-93	.161	.188	.148	40	93	14	15	2	0	6	12	14	0	0	0	43	1	0	.376	.271
2-team total (17 Houston)					.185	.245	.155	57	146	23	27	4	1	7	17	21	0	0	0	57	5	1	.370	.287
Galvis, Freddy	B-R	5-10	185	11-14-89	.267	.281	.259	115	450	55	120	24	1	18	54	21	0	1	1	112	4	1	.444	.299
Grichuk, Randal	R-R	6-2	213	8-13-91	.232	.250	.224	151	586	75	136	29	5	31	80	35	5	0	2	163	2	1	.457	.280
Guerrero Jr., Vladimir	R-R	6-2	250	3-16-99	.272	.215	.293	123	464	52	126	26	2	15	69	46	2	0	2	91	0	1	.433	.339
Gurriel Jr., Lourdes	R-R	6-3	215	10-10-93	.277	.300	.265	84	314	52	87	19	2	20	50	20	5	1	3	86	6	4	.541	.328
Hanson, Alen	B-R	6-0	170	10-22-92	.163	.191	.136	18	43	5	7	0	0	0	4	3	1	0	1	17	1	0	.163	.229
Hernandez, Teoscar	R-R	6-2	205	10-15-92	.230	.247	.222	125	417	58	96	19	2	26	65	45	1	0	1	153	6	3	.472	.306
Jansen, Danny	R-R	6-2	230	4-15-95	.208	.224	.199	107	347	41	72	12	1	13	43	31	4	1	1	79	0	1	.360	.279
Maile, Luke	R-R	6-3	225	2-6-91	.151	.057	.191	44	119	9	18	2	1	2	9	8	0	2	0	33	1	0	.235	.205
McGuire, Reese	L-R	6-0	215	3-2-95	.299	.238	.316	30	97	14	29	7	0	5	11	7	0	0	0	18	0	0	.526	.346
McKinney, Billy	L-L	6-1	205	8-23-94	.215	.196	.220	84	251	37	54	14	1	12	28	19	2	2	2	73	0	2	.422	.274
Pillar, Kevin	R-R	6-0	210	1-4-89	.063	.000	.100	5	16	1	1	0	0	0	1	0	0	0	1	3	0	0	.063	.059
Smoak, Justin	B-L	6-4	220	12-5-86	.208	.220	.202	121	414	54	86	16	0	22	61	79	6	0	1	106	0	0	.406	.342
Sogard, Eric	L-R	5-10	185	5-22-86	.300	.287	.305	73	287	45	86	17	2	10	30	29	1	3	3	47	6	0	.477	.363
2-team total (37 Tampa Bay)					.290	.279	.295	110	396	59	115	23	2	13	40	38	2	3	3	63	8	0	.457	.353
Taylor, Beau	L-R	5-11	205	2-13-90	.000	--	.000	1	2	0	0	0	0	0	0	0	0	0	0	1	0	0	.000	.000
2-team total (10 Oakland)					.160	.000	.174	11	25	3	4	0	0	2	2	4	1	0	0	7	0	0	.400	.300
Tellez, Rowdy	L-L	6-4	255	3-16-95	.227	.270	.208	111	370	49	84	19	0	21	54	29	7	0	3	116	1	1	.449	.293
Urena, Richard	B-R	6-0	195	2-26-96	.243	.231	.250	30	74	4	18	4	0	0	4	2	1	3	0	23	0	0	.324	.273
Valera, Breyvic	B-R	5-11	160	1-8-92	.267	.167	.333	5	15	2	4	1	0	1	3	0	0	0	0	2	0	0	.533	.267
2-team total (12 New York)					.234	.267	.219	17	47	7	11	2	1	1	6	4	1	0	0	7	0	0	.383	.308

Pitching	B-T	HT	WT	DOB	W	L	ERA	G	GS	CG	SV	IP	H	R	ER	HR	BB	SO	AVG	vLH	vRH	K/9	BB/9
Adam, Jason	R-R	6-4	225	8-4-91	3	0	2.91	23	0	0	0	22	15	8	7	1	10	18	.200	.133	.244	7.48	4.15
Biagini, Joe	R-R	6-5	235	5-29-90	3	1	3.78	50	0	0	1	50	50	22	21	8	17	50	.259	.286	.241	9.00	3.06
2-team total (13 Houston)					3	2	4.59	63	0	0	1	65	71	35	33	14	26	60	.281	.320	.253	8.35	3.62
Borucki, Ryan	L-L	6-4	215	3-31-94	0	1	10.80	2	2	0	0	7	15	10	8	2	6	6	.441	.571	.407	8.10	8.10
Boshers, Buddy	L-L	6-3	222	5-9-88	0	3	4.05	28	1	0	0	20	20	10	9	3	10	26	.253	.257	.250	11.70	4.50
Buchholz, Clay	L-R	6-3	190	8-14-84	2	5	6.56	12	12	0	0	59	72	44	43	13	16	39	.306	.310	.302	5.95	2.44
Cordero, Jimmy	R-R	6-4	222	10-19-91	0	1	6.75	1	0	0	0	1	2	1	1	1	0	0	.400	.000	.667	0.00	0.00
2-team total (30 Chicago)					1	1	2.89	31	0	0	0	37	26	12	12	4	13	31	.197	.163	.217	7.47	2.65
Diaz, Yennsy	R-R	6-1	202	11-15-96	0	0	27.00	1	0	0	0	1	1	2	2	0	4	0	.333	.000	1.000	0.00	54.00
Dull, Ryan	R-R	5-9	185	10-2-89	0	0	6.75	1	0	0	0	1	1	1	1	1	0	3	.200	.500	.000	20.25	0.00
3-team total (3 New York, 7 Oakland)					0	0	12.79	11	0	0	0	13	25	19	18	5	7	15	.410	.400	.417	10.66	4.97
Feierabend, Ryan	L-L	6-3	225	8-22-85	0	1	11.12	2	1	1	0	6	11	7	7	2	1	4	.393	.571	.333	6.35	1.59
Font, Wilmer	R-R	6-4	250	5-24-90	2	3	3.66	23	14	0	0	39	34	16	16	7	11	53	.230	.266	.202	12.13	2.52
2-team total (10 Tampa Bay)					3	3	4.22	33	14	0	0	53	49	25	25	9	16	71	.241	.296	.200	11.98	2.70
Gaviglio, Sam	R-R	6-2	205	5-22-90	4	2	4.61	52	0	0	0	96	85	51	49	18	22	88	.235	.277	.206	8.28	2.07
Giles, Ken	R-R	6-3	210	9-20-90	2	3	1.87	53	0	0	23	53	36	11	11	5	17	83	.189	.174	.202	14.09	2.89
Godley, Zack	R-R	6-3	240	4-21-90	1	0	3.94	6	0	0	0	16	15	7	7	2	7	12	.246	.179	.303	6.75	3.94
Guerra, Javy	R-R	6-1	216	10-31-85	0	0	3.86	11	0	0	1	14	12	6	6	1	5	15	.231	.222	.240	9.64	3.21
Hudson, Daniel	R-R	6-3	225	3-9-87	6	3	3.00	45	0	1	2	48	38	18	16	5	23	48	.215	.224	.208	9.00	4.31
Jackson, Edwin	R-R	6-2	215	9-9-83	1	5	11.12	8	5	0	0	28	49	41	35	12	13	19	.380	.322	.429	6.04	4.13
2-team total (10 Detroit)					3	10	9.58	18	13	0	0	68	105	81	72	23	32	52	.351	.326	.373	6.92	4.26
Kay, Anthony	L-L	6-0	218	3-21-95	1	0	5.79	3	2	0	0	14	15	9	9	0	5	13	.263	.182	.283	8.36	3.21
Kingham, Nick	R-R	6-5	235	11-8-91	3	1	3.00	11	0	0	0	21	24	7	7	4	8	14	.296	.290	.302	6.00	3.43

Name	B-T	HT	WT	DOB	W	L	ERA	G	GS	CG	SV	IP	H	R	ER	HR	BB	SO	AVG	vLH	vRH	K/9	BB/9
Law, Derek	R-R	6-3	215	9-14-90	1	2	4.90	58	4	0	5	61	61	36	33	8	40	67	.256	.237	.275	9.94	5.93
Luciano, Elvis	R-R	6-3	200	2-15-00	1	0	5.35	25	0	0	0	34	36	20	20	4	24	27	.275	.268	.280	7.22	6.42
Maile, Luke	R-R	6-3	225	2-6-91	0	0	0.00	2	0	0	0	2	1	0	0	0	0	3	.143	.000	.167	13.50	0.00
Mayza, Tim	L-L	6-3	220	1-15-92	1	3	4.91	68	0	0	0	51	45	29	28	8	27	55	.230	.211	.248	9.64	4.73
Pannone, Thomas	L-L	6-0	200	4-28-94	3	6	6.16	37	7	0	0	73	73	51	50	13	31	69	.255	.224	.269	8.51	3.82
Phelps, David	R-R	6-3	200	10-9-86	0	0	3.63	17	1	0	0	17	14	7	7	3	7	18	.222	.217	.225	9.35	3.63
Ramirez, Neil	R-R	6-4	215	5-25-89	0	2	5.40	6	1	0	0	8	8	5	5	2	6	6	.258	.313	.200	6.48	6.48
2-team total (16 Cleveland)					0	1	5.40	22	1	0	0	25	26	16	15	7	15	24	.274	.296	.255	8.64	5.40
Reid-Foley, Sean	R-R	6-3	220	8-30-95	2	4	4.26	9	6	0	0	32	33	20	15	5	21	28	.262	.274	.250	7.96	5.97
Richard, Clayton	L-L	6-5	240	9-12-83	1	5	5.96	10	10	0	0	45	53	33	30	9	18	22	.298	.212	.317	4.37	3.57
Romano, Jordan	R-R	6-4	200	4-21-93	0	2	7.63	17	0	0	0	15	17	14	13	4	9	21	.274	.192	.333	12.33	5.28
Rosscup, Zac	R-L	6-2	220	6-9-88	0	0	27.00	2	0	0	0	1	3	4	3	0	2	2	.500	.667	.333	18.00	18.00
2-team total (19 Seattle)					2	0	4.80	21	0	0	0	15	16	12	8	1	16	22	.262	.154	.343	13.20	9.60
Sanchez, Aaron	R-R	6-4	210	7-1-92	3	14	6.07	23	23	0	0	113	131	82	76	15	59	99	.291	.279	.304	7.91	4.71
2-team total (4 Houston)					5	14	5.89	27	27	0	0	131	145	92	86	20	68	115	.278	.277	.277	7.88	4.66
Shafer, Justin	R-R	6-2	195	9-18-92	2	1	3.86	34	0	0	1	40	41	19	17	6	25	39	.265	.265	.264	8.85	5.67
Shoemaker, Matt	R-R	6-2	225	9-27-86	3	0	1.57	5	5	0	0	29	16	7	5	3	9	24	.163	.189	.148	7.53	2.83
Stewart, Brock	R-R	6-3	215	10-3-91	4	0	8.31	10	0	0	0	22	28	21	20	9	6	16	.304	.346	.250	6.65	2.49
Stroman, Marcus	R-R	5-7	180	5-1-91	6	11	2.96	21	21	0	0	125	118	50	41	10	35	99	.248	.272	.224	7.15	2.53
Tepera, Ryan	R-R	6-1	195	11-3-87	0	2	4.98	23	1	0	0	22	20	12	12	5	8	14	.250	.290	.225	5.82	3.32
Thornton, Trent	R-R	6-0	195	9-30-93	6	9	4.84	32	29	0	0	154	156	87	83	24	61	149	.259	.248	.270	8.69	3.56
Urena, Richard	B-R	6-0	195	2-26-96	0	0	36.00	1	0	0	0	1	4	4	4	1	1	0	.571	.667	.500	0.00	9.00
Waguespack, Jacob	R-R	6-6	235	11-5-93	5	5	4.38	16	13	0	0	78	75	43	38	12	29	63	.249	.208	.281	7.27	3.35
Zeuch, T.J.	R-R	6-7	225	8-1-95	1	2	4.76	5	3	0	0	23	22	13	12	2	11	20	.250	.286	.217	7.94	4.37

Fielding

Catcher	PCT	G	PO	A	E	DP	PB
Jansen	.995	103	803	47	4	8	4
Maile	.989	44	316	28	4	3	4
McGuire	.992	30	226	16	2	1	1
Taylor	1.000	1	6	0	0	0	0

First Base	PCT	G	PO	A	E	DP
Biggio	.974	8	35	2	1	5
Drury	1.000	12	95	6	0	6
Gurriel Jr.	1.000	3	5	1	0	0
Hanson	1.000	2	9	2	0	1
McKinney	1.000	9	19	4	0	4
Smoak	.995	89	686	42	4	64
Tellez	.996	57	451	41	2	40

Second Base	PCT	G	PO	A	E	DP
Biggio	.989	85	144	205	4	44
Drury	.981	16	22	30	1	10

	PCT	G	PO	A	E	DP
Galvis	1.000	5	5	7	0	1
Gurriel Jr.	.917	9	11	11	2	3
Hanson	1.000	8	11	13	0	5
Sogard	.988	43	61	105	2	21
Urena	1.000	9	8	12	0	1
Valera	1.000	2	4	1	0	0

Third Base	PCT	G	PO	A	E	DP
Drury	.975	65	52	104	4	9
Guerrero Jr.	.936	96	66	182	17	23
Sogard	1.000	6	5	10	0	3
Urena	.917	6	3	8	1	3
Valera	1.000	1	1	4	0	0

Shortstop	PCT	G	PO	A	E	DP
Bichette	.959	42	58	106	7	23
Drury	1.000	5	6	11	0	0
Galvis	.986	103	133	284	6	63
Sogard	.909	4	6	4	1	0

	PCT	G	PO	A	E	DP
Urena	.971	13	9	25	1	2
Valera	1.000	2	0	3	0	1

Outfield	PCT	G	PO	A	E	DP
Alford	.944	13	17	0	1	1
Biggio	1.000	8	13	0	0	0
Brito	.929	17	26	0	2	0
Davis	.982	35	55	0	1	0
Drury	1.000	25	44	0	0	0
Fisher	.950	33	56	1	3	1
Grichuk	.993	140	268	6	2	2
Gurriel Jr.	1.000	63	97	9	0	1
Hanson	.909	6	10	0	1	0
Hernandez	.989	118	261	9	3	4
McKinney	.966	69	112	2	4	0
Pillar	1.000	4	11	0	0	0
Sogard	1.000	7	15	0	0	0
Urena	1.000	1	1	0	0	0

BUFFALO BISONS   TRIPLE-A
INTERNATIONAL LEAGUE

Batting	B-T	HT	WT	DOB	AVG	vLH	vRH	G	AB	R	H	2B	3B	HR	RBI	BB	HBP	SH	SF	SO	SB	CS	SLG	OBP
Alford, Anthony	R-R	6-1	215	7-20-94	.259	.227	.273	76	282	46	73	16	3	7	37	31	5	1	0	94	22	8	.411	.343
Bichette, Bo	R-R	6-0	185	3-5-98	.275	.313	.264	56	222	34	61	16	2	8	32	19	1	1	1	48	15	5	.473	.333
Biggio, Cavan	L-R	6-2	200	4-11-95	.312	.278	.324	43	138	23	43	8	1	6	27	34	1	0	1	28	5	1	.515	.448
Brito, Socrates	L-L	6-2	205	9-6-92	.282	.291	.278	97	394	66	111	28	7	16	67	29	0	1	4	97	11	7	.510	.328
Burns, Andy	R-R	6-2	205	8-7-90	.275	.315	.260	118	411	60	113	17	3	19	63	57	2	0	3	83	6	6	.470	.364
Cantwell, Patrick	R-R	6-2	210	4-10-90	.217	.100	.265	22	69	6	15	4	0	0	5	9	1	1	0	24	1	0	.275	.317
Davis, Jonathan	R-R	5-8	190	5-12-92	.262	.253	.266	82	294	64	77	19	3	10	36	40	17	1	0	83	13	4	.449	.382
De La Cruz, Michael	B-R	5-10	190	5-15-93	.278	.217	.314	52	162	23	45	12	0	5	26	26	1	2	1	33	1	0	.444	.379
Espinal, Santiago	R-R	5-10	175	11-13-94	.317	.267	.338	28	104	11	33	6	0	2	14	7	0	1	0	23	2	2	.433	.360
Fields, Roemon	L-L	5-11	180	11-28-90	.254	.200	.274	98	299	42	76	8	3	2	22	31	2	4	4	52	16	8	.321	.324
Guerrero Jr., Vladimir	R-R	6-2	250	3-16-99	.367	.500	.318	9	30	7	11	1	0	3	8	4	0	0	0	2	1	0	.700	.441
Guillotte, Andrew	R-R	5-8	170	3-30-93	.159	.227	.133	25	82	7	13	2	1	0	3	4	1	1	0	28	3	0	.207	.207
Gurriel Jr., Lourdes	R-R	6-3	215	10-10-93	.276	.257	.284	31	123	18	34	13	0	4	26	3	3	0	1	23	0	2	.480	.308
Hanson, Alen	B-R	6-0	170	10-22-92	.187	.151	.204	48	166	19	31	3	1	3	18	9	1	3	1	39	7	2	.271	.232
Heidt, Gunnar	R-R	6-0	200	9-12-92	.042	.000	.056	7	24	2	1	0	0	0	1	1	0	0	0	19	0	0	.042	.080
Hernandez, Teoscar	R-R	6-2	205	10-15-92	.253	.556	.158	19	19	11	19	0	1	5	16	1	0	1	21	3	0	.480	.313
Kivlehan, Patrick	R-R	6-2	223	12-22-89	.247	.220	.257	90	328	48	81	13	3	25	66	37	8	0	2	105	0	1	.534	.336
2-team total (24 Indianapolis)					.240	.230	.243	114	413	59	99	18	3	29	75	45	9	1	2	132	0	1	.509	.326
Knight, Nash	B-R	6-0	195	10-20-92	.333	.333	.000	3	3	1	1	0	0	1	1	0	0	0	0	5	0	0	.167	.154
McGuire, Reese	L-R	6-0	215	3-2-95	.247	.328	.218	72	243	30	60	12	1	5	29	25	2	2	5	44	4	0	.366	.316
McKinney, Billy	L-L	6-1	205	8-23-94	.271	.269	.272	36	129	17	35	8	4	4	20	22	2	0	1	25	1	1	.488	.383
Patterson, Jordan	L-L	6-4	227	2-12-92	.234	.214	.240	104	359	61	84	19	2	16	47	24	15	2	1	129	3	1	.432	.308
Pompey, Dalton	B-R	6-2	200	12-11-92	.203	.000	.318	8	27	1	7	0	0	0	6	0	0	1	7	0	0		.259	.382
Revere, Ben	L-R	5-9	175	5-3-88	.286	.143	.321	9	35	4	10	3	0	0	6	0	0	0	0	3	1	0	.371	.286
Sogard, Eric	L-R	5-10	185	5-22-86	.267	.250	.269	9	30	7	8	2	0	1	6	7	0	0	1	4	0	0	.433	.395

Player	B-T	HT	WT	DOB	AVG	OBP	SLG	G	AB	R	H	2B	3B	HR	RBI	BB	HBP	SH	SF	SO	SB	CS	SLG	OBP
Sotillo, Andres	R-R	5-11	180	12-28-93	.000	.000	--	1	2	0	0	0	0	0	0	1	0	0	0	1	0	0	.000	.333
Taylor, Beau	L-R	5-11	205	2-13-90	.188	.500	.115	10	32	5	6	2	0	0	4	5	0	0	2	8	0	0	.250	.282
Tellez, Rowdy	L-L	6-4	255	3-16-95	.366	.345	.375	26	93	20	34	9	0	7	21	14	1	0	1	25	0	0	.688	.450
Urena, Richard	B-R	6-0	195	2-26-96	.274	.212	.296	98	369	43	101	18	4	6	52	23	1	4	5	85	3	2	.393	.314
Vicuna, Kevin	R-R	6-0	140	1-14-98	.429	.500	.400	3	7	3	3	0	1	0	0	1	0	1	0	1	1	0	.714	.500
Wall, Forrest	L-R	6-1	195	11-20-95	.255	.417	.200	14	47	9	12	3	0	2	4	6	0	0	0	14	1	0	.447	.340

Pitching	B-T	HT	WT	DOB	W	L	ERA	G	GS	CG	SV	IP	H	R	ER	HR	BB	SO	AVG	vLH	vRH	K/9	BB/9
Adam, Jason	R-R	6-4	225	8-4-91	1	3	2.57	11	0	0	1	14	10	7	4	2	5	20	.200	.318	.107	12.86	3.21
Baker, Bryan	R-R	6-6	220	12-2-94	1	1	3.68	18	0	0	3	22	17	9	9	1	16	31	.207	.177	.229	12.68	6.55
Barnes, Danny	L-R	6-1	215	10-21-89	0	2	11.74	7	0	0	1	8	9	10	10	1	3	9	.281	.300	.273	10.57	3.52
Bergen, Travis	L-L	6-1	205	10-8-93	0	0	3.00	3	0	0	1	3	3	1	1	0	0	6	.250	.333	.222	18.00	0.00
Borucki, Ryan	L-L	6-4	215	3-31-94	1	0	4.91	2	2	0	0	11	11	7	6	4	3	9	.262	.231	.276	7.36	2.45
Boshers, Buddy	L-L	6-3	222	5-9-88	0	2	2.78	25	0	0	5	32	27	13	10	3	14	35	.233	.214	.243	9.74	3.90
Buchholz, Clay	L-R	6-3	190	8-14-84	0	1	5.40	1	1	0	0	5	4	5	3	4	0	5	.200	.222	.182	9.00	0.00
Cheshire, Jonathan	L-R	6-1	185	11-15-94	0	0	2.16	4	0	0	0	8	6	2	2	0	3	4	.207	.250	.177	4.32	3.24
Copping, Corey	R-R	6-1	205	1-11-94	2	2	6.75	22	0	0	0	32	37	25	24	6	22	33	.289	.170	.373	9.28	6.19
Cordero, Jimmy	R-R	6-4	222	10-19-91	1	0	0.00	1	0	0	0	1	0	0	0	0	0	2	.000	.000	.000	18.00	0.00
2-team total (13 Charlotte)					4	1	0.48	14	0	0	4	19	14	1	1	0	2	16	.206	.214	.200	7.71	0.96
Dermody, Matt	R-L	6-5	190	7-4-90	2	1	5.48	15	0	0	0	23	29	17	14	4	3	23	.296	.357	.271	9.00	1.17
Feierabend, Ryan	L-L	6-3	225	8-22-85	6	5	5.53	14	12	0	0	68	77	47	42	19	21	53	.283	.326	.263	6.98	2.77
Fields, Roemon	L-L	5-11	180	11-28-90	0	0	0.00	1	0	0	0	1	0	0	0	0	2	1	.000	--	.000	9.00	18.00
Fisk, Conor	R-R	6-2	220	4-4-92	5	7	5.10	32	15	0	0	97	105	59	55	20	31	92	.269	.268	.270	8.54	2.88
Garner, David	R-R	6-1	180	9-21-92	1	1	13.50	4	0	0	0	5	9	8	8	2	2	9	.346	.364	.333	15.19	3.38
Guerra, Javy	R-R	6-1	216	10-31-85	0	1	2.45	5	0	0	1	7	4	2	2	0	4	6	.167	.143	.177	7.36	4.91
Isaacs, Dusty	R-R	6-1	190	8-7-91	1	0	5.81	17	0	0	0	26	27	17	17	3	7	36	.257	.156	.301	12.30	2.39
Jackson, Edwin	R-R	6-2	215	9-9-83	1	0	4.50	3	0	0	0	4	1	2	2	1	1	3	.077	.250	.000	6.75	2.25
2-team total (2 Toledo)					1	2	5.40	5	0	0	0	12	12	10	7	2	5	5	.267	.400	.200	3.86	3.86
Jackson, Zach	R-R	6-4	230	12-25-94	9	0	3.97	46	0	0	1	68	56	35	30	10	34	68	.225	.217	.229	9.00	4.50
Kay, Anthony	L-L	6-0	218	3-21-95	2	2	2.50	7	7	0	0	36	33	21	10	3	22	39	.244	.129	.279	9.75	5.50
2-team total (7 Syracuse)					3	5	4.41	14	14	0	0	67	73	44	33	10	33	65	.283	.218	.301	8.69	4.41
Kingham, Nick	R-R	6-5	235	11-8-91	0	1	22.50	1	1	0	0	2	6	5	5	2	2	1	.500	.444	.667	4.50	9.00
Larkins, Turner	R-R	6-3	200	11-6-95	0	1	10.50	1	1	0	0	6	8	7	7	3	2	3	.320	.200	.350	4.50	3.00
Law, Derek	R-R	6-3	215	9-14-90	2	1	1.69	8	0	0	2	11	7	3	2	1	3	17	.180	.167	.185	14.34	2.53
Logue, Zach	L-L	6-0	165	4-23-96	1	0	5.40	1	0	0	0	3	5	2	2	0	4	4	.333	.667	.111	10.80	10.80
McClelland, Jackson	R-R	6-5	220	7-19-94	0	0	6.00	11	0	0	0	15	12	10	10	2	11	14	.226	.200	.242	8.40	6.60
Morimando, Shawn	L-L	6-0	206	11-20-92	2	5	6.01	16	14	0	0	70	78	50	47	13	33	76	.283	.273	.286	9.73	4.22
Ouellette, William	R-R	6-1	195	6-30-93	1	0	4.76	5	0	0	0	11	11	6	6	2	9	9	.262	.273	.258	7.15	0.00
Pannone, Thomas	L-L	6-0	200	4-28-94	3	1	3.21	8	6	0	0	34	25	12	12	4	15	41	.203	.161	.217	10.96	4.01
Patterson, Jordan	L-L	6-4	227	2-12-92	0	0	9.00	1	0	0	0	1	1	1	1	0	2	1	.250	.000	.333	9.00	18.00
Paulino, David	R-R	6-6	240	2-6-94	1	1	3.45	7	7	0	0	29	30	14	11	2	11	27	.275	.257	.284	8.48	3.45
Pearson, Nate	R-R	6-6	245	8-20-96	1	0	3.00	3	3	0	0	18	12	6	6	2	3	15	.185	.136	.209	7.50	1.50
Phelps, David	R-R	6-3	200	10-9-86	1	0	0.00	1	0	0	0	2	2	0	0	0	2	3	.222	.333	.167	11.57	0.00
Pulido, Joey	R-R	5-10	185	9-25-95	0	1	13.50	1	0	0	0	3	3	4	4	1	1	2	.273	.143	.500	6.75	3.38
Ramirez, Neil	R-R	6-4	215	5-25-89	0	0	0.00	1	0	0	0	1	1	0	0	0	1	2	.000	.000	.000	18.00	0.00
2-team total (25 Columbus)					2	1	4.75	26	0	0	2	30	29	17	16	7	11	47	.244	.163	.300	13.95	3.26
Reid-Foley, Sean	R-R	6-3	220	8-29-95	3	5	6.47	20	19	0	0	89	78	71	64	13	65	105	.232	.234	.231	10.62	6.57
Richard, Clayton	L-L	6-5	240	9-12-83	0	0	5.06	2	2	0	0	5	4	3	3	1	3	5	.211	.000	.250	8.44	5.06
Rios, Francisco	R-R	6-1	180	5-6-95	0	0	7.71	2	0	0	0	2	4	2	2	2	1	1	.364	.667	.250	3.86	3.86
Romano, Jordan	R-R	6-4	200	4-21-93	2	2	5.73	24	3	0	5	38	37	26	24	8	14	53	.252	.275	.240	12.66	3.35
Saucedo, Tayler	L-L	6-5	185	6-18-93	6	1	4.85	24	7	0	0	56	70	39	30	5	20	46	.307	.254	.339	7.44	3.23
Shafer, Justin	R-R	6-2	195	9-18-92	0	2	3.52	24	0	0	7	31	29	14	12	3	8	35	.246	.255	.239	10.27	2.35
Snead, Kirby	L-L	6-0	200	10-7-94	5	2	3.98	41	0	0	2	52	54	25	23	6	19	54	.266	.197	.296	9.35	3.29
Sopko, Andrew	R-R	6-2	205	8-7-94	1	6	7.12	13	12	0	0	54	63	50	43	14	28	41	.286	.277	.294	6.79	4.64
Spraker, Graham	R-R	6-3	200	3-19-95	0	0	1.69	1	1	0	0	5	3	1	1	0	2	5	.150	.158	.000	8.44	3.38
Stewart, Brock	L-R	6-3	215	10-3-91	1	1	7.56	7	1	0	0	8	13	7	7	3	3	6	.371	.250	.533	6.48	3.24
Tepera, Ryan	R-R	6-1	195	11-3-87	0	0	3.60	5	1	0	0	5	4	2	1	2	4	.200	.167	.214	7.20	3.60
Tice, Ty	L-R	5-9	170	7-9-97	2	1	3.27	26	0	0	4	33	30	14	12	2	21	41	.236	.200	.250	11.18	5.73
Waguespack, Jacob	R-R	6-6	235	11-5-93	2	6	5.30	12	11	0	0	53	57	33	31	9	25	52	.278	.300	.263	8.89	4.27
Young, Danny	L-L	6-3	200	5-27-94	0	1	7.27	9	0	0	0	9	12	7	7	1	6	10	.316	.333	.308	10.38	6.23
Zeuch, T.J.	R-R	6-7	225	8-1-95	4	3	3.69	13	13	1	0	78	70	35	32	6	32	39	.238	.289	.202	4.50	3.69

Fielding

Catcher	PCT	G	PO	A	E	DP	PB
Cantwell	.976	22	188	13	5	1	0
De La Cruz	.989	40	348	24	4	0	4
McGuire	.995	71	605	21	3	5	10
Sotillo	1.000	1	4	2	0	0	1
Taylor	1.000	9	73	2	0	0	2

First Base	PCT	G	PO	A	E	DP
Biggio	1.000	7	41	1	0	3
Burns	1.000	13	84	5	0	12
De La Cruz	1.000	1	7	0	0	1
Heidt	1.000	3	22	1	0	1
Kivlehan	1.000	30	197	14	0	19
McKinney	1.000	4	21	1	0	3
Patterson	.994	64	435	49	3	44
Tellez	.980	26	183	14	4	22

Second Base	PCT	G	PO	A	E	DP
Bichette	1.000	1	0	3	0	0
Biggio	.976	22	33	47	2	9
Burns	.990	29	37	62	1	16
Espinal	.977	18	29	56	2	14
Gurriel Jr.	.946	12	17	18	2	6
Hanson	.973	22	32	39	2	15
Sogard	1.000	2	3	8	0	2
Urena	.971	39	54	79	4	24

Third Base	PCT	G	PO	A	E	DP
Biggio	1.000	7	3	13	0	2
Burns	.939	62	41	114	10	14
Guerrero Jr.	1.000	7	4	9	0	0
Guillotte	1.000	1	0	2	0	0
Hanson	.902	20	14	32	5	6
Heidt	1.000	3	2	4	0	0
Kivlehan	.944	34	31	53	5	7
Knight	.900	3	5	4	1	0

Sogard	.938	5	1	14	1	1
Urena	1.000	1	0	1	0	0

Shortstop	PCT	G	PO	A	E	DP
Bichette	.951	51	59	115	9	30
Espinal	.943	11	9	24	2	3
Guillotte	.950	13	17	21	2	7
Gurriel Jr.	1.000	7	13	9	0	3
Hanson	1.000	2	1	8	0	2
Heidt	1.000	1	0	1	0	0

Urena	.934	57	59	153	15	29
Vicuna	1.000	3	4	4	0	2

Outfield	PCT	G	PO	A	E	DP
Alford	.968	62	120	2	4	1
Biggio	1.000	5	14	0	0	0
Brito	.994	84	157	7	1	1
Burns	.000	1	0	0	0	0
Davis	.979	71	135	3	3	0
Fields	.975	90	186	9	5	4

Guillotte	.900	11	18	0	2	0
Gurriel Jr.	.889	7	8	0	1	0
Hernandez	.935	14	28	1	2	0
McKinney	1.000	24	42	5	0	1
Patterson	.978	37	87	4	2	1
Pompey	.882	5	15	0	2	0
Revere	1.000	6	9	1	0	1
Wall	1.000	12	21	0	0	0

NEW HAMPSHIRE FISHER CATS

DOUBLE-A

EASTERN LEAGUE

Batting	B-T	HT	WT	DOB	AVG	vLH	vRH	G	AB	R	H	2B	3B	HR	RBI	BB	HBP	SH	SF	SO	SB	CS	SLG	OBP
Adams, Riley	R-R	6-4	225	6-26-96	.258	.255	.260	81	287	46	74	15	2	11	39	32	10	0	3	105	3	1	.439	.349
Brodt, Jake	R-R	6-5	235	1-23-96	.000	.000	.000	2	6	0	0	0	0	0	0	0	0	0	0	2	0	0	.000	.000
Capra, Vinny	R-R	5-8	175	7-7-96	.229	.215	.236	110	388	53	89	20	1	3	33	33	5	3	4	83	15	4	.309	.295
Clemens, Kacy	L-R	6-2	200	7-27-94	.145	.177	.136	24	83	8	12	2	0	0	7	11	1	0	2	29	0	0	.169	.247
Espinal, Santiago	R-R	5-10	175	11-13-94	.278	.278	.278	94	367	46	102	21	1	5	57	35	2	4	1	50	10	11	.382	.343
Grudzielanek, BrandonR-R	6-0	205	5-26-95	.156	.091	.177	13	45	5	7	1	0	0	1	1	1	2	0	20	0	0	.178	.192
Heidt, Gunnar	R-R	6-0	200	9-12-92	.177	.091	.200	14	51	9	9	3	0	1	3	5	1	0	0	20	7	0	.294	.263
Hissey, Ryan	L-R	6-0	190	4-8-94	.225	.125	.250	12	40	7	9	1	0	1	2	6	1	0	0	14	1	1	.325	.340
Kivlehan, Patrick	R-R	6-2	223	12-22-89	.421	.412	.429	11	38	5	16	5	0	3	9	4	1	0	1	3	1	1	.790	.477
Knight, Nash	B-R	6-0	195	9-20-92	.252	.298	.228	102	349	46	88	22	1	7	36	53	10	0	2	86	4	8	.381	.365
Large, Cullen	B-R	6-1	175	1-22-96	.234	.200	.250	24	94	7	22	3	3	0	9	1	4	0	0	31	2	0	.330	.273
Lundquist, Brock	L-R	5-11	190	1-23-96	.232	.162	.265	108	370	44	86	20	3	6	50	37	4	0	2	105	7	5	.351	.308
Mineo, Alberto	L-R	5-10	170	7-23-94	.220	.198	.229	83	300	27	66	9	2	5	38	29	5	1	4	101	1	1	.313	.296
Palacios, Josh	L-R	6-1	193	7-30-95	.266	.358	.229	82	286	43	76	18	2	7	38	45	5	1	4	70	15	5	.416	.371
Smith, Kevin	R-R	5-11	188	7-4-96	.209	.235	.197	116	430	49	90	22	2	19	61	29	4	1	4	151	11	6	.402	.263
Sotillo, Andres	R-R	5-11	180	12-28-93	.205	.188	.214	13	44	5	9	1	0	0	2	2	1	0	1	8	0	0	.227	.250
Spanberger, Chad	L-R	6-3	235	11-1-95	.237	.213	.247	122	431	46	102	29	1	13	59	43	3	0	3	117	4	3	.399	.308
Wall, Forrest	L-R	6-1	195	11-20-95	.270	.191	.305	109	415	70	112	27	4	9	41	49	4	1	0	109	13	8	.419	.353
Warmoth, Logan	R-R	6-0	190	9-6-95	.200	.155	.222	65	220	20	44	11	3	0	15	22	7	2	3	74	12	2	.277	.290
Williams, Christian	L-R	6-3	210	9-14-96	.228	.253	.216	79	281	24	64	14	3	4	24	16	3	0	1	113	1	1	.342	.276

Pitching	B-T	HT	WT	DOB	W	L	ERA	G	GS	CG	SV	IP	H	R	ER	HR	BB	SO	AVG	vLH	vRH	K/9	BB/9
Baker, Bryan	R-R	6-6	220	12-2-94	2	5	2.81	31	0	0	9	32	18	14	10	2	20	40	.164	.167	.161	11.25	5.63
Case, Andrew	R-R	6-2	230	1-6-93	0	0	5.40	3	0	0	0	7	10	4	4	1	2	3	.357	.333	.400	4.05	2.70
Cheshire, Jonathan	L-R	6-1	185	11-15-94	1	1	4.63	6	0	0	0	12	16	8	6	1	2	7	.320	.308	.333	5.40	1.54
Copping, Corey	R-R	6-1	205	1-11-94	1	2	3.86	13	0	0	1	19	18	8	4	7	16	.261	.229	.294	7.71	3.38
Cuevas, Adams	R-R	6-0	192	2-2-96	0	0	3.00	2	0	0	0	3	2	1	1	0	1	4	.182	.167	.200	12.00	3.00
Diaz, Yennsy	R-R	6-1	202	11-15-96	11	9	3.74	26	24	1	0	144	125	71	60	12	53	116	.234	.232	.235	7.23	3.30
Dillon, Justin	R-R	6-3	225	9-5-93	5	3	3.32	13	9	0	1	57	51	27	21	5	17	42	.236	.266	.193	6.63	2.68
Ellenbest, Mike	R-R	6-4	220	8-20-94	0	0	1.42	3	0	0	0	6	5	1	1	1	1	1	.238	.111	.333	1.42	1.42
Feierabend, Ryan	L-L	6-3	225	8-22-85	0	1	18.00	1	1	0	0	3	10	6	6	0	2	3	.625	.600	.636	9.00	6.00
Fishman, Jake	L-L	6-3	195	2-8-95	1	1	3.45	42	0	0	4	63	61	28	24	4	18	74	.251	.223	.275	10.63	2.59
Harris, Jon	R-R	6-4	175	10-16-93	2	1	6.08	4	3	0	0	13	18	9	9	2	2	12	.321	.208	.406	8.10	1.35
Hatch, Thomas	R-R	6-1	200	9-29-94	2	3	2.80	6	6	1	0	35	25	11	11	5	2	34	.205	.292	.080	8.66	0.51
Jimenez, Dany	R-R	6-3	190	12-23-93	2	2	1.87	25	0	0	6	34	22	8	7	4	12	46	.183	.200	.167	12.30	3.21
Knight, Nash	B-R	6-0	195	9-20-92	0	1	27.00	1	0	0	0	1	2	1	1	0	0	0	.500	--	.500	0.00	0.00
Larkins, Turner	R-R	6-3	200	11-6-95	0	0	0.00	1	0	0	0	1	1	0	0	0	1	1	.250	.500	.000	9.00	9.00
Logue, Zach	L-L	6-0	165	4-23-96	3	7	4.10	19	18	0	0	101	95	48	46	15	32	79	.247	.255	.242	7.04	2.85
Lundquist, Brock	L-R	5-11	190	1-23-96	0	0	0.00	1	0	0	0	0	0	0	0	0	0	0	.000	.000	--	0.00	0.00
McClelland, Jackson	R-R	6-5	220	7-19-94	0	2	2.98	32	0	0	1	42	33	18	14	4	21	42	.212	.187	.235	8.93	4.46
Murphy, Patrick	R-R	6-4	220	6-10-95	4	7	4.71	18	18	0	0	84	75	53	44	7	27	86	.227	.227	.228	9.21	2.89
Murray, Joey	R-R	6-2	195	9-23-96	2	4	3.50	9	8	0	0	44	37	17	17	4	18	52	.231	.218	.244	10.72	3.71
Nittoli, Vinny	R-R	6-1	210	11-11-90	3	2	3.80	29	0	0	2	43	37	27	18	4	8	27	.247	.200	.253	8.44	1.69
Ortiz, Willy	R-R	6-1	180	7-20-95	3	5	5.83	16	4	0	0	54	53	36	35	7	24	44	.259	.280	.241	7.33	4.00
Ouellette, William	R-R	6-1	195	6-30-93	3	2	3.71	20	1	0	0	44	46	19	18	3	10	24	.274	.286	.262	4.95	2.06
Pearson, Nate	R-R	6-6	245	8-20-96	1	4	2.59	16	16	0	0	63	41	18	18	4	21	69	.186	.160	.207	9.91	3.02
Perez, Hector	R-R	6-3	218	6-6-96	7	6	4.60	26	24	0	0	121	130	65	62	9	67	117	.280	.298	.260	6.48	4.97
Pulido, Joey	R-R	5-10	185	9-25-95	0	1	3.18	3	0	0	0	6	3	2	1	4	8	.191	.273	.100	12.71	6.35
Rios, Francisco	R-R	6-1	180	5-6-95	0	0	5.93	7	0	0	0	14	17	12	9	0	3	9	.315	.310	.320	5.93	1.98
Saucedo, Tayler	L-L	6-5	185	6-18-93	2	1	1.01	12	1	0	0	27	17	6	3	1	16	23	.183	.103	.241	7.76	5.40
Snead, Kirby	L-L	6-0	200	10-7-94	2	0	0.84	9	0	0	5	11	4	3	1	0	1	14	.108	.100	.118	11.81	0.00
Sopko, Andrew	R-R	6-2	205	8-7-94	2	2	2.34	6	6	0	0	35	23	9	9	3	8	26	.184	.140	.221	6.75	2.08
Tice, Ty	R-R	5-9	170	7-4-96	1	3	1.09	20	0	0	4	25	13	9	3	0	8	23	.141	.174	.100	8.39	2.92
Wilson, Brad	R-R	6-1	260	8-15-96	2	0	3.50	11	0	0	0	18	17	7	7	1	6	17	.246	.182	.306	8.50	3.00
Young, Danny	L-L	6-3	200	5-27-94	1	1	1.79	20	0	0	3	40	29	10	8	2	20	32	.204	.179	.227	7.14	4.46

Fielding

Catcher	PCT	G	PO	A	E	DP	PB
Adams	.996	57	422	35	2	2	8
Hissey	1.000	10	88	11	0	1	0

Mineo	.993	61	493	65	4	6	14
Sotillo	1.000	11	84	6	0	0	1

First Base	PCT	G	PO	A	E	DP

Brodt	1.000	2	22	3	0	2
Clemens	.988	20	163	7	2	7
Heidt	1.000	7	56	10	0	5

Kivlehan	1.000	2	23	3	0	0
Knight	.991	30	212	17	2	19
Spanberger	.989	13	85	9	1	8
Williams	.989	70	510	41	6	51

Second Base	PCT	G	PO	A	E	DP
Capra	.971	45	62	107	5	24
Espinal	.979	52	92	141	5	31
Grudzielanek	1.000	1	4	4	0	0
Heidt	1.000	1	2	0	0	0
Smith	1.000	5	6	8	0	2
Warmoth	.987	36	57	90	2	16

Third Base	PCT	G	PO	A	E	DP
Capra	.967	41	24	63	3	9
Espinal	1.000	1	1	2	0	0
Grudzielanek	.909	11	11	19	3	2
Heidt	1.000	3	1	1	0	1
Kivlehan	.833	4	2	3	1	1
Knight	.938	41	25	51	5	8
Large	.972	21	11	24	1	5
Smith	.911	18	12	29	4	2
Warmoth	.500	1	0	1	1	0

Shortstop	PCT	G	PO	A	E	DP
Capra	.944	9	16	18	2	2
Espinal	.944	22	31	53	5	6

| Smith | .964 | 87 | 138 | 208 | 13 | 36 |
| Warmoth | .960 | 21 | 31 | 41 | 3 | 12 |

Outfield	PCT	G	PO	A	E	DP
Capra	1.000	4	5	0	0	0
Espinal	1.000	12	30	2	0	2
Heidt	1.000	3	6	0	0	0
Kivlehan	1.000	4	5	0	0	0
Knight	.950	14	19	0	1	0
Large	1.000	1	1	0	0	0
Lundquist	.984	104	182	2	3	1
Palacios	.994	76	155	5	1	0
Spanberger	.969	97	182	8	6	2
Wall	.984	106	246	5	4	0
Warmoth	1.000	4	6	0	0	0

DUNEDIN BLUE JAYS
FLORIDA STATE LEAGUE

HIGH CLASS A

Batting	B-T	HT	WT	DOB	AVG	vLH	vRH	G	AB	R	H	2B	3B	HR	RBI	BB	HBP	SH	SF	SO	SB	CS	SLG	OBP
Adams, Riley	R-R	6-4	225	6-26-96	.277	.200	.291	19	65	12	18	3	0	3	12	14	4	0	0	18	1	0	.462	.434
Bec, Christopher	R-R	5-11	190	12-30-95	.232	.409	.206	54	168	22	39	9	1	2	24	28	1	1	1	42	16	3	.333	.343
Bichette, Bo	R-R	6-0	185	3-5-98	.546	--	.546	4	11	4	6	2	0	0	1	5	0	0	0	3	1	0	.727	.688
Brito, Ronny	R-R	6-0	165	3-22-99	.308	.667	.200	4	13	1	4	1	0	0	0	2	0	0	0	5	0	0	.385	.400
Cardona, Hugo	R-R	5-11	145	9-5-99	.000	.000	.000	4	7	2	0	0	0	0	0	1	1	0	0	4	0	0	.000	.222
Clemens, Kacy	L-R	6-2	200	7-27-94	.204	.217	.202	88	294	38	60	9	2	10	38	39	0	0	4	95	5	0	.350	.294
Davis, Jonathan	R-R	5-8	190	5-12-92	.000	.000	.000	2	7	1	0	0	0	0	0	2	0	0	0	4	0	0	.000	.222
De Los Santos, Luis	R-R	6-1	160	6-9-98	.231	.500	.182	5	13	3	3	1	0	1	1	1	0	0	0	4	0	0	.539	.286
Guerrero Jr., Vladimir	R-R	6-2	250	3-16-99	.267	.333	.250	4	15	2	4	1	0	0	1	1	1	0	0	2	0	0	.333	.353
Hernandez, Javier	R-R	6-1	180	7-21-96	.083	.200	.000	5	12	0	1	0	0	0	1	1	0	0	1	5	0	0	.083	.143
Kirk, Alejandro	R-R	5-9	220	11-6-98	.288	.364	.266	71	233	26	67	25	0	4	36	38	4	0	1	31	2	0	.446	.395
Large, Cullen	R-R	6-1	175	1-22-96	.269	.339	.249	84	294	51	79	23	3	4	40	39	6	0	5	91	3	3	.408	.361
Navarro, Jesus	R-R	5-11	160	1-13-98	.198	.105	.216	41	121	12	24	2	1	0	13	13	1	1	2	29	1	1	.231	.277
Noda, Ryan	L-L	6-3	217	3-30-96	.238	.212	.244	117	378	62	90	27	1	13	74	74	10	1	6	138	14	2	.418	.372
Obeso, Norberto	L-R	6-0	175	7-9-95	.262	.220	.272	82	271	32	71	14	4	1	32	32	1	1	1	53	4	4	.354	.341
Orimoloye, Demi	R-R	6-4	225	1-6-97	.240	.247	.239	113	412	62	99	18	3	12	64	25	6	0	3	125	22	4	.386	.292
Podkul, Nick	R-R	6-1	200	4-11-97	.227	.278	.217	37	110	12	25	3	1	1	15	17	1	2	2	22	5	2	.300	.331
Pompey, Dalton	B-R	6-2	200	12-11-92	.125	.000	.182	5	16	2	2	0	0	0	1	3	0	0	0	5	0	1	.125	.263
Pruitt, Reggie	R-R	6-0	180	5-7-97	.230	.333	.215	21	74	10	17	5	2	0	7	7	0	0	0	23	8	0	.351	.296
Steinmetz, Hunter	L-L	5-9	175	12-13-96	.167	--	.167	5	12	2	2	0	0	1	3	0	2	0	0	6	0	0	.417	.286
Stevenson, Cal	L-L	5-10	175	9-12-96	.298	.293	.299	90	336	59	100	9	4	5	50	50	0	3	1	52	11	6	.393	.388
Taylor, Samad	R-R	5-10	160	7-11-98	.216	.155	.230	108	319	48	69	23	7	3	38	49	6	3	7	107	26	10	.364	.326
Vicuna, Kevin	R-R	6-0	140	1-14-98	.250	.198	.265	112	396	55	99	19	4	1	36	30	8	2	2	82	19	9	.326	.314
Warmoth, Logan	R-R	6-0	190	9-6-95	.292	.323	.283	36	137	27	40	7	1	3	16	19	1	0	1	41	2	1	.423	.380
Williams, Christian	L-R	6-3	210	9-14-94	.301	.241	.321	29	113	11	34	5	0	2	11	15	1	0	0	44	0	1	.398	.368
Young, Chavez	B-R	6-0	195	7-8-97	.247	.203	.258	111	401	53	99	17	4	6	43	35	6	2	3	102	24	11	.354	.315

Pitching	B-T	HT	WT	DOB	W	L	ERA	G	GS	CG	SV	IP	H	R	ER	HR	BB	SO	AVG	vLH	vRH	K/9	BB/9
Adam, Jason	R-R	6-4	225	8-4-91	0	0	0.00	1	1	0	0	2	0	0	0	0	1	3	.000	.000	.000	13.50	4.50
Allgeyer, Nick	L-L	6-3	210	2-3-96	10	6	3.95	23	22	0	0	118	113	57	52	10	29	104	.247	.209	.262	7.91	2.21
Borucki, Ryan	L-L	6-4	215	3-31-94	0	0	0.00	1	1	0	0	4	1	0	0	0	0	4	.083	.000	.143	9.00	0.00
Buchholz, Clay	L-R	6-3	190	8-14-84	0	0	2.25	1	1	0	0	4	4	1	1	0	0	7	.250	.273	.200	15.75	0.00
Buffo, Maverik	R-R	6-2	200	9-15-95	0	2	6.16	11	1	0	1	19	23	15	13	2	12	16	.307	.368	.243	7.58	5.68
Burland, Gage	R-R	6-2	195	6-27-95	1	0	16.88	3	0	0	0	3	6	5	5	0	2	4	.462	.250	.800	13.50	6.75
Castillo, Maximo	R-R	6-2	256	5-4-99	11	5	2.69	24	24	0	0	130	115	46	39	8	28	114	.235	.207	.263	7.87	1.93
Cheshire, Jonathan	L-R	6-1	185	11-15-94	2	0	2.84	4	0	0	1	6	6	2	2	0	4	4	.261	.400	.154	5.68	5.68
Dillon, Justin	R-R	6-3	225	9-5-93	5	1	3.90	13	11	0	0	67	66	31	29	9	13	61	.262	.221	.295	8.19	1.75
Ellenbest, Mike	R-R	6-4	220	8-20-94	1	4	2.42	22	1	0	2	48	49	19	13	0	24	35	.272	.256	.287	6.52	4.47
Finfrock, Cre	B-R	5-11	185	6-26-96	0	0	0.00	1	0	0	1	1	1	0	0	0	0	2	.250	.500	.000	18.00	0.00
Harris, Jon	R-R	6-4	175	10-16-93	0	1	23.63	1	1	0	0	3	9	7	7	3	1	6	.563	.250	.667	20.25	3.38
Jimenez, Dany	R-R	6-3	190	12-23-93	5	1	3.55	20	0	0	4	25	23	11	10	2	9	47	.240	.163	.319	16.70	3.20
Jimenez, Emerson	R-R	6-1	160	12-16-94	6	1	2.84	38	0	0	3	57	52	28	18	1	24	39	.243	.283	.209	6.16	3.79
Johnston, Kyle	R-R	6-0	190	7-17-96	1	3	10.07	6	4	0	0	20	18	23	22	2	20	13	.273	.200	.355	5.95	9.15
Larkins, Turner	R-R	6-3	200	11-6-95	5	5	4.13	23	13	0	0	89	107	44	41	5	25	76	.296	.280	.312	7.66	2.52
Law, Connor	R-R	6-4	220	4-27-94	1	0	2.86	31	0	0	4	44	46	15	14	0	24	51	.272	.273	.272	10.43	4.91
Merryweather, Julian	R-R	6-4	215	10-14-91	0	0	9.00	1	1	0	0	4	5	4	4	1	2	4	.294	.250	.333	9.00	4.50
Murray, Joey	R-R	6-1	195	9-23-96	5	2	1.71	12	11	0	1	63	40	12	12	3	19	77	.179	.202	.160	11.00	2.71
Ouellette, William	R-R	6-1	195	6-30-93	1	0	2.30	9	0	0	0	16	10	5	4	2	1	20	.172	.160	.182	11.49	0.57
Pearson, Nate	R-R	6-6	245	8-20-96	3	0	0.86	6	6	0	0	21	10	2	2	2	3	35	.139	.147	.132	15.00	1.29
Phelps, David	R-R	6-3	200	10-9-86	0	0	0.00	1	0	0	0	1	1	0	0	0	0	1	.250	.000	.333	9.00	0.00
Rackoski, Sean	R-R	6-7	225	5-12-95	0	0	2.30	8	0	0	0	16	12	4	4	1	2	19	.207	.231	.188	10.34	1.15
Ramirez, Neil	R-R	6-4	215	5-25-89	0	0	0.00	1	0	0	0	1	0	0	0	0	0	1	.000	.000	.000	9.00	0.00
Rees, Jackson	R-R	6-4	210	7-30-94	3	2	0.99	25	0	0	7	36	27	12	4	1	11	44	.205	.270	.145	10.90	2.72
Sanderson, Blake	L-R	6-0	176	11-1-95	0	0	16.20	1	0	0	0	2	3	3	3	0	2	1	.375	.500	.250	5.40	10.80
Shannon, Matt	R-R	6-3	220	5-31-95	0	3	4.74	20	0	0	4	25	33	16	13	1	11	30	.314	.304	.322	10.58	4.01
Spraker, Graham	R-R	6-3	200	3-19-95	7	5	2.90	24	16	1	1	109	99	37	35	6	28	74	.247	.292	.204	6.13	2.32

	B-T	HT	WT	DOB	W	L	ERA	G	GS	CG	SV	IP	H	R	ER	HR	BB	SO	AVG	vLH	vRH	K/9	BB/9
Tepera, Ryan	R-R	6-1	195	11-3-87	0	0	0.00	2	1	0	0	2	0	0	0	0	1	2	.000	.000	.000	9.00	4.50
Townsend, Grant	R-R	6-0	190	8-9-97	1	0	7.20	1	1	0	0	5	5	4	4	0	2	2	.278	.167	.500	3.60	3.60
Watson, Troy	R-R	6-2	180	6-11-97	0	0	6.00	1	1	0	0	6	10	4	4	0	2	3	.400	.357	.455	4.50	3.00
Weatherly, Kyle	R-R	6-4	200	10-3-94	4	4	3.81	37	0	0	1	59	52	28	25	3	33	62	.234	.200	.260	9.46	5.03
Wilson, Brad	R-R	6-1	260	8-15-96	1	3	1.42	28	0	0	9	38	22	13	6	0	10	49	.162	.150	.171	11.61	2.37
Winckowski, Josh	R-R	6-4	202	6-28-98	4	5	3.19	11	10	0	1	54	48	24	19	5	17	37	.232	.236	.227	6.20	2.85
Woods Richardson, Simeon	R-R	6-3	210	9-27-00	3	2	2.54	6	6	0	0	28	18	8	8	1	7	29	.182	.163	.196	9.21	2.22
Zeuch, T.J.	R-R	6-7	225	8-1-95	0	0	4.15	2	2	0	0	9	7	4	4	0	2	12	.206	.357	.100	12.46	2.08

Fielding

Catcher	PCT	G	PO	A	E	DP	PB
Adams	.989	19	157	18	2	0	2
Bec	.986	51	386	25	6	1	7
Hernandez	1.000	4	22	2	0	0	1
Kirk	.991	68	501	59	5	2	6

First Base	PCT	G	PO	A	E	DP
Clemens	.985	66	478	36	8	55
Large	1.000	2	7	1	0	1
Noda	.992	49	350	23	3	38
Williams	.994	20	152	6	1	8

Second Base	PCT	G	PO	A	E	DP
Cardona	.000	1	0	0	0	0
Large	.857	7	2	10	2	0
Navarro	1.000	6	7	10	0	1
Podkul	1.000	7	10	19	0	6

	PCT	G	PO	A	E	DP
Taylor	.969	91	143	201	11	47
Vicuna	.955	13	23	41	3	10
Warmoth	.984	14	23	37	1	10

Third Base	PCT	G	PO	A	E	DP
Bec	.000	1	0	0	1	0
Brito	.714	2	1	4	2	1
De Los Santos	.000	1	0	0	0	0
Guerrero Jr.	1.000	4	1	3	0	0
Large	.963	64	44	85	5	8
Navarro	.974	22	16	21	1	1
Podkul	.955	30	16	47	3	5
Taylor	.947	13	5	13	1	1
Vicuna	1.000	5	2	13	0	0

Shortstop	PCT	G	PO	A	E	DP
Bichette	.778	3	2	5	2	1
Brito	1.000	1	3	5	0	1

	PCT	G	PO	A	E	DP
Cardona	1.000	3	2	7	0	2
De Los Santos	.846	2	2	9	2	3
Navarro	.966	13	25	31	2	12
Taylor	.913	4	6	15	2	5
Vicuna	.943	94	126	222	21	46
Warmoth	.987	21	27	50	1	8

Outfield	PCT	G	PO	A	E	DP
Davis	1.000	2	3	0	0	0
Noda	.978	53	88	3	2	0
Obeso	.990	52	97	5	1	0
Orimoloye	.971	83	157	8	5	3
Pompey	1.000	3	5	0	0	0
Pruitt	1.000	20	38	1	0	0
Steinmetz	1.000	3	8	0	0	0
Stevenson	1.000	85	173	19	0	3
Young	.988	108	240	13	3	0

LANSING LUGNUTS
MIDWEST LEAGUE
LOW CLASS A

Batting	B-T	HT	WT	DOB	AVG	vLH	vRH	G	AB	R	H	2B	3B	HR	RBI	BB	HBP	SH	SF	SO	SB	CS	SLG	OBP
Abbadessa, Dominic	R-R	5-10	185	12-8-97	.189	.300	.157	26	90	11	17	3	2	0	5	12	3	0	0	28	3	3	.267	.305
Aiello, Johnny	R-R	6-2	215	2-14-97	.258	.296	.243	77	260	35	67	18	0	8	32	25	14	0	2	96	4	2	.419	.352
Brito, Ronny	R-R	6-0	165	3-22-99	.200	.200	.200	5	15	1	3	1	0	0	0	0	0	0	0	7	0	0	.267	.200
Brodt, Jake	R-R	6-5	235	1-23-96	.238	.202	.249	96	349	38	83	14	3	13	45	45	4	0	2	133	12	4	.407	.330
Conine, Griffin	L-R	6-1	200	7-11-97	.283	.259	.292	80	304	59	86	19	2	22	64	38	5	0	1	125	2	0	.576	.371
Contreras, Mc Gregory	R-R	6-1	170	8-30-98	.211	.258	.193	32	114	13	24	6	2	1	11	9	0	1	0	51	0	1	.325	.268
Danner, Hagen	R-R	6-2	210	9-30-98	.170	.241	.141	80	271	31	46	8	5	12	33	27	5	0	4	96	4	1	.369	.254
De Los Santos, Luis	R-R	6-1	160		.255	.227	.196	25	78	11	16	4	1	0	2	6	0	0	0	19	1	2	.282	.262
Gold, Ryan	L-R	5-11	215	10-10-97	.239	.229	.242	99	368	35	88	25	5	7	51	26	8	1	3	87	3	2	.391	.301
Groshans, Jordan	R-R	6-3	205	11-10-99	.337	.409	.312	23	83	12	28	6	0	2	13	13	0	0	0	21	1	1	.482	.427
Hiraldo, Miguel	R-R	5-11	170	9-5-00	.250	.000	.333	1	4	0	1	0	1	0	0	0	0	0	0	0	0	0	.750	.250
Jimenez, Leonardo	R-R	5-11	160	5-17-01	.167	.500	.000	2	6	1	1	0	0	0	0	0	0	0	0	2	0	0	.167	.167
Kirk, Alejandro	R-R	5-9	220	11-6-98	.299	.200	.346	21	77	15	23	6	1	3	8	18	0	0	1	8	1	0	.520	.427
Kirwer, Tanner	R-R	6-0	180	3-15-96	.260	.318	.241	52	181	28	47	5	2	1	11	20	6	2	0	49	18	2	.326	.353
Lantigua, Rafael	R-R	5-8	153	4-28-98	.254	.213	.265	95	335	36	85	16	6	4	31	23	2	0	4	58	9	8	.373	.302
Lopez, Jesus	R-R	5-11	170	10-5-96	.625	.500	.667	3	8	1	5	1	0	0	2	1	0	0	0	0	0	0	.750	.667
Lopez, Otto	R-R	5-10	160	10-1-98	.324	.294	.333	108	447	61	145	20	5	5	50	34	2	4	5	63	20	15	.425	.371
Moreno, Gabriel	R-R	5-11	160	2-14-00	.280	.317	.267	82	307	47	86	17	5	12	52	22	7	0	5	38	7	1	.485	.337
Neal, Jc	R-R	6-3	220	1-11-97	.238	.269	.226	84	282	38	67	7	1	4	30	19	2	2	2	74	16	9	.312	.289
Podkul, Nick	R-R	6-1	200	4-11-97	.254	.304	.235	57	201	32	51	13	2	2	20	33	5	0	2	41	12	1	.368	.369
Pruitt, Reggie	R-R	6-0	180	5-7-97	.273	.238	.284	88	337	55	92	12	8	1	22	40	3	1	3	101	40	13	.365	.353
Rodriguez, Yorman	R-R	5-10	160	7-23-97	.344	.316	.351	22	96	17	33	7	2	1	19	2	0	0	1	6	2	1	.490	.354
Severino, Jesus	R-R	6-1	175	6-11-97	.125	.182	.103	12	40	2	5	1	1	0	2	4	0	0	0	11	0	0	.200	.205
Steinmetz, Hunter	L-L	5-9	175	12-13-96	.216	.178	.225	75	236	38	51	11	2	2	25	30	4	2	3	61	14	4	.305	.311
Talley, LJ	L-R	6-2	203	5-7-97	.191	.088	.215	52	183	25	35	6	1	6	27	18	2	1	4	39	1	0	.333	.266

Pitching	B-T	HT	WT	DOB	W	L	ERA	G	GS	CG	SV	IP	H	R	ER	HR	BB	SO	AVG	vLH	vRH	K/9	BB/9
De Paula, Juan	R-R	6-3	165	9-22-97	3	6	9.17	14	10	0	0	52	77	57	53	3	34	32	.348	.385	.308	5.54	5.88
Espada, Jose	R-R	6-0	170	2-22-97	0	0	4.70	6	0	0	0	8	7	5	4	2	1	9	.233	.400	.150	10.57	1.17
Finfrock, Cre	B-R	5-11	185	6-26-96	1	1	3.99	33	0	0	17	38	30	18	17	5	16	50	.216	.215	.216	11.74	3.76
Gold, Ryan	L-R	5-11	215	10-10-97	0	0	0.00	1	0	0	0	1	2	3	0	0	2	0	.400	.500	.333	0.00	18.00
Hiatt, Josh	R-R	5-11	195	3-27-97	2	3	3.64	25	8	0	1	77	73	40	31	4	37	61	.253	.260	.247	7.16	4.34
Johnson, Cobi	R-R	6-4	225	11-6-95	3	9	5.24	25	16	0	0	100	84	66	58	13	56	95	.228	.210	.243	8.58	5.06
Law, Connor	R-R	6-4	220	4-27-94	1	0	0.00	4	0	0	1	7	7	1	0	0	1	13	.259	.333	.111	16.71	1.29
McAffer, Will	R-R	6-2	205	5-30-97	4	3	4.34	31	0	0	1	56	42	30	27	4	39	70	.200	.250	.125	11.25	6.27
McGuire, Andy	R-R	6-0	178	12-2-94	0	1	3.98	11	0	0	0	20	22	10	9	0	11	8	.286	.241	.313	3.54	4.87
Miller, Troy	R-R	6-4	210	2-13-97	6	8	4.81	23	22	0	0	103	108	67	55	10	50	75	.271	.249	.295	6.55	4.37
Murray, Joey	R-R	6-2	195	9-23-96	3	1	3.82	6	6	0	0	31	28	15	13	3	12	40	.239	.188	.313	11.74	3.52
Nunez, Juan	R-R	6-2	185	1-23-96	0	1	5.40	16	0	0	1	22	23	15	13	5	8	27	.267	.279	.256	11.22	3.32
Pardinho, Eric	R-R	5-10	155	1-5-01	1	1	2.41	7	7	0	0	34	29	10	9	1	13	30	.240	.214	.262	8.02	3.48
Pascoe, Mike	R-R	5-10	180	1-17-98	1	2	5.34	21	0	0	0	32	30	23	19	6	23	29	.246	.232	.258	8.16	6.47
Paulino, Naswell	L-L	5-11	160	4-17-00	1	0	0.00	1	0	0	0	2	0	0	0	0	0	2	.400	.500	.333	18.00	0.00
Pondler, Randy	L-L	6-2	160	11-8-96	0	0	5.25	6	0	0	1	12	19	8	7	3	5	12	.352	.500	.278	9.00	3.75

Name	B-T	HT	WT	DOB	W	L	ERA	G	GS	CG	SV	IP	H	R	ER	HR	BB	SO	AVG	vLH	vRH	K/9	BB/9
Pulido, Joey	R-R	5-10	185	9-25-95	2	4	6.08	23	0	0	0	40	41	29	27	7	20	37	.268	.268	.268	8.33	4.50
Rackoski, Sean	R-R	6-7	225	5-12-95	2	2	2.87	28	0	0	5	47	36	18	15	1	18	49	.207	.188	.223	9.38	3.45
Rees, Jackson	R-R	6-4	210	7-30-94	2	0	0.36	14	0	0	2	25	13	3	1	0	4	44	.149	.081	.200	15.63	1.42
Reyes, Marcus	L-L	5-11	180	3-10-95	7	3	2.56	39	0	0	2	77	73	30	22	2	18	56	.248	.241	.251	6.52	2.09
Rodning, Brody	R-L	6-1	185	1-14-96	2	0	2.08	7	0	0	1	9	7	3	2	0	1	9	.219	.200	.227	9.35	1.04
Severino, Jesus	R-R	6-1	175	6-11-97	0	0	0.00	1	0	0	0	0	0	0	0	0	0	0	.000	--	.000	0.00	0.00
Stadler, Fitz	R-R	6-9	245	4-2-97	6	7	4.92	27	16	0	0	106	121	68	58	5	40	94	.289	.284	.292	7.98	3.40
Watson, Troy	R-R	6-2	180	6-11-97	6	5	3.14	19	15	1	0	92	78	39	32	5	37	46	.234	.234	.234	4.52	3.63
Watts, Justin	R-R	6-3	215	9-8-93	0	0	3.21	11	0	0	1	14	10	9	5	1	6	18	.189	.217	.167	11.57	3.86
Winckowski, Josh	R-R	6-4	202	6-28-98	6	3	2.32	13	13	0	0	74	62	20	19	3	26	71	.230	.260	.201	8.67	3.18
Wymer, Sean	R-R	6-1	205	3-19-97	9	11	5.43	28	26	1	0	138	173	89	83	11	36	93	.311	.282	.334	6.08	2.35

Fielding

Catcher	PCT	G	PO	A	E	DP	PB
Danner	.983	23	159	17	3	3	9
Gold	.982	47	359	32	7	4	2
Kirk	.994	17	159	14	1	2	0
Lopez	1.000	1	10	1	0	0	0
Moreno	.993	54	390	56	3	1	11

First Base	PCT	G	PO	A	E	DP
Brodt	.997	91	741	49	2	70
Danner	1.000	21	152	7	0	15
Gold	.988	10	74	9	1	6
Podkul	1.000	2	6	0	0	0
Rodriguez	.994	18	150	14	1	19
Talley	1.000	3	16	0	0	0

Second Base	PCT	G	PO	A	E	DP
Brito	1.000	1	1	0	0	0

	PCT	G	PO	A	E	DP
Hiraldo	.800	1	3	5	2	2
Lantigua	.970	55	99	164	8	39
Lopez	.956	19	31	55	4	13
Podkul	.980	25	30	66	2	7
Talley	.967	46	73	131	7	26

Third Base	PCT	G	PO	A	E	DP
Aiello	.961	75	64	107	7	17
Brito	.000	1	0	0	0	0
Brodt	.000	1	0	0	0	0
De Los Santos	.952	9	4	16	1	0
Lantigua	.953	18	15	26	2	5
Podkul	.968	30	16	44	2	2
Severino	.917	11	5	17	2	0

Shortstop	PCT	G	PO	A	E	DP
Brito	.714	3	1	4	2	0
De Los Santos	.981	15	18	34	1	13

	PCT	G	PO	A	E	DP
Groshans	.909	20	27	43	7	6
Jimenez	1.000	2	1	2	0	1
Lantigua	.963	23	21	56	3	18
Lopez	.925	82	113	194	25	41
Podkul	1.000	2	2	1	0	0

Outfield	PCT	G	PO	A	E	DP
Abbadessa	.949	25	35	2	2	0
Brodt	1.000	1	3	1	0	0
Conine	.950	74	144	9	8	3
Contreras	.977	28	39	4	1	1
Kirwer	.968	49	87	3	3	0
Lantigua	1.000	1	1	0	0	0
Lopez	1.000	12	20	0	0	0
Neal	.977	82	163	8	4	1
Pruitt	.953	85	181	2	9	0
Steinmetz	.981	72	152	5	3	1

VANCOUVER CANADIANS

SHORT SEASON

NORTHWEST LEAGUE

Batting	B-T	HT	WT	DOB	AVG	vLH	vRH	G	AB	R	H	2B	3B	HR	RBI	BB	HBP	SH	SF	SO	SB	CS	SLG	OBP
Abbadessa, Dominic	R-R	5-10	185	12-8-97	.184	.125	.195	44	147	15	27	1	2	0	8	12	1	3	0	30	10	2	.218	.250
Brito, Ronny	R-R	6-0	165	3-22-99	.216	.298	.189	56	190	19	41	6	1	4	16	21	0	0	1	82	0	2	.321	.293
Clarke, Philip	L-R	5-11	190	3-24-98	.257	.276	.252	37	144	24	37	5	0	2	16	21	2	0	0	21	1	0	.333	.359
Contreras, Mc Gregory	R-R	6-1	170	8-30-98	.211	.220	.208	63	251	26	53	12	3	3	29	11	6	1	1	88	3	3	.319	.260
De Los Santos, Luis	R-R	6-1	160	6-9-98	.215	.213	.216	59	228	24	49	12	0	2	21	11	2	1	2	43	3	1	.294	.255
Eden, Cameron	R-R	6-1	181	3-31-98	.220	.220	.220	56	218	22	48	7	2	1	11	19	3	0	0	56	8	2	.284	.292
Horwitz, Spencer	L-R	6-0	190	11-14-97	.191	.200	.189	9	42	6	8	1	0	1	3	1	1	0	0	6	0	0	.286	.227
Lopez, Jesus	R-R	5-11	170	10-5-96	.256	.297	.240	36	137	13	35	9	0	1	15	6	2	1	4	27	1	0	.343	.289
Morris, Tanner	L-R	6-2	190	7-30-97	.246	.156	.267	64	240	37	59	16	1	2	28	49	5	0	0	56	4	2	.346	.384
Ramos, Adrian	R-R	5-10	160	6-18-98	.104	.048	.117	42	115	16	12	1	1	1	14	25	5	1	0	40	9	4	.157	.290
Robertson, Will	L-L	6-2	215	12-26-97	.268	.261	.269	61	228	33	61	11	1	6	33	31	4	0	1	49	1	2	.404	.365
Rodriguez, Yorman	R-R	5-10	160	7-23-97	.383	.514	.320	40	157	25	58	6	2	4	21	9	2	0	2	12	2	2	.510	.406
Schneider, Davis	R-R	5-10	190	1-26-99	.146	.000	.178	17	55	2	8	3	0	0	7	8	2	0	1	18	0	1	.200	.273
Schwecke, Trevor	R-R	6-1	185	12-18-97	.231	.227	.232	61	221	24	51	10	1	2	23	34	2	1	2	68	5	3	.312	.336
Sloniger, Ryan	L-R	5-11	200	3-20-97	.255	.286	.250	13	51	5	13	4	0	1	11	5	0	0	0	14	0	0	.392	.321
Wright, Brett	R-R	6-0	210	8-5-95	.192	.241	.178	41	130	12	25	8	0	2	15	18	1	0	3	35	3	2	.300	.333

Pitching	B-T	HT	WT	DOB	W	L	ERA	G	GS	CG	SV	IP	H	R	ER	HR	BB	SO	AVG	vLH	vRH	K/9	BB/9
Almonte, Josh	R-R	6-3	210	1-28-94	1	2	5.32	20	0	0	1	24	15	17	14	0	29	32	.179	.217	.164	12.17	11.03
Burland, Gage	R-R	6-2	195	6-27-95	0	2	7.32	18	0	0	0	20	28	19	16	0	15	24	.337	.310	.352	10.98	6.86
Caracci, Parker	R-R	6-0	205	9-13-96	2	4	3.03	21	0	0	0	30	25	13	10	0	19	36	.229	.260	.203	10.92	5.76
Castaneda, Felipe	R-R	6-1	194	1-4-00	0	0	9.00	1	0	0	0	2	3	4	2	0	4	2	.333	.500	.286	9.00	18.00
Cuevas, Adams	R-R	6-0	192	2-2-96	0	1	7.56	5	0	0	0	8	7	7	7	1	3	7	.226	.333	.200	7.56	3.24
Diaz, Juan	L-L	6-0	175	6-19-98	3	5	4.31	12	12	0	0	63	64	36	30	5	18	45	.263	.366	.243	6.46	2.59
DiCesare, Jared	R-R	6-0	185	4-21-98	2	0	3.67	7	2	0	0	27	26	12	11	5	5	23	.248	.300	.215	7.67	1.67
Fraze, Nick	R-R	6-3	180	10-24-97	1	1	2.12	12	0	0	0	34	21	8	8	1	10	27	.178	.283	.111	7.15	2.65
Garcia, Winder	R-R	5-10	165	10-11-01	0	0	1.80	1	1	0	0	5	4	1	1	1	2	4	.222	.286	.182	7.20	3.60
Gaston, William	R-R	6-5	190	5-19-96	3	3	3.23	13	5	0	0	47	43	24	17	4	32	40	.239	.220	.255	7.61	6.08
Gillingham, Luke	L-L	6-3	200	3-4-94	3	1	2.65	24	0	0	3	34	22	11	10	3	14	46	.182	.194	.178	12.18	3.71
Huckaby, Kyle	R-L	5-10	190	6-16-96	0	1	0.00	1	0	0	0	1	2	2	0	0	2	1	.333	.000	.500	9.00	18.00
Huffman, Grayson	L-L	6-2	195	5-6-95	3	1	3.86	25	0	0	4	33	31	15	14	0	20	41	.256	.238	.266	11.30	5.51
Kloffenstein, Adam	R-R	6-5	243	8-25-00	4	4	2.24	13	13	0	0	64	47	23	16	4	23	64	.205	.149	.261	8.95	3.22
Manoah, Alek	R-R	6-6	260	1-9-98	0	1	2.65	6	6	0	0	17	13	5	5	1	5	27	.213	.292	.162	14.29	2.65
McGuire, Andy	R-R	6-0	178	12-2-94	0	1	3.91	12	0	0	1	23	22	10	10	0	7	12	.259	.297	.229	4.70	2.74
Medina, Nicolas	L-L	5-10	160	1-15-00	0	0	6.03	22	0	0	0	34	45	28	23	4	18	35	.310	.379	.293	9.17	4.72
Nolan, Alex	R-R	6-4	225	3-21-96	1	3	3.22	12	6	0	0	59	60	24	21	5	11	35	.264	.227	.292	5.37	1.69
Nunez, Juan	R-R	6-2	185	1-23-96	0	0	0.00	2	0	0	0	4	4	0	0	1	3	.250	.000	.333	6.75	2.25
Pascoe, Mike	R-R	5-10	180	1-17-98	0	2	8.66	18	0	0	1	20	23	18	17	1	20	23	.311	.448	.222	11.72	10.19
Ponce, Gabriel	R-R	6-2	205	4-29-99	0	3	4.66	13	10	0	0	39	44	24	20	4	16	36	.288	.229	.314	8.38	3.72
Pondler, Randy	L-L	6-2	160	11-8-96	3	3	7.83	7	0	0	0	23	30	22	20	3	13	16	.333	.409	.309	6.26	5.09

	B-T	HT	WT	DOB	W	L	ERA	G	GS	CG	SV	IP	H	R	ER	HR	BB	SO	AVG	vLH	vRH	K/9	BB/9
Pulido, Joey	R-R	5-10	185	9-25-95	0	0	0.00	2	0	0	0	2	2	0	0	0	0	2	.222	.000	.500	7.71	0.00
Quinones, Luis	R-R	6-0	205	7-2-97	2	2	2.97	10	4	0	0	30	16	12	10	2	17	47	.155	.119	.180	13.95	5.04
Townsend, Grant	R-R	6-0	190	8-9-97	2	3	3.56	8	7	0	0	30	24	13	12	2	13	39	.224	.275	.194	11.57	3.86

Fielding

C: Clarke 25, Lopez 9, Rodriguez 6, Sloniger 8, Wright 30. **1B:** Brito 8, Horwitz 6, Rodriguez 33, Schwecke 26, Wright 7. **2B:** Brito 12, De Los Santos 14, Eden 3, Horwitz 2, Morris 29, Schneider 10, Schwecke 8. **3B:** Brito 20, De Los Santos 15, Eden 3, Lopez 23, Morris 1, Schneider 3, Schwecke 14. **SS:** Brito 11, De Los Santos 26, Eden 1, Morris 29, Schwecke 10. **OF:** Abbadessa 41, Contreras 53, Eden 44, Ramos 39, Robertson 54.

BLUEFIELD BLUE JAYS
APPALACHIAN LEAGUE
ROOKIE ADVANCED

Batting	B-T	HT	WT	DOB	AVG	vLH	vRH	G	AB	R	H	2B	3B	HR	RBI	BB	HBP	SH	SF	SO	SB	CS	SLG	OBP
Ammons, Justin	L-R	5-10	180	3-16-98	.382	.474	.361	25	102	21	39	11	0	0	8	9	2	0	0	12	3	4	.490	.443
Barger, Addison	L-R	6-0	175	11-12-99	.283	.091	.333	13	53	13	15	2	0	2	8	5	0	0	0	13	0	2	.434	.345
Berroa, Steward	B-R	5-10	178	6-5-99	.236	.205	.248	50	161	25	38	7	1	2	13	28	0	0	0	54	14	5	.329	.349
Bradley, Scotty	L-R	6-2	207	4-6-97	.192	.182	.196	36	125	15	24	4	0	2	15	16	1	0	1	40	0	0	.272	.287
Camacho, Angel	R-R	6-3	200	6-13-97	.252	.207	.267	29	115	13	29	5	0	3	18	9	3	0	2	30	0	1	.374	.318
Daniels, D.J.	R-R	6-3	205	12-17-97	.210	.125	.245	41	138	18	29	9	1	7	21	12	2	0	1	63	2	1	.442	.281
Guerra, Andres	R-R	5-11	175	6-3-97	.215	.280	.195	30	107	15	23	4	0	1	14	11	4	0	0	34	0	1	.280	.312
Hiraldo, Miguel	R-R	5-11	170	9-5-00	.300	.370	.279	56	237	43	71	20	1	7	37	14	4	0	1	36	11	3	.481	.348
Horwitz, Spencer	L-R	6-0	190	11-14-97	.330	.311	.335	51	206	31	68	18	1	3	49	23	1	0	3	24	5	0	.471	.395
Jimenez, Leonardo	R-R	5-11	160	5-17-01	.298	.217	.320	56	215	34	64	13	2	0	22	21	7	1	1	42	2	1	.377	.377
Morales, Anthony	B-R	6-0	175	11-13-98	.153	.120	.170	21	72	7	11	3	0	0	2	5	1	0	0	16	0	1	.194	.218
Morris, PK	L-L	6-1	195	11-30-98	.253	.283	.243	52	190	37	48	7	0	8	43	35	2	0	3	54	2	0	.416	.370
Reyes, Joseph	B-R	6-3	195	1-24-98	.150	.121	.158	45	153	21	23	2	0	8	21	21	7	0	1	56	2	2	.320	.280
Rivera, Eric	R-R	6-0	185	9-19-97	.284	.279	.285	53	208	42	59	6	4	0	19	30	4	2	4	28	7	0	.351	.378
Schneider, Davis	R-R	5-10	190	1-26-99	.313	.333	.306	34	131	24	41	13	0	6	24	14	2	0	3	39	0	1	.550	.380
Sloniger, Ryan	L-R	5-11	200	3-20-97	.327	.294	.333	30	107	22	35	3	1	9	20	11	3	0	0	21	0	1	.626	.405

Pitching	B-T	HT	WT	DOB	W	L	ERA	G	GS	CG	SV	IP	H	R	ER	HR	BB	SO	AVG	vLH	vRH	K/9	BB/9
Acosta, Juan	R-R	6-2	185	4-5-00	3	2	7.49	16	0	0	1	34	40	34	28	9	16	28	.288	.303	.270	7.49	4.28
Alvarez, Luis	R-R	6-0	170	2-8-00	3	1	2.36	14	0	0	1	27	21	10	7	1	7	17	.212	.220	.204	5.74	2.36
Caballero, Elixon	R-R	5-9	160	7-9-00	0	0	2.70	1	1	0	0	3	1	1	1	1	0	2	.091	.000	.125	5.40	0.00
Castaneda, Felipe	R-R	6-1	194	1-4-00	3	4	5.10	11	10	0	0	48	48	30	27	3	26	41	.267	.261	.272	7.74	4.91
Concepcion, Jol	R-R	6-5	195	9-17-98	2	3	3.18	9	9	0	0	34	35	15	12	3	9	31	.257	.175	.317	8.21	2.38
Cuevas, Adams	R-R	6-0	192	2-2-96	2	2	3.45	12	0	0	1	31	29	16	12	5	9	42	.228	.254	.196	12.06	2.59
De Paula, Juan	R-R	6-3	165	9-22-97	0	0	0.00	1	1	0	0	4	1	0	0	0	2	3	.077	.000	.125	6.75	4.50
DiCesare, Jared	R-R	6-3	185	4-21-98	2	1	3.60	4	2	0	0	15	15	6	6	0	0	12	.263	.258	.269	7.20	0.00
Estrada, Lazaro	R-R	5-10	180	4-24-99	2	3	5.85	11	9	0	0	48	58	37	31	9	10	39	.293	.315	.280	7.36	1.89
Havekost, Austin	R-R	6-3	215	7-22-96	2	0	0.60	10	0	0	2	15	8	5	1	0	4	17	.143	.160	.129	10.20	2.40
Hernandez, Roither	R-R	6-4	185	3-5-98	4	4	5.56	12	12	0	0	44	48	42	27	3	21	42	.270	.202	.391	8.66	4.33
Hinojosa, Yunior	R-R	6-2	190	12-21-99	1	1	5.10	17	0	0	3	30	28	24	17	2	15	27	.246	.309	.186	8.10	4.50
Huckaby, Kyle	R-L	5-10	190	6-16-96	1	1	5.11	18	0	0	3	25	22	14	14	2	11	25	.242	.129	.300	9.12	4.01
Magdaniel, Ronald	R-R	6-1	170	11-15-96	0	0	10.80	2	0	0	0	2	3	4	2	0	4	1	.429	.600	.000	5.40	21.60
McInvale, Andrew	R-R	6-5	195	11-3-96	1	0	6.23	3	0	0	0	9	12	6	6	1	5	8	.343	.526	.125	8.31	5.19
Melean, Alejandro	R-R	6-0	175	10-11-00	1	1	5.57	7	6	0	0	21	20	18	13	2	15	25	.250	.242	.255	10.71	6.43
Ovando, Aldo	R-R	6-5	195	4-6-97	1	5	8.89	18	0	0	1	26	34	31	26	3	17	18	.330	.256	.375	6.15	5.81
Paulino, Naswell	L-L	5-11	160	4-17-00	1	1	4.05	11	5	0	2	40	48	24	18	4	17	34	.284	.261	.293	7.65	3.83
Quinones, Luis	R-R	6-0	205	7-2-97	0	0	2.84	2	0	0	1	6	1	2	2	0	2	10	.050	.000	.091	14.21	2.84
Ramirez, Gaudy	R-R	6-2	175	9-11-97	1	1	10.64	8	1	0	0	11	16	18	13	4	11	15	.327	.429	.191	12.27	9.00
Reyes, Meliton	R-R	6-2	180	7-31-97	0	1	4.93	17	0	0	1	35	41	29	19	6	7	16	.299	.258	.333	4.15	1.82
Robbins, Jimmy	L-L	6-3	175	12-22-97	0	2	4.50	4	3	0	0	12	16	12	6	1	3	14	.314	.389	.273	10.50	2.25
Ryan, Sam	R-R	6-3	205	9-22-98	1	1	6.31	11	8	0	0	41	57	38	29	4	8	35	.330	.379	.269	7.62	1.74
Valdez, Julian	R-R	6-2	192	12-13-98	0	0	1.19	9	0	0	0	23	8	3	3	2	7	17	.108	.143	.077	6.75	2.78

Fielding

C: Guerra 30, Morales 19, Sloniger 20. **1B:** Bradley 7, Horwitz 20, Morris 40. **2B:** Barger 3, Berroa 1, Hiraldo 29, Jimenez 17, Schneider 19. **3B:** Barger 4, Camacho 24, Jimenez 1, Reyes 27, Schneider 15. **SS:** Barger 6, Hiraldo 22, Jimenez 39, Schneider 1. **OF:** Ammons 23, Berroa 48, Bradley 17, Daniels 35, Horwitz 18, Reyes 16, Rivera 52.

GCL BLUE JAYS
GULF COAST LEAGUE
ROOKIE

Batting	B-T	HT	WT	DOB	AVG	vLH	vRH	G	AB	R	H	2B	3B	HR	RBI	BB	HBP	SH	SF	SO	SB	CS	SLG	OBP
Acevedo, Hanley	R-R	6-0	185	9-28-99	.190	.125	.235	24	58	8	11	3	0	0	6	9	2	1	2	25	4	1	.241	.310
Alford, Anthony	R-R	6-1	215	7-20-94	.385	.667	.300	4	13	3	5	2	1	1	3	2	0	0	1	0	0	0	.923	.467
Ammons, Justin	L-R	5-10	180	3-16-98	.556	.500	.571	3	9	4	5	1	0	0	0	1	1	0	0	1	0	0	.667	.636
Brown, Dasan	R-R	6-0	185	9-25-01	.222	.154	.250	14	45	8	10	2	2	0	5	9	9	0	0	17	6	2	.356	.444
Cantwell, Patrick	R-R	6-2	210	4-10-90	.000	.000	.000	4	5	2	0	0	0	0	0	0	3	2	0	1	2	0	.000	.375
Cardona, Hugo	R-R	5-11	145	9-5-99	.229	.204	.240	41	153	34	35	6	2	0	12	20	5	3	1	40	21	3	.294	.335
Celedonio, Erickvi	L-L	6-0	169	12-15-00	.197	.208	.192	33	76	11	15	3	0	0	4	11	3	0	0	23	7	5	.237	.322
D'Orazio, Javier	R-R	6-0	170	12-28-01	.241	.324	.200	34	116	8	28	5	0	0	11	3	1	0	1	36	2	4	.285	.265
Hernandez, Jesus	R-R	6-0	175	10-30-99	.160	.125	.177	14	25	5	4	1	0	0	1	7	1	2	0	8	0	0	.200	.364
Hurtado, Pedro	R-R	5-10	178	6-29-00	.154	.125	.167	28	78	4	12	2	1	0	6	11	0	1	1	18	3	0	.205	.256
Jimenez, Geyber	R-R	5-11	194	1-17-01	.292	.182	.385	15	24	2	7	3	0	0	4	5	0	2	1	5	0	0	.417	.400

	B-T	HT	WT	DOB	AVG	vLH	vRH	G	AB	R	H	2B	3B	HR	RBI	BB	HBP	SH	SF	SO	SB	CS	SLG	OBP
Kirwer, Tanner	R-R	6-0	180	3-15-96	.167	.000	.182	4	12	4	2	1	0	0	2	3	0	0	0	3	2	0	.250	.333
Large, Cullen	B-R	6-1	175	1-22-96	.250	.000	.500	2	4	0	1	0	0	0	0	0	0	0	0	3	0	0	.250	.250
Martinez, Orelvis	R-R	6-1	188	11-19-01	.275	.302	.263	40	142	20	39	8	5	7	32	14	4	0	2	29	2	0	.549	.352
Nunez, Rainer	R-R	6-3	180	12-4-00	.173	.125	.194	39	133	21	23	6	0	3	20	12	3	0	5	32	0	4	.286	.248
Perez, Yhon	R-R	5-9	150	5-5-00	.302	.257	.328	36	96	13	29	8	0	0	15	14	2	1	0	14	7	3	.385	.402
Pompey, Dalton	B-R	6-2	200	12-11-92	.300	.500	.250	4	10	3	3	1	1	0	1	1	0	0	0	4	1	0	.600	.364
Rivas, Jose	R-R	5-9	165	9-5-00	.284	.323	.269	32	109	21	31	8	0	2	13	11	4	0	1	24	5	3	.413	.368
Rodriguez, Alberto	L-L	5-11	180	10-6-00	.301	.309	.297	47	173	19	52	13	1	2	29	19	0	0	3	32	13	2	.422	.364
Ruiz, Francisco	R-R	6-0	195	1-29-00	.219	.182	.238	15	32	6	7	4	0	0	1	4	2	1	0	12	0	0	.344	.342
Solarte, Jhon	B-R	6-0	165	12-9-00	.275	.237	.295	49	171	25	47	4	2	3	28	26	3	0	4	41	11	9	.374	.373
Zepeda, Jose	R-R	5-11	155	10-1-00	.225	.278	.208	27	71	15	16	4	0	1	15	21	2	2	2	14	6	0	.324	.406

Pitching	B-T	HT	WT	DOB	W	L	ERA	G	GS	CG	SV	IP	H	R	ER	HR	BB	SO	AVG	vLH	vRH	K/9	BB/9
Adam, Jason	R-R	6-4	225	8-4-91	0	0	0.00	2	0	0	0	1	1	0	0	0	2	1	.200	--	.200	6.75	13.50
Alvarado, Wilgenis	L-L	6-1	160	5-18-00	1	1	5.20	8	4	0	0	28	28	20	16	2	12	22	.257	.261	.256	7.16	3.90
Axford, Jason	R-R	6-5	234	4-1-83	0	0	0.00	1	1	0	0	1	0	0	0	0	1	0	.000	.000	.000	9.00	9.00
Barnes, Danny	L-R	6-1	215	10-21-89	0	0	0.00	1	0	0	0	0	0	0	0	0	1	0	.000	--	.000	9.00	0.00
Bello, Eliezer	R-R	6-5	230	2-12-99	0	2	10.97	13	0	0	3	11	9	13	13	0	19	10	.243	.333	.182	8.44	16.03
Borucki, Ryan	L-L	6-4	215	3-31-94	0	0	0.00	1	1	0	0	3	0	0	0	0	0	6	.000	.000	.000	18.00	0.00
Brito, Jose	R-R	6-1	168	9-19-99	0	2	13.97	13	0	0	1	10	10	17	15	1	19	5	.256	.143	.281	4.66	17.69
Buchholz, Clay	L-R	6-3	190	8-14-84	0	0	3.60	2	2	0	0	5	5	2	2	1	0	4	.263	.000	.455	7.20	0.00
Buffo, Maverik	R-R	6-2	200	9-15-95	0	1	3.00	3	2	0	0	6	5	2	2	0	0	8	.208	.375	.125	12.00	0.00
Caballero, Elixon	R-R	5-9	160	7-9-00	0	0	0.00	1	0	0	1	1	1	0	0	0	1	1	.333	.000	.500	13.50	13.50
Carmona, Alexis	R-R	6-4	160	3-24-01	1	1	5.81	8	5	0	0	31	44	22	20	2	9	15	.344	.321	.360	4.35	2.61
Casimiri, Jiorgeny	R-R	6-1	160	7-12-01	0	0	2.57	9	0	0	0	14	11	4	4	1	2	13	.212	.208	.214	8.36	1.29
Castro, Juanfer	R-R	6-1	175	7-22-01	0	1	1.50	7	0	0	0	12	6	5	2	0	8	9	.146	.067	.192	6.75	6.00
De Paula, Juan	R-R	6-3	165	9-22-97	0	0	3.60	2	1	0	0	5	4	2	2	1	2	5	.211	.286	.167	9.00	3.60
Dominguez, Michael	R-R	5-10	175	8-17-00	1	0	1.13	9	0	0	0	24	13	4	3	1	10	29	.153	.129	.167	10.88	3.75
Espada, Jose	R-R	6-0	170	2-22-97	0	0	0.00	4	2	0	0	4	1	0	0	0	2	4	.091	.333	.000	9.00	4.50
Garcia, Winder	R-R	5-10	165	10-11-01	2	0	3.15	5	3	0	0	20	13	8	7	1	5	18	.186	.208	.174	8.10	2.25
Govea, Ronald	R-R	6-3	175	10-10-00	0	0	13.50	3	0	0	0	2	5	3	3	2	0	2	.455	.500	.429	9.00	0.00
Harris, Jon	R-R	6-4	175	10-16-93	0	0	9.00	1	1	0	0	1	3	1	1	0	0	2	.500	.500	.500	18.00	0.00
Havekost, Austin	R-R	6-3	215	7-22-96	1	2	6.75	6	1	0	0	7	6	5	5	1	1	5	.240	.333	.188	6.75	1.35
Hernandez, Adrian	R-L	5-9	161	1-22-00	3	2	8.02	16	0	0	1	21	28	21	19	1	8	15	.326	.455	.281	6.33	3.38
Lebron, Jackxarel	R-R	6-3	175	9-8-00	2	2	11.32	7	0	0	0	10	11	14	13	1	9	7	.268	.133	.346	6.10	7.84
Maese, Justin	R-R	6-3	190	10-24-96	0	0	7.20	3	1	0	0	5	6	5	4	0	2	4	.286	.250	.308	7.20	3.60
McInvale, Andrew	R-R	6-2	195	11-3-96	0	0	6.48	4	2	0	0	8	6	6	6	2	5	10	.200	.333	.143	10.80	5.40
Mejia, Brayan	R-R	6-2	165	6-1-00	1	1	21.60	8	0	0	1	7	14	17	16	2	7	4	.424	.500	.400	5.40	9.45
Merryweather, Julian	R-R	6-4	215	10-14-91	0	0	9.00	1	1	0	0	2	4	2	2	0	0	3	.400	.667	.000	13.50	0.00
Monsion, Rafael	L-L	6-3	185	8-16-99	5	0	1.77	10	5	0	0	41	30	8	8	3	9	37	.207	.200	.209	8.19	1.99
Moreno, Santos	R-R	5-9	165	2-17-00	1	1	3.41	8	3	0	0	34	35	16	13	2	5	25	.252	.220	.265	6.55	1.31
Moreno, Williams	R-R	6-4	198	3-17-98	3	3	4.05	14	0	0	2	20	22	12	9	1	13	16	.282	.304	.273	7.20	5.85
Olivo, Miguel	R-R	6-4	188	11-19-99	1	0	0.69	11	0	0	0	13	7	1	1	0	3	12	.156	.071	.194	8.31	2.08
Pardinho, Eric	R-R	5-10	155	1-5-01	1	0	0.00	1	0	0	0	4	1	0	0	0	3	5	.091	.200	.000	11.25	6.75
Perez, Yhon	R-R	5-9	150	5-5-00	0	0	9.00	1	0	0	0	1	2	1	1	0	1	1	.400	.333	.500	9.00	9.00
Robberse, Sem	R-R	6-1	160	10-12-01	2	0	0.87	5	3	0	0	10	11	1	1	0	0	9	.275	.333	.240	7.84	0.00
Robbins, Jimmy	L-L	6-3	175	12-22-97	0	0	0.00	3	0	0	0	7	6	0	0	0	0	7	.240	.600	.150	12.86	0.00
Rodning, Brody	R-L	6-1	185	1-14-96	1	0	2.70	3	0	0	0	3	4	2	1	0	0	5	.250	.333	.231	13.50	0.00
Romano, Jordan	R-R	6-4	200	4-21-93	0	0	0.00	1	0	0	0	1	0	0	0	0	0	0	.000	.000	.000	0.00	0.00
Sanderson, Blake	L-R	6-0	176	11-1-95	0	1	1.38	5	1	0	0	13	8	3	2	0	3	16	.174	.063	.233	11.08	2.08
Shannon, Matt	R-R	6-3	220	5-31-95	1	1	0.00	2	0	0	0	3	1	2	0	0	4	4	.100	.000	.125	12.00	12.00
Sopko, Andrew	R-R	6-2	205	8-7-94	0	0	2.57	2	2	0	0	7	6	2	2	0	0	4	.222	.231	.214	5.14	0.00
Valdez, Julian	R-R	6-2	192	12-13-98	0	1	3.00	7	0	0	1	6	5	4	2	0	3	1	.238	.143	.286	1.50	4.50
Valdez, Warnel	L-L	5-10	150	3-16-99	0	1	27.00	3	0	0	0	2	5	6	6	2	1	0	.455	.333	.600	0.00	4.50
Williams, Kendall	R-R	6-6	205	8-24-00	0	0	1.13	6	5	0	0	16	6	4	2	0	7	19	.111	.120	.103	10.69	3.94

Fielding

C: Cantwell 4, D'Orazio 27, Hernandez 12, Jimenez 13, Ruiz 10. 1B: Hernandez 1, Hurtado 14, Nunez 37. 2B: Cardona 16, Hurtado 6, Perez 9, Rivas 26, Zepeda 2. 3B: Hurtado 5, Large 1, Martinez 11, Perez 13, Rivas 2, Zepeda 23. SS: Cardona 28, Martinez 26, Perez 1, Rivas 1. OF: Acevedo 23, Alford 3, Ammons 3, Brown 12, Celedonio 30, Kirwer 3, Perez 5, Pompey 2, Rodriguez 42, Solarte 42.

DSL BLUE JAYS   ROOKIE
DOMINICAN SUMMER LEAGUE

Batting	B-T	HT	WT	DOB	AVG	vLH	vRH	G	AB	R	H	2B	3B	HR	RBI	BB	HBP	SH	SF	SO	SB	CS	SLG	OBP
Astudillo, Willfrann	R-R	5-10	165	8-5-01	.239	.200	.244	47	130	22	31	3	0	1	18	17	6	0	0	16	7	1	.285	.353
Brazoban, Amell	R-R	6-2	170	10-9-01	.181	.125	.185	56	216	26	39	8	2	2	19	10	6	0	1	61	13	3	.264	.236
Callez, Leonel	R-R	5-11	165	1-25-01	.272	.250	.274	50	173	22	47	9	1	1	18	10	8	0	3	29	6	5	.353	.335
D'Orazio, Javier	R-R	6-0	170	12-28-01	.375	.333	.381	13	48	4	18	3	1	0	6	0	0	0	11	1	0	.479	.444
David, Gary	R-R	6-0	170	11-23-01	.248	.250	.247	38	105	13	26	1	0	1	10	11	4	0	0	16	1	0	.286	.342
De La Rosa, Marcos	B-R	5-11	160	1-28-02	.250	.000	.278	7	20	8	5	0	1	0	1	7	0	0	0	10	2	0	.350	.444
Fajardo, Francisco	R-R	5-10	163	5-26-00	.300	.200	.317	44	140	28	42	6	2	1	11	14	1	1	0	15	24	4	.393	.368
Gutierrez, Gustavo	R-R	5-8	150	4-17-02	.227	.143	.245	37	119	17	27	3	2	1	11	10	3	2	1	24	9	5	.311	.301
Jimenez, Yeison	R-R	6-1	180	1-9-01	.252	.067	.278	39	123	20	31	8	4	1	15	15	2	0	2	42	4	.1	.407	.338
Martinez, Gabriel	R-R			7-24-02	.239	.125	.254	58	213	30	51	13	2	2	28	21	5	2	4	26	8	9	.347	.317
Montero, Adrian	R-R	5-9	150	8-23-01	.322	.180	.333	39	118	27	38	7	1	0	17	24	6	0	0	11	17	5	.398	.460

Name	B-T	HT	WT	DOB	AVG	vLH	vRH	G	AB	R	H	2B	3B	HR	RBI	BB	SO	SB	CS	OBP	SLG
Oliva, Daniel	R-R	6-0	180	9-14-01	.273	.095	.298	51	172	29	47	9	1	1	23	32	11	2	0	55 15 3	.355	.419
Pizarro, Juan	L-L	5-11	150	1-18-02	.284	.304	.281	51	190	30	54	5	5	1	25	15	3	0	0	44 24 9	.379	.346
Ramos, Junior	R-R	6-0	170	10-5-01	.184	.462	.149	35	114	10	21	5	0	0	16	7	1	0	3	19 3 1	.228	.232
Ruiz, Gustavo	R-R	6-0	175	3-22-00	.200	.294	.183	34	110	11	22	8	0	0	11	9	2	1	2	18 3 1	.273	.268
Sanchez, Emmanuel	R-R	6-0	170	5-30-01	.264	.286	.261	47	174	24	46	7	3	0	25	20	3	0	3	23 7 5	.339	.345
Santiago, Glenn	R-R	6-0	165	12-14-00	.237	.267	.233	35	131	29	31	7	4	0	17	19	7	2	1	23 13 2	.351	.361

Pitching	B-T	HT	WT	DOB	W	L	ERA	G	GS	CG	SV	IP	H	R	ER	HR	BB	SO	AVG	vLH	vRH	K/9	BB/9
Alvarado, Wilgenis	L-L	6-1	160	5-18-00	1	1	2.63	4	4	0	0	14	14	5	4	1	4	6	.275	.286	.273	3.95	2.63
Bernal, Jonatan	R-R	6-1	194	6-29-02	1	3	3.27	9	8	0	0	33	30	22	12	3	5	21	.240	.200	.263	5.73	1.36
Castro, Edgar	R-R	6-1	165	2-7-02	2	0	4.65	10	0	0	0	31	28	16	16	2	7	32	.248	.167	.286	9.29	2.03
Castro, Juanfer	R-R	6-1	175	7-22-01	2	4	5.13	9	7	0	0	33	40	20	19	3	12	24	.299	.539	.273	6.48	3.24
Chacon, Fernando	R-R	5-10	160	11-16-01	4	5	3.83	16	11	0	0	52	65	27	22	2	29	41	.319	.375	.305	7.14	5.05
Civit, Marc	L-L	6-0	150	6-23-02	2	1	3.13	15	0	0	1	32	31	18	11	0	15	24	.250	.250	.250	6.82	4.26
Garcia, Andres	R-R	5-10	165	7-30-02	2	0	5.68	19	0	0	1	32	39	25	20	2	21	16	.289	.250	.320	4.55	5.97
Garcia, Winder	R-R	5-10	165	10-11-01	4	1	2.54	12	1	0	3	28	26	10	8	1	10	33	.245	.280	.235	10.48	3.18
Gonzalez, Jorman	R-R	6-3	183	10-10-01	1	1	10.55	16	0	0	0	21	27	26	25	1	20	16	.310	.158	.353	6.75	8.44
Govea, Ronald	R-R	6-3	175	10-10-00	1	0	0.00	2	0	0	0	3	4	0	0	0	2	1	.364	.500	.286	3.38	6.75
Guzman, Junior A.	L-L	5-11	185	7-19-99	4	0	5.33	11	1	0	3	25	33	16	15	0	8	29	.314	.310	.316	10.30	2.84
Martinez, Juan	R-R	6-3	178	6-19-99	2	2	4.35	19	0	0	1	31	22	19	15	0	24	16	.206	.182	.222	4.65	6.97
Martinez, Soenni	L-L	6-0	180	5-26-01	1	2	5.26	13	13	0	0	51	61	34	30	1	17	50	.289	.289	.289	8.77	2.98
Mercedes, Francis	R-R	5-11	200	3-5-00	1	0	7.14	16	0	0	2	29	31	27	23	2	29	31	.274	.300	.269	9.62	9.00
Meza, Bejardi	R-R	5-11	145	11-16-00	4	1	2.61	17	8	0	5	52	41	21	15	1	22	28	.215	.283	.188	4.88	3.83
Ortiz, Argeny	L-L	6-3	190	9-26-00	0	0	0.00	1	0	0	0	1	0	0	0	0	2	0	.000	--	.000	0.00	18.00
Perdomo, Yaifer	L-L	5-10	160	8-16-01	2	1	2.89	13	13	0	0	53	48	20	17	0	21	52	.253	.180	.287	8.83	3.57
Polonia, Joneivy	R-R	5-11	160	3-30-02	0	2	6.30	19	0	0	3	20	20	25	14	2	23	10	.256	.308	.231	4.50	10.35
Pontes, Alcindo	L-L	6-1	162	5-16-02	0	2	14.66	13	0	0	0	12	9	19	19	0	19	7	.214	.000	.257	5.40	14.66
Quintana, Jose	R-R	6-1	160	3-19-02	0	5	3.78	17	4	0	5	33	24	23	14	1	31	24	.205	.220	.197	6.48	8.37
Sanchez, Raudy	R-R	5-11	196	8-4-00	1	0	11.77	15	0	0	0	13	12	19	17	0	30	8	.250	.273	.243	5.54	20.77
Santana, Gerardo	R-R	6-2	200	9-12-99	0	4	15.00	12	0	0	1	9	7	18	15	0	23	3	.206	.250	.182	3.00	23.00

Fielding

C: Astudillo 1, D'Orazio 10, David 9, Ramos 28, Ruiz 30. **1B:** Astudillo 23, Callez 35, David 19, Ruiz 5. **2B:** Astudillo 5, De La Rosa 3, Fajardo 24, Gutierrez 10, Montero 36, Sanchez 2. **3B:** Astudillo 7, Callez 15, De La Rosa 2, Fajardo 16, Gutierrez 26, Sanchez 12. **SS:** Astudillo 11, De La Rosa 2, Fajardo 3, Gutierrez 1, Sanchez 30, Santiago 31. **OF:** Astudillo 7, Brazoban 52, Jimenez 36, Martinez 53, Oliva 39, Pizarro 37.

Washington Nationals

SEASON IN A SENTENCE: The 2019 season will be one that Nationals fans never forget. After starting the season 19-31, Washington rallied to make the playoffs and eventually beat the heavily favored Astros in seven games to win the franchise's first-ever World Series.

HIGH POINT: Did you miss that part about winning the first World Series in franchise history? That would be the high point of the season, which came from an incredibly resilient effort in October. The Nationals trailed in five separate elimination games that they would come back to win in order to to keep the dream alive and eventually put a curly "W" in the books for the final game of the year.

LOW POINT: On May 23, the Nationals were sitting on a five-game losing streak after getting swept in a four-game series to the Mets. With a 19-31 record that had them sitting in fourth place in the NL East and 10 games behind the Braves, it was starting to look like the club would miss the playoffs in back-to-back seasons.

NOTABLE ROOKIES: Outfielder Victor Robles became the team's everday center fielder, and while he was a slightly below-average hitter (.255/.326/.419), he immediately became one of the best outfielders in baseball and led all outfielders in Outs Above Average. Righthander Wander Suero threw 71.1 innings of relief and fellow righty Tanner Rainey showed huge strikeout potential (13.8 K/9) but struggled with his control in 48.1 innings out of the bullpen.

KEY TRANSACTIONS: The Nationals continued to be big players in free agency during the offseason. The team signed Patrick Corbin to a six-year, $140 million contract and watched him go 14-7, 3.25 and handle a 200-inning season for the second straight year. Catcher Kurt Suzuki signed a two-year, $10 million deal and provided solid offensive production (.264/.324/.486), while a deadline trade for righthander Daniel Hudson (9-3, 2.47) gave the team a reliable bullpen arm.

DOWN ON THE FARM: Washington's farm system isn't deep, but they continue to add important major league contributers every year. Shortstop Carter Kieboom is likely next on the horizon. He hit .303/.409/.493 in Triple-A Fresno and should be ready to fixture in the Nationals' lineup next season. Shortstop Luis Garcia is further away and struggled a bit in Double-A, but he was one of the youngest players in the league as a 19-year-old.

OPENING DAY PAYROLL: $181,400,409 (4th).

PLAYERS OF THE YEAR

MARY DECICCO

MAJOR LEAGUE	MINOR LEAGUE
Anthony Rendon	**Carter Kieboom**
3B	**SS**
.319/.412/.598	(Triple-A)
MLB-best 126 RBIs,	.306/.409/.493
led NL with 44 2B	16 HR, 24 2B

ORGANIZATION LEADERS

Batting		*Minimum 250 AB
MAJORS		
* AVG	Howie Kendrick	.344
* OPS	Anthony Rendon	1.001
HR	Anthony Rendon	34
HR	Juan Soto	34
RBI	Anthony Rendon	126
MINORS		
* AVG	Yadiel Hernandez, Fresno	.324
* OBP	Carter Kieboom, Fresno	.409
* SLG	Yadiel Hernandez, Fresno	.604
* OPS	Yadiel Hernandez, Fresno	1.009
R	Yadiel Hernandez, Fresno	87
H	Yadiel Hernandez, Fresno	142
TB	Yadiel Hernandez, Fresno	265
2B	Aldrem Corredor, Fredericksburg	34
3B	Daniel Marte, DSL Nationals	9
HR	Yadiel Hernandez, Fresno	33
RBI	Yadiel Hernandez, Fresno	90
BB	Carter Kieboom, Fresno	68
SO	Brandon Snyder, Fresno	153
SB	Cole Freeman, Fredericksburg	31

Pitching		#Minimum 75 IP
MAJORS		
W	Stephen Strasburg	18
# ERA	Max Scherzer	2.92
SO	Stephen Strasburg	251
SV	Sean Doolittle	29
MINORS		
W	Joan Adon, Hagerstown	11
W	Tim Cate, Hagerstown, Fredericksburg	11
W	Nick Raquet, Fredericksburg	11
L	Tomas Alastre, Hagerstown	12
# ERA	Steven Fuentes, Fredericksburg	2.23
G	Aaron Barrett, Harrisburg	50
GS	Tim Cate, Hagerstown, Fredericksburg	26
GS	Ben Braymer, Harrisburg, Fresno	26
GS	Wil Crowe, Harrisburg, Fresno	26
SV	Aaron Barrett, Harrisburg	31
IP	Wil Crowe, Harrisburg, Fresno	149
BB	Scott Copeland, Fresno	62
SO	Tim Cate, Hagerstown	139
# AVG	Andrew Lee, Fredericksburg, Harrisburg	.204

2019 PERFORMANCE

General Manager: Mike Rizzo. **Farm Director:** Doug Harris. **Scouting Director:** Kris Kline.

Class	Team	League	W	L	PCT	Finish	Manager
Majors	Washington Nationals	National	93	69	.574	3rd (15)	Dave Martinez
Triple-A	Fresno Grizzlies	Pacific Coast	65	75	.464	11th (14)	Randy Knorr
Double-A	Harrisburg Senators	Eastern	76	63	.547	4th (12)	Matthew LeCroy
High A	Potomac Nationals	Carolina	70	67	.511	5th (10)	Tripp Keister
Low A	Hagerstown Suns	South Atlantic	65	75	.464	t-10th (14)	Patrick Anderson
Short season	Auburn Doubledays	New York-Penn	30	46	.395	14th (14)	Rocket Wheeler
Rookie	GCL Nationals	Gulf Coast	26	23	.531	8th (18)	Mario Lisson
Overall 2019 Minor League Record			332	349	.488	20th (30)	

ORGANIZATION STATISTICS

WASHINGTON NATIONALS
NATIONAL LEAGUE

Batting	B-T	HT	WT	DOB	AVG	vLH	vRH	G	AB	R	H	2B	3B	HR	RBI	BB	HBP	SH	SF	SO	SB	CS	SLG	OBP
Adams, Matt	L-R	6-3	245	8-31-88	.226	.210	.230	111	310	42	70	14	0	20	56	20	2	0	1	115	0	0	.465	.276
Barrera, Tres	R-R	6-0	215	9-15-94	.000	--	.000	2	2	0	0	0	0	0	0	0	0	0	0	0	0	0	.000	.000
Cabrera, Asdrubal	B-R	6-0	205	11-13-85	.323	.407	.299	38	124	24	40	10	1	6	40	19	0	0	3	18	0	0	.565	.404
Difo, Wilmer	B-R	5-11	200	4-2-92	.252	.321	.233	43	131	15	33	2	0	2	8	12	0	1	0	29	0	1	.313	.315
Dozier, Brian	R-R	5-11	200	5-15-87	.238	.280	.222	135	416	54	99	20	0	20	50	61	4	0	1	105	3	4	.430	.340
Eaton, Adam	L-L	5-9	176	12-6-88	.279	.290	.276	151	566	103	158	25	7	15	49	65	13	9	3	106	15	3	.428	.365
Gomes, Yan	R-R	6-2	215	7-19-87	.223	.261	.212	97	314	36	70	16	0	12	43	38	5	0	1	84	2	0	.389	.316
Kendrick, Howie	R-R	5-11	220	7-12-83	.344	.376	.327	121	334	61	115	23	1	17	62	27	4	0	5	49	2	1	.572	.395
Kieboom, Carter	R-R	6-2	190	9-3-97	.128	.143	.125	11	39	4	5	0	0	2	2	4	0	0	0	16	0	0	.282	.209
Noll, Jake	R-R	6-2	195	3-8-94	.167	.000	.182	8	12	1	2	1	0	0	2	1	0	0	0	4	0	0	.250	.231
Parra, Gerardo	L-L	5-11	210	5-6-87	.250	.180	.269	89	188	30	47	11	1	8	42	11	3	1	1	41	6	2	.447	.301
2-team total (30 San Francisco)					.234	.226	.236	119	274	38	64	14	1	9	48	19	5	1	2	59	8	3	.391	.293
Read, Raudy	R-R	6-0	170	10-29-93	.091	.000	.125	6	11	0	1	0	0	0	0	0	0	0	0	5	0	0	.091	.091
Rendon, Anthony	R-R	6-1	200	6-6-90	.319	.316	.320	146	545	117	174	44	3	34	126	80	12	0	9	86	5	1	.598	.412
Robles, Victor	R-R	6-0	190	5-19-97	.255	.248	.257	155	546	86	139	33	3	17	65	35	25	6	5	140	28	9	.419	.326
Sanchez, Adrian	R-R	6-0	210	8-16-90	.226	.250	.217	28	31	3	7	0	0	0	1	1	0	0	0	10	0	0	.226	.250
Soto, Juan	L-L	6-1	185	10-25-98	.282	.285	.281	150	542	110	153	32	5	34	110	108	3	0	6	132	12	1	.548	.401
Stevenson, Andrew	L-L	6-0	192	6-1-94	.367	1.000	.345	30	30	4	11	1	1	0	6	1	0	0	1	11	0	1	.467	.487
Suzuki, Kurt	R-R	5-11	210	10-4-83	.264	.343	.239	85	280	37	74	11	0	17	63	20	6	0	3	36	0	1	.486	.324
Taylor, Michael A.	R-R	6-4	212	3-26-91	.250	.278	.231	53	88	10	22	7	0	1	3	7	0	2	0	34	6	0	.364	.305
Turner, Trea	R-R	6-2	185	6-30-93	.298	.316	.292	122	521	96	155	37	5	19	57	43	3	0	2	113	35	5	.497	.353
Zimmerman, Ryan	R-R	6-3	215	9-28-84	.257	.367	.213	52	171	20	44	9	0	6	27	17	0	0	2	39	0	0	.415	.321

Pitching	B-T	HT	WT	DOB	W	L	ERA	G	GS	CG	SV	IP	H	R	ER	HR	BB	SO	AVG	vLH	vRH	K/9	BB/9
Adams, Austin	R-R	6-3	225	5-5-91	0	0	9.00	1	0	0	0	1	0	1	1	0	2	2	.000	.000	.000	18.00	18.00
Barraclough, Kyle	R-R	6-3	225	5-23-90	1	2	6.66	33	0	0	0	26	33	21	19	8	12	30	.303	.257	.324	10.52	4.21
2-team total (10 San Francisco)					1	2	5.61	43	0	0	0	34	38	24	21	9	21	40	.273	.235	.296	10.69	5.61
Barrett, Aaron	R-R	6-3	230	1-2-88	0	0	15.43	3	0	0	0	2	5	4	4	1	4	1	.417	.400	.429	3.86	15.43
Blazek, Michael	R-R	6-0	205	3-16-89	0	0	7.20	4	0	0	0	5	6	4	4	1	5	0	.286	.200	.364	0.00	9.00
Bourque, James	R-R	6-4	215	7-9-93	0	0	54.00	1	0	0	0	1	3	4	4	0	2	0	.750	1.000	.667	0.00	27.00
Corbin, Patrick	L-L	6-3	210	7-19-89	14	7	3.25	33	33	1	0	202	169	81	73	24	70	238	.227	.190	.235	10.60	3.12
Doolittle, Sean	L-L	6-2	204	9-26-86	6	5	4.05	63	0	0	29	60	63	27	27	11	15	66	.260	.221	.279	9.90	2.25
Dozier, Brian	R-R	5-11	200	5-15-87	0	0	18.00	1	0	0	0	1	2	2	2	1	0	0	.400	.500	.333	0.00	0.00
Elias, Roenis	L-L	6-1	205	8-1-88	0	0	9.00	4	0	0	0	3	5	4	3	2	1	2	.417	.500	.333	6.00	3.00
Fedde, Erick	R-R	6-4	195	2-25-93	4	2	4.50	21	12	0	0	78	81	39	39	11	33	41	.277	.333	.217	4.73	3.81
Grace, Matt	L-L	6-4	215	12-14-88	1	2	6.36	51	1	0	0	47	61	34	33	11	10	35	.319	.322	.317	6.75	1.93
Guerra, Javy	R-R	6-1	216	10-31-85	3	1	4.86	40	0	0	1	54	55	30	29	9	12	42	.256	.282	.239	7.04	2.01
Hellickson, Jeremy	R-R	6-1	190	4-8-87	2	3	6.23	9	8	0	0	39	47	31	27	9	20	30	.294	.329	.264	6.92	4.62
Hudson, Daniel	R-R	6-3	225	3-9-87	3	0	1.44	24	0	0	6	25	18	7	4	3	4	23	.200	.171	.225	8.28	1.44
Jennings, Dan	L-L	6-3	215	4-17-87	1	2	13.50	8	0	0	0	5	8	8	7	1	7	9	.333	.231	.455	17.36	13.50
McGowin, Kyle	R-R	6-3	195	11-27-91	0	0	10.13	7	1	0	1	16	22	19	18	7	4	18	.319	.333	.306	10.13	2.25
Miller, Justin	R-R	6-3	215	6-13-87	1	0	4.02	17	0	0	0	16	16	8	7	5	4	11	.276	.250	.290	6.32	2.30
Parra, Gerardo	L-L	5-11	210	5-6-87	0	0	--	1	0	0	0	1	0	0	0	0	0	0	1.000	1.000	--	--	--
Rainey, Tanner	R-R	6-2	235	12-25-92	2	3	3.91	52	0	0	0	48	32	22	21	6	38	74	.188	.261	.139	13.78	7.08
Rodney, Fernando	R-R	5-11	240	3-18-77	0	3	4.05	38	0	0	2	33	29	16	15	3	16	35	.234	.234	.233	9.45	4.32
Rosenthal, Trevor	R-R	6-2	230	5-29-90	0	1	22.74	12	0	0	0	6	8	16	16	0	15	5	.333	.250	.375	7.11	21.32
Ross, Joe	R-R	6-4	220	5-21-93	4	4	5.48	27	9	0	0	64	74	41	39	7	33	57	.291	.314	.272	8.02	4.64
Sanchez, Anibal	R-R	6-0	205	2-27-84	11	8	3.85	30	30	0	0	166	153	77	71	22	58	134	.237	.248	.226	7.27	3.14
Scherzer, Max	R-R	6-3	215	7-27-84	11	7	2.92	27	27	0	0	172	144	59	56	18	33	243	.222	.255	.193	12.69	1.72
Sipp, Tony	L-L	6-0	190	7-12-83	1	2	4.71	36	0	0	0	19	12	11	1	9	18	.241	.255	.219	7.71	3.86
Strasburg, Stephen	R-R	6-5	235	7-20-88	18	6	3.32	33	33	0	0	209	161	79	77	24	56	251	.210	.192	.224	10.81	2.41
Strickland, Hunter	R-R	6-3	225	9-24-88	2	0	5.14	24	0	0	0	21	20	12	12	5	8	15	.247	.333	.188	6.43	3.43

Name	B-T	HT	WT	DOB	W	L	ERA	G	GS	CG	SV	IP	H	R	ER	HR	BB	SO	AVG	vLH	vRH	K/9	BB/9
Suero, Wander	R-R	6-4	211	9-15-91	6	9	4.54	78	0	0	1	71	64	36	36	5	26	81	.242	.279	.207	10.22	3.28
Venters, Jonny	L-L	6-3	200	3-20-85	0	1	5.40	3	0	0	0	3	3	3	2	0	2	5	.214	.200	.222	13.50	5.40
2-team total (9 Atlanta)					0	1	12.38	12	0	0	1	8	12	16	11	3	10	12	.324	.294	.350	13.50	11.25
Voth, Austin	R-R	6-2	201	6-26-92	2	1	3.30	9	8	0	0	44	33	16	16	5	13	44	.213	.263	.165	9.07	2.68
Williams, Austen	R-R	6-3	220	12-19-92	0	0	162.00	2	0	0	0	0	5	6	2		1	1	.833	1.000	.500	27.00	27.00

Fielding

Catcher

Catcher	PCT	G	PO	A	E	DP	PB
Barrera	.000	1	0	0	0	0	0
Gomes	.995	93	842	41	4	3	10
Read	1.000	4	20	1	0	0	0
Suzuki	.996	75	666	27	3	1	6

First Base

First Base	PCT	G	PO	A	E	DP
Adams	.991	79	502	51	5	40
Cabrera	1.000	3	19	2	0	2
Gomes	1.000	1	1	0	0	0
Kendrick	.997	48	276	27	1	25
Noll	.833	2	5	0	1	0
Parra	.990	14	85	14	1	11
Sanchez	1.000	1	8	0	0	0
Zimmerman	.991	44	307	20	3	24

Second Base

Second Base	PCT	G	PO	A	E	DP
Cabrera	1.000	31	32	59	0	13
Difo	1.000	2	2	3	0	2
Dozier	.987	123	145	248	5	61
Kendrick	.987	23	27	49	1	8
Parra	.000	1	0	0	0	0
Rendon	.000	1	0	0	0	0
Sanchez	1.000	4	0	1	0	0
Sanchez	.857	6	1	5	1	1

Third Base

Third Base	PCT	G	PO	A	E	DP
Cabrera	1.000	5	0	1	0	0
Difo	.900	6	2	7	1	1
Kendrick	1.000	15	5	15	0	2
Noll	1.000	1	2	1	0	0
Parra	.000	1	0	0	0	0
Rendon	.969	146	95	249	11	31

Shortstop

Shortstop	PCT	G	PO	A	E	DP
Difo	.990	33	30	68	1	11
Kieboom	.900	10	15	21	4	4
Sanchez	1.000	2	0	1	0	0
Turner	.971	122	130	298	13	57

Outfield

Outfield	PCT	G	PO	A	E	DP
Eaton	.979	145	277	3	6	1
Parra	1.000	34	59	3	0	1
Robles	.984	152	348	12	6	2
Sanchez	.000	1	0	0	0	0
Soto	.993	150	273	0	2	0
Stevenson	1.000	5	1	0	0	0
Taylor	.971	31	32	2	1	1

FRESNO GRIZZLIES

PACIFIC COAST LEAGUE   **TRIPLE-A**

Batting

Batting	B-T	HT	WT	DOB	AVG	vLH	vRH	G	AB	R	H	2B	3B	HR	RBI	BB	HBP	SH	SF	SO	SB	CS	SLG	OBP
Cowgill, Collin	R-L	5-9	190	5-22-86	.228	.247	.215	84	241	54	55	11	2	12	34	29	8	1	1	90	8	3	.440	.330
Difo, Wilmer	B-R	5-11	200	4-2-92	.300	.256	.323	61	233	48	70	14	3	4	30	25	1	1	1	51	13	5	.438	.369
Dominguez, Chris	R-R	6-4	235	11-22-86	.304	.250	.333	7	23	2	7	2	0	1	7	1	0	0	0	6	0	0	.522	.333
Gonzalez, Bengie	B-R	5-11	160	1-16-90	.188	.348	.040	25	48	6	9	3	0	0	6	5	0	0	1	11	0	1	.250	.259
Gushue, Taylor	B-R	6-1	233	12-19-93	.312	.305	.316	74	263	35	82	19	1	11	39	20	1	0	4	63	0	0	.517	.358
Hernandez, Yadiel	L-R	5-9	185	10-9-87	.324	.338	.316	126	439	87	142	22	1	33	90	63	1	0	5	106	7	5	.604	.406
Jones, Hunter	R-R	6-2	185	8-17-91	.250	.000	.333	2	4	1	1	0	0	0	1	0	0	0	0	1	1	0	.250	.400
Keller, Alec	R-R	6-2	200	5-13-92	.302	.321	.294	119	381	63	115	19	2	3	45	25	3	2	4	61	10	0	.386	.346
Kieboom, Carter	R-R	6-2	190	9-3-97	.303	.374	.267	109	412	79	125	24	3	16	79	68	9	0	5	100	5	2	.493	.409
Marmolejos, Jose	L-L	6-1	225	1-2-93	.315	.281	.333	101	352	53	111	29	2	16	63	28	1	0	1	80	1	0	.546	.367
Noll, Jake	R-R	6-2	195	3-8-94	.285	.270	.293	118	456	69	130	24	0	11	54	26	4	0	3	89	5	2	.410	.327
Read, Raudy	R-R	6-0	170	10-29-93	.275	.318	.250	82	306	52	84	17	3	20	60	17	3	0	2	58	1	1	.546	.317
Reistetter, Matt	L-R	5-10	180	5-5-92	.238	.000	.333	9	21	2	5	2	0	1	3	3	0	0	0	3	0	0	.476	.333
Reynolds, Matt	R-R	6-1	200	12-3-90	.295	.297	.294	111	376	65	111	29	4	16	55	64	4	3	2	95	8	2	.521	.401
Sardinas, Luis	B-R	6-1	180	5-16-93	.333	.280	.371	21	60	6	20	2	1	0	7	3	1	1	1	12	0	1	.400	.369
Snyder, Brandon	R-R	6-2	225	11-23-86	.257	.277	.246	116	417	75	107	24	0	31	80	26	11	0	4	153	3	1	.537	.314
Stevenson, Andrew	L-L	6-0	192	6-1-94	.334	.313	.347	73	302	50	101	17	8	6	44	24	1	4	2	76	10	4	.503	.383
Taylor, Chuck	B-L	5-9	190	9-21-93	.221	.240	.208	40	122	13	27	8	0	4	10	18	1	0	0	30	0	1	.385	.326
Ward, Drew	L-R	6-3	215	11-25-94	.288	.189	.338	30	111	17	32	6	0	8	23	6	0	0	0	46	1	0	.559	.325
Wilson, Jacob	R-R	5-11	205	7-29-90	.310	.319	.305	55	197	40	61	12	1	15	48	31	1	2	1	43	1	0	.609	.404

Pitching

Pitching	B-T	HT	WT	DOB	W	L	ERA	G	GS	CG	SV	IP	H	R	ER	HR	BB	SO	AVG	vLH	vRH	K/9	BB/9
Adams, Austin	R-R	6-3	225	5-5-91	0	1	2.70	8	0	0	1	10	7	4	3	0	3	20	.189	.182	.200	18.00	2.70
2-team total (4 Tacoma)					0	1	1.88	12	0	0	1	14	8	4	3	0	3	27	.157	.138	.182	16.95	1.88
Alvarez III, Henderson	R-R	6-0	205	4-18-90	1	4	5.94	24	4	0	0	53	68	39	35	15	18	37	.311	.293	.327	6.28	3.06
Bacus, Dakota	R-R	6-2	200	4-2-91	5	5	3.58	46	0	0	9	55	50	28	22	3	28	52	.239	.248	.232	8.46	4.55
Baez, Joan	R-R	6-3	190	12-26-94	1	2	4.36	24	0	0	0	33	32	20	16	4	20	18	.258	.319	.221	4.91	5.45
Blazek, Michael	R-R	6-0	205	3-16-89	2	2	6.05	34	1	0	1	39	44	31	26	9	16	42	.282	.301	.269	9.78	3.72
Bonnell, Bryan	L-R	6-5	240	9-28-93	1	0	6.00	1	0	0	0	3	5	2	2	1	1	3	.333	.364	.250	9.00	3.00
Bourque, James	R-R	6-4	215	7-9-93	4	1	5.56	33	0	0	3	44	41	29	27	6	30	53	.247	.284	.222	10.92	6.18
Braymer, Ben	L-L	6-2	215	4-28-94	0	6	7.20	13	13	0	0	60	81	50	48	18	35	47	.328	.358	.317	7.05	5.25
Buchanan, Jake	R-R	6-0	232	9-24-89	0	0	9.64	4	0	0	0	5	8	5	5	0	2	3	.421	.000	.471	5.79	3.86
2-team total (20 Las Vegas)					3	6	6.32	24	20	0	0	104	133	80	73	24	36	74	.317	.287	.339	6.40	3.12
Copeland, Scott	R-R	6-3	220	12-15-87	6	5	6.22	31	19	0	0	114	126	86	79	20	62	102	.279	.324	.239	8.03	4.88
Cordero, Jimmy	R-R	6-4	222	10-19-91	0	1	6.00	12	0	0	3	15	17	12	10	3	9	17	.274	.424	.103	10.20	5.40
Crowe, Wil	R-R	6-2	240	9-9-94	0	4	6.17	10	10	0	0	54	66	43	37	7	26	41	.303	.347	.280	6.83	4.33
Dragmire, Brady	R-R	6-1	185	2-5-93	0	3	11.48	6	2	0	0	18	28	22	17	3	6	4	.431	.452	.412	2.70	4.05
Espino, Paolo	R-R	5-10	215	1-10-87	8	4	5.65	17	17	0	0	92	97	61	58	15	24	93	.266	.264	.267	9.06	2.34
Fedde, Erick	R-R	6-4	195	2-25-93	1	1	12.60	2	2	0	0	10	19	14	14	5	4	10	.413	.464	.333	9.00	3.60
2-team total (35 Salt Lake)					1	1	6.29	40	0	0	3	59	81	48	41	11	30	53	.336	.308	.350	8.13	4.60
Gonzalez, Bengie	R-R	5-11	160	1-16-90	0	0	0.00	2	0	0	0	2	1	0	0	0	1	1	.143	.333	.000	4.50	4.50
Guilbeau, Taylor	L-L	6-4	180	5-12-93	2	0	5.19	7	0	0	0	9	10	5	5	0	6	5	.303	.300	.304	6.23	5.19
2-team total (5 Tacoma)					2	0	3.95	12	0	0	0	14	13	6	6	0	11	11	.260	.294	.242	7.24	4.61
Hoover, J.J.	R-R	6-3	240	8-13-87	6	6	8.47	30	16	0	0	96	127	97	90	26	40	89	.315	.341	.296	8.37	3.76
Kontos, George	R-R	6-3	225	6-12-85	2	1	6.07	31	1	0	0	46	60	36	31	7	18	37	.316	.357	.283	7.24	3.52
Lucas, Josh	R-R	6-6	185	11-5-90	0	0	6.00	3	0	0	0	3	3	2	1	1	3		.250	.000	.333	9.00	3.00
Marmolejos, Jose	L-L	6-1	225	1-2-93	0	0	0.00	1	0	0	0	1	1	0	0	2	1		.200	.000	.250	9.00	18.00

	B-T	HT	WT	DOB	W	L	ERA	G	GS	CG	SV	IP	H	R	ER	HR	BB	SO	AVG	vLH	vRH	K/9	BB/9
McGowan, Kevin	R-R	6-5	233	10-18-91	1	1	5.19	5	5	0	0	26	28	17	15	6	13	18	.277	.292	.264	6.23	4.50
McGowin, Kyle	R-R	6-3	195	11-27-91	7	2	3.86	11	11	0	0	61	59	28	26	8	17	68	.252	.291	.221	10.09	2.52
Miller, Justin	R-R	6-3	215	6-13-87	0	0	2.84	9	0	0	0	13	9	4	4	3	3	16	.192	.211	.179	11.37	2.13
Mills, Jordan	L-L	6-5	215	5-11-92	0	2	8.50	16	0	0	0	18	25	22	17	2	12	19	.317	.206	.400	9.50	6.00
Nuno III, Vidal	L-L	5-11	210	7-26-87	1	1	7.25	18	1	0	2	22	27	19	18	5	12	25	.300	.256	.333	10.07	4.84
Ondrusek, Logan	R-R	6-8	230	2-13-85	4	6	6.96	19	14	0	1	76	97	62	59	19	30	67	.311	.355	.268	7.90	3.54
Pena, Ronald	R-R	6-4	195	9-19-91	0	0	12.00	13	0	0	0	15	24	21	20	3	13	17	.364	.348	.372	10.20	7.80
Rainey, Tanner	R-R	6-2	235	12-25-92	2	2	4.00	16	0	0	2	18	16	8	8	1	12	32	.232	.243	.219	16.00	6.00
Reistetter, Matt	L-R	5-10	180	5-5-92	0	0	13.50	2	0	0	0	2	5	3	3	1	0	0	.455	.500	.400	0.00	0.00
Reynolds, Matt	R-R	6-1	200	12-3-90	0	0	9.00	2	0	0	0	2	4	2	2	0	3	0	.444	.200	.750	0.00	13.50
Rodney, Fernando	R-R	5-11	240	3-18-77	0	2	4.50	9	0	0	8	8	5	4	1	9	11	.250	.238	.273	12.38	10.13
Ross, Joe	R-R	6-4	220	5-21-93	2	3	4.28	8	8	0	0	40	48	21	19	2	8	32	.310	.306	.313	7.20	1.80
Sanchez, Mario	R-R	6-1	166	10-31-94	0	2	11.85	4	3	0	0	14	26	21	18	4	6	7	.406	.577	.290	4.61	3.95
Self, Derek	R-R	6-3	205	1-14-90	4	2	5.91	48	1	0	8	75	96	57	49	15	16	55	.310	.317	.303	6.63	1.93
Snyder, Brandon	R-R	6-2	225	11-23-86	1	1	4.00	7	0	0	0	9	4	4	4	1	2	6	.143	.182	.118	6.00	2.00
Voth, Austin	R-R	6-2	201	6-26-92	3	5	4.40	12	12	0	0	61	68	34	30	7	15	68	.272	.325	.221	9.98	2.20
Williams, Austen	R-R	6-3	220	12-19-92	0	0	15.43	3	0	0	0	2	3	4	4	1	2	3	.333	.000	.429	11.57	7.71

Fielding

Catcher	PCT	G	PO	A	E	DP	PB
Gushue	.991	69	538	30	5	4	7
Read	.993	67	546	41	4	4	4
Reistetter	1.000	7	56	3	0	0	0
Snyder	.800	1	4	0	1	0	1

First Base	PCT	G	PO	A	E	DP
Dominguez	1.000	4	28	5	0	2
Gushue	1.000	2	1	0	0	0
Marmolejos	.991	48	311	26	3	43
Noll	.994	51	309	22	2	31
Read	1.000	10	49	4	0	6
Snyder	.985	49	303	25	5	35
Ward	1.000	6	45	3	0	6
Wilson	1.000	2	7	0	0	0

Second Base	PCT	G	PO	A	E	DP
Difo	.939	20	24	53	5	12
Gonzalez	1.000	6	9	16	0	5
Keller	1.000	1	1	1	0	1
Kieboom	.969	41	75	113	6	25
Noll	.938	11	13	17	2	4
Reynolds	.958	30	41	73	5	19
Sardinas	.947	7	10	8	1	4
Snyder	.971	36	51	85	4	21
Wilson	.981	13	20	33	1	10

Third Base	PCT	G	PO	A	E	DP
Difo	1.000	10	4	11	0	2
Dominguez	1.000	3	1	2	0	0
Kieboom	.875	10	12	16	4	3
Noll	.878	51	38	70	15	7
Reynolds	.750	3	0	3	1	0
Snyder	.909	21	7	33	4	6
Ward	.944	24	8	43	3	0
Wilson	.941	37	21	43	4	4

Shortstop	PCT	G	PO	A	E	DP
Difo	.950	32	37	77	6	19
Gonzalez	.964	12	9	18	1	3
Kieboom	.975	62	91	140	6	44
Reynolds	.975	35	44	74	3	18
Sardinas	.982	13	24	31	1	11
Snyder	1.000	1	1	4	0	1
Wilson	.000	1	0	0	0	0

Outfield	PCT	G	PO	A	E	DP
Cowgill	1.000	68	148	1	0	1
Hernandez	.987	97	150	7	2	2
Jones	.000	1	0	0	0	0
Keller	.981	99	206	1	4	0
Marmolejos	.958	37	68	1	3	0
Noll	.833	4	5	0	1	0
Reynolds	.989	43	85	3	1	0
Snyder	1.000	17	35	1	0	0
Stevenson	.984	70	124	2	2	1
Taylor	1.000	30	40	1	0	0
Wilson	.000	1	0	0	0	0

HARRISBURG SENATORS
DOUBLE-A
EASTERN LEAGUE

Batting	B-T	HT	WT	DOB	AVG	vLH	vRH	G	AB	R	H	2B	3B	HR	RBI	BB	HBP	SH	SF	SO	SB	CS	SLG	OBP
Banks, Nick	L-L	6-0	215	11-18-94	.289	.292	.287	45	156	19	45	12	2	1	21	15	2	0	0	41	6	0	.410	.358
Barrera, Tres	R-R	6-0	215	9-15-94	.249	.259	.245	101	357	42	89	23	0	8	46	36	5	1	4	69	1	2	.381	.323
Bautista, Rafael	R-R	6-2	194	3-8-93	.143	.267	.050	11	35	3	5	0	0	0	3	4	1	0	0	7	2	0	.143	.250
Bichette, Dante	R-R	6-1	210	9-26-92	.297	.304	.293	73	256	31	76	13	4	2	33	19	2	1	2	38	3	1	.402	.348
Collier, Zach	L-L	6-2	200	9-8-90	.217	.167	.235	9	23	3	5	0	1	1	2	4	1	0	0	5	0	2	.435	.357
Davidson, Austin	L-R	6-0	180	1-3-93	.225	.275	.210	75	213	33	48	16	0	4	21	29	3	0	1	50	0	3	.357	.325
Dickson, O'Koyea	R-R	5-11	220	2-9-90	.000	.000	.000	3	7	1	0	0	0	0	0	2	0	0	3	0	0	.000	.222
Dominguez, Chris	R-R	6-4	235	11-22-86	.143	.333	.000	2	7	1	1	0	0	1	0	0	1	0	0	2	0	0	.286	.250
Garcia, Luis	L-R	6-2	190	5-16-00	.257	.249	.261	129	525	66	135	22	4	4	30	17	1	7	3	86	11	5	.337	.280
Goeddel, Tyler	R-R	6-4	180	10-20-92	.208	.164	.234	69	197	21	41	9	2	1	16	23	4	0	3	70	1	2	.289	.300
Jones, Hunter	R-R	6-2	185	8-17-91	.168	.216	.144	55	155	18	26	4	0	3	10	14	4	0	1	49	4	2	.252	.253
Kieboom, Spencer	R-R	6-0	210	3-16-91	.196	.169	.214	52	168	12	33	7	0	1	14	18	0	0	2	35	0	0	.256	.271
Lowery, Jake	L-R	6-0	200	7-21-90	.222	.250	.211	12	27	3	6	3	0	0	2	6	0	0	0	10	0	0	.333	.364
Marmolejos, Jose	L-L	6-1	225	1-2-93	.308	.273	.321	11	39	8	12	2	0	2	10	4	0	0	0	6	0	0	.513	.352
Masters, David	R-R	6-1	185	4-23-93	.261	.077	.304	24	69	10	18	5	0	1	10	8	0	1	1	18	0	0	.377	.333
Mejia, Bryan	B-R	6-1	170	3-2-94	.182	.077	.235	30	77	14	14	2	2	1	4	1	0	1	0	29	3	0	.299	.192
Rivera, T.J.	R-R	6-1	203	10-27-88	.237	.250	.231	15	38	4	9	3	0	0	4	3	0	0	0	8	0	0	.316	.293
Sagdal, Ian	L-R	6-3	190	1-6-93	.271	.283	.265	128	447	58	121	31	3	8	62	42	1	0	2	88	1	1	.407	.333
Sanchez, Adrian	R-R	6-0	216	8-16-90	.316	.300	.324	69	256	43	81	19	1	6	36	19	3	0	4	39	11	5	.469	.365
Sardinas, Luis	B-R	6-1	180	5-16-93	.198	.209	.190	61	167	18	33	8	0	1	14	18	1	3	3	25	1	4	.264	.275
Stevenson, Andrew	L-L	6-0	192	6-1-94	.250	.143	.286	20	84	12	21	4	0	1	5	3	1	0	0	24	3	0	.333	.284
Taylor, Chuck	B-L	5-9	190	7-24-92	.247	.210	.247	80	271	34	63	10	1	8	34	26	2	1	1	67	1	0	.365	.303
Taylor, Michael A.	R-R	6-4	212	3-26-91	.248	.274	.237	57	218	36	54	16	2	9	35	25	1	0	3	69	10	6	.463	.324
Ward, Drew	L-R	6-3	215	11-25-94	.265	.200	.296	53	185	27	49	14	1	9	36	15	3	0	2	74	0	0	.497	.327
Wiseman, Rhett	L-L	6-0	200	6-22-94	.271	.283	.209	105	335	40	72	17	2	15	57	36	5	1	3	123	6	5	.412	.298
Zimmerman, Ryan	R-R	6-3	215	9-28-84	.200	.091	.333	7	20	0	4	0	0	0	1	2	1	0	0	2	0	0	.200	.304

Pitching	B-T	HT	WT	DOB	W	L	ERA	G	GS	CG	SV	IP	H	R	ER	HR	BB	SO	AVG	vLH	vRH	K/9	BB/9
Bacus, Dakota	R-R	6-2	200	4-2-91	0	0	0.00	1	0	0	0	1	0	0	0	0	0	1	.000	.000	.000	9.00	0.00
Baez, Joan	R-R	6-3	190	12-26-94	3	1	2.35	22	0	0	5	31	23	10	8	2	12	32	.200	.170	.232	9.39	3.52
Barraclough, Kyle	R-R	6-3	225	5-23-90	0	1	1.86	7	0	0	0	10	4	2	2	0	5	14	.125	.100	.136	13.03	4.66
Barrett, Aaron	R-R	6-3	210	1-2-88	2	2	2.75	50	0	0	31	52	39	20	16	6	16	64	.199	.218	.184	10.66	2.75

Pitcher	B-T	HT	WT	DOB	W	L	ERA	G	GS	CG	SV	IP	H	R	ER	HR	BB	SO	AVG	vLH	vRH	SO/9	BB/9
Bonnell, Bryan	L-R	6-5	240	9-28-93	3	6	2.83	27	1	0	0	41	33	19	13	5	9	39	.223	.281	.179	8.49	1.96
Bourque, James	R-R	6-4	215	7-9-93	3	0	1.33	14	0	0	6	20	17	5	3	1	6	33	.224	.257	.195	14.61	2.66
Boxberger, Brad	R-R	6-2	205	5-27-88	1	1	1.04	8	0	0	1	9	6	2	1	0	3	11	.194	.100	.238	11.42	3.12
Braymer, Ben	L-L	6-2	215	4-28-94	4	4	2.51	13	13	0	0	79	56	28	22	7	21	69	.194	.216	.180	7.86	2.39
Condra-Bogan, Jacob	R-R	6-3	220	8-30-94	7	4	3.61	38	1	0	1	62	52	28	25	6	11	50	.228	.190	.258	7.22	1.59
Crowe, Wil	R-R	6-2	240	9-9-94	7	6	3.87	16	16	0	0	95	85	43	41	8	22	89	.242	.214	.268	8.40	2.08
Dragmire, Brady	R-R	6-1	185	2-5-93	0	1	6.55	5	0	0	0	11	8	8	1	3	1	8	.408	.435	.385	1.64	2.45
Fedde, Erick	R-R	6-4	195	2-25-93	2	0	2.55	5	4	0	0	25	18	9	7	2	5	27	.200	.304	.164	9.85	1.82
Fletcher, Aaron	L-L	6-0	220	2-25-96	0	0	4.26	5	0	0	0	6	7	3	3	0	2	9	.280	.417	.154	12.79	2.84
Fuentes, Steven	R-R	6-2	175	5-4-97	5	4	2.69	15	11	0	0	64	63	22	19	1	15	63	.252	.267	.235	8.91	2.12
German, Jhonatan	R-R	6-4	215	1-24-95	2	0	2.08	9	0	0	2	13	11	4	3	0	1	9	.234	.350	.148	6.23	0.69
Guilbeau, Taylor	L-L	6-4	180	5-12-93	1	2	2.31	27	0	0	0	35	27	10	9	1	10	44	.213	.246	.186	11.31	2.57
Holland, Greg	R-R	5-10	205	11-20-85	1	0	0.00	8	0	0	0	9	4	1	0	0	3	9	.129	.000	.191	9.00	3.00
Istler, Andrew	R-R	5-11	195	9-18-92	0	0	0.79	10	0	0	2	11	10	1	1	0	5	12	.238	.222	.250	9.53	3.97
Jennings, Dan	L-L	6-3	215	4-17-87	1	0	2.45	3	0	0	0	4	4	1	1	0	0	2	.308	.167	.429	4.91	0.00
Lee, Andrew	L-R	6-5	225	12-2-93	0	1	2.56	11	4	0	0	39	27	15	11	3	17	30	.196	.230	.169	6.98	3.96
Mapes, Tyler	R-R	6-2	205	7-18-91	6	7	5.00	25	25	0	0	133	157	85	74	14	43	106	.289	.288	.290	7.16	2.90
McGowan, Kevin	R-R	6-5	233	10-18-91	2	3	4.26	7	7	0	0	38	30	20	18	4	14	32	.219	.167	.260	7.58	3.32
McGowin, Kyle	R-R	6-3	195	11-27-91	1	1	2.51	6	6	0	0	32	22	10	9	2	9	36	.195	.172	.218	10.02	2.51
Miller, Justin	R-R	6-3	215	6-13-87	0	1	3.18	6	0	0	0	6	3	3	2	1	0	6	.150	.286	.077	9.53	0.00
Mills, Jordan	L-L	6-5	215	5-11-92	6	1	2.72	29	0	0	6	36	30	13	11	2	13	52	.219	.208	.226	12.88	3.22
Ondrusek, Logan	R-R	6-8	230	2-13-85	0	0	5.14	3	1	0	0	7	5	4	4	2	2	4	.185	.200	.143	5.14	2.57
Pena, Ronald	R-R	6-4	195	9-19-91	1	1	3.44	25	0	0	0	34	32	16	13	3	15	40	.256	.239	.266	10.59	3.97
Rosenthal, Trevor	R-R	6-2	230	5-29-90	0	1	5.79	10	0	0	0	9	6	6	6	2	7	11	.243	.300	.177	10.61	6.75
Sanchez, Mario	R-R	6-1	166	10-31-94	10	5	2.85	23	19	1	0	114	94	40	36	16	17	111	.224	.255	.197	8.79	1.35
Sharp, Sterling	R-R	6-3	170	5-30-95	5	3	3.99	9	9	0	0	50	56	23	22	1	14	45	.284	.204	.356	8.15	2.54
Tetreault, Jackson	R-R	6-5	189	6-3-96	4	5	4.73	18	18	0	0	86	98	54	45	8	40	63	.292	.295	.288	6.62	4.20
Venters, Jonny	L-L	6-3	200	3-20-85	0	0	1.29	10	0	0	0	7	6	1	1	0	6	4	.222	.100	.294	5.14	7.71
Vera, Eduardo	R-R	6-2	195	7-3-94	0	0	7.20	3	1	0	0	15	21	12	12	4	5	7	.339	.355	.323	4.20	3.00
Voth, Austin	R-R	6-2	201	6-26-92	1	1	4.76	3	3	0	0	11	11	6	6	1	2	11	.275	.286	.269	8.74	1.59
Williams, Austen	R-R	6-3	220	12-19-92	0	1	10.13	5	0	0	0	5	8	6	6	0	3	7	.348	.286	.444	11.81	5.06

Fielding

Catcher	PCT	G	PO	A	E	DP	PB
Barrera	.991	93	736	66	7	3	4
Davidson	.000	1	0	0	0	0	0
Kieboom	.986	42	336	23	5	0	5
Lowery	.968	7	54	6	2	0	1
Masters	1.000	8	11	16	0		3
Mejia	.976	22	27	53	2		9
Sanchez	.986	33	64	80	2		17
Sardinas	.944	26	30	55	5		13
Sardinas	.956	28	34	53	4		11

First Base	PCT	G	PO	A	E	DP
Bichette	.994	27	168	11	1	15
Davidson	.991	42	318	23	3	32
Kieboom	.988	10	75	4	1	5
Rivera	1.000	6	35	2	0	3
Sagdal	.984	56	406	33	7	33
Sardinas	.000	1	0	0	0	0
Ward	1.000	4	27	5	0	0
Zimmerman	.980	6	49	0	1	5

Second Base	PCT	G	PO	A	E	DP
Bichette	.980	27	42	55	2	8
Garcia	1.000	38	61	83	0	16

Third Base	PCT	G	PO	A	E	DP
Bichette	.750	3	5	1	2	0
Davidson	1.000	2	1	1	0	0
Dominguez	.714	2	2	3	2	0
Masters	.962	10	11	14	1	3
Rivera	1.000	3	2	2	0	0
Sagdal	.919	63	38	86	11	7
Sanchez	.952	21	10	30	2	3
Sardinas	.800	3	0	4	1	0
Ward	.936	45	17	71	6	6

Shortstop	PCT	G	PO	A	E	DP
Garcia	.958	93	133	229	16	56
Masters	.933	4	7	7	1	2
Sanchez	.944	18	30	55	5	14

Outfield	PCT	G	PO	A	E	DP
Banks	.989	41	90	2	1	2
Bautista	.920	11	22	1	2	1
Bichette	.955	14	19	2	1	0
Collier	1.000	8	16	0	0	0
Davidson	1.000	7	11	0	0	0
Dickson	1.000	2	5	0	0	0
Goeddel	1.000	62	117	1	0	0
Jones	.964	45	78	3	3	0
Marmolejos	1.000	7	13	0	0	0
Mejia	1.000	3	4	0	0	0
Rivera	.000	1	0	0	0	0
Sanchez	.000	1	0	0	0	0
Stevenson	.979	18	44	3	1	1
Taylor	.992	70	117	2	1	0
Taylor	.984	48	120	1	2	0
Wiseman	.994	95	160	5	1	1

POTOMAC NATIONALS
CAROLINA LEAGUE

HIGH CLASS A

Batting	B-T	HT	WT	DOB	AVG	vLH	vRH	G	AB	R	H	2B	3B	HR	RBI	BB	HBP	SH	SF	SO	SB	CS	SLG	OBP
Abreu, Osvaldo	R-R	6-0	195	6-13-94	.265	.272	.261	102	359	45	95	23	0	5	41	35	8	2	0	99	9	6	.371	.343
Agustin, Telmito	L-L	5-10	160	10-9-96	.236	.267	.220	112	394	39	93	19	3	9	42	30	1	3	4	107	9	6	.368	.289
Banks, Nick	L-L	6-0	215	11-18-94	.271	.312	.251	69	280	41	76	21	0	9	35	19	4	1	0	54	2	2	.443	.327
Canning, Gage	L-R	5-10	175	4-23-97	.239	.307	.208	101	369	44	88	17	6	3	40	32	6	3	0	114	8	4	.342	.310
Corredor, Aldrem	L-L	6-0	202	10-27-95	.283	.253	.298	127	495	60	140	34	0	9	89	36	4	1	5	104	2	2	.406	.333
Davidson, Austin	L-R	6-0	180	1-3-93	.236	.259	.226	24	89	10	21	5	0	0	8	11	1	0	0	19	1	2	.292	.327
Dunlap, Alex	R-R	6-2	195	10-6-94	.231	.239	.227	59	186	19	43	11	0	3	22	32	3	0	1	62	0	0	.339	.351
Franco, Anderson	R-R	6-3	190	8-15-97	.218	.232	.212	53	174	17	38	8	0	0	16	20	1	0	1	41	1	0	.264	.310
Freeman, Cole	R-R	5-9	175	9-27-94	.311	.268	.333	123	453	82	141	27	3	3	49	53	11	14	3	60	31	6	.404	.394
Harrison, KJ	R-R	6-0	208	8-11-96	.244	.298	.208	101	357	49	87	21	1	11	47	51	4	0	1	98	2	1	.401	.344
Lara, Gilbert	R-R	6-4	198	10-30-97	.232	.182	.261	52	185	20	43	10	1	4	19	3	1	2	2	52	1	0	.362	.246
Marinconz, Kyle	L-R	5-10	185	5-24-96	.174	.286	.125	7	23	2	4	0	0	0	2	0	1	0	0	6	0	0	.174	.208
Masters, David	R-R	6-1	185	4-23-93	.260	.333	.229	49	169	29	44	10	0	11	34	20	3	0	0	42	0	0	.515	.349
Mejia, Bryan	B-R	6-1	170	3-2-94	.144	.097	.162	28	97	8	14	3	2	1	10	2	0	2	0	22	1	0	.247	.162
Meregildo, Omar	R-R	6-1	185	8-18-97	.228	.230	.227	60	184	26	42	11	1	5	23	14	1	0	3	54	1	3	.380	.327
Reetz, Jakson	R-R	6-0	195	1-3-96	.253	.252	.254	96	324	54	82	18	2	13	55	46	15	1	1	95	3	1	.441	.371
Sundberg, Jack	L-R	5-11	195	7-21-93	.263	.255	.266	49	175	30	46	2	0	1	8	22	4	4	0	32	6	4	.291	.358

	B-T	HT	WT	DOB	AVG	vLH	vRH	G	AB	R	H	2B	3B	HR	RBI	BB	HBP	SH	SF	SO	SB	CS	SLG	OBP
Turner, Trea	R-R	6-2	185	6-30-93	.125	.000	.167	2	8	1	1	0	0	0	0	1	0	0	0	4	0	0	.125	.222
Upshaw, Armond	B-L	6-0	190	6-20-96	.194	.243	.167	36	103	18	20	1	2	0	5	19	5	3	0	38	9	5	.243	.347
Zimmerman, Ryan	R-R	6-3	215	9-28-84	.429	.500	.385	6	21	4	9	3	0	0	5	4	0	0	1	4	0	0	.571	.500

Pitching	B-T	HT	WT	DOB	W	L	ERA	G	GS	CG	SV	IP	H	R	ER	HR	BB	SO	AVG	vLH	vRH	K/9	BB/9
Acevedo, Carlos	R-R	6-3	200	9-27-94	0	0	11.57	3	0	0	0	7	10	10	9	1	2	5	.333	.273	.368	6.43	2.57
Barraclough, Kyle	R-R	6-3	225	5-23-90	0	0	9.00	2	0	0	0	2	2	2	2	0	5	.250	.333	.200	22.50	0.00
Bartow, Frankie	R-R	6-3	180	2-26-97	2	2	1.86	37	0	0	10	53	41	13	11	2	16	33	.215	.216	.214	5.57	2.70
Bogucki, A.J.	R-R	6-3	187	5-2-95	0	0	5.17	9	0	0	0	16	20	9	9	1	12	19	.303	.333	.292	10.91	6.89
Bonnell, Bryan	L-R	6-5	240	9-28-93	0	1	4.26	4	0	0	2	6	6	3	3	0	3	5	.261	.250	.273	7.11	4.26
Borne, Grant	L-L	6-5	205	4-6-94	1	3	6.63	10	7	0	0	38	47	31	28	4	8	32	.311	.286	.324	7.58	1.89
Cate, Tim	L-L	6-0	185	9-30-97	4	3	3.31	13	13	1	0	73	71	30	27	4	19	66	.255	.250	.258	8.10	2.33
Doolittle, Sean	L-L	6-2	204	9-26-86	0	0	0.00	1	0	0	0	1	0	0	0	0	0	0	.000	.000	.000	0.00	0.00
Fletcher, Aaron	L-L	6-0	220	2-25-96	3	1	1.38	12	0	0	0	26	15	7	4	1	8	32	.165	.188	.153	11.08	2.77
Fuentes, Steven	R-R	6-2	175	5-4-97	1	1	0.53	8	0	0	0	17	8	3	1	0	7	26	.136	.211	.100	13.76	3.71
German, Jhonatan	R-R	6-4	215	1-24-95	2	2	3.51	23	0	0	6	33	25	14	13	4	8	27	.210	.180	.232	7.29	2.16
Guillen, Angel	R-R	6-2	150	1-24-97	0	0	3.07	7	0	0	1	15	14	6	5	0	4	14	.241	.192	.281	8.59	2.45
Howard, Hayden	R-L	6-5	193	3-26-94	4	2	3.12	36	0	0	3	61	62	23	21	4	19	59	.271	.207	.306	8.75	2.82
Howell, Jacob	R-R	6-3	180	8-9-95	0	1	15.26	6	0	0	0	8	13	15	13	1	4	10	.382	.313	.444	11.74	4.70
Istler, Andrew	R-R	5-11	175	9-18-92	1	2	0.73	16	0	0	0	25	20	5	2	0	5	35	.215	.233	.206	12.77	1.82
Johnston, Kyle	R-R	6-0	190	7-17-96	9	9	4.03	20	20	0	0	105	92	52	47	7	37	100	.235	.223	.245	8.57	3.17
Klobosits, Gabe	L-R	6-7	270	5-16-95	0	0	0.00	7	0	0	0	12	6	0	0	0	4	8	.150	.059	.217	5.84	2.92
Lee, Andrew	L-R	6-5	225	12-2-93	2	5	3.45	16	11	0	0	70	53	32	27	4	33	76	.200	.239	.185	9.73	4.22
McKinney, Jeremy	R-R	6-0	190	12-8-94	1	1	6.68	20	0	0	0	32	33	25	24	5	19	29	.273	.250	.290	8.07	5.29
Miller, Justin	R-R	6-3	215	6-13-87	0	0	9.00	1	0	0	0	1	2	1	1	1	0	2	.400	.500	.000	18.00	0.00
Pantoja, Jorge	R-R	6-5	215	3-26-94	0	0	2.59	21	0	0	1	31	32	11	9	2	12	25	.274	.357	.227	7.18	3.45
Peguero, Francys	R-R	6-2	170	10-4-95	1	1	3.28	9	4	0	0	25	24	10	9	4	9	24	.247	.188	.306	8.76	3.28
Pena, Malvin	R-R	6-2	180	6-24-97	5	9	6.20	23	23	1	0	107	112	86	74	20	38	87	.265	.267	.264	7.30	3.19
Raquet, Nick	R-L	6-0	215	12-12-95	11	9	4.07	25	25	1	0	130	129	72	59	12	43	122	.257	.209	.275	8.42	2.97
Reyes, Luis	R-R	6-2	175	9-26-94	5	5	4.81	31	7	0	0	77	69	46	41	2	35	78	.236	.244	.231	9.16	4.11
Romero, Jhon	R-R	5-10	195	1-17-95	3	1	6.59	9	0	0	0	14	17	11	10	2	4	7	.321	.231	.407	4.61	2.63
Sipp, Tony	L-L	6-0	190	7-12-83	0	0	0.00	1	0	0	0	1	1	0	0	0	0	2	.250	.000	.333	18.00	0.00
Tapani, Ryan	R-R	6-0	180	6-28-94	1	3	5.72	9	4	0	0	28	33	20	18	2	8	29	.285	.304	.267	9.21	2.54
Teel, Carson	L-L	6-0	160	12-17-95	7	3	3.12	25	16	0	0	104	88	41	36	4	32	93	.233	.187	.258	8.05	2.77
Tetreault, Jackson	R-R	6-5	189	6-3-96	4	2	1.91	7	7	0	0	38	29	8	8	0	13	29	.213	.177	.250	6.93	3.11

Fielding

Catcher	PCT	G	PO	A	E	DP	PB
Dunlap	.995	50	352	23	2	1	2
Harrison	1.000	3	29	0	0	0	0
Reetz	.990	86	706	53	8	5	6

First Base	PCT	G	PO	A	E	DP
Corredor	.995	86	594	48	3	48
Harrison	.997	49	344	20	1	44
Meregildo	1.000	2	6	2	0	0
Sundberg	1.000	1	2	0	0	0
Zimmerman	.977	5	39	4	1	3

Second Base	PCT	G	PO	A	E	DP
Abreu	.972	47	79	127	6	30
Davidson	.976	12	22	19	1	7
Freeman	.952	54	130	110	12	28
Marinconz	.947	4	7	11	1	4

	PCT	G	PO	A	E	DP
Masters	1.000	2	2	4	0	0
Mejia	.973	17	33	38	2	9
Meregildo	1.000	3	6	8	0	4

Third Base	PCT	G	PO	A	E	DP
Abreu	.914	10	6	26	3	1
Davidson	.952	8	7	13	1	3
Franco	.915	50	24	83	10	3
Marinconz	.889	3	3	5	1	0
Masters	1.000	5	2	6	0	1
Mejia	.903	9	6	22	3	1
Meregildo	.917	55	37	84	11	11

Shortstop	PCT	G	PO	A	E	DP
Abreu	.976	41	28	94	3	15
Lara	.970	52	70	153	7	30
Masters	.949	40	47	103	8	17
Mejia	1.000	2	2	2	0	1
Turner	.923	2	4	8	1	3

Outfield	PCT	G	PO	A	E	DP
Agustin	.969	101	147	10	5	2
Banks	1.000	68	153	2	0	1
Canning	.986	99	195	10	3	0
Corredor	1.000	15	22	2	0	0
Freeman	.992	47	122	2	1	0
Harrison	1.000	1	3	0	0	0
Meregildo	.000	1	0	0	0	0
Sundberg	.969	48	92	2	3	0
Upshaw	.979	36	94	0	2	0

HAGERSTOWN SUNS
SOUTH ATLANTIC LEAGUE

LOW CLASS A

Batting	B-T	HT	WT	DOB	AVG	vLH	vRH	G	AB	R	H	2B	3B	HR	RBI	BB	HBP	SH	SF	SO	SB	CS	SLG	OBP
Bautista, Rafael	R-R	6-2	194	3-8-93	.185	.200	.182	6	27	1	5	1	0	0	2	3	0	0	0	3	2	0	.222	.267
Blash, Jamori	R-R	6-4	225	11-9-95	.190	.217	.179	21	79	9	15	6	1	2	8	3	2	0	1	32	0	0	.367	.235
Canning, Gage	L-R	5-10	175	4-23-97	.244	.231	.250	10	41	7	10	1	0	1	5	3	0	0	0	13	6	0	.342	.296
Caulfield, Phil	L-R	5-8	170	12-30-94	.250	.222	.255	35	120	12	30	5	1	4	26	7	3	4	1	29	1	2	.408	.305
Cluff, Jackson	L-R	6-0	185	12-3-96	.229	.240	.226	62	240	33	55	8	5	5	19	26	8	2	4	63	11	5	.367	.320
Connell, Justin	R-R	6-1	185	3-11-99	.249	.268	.244	120	433	59	108	20	1	3	38	49	10	14	4	75	13	10	.321	.337
Cropley, Tyler	R-R	5-11	185	12-10-95	.187	.226	.174	41	123	14	23	5	0	2	8	12	7	2	1	32	1	2	.276	.294
Daily, Cole	L-R	5-11	170	11-28-96	.251	.250	.251	71	243	24	61	9	0	0	16	26	2	4	2	47	8	9	.288	.326
Harrison, KJ	R-R	6-0	208	8-11-96	.404	.412	.400	16	57	11	23	8	1	2	16	8	1	0	0	10	0	0	.649	.485
Lara, Gilbert	R-R	6-4	198	10-30-97	.248	.183	.270	81	319	40	79	12	2	9	49	22	1	1	0	71	2	3	.382	.298
Marinconz, Kyle	L-R	5-10	185	5-24-96	.247	.242	.249	106	372	58	92	20	2	5	39	45	6	3	3	76	13	6	.352	.336
Mendez, Ricardo	L-L	6-0	155	1-24-00	.194	.154	.203	23	72	11	14	1	1	0	5	8	1	0	0	20	5	0	.236	.284
Mendoza, Drew	L-R	6-5	230	10-10-97	.264	.257	.265	55	201	23	53	12	0	4	25	34	3	0	1	57	3	0	.383	.377
Meregildo, Omar	R-R	6-1	185	8-18-97	.234	.304	.211	29	94	13	22	7	0	3	14	18	1	0	2	35	0	0	.404	.357
O'Connor, Pablo	R-R	6-0	195	9-6-95	.267	.130	.313	26	90	12	24	5	0	0	8	11	0	1	1	28	2	0	.322	.343
Pascal, Juan	R-R	6-1	175	11-6-97	.181	.077	.203	23	72	8	13	0	0	0	5	7	1	1	0	19	2	0	.181	.263

	B-T	HT	WT	DOB	AVG	vLH	vRH	G	AB	R	H	2B	3B	HR	RBI	BB	HBP	SH	SF	SO	SB	CS	SLG	OBP
Perkins, Nic	R-R	6-4	215	2-19-96	.209	.180	.219	63	201	16	42	16	1	0	20	36	3	1	1	59	2	1	.299	.336
Pineda, Israel	R-R	5-11	190	4-3-00	.217	.205	.220	101	374	48	81	12	0	7	35	30	3	1	3	102	1	2	.305	.278
Rhinesmith, Jacob	L-L	6-2	195	5-23-96	.264	.250	.268	133	489	72	129	33	3	10	67	60	8	1	4	85	19	6	.405	.351
Sanchez, Jose	R-R	5-11	155	7-12-00	.181	.276	.149	37	116	9	21	2	0	0	6	10	2	1	1	36	0	2	.198	.256
Upshaw, Armond	B-L	6-0	190	6-20-96	.215	.311	.189	62	209	22	45	4	4	2	28	22	3	3	2	66	18	5	.301	.297
Vickers, Trey	R-R	6-1	185	9-17-95	.204	.159	.220	83	274	18	56	10	1	3	27	19	7	6	1	54	1	2	.281	.272
Wilson, Cody	R-R	6-2	200	7-4-96	.216	.169	.234	77	297	49	64	9	4	5	23	37	5	7	2	96	22	5	.323	.311

Pitching	B-T	HT	WT	DOB	W	L	ERA	G	GS	CG	SV	IP	H	R	ER	HR	BB	SO	AVG	vLH	vRH	K/9	BB/9
Miller, Justin	R-R	6-4	183	5-17-98	0	0	0.00	1	0	0	0	1	2	2	0	0	0	0	.400	.500	.000	0.00	0.00
Adon, Joan	R-R	6-2	185	8-12-98	11	3	3.86	22	21	0	0	105	93	47	45	8	44	90	.237	.266	.218	7.71	3.77
Alastre, Tomas	R-R	6-4	170	6-11-98	5	12	5.28	25	25	1	0	123	128	81	72	17	54	117	.271	.298	.254	8.58	3.96
Brasher, Jared	R-R	6-1	200	1-3-95	1	1	2.77	18	0	0	1	26	20	13	8	3	17	29	.217	.212	.220	10.04	5.88
Cate, Tim	L-L	6-0	185	9-30-97	4	5	2.82	13	13	0	0	70	61	29	22	2	13	73	.232	.167	.247	9.34	1.66
Cronin, Matt	L-L	6-2	195	9-20-97	0	0	0.82	17	0	0	1	22	11	3	2	1	11	41	.153	.067	.175	16.77	4.50
Day, Chandler	R-R	6-5	175	5-24-97	3	4	4.30	31	0	0	1	67	72	36	32	4	24	56	.279	.289	.274	7.52	3.22
Fletcher, Aaron	L-L	6-0	220	2-25-96	2	3	1.61	15	0	0	1	28	14	14	5	0	5	28	.149	.065	.191	9.00	1.61
German, Jhonatan	R-R	6-4	215	1-24-95	1	1	1.96	12	0	0	3	18	12	5	4	1	5	22	.188	.172	.200	10.80	2.45
Gomez, Niomar	R-R	6-3	173	9-9-98	0	1	19.64	1	1	0	0	4	8	8	8	2	1	2	.444	.250	.500	4.91	2.45
Guillen, Angel	R-R	6-2	150	1-24-97	1	3	3.32	22	2	0	5	62	50	28	23	4	21	73	.213	.174	.235	10.54	3.03
Hernandez, Alfonso	L-L	5-11	162	8-3-99	1	2	5.00	6	0	0	1	18	17	10	10	0	6	16	.250	.143	.278	8.00	3.00
Howell, Jacob	R-R	6-3	180	8-9-95	1	1	2.67	18	0	0	2	30	22	9	9	0	10	36	.214	.156	.239	10.68	2.97
Irvin, Jake	R-R	6-6	225	2-18-97	8	8	3.79	25	25	0	0	128	122	64	54	14	38	113	.250	.273	.232	7.92	2.66
Klobosits, Gabe	L-R	6-7	270	5-16-95	0	0	0.00	4	0	0	0	5	1	0	0	0	3	5	.063	.125	.000	9.00	5.40
McMahan, Pearson	L-R	6-2	190	7-1-96	0	2	1.98	8	0	0	0	14	8	3	3	1	1	12	.167	.250	.125	7.90	0.66
Miller, Justin	R-R	6-3	215	6-13-87	0	0	0.00	1	0	0	0	1	2	2	0	0	0	0	.400	.500	.000	0.00	0.00
Peguero, Francys	R-R	6-2	170	10-4-95	2	8	2.95	17	17	0	0	92	96	40	30	12	19	80	.265	.229	.287	7.85	1.87
Rutledge, Jackson	R-R	6-8	250	4-1-99	2	0	2.30	6	6	0	0	27	14	9	7	0	11	31	.151	.213	.087	10.21	3.62
Schaller, Reid	R-R	6-3	210	4-2-97	3	3	3.29	12	12	0	0	52	38	21	19	5	25	47	.205	.194	.212	8.13	4.33
Stoeckinger, Jackson	L-L	6-3	210	2-13-96	2	3	3.51	29	0	0	5	90	93	40	35	9	22	69	.271	.268	.272	6.93	2.21
Strom, Leif	R-R	6-6	215	5-17-97	0	0	18.00	4	1	0	0	6	11	12	12	2	11	9	.393	.167	.455	13.50	16.50
Tapani, Ryan	R-R	6-0	180	6-28-94	5	5	3.32	19	5	0	0	65	63	29	24	6	18	73	.252	.329	.216	10.11	2.49
Teel, Carson	L-L	6-0	160	12-17-95	1	1	1.50	3	0	0	0	6	5	2	1	0	1	10	.217	.250	.200	15.00	1.50
Troop, Alex	L-L	6-5	210	7-19-96	1	3	2.18	11	0	0	0	33	22	11	8	2	3	34	.193	.161	.205	9.27	0.82
Turner, Trey	R-R	6-1	195	6-15-96	1	3	3.80	16	0	0	0	21	17	10	9	1	14	35	.215	.250	.192	14.77	5.91
Vann, Christian	L-L	6-2	195	6-25-96	4	2	1.57	20	0	0	2	29	14	10	5	0	16	28	.147	.300	.107	8.79	5.02
Wells, Nick	L-L	6-5	185	2-21-96	1	0	2.19	6	0	0	1	12	13	4	3	0	7	11	.265	.438	.182	8.03	5.11
Williamson, Ryan	L-L	6-2	190	4-28-95	4	1	3.84	23	2	0	2	61	57	32	26	5	22	61	.245	.153	.276	9.00	3.25

Fielding

Catcher	PCT	G	PO	A	E	DP	PB
Cropley	.991	25	186	28	2	0	1
Perkins	.980	36	315	24	7	2	7
Pineda	.995	84	655	88	4	4	26

	PCT	G	PO	A	E	DP
Daily	.976	48	65	101	4	20
Marinconz	.957	57	107	115	10	34
Pascal	.964	13	24	30	2	8
Sanchez	.971	9	20	13	1	1

	PCT	G	PO	A	E	DP
Daily	1.000	4	6	10	0	4
Lara	.954	45	61	124	9	19
Sanchez	.896	28	32	80	13	15
Vickers	1.000	5	14	13	0	5

First Base	PCT	G	PO	A	E	DP
Blash	.942	12	92	5	6	11
Daily	.964	7	51	2	2	5
Harrison	1.000	13	93	5	0	7
Mendoza	.989	44	333	18	4	33
Meregildo	.987	25	207	13	3	15
Perkins	1.000	19	129	5	0	8
Vickers	.994	22	176	4	1	15

Second Base	PCT	G	PO	A	E	DP
Caulfield	.933	15	21	35	4	9
Cluff	1.000	1	2	3	0	1

Third Base	PCT	G	PO	A	E	DP
Daily	.750	10	3	6	3	0
Lara	.918	36	23	66	8	4
Marinconz	.978	24	20	25	1	1
Mendoza	.938	6	2	13	1	1
Meregildo	1.000	3	1	4	0	0
Pascal	.947	9	4	14	1	0
Sanchez	.000	1	0	0	0	0
Vickers	.966	56	38	103	5	8

Shortstop	PCT	G	PO	A	E	DP
Cluff	.971	59	78	153	7	32

Outfield	PCT	G	PO	A	E	DP
Bautista	1.000	6	15	1	0	0
Canning	1.000	10	17	1	0	0
Connell	.985	110	192	11	3	3
Cropley	.923	5	12	0	1	0
Daily	1.000	2	1	0	0	0
Mendez	.944	20	33	1	2	0
O'Connor	1.000	12	24	1	0	0
Rhinesmith	.979	119	231	5	5	3
Upshaw	.986	61	134	8	2	1
Wilson	.990	76	186	6	2	0

AUBURN DOUBLEDAYS
NEW YORK-PENN LEAGUE

SHORT SEASON

Batting	B-T	HT	WT	DOB	AVG	vLH	vRH	G	AB	R	H	2B	3B	HR	RBI	BB	HBP	SH	SF	SO	SB	CS	SLG	OBP
Alu, Jake	L-R	5-10	175	4-6-97	.257	.323	.239	45	144	13	37	5	2	1	25	7	0	0	1	32	3	1	.340	.290
Arruda, J.T.	L-R	5-10	180	10-20-97	.245	.244	.245	61	196	22	48	10	5	0	20	30	2	1	0	50	6	3	.347	.351
Bautista, Rafael	R-R	6-2	194	3-8-93	.208	.333	.152	12	48	9	10	1	0	2	4	2	1	0	0	7	3	0	.354	.255
Carrillo, Adalberto	R-R	5-11	185	6-1-95	.258	.375	.232	42	132	24	34	10	1	3	20	16	0	0	1	34	2	1	.417	.336
Caulfield, Phil	L-R	5-8	170	12-30-94	.346	.375	.333	8	26	4	9	2	0	1	3	2	0	0	1	5	0	0	.539	.379
Collier, Zach	L-L	6-2	200	9-8-90	.125	.000	.167	5	16	3	2	1	0	0	1	5	0	0	0	0	0	0	.188	.333
Dunn, Jack	R-R	6-2	185	9-5-96	.255	.262	.252	52	157	22	40	2	0	1	11	16	6	2	1	30	3	0	.287	.344
Martina, Junior	R-R	5-11	190	12-12-97	.177	.375	.000	4	17	3	3	0	0	0	3	1	0	0	0	5	0	1	.177	.222
Masters, David	R-R		185	4-23-93	.214	.125	.250	9	28	6	6	2	0	1	6	5	1	0	0	9	0	0	.393	.353
Mendez, Ricardo	L-L	6-0	155	1-24-00	.264	.273	.273	38	129	21	34	4	0	1	8	16	2	0	2	25	5	8	.318	.349
Morales, Jesus	R-R	5-10	173	12-22-97	.200	.000	.231	4	15	2	3	1	0	0	1	0	0	0	3	0	1		.267	.200
Pena, Landerson	R-R	6-1	194	10-14-97	.226	.083	.268	40	106	13	24	4	1	4	11	6	1	0	0	36	3	1	.396	.274
Perez, Wilmer	R-R	5-10	186	4-16-98	.221	.180	.236	40	145	16	32	6	0	3	16	10	2	0	2	18	2	1	.324	.277
Peroni, Anthony	R-R	5-11	175	12-12-96	.216	.152	.253	41	125	15	27	6	0	2	13	16	2	1	0	27	0	0	.312	.315

	B-T	HT	WT	DOB	AVG	vLH	vRH	G	AB	R	H	2B	3B	HR	RBI	BB	HBP	SH	SF	SO	SB	CS	SLG	OBP
Pogue, Colton	R-R	6-1	195	2-1-96	.250	.400	.200	6	20	2	5	1	0	0	1	0	0	0	1	4	0	0	.300	.238
Pratt, Andrew	R-R	6-3	225	7-24-96	.161	.171	.157	34	118	10	19	3	1	2	7	12	2	0	1	46	0	0	.254	.248
Randa, Jake	L-L	6-1	195	12-14-98	.236	.327	.201	53	191	26	45	8	1	3	18	19	5	1	0	36	3	1	.335	.321
Sanchez, Jose	R-R	5-11	155	7-12-00	.182	.098	.214	60	220	19	40	9	0	0	16	18	4	2	1	56	1	1	.223	.255
Sanfler, Caldioli	L-R	6-2	185	12-7-97	.270	.220	.289	48	178	19	48	9	1	3	15	12	2	1	0	46	9	4	.382	.323
Senior, Eric	R-R	6-2	170	9-29-97	.252	.191	.267	34	107	13	27	4	4	2	18	5	7	0	1	22	0	1	.421	.325
Vega, Onix	R-R	5-10	200	9-7-98	.267	.316	.260	39	150	10	40	6	1	0	20	12	1	0	3	23	2	3	.320	.319
Ward, Drew	L-R	6-3	215	11-25-94	.208	.250	.167	7	24	1	5	2	0	1	7	2	0	0	0	10	0	0	.417	.269
Wilson, Cody	R-R	6-2	200	7-4-96	.286	.500	.154	5	21	4	6	0	2	0	3	2	0	0	0	6	0	0	.476	.348
Wiseman, Rhett	L-R	6-0	200	6-22-94	.308	.000	.400	4	13	4	4	0	0	3	1	2	0	0	3	1	0	1.00	.438
Ydens, Jeremy	R-R	6-2	200	7-3-97	.151	.059	.179	41	146	13	22	6	1	1	8	6	7	0	2	43	2	1	.226	.217

Pitching	B-T	HT	WT	DOB	W	L	ERA	G	GS	CG	SV	IP	H	R	ER	HR	BB	SO	AVG	vLH	vRH	K/9	BB/9
Beasley, Dylan	R-R	6-3	201	12-2-97	1	0	0.00	4	0	0	0	6	5	0	0	0	1	5	.227	.111	.308	7.50	1.50
Bocko, Jordan	R-R	5-11	195	1-10-97	1	1	1.96	12	0	0	0	23	16	6	5	1	6	11	.200	.147	.239	4.30	2.35
Chu, Gilberto	L-L	5-11	160	11-19-97	3	2	2.68	15	2	0	1	44	34	13	13	1	14	42	.213	.239	.202	8.66	2.89
Dragmire, Brady	R-R	6-1	185	2-5-93	0	0	0.00	2	0	0	0	3	1	0	0	0	0	4	.100	.000	.000	12.00	0.00
Dyson, Tyler	R-R	6-3	210	12-24-97	2	1	1.14	8	8	0	0	32	20	8	4	1	8	14	.192	.275	.141	3.98	2.27
Galindez, Nelson	L-L	6-3	220	7-26-98	0	0	9.92	7	2	0	0	16	25	18	18	1	15	6	.368	.316	.388	3.31	8.27
Gomez, Niomar	R-R	6-3	173	9-9-98	1	5	4.26	12	12	0	0	57	63	37	27	4	27	67	.276	.196	.331	10.58	4.26
Gomez, Rafael	R-R	6-0	178	6-15-98	2	6	6.36	13	10	0	0	58	80	43	41	5	23	36	.333	.429	.275	5.59	3.57
Gonzalez, Pedro	R-R	6-2	183	7-16-00	1	4	9.69	5	5	0	0	13	19	20	14	0	7	9	.307	.393	.235	6.23	4.85
Hernandez, Alfonso	L-L	5-11	162	8-3-99	3	1	2.51	10	1	0	0	32	30	12	9	0	5	33	.254	.387	.207	9.19	1.39
Knowles, Lucas	L-L	6-1	175	3-14-98	1	1	4.00	6	2	0	0	18	15	11	8	2	2	13	.217	.167	.235	6.50	1.00
Lee, Evan	L-L	6-1	200	6-18-97	3	2	2.65	12	3	0	0	34	30	13	10	2	17	44	.240	.214	.253	11.65	4.50
Martinez, Adrian	R-R	6-0	192	8-2-98	1	0	1.50	4	0	0	1	6	3	2	1	0	5	6	.130	.250	.000	9.00	7.50
McMahan, Pearson	R-R	6-2	190	7-1-96	1	2	3.52	11	0	0	3	15	9	9	6	1	8	12	.164	.192	.138	7.04	4.70
McMahon, Hunter	R-R	6-3	185	4-9-98	0	1	1.13	7	0	0	2	8	5	1	1	0	2	14	.185	.167	.200	15.75	2.25
Milacki, Bobby	R-R	6-2	210	11-6-96	3	2	3.70	15	0	0	1	24	28	14	10	0	17	24	.295	.361	.254	8.88	6.29
Moore, Davis	R-R	6-4	220	3-4-98	0	1	6.00	10	0	0	0	12	12	9	8	0	9	11	.279	.412	.192	8.25	6.75
Peguero, Jairon	L-L	6-0	177	6-14-97	0	0	0.00	4	0	0	1	5	4	0	0	0	1	4	.200	.200	.200	7.71	3.86
Perez, Fray	R-R	5-11	170	8-22-96	0	1	7.71	3	0	0	0	5	6	4	4	1	1	4	.300	.000	.429	7.71	1.93
Peterson, Todd	R-R	6-5	230	1-22-98	2	1	3.19	9	5	0	0	37	34	18	13	2	11	24	.243	.246	.241	5.89	2.70
Romero, Carlos	R-R	6-6	179	7-15-99	0	5	5.25	11	10	0	0	48	59	39	28	4	25	41	.303	.247	.336	7.69	4.69
Rutledge, Jackson	R-R	6-8	250	4-1-99	0	0	3.00	3	3	0	0	9	4	4	3	2	3	6	.133	.133	.133	6.00	3.00
Segura, Fausto	R-R	6-3	191	10-24-96	2	0	3.21	17	0	0	3	28	15	14	10	3	21	33	.156	.250	.109	10.61	6.75
Seijas, Karlo	R-R	6-1	185	9-6-00	0	0	4.50	1	0	0	1	4	4	3	2	0	0	5	.267	.200	.300	11.25	0.00
Sharp, Sterling	R-R	6-3	170	5-30-95	0	1	1.29	2	2	0	0	7	4	1	1	0	1	5	.191	.250	.154	6.43	1.29
Strom, Leif	R-R	6-6	215	5-17-97	2	0	4.66	4	4	0	0	19.1	14	11	10	5	9	17	.203	.174	.217	7.91	4.19
Troop, Alex	L-L	6-5	210	7-19-96	0	0	0.00	3	0	0	0	11	4	0	0	0	0	15	.108	.000	.154	12.27	0.00
Turner, Trey	R-R	6-1	195	6-15-96	0	1	5.50	11	0	0	2	18	9	11	11	1	16	27	.150	.111	.182	13.50	8.00
Willingham, Amos	R-R	6-4	217	8-21-98	1	4	3.67	12	2	0	1	27	28	11	11	1	4	18	.264	.177	.346	6.00	1.33
Yankosky, Tyler	L-R	6-6	225	5-28-98	2	3	5.82	15	0	0	1	22	22	16	14	0	14	11	.262	.314	.225	4.57	5.82
Yean, Eddy	R-R	6-1	180	6-25-01	1	1	2.45	2	2	1	0	11	7	4	3	0	5	7	.180	.267	.125	5.73	4.09

Fielding

C: Carrillo 2, Perez 22, Peroni 2, Pratt 26, Vega 26, Ydens 1. **1B:** Carrillo 39, Peroni 39. **2B:** Alu 30, Arruda 25, Caulfield 7, Dunn 1, Martina 2, Masters 4, Morales 1, Sanchez 11. **3B:** Alu 13, Arruda 8, Carrillo 1, Dunn 46, Martina 2, Masters 2, Morales 1, Pogue 5, Ward 6. **SS:** Arruda 27, Dunn 3, Masters 1, Morales 3, Sanchez 46. **OF:** Bautista 10, Collier 5, Mendez 33, Pena 37, Randa 43, Sanfler 41, Senior 32, Vega 1, Wilson 5, Wiseman 2, Ydens 36.

GCL NATIONALS ROOKIE
GULF COAST LEAGUE

Batting	B-T	HT	WT	DOB	AVG	vLH	vRH	G	AB	R	H	2B	3B	HR	RBI	BB	HBP	SH	SF	SO	SB	CS	SLG	OBP
Antuna, Yasel	B-R	6-0	170	10-26-99	.167	--	.167	3	6	1	1	0	0	0	0	2	0	0	1	0	0	.167	.375
Arias, Andry	L-L	6-3	180	6-19-00	.195	.154	.207	32	113	19	22	4	0	3	10	19	2	0	0	39	7	0	.310	.321
Berrios, Allan	R-R	5-10	168	8-9-97	.237	.333	.229	12	38	7	9	2	0	0	2	4	1	1	0	6	1	0	.290	.326
De La Rosa, Jeremy	L-L	5-11	160	1-16-02	.232	.067	.269	26	82	14	19	1	2	2	10	13	0	2	0	29	3	2	.366	.343
Diaz, Geraldi	L-R	6-0	196	7-8-00	.280	.182	.297	24	75	16	21	4	0	1	7	13	5	1	1	11	1	2	.373	.415
Difo, Wilmer	B-R	5-11	200	4-2-92	.056	.000	.071	6	18	2	1	0	0	0	2	5	1	0	0	5	0	1	.056	.292
Doolittle, Mason	R-R	6-4	210	7-10-98	.262	.231	.276	13	42	6	11	6	0	1	8	7	1	0	0	18	1	0	.476	.380
Emiliani, Leandro	L-L	6-1	180	3-22-00	.299	.188	.337	39	127	20	38	11	0	4	28	33	7	0	0	42	0	1	.480	.467
Fernandez, Braian	R-L	6-1	170	4-15-99	.245	.167	.262	30	102	10	25	4	1	1	12	11	0	0	0	24	5	2	.333	.319
Gomez, Anthony	R-R	6-1	185	10-2-96	.220	.201	.225	21	59	8	13	3	0	0	2	8	0	0	1	5	2	0	.271	.313
Hubbard, Jaylen	R-R	5-11	200	7-24-96	.179	.100	.213	24	67	14	12	1	1	1	12	13	3	0	0	17	5	0	.269	.337
Hurtado, Jorge	R-R	6-1	165	10-15-00	.272	.286	.267	31	114	15	31	12	2	1	14	10	1	0	1	40	4	2	.439	.333
Martina, Junior	R-R	5-11	190	12-12-97	.338	.258	.362	39	136	33	46	6	3	4	20	20	11	0	0	28	4	2	.515	.461
Matos, Wilfrido	R-R	5-11	160	9-28-00	.204	.188	.208	30	93	10	19	6	0	1	17	12	3	0	0	18	6	3	.301	.315
Murzi, Ivan	R-R	6-0	165	5-28-01	.400	.000	.667	2	5	2	2	0	0	0	1	1	1	0	0	2	0	0	.400	.571
Pena, Viandel	B-R	5-8	148	11-22-00	.359	.480	.330	37	131	27	47	10	3	0	15	21	2	0	0	31	6	3	.481	.455
Perkins, Nic	R-R	6-1	215	2-19-96	.375	.500	.333	3	8	0	3	0	0	1	2	0	0	0	2	0	0	.750	.500
Quinn, Parker	R-R	6-3	220	7-19-96	.163	.000	.206	16	43	5	7	2	0	0	1	4	1	0	0	12	1	0	.209	.250
Russo, Paul	L-R	5-9	160	10-24-95	.250	.167	.275	15	52	8	13	3	0	0	6	3	0	0	1	18	0	0	.308	.316
Strohschein, Kevin	R-R	6-1	215	7-25-97	.302	.333	.293	14	53	7	16	2	1	1	7	6	0	0	1	11	1	1	.434	.373
Sundberg, Jack	L-R	5-11	195	7-21-93	.219	.000	.241	9	32	3	7	0	0	0	3	6	0	0	1	7	1	0	.219	.278
Tovar, Edangel	R-R	5-10	150	7-26-00	.200	.177	.210	33	115	13	23	4	0	1	10	7	1	0	0	38	4	0	.261	.252

Batting	B-T	HT	WT	DOB	AVG	vLH	vRH	G	AB	R	H	2B	3B	HR	RBI	BB	HBP	SH	SF	SO	SB	CS	SLG	OBP
Turbi, Frailin	R-R	6-0	165	10-19-00	.254	.417	.218	20	67	7	17	2	0	0	12	4	6	1	0	12	1	0	.284	.351
Wilson, Cody	R-R	6-2	200	7-4-96	.267	.500	.231	4	15	2	4	0	0	0	2	2	1	0	0	2	1	1	.267	.389

Pitching	B-T	HT	WT	DOB	W	L	ERA	G	GS	CG	SV	IP	H	R	ER	HR	BB	SO	AVG	vLH	vRH	K/9	BB/9
Alvarado, Elvis	R-R	6-4	183	2-23-99	2	2	6.00	7	2	0	0	15	10	12	10	0	16	19	.185	.214	.175	11.40	9.60
Amoroso, Thony	R-R	6-0	154	8-2-98	0	0	0.00	3	0	0	2	5	2	1	0	0	2	5	.125	.500	.071	9.64	3.86
Barnett, Jake	L-L	6-2	190	7-30-94	1	0	0.00	4	1	0	0	4	6	0	0	0	1	3	.316	.250	.333	6.23	2.08
Barraclough, Kyle	R-R	6-3	225	5-23-90	0	0	0.00	1	1	0	0	1	2	0	0	0	0	1	.500	1.000	.333	9.00	0.00
Beasley, Dylan	R-R	6-3	201	12-2-97	0	0	3.00	7	0	0	1	12	11	5	4	1	4	8	.256	.250	.258	6.00	3.00
Cuevas, Michael	R-R	6-2	150	6-29-01	1	0	0.59	8	1	0	1	15	10	1	1	0	8	9	.200	.333	.158	5.28	4.70
De Los Santos, Jose	R-R	6-3	190	1-14-97	1	0	1.69	4	0	0	0	5	8	3	1	0	5	1	.400	.400	.400	1.69	8.44
Denaburg, Mason	R-R	6-4	195	8-8-99	1	1	7.52	7	4	0	0	20	23	22	17	1	14	19	.288	.174	.333	8.41	6.20
Dyson, Tyler	R-R	6-3	210	12-24-97	0	0	0.00	1	1	0	0	2	0	0	0	0	0	3	.000		.000	13.50	0.00
Espino, Paolo	R-R	5-10	215	1-10-87	0	0	4.15	2	0	0	0	4	4	2	2	0	1	9	.250	.250	.250	18.69	2.08
Ferrer, Jose A.	L-L	5-11	180	3-3-00	2	3	2.91	9	2	0	0	22	13	8	7	0	13	24	.173	.154	.177	9.97	5.40
Gonzalez, Pedro	R-R	6-2	183	7-16-00	1	2	3.81	8	2	0	2	28	25	15	12	1	15	21	.245	.241	.247	6.67	4.76
Hellickson, Jeremy	R-R	6-1	190	4-8-87	1	1	2.16	5	4	0	0	17	11	4	4	1	2	22	.180	.087	.237	11.88	1.08
Hiraldo, Abrahan	R-R	6-0	171	10-7-98	0	3	1.99	6	3	0	0	23	19	12	5	1	13	13	.224	.258	.204	5.16	5.16
Jameson, Charls	R-R	6-1	175	1-27-01	2	0	6.48	11	0	0	1	17	23	13	12	1	10	16	.338	.333	.339	8.64	5.40
Klobosits, Gabe	L-R	6-7	270	5-16-95	0	0	5.79	7	0	0	0	9	6	6	1	4	6	.250	.250	.250	5.79	3.86
Knowles, Lucas	L-L	6-1	175	3-14-98	0	0	0.00	2	0	0	0	4	3	0	0	0	3		.214	.333	.182	6.75	0.00
Martinez, Adrian	R-R	6-2	192	8-2-98	1	2	2.84	11	0	0	3	13	9	6	4	0	3	11	.200	.177	.214	7.82	2.13
McGowan, Kevin	R-R	6-5	233	10-18-91	0	1	3.97	5	5	0	0	11	14	6	5	0	1	13	.304	.231	.333	10.32	0.79
McMahon, Hunter	R-R	6-3	185	4-9-98	2	0	0.00	2	0	0	0	5	4	1	0	0	0	4	.235	.000	.267	7.71	0.00
Miller, Justin	R-R	6-3	215	6-13-87	0	0	0.00	2	1	0	0	2	0	0	0	0	0	5	.000	.000	.000	22.50	0.00
Moore, Davis	R-R	6-4	220	3-4-98	0	0	18.00	1	0	0	0	1	2	2	2	0	1	2	.333	.333	.333	18.00	9.00
Peguero, Jairon	L-L	6-0	177	6-14-97	0	1	2.70	8	0	0	1	13	9	5	4	1	4	14	.192	.200	.191	9.45	2.70
Pena, Bryan	L-L	6-1	175	1-10-00	2	2	0.92	11	2	0	0	29	24	4	3	0	11	34	.231	.278	.221	10.43	3.38
Peterson, Todd	R-R	6-5	230	1-22-98	0	0	9.00	1	0	0	0	2	4	2	2	0	0	2	.400	--	.400	9.00	9.00
Pozo, Miguel	R-R	6-4	185	10-11-99	0	0	8.10	5	1	0	0	17	22	18	15	2	15	11	.328	.438	.294	5.94	8.10
Ribalta, Orlando	R-R	6-7	245	3-5-98	2	0	3.18	9	0	0	0	17	11	7	6	1	13	19	.196	.143	.214	10.06	6.88
Russo, Paul	L-R	5-9	160	10-24-95	1	0	0.00	1	0	0	0	1	1	1	0	0	1	1	.250	.000	.333	9.00	9.00
Rutledge, Jackson	R-R	6-8	250	4-1-99	0	0	27.00	1	1	0	0	1	4	3	3	0	1	2	.571	--	.571	18.00	9.00
Seijas, Karlo	R-R	6-1	185	9-6-00	3	1	2.76	10	2	0	0	33	24	10	10	4	6	30	.207	.162	.228	8.27	1.65
Severino, Wilson	R-R	6-4	188	6-7-98	1	0	5.84	8	0	0	1	12	10	8	8	0	14	6	.222	.222	.222	4.38	10.22
Sharp, Sterling	R-R	6-3	170	5-30-95	0	0	0.00	1	0	0	0	2	1	0	0	0	0	2	.167		.500	9.00	0.00
Strom, Leif	R-R	6-6	215	5-17-97	0	0	20.25	1	0	0	0	1	4	3	3	0	1	1	.500	.500	.500	6.75	6.75
Taveras, Felix	R-R	6-2	155	7-11-95	1	2	10.24	5	3	0	0	10	13	12	11	1	5	7	.317	.214	.370	6.52	4.66
Vallejo, Alejandro	R-R	6-3	184	11-4-98	0	0	10.80	2	0	0	0	2	2	2	2	0	5	2	.000	.000	.000	10.80	27.00
Voth, Austin	R-R	6-2	201	6-26-92	0	0	0.00	1	1	0	0	2	1	0	0	0	0	1	.143	.333	.000	4.50	0.00
Williams, Austen	R-R	6-3	220	12-19-92	0	0	0.00	3	0	0	0	6	6	0	0	0	0	6	.250	.286	.222	13.50	0.00
Yean, Eddy	R-R	6-1	180	6-25-01	1	2	3.82	8	8	0	0	35	30	17	15	3	12	36	.233	.237	.231	9.17	3.06

Fielding

C: Berrios 11, Diaz 18, Doolittle 4, Murzi 2, Perkins 2, Turbi 17. **1B**: Emiliani 38, Hubbard 1, Quinn 14. **2B**: Difo 1, Gomez 9, Martina 19, Matos 2, Pena 16, Russo 8. **3B**: Gomez 6, Hubbard 22, Martina 13, Pena 8, Russo 3. **SS**: Antuna 3, Difo 4, Gomez 2, Martina 5, Matos 27, Pena 15. **OF**: Arias 31, De La Rosa 25, Fernandez 30, Hurtado 19, Strohschein 11, Sundberg 8, Tovar 32, Wilson 4.

DSL NATIONALS   ROOKIE
DOMINICAN SUMMER LEAGUE

Batting	B-T	HT	WT	DOB	AVG	vLH	vRH	G	AB	R	H	2B	3B	HR	RBI	BB	HBP	SH	SF	SO	SB	CS	SLG	OBP
Acosta, Jeisel	R-R	6-0	170	9-4-01	.227	.231	.226	33	119	15	27	7	1	0	14	15	3	0	0	27	1	1	.303	.329
Amparo, Yeuri	R-R	6-2	170	9-25-01	.195	.186	.198	45	154	21	30	4	0	0	6	15	5	1	0	42	13	2	.221	.287
Basanta, Delkis	R-R	6-3	175	2-4-02	.130	.158	.121	27	77	10	10	4	1	0	8	4	1	0	1	18	0	0	.208	.181
Castillo, Isan	R-R	6-1	160	12-3-01	.212	.172	.221	47	165	27	35	6	2	0	11	24	5	1	1	50	11	5	.273	.328
Colmenares, Jose	R-R	5-10	165	8-23-02	.143	.250	.118	15	42	3	6	0	0	0	5	2	4	0	2	5	0	1	.143	.240
Cotes, Dariel	L-L	5-11	155	2-4-02	.046	.000	.071	8	22	4	1	0	0	0	2	1	0	0	0	11	1	0	.046	.160
De La Cruz, Christopher	L-L	5-11	145	3-29-01	.243	.257	.239	48	169	23	41	5	3	1	14	23	2	0	1	25	14	2	.325	.339
Francois, Oliver	L-L	6-0	160	7-11-02	.190	.154	.200	19	58	11	11	1	1	0	3	10	2	0	0	11	1	3	.241	.329
Geraldo, Angel	R-R	6-1	160	6-14-01	.282	.385	.248	55	213	23	60	16	1	1	30	6	5	2	2	36	4	3	.380	.314
Gomez, Raymi	B-R	6-0	150	10-28-99	.256	.318	.234	49	172	24	44	9	4	5	32	22	6	0	2	47	1	3	.442	.356
Joseph, Diony	L-L	6-3	165	9-23-00	.143	.000	.200	5	14	1	2	0	0	0	1	0	0	1	0	4	2	1	.143	.143
Marte, Daniel	R-R	6-0	165	1-14-02	.257	.268	.254	55	210	32	54	7	9	5	29	11	6	0	2	67	10	1	.448	.310
Matias, Addiel	R-R	6-1	170	10-17-00	.189	.152	.200	39	148	25	28	9	0	1	16	9	0	0	3	48	1	0	.270	.245
Mercedes, Edwin	R-R	6-1	180	10-26-01	.098	.333	.058	22	61	4	6	3	0	0	1	8	1	0	0	26	1	1	.148	.214
Murzi, Ivan	R-R	6-0	165	12-8-01	.217	.286	.188	30	97	14	21	2	0	5	13	6	5	1	0	25	3	1	.392	.296
Rivero, Yoander	R-R	5-9	155	11-22-01	.249	.143	.277	53	197	25	49	4	3	2	23	23	2	2	4	26	8	6	.330	.327
Sanchez, Bryanth	B-R	5-10	165	2-2-01	.212	.143	.237	19	52	3	11	0	0	2	1	3	0	0	6	0	0	.212	.268
Tatis, Guillermo	R-R	6-1	180	6-3-00	.159	.000	.208	18	63	4	10	3	2	0	6	1	1	0	21	1	0	.270	.221
Tejeda, Erick	R-R	6-4	162	12-26-01	.215	.097	.253	38	130	9	28	1	1	0	11	13	1	2	4	26	3	3	.239	.292

Pitching	B-T	HT	WT	DOB	W	L	ERA	G	GS	CG	SV	IP	H	R	ER	HR	BB	SO	AVG	vLH	vRH	K/9	BB/9
Amoroso, Thony	R-R	6-0	154	8-2-98	0	0	0.00	4	0	0	0	7	2	0	0	0	1	9	.091	.000	.154	11.57	1.29
Atencio, Jose	R-R	5-11	165	9-18-01	0	0	27.00	1	0	0	0	0	1	1	1	0	0	1	.500	--	.500	27.00	0.00
Basanta, Delkis	R-R	6-3	175	2-4-02	0	0	0.00	2	0	0	0	2	0	0	0	0	0	2	.000	.000	.000	9.00	0.00

WASHINGTON NATIONALS

				W	L	ERA	G	GS	CG	SV	IP	H	R	ER	HR	BB	SO	AVG	vLH	vRH	SO/9	BB/9
Blanco, Mirton	R-R	6-5	181	7-10-02	1	1	4.71	13	3	0	0	29	17	19	15	0	36	27	.175	.211	.153	8.48	11.30
Caceres, Bryan	R-R	6-1	170	2-19-00	3	5	4.11	19	0	0	2	35	34	23	16	0	19	39	.258	.314	.222	10.03	4.89
Castro, Andres	R-R	6-2	185	10-15-00	0	3	5.80	12	11	0	0	40	40	33	26	2	38	33	.261	.169	.330	7.36	8.48
Cedeno, Jose	R-R	6-3	170	10-5-01	3	3	3.41	11	7	0	0	34	29	18	13	3	11	32	.228	.257	.217	8.39	2.88
De La Rosa, Manuel	R-R	6-3	182	6-8-99	2	2	6.27	17	0	0	1	33	23	27	23	0	17	37	.198	.209	.192	10.09	4.64
Francisco, Michael	R-R	6-1	163	5-13-01	0	1	0.00	8	0	0	2	12	8	2	0	0	1	11	.195	.294	.125	8.25	0.75
Gomez, Miguel	R-R	6-3	170	9-10-01	0	0	3.45	14	0	0	1	29	29	17	11	1	13	22	.266	.320	.220	6.91	4.08
Hiraldo, Bernardo	R-R	6-2	160	5-20-00	2	6	4.86	12	12	0	0	54	71	42	29	1	7	40	.311	.303	.316	6.71	1.17
Jimenez, Luis	R-R	6-2	165	7-6-01	3	2	7.71	15	0	0	0	28	29	26	24	2	27	31	.279	.265	.291	9.96	8.68
Marcano, Eliel	R-R	6-1	170	7-9-02	1	0	3.09	6	0	0	2	12	11	4	4	0	3	6	.244	.154	.281	4.63	2.31
Marquez, Jose	R-R	6-6	196	12-1-01	0	0	4.00	5	0	0	0	9	9	9	4	0	5	4	.243	.200	.273	4.00	5.00
Mercedes, Jose	R-R	6-5	178	6-2-00	0	5	5.11	13	9	0	1	49	49	36	28	1	34	36	.272	.272	.273	6.57	6.20
Montero, Ronni	R-R	6-3	190	11-2-01	1	3	2.36	13	6	0	0	42	38	23	11	1	16	33	.235	.284	.200	7.07	3.43
Olivero, Sebastian	R-R	6-2	180	1-28-02	1	0	8.46	13	0	0	0	28	27	27	26	1	21	16	.262	.375	.191	5.20	6.83
Otanez, Johan	R-R	6-1	168	2-19-02	1	4	5.02	11	9	0	0	43	37	28	24	2	28	23	.234	.309	.194	4.81	5.86
Rodriguez, Kevin	R-R	6-1	145	8-13-00	2	3	2.67	15	1	0	0	30	26	21	9	2	16	35	.228	.325	.176	10.38	4.75
Sanchez, Bryan	R-R	6-1	175	8-12-02	1	1	5.63	13	5	0	0	24	18	19	15	1	20	23	.205	.175	.229	8.63	7.50
Vallejo, Alejandro	R-R	6-3	184	11-4-98	1	2	3.57	17	1	0	1	23	18	11	9	0	23	31	.222	.273	.188	12.31	9.13

Fielding

C: Acosta 25, Colmenares 7, Mercedes 12, Murzi 26, Sanchez 6. **1B:** Colmenares 3, De La Cruz 14, Francois 1, Joseph 2, Mercedes 1, Sanchez 10, Tatis 16, Tejeda 23. **2B:** Castillo 25, Geraldo 28, Matias 2, Rivero 12. **3B:** Geraldo 13, Matias 37, Rivero 1, Tatis 1, Tejeda 14. **SS:** Castillo 11, Geraldo 14, Rivero 39. **OF:** Amparo 37, Basanta 20, Cotes 7, De La Cruz 30, Francois 13, Gomez 41, Joseph 2, Marte 55.

MINOR
LEAGUES

Home Runs, Looming PBA Pockmark Minor Leagues

BY JOSH NORRIS

Before the season began, Minor League Baseball announced that its Triple-A affiliates would use the same baseball as their parent clubs in the major leagues. At the time, the change seemed fairly innocuous: it was a move designed to get players a step away from the big leagues used to the baseball they would use at the next level, and would keep teams from having to shift baseballs whenever a major leaguer came down for a few days of rehabilitation.

It quickly became obvious that a simple shift in equipment was producing seismic results. Balls flew out of parks at rates never before seen and quickly became the hottest topic of the summer. By season's end, the results were undeniable: The Pacific Coast and International League hit a combined 3,652 home runs in 2018. In 2019, that figure jumped by 2,100, all the way to 5,752. Put another way, the Triple-A home run output increased by more home runs than the International League hit in all of 2018.

The home run surge was best exemplified by the El Paso Chihuahuas, the Padres' Triple-A affiliate in the PCL. Armed with a roster full of already powerful hitters, they assaulted the record books from Opening Day until season's end. In 2018, Salt Lake and Las Vegas led the league with 173 home runs apiece.

El Paso eclipsed that total on June 30. The Chihuahuas' 174th home run was a perfect encapsulation of the degree to which the new, livelier ball was inflating the power not only of entire teams, but also of individual players.

The home run was hit by outfielder Matthew Batten, a 24-year-old outfielder selected from Quinnipiac in the 32nd round of the 2017 draft. In 127 career games over two pro seasons, Batten had three home runs. The blast he hit for El Paso's 174th of the year was his fourth of the season—in his 61st game. Batten finished the year with six home runs, meaning he'd doubled his career total in a season with the new baseball. Not only that, the six home runs drew Batten just one shy from the seven he'd hit in four seasons in at Quinnipiac.

And while the new baseball was an obvious boon for hitters, it was a nightmare for pitchers. Righthander Tyler Danish was a perfect example of the havoc the change created.

Ty France and the El Paso Chihuahuas saw benefits from the livelier MLB baseballs

STEPHEN SMITH/FOUR SEAM

After a successful 2018 that saw him get his first big league callups, Danish signed in 2019 with the Mariners as a minor league free agent. He moved into the rotation at Triple-A Tacoma, which has a reputation as one of the friendliest environments for pitchers in the otherwise hitter's haven of the PCL.

In his first start of the season, Danish gave up nine hits and 10 runs (all earned) in just 1.2 innings at Sacramento. Five days later, he gave up 10 hits and six runs in five innings as Tacoma hosted El Paso.

That was his best outing of his time with Tacoma. By the time he was released in late May, Danish had given up 44 hits, 41 runs (37 earned) and nine home runs in only 15.2 innings. As rough as his 21.26 ERA was, his .502 opponent average was even tougher to fathom. He finished the year with the New Britain Bees of the independent Atlantic League.

Change Is Coming

For several years, the whispers about a potential minor league shakeup coinciding with a new Professional Baseball Agreement have gotten louder. They reached their highest volume in mid-October, when Baseball America reported a proposal that would radically realign the minor leagues. In doing so, 42 teams would lose their affiliations.

At the core of the negotiations, MLB is looking to dramatically improve Minor League Baseball's stadium facilities and take control over how the minor leagues are organized as far as affiliations and the geography of leagues. Those areas have been under the control of MiLB for the past 100-plus years and would lead to a dramatic restructuring of how MiLB is governed and operates.

In the view of some MLB owners and front office officials, the current system, in which MLB teams and MiLB clubs negotiate every two years to sign two-year Player Development Contracts, leaves MLB clubs in undesirable situations from facilities and geographical standpoints.

In the view of some MLB owners and front office officials, the current system, where MLB teams and MiLB clubs negotiate every two years to sign two-year Player Development Contracts, leaves MLB clubs in undesirable situations from facilities and geographical standpoints. In a number of cases over the past decade, MLB owners have ended up purchasing MiLB teams to avoid ending up in what are viewed as some of the worst stadiums around minor league baseball.

An example of both of these situations can be found in 2017, when the Mets purchased the Syracuse affilate in the International League outright. That move meant the Mets would no longer have to participate in the bi-annual Affiliation Shuffle, and ultimately led to the Nationals having to send their Triple-A players to Fresno of the Pacific Coast League. That result made it incredibly inconvenient and costly for the Nationals to move recall a player to the majors or promote one to Fresno from their Double-A affiliate in Harrisburg, Pa

In MLB's view, roughly a quarter of all current MiLB clubs' facilities fail to meet the standard needed for their minor league players. MLB has put the onus on MiLB to find a way to guarantee those stadiums will reach acceptable standards in the near future. If MiLB cannot, then MLB has a proposal to reduce the number of affiliated minor league teams going forward to the 75 percent of MiLB clubs that MLB deems capable of meeting their facility standards.

MLB would work with MiLB and others to ensure the remaining 25 percent of clubs have teams, but they would no longer be affiliated MiLB clubs.

MLB also wants to completely rework the Player Development Contract process to ensure MLB clubs can have MiLB affiliates that meet their desires geographically. To do so, they want to eliminate the current two-year PDC process and replace it with much longer-lasting MLB-MiLB franchise agreements. Doing so would give MLB clubs much more certainty, but it would also eliminate the negotiating leverage MiLB teams currently have every two years.

At the root of the disagreement is a preliminary proposal MLB has offered to reduce its number of PDCs from 160 to 120. That reduction would eliminate the four, non-complex Rookie-level and short-season classifications.

The proposal also completely reorganizes the full-season minor leagues. Triple-A, Double-A, high Class A and low Class A, those four levels would be reworked to make the leagues much more geographically compact. In Triple-A, the Pacific Coast League would shift from 16 teams to 10. The International League would grow to 20 teams. The 14-team low Class A South Atlantic League would be turned into a six-team league with a new Mid-Atlantic league springing up.

The short-season Northwest League would move to full-season ball.

MINOR LEAGUES

A later draft would keep players like Dansby Swanson from being selected while they are in the NCAA playoffs.

The Resulting Backdraft

If the MLB gets its way in the next set of Professional Baseball Agreement negotiations with Minor League Baseball and the number of teams outside the Gulf Coast and Arizona Leagues reduces to 120, then it stands to reason that there would be fewer players needed. With that in mind, the draft would move from 40 rounds to somewhere between 20-25 rounds.

The draft would also move to later in the summer, which would eliminate the awkward situation college players face when they are drafted during the NCAA Tournament's regional rounds while they are focused on trying to get their teams to the College World Series.

Moving the draft later would likely have significant effects.

Without short-season, Appalachian or Pioneer League teams, drafted players would likely not play official games during their draft year. Instead, they would probably play in scrimmages and instructional league-type games in August and September similar to the informal Tricky League where international players go after they sign their first pro contracts.

The next spring, college players would likely head to low Class A in their first full pro seasons, while high school draftees would join international signees in the complex leagues.

ORGANIZATION STANDINGS

Cumulative domestic farm club records for major league organizations, with winning percentages going back five years. Most organizations have six affiliates.

		2019					
		W	L	PCT	2018	2017	2016	2015
1.	Rays	428	319	.573	.591	.536	.529	.502
2.	Dodgers	416	324	.562	.552	.546	.527	.529
3.	Rangers	382	301	.559	.466	.467	.491	.518
4.	D-backs	422	336	.557	.541	.515	.507	.509
5.	Twins	361	309	.539	.511	.581	.540	.534
6.	Padres	396	345	.534	.502	.505	.463	.476
7.	Pirates	379	338	.529	.499	.499	.490	.547
8.	Astros	358	321	.527	.576	.521	.513	.565
9.	Orioles	359	323	.526	.471	.482	.455	.524
10.	Yankees	411	382	.518	.500	.602	.595	.542
11.	Giants	384	360	.516	.457	.446	.483	.504
12.	Indians	377	364	.509	.529	.493	.550	.509
13.	Marlins	340	332	.506	.465	.483	.454	.427
14.	Blue Jays	370	376	.496	.523	.505	.507	.485
15.	Royals	372	380	.495	.492	.466	.452	.497
16.	Phillies	358	366	.494	.549	.528	.595	.542
17.	Mets	369	379	.493	.472	.456	.480	.532
18.	Brewers	367	377	.493	.502	.504	.443	.439
19.	White Sox	331	345	.490	.515	.438	.427	.504
20.	Nationals	332	349	.488	.481	.456	.508	.469
21.	Mariners	335	353	.487	.469	.487	.581	.435
22.	Athletics	354	388	.477	.515	.494	.488	.483
23.	Cubs	352	387	.476	.459	.504	.539	.540
24.	Rockies	334	373	.472	.482	.496	.477	.466
25.	Tigers	340	386	.468	.505	.502	.474	.472
26.	Braves	311	359	.464	.471	.471	.468	.489
27.	Red Sox	313	369	.459	.476	.497	.526	.469
28.	Reds	336	413	.449	.453	.456	.502	.512
29.	Cardinals	334	412	.448	.534	.546	.520	.512
30.	Angels	282	404	.411	.430	.492	.451	.459

POSTSEASON RESULTS

League	Champion	Runner-Up
International	Columbus	Durham
Pacific Coast	Sacramento	Round Rock
Eastern	Trenton	Bowie
Southern	Jackson	Biloxi
Texas	Amarillo	Tulsa
California	Visalia	Lake Elsinore
Carolina	Wilmington	Fayetteville
Florida State	Postseason cancelled due to Hurricane Dorian	
Midwest	South Bend	Clinton
South Atlantic	Lexington	Hickory
New York-Penn	Brooklyn	Lowell
Northwest	Hillsboro	Tri-City
Appalachian	Johnson City	Burlington
Pioneer	Idaho Falls	Ogden
Arizona	AZL Rangers	AZL Indians Blue
Gulf Coast	Postseason cancelled due to Hurricane Dorian	

The draft currently is held at the end of most states' high school baseball seasons and the final month of the college baseball season. If the draft moved to July it could reshape the summer showcase circuit, because high school seniors would have more time post-graduation to try to impress scouts, and might rework summer college wood-bat leagues as well.

Attendance Rises

A year after MiLB posted its smallest total attendance in 14 seasons, MiLB reported that 41,504,077 fans passed through its turnstiles in 2019. That figured marked an increase of 2.6 percent from 2018.

The numbers appear to show was that 2018's attendance drop was not a sign of a developing trend. While MiLB's record attendance of 43.2 million, set in 2008, seems far out of reach, the league has found a solid equilibrium. This was the 14 consecutive season in which MiLB has drawn more than 40 million fans, and its average of 4,044 fans per game is slightly above its average attendance per game for the past decade.

Whether the 2019 season is viewed as a jump from 2018 or a return to normalcy when compared to the rest of the decade, MiLB can confidently state that its attendance is bucking current trends.

"We are one of, if not the only sports property experiencing an increase in attendance. That has not been the trend in pro sports in this country," MiLB President Pat O'Conner said.

MiLB saw significant success with its Copa de la Diversion initiative, in which teams created events to honor the local Latino community, and Pride events aimed at honoring the LGBTQ community.

According to MiLB, Copa games drew crowds 20 percent above average attendance, while Pride events drew crowds 12 percent larger than normal.

The arrival of new teams and new ballparks also made a massive difference. New ballparks in Amarillo, Texas; Fayetteville, N.C. and Las Vegas made an impact.

The new ballpark in Las Vegas was a massive success. The Aviators drew 318,710 more fans than the Las Vegas 51s did in 2018 in the team's old ballpark. Las Vegas averaged 9,299 fans per game, which was the highest average attendance any U.S. team in the minor leagues has seen since Charlotte drew 9,428 fans per game in 2015.

Similarly, Fayetteville drew nearly 223,000 more fans than Buies Creek drew in 2018, and Amarillo drew 165,000 more fans than Colorado Springs did in 2018.

The Rocky Mountain Vibes, which replaced the Helena Brewers, drew 106,208 more fans than Helena did in 2018. Rocky Mountain's average per game attendance (3,923 per game) was nearly 2,000 more fans than Helena drew for its biggest draw of the 2018 season.

The league will look for similar spikes in 2020 from new stadiums in Madison, Ala., Fredericksburg, Va. and Wichita, Kan.

Teams saw big-time attendance spikes in their Copa de la Diversion games.

Hurricanes Strike Again

For the third straight season, the minor league playoffs were affected by hurricanes.

In 2017, Hurricane Irma played havoc in the Carolina, Florida State and Southern leagues. A year later, Hurricane Florence's presence pushed the entire International League Championship Series to Moosic, Pa., home of the Scranton/Wilkes-Barre RailRiders. Similarly, the 2018 Carolina League Championship Series went from three games to a winner-take-all game, won by the Buies Creek Astros in their last game before the club moved to its new home in Fayetteville, N.C.

This time, Hurricane Dorian's path led to the Florida State League cancelling the final few games of its regular season and the entirety of its playoffs. The move left the league without a champion for the first time in history. There were three occasions when the league finished with co-champions (hurricanes in 2017 and 2014 and the Sept. 11 terrorist attacks in 2001), but 2019 marked the only time that league's championship trophy would go without having a new name engraved.

The Gulf Coast League's playoffs were also cancelled by the hurricane, and 2019 marked the first time the GCL did not crown a champion.

CONTINUED ON PAGE 358

Gavin Lux Transforms Into Star Prospect

BY KYLE GLASER

When Trey Magnuson first saw Gavin Lux in the summer of 2015, the Dodgers' area scout for the upper midwest was immediately drawn to Lux's athleticism and lefthanded bat.

The actions he showed at shortstop were rare in a teenager from cold-weather Wisconsin. Even more rare was his advanced feel to hit and comfort facing velocity.

As Magnuson began getting to know Lux in the ensuing months, however, something began to stand out even more.

"You put a little obstacle in front of him, he was going to prove he could get through it," Magnuson said. "He has that resilience. He has that maturity."

Lux would prove Magnuson's assessment spot-on, overcoming a rough first full pro season and years of throwing issues to become one of the minors' top performers in 2019.

Gavin Lux

The Dodgers' 21-year-old shortstop thrived the two highest levels of the minors on his way to his first major league callup in September.

In 113 games at Double-A Tulsa and Triple-A Oklahoma City, Lux hit .347 to rank fourth in the minors, while his .421 on-base percentage ranked 10th and his .607 slugging percentage placed sixth. In terms of OPS, he ranked fourth (1.028), behind Kevin Cron, Jared Walsh and Mark Payton, older players at Triple-A.

Lux put together a 50-game on-base streak from early June to mid-August and slashed his errors from 27 to 13.

For his performance, Lux is Baseball America's Minor League Player of the Year.

"Obviously I feel like I always believed in myself, but I don't think I would have expected two years ago to play like how I am now, I guess you could say," Lux said.

For the practical purposes of his development, Lux's ability to conquer any setback or challenge allowed for rapid gains.

"Each year in spring training we lay out some goals (for our players) for the year," Dodgers president of baseball operations Andrew Friedman said.

"The idea behind that concept is: You lay out goals, you kind of revisit it throughout the year, and the next year you rip up those goals and you set the bar higher.

"It's great in theory. It rarely plays out in practice, but it truly did with Gavin. Every time we gave him goals and things to work on, he poured himself into it and has steadily gotten better at all aspects of his game."

Lux's most striking improvement is his power. The added 25 pounds of muscle over two years are visible in his arms, chest and shoulders, to the point he barely resembles the skinny teenager scouts first saw in 2015.

Lux jumped from seven home runs in 2017 to 15 homers in 2018 to 26 home runs this year. His slugging percentage jumped from .362 to .514 to .607.

"I never used to be able to hit the ball out of the yard the other way, and this year that's kind of changed for me a little bit," Lux said.

That strength wouldn't mean much without an approach to make the most of it. That, more than any individual statistical accomplishment, is where Lux stands out most to the Dodgers' top decision-makers.

"His approach in the box is the most mature I've ever been around in someone this age," Friedman said. "It's very rare to be able to see someone his age to be able to slow down the game and understand that cat-and-mouse game between the hitter and the pitcher in such an advanced way."

PREVIOUS WINNERS

2009: Jason Heyward, Myrtle Beach/Mississippi (Braves)
2010: Jeremy Hellickson, Montgomery/Durham (Rays)
2011: Mike Trout, Arkansas (Angels)
2012: Wil Myers, Northwest Arkansas/Omaha (Royals)
2013: Byron Buxton, Cedar Rapids/Fort Myers (Twins)
2014: Kris Bryant, Iowa (Cubs)
2015: Blake Snell, Charlotte/Montgomery/Durham (Rays)
2016: Yoan Moncada, Salem/Portland (Red Sox)
2017: Ronald Acuna Jr., Florida/Mississippi/Gwinnett (Braves)
2018: Vladimir Guerrero Jr., New Hampshire/Buffalo (Blue Jays)
Full list: BaseballAmerica.com/awards

MINOR LEAGUES

Don Logan's Dreams Became Reality

BY J.J. COOPER

There were plenty of times when Don Logan's quest seemed to be impossible. As the Las Vegas 51's general manager from 1991-1999 and its president since 2000, Logan knew that the team needed a replacement for Cashman Field. But every attempt to find a site and a stadium seemed to fall apart.

There were attempts to bring MLB spring training to Las Vegas. There was an attempt to pair with Reno to get new stadiums. There were mock-ups and proposals at a variety of sites.

But Logan always knew that a new ballpark was built in Las Vegas would make a dramatic difference.

Logan has spent 36 seasons with the Las Vegas club. He's worked for an array of owners and worked through an even larger number of stadium proposals. Year after year, the 51s soldiered on in a ballpark which was long past its prime.

In 2019, his efforts finally paid off, as the club exceeded expectations.

Las Vegas has a new nickname (the Aviators). They have a new logo. They have a new affiliate (Oakland). And they now have best ballpark in the minor leagues.

And they have the success that he had long predicted would arrive with a new ballpark.

Las Vegas drew 332,224 fans in 2018, an average of 4,746 fans per game. In 2019,

they were the largest drawing club in Minor League Baseball. More than 650,000 fans came through the turnstiles for an average of 9,299 fans per night. Las Vegas' 2019 attendance was almost as much as the club's 2017 and 2018 attendance combined.

Las Vegas not only led the minors in attendance, it also finished with an average of less than 1,000 fans per night behind the Marlins in that category.

The Aviators' success is part of a slew of initiatives that have emphasized Las Vegas' appeal. The NFL's Raiders are moving to town for 2020. The NHL's Golden Knights made it to the Stanley Cup Finals in their first season as an expansion team.

And next year, Las Vegas Ballpark will host the 2020 Triple-A Championship game.

CONTINUED FROM PAGE 356

First Time's The Charm

One of the biggest changes after the dust cleared on the 2018 Affiliation Shuffle was the addition of Amarillo to the Texas League. The team filled the void left by San Antonio reclassifying into the Triple-A Pacific Coast League and gave the TL a shiny new stadium called Hodgetown.

The park proved to be one of the best hitter's atmospheres in the minor leagues in its first season. The 206 home runs hit at Amarillo ranked 12th overall in the minor leagues. The figure also ranked second in among teams outside of Triple-A, which was using the livelier ball utilized in the major leagues.

Beyond all the offense, the Sod Poodles experienced plenty of success on the field, too. Boosted by late-season appearances from top Padres prospects like lefty MacKenzie Gore (who checked in at No. 4 on Baseball America's season-ending Top 100 list), righty Luis Patino (No. 29) and trade-deadline addition Taylor Trammell (No. 48). Trammell's go-ahead grand slam helped send his team to the Texas League title in its first season.

The Carolina League also gained a new affiliate when the Fayetteville Woodpeckers moved away from Campbell University, shed its Buies Creek name and moved into shiny new Segra Stadium. The Woodpeckers finished third in the Carolina League attendance race, and advanced to the championship series in its first year before falling to Wilmington in the decisive fifth game.

Ragsdale Pulls Double-Duty For Texas

BY JOSH NORRIS

PREVIOUS WINNERS

2009: Charlie Montoyo, Durham (Rays)
2010: Mike Sarbaugh, Columbus (Indians)
2011: Ryne Sandberg, Lehigh Valley (Phillies)
2012: Dave Miley, Scranton/Wilkes-Barre (Yankees)
2013: Gary DiSarcina, Pawtucket (Red Sox)
2014: Mark Johnson, Kane County (Cubs)
2015: Tony DeFrancesco, Fresno (Astros)
2016: Dave Wallace, Akron (Indians)
2017: Stubby Clapp, Memphis (Cardinals)
2018: Drew Saylor, Rancho Cucamonga (Dodgers)
Full list: BaseballAmerica.com/awards

Corey Ragsdale had a tough job in 2019. Actually, he had two of them.

In addition to managing the high Class A Down East Wood Ducks, Ragsdale, a veteran of the Rangers player-development department, was also cast as the organization's field coordinator.

That meant even longer hours, conference calls and meetings with fellow members of the team's player-development, in addition to trying to make sure all the players under his charge were put in the best position to achieve their goals.

"Going into 2019, we knew that we had talent, but the bulk of that talent was at our lower levels. We kind of knew that going into it," Ragsdale said. "Especially at the two A-ball clubs. So, knowing that, we kind of talked through that and thought about how we were going to set everything up and in instructional league (in 2018), J.D. (Rangers GM Jon Daniels) and (assistant GM) Mike (Daly) came to me and basically asked if I would be willing to do both, just for one year. I think, in their mind, it was like 'How can we make the biggest impact?' And that's how it came up."

The job entailed running spring training and instructional league, as well has helping implement the organization's philosophies throughout the system.

That's a huge workload in and of itself, but there was still the task of actually managing his team in Down East, which included plenty of talented players during the first and second halves of the season.

So, how did those players do? Catcher Sam Huff crushed 13 home runs in 97 games and was named MVP of the Futures Game. Their team pitching worked to an ERA of 3.00, which tied league-champion Wilmington for the best on the circuit. That group was paced by Sal Mendez, a lefthander who worked to a 7-2, 2.37 mark in 117.2 innings.

In all, the Wood Ducks, in their second year in the Carolina League after the franchise moved from the California League, won a league-best 87 games but fell to Fayetteville—which was in its first year in the CL—in the Division Series

Not bad for a guy pulling double-duty.

Fresno Faux Pas

Normally, the Fresno Grizzlies stand as one of the top promotional teams in the minor leagues. Their Taco Tuesday promotions have been a hit for years, and they are constant source of original, popular theme nights that earn praise from around the sport.

This year, however, a pair of missteps brought the Grizzlies the wrong kind of national attention. The first came on Memorial Day weekend, when the team aired a YouTube video that cast congresswoman Alexandria Ocasio-Cortez (D-N.Y.) among North Korea's Kim-Jong Un, Cuba's Fidel Castro as "the enemies of freedom, those who are potential adversaries."

The reaction on social media was swift, and forced the team to issue an apology. Two sponsors—Dos Equis and Tecate beers—announced that they'd dropped their sponsorships with the team as a result of the video.

The team was forced to issue a second public statement three months later, after its annual taco-eating contest. Dana Hutchings, 41, of Fresno, collapsed during the contest and was pronounced dead upon arrival at a local hospital shortly thereafter. The event served as a precursor to its annual Taco Truck Throwdown, which went on as scheduled a few days later, but the competitive-eating portion of the event was cancelled.

The Toledo Mudhens also found negative headlines when a dog died during postgame fireworks following the team's annual "Hens and Hounds" event at Fifth Third Field.

MINOR LEAGUES

TRIPLE-A

Pos	Player	Age	AVG	OBP	SLG	G	AB	H	2B	3B	HR	BB	SO	SB
C	Austin Allen, El Paso (Padres)	25	.330	.379	.663	67	270	89	27	0	21	22	56	0
1B	Kevin Cron, Reno (D-backs)	26	.331	.449	.777	82	305	101	20	1	38	61	77	1
2B	Keston Hiura, San Antonio (Brewers)	22	.329	.407	.681	57	213	70	16	1	19	23	64	7
3B	Ty France, El Paso (Padres)	25	.399	.477	.770	76	296	118	27	1	27	30	51	1
SS	Gavin Lux, Oklahoma City (Dodgers)	21	.392	.478	.719	49	199	78	18	4	13	33	42	3
OF	Yordan Alvarez, Round Rock (Astros)	22	.343	.443	.742	56	213	73	16	0	23	38	50	2
OF	Randy Arozarena, Memphis (Cardinals)	24	.358	.435	.593	64	246	88	18	2	12	24	48	9
OF	Jaylin Davis, Rochester/Sacramento (Twins/Giants)	25	.332	.410	.699	68	256	85	17	1	25	29	74	3
DH	Jared Walsh, Salt Lake (Angels)	26	.325	.423	.686	98	382	124	30	0	36	59	115	0

Pos	Pitcher	Age	W	L	ERA	G	GS	SV	IP	H	HR	BB	SO	WHIP
SP	Zac Gallen, New Orleans (Marlins)	23	9	1	2.07	14	14	0	91	48	10	17	112	0.71
SP	Mitch Keller, Indianapolis (Pirates)	22	7	5	3.56	19	19	0	104	94	9	35	123	1.24
SP	Corey Oswalt, Syracuse (Mets)	25	10	4	2.91	16	16	0	87	84	9	15	79	1.14
SP	Devin Smeltzer, Rochester (Twins)	23	1	4	3.63	15	14	0	74	68	14	19	71	1.17
SP	Bryse Wilson, Gwinnett (Braves)	21	10	7	3.42	21	21	0	121	120	12	26	118	1.21
RP	Trevor Kelley, Pawtucket (Red Sox)	25	5	5	1.79	52	0	12	65	51	8	21	63	1.10

DOUBLE-A

Pos	Player	Age	AVG	OBP	SLG	G	AB	H	2B	3B	HR	BB	SO	SB
C	Daulton Varsho, Jackson (D-backs)	23	.301	.378	.520	108	396	119	25	4	18	42	63	21
1B	Evan White, Arkansas (Mariners)	23	.293	.350	.488	92	365	107	13	2	18	29	92	2
2B	Owen Miller, Amarillo (Padres)	22	.290	.355	.430	130	507	147	28	2	13	46	86	5
3B	Abraham Toro, Corpus Christi (Astros)	22	.306	.393	.513	98	376	115	22	4	16	48	77	4
SS	Gavin Lux, Tulsa (Dodgers)	21	.313	.375	.521	64	259	81	7	4	13	28	60	7
OF	Dylan Carlson, Springfield (Cardinals)	20	.281	.364	.518	108	417	117	24	6	21	52	98	18
OF	Jake Fraley, Arkansas (Mariners)	24	.313	.386	.539	61	230	72	15	2	11	23	55	16
OF	Luis Robert, Birmingham (White Sox)	22	.314	.362	.518	56	226	71	16	3	8	13	54	21
DH	Seth Beer, Corpus/Jackson (Astros/D-backs)	22	.273	.378	.481	87	322	88	16	0	17	32	83	0

Pos	Pitcher	Age	W	L	ERA	G	GS	SV	IP	H	HR	BB	SO	WHIP
SP	Ian Anderson, Mississippi (Braves)	21	7	5	2.68	21	21	0	111	82	8	47	147	1.16
SP	Tucker Davidson, Mississippi (Braves)	23	7	6	2.03	21	21	0	111	88	5	45	122	1.20
SP	Zac Lowther, Bowie (Orioles)	23	13	7	2.55	26	26	0	148	102	8	63	154	1.11
SP	Matt Manning, Erie (Tigers)	21	11	5	2.56	24	24	0	134	93	7	38	148	0.98
SP	Sixto Sanchez, Jacksonville (Marlins)	21	8	4	2.53	18	18	0	103	87	5	19	97	1.03
RP	Drew Carlton, Erie (Tigers)	22	4	3	1.46	45	0	19	68	48	3	18	65	0.97

HIGH CLASS A

Pos	Player	Age	AVG	OBP	SLG	G	AB	H	2B	3B	HR	BB	SO	SB
C	Luis Campusano, Lake Elsinore (Padres)	20	.325	.396	.509	110	422	137	31	1	15	52	57	0
1B	Lewin Diaz, Fort Myers (Twins)	22	.290	.333	.533	57	214	62	11	1	13	14	40	0
2B	Devin Mann, R. Cucamonga (Dodgers)	22	.278	.358	.496	98	367	102	19	2	19	45	93	5
3B	Nolan Jones, Lynchburg (Indians)	21	.286	.435	.425	77	252	72	12	1	7	65	85	5
SS	Jeter Downs, R. Cucamonga (Dodgers)	21	.269	.354	.507	107	412	111	33	4	19	54	97	23
OF	Jarren Duran, Salem (Red Sox)	22	.387	.456	.543	50	199	77	13	3	4	23	44	18
OF	Heliot Ramos, San Jose (Giants)	19	.306	.385	.500	77	294	90	18	0	13	32	85	6
OF	Trevor Larnach, Fort Myers (Twins)	22	.316	.382	.459	84	320	101	26	1	6	35	74	4
DH	Curtis Terry, Down East (Rangers)	22	.322	.395	.515	67	239	77	12	2	10	23	50	0

Pos	Pitcher	Age	W	L	ERA	G	GS	SV	IP	H	HR	BB	SO	WHIP
SP	Kris Bubic, Wilmington (Royals)	22	7	4	2.30	17	17	0	102	76	3	27	110	1.01
SP	Logan Gilbert, Modesto (Mariners)	22	5	3	1.73	26	26	0	62	52	3	12	73	1.03
SP	MacKenzie Gore, Lake Elsinore (Padres)	20	7	1	1.02	15	15	0	79	36	4	20	110	0.71
SP	Josh Green, Visalia (D-backs)	23	9	1	1.73	14	14	0	78	69	1	13	69	1.05
SP	Joe Ryan, Charlotte (Rays)	23	7	2	1.42	15	13	0	83	47	3	12	112	0.71
RP	Mack Lemieux, Visalia (D-backs)	22	4	1	1.54	0	0	1	53	32	3	22	72	1.03

Coming in 2020

The biggest storyline in the minors in 2020 will obviously involve which teams will be on the chopping block and what the league will look like once the negotiations between Major League and Minor League Baseball reach their conclusion.

Beyond that, the biggest headlines will come from a pair of two new teams in new stadiums. After a season of anticipation and success at the merchandise stand, the Mobile BayBears will move north and become the Rocket City Trash Pandas. The team's name has been a hit since it was announced, but now it will get a chance to show

LOW CLASS A

Pos	Player	Age	AVG	OBP	SLG	G	AB	H	2B	3B	HR	BB	SO	SB
C	Ivan Herrera, Peoria (Cardinals)	19	.286	.381	.423	69	248	71	10	0	8	35	56	1
1B	Mason Martin, Greensboro (Pirates)	20	.262	.361	.575	82	301	79	19	3	23	46	103	8
2B	Xavier Edwards, Fort Wayne (Padres)	20	.336	.392	.414	77	307	103	13	4	1	30	35	20
3B	Miguel Vargas, Great Lakes (Dodgers)	19	.325	.399	.464	70	280	91	20	2	5	35	43	9
SS	Wander Franco, Bowling Green (Rays)	18	.318	.390	.506	62	233	74	16	5	6	30	20	14
OF	Griffin Conine, Lansing (Blue Jays)	22	.283	.371	.576	80	304	86	19	2	22	38	125	2
OF	Canaan Smith, Charleston (Yankees)	20	.307	.405	.465	124	449	138	32	3	11	74	108	16
OF	Alek Thomas, Kane County (D-backs)	19	.312	.393	.479	91	353	110	21	7	8	43	72	11
DH	Will Benson, Lake County (Indians)	21	.272	.371	.604	62	217	59	12	3	18	37	78	18

Pos	Pitcher	Age	W	L	ERA	G	GS	SV	IP	H	HR	BB	SO	WHIP
SP	Joey Cantillo, Fort Wayne (Padres)	20	9	3	1.93	19	19	0	98	58	3	27	128	0.89
SP	Seth Corry, Augusta (Giants)	20	9	3	1.76	27	26	0	123	73	4	58	172	1.07
SP	Levi Kelly, Kane County (D-backs)	20	5	1	2.15	22	22	0	100	72	4	39	126	1.11
SP	Max Lazar, Wisconsin (Brewers)	20	7	3	2.39	19	10	1	79	67	5	15	109	1.04
SP	Grayson Rodriguez, Delmarva (Orioles)	19	10	4	2.68	20	20	0	94	57	4	36	129	0.99
RP	Dayeison Arias, W. Virginia (Mariners)	22	2	1	1.32	39	0	14	48	25	3	13	70	0.80

SHORT-SEASON

Pos	Player	Age	AVG	OBP	SLG	G	AB	H	2B	3B	HR	BB	SO	SB
C	Bryan Lavastida, M. Valley (Indians)	20	.335	.410	.481	58	209	70	19	3	2	25	27	3
1B	Blaine Crim, Spokane (Rangers)	22	.335	.411	.543	53	212	71	15	1	8	19	28	1
2B	Ezequiel Duran, Staten Island (Yankees)	20	.256	.329	.496	66	246	63	12	4	13	25	77	11
3B	Aaron Schunk, Boise (Rockies)	22	.306	.370	.503	46	173	53	12	2	6	14	25	4
SS	Greg Jones, Hudson Valley (Rays)	21	.335	.413	.461	48	191	64	13	4	1	22	56	19
OF	Alexander Canario, Salem-Keizer (Giants)	19	.301	.365	.539	49	193	58	17	1	9	18	71	3
OF	Gilberto Jimenez, Lowell (Red Sox)	19	.359	.393	.470	59	234	84	11	3	3	13	38	14
OF	Kristian Robinson, Hillsboro (D-backs)	18	.319	.407	.558	44	163	52	10	1	9	23	47	14
DH	Franklin Labour, Salem-Keizer (Giants)	21	.307	.392	.639	41	166	51	9	2	14	18	43	2

Pos	Pitcher	Age	W	L	ERA	G	GS	SV	IP	H	HR	BB	SO	WHIP
SP	Valente Bellozo, Tri-City (Astros)	19	6	0	1.39	11	4	0	45	25	7	10	58	0.77
SP	Luis Frias, Hillsboro (D-backs)	21	3	3	1.99	10	10	0	50	36	0	17	72	1.07
SP	Edisson Gonzalez, Hudson Valley (Rays)	19	4	2	2.45	13	11	0	61	55	6	13	77	1.09
SP	Ethan Hankins, M. Valley (Indians)	19	0	0	1.4	9	8	0	39	23	4	18	43	1.06
SP	Adam Kloffenstein, Vancouver (Blue Jays)	19	4	4	2.34	13	13	0	64	47	4	23	64	1.09
RP	Jacob Wallace, Boise (Rockies)	21	0	0	1.29	0	0	12	21	9	1	9	29	0.86

ROOKIE

Pos	Player	Age	AVG	OBP	SLG	G	AB	H	2B	3B	HR	BB	SO	SB
C	Francisco Alvarez, Kingsport (Mets)	17	.312	.407	.510	42	157	49	10	0	7	21	37	1
1B	Bryce Ball, Danville (Braves)	22	.324	.410	.676	41	145	47	12	0	13	26	30	0
2B	Jeremiah Jackson, Orem (Angels)	19	.266	.333	.605	65	256	68	14	2	23	24	96	5
3B	Brandon Lewis, Ogden (Dodgers)	20	.333	.398	.608	44	171	57	11	0	12	15	43	0
SS	CJ Abrams, AZL Padres	18	.401	.442	.662	32	142	57	12	8	3	10	14	14
OF	Heriberto Hernandez, AZL Rangers	19	.344	.433	.646	50	192	66	17	4	11	27	57	3
OF	Andy Pages, Ogden (Dodgers)	18	.298	.398	.651	63	235	70	22	2	19	26	79	7
OF	Jhon Torres, Johnson City (Cardinals)	19	.286	.391	.527	33	112	24	9	0	6	19	36	0
DH	Marco Luciano, AZL Giants	17	.322	.438	.616	38	146	47	9	2	10	27	39	8

Pos	Pitcher	Age	W	L	ERA	G	GS	SV	IP	H	HR	BB	SO	WHIP
SP	Adran Alcantara, Burlington (Royals)	20	3	4	2.57	13	11	0	56	30	2	19	61	0.88
SP	Cody Laweryson, Elizabethton (Twins)	20	1	1	1.76	10	6	1	41	25	2	9	59	0.83
SP	Luis Palacios, GCL Marlins	19	1	0	1.12	10	4	1	40	25	2	2	42	0.67
SP	Jorge Rodriguez, GCL Red Sox	19	6	2	1.91	11	6	0	47	35	2	9	58	0.94
SP	Avery Weems, Great Falls (White Sox)	22	5	4	2.09	14	14	0	50	53	1	10	74	1.06
RP	Melvin Jimenez, Ogden (Dodgers)	20	5	0	2.25	10	1	0	20	8	0	6	43	0.70

MINOR LEAGUES

what it can do under the lights in Madison, Ala.

The Nationals' high Class A affiliate will also move from Woodbridge, Va. into a brand-new stadium in Fredericksburg, Va. They will stick with their current name, however, and simply go from the Potomac Nationals to the Fredericksburg Nationals.

There will also be plenty of eyes on Triple-A, where the offensive atmosphere will be under scrutiny after the outburst in 2019. If it turns out that the homer-happy conditions are the new normal, pitchers may be clamoring to stay in Double-A to keep their statistics as respectable as possible before moving to the major leagues.

Rays top prospect Wander Franco dazzled at two levels of Class A in 2019.

Righthander Logan Gilbert led a pack of promising Mariners pitchers.

FIRST TEAM

Pos	Player, Organization (Highest Level)	Age	AVG	OBP	SLG	AB	R	H	HR	RBI	BB	SO
C	Daulton Varsho, D-backs (AA)	23	.301	.378	.520	396	85	119	18	58	42	63
1B	Seth Beer, Astros/D-backs (AA)	22	.289	.388	.516	450	72	113	26	103	46	113
2B	Gavin Lux, Dodgers (AAA)	21	.347	.421	.607	458	99	159	26	76	61	102
3B	Ty France, Padres (AAA)	25	.399	.477	.770	296	83	118	27	89	30	51
SS	Wander Franco, Rays (A+)	18	.327	.398	.487	425	82	139	9	53	56	35
OF	Dylan Carlson, Cardinals (AAA)	20	.292	.372	.542	489	95	143	26	68	58	116
OF	Jarred Kelenic, Mariners (AA)	20	.291	.364	.540	443	80	129	23	68	50	111
OF	Luis Robert, White Sox (AAA)	22	.328	.376	.624	503	108	165	32	92	28	129
DH	Kevin Cron, D-backs (AAA)	26	.329	.446	0.777	310	82	102	39	107	61	79

Pos	Pitcher, Organization (Highest Level)	Age	W	L	ERA	G	GS	IP	H	BB	SO	AVG
SP	Seth Corry, Giants (A)	20	9	3	1.76	27	26	123	73	58	172	.171
SP	Zac Gallen, Marlins/D-backs (AAA)	24	9	1	1.77	14	14	91	48	17	112	.153
SP	Logan Gilbert, Mariners (AA)	22	10	5	2.13	26	26	135	95	33	165	.198
SP	MacKenzie Gore, Padres (AA)	20	9	2	1.69	20	20	101	56	28	135	.164
SP	Brendan McKay, Rays (AAA)	23	6	0	1.15	15	15	74	42	18	102	.165
RP	Demarcus Evans, Rangers (AA)	22	6	0	0.90	47	0	60	23	39	100	.119

SECOND TEAM

Pos	Player (High Level)	Age	AVG	OBP	SLG	AB	R	H	HR	RBI	BB	SO
C	Luis Campusano, Padres (A+)	20	.325	.396	.509	422	63	137	15	81	52	57
1B	Jared Walsh, Angels (AAA)	26	.325	.423	.686	382	90	124	36	86	59	115
2B	Josh Rojas, Astros/D-backs (AAA)	25	.332	.418	.606	416	89	138	23	83	57	70
3B	Alec Bohm, Phillies (AA)	23	.305	.378	.518	475	76	145	21	80	57	73
SS	Jeter Downs, Dodgers (AA)	21	.276	.362	.526	460	92	127	24	86	60	107
OF	Trent Grisham, Brewers (AAA)	22	.300	.407	.603	370	71	111	26	71	67	72
OF	Trevor Larnach, Twins (AA)	22	.309	.384	.458	476	59	147	13	66	57	124
OF	Drew Waters, Braves (AAA)	20	.309	.360	.459	527	80	163	7	52	39	164
DH	Kyle Tucker, Astros (AAA)	22	.266	.354	.555	463	92	123	34	97	60	116

Pos	Pitcher (Highest Level)	Age	W	L	ERA	G	GS	IP	H	BB	SO	AVG
SP	Nate Pearson, Blue Jays (AAA)	23	5	4	2.30	25	25	102	63	27	119	.176
SP	Matt Manning, Tigers (AA)	21	11	5	2.86	24	24	134	93	38	148	.192
SP	Joe Ryan, Rays (AA)	23	9	4	1.96	24	22	124	77	27	183	.173
SP	Tarik Skubal, Tigers (AA)	22	6	8	2.42	24	24	123	87	37	179	.196
SP	Kris Bubic, Royals (A+)	21	11	5	2.23	26	26	149	103	42	185	.199
RP	Sam Delaplane, Mariners (AA)	24	6	3	2.23	46	0	69	35	23	120	.152

Amarillo Title Hints At Big Future

BY JEFF SANDERS

Phillip Wellman guided Double-A Mississippi to a Southern League title more than a decade ago before his Double-A Amarillo Sod Poodles claimed a Texas League championship in September.

At this point in a career in player development that's spanned four decades, perhaps only one accomplishment can trump the feeling the 57-year-old manager had as he celebrated on the field in Tulsa, Okla.

"I'm ready to see the big league club win," Wellman admitted. "We've got to get some of these young stallions, some of this talent translated into big league wins. As happy as I was for us and the kids who came through here at this age, I still work for the San Diego Padres. I want to come in after our game and watch the last three or four innings of the game in San Diego, see that we're 20 games over .500 and go, 'Hell yeah.'

"I think it's coming."

Wellman would know.

He led the Padres' Double-A affiliates into the playoffs the previous two seasons before Double-A Amarillo's championship run in 2019, with a good portion of the nucleus of all those teams made up with the sort of home-grown talent that General Manager A.J. Preller has doubled down on after his initial all-in effort in San Diego crumbled.

Thirteen of Baseball America's midseason top-30 Padres prospects suited up this year for Amarillo, although Fernando Tatis Jr.'s stay was on a rehab assignment after jumping all the way to the majors in 2019 after only half a season in the Texas League the previous year.

Even top pitching prospects MacKenzie Gore and Luis Patino arrived after the Sod Poodles won a first-half title and hit their innings caps before the Texas League playoffs, leaving the sheer depth of arguably baseball's best farm system to fuel a championship run for a city deprived of affiliated baseball for 37 years.

In fact, the Sod Poodles sold out their new downtown ballpark 40 times in their inaugural campaign, including 23 straight home games from June into August, en route to drawing 427,791 in the regular season, second among all Double-A teams in 2019.

Credit both the allure of baseball's return to the Texas panhandle and the quality of players trotted onto the Amarillo diamond. From Opening Day to the final dogpile, a steady stream of promising players came through Amarillo. And many moved on to San Diego.

Righthander Pedro Avila, called up for a spot start in April, was the first Sod Poodle called up directly to the majors. Luis Torrens was the last as a September call-up after leading upper-level minor league catchers 25 and under with 11 defensive runs saved.

In between, the likes of Andres Munoz, Michel Baez, Adrian Morejon, Ronald Bolanos and David Bednar made their big league debuts after pitching in Amarillo in 2019. Even lefthander Nick Margevicius and right-handers Trey Wingenter, Javy Guerra, Miguel Diaz, Jacob Nix and Kazuhisa Makita had big league resumes before making pit-stops at Amarillo this year.

"That was a very strong Double-A lineup and a very aggressive group of relief arms," Padres farm director Sam Geaney said. "We graduated a lot of players off that club. It's a testament to their talent and the work that they did that they continued to play very good baseball."

TEAM OF THE YEAR

Taylor Trammell

PREVIOUS WINNERS

2009: Akron/Eastern League (Indians)
2010: Northwest Arkansas/Texas League (Royals)
2011: Mobile BayBears/Southern League (Diamondbacks)
2012: Springfield Cardinals/Texas League (Cardinals)
2013: Daytona Cubs/Florida State League (Cubs)
2014: Portland Sea Dogs/Eastern League (Red Sox)
2015: Biloxi Shuckers/Southern League (Brewers)
2016: Rome Braves/South Atlantic League (Braves)
2017: Midland RockHounds/Texas League (Athletics)
2018: Bowling Green Hot Rods/Midwest League (Rays)
Full list: BaseballAmerica.com/awards

MINOR LEAGUES

JOHN E. MOORE III/GETTY IMAGES

BY KYLE GLASER

The Futures Game was guaranteed to be different in 2019.

For the first time, the game was played as an American League vs. National League matchup rather than United States vs. the World. It was a reduced to a seven-inning contest rather than a full nine-inning game, the first time that had happened since 1999.

The 2019 Futures Game will be remembered for another first as well—the first tie.

Sam Huff hit the tying two-run home run in the bottom of the seventh inning, and the game ended in a 2-2 tie at Cleveland's Progressive Field.

Huff, a fast-rising Rangers prospect, launched his home run 417 feet off of Rockies lefthanded reliever Ben Bowden with one out in the bottom of the seventh to tie the score.

Neither team scored in an eighth inning played under international tiebreaker rules and the game was declared a tie at the eighth inning's conclusion.

Huff was named the game's MVP.

"I was just trying to hit a ball up the middle, get a good pitch," Huff said. "I didn't really want to try to hit a home run or anything. I just wanted to hit the ball hard."

Taylor Trammell and Dylan Carlson each had an RBI single in the fourth inning to provide the scoring for the National League. Jo Adell reached base three times and had a game-saving catch in extra innings to lead the AL.

The NL held onto its early 2-0 lead without much trouble until the seventh.

Adell walked to lead off the inning against Bowden. Jarred Kelenic followed with a flyout to left, bringing Huff to the plate with the AL down to its final two outs.

The 6-foot-4, 230-pound masher took a changeup in the dirt for ball one before unloading on a 94 mph fastball, sending a towering shot deep onto the left-field concourse to even the score.

"When I saw it go my heart started going and then I started in my head just smiling," Huff said. "I just felt it was something I (never) thought I was going to experience or do in my life."

Isaac Paredes followed Huff's homer with a double into the right-center gap off Bowden and Jarren Duran's bloop single fell into left field to put runners on the corners. With the

winning run 90 feet away, Patino entered in relief of Bowden and struck out Ronaldo Hernandez and Royce Lewis swinging to preserve the tie.

Neither team scored in the eighth under international tiebreaker rules. Adell made a diving catch in right field for the AL to prevent a potential-run scoring single in the top of the inning and Patino retired the side in the bottom of the eighth, including striking out Adell on a 98 mph fastball to end the game.

FUTURES GAME BOX SCORE

NATIONAL LEAGUE 2, AMERICAN LEAGUE 2
JULY 7 IN CLEVELAND

NL	AB	R	H	RBI	AL	AB	R	H	RBI
Pache, CF-RF	4	0	0	0	Franco, SS	2	0	1	0
Kieboom, SS	2	1	1	0	Lewis, SS	2	0	1	0
Bart, C	2	0	0	0	Madrigal, 2B	2	0	0	0
Diaz, 2B	3	0	0	0	Mateo, 2B	2	0	1	0
Bohm, 3B-1B	4	1	1	0	Robert, CF	4	0	0	0
Trammell, LF	2	0	1	1	Adell, RF	2	1	1	0
Ramos, CF	1	0	1	1	Kelenic, LF	3	0	0	0
Craig, 1B	0	0	0	0	White, 1B	1	0	0	0
Gorman, PR-3B	1	0	0	0	Huff, 1B	2	1	1	2
Carlson, RF	2	0	0	1	Jones, 3B	1	0	0	0
Thomas, PR-RF	1	0	0	0	Paredes, 3B	2	0	1	0
Varsho, DH	3	0	0	0	Johnson, DH	1	0	0	0
Amaya, C	1	0	0	0	Duran, PH-DH	2	0	1	0
Lux, PH-SS	1	0	0	0	Rogers, C	1	0	0	0
					Hernandez, C	2	0	0	0
Totals	**28**	**2**	**5**	**2**	**Totals**	**29**	**2**	**7**	**2**

					R	H	E
NATIONAL LEAGUE	000	200	00		2	5	0
AMERICAN LEAGUE	000	401	20		2	7	1

NL: RBI: Carlson (1); Trammell (1); Basabe (2). **Team RISP:** 3-for-9. **Team LOB:** 6. **CS:** Trammell (1, home by Bubic/Rogers) Pache (1, second by Balazovic/Hernandez). **PICKOFFS:** Gore (Adell at 1st base).

U.S.: 2B: Paredes (1, Bowden). **HR:** Huff (1, 7th inn off Bowden, 1 on, 1 out). **RBI:** Huff 2 (2). **Team RISP:** 1-for-8. **Team LOB:** 6. **SB:** Duran (1, 2nd base off Patino/Bart). **E:** Lewis (1, fielding).

NL	IP	H	R	ER	BB	SO	U.S.	IP	H	R	ER	BB	SO
Anderson	1	0	0	0	0	1	Garcia, D	1	0	0	0	0	1
Gore	1	0	0	0	1	0	Dunn	1	0	0	0	0	1
May	1	0	0	0	0	0	Hall	1	0	0	0	0	0
Kay	1	1	0	0	0	1	Manning	0.1	3	2	2	0	0
Sanchez	0.2	1	0	0	0	1	Bubic	0.2	1	0	0	0	1
Williams	0.1	0	0	0	0	1	Pearson	1	0	0	0	0	2
Morejon	1	2	0	0	0	0	Singer	1	1	0	0	1	2
Bowden	0.1	3	2	2	1	2	Balazovic	1	0	0	0	0	0
Patino	1.2	0	0	0	0	3	Rodriguez	1	0	0	0	0	0
Totals	**8**	**7**	**2**	**2**	**2**	**10**	**Totals**	**8**	**5**	**2**	**2**	**1**	**7**

WP: Morejon. **HBP:** Craig 2 (by Dunn, by Manning). **Pitches-strikes:** Anderson, 14-10; Gore, 11-4; May, 8-5; Kay, 8-5; Sanchez, 13-7; Williams, 3-2; Morejon 9-6; Bowden, 25-12; Patino, 24-16; Garcia 14-10; Dunn, 13-8; Hall, 12-8; Manning, 22-16; Bubic 7-5; Pearson, 13-11; Singer, 22-16; Balazovic,12-8; Rodriguez, 11-6. **Inherited runners-scored:** Williams 1-0; Patino 2-0; Bubic 3-1. **T:** 2:39

TRIPLE-A: This game was played at El Paso's Southwest University Park, which had transformed into one of the minor leagues' most homer-happy environments, so it was no surprise when a pair of hometown heroes stole the show. Chihuahuas regulars Luis Urias and Ty France each homered and France made a stellar play in the field to lead the Pacific Coast League past the International League by a 9-3 final.

EASTERN: Richmond's Jacob Heyward earned the day's MVP award for his sixth-inning home run that pushed the Western Division's lead to its final margin in a 5-0 win at his home park. Heyward's teammates limited the Eastern Division to just two singles in the shutout while working around a half-dozen walks.

SOUTHERN: White Sox super prospect Luis Robert doubled, tripled and drove in two runs to help his Northern Division team topple the Southern Division 7-3 in a game played at Biloxi's MGM Park. Robert's effort shone the brightest in a game filled with top prospects. Jesus Sanchez (Marlins), Josh Lowe (Rays), Cristian Pache (Braves), Drew Waters (Braves) and Trent Grisham each made the game, and that's saying nothing of the pitchers. Waters hit the game's only home run.

TEXAS: Midland's Luis Barrera went 3-for-5 with a triple and two runs scored as the South Division topped the North, 5-1. Corpus Christi righthander Bryan Abreu (who finished the season on the Astros' postseason roster) got the win for his scoreless third inning. Arkansas first baseman Evan White (Mariners) went 2-for-4 with a double in the North's loss.

CALIFORNIA: Visalia's Mark Karaviotis went 3-for-5 with two runs and two RBIs in his North Division team's 7-1 win over the South at Inland Empire's San Manuel Stadium. Karaviotis was the game's only player with multiple hits. The South got its only score on a home run from Lake Elsinore second baseman Esteury Ruiz. North starter Ljay Newsome got the win.

CAROLINA: Potomac outfielder Nick Banks went 3-for-4 with a huge three-run home run in the eighth inning in the North Division's dramatic 8-7 win over the South. Banks' blast came off of Myrtle Beach right-hander Paul Richan and gave the North the edge it needed to withstand a comeback effort from the South in the top of the ninth. Fayetteville outfielder Corey Julks hit a two-run homer that cut the North's lead to one run, but Tyler Zuber followed with a strikeout of Diosbel Arias to close the game.

FLORIDA STATE: A Lewin Diaz sacrifice fly and a Travis Swaggerty home run provided all the offense the South Division needed in a 2-0 shutout win over the North at Tampa's George Steinbrenner Field. The South's pitching held the North hitless until the seventh inning, when Tampa's Dermis Garcia hit a single to break up history.

MIDWEST: The regularly played game finished in a 3-3 tie, but the East scored a fun-filled victory when Bowling Green's Chris Betts won a sudden-death home run derby after nine innings. Betts had won the game's actual home run derby earlier in the day, besting Kane County's Alek Thomas by a tally of 8-7 in the final round.

SOUTH ATLANTIC: A five-run eighth inning led the North Division to a 6-2 win over the counterparts from the South in a game played at West Virginia's Appalachian Power Park. With the game tied after a strikeout and a wild pitch, Delmarva's Doran Turchin and Greensboro's Lolo Sanchez smacked a pair of doubles over a three-hitter span to bring four more runs home.

NEW YORK-PENN: The Blue Team got a mid-game boost from a Nathan Perry (Tri-City) solo home run and a Brayan Rocchio steal home in its 7-4 win over the Red Team. The Red Team got a home run from Staten Island's Josh Stowers in the loss.

NORTHWEST-PIONEER: A grand slam from Orem's Jeremiah Jackson kickstarted the Pioneer League in its 11-7 win over the Northwest League in a game played at the home of the NWL's Boise Hawks.

Luis Robert

HANNAH STONE

MINOR LEAGUES

2019 OVERALL MINOR LEAGUE DEPARTMENT LEADERS

WINS

Delmarva (South Atlantic)	90
Montgomery (Southern)	88
Down East (Carolina)	87
Round Rock Express (Pacific Coast)	84
Las Vegas (Pacific Coast)	83
Visalia (California)	83
Hickory (South Atlantic)	83

LONGEST WINNING STREAK

Visalia (California)	14
El Paso (Pacific Coast)	12
Dunedin (Florida State)	11
Great Lakes (Midwest)	10
Charlotte (Florida State)	10
Dayton (Midwest)	10
Delmarva (South Atlantic)	10
Syracuse (International)	10
Biloxi (Southern)	10
Down East (Carolina)	10

LOSSES

West Michigan (Midwest)	90
Mobile (Southern)	86
Peoria (Midwest)	85
Richmond (Eastern)	84
Beloit (Midwest)	84
Frederick (Carolina)	84
Columbia (South Atlantic)	84

LONGEST LOSING STREAK*

Chattanooga (Southern)	14
St. Lucie (Florida State)	14
Memphis (Pacific Coast)	12
Peoria (Midwest)	12
Springfield (Texas)	11
Jupiter (Florida State)	11

BATTING AVERAGE*

El Paso (Pacific Coast)	.299
Las Vegas (Pacific Coast)	.298
Fresno (Pacific Coast)	.289
Albuquerque (Pacific Coast)	.287
Round Rock (Pacific Coast)	.283

RUNS

El Paso (Pacific Coast)	968
Las Vegas (Pacific Coast)	959
Reno (Pacific Coast)	918
Salt Lake (Pacific Coast)	891
Round Rock (Pacific Coast)	890

HOME RUNS

El Paso (Pacific Coast)	258
Las Vegas (Pacific Coast)	250
Reno (Pacific Coast)	242
Sacramento (Pacific Coast)	228
Salt Lake (Pacific Coast)	222

STOLEN BASES

Northwest Arkansas (Texas)	218
Montgomery (Southern)	213
Rancho Cucamonga (California)	178
Quad Cities (Midwest)	171
Lansing (Midwest)	170

EARNED RUN AVERAGE*

Charlotte (Florida State)	2.76
Kane County (Midwest)	2.81
Wilmington (Carolina)	3.00
Down East (Carolina)	3.00
Delmarva (South Atlantic)	3.00

STRIKEOUTS

Rancho Cucamonga (California)	1497
Modesto (California)	1479
Fayetteville (Carolina)	1476
Corpus Christi (Texas)	1453
Delmarva (South Atlantic)	1389

INDIVIDUAL BATTING

BATTING AVERAGE

CJ Abrams (AZL Padres, Fort Wayne)	.393
David Freitas (Tacoma, San Antonio)	.381
Corban Joseph (Las Vegas)	.371
Yonathan Daza (Albuquerque)	.364
Gavin Lux (Tulsa, Oklahoma City)	.347

RUNS

Sam Hilliard (Albuquerque)	109
Luis Robert (W-Salem, Birmingham, Charlotte)	108
Luis Castro (Lancaster, Hartford)	106
Taylor Ward (Salt Lake)	102
Seth Brown (Las Vegas)	101

HITS

Luis Robert (W-Salem, Birmingham, Charlotte)	165
Drew Waters (Mississippi, Gwinnett)	163
Xavier Edwards (Fort Wayne, Lake Elsinore)	162
Ryan Mountcastle (Norfolk)	162
Matt Hearn (Lancaster)	160

TOP HITTING STREAKS

Evan White (Arkansas)	23
L.T. Tolbert (Visalia)	23
Aristides Aquino (Louisville)	22
Cal Stevenson (Dunedin)	22
Wilbis Santiago (Lynchburg)	20
Ian Dawkins (Kannapolis)	20

MOST HITS (ONE GAME)

Drew Ferguson (Round Rock)	6
Clay Dugan (Idaho Falls)	6
Olivber Moreno (DSL Royals)	6
Parker Phillips (GCL Twins)	6
123 others	5

TOTAL BASES

Luis Robert (W-Salem, Birmingham, Charlotte)	314
Jose Rojas (Salt Lake)	297
Seth Brown (Las Vegas)	286
Sam Hilliard (Albuquerque)	279
Gavin Lux (Tulsa, Oklahoma City)	278

EXTRA-BASE HITS

Jose Rojas (Salt Lake)	77
Luis Robert (W-Salem, Birmingham, Charlotte)	74
Seth Brown (Las Vegas)	72
Mason Martin (Greensboro, Bradenton)	71
Sam Hilliard (Albuquerque)	71

DOUBLES

David Fry (Wisconsin)	41
Mike Gerber (Sacramento)	41
Drew Waters (Mississippi, Gwinnett)	40
Zander Wiel (Rochester)	40
Jose Rojas (Salt Lake)	39
Nick Tanielu (Round Rock)	39

TRIPLES

Jorge Mateo (Las Vegas)	14
Mickey Moniak (Reading)	13
Brett Phillips (Omaha)	13
Dairon Blanco (Midland, Northwest Arkansas)	13
Luis Robert (W-Salem, Birmingham, Charlotte)	11
Brock Deatherage (Lakeland)	11
Johan Rojas (GCL Phillies, Williamsport)	11
Luis Barrera (Midland)	11

HOME RUNS

Kevin Cron (Reno, AZL D-backs)	39
Seth Brown (Las Vegas)	37
Jared Walsh (Salt Lake)	36
Mason Martin (Greensboro, Bradenton)	35
Jaylin Davis (Pensacola, Rochester, Sacramento)	35
Sam Hilliard (Albuquerque)	35

RUNS BATTED IN

Mason Martin (Greensboro, Bradenton)	129
Kevin Cron (Reno Aces, AZL D-backs)	107
Jose Rojas (Salt Lake)	107
Luis Castro (Lancaster, Hartford)	105
Roberto Ramos (Albuquerque)	105

MOST RBIS (ONE GAME)

Brian Rey (Dayton)	8
Adolis Garcia (Memphis)	8
Brian O'Grady (Louisville)	8
Yasmany Tomas (Reno)	8
Josh VanMeter (Louisville)	8
Roberto Ramos (Albuquerque)	8
Will Benson (Lake County)	8

WALKS

Nolan Jones (Lynchburg, Akron)	96
John Andreoli (Rochester, Tacoma)	90
Jeisson Rosario (Lake Elsinore)	87
Brice Turang (Wisconsin, Carolina)	83
Jacob Heyward (Richmond, Sacramento)	83

INTENTIONAL WALKS

Yordan Alvarez (Round Rock)	11
Vimael Machin (Tennessee, Iowa)	10
Seth Beer (Fayetteville, Corpus Christi, Jackson)	6
Bobby Dalbec (Portland, Pawtucket)	6
Darick Hall (Reading)	6
Rhett Wiseman (Harrisburg, Auburn)	6
Lazaro Alonso (Jupiter, Jacksonville)	6
Ryan Flaherty (Columbus)	6

Kevin Cron

ROBERT BINDER

STRIKEOUTS

Lazaro Armenteros (Stockton)	227
Collin Theroux (Midland, Las Vegas)	190
Sean Reynolds (Clinton, Batavia)	184
Luis Curbelo (Kannapolis, Great Falls)	181
Jeremy Eierman (Stockton)	177

STOLEN BASES

Nick Heath (Northwest Arkansas, Omaha)	60
Khalil Lee (Northwest Arkansas)	53
Johneshwy Fargas (Richmond)	50
Vidal Brujan (Charlotte, Montgomery)	48
Reggie Pruitt (Lansing, Dunedin)	48

CAUGHT STEALING

Yonny Hernandez (Down East, Frisco)	18
Francisco Palma (DSL Colorado)	17
J.D. Orr (Batavia)	17
Will Golsan (Asheville)	17
Andres Gimenez (Binghamton)	16
Tucupita Marcano (Fort Wayne)	16
Josh Stowers (Charleston)	16

ON-BASE PERCENTAGE*

Kyle Mottice (Greensboro, West Virginia)	.467
David Freitas (Tacoma, San Antonio)	.461
Jimmy Govern (AZL Royals, Omaha, Idaho Falls)	.457
Kevin Cron (Reno, AZL D-backs)	.446
CJ Abrams (AZL Padres, Fort Wayne)	.436

SLUGGING PERCENTAGE*

Kevin Cron (Reno, AZL D-backs)	.777
Jared Walsh (Salt Lake)	.686
Mark Payton (Las Vegas)	.653
CJ Abrams (AZL Padres, Fort Wayne)	.647
Austin Dean (New Orleans, GCL Marlins)	.635

ON-BASE PLUS SLUGGING (OPS)*

Kevin Cron (Reno, AZL D-backs)	1.223
Jared Walsh (Salt Lake)	1.109
CJ Abrams (AZL Padres, Fort Wayne)	1.083
Jimmy Govern (AZL Royals, Omaha, Idaho Falls)	1.060
Mark Payton (Las Vegas)	1.053

HIT BY PITCH

Dwanya Williams-Sutton (Fort Wayne)	32
Seth Beer (Fayetteville, Corpus Christi, Jackson)	31
Andy Young (Jackson, Reno)	31
Arturo Guerrero (DSL Mariners)	26
Greg Cullen (Rome)	25

SACRIFICE BUNTS

Cole Freeman (Fredericksburg)	14
Kyle Holder (Trenton)	14
Justin Connell (Hagerstown)	14
Angelo Castellano (Wilmington, NW Arkansas)	13
Jecksson Flores (Omaha)	13

SACRIFICE FLIES

Ryan Vilade (Lancaster)	13
Michael Chirinos (DSL Rangers)	12
Wander Franco (Bowling Green, Charlotte)	12
Christian Colon (Louisville)	12
Luis Castro (Lancaster, Hartford)	11
Josh Lester (Erie, Toledo)	11
Brady Whalen (Peoria)	11

GROUNDED INTO DOUBLE PLAY

Jose Azocar (Erie)	22
Andretty Cordero (Frisco)	22
Ryan Vilade (Lancaster)	20
Gilberto Celestino (Cedar Rapids, Fort Myers)	20
Christian Colon (Louisville)	20
Danny Mendick (Charlotte)	20

BATTING AVERAGE * By Position

CATCHERS
David Freitas (Tacoma, San Antonio)	.381
Logan Porter (Burlington)	.352
Heriberto Hernandez (AZL Rangers, Spokane)	.345
Yainer Diaz (AZL Indians, Mahoning Valley)	.341
Luis Leon (Princeton, Hudson Valley)	.332

FIRST BASEMEN
Blaine Crim (AZL Rangers, Spokane)	.348
Brian Mundell (Albuquerque)	.333
Bryce Ball (Danville, Rome)	.329
Kevin Cron (Reno, AZL D-backs)	.329
Kyle Mottice (Greensboro, West Virginia)	.325
Jared Walsh (Salt Lake)	.325

SECOND BASEMEN
Corban Joseph (Las Vegas)	.371
Jimmy Govern (AZL Royals, Omaha, Idaho Falls)	.344
Otto Lopez (Lansing)	.324
Wilmer Reyes (Brooklyn)	.323
Jake Elmore (Indianapolis)	.322

THIRD BASEMEN
Josh Rojas (Corpus Christi, Round Rock, Reno)	.332
Toby Welk (Aberdeen, Delmarva)	.330
Abraham Toro (Corpus Christi, Round Rock)	.324
Ali Castillo (Reading, Lehigh Valley)	.322
Pat Valaika (Albuquerque)	.320

SHORTSTOPS
CJ Abrams (AZL Padres, Fort Wayne)	.393
Clay Dungan (Idaho Falls)	.357
Gavin Lux (Tulsa, Oklahoma City)	.347
Greg Jones (Hudson Valley)	.335
Jake Cronenworth (Durham, GCL Rays)	.329

OUTFIELDERS
Nelson Maldonado (AZL Cubs, Eugene, South Bend)	.332
Rob Refsnyder (Reno, Louisville, AZL Reds)	.312
Ryan LaMarre (Gwinnett)	.311
Johnny Rizer (Aberdeen, Delmarva)	.308
Mason Williams (Norfolk)	.308

INDIVIDUAL PITCHING

EARNED RUN AVERAGE*
Cristian Javier (Fayetteville, Corpus Christi, Round Rock)	1.74
Seth Corry (Augusta)	1.76
Michael Plassmeyer (Bowling Green, Charlotte, Durham)	1.91
Joe Ryan (Bowling Green, Charlotte, Montgomery)	1.97
Daniel McGrath (Portland, Pawtucket)	1.98

WORST ERA*
Jerry Keel (El Paso)	6.78
Dietrich Enns (El Paso)	6.70
Scott Copeland (Fresno)	6.22
Emmanuel Ramirez (Amarillo, El Paso)	6.19
Justin Nicolino (Rochester, Charlotte)	6.12

WINS
James Marvel (Altoona, Indianapolis)	16
Dylan File (Carolina, Biloxi)	15
Colin Rea (Iowa)	14
Ronald Bolanos (Lake Elsinore, Amarillo)	13
Ian McKinney (Modesto, Arkansas)	13
Zac Lowther (Bowie)	13
Paul Campbell (Charlotte, Montgomery)	13
Tommy Romero (Charlotte, Montgomery)	13

LOSSES
Edgar Gonzalez (Palm Beach, Memphis)	15
Keury Mella (Louisville)	14
Xavier Altamirano (Stockton)	13
Alex Lange (Myrtle Beach, Tennessee, Erie)	13
Adam Scott (Lynchburg, Akron)	13
Matt Smith (Carolina)	13
Sean Brady (Akron, Columbus, Altoona)	13
Rony Garcia (Tampa, Trenton)	13
Kyle Hart (Portland, Pawtucket)	13
Thomas Hatch (Tennessee, New Hampshire)	13

GAMES
Addison Russ (Reading)	55
Lucas Luetge (Jackson, Reno)	55
Kevin Quackenbush (Oklahoma City)	54
PJ Poulin (Asheville)	54
John Schreiber (Erie, Toledo)	53

GAMES STARTED
Clay Chandler (West Virginia, Modesto)	28
Lucas Gilbreath (Lancaster)	28
Sean Hjelle (Augusta, San Jose, Richmond)	28
Ian McKinney (Modesto, Arkansas)	28
Ljay Newsome (Modesto, Tacoma, Arkansas)	28
James Marvel (Altoona, Indianapolis)	28
Domingo Robles (Bradenton, Altoona)	28
Packy Naughton (Daytona, Chattanooga)	28
Johan Oviedo (Palm Beach, Springfield)	28
Angel Rondon (Palm Beach, Springfield)	28

COMPLETE GAMES
Nolan Kingham (Rome, Florida, Mississippi)	4
Domingo Robles (Bradenton, Altoona)	3
Will Stewart (Jupiter)	3
Josh Fleming (Montgomery, Durham)	3
28 others	2

SHUTOUTS
Nolan Kingham (Rome, Florida, Mississippi)	3
Michael Baumann (Frederick, Bowie)	2
James Marvel (Altoona, Indianapolis)	2
Domingo Robles (Bradenton, Altoona)	2
Bruce Zimmermann (Bowie, Norfolk)	2

GAMES FINISHED
Tim Naughton (Delmarva, Frederick, Bowie)	44
Daniel Alvarez (Trenton, Scranton/Wilkes-Barre)	43
Aaron Barrett (Harrisburg)	43
Alexander Martinez (Asheville)	41
Tyler Zuber (Wilmington, Northwest Arkansas)	39

HOLDS
Holden Capps (Wilmington, Northwest Arkansas)	15
Matt De La Rosa (Delmarva, Frederick)	13
Phillip Diehl (Hartford, Albuquerque)	13
Sam Moll (Sacramento, Richmond)	13
Deolis Guerra (San Antonio)	13
Jack Anderson (Arkansas)	13

SAVES
Aaron Barrett (Harrisburg)	31
Tad Ratliff (Wilmington)	23
Matt Eckelman (Altoona, Indianapolis)	23
Addison Russ (Reading)	22
Nate Griep (Biloxi, San Antonio)	22

INNINGS PITCHED
Tommy Parsons (Peoria, Palm Beach, Springfield, Memphis)	166
Nolan Kingham (Rome, Florida, Mississippi)	165
Domingo Robles (Bradenton, Altoona)	165
Steven Moyers (West Virginia, Modesto)	164
Sean Brady (Akron, Columbus, Altoona)	162
James Marvel (Altoona, Indianapolis)	162

WALKS
Johan Oviedo (Palm Beach, Springfield)	76
Aiden McIntyre (Beloit)	76
Jake Woodford (Memphis)	75
Lucas Gilbreath (Lancaster)	74
Yohan Ramirez (Fayetteville, Corpus Christi)	74

STRIKEOUTS
Kris Bubic (Lexington, Wilmington)	185
Joe Ryan (Bowling Green, Charlotte, Montgomery)	183
Tarik Skubal (Lakeland, Erie)	179
Ian Anderson (Mississippi, Gwinnett)	172
Seth Corry (Augusta)	172

HITS ALLOWED
Jerry Keel (El Paso)	207
Will Gaddis (Lancaster)	189
Steven Moyers (West Virginia, Modesto)	188
Dietrich Enns (El Paso)	182
Matt Swarmer (Iowa)	181

HOME RUNS ALLOWED
Dietrich Enns (El Paso)	37
Justin Nicolino (Rochester, Charlotte)	36
Matt Swarmer (Iowa)	36
Pat Dean (Albuquerque)	34
Tommy Parsons (Peoria, Palm Beach, Springfield, Memphis)	30

STRIKEOUTS PER NINE INNINGS (STARTERS)*
Cristian Javier (Fayetteville, Corpus Christi, Round Rock)	13.5
Deivi Garcia (Tampa, Trenton, Scranton/W-B)	13.3
Joe Ryan (Bowling Green, Charlotte, Montgomery)	13.3
Tarik Skubal (Lakeland, Erie)	13.1
Luis Contreras (AZL Brewers, Wisconsin, Biloxi)	13.1

STRIKEOUT PER NINE INNINGS (RELIEVERS)*
James Karinchak (Akron, Columbus, AZL Indians)	22.0
Kevin Ginkel (Jackson, Reno, AZL D-backs)	16.0
Sam Delaplane (Modesto, Arkansas)	15.7
Michael Kohn (Jackson, Reno, AZL D-backs)	15.5
Demarcus Evans (Down East, Frisco)	15.0

BATTING AVERAGE AGAINST (STARTERS)*
Cristian Javier (Fayetteville, Corpus Christi, Round Rock)	.130
Garrett Hill (West Michigan, Lakeland)	.169
Seth Corry (Augusta)	.171
Joe Ryan (Bowling Green, Charlotte, Montgomery)	.173
Brusdar Graterol (Pensacola, GCL Twins, Rochester)	.179

BATTING AVERAGE AGAINST (RELIEVERS)*
Demarcus Evans (Down East, Frisco)	.119
Luke Barker (Biloxi, San Antonio)	.122
Cristian Javier (Fayetteville, Corpus Christi, Round Rock)	.130
Adam Stauffer (Aberdeen, Delmarva)	.143
Brandon Hughes (AZL Cubs, Eugene, South Bend)	.148

MOST STRIKEOUTS (ONE GAME)
Philip Pfeifer (Florida)	17
Randy Wynne (Greeneville)	17
Cody Laweryson (Elizabethton)	15
Elliot Ashbeck (Lake Elsinore)	15
Deivi Garcia (Trenton)	15

WILD PITCHES
Luis Medina (Charleston, Tampa)	27
Victor Martinez (DSL D-backs)	25
Tomas Alastre (Hagerstown)	24
Justin Martinez (DSL D-backs, AZL D-backs, Missoula)	23
Hector Guance (Delmarva)	23

BALKS
Enmanuel Solan (Palm Beach, State College)	10
Austin Smith (Fort Wayne)	9
Nathanael Heredia (State College, GCL Cardinals)	8
Blayne Enlow (Cedar Rapids, Fort Myers)	7
Dennis Herrera (AZL Athletics)	6
Chad Hockin (AZL Cubs, Myrtle Beach)	6
Steven Moyers (West Virginia, Modesto)	6
Huascar Ynoa (Florida, Mississippi, Gwinnett)	6
Vladimir Gutierrez (Louisville)	6

HIT BATTERS
Alex Royalty (Lake County)	21
Damon Casetta-Stubbs (Modesto, West Virginia, Everett)	20
Tom Hackimer (Fort Myers, Pensacola)	20
Tim Dillard (Nashville)	20
Jhonathan Diaz (Salem)	19

GROUND BALL DOUBLE PLAYS
Josh Green (Visalia, Jackson)	25
Jerry Keel (El Paso)	24
Sean Brady (Akron, Columbus, Altoona)	22
Paul Blackbu (Las Vegas)	22
Sean Hjelle (Augusta, San Jose, Richmond)	21
Matt Peacock (Jackson)	21

INDIVIDUAL FIELDING

ERRORS
Christopher Torres (Clinton)	39
Juan Martinez (Dayton)	38
Ryan Vilade (Lancaster)	37
James Nelson (Jupiter)	35
Osmy Gregorio (Bowling Green)	33
Wenceel Perez (West Michigan)	33
Jeison Guzman (Lexington)	33

MINOR LEAGUES

BY KEGAN LOWE

After posting the league's best regular-season record at 81-59, the Columbus Clippers (Indians) continued their winning ways in the IL playoffs. The Clippers topped Gwinnett (Braves), three games to one, in the league semifinals and then swept two-time defending champion Durham (Rays) in the best-of-five championship series. The title marked Columbus' 11th Governors' Cup, breaking a tie with Rochester (Twins) for the most International League titles. Columbus, which last won an IL championship in 2015, has won four Governors' Cups this decade, and is the second franchise to win four IL titles in a single decade.

While Columbus was enjoying the league's most team success, Norfolk's Ryan Mountcastle (Orioles) was named International League MVP. The 22-year-old infielder played in 127 games for the Tides, hitting .312/.344/.527 with 25 home runs and 83 RBIs. On the mound, Indianapolis righthander Mitch Keller (Pirates) took home IL pitcher of the year honors after going 7-5, 3.56 with 123 strikeouts and 35 walks in 103.2 innings. Keller, who was called up to Pittsburgh three times throughout the season, limited Triple-A hitters to a .243 average and posted a 1.24 WHIP in the league.

In terms of overall prospect talent, the league was top-heavy with young power hitters who showcased the ability to make adjustments while continuing to put up impressive numbers. With both Triple-A leagues adopting the major league baseball prior to the start of the 2019 season, offensive numbers were up across the board in the International League, led by No. 1 prospect Luis

Robert (White Sox). The then-21-year-old outfielder hit 16 homers and drove in 39 runs despite starting the season in the high Class A Carolina League and playing in just 47 games for Triple-A Charlotte. Several hitters, such as Buffalo's Bo Bichette (Blue Jays) and Gwinnett's Austin Riley (Braves), made their major league debuts in 2019. Bichette set a major league record with 13 extra-base hits in his first 11 big league games, while Riley, who hit 10 home runs in his first 26 games, became the fastest Braves player in the modern era to reach double-digit home runs.

There was plenty of pitching talent in the International League, as well. Gwinnett righthander Bryse Wilson (Braves) led all qualified pitchers with a 3.42 ERA, while Norfolk lefthander Keegan Akin (Orioles) led all starters with 131 strikeouts.

TOP 20 PROSPECTS

1. Luis Robert, OF, Charlotte (White Sox)
2. Bo Bichette, SS, Buffalo (Blue Jays)
3. Brendan McKay, LHP/DH, Durham (Rays)
4. Austin Riley, 3B/OF, Gwinnett (Braves)
5. Oscar Mercado, OF, Columbus (Indians)
6. Mitch Keller, RHP, Indianapolis (Pirates)
7. Ryan Mountcastle, 1B/OF, Norfolk (Orioles)
8. Ke'Bryan Hayes, 3B, Indianapolis (Pirates)
9. Kyle Wright, RHP, Gwinnett (Braves)
10. Aristides Aquino, OF, Louisville (Reds)
11. Bryse Wilson, RHP, Gwinnett (Braves)
12. Dylan Cease, RHP, Charlotte (White Sox)
13. Bobby Bradley, 1B, Columbus (Indians)
14. Nate Lowe, 1B, Durham (Rays)
15. Kolby Allard, LHP, Gwinnett (Braves)
16. Nick Solak, 2B/OF, Durham (Rays)
17. Jaylin Davis, OF, Rochester (Twins)
18. Cole Tucker, SS, Indianapolis (Pirates)
19. Jake Cronenworth, SS, Durham (Rays)
20. Keegan Akin, LHP, Norfolk (Orioles)

OVERALL STANDINGS

North Division	W	L	PCT	GB	Manager(s)	Attendance	Average	Last Pennant
Scranton/W-B RailRiders (Yankees)	76	65	.539	—	Jay Bell	414,891	5,943	2016
Syracuse Mets (Mets)	75	66	.532	1	Tony DeFrancesco	327,478	4,734	1976
Buffalo Bisons (Blue Jays)	71	69	.507	4½	Bob Meacham	518,741	7,523	2004
Rochester Red Wings (Twins)	70	70	.500	5½	Joel Skinner	451,853	6,631	1997
Lehigh Valley IronPigs (Phillies)	66	74	.471	9½	Gary Jones	585,110	8,491	1995
Pawtucket Red Sox (Red Sox)	59	81	.421	16½	Billy McMillon	331,010	4,759	2014
South Division								
Gwinnett Stripers (Braves)	80	59	.576	—	Damon Berryhill	212,342	3,092	2007
Charlotte Knights (White Sox)	75	64	.540	5	Mark Grudzielanek	581,006	8,307	1985
Durham Bulls (Rays)	75	64	.540	5	Brady Williams	529,105	7,542	2018
Norfolk Tides (Orioles)	60	79	.432	20	Gary Kendall	350,086	5,147	1999
West Division								
Columbus Clippers (Indians)	81	59	.579	—	Tony Mansolino	590,504	8,588	2019
Indianapolis Indians (Pirates)	66	74	.471	15	Brian Esposito	586,860	8,341	2000
Toledo Mud Hens (Tigers)	66	74	.471	15	Doug Mientkiewicz	481,496	6,976	2006
Louisville Bats (Reds)	59	81	.421	22	Jody Davis	485,356	6,934	2001

Semifinals: Durham defeated Scranton/W-B 3-0 and Columbus defeated Gwinnett 3-1 in best-of-five series. **Finals:** Columbus defeated Durham 3-0 in a best-of-five series.

MINOR LEAGUES

CLUB BATTING

	AVG	G	AB	R	H	2B	3B	HR	RBI	BB	SO	SB	OBP	SLG
Rochester	.278	140	4780	790	1330	299	26	174	753	455	1179	75	.350	.461
Scranton/W-B	.277	141	4714	786	1306	296	22	212	741	496	1056	77	.351	.484
Toledo	.274	140	4789	749	1314	256	39	155	709	481	1234	128	.347	.441
Norfolk	.271	139	4702	702	1275	270	24	146	654	438	1042	67	.337	.432
Charlotte	.270	139	4641	792	1255	268	22	208	751	560	1189	72	.352	.472
Lehigh Valley	.270	140	4722	702	1273	254	28	160	665	494	1299	68	.344	.437
Durham	.269	139	4653	738	1250	259	29	177	702	560	1193	78	.353	.451
Gwinnett	.269	139	4715	781	1269	254	25	200	740	498	1265	63	.348	.461
Louisville	.262	140	4688	650	1229	257	26	163	649	456	1200	92	.333	.432
Buffalo	.261	140	4588	688	1198	243	40	156	655	481	1153	120	.337	.434
Columbus	.256	140	4746	749	1217	265	32	213	723	564	1392	104	.341	.460
Syracuse	.255	141	4600	721	1172	255	20	177	678	517	1338	123	.338	.434
Indianapolis	.253	140	4624	616	1170	275	27	133	567	456	1198	69	.327	.410
Pawtucket	.251	140	4563	646	1146	240	12	166	607	475	1186	69	.327	.418

CLUB PITCHING

	ERA	G	CG	SHO	SV	IP	H	R	ER	HR	BB	SO	AVG
Gwinnett	4.29	139	0	5	35	1218	1195	641	580	134	449	1203	.257
Syracuse	4.51	141	1	8	39	1209	1296	662	606	160	420	1060	.274
Columbus	4.71	140	1	7	35	1233	1205	689	645	198	491	1291	.255
Pawtucket	4.71	140	5	3	39	1190	1206	700	623	177	529	1061	.265
Durham	4.74	139	1	10	38	1206	1234	698	635	190	443	1329	.263
Indianapolis	4.82	140	1	6	43	1213	1214	695	650	158	528	1244	.262
Louisville	4.91	140	1	7	29	1222	1270	741	667	157	554	1143	.268
Rochester	4.91	140	0	2	32	1195	1222	719	652	161	486	1285	.264
Buffalo	4.93	140	1	8	33	1197	1194	738	655	189	529	1196	.257
Scranton/W-B	4.94	141	3	6	35	1204	1207	732	661	178	485	1319	.260
Toledo	4.94	140	2	10	26	1217	1252	728	668	168	482	1267	.265
Lehigh Valley	5.23	140	1	3	35	1206	1210	790	701	179	577	1183	.259
Charlotte	5.37	139	2	7	41	1198	1383	775	715	203	454	1148	.291
Norfolk	5.58	139	1	9	32	1196	1316	802	741	188	504	1195	.278

CLUB FIELDING

	PCT	PO	A	E	DP		PCT	PO	A	E	DP
Columbus	.983	3698	1200	85	103	Syracuse	.981	3627	1263	96	136
Indianapolis	.983	3640	1231	86	125	Scranton/W-B	.980	3612	1147	95	99
Charlotte	.982	3593	1321	91	136	Norfolk	.979	3588	1223	103	109
Louisville	.982	3667	1318	90	134	Rochester	.979	3585	1239	101	115
Pawtucket	.982	3570	1240	88	128	Gwinnett	.978	3654	1235	109	134
Toledo	.982	3651	1127	86	113	Lehigh Valley	.977	3618	1214	116	121
Durham	.981	3617	1137	92	103	Buffalo	.976	3590	1162	116	118

INDIVIDUAL BATTING

Batter, Club	AVG	G	AB	R	H	2B	3B	HR	RBI	BB	SO	SB
Jake Cronenworth, Durham	.334	88	344	75	115	26	4	10	45	49	62	12
Jake Elmore, Indianapolis	.322	109	367	56	118	31	0	6	35	37	56	4
Ali Castillo, Lehigh Valley	.316	113	415	60	131	22	4	7	58	27	55	4
Ryan McBroom, Scranton/W-B	.315	117	413	87	130	29	0	26	66	58	100	2
Ryan Mountcastle, Norfolk	.312	127	520	81	162	35	1	25	83	24	130	2
Ryan LaMarre, Rochester	.311	112	405	55	126	24	8	9	53	38	118	19
Mason Williams, Norfolk	.308	121	442	62	136	15	3	18	67	46	86	4
Kean Wong, Durham	.307	113	453	71	139	29	6	10	63	42	112	6
Daniel Johnson, Columbus	.306	84	337	51	103	27	5	9	44	34	79	6
Willi Castro, Toledo	.301	119	465	75	140	28	8	11	62	37	110	17

INDIVIDUAL PITCHING

Pitcher, Club	W	L	ERA	G	GS	CG	SV	IP	H	R	ER	BB	SO
Bryse Wilson, Gwinnett	10	7	3.42	21	21	0	0	121	120	59	46	26	118
Odrisamer Despaigne, Charlotte	8	6	3.47	24	22	0	0	124	123	52	48	44	124
Teddy Stankiewicz, Pawtucket	6	7	3.85	24	23	1	0	131	138	62	56	39	106
Michael Peoples, Columbus	10	6	3.98	25	22	0	0	145	157	67	64	29	122
Kyle Wright, Gwinnett	11	4	4.17	21	21	0	0	112	107	55	52	35	116
Keegan Akin, Norfolk	6	7	4.73	25	24	0	0	112	100	64	59	61	131
Erasmo Ramirez, Pawtucket	6	8	4.74	27	24	1	0	125	125	75	66	43	95
Keury Mella, Louisville	8	14	5.05	27	27	0	0	143	160	93	80	56	102
Aaron Slegers, Durham	6	7	5.05	26	15	1	0	112	130	72	63	28	80
Shao-Ching Chiang, Columbus	9	9	5.15	26	26	1	0	131	144	86	75	57	128

ALL-STAR TEAM

C: Eric Haase, Columbus. **1B:** Ryan Mountcastle, Norfolk. **2B:** Jake Elmore, Indianapolis. **3B:** Kean Wong, Durham. **SS:** Jake Cronenworth, Durham. **OF:** Aristides Aquino, Louisville; Brandon Barnes, Columbus/Rochester; Adam Duvall, Gwinnett. **DH:** Bobby Bradley, Columbus. **UT:** Ryan McBroom, Scranton/Wilkes-Barre. **SP:** Mitch Keller, Indianapolis. **RP:** Trevor Kelley, Pawtucket. **Most Valuable Player:** Ryan Mountcastle, Norfolk. **Most Valuable Pitcher:** Mitch Keller, Indianapolis. **Rookie of the Year:** Aristides Aquino, Louisville. **Manager of the Year:** Damon Berryhill, Gwinnett.

DEPARTMENT LEADERS

BATTING

OBP	Cronenworth, Jake, Durham	.429
SLG	Duvall, Adam, Gwinnett	.602
OPS	McBroom, Ryan, Scranton/W-B	.976
R	McBroom, Ryan, Scranton/W-B	87
H	Mountcastle, Ryan, Norfolk	162
TB	Mountcastle, Ryan, Norfolk	274
XBH	Wiel, Zander, Rochester	69
2B	Wiel, Zander, Rochester	40
3B	Castro, Willi, Toledo	8
3B	LaMarre, Ryan, Gwinnett	8
HR	Bradley, Bobby, Columbus	33
RBI	Barnes, Brandon, Columbus/Rochester	95
SAC	Canelo, Malquin, Lehigh Valley	10
BB	Ockimey, Josh, Pawtucket	82
HBP	Maggi, Drew, Rochester	20
SO	Taijeron, Travis, Syracuse	165
SB	Robson, Jacob, Toledo	25
CS	Colon, Christian, Louisville	13
AB/SO	Colon, Christian, Louisville	8.569

FIELDING

C PCT	Rivera, Rene, Syracuse	.999
PO	Haase, Eric, Columbus	821
A	Telis, Tomas, Rochester	57
DP	Rivera, Rene, Syracuse	8
E	Jackson, Alex, Gwinnett	12
CS	Rivera, Rene, Syracuse	30
CS	Haase, Eric, Columbus	30
SB	Grullon, Deivy, Lehigh Valley	78
PB	Centeno, Juan, Pawtucket	12
PB	Grullon, Deivy, Lehigh Valley	12
1B PCT	Craig, Will, Indianapolis	.999
PO	Craig, Will, Indianapolis	828
A	Wiel, Zander, Rochester	62
DP	Craig, Will, Indianapolis	92
E	Bradley, Bobby, Columbus	9
2B PCT	Blanco, Andres, Gwinnett	.985
PO	Blanco, Andres, Gwinnett	163
A	Blanco, Andres, Gwinnett	237
DP	Blanco, Andres, Gwinnett	69
E	Bostick, Christopher, Norfolk	15
3B PCT	Hayes, Ke'Bryan, Indianapolis	.989
PO	Witte, Jantzen, Pawtucket	72
A	Hayes, Ke'Bryan, Indianapolis	208
DP	Colon, Christian, Louisville	27
E	Herrera, Dilson, Syracuse	14
SS PCT	Canelo, Malquin, Lehigh Valley	.956
PO	Castro, Willi, Toledo	135
A	Castro, Willi, Toledo	227
DP	Castro, Willi, Toledo	52
E	Castro, Willi, Toledo	22
OF PCT	Blanco, Gregor, Syracuse	.990
PO	Cameron, Daz, Toledo	256
A	Williams, Mason, Norfolk	12
DP	Fields, Roemon, Buffalo	4
E	Aquino, Aristides, Louisville	8

PITCHING

G Kelley, Trevor, Pawtucket		52
GS Gutierrez, Vladimir, Louisville		27
GS Mella, Keury, Louisville		27
GF Kelley, Trevor, Pawtucket		31
GF Vieira, Thyago, Charlotte		31
SV Kelley, Trevor, Pawtucket		12
SV Milner, Hoby, Durham		12
W Wright, Kyle, Gwinnett		11
L Mella, Keury, Louisville		14
IP Peoples, Michael, Columbus		145
H Mella, Keury, Louisville		160
R Nicolino, Justin, Rochester/Charlotte		102
ER Gutierrez, Vladimir, Louisville		92
ER Nicolino, Justin, Rochester/Charlotte		92
HB Gutierrez, Vladimir, Louisville		13
BB Reid-Foley, Sean, Buffalo		65
SO Akin, Keegan, Norfolk		131
SO/9 Akin, Keegan, Norfolk		10.50
SO/9 (RP) Feyereisen, J.P., Scranton/W-B		13.79
BB/9 Peoples, Michael, Columbus		1.8
WP Chiang, Shao-Ching, Columbus		17
WP Dohy, Kyle, Lehigh Valley		17
BK Gutierrez, Vladimir, Louisville		6
HRA Nicolino, Justin, Rochester/Charlotte		36
BAA Wright, Kyle, Gwinnett		.252

MINOR LEAGUES

BY KYLE GLASER

When the Triple-A leagues announced they would begin using the major league ball for 2019, many expected the change would result in increased levels of offense.

That increase, it turns out, would be more extreme than anyone could have imagined.

The Pacific Coast League, already hitter-friendly, turned into an offensive environment unprecedented in minor league history with the introduction of the major league ball. The number of home runs in the league increased from 2,097 in 2018 to 3,312 in 2019. The average ERA jumped from 4.60 to 5.43. The league's average slugging percentage was .477. In the 16-team PCL, 66 qualified hitters slugged .500 or better. That was more than every other full-season minor league—a total of 104 teams—combined. It made for a miserable year for pitchers in the league. Of the 24 pitchers to throw at least 100 innings, just three managed an ERA below 4.00.

In such an environment, offensive accomplishments came left and right. El Paso third baseman Ty France hit .399, falling just short of becoming the first player to bat .400 in the a full-season league since Erubiel Durazo hit .404 in 1999. Reno first baseman Kevin Cron led the minors with 38 home runs in just 82 games. Salt Lake first baseman Jared Walsh led the league with a 1.109 OPS, the highest OPS in the full-season minors since Todd Linden's 1.120 mark in 2005.

While the Astros ran away with the best record in the majors during the season, their Triple-A

TOP 20 PROSPECTS

1. Yordan Alvarez, OF, Fresno (Astros)
2. Keston Hiura, 2B, San Antonio (Brewers)
3. Gavin Lux, SS/2B, Oklahoma City (Dodgers)
4. Carter Kieboom, SS/2B, Fresno (Nationals)
5. Kyle Tucker, OF, Round Rock (Astros)
6. Sean Murphy, C, Las Vegas (Athletics)
7. Zac Gallen, RHP, New Orleans (Marlins)
8. Will Smith, C, Oklahoma City (Dodgers)
9. Brendan Rodgers, 2B/SS, Albuquerque (Rockies)
10. Luis Urias, SS/2B, El Paso (Padres)
11. Tommy Edman, 2B/SS, Memphis (Cardinals)
12. Tyler O'Neill, OF, Memphis (Cardinals)
13. Josh Naylor, OF, El Paso (Padres)
14. Peter Lambert, RHP, Albuquerque (Rockies)
15. Mauricio Dubon, SS, San Antonio (Brewers)/Sacramento (Giants)
16. Trent Grisham, OF, San Antonio (Brewers)
17. Lane Thomas, OF, Memphis (Cardinals)
18. Patrick Sandoval, LHP, Salt Lake (Angels)
19. Isan Diaz, 2B, New Orleans (Marlins)
20. Justus Sheffield, LHP, Tacoma (Mariners)

affiliate Round Rock posted the best record in the PCL at 84-56. Many of the key contributors, such as Yordan Alvarez, Kyle Tucker and Jose Urquidy, went on to help the Astros reach the World Series.

Round Rock cruised into the PCL championship series but fell to Giants affiliate Sacramento. Shortstop Abiatal Avelino played hero for the River Cats, stroking a walk-off RBI single in the bottom of the ninth to win Game 1 and delivering a go-ahead, two-run single in the eighth inning of Game 3 to complete a three-game sweep.

Sacramento then won the Triple-A National Championship with a 4-0 win over International League champion Columbus (Indians).

OVERALL STANDINGS

American Northern	W	L	PCT	GB	Manager(s)	Attendance	Average	Last Pennant
Iowa Cubs (Cubs)	75	65	.536	—	Marty Pevey	489,173	7,137	Never
Memphis Redbirds (Cardinals)	69	71	.493	6	Ben Johnson	327,753	4,671	2018
Nashville Sounds (Rangers)	66	72	.478	8	Jason Wood	578,291	8,225	2005
Omaha Storm Chasers (Royals)	59	80	.424	15 ½	Brian Poldberg	328,307	4,774	2014

American Southern	W	L	PCT	GB	Manager(s)	Attendance	Average	Last Pennant
Round Rock Express (Astros)	84	56	.600	—	Mickey Storey	597,928	8,542	Never
San Antonio Missions (Brewers)	80	60	.571	4	Rick Sweet	337,484	4,831	Never
New Orleans Baby Cakes (Marlins)	73	65	.529	10	Keith Johnson	188,092	2,851	2001
Oklahoma City (Dodgers)	62	77	.446	21 ½	Travis Barbary	444,131	6,335	1965

American Southern	W	L	PCT	GB	Manager(s)	Attendance	Average	Last Pennant
Sacramento River Cats (Giants)	73	67	.521	—	Dave Brundage	549,440	7,849	2019
Reno Aces (D-backs)	66	74	.471	7	Chris Cron	336,215	4,803	2012
Fresno Grizzlies (Nationals)	65	75	.464	8	Randy Knorr	380,090	5,462	Never
Tacoma Rainiers (Mariners)	61	78	.439	11 ½	Daren Brown	347,378	5,063	2010

Pacific Southern	W	L	PCT	GB	Manager(s)	Attendance	Average	Last Pennant
Las Vegas Aviators (Athletics)	83	57	.593	—	Fran Riordan	650,934	9,299	1998
El Paso Chihuahuas (Padres)	80	60	.571	3	Edwin Rodriguez	522,894	7,474	2016
Salt Lake Bees (Angels)	60	79	.432	22 ½	Lou Marson	433,596	6,279	1979
Albuquerque Isotopes (Rockies)	60	80	.429	23	Glenallen Hill	542,832	7,726	1994

Semifinals: Round Rock defeated Iowa 3-2 and Sacramento defeated Las Vegas 3-2 in best-of-five series. **Finals:** Sacramento defeated Round Rock 3-0 in a best-of-five series.

CLUB BATTING

	AVG	G	AB	R	H	2B	3B	HR	RBI	BB	SO	SB	OBP	SLG
El Paso	.299	140	5011	968	1496	320	33	258	926	504	1214	62	.367	.530
Las Vegas	.298	140	4994	959	1487	314	50	250	926	554	1267	82	.371	.531
Fresno	.289	140	4929	823	1424	289	31	208	783	489	1228	74	.357	.487
Albuquerque	.287	140	4904	854	1409	311	47	212	811	492	1240	78	.355	.500
Round Rock	.283	140	4752	890	1344	287	28	220	840	623	1074	143	.370	.494
Salt Lake	.282	139	4822	891	1358	299	39	222	840	637	1214	55	.370	.498
Reno	.281	140	4906	918	1379	305	44	242	881	562	1196	49	.362	.509
Sacramento	.280	140	4860	825	1360	286	25	228	780	498	1281	53	.351	.490
Memphis	.278	140	4731	803	1314	251	30	200	761	509	1166	86	.358	.470
New Orleans	.270	138	4630	719	1249	236	30	202	661	416	1199	140	.337	.465
Tacoma	.270	139	4767	730	1289	279	32	160	691	530	1190	123	.348	.443
San Antonio	.268	140	4724	775	1267	273	18	195	740	552	1261	117	.352	.457
Oklahoma City	.262	139	4636	786	1215	267	29	203	746	573	1266	43	.352	.464
Omaha	.262	139	4693	697	1231	195	43	156	639	479	1110	150	.335	.422
Nashville	.261	138	4698	708	1224	216	20	179	658	494	1179	87	.338	.429
Iowa	.253	140	4565	708	1154	259	25	177	669	519	1209	79	.334	.437

CLUB PITCHING

	ERA	G	CG	SHO	SV	IP	H	R	ER	HR	BB	SO	AVG
San Antonio	4.15	140	0	14	31	1226	1139	643	565	159	476	1276	.245
New Orleans	4.43	138	1	8	42	1202	1142	659	591	196	446	1246	.251
Iowa	4.67	140	2	6	37	1203	1162	688	625	191	552	1247	.252
Memphis	4.87	140	1	8	27	1209	1170	707	654	167	607	1228	.255
Sacramento	5.03	140	5	3	33	1237	1298	773	692	189	465	1270	.268
Las Vegas	5.20	140	1	6	36	1229	1323	789	710	224	482	1163	.274
Round Rock	5.24	140	3	12	34	1227	1225	760	714	206	525	1265	.260
Omaha	5.39	139	1	6	26	1208	1322	803	723	216	574	1044	.278
Nashville	5.46	138	1	2	39	1208	1339	814	732	175	503	1158	.280
El Paso	5.66	140	0	4	35	1240	1453	855	780	235	471	1211	.292
Oklahoma City	5.83	139	1	3	30	1190	1329	856	771	200	573	1287	.282
Fresno	6.06	140	0	5	31	1225	1442	920	824	223	525	1134	.292
Tacoma	6.07	139	2	9	31	1205	1328	878	812	226	528	1243	.277
Albuquerque	6.38	140	0	2	19	1218	1545	938	864	252	524	1114	.309
Reno	6.48	140	0	3	28	1230	1480	968	885	235	587	1217	.297
Salt Lake	6.77	139	1	2	32	1196	1503	1003	900	218	593	1191	.306

CLUB FIELDING

	PCT	PO	A	E	DP		PCT	PO	A	E	DP
Round Rock	.986	3681	1212	69	117	Reno	.978	3690	1314	110	106
Iowa	.984	3610	1181	79	101	San Antonio	.978	3677	1285	112	127
Memphis	.983	3626	1128	82	112	Fresno	.977	3674	1270	114	136
El Paso	.981	3719	1367	100	128	Omaha	.977	3625	1324	116	128
Las Vegas	.981	3687	1364	98	134	New Orleans	.976	3606	1194	117	122
Tacoma	.981	3614	1178	91	107	Sacramento	.975	3711	1278	128	126
Albuquerque	.980	3655	1395	101	146	Oklahoma City	.974	3569	1173	127	120
Nashville	.979	3623	1273	103	119	Salt Lake	.974	3589	1219	129	121

INDIVIDUAL BATTING

Batter, Club	AVG	G	AB	R	H	2B	3B	HR	RBI	BB	SO	SB
David Freitas, San Antonio	.381	91	328	55	125	23	0	12	81	47	55	0
Corban Joseph, Las Vegas	.371	97	383	63	142	35	4	13	73	33	46	0
Yonathan Daza, Albuquerque	.364	89	387	67	141	30	4	11	48	25	52	12
Mark Payton, Las Vegas	.334	118	395	80	132	30	3	30	97	45	76	7
Brian Mundell, Albuquerque	.333	110	390	69	130	32	4	11	61	42	84	1
Jared Walsh, Salt Lake	.325	98	382	90	124	30	0	36	86	59	115	0
Yadiel Hernandez, Fresno	.323	126	439	87	142	22	1	33	90	63	106	7
Pat Valaika, Albuquerque	.320	84	350	60	112	26	1	22	75	27	90	5
Sheldon Neuse, Las Vegas	.317	126	498	99	158	31	2	27	102	56	132	3
Seth Mejias-Brean, El Paso	.316	117	411	69	130	18	3	11	66	33	79	4

INDIVIDUAL PITCHING

Pitcher, Club	W	L	ERA	G	GS	CG	SV	IP	H	R	ER	BB	SO
Hector Noesi, New Orleans	11	4	3.82	21	21	0	0	125	112	54	53	30	133
Colin Rea, Iowa	14	4	3.95	26	26	1	0	148	142	74	65	60	120
Jake Woodford, Memphis	9	8	4.15	26	26	0	0	152	124	75	70	75	131
Paul Blackburn, Las Vegas	11	3	4.34	24	22	0	0	133	133	70	64	34	92
Thomas Jankins, San Antonio	10	5	4.38	23	21	0	0	123	137	67	60	32	88
Tim Dillard, Nashville	9	9	4.75	33	21	1	0	153	169	93	81	37	103
Daniel Corcino, Oklahoma City	8	8	4.90	24	21	1	0	119	112	69	65	61	105
Bubba Derby, San Antonio	7	8	4.99	27	18	0	1	115	117	68	64	49	104
Jake Kalish, Omaha	8	8	5.16	24	10	0	1	119	131	77	68	25	89
Foster Griffin, Omaha	8	6	5.23	25	25	0	0	131	134	86	76	64	111

ALL-STAR TEAM

C: David Freitas, San Antonio. **1B:** Kevin Cron, Reno. **2B:** Isan Diaz, New Orleans. **3B:** Ty France, El Paso. **SS:** Carter Kieboom, Fresno. **OF:** Yonathan Daza, Albuquerque; Sam Hilliard, Albuquerque; Kyle Tucker, Round Rock. **DH:** Jared Walsh, Reno. **RHP:** Colin Rea, Iowa. **LHP:** Foster Griffin, Omaha. **RP:** David Carpenter, Nashville. **Most Valuable Player:** Ty France, El Paso. **Pitcher of the Year:** Colin Rea, Iowa. **Rookie of the Year:** Ty France, El Paso. **Manager of the Year:** Fran Riordan, Las Vegas.

DEPARTMENT LEADERS

BATTING

OBP	Freitas, David, Tacoma/San Antonio	.461
SLG	Walsh, Jared, Salt Lake Bees	.686
OPS	Hilliard, Sam, Albuquerque	.893
R	Neuse, Sheldon, Las Vegas	158
H	Rojas, Jose, Salt Lake	297
TB	Rojas, Jose, Salt Lake Bees	77
XBH	Gerber, Mike, Sacramento	41
2B	Gerber, Mike, Sacramento	41
3B	Mateo, Jorge, Las Vegas	14
HR	Cron, Kevin, Reno	38
RBI	Rojas, Jose, Salt Lake	107
SAC	Flores, Jecksson, Omaha	13
BB	Ward, Taylor, Salt Lake	80
HBP	Orf, Nate, San Antonio	22
SO	Gettys, Michael, El Paso	168
SB	Tucker, Kyle, Round Rock	30
CS	Granite, Zack, Nashville	13
AB/SO	Granite, Zack, Nashville	11.2

FIELDING

C	PCT	Lobaton, Jose, Tacoma/Oklahoma City	.991
	PO	Lobaton, Jose, Tacoma/Oklahoma City	727
	A	Lobaton, Jose, Tacoma/Oklahoma City	47
	A	Heineman, Tyler, Reno/New Orleans	47
	DP	Dini, Nick, Omaha	6
	E	Lobaton, Jose, Tacoma/Oklahoma City	7
	E	Castillo, Wilkin, New Orleans	7
	E	Fernandez, Xavier, Omaha	7
	CS	Knizner, Andrew, Memphis	25
	SB	Gushue, Taylor, Fresno	63
	PB	Nottingham, Jacob, San Antonio	10
1B	PCT	Nogowski, John, Memphis	.997
	PO	Ramos, Roberto, Albuquerque	809
	A	Nogowski, John, Memphis	69
	DP	Ramos, Roberto, Albuquerque	81
	E	Ramos, Roberto, Albuquerque	10
2B	PCT	Diaz, Isan, New Orleans	.978
	PO	Diaz, Isan, New Orleans	180
	A	Diaz, Isan, New Orleans	217
	DP	Diaz, Isan, New Orleans	65
	E	Diaz, Isan, New Orleans	9
3B	PCT	Neuse, Sheldon, Las Vegas	.965
	PO	Neuse, Sheldon, Las Vegas	76
	A	Neuse, Sheldon, Las Vegas	198
	A	Fuentes, Josh, Albuquerque	198
	DP	Fuentes, Josh, Albuquerque	25
	E	Wisdom, Patrick, Nashville	15
	E	Noll, Jake, Fresno	15
SS	PCT	Dubon, Mauricio, San Antonio/Sacramento	.968
	PO	Avelino, Abiatal, Sacramento	142
	A	Mateo, Jorge, Las Vegas	304
	DP	Mateo, Jorge, Las Vegas	76
	E	Mateo, Jorge, Las Vegas	20
OF	PCT	Payton, Mark, Las Vegas	.995
	PCT	Tucker, Kyle, Round Rock	.995
	PO	Garcia, Adolis, Memphis	257
	A	Garcia, Adolis, Memphis	17
	DP	Daza, Yonathan, Albuquerque	4
	DP	Fowler, Dustin, Las Vegas	4
	E	Gettys, Michael, El Paso	10

PITCHING

G	Quackenbush, Kevin, Oklahoma City	54
GS	Keel, Jerry, El Paso	26
GS	Rea, Colin Iowa	26
GS	Woodford, Jake, Memphis	26
GF	Carpenter, David, Nashville	38
SV	Carpenter, David, Nashville	21
W	Rea, Colin, Iowa	14
L	Dean, Pat, Albuquerque	13
IP	Dillard, Tim, Nashville	153
H	Keel, Jerry, El Paso	207
R	Keel, Jerry, El Paso	127
ER	Keel, Jerry, El Paso	114
HB	Dillard, Tim, Nashville	20
BB	Woodford, Jake, Memphis	75
SO	Swarmer, Matt, Iowa	137
SO/9	Noesi, Hector, New Orleans	9.6
SO/9 (RP)	Quackenbush, Kevin, Oklahoma City	13.0
BB/9	Maness, Seth, Nashville	1.23
WP	Copeland, Scott, Fresno	15
BK	Dunshee, Parker, Las Vegas	3
HRA	Enns, Dietrich, El Paso Chihuahuas	37
BAA	Woodford, Jake, Memphis	.223

MINOR LEAGUES

MINOR LEAGUES

BY JUSTIN COLEMAN

The Reading Fightin' Phils (Phillies) won a league-best 80 games in 2019, but they did not take home the Eastern League Championship. After winning the Eastern Division in the second half of the season, the Phils lost in the first round of the playoffs to Trenton (Yankees). The Thunder boasted prominent righthanders Deivi Garcia and Albert Abreu, while league MVP Chris Gittens hit .281/.393/.500 with 23 home runs and 77 RBIs to anchor their offensive attack. The Thunder went on to win the Eastern League championship. It was their fourth title in team history, and their first since 2013.

The Erie Seawolves (Tigers) did not make the postseason, but the 77-win team featured one of the most dynamic rotations in recent memory. Casey Mize, the No. 1 overall pick in 2018, made his presence felt immediately after being promoted to the Eastern League in late April. The righthander spun a no-hitter against Altoona (Pirates), allowing just one walk while fanning seven batters. Rotation-mate Matt Manning was voted the Eastern League's pitcher of the year. The duo was joined by lefthander Tarik Skubal, who dominated the league after being promoted on July 5. He allowed just 25 hits in 42.1 innings and struck out an impressive 82 batters across that span. Righthander Alex Faedo, a 2017 first-round pick who regained his velocity from his time at Florida and pitched to a 3.90 ERA in 115.1 innings, rounded out the group.

A pair of third basemen stuck out in the Eastern League. Reading third baseman Alec Bohm smashed 14 home runs, which was second only to teammate Darick Hall (20), while Nolan Jones (Indians) was among the league leaders in on-base percentage (.370) for players who had at least 200 plate appearances. Both were prominent talents and ranked as the league's top two position players in a league that was flush with top-end pitching.

TOP 20 PROSPECTS

1. Nate Pearson, RHP, New Hampshire (Blue Jays)
2. Casey Mize, RHP, Erie (Tigers)
3. Matt Manning, RHP, Erie (Tigers)
4. Alec Bohm, 3B, Reading (Phillies)
5. Deivi Garcia, RHP, Trenton (Yankees)
6. Nolan Jones, 3B, Akron (Indians)
7. Bryan Mata, RHP, Portland (Red Sox)
8. Bobby Dalbec, 3B, Portland (Red Sox)
9. Andres Gimenez, SS, Binghamton (Mets)
10. Isaac Paredes, 3B/SS, Erie (Tigers)
11. Anthony Kay, LHP, Binghamton (Mets)
12. Alex Faedo, RHP, Erie (Tigers)
13. Jarren Duran, OF, Portland (Red Sox)
14. Yusniel Diaz, OF, Bowie (Orioles)
15. Michael Baumann, RHP, Bowie (Orioles)
16. Luis Garcia, SS, Harrisburg (Nationals)
17. Albert Abreu, RHP, Trenton (Yankees)
18. Adonis Medina, RHP, Reading (Phillies)
19. Adam Haseley, OF, Reading (Phillies)
20. Patrick Murphy, RHP, New Hampshire (Blue Jays)

STANDINGS: SPLIT SEASON

FIRST HALF

Eastern	W	L	PCT	GB	Western	W	L	PCT	GB
Reading	39	28	.582	—	Harrisburg	42	28	.600	—
Trenton	38	28	.576	½	Altoona	36	32	.529	5
Hartford	37	30	.552	2	Akron	34	35	.493	7 ½
Binghamton	35	29	.547	2 ½	Erie	31	35	.470	9
New Hamp.	31	36	.463	8	Bowie	30	38	.441	11
Portland	27	40	.403	12	Richmond	23	44	.343	17 ½

SECOND HALF

Eastern	W	L	PCT	GB	Western	W	L	PCT	GB
Reading	41	31	.569	—	Bowie	46	26	.639	—
Trenton	38	34	.528	3	Erie	46	26	.639	—
Hartford	36	36	.500	5	Harrisburg	34	35	.493	10 ½
Portland	35	37	.486	6	Altoona	33	39	.458	13
New Hamp.	32	40	.444	9	Richmond	32	40	.444	14
Binghamton	32	44	.421	11	Akron	27	44	.380	18 ½

Playoffs—Semifinals: Trenton defeated Reading 3-0 and Bowie defeated Harrisburg 3-1 in best-of-five series. **Finals:** Trenton defeated Bowie 3-1 in a best-of-five series.

New Hampshire righthander Nate Pearson (Blue Jays) was selected as the top prospect in the Eastern League. Pearson posted a 2.59 ERA across 62.2 innings for the Fisher Cats before receiving a promotion to Triple-A Buffalo in late August.

OVERALL STANDINGS

Eastern Division	W	L	PCT	GB	Manager(s)	Attendance	Average	Last Pennant
Reading Fightin Phils (Phillies)	80	59	.576	—	Shawn Williams	398,314	5,578	2001
Trenton Thunder (Yankees)	76	62	.551	3 ½	Pat Osborn	340,705	4,930	2019
Hartford Yard Goats (Rockies)	73	66	.525	7	Warren Schaeffer	414,946	5,903	2001
Binghamton Rumble Ponies (Mets)	67	73	.479	13 ½	Kevin Boles	182,990	2,735	1994
New Hampshire Fisher Cats (Blue Jays)	63	76	.453	17	Mike Mordecai	306,511	4,486	2018
Portland Sea Dogs (Red Sox)	62	77	.446	18	Joe Oliver	357,647	5,131	2006

Western Division	W	L	PCT	GB	Manager(s)	Attendance	Average	Last Pennant
Erie SeaWolves (Tigers)	77	61	.558	—	Mike Rabelo	215,444	3,129	Never
Harrisburg Senators (Nationals)	76	63	.547	1 ½	Matthew LeCroy	258,909	3,708	1999
Bowie Baysox (Orioles)	76	64	.543	2	Buck Britton	224,686	3,226	Never
Altoona Curve (Pirates)	69	71	.493	9	Michael Ryan	308,464	4,280	2017
Akron RubberDucks (Indians)	61	79	.436	17	Rouglas Odor	340,187	4,884	2016
Richmond Flying Squirrels (Giants)	55	84	.396	22 ½	Willie Harris	400,321	5,767	2014

CLUB BATTING

	AVG	G	AB	R	H	2B	3B	HR	RBI	BB	SO	SB	OBP	SLG
Erie	.249	138	4520	589	1125	207	33	116	542	411	1126	82	.317	.386
Bowie	.246	140	4593	588	1128	246	32	96	545	422	1050	97	.314	.376
Binghamton	.243	140	4463	525	1084	232	20	87	490	478	1065	95	.323	.362
Altoona	.241	140	4488	544	1081	218	31	85	503	387	1222	87	.308	.360
Harrisburg	.241	139	4488	566	1082	243	25	88	514	402	1113	65	.307	.365
Trenton	.241	138	4386	543	1055	195	32	102	513	472	1171	106	.320	.369
Akron	.238	140	4606	547	1094	217	29	102	509	425	1071	76	.307	.364
New Hampshire	.238	139	4526	560	1077	244	28	94	524	453	1292	107	.315	.367
Hartford	.234	139	4406	526	1031	221	18	115	482	392	1114	114	.302	.371
Reading	.234	139	4438	586	1039	224	47	119	540	503	1179	115	.318	.386
Portland	.233	139	4425	516	1033	220	16	94	476	409	1291	104	.306	.354
Richmond	.219	139	4455	458	975	188	29	84	430	454	1225	130	.296	.331

CLUB PITCHING

	ERA	G	CG	SHO	SV	IP	H	R	ER	HR	BB	SO	AVG
Bowie	3.18	140	5	16	36	1222	1027	504	432	120	414	1167	.226
Erie	3.29	138	2	16	35	1200	1017	501	439	99	422	1262	.230
Hartford	3.29	139	2	11	50	1202	1137	506	440	107	340	1163	.252
Harrisburg	3.43	139	1	9	48	1201	1088	533	458	103	356	1142	.240
Akron	3.46	140	1	14	33	1216	1102	556	468	94	473	1155	.241
Richmond	3.58	139	1	8	35	1210	1076	594	481	73	513	1167	.238
Binghamton	3.59	140	3	13	35	1190	1067	548	475	106	416	1171	.239
New Hampshire	3.62	139	2	11	36	1199	1054	558	482	108	433	1104	.235
Trenton	3.67	138	3	16	40	1168	1019	547	476	83	492	1214	.233
Altoona	3.69	140	6	18	37	1206	1126	563	494	108	398	964	.249
Reading	3.73	139	0	6	42	1203	1049	574	498	102	442	1271	.235
Portland	3.80	139	2	16	41	1179	1042	564	498	79	509	1139	.238

CLUB FIELDING

	PCT	PO	A	E	DP		PCT	PO	A	E	DP
Altoona	.982	3617	1335	89	134	Akron	.979	3647	1276	108	105
Reading	.982	3608	1171	87	106	Binghamton	.979	3570	1186	101	92
Erie	.981	3600	1159	90	104	Bowie	.979	3665	1159	103	88
Hartford	.980	3606	1217	100	118	Harrisburg	.978	3602	1215	107	105
New Hampshire	.980	3597	1222	97	103	Trenton	.978	3504	1128	102	80
Portland	.980	3538	1157	95	104	Richmond	.973	3631	1294	139	118

INDIVIDUAL BATTING

Batter, Club	AVG	G	AB	R	H	2B	3B	HR	RBI	BB	SO	SB
C.J. Chatham, Portland	.297	90	350	39	104	26	1	3	36	18	66	7
Jose Azocar, Erie	.286	129	504	65	144	21	3	10	58	21	132	10
Isaac Paredes, Erie	.282	127	478	65	135	23	1	13	66	57	61	5
Chris Gittens, Trenton	.281	115	398	58	112	16	1	23	77	71	139	0
Santiago Espinal, New Hampshire	.278	94	367	46	102	21	1	5	57	35	50	10
Jared Oliva, Altoona	.277	123	447	70	124	24	6	6	42	42	104	36
Connor Marabell, Akron	.273	111	421	51	115	23	1	8	50	28	52	7
Hoy Jun Park, Trenton	.272	113	416	60	113	20	6	3	41	57	91	20
Josh Stephen, Reading	.271	113	362	48	98	29	6	12	47	39	110	7
Ian Sagdal, Harrisburg	.271	128	447	58	121	31	3	8	62	42	88	1

INDIVIDUAL PITCHING

Pitcher, Club	W	L	ERA	G	GS	CG	SV	IP	H	R	ER	BB	SO
Daniel McGrath, Portland	7	1	1.68	27	15	0	1	112	72	25	21	45	113
Zac Lowther, Bowie	13	7	2.55	26	26	0	0	148	102	46	42	63	154
Matt Manning, Erie	11	5	2.56	24	24	0	0	134	93	42	38	38	148
Pedro Vasquez, Altoona	8	5	2.71	24	23	1	0	123	107	46	37	29	91
Mario Sanchez, Harrisburg	10	5	2.85	23	19	1	0	114	90	40	36	17	111
Alex Wells, Bowie	8	6	2.95	24	24	1	0	137	123	50	45	24	105
Mickey Jannis, Binghamton	7	5	3.10	20	18	1	0	119	123	48	41	31	105
Caleb Baragar, Richmond	5	5	3.45	22	21	1	0	120	83	52	46	43	107
Brandon Gold, Hartford	12	6	3.56	26	26	0	0	144	166	64	57	22	115
Jack Wynkoop, Hartford	7	13	3.56	24	24	2	0	149	155	64	59	22	99

ALL-STAR TEAM

C: Patrick Mazeika, Binghamton. 1B: Chris Gittens, Trenton. 2B: Santiago Espinal, New Hampshire. 3B: Bobby Dalbec, Portland. SS: C.J. Chatham, Portland. OF: Jose Azocar, Erie; Mickey Moniak, Reading; Jared Oliva, Altoona. DH: Isaac Paredes, Erie. UT: Darick Hall, Reading. RHP: Matt Manning, Erie. LHP: Zac Lowther, Bowie. RP: Aaron Barrett, Harrisburg. Most Valuable Player: Chris Gittens, Trenton. Pitcher of the Year: Matt Manning, Erie. Rookie of the Year: Jose Azocar, Erie. Manager of the Year: Buck Britton, Bowie.

DEPARTMENT LEADERS

BATTING

OBP	Gittens, Chris, Trenton	.393
SLG	Gittens, Chris, Trenton	.500
OPS	Gittens, Chris, Trenton	.893
R	Hill, Derek, Erie	78
R	McKenna, Ryan, Bowie	78
H	Azocar, Jose, Erie	144
TB	Hall, Darick, Reading	207
XBH	Hall, Darick, Reading	59
2B	Hall, Darick, Reading	38
3B	Moniak, Mickey, Reading	13
HR	Gittens, Chris, Trenton	23
RBI	Gittens, Chris, Trenton	77
SAC	Holder, Kyle, Trenton	14
BB	Heyward, Jacob, Richmond	80
HBP	Hall, Darick, Reading	17
SO	Smith, Kevin, New Hampshire	151
SB	Fargas, Johneshwy, Richmond	50
CS	Fargas, Johneshwy, Richmond	23
AB/SO	Clement, Ernie, Akron	11.9

FIELDING

C PCT	Pabst, Arden, Altoona	.998
PO	Barrera, Tres, Harrisburg	736
A	Serven, Brian, Hartford	86
DP	Serven, Brian, Hartford	7
E	Nunez, Jhon, Portland	9
CS	Mineo, Alberto, New Hampshire	33
CS	Serven, Brian, Hartford	33
SB	Barrera, Tres, Harrisburg	74
PB	Mineo, Alberto, New Hampshire	14
PB	Mazeika, Patrick, Binghamton	14
1B PCT	Hall, Darick, Reading	.996
PO	Suiter, Jerrick, Altoona	871
A	Suiter, Jerrick, Altoona	67
DP	Suiter, Jerrick, Altoona	97
E	Nevin, Tyler, Hartford	11
2B PCT	Netzer, Brett, Portland	.984
PO	Miller, Jalen, Richmond	194
A	Miller, Jalen, Richmond	321
DP	Miller, Jalen, Richmond	69
E	Miller, Jalen, Richmond	13
3B PCT	Dalbec, Bobby, Portland	.928
PO	Dalbec, Bobby, Portland	57
A	Dalbec, Bobby, Portland	137
DP	Owen, Hunter, Altoona	16
E	Dalbec, Bobby, Portland	15
SS PCT	Gamboa, Arquimedes, Reading	.980
PO	Gamboa, Arquimedes, Reading	165
A	Gimenez, Andres, Binghamton	255
DP	Garcia, Luis, Harrisburg	56
E	Clement, Ernie, Akron	22
OF PCT	Oliva, Jared, Altoona	1
PO	Oliva, Jared, Altoona	288
A	Fargas, Johneshwy, Richmond	14
DP	Jackson, Bralin, Altoona	4
DP	Melendez, Manuel, Hartford	4
DP	Moniak, Mickey, Reading	4
E	Crawford, Rashad, Trenton	6
E	Brodey, Quinn, Binghamton	6
E	Spanberger, Chad, New Hampshire	6

PITCHING

G	Russ, Addison, Reading	55
GS	Gold, Brandon, Hartford	26
GS	Gutierrez, Alfred, Richmond	26
GS	Hentges, Sam, Akron	26
GS	Lowther, Zac, Bowie	26
GS	Reyes, Denyi, Portland	26
GF	Russ, Addison, Reading	50
SV	Barrett, Aaron, Harrisburg	31
W	Lowther, Zac, Bowie	13
L	Brady, Sean, Akron	13
L	Hentges, Sam, Akron	13
L	Wynkoop, Jack, Hartford	13
IP	Brady, Sean, Akron	152
H	Gold, Brandon, Hartford	166
R	Hentges, Sam, Akron	89
ER	Mapes, Tyler, Harrisburg	74
HB	Williams, Garrett, Richmond	15
BB	Perez, Hector, New Hampshire	67
SO	Lowther, Zac, Bowie	154
SO/9	Faedo, Alex, Erie	10.5
SO/9 (RP)	Russ, Addison, Reading	12.9
BB/9	Wynkoop, Jack, Hartford	1.3
WP	Johnson, Chase, Richmond	19
BK	Garcia, Deivi, Trenton	3
BK	Garcia, Rony, Trenton	3
BK	Holder, Heath, Hartford	3
BK	Santos, Antonio, Hartford	3
BK	Wilson, Tommy, Binghamton	3
HRA	Wynkoop, Jack, Hartford	18
BAA	McGrath, Daniel, Portland	.184

MINOR LEAGUES

BY MATT EDDY

The Southern League was stacked in 2019, with perhaps its greatest quantity and variety of position prospects in a long time.

Despite being a 10-team league, the Southern League's embarrassment of riches included 15 players who qualified for our Top 20 Prospects ranking who were first- or supplemental first-round picks, while at least 20 players who ranked as Top 100 Prospects played in the league long enough to qualify for our ranking.

Mobile right fielder Jo Adell, the league's No. 1 prospect, missed April and most of May because of hamstring and ankle injuries suffered in spring training. He quickly caught up to speed and recorded a .944 OPS that led all SL batters who qualified for our Top 20 Prospects ranking.

Center fielders Luis Robert of Birmingham and Cristian Pache of Mississippi rounded out the league's trio of top prospects. Robert spent about half the season in the SL and shined. Overall, he hit 32 home runs and stole 36 bases as one of two 30-30 minor leaguers. Pache is perhaps the finest defensive center fielder in the minors. He ranked second in the SL in extra-base hits (47), fourth in slugging (.474) and sixth in OPS (.814).

Pache's Mississippi teammate Drew Waters claimed the league's MVP. The outfielder led the league in average (.319), hits (134), doubles (35) and triples (nine) while placing second in slugging (.481) and OPS (.847).

Frontline starters were in shorter supply in the SL, but righthanders Sixto Sanchez, Ian Anderson and Brusdar Graterol and lefty Brendan McKay were all top 30 overall prospects.

The SL regular-season standings held little intrigue. Montgomery (North) and Biloxi (South) convincingly won their divisions in both halves of the season. The Biscuits had the league's youngest roster and were stocked with Rays prospects, especially on the batting side. Montgomery led the league in runs (4.63 per game) and OPS (.732).

Jackson captured its second straight Southern League crown, and the Generals have won three of the past four titles. Jackson catcher/center fielder Daulton Varsho claimed MVP honors during the finals by going 6-for-15 with four runs and three RBIs. Righthander Emilio Vargas allowed one run in seven innings in Jackson's Game 5 clincher.

TOP 20 PROSPECTS

1. Jo Adell, OF, Mobile (Angels)
2. Luis Robert, OF, Birmingham (White Sox)
3. Cristian Pache, OF, Mississippi (Braves)
4. Sixto Sanchez, RHP, Jacksonville (Marlins)
5. Drew Waters, OF, Mississippi (Braves)
6. Brendan McKay, LHP/DH, Montgomery (Rays)
7. Jazz Chisholm, SS, Jackson (D-backs)/Jacksonville (Marlins)
8. Ian Anderson, RHP, Mississippi (Braves)
9. Brusdar Graterol, RHP, Pensacola (Twins)
10. Brandon Marsh, OF, Mobile (Angels)
11. Trevor Larnach, OF, Pensacola (Twins)
12. Alex Kirilloff, OF/1B, Pensacola (Twins)
13. Lewin Diaz, 1B, Pensacola (Twins)/Jacksonville (Marlins)
14. Daulton Varsho, C/OF, Jackson (D-backs)
15. Nico Hoerner, SS/2B, Tennessee (Cubs)
16. Taylor Trammell, OF, Chattanooga (Reds)
17. Nick Madrigal, 2B, Birmingham (White Sox)
18. Royce Lewis, SS, Pensacola (Twins)
19. Jesus Sanchez, OF, Montgomery (Rays)
20. Josh Lowe, OF, Montgomery (Rays)

STANDINGS: SPLIT SEASON

FIRST HALF

North	W	L	PCT	GB	South	W	L	PCT	GB
Montgomery	44	26	.629	—	Biloxi	41	29	.586	—
Jackson	39	31	.557	5	Pensacola	38	32	.543	3
Chattanooga	36	33	.522	7½	Mississippi	33	36	.478	7½
Tennessee	33	36	.478	10½	Jacksonville	29	41	.414	12
Birmingham	27	42	.391	16½	Mobile	27	41	.397	13

SECOND HALF

North	W	L	PCT	GB	South	W	L	PCT	GB
Montgomery	44	24	.647	—	Biloxi	41	28	.594	—
Jackson	39	26	.600	3½	Jacksonville	37	30	.552	3
Birmingham	37	30	.552	6½	Pensacola	38	31	.551	3
Chattanooga	25	42	.373	18½	Mississippi	31	39	.443	10½
Tennessee	25	45	.357	20	Mobile	23	45	.338	17½

Playoffs—Semifinals: Jackson defeated Montgomery 3-1 and Biloxi defeated Pensacola 3-2 in best-of-five series. **Finals:** Jackson defeated Biloxi 3-2 in best-of-five series.

OVERALL STANDINGS

Northern Division	W	L	PCT	GB	Manager	Attendance	Average	Last Pennant
Montgomery Biscuits (Rays)	88	50	.638	—	Morgan Ensberg	216,839	3,041	2007
Jackson Generals (D-backs)	78	57	.578	8½	Blake Lalli	107,131	1,697	2019
Birmingham Barons (White Sox)	64	72	.471	23	Omar Vizquel	379,707	5,424	2013
Chattanooga Lookouts (Reds)	61	75	.449	26	Pat Kelly	228,662	3,459	2017
Tennessee Smokies (Cubs)	58	81	.417	30½	Jimmy Gonzalez	280,708	3,977	2004

Southern Division	W	L	PCT	GB	Manager	Attendance	Average	Last Pennant
Biloxi Shuckers (Brewers)	82	57	.590	—	Mike Guerrero	146,845	2,117	Never
Pensacola Blue Wahoos (Twins)	76	63	.547	6	Ramon Borrego	296,095	4,217	2017
Jacksonville Jumbo Shrimp (Marlins)	66	71	.482	15	Kevin Randel	327,388	4,733	2014
Mississippi Braves (Braves)	64	75	.460	18	Chris Maloney	163,841	2,327	2008
Mobile BayBears (Angels)	50	86	.368	30½	David Newhan	95,087	1,401	2012

CLUB BATTING

	AVG	G	AB	R	H	2B	3B	HR	RBI	BB	SO	SB	OBP	SLG
Chattanooga	.259	136	4479	621	1159	208	26	104	564	443	1129	93	.332	.386
Birmingham	.252	136	4437	549	1116	213	23	73	516	408	1078	113	.320	.359
Montgomery	.251	138	4413	639	1106	211	46	115	568	522	1046	213	.334	.397
Tennessee	.245	139	4549	536	1113	214	29	48	491	469	1043	118	.320	.336
Biloxi	.244	139	4484	597	1093	212	25	120	553	494	1250	118	.325	.382
Jackson	.238	135	4336	606	1034	211	36	128	562	459	1142	72	.321	.392
Mobile	.238	136	4341	483	1032	217	18	70	449	434	1154	75	.313	.344
Mississippi	.236	139	4474	483	1055	202	38	87	448	399	1274	94	.305	.356
Pensacola	.234	139	4496	573	1053	195	25	126	525	461	1214	91	.313	.373
Jacksonville	.233	137	4450	454	1037	187	25	63	420	336	1125	97	.295	.329

CLUB PITCHING

	ERA	G	CG	SHO	SV	IP	H	R	ER	HR	BB	SO	AVG
Mississippi	3.22	139	4	16	35	1192	1017	491	427	78	460	1146	.231
Biloxi	3.25	139	3	16	43	1203	961	496	434	87	448	1230	.219
Jacksonville	3.26	137	2	10	37	1193	958	473	432	107	416	1194	.220
Montgomery	3.30	138	4	19	49	1204	1082	497	441	80	410	1060	.241
Jackson	3.36	135	6	14	41	1156	1045	490	432	74	416	1089	.241
Pensacola	3.44	139	3	17	43	1206	1077	528	461	75	440	1270	.239
Birmingham	4.03	136	2	10	30	1173	1150	609	525	111	432	1072	.257
Tennessee	4.10	139	0	2	34	1216	1131	635	554	115	487	1209	.248
Mobile	4.15	136	2	9	32	1142	1161	637	527	91	472	1148	.262
Chattanooga	4.61	136	2	5	32	1160	1216	685	594	116	444	1037	.268

CLUB FIELDING

	PCT	PO	A	E	DP		PCT	PO	A	E	DP
Pensacola	.982	3619	1275	90	116	Tennessee	.979	3648	1207	106	100
Jacksonville	.981	3578	1178	94	91	Mississippi	.978	3576	1253	107	120
Jackson	.980	3469	1268	98	131	Birmingham	.977	3518	1271	114	117
Biloxi	.979	3608	1194	102	103	Mobile	.973	3426	1231	129	107
Montgomery	.979	3611	1297	105	122	Chattanooga	.972	3481	1143	131	91

INDIVIDUAL BATTING

Batter, Club	AVG	G	AB	R	H	2B	3B	HR	RBI	BB	SO	SB
Drew Waters, Mississippi	.319	108	420	63	134	35	9	5	41	28	121	13
Patrick Leonard, Biloxi	.301	99	355	54	107	22	2	10	45	42	109	9
Daulton Varsho, Jackson	.301	108	396	85	119	25	4	18	58	42	118	21
Brandon Marsh, Mobile	.300	96	360	48	108	21	2	7	43	47	92	18
Miles Mastrobuoni, Montgomery	.299	107	381	57	114	10	6	4	34	42	82	15
Vimael Machin, Tennessee	.294	117	422	47	124	26	1	6	61	63	57	8
Pavin Smith, Jackson	.291	123	440	62	128	29	6	12	67	59	61	2
Alfredo Rodriguez, Chattanooga	.286	104	409	50	117	18	2	1	25	22	62	13
Alex Kirilloff, Pensacola	.283	94	375	47	106	18	2	9	43	29	76	7
Brett Sullivan, Montgomery	.280	102	364	53	102	25	5	10	51	32	48	21

INDIVIDUAL PITCHING

Pitcher, Club	W	L	ERA	G	GS	CG	SV	IP	H	R	ER	BB	SO
Trey Supak, Biloxi	11	4	2.20	20	20	1	0	123	84	33	30	23	91
Matt Peacock, Jackson	8	4	2.97	21	20	2	0	115	96	41	38	43	81
Cory Abbott, Tennessee	8	8	3.01	26	26	0	0	147	112	57	49	52	166
Kenny Rosenberg, Montgomery	11	4	3.29	25	16	0	0	134	118	52	49	55	108
Josh Fleming, Montgomery	11	4	3.31	21	17	3	0	128	127	57	47	19	92
Alec Bettinger, Biloxi	5	7	3.44	26	26	1	0	146	121	62	56	35	157
Jorge Guzman, Jacksonville	7	11	3.50	25	24	1	0	139	96	54	54	71	127
Bo Takahashi, Jackson	9	7	3.72	23	23	0	0	119	108	52	49	38	104
Bowden Francis, Biloxi	7	8	3.99	25	24	0	0	129	111	61	57	49	145
Tanner Banks, Birmingham	5	7	4.23	28	21	0	1	123	131	67	58	21	85

ALL-STAR TEAM

C: Daulton Varsho, Jacksonville. **1B:** Patrick Leonard, Biloxi. **2B:** Travis Blankenhorn, Pensacola. **3B:** Drew Ellis, Jackson. **SS:** Jazz Chisholm, Jacksonville. **OF:** Brandon Marsh, Mobile; Cristian Pache, Mississippi; Pavin Smith, Jackson; Drew Waters, Mississippi. **DH:** Ibandel Isabel, Chattanooga. **UT:** Miles Mastrobuoni, Montgomery. **RHP:** Trey Supak, Biloxi. **LHP:** Tucker Davidson, Mississippi. **RP:** Nate Griep, Biloxi. **Most Valuable Player:** Drew Waters, Mississippi. **Most Outstanding Pitcher:** Trey Supak, Biloxi. **Manager of the Year:** Morgan Ensberg, Montgomery.

DEPARTMENT LEADERS

BATTING

OBP	Machin, Vimael, Tennessee	.386
SLG	Varsho, Daulton, Jackson	.520
OPS	Varsho, Daulton, Jackson	.899
R	Varsho, Daulton, Jackson	85
H	Waters, Drew, Mississippi	134
TB	Varsho, Daulton, Jackson	206
XBH	Waters, Drew, Mississippi	49
2B	Waters, Drew, Mississippi	35
3B	Waters, Drew, Mississippi	9
HR	Isabel, Ibandel, Chattanooga	26
RBI	Sheets, Gavin, Birmingham	83
SAC	Donahue, Christian, Tennessee	7
BB	Ellis, Drew, Jackson	63
BB	Machin, Vimael, Tennessee	63
HBP	Young, Andy, Jackson	19
SO	Isabel, Ibandel, Chattanooga	153
SB	Fox, Lucius, Montgomery	37
CS	Caro, Roberto, Tennessee	13
CS	Mastrobuoni, Miles, Montgomery	13
AB/SO	Sullivan, Brett, Montgomery	7.6

FIELDING

C PCT	Pereda, Jhonny, Tennessee	.996
PO	McDowell, Max, Biloxi	803
A	Pereda, Jhonny, Tennessee	79
DP	Varsho, Daulton, Jackson	9
E	Contreras, William, Mississippi	10
E	Nolan, Nate, Birmingham	10
CS	Pereda, Jhonny, Tennessee	44
SB	Pereda, Jhonny, Tennessee	88
PB	Pereda, Jhonny, Tennessee	13
1B PCT	Leonard, Patrick, Biloxi	.999
PO	Sheets, Gavin, Birmingham	839
A	Sheets, Gavin, Birmingham	68
DP	Casteel, Ryan, Mississippi	80
E	Smith, Pavin, Jackson	7
2B PCT	Hinojosa, C.J., Biloxi	.981
PCT	Salazar, Alejandro, Mississippi	.981
PO	Hinojosa, C.J., Biloxi	176
A	Salazar, Alejandro, Mississippi	285
DP	Salazar, Alejandro, Mississippi	67
E	Daal, Calten, Chattanooga	16
3B PCT	Ellis, Drew, Jackson	.960
PO	Ellis, Drew, Jackson	80
A	Ellis, Drew, Jackson	183
DP	Ellis, Drew, Jackson	27
E	Forbes, Ti'Quan, Birmingham	18
SS PCT	Rodriguez, Alfredo, Chattanooga	.981
PO	Rivera, Laz, Birmingham	154
A	Chisholm, Jazz, Jackson/Jacksonville	249
DP	Rivera, Laz, Birmingham	62
E	Aviles Jr., Luis, Biloxi	21
OF PCT	Miller, Brian, Jacksonville	.995
PO	Lowe, Josh, Montgomery	275
A	Baez, Jeffrey, Jackson	15
DP	Rutherford, Blake, Birmingham	5
E	Trammell, Taylor, Chattanooga	9

PITCHING

G	Boyles, Ty, Chattanooga	47
GS	Abbott, Cory, Tennessee	26
GS	Bettinger, Alec, Biloxi	26
GF	Griep, Nate, Biloxi	37
SV	Griep, Nate, Biloxi	22
W	Fleming, Josh, Montgomery	11
W	Rosenberg, Kenny, Montgomery	11
W	Supak, Trey, Biloxi	11
L	Guzman, Jorge, Jacksonville	11
IP	Abbott, Cory, Tennessee	147
H	Banks, Tanner, Birmingham	131
R	Alcala, Jorge, Pensacola	68
ER	Alcala, Jorge, Pensacola	67
HB	Hackimer, Tom, Pensacola	15
BB	Guzman, Jorge, Jacksonville	71
SO	Abbott, Cory, Tennessee	166
SO/9	Abbott, Cory, Tennessee	10.2
SO/9 (RP)	Anderson, Ian, Mississippi	11.9
BB/9	Fleming, Josh, Montgomery	1.3
WP	Muller, Kyle, Mississippi	16
BK	Guzman, Jorge, Jacksonville	4
HRA	Abbott, Cory, Tennessee	15
BAA	Supak, Trey, Biloxi	.192

MINOR LEAGUES

BY KEGAN LOWE

In the expansion franchise's first season, the Amarillo Sod Poodles (Padres) won the Texas League championship. Amarillo defeated Dodgers affiliate Tulsa, 8-3, in Game 5 of the best-of-five championship series, capping off a season that also included a first-half division title. Before topping Tulsa in the finals, Amarillo defeated Midland, also by a three games to two tally, in the league semifinals.

Led by many of the same prospects who helped the Padres' farm system become the second-ranked system in baseball, Amarillo received contributions from Top 100 prospects MacKenzie Gore, Adrian Morejon, Luis Patiño and Taylor Trammell. Speaking to the depth of the Padres' system, none of the four aforementioned players qualified for the Texas League Top 20 Prospects list due to a lack of innings or at-bats, but Amarillo contributors such as outfielder Edward Olivares, second baseman Owen Miller and righthander Ronald Bolaños all managed to crack the TL's Top 20.

Other top prospects who fell short of enough playing time in the Texas League to qualify for the list include Arkansas outfielder Jarred Kelenic (Mariners), Corpus Christi righthander Forrest Whitley (Astros), Tulsa righthander Josiah Gray and shortstop Jeter Downs (Dodgers), as well as Midland lefthander A.J. Puk (Athletics.)

Even without including those names, the Texas League had yet another strong crop of prospects in 2019. Seven of the league's top 20 prospects went on to to reach the majors, including BA Minor League Player of the Year Gavin Lux (Dodgers). Before making his big league debut on Sept. 2, Lux started his 2019 campaign in Tulsa with the Drillers. In 64 games in the Texas League, Lux hit .313/.375/.521 with 13 home runs and 37 RBIs. Tulsa teammate Dustin May (Dodgers) was the top-ranked pitcher in the Texas League, posting a 3-5, 3.74 record with 86 strikeouts in 79.1 innings before eventually making his major league debut on Aug. 2.

Springfield outfielder Dylan Carlson (Cardinals) was named the Texas League's player of the year after hitting .281/.364/.518 with 21 home runs, 59 RBIs and 18 stolen bases in 108 games. Tacoma righthander Darren McCaughan (Mariners) was selected as the league's pitcher of the year following a 7-5, 2.89 campaign with 89 strikeouts in 102.2 innings. Both Carlson and McCaughan ended the year in the Triple-A Pacific Coast League.

TOP 20 PROSPECTS

1. Gavin Lux, SS, Tulsa (Dodgers)
2. Dylan Carlson, OF, Springfield (Cardinals)
3. Dustin May, RHP, Tulsa (Dodgers)
4. Logan Gilbert, RHP, Arkansas (Mariners)
5. Justus Sheffield, LHP, Arkansas (Mariners)
6. Evan White, 1B, Arkansas (Mariners)
7. Keibert Ruiz, C, Tulsa (Dodgers)
8. Justin Dunn, RHP, Arkansas (Mariners)
9. Brady Singer, RHP, Northwest Arkansas (Royals)
10. Jackson Kowar, RHP, Northwest Arkansas (Royals)
11. Seth Beer, 1B, Corpus Christi (Astros)
12. Elehuris Montero, 3B, Springfield (Cardinals)
13. Abraham Toro, 3B, Corpus Christi (Astros)
14. Leody Taveras, OF, Frisco (Rangers)
15. Daulton Jefferies, RHP, Midland (Athletics)
16. Khalil Lee, OF, Northwest Arkansas (Royals)
17. Jake Fraley, OF, Arkansas (Mariners)
18. Edward Olivares, OF, Amarillo (Padres)
19. Owen Miller, 2B, Amarillo (Padres)
20. Ronald Bolaños, RHP, Amarillo (Padres)

STANDINGS: SPLIT SEASON

FIRST HALF

North	W	L	PCT	GB	South	W	L	PCT	GB
Arkansas	43	25	.632	—	Amarillo	34	34	.500	—
Tulsa	37	32	.536	6 ½	Midland	34	35	.493	½
NW Arkansas	31	37	.456	12	Corpus Christi	33	36	.478	1 ½
Springfield	30	40	.429	14	Frisco	33	36	.478	1 ½

SECOND HALF

North	W	L	PCT	GB	South	W	L	PCT	GB
Tulsa	41	29	.586	—	Midland	39	31	.557	—
Arkansas	38	32	.543	3	Amarillo	38	32	.543	1
Springfield	30	40	.429	11	Frisco	35	35	.500	4
NW Arkansas	26	44	.371	15	Corpus Christi	33	37	.471	6

Playoffs—Semifinals: Amarillo defeated Midland 3-2 and Tulsa defeated Arkansas 3-2 in best-of-five series. **Finals:** Amarillo defeated Tulsa 3-2 in a best-of-five series.

OVERALL STANDINGS

North Division	W	L	PCT	GB	Manager(s)	Attendance	Average	Last Pennant
Arkansas Travelers (Mariners)	81	57	.587	—	M. Canham/C. Nicolas	311,021	4,450	2009
Tulsa Drillers (Dodgers)	78	61	.561	3 ½	Scott Hennessey	374,501	5,352	2018
Springfield Cardinals (Cardinals)	60	80	.429	22	Joe Kruzel	328,217	4,693	2012
Northwest Arkansas Naturals (Royals)	57	81	.413	24	Darryl Kennedy	284,829	4,112	2010

South Division	W	L	PCT	GB	Manager(s)	Attendance	Average	Last Pennant
Midland RockHounds (Athletics)	73	66	.525	—	Scott Steinmann	285,368	4,137	2017
Amarillo Sod Poodles (Padres)	72	66	.522	½	Phillip Wellman	427,791	6,291	2019
Frisco RoughRiders (Rangers)	68	71	.489	5	Joe Mikulik	455,765	6,506	2004
Corpus Christi Hooks (Astros)	66	73	.475	7	Omar Lopez	323,688	4,624	2006

CLUB BATTING

	AVG	G	AB	R	H	2B	3B	HR	RBI	BB	SO	SB	OBP	SLG
Tulsa	.263	139	4647	664	1220	186	24	169	626	471	1288	66	.335	.422
Amarillo	.262	138	4649	664	1220	229	22	139	613	440	1128	119	.331	.411
Frisco	.250	139	4620	600	1154	196	20	98	559	443	1101	70	.322	.365
Arkansas	.248	138	4626	573	1149	195	24	114	520	463	1330	100	.322	.375
Corpus Christi	.248	139	4689	671	1161	212	39	163	622	490	1351	123	.331	.414
Midland	.245	139	4643	621	1136	211	47	91	574	545	1356	105	.330	.369
NW Arkansas	.243	138	4498	533	1094	177	35	85	486	378	1293	218	.309	.355
Springfield	.237	140	4642	609	1101	203	17	140	558	449	1189	85	.313	.379

CLUB PITCHING

	ERA	G	CG	SHO	SV	IP	H	R	ER	HR	BB	SO	AVG
Arkansas	3.09	138	3	11	41	1217	1051	468	418	90	318	1324	.232
Tulsa	3.45	139	1	10	33	1215	1074	563	466	111	472	1240	.235
Midland	3.92	139	1	11	36	1227	1268	596	535	108	362	1092	.270
NW Arkansas	3.96	138	2	6	30	1198	1199	644	527	109	445	1142	.260
Frisco	4.22	139	0	9	35	1220	1115	623	572	119	476	1214	.243
Corpus Christi	4.27	139	1	8	38	1230	1009	649	584	128	646	1453	.221
Amarillo	4.45	138	0	9	38	1216	1236	687	601	160	450	1308	.264
Springfield	4.79	140	0	5	35	1226	1283	705	652	174	510	1263	.269

CLUB FIELDING

	PCT	PO	A	E	DP		PCT	PO	A	E	DP
Arkansas	.985	3652	1172	75	105	Midland	.982	3682	1378	93	134
Springfield	.985	3677	1169	76	109	Corpus Christi	.980	3690	1044	95	85
Amarillo	.982	3649	1257	92	99	Tulsa	.973	3644	1113	131	89
Frisco	.982	3661	1249	92	129	NW Arkansas	.970	3595	1300	151	136

INDIVIDUAL BATTING

Batter, Club	AVG	G	AB	R	H	2B	3B	HR	RBI	BB	SO	SB
Ivan Castillo, Amarillo	.313	104	432	62	135	30	5	8	57	20	59	15
Abraham Toro, Corpus Christi	.306	98	376	65	115	22	4	16	70	48	77	4
Cristian Santana, Tulsa	.301	102	399	45	120	22	1	10	57	10	88	0
Luis Torrens, Amarillo	.300	97	350	50	105	23	1	15	62	42	67	1
Donnie Walton, Arkansas	.300	124	480	72	144	22	3	11	50	63	72	10
Evan White, Arkansas	.293	92	365	61	107	13	2	18	55	29	92	2
Juremi Profar, Frisco	.290	90	348	46	101	24	0	10	53	31	53	0
Owen Miller, Amarillo	.290	130	507	76	147	28	2	13	68	46	86	5
Edward Olivares, Amarillo	.283	127	488	85	138	25	2	18	77	43	98	35
Dylan Carlson, Springfield	.281	108	417	81	117	24	6	21	59	52	98	18

INDIVIDUAL PITCHING

Pitcher, Club	W	L	ERA	G	GS	CG	SV	IP	H	R	ER	BB	SO
Angel Rondon, Springfield	6	6	3.21	20	20	0	0	115	99	45	41	42	112
Brian Howard, Midland	8	8	3.25	23	23	0	0	130	137	54	47	39	118
Kyle Friedrichs, Midland	6	7	3.43	20	19	0	0	113	121	45	43	31	81
Justin Dunn, Arkansas	9	5	3.55	25	25	0	0	132	118	62	52	39	158
Gerson Garabito, Northwest Arkansas	6	12	3.77	26	26	0	0	141	148	64	59	60	113
Lake Bachar, Amarillo	8	4	3.98	24	19	0	0	127	121	62	56	58	126
Ofreidy Gomez, Northwest	7	8	4.05	22	20	1	0	116	110	62	52	45	111
Ricardo Sanchez, Arkansas	8	12	4.44	27	27	0	0	146	157	77	72	38	135
Matt Milburn, Midland	8	9	4.90	26	25	1	0	151	179	89	82	37	86
Jesse Scholtens, Amarillo	5	7	5.40	24	20	0	0	125	145	81	75	40	129

ALL-STAR TEAM

C: Luis Torrens, Amarillo. **1B:** Evan White, Arkansas. **2B:** Ivan Castillo, Amarillo. **3B:** Abraham Toro, Corpus Christi. **SS:** Gavin Lux, Tulsa. **OF:** Edward Olivares, Amarillo; Jake Fraley, Arkansas; Dylan Carlson, Springfield. **P:** Dustin May, Tulsa; Lake Bachar, Amarillo; Justin Dunn, Arkansas; Darren McCaughan; Justus Sheffield, Arkansas; Art Warren, Arkansas; Emmanuel Clase, Frisco; Brian Howard, Midland. **Player of the Year:** Dylan Carlson, Springfield. **Pitcher of the Year:** Darren McCaughan, Arkansas. **Manager of the Year:** Phillip Wellman, Amarillo.

DEPARTMENT LEADERS

BATTING

OBP	Toro, Abraham, Corpus Christi	.393
SLG	Carlson, Dylan, Springfield	.518
OPS	Toro, Abraham, Corpus Christi	.906
R	Olivares, Edward, Amarillo	85
H	Miller, Owen, Amarillo	147
TB	Olivares, Edward, Amarillo	221
XBH	Diaz, Edwin, Midland	57
2B	Diaz, Edwin, Midland	36
3B	Blanco, Dairon, Midland/NW Arkansas	13
HR	Thomas, Cody, Tulsa	23
RBI	Cordero, Andretty, Frisco	82
SAC	Castellano, Angelo, NW Arkansas	11
BB	Lee, Khalil, NW Arkansas	65
HBP	Beer, Seth, Corpus Christi	20
SO	Theroux, Collin, Midland	178
SB	Lee, Khalil, NW Arkansas	53
CS	Blanco, Dairon, Midland/NW Arkansas	13
CS	Walton, Donnie, Arkansas	13
AB/SO	De Leon, Michael, Frisco	7.7

FIELDING

C PCT	O'Keefe, Brian	.996
PO	Robinson, Chuckie	898
A	Torrens, Luis	90
DP	Sanchez, Tony	9
DP	Odom, Joseph	9
DP	Robinson, Chuckie	9
E	Theroux, Collin	8
CS	Torrens, Luis	42
SB	Odom, Joseph	70
PB	Robinson, Chuckie	18
1B PCT	White, Evan	.993
PO	White, Evan	644
A	Zunica, Brad	35
DP	White, Evan	57
E	Zunica, Brad	9
2B PCT	Cowan, Jordan	.995
PO	Mondou, Nate	193
A	Mondou, Nate	298
DP	Mondou, Nate	68
E	Estevez, Omar	10
3B PCT	Rivera, Emmanuel	.928
PO	Rivera, Emmanuel	72
A	Rivera, Emmanuel	185
DP	Rivera, Emmanuel	30
E	Rivera, Emmanuel	20
SS PCT	Walton, Donnie	.990
PO	Merrell, Kevin	170
A	Merrell, Kevin	293
DP	Merrell, Kevin	72
E	Featherston, Taylor	19
PCT	Carlson, Dylan	.995
OF PO	Thomas, Cody	269
A	Reed, Buddy	18
DP	Thomas, Cody	4
DP	Davis, Brendon	4
E	Mieses, Johan	10

PITCHING

G	Patterson, Jacob, Springfield	51
GS	Sanchez, Ricardo, Arkansas	27
GF	Bednar, David, Amarillo	33
SV	Warren, Art, Arkansas	15
W	Dunn, Justin, Arkansas	9
L	Garabito, Gerson, NW Arkansas	12
L	Sanchez, Ricardo, Arkansas	12
IP	Milburn, Matt, Midland	151
H	Milburn, Matt, Midland	179
R	Milburn, Matt, Midland	89
ER	Milburn, Matt, Midland	82
HB	Gomez, Ofreidy, NW Arkansas	14
BB	Oviedo, Johan, Springfield	64
SO	Dunn, Justin, Arkansas	158
SO/9	Dunn, Justin, Arkansas	10.8
SO/9 (RP)	Javier, Cristian, Corpus Christi	13.9
BB/9	Milburn, Matt, Midland	2.2
WP	Greene, Conner, NW Arkansas	17
WP	Valdez, Dauris, Amarillo	17
BK	Sanchez, Ricardo, Arkansas	5
HRA	Parsons, Tommy, Springfield	26
BAA	Rondon, Angel, Springfield	.230

MINOR LEAGUES

BY KYLE GLASER

After 40 years of heartbreak, Visalia finally broke the curse of Joe Charboneau's pet alligator. The Rawhide (D-backs) went 83-53 during the season and steamrolled through the California League playoffs, beating Lake Elsinore (Padres) to win the franchise's first championship since 1978.

Visalia had lost its last 11 championship series appearances, including in 2014, 2016 and 2018. Fans commonly attributed the drought to the curse of Chopper, Charboneau's pet alligator. Legend holds Chopper died trying to escape his tank days after Visalia won its 1978 championship, and that his spirit haunted the franchise ever since.

The 2019 Rawhide, featuring many of the D-backs' top prospects, broke the curse with a series of thrilling finishes.

After sweeping San Jose, 3-0, in the North Division finals, Visalia dropped the first game of the championship series in Lake Elsinore before rallying. Yoel Yanqui hit the tie-breaking RBI single in the fifth inning of Game 2, and reliever Breckin Williams stranded the tying runs in both the eighth and ninth innings to secure a tense 2-1 win and even the series.

Back home in Visalia for Game 3, Luis Alejandro Basabe hit the tie-breaking RBI single in the eighth inning to end a stalemate and lift the Rawhide to a 4-2 win. One win away from the title, Visalia finished the series in grand fashion in Game 4.

After the Rawhide blew a 3-0 lead and the curse again looked to be rearing its ugly head, Geraldo Perdomo walked to lead off the bottom of the 10th inning and Alek Thomas brought him home with a walk-off RBI double down the line, giving Visalia the championship.

While the Rawhide were the best team, the best year belonged to Lake Elsinore lefthander MacKenzie Gore. The Padres prospect delivered a 1.02 ERA before being promoted to Double-A in July, the lowest ERA by a starter with at least 70 innings pitched in Cal League history.

Lake Elsinore catcher Luis Campusano, Gore's battery-mate, won league co-MVP with Lancaster first baseman Luis Castro. Campusano hit .326 to win the batting title while Castro led the league with 25 home runs and 86 RBI.

Modesto lefthander Ian McKinney won pitcher of the year after leading the league in wins (12) and ERA (2.84) and finishing second in strikeouts (148) and WHIP (1.19).

TOP 20 PROSPECTS

1. MacKenzie Gore, LHP, Lake Elsinore (Padres)
2. Joey Bart, C, San Jose (Giants)
3. Jarred Kelenic, OF, Modesto (Mariners)
4. Luis Patiño, RHP, Lake Elsinore (Padres)
5. Heliot Ramos, OF, San Jose (Giants)
6. Josiah Gray, RHP, Rancho Cucamonga (Dodgers)
7. Logan Gilbert, RHP, Modesto (Mariners)
8. Luis Campusano, C, Lake Elsinore (Padres)
9. Jeter Downs, SS, Rancho Cucamonga (Dodgers)
10. Xavier Edwards, 2B, Lake Elsinore (Padres)
11. Sean Hjelle, RHP, San Jose (Giants)
12. Gabriel Arias, SS, Lake Elsinore (Padres)
13. Ryan Rolison, LHP, Lancaster (Rockies)
14. Cal Raleigh, C, Modesto (Mariners)
15. Josh Green, RHP, Visalia (D-backs)
16. Ronald Bolaños, RHP, Lake Elsinore (Padres)
17. Nick Allen, SS, Stockton (Athletics)
18. Devin Mann, 2B/3B, Rancho Cucamonga (Dodgers)
19. Oliver Ortega, RHP, Inland Empire (Angels)
20. Ryan Vilade, SS/3B, Lancaster (Rockies)

STANDINGS: SPLIT SEASON

FIRST HALF

North	W	L	PCT	GB	South	W	L	PCT	GB
Visalia	44	22	.667	—	R. Cucamonga	41	27	.603	—
Stockton	33	35	.485	12	Lake Elsinore	35	33	.515	6
San Jose	30	39	.435	15½	Lancaster	34	34	.500	7
Modesto	30	40	.429	16	Inland Empire	26	43	.377	15½

SECOND HALF

North	W	L	PCT	GB	South	W	L	PCT	GB
Visalia	39	31	.557	—	R. Cucamonga	40	30	.571	—
San Jose	36	34	.514	3	Lake Elsinore	38	32	.543	2
Modesto	35	35	.500	4	Lancaster	34	36	.486	6
Stockton	27	43	.386	12	Inland Empire	31	39	.443	9

Playoffs—Semifinals: Lake Elsinore defeated Rancho Cucamonga 3-1 and Visalia defeated San Jose 3-0 in best-of-five series. **Finals:** Visalia defeated Lake Elsinore 3-1 in a best-of-five series.

OVERALL STANDINGS

North Division	W	L	PCT	GB	Manager(s)	Attendance	Average	Last Pennant
Visalia Rawhide (D-backs)	83	53	.610	—	Shawn Roof	129,118	1,899	2019
San Jose Giants (Giants)	66	73	.475	18½	B. Hayes/H. Borg	155,253	2,277	2010
Modesto Nuts (Mariners)	65	75	.464	20	Denny Hocking	139,762	1,970	2017
Stockton Ports (Athletics)	60	78	.435	24	Webster Garrison	179,465	2,601	2008

South Division	W	L	PCT	GB	Manager(s)	Attendance	Average	Last Pennant
Rancho Cucamonga Quakes (Dodgers)	81	57	.587	—	Mark Kertenian	162,085	2,384	2018
Lake Elsinore Storm (Padres)	73	65	.529	8	Tony Tarasco	172,280	2,521	2011
Lancaster JetHawks (Rockies)	68	70	.493	13	Scott Little	161,595	2,326	2014
Inland Empire 66ers (Angels)	57	82	.410	24½	Ryan Barba	181,253	2,606	2013

MINOR LEAGUES

CLUB BATTING

	AVG	G	AB	R	H	2B	3B	HR	RBI	BB	SO	SB	OBP	SLG
Lancaster	.271	138	4778	757	1294	253	46	148	684	490	1344	154	.345	.436
Lake Elsinore	.259	138	4668	628	1211	203	51	85	579	484	1102	155	.333	.379
Visalia	.254	136	4523	631	1147	229	29	86	561	513	1200	162	.335	.374
San Jose	.250	139	4706	628	1176	223	31	115	576	434	1374	108	.321	.384
Stockton	.249	138	4654	587	1158	239	40	84	527	463	1365	91	.325	.372
R. Cucamonga	.245	138	4636	740	1136	230	69	165	675	554	1529	178	.331	.431
Modesto	.244	140	4781	657	1166	245	40	122	600	482	1351	98	.320	.388
Inland Empire	.234	139	4667	578	1092	186	43	103	516	537	1446	61	.321	.358

CLUB PITCHING

	ERA	G	CG	SHO	SV	IP	H	R	ER	HR	BB	SO	AVG
Lake Elsinore	3.34	138	0	12	24	1216	1074	551	451	98	431	1372	.234
Modesto	3.68	140	2	9	26	1259	1161	623	515	74	478	1479	.244
Visalia	3.68	136	0	10	44	1203	1126	573	492	120	398	1332	.247
R. Cucamonga	3.71	138	1	7	36	1236	1154	611	510	87	586	1497	.246
San Jose	3.95	139	2	10	30	1229	1115	621	539	97	554	1308	.242
Inland Empire	4.28	139	0	4	23	1229	1159	688	585	106	537	1368	.249
Stockton	4.49	138	0	10	24	1210	1166	686	604	148	488	1220	.252
Lancaster	5.36	138	0	3	33	1227	1425	853	731	178	485	1135	.289

CLUB FIELDING

	PCT	PO	A	E	DP		PCT	PO	A	E	DP
Stockton	.981	3630	1201	95	106	Modesto	.971	3778	1188	147	99
Visalia	.981	3608	1233	94	109	R. Cucamonga	.971	3709	1138	146	110
San Jose	.978	3687	1122	110	116	Lake Elsinore	.968	3648	1124	159	89
Inland Empire	.975	3688	1220	128	99	Lancaster	.968	3681	1268	163	126

INDIVIDUAL BATING

Batter, Club	AVG	G	AB	R	H	2B	3B	HR	RBI	BB	SO	SB
Luis Campusano, Lake Elsinore	.325	110	422	63	137	31	1	15	81	52	57	0
Luis Castro, Lancaster	.317	106	385	93	122	24	2	25	98	61	98	14
Ryan Vilade, Lancaster	.303	128	509	92	154	27	10	12	71	56	95	24
Gabriel Arias, Lake Elsinore	.302	120	477	62	144	21	4	17	75	25	128	8
Allen Cordoba, Lake Elsinore	.301	105	422	68	127	20	6	5	43	31	77	32
Joe Rizzo, Modesto	.295	129	518	77	153	30	3	10	63	45	94	0
Luis Alejandro Basabe, Visalia	.293	117	420	70	123	21	4	4	51	75	106	16
Matt Hearn, Lancaster	.292	130	548	86	160	24	6	1	39	56	97	45
Alfonso Rivas, Stockton	.283	114	431	60	122	24	3	8	55	66	113	2
Matt McLaughlin, Lancaster	.279	110	398	55	111	20	2	1	42	48	95	12

INDIVIDUAL PITCHING

Pitcher, Club	W	L	ERA	G	GS	CG	SV	IP	H	R	ER	BB	SO
Ian McKinney, Modesto	12	5	2.84	25	25	1	0	136	108	53	43	54	148
Aaron Leasher, Lake Elsinore	10	7	3.15	22	19	0	0	120	113	44	42	34	113
Matt Frisbee, San Jose	9	8	3.17	22	20	1	0	116	102	47	41	22	131
Justin Vernia, Visalia	8	3	3.65	22	18	0	1	113	117	57	46	34	103
Jeff Bain, Visalia	6	8	3.95	23	22	0	0	121	115	63	53	38	152
Mitchell Jordan, Stockton	10	7	4.41	27	22	0	0	141	141	75	69	39	131
Brady Feigl, Stockton	5	11	4.42	27	25	0	0	134	148	83	66	35	119
Cooper Criswell, Inland Empire	4	8	4.60	25	21	0	0	117	133	69	60	35	111
Aaron Phillips, San Jose	8	7	4.62	25	21	1	0	115	119	66	59	43	101
Austin Hutchison, Modesto	5	12	4.64	26	24	0	0	130	144	79	67	53	136

ALL-STAR TEAM

C: Luis Campusano, Lake Elsinore. **1B:** Luis Castro, Lancaster. **2B:** Devin Mann, Rancho Cucamonga. **3B:** Luis Alejandro Basabe, Visalia. **SS:** Ryan Vilade, Lancaster. **OF:** Matt Hearn, Lancaster; Donovan Casey, Rancho Cucamonga; Heliot Ramos, San Jose. **DH:** Cal Raleigh, Modesto. **UT:** Jeter Downs, Rancho Cucamonga. **P:** Ian McKinney, Modesto; Ljay Newsome, Modesto; MacKenzie Gore, Lake Elsinore; Tommy Doyle, Lancaster. **Most Valuable Players:** Luis Campusano, Lake Elsinore; Luis Castro, Lancaster. **Pitcher of the Year:** Ian McKinney, Modesto. **Rookie of the Year:** Cal Raleigh, Modesto. **Manager of the Year:** Shawn Roof, Visalia.

DEPARTMENT LEADERS

BATTING

OBP	Castro, Luis, Lancaster	.425
SLG	Castro, Luis, Lancaster	.584
OPS	Castro, Luis, Lancaster	1.010
R	Castro, Luis, Lancaster	93
H	Hearn, Matt, Lancaster	160
TB	Vilade, Ryan, Lancaster	237
XBH	Downs, Jeter, R. Cucamonga	56
2B	Downs, Jeter, R. Cucamonga	33
3B	Kendall, Jeren, R. Cucamonga	10
3B	Vilade, Ryan, Lancaster	10
HR	Castro, Luis, Lancaster	25
RBI	Castro, Luis, Lancaster	98
SAC	McPherson, Kyle, San Jose	10
BB	Rosario, Jeisson, Lake Elsinore	87
HBP	Castro, Luis, Lancaster	19
HBP	Chiu, Marcus, R. Cucamonga	19
SO	Armenteros, Lazaro, Stockton	227
SB	Hearn, Matt, Lancaster	45
CS	Hearn, Matt, Lancaster	15
AB/SO	Campusano, Luis, Lake Elsinore	7.4

FIELDING

C	PCT	Devencenzi, Jordan, Stockton	.997
	PO	Campusano, Luis, Lake Elsinore	786
	A	Bernard, Austin, Lancaster	67
	DP	Susnara, Tim, Visalia	8
	E	Bernard, Austin, Lancaster	13
	CS	Bernard, Austin, Lancaster	31
	CS	Washington, Jalen, Lake Elsinore	31
	SB	Campusano, Luis, Lake Elsinore	75
	PB	Torres, Franklin, Inland Empire	17
1B	PCT	Rivas, Alfonso, Stockton	.995
	PO	Rivas, Alfonso, Stockton	724
	A	Davis, Devin, Inland Empire	45
	DP	Rivas, Alfonso, Stockton	70
	E	Castro, Luis, Lancaster	10
2B	PCT	McPherson, Kyle, San Jose	.978
	PO	McPherson, Kyle, San Jose	183
	A	McPherson, Kyle, San Jose	216
	DP	McPherson, Kyle, San Jose	58
	E	Ruiz, Esteury, Lake Elsinore	16
3B	PCT	Bride, Jonah, Stockton	.969
	PO	Bride, Jonah, Stockton	69
	A	Villar, David, San Jose	167
	DP	Villar, David, San Jose	20
	E	Rosario, Eguy, Lake Elsinore	17
SS	PCT	Geraldo, Manuel, San Jose	.964
	PO	Adams, Johnny, Modesto	147
	A	Geraldo, Manuel, San Jose	256
	DP	Geraldo, Manuel, San Jose	59
	E	Arias, Gabriel, Lake Elsinore	26
OF	PCT	Grier, Anfernee, Visalia	.995
	PO	Hearn, Matt, Lancaster	314
	A	Rosario, Jeisson, Lake Elsinore	15
	DP	Rosario, Jeisson, Lake Elsinore	6
	E	Rosario, Jeisson, Lake Elsinore	13

PITCHING

G	Moore, Austin, Lancaster	48
GS	Gilbreath, Lucas, Lancaster	28
GF	Doyle, Tommy, Lancaster	32
SV	Doyle, Tommy, Lancaster	19
W	McKinney, Ian, Modesto	12
L	Altamirano, Xavier, Stockton	13
IP	Gaddis, Will, Lancaster	146
H	Gaddis, Will, Lancaster	189
R	Gaddis, Will, Lancaster	109
R	Gilbreath, Lucas, Lancaster	109
ER	Gaddis, Will, Lancaster	95
HB	Carrillo, Gerardo, R. Cucamonga	17
BB	Gilbreath, Lucas, Lancaster	74
SO	Bain, Jeff, Visalia	152
SO/9	Bain, Jeff, Visalia	11.3
SO/9 (RP)	Gamboa, Max, R. Cucamonga	14.4
BB/9	Frisbee, Matt, San Jose	1.7
WP	Carrillo, Gerardo, R. Cucamonga	17
WP	Herrin, Travis, Inland Empire	17
BK	Harris, Nate, Lancaster	3
BK	Montgomerie, Wills, R. Cucamonga	3
BK	Murfee, Penn, Modesto	3
BK	Rolison, Ryan, Lancaster	3
HRA	Jordan, Mitchell, Stockton	24
BAA	McKinney, Ian, Modesto	.218

MINOR LEAGUES

BY J.J. COOPER

During the regular season, Wilmington catcher M.J. Melendez ranked dead last among all full-season minor league hitters with a .163 batting average. Come playoff time, Melendez was the unlikely star, as he went 5-for-15 with a home run and three RBIs to earn playoff MVP honors.

Wilmington, a Royals affiliate, tied Down East for the league's best ERA and allowed the league's fewest earned runs, but it also hit just .219 during the regular season, ranking dead last in runs scored. All season, Wilmington struggled to score runs but also was extremely good at shutting down opposing lineups.

In the first half of the season, Brady Singer, Jackson Kowar and Daniel Lynch shut down Carolina League hitters. Singer and Kowar moved up to Double-A Northwest Arkansas, but Kris Bubic and Jonathan Bowlan provided a second wave of pitching prospects for Wilmington.

Wilmington also showed that it could survive pressure during the playoffs.

Salem won the first two games of their first-round series, but Wilmington won three consecutive elimination games to advance. Fayetteville jumped out a two-games-to-one lead in the championship series as well, but Austin Cox and Rito Lugo spearheaded back-to-back shutouts. This was Wilmington's first Mills Cup title since 1999, when they shared the crown because a hurricane cancelled the championship series. It was the club's first outright title since 1997.

Wilmington won the title, but Down East, the Rangers' affiliate, was the most impressive team during the regular season. Down East ran away with the South Division's first-half title, becoming the first Carolina League team to win 50 games in one half of the split-season schedule in at least 35 years.

After two years at a temporary home in Buies Creek, the Fayetteville Woodpeckers had a suc-cessful debut season, making it to the championship series while finishing second in the league in attendance.

Wilmington outfielder Brewer Hicklen had the league's only three-home run game. Bowlan no-hit the Carolina Mudcats on July 15.

TOP 20 PROSPECTS

1. DL Hall, LHP, Frederick (Orioles)
2. Nolan Jones, 3B, Lynchburg (Indians)
3. Jackson Kowar, RHP, Wilmington (Royals)
4. Nick Madrigal, 2B, Winston-Salem (White Sox)
5. Sam Huff, C/1B, Down East (Rangers)
6. Daniel Lynch, LHP, Wilmington (Royals)
7. Jarren Duran, OF, Salem (Red Sox)
8. Bryan Mata, RHP, Salem (Red Sox)
9. Brady Singer, RHP, Wilmington (Royals)
10. Tyler Freeman, SS, Lynchburg (Indians)
11. Miguel Amaya, C, Myrtle Beach (Cubs)
12. Kris Bubic, LHP, Wilmington (Royals)
13. Leody Taveras, OF, Down East (Rangers)
14. Mario Feliciano, C, Carolina (Brewers)
15. Tim Cate, LHP, Potomac (Nationals)
16. Brice Turang, SS, Carolina (Brewers)
17. Kyle Isbel, OF, Wilmington (Royals)
18. Payton Henry, C, Carolina (Brewers)
19. Shawn Dubin, RHP, Fayetteville (Astros)
20. Steele Walker, OF, Winston-Salem (White Sox)

STANDINGS: SPLIT SEASON

FIRST HALF

North	W	L	PCT	GB	South	W	L	PCT	GB
Wilmington	44	25	.638	—	Down East	50	20	.714	—
Lynchburg	32	35	.478	11	W-Salem	38	26	.594	9
Potomac	30	37	.448	13	Carolina	39	30	.565	10 ½
Frederick	29	40	.420	15	Fayetteville	31	38	.449	18 ½
Salem	25	42	.373	18	Myrtle Beach	21	46	.313	27 ½

SECOND HALF

North	W	L	PCT	GB	South	W	L	PCT	GB
Salem	42	28	.600	—	Fayetteville	41	29	.586	—
Potomac	40	30	.571	2	Down East	37	32	.536	3 ½
Wilmington	38	31	.551	3 ½	Myrtle Beach	34	35	.493	6 ½
Lynchburg	30	38	.441	11	W-Salem	34	35	.493	6 ½
Frederick	24	44	.353	17	Carolina	26	44	.371	15

Playoffs—Semifinals: Fayetteville defeated Down East 3-2 and Wilmington defeated Salem 3-2 in best-of-five series. **Finals:** Wilmington defeated Fayetteville 3-2 in a best-of-five series.

OVERALL STANDINGS

Northern Division	W	L	PCT	GB	Manager(s)	Attendance	Average	Last Pennant
Wilmington Blue Rocks (Royals)	82	56	.594	—	Scott Thorman	231,325	3,382	2019
Potomac Nationals (Nationals)	70	67	.511	11 ½	Tripp Keister	192,474	2,745	2014
Salem Red Sox (Red Sox)	67	70	.489	14 ½	Corey Wimberly	171,866	2,466	2013
Lynchburg Hillcats (Indians)	62	73	.459	18 ½	Jim Pankovits	117,029	1,776	2017
Frederick Keys (Orioles)	53	84	.387	28 ½	Ryan Minor	263,528	3,489	2011

Southern Division	W	L	PCT	GB	Manager(s)	Attendance	Average	Last Pennant
Down East Wood Ducks (Rangers)	87	52	.626	—	Corey Ragsdale	110,619	1,602	2017
Winston-Salem Dash (White Sox)	72	61	.541	12	Justin Jirschele	264,879	3,993	2003
Fayetteville Woodpeckers (Astros)	72	67	.518	15	Nate Shaver	246,961	3,472	2018
Carolina Mudcats (Brewers)	65	74	.468	22	Joe Ayrault	193,568	2,708	2006
Myrtle Beach Pelicans (Cubs)	55	81	.404	30 ½	Steven Lerud	226,247	3,193	2016

MINOR LEAGUES

CLUB BATTING

	AVG	G	AB	R	H	2B	3B	HR	RBI	BB	SO	SB	OBP	SLG
Salem	.258	137	4392	582	1131	252	29	60	530	397	1084	90	.326	.369
Potomac	.254	137	4445	598	1127	244	21	87	550	464	1112	85	.333	.377
Frederick	.252	137	4434	497	1116	204	15	73	458	362	988	58	.315	.354
Lynchburg	.251	135	4435	538	1114	240	30	65	483	467	1006	71	.327	.363
Winston-Salem	.248	133	4371	587	1086	226	32	92	527	458	1101	93	.327	.378
Down East	.245	139	4479	576	1098	179	30	93	520	482	1209	156	.326	.361
Fayetteville	.245	139	4445	622	1090	248	20	123	600	532	1224	69	.335	.393
Carolina	.227	139	4426	557	1003	215	23	92	507	460	1412	73	.312	.348
Myrtle Beach	.227	136	4274	518	972	190	24	73	463	499	1093	136	.317	.334
Wilmington	.219	138	4181	481	915	176	33	62	423	420	1249	155	.296	.321

CLUB PITCHING

	ERA	G	CG	SHO	SV	IP	H	R	ER	HR	BB	SO	AVG
Down East	3.00	139	3	18	51	1215	987	457	405	65	507	1164	.225
Wilmington	3.00	138	4	16	49	1185	1048	464	395	66	354	1118	.239
Fayetteville	3.50	139	1	14	30	1196	923	546	465	77	547	1476	.211
Winston-Salem	3.51	133	1	8	40	1160	1091	539	452	87	389	1038	.249
Salem	3.75	137	3	11	32	1158	1109	573	482	71	452	1114	.254
Lynchburg	3.79	135	0	8	32	1163	1104	598	490	82	478	1183	.251
Carolina	3.85	139	4	9	35	1181	1140	578	505	82	410	1103	.254
Myrtle Beach	3.96	136	2	10	26	1171	1141	585	516	93	385	1083	.256
Potomac	3.98	137	3	9	25	1157	1074	580	511	89	402	1079	.246
Frederick	4.52	137	4	10	34	1138	1035	636	571	108	617	1120	.243

CLUB FIELDING

	PCT	PO	A	E	DP		PCT	PO	A	E	DP
Down East	.982	3646	1308	91	126	Myrtle Beach	.975	3514	1234	121	117
Frederick	.979	3413	1165	98	113	Salem	.975	3474	1223	120	116
Carolina	.978	3543	1195	109	98	Lynchburg	.973	3488	1207	129	104
Potomac	.976	3470	1206	114	101	Fayetteville	.972	3587	1055	133	80
Wilmington	.976	3556	1316	122	125	Winston-Salem	.971	3481	1338	143	129

INDIVIDUAL BATTING

Batter, Club	AVG	G	AB	R	H	2B	3B	HR	RBI	BB	SO	SB
Oscar Gonzalez, Lynchburg	.319	96	385	46	123	22	3	8	61	12	66	7
Cole Freeman, Potomac	.311	123	453	82	141	27	3	3	49	53	60	33
Zach Remillard, Winston-Salem	.289	95	357	50	103	15	1	5	37	33	89	6
Zach Jarrett, Frederick	.286	96	353	53	101	14	1	11	39	27	84	7
Aldrem Corredor, Potomac	.283	127	495	60	140	34	0	9	89	36	104	2
Jomar Reyes, Frederick	.283	100	389	35	110	24	0	8	47	11	73	1
Steven Kwan, Lynchburg	.280	123	479	68	134	26	7	3	39	53	51	11
Pedro Castellanos, Salem	.276	117	446	61	123	23	2	9	71	22	71	10
Victor Acosta, Salem	.274	100	350	45	96	17	1	3	46	38	42	5
Mario Feliciano, Carolina	.273	116	440	62	120	25	4	19	81	29	139	2

INDIVIDUAL PITCHING

Pitcher, Club	W	L	ERA	G	GS	CG	SV	IP	H	R	ER	BB	SO
Sal Mendez, Down East	7	2	2.37	26	16	0	1	118	107	38	31	37	89
Noah Zavolas, Carolina	6	5	2.98	22	22	1	0	133	128	52	44	23	102
Jorgan Cavanerio, Winston-Salem	9	3	3.13	20	19	0	0	112	102	43	39	22	73
Enmanuel De Jesus, Salem	9	9	3.58	24	24	1	0	131	140	66	52	42	122
Matt Smith, Carolina	4	13	3.67	28	22	0	0	115	117	54	47	32	91
Juan Hillman, Lynchburg	6	12	3.85	25	25	0	0	140	147	77	60	41	99
Jhonathan Diaz, Salem	9	8	3.86	27	27	0	0	128	121	63	55	54	118
Javier Assad, Myrtle Beach	4	10	3.87	22	22	0	0	116	108	53	50	41	91
Reid Anderson, Down East	6	8	3.92	24	24	1	0	126	120	61	55	64	109
Nick Raquet, Potomac	11	9	4.07	25	25	1	0	130	129	72	59	43	122

ALL-STAR TEAM

C: Mario Feliciano, Carolina. **1B:** Aldrem Corredor, Potomac. **2B:** Cole Freeman, Potomac. **3B:** Nolan Jones, Lynchburg. **SS:** Ryan Fitzgerald, Salem. **OF:** Oscar Gonzalez, Lynchburg; Steele Walker, Winston-Salem; Brewer Hicklen, Wilmington. **DH:** Sam Huff, Down East. **UT:** Zach Remillard, Winston-Salem; Zach Jarrett, Frederick. **P:** Noah Zavolas, Carolina; Sal Mendez, Down East; Kris Bubic, Wilmington. **Most Valuable Player:** Mario Feliciano, Carolina. **Pitcher of the Year:** Noah Zavolas, Carolina. **Manager of the Year:** Corey Ragsdale, Down East.

DEPARTMENT LEADERS

BATTING

OBP	Aguilar, Ryan, Carolina	.403
SLG	Feliciano, Mario, Carolina	.477
OPS	Aguilar, Ryan, Carolina	.812
R	Freeman, Cole, Potomac	82
H	Freeman, Cole, Potomac	141
TB	Dedelow, Craig, Winston-Salem	213
XBH	Dedelow, Craig, Winston-Salem	49
2B	Corredor, Aldrem, Potomac	34
3B	Dedelow, Craig, Winston-Salem	10
HR	Feliciano, Mario, Carolina	19
RBI	Corredor, Aldrem, Potomac	89
SAC	Freeman, Cole, Potomac	14
BB	Fisher, Jameson, Winston-Salem	72
HBP	Henry, Payton, Carolina	22
HBP	Manea, Scott, Fayetteville	22
SO	Melendez, MJ, Wilmington	165
SB	Hicklen, Brewer, Wilmington	39
CS	Hernandez, Yonny, Down East	14
CS	Hicklen, Brewer, Wilmington	14
AB/SO	Pozo, Yohel, Down East	10.4

FIELDING

C PCT	Melendez, MJ, Wilmington	.991
PO	Amaya, Miguel, Myrtle Beach	729
A	Amaya, Miguel, Myrtle Beach	78
DP	Papierski, Michael, Fayetteville	8
E	Rivero, Sebastian, Wilmington	12
CS	Amaya, Miguel, Myrtle Beach	46
SB	Amaya, Miguel, Myrtle Beach	86
PB	Sciortino, Nick, Salem	16
1B PCT	Pratto, Nick, Wilmington	.992
PO	Pratto, Nick, Wilmington	936
A	Pratto, Nick, Wilmington	78
DP	Pratto, Nick, Wilmington	100
E	Fisher, Jameson, Winston-Salem	11
2B PCT	Sepulveda, Carlos, Myrtle Beach	.995
PO	Sepulveda, Carlos, Myrtle Beach	153
A	Aracena, Ricky, Wilmington	218
A	Sepulveda, Carlos, Myrtle Beach	218
DP	Aracena, Ricky, Wilmington	61
DP	Sepulveda, Carlos, Myrtle Beach	61
E	Nishioka, Tanner, Salem	12
E	Freeman, Cole, Fredericksburg	12
3B PCT	Silva, Eddie, Carolina	.920
PO	Silva, Eddie, Carolina	75
A	Yrizarri, Yeyson, Winston-Salem	221
DP	Yrizarri, Yeyson, Winston-Salem	26
E	Yrizarri, Yeyson, Winston-Salem	31
SS PCT	Perez, Cristian, Wilmington	.977
PO	Fitzgerald, Ryan, Salem	156
A	Perez, Cristian, Wilmington	306
DP	Perez, Cristian, Wilmington	74
E	Ademan, Aramis, Myrtle Beach	24
OF PCT	Henry, Rob, Carolina	.989
PO	Kwan, Steven, Lynchburg	248
A	Carter, Jodd, Lynchburg	13
A	Perez, Yanio, Down East	13
A	Henry, Rob, Carolina	13
DP	7 players	3
E	Julks, Corey, Fayetteville	7

PITCHING

G	Teaney, Jonathan, Lynchburg	46
GS	Diaz, Jhonathan, Salem	27
GF	Ratliff, Tad, Wilmington	36
SV	Ratliff, Tad, Wilmington	23
W	Hernandez, Nelson, Carolina	11
W	Raquet, Nick, Potomac	11
L	Smith, Matt, Carolina	13
IP	Gonzalez, Daniel, Salem	151
H	Gonzalez, Daniel, Salem	164
R	Lewis, Zach, Winston-Salem	80
R	Pena, Malvin, Potomac	80
ER	Hernandez, Nelson, Carolina	74
ER	Pena, Malvin, Potomac	74
HB	Diaz, Jhonathan, Salem	19
BB	Anderson, Reid, Down East	64
SO	Dubin, Shawn, Fayetteville	132
SO/9	Bishop, Cameron, Frederick	8.6
SO/9 (RP)	Garcia, Luis, Fayetteville	14.8
BB/9	Zavolas, Noah, Carolina	1.6
WP	Dietz, Matthias, Frederick	19
BK	Hockin, Chad, Myrtle Beach	4
HRA	Pena, Malvin, Potomac	20
BAA	Cavanerio, Jorgan, Winston-Salem	.242

BY JOSH NORRIS

Once again, the Florida State League's playoffs (not to mention the last few days of the regular season) were cancelled by an incoming hurricane. This time it was Hurricane Dorian, which was projected to cut such a wide, staggered swath across Florida that the league saw fit to abruptly end the year out of an abundance of caution.

The storm nipped in the bud a remarkable second-half run by the Charlotte Stone Crabs, which housed one of the most prospect-laden and productive rosters in the minor leagues.

Their enviable roster started with the game's No. 1 prospect, stud shortstop Wander Franco. After tearing up low Class A Bowling Green for a half-season, Franco was promoted to the FSL at just 18 years old. He didn't skip a beat.

Franco finished his turn with the Stone Crabs as the league's easy top prospect thanks to a well-rounded tool set and the production—including a .408 on-base percentage—to back it up. He was flanked by a squad of excellent pitchers, including lefthanders Shane McClanahan and Michael Plassmeyer and righties Joe Ryan, Riley O'Brien and Tommy Romero.

The league's other uber-talented team, Fort Myers, featured one of the game's most talented but polarizing prospects in shortstop Royce Lewis. All season, scouts were at divided on his future. The athletic gifts were clear, but high-maintenance mechanics meant there were plenty of questions about whether he'd hit enough to live up to his pedigree as the No. 1 overall pick from 2017.

Nonetheless, Lewis was selected to the Futures Game, then got hot enough upon his return to earn a promotion to Double-A. He was flanked in Fort Myers by a host of talented Twins prospects, including outfielder Trevor Larnach, catcher Ryan Jeffers and righthander Jhoan Duran.

Buoyed by that star power, Fort Myers and

Charlotte were on track for what could have been an epic first round of the playoffs before one advanced to the championship series.

Then the rains came and washed it all away.

TOP 20 PROSPECTS

1. Wander Franco, SS, Charlotte (Rays)
2. Alec Bohm, 3B, Clearwater (Phillies)
3. Trevor Larnach, OF, Fort Myers (Twins)
4. Tarik Skubal, LHP, Lakeland (Tigers)
5. JJ Bleday, OF, Jupiter (Marlins)
6. Edward Cabrera, RHP, Jupiter (Marlins)
7. Oneil Cruz, SS, Bradenton (Pirates)
8. Nolan Gorman, 3B, Palm Beach (Cardinals)
9. Jordan Balazovic, RHP, Fort Myers (Twins)
10. Joe Ryan, RHP, Charlotte (Rays)
11. Shane McClanahan, LHP, Charlotte (Rays)
12. Clarke Schmidt, RHP, Tampa (Yankees)
13. Royce Lewis, SS, Fort Myers (Twins)
14. Jhoan Duran, RHP, Fort Myers (Twins)
15. Vidal Brujan, 2B, Charlotte (Rays)
16. Jose Garcia, SS, Daytona (Reds)
17. Lewin Diaz, 1B, Fort Myers (Twins)
18. Jonathan India, 3B, Daytona (Reds)
19. Ryan Jeffers, C, Fort Myers (Twins)
20. Ronaldo Hernandez, C, Charlotte (Rays)

STANDINGS: SPLIT SEASON

FIRST HALF

North	W	L	PCT	GB	South	W	L	PCT	GB
Dunedin	41	24	.631	—	Fort Myers	39	27	.591	—
Clearwater	36	30	.545	5 ½	Palm Beach	35	29	.547	3
Daytona	35	30	.538	6	Bradenton	36	30	.545	3
Lakeland	29	36	.446	12	Charlotte	35	31	.530	4
Tampa	28	38	.424	13 ½	St. Lucie	32	34	.485	7
Florida	25	41	.379	16 ½	Jupiter	21	42	.333	16 ½

SECOND HALF

North	W	L	PCT	GB	South	W	L	PCT	GB
Dunedin	39	31	.557	—	Charlotte	47	22	.681	—
Tampa	36	33	.522	2 ½	Bradenton	37	32	.536	10
Lakeland	36	34	.514	3	St. Lucie	36	32	.529	10 ½
Clearwater	32	38	.457	7	Fort Myers	35	32	.522	11
Daytona	31	38	.449	7 ½	Jupiter	33	36	.478	14
Florida	29	41	.414	10	Palm Beach	22	44	.323	23 ½

Playoffs—The entire Florida State League postseason was cancelled due to Hurricane Dorian.

OVERALL STANDINGS

North Division	W	L	PCT	GB	Manager(s)	Attendance	Average	Last Pennant
Dunedin Blue Jays (Blue Jays)	80	55	.593	—	Cesar Martin	11,757	187	2017
Clearwater Threshers (Phillies)	68	68	.500	12 ½	Marty Malloy	180,069	2,507	2007
Daytona Tortugas (Reds)	66	68	.493	13 ½	Ricky Gutierrez	137,570	2,027	2011
Lakeland Flying Tigers (Tigers)	65	70	.481	15	Andrew Graham	50,770	774	2012
Tampa Tarpons (Yankees)	64	71	.474	16	Aaron Holbert	61,290	885	2010
Florida Fire Frogs (Braves)	54	82	.397	26 ½	Barrett Kleinknecht	19,615	284	Never

South Division	W	L	PCT	GB	Manager(s)	Attendance	Average	Last Pennant
Charlotte Stone Crabs (Rays)	82	53	.607	—	Jeff Smith	91,349	1,306	2015
Fort Myers Miracle (Twins)	74	59	.556	7	Toby Gardenhire	108,800	1,697	2018
Bradenton Marauders (Pirates)	73	62	.541	9	Wyatt Toregas	71,284	1,072	1963
St. Lucie Mets (Mets)	68	66	.507	13 ½	Chad Kreuter	82,581	1,266	2006
Palm Beach Cardinals (Cardinals)	57	73	.438	22 ½	Dann Bilardello	57,418	855	2017
Jupiter Hammerheads (Marlins)	54	78	.409	26 ½	Todd Pratt	62,684	984	1991

CLUB BATTING

	AVG	G	AB	R	H	2B	3B	HR	RBI	BB	SO	SB	OBP	SLG
Daytona	.252	134	4474	548	1129	186	39	67	490	395	1067	108	.324	.356
Charlotte	.250	135	4396	573	1098	204	39	72	514	426	1129	160	.323	.363
Dunedin	.249	135	4228	609	1052	220	34	76	557	536	1133	165	.339	.371
Bradenton	.245	135	4340	559	1065	219	24	107	512	401	1276	109	.318	.381
Clearwater	.243	136	4377	498	1064	207	33	90	467	342	1034	92	.305	.367
St. Lucie	.243	134	4244	520	1030	193	26	51	468	435	1006	129	.320	.336
Lakeland	.239	135	4286	491	1025	162	58	67	438	360	1087	151	.306	.351
Palm Beach	.239	130	4157	464	994	184	16	67	427	386	1021	23	.310	.339
Tampa	.239	135	4304	532	1030	197	11	93	489	343	1079	106	.303	.355
Jupiter	.238	132	4190	429	996	178	20	56	395	371	1093	77	.305	.330
Fort Myers	.236	133	4276	504	1008	216	22	91	465	392	1043	91	.305	.360
Florida	.230	136	4300	452	989	179	22	59	414	375	1162	51	.296	.323

CLUB PITCHING

	ERA	G	CG	SHO	SV	IP	H	R	ER	HR	BB	SO	AVG
Charlotte	2.76	135	2	20	45	1170	997	440	359	67	370	1081	.231
Fort Myers	3.11	133	0	18	45	1139	986	476	394	53	369	1188	.234
Dunedin	3.29	135	1	19	37	1134	1041	484	415	69	369	1086	.243
St. Lucie	3.39	134	2	12	36	1148	1068	517	432	76	422	1040	.246
Bradenton	3.42	135	4	5	35	1147	1011	491	436	96	382	980	.233
Jupiter	3.43	132	6	12	25	1108	991	502	422	78	352	1082	.237
Clearwater	3.47	136	2	11	42	1171	1035	516	452	96	424	1180	.238
Lakeland	3.52	135	3	13	29	1142	1008	509	447	78	391	1088	.236
Tampa	3.64	135	3	11	28	1145	1048	576	463	64	464	1186	.244
Palm Beach	3.68	130	1	13	26	1097	1059	528	449	67	417	1021	.254
Florida	3.72	136	11	17	22	1141	1085	555	471	54	404	1079	.251
Daytona	3.98	134	1	5	38	1171	1151	585	518	98	398	1119	.257

CLUB FIELDING

	PCT	PO	A	E	DP		PCT	PO	A	E	DP
Clearwater	.982	3514	1262	87	103	Daytona	.976	3514	1223	118	113
Bradenton	.978	3442	1198	106	81	Fort Myers	.974	3416	1184	122	103
Florida	.978	3423	1205	103	98	Palm Beach	.974	3291	1143	118	110
Charlotte	.977	3509	1176	112	127	Jupiter	.973	3325	1227	126	86
Dunedin	.977	3403	1178	108	108	St. Lucie	.972	3443	1168	131	109
Lakeland	.977	3425	1094	105	98	Tampa	.968	3435	1201	151	125

INDIVIDUAL BATTING

Batter, Club	AVG	G	AB	R	H	2B	3B	HR	RBI	BB	SO	SB
Trevor Larnach, Fort Myers	.316	84	320	33	101	26	1	6	44	35	74	4
Cal Stevenson, Dunedin	.298	90	336	59	100	9	4	5	50	50	52	11
Andy Sugilio, Daytona	.294	118	456	57	134	11	5	3	39	24	92	23
Lazaro Alonso, Jupiter	.294	114	385	40	113	21	0	11	57	61	105	0
Simon Muzziotti, Clearwater	.287	110	425	52	122	21	3	3	28	32	60	21
Alejo Lopez, Daytona	.287	124	481	67	138	17	3	2	50	38	80	9
Riley Delgado, Florida	.282	131	511	49	144	15	3	0	33	28	42	1
Lucas Tancas, Bradenton	.280	106	389	47	109	28	1	9	58	29	142	3
Jose Garcia, Daytona	.280	104	404	58	113	37	1	8	55	25	83	15
Jeremy Vasquez, St. Lucie	.277	125	444	44	123	26	2	5	61	55	76	3

INDIVIDUAL PITCHING

Pitcher, Club	W	L	ERA	G	GS	CG	SV	IP	H	R	ER	BB	SO
Tommy Romero, Charlotte	12	4	1.89	23	18	1	0	119	86	28	25	36	103
Miguel Yajure, Tampa	8	6	2.26	22	18	1	0	128	110	47	32	28	122
Maximo Castillo, Dunedin	11	5	2.69	24	24	0	0	130	115	46	39	28	114
Hayden Deal, Florida	5	10	3.24	23	22	1	0	119	119	51	43	32	99
Aaron Shortridge, Bradenton	9	5	3.25	24	24	1	0	136	129	50	49	25	104
Tyler Watson, Fort Myers	1	5	3.62	23	18	0	1	112	105	50	45	31	88
Mac Sceroler, Daytona	5	4	3.69	26	20	0	0	117	101	54	48	29	127
Elvin Rodriguez, Lakeland	11	9	3.77	24	23	1	0	134	113	60	56	44	112
Nick Allgeyer, Dunedin	10	6	3.95	23	22	0	0	118	113	57	52	29	104
Nolan Kingham, Florida	4	8	4.43	18	18	3	0	114	120	63	56	25	84

ALL-STAR TEAM

C: Ronaldo Hernandez, Charlotte; Brady Policelli, Lakeland. **1B:** Lazaro Alonso, Jupiter. **2B:** Carlos Cortes, St. Lucie. **3B:** Dylan Busby, Bradenton. **SS:** Wander Franco, Charlotte. **UT:** Riley Delgado, Florida. **OF:** Trevor Larnach, Fort Myers; Simon Muzziotti, Clearwater; Ryan Noda, Dunedin; Cal Stevenson, Dunedin. **DH:** Dermis Garcia, Tampa. **SP:** Maximo Castillo, Dunedin; Trevor Rogers, Jupiter; Tommy Romero, Charlotte; Miguel Yajure, Tampa. **RP:** Keylan Killgore, Clearwater; Brad Wilson, Dunedin. **Player of the Year:** Trevor Larnach, Fort Myers. **Coaches of the Year:** Toby Gardenhire, Fort Myers; Jeff Smith, Charlotte.

DEPARTMENT LEADERS

BATTING

OBP	Alonso, Lazaro, Jupiter	.393
SLG	Larnach, Trevor, Fort Myers	.459
OPS	Larnach, Trevor, Fort Myers	.842
R	Swaggerty, Travis, Bradenton	79
H	Delgado, Riley, Florida	144
TB	Mitchell, Cal, Bradenton	183
TB	Policelli, Brady, Lakeland	183
XBH	Garcia, Jose, Daytona	46
2B	Garcia, Jose, Daytona	37
3B	Deatherage, Brock, Lakeland	11
HR	Busby, Dylan, Bradenton	22
RBI	Noda, Ryan, Dunedin	74
SAC	Hampton, Reece, Lakeland	7
SAC	Moreno, Hansel, St. Lucie	7
BB	Noda, Ryan, Dunedin	74
HBP	Olivares, Pablo, Tampa	20
SO	Lugbauer, Drew, Florida	169
SB	Deatherage, Brock, Lakeland	45
CS	Olivares, Pablo, Tampa	13
AB/SO	Delgado, Riley, Florida	12.2

FIELDING

C	PCT	Kirk, Alejandro, Dunedin	.991
	PO	Hernandez, Ronaldo, Charlotte	634
	A	Duran, Rodolfo, Clearwater	65
	A	Meyer, Nick, St. Lucie	65
	DP	Meyer, Nick, St. Lucie	13
	E	Lopez, Jason, Tampa	11
	CS	Lopez, Jason, Tampa	33
	CS	Meyer, Nick, St. Lucie	33
	SB	Fortes, Nick, Jupiter	79
	PB	Hernandez, Raul, Bradenton	15
1B	PCT	Vasquez, Jeremy, St. Lucie	.994
	PO	Yari, Bruce, Daytona	842
	A	Alonso, Lazaro, Jupiter	60
	DP	Yari, Bruce, Daytona	83
	E	Alonso, Lazaro, Jupiter	14
2B	PCT	Clemens, Kody, Lakeland	.990
	PO	Clemens, Kody, Lakeland	161
	A	Langhorne, Brett, Florida	272
	DP	Langhorne, Brett, Florida	54
	E	Cortes, Carlos, St. Lucie	17
3B	PCT	Busby, Dylan, Bradenton	.937
	PO	Nelson, James, Jupiter	65
	A	Nelson, James, Jupiter	207
	DP	Bohanek, Cody, St. Lucie	15
	E	Nelson, James, Jupiter	35
SS	PCT	Delgado, Riley, Florida	.975
	PO	Rodriguez, Manny, St. Lucie	173
	A	Garcia, Jose, Daytona	263
	DP	Garcia, Jose, Daytona	60
	E	Garcia, Jose, Daytona	25
	E	Rodriguez, Manny, St. Lucie	25
OF	PCT	Whitley, Garrett, Charlotte	.995
	PO	Swaggerty, Travis, Bradenton	312
	A	Stevenson, Cal, Dunedin	19
	DP	Brodey, Quinn, St. Lucie	4
	DP	Gilliam, Isiah, Tampa	4
	DP	Olivares, Pablo, Tampa	4
	DP	Nootbaar, Lars, Palm Beach	4
	DP	Policelli, Brady, Lakeland	4
	E	Wilson, Izzy, Florida	8

PITCHING

G	Dayton, Patrick, Palm Beach	42
GS	Orewiler, Austin, Daytona	26
GF	Zurak, Kyle, Tampa	30
SV	Killgore, Keylan, Clearwater	11
W	Romero, Tommy, Charlotte	12
L	Gonzalez, Edgar, Palm Beach	15
IP	Shortridge, Aaron, Bradenton	136
H	Orewiler, Austin, Daytona	138
R	Stewart, Will, Jupiter	86
ER	Stewart, Will, Jupiter	78
HB	Roberts, Griffin, Palm Beach	17
BB	Holloway, Jordan, Jupiter	66
SO	Sceroler, Mac, Daytona	127
SO/9	Rogers, Trevor, Jupiter	10.0
SO/9 (RP)	Jones, Damon, Clearwater	13.6
BB/9	Shortridge, Aaron, Bradenton	1.7
WP	Gonzalez, Edgar, Palm Beach	18
BK	Enlow, Blayne, Fort Myers	3
HRA	Lillie, Ryan, Daytona	15
HRA	Wallace, Gavin, Bradenton	15
BAA	Romero, Tommy, Charlotte	.205

MINOR LEAGUES

BY KEGAN LOWE

There were six teams with better regular season records than the South Bend Cubs in 2019, but once the Midwest League playoffs began, the Cubs' low Class A affiliate was in a league of its own. South Bend went a perfect 7-0 during its run to the MWL championship, topping Great Lakes (Dodgers), two games to none, in the league semifinals before sweeping Clinton (Marlins) in the best-of-five championship series. Both clubs accumulated more regular-season wins than the Cubs, including Great Lakes, which was one of three teams—alongside Bowling Green (Rays) and Kane County (D-backs)—to win 81 games during the regular season. It was the South Bend's first Midwest League championship since 2005 and its first title since becoming the Cubs' low Class A affiliate prior to the 2015 season.

From a pure talent point of view, the league was graced with the presence of the sport's No. 1 overall prospect, shortstop Wander Franco (Rays), for nearly three months before the 18-year-old wunderkind was pushed to high Class A Charlotte in late June. In his time in the Midwest League, Franco hit .318/.390/.506 with 27 extra-base hits and more walks (30) than strikeouts (20) despite the fact that he was the youngest player in the league by nearly nine months on Opening Day.

Bowling Green also rostered lefthander Matthew Liberatore, the league's top-ranked pitching prospect who went 6-2, 3.10 with 76 strikeouts in 78.1 innings for the Hot Rods. Between Franco, Liberatore, righthander Shane Baz and lefthander Shane McClanahan, Bowling Green featured four of the five best prospects in the Midwest League in 2019, and that quartet is a major reason why the Rays finished the year with the No. 1-ranked farm system in all of baseball.

TOP 20 PROSPECTS

1. Wander Franco, SS, Bowling Green (Rays)
2. Matthew Liberatore, LHP, Bowling Green (Rays)
3. Brailyn Marquez, LHP, South Bend (Cubs)
4. Shane Baz, RHP, Bowling Green (Rays)
5. Shane McClanahan, LHP, Bowling Green (Rays)
6. Xavier Edwards, SS, Fort Wayne (Padres)
7. Tyler Freeman, SS, Lake County (Indians)
8. Nolan Gorman, 3B, Peoria (Cardinals)
9. Alek Thomas, OF, Kane County (D-backs)
10. Brennan Davis, OF, South Bend (Cubs)
11. Joey Cantillo, LHP, Fort Wayne (Padres)
12. Gabriel Moreno, C, Lansing (Blue Jays)
13. Geraldo Perdomo, SS, Kane County (D-backs)
14. Miguel Vargas, 3B, Great Lakes (Dodgers)
15. Levi Kelly, RHP, Kane County (D-backs)
16. Ryan Weathers, LHP, Fort Wayne (Padres)
17. Brice Turang, SS, Wisconsin (Brewers)
18. Otto Lopez, 2B, Lansing (Blue Jays)
19. Riley Thompson, RHP, South Bend (Cubs)
20. Will Benson, OF, Lake County (Indians)

STANDINGS: SPLIT SEASON

FIRST HALF

Eastern	W	L	PCT	GB	Western	W	L	PCT	GB
Great Lakes	43	24	.642	—	Quad Cities	43	23	.652	—
Lake County	40	29	.580	4	Burlington	39	31	.557	6
B. Green	39	31	.557	5½	Cedar Rapids	39	31	.557	6
South Bend	37	31	.544	6½	Kane County	35	34	.507	9½
Fort Wayne	33	35	.485	10½	Clinton	33	36	.478	11½
Lansing	32	37	.464	12	Wisconsin	31	38	.449	13½
Dayton	28	42	.400	16½	Peoria	30	39	.435	14½
W. Michigan	21	48	.304	23	Beloit	27	41	.397	17

SECOND HALF

Eastern	W	L	PCT	GB	Western	W	L	PCT	GB
B. Green	42	27	.609	—	Kane County	46	24	.657	—
South Bend	39	30	.565	3	Clinton	45	25	.643	1
Great Lakes	38	31	.551	4	Cedar Rapids	39	31	.557	7
Lansing	36	34	.514	6½	Wisconsin	38	32	.543	8
Lake County	34	35	.493	8	Quad Cities	36	34	.514	10
Dayton	30	40	.429	12½	Beloit	27	43	.386	19
Fort Wayne	29	41	.414	13½	Burlington	27	43	.386	19
W. Michigan	28	42	.400	14½	Peoria	24	46	.343	22

Playoffs—Semifinals: South Bend defeated Great Lakes 2-0 and Clinton defeated Cedar Rapids 2-1 in best-of-three series. **Finals:** South Bend defeated Clinton 3-0 in a best-of-five series.

OVERALL STANDINGS

Eastern Division	W	L	PCT	GB	Manager(s)	Attendance	Average	Last Pennant
Great Lakes Loons (Dodgers)	81	55	.596	—	John Shoemaker	195,904	2,827	2017
Bowling Green Hot Rods (Rays)	81	58	.583	1½	Reinaldo Ruiz	190,877	2,717	2018
South Bend Cubs (Cubs)	76	61	.555	5½	Buddy Bailey	319,616	4,621	2019
Lake County Captains (Indians)	74	64	.536	8	Luke Carlin	200,756	2,957	2010
Lansing Lugnuts (Blue Jays)	68	71	.489	14½	Dallas McPherson	311,028	4,443	2003
Fort Wayne TinCaps (Padres)	62	76	.449	20	Anthony Contreras	371,259	5,503	2009
Dayton Dragons (Reds)	58	82	.414	25	Luis Bolivar	545,108	7,790	Never
West Michigan Whitecaps (Tigers)	49	90	.353	33½	Lance Parrish	360,295	5,180	2015

Western Division	W	L	PCT	GB	Manager(s)	Attendance	Average	Last Pennant
Kane County Cougars (D-backs)	81	58	.583	—	Vince Harrison	350,305	5,149	2014
Quad Cities River Bandits (Astros)	79	57	.581	½	Ray Hernandez	150,905	2,446	2013
Clinton LumberKings (Marlins)	78	61	.561	3	Mike Jacobs	121,325	1,794	2016
Cedar Rapids Kernels (Twins)	78	62	.557	3½	Brian Dinkelman	150,278	2,176	1994
Wisconsin Timber Rattlers (Brewers)	69	70	.496	12	Matt Erickson	218,037	3,147	2012
Burlington Bees (Angels)	66	74	.471	15½	Jack Howell	67,369	957	2008
Beloit Snappers (Athletics)	54	84	.391	26½	Lloyd Turner	73,200	1,060	1995
Peoria Chiefs (Cardinals)	54	85	.388	27	Erick Almonte	198,545	2,732	2002

MINOR LEAGUES

CLUB BATTING

	AVG	G	AB	R	H	2B	3B	HR	RBI	BB	SO	SB	OBP	SLG
South Bend	.260	137	4501	585	1172	253	39	59	517	412	979	82	.328	.373
Lansing	.254	139	4672	641	1185	226	57	106	555	465	1215	170	.328	.394
Great Lakes	.247	136	4573	712	1128	244	37	113	638	597	1224	104	.339	.390
Peoria	.247	139	4515	563	1113	226	19	68	511	416	1115	70	.319	.350
Bowling Green	.245	139	4544	625	1112	206	41	94	569	517	1124	125	.329	.370
Fort Wayne	.245	138	4549	600	1116	228	29	64	526	514	1087	113	.332	.350
Kane County	.245	139	4591	626	1127	214	32	78	559	545	1174	107	.335	.357
Quad Cities	.245	136	4395	593	1076	207	39	64	534	457	1104	171	.324	.353
Clinton	.242	139	4627	630	1118	223	28	93	563	431	1448	130	.316	.362
West Michigan	.239	139	4512	551	1078	189	25	65	475	439	1197	109	.312	.335
Dayton	.236	140	4582	533	1080	186	34	77	461	388	1175	120	.303	.342
Lake County	.235	138	4458	620	1046	206	47	102	554	479	1201	149	.318	.371
Beloit	.230	138	4412	547	1014	215	19	52	476	524	1198	121	.320	.323
Cedar Rapids	.227	140	4502	575	1020	193	36	109	514	517	1279	94	.312	.358
Wisconsin	.226	139	4401	551	996	192	36	65	479	538	1196	152	.317	.331
Burlington	.215	140	4368	532	941	167	29	89	483	588	1395	97	.319	.328

CLUB PITCHING

	ERA	G	CG	SHO	SV	IP	H	R	ER	HR	BB	SO	AVG
Kane County	2.81	139	0	11	44	1228	1046	490	383	54	420	1189	.229
Clinton	3.14	139	3	8	40	1219	1055	518	425	61	458	1155	.232
Bowling Green	3.16	139	1	10	40	1215	1060	515	427	84	419	1262	.232
Quad Cities	3.25	136	2	19	39	1178	900	493	426	67	567	1372	.210
Cedar Rapids	3.37	140	3	11	38	1209	1000	555	453	77	455	1240	.223
South Bend	3.54	137	0	13	38	1184	1014	566	466	95	488	1129	.230
Burlington	3.63	140	2	9	36	1191	981	575	480	73	567	1337	.224
Lake County	3.73	138	3	11	44	1191	1083	580	494	84	503	1207	.242
Wisconsin	3.75	139	1	12	33	1189	1087	568	495	97	442	1215	.244
Great Lakes	3.83	136	0	10	44	1200	1085	591	511	78	470	1116	.240
Beloit	4.10	138	0	5	36	1185	1080	652	540	80	544	1181	.241
Dayton	4.14	140	1	8	34	1214	1209	671	559	101	501	1196	.257
Fort Wayne	4.22	138	1	10	28	1191	1188	660	559	87	388	1206	.259
West Michigan	4.27	139	0	7	29	1182	1166	661	561	76	481	1100	.254
Lansing	4.28	139	2	8	33	1214	1197	676	576	84	514	1070	.258
Peoria	4.74	139	3	13	28	1185	1171	713	624	90	610	1136	.259

CLUB FIELDING

	PCT	PO	A	E	DP		PCT	PO	A	E	DP
Quad Cities	.977	3535	1118	111	91	South Bend	.970	3552	1245	147	91
Wisconsin	.975	3568	1257	124	128	Clinton	.968	3656	1174	161	98
Cedar Rapids	.972	3627	1278	143	113	Fort Wayne	.968	3574	1271	162	118
Lansing	.972	3643	1315	141	122	Kane County	.968	3683	1306	167	126
Bowling Green	.971	3644	1270	149	106	West Michigan	.968	3547	1212	157	98
Great Lakes	.971	3600	1256	145	101	Burlington	.967	3572	1098	159	96
Peoria	.971	3556	1227	143	111	Lake County	.967	3573	1263	166	102
Beloit	.970	3555	1267	148	108	Dayton	.964	3643	1192	179	108

INDIVIUAL BATTING

Batter, Club	AVG	G	AB	R	H	2B	3B	HR	RBI	BB	SO	SB
Otto Lopez, Lansing	.324	108	447	61	145	20	5	5	50	34	63	20
Alek Thomas, Kane County	.312	91	353	63	110	21	7	8	48	43	72	11
Jose Fermin, Lake County	.293	105	393	75	115	12	2	6	41	42	40	28
Ford Proctor, Bowling Green	.290	121	458	76	133	29	2	6	53	69	90	11
Gilberto Celestino, Cedar Rapids	.276	117	450	52	124	24	3	10	51	48	81	14
Andy Weber, South bend	.275	127	487	65	134	36	8	3	59	43	110	5
Reggie Pruitt, Lansing	.273	88	337	55	92	12	8	1	22	40	101	40
Ruben Cardenas, Bowling Green	.271	114	431	58	117	24	7	13	70	40	90	11
Ulrich Bojarski, West Michigan	.271	104	384	52	104	17	3	10	55	16	87	6
Leandro Cedeno, Peoria	.270	100	366	35	99	24	2	6	44	18	101	4

INDIVIDUAL PITCHING

Pitcher, Club	W	L	ERA	G	GS	CG	SV	IP	H	R	ER	BB	SO
Josh Winder, Cedar Rapids	7	2	2.65	21	21	2	0	126	93	43	37	30	118
Caleb Sampen, Bowling Green	9	4	2.68	22	21	0	0	121	91	39	36	32	104
Alan Strong, Bowling Green	10	4	2.85	22	18	0	0	126	114	46	40	24	109
Alberto Guerrero, Clinton	9	6	3.13	26	24	0	1	132	127	57	46	53	104
Tanner Andrews, Clinton	8	5	3.52	22	18	0	2	128	100	55	50	38	110
Andrew Cabezas, Cedar Rapids	5	7	3.54	23	22	1	0	114	95	51	45	40	90
Faustino Carrera, South Bend	8	7	3.62	22	21	0	0	117	113	57	47	29	105
Easton McGee, Bowling Green	7	5	3.67	24	22	0	0	125	129	57	51	25	95
George Soriano, Clinton	4	7	3.91	23	20	2	1	120	108	62	52	50	99
Adam Hill, Wisconsin	7	9	3.92	26	23	0	0	122	113	61	53	55	109

ALL-STAR TEAM

C: David Fry, Wisconsin. **1B:** Gabe Snyder, Cedar Rapids. **2B:** Xavier Edwards, Fort Wayne. **3B:** Miguel Vargas, Great Lakes. **SS:** Wander Franco, Bowling Green. **OF:** Will Benson, Lake County; Griffin Conine, Lansing; Alek Thomas, Kane County. **DH:** Chris Betts, Bowling Green. **RHP:** Caleb Sampen, Bowling Green; Cre Finfrock, Lansing. **LHP:** Joey Cantillo, Fort Wayne; Skylar Arias, Lake County. **Most Valuable Player:** Alek Thomas, Kane County. **Prospect of the Year:** Wander Franco, Bowling Green. **Manager of the Year:** John Shoemaker, Great Lakes.

DEPARTMENT LEADERS

BATTING

OBP	Williams-Sutton, Dwanya, Fort Wayne	.411
SLG	Thomas, Alek, Kane County	.479
OPS	Thomas, Alek, Kane County	.872
R	Torres, Christopher, Clinton	82
H	Lopez, Otto, Lansing	145
TB	Fry, David, Wisconsin	224
XBH	Fry, David, Wisconsin	59
2B	Fry, David, Wisconsin	41
3B	Naylor, Bo, Lake County	10
HR	Conine, Griffin, Lansing	22
RBI	Whalen, Brady, Peoria	81
SAC	Hernandez, Miguel, Dayton	9
SAC	McVey, Connor, Wisconsin	9
BB	Torres, Christopher, Clinton	75
HBP	Williams-Sutton, Dwanya, Fort Wayne	32
SO	Williams, Nonie, Burlington	166
SB	Siani, Michael, Dayton	45
CS	Marcano, Tucupita, Fort Wayne	16
AB/SO	Marcano, Tucupita, Fort Wayne	10.2

FIELDING

C PCT	Hunt, Blake, Fort Wayne	.990
PO	Banfield, Will, Clinton	788
A	Banfield, Will, Clinton	83
DP	Betts, Chris, Bowling Green	8
E	Banfield, Will, Clinton	14
CS	Naylor, Bo, Lake County	47
SB	Naylor, Bo, Lake County	81
PB	Weber, Skyler, Beloit	18
PB	Almond, Zachery, Kane County	18
1B PCT	Snyder, Gabe, Cedar Rapids	.992
PO	Snyder, Gabe, Cedar Rapids	827
A	Paulson, Dillon, Great Lakes	51
DP	Brodt, Jake, Lansing	70
E	Solomon, Lee, Fort Wayne	12
2B PCT	Donovan, Brendan, Peoria	.977
PO	Pena, Joseph, Beloit	167
A	Pena, Joseph, Beloit	234
DP	Donovan, Brendan, Peoria	52
E	Pena, Joseph, Beloit	13
3B PCT	Martinez, Juan, Dayton	.866
PO	Vance, Cobie, Beloit	79
A	Martinez, Juan, Dayton	180
DP	Aiello, Johnny, Lansing	17
E	Martinez, Juan, Dayton	38
SS PCT	Perez, Delvin, Peoria	.947
PO	Perez, Wenceel, West Michigan	175
A	Weber, Andy, South Bend	292
DP	Hernandez, Miguel, Dayton	67
E	Torres, Christopher, Clinton	36
OF PCT	Foyle, Devin, Beloit	.989
PO	Siani, Michael, Dayton	314
A	Siani, Michael, Dayton	18
DP	Siani, Michael, Dayton	6
E	Adams, Jordyn, Burlington	13

PITCHING

G	Quezada, Jose, Fort Wayne	48
GS	Richardson, Lyon, Dayton	26
GS	Wymer, Sean, Lansing	26
GF	Reyes, Angel, West Michigan	37
SV	Finfrock, Cre, Lansing	17
W	Chacin, Jose, Great Lakes	11
L	De Jesus, Jhon, Dayton	13
IP	Wymer, Sean, Lansing	138
H	Wymer, Sean, Lansing	173
R	Brettell, Michael, Peoria	89
R	Wymer, Sean, Lansing	89
ER	Wymer, Sean, Lansing	83
HB	Royalty, Alex, Lake County	21
BB	McIntyre, Aiden, Beloit	76
SO	McIntyre, Aiden, Beloit	150
SO/9	McIntyre, Aiden, Beloit	12.0
SO/9 (RP)	Muller, Chris, Bowling Green	13.9
BB/9	Strong, Alan, Bowling Green	1.7
WP	McIntyre, Aiden, Beloit	18
WP	Soriano, George, Clinton	18
BK	Smith, Austin, Fort Wayne	9
HRA	Ponticelli, Thomas, Lake County	15
BAA	Winder, Josh, Cedar Rapids	.205

MINOR LEAGUES

BY J.J. COOPER

The Lexington Legends had a stacked team in 2018, so when they won their first South Atlantic League title since 2001, it wasn't much of a surprise.

The Legends' title defense was less expected. The Legends won the South Division's first-half title, but lefthander Kris Bubic and righthander Jonathan Bowlan, two of the team's top pitchers, moved up to the Carolina League. Wilmington finished seven games under .500 in the second half of the season.

But the Legends rallied in the playoffs. Lexington first baseman Reed Rohlman hit a walk-off, two-run home run in the bottom of the 13th inning to win Game 4 and clinch Lexington's second straight league championship.

Delmarva was knocked out by Hickory in the first round of the playoffs, but the Shorebirds were the league's most impressive team during the regular season. Delmarva became the first Sally League team to win 90 or more games since Augusta won 92 in 2006. The Shorebirds had the league's best pitching staff, led by righthander Grayson Rodriguez.

On the mound, Augusta lefthander Seth Corry strung together one of the most impressive seasons in recent South Atlantic League history. Corry led the league in ERA (1.76) and opponents' batting average (.171). He also had the league's most strikeouts (172) and best strikeout rate (12.2 strikeouts per nine innings). Corry at one point had a 31-inning scoreless streak.

Charleston outfielder Canaan Smith hit for the cycle on May 12 against Hickory. Greensboro catcher Grant Koch had a three-home run game against West Virginia on Aug. 30.

TOP 20 PROSPECTS

1. Jarred Kelenic, OF, West Virginia (Mariners)
2. Julio Rodriguez, OF, West Virginia (Mariners)
3. Grayson Rodriguez, RHP, Delmarva (Orioles)
4. Triston Casas, 1B, Greenville (Red Sox)
5. Ronny Mauricio, SS, Columbia (Mets)
6. Seth Corry, LHP, Augusta (Giants)
7. Simeon Woods-Richardson, RHP, Columbia (Mets)
8. Kris Bubic, LHP, Lexington (Royals)
9. Braden Shewmake, SS, Rome (Braves)
10. Josh Jung, 3B, Hickory (Rangers)
11. Cole Winn, RHP, Hickory (Rangers)
12. Roansy Contreras, RHP, Charleston (Yankees)
13. Alexander Vizcaino, RHP, Charleston (Yankees)
14. Luis Gil, RHP, Charleston (Yankees)
15. Luis Medina, RHP, Charleston (Yankees)
16. Sherten Apostel, 3B, Hickory (Rangers)
17. Hans Crouse, RHP, Hickory (Rangers)
18. Ji-Hwan Bae, 2B/SS, Greensboro (Pirates)
19. Trey Harris, OF, Rome (Braves)
20. Canaan Smith, OF, Charleston (Yankees)

STANDINGS: SPLIT SEASON

FIRST HALF

North	W	L	PCT	GB	South	W	L	PCT	GB
Delmarva	48	21	.696	—	Lexington	37	32	.536	—
Greensboro	44	25	.638	4	Augusta	36	32	.529	½
Hickory	41	25	.621	5½	Charleston	37	33	.529	½
West Virginia	37	33	.529	11½	Greenville	32	38	.457	5½
Hagerstown	30	40	.429	18½	Rome	30	39	.435	7
Lakewood	29	41	.414	19½	Asheville	29	41	.414	8½
Kannapolis	28	40	.412	19½	Columbia	24	42	.364	11½

SECOND HALF

North	W	L	PCT	GB	South	W	L	PCT	GB
Delmarva	42	27	.609	—	Augusta	41	29	.586	—
Hickory	42	27	.609	—	Asheville	39	31	.557	2
Kannapolis	36	34	.514	6½	Charleston	36	33	.522	4½
Greensboro	35	34	.507	7	Rome	35	35	.500	6
Hagerstown	35	35	.500	7½	Lexington	31	38	.449	9½
West Virginia	32	37	.464	10	Columbia	28	42	.400	13
Lakewood	29	39	.426	12½	Greenville	24	44	.353	16

Playoffs—Semifinals: Hickory defeated Delmarva 2-0 and Lexington defeated Augusta 2-0 in best-of-three series. **Finals:** Lexington defeated Hickory 3-1 in a best-of-five series.

OVERALL STANDINGS

Northern Division	W	L	PCT	GB	Manager(s)	Attendance	Average	Last Pennant
Delmarva Shorebirds (Orioles)	90	48	.652	—	Kyle Moore	218,704	3,120	2001
Hickory Crawdads (Rangers)	83	52	.615	5½	Matt Hagen	137,546	2,084	2015
Greensboro Grasshoppers (Pirates)	79	59	.572	11	Miguel Perez	306,136	4,483	2011
West Virginia Power (Mariners)	69	70	.496	21½	Dave Berg	118,444	1,711	1990
Hagerstown Suns (Nationals)	65	75	.464	26	Patrick Anderson	59,682	825	Never
Kannapolis Intimidators (White Sox)	64	74	.464	26	Ryan Newman	75,931	1,078	2005
Lakewood BlueClaws (Phillies)	58	80	.420	32	Mike Micucci	308,318	4,539	2010

Southern Division	W	L	PCT	GB	Manager(s)	Attendance	Average	Last Pennant
Augusta GreenJackets (Giants)	77	61	.558	—	Carlos Valderrama	266,569	3,866	2008
Charleston RiverDogs (Yankees)	73	66	.525	4½	Julio Mosquera	301,320	4,367	Never
Lexington Legends (Royals)	68	70	.493	9	Brooks Conrad	270,221	3,873	2019
Asheville Tourists (Rockies)	68	72	.486	10	Robinson Cancel	187,718	2,703	2014
Rome Braves (Braves)	65	74	.468	12½	Matt Tuiasosopo	152,874	2,181	2016
Greenville Drive (Red Sox)	56	82	.406	21	Iggy Suarez	329,733	4,849	2017
Columbia Fireflies (Mets)	52	84	.382	24	Pedro Lopez	245,522	3,560	2013

CLUB BATTING

	AVG	G	AB	R	H	2B	3B	HR	RBI	BB	SO	SB	OBP	SLG
Asheville	.253	140	4534	672	1145	275	20	102	592	481	1178	157	.334	.390
Hickory	.251	135	4444	652	1117	243	33	142	607	436	1106	134	.325	.417
Rome	.249	139	4667	617	1164	226	45	66	544	425	1273	123	.326	.360
Greensboro	.245	138	4492	700	1099	235	33	127	626	507	1206	150	.331	.396
Delmarva	.243	138	4544	610	1106	216	32	74	540	469	1260	106	.324	.354
Charleston	.242	139	4573	606	1107	240	21	90	543	498	1281	138	.325	.363
Kannapolis	.238	138	4625	560	1103	268	32	96	504	417	1376	79	.309	.373
Lexington	.236	138	4555	577	1076	223	31	90	526	434	1297	131	.311	.358
Augusta	.234	138	4551	600	1065	201	27	79	537	401	1159	61	.307	.342
Hagerstown	.234	140	4543	569	1065	206	26	67	489	496	1108	132	.318	.335
Greenville	.232	138	4511	551	1045	236	38	79	491	481	1334	89	.313	.351
West Virginia	.231	139	4587	589	1058	232	22	103	542	440	1299	46	.307	.358
Lakewood	.227	138	4430	489	1007	188	22	75	423	403	1263	146	.297	.330
Columbia	.226	136	4413	494	997	199	29	76	430	342	1211	55	.291	.336

CLUB PITCHING

	ERA	G	CG	SHO	SV	IP	H	R	ER	HR	BB	SO	AVG
Delmarva	3.00	138	0	20	53	1211	898	475	404	67	526	1389	.205
Augusta	3.23	138	0	9	47	1212	1010	527	435	71	462	1358	.226
Hickory	3.35	135	1	9	36	1194	1011	501	444	82	411	1224	.230
Rome	3.38	139	2	10	36	1216	1137	575	457	78	436	1069	.248
Hagerstown	3.52	140	1	6	27	1215	1084	572	475	99	422	1201	.239
Greensboro	3.65	138	1	12	41	1202	1054	568	487	107	392	1218	.234
Lexington	3.65	138	1	5	31	1217	1100	617	494	102	419	1276	.238
Kannapolis	3.73	138	1	9	37	1215	1089	607	504	94	442	1298	.236
Charleston	3.84	139	1	9	36	1225	1017	602	523	77	465	1239	.225
Lakewood	3.84	138	0	9	30	1190	1017	594	508	79	516	1183	.231
West Virginia	4.10	139	4	13	34	1218	1171	655	555	118	401	1270	.251
Columbia	4.11	136	0	5	33	1171	1131	646	535	88	422	1159	.254
Greenville	4.11	138	3	9	26	1203	1167	656	550	103	477	1209	.252
Asheville	4.49	140	3	9	33	1207	1268	691	602	101	439	1258	.270

CLUB FIELDING

	PCT	PO	A	E	DP		PCT	PO	A	E	DP
Hickory	.980	3581	1252	101	106	Charleston	.972	3676	1324	144	93
Delmarva	.979	3632	1185	102	80	Lakewood	.972	3571	1182	139	127
Greensboro	.975	3606	1238	125	111	Rome	.972	3647	1385	146	118
Hagerstown	.975	3646	1288	128	103	Augusta	.971	3636	1292	149	103
West Virginia	.974	3655	1114	127	86	Kannapolis	.970	3646	1179	147	102
Greenville	.973	3609	1242	134	97	Columbia	.969	3513	1248	150	110
Asheville	.972	3620	1361	144	116	Lexington	.969	3651	1304	161	92

INDIVIDUAL BATTING

Batter, Club	AVG	G	AB	R	H	2B	3B	HR	RBI	BB	SO	SB
Ji-Hwan Bae, Greensboro	.323	86	328	69	106	25	5	0	38	43	77	31
Terrin Vavra, Asheville	.318	102	374	79	119	32	1	10	52	62	62	18
Canaan Smith, Charleston	.307	124	449	67	138	32	3	11	74	74	108	16
Ian Dawkins, Kannapolis	.298	131	533	75	159	38	1	4	36	37	95	23
Adam Hall, Delmarva	.298	122	463	78	138	22	4	5	45	45	117	33
Alex Destino, Kannapolis	.298	112	420	63	125	20	2	17	64	49	116	0
Diego Rincones, Augusta	.295	105	400	48	118	25	4	5	57	27	56	0
Ismael Munguia, Augusta	.286	100	388	67	111	22	5	1	39	24	41	13
Kyle Datres, Asheville	.286	96	315	70	90	27	4	15	46	47	81	21
Devlin Granberg, Greenville	.286	99	357	57	102	19	5	8	45	45	79	6

INDIVIDUAL PITCHING

Pitcher, Club	W	L	ERA	G	GS	CG	SV	IP	H	R	ER	BB	SO
Seth Corry, Augusta	9	3	1.76	27	26	0	0	123	73	35	24	58	172
Dilmer Mejia, Rome	8	5	2.66	27	14	0	1	118	108	44	35	24	96
Jon Heasley, Lexington	8	5	3.12	25	20	0	0	113	93	47	39	34	120
Keaton Winn, Augusta	7	7	3.32	26	20	0	0	127	123	54	47	26	99
Roansy Contreras, Charleston	12	5	3.33	24	24	0	0	132	105	55	49	36	113
Alex Manasa, Greensboro	9	5	3.48	25	25	1	0	140	134	57	54	32	120
Jose Butto, Columbia	4	10	3.62	27	25	0	0	112	100	53	45	31	109
Odalvi Javier, Rome	3	8	3.78	22	22	0	0	121	112	56	51	45	101
Jake Irvin, Hagerstown	8	8	3.79	25	25	0	0	128	122	64	54	38	113
Steven Moyers, West Virginia	7	4	3.86	19	18	0	0	112	123	54	48	17	110

ALL-STAR TEAM

C: Willie MacIver, Asheville. **1B:** Mason Martin, Greensboro. **2B:** Greg Cullen, Rome. **3B:** Bobby Honeyman, West Virginia. **SS:** Terrin Vavra, Asheville. **OF:** Canaan Smith, Charleston; Ian Dawkins, Kannapolis; Justin Dean, Rome. **UT:** Adam Hall, Delmarva; Alex Destino, Kannapolis. **RHP:** Grayson Rodriguez, Delmarva. **LHP:** Seth Corry, Augusta. **RP:** Jesus Tona, Augusta. **Most Valuable Player:** Terrin Vavra, Asheville. **Most Outstanding Pitcher:** Seth Corry, Augusta. **Most Outstanding Prospect:** Grayson Rodriguez, Delmarva. **Manager of the Year:** Kyle Moore, Delmarva.

DEPARTMENT LEADERS

BATTING

OBP	Vavra, Terrin, Asheville	.409
SLG	Datres, Kyle, Asheville	.540
OPS	Datres, Kyle, Asheville	.937
R	Dean, Justin, Rome	85
H	Dawkins, Ian, Kannapolis	159
TB	Dawkins, Ian, Kannapolis	211
TB	Tostado, Frankie, Augusta	211
XBH	Lockridge, Brandon, Charleston	50
2B	Dawkins, Ian, Kannapolis	38
3B	Dean, Justin, Rome	9
HR	Gonzalez, Pedro, Hickory	23
HR	Martin, Mason, Greensboro	23
RBI	Montes, Coco, Asheville	89
SAC	Connell, Justin, Hagerstown	14
BB	Smith, Canaan, Charleston	74
HBP	Cullen, Greg, Rome	25
SO	Sharp, Brian, Columbia	168
SB	Dean, Justin, Rome	47
CS	Golsan, Will, Asheville	17
AB/SO	Munguia, Ismael, Augusta	9.5

FIELDING

C PCT	Pineda, Israel, Hagerstown	.995
PO	Koch, Grant, Greensboro	802
A	Whatley, Matt, Hickory	99
DP	Gutierrez, Abrahan, Lakewood	8
E	Marrero, Alan, Greenville	13
CS	Angulo, Andres, Augusta	33
CS	Senger, Hayden, Columbia	33
CS	Whatley, Matt, Hickory	33
SB	Koch, Grant, Greensboro	79
PB	Pineda, Israel, Hagerstown	26
1B PCT	Benson, Griffin, Rome	.998
PO	Rohlman, Reed, Lexington	919
A	Lavigne, Grant, Asheville	72
DP	Lavigne, Grant, Asheville	90
E	Lavigne, Grant, Asheville	18
2B PCT	Cullen, Greg, Rome	.976
PO	Cullen, Greg, Rome	214
A	Cullen, Greg, Rome	317
DP	Cullen, Greg, Rome	81
E	Beltre, Ramon, Kannapolis	14
3B PCT	Honeyman, Bobby, West Virginia	.955
PO	Honeyman, Bobby, West Virginia	79
A	Eaton, Nathan, Lexington	209
DP	Vientos, Mark, Columbia	19
E	Vientos, Mark, Columbia	23
E	Howlett, Brandon, Greenville	23
E	Eaton, Nathan, Lexington	23
SS PCT	Williams, Grant, Greenville	.975
PO	Sosa, Lenyn, Kannapolis	158
A	Guzman, Jeison, Lexington	317
DP	Sosa, Lenyn, Kannapolis	59
E	Guzman, Jeison, Lexington	33
OF PCT	Aparicio, Miguel, Hickory	.996
PO	Dawkins, Ian, Kannapolis	278
A	Brannen, Cole, Greenville	16
DP	Brannen, Cole, Greenville	5
E	Gonzalez, Pedro, Hickory	8
E	Suarez, Kervin, Greenville	8

PITCHING

G	Poulin, PJ, Asheville	54
GS	Jennings, Steven, Greensboro	27
GS	Martin, Davis, Kannapolis	27
GS	Neuweiler, Charlie, Lexington	27
GF	Martinez, Alexander, Asheville	41
SV	Tona, Jesus, Augusta	16
W	Contreras, Roansy, Charleston	12
L	Alastre, Tomas, Hagerstown	12
L	Jennings, Steven, Greensboro	12
L	Scherff, Alex, Greenville	12
IP	Neuweiler, Charlie, Lexington	149
H	Martin, Davis, Kannapolis	152
R	Martin, Davis, Kannapolis	94
ER	Martin, Davis, Kannapolis	81
HB	Guance, Hector, Delmarva	18
BB	Medina, Luis, Charleston	67
SO	Corry, Seth, Augusta	172
SO/9	Corry, Seth, Augusta	12.6
SO/9 (RP)	Rodriguez, Grayson, Delmarva	12.4
BB/9	Olague, Jose, Rome	1.4
WP	Medina, Luis, Charleston	26
BK	Mora, Luis, Rome	4
BK	Moyers, Steven, West Virginia	4
BK	Noguera, Gabriel, Rome	4
HRA	Taveras, Willy, Columbia	19
BAA	Corry, Seth, Augusta	.171

MINOR LEAGUES

MINOR LEAGUES

BY JUSTIN COLEMAN

While the team was notably thin on prospects in 2019, the Brooklyn Cyclones (Mets) took home the New York-Penn League championship for the first time since 2001, defeating Lowell (Red Sox) in the best-of-three championship series.

Brooklyn won the first game of the finals in a 2-1 pitchers' duel, but Lowell quickly answered to take Game 2. Third baseman Yoel Romero laced an RBI single in the seventh inning of Game 3 to put Brooklyn ahead for good. The Cyclones finished the victory and claimed their third NYPL championship.

Outside of ranking second in the league for batting average (.242), Brooklyn did not win because of a high-powered offense. The Cyclones' pitching staff was stingy all season long, ranking among the top five in WHIP (1.14) and ERA (3.25) while also allowing the third-fewest hits at 502. Righthanders Garrison Bryant and Matt Cleveland anchored the front of the rotation, posting 2.39 and 3.78 ERAs, respectively. The Cyclones went on to win a league-high 43 games and were 24-14 at home, also best in the league.

Catcher Adley Rutschman, the No. 1 overall pick in the 2019 draft, made quite the first impression. He hit .325/.413/.481 through 20 games for Aberdeen (Orioles). The best prospect in the league ended his New York-Penn League stint with a 10-game hitting streak, culminating in a 5-for-5 performance against Vermont (Athletics) with a home run and four RBIs before receiving a promotion to low Class A Delmarva.

The league was infused with plenty of high-end 2019 draft talent. Besides Rutschman, 2019 first-rounders Riley Greene (Tigers) and Greg Jones (Rays) both made immediate impacts for their teams. Greene hit .295/.380/.386 in 88 at-bats for Connecticut, while Jones ranked among the NYPL leaders in batting average (.335), on-base percentage (.413) and stolen bases (19).

On the pitching front, righthander Noah Song (Red Sox) generated the most buzz. The Naval Academy graduate may have military service time to complete, which could slow down his timeline to the big leagues, but his stuff showed glimpses of why he could be suitable for a big league rotation down the road. Righthander Ethan Hankins (Indians) dominated in his nine appearances in the league, while fellow righthander Leonardo Rodriguez (Orioles) ranked among league leaders in ERA (2.65), strikeouts (80) and WHIP (1.01).

TOP 20 PROSPECTS

1. Adley Rutschman, C, Aberdeen (Orioles)
2. Riley Greene, OF, Connecticut (Tigers)
3. Greg Jones, SS, Hudson Valley (Rays)
4. Gilberto Jimenez, OF, Lowell (Red Sox)
5. Brayan Rocchio, SS/2B, Mahoning Valley (Indians)
6. George Valera, OF, Mahoning Valley (Indians)
7. Ezequiel Duran, 2B, Staten Island (Yankees)
8. Jordan Diaz, 3B, Vermont (Athletics)
9. Ethan Hankins, RHP, Mahoning Valley (Indians)
10. Leonardo Rodriguez, RHP, Aberdeen (Orioles)
11. Bryson Stott, SS, Williamsport (Phillies)
12. Tyler Baum, RHP, Vermont (Athletics)
13. John Doxakis, LHP, Hudson Valley (Rays)
14. Oswald Peraza, SS, Staten Island (Yankees)
15. Kendall Simmons, 2B, Williamsport (Phillies)
16. Josh Smith, 2B, Staten Island (Yankees)
17. Korey Lee, C, Tri-City (Astros)
18. Aldo Ramirez, RHP, Lowell (Red Sox)
19. Dalvy Rosario, SS, Batavia (Marlins)
20. Eliezer Alfonzo, C, Connecticut (Tigers)

OVERALL STANDINGS

McNamara Division	W	L	PCT	GB	Manager(s)	Attendance	Average	Last Pennant
Brooklyn Cyclones (Mets)	43	32	.573	—	Edgardo Alfonzo	174,522	4,629	2019
Hudson Valley Renegades (Rays)	43	32	.573	—	Blake Butera	148,158	3,916	2017
Aberdeen IronBirds (Orioles)	42	33	.560	1	Kevin Bradshaw	118,357	3,055	1983
Staten Island Yankees (Yankees)	40	36	.526	3 ½	David Adams	66,520	1,686	2011

Pinckney Division	W	L	PCT	GB	Manager(s)	Attendance	Average	Last Pennant
Batavia Muckdogs (Marlins)	41	35	.539	—	Tom Lawless	43,118	1,165	2008
West Virginia Black Bears (Pirates)	40	36	.526	1	Drew Saylor	62,846	1,628	2015
State College Spikes (Cardinals)	39	36	.520	1 ½	Jose Leon	119,120	3,073	2016
Mahoning Valley Scrappers (Indians)	37	39	.487	4	Dennis Malave	98,833	2,553	2004
Williamsport Crosscutters (Phillies)	32	43	.427	8 ½	Pat Borders	64,148	1,731	2003
Auburn Doubledays (Nationals)	30	46	.395	11	Rocket Wheeler	39,381	1,082	2007

Stedler Division	W	L	PCT	GB	Manager(s)	Attendance	Average	Last Pennant
Lowell Spinners (Red Sox)	42	34	.553	—	Luke Montz	100,687	2,788	Never
Connecticut Tigers (Tigers)	34	42	.447	8	Brayan Pena	66,532	1,674	1998
Vermont Lake Mosnters (Athletics)	33	42	.440	8 ½	Aaron Nieckula	83,122	2,212	1996
Tri-City ValleyCats (Astros)	32	42	.432	9	Ozney Guillen	131,529	3,594	2018

Semifinals: Brooklyn defeated Hudson Valley 2-1 and Lowell defeated Batavia 2-1 in best-of-three series. **Finals:** Brooklyn defeated Lowell 2-1 in a best-of-three series.

CLUB BATTING

	AVG	G	AB	R	H	2B	3B	HR	RBI	BB	SO	SB	OBP	SLG
State College	.247	76	2533	353	626	135	17	42	314	293	637	38	.331	.364
Brooklyn	.242	75	2398	324	581	99	16	37	286	202	610	82	.310	.343
Batavia	.241	76	2450	325	590	116	20	33	274	260	685	85	.323	.345
Hudson Valley	.241	75	2418	347	583	98	27	20	289	284	654	118	.332	.329
Lowell	.238	76	2425	316	578	114	31	38	285	237	692	49	.314	.358
Aberdeen	.237	75	2444	315	579	115	16	42	276	255	650	61	.323	.349
Williamsport	.234	76	2363	270	553	106	24	37	241	214	648	111	.306	.346
Auburn	.231	76	2472	294	570	102	20	34	258	221	574	45	.304	.329
West Virginia	.231	76	2466	329	569	128	24	24	286	298	648	55	.321	.331
Mahoning Valley	.229	76	2441	314	559	118	27	38	282	251	637	60	.308	.346
Staten Island	.225	76	2418	308	543	99	16	52	271	293	732	59	.315	.343
Connecticut	.221	76	2384	267	527	99	17	15	224	244	652	37	.303	.296
Tri-City	.216	74	2305	270	499	84	13	47	230	254	623	90	.302	.325
Vermont	.211	75	2441	275	514	100	11	41	249	248	729	20	.293	.311

CLUB PITCHING

	ERA	G	CG	SHO	SV	IP	H	R	ER	HR	BB	SO	AVG
Aberdeen	2.38	75	2	12	18	650	493	223	172	25	226	702	.210
Hudson Valley	2.93	75	0	4	24	654	558	258	213	34	194	672	.226
Williamsport	3.14	76	0	8	18	637	581	294	222	27	247	661	.241
Brooklyn	3.25	75	0	6	24	642	502	270	232	33	233	666	.213
Staten Island	3.35	76	1	11	20	652	527	291	243	36	209	713	.218
Lowell	3.40	76	0	4	23	648	566	305	245	46	252	664	.233
Connecticut	3.55	76	1	6	22	643	570	297	254	37	311	601	.239
State College	3.62	76	1	3	19	662	596	346	266	38	250	636	.237
Batavia	3.67	76	1	7	23	657	611	322	268	38	220	654	.243
Mahoning Valley	3.71	76	2	10	24	650	559	331	268	32	253	620	.231
West Virginia	3.73	76	0	1	20	657	601	324	272	45	253	612	.244
Vermont	3.79	75	0	3	22	659	598	337	278	46	260	680	.241
Auburn	3.92	76	1	2	17	652	608	354	284	37	278	568	.248
Tri-City	4.03	74	0	3	14	627	501	355	281	26	368	722	.217

CLUB FIELDING

	PCT	PO	A	E	DP		PCT	PO	A	E	DP
Brooklyn	.977	1927	669	61	48	Auburn	.968	1955	718	87	66
Aberdeen	.976	1950	678	64	46	State College	.967	1985	711	91	53
West Virginia	.975	1971	708	68	72	Tri-City	.967	1881	618	86	58
Connecticut	.974	1930	651	70	56	Vermont	.967	1978	660	91	60
Hudson Valley	.972	1963	647	76	40	Williamsport	.967	1910	654	88	64
Batavia	.970	1970	654	82	46	Mahoning Valley	.965	1949	710	96	72
Staten Island	.969	1957	741	85	48	Lowell	.964	1945	657	98	67

INDIVIDUAL BATTING

Batter, Club	AVG	G	AB	R	H	2B	3B	HR	RBI	BB	SO	SB
Gilberto Jimenez, Lowell	.359	59	234	35	84	11	3	3	19	13	38	14
J.D. Orr, Batavia	.352	64	213	57	75	9	3	0	18	44	30	29
Greg Jones, Hudson Valley	.335	48	191	39	64	13	4	1	24	22	56	19
Bryan Lavastida, Mahoning Valley	.335	58	209	39	70	19	3	2	38	25	27	3
Wilmer Reyes, Brooklyn	.323	61	229	32	74	8	2	5	33	8	41	12
Milton Smith II, Batavia	.305	60	200	31	61	1	1	0	17	23	38	11
Pedro Pages, State College	.291	50	179	29	52	17	1	2	21	28	39	1
Nick Sogard, Hudson Valley	.290	63	214	36	62	5	0	0	21	39	43	20
David Vinsky, State College	.284	56	236	34	67	14	2	1	19	19	44	9
Troy Johnston, Batavia	.277	59	213	34	59	15	1	3	35	29	51	1

INDIVIDUAL PITCHING

Pitcher, Club	W	L	ERA	G	GS	CG	SV	IP	H	R	ER	BB	SO
Kevin Magee, Aberdeen	5	6	2.04	15	15	1	0	71	59	18	16	13	79
Garrison Bryant, Brooklyn	5	1	2.39	14	12	0	0	75	49	21	20	14	75
Edisson Gonzalez, Hudson Valley	4	2	2.45	13	11	0	0	62	55	19	17	13	77
Edgar Martinez, Batavia	4	4	2.50	15	13	1	0	72	53	26	20	22	62
Anderson Munoz, Staten Island	7	2	2.60	13	10	0	0	62	46	21	18	23	63
Ryan Conroy, Aberdeen	5	5	2.64	15	15	1	0	78	73	30	23	20	71
Leonardo Rodriguez, Aberdeen	2	2	2.65	14	13	0	0	71	47	27	21	25	80
Yusniel Padron-Artilles, Lowell	7	1	2.67	13	9	0	0	64	55	22	19	14	84
Richard Morban, Vermont	2	1	2.67	15	9	0	0	71	63	24	21	26	69
Julio Frias, Batavia	5	4	2.83	14	14	0	0	70	62	30	22	23	73

DEPARTMENT LEADERS

BATTING

OBP	Orr, J.D., Batavia	.469
SLG	Simmons, Kendall, Williamsport	.521
OPS	Welk, Toby, Aberdeen	.897
R	Orr, J.D., Batavia	57
H	Jimenez, Gilberto, Lowell	84
TB	Ready, Nic, Batavia	133
XBH	Ready, Nic, Batavia	42
2B	Ready, Nic, Batavia	30
3B	Rojas, Johan, Williamsport	6
HR	Duran, Ezequiel, Staten Island	13
RBI	Diaz, Jordan, Vermont	47
RBI	Ready, Nic, Batavia	47
SAC	Rosario, Dalvy, Batavia	11
BB	Orr, J.D., Batavia	44
HBP	Turner, Andrew, Batavia	11
SO	Butler, Lawrence, Vermont Lake	90
SB	Williams, Corbin, Williamsport	30
CS	Orr, J.D., Batavia	17
AB/SO	Lavastida, Bryan, Mahoning Valley	7.7

FIELDING

C	PCT	Alfonzo, Eliezer, Connecticut	.994
	PO	Rivas, Jose, Vermont	391
	A	Narvaez, Carlos, Staten Island	53
	DP	Lee, Korey, Tri-City	7
	E	Rivas, Jose, Vermont	11
	E	Narvaez, Carlos, Staten Island	11
	CS	Rivas, Jose, Vermont	24
	SB	Rivas, Jose, Vermont	50
	PB	Wilkie, Kyle, West Virginia	11
1B	PCT	Holton, Jake, Connecticut	.993
	PO	McGowan, Jacson, Hudson Valley	534
	A	McGowan, Jacson, Hudson Valley	29
	DP	Cooper, Michael, Mahoning Valley	49
	E	Gomez, Dariel, State College	9
2B	PCT	Duran, Ezequiel, Staten Island	.969
	PO	Duran, Ezequiel, Staten Island	100
	A	Duran, Ezequiel, Staten Island	152
	DP	Ritter, Luke, Brooklyn	29
	E	Suarez, Kervin, Lowell	11
3B	PCT	Northcut, Nicholas, Lowell	.912
	PO	Diaz, Jordan, Vermont	33
	PO	Northcut, Nicholas, Lowell	33
	A	Diaz, Jordan, Vermont	100
	DP	Northcut, Nicholas, Lowell	16
	E	Diaz, Jordan, Vermont	15
SS	PCT	Kreidler, Ryan, Connecticut	.972
	PO	Kreidler, Ryan, Connecticut	99
	A	Rocchio, Brayan, Mahoning Valley	167
	DP	Rocchio, Brayan, Mahoning Valley	39
	E	Rocchio, Brayan, Mahoning Valley	20
OF	PCT	Quiggle, Kona, Connecticut	1.000
	PCT	Alexander, Hill, Hudson Valley	1.000
	PCT	Vinsky, David, State College	1.000
	PO	Vinsky, David, State College	136
	A	Duplantis, Antoine, Brooklyn	8
	A	Rodriguez, Johnathan, Mahoning Valley	8
	A	Hearn, Hunter, Williamsport	8
	DP	Valera, George, Mahoning Valley	4
	E	Orr, J.D., Batavia	7

PITCHING

G	Blanco, Fabian, State College	22
G	Jackson, Kris, Lowell	22
G	Suriel, Edison, Batavia	22
GS	Conroy, Ryan, Aberdeen	15
GS	Magee, Kevin, Aberdeen	15
GS	Miller, Andrew, Batavia	15
GS	Vargas, Carlos, Mahoning Valley	15
GF	Jackson, Kris, Lowell	20
SV	Brabrand, Evan, Batavia	13
W	Munoz, Anderson, Staten Island	7
W	Padron-Artilles, Yusniel, Lowell	7
L	Ashcraft, Braxton, West Virginia	9
IP	Solano, Enmanuel, State College	82
H	Gomez, Rafael, Auburn	80
R	Gonzalez, Junior, State College	46
ER	Gomez, Rafael, Auburn	41
HB	Rodriguez, Leonardo, Aberdeen	12
HB	Schlesener, Jacob, State College	12
BB	Ramirez, Manny, Tri-City	40
SO	Padron-Artilles, Yusniel, Lowell	84
SO/9	Padron-Artilles, Yusniel, Lowell	11.8
SO/9 (RP)	Blanton, Bryan, Staten Island	14.5
BB/9	Magee, Kevin, Aberdeen	1.7
WP	Concepcion, Xavier, West Virginia	15
BK	Solano, Enmanuel, State College	10
HRA	Rose, Jackson, Batavia	10
BAA	Bryant, Garrison, Brooklyn	.180

MINOR LEAGUES

BY JOSH NORRIS

In the regular season, the Hillsboro Hops were powered by outfielder Kristian Robinson and righthander Luis Frias.

The precocious teenager and the fireballer ran roughshod over the competition, helping boost the Hops to their sixth straight playoff appearance. Both were promoted to low Class A before the postseason began, however, in a pair of transactions that would have hamstrung the title hopes of many other teams.

The D-backs had just added a bounty of talent through the draft, however, and replaced Robinson and Frias with a glut of high picks, including outfielder Corbin Carroll, lefthander Blake Walston and righthander Ryne Nelson. They also received talented shortstop Liover Peguero from their affiliate in the Pioneer League.

With its new weapons, Hillsboro bullied past Salem-Keizer—which had convincingly won the first half on the strength of Franklin Labour's white-hot early-season stretch—in the division series. The Hops faced more resistance in the finals but eventually prevailed, three games to two, over Tri-City to claim their third NWL championship in eight seasons.

Besides the Hops' dominance, the 2019 Northwest League was marked by its youth. Robinson starred in the league as a teenager, and Carroll arrived just before his 18th birthday as well.

Those two were old maids compared to Boise infielders Ezequiel Tovar and Bladimir Restituyo, who each made their NWL debuts as 17-year-olds.

The same was true for Salem-Keizer shortstop Marco Luciano, who made it all the way to short-season ball in his first season as a pro after dominating the Rookie-level Arizona League. An injury ended Luciano's season before he could qualify for the league's Top 20 prospect ranking, but his presence in the league by itself hints at his extremely high ceiling.

Besides Luciano and Labour, Salem-Keizer also was home to a host of talented outfielders, including Giants' first-rounder Hunter Bishop, as well as seventh-rounder Armani Smith and the toolsy Alexander Canario.

Vancouver's Adam Kloffenstein ran a close second to Frias as the league's top arm, and Spokane's Ricky Vanasco used his electric fastball to build on the buzz he'd created in extended spring training back at the Rangers' complex in Arizona.

Above all, though, 2019 belonged to Hillsboro.

TOP 20 PROSPECTS

1. Kristian Robinson, OF, Hillsboro (D-backs)
2. Luis Frias, RHP, Hillsboro (D-backs)
3. Hunter Bishop, OF, Salem-Keizer (Giants)
4. Aaron Schunk, 3B, Boise (Rockies)
5. Adam Kloffenstein, RHP, Vancouver (Blue Jays)
6. Chase Strumpf, 2B, Eugene (Cubs)
7. Ezequiel Tovar, SS, Boise (Rockies)
8. Liover Peguero, SS, Hillsboro (D-backs)
9. Alexander Canario, OF, Salem-Keizer (Giants)
10. Ricky Vanasco, RHP, Spokane (Rangers)
11. Michael Toglia, 1B, Boise (Rockies)
12. David Garcia, C, Spokane (Rangers)
13. Kohl Franklin, RHP, Eugene (Cubs)
14. Logan Wyatt, 1B, Salem-Keizer (Giants)
15. Edmond Americaan, OF, Eugene (Cubs)
16. Austin Shenton, 3B, Everett (Mariners)
17. Armani Smith, OF, Salem-Keizer (Giants)
18. Franklin Labour, OF, Salem-Keizer (Giants)
19. Pedro Martinez, SS, Eugene (Cubs)
20. Bladimir Restituyo, 2B/OF, Boise (Rockies)

STANDINGS: SPLIT SEASON

FIRST HALF

North	W	L	PCT	GB	South	W	L	PCT	GB
Spokane	22	16	.579	—	Salem-Keizer	26	12	.684	—
Everett	18	20	.474	4	Hillsboro	24	14	.632	2
Tri-City	16	22	.421	6	Eugene	16	22	.421	10
Vancouver	15	23	.395	7	Boise	15	23	.395	11

SECOND HALF

North	W	L	PCT	GB	South	W	L	PCT	GB
Spokane	23	15	.605	—	Hillsboro	24	14	.632	—
Tri-City	22	16	.579	1	Salem-Keizer	20	18	.526	4
Everett	19	19	.500	4	Eugene	17	21	.447	7
Vancouver	15	23	.395	8	Boise	12	26	.316	12

Playoffs—Semifinals: Tri-City defeated Spokane 2-1 and Hillsboro defeated Salem-Keizer 2-0 in best-of-three series. **Finals:** Hillsboro defeated Tri-City 3-2 in a best-of-five series.

OVERALL STANDINGS

North Division	W	L	PCT	GB	Manager(s)	Attendance	Average	Last Pennant
Spokane Indians (Rangers)	45	31	.592	—	Kenny Hook	200,273	5,270	2008
Tri-City Dust Devils (Padres)	38	38	.500	7	Mike McCoy	87,021	2,290	Never
Everett AquaSox (Mariners)	37	39	.487	8	J. Moreno/L. Boyd	116,630	3,069	2010
Vancouver Canadians (Blue Jays)	30	46	.395	15	Casey Candaele	235,980	6,210	2017

South Division	W	L	PCT	GB	Manager(s)	Attendance	Average	Last Pennant
Hillsboro Hops (D-backs)	48	28	.632	—	Javier Colina	133,605	3,516	2019
Salem-Keizer Volcanoes (Giants)	46	30	.605	2	Mark Hallberg	80,833	2,127	2009
Eugene Emeralds (Cubs)	33	43	.434	15	Lance Rymel	131,467	3,460	2018
Boise Hawks (Rockies)	27	49	.355	21	Steve Soliz	129,805	3,416	2004

CLUB BATTING

	AVG	G	AB	R	H	2B	3B	HR	RBI	BB	SO	SB	OBP	SLG
Salem-Keizer	.263	76	2644	425	695	148	19	73	386	317	703	52	.348	.416
Hillsboro	.249	76	2511	373	625	128	23	39	325	311	587	96	.343	.365
Everett	.241	76	2510	385	606	121	23	52	343	347	743	81	.344	.370
Eugene	.238	76	2533	321	603	136	25	26	277	250	669	92	.315	.342
Tri-City	.237	76	2549	330	604	128	27	40	284	299	713	75	.323	.355
Boise	.235	76	2515	299	592	109	18	36	250	242	673	74	.311	.336
Spokane	.235	76	2553	389	600	126	13	50	335	294	759	67	.327	.353
Vancouver	.229	76	2554	303	585	112	14	32	271	281	646	50	.315	.321

CLUB PITCHING

	ERA	G	CG	SHO	SV	IP	H	R	ER	HR	BB	SO	AVG
Hillsboro	2.87	76	0	11	22	671	498	245	214	31	294	742	.205
Spokane	3.46	76	0	4	19	678	568	312	261	43	294	745	.225
Eugene	3.84	76	0	6	17	672	594	341	287	43	327	707	.235
Tri-City	3.94	76	0	5	20	674	605	375	295	42	325	789	.237
Vancouver	3.95	76	0	6	10	671	621	348	294	46	317	667	.246
Salem-Keizer	4.40	76	0	4	24	680	645	388	332	39	283	621	.248
Everett	4.50	76	0	2	15	671	664	404	336	68	251	629	.255
Boise	4.78	76	0	4	15	665	715	412	353	36	250	593	.273

CLUB FIELDING

	PCT	PO	A	E	DP		PCT	PO	A	E	DP
Hillsboro	.978	2012	701	61	60	Boise	.968	1994	813	93	68
Salem-Keizer	.975	2039	721	72	46	Vancouver	.968	2012	686	88	57
Eugene	.970	2016	658	82	50	Everett	.966	2014	721	95	57
Spokane	.969	2035	664	87	57	Tri-City	.960	2022	662	113	55

INDIVIDUAL BATTING

Batter, Club	AVG	G	AB	R	H	2B	3B	HR	RBI	BB	SO	SB
Blaine Crim, Spokane	.335	53	212	34	71	15	1	8	45	19	28	1
Kelvin Melean, Tri-City	.308	50	185	21	57	14	0	1	27	22	37	5
Patrick Frick, Everett	.302	60	215	46	65	12	0	0	21	41	40	7
Cade Marlowe, Everett	.301	62	219	29	66	15	3	3	30	26	62	10
Alexander Canario, Salem-Keizer	.301	49	193	38	58	17	1	9	40	18	71	3
Tristin English, Hillsboro	.290	50	193	32	56	12	2	7	30	13	24	1
Cesar Izturis Jr., Everett	.285	60	214	29	61	10	1	0	32	23	41	11
Ricky Martinez, Hillsboro	.283	62	240	34	68	10	0	0	16	26	45	15
Edmond Americaan, Eugene	.282	66	255	38	72	17	5	4	32	19	65	16
Kellen Strahm, Spokane	.278	50	194	40	54	5	1	5	24	32	46	12

INDIVIDUAL PITCHING

Pitcher, Club	W	L	ERA	G	GS	CG	SV	IP	H	R	ER	BB	SO
Deyni Olivero, Hillsboro	8	3	2.09	15	8	0	0	65	50	18	15	20	42
Adam Kloffenstein, Vancouver	4	4	2.24	13	13	0	0	64	47	23	16	23	64
Marcos Tineo, Hillsboro	6	4	2.57	15	8	0	0	67	62	25	19	19	66
Kervin Castro, Salem-Keizer	5	3	2.66	14	14	0	0	68	52	24	20	13	61
Travis Perry, Salem-Keizer	5	2	3.82	14	9	0	0	64	56	31	27	25	47
Damon Casetta-Stubbs, Everett	3	3	4.11	15	15	0	0	70	52	37	32	27	67
Juan Diaz, Vancouver	3	5	4.31	12	12	0	0	63	64	36	30	18	45

ALL-STAR TEAM

C: David Garcia, Spokane. **1B:** Blaine Crim, Spokane. **2B:** Kevin Melean, Tri-City. **3B:** Aaron Schunk, Boise. **SS:** Patrick Frick, Everett. **OF:** Edmond Americaan, Eugene; Alexander Canario, Salem-Keizer, Kristian Robinson, Hillsboro. **DH:** Franklin Labour, Salem-Keizer. **P:** Deyni Olivero, Hillsboro; Marcos Tineo, Hillsboro; Kervin Castro, Salem-Keizer; Adam Kloffenstein, Vancouver; Werner Leal, Spokane. **Most Valuable Player:** Blaine Crim, Spokane. **Pitcher of the Year:** Deyni Olivero, Hillsboro. **Manager of the Year:** Kenny Hook, Spokane.

DEPARTMENT LEADERS

BATTING

OBP	Frick, Patrick, Everett	.431
SLG	Canario, Alexander, Salem-Keizer	.539
OPS	Crim, Blaine, Spokane	.927
R	Marriaga, Jesus, Hillsboro	51
H	Americaan, Edmond, Eugene	72
TB	Barley, Jordy, Tri-City	118
XBH	Canario, Alexander, Salem-Keizer	27
2B	Americaan, Edmond, Eugene	17
2B	Canario, Alexander, Salem-Keizer	17
3B	Barley, Jordy, Tri-City	6
HR	Labour, Franklin, Salem-Keizer	14
RBI	Crim, Blaine, Spokane	45
SAC	Tovar, Ezequiel, Boise	6
BB	Tingelstad, Trent, Everett	51
HBP	Bins, Carter, Everett	14
HBP	Kapers, Scott, Spokane	14
SO	Perez, Miguel, Everett	103
SB	Ilarraza, Reinaldo, Tri-City	26
CS	Barley, Jordy, Tri-City	8
CS	Martinez, Ricky, Hillsboro	8
CS	Whiteman, Simon, Salem-Keizer	8
AB/SO	English, Tristin, Hillsboro	8.0

FIELDING

C PCT	Soto, Jonathan, Eugene	.989
PO	Bins, Carter, Everett	385
A	Garcia, David, Spokane	48
DP	Homza, Jonny, Tri-City	6
E	Garcia, David, Spokane	9
CS	Genoves, Ricardo, Salem-Keizer	20
CS	Quintero, Alison, Tri-City	20
SB	Quijada, Bryant, Boise	46
PB	Soto, Jonathan, Eugene	19
1B PCT	Yerzy, Andy, Hillsboro	.989
PO	Yerzy, Andy, Hillsboro	426
A	Yerzy, Andy, Hillsboro	30
DP	Yerzy, Andy, Hillsboro	45
E	Perez, Robert, Everett	9
2B PCT	Hoover, Jake, Spokane	.984
PO	Rodriguez, Yorlis, Salem-Keizer	76
A	Rodriguez, Yorlis, Salem-Keizer	84
DP	Grande, Nick, Hillsboro	20
E	Rodriguez, Yorlis, Salem-Keizer	13
3B PCT	Schunk, Aaron, Boise	.977
PO	Schunk, Aaron, Boise	33
A	Schunk, Aaron, Boise	95
DP	Schunk, Aaron, Boise	9
E	Luis, Carlos, Tri-City	10
SS PCT	Vazquez, Luis, Eugene	.964
PO	Vazquez, Luis, Eugene	102
A	Tovar, Ezequiel, Boise	175
DP	Tovar, Ezequiel, Boise	31
E	Barley, Jordy, Tri-City	23
OF PCT	Carter, Tre, Tri-City	1.000
PCT	Barrosa, Jorge, Hillsboro	1.000
PO	Kelli, Fernando, Eugene	147
A	Tingelstad, Trent, Everett	10
DP	Kelli, Fernando, Eugene	3
E	Kelli, Fernando, Eugene	6
E	Boone, Trevor, Boise	6

PITCHING

G	Condreay, Joel, Boise	27
GS	Casetta-Stubbs, Damon, Everett	15
GF	Gillingham, Luke, Vancouver	19
SV	Wallace, Jacob, Boise	12
W	Olivero, Deyni, Hillsboro	8
L	Ocando, Jeffri, Boise	8
IP	Casetta-Stubbs, Damon, Everett	70
H	Ocando, Jeffri, Boise	79
R	Ocando, Jeffri, Boise	55
ER	Ocando, Jeffri, Boise	46
HB	Casetta-Stubbs, Damon, Everett	13
BB	Benitez, Jorge, Everett	38
BB	Vargas, Didier, Eugene	38
SO	Frias, Luis, Hillsboro	72
SO/9	Kloffenstein, Adam, Vancouver	8.9534
SO/9 (RP)	Holton, Tyler, Hillsboro	14.1959
BB/9	Castro, Kervin, Salem-Keizer	1.7291
WP	Cabrera, Wander, Boise	12
BK	12 players	2
HRA	Florido, Deivy, Everett	9
HRA	Ocando, Jeffri, Boise	9
BAA	Kloffenstein, Adam	.205

MINOR LEAGUES

MINOR LEAGUES

BY CARLOS COLLAZO

Johnson City won the Rookie-level Appalachian League title for the fifth time this decade, topping Burlington, two games to one, in the league final. The 2019 championship gave the Cardinals' Rookie-level affiliate its 12th championship of all time and its first since 2016.

The Cardinals won the championship despite ranking as a middling team in the league in both hitting and pitching. Johnson City was sixth in the league in runs scored (5.19 per game) among the ten teams, and eighth in the league in runs allowed (5.57 per game).

Despite those season-long stats, the team went on to a terrific streak at the end of the regular season, needing to win its final two games just to qualify for the playoffs. After that, Johnson City lost the opening game in both the semifinals and finals before winning back-to-back elimination games in both series to clinch the championship.

Like a year ago, when the championship team placed just one player on the league top 20 list, Johnson City's lone representative is outfielder Jhon Torres (No. 4), who was second on the team with a .918 OPS, behind only Chandler Freeman among qualified batters, who's three years his elder.

The prospect talent in the Appy League is down from the 2018, as last year's list was led by one of the best prospects in baseball in Wander Franco. The pitching depth in particular was down, as just five pitchers made the top 20, and only one arm—Pulaski righthander Yoendrys Gomez (No. 9)—landed among the top 10.

As usual, there were plenty of high-profile draft picks in the league, including 2019 draftees third baseman Brett Baty (Mets), outfielder Matt Wallner (Twins), shortstop Anthony Volpe (Yankees) and infielder Tyler Callihan (Reds), among others. The league also featured a number of exciting international prospects, including six

players from a strong 2017 class. The top prospect in the league, Mets catcher Francisco Alvarez, showed solid offensive ability and remarkable refinement as a defender for a 17-year-old and has scouts and managers alike excited for his future.

Danville first baseman Bryce Ball was the league's player of the year and ranked as the No. 15 prospect in the league. A 2019 draft pick in the 24th round, Ball showed big power potential and hit .324/.410/.676 with 13 home runs and the second-best OPS (1.086) in the league. Danville was also responsible for the league's pitcher of the year, as 24-year-old lefthander Mitch Stallings went 3-5, 2.25 with 69 strikeouts and 11 walks over 56 innings.

Pulaski was named the league's organization of the year after leading the league in attendance for the fifth straight season. The club also had the best regular-season record in the league, going 42-26 before falling to Burlington in the semifinals and seeing their season come to an end.

TOP 20 PROSPECTS

1. Francisco Alvarez, C, Kingsport (Mets)
2. Brett Baty, 3B, Kingsport (Mets)
3. Miguel Hiraldo, SS/2B, Bluefield (Blue Jays)
4. Jhon Torres, OF, Johnson City (Cardinals)
5. Antonio Cabello, OF, Pulaski (Yankees)
6. Matt Wallner, OF, Elizabethton (Twins)
7. Anthony Volpe, SS, Pulaski (Yankees)
8. Nick Schnell, OF, Princeton (Rays)
9. Yoendrys Gomez, RHP, Pulaski (Yankees)
10. Jaylen Palmer, SS/3B, Kingsport (Mets)
11. Tyler Callihan, 3B/2B, Greeneville (Reds)
12. Junior Santos, RHP, Kingsport (Mets)
13. Ivan Johnson, SS/2B, Greeneville (Reds)
14. Leonardo Jimenez, SS/2B, Bluefield (Blue Jays)
15. Bryce Ball, 1B, Danville (Braves)
16. Spencer Steer, SS/2B, Elizabethton (Twins)
17. Ryder Green, OF, Pulaski (Yankees)
18. Adrian Alcantara, RHP, Burlington (Royals)
19. Tahnaj Thomas, RHP, Bristol (Pirates)
20. Jose Salvador, LHP, Greeneville (Reds)

OVERALL STANDINGS

Eastern Division	W	L	PCT	GB	Manager(s)	Attendance	Average	Last Pennant
Pulaski Yankees (Yankees)	42	26	.618	—	Luis Dorante	95,897	2,782	2013
Burlington Royals (Royals)	39	29	.574	3	Chris Widger	40,142	1,177	1993
Princeton Rays (Rays)	34	34	.500	8	Danny Sheaffer	24,133	731	1994
Bluefield Blue Jays (Blue Jays)	31	36	.463	10 ½	Luis Hurtado	20,909	609	2001
Danville Braves (Braves)	30	38	.441	12	Anthony Nunez	30,007	873	2009

Western Division	W	L	PCT	GB	Manager(s)	Attendance	Average	Last Pennant
Johnson City Cardinals (Cardinals)	35	33	.515	—	Roberto Espinoza	80,612	2,419	2019
Birstol Pirates (Pirates)	34	33	.507	½	Kieran Mattison	18,750	598	2002
Kingsport Mets (Mets)	34	34	.500	1	Rich Donnelly	29,553	868	1995
Elizabethton Twins (Twins)	33	34	.493	1 ½	Ray Smith	27,569	811	2018
Greeneville Reds (Reds)	26	41	.388	8 ½	Gookie Dawkins	43,617	1,185	2015

Semifinals: Johnson City defeated Bristol 2-1 and Burlington defeated Pulaski 2-1 in best-of-three series. **Finals:** Johnson City defeated Burlington 2-1 in a best-of-three series.

CLUB BATTING

	AVG	G	AB	R	H	2B	3B	HR	RBI	BB	SO	SB	OBP	SLG
Princeton	.269	68	2318	368	623	111	19	47	324	207	578	68	.339	.394
Bluefield	.266	67	2320	381	617	127	11	58	334	264	562	48	.349	.405
Bristol	.266	67	2223	351	592	125	11	33	316	221	502	58	.345	.377
Kingsport	.255	68	2323	348	593	110	24	62	306	221	673	28	.327	.403
Elizabethton	.251	67	2280	350	572	115	13	71	314	250	621	32	.342	.406
Burlington	.243	68	2251	361	547	109	18	49	311	310	649	81	.347	.373
Johnson City	.242	68	2210	353	534	116	12	63	311	263	696	54	.330	.390
Danville	.232	68	2210	291	513	98	6	42	246	240	579	51	.317	.339
Pulaski	.230	68	2219	344	511	106	19	71	296	234	671	67	.310	.391
Greeneville	.226	67	2208	284	499	98	23	51	257	182	684	44	.295	.361

CLUB PITCHING

	ERA	G	CG	SHO	SV	IP	H	R	ER	HR	BB	SO	AVG
Burlington	3.48	68	0	6	13	600	479	267	232	49	260	654	.219
Pulaski	3.89	68	0	8	15	593	490	294	256	50	225	663	.224
Elizabethton	4.04	67	0	1	16	591	579	331	265	52	214	731	.253
Bristol	4.06	67	1	4	24	581	540	312	262	51	253	599	.244
Princeton	4.30	68	0	3	13	586	568	351	280	68	226	615	.250
Danville	4.35	68	0	2	13	588	540	339	284	53	294	639	.242
Greeneville	4.58	67	1	8	12	585	568	351	298	43	204	656	.249
Johnson City	4.76	68	1	1	19	584	628	379	309	63	213	578	.272
Kingsport	4.78	68	0	1	18	587	599	388	312	53	277	561	.262
Bluefield	4.88	67	0	3	16	582	610	419	316	65	226	519	.266
Billings	3.88	76	0	6	16	664	636	358	286	65	220	724	.249

CLUB FIELDING

	PCT	PO	A	E	DP		PCT	PO	A	E	DP
Burlington	.975	1799	658	64	52	Danville	.965	1764	584	84	45
Bristol	.972	1744	620	68	44	Greeneville	.963	1755	543	88	27
Pulaski	.972	1779	638	70	51	Kingsport	.961	1762	578	95	57
Princeton	.971	1757	590	70	45	Johnson City	.960	1751	568	96	40
Bluefield	.966	1747	604	82	54	Elizabethton	.956	1772	557	108	39

INDIVIDUAL BATTING

Batter, Club	AVG	G	AB	R	H	2B	3B	HR	RBI	BB	SO	SB
Logan Porter, Burlington	.352	44	145	26	51	14	1	9	37	31	34	0
Luis Leon, Princeton	.341	43	173	29	59	12	1	5	30	11	40	0
Spencer Horwitz, Bluefield	.330	51	206	31	68	18	1	3	49	23	24	5
Jake Guenther, Princeton	.320	48	175	29	56	10	1	2	30	23	26	2
Miguel Hiraldo, Bluefield	.300	56	237	43	71	20	1	7	37	14	36	11
Leonardo Jimenez, Bluefield	.298	56	215	34	64	13	2	0	22	21	42	2
Vinnie Pasquantino, Burlington	.294	57	211	43	62	17	2	14	53	27	40	0
Francisco Acuna, Bristol	.293	53	181	31	53	20	1	1	30	13	34	9
Andres Regnault, Kingsport	.292	44	178	26	52	11	0	8	49	8	36	0
Jesus Valdez, Bristol	.292	55	209	38	61	12	1	5	34	21	42	7

INDIVIDUAL PITCHING

Pitcher, Club	W	L	ERA	G	GS	CG	SV	IP	H	R	ER	BB	SO
Mitch Stallings, Danville	3	5	2.25	11	9	0	0	56	53	22	14	11	69
Randy Vasquez, Pulaski	4	1	3.29	11	11	0	0	55	36	23	20	28	53
Jhonatan Munoz, Pulaski	5	3	4.13	11	11	0	0	57	52	34	26	18	68
Julio Puello, Johnson City	5	4	5.40	13	13	0	0	72	77	45	43	18	68

ALL-STAR TEAM

C: Luis Leon, Princeton. **1B:** Bryce Ball, Danville. **2B:** Francisco Acuna, Bristol. **3B:** Miguel Hiraldo, Bluefield. **SS:** Maikel Garcia, Burlington. **OF:** Spencer Horwitz, Bluefield; Diego Infante, Princeton; Max Smith, Elizabethton. **DH:** Logan Porter, Burlington. **UT:** Vinnie Pasquantino, Burlington; Nick Schnell, Princeton. **RHP:** Adrian Alcantara, Burlington. **LHP:** Mitch Stallings, Danville. **RP:** Reyson Santos, Kingsport. **Most Valuable Player:** Bryce Ball, Danville. **Pitcher of the Year:** Mitch Stallings, Danville. **Manager of the Year:** Luis Dorante, Pulaski.

DEPARTMENT LEADERS

BATTING

OBP	Porter, Logan, Burlington	.481
SLG	Porter, Logan, Burlington	.648
OPS	Porter, Logan, Burlington	1.129
R	Green, Ryder, Pulaski	45
H	Hiraldo, Miguel, Bluefield	71
TB	Pasquantino, Vinnie, Burlington	125
XBH	Pasquantino, Vinnie, Burlington	33
2B	Acuna, Francisco, Bristol	20
2B	Hiraldo, Miguel, Bluefield	20
3B	Callihan, Tyler, Greeneville	5
3B	Lantigua, Danny, Greeneville	5
3B	Ota, Scott, Kingsport	5
HR	Pasquantino, Vinnie, Burlington	14
RBI	Pasquantino, Vinnie, Burlington	53
SAC	Gethings, Jack, Burlington	6
BB	Milligan, Cody, Danville	44
HBP	Means, Jake, Burlington	17
SO	Palmer, Jaylen, Kingsport	108
SB	Sanchez, Aldenis, Princeton	21
CS	Rivero, Daniel, Bristol	9
AB/SO	Horwitz, Spencer, Bluefield	8.6

FIELDING

C PCT	Hancock, William, Burlington	.998
PO	Hancock, William, Burlington	424
A	Hancock, William, Burlington	48
DP	Wilson, Eli, Bristol	5
E	De Hoyos, Victor, Danville	5
E	Antonini, Aaron, Johnson City	5
CS	Hancock, William, Burlington	21
SB	Wilson, Eli, Bristol	28
PB	Guerra, Andres, Bluefield	16
1B PCT	Pasquantino, Vinnie, Burlington	.995
PO	Pasquantino, Vinnie, Burlington	367
A	Guenther, Jake, Princeton	31
DP	Pujols, Cristopher, Kingsport	37
E	Pujols, Cristopher, Kingsport	13
2B PCT	Bissonette, Josh, Bristol	.995
PO	Bissonette, Josh, Bristol	84
A	Guerrero, Gregory, Kingsport	135
DP	Guerrero, Gregory, Kingsport	27
E	Wisely, Brett, Princeton	12
3B PCT	Bell, Chad, Bristol	.951
PO	Birdsong, Cody, Danville	39
A	Means, Jake, Burlington	114
DP	Reyes, Joseph, Bluefield	9
E	Means, Jake, Burlington	13
SS PCT	Garcia, Maikel, Burlington	.954
PO	Gil, Mateo, Johnson City	92
A	Garcia, Maikel, Burlington	136
DP	Garcia, Maikel, Burlington	37
E	Espino, Sebastian, Kingsport	19
OF PCT	Rivero, Daniel, Bristol	1.000
PO	Rivera, Eric, Bluefield	134
A	Soler, Carlos, Johnson City	8
A	Fletcher, Trejyn, Johnson City	8
DP	6 players	2
E	Wallner, Matt, Elizabethton	7

PITCHING

G	Rodriguez, Hector, Kingsport	22
G	Santos, Reyson, Kingsport	22
GS	Santos, Junior, Kingsport	14
GF	Santos, Reyson, Kingsport	17
SV	Abernathy, Samson, Bristol	8
SV	Santos, Reyson, Kingsport	8
W	Escorcha, Jefferson, Kingsport	7
L	Abril, Juan Manuel, Greeneville	7
L	Widell, Ryley, Elizabethton	7
IP	Puello, Julio, Johnson City	72
H	Moreno, Jose, Johnson City	93
R	Moreno, Jose, Johnson City	60
ER	Moreno, Jose, Johnson City	50
HB	Puello, Julio, Johnson City	11
BB	Pestana, Leonardo, Pulaski	32
BB	Van Buren, Malcolm, Burlington	32
SO	Stallings, Mitch, Danville	69
SO/9	Stallings, Mitch, Danville	11.1
	SO/9 (RP) Waldichuk, Ken, Pulaski	15.0
BB/9	Stallings, Mitch, Danville	1.8
WP	Allain, Ryan, Princeton	13
BK	Hodgson, Alger, Danville	4
HRA	4 players	9
BAA	Vasquez, Randy, Pulaski	.188

MINOR LEAGUES

BY BILL MITCHELL

The Idaho Falls Chukars (Royals) overcame a one-game deficit to capture the Pioneer League championship in a three-game series against the Ogden Raptors (Dodgers). The Chukars were the third Royals club to win a league championship in a three-day span, joining low Class A Lexington and high Class A Wilmington, were certainly the surprise of the year. After posting the North Division's best record (21-16) in the first half of the season, Idaho Falls went just 13-25 in the second half and seemed to be limping into the playoffs. Ogden, meanwhile, posted the league's best regular-season record at 54-22, tying the Pioneer League record for wins in a season.

Grand Junction catcher Colin Simpson (Rockies) was named the league's most valuable player after the Oklahoma State product posted a .309/.383/.667 slash line in his first professional season. Billings righthander Miguel Medrano (Reds) earned accolades as the league's pitcher of the year with a solid season in which he posted a 3.13 ERA and struck out 66 batters in 60.1 innings. Orem infielder Jeremiah Jackson (Angels) tied the 22-year-old league record of 23 home runs while also pacing all hitters with 60 RBIs. Grand Junction outfielder Brenton Doyle recovered from an early-season injury to lead the league in average (.383), on-base percentage (.477) and OPS (1.088), and Ogden skipper Austin Chubb was awarded manager of the year honors.

The Pioneer League wasn't loaded with many top prospects, but that is largely due to the growing trend of organizations adding a third Rookie ball affiliate and therefore thinning out the distribution of talent. But enough sleepers, especially teenaged Latin talent, emerged to make it a reasonably good year, prospect-wise, for the eight-team league. Missoula (D-backs) shortstop Liover Peguero emerged and was named the league's top prospect in his first season above complex-level leagues. Orem infielder Will Wilson (Angels) was the only true first-round pick to accrue enough playing time to rank on the league's prospect list.

TOP 20 PROSPECTS

1. Liover Peguero, SS, Missoula (D-backs)
2. Andy Pages, OF, Ogden (Dodgers)
3. Jeremiah Jackson, SS/2B, Orem (Angels)
4. Helcris Olivarez, LHP, Grand Junction (Rockies)
5. Will Wilson, SS/2B, Orem (Angels)
6. Brenton Doyle, OF, Grand Junction (Rockies)
7. Alec Marsh, RHP, Idaho Falls (Royals)
8. Noah Davis, RHP, Billings (Reds)
9. Carlos Rodriguez, OF, Rocky Mountain (Brewers)
10. Miguel Medrano, RHP, Billings (Reds)
11. Brady McConnell, SS, Idaho Falls (Royals)
12. Julio Carreras, 3B/SS, Grand Junction (Rockies)
13. Eddy Davis, SS/2B, Grand Junction (Rockies)
14. Mitchell Kilkenny, RHP, Grand Junction (Rockies)
15. Brandon Lewis, 3B/1B, Ogden (Dodgers)
16. Christian Koss, INF, Grand Junction (Rockies)
17. Ezequiel Tovar, SS, Grand Junction (Rockies)
18. Nick Kahle, C, Rocky Mountain (Brewers)
19. Eric Yang, C, Billings (Reds)
20. Grant Gambrell, RHP, Idaho Falls (Royals)

STANDINGS: SPLIT SEASON

FIRST HALF

North	W	L	PCT	GB	South	W	L	PCT	GB
Idaho Falls	21	16	.568	—	Ogden	31	7	.816	—
Missoula	20	18	.526	1 ½	Grand Junct.	19	19	.500	12
Great Falls	15	22	.405	6	Rocky Mount.	17	21	.447	14
Billings	15	23	.395	6 ½	Orem	13	25	.342	18

SECOND HALF

North	W	L	PCT	GB	South	W	L	PCT	GB
Billings	24	14	.632	—	Ogden	23	15	.605	—
Missoula	20	18	.526	4	Grand Junct.	19	17	.528	3
Great Falls	19	18	.514	4 ½	Orem	17	21	.447	6
Idaho Falls	13	25	.342	11	Rocky Mount.	15	22	.405	7 ½

Playoffs—Semifinals: Idaho Falls defeated Billings 2-0 and Ogden defeated Grand Junction 2-0 in best-of-three series. **Finals:** Idaho Falls defeated Ogden 2-1 in a best-of-three series.

This season also marked the first year for the Brewers' new short-season affiliate in Colorado Springs, Colo., re-branded as the Rocky Mountain Vibes to replace the franchise formerly in Helena, Mont.. The Vibes had a successful first season in what had long been a Triple-A market, ranking second in the league in average attendance with just more than 3,600 fans per game after drawing only 840 per home outing in Helena's final year in 2018.

OVERALL STANDINGS

North Division	W	L	PCT	GB	Manager(s)	Attendance	Average	Last Pennant
Missoula Osprey (D-backs)	40	36	.526	—	Juan Francia	57,076	1,587	2015
Billings Mustangs (Reds)	39	37	.513	1	Bryan LaHair	96,594	2,549	2014
Great Falls Voyagers (White Sox)	34	40	.459	5	Tim Esmay	47,240	1,298	2018
Idaho Falls Chukars (Royals)	34	41	.453	5 ½	Omar Ramirez	102,859	2,695	2019

South Division	W	L	PCT	GB	Manager(s)	Attendance	Average	Last Pennant
Ogden Raptors (Dodgers)	54	22	.711	—	Austin Chubb	146,201	3,801	2017
Grand Junction Rockies (Rockies)	38	36	.514	15	Jake Opitz	88,476	2,313	Never
Rocky Mountain Vibes (Brewers)	32	43	.427	21 ½	Nestor Corredor	137,294	3,653	Never
Orem Owlz (Angels)	30	46	.395	24	Jack Santora	45,561	1,148	2016

CLUB BATTING

	AVG	G	AB	R	H	2B	3B	HR	RBI	BB	SO	SB	OBP	SLG
Ogden	.292	76	2570	548	751	169	22	103	492	342	702	62	.385	.495
Grand Junction	.267	74	2490	416	664	126	33	68	363	291	685	107	.350	.426
Billings	.265	76	2570	371	682	123	26	51	326	238	651	38	.337	.393
Idaho Falls	.258	75	2490	397	643	133	30	66	359	240	807	82	.332	.415
Rocky Mountain	.256	75	2490	360	637	138	22	56	305	215	638	78	.322	.396
Orem	.255	76	2541	386	647	128	27	87	338	273	807	45	.339	.429
Missoula	.254	76	2544	374	645	116	28	62	317	221	636	51	.323	.394
Great Falls	.249	74	2410	315	601	127	28	45	284	174	729	21	.308	.381

CLUB PITCHING

	ERA	G	CG	SHO	SV	IP	H	R	ER	HR	BB	SO	AVG
Ogden	4.01	76	1	5	16	657	606	344	293	59	243	775	.242
Missoula	4.41	76	0	4	21	663	638	379	325	61	223	777	.250
Great Falls	4.47	74	4	3	19	618	646	368	307	48	177	622	.267
Idaho Falls	4.78	75	1	5	16	634	716	414	337	64	236	687	.281
Grand Junction	4.87	74	0	4	18	645	698	422	349	84	243	638	.276
Rocky Mountain	4.87	75	0	2	15	642	632	405	347	77	325	696	.260
Orem	5.39	76	0	2	15	654	698	477	392	80	327	736	.272

CLUB FIELDING

	PCT	PO	A	E	DP		PCT	PO	A	E	DP
Missoula	.971	1990	701	81	59	Grand Junction	.963	1935	768	105	75
Rocky Mountain	.967	1925	654	87	69	Great Falls	.963	1854	729	99	70
Billings	.966	1991	672	94	48	Ogden	.963	1972	641	101	61
Idaho Falls	.964	1902	678	97	62	Orem	.958	1963	709	118	58

INDIVIDUAL BATTING

Batter, Club	AVG	G	AB	R	H	2B	3B	HR	RBI	BB	SO	SB
Brenton Doyle, Grand Junction	.383	51	180	42	69	11	3	8	33	31	47	17
Clay Dungan, Idaho Falls	.357	65	255	57	91	19	5	2	38	28	32	9
Christian Koss, Grand Junction	.332	53	190	45	63	11	4	11	51	35	43	10
Zac Ching, Ogden	.316	49	177	45	56	13	1	4	38	28	47	1
Rhett Aplin, Idaho Falls	.310	68	239	43	74	14	1	10	42	37	52	0
Jose Marquez, Idaho Falls	.310	64	252	45	78	12	5	1	28	28	48	13
Colin Simpson, Grand Junction	.309	56	207	47	64	12	4	18	49	25	69	5
Jonathan Willems, Billings	.300	60	230	29	69	12	4	0	26	10	41	2
Andy Pages, Ogden	.298	63	235	57	70	22	2	19	55	26	79	7
Julio Carreras, Grand Junction	.294	67	262	51	77	14	8	5	38	25	63	14

INDIVIDUAL PITCHING

Pitcher, Club	W	L	ERA	G	GS	CG	SV	IP	H	R	ER	BB	SO
Carlos Luna, Rocky Mountain	3	4	3.58	14	14	0	0	70	70	33	28	10	70
Jeronimo Castro, Ogden	4	2	3.62	15	15	1	0	70	63	35	28	15	74
Matt Leon, Orem	4	4	3.64	14	11	0	0	64	55	31	26	20	68
Alfredo Tavarez, Ogden	1	3	3.65	15	15	0	0	67	62	32	27	26	70
Anderson Amarista, Grand Junction	5	4	4.02	13	13	0	0	69	68	34	31	17	49
Nathan Webb, Idaho Falls	4	3	4.55	13	12	1	0	63	72	43	32	27	77
Jason Morgan, Great Falls	3	6	4.68	14	14	1	0	75	83	52	39	20	33
Justin McGregor, Billings	3	6	4.78	15	14	0	0	70	95	52	37	7	56
Emilker Guzman, Orem	3	7	4.82	15	12	0	0	62	63	42	33	14	59
Antonio Hernandez, Ogden	4	2	4.94	15	14	0	0	62	71	35	34	16	54

ALL-STAR TEAM

C: Michael Emodi, Idaho Falls. **1B:** Rhett Aplin, Idaho Falls. **2B:** Clay Dungan, Idaho Falls. **3B:** Christian Koss, Grand Junction. **SS:** Liover Peguero, Missoula. **OF:** Andy Pages, Ogden; Colin Simpson, Grand Junction; Quin Cotton, Billings. **DH:** Jeremiah Jackson, Orem. **P:** Miguel Medrano, Billings; Jeronimo Castro, Ogden; Omar Conoropo, Billings; Alfredo Tavarez, Ogden; Avery Weems, Great Falls. **Most Valuable Player:** Colin Simpson, Grand Junction. **Pitcher of the Year:** Miguel Medrano, Billings. **Manager of the Year:** Austin Chubb, Ogden.

DEPARTMENT LEADERS

BATTING

OBP	Doyle, Brenton, Grand Junction	.477
SLG	Simpson, Colin, Grand Junction	.667
OPS	Doyle, Brenton, Grand Junction	1.088
R	Dungan, Clay, Idaho Falls	57
R	Pages, Andy, Ogden	57
H	Dungan, Clay, Idaho Falls	91
TB	Jackson, Jeremiah, Orem	155
XBH	Pages, Andy, Ogden	43
2B	Pages, Andy, Ogden	22
3B	Carreras, Julio, Grand Junction	8
HR	Jackson, Jeremiah, Orem	23
RBI	Jackson, Jeremiah, Orem	60
SAC	Carreras, Julio, Grand Junction	6
SAC	Sano, Edwin, Rocky Mountain	6
BB	Aplin, Rhett, Idaho Falls	37
HBP	Yang, Eric, Billings	19
SO	Rodriguez, Ismaldo, Idaho Falls	111
SB	Torres, Bryan, Rocky Mountain	21
CS	Diaz, Eddy, Grand Junction	9
AB/SO	Coursey, Cam, Missoula	8.5

FIELDING

C PCT	Yang, Eric, Billings	.995
PO	Valbuena, Luvin, Missoula	370
A	Mulrine, Anthony, Orem	54
DP	Emodi, Michael, Idaho Falls	6
DP	Mulrine, Anthony, Orem	6
E	Sanchez, Kleyder, Great Falls	6
CS	Mulrine, Anthony, Orem	31
SB	Mulrine, Anthony, Orem	30
PB	Emodi, Michael, Idaho Falls	9
1B PCT	Aplin, Rhett, Idaho Falls	.984
PO	Clawson, David, Orem	429
A	Brickhouse, Spencer, Missoula	37
DP	Mendoza, Harvin, Great Falls	43
E	Clawson, David, Orem	11
2B PCT	Willems, Jonathan, Billings	.958
PO	Egnatuk, Nick, Rocky Mountain	88
A	Coursey, Cam, Missoula	108
DP	Egnatuk, Nick, Rocky Mountain	31
E	Egnatuk, Nick, Rocky Mountain	10
3B PCT	Ruiz, Victor, Billings	.866
PO	Curbelo, Luis, Great Falls	32
A	Ruiz, Victor, Billings	80
DP	Lao, Sauryn, Ogden	8
DP	Ruiz, Victor, Billings	8
E	Ruiz, Victor, Billings	16
SS PCT	Dungan, Clay, Idaho Falls	.958
PO	Pinero, Antonio, Rocky Mountain	69
A	Dungan, Clay, Idaho Falls	123
DP	Pinero, Antonio, Rocky Mountain	28
E	McConnell, Brady, Idaho Falls	16
OF PCT	White, Brandon, Orem	1.000
PO	Cotton, Quin, Billings	123
A	Ozuna, Reniel, Billings	10
DP	Knowles, D'Shawn, Orem	3
DP	Yalowitz, Jack, Grand Junction	3
E	Rodriguez, Ismaldo, Idaho Falls	8

PITCHING

G	Hepple, Eric, Grand Junction	25
G	Carreno, Carlos, Billings	15
G	Castro, Jeronimo, Ogden	15
G	Tavarez, Alfredo, Ogden	15
GS	Vassalotti, Michele, Rocky Mountain	15
GF	Hepple, Eric, Grand Junction	20
SV	Arroyo, Mailon, Missoula	7
SV	Hollowell, Gavin, Grand Junction	7
W	Bido, Anderson, Grand Junction	6
W	Dunne, Ryan, Billings	6
L	Guzman, Emilker, Orem	7
L	Thompson, Sean, Great Falls	7
IP	Thompson, Sean, Great Falls	80
H	Thompson, Sean, Great Falls	101
R	Thompson, Sean, Great Falls	59
ER	Thompson, Sean, Great Falls	54
HB	Webb, Nathan, Idaho Falls	11
BB	Walters, Nash, Rocky Mountain	32
SO	Ridings, Stephen, Idaho Falls	88
SO/9	Webb, Nathan, Idaho Falls	10.9
SO/9 (RP)	Schanuel, Brady, Rocky Mountain	15.9
BB/9	McGregor, Justin, Billings	0.9
WP	Johnson, Bryar, Idaho Falls	12
BK	Thompson, Sean, Great Falls	4
HRA	Amarista, Anderson, Grand Junction	12
HRA	Vassalotti, Michele, Rocky Mountain	12
BAA	Leon, Matt, Orem	.230

MINOR LEAGUES

BY BILL MITCHELL

The Rookie-level Arizona League continued its rapid growth in 2019. Three new teams expanded the league to 21, when just 10 years ago there were 11 teams in the complex league. Seven of the 14 organizations making up the league now have two affiliates, with the Athletics, Brewers and Dodgers adding second squads before the season.

The top prospect was Padres shortstop C.J. Abrams, the No. 6 overall pick in the 2019 draft. Lauded by scouts for his elite-level athleticism and advanced hitting instincts, Abrams was named the league's most valuable player and led all hitters with a .401 batting average. Giants Orange slugger Connor Cannon led the league in home runs (13) and slugging percentage (.689), while Royals infielder Jimmy Govern led all hitters in OPS (1.121) and on-base percentage (.492).

Dodgers Lasorda reliever Adolfo Ramirez posted the best ERA among qualifying pitchers at 0.73, and Luis D. Garcia (Indians Blue) and Juan Sanchez (Giants Orange) both won a league-high seven games.

The AZL Rangers, with first-year manager Carlos Cardoza skippering one of the league's youngest teams, raced through the postseason undefeated to capture the league championship, sweeping Indians Blue in the best-of-three championship series. Giants Orange compiled the league's best record at 43-13, setting an Arizona League record for most wins in a single season and earning former major league shortstop Alvaro Espinoza the league's manager of the year award.

TOP 20 PROSPECTS

1. CJ Abrams, SS, Padres
2. Marco Luciano, SS, Giants
3. Bobby Witt Jr., SS, Royals
4. Corbin Carroll, OF, D-backs
5. Diego Cartaya, C, Dodgers
6. Kody Hoese, 3B, Dodgers
7. Antoine Kelly, LHP, Brewers
8. Aaron Bracho, 2B, Indians
9. Wilderd Patiño, OF, D-backs
10. Hudson Head, OF, Padres
11. Alex De Jesus, SS, Dodgers
12. Keithron Moss, 2B/3B, Rangers
13. Hyun-il Choi, RHP, Dodgers
14. H. Hernandez, OF/C/1B, Rangers
15. Jose Tena, SS, Indians
16. Luis Toribio, 3B, Giants
17. Jairo Pomares, OF, Giants
18. Pedro Martinez, SS/2B, Cubs
19. Brayan Buelvas, OF, Athletics
20. Joshua Mears, OF, Padres

STANDINGS: SPLIT SEASON

FIRST HALF

East	W	L	PCT	GB	West	W	L	PCT	GB
Giants Orange	22	6	.786	—	Rangers	19	9	.679	—
Athletics Gold	16	12	.571	6	Padres 1	17	11	.607	2
Cubs 1	15	13	.536	7	Royals	17	11	.607	2
Cubs 2	13	15	.464	9	Dodgers Mota	15	13	.536	4
D-backs	13	15	.464	9	Indians Reds	14	14	.500	5
Giants Black	12	16	.429	10	Mariners	14	14	.500	5
Athletics Green	11	17	.393	11	Brewers Blue	10	18	.357	9
Angels	8	20	.286	14					
Central	**W**	**L**	**PCT**	**GB**					
Indians Blue	19	9	.679	—					
Padres 2	18	10	.643	1					
Dodgers Laso.	12	16	.429	7					
White Sox	11	17	.393	8					
Reds	10	18	.357	9					
Brewers Gold	8	20	.286	11					

SECOND HALF

East	W	L	PCT	GB	West	W	L	PCT	GB
Giants Orange	21	7	.750	—	Dodgers Mota	18	10	.643	—
Cubs 2	18	10	.643	3	Royals	16	12	.571	2
Athletics Gold	15	13	.536	6	Padres 1	15	12	.556	2½
D-backs	13	15	.464	8	Rangers	14	14	.500	4
Giants Black	12	16	.429	9	Brewers Blue	13	15	.464	5
Angels	11	17	.393	10	Indians Red	13	15	.464	5
Cubs 1	9	18	.333	11½	Mariners	8	20	.286	10
Athletics Green	9	19	.321	12					
Central	**W**	**L**	**PCT**	**GB**					
Padres 2	21	7	.750	—					
Reds	17	11	.607	4					
Indians Blue	16	12	.571	5					
Dodgers Laso.	15	13	.536	6					
White Sox	11	17	.393	10					
Brewers Gold	8	20	.286	13					

Playoffs—Semifinals: Rangers defeated Giants Orange and Indians Blue defeated Padres 2 in one-game playoffs. **Finals:** Rangers defeated Indians Blue 2-0 in a best-of-three series.

OVERALL STANDINGS

East Division	W	L	PCT	GB	Manager(s)	Last Pennant
Giants Orange	43	13	.768	—	Alvaro Espinoza	Never
Athletics Gold	31	25	.554	12	Hiram Bocachica	Never
Cubs 2	31	25	.554	12	Ricardo Medina	Never
D-backs	26	30	.464	17	Wellington Cepeda	Never
Cubs 1	24	31	.436	18½	Carmelo Martinez	2017
Giants Black	24	32	.429	19	Michael Johnson	2013
Athletics Green	20	36	.357	23	Eddie Menchaca	2001
Angels	19	37	.339	24	Dave Stapleton	Never

Central Division	W	L	PCT	GB	Manager(s)	Last Pennant
Padres 2	39	17	.696	—	Aaron Levin	Never
Indians Blue	35	21	.625	4	Larry Day	Never
Dodgers Lasorda	27	29	.482	12	Danny Dorn	2018
Reds	27	29	.482	12	Jose Nieves	Never
White Sox	22	34	.393	17	Ever Magallanes	2015
Brewers Gold	16	40	.286	23	Liu Rodriguez	Never

West Division	W	L	PCT	GB	Manager(s)	Last Pennant
Dodgers Mota	33	23	.589	—	Jair Fernandez	Never
Rangers	33	23	.589	—	Carlos Cardoza	2019
Royals	33	23	.589	—	Tony Pena Jr.	Never
Padres 1	32	23	.582	½	Vinny Lopez	2006
Indians Red	27	29	.482	6	Jerry Owens	2014
Brewers Blue	23	33	.411	10	Rafael Neda	2010
Mariners	22	34	.393	11	Zac Livingston	2016

MINOR LEAGUES

CLUB BATTING

	AVG	G	AB	R	H	2B	3B	HR	RBI	BB	SO	SB	OBP	SLG
Rangers	.291	56	1996	391	581	91	43	48	323	260	532	85	.377	.452
Padres 2	.287	56	1978	369	567	95	25	32	304	256	528	87	.374	.408
Indians Blue	.282	56	1949	373	550	126	25	48	318	234	499	63	.365	.446
Royals	.275	56	1914	309	526	79	25	22	272	219	434	76	.356	.377
Cubs 1	.273	55	1888	332	516	103	18	33	291	226	520	92	.357	.399
Dodgers Mota	.273	56	1947	316	531	93	28	36	266	190	510	101	.343	.405
Athletics Gold	.272	56	1921	366	523	85	20	22	298	287	484	49	.374	.372
Padres 1	.269	55	1901	313	511	90	31	27	255	241	530	68	.357	.391
Giants Orange	.266	56	1847	362	491	102	20	46	291	268	546	119	.372	.417
Reds	.260	56	1967	321	512	95	32	32	263	182	580	54	.336	.390
White Sox	.258	56	1987	274	513	101	15	38	235	137	619	42	.336	.381
Diamondbacks	.252	56	1906	290	480	85	31	16	231	232	528	132	.338	.354
Giants Black	.251	56	1873	267	470	90	24	24	229	205	578	67	.332	.363
Cubs 2	.249	56	1882	307	468	92	13	31	267	222	474	60	.332	.361
Dodgers Lasorda	.248	56	1955	293	484	88	20	41	256	219	545	39	.333	.376
Athletics Green	.240	56	1870	259	449	88	23	14	221	223	626	63	.328	.334
Brewers Blue	.240	56	1898	273	456	78	26	27	210	193	629	120	.325	.351
Angels	.237	56	1901	277	451	88	24	16	227	235	599	44	.328	.334
Indians Red	.234	56	1871	271	438	69	14	22	212	219	510	79	.320	.321
Mariners	.232	56	1879	242	436	79	23	29	201	190	603	55	.311	.345
Brewers Gold	.228	56	1894	220	432	85	14	16	184	195	571	73	.310	.313

CLUB PITCHING

	ERA	G	CG	SHO	SV	IP	H	R	ER	HR	BB	SO	AVG
Giants Orange	3.12	56	0	3	18	496	437	218	172	15	200	547	.237
Padres 1	3.60	55	0	4	14	488	473	269	195	24	154	570	.251
Cubs 2	3.74	56	0	1	14	493	454	271	205	21	208	492	.243
Indians Blue	3.76	56	0	0	16	497	479	294	208	27	173	570	.248
Mariners	4.01	56	0	1	11	492	469	270	219	28	180	521	.250
Diamondbacks	4.02	56	0	0	14	492	432	281	220	17	249	577	.234
Dodgers Mota	4.02	56	0	3	13	497	462	272	222	39	203	582	.244
Brewers Blue	4.11	56	0	7	9	502	519	283	229	31	195	507	.269
Royals	4.11	56	0	3	13	499	509	274	228	40	183	516	.263
Padres 2	4.14	56	0	5	18	507	460	303	233	35	275	570	.240
Dodgers Lasorda	4.15	56	0	8	8	507	490	293	234	37	193	554	.252
Rangers	4.31	56	0	1	15	497	477	286	238	40	204	564	.251
Indians Red	4.34	56	0	1	11	495	510	307	239	36	247	551	.267
White Sox	4.46	56	0	1	12	500	562	331	248	45	197	544	.280
Giants Black	4.66	56	0	5	12	487	511	313	252	18	222	490	.267
Athletics Gold	4.75	56	0	3	11	496	497	315	262	22	191	598	.261
Brewers Gold	5.11	56	0	0	9	495	567	350	281	25	244	586	.287
Reds	5.27	56	0	4	14	498	563	376	292	41	236	508	.281
Athletics Green	5.31	56	0	7		487	527	375	287	24	260	526	.274
Angels	5.35	56	0	0	8	495	501	391	294	24	360	562	.261
Cubs 1	5.58	55	0	4	10	488	486	353	303	31	259	510	.257

CLUB FIELDING

	PCT	PO	A	E	DP		PCT	PO	A	E	DP
Dodgers Lasorda	.966	1521	528	73	51	Padres 2	.956	1521	509	93	46
Giants Orange	.965	1488	564	75	53	Diamondbacks	.955	1477	520	94	40
Royals	.963	1498	540	79	47	Padres 1	.954	1464	537	96	42
Athletics Gold	.962	1489	554	80	53	White Sox	.953	1500	528	99	48
Dodgers Mota	.962	1492	494	78	40	Brewers Gold	.952	1486	504	101	43
Brewers Blue	.960	1505	571	86	70	Cubs 2	.949	1478	580	111	49
Cubs 1	.960	1465	507	83	43	Indians Blue	.945	1492	499	116	45
Mariners	.960	1476	531	84	53	Athletics Green	.943	1460	564	122	54
Rangers	.959	1492	526	86	54	Reds	.943	1495	481	120	44
Indians Red	.957	1486	491	88	33	Angels	.939	1484	539	132	38
Giants Black	.956	1460	516	92	48						

INDIVIDUAL BATTING

Batter, Club	AVG	G	AB	R	H	2B	3B	HR	RBI	BB	SO	SB
CJ Abrams, Padres 1	.401	32	142	40	57	12	8	3	22	10	14	14
Jairo Pomares, Giants Black	.368	37	155	17	57	10	4	3	33	10	26	5
Jimmy Govern, Royals	.365	46	156	33	57	17	3	6	33	34	20	6
Yeison Santana, Padres 2	.346	41	162	38	56	5	5	3	30	23	38	4
Heriberto Hernandez, Rangers	.344	50	192	42	66	17	4	11	48	27	57	3
Taylor Lomack, Padres	.343	39	137	30	47	3	3	0	14	15	30	11
Joshwan Wright, Athletics gold	.330	50	191	37	63	9	4	0	37	17	25	4
Cristopher Cespedes, Indians Blue	.326	48	184	38	60	18	2	6	33	18	54	4
Fabian Pertuz, Cubs 2	.325	49	197	33	64	14	1	2	25	9	46	9
Jose Tena, Indians Blue	.325	44	191	30	62	7	6	1	18	6	44	6

INDIVIDUAL PITCHING

Pitcher, Club	W	L	ERA	G	GS	CG	SV	IP	H	R	ER	BB	SO
Adolfo Ramirez, Dodgers Lasorda	3	0	0.73	14	0	0	1	49	24	5	4	9	61
Gabriel Morales, Padres 2	4	0	1.66	11	6	0	0	48.2	32	10	9	14	58
Jasier Herrera, Giants Black	6	1	1.99	10	7	0	0	54.1	53	18	12	8	48
Carlos Guarate, Padres 2	6	1	2.22	11	9	0	0	44.2	41	17	11	12	38
Jeisson Cabrera, Dodgers Mota	4	2	2.31	14	7	0	0	50.2	28	16	13	25	63
Woo-Young Jin, Royals	6	2	2.35	14	1	0	2	46	33	14	12	13	54
Manuel Espinoza, Cubs 2	5	2	2.49	11	7	0	0	47	52	21	13	9	37
Emilio Marquez, Royals	5	1	2.51	13	6	0	0	46.2	39	16	13	7	63
Juan Morillo, Dodgers Lasorda	2	1	2.56	13	1	0	0	45.2	39	20	13	13	58
Luis D. Garcia, Indians Blue	7	0	2.58	13	11	0	0	66.1	53	26	19	15	44

ALL-STAR TEAM

C: Yainer Diaz, Indians 2. **1B:** Stanley Martinez, Rangers. **2B:** Tucupita Marcano, Padres 2. **3B:** Fidel Mejia, Cubs 2. **SS:** Frainyer Chavez, Rangers; Brayan Rocchio, Indians 2. **OF:** Miguel Jerez, Indians 1; Ruben Cardenas, Indians 1; Anderson Comas, White Sox. **DH:** Nick Gatewood, Padres 1. **RHP:** Richard Morban, Athletics; Tom Colletti, Padres 1. **LHP:** Taylor Varnell, White Sox; Rigo Fernandez, White Sox. **Most Valuable Player:** Miguel Jerez, Indians 1. **Manger of the Year:** Carmelo Martinez, Cubs 1.

DEPARTMENT LEADERS

BATTING

OBP	Govern, Jimmy, Royals	.493
SLG	Abrams, CJ, Padres 1	.662
OPS	Govern, Jimmy, Royals	1.121
R	Luciano, Marco, Giants Orange	46
H	Hernandez, Heriberto, Rangers	66
TB	Hernandez, Heriberto, Rangers	124
XBH	Hernandez, Heriberto, Rangers	32
2B	Cespedes, Cristopher, Indians Blue	18
3B	Abrams, CJ, Padres 1	8
3B	Diaz, Luis Yanel, Dodgers Mota	8
HR	Cannon, Connor, Giants Orange	13
RBI	Hernandez, Heriberto, Rangers	48
SAC	11 players	3
BB	Toribio, Luis, Giants Orange	45
HBP	Reyes, Ripken, Padres 2	15
SO	Gil, Edwin, Mariners	83
SB	Curpa, Jose, D-backs	28
CS	McCray, Grant, Giants Black	13
AB/SO	Abrams, CJ, Padres 1	10.1

FIELDING

C	PCT	Betancourt, Marcos, Athletics	.997
	PO	Chalo, Wladimir, Dodgers Lasorda	337
	A	Vizcarra, Gilberto, Padres 2	56
	DP	Lopez, Hansen, Athletics Green	6
	E	Melendez, Andres, Brewers Gold	8
	E	Hernandez, Omar, Royals	8
	E	Torres, Victor, White Sox	8
	CS	Marcano, Marlon, Angels	23
	SB	Lopez, Hansen, Athletics Green	48
	PB	Torres, Victor, White Sox	14
1B	PCT	Gil, Edwin, Mariners	.989
	PO	Gomez, Cristian, Angels	412
	A	Gil, Edwin, Mariners	27
	DP	Maican, Diego, Royals	36
	DP	Gil, Edwin, Mariners	36
	E	Jimenez, Rafael, D-backs	12
2B	PCT	Hill Jr., Glenallen, D-backs	.975
	PO	Alvarez, Wilson, Athletics	74
	A	Hill Jr., Glenallen, D-backs	102
	DP	Reyes, Ripken, Padres 2	25
	DP	Grosse, Cody, Mariners	25
	E	Cruz, Rochest, Cubs 2	10
3B	PCT	Perez, Nolan, Mariners	.965
	PO	Diaz, Luis Yanel, Dodgers Mota	36
	A	Perez, Nolan, Mariners	79
	DP	Wright, Joshwan, Athletics Gold	15
	E	Pena, Jean, Giants Black	15
SS	PCT	De Jesus, Alex, Dodgers Mota	.950
	PO	Santana, Yeison, Padres 2	63
	A	Peralta, Elvis, Athletics Gold	106
	DP	Paulino, Jhoan, Athletics Green	27
	E	Rosario, Dilan, Giants Black	21
OF	PCT	Ochoa, Sebastian, Mariners	.988
	PO	Montero, Jean, Indians Red	113
	PO	Pagan, Ezequiel, Cubs	113
	A	Castro, Fidel, Reds	10
	DP	Castro, Fidel, Reds	5
	DP	Pagan, Ezequiel, Cubs	5
	E	Reyes, Jose, Angels	10

PITCHING

	G	Parra, Jose, Brewers Gold	21
	G	Tavarez, Eddy, Brewers Blue	21
	G	Vennaro, Zach, Brewers Gold	21
	GS	Herrera, Dennis, Ahtletic Green	13
	GF	Hunter, Leon, Rangers	16
	GF	Rodriguez, Jhan, Indians Red	16
	SV	Baker, Blake, Padres 2	8
	SV	Hunter, Leon, Rangers	8
	W	Garcia, Luis D., Indians Blue	7
	W	Sanchez, Juan, Giants Orange	7
	L	Acosta, Hector, White Sox	8
	IP	Garcia, Luis D., Indians Blue	66
	H	Paulino, Anderson, Royals	75
	R	Acosta, Hector, White Sox	52
	ER	Salaya, Brayan, Brewers Gold	39
	HB	Chaney, Chase, Angels	10
	HB	Ramos, Luis, Cubs 2	10
	BB	Duran, Emmanuel, Angels	43
	SO	Choi, Hyun-il, Dodgers Mota	71
	SO/9	Marquez, Emilio, Royals	12.2
	SO/9 (RP)	Carrasco, Martin, Padres 1	15.0
	BB/9	Manuel, Maiker, Reds	1.2
	WP	Chaney, Chase, Angels	21
	BK	Herrera, Dennis, Ahtletic Green	6
	HRA	Valdez, Joan, Dodgers Lasorda	10
	BAA	Ramirez, Adolfo, Dodgers Lasorda	.146

BY BEN BADLER

The Orioles breezed through the Rookie-level Gulf Coast League with a 38-15 record, a .717 winning percentage that was the best in the league during the regular season.

They didn't get a chance to bring back the league championship, however, because the league cancelled the final two games of the season and the playoffs due to Hurricane Dorian. The Orioles won the South division, the Marlins finished first in the East and the Phillies West club captured the North division title.

The Orioles' team included Gunnar Henderson, Baltimore's second-round pick (No. 43 overall) and the No. 3 prospect in the league. The Marlins' talent included 17-year-old outfielder Victor Mesa Jr. making his pro debut after signing in 2018 out of Cuba, and they received strong defense at shortstop from second-round pick Nasim Nuñez. Catcher Andrick Nava, 17, made an impact for the Phillies West in his first season, showing an advanced offensive approach to hit .314/.349/.372 in 44 games.

While the other complex league in Arizona was stacked with talent in 2019, the caliber of prospects who qualified for the GCL prospect rankings was well below normal. The best prospect in the league was Blue Jays shortstop Orelvis Martinez, a 17-year-old who made his pro debut after signing in 2018 for $3.51 million, the largest bonus for a 16-year-old in the 2018-19 international signing class. Martinez batted .275/.352/.549, showing an impressive balance of hitting ability and power.

The Pirates had a pair of top 2019 draft picks

who stood out in righthander Quinn Priester (No. 18 overall) and outfielder Sammy Siani (No 37), with Priester in particular looking sharp with a 3.03 ERA and a 37-to-10 strikeout-to-walk ratio in 32.2 innings. The Yankees had a slew of young Latin American prospects who didn't necessarily perform well but impressed scouts with their tools and actions, including catcher Antonio Gomez and shortstop Alexander Vargas.

Tigers West outfielder Kerry Carpenter won the league's MVP award, batting .319/.408/.625 in 43 games. At 21, Carpenter was old for a league that's heavy on first-year high school players and young international talent, but it was a promising start for the 19th-round pick out of Virginia Tech.

TOP 20 PROSPECTS

1. Orelvis Martinez, SS/3B, Blue Jays
2. Quinn Priester, RHP, Pirates
3. Gunnar Henderson, SS, Orioles
4. Sammy Siani, OF, Pirates
5. Antonio Gomez, C, Yankees
6. Andrick Nava, C, Phillies
7. Victor Mesa Jr., OF, Marlins
8. Kevin Alcantara, OF, Yankees
9. Alexander Vargas, SS, Yankees
10. Nasim Nuñez, SS, Marlins
11. Raimfer Salinas, OF, Yankees
12. Jairo Lopez, RHP, Astros
13. Keoni Cavaco, SS, Twins
14. Matthew Lugo, SS, Red Sox
15. Michael Harris, OF, Braves
16. Evan Fitterer, RHP, Marlins
17. Alberto Rodriguez, Blue Jays
18. Jeremy de la Rosa, OF, Nationals
19. Dasan Brown, OF, Blue Jays
20. Viandel Pena, INF, Nationals

OVERALL STANDINGS

East Division	W	L	PCT	GB	Manager(s)	Last Pennant
Marlins	28	22	.560	—	Robert Rodriguez	Never
Mets	30	24	.556	—	David Davalillo	Never
Nationals	26	23	.531	1 ½	Mario Lisson	2009
Astros	25	26	.490	3 ½	Wladimir Sutil	Never
Cardinals	20	34	.370	10	Josh Lopez	2016

North Division	W	L	PCT	GB	Manager(s)	Last Pennant
Phillies West	33	15	.668	—	Milver Reyes	Never
Tigers West	30	20	.600	4	Gary Cathcart	2018
Blue Jays	27	23	.540	7	Dennis Holmberg	Never
Yankees West	22	27	.449	11 ½	Nick Ortiz	2011
Phillies East	21	27	.438	12	Roly de Armas	2010
Tigers East	19	29	.396	14	Luis Lopez	Never
Yankees East	18	29	.383	14 ½	Dan Fiorito	2017

South Division	W	L	PCT	GB	Manager(s)	Last Pennant
Orioles	38	15	.717	—	Alan Mills	Never
Twins	30	21	.588	7	Robbie Robinson	Never
Red Sox	27	25	.519	10 ½	Tom Kotchman	2015
Rays	25	28	.472	13	Rafael Valenzuela	Never
Braves	18	31	.367	18	Nestor Perez	2003
Pirates	18	36	.333	20 ½	Gera Alvarez	2012

Playoffs—The entire Gulf Coast League postseason was cancelled due to Hurricane Dorian.

CLUB BATTING

	AVG	G	AB	R	H	2B	3B	HR	RBI	BB	SO	SB	OBP	SLG
Phillies West	.260	48	1563	246	407	89	19	25	212	167	338	41	.337	.390
Mets	.255	54	1714	291	437	95	10	29	244	245	411	58	.365	.373
Nationals	.255	49	1593	249	407	86	13	21	205	224	424	53	.364	.365
Orioles	.254	53	1619	264	412	74	13	26	227	229	420	84	.356	.364
Tigers West	.247	50	1586	277	392	92	12	37	242	236	334	40	.356	.390
Blue Jays	.246	50	1555	237	382	85	15	19	206	203	383	92	.345	.356
Phillies East	.243	48	1509	197	367	65	17	16	159	134	353	60	.309	.341
Astros	.238	51	1650	227	392	79	9	25	181	214	453	52	.338	.342
Marlins	.237	50	1597	245	379	73	15	16	210	231	392	86	.345	.332
Red Sox	.236	52	1633	229	385	73	15	19	203	228	481	37	.343	.334
Pirates	.233	54	1673	190	389	58	24	10	148	189	446	71	.325	.314
Rays	.233	53	1633	198	381	59	22	7	155	132	392	41	.299	.309
Tigers East	.233	48	1500	198	349	70	5	16	171	164	328	51	.318	.318
Braves	.224	49	1498	188	335	64	10	22	167	182	461	33	.315	.324
Yankees East	.224	47	1448	192	325	66	16	15	162	151	370	42	.308	.323
Cardinals	.223	54	1723	221	384	90	15	35	195	205	510	32	.318	.353
Twins	.220	51	1557	212	342	65	16	23	176	195	456	39	.317	.326
Yankees West	.219	49	1509	219	330	70	14	32	196	246	457	55	.340	.347

CLUB PITCHING

	ERA	G	CG	SHO	SV	IP	H	R	ER	HR	BB	SO	AVG
Orioles	2.54	53	0	11	17	432	332	165	122	11	171	443	.211
Phillies West	3.17	48	0	7	13	406	291	173	143	13	180	433	.200
Red Sox	3.19	52	0	8	11	434	379	185	154	21	135	455	.231
Tigers West	3.19	50	0	10	10	423	383	199	150	21	143	374	.240
Rays	3.36	53	0	4	9	429	345	202	160	16	233	471	.221
Twins	3.47	51	0	5	9	420	359	199	162	15	172	483	.230
Marlins	3.50	50	0	3	15	426	359	209	166	25	198	422	.226
Mets	3.55	54	0	1	11	462	410	229	182	16	204	465	.237
Nationals	3.76	49	0	0	12	417	370	211	174	19	201	391	.241
Yankees East	4.12	47	1	4	7	380	351	233	174	25	193	360	.244
Astros	4.19	51	0	2	13	434	363	257	202	29	263	496	.227
Phillies East	4.26	48	0	4	2	393	345	223	186	19	213	356	.232
Braves	4.31	49	0	2	8	399	384	243	191	13	184	385	.249
Blue Jays	4.34	50	0	2	10	421	383	235	203	27	176	367	.240
Yankees West	4.53	49	0	2	13	408	393	251	205	31	182	346	.251
Tigers East	4.72	48	0	1	7	397	410	254	208	24	215	330	.265
Pirates	4.90	54	0	2	9	448	445	287	244	31	260	419	.257
Cardinals	5.17	54	0	2	12	466	497	327	268	37	253	416	.273

CLUB FIELDING

	PCT	PO	A	E	DP		PCT	PO	A	E	DP
Phillies West	.975	1218	402	42	30	Phillies East	.964	1179	419	59	30
Blue Jays	.971	1263	391	50	41	Rays	.964	1287	457	66	39
Twins	.971	1261	453	52	31	Nationals	.963	1250	431	65	48
Pirates	.968	1344	484	61	36	Tigers West	.963	1269	445	66	34
Orioles	.967	1295	499	61	36	Cardinals	.961	1399	478	77	48
Red Sox	.967	1303	476	60	31	Braves	.960	1197	438	68	36
Tigers East	.966	1190	423	57	37	Mets	.960	1385	466	77	44
Astros	.965	1302	444	63	42	Yankees East	.957	1132	405	69	29
Marlins	.964	1279	425	63	32	Yankees West	.954	1223	423	80	39

INDIVIDUAL BATTING

Batter, Club	AVG	G	AB	R	H	2B	3B	HR	RBI	BB	SO	SB
Viandel Pena, Nationals	.359	37	131	27	47	10	3	0	15	21	31	6
Junior Martina, Nationals	.338	39	136	33	46	6	3	4	20	20	28	4
Edgar Made, Phillies West	.333	42	165	31	55	12	4	3	34	13	26	5
Warren Saunders, Mets	.323	33	127	25	41	5	0	1	20	10	23	3
Kerry Carpenter, Tigers West	.319	43	160	33	51	16	3	9	34	22	18	6
Andrick Nava, Phillies West	.314	44	156	25	49	6	0	1	20	8	20	1
Kenedy Corona, Mets	.311	42	151	35	47	9	1	5	21	17	25	11
Alberto Rodriguez, Blue Jays	.301	47	173	19	52	13	1	2	29	19	32	13
Leandro Emiliani, Nationals	.299	39	127	20	38	11	0	4	28	33	42	0
Rixon Wingrove, Phillies West	.298	48	178	28	53	17	2	5	37	22	38	0

INDIVIDUAL PITCHING

Pitcher, Club	W	L	ERA	G	GS	CG	SV	IP	H	R	ER	BB	SO
Jorge Rodriguez, Red Sox	6	2	1.91	11	6	0	0	47	35	13	10	9	58
Jose Appleton, Tigers West	6	2	2.66	11	7	0	0	44	33	17	13	25	34
Matt Givin, Marlins	5	1	2.74	10	5	0	1	46	36	18	14	15	35
Edward Paredes, Yankees West	3	4	2.74	10	7	0	0	43	42	22	13	13	33
Emmanuel Quinones, Tigers West	4	3	3.47	11	11	0	0	47	47	24	18	10	34
Anthony Escobar, Twins	5	2	3.83	11	6	0	0	42	33	18	18	13	37
Nathanael Heredia, Cardinals	5	4	3.83	12	7	0	0	49	43	27	21	35	48
Ludwin Jimenez, Cardinals	4	4	4.59	10	7	0	0	51	48	29	26	24	51
Blas Castano, Yankees West	2	5	4.67	11	7	0	0	52	67	31	27	11	30
Francis Ventura, Cardinals	1	2	5.18	11	5	0	0	49	65	36	28	19	31

ALL-STAR TEAM

C: Yoandy Rea, Tigers. **1B:** Rixon Wingrove, Phillies. **2B:** Junior Martina, Nationals. **3B:** Edgar Made, Phillies. **SS:** Orelvis Martinez, Blue Jays. **OF:** Kerry Carpenter, Tigers; Matthew Jarecki, Tigers; Alberto Rodriguez, Blue Jays. **DH:** Leandro Emiliani, Nationals. **RHP:** Matt Givin, Marlins. **LHP:** Jorge Rodriguez, Red Sox. **RP:** Kevin Milam, Yankees. **Most Valuable Player:** Kerry Carpenter, Tigers. **Manager of the Year:** Alan Mills, Orioles.

DEPARTMENT LEADERS

BATTING

OBP	Emiliani, Leandro, Nationals	.467
SLG	Carpenter, Kerry, Tigers West	.625
OPS	Carpenter, Kerry, Tigers West	1.033
R	Mesa Jr., Victor, Marlins	39
H	Made, Edgar, Phillies West	55
TB	Carpenter, Kerry, Tigers West	100
XBH	Carpenter, Kerry, Tigers West	28
2B	Wingrove, Rixon, Phillies West	17
3B	Martinez, Orelvis, Blue Jays	5
3B	Rojas, Johan, Phillies West	5
3B	Vargas, Alexander, Yankees East	5
HR	Carpenter, Kerry, Tigers West	9
RBI	Wingrove, Rixon, Phillies West	37
SAC	Corona, Kenedy, Mets	4
SAC	Flores, Wilfredo, Phillies East	4
BB	Rojas, Ronny, Yankees	36
HBP	Foster, Kaleb, Pirates	12
HBP	Shinn, Ryan, Mets	12
SO	Rojas, Ronny, Yankees	69
SB	Nunez, Nasim, Marlins	28
CS	Solarte, Jhon, Blue Jays	9
AB/SO	Carpenter, Kerry, Tigers West	8.9

FIELDING

C PCT	D'Orazio, Javier, Blue Jays	.988
PO	Meza, Julio, Rays	257
A	Longa, Cristhian, Cardinals	31
DP	Diaz, Geraldi, Nationals	4
DP	Meza, Julio, Rays	4
DP	O'Neill, Matt, Mets	4
E	Ascanio, Enyerberth, Yankees West	6
CS	Longa, Cristhian, Cardinals	18
SB	Shockley, Dylan, Pirates	33
PB	Morales, Jeferson, Twins	12
1B PCT	Zabowski, Cole, Tigers West	1
PO	Wingrove, Rixon, Phillies West	336
A	Wingrove, Rixon, Phillies West	17
DP	Emiliani, Leandro, Nationals	27
E	Wingrove, Rixon, Phillies West	8
2B PCT	Stevens, Eliezel, Braves	.949
PO	Burks, Jeremiah, Tigers West	61
PO	Mendoza, Ramon, Cardinals	61
A	Stevens, Eliezel, Braves	86
DP	Burks, Jeremiah, Tigers West	19
E	Stevens, Eliezel, Braves	7
3B PCT	Hernandez, Francisco, Cardinals	.896
PO	Hernandez, Francisco, Cardinals	31
A	Hernandez, Francisco, Cardinals	64
DP	Rojas, Ronny, Yankees	11
E	Rojas, Ronny, Yankees	14
SS PCT	Vargas, Alexander, Yankees East	.957
PO	Nunez, Nasim, Marlins	74
A	Nunez, Nasim, Marlins	128
DP	Grissom, Vaughn, Braves	22
E	Nunez, Nasim, Marlins	16
OF PCT	5 players	1.000
PO	Rodriguez, Alberto, Blue Jays	107
A	Maita, Angel, Red Sox	7
DP	12 players	2
E	Hurtado, Jorge, Nationals	5

PITCHING

G	Colon, Jeffrey, Mets	19
GS	Quinones, Emmanuel, Tigers West	11
GF	Schneider, Zach, Red Sox	14
SV	Milam, Kevin, Yankees West	8
W	Appleton, Jose, Tigers West	6
W	Rodriguez, Jorge, Red Sox	6
L	Carela, Juan, Yankees East	7
IP	Castano, Blas, Yankees West	52
H	Castano, Blas, Yankees West	67
R	Paniagua, Inohan, Cardinals	40
ER	Paniagua, Inohan, Cardinals	33
HB	Larrondo, Denny, Yankees	10
BB	Heredia, Nathanael, Cardinals	35
SO	Rodriguez, Jorge, Red Sox	58
SO/9	Rodriguez, Jorge, Red Sox	11.1
SO/9 (RP)	Robaina, Julio, Astros	12.7
BB/9	Palacios, Luis, Marlins	0.4
WP	Carela, Juan, Yankees East	14
BK	Heredia, Nathanael, Cardinals	6
HRA	Torres, Bryan, Pirates	7
BAA	Palacios, Luis, Marlins	0.180

MINOR LEAGUES

MINOR LEAGUES

	INTERNATIONAL LEAGUE	PACIFIC COAST LEAGUE	EASTERN LEAGUE	SOUTHERN LEAGUE	TEXAS LEAGUE	CALIFORNIA LEAGUE	CAROLINA LEAGUE	FLORIDA STATE LEAGUE	MIDWEST LEAGUE	SOUTH ATLANTIC LEAGUE
Best Batting Prospect	Jake Cronenworth, Durham	Yordan Alvarez, Round Rock	Colton Welker, Hartford	Drew Waters, Mississippi	Gavin Lux, Tulsa	Luis Campusano, Lake Elsinore	Jarren Duran, Salem	Trevor Larnach, Fort Myers	Wander Franco, Bowling Green	Canaan Smith, Charleston
Best Power Prospect	Bobby Bradley, Columbus	Yordan Alvarez, Round Rock	Bobby Dalbec, Portland	Luis Robert, Birmingham	Cody Thomas, Tulsa	Heliot Ramos, San Jose	Sam Huff, Down East	Dennis Garcia, Tampa	Will Benson, Lake County	Sam Huff, Hickory
Best Strike-Zone Judgment	LaMonte Wade, Rochester	Matt Thaiss, Salt Lake	Bobby Dalbec, Portland	Taylor Trammell, Chattanooga	Chas McCormick, Corpus Christi	Luis Gastro, Lancaster	Nolan Jones, Lynchburg	Taylor Walls, Charlotte	Wander Franco, Bowling Green	Terrin Vavra, Asheville
Best Baserunner	Anthony Alford, Buffalo	Kyle Tucker, Round Rock	Sam Haggerty, Binghamton	Luis Aviles Jr., Biloxi	Nick Heath, NW Arkansas	Jose Caballero, Visalia	Zach Davis, Myrtle Beach	Vidal Brujan, Charlotte	Reggie Pruitt, Lansing	Michael Gigliotti, Lexington
Fastest Baserunner	Oscar Mercado, Columbus	Jorge Mateo, Las Vegas	Johneshwy Fargas, Richmond	Magneuris Sierra, Jacksonville	Nick Heath, NW Arkansas	Matt Hearn, Lancaster	Jarren Duran, Salem	Vidal Brujan, Charlotte	Reggie Pruitt, Lansing	Michael Gigliotti, Lexington
Best Pitching Prospect	Mitch Keller, Indianapolis	Corbin Martin, Round Rock	Deivi Garcia, Trenton	Brusdar Graterol, Pensacola	Dustin May, Tulsa	MacKenzie Gore, Lake Elsinore	Jackson Kowar, Wilmington	Edward Cabrera, Jupiter	Humberto Mejia, Clinton	Luis Gil, Charleston
Best Fastball	Dylan Cease, Charlotte	Andres Munoz, El Paso	Melvin Adon, Richmond	Brusdar Graterol, Pensacola	Andres Munoz, Amarillo	Josiah Gray, Rancho Cucamonga	Jackson Kowar, Wilmington	Nate Pearson, Dunedin	Brailyn Marquez, South Bend	Luis Gil, Charleston
Best Breaking Pitch	Mitch Keller, Indianapolis	Dillon Maples, Iowa	Matt Manning, Erie	Brusdar Graterol, Pensacola	Dustin May, Tulsa	MacKenzie Gore, Lake Elsinore	DeMarcus Evans, Down East	Braxton Garrett, Jupiter	Jose Soriano, Burlington	Grayson Rodriguez, Delmarva
Best Changeup	Kolby Allard, Gwinnett	Jesus Luzardo, Las Vegas	Rico Garcia, Hartford	Sixto Sanchez, Jacksonville	Jackson Kowar, NW Arkansas	Garrett Schilling, Lancaster	Jackson Kowar, Wilmington	Junior Fernandez, Palm Beach	Joey Cantillo, Fort Wayne	Jesus Tona, Augusta
Best Control	Brendan McKay, Durham	Zac Gallen, New Orleans	Casey Mize, Erie	Brendan McKay, Montgomery	Darren McCaughan, Arkansas	Ljay Newsome, Modesto	Noah Zavolas, Carolina	Jordan Balazovic, Fort Myers	Alan Strong, Bowling Green	Jose Olaque, Rome
Best Reliever	Trevor Kelley, Pawtucket	Jimmie Sherfy, Reno	Ben Bowden, Hartford	Joel Kuhnel, Chattanooga	Andres Munoz, Amarillo	Tommy Doyle, Lancaster	Joe Barlow, Down East	Ryan Nutof, Daytona	Connor Bennett, Dayton	Jesus Tona, Augusta
Best Defensive C	Jake Rogers, Toledo	Andrew Knizner, Memphis	Jake Rogers, Erie	Tyler Stephenson, Chattanooga	Luis Torrens, Amarillo	Joey Bart, San Jose	Payton Henry, Carolina	Ben Rortvedt, Fort Myers	Will Banfield, Clinton	Rafael Marchan, Lakewood
Best Defensive 1B	Brian O'Grady, Louisville	John Nogowski, Memphis	Chris Gittens, Trenton	Dalton Kelly, Montgomery	Evan White, Arkansas	Yoel Yanqui, Visalia	Ryan Aguilar, Carolina	Lewin Diaz, Fort Myers	Brady Whalen, Peoria	Triston Casas, Greenville
Best Defensive 2B	Luis Arraez, Rochester	Isan Diaz, New Orleans	Sam Haggerty, Binghamton	Nick Madrigal, Birmingham	Jordan Cowan, Arkansas	Connor Kopach, Modesto	Yonny Hernandez, Down East	Vidal Brujan, Charlotte	Xavier Edwards, Fort Wayne	Greg Cullen, Rome
Best Defensive 3B	Ke'Bryan Hayes, Indianapolis	Sheldon Neuse, Las Vegas	Hunter Owen, Altoona	Drew Ellis, Jackson	Edwin Diaz, Midland	Joe Rizzo, Modesto	Ryan Dorow, Down East	Jonathan India, Daytona	Nolan Gorman, Peoria	Bobby Honeyman, West Virginia
Best Defensive SS	Jake Cronenworth, Durham	Luis Urias, El Paso	Andres Gimenez, Binghamton	Jazz Chisholm, Jackson	Gavin Lux, Tulsa	Nick Allen, Stockton	Anderson Tejeda, Down East	Cole Peterson, Lakeland	Jeremy Pena, Quad Cities	Ronny Mauricio, Columbia
Best Infield Arm	Jake Cronenworth, Durham	Jorge Mateo, Las Vegas	Bobby Dalbec, Portland	Jordan Gore, Pensacola	Edwin Diaz, Midland	Gabriel Arias, Lake Elsinore	Anderson Tejeda, Down East	Royce Lewis, Fort Myers	Justin Lopez, Fort Wayne	Nathan Eaton, Lexington
Best Defensive OF	Oscar Mercado, Columbus	Yonathan Daza, Albuquerque	Derek Hill, Erie	Cristian Pache, Mississippi	Dylan Carlson, Springfield	Heliot Ramos, San Jose	Leody Taveras, Down East	Aaron Whitefield, Fort Myers	Alek Thomas, Kane County	Justin Dean, Rome
Best Outfield Arm	Aristides Aquino, Louisville	Adolis Garcia, Memphis	Jose Azocar, Erie	Cristian Pache, Mississippi	Buddy Reed, Amarillo	Donovan Casey, Rancho Cucamonga	Seuly Matias, Wilmington	Travis Swaggerty, Bradenton	Jerar Encarnacion, Clinton	Hansel Moreno, Columbia
Most Exciting Player	Jake Cronenworth, Durham	Jorge Mateo, Las Vegas	Bobby Dalbec, Portland	Jo Adell, Mobile	Gavin Lux, Tulsa	Heliot Ramos, San Jose	Jarren Duran, Salem	Vidal Brujan, Charlotte	Wander Franco, Bowling Green	Canaan Smith, Charleston
Best Manager Prospect	Brady Williams, Durham	Fran Riordan, Las Vegas	Warren Schaeffer, Hartford	Blake Lalli, Jackson	Phillip Wellman, Amarillo	Denny Hocking, Modesto	Corey Ragsdale, Down East	Jeff Smith, Charlotte	Ray Hernandez, Quad Cities	Brooks Conrad, Lexington

BY BEN BADLER

Pitching fueled the Royals1 squad during the regular season. It also carried them in the decisive Game 5 of the DSL championship, with three pitchers combining for 14 strikeouts in a 1-0 shutout of the D-backs2 to win the title.

As a staff, the Royals issued the fewest walks in the league and had a team ERA of 3.10 that ranked third in the DSL. Righthander Luis de la Rosa, who turned 17 during the season, made an impact in his first year, striking out 52 batters and posting a 2.33 ERA in 38.2 innings.

Wilmin Candelario, who was Kansas City's top international signing in 2018, played for the Royals' other DSL team and was one of the standout prospects in the league. Candelario, a 17-year-old who signed for $847,500 out of

the Dominican Republic, showed tremendous defensive actions at shortstop while also hitting .315/.396/.505 in 49 games.

Rangers1 posted the best record in the league during the regular season and won the North division, thanks in large part to shortstop Luisangel Acuña, the younger brother of Braves outfielder Ronald Acuña Jr. The 17-year-old Acuña batted .342/.438/.455 in his first season.

Pirates 2 had the second-best regular season record to win the Northeast division, with third baseman Alexander Mojica batting .351/.468/.580 in his first year.

Other standout prospects in the league included Mariners shortstop Noelvi Marte, Twins outfielder Misael Urbina, Indians shortstop Angel Martinez and Dodgers righthander Jerming Rosario.

PLAYOFFS—Semifinals: Royals 1 defeated Rangers 1 2-1 and D-backs 2 defeated Pirates 2 2-0 in best-of-three series. **Finals:** Royals 1 defeated D-backs 2 3-2 in a best-of-five series.

MINOR LEAGUES

NORTH

Team	W	L	PCT	GB
Rangers 1	55	15	.786	—
Rays 2	46	24	.657	9
Dodgers Shoemaker	35	34	.507	19 ½
Pirates 1	34	36	.486	21
Cubs 1	34	37	.479	21 ½
Red Sox 2	31	39	.443	24
Indians	26	41	.388	27 ½
Indians/Brewers	17	52	.246	37 ½

NORTHWEST

Team	W	L	PCT	GB
Royals 1	41	29	.586	—
Astros	38	31	.551	2 ½
Dodgers Bautista	37	32	.536	3 ½
Red Sox 1	38	33	.535	3 ½
Braves	36	34	.514	5
Marlins	34	36	.486	7
Athletics	29	41	.414	12
Rays 1	27	44	.380	14 ½

SAN PEDRO

Team	W	L	PCT	GB
D-backs 2	45	26	.634	—
Phillies White	41	30	.577	4
Cubs 2	40	31	.563	5
Brewers	36	36	.500	9 ½
Mets 2	33	38	.465	12
Cardinals Red	32	39	.451	13
Rangers 2	30	41	.423	15
Tigers 1	28	44	.389	17 ½

SOUTH

Team	W	L	PCT	GB
Rockies	43	21	.672	—
Cardinals Blue	41	23	.641	2
Phillies Red	38	35	.603	4 ½
Mets 1	34	30	.531	9
Yankees	33	31	.516	10
Orioles 2	28	34	.452	14
Twins	24	40	.375	19
Angels	23	40	.365	19 ½
Nationals	22	42	.344	21

BASEBALL CITY

Team	W	L	PCT	GB
Reds	47	24	.662	—
White Sox	36	34	.514	10 ½
Blue Jays	35	35	.500	11 ½
Orioles 1	34	36	.486	12 ½
Padres	30	41	.423	17
D-backs 1	29	41	.414	17 ½

NORTHEAST

Team	W	L	PCT	GB
Pirates 2	56	16	.778	—
Mariners	35	37	.486	21
Tigers 2	34	38	.472	22
Giants	31	41	.431	25
Royals 2	30	41	.423	25 ½
Colorado	29	42	.408	26 ½

INDIVIDUAL BATTING LEADERS

Player, Team	AVG	G	AB	R	H	2B	3B	HR	RBI	BB	SO	SB
Jose Acosta, Reds	.403	43	149	48	60	12	5	3	24	30	32	24
Randy Romero, Pirates2	.376	62	218	52	82	13	5	1	35	17	15	36
Luis Matos, Giants	.362	55	235	60	85	24	2	7	47	19	30	20
Yohendrick Pinango, Cubs1	.358	62	240	43	86	20	0	0	36	27	20	27
Jeferson Espinal, D-backs1	.358	47	187	36	67	9	2	2	14	15	45	22
Johnabiell Laureano, White Sox	.357	59	210	43	75	15	3	6	36	28	43	6
Darlin Guzman, Reds	.357	47	185	40	66	18	6	6	41	10	44	5
Alexander Mojica, Pirates2	.351	55	174	37	61	14	1	8	46	37	34	2
Victor Bericoto, Giants	.344	60	227	58	78	15	1	5	41	53	56	10
Luisangel Acuna, Rangers1	.342	51	202	61	69	11	3	2	29	34	26	17

INDIVIDUAL PITCHING LEADERS

Player, Team	W	L	ERA	G	GS	CG	SV	IP	H	R	ER	BB	SO
Manuel Urias, Phillies Red	3	3	1.48	13	13	0	0	61	38	13	10	8	55
Juan Pichardo, Twins	4	1	1.69	14	11	0	0	59	55	17	11	9	65
Wilberson Liendo, Phillies Red	5	1	1.86	16	8	0	1	58	44	16	12	22	59
Martin Buitimea, Rangers1	5	3	1.89	12	12	0	0	62	44	13	13	16	59
Israel Puello, Phillies White	2	1	1.92	15	15	0	0	66	44	16	14	19	83
Angel Cuenca, Cardinals Red	5	1	2.00	12	12	0	0	63	40	21	14	18	60
Jesus Lugo, Padres	7	1	2.12	14	11	0	0	68	46	28	16	17	69
Kelvin Feliz, Cubs2	2	2	2.12	13	13	0	0	59	50	17	14	27	54
Cesar Angomas, Orioles1	2	5	2.14	14	14	0	0	63	55	29	15	32	64
Sergio Umana, Pirates2	9	1	2.39	13	13	0	0	64	63	22	17	8	59

Franchises Worth Honoring

Triple-A

NASHVILLE (PACIFIC COAST)

They are still the Nashville Sounds, just as they have been since the team arrived in 1978.

But there was a logical reason for the team to dub its 2019 theme as "Nashville Sounds Remastered." The Sounds adopted new logos and a new color scheme, and they added the Rangers as a new affiliate.

The Sounds rebranded without saying goodbye to their old nickname. It appears to have made a difference.

Many teams get a big boost from a new ballpark and then struggle to maintain that improvement. The Sounds are drawing more fans per game to First Tennessee Park than they did when the ballpark first opened in 2015. In 2019, 578,921 fans came to see the Sounds at home, an average of 8,631 fans per game. That was third-best in the minors and more than 600 more fans per game than they drew in 2015.

Double-A

TULSA (TEXAS)

The Tulsa Drillers' ONEOK Field has been one of the best in Double-A ever since it opened in 2010. But the Drillers have worked hard to ensure that the field remains as fresh and new as it was when it opened.

Even the best ballparks can start to grow a little stale to regular fans if there aren't measures to improve and update. ONEOK Field has the kids zones, upscale club seating and patio areas that fans expect. The club was one of the first teams in Double-A to have a ribbon board that went along the club level. In 2020, the team will update that ribbon board, add another one in right field and put in place a 2,100-square foot LED scoreboard as the cherry on top.

Class A

LEXINGTON (SOUTH ATLANTIC)

One of the Lexington Legends' core values is to give the community more than it expects.

The team strives to exceed those expectations. Like many teams, the Legends continually work in the community. They hold reading programs for local students, camping trips for Boy Scouts and Girl Scouts, as well as a variety of other programs to benefit charities around Lexington and its surrounding areas.

Living up to those values is easy because the Legends front office has developed deep roots in the community.

President and CEO Andy Shea began his time in Lexington as a ticket sales rep in 2005, rising to GM in 2008 and president in 2011. Executive vice president Gary Durbin has been working for the Legends since the team was founded in 2001. So has Shannon Kidd, the vice president for operations.

Short-Season

HUDSON VALLEY (NEW YORK-PENN)

At first glance, the Hudson Valley Renegades are your typical New York-Penn League team. They have a solid stadium that is maintained well, but Dutchess Stadium is 25 years old. They have a picturesque view, with trees and mountains visible beyond the outfield walls, but so do other parks.

What has made the Renegades one of the most successful franchises in the New York-Penn League are the deep connections between team and community. In addition to the fans who check out a game or two a year, the Renegades have a solid group of regulars at most every game. Hudson Valley was one of two teams in the league to top 4,000 fans per game in 2019. The Renegades have cleared that mark in nine of the past 10 seasons.

PREVIOUS 10 WINNERS

	TRIPLE-A	DOUBLE-A	CLASS A	SHORT-SEASON
2009:	Iowa (Pacific Coast)	New Hamshire (Eastern)	San Jose (California)	Tri-City (New York-Penn)
2010:	Louisville (International)	Corpus Christi (Texas)	Lynchburg (Carolina)	Idaho Falls (Pioneer)
2011:	Colo. Springs (Pacific Coast)	Harrisburg (Eastern)	Fort Wayne (Midwest)	Vancouver (Northwest)
2012:	Lehigh Valley (International)	N-West Arkansas (Texas)	Greenville (South Atlantic)	Billings (Pioneer)
2013:	Indianapolis (International)	Tulsa (Texas)	Clearwater (Florida State)	State College (NY-Penn)
2014:	Charlotte (International)	Montgomery (Southern)	West Michigan (Midwest)	Brooklyn (NY-Penn)
2015:	Salt Lake (Pacific Coast)	Richmond (Eastern)	Myrtle Beach (Carolina)	Grand Junction (Pioneer)
2016:	Round Rock (Pacific Coast)	Pensacola (Southern)	San Bernardino (California)	Pulaski (Appalachian)
2017:	Fresno (Pacific Coast)	Reading (Eastern)	Charleston (South Atlantic)	Hillsboro (Northwest)
2018:	Oklahoma City (Pacific Coast)	2008: Tennessee (Southern)	Lexington (South Atlantic)	Hudson Valley (NY-P)

BY KYLE GLASER & BILL MITCHELL

As is customary, the Arizona Fall League, which completed its 28th season in 2019, brought many of the game's brightest prospects to the desert. Twenty-two players on Baseball America's year-end Top 100 Prospects list populated the AFL's six rosters.

The significant changes brought to Major League Baseball's premier developmental league in 2019 were even more notable. This season, the AFL began play on Sept. 18, three weeks earlier than the customary Opening Day. This change was made to allow pitchers to more seamlessly transition from the regular season and to give players more of an offseason by finishing earlier in the fall. The downside of this change was an attendance decline for the season's first couple of weeks, with MLB's regular season still in progress in addition to the effects of the lingering summer heat and the lack of the customary winter visitors who don't arrive in the Phoenix area until later in the fall. The league's showcase events—the Fall Stars Game and Championship Game, which in past years were held after the World Series—could not be broadcast on the MLB Network due to programming conflicts.

Another change for the 2019 season was the inclusion of Mexican Pacific League teams in the early weeks of the schedule. That decision is likely to be re-evaluated after four of the 12 scheduled games were cancelled due to insufficient roster depth on the Mexican rosters in what was the early portion of their preseason.

The Salt River Rafters captured the league crown with a 5-1 victory over the Surprise Saguaros, highlighted by a fourth-inning grand slam off the bat of Salt River outfielder Jerar Encarnacion (Marlins), capping a breakout season by the Dominican native. Encarnacion's home run off Surprise reliever Sterling Sharp (Nationals) left his bat at 109.6 mph and traveled 418 feet, according to Statcast, and landed high up the grassy knoll beyond the left-field fence.

"I was talking to our hitting coach and he was giving me tips about that pitcher," Encarnacion said. "That he always keeps the ball down and I was looking for something up in the zone so I could make some good contact on it."

Encarnacion's slam overshadowed a dominant start by Surprise's Daniel Lynch (Royals). The 22-year-old lefty pitched three scoreless innings, allowed one hit, walked none and struck out three while allowing only one ball to leave the infield.

Lynch overpowered hitters with a 93-98 mph fastball and 84-88 mph power slider and slowed them down with an 81-84 mph changeup. He pounded the strike zone with all of his offerings, throwing 27 of 36 pitches for strikes and departed with a 1-0 lead.

Salt River struck once Lynch left the game, and its bullpen took care of the rest.

After starter Dakota Chalmers (Twins) walked the leadoff hitter in each of his three innings and was pulled with one out in the third, Ashton Goudeau (Rockies) tossed 2.2 scoreless innings of relief and fellow righthander Antonio Santos (Rockies) followed with two scoreless innings of his own. Alex Valverde (Rays) and Zach Neff (Twins) took care of the eighth, and Alex Vesia (Marlins) retired the side in the ninth to wrap up 6.2 scoreless innings from the Salt River bullpen.

Fall League Superlatives

Royce Lewis (Twins) was presented with the league's most valuable player award prior to the championship game, the second honor of the fall for the Salt River infielder. Lewis also earned MVP honors at the annual Fall Stars Game. Lewis batted .353/.411/.565 with three home runs in 85 at-bats in the AFL.

Having the chance to display his versatility by playing multiple positions for the Rafters was perhaps an even more significant accomplishment for Lewis. Primarily a shortstop through his three minor league seasons, Lewis saw most of his action in Arizona at third base, as well as a few games at second base and center field.

Glendale catcher Tyler Stephenson (Reds) was awarded the AFL's Dernell Stenson Sportsmanship Award prior to the championship game. Named in memory of the former AFL player who was murdered in 2003 while playing in the AFL with Scottsdale, the award has been given annually since 2004 to the league's player who best exemplifies unselfishness, hard work and leadership.

Scottsdale shortstop Andres Gimenez (Mets) was awarded the EyePromise Vizual EDGE Award as the league's leading hitter. In his second AFL season, the lefthanded hitter batted .371 in the fall, also leading all hitters in OPS at .999.

Mesa outfielder Greg Deichmann (Athletics) paced all hitters with nine home runs, while Surprise first baseman Brandon Wagner (Yankees) led in RBIs with 21. Salt River righthander Ashton Goudeau (Rockies) did not allow an earned run in 13 innings to top all qualifying pitchers in ERA.

MINOR LEAGUES

STANDINGS

East

	W	L	PCT	GB
Salt River Rafters	17	11	.607	-
Mesa Solar Sox	15	13	.536	2
Scottsdale Scorpions	12	17	.414	5.5

West

	W	L	PCT	GB
Surprise Saguaros	17	12	.586	-
Glendale Desert Dogs	14	15	.483	3
Peoria Javelinas	14	15	.483	3

INDIVIDUAL BATTING LEADERS
(Minimum 2 Plate Appearances/League Games)

Player, Team	AVG	G	AB	R	H	HR	RBI
Andres Gimenez, Scottsdale	.371	18	70	11	26	2	15
Alec Bohm, Scottsdale	.361	19	72	6	26	2	9
Royce Lewis, Salt River	.353	22	85	21	30	3	20
Brandon Marsh, Mesa	.328	19	67	13	22	2	11
Geraldo Perdomo, Salt River	.316	21	79	17	25	1	5
Seth Beer, Salt River	.315	19	73	9	23	1	12
Kyle Isbel, Surprise	.315	21	73	8	23	1	16
Jared Oliva, Peoria	.312	26	93	18	29	0	10
Alfonso Rivas, Mesa	.306	15	49	8	15	0	7
Ernie Clement, Mesa	.303	18	66	5	20	0	5

INDIVIDUAL PITCHING LEADERS
(Minimum .4 Innings Pitched/League Games)

Player, Team	W	L	ERA	IP	H	BB	SO
Ashton Goudeau, Salt River	1	0	0.00	13	4	0	18
Alex Wells, Surprise	3	0	0.57	16	15	2	15
Erich Uelmen, Mesa	1	0	0.75	12	5	3	9
Connor Seabold, Scottsdale	1	0	1.06	17	7	3	22
Penn Murfee, Peoria	2	1	1.23	22	16	5	30
Nick Neidert, Salt River	2	0	1.25	22	16	2	19
Andrew Lee, Surprise	0	0	1.38	13	9	2	12
Zach Neff, Salt River	1	0	1.38	13	6	1	12
Sterling Sharp, Surprise	2	1	1.50	24	11	11	24
Glenn Otto, Surprise	3	1	1.88	24	10	13	26

GLENDALE DESERT DOGS

Name	AVG	AB	R	H	2B	3B	HR	RBI	BB	SO	SB
Justin Yurchak	.375	8	2	3	2	0	0	1	1	1	0
Stuart Fairchild	.353	34	5	12	4	0	0	6	3	9	1
Tyler Stephenson	.347	49	9	17	7	0	0	6	5	7	0
Ivan Herrera	.324	34	3	11	2	0	0	6	5	4	0
David Fry	.300	50	7	15	5	0	1	6	5	13	0
Kramer Robertson	.269	26	5	7	1	0	0	4	7	4	0
Conner Capel	.266	79	12	21	3	0	3	9	7	20	1
Gavin Sheets	.250	72	9	18	5	0	0	8	8	23	0
Omar Estevez	.247	77	9	19	2	0	0	10	9	16	0
Michael Busch	.231	13	6	3	0	0	1	1	9	4	1
Jose Garcia	.213	61	8	13	3	0	1	9	5	12	3
Jeren Kendall	.210	62	4	13	1	0	2	9	4	31	4
Clayton Andrews	.200	10	1	2	0	0	0	2	0	1	0
Elehuris Montero	.200	50	5	10	3	1	0	3	9	17	1
Devin Mann	.191	47	8	9	4	0	1	6	11	11	0
Blake Rutherford	.179	78	12	14	4	3	2	7	11	21	1
Micker Adolfo	.167	54	5	9	0	0	4	6	5	27	0
Pablo Abreu	.146	41	2	6	1	0	0	2	0	23	0
Jake Gatewood	.143	42	6	6	1	0	0	1	4	15	0
Jonathan India	.133	60	5	8	1	1	3	10	8	21	1

Name	W	L	ERA	G	GS	SV	IP	H	BB	SO	AVG
Brett de Geus	0	0	0.00	8	0	2	9	2	2	11	.074
Kodi Whitley	0	1	1.64	9	0	4	11	8	1	13	.205
Victor Castaneda	3	1	1.99	6	5	0	23	13	6	29	.165
Quintin Torres-Costa	0	0	2.00	9	0	0	9	6	7	15	.188
Roel Ramirez	2	0	2.03	9	3	0	13	12	3	16	.222
Gerardo Carrillo	0	2	2.22	7	5	0	24	16	13	25	.193
Seth Elledge	0	1	3.00	8	0	1	9	9	2	12	.265
Marshall Kasowski	1	1	3.00	9	0	1	9	7	10	13	.206
Griffin Roberts	0	1	3.07	4	4	0	15	18	2	18	.300
Clayton Andrews	1	1	3.09	10	0	1	12	6	7	20	.146
Tyler Johnson	0	0	3.12	9	0	0	9	6	7	3	.200
Jordan Johnson	1	2	3.32	5	4	0	19	17	7	18	.230
Dauri Moreta	1	0	4.22	10	0	1	11	8	3	9	.211

Name	W	L	ERA	G	GS	SV	IP	H	BB	SO	AVG
Cory Thompson	1	0	5.06	9	0	0	11	13	3	8	.310
Bennett Sousa	1	0	5.59	9	0	0	10	11	1	12	.282
Robbie Hitt	1	0	5.73	8	0	0	11	8	6	14	.195
Vince Arobio	0	0	6.75	9	0	0	11	11	8	7	.256
Bernardo Flores	1	3	7.97	6	6	0	20	32	5	19	.360
Diomar Lopez	0	0	9.53	10	0	0	11	19	4	11	.373
Mitchell White	0	1	13.50	6	0	0	5	7	4	4	.333
Bobby Wahl	1	1	14.40	6	2	0	5	8	4	7	.348

MESA SOLAR SOX

Name	AVG	AB	R	H	2B	3B	HR	RBI	BB	SO	SB
Brandon Marsh	.328	67	13	22	5	1	2	11	7	15	4
Alfonso Rivas	.306	49	8	15	7	0	0	7	10	17	0
Ernie Clement	.303	66	5	20	2	1	0	5	6	13	1
Jahmai Jones	.302	53	9	16	5	0	2	10	6	16	7
Jose Azocar	.279	61	4	17	1	0	0	7	7	17	5
Jo Adell	.273	99	15	27	8	0	3	9	11	29	3
Greg Deichmann	.256	82	15	21	2	1	9	20	10	29	2
Derek Hill	.254	59	8	15	4	0	3	6	5	21	6
Zack Short	.234	77	9	18	4	0	1	4	15	26	3
Miguel Amaya	.224	49	5	11	3	0	0	7	5	12	0
Isaac Paredes	.208	53	11	11	2	1	2	8	12	13	0
Nolan Jones	.200	60	8	12	2	0	4	8	8	31	1
Jared Young	.196	46	4	9	2	0	1	4	7	8	2
Nick Allen	.194	62	4	12	1	0	0	6	4	18	0
Gavin Collins	.162	37	7	6	2	0	1	5	3	8	1
Franklin Torres	.118	17	1	2	0	0	0	0	3	9	0

Name	W	L	ERA	G	GS	SV	IP	H	BB	SO	AVG
Billy Lescher	0	0	0.00	4	0	0	4	2	3	6	.143
Jhenderson Hurtado	0	0	0.00	8	0	0	11	4	2	12	.114
Erich Uelmen	1	0	0.75	7	0	0	12	5	3	9	.135
Austin Warren	0	0	1.54	9	0	1	12	8	2	15	.186
Isaac Mattson	0	2	1.69	7	0	0	11	9	3	12	.237
Wladimir Pinto	0	0	1.80	4	0	0	5	3	1	5	.158
Scott Effross	0	0	1.80	8	0	0	10	12	1	9	.308
Jordan Minch	0	1	1.80	8	0	0	10	8	1	14	.216
Brady Feigl	1	1	1.86	8	0	0	10	13	2	14	.325
Daniel Gossett	3	1	2.57	5	5	0	14	10	3	12	.204
Kirk McCarty	2	1	3.00	6	5	0	24	17	6	19	.202
Jesus Zambrano	1	0	3.27	9	0	2	11	10	3	10	.238
Aaron Hernandez	2	0	3.38	6	6	0	19	19	6	25	.264
Alex Lange	0	1	3.72	8	0	0	10	8	3	13	.229
Anthony Castro	3	2	4.58	6	6	0	20	13	8	20	.188
Keegan Thompson	1	1	4.62	7	7	0	25	20	6	26	.217
Jonathan Teaney	0	0	5.23	8	0	0	10	12	9	11	.279
Argenis Angulo	0	0	5.68	8	0	2	6	7	5	7	.292
Nathan Bates	0	0	6.48	7	0	0	8	7	5	10	.226
Manuel Alvarez	1	0	8.53	7	0	1	6	4	8	7	.174
Will Vest	0	2	8.74	9	0	2	11	15	6	10	.326

PEORIA JAVELINAS

Name	AVG	AB	R	H	2B	3B	HR	RBI	BB	SO	SB
Marcus Wilson	.333	30	4	10	1	0	1	8	3	7	2
Logan Driscoll	.316	19	4	6	0	0	2	3	2	3	0
Jared Oliva	.312	93	18	29	11	2	0	10	14	19	11
Jarred Kelenic	.300	10	2	3	0	0	0	2	1	2	0
Julio Rodriguez	.288	52	7	15	4	0	0	10	8	10	4
Jarren Duran	.267	90	15	24	5	2	1	9	10	20	7
J.J. Matijevic	.255	102	9	26	2	1	4	17	8	35	1
C.J. Chatham	.243	70	12	17	5	0	0	9	5	16	4
Brett Netzer	.200	20	1	4	1	0	0	1	2	10	0
Joe Rizzo	.200	45	4	9	1	0	1	4	5	11	0
Jose Caballero	.190	63	8	12	2	0	1	2	9	21	8
Oneil Cruz	.190	42	6	8	1	0	0	1	7	21	1
Jeremy Pena	.183	93	11	17	5	1	1	10	6	35	2
Hudson Potts	.182	44	2	8	1	1	0	3	1	14	0
Owen Miller	.176	68	7	12	1	0	1	7	2	15	1
Colton Shaver	.175	57	4	10	4	1	1	6	9	23	0
Jason Delay	.094	32	3	3	1	0	0	1	4	9	0
Luis Campusano	.077	13	1	1	0	0	0	2	2	6	0

Name	W	L	ERA	G	GS	SV	IP	H	BB	SO	AVG
Adrian Morejon	0	0	0.00	1	1	0	2	1	1	3	.143
Nick Mears	0	0	0.00	8	0	1	9	2	5	11	.077
Aaron Fletcher	0	0	0.00	8	0	1	9	6	1	15	.194

Name	W	L	ERA	G	GS	SV	IP	H	BB	SO	AVG
Reggie Lawson	1	0	0.82	3	2	0	11	3	2	14	.083
Blake Cederlind	1	1	1.13	8	0	0	8	4	7	9	.143
Sam Delaplane	0	1	1.13	6	0	2	8	5	1	15	.172
Penn Murfee	2	1	1.23	6	6	0	22	16	5	30	.195
Raymond Kerr	0	0	1.93	6	0	0	9	6	6	9	.143
Cody Ponce	2	1	2.35	5	5	0	23	26	3	27	.283
Forrest Whitley	3	2	2.88	6	6	0	25	22	9	32	.237
Elliot Ashbeck	2	0	2.92	6	0	0	12	7	4	13	.163
Beau Sulser	0	1	3.14	6	2	0	14	14	9	13	.250
Jacob Nix	0	0	3.38	1	1	0	3	5	1	3	.357
Jojanse Torres	0	1	3.38	7	0	3	8	7	5	16	.250
Tanner Houck	3	2	3.47	6	6	0	23	20	12	26	.238
Reiss Knehr	0	2	4.09	7	0	0	11	10	10	14	.250
Jhonathan Diaz	0	0	4.35	8	0	0	10	11	6	16	.282
Bryan Mata	0	0	5.23	8	0	1	10	5	11	10	.156
Yoan Aybar	0	1	6.75	7	0	0	8	5	6	9	.172
Cody Deason	0	1	6.75	6	0	0	8	11	6	10	.355
Carlos Sanabria	0	0	9.00	8	0	0	9	13	4	12	.325
Osvaldo Hernandez	0	1	15.63	6	0	0	6	13	7	7	.406

SALT RIVER RAFTERS

Name	AVG	AB	R	H	2B	3B	HR	RBI	BB	SO	SB
Ronaldo Hernandez	.359	39	5	14	3	0	1	5	2	9	0
Royce Lewis	.353	85	21	30	9	0	3	20	9	22	5
Josh Lowe	.327	52	11	17	4	1	2	11	5	16	4
Geraldo Perdomo	.316	79	17	25	3	1	1	5	13	21	2
Seth Beer	.315	73	9	23	5	1	1	12	5	14	1
Brian Serven	.283	46	4	13	3	1	2	9	0	13	0
Victor Victor Mesa	.271	70	10	19	4	0	0	6	3	12	3
Jerar Encarnacion	.269	67	10	18	2	0	3	16	5	28	0
Jake McCarthy	.265	68	8	18	4	1	1	6	6	20	4
Jose Devers	.262	42	5	11	3	0	0	1	1	15	5
Vidal Brujan	.256	82	12	21	3	4	2	10	15	17	4
Luke Raley	.244	82	14	20	5	1	3	14	4	21	0
Colton Welker	.229	83	10	19	2	0	0	7	12	13	3
Freddy Fermin	.188	16	1	3	0	0	0	1	0	4	0
Roberto Ramos	.162	37	6	6	0	0	2	7	6	16	0
Ben Rortvedt	.111	9	0	1	0	0	0	0	0	2	0
Bret Boswell	.098	41	3	4	1	0	0	1	5	16	0

Name	W	L	ERA	G	GS	SV	IP	H	BB	SO	AVG
Alex Vesia	0	0	0.00	9	0	1	10	4	2	16	.114
Ashton Goudeau	1	0	0.00	6	0	0	13	4	0	18	.095
Alexander Guillen	2	0	0.90	7	0	2	10	6	1	13	.171
Alex Valverde	1	0	0.90	9	0	1	10	4	3	10	.129
Matt Brill	0	0	0.93	9	0	0	10	6	2	4	.188
Nick Neidert	2	0	1.25	5	5	0	22	16	2	19	.205
Zach Neff	1	0	1.38	9	0	1	13	6	1	12	.133
Simon Rosenblum-Larson	0	0	2.13	9	0	0	13	9	10	12	.196
Ryan Castellani	1	0	2.16	5	5	0	17	16	7	20	.242
Antonio Santos	1	1	2.77	8	0	0	13	18	2	16	.321
Miguel Aguilar	1	0	2.92	10	0	3	12	14	1	17	.275
Emilio Vargas	1	0	3.00	3	1	0	6	5	0	9	.208
Cody Reed	1	1	4.09	5	4	0	11	15	4	17	.306
Dakota Chalmers	1	2	5.09	6	6	0	18	17	12	25	.239
Matt Peacock	1	0	6.00	1	1	0	3	5	0	4	.357
Drew Strotman	2	2	6.43	6	6	0	21	24	8	18	.279
Moises Gomez	0	1	6.55	9	0	0	11	14	9	15	.298
Jovani Moran	0	1	7.00	9	0	0	9	7	12	14	.219
Shane Baz	0	2	8.18	8	1	0	11	13	8	14	.310
C.J. Carter	0	0	8.18	8	0	0	11	12	3	12	.273
Vincenzo Aiello	1	1	10.64	9	0	0	11	15	8	11	.341

SCOTTSDALE SCORPIONS

Name	AVG	AB	R	H	2B	3B	HR	RBI	BB	SO	SB
Andres Gimenez	.371	70	11	26	5	2	2	15	4	15	2
Alec Bohm	.361	72	6	26	6	0	2	9	5	16	0
Joey Bart	.333	30	9	10	1	0	4	10	9	7	0
Nick Maton	.333	12	1	4	1	0	1	2	1	6	0
Logan Warmoth	.295	61	10	18	6	0	1	8	9	22	1
Trey Harris	.281	57	7	16	4	0	2	5	7	12	2
Ali Sanchez	.262	42	5	11	2	0	0	5	6	8	0
Josh Stephen	.250	36	4	9	0	1	0	2	3	7	0
Cullen Large	.230	61	5	14	3	0	1	8	7	12	0
Greyson Jenista	.214	42	6	9	2	0	0	3	6	20	0
Justin Dean	.200	45	7	9	0	0	0	3	7	18	3
Jalen Miller	.188	32	2	6	1	0	1	1	1	14	1

Name	AVG	AB	R	H	2B	3B	HR	RBI	BB	SO	SB
Luis Carpio	.188	32	4	6	2	0	0	0	4	8	0
Mickey Moniak	.186	70	5	13	4	2	0	5	4	17	3
Heliot Ramos	.185	65	9	12	2	0	1	6	5	23	1
Jacob Heyward	.184	38	1	7	4	1	1	4	6	18	1
Patrick Mazeika	.174	46	2	8	1	1	0	6	2	12	0
Jose Gomez	.120	25	0	3	0	0	0	1	0	10	0
Garrison Schwartz	.103	29	3	3	0	0	0	6	0	15	0
Kevin Smith	.095	63	3	6	2	1	0	0	3	38	1
Ricardo Genoves	.071	14	0	1	1	0	0	1	0	8	0

Name	W	L	ERA	G	GS	SV	IP	H	BB	SO	AVG
Jordan Humphreys	1	0	0.77	4	0	0	12	8	4	8	.222
JoJo Romero	1	0	0.84	8	0	0	11	6	4	5	.158
Ryley Gilliam	0	0	0.96	7	0	0	9	8	2	11	.205
Connor Seabold	1	0	1.06	4	4	0	17	7	3	22	.125
Mike Ellenbest	0	0	1.59	8	0	0	11	9	6	9	.225
Bradley Roney	1	0	1.59	8	0	1	11	3	7	16	.088
Frank Rubio	0	1	1.64	9	2	1	11	10	0	9	.238
Blake Taylor	0	1	2.00	7	0	2	9	5	2	11	.156
Spencer Howard	1	1	2.11	6	6	0	21	10	10	27	.137
Bryce Tucker	1	1	3.00	6	0	0	9	8	6	14	.242
Jackson Rees	1	0	3.24	7	0	1	8	9	1	13	.265
Connor Johnstone	2	3	3.27	6	6	0	22	24	4	19	.289
David Peterson	0	1	3.46	4	4	0	13	18	8	13	.327
Tristan Beck	1	2	3.63	6	6	0	22	24	7	23	.282
Zach Warren	0	0	3.86	5	0	1	5	1	4	7	.063
Julian Merryweather	0	1	4.50	4	0	0	6	4	2	8	.190
Daysbel Hernandez	0	0	4.76	8	0	1	11	9	10	6	.225
Tyler Schimpf	0	0	5.40	7	1	0	10	9	8	10	.231
Graham Spraker	2	2	5.68	8	0	0	13	16	6	13	.296
Brandon White	0	1	8.31	7	0	1	9	12	10	7	.324
Maverik Buffo	0	3	14.46	8	0	0	9	16	10	9	.372

SURPRISE SAGUAROS

Name	AVG	AB	R	H	2B	3B	HR	RBI	BB	SO	SB
Jakson Reetz	.333	27	5	9	2	0	1	4	4	9	1
Kyle Isbel	.315	73	8	23	4	1	1	16	14	20	6
Matt Whatley	.281	32	4	9	1	1	0	6	5	11	1
Luis Garcia	.276	76	6	21	4	2	0	6	8	13	2
T.J. Nichting	.273	22	3	6	1	0	0	0	1	3	1
Bubba Thompson	.254	71	13	18	1	0	3	9	8	25	5
Nick Banks	.250	56	9	14	3	0	3	8	3	20	2
Cole Freeman	.233	43	8	10	1	0	0	5	3	9	1
Mason McCoy	.219	64	8	14	2	1	0	5	11	18	1
Brandon Wagner	.214	70	10	15	4	0	2	21	12	27	0
Donny Sands	.204	54	5	11	3	0	1	9	8	12	0
Rylan Bannon	.200	85	9	17	1	0	1	9	6	18	3
Travis Jones	.200	40	6	8	1	0	0	3	11	20	2
Jax Biggers	.169	59	14	10	0	0	0	2	12	11	6
Brewer Hicklen	.149	47	6	7	1	0	1	3	8	26	4
Josh Stowers	.131	61	6	8	0	0	0	5	13	27	4
KJ Harrison	.125	16	2	2	0	0	1	1	2	4	0
Gabriel Cancel	.094	32	1	3	0	0	0	1	2	10	0

Name	W	L	ERA	G	GS	SV	IP	H	BB	SO	AVG
Pearson McMahan	0	0	0.00	2	0	0	2	2	1	4	.222
Jacob Condra-Bogan	0	0	0.00	6	0	3	7	2	4	5	.091
Josh Advocate	0	0	0.00	9	0	0	3	1	3	9	.081
Alex Wells	3	0	0.57	9	1	0	16	15	2	15	.263
Aaron McGarity	1	0	0.79	10	0	0	11	6	1	15	.150
Tad Ratliff	0	0	1.08	9	0	2	8	6	0	10	.188
Andrew Lee	0	0	1.38	9	0	0	13	9	2	12	.196
Sterling Sharp	2	1	1.50	6	6	0	24	11	11	24	.143
Glenn Otto	3	1	1.88	6	6	0	24	10	13	26	.128
Cody Carroll	0	0	2.08	9	0	0	9	7	7	11	.219
Dean Kremer	1	1	2.37	6	5	0	19	13	4	23	.206
Cole Uvila	2	0	2.53	9	0	0	11	10	7	16	.244
David Lebron	0	0	3.29	9	0	1	14	9	5	12	.188
Daniel Lynch	1	1	3.86	4	4	0	14	16	4	19	.276
Daniel Bies	0	1	3.97	10	0	0	11	14	2	14	.304
Trevor Oaks	0	2	4.50	7	1	0	12	14	3	11	.304
Nick Snyder	2	0	5.40	9	0	1	10	8	4	7	.216
A.J. Alexy	0	2	6.75	3	3	0	8	11	6	6	.367
Daniel Tillo	1	1	6.94	10	0	1	12	12	7	11	.273
Derek Craft	0	0	7.71	3	0	0	2	4	2	0	.400
Nick Raquet	0	2	8.49	9	0	0	12	14	9	12	.311
Noah Bremer	1	0	9.95	3	3	0	6	11	7	7	.393

INDEPENDENT
LEAGUES

Merger Marks End Of An Era For Indy Ball

BY J.J. COOPER

Not long ago it seemed reasonable to think that the biggest four independent leagues—American Association, Atlantic, Can-Am and Frontier—might one day field close to 60 teams.

When the 2020 season begins, however, those leagues will be fortunate if they field 40 teams, combined.

The Kansas City T-Bones, a long-running stalwart of the American Association, were battling being evicted from their stadium because of more than $700,000 in back-rent and utility payments. The Can-Am League's Ottawa Champions had their lease cancelled because of more than $400,000 in unpaid rent.

And the Frontier League crowned the River City Rascals as the league champions in a celebration that was also a fond farewell. The Rascals owners announced in August that they were shutting down at the end of the season.

Coming into the 2010s, indy ball seemed to be growing expeditiously. Coming into the 2020s, the picture is much less promising.

In the 1990s, indy ball flourished by coming into markets that were no longer viable affiliated markets, either because of territorial restrictions or because their ballparks were no longer sufficient to meet required standards.

Now, the tables have turned. Year after year, indy ball owners are deciding that the finances of collegiate wood-bat leagues are more attractive. While there are fewer home games in a shorter season, the college players are unpaid and worker's compensation costs are dramatically reduced. Over the past few years, an announcement of an indy ball team's departure is often followed by the announcement of a wood-bat team filling the stadium.

That has led to the biggest shakeup indy ball has seen since the American Association split from the Northern League prior to 2006. Ever since the Northern League folded after the 2010 season, there have been four big indy leagues in terms of attendance. Now, there are three. The Can-Am League and the Frontier League announced that they will merge for the 2020 season. The combined, 14-team league will continue to operate under the Frontier League banner.

The River City Rascals won the Frontier League title in their final season.

COURTESY OF RIVER CITY RASCALS

The move provides stability going forward that would have been lacking without the merger. The footprint of the league grows significantly—which also opens wider possibilities for expansion. The trade-off will be likely higher travel costs.

The move was needed for both leagues, but especially for the Can-Am League. A decade ago, the league had expanded to seven teams (with an eighth slot filled by a New York State League all-star team). Going into 2020, with Ottawa losing the lease to its stadium because of unpaid bills, the league was looking at potentially having just five teams. The Frontier League once had 13 franchises, but it was looking at a nine-team league for 2020. The merger makes this the largest league in independent baseball.

The news wasn't all bad in 2019. The Atlantic League welcomed the High Point Rockers, and the American Association saw the Milwaukee Milkmen debut. The United States Professional Baseball League continued succeeding at developing players. Righthander Randy Dobnak became the league's biggest success story. Signed by the Twins out of the USPBL in 2018, Dobnak made his MLB debut in 2019 and started a playoff game.

INDEPENDENT LEAGUES

Keon Barnum Rediscovers His Power

When Keon Barnum was in high school, he was the hitter pitchers feared. He had the power to change a game with one long fly ball.

But during his time in the White Sox system, Barnum stopped being the batter who pitchers had to worry about. Early in his pro career, he struck out like a power hitter, but his near top-of-the-scale raw power rarely played in games. He didn't reach double-digits in home runs in a season until his sixth season in pro ball. And while he did hit 18 home runs in 2017 and 16 with Double-A Birmingham in 2018, the improved power came with batting averages that hovered around .200.

Keon Barnum

So it wasn't all that surprising that, when Barnum reached minor league free agency after the 2018 season, no affiliated professional teams called.

That didn't stop Chicago Dogs manager Butch Hobson, who wanted Barnum. And as a result, the Dogs watched him revert into a middle-of-the-order masher once more.

After hitting 63 home runs in 606 minor league games, Barnum hit 31 homers in just 98 independent league games this year. He broke the American Association's single-season home run record while cutting his strikeout rate and raising his batting average to .311. For that, Barnum is Baseball America's 2019 Independent League Player of the Year.

"A lot of guys go to their first year of independent ball and they relax," Hobson said.

"I think, in my evaluation of him, he relaxed enough to be able to accept, 'This is the kind of hitter I need to become.' I give a great deal of credit to (hitting coach) D.J. Boston. He and Keon clicked."

When he felt lost at the plate, Barnum went back to what had worked for him in high school. Barnum went back to a version of the stance that worked for him when he was playing travel ball as an amateur. The bat rests on his shoulder in an upright stance. Then, as the pitcher begins his delivery, Barnum sinks into his legs to begin his load.

That sinking action started to get Barnum more on time with his swing. Working with Boston helped as well, as the 6-foot-5 Barnum was able to relate to the 6-foot-7 Boston, who knows the challenges of being a big man with a big swing.

Even more important was Barnum's newfound opposite-field power. The book on Barnum used to be simple: Pitch him so far inside with fastballs that a swing was, at worst, a long foul ball and a harmless strike. And once he swung at that, go soft and away and watch him turn himself into a corkscrew.

Now that he's developed the ability to stay back and drive the outside pitch to the opposite field, his plate coverage has significantly improved.

In 2018, just two of his home runs were opposite-field shots. In 2019, more than half of his home runs were to left or left-center

PREVIOUS WINNERS

1996: Darryl Motley, OF, Fargo-Moorhead (Northern)
1997: Mike Meggers, OF, Winnipeg/Duluth (Northern)
1998: Morgan Burkhart, 1B, Richmond (Frontier)
1999: Carmine Cappucio, OF, New Jersey (Northeast)
2000: Anthony Lewis, 1B, Duluth-Superior (Northern)
2001: Mike Warner, OF, Somerset (Atlantic)
2002: Bobby Madritsch, LHP, Winnipeg (Northern)
2003: Jason Shelley, RHP, Rockford (Frontier)
2004: Victor Rodriguez, SS, Somerset (Atlantic)
2005: Eddie Lantigua, 3B, Quebec (Can-Am)
2006: Ian Church, OF, Kalamazoo (Frontier)
2007: Darryl Brinkley, OF, Calgary (Northern)

2008: Patrick Breen, OF, Orange County (Golden)
2009: Greg Porter, OF, Wichita (American Association)
2010: Beau Torbert, OF, Sioux Falls (American Association)
2011: Chris Collabello, 1B, Worcester (Can-Am League)
2012: Blake Gailen, OF, Lancaster (Atlantic)
2013: C.J. Ziegler, 1B, Wichita (American Association)
2014: Balbino Fuenmayor, 1B, Quebec (Can-Am League)
2015: Joe Maloney, OF, Rocland (Can-Am League)
2016: Art Charles, 1B, New Jersey (Can-Am League)
2017: Alonzo Harris, OF, York (Atlantic League)
2018: Jordany Valdespin, INF, Long Island (Atlantic League)

INDEPENDENT LEAGUES

AMERICAN ASSOCIATION

The St. Paul Saints lost in the American Association championship series four times, including a loss to Kansas City in 2018. St. Paul finally got to celebrate its first American Association crown, as the flagship franchise of the league swept Sioux City in the league championship series. The Saints also finished with the best record in the regular season while drawing more than 8,000 fans per game in their second season in their new ballpark.

North Division	W	L	PCT	GB
St. Paul Saints	64	36	.640	—
Fargo-Moorhead Redhawks	63	37	.630	1
Chicago Dogs	59	41	.590	5
Winnipeg Goldeyes	57	43	.570	7
Gary SouthShore RailCats	40	59	.404	23.5
Milwaukee Milkmen	38	62	.380	26

South Division	W	L	PCT	GB
Kansas City T-Bones	58	42	.580	—
Cleburne Railroaders	57	43	.570	1
Sioux City Explorers	57	43	.570	1
Lincoln Saltdogs	40	59	.404	17.5
Sioux Falls Canaries	38	62	.380	20
Texas AirHogs	28	72	.280	20

PLAYOFFS—Semifinals: St. Paul defeated Fargo-Moorhead 3-2 and Sioux City defeated by Kansas City 3-1 in best-of-five series. **Finals:** St. Paul defeated Sioux City 3-0 in best-of-five series.

Attendance: St. Paul Saints 394,970; Winnipeg Goldeyes 195,787; Lincoln Saltdogs 168,394; Gary SouthShore RailCats 167,887; Chicago Dogs 166,672; Fargo-Moorhead RedHawks 161,857; Kansas City T-Bones 156,058; Sioux Falls Canaries 114,452; Cleburne Railroaders 78,624; Texas AirHogs 59,471; Milwaukee Milkmen 59,459; Sioux City Explorers 51,618.

All-Star Team: C: John Nester, Cleburne Railroaders. **1B:** Keon Barnum, Chicago Dogs. **2B:** Alay Lago, Sioux Falls Canaries. **SS:** Nate Samson, Sioux City Explorers. **3B:** Chase Simpson, Cleburne Railroaders. **OF:** Tim Colwell, Fargo-Moorhead RedHawks,Dan Motl, St. Paul Saints and Victor Roache, Chicago Dogs. **DH:** Brady Shoemaker, St. Paul Saints. **SP:** Mitchell Lambson, Winnipeg Goldeyes. **RP:** Geoff Broussard, Fargo-Moorhead. **Player of the Year:** Keon Barnum, 1B, Chicago. **Manager of the Year:** Jim Bennett, Fargo-Moorhead. **Rookie of the Year:** Mike Hart, Sioux Falls.

BATTING LEADERS

Player, Team	Team	AVG	AB	R	H	HR	RBI
Daniel Robertson	CLE	.339	289	73	98	6	53
Alay Lago	SF	.339	369	58	125	13	57
Jonathan Moroney	2 teams	.331	296	44	98	6	34
Dan Motl	StP	.328	366	74	120	4	42
Nate Samson	SC	.324	404	60	131	6	67
Leobaldo Pina	F-M	.323	368	53	119	10	61
Tim Colwell	F-M	.321	405	71	130	5	54
Brady Shoemaker	StP	.319	357	70	114	18	71
Wes Darvill	WPG	.317	350	66	111	7	34
Dylan Tice	KC	.316	358	64	113	4	38

PITCHING LEADERS

Player, Team	Team	W	L	ERA	IP	H	BB	SO
Justin Sinibaldi	GARY	6	7	2.75	118	106	45	76
Angel Ventura	MIL	6	10	2.76	131	111	36	108
Luke Westphal*	CHI	11	2	2.82	89	62	35	123
Ryan Williams	F-M	8	1	2.93	80	90	6	51
Mitchell Lambson*	WPG	13	4	3.11	151	153	33	133
Michael Tamburino	F-M	7	6	3.12	113	97	30	110
D.J. Snelten*	CHI	7	3	3.12	118	99	43	112
Tyler Pike*	F-M	8	3	3.20	87	82	34	92
Carlos Sierra	SC	8	1	3.21	95	71	40	96
Jesus Sanchez	CLE	10	4	3.31	128	140	15	78

CHICAGO DOGS

Name	AVG	AB	R	H	HR	RBI	BB	SO	SB
Brett Milazzo*	.385	13	3	5	0	1	3	2	0
Kelly Dugan*	.313	208	36	65	6	35	21	40	0
Keon Barnum*	.311	373	67	116	31	90	52	91	0
Victor Roache	.309	362	67	112	24	79	47	106	5
Gustavo Pierre	.308	237	34	73	7	33	22	52	13
David Olmedo-Barrera*	.300	353	69	106	9	47	27	61	10
Jordan Dean	.296	371	61	110	15	55	30	60	12
Edwin Arroyo#	.291	357	60	104	2	55	37	39	3
Trey Vavra	.279	340	66	95	7	56	40	48	7
Tony Rosselli	.269	309	51	83	12	48	25	82	4
Larry Balkwill	.240	50	7	12	1	5	3	13	0
Rey Gonzalez	.225	178	32	40	4	20	21	48	1
Mitchell Kranson*	.221	131	13	29	2	15	12	17	0
Harrison Smith	.207	116	23	24	2	12	12	48	2

Name	W	L	ERA	G	SV	IP	H	BB	SO
Kyle Halbohn	2	0	1.98	36	14	41	30	12	46
Casey Crosby*	3	1	1.99	36	0	41	24	30	64
Rich Mascheri	6	3	2.52	44	1	50	39	26	54
Justin Goossen-Brown	1	1	2.73	14	0	33	37	6	18
Luke Westphal*	11	2	2.82	17	0	89	62	35	123
D.J. Snelten*	7	3	3.12	20	0	118	99	43	112
Harrison Smith	0	0	3.48	20	0	21	16	12	18
Austin Wright*	7	8	4.08	20	0	104	91	47	135
Pedro Echemendia	0	1	4.32	8	0	17	22	4	14
Jake Dahlberg*	9	6	4.49	19	0	110	109	31	100
Carlos Zambrano	4	1	5.16	35	0	61	78	18	51
Josh Goossen-Brown	2	3	6.84	22	4	26	40	17	20
Luke Wilkins	2	2	7.29	16	0	21	28	8	25
Ben Allison	0	2	7.50	20	1	30	38	16	23
Brandon Shimo	1	0	7.71	13	0	12	12	7	20
Trevor Simms	1	4	7.71	10	0	35	42	20	31
Wes Torrez	1	4	7.91	9	0	39	50	11	24

CLEBURNE RAILROADERS

Name	AVG	AB	R	H	HR	RBI	BB	SO	SB
Daniel Robertson	.339	289	73	98	6	53	42	38	21
Jared Reaves	.308	26	4	8	0	1	5	3	0
Angel Reyes	.306	160	35	49	8	33	28	26	11
Jonathan Rodriguez	.287	94	14	27	2	14	11	24	1
Zach Nehrir	.285	382	71	109	12	60	45	102	13
Grant Buck*	.280	218	38	61	1	32	23	64	0
John Nester	.277	321	55	89	16	63	31	80	0
KC Huth	.276	272	44	75	6	43	17	64	8
Chase Simpson#	.272	364	64	99	20	93	72	99	8
Nick Rotola	.265	249	47	66	1	30	18	68	19
Logan Trowbridge	.259	220	33	57	0	25	35	43	7
Ryan Brett#	.257	249	37	64	8	28	15	39	7
Kenny Meimerstorf	.231	130	16	30	3	20	21	33	0
Angel Rosa	.227	128	20	29	3	13	10	34	3
Hunter Clanin	.227	247	38	56	12	42	19	74	6
Audie Afenir	.222	27	4	6	2	4	1	7	0

Name	W	L	ERA	G	SV	IP	H	BB	SO
Tyler Wilson	3	2	1.71	41	24	42	33	17	59
John Shull	0	0	2.38	8	0	11	12	2	9
Michael Gunn*	5	0	3.12	15	0	78	67	30	63
Jesus Sanchez	10	4	3.31	21	0	128	140	15	78
Daniel Hurtado	1	0	3.48	17	0	21	13	10	20
Charlie Gillies	6	7	3.54	18	0	109	118	25	89
Nefi Ogando	4	5	3.56	34	0	66	68	30	61
Martire Garcia*	2	2	3.68	27	2	37	26	28	47
Edward Cruz	0	3	3.86	19	1	21	15	20	30
Bryan Saucedo	2	2	3.97	12	0	23	25	17	21
D.J. Sharabi	0	2	4.17	30	1	41	40	13	44
Eudis Idrogo*	9	5	4.46	22	0	113	127	42	102
Stephen Johnson	8	3	4.52	12	0	64	62	25	48
Jared Wilson	0	1	5.11	10	0	12	6	13	12
Braden Pearson*	3	3	5.14	45	0	42	50	10	33
Greyfer Eregua	3	2	5.80	9	0	36	46	6	26
Hayden Shenefield	0	2	7.50	12	0	12	16	6	10

FARGO-MOORHEAD REDHAWKS

Name	AVG	AB	R	H	HR	RBI	BB	SO	SB
Leobaldo Pina	.323	368	53	119	10	61	34	66	6
Tim Colwell*	.321	405	71	130	5	54	41	50	20
Brennan Metzger	.314	388	69	122	8	41	60	77	18

INDEPENDENT LEAGUES

Name	AVG	AB	R	H	HR	RBI	BB	SO	SB
Correlle Prime	.312	385	78	120	18	77	28	85	7
Devan Ahart*	.308	399	67	123	7	64	39	43	14
Chris Jacobs	.300	350	63	105	17	76	39	101	1
T.J. Bennett*	.283	314	47	89	12	54	36	81	4
Carlos Garcia#	.264	53	7	14	2	8	4	9	3
Brian Olson	.251	219	27	55	2	26	33	58	1
Yhoxian Medina	.250	292	44	73	4	30	18	44	4
Daniel Comstock	.238	151	23	36	10	28	14	46	0
Wilfredo Gimenez	.229	35	4	8	1	2	2	12	0
Joe Becht*	.220	50	10	11	2	4	9	17	0

Name	W	L	ERA	G	SV	IP	H	BB	SO
Geoff Broussard	1	2	1.81	42	28	45	40	15	47
Ryan Williams	8	1	2.93	13	0	80	90	6	51
Brent Jones	0	4	3.10	39	0	41	33	18	53
Michael Tamburino	7	6	3.12	19	0	113	97	30	110
Tyler Pike*	8	3	3.19	15	0	87	82	34	92
Carter Hope	2	1	3.42	40	1	55	53	17	36
Joe Filomeno*	6	3	3.44	44	4	55	50	21	64
Michael Hope	8	0	3.47	31	1	60	54	25	46
J.R. Bunda	0	1	3.94	13	1	16	19	4	11
Bret Helton	6	7	4.40	17	0	90	92	47	64
Luke Wilkins	4	2	4.46	14	1	36	39	8	35
Sebastian Kessay*	8	1	4.75	22	0	91	88	58	96
Taylor Bloye	4	3	4.76	19	0	57	69	32	39
Will Solomon*	1	2	5.63	7	0	32	49	12	26

GARY SOUTHSHORE RAILCATS

Name	AVG	AB	R	H	HR	RBI	BB	SO	SB
Marcus Mooney	.310	284	49	88	3	41	28	24	9
Colin Willis*	.302	328	65	99	10	60	69	64	16
Tom Walraven	.300	203	35	61	6	31	35	32	6
Tommy McCarthy	.286	14	1	4	0	1	5	3	0
Danny De la Calle	.276	174	24	48	3	20	12	53	2
Edgar Corcino#	.250	16	1	4	0	2	3	5	0
Hayden Schilling*	.246	65	5	16	0	6	11	17	7
Wilfredo Gimenez	.246	203	17	50	2	22	12	28	3
Alex Crosby*	.241	319	35	77	6	29	28	42	7
Chase Dawson*	.237	38	3	9	0	10	8	11	1
Will Savage	.236	123	25	29	0	5	16	30	5
Andy DeJesus#	.234	304	33	71	4	25	17	75	9
John Price	.234	124	15	29	3	20	2	25	0
Randy Santiesteban	.228	281	26	64	2	39	33	49	1
Ray Jones*	.215	209	17	45	3	28	23	41	0
Evan Marzilli*	.203	153	22	31	0	13	31	40	7
MJ Rookard*	.180	89	15	16	1	8	16	20	5
Zach Welz	.169	89	10	15	0	4	18	35	4
Sean Guida*	.135	74	7	10	0	9	12	25	1
Dan Gardner*	.122	74	3	9	0	7	6	16	2
Michael Blatchford*	.115	26	2	3	0	0	2	5	0

Name	W	L	ERA	G	SV	IP	H	BB	SO
Sandy Lugo	2	2	1.27	24	11	28	16	16	44
Ryan Thurston*	3	1	2.73	34	4	53	40	26	48
Justin Sinibaldi	6	7	2.75	25	1	118	106	45	76
Felix Carvallo*	2	4	2.93	32	5	46	45	18	30
Nile Ball	2	3	3.49	10	0	39	42	10	31
Darin May	0	0	3.55	6	0	13	9	7	5
David Griffin	2	1	3.58	12	0	28	20	17	22
Jack Alkire	1	4	3.71	22	1	34	38	19	44
Andrew Cartier	3	0	4.09	10	0	11	9	4	9
Eric Morell	0	1	4.15	3	0	13	11	4	7
Kaleb Fontenot	1	4	4.50	10	0	24	24	6	18
Trevor Lubking*	6	11	4.53	24	0	139	134	54	108
Nick Floyd	0	1	4.94	12	0	24	30	6	18
Seth Hougesen*	3	3	5.04	12	0	55	60	20	33
Jumpei Akanuma	2	2	5.05	16	0	36	41	16	22
Christian DeLeon	1	4	5.16	14	1	30	33	9	18
Lars Liguori*	4	5	6.22	12	0	68	97	20	34
Frankie Moscatiello	0	2	6.55	15	0	34	51	15	27
Robbie Coursel	1	2	9.55	11	0	27	36	17	19

KANSAS CITY T-BONES

Name	AVG	AB	R	H	HR	RBI	BB	SO	SB
Dylan Tice#	.316	358	64	113	4	38	37	53	20
Roy Morales	.310	216	37	67	3	25	22	34	2

Name	AVG	AB	R	H	HR	RBI	BB	SO	SB
Mason Davis#	.309	220	31	68	2	20	23	30	19
Shawn O'Malley#	.307	303	52	93	5	40	28	63	10
Stewart Ijames*	.296	54	11	16	2	6	1	11	0
Chris Colabello	.294	221	34	65	9	34	27	52	1
Forrestt Allday*	.290	62	7	18	1	11	15	12	1
Daniel Nava*	.288	274	39	79	7	46	40	33	2
Darnell Sweeney#	.288	80	15	23	4	9	17	28	6
Carlos Franco*	.286	70	11	20	1	8	8	16	1
Danny Mars#	.280	332	39	93	4	35	24	43	14
Ramsey Romano	.273	260	28	71	3	34	10	63	7
Omar Carrizales*	.268	56	9	15	2	8	3	20	2
Casey Gillaspie#	.257	358	52	92	14	69	52	109	4
Daniel Robertson	.250	36	3	9	1	4	9	9	0
Christian Correa	.249	197	19	49	4	33	19	39	1
Ryan Brett#	.238	84	17	20	2	5	3	25	2
Tyler Marincov	.236	72	10	17	3	11	7	21	1
Mikey Reynolds	.211	57	7	12	0	5	4	12	3
Taylor Sparks	.140	86	9	12	2	10	3	36	0

Name	W	L	ERA	G	SV	IP	H	BB	SO
Randall Delgado	2	0	0.00	2	0	10	6	2	14
Brian Ellington	0	0	0.60	12	1	15	6	2	15
Ramsey Romano	1	0	0.82	8	0	11	7	4	5
Carlos Diaz*	1	2	2.10	30	13	30	13	21	51
Hunter Smith	1	0	2.30	11	2	16	12	5	19
Nick Lee*	1	1	2.60	26	2	28	18	17	37
Akeem Bostick	2	1	3.12	4	0	17	15	7	17
Dylan Baker	4	5	3.36	14	0	80	74	29	66
T.J. House*	2	0	3.52	3	0	15	18	4	22
Christian Binford	4	3	3.55	10	0	51	49	12	47
Tommy Collier	10	5	3.58	20	0	118	127	31	109
Jon Perrin	7	2	3.92	14	0	85	72	33	90
Evan Korson*	1	1	4.22	20	0	21	19	17	26
Robert Calvano	3	2	4.37	42	2	56	55	27	51
Henry Owens*	4	2	4.69	21	2	56	39	45	72
Jose Mesa Jr.	3	2	4.78	12	0	49	48	23	63
Nathan Foriest*	0	1	5.84	10	0	12	12	16	7
Kenny Koplove	2	3	6.37	6	0	30	36	12	28
Jackson Lowery	0	2	6.65	16	1	22	27	16	28
Marc Magliaro	4	2	6.81	16	0	38	46	21	28
Erik Manoah	2	1	7.30	7	0	25	23	16	19
Dustin Hurlbutt	0	3	7.63	4	0	15	16	11	13
Kevin Hamann	1	3	8.00	21	0	36	44	29	23

LINCOLN SALTDOGS

Name	AVG	AB	R	H	HR	RBI	BB	SO	SB
Forrestt Allday*	.311	148	26	46	1	9	20	27	3
Curt Smith	.288	368	55	106	14	58	30	73	2
Randolph Oduber	.284	317	39	90	9	41	12	78	4
Josh Mazzola	.263	198	21	52	5	24	9	42	5
Teodoro Martinez	.259	81	3	21	0	5	5	14	3
Christian Ibarra	.254	335	58	85	16	43	62	74	2
Joe Lytle*	.243	37	6	9	0	1	7	6	0
Tyler Moore*	.243	313	38	76	7	40	26	78	1
Cody Regis*	.237	367	48	87	16	56	48	110	3
Ivan Marin	.231	294	35	68	2	23	46	46	4
John Sansone	.225	178	18	40	6	18	13	55	4
Nick Schulz	.225	187	16	42	6	20	28	65	1
DonAndre Clark#	.214	56	3	12	0	0	5	12	3
Daniel Herrera##	.208	216	17	45	3	19	16	61	0
Auggie Francis	.200	35	2	7	0	3	3	17	0
Colton Burns*	.106	47	4	5	0	3	2	20	1
Steve Pascual	.078	51	2	4	0	0	2	21	0

Name	W	L	ERA	G	SV	IP	H	BB	SO
Evan Korson*	2	0	1.35	17	0	20	10	11	17
Reese Gregory	1	0	1.57	18	4	29	23	5	19
Austin Boyle	4	2	1.88	40	2	48	30	25	65
Martire Garcia*	2	1	2.70	18	0	17	14	7	14
Josh Norwood*	0	1	3.12	9	0	17	20	10	13
John Brownell	8	5	3.70	19	0	122	117	34	90
Kyle Kinman*	1	4	3.71	14	0	70	64	35	68
Austin Pettibone	1	4	4.32	33	2	42	49	20	20
Jake Hohensee	4	8	4.68	31	1	85	89	24	62
Nick Tepesch	6	4	4.84	10	0	61	75	22	42
Tyler Anderson*	3	1	4.89	30	0	50	60	27	31
Brad Thoutt	0	2	4.91	7	0	37	45	14	32

INDEPENDENT LEAGUES

Name	W	L	ERA	G	SV	IP	H	BB	SO
Cameron McVey	0	4	5.12	26	1	19	23	12	28
Spencer Herrmann*	2	4	5.14	8	0	42	50	11	27
Ricky Knapp	4	10	5.80	20	1	102	126	35	60
Shairon Martis	2	7	6.44	22	2	66	70	29	38
Tyson Cronin	0	2	6.84	8	0	25	34	9	16

MILWAUKEE MILKMEN

Name	AVG	AB	R	H	HR	RBI	BB	SO	SB
Teodoro Martinez	.305	105	15	32	1	9	4	14	7
Taisei Fukuhara*	.280	25	2	7	0	4	1	9	1
Manuel Boscan#	.277	339	46	94	9	51	49	64	10
Derek Reddy	.264	125	17	33	0	3	18	29	5
Daniel Ward	.255	271	25	69	7	28	17	80	1
Adam Walker	.249	362	54	90	22	64	24	114	8
Jose Rosario	.246	329	32	81	8	35	17	77	7
Glen McClain	.245	220	17	54	3	12	17	36	3
Garrett Copeland*	.237	363	49	86	5	36	50	108	12
Riley Pittman*	.236	161	15	38	4	12	16	42	0
Sam Dexter	.234	320	25	75	1	23	23	52	5
Cesar Valera	.218	211	24	46	1	11	23	50	10
Nolan Earley*	.218	252	32	55	7	27	31	52	4
Christ Conley*	.209	134	14	28	1	11	21	39	1
Jeff Chandler	.176	34	3	6	1	2	2	11	1

Name	W	L	ERA	G	SV	IP	H	BB	SO
Tanner Kiest	1	1	1.72	31	0	31	24	17	41
Myles Smith	1	4	2.20	36	17	41	33	11	61
Jake Joyce	1	1	2.59	28	1	31	16	33	36
Angel Ventura	6	10	2.76	20	0	131	111	36	108
Zach Hartman	3	3	3.61	42	0	52	55	22	46
Jordan Kraus	7	5	3.64	19	0	99	99	36	58
T.J. House*	7	9	4.35	17	0	112	116	31	78
Colby Morris	0	0	4.50	9	0	10	5	7	12
Carlos Diaz*	1	1	4.58	30	1	37	37	28	39
Manny Corpas	1	0	4.63	9	0	12	15	5	7
Kurt Heyer	6	11	4.76	21	0	125	151	26	91
Joey Wagman	1	4	4.79	7	0	36	46	14	21
Jake Matthys	0	1	4.91	2	0	11	14	2	6
Javon Rigsby	0	1	6.23	5	0	13	16	16	5
Zac Westcott	1	3	6.23	8	0	39	48	19	24
Mike Scimanico*	1	1	6.57	14	0	12	17	13	18
Cody Dickson*	0	2	6.89	3	0	16	10	10	13
K. Johnson-Battilana	1	2	8.50	10	0	18	25	13	9
Derek Heffel	0	3	13.21	9	0	16	32	12	17

SIOUX CITY EXPLORERS

Name	AVG	AB	R	H	HR	RBI	BB	SO	SB
Nate Samson	.324	404	60	131	6	67	30	25	21
Kyle Wren*	.298	373	75	111	8	44	43	88	27
Dylan Kelly*	.287	310	35	89	3	29	31	37	3
Michael Lang	.279	258	47	72	5	18	25	51	13
Drew Stankiewicz*	.278	316	50	88	5	52	41	71	19
Sebastian Zawada	.263	274	37	72	11	48	17	59	0
Jose Sermo#	.260	362	55	94	13	77	62	114	21
Dexture McCall	.258	353	48	91	4	45	52	76	4
Luke Bonfield	.253	87	8	22	1	12	7	19	0
Jeremy Hazelbaker*	.248	133	24	33	5	18	16	38	7
Dean Green*	.244	45	5	11	1	10	11	7	0
Adam Sasser*	.223	269	28	60	4	31	26	82	0
Hunter Wood#	.222	27	4	6	0	6	1	7	2
Nelson Ward*	.175	57	5	10	0	2	2	17	1
Justin Felix	.170	53	12	9	5	6	11	23	0
Daytona Bryden	.158	38	4	6	5	5	8	10	1

Name	W	L	ERA	G	SV	IP	H	BB	SO
Jose Velez*	2	1	1.65	32	0	33	24	11	47
Nate Gercken	4	2	1.91	42	0	47	30	23	44
Jason Garcia	8	1	2.73	9	0	56	50	20	51
Tyler Fallwell	8	5	3.13	36	1	75	56	35	104
Peter Tago	6	3	3.16	11	0	74	69	24	88
Matt Pobereyko	1	4	3.18	47	24	51	31	14	74
Carlos Sierra	3	1	3.21	25	0	70	71	40	96
Sam Held	3	1	3.86	11	0	30	33	10	25
Taylor Jordan	6	10	4.49	20	0	124	120	36	95
Ryan Flores	2	1	4.72	27	0	34	28	24	42
Eric Karch	6	6	5.09	20	0	122	133	41	83

Name	W	L	ERA	G	SV	IP	H	BB	SO
Juan Aguilera	0	0	5.40	16	0	23	25	15	23
Max Duval	1	6	6.96	10	0	54	75	20	49
Andrew Chin*	1	0	7.30	4	0	12	19	11	4
Zach Jemiola	0	2	7.40	5	0	24	27	17	11

SIOUX FALLS CANARIES

Name	AVG	AB	R	H	HR	RBI	BB	SO	SB
Alay Lago	.339	369	58	125	13	57	29	55	14
Kevin Taylor*	.305	361	50	110	7	51	42	31	1
Mike Hart*	.297	269	42	80	11	41	29	77	3
Clint Coulter	.294	374	69	110	18	72	35	90	2
Graham Low	.282	220	36	62	4	27	20	59	1
Andrew Ely*	.279	340	42	95	8	46	37	76	4
Brett Vertigan*	.279	401	58	112	2	32	44	62	13
Jordan Ebert	.274	285	43	78	2	42	25	36	16
Adrian Nieto#	.269	130	21	35	4	24	14	24	2
Mitch Glasser	.264	311	52	82	3	38	43	41	4
Burt Reynolds	.230	204	35	47	9	35	21	85	15
Trae Santos*	.224	67	8	15	4	9	7	21	0
Josh Rehwaldt*	.219	96	13	21	2	14	9	42	1

Name	W	L	ERA	G	SV	IP	H	BB	SO
Taylor Hill	6	3	2.52	12	0	75	70	16	58
Tyler Herron	1	3	3.78	7	0	50	60	7	37
Luis Pollorena*	6	3	3.82	35	3	61	56	20	59
Ryan Froom	0	2	4.11	14	0	31	32	21	25
Trevor Jaunich	1	1	4.12	19	0	20	19	7	13
Brian Heldman	0	0	5.11	9	0	12	19	7	5
Connor Leedholm	0	0	5.52	12	3	15	18	0	9
Keaton Steele	3	9	5.89	21	0	115	148	40	84
Alex Boshers	6	9	6.20	22	0	119	155	30	89
Sam Bragg	4	6	6.68	35	7	67	86	14	60
Harrison Cooney	0	1	6.97	11	0	10	15	7	9
Will Solomon*	4	4	7.03	23	0	40	56	19	25
Tyler Lesley	0	1	7.31	9	0	16	19	7	9
Mark Seyler	3	10	7.33	23	0	101	142	35	55
Spencer Herrmann*	0	1	7.42	10	0	30	45	22	30
Alex Ogren	0	1	7.48	22	0	28	36	16	31
Reilly Hovis	1	3	8.76	22	4	25	33	12	33

ST. PAUL SAINTS

Name	AVG	AB	R	H	HR	RBI	BB	SO	SB
Max Murphy	.343	213	44	73	17	43	17	48	12
Dan Motl	.328	366	74	120	4	42	47	71	24
Brady Shoemaker	.319	357	70	114	18	71	80	56	0
Devon Rodriguez*	.286	185	28	53	5	26	11	22	0
Jeremy Martinez	.284	296	45	84	11	41	54	46	1
Josh Allen	.272	342	58	93	17	58	36	80	7
Michael Lang	.272	147	26	40	6	18	12	40	8
Chesny Young	.263	342	52	90	6	48	48	57	2
Chris Baker	.243	152	15	37	3	31	12	49	1
Blake Schmit	.242	244	42	59	3	32	22	46	10
John Silviano*	.241	220	32	53	13	38	28	74	0
Mike Aiello*	.229	35	5	8	0	4	9	10	0
Burt Reynolds	.228	136	17	31	3	17	15	47	5
Joey Wong*	.218	124	15	27	0	18	19	30	0
Jhonatan Solano	.213	47	2	10	0	3	1	7	0
Josh Romanski*	.200	30	3	6	0	2	2	7	0
Matt Morales#	.200	55	7	11	0	5	2	12	2
Troy Alexander*	.200	40	4	8	0	7	2	14	0
Jabari Henry	.183	60	9	11	2	12	8	13	0

Name	W	L	ERA	G	SV	IP	H	BB	SO
Nick Belzer	2	0	1.32	5	0	27	17	9	17
Spencer Jones	1	0	1.34	7	0	34	23	11	29
Mike Devine	4	3	2.00	37	3	54	41	20	50
Kenny Frosch*	2	4	2.87	46	0	38	36	12	40
Karch Kowalczyk	3	1	3.21	29	2	42	36	17	25
Tanner Kiest	0	1	3.38	13	9	16	12	11	25
Eddie Medina	10	3	3.45	19	0	115	93	66	101
Landon Beck	5	2	3.84	38	1	68	68	36	67
Jordan Jess*	7	1	3.84	38	0	75	78	23	69
Chris Lee*	3	0	4.10	12	0	26	21	10	32
Ryan Zimmerman	7	3	4.16	23	0	110	96	65	105
Todd Van Steensel	3	2	4.33	31	16	35	38	20	63
Dustin Crenshaw	4	5	4.96	13	0	82	102	14	34

	W	L	ERA	G	SV	IP	H	BB	SO
Ryan Schlosser	2	2	5.23	22	0	33	41	10	16
Jake Matthys	8	4	5.42	15	0	83	99	30	39
Benji Waite	1	2	5.66	4	0	21	23	12	12
Tom Curtin	0	1	6.63	6	0	19	27	8	9

TEXAS AIRHOGS

Name	AVG	AB	R	H	HR	RBI	BB	SO	SB
Jonathan Moroney	.315	257	38	81	3	26	11	57	12
Na Chuang*	.314	51	5	16	0	7	0	8	0
Josh Prince	.307	153	29	47	2	12	27	31	18
Li Ning*	.285	277	39	79	0	19	43	54	7
Javion Randle	.280	293	33	82	1	33	33	75	16
Stewart Ijames*	.278	281	39	78	10	50	45	70	2
Justin Byrd*	.272	81	18	22	1	5	8	23	5
Chen Junpeng*	.249	261	27	65	2	33	20	51	0
Matt Dean	.245	163	16	40	2	14	19	49	1
Yang Jin*	.230	269	15	62	0	27	11	71	1
Erik Manoah	.226	53	4	12	1	6	1	22	0
Luo Jinjun	.223	264	25	59	0	19	19	72	12
Luan Chenchen*	.188	117	6	22	0	5	6	30	0
Song Yunqi	.182	33	4	6	1	2	1	13	1
Han Xiao*	.180	89	8	16	1	10	4	27	5
Al Reda	.176	17	1	3	0	1	1	6	0
Cao Jie	.175	143	4	25	0	7	6	49	1
Brett Eibner	.167	72	13	12	3	5	15	23	0
Stephen Haviar	.157	153	13	24	1	13	11	46	1
Du Nan	.154	26	0	4	0	1	0	14	0
Lu YuHeng*	.146	82	6	12	0	1	8	37	4
Li Xuhong	.116	43	2	5	0	1	0	21	0
Will Baker	.087	23	2	2	0	0	1	7	0

Name	W	L	ERA	G	SV	IP	H	BB	SO
Brett Eibner	3	0	1.00	16	3	18	9	6	27
Carlos Contreras	1	0	1.62	17	4	17	10	5	12
Pete Perez	2	2	2.51	23	0	32	29	10	30
Tyler Matzek*	5	4	2.64	22	3	31	26	19	53
Zhang Tao	4	6	4.02	13	0	69	62	36	47
Kevin Hilton	3	8	4.62	15	0	97	112	29	55
Travis Ballew	1	12	4.82	24	1	93	104	50	71
Erik Manoah	2	6	4.93	12	0	69	70	25	70
Tu Jialun*	1	2	5.01	20	0	32	36	16	26
Liu Guoqing	0	1	5.53	19	2	28	35	13	18
Gan Quan	1	7	5.94	16	0	73	65	47	54
Zech Lemond	1	13	7.02	19	0	99	122	37	83
Taylor Wright	1	2	7.82	15	0	38	51	13	25
Sean Stutzman*	2	1	8.17	16	0	36	58	16	36
Cui Enting	0	2	8.21	18	0	34	50	16	14
Mi Jia Hong*	0	0	8.42	16	0	26	32	23	21
Stewart Ijames	0	0	8.44	7	0	11	18	7	10
Ryan Smith	1	4	11.95	16	0	20	36	8	22

WINNIPEG GOLDEYES

Name	AVG	AB	R	H	HR	RBI	BB	SO	SB
Jonathan Moroney	.436	39	6	17	3	8	3	4	1
Tyler Hill	.375	168	32	63	4	28	19	18	16
Kevin Lachance	.372	43	8	16	2	7	12	11	3
Wes Darvill*	.317	350	66	111	7	34	36	59	26
Willy Garcia	.310	336	58	104	17	73	34	97	2
Dominic Ficociello#	.292	308	48	90	10	52	24	75	5
James Harris	.280	257	39	72	3	38	42	45	13
Kyle Martin*	.275	287	60	79	14	67	44	44	8
Carlos Garcia#	.271	48	8	13	1	4	6	8	7
Josh Romanski*	.266	128	14	34	0	8	12	13	5
Tyler Marincov	.262	65	9	17	0	4	7	25	1
Reggie Abercrombie	.256	379	64	97	16	70	23	96	11
Adrian Marin	.240	175	22	42	0	16	20	27	6
Kevin Garcia#	.233	266	29	62	4	33	22	34	4
Alex Perez*	.211	337	47	71	0	36	66	65	7
Cody Young	.194	67	6	13	0	2	2	18	0
Jordan Hovey*	.190	42	7	8	0	3	7	16	1
John Price	.143	21	4	3	0	0	0	6	0
Rey Pastrana	.132	38	2	5	0	2	0	10	0

Name	W	L	ERA	G	SV	IP	H	BB	SO
Cameron McVey	0	0	1.72	20	1	16	8	11	18
Justin Kamplain*	2	1	2.08	14	0	17	13	11	14

	W	L	ERA	G	SV	IP	H	BB	SO
Mitchell Lambson*	13	4	3.11	21	0	151	153	33	133
Victor Capellan	1	1	3.16	46	27	43	36	13	53
Kevin Hilton	2	2	3.79	5	0	36	33	13	22
Kevin McGovern*	12	7	3.85	21	0	126	129	39	95
Christian Torres*	1	1	4.33	35	1	54	49	24	38
Mitchell Aker	2	2	4.50	33	0	32	37	22	20
Tyler Garkow	4	0	4.91	32	1	44	39	16	46
Ryan Johnson*	1	4	5.00	9	0	45	48	31	19
Joel Bender*	2	3	5.24	26	0	46	53	12	24
Parker French	6	6	5.32	22	0	108	127	49	51
Brandon Bingel	3	2	5.44	28	0	41	38	14	34
Harrison Cooney	2	2	6.97	9	0	21	17	18	17
Joel Seddon	2	5	6.99	12	0	66	86	28	34
Marcus Crescentini	4	3	8.44	25	0	21	23	16	33

ATLANTIC LEAGUE

For the third time in four seasons, Sugar Land and Long Island faced off for the Atlantic League title. This time, the Ducks finally broke through, edging the Skeeters thanks to Vin Mazarro's solid outing in the deciding Game 5 of the championship series.

The Ducks had finished as league runners-up for three consecutive seasons. This was their fourth Atlantic League title and the team's first since 2013.

Freedom Division	W	L	PCT	GB
&York Revolution	75	65	.536	—
*Sugar Land Skeeters	72	66	.522	2
Southern Maryland Blue Crabs	59	81	.421	16
Lancaster Barnstormers	51	89	.364	24

Liberty Division	W	L	PCT	GB
*Long Island Ducks	86	54	.614	—
^High Point Rockers	74	66	.529	12
New Britain Bees	72	68	.514	14
Somerset Patriots	69	69	.500	16

*First-half champion. & Second-half champion. ^Wild-Card

Playoffs—Semifinals: Long Island defeated High Point 3-0 and Sugar Land defeated York 3-1 in best-of-five series. **Finals:** Lion Long Island defeated Sugar Land 3-2 in best-of-five series.

Attendance: Somerset 344,641; Long Island 328,194; Sugar Land 304,753; Lancaster 285,441; Southern Maryland 200,889; York 199,045; High Point 144,486; New Britain 133,141.

All-Star Team: C-Isaias Tejeda, York. **1B:** Telvin Nash, York. **2B:** Jonathan Galvez, New Britain. **3B:** Will Kengor, Somerset. **SS:** Edwin Garcia, Southern Maryland. **OF:** Caleb Gindl, Lancaster; Stephen Cardullo, High Point; Melky Mesa, York. **DH:** Jason Rogers, New Britain. **SP:** Daryl Thompson, Southern Maryland. **RP:** Mat Latos, Southern Maryland. **CL:** Jim Fuller, New Britain. **Player of the Year:** Telvin Nash, York.
Pitcher of the Year: Daryl Thompson, Southern Maryland. **Defensive Player of the Year:** Edwin Garcia, Southern Maryland. **Manager of the Year:** Wally Backman, Long Island.

BATTING LEADERS

Player	Team	AVG	AB	R	H	HR	RBI
Isaias Tejeda	YOR	.338	131	562	86	0	23
Will Kengor	SOM	.321	129	544	70	2	15
Welington Dotel	YOR	.313	125	530	71	5	13
Jonathan Galvez	NBR	.305	127	495	63	4	17
Melky Mesa	YOR	.298	113	484	66	4	20
Telvin Nash	YOR	.294	137	603	107	1	41
Joey Terdoslavich	LAN	.294	125	532	71	0	22
L.J. Mazzilli	LI	.293	120	508	66	0	13
Juan Silverio	SLS	.293	128	543	79	5	14
Henry Castillo	YOR	.293	109	441	56	4	14

PITCHING LEADERS

Player	Team	W	L	ERA	IP	H	BB	SO
Joe Van Meter	HP	10	6	2.30	145	107	32	131
Mitch Atkins	YOR	11	6	2.81	157	137	31	129
Liam O'Sullivan	SOM	7	9	2.96	158	151	37	113
Daryl Thompson	SMD	15	8	3.13	193	168	27	162
John Anderson	LAN	11	8	3.83	150	150	51	140
Dallas Beeler	SLS	9	7	3.86	145	167	53	97
Seth Simmons	LI	8	8	3.86	140	110	67	119
Jared Lakind	LAN	7	9	4.82	142	157	63	98

HIGH POINT ROCKERS

Name	AVG	AB	R	H	HR	RBI	BB	SO	SB
Dante Bichette	.386	140	23	54	3	23	7	13	3
Brett Austin#	.321	84	16	27	4	18	10	21	0
Hector Gomez	.291	464	69	135	12	76	23	53	20
Michael Russell	.287	258	31	74	4	26	25	32	21
Shane Opitz*	.286	14	3	4	0	1	4	4	1
Breland Almadova	.278	108	12	30	1	13	3	28	3
Stephen Cardullo	.266	511	96	136	22	70	74	94	20
Quincy Latimore	.264	402	57	106	21	72	46	86	12
Tyler Ladendorf	.256	347	56	89	13	44	37	78	12
Tyler Marincov	.250	132	19	33	4	15	12	37	7
Giovanny Alfonzo	.248	367	39	91	0	30	21	87	13
Michael Baca	.245	49	6	12	0	2	8	14	1
Myles Schroder#	.235	443	59	104	8	45	40	105	9
Richie Shaffer	.235	353	57	83	27	72	58	141	2
Jared Mitchell*	.232	181	25	42	6	21	22	46	10
Viosergy Rosa*	.227	286	38	65	11	35	36	81	2
Matt Jones	.208	183	28	38	4	23	21	48	2
Kalian Sams	.203	64	6	13	1	9	6	21	2
Josh Mazzola	.182	44	3	8	2	6	2	11	0
John Nester	.154	26	2	4	1	5	3	11	0
Frank Nigro	.117	103	9	12	1	5	6	27	0
C.J. Retherford	.111	27	1	3	0	0	0	8	0

Name	W	L	ERA	G	SV	IP	H	BB	SO
John Brownell	2	0	1.31	3	0	21	15	7	15
John Richy	0	1	1.80	3	0	10	14	2	5
Kyle Halbohn	1	0	1.89	15	0	19	21	5	16
Alberto Baldonado*	0	1	1.98	13	1	14	7	6	19
Kyle Hansen	0	1	2.08	24	0	26	15	8	16
Brian Clark*	3	3	2.27	45	0	48	34	16	44
Joe Van Meter	10	6	2.30	24	0	145	107	32	131
Michael Bowden	2	4	2.93	9	0	43	38	8	53
Ashur Tolliver*	8	1	2.94	38	0	49	38	17	38
Chase Huchingson*	5	4	2.98	56	1	54	37	28	53
Chris Pennell	2	1	3.00	11	0	42	30	17	24
Craig Stem	1	2	3.33	4	0	24	16	8	28
Edwin Carl	5	5	3.35	21	0	94	98	35	87
Daniel Gibson*	1	0	3.48	12	0	10	7	4	8
Dominic DeMasi	7	3	3.57	13	0	81	71	26	74
Ryan Kelly	2	2	3.75	25	13	24	18	6	24
Seth Simmons	5	4	4.21	13	0	68	55	31	48
Akeel Morris	1	0	4.23	22	1	28	24	11	23
Trevor Frank	3	4	4.33	50	13	52	55	16	55
Ryan Williams	1	2	4.43	5	0	22	31	7	15
Matt Sergey	3	4	4.47	10	0	48	41	26	38
Sam Runion	3	2	4.55	48	1	55	55	10	47
Stephen Johnson	3	3	5.02	8	0	43	44	17	29
Dusty Isaacs	1	3	5.55	23	0	24	23	13	32
Luke Irvine	0	0	5.68	10	0	25	37	10	21
Tyler Herron	2	7	6.05	17	0	94	128	21	57
Paul Clemens	2	2	6.67	21	0	28	33	11	26

LANCASTER BARNSTORMERS

Name	AVG	AB	R	H	HR	RBI	BB	SO	SB
Dan Gamache*	.303	264	46	80	6	46	26	52	0
Joey Terdoslavich#	.294	473	71	139	22	75	50	81	9
Caleb Gindl*	.289	492	82	142	22	91	82	100	2
Gift Ngoepe	.289	38	6	11	3	7	2	18	0
Andrew Aplin*	.286	185	24	53	6	34	25	34	9
Anderson De La Rosa	.275	265	28	73	5	34	20	58	1
Greg Golson	.267	176	21	47	2	16	8	56	3
Melvin Mercedes#	.264	193	24	51	2	15	17	25	6
Michael Martinez#	.252	377	56	95	9	42	24	64	8
Parker Morin*	.251	235	16	59	5	22	16	72	1
Darian Sandford#	.234	423	70	99	0	27	48	73	74
Devon Torrence#	.227	242	37	55	2	23	21	83	26
Destin Hood	.224	210	26	47	9	42	14	73	3
Josh Bell#	.213	287	27	61	4	24	52	102	6
K.C. Hobson*	.205	469	56	96	19	66	53	150	3
Zach Shank	.199	226	31	45	0	9	20	54	4
Brian Mayer	.167	24	2	4	0	2	0	12	0

Name	W	L	ERA	G	SV	IP	H	BB	SO
Pedro Echemendia	3	0	2.57	32	0	35	28	18	31
Scott Shuman	3	1	2.62	33	3	34	24	15	40
Buddy Baumann*	4	8	3.48	17	0	101	80	34	92
John Anderson*	11	8	3.83	30	0	150	150	51	140
Connor Overton	3	5	4.02	9	0	54	46	15	56
Kyle Davies	4	9	4.44	15	0	95	103	26	68
Jonathan Albaladejo	3	12	4.77	19	0	109	123	29	69
Jared Lakind*	7	9	4.82	29	0	142	157	63	98
Nate Reed*	4	5	4.97	12	0	63	76	18	56
Garrett Granitz	0	2	5.06	45	0	59	60	32	24
Bryan Harper*	0	5	5.17	37	0	31	25	24	32
Cody Eppley	1	6	5.25	50	17	48	74	12	36
Jake McCasland	1	5	5.35	6	0	34	39	8	32
Alejandro Chacin	1	4	5.50	41	0	56	53	38	52
Logan Sawyer	2	1	5.66	41	0	41	46	29	31
Matt Marksberry*	4	4	5.69	54	1	55	58	29	64
Andury Acevedo	0	1	6.53	22	0	21	17	21	15
Caleb Gindl*	0	2	6.62	19	0	18	16	19	18
Kelvin Vasquez	0	2	7.23	9	0	19	22	21	11

LONG ISLAND DUCKS

Name	AVG	AB	R	H	HR	RBI	BB	SO	SB
Ivan De Jesus	.306	36	5	11	0	5	7	4	0
Lew Ford	.303	297	43	90	4	35	18	57	1
Ezequiel Carrera*	.301	173	28	52	1	10	23	20	8
L.J. Mazzilli	.293	460	66	135	13	74	40	72	15
D'Arby Myers	.277	267	43	74	2	21	18	38	33
Hector Sanchez#	.273	352	37	96	9	58	18	49	0
Clint Freeman*	.270	89	12	24	2	14	9	21	0
T.J. Rivera	.270	89	12	24	4	16	7	10	0
Deibinson Romero	.268	246	33	66	11	46	18	48	0
Matt den Dekker*	.268	112	18	30	2	12	10	30	4
Steve Lombardozzi#	.262	275	36	72	2	33	34	34	4
Kirk Nieuwenhuis*	.259	220	35	57	11	41	21	63	7
Rey Fuentes*	.258	364	65	94	14	47	36	86	18
Ramon Cabrera#	.249	237	21	59	7	25	10	28	1
Rando Moreno#	.245	98	7	24	0	12	5	16	3
Daniel Fields*	.244	287	44	70	14	36	32	113	11
David Washington*	.237	346	59	82	23	60	49	152	19
Vladimir Frias#	.237	417	53	99	8	34	36	73	28
Cade Gotta	.200	20	4	4	0	0	4	5	4
John Apostolo	.185	124	17	23	1	8	13	28	4
Nick Garland	.094	32	3	3	0	2	4	8	1
Mike Olt	.082	73	8	6	0	5	11	32	0

Name	W	L	ERA	G	SV	IP	H	BB	SO
Michael Tonkin	3	2	0.34	22	7	27	10	9	31
Jose Cuas	0	0	0.71	10	1	13	5	4	16
Tim Melville	2	0	0.75	2	0	12	7	3	13
Josh Lueke	0	1	0.77	12	6	12	5	4	17
Sean Nolin*	6	0	1.10	8	0	41	30	8	45
Tim Adleman	2	0	1.64	3	0	11	6	1	14
Travis Banwart	3	1	1.91	6	0	38	26	10	36
Enrique Burgos	4	2	2.43	29	13	30	18	14	49
Cody Mincey	7	1	2.53	49	5	68	54	26	96
Darin Downs*	3	3	2.63	21	0	110	85	35	140
Brandon Beachy	6	0	2.85	9	0	41	30	20	38
Joe Iorio	6	3	3.09	32	0	128	124	32	92
Alec Asher	3	1	3.12	7	0	35	30	13	21
Bennett Parry*	1	0	3.38	5	0	27	27	12	32
Seth Simmons	3	4	3.52	13	0	72	55	36	71
Vin Mazzaro	11	4	3.61	39	1	92	95	27	84
Rob Rogers	2	3	3.62	35	0	37	43	27	34
Mariel Checo	1	2	3.95	26	0	43	27	18	37
Brian Matusz*	2	3	4.05	9	0	47	39	15	45
Zack Weiss	4	1	4.68	16	1	25	23	12	34
Alex Katz*	0	0	4.70	13	0	15	18	7	13
Ismael Cabrera	1	0	4.74	15	0	19	17	9	20
Jake Fisher*	4	6	4.99	13	0	70	84	18	50
Clint Freeman*	0	0	5.29	15	0	17	23	10	13
Anderson DeLeon	1	2	5.29	7	0	17	14	10	14
Pedro Beato	3	3	5.81	21	9	48	59	14	46
Brett Marshall	1	3	9.00	7	0	21	25	15	19
Kevin McAvoy	0	5	9.32	9	0	28	34	21	22

INDEPENDENT LEAGUES

NEW BRITAIN BEES

Name	AVG	AB	R	H	HR	RBI	BB	SO	SB
Alejandro De Aza*	.346	269	45	93	6	42	25	52	4
Jonathan Galvez	.305	452	63	138	17	76	31	87	2
Jason Rogers	.289	481	80	139	15	91	85	67	10
Bijan Rademacher*	.286	329	63	94	15	45	69	55	18
Taylor Motter	.282	117	15	33	5	28	22	28	6
Alexi Amarista*	.270	241	35	65	11	31	19	20	4
Deibinson Romero	.266	143	12	38	3	12	20	28	1
Darren Ford	.265	430	81	114	6	37	49	92	50
Ryan Jackson	.262	191	21	50	0	19	18	26	5
Mike Carp*	.260	200	16	52	6	39	19	41	1
Jared James*	.259	355	47	92	4	35	40	81	8
Zach Collier*	.237	173	27	41	6	19	20	47	14
Jovan Rosa	.231	26	1	6	1	3	2	3	0
Osvaldo Martinez	.227	362	52	82	3	27	34	65	4
Rando Moreno#	.219	265	38	58	4	28	24	64	13
Logan Moore*	.210	366	47	77	15	66	52	111	3
Joe Poletsky	.180	50	5	9	1	3	3	17	1
Tyler Clark#	.155	97	9	15	3	11	8	38	2
Brian Mayer	.091	22	1	2	0	2	1	9	0
Vinny Siena	.071	28	2	2	0	0	7	11	1

Name	W	L	ERA	G	SV	IP	H	BB	SO
Jim Fuller*	7	2	1.03	57	25	61	30	14	68
Dakota Smith	1	0	1.38	10	0	13	10	7	13
Michael Johnson*	1	2	2.94	35	1	34	32	10	27
Christian Friedrich*	5	1	3.00	11	0	63	64	15	63
Jose Rosario	3	2	3.02	47	7	48	46	17	42
Giovanni Soto*	3	1	3.14	27	2	49	39	16	58
Brandon Fry*	1	1	3.34	31	1	35	36	20	33
David Roseboom*	4	3	3.63	15	0	67	62	23	68
Brady Dragmire	2	1	4.34	27	0	29	29	15	20
Sammy Gervacio	5	6	4.41	54	0	69	74	30	55
Grant Black	1	1	4.63	12	1	12	16	4	13
Devin Burke	3	7	4.80	28	0	116	132	36	86
Chris Reed*	2	0	4.84	15	0	22	23	19	13
Akeel Morris	7	4	4.94	16	0	75	70	37	52
Anthony Marzi*	1	1	4.96	6	0	33	34	8	36
Rainy Lara	8	12	5.84	26	0	136	160	39	86
Cory Riordan	8	8	5.84	22	0	114	150	24	39
Tyler Danish	4	2	6.08	19	0	24	27	12	19
Zach Stewart	0	1	6.50	5	0	18	26	12	9
Christopher De Leon	1	0	6.75	11	0	17	16	10	13
Kyle Simon	1	3	7.43	12	0	40	58	16	19
Jed Bradley*	3	8	7.75	23	0	72	105	40	65
Anthony Alicki	0	0	11.57	11	0	23	32	28	12

SOMERSET PATRIOTS

Name	AVG	AB	R	H	HR	RBI	BB	SO	SB
Will Kengor*	.321	474	70	152	15	65	60	111	22
Ramon Flores*	.308	305	46	94	6	47	43	51	10
Olmo Rosario	.302	53	9	16	1	3	2	1	2
Justin Pacchioli	.282	266	53	75	1	19	31	51	38
Alfredo Rodriguez	.267	468	55	125	4	48	59	68	20
Jimmy Paredes#	.265	249	30	66	13	45	14	60	6
Yovan Gonzalez	.263	240	32	63	3	26	27	50	0
Mike Ohlman	.260	362	47	94	10	58	47	92	2
Edwin Espinal	.253	435	41	110	7	62	35	64	0
Craig Massey	.242	343	44	83	3	36	41	71	28
Rey Navarro#	.240	300	32	72	5	24	13	48	2
Mike Crouse	.237	245	45	58	10	25	29	93	29
Scott Kelly	.228	202	25	46	0	18	27	35	14
D'Arby Myers	.214	84	8	18	0	3	4	17	5
Teodoro Martinez	.208	120	11	25	4	19	7	18	5
Dario Pizzano*	.200	45	5	9	0	4	4	8	0
Mike Fransoso*	.195	154	19	30	3	22	14	38	1
Gabriel Bracamonte	.190	84	15	16	3	14	14	23	1
Steve Nyisztor	.140	43	6	6	0	2	8	1	0

Name	W	L	ERA	G	SV	IP	H	BB	SO
Jonathan Cheshire	0	1	0.55	15	4	16	10	3	19
Dave Kubiak	7	1	1.76	12	0	82	50	24	82
Jeff Kinley	0	1	2.25	16	0	16	14	10	17
Thomas Dorminy*	6	6	2.72	16	0	93	90	28	97

Name	W	L	ERA	G	SV	IP	H	BB	SO
Mike Antonini*	2	4	2.75	38	29	36	27	15	36
Mike Broadway	1	4	2.84	31	1	32	22	5	45
Liam O'Sullivan	7	9	2.96	25	0	158	151	37	113
Tyler Cloyd	1	3	3.48	15	2	44	41	6	39
Brett Oberholtzer*	7	1	3.49	14	0	77	79	24	70
Luis Cruz*	2	4	3.58	52	3	55	49	21	62
James Pugliese	4	1	3.62	45	1	60	59	17	59
Ryan Kussmaul	3	3	3.63	7	0	40	38	8	29
Rick Teasley*	6	3	4.20	17	0	96	108	26	68
Zack Dodson*	3	2	4.35	7	0	41	44	12	25
Jake Joyce	3	2	4.96	16	0	16	16	9	14
Nate Roe	3	2	4.96	43	1	49	62	24	40
Logan Darnell*	1	1	5.02	6	0	14	13	2	14
David Holmberg*	2	8	5.17	20	0	87	105	29	66
Bobby Blevins	0	2	5.54	2	0	13	16	2	6
Zech Zinicola	4	2	5.93	30	0	30	31	15	22
Duane Below*	2	2	6.08	22	0	27	40	2	30
Vince Molesky	4	4	6.37	27	1	71	89	21	51

SOUTHERN MARYLAND BLUE CRABS

Name	AVG	AB	R	H	HR	RBI	BB	SO	SB
Dean Green*	.304	135	16	41	4	27	13	27	0
Josh McAdams	.279	272	27	76	7	32	19	109	1
Angelys Nina	.277	101	11	28	0	4		17	0
Edwin Garcia	.269	479	52	129	5	52	40	65	6
Tony Thomas	.268	466	66	125	17	68	33	125	20
Charlie Valerio#	.262	382	35	100	11	46	18	92	2
Cory Vaughn	.258	418	55	108	23	59	58	124	5
Rubi Silva*	.250	484	57	121	12	44	12	90	16
Kent Blackstone*	.237	379	55	90	4	24	50	96	25
Frank Martinez#	.235	226	23	53	5	29	15	43	1
Jon Griffin	.231	325	29	75	8	33	17	97	0
Joe Benson	.219	361	38	79	4	28	29	88	12
Jose Julio-Ruiz*	.200	120	15	24	2	7	6	19	0
Matt Dean	.179	28	4	5	0	5	2	7	1
Mike Falsetti	.176	153	11	27	1	9	13	70	1
Travis Witherspoon	.170	94	12	16	3	7	6	35	3
Rian Kiniry*	.160	25	3	4	1	4	0	5	1
Craig Maddox*	.136	103	4	14	1	8	1	32	0

Name	W	L	ERA	G	SV	IP	H	BB	SO
Pat Dean*	1	0	0.82	2	0	11	11	2	17
Mat Latos	4	5	1.06	50	25	51	24	9	39
Mitchell Lambson*	3	1	1.35	4	0	27	17	9	25
Josh McAdams	0	0	1.54	7	0	12	7	8	8
Adam Choplick*	3	2	2.15	50	0	54	46	23	66
Kevin McGovern*	1	2	2.16	4	0	25	18	11	22
Kevin Munson	2	3	2.60	34	0	45	42	18	35
Craig Stem	4	3	2.74	12	0	72	69	20	56
Daryl Thompson	15	8	3.13	28	0	193	168	27	162
James Dykstra	3	3	3.28	39	2	47	39	15	50
Dusten Knight	3	6	3.78	13	0	79	63	24	92
Brandon Cumpton	5	8	4.88	15	0	83	103	34	73
Kyle Simon	3	10	4.97	15	0	96	106	30	57
John Hayes	3	6	5.00	34	0	94	104	61	57
Ryan Chaffee	3	4	5.19	41	1	69	67	52	65
Michael Kelly	3	8	5.34	20	0	89	85	63	83
Tommy Thorpe*	3	7	7.05	27	1	75	95	58	54
Brandon Shimo	0	0	8.44	14	0	16	16	19	9
El'Hajj Muhammad	0	1	12.41	11	0	12	19	16	13

SUGAR LAND SKEETERS

Name	AVG	AB	R	H	HR	RBI	BB	SO	SB
C.J. McElroy*	.365	63	10	23	0	7	5	9	5
Wynton Bernard	.314	245	46	77	6	36	17	38	32
D.J. Peterson	.305	141	27	43	8	20	17	28	0
Juan Silverio	.293	488	79	143	14	68	42	87	18
Will Maddox*	.286	21	1	6	0	2	1	3	2
Rico Noel	.284	197	42	56	1	15	28	33	45
James Loney*	.278	36	4	10	0	3	4	4	0
Zach Borenstein*	.267	360	48	96	16	67	44	103	3
Albert Cordero#	.263	361	40	95	15	65	21	61	3
Denis Phipps	.261	448	77	117	21	81	61	107	7
Jared Mitchell*	.258	229	29	59	6	28	35	43	22
Willy Taveras	.255	98	13	25	0	6	7	22	7

Name	AVG	AB	R	H	HR	RBI	BB	SO	SB
Anthony Giansanti	.252	421	61	106	9	51	26	74	19
Cody Stanley*	.251	342	38	86	5	43	26	56	5
Ryan Jackson	.251	171	14	43	2	14	23	30	6
Cody Asche*	.250	20	4	5	1	3	2	4	1
Jabari Henry	.250	48	5	12	1	4	7	9	1
Ryan Court	.250	24	3	6	1	4	5	10	0
Blair Beck	.234	158	16	37	5	18	12	56	0
Javier Betancourt	.229	140	8	32	0	12	11	24	8
Jason Martinson	.210	372	64	78	15	50	76	145	14
Alvaro Rondon#	.197	71	10	14	0	3	9	20	7
Chris Colabello	.195	82	13	16	1	6	10	26	0
O'Koyea Dickson	.185	27	2	5	0	1	3	7	0
Josh Prince	.133	45	2	6	1	5	6	4	0

Name	W	L	ERA	G	SV	IP	H	BB	SO
Nick Rumbelow	3	0	0.81	21	7	22	16	3	31
Dan Runzler*	1	0	1.15	16	2	16	17	3	17
Kevin McGowan	2	2	2.29	4	0	20	13	8	18
Daniel Gibson*	2	2	2.41	36	0	34	24	7	37
Mike Hauschild	4	0	2.50	9	0	50	53	11	40
Ricardo Gomez	1	1	2.72	35	1	43	21	21	48
Matt West	2	3	3.00	50	4	48	37	24	57
Michael Mariot	3	0	3.00	8	0	36	34	11	40
Felipe Paulino	2	1	3.08	26	15	26	17	13	37
Konner Wade	0	2	3.38	5	0	27	33	3	17
Cesar Cabral*	1	1	3.46	12	0	13	15	12	6
Troy Scribner	6	7	3.68	22	0	122	113	49	127
Roy Merritt*	2	3	3.70	11	0	56	62	20	32
James Dykstra	1	0	3.75	14	1	12	14	6	6
Josh Martin	3	0	3.77	25	0	29	21	10	29
Dallas Beeler	9	7	3.86	26	0	145	167	53	97
Carlos Pimentel	6	4	3.92	18	0	78	65	35	71
Mitch Talbot	1	3	3.93	7	0	34	38	8	28
Daniel Schlereth*	2	2	4.07	28	1	24	23	15	35
Jeff Ames	2	1	4.20	15	0	15	11	9	28
Kevin Comer	2	5	4.44	43	1	47	39	19	55
Joe Lienhard	1	0	4.50	5	0	14	15	5	8
Chase De Jong	4	4	5.56	12	0	66	81	14	53
Matt Purke*	5	8	5.62	31	0	90	109	39	48
Luke Irvine	2	2	6.35	15	0	34	36	23	15
Jean Machi	2	2	6.75	25	1	24	32	5	15
Mark Lowe	2	1	8.35	14	0	18	26	9	21
Christian Bergman	0	2	8.53	5	0	19	33	5	11
Roger Bernal	0	1	11.12	3	0	11	25	9	8

YORK REVOLUTION

Name	AVG	AB	R	H	HR	RBI	BB	SO	SB
Isaias Tejeda	.338	500	86	169	23	87	53	73	1
Carlos Franco*	.319	317	54	101	13	55	35	70	0
Welington Dotel	.313	480	71	150	13	79	31	130	34
J.P. Sportman	.304	204	30	62	3	24	6	38	9
Ryan Dent	.302	308	47	93	10	50	37	86	0
Alexi Casilla#	.300	130	18	39	3	9	6	15	1
Melky Mesa	.298	460	66	137	20	70	17	102	6
Telvin Nash	.294	486	107	143	41	100	105	122	0
Henry Castillo#	.293	400	56	117	14	67	36	111	4
Angelys Nina	.286	248	36	71	4	41	19	27	0
James Skelton*	.281	331	62	93	9	49	72	96	11
DJ Jenkins	.267	15	2	4	0	0	3	6	1
Justin Trapp	.260	415	57	108	5	39	28	89	18
Zach Sullivan	.242	128	25	31	5	13	5	48	8
Alvaro Rondon#	.231	169	19	39	0	13	14	36	10
Nate Coronado	.230	122	17	28	2	10	9	19	0
Corey Bass	.222	18	3	4	1	3	1	9	0
Emmanuel Marrero#	.211	38	6	8	1	3	3	13	0

Name	W	L	ERA	G	SV	IP	H	BB	SO
Jameson McGrane	4	2	1.33	59	24	61	35	34	79
Victor Capellan	1	0	1.69	11	0	11	5	2	8
Ross Detwiler*	0	0	2.81	3	0	16	18	2	7
Mitch Atkins	11	6	2.81	25	0	157	137	31	129
Josh Judy	7	2	3.20	54	7	51	53	19	42
Duke von Schamann	10	7	3.51	22	0	128	153	16	93
Cesar Cabral*	2	0	3.71	28	0	27	18	7	20
Matthew Grimes	1	5	3.72	8	0	46	45	14	27
Robert Carson*	5	1	3.91	48	0	48	48	9	27

Name	W	L	ERA	G	SV	IP	H	BB	SO
Julio Perez	5	2	4.13	48	4	48	40	34	35
Peter Tago	3	1	4.26	28	0	25	20	13	27
Orleny Quiroz*	3	2	4.46	38	0	34	47	18	27
Pat Young	0	2	4.82	22	2	19	6	16	24
Ian Thomas*	3	2	4.96	21	0	49	54	24	48
Dan Minor	8	9	4.99	26	0	126	151	21	108
Philip Walby	0	2	5.12	31	0	39	48	17	23
Ricky Schafer	2	2	5.16	8	0	23	28	13	19
Austin Steinfort	3	1	5.33	6	0	27	22	21	19
Corey Walter	4	3	5.71	11	0	52	76	22	18
Josh Smoker*	0	1	6.05	11	0	19	21	12	17
Jalen Miller	1	1	6.75	7	0	16	23	11	21
Jake Welch	0	0	6.88	3	0	17	19	6	20
Jeffrey Rosa	0	2	7.20	13	0	15	11	12	9
Julio Eusebio	0	3	7.22	11	0	29	40	19	20
Troy Terzi	1	3	7.22	7	0	29	37	14	24
Jarret Martin*	0	1	7.71	19	0	16	15	15	16
Sam Burton	0	0	7.90	9	0	14	17	15	11
Joe Jones	1	1	8.38	12	0	19	25	14	7

CAN-AM LEAGUE

The final season of the Can-Am League brought with it a new champion. The New Jersey Jackals had lost in the championship series five straight seasons at one point, but they had not won a title. The Jackals received the final Can-Am League championship trophy by topping Sussex County.

Can-Am Division	W	L	PCT	GB
Sussex County Miners	61	33	.649	--
Trois-Rivieres Aigles	58	36	.617	3
New Jersey Jackals	48	46	.511	13
Rockland Boulders	42	50	.457	18
Ottawa Champions	41	54	.432	20.5
Les Capitales de Quebec	36	59	.379	25.5

Guests Division	W	L	PCT	GB
Cuban National Team	8	7	.533	--
Empire League	0	4	.000	2.5
Shikoku Island All-Stars	7	12	.368	3

Playoffs—Semifinals: Sussex County defeated Rockland 3-1 and New Jersey defeated Trois Rivieres 3-2 in best-of-five series. **Finals:** New Jersey defeated Sussex County 3-1 in best-of-five series.

Attendance: Rockland 123,999; Quebec 119,060; Ottawa 88,119; Trois-Rivieres 85,506; New Jersey 76,658; Sussex County 72,594.

BATTING LEADERS

Player	Team	AVG	AB	R	H	HR	RBI
Audy Ciriaco	SC	.328	351	57	115	9	70
Blake Grant-Parks	ROC	.327	251	35	82	10	44
Trey Hair	SC	.324	318	60	103	8	62
Conrad Gregor	NJ	.322	326	85	105	12	67
Juan Kelly	TR	.321	221	45	71	10	46
Matt Oberste	ROC	.320	297	50	95	13	45
Ryne Birk	ROC	.317	268	42	85	5	39
John Brontsema	ROC	.314	264	39	83	4	34
Alfredo Marte	NJ	.311	350	68	109	16	88
Jay Gonzalez	NJ	.310	242	52	75	0	15

PITCHING LEADERS

Player	Team	W	L	ERA	IP	H	BB	SO
Andrew Gist	SC	9	1	2.62	86	98	25	61
Phillippe Aumont	OTT	8	4	2.65	119	109	23	145
Frank Duncan	SC	10	6	3.05	133	113	16	111
Tom Burns	SC	8	1	3.29	88	84	31	71
Brandon Barker	TR	7	3	3.39	101	99	32	107
Brendan Butler	NJ	6	3	3.55	101	81	41	93
Jeff Thompson	SC	11	3	3.68	117	120	40	96
Eduard Reyes	NJ	9	4	3.71	107	101	40	88
Garrett Harris	TR	9	3	3.75	98	83	39	105
Jared Mortensen	OTT	7	8	3.96	109	109	36	97

CUBAN NATIONAL TEAM

Name	AVG	AB	R	H	HR	RBI	BB	SO	SB
Carlos Perez	.400	15	3	6	1	4	2	5	0
Raul Gonzalez	.389	36	8	14	0	4	8	7	0

INDEPENDENT LEAGUES

Name	AVG	AB	R	H	HR	RBI	BB	SO	SB
Cesar Prieto*	.322	59	8	19	1	6	2	10	4
Frank Morejon	.300	10	1	3	0	1	0	3	0
Yuniesky Larduet	.300	50	8	15	0	7	5	8	5
Yosvany Alacorn	.283	46	3	13	2	9	1	6	1
Orlando Aceby	.280	25	1	7	0	3	0	4	1
Yordanis Samon	.259	54	8	14	3	7	1	7	2
Andres Hernandez	.235	17	0	4	0	1	2	5	1
Yoelkis Stevens*	.222	54	8	12	2	4	5	9	1
Alfredo Fradaga	.182	11	0	2	0	0	1	4	0
Frederich Cepeda#	.176	34	5	6	1	3	6	12	0
Yoelquis Cespedes	.167	18	1	3	0	0	0	6	1
Jorge Aloma	.154	26	2	4	0	0	1	7	0

Name	W	L	ERA	G	SV	IP	H	BB	SO
Lazaro Blanco	2	0	0.79	2	0	11	4	5	9
Freddy Alvarez	1	0	0.82	2	0	11	9	2	8
Yosimar Cousin	0	1	2.38	3	0	11	15	5	11
Pedro Jiminez?	0	1	2.63	6	1	14	15	4	12
Yariel Rodriguez	1	0	2.84	3	0	13	8	6	19
Misael Villa*	0	2	4.35	4	0	10	15	6	8
Frank Medina	1	1	4.50	6	1	10	10	6	10
Wilson Paredes	2	0	5.93	7	1	14	12	8	10

NEW JERSEY JACKALS

Name	AVG	AB	R	H	HR	RBI	BB	SO	SB
David Harris	.342	111	14	38	2	22	11	22	4
Conrad Gregor*	.322	326	85	105	12	67	82	71	49
Alfredo Marte	.311	350	68	109	16	88	44	49	12
Jay Gonzalez*	.310	242	52	75	0	15	41	57	11
Santiago Chirino	.308	279	50	86	0	30	20	28	0
Richard Stock*	.281	292	34	82	9	64	22	52	2
Emilio Guerrero	.270	159	22	43	4	24	12	40	6
Isaac Wenrich*	.268	168	25	45	2	18	23	34	2
Jason Agresti	.268	224	19	60	2	26	14	50	1
Nelson Ward*	.268	235	41	63	2	22	41	55	19
Sthervin Matos	.263	57	7	15	1	10	1	12	1
Demetrius Moorer	.247	194	32	48	0	14	40	49	26
Chase Smartt	.240	146	16	35	1	15	17	27	1
Gregg Veneklasen	.215	107	7	23	1	10	3	41	0
Andrew Dundon	.211	109	18	23	2	12	4	28	4
Rylan Sandoval	.088	34	4	3	0	1	6	16	0
Ronnie Mitchell*	.050	40	4	2	0	1	4	9	4

Name	W	L	ERA	G	SV	IP	H	BB	SO
Dylan Brammer	1	3	1.29	31	9	42	30	21	49
Javier Reynoso*	2	1	2.31	9	0	12	5	5	17
Reece Karalus	6	4	3.25	35	4	55	40	22	56
Brendan Butler	6	3	3.55	17	0	101	81	41	93
Eduard Reyes	9	4	3.71	17	0	107	101	40	88
Matt Vogel	2	4	3.86	16	0	51	41	49	66
Ismael Cabrera	3	1	3.86	8	0	14	11	8	11
Matt Dallas	3	0	4.86	11	0	17	15	10	21
Jeffrey Rosa	0	1	4.87	9	0	20	16	18	20
Lendy Castillo	4	5	5.13	23	3	79	82	50	82
Justin Brantley	7	6	5.40	18	0	100	116	34	77
Nick Bozman*	0	0	5.73	13	0	22	27	18	32
David Richardson	0	3	5.79	10	1	19	17	13	19
Will Landsheft	1	1	5.97	16	0	32	49	17	33
Jorge Perez	0	1	6.11	10	0	18	21	17	14
Anthony Auletta*	0	1	6.17	4	0	12	14	11	6
Anthony Fernandez*	1	3	6.89	7	0	31	45	15	30
Lars Liguori*	1	3	7.14	5	0	29	48	11	17

OTTAWA CHAMPIONS

Name	AVG	AB	R	H	HR	RBI	BB	SO	SB
Michael Baca	.348	66	10	23	0	11	6	10	5
Larry Balkwill	.141	85	15	12	3	10	19	32	0
Chris Bosco	.119	42	10	5	0	1	8	16	1
Steve Brown	.302	288	55	87	7	54	32	58	17
Jordan Caillouet	.219	247	20	54	5	34	11	47	4
Adron Chambers*	.187	75	10	14	1	9	11	14	2
Malik Collymore	.269	327	55	88	4	31	38	70	52
Nick DeTringo	.223	121	15	27	0	9	16	26	5
Matt Foley	.231	52	6	12	0	3	7	22	0
Maikol Gonzalez	.269	286	46	77	2	27	32	30	9

Name	AVG	AB	R	H	HR	RBI	BB	SO	SB
Vinny Guglietti*	.257	191	26	49	6	28	16	40	3
Trey Martin	.235	34	8	8	1	4	8	12	3
Andy Mocahbee	.225	129	13	29	4	10	16	35	0
Stephen Octave	.286	35	4	10	0	4	2	8	1
Eduard Pinto*	.290	207	27	60	3	26	19	17	4
Brian Portelli	.263	274	34	72	6	51	25	77	1
Leonardo Reginatto	.300	337	52	101	0	37	41	60	8
Jiandido Tromp	.264	318	47	84	7	53	39	65	8

Name	W	L	ERA	G	SV	IP	H	BB	SO
Zach Vennaro	1	0	0.77	10	2	12	7	5	16
Phillippe Aumont	8	4	2.65	18	0	119	109	23	145
Dakota Freese	0	1	2.84	3	0	13	4	9	13
Evan Rutckyj*	2	2	3.03	29	3	36	27	26	53
Zac Westcott	2	5	3.54	8	0	53	52	10	44
Matt Valin*	0	0	3.78	15	0	17	12	14	23
Jared Mortensen	7	8	3.96	20	0	109	109	36	97
Danny Garcia*	6	6	4.23	19	0	113	106	36	120
Austin Glorius	4	3	4.25	35	11	36	34	22	41
Miles Sheehan	1	3	5.03	25	1	39	40	16	47
Austin Chrimson	2	3	5.06	9	0	48	64	17	38
Jordan Kurokawa	2	5	5.12	16	0	65	77	29	38
Heath Bowers	2	7	5.34	26	0	61	54	43	82
Jesse Lepore	2	4	7.11	13	0	32	36	30	26
Andrew Cooper	0	1	8.41	25	2	35	47	16	27
Kida De La Cruz	1	2	12.41	13	0	12	15	13	15

QUEBEC CAPITALES

Name	AVG	AB	R	H	HR	RBI	BB	SO	SB
Josue Peley	.409	22	0	9	0	3	0	2	0
Yordan Manduley	.350	214	30	75	1	27	9	13	8
Stayler Hernandez*	.319	204	32	65	4	30	13	32	1
Zach Wilson	.305	82	11	25	1	14	1	20	0
Kody Ruedisili	.293	92	12	27	2	8	9	35	3
Joe Lytle*	.288	80	11	23	0	10	11	15	1
T.J. White	.274	223	35	61	10	44	26	57	2
Connor Panas*	.271	96	15	26	1	10	4	16	2
Jhalan Jackson	.271	218	35	59	13	39	26	58	1
David Salgueiro	.269	268	48	72	1	21	45	58	21
Tyson Gillies*	.263	137	24	36	5	18	17	38	1
Brandon Fischer	.254	244	43	62	3	24	44	64	10
Michael Baca	.252	119	19	30	1	14	11	23	6
J.D. Williams	.247	77	11	19	0	7	9	26	8
Jesse Hodges	.233	202	24	47	4	30	13	55	1
Rian Kiniry*	.229	188	30	43	5	28	27	45	2
Alan Mocahbee	.228	101	10	23	1	15	12	29	0
Chris Shaw	.207	164	12	34	2	22	9	39	1
Melvin Rodriguez*	.207	58	4	12	0	7	3	12	0
Andrew Godbold	.204	54	3	11	0	5	1	16	0
Corey Bass	.195	195	18	38	3	18	31	74	2
Brandon Brosher	.192	26	3	5	0	2	1	9	1
Rylan Sandoval	.150	20	1	3	0	0	1	10	0
Brett Siddall*	.136	44	5	6	0	4	12	18	0

Name	W	L	ERA	G	SV	IP	H	BB	SO
Reilly Hovis	2	0	1.23	15	0	22	11	14	31
Jonathan de Marte	3	2	2.23	35	5	40	27	15	42
Dustin Molleken	2	1	2.51	28	7	47	42	14	46
David Richardson	2	4	3.09	12	0	55	49	18	51
Nate Antone	0	1	3.86	11	0	23	25	12	16
Matt Marsh	0	2	4.09	5	0	22	22	8	21
Jack Charleston	3	5	4.13	43	0	52	58	12	38
Scott Richmond	5	5	4.24	17	0	102	102	28	86
Karl Gelinas	2	8	4.54	13	0	77	93	23	61
Seth Davis*	2	2	5.01	30	0	32	29	21	37
Dany Paradis Giroux	2	3	5.54	25	0	52	67	14	32
Sean Cruz	0	3	5.76	6	0	25	37	9	19
Arik Sikula	6	8	5.79	21	0	110	132	42	93
Max Kuhns	1	2	6.00	18	0	18	25	11	14
Austin Chrimson	3	2	6.23	8	0	43	57	19	30
Levi MaVorhis	0	1	7.07	11	0	14	18	4	11
Vladimir Garcia	1	4	7.66	8	0	25	33	7	22
Lachlan Fontaine	0	2	8.71	18	0	31	43	15	25
Marvin Gorgas	1	3	9.53	10	0	11	17	8	15

ROCKLAND BOULDERS

Name	AVG	AB	R	H	HR	RBI	BB	SO	SB
Katsuya Senoo*	.339	118	19	40	0	7	9	17	3
Blake Grant-Parks	.327	251	35	82	10	44	17	51	1
Matt Oberste	.320	297	50	95	13	45	19	54	1
Ryne Birk*	.317	268	42	85	5	39	34	54	6
John Brontsema	.314	264	39	83	4	34	16	58	14
Ezequiel Carrera*	.267	15	4	4	0	0	4	4	1
Marcos Almonte	.257	148	17	38	1	11	3	34	6
Adam Ehrlich*	.253	285	27	72	2	40	34	65	0
Angelo Mora#	.238	21	2	5	0	0	3	7	1
Grant Heyman*	.237	283	41	67	12	44	15	84	6
Richie Fecteau*	.236	271	47	64	16	38	23	68	5
Collin Ferguson*	.224	304	31	68	6	39	32	83	2
Chase Harris	.218	293	40	64	5	27	25	85	26
Steven Figueroa*	.217	23	3	5	0	0	1	7	0
Craig Maddox*	.214	14	1	3	0	0	1	6	0
Cito Culver	.188	64	6	12	0	5	7	34	0
Mitch Piatnik	.178	101	7	18	1	6	4	35	8
Jordan Hinshaw	.171	41	3	7	0	2	5	16	1

Name	W	L	ERA	G	SV	IP	H	BB	SO
Josh Turner	0	0	1.00	12	0	18	12	9	20
James Mulry*	3	1	1.82	52	1	40	27	23	41
Luis Cedeno	1	2	2.57	9	0	35	23	19	40
Jake Zokan*	5	4	2.65	22	2	54	47	22	50
Landon Holifield	1	1	2.79	27	0	42	36	13	53
Robbie Gordon	5	2	3.05	42	12	41	22	32	59
Edgar De La Rosa	2	2	3.52	5	0	31	22	13	27
Tim Ponto	2	3	3.74	49	0	67	70	28	50
Brett Schneider	1	1	3.98	6	0	20	20	7	27
Nick Kennedy	3	3	4.14	59	0	67	67	18	45
Alex Fishberg	0	0	4.44	14	0	24	19	15	33
J.D. Busfield	7	3	4.45	16	0	89	104	17	67
Reinaldo Lopez	5	7	4.70	15	0	75	100	24	36
Justin Valdespina	1	2	5.33	7	0	27	28	25	17
Zach Jemiola	1	4	5.40	15	0	28	35	22	23
Pasquale Mazzoccoli	2	4	5.60	9	0	45	45	25	23
Tommy Shirley*	2	7	5.62	15	0	58	69	18	43
Edilson Alvarez	1	2	7.53	3	0	14	20	11	14

SHIKOUKU ALL-STARS

Name	AVG	AB	R	H	HR	RBI	BB	SO	SB
Sendo Katsuya*	.373	67	12	25	1	13	3	10	7
Nakamura Michitaro	.328	58	8	19	0	4	5	5	1
Kishi Junichiro	.321	81	14	26	1	6	3	13	4
Hirima Hayato	.318	66	8	21	0	9	8	15	10
Takai Yuka	.318	44	3	14	0	10	1	12	1
Takai Yuka	.318	44	3	14	0	10	1	12	1
Hama Shonosuke	.317	41	3	13	0	4	0	11	0
Ota Naoya	.294	34	3	10	0	3	2	12	2
Shirakata Katsuya	.286	56	14	16	0	6	9	9	7
Miyoshi Issei	.273	33	4	9	0	5	0	11	0
Yokomizo Takuya	.219	32	4	7	0	7	2	6	1
Kawabata Koki	.214	28	3	6	0	2	0	11	2
Morita Kyuto	.214	14	1	3	0	3	3	6	0
Okamura Mizuki	.196	51	7	10	0	4	5	15	4
Mayama Katsunori	.179	28	2	5	0	2	2	2	1

Name	W	L	ERA	G	SV	IP	H	BB	SO
Ishi Daichi	2	2	3.09	4	0	23	23	11	35
Shodi Itsuki*	1	0	3.60	3	0	15	13	1	6
Michihara Junya*	1	1	3.95	6	0	14	13	13	6
Hayashi Yudai?	0	0	4.63	9	0	12	7	10	6
Furuya Tsuyoshi	0	0	4.85	11	0	13	12	11	8
Fukuda Yuji	0	1	5.06	5	0	16	16	8	11
Yamazaki Katsuya*	0	1	7.84	6	0	10	17	6	4
Otaka Ayumi*	0	0	11.32	8	0	10	21	12	11

SUSSEX COUNTY MINERS

Name	AVG	AB	R	H	HR	RBI	BB	SO	SB
Angel Reyes	.373	59	17	22	2	13	3	6	9
Nate Coronado	.336	131	24	44	4	20	15	24	13
Audy Ciriaco	.328	351	57	115	9	70	24	45	21

Name	AVG	AB	R	H	HR	RBI	BB	SO	SB
Trey Hair*	.324	318	60	103	8	62	60	81	27
Jose Brizuela*	.302	285	62	86	9	44	63	69	13
Nick Zaharion	.295	146	22	43	2	21	24	31	2
Kalian Sams	.278	90	19	25	1	16	11	30	6
Mikey Reynolds	.274	259	54	71	6	32	36	33	40
Jordan Scott#	.273	55	12	15	1	8	8	15	3
Jarred Mederos	.253	265	46	67	2	37	39	79	10
Gavin Stupienski*	.248	117	15	29	1	13	18	28	5
Cito Culver	.242	215	25	52	2	31	16	45	4
Noah Cummings	.232	112	25	26	4	14	15	31	6
Brian Mayer	.222	18	1	4	0	1	1	7	0
Brandon Downes	.214	196	31	42	4	25	26	91	9
Breland Almadova	.211	71	12	15	1	5	10	21	1
Andy Paz	.208	48	6	10	2	15	4	14	1
D.K. Carey	.178	45	6	8	0	6	9	18	3
Troy Dixon*	.175	57	8	10	1	8	10	15	1
Yordany Salva#	.154	26	1	4	0	4	2	9	1
C.J. Retherford	.125	32	1	4	0	3	3	7	0

Name	W	L	ERA	G	SV	IP	H	BB	SO
Jose Jose*	6	2	1.58	37	6	46	40	6	54
Ryan Newell	0	3	1.75	38	19	36	29	13	60
Andrew Gist*	9	1	2.62	20	0	86	98	25	61
Frank Duncan	10	6	3.05	19	0	133	113	16	111
Tommy Burns	8	1	3.29	21	0	88	84	31	71
Cory Jones	2	2	3.56	11	0	48	43	23	34
Jeff Thompson	11	3	3.68	19	0	117	120	40	96
Scott Kuzminsky	1	2	4.02	15	0	31	32	26	16
Kevin Grendell*	5	5	4.11	37	0	50	39	29	58
David Palladino	7	2	4.53	19	0	95	95	58	90
James Campbell	2	1	5.40	15	0	30	19	21	30
Ty Mondile	0	2	6.75	4	0	13	18	4	6

TROIS-RIVIERES AIGLES

Name	AVG	AB	R	H	HR	RBI	BB	SO	SB
Brandon Bednar	.357	14	2	5	0	1	1	5	0
Francis Desilets*	.333	30	4	10	0	3	0	3	1
Juan Kelly#	.321	221	45	71	10	46	34	37	4
Raphael Gladu*	.302	258	47	78	8	64	25	38	7
David Glaude*	.290	365	78	106	13	49	51	71	16
Tucker Nathans*	.289	377	64	109	12	56	54	104	30
Alberth Martinez	.284	215	41	61	6	40	30	43	0
Thomas Roulis#	.263	217	25	57	1	26	20	48	6
Anthony Hermelyn	.257	276	59	71	9	41	65	84	1
Parker Sniatynski	.257	167	29	43	2	17	18	47	6
Michael Suchy	.250	312	40	78	7	47	39	90	8
Taylor Brennan	.246	341	61	84	15	60	59	133	6
LeVon Washington*	.220	164	25	36	6	25	21	43	0
Joe DeLuca#	.199	156	21	31	7	26	25	70	1
Brandon Brosher	.167	30	2	5	0	2	4	17	2

Name	W	L	ERA	G	SV	IP	H	BB	SO
Garrett Mundell	2	2	2.32	39	20	43	31	12	52
Bubby Rossman	3	0	2.41	29	1	34	30	15	48
Domenic Mazza*	5	2	2.62	10	0	55	53	9	60
Cortland Cox	2	3	3.14	45	1	49	42	19	50
Brandon Barker	7	3	3.39	19	0	101	99	32	107
Brandon Brosher	0	2	3.71	24	1	34	33	16	35
Garrett Harris	9	3	3.75	20	0	98	83	39	105
Chris Murphy	8	5	4.35	20	0	114	141	31	86
El'Hajj Muhammad	2	0	4.63	22	0	23	25	12	17
Tyler Ferguson	3	5	4.75	45	2	55	44	34	55
Cam LaFleur*	5	3	4.82	25	0	56	55	32	44
Kevin McNorton	10	7	5.02	22	0	115	164	22	73
Colby Morris	2	0	5.40	3	0	12	14	4	6
Andrew Cohen	0	1	9.28	7	0	11	10	10	9

FRONTIER LEAGUE

River City said goodbye in fine fashion. A month after the owners announced the team would shut down at the end of the season, the Rascals won the Frontier League title. They relied on a little help from their friends—the team's booster club paid for the team to stay in hotel rooms before the deciding Game 5 of the finals.

INDEPENDENT LEAGUES

East Division	W	L	PCT	GB
Lake Erie Crushers	54	42	.563	--
Schaumburg Boomers	47	49	.490	7
Windy City ThunderBolts	42	54	.438	12
Joliet Slammers	39	56	.411	14.5
Washington WildThings	37	59	.385	17

West Division	W	L	PCT	GB
Evansville Otters	57	39	.594	--
Florence Freedom	57	39	.594	--
River City Rascals	53	42	.558	3.5
Southern Illinois Miners	53	43	.552	4
Gateway Grizzlies	39	56	.411	17.5

Division Champ. ^Wild Card

Playoffs—Semifinals: River City defeated Evansville 3-0 and Florence defeated Lake Erie 3-0 in best-of-five series. **Finals:** River City defeated Florence 3-2 in best-of-five series.

Attendance: Schaumburg 156,383; Joliet 121,730; Gateway 112,252; Southern Illinois 101,441; Lake Erie 100,915; Evansville 100,051; Florence 99,308; Washington 90,638; Windy City 79,171; River City 66,832. .

All-Star Team: C: Skyler Ewing, Florence. **1B:** Chris Iriart, Normal. **2B:** Jack Parenty, Schaumburg. **3B:** Ryan Long, Evansville. **SS:** Santiago Chirino, Normal. **OF:** Derrick Loveless, Normal; James Harris, Washington; Andrew Godbold, Normal. **DH:** Paul Kronenfeld, River City. **SP:** Thomas Dorminy, Washington. **RP:** Cody Mincey, River City. **Most Valuable Player:** James Harris, Washington. **Pitcher of the Year:** Thomas Dorminy. **Rookie of the Year:** Aaron Hill, Lake Erie.

BATTING LEADERS

Player	Team	AVG	AB	R	H	HR	RBI
Quincy Nieporte	SCH	.315	324	46	102	13	71
Gianfranco Wawoe	S. ILL	.306	337	49	103	10	43
Steven Kraft	LE	.293	300	42	88	2	38
Keith Grieshaber	Evan	.291	351	48	102	2	42
Jamey Smart	S. ILL	.290	331	44	96	5	55
Ricky Ramirez	FLOR	.289	311	56	90	7	54
Emmanuel Marrero	LE	.288	382	56	110	16	50
Hector Roa	WASH	.288	382	58	110	18	70
Jack Parenty	SCH	.288	392	55	113	1	28
Ryan Long	EVAN	.285	347	54	99	14	78

PITCHING LEADERS

Player	Team	W	L	ERA	IP	H	BB	SO
Brendan Feldmann	RC	7	1	1.97	87	74	14	87
Jared Koenig	LE	7	2	2.24	104	87	34	133
Patrick Ledet	LE	6	4	2.34	119	93	27	109
Gunnar Kines	SCH	6	2	2.36	103	85	20	112
Tyler Beardsley	EVAN	9	4	2.56	130	105	37	116
Mike Castellani	FLOR	9	2	2.66	129	133	25	72
Tyler Thornton	WC	7	3	2.69	100	81	27	107
Tyler Vail	EVAN	5	5	2.78	81	60	29	84
Jake Welch	WC	8	5	2.93	129	125	38	127
Daren Osby	JOL	4	6	2.95	116	101	30	122

EVANSVILLE OTTERS

Name	AVG	AB	R	H	HR	RBI	BB	SO	SB
Elijah MacNamee	.309	139	19	43	1	17	21	31	3
Keith Grieshaber	.291	351	48	102	2	42	17	92	23
David Cronin*	.285	358	65	102	3	34	50	54	20
Ryan Long*	.285	347	54	99	14	78	51	93	9
Carlos Castro	.276	257	32	71	11	31	8	63	2
Hunter Cullen*	.261	249	43	65	8	34	27	59	16
Rob Calabrese	.257	210	30	54	10	26	34	57	5
Taylor Lane	.252	111	11	28	0	22	8	24	4
Mike Rizzitello	.249	181	24	45	1	11	23	33	7
Anthony Maselli*	.242	33	4	8	1	2	2	9	3
Dakota Phillips*	.233	219	24	51	7	32	21	95	0
Tanner Wetrich	.227	66	11	15	0	7	9	20	2
Jack Meggs*	.221	298	33	66	2	26	22	59	22
J.J. Gould	.188	208	32	39	5	24	32	65	3
Justin Erby	.185	27	3	5	0	0	4	12	2
Mitchell Hansen*	.159	63	9	10	2	5	5	22	3

Name	W	L	ERA	G	SV	IP	H	BB	SO
Taylor Wright	3	0	0.92	38	18	49	31	16	56

Name	W	L	ERA	G	SV	IP	H	BB	SO
Patrick McGuff	5	0	1.05	6	0	43	22	17	60
Danny Hrbek	1	2	1.08	15	5	17	9	5	27
Brandyn Sittinger	2	2	1.42	7	1	38	24	20	52
Tyler Beardsley	9	4	2.56	20	0	130	105	37	116
Cam Opp*	4	2	2.70	21	2	27	22	11	35
Tyler Vail	5	5	2.78	18	0	81	60	29	84
Drew Beyer	3	3	2.83	26	1	29	28	9	32
Jake Welch	8	5	2.93	20	0	129	125	38	127
Randy Wynne	5	2	3.42	7	0	50	49	8	47
Matt Quintana	2	0	4.22	3	0	21	16	5	19
Austin Nicely*	6	7	4.32	17	0	92	98	36	66
Abraham Almonte*	0	0	4.38	14	1	12	4	10	13
Anthony Arias*	2	2	4.56	9	0	26	20	15	31
Chris Cepeda	1	0	5.02	13	0	14	14	7	14
Matt Rowland	0	1	5.40	10	0	10	4	14	16
Malcolm Grady	0	0	6.97	9	0	10	14	7	13
Michael Gizzi	0	2	7.31	17	0	16	16	10	22

FLORENCE FREEDOM

Name	AVG	AB	R	H	HR	RBI	BB	SO	SB
Tyler Reichenborn	.319	72	12	23	3	15	5	12	2
Andre Mercurio*	.291	199	33	58	3	23	15	31	14
Kenny Meimerstorf	.290	31	2	9	0	6	3	10	2
Ricky Ramirez*	.289	311	56	90	7	54	54	56	6
Isaac Benard*	.280	347	45	97	5	45	35	79	16
Brandon Pugh*	.276	170	28	47	2	14	17	36	27
Luis Pintor	.268	365	55	98	6	37	32	90	27
Michael Gulino	.268	56	10	15	1	12	16	16	3
Austin Wobrock*	.267	329	42	88	1	50	34	81	14
Caleb Lopes	.265	351	59	93	9	40	45	70	8
Connor Crane	.260	269	43	70	11	61	29	93	18
Ryan Rinsky	.204	98	8	20	0	8	16	28	6
Jackson Pritchard	.194	144	22	28	4	22	13	50	5
Taylor Bryant	.182	220	35	40	6	22	53	76	6
Trevor Craport	.167	78	6	13	1	6	4	18	3

Name	W	L	ERA	G	SV	IP	H	BB	SO
Karl Craigie*	5	3	0.93	37	10	39	25	15	48
Johnathon Tripp	4	3	1.06	27	13	42	28	10	41
Jared Cheek	1	1	1.84	10	1	15	11	4	19
Frank Valentino	4	3	2.10	8	0	51	41	16	49
Mike Castellani*	9	2	2.66	21	0	129	133	25	72
Zak Spivy	2	5	2.86	18	0	66	55	25	28
Scott Sebald*	7	1	3.40	18	0	114	87	34	105
Tyler Gibson	7	2	3.51	12	0	74	74	11	60
Brian McKenna	1	2	3.63	20	3	22	18	0	34
Reece Calvert	0	0	3.75	3	0	12	13	0	13
John LaRossa	0	0	4.38	9	0	12	14	7	8
Hayden Wheeler*	1	2	4.81	19	1	34	29	16	29
Ryan Mordecai	4	4	4.85	26	1	26	26	14	23
Daniel Williams	3	3	5.19	9	0	50	58	11	37
Sean Watkins	1	0	5.27	13	0	14	14	14	12
George Faue*	3	4	5.32	7	0	44	47	14	36
Ryan Hill	1	0	5.93	3	0	14	16	8	6
Chris Amend	0	1	16.20	4	0	12	16	12	4

GATEWAY GRIZZLIES

Name	AVG	AB	R	H	HR	RBI	BB	SO	SB
Tyler Plantier	.438	16	2	7	1	6	0	2	0
Wesley Jones	.343	67	4	23	0	6	3	13	0
Jamey Smart*	.276	116	14	32	1	25	14	23	0
Connor Owings*	.265	347	45	92	12	52	53	112	12
Luis Roman*	.265	117	12	31	0	15	13	29	2
Brent Sakurai	.261	371	52	97	5	26	40	70	22
Luke Lowery	.256	266	27	68	12	33	20	79	13
Anthony Ray*	.250	180	16	45	1	8	13	47	9
Shawon Dunston*	.250	340	45	85	9	39	33	65	36
Andrew Daniel	.246	256	35	63	9	38	30	63	6
Zak Taylor	.246	203	17	50	2	19	8	39	0
Cody Brickhouse	.225	40	6	9	0	2	5	14	0
Stoney O'Brien	.225	40	6	9	1	3	2	13	0
Dustin Woodcock*	.221	199	27	44	12	27	22	48	3
Cletis Avery	.216	51	4	11	0	4	7	15	5
Greg White	.211	57	6	12	1	7	3	18	1
Gunnar Buhner	.211	185	24	39	4	17	19	66	7

Matt Brown	.207	116	12	24	1	16	18	49	0
Matt McPhearson*	.206	68	9	14	0	6	6	15	0
Rafael Valera	.200	70	14	14	1	7	9	18	1
Ryan Kirby*	.163	49	2	8	0	2	2	17	0

Name	W	L	ERA	G	SV	IP	H	BB	SO
Geoff Bramblett	2	3	0.50	44	14	54	25	17	61
Jason Seever*	2	1	2.34	45	0	50	38	15	54
Grant Black	1	6	2.41	51	9	52	36	16	65
Dakota Smith	1	2	3.47	45	0	49	46	19	53
Reign Letkeman	4	5	3.74	14	0	65	53	28	62
Chris Carden	8	5	4.00	19	0	106	95	51	90
Thomas Nicoll	3	3	4.01	20	0	61	53	18	73
Dom Topoozian	6	7	4.23	17	0	100	109	22	57
Jordan Barrett*	4	6	4.38	18	0	97	88	62	108
Ian Kahaloa	3	7	4.67	18	0	62	67	26	73
Luke Lanphere	2	4	4.94	20	0	55	52	19	58
Patrick Boyle*	0	3	5.36	44	0	40	24	39	55
Cody Luther	2	1	5.52	3	0	15	19	4	10

JOLIET SLAMMERS

Name	AVG	AB	R	H	HR	RBI	BB	SO	SB
Clayton Harp*	.313	147	14	46	4	17	10	30	3
Jacob Crum	.302	43	7	13	0	5	4	11	1
Riley Krane*	.280	368	52	103	8	31	22	68	6
Dash Winningham*	.264	235	20	62	8	35	14	51	0
Brian Parreira*	.262	107	8	28	2	13	8	14	0
Harrison Bragg	.260	235	24	61	7	30	14	77	0
Oliver Nunez#	.231	143	16	33	1	6	14	23	12
Peyton Isaacson*	.218	202	15	44	4	28	16	67	0
Milton Ramos	.215	65	2	14	1	6	2	16	3
Jose Camacho*	.213	61	6	13	0	2	4	18	3
London Lindley	.208	264	29	55	0	17	15	46	21
Chaz Meadows	.203	300	35	61	4	20	37	90	10
Jimmy Roche	.197	137	15	27	3	11	13	41	0
Tyler Coolbaugh#	.186	118	6	22	0	9	9	28	0
Jared Morello*	.185	151	12	28	1	8	14	42	8
Tyler Bordner	.179	56	3	10	0	2	1	15	0
L.J. Kalawaia*	.178	118	10	21	0	5	10	34	2
Ridge Hoopii-Haslam	.174	121	7	21	0	8	10	37	7
Frank Podkul	.154	13	1	2	0	0	2	8	0
Travis Bolin	.146	41	5	6	0	0	4	18	5
Luis Touron#	.136	22	1	3	0	0	0	10	0
Tommy LaCongo	.111	45	3	5	0	0	5	13	0
Cody Clark	.064	47	2	3	1	2	7	27	0

Name	W	L	ERA	G	SV	IP	H	BB	SO
Ryan Koziol	4	3	1.21	37	23	45	41	5	47
Mario Samuel*	3	4	2.47	31	3	51	32	23	48
Matt Quintana	6	3	2.85	16	0	88	68	34	105
Daren Osby	4	6	2.95	18	0	116	101	30	122
Drew Peden	2	4	3.00	33	0	42	36	17	34
Tyler Jandron*	4	4	3.59	14	0	85	77	30	97
Scot Hoffman	5	4	3.64	14	0	77	70	16	40
Kit Fowler	1	1	3.79	3	0	19	15	6	14
Tyler Jones	2	4	4.60	10	0	43	42	18	29
Keegan Long	3	11	4.67	18	0	104	94	52	81
Wes Albert	1	3	4.74	17	0	49	46	31	42
Isaac Sanchez	2	6	5.28	29	0	44	50	18	39
Mitch McIntyre	0	0	5.32	17	0	24	27	12	14
Cody Clark	2	2	9.43	14	1	21	31	9	25

LAKE ERIE CRUSHERS

Name	AVG	AB	R	H	HR	RBI	BB	SO	SB
Logan Farrar*	.308	78	11	24	3	9	5	15	0
Steven Kraft	.293	300	42	88	2	38	47	59	25
Emmanuel Marrero#	.288	382	56	110	16	50	27	90	6
Zach Racusin	.274	358	31	98	2	33	15	36	6
Aaron Hill	.269	346	65	93	12	33	58	108	24
Jake Vieth*	.254	284	38	72	18	57	34	98	0
James Davison*	.240	175	25	42	6	22	6	38	16
Bodie Bryan	.238	63	6	15	0	7	7	24	3
Dale Burdick	.233	317	47	74	12	45	46	94	8
Brody Wofford*	.229	170	23	39	3	12	16	50	1
John Cable*	.221	140	11	31	0	9	14	50	0
Bryan De La Rosa	.203	232	26	47	3	23	25	63	6

Dondrei Hubbard	.200	65	6	13	2	5	5	18	2
Kody Ruedisili	.190	21	0	4	0	3	1	9	0
Karl Ellison	.152	99	7	15	4	17	6	42	0
Sebastian Diaz	.146	41	4	6	2	5	6	14	1
Dane Hutcheon*	.133	45	3	6	0	1	1	18	1

Name	W	L	ERA	G	SV	IP	H	BB	SO
Michael Stryffeler	1	0	0.00	11	0	14	10	8	16
Augie Gallardo	5	2	0.85	39	0	53	33	21	60
Dalton Geekie	2	2	1.09	27	3	25	14	7	32
Seth Lucio	1	0	1.57	22	6	23	5	11	37
Kent Hasler	7	4	2.01	38	7	67	43	30	89
Sean Johnson	4	0	2.08	5	0	26	17	7	22
Sam Curtis	2	1	2.13	5	0	25	21	8	20
Evy Ruibal	1	3	2.20	13	1	16	13	3	14
Jared Koenig*	7	2	2.24	20	0	104	87	34	133
Paddy Ledet*	6	4	2.34	19	0	119	93	27	109
Dylan Mouzakes	4	3	2.44	11	0	59	46	15	45
Paul Hall*	1	2	2.53	8	0	43	41	14	42
Logan Lombana	1	3	3.28	24	10	25	23	5	31
Alex Romero	3	2	3.68	12	0	66	60	29	73
Jack Maynard	0	0	4.85	9	1	13	11	10	23
Jake Repavich*	6	6	4.89	27	0	92	100	32	76
Greyfer Eregua	0	3	5.06	6	0	27	24	8	18
Chris Pennell	0	0	7.98	9	0	15	15	6	12

RIVER CITY RASCALS

Name	AVG	AB	R	H	HR	RBI	BB	SO	SB
Tanner Wetrich	.357	14	2	5	0	1	2	6	2
L.J. Kalawaia*	.295	166	19	49	2	24	7	34	6
Andrew Penner	.282	333	49	94	4	45	33	56	7
James Morisano	.282	163	24	46	7	24	19	40	7
Braxton Martinez	.275	309	60	85	13	75	82	74	2
Kameron Esthay*	.267	348	56	93	8	45	27	90	6
Trevor Achenbach	.259	301	55	78	14	45	34	75	7
Nolan Meadows*	.253	328	45	83	10	60	49	89	1
J.D. Hearn	.249	189	30	47	6	23	23	68	7
Nick Anderson	.242	161	24	39	0	10	13	34	4
Zach Lavy*	.225	227	34	51	15	38	19	77	6
Tanner Murphy	.221	190	20	42	6	25	24	43	0
Artemis Kadkhodaian	.212	137	13	29	3	16	12	49	3
Cody Livesay*	.212	137	23	29	0	5	12	27	18
Ross Haffey	.176	17	0	3	0	0	1	6	0
Alvin Swoope	.160	25	5	4	0	1	4	12	1

Name	W	L	ERA	G	SV	IP	H	BB	SO
Jackson Sigman	1	1	0.77	11	7	12	7	4	18
Dalton Roach	4	0	1.13	5	0	32	17	6	37
Micah Kaczor	2	1	1.46	4	0	25	20	3	15
Brendan Feldmann	7	1	1.97	14	0	87	74	14	87
Jason Zgardowski	2	1	2.39	30	12	49	45	22	53
Anthony Herrera	3	2	2.59	42	0	42	38	18	46
Taylor Sugg	2	2	2.65	13	1	17	11	11	20
Taylor Purus*	1	2	2.70	29	0	20	23	6	30
Andrew Vernon	4	2	2.95	31	2	40	38	17	46
Austin Dubsky	1	1	3.00	8	0	39	35	16	43
Taylor Ahearn	2	5	3.04	12	0	74	57	17	72
Alex Winkelman*	7	2	3.63	18	0	74	59	55	86
Yeison Medina	6	4	4.08	38	3	46	50	13	37
Tanner Cable	1	4	4.54	25	0	38	37	21	44
Alec Byrd*	2	1	4.70	6	0	31	27	15	35
Travis McQueen	5	2	5.17	18	1	85	106	22	76
Michael McCraith	0	0	5.23	2	0	10	12	2	9
Keenan Bartlett	2	3	5.25	7	0	36	34	13	28
Kyle Fimbrez	0	1	6.88	14	0	17	25	11	5

SCHAUMBURG BOOMERS

Name	AVG	AB	R	H	HR	RBI	BB	SO	SB
Luis Roman*	.323	62	12	20	2	5	4	22	1
Quincy Nieporte	.315	324	46	102	13	71	28	46	1
Jack Parenty*	.288	392	55	113	1	28	30	45	7
Nick Oddo*	.274	307	30	84	5	34	17	54	2
Clint Hardy	.261	299	31	78	8	38	21	70	7
Dylan Jones*	.259	220	24	57	4	27	16	48	5
Rayden Sierra	.245	94	9	23	0	7	9	22	1
Matt Rose	.225	311	42	70	15	40	36	98	0

INDEPENDENT LEAGUES

Zach Taylor	.222	27	2	6	0	4	4	8	0
Julio Gonzalez*	.220	109	15	24	0	3	26	22	2
Connor Oliver*	.219	297	32	65	3	30	30	89	4
Alex Polston	.202	218	22	44	0	15	38	62	2
Brock Carpenter	.200	90	9	18	2	9	9	29	2
Wilkyns Jimenez	.196	56	3	11	0	1	3	16	0
Jimmy Galusky	.191	230	19	44	4	18	12	80	0
Gian Martellini	.188	32	3	6	0	0	5	12	0
Chase Dawson*	.185	146	16	27	1	9	15	28	2

Name	W	L	ERA	G	SV	IP	H	BB	SO
Jake Cousins	1	2	0.47	15	2	19	12	3	18
Orlando Rodriguez	0	0	2.03	2	0	13	9	6	12
Gunnar Kines*	6	6	2.36	17	0	103	85	20	112
Dylan Stutsman	6	3	2.40	44	0	49	30	19	67
Jack Landwehr	0	0	2.50	3	0	18	20	2	12
Darrell Thompson*	4	0	2.58	43	0	45	24	20	62
Connor Eller	5	4	2.63	43	22	48	40	7	52
Devin Rose	0	1	3.07	6	0	15	11	11	12
Jumpei Akanuma	1	0	3.25	10	1	28	25	8	19
Christian Aragon*	3	0	3.27	16	0	22	18	14	18
Erik Martinez	0	2	3.58	25	1	60	56	19	67
Aaron Rozek*	7	5	3.60	20	0	120	131	24	99
Payton Lobdell	3	9	3.70	14	0	75	83	17	51
Joe Dougherty	0	0	3.94	13	0	16	16	13	16
Connor Reed*	5	8	4.33	18	0	81	106	15	59
Taylor Goshen	1	2	4.38	7	0	25	30	4	18
Matt Miller	3	6	4.73	13	0	65	67	24	70
Trevin Eubanks	1	0	5.27	10	0	14	15	8	13
Michael McCraith	0	1	7.71	6	0	14	19	7	11

SOUTHERN ILLINOIS MINERS

Name	AVG	AB	R	H	HR	RBI	BB	SO	SB
Anthony Brocato	.400	40	7	16	2	10	4	13	0
Bryant Flete*	.360	150	30	54	1	11	22	30	3
Yeltsin Gudino	.321	134	28	43	1	19	10	19	3
Gianfranco Wawoe	.306	337	49	103	10	43	33	36	0
Jamey Smart*	.298	215	30	64	4	30	25	26	0
Kyle Davis	.280	347	56	97	15	62	39	96	0
Ryan Stacy*	.275	40	3	11	0	5	3	8	0
Cletis Avery	.273	128	18	35	4	25	10	36	4
Steve Lohr	.257	191	23	49	1	30	43	41	0
Andy Cosgrove	.256	195	26	50	0	21	18	49	1
Arturo Nieto	.256	180	25	46	3	21	21	40	0
Joe Duncan	.248	323	31	80	1	39	30	56	4
Alex Santana	.243	74	9	18	3	8	10	28	0
Anthony Jimenez	.239	92	18	22	2	8	15	28	7
Jarrod Watkins*	.236	165	17	39	0	12	9	21	0
Jonathan Pryor*	.229	48	3	11	0	3	6	18	0
Omar Obregon#	.220	50	8	11	0	4	6	11	1
Colton Pogue	.214	14	1	3	0	1	0	6	0
Taylor Sparks	.209	139	21	29	10	25	7	70	1
Kirvin Moesquit#	.203	79	13	16	0	5	10	11	3
Joe Moran*	.161	31	6	5	0	1	1	8	2
Brett Siddall*	.101	69	5	7	1	5	19	38	0
Chris Iriart	.101	109	11	11	2	8	13	54	0
Jhombeyker Morales	.080	25	1	2	0	0	2	7	0

Name	W	L	ERA	G	SV	IP	H	BB	SO
Nick Duron	2	0	1.35	10	2	13	6	5	18
Jake Godfrey	2	1	1.50	16	2	18	6	16	21
Will Headean*	3	1	1.75	24	0	26	20	7	34
Steven Ridings	1	1	1.86	6	0	29	17	6	24
Jordan Brink	2	3	2.04	31	6	35	23	13	55
Gabe Gentner	2	4	2.17	44	13	46	32	17	52
Benjamin Dum	1	0	2.75	19	2	20	13	2	24
Marty Anderson*	5	5	2.95	17	0	88	71	59	90
Chase Cunningham	10	5	3.23	22	0	137	116	40	132
Jake Waters	0	0	3.60	4	0	10	9	4	8
Andrew Bernstein	3	2	3.62	28	0	65	65	26	41
Ryan McAuliffe	6	4	3.68	13	0	73	72	11	46
Frankie Moscatiello	2	0	3.74	4	0	22	20	12	25
Heath Renz	1	1	3.86	39	1	51	50	30	56
Cole Cook*	1	1	3.92	5	0	21	28	4	15
Cody Thompson	3	2	4.97	16	0	42	45	24	32
Nick Stroud	1	2	5.17	4	0	16	10	17	23

Tyson Cronin	0	1	5.40	3	0	15	21	9	5
Austin Dubsky	4	3	6.50	10	0	46	64	18	38
Nick Durazo*	2	1	6.60	13	0	15	17	10	12
Greg Marino	1	1	7.27	4	0	17	23	9	17

WASHINGTON WILD THINGS

Name	AVG	AB	R	H	HR	RBI	BB	SO	SB
Lucas Herbert	.290	62	7	18	1	10	6	14	0
Hector Roa	.288	382	58	110	18	70	8	85	8
Wander Franco	.283	127	16	36	4	16	5	18	0
Cody Erickson	.274	237	33	65	7	39	12	44	1
J.R. Davis	.273	150	14	41	1	19	6	20	3
Jorge Fernandez	.254	339	41	86	6	36	41	90	18
Blake Adams	.249	253	33	63	7	18	20	80	4
Shaine Hughes*	.248	302	36	75	5	32	27	61	2
Alex Murphy	.244	86	14	21	3	7	8	26	0
Terrence Pinkston	.235	34	4	8	0	2	2	7	1
Saige Jenco	.226	155	30	35	6	18	19	49	6
Ryan Cox*	.223	220	25	49	0	20	20	47	4
Cameron Baranek*	.222	180	29	40	8	33	16	49	7
Brett Marr	.218	216	21	47	1	20	22	39	2
Steve Lohr	.204	93	11	19	2	7	13	32	0
Mikael Mogues*	.200	85	12	17	5	15	11	42	1
Drew Bene	.191	115	13	22	0	11	8	40	0
Javier Betancourt	.189	37	3	7	0	1	3	4	0
Preston Scott	.172	29	3	5	1	2	0	9	0
Mick Fennell*	.171	41	4	7	0	3	4	10	1
Chase Sudduth	.161	31	1	5	0	2	5	5	0
Chase Slone	.118	34	4	4	0	2	0	3	0

Name	W	L	ERA	G	SV	IP	H	BB	SO
Zach Strecker	2	5	1.29	44	11	56	45	16	43
Zach Reid*	0	0	1.80	10	0	15	10	5	12
Jesus Balaguer	5	3	2.33	35	0	46	32	16	55
James Meeker	2	3	3.17	40	1	54	44	14	57
John Havird*	6	7	3.19	17	0	104	96	30	93
B.J. Sabol*	1	2	3.24	44	1	42	36	17	56
Carter Johnson	2	2	3.83	20	0	45	48	15	28
Nick Wegmann*	6	8	3.85	19	0	112	117	42	86
Michael Austin	6	8	4.08	20	0	117	118	46	76
Nick Durazo*	2	2	4.18	18	0	32	34	9	33
Nick Gallagher	2	4	4.69	8	0	40	39	13	31
A.J. Bogucki	2	4	5.80	13	0	64	70	40	69
Eric Morell	1	1	6.05	4	0	19	25	9	12
Josh Lapiana*	0	5	6.31	17	0	51	62	19	32
Ty Mondile	0	2	13.50	3	0	12	23	8	10

WINDY CITY THUNDERBOLTS

Name	AVG	AB	R	H	HR	RBI	BB	SO	SB
Tanner Gardner*	.311	106	19	33	4	16	8	25	2
Michael Mateja	.292	96	15	28	5	16	9	25	3
Brynn Martinez#	.283	361	46	102	5	29	23	66	26
Nate Montgomery	.278	18	2	5	0	3	1	5	0
Taisei Fukuhara*	.268	112	10	30	1	11	10	26	5
Omar Obregon#	.254	126	12	32	0	10	16	27	2
Shane Carrier	.247	166	16	41	5	16	8	48	1
Dash Winningham*	.246	122	10	30	6	19	8	22	2
Micah Coffey	.246	187	18	46	1	17	17	51	2
Tyler Alamo	.244	332	45	81	16	52	22	81	1
Trey Fulton	.232	56	2	13	0	5	7	8	0
David Oppenheim*	.231	65	8	15	0	6	15	11	2
Chase Cockrell	.229	166	21	38	3	21	14	61	1
Tyler Straub	.211	318	28	67	3	23	25	92	3
Randy Perez	.206	136	11	28	3	13	11	48	1
Manuel Mesa#	.204	54	5	11	0	0	4	14	3
Patrick Mathis*	.203	143	14	29	4	17	8	37	1
Joe Becht*	.194	31	3	6	0	1	3	10	2
Blair Beck	.184	98	11	18	0	10	13	32	4
Jordan Swiss	.180	61	3	11	0	5	2	18	0
Brett Coffel	.167	72	6	12	0	5	5	20	0
Cal Aldridge	.167	30	3	5	0	2	3	10	0
Christian Funk*	.157	108	16	17	2	9	18	46	0
Zach Rheams*	.139	72	7	10	1	5	11	42	0
Justin Smith	.119	42	4	5	0	1	4	17	2
Zach Taylor	.118	51	3	6	0	1	2	25	0

Name	W	L	ERA	G	SV	IP	H	BB	SO
Dylan Prohoroff	2	0	0.00	11	7	13	3	1	12
Adam Oller	2	1	0.67	4	0	27	15	2	45
Colby Blueberg	4	2	2.16	29	8	33	23	15	44
Tyler Thornton	7	3	2.69	18	0	100	81	27	107
Connor Mayes	1	4	2.79	31	1	42	36	10	39
Joel Toribio	4	2	2.98	38	1	54	46	33	60
Randy Perez	0	0	3.38	8	1	13	8	12	20
Blake Hickman	4	3	3.42	38	4	50	33	26	60
Christian Morris	3	4	3.66	15	0	52	58	21	44
Chris Washington*	4	8	3.71	19	0	112	131	19	90
Kenny Mathews*	4	9	4.27	20	0	116	132	15	114
Sean Leland	1	3	4.43	19	0	43	47	16	47
Justin Miller	1	1	5.23	23	0	33	30	30	31
Cole Bellair	3	7	5.65	12	0	65	78	23	40
Austin Jones	1	4	6.20	11	0	41	43	8	53
Hayden Shenefield	1	3	6.64	9	0	41	55	12	33

PACIFIC ASSOCIATION

Sonoma once again led the Pacific Association during the regular season. A year after setting a league record for wins, the Stompers led the league with a .703 winning percentage, but once again the Stompers were stymied by the San Rafael Pacifics in the postseason. San Rafael edged Sonoma for its fifth league title in eight seasons.

Team	W	L	PCT	GB
*Sonoma Stompers	45	19	.703	--
^San Rafael Pacifics	38	26	.594	7
^Vallejo Admirals	34	30	.531	11
^Napa Silverados	29	35	.453	16
Salina Stockade	14	50	.219	

*Regular season champion. ^Wild Card

Playoffs—Finals: San Rafael defeated Sonoma 2-1 in best-of-five series.

Attendance: San Rafael 17,334; Sonoma 15,875; Vallejo 8,080; Napa 3,950.

BATTING LEADERS

Player	Team	AVG	AB	R	H	HR	RBI
Raul Navarro	SRF	.372	247	66	92	6	41
Dondrei Hubbard	SON	.364	173	45	63	16	55
Nick Gotta	SON	.362	210	71	76	5	39
William Salas	NAPA	.339	227	45	77	5	37
Ermido Escobar	SRF	.332	223	41	74	8	34
Nick Ultsch	NAPA	.320	241	45	77	12	54
Chris Kwitzer	SON	.309	236	50	73	9	56
Brent Gillespie	SON	.307	176	41	54	16	53
Pedro Barrios	SON	.305	197	42	60	5	40
Mike Annone	SRF	.304	161	34	49	8	27

PITCHING LEADERS

Player	Team	W	L	ERA	IP	H	BB	SO
Dakota Freese	VAL	7	5	2.91	77	49	45	94
Nick Barnese	SON	7	1	3.68	64	61	28	73
Vijay Patel	SON	7	1	4.3	67	52	41	78
Skylar Janisse	VAL	3	1	4.34	56	63	16	51
Mike Melendez	VAL	5	4	4.84	67	75	38	52
Chip White	SRF	3	6	5.2	62	59	54	51
Tre Hobbs	NAPA	3	2	5.43	70	79	34	77
Konner Arnold	SON	6	5	5.51	67	81	37	65
Neil Lang	NAPA	1	4	5.56	70	84	24	65
Jesse Remington	VAL	5	4	5.63	70	95	39	51

PECOS LEAGUE

A year after Bakersfield beat Alpine in the Pecos League final, the Cowboys got their revenge by sweeping Bakersfield in the 2019 Pecos League finals.

Mountain Division	W	L	PCT	GB
*Alpine Cowboys	41	16	.719	--
Garden City Wind	41	19	.683	1.5
Roswell Invaders	37	20	.649	4
Santa Fe Fuego	27	31	.466	14.5
Trinidad Triggers	24	30	.444	15.5
White Sands Pupfish	8	50	.138	33.5
Pacific Division	W	L	PCT	GB
*High Desert Yardbirds	46	18	.719	--
Monterey Amberjacks	36	25	.590	8.5
Bakersfield Train Robbers	37	26	.587	8.5
Tucson Saguaros	30	30	.500	14
Wasco Reserves	19	43	.306	26
California City Whiptails	12	48	.200	32

Playoffs—Semifinals: Alpine defeated Roswell 2-0 and Bakersfield defeated High Desert 2-1 in best-of-three series. **Finals:** Alpine defeated Bakersfield 2-0 in best-of-three series.

U.S. PRO BASEBALL LEAGUE

After trailing by three runs heading into the seventh inning, Utica rallied to score four unanswered runs to top Westside, 6-5, in the USPBL championship game. The USPBL had 62 sellouts over its season, with an announced attendance for the four teams of 259,000.

East Division	W	L	PCT	GB
Utica Unicorns	27	22	.551	—
Eastside Diamond Hoppers	18	29	.388	8
West Division	W	L	PCT	GB
Westside Woolly Mammoths	28	21	.571	—
Birmingham Bloomfield Beavers	23	24	.490	4

Playoffs—Semifinals: Utica defeated Bloomfield and Birmingham defeated Eastside. **Finals:** Utica defeated Westside.

All-Star Team: C: Adam Gauthier, Beavers. **1B:** Ross Haffey, Beavers. **2B:** Freddy Jehle, Hoppers. **SS:** Ryan Dobson, Mammoths. **3B:** TJ Ward, Beavers. **OF:** Pat Adams, Hoppers; Sonny Cortez, Mammoths; Ethan Wiskur, Mammoths. **SP:** Matt Cronin, Mammoths; Donald Goodson, Unicorns; Garrett Christman, Beavers. **RP:** Joey Beals, Hoppers; Nolan Clenney, Unicorns; Thomas Muratore, Mammoths. **UT:** Colie Currie, Unicorns; Jimmy Latona, Unicorns; Collin Ridout, Unicorns. **Most Valuable Player:** Ethan Wiskur, Westside. **Pitcher of the Year:** Matt Cronin, Westside.

BATTING LEADERS

Player	Team	AVG	AB	R	H	HR	RBI
Pat Adams	East	.317	164	34	52	4	22
Sonny Cortez	WWM	.311	180	45	56	2	28
Ethan Wiskur	WWM	.307	179	36	55	14	46
Ryan Dobson	WWM	.305	197	32	60	1	18
Colin Ridout	UU	.301	186	18	56	1	26
Adam Gauthier	BBB	.301	173	41	52	7	37
Ross Haffey	BBB	.299	167	30	50	10	39
TJ Ward	BBB	.290	193	25	56	5	30
Colie Currie	UU	.288	184	20	53	2	13
Dan Elliott	UU	.284	183	28	52	6	27

PITCHING LEADERS

Player	Team	W	L	ERA	IP	H	BB	SO
Matt Cronin	WWM	7	0	2.47	73	62	22	66
Donald Goodson	UU	3	2	2.71	90	56	66	64
Thomas Muratore	WWM	4	4	2.77	65	58	28	62
N. Gotsis	DH	4	2	3.35	51	53	8	50
Ben McKendall	WWM	5	4	3.38	56	59	21	46
Gerry Salisbury	BBB	4	5	3.39	61	56	20	55
Garrett Christman	BBB	7	4	4.88	98	114	20	73
Ty Hensley	UU	4	5	5.42	78	64	49	75
Nate Sweeney	DH	2	6	6.43	58	72	32	34

INDEPENDENT LEAGUES

INTERNATIONAL

Japan Wins Premier 12 As U.S. Falls To Fourth

BY KYLE GLASER AND J.J. COOPER

For several years, Japan stood atop the World Baseball Softball Confederation's rankings even as the U.S. racked up tournament win after tournament win.

The WBSC rankings are weighted toward participation, so even when the U.S. was winning multiple World Cups and other international tournaments each year, Japan remained atop the rankings. It wasn't until the U.S. won the World Baseball Classic, 12U World Cup, 15U World Cup and 18U World Cup in the span of 18 months that the U.S. climbed to the top of the rankings.

Japan has returned to the top spot, but this time they did it by beating the U.S. on the field. Japan entered Premier12, the WBSC's biggest event of 2019, as both the tournament host and favorite. Aside from one slight hiccup, its supremacy was never seriously challenged.

Japan beat defending-champion South Korea 5-3 in the Premier12 gold medal game in Tokyo to win the tournament, which served as a qualifier for the 2020 Olympics.

South Korea scored three runs in the first inning on a two-run homer by Ha Seong Kim and a solo homer by Hyun-Soo Kim, but Japan quickly erased the deficit. Tournament MVP Seiya Suzuki delivered an RBI double in the bottom of the first to cut the deficit to 3-1, and Tetsuto Yamada put Japan ahead for good with a three-run homer in the second. Hideto Asamura added an insurance run with an RBI single in the seventh.

Japan entered Premier12 as the top-ranked team in the event and went 7-1 overall. Its only loss came to Team USA in the Super Round.

Japan already received an automatic berth to the 2020 Tokyo Olympics as the host nation, so South Korea received the Olympics bid reserved for the top finisher at Premier12 from Asia/Oceania.

"Since I became manager of the Japanese National Team two years ago our goal has been to win the Premier12 and the Olympics next year," Japan manager Atusnori Inaba said. "I think all the players on our team had the same determination to become world No. 1."

While Japan and South Korea finished 1-2 at Premier12 as expected, what happened beyond

Japan's Seiya Suzuki was named the MVP of the WBSC's Premier 12 Tournament

them was surprising.

Mexico beat Team USA 3-2 in 10 innings in the bronze medal game to clinch the Olympic berth reserved for the highest-finishing team from the Americas at Premier12. It marked Mexico's first time qualifying for the Olympics in baseball. Team USA, as a result, failed to qualify for the Olympics with the loss. It gets another shot at an Americas qualifier in Arizona in March 2020.

Team USA was three outs away from beating Mexico and clinching the Olympic bid, but Matt Clark led off the bottom of ninth inning with a solo home run for Mexico to tie the score 2-2 and send it to extra innings.

With the international tiebreaker rule in effect placing runners on first and second base to start each inning, Bobby Dalbec led off the top of the 10th with a sacrifice bunt and Drew Waters was intentionally walked to load the bases with one out for Team USA. But Alec Bohm struck out swinging and Jake Cronenworth flied out to leave the bases loaded.

A sacrifice bunt by Jonathan Jones and an inten-

INTERNATIONAL

SUPER ROUND IN JAPAN

STANDINGS

Team	W	L	Team	W	L
Japan	7	1	Canada	1	2
Korea	5	3	Dominican Republic	1	2
Mexico	6	2	Venezuela	1	2
USA	4	4	Cuba	1	2
Taiwan	4	3	Netherlands	0	3
Australia	2	5	Puerto Rico	0	3

Top six teams advanced to Super Round. Japan defeated Korea 5-3 in gold medal game. Mexico defeated USA 3-2 (10) in bronze medal game.

BATTING LEADERS

PLAYER	TEAM	AVG	AB	R	H	HR	RBI	TB
Seiya Suzuki	JAP	.444	27	9	12	3	13	28
Jordon Adell	USA	.394	33	4	13	3	5	23
Jung-Ho Lee	KOR	.385	26	5	10	0	4	15
Erik Kratz	USA	.381	21	5	8	2	3	15
Jonathan Jones	MEX	.367	30	9	11	3	6	21
Hideto Asamura	JAP	.360	25	1	9	0	6	12
Chin-Lung Ho	TAI	.350	20	2	7	1	2	10
Hyun-Soo Kim	KOR	.348	23	5	8	1	6	13
Ryosuke Kikuchi	JAP	.333	24	5	8	0	4	10
Ha Seong Kim	KOR	.333	27	7	9	1	6	13

PITCHING LEADERS

PLAYER	TEAM	W	L	ERA	G	IP	H	BB	SO
Yi Chang	TAI	2	0	0.00	2	13	8	6	10
Chih-Wei Hu	TAI	0	0	0.00	2	8	6	2	9
Phillippe Aumont	CAN	1	0	0.00	1	8	2	1	9
Manuel Barreda	MEX	1	0	0.00	3	7	1	4	7
Arturo Reyes	MEX	1	0	0.68	3	13	6	4	13
Eduardo Vera	MEX	1	0	0.77	3	11	9	2	8
Shota Imanaga	JPN	1	0	1.00	2	9	5	1	12
Young-Ha Lee	KOR	1	0	1.08	5	8	5	3	6
Rei Takahashi	JPN	2	1	1.50	3	12	6	4	5
Steven Kent	AUS	0	0	1.59	4	11	8	2	11

Premier 12 All-World Team

C: Erik Kratz (USA). **1B:** Bobby Dalbec (USA). **2B:** Kikuchi Ryosuke (Japan). **3B:** Wang Wei-Chen (Taiwan), **SS:** Kim Ha Seong (Korea).**OFs:** Seiya Suzuki, Jonathan Jones (Mexico), Lee Jung-Ho (Korea). **DH:** Brent Rooker (USA).
SP: Chang-Yi (Taiwan). **P:** Brandon Dickson (USA).
MVP: Seiya Suzuki (Japan).

FINAL STANDINGS

Team	W	L	Team	W	L
Taiwan	8	1	USA	6	2
Japan	7	2	Czech Republic	4	4
Cuba	7	2	Italy	3	5
South Korea	4	5	Australia	2	6
Mexico	5	3	South Africa	1	7
Venezuela	3	5	Fiji	0	8

Top six teams advanced to Super Round, while other six teams continued in consolation round.

Gold Medal Game: Taiwan defeated Japan 4-0.

Bronze Medal Game: Cuba defeated South Korea 2-1.

MVP: Kai-Sheng Chen (Taiwan).

All-World Team: C: Shinsuke Kuwamoto (Japan). **1B:** Christian Saez (Cuba). **2B:** Kazuki Takahata (Japan). **3B:** Tien-Szu Huang (Taiwan). **SS:** Johan Rodriguez (Cuba). **LF:** Tsung-Chun Chiang (Taiwan). **CF:** Alejandro Prieto (Cuba). **RF:** Taeoh Lee (South Korea). **DH:** Leonel Dominguez. **P:** Kai-Sheng Chen (Taiwan). **RP:** Sakuma Aoki (Japan).

---

tional walk to Esteban Quiroz loaded the bases for Mexico with one out in the bottom of the 10th, and Efren Navarro finished an eight-pitch at-bat against Caleb Thielbar with a broken-bat flare into center field to bring home Noah Perio with the winning run.

Mexico held its own throughout the tournament. It started 5-0—including an 8-2 win over Team USA in group play—and was one win away from reaching the gold medal game before losing its final two games of the Super Round to Japan and South Korea.

Team USA, meanwhile, was fortunate to even get to the bronze medal game. After going 2-1 in group play, Team USA dropped two of its first three games of the Super Round, including a listless 2-1 defeat to Australia. Team USA's only path to an Olympic bid after that required Japan to beat Mexico, Team USA to beat Taiwan in its finale, South Korea to beat Mexico and Taiwan to beat Australia. All four of those things happened over a thrilling final two days of the Super Round to push Team USA into the bronze medal game against Mexico, but it came up short in its quest to wrap up an Olympic berth.

Team USA went 4-4 overall at Premier12 and finished in fourth place. Team USA's offense scored just 32 runs in its eight games, an average of four runs per game.

Nineteen of those runs came in Team USA's opening-round wins against the Netherlands (9-0) and the Dominican Republic (10-2). Against teams who advanced past the opening round, Team USA managed just 13 runs in six games.

Jo Adell hit .394/.429/.697 with a tournament-high 13 hits and tied for the tournament lead with three home runs. Dalbec (2 HR, 8 RBIs), Brent Rooker (3 HR), Erik Kratz (.381/.435/.714) and Brandon Dickson (3 SV, 11 K) were named to the all-Premier12 team.

Suzuki, the Nippon Pro Baseball Central League batting champion, hit a tournament-best .444, tied for the tournament lead with three home runs and led the tournament with 13 RBIs to win MVP. He also led the tournament in triples (2) and total bases (28) and tied for the lead in runs (9).

South Korea and Mexico joined Japan and Israel in the 2020 Olympic field.

In addition to clinching its first Olympic berth, Mexico also carried the banner for Latin America in an otherwise dismal showing for the region. Puerto Rico, Cuba, Venezuela and the Dominican Republic all failed to get out of the opening round and went a combined 3-9.

18U WORLD CUP

STANDINGS

Team	W	L	Team	W	L
Taiwan	7	2	Netherlands	6	2
USA	7	2	Spain	3	5
Korea	6	3	Panama	3	5
Australia	4	5	Nicaragua	3	5
Japan	5	3	China	2	6
Canada	4	4	South Africa	0	8

Format: Top six teams advanced to Super Round, while the other six teams continued in consolation round. **Bronze Medal Game:** Korea defeated Japan 6-5. **Gold Medal Game:** Taiwan defeated USA 2-1.

BATTING LEADERS

PLAYER	COUNTRY	AVG	AB	R	H	HR	RBI
Abrego Danilo	PAN	.412	17	2	7	0	5
Aburto Enmanuel	NCA	.269	26	3	7	0	4
Anasagasti Leandro	NED	.200	20	2	4	0	1
Arana Gustavo	NCA	.250	20	1	5	0	2
Armstrong Byron	AUS	.333	27	6	9	0	6
Arnaez Jean	PAN	.250	24	5	6	0	4
Bailey Benyamin	PAN	.333	21	1	7	0	7
Bassett Anthony	NCA	.048	21	2	1	0	0
Bazzana Travis	AUS	.171	35	3	6	0	4
Bentura Nathaniel	NED	.231	26	3	6	1	7

PITCHING LEADERS

PLAYER	COUNTRY	W	L	ERA	G	IP	H	BB	SO
HARRISON Kyle	USA	1	0	0.00	3	10	8	4	12
YU Chien	TPE	1	0	0.00	3	10	4	0	15
LIN Yu-Min	TPE	2	0	0.64	4	14	3	6	15
TER BEEK Luuk	NED	2	0	0.64	3	14	9	3	10
MENDOZA Samuel	NCA	1	0	0.90	3	10	5	4	5
CHEN Po-Yu	TPE	2	0	1.29	3	14	9	3	12
SO Hyeongjun	KOR	0	0	1.32	3	13.2	10	1	15
NISHI Junya	JPN	2	0	1.35	4	13.1	11	3	17
RAJCIC Maxwel	USA	1	0	1.35	2	13.1	8	1	10
BIDOIS Brandan	AUS	2	0	1.38	2	13	4	4	9

All-World Team: C: Juan Gonzalez (Spain). **1B:** Yuya Nirasawa (Japan). **2B:** Jichan Kim (South Korea). **3B:** Wang Shun-Ho (Taiwan). **SS:** Austin Gomm (Canada). **LF:** Darryl Collins (Netherlands). **CF:** Pete Crow-Armstrong (USA). **RF:** Robert Hassell (USA). **DH:** Tyler Soderstrom (USA). **P:** Yansunobu Okugawa (Japan). **RP:** Alejandro Rosario (USA). **Most Valuable Player:** Yu Chien, Taiwan.

Team USA Can't Match 2018 Success

If 2018 was the year where USA Baseball stood clearly at the pinnacle of international baseball, 2019 was the year that the world fought back.

A year after the U.S. won four different world championships, it lost in the championship game of the 18U World Cup to Taiwan. The U.S. had won the previous four 18U World Cup championships and its 18U team had won gold at its last nine major international competitions.

That was a better result than the USA 12U team, which failed to advance to the Super Round at the 12U World Cup. Team USA's 12U team had won the previous two World Cups. Alexander Mercurius and Brenden Lewis did combine to no-hit South Africa in Team USA's final game of the

Blake Gailen and Team Israel earned a spot in the 2020 Olympics

consolation round.

The U.S. 15U team did win its Americas World Cup qualifier, going 4-1 and avenging its only loss by beating Panama in the gold medal game.

Israel Earns An Olympic Spot

With only a six-team field, baseball's return to the Olympics will leave a lot of quality teams sitting at home. Japan was guaranteed a spot as the host country. The second team to earn an Olympic qualifying bid was a bit of a surprise. Israel, a country that has never played in an Olympic baseball tournament before, won the European/African Olympic qualifier by going 4-1 in a five-game round-robin tournament in Italy in September 2019.

The Israeli baseball team had qualified for the World Baseball Classic in 2017 and then pulled off a surprising run to the second round. That laid the groundwork for the team's success in 2019. Much like the WBC team, Israel got plenty of help from U.S. born players who meet all the qualifications needed to play for the Israeli team. Former big leaguer Danny Valencia led the tournament with three home runs to provide plenty of power in the middle of Israel's lineup. U.S. minor leaguer Jon Moscot and indy leagues pitcher Joseph Wagman were Israel's aces on the mound.

The key game of the qualifier proved to be Israel's 8-1 win over the Netherlands. Moscot and three relievers combined to limit the Dutch team to five hits while catcher Nick Rickels homered and Valencia had two hits, a run scored and an RBI.

New Ball Boosts Offenses To New Heights

A switch to a new brand of baseball boosted the already high-octane Mexican League offenses to an entirely new level.

Over the first half of the season, Felix Pie and several other hitters flirted with hitting .400. More than half of the league's teams posted ERAs above 6.00 in the first two months of the season.

Eventually the ball was detuned at least a little, but when the season was over, the home run rate had gone from one every 39 at-bats in 2018 to one every 27 at-bats in 2019. The league ERA jumped by three-quarters of a run to 5.79.

Former Astros slugger Chris Carter had a monstrous season, easily winning the home run crown with 49 homers for Monclova. Carter hit an additional seven home runs in the playoffs to help push the Acereros to their first LMB title. Francisco Peguero added six postseason home runs for the Acereros.

Monclova managed to win five do-or-die games in the playoffs. All three of Monclova's playoff series went to seven games. In the deciding Game 7 of the championship series, Monclova quickly fell behind by three runs. A three-run home run by Erick Aybar tied the game in the fifth. Aybar then doubled in another run in the sixth to give Monclova a lead it would never relinquish. Three more insurance runs in the late innings gave the Acereros a 9-5 win.

Ex-Oregon State lefthander Luke Heimlich also made his pro debut in the league. Heimlich had been left undrafted and unsigned by U.S. teams because he had pled guilty to a count of child molestation while he was a minor. He had also tried to sign with a Taiwanese team, but that contract was also disallowed. His contract with Laredo was held up, but eventually was approved by the league.

After experimenting with a two-season format in 2018—there was a spring season that culminated with a champion and another summer season that also finished with playoffs that determined a champ—the league returned to its normal one-season format in 2019. The league drew 5.1 million fans in 2019, up nearly half a million from 2018's attendance.

FIRST-HALF STANDINGS

Northern Division	W	L	PCT	GB
Sultanes de Monterrey	40	20	.667	—
Toros de Tijuana	40	20	.667	—
Acereros del Norte (Monclova)	39	21	.650	1
Tecolotes de los Dos Laredos	33	27	.550	7
Saraperos de Saltillo	28	32	.467	12
Generales de Durango	26	34	.433	14
Rieleros de Aguascalientes	26	34	.433	14
Algodoneros Union Laguna	20	37	.351	18.5

Southern Division	W	L	PCT	GB
Guerreros de Oaxaca	37	23	.617	—
Diablos Rojos del Mexico	32	24	.571	3
Pericos de Puebla	34	26	.567	3
Bravos de Leon	27	32	.458	9.5
Leones de Yucatan	26	32	.448	10
Tigres de Quintana Roo	25	35	.417	12
Olmecas de Tabasco	21	39	.350	16
Piratas de Campeche	20	38	.345	16

SECOND HALF STANDINGS

Northern Division	W	L	PCT	GB
Saraperos de Saltillo	38	21	.644	—
Acereros del Norte (Monclova)	36	24	.600	2.5
Toros de Tijuana	35	25	.583	3.5
Sultanes de Monterrey	32	26	.552	5.5
Rieleros de Aguascalientes	28	31	.475	10
Tecolotes de los Dos Laredos	27	33	.450	11.5
Generales de Durango	21	38	.356	17
Algodoneros Union Laguna	17	42	.288	21

Southern Division	W	L	PCT	GB
Leones de Yucatan	40	20	.667	—
Tigres de Quintana Roo	37	22	.627	2.5
Diablos Rojos del Mexico	35	25	.583	5
Guerreros de Oaxaca	31	28	.525	8.5
Piratas de Campeche	27	30	.474	11.5
Olmecas de Tabasco	24	33	.421	14.5
Pericos de Puebla	22	34	.393	16
Bravos de Leon	20	38	.345	19

Playoffs—Quarterfinals: Tijuana defeated Saltillo 4-2; Mexico defeated Oaxaca 4-1; Mexico defeated Quintana Roo 4-3 and Monclova defeated Monterrey 4-3 in best-of-seven series. **Semifinals:** Monclova defeated Tijuana 4-3 and Yucatan defeated Mexico 4-0 in best-of-seven series. **Finals:** Monclova defeated Yucatan 4-3 in best-of-seven series.

BATTING LEADERS

Batter	Team	AVG	G	AB	R	H	HR	RBI
Mayora, Daniel	DUR	.391	115	453	89	177	19	92
Pie, Felix	LEO	.381	93	328	70	125	22	80
Peguero, Francisco	MVA	.380	115	463	123	176	31	106
Mendoza, Victor	MTY	.375	114	424	98	159	26	101
Urrutia, Henry	SAL	.370	110	422	95	156	33	100
Fabela, Jesus	MEX	.368	114	454	104	167	9	62
Avila, Emmanuel	MEX	.367	108	406	73	149	16	76
Mustelier, Ronnier	TAB	.366	106	396	63	145	13	73
Castro, Leandro	TIJ	.361	111	429	84	155	27	92
Rodriguez, Erick	OAX	.356	87	298	48	106	12	47

PITCHING LEADERS

Pitcher	Team	W-L	ERA	IP	H	BB	SO
Valdez, Cesar	YUC	15-2	2.26	148	140	17	122
Negrin, Yoanner	YUC	13-6	3.22	148	133	49	124
Oramas, Juan Pablo	TAB	6-10	3.85	140	146	52	145
Samayoa, Jose	YUC	9-5	4.05	116	118	33	109
Boscan, Wilfredo	TIG	9-4	4.22	109	107	26	67
Vargas, Cesar	MTY	8-6	4.34	114	137	27	92
Barreda, Manny	TIJ	8-3	4.40	104	116	42	95
Heimlich, Luke	LAR	8-7	4.58	118	141	39	109
Doubront, Felix	SAL	8-6	4.58	126	151	26	108
Castillo, Jorge	TIG	11-8	4.60	119	122	39	110

INTERNATIONAL

Fukuoka Wins Third Straight Title

There's no question that the Fukuoka SoftBank Hawks are the team of the decade in Nippon Professional Baseball. The only real question remaining is whether they are in the midst of the most dominant stretch in NPB history.

The Hawks won their third consecutive title, their fifth in six years and their sixth of the decade, winning 10 of 11 postseason games. Fukuoka swept Yomiuri in the Japan Series and won all four games against Seibu in the Climax Series, although Seibu began the series with a 1-0 lead thanks to its Pacific League regular season title.

Yurisbel Gracial was named the Japan Series MVP. He hit three home runs in four games.

Over those six titles, Fukuoka has faced all six Central League teams in the Japan Series. It has beaten them all.

Fukuoka's six titles in a decade is one behind Yomiuri's seven titles in the 1960s for the most in NPB history. Seibu won six titles from 1986-1992 in the other stretch of dominance that compares favorably to the Hawks.

Fukuoka's dominance was the story of the season, but the return to prominence of the Yomiuri Giants was hailed by many fans. The Giants are the most dominant team in NPB history with 22 titles, but this was their first Central League title since 2014 and their first Japan Series appearance since 2013.

BayStars slugger Neftali Soto, once a Reds minor league prospect, led the Central League with 43 home runs. He was equaled by Seibu's Hotaka Yamakawa, who led the Pacific League with 43 home runs.

The Giants successful season was also a fitting end for catcher Shinnosuke Abe. Abe announced his retirement after a 19-year NPB career. He leaves the field as one of the best catchers Japan has ever seen. He provided both exceptional defense (he won four Gold Gloves) and a potent bat (he hit 406 home runs, finished with more than 2,000 hits and won a batting title in 2012).

Hanshin righthander Randy Messenger also announced his retirement. The 38-year-old had spent a decade with the Tigers, going 98-84, 3.13. He was the Central League's wins leader in

Shinnosuke Abe

KOJI WATANABE/GETTY IMAGES

2014. Yomiuri righthander Scott Mathieson, 35, also announced his retirement from professional baseball. Mathieson had spent the past eight seasons with the Giants. Mathieson, a one-time Phillies prospect, said he still hopes to pitch for Team Canada if Canada reaches the 2020 Olympics.

Yokohama outfielder Yoshitomo Tsutsugo and Seibu outfielder Shogo Akiyama both announced at the end of the season their intent to try to come to the U.S. to play in 2020.

There was no Sawamura Award given out in 2019. Japan's version of the Cy Young award was not handed out because the selection committee said it felt no pitcher met the standards they hold for the award. The main complaint was that the top candidates did not throw enough innings and finish enough games to meet the awards standards.

CENTRAL LEAGUE

Team	W	L	T	PCT	GB
Yomiuri Giants	77	64	2	.546	--
Yokohama DeNA BayStars	71	69	3	.507	5.5
Hanshin Tigers	69	68	6	.504	6
Hiroshima Toyo Carp	70	70	3	.500	6.5
Chunichi Dragons	68	73	2	.482	9
Yakult Swallows	59	82	2	.418	18

Playoffs—First round: Hanshin defeated Yokohama 2-1 in best-of-three series. **Climax Series:** Yomiuri defeated Hanshin 4-1 in best-of-seven series. **Japan Series:** Fukuoka defeated Hiroshima 4-2 in best-of-seven series.

CENTRAL LEAGUE BATTING LEADERS

Player, Team	AVG	AB	R	H	HR	RBI	SB
Seiya Suzuki, Carp	.335	499	112	167	28	87	25
Dayan Viciedo, Dragons	.315	534	56	168	18	93	2
Yoshio Itoi, Tigers	.314	382	45	120	5	42	9
Yohei Oshima, Dragons	.312	558	89	174	3	45	30
Hayato Sakamoto, Giants	.312	555	103	173	40	94	5
Ryoma Nishikawa, Carp	.297	535	70	159	16	64	6
Norichika Aoki, Swallows	.297	489	84	145	16	58	1
Shuhei Takahashi, Dragons	.293	430	50	126	7	59	3
Yoshihiro Maru, Giants	.292	535	82	156	27	89	12
Toshiki Abe, Dragons	.291	447	51	130	7	59	1
Yoshiyuki Kamei, Giants	.284	450	67	128	13	55	9
Toshiro Miyazaki, BayStars	.284	433	54	123	15	49	0
Wladimir Balentien, Swallows	.280	410	65	115	33	93	0
Kazuki Kamizato, BayStars	.279	427	62	119	6	35	15
Tsubasa Aizawa, Carp	.277	376	38	104	12	63	2
Yuhei Takai, Swallows	.273	447	55	122	12	56	4
Yoshitomo Tsutsugo, BayStars	.272	464	74	126	29	79	0
Koji Chikamoto, Tigers	.271	586	81	159	9	42	36
Tetsuto Yamada, Swallows	.271	520	102	141	35	98	33
Neftali Soto, BayStars	.269	516	82	139	43	108	0

INTERNATIONAL

OTHER NOTABLE HITTERS

Player, Team	AVG	AB	R	H	HR	RBI	SB
Shinnosuke Abe, Giants	.297	158	15	47	7	27	0
Jose Lopez, BayStars	.241	551	69	133	31	84	0
Alex Guerrero, Giants	.237	287	33	68	21	54	1
Munetaka Murakami, Swallows	.231	511	76	118	36	96	5

CENTRAL LEAGUE PITCHING LEADERS

Pitcher, Team	W	L	ERA	IP	H	HR	BB	SO
Yudai Ono, Dragons	9	8	2.58	178	132	18	43	156
Kris Johnson, Carp	11	8	2.59	157	132	12	58	132
Shun Yamaguchi, Giants	15	4	2.91	170	137	8	60	188
Shota Imanaga, BayStars	13	7	2.91	170	128	18	56	186
Yuki Nishi, Tigers	10	8	2.92	172	159	12	36	112
Koyo Aoyagi, Tigers	9	9	3.14	143	145	14	42	100
Daichi Osera, Carp	11	9	3.53	173	176	22	35	136
Yuya Yanagi, Dragons	11	7	3.53	171	165	21	38	146
Yasuhiro Ogawa, Swallows	5	12	4.57	160	173	26	36	132

OTHER NOTABLE PITCHERS

Pitcher, Team	W	L	ERA	IP	H	HR	BB	SO
Suguru Iwazaki, Tigers	3	0	1.01	54	24	5	17	58
Pierce Johnson, Tigers	2	3	1.38	59	34	2	13	91
Joely Rodriguez, Dragons	3	4	1.64	60	42	3	14	77
Kyuji Fujikawa, Tigers	4	1	1.77	56	29	3	32	83
Kyuji Fujikawa, Tigers	4	1	1.77	56	29	3	32	83
Yasuaki Yamasaki, BayStars	3	2	1.95	60	44	6	19	54
Rafael Dolis, Tigers	5	4	2.11	55	36	1	11	50
Kota Nakagawa, Giants	4	3	2.37	65	57	3	18	74
Edwin Escobar, BayStars	5	4	2.51	75	60	7	24	88
Taichi Ishiyama, Swallows	2	2	2.73	33	30	2	8	31
Geronimo Franzua, Carp	8	6	2.76	72	55	8	32	94
Geronimo Franzua, Carp	8	6	2.76	72	55	8	32	94
Scott McGough, Swallows	6	3	3.15	69	71	2	22	64
Scott McGough, Swallows	6	3	3.15	69	71	2	22	64
Toshiya Okada, Dragons	3	2	3.58	50	44	8	14	53
Yugo Umeno, Swallows	2	3	3.72	68	55	7	25	77
Dave Huff, Swallows	1	5	3.97	66	58	6	21	58
Shota Nakazaki, Carp	3	3	4.08	35	44	3	17	23
Hiroshi Suzuki, Dragons	0	2	4.32	25	29	1	15	16
Kazuki Mishima, BayStars	5	4	4.33	73	67	10	31	62

OTHER NORTH AMERICAN PITCHERS

Pitcher, Team	W	L	ERA	IP	H	HR	BB	SO
Casey Lawrence, Carp	3	4	1.64	60	42	3	14	77
Kyle Regnault, Carp	5	4	2.11	55	36	1	11	50
David Buchanan, Swallows	1	0	2.25	24	16	4	5	32
Dave Huff, Swallows	5	4	2.51	75	60	7	24	88
Scott McGough, Swallows	6	3	3.15	69	71	2	22	64
Scott Mathieson, Giants	6	3	3.30	59	53	7	34	67
Cristopher Mercedes, Giants	8	8	3.52	120	137	12	28	89
Ryan Cook, Giants	1	5	3.97	66	58	6	21	58
Rubby De La Rosa, Giants	8	10	4.26	116	106	19	55	105
Edwin Escobar, BayStars	2	2	4.37	23	28	2	9	19
Spencer Patton, BayStars	3	7	4.67	79	71	11	38	55
Joely Rodriguez, Dragons	6	8	4.69	104	123	8	40	79
Enny Romero, Dragons	4	6	4.79	100	118	10	33	58
Onelki Garcia, Tigers	0	2	4.80	15	19	2	6	9
Randy Messenger, Tigers	0	3	5.15	37	38	4	22	45
Rafael Dolis, Tigers	0	1	10.80	5	4	1	4	3

PACIFIC LEAGUE

Team	W	L	T	PCT	GB
Saitama Seibu Lions	80	62	1	.563	--
Fukuoka SoftBank Hawks	76	62	5	.551	2
Tohoku Rakuten Golden Eagles	71	68	4	.511	7.5
Chiba Lotte Marines	69	70	4	.496	9.5
Hokkaido Nippon-Ham Fighters	65	73	5	.471	13
Orix Buffaloes	61	75	7	.449	16

Playoffs: First round: Fukuoka defeated Rakuten 2-1 in best-of-three series. **Climax Series:** Fukuoka defeated Seibu 4-1 in best-of-seven series. **Japan Series:** Fukuoka defeated Yomiuri 4-0 in best-of-seven series.

PACIFIC LEAGUE BATTING LEADERS

Player, Team	AVG	AB	R	H	HR	RBI	SB
Tomoya Mori, Lions	.329	492	96	162	23	105	3
Masataka Yoshida, Buffaloes	.322	521	92	168	29	85	5
Takashi Ogino, Marines	.315	508	76	160	10	46	28
Ginji Akaminai, Eagles	.304	529	56	161	5	56	2
Shogo Akiyama, Lions	.303	590	112	179	20	62	12
Kensuke Kondo, Fighters	.302	490	74	148	2	59	1
Taishi Ota, Fighters	.289	557	79	161	20	77	6
Daichi Suzuki, Marines	.288	527	76	152	15	68	3
Haruki Nishikawa, Fighters	.288	548	88	158	5	41	19
Hiroaki Shimauchi, Eagles	.287	506	68	145	10	57	3
Takeya Nakamura, Lions	.286	496	69	142	30	123	2
Eigoro Mogi, Eagles	.282	568	86	160	13	55	7
Sosuke Genda, Lions	.274	540	90	148	2	41	30
Shuta Tonosaki, Lions	.274	533	96	146	26	90	22
Hideto Asamura, Eagles	.263	529	93	139	33	92	1
Ryo Watanabe, Fighters	.262	481	60	126	11	58	0
Jabari Blash, Eagles	.261	426	66	111	33	95	2
Nobuhiro Matsuda, Hawks	.260	534	64	139	30	76	5
Takuya Kai, Hawks	.260	377	42	98	11	43	9
Alfredo Despaigne, Hawks	.259	448	61	116	36	88	0

OTHER NOTABLE HITTERS

Player, Team	AVG	AB	R	H	HR	RBI	SB
Hotaka Yamakawa, Lions	.256	524	93	134	43	120	1
Nobuhiro Matsuda, Hawks	.260	534	64	139	30	76	5
Seiya Inoue, Marines	.252	429	60	108	24	65	0
Brandon Laird, Marines	.248	487	59	121	32	89	0

PACIFIC LEAGUE PITCHING LEADERS

Pitcher, Team	W	L	ERA	IP	H	HR	BB	SO
Yoshinobu Yamamoto, Buffaloes	8	6	1.95	143	101	8	36	127
Kohei Arihara, Fighters	15	8	2.46	164	111	14	40	161
Kodai Senga, Hawks	13	8	2.79	180	134	19	75	227
Rei Takahashi, Hawks	12	6	3.34	143	114	10	49	73
Taisuke Yamaoka, Buffaloes	13	4	3.71	170	154	16	45	154
Manabu Mima, Eagles	8	5	4.01	144	146	19	24	112

OTHER NOTABLE PITCHERS

Pitcher, Team	W	L	ERA	IP	H	HR	BB	SO
Yuki Matsui, Eagles	2	8	1.94	70	40	5	24	107
Yuito Mori, Hawks	2	3	2.21	53	40	5	13	59
Tatsushi Masuda, Lions	4	1	1.81	70	51	5	10	74
Naoya Masuda, Marines	4	5	2.15	59	36	5	22	56
Ryo Akiyoshi, Fighters	0	5	2.96	52	38	6	19	48
Brandon Dickson, Buffaloes	2	1	3.03	36	29	1	18	38
Hirotoshi Masui, Buffaloes	1	4	4.83	50	51	5	24	64
Hiroshi Kaino, Hawks	2	5	4.14	59	49	6	34	73
Naoya Ishikawa, Fighters	3	2	3.31	54	39	6	16	75
Livan Moinelo, Hawks	3	1	1.52	59	37	4	25	86
Naoki Miyanishi, Fighters	1	2	1.71	47	32	1	6	51
Katsunori Hirai, Lions	5	4	3.50	82	77	6	32	66
Livan Moinelo, Hawks	3	1	1.52	59	37	4	25	86
Kohei Morihara, Eagles	4	2	1.97	64	47	3	18	65
Alan Busenitz, Eagles	4	3	1.94	51	46	1	20	45
Hiroshi Kaino, Hawks	2	5	4.14	59	49	6	34	73
Chia-Hao Sung, Eagles	3	2	2.18	45	34	2	23	40
Takahiro Matsunaga, Marines	2	3	2.60	35	25	3	17	32
Frank Herrmann, Eagles	5	3	3.04	47	31	5	16	49
Taisuke Kondo, Buffaloes	4	6	3.44	50	39	4	22	61

OTHER NORTH AMERICAN PITCHERS

Pitcher, Team	W	L	ERA	IP	H	HR	BB	SO
Deunte Heath, Lions	2	3	3.73	31	26	2	14	34
Ariel Miranda, Hawks	7	5	4.19	86	80	13	48	58
Rick van den Hurk, Hawks	2	0	3.10	17	13	2	2	22
Johnny Barbato, Fighters	2	2	5.63	32	35	5	21	22
Bryan Rodriguez, Fighters	6	7	3.25	91	89	7	27	55
Brandon Dickson, Buffaloes	2	1	3.03	36	29	1	18	38
Tyler Eppler, Buffaloes	4	4	4.02	31	41	2	9	25
Andrew Albers, Buffaloes	2	6	5.83	63	84	12	10	45
Mike Bolsinger, Marines	4	6	4.63	103	105	14	52	86
Brandon Mann, Marines	0	2	3.94	16	16	1	12	20
Alan Busenitz, Eagles	4	3	1.94	51	46	1	20	45

KOREA

Doosan Rallies

With a little over a month to go in the KBO season, the Doosan Bears seemed to be an afterthought. The Bears rallied from nine games down in the standings on Aug. 15 to catch the SK Wyverns for the regular season crown on the final day of the season. The two clubs finished with identical records, but the Bears won the regular season crown because they won the head-to-head series against the Wyverns.

By doing so, the Bears earned a bye to the Korean Series finals. The Bears swept the Kiwoom Heroes in the Korean Series finals for their first title since 2016 and their sixth overall.

Offense was down precipitously after a new larger and softer baseball was adopted. There were only 1,014 home runs in 2019 down from a record 1,756 in 2018. Coincidentally or not, KBO attendance also dipped by nearly 800,000 fans from 8.1 million to 7.3 million.

STANDINGS & LEADERS

Team	W	L	T	PCT	GB
Doosan Bears	88	55	1	.615	—
SK Wyverns	88	55	1	.615	—
Kiwoom Heroes	86	57	1	.601	2
LG Twins	79	64	1	.552	9
NC Dinos	73	69	2	.514	14.5
KT Wiz	71	71	2	.500	16.5
Kia Tigers	62	80	2	.437	25.5
Samsung Lions	60	83	1	.420	28
Hanwha Eagles	58	86	0	.403	30.5
Lotte Giants	48	93	3	.340	39

Playoffs—First Round: Kiwoom defeated LG 3-1 in best-of-five series. **Semifinals**: Kiwoom defeated SK 3-0 in best-of-five series. **Finals:** Doosan defeated Kiwoom 4-0 in best-of-seven series.

BATTING LEADERS

Player, Team	AVG	AB	R	H	HR	RBI	SB
Eui Ji Yang, NC	.354	390	61	138	20	68	4
Jose Fernandez, DOOSAN	.344	572	87	197	15	88	1
Min Woo Park, NC	.344	468	89	161	1	45	18
Jung Hoo Lee, KIWOOM	.336	574	91	193	6	68	13
Baek Ho Kang, KT	.336	438	72	147	13	65	9
Jong Wook Ko, SK	.323	492	76	159	3	56	31
Mel Rojas Jr., KT	.322	521	68	168	24	104	4
Kun Woo Park, DOOSAN	.319	458	83	146	10	64	12
Han Joon Yoo, KT	.317	501	61	159	14	86	3
Eun Seong Chae, LG	.315	470	59	148	12	72	2

PITCHING LEADERS

Player, Team	W	L	ERA	IP	H	HR	BB	SO
Hyeon Jong Yang, KIA	16	8	2.29	185	165	6	33	163
Josh Lindblom, DOOSAN	20	3	2.50	195	165	13	29	189
Kwang Hyun Kim, SK	17	6	2.51	190	198	13	38	180
Casey Kelly, LG	14	12	2.55	180	164	7	41	126
Angel Sanchez, SK	17	5	2.62	165	151	2	42	148
Tyler Wilson, LG	14	7	2.92	185	171	7	44	137
Jake Brigham, KIWOOM	13	5	2.96	158	148	5	46	130
Drew Rucinski, NC	9	9	3.05	177	164	13	45	119
Eric Jokisch, KIWOOM	13	9	3.13	181	166	9	39	141
Hee Kwan Yoo, DOOSAN	11	8	3.25	166	171	8	42	64

TAIWAN

Lamigo Wins One Last Title

The Lamigo Monkeys draw the largest crowds in the CPBL. To celebrate the league's 30th season, they wrapped up their third straight CPBL title. The deciding Game 5 of the championship was a laugher, as the Monkeys beat the Chinatrust Brothers 20-3.

And now the Monkeys are no more. The team will continue to play in Taoyuan but the team's owners sold the club to Rakuten, a Japanese e-commerce company, which said that it will rename the team for the 2020 season. The club gave its old moniker a fitting send-off, averaging 11 runs a game during the championship series.

The woeful state of the basement-dwelling Uni President 7-Eleven Lions meant that the league's other three teams all had winning records.

Chinatrust's Cheng-Ming Peng announced his retirement at the end of the season after a 19-year career. Peng picked up his 2,000th career hit late in his final season.

Wei-Lun Pan also reached a milestone as the veteran UniLions pitcher broke the league's career wins record with his 142nd win. Pan has been pitching for the Lions since 2003.

STANDINGS & LEADERS

Team	W	L	T	PCT	GB
&Lamigo Monkeys	63	55	2	.534	—
Fubon Guardians	63	55	2	.534	—
*Chinatrust Brothers	62	56	2	.525	1
Uni President 7-Eleven Lions	28	70	2	.407	15

* First half champion &Second half champion
Finals: Lamigo defeated the UniLions 4-2 in best-of-seven series.

BATTING LEADERS

Player, Team	AVG	OBP	SLG	AB	R	H	HR	RBI	SB
Lin Li, Lamigo	.389	.438	.639	388	97	151	20	81	9
Chen Jun Shue, Lamigo	.381	.449	.619	381	87	145	22	89	2
Chan Tsu Shen, Chinatrust	.351	.402	.638	348	74	122	26	75	6
Lin Hong Yue, Lamigo	.350	.416	.585	434	106	152	26	95	0
Chu Yue Shen, Lamigo	.347	.394	.605	458	93	159	30	105	0
Hu Jin Long, Fubon	.342	.374	.482	427	69	146	13	60	6
Lin Yi Chyuan, Fubon	.325	.373	.573	431	71	140	27	108	1
Kuo Yan Wen, Lamigo	.324	.368	.505	426	59	138	17	94	0
Lan Yin Lun, Laimgo	.318	.364	.447	443	73	141	10	65	7
Wang Wei Chen, Chinatrust	.317	.349	.370	451	64	143	1	45	27

PITCHING LEADERS

Player, Team	W	L	ERA	G	IP	H	BB	SO
Mike Loree, Lamigo	12	9	2.78	26	172	142	30	167
Mitch Lively, Chinatrust	10	11	3.23	31	167	178	46	140
Chen Shi Peng, Fubon	11	8	3.48	23	124	151	35	73
Michael Nix, Lamigo	11	9	3.86	29	177	184	51	141
Radhames Liz, Lamigo	16	6	4.18	30	162	155	58	179
Wang Yi Zheng, Lamigo	12	5	4.54	25	139	171	33	113
Pan Wei Lun, UniLions	8	7	5.10	23	120	157	20	52

INTERNATIONAL

Bologna Wins Serie A1 Again

BY HARVEY SAHKER

Bologna's domination of Series A1 continued in 2019 as the most successful club in Italian baseball in the 21st century dominated the regular season and won yet another title.

Bologna swept San Marino three games to none in the Italy Series. It was Bologna's thirteenth national championship and their fourth in the last six years. Bologna lost the first two games of their best-of-five semi-final at home against Parma, then won two on the road and the decisive fifth game at home. San Marino defeated Nettuno in the other semi-final, three games to one. In this series, too, the visiting team prevailed in all but the final game.

The Rimini Pirates, one of Italy's most successful clubs, dropped out of Serie A1 shortly before the beginning of the season. Club president Simone Pillisio had left the club in January and joined Nettuno, taking no fewer than five Rimini regulars with him. Left with gaping holes both on and off the field, Rimini were forced to opt out of the league. The Pirates had won thirteen Italian titles of their own. Their first came in 1975. Their most recent was in 2017.

One of the few Rimini regulars who did not move to Nettuno was 2018 batting king Alex Romero. The former Arizona Diamondback outfielder signed with San Marino and batted .357 for his new club, good enough for ninth in the league.

Bologna bolstered their roster by signing former Giants farmhand John Polonius in April. The 28-year old Curacao native spent seven seasons in the San Francisco organization and played as high as AAA. Polonius hit .316 with five homers for Bologna. After the Serie A1 season, Polonius played for the Netherlands in the European Championships.

The Bologna lineup got another boost in June when catcher Andy Paz joined the club. Paz, 26, played in the Oakland system from 2011 to 2017. He spent part of the 2019 campaign in the Can-Am League. The Havana native hit a Serie A1 leading four triples for Bologna in just nine games.

Bologna also won the 2019 European Champions Cup. They captured the continental club championship after defeating the Amsterdam Pirates 8-0 in the tournament final.

Renzo Martini of Redipuglia hit .413 and won the Serie A1 batting title. The 27-year old Venezuelan also topped the league in homers (7), slugging (.763), on-base percentage (.500) and total bases (61). A newcomer to Italian baseball in 2019, Martini was in the Yankees chain between 2011 and 2015.

Alex Romero

Angelo Palumbo pitched a seven-inning perfect game as Bolzano defeated the Toselli Yankees 15-0 in a mid-July Serie A2 game. Palumbo had 14 strikeouts in the second tier contest. The Yankees failed to hit the ball out of the infield. The remaining seven outs were groundouts. The ten-run "mercy rule" was invoked after the Yankees batted in the seventh inning.

STANDINGS

Team	W	L	PCT	GB
Bologna	21	3	.875	—
Nettuno	15	9	.625	6
San Marino	14	9	.609	6.5
Parma	12	11	.522	8.5
Redipuglia	9	14	.391	11.5
Godo	6	18	.250	15
Castenaso	5	18	.217	15.5

Playoffs—Semifinals: Bologna beat Parma 3-2 and San Marino beat Nettuno 3-1 in best-of-five series. **Italy Series:** Bologna beat San Marino 3-0 in best-of-five series.

INDVIDUAL BATTING LEADERS

Player, Team	AVG	AB	R	H	2B	3B	HR	RBI	SB
Martini, Renzo G., RNG	.413	80	17	33	7	0	7	19	1
Poma, Sebastiano, PAR	.380	92	19	35	10	2	4	26	3
Ferrini, C. Jose L., BOL	.379	87	19	33	4	1	1	21	5
Giordani, Federico, RSM	.375	104	23	39	5	1	5	14	2
Leonora, Ericson N., BOL	.375	88	26	33	6	1	5	23	3
Flores, Jose, RSM	.371	89	15	33	13	1	3	27	4
Angulo, Oscar D., NETC	.368	95	23	35	4	1	1	12	1
Loardi, Niccolo' M., CAE	.354	82	12	29	8	1	0	13	2
Romero, Alex, RSM	.351	57	17	20	2	0	3	13	0
Mazzanti, Giuseppe, NETC	.329	82	24	27	8	0	5	22	1

INDIVIDUAL PITCHING LEADERS

Player	W	L	ERA	IP	H	R	ER	BB	SO
Rivero, Raul, BOL	4	0	1.35	53	33	8	8	7	87
Noguera, Antonio, BOL	2	1	2.42	22	18	8	6	7	27
Habeck, Marc-Andre', PAR	1	2	2.48	29	20	10	8	11	38
Di Raffaele, Luca, GOD	1	3	2.57	21	15	13	6	12	22
Casanova, Erly, PAR	2	3	3.02	51	46	22	17	22	52
Hernandez, Ricardo, NETC	4	1	3.18	51	41	20	18	24	49
Brolo Gouvea, Murilo, BOL	3	0	3.20	25	19	9	9	6	34
Lopez, Aliangel, CAE	3	6	3.31	68	60	28	25	30	97
Quevedo, Carlos, RSM	6	2	3.32	57	52	22	21	13	73
Maestri, Alessandro, RSM	5	4	3.34	59	37	24	22	27	65

Amsterdam Edges Neptunus

BY HARVEY SAHKER

The Amsterdam Pirates came back from a three-game deficit to defeat Neptunus in the Holland Series. It was Amsterdam's fifth Dutch Major League championship and its first since 2011. The Pirates are the first club in DML history to win the Holland Series in seven games after losing the first three. The margin of victory was one run in four of the seven games.

Neptunus was one inning away from winning the Series in Game Six, in Amsterdam. After eight frames, they had a slender 3-2 lead over the Pirates. But Amsterdam scored twice in the bottom of the ninth to even the Series at three games apiece. The winning run came on a bases loaded walk.

Amsterdam infielder Delano Selassa won the Holland Series MVP award. Selassa came into Games One and Two as a substitute. He went 7 for 15 in the Pirates' four victories and hit a key bases-loaded double in the Pirates' 6-0 Game Seven win. Selassa was 8 for 20 in the Series.

Both of the DML best-of-five semi-finals were one-sided. Amsterdam and Neptunus swept HCAW and the Hoofddorp Pioniers, respectively, in three games. The victors outscored their opponents 33-4 in the six games.

In April, Misja Harcksen pitched a perfect game for Neptunus. Harcksen had ten strikeouts and made just 97 pitches in the game, a 4-0 win against the Oosterhout Twins. It was the third perfect game in DML history. Harcksen's gem was against his old team. He left the Twins and joined Neptunus after the 2018 season.

Later that month, Lars Huijer pitched a seven-inning no-hitter for the Hoofddorp Pioniers in a 12-0 decision against The Hague Storks. Huijer walked three Storks in the game. It was the fiftieth no-hitter in Holland's top league.

Also in April, Amsterdam's Rob Cordemans, 44, became the first DML pitcher to log 2,000 regular season strikeouts. In early May, Kit Gijsbers of the Pirates became the first player to hit a grand slam on the first pitch of his DML career. Gijsbers hit the historic round tripper in a 20-1 rout of DSS.

Infielder Sharlon Schoop joined the Amsterdam Pirates in late May. Schoop had a thirteen year minor league career in the Giants, Royals and Orioles farm systems. Schoop batted .357 for the Pirates in the regular season and .308 in the post-season.

Oosterhout Twins catcher Jason Halman returned to the DML after an absence of seven years. After the 2011 season, Halman was accused of murdering his brother, Gregory, then a member of the Seattle Mariners. Jason was acquitted by reason of temporary insanity. He hit .305 for the Twins in 2019 (ninth in the league) and threw out nine would be base stealers (tied for second). He also led the DML with 17 doubles.

In September, the Dutch national team won their twenty-third European Championship. The Netherlands defeated Italy 5-1 in the tournament finale, at Bonn.

Sharlon Schoop

ROBERT SARGENT/WBCI

STANDINGS

Team	W	L	T	GB
Neptunus	36	6	0	-
Amsterdam Pirates	34	8	0	2
HCAW	22	18	2	13
Hoofddorp Pioniers	20	20	2	15
Amersfoort	17	25	0	19
Oosterhout Twins	17	25	0	19
DSS	13	29	0	23
The Hague Storks	7	35	0	29

Playoffs—Semifinals: Neptunus defeated Hoofddorp 3-0 and Amsterdam defeated HCAW 3-0 in best-of-five series. **Holland Series:** Amsterdam defeated Neptunus 4-3 in best-of-seven series.

INDIVIDUAL BATTING LEADERS

Player, Team	AVG	AB	R	H	2B	3B	HR	RBI	SB
Richardson, Denzel, AMS	.388	134	24	52	13	3	4	38	13
Lampe, Gilmer, AMS	.382	136	38	52	14	3	4	36	16
Kemp, Dwayne, NEP	.364	176	32	64	12	4	4	40	22
Daantji, Shaldimar, NEP	.358	137	29	49	3	2	2	21	10
Leonora, Dudley, NEP	.335	158	32	53	12	0	0	28	11
Engelhardt, Rachid, QUI	.333	174	34	58	6	2	1	23	6
Dille, Benjamin, NEP	.320	128	35	41	3	2	1	22	7
Meer, vd Stijn, NEP	.309	165	39	51	10	1	0	19	6
Halman, Jason, TWI	.305	164	24	50	17	0	3	27	1
Daal, Rodney, HCA	.304	138	24	42	7	1	5	25	6

INDIVIDUAL PITCHING LEADERS

Player, Team	W	L	ERA	IP	H	R	ER	BB	SO
Huijer, Lars, PIO	4	2	0.77	93	42	16	8	25	112
Rifaele, Jhan, AMS	4	1	1.19	38	24	7	5	19	35
Pfau, Chris, HCA	8	4	1.61	90	52	21	16	41	105
Markwell, Diegomar, NEP	11	1	1.69	85	69	19	16	23	64
Ploeger, Jim, AMS	9	2	1.82	79	56	19	16	23	77
Robberse, Sem, QUI	6	3	1.83	64	50	24	13	9	62
Harcksen, Misja, NEP	11	2	1.95	65	45	18	14	23	64
Kirkpatrick, Paul, PIO	3	4	1.98	59	40	17	13	25	50
Cordemans, Rob, AMS	6	1	2.11	55	47	15	13	13	58
Yntema, Orlando, NEP	8	1	2.22	77	51	22	19	25	94

INTERNATIONAL

Las Tunas Wins First Title

F or years, Las Tunas was a team that struggled to compete in Serie Nacional. Winning a title was simply an impossible dream. The Lumberjacks had entered Serie Nacional in 1977. They had zero titles to their name.

For the long-suffering Lumberjacks fans, the 2018-2019 season ended the drought. Outfielder Jorge Johnson was named the playoff MVP. Johnson hit .478 (11-for-23) in the playoffs with two home runs, that came after a regular season where he won the batting title, hitting .419.

The other big news for Cuban baseball was an announcement that MLB and Cuba reached an agreement to allow Cuban players to be posted to come to play in the U.S. But the U.S. government then nixed the proposal before it was implemented.

STANDINGS

Team	W	L	PCT	GB
Las Tunas	34	26	.567	-
Santi Spiritus	32	28	.534	2
Villa Clara	31	29	.517	3
Ciego de Avila	31	29	.517	3
Industriales	30	30	.500	4
Holguin	22	38	.367	12

ELIMINATED IN FIRST HALF

Team	W	L	PCT	GB
Santiago de Cuba	25	20	.556	3
Mayabeque	24	21	.534	4
Isla de la Juventud	23	22	.512	5
Pinar del Rio	21	24	.467	7
Artemisa	20	23	.466	7
Camaguey	19	26	.423	9
Granma	18	25	.419	9
Guantanamo	17	28	.378	11
Cienfuegos	16	28	.364	11.5
Matanzas	14	30	.319	13.5

Wild Card: Industriales defeated Mayabeque 2-0 and Santi Spiritus defeated Santiago 2-0 in best-of-3 series ensuring the two teams advanced to the second phase of the season.
Playoffs: Semifinals: Villa Clara defeated Santi Spiritus and Las Tunas defeated Ciego de Avila. Finals: Las Tunas defeated Villa Clara 4-1 in best-of-7 series.

BATTING LEADERS

Player, Team	AVG	AB	R	H	2B	3B	HR	RBI
Jorge Antonio Johnson,LTU	.419	167	35	70	8	2	1	37
Maikel Caceres,HOL	.416	185	44	77	19	1	10	41
Jorge Enrique Alomá,ART	.394	137	34	54	8	0	7	31
Carlos Benítez,GRA	.389	131	14	51	7	0	5	28
Lázaro Hernández,ART	.384	99	24	38	6	1	7	30
Yordanis Samón,IND	.384	172	42	66	16	2	6	29
Yosvani Alarcón,LTU	.379	161	30	61	10	0	12	43
Cesar Prieto,CFG	.379	182	35	69	9	1	5	28
Edilse Silva La,SCU	.377	138	26	52	7	0	6	34

Player, Team	AVG	AB	R	H	2B	3B	HR	RBI
Alexander Ayala,CMG	.373	126	25	47	10	0	4	27
Pedro Manuel Leon,MAY	.371	132	33	49	7	0	15	36
Norel González,VCL	.370	146	31	54	7	0	3	23
Yunier Mendoza,SSP	.359	181	24	65	6	0	3	30
Yoan Moreno,ART	.358	109	27	39	9	2	1	11
Dayán García,ART	.356	163	25	58	9	0	5	39
Andrés Hernández,IND	.352	108	14	38	8	0	2	17
Jhony Hardy,IJV	.352	125	22	44	7	2	0	15
Alberto Calderón,IJV	.352	142	24	50	4	1	0	16
Stayler Hernández,IND	.352	165	35	58	10	0	10	48
Yuniesky Larduert,LTU	.350	180	43	63	11	3	0	20
Dayron Blanco,ART	.342	161	45	55	4	6	4	22
Ariel Sánchez,MTZ	.339	127	21	43	4	0	1	13
Dunieski Ramón Barroso,SSP	.339	171	20	58	8	0	5	31
Santiago Torres,SCU	.338	154	36	52	7	2	4	23
Orlando Acebey,SSP	.337	181	24	61	10	1	4	25
Marnolki Aguiar,HOL	.333	102	18	34	5	2	3	28
Orlando Lavandera,MAY	.333	105	11	35	7	1	2	14
Yoelkis Guibert,SCU	.333	174	36	58	12	1	5	33
Wilfredo Yasel Aroche,IND	.333	195	28	65	9	2	1	20
Edain Román,MAY	.329	143	25	47	5	0	2	17
Robert Luis Delgado,GTM	.329	161	24	53	10	0	4	15
Yordanis Alarcón,LTU	.325	126	16	41	3	0	3	19
Daykel Manso Del,GTM	.324	148	18	48	9	1	3	24
Leonelkis Escalante,GTM	.324	179	24	58	7	0	1	20
Yunior Paumier,HOL	.320	150	32	48	13	0	7	29
Andy Cosme,ART	.319	135	21	43	6	0	2	14
Juan Carlos Arencibia,PRI	.319	135	22	43	6	0	1	10
Yurién Vizcaino,VCL	.319	138	20	44	11	0	5	38
Geidy Soler,HOL	.319	166	30	53	6	1	9	34
Pedro Luis Rodríguez,PRI	.316	117	20	37	9	0	3	16

PITCHING LEADERS

Player, Team	W	L	ERA	G	IP	H	HR	BB	SO
Frank Luis Medina,PRI	4	4	1.46	10	62	2	56	14	33
Vladimir García,CAV	4	1	1.63	8	50	0	32	13	48
Alberto Bicet,SCU	9	2	1.64	14	77	4	82	19	34
Yosbel José Zulueta,VCL	4	4	1.96	10	55	1	36	35	47
Pablo Luis Guillén,VCL	4	2	2.00	10	45	1	41	28	36
Yoanni Yera,MTZ	5	2	2.41	9	52	1	36	16	61
Yadián Martínez,MAY	5	2	2.45	13	88	3	69	30	52
Yamichel Pérez,SSP	5	3	2.47	13	58	2	60	9	33
Fredy Asiel Alvarez,VCL	3	4	2.48	10	58	2	51	10	30
Frank Montieth,IND	4	0	2.62	8	45	4	38	9	24
Geonel Gutiérrez,ART	4	2	2.64	8	44	2	35	18	30
Yaifredo Domínguez,PRI	5	2	2.68	10	57	4	52	20	21
Alain Sánchez,VCL	5	2	2.71	10	66	2	74	13	41
Wilson Paredes,HOL	8	0	2.74	17	62	4	60	22	54
Joel Mojena,GRA	5	2	2.84	17	44	1	28	20	33
Maikel Folch,CAV	4	2	2.89	9	56	3	51	22	35
Raicol Suárez,CFG	3	2	3.02	21	45	3	46	21	28
Yariel Rodríguez,CMG	3	2	3.10	11	70	6	62	35	55
Miguel Angel Lastra,IJV	5	1	3.12	21	52	3	47	20	43
Carlos A. Santiesteban,HOL	3	3	3.18	11	65	2	48	22	35
Rafael Sanchez,HOL	5	2	3.27	22	44	3	45	24	23
Yander Guevara,CAV	6	2	3.27	9	63	5	68	18	26
Rubén Rodríguez,HOL	6	1	3.31	13	54	5	50	16	13
Yunier Gamboa,IJV	3	3	3.32	13	60	3	66	26	23
Yoen Socorrás,SSP	4	6	3.39	13	69	4	65	24	38
Ricardo Martínez,ART	4	4	3.44	9	50	3	50	23	20
Pedro Angel Alvarez,SSP	4	2	3.45	13	73	4	67	30	44
Frank Navarro,GTM	2	3	3.50	8	46	3	44	12	23
Yeinel Alberto Zayas,IJV	4	4	3.51	11	59	1	51	24	33
Adrián Rajiv Sosa,IND	3	2	3.63	13	45	3	41	16	21
César García,GRA	3	5	3.70	10	58	4	65	22	23
Pedro Enrique Aguero,GTM	2	5	3.72	12	56	5	54	25	19
Dariel Góngora De La,CMG	6	4	3.74	10	65	4	65	27	42
Norge Vera,SCU	2	3	3.79	11	55	3	56	32	37
Yudier Rodríguez,LTU	5	2	3.84	11	66	5	63	21	44
Danny Betancourt,SCU	4	4	3.99	18	56	6	50	22	40
Frank Madan,CMG	3	4	4.08	10	57	2	59	18	31
Dayron Alexis Riera,GTM	4	5	4.25	11	55	4	62	28	24
Yosvani Torres,PRI	4	5	4.31	9	63	4	69	14	36
Alyanser álvarez Del,MAY	3	5	4.33	21	44	0	41	18	17

Panama topped Cuba in the final round of the 2019 Caribbean Series, winning the country's first tournament title since 1950.

Panama Wins Caribbean Series For First Time In 69 Years

Panama City was selected as the replacement hosting location for the 2019 Caribbean Series due to security concerns in Venezuela. Panama would go on to win the championship, defeating Cuba, 3-1, in the final round. Panama, which had not even participated in the tournament since 1960, won its first Caribbean Series title since 1950.

Panama's Javy Guerra was named the tournament's Most Valuable Player. After starting his career as a minor league shortstop, Guerra has recently transitioned to the mound as a right-handed pitcher. He made his major league debut on Sept. 2, and he went on to pitch 8.2 innings across eight relief appearances in 2019.

Despite winning this year's tournament, Panama's presence in next year's series is still questionable as the competition will be hosted in San Juan, Puerto Rico.

INDIVIDUAL BATTING LEADERS

Player, Team	AVG	AB	R	H	2B	3B	HR	RBI	BB	SO	SB
Fransoso, Michael, CAN	.430	100	20	43	9	2	5	18	16	20	2
Ngoepe, Gift, SYD	.379	132	26	50	9	4	6	32	20	33	9
Reynolds, Mikey, ADE	.366	101	22	37	10	0	2	15	11	10	11
Glendinning, Robbie, PER	.364	99	18	36	9	0	3	25	21	27	0
Kemp, Dwayne, SYD	.348	158	25	55	10	1	2	24	10	15	6
Campbell, Michael, SYD	.339	127	18	43	8	0	0	15	12	26	1
Burt, D.J., MEL	.338	133	26	45	7	2	2	18	21	19	18
Kennelly, Tim, PER	.338	160	38	54	11	1	6	24	21	22	8
Wilson, Zach, CAN	.331	148	31	49	10	2	12	30	11	23	0
George, Darryl, MEL	.329	149	29	49	7	1	7	17	6	35	7

INDIVIDUAL PITCHING LEADERS

Player, Team	W	L	ERA	G	SV	IP	H	BB	SO	AVG
Imanaga, Shota, CAN	4	0	0.51	6	0	35	14	1	57	.118
Solbach, Markus, ADE	5	3	1.10	10	0	65	41	13	74	.178
Anderson, Craig, SYD	2	1	2.25	10	2	40	37	11	30	.245
Guyer, Josh, SYD	7	1	2.60	10	0	55	55	10	54	.264
Schmidt, Daniel, PER	2	0	2.81	11	0	32	31	6	21	.248
Ruzic, Dushan, MEL	5	1	2.82	9	0	51	49	17	46	.247
Atherton, Tim, BRI	7	0	2.87	10	0	60	47	11	67	.208
Kent, Steven, CAN	7	1	2.90	11	0	62	47	13	76	.211
Maestri, Alex, SYD	5	4	2.93	10	0	58	52	18	78	.234
Blackley, Travis, BRI	2	2	3.00	10	0	57	59	12	47	.273

AUSTRALIAN BASEBALL LEAGUE

Team	W	L	PCT	GB
Brisbane Bandits	25	15	.625	—
Sydney Blue Sox	25	15	.625	—
Perth Heat	24	16	.600	1
Melbourne Aces	23	17	.575	2
Canberra Cavalry	23	17	.575	2
Adelaide Bite	19	21	.475	6
Auckland Tuatara	14	26	.350	11
Geelong-Korea	7	33	.175	18

Playoffs—Semifinals: Brisbane defeated Canberra 2-1 and Perth defeated Sydney 2-1 in best-of-three series. **Finals:** Brisbane defeated Perth 2-0 in a best-of-three series.

DOMINICAN LEAGUE

TEAM	W	L	PCT	GB
Estrellas Orientales	29	21	.580	—
Leones del Escogido	27	23	.540	2
Tigres del Licey	27	23	.540	2
Toros del Este	25	25	.500	4
Aguilas Cibaenas	22	28	.440	7
Gigantes del Cibao	20	30	.400	9

Playoffs—Round Robin: Estrellas Orientales and Toros del Este advance. **Finals:** Estrellas Orientales defeated Toros del Este 5-1 in best-of-nine series.

INDIVIDUAL BATTING LEADERS

Player, Team	AVG	AB	R	H	2B	3B	HR	RBI	BB	SO	SB
Valdespin, Jordany, TOR	.349	166	30	58	6	0	2	20	20	21	14
Alberto, Hanser, GIG	.322	171	16	55	9	0	1	16	10	15	2
Sosa, Ruben, TOR	.297	158	30	47	3	1	0	15	16	28	13
Lake, Junior, EST	.289	173	31	50	7	0	4	24	31	31	13
Siri, Jose, EST	.275	131	24	36	7	2	3	11	8	39	13
Valenzuela, Luis, ESC	.273	165	21	45	6	2	1	18	7	26	2
Sierra, Moises, LIC	.268	153	19	41	10	1	2	13	25	30	3
Reyes, Pablo, LIC	.261	142	13	37	5	1	1	14	19	27	6
Avelino, Abiatal, EST	.253	162	20	41	3	0	2	9	14	29	7
Torres, Ramon, GIG	.246	142	6	35	5	0	1	15	9	20	2

INDIVIDUAL PITCHING LEADERS

Player, Team	W	L	ERA	G	SV	IP	H	BB	SO	AVG
Romero, Enny, ESC	2	1	1.33	10	0	54	32	15	54	.175
Cortes, Nestor, EST	2	0	1.71	8	0	42	26	10	45	.177
Lowey, Josh, ESC	6	2	2.10	12	0	56	50	22	48	.244
Alexander, Tyler, ESC	2	3	2.68	11	0	50	34	10	48	.192
Liz, Radhames, EST	2	3	2.98	11	0	45	33	15	42	.200
Valdes, Raul, TOR	4	4	3.05	11	0	65	45	20	53	.192
Rogers, Esmil, LIC	2	4	3.24	10	0	42	54	12	30	.316
Maya, Yunesky, EST	2	1	3.60	10	0	45	42	12	37	.249

MEXICAN PACIFIC LEAGUE

Team	W	L	PCT	GB
Naranjeros de Hermosillo	33	25	.569	—
Tomateros de Culiacan	33	25	.569	—
Yaquis de Obregon	30	26	.536	2
Charros de Jalisco	28	29	.491	4
Caneros de los Mochis	28	30	.483	5
Venados de Mazatlan	27	31	.466	6
Mayos de Navojoa	26	31	.456	6
Aguilas de Mexicali	24	32	.429	8

Playoffs—Semifinals: Charros de Jalisco defeated Venados de Mazatlan 4-1 and Yaquis de Obregon defeated Caneros de los Mochis 4-3 in best-of-seven series. **Finals:** Charros de Jalisco defeated Yaquis de Obregon 4-2 in a best-of-seven series.

INDIVIDUAL BATTING LEADERS

Player, Team	AVG	AB	R	H	2B	3B	HR	RBI	BB	SO	SB
Peguero, Francisco, HER	.352	216	27	76	15	2	6	44	9	43	0
Atondo, Jasson, HER	.351	231	39	81	10	0	0	21	11	21	1
Valdez, Jesus, OBR	.325	240	30	78	13	1	6	43	33	41	2
Mendoza, Victor, OBR	.323	186	29	60	15	1	6	30	29	29	0
Rodriguez Salazar, Isaac, MOC	.318	245	41	78	11	2	1	18	37	32	9
Urias, Ramon, MOC	.318	173	31	55	7	0	10	34	34	35	5
Alvarez, Dariel, JAL	.315	219	33	69	12	1	14	38	18	22	0
Rodriguez, Manny, JAL	.313	256	41	80	9	0	13	52	22	37	2
Castro, Leandro, MOC	.303	241	49	73	15	2	13	45	36	42	12
Harris, Alonzo, JAL	.302	248	51	75	10	1	7	22	32	55	28

INDIVIDUAL PITCHING LEADERS

Player, Team	W	L	ERA	G	SV	IP	H	BB	SO	AVG
Leyva, Elian, JAL	6	2	2.02	14	0	76	59	23	67	.219
Barreda, Manny, CUL	5	3	2.65	12	0	68	56	21	42	.228
Lugo, Jaime, MOC	5	3	2.75	13	0	79	72	18	46	.248
Carrillo, Marco, NAV	5	4	3.08	15	0	79	68	21	48	.239
Oliver, William, JAL	5	4	3.24	13	0	78	90	20	53	.298
Reyes, David, CUL	1	7	3.25	13	0	69	58	20	67	.224
Solano, Javier, MXC	3	5	3.42	14	0	82	83	13	63	.269
Lara, Orlando, JAL	3	5	3.98	13	0	72	71	21	62	.254
Quiala, Yoanys, MOC	3	5	4.37	18	1	68	67	30	53	.250
Mendoza, Luis, HER	4	5	4.85	14	0	69	82	21	53	.298

PUERTO RICAN LEAGUE

Team	W	L	PCT	GB
Indios de Mayaguez	21	14	.600	—
Gigantes de Carolina	17	18	.486	4
Cangrejeros de Santurce	17	19	.472	4.5
Criollos de Caguas	16	20	.444	5½

Playoffs—Round Robin: Cangrejeros de Santurce and Indios de Mayaguez advance. **Finals:** Cangrejeros de Santurce defeated Indios de Mayaguez 4-0 in a best-of-seven series.

INDIVIDUAL BATTING LEADERS

Player, Team	AVG	AB	R	H	2B	3B	HR	RBI	BB	SO	SB
Vargas, Kennys, MAY	.376	93	20	35	5	0	6	20	27	20	0
Lopez, Jack, CAG	.355	107	22	38	9	4	0	15	7	13	2
Gonzalez, Jay, MAY	.348	92	22	32	6	2	0	7	13	23	5
De Jesus Jr., Ivan, SAN	.344	122	15	42	5	1	1	11	12	19	1
Blanco, Dairon, CAG	.314	86	14	27	6	1	0	5	13	18	6
Machin, Vimael, CAG	.314	118	12	37	6	2	2	14	19	15	4
Ramos, Henry, MAY	.295	105	16	31	2	2	4	21	12	9	1
Gonzalez, Yariel, MAY	.294	119	17	35	7	0	1	23	6	7	0
Hernandez, Jan, SAN	.277	112	16	31	11	0	1	12	13	28	4
Burgos, Aldemar, CAR	.276	98	15	27	5	1	3	12	3	12	2

INDIVIDUAL PITCHING LEADERS

Player, Team	W	L	ERA	G	SV	IP	H	BB	SO	AVG
Cabrera, Fernando, SAN	3	2	2.09	7	0	43	32	10	22	.203
Maldonado, Ivan, CAG	2	2	2.20	6	0	33	28	9	12	.228
Oquendo, Enrique, SAN	1	3	2.30	8	0	31	26	18	26	.230
Cruz, Fernando, SAN	5	2	2.81	12	1	51	46	10	37	.232
Hernandez, Hector, SAN	2	4	2.86	7	0	35	39	13	16	.300
Romero, Alex, MAY	2	2	3.57	8	0	35	28	11	20	.217
Sanchez, Jonathan, MAY	1	1	3.72	7	0	29	30	12	17	.268
Rivera, Raul, CAG	3	2	4.31	7	0	31	38	3	17	.304
Martinez, Miguel, CAR	2	5	4.46	11	0	40	51	9	22	.319

VENEZUELAN LEAGUE

Team	W	L	PCT	GB
Navegantes del Magallanes	36	27	.571	—
Cardenales de Lara	35	28	.556	1
Leones del Caracas	34	29	.540	2
Tigres de Aragua	33	30	.524	3
Bravos de Margarita	32	31	.508	4
Caribes de Anzoategui	31	32	.492	5
Tiburones de La Guaira	28	33	.459	7
Aguilas del Zulia	21	40	.344	14

Playoffs—Semifinals: Leones del Caracas defeated Caribes de Anzoategui 4-1 and Cardenales de Lara defeated Navegantes del Magallanes 4-2 in best-of-seven series. **Finals:** Cardenales de Lara defeated Leones del Caracas 4-1 in a best-of-seven series.

INDIVIDUAL BATTING LEADERS

Player, Team	AVG	AB	R	H	2B	3B	HR	RBI	BB	SO	SB
Ramirez, Harold, CAR	.381	160	28	61	12	2	4	31	19	20	5
Barreto, Franklin, ARA	.352	199	37	70	12	1	7	38	20	35	7
Castro, Harold, CAR	.343	245	38	84	13	2	3	27	13	30	6
De Aza, Alejandro, LAR	.338	204	34	69	8	1	5	23	21	30	1
Castillo, Ali, LAR	.335	245	40	82	10	3	3	21	12	21	10
Valera, Cesar, ORI	.330	185	27	61	15	0	1	25	23	35	2
Carrera, Ezequiel, ARA	.328	189	36	62	10	1	2	23	28	36	11
Astudillo, Willians, ORI	.325	234	33	76	9	1	10	46	13	4	3
Chavez, Endy, MAG	.319	185	21	59	9	0	1	18	16	14	1
Arteaga, Humberto, ARA	.318	195	24	62	8	4	1	19	7	22	2

INDIVIDUAL PITCHING LEADERS

Player, Team	W	L	ERA	G	SV	IP	H	BB	SO	AVG
Bencomo, Omar, MAR	6	1	1.25	9	0	50	47	15	29	.246
Martinez, Jorge, LAR	5	3	2.26	12	0	60	52	6	40	.233
Boscan, Wilfredo, MAG	5	4	2.51	13	0	57	61	12	24	.274
Kubiak, David, MAR	4	3	2.53	14	0	64	55	22	48	.233
Perez, Williams, LAR	6	1	2.67	12	0	61	57	11	37	.253
Ledezma, Wilfredo, ORI	3	1	2.89	13	0	56	56	17	33	.258
Duran, Logan, MAG	3	4	2.99	13	0	69	69	22	52	.263
Moscoso, Guillermo, ARA	5	3	3.08	12	0	61	61	14	36	.262
Martinez, David, LAR	3	2	3.23	12	0	53	53	9	21	.260
Diaz, Luis, CAR	2	1	3.36	12	0	56	53	18	36	.249

INTERNATIONAL

COLLEGE

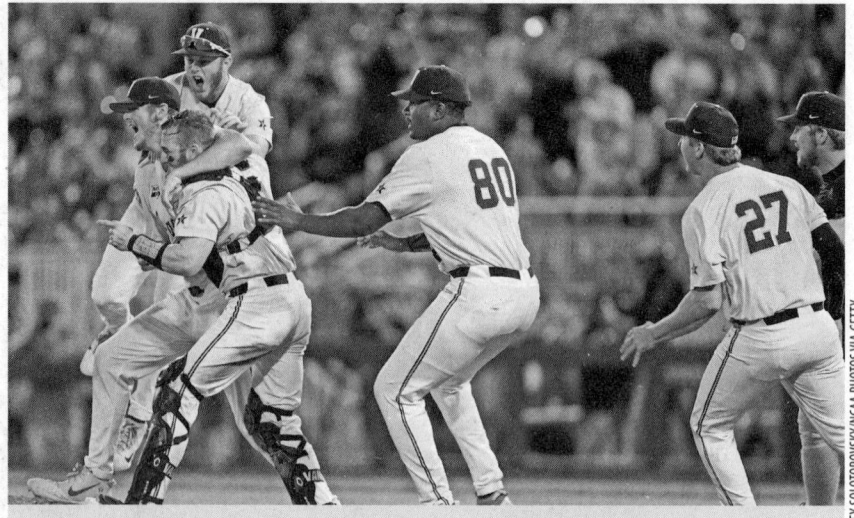

The Vanderbilt Commodores celebrated in Omaha after winning the College World Series.

COREY SOLOTOROVSKY/NCAA PHOTOS VIA GETTY

Vanderbilt Provides Gold Standard

BY TEDDY CAHILL

Vanderbilt wore its gold uniforms for Game 3 of the College World Series finals. It wasn't a coronation, not with a strong Michigan team on a magical postseason run in the opposite dugout, but the Commodores were dressed for success.

Vanderbilt had started the season No. 1 and that's where it was going to finish. The Commodores had played like the best team in the country throughout the second half of the season and while they had been pushed during the NCAA Tournament, losing the first game of super regionals to Duke and the first game of the College World Series finals to Michigan, they never buckled.

Vanderbilt had the nation's home run king in JJ Bleday. It had the Freshman of the Year in Kumar Rocker. It had a catalyst at the top of the lineup in Austin Martin, a premium closer in Tyler Brown and a committed, experienced senior class that had stuck together through a trying four years. It led the nation in wins, won the SEC and the SEC Tournament and had beaten every other SEC team.

Vanderbilt had come this far, and it wasn't going to be denied in Omaha. It was too deep, too talented, too well built for this stage. Vanderbilt, which had been an unstoppable battleship for the last three months, cruised to an 8-2 victory against Michigan to claim the national championship.

"I'm just happy for our team," coach Tim Corbin said. "I'm happy for the boys. It's fun to watch this thing come full-circle for them."

Vanderbilt won everything it possibly could have this season, but Corbin said the team hadn't talked much about championships. That approach led to a trophy case full of them, including the Commodores' second national championship in program history and first since 2014. They finished 59-12, setting an SEC record for wins

Only one team this century won more games than Vanderbilt did this season–Florida State bested it by one win in 2002. North Carolina's 2013 team also won 59 games. No one else has reached that number. And neither 2002 Florida State nor 2013 North Carolina finished the job with a national championship.

Vanderbilt won more games than any national champion since 1989 when Wichita State won 68 games. Five national champions have won more games than Vanderbilt did this season–1989 Wichita State, 1985 Miami (64), 1984 Cal State Fullerton (66), 1983 Texas (66) and 1979

COACHING CAROUSEL

School	In (Previous Job)	Out (Reason/New Job)
Bryant	Ryan Klosterman (Central Florida assistant)	Steve Owens (Rutgers head coach)
Cal State Northridge	Dave Serrano (Baseball America analyst)	Greg Moore (fired)
Charlotte	Robert Woodard (North Carolina assistant)	Loren Hibbs (Wichita St. assistant athletic director)
Fairleigh Dickinson	Rob DiToma (Fordham assistant)	Justin McKay (interim)
Florida State	Mike Martin Jr. (Florida State assistant)	Mike Martin (retired)
Gardner-Webb	Jim Chester (Barton (N.C.) head coach)	Rusty Stroupe (retired)
Georgia State	Brad Stromdahl (Georgia Gwinnett head coach)	Greg Frady (fired)
Incarnate Word	Ryan Shotzberger (Houston assistant)	Pat Hallmark (UTSA head coach)
Long Beach State	Eric Valenzuela (Saint Mary's head coach)	Troy Buckley (fired)
Louisiana-Lafayette	Matt Deggs (Sam Houston State head coach)	Tony Robichaux (deceased)
Loyola Marymount	Nathan Choate (LMU assistant)	Jason Gill (Southern California head coach)
Maryland-Baltimore County	Liam Bowen (UMBC assistant)	Bob Mumma (fired)
Morehead State	Mik Aoki (Notre Dame head coach)	Mike McGuire (USC-Upstate head coach)
Nebraska	Will Bolt (Texas A&M assistant)	Darin Erstad (resigned)
New Mexico State	Mike Kirby (Nebraska assistant)	Brian Green (Washington State head coach)
Notre Dame	Link Jarrett (UNC Greensboro head coach)	Mik Aoki (fired)
Oregon	Mark Wasikowski (Purdue head coach)	George Horton (fired)
Oregon State	Mitch Canham (Double-A Arkansas manager)	Pat Bailey (interim)
Purdue	Greg Goff (Purdue assistant)	Mark Wasikowski (Oregon head coach)
Purdue-Fort Wayne	Doug Schreiber (former Purdue head coach)	Bobby Pierce (resigned)
Radford	Karl Kuhn (Virginia assistant)	Joe Raccuia (resigned)
Rutgers	Steve Owens (Bryant head coach)	Joe Litterio (fired)
Saint Mary's	Greg Moore (Cal State Northridge head coach)	Eric Valenzuela (Long Beach State head coach)
Saint Peter's	Lou Proietti (Stonehill (Mass.) head coach)	Danny Ramirez (resigned)
Sam Houston State	Jay Sirianni (Sam Houston State assistant)	Matt Deggs (Louisiana-Lafayette head coach)
South Carolina-Upstate	Mike McGuire (Morehead State head coach)	Matt Fincher (resigned)
Southern California	Jason Gill (Loyola Marymount head coach)	Dan Hubbs (fired)
Southern Illinois	Lance Rhodes (Missouri assistant)	Ken Henderson (resigned)
Texas State	Steven Trout (Texas State assistant)	Ty Harrington (retired)
Toledo	Rob Reinstetle (Western Kentucky assistant)	Cory Mee (resigned)
UNC Greensboro	Billy Godwin (Yankees scout)	Link Jarrett (Notre Dame head coach)
UNC Wilmington	Randy Hood (UNCW assistant)	Mark Scalf (retired)
UTSA	Pat Hallmark (Incarnate Word head coach)	Jason Marshall (resigned)
Washington State	Brian Green (New Mexico State head coach)	Marty Lees (fired)
Western Illinois	Andy Pascoe (Butler assistant)	Ryan Brownlee (American Baseball Coaches Assoc.)
Wichita State	Eric Wedge (Blue Jays front office)	Todd Butler (fired)

Fullerton (60)—and all did so in a different era of college baseball.

Before 1992, the NCAA allowed teams to play about 70 regular-season games and many teams regularly played schools from outside of Division I. Now, teams are limited to 56 regular-season games and upper-echelon teams don't often play teams in Division II and below.

Vanderbilt came into the season ranked No. 1, but it evolved throughout the season. Early on, its offense led the way. Bleday's power surge made him an All-American and the No. 4 overall pick in the draft. Martin also earned first-team All-America honors and established himself as a premium prospect in the 2020 draft. Seniors Ethan Paul and Stephen Scott anchored the lineup and the Commodores averaged more than eight runs per game.

But in Omaha, where TD Ameritrade Park's dimensions have often deadened offenses over the last decade, the Commodores' bats weren't as potent. They hit .221 as a team, the lowest batting average for a national champion since 1972

Southern California—two years before college base-ball switched to metal bats.

That partially was a result of broader changes to baseball in 2019, when batting averages were down and power was up, but it meant more was required more of Vanderbilt's pitching staff. In six games at the College World Series, it allowed 16 runs, nearly half of which came in a loss to Michigan in Game 1 of the finals.

Rocker twice delivered outstanding starts to finish off a spectacular freshman season that lived up to the considerable hype that preceded him. He became the first freshman since Jorge Reyes from Oregon State in 2007 to be named Most Outstanding Player.

Vanderbilt also benefitted from a mature, veteran core. The Commodores last season nearly reached the College World Series, falling just short in a back-and-forth super regional against Mississippi State. Nearly that entire team returned this season, including five seniors, an unusual luxury for Vanderbilt.

But that group, including Paul, Scott, first baseman Julian Infante, righthander Patrick Raby and outfielder Walker Grisanti, stuck together and was rewarded with a championship.

Paul said while the national title made his decision to return easier in retrospect, it wasn't their sole aim when they chose to return for his senior year.

"Our No. 1 reason to come back to school wasn't to have this outlandish season or anything like that," he said. "I think that we all wanted to just be a part of something special.

"It's great to win a national championship, it's great to do all those things, but the program means so much more to us than just winning."

Paul and the rest of Vanderbilt's four-year players have been through a lot during their college careers. When the class of 2015 came to Nashville, Vanderbilt was coming off back-to-back College World Series finals appearances against Virginia, winning in 2014 and losing in 2015. They were the top-ranked recruiting class in the country, loaded with premium talent. At the heart of it all, was Donny Everett, a powerful righthander from Tennessee who was a first-round talent but chose

to instead play for Vanderbilt.

The Commodores were getting ready for regionals the next spring when Everett tragically drowned while he and some teammates were fishing. Everett's memory has been kept alive in the program in the years since. His parents, Teddy and Susan, are often around the team and were on the field at TD Ameritrade Park for the national championship celebration, even joining the team on stage for the trophy presentation.

"Those two mean so much to this program and all the players and the seniors," Paul said. "To this day, every time I look at Teddy, I think of Donny. Just being able to share that moment with them was something that I think—I can speak for the seniors, but probably the whole team—is something that we've all really wanted to do."

Vanderbilt has come full-circle in the last six years. Again, the Commodores are atop the college baseball world, steady and unflinching as champions. And on that night in Omaha when they reclaimed that spot, gold was an appropriate choice as they took their place among college baseball's all-time greats.

COLLEGE WORLD SERIES CHAMPIONS

Year	Champion	Coach	Record	Runner-Up	Most Outstanding Player
1948	Southern California	Sam Barry	40-12	Yale	None selected
1949	Texas*	Bibb Falk	23-7	Wake Forest	Charles Teague, 2B, Wake Forest
1950	Texas	Bibb Falk	27-6	Washington State	Ray VanCleef, OF, Rutgers
1951	Oklahoma*	Jack Baer	19-9	Tennessee	Sid Hatfield, 1B/P, Tennessee
1952	Holy Cross	Jack Barry	21-3	Missouri	Jim O'Neill, P, Holy Cross
1953	Michigan	Ray Fisher	21-9	Texas	J.L. Smith, P, Texas
1954	Missouri	Hi Simmons	22-4	Rollins	Tom Yewcic, C, Michigan State
1955	Wake Forest	Taylor Sanford	29-7	Western Michigan	Tom Borland, P, Oklahoma State
1956	Minnesota	Dick Siebert	33-9	Arizona	Jerry Thomas, P, Minnesota
1957	California*	George Wolfman	35-10	Penn State	Cal Emery, 1B/P, Penn State
1958	Southern California	Rod Dedeaux	35-7	Missouri	Bill Thom, P, Southern California
1959	Oklahoma State	Toby Greene	27-5	Arizona	Jim Dobson, 3B, Oklahoma State
1960	Minnesota	Dick Siebert	34-7	Southern California	John Erickson, 2B, Minnesota
1961	Southern California*	Rod Dedeaux	43-9	Oklahoma State	Littleton Fowler, P, Oklahoma State
1962	Michigan	Don Lund	31-13	Santa Clara	Bob Garibaldi, P, Santa Clara
1963	Southern California	Rod Dedeaux	37-16	Arizona	Bud Hollowell, C, Southern California
1964	Minnesota	Dick Siebert	31-12	Missouri	Joe Ferris, P, Maine
1965	Arizona State	Bobby Winkles	54-8	Ohio State	Sal Bando, 3B, Arizona State
1966	Ohio State	Marty Karow	27-6	Oklahoma State	Steve Arlin, P, Ohio State
1967	Arizona State	Bobby Winkles	53-12	Houston	Ron Davini, C, Arizona State
1968	Southern California*	Rod Dedeaux	45-14	Southern Illinois	Bill Seinsoth, 1B, Southern California
1969	Arizona State	Bobby Winkles	56-11	Tulsa	John Dolinsek, OF, Arizona State
1970	Southern California	Rod Dedeaux	51-13	Florida State	Gene Ammann, P, Florida State
1971	Southern California	Rod Dedeaux	53-13	Southern Illinois	Jerry Tabb, 1B, Tulsa
1972	Southern California	Rod Dedeaux	50-13	Arizona State	Russ McQueen, P, Southern California
1973	Southern California*	Rod Dedeaux	51-11	Arizona State	Dave Winfield, OF/P, Minnesota
1974	Southern California	Rod Dedeaux	50-20	Miami	George Milke, P, Southern California
1975	Texas	Cliff Gustafson	56-6	South Carolina	Mickey Reichenbach, 1B, Texas
1976	Arizona	Jerry Kindall	56-17	Eastern Michigan	Steve Powers, DH/P, Arizona
1977	Arizona State	Jim Brock	57-12	South Carolina	Bob Horner, 3B, Arizona State
1978	Southern California*	Rod Dedeaux	54-9	Arizona State	Rod Boxberger, P, Southern California
1979	Cal State Fullerton	Augie Garrido	60-14	Arkansas	Tony Hudson, P, Cal State Fullerton
1980	Arizona	Jerry Kindall	45-21	Hawaii	Terry Francona, OF, Arizona
1981	Arizona State	Jim Brock	55-13	Oklahoma State	Stan Holmes, OF, Arizona State
1982	Miami	Ron Fraser	57-18	Wichita State	Dan Smith, P, Miami
1983	Texas	Cliff Gustafson	66-14	Alabama	Calvin Schiraldi, P, Texas

Michigan Returns Big Ten To Center Stage

The entire trajectory of Michigan's season changed in the postseason as the Wolverines finally got the breakthrough they had been looking for all season. They were one of the last four teams the selection committee placed in the Field of 64 after an up-and-down regular season.

But once in the postseason, no moment was too big for the Wolverines. Ultimately, they rode a wave of momentum to the College World Series finals.

While Michigan ultimately fell to Vanderbilt in the finals, it was the first time the Wolverines played for the national championship since 1962. It was also their first trip to Omaha in 35 years.

It wasn't quite uncharted territory for the program, which won the national championship in 1953 and 1962, but it has been a long time since the Wolverines or any Big Ten team has made it this far in Omaha. Since Ohio State won the national title in 1966, no Big Ten team has played for the national title.

But Michigan was never overwhelmed by the moment in the postseason, and got to Omaha only after winning the Corvallis Regional and then upsetting top-seeded UCLA on the road in super regionals.

In Omaha, the Wolverines rode the trio of lefthander Tommy Henry and righthanders Jeff Criswell and Karl Kauffman for much of the tournament, using just the three of them to reach the finals. Their lineup featured Big Ten player of the year Jordan Brewer and a strong core of sophomores who were a part of Michigan's historic 2017 recruiting class, the first Big Ten class to rank in the top 10.

It also included first baseman Jimmy Kerr, whose grandfather and father also played for Michigan teams that reached Omaha. The Wolverines drew inspiration from the 1962 team Kerr's grandfather played on and ultimately joined them in Michigan lore.

"Teams that win together, stay together," coach Erik Bakich said. "That team will forever be bookmarked in the Michigan history book and, ultimately, I think that's what this team wants to do as well."

Year	Champion	Coach	Record	Runner-Up	MOST OUTSTANDING PLAYER
1984	Cal State Fullerton	Augie Garrido	66-20	Texas	John Fishel, OF, Cal State Fullerton
1985	Miami*	Ron Fraser	64-16	Texas	Greg Ellena, DH, Miami
1986	Arizona	Jerry Kindall	49-19	Florida State	Mike Senne, OF, Arizona
1987	Stanford	Mark Marquess	53-17	Oklahoma State	Paul Carey, OF, Stanford
1988	Stanford	Mark Marquess	46-23	Arizona State	Lee Plemel, P, Stanford
1989	Wichita State	Gene Stephenson	68-16	Texas	Greg Brummett, P, Wichita State
1990	Georgia	Steve Webber	52-19	Oklahoma State	Mike Rebhan, P, Georgia
1991	Louisiana State*	Skip Bertman	55-18	Wichita State	Gary Hymel, C, Louisiana State
1992	Pepperdine*	Andy Lopez	48-11	Cal State Fullerton	Phil Nevin, 3B, Cal State Fullerton
1993	Louisiana State	Skip Bertman	53-17	Wichita State	Todd Walker, 2B, Louisiana State
1994	Oklahoma*	Larry Cochell	50-17	Georgia Tech	Chip Glass, OF, Oklahoma
1995	Cal State Fullerton*	Augie Garrido	57-9	Southern California	Mark Kotsay, OF/P, Cal State Fullerton
1996	Louisiana State*	Skip Bertman	52-15	Miami	Pat Burrell, 3B, Miami
1997	Louisiana State*	Skip Bertman	57-13	Alabama	Brandon Larson, SS, Louisiana State
1998	Southern California	Mike Gillespie	49-17	Arizona State	Wes Rachels, 2B, Southern California
1999	Miami*	Jim Morris	50-13	Florida State	Marshall McDougall, 2B, Florida State
2000	Louisiana State*	Skip Bertman	52-17	Stanford	Trey Hodges, P, Louisiana State
2001	Miami*	Jim Morris	53-12	Stanford	Charlton Jimerson, OF, Miami
2002	Texas*	Augie Garrido	57-15	South Carolina	Huston Street, P, Texas
2003	Rice	Wayne Graham	58-12	Stanford	John Hudgins, P, Stanford
2004	Cal State Fullerton	George Horton	47-22	Texas	Jason Windsor, P, Cal State Fullerton
2005	Texas*	Augie Garrido	56-16	Florida	David Maroul, 3B, Texas
2006	Oregon State	Pat Casey	50-16	North Carolina	Jonah Nickerson, P, Oregon State
2007	Oregon State*	Pat Casey	49-18	North Carolina	Jorge Reyes, P, Oregon State
2008	Fresno State	Mike Batesole	47-31	Georgia	Tommy Mendonca, 3B, Fresno State
2009	Louisiana State	Paul Mainieri	56-17	Texas	Jared Mitchell, OF, Louisiana State
2010	South Carolina	Ray Tanner	54-16	UCLA	Jackie Bradley Jr., OF, South Carolina
2011	South Carolina*	Ray Tanner	55-14	Florida	Scott Wingo, 2B, South Carolina
2012	Arizona*	Andy Lopez	48-17	South Carolina	Robert Refsnyder, OF, Arizona
2013	UCLA*	John Savage	49-17	Mississippi State	Adam Plutko, P, UCLA
2014	Vanderbilt	Tim Corbin	51-21	Virginia	Dansby Swanson, 2B, Vanderbilt
2015	Virginia	Brian O'Connor	44-24	Vanderbilt	Josh Sborz, P, Virginia
2016	Coastal Carolina	Gary Gilmore	55-18	Arizona	Andrew Beckwith, P, Coastal Carolina
2017	Florida	Kevin O'Sullivan	52-19	Louisiana State	Alex Faedo, P, Florida
2018	Oregon State	Pat Casey	55-12-1	Arkansas	Adley Rutschman, C, Oregon State
2019	Vanderbilt	Tim Corbin	59-12	Michigan	Kumar Rocker, RHP, Vanderbilt

Martin's Legendary Career Comes To A Close

When Florida State's magical postseason run came to an end with a loss to Texas Tech in the College World Series, Mike Martin's storied career also came to a close after 40 years as the Seminoles coach.

He is the winningest coach in college sports and finishes with a record of 2,029-736-4. In all 40 years of his head coaching career, he has led the Seminoles to at least 40 wins and an appearance in the NCAA Tournament. He reached the College World Series 17 times in his career and twice played for a national championship. His consistency is unparalleled, and his wins record is unbreakable. Martin does, however, finish without a national championship, the one thing his trophy case is missing.

Martin was an assistant coach at Florida State 40 years ago when Dick Howser, then the head coach, was hired away by George Steinbrenner to manage the Yankees. Martin, who had been passed over for the job two years earlier in favor of Howser, was promoted and he has been head coach ever since. All he wanted was an opportunity and once Florida State gave it to him, he ran with it. He elevated the program into a national powerhouse and perennial contender.

Earlier in the season, Martin was his 2,000th game as head coach, an unprecedented number in college sports. His career wins record is unlikely to ever be matched and his winning percentage ranks in the top 20 all-time.

Kids grew up dreaming of playing for Martin and this year the Seminoles did that for the last time. In the locker room after the Texas Tech loss, they cried and exchanged hugs, their season over. Third baseman Drew Mendoza, one of the team's captains, said it was an honor to play for Martin.

"To have the success that we've had in the last three years, the ACC championships, two trips to Omaha, 40 wins every year, just to experience that with him and be a part of his legacy, it's been a dream come true," Mendoza said. "Just to be with him day in and day out and just know the kind of person he is and to grow as a man with him at the helm, it's been everything that I could have dreamed of."

Assistant coach Mike Martin Jr., who worked on his father's staff for 22 years, said the clubhouse was more emotional this year.

"This one was a little more because they loved him," Martin Jr., said, before correcting himself. "Shouldn't act like he's dead, they love him. It's hard on everybody."

RPI RANKINGS

The Ratings Percentage Index is an important tool used by the NCAA in selecting at-large teams for the 64-team Division I tournament. These were the top 100 finishers for 2019. A team's rank in the final Baseball America Top 25 is indicated in parentheses, and College World Series teams are bolded.

Rank School	Record	Rank School	Record
1. Vanderbilt (1)	59-12	51. Kentucky	26-29
2. UCLA (6)	52-11	52. Arizona	32-24
3. Mississippi St. (5)	52-15	53. Texas State	36-20
4. Georgia (16)	46-17	54. Wake Forest	31-26
5. Louisville (3)	51-18	55. Texas Christian	34-28
6. East Carolina (12)	47-18	56. Boston College	31-27
7. Oklahoma St. (11)	40-21	57. UC Irvine	37-17
8. Texas Tech (4)	46-20	58. Loyola Marymount	34-25
9. Arkansas (8)	46-20	59. VCU	39-19
10. Stanford (10)	45-14	60. Coastal Carolina	36-26-1
11. Auburn (9)	38-28	61. Louisiana Tech	34-24
12. Georgia Tech (17)	43-19	62. Central Michigan	44-13
13. Tennessee	40-21	63. Saint Mary's	35-22
14. North Carolina (14)	46-19	64. Minnesota	27-27
15. Miami (22)	41-20	65. Virginia Tech	26-27
16. Mississippi (13)	41-27	66. Xavier	27-31
17. Texas A&M (23)	39-23-1	67. Pepperdine	24-25
18. West Virginia (20)	38-22	68. Texas	27-27
19. **Michigan** (2)	50-22	69. Kansas	32-26
20. Creighton (25)	41-13	70. Oregon	27-29
21. Louisiana St. (15)	40-26	71. Georgia Southern	35-24
22. N.C. State	42-19	72. Samford	41-19
23. Indiana State	43-18	73. Maryland	29-29
24. Illinois State	36-26	74. Washington	28-24
25. UCSB (24)	45-11	75. Gonzaga	31-24
26. Dallas Baptist	43-20	76. Sam Houston State	31-25
27. Connecticut	39-25	77. S. California	25-29-1
28. Fresno State (21)	40-16-1	78. Jacksonville	32-27
29. Oregon St. (19)	36-20-1	79. San Diego State	32-25
30. Florida	34-26	80. Old Dominion	35-21
31. Missouri	34-22-1	81. Jacksonville State	39-23
32. Duke (18)	35-27	82. South Carolina	28-28
33. **Florida State** (7)	42-23	83. Wichita State	28-31
34. Baylor	35-19	84. SE Louisiana	33-27
35. Illinois	36-21	85. William & Mary	33-22
36. California	32-20	86. Morehead State	40-21
37. Florida Atlantic	41-21	87. Bryant	40-20
38. Indiana	37-23	88. UNC Greensboro	34-20
39. Arizona State	38-19	89. Wright State	40-17
40. Nebraska	32-24	90. McNeese State	35-26
41. Clemson	35-26	91. Cincinnati	31-31
42. Liberty	43-21	92. Charleston	36-21
43. Southern Miss.	40-21	93. San Diego	32-21
44. Alabama	30-26	94. Texas-Arlington	32-26
45. Houston	32-24	95. Evansville	24-29
46. Oklahoma	33-23	96. Ark.-Little Rock	29-28
47. Brigham Young	36-17	97. Kansas State	25-33
48. Central Florida	36-22	98. Tulane	32-26
49. Virginia	32-24	99. Elon	33-24
50. Campbell	37-21	100. Bradley	25-19

The game has changed around Martin, but he has not. He is esteemed by his peers for his consistency, his approach to coaching, his graciousness, for the model he has set. As the winningest coach in history, he is a true legend of the game, but he doesn't want that to be his legacy.

"I want to be remembered as a guy that did it right, that put education first, that made sure that guys understood what's expected of them, that

COLLEGE ALL-AMERICA TEAM

FIRST TEAM

Pos. Name	Year	AVG	OBP	SLG	AB	R	H	HR	RBI	BB	SO	SB
C Adley Rutschman, Oregon State	Jr.	.411	.575	.751	185	57	76	17	58	76	38	0
1B Andrew Vaughn, California	Jr.	.381	.544	.716	176	49	67	15	50	59	33	2
2B Cameron Cannon, Arizona	Jr.	.397	.478	.651	232	71	92	8	56	35	29	0
3B Kody Hoese, Tulane	Jr.	.391	.486	.779	235	72	92	23	61	39	34	4
SS Will Wilson, North Carolina State	Jr.	.335	.425	.661	221	55	74	16	57	33	46	1
OF Hunter Bishop, Arizona State	Jr.	.342	.479	.748	222	67	76	22	63	50	61	12
OF JJ Bleday, Vanderbilt	Jr.	.350	.464	.717	254	77	89	26	69	54	53	1
OF Matt Wallner, Southern Mississippi	Jr.	.323	.446	.681	226	58	73	23	60	48	50	2
DH Austin Martin, Vanderbilt	So.	.410	.503	.619	244	83	100	8	42	38	31	18
UTL Aaron Schunk, Georgia	Jr.	.339	.373	.604	230	49	78	15	58	14	29	3

	Year	W	L	ERA	G	CG	SV	IP	H	BB	SO	AVG
SP Ryan Garcia, UCLA	Jr.	10	1	1.44	16	1	0	94	52	26	117	.160
SP Alek Manoah, West Virginia	Jr.	9	4	2.08	16	2	0	108.1	71	27	144	.186
SP Ethan Small, Mississippi State	R-Jr.	10	2	1.76	17	0	0	102	58	29	168	.164
SP Noah Song, Navy	Sr.	11	1	1.44	14	6	0	94	55	31	161	.171
RP Kyle Hill, Baylor	Sr.	6	0	0.00	23	0	7	29.1	10	10	35	.109
RP Jacob Wallace, Connecticut	Jr.	3	1	0.64	30	0	16	42	20	10	68	.140
UTL Aaron Schunk, Georgia	Jr.	1	2	2.49	17	0	12	21.2	15	7	18	0.19

SECOND TEAM

Pos. Name	Year	AVG	OBP	SLG	AB	R	H	HR	RBI	BB	SO	SB
C Eric Yang, UC Santa Barbara	Jr.	.368	.479	.545	209	48	77	7	45	30	29	6
1B Spencer Torkelson, Arizona State	So.	.351	.446	.707	242	69	85	23	66	41	45	1
2B Nick Gonzales, New Mexico State	So.	.432	.532	.773	220	80	95	16	80	45	30	7
3B Drew Mendoza, Florida State	Jr.	.319	.484	.620	213	60	68	16	56	69	69	2
SS Josh Jung, Texas Tech	Jr.	.342	.476	.636	225	62	77	14	56	52	39	1
OF Peyton Burdick, Wright State	R-Jr.	.407	.538	.729	214	79	87	15	72	60	35	24
OF Jake Mangum, Mississippi State	Sr.	.355	.411	.462	290	72	103	1	39	22	24	22
OF Jake Sanford, Western Kentucky	Jr.	.398	.483	.805	221	65	88	22	66	33	50	6
DH Kyle McCann, Georgia Tech	Jr.	.299	.468	.674	221	58	66	23	70	62	77	0
UTL J.C. Flowers, Florida State	Jr.	.271	.372	.511	225	45	61	13	53	30	64	11

	Year	W	L	ERA	G	CG	SV	IP	H	BB	SO	AVG
SP Jake Agnos, East Carolina	Jr.	11	3	2.29	17	0	0	102	74	43	145	.198
SP Isaiah Campbell, Arkansas	R-Jr.	12	1	2.26	17	0	0	111.1	82	20	115	.205
SP Emerson Hancock, Georgia	So.	8	3	1.99	14	1	0	90.1	58	18	97	.185
SP TJ Sikkema, Missouri	Jr.	7	4	1.32	17	2	2	88.2	54	31	101	.175
RP Matt Cronin, Arkansas	Jr.	1	0	2.00	23	0	12	27	15	14	40	.163
RP Holden Powell, UCLA	So.	4	3	1.84	40	0	17	49	19	27	65	.121
UTL J.C. Flowers, Florida State	Jr.	0	0	1.40	21	0	12	25.2	17	11	23	.185

THIRD TEAM

Pos. Name	Year	AVG	OBP	SLG	AB	R	H	HR	RBI	BB	SO	SB
C Korey Lee, California	Jr.	.338	.419	.626	198	34	67	15	57	26	42	1
1B Aaron Sabato, North Carolina	Fr.	.342	.454	.676	225	45	77	16	60	39	54	0
2B Justin Foscue, Mississippi State	So.	.338	.402	.582	263	65	89	14	59	29	31	2
3B Davis Wendzel, Baylor	Jr.	.367	.484	.610	177	38	65	8	42	31	37	11
SS Bryson Stott, Nevada-Las Vegas	Jr.	.356	.486	.599	222	65	79	10	36	55	39	16
OF Zach Ashford, Fesno State	Sr.	.381	.488	.526	215	67	82	4	21	40	22	10
OF Jordan Brewer, Michigan	Jr.	.338	.396	.586	222	55	75	12	55	22	48	24
OF Kevin Strohschein, Tennessee Tech	Jr.	.382	.447	.691	233	57	89	15	47	26	45	2
DH Cameron Warren, Texas Tech	Sr.	.354	.448	.664	229	60	81	17	76	37	28	1
UTL Tristin English, Georgia Tech	R-Jr.	.346	.427	.710	214	58	74	18	71	17	30	0

	Year	W	L	ERA	G	CG	SV	IP	H	BB	SO	AVG
SP John Doxakis, Texas A&M	Jr.	7	4	2.06	16	0	0	104.2	80	26	115	.207
SP George Kirby, Elon	Jr.	8	2	2.75	14	3	0	88.1	73	6	107	.221
SP Nick Lodolo, Texas Christian	Jr.	6	6	2.36	16	1	0	103	76	25	131	.203
SP Zack Thompson, Kentucky	Jr.	6	1	2.40	14	2	0	90	59	34	130	.184
RP Brandon Eisert, Oregon State	Jr.	8	2	2.03	14	0	0	62	59	13	74	.255
RP Andrew Magno, Ohio State	Jr.	5	3	2.09	31	0	14	64.2	45	36	75	.205
UTL Tristin English, Georgia Tech	R-Jr.	3	0	3.70	15	0	6	24.1	19	7	20	.221

they're coming to Florida State to get a degree first," he said.

"We're not a school that just wants baseball players. We're a university that demands that you do what you're supposed to do in the classroom, and that's give it your best shot."

Third Assistant Coach Proposal Defeated By Division I Council

After a long, protracted fight, college baseball's bid to pass NCAA legislation to transform the volunteer assistant coach position into a third, full-time, paid assistant coach in April failed in a close vote of the Division I council.

The proposal has long been championed by the American Baseball Coaches Association, which began working on the campaign three years ago. The proposal has held wide support of head coaches, initially polling at more than 85 percent in favor in the fall of 2015, but they were unable to convince the athletic directors that form the Division I council of the need for an extra assistant coach. The legislation, which was sponsored by the SEC, would have also allowed for another assistant coach in softball.

Baseball's revised recruiting calendar, which shortens the number of days coaches are allowed on the road with the creation of additional dead and quiet periods, passed the Division I council.

The proposed third assistant had been ABCA's key legislative push over the last few years, even while it passed the revised recruiting calendar and a proposal last year to allow for two fall exhibition games that don't count to the 56-game maximum. In a sport that has seen significant growth in revenue at the College World Series and increased prominence with the rise of conference networks, it was a tough psychological blow.

The legislative journey of the third assistant proposal was fraught from the start. Initially, the idea was baseball-specific and would have added a coach to the staff, which would have then been a head coach, three full-time, paid assistant coaches and a volunteer. Baseball has one of the worst ratio of paid coaches to players in college sports at 1:12 and improving that was one of the ABCA's chief arguments for an additional paid coach.

But as the proposal advanced, it was changed to, instead of adding a coach to the staff, transforming the volunteer assistant coach position to a full-time position. While that would still improve the full-time coach to player ratio, that argument was devalued with the change. The proposal was also changed to add softball to the mix. That decision came as a result of discussions that led the legislation's backers to believe it needed a gender-equity component to pass. Ultimately, that proved not to be the case.

The Division I Council did pass a rule change allowing any player who is not (and has not previously been) on an athletic scholarship can transfer and be immediately eligible. That came in the

same year as the NCAA created the transfer portal, which allows players an easier way to declare their intent to transfer and subsequently talk to coaches at other schools.

The combination of the two changes led to some confusion and at least the feeling among many coaches that the summer has had a more robust transfer market. It also created some confusion among coaches and players as they got used to the new rules. The long-term impact of the rule changes remains to be seen, but college baseball will have to adjust moving forward.

COLLEGE WORLD SERIES

STANDINGS

Bracket One	W	L
Michigan	3	0
Texas Tech	2	2
Florida State	1	2
Arkansas	0	2

Bracket Two	W	L
Vanderbilt	3	0
Louisville	2	2
Mississippi State	1	2
Auburn	0	2

CWS FINALS (BEST OF THREE)

June 24: Michigan 7, Vanderbilt 4
June 25: Vanderbilt 4, Michigan 1
June 26: Vanderbilt 8, Michigan 2

ALL-TOURNAMENT TEAM

C: Phillip Clarke, Vanderbilt. **1B:** Jimmy Kerr, Michigan. **2B:** Ako Thomas, Michigan. **3B:** Austin Martin, Vanderbilt. **SS:** Jack Blomgren, Michigan. **OF:** JJ Bleday, Vanderbilt; Drew Campbell, Louisville; Jesse Franklin, Michigan. **DH:** Cameron Warren, Texas Tech. **P:** Tommy Henry, Michigan; *Kumar Rocker, Vanderbilt.

Named Most Outstanding Player.

BATTING
(Minimum 8 PA)

Player	AVG	R	H	2B	3B	HR	RBI	SB
Edouard Julien, Auburn	.667	2	4	0	0	1	3	0
Christian Franklin, Ark.	.571	1	4	1	0	0	0	1
Drew Campbell, Lou.	.462	1	6	1	0	0	3	0
Jake Mangum, MSU	.417	3	5	2	0	0	0	0
Easton Murrell, TTU	.400	1	4	0	0	1	2	0
Cameron Warren, TTU	.385	3	5	1	0	1	3	0
Braxton Fullford, TTU	.385	0	5	1	0	0	1	0
Matt Scheffler, Auburn	.375	3	3	1	0	0	0	0
Conor Davis, Auburn	.375	1	3	2	0	1	2	0
Matheu Nelson, FSU	.375	0	3	1	0	0	0	0

PITCHING
(Minimum 6 IP)

Pitcher	W-L	ERA	G	SV	IP	H	BB	SO
Drew Parrish, FSU	1-0	0.00	1	0	8	5	2	9
Isaiah Campbell, Ark.	0-0	0.00	1	0	7	5	2	10
J.T. Ginn, MSU	0-0	0.00	1	0	6	3	1	2
Taylor Floyd, TTU	0-0	0.00	3	2	6	3	4	9
Mason Hickman, Vandy	1-0	0.75	2	0	12	6	5	13
Kumar Rocker, Vandy	2-0	1.46	2	0	12	8	3	17
Reid Detmers, Lou.	1-0	1.50	2	0	6	3	6	5
Tommy Henry, Michigan	2-0	1.56	2	0	17	10	1	18
Jeff Criswell, Michigan	0-0	2.53	4	2	11	8	5	17
Luke Smith, Lou.	0-1	3.24	1	0	8	4	2	10

REGIONALS

MAY 31-JUNE 3
64 teams, 16 four-team, double-elimination tournaments. Winners advance to super regionals.

LOS ANGELES
Host: UCLA (No. 1 national seed).
Participants: No. 1 UCLA (47-8), No. 2 Baylor (34-17), No. 3 Loyola Marymount (32-23), No. 4 Nebraska-Omaha (31-22-1).
Champion: UCLA (4-1).
Runner-up: Loyola Marymount (2-2).
Outstanding player: Chase Strumpf, 2B, UCLA.

NASHVILLE
Host: Vanderbilt (No. 2 national seed).
Participants: No. 1 Vanderbilt (49-10), No. 2 Indiana State (41-16), No. 3 McNeese State (35-24), No. 4 Ohio State (35-25).
Champion: Vanderbilt (3-0).
Runner-up: Indiana State (2-2).
Outstanding player: Julian Infante, 1B, Vanderbilt.

ATLANTA
Host: Georgia Tech (No. 3 national seed).
Participants: No. 1 Georgia Tech (41-17), No. 2 Auburn (33-25), No. 3 Coastal Carolina (35-24-1), No. 4 Florida A&M (27-32).
Champion: Auburn (3-0).
Runner-up: Georgia Tech (2-2).
Outstanding player: Steven Williams, OF, Auburn.

ATHENS, GA.
Host: Georgia (No. 4 national seed).
Participants: No. 1 Georgia (44-15), No. 2 Florida Atlantic (40-19), No. 3 Florida State (36-21), No. 4 Mercer (35-27).
Champion: Florida State (3-0).
Runner-up: Georgia (2-2).
Outstanding player: Mike Salvatore, SS, Florida State.

FAYETTEVILLE, ARK.
Host: Arkansas (No. 5 national seed).
Participants: No. 1 Arkansas (41-17), No. 2 California (32-18), No. 3 Texas Christian (32-26), No. 4 Central Connecticut State (30-21).
Champion: Arkansas (3-0).
Runner-up: Texas Christian (2-2).
Outstanding player: Isaiah Campbell, RHP, Arkansas.

STARKVILLE, MISS.
Host: Mississippi State (No. 6 national seed).
Participants: No. 1 Mississippi State (46-13), No. 2 Miami (39-18), No. 3 Central Michigan (46-12), No. 4 Southern (32-22).
Champion: Mississippi State (3-0).
Runner-up: Miami (2-2).
Outstanding player: Rowdey Jordan, OF, Mississippi State.

LOUISVILLE
Host: Louisville (No. 7 national seed).
Participants: No. 1 Louisville (43-15),

No. 2 Indiana (36-21), No. 3 Illinois State (34-24), No. 4 Illinois-Chicago (29-21).
Champion: Louisville (4-1).
Runner-up: Illinois State (2-2).
Outstanding player: Eric Snider, OF, Louisville.

LUBBOCK, TEXAS
Host: Texas Tech (No. 8 national seed).
Participants: No. 1 Texas Tech (39-17), No. 2 Dallas Baptist (41-18), No. 3 Florida (33-24), No. 4 Army (35-24).
Champion: Texas Tech (3-0).
Runner-up: Dallas Baptist (2-2).
Outstanding player: Cameron Warren, 1B, Texas Tech.

OKLAHOMA CITY
Host: Oklahoma State (No. 9 national seed).
Participants: No. 1 Oklahoma State (36-18), No. 2 Connecticut (36-23), No. 3 Nebraska (31-22), No. 4 Harvard (27-14).
Champion: Oklahoma State (3-1).
Runner-up: Connecticut (2-2).
Outstanding player: Trevor Boone, OF, Oklahoma State.

GREENVILLE, N.C.
Host: East Carolina (No. 10 national seed).
Participants: No. 1 East Carolina (43-15), No. 2 North Carolina State (42-17), No. 3 Campbell (35-19), No. 4 Quinnipiac (29-17).
Champion: East Carolina (4-1).
Runner-up: Campbell (2-2).
Outstanding player: Jake Washer, C, East Carolina.

STANFORD, CALIF.
Host: Stanford (No. 11 national seed).
Participants: No. 1 Stanford (41-11), No. 2 UC Santa Barbara (45-9), No. 3 Fresno State (38-14-1), No. 4 Sacramento State (39-23).
Champion: Stanford (4-1).
Runner-up: Fresno State (2-2).
Outstanding player: Maverick Handley, C, Stanford.

OXFORD, MISS.
Host: Mississippi (No. 12 national seed).
Participants: No. 1 Mississippi (37-25), No. 2 Illinois (36-19), No. 3 Clemson (34-24), No. 4 Jacksonville State (37-21).
Champion: Mississippi (3-0).
Runner-up: Jacksonville State (2-2).
Outstanding player: N/A.

BATON ROUGE, LA.
Host: Louisiana State (No. 13 national seed).
Participants: No. 1 Louisiana State (37-24), No. 2 Arizona State (37-17), No. 3 Southern Mississippi (38-19), No. 4 Stony Brook (31-21).
Champion: Louisiana State (3-0).
Runner-up: Southern Mississippi (2-2).
Outstanding player: Saul Garza, C, LSU; Gabe Montenegro, OF, Southern Miss..

CHAPEL HILL, N.C.
Host: North Carolina (No. 14 national

seed).
Participants: No. 1 North Carolina (42-17), No. 2 Tennessee (38-19), No. 3 Liberty (42-19), No. 4 UNC Wilmington (32-29).
Champion: North Carolina (3-0).
Runner-up: Tennessee (2-2).
Outstanding player: N/A.

MORGANTOWN, W.V.
Host: West Virginia (No. 15 national seed).
Participants: No. 1 West Virginia (37-20), No. 2 Texas A&M (37-27-1), No. 3 Duke (31-25), No. 4 Fordham (38-22).
Champion: Duke (3-0).
Runner-up: Texas A&M (2-2).
Outstanding player: Bryce Jarvis, RHP, Duke.

CORVALLIS, ORE.
Host: Oregon State (No. 16 national seed).
Participants: No. 1 Oregon State (36-18-1), No. 2 Creighton (38-11), No. 3 Michigan (41-18), No. 4 Cincinnati (30-29).
Champion: Michigan (3-1).
Runner-up: Creighton (3-2).
Outstanding player: Jimmy Kerr, 1B, Michigan.

SUPER REGIONALS

JUNE 7-10
16 teams, best-of-three series. Winners advance to College World Series.

MICHIGAN AT UCLA
Site: Los Angeles
Michigan wins 2-1, advances to CWS.

DUKE AT VANDERBILT
Site: Nashville
Vanderbilt wins 2-1, advances to CWS.

AUBURN AT NORTH CAROLINA
Site: Chapel Hill, N.C.
Auburn wins 2-1, advances to CWS.

FLORIDA STATE AT LOUISIANA STATE
Site: Baton Rouge, La..
Florida State wins 2-0, advances to CWS.

MISSISSIPPI AT ARKANSAS
Site: Fayetteville, Ark.
Arkansas wins 2-1, advances to CWS.

STANFORD AT MISSISSIPPI STATE
Site: Starkville, Miss.
Mississippi State wins 2-0, advances to CWS.

EAST CAROLINA AT LOUISVILLE
Site: Louisville.
Louisville wins 2-0, advances to CWS.

OKLAHOMA STATE AT TEXAS TECH
Site: Lubbock, Texas.
Texas Tech wins 2-1, advances to CWS.

Rutschman Rises To Top

PLAYER OF THE YEAR

BY TEDDY CAHILL

After a sensational performance last year in the College World Series that saw him earn Most Outstanding Player honors and led Oregon State to the national title, catcher Adley Rutschman came into this season with all of baseball watching.

Those in the college game wanted to see how he would respond to taking over as the Beavers' unquestioned leader after the veterans from their 2018 national championship team had moved on to the minor leagues. Those in pro ball were closely watching him as a potential first overall pick in the draft.

The pressure didn't bother him. Rutschman never wavered and he went wire-to-wire as both college baseball's best player and the draft's best prospect. The Orioles made him the first overall pick in the draft. Now, Rutschman wins Baseball America's College Player of the Year award for his sensational all-around season.

Rutschman hit .411/.575/.751 with 17 home runs, 76 walks and 38 strikeouts. He led the nation in on-base percentage and walks, ranks fifth in batting average and sixth in slugging percentage. He averaged 1.33 walks per game, the most since Florida's Brad Wilkerson did so in 1998, the height of Gorilla Ball. Those impressive offensive numbers came while he was playing excellent defense behind the plate for the Beavers and was named the Pac-12's co-defensive player of the year.

Rutschman also left his mark on the Oregon State record book. He set the program's career walks record (156), ranks second in RBIs (174), third in runs (151) and is in the top 10 of nearly every major offensive category. He became the first Beaver to be drafted first overall, surpassing the likes of Michael Conforto and Nick Madrigal as the highest drafted player in program history.

Adley Rutschman

KARL MAASDAM

Rutschman said it was the kind of career he envisioned having when he committed to Oregon State.

"It's something you dream of and hope happens when you come to Oregon State," Rutschman said. "I remember watching Conforto and you want to be that guy who has a huge impact. Having that opportunity is a true blessing."

Rutschman is the fourth catcher to win Baseball America's Player of the Year award, joining Florida's Mike Zunino (2012), Florida State's Buster Posey (2008) and Georgia Tech's Jason Varitek (1994). He is the first Oregon State player to win the award and the first Pac-12 player to do so since UCLA righthander Trevor Bauer in 2011.

Rutschman made his mark on college baseball, winning everything there is to win. His ability as a player was unparalleled in the country this spring, but his legacy as a winner and a leader will stand the test of time.

PREVIOUS WINNERS

1982: Jeff Ledbetter, OF/LHP Florida St.
1983: Dave Magadan, 1B, Alabama
1984: Oddibe McDowell, OF, Arizona St.
1985: Pete Incaviglia, OF, Oklahoma State
1986: Casey Close, OF, Michigan
1987: Robin Ventura, 3B, Oklahoma State
1988: John Olerund, 1B/LHP, Washington St.
1989: Ben McDonald, RHP, Louisiana State
1990: Mike Kelly, OF, Arizona State
1991: David McCarthy, 1B, Stanford
1992: Phil Nevin, 3B, Cal State Fullerton
1993: Brooks Kieschnick, DH/RHP, Texas
1994: Jason Varitek, C, Georgia Tech

1995: Todd Helton, 1B/LHP, Tennessee
1996: Kris Benson, RHP, Clemson
1997: J.D. Drew, OF, Florida State
1998: Jeff Austin, RHP, Stanford
1999: Jason Jennings, RHP, Baylor
2000: Mark Teixeira, 3B, Georgia Tech
2001: Mark Prior, RHP, S. California
2002: Khalil Greene, SS, Clemson
2003: Rickie Weeks, 2B, Southern
2004: Jered Weaver, RHP, Long Beach St.
2005: Alex Gordon, 3B, Nebraska
2006: Andrew Miller, LHP, North Carolina
2007: David Price, LHP, Vanderbilt

2008: Buster Posey, C/RHP, Florida State
2009: Stephen Strasburg, RHP, San Diego St.
2010: Anthony Rendon, 3B, Rice
2011: Trevor Bauer, RHP, UCLA
2012: Mike Zunino, C, Florida
2013: Kris Bryant, 3B, San Diego
2014: A.J. Reed, 1B/LHP, Kentucky
2015: Andrew Benintendi, OF, Arkansas
2016: Klye Lewis, OF, Mercer
2017: Brendan McKay, LHP/1B, Louisville
2018: Brady Singer, RHP, Florida

Martin Finishes Historic Career In Style

COACH OF THE YEAR

BY TEDDY CAHILL

For his strong coaching job this season and in recognition of an unparalleled career, Mike Martin is the 2019 Coach of the Year.

As Martin now heads into retirement after 40 seasons at Florida State—his alma mater—the sport is unlikely to ever see another coach like him. His consistency is without equal, as is his winning. No college coach in any sport had ever won more than 2,000 games, a milestone he passed early in the season. He finished his career with a record of 2,029-736-4, a record that will never be broken. He has taken 17 teams to the College World Series and never missed an NCAA Tournament.

DON JUAN MOORE

Mike Martin

Florida State's regionals streak was in some doubt at times this season because the Seminoles often played with three freshmen in their lineup and leaned heavily on underclassmen throughout the team. Florida State's RPI in April approached 100, well outside the range required for an at-large berth in the NCAA Tournament. But Martin and the Seminoles righted the ship in the second half and then embarked on an impressive postseason run. They swept through the Athens

Regional, defeating No. 4 overall seed Georgia twice along the way, and then swept LSU, the No. 13 overall seed, in Baton Rouge to make it back to Omaha.

At the College World Series, Florida State began with a 1-0 victory against Arkansas, the No. 5 national seed, before losses to Michigan and Texas Tech ended its season.

Martin previously won Coach of the Year in 2012 and is the sixth man to win the Coach of the Year award twice, joining Skip Bertman, Augie Garrido, Dave Snow, Gene Stephenson and Ray Tanner.

Martin is quick to spread credit for the Seminoles' success throughout the program. He believes the key to their long-term consistency goes well beyond the field. He credits his assistant coaches over the years, as well as the support from the university and fans. It all goes to create an atmosphere that has kept propelling FSU to success year after year.

"It truly is a family atmosphere," he said. "If that sounds a little corny, it's nothing more than the truth."

Whatever the secret was, it worked. This year, the season never spun out of control even while the Seminoles went through a midseason slump as their young players adjusted to the rigors of ACC play. They figured it out at just the right time and played their best baseball in June, the most important time of the college baseball season. It was enough to carry Florida State to the College World Series for the 17th time under Martin.

PREVIOUS WINNERS

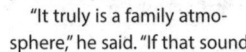

1982: Gene Stephenson, Wichita State	**1995:** Pat Murphy, Arizona State	**2008:** Mike Fox, North Carolina
1983: Barry Shollenberger, Alabama	**1996:** Skip Bertman, Louisiana State	**2009:** Paul Mainieri, Louisiana State
1984: Augie Garrido, Cal State Fullerton	**1997:** Jim Wells, Alabama	**2010:** Ray Tanner, South Carolina
1985: Ron Polk, Mississippi State	**1998:** Pat Murphy, Arizona State	**2011:** Kevin O'Sullivan, Florida
1986: Skip Bertman, LSU/Dave Snow, LMU	**1999:** Wayne Graham, Rice	**2012:** Mike Martin, Florida State
1987: Mark Marquess, Stanford	**2000:** Ray Tanner, South Carolina	**2013:** John Savage, UCLA
1988: Jim Brock, Arizona State	**2001:** Dave Van Horn, Nebraska	**2014:** Tim Corbin, Vanderbilt
1989: Dave Snow, Long Beach State	**2002:** Augie Garrido, Texas	**2015:** Brian O'Connor, Virginia
1990: Steve Webber, Georgia	**2003:** George Horton, Cal State Fullerton	**2016:** Jim Schlossnagle, Texas Christian
1991: Jim Hendry, Creighton	**2004:** David Perno, Georgia	**2017:** Dan McDonnell, Louisville
1992: Andy Lopez, Pepperdine	**2005:** Rick Jones, Tulane	**2018:** David Pierce, Texas
1993: Gene Stephenson, Wichita State	**2006:** Pat Casey, Oregon State	
1994: Jim Morris, Miami	**2007:** Dave Serrano, UC Irvine	

Rocker Lives Up To Hype

FRESHMAN OF THE YEAR

BY TEDDY CAHILL

Kumar Rocker last fall came to Vanderbilt to much fanfare. He had ranked No. 13 on the 2018 BA 500 and was the highest-ranked player ever to make it to campus.

Ultimately, Rocker exceeded even those lofty expectations. He opened the season in the weekend rotation and stayed there nearly the whole year, a rarity among Vanderbilt's elite pitchers. And while the start of his season was a bit rocky, it ended on the highest of highs, with him helping Vanderbilt to the national championship and being named College World Series Most Outstanding Player.

Rocker went 12-5, 3.25 with 114 strikeouts and 21 walks in 99.2 innings this season. In the NCAA Tournament alone, he was 4-0, 0.96

Kumar Rocker

JOE HOWELL

with 44 strikeouts and five walks in 28 innings. When the Commodores needed him the most, he stepped up. Facing elimination against Duke in the Nashville Super Regional, Rocker delivered the best performance, not only of his season, but of any pitcher in college baseball in 2019. He threw the first no-hitter ever in super regionals and struck out 19 batters. He did it again in the CWS finals, striking out 11 batters in 6.1 innings against Michigan.

As a result of his outstanding season, Rocker is the 2019 Freshman of the Year.

The award is especially fitting because beyond having a great season, Rocker enjoyed being a freshman—a year most are happy to leave behind.

"I like being a freshman one more time," he said. "Being a high school freshman was fun and being a college freshman is a whole different experience. No one says that a lot, but it's fun."

PREVIOUS WINNERS

1990: Jeffrey Hammonds, OF, Stanford
1991: Brooks Kieschnick, RHP/DH, Texas
1992: Todd Walker, 2B, Louisiana State
1993: Brett Laxton, RHP, Louisiana State
1994: R.A. Dickey, RHP, Tennessee
1995: Kyle Peterson, RHP, Stanford
1996: Pat Burrell, 3B, Miami
1997: Brian Roberts, SS, North Carolina
1998: Xavier Nady, 2B, California
1999: James Jurries, 2B, Tulane
2000: Kevin Howard, 3B, Miami
2001: Michael Aubrey, OF/LHP, Texas
2002: Stephen Drew, SS, Florida State
2003: Ryan Braun, SS, Miami
2004: Wade LeBlanc, LHP, Alabama
2005: Joe Savery, LHP, Rice
2006: Pedro Alvarez, 3B, Vanderbilt
2007: Dustin Ackley, 1B, North Carolina
2008: Chris Hernandez, LHP, Miami
2009: Anthony Rendon, 3B, Rice
2010: Matt Purke, LHP, Texas Christian
2011: Colin Moran, 3B, North Carolina
2012: Carlos Rodon, LHP, N.C. State
2013: Alex Bregman, SS, Louisiana State
2014: Zack Collins, C, Miami
2015: Brendan McKay, LHP/1B, Louisville
2016: Seth Beer, OF, Clemson
2017: Matt Wallner, OF/RHP, Southern Miss
2018: Kevin Abel, RHP, Oregon State
Full list of winners can be found at BaseballAmerica.com/Stories/Baseball-America-Awards

FRESHMAN ALL-AMERICA TEAMS

FIRST TEAM

Pos.		AVG	OBP	SLG	AB	R	H	HR	RBI	SB
C	Austin Wells, Arizona	.353	.462	.552	221	73	78	5	60	6
1B	Aaron Sabato, North Carolina	.343	.453	.696	230	47	79	18	63	0
2B	Cody Morissette, Boston Col.	.320	.371	.476	231	27	74	4	41	8
3B	Alex Binelas, Louisville	.301	.390	.638	196	52	59	14	59	3
SS	Josh Hood, Pennsylvania	.331	.411	.580	181	42	60	8	42	1
OF	Hunter Goodman, Memphis	.326	.367	.573	239	51	78	13	67	11
OF	Tyler McDonough, N.C. State	.320	.392	.452	250	38	80	5	47	10
OF	Ethan Wilson, South Alabama	.345	.453	.686	220	59	76	17	51	6
DH	Adrian Del Castillo, Miami	.331	.418	.576	236	58	78	12	72	3
UT	Davis Sharpe, Clemson	.264	.377	.364	129	22	34	3	18	3

Pos.		W	L	ERA	G	SV	IP	H	BB	SO	BAA
SP	JT Ginn, Mississippi State	8	4	3.36	16	0	80	69	18	103	.223
SP	Doug Nikhazy, Mississippi	9	3	3.31	20	1	90	78	33	86	.237
SP	Kumar Rocker, Vanderbilt	12	5	3.25	19	0	100	88	21	114	.233
SP	Tyler Thornton, Saint Mary's	10	2	2.71	15	0	76	47	27	94	.175
RP	Will Dion, McNeese State	5	0	1.98	29	6	50	26	14	62	.155
RP	Michael McGreevy, UCSB	5	1	1.94	29	6	60	52	13	53	.234
UT	Davis Sharpe, Clemson	7	4	3.20	15	0	84	61	33	84	.205

SECOND TEAM

C: Taylor Smith, Incarnate Word. **1B:** Sonny DiChiara, Samford. **2B:** Tyler Black, Wright State. **3B:** John Dempsey, Wofford. **SS:** Ethan Murray, Duke. **OF:** Colton Cowser, Sam Houston State; Andy Garriolla, Old Dominion; Hudson Haskin, Tulane. **DH:** Dayton Dooney, Arizona. **UT:** Isaac Coffey, Oral Roberts. **SP:** Rodney Boone, UC Santa Barbara; Seth Lonsway, Ohio State; Chris Weber, Texas A&M; Alex Wiliams, Stanford. **RP:** Clayton Beeter, Texas Tech; Danny Garcia, Stetson.

HITTING (MINIMUM 140 AT-BATS)

BATTING AVERAGE

Rk.	Player, Team	Class	AVG	OBP	SLG	G	AB	2B	3B	HR	RBI	BB	SO	SB
1.	Nick Gonzales, New Mexico St.	So.	.432	.532	.773	55	220	19	4	16	80	45	30	7
2.	Dominic D'Alessandro, George Washington	Sr.	.423	.506	.668	53	208	12	0	13	56	33	40	2
3.	Joey Ortiz, New Mexico St.	Jr.	.422	.474	.697	55	251	25	10	8	84	21	26	12
4.	Mitchell Berryhill, Cal St. Fullerton	Sr.	.415	.493	.487	53	195	8	3	0	27	23	29	17
5.	Adley Rutschman, Oregon St.	Jr.	.411	.575	.751	57	185	10	1	17	58	76	38	0
6.	Luis Trevino, Abilene Christian	R-Sr.	.408	.504	.743	52	191	13	3	15	63	39	15	1
7.	Peyton Burdick, Wright St.	R-Jr.	.407	.538	.729	59	214	18	3	15	72	60	35	24
8.	Ben Carew, Kent St.	R-So.	.406	.474	.525	54	219	13	2	3	31	25	31	24
9.	Daniel Lingua, Prairie View		.406	.506	.540	52	202	11	5	2	49	39	27	37
10.	Matt O'Neill, Penn	Sr.	.405	.527	.620	40	158	15	2	5	40	40	36	2
11.	Javeyan Williams, Southern	Sr.	.404	.478	.612	55	188	13	7	4	44	25	36	26
12.	Patrick Causa, Mount St. Mary's	Sr.	.402	.521	.710	47	169	12	2	12	39	39	22	9
13.	Tristan Peterson, New Mexico St.	Jr.	.400	.510	.769	53	195	10	1	20	90	38	47	0
14.	Jake Sanford, Western Kentucky	Jr.	.398	.483	.805	56	221	20	2	22	66	33	50	6
15.	Cameron Cannon, Arizona	Jr.	.397	.478	.651	56	232	29	3	8	56	35	29	0
16.	Justin Banks, Coppin St.	Jr.	.394	.493	.588	45	165	17	0	5	43	30	32	0
17.	Matthew Dyer, Arizona	Jr.	.393	.480	.571	42	168	10	4	4	28	22	28	5
18.	Austin Martin, Vanderbilt	So.	.392	.486	.604	65	268	19	4	10	46	40	34	18
19.	Kody Hoese, Tulane	Jr.	.391	.486	.779	58	235	20	1	23	61	39	34	4
20.	Patrick McColl, Harvard	Sr.	.387	.448	.707	43	181	16	3	12	47	17	33	5
21.	Jake Holton, Creighton	Jr.	.386	.488	.681	54	207	15	2	14	58	32	40	1
22.	Mike Antico, St. John's	Jr.	.386	.500	.598	51	184	13	4	6	29	38	46	20
23.	Tyler Wilber, Southeast Missouri St.	So.	.383	.480	.531	55	209	19	3	2	40	37	24	1
24.	Rudy Rott, Ohio	Sr.	.382	.464	.618	54	212	18	1	10	47	28	29	6
25.	Kevin Stohschein, Tennessee Tech	Sr.	.382	.447	.691	54	233	23	2	15	47	26	45	2
26.	Kellen Strahm, San Jose St.	R-Sr.	.382	.487	.546	43	152	5	1	6	28	27	21	14
27.	Ryan Ward, Bryant	R-So.	.382	.450	.614	58	249	15	2	13	51	30	17	12
28.	Christian Pena, Eastern Illinois	Jr.	.381	.457	.490	51	194	7	1	4	42	30	17	1
29.	Zach Ashford, Fresno St.	Sr.	.381	.488	.526	56	215	11	4	4	21	40	22	10
30.	Jaylyn Williams, Jackson St.	Jr.	.381	.487	.540	52	189	15	0	5	55	30	14	10
31.	Alsander Womack, Norfolk St.	So.	.377	.441	.503	42	167	10	1	3	31	19	16	10
32.	Bobby Seymour, Wake Forest	So.	.377	.439	.576	57	236	20	0	9	92	26	44	3
33.	Tyler LaPorte, Southern	Sr.	.377	.421	.560	56	252	18	5	6	65	16	24	21
34.	Enrique Sanchez Jr., Texas A&M-Corpus Christi	Sr.	.377	.442	.485	57	231	16	3	1	45	24	16	8
35.	Harrison Freed, Butler	Jr.	.376	.448	.683	52	218	10	3	17	73	23	36	8
36.	Shane Marshall, Binghamton	So.	.376	.423	.584	42	173	12	3	6	35	12	27	8
37.	Tyler Bordner, Milwaukee	Sr.	.376	.439	.598	48	189	15	3	7	52	20	32	3
38.	Jacob Hurtubise, Army West Point	Jr.	.375	.541	.445	61	200	6	4	0	26	69	26	45
39.	Andrew Vaughn, California	Jr.	.374	.539	.704	52	179	14	0	15	50	60	33	2
40.	Mason Mallard, Louisiana Tech	R-Sr.	.374	.470	.545	58	222	15	1	7	34	33	28	20
41.	Blake Dunn, Western Michigan	So.	.374	.467	.521	49	190	9	2	5	29	23	38	30
42.	Ryan Stacy, UTSA	Sr.	.374	.440	.589	48	190	14	3	7	33	12	39	5
43.	Jordan Cannon, Sam Houston St.	So.	.372	.455	.521	53	188	12	2	4	37	18	27	14
44.	Jake Suddleson, Harvard	Jr.	.372	.423	.651	43	172	11	2	11	53	8	36	3
45.	Hudson Haskin, Tulane	Fr.	.372	.459	.647	56	207	19	4	10	52	26	29	4
46.	Nate Fassnacht, George Washington	Jr.	.372	.453	.655	54	226	23	4	11	60	30	23	12
47.	Tristen Carranza, New Mexico St.	Sr.	.371	.500	.719	55	210	7	6	18	73	40	39	3
48.	Alec Burleson, East Carolina	So.	.370	.399	.573	64	246	23	0	9	61	14	24	3
49.	Zavier Warren, Central Michigan	So.	.369	.502	.578	61	244	23	2	8	70	59	56	14
50.	J.J. Shimko, USC Upstate	R-Sr.	.369	.461	.481	45	160	15	0	1	27	25	19	5
51.	Eric Yang, UC Santa Barbara	Jr.	.368	.479	.545	56	209	16	0	7	45	30	30	6
52.	Logan Bottrell, New Mexico St.	Sr.	.367	.482	.446	49	177	10	2	0	28	29	16	17
53.	Davis Wendzel, Baylor	Jr.	.367	.484	.612	46	179	19	0	8	42	31	37	11
54.	Oliver Dunn, Utah	Jr.	.366	.450	.567	49	194	22	4	3	28	30	44	9
55.	Ripken Reyes, San Diego	Sr.	.366	.462	.500	53	194	11	3	3	33	10	28	3
56.	Liam Hibbits, Virginia Commonwealth	So.	.366	.450	.546	57	205	17	1	6	60	21	27	4
57.	Tyler Kapuscinski, Marist	R-Jr.	.366	.469	.531	40	145	10	1	4	29	24	17	1
58.	Jared Mang, New Mexico	Sr.	.365	.441	.587	52	208	23	4	5	51	27	29	15
59.	Cameron Eden, California	Jr.	.365	.435	.555	50	200	8	3	8	36	22	45	20
60.	Myles Nicholson, Mount St. Mary's	So.	.365	.444	.514	44	181	10	4	3	23	15	24	37
61.	Dean Miller, UC Riverside	Sr.	.365	.401	.650	52	203	16	0	14	49	12	55	2
62.	Tanner Murray, UC Davis	So.	.364	.416	.503	49	195	16	4	1	31	14	15	12
63.	Jack Gethings, Fairfield	Sr.	.364	.436	.492	60	242	14	7	1	36	31	38	8
64.	Adam Frank, Fairleigh Dickinson	R-So.	.363	.419	.508	46	179	15	1	3	27	14	31	8
65.	Sean Phelan, Penn	Sr.	.363	.458	.564	41	179	18	0	6	37	21	15	0
66.	Griffin Dey, Yale	Sr.	.362	.482	.651	41	152	5	3	11	44	35	38	6

#	Player, Team	Class	AVG	OBP	SLG	G	AB							
67.	Spencer Henson, Oral Roberts	Jr.	.362	.509	.768	50	177	11	2	19	51	51	52	2
68.	Colton Cowser, Sam Houston State	Fr.	.361	.450	.602	56	216	17	7	7	54	26	29	9
69.	Matthew Koehler, Western Carolina	R-Sr.	.361	.445	.649	51	205	10	5	13	45	23	40	17
70.	Jeff Taylor, South Carolina-Upstate	So.	.360	.433	.547	42	150	13	3	3	29	19	36	3
71.	Patrick Frick, Wake Forest	Jr.	.360	.457	.481	55	214	14	0	4	38	38	24	7
72.	Peyton Sorrels, La Salle	Sr.	.359	.429	.502	53	217	11	4	4	28	27	46	25
73.	Lawson Hill, Wofford	So.	.359	.420	.411	61	231	8	2	0	46	26	20	9
74.	Equon Smith, Jackson St.	Jr.	.359	.409	.421	54	209	8	1	1	36	16	15	39
75.	Drew Devine, Western Michigan	Jr.	.359	.400	.484	49	184	15	1	2	31	9	41	4
76.	Connor Mang, New Mexico	R-Jr.	.359	.439	.530	51	198	16	3	4	47	26	43	11
77.	Bryant Packard, East Carolina	Jr.	.358	.444	.550	58	218	19	1	7	40	29	44	5
78.	Jake Mangum, Mississippi St.	Sr.	.358	.417	.467	67	302	24	3	1	39	22	24	22
79.	Ian Fair, Northeastern	R-So.	.357	.419	.520	49	196	6	1	8	33	21	31	8
80.	Eddy Gonzalez, Incarnate Word	Sr.	.357	.431	.495	53	196	13	4	2	28	20	13	9
81.	Elvis Peralta Jr., Marshall	R-Jr.	.357	.425	.571	57	224	15	3	9	42	21	50	12
82.	Alerick Soularie, Tennessee	So.	.357	.466	.602	60	196	13	1	11	46	37	39	8
83.	Scott Ota, UIC	Sr.	.357	.458	.749	52	199	14	2	20	64	33	23	5
84.	Itchy Burts, Texas A&M-Corpus Christi	Jr.	.356	.412	.494	57	233	15	4	3	33	20	33	10
85.	McCarthy Tatum, Fresno St.	R-Sr.	.356	.397	.606	57	236	16	2	13	77	14	32	5
86.	Rigsby Mosley, Troy	R-Jr.	.356	.430	.554	55	222	19	2	7	34	29	27	8
87.	Bryson Stott, UNLV	Jr.	.356	.486	.599	58	222	20	2	10	36	55	39	16
88.	Alex Baratta, Binghamton	R-Jr.	.356	.426	.479	44	163	9	1	3	33	17	24	4
89.	Justice Bigbie, Western Carolina	So.	.355	.446	.578	53	211	11	0	12	51	29	43	2
90.	Cameron Warren, Texas Tech	Sr.	.355	.451	.665	66	242	17	2	18	79	40	30	1
91.	Jake Wright, Coastal Carolina	R-So.	.355	.516	.601	61	183	8	2	11	49	45	37	1
92.	Michael Guldberg, Georgia Tech	So.	.355	.441	.418	60	220	7	2	1	32	31	32	7
93.	Connor Aube, Texas-Arlington	Jr.	.354	.402	.529	49	206	18	3	4	29	13	26	16
94.	Gaby Cruz, Bryant	Jr.	.354	.449	.592	48	147	6	1	9	37	20	38	0
95.	Nico Popa, Pittsburgh	Jr.	.353	.424	.581	55	215	15	5	8	39	16	42	14
96.	Tyler Black, Wright St.	Fr.	.353	.469	.600	52	170	11	5	7	41	38	18	8
97.	Nick Howie, Eastern Kentucky	Jr.	.353	.474	.557	59	221	12	0	11	45	46	51	16
98.	Austin Wells, Arizona	Fr.	.353	.462	.552	56	221	15	7	5	60	46	43	6
99.	Trent Tingelstad, Louisiana-Monroe	Jr.	.353	.471	.585	56	207	19	4	7	46	43	32	5
100.	Raul Hernandez, Jackson St.	Sr.	.352	.429	.554	54	213	14	1	9	56	25	38	4

ON-BASE PERCENTAGE

Rank Player, Pos., Team	OBP
1. Adley Rutschman, C, Oregon State	.575
2. Jacob Hurtubise, OF, Army	.541
3. Andrew Vaughn, 1B, California	.539
4. Peyton Burdick, OF, Wright St.	.538
5. Nick Gonzales, 2B, New Mexico St.	.532
6. Matt O'Neill, C, Pennsylvania	.527
7. Patrick Causa, SS, Mount St. Mary's	.521
8. Jake Wright, OF, Coastal Carolina	.516
9. Tristan Peterson, INF, New Mexico St.	.510
10. Spencer Henson, UT, Oral Roberts	.509

SLUGGING PERCENTAGE

Rank Player, Pos., Team	SLG
1. Jake Sanford, OF, Western Kentucky	.805
2. Kody Hoese, 3B, Tulane	.779
3. Nick Gonzales, 2B, New Mexico St.	.773
4. Tristan Peterson, INF, New Mexico St.	.769
5. Spencer Henson, UT, Oral Roberts	.768
6. Adley Rutschman, C, Oregon St.	.751
7. Scott Ota, OF, Illinois-Chicago	.749
8. Hunter Bishop, OF, Arizona St.	.748
9. Luis Trevino, C, Abilene Christian	.743
10. Parker Phillips, 1B, Austin Peay	.732

RUNS BATTED IN

Rank Player, Pos., Team	RBI
1. Bobby Seymour, 1B, Wake Forest	92
2. Tristan Peterson, INF, New Mexico St.	90
3. Joey Ortiz, SS, New Mexico St.	84
4. Zach Biermann, 1B, Coastal Carolina	82
5. Nick Gonzales, 2B, New Mexico St.	80
6. Cameron Warren, OF, Texas Tech	79
7. Nick Quintana, 3B, Arizona	77
8. McCarthy Tatum, 3B, Fresno St.	77
9. Griffin Lockwood-Powell, C, Central Michiwgan	74
10. Tristen Carranza, OF, New Mexico St.	73
11. Harrison Freed, OF, Butler	73
12. Ethan Paul, SS, Vanderbilt	73

HOME RUNS

Rank Player, Pos., Team	HR
1. JJ Bleday, OF, Vanderbilt	27
2. Parker Phillips, 1B, Austin Peay	25
3. Jason Hinchman, INF, Tenn. Tech	24
4. Alejandro Toral, 1B, Miami	24
5. Kody Hoese, 3B, Tulane	23
6. Kel Johnson, OF, Mercer	23
7. Kyle McCann, C, Georgia Tech	23
8. Spencer Torkelson, 1B, Arizona St.	23
9. Matt Wallner, OF, Southern Miss.	23
10. Hunter Bishop, OF, Arizona St.	22
11. Jake Sanford, OF, Western Kentucky	22

DOUBLES

Rank Player, Pos., Team	2B
1. Cameron Cannon, SS, Arizona	29
2. Jake Garella, INF, Saint Louis	27
3. Troy Johnston, OF, Gonzaga	27
4. Trevor Ezell, 1B, Arkansas	25
5. Anthony Giachin, INF, Army	25
6. Darius Hill, OF, West Virginia	25
7. Joey Ortiz, SS, New Mexico St.	25
8. Aaron Sabato, 1B, North Carolina	25
9. Dominic Fletcher, OF, Arkansas	24
10. Jake Mangum, OF, Mississippi St.	24

TRIPLES

Rank Player, Pos., Team	3B
1. Garrett Mitchell, OF, UCLA	12
2. Joey Ortiz, SS, New Mexico St.	10
3. Chris Prentiss, INF, Jackson St.	10
4. Greg Jones, SS, UNC Wilmington	9
5. Jacob Crum, OF, Central Michigan	8
6. Erik Rodriguez, OF, Marshall	8
7. Armani Smith, UT, UC Santa Barbara	8
8. Eight players tied	

STOLEN BASES

Rank Player, Pos., Team	SB
1. JD Orr, OF, Wright St.	60
2. Jess Davis, OF, UAB	48
3. Jacob Hurtubise, OF, Army	45
4. Jake MacKenzie, INF, Fordham	43
5. Greg Jones, SS, UNC Wilmington	42
6. Jay Charleston, UT, Tennessee	41
7. Tyler Tolbert, UT, UAB	41
8. Dupree Hart, 2B, Col. of Charleston	40
9. Equon Smith, OF, Jackson St.	39
10. Mike Brown, OF, Wofford	38

RUNS

Rank Player, Pos., Team	R
1. Austin Martin, 3B, Vanderbilt	87
2. Joey Ortiz, SS, New Mexico St.	85
3. JD Orr, OF, Wright St.	83
4. JJ Bleday, OF, Vanderbilt	82
5. Nick Gonzales, 2B, New Mexico St.	80
6. Peyton Burdick, OF, Wright St.	79
7. Michael Busch, 1B, North Carolina	78
8. Jake Mangum, OF, Mississippi St.	75
9. Zavier Warren, C, Central Michigan	73
10. Austin Wells, C, Arizona	73

HITS

Rank Player, Pos., Team	H
1. Jake Mangum, OF, Mississippi St.	108
2. Joey Ortiz, SS, New Mexico St.	106
3. Austin Martin, 3B, Vanderbilt	105
4. Tanner Allen, OF, Mississippi St.	96
5. JJ Bleday, OF, Vanderbilt	95
6. Nick Gonzales, 2B, New Mexico St.	95
7. Tyler LaPorte, INF, Southern	95
8. Ryan Ward, OF, Bryant	95
9. Cameron Cannon, SS, Arizona	92

10. Kody Hoese, 3B, Tulane — 92
11. Connor Pauly, OF, Morehead St. — 92

TOTAL BASES

Rank	Player, Pos., Team	TB
1.	JJ Bleday, OF, Vanderbilt	192
2.	Kody Hoese, 3B, Tulane	183
3.	Jake Sanford, OF, Western Kentucky	178
4.	Joey Ortiz, SS, New Mexico St.	175
5.	Spencer Torkelson, 1B, Arizona St.	171
6.	Nick Gonzales, 2B, New Mexico St.	170
7.	Hunter Bishop, OF, Arizona St.	166
8.	Austin Martin, 3B, Vanderbilt	162
9.	Kevin Strohschein, OF, Tenn. Tech	161
10.	Cameron Warren, 1B, Texas Tech	161

WALKS

Rank	Player, Pos., Team	BB
1.	Adley Rutschman, C, Oregon St.	76
2.	Drew Mendoza, 3B, Florida St.	70
3.	Jacob Hurtubise, OF, Army	69
4.	Logan Wyatt, 1B, Louisville	69
5.	Kyle McCann, C, Georgia Tech	62
6.	JJ Bleday, OF, Vanderbilt	61
7.	Michael Busch, 1B, North Carolina	61
8.	Thomas Dillard, C, Mississippi	61
9.	Jordan Lala, OF, Miami	61
10.	Peyton Burdick, OF, Wright St.	60
11.	Andrew Vaughn, 1B, California	60
12.	Cory Wood, 2B, Coastal Carolina	60

TOUGHEST TO STRIKE OUT

Rank	Player, Pos., Team	AB/SO
1.	Will Brennan, UTL, Kansas St.	18.6
2.	Luke Manzo, SS, Col. of Charleston	17.9
3.	Ernie Yake, SS, Gonzaga	17.3
4.	Bryce Windham UTL, Old Dominion	16.6
5.	Dakota Julylia, SS, Jacksonville	15.6
6.	Eddy Gonzalez, OF, incarnate Word	15.1
7.	Zachary Ardito, 3B, Hartford	14.8
8.	Ryan Ward, OF, Bryant	14.6
9.	Enrique Sanchez Jr., 3B, Texas A&M-CC	14.4
10.	John Weglarz, 2B, Delaware St.	14.2

HIT BY PITCH

Rank	Player, Pos., Team	HBP
1.	Michael Cleary, OF, Dayton	28
2.	Ripken Reyes, 3B, San Diego	27
3.	Ryan Smoot, C, Virginia Military	25
4.	Trevon Dabney, 3B, James Madison	24
5.	Octavien Moyer, 2B, Florida A&M	24
6.	Mitchell Garrity, OF, Dayton	23
7.	James Cosentino, 2B, Kentucky	22
8.	Matthew Guidry, 2B, Southern Miss.	22
9.	Five tied	21

SACRIFICE BUNTS

Rank	Player, Pos., Team	SAC
1.	Andres Alvarez, SS, Washington St.	16
2.	Kyle Dockus, 2B, Mercer	15
3.	Max Foxcroft, 2B, Oregon	15

4. Brady Lloyd, 2B, East Carolina — 15
5. Equon Smith, OF, Jackson St. — 15
6. Brooks Stotler, OF, Long Beach St. — 15
7. Chris Clary, OF, Gardner-Webb — 15
8. Kyle Lovelace, C, Houston — 15
9. Christian Reyes, SS, Little Rock — 15
10. Five tied — 14

SACRIFICE FLYS

Rank	Player, Pos., Team	SF
1.	Brian Klein, 2B, Texas Tech	11
2.	Tristian English, 1B, Georgia Tech	10
3.	Evan Lowery, OF, Navy	10
4.	Riley Pittman, DH, Little Rock	10
5.	Ryan Kreidler, SS, UCLA	9
6.	Todd Lott, OF, Louisiana-Lafayette	9
7.	Jack Stronach, 3B, UCLA	9
8.	17 tied	8

PITCHING (MINIMUM 40 INNINGS PITCHED)

Rk.	Pitcher, Team	Class	W	L	ERA	G	GS	SV	IP	H	R	ER	BB	SO
1.	Chad Sykes, UNC Greensboro	R.-Sr.	6	3	0.96	27	0	11	56	36	7	6	22	68
2.	Danny Garcia, Stetson	Fr.	5	1	1.22	28	0	2	59	39	13	8	18	32
3.	T.J. Sikkema, Missouri	Jr.	7	4	1.32	17	13	2	88.2	54	23	13	31	101
4.	Ryan Garcia, UCLA	Jr.	10	1	1.44	16	13	0	94	52	24	15	26	117
5.	Noah Song, Navy	Sr.	11	1	1.44	14	14	0	94	55	15	15	31	161
6.	John Stankiewicz, Fordham	So.	8	4	1.47	17	13	0	92	62	21	15	20	102
7.	Joe LaSorsa, St. John's	Jr.	6	5	1.66	15	14	1	86.2	62	31	16	33	67
8.	Chris Clements, Portland	R.-Sr.	7	1	1.69	13	12	0	85.1	54	19	16	18	76
9.	Steve Theetge, Bryant	Sr.	9	2	1.75	16	16	0	102.2	81	30	20	30	96
10.	Trenton Denholm, UC Irvine	So.	9	4	1.81	15	14	0	99.2	61	21	20	20	93
11.	Griffin McLarty, Col. of Charleston	Jr.	8	4	1.87	15	15	0	101	66	28	21	20	116
12.	Codie Paiva, Loyola Marymount	Sr.	8	5	1.91	16	15	0	103.2	86	25	22	18	90
13.	Adrian Mardueno, San Diego St.	Jr.	5	2	1.93	26	3	2	65.1	44	21	14	28	75
14.	Ethan Small, Mississippi St.	R.-Jr.	10	2	1.93	18	18	0	107	61	26	23	32	176
15.	Michael McGreevy, UC Santa Barbara	Fr.	5	1	1.94	29	0	6	60.1	52	15	13	13	53
16.	Payton Kinney, Nebraska-Omaha	Sr.	11	2	1.96	17	17	0	115	75	25	25	38	111
17.	Garrett Lawson, Deleware St.	Jr.	6	5	1.96	14	14	0	82.2	63	33	18	32	102
18.	Cody Davenport, Central Arkansas	Sr.	7	4	1.98	16	15	1	104.2	79	34	23	21	95
19.	Emerson Hancock, Georgia	So.	8	3	1.99	14	14	0	90.1	58	21	20	18	97
20.	Dylan Thomas, Hawaii	R.-Jr.	4	4	2.01	20	3	4	53.2	40	18	12	13	59
21.	Cole Cook, Bradley	Sr.	5	2	2.03	19	4	0	62	48	14	14	17	38
22.	Brandon Eisert, Oregon St.	Jr.	8	2	2.03	14	7	0	62	59	15	14	13	74
23.	Mason Hickman, Vanderbilt	So.	9	0	2.05	20	13	3	96.2	64	24	22	28	129
24.	Jared Horn, California	Jr.	6	2	2.06	12	12	0	74.1	55	23	17	21	62
25.	Mitch Janssen, Bradley	Sr.	4	2	2.06	16	15	0	74.1	54	22	17	35	71
26.	John Doxakis, Texas A&M	Jr.	7	4	2.06	16	16	0	104.2	80	31	24	26	115
27.	Alek Manoah, West Virginia	Jr.	9	4	2.08	16	16	0	108.1	71	32	25	27	144
28.	Andrew Magno, Ohio St.	Jr.	5	3	2.09	31	0	14	64.2	45	17	15	36	75
29.	Bernie Martinez, Incarnate Word	Sr.	9	2	2.11	22	3	7	81	66	27	19	34	7
30.	Max Meyer, Minnesota	So.	5	3	2.11	16	11	2	76.2	58	21	18	20	87
31.	Isaiah Campbell, Arkansas	R.-Jr.	12	1	2.13	18	18	0	118.1	87	36	28	22	125
32.	Asa Lacy, Texas A&M	So.	8	4	2.13	15	15	0	88.2	49	23	21	43	130
33.	Micah Kaczor, East Tennessee St.	Sr.	12	6	2.13	16	15	0	101.1	83	31	24	20	85
34.	John Baker, Ball St.	Jr.	7	2	2.13	14	14	0	71.2	48	27	17	35	90
35.	Kade Mechals, Grand Canyon	Jr.	11	1	2.16	16	15	0	91.2	64	24	22	35	100
36.	Zach Hester, Samford	Jr.	7	4	2.17	15	15	0	83	66	21	20	12	82
37.	Alek Jacob, Gonzaga	So.	7	3	2.17	25	4	12	78.2	56	23	19	31	87
38.	Benjamin Dum, Virginia Commonwealth	Sr.	5	7	2.18	21	0	4	70.1	48	24	17	15	63

#	Pitcher, Team	Class	W	L	ERA	G	GS	SV	IP	H	R	ER	BB	SO
39.	Easton Walker, Brigham Young	So.	7	2	2.2	19	10	1	77.2	67	24	19	14	48
40.	Brennan Lewis, Abilene Christian	Sr.	2	1	2.21	24	1	10	57	49	20	14	5	34
41.	Bodie Sheehan, William & Mary	Sr.	5	2	2.26	14	14	0	91.2	83	25	23	16	56
42.	Alex Palmer, Stephen F. Austin	Jr.	7	6	2.27	15	15	0	107	70	31	27	31	109
43.	Connor Schultz, Butler	So.	6	1	2.29	13	13	0	78.2	70	24	20	21	79
44.	Fred Villarreal, Houston	Jr.	5	4	2.29	33	0	10	59	45	18	15	19	44
45.	Jake Agnos, East Carolina	Jr.	11	3	2.29	17	17	0	102	74	29	26	43	145
46.	Dan Metzdorf, Boston College	Sr.	8	2	2.3	12	12	0	82.1	59	26	21	32	72
47.	Kyle Gruller, Houston Baptist	Jr.	3	3	2.3	12	12	0	74.1	56	24	19	39	85
48.	Stevie Emanuels, Washington	So.	2	3	2.35	31	0	6	53.2	43	20	14	22	65
49.	Nick Lodolo, Texas Christian	Jr.	6	6	2.36	16	16	0	103	76	38	27	25	131
50.	Tim Elliott, Georgia	Jr.	7	3	2.38	15	15	0	75.2	42	24	20	24	72
51.	Zack Thompson, Kentucky	Jr.	6	1	2.4	14	14	0	90	59	29	24	34	130
52.	Matthew Brash, Niagara	Jr.	4	5	2.43	14	14	0	85.1	61	33	23	29	121
53.	Mason Mellott, Penn St.	Jr.	6	3	2.43	21	0	6	63	59	25	17	14	52
54.	Brad Depperman, North Florida	Sr.	6	5	2.46	15	15	0	95	76	29	26	24	108
55.	Jack Dashwood, UC Santa Barbara	So.	9	2	2.48	15	15	0	90.2	79	32	25	17	93
56.	Casey Sutherland, Davidson	Sr.	8	1	2.49	13	11	0	79.2	81	31	22	7	66
57.	Connor Gillispie, Virginia Commonwealth	Jr.	5	3	2.5	20	20	0	86.1	58	27	24	24	118
58.	Justin Slaten, New Mexico	Jr.	5	5	2.51	13	13	0	82.1	65	31	23	36	98
59.	Tony Locey, Georgia	Jr.	11	2	2.53	16	15	0	89	51	28	25	45	97
60.	Jake Gilbert, Air Force	Sr.	6	3	2.55	15	10	1	67	72	28	19	23	53
61.	Dante Biasi, Penn St.	R.-So.	3	6	2.55	14	14	0	74	52	28	21	33	102
62.	Alex Williams, Stanford	Fr.	8	1	2.56	14	14	0	63.1	53	23	18	8	43
63.	Garrett Farmer, Jacksonville St.	R.-Jr.	2	2	2.56	16	16	0	105.1	89	38	30	16	110
64.	Corey Gaconi, Southeastern Louisiana	Sr.	7	3	2.57	16	16	0	108.2	100	34	31	11	95
65.	Donovan Moffat, St. Bonaventure	Jr.	4	4	2.58	21	4	4	59.1	49	22	17	13	53
66.	Nathan Price, Air Force	Fr.	6	3	2.59	22	0	5	62.2	51	21	18	18	32
67.	Scott Randall, Sacramento St.	So.	8	2	2.59	17	15	0	93.2	86	36	27	33	76
68.	Mason Studstill, Florida Gulf Coast	Jr.	5	2	2.6	15	15	0	86.2	53	30	25	43	96
69.	Landon Knack, East Tennessee St.	Jr.	9	4	2.6	15	15	0	97	90	34	28	16	94
70.	Kevin Perez, Jackson St.	Jr.	5	4	2.6	21	3	1	62.1	55	21	18	20	74
71.	Jordan Martinson, Dallas Baptist	Sr.	8	4	2.61	16	16	0	100	79	30	29	29	115
72.	Michael Horrell, Campbell	Sr.	10	3	2.62	15	13	0	89.1	79	36	26	13	85
73.	Christian Scafidi, Pennsylvania	Jr.	6	1	2.62	10	9	0	68.2	60	29	20	19	59
74.	Brett Kerry, South Carolina	Fr.	4	1	2.62	22	2	7	58.1	43	17	17	13	65
75.	Nick Snyder, West Virginia	Jr.	9	1	2.65	16	13	0	68	42	22	20	34	103
76.	Hayes Heinecke, Wofford	Fr.	10	2	2.65	16	15	0	88.1	82	35	26	15	84
77.	Jack Ralston, UCLA	R.-Jr.	11	1	2.66	17	17	0	101.1	79	35	30	33	110
78.	Harrison Smith, High Point	R.-Jr.	2	4	2.67	13	12	0	64	50	34	19	27	68
79.	Andre Pallante, UC Irvine	Jr.	10	4	2.68	15	15	0	94	73	38	28	29	89
80.	Tyler Thornton, St. Mary's	Fr.	10	2	2.71	15	13	0	76.1	47	23	23	27	94
81.	Chase Smith, Pittsburgh	So.	4	6	2.72	33	0	5	59.2	54	23	18	17	55
82.	Jeff Criswell, Michigan	So.	7	1	2.72	22	17	3	106	88	40	32	50	116
83.	Grant Judkins, Iowa	Jr.	4	7	2.72	15	15	0	82.2	70	38	25	31	65
84.	Nick Stewart, James Madison	So.	4	5	2.74	15	15	0	72.1	56	31	22	33	61
85.	Michael Clark, Cal Poly	Sr.	6	3	2.74	32	0	8	69	58	27	21	23	52
86.	Max Loven, North Dakota St.	Fr.	4	2	2.74	13	13	0	88.2	78	30	27	15	75
87.	Chance Hroch, New Mexico St.	Jr.	10	1	2.74	15	15	0	85.1	82	47	26	30	69
88.	George Kirby, Elon	Jr.	8	2	2.75	14	14	0	88.1	73	34	27	6	107
89.	Jack Owen, Auburn	So.	4	2	2.75	14	10	0	68.2	64	22	21	14	59
90.	MD Johnson, Dallas Baptist	Sr.	10	2	2.76	16	16	0	98	71	35	30	29	110
91.	Ben Anderson, Binghamton	Jr.	9	4	2.76	15	15	0	88	79	29	27	27	108
92.	Chris Gerard, Virginia Tech	Fr.	3	1	2.77	12	12	0	55.1	55	22	17	25	44
93.	Rodney Boone, UC Santa Barbara	Fr.	8	0	2.78	14	14	0	81	58	26	25	29	80
94.	Nathan Jones, Northwestern St.	Sr.	7	4	2.78	14	14	0	81	60	29	25	25	80
95.	Reid Detmers, Louisville	So.	13	4	2.78	19	18	0	113.1	71	35	35	33	167
96.	Matt Canterino, Rice	Jr.	6	5	2.81	15	15	0	99.1	73	35	31	23	121
97.	Walker Powell, Southern Mississippi	Jr.	6	2	2.81	16	16	0	99.1	99	35	31	13	73
98.	Arman Sabouri, California	Jr.	2	2	2.81	26	16	4	57.2	44	21	18	17	71
99.	Tanner Burns, Auburn	So.	4	4	2.82	16	15	0	79.2	65	35	25	23	101
100.	Grant Gambrell, Oregon St.	Jr.	5	3	2.83	13	13	0	70	59	26	22	25	80

WINS

Rank Pitcher, Team	W
1. Drake Fellows, Vanderbilt	13
Reid Detmers, Louisville	13
3. Isaiah Campbell, Arkansas	12
Ryan Jensen, Fresno St.	12
Tommy Henry, Michigan	12
Kumar Rocker, Vanderbilt	12
Karl Kauffmann, Michigan	12
8. Nine tied	11

SAVES

Rank Pitcher, Team	SV
1. Garrett Acton, Illinois	19
2. Tyler Brown, Vanderbilt	17
Andrew Gross, Texas-Arlington	17
Holden Powell, UCLA	17
5. Zach Schneider, Florida Atlantic	16
Jacob Wallace, Connecticut	16
7. Grant Leonard, Iowa	14
Trey McDaniel, Southern Illinois	14
Reeves Martin, New Orleans	14
Andrew Magno, Ohio St.	14

STRIKEOUTS

Rank Pitcher, Team	SO
1. Ethan Small, Mississippi St.	176
2. Reid Detmers, Louisville	167
3. Noah Song, Navy	161
4. Drey Jameson, Ball St.	146
5. Jake Agnos, East Carolina	145
6. Alek Manoah, West Virginia	144
7. Tommy Henry, Michigan	135
8. Drake Fellows, Vanderbilt	133
9. Zak Kent, Virginia Military	132
10. Nick Lodolo, Texas Christian	131

STRIKEOUTS PER NINE

Rank Pitcher, Team	SO/9
1. Noah Song, Navy	15.41
2. Ethan Small, Mississippi St.	14.80
3. Ryan Pepiot, Butler	14.54
4. Ryne Nelson, Oregon	14.40
5. Drey Jameson, Ball St.	14.33
6. Nick Snyder, West Virginia	13.63
7. Reid Detmers, Louisville	13.26
8. Asa Lacy, Texas A&M	13.20
9. Chris Micheles, Washington	13.07
10. Zack Thompson, Kentucky	13.00

FEWEST HITS PER NINE

Rank Pitcher, Team	H/9
1. Asa Lacy, Texas A&M	4.97
2. Ryan Garcia, UCLA	4.98
3. Tim Elliott, Georgia	5.00
4. Spencer Koelewyn, Nebraska-Omaha	5.05
5. Ethan Small, Mississippi St.	5.13
6. Tony Locey, Georgia	5.16
7. Noah Song, Navy	5.27

8. T.J. Sikkema, Missouri	5.48
9. Mason Studstill, Florida Gulf Coast	5.50
10. Trenton Denholm, UC Irvine	5.51

FEWEST WALKS PER NINE

Rank Pitcher, Team	BB/9
1. George Kirby, Elon	0.61
2. Matt Waldron, Nebraska	0.63
3. Brennan Lewis, Abilene Christian	0.79
4. Casey Sutherland, Davidson	0.79
5. Corey Gaconi, Southeastern Louisiana	0.91
6. Brett Wicklund, Illinois St.	1.13
7. Alex Williams, Stanford	1.14
8. Walker Powell, Southern Miss.	1.18
9. Ryan Shreve, Pacific	1.25
10. Isaiah Nunez, Cal St. Northridge	1.25

TEAM LEADERS

SCORING

Rank Team	G	R	R/G
1. New Mexico St.	55	610	11.1
2. Arizona	56	548	9.8
3. Pennsylvania	41	354	8.6
4. Wright St.	59	501	8.5
5. Central Michigan	61	511	8.4
6. Coastal Carolina	63	525	8.3
7. Arizona St.	57	469	8.2
8. Vanderbilt	71	578	8.1
9. Bryant	60	487	8.1
10. Southern	56	443	7.9
11. Mississippi St.	67	530	7.9
12. Wake Forest	57	447	7.8
13. Tulane	58	446	7.7
14. Miami	61	459	7.5
15. Alabama St.	54	406	7.5
16. Georgia Tech	62	464	7.5
17. Arkansas	66	491	7.4
18. Louisville	69	512	7.4
19. Wisconsin-Milwaukee	57	419	7.4
20. Wofford	61	448	7.3
21. Texas Tech	66	482	7.3
22. Grambling	52	379	7.3
23. North Carolina St.	61	444	7.3
24. Jackson St.	55	400	7.3
25. Eastern Kentucky	59	429	7.3
26. North Carolina	65	472	7.3
27. Austin Peay	57	413	7.2
28. Virginia Commonwealth	58	417	7.2
29. Fresno St.	57	407	7.1
30. Baylor	54	385	7.1
31. UC Santa Barbara	56	395	7.1
32. Morehead St.	61	430	7.0
33. George Washington	54	380	7.0
34. Creighton	54	379	7.0
35. Mississippi	68	475	7.0
36. Southern Mississippi	61	426	7.0
37. Campbell	58	405	7.0
38. Dallas Baptist	63	439	7.0
39. Indiana	60	418	7.0
40. Old Dominion	56	390	7.0
41. Florida Atlantic	62	431	7.0
42. Kent St.	54	374	6.9
43. Florida	60	409	6.8
44. Tennessee Tech	54	368	6.8
45. Georgia Southern	59	400	6.8
46. Michigan	72	487	6.8
47. Texas St.	56	377	6.7
48. Eastern Illinois	56	377	6.7
49. Incarnate Word	59	397	6.7
50. Richmond	54	363	6.7

BATTING AVERAGE

Rank Team	AVG
1. New Mexico St.	.356
2. Pennsylvania	.334
3. Arizona	.326
4. Jackson St.	.315
5. Mississippi St.	.315
6. Bryant	.311
7. Souther	.311
8. Vanderbilt	.310
9. Baylor	.310
10. Arizona St.	.310

HOME RUNS

Rank Team	HR
1. Vanderbilt	100
2. Indiana	95
3. Arizona St.	94
4. Oklahoma St.	93
5. Coastal Carolina	91
6. Tulane	89
7. Arkansas	88
8. Stanford	88
9. Tennessee Tech	87
10. Miami	85

DOUBLES

Rank Team	2B
1. Mississippi St.	166
2. Vanderbilt	164
3. Arizona	154
4. Michigan	150
5. Grand Canyon	148
6. Arkansas	142
7. Louisville	140
8. Texas Tech	136
9. Wofford	135
10. Tulane	132
11. North Carolina	132

TRIPLES

Rank Team	3B
1. New Mexico St.	34
2. Arizona	32
3. UCLA	31
4. UC Santa Barbara	29
Miami (Ohio)	29
6. Ball St.	28
7. Incarnate Word	24
Central Michigan	24
UNC Wilmington	24
10. Southern	23
Kansas	23
Wright St.	23
Northeastern	23

SLUGGING PERCENTAGE

Rank Team	SLG
1. New Mexico St.	.573
2. Arizona	.533
3. Arizona St.	.519
4. Tulane	.518
5. Vanderbilt	.513
6. Coastal Carolina	.503
7. Pennsylvania	.497
8. UC Santa Barbara	.494
9. California	.490
10. Akransas	.489

STOLEN BASES

Rank Team	SB
1. Fordham	178
2. Wright St.	169
3. Wofford	155
4. UAB	147
5. Southern Illinois	144
6. Southern	137
7. Eastern Kentucky	129
8. Norfolk St.	124
Army	124
10. Col. of Charleston	118

WALKS

Rank Team	BB
1. North Carolina	406
2. Vanderbilt	389
3. Central Michigan	386
4. Florida St.	383
5. Wright St.	368
6. Texas Tech	358
7. Georgia Tech	357
8. Michigan	354
9. North Carolina State	351
Mississippi	351

PITCHING

EARNED RUN AVERAGE

Rank Team	ERA
1. UCLA	2.60
2. Oregon St.	3.02
3. Texas A&M	3.21
4. Georgia	3.24
5. Missouri	3.24
6. Fordham	3.26
7. UC Santa Barbara	3.30
8. Bradley	3.37
9. Virginia Commonwealth	3.42
10. Michigan	3.46
11. East Tennessee St.	3.48
12. Central Arkansas	3.50
13. Samford	3.50
14. Loyola Marymount	3.50
15. Mississippi St.	3.51
16. Nicholls St.	3.53
17. Louisville	3.53
18. UC Irvine	3.54
19. Tennessee	3.59
20. Stanford	3.62
21. Liberty	3.63
22. Brigham Young	3.65
23. James Madison	3.69
24. West Virginia	3.70
25. Vanderbilt	3.72
26. North Carolina A&T	3.74
27. Saint Mary's	3.76
28. Indiana St.	3.76
29. Illinois-Chicago	3.78
30. Illinois	3.78
31. Bryant	3.79
32. Indiana	3.81
33. Navy	3.82
34. Houston	3.82
35. North Florida	3.84
36. Miami	3.84
37. Fresno St.	3.84
38. William & Mary	3.84
39. College of Charleston	3.84
40. Fairfield	3.88
41. Sacramento St.	3.88
42. St. John's	3.89
43. Arkansas	3.90
44. Oklahoma	3.92
45. East Carolina	3.96
46. Virginia Tech	3.98
47. Texas Tech	4.01
48. Connecticut	4.01
49. Dallas Baptist	4.01
50. Miami (Ohio)	4.02

STRIKEOUTS PER NINE

Rank Team	SO/9
1. Ball St.	11.1
2. Texas A&M	10.9
3. Vanderbilt	10.9
4. Mississippi St.	10.8
5. Florida St.	10.4
6. Louisville	10.4
7. UCLA	10.2
8. West Virginia	10.1
9. Penn St.	10.1
10. Navy	10

FEWEST WALKS PER NINE

Rank Team	BB/9
1. UC Irvine	2.62
2. Central Arkansas	2.64
3. Wofford	2.89
4. Virginia Commonwealth	2.90
5. UC Santa Barbara	2.94
6. East Tennessee St.	3.00
7. Brigham Young	3.04
8. Saint Mary's	3.05
9. Southeastern Louisiana	3.05
10. Pepperdine	3.06

FIELDING

FIELDING PERCENTAGE

Rank Team	PCT
1. Nebraska-Omaha	.984
2. Illinois	.982
3. UCLA	.982
4. Xavier	.982
5. Creighton	.982
6. Navy	.981
7. Wright St.	.981
8. UC Irvine	.981
9. Cal St. Fullerton	.980
10. Vanderbilt	.980
11. Georgia	.980
12. NC State	.980
13. Yale	.979
14. Tennessee	.979
15. Oklahoma	.979
16. Stony Brook	.979
17. Virginia Commonwealth	.979
18. Gonzaga	.978
19. Cincinnati	.978
20. Indiana St.	.978
21. Alabama	.978
22. Mississippi	.978
23. Old Dominion	.978
24. Louisville	.978
25. Kansas	.978
26. Baylor	.978
27. San Francisco	.978
28. Saint Mary's	.977
29. Texas St.	.977
30. Binghamton	.977
31. Incarnate Word	.977
32. East Carolina	.977
33. UC Santa Barbara	.977
34. Tulane	.977
35. Virginia	.977
36. George Mason	.977
37. Charlotte	.977
38. McNeese St.	.977
39. Stanford	.977
40. Louisiana State	.977
41. South Alabama	.977
42. Jacksonville	.977
43. Seton Hall	.977
44. Grand Canyon	.977
45. Oregon St.	.977
46. Southeastern Louisiana	.976
47. Texas Tech	.976
48. Liberty	.976
49. College of Charleston	.976
50. Arizona St.	.976

DOUBLE PLAYS

Rank Team	DP
1. San Diego St.	71
2. Texas Tech	68
3. UNLV	65
4. Arizona St.	61
5. William & Mary	58
Southern Mississippi	58
7. Cincinnati	57
Western Caro.	57
9. Hofstra	56
10. Four tied	55

1. VANDERBILT

Coach: Tim Corbin. **Record:** 59-12

Player, Pos., Year	AVG	OBP	SLG	AB	R	2B	3B	HR	RBI	SB
Bleday, JJ, OF, Jr.	.347	.465	.701	274	82	14	1	27	72	1
Clarke, Philip, C,So.	.308	.388	.480	279	49	13	4	9	70	3
Davis, Cooper, OF, So.	.331	.441	.421	121	26	7	2	0	19	6
DeMarco, Pat, OF, So.	.290	.376	.512	207	49	19	3	7	49	7
Duvall, Ty, C, Jr.	.275	.418	.413	189	35	11	0	5	42	0
Fentress, Kiambu, OF, R-Jr.	.125	.417	.125	8	5	0	0	0	0	2
Gonzalez, Jayson, INF, So.	.357	.471	.446	56	14	2	0	1	10	2
Gristanti, Walker, OF, Sr.	.333	.462	.667	21	5	2	1	1	6	0
Hayes, Sterling, INF, Fr.	.000	.500	.000	2	2	0	0	0	0	0
Hogan, Matt, OF, Fr.	.000	.200	.000	4	1	0	0	0	0	0
Infante, Julian, 1B, Sr.	.231	.326	.457	199	34	9	0	12	39	3
Keegan, Dominic, UT, Fr.	.227	.320	.273	22	3	1	0	0	1	0
Kolwyck, Tate, INF, Fr.	.667	.750	1.333	3	1	2	0	0	1	0
Malcom, John, UT, Fr.	.000	.000	.000	3	0	0	0	0	1	0
Malloy, Justyn-Henry, UT,Fr.	.067	.364	.067	15	3	0	0	0	2	0
Martin, Austin, 3B, So.	.392	.486	.604	268	87	19	4	10	46	18
Paul, Ethan, SS, Sr.	.314	.386	.495	287	55	23	1	9	73	11
Ray, Harrison, 2B/3B, Jr.	.276	.358	.397	232	50	18	2	2	38	21
Scott, Stephen, OF, Sr.	.325	.445	.583	252	68	21	1	14	61	5
Thomas, Isaiah, OF, So.	.368	.405	.684	38	9	3	0	3	10	1

Pitcher, Year	W	L	ERA	G	GS	SV	IP	H	BB	SO
Becker, Austin, Fr.	0	0	6.75	2	0	1	4	3	4	9
Brown, Tyler, So.	3	1	2.19	31	0	17	49.1	35	9	65
Eder, Jake, So.	2	0	2.97	19	0	4	39.1	28	16	41
Fellows, Drake, Jr.	13	2	4.09	19	19	0	116.2	111	47	133
Fisher, Hugh, So.	2	0	4.41	22	0	4	34.2	31	21	46
Franklin, AJ, R-Jr.	1	0	10.43	14	0	0	14.2	16	13	17
Gillis, Jackson, Jr.	1	1	5.14	7	0	0	7	7	5	7
Gobillot, Joe, R-Fr.	0	0	13.50	2	0	0	2	2	3	4
Hickman, Mason, So.	9	0	2.05	20	13	3	96.2	64	28	129
Huff, Chance, Fr.	2	0	6.38	8	4	0	18.1	16	16	21
Kalser, Erik, So.	0	0	12.00	1	1	0	3	4	0	4
King, Zach, Jr.	0	2	6.18	22	3	3	39.1	40	22	47
Raby, Patrick, Sr.	10	1	3.08	18	15	0	76	75	46	81
Rocker, Kumar, Fr.	12	5	3.25	19	16	0	99.2	88	21	114
Smith, Ethan, Fr.	4	0	3.27	17	0	0	33	17	17	47

2. MICHIGAN

Coach: Erik Bakich. **Record:** 50-22

Player, Pos., Year	AVG	OBP	SLG	AB	R	2B	3B	HR	RBI	SB
Bertram, Riley, INF, Fr.	.385	.515	.538	26	4	4	0	0	7	1
Blomgren, Jack, INF, So.	.314	.417	.401	242	40	8	2	3	47	7
Brewer, Jordan , OF, Jr.	.329	.389	.557	246	58	20	0	12	59	25
Buckley, Casey, C, Fr.	.000	.000	.000	14	0	0	0	0	0	0
Bullock, Christian, OF, Jr.	.263	.385	.407	118	27	7	2	2	14	14
Carattini, Keaton, RHP, Fr.	.000	.500	.000	1	0	0	0	0	0	0
Clementi, Dominic, OF, Jr.	.195	.276	.299	87	13	4	1	1	6	2
Donovan, Joe, C, So.	.234	.314	.421	209	40	12	0	9	37	0
Franklin, Jesse, OF, So.	.262	.388	.477	260	61	15	1	13	55	4
Kerr, Jimmy, 1B, Sr.	.268	.364	.500	268	52	15	1	15	63	4
Lewis, Miles, OF, R-Sr.	.265	.364	.408	223	43	16	2	4	31	10
Nelson, Blake, 3B, Sr.	.297	.391	.390	236	42	17	1	1	39	18
Nwogu, Jordan, OF, So.	.321	.435	.557	246	58	14	4	12	46	16
Salter, Harrison, C, R-So.	.265	.357	.294	34	4	1	0	0	8	0
Schmidt, Matthew, INF, Sr.	.167	.389	.250	12	4	1	0	0	2	2
Thomas, Ako, 2B, Sr.	.267	.2366	.373	225	38	16	1	2	32	2
Van Remortel, Jack, INF, Fr.	.167	.375	.167	12	3	0	0	0	1	0

Pitcher, Year	W	L	ERA	G	GS	SV	IP	H	BB	SO
Beers, Blake, So.	1	1	6.04	14	2	1	22.1	26	10	15
Bredeson, Jack, Sr.	0	0	6.75	4	0	0	2.2	3	5	6
Carattini, Keaton, Fr.	0	0	12	4	0	0	3	5	3	3
Cleveland, Walker, Fr.	5	3	4.23	15	3	0	38.1	30	15	19
Criswell, Jeff, So.	7	1	2.72	22	17	3	106	88	50	116
Henry, Tommy, Jr.	12	5	3.27	20	19	0	124	102	26	135
Kauffman, Karl, Jr.	12	7	3.03	21	20	0	130.2	107	39	111

Player, Pos., Year	AVG	OBP	SLG	AB	R	2B	3B	HR	RBI	SB
Keizer, Benjamin, R.-Jr.	4	1	4.3	34	1	2	44	31	21	48
Pace, Joe, R.-Jr.	0	0	3.86	9	1	0	9.1	8	5	14
Paige, Isaiah, R.-Fr.	3	1	2.75	26	5	1	52.1	43	16	33
Smith, Angelo, So.	1	0	4.6	23	4	0	31.1	34	20	39
Weisenburger, Jack, Jr.	3	1	4.25	25	0	1	29.2	23	23	31
Weiss, Willie, Fr.	2	2	2.97	27	0	9	39.1	25	32	50
White, Jack, Fr.	0	0	0	2	0	0	2	0	2	1

3. LOUISVILLE

Coach: Dan McDonnell. **Record:** 51-18

Player, Pos., Year	AVG	OBP	SLG	AB	R	2B	3B	HR	RBI	SB
Binelas, Alex, 3B, Fr.	.291	.383	.612	206	54	14	5	14	59	3
Britton, Zach, C, So.	.288	.368	.470	132	26	7	1	5	28	2
Campbell, Drew, OF, Jr.	.309	.388	.431	188	30	15	1	2	39	9
Davis, Henry, C, Fr.	.280	.345	.386	132	15	5	0	3	23	0
Dunn, Lucas, INF, So.	.309	.399	.398	191	48	10	2	1	25	15
Elliott, Adam, UT, Jr.	.000	.000	.000	3	0	0	0	0	0	0
Fitzgerald, Tyler, SS, Jr.	.315	.391	.483	267	64	15	3	8	65	18
Lavey, Justin, INF, Jr.	.286	.361	.366	227	34	9	0	3	33	20
Leonard, Trey, OF, So.	.264	.365	.377	53	25	1	1	1	9	14
Masterman, Cameron, INF, So.	.286	.310	.536	28	6	2	1	1	5	0
Metzinger, Ben, C, Fr.	.312	.389	.375	16	3	1	0	0	4	0
Oriente, Danny, OF, Jr.	.332	.404	.435	193	29	17	0	1	49	0
Pinkham, Zeke, C, Sr.	.324	.454	.431	102	20	8	0	1	16	2
Poland, Jared, INF, Fr.	.211	.270	.368	57	8	4	1	1	18	0
Rumoro, Jack, SS, Jr.	.143	.308	.143	21	3	0	0	0	3	0
Snider, Jake, INF, Jr.	.283	.383	.385	265	64	16	4	1	34	13
Stringer, Ethan, OF, So.	.218	.344	.308	78	11	4	0	1	8	4
Wyatt, Logan, 1B, Jr.	.283	.445	.449	247	72	12	1	9	53	8

Pitcher, Year	W	L	ERA	G	GS	SV	IP	H	BB	SO
Albanese, Glenn, Jr.	1	1	3.72	8	2	0	9.2	15	3	10
Bennett, Nick, Jr.	7	3	4.40	16	16	0	77.2	77	32	76
Detmers, Reid, So.	13	4	2.78	19	18	0	113.1	71	33	167
Dickey, Austin, Jr.	0	0	6.35	5	0	0	5.2	4	5	5
Elliott, Adam, Jr.	3	2	2.48	23	0	0	32.2	25	18	33
Hoeing, Bryan, Sr.	3	4	3.00	22	5	1	63	55	17	75
Kirian, Michael, So.	3	1	1.69	26	0	5	32	26	9	42
Lohman, Carter, Jr.	0	0	4.66	11	1	0	9.2	5	8	8
McAvene, Michael, Jr.	2	0	2.73	23	0	7	33	23	11	50
Miller, Bobby, So.	7	1	3.83	20	12	2	80	59	38	86
Perkins, Jack, Fr.	3	0	4.18	16	4	1	32.1	24	18	37
Poland, Jared, Fr.	2	1	4.12	16	0	0	19.2	13	11	25
Schmeltz, Garrett, Fr.	0	0	3.55	15	0	0	12.2	13	4	13
Smiddy, Shay, Jr.	1	0	2.31	19	0	0	23.1	11	18	28
Smith, Luke, Jr.	6	1	4.24	18	10	0	68	56	24	53
Wright, Kerry, Fr.	0	0	10.61	10	1	0	9.1	8	13	8

4. TEXAS TECH

Coach: Tim Tadlock. **Record:** 46-20

Player, Pos., Year	AVG	OBP	SLG	AB	R	2B	3B	HR	RBI	SB
Baker, Dru, INF, Fr.	.321	.395	.445	137	30	6	1	3	25	3
Facendo, Doug, UT, Jr.	.231	.380	.410	39	9	4	0	1	8	0
Fulford, Braxton, INF, So.	.298	.388	.419	191	35	9	1	4	34	0
Holt, Gabe, OF, So.	.318	.409	.433	261	53	15	3	3	35	28
Jung, Josh, 3B, Jr.	.343	.474	.636	239	65	23	1	15	58	1
Kelly, Parker, INF, So.	.200	.277	.306	85	12	6	0	1	4	0
Klein, Brian , 2B, Jr.	.315	.406	.440	257	54	19	2	3	57	0
Marusak, Max, OF, Fr.	.233	.298	.350	103	20	1	4	1	12	10
Masters, Cody, OF, So.	.292	.373	.458	144	23	7	1	5	28	5
Minzey, Mason, C, Fr.	.091	.286	.091	11	0	0	0	0	0	0
Murrell, Easton, INF, So.	.262	.436	.381	42	8	2	0	1	9	0
Neuse, Dylan, OF/SS, So.	.298	.408	.494	245	58	12	6	8	51	18
O'Tremba, Tanner, OF, Fr.	.261	.367	.402	92	18	7	0	2	20	2
Stilwell, Cole, C, Fr.	.268	.408	.407	123	23	6	1	3	22	1
Warren, Cameron, 1B, Sr.	.355	.451	.665	242	63	17	2	18	79	1
Wilson, Kurt, INF, Jr.	.227	.317	.386	88	11	2	0	4	17	2

Pitcher, Year	W	L	ERA	G	GS	SV	IP	H	BB	SO
Beeter, Clayton, Fr.	0	3	3.48	21	0	8	20.2	12	20	40
Bonnin, Bryce, So.	7	1	4.08	15	13	0	64	50	45	65
Dallas, Micah, Fr.	7	2	4.03	19	13	0	76	74	28	84
Dobbins, Hunter, Fr.	2	1	4.44	14	2	1	26.1	25	11	24
Farr, Cade, Fr.	0	0	21.6	4	0	0	1.2	3	1	2
Floyd, Taylor, Jr.	5	3	2.51	31	0	5	57.1	46	27	88
Freeman, Caleb, Jr.	2	0	6.61	18	0	16.1	26	15	15
Garlett, Trey, Fr.	1	0	4.22	8	1	0	10.2	9	6	5
Haveman, Dane, Jr.	2	1	3.02	34	0	3	44.2	48	9	59
Huerta, Noah, Fr.	0	0	18	1	0	0	1	4	0	1
Keese, Ryan, Jr.	0	0	7.2	11	0	0	5	6	1	3
Kilan, Caleb, Jr.	8	3	3.92	17	17	0	96.1	86	20	89
Lanning, Erikson, Jr.	0	1	4.81	13	11	0	39.1	49	6	25
McMillon, John, Jr.	4	3	3.40	24	0	3	47.2	35	35	67
Montgomery, Mason, Fr.	3	1	5.14	12	9	0	35	32	26	24
Queen, Connor, Jr.	4	0	1.06	11	0	0	17	15	7	13
Sublette, Ryan, So.	1	0	4.76	14	0	1	17	18	13	16
Wilson, Kurt, So.	0	1	6.14	12	0	0	14.2	14	8	12

5. MISSISSIPPI STATE

Coach: Chris Lemonis. **Record:** 52-15

Player, Pos., Year	AVG	OBP	SLG	AB	R	2B	3B	HR	RBI	SB
Allen, Tanner, 1B, So.	.349	.426	.516	275	56	23	1	7	66	1
Bell, Benjamin, OF, Fr.	.000	.000	.000	1	3		0	0	0	0
Brock, Bryce, UT, Fr.	.500	.500	.500	2	1	0	0	0	0	0
Cumbest, Brad, OF, Fr.	.286	.345	.429	49	9	4	0	1	11	0
Foscue, Justin, INF, So.	.331	.395	.564	275	66	22	0	14	60	2
Gilbert, Marshall, C, Sr.	.313	.432	.493	134	25	6	0	6	18	0
Ginn, JT, 1B/RHP, Fr.	.000	.000	.000	3	0	0	0	0	0	0
Halter, Gunner, INF, Jr.	.287	.364	.530	143	36	6	0	1	19	3
Hancock, Luke, C, Fr.	.326	.483	.419	43	9	4	0	0	14	0
Hatcher, Josh, INF/OF, So.	.321	.379	.500	106	15	6	2	3	21	3
Jones, Hayden, C, Fr.	.224	.269	.367	49	5	4	0	1	5	1
Jordan, Landon, INF, Fr.	.328	.397	.426	61	17	3	9	1	11	4
Jordan, Rowdey, OF, So.	.290	.370	.420	255	55	10	6	0	49	11
MacNamee, Elijah, OF, Sr.	.286	.398	.475	217	51	20	0	7	52	4
Mangum, Jake, OF, Sr.	.358	.417	.467	302	75	24	3	1	39	22
Skelton, Dustin, C, Jr.	.314	.385	.505	220	39	8	2	10	55	3
Westburg, Jordan, SS, So.	.294	.402	.457	265	68	21	2	6	61	7

Pitcher, Year	W	L	ERA	G	GS	SV	IP	H	BB	SO
Barlow, Trysten, Jr.	3	1	6.00	28	0	0	24	21	13	32
Breaux, Kale, Jr.	0	0	0.00	1	0	0	0.1	1	1	1
Brock, Bryce, Fr.	0	0	7.56	7	0	0	8.1	16	6	12
Cerantola, Eric, Fr.	3	0	4.3	11	4	0	14.2	8	11	21
Eagan, Jack, Jr.	1	0	3.09	18	1	0	23.1	12	17	34
Ginn, JT, Fr.	8	4	3.13	17	17	0	86.1	72	19	105
Gordon, Cole, Sr.	5	1	3.8	30	0	11	42.2	34	24	69
James, Keegan, Jr.	4	1	5.02	18	8	0	43	44	31	41
Liebelt, Jared, Sr.	2	0	2.96	34	0	5	54.2	57	11	38
Plumlee, Peyton, Sr.	7	5	3.8	21	16	0	85.1	67	28	68
Price, Spencer, Jr.	0	0	3.09	12	0	0	11.2	10	7	11
Self, Riley, Jr.	2	0	4.91	23	0	0	25.2	37	9	18
Small, Ethan, R-Jr.	10	2	1.93	18	18	0	107	61	32	176
Smith, Brandon, Fr.	3	-	3.93	26	3	0	36.2	43	6	31
Spring, Tyler, Jr.	1	0	2.61	10	0	0	10.1	7	8	13
White, Colby, Jr.	3	1	3.12	27	0	0	26	16	9	48

6. UCLA

Coach: John Savage. **Record:** 52-11

Player, Pos., Year	AVG	OBP	SLG	AB	R	2B	3B	HR	RBI	SB
Cardenas, Noah, C, Fr.	.375	.476	.500	135	27	6	1	3	18	0
Cueller, Kyle, INF, Jr.	.182	.269	.318	22	3	3	0	0	4	0
Filby, Jack, INF, Fr.	.400	.400	.400	5	0	0	0	0	1	0
Hirabayashi, Jake, C, Sr.	.190	.296	.310	58	6	4	0	1	11	1
Kendall, Kevin, INF, So.	.258	.331	.298	124	23	5	0	0	13	9
Kreidler, Ryan, INF, Jr.	.300	.370	.502	243	50	18	2	9	45	12
McInerny, Will, C, Jr.	.205	.339	.250	44	4	2	0	0	4	1
McLain, Matt, OF, Fr.	.203	.276	.355	217	28	9	6	4	30	6
Mitchell, Garrett, OF, So.	.349	.418	.566	258	57	14	12	6	41	18
Moberg, Jake, INF, Jr.	.143	.250	.214	14	3	1	0	0	0	0
Perez, Mikey, INF, Fr.	.200	.385	.300	10	1	1	0	0	1	0

Pitcher, Year	W	L	ERA	G	GS	SV	IP	H	BB	SO
Prendiz, Jordan, OF, R-So.	.000	.000	.000	3	6	0	0	0	0	1
Pries, Jake, OF, Sr.	.282	.388	.533	195	40	7	3	12	41	2
Silva, Jarron, OF, R-So.	.238	.327	.405	42	9	4	0	1	9	0
Stronach, Jack, INF, Jr.	.317	.378	.418	189	27	11	1	2	34	2
Strumpf, Chase, 2B, Jr.	.279	.416	.472	233	53	14	2	9	44	3
Teijeiro, RJ, INF, So.	.250	.400	.250	4	0	0	0	0	1	1
Toglia, Michael, 1B, Jr.	.314	.392	.624	242	50	16	4	17	65	1
Ydens, Jeremy, OF, Jr.	.273	.354	.443	88	15	6	0	3	11	6

Pitcher, Year	W	L	ERA	G	GS	SV	IP	H	BB	SO
Bergin, Jesse, Fr.	5	0	4.43	17	15	0	67	57	25	76
Colwell, Daniel, Fr.	0	0	0.00	2	0	0	2	2	0	0
Filby, Jack, Fr.	2	0	4.05	23	0	0	20	19	7	25
Garcia, Ryan, Jr.	10	1	1.44	16	13	0	94	52	26	117
Hadley, Nathan, R-Sr.	8	1	2.33	41	0	0	46.1	22	19	55
Hooper, Justin, R-Jr.	0	0	0.00	1	0	0	0.2	0	2	0
Mora, Kyle, Jr.	3	3	2.09	47	0	1	56	40	18	67
Mullen, Sean, Fr.	1	0	0.00	4	1	0	6.1	5	5	6
Nastrini, Nick, Fr.	1	0	1.37	5	4	0	19.2	10	7	28
Pettway, Zach, So.	2	2	4.55	10	10	0	63.1	57	22	60
Powell, Holden, So.	4	3	1.84	40	0	17	49	19	27	65
Ralston, Jack, R-Jr.	11	1	2.66	17	17	0	101.1	79	33	110
Rubi, Felix, Jr.	2	0	1.31	11	3	0	20.2	12	7	9
Townsend, Michael, So.	3	0	1.85	20	0	0	24.1	18	9	29

7. FLORIDA STATE

Coach: Mike Martin. **Record:** 42-23

Player, Pos., Year	AVG	OBP	SLG	AB	R	2B	3B	HR	RBI	SB
Albert, Reese, OF, So.	.283	.390	.518	166	33	6	3	9	35	2
Baldor, Nico, INF, Jr.	.173	.277	.252	127	13	7	0	1	16	2
Becker, Tim, OF, Sr.	.246	.362	.456	57	17	3	0	3	13	0
Cabell, Elijah, OF, Fr.	.220	.404	.415	164	37	9	1	7	25	9
De Sedas, Nander, INF, Fr.	.231	.353	.337	208	38	4	1	4	32	3
Flowers, J.C., OF/RHP, Jr.	.266	.371	.498	233	46	11	2	13	53	11
Foster, Jonathan, C, Sr.	.194	.398	.323	62	19	2	0	2	7	0
Haney, Chase, RHP, Jr.	1.000	1.000	1.000	2	0	0	0	0	0	0
Hutchinson, Gage, UT, Fr.	.000	.000	.000	1	0	0	0	0	0	0
Martin, Robby, OF, Fr.	.315	.398	.449	216	34	17	0	4	54	2
Mendoza, Drew, 3B, Jr.	.308	.471	.594	224	34	12	2	16	56	2
Nelson, Matheu, C, Fr.	.282	.442	.442	156	32	7	0	6	29	4
Salvatore, Mike, SS, Sr.	.340	.432	.536	265	55	23	4	7	51	6
Sanchez, Alec, INF,Fr.	.225	.291	.239	71	10	1	0	0	6	2
Smith, Carter, C, Jr.	.245	.360	.362	94	18	5	0	2	10	0
Swanson, Cooper, INF, So.	.159	.362	.409	88	17	1	0	7	14	4
Velez, Antonio, UT, Jr.	.000	.000	.000	1	0	0	0	0	0	0
Weaver, McGuire, INF, Jr.	.313	.313	.438	16	4	2	0	0	4	0

Pitcher, Year	W	L	ERA	G	GS	SV	IP	H	BB	SO
Ahearn, Tyler, So.	1	0	9.72	16	2	0	16.2	17	15	16
Anderson, Jack, Fr.	0	1	7.04	6	1	0	7.2	10	5	10
Drohan, Shane, So.	3	1	3.66	16	11	0	51.2	47	48	71
Flowers, JC, Jr.	0	0	1.69	23	1	13	26.2	20	11	25
Grady, Conor, So.	9	6	3.64	25	8	0	64.1	54	26	71
Haney, Chase, Jr.	2	2	2.41	31	0	1	37.1	23	11	36
Hungate, Cade, Fr.	0	0	7.88	8	0	0	8	8	9	4
Hutchinson, Gage, Sr.	0	0	5.06	10	0	0	10.2	13	5	10
Kwiatkowski, Clayton, Jr.	0	0	4.00	23	1	0	36	38	16	40
Parrish, Drew, Jr.	9	5	4.67	19	18	0	94.1	89	32	125
Pollock, Austin, So.	0	0	10.22	16	2	0	24.2	34	19	18
Scolaro, Jonah, So.	3	2	4.69	26	1	2	48	35	23	52
Van Eyk, CJ, So.	10	4	3.81	18	18	0	99.1	89	41	129
Velez, Antonio, Jr.	5	2	4.17	22	3	1	45.1	46	11	50

8. ARKANSAS

Coach: Dave Van Horn. **Record:** 46-20

Player, Pos., Year	AVG	OBP	SLG	AB	R	2B	3B	HR	RBI	SB
Ezell, Trevor, INF, R.-Sr.	.329	.435	.561	255	72	35	2	10	49	19
Fletcher, Dominic, OF, Jr.	.313	.385	.528	265	56	24	0	11	61	2
Franklin, Christian, OF, Fr.	.274	.361	.413	201	42	8	1	6	34	12
Goodheart, Matt, 1B, So.	.345	.444	.517	203	35	16	2	5	47	5
Harris, Trey, OF, Fr.	.257	.341	.343	35	5	3	0	0	6	0
Kenley, Jack, INF, Jr.	.311	.428	.553	235	55	10	4	13	54	8
Kjerstad, Heston, OF, So.	.327	.400	.575	266	53	13	1	17	51	5

Player, Pos., Year	AVG	OBP	SLG	AB	R	2B	3B	HR	RBI	SB
Martin, Casey, SS, So.	.286	.364	.548	283	67	21	4	15	57	10
McFarland, Jordan, INF, Jr.	.238	.320	.349	63	14	1	0	2	12	2
Nesbit, Jacob, INF, R.-Fr.	.255	.333	.344	212	35	10	0	3	42	7
Opitz, Casey, C, So.	.243	.379	.311	177	31	3	0	3	33	7
Plunkett, Zack, C, R.-Sr.	.260	.451	.480	50	12	5	0	2	9	0
Washington, Curtis, OF, Fr.	.353	.476	.588	34	14	3	1	1	3	4

Pitcher, Year	W	L	ERA	G	GS	SV	IP	H	BB	SO
Burton, Jacob, Fr.	0	0	4.82	11	0	0	9.1	10	6	7
Campbell, Isaiah, Jr.	12	1	2.13	18	18	0	118.1	87	22	125
Cronin, Matt, Jr.	1	0	1.86	25	0	12	29	16	14	42
Denton, Marshall, So.	2	0	4.5	24	4	1	30	30	5	31
Henry, Liam, Fr.	0	1	4.32	9	0	0	8.1	6	8	7
Kopps, Kevin, Jr.	6	3	3.89	30	0	0	41.2	38	14	52
Kostyshock, Jacob, Jr.	1	3	2.64	22	1	1	30.2	24	10	29
Monke, Caden, Fr.	0	0	18.00	6	0	0	3	3	5	5
Noland, Connor, Fr.	3	5	4.02	20	19	0	78.1	73	14	55
Ramage, Kole, So.	7	1	5.25	24	2	0	60	61	29	53
Scroggins, Cody, Jr.	3	2	4.01	19	7	0	49.1	40	26	62
Sells, Carter, Fr.	0	0	18.00	3	0	0	2	1	7	1
Taylor, Collin, So.	0	0	4.05	7	0	0	6.2	4	6	3
Taylor, Evan, Fr.	0	0	6.43	8	0	0	7	3	9	13
Trest, Elijah, Fr.	1	1	7.58	15	0	0	19	18	17	19
Vermillion, Zebulon, So.	4	1	3.63	20	0	1	22.1	21	9	21
Wicklander, Patrick, Fr.	6	2	4.32	22	15	0	66.2	50	37	90

9. AUBURN

Coach: Butch Thompson. **Record:** 38-28

Player, Pos., Year	AVG	OBP	SLG	AB	R	2B	3B	HR	RBI	SB
Bliss, Ryan, 2B, Fr.	.281	.367	.369	249	50	11	1	3	37	11
Davis, Conor, OF, Jr.	.290	.351	.448	252	35	14	1	8	36	2
Eaton, Jarrett, OF, Fr.	.000	.000	.000	3	6	0	0	0	0	2
Hall, Chase, C, R-Jr.	.160	.250	.250	25	2	1	0	0	3	0
Henderson, Jackson, INF, Jr.	.000	.000		2	1	0	0	0	0	0
Holland, Will, SS, Jr.	.246	.376	.401	232	48	9	0	9	32	15
Howell, Kason, OF, Fr.	.262	.340	.307	225	31	10	0	0	28	14
Johnson, Ed, INF, Fr.	.286	.375	.286	7	0	0	0	0	0	0
Julien, Edouard, 3B, So.	.258	.388	.453	236	52	14	1	10	57	3
Lau, Everett, INF, Jr.	.250	.333	.375	40	7	2	0	1	8	1
Moore, Brody, INF, Fr.	.333	.379	.444	27	6	1	1	0	4	0
Olson, Brett, INF, R-Sr.	1.000	1.000	1.000	1	0	0	0	0	0	0
Scheffler, Matt, C, Jr.	.260	.331	.342	219	30	12	0	2	28	5
Ward, Judd, OF, So.	.272	.377	.393	257	42	12	2	5	34	5
Warner, Devin, OF, Fr.	.267	.312	.267	15	1	0	0	0	3	0
Williams, Steven, OF, So.	.247	.355	.413	235	40	8	2	9	36	3
Woley, Rankin, INF, Jr.	.277	.336	.387	256	36	17	1	3	45	2

Pitcher, Year	W	L	ERA	G	GS	SV	IP	H	BB	SO
Anderson, Elliott, Jr.	7	2	4.15	30	3	0	65	64	30	67
Burns, Tanner, So.	4	4	2.82	16	15	0	79.2	65	23	101
Daniel, Davis, Jr.	0	0	4.50	1	1	0	2	4	0	4
Fitts, Richard, Fr.	5	3	5.31	21	5	0	62.2	78	17	47
Fuller, Brooks, Fr.	2	2	4.50	20	8	2	44	39	35	36
Glavine, Peyton, So.	1	0	5.62	9	0	0	8	10	8	12
Gray, Kyle, R-Jr.	2	4	4.98	15	3	0	21.2	21	16	17
Greenhill, Cody, So.	2	3	3.45	28	0	12	57.1	53	18	44
Horn, Bailey, R-So.	4	2	5.97	18	5	0	37.2	34	20	31
Morrison, Will, Fr.	0	0	4.56	24	0	0	25.2	24	11	15
Owen, Jack, So.	4	2	2.75	4	10	0	68.2	64	14	59
Schillechi, Blake, Sr.	0	2	7.41	12	0	0	17	23	7	15
Skipper, Carson, Fr.	3	3	7.46	17	8	2	35	45	23	38
Wade, Garrett, Fr.	3	0	4.86	5	7	0	33.1	33	27	41
Watson, Ryan, Jr.	1	1	4.87	24	1	0	40.2	44	18	41

10. STANFORD

Coach: David Esquer. **Record:** 45-14

Player, Pos., Year	AVG	OBP	SLG	AB	R	2B	3B	HR	RBI	SB
Bellafronto, Nick, INF, R.-Jr.	.258	.383	.492	132	32	13	0	6	32	1
Bruesser, Nick, INF, So.	.224	.355	.365	85	11	6	0	2	16	2
Burton, Grant, OF, Fr.	.000	.250	.000	2	1	0	0	0	1	0
Daschbach, Andrew, 1B, Jr.	.289	.382	.602	211	55	11	2	17	46	1
Dieter, Brandon, INF, Fr.	.208	.284	.278	72	7	2	0	1	12	0
Handley, Maverick, C, Jr.	.290	.393	.442	224	45	13	3	5	24	12

Player, Pos., Year	AVG	OBP	SLG	AB	R	2B	3B	HR	RBI	SB
Kinamon, Duke, INF, R.-Jr.	.303	.348	.465	185	39	12	0	6	32	12
Kretzschmar, Austin, INF, Fr.	.500	.538	.667	12	3	5	1	1	0	0
Martinez, Vincent, C, Fr.	.250	.250	.250	8	0	0	0	0	2	0
Matthiessen, Will, UT, Jr.	.310	.389	.532	216	46	12	0	12	52	1
Molfetta, Christian, OF, R.-Jr.	.167	.231	.417	12	2	0	0	1	1	0
Oar, Nickolas, OF, R.-Jr.	.294	.333	.471	17	3	0	0	1	2	0
Robinson, Christian, OF, So.	.287	.386	.370	108	16	9	0	0	15	8
Sehgal, Zach, INF, R.-Fr.	.000	.000	.000	1	0	0	0	0	0	0
Stowers, Kyle, OF, Jr.	.303	.369	.523	218	39	19	1	9	39	13
Tawa, Tim, INF, So.	.253	.284	.410	217	35	10	0	8	37	6
Wilson, Alec, OF, Sr.	.176	.283	.314	51	8	4	0	1	7	1
Wulff, Brandon, OF, Sr.	.272	.398	.592	206	54	7	1	19	42	6

Pitcher, Year	W	L	ERA	G	GS	SV	IP	H	BB	SO
Baggett, Ben, R.-So.	0	0	36.00	2	0	0	1	2	3	0
Beck, Brendan, So.	5	4	3.63	17	16	0	91.2	102	25	83
Dieter, Brandon, Fr.	0	0	0.00	1	0	0	1.1	0	0	1
Grech, Jach, Jr.	2	0	3.68	32	0	1	44	47	7	28
Jensen, Cody, Fr.	1	0	3.55	20	2	1	33	28	11	32
Little, Jack, Jr.	3	2	3.37	25	0	12	42.2	35	11	55
Lopez, Nicolas, Fr.	1	0	15.00	3	0	0	3	4	3	4
Matthiessen, Will, Jr.	6	2	3.83	16	8	1	54	48	19	56
Miller, Erik, Jr.	8	3	3.48	16	16	0	82.2	68	46	102
Palisch, Jacob, So.	5	2	4.79	26	7	0	56.1	67	21	48
Rudd, Carson, So.	0	0	2.95	15	0	0	21.1	17	11	14
Weiermiller, Austin, So.	6	0	2.45	25	0	2	33	25	17	41
Williams, Alex, Fr.	8	1	2.56	14	10	0	63.1	53	8	43

11. OKLAHOMA STATE

Coach: Matt Holliday. **Record:** 40-21

Player, Pos., Year	AVG	OBP	SLG	AB	R	2B	3B	HR	RBI	SB
Becker, Adam, INF, Fr.	.000	.000	.000	4	1	0	0	0	0	0
Boone, Trevor, OF, So.	.290	.364	.633	221	41	9	2	21	57	6
Cabbiness, Cade, OF, Jr.	.234	.307	.406	197	34	8	1	8	27	4
Carter, Bryce, C, Sr.	.255	.372	.376	157	23	7	0	4	30	0
Factor, Cross, INF, So.	.000	.000	.000	5	0	0	0	0	0	0
Funk, Christian, INF, Sr.	.237	.381	.460	211	45	11	0	12	41	1
Garcia, Alix, INF, Jr.	.294	.388	.485	163	19	7	0	8	25	0
Gardner, Dylan, INF, So.	.250	.400	.312	16	5	1	0	0	2	1
Hewitt, Max, INF, Jr.	.303	.472	.348	66	13	0	0	1	9	5
McCusker, Carson, OF, Jr.	.311	.383	.520	196	36	17	3	6	40	2
Morrill, Hueston, INF, Fr.	.282	.390	.386	220	47	17	0	2	20	12
Navigato, Andrew, INF, Jr.	.288	.367	.515	233	56	15	1	12	42	7
Provost, Dayton, INF, Jr.	.000	.500	.000	1	2	0	0	0	0	0
Sifrit, Noah, UT, So.	.265	.405	.353	34	13	1	1	0	3	3
Simpson, Colin, C, Sr.	.245	.348	.519	233	41	13	0	17	57	5
Taylor, Jake, C, Jr.	.217	.327	.313	83	10	2	0	2	4	0

Pitcher, Year	W	L	ERA	G	GS	SV	IP	H	BB	SO
Basso, Brady, Jr.	1	0	1.64	14	0	0	11	6	8	16
Battenfield, Peyton, Jr.	4	3	3.28	30	0	5	60.1	44	21	74
Belden, Brayden, Fr.	0	0	0.00	1	0	0	1	1	1	0
Elliott, Jensen, Sr.	10	4	3.56	17	17	0	98.2	81	37	62
Gragg, Logan, Jr.	3	3	5.10	24	4	2	42.1	49	19	36
Kelly, John, Fr.	1	0	1.59	6	0	0	5.2	4	5	9
Leeper, Ben, Jr.	4	4	4.31	29	0	7	31.1	24	23	43
Lienhard, Joe, Sr.	4	1	4.39	21	8	0	53.1	60	22	41
Lyons, Jake, Jr.	5	2	4.89	20	2	1	49.2	47	16	51
Peterson, Nate, Fr.	0	0	3.46	11	0	1	13	18	7	16
Scott, Parker, So.	3	1	2.18	15	8	0	45.1	42	14	51
Sifrit, Noah, So.	0	0	3.60	5	0	0	5	0	5	5
Sparks, Tanner, Fr.	0	0	13.50	3	0	0	2	2	6	3
Standlee, Brett, R-Fr.	3	2	4.46	19	12	1	72.2	88	23	55
Stone, Mitchell, R-Fr.	2	1	4.88	9	5	1	27.2	23	14	19
Varela, C.J., Jr.	0	0	6.38	10	5	0	24	25	18	24

12. EAST CAROLINA

Coach: Cliff Godwin. **Record:** 47-18

Player, Pos., Year	AVG	OBP	SLG	AB	R	2B	3B	HR	RBI	SB
Baker, Dusty, OF, Jr.	.250	.343	.380	92	17	9	0	1	11	3
Barber, Nick, INF, Jr.	.235	.316	.324	68	17	3	0	1	7	2
Brickhouse, Spencer, 1B, Jr.	.335	.467	.626	206	57	14	2	14	56	2
Brown, Turner, INF, Sr.	.294	.387	.399	228	39	11	2	3	33	11

Player, Pos., Year	AVG	OBP	SLG	AB	R	2B	3B	HR	RBI	SB
Burleson, Alec, UT, So.	3.70	.399	.573	246	38	23	0	9	61	3
Caddell, Seth, C, So.	.241	.284	.434	83	8	2	1	4	13	0
Francisco, Thomas, INF, Fr.	.319	.451	.478	113	13	4	1	4	6	0
Giles, Ryder, INF, Fr.	.242	.385	.295	149	29	5	0	1	26	2
Hoover, Lane, OF, Fr.	.328	.448	.358	134	31	4	0	0	15	7
Jayne, Christian, OF, Fr.	.111	.333	.167	18	13	1	0	0	2	0
Jenkins, Chandler, OF, Sr.	.203	.288	.356	59	10	0	0	3	8	0
Kuchmaner, Jake, UT, So.	.000	.000	.000	3	0	0	0	0	0	0
Lloyd, Brady, INF, Sr.	.248	.343	.284	218	36	3	1	1	23	10
Norby, Connor, INF, Fr.	.194	.286	.290	31	5	0	0	1	6	0
Packard, Bryant, OF, Jr.	.358	.444	.550	218	56	19	1	7	40	5
Saylor, Garrett, UT, Fr.	.000	.000	.000	1	0	0	0	0	0	0
Smallwood, Christian, OF, Jr.	.133	.28	.200	15	2	1	0	0	1	0
Washer, Jake, C, Jr.	.301	.393	.597	206	40	10	0	17	55	2
Wilmer, Stephen, UT, Fr.	.000	.333	.000	2	0	0	0	0	0	0
Worrell, Bryson, UT, So.	.253	.327	.442	95	24	3	0	5	19	5

Pitcher, Year	W	L	ERA	G	GS	SV	IP	H	BB	SO
Agnos, Jake, Jr.	11	3	2.29	17	17	0	102	74	43	145
Barnes, Zach, Sr.	2	2	6.49	29	0	1	34.2	54	6	29
Benton, Trey, Jr.	4	0	4.01	13	3	0	24.2	29	9	28
Burleson, Alec, So.	6	2	3.28	24	9	5	60.1	56	26	68
Colmore, Cam, Jr.	1	0	4.91	26	0	0	25.2	34	13	24
Giles, Ryder, Fr.	1	0	3.75	20	1	1	24	22	5	20
Kuchmaner, Jake, So.	7	2	2.99	17	14	0	87.1	63	26	73
Lanier, Sam, Sr.	1	0	2.43	21	0	2	29.2	21	10	31
Odum, Evan, So.	0	0	7.43	11	1	0	13.1	20	4	12
Saylor, Garrett, Fr.	0	0	3.52	9	0	1	7.2	11	2	5
Smith, Tyler, Jr.	7	1	5.57	16	15	0	74.1	86	28	49
Spivey, Carter, Fr.	1	0	19.50	7	0	0	6	12	4	5
Voliva, Evan, Sr.	5	4	3.19	32	0	4	36.2	24	14	49
Williams, Gavin, So.	1	4	4.56	21	5	1	49.1	40	23	56
Wilmer, Stephen, Fr.	0	0	0.00	1	0	0	0.1	1	0	0

13. MISSISSIPPI

Coach: Mike Bianco. Record: 41-27

Player, Pos., Year	AVG	OBP	SLG	AB	R	2B	3B	HR	RBI	SB
Adams, Jacob, INF, Sr.	.222	.365	.257	144	24	5	0	0	19	4
Bench, Justin, INF, Fr.	.200	.368	.200	15	3	0	0	0	4	0
Cockrell, Chase, INF, Jr.	.214	.353	.274	84	11	5	0	0	11	0
Dillard, Thomas, OF, Jr.	.310	.450	.541	242	61	10	2	14	61	14
Elko, Tim, INF, So.	.212	.316	.364	66	10	2	1	2	9	1
Fitzsimmons, Michael, INF, R-Sr.	.154	.298	.154	39	4	0	0	0	1	0
Gindl, Carl, OF, So.	.235	.308	.265	34	12	1	0	0	6	2
Graham, Kevin, INF, Fr.	.250	.324	.507	152	28	7	1	10	34	0
Hall, Josh, OF, Fr.	.171	.310	.314	35	12	0	1	1	7	10
Johnson, Cooper, C, Jr.	.271	.371	.449	207	39	13	0	8	32	3
Keenan, Tyler, INF, So.	.285	.420	.506	253	39	7	2	15	66	2
Kessinger, Grae, SS, Jr.	.330	.430	.474	270	67	18	0	7	50	16
Loposer, Knox, C, Fr.	.213	.302	.319	47	9	2	0	1	9	0
Nabors, Hunter, C, Jr.	.000	.000	.000	1	0	0	0	0	0	0
Olenek, Ryan, OF, Sr.	.329	.404	.410	234	44	14	1	1	33	10
Servideo, Anthony, INF, So.	.287	.429	.388	209	62	10	1	3	26	24
Zabowski, Cole, 1B, Jr.	.318	.375	.517	261	50	16	0	12	51	7

Pitcher, Year	W	L	ERA	G	GS	SV	IP	H	BB	SO
Broadway, Taylor, Jr.	1	0	6.56	15	0	0	23.1	32	3	23
Caracci, Parker, R-Jr.	3	3	6.12	24	0	11	32.1	28	19	38
Cioffi, Maxwell, So.	2	2	4.45	16	1	0	30.1	31	9	38
Ethridge, Will, Jr.	7	7	3.39	17	16	0	93	87	24	73
Falk, Ray, R-Jr.	0	0	36.00	2	0	0	1	2	2	1
Fowler, Jordan, So.	1	0	6.87	9	4	0	18.1	16	12	18
Green, Connor, Sr.	3	2	4.81	19	0	0	24.1	27	11	24
Hill, Kaleb, Fr.	0	0	7.71	14	0	0	11.2	15	8	14
Hogland, Gunnar, Fr.	3	3	5.29	17	16	0	68	77	45	40
Holston, Greer, Jr.	0	0	0.00	1	0	0	1	0	1	1
Miller, Austin, Jr.	5	3	3.15	32	0	2	54.1	40	25	62
Myers, Tyler, Jr.	2	0	4.97	23	0	1	38	41	9	34
Nikhazy, Doug, Fr.	9	3	3.31	20	14	1	89.2	78	33	86
Olenek, Ryan, Sr.	0	0	1.50	7	0	2	6	3	3	6
Phillips, Zack, Jr.	4	3	4.99	19	13	0	61.1	62	25	52
Roth, Houston, Jr.	1	1	3.67	21	4	1	41.2	47	17	47
Smith, Pierce, Sr.	0	0	0.00	1	0	0	1	0	1	1

14. NORTH CAROLINA

Coach: Mike Fox. Record: 46-19

Player, Pos., Year	AVG	OBP	SLG	AB	R	2B	3B	HR	RBI	SB
Brantley, Cameran, OF, Fr.	.143	.222	.143	7	1	0	0	0	1	0
Busch, Michael, 1B, Jr.	.284	.436	.547	243	78	14	1	16	57	4
Casparius, Ben, INF, So.	.179	.261	.205	39	3	1	0	0	9	0
Caufield, Tom, INF, Fr.	.286	.286	.286	7	5	0	0	0	2	0
Enwiller, Dylan, OF/INF, Sr.	.256	.331	.444	133	34	6	2	5	29	11
Freeman, Ike, INF, Jr.	.293	.436	.427	232	45	9	2	6	52	2
Harris, Dylan, OF, Jr.	.268	.397	.423	246	62	15	1	7	29	5
Hesterlee, Jackson, OF, Sr.	.294	.393	.555	119	24	9	2	6	26	0
Holtzapple, Jake, INF, R-So.	.000	.250	.000	6	0	0	0	0	1	0
Illies, Brendan, C, Sr.	.182	.357	.545	11	1	1	0	1	1	0
Inclan, Clemente, INF, So.	.227	.394	.273	22	3	1	0	0	4	0
Matorano, Brandon, C, Jr.	.249	.364	.406	217	37	10	0	8	43	2
McGee, Ashton, OF/INF, Jr.	.278	.419	.440	216	48	12	1	7	46	2
Roberts, Caleb, C/OF, Fr.	.227	.374	.280	150	23	8	0	0	17	7
Sabato, Aaron, 1B, Fr.	.343	.453	.696	230	47	25	1	18	63	2
Schroeder, Wil, OF, Fr.	.143	.429	.143	14	3	0	0	0	1	0
Semper, Earl, OF, So.	.250	.400	.250	8	2	0	0	0	1	1
Serretti, Danny, INF, Fr.	.299	.373	.424	231	36	18	1	1	45	0
Tessar, Dallas, OF, R-Jr.	.213	.324	.311	61	14	3	0	0	7	4
Zarate, Angel, UT, R-Fr.	.100	.182	.100	10	6	0	0	0	0	4

Pitcher, Year	W	L	ERA	G	GS	SV	IP	H	BB	SO
Baum, Tyler, Jr.	7	3	3.87	17	16	0	93	94	25	99
Bergner, Austin, Jr.	6	1	4.94	16	16	0	82	91	31	77
Blendinger, Kyle, So.	0	0	4.00	9	0	0	9	5	4	8
Butler, Hansen, R-Sr.	5	0	3.86	21	0	1	21	18	18	31
Casparius, Ben, So.	0	0	4.41	12	0	1	16.1	17	7	14
Dalatri Gianluca, Jr.	1	1	2.25	6	6	0	32	29	8	35
Dotson, Josh, Fr.	3	0	4.50	25	2	0	34	32	18	27
Grogan, Andrew, Jr.	4	2	4.84	21	7	0	44.2	46	22	34
Lancellotti, Joey, So.	6	4	3.12	27	2	3	52	47	29	56
Love, Austin, R-Fr.	8	4	3.18	36	0	5	67.3	53	25	67
Nance, Bennett, Jr.	0	0	0.00	4	0	0	1	2	2	1
O'Brien Caden, Jr.	1	1	5.13	30	0	2	33.1	27	22	29
Ollio, Connor, Fr.	3	1	4.58	22	5	0	37.1	38	16	44
Pry, Nick, Fr.	0	0	18.00	5	0	0	4	6	0	7
Sandy, Will, Fr.	2	2	5.52	22	11	0	58.2	63	31	41

15. LOUISIANA STATE

Coach: Paul Mainieri. Record: 40-26

Player, Pos. Year	AVG	OBP	SLG	AB	R	2B	3B	HR	RBI	SB
Beloso, Cade, INF, Fr.	.279	.339	.429	219	30	3	0	10	52	1
Bianco, Drew, INF, Fr.	.176	.348	.353	68	16	3	0	3	14	1
Broussard, Brandt, INF, Sr.	.255	.324	.309	165	32	4	1	1	20	10
Cabrera, Daniel, OF, So.	.284	.359	.516	225	40	12	2	12	50	1
DiGiacoma, Giovanni, OF, Fr.	.275	.376	.333	138	31	3	1	1	15	6
Doughty, Braden, C, So.	.077	.250	.077	13	2	0	0	0	0	0
Dugas, Gavin, INF, Fr.	.186	.265	.233	43	1	2	0	0	6	1
Duplantis, Antoine, OF, Sr.	.324	.376	.505	281	63	9	3	12	68	6
Garza, Saul, C, So.	.303	.358	.476	145	20	10	0	5	27	0
Hughes, Hal, INF, So.	.174	.289	.188	149	20	2	0	0	11	2
Mathis, Brock, C, So.	.164	.291	.287	122	19	4	1	3	12	0
Reid, Chris, INF, Sr.	.255	.382	.339	165	31	11	0	1	33	1
Smith, Josh, SS, Jr.	.346	.433	.533	257	72	17	2	9	41	20
Watson, Zach, OF, Jr.	.308	.378	.468	237	52	17	0	7	42	11
Willis, CJ, UT, Fr.	.212	.311	.288	52	8	4	0	0	7	1

Pitcher, Year	W	L	ERA	G	GS	SV	IP	H	BB	SO
Beck, Matthew, Jr.	3	0	2.05	27	0	0	44	30	25	39
Costello, Chase, Fr.	0	1	8.84	14	1	0	19.1	26	12	10
Fontenot, Devin, So.	5	4	3.71	28	3	7	51	33	25	54
George, Aaron, Jr.	3	1	6.49	21	0	0	26.1	31	19	31
Gunter, Rye, Fr.	0	0	6.75	6	0	0	6.2	7	7	6
Henry, Cole, Fr.	4	2	3.39	14	11	0	58.1	50	18	72
Hess, Zack, Jr.	4	5	4.71	19	10	2	70.2	80	35	82
Hill, Jaden, Fr.	1	0	1.80	2	2	0	10	6	3	11
Hilliard, Ma'Khail, So.	4	5	5.32	21	6	0	44	43	16	57
Marceaux, Landon, Fr.	5	2	4.66	15	14	0	58	68	20	43
Moffitt, Clay, Sr.	2	0	3.26	12	3	0	19.1	12	7	16
Peterson, Todd, Jr.	5	2	3.86	29	1	3	49	43	18	44

Pitcher, Year	W	L	ERA	G	GS	SV	IP	H	BB	SO
Ripoll, Will, Fr.	0	0	6.48	10	0	0	16.2	18	10	18
Threadgill, Riggs, Fr.	0	0	7.24	11	0	0	13.2	17	10	12
Vietmeier, Trent, So.	3	1	5.24	25	0	1	34.1	36	11	34
Walker, Eric, Jr.	5	4	5.47	18	15	0	72.1	67	32	56

16. GEORGIA

Coach: Scott Stricklin. **Record:** 46-17

Player, Pos., Year	AVG	OBP	SLG	AB	R	2B	3B	HR	RBI	SB
Biggar, Austin, C, Jr.	.255	.397	.451	51	6	4	0	2	9	1
Bradley, Tucker, OF, Jr.	.222	.300	.444	9	1	0	1	0	3	0
Cable, John , C/INF, Jr.	.314	.407	.524	185	30	15	0	8	47	1
Jernigan, Randon, OF, Fr.	.248	.338	.301	113	24	3	0	1	12	11
King, Riley, INF, R-So.	.295	.403	.440	241	58	9	1	8	43	5
Marshall, Shane, C, Fr.	.258	.432	.371	62	12	2	1	1	10	0
Maxwell, Tucker, OF, Jr.	.251	.387	.525	183	45	9	1	13	39	21
Meadows, Mason, C, R-So.	.180	.322	.295	122	23	3	1	3	15	1
Minter, Steven, INF, R-Fr.	.000	.333	.000	4	1	0	0	0	0	0
Moody, Logan, UT, R-Jr.	.000	.000	.000	1	0	0	0	0	0	0
Pasqua, Darryn, UT, So.	.000	.000	.000	1	0	0	0	0	0	0
Rogers, Chaney, OF, R-Fr.	.256	.379	.338	133	25	8	0	1	13	0
Schunk, Aaron, UT, Jr.	.339	.373	.604	230	49	12	2	15	58	3
Shepherd, Cam, SS, Jr.	.231	.333	.386	251	46	13	1	8	33	7
Smith, C.J., UT, So.	.111	.273	.222	27	5	0	0	1	3	0
Sullivan, Patrick, INF, R-Jr.	.263	.350	.360	175	16	8	0	3	24	0
Talley, LJ, INF, Sr.	.332	.435	.489	235	51	11	1	8	41	5
Tate, Cole, INF, So.	.192	.300	.231	26	3	1	0	0	5	0
Tate, Connor, INF, R-Fr.	.270	.304	.459	74	6	5	0	3	19	0
Williams, James, UT, R-So.	.000	.000	.000	1	0	0	0	0	0	0

Pitcher, Year	W	L	ERA	G	GS	SV	IP	H	BB	SO
Elliott, Tim, Jr.	7	3	2.38	15	14	0	75.2	42	24	72
Glover, Justin, Jr.	1	0	2.79	25	0	0	29	15	15	28
Goodman, Adam, Sr.	1	1	5.79	15	0	0	14	15	10	21
Gowen, Jack, Fr.	0	1	9.35	9	0	0	8.2	7	10	10
Hancock, Emerson, So.	8	3	1.99	14	14	0	90.1	58	18	97
Kristofak, Zac, Jr.	5	0	3.80	24	0	6	47.1	45	15	63
Locey, Tony, Jr.	11	2	2.53	16	15	0	89	51	45	97
Moody, Logan, R-Jr.	1	0	4.07	11	3	0	24.1	15	14	33
Pasqua, Darryn, So.	1	0	1.20	9	0	0	15	13	4	11
Proctor, Will, Jr.	3	0	4.35	3	2	0	10.1	10	5	15
Ryder, Christian, Jr.	0	0	10.80	5	0	0	3.1	2	2	3
Schunk, Aaron , Jr.	1	2	2.49	17	0	12	21.2	15	7	18
Smith, C.J., So.	3	3	4.30	11	9	0	46	38	20	38
Webb, Ryan, So.	1	0	3.75	16	0	1	24	19	11	27
Wilcox, Cole, Fr.	3	2	4.07	19	6	0	59.2	46	38	64
Williams, James, R-So.	0	0	6.35	5	0	0	5.2	10	4	4

17. GEORGIA TECH

Coach: Danny Hall. **Record:** 43-19

Player, Pos., Year	AVG	OBP	SLG	AB	R	2B	3B	HR	RBI	SB
Benson, Charlie, INF, Fr.	.222	.533	.222	9	2	0	0	0	1	1
Carpenter, Micah, UT, Sr.	.500	.500	.500	2	0	0	0	0	0	0
English, Tristin, UT, R-Jr.	.346	.427	.710	214	58	20	2	18	71	0
Guldberg, Michael, INF, So.	.355	.441	.418	220	61	7	2	1	32	7
Hall, Colin, OF, R-Jr.	.307	.363	.432	241	44	18	0	4	41	4
McCann, Kyle, C, Jr.	.299	.468	.674	221	58	12	1	23	70	0
Miller, Ryan, INF, Fr.	.000	.000	.000	4	0	0	0	0	0	0
Murray, Chase, OF, Jr.	.235	.293	.353	85	15	2	1	2	7	3
Neuber, Cole, OF, So.	.077	.294	.308	13	1	0	0	1	4	0
Radcliff, Baron, OF, So.	.257	.403	.503	183	40	9	0	12	44	6
Rigby, Paxton, INF, Jr.	.111	.100	.111	9	0	0	0	0	1	0
Serratos, Oscar, INF, So.	.246	.315	.338	130	17	4	1	2	20	4
Taylor, Jamie, C, So.	.167	.231	.333	12	1	0	1	0	3	0
Turley, Cameron , C, So.	.000	.364	.000	6	2	0	0	1	0	0
Waddell, Luke, SS, So.	.322	.436	.416	233	57	12	2	2	34	7
Webb, Jackson, INF, R-Jr.	.312	.437	.408	125	26	5	2	1	19	13
Willhite, Austin, INF, Jr.	.266	.369	.349	218	43	11	2	1	32	12
Willhite, Nick, OF, Jr.	.311	.427	.383	209	39	7	1	2	41	8
Zinnershine, Billy, INF, Fr.	.000	.500	.000	1	0	0	0	0	0	0

Pitcher, Year	W	L	ERA	G	GS	SV	IP	H	BB	SO
Barlow, Walker, Fr.	0	0	6.23	7	0	0	4.1	4	1	1
Bartnicki, Luke, Fr.	2	2	6.40	29	0	1	32.1	46	21	32
Brace, Jake, So.	0	0	7.11	5	1	0	6.1	10	3	3
Carpenter, Micah, Sr.	1	2	5.47	19	0	1	24.2	32	12	36
Chapman, Hugh, So.	2	0	4.15	12	0	0	13	12	2	10
Curry, Xzavion, Jr.	4	2	4.08	11	10	0	57.1	58	16	66
English, Tristin, R-Jr.	3	0	3.70	15	0	6	24.1	19	7	20
Gibson, Keyton, Sr.	1	2	6.21	20	3	1	29	23	21	33
Hughes, Jonathan, R-Jr.	9	2	5.09	26	0	0	53	61	23	48
Hurter, Brant, So.	2	2	2.42	10	9	0	48.1	37	14	58
Lee, Jake, Sr.	0	1	5.25	19	0	0	12	10	10	17
Mannelly, Joseph, So.	0	0	0.00	3	0	0	2.2	2	0	2
Roedig, Cort, Fr.	2	2	4.88	15	10	0	48	36	24	47
Shirah, Will, So.	0	0	9.53	7	0	0	5.2	8	6	2
Thomas, Connor, Jr.	9	2	3.11	16	16	0	113	118	19	103
Willingham, Amos, Jr.	8	2	5.19	18	13	0	69.1	78	19	42
Winborne, Robert, Sr.	0	0	4.63	10	0	0	11.2	12	6	7

18. DUKE

Coach: Chris Pollard. **Record:** 35-27

Player, Pos., Year	AVG	OBP	SLG	AB	R	2B	3B	HR	RBI	SB
Cheek, Chase, OF, Jr.	.293	.380	.403	181	35	11	3	1	24	20
Crabtree, Chris, INF, So.	.263	.356	.394	198	30	15	1	3	32	7
Gallagher, Kyle, OF, Sr.	.258	.347	.435	209	38	9	2	8	31	1
Hoyle, Wil, INF, So.	.097	.222	.097	31	5	0	0	0	1	0
Loperfido, Joey, INF, So.	.261	.361	.389	157	29	6	1	4	18	8
Lux, Damon, OF, Fr.	.000	.200	.000	8	0	0	0	0	0	0
Mann, Steve, OF, So.	.077	.143	.077	13	1	0	0	0	0	0
Maxwell, Rudy, C, Fr.	.257	.353	.439	148	27	9	3	4	21	4
Mervis, Matt, UT, Jr.	.274	.357	.421	190	33	8	1	6	31	2
Murray, Ethan, SS, Fr.	.305	.391	.445	200	48	9	2	5	40	6
Nichols, Erikson, INF, Jr.	.255	.325	.318	239	25	9	0	2	38	2
Rothenburg, Michael, C, So.	.269	.390	.481	212	44	10	1	11	52	3
Schreck, RJ, OF. Fr.	.182	.284	.260	77	4	4	1	0	5	0
Stinebiser, Matt, C, Fr.	.267	.267	.333	15	0	1	0	0	2	0
Taylor, Kennie, OF, Sr.	.317	.384	.498	259	51	19	5	6	39	10
Therien, Aaron, C, Sr.	.000	.000	.000	2	0	0	0	0	0	0
Wardwell, Tyler, INF, So.	.100	.419	.150	20	7	1	0	0	0	1

Pitcher, Year	W	L	ERA	G	GS	SV	IP	H	BB	SO
Beasley, Aaron, Fr.	0	0	5.68	10	0	9	12.2	18	10	13
Carey, Jack, Fr.	4	1	5.14	23	0	1	42	46	20	32
Chillari, Bill, Jr.	2	4	5.35	19	16	0	67.1	75	30	48
Davis, Hunter, Sr.	1	2	1.59	20	0	2	39.2	24	25	42
Dockman, Matt, So.	6	1	3.80	25	0	2	42.2	44	9	39
Girard, Thomas, So.	1	5	2.33	28	0	9	46.1	28	18	61
Gross, Ben, Gr.	8	4	4.40	20	13	0	75.2	63	35	76
Herrick, Eli, Jr.	2	2	4.50	26	0	1	38	36	17	49
Jarvis, Bryce, So.	5	2	3.81	19	11	1	75.2	70	37	94
Laskey, Adam, Jr.	1	0	6.00	6	3	0	12	13	13	10
Mervis, Matt, Jr.	1	0	2.16	7	0	0	8.1	13	5	8
Nifong, Josh, So.	0	0	27.00	1	0	0	0.2	3	1	1
Pesto, Al, Sr.	0	0	0.00	4	0	0	6	5	2	7
Salley, Kyle, Fr.	1	0	5.11	11	0	0	12.1	14	10	14
Stinson, Cooper, Fr.	1	4	5.47	18	14	1	54.1	58	43	78
Stinson, Graeme, Jr.	2	2	4.58	5	5	0	19.2	12	9	26

19. OREGON STATE

Coach: Pat Bailey. **Record:** 36-20-1

Player, Pos., Year	AVG	OBP	SLG	AB	R	2B	3B	HR	RBI	SB
Armstrong, Andy, INF, Jr.	.248	.304	.328	125	10	5	1	1	13	3
Casey, Joe, OF, R-So.	.254	.347	.400	130	26	8	1	3	13	4
Claunch, Troy, C, So.	.264	.333	.347	72	7	3	0	1	9	1
Dukart, Jake, INF, Fr.	.210	.320	.247	81	6	3	0	0	12	0
Fuchs, Greg, OF, Fr.	.167	.306	.200	30	1	1	0	0	4	0
Gretler, Matthew, INF, Fr.	.269	.328	.365	52	7	2	0	1	9	1
Harvey, Jake, INF, Fr.	.255	.354	.347	98	23	4	1	1	8	4
Jones, Preston, OF, Jr.	.228	.338	.325	123	23	6	0	2	16	7
Malone, Tyler, INF, Jr.	.213	.383	.287	150	20	8	0	1	19	1
McGarry, Alex, OF, R-So.	.293	.401	.478	157	36	5	0	8	29	3
McMahan, Kyler, INF, So.	.245	.303	.350	143	24	10	1	1	15	4
Meckler, Wade, INF, Fr.	.100	.400	.100	10	5	0	0	0	2	1

Player	AVG	OBP	SLG	AB	R	2B	3B	HR	RBI	SB
Mendazona, George, INF, R-So.	.217	.316	.287	115	11	5	0	1	12	0
Ober, Ryan, INF, So.	.266	.371	.392	143	21	9	0	3	22	1
Philip, Beau, SS, Jr.	.311	.369	.486	177	32	14	1	5	31	6
Rutschman, Adley, C, Jr.	.411	.575	.751	185	57	10	1	17	58	0
Taylor, Zak, C, Sr.	.153	.200	.208	72	6	1	0	1	9	0
Willy, Elliot, OF, R-So.	.174	.240	.261	23	3	2	0	0	4	0
Zalesky, Zack, C, R-So.	.207	.281	.345	29	3	1	0	1	7	1

Pitcher, Year	W	L	ERA	G	GS	SV	IP	H	BB	SO
Abel, Kevin, So.	2	0	3.86	3	3	0	16.1	8	9	25
Burns, Nathan, So.	2	0	3.32	10	1	0	21.2	16	15	19
Chamberlain, Christian, So.	3	4	3.83	23	3	2	42.1	35	19	57
Eisert, Brandon, Jr.	8	2	2.03	14	7	0	62	59	13	74
Fehmel, Bryce, Sr.	7	3	3.53	16	16	0	99.1	88	20	71
Gambrell, Grant, Jr.	5	3	2.83	13	13	0	70	59	25	80
Mulholland, Jake, Jr.	3	3	1.93	28	0	8	46.2	40	11	41
Mundt, Joey, Fr.	0	0	1.93	8	0	1	14	8	8	15
Pearce, Dylan, Fr.	3	2	3.34	22	4	0	56.2	45	27	51
Pfennigs, Jake, Sr.	1	1	4.55	17	3	1	31.2	30	16	22
Tweedt, Sam, R-Sr.	1	2	4.03	9	7	0	29	35	11	24
Verburg, Mitchell, R-So.	1	0	1.40	16	0	2	25.2	15	7	38
Walling, Andrew, Fr.	0	0	0.00	7	0	0	6.2	2	7	3

20. WEST VIRGINIA
Coach: Randy Mazey. Record: 38-22

Player, Pos., Year	AVG	OBP	SLG	AB	R	2B	3B	HR	RBI	SB
Brophy, Kevin, INF, Jr.	.204	.267	.401	167	23	6	0	9	35	1
Davis, Austin , INF/OF, Jr.	.220	.313	.237	59	14	1	0	0	3	12
Doanes, Tyler, INF, So.	.316	.398	.500	228	40	21	3	5	32	20
Dull, Phillip, UT, Fr.	.245	.355	.283	53	8	2	0	0	5	2
Gonzalez, Ivan, C/INF, Jr.	.294	.397	.407	214	39	15	0	3	31	5
Hamilton, Connor, C, So.	.063	.211	.063	16	0	0	0	0	0	0
Hill, Darius, OF, Sr.	.315	.376	.521	238	47	25	3	6	41	4
Hudson, Tristen, UT, So.	.125	.178	.150	40	5	1	0	0	5	3
Inman, Marques, INF, R-Jr.	.262	.338	.451	206	36	10	1	9	41	1
Lake, TJ, OF/INF, R-Jr.	.259	.319	.381	147	21	9	0	3	21	3
Lowe, Trey, OF, So.	.000	.000	.000	2	0	0	0	0	0	0
McIntosh, Paul, C, So.	.277	.359	.497	191	28	10	1	10	34	1
Tucker, Tevin, INF, Fr.	.199	.365	.282	156	37	10	0	1	21	19
White, Brandon, UT, Jr.	.272	.387	.308	195	37	5	1	0	26	26
Zitel, Andrew, INF, Sr.	.188	.269	.377	69	11	4	0	3	11	1

Pitcher, Year	W	L	ERA	G	GS	SV	IP	H	BB	SO
Bergert, Ryan, Fr.	2	0	1.85	17	2	0	34	23	8	38
Dull, Phillip, Fr.	0	0	0.00	4	0	0	2	0	4	1
Helverson, Brock, Fr.	0	1	6.75	12	1	0	16	17	11	14
Hudson, Tristen, So.	1	0	5.23	15	0	0	10.1	7	8	14
Jeffrey, Madison, Fr.	0	1	6.55	12	0	0	11	4	12	12
Kessler, Sam, Jr.	4	3	3.19	24	0	8	36.2	30	11	46
Kurtzhals, Gabe, Fr.	2	0	3.38	13	0	0	16	13	6	7
Lowery, Beau, Fr.	0	2	4.61	13	0	2	13.2	15	11	14
Manoah, Alek, Jr.	9	4	2.08	16	16	0	108.1	71	27	144
Meadows, Dillon, R-Jr.	0	0	5.63	17	0	2	24	17	11	30
Ottinger, Zach, Fr.	2	0	4.50	14	0	1	20	18	6	19
Reid, Zach, R-Sr.	2	0	2.40	19	0	1	15	19	8	16
Snyder, Nick, Jr.	9	1	2.65	16	13	0	68	42	34	103
Strowd, Kade, Jr.	5	6	4.73	16	15	1	83.2	67	59	87
Wolf, Jackson, So.	2	4	5.17	15	13	0	69.2	79	31	50

21. FRESNO STATE
Coach: Mike Batesole. Record: 40-16-1

Player, Pos., Year	AVG	OBP	SLG	AB	R	2B	3B	HR	RBI	SB
Andrews, EJ, OF, Fr.	.290	.402	.362	69	13	5	0	0	2	1
Arruda, JT, INF, R-So.	.338	.448	.531	213	56	15	1	8	45	8
Ashford, Zach, OF, Sr.	.381	.488	.526	215	67	11	4	4	21	10
Bins, Carter, C, Jr.	.280	.385	.427	218	58	14	0	6	28	7
Chastain, Auston, OF, Jr.	.205	.290	.229	83	12	2	0	0	6	4
Dempsey, Nolan, INF, Sr.	.332	.387	.539	217	41	17	2	8	57	4
Higgins, Ryan, INF, Fr.	.320	.393	.460	50	7	4	0	1	9	1
Jamison, Jeff, INF, Jr.	.227	.292	.303	66	12	3	1	0	7	3
Johnson, Dylan, OF, R-Fr.	.231	.286	.231	26	2	0	0	0	1	0
Nogales, Emilio, INF, So.	.290	.413	.428	138	16	11	1	2	27	0
Ottino, Matt, INF, Fr.	.360	.429	.480	25	6	1	1	0	7	1

Player	AVG	OBP	SLG	AB	R	2B	3B	HR	RBI	SB
Pena, Eddie, INF, Sr.	.200	.273	.200	10	2	0	0	0	1	0
Presno, Zach, C, So.	.221	.328	.409	208	32	9	0	10	45	0
Tatum, McCarthy, UT, R-Sr.	.356	.397	.606	236	54	16	2	13	77	5
Thimjon, Nate, OF, So.	.267	.310	.379	161	21	7	1	3	27	4
Tomczak, Miles, OF, So.	.167	.250	.259	54	8	2	0	1	4	1

Pitcher, Year	W	L	ERA	G	GS	SV	IP	H	BB	SO
Arias, Jaime, So.	1	3	3.28	28	2	12	46.2	40	14	59
Cardinal, Nik, Jr.	2	0	4.29	16	2	0	21	22	5	25
Carvajal, Oscar, R-So.	4	0	2.68	28	0	2	40.1	37	10	48
Hill, Jamison, So.	2	2	4.97	19	4	1	38	38	24	39
Jensen, Ryan, Jr.	12	1	2.88	16	15	1	100	82	27	107
Jones, Tiegen, R-So.	1	1	2.84	18	0	0	12.2	14	8	7
Larson, Kevin, R-Fr.	2	1	4.06	28	0	0	31	29	24	43
Mitchell, Nikoh, So.	3	4	5.23	19	15	0	62	75	37	51
Moore, Davis, Jr.	10	1	3.91	16	15	0	89.2	85	34	91
Peters, Robbie, R-Fr.	0	0	5.51	19	0	0	16.1	20	5	12
Pruhsmeier, Kyle, Fr.	1	1	6.35	9	1	0	11.1	8	6	14
Sullivan, Ryan, R-Jr.	2	2	3.27	22	0	1	22	21	11	17
Tatum, McCarthy, R-Sr.	0	0	2.53	6	3	0	10.2	11	4	4

22. MIAMI
Coach: Gino DiMare. Record: 41-20

PLAYER, POS., YEAR	AVG	OBP	SLG	AB	R	2B	3B	HR	RBI	SB
Amditis, Michael, C, R-So.	.273	.375	.436	165	28	6	0	7	24	1
Cloonan, Dylan, UT, So.	.244	.271	.356	45	5	2	0	1	4	1
Crosbie, Chad, OF, Jr.	.200	.296	.243	70	11	0	0	1	7	4
Del Castillo, Adrian, C, Fr.	.331	.418	.576	236	58	22	0	12	72	3
Escala, Willy, INF, So.	.257	.350	.357	70	18	5	1	0	8	4
Gates, JP, UT, Fr.	.340	.371	.510	147	21	9	2	4	31	0
Gil, Raymond, 3B, So.	.318	.396	.565	214	39	14	0	13	44	1
Jenkins, Tony, OF, So.	.268	.392	.330	97	28	4	1	0	12	9
Lala, Jordan, OF, Fr.	.276	.446	.386	210	68	9	1	4	18	28
Moore, Chet, OF, Fr.	.185	.258	.185	27	2	0	0	0	3	0
Paige, Tyler, INF, So.	.111	.200	.222	9	3	1	0	0	1	0
Pollack, Austin, OF, Fr.	.167	.167	.167	6	0	0	0	0	0	1
Quinones, Isaac, C, So.	.200	.333	.400	20	4	1	0	1	4	0
Rivera, Gabe, OF, So.	.290	.374	.590	100	29	5	2	7	31	6
Toral, Alex, 1B, So.	.293	.400	.656	215	47	6	0	24	67	1
Tuero, Luis, INF, Fr.	.333	.400	.414	36	6	3	0	0	2	1
Vilar, Anthony, INF, Fr.	.291	.416	.414	237	49	12	1	5	39	0
Zamora, Freddie, SS, So.	.296	.393	.447	199	43	12	0	6	46	13

Pitcher, Year	W	L	ERA	G	GS	SV	IP	H	BB	SO
Cecconi, Slade, Fr.	5	4	4.16	17	13	0	80	79	18	89
Cook, Jeremy, So.	0	1	5.11	15	0	0	12.1	12	9	6
Federman, Daniel, So.	3	5	3.51	35	0	7	48.2	45	19	60
Gates, JP, Fr.	1	1	5.82	20	1	0	17	19	18	18
Keysor, Tyler, Jr.	6	1	3.78	22	5	0	47.2	52	16	38
Mantilla, Bailey, Fr.	0	0	8.79	14	0	0	14.1	22	9	15
Maury, Albert, R-So.	1	0	5.87	20	1	0	23	22	15	21
McKendry, Evan, Jr.	7	2	4.41	13	13	0	67.1	70	19	72
McMahon, Chris, So.	3	2	3.73	12	12	0	60.1	50	23	67
Mixon, Mark, Jr.	3	1	2.33	26	0	0	27	26	11	28
Ruiz, Alex, R-Fr.	0	0	1.04	8	0	0	8.2	6	3	6
Van Belle, Brian, R-Jr.	10	2	3.30	16	16	0	95.1	91	24	84
Veliz, Greg, Jr.	2	1	2.55	30	0	9	42.1	30	21	69

23. TEXAS A&M
Coach: Rob Childress. Record: 39-23-1

Player, Pos., Year	AVG	OBP	SLG	AB	R	2B	3B	HR	RBI	SB
Ashy, Brandon, C, Jr.	.000	.000	.000	6	0	0	0	0	0	0
Blake, Cam, OF, Jr.	.260	.324	.349	169	23	6	3	1	26	7
Blaum, Bryce, INF, Jr.	.292	.394	.464	233	53	9	2	9	32	17
Brown, Brett, INF/OF, Jr.	.077	.143	.077	13	1	0	0	0	1	0
Coleman, Hunter, C, Jr.	.244	.390	.537	82	18	7	1	5	18	1
Coleman, Ty, INF, Fr.	.241	.301	.340	191	28	4	0	5	33	1
Condel, Ty, OF, Jr.	.243	.284	.257	70	12	1	0	0	4	0
Corbett, Mason, INF, So.	.250	.250	.500	4	4	1	0	0	0	0
DeLoach, Zach, OF, So.	.200	.318	.294	160	27	4	1	3	16	1
Ducoff, Jonathan, OF, Sr.	.229	.262	.356	118	20	6	0	3	27	3
Foster, Logan, OF, Jr.	.263	.329	.390	213	36	10	1	5	37	3
Frizzell, Will, INF, So.	.215	.305	.300	130	17	5	0	2	18	0

Player, Pos., Year	AVG	OBP	SLG	AB	R	2B	3B	HR	RBI	SB
Hoehner, Mikey, C, Jr.	.292	.381	.380	216	35	10	0	3	30	2
Menefee, Joseph, UT, Fr.	.167	.231	.250	12	1	1	0	0	3	0
Morris, Chandler, UT, Sr.	.156	.333	.156	45	5	0	0	0	5	2
Shewmake Braden, SS, Jr.	.313	.374	.474	249	45	14	4	6	47	9
Walters, Aaron, C, So.	.197	.296	.211	71	7	1	0	0	7	0
Watson, Hunter, INF, Fr.	.158	.238	.184	38	7	1	0	0	3	0
Wingate, Allonte, OF, Sr.	.189	.246	.189	53	7	0	0	0	4	0

Pitcher, Year	W	L	ERA	G	GS	SV	IP	H	BB	SO
Birdsell, Brandon, Fr.	1	0	6.43	9	0	0	7	6	6	8
Childress, Jonathan, Fr.	0	1	2.13	3	3	0	12.2	7	1	8
Cole, Mason, R-So.	0	0	5.40	6	0	0	8.1	10	4	9
Doxakis, John, Jr.	7	4	2.06	16	16	0	104.2	80	26	115
Geisler, Colson, Fr.	0	0	0.00	2	0	0	0.2	1	1	1
Jozwiak, Chandler, So.	4	5	4.76	26	5	1	58.2	57	25	80
Kalich, Kasey, So.	3	1	3.18	28	0	12	34	32	13	51
Lacy, Asa, So.	8	4	2.13	15	15	0	88.2	49	43	130
Menefee, Joseph, Fr.	3	2	3.75	26	1	0	36	28	14	51
Miller, Bryce, So.	4	2	3.68	33	0	1	43.3	38	18	57
Nelson, Jake, Jr.	0	0	0.87	10	0	0	10.1	7	1	12
Richardson, Kyle, Jr.	0	0	5.19	11	0	0	8.2	10	5	10
Roa, Christian, So.	3	2	3.56	17	10	1	48	48	11	46
Saenz, Dustin, So.	2	1	4.85	15	5	1	29.2	36	14	17
Weber, Chris, Fr.	4	1	3.18	23	8	0	65	59	20	78

24. UC SANTA BARBARA
Coach: Andrew Checketts. **Record:** 45-11

Player, Pos., Year	AVG	OBP	SLG	AB	R	2B	3B	HR	RBI	SB
Castanon, Marcos, INF, So.	.324	.358	.459	74	14	4	0	2	11	3
Eng, Mason, C, Fr.	.333	.500	.333	3	0	0	0	0	0	0
Fariss, Ben, UT, So.	.000	.222	.000	7	1	0	0	0	1	0
Greene, Jarred, UT, Fr.	.111	.273	.444	9	2	0	0	1	1	0
Jew, Tommy, OF, Jr.	.283	.352	.530	219	49	9	6	11	40	20
Johnson, Kyle, INF, R-Fr.	.223	.284	.355	121	13	3	2	3	20	1
Kirtley, Christian, INF, Fr.	.244	.349	.300	90	19	5	0	0	16	0
Marquez, Mason, INF, Fr.	.000	.200	.000	4	5	0	0	0	0	0
Martinez, Andrew, INF, So.	.285	.402	.495	200	47	14	2	8	47	7
Martinez, Chazz, UT, Fr.	.200	.333	.400	5	0	1	0	0	0	0
McAdoo, Michael, OF, Sr.	.333	.333	.333	9	1	0	0	0	2	1
Mitchell, Tevin, INF, Sr.	.277	.373	.451	184	49	11	3	5	37	20
Mueller, Cole, INF, So.	.246	.342	.393	61	9	6	0	1	12	0
O'Connor, McClain, INF, Jr.	.325	.393	.503	151	25	12	3	3	17	13
Rowan, Thomas, C, Sr.	.327	.407	.593	214	43	14	2	13	46	5
Smith, Armani, OF, Jr.	.323	.393	.631	217	53	18	8	11	45	3
Troye, Christopher, UT, So.	.000	.000	.000	1	0	0	0	0	0	0
Willow, Jason, UT, So.	.267	.378	.392	120	17	6	3	1	20	5
Yang, Eric, C, Jr.	.368	.479	.545	209	28	16	0	7	45	6

Pitcher, Year	W	L	ERA	G	GS	SV	IP	H	BB	SO
Arellano, Jr., Jorge, R-Fr.	4	1	2.30	9	7	0	31.1	26	16	21
Barry, Shea, Jr.	0	2	6.84	18	0	0	26.1	23	12	32
Beer, Trevor, Fr.	0	0	0.00	9	0	0	3	4	1	3
Boone, Rodney, Fr.	8	0	2.78	14	14	0	81	58	29	80
Brecht, Ben, Jr.	10	2	4.10	16	16	0	90	90	18	101
Candau, Josh, So.	0	0	6.75	6	0	0	4	9	2	4
Chandler, Kevin, Sr.	0	1	5.65	10	0	0	14.1	13	9	14
Dand, Conner, Jr.	3	0	2.76	13	0	0	16.1	10	7	12
Dashwood, Jack, So.	9	2	2.48	15	15	0	90.2	79	17	93
Lincoln, Chris, Jr.	4	1	3.57	24	0	13	35.1	32	10	40
McGreevy, Michael, Fr.	5	1	1.94	29	0	6	60.1	52	13	53
Newton, Grant, Fr.	0	0	0.00	1	0	0	1	1	1	1
Patterson, Alex, Sr.	0	0	3.43	15	0	0	21	13	10	23
Steigerwald, Liam, Jr.	0	0	4.50	6	0	0	6	7	1	4
Troye, Chris, So.	2	1	4.42	13	4	0	18.1	10	17	26

25. CREIGHTON
Coach: Ed Servais. **Record:** 41-13

Player, Pos., Year	AVG	OBP	SLG	AB	R	2B	3B	HR	RBI	SB
Allbery, Jason, OF, Jr.	.216	.345	.330	97	18	8	0	1	11	6
Berney, Jackson, UT, R-Fr.	.333	.333	.333	3	0	0	0	0	1	0
Collins, Isaac, INF, Jr.	.293	.366	.479	242	49	13	7	6	34	13
Gilbert, Garrett, C, So.	.200	.318	.400	55	11	2	0	3	11	0
Hanafan, Will, OF, So.	.279	.364	.312	154	20	2	0	1	20	4
Holton, Jake, INF, Jr.	.386	.488	.681	207	55	15	2	14	58	1
Hovey, Jordan, INF, So.	.267	.388	.455	191	33	11	2	7	33	11
Meggs, Andrew, INF, R-Fr.	.241	.324	.241	29	5	0	0	0	3	1
Robertson, Will, OF, Jr.	.311	.408	.599	222	53	19	0	15	67	1
Spry, Evan, INF, So.	.190	.227	.238	21	1	1	0	0	2	0
Strunc, Jack, INF, Jr.	.294	.347	.440	218	24	20	0	4	34	4
Upton ,Parker, INF, Jr.	.324	.483	.603	179	65	14	3	10	34	9
Vilches, David, C, So.	.227	.366	.429	119	25	7	1	5	17	1
Wegner, Jared, OF, Fr.	.264	.369	.336	125	20	6	0	1	20	7

Pitcher, Year	W	L	ERA	G	GS	SV	IP	H	BB	SO
Bergstorm, Paul, Fr.	1	0	5.23	15	0	0	10.1	15	7	5
Boyer, Mitchell, Jr.	0	1	9.00	18	0	0	14	16	13	10
Connolly, Ryan, Jr.	0	1	7.02	22	0	0	16.2	15	14	26
Dotzler, Ben, Jr.	1	0	3.10	18	2	0	40.2	36	15	29
Hovey, Jordan, Sr.	0	0	13.50	2	0	0	1.1	4	0	1
Hull, Denson, Sr.	5	4	5.75	19	18	0	72	65	39	58
Johnson, Evan, Sr.	9	2	3.26	17	14	0	77.1	55	42	74
Kametas, Bobby, Sr.	3	0	2.36	21	0	9	26.2	10	16	28
Ragan, Mitch , Sr.	8	3	4.17	17	17	0	99.1	96	18	95
Sakowski, John, Jr.	7	1	2.83	29	0	3	47.2	28	12	44
Shoemaker, Nate, Fr.	0	0	10.80	4	0	0	1.2	0	5	1
Smith, Jonah, Jr.	4	0	4.89	24	0	1	35	38	15	30
Swafford, Thomas, Fr.	0	0	99.00	2	0	0	0	2	0	0
Tebrake, Dylan, Fr.	2	1	3.90	15	3	1	30	26	6	16
Wick, Justin, Jr.	0	0	9.00	9	0	0	3	3	3	5
Windham, Ryan, Fr.	1	0	7.56	10	0	0	8.1	12	9	4

CONFERENCE STANDINGS & LEADERS

NCAA regional teams in bold. Conference category leaders in bold.
*Team won conference's automatic regional bid. #Category leader who did not qualify for batting or pitching title.

AMERICA EAST CONFERENCE

	Conference		Overall	
	W	L	W	L
*Stony Brook	15	9	31	23
Albany	14	9	28	23
Binghamton	12	9	26	24
Massachusetts-Lowell	12	12	20	36
Maine	11	12	15	34
Hartford	11	13	23	34
Maryland-Baltimore County	6	17	22	31

ALL-CONFERENCE TEAM: C: Ciaran Devenney, Jr., UMass-Lowell. **1B:** Chris Hamilton, Jr., Stony Brook. **2B:** Alex Baratta, Jr. Binghamton. **3B:** Zach Ardito, Jr. Hartford. **SS:** Nick Grande, Jr., Stony Brook. **OF:** Michael Wilson, Jr., Stony Brook; Hernen Sardinas, Jr., Maine; Shane Marshall, So., Binghamton. **DH:** Danny Casals, Sr., Maine. **UTL:** Nick Kondo, Jr., Albany. **SP:** Dominic Savino, Sr., Albany; Ben Anderson, Jr., Binghamton; Nick Rand, Sr., UMass-Lowell; Cody Laweryson, Jr., Maine. **RP:** Joe Kruszka, Jr., Albany. **Player of the Year:** Nick Grande, Stony Brook. **Pitcher of the Year:** Ben Anderson, Binghamton. **Coach of the Year:** Jon Mueller, Albany. **Rookie of the Year:** Thomas Babalis, Binghamton.

INDIVIDUAL BATTING LEADERS
(Minimum 140 at-bats)

	AVG	OBP	SLG	AB	2B	3B	HR	RBI	SB
Shane Marshall, Binghamton	.376	.423	.584	173	12	3	6	35	8
Alex Baratta, Binghamton	.356	.426	.479	163	9	1	3	33	4
Brandon Alamo, Stony Brook	.335	.423	.530	185	22	1	4	33	3
Oscar Marchena, UMass-Lowell	.333	.385	.458	192	11	2	3	41	4
Nick Grande, Stony Brook	.332	.440	.505	208	17	2	5	24	19
Michael Wilson, Stony Brook	.331	.384	.611	175	13	3	10	45	6
Daniel Franchi, Binghamton	.330	.387	.431	197	9	1	3	24	10
Chris Hamilton, Stony Brook	.325	.395	.535	200	16	1	8	42	6
Nich Kondo, Albany	.324	.432	.438	185	11	2	2	22	17
Brad Malm, Albany	.319	.390	.444	135	9	1	2	24	3
Raven Beenman, UMBC	.314	.394	.479	140	8	0	5	15	3
Terrence Pinkston, UMBC	.312	.429	.503	189	17	2	5	32	27
Jackson Olson, Hartford	.306	.345	.396	222	13	2	1	21	8
Marc Wangenstein, Albany	.304	.382	.513	191	8	4	8	51	4
Hernen Sardinas, Maine	.298	.353	.556	198	14	2	11	34	6
Joe Bramanti, Maine	.296	.404	.426	169	13	0	3	31	5
Travis Collins, Albany	.292	.397	.363	171	4	1	2	27	6
Christian Torres, UMBC	.286	.375	.443	185	11	3	4	36	5
Ashton Bardzell, Hartford	.283	.413	.561	198	14	7	9	40	10
Danny Casals, Maine	.282	.399	.500	170	13	0	8	25	11
Patrick Lagravinese, Albany	.282	.358	.446	177	12	7	1	25	7
AJ Wright, UMBC	.280	.397	.516	186	22	2	6	43	13
Sean Trenholm, Binghamton	.279	.362	.421	140	5	0	5	31	4
Zachary Ardito, Hartford	.275	.359	.363	193	9	4	0	22	9
John Thrasher, Hartford	.274	.356	.369	157	6	0	3	24	13
Drew DeMartino, Hartford	.266	.352	.370	184	10	0	3	24	5
Chris Sullivan, Hartford	.264	.343	.377	212	15	0	3	38	0
Blaze O'Saben, UMBC	.262	.360	.351	191	8	3	1	20	25
Colin Casey, UMBC	.259	.305	.435	170	6	3	6	36	0
Sean Buckhout, Stony Brook	.259	.353	.342	158	10	0	1	22	6

INDIVIDUAL PITCHING LEADERS
(Minimum 40 innings pitched)

	W	L	ERA	G	SV	IP	H	BB	SO
Ben Anderson, Binghamton	9	4	2.76	15	0	88	79	27	108
Cody Laweryson, Maine	5	5	2.85	14	0	73	59	23	79
Dominic Savino, Albany	4	5	3.59	13	0	78	74	19	58
Nick Rand, UMass-Lowell	5	6	4.04	16	0	91	81	54	81
Nick Gallagher, Binghamton	4	6	4.32	16	0	81	76	38	82
Bret Clarke, Stony Brook	8	1	4.42	15	0	71	66	41	51
Sebastian DiMauro, Hartford	3	4	4.60	15	0	59	67	21	44
Nicholas Dombkowski, Hartford	3	6	4.97	14	0	83	90	24	78
John Clayton, Albany	6	3	5.12	13	0	63	65	15	51

Outfielder Bryant Packard helped East Carolina win the AAC championship.

Greg Marino, Stony Brook	5	5	5.32	15	0	88	90	18	77
Nick Silva, Maine	4	6	5.45	16	0	73	67	36	59
Peter Kemble, Maine	3	7	6.37	16	0	54	56	27	31
Billy DeVito, Hartford	4	3	6.71	14	0	60	66	28	65

AMERICAN ATHLETIC CONFERENCE

	Conference		Overall	
	W	L	W	L
*East Carolina	20	4	47	18
*Cincinnati	13	11	31	31
Tulane	12	11	32	26
Connecticut	12	12	39	25
Houston	12	12	32	24
Central Florida	11	13	36	22
Memphis	10	13	27	28
Wichita State	9	15	28	31
South Florida	8	16	26	27

ALL-CONFERENCE TEAM: C: Jake Washer, Jr., East Carolina. **1B:** Joe Genord, Sr., South Florida. **2B:** Matthew Mika, Sr., Central Florida. **3B:** Kody Hoese, Jr., Tulane. **SS:** Anthony Prato, Jr., Connecticut. **OF:** Alec Burleson, So., East Carolina; Bryant Packard, Jr., East Carolina; Hunter Goodman, Fr., Memphis. **DH:** Spencer Brickhouse, Jr., East Carolina. **UTL:** Luke Ritter, Sr., Wichita State. **SP:** Mason Feole, Jr., Connecticuit; Jake Agnos, Jr., East Carolina; Jake Kuchmaner, So., East Carolina; Clay Aguilar, Jr., Houston. **RP:** Jacob Wallace, Jr., UConn. **Player of the Year:** Kody Hoese, Tulane. **Pitcher of the Year:** Jake Agnos, East Carolina. **Coach of the Year:** Cliff Godwin, East Carolina. **Rookie of the Year:** Hunter Goodman, Memphis; Devon Roedahl, Houston .

INDIVIDUAL BATTING LEADERS
(Minimum 140 at-bats)

	AVG	OBP	SLG	AB	2B	3B	HR	RBI	SB
Kody Hoese, Tulane	.391	.486	.779	235	20	1	23	61	4
Hudson Haskin, Tulane	.372	.459	.647	207	19	4	10	52	4
Alec Burleson, East Carolina	.370	.399	.573	246	23	0	9	61	3
Bryant Packard, East Carolina	.358	.444	.550	218	19	1	7	40	5
Spencer Brickhouse, East Carolina	.335	.467	.626	206	14	2	14	56	2
Luke Ritter, Wichita State	.333	.458	.545	222	16	2	9	40	12
Joe Genord, South Florida	.333	.446	.618	186	14	0	13	52	4
Jared Triolo, Houston	.332	.420	.512	217	18	0	7	44	13
Trevor Jensen, Tulane	.327	.413	.486	245	16	1	7	39	2
Hunter Goodman, Memphis	.326	.367	.573	239	16	2	13	67	11
John Toppa, Connecticut	.326	.433	.438	233	14	0	4	35	15
Michael Woodworth, Connecticut	.325	.413	.430	249	10	3	5	42	16
Anthony Prato, Connecticut	.324	.441	.430	244	17	0	3	35	14
Tyler Osik, Central Florida	.320	.406	.573	203	14	0	10	39	9
Matthew Mika, Central Florida	.319	.448	.502	213	16	1	7	34	31
Grant Matthews, Tulane	.319	.392	.527	226	13	2	10	55	2
Pat Winkel, Connecticut	.318	.361	.486	173	8	0	7	38	0
Frankie Niemann, Tulane	.318	.432	.493	148	14	0	4	36	1
Dallas Beaver, Central Florida	.316	.455	.545	209	12	0	12	56	4
Payton Marshall, Memphis	.313	.422	.465	144	11	1	3	32	5
Jonathon Artigues, Tulane	.310	.450	.433	203	9	5	2	27	8
Jake Sullivan, South Florida	.309	.421	.430	149	6	0	4	21	0
Kyle Phillips, South Florida	.308	.368	.429	224	12	3	3	29	8
Jordan Boyer, Witchita State	.308	.388	.475	221	16	3	5	38	7
Jake Washer, East Carolina	.301	.393	.597	206	10	0	17	55	2
Ray Alejo, Central Florida	.296	.363	.496	250	18	4	8	29	17
Kyle Ouellette, Memphis	.295	.387	.410	166	8	1	3	24	11
Joe Davis, Houston	.295	.426	.605	200	8	0	18	57	0
Dalton Wingo, Central Florida	.294	.373	.448	221	9	2	7	44	8
Turner Brown, East Carolina	.294	.387	.399	228	11	2	3	33	11

INDIVIDUAL PITCHING LEADERS
(Minimum 40 innings pitched)

	W	L	ERA	G	SV	IP	H	BB	SO
Fred Villarreal, Houston	5	4	2.29	33	10	59	45	19	44
Jake Agnos, East Carolina	11	3	2.29	17	0	102	74	43	145
Jake Kuchmaner, East Carolina	7	2	2.99	17	0	87	63	26	73
Jordan Spicer, Central Florida	3	0	3.14	14	0	63	52	35	47
Clay Aguilar, Houston	6	4	3.19	16	0	68	61	21	73
Lael Lockhart, Houston	4	6	3.58	15	0	83	74	31	76
Collin Sullivan, South Florida	4	5	3.86	14	0	82	63	40	73
Clayton McGinness, Wich. State	6	4	3.89	18	0	74	77	46	83
Devon Roedahl, Houston	7	2	3.94	30	4	62	53	23	60
Grant Schuermann, C. Florida	6	5	3.97	15	0	91	85	21	56
Chris Durham, Memphis	4	4	3.98	14	0	72	78	24	75
Alex Hicks, Memphis	4	3	4.07	16	0	84	95	19	88
Mason Feole, Connecticut	3	4	4.32	14	0	77	73	46	83
Kaleb Roper, Tulane	7	4	4.60	15	0	88	86	31	90
Ryan Randel, Houston	4	2	4.72	14	0	61	61	24	39

ATLANTIC COAST CONFERENCE

	Conference		Overall	
Atlantic Division	W	L	W	L
*Louisville	21	9	51	18
*North Carolina State	18	12	42	19
*Florida State	17	13	42	23
*Clemson	15	15	35	26
Wake Forest	14	16	31	26
Notre Dame	13	17	24	30
Boston College	12	18	31	27

	Conference		Overall	
Coastal Division	W	L	W	L
*Georgia Tech	19	11	43	19
*Miami	18	12	40	20
*North Carolina	17	13	46	19
*Duke	15	15	35	27
Virginia	14	16	32	24
Virginia Tech	9	21	26	27
Pittsburgh	8	22	21	34

ALL-CONFERENCE TEAM:
C: Kyle McCann, Jr., Georgia Tech; Patrick Bailey, So., North Carolina State. **1B:** Tristin English, R-Jr., Georgia Tech; Bobby Seymour, So., Wake Forest. **2B:** Nic Kent, Fr., Virginia. **3B:** Drew Mendoza, Jr., Florida State. **SS:** Will Wilson, Jr., North Carolina State. **OF:** Grayson Byrd, Sr., Clemson; Kennie Taylor, Sr., Duke; Michael Busch, Jr., North Carolina, Chris Lanzilli, So., Wake Forest. **DH/UTL:** Aaron Sabato, Fr., North Carolina. **SP:** Reid Detmers, So., Louisville; Connor Thomas, Jr., Georgia Tech; Dan Metzdorf, Sr., Boston College. **RP:** J.C. Flowers, Jr., Florida State. **Player of the Year:** Bobby Seymour, Wake Forest. **Pitcher of the Year:** Reid Detmers, Louisville. **Coach of the Year:** Reid Detmers, Louisville. **Rookie of the Year:** Aaron Sabato, North Carolina.

INDIVIDUAL BATTING LEADERS
(Minimum 140 at-bats)

	AVG	OBP	SLG	AB	2B	3B	HR	RBI	SB
Bobby Seymour, Wake Forest	.377	.439	.576	236	20	0	9	92	3
Sal Frelick, Boston College	.361	.445	.514	144	8	1	4	31	18
Michael Guldberg, Ga. Tech	.361	.448	.000	.426	216	7	2	1	32	7
Patrick Frick, Wake Forest	.360	.457	.481	214	14	0	4	38	7
Nico Popa, Pittsburgh	.353	.424	.581	215	15	5	8	39	14
Aaron Sabato, North Carolina	.348	.458	.710	224	25	1	18	62	0
Chris Lanzilli, Wake Forest	.347	.409	.620	245	19	0	16	67	3
Jake Alu, Boston College	.346	.416	.485	231	18	1	4	39	11
Tristin English, Georgia Tech	.346	.429	.701	211	20	2	17	70	0
Tanner Morris, Virginia	.345	.452	.507	223	21	0	5	38	3
Mike Salvatore, Florida State	.341	.432	.541	255	22	4	7	51	5
JP Gates, Miami	.340	.371	.510	147	9	2	4	31	0
Nic Kent, Virginia	.337	.417	.455	202	9	3	3	42	17
Will Wilson, NC State.	.335	.425	.661	221	20	2	16	57	1
Danny Oriente, Louisville	.332	.404	.435	193	17	0	1	49	0
Kennie Taylor, Duke	.331	.396	.525	242	19	5	6	39	10
Adrian Del Castillo, Miami	.331	.418	.576	236	22	0	12	72	3
Evan Edwards, NC State	.330	.455	.604	230	17	2	14	60	7
Luke Waddell, Georgia Tech	.328	.442	.424	229	12	2	2	34	7
Robby Martin, Florida State	.325	.408	.466	206	17	0	4	54	2
Jack Owens, Virginia Tech	.323	.456	.415	164	9	0	2	12	5
Cody Morissette, BC	.323	.374	.482	226	20	2	4	41	8
Brendan Rivoli, Virginia	.320	.386	.466	206	13	1	5	42	5
Tyler McDonough, NC State	.320	.392	.452	250	14	2	5	48	10
Raymond Gil, Miami	.318	.396	.565	214	14	0	13	44	1
Kevin Madden, Virginia Tech	.316	.362	.423	196	10	1	3	23	3
Ethan Murray, Duke	.316	.403	.458	190	8	2	5	37	6
Nick Wilhite, Georgia Tech	.316	.432	.388	206	7	1	2	41	8
Grayson Byrd, Clemson	.316	.394	.588	250	16	2	16	59	4
Tyler Fitzgerald, Louisville	.315	.391	.483	267	15	3	8	65	18

INDIVIDUAL PITCHING LEADERS
(Minimum 40 innings pitched)

	W	L	ERA	G	SV	IP	H	BB	SO
Dan Metzdorf, Boston College	8	2	2.13	11	0	76	55	29	67
Chase Smith, Pittsburgh	4	6	2.72	36	5	60	54	17	55
Chris Gerard, Virginia Tech	3	2	2.77	12	0	55	55	25	44
Reid Detmers, Louisville	13	4	2.78	19	0	113	71	33	167
Austin Love, North Carolina	8	4	2.78	36	5	65	51	23	64
Connor Thomas, Georgia Tech	9	2	3.11	16	0	113	118	19	103
Davis Sharpe, Clemson	7	4	3.20	15	0	84	61	33	84
Mat Clark, Clemson	9	3	3.21	14	0	73	53	23	60
Brian Van Belle, Miami	10	2	3.30	16	0	95	91	24	84
Chesdin Harrington, Virginia	5	1	3.49	23	0	59	65	16	64
Mason Pelio, Boston College	4	3	3.63	13	0	72	48	37	62
Reid Johnston, NC State	6	2	3.71	17	0	78	80	27	65
Billy Corcoran, Pittsburgh	2	6	3.80	20	0	69	64	26	54
Tyler Baum, North Carolina	7	3	3.80	16	0	88	85	22	95
C.J. Van Eyk, Florida State	10	3	3.80	17	0	95	82	39	120

ATLANTIC SUN CONFERENCE

	Conference W	L	Overall W	L
Florida Guf Coast	16	7	34	21
*Liberty	15	9	43	21
Lipscomb	14	10	30	25
Jacksonville	13	11	32	27
North Florida	12	11	32	25
Stetson	11	12	27	32
Kennesaw State	11	13	27	29
North Alabama	7	16	16	38
NJIT	7	17	17	27

ALL-CONFERENCE TEAM: C: Jonathan Embry, Jr., Liberty. **1B:** Jake Franklin, Sr., Kennesaw State. **2B:** Will Wagner, So., Liberty; Jay Prather, Sr., North Florida. **3B:** Angel Camacho, Sr., Jacksonville. **SS:** Dakota Julylia, Jr., Jacksonville. **OF:** Tanner Murphy, Jr., North Florida; Terence Norman, Jr., Kennesaw State; Tevin Symonette, Sr., Lipscomb. **DH:** Justin Russell, Jr., Kennesaw State. **SP:** Brad Deppermann, Sr., North Florida; Chris Kachmar, Sr., Lipscomb; Mason Studstill, Jr., Florida Gulf Coast. **RP:** Evan Brabrand, Sr., Liberty. **Player of the Year:** Jonathan Embry, Liberty. **Pitcher of the Year:** Brad Deppermann, North Florida. **Coach of the Year:** Dave Tollett, Florida Gulf Coast. **Rookie of the Year:** Daniel Paret, Stetson.

INDIVIDUAL BATTING LEADERS
(Minimum 140 at-bats)

	AVG	OBP	SLG	AB	2B	3B	HR	RBI	SB
Terence Norman, Kennesaw St.	.350	.431	.481	214	13	0	5	40	2
Maddox Houghton, Lipscomb	.342	.400	.482	193	7	4	4	34	20
Keith Stevens, FGCU	.337	.450	.446	184	11	0	3	29	0
David Maberry, North Florida	.327	.390	.434	159	14	0	1	38	0
Brett Helmkamp, NJIT	.325	.420	.387	163	7	0	1	25	6
Jake Franklin, Kennesaw St.	.324	.413	.562	219	18	2	10	49	9
Joe Kinker, Florida Gulf Coast	.324	.461	.492	179	9	0	7	39	1
Alex Brait, Florida Gulf Coast	.322	.396	.411	236	7	1	4	29	11
Angel Camacho, Jacksonville	.317	.407	.480	227	7	0	10	41	2
Jay Hayes, Florida Gulf Coast	.316	.451	.575	193	18	1	10	52	0
Chris Berry, North Florida	.316	.451	.458	190	8	2	5	36	7
John Cassala, Jacksonville	.315	.395	.418	165	5	0	4	29	5
David Marcano, NJIT	.314	.402	.416	185	5	1	4	15	11
Dakota Julylia, Jacksonville	.313	.379	.378	217	9	1	1	28	6
Jonathan Embry, Liberty	.312	.451	.538	221	16	2	10	42	8
Julio Marcano, NJIT	.309	.415	.509	165	9	0	8	31	3
Will Wagner, Liberty	.308	.387	.458	227	14	1	6	42	9
Justin Russell, Kennesaw St.	.308	.374	.609	156	9	1	12	37	3
Scott Dubrule, Jacksonville	.307	.404	.359	231	10	1	0	29	5
Jay Prather, North Florida	.307	.384	.377	228	10	0	2	29	5
Brandon Rohrer, Liberty	.305	.424	.350	203	7	1	0	28	3
Cade Sorrells, Lipscomb	.305	.418	.433	187	9	0	5	51	7
Chris Bashlor, Lipscomb	.302	.413	.447	179	12	1	4	29	1
Tyler Simon, Kennesaw St.	.301	.383	.416	219	12	2	3	33	6
Gray Betts, Liberty	.299	.441	.338	157	6	0	0	21	2
Kevin Brenning, N. Alabama	.294	.351	.429	119	7	0	3	18	11
Ben Kiefer, North Alabama	.293	.354	.328	174	6	0	0	14	7
Garry Hodges, Kennesaw St.	.293	.377	.428	215	8	0	7	36	5
Nick Hussey, NJIT	.291	.357	.430	165	11	0	4	23	1
Kohl Gilmore, FGCU	.290	.395	.435	186	10	1	5	45	1

INDIVIDUAL PITCHING LEADERS
(Minimum 40 innings pitched)

	W	L	ERA	G	SV	IP	H	BB	SO
Danny Garcia, Stetson	5	1	1.22	28	2	59	39	18	32
Brad Deppermann, N. Florida	6	5	2.46	15	0	95	76	24	108
Mason Studstill, FGCU	5	2	2.60	15	0	87	53	43	96
Garret Price, Liberty	7	3	3.29	28	3	63	42	23	68
AJ Jones, Jacksonville	7	4	3.30	15	0	87	74	31	77
Chris Gonzalez, Stetson	7	3	3.40	17	0	93	98	22	73
Andrew McInvale, Liberty	9	2	3.46	15	0	91	78	35	93
Joshua Colon, Lipscomb	5	4	3.55	12	0	66	69	25	32
Bryant Claunch, N. Alabama	5	2	3.57	22	1	58	56	19	62
Chris Kachmar, Lipscomb	9	3	3.61	15	0	95	74	41	94
Daniel Paret, Stetson	5	4	3.61	19	0	95	74	47	102
Noah Skirrow, Liberty	5	6	3.76	16	0	77	64	35	98
Joseph Adametz, Liberty	7	2	3.79	15	0	74	77	27	54
Evan Lumbert, FGCU	5	3	4.03	13	0	67	58	39	58
Robbie Peto, Stetson	1	9	4.11	15	0	72	75	28	78

ATLANTIC 10 CONFERENCE

	Conference W	L	Overall W	L
Virginia Commonwealth	19	5	39	19
Davidson	14	6	29	21
Dayton	16	8	32	25
*Fordham	15	9	37	24
Richmond	13	8	28	25
Rhode Island	14	9	24	29
Saint Louis	13	11	25	29
Saint Joseph's	13	11	21	28
George Washington	11	13	30	24
Massachusetts	8	14	16	27
St. Bonaventure	6	18	13	32
George Mason	5	19	19	35
La Salle	4	20	25	31

ALL-CONFERENCE TEAM: C: Logan Driscoll, Jr., George Mason. **1B:** Dominic D'Alessandro, Sr., George Washington. **2B:** Paul Witt, Jr., VCU. **3B:** Tyler Plantier, Sr., Richmond. **SS:** Nate Fassnacht, Jr., George Washington. **OF:** Anthony Forte, Jr., Richmond; Jake Garella, Jr., Saint Louis; Corrigan Bartlett, Jr., Saint Louis. **DH:** Liam Hibbits, So., VCU. **SP:** John Stankiewicz, So., Fordham; Connor Gillispie, Jr., VCU. **RP:** Kyle Martin, Jr., Fordham. **Player of the Year:** Nate Fassnacht, George Washington. **Pitcher of the Year:** John Stankiewicz, Fordham. **Coach of the Year:** Shawn Stiffler, VCU. **Rookie of the Year:** Noach Levin, George Washington; Tatem Levins, La Salle.

INDIVIDUAL BATTING LEADERS
(Minimum 140 at-bats)

	AVG	OBP	SLG	AB	2B	3B	HR	RBI	SB
Dom D'Alessandro, G. Wash.	.423	.506	.668	208	12	0	13	56	2
Nate Fassnacht, G. Wash.	.370	.453	.652	227	23	4	11	60	12
Liam Hibbits, VCU	.366	.450	.546	205	17	1	6	60	4
Logan Driscoll, George Mason	.360	.482	.647	150	12	2	9	33	5
Peyton Sorrels, La Salle	.359	.429	.502	217	11	4	4	28	25
Eric Jones, Davidson	.351	.432	.579	202	17	1	9	26	3
Kyle Schmidt, Richmond	.347	.415	.488	170	12	0	4	37	0
Jake Garella, Saint Louis	.341	.415	.547	214	26	0	6	44	1
Paul Witt, VCU	.336	.437	.471	223	16	1	4	50	9
Sam Fuller, St. Bonaventure	.325	.433	.485	163	9	7	1	13	16
Tatem Levins, La Salle	.321	.385	.556	187	17	0	9	50	2
Tyler Plantier, Richmond	.320	.415	.543	197	8	0	12	50	1
Corrigan Bartlett, Saint Louis	.319	.409	.431	204	12	4	1	26	4
Cam Redding, Saint Louis	.318	.436	.377	154	7	1	0	24	1
Cole Dubet, Saint Louis	.316	.356	.466	206	11	1	6	35	11
Dominic Cuoci, Saint Joseph's	.311	.410	.475	177	11	0	6	39	0
Zac Ching, VCU	.310	.404	.502	229	22	2	6	42	17
Brett Norwood, VCU	.310	.427	.455	200	11	0	6	37	25
Jake Baker, Fordham	.309	.366	.352	152	4	1	1	25	17
Brendan Hueth, Saint Joseph's	.308	.366	.380	221	7	3	1	18	24
Tyler Hix, G. Wash.	.307	.379	.474	215	21	3	3	42	6
Jake Mackenzie, Fordham	.305	.361	.451	246	15	6	3	28	43
Noah Levin, G. Wash.	.305	.385	.460	174	11	2	4	43	0
Colin Shapiro, Massachusetts	.301	.450	.397	156	8	2	1	22	10
Sage Bruhl, Richmond	.300	.424	.371	210	12	0	1	22	3
James McConnon, Saint Joseph's	.300	.415	.347	170	5	0	1	27	1
Xavier Vargas, Rhode Island	.300	.347	.406	217	9	1	4	38	1
Austin White, Rhode Island	.298	.416	.367	188	6	2	1	16	13
Anthony Videtto, Rhode Island	.296	.421	.420	162	11	0	3	29	6
Kevin McGowan, La Salle	.296	.380	.393	206	16	2	0	35	5

INDIVIDUAL PITCHING LEADERS
(Minimum 40 innings pitched)

	W	L	ERA	G	SV	IP	H	BB	SO
John Stankiewicz, Fordham	8	4	1.47	17	0	92	62	20	102
Benjamin Dum, VCU	5	7	2.18	21	4	70	48	15	63
Casey Sutherland, Davidson	8	1	2.49	13	0	80	81	7	66
Connor Gillispie, VCU	5	3	2.50	20	0	86	58	24	118

	W	L	ERA	G	SV	IP	H	BB	SO
Donovan Moffat, St. Bona.	4	4	2.58	21	4	59	49	13	53
Cole Stetzar, Saint Joseph's	3	2	2.92	22	3	52	52	21	43
Justin Cherry, Rhode Island	3	1	2.93	15	0	55	55	19	56
Cody Luther, Saint Louis	8	3	2.96	14	0	85	71	22	82
Jackson Wark, Saint Louis	3	5	3.12	18	2	61	52	26	68
Tim Miller, Richmond	5	2	3.21	14	0	76	63	34	65
Sean Harney, Massachusetts	3	5	3.27	12	0	66	55	33	48
Anthony Dimeglio, Fordham	6	4	3.38	17	0	67	60	25	64
Justin Sorokowski, VCU	4	2	3.42	20	0	74	61	16	73
Allen Barry, Davidson	7	3	3.63	12	0	57	53	19	64
Josh Hudson, Davidson	5	2	3.63	14	0	69	66	26	66

	W	L	ERA	G	SV	IP	H	BB	SO
Ryan Pepiot, Butler	4	4	3.92	14	0	88	55	44	126
Connor Grammes, Xavier	5	5	3.95	14	0	68	48	46	79
Jimmy Kingsbury, Villanova	5	5	4.13	19	1	85	75	35	56
Mitch Ragan, Creighton	8	3	4.17	17	0	99	96	18	95
Noah Thompson, Seton Hall	4	3	4.20	13	0	64	46	29	73
David Festa, Seton Hall	3	4	4.42	14	0	53	49	25	58
Nick Morreale, Georgetown	4	5	4.63	15	1	68	70	39	82
Jeremiah Burke, Georgetown	2	8	4.66	14	0	85	83	25	86
Gordon Graceffo, Villanova	3	8	4.88	17	0	72	82	25	47

BIG EAST CONFERENCE

	Conference		Overall	
	W	L	W	L
*Creighton	14	4	41	13
Xavier	12	4	27	31
St. John's	9	9	31	23
Seton Hall	9	9	25	28
Georgetown	7	11	22	34
Butler	6	11	26	26
Villanova	4	13	13	38

ALL-CONFERENCE TEAM: C: Wyatt Mascarella, Sr., St. John's. **1B:** Jake Holton, Jr., Creighton. **2B:** Isaac Collins, Jr., Creighton. **3B:** Eddie McCabe, So., Georgetown. **SS:** Chris Givin, Sr., Xavier. **OF:** Harrison Freed, Jr., Butler; Mike Antico, Jr., St. John's; Tyler Shedler-McAvoy, Jr., Seton Hall. **DH:** Connor Grammes, Jr., Xavier. **SP:** Connor Schultz, So., Butler; Mitch Ragan, Sr., Creighton; Joe LaSorsa, Jr., St. John's. **RP:** Gavin Hollowell, Jr., St. John's. **Player of the Year:** Jake Holton, Jr., Creighton. **Pitcher of the Year:** Mitch Ragan, Sr., Creighton. **Coach of the Year:** Ed Servais, Creighton. **Rookie of the Year:** Nick Lorusso, Fr., Villanova.

INDIVIDUAL BATTING LEADERS
(Minimum 140 at-bats)

	AVG	OBP	SLG	AB	2B	3B	HR	RBI	SB
Jake Holton, Creighton	.386	.488	.681	207	15	2	14	58	1
Mike Antico, St. John's	.386	.500	.598	184	13	4	6	29	20
Harrison Freed, Butler	.376	.448	.683	218	10	3	17	73	9
Eddie McCabe, Georgetown	.345	.448	.453	203	7	0	5	32	2
Connor Grammes, Xavier	.330	.428	.524	227	14	3	8	28	12
Parker Upton, Creighton	.324	.483	.603	179	14	3	10	34	9
Tyler Shedler-McAvoy, S. Hall	.324	.406	.471	204	12	6	2	37	22
Will Robertson, Creighton	.311	.408	.599	222	19	0	15	67	1
Kyle Smith, Butler	.309	.475	.584	178	13	3	10	35	10
Chris Givin, Xavier	.306	.369	.471	242	11	4	7	35	6
Nick Lorusso, Villanova	.302	.408	.425	179	8	1	4	29	2
Jack Strunc, Creighton	.298	.351	.445	218	20	0	4	34	4
Isaac Collins, Creighton	.293	.366	.479	242	13	7	6	34	13
Ryan Markey, St. John's	.291	.365	.407	172	13	2	1	36	5
Matt Toke, Seton Hall	.290	.394	.398	186	8	0	4	29	3
Ryan Weisenberg, G'town	.289	.385	.378	180	13	0	1	22	4
Jake Shepski, Xavier	.286	.388	.385	213	13	1	2	43	5
Christian Del Castillo, S. Hall	.286	.364	.505	182	17	4	5	35	3
Mitchell Henshaw, St. John's	.284	.352	.376	141	4	0	3	25	0
Allbry Major, Xavier	.281	.341	.488	203	15	3	7	34	4
Steve Grober, Seton Hall	.280	.339	.421	164	6	4	3	33	1
Will Hanafan, Creighton	.279	.364	.312	154	2	0	1	20	4
Brandon Miller, St. John's	.279	.361	.364	129	8	0	1	15	5
Jack Housinger, Xavier	.275	.407	.357	171	12	1	0	21	5
Kyle Ruedisili, Georgetown	.269	.326	.575	193	16	2	13	34	15
James Gargano, Butler	.268	.364	.381	168	11	1	2	20	9
Jordan Hovey, Creighton	.267	.388	.455	191	11	2	7	33	11
Carson Bartels, St. John's	.264	.357	.330	212	11	0	1	30	8

INDIVIDUAL PITCHING LEADERS
(Minimum 40 innings pitched)

	W	L	ERA	G	SV	IP	H	BB	SO
Joe LaSorsa, St. John's	6	5	1.66	15	1	87	62	33	67
Connor Schultz, Butler	6	1	2.29	13	0	79	70	21	79
Jack Cushing, Georgetown	4	5	3.06	15	0	79	72	20	87
Evan Johnson, Creighton	9	2	3.26	17	0	77	55	42	74
Ricky Devito, Seton Hall	2	5	3.92	12	0	64	73	31	68

BIG SOUTH CONFERENCE

	Conference		Overall	
	W	L	W	L
*Campbell	19	7	37	21
Radford	19	8	30	27
Winthrop	18	9	34	23
Presbyterian	16	11	20	29
Gardner-Webb	14	13	25	26
High Point	14	13	27	27
Charleston Southern	11	16	23	36
USC Upstate	9	17	23	30
UNC Asheville	9	18	16	36
Longwood	5	22	11	41

ALL-CONFERENCE TEAM: C: Justin Kunz, Sr., Gardner-Webb. **INF:** Chandler Redmond, Sr., Gardner-Webb; Ryan Stoudermire, Jr., Charleston Southern; Luis Gimenez, Sr., Campbell; Brandon Lankford, Jr., UNC Asheville. **OF:** Matthew Barefoot, R-Jr., Campbell; Hunter Lipscomb, So., Winthrop; Jeff Taylor, So., USC Upstate. **DH:** J.D. Mundy, Jr., Radford. **UTL:** Kyle Butler, R-Sr., Radford. **SP:** Michael Horrell, Sr., Campbell; Ryan Chasse, Fr., Campbell; Nate Pawelczyk, Sr., Winthrop. **RP:** RJ Petit, Fr., Charleston Southern; Colten Rendon, Jr., Winthrop. **Player of the Year:** Chandler Redmond, Gardner-Webb. **Pitcher of the Year:** Michael Horrell, Campbell. **Coach of the Year:** Rusty Stroupe, Gardner-Webb. **Rookie of the Year:** Ryan Chasse, Campbell.

INDIVIDUAL BATTING LEADERS
(Minimum 140 at-bats)

	AVG	OBP	SLG	AB	2B	3B	HR	RBI	SB
J.J. Shimko, USC Upstate	.369	.461	.481	160	15	0	1	27	5
Jeff Taylor, USC Upstate	.360	.433	.547	150	13	3	3	29	3
Hunter Lipscomb, Winthrop	.332	.444	.482	199	12	0	6	45	8
Greg Gasparro, UNC Asheville	.329	.434	.425	146	10	2	0	13	5
Zacchaeus Rasberry, Presbyterian	.327	.405	.496	226	9	4	7	34	23
Spencer Yankle, Winthrop	.326	.397	.471	221	11	3	5	37	0
Grant English, Winthrop	.324	.403	.502	213	14	3	6	50	23
Joe Johnson, High Point	.324	.366	.435	207	9	1	4	40	8
Travis Holt, High Point	.323	.349	.448	232	14	0	5	19	4
Spencer Packard, Campbell	.323	.436	.455	198	20	0	2	46	1
Jimmy Marcelli, Presbyterian	.321	.386	.460	224	14	1	5	48	7
Andres Kim, USC Upstate	.321	.404	.402	184	10	1	1	25	0
Julian Rip, USC Upstate	.319	.417	.500	166	12	3	4	30	2
Justin Kunz, Gardner Webb	.319	.383	.554	213	15	1	11	38	3
Corey Howard, Gardner Webb	.316	.383	.445	209	15	0	4	37	4
Alex Raines, Winthrop	.314	.360	.363	204	7	0	1	20	2
Luis Gimenez, Campbell	.312	.392	.422	237	15	1	3	44	26
Scout McFalls, Winthrop	.312	.407	.376	189	6	0	2	23	15
Jason Matthews, USC Upstate	.311	.398	.347	167	6	0	0	15	2
Matthew Barefoot, Campbell	.311	.407	.570	235	13	3	14	48	25
Chandler Redmon, G. Webb	.309	.412	.660	191	11	1	18	59	1
Andrew Szamski, Radford	.307	.377	.496	228	11	1	10	53	5
Brandon Fite, Winthrop	.307	.348	.363	163	5	2	0	23	4
Jonathan White, Presbyterian	.305	.421	.414	203	7	0	5	31	12
J.D. Mundy, Radford	.304	.412	.588	204	17	1	13	55	4
Danny Wilson, UNC Asheville	.302	.398	.469	192	12	1	6	48	5
Ryan Stoudemire, C. Southern	.298	.381	.544	215	11	0	14	45	2
Matther Mulkey, Winthrop	.294	.340	.463	218	17	1	6	48	23
Collin Wolf, Campbell	.293	.411	.466	208	11	2	7	48	11

CRchristian; Caleb Kilian, Jr., Texas Tech; Alek Manoah, Jr., West Virginia. **RP:** Kyle Hill, Sr., Baylor; Taylor Floyd, Jr., Texas Tech. **Player of the Year:** Davis Wendzel, Baylor; Josh Jung, Texas Tech. **Pitcher of the Year:** Alek Manoah, West Virginia. **Coach of the Year:** Randy Mazey, West Virginia. **Newcomers of the Year:** Jordan Wicks, Kansas State.

INDIVIDUAL BATTING LEADERS
(Minimum 2.5 at-bats per team game)

	AVG	OBP	SLG	AB	2B	3B	HR	RBI	SB
Davis Wendzel, Baylor	.361	.480	.606	180	20	0	8	44	11
Cameron Warren, Texas Tech	.356	.450	.669	239	17	2	18	79	1
Andy Thomas, Baylor	.349	.428	.554	186	23	0	5	36	1
Jake Guenther, TCU	.345	.462	.576	203	13	2	10	42	14
Josh Jung, Texas Tech	.343	.473	.640	236	23	1	15	58	1
Jaxx Groshans, Kansas	.340	.475	.604	197	14	1	12	46	0
Richard Cunningham, Baylor	.333	.395	.496	234	15	4	5	33	6
Shae Langeliers, Baylor	.332	.397	.604	187	10	1	13	53	4
Nick Loftin, Baylor	.331	.391	.517	236	20	3	6	43	6
Zach Kokoska, Kansas St.	.330	.408	.522	182	7	2	8	31	8
Josh Watson, TCU	.324	.424	.528	250	21	0	10	42	10
Cole Haring, Baylor	.321	.377	.539	193	4	1	12	44	6
Brian Klein, Texas Tech	.320	.412	.447	253	19	2	3	57	0
Gabe Holt, Texas Tech	.318	.409	.433	261	15	3	3	35	28
Tyler Doanes, West Virginia	.316	.398	.500	228	21	3	5	32	20
Darius Hill, West Virginia	.315	.376	.521	238	25	3	6	41	4
Carson McCusker, Oklahoma St.	.313	.385	.526	192	17	3	6	39	2
Johnny Rizer, TCU	.311	.380	.531	241	16	2	11	39	8
Eric Kennedy, Texas	.310	.382	.418	184	8	3	2	28	9
Tyler Hardman, Oklahoma	.306	.394	.457	219	13	1	6	42	0
Benjamin Sems, Kansas	.305	.414	.437	197	12	1	4	39	14
Dylan Neuse, Texas Tech	.304	.415	.504	240	12	6	8	51	18
Brylie Ware, Oklahoma	.299	.405	.450	211	12	1	6	35	0
Chase Wehsener, Baylor	.298	.386	.348	181	7	1	0	21	2
Conner Shepherd, TCU	.297	.389	.465	185	9	2	6	22	5
Braxton Fulford, Texas Tech	.296	.387	.418	189	9	1	4	33	0

Michigan outfielder Jordan Brewer was the Big Ten player of the year

INDIVIDUAL PITCHING LEADERS
(Minimum 40 innings pitched)

	W	L	ERA	G	SV	IP	H	BB	SO
Michael Horrell, Campbell	10	3	2.62	15	0	89	79	13	85
Harrison Smith, High Point	2	4	2.67	13	0	64	50	27	68
Ryan Chasse, Campbell	7	2	2.95	15	0	76	61	27	58
Andrew Nardi, Radford	5	4	3.60	16	5	65	68	11	37
Jackson Dean, Presbyterian	6	5	3.70	19	0	92	121	14	50
Grey Little, High Point	7	3	3.72	17	3	58	36	25	65
Cody Maw, C. Southern	4	5	3.74	15	0	84	76	13	62
Landon Mitchell, G. Webb	7	6	3.80	15	0	83	96	27	70
Tyler Morgan, Longwood	2	6	3.83	10	0	56	53	27	71
Zack Ridgely, Radford	4	3	3.86	15	0	82	84	19	50
Nate Pawelczyk, Winthrop	9	4	3.90	15	0	92	90	29	83
Eric Miles, Presbyterian	7	4	3.97	15	0	93	102	20	84
Zach Peek, Winthrop	7	3	4.02	14	0	87	80	35	91

INDIVIDUAL PITCHING LEADERS
(Minimum 40 innings pitched)

	W	L	ERA	G	SV	IP	H	BB	SO
Alek Manoah, West Virginia	9	4	2.08	16	0	108	71	27	144
Nick Lodolo, TCU	6	6	2.36	16	0	103	76	25	131
Nick Snyder, West Virginia	9	1	2.65	16	0	68	42	34	103
Bryce Elder, Texas	2	4	2.93	13	0	83	70	33	86
Levi Prater, Texas	7	4	3.26	16	0	80	60	43	97
Cade Cavalli, Oklahoma	5	3	3.28	12	0	60	53	35	59
Blair Henley, Texas	6	4	3.54	13	0	74	74	34	62
Charles King, TCU	6	3	3.54	21	1	86	90	15	54
Micah Dallas, Texas Tech	7	1	3.60	18	0	75	69	27	84
Jordan Wicks, Kansas St.	6	2	3.61	15	0	85	92	26	86
Jensen Elliott, Oklahoma St.	9	4	3.79	16	0	93	79	36	58
Caleb Kilian, Texas Tech	8	3	3.92	17	0	96	86	20	89
Ryan Zeferjahn, Kansas	5	2	3.97	15	0	68	60	44	107
Jimmy Winston, Baylor	5	2	4.10	18	0	68	59	29	38
Brandon Williamson, TCU	4	5	4.19	16	0	77	82	36	89

BIG 12 CONFERENCE

	Conference W	L	Overall W	L
*Texas Tech	16	8	46	20
*Baylor	14	8	35	19
*Oklahoma State	14	9	40	21
*West Virginia	13	11	38	22
Kansas	12	12	32	26
*Texas Christian	11	13	34	28
Oklahoma	11	13	33	23
Kansas State	8	16	25	33
Texas	7	16	27	27

ALL-CONFERENCE TEAM: C: Shea Langeliers, Jr., Baylor. **INF:** Nick Loftin, So., Baylor; Davis Wendzel, Jr., Baylor; Jake Guenther, R-Jr., Texas Christian; Josh Jung, Jr., Texas Tech; Cameron Warren, Jr., Texas Tech. **OF:** Richard Cunningham, Sr., Baylor; Trevor Boone, Jr., Oklahoma State; Gabe Holt, So., Texas Tech. **DH:** Andy Thomas, Jr., Baylor. **UTL:** Cade Cavalli, So., Oklahoma. **SP:** Ryan Zeferjahn, Jr., Kansas; Nick Lodolo, Jr., Texas

BIG TEN CONFERENCE

	Conference W	L	Overall W	L
*Indiana	17	7	36	21
*Michigan	16	7	50	22
*Illinois	15	9	36	21
*Nebraska	15	9	32	24
Minnesota	15	9	29	27
*Ohio State	12	12	36	27
Iowa	12	12	31	24
Maryland	12	12	29	29
Northwestern	11	13	24	27
Rutgers	9	14	20	31
Michigan State	8	15	20	34
Purdue	7	16	20	34
Penn State	4	18	22	27

ALL-CONFERENCE TEAM: C: Eli Wilson, Jr., Minnesota. **1B:** Maxwell Costes, Fr., Maryland. **2B:** Michael Massey, Jr., Illinois. **3B:** Alex Erro, Jr., Northwestern. **SS:** Jack Dunn, Jr., Northwestern. **OF:** Zac Taylor, R-Sr., Illinois; Jordan Brewer, Jr., Michigan; Dominic Canzone, Jr., Ohio State. **DH:** Jordan Nwogu, So., Michigan. **SP:** Andy Fisher, R-Sr., Illinois; Andrew Saalfrank, Jr., Indiana; Jeff Criswell, So., Michigan. **RP:** Garrett Acton, Jr., Illinois. **Player of the Year:** Jordan Brewer, Michigan. **Pitcher of the Year:** Andrew Saalfrank, Indiana. **Coach of the Year:**Jeff Mercer, Indiana. **Rookie of the Year:** Maxwell Costes, Maryland.

INDIVIDUAL BATTING LEADERS
(Minimum 140 at-bats)

	AVG	OBP	SLG	AB	2B	3B	HR	RBI	SB
Grant Van Scoy, Illinois	.347	.442	.466	176	13	1	2	22	1
Jack Dunn, Northwestern	.346	.438	.410	188	10	1	0	36	11
Dominic Canzone, Ohio State	.345	.444	.620	255	18	2	16	43	8
Jordan Brewer, Michigan	.329	.389	.557	246	20	0	12	59	25
Alex Erro, Northwestern	.324	.372	.459	207	12	2	4	34	8
Jordan Nwogu, Michigan	.321	.435	.557	246	14	4	12	46	16
Zac Taylor, Illinois	.321	.405	.612	165	12	3	10	29	23
Aaron Palensky, Nebraska	.320	.420	.482	222	11	2	7	35	6
Cole McKenzie, Purdue	.317	.407	.371	205	6	1	1	21	10
Michael Massey, Illinois	.317	.459	.472	218	14	1	5	28	2
AJ Lee, Maryland	.317	.443	.497	189	13	0	7	36	10
Jack Blomgren, Michigan	.314	.417	.401	242	8	2	3	47	7
Brady Cherry, Ohio State	.314	.386	.563	261	15	1	16	82	2
Jordan Bowersox, Penn State	.309	.379	.393	191	8	1	2	15	9
Skyler Hunter, Purdue	.307	.385	.472	199	10	6	0	17	7

INDIVIDUAL PITCHING LEADERS
(Minimum 40 innings pitched)

	W	L	ERA	G	SV	IP	H	BB	SO
Andrew Magno, Ohio State	5	3	2.09	31	14	65	45	36	75
Max Meyer, Minnesota	5	3	2.11	16	2	77	58	20	87
Mason Mellott, Penn State	6	3	2.43	21	5	63	59	14	52
Dante Biasi, Penn State	3	6	2.55	14	0	74	52	33	102
Andrews Saalfrank, Indiana	8	1	2.58	14	0	70	61	23	96
Jeff Criswell, Michigan	7	1	2.72	22	3	106	88	50	116
Grant Judkins, Iowa	4	7	2.72	15	0	83	70	31	65
Andy Fisher, Illinois	7	1	2.75	16	0	101	76	35	95
Trent Johnson, Purdue	3	3	2.83	22	1	60	43	19	73
Tevin Murray, Rutgers	4	5	3.01	17	0	69	50	36	81

BIG WEST CONFERENCE

	Conference		Overall	
	W	L	W	L
*UC Santa Barbara	19	5	45	11
UC Irvine	17	7	37	17
Cal Poly	17	7	28	28
Cal State Fullerton	13	11	27	26
Cal State Northridge	9	15	23	32
UC Davis	9	15	19	31
Hawaii	8	16	20	30
UC Riverside	8	16	20	36
Long Beach State	8	16	14	41

ALL-CONFERENCE TEAM: C: Eric Yang, Jr., UC Santa Barbara. **1B:** Adrian Damla, Jr., UC Irvine. **2B:** Andrew Martinez, So., UC Santa Barbara. **3B:** Brandon Lewis, Jr., UC Irvine. **SS:** Tanner Murray, So., UC Davis. **OF:** Mitchell Berryhill, Sr., Cal State Fullerton; Tommy Jew, Jr., UC Santa Barbara; Dean Miller, Sr., UC Riverside; Armani Smith, Jr., UC Santa Barbara. **DH:** Connor Cannon, Jr., UC Riverside; Thomas Rowan, Sr., UC Santa Barbara. **UTL:** Maaki Yamazaki, Sr., Hawaii. **SP:** Bobby Ay, Jr., Cal Poly; Jack Dashwood, So., UC Santa Barbara; Trenton Denholm, So., UC Irvine. **RP:** Taylor Dollard, So., Cal Poly; Michael McGreevy, Fr., UC Santa Barbara. **Player of the Year:** Eric Yang, UC Santa Barbara. **Pitcher of the Year:** Trenton Denholm, UC Irvine. **Coach of the Year:** Andrew Checketts, UC Santa Barbara. **Rookie of the Year:** Scotty Scott, Hawaii; Rodbey Boone, UC Santa Barbara.

INDIVIDUAL BATTING LEADERS
(Minimum 140 at-bats)

	AVG	OBP	SLG	AB	2B	3B	HR	RBI	SB
Mitchell Berryhill, CS Fullerton	.415	.493	.487	195	8	3	0	27	17
Eric Yang, UC Santa Barbara	.368	.479	.545	209	16	0	7	45	6
Dean Miller, UC Riverside	.365	.401	.650	203	16	0	14	49	2
Tanner Murray, UC Davis	.364	.416	.503	195	16	4	1	31	12
Kyle Barret, CS Northridge	.333	.419	.502	207	19	2	4	32	10
Travis Bohall, UC Riverside	.331	.382	.384	151	4	2	0	9	16
Thomas Rowan, UCSB	.327	.407	.593	214	14	2	13	46	5
McClain O'Connor UCSB	.325	.393	.503	151	12	3	3	17	13
Jacob Hughey, Long Beach St.	.324	.387	.404	188	13	1	0	26	4
Isaiah Garcia, CS Fullerton	.323	.394	.437	167	9	2	2	39	2
Armani Smith, UCSB	.323	.393	.631	217	18	8	11	45	3
Connor Cannon, UC Riverside	.319	.426	.660	188	10	0	18	44	2
Brandon Lewis, UC Irvine	.315	.408	.598	219	20	0	14	54	5
Mike Peabody, UC Irvine	.312	.434	.416	173	11	2	1	28	6
Yeager Taylor, UC Riverside	.311	.347	.426	209	8	2	4	38	1
Daylen Calicdan, Hawai'i	.310	.367	.399	168	10	1	1	19	3
Maaki Yamazaki, Hawai'i	.308	.379	.368	182	5	0	2	24	1
Jake Palmer, UC Irvine	.307	.460	.359	153	5	0	1	22	3
Christian Koss, UC Irvine	.307	.397	.490	202	12	5	5	30	11
Hank LoForte, CS Fullerton	.302	.394	.405	205	9	6	0	29	6
Cooper Morrison, UC Davis	.302	.371	.381	189	12	0	1	21	14
Adrian Damla, UC Irvine	.299	.419	.367	177	9	0	1	39	1
Tate Samuelson, Cal Poly	.298	.388	.395	205	5	0	5	39	2
Logan Denholm, UC Davis	.295	.398	.452	146	14	0	3	25	3
Scotty Scott, Hawai'i	.291	.381	.360	203	6	4	0	20	6
Andrew Martinez, UCSB	.285	.402	.495	200	14	2	8	47	7
Bradlee Beesley, Cal Poly	.283	.351	.374	219	15	1	1	35	8
Tommy Jew, UCSB	.283	.352	.530	219	9	6	11	40	20
Alex Baeza, Hawai'i	.278	.368	.394	180	7	1	4	27	1
Tevin Mitchell, UCSB	.277	.373	.451	184	11	3	5	37	20

INDIVIDUAL PITCHING LEADERS
(Minimum 40 innings pitched)

	W	L	ERA	G	SV	IP	H	BB	SO
Trenton Denholm, UC Irvine	9	4	1.81	15	0	100	61	20	93
Michael McGreevy, UCSB	5	1	1.94	29	6	60	52	13	53
Dylan Thomas, Hawai'i	4	4	2.01	20	4	54	40	13	59
Jack Dashwood, UCSB	9	2	2.48	15	0	91	79	17	93
Andre Pallante, UC Irvine	10	4	2.68	15	0	94	73	29	89
Michael Clark, UC Irvine	6	3	2.74	32	8	69	58	23	52
Rodney Boone, UCSB	8	0	2.78	14	0	81	58	29	80
Tanner Brubaker, UC Irvine	5	3	2.99	12	0	72	64	17	50
Isaiah Nunez, CS Northridge	8	4	3.09	15	0	93	106	13	66
Bobby Ay, Cal Poly	9	1	3.27	15	0	85	82	35	74
Adam Seminaris, LB State	4	9	3.35	15	0	94	98	24	74
Brett Erwin, UC Davis	5	5	3.70	14	0	73	76	23	29
Nick Avila, LB State	0	5	3.99	12	0	56	56	19	38
Ben Brecht, UC Santa Barbara	10	2	4.10	16	0	90	90	18	101
Timothy Josten, CS Fullerton	3	4	4.14	19	0	67	65	23	51

COLONIAL ATHLETIC ASSOCIATION

	Conference		Overall	
	W	L	W	L
Elon	19	5	33	24
Charleston	16	8	36	21
William & Mary	12	12	33	22
*UNC-Wilmington	12	12	32	31
Northeastern	12	12	28	29
James Madison	11	13	31	26
Hofstra	10	14	18	31
Delaware	9	15	21	33
Towson	7	17	14	39

ALL-CONFERENCE TEAM: C: Danny Wondrack, Sr., Charleston. **1B:** Joe Satterfield, Jr., Elon. **2B:** Dupree Hart, Sr., Charleston . **3B:** Cole Weiss, Jr., UNC Wilminton. **SS:** Greg Jones, So., UNC Wilmington. **OF:** Kep Brown, Jr., UNC Wilmington; Bradley Dixon, Sr., Charleston; Jordan Hutchins, So., Delaware. **DH:** Ian Fair, So., Northeastern. **UTL:** Fox Semones, Jr., James Madison. **SP:** George Kirby, Jr., Elon; Griffin McLarty, Jr., Charleson. **RP:**

Nick Robertson, So., James Madison. **Player of the Year:** Greg Jones, UNC Wilmington. **Pitcher of the Year:** George Kirby, Elon. **Coach of the Year:** Mike Kennedy, Elon. **Rookie of the Year:** Joseph Carpenter, Delaware.

INDIVIDUAL BATTING LEADERS
(Minimum 140 at-bats)

	AVG	OBP	SLG	AB	2B	3B	HR	RBI	SB
Ian Fair, Northeastern	.357	.419	.520	196	6	1	8	33	8
Greg Jones, UNC Wilmington	.341	.491	.543	223	12	9	5	36	42
Cam Devanney, Elon	.335	.435	.592	206	17	3	10	52	3
Joe Satterfield, Elon	.325	.438	.476	212	14	3	4	35	3
Jake Farrell, Northeastern	.322	.382	.581	227	17	6	10	51	2
Danny Wondrack, Charleston	.318	.404	.593	214	12	1	15	51	3
Vito Friscia, Hofstra	.317	.422	.530	183	15	0	8	31	3
Bradley Dixon, Charleston	.308	.360	.368	185	7	2	0	17	22
Trevon Dabney, James Madison	.308	.457	.494	180	14	1	6	29	17
Dupree Hart, Charleston	.305	.386	.389	226	9	2	2	44	40
Cole Weiss, UNC Wilmington	.305	.387	.434	256	13	4	4	49	4
Kyle Novak, James Madison	.303	.389	.378	188	9	1	1	28	3
Joseph Carpenter, Delaware	.302	.372	.465	202	10	4	5	37	0
Zach Pearson, William & Mary	.301	.336	.411	209	14	3	1	32	9
Brady Harju, James Madison	.295	.358	.469	207	9	0	9	43	3
Corey DiLoreto, James Madison	.287	.391	.392	209	11	4	1	34	6
Javon Fields, Towson	.286	.383	.391	192	10	5	0	17	14
Matthew Trehub, William & Mary	.282	.397	.403	149	8	2	2	20	2
Chaz Davey, Charleston	.281	.325	.434	221	12	2	6	44	6
Luke Manzo, Charleston	.280	.428	.335	161	3	3	0	24	15
Jordan Hutchins, Delaware	.279	.383	.431	197	16	1	4	42	11
Anthony Galason, Elon	.274	.345	.367	226	18	0	1	25	2
Hunter Smith, William & Mary	.274	.376	.514	212	13	1	12	40	0
Kep Brown, UNC Wilmington	.273	.343	.449	245	15	2	8	54	4
Brandon Raquet, William & Mary	.269	.402	.531	145	6	4	8	31	5
Austin Gauthier, Hofstra	.269	.373	.374	171	8	2	2	22	12
Brad Powers, Towson	.268	.391	.471	157	9	1	7	26	2
Jeff Costello, Northeastern	.267	.348	.351	202	10	1	2	29	19
Logan McRae, Charleston	.264	.374	.486	208	17	1	9	35	5
Noah Bridges, UNC Wilmington	.263	.324	.390	228	11	3	4	45	17

INDIVIDUAL PITCHING LEADERS
(Minimum 40 innings pitched)

	W	L	ERA	G	SV	IP	H	BB	SO
Griffin McLarty, Charleston	8	4	1.87	15	0	101	65	20	116
Bodie Sheehan, William & Mary	5	2	2.26	14	0	92	83	16	56
Nick Stewart, James Madison	4	5	2.74	15	0	72	56	33	61
George Kirby, Elon	8	2	2.75	14	0	88	73	6	107
Jared Wetherbee, Elon	7	4	3.00	19	1	84	67	23	98
Sean Mellen, Northeastern	5	2	3.10	15	0	90	69	38	112
Gavin Weyman, Towson	4	7	3.25	12	0	72	69	25	54
Kevin Kelly, James Madison	7	7	3.26	15	0	88	75	24	94
Josh Price, Charleston	7	5	3.33	35	1	81	78	23	54
Landen Roupp, UNC Wilmington	6	3	3.47	22	2	80	72	31	91
Luke Gesell, UNC Wilmington	5	5	3.59	17	0	93	74	27	72
Zach Tsakounis, William & Mary	4	2	3.60	16	1	65	66	22	52
Wade Strain, William & Mary	6	4	3.61	14	0	82	71	26	63
Kyle Brnovich, Elon	7	3	3.66	14	0	86	66	42	110
Brandon Walter, Delaware	5	6	4.08	13	0	79	68	27	94

CONFERENCE USA

	Conference W L		Overall W L	
*Florida Atlantic	22	8	41	21
*Southern Mississippi	20	10	40	21
Louisiana Tech	17	13	34	24
Western Kentucky	16	13	26	29
Old Dominion	16	14	35	21
Marshall	14	15	29	28
Rice	14	16	26	33
Texas-San Antonio	13	16	28	30
Alabama-Birmingham	12	18	27	29
Florida International	12	18	23	32
Charlotte	11	18	21	31

Middle Tennessee — 11 19 — 18 37

ALL-CONFERENCE TEAM: C: Harris Yett, Sr., Charlotte. **INF:** Bryan Arias, Sr., Texas-San Antonio; Mason Mallard, Sr., Louisiana Tech; Elvis Peralta, Jr., Marshall; Vinnie Pasquantino, Jr., Old Dominion. **OF:** Andy Garriola, Fr., Old Dominion; Jake Sanford, Jr., Western Kentucky; Matt Wallner, Jr., Southern Mississippi. **DH:** Andrew Dunlap, Sr., Rice. **UTL:** Logan Allen, So., Florida International. **SP:** Matt Canterino, Jr., Rice; Karan Patel, Sr., Texas-San Antonio; Walker Powell, Jr., Southern Mississippi; Blake Sanderson, Sr., Florida Atlantic. **RP:** Braxton Smith, Sr., Louisiana Tech; Zach Schneider, Sr., Florida Atlantic. **Player of the Year:** Jake Sanford, Western Kentucky. **Pitcher of the Year:** Matt Canterino, Rice. **Coach of the Year:** John McCormack, Florida Atlantic. **Newcomer of the Year:** Andy Garriolam, Old Dominion.

INDIVIDUAL BATTING LEADERS
(Minimum 140 at-bats)

	AVG	OBP	SLG	AB	2B	3B	HR	RBI	SB
Jake Sanford, W. Kentucky	.398	.483	.805	221	20	2	22	66	6
Mason Mallard, Louisiana Tech	.374	.470	.545	222	15	1	7	34	20
Ryan Stacy, UTSA	.357	.422	.566	182	114	3	6	29	5
Elvis Peralta, Marshall	.357	.425	.571	224	15	3	9	42	12
Gabe Montenegro, So. Miss.	.342	.455	.494	237	10	4	6	25	2
Bryant Bowen, So. Miss.	.341	.403	.563	208	11	1	11	51	1
Bryce Windham, Old Dominion	.338	.463	.417	216	4	2	3	25	9
Todd Elwood, Charlotte	.333	.384	.385	174	9	0	0	13	5
Eric Rivera, Fla. Atlantic	.332	.434	.435	262	9	0	6	48	11
Austin Shenton, Florida Intl.	.330	.425	.513	197	11	2	7	47	4
Andy Garriola, Old Dominion	.328	.378	.559	229	19	2	10	62	6
Zack Davis, UAB	.328	.417	.570	186	15	3	8	47	5
Harris Yett, Charlotte	.325	.392	.552	212	22	1	8	39	0
Dylan Rock, UTSA	.324	.420	.457	219	19	2	2	37	7
Matt Wallner, Marshall	.323	.446	.681	226	12	0	23	60	2
Francisco Urbaez, Fla. Atlantic	.322	.432	.519	233	12	2	10	41	2
Mitchell Hartigan, FAU	.322	.404	.514	177	14	1	6	33	3
Tucker Linder, Marshall	.322	.366	.465	245	15	1	6	50	7
Joe Montes, FAU	.321	.373	.500	240	14	1	9	53	0
Alvarez Willfredo, FAU	.320	.396	.395	147	8	0	1	21	3
Bryan Arias, UTSA	.319	.445	.536	207	14	2	9	36	10
Derek Cartaya, FIU	.316	.395	.374	190	11	0	0	28	20
Taylor Young, LA Tech	.316	.443	.396	212	8	0	3	25	9
Colton Schultz, UAB	.315	.420	.493	203	12	3	6	43	10
Bobby Morgensen, FAU	.312	.408	.535	202	8	2	11	46	0
Bryan Sturges, UTSA	.312	.462	.505	186	18	0	6	44	8
Pedro Pages, FAU	.310	.423	.438	226	11	0	6	43	0
Nick Thornquist, UTSA	.310	.389	.555	155	19	2	5	34	1
Cade Edwards, Rice	.308	.360	.498	221	16	4	6	38	6

INDIVIDUAL PITCHING LEADERS
(Minimum 40 innings pitched)

	W	L	ERA	G	SV	IP	H	BB	SO
Walker Powell, Marshall	6	2	2.72	16	0	99	98	13	73
Karan Patel, UTSA	4	5	2.74	15	0	92	83	36	104
Matt Canterino, Rice	6	5	2.81	15	0	99	73	23	121
Slater Foust, UTSA	8	2	2.96	16	0	85	74	23	45
Logan Allen, FIU	4	6	3.21	39	0	84	71	25	120
Evan Kravetz, Rice	6	2	3.24	14	0	81	58	32	108
Matt Miller, LA Tech	6	1	3.40	18	1	85	71	34	99
David Zoz, Middle Tennessee	2	3	3.44	20	2	55	55	30	51
Joshua Shapiro, Marshall	5	3	3.61	16	0	85	71	44	80
Ryne Moore, Old Dominion	6	4	3.78	16	1	83	82	24	57
Cody Carroll, So. Miss.	3	2	3.86	27	1	63	73	18	50
Nick MacDonald, FIU	4	5	3.91	15	0	76	97	18	68
Franco Aleman, FIU	3	5	3.98	14	0	66	76	20	53
Nick Pantos, Old Dominion	4	3	4.05	16	0	80	63	38	74
Hunter Gregory, Old Dominion	7	3	4.05	28	2	60	61	27	85

HORIZON LEAGUE

	Conference W L	Overall W L
Wright State	21 8	41 15
*Illinois-Chicago	18 11	30 23
Milwaukee	18 11	36 22
Northern Kentucky	12 17	15 40
Oakland	9 18	11 37
Youngstown State	7 20	13 41

ALL-CONFERENCE TEAM: C: Tyler Bordner, Sr., Milwaukee. **1B:** Joe Vyskocil, R-Jr., Milwaukee. **2B:** Tyler Black, Fr., Wright State. **3B:** Seth Gray, Jr., Wright State. **SS:** Trevor Schwecke, Jr., Wright State. **OF:** JD Orr, Sr., Wright State; Zach Weatherford, R-Sr., Wright State; Peyton Burdick, R-Jr., Wright State. **DH:** Ryan Hampe, Fr., Illinois-Chicago. **SP:** Jacob Key, Jr., Illinois-Chicago; Bear Bellomy, Sr., Wright State; Beau Keathley, So., Oakland. **RP:** Alex Padilla, R-Sr., Illinois-Chicago. **Player of the Year:** Gabe Snyder, Wright State. **Pitcher of the Year:** Jacob Key, Jr., Illinois-Chicago. **Coach of the Year:** Alex Sogard, Wright State. **Rookie of the Year:** Tyler Black, Wright State.

INDIVIDUAL BATTING LEADERS
(Minimum 140 at-bats)

	AVG	OBP	SLG	AB	2B	3B	HR	RBI	SB
Peyton Burdick, Wright State	.407	.538	.729	214	18	3	15	72	23
Tyler Bordner, Milwaukee	.376	.439	.598	189	15	3	7	52	3
Scott Ota, Ill.-Chicago	.357	.458	.749	199	14	2	29	64	5
Tyler Black, Wright State	.353	.469	.600	170	11	5	7	41	8
Ryan Hampe, UIC	.351	.401	.524	168	14	0	5	48	0
Seth Gray, Wright State	.351	.483	.630	208	13	6	11	70	6
Zach Weatherford, Wright St.	.345	.424	.553	226	12	4	9	66	21
Trevor Schwecke, Milwaukee	.335	.416	.507	221	20	3	4	54	8
Joe Vyskocil, Milwaukee	.330	.403	.527	203	14	1	8	39	2
JD Orr, Wright State	.330	.464	.404	230	14	1	8	39	56
Matt Dileo, Oakland	.313	.431	.464	166	3	2	6	26	11
Devin Rybacki, Milwaukee	.312	.414	.416	231	14	2	2	33	7
Damon Dues, Wright State	.307	.466	.448	163	9	1	4	33	28
Marion Camilletti, Oakland	.306	.457	.400	170	10	0	2	25	10
Will Haueter, N. Kentucky	.304	.394	.495	214	12	1	9	39	6
Joshua Figueroa, UIC	.294	.353	.406	170	10	0	3	34	0
Jeff Wehler, Youngstown St.	.290	.373	.441	186	10	0	6	27	30
Blake Griffith, Oakland	.284	.380	.457	162	8	1	6	31	4
Ryan Lin-Peistrup, UIC	.282	.367	.389	149	11	1	1	28	1
Trevor Wiersma, Y'town St.	.281	.399	.449	185	9	2	6	29	2
Matt Bottcher, UIC	.279	.356	.322	183	4	2	0	10	7
Matt Quartel, Milwaukee	.277	.399	.422	166	7	1	5	30	4

INDIVIDUAL PITCHING LEADERS
(Minimum 40 innings pitched)

	W	L	ERA	G	SV	IP	H	BB	SO
Bear Bellomy, Wright State	9	3	3.58	15	0	96	93	21	74
Jacob Key, UIC	7	8	3.75	16	0	106	102	25	90
Beau Keathley, Oakland	3	7	3.77	16	0	72	47	42	83
Mike Edwards, Milwaukee	4	4	3.93	13	0	69	75	29	45
Bradley Brehmer, Wright State	7	0	4.50	15	0	72	68	23	42
Joey Fredrickson, UIC	6	5	4.57	15	0	85	102	19	45
Zane Collins, Wright State	8	4	5.72	15	0	74	74	46	65
Jared Reklaitis, Milwaukee	9	5	6.43	20	0	99	120	34	104

IVY LEAGUE

	Conference W L	Overall W L
*Harvard	14 7	27 16
Columbia	13 8	19 23
Yale	12 8	18 23
Pennsylvania	11 10	23 18
Brown	9 12	12 27
Princeton	8 12	14 26
Cornell	8 13	14 24
Dartmouth	8 13	15 26

ALL-CONFERENCE TEAM: C: Matt O'Neill, Sr., Pennsylvania. **1B:** Patrick McColl, Sr., Harvard. **2B:** Sean Sullivan, Sr., Dartmouth. **3B:** Seteffen Torgersen, Sr., Dartmouth . **SS:** Joe Engel, Sr., Columbia; Josh Hood, Fr., Pennsylvania. **OF:** Joe Lomuscio, So., Brown; Jake Suddleson, Jr., Harvard; Peter Matt, Pennsylvania. **DH:** Hunter Bigge, Jr., Harvard. **UTL:** Mark Sluys, Sr., Brown. **SP:** Christian Scafidi, Jr., Pennsylvania; Kumar Nambiar, Sr., Yale; Alex Stiegler, Jr., Yale. **RP:** John Natoli, Jr., Cornell. **Player of the Year:** Jake Suddleson, Harvard. **Pitcher of the Year:** Christian Scafidi, Pennsylvania. **Coach of the Year:** Bill Decker, Harvard. **Rookie of the Year:** Josh Hood, Pennsylvania.

INDIVIDUAL BATTING LEADERS
(Minimum 140 at-bats)

	AVG	OBP	SLG	AB	2B	3B	HR	RBI	SB
Matt O'Neill, Penn	.405	.527	.620	158	15	2	5	40	2
Patrick McColl, Harvard	.391	.454	.724	174	16	3	12	48	5
Jake Suddleson, Harvard	.378	.436	.652	164	11	2	10	51	2
Sean Phelan, Penn	.363	.458	.564	179	18	0	6	37	0
Griffin Dey, Yale	.351	.474	.649	148	5	3	11	43	6
Steffen Torgersen, Dartmouth	.344	.438	.477	151	6	4	2	13	3
Joe Lomuscio, Brown	.339	.385	.483	174	9	2	4	26	2
Simon Whiteman, Yale	.337	.388	.465	187	17	2	1	20	34
Josh Hood, Penn	.331	.411	.580	181	13	4	8	42	1
Joe Engel, Colgate	.329	.429	.439	173	10	3	1	18	2
Peter Matt, Penn	.328	.391	.456	195	10	6	1	35	14
Mason LaPlante, Yale	.326	.423	.404	141	9	1	0	18	28
Craig Larsen, Penn	.322	.402	.517	174	14	1	6	44	4
Matt Fienstein, Dartmouth	.321	.383	.524	168	10	3	6	28	0
Hunter Bigge, Harvard	.318	.367	.527	148	7	0	8	35	1
Ben Skinner, Harvard	.317	.384	.451	142	7	3	2	17	2
Tommy Courtney, Penn	.316	.396	.439	171	11	2	2	27	4
Julian Bury, Colgate	.313	.354	.411	192	16	0	1	18	2
Jake Boone, Princeton	.312	.342	.393	173	11	0	1	18	6
Chad Minato, Harvard	.311	.386	.391	151	6	0	2	15	6
Jake Gehri, Yale	.309	.382	.530	149	10	1	7	35	3
Josh Nicoloff, Colgate	.307	.372	.405	163	9	2	1	20	8
Will Simoneit, Cornell	.301	.358	.500	146	11	0	6	21	6
Nate Ostmo, Dartmouth	.301	.385	.514	146	11	1	6	33	2
Parke Phillips, Brown	.293	.391	.388	147	8	0	2	29	1
Liam McGill, Colgate	.292	.386	.429	161	10	0	4	24	0

INDIVIDUAL PITCHING LEADERS
(Minimum 40 innings pitched)

	W	L	ERA	G	SV	IP	H	BB	SO
Christian Safidi, Penn	6	1	2.62	11	0	69	60	19	59
John Alan Kendrick, Penn	0	2	3.07	11	0	59	58	19	46
Josh Simpson, Colgate	4	4	3.15	11	0	69	58	22	62
Enzo Stefanoni, Harvard	5	1	3.16	19	0	43	37	12	34
Ryan Smith, Princeton	5	4	3.45	12	0	76	70	35	76
Scott Politz, Yale	6	3	3.46	11	0	83	91	18	56
Alex Stiegler, Yale	6	4	3.52	11	0	77	75	21	76
Mitchell Holcomb, Penn	6	1	3.76	11	0	65	66	28	51
Colby Wyatt, Cornell	3	5	3.84	12	0	59	68	17	32
Kumar Nambiar, Yale	3	2	3.90	10	0	60	57	26	57
Ben Wereski, Colgate	4	3	4.18	10	0	52	48	33	53
Hunter Bigge, Harvard	8	1	4.29	12	0	78	71	38	74

METRO ATLANTIC ATHLETIC CONFERENCE

	Conference W L	Overall W L
Canisius	17 7	24 29
*Quinnipiac	17 7	30 29
Fairfield	15 9	35 25
Marist	15 9	27 26
Manhattan	15 9	26 33
Monmouth	13 11	27 29
Siena	12 12	18 33
Niagara	9 15	15 33
Iona	8 16	14 38
Rider	8 16	17 36
Saint Peter's	3 21	5 46

ALL-CONFERENCE TEAM: C: Matt Padre, So., Manhattan. **1B:** Anthony Boselli, Sr., Fairfield. **2B:** Anthony Lazar, Sr., Marist. **3B:** Robbie Armitage, So., Marist. **SS:** Jack Gethings, Sr., Fairfield. **OF:** Nick Cimillo, Fr., Manhattan; Frankie Gregoire, Sr., Marist; Andre Marrero, Jr., Quinnipiac. **DH:** Tyler Kapuscinski, R-Jr., Marist. **UTL:** Ian Ostberg, So., Quinnipiac. **SP:** Matthew Brash, Jr., Niagara; Tyler Poulin, Sr., Quinnipiac. **RP:** Brendan White, Jr., Siena. **Player of the Year:** Brendan White, Jr., Siena. **Pitcher of the Year:** Matthew Brash, Niagara. **Coach of the Year:** Matt Mazurek, Canisius. **Rookie of the Year:** Nick Cimillo, Manhattan.

INDIVIDUAL BATTING LEADERS
(Minimum 140 at-bats)

	AVG	OBP	SLG	AB	2B	3B	HR	RBI	SB
Tyler Kapuscinski, Marist	.366	.469	.531	145	10	1	4	29	1
Jack Gethings, Fairfield	.364	.436	.492	242	14	7	1	36	8
Nick Cimillo, Manhattan	.350	.417	.498	223	12	0	7	36	0
Anthony Boselli, Fairfield	.335	.415	.442	233	16	0	3	55	6
Anthony Lazar, Marist	.333	.402	.516	213	16	1	7	27	19
Colton Bender, Quinnipiac	.322	.373	.429	205	14	1	2	32	3
Ian Ostberg, Quinnipiac	.320	.383	.429	225	11	2	3	35	18
Michael Gabriele, Niagra	.318	.379	.376	157	9	0	0	19	1
Robbie Armitage, Marist	.318	.373	.512	211	6	4	9	50	7
Andre Marrero, Quinnipiac	.316	.383	.538	234	14	4	10	48	20
Randy Taveras, Marist	.316	.414	.386	171	7	1	1	22	18
Dan Ryan, Fairfield	.315	.391	.437	213	21	1	1	36	4
Riley Mihalik, Rider	.313	.408	.573	192	8	3	12	41	0
Brian Kelly, Siena	.305	.425	.368	174	11	0	0	25	5
Zach Durfee, Siena	.304	.419	.405	158	11	1	1	18	7
Zach Schild, Monmouth	.303	.344	.394	208	10	0	3	36	4
Sam Franco, Manhattan	.301	.373	.432	176	9	1	4	31	12
Sebastian Williamson, Rider	.301	.322	.393	196	12	0	2	26	12
Hunter Mason, Saint Peter's	.300	.379	.453	190	14	3	3	37	13

INDIVIDUAL PITCHING LEADERS
(Minimum 40 innings pitched)

	W	L	ERA	G	SV	IP	H	BB	SO
Matthew Brash, Niagra	4	5	2.43	14	0	85	61	29	121
Brendan White, Siena	4	7	3.00	14	0	90	89	31	93
Austin Pope, Fairfield	4	3	3.16	14	0	77	56	35	79
Stephen Hansen, Iona	4	6	3.23	14	0	95	107	14	93
Nolan Hunt, Canisus	5	4	3.28	14	0	71	71	18	49
Chris Enns, Quinnipiac	7	5	3.47	15	0	80	74	24	77
Colin Donnelly, Quinnipiac	6	1	3.79	29	1	59	62	19	51
Rob Hensey, Monmouth	4	5	3.88	14	0	63	52	23	51
Tyler Poulin, Quinnipiac	7	2	3.93	15	0	87	86	30	82
Mike Coss, Marist	5	2	3.38	27	8	48	38	15	54
Jordan Silverman, Rider	2	4	5.72	25	2	61	80	5	34

MID-AMERICAN CONFERENCE

	Conference W	L	Overall W	L
*Central Michigan	22	5	46	12
Ball State	20	5	38	19
Kent State	17	8	30	24
Miami (Ohio)	15	11	37	19
Northern Illinois	14	12	20	36
Ohio	12	14	20	34
Western Michigan	11	14	18	31
Bowling Green	8	18	16	33
Eastern Michigan	6	21	11	43
Toledo	4	21	17	36

ALL-CONFERENCE TEAM: C: Griffin Lockwood-Powell, So., Central Michigan; Michael Turner, So., Kent State. **1B:** Rudy Rott, Sr., Ohio. **2B:** Landon Stephens, Jr., Miami (Ohio). **3B:** Kian O'Brien, Sr., Kent State. **SS:** Zavier Warren, So., Central Michigan. **OF:** Ben Carew, R-So., Kent State, Blake Dunn, So., Western Michigan, Jacob Crum, Sr., Central Michigan. **DH:** Cole Andrews, Fr., Miami (Ohio). **SP:** Drey Jameson, So., Ball State; Pat Leatherman, Sr., Central Michigan; John Baker, Jr., Ball State, Sam Bachman, Fr., Miami (Ohio). **RP:** Nick Floyd, Sr., Ball State. **Player of the Year:** Rudy Rott, Ohio. **Pitcher of the Year:** Drey Jameson, Ball State. **Coach of the Year:** Jordan Bischel, Central Michigan. **Rookie of the Year:** Justin Kirby, Kent State; Sam Bachman, Miami (Ohio).

INDIVIDUAL BATTING LEADERS
(Minimum 140 at-bats)

	AVG	OBP	SLG	AB	2B	3B	HR	RBI	SB
Ben Carew, Kent State	.406	.474	.525	219	13	2	3	31	24
Rudy Rott, Ohio	.382	.464	.618	212	18	1	10	47	6
Blake Dunn, W. Michigan	.374	.467	.521	190	2	5	29	99	30
Zavier Warren, C. Michigan	.369	.502	.578	244	23	2	8	70	14
Drew Devine, W. Michigan	.359	.400	.484	184	15	1	2	31	4
Zach Gilles, C. Michigan	.351	.447	.430	242	7	6	0	34	20
Zachary Owings, E. Michigan	.345	.395	.527	220	18	5	4	34	14
Cam Touchette, Kent State	.345	.445	.429	168	7	2	1	27	19
Gri Lockwood-Powell, C. Mich.	.341	.449	.580	226	17	2	11	74	0
Cristian Tejada, Miami (Ohio)	.339	.453	.497	183	14	6	1	26	19
Brad Boss, Toledo	.332	.431	.495	214	18	1	5	41	6
Jacob Crum, C. Michigan	.332	.413	.589	214	18	8	7	57	10
Darryn Davis, Toledo	.329	.373	.414	210	9	0	3	33	2
William Baker, Ball State	.324	.377	.454	207	14	5	1	31	7
Neil Lambert, Bowling Green	.322	.441	.389	149	10	0	0	17	12
Aaron Simpson, Ball State	.321	.413	.502	221	10	6	6	44	14
Brad Croy, Bowling Green	.319	.353	.410	144	7	0	2	24	0
Jordan Stephens, Miami (Ohio)	.316	.402	.415	171	9	1	2	31	4
Ross Messina, Ball State	.316	.380	.547	225	22	3	8	50	5
Kian O'Brien, Kent State	.313	.402	.530	166	11	2	7	45	6
Justin Kirby, Kent State	.313	.398	.619	147	14	2	9	30	9
Zach Heeke, C. Michigan	.311	.437	.377	244	14	1	0	38	6
Landon Stephens, Miami (Ohio)	.310	.407	.555	229	21	4	9	46	12
John Ricotta, Ball State	.308	.382	.520	221	17	0	10	48	0
Cal Evers, Miami (Ohio)	.306	.394	.482	170	13	1	5	29	5
Jason Sullivan, C. Michigan	.305	.404	.399	233	14	1	2	50	14

INDIVIDUAL PITCHING LEADERS
(Minimum 40 innings pitched)

	W	L	ERA	G	SV	IP	H	BB	SO
John Baker, Ball State	7	2	2.14	16	0	72	48	35	90
Pat Leatherman, S. Michigan	10	1	2.86	16	0	88	71	28	86
Brady Miller, W. Michigan	5	2	3.10	15	0	61	59	11	49
Andrew Abrahamowicz, B. Green	2	5	3.11	17	0	75	82	26	61
Jack Corbell, Miami (Ohio)	5	3	3.13	16	0	78	73	35	50
Cameron Brown, C. Michigan	10	1	3.20	16	0	98	89	30	79
Drey Jameson, Ball State	6	3	3.24	16	0	92	74	32	146
Layne S.P., Toledo	2	6	3.28	10	0	60	50	28	46
Jack Liberatore, Ohio	8	5	3.61	15	0	77	70	39	63
Eddie Kutt, Ohio	3	5	3.64	24	1	77	71	30	67
Sam Bachman, Miami (Ohio)	7	1	3.93	15	0	76	64	39	75
Michael Lasiewicz, N. Illinois	6	4	3.94	13	0	75	70	39	77
Spencer Mraz, Miami (Ohio)	5	6	4.03	15	1	76	67	29	72
Connor Wollersheim, Kent State	6	6	4.20	15	0	84	79	39	97

MID-EASTERN ATHLETIC CONFERENCE

	Conference W	L	Overall W	L
Northern Division	**W**	**L**	**W**	**L**
Norfolk State	17	7	24	26
Coppin State	15	9	24	24
Delaware State	12	12	20	25
Maryland Eastern-Shore	4	20	10	43
Southern Division	**W**	**L**	**W**	**L**
North Carolina A&T	16	8	29	24
*Florida A&M	14	10	27	34
North Carolina Central	10	14	21	28
Savannah State	10	14	13	27
Bethune-Cookman	10	14	17	38

ALL-CONFERENCE TEAM: C: Ryne Stanley, Jr., North Carolina A&T. **1B:** Justin Banks, Jr., Coppin State. **2B:** Joe Fernando, Sr., Bethune-Cookman. **3B:** Jared Gillis, Jr., Delaware State. **SS:** Corey Joyce, Jr., North Carolina Central. **OF:** Carter Williams Jr., North Carolina Central; Justin Hayes, R-Sr., Norfolk State; Dawnoven Smith, Sr., North Carolina A&T. **UTL:** Alsander Womack, So., Norfolk State. **SP:** Garrett Lawson, Jr., Delaware State; Tim Luth, Sr., North Carolina A&T. **RP:** Jeremiah McCullom, So., Florida A&M. **Player of the Year:** Corey Joyce, North Carolina Central. **Pitcher of the Year:** Garrett Lawson, Delaware State.

Coach of the Year: Keith Shumate, Norfolk State. **Rookie of the Year:** Ryan Miller, North Carolina Central.

INDIVIDUAL BATTING LEADERS
(Minimum 140 at-bats)

	AVG	OBP	SLG	AB	2B	3B	HR	RBI	SB
Justin Banks, Coppin State	.394	.493	.588	165	17	0	5	43	0
Alsander Womack, Norfolk State	.377	.441	.503	167	10	1	3	31	10
Corey Joyce, N.C. Central	.343	.444	.527	169	8	4	5	32	12
John Weglarz, Delaware State	.342	.391	.440	184	10	4	0	23	4
Carter Williams, N.C. Central	.328	.394	.475	198	14	0	5	42	14
Dustin Baber, N.C. A&T	.328	.402	.436	195	15	0	2	30	13
Joseph Fernando, B-Cookman	.324	.373	.443	210	11	1	4	26	15
Jalen Atterbury, Savannah St.	.323	.398	.372	164	8	0	0	24	26
Stephen Baughan, Norfolk St.	.314	.393	.560	175	22	3	5	27	3
Octavi Moyer, Florida A&M	.310	.414	.452	239	14	1	6	27	6
Nazier McIlwain, Coppin State	.309	.412	.427	178	10	1	3	25	1
Jared Gillis, Delaware State	.307	.399	.428	166	12	1	2	37	3
Vinny Bailey, N.C. Central	.305	.431	.470	164	10	1	5	31	2
Justin Hayes, Norfolk St.	.301	.364	.393	196	7	4	1	22	30
Sey Lawerence, Florida A&M	.296	.363	.367	226	13	0	1	27	14
Joseph Roberson, Savannah St.	.293	.414	.408	147	5	0	4	28	1
Tommy Jordan, Delaware St.	.293	.410	.415	147	12	0	2	14	5
Caleb Ward, Norfolk St.	.290	.368	.457	186	12	2	5	44	13
Rob Robinson, Florida A&M	.288	.386	.346	153	6	0	1	23	5
Josten Heron, B-Cookman	.287	.398	.378	164	10	1	1	18	9

INDIVIDUAL PITCHING LEADERS
(Minimum 40 innings pitched)

	W	L	ERA	G	SV	IP	H	BB	SO
Leon Davidson, N.C. A&T	5	0	0.67	33	4	40	21	9	26
Garrett Lawson, Delaware St.	6	5	1.96	14	0	83	63	32	102
Ethan Chavis, N.C. A&T	2	2	2.98	19	0	57	54	20	34
Branden Redfern, Coppin State	3	2	3.11	22	2	46	49	19	52
Darnell Maisonet, Delaware St.	3	2	3.12	8	0	43	37	10	46
Ryan Miller, N.C. Central	6	4	3.15	17	1	71	73	13	73
Michael Johnson, N.C. A&T	4	5	3.22	15	0	81	92	13	46
Devin Rivera Ozuna, Coppin St.	8	3	3.36	12	0	75	70	24	74
Tim Luth, N.C. A&T	7	3	3.51	16	1	90	88	21	43
Kyle Coleman, Florida A&M	6	6	3.52	17	0	100	106	40	81
Anthony Maldonado, B--Cook	3	5	3.76	14	0	81	62	30	97
Jonathan Mahoney, Norfolk St.	6	4	3.99	14	0	88	101	32	74
Evan Gates, N.C. A&T	4	4	4.05	17	1	67	58	24	65

MISSOURI VALLEY CONFERENCE

Team	Conference		Overall	
	W	L	W	L
*Dallas Baptist	14	7	43	20
Illinois State	14	7	36	26
*Indiana State	13	8	43	18
Bradley	11	10	31	19
Evansville	11	10	24	29
Missouri State	10	11	20	36
Valparasio	6	15	14	36
Southern Illinois	5	16	26	29

ALL-CONFERENCE TEAM: C: Drew Millas, Jr., Missouri State. **1B:** Connor O'Brien, Fr., Bradley. **2B:** Jarrod Watkins, Sr., Indiana State. **3B:** Joe Butler, Jr., Illinois State. **SS:** Jimmy Glowenke, So., Dallas Baptist. **OF:** Joe Aeilts, Jr., Illinois State; Luke Bandy, Jr., Dallas Baptist; Dakota Kotowski, Fr., Missouri State; John Rave, Jr., Illinois State. **DH:** Bryce Ball, Jr., Dallas Baptist. **SP:** Bryce Ball, Jr., Dallas Baptist. **RP:** Burl Carraway, So., Dallas Baptist; Tyler Grauer, Jr., Indiana State. **Player of the Year:** Joe Aeilts, Illinois State. **Pitcher of the Year:** Brent Headrick, Illinois State. **Coach of the Year:** Steve Holm, Illinois State. **Rookie of the Year:** Dakota Kotowski, Missouri State.

INDIVIDUAL BATTING LEADERS
(Minimum 140 at-bats)

	AVG	OBP	SLG	AB	2B	3B	HR	RBI	SB
Joe Aeilts, Illinois St.	.346	.408	.559	254	16	4	10	49	14
Luke Shadid, Bradley	.344	.421	.574	209	12	3	10	42	7
Luke Bandy, Dallas Baptist	.338	.424	.505	198	11	2	6	32	26
Jimmy Glowenke, Dallas Baptist	.328	.429	.467	244	16	0	6	43	2
Dan Bolt, Bradley	.327	.453	.595	168	8	2	11	40	7
Bryce Ball, Dallas Baptist	.325	.443	.614	228	12	0	18	54	3
Chase Dawson, Valparasio	.324	.390	.506	170	9	5	4	28	6
Joe Butler, Illinois St.	.319	.370	.450	251	14	2	5	44	12
Nate Reeder, Evansville	.309	.411	.438	194	10	0	5	37	5
Jarrod Watkins, Indiana St.	.306	.375	.396	235	13	1	2	33	2
Blake Billinger, Valparasio	.306	.407	.544	180	14	1	9	40	1
Clay Dungan, Indiana St.	.305	.406	.481	243	10	3	9	38	8
Jack Butler, Illinois St.	.304	.370	.444	171	15	0	3	25	1
Jack Duffy, Missouri St.	.303	.391	.424	198	13	1	3	20	5
Jordan Libman, Illinois St.	.299	.421	.376	234	12	0	2	28	4
John Rave, Illinois St.	.297	.377	.502	273	14	3	12	48	12
Max Wright, Indiana St.	.296	.380	.394	203	8	0	4	36	2
Jackson Glenn, Dallas Baptist	.292	.372	.460	250	19	1	7	54	3
Riley Dent, Valparasio	.290	.379	.341	176	5	2	0	11	4
Derek Parola, Illinois St.	.289	.341	.406	266	11	1	6	42	14
Jake Means, Indiana St.	.286	.417	.404	213	10	0	5	42	4
Roby Enriquez, Indiana St.	.285	.369	.397	239	12	0	5	33	3
Tanner Craig, Evansville	.284	.374	.442	197	14	1	5	32	0
Brendan Dougherty, Bradley	.283	.363	.415	205	11	5	2	26	1
Connor O'Brien, Bradley	.282	.352	.404	156	7	0	4	25	5
Herbert, Iser, Dallas Baptist	.280	.347	.490	157	12	0	7	34	0
CJ Huntley, Indiana St.	.280	.342	.393	168	9	2	2	29	4

INDIVIDUAL PITCHING LEADERS
(Minimum 40 innings pitched)

	W	L	ERA	G	SV	IP	H	BB	SO
Cole Cook, Bradley	5	2	2.03	19	0	62	48	17	38
Mitch Janssen, Bradley	4	2	2.06	16	0	74	54	35	71
Jordan Martinson, Dallas Baptist	8	4	2.61	16	0	100	79	29	115
MD Johnson, Dallas Baptist	10	2	2.76	16	0	98	71	29	110
Triston Polley, Indiana St.	8	1	2.84	16	0	105	84	40	90
Collin Liberatore, Indiana St.	10	2	2.96	16	0	103	75	35	80
Tyler Whitbread, Indiana St.	9	2	3.23	15	0	84	77	16	66
Brent Headrick, Illinois St.	9	3	3.47	16	0	96	74	31	115
Logan Wiley, Missouri St.	5	5	3.47	15	0	91	92	22	82
Sam Lund, Bradley	5	4	3.76	15	0	55	50	16	44
Shane Gray, Evansville	3	1	4.25	22	0	53	50	17	44
Nathan Croner, Evansville	5	6	4.28	15	0	82	85	30	65
Brooks Gosswein, Bradley	4	4	4.38	16	0	64	50	36	51
Brett Wicklund, Illinois St.	4	4	4.50	15	0	64	76	8	28
Justin Hayden, Evansville	3	3	4.53	12	0	56	51	16	42

MOUNTAIN WEST CONFERENCE

	Conference		Overall	
	W	L	W	L
*Fresno State	20	8	40	16
San Diego State	16	13	32	25
Nevada	14	16	30	26
UNLV	14	16	29	29
Air Force	12	14	26	26
San Jose State	13	17	20	34
New Mexico	11	16	23	28

ALL-CONFERENCE TEAM: C: Rob Dau, Sr., Air Force. **2B:** Nolan Dempsey, Sr., Fresno State. **3B:** McCarthy Tatum, Sr., Fresno State. **SS:** JT Arruda, So., Fresno State; Bryson Stott, Jr., UNLV. **OF:** Zach Ashford, Sr., Fresno State; Jaylon McLaughlin, Jr., Nevada; Jared Mang, Sr., New Mexico; Matt Rudick, So., San Diego State; Kellen Strahm, Sr., San Jose State. **SP:** Ryan Jensen, Jr., Fresno State; Ryan Hare, Jr., UNLV. **RP:** Jamie Arias, So., Fresno State; Adrian Mardueno, Jr., San Diego State. **Player of the Year:** McCarthy Tatum, Fresno State; Bryson Stott, UNLV. **Pitcher of the Year:** Ryan Jensen, Fresno State. **Coach of the Year:** Mike Batesole, Fresno State. **Rookie of the Year:** Jaden Fein, San Diego State; Edarian Williams, UNLV.

INDIVIDUAL BATTING LEADERS
(Minimum 140 at-bats)

	AVG	OBP	SLG	AB	2B	3B	HR	RBI	SB
Kellen Strahm, San Jose St.	.382	.487	.546	152	5	1	6	28	14
Zach Ashford, Fresno St.	.381	.488	.526	215	11	4	4	21	10
Connor Mang, New Mexico	.369	.447	.542	203	17	3	4	50	11
Bryson Stott, UNLV	.360	.488	.605	228	22	2	10	36	17
Jared Mang, New Mexico	.358	.436	.575	212	23	4	5	52	15
McCarthy Tatum, Fresno St,	.356	.397	.606	236	16	2	13	77	5
Edarian Williams, UNLV	.350	.408	.425	240	13	1	1	39	2
Jack-Thomas Wold, UNLV	.341	.414	.518	170	9	0	7	35	1
Jaylon McLaughlin, Nevada	.339	.385	.456	180	8	2	3	24	25
JT Arruda, Fresno St.	.338	.448	.531	213	15	1	8	45	8
Nolan Dempsey, Fresno St.	.332	.387	.539	217	17	2	8	57	4
Dillon Johnson, UNLV	.329	.404	.401	237	11	0	2	36	2
Ashton Easley, Air Force	.327	.377	.545	202	15	4	7	30	30
Blake Berry, San Jose St.	.323	.406	.423	201	15	1	1	30	5
Hayden Schilling, New Mexico	.322	.407	.454	205	14	5	1	32	16
Justin Watari, New Mexico	.321	.451	.414	162	11	2	0	14	5
Joshua Zamora, Nevada	.320	.381	.511	219	14	2	8	38	3
Matt Rudick, San Diego St.	.320	.403	.394	241	12	3	0	28	6
Casey Schmitt, San Diego St.	.315	.415	.450	200	8	2	5	36	4
Colby Brown, Air Force	.309	.378	.376	178	10	1	0	27	2
Angelo Armenta, San Diego St.	.307	.412	.415	212	15	1	2	39	6
Rob Dau, Air Force	.305	.364	.446	177	14	1	3	37	3
Jeff Deimling, New Mexico	.305	.382	.455	154	8	0	5	39	2
Max Smith, UNLV	.303	.396	.509	228	17	0	10	51	5
Weston Hatten, Nevada	.300	.416	.550	200	14	3	10	32	8
Gabe Martinez, Air Force	.297	.409	.531	175	11	0	10	45	2
Nic Ready, Air Force	.297	.351	.589	219	19	3	13	44	8
James Shimashite, San Jose St.	.295	.374	.352	193	8	0	1	34	6
Tyler Bosetti, Nevada	.293	.348	.433	164	7	2	4	25	0
Jaden Fein, San Diego St.	.293	.354	.473	150	11	2	4	20	2

INDIVIDUAL BATTING LEADERS
(Minimum 140 at-bats)

	AVG	OBP	SLG	AB	2B	3B	HR	RBI	SB
Patrick Causa, Mount St. Mary's	.402	.521	.710	169	12	2	12	39	9
Ryan Ward, Bryant	.382	.450	.614	249	15	2	13	51	12
TT Bowens, C. Connecticut	.376	.459	.640	125	12	3	5	26	0
Myles Nicholson, Mount St. Mary's	.365	.444	.514	181	10	4	3	23	37
Adam Frank, FDU	.363	.419	.508	179	15	1	3	27	8
Gaby Cruz, Bryant	.354	.449	.592	147	6	1	9	37	0
Zack Costello, Mount St. Mary's	.346	.429	.497	153	6	1	5	30	4
Jimmy Titus, Bryant	.343	.423	.571	233	13	2	12	63	4
Will Johnson, Wagner	.337	.451	.415	193	10	1	1	29	2
Nick Angelini, Bryant	.336	.400	.531	226	12	1	10	52	12
Jake Frasca, Sacred Heart	.332	.403	.439	205	13	0	3	29	2
Sam Owens, Bryant	.326	.431	.497	181	11	1	6	37	4
Evan McDonald, FDU	.319	.423	.548	188	13	0	10	37	1
Nate Brodsky, FDU	.318	.373	.495	192	12	2	6	29	2
Isiah Daubon, Sacred Heart	.317	.396	.423	142	6	0	3	22	3
Freddy Sabido, Wagner	.317	.396	.477	199	6	4	6	34	6
Justin Jordan, Sacred Heart	.314	.416	.407	172	8	1	2	21	12
Salvatore Monticciolo, FDU	.305	.370	.568	190	11	0	13	46	0
Joe Silvestrone, Wagner	.302	.362	.446	202	9	4	4	28	4
Dave Matthews, C. Connecticut	.301	.403	.505	196	19	0	7	43	1
Gregory Vaughn Jr., LIU Brooklyn	.298	.415	.430	151	4	2	4	24	4
Chris Wright, Bryant	.297	.388	.441	236	14	1	6	51	1
Tyler Sanfilippo, Wagner	.295	.423	.455	176	14	4	2	36	3
Rob Griswold, LIU Brooklyn	.294	.391	.355	197	12	0	0	19	11
Anthony Pecora, Wagner	.293	.357	.488	215	14	5	6	37	6
Jake Gustin, Bryant	.287	.396	.363	171	8	1	1	27	3

INDIVIDUAL PITCHING LEADERS
(Minimum 40 innings pitched)

	W	L	ERA	G	SV	IP	H	BB	SO
Steve Theetge, Bryant	9	2	1.75	16	0	103	81	30	96
Jared Gallagher, C. Connecticut	3	0	2.47	25	10	40	25	17	39
Nathan Wrighter, Bryant	4	2	2.77	26	3	49	41	26	52
Mike Appel, C. Connecticut	6	1	3.02	16	2	45	39	19	44
Noah Smith, Mount St. Mary's	2	1	3.28	18	1	47	47	21	26
Tyler Mattison, Bryant	9	1	3.47	15	0	80	83	30	67
Tom Curtin, C. Connecticut	6	3	3.86	15	0	96	105	25	53
John Cerrretani, Sacred Heart	4	1	4.08	18	0	46	49	15	25
Justin Beyer, Wagner	3	4	4.24	17	0	51	53	25	44
Brandon Fox, C. Connecticut	3	6	4.35	16	0	89	118	24	44
Ryan Lauk, Wagner	4	4	4.46	20	0	40	33	34	36
McCae Allen, Wagner	4	6	4.53	13	0	52	57	35	52
Jackson Svete, LIU Brooklyn	1	5	4.57	16	0	65	68	32	51
Alec Huertas, LIU Brooklyn	4	4	4.58	14	0	57	72	25	51

INDIVIDUAL PITCHING LEADERS
(Minimum 40 innings pitched)

	W	L	ERA	G	SV	IP	H	BB	SO
Adrian Mardueno, SD State	5	2	1.93	29	2	65	44	28	75
Justin Slaten, New Mexico	5	5	2.51	13	0	82	65	36	98
Jake Gilbert, Air Force	6	3	2.55	16	1	67	72	23	53
Nathan Price, Air Force	6	3	2.59	23	5	63	51	18	32
Ryan Jensen, Fresno St.	12	1	2.88	16	1	100	82	27	107
Ryan HAre, UNLV	8	3	3.61	18	0	82	67	26	55
Justin Goossen-Brown, SD State	6	5	3.80	21	0	95	93	27	73
Davis Moore, Fresno St.	10	1	3.91	16	0	90	85	34	91
Aaron Eden, San Diego St.	4	2	4.01	19	0	74	90	19	41
Dalton Gomez, Nevada	5	2	4.43	22	0	61	65	26	39
Andrew Mitchell, San Jose St.	4	5	4.57	15	0	85	63	58	112
Ryan Anderson, Nevada	4	5	4.84	14	0	71	63	30	64
Nathaniel Garley, New Mexico	6	4	4.92	13	0	75	96	24	47
Cameron Jabara, UNLV	2	7	5.09	15	0	88	109	25	59

NORTHEAST CONFERENCE

	Conference W	L	Overall W	L
Bryant	19	5	40	20
*Central Connecticut	16	8	31	23
Wagner	11	13	19	32
Sacred Heart	11	13	19	34
Long Island-Broooklyn	10	14	20	33
Fairleigh Dickinson	9	15	15	37
Mount St. Mary's	8	16	15	35

ALL-CONFERENCE TEAM: C: Evan McDonald, Sr., Fairleigh Dickinson. 1B: Chris Wright, Jr., Fairleigh Dickinson. 2B: Nate Brodsky, Fr., Fairleigh Dickinson. 3B: Jake Frasca, Jr., Sacred Heart. SS: Partick Causa, Sr., Mount St. Mary's. OF: Ryan Ward, So., Bryant; Nick Angelini, Sr., Bryant; Myles Nicholson, So., Mount St. Mary's. DH: Gaby Cruz, Jr., Bryant. SP: Steve Theetge, Sr., Bryant; Tyler Matticon, So., Bryant; Patrick Mitchell, Jr., Central Connecticut. RP: Chris Wright, Jr., Bryant. Player of the Year: Partick Causa, Mount St. Mary's. Pitcher of the Year: Steve Theetge, Bryant. Coach of the Year: Steve Owens, Bryant. Rookie of the Year: Salvatore Monticciolo, Fairleigh Dickinson.

OHIO VALLEY CONFERENCE

	Conference W	L	Overall W	L
*Jacksonville State	22	8	39	23
Morehead State	19	11	40	21
Austin Peay	19	11	32	25
Eastern Kentucky	18	12	27	30
Murray State	16	14	24	30
Eastern Illinois	13	17	26	30
Tennessee-Martin	12	18	25	31
SIU Edwardsville	11	19	19	32
Southeast Missouri State	10	20	23	32
Tennessee Tech	9	21	22	32

ALL-CONFERENCE TEAM: C: Nic Gaddis, Sr., Jacksonville State. 1B: Jason Hinchman, So., Tennessee Tech. 2B: Jimmy Govern, Sr., Eastern Illinois. 3B: Christian Pena, Jr., Eastern Illinois. SS: Tyler Wilber, So., Southeast Missouri. OF: Kevin Strohschein, Sr., Tennessee Tech; Connor Pauly, Sr., Morehead State; Nick Howie, Jr., Eastern Kentucky. DH: John Dyer, Fr., Tennessee Tech; Alex Webb, Jr., Jacksonville State. UTL: Parker Phillips, Jr., Austin Peay. SP: Garrett Farmer, Jr., Jacksonville State; Jacques Pucheu, Sr., Austin Peay; Dalton Stambaugh, Jr., Morehead State. RP: Aaron Ochsenbein, Jr., Eastern Kentucky. Player of the Year: Kevin Strohschein, Tennessee Tech. Pitcher of the Year: Garrett Farmer, Jacksonville State. Coach of the Year: Jim Case, Jacksonville State.

Rookie of the Year: Garrett Spain, Austin Peay.

INDIVIDUAL BATTING LEADERS
(Minimum 140 at-bats)

	AVG	OBP	SLG	AB	2B	3B	HR	RBI	SB
Tyler Wilber, SE Missouri State	.383	.480	.531	209	19	3	2	40	1
Kevin Strohschein, Tenn. Tech	.382	.447	.691	233	23	2	15	47	2
Christian Pena, Eastern Illinois	.381	.457	.490	194	7	1	4	42	1
Nick Howie, E. Kentucky	.353	.474	.557	221	12	0	11	45	16
Grant Emme, Eastern Illinois	.349	.426	.497	189	12	2	4	30	14
Connor Pauly, Morehead St.	.348	.404	.557	264	13	3	12	64	12
David Martinez, Austin Peay	.345	.427	.527	203	9	2	8	44	2
Jake Hammon, Morehead St.	.339	.415	.445	245	14	0	4	42	14
Ryan Knernschield, Eastern Illinois	.335	.420	.430	200	14	1	1	35	1
Garrett Spain, Austin Peay	.333	.412	.502	219	8	4	7	52	6
Hunter Fain, Morhead St.	.332	.456	.533	199	11	1	9	38	0
John Dyer, Tenn. Tech	.330	.420	.581	191	13	1	11	54	2
Nic Gaddis, Jacksonville St.	.329	.441	.584	231	17	0	14	44	8
Stephen Hill, Morehead St.	.327	.428	.462	208	10	0	6	37	2
Reid Leonard, Morehead St.	.327	.419	.426	251	16	0	3	32	9
Jimmy Govern, Eastern Illinois	.326	.404	.609	233	16	1	16	52	6
Jordan Stoner, Tenn.-Martin	.323	.402	.452	217	17	1	3	30	7
Parker Phillips, Austin Peay	.316	.450	.732	209	12	0	25	64	7
Casey Harford, Tenn.-Martin	.312	.356	.463	205	12	2	5	45	4
Ryland Kerr, E. Kentucky	.311	.391	.429	238	16	3	2	35	16
Garrett Kueber, Austin Peay	.304	.409	.416	214	10	1	4	26	11
Alex Web, Jacksonville St.	.304	.367	.513	240	21	1	9	57	3
Will Johnson, E. Kentucky	.303	.440	.593	231	13	3	16	47	26
A.J. Lewis, E. Kentucky	.303	.434	.521	188	10	2	9	49	17
Logan Thomason, E. Kentucky	.302	.374	.479	192	11	1	7	38	4
Tyler Duke, Murray St.	.299	.374	.532	154	9	3	7	26	19
Brock Weimer, SIU Edwardsville	.298	.384	.580	188	15	1	12	48	1
Nathan McMeans, Ten. Tech	.294	.374	.365	170	12	0	0	17	2

INDIVIDUAL PITCHING LEADERS
(Minimum 40 innings pitched)

	W	L	ERA	G	SV	IP	H	BB	SO
Garrett Farmer, Jacksonville St.	5	2	2.56	16	0	105	89	16	110
Kaven Brown, E. Kentucky	8	1	3.06	10	0	62	55	28	57
Jacques Pucheu, Austin Peay	8	4	3.07	16	0	97	69	37	108
Noah Niznik, SE Missouri St.	3	4	3.63	13	0	62	59	17	49
Dalton Stambaugh, Morehead St.	7	4	3.84	15	0	91	78	29	104
Shane Burns, Murray St.	3	3	3.89	14	0	66	55	27	60
Joshua South, Belmont	4	5	3.89	14	0	90	92	22	77
Dylan Hathcock, Jacksonville St.	3	0	4.02	19	0	65	74	24	34
Austen Bullington, Tenn.-Martin	4	8	4.15	16	0	85	91	26	49
Casey Queener, Belmont	6	3	4.17	15	0	91	76	36	119
Josh Rye, Austin Peay	7	3	4.21	16	0	68	67	29	66
Jason Goe, Morehead St.	7	2	4.48	15	0	68	76	11	65
Sam Folks, Tenn.-Martin	5	6	4.63	16	0	84	82	39	59
Collin Baumgartner, SIU Edwards.	2	5	4.72	15	0	74	79	30	82
Brennan Kelly, E. Kentucky	4	4	4.95	15	0	80	98	34	51

PACIFIC-12 CONFERENCE

	Conference		Overall	
	W	L	W	L
*UCLA	24	5	52	11
*Stanford	22	7	45	14
*Oregon State	21	8	36	20
*California	17	11	32	20
*Arizona State	16	13	38	19
Arizona	15	14	32	24
Southern California	13	15	25	29
Washignton	12	17	28	24
Oregon	10	19	27	29
Utah	6	24	16	33
Washington State	3	26	11	42

ALL-CONFERENCE TEAM: C: Maverick Handley, Jr., Stanford; Nick Kahle, Jr., Washington; Korey Lee, Jr., California; Lyle Lin, Jr., Arizona State. **C/INF:** Clay Owens, Fr., Southern California; Adley Rutschman, Jr., Oregon State. **INF:** Cameron Cannon, Jr., Arizona; Oliver Dunn, Jr., Utah; Ryan Kreidler, Jr., UCLA; Nick Quintana, Jr., Arizona; Quentin Selma, So., California; Spencer Steer, Jr., Oregon; Chase Strumpfm Jr., UCLA; Michael Toglia, Jr., UCLA; Spencer Torkelson, So., Arizona State; Andrew Vaughn, Jr., California. **INF/OF:** Andrew Daschbach, Jr., Stanford; Alex McGarry, So., Oregon State. **OF:** Hunter Bishop, Jr., Arizona State; Garrett Mitchell, So., UCLA; Jack Stronach, Jr., UCLA; Brandon Wuff, Sr., Stanford. **P/INF:** Will Matthiessen, Jr., Stanford. **RHP:** Chris Clarke, Jr., Southern California; Ryan Garcia, Jr., UCLA; Jared Horn, Jr., California; Jack Little, Jr., Stanford; Connor Lunn, Jr., USC; Alec Marsh, Jr., Arizona State; Ryne Nelson, Jr., Oregon; Holden Powell, So., UCLA; Jack Ralston, Jr., UCLA. **LHP:** Jake Mulholland, Jr., Oregon State. **Player of the Year:** Adley Rutschman, Oregon State. **Pitcher of the Year:** Ryan Garcia, UCLA. **Coach of the Year:** John Savage, UCLA. **Rookie of the Year:** Austin Wells, Arizona.

INDIVIDUAL BATTING LEADERS
(Minimum 140 at-bats)

	AVG	OBP	SLG	AB	2B	3B	HR	RBI	SB
Adley Rutschman, Oregon St.	.411	.575	.751	185	10	1	17	58	
Cameron Cannon Arizona	.397	.478	.651	232	29	3	8	56	
Matthew Dyer, Arizona	.393	.480	.571	168	10	4	4	28	
Andrew Vaughn, Calif.	.374	.539	.704	179	14	0	15	50	
Oliver Dunn, Utah	.366	.450	.567	194	22	4	3	28	
Cameron Eden, Calif.	.365	.435	.555	200	8	3	8	36	
Austin Wells, Arizona	.353	.462	.552	221	15	7	5	60	
Spencer Torkelson, Arizona St.	.351	.446	.707	242	17	0	23	66	
Garrett Mitchell, UCLA	.349	.418	.566	258	14	12	6	41	
Spencer Steer, Oregon	.349	.456	.502	215	13	1	6	57	
Hunter Bishop, Arizona State	.342	.479	.748	222	16	4	22	63	
Nick Quintana, Arizona	.342	.462	.626	222	18	0	15	77	
Nick Kahle, Washington	.339	.506	.532	171	9	0	8	50	
Trevor Hauver, Arizona St.	.339	.433	.574	242	16	1	13	50	
Korey Lee, Calif.	.337	.416	.619	202	12	0	15	57	
Alika Williams, Arizona St.	.333	.429	.474	213	12	3	4	53	
Gage Workman, Arizona St.	.330	.413	.528	218	11	4	8	42	
Danny Sinatro, Washington St.	.325	.416	.401	197	5	5	0	16	
Dayton Dooney, Arizona	.323	.417	.596	161	14	0	10	53	
Braiden Ward, Washington	.321	.412	.446	193	11	5	1	26	
Matthew Acosta, S. California	.319	.417	.482	191	10	0	7	40	
Jack Stronach, UCLA	.317	.378	.418	189	11	1	2	34	
Michael Toglia, UCLA	.314	.392	.624	242	16	4	17	65	
Beau Philip, Oregon St.	.311	.369	.486	177	14	1	5	31	
Quentin Selma, Calif,	.311	.366	.584	161	14	0	10	27	
Will Matthiessen, Stanford	.310	.389	.532	216	12	0	12	52	
Darren Baker, Calif.	.306	.367	.335	206	4	1	0	19	
Kyle Stowers, Stanford	.303	.369	.523	218	19	1	9	39	

INDIVIDUAL PITCHING LEADERS
(Minimum 40 innings pitched)

	W	L	ERA	G	SV	IP	H	BB	SO
Ryan Garcia, UCLA	10	1	1.44	16	0	94	52	26	117
Brandon Eisert, Oregon St.	8	2	2.03	14	0	62	59	13	74
Jared Horn, Calif.	6	2	2.06	12	0	74	55	21	62
Stevie Emanuels, Washington	2	3	2.35	31	6	54	43	22	65
Alex Williams, Stanford	8	1	2.56	14	0	63	53	8	43
Jack Ralston, UCLA	11	1	2.66	17	0	101	79	33	110
Arman Sabouri, Calif.	2	2	2.81	26	4	58	44	17	71
Grant Gambrell, Oregon St.	5	3	2.83	13	0	70	59	25	80
Rogelio Reyes, Calif	4	3	3.38	20	1	61	59	25	57
Alec Marsh, Arizona St.	9	4	3.46	17	0	101	91	36	99
Erik Miller, Stanford	8	3	3.48	16	0	83	68	46	102
Bryce Fehmel, Oregon St.	7	3	3.53	16	0	99	88	20	71
Brendan Beck, Stanford	5	4	3.63	17	0	92	102	25	83
Connor Lunn, S. California	7	4	3.69	15	1	83	68	27	79
Robert Ahlstrom, Oregon	5	7	3.93	16	0	73	70	20	61

PATRIOT LEAGUE

	Conference		Overall	
	W	L	W	L
Navy	18	7	39	17
Holy Cross	15	10	22	32
*Army	15	10	35	26
Lafayette	12	13	19	33
Lehigh	9	16	21	28

Bucknell 6 19 14 33

ALL-CONFERENCE TEAM: C: Christian Hodge, Sr., Navy. **1B:** Tany Gallo, Jr., Lehigh. **2B:** Zach Biggers, Jr., Navy. **3B:** Anthony Giachin, So., Army. **SS:** Trey Martin, Sr., Army; Justin Johnson, Fr., Lafayette. **OF:** Jacon Hurtubisem Jr., Army; Trey Durrah, Jr., Lafayette; Tyler Wincig, Jr., Bucknell; Ryan Malloy, Sr., Lehigh. **DH:** Evan Blum, So., Holy Cross. **SP:** Noah Song, Sr., Navy; Liam Dvorak, So., Holy Cross; Daniel Burggraaf, Sr., Army West; Declan Cronin, Sr., Holy Cross. **RP:** Trey Braithwaite, So., Navy. **Player of the Year:** Christian Hodge, Navy. **Pitcher of the Year:** Noah Song, Navy. **Coach of the Year:** Paul Kostacopoulos, Navy. **Rookie of the Year:** Justin Johnson, Lafayette.

INDIVIDUAL BATTING LEADERS
(Minimum 140 at-bats)

	AVG	OBP	SLG	AB	2B	3B	HR	RBI	SB
Jacob Hurtubise, Army	.375	.541	.445	200	6	4	0	26	45
Tony Gallo, Lehigh	.321	.413	.509	165	8	1	7	42	4
Zach Stevens, Navy	.319	.409	.519	160	11	3	5	28	0
Anthony Giachin, Army	.316	.405	.509	234	25	1	6	67	5
Austin Masel, Holy Cross	.312	.352	.454	205	13	5	2	31	12
Ryan Malloy, Lehigh	.309	.396	.551	178	15	2	8	41	2
Liam Lowery, Navy	.303	.401	.495	198	13	2	7	46	1
Trey Martin, Army	.302	.377	.503	189	11	3	7	41	7
Dominic Toso, Bucknell	.300	.370	.441	170	14	2	2	26	3
Christian Hodge, Navy	.298	.388	.507	205	7	0	12	52	0
Zach Biggers, Navy	.295	.369	.405	220	11	5	1	43	7
Michael Coritz, Navy	.289	.385	.330	197	3	1	1	26	2
Gerard Sweeney, Lehigh	.289	.395	.394	180	11	2	3	32	4
Jeff Shanfeldt, Lehigh	.285	.428	.515	165	14	0	8	46	2
Justin Johnson, Lafayette	.284	.371	.407	194	16	1	2	18	9
Caleb Broughton, Bucknell	.282	.352	.309	110	3	0	0	10	4
Ben Malgeri, Holy Cross	.282	.385	.390	177	11	1	2	17	9
Richard Villa, Lafayette	.278	.345	.432	176	9	0	6	33	1
Andre Walden, Army	.275	.398	.420	200	10	2	5	42	25
Evan Lowery, Navy	.275	.346	.350	200	11	2	0	34	1
Dan Leckie, Lafayette	.274	.318	.430	179	9	2	5	26	8
Treay Durrah, Lafayette	.273	.358	.409	176	9	0	5	44	3
Matt Hand, Lehigh	.262	.404	.403	149	10	1	3	24	4
Evan Blum, Holy Cross	.257	.372	.326	144	10	0	0	16	2
Evan Madigan, Bucknell	.255	.354	.328	137	6	2	0	18	16
Spencer Rouse, Lafayette	.250	.386	.372	172	9	0	4	17	11
John McKenna, Army	.249	.403	.370	181	15	2	1	31	4

INDIVIDUAL PITCHING LEADERS
(Minimum 40 innings pitched)

	W	L	ERA	G	SV	IP	H	BB	SO
Noah Song, Navy	11	1	1.44	14	0	94	55	31	161
Jared Leins, Navy	3	1	3.27	13	0	72	58	20	73
Daniel Burggraaf, Army	5	3	3.32	14	0	84	73	21	83
Levi Stoudt, Lehigh	3	4	3.53	11	0	64	53	21	69
Liam Dvorak, Holy Cross	6	5	3.58	14	1	75	68	34	83
Charlie Connolly, Navy	4	3	3.69	14	1	61	41	39	70
Tyler Giovinco, Army	8	6	3.98	17	0	93	103	21	66
Declan Cronin, Holy Cross	6	4	4.06	15	0	71	78	31	61
Sam Messina, Army	8	4	4.46	17	0	77	57	44	70
Brett Kreyer, Lafayette	4	5	4.59	13	0	71	78	44	51
Nate Grisius, Bucknell	2	6	5.01	14	0	50	44	31	40
Luke Rettig, Lehigh	2	4	5.04	12	0	50	48	21	47
Jason Reynolds, Lehigh	2	6	5.76	13	1	50	56	24	49
JP Woodward, Lafayetter	5	7	5.90	12	0	69	72	29	69
Pat McGowan, Holly Cross	2	9	5.94	15	0	70	83	30	57

SOUTHEASTERN CONFERENCE

East Division	Conference W	L	Overall W	L
*Vanderbilt	23	7	49	10
*Georgia	21	9	44	15
*Tennessee	14	16	38	19
Missouri	13	16	34	22
Florida	13	17	33	24
South Carolina	8	22	28	28
Kentucky	7	23	26	29

West Division	Conference W	L	Overall W	L
*Mississippi State	20	10	46	13
*Arkansas	20	10	41	17
*LSU	17	13	37	24
Texas A&M	16	13	37	21
*Ole Miss	16	14	37	25
*Auburn	14	16	33	25
Alabama	7	23	30	26

ALL-CONFERENCE TEAM: C: Philip Clarke, So., Vanderbilt. **1B:** Tanner Allen, So., Mississippi State. **2B:** Justin Foscue, So., Mississippi State. **3B:** Austin Martin, So., Vanderbilt. **SS:** Grae Kessinger, Jr., Ole Miss. **OF:** JJ Bleday, Jr., Vanderbilt; Jake Mangum, Sr., Mississippi State; Alerick Soularie, Jr., Tennessee. **DH:** Nelson Maldonado, Sr., Florida. **SP:** Ethan Small, Mississippi State; Emerson Hancock, So., Georgia. **RP:** Tyler Brown, So., Vanderbilt. **Player of the Year:** JJ Bleday, Vanderbilt. **Pitcher of the Year:** Ethan Small, Mississippi State. **Coach of the Year:** Tim Corbin, Vanderbilt. **Rookie of the Year:** JT Ginn, Mississippi State.

INDIVIDUAL BATTING LEADERS
(Minimum 140 at-bats)

	AVG	OBP	SLG	AB	2B	3B	HR	RBI	SB
Austin Martin, Vanderbilt	.392	.486	.604	268	19	4	10	46	18
Jake Mangum, Mississippi St.	.358	.417	.467	302	24	3	1	39	22
Alerick Soularie, Tennessee	.357	.466	.602	196	13	1	11	46	8
Tanner Allen, Mississippi St.	.349	.426	.516	275	23	1	7	66	1
JJ Bleday, Vanderbilt	.347	.465	.701	274	14	1	27	72	1
Josh Smith, LSU	.346	.433	.533	257	17	2	9	41	20
Matt Goodheart, Arkansas	.345	.444	.517	203	16	2	5	47	5
Nelson Maldonado, Florida	.343	.408	.575	207	14	2	10	43	4
Aaron Schunk, Georgia	.339	.373	.604	230	12	2	15	58	3
LJ Talley, Georgia	.332	.385	.489	235	11	1	8	41	5
Brady McConnell, Florida	.332	.385	.576	229	11	0	15	48	6
Justin Foscue, Mississippi St.	.331	.395	.564	275	22	0	14	60	2
Grae Kessinger, Ole Miss	.330	.430	.474	270	18	0	7	50	16
Trevor Ezell, Arkansas	.329	.435	.561	255	25	2	10	49	19
Ryan Olenek, Ole Miss	.329	.404	.410	234	14	1	1	33	10
Heston Kjerstad, Arkansas	.327	.400	.575	266	13	1	17	51	5
Chris Cornelius, Missouri	.326	.385	.471	227	12	0	7	41	4
Stephen Scott, Vanderbilt	.325	.445	.583	252	21	1	14	61	5
Antoine Duplantis, LSU	.324	.376	.505	281	9	3	12	68	6
Cole Zabowski, Ole Miss	.318	.375	.517	261	16	0	12	51	7
Ethan Paul, Vanderbilt	.315	.386	.497	286	23	1	9	73	11
Dustin Skelton, Mississippi St.	.314	.385	.505	220	8	2	10	55	3
John Cable, Georgia	.314	.407	.524	185	15	0	8	47	1
Brandon Shewmake, Texas A&M	.313	.374	.474	249	14	4	6	47	9
Dominic Fletcher, Texas A&M	.313	.385	.528	265	24	0	11	61	2
Jacob Young, Florida	.311	.383	.404	183	6	0	3	26	7
Jack Kenley, Arkansas	.311	.428	.553	235	10	4	13	54	8
Thomas Dillard, Ole Miss	.310	.450	.541	242	10	2	14	61	14
Tyler Gentry, Ole Miss	.310	.378	.552	210	12	0	13	42	7
Andrew Eyster, South Carolina	.309	.389	.576	165	12	1	10	32	0

INDIVIDUAL PITCHING LEADERS
(Minimum 40 innings pitched)

	W	L	ERA	G	SV	IP	H	BB	SO
TJ Sikkema, Missouri	7	4	1.32	17	2	89	54	31	101
Redmond Walsh, Tennessee	2	2	1.38	27	9	46	38	13	48
Ian Bedell, Missouri	3	1	1.56	18	5	40	28	12	36
Ethan Small, Mississippi St.	10	2	1.93	18	0	107	61	32	176
Emerson Hancock, Georgia	8	3	1.99	14	0	90	58	18	97
Matthew Beck, Louisiana St.	3	0	2.05	27	0	44	30	25	39
Mason Hickman, Vanderbilt	9	0	2.05	20	3	97	64	28	129
John Doxakis, Texas A&M	7	4	2.06	16	0	105	80	26	115
Isaiah Campbell, Arkansas	12	1	2.13	18	0	118	87	22	125
Asa Lacy, Texas A&M	8	4	2.13	15	0	89	49	43	130
Camden Sewell, Tennessee	4	1	2.18	20	1	45	29	22	43
Tyler Brown, Vanderbilt	3	1	2.19	31	17	49	35	9	65
Tim Elliott, Georgia	7	3	2.38	15	0	76	42	24	72
Tyler LaPlante, Missouri	1	1	2.38	8	0	45	35	8	34
Zack Thompson, Kentucky	6	1	2.40	14	0	90	59	34	130

SOUTHERN CONFERENCE

	Conference		Overall	
	W	L	W	L
Samford	19	5	41	19
Wofford	14	9	36	25
UNC Greensboro	14	10	34	20
*Mercer	14	10	35	29
Furman	13	11	26	31
East Tennessee State	11	12	34	21
Virginia Military Institute	9	15	17	41
Western Carolina	8	16	21	32
The Citadel	5	19	12	43

ALL-CONFERENCE TEAM: C: Jackson Greer, Jr., East Tennessee State. **1B:** Sonny DiChiara, Fr., Samford. **2B:** Brett Rodriguez, Jr., Wofford. **3B:** Justice Bigbie, So., Western Carolina. **SS:** Brandon Fryman, Jr., Samford. **OF:** Matthew Koehler, R-Sr., Western Carolina; Kel Johnson, Gr., Mercer; Jordan Fucci, R-Jr., Samford. **DH:** Brooks Carlson, So., Samford. **SP:** Micah Kaczor, Sr., East Tennessee State; Zach Hesterm Jr., Samford. **RP:** Chad Sykes, R-Sr., UNC Greensboro. **Player of the Year:** Justice Bigbie, Western Carolina. **Pitcher of the Year:** Chad Sykes, UNC Greensboro. **Coach of the Year:** Casey Dunn, Samford. **Rookie of the Year:** Hayes Heinecke, Wofford.

INDIVIDUAL BATTING LEADERS
(Minimum 140 at-bats)

	AVG	OBP	SLG	AB	2B	3B	HR	RBI	SB
Matthew Koehler, WCU	.361	.445	.649	205	10	5	13	45	17
Lawson Hill, Wofford	.359	.420	.411	231	8	2	0	46	9
Justice Bigbie, WCU	.355	.446	.578	211	11	0	12	51	2
Brooks Carlson, Samford	.345	.429	.518	226	17	2	6	41	0
Greg Hardison, UNCG	.340	.413	.475	162	14	1	2	22	4
Tyler Corbitt, Citadel	.333	.376	.430	207	15	1	1	22	9
Mike Brown, Wofford	.330	.441	.435	209	12	5	0	36	38
Jabari Richards, Furman	.329	.420	.609	161	10	4	9	33	14
Caleb Webster, UNCG	.327	.376	.464	220	16	1	4	32	11
Hudson Byorick, Wofford	.326	.443	.436	218	18	0	2	45	8
John Dempsey, Wofford	.324	.387	.536	222	22	2	7	41	3
Brett Rodriguez, Wofford	.324	.435	.469	241	14	3	5	43	33
Branden Fryman, Samford	.323	.385	.407	226	7	0	4	29	19
Kyle Dockus, Mercer	.323	.421	.383	248	12	0	1	24	17
Callen Nuccio, VMI	.321	.401	.404	240	16	2	0	29	10
Daylan Nanny, WCU	.320	.403	.515	206	19	0	7	31	4
John Michael Boswe, Furman	.315	.354	.497	149	9	0	6	32	0
Jackson Greer, ETSU	.314	.434	.541	207	15	1	10	42	0
Trent Alley, Furman	.310	.368	.476	145	13	1	3	27	2
Jordan Fucci, Samford	.308	.387	.589	224	14	2	15	49	4
Cullen Smith, ETSU	.304	.427	.473	207	14	0	7	30	7
Colin Davis, Wofford	.302	.361	.471	225	15	1	7	41	11
Ben Peden, Citadel	.299	.378	.518	197	15	2	8	36	5
Luke Robinson, WCU	.299	.380	.557	201	11	4	11	44	3
Trevor Austin, Mercer	.294	.352	.329	231	4	2	0	29	7
Jake Huggins, VMI	.293	.380	.466	232	12	2	8	44	5
Sonny DiChiara, Samford	.293	.407	.646	198	7	0	21	55	0
Kel Johnson, Mercer	.290	.389	.622	241	9	1	23	65	0
Angelo DiSpigna, Mercer	.289	.396	.509	228	11	0	13	43	2
Jalen Jones, WCU	.289	.352	.376	149	9	2	0	16	5

INDIVIDUAL PITCHING LEADERS
(Minimum 40 innings pitched)

	W	L	ERA	G	SV	IP	H	BB	SO
Chad Sykes, UNCG	6	3	0.96	27	11	56	36	22	68
Micah Kaczor, ETSU	7	2	2.13	16	0	101	83	20	85
Zach Hester, Samford	7	4	2.17	15	0	83	66	12	82
Reese Maniscalco, Wofford	4	1	2.55	21	6	42	30	22	60
Landon Knack, ETSU	9	4	2.60	15	0	97	90	16	94
Hayes Heinecke, Wofford	10	2	2.65	16	0	88	82	15	84
Connor Radcliff, Samford	2	2	2.70	31	2	43	35	14	39
Jesse McCord, Samford	6	1	2.88	13	0	69	66	21	54
Daniel Sweeney, ETSU	6	3	3.23	14	0	78	73	13	71
Nick Spear, Mercer	2	1	3.25	36	9	55	53	18	63
Austin Koehn, UNCG	4	3	3.49	15	0	77	67	22	67
David Yourke, Wofford	1	5	3.77	14	0	45	42	14	27
Kevin Coulter, Mercer	5	3	3.90	21	3	83	104	19	66

| Alex Bialakis, Citadel | 0 | 6 | 4.00 | 31 | 0 | 45 | 43 | 24 | 41 |
| Samuel Strickland, Samford | 7 | 3 | 4.00 | 15 | 0 | 70 | 79 | 20 | 57 |

SOUTHLAND CONFERENCE

	Conference		Overall	
	W	L	W	L
Sam Houston State	20	10	31	25
Southeastern Louisiana	19	11	33	27
Central Arkansas	19	11	32	27
Incarnate Word	18	12	37	22
*McNeese	16	14	35	26
Stephen F. Austin	16	14	25	33
Northwestern State	15	15	30	25
Texas A&M-Corpus Christi	14	16	31	26
New Orleans	13	17	29	27
Nicholls St.	13	17	27	28
Houston Baptist	10	20	18	35
Lamar	9	21	18	36

ALL-CONFERENCE TEAM: C: Luis Trevino, R-Sr., Abilene Christian. **1B:** Hunter Hearn, Sr., Sam Houston State. **2B:** Riley McKnight, Sr., Sam Houston State. **3B:** Enrique Sanchez, Sr., Texas A&M-Corpus Christi. **SS:** Ryan Gonzalez, Sr., Incarnate Word. **OF:** Colton Cowser, Fr., Sam Houston State; Eddy Gonzalez, Sr., Incarnate Word; Sean Arnold, Jr., Incarnate Word. **DH:** Itchy Burts, Jr., Texas A&M-Corpus Christi. **SP:** Corey Gaconi, Sr., Southeastern Louisiana; Hayden Wesneski, Jr., Sam Houston State, Alex Palmer, Jr., Stephen F. Austin. **RP:** Reeves Martin, Jr., New Orleans. **Player of the Year:** Luis Trevino, Abilene Christian. **Pitcher of the Year:** Corey Gaconi, Southeastern Louisiana. **Coach of the Year:** Patrick Hallmark, Incarnate Word. **Newcomer of the Year:** Taylor Smith, Incarnate Word.

INDIVIDUAL BATTING LEADERS
(Minimum 140 at-bats)

	AVG	OBP	SLG	AB	2B	3B	HR	RBI	SB
Luis Trevino, Abilene Christian	.408	.504	.743	191	13	3	15	63	1
Jordan Cannon, S. Houston St.	.372	.455	.521	188	12	2	4	37	14
Enrique Sanchez, Texas A&M-CC	.372	.438	.481	231	16	3	1	45	8
Colton Cowser, S. Houston St.	.361	.450	.602	216	17	7	7	54	9
Eddy Gonzalez, UIW	.357	.431	.495	196	13	4	2	28	9
Itchy Burns, Texas A&M-CC	.356	.412	.494	233	15	4	3	33	10
Ryan Gonzalez, UIW	.347	.404	.574	216	18	5	7	42	3
Hunter Hearn, S. Houston St.	.336	.382	.593	226	17	4	11	51	3
Ryan Flores, UIW	.335	.355	.608	212	18	2	12	42	1
JC Correa, Lamar	.332	.381	.529	223	14	0	10	44	1
Logan Berlof, Lamar	.331	.394	.483	145	8	1	4	20	1
Gaige Howard, New Orleans	.330	.432	.414	191	8	1	2	29	2
Sean Arnold, UIW	.325	.425	.495	200	11	4	5	35	8
Clayton Harp, S. Houston St.	.322	.368	.449	214	9	0	6	41	7
Taylor Smith, UIW	.322	.447	.615	208	13	0	16	57	2
Avery George, Lamar	.321	.387	.339	224	2	1	0	17	12
Brandon Bena, Houston Bapt.	.313	.372	.453	192	12	0	5	36	3
Jake Dickerson, McNeese St.	.313	.416	.413	208	10	1	3	35	11
Sam Taylor, Northwestern St.	.311	.380	.413	206	13	1	2	28	12
Erik Voller, Houston Bapt.	.309	.392	.457	162	10	1	4	28	0
Caleb Ricca, Northwestern St.	.309	.405	.484	217	17	3	5	35	24
Collina Morrill, New Orleans	.309	.389	.496	230	20	1	7	35	0
Dalon Farkas, Abilene Christian	.308	.374	.464	211	16	1	5	46	4
Jack Rogers, Sam Houston St.	.304	.377	.541	194	20	1	8	30	7
Nate Fisbeck, McNeese St.	.304	.378	.541	257	21	2	12	50	6
Clayton Rasbeary, McNeese St.	.304	.401	.507	227	16	0	10	49	5
Antonio Valdez, UIW	.302	.388	.479	215	14	6	4	31	10
Kyle Schimpf, SE Louisiana	.299	.408	.482	224	11	0	10	49	2
Riley McKnight, S. Houston St.	.298	.362	.414	191	8	4	2	22	3
Nick Anderson, Texas A&M-CC	.298	.392	.400	215	10	3	2	30	7

INDIVIDUAL PITCHING LEADERS
(Minimum 40 innings pitched)

	W	L	ERA	G	SV	IP	H	BB	SO
Cody Davenport, C. Arkansas	7	4	1.98	16	1	105	79	21	95
Bernie Martinez, UIW	9	2	2.11	22	7	81	66	34	74
Kyle Gruller, Houston Bapt.	3	3	2.18	12	0	74	55	39	85
Brennan Lewis, Abilene Christian	2	1	2.21	27	10	57	49	5	34
Alex Palmer, Stephen F. Austin.	7	6	2.27	15	0	107	70	31	109
Corey Gaconi, SE Louisiana	7	3	2.57	16	0	109	100	11	95
Nathan Jones, Northwestern St.	7	4	2.78	14	0	81	60	25	80
Noah Cameron, C. Arkansas	6	2	2.95	14	0	95	83	19	91
Jacob Bedevian, Nicholls St.	4	2	2.99	15	0	102	96	19	61
Jason Blanchard, Lamar	5	4	3.12	14	0	89	76	27	87
Aidan Anderson, McNeese St.	7	6	3.29	30	7	79	70	30	66
Hayden Wesneski, S. Houston St.	8	4	3.32	15	0	106	98	21	110
Parker White, Nicholls St.	4	4	3.32	20	0	60	58	24	43
Shane Mejia, Nicholls St.	4	2	3.51	14	0	59	67	20	43
Luke Taggart, UIW	7	5	3.68	19	1	88	82	17	76

SOUTHWESTERN ATHLETIC CONFERENCE

East Division	Conference		Overall	
	W	L	W	L
Alabama State	17	5	27	26
Jackson State	15	9	31	24
Alabama A&M	11	11	15	35
Alcorn State	7	15	14	29
Mississippi Valley State	6	16	8	26

West Division	Conference		Overall	
	W	L	W	L
*Southern	15	5	30	19
Grambling State	16	8	26	25
Texas Southern	13	11	19	34
Prairie View	9	14	18	35
Arkansas-Pine Bluff	3	19	8	42

ALL-CONFERENCE TEAM: C: Santiago Garcia, So., Alabama State. **1B:** Raul Hernandez, Sr., Jackson State. **2B:** Eriq White, R-Jr., Alabama State. **3B:** Tyler LaPorte, Sr., Southern. **SS:** Malik Blaise, Sr., Southern. **OF:** Yamil Pagan, Sr., Alabama State; O.J. Oloruntimilehin, Jr., Texas Southern; Javeyan Williams, Sr., Southern. **DH:** Chris Prentiss, Jr., Jackson State. **SP:** Aron Solis, Sr., Texas Southern; Darren Kelly, R-Sr., Alabama State. **RP:** Connor Whalen, Sr., Southern. **Player of the Year:** Tyler LaPorte, Southern; Yamil Pagan, Alabama State. **Pitcher of the Year:** Darren Kelly, Alabama State. **Coach of the Year:** Kerrick Jackson, Southern. **Newcomers of the Year:** Ricardo Rivera, Alabama State.

INDIVIDUAL BATTING LEADERS
(Minimum 140 at-bats)

	AVG	OBP	SLG	AB	2B	3B	HR	RBI	SB
Daniel Lingua, Prairie View A&M	.397	.500	.515	194	10	5	1	42	36
Tyler LaPorte, Southern	.389	.434	.577	239	17	5	6	64	21
Javeyan Williams, Southern	.388	.470	.584	178	9	7	4	41	26
Chris Prentiss, Jackson St.	.378	.441	.564	156	6	10	1	30	10
Jonathan Smith II, Alabama A&M	.369	.500	.477	149	11	1	1	23	22
Jaylyn Williams, Jackson St.	.368	.471	.527	182	14	0	5	49	9
Raul Hernandez, Jackson St.	.357	.435	.565	207	14	1	9	54	3
Nick Kreutze, Arkansas-PB	.352	.448	.626	179	16	0	11	51	4
Tristin Garcia, Alcorn St.	.348	.413	.503	161	10	3	3	25	5
Johnny Johnson, Southern	.347	.430	.485	167	10	2	3	36	18
Yamil Pagan, Alcorn St.	.346	.461	.598	214	4	4	14	53	12
Kevin Whitaker Jr., Gramb. St.	.340	.408	.471	153	8	3	2	34	9
Equon Smith, Jackson St.	.340	.391	.405	200	8	1	1	34	36
Santiago Garcia, Alcorn St.	.335	.388	.509	224	15	0	8	60	1
Isaiah Torres, Grambling St.	.330	.459	.454	194	15	3	1	38	12
Alex Martinez, Prairie View A&M	.330	.391	.558	197	13	1	10	55	3
Drexler Macaay, Gramb. St.	.328	.446	.539	180	12	1	8	40	2
Noel Cheneau, Alcorn St.	.323	.387	.533	229	9	6	9	57	20
Tyson Thompson, Texas Sou.	.311	.417	.383	167	8	2	0	19	15
Kirt Cormier, Alcorn St.	.309	.436	.448	165	10	2	3	28	3
Malik Blaise, Southern	.309	.372	.412	194	17	0	1	29	11

Tyler Culpepper, Jackson St.	.306	.401	.429	147	9	3	1	32	7
OJ Oloruntimilehin, Texas Sou.	.304	.414	.603	194	10	3	14	41	13
Justin Robinson, Arkansas-P-B	.303	.363	.400	145	8	3	0	12	24
Eriq White, Alcorn St.	.302	.386	.433	215	15	2	3	39	8
Ashanti Wheatley, Southern	.302	.431	.475	162	10	3	4	26	19
Kvan Kuren, Texas Southern	.291	.369	.442	206	15	2	4	44	16
Garratt Smith, Grambling St.	.289	.436	.380	142	8	1	1	26	0
Ryan Diaz, Texas Southern	.288	.394	.340	153	6	1	0	12	33
Wesley Reyes, Jackson St.	.288	.330	.382	191	10	1	2	30	10

INDIVIDUAL PITCHING LEADERS
(Minimum 40 innings pitched)

	W	L	ERA	G	SV	IP	H	BB	SO
Kevin Perez, Jackson St.	5	4	2.60	22	1	62	55	20	74
Darren Kelly, Alcorn St.	6	2	3.05	12	0	65	43	17	55
Bryan Delgado, Grambling St.	6	3	3.29	14	0	82	79	24	66
Garth Cahill, Jackson St.	6	1	3.45	21	1	78	68	17	47
Alex Olguin, Texas Southern	5	3	3.63	18	1	72	92	21	42
Nikelle Galatas, Jackson St.	6	5	4.35	21	2	97	90	33	75
Mario Lopez, Jackson St.	4	4	4.45	22	1	59	68	12	38
Eli Finney, Southern	6	2	4.45	14	0	65	65	23	49
Tyler Laux, Prairie View A&M	3	4	4.61	21	0	68	87	27	49
Jorge Rivera, Alcorn St.	7	4	4.93	21	2	66	83	24	60
Aron Solis, Texas Southern	5	3	5.03	15	2	91	102	28	89
Nicholas Johnson, Miss. Valley St.	3	5	5.09	12	0	69	91	18	30
Peyton Baker, Alabama A&M	4	3	5.14	13	0	49	60	21	38
Ricardo Rivera, Alcorn St.	6	3	5.16	13	1	59	64	37	46
Anthony Becerra, Jackson St.	3	6	5.18	16	0	73	73	42	71

SUMMIT LEAGUE

	Conference		Overall	
	W	L	W	L
*Omaha	20	10	31	24
South Dakota State	19	10	28	22
Oral Roberts	17	12	29	26
Western Illinois	16	14	22	31
North Dakota State	15	15	19	24
Fort Wayne	2	28	7	45

ALL-CONFERENCE TEAM: C: C.J. Schaeffer, Sr., Western Illinois. **1B:** Spencer Henson, Jr., Oral Roberts. **2B:** Hunter Wilson, Sr., Oral Roberts. **3B:** Breyden Eckhout, Jr., Omaha. **SS:** Gus Steiger, So., South Dakota State. **OF:** Drue Galassi, Jr., Western Illinois; Parker Smejkal, Jr., Omaha; Nick Smith, Jr., South Dakota State. **DH:** Josh Falk, Jr., South Dakota State. **UTL:** Isaac Coffey, Fr., Oral Roberts. **SP:** Javin Drake, Jr., Western Illinois; Payton Kinney, Sr., Omaha; Max Loven, Fr., North Dakota State. **RP:** Brett Barnett, So., South Dakota State. **Player of the Year:** Spencer Henson, Oral Roberts. **Pitcher of the Year:** Payton Kinney, Omaha. **Coach of the Year:** Evan Porter, Omaha. **Rookie of the Year:** Max Loven, North Dakota State.

INDIVIDUAL BATTING LEADERS
(Minimum 140 at-bats)

	AVG	OBP	SLG	AB	2B	3B	HR	RBI	SB
Spencer Henson, Oral Roberts	.362	.509	.768	177	11	2	19	51	2
Parker Smejkal, Omaha	.329	.457	.561	164	15	1	7	43	0
Gus Steiger, South Dakota St.	.324	.372	.449	225	13	0	5	43	18
Nick Smith, South Dakota St.	.324	.453	.398	176	4	3	1	24	8
Hunter Wilson, Oral Roberts	.302	.361	.377	212	8	1	2	33	12
Drue Galassi, W. Illinois	.298	.379	.527	188	9	2	10	51	14
Breyden Eckhout, Omaha	.293	.409	.426	188	11	1	4	21	6
Isaac Coffey, Oral Roberts	.292	.372	.472	161	11	0	6	32	0
Kevin Raisbeck, W. Illinois	.291	.395	.341	179	9	0	0	24	10
Blake Hall, Oral Roberts	.289	.366	.522	180	11	2	9	32	3
Garrett Mohler, Purdue FW	.285	.360	.464	179	8	3	6	26	1
CJ Schaeffer Jr., W. Illinois	.283	.343	.417	180	10	1	4	35	6
Braeden Brown, SD State	.282	.384	.346	188	4	1	2	27	7
Jack Simonsen, ND State	.280	.381	.336	143	5	0	1	28	3
Logan Holtz, SD State	.278	.387	.389	162	2	2	4	22	1
Andrew Pace, Oral Roberts	.277	.341	.364	206	12	0	2	27	1
Brock Anderson, ND State	.277	.437	.340	141	4	1	1	21	8
Drew Beazley, SD State	.275	.420	.443	149	11	1	4	21	2
Brandon Yoho, Purdue FW	.273	.348	.345	165	6	0	2	7	3

Thomas Debonville, Omaha	.272	.317	.442	224	8	6	6	36	10
Riley Keizor, Oral Roberts	.272	.387	.389	180	10	1	3	48	1
Landon Badger, SD State	.270	.376	.414	152	12	2	2	22	6
Peter Brookshaw, ND State	.266	.375	.349	169	12	1	0	25	10
Hunter Swift, Oral Roberts	.263	.404	.375	152	5	3	2	18	5
Alec Brunson, Purdue FW	.260	.321	.337	169	10	0	1	18	3
Keil Krumwiede, Omaha	.260	.383	.351	208	11	1	2	37	1
Max Gamm, Omaha	.259	.353	.299	147	4	1	0	12	13
Josh Falk, SD St.	.257	.379	.446	175	9	0	8	38	2
Braden Rogers, Omaha	.256	.328	.345	203	6	0	4	30	2
Robert Young III, Purdue FW	.253	.346	.344	154	5	3	1	19	5

INDIVIDUAL PITCHING LEADERS
(Minimum 40 innings pitched)

	W	L	ERA	G	SV	IP	H	BB	SO
Payton Kinney, Omaha	11	2	1.96	17	0	115	75	39	111
Max Loven, ND State	4	2	2.74	13	0	89	78	15	75
Ben Smith, ND State	4	3	3.26	12	0	61	60	21	38
Tyler Olmstead, SD State	4	4	3.30	15	0	95	83	31	92
Isaac Coffey, Oral Roberts	3	2	3.82	14	0	61	61	17	56
Nic McCay, SD State	6	1	4.08	14	0	79	69	30	83
Ryan Froom, SD State	6	5	4.09	16	0	77	78	45	50
Javin Drake, W. Illinois	7	6	4.37	17	0	103	99	42	109
Jace Warkentien, W. Illinois	3	4	4.41	18	2	88	91	41	74
Joey Machado, Omaha	6	3	4.65	14	0	70	69	31	64
Josh McMinn, Oral Roberts	7	5	4.75	15	0	91	102	30	92
Matt Gaskins, Oral Roberts	5	5	5.13	15	0	79	84	35	53
Zach Smith, ND State	1	5	5.56	13	0	66	85	25	47
Spencer Koelewyn, Omaha	4	2	5.68	15	0	57	32	63	79
Jack Carberry, W. Illinois	5	4	6.67	16	0	55	61	33	47

SUN BELT CONFERENCE

	Conference		Overall	
East Division	**W**	**L**	**W**	**L**
Georgia Southern	18	12	35	24
*Coastal Carolina	15	13	36	26
South Alabama	16	14	30	26
Troy	16	14	31	29
Appalachian State	13	16	22	31
Georgia State	6	24	15	41

	Conference		Overall	
West Division	**W**	**L**	**W**	**L**
Texas State	20	10	36	20
Little Rock	18	11	29	28
Texas-Arlington	17	12	32	26
Louisiana	15	15	28	31
Louisiana-Monroe	12	17	27	31
Arkansas State	11	19	26	29

ALL-CONFERENCE TEAM: C: Chase Smartt, Sr., Troy. **1B:** Zach Biermann, Sr., Coastal Carolina. **2B:** Jaxon Williams, Jr., Texas State. **3B:** Chad Bell, Sr., Louisiana-Monroe. **SS:** Hayden Cantrelle, So., Louisiana. **OF:** Parker Chavers, So., Coastal Carolina; Mason McWhorter, Jr., Georgia Southern; Ethan Wilson, Fr., South Alabama. **DH:** Riley Pittman, Sr., Little Rock. **UTL:** Todd Lott, Jr., Louisiana. **SP:** Seth Shuman, Sr., Georgia Southern; Chandler Fidel, Jr., Little Rock; Connor Reich, Sr., Texas State. **RP:** Zach Greene, Sr., South Alabama. **Player of the Year:** Ethan Wilson, South Alabama. **Pitcher of the Year:** Connor Reich, Texas State. **Coach of the Year:** Ty Harrington, Texas State. **Newcomer of the Year:** Jake Wright, Coastal Carolina.

INDIVIDUAL BATTING LEADERS
(Minimum 140 at-bats)

	AVG	OBP	SLG	AB	2B	3B	HR	RBI	SB
Jake Wright, CCU	.374	.532	.662	198	8	2	15	59	1
Trent Tingelstad, ULM	.357	.473	.588	221	22	4	7	47	5
Rigsby Mosley, Troy	.356	.430	.554	222	19	2	7	34	8
Connor Aube, Texas-Arlington	.354	.402	.529	206	18	3	4	29	16
Parker Chavers, CCU	.353	.457	.670	215	9	4	17	59	10
Ethan Wilson, South Ala.	.346	.453	.675	228	16	4	17	52	6
Scott McKeon, CCU	.343	.402	.500	268	19	7	3	42	6
Chase Smartt, Troy	.343	.406	.523	216	21	0	6	41	0

Steven Curry, Ga. Southern	.341	.463	.431	232	16	1	1	33	3
Luke Drumheller, App. St.	.340	.405	.458	203	16	1	2	38	3
Hunter Kasuls, Louisiana	.338	.404	.502	225	10	3	7	38	11
Chad Bell, ULM	.336	.405	.692	250	16	2	23	67	2
Ryan Benavidez, Arkansas-LR	.335	.440	.530	230	11	2	10	38	4
Todd Lott, Louisiana	.332	.395	.505	202	9	1	8	48	12
Dalton Shuffield, Texas St.	.330	.393	.427	218	12	3	1	26	10
Michael Sandle, South Ala.	.326	.402	.514	181	12	2	6	41	8
Kieton Rivers, CCU	.326	.428	.628	242	16	3	17	76	9
Riley Pittman, Arkansas-LR	.325	.400	.604	212	15	1	14	53	2
Jaylen Hubbard, Texas St.	.323	.438	.548	217	17	4	8	30	9
Will Hollis, Texas St.	.320	.452	.520	200	20	1	6	47	1
Mason McWhorter, Ga. Southern	.319	.384	.562	226	15	2	12	57	3
Zach Biermann, CCU	.319	.411	.572	276	13	0	19	87	2
Jaxon Williams, Texas St.	.318	.432	.425	214	8	0	5	29	5
Drew Frederic, Troy	.318	.410	.527	245	16	1	11	36	20
Sky-Lar Culver, App. St.	.316	.398	.493	209	14	1	7	45	0
Kendall McGowan, App. St.	.313	.375	.526	192	9	4	8	38	11
John Wuthrich, Texas St.	.311	.402	.565	161	11	3	8	40	0
Kyle Skeels, CCU	.311	.442	.524	206	14	0	10	59	4
Brandon Bell, Georgia St.	.310	.380	.398	216	13	0	2	24	4
Cory Wood, CCU	.310	.468	.435	248	23	1	2	37	20

INDIVIDUAL PITCHING LEADERS
(Minimum 40 innings pitched)

	W	L	ERA	G	SV	IP	H	BB	SO
Zach Greene, South Ala.	3	0	1.53	32	13	59	37	12	79
Kaleb Bowman, App. St.	6	2	3.00	29	4	63	52	30	53
Drake Nightengale, South Ala.	7	2	3.43	16	1	79	51	41	102
Drew Gooch, Texas-Arlington	3	3	3.47	18	0	62	76	24	42
Jacob Schultz, ULM	3	3	3.51	24	2	67	61	32	60
Matt Eardensohn, CCU	8	1	3.56	28	1	78	76	22	73
Chandler Fidel, Arkansas-LR	5	4	3.65	16	0	101	91	31	101
Trey Jeans, Louisiana-Monroe	5	8	3.76	15	0	79	61	37	69
Seth Shuman, Ga. Southern	6	5	3.83	16	0	92	81	27	114
Hayden Arnold, Arkansas-LR	5	3	4.17	21	1	69	65	26	68
Levi Thomas, Troy	8	2	4.24	15	0	81	79	31	87
Tyler Owens, Ga. Southern	7	1	4.26	14	0	63	71	18	53
David Moffat, Texas-Arlington	4	4	4.33	16	0	81	89	18	52
Cory Gill, Troy	7	3	4.44	19	5	73	75	25	75
Zach Jackson, App. St.	6	5	4.46	14	0	77	93	20	61

WEST COAST CONFERENCE

	Conference		Overall	
	W	**L**	**W**	**L**
New Mexico State	19	8	38	17
California Baptist	19	8	35	20
Texas-Rio Grande Valley	19	8	34	21
*Sacramento State	18	9	40	25
Grand Canyon	18	9	36	24
Cal State Bakersfield	12	15	24	35
Utah Valley	9	18	15	41
Northern Colorado	8	19	12	35
Seattle	8	19	13	39
Chicago State	5	22	10	41

ALL-CONFERENCE TEAM: C: Dawsen Bach, So., Sacramento State. **INF:** Tristian Peterson, Jr., New Mexico State; Nick Gonzales, So., New Mexico State; Tyler Wyatt, Sr., Grand Canyon; Joey Ortiz, Jr., New Mexico State. **OF:** Tristen Carranza, Sr., New Mexico State; Jack Pauley, Sr., Northern Colorado; Matt Smith, Jr., Saramento State. **UTL/DH:** Ryan Mota, Jr., California Baptist. **SP:** Kade Mechals, Jr., Grand Canyon; Logan Rinehart, Jr., California Baptist. **RP:** Ryan Jackson, Sr., Texas-Rio Grande Valley. **Player of the Year:** Joey Ortiz, New Mexico State. **Pitcher of the Year:** Logan Rinehart, California Baptist. **Coach of the Year:** Derek Matlock, Texas-Rio Grande Valley. **Rookie of the Year:** Pierson Ohl, Grand Canyon.

INDIVIDUAL BATTING LEADERS
(Minimum 140 at-bats)

	AVG	OBP	SLG	AB	2B	3B	HR	RBI	SB
Nick Gonzales, NM State	.432	.532	.773	220	19	4	16	80	7
Joseph Ortiz, NM State	.422	.474	.697	251	25	10	8	84	12
Tristan Peterson, NM State	.400	.510	.769	195	10	1	20	90	0
Luke Navigato, CSBU	.372	.443	.549	215	15	1	7	33	7
Tristen Carranza, NM State	.371	.500	.719	210	7	6	18	73	3
Logan Bottrell, NM State	.367	.482	.446	177	10	2	0	28	17
Jack Pauley, Northern Colo.	.344	.441	.611	157	13	1	9	36	8
Cuba Bess, Grand Canyon	.341	.476	.632	182	18	1	11	40	2
Chad Castillo, Cal. Baptist	.335	.385	.423	194	8	3	1	27	2
Eric Mingus, NM State	.332	.456	.497	187	10	3	5	53	3
Ryan Eastburn, Utah Valley	.331	.452	.424	151	8	0	2	26	1
Quin Cotton, Grand Canyon	.331	.406	.494	251	21	4	4	37	8
Jake Ortega, CSUB	.326	.418	.400	190	9	1	1	25	13
Tyler Jorgensen, CSUB	.323	.391	.411	192	9	1	2	30	2
Michael Beltran, Utah Valley	.320	.433	.437	222	9	4	3	21	2
Conrado Diaz, UTRGV	.319	.434	.386	207	11	0	1	31	2
Pikai Winchester, G. Canyon	.315	.427	.479	165	15	0	4	32	1
John Glenn, Cal. Bakersfield	.314	.364	.476	210	10	0	8	44	4
Anthony Gomez, UTRGV	.312	.389	.430	221	10	2	4	49	5
Matt Smith, Sacremento St.	.311	.378	.478	228	9	4	7	38	8
Sam Leach, Northern Colo.	.311	.396	.451	164	10	2	3	19	5
Kona Quiggle, G. Canyon	.311	.390	.583	225	20	4	12	62	4
Kyle Sherick, Seattle	.310	.355	.450	200	7	3	5	21	10
Jake Gitter, Northern Colo.	.310	.441	.535	142	15	1	5	25	4
Tyler Torres, UTRGV	.300	.417	.371	170	3	0	3	29	2
Austin Lively, Seattle	.298	.381	.426	141	6	0	4	20	3
Logan Ehnes, NM State	.297	.439	.410	212	12	3	2	50	12
Alexander Marco, Utah Valley	.297	.414	.450	202	13	0	6	42	0
Jesse Rowley, CSUB	.296	.373	.392	199	6	2	3	30	7
Ryan Mota, Cal. Baptist	.295	.370	.600	210	10	0	18	53	1

INDIVIDUAL PITCHING LEADERS
(Minimum 40 innings pitched)

	W	L	ERA	G	SV	IP	H	BB	SO
Ryan Jackson, UTRGV	5	4	1.74	28	8	47	46	13	61
Andrew Bash, Cal. Baptist	6	4	1.98	15	1	77	58	24	77
Matt Mogollon, Cal. Baptist	1	1	2.05	24	7	44	27	17	56
Tanner Dalton, Sac. State	5	2	2.14	29	6	59	36	19	67
Kade Mechals, Grand Canyon	11	1	2.16	16	0	92	64	35	100
Scott Randall, Sac. State	8	2	2.59	17	0	94	86	33	76
Chance Hroch, NM State	10	1	2.74	15	0	85	82	30	69
Jack Schneider, Grand Canyon	3	2	2.83	12	0	60	57	18	38
Austin Roberts, Sac. State	5	4	3.18	22	6	74	64	30	84
Travis Booth, Cal. Baptist	3	4	3.18	16	0	45	45	19	45
Logan Rinehart, Cal. Baptist	9	0	3.20	12	0	65	52	27	68
Matt Amrhein, Cal. Baptist	4	1	3.43	25	6	45	44	20	38
Pierson Ohl, Grand Canyon	7	5	3.45	16	0	91	93	19	66
Travis Martizia, Sac. State	4	1	3.49	31	2	57	57	13	31
Trevelle Hill, UTRGV	7	5	3.60	15	0	95	91	35	73

WESTERN ATHLETIC CONFERENCE

	Conference		Overall	
	W	L	W	L
Brigham Young	19	8	36	17
Gonzaga	18	9	31	24
Saint Mary's	17	10	35	22
*Loyola Marymount	15	12	34	25
San Francisco	15	12	30	26
San Diego	14	13	32	21
Pepperdine	14	13	24	24
Pacific	10	16	23	26
Portland	7	19	25	27
Santa Clara	5	22	12	40

ALL-CONFERENCE TEAM: C: James Free, Jr., Pacific. **INF:** Jackson Cluff, So., Brigham Young; Ripken Reyes, Gr., San Diego; Nick Sogard, Fr., Loyola Marymount. **OF:** Jon Allen, Sr., San Francisco; Brock Hale, Sr., Brigham Young; Troy Johnston, Jr., Gonzaga; Jor Vranesh, Jr., Saint Mary's. **RHP:** Chris Clements, Sr., Portland; Alek Jacob, So., Gonzaga; Codie Paiva, Sr., Loyola Marymount; Tyler Thornton, Fr., Saint Mary's. **LHP:** Ken

Waldichuk, Jr., Saint Mary's. **Player of the Year:** Brock Hale, Brigham Young. **Pitcher of the Year:** Codie Paiva, Loyola Marymont. **Coach of the Year:** Mike Littlewood, Brigham Young. **Rookie of the Year:** Tyler Thornton, Saint Mary's.

INDIVIDUAL BATTING LEADERS
(Minimum 140 at-bats)

	AVG	OBP	SLG	AB	2B	3B	HR	RBI	SB
Ripken Reyes, San Diego	.366	.462	.500	194	11	3	3	33	3
Jeffrey Houghtby, San Diego	.341	.438	.512	170	12	1	5	38	4
James Free II, Pacific	.335	.412	.541	194	14	1	8	39	1
Brock Hale, Brigham Young	.330	.460	.571	203	14	1	11	45	3
Troy Johnston, Gonzaga	.330	.402	.610	218	27	2	10	46	0
Ryan Novis, Saint Mary's	.328	.372	.402	229	7	2	2	41	13
Joe Vranesh, Saint Mary's	.327	.437	.640	214	16	3	15	56	4
Jackson Cluff, Brigham Young	.325	.458	.515	200	20	3	4	56	12
Bryce Willits, Saint Mary's	.325	.377	.448	154	10	0	3	18	4
Shane McGuire, San Diego	.325	.444	.401	197	12	0	1	31	3
Brian Hsu, Brigham Young	.321	.407	.388	196	4	0	3	20	2
Robert Emery, San Francisco	.320	.386	.479	194	16	0	5	40	1
Wyatt Young, Pepperdine	.315	.351	.366	213	3	1	2	22	5
Nick Sogard, Loyola Marymount	.310	.418	.345	229	8	0	0	19	30
Quincy McAfee, Pepperdine	.310	.396	.433	187	15	1	2	23	4
Kevin Milam, Saint Mary's	.308	.416	.488	211	17	0	7	43	1
Noah Hill, Brigham Young	.307	.418	.340	153	3	1	0	15	0
Guthrie Morrison, Gonzaga	.306	.351	.392	232	13	2	1	24	5
Brett Harris, Gonzaga	.305	.366	.444	151	12	0	3	26	3
Brandon Shearer, Loyola Marymount	.304	.401	.392	227	12	1	2	31	8
Nick Nyquist, Gonzaga	.302	.392	.558	172	12	1	10	51	6
Ernie Yake, Gonzaga	.302	.378	.413	225	12	2	3	30	3
Daniel Fredrickson, Gonzaga	.301	.338	.427	143	11	2	1	19	1
Matthew Kanfer, Pepperdine	.301	.356	.429	196	10	3	3	36	4
Jack Winkler, San Francisco	.300	.379	.454	227	17	0	6	38	9
Mitch McIntyre, Brigham Young	.291	.414	.508	189	14	3	7	38	8
Tora Otsuka, San Diego	.287	.402	.374	171	7	1	2	34	3
Tyler Villaroman, San Francisco	.285	.364	.337	193	3	2	1	18	21
Chad Stevens, Portland	.284	.350	.422	218	13	1	5	27	12
Austin Chauvin, Saint Mary's	.281	.392	.419	167	5	3	4	28	1

INDIVIDUAL PITCHING LEADERS
(Minimum 40 innings pitched)

	W	L	ERA	G	SV	IP	H	BB	SO
Chris Clements, Portland	7	1	1.69	13	0	85	54	18	76
Codie Paiva, Loyola Marymount	8	5	1.91	16	0	104	86	18	90
Alek Jacob, Gonzaga	7	3	2.17	25	12	79	56	31	87
Easton Walker, Brigham Young	7	2	2.20	19	1	78	67	14	68
Nick Frasso, Loyola Marymount	2	2	2.22	19	10	57	30	17	73
Trevor Kniskern, Pepperdine	4	5	2.42	14	0	45	41	19	37
Reid McLaughlin, Brigham Young	7	1	2.61	25	4	52	46	11	46
Tyler Thornton, Saint Mary's	10	2	2.71	15	0	76	47	27	94
Connor Knutson, Portland	3	3	2.85	24	10	41	37	12	38
Justin Sterner, Brigham Young	8	3	2.92	15	0	71	56	23	71
Carlos Lomeli, Saint Mary's	10	3	3.05	16	0	89	81	13	58
Cooper Chandler, Pepperdine	3	1	3.07	7	0	44	37	7	24
Ryan Shreve, Pacific	4	5	3.08	12	0	79	57	11	56
Christian Peters, Portland	2	4	3.12	26	1	43	25	21	45
Anthony Donatella, San Diego	4	1	3.23	18	0	53	46	22	41

NCAA DIVISION II

Tampa completed a perfect postseason by sweeping through the College World Series, beating Colorado Mesa, 3-1, in the championship game. Tampa and Colorado Mesa were the top two seeds in the CWS.

The Spartans are one of the heavyweights of DII and won their eighth national championship. Five of those titles have come since 2006 under the direction of coach Joe Urso.

"To be remembered as a Spartan, you have to win a national championship," Urso told reporters after the championship game. "No one remembers who was runner-up. That's how big this is for our program."

Righthander Jacinto Arredondo was named MVP after throwing 8.1 scoreless innings in the CWS and appearing in all four of Tampa's games. He threw the final two innings of the championship game.

DIVISION II WORLD SERIES

Site: Cary, N.C.
Participants: 1. Colorado Mesa; 2. Tampa; 3. Catawba (N.C.); 4. Ashland (Ohio); 5. Central Missouri; 6. UC San Diego; 7. Mercyhurst (Pa.); 8. New York Tech.
Champion: Tampa.
Runner-up: Colorado Mesa.

LEADERS: BATTING AVERAGE
(Minimum 140 at bats)

Rk. Player, Pos., Team	Class	AVG	OBP	SLG
1. Josh Elvir, OF, Angelo State (Texas)	Jr.	.458	.584	.989
2. Eddie Nevins, C, Wilmington (Del.)	R-Jr.	.440	.548	.720
3. Jared Melone, 1B, West Chester (Pa.)	Sr.	.438	.520	.784
4. Tyler Thompson, OF, Carson-Newman (Tenn.)	So.	.438	.528	.756
5. Ej Cumbo, OF, New York Tech	R-Fr.	.437	.510	.665
6. Jahleel Sewer, OF, Virginia State	Sr.	.436	.527	.729
7. Augie Francis, OF, New Mexico Highlands	Sr.	.434	.524	.751
8. Trevor Kehe, OF, Colorado School of Mines	Jr.	.431	.533	.822
9. Payton Eeles, 2B, Cedarville (Ohio)	Fr.	.429	.508	.535
10. Jared Carr, INF, Shepherd (Pa.)	So.	.428	.477	.647

EARNED RUN AVERAGE
(Minimum 40 innings pitched)

Rk. Pitcher, Team	Class	W	L	ERA
1. Ed Baram, Adelphi (N.Y.)	Sr.	7	2	1.32
2. Josh Loeschorn, Long Island-Post (N.Y.)	Fr.	10	0	1.34
3. Dan Wirchansky, Pace (N.Y.)	Sr.	6	2	1.38
4. Quinton Driggers, Newberry (S.C.)	Jr.	9	0	1.40
5. Derek Duffy, Franklin Pierce (N.H.)	Jr.	6	2	1.59
6. Cam Monagle, Merrimack (Mass.)	Sr.	7	1	1.63
7. Dominic Austing, St. Cloud State (Minn.)	Sr.	8	0	1.79
8. Kris Priddy, Henderson State (Ark.)	Sr.	1	0	1.86
9. Hunter Riggins, Delta State (Miss.)	So.	11	4	1.88
10. Lorenzo Russo, Pace (N.Y.)	Jr.	2	2	1.93

CATEGORY LEADERS: BATTING
*Minimum 140 at bats

Dept.	Player, Pos., Team	Class	G	Total
OBP*	Josh Elvir, OF, Angelo State (Texas)	Jr.	55	.584
SLG*	Josh Elvir, OF, Angelo State (Texas)	Jr.	55	.985
R	Brenton Doyle, OF, Shepherd (Pa.)	Jr.	52	79
	John Sechen, C, Springfield (Ill.)	Sr.	59	79
H	Mason Janvrin, OF, Central Missouri	Jr.	62	114

2B	Erik Webb, OF, Central Missouri	Jr.	61	26
3B	Ryan McPhail, OF, St. Edward's (Texas)	Sr.	43	11
HR	Cole Kleszcz, OF, Azusa Pacific (Calif.)	Jr.	55	27
RBI	Josh Elvir, OF, Angelo State (Texas)	Jr.	55	81
SB	Brandon O'Connor, OF, Benedict (S.C.)	So.	34	47

CATEGORY LEADERS: PITCHING
*Minimum 40 innings

Dept.	Pitcher, Team	Class	Total
W	Tucker Burgess, North Greenville (S.C.)	Sr.	13
	Ryan Johnson, Lubbock Christian (Texas)	Sr.	13
	Kevin Pimentel, Tampa	Sr.	13
	Chris Slavic, Ashland (Ohio)	Sr.	13
SV	Will Dixon, Colorado Mesa	Sr.	16
G	Junior Obeso, Central Oklahoma	Sr.	37
IP	Kevin Pimentel, Tampa	Sr.	120
SO	Charles Hall, Tusculum (Tenn.)	Sr.	148
SO/9*	Matthew Minnick, Mercyhurst (Pa.)	Sr.	15.64
BB/9*	Derek Duffy, Franklin Pierce (N.H.)	Jr.	0.72
WHIP*	Joshua Loeschorn, Long Island-Post (N.Y.)	Fr.	0.74

NCAA Division III

Chapman (Calif.) swept Birmingham-Southern in the finals of the Division III College World Series to win the national championship. It was the Panthers' second ever national championship and first since 2003.

First baseman Henry Zeisler wsa named the tournament MVP after going 14-for-26 and scoring 10 runs in six games.

The DIII CWS was held in Cedar Rapids, Iowa, for the first time after a 19-year run in Appleton, Wisc. It will remain in Cedar Rapids through 2022.

DIVISION III WORLD SERIES

Site: Cedar Rapids, Iowa
Participants: Babson (Mass.); Birmingham-Southern; Chapman (Calif.); Heidelberg (Ohio); Johns Hopkins (Md.); Massachusetts-Boston; Washington & Jefferson (Pa.); Webster (Mo.).
Champion: Chapman (Calif.).
Runner-up: Birmingham-Southern.

LEADERS: BATTING AVERAGE
(Minimum 120 at bats)

RK. Player, Pos., Team	Class	AVG	OBP	SLG
1. Toby Welk, 3B, Penn State-Berks	Sr.	.483	.555	.938
2. Matthew Putman, INF, Carroll (Wisc.)	Sr.	.472	.557	.593
3. Connor Harding, INF, Scranton (N.J.)	So.	.464	.517	.695
4. Patrick Keohane, OF, John Carroll (Ohio)	Sr.	.459	.523	.662
5. Will Welsh, OF, Lancaster Bible (Pa.)	Sr.	.453	.520	.781
6. Nathan Sides, INF, Alvernia (Pa.)	Sr.	.453	.507	.632
7. Dylan Nolan, C, Wells (N.Y.)	Jr.	.452	.517	.742
8. Nick Fowkes, OF, Thiel (Pa.)	Sr.	.447	.494	.673
9. Davis Mikell, 1B, Castleton (Vt.)	Jr.	.446	.552	.676
10. Mitch Walker, C, Rowan (N.J.)	Jr.	.444	.510	.621

EARNED RUN AVERAGE
(Minimum 30 innings pitched)

Rk. Pitcher, Team	Class	W	L	ERA
1. Nick Garcia, Chapman (Calif.)	So.	9	0	0.64
2. Lake Summers, Fontbonne (Mo.)	Jr.	11	2	0.67
3. Jonathan Cole, Franklin & Marshall (Pa.)	Jr.	7	2	1.02
4. Ethan Osgood, Washington (Md.)	So.	5	1	1.03
5. Kyle Petri, Chicago	Fr.	6	0	1.12
6. Gage Smart, Buena Vista (Iowa)	Jr.	5	1	1.14

7.	John Howard, Washington-St. Louis	Sr.	11	1	1.23
8.	Andrew Spinnenweber, Merchant Marine	Sr.	6	0	1.31
9.	Ben Lambert, Southern Maine	Jr.	10	1	1.38
10.	Tim Woodford, Saint Joseph's (N.Y.)	Jr.	6	1	1.40

CATEGORY LEADERS: BATTING
Minimum 120 at bats

Dept.	Player, Pos., Team	Class	G	Total
OBP*	Ryan Grubbs, C, Christopher Newport (N.J.)	Sr.	38	.607
SLG*	Toby Welk, 3B, Penn State-Berks	Sr.	39	.938
R	Bret Williams, OF, Penn State-Harrisburg	Jr.	49	75
H	Bret Williams, OF, Penn State-Harrisburg	Jr.	49	88
2B	Eddie Riley, INF, Massachusetts-Boston	Sr.	51	24
	Scott Sada, INF, Penn State-Behrend	Sr.	41	24
3B	Nick Herzog, OF, Massachusetts-Boston	Sr.	51	12
	Noah Payne, INF, Howard Payne (Texas)	Sr.	40	12
HR	Nicholas Baham, INF, Christopher Newport (N.J.)	Sr.	45	19
RBI	Travis Van Houten, P, Penn State-Harrisburg	Sr.	49	71
SB	Jose Mercado, SS, Concordia Chicago	Sr.	52	46

CATEGORY LEADERS: PITCHING
Minimum 30 innings

Dept.	Pitcher, Team	Class	Total
W	Jack Bunting, Johns Hopkins (Md.)	Sr.	13
SV	Gerard DePhillips, Shenandoah (Va.)	Jr.	13
	Bobby Tramondozzi, Massachusetts-Boston	Sr.	13
IP	Jonathan Hernandez, Chapman (Calif.)	Sr.	114
	Tyler Peck, Chapman (Calif.)	Sr.	114
SO	Tyler Peck, Chapman (Calif.)	Sr.	155
SO/9*	Danny Serreino, Rowan (N.J.)	Sr.	14.81
BB/9*	Will Carey, Susquehanna (Pa.)	So.	0.56
WHIP*	Gage Smart, Buena Vista (Iowa)	Jr.	0.70

NAIA

Tennessee Wesleyan defeated St. Thomas (Fla.), 6-2, in the championship game of the NAIA World Series to claim the national title.

The Bulldogs were the top-seeded team in the tournament and their 56 wins were the most in program history. Second baseman Bryce Giles was named tournament MVP.

NAIA WORLD SERIES
Site: Lewiston, Idaho.
Participants: 1. Tennessee Wesleyan; 2. Science & Arts (Okla.); 3. Southeastern (Fla.); 4. Faulkner (Ala.); 5. Georgia Gwinnett; 6. St. Thomas (Fla.); 7. Feed-Hardeman (Tenn.); 8. Indiana Tech; 9. Bellevue (Neb.); 10. Lewis-Clark State (Idaho).
Champion: Tennessee Wesleyan.
Runner-up: St. Thomas (Fla.).

LEADERS: BATTING AVERAGE
(Minimum 140 at bats)

RK.	Player, Pos., Team	Class	AVG	OBP	SLG
1.	Blaine Milheim, OF, Concordia (Mich.)	Sr.	.482	.565	.660
2.	Cam Coursey, INF, Georgia Gwinnett	Jr.	.458	.535	.687
3.	Mitchell Lundholm, 1B, Fisher (Mass.)	Jr.	.454	.502	.619
4.	Austin Sojka, SS, Oklahoma Wesleyan	Sr.	.447	.556	.769
5.	Garrett Hall, INF, Keiser (Fla.)	Jr.	.441	.524	.726

EARNED RUN AVERAGE
(Minimum 40 innings pitched)

Rk.	Pitcher, Team	Class	W	L	ERA
1.	Ray Diaz, Marymount California	Sr.	4	2	1.26
2.	Colton Williams, Science & Arts (Okla.)	Jr.	16	0	1.33
3.	Matt Burleton, Marian (Ind.)	Sr.	8	2	1.37
4.	Cole Bellair, Tennessee Wesleyan	Sr.	13	2	1.67
5.	Evan Gillespie, Faulkner (Ala.)	Jr.	11	1	1.68

CATEGORY LEADERS: BATTING
Minimum 140 at bats

Dept.	Player, Pos., Team	Class	G	Total
OBP*	Blaine Milheim, OF, Concordia (Mich.)	Sr.	59	.565
SLG*	Aaron Shackleford, INF, The Master's (Calif.)	Sr.	52	1.096
HR	Aaron Shackleford, INF, The Master's (Calif.)	Sr.	52	36
RBI	Aaron Shackleford, INF, The Master's (Calif.)	Sr.	52	99
SB	Collin Baber, OF, Freed-Hardeman (Tenn.)	Jr.	52	47

CATEGORY LEADERS: PITCHING

Dept.	Pitcher, Team	Class	Total
W	Colton Williams, Science & Arts (Okla.)	Jr.	16
SV	Hunter Avery, Mobile (Ala.)	Sr.	12
	River Carbone, Arizona Christian	Sr.	12
IP	Zak Spivy, Webber International (Fla.)	Sr.	124
SO	Colton Williams, Science & Arts (Okla.)	Jr.	136

NJCAA Division I

Central Arizona defeated Iowa Western, 13-8, in the championship game of the DI Junior College World Series. After falling behind 7-0 in the top of the first inning, the Vaqueros quickly launched a comeback and held off the Reivers for the national championship.

Central Arizona won its third national title and first since 2002. Outfielder Hunter Jump was named tournament MVP. He hit .545 with two home runs during the World Series, including one in the championship game.

NJCAA DIVISION I WORLD SERIES
Site: Grand Junction, Colo.
Participants: Central Arizona; Chattahoochee Valley (Ala.); Chipola (Fla.); Connors State (Okla.); Cowley (Kan.); Iowa Western; Monroe (N.Y.); Navarro (Texas); New Mexico; Walters State (Tenn.).
Champion: Central Arizona.
Runner-up: Iowa Western.

LEADERS: BATTING AVERAGE
Minimum 140 at bats)

Rk.	Player, Pos., Team	Class	AVG	OBP	SLG
1.	Cael Baker, 1B, Wabash Valley (Ill.)	So.	.506	.596	1.051
2.	Anthony Amicangelo, OF, Seminole St. (Okla.)	So.	.492	.556	.768
3.	Nathan Collins, INF, Vernon (Texas)	So.	.477	.525	.693
4.	Noah Fitzgerald, SS, Chattanooga St. (Tenn.)	So.	.470	.522	.705
5.	James Nix, OF, Central Florida	Fr.	.462	.593	.739

EARNED RUN AVERAGE
(Minimum 40 innings pitched)

Rk.	Pitcher, Team	Class	W	L	ERA
1.	Jackson Rutledge, San Jacinto (Texas)	So.	9	2	0.87
2.	Kobe Foster, Motlow State (Tenn.)	So.	8	2	1.19
3.	Lucas Knowles, Central Arizona	So.	9	2	1.23
4.	Chris Koeiman, Arizona Western	So.	12	2	1.44
5.	Robert Gonzalez, Arizona Western	So.	9	3	1.49

CATEGORY LEADERS: BATTING
Minimum 140 at bats

		Dept.	Player,
Pos., Team		Class	G	Total
OBP*	Cael Baker, 1B, Wabash Valey (Ill.)	So.	58	.596
SLG*	Cael Baker, 1B, Wabash Valley (Ill.)	So.	58	1.051
HR	Cael Baker, 1B, Wabash Valley (Ill.)	So.	58	25
RBI	Cael Baker, 1B, Wabash Valley (Ill.)	So.	58	101
SB	Noah Myers, OF, Wabash Valley (Ill.)	So.	59	77

CATEGORY LEADERS: PITCHING

Dept.	Pitcher, Team	Class	Total

W	Zachary Ebert, Johnson County (Kan.)	So.	12
	Chris Koeiman, Arizona Western	So.	12
	Ryan O'Connell, Wabash Valley (Ill.)	So.	12
SV	Trystan Kimmell, Iowa Western	So.	18
IP	Anthony Durbano, Trinidad State (Colo.)	So.	98
SO	Jake Hamilton, Rose State (Okla.)	So.	137

NJCAA Division II

Northeast Oklahoma Enid won its first-ever national title thanks to a Dylan Caplinger ninth-inning home run. The Jets topped Mesa (Ariz.), 5-4, in the title game.

NEO Enid reliever Brandon Hudson worked 2.2 innings of relief to pick up the win. Hudson was also named the player of the tournament.

NJCAA DIVISION II WORLD SERIES
Site: Enid, Okla.
Participants: 1. Pearl River (Miss.); 2. Madison (Wisc.); 3. Mesa (Ariz.); 4. Kellogg (Mich.); 5. Northern Oklahoma Enid; 6. Lincoln Land (Ill.); 7. Northeast (Neb.); 8. Pasco-Hernando State (Fla.); 9. Lackawanna (Pa.); 10. Monroe (N.Y.).
Champion: Northeast Oklahoma Enid.
Runner-up: Mesa.

LEADERS: BATTING AVERAGE
(Minimum 120 at bats)

RK. Player, Pos., Team	Class	AVG	OBP	SLG
1. Dan Pruitt, 1B, Western Oklahoma State	So.	.481	.573	1.016
2. Ryan Moormeier, 1B, Bismarck State (N.D.)	So.	.480	.565	.843
3. Drew Smith, INF, Northeast (Neb.)	So.	.465	.538	.897
4. Trent Quartermaine, INF, Kalamazoo Valley (Mich)	So.	.463	.562	.846
5. Adam Henderson, OF, Kellogg (Mich.)	So.	.457	.548	.790

EARNED RUN AVERAGE
(Minimum 40 innings pitched)

Rk. Pitcher, Team	Class	W	L	ERA
1. Dylan Patrick, Pitt (N.C.)	So.	5	0	0.35
2. Logan Bender, Catawba Valley (N.C.)	So.	7	0	0.78
3. Blake Dockery, Catawba Valley (N.C.)	Fr.	6	2	0.92
4. Ty Rybarczyk, Parkland (Ill.)	Fr.	8	1	0.96
5. Spencer Walker, Lincoln Land (Ill.)	Fr.	8	1	1.26

CATEGORY LEADERS: BATTING
*Minimum 120 at bats

Dept.	Player, Pos., Team	Class	G	Total
OBP*	Ryan Parquette, C, McHenry County (Ill.)	So.	51	.585
SLG*	Dan Pruitt, 1B, Western Oklahoma State	So.	55	1.016
HR	Fox Leum, 1B, North Iowa Area	R-So.	58	24
RBI	Mike Sears, INF, Sinclair (Mich.)	Fr.	61	86
SB	Gary Mattis, INF, GateWay (Ariz.)	So.	58	64

CATEGORY LEADERS: PITCHING

Dept.	Pitcher, Team	Class	Total
W	Dane Dixon, LSU-Eunice	R-So.	13
SV	Kyle Amendt, Southeastern (Iowa)	Fr.	14
IP	Carter Robinson, Mesa (Ariz.)	R-So.	112
SO	Brock Begue, Cuyahoga (Ohio)	So.	130

NJCAA Division III

Cumberland (N.J.) topped Rowan Gloucester (N.J.), 11-7, in an all-New Jersey affair for the title.

The win is Cumberland's first national championship in any sport. Michael Miles picked up the complete-game win. He shouldered a massive workload on the road to the title, pitching 14.1 innings over three games in five days, and was named tournament MVP.

NJCAA DIVISION III WORLD SERIES
Site: Greeneville, Tenn.
Participants: 1. Rowan Gloucester (N.J.); 2. Brookhaven (Texas); 3. Cumberland County (N.J.); 4. Herkimer (N.Y.); 5. Oakton (Ill.); 6. Century (Minn.); 7. Rockingham (N.C.); 8. Rhode Island.
Champion: Cumberland County.
Runner-up: Rowan Gloucester.

LEADERS: BATTING AVERAGE
(Minimum 120 at bats)

RK. Player, Pos., Team	Class	AVG	OBP	SLG
1. Billy Rogers, OF, Cedar Valley (Texas)	So.	.488	.557	.714
2. Spencer Brown, INF, Northern Essex (Mass.)	Fr.	.486	.512	1.000
3. Alan Pietila, OF, Central Lakes (Minn.)	So.	.468	.522	.604
4. Kyle Lauria, 3B, Ocean County (N.J.)	So.	.459	.526	.759
5. Adrian Urena, Bronx (N.Y.)	Fr.	.458	.472	.583

EARNED RUN AVERAGE
(Minimum 40 innings pitched)

Rk. Pitcher, Team	Class	W	L	ERA
1. Jared Naida, Lorain County (Ohio)	So.	3	3	0.67
2. Joseph Valentino, Suffolk County (N.Y.)	So.	8	0	1.12
3. Price Hargett, Surry (N.C.)	So.	2	1	1.28
4. Noah Weber, Northampton (Pa.)	Fr.	9	1	1.61
5. Tanner Cooper, Finger Lakes (N.Y.)	So.	8	4	1.62

California Junior Colleges

Orange Coast defeated El Camino, 8-7, on a walk-off single to win the California CC Athletic Association state championship.

OCC had to come out of the losers' bracket to win its seventh state title and won three games in the final two days of the tournament. None, however, was as dramatic as the final, when Joey Fregosi delivered the game-winner.

Righthander Cole Van Den Helder was named tournament MVP.

CALIFORNIA CC ATHLETIC ASSOCIATION
Site: Fresno.
Participants: El Camino, Orange Coast, Sacramento City, San Joaquin Delta.
Champion: Orange Coast.
Runner-up: El Camino.

LEADERS: BATTING AVERAGE
(Minimum 140 at bats)

RK. Player, Pos., Team	Class	AVG	OBP	SLG
1. Chet Allison, OF, Fresno City	So.	.446	.548	.831
2. Trent MacKinney, UTL, Glendale	Fr.	.430	.489	.617
3. Nick Henry, C, Canyons	Fr.	.419	.521	.671
4. Judah Wilbur, INF, Barstow	So.	.416	.485	.711
5. Wyatt Hendrie, C, Antelope Valley	Fr.	.410	.479	.660

EARNED RUN AVERAGE
(Minimum 40 innings pitched)

Rk. Pitcher, Team	Class	W	L	ERA
1. Clayton Hall, Merced	Fr.	1	1	0.21
2. Devin Kirby, Santa Rosa	So.	3	2	1.09
3. Josh Ibarra, Golden West	So.	4	1	1.62
4. Jacob Miller, Feather River	So.	7	0	1.66
4. Steven Silvas, Mt. San Jacinto	Fr.	3	3	1.66

Pitching and defense were a constant theme for USA Baseball's Collegiate National Team this summer. Over 14 international games, Team USA posted a 3.06 ERA and a .981 fielding percentage, helping it to an 8-6 record.

Team USA faced a tough slate as it hosted Cuba before heading to Asia to play Taiwan and Japan. The CNT went 4-1 against Cuba to win the series for the fifth straight year. Its four wins in the series was the most since 2013.

After the Cuba series, the CNT traveled to Asia. It went 2-1 in its series at Taiwan, giving it a chance to win all of its series for the third straight season. But standing in its way was Japan, which has traditionally been Team USA's toughest opponent.

Japan won the series opener, but Team USA stormed back with two tight victories. In the first, Alec Burleson hit a walk-off homer for a 3-2 victory. The CNT followed that up with a 2-0 victory as three pitchers combined for a one-hitter. But it was unable to close out what would have been its first series win in Japan in 40 years.

Still, it was a successful summer all-around for Team USA.

"We live in a great country," coach Dan McDonnell (Louisville) said. "It was an honor to coach the 24 best players in our country."

Lefthander Reid Detmers (Louisville) and righthander Max Meyer (Minnesota) led the CNT's pitching staff. Both threw 13 innings and allowed just one earned run apiece to finish the summer with matching 0.69 ERAs. Lefthanders Andrew Abbott (Virginia) and Burl Carraway (Dallas Baptist) led a strong bullpen. Abbott appeared in a team-high seven games and struck out 12 batters in 12 innings, while Carraway held opponents scoreless in 4.1 innings over five appearances.

Team USA had some strong hitters, including sluggers Heston Kjerstad (Arkansas) and Spencer Torkelson (Arizona State). Kjerstad hit .395/.426/.651 to lead the team in all three categories, and he and Torkelson each hit a team-high two home runs.

Beyond that offensive output, however, Team USA impressed in the field. Shortstops Nick Loftin (Baylor) and Alika Williams (Arizona State) anchored the infield, while Luke Waddell (Georgia Tech) impressed at third base and Austin Martin (Vanderbilt) took over in center field.

"They're attacking the zone with the fastball," McDonnell said. "With the defense, I think our pitchers get a good feeling looking at the guys behind them and going, 'Wow, those are some nice plays,'"

COLLEGIATE NATIONAL TEAM STATS

Player, Pos.	Year	School	AVG	OBP	SLG	G	AB	R	H	2B	3B	HR	RBI	BB	SO	SB
Heston Kjerstad, OF	Jr.	Arkansas	.395	.426	.651	14	43	8	17	*Year indicates 2018-19 class standing*						
Alika Williams, SS	Jr.	Arizona State	.364	.370	.545	14	44	8	16	1	2	1	10	1	5	0
Luke Waddell, 3B	Jr.	Georgia Tech	.320	.404	.380	14	50	8	16	3	0	0	5	7	6	4
Tanner Allen, 1B	Jr.	Mississippi State	.308	.357	.359	13	39	3	12	2	0	0	3	3	10	0
Nick Loftin, SS	Jr.	Baylor	.292	.280	.583	11	24	8	7	2	1	1	5	0	6	1
Colton Cowser, OF	So.	Sam Houston State	.273	.390	.303	13	33	9	9	1	0	0	3	5	11	1
Alec Burleson, 1B/LHP	Jr.	East Carolina	.267	.353	.467	8	15	1	4	0	0	1	3	1	4	0
Spencer Torkelson, 1B	Jr.	Arizona State	.260	.361	.440	14	50	7	13	3	0	2	8	8	11	1
Justin Foscue, 2B	Jr.	Mississippi State	.255	.288	.362	14	47	2	12	3	1	0	5	3	8	1
Austin Martin, OF	Jr.	Vanderbilt	.250	.321	.396	12	48	6	12	2	1	1	8	2	7	1
Patrick Bailey, C	Jr.	North Carolina State	.231	.333	.308	9	26	3	6	0	1	0	4	3	12	1
Lucas Dunn, OF	Jr.	Louisville	.217	.308	.261	10	23	3	5	1	0	0	0	3	5	1
Casey Opitz, C	Jr.	Arkansas	.056	.292	.056	6	18	2	1	0	0	0	1	6	1	0

Pitcher, Pos.	Year	School	W	L	ERA	G	SV	IP	H	R	ER	BB	SO	AVG
Burl Carraway, LHP	Jr.	Dallas Baptist	0	0	0.00	5	0	4	3	0	0	2	7	.200
Nick Frasso, RHP	Jr.	Loyola Marymount	1	0	0.00	1	0	4	2	0	0	0	1	.167
Max Meyer, RHP	Jr.	Minnesota	1	2	0.69	3	0	13	13	4	1	2	10	.260
Reid Detmers, LHP	Jr.	Louisville	2	0	0.69	3	0	13	5	1	1	7	10	.128
Andrew Abbott, LHP	Jr.	Virginia	2	1	2.25	7	1	12	10	5	3	4	12	.244
Chris McMahon, RHP	Jr.	Miami	0	0	2.25	3	1	12	6	3	3	6	15	.154
Asa Lacy, LHP	Jr.	Texas A&M	0	0	2.25	3	0	12	9	3	3	5	9	.220
Jeff Criswell, RHP	Jr.	Michigan	0	0	2.35	3	1	8	3	2	2	4	4	.120
Alec Burleson, 1B/LHP	Jr.	East Carolina	0	0	2.53	3	0	11	9	4	3	4	8	.237
Cole Wilcox, RHP	So.	Georgia	1	0	2.57	4	0	7	5	3	2	4	7	.217
Cade Cavalli, RHP	Jr.	Oklahoma	0	0	3.38	1	0	3	3	1	1	2	1	.273
Doug Nikhazy, LHP	So.	Mississippi	0	0	5.14	4	0	7	5	4	4	5	6	.217
Tyler Brown, RHP	Jr.	Vanderbilt	1	1	7.56	5	1	8	9	7	7	4	12	.300
Logan Allen, LHP	Jr.	Florida International	0	1	10.80	3	0	10	19	12	12	1	11	.413

Cotuit Wins Cape Title

Led by MVP and No. 1 prospect Nick Gonzales, Cotuit ran off six straight wins in the Cape Cod League playoffs to win its 17th championship, the most in league history. The Kettleers beat Harwich in the finals.

Cotuit was a .500 team during the regular season and lost the first game of its best-of-three opening round playoff series against Wareham. But the Kettleers roared back the next day for a 22-2 victory that sparked a six-game winning streak and run to the championship. Along the way, Cotuit knocked out the defending champions (Wareham) and the division winner (Falmouth).

That set up a championship series against Harwich, which also had been a .500 team in the regular season before getting hot in the playoffs. The first game of the series was an instant classic that lasted 15 innings before Cotuit won, 7-6. After giving up two runs in the bottom of the eighth inning, the Kettleers had to score twice in the top of the ninth against hard-throwing Joe Boyle to extend the game and the two teams then battled through five scoreless extra innings before Gonzales drove in what proved to be the winning run in the 15th inning.

Cotuit clinched the championship the next day in less dramatic fashion, with a 10-3 victory. The Kettleers jumped out to a lead in the first inning and never looked back, blowing the game open with a six-run fifth inning. Third baseman/righthander Casey Schmitt was named MVP of the championship series after going 4-for-10 with two home runs and throwing a scoreless ninth inning of the decisive game to clinch the title.

Overall, offense continued to be up on the Cape. Some larger trends, such as emphasis on launch angle, have helped scoring tick up, but like summer leagues across the country, the Cape is also dealing with pitchers who are more limited in how many innings they can throw during the summer.

That trend showed in the top prospects list, as six of the top seven players in the league were position players. Still, the league figures to again produce several first-round picks for the 2020 draft.

Summer League Roundup

Morehead City, the defending champions, again claimed the Petit Cup and the Coastal Plains League title, defeating Macon in the championship series. The Marlins entered the playoffs as the No. 1 seed in the East Division after topping the standings in both halves of the season. After splitting the first two games of the series, Morehead City claimed the title with a 6-2 victory in the decisive third game.

Righthander Leo Perez (Texas A&M-Corpus Christi) started on the mound for the Marlins and kept them in the game until their hot offense took over. A dominant relief performance by Jack Myers (Butler) silenced a Macon comeback, as the Marlins took the 6-2 victory and championship title, asserting their reign as back to back champs of the CPL.

Santa Barbara, again loaded with talent in the California Collegiate League, headed into the postseason with the league's best record (27-8) and emerged as the champion. The Foresters defeated the Healdsburg Prune Packers in three games. Santa Barbara advanced to the National Baseball Congress World Series, which it won in 2012. After going 3-0 in pool play, the Foresters were knocked out in tournament play by the Seattle Studs, the eventual champions.

The Keene Swampbats swept the best-of-three series against the Martha's Vineyard Sharks to claim the Fay Vincent Sr. Cup in the New England Collegiate Baseball League. Keene won its fifth championship in team history and its first since 2013.

For just the second time in the last five years, the Northwoods League saw a 50-win team: the 52-win Traverse City Pit Spitters, which got by with excellent starting pitching in what was a hitter-dominant league. They rode their regular season momentum to the title in their first season in the league. Traverse City won the title in dramatic fashion, defeating the Eau Clair Express, 3-2, on a walk-off error. The Pit Spitters entered the ninth inning trailing, 2-1, but were able to erase that deficit. Ultimately, they claimed the first-half, second-half, overall and playoff titles. Their 52 wins also tied the single-season league record.

In the Alaska Baseball League, it was an all-Anchorage championship series as the Bucs beat the Pilots in three games. The Bucs, which also finished first in the regular season, broke through for their ninth championship after falling short in the finals in the last two seasons.

In the Perfect Game Collegiate League, the Amsterdam Mohawks swept the Adirondack Trail Blazers in the championship series to win their first title since 2016. The Mohawks went undefeated in the playoffs and Maxwell Costes starred in the finals and was named playoff MVP.

The Corvallis Knights built on their West Coast League dynasty with another championship. Corvallis defeated the Victoria HarbourCats in the finals for a record fourth straight league title. The Knights, who have won seven titles since 2008, also tied a franchise record with 54 wins and set a WCL record with 42 league wins.

COLLEGE SUMMER LEAGUES

For players who qualified for multiple teams: 1: Stats with first team. 2: Stats with second team. 3: Stats with third team. T: combined stats.

Zach DeLoach this summer hit .353 to win the Cape Cod League batting title.

COURTESY OF MEGHAN MURPHY/FALMOUTH COMMODORES

CAPE COD LEAGUE

East Division	W	L	T	PTS
Orleans Firebirds	23	17	4	50
Chatham Anglers	24	18	2	50
Yarmouth-Dennis Red Sox	22	19	3	47
Harwich Mariners	21	21	2	44
Brewster Whitecaps	18	22	4	40

West Division	W	L	T	PTS
Falmouth Commodores	27	15	2	56
Wareham Gatemen	24	18	2	50
Cotuit Kettleers	20	20	4	44
Bourne Braves	18	24	2	38
Hyannis Harbor Hawks	9	32	3	21

CHAMPIONSHIP: Cotuit Kettleers defeated Harwich Mariners, 2-0, in best-of-three championship series.

TOP 50 PROSPECTS: 1. Nick Gonzales, 2B, Cotuit (Jr., New Mexico State). **2.** Carmen Mlodzinski, RHP, Falmouth (R-So., South Carolina). **3.** Austin Wells, C/1B, Yarmouth-Dennis (So., Arizona). **4.** Jordan Westburg, SS, Hyannis (Jr., Mississippi State). **5.** Daniel Cabrera, OF, Harwich (Jr., Louisiana State). **6.** Gage Workman, SS/3B, Brewster (Jr., Arizona State). **7.** Matt McLain, UTL, Wareham (So., UCLA). **8.** Logan Allen, LHP, Harwich (Jr., Florida International). **9.** Ian Seymour, LHP, Yarmouth-Dennis (Jr., Virginia Tech). **10.** Noah Campbell, 2B/OF, Yarmouth-Dennis (Jr., South Carolina). **11.** Jake Eder, LHP, Orleans (Jr., Vanderbilt). **12.** RJ Dabovich, RHP, Chatham (Jr., Arizona State). **13.** Adrian Del Castillo, C/OF, Wareham (So., Miami). **14.** Zach DeLoach, OF, Falmouth (Jr., Texas A&M). **15.** Hayden Cantrelle, 2B/SS, Falmouth (Jr., Louisiana-Lafayette). **16.** Joe Boyle, RHP, Harwich (Jr., Notre Dame). **17.** Jud Fabian, OF, Bourne (So., Florida). **18.** Jesse Franklin, OF, Brewster (Jr., Michigan). **19.** Joey Wiemer, OF, Harwich (Jr., Cincinnati). **20.** Ian Bedell, RHP, Wareham (Jr., Missouri). **21.** Casey Schmitt, 3B/RHP, Cotuit (Jr., San Diego State). **22.** Jack Leftwich, RHP, Yarmouth-Dennis (Jr.,

Florida). **23.** Parker Chavers, OF, Cotuit (Jr., Coastal Carolina). **24.** Brady Smith, C, Chatham (Jr., Florida). **25.** Zach Brzykcy, RHP, Falmouth (Jr., Virginia Tech). **26.** Franco Aleman, RHP, Falmouth (So., St. Johns River State (Fla.) JC). **27.** Tyler Mattison, RHP, Hyannis (Jr., Bryant). **28.** Seth Lonsway, LHP, Brewster (R-So., Ohio State). **29.** Sean Sullivan, RHP, Cotuit (So., California). **30.** Nick Nastrini, RHP, Falmouth (So., UCLA). **31.** Wyatt Young, SS, Yarmouth-Dennis (So., Pepperdine). **32.** Jacob Palisch, LHP, Harwich (Jr., Stanford). **33.** Jimmy Glowenke, SS, Bourne (Jr., Dallas Baptist). **34.** Jared Shuster, LHP, Orleans (Jr., Wake Forest). **35.** Koby Kubichek, RHP, Chatham (So., Texas). **36.** Aidan Maldonado, RHP, Falmouth (So., Illinois). **37.** Mason Black, RHP, Brewster (So., Lehigh). **38.** Ben Ramirez, SS, Chatham (Jr., Southern California). **39.** Taylor Dollard, RHP, Yarmouth-Dennis (Jr., Cal Poly). **40.** Trei Cruz, SS, Falmouth (Jr., Rice). **41.** Kaden Polcovich, OF/2B (Jr., Oklahoma State). **42.** Ty Madden, RHP, Chatham (So., Texas). **43.** Luke Bartnicki, LHP, Chatham (So., Georgia Tech). **44.** Allbry Major, OF, Cotuit (Jr., Xavier). **45.** Cody Morissette, 2B, Bourne (So., Boston College). **46.** Darren Baker, 2B, Wareham (Jr., California). **47.** Jamal O'Guinn, OF/1B, Chatham (Jr., Southern California). **48.** Zach McCambley, RHP, Cotuit (Jr., Coastal Carolina). **49.** Kyle Nicholas, RHP, Cotuit (Jr., Ball State). **50.** Trey Dillard, RHP, Wareham (Jr., Misouri).

INDIVIDUAL BATTING LEADERS

	AVG	AB	R	H	2B	3B	HR	RBI	SB
Zach DeLoach, OF, Falmouth	.353	133	22	47	8	1	5	23	8
Nick Gonzales, 2B, Cotuit	.351	154	39	54	14	4	7	33	6
Max Troiani, OF, Orleans	.345	142	17	49	2	0	0	19	5
Darren Baker, 2B, Wareham	.342	117	16	40	2	1	0	8	12
Wyatt Young, SS, Y-D	.338	130	26	44	7	2	1	23	9
Noah Campbell, 2B/OF, Y-D	.324	102	18	33	0	1	3	19	6
Riley King, 3B, Y-D	.323	124	16	40	4	0	3	10	3
Zavier Warren, INF, Bourne	.315	149	19	47	8	1	3	24	2
Hayden Cantrelle, 2B, Falmouth	.315	130	29	41	7	0	3	14	19
Austin Wells, C/1B, Y-D	.308	156	23	48	13	0	7	26	8

INDIVIDUAL PITCHING LEADERS

Player, Team	W	L	ERA	G	SV	IP	H	BB	SO
Logan Allen, Harwich	2	0	0.00	3	0	15	7	3	24
Ian Bedell, Wareham	4	0	0.59	6	0	31	17	3	36
Will Heflin, Harwich	2	0	0.75	9	2	24	17	7	29
Jacob Palisch, Harwich	5	1	0.77	6	0	35	24	5	38
Koby Kubichek, Chatham	2	2	0.90	8	0	30	16	9	34
Levi Prater, Wareham	2	1	0.92	7	0	20	9	8	21
Jacob Winger, Y-D	0	0	1.04	11	0	17	9	6	22
Connor McCullough, Harwich	2	0	1.05	6	0	26	16	8	29
Franco Aleman, Falmouth	2	0	1.16	6	0	31	25	2	27
Jacob Eder, Orleans	1	1	1.20	4	0	15	12	4	15

BOURNE

Batting	AVG	AB	R	H	2B	3B	HR	RBI	SB
Cade Beloso, 1B	.222	90	11	20	4	0	1	10	0
Noah Bridges, OF	.200	25	1	5	1	0	0	1	1
Nick Brueser, 1B	.237	59	6	14	3	2	0	3	0
Alec Burleson, 1B/LHP	.148	27	3	4	2	0	0	3	0
Peter Burns, C	.333	9	1	3	0	0	0	1	0
Jacob Campbell, C	.136	22	1	3	1	0	0	1	0
Robert Carmody, C	.118	17	2	2	0	0	0	1	0
Cal Christofori, C	.286	7	0	2	0	0	0	0	0
A.J Curtis, 1B/OF	.235	34	3	8	0	1	0	2	0
Henry Davis, C	.133	15	2	2	0	0	1	4	0
Giovanni DiGiacomo, OF	.308	39	8	12	1	0	0	1	4
Jud Fabian, OF	.290	124	23	36	8	0	6	16	1
Kyler Fedko, INF	.171	76	7	13	4	0	0	3	0
Jimmy Glowenke, SS	.296	135	14	40	6	0	2	24	1
Paul Gozzo, C	.188	16	2	3	2	0	0	1	0
Jackson Greer, C	.224	49	10	11	5	0	1	8	0
Kyle Hess, OF	.203	79	9	16	2	0	1	11	1
Jake Mackenzie, SS	.291	79	16	23	4	1	3	7	9
Joshua Madole, 1B	.286	7	1	2	0	0	0	0	0
Cody Morissete, 2B	.252	123	13	31	6	3	0	15	0
Shane Muntz, C	.429	7	1	3	1	0	0	0	0
Jared Poland, 2B/RHP	.271	59	6	16	4	0	0	7	0
Brendan Rivoli, OF	.262	84	7	22	5	0	0	11	0
Zavier Warren, INF	.315	149	19	47	8	1	3	24	2
Alika Williams, SS	.286	35	5	10	1	0	0	1	0
Ernie Yake, 3B	.250	4	0	1	0	0	0	0	0

Pitching	W	L	ERA	G	SV	IP	H	BB	SO
Tyler Brosius	0	0	6.46	12	4	15	16	5	19
Blake Burzell	0	1	4.11	11	0	15	21	4	9
Erubiel Candelario	0	0	0.00	1	0	1	0	0	2
Joshua Culliver	0	3	7.53	10	0	20	28	7	12
Ryan Cusick	3	3	3.79	7	0	36	28	7	33
Nick Dombkowski	3	2	2.48	8	0	36	35	11	29
Colby Dunlop	0	2	5.52	5	0	15	20	2	12
Nicholas Grabek	0	0	2.25	1	0	4	4	1	2
Sean Harney	1	1	4.95	10	0	20	21	12	14
Karl Johnson	2	1	3.10	11	1	20	20	3	20
Haydn King	0	1	4.05	5	0	13	9	7	9
Mac Lardner	2	2	2.25	6	0	32	25	3	31
Shane Muntz	0	0	36.00	1	0	1	3	2	0
Jared Poland	3	1	3.38	8	0	11	13	4	18
Nicholas Richmond	0	0	4.50	1	0	2	1	1	1
Braxton Roxby	0	0	0.00	3	0	4	1	1	6
Harrison Rutkowski	3	2	2.38	7	0	34	34	5	21
Adam Schwartz	0	0	13.5	1	0	1	4	1	1
Kieran Shaw	1	0	1.32	14	5	14	7	3	20
Wesley Tobin	0	0	2.25	2	0	4	4	3	2
Nick Trogrlic-Iverson	0	1	4.43	12	1	20	19	7	8
Jacob Winger	0	0	0.00	2	0	2	2	1	0
JP Woodward	0	3	6.53	10	0	21	29	14	15
Kerry Wright	0	1	6.35	7	0	11	5	12	11

BREWSTER

Batting	AVG	AB	R	H	2B	3B	HR	RBI	SB
Brett Auerbach, C	.297	145	25	43	3	0	3	11	11
Luke Berryhill, C	.333	15	2	5	2	0	0	0	0
Ryan Bliss, SS	.286	42	8	12	2	1	1	2	5
Coby Boulware, 2B	.050	20	1	1	0	0	0	0	0
Marcos Castanon, INF	.189	106	15	20	5	0	2	18	1
T.J. Collett, 1B	.281	128	19	36	6	0	9	32	1
Joshua Crouch, C	.167	18	2	3	0	0	0	0	0
Colin Davis, OF	.368	19	4	7	4	1	1	4	3
Ciaran Devenney, C	.250	12	1	3	0	0	0	2	0
Noah Dickerson, OF	.000	4	0	0	0	0	0	0	0
Mason Dodd, INF	.167	54	7	9	2	0	2	5	0
Damon Dues, SS	.231	26	2	6	0	0	0	0	1
Duke Ellis, OF	.213	61	15	13	3	0	0	3	6
Eric Foggo, 1B	.179	56	6	10	1	0	2	5	1
Jesse Franklin, OF	.282	71	9	20	4	0	1	9	2
Tyler Gentry, OF	.267	150	17	40	11	3	2	22	3
Tyler Hardman, 3B	.262	130	18	34	5	0	8	17	0
Ben LaSpaluto, SS	.250	4	0	1	0	0	0	0	0
Cameron Locklear, SS	.200	15	1	3	1	0	0	1	1
Christian Molfetta, C	.310	58	11	18	3	0	2	12	0
Brennan Reback, OF	.000	6	0	0	0	0	0	0	1
Alerick Soularie, OF	.207	29	7	6	1	0	1	2	1
Dominic Toso, INF	.571	7	2	4	0	0	0	3	0
Justin Vought, C	.194	36	4	7	2	0	2	3	0
Kurt Wilson, OF/RHP	.333	9	1	3	1	0	1	3	0
Gage Workman, SS	.266	154	19	41	5	4	1	20	7

Pitching	W	L	ERA	G	SV	IP	H	BB	SO
Peyton Alford	1	1	4.28	12	0	27	25	14	23
Mason Black	3	0	1.49	8	0	36	27	12	39
Carson Coleman	0	0	5.40	6	2	5	4	3	9
Brian Craven	0	0	0.00	2	0	3	0	3	2
Stephen Emanuels	0	1	3.68	7	0	22	26	6	28
Sean Fisher	3	0	2.84	12	3	25	22	4	15
Tyler Follis	1	0	2.00	6	0	18	15	2	17
Daniel Harper	0	3	11.32	7	0	21	40	11	14
Chance Huff	1	2	10.13	4	0	8	10	11	8
Sean Hunley	1	1	11.85	7	1	14	30	5	14
Chandler Jozwiak	1	2	1.74	4	0	21	20	10	19
Seth Lonsway	2	0	4.50	7	1	12	6	12	10
William McKay	3	3	4.91	12	1	18	26	6	11
Matthew Mikulski	1	1	1.86	5	0	19	12	13	26
Jimmy Ramsey	0	1	7.13	9	0	24	32	11	21
Sean Roberts	0	0	0.00	2	0	4	2	1	3
Connor Shamblin	0	2	3.10	8	0	29	20	26	22
Jonah Smith	0	0	10.13	3	0	3	5	2	4
Cam Tringali	1	3	3.21	8	0	34	30	15	36
Kurt Wilson	0	2	7.36	5	1	7	6	6	10
Aaron Winkler	0	0	7.50	4	0	6	6	4	9

CHATHAM

Batting	AVG	AB	R	H	2B	3B	HR	RBI	SB
Jorge Arenas, SS	.222	90	10	20	6	0	1	7	4
Vincenzo Bologna, OF	.100	10	1	1	0	0	0	0	1
Cade Cabbiness, OF	.188	48	5	9	2	0	2	9	2
Kendrick Calilao, OF/1B	.157	51	4	8	1	0	0	1	0
Cooper Davis, OF	.240	50	7	12	0	0	0	2	3
Tyler Doanes, 2B	.234	77	17	18	1	1	0	5	9
Adan Fernandez, OF	.125	16	0	2	1	0	0	3	0
Saul Garza, C	.333	15	3	5	1	0	1	2	0
Andrew Hague, SS	.500	2	1	1	0	0	0	0	2
Colin Hall, OF	.198	91	10	18	1	0	0	6	3
Zack Miller, C	.250	4	0	1	0	0	0	1	0
Hueston Morrill, INF	.247	77	13	19	5	0	0	2	2
Jamal O'Guinn, OF	.259	116	16	30	8	0	3	20	3
Drenis Ozuna, OF	.192	26	5	5	3	0	0	0	1
Aaron Palensky, OF	.200	5	0	1	0	0	0	0	0
Kaden Polcovich, INF	.305	131	30	40	8	1	4	28	6
Ben Ramirez, SS	.279	122	15	34	5	0	2	12	7

	AVG	AB	R	H	2B	3B	HR	RBI	SB
Keaton Rice, C	.214	42	2	9	1	1	0	6	1
Brady Smith, C	.233	60	8	14	4	0	2	7	0
Cooper Swanson, SS	.000	5	0	0	0	0	0	0	1
Alex Toral, 1B	.200	95	10	19	4	0	2	17	1
Spencer Torkelson, 1B	.385	13	4	5	2	0	2	7	0
Anthony Vilar, 2B	.172	64	6	11	1	0	1	7	2
Paxton Wallace, 3B	.209	67	8	14	4	1	2	8	0
Charles Welch, C	.197	61	9	12	2	0	3	10	1

Pitching	W	L	ERA	G	SV	IP	H	BB	SO
Dane Acker	0	1	6.75	4	0	11	13	3	12
Jorge Arenas	0	1	5.40	3	1	3	3	2	4
Cole Ayers	2	2	4.28	8	0	34	37	12	29
Luke Bartnicki	3	1	3.20	8	1	25	22	17	30
Riley Boyd	0	1	8.44	2	0	5	7	2	1
Zach Cable	1	0	4.50	6	0	10	8	7	10
Burl Carraway	0	0	0.00	1	0	1	0	1	2
Jack Conlon	0	0	8.44	3	0	5	4	9	5
RJ Dabovich	1	0	3.32	7	0	19	16	5	29
Cooper Davis	0	0	27.00	1	0	1	2	1	0
Daniel Federman	1	3	5.76	7	1	25	30	7	24
Hugh Fisher	1	0	7.27	6	1	9	14	6	13
Colin Hall	0	0	0.00	1	0	1	1	0	0
Jake Hamilton	0	0	0.00	3	0	5	3	3	4
Mason Hazelwood	2	0	1.80	9	0	25	15	18	32
Dane Kapande	0	0	20.25	1	0	1	2	1	1
Haydn King	0	1	10.80	3	0	5	5	3	4
Nick Krauth	0	0	3.86	1	0	7	8	1	2
Kolby Kubichek	2	2	0.90	8	0	30	16	9	34
Ty Madden	1	1	3.33	8	0	27	24	14	28
Dawson Merryman	2	0	3.52	15	4	15	15	9	15
Hueston Morrill	0	0	10.80	2	0	3	4	1	5
Jack Owen	1	2	7.07	5	0	14	18	2	14
Kaden Polcovich	0	0	0.00	1	0	1	2	1	1
Keaton Rice	0	0	0.00	1	0	1	0	1	0
Parker Scott	2	0	0.00	3	0	14	9	1	17
Zarion Sharpe	0	2	1.35	5	0	20	12	6	24
Austin Vernon	3	0	3.92	8	0	21	26	9	31
Paxton Wallace	0	0	18.00	1	0	1	3	0	0
Jeremy Wu-Yelland	2	1	3.16	10	1	26	20	15	26

COTUIT

Batting	AVG	AB	R	H	2B	3B	HR	RBI	SB
Oraj Anu, OF	.248	105	14	26	2	1	6	21	1
Richard Brereton, INF/RHP	.000	2	0	0	0	0	0	0	0
Joe Casey, OF	.000	4	0	0	0	0	0	0	0
Parker Chavers, OF	.270	122	19	33	9	0	5	18	3
Andrew Czech, 1B	.143	7	0	1	0	0	0	0	0
Colin Davis, OF	.250	4	0	1	1	0	0	0	0
Mason Dodd, 2B	.222	36	6	8	1	1	1	5	0
Matthew Donlan, C	.000	3	0	0	0	0	0	0	0
Duke Ellis, OF	.235	17	2	4	0	0	0	1	1
Sam Ferri, C	.083	12	0	1	0	0	0	0	0
Nick Gonzales, 2B	.351	154	39	54	14	4	7	33	6
Cameron Hill, OF	.221	77	16	17	2	0	0	2	11
Grant Holman, 1B	.000	2	0	0	0	0	0	0	0
Coltyn Kessler, C	.138	65	8	9	1	1	1	5	0
GeonHyoung Kim, OF	.500	2	1	1	0	0	0	0	0
Joey Loperfido, INF	.280	75	9	21	3	1	2	9	4
Allbry Major, OF	.407	59	7	24	7	0	0	10	2
Robbie Martin, OF	.167	30	2	5	0	1	0	0	0
Mason McWhorter, OF	.241	79	10	19	4	0	0	13	1
Matt Mervis, INF/RHP	.325	77	15	25	7	0	4	24	0
Adam Oviedo, SS	.252	127	21	32	4	0	3	22	3
Cody Pasic, C	.206	68	8	14	0	0	0	5	0
Christian Robinson, OF	.185	65	10	12	2	0	0	9	0
Casey Schmitt, 3B/RHP	.248	129	21	32	6	0	5	18	1
Ronald Sweeny, 1B	.000	2	0	0	0	0	0	0	0
Camryn Williams, SS	.143	14	2	2	0	0	1	2	0
Donta Williams, OF	.190	58	14	11	0	0	2	3	2

Pitching	W	L	ERA	G	SV	IP	H	BB	SO
Cole Beavin	0	1	15.75	2	0	4	8	0	2
Richard Brereton	1	0	5.79	11	2	23	31	8	24
Parker Chavers	0	0	6.75	1	0	1	3	1	1
Kevin Conley	0	0	9.00	2	0	3	2	8	1
Christopher Farrell	0	1	5.91	8	0	21	24	19	16
Cameron Hill	1	0	2.25	1	0	4	5	1	2
Bo Hofstra	4	1	6.32	10	1	16	17	11	20
Christopher Holcomb	1	2	2.50	10	0	18	21	11	14
Trey Holland	1	0	4.50	3	0	12	14	2	10
Reid Johnston	2	0	1.82	6	0	25	22	5	17
Nick Jones	0	1	54.00	1	0	1	1	6	4
Evan Justice	0	3	6.75	8	0	20	23	16	9
Coltyn Kessler	0	0	0.00	1	0	2	2	2	2
Zach McCambley	1	0	1.74	5	0	21	15	7	24
Matt Mervis	1	2	3.24	9	1	17	15	2	16
Matt Moore	1	0	0.68	9	0	13	8	5	11
Joe Nahas	1	1	1.50	5	1	18	8	6	27
Kyle Nicolas	1	2	6.29	12	4	24	20	21	31
Cody Pasic	0	1	22.50	1	0	2	4	1	2
Holden Powell	0	0	0.00	1	0	3	0	1	3
Kole Ramage	0	0	3.60	4	0	10	14	3	8
Casey Schmitt	1	0	2.46	11	3	22	17	10	26
Sean Sullivan	0	2	1.97	8	0	32	25	6	37
Nick Swiney	1	0	2.70	2	0	3	5	1	4
Joey Walsh	1	0	8.31	4	0	4	7	1	6
Beck Way	2	2	3.29	11	0	14	14	11	18
Donta Williams	0	0	0.00	1	0	2	1	2	1
Jackson Wolf	0	1	3.04	7	0	27	18	11	27

FALMOUTH

Batting	AVG	AB	R	H	2B	3B	HR	RBI	SB
Ryan Berardino, 1B	.000	2	0	0	0	0	0	0	0
Hayden Cantrelle, 2B	.315	130	29	41	7	0	3	14	19
Ben Casparius, INF/RHP	.308	13	2	4	0	0	0	4	1
Troy Claunch, C	.226	62	4	14	2	0	1	8	0
Jackson Coutts, 1B	.29.	75	7	22	3	1	0	12	0
Trei Cruz, SS	.307	140	23	43	6	1	3	22	11
Zach DeLoach, OF	.353	133	22	47	8	1	5	23	8
Blake Dunn, OF	.229	131	15	30	3	0	2	18	14
Max Ferguson, INF	.143	7	0	1	0	0	0	0	0
Jake Frasca, 3B	.000	6	0	0	0	0	0	0	0
Sean Harrington, C	.111	9	1	1	0	0	0	1	0
Maddux Houghton, OF	.333	12	2	4	0	0	0	0	2
Kevin Kendall, SS	.188	69	9	13	1	0	2	8	2
Austin Langworthy, OF/LHP	.197	71	12	14	2	0	0	4	2
Austin Masel, OF	.371	62	12	23	3	0	1	6	4
Steven Moretto, 3B	.175	97	10	17	2	0	3	12	1
Matheu Nelson, C	.163	43	7	7	0	0	1	2	0
Baron Radcliff, OF	.237	93	12	22	4	1	6	22	3
Tyler Ras, RHP/OF	.200	35	3	7	4	0	0	2	1
Chris Rinaldi, SS	.167	6	1	1	0	0	0	1	0
Taylor Smith, C	.167	60	12	10	1	0	5	9	1
Tim Tawa, OF	.221	86	7	19	4	0	1	8	4
Michael Turner, C	.267	15	1	4	2	0	0	4	0
Alex Volpi, 1B	.000	4	1	0	0	0	0	0	0

Pitching	W	L	ERA	G	SV	IP	H	BB	SO
Robert Ahlstrom	0	1	5.56	6	1	11	14	3	13
Franco Aleman	2	0	1.16	6	0	31	25	2	27
Brant Brown	2	0	2.00	3	0	9	6	2	4
Zachary Brzykcy	1	0	1.80	10	7	10	4	1	14
Steven Casey	0	0	2.25	2	0	4	5	1	2
Ben Casparius	0	0	0.00	1	0	1	0	1	0
Javin Drake	0	0	0.00	2	0	3	3	1	3
Shane Drohan	0	0	18.90	3	0	3	7	4	2
Christian Edwards	1	0	0.00	2	0	4	1	1	8
Justin Foy	0	0	32.40	1	0	2	4	2	0
Thomas Girard	0	1	2.57	5	3	7	3	4	8
Chris Gonzalez	2	4	5.60	8	0	35	42	9	24
Kenneth Haus	0	1	9.00	1	0	3	6	0	2
Logan Hoffman	3	0	3.38	10	0	16	11	7	22
Austin Langworthy	1	0	5.19	7	2	9	12	2	9

Batting	AVG	AB	R	H	2B	3B	HR	RBI	SB
Bradley Littleton	0	0	1.69	3	0	5	6	1	7
Aidan Maldonado	2	1	3.12	10	2	17	15	6	30
Bryce Miller	0	0	3.00	4	1	6	6	3	10
Carmen Mlodzinski	2	0	2.15	6	0	29	15	4	40
Sean Mullen	0	0	7.43	9	1	13	15	4	18
Nick Nastrini	2	1	2.63	6	0	27	26	8	30
Tyler Ras	2	0	4.34	7	0	19	17	8	19
Hayden Rosenkrantz	0	0	8.10	2	0	3	4	2	2
Tommy Sheehan	0	0	2.16	2	0	8	10	0	7
Samuel Strickland	2	1	2.70	4	0	20	19	5	13
Luke Sutko	0	0	0.00	1	0	2	4	1	2
Noah Thompson	0	1	2.25	1	0	4	4	2	2
Sam Weatherly	0	1	3.45	10	0	16	7	11	17
Justin Wrobleski	3	1	6.17	9	0	23	24	15	22
Caleb Wurster	2	2	5.40	11	0	17	22	5	14

HARWICH

Batting	AVG	AB	R	H	2B	3B	HR	RBI	SB
Cory Acton, INF	.254	59	11	15	0	1	3	12	0
Ben Brooks, INF	.000	1	0	0	0	0	0	1	0
Daniel Cabrera, OF	.287	115	20	33	5	1	2	14	10
Brian Dempsey, INF	.176	17	0	3	1	0	0	3	0
Christian Fedko, INF	.271	107	19	29	5	1	1	9	1
Chris Galland, OF	.287	108	14	31	3	1	2	16	13
Jackson Greer, C	.400	10	3	4	0	0	1	1	0
Sean Harrington, C	.500	2	1	1	0	0	0	0	0
Daniel Harris, INF	.091	11	0	1	1	0	0	0	0
Hal Hughes, SS	.170	88	7	15	1	0	0	6	2
Jacob Hurtubise, OF	.154	13	1	2	0	0	0	0	1
Niko Kavadas, 1B	.252	131	19	33	6	1	9	30	0
Tyler Keenan, 3B	.300	30	6	9	2	0	1	4	0
Matt Koperniak, INF	.000	3	1	0	0	0	0	0	0
Chris Lanzilli, OF	.293	92	15	27	4	0	4	18	2
Joseph Lomuscio, OF	.286	7	2	2	1	0	0	1	1
Michael Ludowig, OF	.256	90	6	23	2	0	0	3	0
Eduardo Malinowski, INF	.000	8	0	0	0	0	0	0	0
Max Marusak, OF	.145	55	9	8	1	0	0	1	10
Dylan Neuse, UTL	.197	76	12	15	3	0	2	10	6
Matt Oldham, C	.000	7	0	0	0	0	0	0	0
Michael Rothenberg, C	.200	55	3	11	1	0	0	4	1
Bobby Seymour, 1B	.250	32	2	8	1	0	0	2	0
Cameron Thompson, INF	.154	39	2	6	1	0	0	2	2
Riley Tirotta, 3B	.222	18	4	4	2	0	0	1	2
Joey Wiemer, OF	.273	99	17	27	5	0	1	17	8
Patrick Winkel, C	.167	78	8	13	1	0	1	9	0
Pitching	**W**	**L**	**ERA**	**G**	**SV**	**IP**	**H**	**BB**	**SO**
Logan Allen	2	0	0.00	3	0	15	7	3	24
Cam Baumann	1	0	4.96	8	0	16	21	4	14
Joe Boyle	1	2	1.93	10	2	14	5	12	28
Jordan Butler	1	1	5.52	4	0	15	22	3	10
Devin Dunn	0	0	0.00	1	0	2	3	0	1
Blake Espinal	0	1	5.93	7	0	14	12	6	12
Buddy Hayward	0	1	3.12	2	0	9	3	5	10
Will Heflin	2	0	0.75	9	2	24	17	7	29
Connor McCullough	2	0	1.05	6	0	26	16	8	29
Antonio Menendez	0	2	3.72	7	0	29	29	8	25
Caden O'Brien	0	0	0.00	2	0	3	2	1	2
Devin Ortiz	0	0	10.80	2	0	3	6	0	1
Jacob Palisch	5	1	0.77	6	0	35	24	5	38
Connor Sechler	3	2	2.77	6	0	26	19	9	29
Carson Seymour	0	3	5.06	7	0	27	26	15	20
Evan Shawver	1	1	7.11	2	0	6	10	3	8
Nick Stewart	2	1	4.68	8	3	25	21	9	32
Wade Strain	0	1	6.75	1	0	4	7	1	1
John Teehan	0	0	0.00	1	0	5	1	0	5
Greg Tobin	0	0	9.00	1	0	4	7	1	2
Tommy Vail	1	1	4.37	8	1	17	10	11	31
Hunter Waldis	0	0	27.00	1	0	1	4	0	0
Jared Wetherbee	0	1	3.09	9	2	12	9	7	14
Connor Yoder	0	0	0.00	1	0	2	0	2	1
Nick Zwack	0	3	5.11	7	0	25	27	9	20

HYANNIS

Batting	AVG	AB	R	H	2B	3B	HR	RBI	SB
Brooks Carlson, INF	.159	82	5	13	2	0	2	6	1
Jared DeSantolo, 3B	.301	113	22	34	3	0	4	13	4
Lucas Dunn, 2B	.286	42	5	12	0	0	0	3	2
Ian Fair, 1B	.348	89	11	31	5	1	1	9	1
Hunter Goodman, C/OF	.276	156	21	43	10	0	8	37	2
Adam Hackenberg, C	.169	65	6	11	1	0	2	5	0
Trevor Hauver, OF	.250	120	23	30	4	0	3	16	1
Rowdey Jordan, OF	.128	78	4	10	2	0	0	3	2
Edouard Julien, 3B	.348	23	3	8	5	0	0	5	0
Nick Loftin, SS	.316	38	6	12	2	0	1	3	1
Chad McDaniel, C	.233	43	3	10	4	0	0	6	2
Mitch McIntyre, OF	.185	54	9	10	2	0	0	4	3
Justin Mitchell, C	.333	6	0	2	0	0	0	1	0
Rigsby Mosley, OF	.200	95	10	19	1	1	1	7	1
Jackson Olson, SS	.230	100	7	23	3	0	1	9	2
Fox Semones, 2B	.182	11	1	2	0	0	0	0	0
Anthony Servideo, SS	.149	101	13	15	5	0	1	4	5
Joe Sullivan, C	.000	2	0	0	0	0	0	0	0
Bryce Teodosio, OF	.188	69	7	13	3	0	1	4	1
Jordan Westburg, SS	.326	95	12	31	6	0	4	14	0
Adam Zeratsky, SS	.000	8	1	0	0	0	0	0	0
Pitching	**W**	**L**	**ERA**	**G**	**SV**	**IP**	**H**	**BB**	**SO**
Ben Abram	0	1	4.38	4	0	12	14	4	10
Glenn Albanese	0	1	6.64	6	0	20	29	7	19
Konnor Ash	0	3	5.72	10	0	28	31	17	41
Billy Corcoran	2	0	4.36	3	0	10	13	3	8
Nolan Crisp	1	1	7.94	8	1	17	20	8	19
Trevor DeLaite	0	1	17.61	6	1	8	20	6	11
Tyler Drabick	0	1	4.85	8	0	13	9	8	10
Patrick Fredrickson	1	3	9.72	10	0	25	37	19	24
Alex Garbrick	0	1	15.19	4	0	5	10	8	4
Jonathan Hughes	0	1	4.50	3	0	12	16	2	7
Holt Jones	0	1	22.85	2	0	4	8	5	4
Landon Kelly	0	1	3.77	5	1	14	10	4	10
Nathan Lavender	0	0	0.00	2	0	4	2	4	1
Tyler Mattison	0	1	4.09	5	0	22	23	6	18
Angus McCloskey	0	0	3.38	3	0	5	6	2	4
Tommy McCollum	1	0	2.38	3	0	11	7	6	8
Griff McGarry	0	1	1.69	3	0	5	2	4	8
Mitch McIntyre	1	0	1.80	6	0	10	6	3	7
Nick Mondak	0	0	3.38	5	0	8	6	5	9
David Moore	0	1	11.81	4	0	5	6	9	7
Rigsby Mosley	0	0	0.00	1	0	2	1	1	1
Kyle Murphy	1	2	7.40	10	0	24	34	11	25
Cole Pletka	0	1	7.13	7	0	18	24	6	15
Joseph Quintal	0	1	6.00	6	0	15	14	10	15
Jonah Scolaro	1	3	6.75	7	0	11	13	8	18
TJ Stuart	0	2	10.80	6	0	7	11	4	8
Samuel Thoresen	1	3	5.66	5	0	21	12	19	28
Kyle Whitten	0	2	11.57	11	0	16	26	15	12

ORLEANS

Batting	AVG	AB	R	H	2B	3B	HR	RBI	SB
David Avitia, C	.171	70	4	12	4	0	0	6	0
Zach Britton, OF	.286	98	18	28	6	0	5	19	3
Zach Daniels, OF	.169	77	15	13	1	1	1	7	2
Rob Emery, C	.261	92	16	24	4	0	4	9	0
Trevin Esquerra, OF	.241	58	5	14	1	0	1	6	1
Raymond Gil, 3B	.212	66	8	14	4	0	3	10	1
Matthew Goodheart, OF/1B	.320	25	6	8	1	0	0	3	0
Jacob Hurtubise, OF	.313	64	12	20	3	1	0	2	6
Trevor Johnson, OF	.071	14	1	1	0	0	0	0	0
Dominic Keegan, C	.000	11	0	0	0	0	0	1	0
Zach Kokoska, OF	.231	104	14	24	1	0	1	7	2
Jordan Lala, OF	.220	41	5	9	0	1	0	3	0
AJ Lewis, C	.304	23	2	7	2	0	0	3	0
Julio Marcano, 2B	.256	39	5	10	1	0	1	6	0
Eddie McCabe, SS	.291	103	12	30	3	1	0	14	1

	AVG	AB	R	H	2B	3B	HR	RBI	SB
Tanner Murray, SS	.211	114	15	24	5	0	2	14	5
Danny Serretti, SS	.206	34	3	7	1	0	0	3	0
Max Troiani, OF	.345	142	17	49	2	0	0	19	5
Shay Whitcomb, 3B	.303	109	20	33	9	0	8	17	4
Josh Zamora, INF	.136	88	12	12	0	0	3	9	0

Pitching	W	L	ERA	G	SV	IP	H	BB	SO
Andrew Abbott	1	1	6.00	2	0	6	6	0	6
Donovan Benoit	1	0	0.00	4	0	6	2	0	6
Jake Eder	1	1	1.20	4	0	15	12	4	15
Isaac Esqueda	2	1	2.18	8	1	21	11	3	23
Kamron Fields	0	1	6.75	5	0	8	9	3	9
Nick Frasso	1	0	0.00	2	0	2	0	0	1
Nick Garcia	1	3	3.18	15	1	17	15	11	20
Michael Hobbs	0	0	0.00	5	0	7	8	1	3
Michael Johnson	0	0	10.13	2	0	3	5	0	3
Jared Leins	0	0	5.79	2	0	5	4	2	4
Carter Lohman	0	0	15.43	5	0	2	1	9	3
Austin Love	2	1	2.70	7	0	20	14	11	21
Dawson McCarville	1	0	5.14	9	1	21	25	7	15
Ried McLaughlin	0	0	8.10	2	0	3	3	2	4
Tim Miller	0	0	5.06	3	0	5	8	1	9
Connor Pellerin	0	0	0.00	13	3	13	8	13	24
Jeffrey Praml	0	2	3.12	13	5	17	15	7	18
Benjamin Sears	1	0	0.00	1	0	5	2	0	3
Adam Seminaris	2	1	3.26	7	0	30	30	6	21
Owen Sharts	1	1	4.82	6	0	19	20	6	13
Justin Showalter	0	1	3.86	2	0	7	4	2	6
Jared Shuster	4	0	1.41	7	0	32	20	5	35
Noah Skirrow	1	1	2.76	7	0	29	24	14	40
Angelo Smith	1	1	2.84	7	0	13	9	6	14
David Stiehl	0	0	2.00	5	0	9	5	4	11
Hayden Thomas	0	0	0.00	1	0	4	2	4	5
Mike Vasil	0	1	10.29	2	0	7	9	4	7
Zebulon Vermillion	1	0	5.23	9	0	10	13	8	4
Chase Wallace	2	0	2.74	14	2	23	18	11	26
Cole Wilcox	0	1	6.75	2	0	8	7	6	10

WAREHAM

Batting	AVG	AB	R	H	2B	3B	HR	RBI	SB
Mike Antico, OF	.259	112	19	29	5	0	1	7	8
Darren Baker, 2B	.342	117	16	40	2	1	0	8	12
Dallas Beaver, C	.287	115	11	33	7	0	2	15	0
Jack Blomgren, SS	.200	5	0	1	0	0	0	0	0
Adrian Del Castillo, C/OF	.261	138	19	36	7	0	5	22	0
Pete Derkay, C	.375	16	4	6	0	1	0	4	0
J.P. Gates, 1B/LHP	.000	4	0	0	0	0	0	1	0
Kameron Guangorena, C	.250	44	6	11	3	0	1	7	0
Trey Lipscomb, INF	.333	6	3	2	0	0	1	2	1
Zack Mathis, INF	.227	22	5	5	1	1	1	5	0
Matt McLain, UTL	.274	113	25	31	7	2	2	23	6
Tora Otsuka, OF	.275	69	11	19	2	1	0	8	0
DJ Poteet, OF	.000	4	0	0	0	0	0	0	0
Matthew Rudick, OF	.287	115	25	33	3	1	3	14	5
Quentin Selma, 3B	.167	6	0	1	0	0	0	0	0
Benjamin Sems, SS	.261	115	16	30	3	0	1	16	4
Drew Sims, C	.250	12	3	3	0	0	1	2	0
Chad Stevens, SS	.247	73	9	18	2	0	0	12	2
Jacob Teter	.292	161	21	47	5	1	2	31	2
Andrew Thomas, C	.280	25	5	7	2	0	0	1	1
Braiden Ward, OF	.303	145	26	44	6	0	3	21	27
Sam Wezniak, SS	.000	2	1	0	0	0	0	0	0
Jack Winkler, SS	.214	14	1	3	0	0	0	4	0

Pitching	W	L	ERA	G	SV	IP	H	BB	SO
Joseph Baran	0	0	7.88	5	0	8	10	3	8
Ian Bedell	4	0	0.59	6	0	31	17	3	36
Tanner Bibee	3	1	3.64	9	1	17	19	3	19
Brendan Cellucci	0	0	6.00	3	0	6	6	4	7
Quinn Cleary	0	0	27.00	2	0	2	2	3	0
Coy Cobb	1	0	6.55	7	0	11	17	8	10
Aaron Davenport	0	1	5.68	2	0	6	5	5	10
Trey Dillard	2	0	2.29	9	2	20	11	9	22
Kevin Eaise	1	0	0.00	1	0	5	1	1	3

	W	L	ERA	G	SV	IP	H	BB	SO
Bryce Elder	0	1	4.15	3	0	9	6	5	10
Jack Enger	0	0	5.40	5	0	5	7	4	4
Lane Flamm	0	0	13.50	1	0	2	3	2	3
William Fleming	1	2	5.33	9	0	25	33	6	24
J.P. Gates	0	2	2.86	7	0	22	23	4	20
Brooks Gosswein	0	0	9.00	1	0	1	2	0	0
Garrett Irvin	2	0	1.29	3	0	7	2	3	7
Conor Larkin	0	1	13.50	1	0	2	4	1	1
Cole Larsen	1	0	4.82	3	0	9	11	1	6
Ben Leeper	0	0	3.60	10	2	10	11	8	12
Trey Lipscomb	0	0	0.00	1	0	1	0	0	2
Chris Mauloni	0	0	4.91	3	0	4	2	4	3
Tevin Murray	1	0	0.00	2	0	5	2	3	6
Trent Palmer	1	1	1.45	7	2	19	18	8	21
Brandon Pfaadt	2	1	2.81	9	1	32	19	8	34
Levi Prater	2	1	0.92	7	0	20	9	8	21
David Rhodes	0	1	19.29	1	0	2	5	1	1
Nicholas Richmond	0	0	9.00	1	0	3	5	1	1
Joe Rock	0	0	0.00	2	0	3	0	0	4
Landen Roupp	0	0	3.97	4	1	11	8	4	14
Jason Ruffcorn	0	2	6.23	4	0	4	5	4	3
Cole Stetzar	0	2	5.82	5	0	17	20	4	14
Eric Torres	1	0	4.77	4	0	6	6	1	6
Lukas Veinbergs	1	1	6.30	2	0	10	13	1	3
Michael Webb	1	1	5.54	8	0	13	18	5	17
Austin Weiermiller	0	0	7.50	4	0	6	5	7	6
Jeremy Williams	0	0	1.35	3	1	7	2	2	7
Caleb Wurster	0	0	6.75	1	0	1	2	0	0

YARMOUTH-DENNIS

Batting	AVG	AB	R	H	2B	3B	HR	RBI	SB
Bradlee Beesley, OF	.280	125	21	35	10	0	3	12	3
Eric Bigani, C	.500	8	1	4	0	0	0	0	1
Noah Campbell, 2B/OF	.324	102	18	33	0	1	3	19	6
Noah Cardenas, C	.250	52	5	13	3	0	0	7	1
Jeffrey Costello, OF	.400	10	2	4	1	1	0	2	0
Gavin Dugas, 2B	.115	26	6	3	0	0	0	0	1
William Escala, SS	.333	6	2	2	0	0	0	1	0
Andrew Eyster, OF	.208	77	11	16	2	0	3	13	4
Jackson Greer, C	.333	3	1	1	0	0	0	0	0
Joseph Hall, 2B	.217	46	3	10	2	0	0	4	4
Brendan Hueth, OF	.000	6	0	0	0	0	0	0	0
Adam Kerner, C	.000	6	0	0	0	0	0	0	0
Riley King, 3B	.323	124	16	40	4	0	3	10	3
Jack Leftwich, RHP	.250	4	1	1	0	0	0	0	0
Noah Myers, OF	.000	3	0	0	0	0	0	0	0
Daylan Nanny, OF	.333	12	3	4	0	0	1	0	0
Jake Palmer, OF	.242	66	12	16	1	1	0	2	3
Will Picketts, SS	.200	5	1	1	0	1	0	1	0
Tate Samuelson, 3B	.240	104	8	25	2	0	1	9	3
Jake Suddleson, OF	.250	8	4	2	1	0	0	0	0
Drew Swift, SS	.143	14	2	2	0	0	0	3	1
Carson Taylor, C	.152	33	6	5	0	0	2	6	0
Riley Tirotta, 3B	.130	46	16	6	4	0	0	5	0
Erik Tolman, LHP/OF	.294	17	5	5	1	0	2	5	1
Luke Waddell, SS	.174	23	4	4	0	0	0	2	1
Ronald Washington, OF	.083	12	2	1	0	0	0	0	0
Austin Wells, C/1B	.308	156	23	48	13	0	7	26	8
Jack-Thomas Wold, 1B	.243	111	15	27	7	0	3	20	0
R.J. Yeager, SS	.200	60	6	12	1	0	0	9	1
Wyatt Young, SS	.338	130	26	44	7	2	1	23	9

Pitching	W	L	ERA	G	SV	IP	H	BB	SO
John Beller	1	2	3.52	7	0	31	27	9	32
Oscar Carvajal	2	0	2.89	7	0	9	9	2	15
Brady Corrigan	0	0	5.27	10	0	14	14	11	10
Trenton Denholm	0	0	0.00	2	0	7	3	2	5
Mark DiLuia	0	1	11.57	2	0	2	3	3	3
Taylor Dollard	2	1	1.56	11	5	17	9	1	27
Brandon Dufault	0	1	6.75	10	0	20	26	12	19
Ryan Hare	0	3	4.26	5	0	19	24	9	16
Gordon Ingebritson	1	0	5.23	7	1	10	14	4	13
Adam Jeannette	0	0	6.75	4	0	5	5	5	6

	W	L	ERA	G	SV	IP	H	BB	SO
Jack Jett	1	0	0.00	1	0	4	1	1	3
Cullen Kafka	2	0	7.00	9	0	18	21	13	20
Trevor Kniskern	0	1	5.40	1	0	2	3	2	1
Jack Leftwich	3	1	3.64	6	0	30	21	7	28
Carlos Lomeli	1	3	8.15	9	0	18	28	4	17
Zack Matthews	0	0	13.50	2	1	3	2	2	5
Nolan McCarthy	1	0	2.70	2	0	3	3	1	6
Ryne Moore	0	0	3.00	2	0	3	3	4	2
Andrew Mundy	0	0	4.50	3	0	4	7	0	2
Cole Pletka	0	0	0.00	1	0	2	2	1	5
Ian Seymour	2	2	2.49	5	0	25	20	6	39
Chase Smith	2	0	1.23	5	0	7	4	3	7
Ledgend Smith	1	1	4.50	8	0	26	24	9	29
Cole Stetzar	0	0	0.00	1	0	2	1	1	2
David Stiehl	0	0	0.00	2	0	1	1	0	2
Drew Swift	0	0	18.00	1	0	1	3	0	3
Erik Tolman	1	1	4.00	7	0	27	26	11	31
Boyd Vander Kooi	1	1	4.85	3	1	13	15	7	10
Chase Walter	1	1	9.00	6	0	10	10	9	13
Michael Weisberg	0	0	10.64	11	0	11	16	6	11
Jacob Winger	0	0	1.04	11	0	17	9	6	22

ALASKA LEAGUE

	W	L	PCT	GB
Anchorage Bucs	29	14	.674	-
Matsu Miners	26	18	.591	3.5
Anchorage Glacier Pilots	26	18	.591	3.5
Peninsula Oilers	15	29	.341	14.5
Chugiak Chinooks	13	30	.302	16

CHAMPIONSHIP: Anchorage Bucs defeated Anchorage Glacier Pilots, 2-1, in best-of-three championship series.

INDIVIDUAL BATTING LEADERS

	AVG	AB	R	H	2B	3B	HR	RBI	SB
Erik Webb, OF, Miners	.368	144	35	53	16	2	4	33	12
Bobby Goodloe, INF, Oilers	.339	127	16	43	9	2	1	18	3
Chad Castillo, OF, Bucs	.335	164	27	55	5	2	1	25	8
Cole Tate, UTL, Bucs	.302	129	26	39	4	4	1	18	6
Travis Bohall, OF, Oilers	.297	111	18	33	3	1	0	11	10
Daniel Mendez, C, Pilots	.296	54	8	16	2	1	2	4	3
Kaden Hopson, C, Bucs	.293	92	9	27	1	0	0	11	1
Camden Vasquez, OF, Oilers	.292	113	22	33	4	0	0	7	7
Damon Keith, OF/RHP, Oilers	.286	56	6	16	2	2	0	13	3
Connor McCord, INF, Oilers	.286	105	13	30	5	0	1	8	0

INDIVIDUAL PITCHING LEADERS

	W	L	ERA	G	SV	IP	H	BB	SO
Hunter Rigsby, Pilots	3	0	0.66	13	4	27	21	11	34
Colton Rendon, Bucs	1	1	0.76	17	9	24	14	4	24
Calvin Farris, Oilers	1	0	0.98	14	2	18	14	5	22
Jacob McNairy, Miners	0	0	1.25	17	9	22	13	2	19
Kyler Bush, Miners	4	0	1.32	7	0	41	23	6	35
Jeremy Cook, Bucs	3	0	1.44	5	0	25	14	13	29
Randy Abshire, Miners	3	1	1.52	10	0	47	22	23	42
Logan Freeman, Pilots	3	0	1.57	6	0	29	18	12	30
Matthew Sanchez, Pilots	3	1	1.77	9	0	46	35	12	51
Owen Lamon, Miners	0	1	1.84	15	0	15	12	5	11

ATLANTIC COLLEGIATE LEAGUE

Wolff Division	W	L	PCT	GB
Allentown	22	11	.662	1
Trenton	20	16	.553	2
Quakertown	17	22	.438	1
Jersey	14	20	.414	1

Kaiser Division	W	L	PCT	GB
North Jersey	21	16	.568	0
New York	17	14	.548	0
Ocean Ospreys	18	17	.514	0
Ocean Gulls	9	22	.297	1

CHAMPIONSHIP: Allentown Railers defeated North Jersey Eagles, 2-1, in best-of-three championship series.

INDIVIDUAL BATTING LEADERS

	AVG	AB	R	H	2B	3B	HR	RBI	SB
David Melfi, C, Phenoms	.406	96	26	39	3	5	4	19	4
Pete Vaccaro, INF, Generals	.378	111	19	42	8	1	1	20	3
Anthony Maisano, OF, Eagles	.366	112	33	41	13	0	3	13	11
Jack Peterson, OF, Pilots	.353	102	12	36	7	1	1	21	7
Ian Csencsits, INF, Railers	.350	80	19	28	5	0	0	11	4
Anthony Viggiano, INF, Blazers	.339	124	24	42	5	4	1	22	8
Matt Ervolina, SS, Railers	.337	83	22	28	7	1	2	12	8
Ryan Mostrangeli, OF, Generals	.336	110	22	37	6	4	3	26	9
Max Felsenstein, OF, Pilots	.330	97	32	32	5	0	0	4	11
TJ Scuderi, OF, Ospreys	.321	112	24	36	8	2	6	28	14

INDIVIDUAL PITCHING LEADERS

	W	L	ERA	G	SV	IP	H	BB	SO
Francis Driscoll, Railers	1	1	1.20	13	5	30	14	9	49
Alex Mack, Eagles	5	1	1.66	7	0	38	26	17	47
Nicholas Marini, Ospreys	4	1	1.69	10	0	27	23	6	21
Frank Doelling, Generals	2	2	1.90	8	0	38	25	25	49
Jack Brodsky, Eagles	3	2	2.18	7	0	33	23	24	29
Blaise Venancio, Ospreys	4	2	2.25	7	0	32	28	7	19
Matthew Devlin, Pilots	4	2	2.73	8	0	36	28	13	45
Ethan Osgood, Pilots	4	2	2.84	8	0	38	40	4	20
JJ Spehrley, Blazers	4	3	3.25	9	1	36	37	12	41
Daniel Frake, Generals	6	1	3.38	10	0	48	40	21	77

CAL RIPKEN COLLEGIATE LEAGUE

	W	L	PCT	GB
Bethesda Big Train	31	7	.816	-
Silver Spring-Takoma T Bolts	20	18	.526	11
D.C. Grays	17	19	.472	13
FCA Braves	16	21	.432	14.5
Gaithersburg Giants	14	22	.389	16
Alexandria Aces	14	25	.359	17.5

CHAMPIONSHIP: Bethesda Big Train defeated Silver Spring-Takoma T Bolts, 2-1, in championship series.

INDIVIDUAL BATTING LEADERS

	AVG	AB	R	H	2B	3B	HR	RBI	SB
Kobe Kato, INF, Big Train	.457	116	41	53	7	0	1	22	27
Jordan Wiley, OF, Grays	.380	108	21	41	9	0	5	27	8
Matt Thomas, OF, Big Train	.366	123	24	45	7	2	0	43	9
Anthony Gallo, INF, T Bolts	.364	99	29	36	6	1	7	33	0
Noah Searcy, OF, Grays	.355	110	29	39	6	1	4	17	3
Cade Doughty, INF, Giants	.346	127	26	44	7	2	5	23	5
Jacob Southern, C, Big Train	.330	106	34	35	12	0	8	31	6
Stephen Hill, INF, Aces	.323	96	22	31	4	0	4	22	2
Davonn Griffin, OF, T Bolts	.322	87	21	28	5	0	2	15	8
Christian Jayne, OF, Big Train	.315	130	25	41	5	2	1	25	11

INDIVIDUAL PITCHING LEADERS

	W	L	ERA	G	SV	IP	H	BB	SO
Reid McLaughlin, Grays	1	0	0.45	5	0	20	10	2	17
Chase Lee, Big Train	1	0	1.04	16	7	26	16	6	51
Ryan Okuda, Big Train	3	0	1.13	5	0	24	16	11	32
Elliot Zoellner, Big Train	1	0	1.20	11	1	15	9	5	15
Carson McClure, Braves	1	1	1.66	11	0	22	14	16	15
Anthony Piccolino, Big Train	1	1	1.90	9	1	19	11	6	25
John Reynols, Braves	1	0	2.08	6	0	22	21	6	19
Jack Cone, Braves	3	2	2.70	9	2	37	27	20	44
Ben Jordan, Giants	1	1	2.70	7	0	27	14	13	36
Brandon McGaw, Aces	2	1	2.86	8	0	28	23	10	27

CALIFORNIA COLLEGIATE LEAGUE

CCL	W	L	PCT	GB
Santa Barbara Foresters	27	8	.771	----
Orange County Riptide	23	12	.657	4
Arroyo Seco Saints	18	17	.514	9
San Luis Obispo Blues	16	19	.457	11
Conejo Oaks	12	23	.343	15

	W	L	PCT	GB
Academy Barons	8	27	.229	19
Affiliate Division	**W**	**L**	**PCT**	**GB**
Healdsburg Prune Packers	19	5	.792	----
Lincoln Potters	14	9	.609	4.5
Solano Mudcats	9	15	.375	10
San Francisco Seals	5	16	.238	12.5

CHAMPIONSHIP: Santa Barbara defeated Healdsburg, 2-1, in best-of-three championship series.

TOP 10 PROSPECTS: 1. Spencer Jones, LHP/OF, Santa Barbara (Fr., Vanderbilt), 2. Nick Jones, LHP, Orange County (Jr., Georgia Southern), 3. Ian Villers, RHP, Healdsburg (So., California), 4. Christian Franklin, OF, Santa Barbara (So., Arkansas), 5. Hunter Breault, RHP, Santa Barbara (Jr., Oregon), 6. Eric Kennedy, OF, Santa Barbara (So., Texas), 7. Ryan Bergert, RHP, Santa Barbara (So., West Virginia), 8. Connor Pavolony, C, Santa Barbara (So., Tennessee), 9. Mike Peabody, OF, Orange County (Jr., UC Irvine), 10. Elijah Trest, RHP, Santa Barbara (So., Arkansas).

INDIVIDUAL BATTING LEADERS

	AVG	AB	R	H	2B	3B	HR	RBI	SB
Eric Kennedy, OF, Foresters	.400	115	28	46	7	3	3	18	21
Hunter Swift, OF, Blues	.361	108	18	39	5	2	1	19	10
Thomas Luevano, SS, Saints	.359	103	23	37	7	0	5	24	11
Niko Lima, 1B, Oaks	.346	107	24	37	4	2	3	14	8
Christian Franklin, OF, Foresters	.343	70	14	24	3	2	4	19	3
Taison Corio, 2B, Blues	.333	123	21	41	4	1	1	26	11
Conor McKenna, OF, Foresters	.333	72	11	24	2	0	1	14	6
Connor Aoki, C, Riptide	.327	98	12	32	6	0	3	17	1
Nick Bellafronto, 3B, Foresters	.317	63	11	20	5	1	4	12	0
Daniel Jung, OF, Riptide	.314	70	6	22	6	0	1	15	2

INDIVIDUAL PITCHING LEADERS

	W	L	ERA	G	SV	IP	H	BB	SO
Brad Demco, Foresters	0	0	0.00	17	0	19	2	11	35
Isaac Coffey, Foresters	1	0	0.98	5	0	18	10	5	23
Colin King, Saints	1	0	1.74	5	0	21	14	8	23
Travis Weston, Oaks	1	0	1.76	7	0	31	21	12	28
Ryan Bergert, Foresters	2	1	1.99	8	3	23	14	8	34
Trevor Beer, Saints	2	0	2.04	5	0	18	13	7	21
Brooks Fuller, Foresters	3	0	2.05	5	0	22	16	7	19
Derek True, Blues	0	1	2.12	6	0	17	11	8	21
Andrew Alvarez, Blues	2	1	2.19	8	0	25	15	15	22
Noah Huerta, Blues	2	1	2.25	8	0	28	16	11	21

COASTAL PLAIN LEAGUE

North Division	**W**	**L**	**PCT**	**GB**
Peninsula Pilots	29	21	.580	—
Wilson Tobs	27	25	.519	3
Edenton Steamers	26	26	.500	4
Martinsville Mustangs	15	31	.326	12
South Division	**W**	**L**	**PCT**	**GB**
Savannah Bananas	35	15	.700	—
Macon Bacon	28	21	.571	6½
Florence RedWolves	22	28	.440	13
Lexington County Blowfish	15	30	.333	17½
East Division	**W**	**L**	**PCT**	**GB**
Morehead City Marlins	37	14	.725	—
Fayetteville SwampDogs	24	26	.480	12½
Wilmington Sharks	20	31	.392	14½
Holly Springs Salamanders	19	32	.373	18½
West Division	**W**	**L**	**PCT**	**GB**
Gastonia Grizzlies	24	12	.667	—
High Point-Thomasville HiToms	18	22	.450	8
Asheboro Copperheads	17	22	.436	8½
Forest City Owls	-	-	-	-

CHAMPIONSHIP: Morehead City Marlins defeated Macon Bacon , 2-1, in best-of-three championship series.

TOP 10 PROSPECTS: 1. Dustin Saenz, LHP, Savannah (Jr., Texas A&M), 2. Jake Plastiak, 3B, Wilmington (So., Wabash Valley (Ill.) JC), 3. Chris Crabtree, 1B, Holly Springs (Jr., Duke), 4. Leo Perez, RHP, Morehead City (Jr., Texas A&M-Corpus Christi), 5. Kendall McGowan, OF, Forest City (Jr., Appalachian State), 6. Josh Hood, SS, Asheboro (Fr., Pennsylvania), 7. Myles Christian, OF, High Point (Jr., Middle Tennessee State), 8. Cort

Roedig, RHP, Macon (So., Georgia Tech), 9. Logan Workman, RHP, High Point (Jr., Lee (Tenn.)), 10. Davis Palermo, RHP, Martinsville (R-Fr., North Carolina).

INDIVIDUAL BATTING LEADERS

	AVG	AB	R	H	2B	3B	HR	RBI	SB
Riley Hogan, 1B, Pilots	.389	157	35	61	14	2	4	47	1
Calvin Estrada, OF, Bacon	.358	165	30	59	25	0	5	43	9
Nick Biddison, INF, Pilots	.354	178	49	63	14	4	6	39	26
Mike Williams, OF, Bananas	.353	170	28	60	5	2	0	23	21
Quincy Hamilton, OF, Steamers	.348	161	41	56	9	2	12	50	17
Nathan Chevalier, OF, Grizzlies	.339	112	25	38	7	0	3	33	16
Alex Kachler, C, SwampDogs	.333	153	33	51	7	0	5	33	4
Jared Miller, INF, Bacon	.333	159	44	53	17	2	3	36	9
Hunter Shepherd, LHP, Marlins	.333	162	27	54	10	0	5	42	7
Josh Hood, SS, Copperheads	.331	139	35	46	13	2	8	31	2

INDIVIDUAL PITCHING LEADERS

	W	L	ERA	G	SV	IP	H	BB	SO
Dustin Saenz, Bananas	4	0	1.16	7	1	31	16	9	41
Luke Davis, HiToms	0	2	1.82	8	0	30	31	12	18
Eric Miles, Marlins	6	0	2.06	10	0	48	31	5	58
Rohan Handa, Grizzlies	6	2	2.11	13	0	47	39	11	31
Jordan Merritt, Bananas	1	0	2.23	9	0	36	35	7	35
Jonathan Cole, SwampDogs	2	3	2.25	6	0	32	19	10	33
Matt Vonderschmidt, SwampDogs	4	2	2.40	22	4	41	33	12	46
Chace Harris, Bacon	4	1	2.68	9	0	37	27	16	47
Leo Perez, Marlins	5	2	2.86	21	3	35	22	18	50
Parker Thode, Salamanders	3	4	2.91	12	0	53	58	13	47

FLORIDA COLLEGIATE SUMMER LEAGUE

	W	L	PCT	GB
Winter Park Diamond Dawgs	30	7	.811	-
DeLand Suns	27	13	.675	4.5
Sanford River Rats	21	16	.568	9
Leesburg Lightning	21	17	.553	9.5
Seminole County Scorpions	8	30	.218	22.5
Winter Garden Squeeze	6	30	.176	23.5

CHAMPIONSHIP: Winter Park Diamond Dawgs defeated Deland Suns, 2-1, in best-of-three championship series.

INDIVIDUAL BATTING LEADERS

	AVG	AB	R	H	2B	3B	HR	RBI	SB
Dalton Shuffield, SS, Squeeze	.365	96	22	35	11	0	1	7	12
Trent Taylor, INF, River Rats	.347	101	24	35	1	2	0	4	26
Justin Farmer, OF, River Rats	.347	95	24	33	6	1	2	9	7
Luis Cabrera, C, Diamond Dawgs	.344	96	13	33	6	0	3	17	3
Luke Reidy, OF, Diamond Dawgs	.341	132	18	45	5	0	4	32	1
Mark Townsend, OF, Suns	.340	144	33	49	9	2	7	30	13
Tate Mathis, OF, Lightning	.333	114	25	38	7	0	1	15	17
Wesley Faison, 1B, Squeeze	.327	107	17	35	5	0	5	17	2
Cage Cox, OF, Lightning	.323	124	30	40	4	0	8	31	0
Parker Pillsbury, OF, Lightning	.323	93	23	30	2	0	5	17	8

INDIVIDUAL PITCHING LEADERS

	W	L	ERA	G	SV	IP	H	BB	SO
Tate Stone-Frisina, Diamond Dawgs	1	3	1.78	12	0	35	22	22	27
Logan Frasier, River Rats	2	1	2.64	11	0	31	28	9	26
Ryan Stuempfig, Diamond Dawgs	3	2	3.08	8	0	38	36	7	32
Nathan Palmer, Suns	5	1	3.40	13	0	42	31	32	53
Steven Swift, Diamond Dawgs	1	3	3.48	10	0	34	25	10	35
Cole Beverlin, Suns	3	0	3.55	7	0	33	27	17	22
Christian Simon, Scorpions	1	3	3.57	8	0	35	36	13	40
Peyton Winebarger, Lightning	3	4	3.73	10	0	31	25	17	36
Brandon Castle, Suns	2	1	3.79	13	1	36	34	17	36
James Hoelle, Diamond Dawgs	3	0	4.22	9	0	32	27	16	28

FUTURES COLLEGIATE LEAGUE

	W	L	PCT	GB
Brockton Rox	31	23	.574	-
Bristol Blues	31	23	.574	-
North Shore Navigators	30	25	.545	1.5
Worcester Bravehearts	30	26	.536	2

	W	L	PCT	GB
Pittsfield Suns	28	27	.509	3.5
Nashua Silver Knights	27	27	.500	4
Westfield Starfires	15	41	.268	17

CHAMPIONSHIP: Worcester Bravehearts defeated Bristol Blues, 2-0, in best-of-three championship series.

INDIVIDUAL BATTING LEADERS

	AVG	AB	R	H	2B	3B	HR	RBI	SB
Thomas Joyce, OF, Westfield	.370	135	26	50	13	0	4	23	6
Sean Lawlor, OF, N. Shore	.351	188	44	66	15	3	8	40	7
Kade Kretzschmar, OF, N. Shore	.348	132	26	46	7	2	4	23	5
Brandon Miller, OF, Bristol	.344	186	33	64	8	2	6	41	28
Zeke Diamond, INF, Bristol	.338	160	27	54	6	2	2	26	4
Matt Malcolm, C, Pittsfield	.336	140	19	47	11	0	3	19	11
Ben Malgeri, OF, N. Shore	.333	153	42	51	12	2	4	27	8
Mark Coley, OF, Pittsfield	.327	150	38	49	15	3	7	29	14
Kyle Sandstrom, OF, Nashua	.320	178	34	57	12	0	1	21	4
Mariano Ricciardi, INF, Worcester	.311	164	34	51	17	2	0	26	2

INDIVIDUAL PITCHING LEADERS

	W	L	ERA	G	SV	IP	H	BB	SO
Matt Svanson, Brockton	3	1	1.45	10	1	43	27	14	47
Scott Creedon, Brockton	2	1	2.27	10	0	44	43	10	33
Nick Sinacola, Brockton	2	0	2.66	10	0	44	33	21	71
Chase Jeter, Westfield	4	4	2.96	9	0	46	57	14	30
Jack Fox, Westfield	2	7	3.24	12	0	67	65	17	79
Evan Christopulos, Nashua	4	4	3.42	10	0	50	45	14	54
Alex Price, Pittsfield	2	1	4.24	9	0	47	52	16	47
Gavin Sullivan, N. Shore	5	2	4.26	10	0	51	48	9	37
James Flood, N. Shore	5	1	4.47	10	0	48	49	21	39
James Judenis, Bristol	1	3	5.32	11	2	46	61	14	34

GREAT LAKES LEAGUE

North Division

	W	L	PCT	GB
Lima Locos	26	15	.634	-
Muskegon Clippers	22	19	.537	4
Michigan Monarchs	20	20	.500	5.5
Grand Lake Mariners	20	21	.488	6
St. Clair Green Giants	19	20	.487	6
Galion Graders	11	29	.275	14.5

South Division

	W	L	PCT	GB
Licking County Settlers	25	17	.595	-
Cincinnati Steam	24	18	.571	1
S. Ohio Copperheads	23	18	.561	1.5
Hamilton Joes	22	18	.550	2
Xenia Scouts	18	24	.429	7
Richmond Jazz	15	26	.366	9.5

CHAMPIONSHIP: Lima Locos defeated Licking County Settlers, 2-1, in best-of-three championship series.

INDIVIDUAL BATTING LEADERS

	AVG	AB	R	H	2B	3B	HR	RBI	SB
Will David, C, Mariners	.394	104	27	41	7	0	1	19	8
Alex Crump, C, Green Giants	.385	91	18	35	6	0	1	21	3
Carson Eddy, 2B, Mariners	.377	130	33	49	7	0	0	17	8
Jordan Schaffer, SS, Monarchs	.367	98	18	36	9	0	0	12	8
Turner Hill, OF, Settlers	.356	132	25	47	2	2	0	16	14
Sebastian Fabik, OF, Copperheads	.345	165	34	57	18	0	5	38	7
Noah Thigpen, 3B, Mariners	.345	139	29	48	11	0	6	31	5
Gephry Pena, OF, Steam	.343	108	33	37	7	2	3	19	18
Randon Jernigan, OF, Locos	.343	108	27	37	3	1	1	12	14
Peter Ahn, INF, Monarchs	.342	152	30	52	9	2	6	33	16

INDIVIDUAL PITCHING LEADERS

	W	L	ERA	G	SV	IP	H	BB	SO
Liam Devine, Settlers	5	0	0.61	15	1	35	18	12	45
Zach Iverson, Copperheads	5	0	1.51	8	0	51	49	7	57
Jesse Heikkinen, Monarchs	2	1	1.68	8	0	50	34	12	49
Sam Benschoter, Monarchs	3	2	1.72	13	0	53	46	12	63
Jackson Mandella, Copperheads	3	2	1.86	6	0	41	36	11	28
Bradley Calhoun, Mariners	3	0	2.08	16	1	34	35	6	27
Cody Kanclerz, Scouts	2	0	2.31	9	0	36	34	11	27

	W	L	ERA	G	SV	IP	H	BB	SO
Braxton Kelly, Copperheads	2	1	2.67	13	4	37	29	17	48
Eric Roberts, Jazz	3	2	2.72	10	0	36	39	14	30
Josh Currier, Mariners	3	3	2.96	10	0	50	55	16	36

HAMPTONS COLLEGIATE LEAGUE

	W	L	T	PTS
Riverhead Tomcats	27	11	2	56
Westhampton Aviators	27	11	2	56
Sag Harbor Whalers	19	21	0	38
Shelter Island Bucks	19	21	0	38
Southampton Breakers	16	23	1	33
Long Island Road Warriors	14	23	3	31
North Fork Ospreys	14	26	0	28

CHAMPIONSHIP: Westhampton Aviators defeated Riverhead Tomcatss, 2-0, in best-of-three championship series.

INDIVIDUAL BATTING LEADERS

	AVG	AB	R	H	2B	3B	HR	RBI	SB
Jason Coules, OF, Tomcats	.407	91	30	37	7	5	3	22	28
Bailey Peterson, INF, Aviators	.368	136	30	50	14	2	5	38	17
Johnny Hipsman, OF, Breakers	.367	128	33	47	8	2	4	17	4
John Marti, INF, Road Warriors	.358	123	25	44	7	1	1	12	14
Landon Gray, C, Aviators	.354	82	23	29	5	0	5	22	5
Michael Ferrara, 1B, Breakers	.351	94	19	33	10	0	3	26	7
Daniel Franchi, OF, Aviators	.340	162	35	55	10	1	4	35	21
Gerard Sweeney, INF, Breakers	.333	102	17	34	4	0	1	20	2
Javier Vaz, INF, Ospreys	.333	87	20	29	4	0	2	10	13
Bryce Willits, INF, Tomcats	.320	128	30	41	14	1	1	23	23

INDIVIDUAL PITCHING LEADERS

	W	L	ERA	G	SV	IP	H	BB	SO
Bobby Vath, Tomcats	4	1	1.44	9	0	44	36	10	59
Brian Hendry, Tomcats	4	1	1.75	8	0	36	21	22	44
Harrison Cohen, Aviators	4	1	1.79	7	0	40	30	11	45
Erubiel Candelario, Aviators	4	0	1.98	7	0	36	27	16	38
Coleton Reitan, Tomcats	6	0	2.13	13	1	38	30	7	46
John LaPointe, Whalers	2	1	2.57	9	0	35	32	18	33
Trevor Olson, Bucks	2	2	2.65	7	0	34	29	15	42
Tristan Amone, Road Warriors	1	1	2.91	8	0	43	40	9	39
Ryan Taurek, Whalers	3	2	2.95	8	0	37	33	21	30
Joseph O'Connell, Bucks	1	1	3.50	10	0	36	33	16	29

MINK LEAGUE

North Division

	W	L	PCT	GB
St. Joseph Mustangs	29	8	.784	-
Chillicothe Mudcats	23	14	.622	6
Sedalia Bombers	20	16	.556	8.5
Clarinda A's	9	28	.243	20

South Division

	W	L	PCT	GB
Ozark Generals	22	14	.611	-
Joplin Outlaws	21	16	.543	1.5
Jefferson City Renegades	12	26	.316	11
Nevada Griffons	12	26	.316	11

CHAMPIONSHIP: St. Joseph Mustangs defeated Ozark Generals, 2-0, in best-of-three championship series.

INDIVIDUAL BATTING LEADERS

	AVG	AB	R	H	2B	3B	HR	RBI	SB
Logan Eickhoff, OF, Mudcats	.408	152	36	62	10	4	0	29	11
Jackson Dierenfeldt, INF, Mustangs	.404	141	45	57	8	0	1	29	24
Zack Ehlen, OF, Outlaws	.396	134	44	53	8	1	2	22	23
Nolan Metcalf, C, Mudcats	.383	141	38	54	13	1	5	33	4
Freilin Cabrera, INF, Outlaws	.382	55	9	21	8	2	0	16	6
AJ Gardner, OF, Bombers	.379	116	28	44	5	3	10	37	9
Peyton Holt, SS, A's	.373	83	23	31	8	0	2	11	12
Will Hanafan, OF, A's	.371	62	18	23	5	0	3	16	10
Jake Lufft, INF, Bombers	.360	86	16	31	10	0	4	26	0
Alex Hoff, INF, Bombers	.358	53	15	19	5	0	1	10	4

INDIVIDUAL PITCHING LEADERS

	W	L	ERA	G	SV	IP	H	BB	SO
Austin Brooks, Mustangs	3	0	1.04	7	1	17	11	7	19
Cam Bendnar, Mustangs	3	0	1.40	6	0	45	31	16	49

	W	L	ERA	G	SV	IP	H	BB	SO
Mack Stephenson, Mustangs	4	0	1.63	8	0	28	18	8	37
Jack McNellis, Mudcats	2	0	1.76	17	6	15	13	0	25
Garrett Presko, Mustangs	1	0	2.00	5	0	18	12	6	17
Shane Fontenot, Renegades	0	3	2.46	14	2	18	17	7	13
Tyson Campbell, Generals	6	3	2.59	10	1	76	62	19	94
Scott Duensing, Mudcats	2	1	2.84	5	0	25	24	8	17
Austin Gottula, Outlaws	3	2	2.93	12	2	28	20	11	26
Damian Acosta, Outlaws	1	0	2.95	6	2	18	16	13	25

NEW ENGLAND COLLEGIATE LEAGUE

Northern Division

	W	L	PCT	GB
Keene Swamp Bats	26	18	.591	-
Valley Blue Sox	25	18	.580	0.5
Vermont Mountaineers	25	19	.568	1
Upper Valley Nighthawks	24	20	.545	2
North Adams SteepleCats	24	20	.545	2
Sanford Mainers	17	27	.386	9
Winnipesaukee Muskrats	13	29	.310	12

Southern Division

	W	L	PCT	GB
Marthas Vineyard Sharks	28	16	.636	-
Newport Gulls	27	17	.614	1
Mystic Schooners	22	21	.511	5.5
Danbury Westerners	19	23	.452	8
Ocean State Waves	19	25	.432	9
New Bedford Bay Sox	14	30	.318	14

CHAMPIONSHIP: Keene Swampbats defeated Martha's Vineyard Sharks, 2-0, in best-of-three championship series.

TOP 10 PROSPECTS: 1. Nander De Sedas, SS, Martha's Vineyard (So., Florida State), 2. Hudson Haskin, OF, Newport (So., Tulane), 3. TT Bowens, 1B, Mystic (R-Jr., Central Connecticut State), 4. Trey McLoughlin, RHP, Mystic (Jr., Fairfield), 5. Randy Bednar, OF, Keene (Jr., Maryland), 6. Elijah Dunham, OF, Ocean State (Jr., Indiana), 7. Justin-Henry Malloy, 3B, Newport (So., Vanderbilt), 8. Thomas Spinelli, LHP, Martha's Vineyard (R-Jr., Florida Southern), 9. David Bedgood, 2B, Keene (Jr., Tulane), 10. Madison Jeffrey, RHP, North Adams (So., West Virginia).

INDIVIDUAL BATTING LEADERS

	AVG	AB	R	H	2B	3B	HR	RBI	SB
Cole Frederick, 3B, Nighthawks	.396	154	29	61	11	3	8	38	9
Greg Cavaliere, OF, Gulls	.378	98	22	37	10	1	1	18	11
Matthew Koperniak, INF, SteepleCats	.376	141	31	53	15	0	5	37	5
Elijah Dunham, OF, Waves	.360	136	25	49	11	0	6	27	8
Richard Constantine, 1B, Blue Sox	.358	159	30	57	7	0	7	37	0
David Beam, OF, Schooners	.357	129	35	46	8	0	3	26	14
Carter Williams, OF, Blue Sox	.353	150	34	53	2	1	1	27	17
Sam Cochrane, OF, Muskrats	.352	159	34	56	10	1	6	38	20
Scott Holzwasser, 2B, Gulls	.346	130	33	45	10	0	5	22	8
Jackson Raper, 3B, Sharks	.345	145	27	50	4	0	6	35	4

INDIVIDUAL PITCHING LEADERS

	W	L	ERA	G	SV	IP	H	BB	SO
Ryan Murphy, Mountaineers	5	2	2.25	8	0	48	44	12	55
Alec Huertas, Mountaineers	2	2	2.25	8	0	36	35	11	35
Nicholas Payero, SteepleCats	5	1	2.25	7	0	36	27	10	34
Kevin Gould, Blue Sox	5	0	2.46	8	0	37	38	9	19
Jordan DiValerio, Nighthawks	3	2	2.50	7	0	40	29	7	48
Trey McLoughlin, Schooners	4	1	2.75	7	0	36	27	6	48
Alex Schwartz, Muskrats	2	2	2.78	7	0	36	41	5	27
Tyler Schoff, Schooners	2	0	3.02	10	0	42	38	14	33
Christian Scafidi, Mountaineers	4	3	3.10	8	0	41	39	15	41
Gordon Graceffo, SteepleCats	4	3	3.10	9	0	49	49	11	47

NORTHWOODS LEAGUE

Great Lakes East Division

	W	L	PCT	GB
Traverse City Pit Spitters	52	20	.722	-
Kalamazoo Growlers	37	35	.514	15
Kenosha Kingfish	34	38	.472	18
Rockford Rivets	33	39	.458	19
Kokomo Jackrabbits	29	42	.408	22.5
Battle Creek Bombers	23	49	.319	29

Great Lakes West Division

	W	L	PCT	GB
Wisconsin Rapids Rafters	46	26	.639	-
Madison Mallards	42	30	.583	4
Fond du Lac Dock Spiders	36	35	.507	9.5
Wisconsin Woodchucks	34	38	.472	12
Green Bay Booyah	33	39	.458	13
Lakeshore Chinooks	32	40	.444	14

Great Plains East Division

	W	L	PCT	GB
Eau Claire Express	40	30	.571	-
La Crosse Loggers	37	35	.514	4
Waterloo Bucks	34	35	.493	5.5
Duluth Huskies	29	38	.433	9.5
Thunder Bay Border Cats	24	47	.338	16.5

Great Plains West Division

	W	L	PCT	GB
St. Cloud Rox	44	28	.611	-
Willmar Stingers	40	32	.556	4
Rochester Honkers	38	34	.528	6
Mankato MoonDogs	36	36	.500	8
Bismarck Larks	32	40	.444	12

CHAMPIONSHIP: Traverse City Pit Spitters defeated Eau Claire Express, 3-2, championship game.

TOP 10 PROSPECTS: 1. Will Klein, RHP, Lakeshore (Jr., Eastern Illinois), 2. T.J. Reeves, OF, Wisconsin (So., Alabama), 3. Luke Little, LHP, Traverse City (So., San Jacinto (Texas) JC), 4. Justice Bigbie, DH, Madison (Jr., East Carolina), 5. Mason Bryant, RHP, Duluth (So., Texas), 6. Jack Filby, RHP/DH, La Crosse (So., UCLA), 7. Logan Michaels, C, Madison (Sr., Virginia), 8. Tristan Peterson, 1B, Rochester (Sr., New Mexico State), 9. Drew Benefield, UTL, Madison (R-Fr., Louisville), 10. Jimmy Burnette, LHP, Rockford (Jr., Illinois).

INDIVIDUAL BATTING LEADERS

	AVG	AB	R	H	2B	3B	HR	RBI	SB
JT Schwatz, INF, Loggers	.378	196	40	74	15	1	1	35	6
Matt Bottcher, INF, Express	.367	229	44	84	10	7	1	40	20
Evan Berkey, SS, Honkers	.358	229	39	82	7	1	2	23	13
Jake Thompson, INF, Chinooks	.355	186	34	66	16	0	2	41	5
Logan Michaels, C, Mallards	.354	192	29	68	11	0	0	27	2
Adam Frank, INF, Woodchucks	.348	224	49	78	4	3	10	42	19
Justice Bigbie, INF, Mallards	.346	283	53	98	16	1	12	70	2
Daryl Myers, INF, Chinooks	.341	167	36	57	14	4	1	28	10
Austin Blazevic, INF, Mallards	.339	186	19	63	6	0	4	36	1
Jake Dunham, C, Rafters	.332	190	27	63	14	0	8	52	1

INDIVIDUAL PITCHING LEADERS

	W	L	ERA	G	SV	IP	H	BB	SO
Andrew Hoffman, Pit Spitters	8	0	1.08	12	0	58	32	22	43
Polo Portela, Stingers	8	0	1.23	10	0	58	43	11	47
Trevor Koenig, Rox	7	1	1.35	10	0	60	35	29	51
Gareth Stroh, Rafters	7	1	1.61	10	0	62	36	17	57
Nathan Hemmerling, Rafters	7	2	2.28	12	0	59	47	25	36
Kyle Jones, Pit Spitters	6	2	2.73	13	0	63	68	15	30
Matt Osterberg, Rafters	6	2	3.10	11	0	58	61	14	47
Aaron Husson, Jackrabbits	7	1	3.16	19	0	68	51	26	69
Brett Newberg, MoonDogs	5	2	3.22	12	2	67	67	18	55
Blaine Traxel, Jackrabbits	1	3	3.47	18	2	57	61	8	57

PERFECT GAME COLLEGIATE LEAGUE

East Division

	W	L	PCT	GB
Amsterdam Mohawks	33	13	.717	-
Albany Dutchmen	28	16	.633	4
Mohawk Valley DiamondDawgs	29	17	.630	4
Saugerties Stallions	26	19	.578	6.5
Oneonta Outlaws	18	28	.394	15
Glens Falls Dragons	13	34	.277	20.5

West Division

	W	L	PCT	GB
Utica Blue Sox	30	16	.652	-
Geneva Red Wings	26	20	.565	4
Elmira Pioneers	20	25	.444	9.5
Adirondack Trail Blazers	19	26	.422	10.5
Newark Pilots	17	31	.354	14
Watertown Rapids	16	30	.348	14

CHAMPIONSHIP: Amsterdam Mohawks defeated Adirondack Trail Blazers, 2-1, in best-of-three championship series.

INDIVIDUAL BATTING LEADERS

	AVG	AB	R	H	2B	3B	HR	RBI	SB
Luis Deleon, INF, Blue Sox	.397	121	34	48	9	3	6	31	7
Kevin Ferrer, OF, Trail Blazers	.385	143	28	55	20	0	1	24	11
Max Costes, INF, Mohawks	.374	123	36	46	11	0	12	36	5
Robbie Young, INF, Blue Sox	.368	152	37	56	14	1	3	29	7
Over Torres, OF, Pilots	.364	118	16	43	9	1	1	32	7
Chris Rotondo, OF, Trail Blazers	.358	106	33	38	9	2	7	21	6
Andy Hague, INF, Trail Blazers	.356	135	34	48	9	1	3	20	16
Allen Murphy, OF/RHP, Pilots	.349	126	32	44	9	4	2	26	4
Tyler Simon, INF, Blue Sox	.340	147	49	50	16	2	1	25	14
Brandon Cooper, OF, Red Wings	.336	122	31	41	7	3	6	28	10

INDIVIDUAL PITCHING LEADERS

	W	L	ERA	G	SV	IP	H	BB	SO
Ray Pacella, Blue Sox	3	1	1.23	17	5	44	48	11	41
Noah Rubino, Pioneers	3	2	2.13	8	0	42	34	19	36
Lane Miller, Stallions	3	1	2.13	9	1	42	28	11	42
Ryan Solimine, Trail Blazers	5	1	2.83	7	0	48	48	5	30
Jacob Maser, Red Wings	5	1	3.12	12	1	40	44	11	36
Steven Miller, Trail Blazers	5	2	3.23	9	0	39	30	23	44
Billy Black, Stallions	2	2	3.40	8	0	40	31	16	29
Cole Miller, DiamondDawgs	4	3	3.48	8	0	44	57	9	33
Greg Tobin, Rapids	0	5	3.89	10	0	39	30	22	45
Ben Seiler, Dutchmen	1	1	4.26	9	0	38	36	24	32

PROSPECT LEAGUE

East Division	W	L	PCT	GB
Danville Dans	40	20	.667	-
Chillicothe Paints	40	20	.667	-
Terre Haute Rex	35	25	.583	5
Lafayette Aviators	34	26	.567	6
Champion City Kings	25	34	.424	14.5
West Virginia Miners	18	42	.300	22
West Division	W	L	PCT	GB
Cape Catfish	43	17	.717	-
DuPage Pistol Shrimp	34	25	.576	8.5
Quincy Gems	34	26	.567	9
Hannibal Hoots	23	37	.383	20
Normal CornBelters	21	39	.350	22
Springfield Sliders	12	48	.200	31

CHAMPIONSHIP: Chillicothe Paints defeated Cape Catfish, 2-1, in best-of-three championship series.

INDIVIDUAL BATTING LEADERS

	AVG	AB	R	H	2B	3B	HR	RBI	SB
Cody Orr, OF/RHP, Paints	.409	181	58	74	9	14	4	44	28
Andrew Stone, INF, Catfish	.397	224	66	89	12	7	16	49	33
Ellison Hanna, OF, Catfish	.382	165	43	63	13	2	14	65	3
Tyler Clark-Chiapparelli, INF, Gems	.373	201	51	75	19	2	15	44	17
Brendan Ryan, INF, Sliders	.360	139	26	50	7	1	3	17	30
Aidan Malm, OF, Dans	.360	164	41	59	10	1	5	30	19
Canyon McWilliams, INF, CornBelters	.357	143	27	51	12	1	3	25	17
Trey Sweeney, INF, Aviators	.354	212	59	75	11	2	7	42	10
Chris Monroe, INF, Aviators	.348	250	57	87	23	0	7	62	6
Max Jung Goldberg, INF, Dans	.348	178	53	62	11	4	9	40	8

INDIVIDUAL PITCHING LEADERS

	W	L	ERA	G	SV	IP	H	BB	SO
Bryan McNeely, Catfish	6	1	2.40	10	0	56	47	6	33
Zach Kendall, Paints	4	0	2.53	10	0	53	44	20	55
Jack Raines, Paints	7	1	3.02	10	0	54	59	18	54
Andrew Rolfsen, CornBelters	2	4	3.42	14	0	50	54	23	40
Jared Hatch, Kings	2	1	3.54	13	1	48	51	19	37
Matt Burleton, Aviators	3	3	3.81	13	0	50	49	13	63
RJ Kuruts, Dans	5	1	4.18	13	0	52	64	14	49
CJ Growney, Miners	3	3	4.86	13	0	50	55	9	52
Tommy Springer, Catfish	4	3	5.00	12	0	54	54	32	61
Nate Gorczyca, CornBelters	3	4	5.29	14	0	51	54	31	44

SOUTH FLORIDA COLLEGIATE LEAGUE

North Division	W	L	PCT	GB
Boynton Beach Buccaneers	20	19	.513	-
Palm Beach Diamond Ducks	18	21	.462	2
Phipps Park Barracudas	16	23	.410	4
Boca Raton Blazers	15	24	.388	5
Delray Beach Lightning	11	26	.297	8
South Division	W	L	PCT	GB
Ft. Lauderdale Knights	30	13	.698	-
West Boca Snappers	29	13	.690	0.5
Palm Beach Xtreme	21	17	.553	6.5
Florida Pokers	19	21	.475	9.5
Pompano Beach Clippers	18	20	.474	9.5

CHAMPIONSHIP: West Boca Snappers defeated Ft. Lauderdale Knights, 2-0, in best-of-three championship series.

INDIVIDUAL BATTING LEADERS

	AVG	AB	R	H	2B	3B	HR	RBI	SB
Derek Cartaya, INF, Snappers	.395	76	19	30	4	0	0	8	14
Ricky Clark, OF, Palm Beach	.380	100	22	38	3	1	0	12	3
Andrew Martinez, OF, Palm Beach	.380	71	17	27	7	1	1	14	4
Logan Stoldt, C, Knights	.375	64	11	24	4	0	0	19	2
Jalen Townsend, OF, Clippers	.373	67	24	25	3	1	0	14	19
Keith Stevens, UTL, Clippers	.370	81	14	30	8	0	1	21	3
Anthony Orta, C, Xtreme	.354	113	18	40	4	1	2	23	2
Jordan Mercado, INF, Palm Beach	.51	97	23	34	6	1	0	11	8
Justin Lara, OF, Pokers	.345	113	30	39	7	4	1	15	24
Alex McCormack, INF, Pokers	.341	85	14	29	5	0	0	9	2

INDIVIDUAL PITCHING LEADERS

	W	L	ERA	G	SV	IP	H	BB	SO
Israel Cordero, Knights	4	0	1.22	7	0	37	30	2	24
Corey Martinez, Snappers	6	0	1.27	8	0	43	30	14	57
Nik Constantakos, Pokers	3	1	1.75	8	0	36	23	13	66
Jean Sapini, Clippers	1	1	2.25	11	0	32	25	8	45
Gus Carter, Snappers	5	2	2.38	8	0	34	19	15	40
Andrew Martinez, Xtreme	2	1	3.19	9	0	31	25	18	41
Max Charnin, Lightning	3	2	3.41	10	0	32	31	8	27
Rich Frommelt, Barracudas	2	3	3.86	8	0	33	40	14	14
Matt Lawlor, Barracudas	2	1	3.93	10	1	37	33	12	36
Cody Sheider, Barracudas	3	2	4.05	8	0	33	29	19	40

SUNBELT LEAGUE

	W	L	PCT	GB
Brookhaven Bucks	21	12	.636	-
Norcross Astros	20	16	.556	2.5
Atlanta Crackers	17	15	.531	3.5
Gwinnett Tides	15	15	.500	4.5
Alpharetta Aviators	11	17	.393	7.5
Marietta Patriots	10	19	.345	9

CHAMPIONSHIP: Brookhaven Bucks defeated Norcross Astros, 2-1, in best-of-three championship series.

INDIVIDUAL BATTING LEADERS

	AVG	AB	R	H	2B	3B	HR	RBI	SB
Matthew Vaccaro, 1B, Patriots	.465	71	10	33	10	1	1	22	1
Chandler Simpson, 2B, Bucks	.402	92	32	37	2	4	0	12	12
DeAngelo Abboud, SS, Tides	.382	76	18	29	8	0	4	21	3
Noah Mendlinger, OF, Bucks	.378	111	31	42	8	1	2	28	3
Drew Compton, 1B, Bucks	.375	80	16	30	8	2	4	25	0
Trenton Jamison, INF, Tides	.367	109	26	40	8	1	4	23	8
Daino Deas, 3B, Bucks	.337	101	21	34	3	0	2	16	3
Andrew Jenkins, C, Bucks	.330	109	27	36	11	0	3	26	0
Nick Clarno, C, Astros	.326	132	19	43	5	1	0	18	2
Reeve Holley, SS, Crackers	.322	87	18	28	4	0	1	13	3

INDIVIDUAL PITCHING LEADERS

	W	L	ERA	G	SV	IP	H	BB	SO
Rafael Acosta, Astros	3	0	0.62	7	0	29	10	5	27
Jet Kern, Aviators	1	0	1.57	13	1	23	16	6	22
James Boatright, Astros	2	4	2.95	9	0	37	36	5	23
James Janco, Aviators	2	0	2.97	9	0	30	25	11	22

Righthander Carmen Mlodzinski starred in the Cape Cod League.

COURTESY OF MEGHAN MURPHY/FALMOUTH COMMODORES

Mykel Page, Aviators	2	2	3.00	6	0	24	21	9	27
Tyler Fairchild, Crackers	7	0	3.18	10	0	51	41	22	57
Luke Sutko, Crackers	1	3	3.38	17	5	27	31	3	36
Darryn Pasqua, Aviators	1	2	3.42	7	0	50	49	1	45
Jeffrey Jenkins, Tides	4	1	3.43	9	0	42	43	9	43
Christopher Bergmoser, Bucks	4	0	3.44	7	0	34	38	13	27

SUNFLOWER COLLEGIATE LEAGUE

East Division	W	L	PCT	GB
Haysville Aviators	22	14	.611	-
Derby Twins	21	14	.600	0.5
Mulvane Patriots	16	18	.471	5
Newton Rebels	16	18	.471	5
El Dorado Broncos	15	19	.441	6
West Division	**W**	**L**	**PCT**	**GB**
Cheney Diamond Dawgs	31	5	.861	-
Hutchinson Monarchs	23	13	.639	8
Great Bend Bat Cats	21	14	.600	9.5
Wichita Sluggers	17	19	.472	14
Andale Warhawks	5	29	.147	25

CHAMPIONSHIP: Cheney Diamond Dawgs defeated Haysville Aviators, 2-0, in best-of-three championship series.

INDIVIDUAL BATTING LEADERS

	AVG	AB	R	H	2B	3B	HR	RBI	SB
Tresten Kennard, OF, Cheney	.433	97	25	42	7	2	3	34	7
Ryan Chargo, OF, Salina	.432	74	22	32	8	4	7	28	3
Brayden Whitchurch, OF, Hutchinson	.404	109	28	44	7	1	3	26	19
Kyler Castillo, OF, Cheney	.404	89	32	36	5	2	0	18	6
Matt Scheurich, OF, Cheney	.400	50	11	20	5	0	4	9	5
Colton Bertus, INF, Wichita	.394	104	29	41	7	2	10	34	4
Blake Rambusch, SS, Cheney	.394	109	26	43	7	3	7	43	1
Keone Givens, OF, Mulvane	.387	111	33	43	8	0	5	26	8
Livane Reinoso, INF, Haysville	.383	60	7	23	2	0	1	7	8
Enzo Bonventre, C, Newton	.380	108	27	41	5	1	2	13	0

INDIVIDUAL PITCHING LEADERS

	W	L	ERA	G	SV	IP	H	BB	SO
Michael Mitchell, Derby	5	1	1.05	6	0	34	15	6	40
Steven Beard, Great Bend	3	0	1.53	3	0	18	15	3	23
Matt Contreras, Newton	3	0	2.08	11	0	17	12	9	18
Zach Curry, Great Bend	3	0	2.10	9	1	39	26	9	51
Weston Murrow, Newton	3	1	2.10	10	0	36	21	8	21
Dakota Rodd, Mulvane	1	2	2.11	10	0	21	20	7	21
Hunter O'Toole, Cheney	1	0	2.21	5	0	20	18	6	14
Derek Schumann, Cheney	2	1	2.42	5	0	22	22	8	31
Nate Postlethwait, Cheney	4	0	2.56	8	0	46	36	6	41
Dawson Linder, Hutchinson	2	0	2.61	7	2	21	18	19	25

VALLEY LEAGUE

North Division	W	L	PCT	GB
Strasburg Express	26	16	.619	-
Woodstock River Bandits	25	17	.595	1
New Market Rebels	19	23	.452	7
Winchester Royals	18	24	.429	8
Purcellville Cannons	15	27	.357	11
Front Royal Cardinals	14	28	.333	12
South Division	**W**	**L**	**PCT**	**GB**
Waynesboro Generals	31	11	.738	-
Charlottesville TomSox	25	17	.595	6
Covington Lumberjacks	21	21	.500	10
Staunton Braves	19	23	.452	12
Harrisonburg Turks	18	24	.429	13

CHAMPIONSHIP: Charlottesville TomSox defeated Strasburg Express, 2-0, in best-of-three championship series.

INDIVIDUAL BATTING LEADERS

	AVG	AB	R	H	2B	3B	HR	RBI	SB
Thomas Francisco, INF, TomSox	.412	114	22	47	8	1	1	30	2
Logan Amiss, C, Lumberjacks	.410	105	22	43	7	0	4	18	4
Aidan Nagle, 1B, River Bandits	.406	160	47	65	10	0	11	33	9
Caleb Ward, OF, River Bandits	.385	122	25	47	9	0	6	30	4
Wes Clarke, C, Generals	.364	121	33	44	14	1	6	29	0
Josh Madole, 1B, Turks	.357	140	22	50	9	0	1	24	1
William Escala, INF, River Bandits	.348	112	23	39	7	2	0	15	8
Cayman Richardson, OF, TomSox	.344	131	36	45	7	1	1	19	4
Andrew Czech, 1B, Braves	.344	157	31	54	15	0	9	47	0
Lael Lockhart, 1B, River Bandits	.342	111	36	38	11	0	7	27	1

INDIVIDUAL PITCHING LEADERS

	W	L	ERA	G	SV	IP	H	BB	SO
Eli Ellington, Turks	1	1	2.31	12	1	35	28	19	54
Shane Scott, Cardinals	3	1	2.44	8	0	44	44	13	27
Reid Celata, Braves	2	0	3.07	11	1	41	40	12	39
Logan Walters, Royals	3	1	3.55	8	0	38	31	11	42
Mason Kenney, Express	3	1	3.64	8	0	35	38	11	24
Dylan Oliver, Express	1	1	3.75	10	0	36	38	9	38
Sam Prince, Rebels	3	3	4.05	18	1	40	41	8	23
Will Brian, Turks	0	3	4.33	8	0	35	33	20	42
Avery Short, TomSox	3	4	4.53	14	0	46	59	23	43
Grant Vurpillat, Lumberjacks	5	2	4.62	11	0	39	38	21	39

WEST COAST LEAGUE

North Division	W	L	PCT	GB
Victoria HarbourCats	21	6	.778	-
Wenatchee AppleSox	17	10	.630	4
Port Angeles Lefties	12	16	.429	9.5
Bellingham Bells	9	16	.360	11
Yakima Valley Pippins	10	18	.357	11.5
Kelowna Falcons	7	19	.269	13.5
South Division	**W**	**L**	**PCT**	**GB**
Corvallis Knights	21	6	.778	
Portland Pickles	15	12	.556	6
Ridgefield Raptors	14	13	.519	7
Cowlitz Black Bears	14	13	.519	7
Walla Walla Sweets	12	14	.462	8.5
Bend Elks	9	18	.333	12

CHAMPIONSHIP: Corvallis Knights defeated Victoria HarbourCats, 2-1, in best-of-three championship series.

INDIVIDUAL BATTING LEADERS

	AVG	AB	R	H	2B	3B	HR	RBI	SB
Jake Holcroft, OF, Knights	.368	223	51	82	7	2	1	33	22
Briley Knight, OF, Knights	.357	182	48	65	18	3	8	42	15
Brooks Lee, SS, Knights	.342	146	33	50	12	0	2	30	12
John Jensen, OF, Pickles	.338	160	32	54	10	2	7	24	14
Blake Klassen, 1B, AppleSox	.338	139	36	47	9	0	1	25	13
Zach Needham, INF, Bend	.331	178	37	59	18	1	6	25	8
Patrick Caufield, OF, Sweets	.328	189	45	62	12	1	5	26	41
Johnny Sage, OF, AppleSox	.327	147	31	48	11	0	1	26	13
Jack Machtolf, OF, Bells	.321	137	22	44	9	2	1	27	2
Michael Hicks, OF, Raptors	.320	178	36	57	12	0	9	50	0

INDIVIDUAL PITCHING LEADERS

	W	L	ERA	G	SV	IP	H	BB	SO
Nick Proctor, Bells	5	2	2.05	11	0	53	33	15	35
Tevita Gerber, Knights	7	1	2.20	10	0	49	43	20	50
Bradley McVay, Pickles	4	2	2.60	10	0	45	35	21	55
Jake Saum, AppleSox	4	1	2.80	9	0	45	30	18	54
Jack Gonzales, Pippins	2	2	3.43	17	1	58	61	19	45
Dwayne Angebrandt, Lefties	4	3	3.52	8	0	46	42	12	37
Joey Martin, Raptors	1	4	3.83	14	1	47	36	52	67
David Watson, Knights	5	1	4.02	11	0	47	45	15	45
Peter Allegro, Raptors	3	3	4.21	11	1	51	51	18	41
Nick Nygard, Falcons	2	3	4.22	13	0	43	42	22	39

HIGH
SCHOOL

Argyle Cements Legacy To Close Out Decade

Argyle (Texas) High won the Texas 4A state championship and finished with a 40-1-1 record.

BY JARED MCMASTERS

The early years of Ricky Griffin's career as head baseball coach at Argyle (Texas) High weren't exactly filled with trophies and accolades.

From the start, he aimed at the long-term goal: develop a program for the future.

In recent years, that vision has become a reality. The Eagles won the 4A state championship in 2015 and added an undefeated season in 2018.

Then, in 2019, they claimed their third state championship on his watch and were named the Baseball America High School Team of the Year.

"We started getting good players, we continued to get them, and they continued to develop," Griffin said. "They did a ton of work on their own . . . to be able to get their talent to where it needed to be, and now we seem to have kids committed to do that every year."

Argyle finished this season with a 40-1-1 record and won its last 28 games, but this season has been rewarding in many ways.

Griffin joined the Argyle coaching staff in 2007, when his son, Storm, was a freshman pitcher on the team. This year, Griffin won his first state championship with Storm by his side on the coaching staff.

"I'm obviously in the fourth quarter of my career," Griffin said. "And to be able to spend the last part of it here with my son coaching next to me means a lot."

Argyle has been one of the most dominant high school teams in the country since 2015. However, the 2019 season will always hold a special place in Griffin's heart thanks to the seniors on the team who have proven their resilience.

"Their sophomore year, we got beat in either the regional quarterfinals or semifinals," Griffin said. "They got together on their own, away from me, and made a commitment to each other that they weren't going to settle for finishing the season before they got to play in the state tournament.

"The next two years, that's what they did. They took us to—and won—two state championships."

Griffin said this year's title was more rewarding because of the expectations they faced.

"We played with a target on our back all year long," Griffin said.

Argyle has 10 players who are either committed to or signed with Division I colleges. The Eagles have been led by seniors Dillon Carter, an outfielder committed to Texas Tech, and second baseman Brenden Dixon, a Texas commit.

Most of the seniors on this year's Argyle team have been with Griffin for all four years. He credits the upperclassmen for being leaders who bring the group together based on a shared desire to win.

"They're such a tight group," Griffin said. "They're all close friends, and they're together off the field."

All of the joy of the 2019 season comes at a price for Griffin. He now has to say goodbye to the players who worked so hard to be successful.

"It was awesome to finish the way we did, but also bittersweet because I'm going to really miss them, both as kids and as players," Griffin said.

"The impact that they've had on our program, you know, I can't say enough."

Florida Burn Repeats At Jupiter

Last year, Florida Burn wasn't expected to win Perfect Game's WWBA World Championship. The team entered the 2018 tournament with low expectations from most people outside of the organization.

They answered by winning every game they played and beating one of the perceived favorites—Canes National—in the championship game.

So, naturally, they would be given more credit a year later, right?

Not the case.

"Coming in, we were the underdogs again," Florida Burn 2020 Platinum catcher Mac Guscette said. "We were the 'dark horse' as they called us. We won the tournament last year and went undefeated as well. We weren't supposed to win a game. I think that really fired us up last year and again this year. It was the same thing."

After the 2018 team won eight straight games and outscored its opponents 25-9, the 2019 version of the club followed the same script. The Burn went 3-0 in group play before storming through the bracket and winning back-to-back WWBA World Championships, topping the Dirtbags, 11-2, in the championship game.

"They're great," Florida Burn general manager Mark Guthrie said about the Dirtbags. "That's a big group of kids and they can swing it," "But when you get this late in tournaments anything can happen. This game could have easily gone the other way. Kids get tired and play five games in two days. We always preach to our guys, 'You have to get off to a good start.' If you can take the wind out of the other team's sails early, it really helps.

"And shoot, their guy hits a leadoff home run so that wasn't going to happen."

In the top of the first inning, Dirtbags leadoff hitter and center fielder Jake DeLeo—who posted a 1.132 OPS after going 10-for-24 with seven walks during the tournament—got his team on the board with a long home run to left field.

But the Burn answered back immediately in the bottom of the frame thanks to an RBI double off the left-field wall from Guscette to even things at 1-1. Shortly thereafter, Guscette would score from third base to give the Burn a 2-1 lead that they later expanded to an 11-1 lead with a game-breaking nine-run effort in the bottom of the third.

For his efforts in the championship game and throughout the entire tournament—both offensively and handling the pitching staff behind the plate—Guscette was named tournament MVP.

The Florida commit went 10-for-22 (.455) with three doubles, two walks, six runs and five RBIs this year, just 12 months after being a part of the championship-winning 2018 Burn team.

"I feel like I came back as a leader," Guscette said. "(The semifinal) game, it was just like our championship game last year, we were tied, 1-1, and then we just stayed up the whole game and knew something was going to happen."

Burn second baseman Vince Smith played the

hero in that semifinal matchup against Padres Scout Team/ECB, hitting a walk-off home run to left field in the bottom of the ninth inning to break a 1-1, extra-inning tie and push the Burn to the final.

"I've just been thinking really small lately," Guscette said. "Just trying to hit the ball hard. I just felt so into the game this weekend—and even all summer and fall. I don't know, I like having these teammates behind me. They always pick me up."

The Burn outscored opponents 43-10 and pitched two shutouts during the tournament. The most runs a team would put up against their pitching staff was three runs—by Team Citius National 2020 during the Burn's third group play game, a 7-3 win—and the the pitching staff managed all that success despite pitching with fastballs in the low 80s for the majority of the tournament.

"Our pitchers, they aren't the hardest throwers, but they just hit their spots," Guscette said. "They know how to pitch, they know how to throw everything for a strike, and they just know how to control the game. This shows that you don't have to throw hard to win."

Four different Florida Burn pitchers threw at least seven innings without allowing an earned run. Righthander Daniel Vassallo threw 8.2 innings with 10 strikeouts and no walks; righthander Jacob Faulkner threw 8.1 innings and struck out six batters; lefthander Sam Drumheller threw eight innings and struck out eight batters; and righthander Trace Goforth threw seven innings with six strikeouts.

The Burn have also showed—in back-to-back years now—that you don't need to have the most star-studded roster to win the most prestigious trophy in travel ball. For them, it's all about the familiarity of the roster. Playing with a group of players who you are comfortable with and who you've played with for years.

"All of us are so close, we all play high school ball together or against each other, and I just feel like whenever someone went down then that person behind them would pick them up," Guscette said. "We'd be in the dugout the entire time cheering them on.

"I think that's good because I like knowing everyone, especially my pitchers. Knowing what I can do to calm them down and even everyone, just being able to talk to everyone and calm them down or pick them up when they need it."

Perhaps other teams will start to follow that model to try and replicate their success. Because regardless of the expectations put on them from others, success is the only thing that Florida Burn

has known for the last two years in Jupiter.

"Man, to tell you the truth, it's even more amazing to come here and win 16 games in a row," Guthrie said. "I don't know if that's happened before.

"I'm just really happy for them, man. You watched last year's team do it, and they were excited about it. A lot of these guys were here last year. And it's a great moment for them. Hopefully something they remember for the rest of their lives and see each other later on and can reminisce over that. It's a really cool thing for these guys, and I'm really happy for them."

Orange Lutheran Wins Third NHSI

USA Baseball's National High School Invitational is getting a bit predictable. In most cases, that wouldn't be the ideal scenario. However, for the players and coaches of Orange (Calif.) Lutheran High, that's exactly how they like it—even if becoming the first team to win the event in three consecutive years wasn't something they just walked in and expected to happen.

"You know, it's still unbelievable," said Orange Lutheran coach Eric Borba, still wet and sticky from both the humid North Carolina air and his third Gatorade shower on the final day of USA Baseball's annual high school tournament. "The odds of coming back here and winning this thing again, it was almost a joke.

"We know we're good enough to do it, but really, the odds of winning this thing three times in a row are slim to none. And somehow, these guys found a way to rally together and defeat the odds."

Since the first year of the NHSI in 2012, California teams have dominated the competition, winning seven of eight championships with 14 of the 16 championship game participants hailing from the state.

"The baseball in Southern California is deeper than anybody can talk about," Borba said. "I don't mean any disrespect toward any teams across the country, but these guys play a lot. With the weather, obviously, we can play year-round, but the quality of the competition and the depth of the teams out there is unbelievable. So I don't think it's a surprise that we see California teams in the final. But it's a tribute to how hard the guys work out there and the number of quality players we have in Southern California."

The 2019 edition of the event saw Orange Lutheran beat fellow Southern California powerhouse Harvard-Westlake (Studio City, Calif.), 6-2, to make history and surpass Mater Dei's back-to-back championship mark from 2012 and 2013.

"I just like how you said 'first team in history,'"

AMATEUR/YOUTH CHAMPIONS 2019

ALL-AMERICAN AMATEUR BASEBALL ASSOCIATION (AAABA)

Event	Site	Champion	Runner-up
World Series (21U)	Johnstown, Pa.	New Orleans Boosters	Johnstown Realty (Altoona, Pa.)

AMERICAN LEGION BASEBALL

Event	Site	Champion	Runner-up
World Series (19U)	Shelby, N.C.	Idaho Falls, Idaho	Fargo, N.D.

BABE RUTH BASEBALL

Event	Site	Champion	Runner-up
Cal Ripken (10U)	Phenix City, Ala.	North Carolina	Alabama
Cal Ripken 12-year-old (60 feet)	Branson, Mo.	Mexico	Hawaii
13-year-old	Demopolis, Ala.	Chandler, Ariz.	Fort Carolina, Fla.
13-15-year-olds	Bismarck, N.D.	Norwalk Revolution	Bismarck, N.D.
16-18-year-olds	Mobile, Ala.	Mobile, Ala.	New England

LITTLE LEAGUE BASEBALL

Event	Site	Champion	Runner-up
Little League (11-12)	South Williamsport, Pa.	Louisiana	Curacao
Junior League (12-14)	Taylor, Mich.	California	Puerto Rico
Senior League (13-16)	Easley, S.C.	Hawaii	Willemstad, Curacao
Intermediate (50-70)	Livermore, Calif.	Southeast	Mexico

NATIONAL AMATEUR BASEBALL FEDERATION (NBAF)

Event	Site	Champion	Runner-up
Rookie (10U)	Tuxedo Park, N.Y.	New York Devil Cats	North Atlantic Select, N.Y.
Freshman (12U)	Tuxedo Park, N.Y.	Paterson, N.J.	Bonnie Robins, N.Y.
Sophomore (14U)	Struthers, Ohio	Astros Falcons, Ohio	Release Baseball, Ohio
Junior (16U)	Struthers, Ohio	Brooklyn Bonnie Cougars, N.Y.	Jackson 96ers White, Miss.
High School (17U)	Jackson, Miss.	Brooklyn Bonnie Cougars, N.Y.	Jackson 96ers White, Miss.
Senior (18U)	Struthers, Ohio	New York Nine	Creekside Fitness, Ohio
College (22U)	Toledo, Ohio	Creekside Crocodiles, Ohio	Stark County Terriers, Ohio

PERFECT GAME/BCS FINALS

Event	Site	Champion	Runner-up
12U	Fort Myers, Fla.	Gulf Coast Monarchs 12U	Elite Squad National
13U	Fort Myers, Fla.	5 Star National 13U Black	Team Elite 13U Premier
14U	Fort Myers, Fla.	Genesis Baseball	Legends Prospects 14U
15U	Fort Myers, Fla.	5 Star National 15U Dobbs	Florida Dodgers Scout Team 2022
16U	Fort Myers, Fla.	Dulins Dodgers-Godwin	Team Elite 16U Prime
17U	Fort Myers, Fla.	Florida Burn 2020 Platinum	East Cobb Astros 17U Navy
18U	Fort Myers, Fla.	Okotok Dawgs 18U Black	SBO 17U

said Orange Lutheran righthander Evan Adolphus after being asked about the trifecta following the victory. "It feels great."

Adolphus, a member of the 2019 class who is committed to Cal State Fullerton, was tabbed the starter for the championship game and rose to the occasion with aplomb, throwing 6.2 innings on 105 pitches and allowing just a pair of runs. Adolphus came out of the gate with a fastball that touched 92 mph early and settled into the 87-90 mph range throughout the outing, pairing it with a devastating, low-80s changeup that kept hitters off-balance and helped him retire the first 13 Harvard-Westlake hitters he faced.

"I think he has one of the best changeups I've ever coached," Borba said.

If Orange Lutheran had allowed more than three runs in the previous three games leading up to the championship, there's a chance Adolphus wouldn't have been in the position to shine in the championship game. He was available in relief

if necessary throughout the tournament, but the quality of the Lancer pitching performances during the week meant he was fresh for the final.

The key to the NHSI is always pitching depth. And this year—like last year and like the year before that—Orange Lutheran had pitching depth and then some. Righthander Max Rajcic threw six dominant innings in a Game 1 win against South Forsyth (Cumming, Ga.). righthander Christian Rodriguez threw a complete game in a 2-1 win over Desert Oasis (Las Vegas) in Game 2, and righthander Jonathan Guzman threw six shutout innings in a blowout, 12-1 win against Monsignore Pace (Miami) in Game 3.

"Sometimes it's hard as a coach, you try to get everybody in there and you can't get them as many innings as you want," Borba said. "But knowing we have opportunities like this where you have a lot of confidence in a guy who can go out and give you 6.2 (innings) against an opponent like Harvard-Westlake and just really dominate the

PERFECT GAME/WORLD WOOD BAT ASSOCIATION SUMMER CHAMPIONSHIPS

Event	Site	Champion	Runner-up
14U	Marietta, Ga.	Team Elite 14U National	Canes National 14U
15U	Marietta, Ga.	Canes National 15U	5 Star National 15U Dobbs
16U	Marietta, Ga.	Team Elite 16U Scout Team	Wilson Sandlot
17U	Marietta, Ga..	Canes National 17	Dallas Patriots 17U Stout
18U	Marietta, Ga.	Team Georgia 17U National	East Cobb Astros 17U Navy

PONY BASEBALL

Event	Site	Champion	Runner-up
Pinto 8U	Mt. Vernon, Ill.	Paradera, Aruba	—
Mustang 9U	Mt. Vernon, Ill.	Stars and Stripes	Aruba
Mustang 10U	Youngsville, La.	Placentia, Calif.	Mexicali, Baja California, Mexico
Bronco 11U	Chesterfield, Va.	Redondo Beach, Calif.	Navojoa, Mexico
Bronco 12U	Laredo, Texas	Taitung City, Taiwan	Tijuana, Mexico
Pony 13U	Whittier, Calif.	Hilo, Hawaii	Johnstown, Pa.
Pony 14U	Washington, Pa.	Taipei City, Taiwan	Bay County, Mich.
Colt 16U	Marion, Ill.	Southern Illinois	Brownsville, Texas
Palomino 18U	Laredo, Texas	Taoyuan County, Taiwan	Guaynabo, P.R.

REVIVING BASEBALL IN INNER CITIES (RBI)

Event	Site	Champion	Runner-up
Junior (13-15)	Vero Beach, Fla.	Chicago White Sox RBI	Miami Marlins RBI
Senior (16-18)	Minnesota	Arizona RBI	Miami Marlins RBI

U.S. SPECIALTY SPORTS ASSOCIATION (USSSA)

Event	Site	Champion	Runner-up
10U/Majors Elite	Viera, Fla.	MVP Hustle Ruiz	Line Drive Elite
11U/Majors Elite	Viera, Fla.	Easton Top Notch National	Texas Canes Elite
12U/Majors Elite	Viera, Fla.	Florida Ballers	Gulf Coast Monarchs
13U/Majors Elite	Viera, Fla.	SBA Futures	Chicago West Englewood Tigers
14U/Majors Elite	Viera, Fla.	YETI Baseball Club Crawdads	Dallas Tigers East Lovell

USA BASEBALL

Event	Site	Champion	Runner-up
14 U West	Peoria, Ariz.	PBA	Tri County Baseball Club
14U East	West Palm Beach, Fla.	Meridian Panthers	Columbus HS Blue
15U West	Peoria, Ari.	GBG Renegades	Team Utah
15U East	Jupiter, Fla.	Gamblers Elite/Team Elite (Co-Champions)	
16U West	Peoria, Ariz.	Sports Academy Dukes	Chino Hills Storm
USA Baseball 14U—East	Jupiter, Fla.	5 Star National Burress	Dallas Tigers 2022-Polk
USA Baseball 14U—West	Peoria, Ariz.	Zoots Baseball Club	CBA Marucci National

whole game. It's pretty awesome, I just thought it was a real gutsy performance by him.

"Having that in the back pocket going into the championship game—we knew we had an advantage going into it."

Orange Lutheran also had the advantage of plugging outfielder Caden Connor into the two-hole of the lineup. Connor was named the MVP of the tournament after going 7-for-10 with two doubles, five singles, five walks and zero strikeouts over 15 plate appearances.

"Through my mind I'm just like, go do my thing," Connor said about playing in the championship. "Just take a breather, be calm. My first at-bat I was a little nervous. I didn't pull the trigger much, and then I just went up there and did my thing. Just glad I found holes, got on base, scored runs for my team."

In the championship game, Connor was as reliable as a coach could hope for, going a perfect 3-for-3 with a double and a pair of singles, tacking on a walk and also scoring four of the team's six runs.

"I can't say enough about this kid," Borba said. "I have to believe he's one of the best uncommitted players in the country, and how nobody wants a guy like this on their team yet is pretty surprising—because I wish he could play for me for another four years. He just does everything you want. And he comes up big in the biggest times."

As a program, Orange Lutheran seems to come up in those clutch moments. They have in each of the past three years. And until something changes, they'll continue to be the favorites on one of the biggest stages in high school baseball.

"You walk (into) USA Baseball's National Training Complex) on the walk of champions," Borba said, referring to the path to the fields that highlights each of the previous NHSI victors. "And to see Orange Lutheran, Orange Lutheran and to think next year it's going to have three of them—it's pretty awesome.

"You get the chills every time you walk into this place as it is, and then you see your name up there and everyone is going to see that as long as this tournament is going on. It's pretty cool."

Bobby Witt Jr. Does It All

BY CARLOS COLLAZO

Back before he even got a chance to play high school baseball, Bobby Witt Jr. put high expectations on himself. Around the time he was 10 years old, he remembers wanting to win a Texas state championship, wanting to get drafted, wanting to follow in his father's footsteps and play pro ball, and some-day, reach the majors.

"I just knew that this is what I wanted to do," Witt Jr. said. "And it was going to take a lot of steps and a lot of hard work. I just kind of instilled that in my brain, and ever since then it has always been just a grind."

Steadily, the grind has been paying off. Witt has been checking off the boxes he laid out for himself as a preteen.

This spring, in the Texas 5A state championship Witt and his Colleyville (Texas) Heritage High teammates were determined to end their season on a high note after three years of falling short.

"It hit home for me (that this was our last shot)," Witt said. "It made me want to work more and work harder—try to get to the best spot at the end, just getting called the state champions. I've always put that in the back of my mind. Whenever I'm working out or hitting or whatever, just have that in the back of my head."

Colleyville beat Mansfield Legacy High in the quarterfinals before sweeping Amarillo in a regional semifinal rematch. Witt sparked the offense with a 2-for-5 game including a home run, two runs and four RBIs in the first game against Amarillo. Over the team's final six games, he went 5-for-17 with a home run, a triple, six walks, six runs and six RBIs en route to a 5A state championship against Georgetown High.

"It's mind-boggling what he's able to do," Colleyville coach Alan McDougal said. "And to be honest, it amazed me that some people continued to pitch to him—but they did."

Witt led the team with a .500 average while hitting 15 home runs, 15 doubles, eight triples and 19 stolen bases. He also pitched in 11 games, recorded five saves and posted a 1.35 ERA with 21 strikeouts in 10.1 innings.

He did all of that with intense scrutiny every game. The Royals—who wound up selecting

PLAYER OF THE YEAR

PREVIOUS WINNERS

1992: Preston Wilson, OF/RHP, Bamberg-Ehrhardt (S.C.) HS
1993: Trot Nixon, OF/LHP, New Hanover HS, Wilmington, N.C.
1994: Doug Million, LHP, Sarasota (Fla.) HS
1995: Ben Davis, C, Malvern (Pa.) Prep
1996: Matt White, RHP, Waynesboro Area (Pa.) HS
1997: Darnell McDonald, OF, Cherry Creek HS, Englewood, Colo.
1998: Drew Henson, 3B/RHP, Brighton (Mich.) HS
1999: Josh Hamilton, OF/LHP, Athens Drive HS, Raleigh, N.C.
2000: Matt Harrington, RHP, Palmdale (Calif.) HS
2001: Joe Mauer, C, Cretin-Derham Hall HS, St. Paul, Minn.
2002: Scott Kazmir, LHP, Cypress Falls HS, Houston
2003: Jeff Allison, RHP, Veterans Memorial HS, Peabody, Mass.
2004: Homer Bailey, RHP, LaGrange (Texas) HS
2005: Justin Upton, SS, Great Bridge HS, Chesapeake, Va.
2006: Adrian Cardenas, SS/2B, Mons. Pace HS, Opa Locka, Fla.
2007: Mike Moustakas, SS, Chatsworth (Calif.) HS
2008: Ethan Martin, RHP/3B, Stephens County HS, Toccoa, Ga.
2009: Bryce Harper, C, Las Vegas HS
2010: Kaleb Cowart, RHP/3B, Cook HS, Adel, Ga.
2011: Dylan Bundy, RHP, Owasso (Okla.) HS
2012: Byron Buxton, OF, Appling County HS, Baxley, Ga.
2013: Clint Frazier, OF, Loganville (Ga.) HS
2014: Alex Jackson, OF, Rancho Bernardo (Calif.) HS
2015: Kyle Tucker, OF, Plant HS, Tampa
2016: Mickey Moniak, OF, La Costa Canyon HS, Carlsbad, Calif.
2017: MacKenzie Gore, LHP, Whiteville (N.C.) HS
2018: Cole Winn, RHP, Orange (Calif.) Lutheran HS

Witt with the No. 2 overall pick of the draft— had scouts bearing down on him for every inning he played and every swing he took in the batter's box.

"It has been kind of surreal watching him go through this whole process," McDougal said. "Especially with the draft being such a big deal, as far as talent evaluators coming in . . .But he is an extraordinary kid with even more talent."

Witt won't just be leaving behind a state championship and a pristine résumé, but a legacy to guide future Colleyville players. He modeled not just how to be a great player, but how to be a better teammate.

"(I'm still) kind of taking it all in," Witt said. "But obviously I want to keep getting better day in and day out. Kind of like how Mike Trout is. He's the best in baseball right now, and he's getting better each and every year. That's what I want to do.

"No matter what step it is in pro ball, try to get better and better and eventually—hope-fully—one day make it up to the big leagues and just play."

2019 HIGH SCHOOL ALL-AMERICA TEAM

CJ Abrams

BILL MITCHELL

Brett Baty

BILL MITCHELL

FIRST TEAM

Pos.	Player, School	YR.	AVG	AB	R	H	2B	3B	HR	RBI	SB	Drafted
C	Ethan Hearn, Mobile (Ala.) Christian HS	Sr.	.482	83	31	40	11	2	11	42	—	Cubs (6)
INF	Brett Baty, Lake Travis HS, Austin	Sr.	.602	98	63	59	6	3	19	50	11	Mets (1)
INF	Bobby Witt Jr., Colleyville (Texas) Heritage HS	Sr.	.482	137	65	66	15	9	15	55	19	Royals (1)
INF	CJ Abrams, Blessed Trinity HS, Roswell, Ga.	Sr.	.410	134	45	55	17	5	3	27	33	Padres (1)
INF	Keoni Cavaco, Eastlake HS, Chula Vista, Calif.	Sr.	.429	84	32	36	13	0	8	21	—	Twins (1)
OF	Riley Greene, HagertyHS, Oviedo, Fla.	Sr.	.422	83	38	35	11	3	8	27	13	Tigers (1)
OF	Corbin Carroll, Lakeside HS, Seattle	Sr.	.540	63	34	38	5	5	9	26	11	D-backs (1)
OF	Hudson Head, Churchill HS, San Antonio	Sr.	.615	91	48	56	12	6	13	54	34	Padres (3)
DH	Gunnar Henderson, Morgan Academy, Selma, Ala.	Sr.	.554	101	69	56	17	9	11	75	31	Orioles (2)

Pos.	Player, School	YR.	W	L	ERA	IP	H	R	ER	BB	SO	Drafted
P	Matthew Allan, Seminole HS, Sanford, Fla.	Sr.	8	2	1.21	63	27	17	11	18	118	Mets (3)
P	Daniel Espino, Ga. Premier Academy, Statesboro, Ga.	Sr.	9	0	0.32	44	10	2	2	9	109	Indians (1)
P	Jack Leiter, Delbarton HS, Morristown, N.J.	Sr.	8	0	0.72	59	27	14	6	23	95	Yankees (20)
P	Brennan Malone, IMG Academy, Bradenton, Fla.	Sr.	11	0	0.27	51	23	6	2	14	69	D-backs (1)
P	Quinn Priester, Cary-Grove HS, Cary, Ill.	Sr.	8	2	1.16	60	32	16	10	14	91	Pirates (1)

SECOND TEAM

Pos.	Player, School	YR.	AVG	AB	R	H	2B	3B	HR	RBI	SB	Drafted
C	Jonathan French, Parkview HS, Lilburn, Ga.	Sr.	.472	106	44	50	12	4	13	61	0	Indians (30)
INF	Cade Doughty, Denham Springs (La.) HS	Sr.	.495	95	43	47	11	3	6	25	15	Tigers (39)
INF	Anthony Volpe, Delbarton HS, Morristown, N.J.	Sr.	.477	88	42	42	5	7	8	36	8	Yankees (30)
INF	Nasim Nunez, Collins Hill HS, Suwanee, Ga.	Sr.	.352	88	36	31	11	2	1	14	31	Marlins (2)
INF	Tyler Callihan, Providence HS, Jacksonville	Sr.	.447	94	42	42	6	1	12	36	11	Reds (3)
OF	Maurice Hampton, Memphis University HS	Sr.	.440	118	51	52	11	0	10	24	40	Padres (23)
OF	Sammy Siani, Penn Charter HS, Philadelphia	Sr.	.457	—	—	—	8	9	6	25	16	Pirates (1s)
OF	James Beard, Loyd Star HS, Brookhaven, Miss.	Sr.	.429	70	46	30	8	1	10	30	26	White Sox (4)
DH	Joshua Mears, Federal Way (Wash.) HS	Sr.	.500	60	26	30	6	1	10	24	15	Padres (2)

Pos.	Player, School	YR.	W	L	ERA	IP	H	R	ER	BB	SO	Drafted
P	Blake Walston, New Hanover HS, Wilmington, N.C.	Sr.	13	0	0.46	75	31	5	5	21	137	D-backs (1)
P	JJ Goss, Cypress Ranch HS, Houston	Sr.	11	2	0.64	87	31	10	8	28	147	Rays (1s)
P	Jacob Meador, Centennial HS, Burleson, Texas	Sr.	10	1	0.63	77	24	9	7	23	162	Mariners (31)
P	Josh Wolf, St. Thomas HS, Houston	Sr.	8	2	1.52	69	33	17	15	21	126	Mets (2)
P	Jared Kelley, Refugio (Texas) HS	Jr.	11	0	0.22	65	12	4	2	24	144	Class of 2020

DRAFT

As Expected, Orioles Take Rutschman No. 1

BY CARLOS COLLAZO

There were rumors, rumors and more rumors leading up to the draft that the Orioles were considering someone other than Oregon State catcher Adley Rutschman with the No. 1 overall pick.

Like 2018 when there were similar rumblings about the Tigers taking someone not named Casey Mize (the consensus top talent) with the first pick, all of those rumors proved to be just noise. The Orioles did what teams had been expecting the entire spring and they took the consensus top talent in the class.

"We spent as much time as possible analyzing every angle of this and we landed at Rutschman," Orioles general manager Mike Elias said. "We're thrilled with the decision, but it's not a decision we came to easily."

After that, the top 10 went largely as expected, with Baseball America nailing nine of the first 10 picks in its final mock draft. Kansas City had long been thought to covet prep shortstop Bobby Witt Jr., and the White Sox continued their recent college-bat trend with California first baseman Andrew Vaughn—getting the top three ranked players off the board in the same order they appeared in the BA 500.

The wire-to-wire top player in the class, Adley Rutschman went No. 1 overall.

BILL MITCHELL

"(Witt) went out and earned this spot in the draft based on how he performed," Royals general manager Dayton Moore said. "We had a scout, sometimes several, at all his games. We saw every inning he played this season. We saw him in

FIRST-ROUND BONUS PROGRESSION

After seeing first-round bonuses fall in 2018 following three successive increases from 2015-2017, first-round bonuses dipped in 2018 before seeing a slight bump in the 2019 draft, with first-round selections averaging $3,791,729. First-round picks during the 2010s averaged $2,970,223. During the 2000s, first-round picks averaged $2,080,070; during the 1990s, first-round picks averaged $913,865; during the 1980s, first-round picks averaged $110,928; during the 1970s, first-round picks averaged $47,202; and during the 1960s, first-round picks averaged $43,440.

After the first draft in 1965, first-round bonuses rose by an average of just 0.6 percent annually for the rest of the 1960s and 5.2 percent per year in the 1970s. Bonus inflation picked up in the 1980s, averaging 10.2 percent annually, and soared to 26.9 percent per year in the 1990s.

Below are the annual averages for first-round bonuses since the draft started in 1965. The 1996 total does not include four players who became free agents through a loophole in the draft rules.

Year	Average	Change	Year	Average	Change	Year	Average	Change	Year	Average	Change
1965	$42,516	—	1979	$68,094	0.20%	1993	$613,037	27.20%	2007	$2,098,083	8.50%
1966	$44,430	4.50%	1980	$74,025	8.70%	1994	$790,357	28.90%	2008	$2,458,714	17.20%
1967	$42,898	-3.40%	1981	$78,573	6.10%	1995	$918,019	16.10%	2009	$2,434,800	-1.00%
1968	$43,850	2.20%	1982	$82,615	5.10%	1996*	$944,404	2.90%	2010	$2,220,966	-8.80%
1969	$43,504	-0.80%	1983	$87,236	5.60%	1997	$1,325,536	40.40%	2011	$2,653,375	19.50%
1970	$45,230	3.90%	1984	$105,391	20.80%	1998	$1,637,667	23.10%	2012	$2,475,167	-6.70%
1971	$45,197	-0.10%	1985	$118,115	12.10%	1999	$1,809,767	10.50%	2013	$2,641,538	6.70%
1972	$44,952	-0.50%	1986	$116,300	-1.60%	2000	$1,872,586	3.50%	2014	$2,612,109	-1.10%
1973	$48,832	8.60%	1987	$128,480	10.50%	2001	$2,154,280	15.00%	2015	$2,774,945	6.23%
1974	$53,333	9.20%	1988	$142,540	10.90%	2002	$2,106,793	-2.20%	2016	$2,897,557	4.42%
1975	$49.33	-7.50%	1989	$176,008	23.50%	2003	$1,765,667	-16.20%	2017	$3,880,723	25.4%
1976	$49,631	0.60%	1990	$252,577	43.50%	2004	$1,958,448	10.90%	2018	$3,754,123	-3.37%
1977	$48,813	-1.60%	1991	$365,396	44.70%	2005	$2,018,000	3.00%	2019	$3,791,729	1.01%
1978	$67,892	39.10%	1992	$481,893	31.90%	2006	$1,933,333	-4.20%			

preseason, workouts . . . It was an easy, natural decision for us."

J.J. Bleday going to the Marlins, Riley Greene going to the Tigers, C.J. Abrams going to the Padres and Nick Lodolo going to the Reds were all somewhat expected, and they were the exact names that had been rumored most heavily to each team in the weeks leading up to the draft.

There were less obvious signs about what Texas was looking to do, and No. 8 was the pick where many sources expected to draft to take a turn. But there was no Kyler Murray scenario in the 2019 draft, where a top-10 team took a player significantly down the board. The Rangers were linked with Texas Tech third baseman Jung, the Braves were tied to Baylor catcher Shea Langeliers and the Giants were linked to Arizona State outfielder Hunter Bishop.

With those 10 players off the board, nine of the top 10 ranked players on the BA 500, plus Jung (ranked No. 17), came off the board with the top 10 picks.

It was as close to chalk as a draft could really get.

A New Low For Pitching

While Lodolo went off the board where we were expecting, the 2019 class still became the first June draft without a pitcher—high school or college—coming off the board as one of the first six selections.

Prior to 2019, the lowest the first pitcher in the draft was selected was in 2005, when the Blue Jays took Cal State Fullerton lefthander Ricky Romero with the sixth pick of the draft.

BA wondered throughout the spring if teams would be able to resist simply pushing an arm up the board, but for the most part the industry took the top college pitchers in line with—or later than—we perceived their talent to fit.

Lodolo was the No. 8-ranked prospect and went to the Reds at No. 7, West Virginia righthander Alek Manoah was ranked No. 13 and went with the 11th pick to the Blue Jays. Kentucky lefthander Zack Thompson was ranked No. 11 and went No. 19 to the Cardinals, while Elon righthander George Kirby (ranked No. 20) went with the 20th pick to the Mariners. San Jacinto (Texas) JC righthander Jackson Rutledge went 17th to the Nationals and was ranked as the 14th-best prospect in the country.

"I think in any class I could be a top pitcher," said Lodolo, whose decision to not sign out of high school three years ago with the Pirates (pick No. 41) paid off in a big way. "I believe in myself and my stuff . . . I was pretty much set on

BONUS SPENDING BY TEAM

Teams combined to spend $316.5 million on draft bonuses in 2019, which sets a new record for draft spending a year after the 2018 draft ($294.6 million) saw teams blow away the 2016 record ($267.4 million). Spending continues to go up as MLB revenues and bonus slot values increase year after year.

The CBA that went into effect in 2012 curtailed spending by instituting harsh penalties for teams that exceeded their bonus pools by more than five percent. It also ended the practice of awarding major league contracts to draftees. But as revenues within the game have increased, so too have the bonus pools MLB allocates to teams for the first 10 rounds. No team has yet been willing to exceed the five percent mark.

The Diamondbacks easily spent more than any other club in 2019, thanks to owning seven Day 1 picks. The team had two first round picks thanks to not signing SS Matt McLain with 25th pick in 2018, and were given picks No. 32 and 33 at the end of the first round after LHP Patrick Corbin and OF AJ Pollock signed with other teams in free agency for more than $50 million. They also received a supplemental second round pick (No. 74) as one of the smallest markets in baseball and traded for the Cardinals supplemental second round pick (No. 75) in the Paul Goldschmidt trade.

TEAM	2019	2018	2017
D-backs	$17,045,500	$5,769,400	$10,330,300
Orioles	$15,168,600	$10,433,500	$6,404,300
Marlins	$14,832,700	$10,415,200	$9,375,000
Royals	$14,452,200	$14,768,200	$8,369,000
Braves	$14,338,000	$5,815,000	$10,372,100
White Sox	$13,633,200	$12,284,400	$7,957,000
Padres	$13,010,900	$12,565,515	$12,354,700
Rangers	$12,858,300	$9,150,500	$7,893,200
Pirates	$12,111,400	$10,402,600	$10,418,300
Tigers	$11,980,800	$14,784,100	$6,837,300
Rays	$11,685,800	$13,786,100	$10,912,800
Reds	$11,273,400	12,952,000	$13,665,300
Twins	$10,892,800	$6,876,700	$14,090,300
Blue Jays	$10,677,000	$9,980,300	$8,642,500
Dodgers	$10,539,300	$5,139,540	$6,048,000
Giants	$10,384,500	$13,935,000	$6,456,400
Angels	$9,751,300	$8,760,000	$8,251,000
Mets	$9,497,000	$11,017,238	$6,064,500
Yankees	$9,327,300	$8,148,400	$6,937,800
Mariners	$8,927,500	$8,655,200	$6,732,800
Phillies	$8,779,800	$11,342,900	$8,933,400
Cardinals	$8,205,000	$9,534,100	$2,248,100
Rockies	$8,073,300	$8,549,000	$4,477,600
Indians	$8,010,505	$11,222,459	$3,828,870
Nationals	$7,683,580	$6,908,000	$5,533,800
Cubs	$6,987,900	$9,218,950	$7,655,100
Brewers	$6,908,200	$7,747,400	$10,968,900
Athletics	$6,696,900	$10,888,200	$11,950,600
Astros	$6,462,099	$6,440,800	$8,913,300
Red Sox	$6,369,200	$7,252,900	$5,927,000
Total	**$316,563,984**	**$294,653,602**	**$248,549,270**
Average	**$10,552,133**	**$9,821,787**	**$8,284,976**

(school) to begin with. I knew that if I signed out of high school, I was not going to go back to do four years of education, and education was really important to me and my family."

Of the 34 first-round picks, just 12 were pitchers, making the first round just as hitter heavy as expected, given the strength of the class.

The Prep Arms Who Slid

Historically, teams are skeptical of high school

pitchers due to a scary track record. The 2019 draft was similar to the 2018 class, in which a handful of first-round prep pitching talents were still available after Day 1.

In 2018, Vanderbilt commit Kumar Rocker was the highest rated player still available after Day 1, and while he was drafted late on Day 3, he wound up on campus. This year, that player seemed to be Matthew Allan, who was the top-rated high school pitcher of the class and was committed to Florida.

With signing-bonus demands that were rumored to be around $4 million, it seemed unlikely that a team would be able to sign him on the second or third day of the draft, and it appeared that Florida would benefit by seeing him get to campus. The Mets thought otherwise and grabbed Allan with their first selection on Day 2 and then dedicated the entirety of their draft to being able to sign him by going after college seniors with every pick during rounds 4-10. It paid off, and the team signed Allan to a $2.5 million bonus. The team spent $62,000 combined on their seven college picks from rounds 4-10, compared to $8.55 million for their first

Prep SS Bobby Witt Jr. was heavily linked to the Royals and went to them at No. 2

HIGHEST BONUSES EVER

Adley Rutschman set the new all-time draft bonus record, topping Gerrit Cole's 2011 bonus by $100,000, despite signing for more than $300,000 under slot. Each of the top five draft picks joined the list of highest bonuses ever, with Bobby Witt Jr., Andrew Vaughn, JJ Bleday and Riley Greene joining Rutschman.

Player, Pos.	Team, Year (Pick)	Bonus
Adley Rutschman, C	Orioles, 2019 (No. 1)	$8,100,000
Gerrit Cole, RHP	Pirates, 2011 (No. 1)	$8,000,000
Bobby Witt Jr., SS	Royals, 2019 (No. 2)	$7,787,400
Stephen Strasburg, RHP	Nationals, 2009 (No. 1)	*$7,500,000
Bubba Starling, OF	Royals, 2011 (No. 5)	+$7,500,000
Casey Mize, RHP	Tigers, 2018 (No. 1)	$7,500,000
Hunter Greene, RHP/SS	Reds, 2017 (No. 2)	$7,230,000
Andrew Vaughn, 1B	White Sox, 2019 (No. 3)	$7,221,200
Joey Bart, C	Giants, 2018 (No. 2)	$7,025,000
Brendan McKay, 1B/LHP	Rays, 2017 (No. 4)	$7,005,000
Kyle Wright, RHP	Braves, 2017 (No. 5)	$7,000,000
Royce Lewis, SS	Twins, 2017 (No. 1)	$6,725,000
Kris Bryant, 3B	Cubs, 2013 (No. 2)	$6,708,400
MacKenzie Gore, LHP	Padres, 2017 (No. 3)	$6,700,000
JJ Bleday, OF	Marlins, 2019 (No. 4)	$6,670,000
Carlos Rodon, LHP	White Sox, 2014 (No. 3)	$6,582,000
Jameson Taillon, RHP	Pirates, 2010 (No. 2)	$6,500,000
Dansby Swanson, SS	D-backs, 2015 (No. 1)	$6,500,000
Nick Madrigal, SS	White Sox, 2018 (No. 4)	$6,411,000
Danny Hultzen, LHP	Marinters, 2011 (No. 2)	*$6,350,000
Mark Appel, RHP	Astros, 2013 (No. 1)	$6,350,000
Donavan Tate, OF	Padres, 2009 (No. 3)	+$6,250,000
Bryce Harper, OF	Nationals, 2010 (No. 1)	*$6,250,000
Buster Posey, C	Giants, 2008 (No. 5)	$6,200,000
Nick Senzel, 3B	Reds, 2016 (No. 2)	$6,200,000
Tim Beckham, SS	Rays, 2008 (No. 1)	+$6,150,000
Riley Greene, OF	Tigers, 2019 (No. 5)	$6,180,700
Justin Upton, SS	D-backs, 2005 (No. 1)	+$6,100,000

*Part of major league contract. +Bonus spread over multiple years under MLB two-sport provisions

three high school players—3B Brett Baty (1), RHP Josh Wolf (2) and Allan.

Similarly, Vanderbilt commit Jack Leiter was rumored to have a high price tag, and didn't get selected until the Yankees took him in the 20th round (he didn't sign), though that was more expected than Allan's absence from Day 1. Along with the two high-upside righthanders, the top lefthander in the class, Hunter Barco (also a Florida commit) was another notable prep pitcher who didn't have his name called.

While Florida didn't wind up getting both Allan and Barco to campus, simply getting one was a huge addition for the Gators and speaks to the fact that you can count on some high school pitchers to slide on draft day.

In 2018, Rocker, Cole Wilcox and Adam Kloffenstein were the notable Day 1 omissions, and while Kloffenstein did wind up getting an overslot bonus in the third round, both Rocker and Wilcox ended up in college at Vanderbilt and Georgia, respectively.

Texas Talent

One of the strengths of the 2019 class was expected to be the enormous amount of talent out of Texas. BA wrote earlier in the spring about how the chance for the Lone Star State to produce more first-round picks than ever before this century. With seven players drafted out of the state before the start of the supplemental first round, the 2019 Texas class is likely to be seen as one of the strongest ever.

Prior to 2019, the most first-round picks Texas has produced was six, back in 2006. During each of the last three years, just two first-round players came out of the state.

Two of the most exciting high school bats came from Texas in the first round in 2019, in

NO. 1 OVERALL PICKS

Year Team: Player, Pos., School	Bonus
1965 Athletics: Rick Monday, OF, Arizona State	$100,000
1966 Mets: Steve Chilcott, C, Antelope Valley HS, Lancaster, Calif.	$75,000
1967 Yankees: Ron Blomberg, 1B, Druid Hills HS, Atlanta	$65,000
1968 Mets: Tim Foli, SS, Notre Dame HS, Sherman Oaks, Calif.	$74,000
1969 Senators: Jeff Burroughs, OF, Centennial HS, Long Beach	$88,000
1970 Padres: Mike Ivie, C, Walker HS, Atlanta	$75,000
1971 White Sox: Danny Goodwin, C, Peoria (Ill.) HS	Did Not Sign
1972 Padres: Dave Roberts, 3B, Oregon	$70,000
1973 Rangers: David Clyde, LHP, Westchester HS, Texas	*$65,000
1974 Padres: Bill Almon, SS, Brown	*$90,000
1975 Angels: Danny Goodwin, C, Southern	*$125,000
1976 Astros: Floyd Bannister, LHP, Arizona State	$100,000
1977 White Sox: Harold Baines, OF, St. Michaels (Md.) HS	$32,000
1978 Braves: Bob Horner, 3B, Arizona State	*$162,000
1979 Mariners: Al Chambers, 1B, Harris HS, Harrisburg, Pa.	$60,000
1980 Mets: Darryl Strawberry, OF, Crenshaw HS, Los Angeles	$152,500
1981 Mariners: Mike Moore, RHP, Oral Roberts	$100,000
1982 Cubs: Shawon Dunston, SS, Jefferson HS, New York	$135,000
1983 Twins: Tim Belcher, RHP, Mount Vernon Nazarene (Ohio)	Did Not Sign
1984 Mets: Shawn Abner, OF, Mechanicsburg (Pa.) HS	$150,500
1985 Brewers: B.J. Surhoff, C, North Carolina	$150,000
1986 Pirates: Jeff King, 3B, Arkansas	$180,000
1987 Mariners: Ken Griffey Jr., OF, Moeller HS, Cincinnati	$160,000
1988 Padres: Andy Benes, RHP, Evansville	$235,000
1989 Orioles: Ben McDonald, RHP, Louisiana State	*$350,000
1990 Braves: Chipper Jones, SS, The Bolles School, Jacksonville	$275,000
1991 Yankees: Brien Taylor, LHP, East Carteret HS, Beaufort, N.C.	$1,550,000
1992 Astros: Phil Nevin, 3B, Cal State Fullerton	$700,000
1993 Mariners: Alex Rodriguez, SS, Westminster Christian HS, Miami	*$1,000,000
1994 Mets: Paul Wilson, RHP, Florida State	$1,550,000
1995 Angels: Darin Erstad, OF, Nebraska	$1,575,000
1996 Pirates: Kris Benson, RHP, Clemson	$2,000,000
1997 Tigers: Matt Anderson, RHP, Tigers	$2,505,000
1998 Phillies: Pat Burrell, 3B, Miami	*$3,150,000
1999 Devil Rays: Josh Hamilton, OF, Athens Drive HS, Raleigh	$3,960,000
2000 Marlins: Adrian Gonzalez, 1B, Eastlake HS, Chula Vista, Calif.	$3,000,000
2001 Twins: Joe Mauer, C, Cretin-Derham Hall, St. Paul	$5,150,000
2002 Pirates: Bryan Bullington, RHP, Ball State	$4,000,000
2003 Devil Rays: Delmon Young, OF, Camarillo (Calif.) HS	*$3,700,000
2004 Padres: Matt Bush, SS, Mission Bay HS, San Diego	$3,150,000
2005 D-backs: Justin Upton, SS, Great Bridge HS, Chesapeake, Va.	$6,100,000
2006 Royals: Luke Hochevar, RHP, Fort Worth (American Assoc.)	*$3,500,000
2007 Devil Rays: David Price, LHP, Vanderbilt	*$5,600,000
2008 Rays: Tim Beckham, SS, Griffin (Ga.) HS	$6,150,000
2009 Nationals: Stephen Strasburg, RHP, San Diego State	*$7,500,000
2010 Nationals: Bryce Harper, OF, JC of Southern Nevada	*$6,250,000
2011 Pirates: Gerrit Cole, RHP, UCLA	$8,000,000
2012 Astros: Carlos Correa, SS, Puerto Rico Baseball Acad., Gurabo, P.R.	$4,800,000
2013 Astros: Mark Appel, RHP, Stanford	$6,350,000
2014 Astros: Brady Aiken, LHP, Cathedral Catholic, San Diego	Did Not Sign
2015 D-backs: Dansby Swanson, SS, Vanderbilt	$6,500,000
2016 Phillies: Mickey Moniak, OF, La Costa Canyon HS, Carlsbad, Calif.	$6,100,000
2017 Twins: Royce Lewis, SS, JSerra Catholic HS, San Juan Capistrano, Calif.	$6,750,000
2018 Tigers: Casey Mize, RHP, Auburn	$7,500,000
2019 Orioles: Adley Rutschman, C, Oregon State	$8,100,000

Part of major league contract.

Witt Jr., Baty, as well as the first pitcher off the board (Lodolo), the highest-rated and first-drafted junior college player (Rutledge) and three college hitters with extensive track records in Jung, Langeliers and Texas A&M shortstop Braden Shewmake, who went No. 21 to the Braves.

The Texas trend continued in the second round as well. While teams are proving reluctant to take prep arms in the first round, they were more than happy to take them in the second. Three Lone Star State prep pitchers were picked in the second and supplemental-second rounds (Matthew Thompson, Wolf and Jimmy Lewis) in addition to three college pitchers (Matt Canterino, Brandon Williamson and John Doxakis).

All together, Texas accounted for 16 Day 1 selections, with the runner-up (California) tallying just nine Day 1 picks and North Carolina coming in third with seven selections.

College Percentage Rises

The 2019 MLB draft reinforced that teams are prioritizing college players at a higher level than ever before.

Fifty-one of the 78 total selections on the first day of the 2019 draft—or roughly 65.4 percent of the pre-third round draft pool—came out of four-year college programs. That is the second-highest rate of four-year players selected in that portion of the draft. Only the 1981 draft (69.2 percent) is higher, and that was at a time when junior college players were selected in a separate January draft.

Teams have begun prioritizing college picks later in the draft as well. That trend is present throughout the top 10 rounds, as well as the entirety of Day 3.

Since the late 1990s there has been a steadily increasing trend of teams selecting more and more college players, and it has come at the expense of the high school and junior college prospects. That's true of drafted players overall, as well as players who are drafted and signed.

Since the 1981 draft, approximately two-thirds of all drafted players who have signed contracts have been products of four-year colleges and universities. High school players make up about 22 percent, and the remaining 11.4 percent consists of JuCo players.

In the last five drafts, the percentage of signed draftees coming out of four-year schools has ranged from 75.5 to 78.3 percent. The 2015 draft saw 715 college players sign contracts, the most of any draft from 1981 to 2018, despite that year's draft only having the fifth-most total signees in that same time frame.

There are a number of reasons for this trend. Multiple teams have told Baseball America that they are more prone to pass on high school pitchers at the top of the draft because of the recent struggles of that demographic.

Teams also have a much more robust data set for college players thanks to a deeper statistical resume and troves of analytical data from TrackMan, etc. The college ranks also provide depth that isn't possible to acquire with high school players. Both of those reasons can push teams to take more college players. The increase in college players taken in the first two rounds this year would seem to indicate there is something to this trend.

But there's another reason that is also speeding up the trend. The current draft system has created an environment that leads teams to sign college players instead of high school players. There's an obvious jump in the percentage of college players that occurs in 2012, which accounts for the current CBA in which teams aggressively take college seniors in rounds six through 10 in order to create more financial flexibility under the current slotting system.

Maybe more importantly for the trend lines, the 2012 draft was the first time when teams were unable to spend freely on Day 3. Under the previous draft systems, if the Reds wanted to give basketball player Amir Garrett $1 million to sign in the 22nd round or the Orioles wanted to hand Zach Davies $575,000 as a 26th rounder, they could. And they did. Garrett would have been an extremely risky early-round pick—there was no guarantee he would sign and he hadn't even played competitive baseball during his senior year of high school. But the Reds were able to spend money, while also spending very little draft capital (only a 22nd-round pick in 2011).

It would be nearly impossible to sign Garrett in a similar situation now, as finding $1 million or more to spend in the late rounds of the draft requires saving significant money on bonuses in the top 10 rounds. In 2011, there were three high school players who received $1 million or larger bonuses after the 10th round. There have been

THE BONUS RECORD

Rick Monday, the No. 1 overall pick in baseball's first draft in 1965, signed with the Athletics for $100,000—a figure that no draftee bettered for a decade. The record has been broken many times since, including in 2019, when Adley Rutschman signed with the Orioles as the No. 1 overall pick for $8,100,000. Rutschman topped the previous record by Gerrit Cole ($8 million) in 2011, which stood for eight years before being topped.

The longest bonus record stretch dates back to Todd Demeter, whose $208,000 bonus in 1979 held the mark for nine years until 1988 when Andy Benes topped him with a $235,000 bonus.

The list below represents only cash bonuses and doesn't include guaranteed money from major league deals, college scholarship plans or incentives. It also considers only players who signed with the clubs that drafted them and doesn't include draft picks who signed after being granted free agency.

Year	Player, Pos. , Club (Round)	Bonus
1965	Rick Monday, OF, Athletics (1)	$100,000
1975	Danny Goodwin, C, Angels (1)	$125,000
1978	Kirk Gibson, OF, Tigers (1)	$150,000
	*Bob Horner, 3B, Braves (1)	$162,000
1979	Todd Demeter, 1B, Yankees (2)	$208,000
1988	Andy Benes, RHP, Padres (1)	$235,000
1989	Tyler Houston, C, Braves (1)	$241,500
	*Ben McDonald, RHP, Orioles (1)	$350,000
	*John Olerud, 1B, Blue Jays (3)	$575,000
1991	Mike Kelly, OF, Braves (1)	$575,000
	Brien Taylor, LHP, Yankees (1)	$1,550,000
1994	Paul Wilson, RHP, Mets (1)	$1,550,000
	Josh Booty, 3B, Marlins (1)	$1,600,000
1996	Kris Benson, RHP, Pirates (1)	$2,000,000
1997	Rick Ankiel, LHP, Cardinals (2)	$2,500,000
	Matt Anderson, RHP, Tigers (1)	$2,505,000
1998	*J.D. Drew, OF, Cardinals (1)	$3,000,000
	*Pat Burrell, 3B, Phillies (1)	$3,150,000
	Mark Mulder, LHP, Athletics (1)	$3,200,000
	Corey Patterson, OF, Cubs (1)	$3,700,000
1999	Josh Hamilton, OF, Devil Rays (1)	$3,960,000
2000	Joe Borchard, OF, White Sox (1)	$5,300,000
2005	Justin Upton, SS, D-backs (1)	$6,100,000
2008	Tim Beckham, SS, Rays (1)	$6,150,000
	Buster Posey, C, Giants (1)	$6,200,000
2009	Donavan Tate, OF, Padres (1)	$6,250,000
	*Stephen Strasburg, RHP, Nationals (1)	$7,500,000
2011	Gerrit Cole, RHP, Pirates (1)	$8,000,000
2019	Adley Rutschman, C, Orioles (1)	$8,100,000

*Part of major league contract.

just two in the past six drafts combined.

What has changed is teams are signing many more college players for less than $500,000. Many high school players with solid college options are hesitant to sign for less than that amount. That has led to a significant increase in the percentage of college draftees and college signees in the draft.

In the past, teams knew that while they would have to spend significant money to land a projectable high school player, in many cases the second wave of top high school players would fall late in the draft. Teams could spend money but little in terms of draft capital to land those players.

But under the current format, where spending more than $500,000 on any player taken after

BONUSES VS. PICK VALUES

The assigned slots for the 2019 draft increased by 3.9 percent from the 2018 slots, reflecting increases in MLB revenue. The first overall pick a year ago was valued at $8,096,300 compared to the Orioles' No. 1 pick in 2019, which was assigned a bonus value of $8,415,300. First overall pick Adley Rutschman signed under slot but still set the all-time bonus record at $8,100,000.

The top-50 bonuses added up to $162,749,200 compared to a slot value of $161,722,500 for those picks. That overage was largely thanks to supplemental first-round and second-round over-slot deals, as all but three first-round picks were either for exactly slot value or under-slot deals. By comparison, when MLB unilaterally determined slot recommendations in the last year of the previous Collective Bargaining Agreement (2011) but had no enforcement mechanism, the total of the first 50 bonuses ($120.5 million) dwarfed that of the top 50 slot values ($70 million).

Player, Pos., Team (Round/Overall Pick)	Bonus	Pick Value
1. Adley Rutschman, C, Oregon State (1st round/No. 1)	$8,100,000	$8,415,300
2. Bobby Witt Jr., SS, Colleyville (Texas) Heritage HS (1st round/No. 2)	$7,787,400	$7,789,900
3. Andrew Vaughn, 1B, California (1st round/No. 3)	$7,221,200	$7,221,200
4. JJ Bleday, OF, Vanderbilt (1st round/No. 4)	$6,670,000	$6,664,000
5. Riley Greene, OF, Hagerty HS, Oviedo, Fla. (1st round/No. 5)	$6,180,000	$6,180,700
6. Nick Lodolo, LHP, Texas Christian (1st round/No. 7)	$5,432,400	$5,432,400
7. CJ Abrams, SS, Blessed Trinity HS, Roswell, Ga. (1st round/No. 6)	$5,200,000	$5,742,900
8. Alek Manoah, RHP, West Virginia (1st round/No. 11)	$5,200,000	$5,742,900
9. Josh Jung, 3B, Texas Tech (1st round/No. 8)	$4,400,000	$5,176,900
10. Hunter Bishop, OF, Arizona State (1st round/No. 10)	$4,097,500	$4,739,900
11. Keoni Cavaco, SS, Eastlake HS, Chula Vista, Calif. (1st round/No. 13)	$4,050,000	$4,197,300
12. Shea Langeliers, C, Baylor (1st round/No. 9)	$3,997,500	$4,949,100
13. Brett Baty, 3B, Lake Travis HS, Austin (1st round/No. 12)	$3,900,000	$4,366,400
14. Bryson Stott, SS, Nevada-Las Vegas (1st round/No. 14)	$3,900,000	$4,036,800
15. Corbin Carroll, OF, Lakeside HS, Seattle (1st round/No. 16)	$3,745,500	$3,745,500
16. Jackson Rutledge, RHP, San Jacinto (Texas) JC (1st round/No. 17)	$3,450,500	$3,609,700
17. Quinn Priester, RHP, Cary-Grove HS, Cary, Ill. (1st round/No. 18)	$3,400,000	$3,481,300
18. Will Wilson, SS, North Carolina State (1st round/No. 15)	$3,397,500	$3,885,800
19. George Kirby, RHP, Elon (1st round/No. 20)	$3,242,900	$3,242,900
20. Braden Shewmake, SS, Texas A&M (1st round/No. 21)	$3,129,800	$3,132,300
21. Greg Jones, SS, UNC-Wilmington (1st round/No. 22)	$3,024,500	$3,027,000
22. Zack Thompson, LHP, Kentucky (1st round/No. 19)	$3,000,000	$3,359,000
23. Hudson Head, OF, Churchill HS, San Antonio (3rd round/No. 84)	$3,000,000	$721,900
24. Kody Hoese, 3B, Tulane (1st round/No. 25)	$2,740,300	$2,740,300
25. Anthony Volpe, SS, Delbarton HS, Morristown, N.J. (1st round/No. 30)	$2,740,300	$2,365,500
26. Michael Toglia, 1B, UCLA (1st round/No. 23)	$2,725,000	$2,365,500
27. Daniel Espino, RHP, Georgia Premier Academy, Statesboro, Ga. (1st round/No. 24)	$2,500,000	$2,831,300
28. Matthew Allan, RHP, Seminole HS, Sanford, Fla. (3rd round/No. 89)	$2,500,000	$667,900
29. Blake Walston, LHP, New Hanover HS, Wilmington, N.C. (1st round/No. 26)	$2,450,000	$2,653,400
30. Logan Davidson, SS, Clemson (1st round/No. 29)	$2,424,600	$2,424,600
31. Michael Busch, 2B, North Carolina (1st round/No. 31)	$2,312,000	$2,312,000
32. Gunnar Henderson, SS, Morgan Academy, Selma, Ala. (2nd round/No. 42)	$2,300,000	$1,771,100
33. Brady McConnell, SS, Florida (2nd round/No. 44)	$2,222,500	$1,689,500
34. Brennan Malone, RHP, IMG Academy, Bradenton, Fla. (1st round/No. 33)	$2,202,200	$2,202,200
35. Nasim Nunez, SS, Collins Hill HS, Suwannee, Ga. (2nd round/No. 46)	$2,200,000	$1,617,400
36. Sammy Siani, OF, Penn Charter HS, Philadelphia (supp. 1st/No. 37)	$2,150,000	$1,999,300
37. Josh Wolf, RHP, St. Thomas HS, Philadelphia (2nd round/No. 53)	$2,150,000	$1,370,400
38. Kameron Misner, OF, Missouri (supp. 1st/No. 35)	$2,115,000	$2,095,800
39. Matthew Thompson, RHP, Cypress Ranch HS, Houston (2nd round/No. 45)	$2,100,000	$1,650,200
40. JJ Goss, RHP, Cypress Ranch HS, Houston (supp. 1st/No. 36)	$2,042,900	$2,045,400
41. Ryan Jensen, RHP, Fresno State (1st round/No. 27)	$2,000,000	$2,570,100
42. Andrew Dalquist, RHP, Redondo Union HS, Redondo Beach, Calif. (3rd round/No. 81)	$2,000,000	$755,300
43. TJ Sikkema, LHP, Missouri (supp. 1st/No. 38)	$1,949,800	$1,952,300
44. Ethan Small, LHP, Mississippi State (1st round/No. 28)	$1,800,000	$2,493,900
45. Matt Wallner, OF, Southern Mississippi (supp. 1st/No. 39)	$1,800,000	$1,906,800
46. Rece Hinds, SS, IMG Academy, Bradenton, Fla. (2nd round/No. 49)	$1,797,500	$1,507,600
47. Korey Lee, C, California (1st round/No. 32)	$1,750,000	$2,257300
48. Seth Johnson, RHP, Campbell (supp. 1st/No. 40)	$1,722,500	$1,856,700
49. Davis Wendzel, 3B, Baylor (supp. 1st/No. 41)	$1,600,000	$1,813,500
50. Nick Quintana, 3B, Arizona (2nd round/No. 47)	$1,580,200	$1,580,200
Total	**$162,749,200**	**$161,722,500**

the middle of the fourth round means going above slot for that pick and taking money from elsewhere in the team's draft pool, teams generally have to spend both money and a relatively high draft pick to land a second-tier prep prospect.

Some of the current shift may result from teams taking a different approach than in past years, but the larger picture is that top high school players are generally looking to receive large signing bonuses out of high school to buy out their chances to play in college. Under the current system, it has become much more difficult to do so, leading to a stronger emphasis on drafting college players.

TOP 100 PICKS

Team, Player, Pos., School	Bonus
1. BAL, Adley Rutschman, C, Oregon State	$8,100,000
2. KC, Bobby Witt Jr., SS, Colleyville (Texas) Heritage HS	7,787,400
3. CWS, Andrew Vaughn, 1B, California	7,221,200
4. MIA, JJ Bleday, OF, Vanderbilt	6,670,000
5. DET, Riley Greene, OF, Hagerty HS, Oviedo, Fla.	6,180,700
6. SDP, CJ Abrams, SS, Blessed Trinity HS, Roswell, Ga.	5,200,000
7. CIN, Nick Lodolo, LHP, Texas Christian	5,432,400
8. TEX, Josh Jung, 3B, Texas Tech	4,400,000
9. ATL, Shea Langeliers, C, Baylor	3,997,500
10. SFG, Hunter Bishop, OF, Arizona State	4,097,500
11. TOR, Alek Manoah, RHP, West Virginia	4,547,500
12. NYM, Brett Baty, 3B, Lake Travis HS, Austin	3,900,000
13. MIN, Keoni Cavaco, SS, Eastlake HS, Chula Vista, Calif.	4,050,000
14. PHI, Bryson Stott, SS, Nevada-Las Vegas	3,900,000
15. LAA, Will Wilson, SS, North Carolina State	3,397,500
16. ARI, Corbin Carroll, OF, Lakeside HS, Seattle	3,745,500
17. WAS, Jackson Rutledge, RHP, San Jacinto (Texas) JC	3,450,000
18. PIT, Quinn Priester, RHP, Cary-Grove HS, Cary, Ill	3,400,000
19. STL, Zack Thompson, LHP, Kentucky	3,000,000
20. SEA, George Kirby, RHP, Elon	3,242,900
21. ATL, Braden Shewmake, SS, Texas A&M	3,129,800
22. TBR, Greg Jones, SS, UNC Wilmington	3,024,500
23. COL, Michael Toglia, 1B, UCLA	2,725,000
24. CLE, Daniel Espino, RHP, Georgia Premier Acad., Statesboro, Ga.	2,500,000
25. LAD, Kody Hoese, 3B, Tulane	2,740,300
26. ARI, Blake Walston, LHP, New Hanover HS, Wilmington, N.C.	2,450,000
27. CHC, Ryan Jensen, RHP, Fresno State	2,000,000
28. MIL, Ethan Small, LHP, Mississippi State	1,800,000
29. OAK, Logan Davidson, SS, Clemson	2,424,600
30. NYY, Anthony Volpe, SS, Delbarton HS, Morristown, N.J	2,740,300
31. LAD, Michael Busch, 2B, North Carolina	2,312,000
32. HOU, Korey Lee, C, California	1,750,000
33. ARI, Brennan Malone, RHP, IMG Acad., Bradenton, Fla.	2,202,200
34. ARI, Drey Jameson, RHP, Ball State	1,400,000
35. MIA, Kameron Misner, OF, Missouri	2,115,000
36. TBR, JJ Goss, RHP, Cypress Ranch HS, Houston	2,042,900
37. PIT, Sammy Siani, OF, Penn Charter HS, Philadelphia	2,150,000
38. NYY, TJ Sikkema, LHP, Missouri	1,949,800
39. MIN, Matt Wallner, OF, Southern Mississippi	1,800,000
40. TBR, Seth Johnson, RHP, Campbell	1,722,500
41. TEX, Davis Wendzel, 3B, Baylor	1,600,000
42. BAL, Gunnar Henderson, SS, Morgan Acad., Selma, Ala.	2,300,000
43. BOS, Cameron Cannon, SS, Arizona	1,300,000
44. KC, Brady McConnell, SS, Florida	2,222,500
45. CWS, Matthew Thompson, RHP, Cypress Ranch HS, Houston	2,100,000
46. MIA, Nasim Nunez, SS, Collins Hill HS, Suwanee, Ga	2,200,000
47. DET, Nick Quintana, 3B, Arizona	1,580,200
48. SDP, Joshua Mears, OF, Federal Way (Wash.) HS	1,000,000
49. CIN, Rece Hinds, SS, IMG Acad., Bradenton, Fla	1,797,500
50. TEX, Ryan Garcia, RHP, UCLA	1,469,900
51. SFG, Logan Wyatt, 1B, Louisville	997,500
52. TOR, Kendall Williams, RHP, IMG Acad., Bradenton, Fla	1,547,500
53. NYM, Josh Wolf, RHP, St. Thomas HS, Houston	2,150,000
54. MIN, Matt Canterino, RHP, Rice	1,100000
55. LAA, Kyren Paris, SS, Freedom HS, Oakley, Calif	1,400,000
56. ARI, Ryne Nelson, RHP, Oregon	1,100,000
57. PIT, Matt Gorski, OF, Indiana	1,000,000
58. STL, Trejyn Fletcher, OF, Deering HS, Portland, Maine	1,500,000
59. SEA, Brandon Williamson, LHP, Texas Christian	925,000
60. ATL, Beau Philip, SS, Oregon State	697,500
61. TBR, John Doxakis, LHP, Texas A&M	1,127,200
62. COL, Aaron Schunk, 3B, Georgia	1,102,700
63. CLE, Yordys Valdes, SS, McArthur HS, Hollywood, Fla	1,001,000
64. CHC, Chase Strumpf, 2B, UCLA	1,050,300
65. MIL, Antoine Kelly, LHP, Wabash Valley (Ill.) JC	1,025,100
66. OAK, Tyler Baum, RHP, North Carolina	900,000

After big uptick in power, Vanderbilt's JJ Bleday was taken No. 4 by the Marlins.

JOHN BYRUM/GETTY

Team, Player, Pos., School	Bonus
67. NYY, Josh Smith, 2B, Louisiana State	976,700
68. HOU, Grae Kessinger, SS, Mississippi	750,000
69. BOS, Matthew Lugo, SS, Beltran Baseball Acad., Florida, P.R	1,100,000
70. KC, Alec Marsh, RHP, Arizona State	904,300
71. BAL, Kyle Stowers, OF, Stanford	884,200
72. PIT, Jared Triolo, 3B, Houston	868,200
73. SDP, Logan Driscoll, C, George Mason	600,000
74. ARI, Tommy Henry, LHP, Michigan	750,000
75. ARI, Dominic Fletcher, OF, Arkansas	700,000
76. SEA, Isaiah Campbell, RHP, Arkansas	850,000
77. COL, Karl Kauffmann, RHP, Michigan	805,600
78. LAD, Jimmy Lewis, RHP, Lake Travis HS, Austin	1,097,500
79. BAL, Zach Watson, OF, Louisiana State	780,400
80. KC, Grant Gambrell, RHP, Oregon State	647,500
81. CWS, Andrew Dalquist, RHP, Redondo Union HS, Redondo Beach, Ca	2,000,000
82. MIA, Peyton Burdick, OF, Wright State	397,500
83. DET, Andre Lipcius, 3B, Tennessee	733,100
84. SDP, Hudson Head, OF, Churchill HS, San Antonio	3,000,000
85. CIN, Tyler Callihan, 2B, Providence HS, Jacksonville	1,497,500
86. TEX, Justin Slaten, RHP, New Mexico	575,000
87. SFG, Grant McCray, OF, Lakewood Ranch HS, Bradenton, Fla	697,500
88. TOR, Dasan Brown, OF, Abbey Park HS, Oakville, Ont	797,500
89. NYM, Matt Allan, RHP, Seminole HS, Sanford, Fla.	2,500,000
90. MIN, Spencer Steer, OF, Oregon	575000
91. PHI, Jamari Baylor, SS, Benedictine HS, Richmond	675,000
92. LAA, Jack Kochanowicz, RHP, Harriton HS, Rosemont, Pa.	1,247,500
93. ARI, Tristin English, 1B, Georgia Tech	500,000
94. WAS, Drew Mendoza, 3B, Florida State	800,000
95. PIT, Matt Fraizer, OF, Arizona	525,000
96. STL, Tony Locey, RHP, Georgia	604,800
97. SEA, Levi Stoudt, RHP, Lehigh	339,000
98. ATL, Michael Harris, LHP/OF, Stockbridge (Ga.) HS	547,500
99. TBR, Shane Sasaki, OF, Iolani HS, Honolulu	472,500
100. COL, Jacob Wallace, RHP, Connecticut	581,600

Order Of Selection In Parentheses | Players Signed In Bold

DRAFT

ARIZONA DIAMONDBACKS (16)

1. Corbin Carroll, OF, Lakeside HS, Seattle
1. Blake Walston, LHP, New Hanover HS, Wilmington, N.C.
1. Brennan Malone, RHP, IMG Academy, Bradenton, Fla.
1. Drey Jameson, RHP, Ball State
2. Ryne Nelson, RHP, Oregon
2s. Tommy Henry, LHP, Michigan
2s. Dominic Fletcher, OF, Arkansas
3. Tristin English, 1B, Georgia Tech
4. Glenallen Hill, SS, Baylor
5. Conor Grammes, RHP, Xavier
6. Andrew Saalfrank, LHP, Indiana
7. Spencer Brickhouse, 1B, East Carolina
8. Dominic Canzone, OF, Ohio State
9. Bobby Ay, RHP, Cal Poly
10. Oscar Santos, C, PJ Educational HS, Carolina, P.R.
11. Nick Snyder, LHP, West Virginia
12. Avery Short, LHP, Southport HS, Indianapolis
13. Cam Coursey, 2B, Georgia Gwinnett
14. Lyle Lin, C, Arizona State
15. Austin Pope, RHP, Fairfield
16. Brock Jones, LHP, W.F. West HS, Chehalis, Wash.
17. Nick Grande, SS, Stony Brook
18. Ricky Martinez, SS, Tennessee
19 Noah Soles, OF, Ledford Senior HS, Thomasville, N.C.
20. Jared Liebelt, RHP, Mississippi State
21. Dustin Lacaze, RHP, Texas A&M-Corpus Christi
22. Jonathan Stroman, RHP, Central Arizona JC
23. Dane Acker, RHP, San Jacinto (Texas) JC
24. Dylan Eskew, RHP, Sickles HS, Tampa
25. Carson Maxwell, 3B, McNeese State
26. Seth Tomczak, RHP, Argonaut HS, Jackson, Calif.
27. Josh McMinn, RHP, Oral Roberts
28. Denson Hull, LHP, Creighton
29. Tyler Poulin, RHP, Quinnipiac
30. Will Childers, RHP, Lakeside HS, Atlanta
31. Jerrion Ealy, OF, Jackson (Miss.) Prep
32. Luke Waddell, 3B, Georgia Tech
33. Phillip Sikes, OF, Pima (Ariz.) JC
34. Luke Bell, RHP, Seton Catholic HS, Chandler, Ariz.
35. Ramsey David, RHP, Buford (Ga.) HS
36. Kyle Smith, C, New Hanover HS, Wilmington, N.C.
37. Mason Greer, 2B, Colleyville (Texas) Heritage HS
38. Ryan Vanderhei, RHP, Estrella Foothills HS, Goodyear, Ariz.
39. Evan Vanek, RHP, Heritage HS, Frisco, Texas
40. Derek Diamond, RHP, Ramona (Calif.) HS

ATLANTA BRAVES (9)

1. Shea Langeliers, C, Baylor
1. Braden Shewmake, SS, Texas A&M
2. Beau Philip, SS, Oregon State
3. Michael Harris, LHP/OF, Stockbridge (Ga.) HS
4. Kasey Kalich, RHP, Texas A&M
5. Stephen Paolini, OF, St. Joseph HS, Trumbull, Conn.
6. Tanner Gordon, RHP, Indiana
7. Darius Vines, RHP, Cal State Bakersfield
8. Ricky DeVito, RHP, Seton Hall
9. Cody Milligan, 2B, Cowley County (Kan.) JC
10. Brandon Parker, OF, Gulf Coast (Miss.) JC
11. Vaughn Grissom, SS, Hagerty HS, Oviedo, Fla.
12. Andy Samuelson, LHP, Wabash Valley (Ill.) JC
13. Tyler Owens, RHP, Trinity Catholic HS, Ocala, Fla.
14. Jared Johnson, RHP, Smithville (Miss.) HS
15. Connor Blair, OF, Washington
16. Joey Estes, RHP, Paraclete HS, Lancaster, Calif.
17. Alec Barger, RHP, North Carolina State
18. Mahki Backstrom, 1B, Serra HS, Gardena, Calif.

19. Kadon Morton, OF, Seguin HS, Arlington, Texas
20. Peyton Williams, RHP, Catawba (N.C.)
21. Javier Valdes, C, Florida International
22. Alex Segal, LHP, Wichita State
23. Drew Campbell, OF, Louisville
24. Bryce Ball, 1B, Dallas Baptist
25. Chad Bryant, RHP, Pensacola State (Fla.) JC
26. Riley King, 3B, Georgia
27. Indigo Diaz, RHP, Michigan State
28. Ben Thompson, RHP, Chandler-Gilbert (Ariz.) JC
29. James Acuna, RHP, Oregon
30. Mitch Calandra, C, Eckerd (Fla.)
31. Greg Leban, RHP, Austin Peay
32. Cody Birdsong, 2B, Quincy (Ill.)
33. Justin Yeager, RHP, Southern Illinois-Carbondale
34. Willie Carter, OF, Webber International (Fla.)
35. Anthony Hall, 1B, Point Loma HS, San Diego
36. Mitchell Jackson, RHP, Marion (Ill.) HS
37. Davis Schwab, LHP, Missouri State
38. Grant Mathews, OF, Tulane
39. Joshua Rolling, SS, Bishop Manogue HS, Reno, Nev.
40. Cade Bunnell, 2B, Indiana

BALTIMORE ORIOLES (1)

1. Adley Rutschman, C, Oregon State
2. Gunnar Henderson, SS, Morgan Academy, Selma, Ala.
2s. Kyle Stowers, OF, Stanford
3. Zach Watson, OF, Louisiana State
4. Joey Ortiz, SS, New Mexico State
5. Darell Hernaiz, SS, Americas HS, El Paso
6. Maverick Handley, C, Stanford
7. Johnny Rizer, OF, Texas Christian
8. Griffin McLarty, RHP, College of Charleston
9. Connor Gillispie, RHP, Virginia Commonwealth
10. Jordan Cannon, C, Sam Houston State
11. Andrew Daschbach, 1B, Stanford
12. Kade Strowd, RHP, West Virginia
13. Dan Hammer, RHP, Pittsburgh
14. Mason Janvrin, OF, Central Missouri
15. Kyle Martin, RHP, Fordham
16. Shelton Perkins, RHP, James Madison
17. Morgan McSweeney, RHP, Wake Forest
18. Malachi Emond, RHP, New Mexico
19. Jensen Elliott, RHP, Oklahoma State
20. Clayton McGinness, RHP, Wichita State
21. Toby Welk, 3B, Pennsylvania State Berks
22. Jake Lyons, RHP, Oklahoma State
23. Shayne Fontana, OF, Lynn (Fla.)
24. Andrew Martinez, SS, UC Santa Barbara
25. Garrett Farmer, RHP, Jacksonville State
26. Nick Roth, RHP, Randolph-Macon (Va.)
27. Dillon McCollough, LHP, Eckerd (Fla.)
28. Jonathan Pendergast, RHP, Pepperdine
29. Houston Roth, RHP, Mississippi
30. Dalton Stambaugh, LHP, Morehead State
31. Jake Prizina, LHP, Seattle
32. Harris Yett, C, Charlotte
33. Craig Lewis, OF, Seton Hill (Pa.)
34. Zach Arnold, SS, Great Oak HS, Temecula, Calif.
35. Justin Miknis, C, Dubois (Pa.) Central Christian HS
36. Trevor Kehe, RHP, Colorado School of Mines, Golden, Colo.
37. Colby Thomas, OF, Valdosta (Ga.) HS
38. Ben Pedersen, RHP, Marshall (Minn.) HS
39. Christian Fagnant, C, East Granby (Conn.) HS
40. Bobby Zmarzlak, OF, Westhill HS, Stamford, Conn.

BOSTON RED SOX (43)

2. Cameron Cannon, SS, Arizona
2. Matthew Lugo, SS, Beltran Baseball Academy, Florida, P.R.
3. Ryan Zeferjahn, RHP, Kansas
4. Noah Song, RHP, Navy
5. Jaxx Groshans, C, Kansas
6. Chris Murphy, LHP, San Diego
7. Brock Bell, RHP, State JC of Florida
8. Wil Dalton, OF, Florida
9. Cody Scroggins, RHP, Arkansas
10. Steve Scott, OF, Vanderbilt
11. Sebastian Keane, RHP, North Andover (Mass.) HS N
12. Brendan Cellucci, LHP, Tulane
13. Blake Loubier, RHP, Oviedo (Fla.) HS
14. Jordan Beck, OF, Hazel Green (Ala.) HS
15. Aaron Roberts, RHP, Desert Oasis HS, Las Vegas
16. Oraj Anu, OF, Wallace (Ala.) JC
17. Alex Erro, 2B, Northwestern
18. Jacob Herbert, C, George Jenkins HS, Lakeland, Fla.
19. Joe Davis, 1B, Houston
20. Reed Harrington, RHP, Spokane Falls (Wash.) JC
21. Dylan Spacke, RHP, Long Beach State
22. Dominic D'Alessandro, 1B, George Washington
23. Leon Paulino, OF, Florida Virtual School
24. Dean Miller, OF, UC Riverside
25. Karson Simas, SS, Clovis West HS, Fresno, Calif.
26. Brandon Walter, LHP, Delaware
27. Devon Roedahl, RHP, Houston
28. Daniel Bakst, SS, Stanford
29. Luke Bandy, OF, Dallas Baptist
30. Nathan Martorella, 1B, Salinas (Calif.) HS
31. Feleipe Franks, RHP, Florida
32. Bradley Blalock, RHP, Grayson HS, Loganville, Ga.
33. Thayer Thomas, OF, North Carolina State
34. Ryan Berardino, 1B, Bentley (Mass.)
35. Chris Mauloni, RHP, Jacksonville
36. Caleb Hill, LHP, Montana
37. Connor Prielipp, LHP, Tomah (Wis.) HS
38. Cameron Meeks, RHP, Sam Houston HS, Lake Charles, La.
39. Trey Faltine, SS, Fort Bend Travis HS, Richmond, Texas
40. Garrett Irvin, LHP, Riverside (Calif.) JC

CHICAGO CUBS (27)

1. Ryan Jensen, RHP, Fresno State
2. Chase Strumpf, 2B, UCLA
3. Michael McAvene, RHP, Louisville
4. Chris Clarke, RHP, Southern California
5. Josh Burgmann, RHP, Washington
6. Ethan Hearn, C, Mobile (Ala.) Christian HS
7. Brad Deppermann, RHP, North Florida
8. D.J. Herz, LHP, Sanford HS, Fayetteville, N.C.
9. Tyler Schlaffer, RHP, Homewood-Flossmoor HS, Flossmoor, Ill.
10. Wyatt Hendrie, C, Antelope Valley (Calif.) JC N
11. Mack Chambers, SS, Seminole (Okla.) JC N
12. Hunter Bigge, RHP, Harvard
13. Porter Hodge, RHP, Cottonwood Senior HS, Murray, Utah
14. Ryan Reynolds, 3B, Texas
15. Zach Bryant, RHP, Jacksonville
16. Johzan Oquendo, RHP, Leadership Christian Academy, P.R.
17. Tanner Dalton, RHP, Sacramento State
18. Alex Moore, RHP, Lander (S.C.)
19. Adam Laskey, LHP, Duke
20. Darius Hill, OF, West Virginia
21. Nelson Maldonado, OF, Florida
22. Elian Almanzar, RHP, Florence-Darlington Tech (S.C.) JC
23. Manny Collier, OF, Westwood HS, Mesa, Ariz.
24. Grayson Byrd, IF, Clemson
25. Zac Taylor, OF, Illinois
26. Jacob Olson, IF, South Carolina
27. Cayne Ueckert, RHP, McNeese State
28. Chris Kachmar, RHP, Lipscomb

29. Jake Washer, C, East Carolina
30. Bryan King, LHP, McNeese State
31. Shane Combs, RHP, Notre Dame
32. Bryce Windham, 2B, Old Dominion
33. Ryan Ritter, SS, Lincoln-Way East HS, Frankfort, Ill.
34. Nolan Letzgus, RHP, Heritage HS, Ringgold, Ga.
35. Hunter Patteson, LHP, Vero Beach (Fla.) HS
36. Jayson Hoopes, RHP, St. Augustine Prep, Richland, N.J.
37. Jaylon McLaughlin, OF, Nevada
38. Marc Davis, 3B, Florida Southwestern State JC
39. Mason Auer, OF, Kickapoo HS, Springfield, Mo.
40. Mac Bingham, OF, Torrey Pines HS, San Diego, Calif.

CHICAGO WHITE SOX (3)

1. Andrew Vaughn, 1B, California
2. Matthew Thompson, RHP, Cypress Ranch HS, Houston
3. Andrew Dalquist, RHP, Redondo Union HS, Calif.
4. James Beard, OF, Loyd Star HS, Brookhaven, Miss.
5. Dan Metzdorf, LHP, Boston College
6. Avery Weems, LHP, Arizona
7. Karan Patel, RHP, Texas-San Antonio
8. Ivan Gonzalez, C, West Virginia
9. Tyson Messer, RHP, Campbell
10. Nate Pawelczyk, RHP, Winthrop
11. Victor Torres, C, International Baseball Academy, P.R.
12. Misael Acosta, OF, Leadership Christian Academy, P.R.
13. Cooper Bradford, RHP, Florida Southern
14. McKinley Moore, RHP, Arkansas-Little Rock
15. Caleb Freeman, RHP, Texas Tech
16. Damon Gladney, 3B, Illiana Christian HS, Lansing, Ill.
17. Jeremiah Burke, RHP, Georgetown
18. Sammy Peralta, LHP, Tampa
19. Joshua Rivera, SS, Chipola (Fla.) JC
20. Cameron Simmons, OF, Virginia
21. Chase Solesky, RHP, Tulane
22. Logan Glass, OF, Mustang (Okla.) HS
23. Pauly Milto, RHP, Indiana
24. Jakob Goldfarb, C, Oregon
25. Hansen Butler, RHP, North Carolina
26. Justin Friedman, RHP, Hope International (Calif.)
27. Tyler Osick, 1B, Central Florida
28. Caeden Trenkle, OF, Hillsboro (Texas) HS
29. Kaleb Roper, RHP, Tulane
30. Daniel Millwee, C, High Point
31. Connor Reich, RHP, Texas State
32. Jonathan Allen, OF, San Francisco
33. Trey Jeans, LHP, Louisiana-Monroe
34. Chase Krogman, OF, Liberty (Mo.) HS
35. Logan Britt, OF, Colleyville (Texas) Heritage HS
36. Declan Cronin, RHP, Holy Cross
37. Garvin Alston, LHP, South Carolina-Aiken
38. Emmet Flood, RHP, Glendale (Ariz.) JC
39. Tom Archer, 2B, Lynn (Fla.)
40. Nick Silva, RHP, Maine

CINCINNATI REDS (7)

1. Nick Lodolo, LHP, Texas Christian
2. Rece Hinds, SS, IMG Academy, Bradenton, Fla.
3. Tyler Callihan, 2B, Providence HS, Jacksonville
4. Ivan Johnson, 2B, Chipola (Fla.) JC
5. Evan Kravetz, LHP, Rice
6. Graham Ashcraft, RHP, Alabama-Birmingham
7. Eric Yang, C, UC Santa Barbara
8. Quin Cotton, OF, Grand Canyon
9. TJ Hopkins, OF, South Carolina
10. Jake Stevenson, RHP, Minnesota
11. Wendell Marrero, OF, Puerto Rico Baseball Academy, P.R.
12. Yan Contreras, SS, Dr. Carlos Gonzalez HS, P.R.
13. Luke Berryhill, C, South Carolina
14. Garrett Wolforth, C, Nova Southeastern (Fla.)
15. Matt Lloyd, OF, Indiana
16. Jason Parker, RHP, North Carolina State

17. **Patrick Raby, RHP, Vanderbilt**
18. Jason Ruffcorn, RHP, Oklahoma
19. **Tyler Garbee, RHP, Mercyhurst (Pa.)**
20. Jose Rodriguez, RHP, Cumberland County (N.J.) JC
21. **Ashton Creal, OF, John A. Logan (Ill.) JC**
22. **Cameron Warren, 1B, Texas Tech**
23. **JC Keys, RHP, Southern Mississippi**
24. **Quinten Sefcik, RHP, Illinois**
25. **Yamil Nieves, C, Puerto Rico Baseball Academy, P.R.**
26. **Quincy McAfee, SS, Pepperdine**
27. **Matt Gill, RHP, Boston College**
28. Michael Miles, RHP, Cumberland County (N.J.) JC
29. **Yassel Pino, 3B, South Miami HS**
30. Ryan Leitch, C, Sinclair SS, Whitby, Ont.
31. **Justin Gomez, C, Azusa Pacific (Calif.)**
32. **Danny Serreino, RHP, Rowan (N.J.)**
33. Trey Clarkson, LHP, Mesquite HS, Glendale, Ariz.
34. Jason Hodges, OF, Marist HS, Chicago
35. **Tanner Cooper, RHP, Finger Lakes (N.Y.) JC**
36. **Alexander Johnson, RHP, McKinley HS, Buffalo**
37. **Caleb Van Blake, 2B, UC Davis**
38. Maxwell Romero, C, Pembroke Pines (Fla.) HS
39. **A.J. Bumpass, OF, Cincinnati**
40. Matt McCormick, C, St Laurence HS, Burbank, Ill.

CLEVELAND INDIANS (24)

1. **Daniel Espino, RHP, Georgia Premier Academy, Ga.**
2. **Yordys Valdes, SS, McArthur HS, Hollywood, Fla.**
3. **Joseph Naranjo, 1B, Ayala HS, Chino Hills, Calif.**
4. **Christian Cairo, SS, Calvary Christian HS, Clearwater, Fla.**
5. **Hunter Gaddis, RHP, Georgia State**
6. **Jordan Brown, SS, Serra HS, Gardena, Calif.**
7. **Xzavion Curry, RHP, Georgia Tech**
8. **Will Brennan, OF, Kansas State**
9. **Will Bartlett, C, IMG Academy, Bradenton, Fla.**
10. **Zach Hart, RHP, Franklin Pierce (N.H.)**
11. **Nick Mikolajchak, RHP, Sam Houston State**
12. **Allan Hernandez, RHP, Miami Christian**
13. **Micah Pries, OF, Point Loma Nazarene (Calif.)**
14. **Ike Freeman, SS, North Carolina**
15. **Trey Benton, RHP, East Carolina**
16. **Jordan Jones, RHP, Washington**
17. **Julian Escobedo, OF, San Diego State**
18. **Matt Waldron, RHP, Nebraska**
19. **Kevin Kelly, RHP, James Madison**
20. **Nic Enright, RHP, Virginia Tech**
21. **Mike Amditis, C, Miami**
22. **Austin Pinorini, C, Gonzaga**
23. **Chandler Fidel, LHP, Arkansas-Little Rock**
24. **Joab Gonzalez, SS, New Mexico JC**
25. **Eric Mock, RHP, Penn State**
26. Armani Sanchez, SS, Reagan HS, San Antonio
27. **Landy Pena, SS, Leadership Christian Academy, P.R.**
28. **Serafino Brito, RHP, Rutgers**
29. **Nate Ocker, RHP, College of Charleston**
30. Jonathan French, C, Parkview HS, Lilburn, Ga.
31. **Jared Janczak, RHP, Texas Christian**
32. **Andrew Misiaszek, LHP, Northeastern**
33. **Kevin Coulter, RHP, Mercer**
34. **Alec Wisely, RHP, South Florida**
35. **Randy Labaut, LHP, Arizona**
36. Ryan Ramsey, LHP, Pascack Hills HS, Montvale, N.J.
37. **Jacob Forrester, RHP, Central Washington**
38. Jake Eissler, RHP, Texas Christian
39. Jake Harrell, LHP, Sanger (Calif.) HS
40. Cy Nielson, LHP, Spanish Fork (Utah) HS

COLORADO ROCKIES (23)

1. **Michael Toglia, 1B, UCLA**
2. **Aaron Schunk, 3B, Georgia**
2s. **Karl Kauffmann, RHP, Michigan**
3. **Jacob Wallace, RHP, Connecticut**

4. **Brenton Doyle, OF, Shepherd (W.Va.)**
5. **Will Ethridge, RHP, Mississippi**
6. **Gavin Hollowell, RHP, St. John's**
7. **Jared Horn, RHP, California**
8. **Jacob Kostyshock, RHP, Arkansas**
9. **Isaac Collins, 2B, Creighton**
10. **Jack Yalowitz, OF, Illinois**
11. **Mike Ruff, RHP, Florida Atlantic**
12. **Christian Koss, SS, UC Irvine**
13. **Daniel Cope, C, Cal State Fullerton**
14. **Joe Aeilts, OF, Illinois State**
15. **Alex Haynes, RHP, Walters State (Tenn.) JC**
16. **Trysten Barlow, LHP, Mississippi State**
17. **Zak Baayoun, LHP, Long Beach State**
18. **Trevor Boone, OF, Oklahoma State**
19. **Turner Brown, SS, East Carolina**
20. **Yorvis Torrealba, OF, Tampa**
21. **Stephen Jones, RHP, Samford**
22. **Fineas Del Bonta-Smith, RHP, San Jose State**
23. **Blair Calvo, RHP, Flagler (Fla.)**
24. **Jordan Spicer, RHP, Central Florida**
25. **Keegan James, RHP, Mississippi State**
26. **Luke Chevalier, RHP, Northern State (S.D.)**
27. **Cameron Enck, RHP, Rollins (Fla.)**
28. **Keven Pimentel, RHP, Tampa**
29. **Colin Simpson, C, Oklahoma State**
30. **Alex Achtermann, OF, Pittsburg State (Kan.)**
31. Michael Curialle, 3B, JSerra Catholic HS, Calif.
32. Tyler Nesbitt, RHP, Labelle (Fla.) HS
33. Hunter Fitz-Gerald, 3B, Stoneman Douglas HS, Fla.
34. Tanner Allen, 1B, Mississippi State
35. Cade Hunter, C, Lenape HS, Medford, N.J.
36. Silas Ardoin, C, Sam Houston HS, Lake Charles, La.
37. Hayden Dunhurst, C, Pearl River Central HS, Miss.
38. Darius Perry, C, La Mirada (Calif.) HS
39. Brady Hill, OF, Mt. Spokane (Wash.) HS
40. Kendal Ewell, OF, Marist HS, Chicago

DETROIT TIGERS (5)

1. **Riley Greene, OF, Hagerty HS, Oviedo, Fla.**
2. **Nick Quintana, 3B, Arizona**
3. **Andre Lipcius, 3B, Tennessee**
4. **Ryan Kreidler, SS, UCLA**
5. **Bryant Packard, OF, East Carolina**
6. **Cooper Johnson, C, Mississippi**
7. **Zack Hess, RHP, Louisiana State**
8. **Jack Kenley, SS, Arkansas**
9. **Austin Bergner, RHP, North Carolina**
10. **Jake Holton, 1B, Creighton**
11. John McMillon, OF, Texas Tech
12. **Corey Joyce, SS, North Carolina Central**
13. **Matt Walker, LHP, Illinois State**
14. **Ted Stuka, RHP, UC San Diego**
15. **Andrew Magno, LHP, Ohio State**
16. **Kona Quiggle, OF, Grand Canyon**
17. Anthony Block, LHP, Washington State
18. **Jared Mang, OF, New Mexico**
19. **Kerry Carpenter, OF, Virginia Tech**
20. **Andrew Navigato, SS, Oklahoma State**
21. Scott McKeon, SS, Coastal Carolina
22. **Cole Zabowski, 1B, Mississippi**
23. **Griffin Dey, 1B, Yale**
24. **Michael Bienlien, RHP, North Carolina State**
25. **Josh Coburn, LHP, Kennesaw State**
26. **Brendan White, RHP, Siena**
27. **Beau Brieske, RHP, Colorado State-Pueblo**
28. **Connor Perry, OF, Pittsburgh**
29. **Elliott Cary, OF, Oklahoma City**
30. **Cordell Dunn, 3B, Grayson (Texas) JC**
31. **Bryce Tassin, RHP, Southeastern Louisiana**
32. **Jack Dellinger, RHP, Virginia Tech**
33. **Jimmy Kerr, 3B, Michigan**

34. Sam Kessler, RHP, West Virginia
35. Robert Klinchock, LHP, Shenandoah (Va.)
36. Pavin Parks, 3B, Kent State
37. Kolton Ingram, LHP, Columbus State (Ga.)
38. Dan Pruitt, 1B, Western Oklahoma State JC
39. Cade Doughty, SS, Denham Springs (La.) HS
40. Luca Dalatri, RHP, North Carolina

HOUSTON ASTROS (32)

1. Korey Lee, C, California
2. Grae Kessinger, SS, Mississippi
3. Jordan Brewer, OF, Michigan
4. Colin Barber, OF, Pleasant Valley HS, Chico, Calif.
5. Hunter Brown, RHP, Wayne State
6. Matthew Barefoot, OF, Campbell
7. Blair Henley, RHP, Texas
8. Luis Guerrero, OF, Miami Dade JC
9. Peyton Battenfield, RHP, Oklahoma State
10. C.J. Stubbs, C, Southern California
11. Ryan Gusto, RHP, Florida Southwestern State JC
12. Garrett Gayle, RHP, Rice
13. Kevin Holcomb, RHP, Glendale (Calif.) JC
14. Derek West, RHP, Pittsburgh
15. Cole McDonald, RHP, Iowa
16. Dexter Jordan, 2B, Pearl River (Miss.) JC
17. Daniel Cody, RHP, Baldwin-Wallace (Ohio)
18. Justin Campbell, RHP, Simi Valley (Calif.) HS
19. Tyler Krabbe, C, Montevallo (Ala.)
20. Alex Palmer, RHP, Stephen F. Austin
21. Davis Vainer, RHP, Alabama
22. Shea Barry, RHP, UC Santa Barbara
23. Zach Biermann, 1B, Coastal Carolina
24. Preston Pavlica, OF, Grand Canyon
25. E.P. Reese, OF, Winston-Salem State (N.C.)
26. Chandler Casey, RHP, Lubbock Christian (Texas)
27. Kevin Dickey, LHP, Seminole (Okla.) JC
28. Bryan Arias, 2B, Texas-San Antonio
29. Whit Drennan, LHP, Rollins (Fla.)
30. Michael Horrell, RHP, Campbell
31. Peyton Plumlee, RHP, Mississippi State
32. Oscar Carvajal, RHP, Fresno State
33. Bryan Martinez, LHP, Connors State (Okla.) JC
34. AJ Lee, SS, Maryland
35. James Nix, OF, Central Florida
36. Chandler Murphy, RHP, Liberty HS, Peoria, Ariz.
37. Maxwell Dias, 3B, Porter (Texas) HS
38. J.C. Correa, SS, Lamar
39. Brock Rudy, C, Northgate HS, Walnut Creek, Calif.
40. Dillon Plew, 1B, Washington State

KANSAS CITY ROYALS (2)

1. Bobby Witt, SS, Colleyville (Texas) Heritage HS
2. Brady McConnell, SS, Florida
2s. Alec Marsh, RHP, Arizona State
3. Grant Gambrell, RHP, Oregon State
4. Michael Massey, 2B, Illinois
5. John Rave, OF, Illinois State
6. Dante Biasi, LHP, Penn State
7. Noah Murdock, RHP, Virginia
8. Drew Parrish, LHP, Florida State
9. Clay Dungan, SS, Indiana State
10. Anthony Veneziano, LHP, Coastal Carolina
11. Vinnie Pasquantino, 1B, Old Dominion
12. Adam Lukas, RHP, Evansville
13. Tyler Tolbert, SS, Alabama Birmingham
14. Justin Hooper, LHP, UCLA
15. Sean Bretz, RHP, Houston
16. Erick Figueroa, RHP, Juan Jose Maunez HS, P.R.
17. A.J. Franklin, LHP, Vanderbilt
18. Burle Dixon, OF, Cosumnes River (Calif.) JC
19. Austin Manning, LHP, Southern California
20. Cody Davenport, RHP, Central Arkansas

21. Matthew Stil, RHP, Rowan-Gloucester (N.J.) JC
22. Jake Means, 3B, Indiana State
23. Elliott Anderson, LHP, Auburn
24. Alex Smith, LHP, Memphis
25. Josh Broughton, 3B, Valdosta State (Ga.)
26. Jay Charleston, 2B, Tennessee
27. Zack Phillips, LHP, Mississippi
28. Riley Boyd, RHP, Jefferson (Mo.) JC
29. Jon Beymer, RHP, Wabash Valley (Ill.) JC
30. Jimmy Govern, 2B, Eastern Illinois
31. Mikey Filia, OF, UC Irvine
32. Saul Garza, C, Louisiana State
33. Patrick Smith, LHP, Purdue
34. Justin Fall, LHP, Brookdale (N.J.) JC
35. Jonah Dipoto, RHP, UC San Diego
36. Andy Martin, OF, Hialeah (Fla.) HS
37. Reggie Crawford, LHP, North Schuylkill HS, Ashland, Pa.
38. Augue Sylk, LHP, Southern California
39. Jorge Corona, C, Killian HS, Miami
40. David Estevez, RHP, Pembroke Pines (Fla.) HS

LOS ANGELES ANGELS (15)

1. Will Wilson, SS, North Carolina State
2. Kyren Paris, SS, Freedom HS, Oakley, Calif.
3. Jack Kochanowicz, RHP, Harriton HS, Rosemont, Pa.
4. Erik Rivera, OF/LHP, Puerto Rico Baseball Academy, P.R.
5. Garrett Stallings, RHP, Tennessee
6. Zach Peek, RHP, Winthrop
7. Davis Daniel, RHP, Auburn
8. Kyle Brnovich, RHP, Elon
9. Zach Linginfelter, RHP, Tennessee
10. Chad Sykes, RHP, UNC Greensboro
11. Brent Killam, LHP, Georgetown
12. Jack Dashwood, LHP, UC Santa Barbara
13. Edwin Sanchez, RHP, B-You Academy, Caguas, P.R.
14. Zac Kristofak, RHP, Georgia
15. Greg Veliz, RHP, Miami
16. Dakota Donovan, RHP, Central Arizona JC
17. Brandon White, OF, West Virginia
18. Ryan Smith, LHP, Princeton
19. Garrett Lawson, LHP, Delaware State
20. Jared Southard, RHP, Rouse HS, Leander, Texas
21. Andrew Blake, RHP, North Carolina State
22. Morgan McCullough, SS, Alabama
23. Matthew Corlew, OF, North Broward Prep HS , Fla.
24. Shane Kelso, RHP, Oklahoma Baptist
25. Anthony Mulrine, C, Samford
26. Kyle Molnar, RHP, UCLA
27. Kenyon Yovan, RHP, Oregon
28. Coleman Crow, RHP, Pike County HS, Zebulon, Ga.
29. Matthew Woods, OF, Rowan (N.J.)
30. Andrew Bash, RHP, California Baptist
31. Spencer Jones, OF, La Costa Canyon HS, Carlsbad, Calif.
32. Chase Walter, RHP, Western Carolina
33. Justin Kunz, C, Gardner-Webb
34. Ridge Chapman, RHP, South Carolina
35. Vincent Bianchi, SS, Red Bank (N.J.) Catholic HS
36. Keaton Weisz, SS, Coastal Carolina
37. Levi Usher, OF, Kirkwood (Iowa) JC
38. Luke Boyd, RHP, Baylor
39. Spencer Brown, SS, Northern Essex (Mass.) JC
40. Tyson Heaton, RHP, Yucaipa (Calif.) HS

LOS ANGELES DODGERS (25)

1. Kody Hoese, 3B, Tulane
1. Michael Busch, 2B, North Carolina
2s. Jimmy Lewis, RHP, Lake Travis HS, Austin
3. Ryan Pepiot, RHP, Butler
4. Brandon Lewis, 3B, UC Irvine
5. Jack Little, RHP, Stanford
6. Aaron Ochsenbein, RHP, Eastern Kentucky
7. Nick Robertson, RHP, James Madison

8. Ryan Ward, OF, Bryant
9. Alec Gamboa, LHP, Fresno JC
10. Zac Ching, SS, Virginia Commonwealth
11. Logan Boyer, RHP, San Diego State
12. Mitchell Tyranski, LHP, Michigan State
13. Jacob Cantleberry, LHP, Missouri
14. Sean Mellen, LHP, Northeastern
15. Joe Vranesh, OF, St. Mary's
16. Andrew Baker, RHP, Chipola (Fla.) JC
17. Brandon Wulff, OF, Stanford
18. Jeff Belge, RHP, St. John's
19. Braidyn Fink, RHP, Oklahoma
20. Zack Plunkett, RHP, Arkansas
21. Trey Lafleur, OF, J.M. Tate HS, Cantonment, Fla.
22. Jimmy Titus, SS, Bryant
23. Cyrillo Watson, RHP, Illinois
24. Chet Allison, OF, Fresno (Calif.) JC
25. Jonny DeLuca, OF, Oregon
26. Mark Mixon, RHP, Miami
27. Parker Brahms, RHP, Sacramento State
28. Brennan Milone, SS, Woodstock (Ga.) HS
29. Breyln Jones, SS, Rutherford (N.J.) HS
30. Josh Ibarra, RHP, Golden West (Calif.) JC
31. Kayler Yates, SS, Dixie HS, St. George, Utah
32. Danny Sinatro, OF, Washington State
33. Julio Carrion, 3B, Chipola (Fla.) JC
34. Francisco Martinez, LHP, Puerto Rico Baseball Academy, P.R.
35. Justin Washington, OF, Savannah State (Ga.)
36. Matthew Kanfer, OF, Pepperdine
37. Tres Gonzalez, OF, Mount Vernon Presbyterian HS, Atlanta
38. Tyler Ryan, C, Pacific
39. Caden MacDonald, LHP, Pantego Christian Academy, Texas
40. Ty Haselman, C, UCLA

MIAMI MARLINS (4)

1. JJ Bleday, OF, Vanderbilt
1s. Kameron Misner, OF, Missouri
2. Nasim Nunez, SS, Collins Hill HS, Suwanee, Ga.
3. Peyton Burdick, OF, Wright State
4. Evan Edwards, 1B, North Carolina State
5. Evan Fitterer, RHP, Aliso Niguel HS, Aliso Viejo, Calif.
6. M.D. Johnson, RHP, Dallas Baptist
7. Bryan Hoeing, RHP, Louisville
8. Tevin Mitchell, OF, UC Santa Barbara
9. Evan Brabrand, RHP, Liberty
10. J.D. Orr, OF, Wright State
11. Anthony Maldonado, RHP, Bethune-Cookman
12. Chris Mokma, RHP, Holland (Mich.) HS
13. Zach King, LHP, Vanderbilt
14. Easton Lucas, LHP, Pepperdine
15. Javeon Cody, OF, Alvin (Texas) JC
16. Andrew Nardi, LHP, Arizona
17. Troy Johnston, OF, Gonzaga
18. Dustin Skelton, C, Mississippi State
19. Nate Rombach, C, Legacy HS, Mansfield, Texas
20. Thomas Rowan, C, UC Santa Barbara
21 Jhonny Felix, RHP, Western Oklahoma State JC
22. Codie Paiva, RHP, Loyola Marymount
23. Nic Ready, 3B, Air Force
24. Jeff Lindgren, RHP, Illinois State
25. Jack Strunc, SS, Creighton
26. Brandon McIlwain, OF, California
27. Casey Combs, C, East Texas Baptist
28. Lorenzo Hampton, OF, Florida International
29. John Baker, RHP, Ball State
30. Joey Steele, RHP, San Francisco
31. Parker Noland, 3B, Farragut HS, Knoxville
32. Josh Simpson, LHP, Columbia
33. Zachary Owings, 1B, Eastern Michigan
34. Brock Love, RHP, Alabama
35. Torin Montgomery, 1B, Lake Washington HS, Wash.
36. Julian Infante, 1B, Vanderbilt

37. Tyler Causey, SS, Nation Ford HS, Fort Mill, S.C.
38. Tyresse Turner, SS, Gahr HS, Cerritos, Calif.
39. Evan Justice, LHP, North Carolina State
40. Kade Mechals, RHP, Grand Canyon

MILWAUKEE BREWERS (28)

1. Ethan Small, LHP, Mississippi State
2. Antoine Kelly, LHP, Wabash Valley (Ill.) JC
4. Nick Kahle, C, Washington
5. Thomas Dillard, C, Mississippi
6. Nick Bennett, LHP, Louisville
7. Gabe Holt, 2B, Texas Tech
8. David Hamilton, SS, Texas
9. Darrien Miller, C, Clovis (Calif.) HS
10. Taylor Floyd, RHP, Texas Tech
11. Brock Begue, LHP, Cuyahoga (Ohio) JC
12. Arman Sabouri, LHP, California
13. Jackson Gillis, LHP, Vanderbilt
14. Paxton Schultz, RHP, Utah Valley
15. Cam Devanney, SS, Elon
16. Michael Wilson, OF, Stony Brook
17. Kelvin Bender, LHP, Serra HS, Gardena, Calif.
18. Ashton McGee, 2B, North Carolina
19. Bryce Milligan, RHP, Oklahoma City
20. Myles Austin, SS, Westlake HS, Atlanta
21. Eddy Tavarez, RHP, Peru State (Neb.)
22. Terence Doston, OF, Hillsborough HS, Tampa
23. Carter Rustad, RHP, Staley HS, Kansas City, Mo.
24. Jose Torres, SS, Calvert Hall College HS, Baltimore
25. Dan Wirchansky, LHP, Pace (N.Y.)
26. Zach Humphreys, C, Texas Christian
27. Zane Zurbrugg, OF, Shoreline (Wash.) JC
28. Andre Nnebe, OF, Santa Clara
29. Jackie Urbaez, 2B, St. Thomas (Fla.)
30. Peyton Long, RHP, Central Methodist (Mo.)
31. Jonathan Jones, RHP, San Jacinto (Texas) JC
32. Jefferson Figueroa, RHP, Florida Virtual School
33. Kevin Hardin, 1B, Maplewoods (Mo.) JC
34. Josh Shapiro, LHP, Marshall
35. Odrick Pitre, SS, Alvin (Texas) JC
36. Keegan McCarville, RHP, Santa Clara
37. Abimael Gonzalez, OF, Leadership Christian Academy, P.R.
38. Eli Nabholz, RHP, Millersville (Pa.)
39. Harrison Beethe, RHP, North Iowa Area JC
40. Tyler Keysor, RHP, Miami

MINNESOTA TWINS (13)

1. Keoni Cavaco, SS, Eastlake HS, Chula Vista, Calif.
1s. Matt Wallner, OF, Southern Mississippi
2. Matt Canterino, RHP, Rice
3. Spencer Steer, SS, Oregon
4. Seth Gray, 3B, Wright State
5. Will Holland, SS, Auburn
6. Sawyer Gipson, RHP, Mercer
7. Anthony Prato, SS, Connecticut
8. Casey Legumina, RHP, Gonzaga
9. Brent Headrick, LHP, Illinois State
10. Ben Gross, RHP, Duke
11. Tanner Brubaker, RHP, UC Irvine
12. Sean Mooney, RHP, St. John's
13. Dylan Thomas, RHP, Hawaii
14. Cody Laweryson, RHP, Maine
15. Louie Varland, RHP, Concordia (Minn.)
16. Ryan Shreve, RHP, Pacific
17. Antoine Jean, LHP, Edouard Montpetit College
18. Eduoard Julien, 2B, Auburn
19. Niall Windeler, LHP, British Columbia
20. Owen Griffith, RHP, Clemson
21. Bradley Hanner, RHP, Patrick Henry (Va.) JC
22. Rogelio Reyes, RHP, California
23. Matthew Swain, RHP, Georgia Gwinnett
24. Trevor Jensen, 1B, Tulane

25. Nate Hadley, RHP, UCLA
26. Blake Robertson, 3B, Santa Fe HS, Edmond, Okla.
27. Parker Phillips, 1B, Austin Peay
28. Travis Phelps, RHP, Alvin (Texas) HS
29. Alex Isola, C, Texas Christian
30. Tyler Beck, RHP, Tampa
31. Max Smith, OF, Nevada-Las Vegas
32. Bryson Gandy, OF, Wallace State (Ala.) JC
33. Kyle Schmidt, C, Richmond
34. Antoine Harris, RHP, Chalmette (La.) HS
35. Drew Gilbert, LHP, Stillwater (Minn.) HS
36. Will Frisch, RHP, Stillwater (Minn.) HS
37. Adrian Colon, OF, Dr. Juan J. Osuna HS, Caguas, P.R.
38. Zack Mathis, C, San Joaquin Delta (Calif.) JC
39. Jake Hirabayashi, 3B, UCLA
40. Logan Steenstra, SS, Cowley County (Kan.) JC

NEW YORK METS (12)

1. Brett Baty, 3B, Lake Travis HS, Austin
2. Josh Wolf, RHP, St. Thomas HS, Houston
3. Matt Allan, RHP, Seminole HS, Sanford, Fla.
4. Jake Mangum, OF, Mississippi State
5. Nathan Jones, RHP, Northwestern State
6. Zach Ashford, OF, Fresno State
7. Luke Ritter, 2B, Wichita State
8. Connor Wollersheim, LHP, Kent State
9. Joe Genord, 1B, South Florida
10. Scott Ota, OF, Illinois-Chicago
11. Jordan Martinson, LHP, Dallas Baptist
12. Antoine Duplantis, OF, Louisiana State
13. Blaine McIntosh, OF, Sycamore HS, Pleasant View, Tenn.
14. Kennie Taylor, OF, Duke
15. Mitch Ragan, RHP, Creighton
16. Nic Gaddis, 3B, Jacksonville State
17. Dan Goggin, RHP, James Madison
18. Tanner Murphy, OF, North Florida
19. Hunter Parsons, RHP, Maryland
20. Matt O'Neill, C, Pennsylvania
21. Branden Fryman, SS, Samford
22. Jace Beck, RHP, Blanchard (Okla.) HS
23. Nick MacDonald, RHP, Florida International
24. Hunter Barco, LHP, Bolles School, Jacksonville
25. Joseph Charles, RHP, TNXL Academy, Fla.
26. Mitchell Senger, LHP, Stetson
27. Dalton Fowler, LHP, Northwest Mississippi JC
28. Jake Ortega, C, Cal State Bakersfield
29. LT Struble, OF, Felician (N.J.)
30. Justin Lasko, RHP, Amherst (Mass.)
31. Andrew Edwards, LHP, New Mexico State
32. Cole Gordon, RHP, Mississippi State
33. Cole Kleszcz, OF, Azusa Pacific (Calif.)
34. Ryan Shinn, OF, Kentucky
35. Daniel Maldonado, OF, Carlos Beltran Baseball Academy, P.R.
36. Tucker Flint, OF, Bishop Hendricken HS, Warwick, R.I.
37. Dilan Lawson, RHP, Madison County HS, Madison, Fla.
38. Casey Slattery, 1B, Glendale (Calif.) JC
39. Nick Conti, 2B, Eckerd (Fla.)
40. Camden Lovrich, RHP, Trinity Presbyterian HS, Ala.

NEW YORK YANKEES (30)

1. Anthony Volpe, SS, Delbarton HS, Morristown, N.J.
1s. TJ Sikkema, LHP, Missouri
2. Josh Smith, 2B, Louisiana State
3. Jake Sanford, OF, Western Kentucky
4. Jake Agnos, LHP, East Carolina
5. Ken Waldichuk, LHP, St. Mary's
6. Hayden Wesneski, RHP, Sam Houston State
7. Nick Paciorek, RHP, Northwestern
8. Zach Greene, RHP, South Alabama
9. Spencer Henson, 1B, Oral Roberts
10. Mitch Spence, RHP, South Carolina-Aiken
11. Oliver Dunn, 2B, Utah

12. Ryan Anderson, LHP, Nevada
13. Nelson Alvarez, RHP, South Florida
14. Kevin Milam, 2B, St. Mary's
15. Edgar Barclay, LHP, Cal State Bakersfield
16. Shaine McNeely, RHP, Hope International (Calif.)
17. Pat DeMarco, OF, Vanderbilt
18. Evan Voliva, RHP, East Carolina
19. Chad Bell, 3B, Louisiana-Monroe
20. Jack Leiter, RHP, Delbarton HS, Morristown, N.J.
21. Zach Kohn, RHP, Central Michigan
22. Garrett Van Zijll, LHP, Alvin (Texas) JC
23. Matt Minnick, LHP, Mercyhurst (Pa.)
24. Jake Pries, OF, UCLA
25. Luke Brown, OF, John A. Logan (Ill.) JC
26. Ryan Brown, RHP, South Salem HS, Salem, Ore.
27. Kyle MacDonald, 1B, Arkansas State
28. Michael Giacone, LHP, North Greenville (S.C.)
29. Chase Illig, C, West Virginia
30. Zachary Maxwell, RHP, North Paulding HS, Dallas, Ga.
31. Chad Knight, C, Staples HS, Westport, Conn.
32. Ethan Hoopingarner, RHP, Aliso Niguel HS, Aliso Viejo, Calif.
33. Francisco Reynoso, SS, Colegio Angel David HS, P.R.
34. Joey Lancellotti, RHP, North Carolina
35. Nathaniel Espelin, LHP, Winchendon (Mass.) School
36. Montana Semmel, RHP, Westhill HS, Stamford, Conn.
37. Bryce Jarvis, RHP, Duke
38. Dontae Mitchell, OF, Lakewood HS, St. Petersburg, Fla.
39. Jake Farrell, 1B, Northeastern
40. Alex Garbrick, RHP, Morehead State N

OAKLAND ATHLETICS (29)

1. Logan Davidson, SS, Clemson
2. Tyler Baum, RHP, North Carolina
3. Marcus Smith, OF, Pembroke Hill HS, Kansas City, Mo.
4. Kyle McCann, C, Georgia Tech
5. Jalen Greer, SS, St. Rita HS, Chicago
6. Seth Shuman, RHP, Georgia Southern
7. Drew Millas, C, Missouri State
8. Jose Dicochea, RHP, Sahuarita (Ariz.) HS
9. Colin Peluse, RHP, Wake Forest
10. Patrick McColl, 1B, Harvard
11. Dustin Harris, SS, St. Petersburg (Fla.) JC
12. TJ Schofield-Sam, SS, North Park SS, Brampton, Ont.
13. Sahid Valenzuela, SS, Cal State Fullerton
14. Peyton Miller, RHP, Tyler (Texas) JC
15. Josh Watson, OF, Texas Christian
16. Brady Basso, LHP, Oklahoma State
17. Vince Coletti, RHP, Florida Atlantic
18. Jorge Romero, OF, Colegio Angel David HS, P.R.
19. Jared McDonald, C, Western Oregon
20. Jack Weisenburger, RHP, Michigan
21. Shane Selman, OF, McNeese State
22. Jack Cushing, RHP, Georgetown
23. Austin Wahl, RHP, Cal State Monterey Bay
24. Trayson Kubo, RHP, Stephen F. Austin
25. Ty Duvall, C, Vanderbilt
26. Elvis Peralta, SS, Marshall
27. Gavin Jones, 3B, State Fair (Mo.) JC
28. Wil Jensen, RHP, Pepperdine
29. Michael Woodworth, 2B, Connecticut
30. Edward Baram, RHP, Adelphi (N.Y.)
31. Matthew Koehler, OF, Western Carolina
32. Marty Bechina, 2B, Michigan State
33. Charles Hall, RHP, Tusculum (Tenn.)
34. Kumar Nambiar, LHP, Yale
35. Zach Rafuse, RHP, South Carolina-Aiken
36. Jake Walkinshaw, RHP, Southern New Hampshire
37. Chase Wheatcroft, RHP, Cal State Stanislaus
38. David Leal, LHP, Louisiana Tech
39. Derek Lee, OF, Richmond
40. Sam Romero Contreras, RHP, Arizona State

PHILADELPHIA PHILLIES (14)

1. Bryson Stott, SS, Nevada-Las Vegas
3. Jamari Baylor, SS, Benedictine HS, Richmond
4. Erik Miller, LHP, Stanford
5. Gunner Mayer, RHP, San Joaquin Delta (Calif.) JC
6. Andrew Schultz, RHP, Tennessee
7. Brett Schulze, RHP, Minnesota
8. Nate Fassnacht, SS, George Washington
9. Rudy Rott, 1B, Ohio
10. McCarthy Tatum, 3B, Fresno State
11. Marcus Lee Sang, OF, Northern HS, Owings, Md.
12. Jadiel Sanchez, OF, Natividad Rodriguez Gonzalez HS, P.R.
13. Hunter Markwardt, OF, Oklahoma Christian
14. Chris Micheles, LHP, Washington
15. Adam Leverett, RHP, Gordon State (Ga.) JC
16. Chris Cornelius, SS, Missouri
17. Hunter Milam, LHP, Gulf Coast (Fla.) JC
18. Nick Lackney, LHP, Minnesota
19. Spencer Van Scoyoc, LHP, Central Oklahoma
20. Keaton Greenwalt, OF, Lubbock Christian (Texas)
21. Hilton Dyar, RHP, Clinton (Miss.) HS
22. Tucker Maxwell, OF, Georgia
23. Herbert Iser, C, Dallas Baptist
24. Jose Ulloa, RHP, ASA College (Miami)
25. Jamie Sara, RHP, William & Mary
26. Hunter Hearn, OF, Sam Houston State
27. Tyler Adams, LHP, Indiana (Pa.)
28. Carlos Francisco, RHP, Hillsborough (Fla.) JC
29. Micah Yonamine, C, Iolani HS, Honolulu
30. Dylan Castaneda, RHP, Salisbury (Conn.) School
31. Shane Murphy, LHP, Hamilton HS, Chandler, Ariz.
32. Logan Koester, RHP, Chaminade HS, Mineola, N.Y.
33. Thomas Little, LHP, Vauxhall HS, Alberta, Canada
34. Jalen Battles, SS, McLennan (Texas) JC
35. Michael Prosecky, LHP, Nazareth Academy, La Grange Park, Ill.
36. Cam Beauchamp, LHP, Indiana
37. Brendan Bell, RHP, Central Florida
38. Josh Hendrickson, LHP, San Diego
39. Austin Crowson, LHP, Western Oregon
40. Vito Friscia, C, Hofstra

PITTSBURGH PIRATES (18)

1. Quinn Priester, RHP, Cary-Grove HS, Cary, Ill.
1s. Sammy Siani, OF, Penn Charter HS, Philadelphia
2. Matt Gorski, OF, Indiana
2s. Jared Triolo, 3B, Houston
3. Matt Fraizer, OF, Arizona
4. J.C. Flowers, RHP, Florida State
5. Grant Ford, RHP, Nevada
6. Will Matthiesen, OF, Stanford
7. Blake Sabol, OF, Southern California
8. Austin Roberts, RHP, Sacramento State
9. Ethan Paul, SS, Vanderbilt
1-. Cameron Junker, RHP, Notre Dame
11. Jase Bowen, OF, Toledo Central Catholic HS
12. Kyle Wilkie, C, Clemson
13. Chase Murray, OF, Georgia Tech
14. Aaron Shackelford, SS, The Masters (Calif.)
15. Garrett Leonard, RHP, Rollins (Fla.)
16. Eli Wilson, C, Minnesota
17. Ryan Harbin, RHP, Bartow (Fla.) HS
18. Will Simpson, 1B, Skyline HS, Sammamish, Wash.
19. Cory Wood, 2B, Coastal Carolina
20. Jake Snider, OF, Louisville
21. Alex Roth, RHP, Western Oregon
22. Andres Alvarez, SS, Washington State
23. Jasiah Dixon, OF, Orange (Calif.) Lutheran HS
24. Trey McGough, LHP, Mount St. Mary's
25. Ethan Goforth, C, Carson-Newman (Tenn.)
26. Ryan Troutman, RHP, Lander (S.C.)
27. Samson Abernathy, RHP, Pacific

28. Bear Bellomy, RHP, Wright State
29. Marshall Gilbert, C, Mississippi State
30. Dawson McCarville, RHP, Glendale (Ariz.) JC
31. Josh Bissonette, 2B, Baylor
32. Jake Wright, OF, Coastal Carolina
33. Erny Ordonez, 3B, Central Arizona JC
34. Dylan Shockley, C, Rio Grande (Ohio)
35. Deion Walker, OF, Hillgrove HS, Powder Springs, Ga.
36. Jake Sweeney, LHP, Pensacola State (Fla.) JC
37. CJ Dandeneau, RHP, Connecticut
38. Christian Gordon, OF, Liberty Christian Academy, Lynchburg, Va.
39. Daniel Ross, RHP, Millersville (Pa.)
40. Elijah Dunham, OF, Indiana

SAN DIEGO PADRES (6)

1. CJ Abrams, SS, Blessed Trinity HS, Roswell, Ga.
2. Joshua Mears, OF, Federal Way (Wash.) HS
2s. Logan Driscoll, C, George Mason
3. Hudson Head, OF, Churchill HS, San Antonio
4. Matt Brash, RHP, Niagara
5. Chris Lincoln, RHP, UC Santa Barbara
6. Drake Fellows, RHP, Vanderbilt
7. Connor Lehmann, RHP, Saint Louis
8. Andrew Mitchel, LHP, San Jose State
9. Jason Blanchard, LHP, Lamar
10. Ethan Elliott, LHP, Lincoln Memorial (Tenn.)
11. Mason Feole, LHP, Connecticut
12. Matthew Acosta, OF, Southern California
13. Brandon Komar, RHP, Madison (Wis.) JC
14. Bodi Rascon, LHP, Decatur (Texas) HS
15. Andre Tarver, OF, Ringgold (Ga.) HS
16. Robert Briley, RHP, Seminole State (Okla.) JC
17. Jared Alvarez-Lopez, C, Cypress Ranch HS, Houston
18. Andrew Dean, LHP, Illinois-Springfield
19. Chris Givin, SS, Xavier
20. Deacon Medders, RHP, Alabama
21. Jack Stronach, 3B, UCLA
22. Joshua Rivera, 3B, IMG Academy, Bradenton, Fla.
23. Maurice Hampton, OF, Memphis University HS
24. Taylor Lomack, OF, Tallahassee (Fla.) JC
25. Blake Baker, RHP, Miami Dade JC
26. Pierce Jones, OF, Marian Catholic HS, Chicago Heights, Ill.
27. Tyler Malone, C, Oregon State
28. Sam Ballard, LHP, Parkland (Ill.) JC
29. Anthony Nunez, SS, Miami Springs (Fla.) HS
30. Ripken Reyes, 2B, San Diego
31. Jason Nelson, RHP, Central Arizona JC
32. Jason Reynolds, RHP, Lehigh
33. Keegan Pulford-Thorpe, LHP, Newmarket HS, Hamilton, Ontario
34. Bryant Salgado, RHP, San Jacinto (Texas) JC
35. Keegan Collett, RHP, Florida Gulf Coast
36. Isaiah Bennett, RHP, Pine Forest HS, Fayetteville, N.C.
37. Owen Cobb, SS, Garfield HS, Seattle
38. Cole Roberts, SS, Santa Fe Christian HS, Solana Beach, Calif.
39. Dylan Hoffman, LHP, Waldorf (Iowa)
40. Koty Fallon, RHP, Western Oregon

SAN FRANCISCO GIANTS (10)

1. Hunter Bishop, OF, Arizona State
2. Logan Wyatt, 1B, Louisville
3. Grant McCray, OF, Lakewood Ranch HS, Bradenton, Fla.
4. Tyler Fitzgerald, SS, Louisville
5. Garrett Frechette, 1B, Orange (Calif.) Lutheran HS
6. Dilan Rosario, SS, Leadership Christian Academy, P.R.
7. Armani Smith, OF, UC Santa Barbara
8. Caleb Kilian, RHP, Texas Tech
9. Simon Whiteman, SS, Yale
10. Jeff Houghtby, SS, San Diego
11. Trevor McDonald, RHP, George County HS, Miss.
12. Chris Wright, LHP, Bryant
13. Harrison Freed, OF, Butler
14. Nick Morreale, RHP, Georgetown

15. Carter Aldrete, 2B, Arizona State
16. Brandon Martorano, C, North Carolina
17. Connor Cannon, 1B, UC Riverside
18. Cole Waites, RHP, West Alabama
19. Kanoa Pagan, RHP, Mission (Calif.) JC
20. Najee Gaskins, OF, St. Cloud State (Minn.)
21. Bryce Fehmel, RHP, Oregon State
22. Javeyan Williams, OF, Southern
23. Taylor Rashi, RHP, UC Irvine
24. Evan Lumbert, RHP, Florida Gulf Coast
25. Richard Rodriguez, 2B, Pro Baseball HS Academy, P.R.
26. Nick Avila, RHP, Long Beach State
27. Connor Beichler, SS, Owasso (Okla.) HS
28. Reese Sharp, RHP, Noblesville (Ind.) HS
29. Brooks Crawford, RHP, Clemson
30. Justin Crump, RHP, UNC Wilmington
31. Tyler Wyatt, RHP, Grand Canyon
32. Dylan Brewer, OF, Latta (S.C.) HS
33. Nolan Dempsey, 2B, Fresno State
34. Morgan Colopy, OF, Centerville (Ohio) HS
35. Brooks Lee, SS, San Luis Obispo (Calif.) HS
36. Cameron Repetti, 3B, Cypress (Calif.) HS
37. Cole Weiss, 3B, UNC Wilmington
38. Will Rigney, RHP, Midway HS, Waco, Texas
39. Chris Lanzilli, OF, Wake Forest
40. Jeff Heinrich, 3B, McHenry County (Ill.) JC

SEATTLE MARINERS (20)

1. George Kirby, RHP, Elon
2. Brandon Williamson, LHP, Texas Christian
2s. Isaiah Campbell, RHP, Arkansas
3. Levi Stoudt, RHP, Lehigh
4. Tim Elliott, RHP, Georgia
5. Austin Shenton, 3B, Florida International
6. Michael Limoncelli, RHP, Horseheads (N.Y.) High
7. Adam Macko, LHP, Vauxhall (Alb.) Academy
8. Ty Adcock, RHP, Elon
9. Mike Salvatore, SS, Florida State
10. Kyle Hill, RHP, Baylor
11. Carter Bins, C, Fresno State
12. Antoine Mistico, OF, Gateway (Ariz.) JC
13. Reid Morgan, RHP, South Carolina
14. Patrick Frick, SS, Wake Forest
15. Anthony Tomczak, RHP, North Broward Prep HS, Fla.
16. Logan Rinehart, RHP, California Baptist
17. Dutch Landis, RHP, Bishop Gorman HS, Las Vegas
18. Tyler Driver, LHP, Crossroads Flex HS, Cary N.C.
19. Travis Kuhn, RHP, San Diego
20. Cade Marlowe, OF, West Georgia
21. Reeves Martin, RHP, New Orleans
22. Trent Tingelstad, OF, Louisiana-Monroe
23. Caleb Ricca, SS, Northwestern State
24. Kipp Rollings, RHP, North Greenville (S.C.)
25. Freddy Villarreal, RHP, Houston
26. Garrett Westberg, RHP, Central Florida
27. Brock Minich, RHP, Nova Southeastern (Fla.)
28. Anthony Lepre, C, The Masters (Calif.)
29. Utah Jones, SS, North Greenville (S.C.)
30. Cody Grosse, SS, Southeastern Louisiana
31. Jacob Meador, RHP, Centennial HS, Burleson, Texas
32. Jackson Tate, OF, Lawson State (Ala.) JC
33. Jarod Bayless, RHP, Dallas Baptist
34. Christian Encarnacion-Strand, 3B, Yavapai (Ariz.) JC
35. Dominic Tamez, C, Lady Bird Johnson HS, San Antonio
36. C.J. Mayhue, LHP, Crest HS, Shelby, N.C.
37. Cole Barr, 3B, Indiana
38. Jackson Lancaster, OF, Itawamba (Miss.) JC
39. Jacob Hurtubise, OF, Army
40. Perry McMichen, 2B, Wyoming (Ohio) HS

ST. LOUIS CARDINALS (19)

1. Zack Thompson, LHP, Kentucky
2. Trejyn Fletcher, OF, Deering HS, Portland, Maine
3. Tony Locey, RHP, Georgia
4. Andre Pallante, RHP, UC Irvine
5. Connor Thomas, LHP, Georgia Tech
6. Pedro Pages, C, Florida Atlantic
7. Jack Ralston, RHP, UCLA
8. Logan Gragg, RHP, Oklahoma State
9. Todd Lott, OF, Louisiana-Lafayette
10. Jake Sommers, RHP, Wisconsin-Milwaukee
11. Connor Lunn, RHP, Southern California
12. Patrick Romeri, OF, IMG Academy, Bradenton, Fla.
13. Tommy Jew, OF, UC Santa Barbara
14. Tyler Statler, RHP, Hononegah HS, Rockton, Ill.
15. David Vinsky, OF, Northwood (Mich.)
16. Thomas Hart, RHP, Wakeland HS, Frisco, Texas
17. Michael YaSenka, RHP, Eastern Illinois
18. Aaron Antonini, C, Middle Tennessee State
19. Zarion Sharpe, LHP, UNC Wilmington
20. Adrian Mardueno, RHP, San Diego State
21. Jack Owen, LHP, Auburn
22. Zade Richardson, C, Wabash Valley (Ill.) JC
23. Brylie Ware, 3B, Oklahoma
24. Will Guay, RHP, Concord (W.Va.)
25. Alex McFarlane, RHP, Habersham Central HS, Mt. Airy, Ga.
26. Jeremy Randolph, RHP, Alabama
27. Eric Lex, RHP, Santa Clara
28. Tyler Peck, RHP, Chapman (Calif.)
29. Scott Politz, RHP, Yale
30. Cameron Dulle, RHP, Missouri
31. Dylan Pearce, RHP, Oregon State
32. Chandler Redmond, 2B, Gardner-Webb
33. Anthony Green, RHP, Jefferson (Mo.) JC
34. Ben Baird, SS, Washington
35. Logan Hofmann, RHP, Colby (Kan.) JC
36. Kyle Skeels, C, Coastal Carolina
37. Chris Newell, OF, Malvern (Pa.) Prep
38. Kurtis Byrne, C, Christian Brothers College HS, St. Louis
39. T.J. McKenzie, SS, Benjamin School, North Palm Beach, Fla.
40. Cash Rugely, SS, Navarro (Texas) JC

TAMPA BAY RAYS (22)

1. Greg Jones, SS, UNC Wilmington
1s. JJ Goss, RHP, Cypress Ranch HS, Houston
1s. Seth Johnson, RHP, Campbell
2. John Doxakis, LHP, Texas A&M
3. Shane Sasaki, OF, Iolani HS, Honolulu
4. Graeme Stinson, LHP, Duke
5. Ben Brecht, LHP, UC Santa Barbara
6. Colby White, RHP, Mississippi State
7. Jake Guenther, 1B, Texas Christian
8. Nathan Wiles, RHP, Oklahoma
9. Evan McKendry, RHP, Miami
10. Jonathan Embry, C, Liberty
11. Ben Troike, SS, Illinois
12. Nick Sogard, SS, Loyola Marymount
13. Zach Huffins, OF, Arizona Western JC
14. Logan Allen, OF, Arkansas-Fort Smith
15. Brett Wisely, 2B, Gulf Coast (Fla.) JC
16. Joe Gobillot, LHP, Vanderbilt
17. Trevor Brigden, RHP, Okanagan College
18. Joe LaSorsa, LHP, St. John's
19. Christian Johnson, OF, Clinton (Miss.) HS
20. Cam Shepherd, SS, Georgia
21. Andrew Peters, RHP, John A. Logan (Ill.) JC
22. Ben Peoples, RHP, Giles County HS, Pulaski, Tenn.
23. Jayden Murray, RHP, Dixie State (Utah) JC
24. Duke Kinamon, SS, Stanford
25. Garrett Hiott, OF, Eckerd (Fla.)
26. Robbie Peto, RHP, Stetson N

DRAFT

27. Mitchell Parker, LHP, San Jacinto (Texas) JC
28. Hill Alexander, OF, Lubbock Christian (Texas)
29. Zach Bravo, RHP, Butler County (Kan.) JC
30. Michael Carpentier, C, Yucaipa (Calif.) HS
31. Brannon Jordan, RHP, Cowley County (Kan.) JC
32. Kody Huff, C, Horizon HS, Scottsdale, Ariz.
33. Carson Coleman, RHP, Kentucky
34. Carter Bach, LHP, Wake Forest
35. Mitchell Walters, RHP, Wichita State
36. Shay Smiddy, RHP, Louisville
37. Addison Moss, RHP, Rice
38. Angelo Armenta, SS, San Diego State
39. Andrew Gross, RHP, Texas-Arlington
40. Luis Trevino, C, Abilene Christian

TEXAS RANGERS (8)

1. Josh Jung, 3B, Texas Tech
1s. Davis Wendzel, 3B, Baylor
2. Ryan Garcia, RHP, UCLA
3. Justin Slaten, RHP, New Mexico
4. Cody Freeman, SS, Etiwanda HS, Calif.
5. Kellen Strahm, OF, San Jose State
6. Cody Bradford, LHP, Baylor
7. Brandon Sproat, RHP, Pace (Fla.) HS N
8. John Matthews, RHP, Kent State
9. Zak Kent, RHP, Virginia Military Institute
10. Joe Corbett, RHP, West Texas A&M
11. Nick Lockhart, RHP, Woodgrove HS, Purcellville, Va.
12. Gavin Collyer, RHP, Mountain View HS, Ga.
13. Ben Anderson, RHP, Binghamton
14. Adam Berghorst, RHP, Zeeland (Mich.) East HS N
15. Randon Hostert, RHP, Bonneville HS, Idaho Falls, Idaho N
16. Triston Polley, LHP, Indiana State
17. Connor Housley, RHP, Sandy Creek HS, Tyrone, Ga.
18. Marc Church, RHP, North Atlanta HS
19. Blaine Crim, 1B, Mississippi College
20. Ken Turner, RHP, Ledyard (Conn.) HS
21. Jake Hamilton, RHP, Rose State (Okla.) JC
22. Cameron Wagoner, RHP, Tecumseh (Mich.) HS
23. Ross Carver, RHP, Crowder (Mo.) JC
24. Luke Schiltz, RHP, Stoneman Douglas HS, Parkland, Fla.
25. Raphael Pelletier, C, Edouard Montpetit HS, Montreal
26. Corey Stone, LHP, Walters State (Tenn.) JC
27. Mason Cole, RHP, Texas A&M
28. Jake Hoover, SS, Hillsdale (Mich.)
29. Eli Saul, RHP, Prince of Wales SS, Vancouver, B.C.
30. Anthony Hoopii-Tuionetoa, RHP, Pierce (Wash.) JC
31. Hunter Bryan, SS, Redwood HS, Visalia, Calif.
32. Michael Brewer, RHP, Hillsboro (Mo.) HS
33. Spencer Mraz, RHP, Miami (Ohio)
34. Nicholas Yoder, RHP, Rowan-Gloucester (N.J.) JC
35. Leon Hunter, RHP, North Carolina A&T
36. Donovan Benoit, RHP, Santa Fe (Fla.) JC
37. Thomas Farr, RHP, Northwest Florida State JC
38. Jamarcus Lang, RHP, Enterprise State (Ala.) JC
39. Adrian Rodriguez, RHP, Florida Virtual School
40. Tyler Myrick, RHP, Florida International

TORONTO BLUE JAYS (11)

1. Alek Manoah, RHP, West Virginia
2. Kendall Williams, RHP, IMG Academy, Bradenton, Fla.
3. Dasan Brown, OF, Abbey Park HS, Oakville, Ont.
4. Will Robertson, OF, Creighton
5. Tanner Morris, SS, Virginia
6. Cameron Eden, SS, California
7. L.J. Talley, 2B, Georgia
8. Angel Camacho, 3B, Jacksonville
9. Philip Clarke, C, Vanderbilt
10. Glenn Santiago, SS, International Baseball Academy, P.R.
11. Nick Neal, OF, Randleman (N.C.) HS
12. Sam Ryan, RHP, Virginia Commonwealth
13. Trevor Schwecke, SS, Wisconsin-Milwaukee

14. Eric Rivera, OF, Florida Atlantic
15. Michael Dominguez, RHP, Jefferson HS, Tampa
16. Jackxarel Lebron, RHP, International Baseball Academy, P.R.
17. Jared DiCesare, RHP, George Mason
18. Brandon Eisert, LHP, Oregon State
19. Gustavo Sosa, C, Tottenville HS, Staten Island, N.Y.
20. Jimmy Robbins, LHP, Rollins (Fla.)
21. Parker Caracci, RHP, Mississippi
22. Nick Fraze, RHP, Texas State
23. Anders Tolhurst, RHP, Grossmont (Calif.) JC
24. Spencer Horwitz, 1B, Radford
25. Nathaniel LaRue, RHP, McGill-Toolen HS, Mobile, Ala.
26. J-C Masson, OF, Cardinal Roy SS, Quebec
27. Roel Garcia, RHP, Rice
28. Gabriel Ponce, RHP, Arizona Western JC
29. Owen Diodati, C, Stamford Collegiate SS, Ont.
30. Noah Myers, OF, Wabash Valley (Ill.) JC
31. Blake Sanderson, RHP, Florida Atlantic
32. Braden Halladay, RHP, Calvary Christian HS, Fla.
33. Daniel Batcher, LHP, George Jenkins HS, Lakeland, Fla.
34. Luis Quinones, RHP, San Jacinto (Texas) JC
35. Connor Phillips, RHP, Magnolia (Texas) West HS
36. Scotty Bradley, 1B, Indiana
37. Andrew McInvale, RHP, Liberty
38. Dalton Sloniger, C, Penn State
39. Octavio Corona, RHP, Otay Ranch HS, Chula Vista, Calif.
40. Miguel Obeso, RHP, Cowley County (Kan.) JC

WASHINGTON NATIONALS (17)

1. Jackson Rutledge, RHP, San Jacinto (Texas) JC
3. Drew Mendoza, 3B, Florida State
4. Matt Cronin, LHP, Arkansas
5. Tyler Dyson, RHP, Florida
6. Jackson Cluff, SS, Brigham Young
7. Todd Peterson, RHP, Louisiana State
8. Jeremy Ydens, OF, UCLA
9. Hunter McMahon, RHP, Texas State
10. Andrew Pratt, C, Lubbock Christian (Texas)
11. J.T. Arruda, SS, Fresno State
12. Orlando Ribalta, RHP, Miami Dade JC
13. Jake Randa, OF, Northwest Florida State JC
14. Lucas Knowles, LHP, Central Arizona JC
15. Davis Moore, RHP, Fresno State
16. Junior Martina, SS, Western Oklahoma State JC
17. Amos Willingham, RHP, Georgia Tech
18. Mason Doolittle, C, Palm Beach (Fla.) JC
19. Tyler Yankosky, RHP, Millersville (Pa.)
20. Jack Dunn, SS, Northwestern
21. Kevin Strohschein, 1B, Tennessee Tech
22. Allan Berrios, C, Western Oklahoma State JC
23. Michael Cuevas, RHP, William J Brennan HS, Texas
24. Jake Alu, 3B, Boston College
25. Parker Quinn, 1B, Hofstra
26. Dupree Hart, 2B, College of Charleston
27. Jaylen Hubbard, 3B, Texas State
28. Jordan Bocko, RHP, UC Irvine
29. Brandon Gonzales, SS, James Madison HS, San Antonio
30. Troy Stainbrook, LHP, Biola (Calif.)
31. Brady Stover, LHP, South Dakota State
32. Dylan Beasley, RHP, Berry (Ga.)
33. Cutter Clawson, LHP, Laguna Beach (Calif.) HS
34. Anthony Gomez, 2B, Texas-Rio Grande Valley
35. Bryce Osmond, RHP, Jenks (Okla.) HS
36. Sam Wibbels, RHP, Hastings (Neb.) HS
37. Trei Cruz, SS, Rice
38. Tyler LaRue, C, Blanco (Texas) HS
39. Jake Bennett, LHP, Bixby (Okla.) HS
40. Jaden Brown, SS, St. Marcellinus SS, Mississauga, Ont.

APPENDIX

■ **Salomon "Sal" Artiaga**, a former Minor League Baseball president who also served in front office roles for the El Paso Sun Kings, Tampa Tarpons and Reds and in player development roles for the White Sox, Phillies and Royals during his 48 years in baseball, died Feb. 15 in Palm Harbor, Fla. He was 72.

■ **Gregory "Greg" Booker**, a righthander who pitched for the Padres, Twins and Giants from 1983-90 and also later served as a bullpen coach, pitching coach and scout for the Padres and Dodgers, died March 30 in Elon, N.C. He was 58.

■ **James "Jim" Bouton**, an all-star righthander who pitched for the Yankees, Seattle Pilots, Astros and Braves for parts of 10 seasons from 1962-78 and was also known for his work as a best-selling author, actor, activist, sportscaster and one of the creators of the popular gum brand Big League Chew, died July 10 in Great Barrington, Mass. He was 80.

Bouton made his major league debut on April 22, 1962. As a member of the Yankees, he was selected to the American League all-star team in 1963, when he also finished 16th in AL MVP voting with a 21-7, 2.53 record and 148 strikeouts in 249.1 innings. In all, Bouton made 304 major league appearances (144 starts) in 10 seasons, finishing with 62 wins and a 4.97 ERA in 1,238.2 innings.

In 1970, Bouton released the book "Ball Four," which was a diary of Bouton's 1969 season, which was split playing with both the expansion Pilots and Astros, as well as some of the early happenings in his Yankees career. Bouton later wrote the sequel "I'm Glad You Didn't Take It Personally," which discussed some of the controversies surrounding his first book, as well as the end of his playing career.

■ **Dave Brazell**, who started the baseball program at Grand Canyon University and served as the school's head baseball coach from 1953-80, died Oct. 17. He was 93.

A two-time NAIA coach of the year in baseball, Brazell also coached Grand Canyon's men's basketball team for 13 seasons from 1951-65, including an undefeated 20-0 season in 1958-59.

■ **Jonathan "John" Briggs**, a righthander who pitched for the Cubs, Indians and Kansas City Athletics from 1956-60, died Dec. 25 in Big Trees, Calif. He was 84.

■ **Richard "Dick" Brodowski,** a righthander who pitched for the Red Sox in 1952 and '55 and for the Washington Senators and Indians from 1955-59, died Jan. 14 in Lynn, Mass. He was 86.

Brodowski made his major league debut as a 19-year-old in June 1952 and appeared in 20 games for the Red Sox during his rookie season before taking a two-year hiatus to serve in the military. Brodowski return to the big leagues in 1955, and he finished his career with a 9-11, 4.76 record and 85 strikeouts in 215.2 innings.

■ **Ernest "Ernie" Broglio,** a righthander who pitched for the Cardinals and Cubs from 1959-66 and finished third in the National League Cy Young Award voting in 1960, died July 16 in San Jose. He was 83.

A 24-year-old Broglio led the NL in wins (21) in 1960, the same year in which he struck out 188 batters. The California native was traded from the Cardinals to the Cubs in the June 1964 deal that sent future Hall of Fame outfielder Lou Brock to St. Louis. In eight major league seasons, Broglio went 77-74, 3.74 with 849 strikeouts in 1,337.1 innings.

■ **Gerald "Jerry" Buchek,** a middle infielder and third baseman who played for the Cardinals and Mets for all or parts of seven seasons from 1961-68, died Jan. 2 in Springfield, Mo. He was 76.

Buchek was a member of the 1964 World Series champion Cardinals, and overall he finished his seven-season major league career with a .220/.269/.325 slash line and 22 home runs in 421 games.

■ **William "Bill" Buckner,** a 1981 all-star and the 1980 National League batting champion who played for the Dodgers, Cubs, Red Sox, California Angels and Royals over 22 big league seasons from 1969-90, died May 27 in Vallejo, Calif. He was 69.

An outfielder and first baseman during his career, Buckner played in more than 2,500 major league games, hitting .289/.321/.408 with 174 home runs, 1,208 RBIs and 183 stolen bases. He finished inside the top 10 in NL MVP voting in both 1981 and 1982, and he led the league in doubles in 1981 and 1983. He hit over .300 in eight different seasons, including a career-best .324 in 1980.

Traded from the Cubs to the Red Sox in the middle of the 1984 season, Buckner started all 162 games for the 1985 Red Sox at first base. He was plagued by a leg injury toward the end of the 1986 season, and he is infamously remembered for a 10th-inning error in Game 6 of the 1986 World Series against the Mets, a series in which the Red Sox went on to lose in seven games. Buckner is one of 21 players to play in the majors in four different decades.

■ **Nicholas "Nick" Cafardo,** a longtime Red Sox beat writer for the Boston Globe who also wrote several books on baseball, including "100 Things Red Sox Fans Should Know & Do Before They Die" and "If These Walls Could Talk: Boston Red Sox", died Feb. 21 in Fort Myers, Fla. He was 62.

■ **Frederick "Fred" Caliguiri,** a righthander who pitched for the Philadelphia Athletics in 1941 and '42, died Nov. 30 in Charlotte. He was 100.

In his two seasons in the majors, Caliguiri made 18 appearances (seven starts) for the A's, going 2-5, 4.52 with 27 strikeouts in 79.2 innings. At the time of his death, he was recognized as the oldest living major leaguer.

■ **Gennaro "Jerry" Casale,** a righthander who pitched for the Red Sox, Angels and Tigers from 1958-62, died Feb. 9 in Paramus, N.J. He was 85.

Casale pitched in 96 major league games, making 49 starts in a five-year career. He won a career-high 13 games for the 1959 Red Sox, when he posted a 4.31 ERA in 179.2 innings over 26 starts. In all, Casale won 17 games and pitched more than 370 innings in the major leagues.

■ **Jose Castillo,** a second baseman who played for the Pirates, Giants and Astros from 2004-08, died Dec. 6 in Yaracuy, Venezuela. He was 37.

Castillo played in nearly 600 games during his five major league seasons, hitting .254/.296/.379 with 39 home runs and 218 RBIs.

■ **Dominick "Dom" Christy Jr.,** who served as a scout for the Royals and Dodgers for more than 20 years, died July 4 in Uniontown, Pa. He was 89.

■ **Truman "Tex" Clevenger,** a righthander who pitched for the Red Sox, Senators, Angels and Yankees in 1954 and from 1956-62, died Aug. 24 in Visalia, Calif. He was 87.

In eight major league seasons, Clevenger won 36 games, recorded a 4.18 ERA and struck out 361 batters in 695 innings across 307 appearances (40 starts).

■ **Michael "Mike" Colbern,** a catcher who played for the White Sox from 1978-79, died March 21 in Tempe, Ariz. He was 63.

An All-American at Arizona State during his collegiate career, Colbern was a second-round pick of the White Sox in 1976. He made his major league debut as a 23-year-old on July 18, 1978, going 1-for-4 against the Brewers. Colbern finished his major league career with 58 hits in 224 at-bats with two home runs and 28 RBIs.

■ **Clinton "Clint" Conatser,** an outfielder who played for the Boston Braves in 1948 and '49, died Aug. 23 in Laguna Hills, Calif. He was 98.

In two major league seasons, Conatser hit .271/.352/.375 with six home runs and 39 RBIs in 376 at-bats. He went 0-for-4 with an RBI in the 1948 World Series as a member of the last Boston-based team to win a National League pennant.

■ **Alex Cosmidis,** who played 12 seasons in the minor leagues from 1950-61, managed in the minors for eight seasons from 1961-70 and spent nearly 30 years scouting for the Angels and White Sox, died June 27 in Raleigh, N.C. He was 90. Cosmidis was the East Coast scout of the year in 2009 and signed James Baldwin, Ray Durham, Bryan Harvey and Roberto Hernandez.

■ **John "Jack" Crimian,** a righthander who pitched for the Cardinals, Kansas City Athletics and Tigers from 1951-52 and 1956-57, died Feb. 11 in Middletown, Del. He was 92.

Crimian pitched in 74 games and made seven starts during his four seasons in the major leagues. He pitched a career-high 129 innings for the 1956 A's, when he went 4-8, 5.51 with 59 strikeouts.

■ **Richard "Rick" Down,** a major league hitting coach for the Yankees, Orioles, Dodgers and Red Sox from 1993-2003 who most recently filled that same role with the Mets from 2005-07, died Jan. 5 in Las Vegas. He was 68.

Before his career as a coach, Down was a minor league first baseman. He played for the Montreal Expos organization from 1969-75 and the Mariners organization in 1978.

■ **Christopher "Chris" Duncan,** a left fielder and first baseman who played for the Cardinals from 2005-09, died Sept. 6 of brain cancer in Tucson. He was 38.

The son of Dave Duncan, a former big league catcher and Tony La Russa's longtime pitching coach with the Athletics and Cardinals, and brother of ex-major leaguer Shelley Duncan, Chris hit .257/.348/.458 with 55 home runs and 175 RBIs in 389 career games. Duncan was a member of the Cardinals' 2006 World Series title team, playing in 10 playoff games and recording three hits and two RBIs in 22 postseason at-bats.

■ **Larry Foss,** a righthander who pitched for the Pirates and Mets in 1961 and '62, died June 15 in Wichita. He was 83. Foss appeared in eight games (four starts) in two major league seasons, ending his career 1-2, 5.33 with 12 strikeouts in 27 innings.

■ **Robert "Bob" Friend,** a four-time all-star and 1960 World Series champion who pitched for the Pirates from 1951-65 and for the Yankees and Mets in 1966, died Feb. 3 in Pittsburgh. He was 88.

Friend won a career-high 22 games in 1958, when he finished third in the NL Cy Young Award voting and sixth in the MVP race. He also led the NL in starts and innings in both 1956 and '57, when he made a combined 80 starts and completed 591.1 innings. In all, Friend finished with 197 wins and struck out 1,734 batters in 3,611 innings over 602 appearances and 497 starts.

■ **Alan "Al" Gallagher,** a third baseman who played for the Giants and California Angels from 1970-73, died Dec. 6 in Fresno. He was 73.

Gallagher played in 442 games during his five-year major league career, hitting .263/.335/.337 with 11 home runs and 130 RBIs in 1,264 at-bats. Gallagher also served as an independent league manager in the Western Baseball and Northern leagues from 1995-2000.

■ **Aubrey Gatewood,** a righthander who pitched for the Angels from 1963-65 and the Braves in '70, died June 5 in North Little Rock, Ark. He was 80.

Gatewood appeared in 68 games (13 starts) over four major league seasons, accumulating an 8-9, 2.78 record with 75 strikeouts and 67 walks in 178.1 innings. He ranked second on the 1965 Angels with 46 appearances, when he completed a career-high 92 innings with a 3.42 ERA.

■ **Joseph "Joe" Gibbon,** a lefthander who pitched for the Pirates, Giants, Reds and Astros from 1960-72 and was a member of the World Series-winning Pirates in 1960, died Feb. 20 in Newton, Miss. He was 83.

A 13-year big league veteran, Gibbon made 419 appearances (127 starts) in the majors. He made his debut on April 17, 1960, and later that season pitched in relief in multiple World Series games against the Yankees.

■ **Robert "Bob" Giggie,** a righthander who pitched for the Milwaukee Braves and Kansas City Athletics in 1959, '60 and '62, died Dec. 9 in Braintree, Mass. He was 85. Giggie appeared in 30 big league games, posting a 3-1, 5.18 record with 32 strikeouts in 57.1 innings.

■ **Thomas "Tommy" Giordano,** a second baseman who played in 11 games for the 1953 Philadelphia Athletics in the midst of an 12-year minor league career from 1948-59, died Feb. 14 in Orlando. He was 93.

■ **Eli Grba,** a righthander who pitched for the Yankees and Angels from 1959-63, died Jan. 14 in Florence, Alabama. He was 84.

Grba won a career-best 11 games in 1961, and he ended his five-year major league career 28-33, 4.48 with 255 strikeouts in 536.1 innings.

■ **Elijah "Pumpsie" Green,** a middle infielder who played for the Red Sox and Mets from 1959-63 and held the distinction of being the first black player to play for the Red Sox, the last of the original 16 major league franchises to integrate, died July 17 in San Leandro, Calif. He was 85. Green appeared in 344 games over five major league seasons, hitting .246/.357/.364 with 13 home runs and 12 stolen bases in 796 career at-bats.

■ **Leonard "Lenny" Green,** a center fielder who played for the Orioles, Washington Senators, Twins, Angels, Red Sox and Tigers from 1957-68, died Jan. 6 in Detroit. He was 86.

A Detroit native and member of the 1968 World Series champion Tigers, Green was a career .267/.351/.379 hitter with 47 home runs, 78 stolen bases and more walks (368) than strikeouts (260) in 1,136 major league games.

■ **Joseph "Joe" Grzenda,** a lefthander who pitched for the Tigers, Kansas City Athletics, Mets, Twins, Washington Senators and Cardinals for parts of eight major league seasons from 1961-72, died July 12 in Covington Township, Pa. He was 82. Grzenda appeared in 219 major league games over his career.

■ **Charles "Chuck" Harmon,** a corner infielder and outfielder who played for the Reds, Cardinals and Phillies from 1954-57, died March 19 in Golf Manor, Ohio. He was 94.

Harmon was the first black player for the Reds when he appeared as a pinch-hitter on April 17, 1954. Over four major league seasons, he hit .238/.294/.326 with seven home runs and 25 stolen bases in 592 at-bats.

■ **Thomas "Tom" Hausman,** a righthander who pitched for the Brewers from 1975-76 and for the Mets and Braves from 1978-82, died Jan. 16 in Las Vegas. He was 65.

Hausman appeared in 160 career games during his seven major league seasons, finishing with a 15-23, 3.80 record and 180 strikeouts in 441 innings. Hausman appeared in a career-high 55 games for the Mets in 1980, when he went 6-5, 3.98 in 122 innings.

■ **John "Johnny" Hetki,** a righthander who pitched for the Reds, St. Louis Browns and Pirates for all or parts of eight seasons from 1945-54, died Jan. 10 in Parma, Ohio. He was 96.

Working primarily in relief, Hetki appeared in 214 games (23 starts) during his eight seasons in the majors. The 6-foot-1 righthander finished his career 18-26, 4.39 with 175 strikeouts in 525.1 innings. He won a career-best six games for the Reds in 1946, and he appeared in a combined 112 games for the Pirates in 1953-54.

■ **Frederick "Fred" Hill,** the head baseball coach at Rutgers for 30 seasons who won more than 1,000 games in his career and also played shortstop in the Nebraska State, Alabama-Florida and Pioneer leagues for the Washington Senators organization from 1957-58, died March 2 in Cedar Grove, N.J. He was 84.

Hill is the winningest coach of any sport in Rutgers' 150-year history, having led the program to 12 regular season conference championships, eight conference tournament titles and 11 NCAA Tournament appearances.

■ **James "Jim" Holt,** a corner outfielder and first baseman who played for the Twins and Athletics from 1968-76, died March 29 in Burlington, N.C. He was 74.

Holt was a member of the World Series-winning '74 A's. For his career, he hit .265/.305/.352 with 19 home runs, eight stolen bases and 177 RBIs.

■ **Fred Hopke,** a minor league first baseman who played for the Phillies, Reds, Cardinals, Washington Senators, Yankees and Tigers organizations from 1956-65, died Oct. 19 in Toms River, N.J.

Hopke also served as the hitting coach at Seton Hall for parts of two decades in the 1980s and '90s. During his Hall of Fame induction speech in 2015, former Seton Hall player Craig Biggio acknowledged Hopke's help and said Hopke was "the first person who taught me how to work myself through an at-bat."

■ **Kenneth "Ken" Howell,** a righthander who pitched for the Dodgers and Phillies from 1984-90, died Nov. 9 in West Bloomfield, Mich. He was 57.

In his seven big league seasons, Howell made 245 appearances (54 starts) and went 38-48, 3.95 with 549 strikeouts in 613.1 innings. He posted career highs in wins (12), innings (204) and strikeouts (164) for the 1989 Phillies.

■ **Alvin "Al" Jackson,** a lefthander who pitched for the Pirates, Mets, Cardinals and Reds in 1959 and from 1961-69, died Aug. 19 in Port St. Lucie, Fla. He was 83.

During his 10-year big league career, Jackson won 67 games, recorded a 3.98 ERA and struck out 738 batters in 1,389 innings across 303 appearances (184 starts).

■ **Ransom "Randy" Jackson,** a two-time all-star third baseman who played for the Cubs, Dodgers and Indians from 1950-59, died March 20 in Athens, Ga. He was 93.

In all, Jackson hit .261/.320/.421 with 103 home runs, 36 stolen bases and 415 RBIs in 3,203 career at-bats.

■ **Thomas "Tom" Jordan,** a catcher who played for the White Sox, Indians and St. Louis Browns in 1944, '46 and '48, died Aug. 26 in Roswell, N.M. He was 99.

Jordan appeared in 39 major league games in his career, hitting .240/.270/.354 with one home run and six RBIs in 96 at-bats. Just before his death, Jordan was the oldest living former major leaguer and the last living major leaguer born in the 1910s.

■ **Larry Keller,** a longtime scout for the Mets, Brewers and Marlins and manager for the Baton Rouge franchise of the independent Southeastern

League in 2003, died Dec. 28 in Germantown, Tenn. He was 64.

■ **Larry Koentopp,** the head baseball coach at Gonzaga from 1970-77 and the minor league general manager and principal owner who brought Triple-A baseball to Las Vegas in 1983, died Jan. 12 in Las Vegas. He was 82.

Koentopp was largely responsible for moving the Triple-A Spokane Indians to Las Vegas in September 1982, and the franchise had near immediate success by winning the Pacific Coast League championship in 1986 and 1988.

As a college head coach, Koentopp produced a 289-138 record at Gonzaga, winning five conference championships and qualifying for four NCAA tournaments in eight seasons. He also served as the athletic director at Gonzaga before stepping down to focus on his minor league ownership.

■ **Gary Kolb,** an outfielder and catcher who played for the Cardinals, Milwaukee Braves, Mets and Pirates in 1960, from 1962-65 and in 1968 and '69, died July 3 in Charleston, W.Va. He was 79.

■ **Donald "Don" Koonce,** a righthanded reliever who pitched in the Mets, Montreal Expos, Tigers and Braves organizations in 1968 and from 1970-74, died July 15 in Fayetteville, N.C. He was 71.

Following his playing career, Koonce spent 12 years working with the Major League Scouting Bureau covering prospects in both North Carolina and South Carolina.

■ **Rocco "Rocky" Krsnich,** a third baseman who played for the White Sox in 1949 and from 1952-53, died Feb. 14 in Overland Park, Kan. He was 91.

Krsnich played in 120 games over his three seasons in the major leagues, hitting .215 with three home runs and 38 RBIs in 275 at-bats.

■ **Arnold "Barry" Latman,** an all-star righthander who pitched for the White Sox, Indians, Angels and Astros from 1957-67, died April 28 in Richmond, Texas.

In 159 appearances (80 starts) over his 11-year big league career, Latman went 59-68, 3.91 with 829 strikeouts and 489 walks in 1,219 innings.

Latman was selected to the All-Star Game as a member of the 1961 Indians, a season in which he finished 13-5, 4.02 with five saves in 108 strikeouts in 176.2 innings.

■ **Alberto Lois,** an outfielder who played for the Pirates from 1978-79, died March 12 in Cosuelo, Dominican Republic. He was 62.

Lois played in 14 major league games over two seasons, going 1-for-4 with a triple in his four plate appearances.

■ **Will Lotter,** who played in and won the first College World Series with California in 1947 and later served as a college baseball, football and men's soccer coach at UC Davis in parts of four different decades from 1952-1987, died May 20 in Davis, Calif. He was 94.

■ **Peter "Pete" Lovrich,** a righthander who pitched for the Kansas City Athletics in 1963, died Dec. 26 in Mokena, Ill. He was 76.

The first former Arizona State baseball player to reach the major leagues, Lovrich appeared in 20 games for the Athletics, making one start. He finished his major league career with a 1-1, 7.84 record and 16 strikeouts in 20.2 innings.

■ **Frank Lucchesi,** a major league manager for the Phillies (1970-72), Rangers (1975-77) and Cubs (1987) who also spent more than two decades as a minor league manager, died June 8 in Arlington, Texas. He was 92.

Over his seven year managerial career in the majors, Lucchesi led the Phillies, Rangers and Cubs to a combined record of 316-399.

As a minor league manager, Lucchesi accumulated 1,319 wins.

■ **William "Billy" MacLeod,** a lefthander who pitched for the Red Sox in 1962, died Dec. 12 in Marblehead, Mass. He was 76.

MacLeod made two big league appearances, striking out two in 1.2 innings.

■ **Peter Magowan,** the president and managing general partner of the Giants from 1992-2008 who was vital in keeping the franchise in San Francisco during the early 1990s, died Jan. 27 in San Francisco. He was 76.

■ **David "Dave" Marshall,** an outfielder who played for the Giants, Mets and Padres from 1967-73, died June 6 in Long Beach, Calif. He was 76.

In seven major league seasons, Marshall hit .246/.333/.338 with 16 home runs and 13 stolen bases in 490 games. Marshall played in a career-high 110 games for the 1969 Giants, and he hit a career-best .286/.390/.388 in his final major league season with the 1973 Padres.

■ **Demie Mainieri,** who won 1,012 games as the head baseball coach at Miami-Dade North JC from 1961-90, died March 13 in Baton Rouge. He was 90.

Mainieri was the first junior college head coach to win more than 1,000 games. His 1964 team won the NJCAA national championship, and he coached three more teams to national runner-up finishes. More than 100 of his players went on to sign professional contracts, and 30 of his former players reached the major leagues.

Mainieri's son, Paul, is the current head baseball coach at Louisiana State.

■ **Richard "Dick" Manville,** a righthander who pitched for the 1950 Boston Braves and 1952 Cubs, died Feb. 13 in Winter Springs, Fla. He was 93.

■ **Walt McKeel,** a catcher and first baseman who played for the Red Sox in 1996 and '97 and for the Rockies in 2002, died Jan. 1 in Statonsburg, N.C. He was 46.

In three major league seasons, McKeel appeared in 11 games and went 4-for-16 with one run scored.

■ **Luis Mercedes,** an outfielder who played for the Orioles and Giants from 1991-93, died June 30 in San Pedro de Macoris, Dominican Republic. He was 51. Mercedes finished his major league career with a .190/.286/.242 slash line.

■ **Glenn Mickens,** a righthander who appeared in four games and made two starts for the 1953 Brooklyn Dodgers, died July 9 in Kapaa, Hawaii. He was 88.

■ **William "Bill" Mills,** a catcher who played for the Philadelphia Athletics for five games in 1944, died Aug. 9 in Gainesville, Fla. He was 99. He was the second-oldest former major leaguer at the time of his death.

■ **David Montgomery,** a former president and later chairman of the Phillies who oversaw the construction of Citizens Bank Park and the organization's 2008 World Series title, died on May 8. He was 72.

■ **Donald "Don" Mossi,** an all-star lefthander

who pitched for the Indians, White Sox and Kansas City Athletics from 1954-65, died July 19 in Nampa, Idaho. He was 90.

In 12 major league seasons, Mossi made 460 appearances (165 starts) and accumulated a 101-80, 3.43 record with 932 strikeouts in 1,548 innings. After finishing 24th in the American League MVP voting in 1955, Mossi was selected as an AL all-star with the Indians in 1957.

■ **Harold "Hal" Naragon,** a catcher who played for the Indians, Senators and Twins in 1951 and from 1954-62, died Aug. 31 in Barberton, Ohio. He was 90.

■ **Ronald Negray,** a righthander who pitched for the Brooklyn Dodgers in 1952, the Phillies from 1955-56 and the Los Angeles Dodgers in 1958, died Nov. 8 in New Franklin, Ohio. He was 88.

■ **Donald "Don" Newcombe,** a righthander who pitched for the Dodgers, Reds and Indians from 1949-60, died Feb. 19 in Santa Monica, Calif. He was 92.

A star in the Negro Leagues before signing with the Dodgers in 1946, Newcombe was the first major league pitcher to win the Rookie of the Year (1949), MVP and Cy Young awards (both 1956). He became the first black pitcher to start a World Series game when as a rookie he took the mound for Brooklyn in the 1949 World Series. In 1951, Newcombe became the first black pitcher to win 20 games in a season.

■ **Alfred "Al" Ogletree,** who won more than 1,000 games over 29 seasons as the head coach of Texas Pan-American from 1969-97, died June 24 in McAllen, Texas. He was 89.

Ogletree led Texas-Pan American to 12 NCAA Tournaments during his tenure, including the program's first-ever College World Series appearance in 1971.

■ **Kelly Paris,** an infielder who played for the Cardinals, Reds, Orioles and White Sox for parts of five major league seasons from 1982-1988, died May 27 in Rock Hill, S.C. He was 61.

■ **Gene Pemberton,** the former director of community development for the Astros who was also the first full-time team chaplain in major league history, died Jan. 27 in Temple, Texas. He was 79.

■ **Ray Peters,** a righthander who appeared in two games (both starts) for the Brewers in 1970, died May 4 in Mesa, Ariz. He was 72.

■ **Harding "Pete" Peterson,** a former catcher, scout, minor league manager, farm director and general manager for the Pirates who spent parts of four decades with the organization, died April 16 in Palm Harbor, Fla. He was 89.

In four major league seasons with the Pirates in 1955 and from 1957-59, Peterson played in 66 games, hitting .273/.344/.391 with three home runs in 161 at-bats.

Peterson took over the Pirates' general manager role in 1976 and is credited with being the architect of the organization's most recent World Series championship in 1979. In all, Peterson spent 35 years in the Pirates organization, and he also served as the Yankees' GM in 1990.

■ **Thomas "Tom" Phoebus,** a righthander who pitched for the Orioles, Padres and Cubs from 1966-72, died on Sept. 5. He was 77.

Phoebus began his major league career by throwing two shutouts for the 1966 Orioles, becoming just the fourth American League pitcher in history to begin his career with back-to-back complete game shutouts. The righthander also threw a no-hitter on April 27, 1968.

In all, Phoebus won 56 games, recorded a 3.33 ERA and struck out 725 batters in 1,030 innings across 201 appearances (149 starts).

■ **Michael "Mike" Roarke,** a catcher who played for the Tigers from 1961-64, died July 27 in West Warwick, R.I. He was 88.

■ **Tony Robichaux,** the winningest coach in both Louisiana-Lafayette and McNeese State program history, died July 3 in New Orleans. He was 57.

Robichaux played at McNeese State from 1983-86 and then became the program's interim head coach immediately following his playing career.

Robichaux was hired by Louisiana-Lafayette prior to the 1995 season and led the Ragin' Cajuns to 12 NCAA Tournament appearances, four super regionals and the 2000 College World Series in 23 seasons. In all, Robichaux accumulated more than 900 career wins at Louisiana-Lafayette, ending his collegiate coaching career with 1,177 total victories.

■ **Frank Robinson**, a first-ballot Hall of Fame right fielder for the Reds, Orioles, Dodgers, California Angels and Indians from 1956-76 who was also the first African-American manager in major league history, died Feb. 7 in Los Angeles. He was 83.

The unanimous 1956 National League Rookie of the Year, Robinson was selected to 14 All-Star Games, and he is the only player in history to win MVP awards in both the National (1961) and American (1966) leagues.

In 1975, Robinson was named player-manager for the Indians, making him the first black manager in the major league history. He later managed the Giants (1981-84), Orioles (1988-91) and Montreal Expos/Washington Nationals (2002-06) and was named AL Manager of the Year in 1989. In total, Robinson finished his managerial career with more than 1,000 career wins.

A career .294/.389/.537 hitter with 2,943 hits, 1,812 RBIs and 204 stolen bases, Robinson was elected to the Hall of Fame with 89.2 percent of the vote in 1982. His No. 20 is retired by the Orioles, Reds and Indians.

■ **John Romano**, a four-time all-star catcher who played for the White Sox, Indians and Cardinals from 1958-67, died Feb. 24 in Naples, Fla. He was 84.

Considered one of the best catchers in the American League during the early 1960s, Romano played in 905 games over his 10-year major league career. He posted an OPS better than .820 in four consecutive seasons from 1959-62.

■ **Joe Russo**, a former player, team captain and head coach at St. John's for more than three decades who was inducted into the American Baseball Coaches Association Hall of Fame in 1997, died on May 26. He was 74. Russo played for St. John's from 1963-66, captaining the '66 squad to the College World Series. He then took over the reins as head coach of the program in 1974, leading the Red Storm to a 612-310 record over the next 22 seasons, including two more College World Series appearances in 1978 and 1980.

■ **Scott Sanderson**, an all-star righthander who pitched for the Montreal Expos, Cubs, Athletics, Yankees, California Angels, Giants and White Sox during his 19-year major league career, died April 11 in Lake Forest, Ill. He was 62.

Sanderson won 163 games and had a 3.84 ERA

while striking out 1,611 hitters in 2,561.2 career innings.

■ **Paul Schramka**, a left fielder who appeared in two games for the 1953 Cubs, died July 8 in Menomonee Falls, Wis. He was 91.

■ **Gerald "Jerry" Schypinski**, a shortstop who played in 22 games for the Kansas City Athletics in 1955, died March 25 in Sterling Heights, Mich. He was 87.

■ **Mike Sheppard**, the head baseball coach at Seton Hall from 1973-2003 who won 998 games over 31 seasons, made 12 NCAA Tournament appearances and qualified for two College World Series in 1974 and '75, died on April 6. He was 82.

Sheppard, whose youngest son Rob is the current head baseball coach at Seton Hall, coached 30 major leaguers during his tenure with the Pirates, including Hall of Famer Craig Biggio and stars Rick Cerone, Mo Vaughn, John Valentin, Matt Morris and Jason Grilli.

■ **Tyler Skaggs**, a lefthander who pitched for the Diamondbacks and Angels from 2012-19, died July 1 in Southlake, Texas. He was 27. He was a member of the Angels' rotation at the time of his death.

In seven major league seasons, Skaggs pitched to a 28-38 record and 4.41 ERA with 476 strikeouts in 520.2 innings. He was the top prospect in the California League in 2011 and ranked as the D-backs' No. 1 prospect entering 2013, when he ranked as high as No. 12 on the Baseball America Top 100 Prospects.

■ **Leroy Stanton**, a right fielder who played for the Mets, California Angels and Mariners from 1970-78, died March 13 in Florence County, S.C. He was 72. Stanton made his major league debut as a 24-year-old on Sept. 10, 1970. In total, Stanton hit .244/.311/.388 with 77 home runs, 36 stolen bases and 358 RBIs in 2,575 career at-bats.

■ **Glenn "Gene" Stephens**, a left fielder who played 12 seasons in the American League with the Red Sox, Orioles, Kansas City Athletics and White Sox from 1952-53 and 1955-1964, died April 27 in Granbury, Texas. He was 86. Over 12 major league seasons, Stephens played in 964 games and hit .240/.325/.355 with 37 home runs and 207 RBIs in 1,913 at-bats.

■ **Mel Stottlemyre**, an all-star righthander who pitched for the Yankees from 1964-74 and also served as a pitching coach for the Mets, Astros and Yankees from 1984-2005 and for the Mariners in 2008, died Jan. 13 in Seattle. He was 77.

A starting pitcher for 11 seasons in the majors, Stottlemyre was selected to five All-Star Games from 1965-70. Stottlemyre ended his career with a 164-139, 2.97 record, and he struck out 1,257 hitters in 2,661.1 innings.

As a pitching coach, Stottlemyre won five World Series championships.

■ **Jerry Streeter**, who played six seasons in the minor leagues from 1953-58, served as the head coach at Modesto (Calif.) JC from 1966-83 and worked as a scout for the Angels from 1994-2000, died July 5 in Hughson, Calif. He was 87.

■ **Nicholas "Nick" Testa**, a catcher who played in one game for the 1958 Giants and then served as a batting practice coach for the Yankees, died Nov. 16 in New York. He was 90.

■ **Luis Valbuena**, a third baseman for the Mariners, Indians, Cubs, Astros and Angels from 2008-18, died Dec. 6 in Yaracuy, Venezuela. He was 33.

Valbuena, who was murdered in a highway robbery gone wrong along with Jose Castillo, played in more than 1,000 major league games during his 11-year career, and he appeared in 96 games for the Angels in 2018.

■ **Federico "Freddie" Velazquez**, a catcher who appeared in a combined 21 major league games for the 1969 Seattle Pilots and 1973 Braves, died May 21 in Villa Altagracia, Dominican Republic. He was 81.

■ **Bruce Winkworth**, a fixture in North Carolina State's baseball program and in Raleigh baseball circles for more than 30 years, died May 17 in Raleigh, N.C. He was 67. Winkworth was also one of Baseball America's earliest staff members, working with founding editor Allan Simpson when BA moved to Durham from Canada in 1982. He served as North Carolina State's sports information director for baseball from 1996-2012.

■ **Kevin Ward,** a left fielder who played for the Padres in 1991 and '92, died March 9 in Coronado, Calif. He was 57. Ward played in 125 major league games over two seasons.

APPENDIX